REVERSE
ACRONYMS AND INITIALISMS
DICTIONARY

OTHER GALE PUBLICATIONS

ACRONYMS AND INITIALISMS DICTIONARY—Third Edition. Contains over 80,000 entries, including many new terms for vital groups, agencies, processes, equipment, developments, and projects.

ENCYCLOPEDIA OF BUSINESS INFORMATION SOURCES—Second Edition. Arranged according to subjects, entries in the first volume contain full references to sources of information important to executives and researchers. The second volume provides the same kinds of details on geographic subjects, on which the arrangement of the volume is based.

NATIONAL FACULTY DIRECTORY—Annual. An alphabetical list of names, with departmental affiliations and full institutional addresses, of nearly 380,000 faculty members at junior colleges, colleges, and universities in the United States.

CONTEMPORARY AUTHORS—Annual. A bio-bibliographical reference offering detailed information on more than 3,000 current authors each year. Distinctive features: unabridged bibliographies, sidelights, critical and biographical sources, work in progress. No duplication among volumes; cumulatively indexed.

AUTHOR BIOGRAPHY SERIES—Reference Book Reprints. Collective biographical works including Allibone, Duyckinck, and others.

ENCYCLOPEDIA OF ASSOCIATIONS—Sixth Edition. Volume 1: National Associations of the United States, detailed descriptions of nearly 14,000 national, nonprofit membership organizations. With 30,000-item keyword/alphabetical index. Volume 2: Geographic-Executive Index, a two-part index to material in Volume 1. Volume 3: **NEW ASSOCIATIONS AND PROJECTS,** quarterly supplements to Volume 1. Cumulatively indexed.

STATISTICS SOURCES—Third Edition. A subject guide to data on industrial, business, social, educational, financial, and other topics for the United States and selected foreign countries. With entries on 11,000 subjects from Abaca to Zoologists.

MANAGEMENT INFORMATION GUIDE SERIES. Authoritative, comprehensive, carefully-indexed guides to the literature of such major business and governmental areas as Accounting, Commercial Law, Computers, Insurance, Communications, Transportation, Public Relations, and Economic and Business History.

BOOKMAN'S PRICE INDEX. The five volumes now available contain listings for over 250,000 antiquarian books and periodicals selected from the catalogs issued by leading rare book sellers, specialist dealers, and O.P. bookmen. Gives all essential details.

DIRECTORY OF SPECIAL LIBRARIES AND INFORMATION CENTERS—Second Edition. Volume 1 contains information about more than 13,000 special libraries, information centers, and documentation centers in the U.S. and Canada. Volume 2: Geographic-Personnel Index. Volume 3: **NEW SPECIAL LIBRARIES,** a periodic supplement to Volume 1.

RESEARCH CENTERS DIRECTORY—Fourth Edition. Covers nearly 6,500 university-related and other nonprofit research units. Entries are indexed by name of research center, sponsoring institution, and research director. **NEW RESEARCH CENTERS,** a quarterly supplement to RCD; each issue averages about 200 listings.

REVERSE ACRONYMS AND INITIALISMS DICTIONARY

First Edition

A Companion Volume to *Acronyms and Initialisms Dictionary*, with Terms Arranged Alphabetically by Meaning of Acronym

Covering: Aerospace, Associations, Biochemistry, Business and Trade, Domestic and International Affairs, Education, Electronics, Genetics, Government, Labor, Medicine, Military, Pharmacy, Physiology, Politics, Religion, Science, Societies, Sports, Technical Drawings and Specifications, Transportation, and Other Fields

Edited By

Ellen T. Crowley
and
Robert C. Thomas

Contributing Editors

Harry Schecter
Former Chairman
Government Printing Office Style Board

Harvey Wolf
Staff Scientist, Data Systems Division
Hughes Aircraft Company

GALE RESEARCH COMPANY · BOOK TOWER · DETROIT, MICHIGAN

GALE EDITORIAL STAFF
for
REVERSE ACRONYMS AND INITIALISMS DICTIONARY

First Edition

Editors

Ellen T. Crowley

and

Robert C. Thomas

Editorial Staff

Dorothy Dockterman   Kathleen Turner

Margaret Fisk   Barbara Tyler

Stephenie Koehn   Mary Wilson

**Library of Congress
Cataloging in Publication Data**

Main entry under title:

Reverse acronyms and initialisms dictionary.

1. Acronyms.   2. English language-Reverse
indexes.   I. Crowley, Ellen T., ed.   II. Thomas,
Robert C., ed.

PE1693.R4   71-165486

CONTENTS

ACKNOWLEDGMENTS

For suggestions, contributions of terms, permission to take material from personal or published sources, and for other courtesies during the preparation of this edition, the editors are indebted to the following:

The contributing editors, named and identified on the title page

O.T. Albertini, Personnel Directorate, Joint Chiefs of Staff, Department of Defense

A. Marjorie Taylor, editor, Language of World War II

Data Processing Division, International Business Machines Corp. (publishers of IBM Glossary for Information Processing)

B-G-R Division, Associated Spring Corp. (publishers of Civilian's Dictionary, a dictionary of wartime abbreviations)

Eric Partridge, author of A Dictionary of Slang and Unconventional English; A Dictionary of Abbreviations, with Special Attention to War-Time Abbreviations; and other books

Edwin B. Steen, Professor of Anatomy and Physiology, Western Michigan University

Mamie Meredith, late Professor of English, University of Nebraska

Robert E. Lacey, journalist

Roy Hubbard, journalist

Morgan Oates, librarian, Detroit Free Press

Miriam M. Steinert, editorial consultant

James Aguirre, staff writer and editor, Quality Evaluation Laboratory, United States Naval Weapons Station, Concord, California

Edith Thompson

Ethel M. Fair

In addition, many suggestions concerning individual terms to be included or subjects to be covered have been received from individual users, and have been most helpful. The editors invite all such comments and suggestions, and will make every effort to incorporate them in future editions.

PREFACE

The use of the acronym, initialism, or other abbreviated letter symbol is perhaps the fastest growing "language" in contemporary society. Whether one views the phenomenon with disdain or delight, it is apparent that the acronymic form has established a lasting and ever-widening influence on both written and spoken communication.

For several years, Gale's ACRONYMS AND INITIALISMS DICTIONARY (AID) has served as a reliable and up-to-date reference, guiding librarians, businessmen, technical writers, and other researchers through the alphabetical maze. Now its scope is broadened with publication of this companion volume, REVERSE ACRONYMS AND INITIALISMS DICTIONARY (RAID). The 80,000 entries of AID's third edition appear in this first edition of RAID, but here the terms are arranged alphabetically by _meaning_ rather than by acronym or initialism.

USEFUL IN SORTING OUT INCONSISTENCIES

If all acronymic terms were as logically formed as Royal Artillery -- RA, there would be little need for a tool such as RAID. The countless exceptions to this generalized formation, however, make a guide essential. Receipt Acknowledged, for instance, is not shortened to RA, but rather to REACK; Sisters of the Most Holy Sacrament is abbreviated as MHS, not SMHS.

Another generality regarding the formation of acronyms and initialisms is that articles, prepositions, etc., are not usually represented in the shortened form: General Agreements on Tariffs and Trade -- GATT. Yet it is becoming more common to find terms in which some or all of these minor words _are_ abbreviated: Research in Laboratory Animal Medicine and Care -- RILAMAC. Another popular practice is to tack on a stray letter which has no connection with the acronym's translation, but which renders it pronounceable or gives it an appropriate meaning: Greater Underwater Propulsive Power (Type of submarine) -- GUPP_Y_.

'MISTAKEN IDENTITY' AVOIDED

An incorrect initialism can not only cause confusion, but may even change the meaning of a term. A Bachelor of Interior Architecture is designated as BI Arch. Writing it as BIA confers on the subject a Bachelor of Industrial Arts degree.

Some commercial firms and associations use their entire corporate name in their initials: Cancer Care, Inc. -- CCI; while others use only the principal part of their name: Perlite Industries, Inc. -- PI. If Cancer Care, Inc., is abbreviated CC, it may indicate Chrysler Corporation;

lengthening the initialism for Perlite Industries, Inc., to PII may result in translation as Printing Industry Institute.

Even terms in the same subject field are not always shortened the same way. The abbreviation for Luggage and Leather Goods Manufacturers of America is formed as one might expect -- LLGMA; however, the Luggage and Leather Goods Salesmen's Association of America is shortened simply to LLG.

A VALUABLE KEY TO SYMBOLS

Both AID and RAID contain a number of letter symbols. These do not meet the criteria of being acronyms or initialisms, but are included as an important part of an alphabetical reference. REVERSE ACRONYMS AND INITIALISMS DICTIONARY is especially valuable in assigning correct symbols to given terms, since the symbol often bears little or no resemblance to what it represents. For example, the meteorological symbol for Hail is A; the Navy symbol for a Heavy Cruiser is CA; the New York Stock Exchange symbol for the Borden Company is BN, etc.

Airport code names may also seem baffling. A few are apparent, such as the symbol for Denver -- DEN. But in many cases the connection between subject and symbol seems remote at best: Michigan's Willow Run Airport is represented by YIP, illogical unless one realizes the airport's proximity to the city of Ypsilanti.

In cases like these, and in countless others, RAID can eliminate guesswork and tiresome searches by providing the correct alphabetical form quickly and accurately.

NOTES ON ARRANGEMENT OF TERMS

Terms are arranged in alphabetical order, according to the meaning of the acronym or initialism. If a particular meaning has more than one initialism representing it, the various initialisms are then arranged alphabetically as in the ACRONYMS AND INITIALISMS DICTIONARY:

LIN . . . . Liquid Nitrogen

LN . . . . Liquid Nitrogen

TREATMENT OF PARENTHESES

Material within parentheses is generally ignored in the alphabetizing, with two exceptions:

--If the meaning includes an acronym or initialism which is followed by a parenthetical translation, then the entry is alphabetized by the translation rather than by the acronym or initialism:

CHARM . . . . CAA (Civil Aeronautics Authority)
High Altitude Remote Monitoring

would be filed under "Civil."

--If the material within parentheses is an integral part of the term or is important to the sensible placement of the term, it is considered in alphabetizing:

COM(D)WA . . . . Commodore (Destroyers) Western
Approaches (British)

would be alphabetized by "(Destroyers)," but not by "(British)," which is simply an explanatory addition. Similarly,

SCL . . . . Sisters of Charity of Leavenworth

comes before

SCN . . . . Sisters of Charity (of Nazareth)

MINOR PARTS OF SPEECH

Articles, conjunctions, prepositions, etc., are also usually ignored in the alphabetizing. Exceptions are:

--those few entries which begin with an article, preposition, etc., when that particular word is also represented in the acronym. Thus:

TAG . . . . The Adjutant General

would be filed under "The," while

AG . . . . The Adjutant General

would be filed under "Adjutant."

--those entries in which the preposition or other minor word is an integral part of the term:

LORBI . . . . Locked-On RADAR Bearing Indicator

for which "On" is considered in alphabetizing, and

CWPEA . . . . Childbirth Without Pain Education
Association,

for which "Without" is considered in alphabetizing.

HYPHENATION

Hyphenated words are treated as two words if each can stand alone as a word (Eye-Bank) and as one word if the first part cannot stand alone (Tri-Butyl).

If a series of entries begins with the same word, sometimes hyphenated, sometimes treated as one word, the entries are all alphabetized as though it were one word:

FAS . . . . Followup Alarm System

FUA . . . . Follow-Up Amplifier

FEA . . . . Followup Error Alarm

INITIALS

Whenever one of the following abbreviations appears in an entry, it has been alphabetized as though spelled out as indicated:

RR as Railroad   St. as Saint

US as United States   USA as United States of America

If an entry consists of the name of a commercial firm which is officially known by a set of initials, that entry is alphabetized as though the initials formed a word:

DWG . . . . DWG Cigar Corporation (NYSE symbol)

FMC . . . . FMC Corporation (NYSE symbol)

Some entries contain acronyms so commonly used in their short forms that they have come to be identified as words. The acronyms appearing in such entries are alphabetized as words, rather than translating them and alphabetizing by translation. Examples of such entries are:

LXD . . . . LASER Transceiver Device

alphabetized under "La..."

RBS . . . . RADAR Bombsight

alphabetized under "Ra...."

When an entry begins with a single letter, that letter is treated as a word and the entry will be found at the beginning of its particular letter section:

ABY . . . . A.M. Byers Company (NYSE symbol)

comes before other A entries, and

MDMR . . . . M-Day Mobilization Requirement

comes before other M entries.

A

ABC . . . . A Better Chance (Scholarship program for the underprivileged)
ACRONYM . . . A Contrived Reduction of Nomenclature Yielding Mnemonics (Humorous interpretation of the term)
ADEPT . . . . . . A Distinctly Empirical Prover of Theorems
AD . . . . A Drink
ABY . . . . A. M. Byers Company (NYSE symbol)
ANT . . . . A. N. Tupolev (Initialism used as designation for Russian aircraft designed by Tupolev)
ANITA . . . . . . A New Inspiration to Arithmetic
APL . . . . A Programming Language (Data processing)
ARESTEM . . . . . A Recording Stray Energy Monitor
BEK . . . . A. S. Beck Shoe Corporation (American Stock Exchange symbol)
AWOL . . . . . . A Wolf on the Loose (Slang)
AI . . . . Aaland Islands
ABA . . . . Aaron Burr Association
AXO . . . . Aaxico Air Lines
ABEX . . . . Ab Extra (From Without)
AUC . . . . Ab Urbe Condita (From the founding of the city, refers especially to Rome)
ABJ . . . . Abacus Fund (NYSE symbol)
ACR . . . . Abandon Call and Retry
ASC . . . . Abbe Sine Condition
ASL . . . . Abbe's Sine Law
ABT . . . . Abbott Laboratories (NYSE symbol)
AER . . . . Abbreviated Effectiveness Report (Air Force)
ABRACADABRA . . Abbreviations and Related Acronyms Associated with Defense, Astronautics, Business and Radio-electronics (Raytheon Company publication)
ABC . . . . ABC Consolidated Corporation (NYSE symbol)
AAS . . . . Aberdeen Art Society
AML . . . . Aberdeen Marine Laboratory
APG . . . . Aberdeen Proving Ground (Army)
APGBRL . . . . . Aberdeen Proving Ground – Ballistics Research Laboratory
ACC . . . . Abilene Christian College (Texas)
AR . . . . Aberdeen & Rockfish R. R. (AAR code)
AS . . . . Abilene & Southern Railway Company (AAR code)
ABB . . . . Ablating Blunt Body
AIS . . . . Ablating Inner Surface
AHS . . . . Ablative Heat Shield
AIP . . . . Ablative Insulative Plastic
ATC . . . . Ablative Thrust Chamber
ATCE . . . . Ablative Thrust Chamber Engine (NASA)
AB . . . . Able-Bodied Seaman
AMR . . . . Abnormal Mission Routine
ARC . . . . Aboriginal Research Club
APS . . . . Aborigines Protection Society
AGS . . . . Abort Guidance System (Air Force)
ASIS . . . . Abort Sensing & Implementation System
AB . . . . Abortion Patient (Medical slang)
A . . . . About
AGL . . . . Above Ground Level
ATH . . . . Above the Horizon
AMSL . . . . Above Mean Sea Level (Navigation)
AN . . . . Above-Named
ANO . . . . Above Named Officer (Army orders)
AP . . . . Above Proof
ASL . . . . Above Sea Level
ATAR . . . . Above Transmitted As Received
AW . . . . Above Water
ABAC . . . . . . Abraham Baldwin Agricultural College (Georgia)
ABLI . . . . Abraham Lincoln Birthplace National Monument
AGA . . . . Abrasive Grain Association

ABC . . . . Abridged Building Classification for Architects, Builders, and Civil Engineers
AJVD . . . . Abrupt Junction Varactor Doubler
A . . . . Absent
AOL . . . . Absent Over Leave (Navy)
HCA . . . . Absent by Reason of Being Held by Civil Authorities (Military)
ATAD . . . . . . Absent on Temporary Additional Duty (Navy)
ATD . . . . Absent (on) Temporary Duty
AWL . . . . Absent with Leave
AWOL . . . . . . Absent Without Official Leave
A . . . . Absolute (Temperature in fahrenheit degrees)
AA . . . . Absolute Altitude (Navigation)
ABAMP . . . . . Absolute Ampere
ABP . . . . Absolute Boiling Point
ACD . . . . Absolute Cardiac Dullness
A/C . . . . Absolute Ceiling (Aerospace)
AEE . . . . Absolute Essential Equipment
AL . . . . Absolute Limen (Psychophysics)
M . . . . Absolute Magnitude (Astronomy)
AST . . . . Absolute Space-Time
ATS . . . . Absolute Temperature Scale
ABF . . . . Absolutely Bloody Final (Especially with reference to a drink)
A . . . . Absolvo (I acquit) (Used by Romans in criminal trials)
APMA . . . . . . Absorbent Paper Manufacturers Association
A/E . . . . Absorptivity-Emissivity (Ratio)
AUN . . . . Absque Ulla Nota (Unmarked; literally, without any marking or note)
ABTICS . . . . . Abstract and Book Title Index Card Service (Iron and Steel Institute) (British)
IAB-ICSU . . . . Abstracting Board – International Council of Scientific Unions
A & I . . . . . Abstracting and Indexing
A . . . . Abstracts
ACR . . . . Abstracts of Classified Reports
AIM . . . . Abstracts of Instructional Materials in Vocational and Technical Education (A periodical of ERIC)
ADD . . . . Abstracts of Declassified Documents
ANWA . . . . . . Abstracts of New World Archaeology
APSE . . . . . . Abstracts of Photographic Science and Engineering Literature
ARM . . . . Abstracts of Research and Related Materials in Vocational and Technical Education (A periodical of ERIC)
AGL . . . . Abteilungsgewerkschaftaleitung
APO . . . . Abteilungsparteiorganisation
A . . . . Abundant (With respect to occurrence of species)
ABC . . . . Academia Brasileira de Ciencias (Brazil)
AAS . . . . Academiae Americanae Socius (Fellow of the American Academy)
AAIP . . . . Academic Administration Internship Program
AIAOS . . . . . . Academic Instructor and Allied Officer School (Military)
AIS . . . . Academic Instructors School (Air Force)
API . . . . Academic Press, Incorporated
A . . . . Academician or Academy
AIC . . . . Academie Internationale de la Ceramique
ADS . . . . Academie des Sciences (Academy of Science)
AAFH . . . . . . Academy of American Franciscan History
AAP . . . . Academy of American Poets
AAO . . . . Academy of Applied Osteopathy
AAS . . . . Academy of Applied Science
ACBFC . . . . . . Academy of Comic-Book Fans and Collectors
ADH . . . . Academy of Dentistry for the Handicapped
ADP . . . . Academy of Denture Prosthetics
AED . . . . Academy for Educational Development
AGD . . . . Academy of General Dentistry
AHC . . . . Academy of Hospital Counselors
AHPR . . . . . . Academy of Hospital Public Relations

REVERSE ACRONYMS AND INITIALISMS DICTIONARY

AHR . . . . Academy of Human Rights
AIMH . . . . . . Academy of International Military History
AIM . . . . Academy of Interscience Methodology
AM . . . . Academy of Management
AMWG . . . . . Academy of Master Wine Growers
AMA . . . . . . Academy of Model Aeronautics
AMPAS . . . . . Academy of Motion Picture Arts and Sciences
ANSP . . . . . . Academy of Natural Science, Philadelphia
ANC . . . . . . Academy of the New Church
AOD . . . . . . Academy of Oral Dynamics
APS . . . . Academy of Political Science
APMC . . . . . . Academy of Psychologists in Marital Counseling
APM . . . . . . Academy of Psychosomatic Medicine
ARA . . . . . . Academy of Rehabilitative Audiology
ARMH . . . . . Academy of Religion and Mental Health
ASUSSR . . . . . Academy of Science (Union of Soviet Socialist Republics)
AS . . . . Academy of Sciences
ATO . . . . . . Academy of Teachers of Occupations
ATAS . . . . . . Academy of Television Arts and Sciences
AUAS . . . . . . Academy of Underwater Arts and Sciences
AWAPA . . . . . Academy of Wind and Percussion Arts
ACAD . . . . . . Acadia National Park
ABCD . . . . . . Accelerated Business Collection and Delivery (US Post Office)
AGA . . . . . . Accelerated Growth Area (Embryology)
AIR . . . . Accelerated Item Reduction (Military)
ALL . . . . . . Accelerated Learning of Logic
ALT . . . . . . Accelerated Life Testing
APC . . . . . . Accelerated Pacification Campaign (South Vietnam)
APW . . . . . . Accelerated Public Works (Program) (Interior Department)
APWP . . . . . Accelerated Public Works Program (Interior Department)
ARD . . . . . . Accelerated Rural Development
ASAPR . . . . . Accelerated Strike Aircraft Program
ATT . . . . . . Accelerated Test Technology
A . . . . Acceleration
ACU . . . . . . Acceleration Compensation Unit
C . . . . Acceleration Correction
ADU . . . . . . Acceleration-Deceleration Unit
AMGS . . . . . Acceleration Monitoring Guidance System
ASV . . . . . . Acceleration Switching Valve
AVC . . . . . . Acceleration Vector Control
AIC . . . . . . Accelerator Information Center (ORNL)
APACHE . . . . Accelerator for Physics and Chemistry of Heavy Metals
APFA . . . . . . Accelerator Pulsed Fast Assembly
ACVE . . . . . . Accelerometer Calibration Vibration Exciter
APS . . . . Accelerometer Parameter Shift
ANVO . . . . . . Accept No Verbal Orders
ADI . . . . Acceptable Daily Intake
ADL . . . . . . Acceptable Defect Level
AERT . . . . . . Acceptable Environmental Range Test
AFR . . . . . . Acceptable Failure Rate
ALD . . . . . . Acceptable Limit for Dispersion
API . . . . Acceptable Periodic Inspection
AQL . . . . . . Acceptable Quality Level (Quality control)
ARL . . . . . . Acceptable Reliability Level (Quality control)
AWF . . . . . . Acceptable Workload Factor (Management)
ACE . . . . . . Acceptance Checkout Equipment (NASA)
ATF . . . . . . Acceptance Test Facility
ATP . . . . . . Acceptance Test Procedure
AT . . . . Acceptance Tester
A & T . . . . . . Acceptance and Transfer
A . . . . Accepted
AADO . . . . . . Accepted Alternative Designation Of
ADR . . . . . . Accepted Dental Remedies (A publication)
AWE . . . . . . Accepted Weight/Estimate (Ships)
AEL . . . . . . Acceptor Energy Level
AA . . . . Access Authorization
ABD . . . . . . Access Block Diagram
AD . . . . Access Door
AFR . . . . . . Access Function Register
AO . . . . Access Opening (Technical drawings)
AP . . . . Access Panel (Technical drawings)
AP . . . . Access Permit or Access Permittee (AEC)
APH . . . . . . Access Permit Holder
ADN . . . . . . Accession Designation Number (Military)
AL . . . . Accession List
AD . . . . Accessions Document (Air Force)
AB . . . . Accessories Bulletin
ABO . . . . . . Accessory Boring Organ (of a gastropod)
AGB . . . . . . Accessory Gear Box
APG . . . . . . Accessory Pedal Ganglia
APS . . . . Accessory Power Supply

AID . . . . Accident, Incident, Deficiencies
ACCI . . . . . . Accident Injury
ACNOT . . . . . Accident Notice (Aviation)
ACPO . . . . . . Accion Cultural Popular (Basic education organization) (Colombia)
AD . . . . Accion Democratica (Democratic Action) (Venezuelan political party)
ACP . . . . . . Accion Democratica Popular (Popular Democratic Action) (Political party in Costa Rica)
ARNE . . . . . . Accion Revolucionaria Nacional Ecuatoriana (National Revolutionary Action) (Political party in Ecuador)
A . . . . Accommodation
ASO . . . . . . Accommodation Sales Order
AAMID . . . . . Accomplishment of Assigned Mission Impeded by Deadline (Army)
AQ . . . . Accomplishment Quotient
AME . . . . . . Accord Monetaire Europeen
ATG . . . . . . Accordion Teachers' Guild
AO . . . . Account of
A/O . . . . . . Account of (Business and trade)
AC . . . . Account Control
A/C . . . . Account Current (Business and Trade)
AP . . . . Account Paid
AR . . . . Account Receivable
AS . . . . Account Sales
ACTPO . . . . . Accountable Property Officer (Army)
APO . . . . . . Accountable Property Officer
AG . . . . Accountant General
AC . . . . Accountants and Controllers
ACC . . . . . . Accounting Careers Council
ACC . . . . . . Accounting Classification Code
ADSN . . . . . . Accounting and Disbursing Station Number (Air Force)
A & F . . . . . . Accounting and Finance
AFO . . . . . . Accounting and Finance Office(r)
APB . . . . . . Accounting Principles Board (American Institute of Certified Public Accountants)
A/C . . . . . . Accounts
ACA . . . . . . Accounts Control Area
AP . . . . Accounts Payable
AFM . . . . . . Accredited Farm Manager (Designation given by American Society of Farm Managers and Rural Appraisers)
AHNA . . . . . . Accredited Home Newspapers of America
AMO . . . . . . Accredited Management Organization (Designation given by Institute of Real Estate Management)
ART . . . . . . Accredited Record Technician
ARA . . . . . . Accredited Rural Appraiser (Designation given by American Society of Farm Managers and Rural Appraisers)
AABC . . . . . . Accrediting Association of Bible Colleges
ACBS . . . . . . Accrediting Commission for Business Schools
AE . . . . Accrued Expenditure
AEP . . . . . . Accrued Expenditure Paid
AEU . . . . . . Accrued Expenditure Unpaid
ACLV . . . . . . Accrued Leave (Military)
AMPS . . . . . . Accrued Military Pay System
ADU . . . . . . Accumulation Distribution Unit
AHPA . . . . . . Accumulator High Pressure Air
ARMA . . . . . . Accumulator Reservoir Manifold Assembly
ACS . . . . . . Accumulator Switch
ADS . . . . . . Accurately Defined Systems (Data processing)
A . . . . Ace
ACT . . . . . . Acetate Cloth Tape
AFT . . . . . . Acetate Film Tape
AHL . . . . . . Acetate Halftone Litho (Du Pont)
Ac Co A . . . . Acetyl Coenzyme A
AAF . . . . . . Acetylaminofluorene
A Ch . . . . . . Acetylcholine
ACHE . . . . . . Acetylcholinesterase
APAD . . . . . . Acetylpyridine-Adenine Dinucleotide
ASA . . . . . . Acetylsalicylic Acid (Aspirin)
ASECH . . . . . Acetylselenocholine
ACF . . . . . . ACF Industries, Inc. (NYSE symbol)
ASPIRE . . . . . Achieve Successful Performance, Intensify Reliability Effort
AA . . . . Achievement Age (Psychology)
AQ . . . . Achievement Quotient
AR . . . . Achievement Ratio
ARCS . . . . . . Achievement Rewards for College Scientists (Foundation)
AT . . . . Achievement Test
ACD . . . . . . Acid Citrate Dextrose
AF . . . . Acid-Fast
AFB . . . . . . Acid-Fast Bacillus
AMP . . . . . . Acid Mucopolysaccharides
AN . . . . Acid Number
AR . . . . Acid Resisting (Technical drawings)
AV . . . . Acid Value

AW . . . . Acid Waste
AP . . . . Acidproof
ACMA . . . . . . Acidproof Cement Manufacturers Association
APF . . . . Acidproof Floor (Technical drawings)
AR . . . . Acknowledgment of Receipt
R . . . . Acknowledgment of Receipt (Message handling)
ASC . . . . Acme Markets, Inc. (NYSE symbol)
ACO . . . . Acme Steel Company (NYSE symbol)
AAM . . . . Acoustic Analysis Memo (Navy)
ACTS . . . . . . Acoustic Control and Telemetry System
ACCORDS . . . . Acoustic Correlation and Detection System
ADAC . . . . . . Acoustic Data Analysis Center
ADL . . . . Acoustic Delay Line
ADF . . . . Acoustic Depth Finder
ADD . . . . Acoustic Discrimination of Decoys
AHT . . . . Acoustic Homing Torpedo
AIR . . . . Acoustic Intercept Receiver
AMOS . . . . . Acoustic, Meteorological & Oceanographic Survey
ANE . . . . Acoustic Noise Environment
ANG . . . . Acoustic Noise Generator
ARE . . . . Acoustic Radiation Element
AR . . . . Acoustic Reflex
ARU . . . . Acoustic Resistance Unit
ASPS . . . . . . Acoustic Ship Positioning System
ATBT . . . . . . Acoustic Telemetry Bathythermometer
ATL . . . . Acoustic Test Laboratory
ATS . . . . Acoustic Transmission System
AWA . . . . Acoustic Wave Analysis
AWAS . . . . . . Acoustic Wave Analysis System
AAC . . . . Acoustical Absorption Coefficient
AAL . . . . Acoustical Absorption Loss
AAC . . . . Acoustical Attenuation Constant
ADI . . . . . . Acoustical Door Institute
ACOUSTINT . . Acoustical Intelligence (Military)
AMA . . . . Acoustical Materials Association
APC . . . . Acoustical Phase Constant
APC . . . . Acoustical Plaster Ceiling (Technical drawings)
APC . . . . Acoustical Propagation Constant
ACSOC . . . . . Acoustical Society of America
ASA . . . . Acoustical Society of America
ATC . . . . Acoustical Test Chamber
ATC . . . . Acoustical Tile Ceiling (Technical drawings)
AL . . . . Acoustics Laboratory
AOJ . . . . Acquire on Jam
AR . . . . Acquisition RADAR
AOS . . . . . . Acquisition of Signal
AOT . . . . Acquisition on Target
ATS . . . . Acquisition Target and Search
ATSS . . . . . . Acquisition and Tracking Seeker Subsystem
ATS . . . . Acquisition and Tracking System
A . . . . Acre
AF . . . . Acre-Foot
ACORN . . . . . Acronym-Oriented Nut
ANGELL . . . . . Acronymic Nonsense Game to Eliminate Lack of Loot
AID . . . . . Acronyms and Initialisms Dictionary (A reference publication)
AT . . . . Across Tape (Curve)
AEI . . . . Acrylic Eye Illustrator (Medical)
AN . . . . Acrylonitrile (Chemical)
ABS . . . . Acrylonitrile Butadiene Styrene (Chemical)
A . . . . Act, Acting, Active, or Activity
AITA . . . . Act Inside the Army (European antiwar group)
AA . . . . Acting Appointment
AAQM . . . . . . Acting Assistant Quartermaster (Marine Corps)
ACTPC . . . . . Acting Pay Clerk
ACTSECNAV . . Acting Secretary of the Navy
ATRO . . . . . . Acting Transportation Officer
Ac . . . . Actinium (Chemical element)
ABCD . . . . . . Action for Boston Community Development
ACC . . . . Action Change Card
ACAAR . . . . . Action Committee on American-Arab Relations
ACNEE . . . . . Action Committee for Narcotics Education and Enforcement
ACO . . . . Action Cut-Out
AG . . . . Action Group (Nigeria)
AICO . . . . . . Action Information Control Officer (Navy)
AIDS . . . . . . Action Information Display System
AIO . . . . Action Information Organization
AITC . . . . . . Action Information Training Center
AIU . . . . Action for Interracial Understanding
ACTO . . . . . . Action Officer (Army)
AO . . . . Action Officer
AP . . . . Action Potential

AR . . . . Action Register
ASH . . . . . . Action on Smoking and Health (Antismoking organization)
AST . . . . Action Sociale Tchadienne (Chadian Social Action)
AS . . . . Action Socialiste (Socialist Action) (Congo)
ASC . . . . Action Socialiste Congolaise (Congolese Socialist Action)
AST . . . . Action Speed Tactical
ASCGW . . . . . Action-Study Center for a Governed World
AT . . . . Action Taken
A/T . . . . Action Taken
A/T . . . . Action Time (Air Force)
APTI . . . . Actions Per Time Interval
AA . . . . Activation Analysis
AWN . . . . . . Activation Work Notice
AAD . . . . Active Acoustic Device
ACM . . . . . . Active Counter Measures
ACDU . . . . . . Active Duty
AD . . . . Active Duty
ADBD . . . . . . Active Duty Base Date (Navy)
ADC . . . . Active Duty Commitment
ADSC . . . . . . Active Duty Service Commitment (Military)
ACDUTRA . . . . Active Duty Training (Military)
ACDUINS . . . . Active Duty Under Instruction (Navy)
AEGIS . . . . . . Active Electronic Gimballess Inertial System
AEA . . . . Active Element Array
AEG . . . . Active Element Group (QCR)
AFCS . . . . . . Active Federal Commissioned Service
AFN . . . . Active Filter Network
AFS . . . . Active Fuzing System
ACT/IC . . . . . Active--In Commission (Vessel status)
ACT/IS . . . . . Active--In Service (Vessel status)
AIM . . . . Active Inert Missile
AI . . . . Active Ingredient
AID . . . . Active Integral Defense
AMDT . . . . . . Active Maintenance Down Time
AMT . . . . Active Maintenance Time
ANS . . . . Active Network Synthesis
AOF . . . . Active Optical Fuze
AOFS . . . . . . Active Optical Fuzing System
ACT/OC . . . . . Active--Out of Commission (Vessel status)
ACT/OS . . . . . Active--Out of Service (Vessel status)
APCN . . . . . . Active Pulse Compression Network
ARS . . . . Active Repeater Satellite (Air Force)
AR . . . . Active Resistance (Occupational therapy)
ARLSEA . . . . . Active-Retired Lighthouse Service Employees' Association
ASAC . . . . . . Active Satellite Attitude Control
ASP . . . . Active SONAR Processor
ASFIR . . . . . . Active Swept-Frequency Interferometer Radar (RADC)
AOT . . . . Active on Target
ATV . . . . Active Tattic Vibration
ATC . . . . Active Thermal Control
ATC . . . . Active Transfer Command
AVIS . . . . . . Active Vibration Isolation System
ADL . . . . Activities of Daily Living (Medicine)
ACTREP . . . . . Activities Report (Shipping)
ABLE . . . . . . Activity Balance Line Evaluation (PERT)
ACN . . . . Activity Control Number
AIO . . . . Activity, Interest, and Opinion (Factor Scores) (Marketing)
AMR . . . . Activity Metabolic Rate
AEA . . . . Actors' Equity Association
AFA . . . . Actors' Fund of America
ACV . . . . Actual Cash Value
AEA . . . . Actual Expenses Allowable (Military)
AGW . . . . . . Actual Gross Weight (Railroads)
AGZ . . . . Actual Ground Zero (Nuclear explosions)
AMW . . . . . . Actual Measurement Weight (Railroad)
ATN . . . . Actual Test Number (NASA)
ATA . . . . Actual Time of Arrival
ATD . . . . Actual Time of Departure
ATF . . . . Actual Time of Fall
ATI . . . . Actual Time of Interception
ATOT . . . . . . Actual Time Over Target
ATP . . . . Actual Time of Penetration (Aviation)
ATRLS . . . . . . Actual Time of Release (Aviation)
ATRO . . . . . . Actual Time of Return to Operation
AW . . . . Actual Weight
A/W . . . . Actual Weight (Business and trade)
ASA . . . . Actuarial Society of America
ARD . . . . Acute Respiratory Disease (Medicine)
ACP . . . . Acyl Carrier Protein
ACAH . . . . . . Acylcholine Acyl-Hydrolase
AF . . . . Ad Finem (At the End; To the End)

AHV . . . . Ad Hanc Vocem (At This Word)
AHGMR . . . . . Ad Hoc Group on Missile Reliability
AI . . . . Ad Interim (In the Meantime)
INT . . . . Ad Interim Specification (Navy)
AMDG . . . . . . Ad Majorem Dei Gloriam (To the Greater Glory of God)
AU . . . . Ad Usum (According to Custom)
AV . . . . Ad Valorem (According to Value)
AGT . . . . Adage Graphics Terminal
ADX . . . . Adams Express Company (NYSE symbol)
ALL . . . . Adams-Millis Corporation (NYSE symbol)
ADAM . . . . . . Adams National Historic Site
ASC . . . . Adams State College (Colorado)
AL . . . . Adaptation Level
AMP . . . . Adaptation Mathematical Processor
AIDE . . . . Adapted Identification Decision Equipment
ASTRA . . . . . Adapted Swimming-Pool Tank Reactor, Austria
ABP . . . . Adapter, Binding Post
AB . . . . Adapter Booster
AB . . . . Adapter, Bulkhead
AC . . . . Adapter Cable
AP . . . . Adapter Panel
ARA . . . . Adapter, Right Angle
AS . . . . Adapter, Straight
ASUT . . . . . . Adapter Sub-Unit Tester
AT . . . . Adapter, Tee
ADAPT . . . . . . Adaption of Automated Program Tools
AEN . . . . Adaption Error Note
AK . . . . Adaption Kit (Army)
ACP . . . . Adaptive Control Process
ACS . . . . Adaptive Control System
AFCS . . . . . . Adaptive Flight Control System
AMNIP . . . . . Adaptive Man-Machine Nonarithmetic Information Processing (Documentation)
APPECS . . . . . Adaptive Pattern Perceiving Electronic Computer System
APAR . . . . . . Adaptive Phase Array RADAR
APACS . . . . . Adaptive Planning and Control Sequence (Marketing)
AIM . . . . Add, Initial, Multiprecision
AMP . . . . Add, Multi-Precision
AOS . . . . Add or Subtract
AS . . . . Add-Subtract
AST . . . . Add-Subtract Time
ALTU . . . . . . Adder, Logical, and Transfer Unit (Computer)
AD . . . . Addict (Drug) (Slang)
AA . . . . Addicts Anonymous
AAFSC . . . . . Additional Air Force Specialty Code
ACM . . . . Additional Crew Member (Military)
ADDU . . . . . . Additional Duty
AMP . . . . Additional Military Production
AP . . . . Additional Premium (Insurance)
ASF . . . . Additional Selection Factor
AMOS . . . . . . Additionally Awarded Military Occupational Specialty
ACP . . . . Additive Color Process
AXT . . . . Address to Index, True
AIG . . . . Address Indicating Group
ALL . . . . Address Locator Logic
APC . . . . Address Plate Cabinet
AMCD . . . . . . Addressograph Multigraph Copier Duplicator
AIN . . . . Addressograph-Multigraph Corporation (NYSE symbol)
AD . . . . Aden Airways
ATUC . . . . . . Aden Trade Union Congress
A . . . . Adenine
ADP . . . . Adenosine Diphosphate
AMP . . . . Adenosine Monophosphate
APS . . . . Adenosine Phosphosulfate
ADT . . . . Adenosine Triphosphate (Chemical)
ATP . . . . Adenosine Triphosphate
AA . . . . Adenylic Acid
ABR . . . . Adhesive Bonding Repair
AIM . . . . Adhesive Insulation Material
ASC . . . . Adhesive and Sealant Council
ABJ . . . . Adhesively Bonded Joint (or Junction)
AMAA . . . . . . Adhesives Manufacturers Association of America
ALICE . . . . . . Adiabatic Low-Energy Injection and Capture Experiment
ADN . . . . Adiponitrile (Chemical)
AHA . . . . Adirondack Historical Association
ATIS . . . . . . Adirondack Trail Improvement Society
AWARE . . . . . Adirondack World Affairs Resources for Education
ACA . . . . Adjacent Channel Attenuation
ACI . . . . Adjacent Channel Interference
ACR . . . . Adjacent Channel Rejection
A . . . . Adjective

ACL . . . . Adjective Check List
AWF . . . . Adjoint Wave Function
Adj A . . . . . . Adjunct in Arts
APF . . . . Adjustable Pawl Fastener
APD . . . . Adjustable Pitch Device
APC . . . . Adjustable Pressure Conveyor
ASA . . . . Adjustable Shock Absorber
ASD . . . . Adjustable Speed Drive
ASK . . . . Adjustable Stroke Kit
ATWS . . . . . . Adjustable Thermal Wire Stripper
AVS . . . . Adjustable Voltage Screwdown
AWS . . . . Adjustable Wire Stripper
AZAR . . . . . . Adjustable Zero Adjustable Range
AAS . . . . Adjusted Air Speed (Navigation)
AGI . . . . Adjusted Gross Income
AC . . . . Adjustment-Calibration
A . . . . Adjutant
AGA . . . . Adjutants General Association of the United States
AGAUS . . . . . Adjutants General Association of United States
AGMIS . . . . . Adjutant General Management Information System
AG . . . . Adjutant General, Office of the
AGP . . . . Adjutant General Pool (for Army officers)
AGWAR . . . . . Adjutant General, War Department
AGC . . . . Adjutant General's Corps
AGD . . . . Adjutant General's Department (Army)
AGO . . . . Adjutant General's Office (Army)
AIG . . . . Adjutant Inspector General (Military)
A . . . . Administration
AATNU . . . . . Administration de l'Assistance Technique des Nations Unies
ADMCEN . . . . Administration Center
AGO . . . . Administration Group Office
AJB . . . . Administration of Justice Branch (US Military Government, Germany)
AO . . . . Administration Office
ARIA . . . . . . Administration, Ryukyu Islands, Army
AT (E) . . . . . . Administration of Territories (Europe)
ADANDAC . . . Administrative and Accounting Purposes
Z . . . . Administrative Aircraft (when a suffix to Navy plane designation)
AAU . . . . Administrative Area Unit (Army)
AA . . . . Administrative Assistant (to the Army Secretary)
AASA . . . . . . Administrative Assistant to the Secretary of the Army
ABDI . . . . . . Administrative Board -- Dress Industry
ADCIR . . . . . Administrative Circular
ADCOM . . . . . Administrative Command
ADCOMPHIBSPAC . . Administrative Command, Amphibious Forces, Pacific Fleet
ADCOMSUBORDCOMPHIBSPAC . . Administrative Command, Amphibious Forces, Pacific Fleet, Subordinate Command
ADCOMINPAC . . Administrative Command, Minecraft, Pacific Fleet
ACD . . . . Administrative Commitment Document
ACA . . . . Administrative Committee on Administration (UN)
ACC . . . . Administrative Committee on Coordination (of the United Nations) (Aviation)
ACUS . . . . . . Administrative Conference of the United States (A federal government body)
ACO . . . . Administrative Contracting Officers (Air Force)
APF . . . . Administrative Flagship (Navy symbol)
AIDS . . . . . . Administrative Information Data System
ADMINI . . . . . Administrative Instructions
ALT . . . . Administrative Lead Time
CAM . . . . Administrative Management Division (Coast Guard)
AMS . . . . Administrative Management Society
AM . . . . Administrative Manual
AMD . . . . Administrative and Miscellaneous Duties (RAF)
AMVM . . . . . . Administrative Motor Vehicle Management
AO-N . . . . . . Administrative Office-Navy
AOND . . . . . . Administrative Office, Navy Department
AOUSC . . . . . Administrative Office of United States Courts
AO . . . . Administrative Operations
AOB . . . . Administrative Operations Branch (CFSTI)
ADMINO . . . . Administrative Orders
APA . . . . Administrative Procedure Act (1946)
AR . . . . Administrative Ruling (US)
ASQ . . . . Administrative Science Quarterly
ASC . . . . Administrative Service Centers
ASO . . . . Administrative Service Office
ASU . . . . Administrative Service Unit
ASG . . . . Administrative Support Group (Army)
ADSOC . . . . . Administrative Support Operations Center
ATS . . . . Administrative Terminal System (IBM)
AUV . . . . Administrative Use Vehicle (Military)
AWL . . . . Administrative Weight Limitation (Military)
A . . . . Admiral

AC . . . . Admiral Commanding
ADL . . . . Admiral Corporation (NYSE symbol)
AF . . . . Admiral of the Fleet
ABQ . . . . Admiralty Berthing Officer (British)
AEL . . . . Admiralty Engineering Laboratory (Great Britain)
AEDU . . . . . . Admiralty Experimental Diving Unit (British)
AI . . . . Admiralty Islands
ALL . . . . Admiralty List of Lights (British)
ALRS . . . . . . Admiralty List of Radio Signals (British)
AML . . . . . . Admiralty Materials Laboratory (British)
AME . . . . Admiralty Mining Establishment (British)
AP . . . . Admiralty Pattern (The right procedure, the correct thing to do) (British)
ARL . . . . Admiralty Research Laboratory (British)
ASRE . . . . . . Admiralty Signal & Radar Establishment (British)
ASWE . . . . . . Admiralty Surface Weapon Establishment (British)
AUWE . . . . . . Admiralty Underwater Weapons Establishment (British)
ALUE . . . . . . Admissible Linear Unbiased Estimator (Statistics)
ART . . . . Admissible Rank Test (Statistics)
AAD . . . . Admission and Disposition (Military)
ARENA . . . . . Adoption Resource Exchange of North America
AC . . . . Adrenal Cortex (Medicine)
ACE . . . . Adrenal Cortical Extract
ACH . . . . Adrenal Cortical Hormone
AWF . . . . . . Adrenal Weight Factor
AC . . . . Adrenocorticoid (Medicine)
ACPP . . . . . . Adrenocorticopolypeptide
ACTH . . . . . . Adrenocorticotropic Hormone
ACTP . . . . . . Adrenocorticotrophic Polypeptide
ADFOR . . . . . Adriatic Force (Military)
A . . . . Adult
ACI . . . . . . Adult-Child Interaction (Test)
ACEF . . . . . . Adult Christian Education Foundation
ACME . . . . . . Adult Community Movement for Equality (Civil rights)
AEA . . . . Adult Education Association of the USA
AEP . . . . Adult Education Program
AH . . . . Adult Heart
HbA . . . . Adult Hemoglobin (Physiology)
AJE . . . . Adult Jewish Education
AO . . . . Adult Operculum
ARIA . . . . . . Adult Reading Improvement Association
ASD . . . . Adult Services Division
AVT . . . . Adult Vocational Training (HEW)
AVTP . . . . . . Adult Vocational Training Program (HEW)
ABSD . . . . . . Advance Base Section Dock (Floating drydock, first used in World War II)
ACTG . . . . . . Advance Carrier Training Group (Navy)
ADCON . . . . . Advance Concepts for Terrain Avoidance
ACS . . . . Advance Count Switch
ADC . . . . Advance Delivery of Correspondence (Military)
ADVDISC . . . . Advance Discontinuance of Allotment
AEMO . . . . . . Advance Engineering Material Order
AEM . . . . . . Advance Engineering Memorandum
AEN . . . . Advance Evaluation Note
AF . . . . Advance Freight (Shipping)
AIL . . . . Advance Information Letter (Military)
AOR . . . . Advance List of Oversea-Returnees for Reassignment (Army)
ADLOG . . . . . Advance Logistical Command (Army)
AMPSS . . . . . . Advance Manned Precision Strike System (Proposed Air Force plane)
AMO . . . . Advance Material Order
AMR . . . . Advance Material Request
AOI . . . . Advance Ordering Information
ADVPMT . . . . . Advance Payment
APMA . . . . . . Advance Payment of Mileage Authorized (Army)
APMALTA . . . Advance Payment of Monetary Allowance in Lieu of Transportation is Authorized (Army)
APSQ . . . . . . Advance Payment of Subsistence and Quarters
APTPDA . . . . . Advance Payment of Travel Per Diem Authorized (Army)
APPI . . . . Advance Planning Procurement Information (Army)
APL . . . . Advance Procurement List
AWASP . . . . . Advance Weapon Ammunition Support Point
AWSCOM . . . . Advance Weapons Support Command
AAFSS . . . . . . Advanced Aerial Fire Support System (Army)
AADS . . . . . . Advanced Air Defense System
AADW . . . . . . Advanced Air Defense Weapon
AADA . . . . . . Advanced Air Depot Area (Air Force)
AABNCP . . . . Advanced Airborne Command Post
AAPO . . . . . . Advanced Aircraft Programs Office
AATB . . . . . . Advanced Amphibious Training Base (Navy)
AAS . . . . Advanced Antenna System (Air Force)
AAAIS . . . . . . Advanced Army Airborne Indicating System
AASR . . . . . . Advanced Army System Requirements

AVB . . . . Advanced Aviation Base Ship (Navy symbol)
ABMDA . . . . . . Advanced Ballistic Missile Defense Agency
ABRES . . . . . . Advanced Ballistic Re-Entry System (BSD)
ABATU . . . . . . Advanced Base Air Task Unit
ABATU . . . . . . Advanced Base Aviation Training Unit (Navy)
ABCCTC . . . . . Advanced Base Combat Communication Training Center (Pearl Harbor)
ABCO . . . . . . Advanced Base Components (Military)
ABCD . . . . . . Advanced Base Construction Depot
ABD . . . . Advanced Base Depot (Navy)
ABDACOM . . . Advanced Base Depot Area Command
ABD . . . . Advanced Base Dock
ABIOL . . . . . . Advanced Base Initial Outfitting List (Military)
ABPA . . . . . . Advanced Base Personnel Administration
ABPO . . . . . . Advanced Base Personnel Officer
ABPU . . . . . . Advanced Base Personnel Unit
ABPG . . . . . . Advanced Base Proving Ground
ABRB . . . . . . Advanced Base Receiving Barracks
ABRD . . . . . . Advanced Base Repair Depot
ABRD . . . . . . Advanced Base Reshipment Depot
ABSD . . . . . . Advanced Base Supply Depot
ABTU . . . . . . Advanced Base Torpedo Unit
ABTU . . . . . . Advanced Base Training Unit
ABAR . . . . . . Advanced (or Alternate) Battery Acquisition RADAR
ABC . . . . Advanced Biological Capsule
ABC . . . . Advanced Biomedical Capsule
ABOSS . . . . . . Advanced Bombardment System
ACR . . . . Advanced Capabilities Radar
Adv Cert in Ed . . Advanced Certificate in Education
Adv Cert in Mus Ed . . Advanced Certificate in Music Education
ACSR . . . . . . Advanced Combat Surveillance RADAR
ACERP . . . . . . Advanced Communications-Electronics Requirements Plan (Air Force)
ACP . . . . Advanced Computational Processor (Data processing)
ACG . . . . Advanced Concepts Group
ACR . . . . Advanced Confidential Report
ACMS . . . . . . Advanced Configuration Management System
ADCP . . . . . . Advanced (Flight) Control Programmer
ACSP . . . . . . Advanced Control Signal Processor (for spacecraft)
ACP . . . . Advanced Cooperative Project (NASA)
ACT . . . . Advanced Core Test
ACIS . . . . Advanced Credit Information System
ADAM . . . . . . Advanced Data Management
ADS . . . . Advanced Data System (DOD)
ADCS . . . . . . Advanced Defense Communications Satellite
ADCSP . . . . . . Advanced Defense Communications Satellite Program
ADSCP . . . . . . Advanced Defense Satellite Communications Project
Ed A2 . . . . . . Advanced Degree in Education
ADAR . . . . . . Advanced Design Array RADAR
ADT . . . . Advanced Design Team
ADM . . . . Advanced Development Model
ADO . . . . Advanced Development Objective (Air Force)
ADP . . . . Advanced Development Plans (Air Force)
ADV . . . . Advanced Development Vehicle
ADS . . . . Advanced Display System
ADS . . . . Advanced Diving System
ADVON . . . . . Advanced Echelon (Marine Corps)
AEA . . . . Advanced Engine Aerospike
AEB . . . . Advanced Engine Bell
AECS . . . . . . Advanced Engine Control System
AEOB . . . . . . Advanced Engine Overhaul Base
AETR . . . . . . Advanced Engineering Test Reactor (AEC)
AETR . . . . . . Advanced Epithermal Thorium Reactor
A-FIRST . . . . Advanced - Far Infrared Search/Track
AFRS . . . . . . Advanced Fighter RADAR System
AFWS . . . . . . Advanced Filament Wound Structure
AFSAS . . . . . . Advanced Fire Support Avionics System
AFXF . . . . . . Advanced Flash X-Ray Facility
AFCP . . . . . . Advanced Flight Control Programmer
AFU . . . . Advanced Flying Unit (Air Force)
AFSR . . . . . . Advanced Foreign System Requirements
AFAADS . . . . . Advanced Forward Area Air Defense System
AFAADW . . . . Advanced Forward Area Air Defense Weapon
AGR . . . . Advanced Gas Cooled Reactor (Nuclear energy) (British)
AG . . . . Advanced Guard
AGS . . . . Advanced Guidance System
AIT . . . . Advanced Individual Training (Army)
AITA . . . . . . Advanced Individual Training Available (Military)
AIMS . . . . . . Advanced Inertial Measurement System
AIS . . . . Advanced Information Systems Company
AIFS . . . . . . Advanced Instruction Flying School
AIDS . . . . . . Advanced Integrated Data System
AILS . . . . . . Advanced Integrated Landing System

REVERSE ACRONYMS AND INITIALISMS DICTIONARY

ADVISOR .... Advanced Integrated Safety and Optimizing Computer
AD INTEL CEN.. Advanced Intelligence Center
ADV INTEL CEN.. Advanced Intelligence Center (Navy)
AIC .... Advanced Intelligence Center
AICPOA ..... Advanced Intelligence Center, Pacific Ocean Areas
AIMS .... Advanced Intercontinental Missile System
AJT .... Advanced Jet Trainer
ALG .... Advanced Landing Ground (Air Force)
ALIS .... Advanced Life Information System (Data processing)
ALPS .... Advanced Linear Programing System
ALPS .... Advanced Liquid Propulsion System (NASA)
ALM .... Advanced List of Materials
ALS .... Advanced Logistics Spacecraft
ALRI .... Advanced Long Range Interceptor
ALO .... Advanced Lunar Operation
ALP .... Advanced Lunar Projects
ALPL .... Advanced Lunar Projects Laboratory
ALTS .... Advanced Lunar Transportation Systems
AMIS .... Advanced Management Information System
AMI .... Advanced Manned Interceptor (US Air Force Artillery Spotting Division Interceptor)
AMP .... Advanced Manned Penetrator
AMPSS ..... Advanced Manned Penetrator Strike System
AMPS ...... Advanced Manned Penetrator System
AMSS ...... Advanced Manned Space Simulator
AMSA ...... Advanced Manned Strategic Aircraft (Air Force)
AMSAS ..... Advanced Manned Strategic Aircraft
AMT .... Advanced Manufacturing Technology
AME .... Advanced Master of Education
AMCA ...... Advanced Materiel Concepts Agency (Army)
AMRC ..... Advanced Metals Research Corporation
AMAS...... Advanced Midcourse Active System
AMWD ..... Advanced Millimeter Wave Device
AMA .... Advanced Minuteman Accelerometer
AMC .... Advanced Minuteman Computer
AMP....... Advanced Minuteman Platform
AMS .... Advanced Minuteman System
AMS ...... Advanced Missile System
AMMR ..... Advanced Multimission RADAR
AMLLV ..... Advanced Multipurpose Large Launch Vehicle
AMSA ..... Advanced Mutual Security Act
ANSR...... Advanced Naval System Requirements
ANTS....... Advanced Naval Training School
AN .... Advanced Navigator (Air Force)
ANDS ...... Advanced Navy Display System
AOB ...... Advanced Operational Base (Navy)
ADVON .... Advanced Operations Unit (Navy)
AOCR...... Advanced Optical Character Reader
AOLO ..... Advanced Orbital Launch Operations
AOAO ..... Advanced Orbiting Astronautical Observatory
AOGO ..... Advanced Orbiting Geophysical Observatory
AOSO ..... Advanced Orbiting Solar Observatory (NASA)
API .... Advanced Performance Interceptor
APS .... Advanced Personnel System
APP .... Advanced Planetary Probe
APSS ...... Advanced Planetary Spacecraft System
APBI........ Advanced Planning Briefing for Industry
APD .... Advanced Planning Document
APDSMS ..... Advanced Point Defense Surface Missile System (Navy)
APOS ...... Advanced Polar Orbiting Satellite
AP .... Advanced Post (Military)
APO....... Advanced Post Office (Military)
APCEF ..... Advanced Power Conversion Experimental Facility
APTR ...... Advanced Pressure Tube Reactor
APP .... Advanced Procurement Plan (Navy)
APE .... Advanced Production Engineering
APD .... Advanced Program Development
APC .... Advanced Programming Course (Data processing)
APC .... Advanced Propulsion Cooling
APPLE...... Advanced Propulsion Packaged Liquid Engine
ARIES ...... Advanced RADAR Information Evaluation System
ARTCS ..... Advanced RADAR Traffic Control System
ARTS ...... Advanced RADAR Traffic Control System (Air Force)
ARIS ...... Advanced Range Instrumentation Ship
ARIS....... Advanced Range Instrumentation Systems
ARTRAC .... Advanced Range Testing, Reporting, and Control
ARMF ...... Advanced Reactivity Measurement Facility (AEC)
ARDA ...... Advanced Reactor Development Associates
ARMS ...... Advanced Receiver Model System
ARS ...... Advanced Reconnaissance Satellite
ARS .... Advanced Record System (Air Force)

ARC .... Advanced Reentry Concepts
ARP .... Advanced Reentry Program (Aerospace)
ARS .... Advanced Reentry System (Aerospace)
ARCON ..... Advanced Research Consultants
ARP ...... Advanced Research Projects
ARPA ...... Advanced Research Projects Agency (Military)
ARENTS ..... ARPA (Advanced Research Projects Agency) Environmental Test Satellites
ALTAIR ...... Advanced Research Projects Agency Long-Range Tracking and Instrument RADAR
AMRAD ..... ARPA (Advanced Research Projects Agency) Measurements RADAR (Raytheon)
AMOS....... ARPA (Advanced Research Projects Agency) Mid-Course Optical Observatory
ARPAT ...... Advanced Research Projects Agency Terminal
ART .... Advanced Research and Technology
ARR .... Advanced Restricted Report
ASI .... Advanced Scientific Instruments
ASBD ...... Advanced Sea Based Deterrent (Navy)
AD SEC ..... Advanced Section (Military)
ADSC ...... Advanced Section Communication Zone (World War II)
ASCR ...... Advanced Sodium Cooled Reactor
ASTEC ..... Advanced Solar Turbo-Electric Conversion
ASLT ...... Advanced Solid Logic Technology
ASTRO ..... Advanced Spacecraft Truck/Trainer/Transport Reusable Orbiter
ASPIRE ..... Advanced Special Projects in Radiation Effects
ASG....... Advanced Studies Group (Air Force)
ASP .... Advanced Study Program
ASST ...... Advanced Supersonic Transport
ASM .... Advanced Surface Missile
ASMS ...... Advanced Surface Missile System
ASR .... Advanced Surveillance RADAR
ASMS ...... Advanced Synchronous Meteorological Satellite
ASCL ...... Advanced System Concepts Laboratory (Army)
ASP .... Advanced System Planning (Air Force)
ASD .... Advanced Systems Division (IBM)
ASL .... Advanced Systems Laboratory
ASR .... Advanced Systems Requirements
ASRD ...... Advanced Systems Research Department
ATAW...... Advanced Tactical Assault Weapon
ATAR ...... Advanced Tactical Avionics RADAR
ATBM ...... Advanced Tactical Ballistic Missile (AMC--Missile)
ATEWS ..... Advanced Tactical Electronic Warfare System
ATR .... Advanced Tactical RADAR
ATEP ...... Advanced Technical Education Program
ATTF ...... Advanced Technical Training Facility (Military)
ATS .... Advanced Technological Satellite
ATG....... Advanced Technology Group (Navy)
ATL .... Advanced Technology Laboratory (Navy)
ATR .... Advanced Test Reactor (AEC)
ATRCE ..... Advanced Test Reactor Critical Experiment (AEC)
AT .... Advanced Trainer (Air Force)
ATU .... Advanced Training Unit
ATPR ...... Advanced Triga Prototype Reactor
ATEGG ..... Advanced Turbine Engine Gas Generator
AUW .... Advanced Underwater Weapons
AUT .... Advanced Unit Training (Army)
AUJS ...... Advanced Universal Jamming System
AVDD ...... Advanced Vehicle Design Department
AVCS ...... Advanced Vidicon Camera System
AVID ...... Advanced Visual Information Display
AV .... Advanced Voyager
AWMC ...... Advanced Weapon Monitoring System
AXF .... Advanced X-Ray Facility
AMDA ...... Advances for Mutual Defense Assistance
ACNY ...... Adventurers Club of New York
AAPC ...... Advertising Agency Production Club of New York
AASI ...... Advertising Agency Service Interchange
AAW ...... Advertising Association of the West
ACB .... Advertising Checking Bureau
AC .... Advertising Council
AEF .... Advertising Educational Foundation
AFA .... Advertising Federation of America
A & MA ..... Advertising and Marketing Association
AMIN....... Advertising and Marketing International Network
AMCEA ..... Advertising Media Credit Executives Association
ARF .... Advertising Research Foundation
ASGA ..... Advertising Specialty Guild of America
ASNA ..... Advertising Specialty National Association
ATC .... Advertising Training Center (New York City)
ATA .... Advertising Typographers Association of America
ATAA ...... Advertising Typographers Association of America

AWNY . . . . . . Advertising Women of New York
A/A . . . . Advice of Allotment
ADVALT . . . . . Advice of Allotment
ADCONSEN . . (With the) Advice and Consent of the Senate
AP . . . . Advice of Payment
ADMAP . . . . . . Advise by Air Mail As Soon As Practicable
ADAML . . . . . Advise by Airmail (Army)
ADAVAL . . . . Advise Availability (Army)
ADCUS . . . . . . Advise Customs (Aviation)
ADARCO . . . . . Advise Date of Reporting in Compliance with Orders (Navy)
ADSPN . . . . . . Advise Disposition (Aviation)
ADHCA . . . . . Advise this Headquarters of Complete Action (Army)
AIA . . . . Advise If Able (Aviation)
AAP . . . . Advise If Able to Proceed (Aviation)
ADNOK . . . . . Advise If Not Correct
ADCON . . . . . Advise or Issue Instructions to All Concerned
ADLATAD . . . Advise Latest Address (Military)
AMBLADS . . . . Advise Method, Bill of Lading, and Date Shipped
APPA . . . . Advise Present Position and Altitude (Aviation)
ADRDE . . . . . . Advise Reason for Delay (Aviation)
ARAT . . . . Advise (names of) Representatives, Accommodations, and Transportation
   (desired) (Army)
ADSHIPDA . . . . Advise Shipping Data
ADSHPDAT . . . Advise Shipping Date
ASWH . . . . Advise Soldier Write Home
ADSTADIS . . . . Advise Status and/or Disposition (Army)
ADSTKOH . . . Advise Stock on Hand (Army)
AWA . . . . Advise When Able
AWE . . . . Advise When Established (Aviation)
ADA . . . . Advisory Area (Aviation)
AC . . . . Advisory Circular
ACIR . . . . Advisory Commission on Intergovernmental Relations
ACABQ . . . . . . Advisory Committee on Administrative and Budgetary Questions (UN)
ACBM . . . . . . Advisory Committee for Biology and Medicine (AEC)
ACCP . . . . Advisory Committee on Civilian Policy (World War II)
ACEP . . . . Advisory Committee on Export Policy
ACMRR . . . . . . Advisory Committee on Marine Resources Research
ACRS . . . . Advisory Committee on Reactor Safeguards (AEC)
ACVFA . . . . . Advisory Committee on Voluntary Foreign Aid (Department of State)
ACWC . . . . . Advisory Committee on Weather Control
ACCC . . . . . . Advisory Council on College Chemistry
ACFR . . . . . . Advisory Council on Federal Reports
ACME . . . . . . Advisory Council on Medical Education
ACNA . . . . . Advisory Council on Naval Affairs
ACONA . . . . Advisory Council on Naval Affairs of the Navy League
ACSP . . . . . Advisory Council on Scientific Policy
ADGRU . . . . . Advisory Group (Military)
AGARD . . . . . Advisory Group for Aerospace Research and Development (NATO)
   (Formerly, Advisory Group for Aeronautical Research and Development)
AGED . . . . . . Advisory Group on Electron Devices (Army)
AGEP . . . . . . Advisory Group on Electronic Parts (Military)
AGET . . . . . . Advisory Group on Electronic Tubes (DOD)
AGMEPS . . . . . Advisory Group on Management of Electronic Parts Specifications
AGREE . . . . . Advisory Group on Reliability of Electronics Equipment (Military)
ADR . . . . Advisory Route (Aviation)
AE . . . . Aeon
ALT . . . . Aer Lingus TTA
ABC . . . . Aerated Bread Company
ATB . . . . Aeration Test Burner (Heating)
AB . . . . Aerial Burst Bombs
ACR . . . . Aerial Combat Reconnaissance
ADLM . . . . . . Aerial Delivered Land Mine
ADS . . . . Aerial Delivery System
AFS . . . . Aerial Fire Support
AFGIS . . . . . . Aerial Free Gunnery Instructions School(s)
AFGU . . . . . . Aerial Free Gunnery Unit
AII . . . . Aerial Inspection Instrument
AMT . . . . Aerial Mail Terminal
ANCOA . . . . . Aerial Nurse Corps of America
APRO . . . . . . Aerial Phenomena Research Organization
APAC . . . . . . Aerial Photographic Analysis Center
APR . . . . Aerial Photographic Reconnaissance
AP . . . . Aerial Port
APOD . . . . . . Aerial Port of Debarkation (Air Force)
APE . . . . Aerial Port of Embarkation
APOE . . . . . . Aerial Port of Embarkation (Air Force)
APOG . . . . . . Aerial Port Group
APLO . . . . . . Aerial Port Liaison Office(r) (Air Force)
ARI . . . . Aerial Radiac Instrument
ARIS . . . . Aerial Radiac Instrument System
ARMS . . . . . . Aerial Radiological Measurements and Survey (Program)

ARMS . . . . . . Aerial Radiological Monitoring System
ARL . . . . Aerial Reconnaissance Laboratory
ARS . . . . Aerial Reconnaissance and Security
ARST . . . . . . Aerial Reconnaissance and Security Troop
ARA . . . . Aerial Rocket Artillery
ASTA . . . . . . Aerial Surveillance and Target Acquisition (Military)
AST . . . . Aerial Survey Team
AT . . . . Aerial Torpedo
ATC . . . . Aerial Tuning Condenser
ATI . . . . Aerial Tuning Inductance
AET . . . . Aerlinte Eireann Teoranta (Irish Air Lines)
ACA . . . . Aero Club of America
AGAC . . . . . . Aero Geo Astro Corporation (Fairchild division)
AITI . . . . Aero Industries Technical Institute
FINNAIR . . . . . Aero O/Y (Finnish Air Lines)
ATHODYD . . . . Aero-Thermo-Dynamic-Duct
ATSA . . . . . . Aero Transportes, SA (Mexican airline)
ARV . . . . Aeroballistic Reentry Vehicle
ABN . . . . Aerodrome Beacon
ARP . . . . Aerodrome Reference Point
AGA . . . . Aerodromes, Air Routes and Ground Aids (Aviation)
AC . . . . Aerodynamic Center
ADDPEP . . . . . . Aerodynamic Deployable Decelerator Performance Evaluation Program
AIC . . . . Aerodynamic-Influence Coefficient
AR . . . . Aerodynamic Report
ASTRO . . . . . Aerodynamic Spacecraft Two Stage Reusable Orbiter
AYC . . . . Aerodynamic Yaw Coupling
AYCP . . . . . . Aerodynamic Yaw Coupling Parameters
AAP . . . . Aerodynamics Advisory Panel (AEC)
AN . . . . Aerodynamics Note
AERL . . . . . . Aero-Elastic Research Laboratory (MIT)
ASRL . . . . . . Aeroelastic and Structures Research Laboratory (MIT)
AWT . . . . Aeroelastic Wind Tunnel
AETD . . . . . . Aero-Electronic Technology Department (Navy)
AERM . . . . . . Aerographer's Mate
AG . . . . Aerographer's Mate (Navy rating)
ADA . . . . Aerojet Differential Analyzer
AG . . . . Aerojet-General Corporation
AGC . . . . Aerojet-General Corporation
AGN . . . . Aerojet-General Nucleonics (of Aerojet-General Corporation)
ANA . . . . Aerojet Network Analyzer
AA . . . . Aerolineas Argentinas (Argentine airline)
ARG . . . . Aerolineas Argentinas (Airline)
ALITALIA . . . . . Aerolinee Italiane Internazionali (Italian International Airline)
AER OF . . . . . Aerological Officer
AMD . . . . Aero-Mechanics Department (Navy)
AMAL . . . . . . Aero-Medical Acceleration Laboratory
AAW . . . . Aeromedical Airlift Wing (Air Force)
AMEL . . . . . . Aero-Medical Equipment Laboratory
AE . . . . Aeromedical Evacuation
AMDLEVAC . . . Aeromedical Evacuation (Later, AME)
AME . . . . Aeromedical Evacuation
AECC . . . . . . Aeromedical Evacuation Control Center (Military)
AECO . . . . . . Aeromedical Evacuation Control Officer (Military)
AELO . . . . . . Aeromedical Evacuation Liaison Officer (Air Force)
AEOO . . . . . . Aeromedical Evacuation Operations Office(r) (Air Force)
AMES . . . . . . Aeromedical Evacuation System
AML . . . . Aero Medical Laboratory
AMLO . . . . . . Aeromedical Liaison Office(r) (Air Force)
AAC . . . . Aeronautical Advisory Council
AAC . . . . Aeronautical Approach Chart (Military)
AC . . . . Aeronautical Approach Charts (Air Force)
AB . . . . Aeronautical Board (Air Force)
AC . . . . Aeronautical Center (FAA)
ACCA . . . . . . Aeronautical Chamber of Commerce of America
ACIC . . . . . . Aeronautical Charting and Information Center (Air Force)
AEROCOM . . . Aeronautical Communications Equipment Corporation
ACL . . . . Aeronautical Computers Laboratory (Navy)
AEEL . . . . . . Aeronautical and Electronic Engineering Laboratory (Navy)
AEL . . . . Aeronautical Engine Laboratory (Navy)
AE . . . . Aeronautical Engineer
AED . . . . Aeronautical Engineering Duty (Navy)
AER . . . . Aeronautical Engineering Report
AERNO . . . . . Aeronautical Equipment Reference Number (Military)
AFS . . . . Aeronautical Fixed Service
AFTN . . . . . . Aeronautical Fixed Telecommunications Network
AIRL . . . . . . Aeronautical Icing Research Laboratory
AIP . . . . Aeronautical Information Publication (FAA)
AIR . . . . Aeronautical (or Aerospace) Information Report
AIS . . . . Aeronautical Information Service
AIL . . . . Aeronautical Instruments Laboratory (Military)

AL . . . . Aeronautical Laboratory
AMPR . . . . . . Aeronautical Manufacturers Planning Report
AMS . . . . Aeronautical Material Specification
AML . . . . Aeronautical Materials Laboratory
AEM . . . . Aeronautical Mobile
AMS . . . . Aeronautical Mobile Service
ANPT . . . . . . Aeronautical National Taper Pipe Threads
ANE . . . . Aeronautical & Navigation Electronics Association
AO . . . . Aeronautical Order
APEL . . . . . . Aeronautical Photographic Experimental Laboratory
APC . . . . Aeronautical Planning Chart (Military)
ARINC . . . . . Aeronautical Radio, Incorporated
ARRL . . . . . . Aeronautical Radio and RADAR Laboratory (Navy)
ARR . . . . Aeronautical Radionavigation RADAR
ARP . . . . Aeronautical (or Aerospace) Recommended Practice
ARAP . . . . . . Aeronautical Research Association of Princeton
ARC . . . . Aeronautical Research Council (British)
ARIS . . . . Aeronautical Research Institute of Sweden
ARL . . . . Aeronautical Research Laboratory (OAR)
ARS . . . . Aeronautical Research Scientist
AS . . . . Aeronautical Standards
AG . . . . Aeronautical Standards (Group), Bureau of Aeronautics (Navy)
ASG . . . . Aeronautical Standards Group (Military)
ASL . . . . Aeronautical Structures Laboratory (Navy)
ASC . . . . Aeronautical Systems Center (Air Force)
ASD . . . . Aeronautical Systems Division (AFSC)
ATO . . . . Aeronautical Telecommunications Operator
ATS . . . . Aeronautical Training Society
ATL . . . . Aeronautical Turbine Laboratory (Navy)
AF . . . . Aeronautically Fixed
AACB . . . . . . Aeronautics and Astronautics Coordinating Board (NASA)
AEROSPACE . . . Aeronautics and Space
AGPDC . . . . . Aeronutronic General Perturbations Differential Correction Program
ADC . . . . Aerophysics Development Corporation
AL . . . . Aerophysics Laboratory
APL . . . . Aero-Propulsion Laboratory (Air Force)
AQP . . . . Aeroquip Corporation (NYSE symbol)
ASS . . . . Aerosol Sampling System
A . . . . Aerospace
AAE . . . . Aerospace Ancillary Equipment
AAVS . . . . . . Aerospace Audio Visual Service (Air Force)
ABES . . . . . . Aerospace Business Environment Simulator (Computer-programmed
                 management game)
ASCAM . . . . . Aerospace Catalog Automated Microfilm, Inc.
AEROSPACECOM . . Aerospace Communications
AIRCOM . . . . . Aerospace Communications Complex (Air Force)
ACP . . . . Aerospace Computer Program (Air Force)
ACE . . . . Aerospace Control Environment (Air Force)
ACEL . . . . . . Aerospace Crew Equipment Laboratory
ADC . . . . Aerospace Defense Command (Air Force) (Formerly Air Defense Command)
ADD . . . . Aerospace Defense Division (Air Force)
ADSO . . . . . . Aerospace Defense Systems Officer (Air Force)
ADD . . . . Aerospace Digital Development
AE . . . . Aerospace Education
AEF . . . . Aerospace Education Foundation
AEI . . . . Aerospace Education Instructor
AES . . . . Aerospace Electrical Society
AES . . . . Aerospace and Electronic Systems
ASESS . . . . . . Aero-Space Environment Simulation System
AFE . . . . Aerospace Facilities Engineer
AFV . . . . Aerospace Flight Vehicle
AGE . . . . Aerospace Ground Equipment
AGED . . . . . . Aerospace Ground Equipment Department
AGEOCP . . . . . Aerospace Ground Equipment Out of Commission for Parts (Air Force)
AG . . . . Aerospace Group
AIA . . . . Aerospace Industries Association of America
AIL . . . . Aerospace Instrumentation Laboratory (Air Force)
AESIR . . . . . . Aerospace Instrumentation Range Station
AIDR . . . . . . Aerospace Internal Data Report (Air Force)
AMOS . . . . . . Aerospace Maintenance and Operational Status
AMC . . . . Aerospace Manufacturers Council
AMS . . . . Aerospace Material Specification
AMI . . . . Aerospace Materials Information
AMIC . . . . . . Aerospace Materials Information Center (Air Force)
ASMA . . . . . . Aerospace Medical Association
AMC . . . . Aerospace Medical Command (Air Force)
AMD . . . . Aerospace Medical Division (Air Force)
AMR . . . . Aerospace Medical Research
AMRL . . . . . . Aerospace Medical Research Laboratory (Air Force)
ANE . . . . Aerospace and Navigational Electronics
APRE . . . . . . Aerospace Photographic Reconnaissance Equipment

ASP . . . . Aerospace Plane
APD . . . . Aerospace Power Division (Air Force)
APC . . . . Aerospace Primus Club
ARP . . . . Aerospace Reference Project (Formerly, Aerospace Technology Division)
                 (Library of Congress)
ARRC . . . . . . Aerospace Rescue and Recovery Center
ARRS . . . . . . Aerospace Rescue and Recovery Service (Air Force)
ARAC . . . . . . Aerospace Research Applications Center (Indiana University)
ARA . . . . Aerospace Research Association
ARC . . . . Aerospace Research Chamber
ARL . . . . Aerospace Research Laboratory (Air Force)
ARPS . . . . . . Aerospace Research Pilot School (Air Force)
ARPSE . . . . . . Aerospace Research Pilot School - Edwards Air Force Base
ARS . . . . Aerospace Research Satellite
ARSP . . . . . . Aerospace Research Support Program (Air Force)
ARV . . . . Aerospace Research Vehicle
ASF . . . . Aerospace Security Force
AS . . . . Aerospace Standards
ASC . . . . Aerospace Static Converter
ASI . . . . Aerospace Static Inverter
ASM . . . . Aerospace Structural Material
AS . . . . Aerospace Studies (AFROTC)
ASI . . . . Aerospace Studies Institute (Air Force)
ASE . . . . Aerospace Support Equipment
AS & C . . . . . . Aerospace Surveillance and Control
ASCS . . . . . . Aerospace Surveillance and Control Squadron (Air Force)
ASS . . . . Aerospace Surveillance System
ASSAW . . . . . Aerospace Surveillance and Warning
ASSS . . . . . . Aerospace System Safety Society
ASSP . . . . . . Aerospace Systems Security Program
ASTR . . . . . . Aerospace Systems Test Reactor (Formerly, Aircraft Shield Test Reactor)
ATIC . . . . . . Aerospace Technical Intelligence Center
AST . . . . Aerospace Technology (NASA)
ATD . . . . Aerospace Technology Division (Formerly, Aerospace Information Division;
                 now, ARP) (Library of Congress)
ATD/LC . . . . . Aerospace Technology Division/Library of Congress
ATE . . . . Aerospace Test Equipment
ATW . . . . Aerospace Test Wing
AV . . . . Aerospace Vehicle
AVDO . . . . . . Aerospace Vehicle Distribution Office(r) (Air Force)
AVE . . . . Aerospace (or Airborne) Vehicle Equipment
ASSET . . . . . . Aerothermodynamic/Elastic Structural Systems Environmental Test
                 (Military)
AEV . . . . Aerothermodynamic Elastic Vehicle
ASV . . . . Aerothermodynamic Structural Vehicle (Air Force)
ASUD . . . . . . Aerovia Sud Americana
AREA . . . . . . Aerovias Ecuatoriana, SA
AVISPA . . . . . Aerovias Interamericanas de Panama, SA
APA . . . . Aerovias Panama Airways
AVENSA . . . . . Aerovias Venezolanas, SA (Venezuelan airline)
AA . . . . Affected Areas
ACA . . . . Affenpinscher Club of America
ABV . . . . Afferent Branchial Vein
ARV . . . . Afferent Renal Vein
AVNG . . . . . . Afferent Vein to Nephridial Gland
AV . . . . Afferent Vessel
ABC . . . . Afghan Border Crusade
AHCA . . . . . . Afghan Hound Club of America
AAAI . . . . . . Affiliated Advertising Agencies International
ACPA . . . . . . Affiliated Chiropodists-Podiatrists of America
ADM . . . . Affiliated Dress Manufacturers, Inc.
ACS . . . . Affinely Connected Space
AFL-CIO DAP . . AFL-CIO Demonstration Arts Project
AIM . . . . Africa Inland Mission
AMET . . . . . . Africa - Middle East Theater (World War II)
ASI . . . . Africa Service Institute of New York
ASOTS . . . . . . Africa South of the Sahara (Military)
AAI . . . . African-American Institute
AALC . . . . . . African-American Labor Center (AFL-CIO)
AACM . . . . . . African Anti-Colonial Movement of Kenya
AEMO . . . . . . African Elected Members Organization
AFHQ . . . . . . African Force Headquarters
AGMK . . . . . . African Green Monkey Kidney (Cells)
AFI . . . . African/Indian Ocean (Aviation)
AME . . . . African Methodist Episcopal (Church)
AMEZ . . . . . . African Methodist Episcopal Zion (Church)
ANC . . . . African National Congress (South Africa; Northern Rhodesia)
ANCYL . . . . . . African National Congress Youth League
ANPM . . . . . . African Nationalist Pioneer Movement
APTU . . . . . . African Postal and Telecommunications Union
AFRO . . . . . . African Regional Organization

ARF . . . . African Research Foundation
ASPAU . . . . . . African Scholarship Program of American Universities (Joint undertaking, headquartered in Cambridge, Mass., to provide aid to African applicants for admission to American universities)
ASA . . . . African Studies Association
ATUC . . . . . . African Trade Union Confederation (Confederation Syndical Africaine)
ATUC(SR) . . . . African Trades Union Congress of Southern Rhodesia
AVSA . . . . . . African Violet Society of America
AWLF . . . . . . African Wildlife Leadership Foundation
ACVV. . . . . . Afrikaanse Christelike Vrouevereniging
AEF . . . . Afrique Equatoriale Francaise (French Equatorial Africa)
AOF. . . . . . . Afrique Occidentale Francaise (French West Africa)
AACHS . . . . . . Afro-American Cultural and Historical Society
AAPSC . . . . Afro-Asian Peoples Solidarity Council
ASP . . . . Afro-Shirazi Party (Zanzibar)
AEA . . . . Aft End Assembly
AP . . . . Aft Perpendicular (Naval engineering)
A . . . . After
AAR . . . . After Action Report (Military)
AB . . . . After Body
ABC . . . . After Bottom Center (Valve position)
ABDC . . . . . After Bottom Dead Center
AC. . . . . After Christ
AD. . . . . After Date
ADF . . . . After Deducting Freight
ADE . . . . After Delivery Economies
AER . . . . After Engine Room
AEF . . . . After England Failed (Soldier slang for American Expeditionary Force in World War I)
ARO . . . . . . After Receipt of Order
AS . . . . After Sight
ATC . . . . After Top Center (Valve position)
AWOL . . . . . . After Women or Liquor (Slang)
AB . . . . Afterburner
A . . . . Afternoon
AFCCM . . . . . AFTN (Aeronautical Fixed Telecommunications Network) Communications
AAR . . . . Against All Risks (Business and trade)
AR . . . . Age Replacement
ARL . . . . Age Run Length
ACLO. . . . . . Agena Class Lunar Orbiter
ACS . . . . Agena Control System (NASA)
ACI . . . . Agence Congolaise d'Information (Congolese Information Agency) (Congo--Brazzaville)
ACP . . . . Agence Congolaise de Presse (Congolese Press Agency) (Leopoldville)
ADP. . . . . . . Agence Dahomeene de Presse (Dahomean Press Agency)
AEA . . . . Agence Europeenne d'Approvisionnement
AEEN . . . . . . Agence Europeenne pour l'Energie Nucleaire
AEP . . . . Agence Europeenne de Productivite
AFP . . . . Agence France Presse (French Press Agency)
AGP. . . . . . . Agence Guineene de Presse (Guinean Press Agency)
AIEA . . . . . . Agence Internationale de l'Energie Atomique
AIP . . . . Agence Ivoirienne de Presse (Ivorian Press Agency)
ANVAR . . . . . Agence Nationale pour la Valorisation de la Recherche (France)
APS . . . . Agence de Presse Senegalese (Senegalese Press Agency)
ANI . . . . Agencia Nacionale de Informacoes (National Information Agency) (Portugal)
ABPW . . . . . . Agency Broadcast Producers Workshop
ABCD . . . . . . Agency for Business and Career Development
AID . . . . Agency for International Development (State Department)
AID/PEP . . . . Agency for International Development/Private Enterprise Promotion
APR . . . . Agency Progress Report
ASECNA . . . . Agency for the Security of Air Navigation
AG. . . . . Agent General
AGG . . . . Agent to the Governor-General (British)
ANSA. . . . . . . Agenzia Nationale Stampa Associata (Associated National Press Agency) (Italy)
AGIT-PROP . . . Agitation and Propaganda (Military)
ASC . . . . Agnes Scott College (Georgia)
AYS . . . . Agni Yoga Society
AD. . . . . Agnus Dei (Lamb of God)
AAA . . . . Agricultural Adjustment Act
AAA . . . . Agricultural Adjustment Administration (or Agency)
AAF . . . . Agricultural Aids Foundation
AAA . . . . Agricultural Aircraft Association
AAI . . . . Agricultural Ammonia Institute
ABLE . . . . . . Agricultural-Biological Literature Exploitation (Systems study of National Agricultural Library)
ACP . . . . Agricultural Conservation Program (Department of Agriculture)
ACCFA . . . . . Agricultural Credit Cooperative Farmers' Association (Philippines)
ADC . . . . Agricultural Development Council
AEC . . . . Agricultural Economics Division (of AMS, Department of Agriculture)

AE . . . . Agricultural Engineer
AE . . . . Agricultural Engineering Research Division (of ARS, Department of Agriculture)
AES . . . . Agricultural Estimates Divsion (of AMS, Department of Agriculture)
AHS. . . . . . . Agricultural History Society
AHA . . . . Agricultural and Horticultural Engineering Abstracts
AI . . . . Agricultural Index
ALI . . . . Agricultural Limestone Institute
AMA . . . . . . Agricultural Marketing Adminisiration (World War II)
AMS . . . . Agricultural Marketing Service (Department of Agriculture)
A & M . . . . . Agricultural and Mechanical (in a college name)
AGPR. . . . . . Agricultural Procurement Regulations
AGPMR. . . . . . Agricultural Property Management Regulations
APA . . . . Agricultural Publishers Association
ARC . . . . Agricultural Relations Council
ARA . . . . Agricultural Research Administration (Department of Agriculture) (Superseded by ARS, 1953)
ARC . . . . Agricultural Research Center (Agriculture Department)
ARCO. . . . . . Agricultural Research Center Operations (of ARS, Department of Agriculture)
ARC . . . . Agricultural Research Council (British)
ARI . . . . Agricultural Research Institute
ARS . . . . Agricultural Research Service (US Department of Agriculture)
ASC . . . . Agricultural Stabilization and Conservation
ASCS . . . . . Agricultural Stabilization and Conservation Service (Department of Agriculture)
ATAF . . . . . . Agricultural Technical Assistance Foundation
AWO . . . . Agricultural Workers' Organization
AWOC . . . . . Agricultural Workers Organizing Committee (AFL-CIO)
ADAM . . . . . Agriculture Department's Automated Manpower
AFDC . . . . . . Agriculture and Fishery Development Corporation (South Korea)
A & F . . . . . . Agriculture and Forestry Committee (US Senate)
A & I . . . . . . Agriculture and Industrial (in a college name)
ALPPA . . . . . Agriculture and Livestock Professional Photographers Association
A & T . . . . . Agriculture and Technical (in a college name)
AIWO. . . . . . Agudas Israel World Organization
AI . . . . Agudat Israel (Union of Israel) (World organization of Orthodox Jews)
AIA . . . . Agudath Israel of America
AW . . . . Ahnapee & Western Railway Company (AAR code)
AABD . . . . . . Aid to the Aged, Blind, or Disabled
AAL . . . . Aid Association for Lutherans
AB . . . . Aid to the Blind
ADC. . . . . . . Aid to Dependent Children
AFDC . . . . . . Aid to Families with Dependent Children
AFDC-UP . . . . Aid to Families With Dependent Children - Unemployed Parents (HEW)
AIM . . . . Aid for International Medicine (An organization)
APTD . . . . . . Aid to the Permanently and Totally Disabled
ADC. . . . . . . Aide-de-Camp (Military)
AVDP . . . . . . Aided Visual Development Program
AVS . . . . Aided Visual System
ALSAC . . . . . Aiding Leukemia Stricken American Children (Fund-raising organization)
ATON . . . . . . Aids to Navigation
ANRAC. . . . . . Aids Navigation Radio Control (Military)
ARC . . . . Aiken Relay Calculator
APM. . . . . . . Aim-Point-Miss
AP . . . . Aiming Point
APD . . . . Aiming Point Determination
A . . . . Air
AAFC . . . . . . Air Accounting and Finance Center (Air Force)
AAG . . . . Air Adjutant-General
AA. . . . . Air-to-Air
A-A . . . . Air-to-Air
A/A . . . . Air-to-Air
ATA . . . . Air to Air
AAGR . . . . . . Air-to-Air Gunnery Range
AAI . . . . Air-to-Air Identification
AAI . . . . Air-to-Air Intercept
AAM . . . . . . Air-to-Air Missile
G . . . . Air or Army National Guard (Military aircraft identification prefix)
AAC. . . . . . . Air Approach Control
AAH. . . . . . . Air Arc Heater
AAHH. . . . . . Air Arc Heater Housing
AAD . . . . Air Assault Division (Army)
ATM . . . . . . Air Atlas/Air Maroc
AIRA . . . . . . Air Attache (Air Force)
AAR . . . . Air Augmented Rocket
AARPS . . . . . Air Augmented Rocket Propulsion System
AB . . . . Air Bags
ABMD . . . . . . Air Ballistics Missile Division (Air Force)
AB . . . . Air Base
AIRBASECOM . . Air Base Commander

ADAM ...... Air Base Damage Assessment Model
ABG........ Air Base Group (Navy)
ABGP ...... Air Base Group (Air Force)
ABS .... Air Base Simulator (Air Force)
ABS .... Air Base Squadron (Air Force)
ABW .... Air Base Wing (Air Force)
ABWG ...... Air Base Wing (Air Force)
AB ONE ..... Air Bases Command, 1st Naval District
ABC .... Air Bath Chamber
ABACUS ..... Air Battle Analysis Center, US Air Force
ABAD ...... Air Battle Analysis Division (Air Force)
ABCB ...... Air-Blast Circuit Breaker
ABL .... Air Blast Loading
ABV .... Air Blast Valve
AB .... Air Bomber
ABTU ...... Air Bombers Training Unit (Navy)
ABA .... Air Brake Association
ABS .... Air-Break Switch
ABS .... Air Breathing System
ABC .... Air Bubble Craft
ABV .... Air Bubble Vehicle
ABE .... Air Burst Effect
ACG .... Air Cargo Express, Inc.
ACG .... Air Cargo Glider
AACP ...... Air Carrier Contract Personnel
ACDO ...... Air Carrier District Office
ACFEA ..... Air Carrier Flight Engineers Association
ACMA...... Air Carrier Mechanic Association
ACSDO..... Air Carrier Safety District Office
ACSC ...... Air Carrier Service Corporation
ACC .... Air Center Commander
AIRCEY..... Air Ceylon Limited (Airline)
ACM .... Air Chief Marshal (British)
ACB .... Air Circuit Breaker
ACTA ...... Air Coach Transport Association
ACES ...... Air Collection Engine System
ACE .... Air Collection and Enrichment
ACES ...... Air Collection & Enrichment System
ACI .... Air Combat Information
ACI .... Air Combat Intelligence (Navy)
ACIO ...... Air Combat Intelligence Office(r) (Navy)
ACM .... Air Combat Maneuvering
ACT .... Air Combat Tactics
ACSEA ..... Air Command, Southeast Asia
ACSC ...... Air Command Staff College (Air Force)
AC & SC .... Air Command and Staff College (of the Air University)
ACSS ...... Air Command and Staff School
AC & SS .... Air Command and Staff School
COMAIRCANLANT .. Air Commander Canadian Atlantic Subarea
COMAIRCENTLANT .. Air Commander Central Atlantic Subarea
CINCAIREASTLANT.. Air Commander-in-Chief Eastern Atlantic Area
COMAIRNORECHAN.. Air-Commander, Nore Subarea Channel
COMAIRNORLANT .. Air Commander Northern Atlantic Subarea
COMAIRPLYMCHAN.. Air-Commander, Plymouth Subarea Channel
ACM .... Air Commerce Manual
A/C........ Air Commodore (RAF and RCAF)
AIRCOMNET .. Air Communications Network
AC & W...... Air Communications and Weather (Group) (Navy)
ACI .... Air Commuter, Incorporated
ACC....... Air Component Command (Air Force)
ACRC ...... Air Compressor Research Council
ARI .... Air-Conditioning and Refrigeration Institute
ARW .... Air-Conditioning and Refrigeration Wholesalers
AC .... Air Conduction
ACC .... Air Control Center (Air Force)
ACP........ Air Control Point
AIR .... Air Control Products, Inc. (NYSE symbol)
ACT .... Air Control Team (Air Force)
ACW .... Air(craft) Control and Warning (Military)
ACI ...... Air-Controlled Interception
AC .... Air Controlman
AC/OC ..... Air Co-operation Command (British Royal Air Force)
ACC........ Air Coordinating Committee (Governmental policy body for civil aviation in US; terminated, 1962)
ACCASP ..... Air Coordinating Committee, Airspace Subcommittee
ACC/COM ... Air Coordinating Committee Communications Subcommittee
ACC/MET ... Air Coordinating Committee Meteorological Subcommittee
AIRCO ..... Air Coordinator (Air Force)
AC .... Air Corps
ACMF....... Air Corps Medical Forces
ACTS .... Air Corps Tactical School

ACTR .... Air Corps Technical Report
ACM .... Air Court Martial
ACEL .... Air Crew Equipment Laboratory (Navy)
ACLG ...... Air-Cushion Landing Gear
ACT .... Air Cushion Trailer
ACV .... Air-Cushion Vehicle
ADC .... Air Data Computers (or Computing)
ADCS ...... Air Data Computing System
ADC .... Air Data Converter
ADM .... Air Decoy Missile
ADO .... Air Defence Officer (British Navy)
AD .... Air Defense (Air Force)
ADASP ..... Air Defense Annual Service Practice
ADA .... Air Defense Area (Army)
ADAR ...... Air Defense Area
ADA .... Air Defense Artillery (Air Force)
ADAC...... Air Defense Artillery Complex
ADAD ...... Air Defense Artillery, Director (Air Force)
ADAOD ..... Air Defense Artillery Operations Detachment
ADAOO ..... Air Defense Artillery Operations Officer
ADC .... Air Defense Command (Air Force)
ADCCC..... Air Defense Command Commendation Certificate
CANAIRDEF... Air Defense Command Headquarters, St. Hubert, Province of Quebec, Canada
ADCP ...... Air Defense Command Post
AIRDEFCOM .. Air Defense Commander
ADCO ...... Air Defense Communications Office
ADCC ...... Air Defense Control Center (Air Force)
ADCAT ..... Air Defense Control and Targets Office (Army)
ADDA ...... Air Defense Defended Area (Army)
ADDP...... Air Defense Defended Point (Army)
ADDC ...... Air Defense Direction Center (Air Force)
ADE .... Air Defense Element
ADX .... Air Defense Exercise
ADFC ...... Air Defense Filter Center (Military)
ADF .... Air Defense Force
ADGB ...... Air Defense of Great Britain
ADGE....... Air Defense Ground Environment
ADG .... Air Defense Group
ADIL ...... Air Defense Identification Line (Air Force)
ADIZ ...... Air Defense Identification Zone (Air Force, FAA)
ADI .... Air Defense Institute
ADI .... Air Defense Intercept (Air Force)
ADIP ...... Air Defense, Interdiction and Photographic
ADIS ...... Air Defense Integrated System (Military)
ADLO....... Air Defense Liaison Officer
ADMO ...... Air Defense Management Office
ADM .... Air Defense Missile
ADOC ...... Air Defense Operations Center (Air Force)
ADPB ...... Air Defense Planning Board
ADP........ Air Defense Position (Military)
ADRDE ..... Air Defense Research and Development Establishment
ADS .... Air Defense Sector (Air Force)
ADS .... Air Defense System
ADSEC ...... Air Defense System Engineering Committee
ADSMO ..... Air Defense System Management Office (Air Force)
ADSC ...... Air Defense Systems Command
ADSID ..... Air Defense Systems Integration Division (Air Force)
ADVUL ...... Air Defense Vulnerability Simulation
ADW .... Air Defense Warning (Air Force)
ADWKP...... Air Defense Warning Key Point
ADW .... Air Defense Weapon
ADAM ..... Air Deflection and Modulation (Air Force)
ADW .... Air Denial Weapon
AD-A .... Air Density A (Explorer satellite)
ADE .... Air Density Explorer (Satellite)
AD/I .... Air Density/Injun (Explorer satellite)
AD......... Air Depot
A/D........ Air Depot
ADEP ...... Air Depot (Army)
ADSAS ..... Air-Derived Separation Assurance System
ADC....... Air Development Center (Air Force)
ADF .... Air Development Force
AIRDEVRON .. Air Development Squadron
ADS .... Air Development Station (Navy)
ADC .... Air Diffusion Council
ADF .... Air Direction Finder
ADLS ...... Air Dispatch Letter Service (Navy)
ADI ...... Air Distribution Institute
AD .... Air Division
A DIV....... Air Division (Air Force)

AD . . . . Air-Dried (Lumber)
ADAA . . . . . . Air Driven Air Amplifier
AES . . . . Air and Earth Shock
AIRELO . . . . . Air Electrical Officer
AEG . . . . Air Encephalogram (Medicine)
AEO . . . . Air Engineer Officer
AIREO . . . . . . Air Engineer Officer
AEDD . . . . . . Air Engineering Development Division (Air Force)
AE & S . . . . . Air Equipment and Support
AE . . . . Air Escape (Technical drawings)
AEVAC . . . . . Air Evacuation
AIREVAC . . . . Air Evacuation
E . . . . Air Evacuation (Military aircraft identification prefix)
AIREVACWING . . Air Evacuation Wing
AESQ . . . . . . Air Explorer Squadron
AXPS . . . . . . Air Express
AEI . . . . Air Express International
AIRFERONS . . . Air Ferry Squadrons (Navy)
AF . . . . Air Filter
AFI . . . . Air Filter Institute
AFMF . . . . . . Air Fleet Marine Force
AFAS . . . . . . Air Flow Actuated Switch
AFI . . . . Air Flow Indicator
AF . . . . Air Force
AFA . . . . . . Air Force Academy
AFAAEC . . . . . Air Force Academy and Aircrew Examining Center
AFAB . . . . . . Air Force Academy Board
AFAFC . . . . . Air Force Accounting and Finance Center
AFADVMC . . . . Air Force Advanced Management Class
AFASD . . . . . . Air Force Aeronautical Systems Division
AFAPL . . . . . . Air Force Aero-Propulsion Laboratory
AFAFFO . . . . . Air Force Aerospace Fuels Field Office
AARS . . . . . . Air Force Aerospace Rescue and Recovery Service
AFAI . . . . Air Force Agent Installation
AFAS . . . . . . Air Force Aid Society
AFAC . . . . . . Air Force Armament Center
AFATL . . . . . . Air Force Armament Technology Laboratory
AFWA . . . . . . Air Force with Army
AFA . . . . Air Force Association
AFA-SEF . . . . . Air Force Association – Space Education Foundation
AIRA . . . . . . Air Force Attache
AFAB . . . . . . Air Force Audit Branch
AFAUX . . . . . . Air Force Auxiliary Field
AFAL . . . . . . Air Force Avionics Laboratory
AFBMA . . . . . Air Force Ballistic Missile Arsenal
AFBMC . . . . . . Air Force Ballistic Missile Committee
AFBMD . . . . . . Air Force Ballistic Missile Division
AFBMTC . . . . . Air Force Ballistic Missiles Training Center
AFBSD . . . . . . Air Force Ballistic Systems Division
AFB . . . . Air Force Base
AFBU . . . . . . Air Force Base Unit
AFBR . . . . . . Air Force Board of Review
AFB . . . . Air Force Bulletin
AFCRC . . . . . . Air Force Cambridge Research Center
AFCRL . . . . . . Air Force Cambridge Research Laboratory
AFCWF . . . . . . Air Force Civilian Welfare Fund
AFCC . . . . . . Air Force Combat Command
AFCCDC . . . . . Air Force Command and Control Development Center
AFCCS . . . . . . Air Force Command and Control System
AFCP . . . . . . Air Force Command Post
AFCM . . . . . . Air Force Commendation Medal
AFCC . . . . . . Air Force Communication Center
AFCOM . . . . . Air Force Communications (Satellite)
AFCOMSEC . . . Air Force Communications Security
AFCSL . . . . . . Air Force Communications Security Letter
AFCOMSECM . . Air Force Communications Security Manual
AFCSM . . . . . Air Force Communications Security Manual
AFCS . . . . . . Air Force Communications Service
AFCOMMSTA . . Air Force Communications Station
AFCSS . . . . . . Air Force Communications Support System
AFCCP . . . . . . Air Force Component Command Post
AFCC . . . . . . Air Force Component Commander
AFCMD . . . . . . Air Force Contract Management Division
AFCOA . . . . . . Air Force Contracting Office Approval
AFCO . . . . . . Air Force Contracting Officer
AFCEL . . . . . . Air Force Contractor Experience List
AFCON . . . . . Air Force Controlled (Units)
AFCRP . . . . . . Air Force Cost Reduction Program
AFC . . . . Air Force Council (Advisory board to Air Force)
AFC . . . . Air Force Cross (British)
AFKAG . . . . . . Air Force Cryptographic Aid, General

AFCD . . . . . . Air Force Cryptologic Depot
AFDATACOM . Air Force Data Communications System
AFDASTA . . . . Air Force Data Station
AFDSDC . . . . . Air Force Data System Design Center
AFDB . . . . . . Air Force Decorations Board
AFDCCO . . . . Air Force Departmental Catalog Coordinating Office
AFDIERSS . . . . Air Force Departmental Industrial Equipment Reserve Storage Site
AFD . . . . Air Force Depot
AFDAT . . . . . . Air Force Directorate of Advanced Technology
AFDRB . . . . . . Air Force Disability Review Board
AFDRB . . . . . . Air Force Discharge Review Board
AFETR . . . . . . Air Force Eastern Test Range
AFERB . . . . . . Air Force Educational Requirements Board
AFERC . . . . . . Air Force Edwards Research Center
AFESD . . . . . . Air Force Electronic Systems Division
AFETS . . . . . . Air Force Engineering and Technical Service
AFEMS . . . . . . Air Force Equipment Management System
AFE . . . . Air Force in Europe
AFES . . . . . . Air Force Exchange Service
AFFE . . . . . . Air Force Far East
AFFLC . . . . . . Air Force Film Library Center
AFFC . . . . . . Air Force Finance Center
AFN . . . . Air Force Finance Center
AFFDL . . . . . . Air Force Flight Dynamics Laboratory
AFFTC . . . . . . Air Force Flight Test Center (AFSC)
AFFTC . . . . . . Air Force Flying Training Command
AFGWRP . . . . . Air Force Global Weather Reconnaissance Program
AFGCM . . . . . Air Force Good Conduct Medal
GW . . . . Air Force Guide for Writing
AFHQ . . . . . . Air Force Headquarters
AFHC . . . . . . Air Force Headquarters Command
CANAIRHED . . . Air Force Headquarters, Ottawa, Ontario, Canada
AFHF . . . . . . Air Force Historical Foundation
AFH . . . . Air Force Hospital
AFIF . . . . Air Force Industrial Fund
AFISR . . . . . . Air Force Industrial Security Regulations
AFIR . . . . Air Force Installation Representative
AFIRO . . . . . . Air Force Installation Representative Officer
AFIT . . . . . . Air Force Institute of Technology
AFICCS . . . . . . Air Force Integrated Command and Control System
AFIC . . . . Air Force Intelligence Center
AIDS . . . . . . Air Force Intelligence Data Handling System (ESD)
AFJ . . . . Air Force Jet
AFJKT . . . . . . Air Force Job Knowledge Test
AFJROTC . . . . . Air Force Junior Reserve Officers Training Corps
AFL . . . . Air Force Letter
AFL . . . . Air Force Liaison
AFLC . . . . . . Air Force Logistics Command
AFLCON . . . . . Air Force Logistics Communications Network
AFLMC . . . . . . Air Force Logistics Management Center
AFLSA . . . . . . Air Force Longevity Service Award
AFM . . . . Air Force Manuals
AFMRB . . . . . . Air Force Material Review Board
AFML . . . . . . Air Force Materials Laboratory
AFM . . . . Air Force Medal (British)
AFMMFO . . . . Air Force Medical Materiel Field Office
AFMPA . . . . . . Air Force Medical Publications Agency
AFMS . . . . . . Air Force Medical Service
AFMSC . . . . . Air Force Medical Specialist Corps
AF -- MIPR . . . Air Force -- Military Interdepartmental Purchase Requests
AFMDC . . . . . . Air Force Missile Development Center (AFSC)
AFMTC . . . . . . Air Force Missile Test Center
AFM . . . . Air Force Museum
AFNRD . . . . . . Air Force National Range Division
AFNA . . . . . . Air Force – Navy
AN . . . . Air Force-Navy
ANA . . . . Air Force-Navy Aeronautical
ANC . . . . Air Force-Navy-Civil
AND . . . . Air Force-Navy Design
AFNETSTA . . . Air Force Networks Station
AFNEA . . . . . . Air Force NOTAM Exchange Area
AFNEO . . . . . . Air Force NOTAM Exchange Office
AF NETF . . . . . Air Force Nuclear Engineering Test Facility (Reactor)
AFNC . . . . . . Air Force Nurse Corps
AFOS . . . . . . Air Force Objective Series (Papers)
AFOAR . . . . . . Air Force Office of Aerospace Research (AFSC)
AFOAS . . . . . . Air Force Office of Aerospace Sciences (AFOAR)
AFOAT . . . . . . Air Force Office of Atomic Energy
AFORA . . . . . . Air Force Office of Research Analysis
AFOSR . . . . . . Air Force Office of Scientific Research
AFOIC . . . . . . Air Force Officer in Charge

REVERSE ACRONYMS AND INITIALISMS DICTIONARY

AFOEP . . . . . . Air Force Officer Education Program
AFOQT . . . . . . Air Force Officer Qualifying Test
AFOREP . . . . . Air Force Operational Report
AFOTC . . . . . . Air Force Operational Test Center
AFOC . . . . . . Air Force Operations Center
AFOSCR . . . . . Air Force Organization Status Change Report
AFOUA . . . . . Air Force Outstanding Unit Award
AFOUAR . . . . . Air Force Outstanding Unit Award Ribbon
AFORD . . . . . . Air Force Overseas Replacement Depot (World War II)
AFORG . . . . . . Air Force Overseas Replacement Group
AFPEA . . . . . . Air Force Packaging Evaluation Agency
AFPL . . . . Air Force Packaging Laboratory
AFP . . . . Air Force Pamphlet
AFPB . . . . Air Force Personnel Board
AFPC . . . . . . Air Force Personnel Council
AFWAR . . . . . . Air Force Personnel on Duty with Army
AFWN . . . . . . Air Force Personnel on Duty with Navy
AFPG . . . . Air Force Personnel Processing Group
AFPT . . . . Air Force Personnel Test
AFPTRC . . . . . Air Force Personnel and Training Research Center
AFPRDS . . . . . . Air Force Petroleum Retail Distribution Station
AFPDAB . . . . . Air Force Physical Disability Appeal Board
AFP . . . . Air Force Plant
AFPR . . . . Air Force Plant Representative
AFPRO . . . . . . Air Force Plant Representative Office
APO . . . . Air Force Post Office
AFPU . . . . Air Force Postal Unit
AFPC . . . . Air Force Procurement Circulars
AFPI . . . . Air Force Procurement Instructions
AFPP . . . . Air Force Procurement Procedures
AFPEB . . . . . . Air Force Professional Entertainment Branch
AFPO . . . . Air Force Property Officer
AFQAR . . . . . . Air Force Quality Assurance Representative
AFQC . . . . . . Air Force Quality Control
AFQCR . . . . . . Air Force Quality Control Representative
AFRC . . . . . . Air Force Records Center
AFRAMS . . . . . Air Force Recoverable Assembly Management System
AFRCE . . . . . . Air Force Regional Civil Engineers
AFR . . . . Air Force Regulations
AFRS . . . . Air Force Rescue Service
AFRD . . . . Air Force Research Division
AFRTD . . . . . . Air Force Research and Technology Division
AFR . . . . Air Force Reserve
AFRES . . . . Air Force Reserve
AFRCSTC . . . . . Air Force Reserve Combat Support Training Center
AFRCTC . . . . . Air Force Reserve Combat Training Center
AFRD . . . . Air Force Reserve Division
AFRFTC . . . . . Air Force Reserve Flying Training Center
AFRESNAVSQ . . Air Force Reserve Navigation Squadron
AFROTC . . . . . Air Force Reserve Officers Training Corps
AFRO . . . . Air Force Reserve Orders
AFRPC . . . . . . Air Force Reserve Policy Committee
AFRR . . . . Air Force Reserve Region
AFRESR . . . . . . Air Force Reserve Regions
AFRESBSGP . . . Air Force Reserve Regions Base Support Group
AFRESRGP . . . . Air Force Reserve Regions Group
AFRS . . . . Air Force Reserve Sector
AFRESS . . . . . . Air Force Reserve Sectors
AFRSTC . . . . . Air Force Reserve Specialist Training Center
AFROIC . . . . . Air Force Resident Officer in Charge
AFRB . . . . Air Force Retiring Board
AFRPL . . . . . . Air Force Rocket Propulsion Laboratories
AFSCF . . . . . . Air Force Satellite Control Facility
AFSAM . . . . . . Air Force School of Aviation Medicine
AFSAB . . . . . . Air Force Scientific Advisory Board
AFSMAAG . . . . Air Force Section, Military Assistance Advisory Group
AFSS . . . . Air Force Security Service
AFSSOP . . . . . Air Force Security Service Office of Production
AFSA . . . . Air Force Sergeants Association
AFSN . . . . Air Force Serial Number
AFSC . . . . Air Force Service Command
AFSN . . . . Air Force Service Number
AFSO . . . . Air Force Service Office
AFSS . . . . Air Force Service Statement
AFSSD . . . . . . Air Force Space Systems Division
AFSTC . . . . . . Air Force Space Test Center (Now, Western Test Range)
AFSAW . . . . . . Air Force Special Activities Wing
AFSCC . . . . . . Air Force Special Communications Center
AFSSO . . . . . . Air Force Special Security Office(r)
AFSWC . . . . . . Air Force Special Weapons Center (AFSC)
AFS . . . . Air Force Specialty

AFSC . . . . Air Force Specialty Code
AFSC . . . . Air Force Staff College
AFSIP . . . . . . Air Force Standard Intelligence Publication
AFS . . . . Air Force Station
AFSF . . . . Air Force Stock Fund
AFSN . . . . Air Force Stock Number
AFSTRIKE . . . . Air Force Strike Command
AFS . . . . Air Force Supply
AFSC . . . . Air Force Supply Catalog
AFSD . . . . Air Force Supply Directive
AFSC . . . . Air Force Systems Command
AFTF . . . . Air Force Task Force
AFTAC . . . . . . Air Force Technical Application Center
AFTO . . . . . . Air Force Technical Order
AFTOSB . . . . . Air Force Technical Order Standardization Board
AFTTH . . . . . . Air Force Technical Training Headquarters
AFTB . . . . Air Force Test Base
AFTU . . . . Air Force Test Unit
AFTRC . . . . . . Air Force Training Command
AFUPO . . . . . . Air Force Unit Post Office
AF . . . . Air Force, United States
AFUS . . . . Air Force of the United States
AFVA . . . . Air Force Visual Aid
AFW . . . . Air Force Weapon
AFWET . . . . . . Air Force Weapons Effectiveness Testing
AFWL . . . . Air Force Weapons Laboratory
AFWOFS . . . . Air Force Weather Observing and Forecasting System
AFWB . . . . . . Air Force Welfare Board
AFWTR . . . . . . Air Force Western Test Range
AFWETS . . . . . Air Force's Weapons Effectiveness Testing System
AIRLANT . . . . Air Forces, Atlantic Fleet (Navy)
AFCENT . . . . . Air Forces, Central Europe
AFEX . . . . Air Forces Europe Exchange
AFICE . . . . Air Forces, Iceland
AIRPAC (ADV) . . Air Forces Pacific Advanced
AIRPAC . . . . . . Air Forces, Pacific Fleet
AIRPAC (PEARL) . . Air Forces Pacific, Pearl Harbor
AIRPACSUBCOMFORD . . Air Forces Subordinate Command, Forward Area
AF . . . . Air France
AFFA . . . . Air Freight Forwarders Association
AFT . . . . Air Freight Terminal
AG . . . . Air Gage
AGW . . . . Air Gap Width
AG . . . . Air Group
AIRGRP . . . . . Air Group
AG . . . . Air-to-Ground (Communications, missiles, etc.)
A/G . . . . Air-to-Ground (Photo, missile, etc.)
ATG . . . . Air-to-Ground (Military)
AGATE . . . . . . Air to Ground Acquisition and Tracking Equipment
AGA . . . . Air-to-Ground-to-Air (Air Force)
A/G/A . . . . . . Air-to-Ground-to-Air
AGACS . . . . . Air-Ground-Air Communications System
AGC . . . . Air Ground Chart
AGCC . . . . . . Air-Ground Communications Channel
AGCO . . . . . . Air-Ground Cooperation Officer
AGCF . . . . . . Air Ground Correlation Factor
AGFRTS . . . . . Air and Ground Forces Resources and Technical Staff (Army)
AGGR . . . . . . Air-to-Ground Gunnery Range
AGIC . . . . . . Air-Ground Information Center
AGIS . . . . . . Air-Ground Integration System
AGLC . . . . . . Air-to-Ground Liaison Code (Air Force)
AGLO . . . . . . Air Ground Liaison Officer (Marine Corps)
AGM . . . . Air-to-Ground Missile
A/G/M . . . . . . Air-to-Ground Missile
AGMTI . . . . . . Air-to-Ground Moving Target Indicator
AGOS . . . . . . Air-Ground Operations Section, School, or System
AGO . . . . Air Gunnery Officer
AHQ . . . . Air Headquarters
AHB . . . . Air Heater Blower
AHSR . . . . . . Air Height Surveillance RADAR
AHP . . . . Air Horsepower (Air Force)
AII . . . . Air-India International (Airline)
ARNO . . . . . . Air Indicator Not Operating (Aviation)
AITA . . . . Air Industries and Transports Association
AID . . . . Air Information Division (Library of Congress)
AIR . . . . Air Injection Reaction
AI . . . . Air Inspector
A/I . . . . Air Inspector
AI . . . . Air Installations
AIP . . . . Air Intake Panel
AIF . . . . Air Intelligence Force

12

AIL . . . . Air Intelligence Liaison (British)
AILO . . . . Air Intelligence Liaison Officer (British)
AINTSEC . . . . Air Intelligence Section (Army)
AIS . . . . Air Intelligence Service
SIA . . . . Air Intelligence Service (Italian)
AITC . . . . Air Intelligence Training Center
AIM . . . . Air Intercept Missile
AIC . . . . Air Interception Control (Common)
AIC . . . . Air Interception Control (RADAR)
AIF . . . . Air Interceptor Fuze
AIM . . . . Air Isolated Monolithic (Circuit)
AJCU . . . . Air Jet Control Unit
AJ . . . . Air Jordan (Airline)
ALAAR . . . . . . Air Launched Air Recoverable Rocket
ALARR . . . . . . Air Launched, Air Recoverable Rocket
ALABM . . . . . . Air Launched Anti-Ballistic Missile
ALBI . . . . Air-Launched Ballistic Intercept
ALBM . . . . Air-Launched Ballistic Missile
ALGM . . . . . . Air-Launched Guided Missile (Military)
ALIM . . . . Air-Launched Intercept Missile
ALM . . . . Air Launched Missile
ALMS . . . . Air-Launched Missile System
ALSAM . . . . . . Air-Launched Ship-Attack Missile
ATR . . . . Air-Launched Trainer Rocket
ALV . . . . Air Launched Vehicle
ALW . . . . Air Launched Weapon
AL . . . . Air Letter
AL . . . . Air Liaison
AIRLO . . . . . . Air Liaison Officer
ALO . . . . Air Liaison Officer (US Air Force, British Navy)
ALP . . . . Air Liaison Party
LN . . . . Air Liban (Lebanese Air Lines)
ALOC . . . . Air Line of Communication (Air Force)
ACEA . . . . Air Line Communication Employees Association
ALCEA . . . . . . Air Line Communication Employees Association
ALDA . . . . Air Line Dispatchers Association
ALEA . . . . Air Line Employees Association, International
ALPA . . . . Air Line Pilots Association
ALPAI . . . . Air Line Pilots Association, International
ALSSAI . . . . . . Air Line Stewards and Stewardesses Association, International
AL . . . . Air Lock (Technical drawings)
ALCORCEN . . . Air Logistic Coordination Center
ALS . . . . Air Logistics Service (or System) (Military)
ALFA . . . . Air Lubricated Free Attitude
ALFA . . . . Air Lubricated Free Axis Trainer (NASA)
AMC . . . . Air Mail Center
AMF . . . . Air Mail Facility (Post Office)
AMF . . . . Air Mail Field
AMP . . . . Air Mail Pioneers
AMS . . . . Air Management Station
AM . . . . Air Marshal (British)
AMS . . . . Air Mass
AMAFA . . . . . . Air Mass and Frontal Analysis (Meteorology)
AMATC . . . . . Air Material Armament Test Center
AMTC . . . . . . Air Material Armament Test Center
AMCCOMNET . Air Material Command Communications Network
CANAIRMAT . . Air Material Command Headquarters, Ottawa, Ontario, Canada
AIMACO . . . . Air Material Computer (Air Force)
AMA . . . . Air Materiel Area (Air Force)
AMC . . . . Air Materiel Command (Later, Air Force Logistics Command)
AIMACC . . . . . Air Materiel Command Compiling (System)
AMCHQ . . . . Air Materiel Command Headquarters
AMCL . . . . . . Air Materiel Command Letter
AMCM . . . . . . Air Materiel Command Manual
AMCR . . . . Air Materiel Command Regulations
AMF . . . . Air Materiel Force
AMFEA . . . . . . Air Materiel Force, European Area
AMFPA . . . . . . Air Materiel Force, Pacific Area
AM . . . . Air Medal (Air Force)
CANAIRLON . . Air Member, Canadian Joint Staff, London, England
CANAIRWASH . . Air Member, Canadian Joint Staff, Washington, DC
AMI . . . . Air Mileage Indicator (Navigation)
AMU . . . . Air Mileage Unit (Navigation)
AMM . . . . Air-Mining Mission (Military)
AM . . . . Air Ministry (British)
AMES . . . . Air Ministry Experimental Station
AMLSU . . . . . . Air Ministry Local Staff Union (Singapore)
AMO . . . . Air Ministry Order (British)
AMU . . . . Air Mission Unit (Air Force)
AMARS . . . . . Air Mobile Aircraft Refueling System
AMTF . . . . . . Air Mobile Task Force

AIRVAN . . . . . Air-mobile Van (Trailer unit for use on ground or in air) (Military)
AMD . . . . Air Movement Data (Air Force)
AMD . . . . Air Movement Designator (Army)
AMR . . . . Air Movement Recorder
AMIS . . . . Air Movements Information Section
AMCA . . . . . . Air Moving and Conditioning Association
AM & CA . . . . . Air Moving and Conditioning Association
ANG . . . . Air National Guard
ANGPC . . . . . Air National Guard Policy Council
ANGUS . . . . . Air National Guard of the United States
ANGLICO . . . . Air and Naval Gunfire Liaison Company (Military)
AN . . . . Air Navigation
ANC . . . . Air Navigation Conference
ANDB . . . . Air Navigation Development Board (Functions absorbed by the FAA)
AND . . . . Air Navigation Device
ANF . . . . Air Navigation Facility
ANO . . . . Air Navigation Office
ANRA . . . . . . Air Navigation Radio Aids
ANTAC . . . . . . Air Navigation and Tactical Control
ANTC . . . . . . Air Navigation Traffic Control
ANTU . . . . . . Air Navigation Training Unit
ANPC . . . . Air-Nitrogen Pressurization Control
AOC . . . . Air Officer Commanding (British)
AOC . . . . Air Officer Commanding (Marine Corps)
AOC in CBAFO . . Air Officer Commanding in Chief British Air Force Occupation
AOD . . . . Air Officer of the Day (Air Force)
AOC . . . . Air Oil Cooler
AOS . . . . Air Oil Separator
AOPV . . . . . . Air-Operated Plastic Valve
AOU . . . . Air Operated Unit
AIROPNET . . . Air Operational Network (Air Force)
OPTRA . . . . . Air Operational Training
AIROPS . . . . . Air Operations
AOC . . . . Air Operations Center (Air Force)
AOR . . . . Air Operations Room
AOB . . . . Air Order of Battle
APP . . . . Air Parcel Post
APM . . . . Air Permeability Meter
APCS . . . . . . Air Photographic and Charting Service
APR . . . . Air Pictorial Service
APS . . . . Air Pictorial Service
APCV . . . . . . Air Piloted Control Valve
APV . . . . Air Piloted Valve
AP . . . . Air Police; by extension, a person who is a member of the Air Police
APCA . . . . . . Air Pollution Control Association
APEX . . . . . . Air Pollution Exercise
APRAC . . . . . Air Pollution Research Advisory Committee
APTIC . . . . . . Air Pollution Technical Information Center (of National Center for Air Pollution Control)
AP . . . . Air Position
API . . . . Air Position Indicator (Air Force)
APO . . . . Air Post Office
APS . . . . Air Pressure Switch
PRIMTRA . . . . Air Primary Training
APRI . . . . Air Priority
APR . . . . Air Priority Rating
APWI . . . . . . Air Prisoner of War Interrogation
APD . . . . Air Procurement Directive (Air Force)
APD . . . . Air Procurement District (Air Force)
APDC . . . . . . Air Procurement District Commander
APO . . . . Air Procurement Office
APRE . . . . . . Air Procurement Region, Europe
APRFE . . . . . . Air Procurement Region, Far East
APD . . . . Air Products & Chemicals, Inc. (NYSE symbol)
APG . . . . Air Proving Ground
APGC . . . . . . Air Proving Ground Center
APGCE . . . . . Air Proving Ground Center - Eglin Air Force Base
APGC . . . . . . Air Proving Ground Command
APM . . . . Air Provost Marshal
AP . . . . Air Publication (Navy)
AQA . . . . Air Quality Act
ARO . . . . Air Radio Officer
ARP . . . . Air Raid Precautions (British) (World War II)
ARPC . . . . . . Air Raid Precautions Controller (British)
ARPO . . . . . . Air Raid Precautions Officer (British)
ARW . . . . Air Raid Warden
ARW . . . . Air Raid Warning (Air Force)
ARE . . . . Air Reactor Experiment
ARLO . . . . . . Air Reconnaissance Liaison Officer
ARSB . . . . . . Air Reconnaissance Support Battalion
AN . . . . Air Reduction Company, Inc. (NYSE symbol)

AR . . . . Air Refueling
ARCP . . . . . . Air Refueling Control Point
ARCT . . . . . . Air Refueling Control Time
AREP . . . . . . Air Refueling Egress Point
ARIP . . . . Air Refueling Ingress Point (FAA)
ARIP . . . . Air Refueling Initial Point (Air Force)
AREFS . . . . . . Air Refueling Squadron
ARCI . . . . . . Aid Refugee Chinese Intellectuals
ARX . . . . Air Regenerative Exhaust
ARR . . . . Air Regional Representative
ARB . . . . Air Registration Board (British)
ARS . . . . Air Regulating Squadron
AR . . . . Air Regulator
AROC . . . . . . Air Rescue Operations Center (Air Force)
ARS . . . . Air Rescue Service (Air Force)
ARB . . . . Air Research Bureau
ARDC . . . . . . Air Research and Development Center (Later, Air Force System Command)
ARDC . . . . . . Air Research and Development Command
ARDCA . . . . . Air Research and Development Command – Andrews Air Force Base
ARC . . . . Air Reserve Center
ARD . . . . Air Reserve District
ARFC . . . . . . Air Reserve Flying Center (Air Force)
ARF . . . . Air Reserve Forces
ARFMSR . . . . Air Reserve Forces Meritorious Service Ribbon
ARFPDS . . . . . Air Reserve Forces Personnel Data System
ARFPC . . . . . Air Reserve Forces Policy Committee
AROTC . . . . . Air Reserve Officers' Training Corps (Air Force)
ARPS . . . . . . Air Reserve Pay System
ARPC . . . . . . Air Reserve Personnel Center (Air Force)
ARRC . . . . . . Air Reserve Records Center
ARSTS . . . . . Air Reserve Specialist Training Squadron
ART . . . . Air Reserve Technician
ARTP . . . . . . Air Reserve Technician Program (Air Force)
ARU . . . . Air Reserve Unit
ARUG . . . . . . Air Reserve Unit (General Training)
ARUSNP . . . . Air Reserve Unit (General Training, Nonpay)
ARUSP . . . . . Air Reserve Unit (General Training, Pay)
ARVSG . . . . . Air Reserve Volunteer Support Group
AR . . . . Air Resistance
ARCS . . . . . . Air Resupply and Communication Service
ARSR . . . . . . Air Route Surveillance RADAR
ARTC . . . . . . Air Route Traffic Control
ARTCC . . . . . Air Route Traffic Control Center
ASB . . . . Air Safety Board
ASS . . . . Air Sampling System
AS . . . . Air Screw
ASR . . . . Air-Sea-Rescue
ASRC . . . . . . Air-Sea Rescue Craft
ASAT . . . . . . Air Search Attack Team (Military)
ASAU . . . . . . Air Search Attack Unit (Military)
ASR . . . . Air Search RADAR
SR . . . . Air Search RADAR Receiver (Shipborne)
AS . . . . Air Section
AS . . . . Air Service
ASAC . . . . . . Air Service Area Command
ASC . . . . Air Service Command
ASG . . . . Air Service Group (Air Force)
ASIC . . . . . . Air Service Information Circular
ASSRON . . . . . Air Service Support Squadron (Army)
ASO . . . . Air Signal Officer
ASI . . . . Air Society, International
ASV . . . . Air Solenoid Valve
AIRSOLS . . . . Air Solomons Command (US)
ASTRA . . . . . . Air Space Transportation
ASTRO . . . . . Air Space Travel Research Organization
AS . . . . Air Speed
AS . . . . Air Staff (Air Force)
ASB . . . . Air Staff Board
ASO . . . . Air Staff Officer
ASO . . . . Air Staff Orientation
ASCC . . . . . . Air Standardization Coordinating Committee
ASCP . . . . . . Air Standardization Coordination Program (NATO)
AS . . . . Air Station
ASWO . . . . . . (Naval) Air Stations Weekly Orders
AIRIS . . . . . . Air Store Issuing Ship
AIRSTORDEP. . . Air Stores Depot (Navy)
ASP . . . . Air Superiority Mission
ASUPP . . . . . . Air Supply
ASC . . . . Air Support Command
ASC . . . . Air Support Control
ASCU . . . . . . Air Support Control Units

ASOC . . . . . . Air Support Operations Center (Air Force)
ASRT . . . . . . Air Support RADAR Team (Marine Corps)
ASTU . . . . . . Air Support Test Unit
ASTU . . . . . . Air Support Training Units
AS & EWD . . . Air, Surface and Electronic Warfare Division (Navy)
ASM . . . . Air-to-Surface Missile (Air Force)
ASV . . . . Air-to-Surface Vessel
ASW . . . . Air to Surface Weapon
AS . . . . Air Surveillance (Air Force)
ASO . . . . Air Surveillance Officer (Air Force)
ASS . . . . Air Surveillance System
AST . . . . Air Surveillance Technician (Air Force)
ASC . . . . Air Systems Command (Navy)
ATDS . . . . . . Air Tactical Data System (Marine Corps)
ATS . . . . Air Tactical School (Air Force)
ATO . . . . Air Tactics Officer (Air Force)
ATMP . . . . . . Air Target Materials Program
ATF . . . . Air Task Force
ATCO . . . . . . Air Taxi-Commercial Operator
ATAD . . . . . . Air Technical Analysis Division
ATI . . . . Air Technical Index
ATI . . . . Air Technical Information (Used by Armed Services Technical Information Agency to accession and identify documents)
ATI . . . . Air Technical Intelligence (Air Force)
ATISC . . . . . . Air Technical Intelligence Services Command (Air Force)
ATIS . . . . Air Technical Intelligence Study (Air Force)
ATSC . . . . . . Air Technical Service Command
TECHTRA . . . . Air Technical Training (Navy)
AT . . . . Air Technician (Air National Guard)
AT . . . . Air Temperature
T . . . . Air Temperature Correction
ATERM . . . . . . Air Terminal
ATO . . . . Air Terminal Officer (Air Force)
ATV . . . . Air Test Vehicle
ATCS . . . . . . Air Traffic Communications Station
ATC . . . . Air Traffic Conference
ATCA . . . . . . Air Traffic Conference of America
ATC . . . . Air Traffic Control (Air Force)
ATCA . . . . . . Air Traffic Control Association
ATCBGS . . . . . Air Traffic Control Beacon Ground Station
ATCBI . . . . . . Air Traffic Control Beacon Interrogator
ATCC . . . . . . Air Traffic Control Center (Air Force)
ATCC . . . . . . Air Traffic Control Communication
ATCEU . . . . . . Air Traffic Control Experimental Unit
ATCF . . . . . . Air Traffic Control Facility
ATCL . . . . . . Air Traffic Control Line
ATCO . . . . . . Air Traffic Control Officer (Air Force)
ATCOR . . . . . . Air Traffic Control Operations Representative
ATCRB . . . . . . Air Traffic Control RADAR Beacon (Air Force)
ATCRBS . . . . . Air Traffic Control RADAR Beacon System
ATCRS . . . . . . Air Traffic Control RADAR System
ATCRU . . . . . . Air Traffic Control RADAR Unit
ATCSS . . . . . . Air Traffic Control Signaling System
ATCS . . . . . . Air Traffic Control Specialist
ATCT . . . . . . Air(port) Traffic Control Tower
ATCT . . . . . . Air Traffic Control Transponder
ATCO . . . . . . Air Traffic Coordinating Officer
ATCOR . . . . . . Air Traffic Coordinator
ATCOREU . . . Air Traffic Coordinator Europe
ATDP . . . . . . Air Traffic Data Processor
ATP . . . . Air Traffic Procedures
ATRC . . . . . . Air Traffic Regulation Center
ATR . . . . Air Traffic Regulations
ATREP . . . . . . Air Traffic Representative
ATS . . . . Air Traffic Section
AT . . . . Air Traffic Service (of FFA) (Also known as ATS)
ATS . . . . Air Traffic Service (of FAA) (Also known as AT)
ATAS . . . . . . Air Traffic (Area) Supervisor
ATT . . . . Air Traffic Transponder
ATAG . . . . . . Air Training Advisory Group
ATC . . . . Air Training Command (Air Force)
ATRC . . . . . . Air Training Command
ATC . . . . Air Training Corps (Royal Air Force) (British)
AIRTRAINRON . . Air Training Squadron (Navy)
AT . . . . Air Transport (Military)
ATA . . . . Air Transport Association of America
ATAA . . . . . . Air Transport Association of America
ATAS . . . . . . Air Transport Auxiliary Service (British)
ATB . . . . Air Transport Bureau (ICAO)
ATC . . . . Air Transport Command (Military)
CANAIRLIFT. . . Air Transport Command Headquarters, Rockcliffe, Ontario, Canada

ATC . . . . Air Transport Committee (ICAO)
ATCORUS . . . . Air Transport Coordinator for the United States
ATMC . . . . . . Air Transport Movement Control Center
ATR . . . . Air Transport Rating
AIRTRANSRON . . Air Transport Squadron
AIRTRANSRONLANT . . Air Transport Squadron, Atlantic
AIRTRANSRONPAC . . Air Transport Squadron, Pacific
AIRTRANSRONWESTCOAST . . Air Transport Squadron, West Coast
ATW . . . . Air Transport Wing
ATRAX . . . . . Air Transportable Communications Complex
ATD . . . . Air Transportable Dispensary
ATH . . . . Air Transportable Hospital
ATS . . . . Air Transportable SONAR
ATSSS . . . . . Air Transportable SONAR Surveillance System
ATSU . . . . Air Travel Security Unit
ATG . . . . Air Turbine Generator
ATM . . . . Air Turbine Motor
ATE . . . . Air-Turbo Exchanger
ATR . . . . Air Turbo Rocket
AUJ . . . . Air-to-Umbilical Junction Box
AUM . . . . Air-to-Underwater Missile (Air Force)
AU . . . . Air University
AUBV . . . . . Air University Board of Visitors
AUL . . . . Air University Library
AUP . . . . Air University Press
AVS . . . . Air Valve Silencer
AVD . . . . Air Velocity Detector
AVM . . . . Air Velocity Meter
AVT . . . . Air Velocity Transducer
AVT . . . . Air Vibrating Table
AVM . . . . Air Vice-Marshal (British)
VNA . . . . Air Vietnam
AWC . . . . Air War College
AWCAP . . . . . . Air War College Associate Program
AWA . . . . Air Warfare Analysis Section (British)
AWAS . . . . Air Warfare Analysis Section (British)
AWD . . . . Air Warfare Division (Navy)
AWRD . . . . . . Air Warfare Research Department (Navy)
AWSA . . . . . Air Warfare Systems Analysis
AW . . . . Air Warning
AWS . . . . Air Warning Service (or System)
AWS . . . . Air Warning Squadron (Marine Corps)
AWS . . . . Air Weapon Systems (Air Force)
AWCS . . . . . Air Weapons Control System (Air Force)
AWS . . . . Air Weather Service (Air Force)
AWSM . . . . . Air Weather Service Manual
AWSTG . . . . . . Air Weather Service Training Guide
AWS . . . . Air Wing Staffs
AB . . . . Airborne
A/B . . . . Airborne
ABN . . . . Airborne
AA . . . . Airborne Alert
AAI . . . . Airborne Alert Indoctrination
AAWS . . . . . . Airborne Alert Weapon System
AAPS . . . . Airborne Angular Position Sensor
AAS . . . . Airborne Antenna System
AASW . . . . Airborne Antisubmarine Warfare
AAIL . . . . Airborne Argon Ion LASER
AAV . . . . Airborne Assault Vehicle
AACS . . . . . . Airborne Astrographic Camera System (Air Force)
AAFC . . . . . . Airborne Audio Frequency Coder
AAMS . . . . Airborne Auxiliary Memory System
ABCCC . . . . . . Airborne Battlefield Command and Control Center
ABLES . . . . . . Airborne Battlefield Light Equipment System (Army)
ABPS . . . . . Airborne Beacon Processing System
ABP . . . . Airborne Beacon Processor
ABETS . . . . . Airborne Beacon Test Set
ABE . . . . Airborne Bombing Evaluation
ACW . . . . Airborne Collision Warning
ABNCP . . . . . Airborne Command Post
ACP . . . . Airborne Command Post (Air Force)
ACRES . . . . . Airborne Communication Relay Station (Air Force)
ACRP . . . . . . Airborne Communications Reconnaissance Program
ACC . . . . Airborne Control Computer
ACI . . . . Airborne Controlled Intercept (Air Force)
ACG . . . . Airborne Coordinating Group
ACOP . . . . . . Airborne Corps Operation Plan (Military)
ACEARTS . . . . . Airborne Countermeasures Environment and RADAR Target Simulation
ADA . . . . Airborne Data Automation
ADL . . . . Airborne Data Link
ADLS . . . . . . Airborne Data Link System

ADP . . . . Airborne Data Processor (Air Force)
ADC . . . . Airborne Digital Computer (Air Force)
ADIS . . . . . . Airborne Digital Instrumentation System
ADPU . . . . . . Airborne Digital Processing Unit
ADR . . . . Airborne Digital Recorder
ADRS . . . . . . Airborne Digital Recording System
ADT . . . . Airborne Digital Timer
ADV . . . . Airborne Digital Voltmeter
AEW . . . . Airborne Early Warning (Station)
AEWA . . . . . . Airborne Early Warning Aircraft
AEW & C . . . . Airborne Early Warning and Control
AEWF . . . . . . Airborne Early Warning Fighter
AEWRON . . . . Airborne Early Warning Squadron
AEWTU . . . . . Airborne Early Warning Training Unit
AEBR . . . . . . Airborne Electron Beam Recorder
AERIS . . . . . . Airborne Electronic Ranging Instrumentation System
AE . . . . Airborne Electronics
AEB . . . . Airborne and Electronics Board (Army)
AEAO . . . . . . Airborne Emergency Actions Officer (SAC)
AED . . . . Airborne Equipment Division
AE . . . . Airborne Equipment Division, Bureau of Aeronautics (Navy)
AEF . . . . Airborne Equipment Failure (Air Force)
AFAR . . . . . . Airborne Fixed Array RADAR
AFTC . . . . . . Airborne Flight Training Command
AFLD . . . . . . Airborne Fraunhofer Line Discriminator
AFMS . . . . . . Airborne Frequency Multiplexing System
AGIL . . . . . . Airborne General Illumination Light
AGFLS . . . . . . Airborne Ground Fire Locating System
AGFL . . . . . . Airborne Ground Fire Locator
AGL . . . . Airborne Gun Laying
AGLR . . . . . . Airborne Gun Laying RADAR
AGLT . . . . . . Airborne Gun Laying for Turrets
AGS . . . . Airborne Gunsight
AHMD . . . . . . Airborne Helmet Mounted Display
AIDS . . . . . . Airborne Inertial Data System
ABNINF . . . . . Airborne Infantry (Military)
AIREW . . . . . . Airborne Infrared Early Warning
AIETA . . . . . . Airborne Infrared Equipment for Target Analysis
AIRGLO . . . . . Airborne Infrared Gunfire Locator
AILS . . . . Airborne Infrared Live Scanner
AIM . . . . Airborne Infrared Mapper
AIRM . . . . . . Airborne Infrared Mapper
AIMI . . . . . . Airborne Infrared Measurement Instrument
AIRS . . . . . . Airborne Infrared Radiometer System
AIS . . . . Airborne Infrared Spectrometer
AISS . . . . . . Airborne Infrared Surveillance Set
AIDE . . . . . . Airborne Insertion Display Equipment
AIP . . . . Airborne Instrumentation Platform
AIL . . . . Airborne Instruments Laboratory (Mineola, New York)
AILAS . . . . . . Airborne Integrated Light Avionics System
AIMS . . . . . . Airborne Integrated Maintenance System
AI . . . . Airborne Intercept (RADAR) (Air Force)
AIFCS . . . . . . Airborne Interception Fire Control System (Air Force)
AIE . . . . Airborne Interceptor Equipment
AIO . . . . Airborne Interceptor Officer
ALERTS . . . . . Airborne LASER Equipment Real Time Surveillance
ALI . . . . Airborne LASER Illuminator
ALIRATS . . . . . Airborne LASER Illuminator Ranging and Tracking System
ALCC . . . . . . Airborne Launch Control Center
ALOT . . . . . . Airborne Lightweight Optical Tracker
ALOTS . . . . . . Airborne Lightweight Optical Tracking System (Air Force)
ALD . . . . Airborne Line Discriminator
ALP . . . . Airborne Line Printer
ALS . . . . Airborne Live Scanner
ALRI . . . . . . Airborne Long Range Input
ALRI . . . . . . Airborne Long-Range RADAR Input
AMR . . . . Airborne Magnetic Recorder
AMS . . . . Airborne Maintenance System
AMCSS . . . . . . Airborne Missile Control Subsystem
AMCS . . . . . . Airborne Missile Control System
AMTI . . . . . . Airborne Moving Target Indicator (Air Force)
ANC . . . . Airborne Navigation Computer
ANS . . . . Airborne Navigation Sensor
AOB . . . . Airborne Optical Beacon
AOR . . . . Airborne Overland RADAR
APAC . . . . . . Airborne Parabolic Arc Computer
APEQS . . . . . . Airborne Photography of the Eclipse of the Quiet Sun
APU . . . . Airborne Processing Unit
APS . . . . Airborne Pulse Search RADAR
ARA . . . . Airborne RADAR Approach (Aviation)
ARAD . . . . . . Airborne RADAR and Doppler

ARIMS . . . . . . Airborne RADAR Inflight Monitoring System
ARODS . . . . . . Airborne RADAR Orbital Determination System
ARP . . . . Airborne RADAR Platform (Air Force)
NAVASCOPE . . Airborne RADARscope Used in NAVAR (Air Force)
ART . . . . Airborne Radiation Thermometer
ARC . . . . Airborne Radio Communicating
ARDF . . . . Airborne Radio Direction Finding
ARN . . . . Airborne Radio Navigation
ARR . . . . Airborne Radio Receiver
ARIS . . . . Airborne Range Instrumentation Station
ARO . . . . Airborne Range Only (RADAR ranging set for use with various gun computers)
AROD . . . . . . Airborne Ranging and Orbit Determination System
ARS . . . . Airborne Ranging System
ARS . . . . Airborne Refrigeration System
ARC . . . . Airborne Research Capsule
ASRS . . . . . . Airborne Satellite Receiving Station
ASR . . . . Airborne Scanning Radiometer
ABSAP . . . . . . Air-Borne Search and Attack Plotter
ASE . . . . Airborne Search Equipment
ASVS . . . . . . Airborne Stabilized Viewing System
ASP . . . . Airborne Support Platform (Army)
ASV . . . . Airborne Surface Vessel Detection (RADAR device)
ASACS . . . . . . Airborne Surveillance And Control System (ASD)
ASR . . . . Airborne Surveillance RADAR
ASS . . . . Airborne Surveillance Set
ASWCR . . . . . . Airborne Surveillance Warning and Control RADAR (ASD/ADC)
ATDPS . . . . . . Airborne Tactical Data Processing System
ABTF . . . . Airborne Task Force
ATDS . . . . . . Airborne Technical Data System
ATE . . . . Airborne Teletypewriter Equipment
ATFRAM . . . . . Airborne Time/Frequency Range/Altitude Monitor
ABTSS . . . . . . Airborne Transponder Subsystem
AVI . . . . Airborne Vehicle Identification
AVID . . . . . . Airborne Vehicle Identification
AVS . . . . Airborne Viewing System
AWACS . . . . . . Airborne Warning and Control System (Air Force)
AWSA . . . . . . Airborne Wave-Guide Slotted Array
AWSAA . . . . . . Airborne Wave-Guide Slot Array Antenna
AWAC . . . . . . Airborne Weapon and Control
AWC . . . . Airborne Weapons Control
AWRS . . . . . . Airborne Weather RADAR System
AM . . . . Aircooled Motor
A . . . . Aircraft, Airman, or Airplane
AC . . . . Aircraft
A/C . . . . Aircraft
P . . . . Aircraft (Wind triangle problems)
VTD . . . . Aircraft (Training) (Navy symbol)
AAB . . . . Aircraft Accident Board
AANP . . . . Aircraft Accident Notification Procedures and Bureau Responsibilities (Manual)
AAR . . . . Aircraft Accident Record (Military)
AAR . . . . Aircraft Accident Report
AAS . . . . Aircraft Airworthiness Section
AIRASDEVLANT . . Aircraft Anti-Submarine Development Detachment, Atlantic Fleet
AAB . . . . Aircraft Armament Bulletin (Navy)
AAC . . . . Aircraft Armament Change
AAD . . . . Aircraft and Armament Development
AIRARMUNIT . . Aircraft, Armament Unit
AAI . . . . Aircraft Armaments, Incorporated
AIRAF . . . . . . Aircraft, Asiatic Fleet
AAP . . . . Aircraft Assembly Plant
AAD . . . . Aircraft Assignment Directive
ABF . . . . Aircraft Battle Force (Navy)
AIRBATFORPAC . . Aircraft Battle Force, Pacific Fleet
A/B . . . . Aircraft Bulletin
CV . . . . Aircraft Carrier
ACGM . . . . . . Aircraft Carrier General Memorandum
ACAL . . . . . . Aircraft Change Application List
ACL . . . . Aircraft Circular Letter
AC . . . . Aircraft Commander
A/C . . . . Aircraft Commander
AIC . . . . Aircraft in Commission
ACCESS . . . . . Aircraft Communication Control and Electronic Signaling System (Air Force)
ACCS . . . . . . Aircraft Communications System
ACS . . . . Aircraft Communications System
ACS . . . . Aircraft Control and Surveillance (Air Force)
ACR . . . . Aircraft Control Room
ACWO . . . . . . Aircraft Control and Warning Officer
ACWRON . . . . Aircraft Control and Warning Squadron (ADC)

AC & WS . . . . . Aircraft Control and Warning Stations (Military)
ACWS . . . . . . Aircraft Control and Warning System (ADC)
ACIS . . . . Aircraft Crew Interphone System
ADSS . . . . . . Aircraft Damage Sensing System
ADU . . . . Aircraft Delivery Unit (Air Force)
ADS . . . . Aircraft Development Service (Air Force)
ADR . . . . Aircraft Direction Room
ADDL . . . . . . Aircraft Dummy Deck Landing (Navy)
AEW . . . . Aircraft Early Warning (Station)
AEK . . . . Aircraft Ejection Kit
AES . . . . Aircraft Ejection Seat
AESS . . . . . . Aircraft Ejection Seat System
AEPS . . . . . . Aircraft Electrical Power System
AES . . . . Aircraft Electrical Society
AEL . . . . Aircraft Engine Laboratory
AEM . . . . Aircraft and Engine Mechanic
AEDO . . . . . . Aircraft Engineering District Office
AEF . . . . Aircraft Engineering Foundation
AEMCO . . . . . Aircraft Engineering Maintenance Company
AE . . . . Aircraft Equipment
AEL . . . . Aircraft Equipment List
AERS . . . . . . Aircraft Equipment Requirement Schedule
AVG . . . . Aircraft Escort Vessel (Navy symbol)
A & F . . . . . . Aircraft and Facilities (Navy appropriation)
AFMFP . . . . . . Aircraft Fleet Marine Force Pacific
AIRFMFPAC . . . Aircraft, Fleet Marine Force, Pacific
ACFT . . . . Aircraft Flying Training
AGT . . . . Aircraft Gas & Turbine
AGS . . . . Aircraft General Standards (British)
ACOG . . . . . . Aircraft on Ground
AOG . . . . Aircraft on Ground (Navy)
AGP . . . . Aircraft Grounded for Lack of Parts
AGD . . . . Aircraft Gunfire Detector
AIMS . . . . . . Aircraft Identification Military System
AIA . . . . Aircraft Industries Association
AIAA . . . . . . Aircraft Industries Association of America
AIC . . . . Aircraft Industry Conference (Navy)
AIDE . . . . . . Aircraft Installation Diagnostic Equipment
AIRF . . . . Aircraft Instrument Repair Facility
AIDS . . . . . . Aircraft Integrated Data System
AI . . . . Aircraft Interception (Air Force)
ALG . . . . Aircraft Landing Gear
ALL . . . . Aircraft Landing Lamp
ALS . . . . Aircraft Landing System
ALASC . . . . . . Aircraft Launching Accessory Service Change
ALB . . . . Aircraft Launching Bulletin
AL . . . . Aircraft Logistics (Division), Bureau of Aeronautics (Navy)
ALPB . . . . . . Aircraft Logistics Planning Board
AIRMG . . . . . . Aircraft, Machine Gunner
AMG . . . . Aircraft Machine Gunner
AMDP . . . . . . Aircraft Maintenance Delayed for Parts (Military)
AMMR . . . . . . Aircraft Maintenance Manpower Requirement
AMSE . . . . . . Aircraft Maintenance Support Equipment
AMA . . . . Aircraft Manufacturers Association
AMC . . . . Aircraft Manufacturers Council
AMPR . . . . . . Aircraft Manufacturer's Progress Report
AMC . . . . Aircraft Manufacturing Company
AMO . . . . Aircraft Material Officer
AMFA . . . . . . Aircraft Mechanics Fraternal Association
AMP . . . . Aircraft-Missile Project
AMC . . . . Aircraft Motion Compensation
AMCS . . . . . . Aircraft Mounted Control System
AMIS . . . . . . Aircraft Movement Information Service (Air Force)
AMI . . . . Aircraft Multiplex Intercommunications
AMIS . . . . . . Aircraft Multiplex Intercommunications System
AMTIDE . . . . . Aircraft Multipurpose Test Inspection & Diagnostic Equipment
AIRNORSOLS . . Aircraft, Northern Solomons
ANCR . . . . . . Aircraft Not Combat Ready
ANFE . . . . . . Aircraft Not Fully Equipped
ANP . . . . Aircraft Nuclear Power
ANP . . . . Aircraft Nuclear-Powered Program (Air Force)
ANP . . . . Aircraft Nuclear Propulsion
ANPD . . . . . . Aircraft Nuclear Propulsion Department (Navy)
ANPO . . . . . . Aircraft Nuclear Propulsion Office (of AEC) (Defunct)
ANPP . . . . . . Aircraft Nuclear Propulsion Program
AOCM . . . . . . Aircraft Out of Commission for Maintenance (Air Force)
AOCP . . . . . . Aircraft Out of Commission for (Lack of) Parts (Military)
AOPA . . . . . . Aircraft Owners and Pilots Association
APICON . . . . . Aircraft Position Information Converter (Air Force)
APRA . . . . . . Aircraft Production Resources Agency
APWD . . . . . . Aircraft Proximity Warning Device

APWS . . . . Aircraft Proximity Warning System
ARB . . . . Aircraft Reactors Brand
ARB . . . . Aircraft Recovery Bulletin
ARE . . . . Aircraft Recovery Equipment
ARPN . . . . . . Aircraft and Related Procurement, Navy
AIREPDIV . . . . Aircraft Repair Division
AIREPDN . . . . Aircraft Repair Division
ARV . . . . Aircraft Repair Ship (Navy symbol)
ARVA . . . . . . Aircraft Repair Ship (Aircraft)
ARVE . . . . . . Aircraft Repair Ship (Engine)
ARSC . . . . Aircraft Repair and Supply Center
ARA . . . . Aircraft Replaceable Assemblies
AIREP . . . . . . Aircraft Report
AVH . . . . Aircraft Rescue Boat (Navy symbol)
AVR . . . . Aircraft Rescue Vessel (Navy symbol)
ARTC . . . . . . Aircraft Research and Testing Committee
ARCO . . . . . . Aircraft Resources Control Office
ASB . . . . Aircraft Safety Beacon
ASU . . . . Aircraft Scheduling Unit
AIRSCOFORPAC . . Aircraft Scouting Force, Pacific Fleet
ASE . . . . Aircraft Search Equipment
A/CS . . . . . . Aircraft Security Vessel
ASC . . . . Aircraft Service Change
AIRSOPAC . . . Aircraft, South Pacific Force
AIRSOWESPAC . . Aircraft, Southwest Pacific Force (Navy)
ASK . . . . Aircraft Station Keeper
ASDG . . . . . . Aircraft Storage & Disposition Group (Air Force)
ASE . . . . Aircraft Stores Establishment (Navy)
ATB . . . . Aircraft Technical Bulletin
ATC . . . . Aircraft Technical Committee
ATO . . . . Aircraft Technical Order
TCTM . . . . . . Aircraft Time Compliance Technical Manuals
ATMU . . . . . . Aircraft Torpedo Maintenance Unit
ATO . . . . Aircraft Transfer Order
YCU . . . . Aircraft Transportation Lighter (Navy symbol)
YCV . . . . Aircraft Transportation Lighter (Navy symbol)
ATR . . . . Aircraft Trouble Report
AUR . . . . Aircraft Utilization Report
AC & W . . . . . Aircraft and Warning (Squadrons)
AWRNCO . . . . Aircraft Warning Company (Marine Corps)
AWS . . . . Aircraft Warning Service (Military)
AWCI . . . . . . Aircraft and Weapons Control Interceptor
AWCIS . . . . . . Aircraft and Weapons Control Interceptor System
ACH . . . . Aircrafthand (British)
AC . . . . Aircraftman (RAF and RCAF)
ACW . . . . . . Aircraftwoman (British)
ACT . . . . Aircrew Classification Test
ACTB . . . . . . Aircrew Classification Test Battery
ARP . . . . Aircrew Respiratory Protection
AD . . . . Airdrome
A/D . . . . Airdrome (or Aerodrome)
ADROBN . . . . Airdrome Battalion (Military)
PARADROP . . . An Airdrop by Parachute
AO . . . . Airdrome Officer
ATZ . . . . Airdrome Traffic Zone
ATCA . . . . . . Airedale Terrier Club of America
APAC . . . . . . Airesearch Parabolic Analog Computer
ACR . . . . Airfield Control RADAR (Air Force)
AH . . . . Airfield Heliport
AOD . . . . . . Airfield Operations Designator
ASMI . . . . . . Airfield Surface Movement Indicator
A/F . . . . Airfile
ACA . . . . Airflow Club of America
AC . . . . Airframe Change
AD . . . . Airframe Design (Division), Bureau of Aeronautics (Navy)
A and E . . . . Airframe and Engine
AMEC . . . . . . Airframe Manufacturing Equipment Committee
A & P . . . . . . Airframe and Powerplant (Aviation)
ASG . . . . Airless Spray Gun
AS . . . . Airless Spraying
ACA . . . . Airlift Clearance Authority
ACP . . . . Airlift Command Post
ALCC . . . . . . Airlift Control Center
ALCE . . . . . . Airlift Control Element
ALCO . . . . . . Airlift Coordinating Office(r)
ALCO . . . . . . Airlift Launch Control Officer (Air Force)
ALCO . . . . . . Airlift Liaison Coordination Officer
AOD . . . . Airlift Operations Directive
ASIF . . . . . . Airlift Service Industrial Fund (Military)
ALTF . . . . . . Airlift Task Force
ATD . . . . Airlift and Training Division (Air Force)

ACG . . . . Airline Carriers of Goods
ACP . . . . Airline Carriers of Passengers
ACS . . . . Airline Charter Service
AFS . . . . Airline Feed System
AGTA . . . . . . Airline Ground Transportation Association
AGIFORS . . . . Airline Group, International Federation of Operational Research Societies
AID . . . . Airline Interline Development
AMDA . . . . . . Airline Medical Directors Association
APA . . . . Airline Passengers Association
ALTA . . . . . . Airline Traffic Association
ALCAC . . . . . . Airlines Communications Administrative Council
ACTS . . . . . . Airlines Computer Tracing System (Luggage retrieving system)
AEEC . . . . . . Airlines Electronic Engineering Committee
AIRLORDS . . . . Airlines Load Optimization Recording and Display System (Airport passenger-moving sidewalk)
ASIA . . . . . . Airlines Staff International Association
AM . . . . Airmail
AA . . . . Airman Apprentice
AB . . . . Airman Basic
A/B . . . . Airman Basic
AECP . . . . . . Airman Education and Commissioning Program
AER . . . . Airman Effectiveness Report (Air Force)
A/1C . . . . . . Airman First Class
AMR . . . . Airman Military Record (Air Force)
APR . . . . Airman Performance Report
APRRB . . . . . . Airman Performance Report Review Board
AQE . . . . Airman Qualifying Examination
AR . . . . Airman Records (Air Force)
AR . . . . Airman Recruit
A/2C . . . . . . Airman Second Class
A/3C . . . . . . Airman Third Class
AIRGI . . . . . . Airman's Guide (A publication)
AIM . . . . Airman's Information Manual (FAA)
ACB . . . . Airmen Classification Battery (Military tests)
APT . . . . Airmen Proficiency Test
AIRAD . . . . . . Airmen's Advisory (A notice to airmen)
AIRMET . . . . . Airmen's Meteorological Information
AP . . . . Airplane
A/P . . . . Airplane
AAEE . . . . . . Airplane & Armament Experimental Establishment (British)
ACA . . . . Airplane Change Analysis
AIRENGPROPACCOVERHAUL . . Airplane Engine, Propeller and Accessory Overhaul (Navy)
AP . . . . Airplane Pilot
ATE . . . . Airplane Test Equipment
AP . . . . Airport
AAS . . . . Airport Advisory Service
AASR . . . . . . Airport and Airways Surveillance RADAR (Air Force)
ADP . . . . Airport Development Program
APDO . . . . . . Airport District Office
AEDS . . . . . . Airport Engineering Data Sheet (FAA)
AID . . . . Airport Information Desk
AOC . . . . Airport Operators Council
ASDR . . . . . . Airport Surface Detection (RADAR)
ASDE . . . . . . Airport Surface Detection Equipment
ASR . . . . Airport Surveillance RADAR
ATC . . . . Airport (or Airway) Traffic Control
AFO . . . . Airports Field Office
AS . . . . Airports Service (of FAA)
ZNH . . . . Airship, Air-Sea Rescue (Navy symbol)
AEC . . . . Airship Experimental Center (Navy)
AIRSHIPGR . . . Airship Group
ZPG . . . . Airship Group (Navy symbol)
ZN . . . . Airship (Nonrigid) (Navy symbol)
AR . . . . Airship Rigger
AIRSHIPRON . . Airship Squadron
AZ . . . . Airship Tender (Navy symbol)
ZNJ . . . . Airship, Utility (Navy symbol)
ZUTRON . . . . . Airship Utility Squadron (Navy symbol)
ASD . . . . Airspace Docket
ARCO . . . . . . Airspace Reservation Coordination Office (Canadian)
ASP . . . . Airspace Subcommittee (ACC)
ASI . . . . Airspeed Indicator (Aviation)
AT . . . . Airtight (Technical drawings)
AFS . . . . Airway Facilities Service (FAA)
ABCD . . . . . . Airway opened, Breathing restored, Circulation restored, and Definitive therapy (Medicine)
AOSAP . . . . . . Airway Operations Specialist (Airport)
AACS . . . . . . Airways and Air Communications Service (Air Force)
AACSM . . . . . . Airways and Air Communications Service Manual
AIRCOM . . . . . Airways Communications System
ADCAD . . . . . Airways Data Collection and Distribution (Data processing)

AENG . . . . . . Airways Engineer
AES . . . . Airways Engineering Society
AFS . . . . Airways Facility Shop
AFINS. . . . . . Airways Flight Inspector
AI . . . . Airways Inspector
AMB. . . . . . . Airways Modernization Board (Functions transferred to FAA)
AOSG . . . . . . Airways Operations Specialist (General)
AOSS . . . . . . Airways Operations Specialist
AOSPV . . . . . Airways Operations Supervisor
ATDO. . . . . . Airways Technical District Office
ATDS . . . . . . Airways Technical District Supervisor
ATFO . . . . . . Airways Technical Field Office
AW . . . . Airwork, Ltd.
AD. . . . . Airworthiness Directive
ARC . . . . Airworthiness Requirements Committee
ASEC . . . . . . Airworthiness Standards Evaluation Committee (FAA)
AJ . . . . A.J. Industries, Inc. (NYSE symbol)
ATV . . . . Akademiet for de Tekniska Videnskaber (Academy of Technical
           Sciences) (Denmark)
ACA . . . . Akita Club of America
ABB . . . . Akron & Barberton Belt R. R. (AAR code)
AKB . . . . Akron Brass Manufacturing Company (NYSE symbol)
ACY . . . . Akron, Canton & Youngstown R. R. (AAR code)
AB . . . . Aktiebolaget (Swedish word for company)
ABA . . . . Aktiebolaget Aero Transport (Swedish Airlines)
ABA . . . . Aktiebolaget Atomenergi (Swedish nuclear development company)
AE . . . . Aktiebolaget Atomenergi (Stockholm)
ABACUS . . . . Aktiebolaget Atomenergi Computer-Based User-Oriented Service
AGFA. . . . . . Aktien Gesellschaft fuer Anilin Farben
AG . . . . Aktiengesellschaft (Joint Stock Company) (Germany)
AL . . . . Alabama
ALC. . . . . . . Alabama Central R. R. (AAR code)
ACHE . . . . . . Alabama Commission on Higher Education
AGA . . . . Alabama Gas Corporation (NYSE symbol)
AGS. . . . . . . Alabama Great Southern R. R. (AAR code)
AGT. . . . . . . Alabama Great Southern R. R. Corporation (NYSE symbol)
API . . . . Alabama Polytechnic Institute
ASC . . . . Alabama State College
ATN. . . . . . . Alabama, Tennessee & Northern R. R. (AAR code)
Ab . . . . Alabamine (Chemical element) (Superseded by astatine)
ABL . . . . Alameda Belt Line (AAR code)
AAFGH. . . . . . Al-Anon Family Group Headquarters
ACP . . . . Alarm Control Panel
AIM . . . . Alarm Indicating Monitor
AMC . . . . Alarm Monitor Computer
AMS . . . . Alarm Monitoring System
ANG . . . . Alarm Network Group
APM. . . . . . . Alarm Panel Monitor
AR . . . . Alarm Reaction (Physiology)
ART . . . . Alarm Reporting Telephone
ASCU . . . . . . Alarm System Control Unit
ASO . . . . Alarm System Operation
AK . . . . Alaska
AAA . . . . Alaska (Officially, name is spelled out); sometimes Alas.
ALK . . . . Alaska Airlines, Inc. (NYSE symbol)
ASA . . . . Alaska Airlines, Inc.
ALCAN. . . . . . Alaska-Canada (Highway)
ALCANUS . . . . Alaska, Canada, United States
ACA . . . . Alaska Coastal Airlines
ALCOM . . . . . Alaska Command (Military)
ACSIF. . . . . . Alaska Communication System Industrial Fund
ADC. . . . . . . Alaska Defense Command (Known to many of the soldiers who served
           in it as "All Damn Confusion") (World War II)
ADFG . . . . . . Alaska Department of Fish and Game
AEC . . . . Alaska Engineering Commission (Later, the Alaska Railroad)
AGC . . . . Alaska Game Commission (Terminated, 1959)
AIFD . . . . . . Alaska Institute for Fisheries Development
AIRHC . . . . . . Alaska International Rail and Highway Commission (Terminated, 1961)
AMH . . . . Alaska Military Highway
ALSK . . . . . . Alaska R. R. (AAR code)
ALST . . . . . . Alaska Standard Time
AYP . . . . Alaska Yukon Pioneers
AAC. . . . . . . Alaskan Air Command (Air Force)
ACC. . . . . . . Alaskan Collectors Club
AC . . . . Alaskan Command (Military)
ACR . . . . Alaskan Communications Region (Air Force)
ACS . . . . Alaskan Communications System (Military)
ALIADS. . . . . . Alaskan Integrated Air Defense System
ALICE. . . . . . Alaskan Integrated Communications Exchange
AMCA . . . . . . Alaskan Malamute Club of America
ASF . . . . Alaskan Sea Frontier (Navy)

AL SEA FRON . . Alaskan Sea Frontier
AL SEC . . . . . . Alaskan Sector
A . . . . Alaskan Standard Time (Aviation)
AANO . . . . . . Albanian-American National Organization
ALN . . . . Albany & Northern Railway Company (AAR code)
APD . . . . Albany Port District R. R. (AAR code)
ASC . . . . Albany State College (Georgia)
AEMC. . . . . . Albert Einstein Medical Center
AM . . . . Albert Medal (British)
AMC . . . . Albertus Magnus College (Connecticut)
AMG . . . . . . Albertus Magnus Guild
ALOO . . . . . . Albuquerque Operations Office
AP . . . . Alco Products, Inc. (NYSE symbol)
AOB. . . . . . . Alcohol on Breath (Police term)
ACE . . . . Alcohol, Chloroform, Ether (An early anesthetic mixture)
ADH . . . . Alcohol Dehydrogenase
ATU . . . . Alcohol Tax Unit (US Treasury Department)
ATTD . . . . . . Alcohol and Tobacco Tax Division (Internal Revenue Service)
ABC . . . . Alcoholic Beverage Control (Board)
AA . . . . Alcoholics Anonymous
AUD. . . . . . . Aldens, Inc. (NYSE symbol)
ABC . . . . Ale, Bread and Cheese
AZA . . . . Aleph Zadik Aleph (Society)
AAS . . . . Alert Area Supervisor (Military)
ACBS . . . . . . Alert Crew Billet Security
ALNOT. . . . . . Alert Notice
ART . . . . Alert Reaction Time
AGBA . . . . . . Alexander Graham Bell Association for the Deaf
ARC . . . . Alexander R. R. (AAR code)
AXS . . . . Alexander Smith, Inc. (NYSE symbol)
AAI . . . . Alfred Adler Institute
APE . . . . Alfven Propulsion Engine (Aerospace)
ALPAK . . . . . . Algebra Package
ALCOM . . . . . Algebraic Compiler (Data processing)
ACT . . . . Algebraic Compiler and Translator
ALIAS. . . . . . Algebraic Logic Investigation of Apollo Systems
ALGOL . . . . . Algebraic Oriented Language
ALTRAN . . . . . Algebraic Translator
ALTAC . . . . . . Algebraic Translator and Compiler
AVV. . . . . . . Algemeen Vrijzinning Vakverbond in Nederland (General Liberal Labor
           Federation) (Netherlands)
ABC . . . . Algemene Bedrijfsgroepen Centrale (General Union of Workers in
           Miscellaneous Industries) (Netherlands)
AKWV . . . . . . Algemene Katholieke Werkgeversvereniging
AKU. . . . . . . Algemene Kunstzidje Unie (Commercial firm) (Netherlands)
AWW . . . . . . Algers, Winslow & Western Railway Company (AAR code)
AED . . . . ALGOL Extended for Design
AC . . . . Algoma Central & Hudson Bay Railway Company (AAR code)
ALABOL . . . . . Algorithmic and Business Oriented Language
ALGOL . . . . . Algorithmic Language (Data processing)
ALGEC . . . . . . Algorithmic Language for Economic Problems
ADR . . . . Alianza Democratica Revolucionaria
AI . . . . Alianza Interamericana
ANAPO . . . . . Alianza Nacional Popular (Colombian political party)
APRA . . . . . . Alianza Popular Revolucionaria Americana (Peruvian political party)
ADI . . . . Alien Declared Intention
AFA . . . . Alien Firearms Act
APUPA . . . . . . Alien, Penumbral, Umbral, Penumbral, Alien
AG . . . . Alignment Group
AP . . . . Alignment Periscope
ATFOS . . . . . . Alignment and Test Facility for Optical Systems (Navy)
AW . . . . Alignment Window
ALIANSA . . . . Alimentos para Animales, SA (Feed plant) (Guatemala)
ALQS. . . . . . . Aliquippa & Southern R. R. (AAR code)
AZ. . . . . ALITALIA (Aerolinee Italiane Internazionali, Italian airline)
AMT. . . . . . . Alkali-Metal Turbine
ALPHA . . . . . . Alkali Plasma Hall Accelerator
AEFC . . . . . . Alkaline Electrolyte Fuel Cell
ABS . . . . Alkyl Benzene Sulfonate (Chemical)
ALANO . . . . . All Accident Notice Offices (Aviation)
AAPC . . . . . . All African Peoples' Conference
AATUF . . . . . . All African Trade Union Federation
AA . . . . All (text) After (specified point) (Message handling)
ALADLO . . . . . All Air Defense Liaison Officers (in region)
ALARTC . . . . . All Air Route Traffic Control Centers (in region)
AAGS . . . . . . All-America Gladiolus Selections
AARS . . . . . . All-America Rose Selections
AAS . . . . All-America Selections
AABC . . . . . . All-American Bronze Club
ALAMCABCO. . All American Cable Company
AACCC . . . . . All-American Conference to Combat Communism

ALCS/C ..... All AT (Air Traffic Service) Combined Station/Centers (in region)
ALCS/T ..... All AT (Air Traffic Service) Combined Station/Towers (in region)
AAI .... All Attitude Indicator
AABS .... All Attitude Indicator Bombing System
AB .... All (text) Before (specified point) (Message handling)
ALBUS ...... All Bureaus (Navy)
ABL .... All Busy Low (AT & T)
ABD .... All But Their Dissertation (PhD candidates)
ACFFTU ..... All Ceylon Federation of Free Trade Unions
ACHDWU ..... All-Ceylon Harbor and Dock Workers' Union
ACFTU ...... All-China Federation of Trade Unions (Communist China)
ALCOM ...... All Commands (A dispatch to all commands in an area) (Navy)
ACN .... All Concerned Notified
ACQ .... All Courses and Quadrants (Aviation)
ADC .... All Damn Confusion
ADF .... All Dielectric Filter
AE .... All England
AELTC ...... All England Lawn Tennis Club
ALFAA ...... All Federal Aviation Agency Field Offices and Personnel
ALFSS ...... All Flight Service Stations (in region)
AIBEA ...... All-India Bank Employees' Association
AIBEF ...... All-India Bank Employees' Federation
AICC .... All-India Congress Committee
AIFEE ...... All-India Federation of Electricity Employees
AIIEA ...... All-India Insurance Employees' Association
AIJWF ...... All-India Jute Textile Workers' Federation
AIPDWF ..... All-India Port and Dock Workers' Federation
AIR .... All-India Radio
AIRF .... All-India Railwaymen's Federation
AITUC ...... All-India Trade Union Congress
AIEC .... All-Industry Electronics Conference
AIGS .... All-Inertial Guidance System
ALIATCS .... All International Air Traffic Communications Stations
ALIFSS ..... All International Flight Service Stations (in region)
AI .... All Iron
AL .... All Lengths (Lumber)
ALMAJCOM ... All Major Commands
ALMILACT ... All Military Activities
ALNAV ...... All Naval Activities
ALLNAVSTAS . All Naval Stations
ALNAVSTA ... All Naval Stations (A dispatch to all Naval stations in an area)
NAVACT ..... (Communication directed to) All Navy Activities
ALNAV ...... All Navy and Marine Corps Activities (A dispatch to all activities in an area)
ANTUF ...... All-Nigeria Trade Union Federation
ANC .... All Numbers Calling (Telephone)
AODS .... All Ordnance Destruct System
APCOL ...... All-Pakistan Confederation of Labor
APPTU ...... All-Pakistan Post and Telegraph Union
APRF .... All-Pakistan Railwaymen's Federation
APA .... All Party Alliance (British)
APN .... All Pass Network
APC .... All Peoples Congress (Sierra Leone)
ALPERSCOM .. All Personnel Communication (Military)
APB .... All Points Bulletin (Police call)
APOAF ...... All Present or Accounted For
ALPURCOMS .. All-Purpose Communications System
APRCAS ..... All Purpose Rocket for Collecting Atmospheric Soundings (Navy)
ARCAS ...... All Purpose Rocket for Collecting Atmospheric Soundings (US Navy)
APR .... All Purpose Room
ALRAFAC .... All RADAR Air Traffic Control Facilities in Region
AR .... All Rail (Railroad)
ARM .... All Risk Management (Insurance)
OK .... All Right (From Old Kinderhook or Oll Korrect)
AR .... All Risks
A/R .... All Risks (Business and trade)
ASD .... All Saints' Day
ASCAS ...... All-Service Close Air Support (Military)
AS & SL .... All Ships and Stations Letters
ASHC .... All States Hobby Club
ASE .... All-Steel Equipment, Inc.
ATV .... All-Terrain Vehicle
ATB .... All Trunks Busy (Communications)
AUCCTU ..... All Union Central Council of Trade Unions (USSR)
AUW .... All Up Weight (Aviation)
AW .... All Water
AWA .... All Wave Antenna
AW .... All-Weather (As applied to fighter aircraft, etc.)
AWADS ...... All Weather Aerial Delivery System
AWA .... All-Weather Attack
ACLS .... All-Weather Carrier Landing System (Navy)

AWF .... All Weather Flare
AGSR .... All-Weather Ground Surveillance RADAR
AWI .... All Weather Interceptor
AWL .... All Weather Landing (Aviation)
AWLS .... All-Weather Landing System
AWOC .... All-Weather Operations Committee (ATA)
AWYDC ...... All Weather Yaw Damper Computer
AW .... All Widths (Lumber)
AHC .... Allan Hancock College (California)
AL .... Allegheny Airlines, Inc.
ABL .... Allegheny Ballistics Laboratory
Y .... Alleghany Corporation (NYSE symbol)
ACTION ..... Allegheny Council to Improve our Neighborhoods
AHRCO ...... Allegheny Housing Rehabilitation Corporation
AG .... Allegheny Ludlum Steel Corporation (NYSE symbol)
ALPO .... Allegheny Portage Railroad National Historic Site
AYP .... Allegheny Power System, Inc. (NYSE symbol)
AYSS .... Allegheny & South Side R. R. (AAR code)
AY .... Allegheny & Western Railway Company (NYSE symbol)
A-B .... Allen-Bradley Company
ANL .... Allen Industries, Inc. (NYSE symbol)
ATC .... Allergic to Combat (A play on the initialism for the Air Transport Command)
AFA .... Allergy Foundation of America
ADN .... Allgemeine Deutsche Nachrichtendienst (General German Press Agency) (East Germany)
AEG .... Allgemeine Elektrizitaets-Gesellschaft (Germany)
ADAC .... Allgemeiner Deutscher Automobil Club (Prewar; Germany)
ABAKWA ..... Alliance de Baboma-Bateke du Kwamouth (Alliance of Baboma-Bateke People of Kwamouth)
ABAKO ...... Alliance des Bakongo (Alliance of the Bakongo People)
AB .... Alliance Balkanique
ABATE ...... Alliance des Bateke (Alliance of Bateke)
ABAZI ...... Alliance des Bayanzi (Alliance of Bayanzis)
ABU .... Alliance Biblique Universelle
ACI .... Alliance Cooperative Internationale
AEAP .... Alliance Europeenne des Agences de Presse
AFNY .... Alliance Francaise de New York
AGI .... Alliance Graphique Internationale
AITU .... Alliance of Independent Telephone Unions
ATU .... Alliance of Independent Telephone Unions
AID .... Alliance Internationale de la Diffusion par Fil (International Alliance for Diffusion by Wire)
AIF .... Alliance Internationale des Femmes, Droits Egaux, Responsabilites Egales
AIT .... Alliance Internationale de Tourisme
AIU .... Alliance Israelite Universelle
AJEUNAL .... Alliance de Jeunesse Angolaise pour la Liberte (Alliance of Angolan Youth for Freedom)
ALA .... Alliance for Labor Action (An organization)
ALIAZO ..... Alliance of Natives of Zombo (Angola)
APART ...... Alliance of Pan American Round Tables
APIC .... Alliance des Patriotes Independants du Congo (Alliance of Independent Patriots of the Congo)
APA .... Alliance of Poles of America
APIC .... Alliance des Proletaires Independents du Congo (Alliance of Independent Proletarians of the Congo)
ARM .... Alliance Reformee Mondiale
ATFP .... Alliance of Television Film Producers
AUOD .... Alliance Universelle des Ouvriers Diamantaires
UCJG .... Alliance Universelle des Unions Chretiennes de Jeunes Gens
AAP .... Allied Administrative Publication
AAPIU ...... Allied Aerial Photographic Interpretation Unit
AAFCE ...... Allied Air Force, Central Europe
AIRCENT .... Allied Air Forces, Central Europe (Formerly AAFCE)
AAFNE ...... Allied Air Force Northern Europe
AIRNORTH ... Allied Air Forces Northern Europe
AAFSE ...... Allied Air Force Southern Europe
AIRSOUTH ... Allied Air Forces Southern Europe
AAHQ .... Allied Air Headquarters
AAIC .... Allied Air Intelligence Center
AASC .... Allied Air Support Command (Mediterranean)
AAI .... Allied Armies in Italy
AAA .... Allied Artists of America
ACIC .... Allied Captured Intelligence Center (US and British)
ACD .... Allied Chemical Corporation (NYSE symbol)
ACLANT ..... Allied Command Atlantic
BALTAP ..... Allied Command Baltic Approaches (NATO)
COMBALTAP .. Allied Command Baltic Approaches (NATO)
ACCHAN ..... Allied Command Channel (NATO)
ACE .... Allied Command Europe (NATO)
ACEUR ...... Allied Command Europe

REVERSE ACRONYMS AND INITIALISMS DICTIONARY

ACEREP......Allied Command Europe Report
ACR........Allied Commission on Reparations
ACP........Allied Communications Publications (Military)
ACSA.......Allied Communications Security Agency
ACAC......Allied Container Advisory Committee
ACA........Allied Control Authority (Allied German Occupation Forces)
ACC........Allied Control Commission (World War II)
AACA.......Allied Control Commission for Austria
AACB.......Allied Control Commission for Bulgaria
AACH.......Allied Control Commission for Hungary
AACI.......Allied Control Commission for Italy
AACR.......Allied Control Commission for Rumania
ACC........Allied Control Council
AACG......Allied Control Council for Germany
AACJ.......Allied Control Council for Japan
AEAF.......Allied Expeditionary Air Force (World War I)
AEF........Allied Expeditionary Force
AXP........Allied Exercise Publication
AFAC.......Allied Finance Adjusters Conference
AFHQ (CIC)....Allied Force Headquarters (Counter Intelligence Corps)
AFHQPS....Allied Force Headquarters Petroleum Section
AFCENT.....Allied Forces Center
AFCE.......Allied Forces Central Europe (Air Force)
AFCENT....Allied Forces in Central Europe (NATO)
AFHQ......Allied Forces Headquarters (Might refer to any theater of war)
                (World War II)
AFMED......Allied Forces Mediterranean (NATO)
AFNE.......Allied Forces Northern Europe
AFNORTH....Allied Forces Northern Europe (NATO)
AFSOUTH....Allied Forces Southern Europe (NATO)
AGS........Allied Geographic Section (Southwest Pacific)
AHMA.......Allied Hat Manufacturers Association
AHQ.......Allied Headquarters
HICOM......Allied High Commission for Germany
AHP........Allied Hydrographic Publication
AIU........Allied Independent Unions (Lebanon)
AIC........Allied Intelligence Committee (London)
AIO........Allied Interrogating Organization
AKD........Allied Kid Company (NYSE symbol)
AK.........Allied Kommandatura
LANDCENT...Allied Land Forces Central Europe
LANDENMARK..Allied Land Forces Denmark
LANDNORWAY..Allied Land Forces Norway
ALFSEA......Allied Land Forces South East Asia
LANDSOUTHEAST..Allied Land Forces Southeastern Europe
ALFSE......Allied Land Forces Southern Europe
LANDSOUTH..Allied Land Forces Southern Europe
ALO........Allied Liaison Office
ALP........Allied Liaison and Protocol
ALDA.......Allied Linens and Domestics Association
ALP........Allied Logistic Publication (Military)
ALLA.......Allied Long Lines Agency
CINCMAIRCHAN..Allied Maritime Air Commander-in-Chief, Channel
AMCEC......Allied Military Communications Electronics Committee
AMG........Allied Military Government (of occupied territory) (Post-World War II)
AMGOT.....Allied Military Government of Occupied Territory
AMLG.......Allied Military Headquarters, Greece
AML........Allied Military Liaison (Balkans) (World War II)
AMSP.......Allied Military Security Publication
AMSC.......Allied Military Staff Conference (Quebec, Yalta, etc.) (World War II)
ADS........Allied Mills, Inc. (NYSE symbol)
AMF........Allied Mobile Force (NATO)
AMF(A)......Allied Mobile Force (Air) (NATO)
AMF(L)......Allied Mobile Force (Land) (NATO)
ANCXF......Allied Naval Commander Expeditionary Forces
NAVCENT....Allied Naval Forces Central Europe
NAVNORTH...Allied Naval Forces, Northern Europe
A/N........Allied/Neutral (Military)
ANF........Allied Nuclear Force
A/P........Allied Papers
APSO.......Allied Petroleum Service Organization
APA........Allied Pilots Association
ADP........Allied Products Corporation (NYSE symbol)
ALE........Allied Products Corporation (NYSE symbol)
ARFA.......Allied Radio Frequency Agency
ARSA.......Allied Railway Supply Association
ARA........Allied Research Association, Inc.
ASEC.......Allied Secretariat (Allied German Occupation Forces)
ASAMPE....Allied States Association of Motion Picture Exhibitors
ASSMPE....Allied States Association of Motion Picture Exhibitors
ALS........Allied Stores Corporation (NYSE symbol)

ASU........Allied Supermarkets, Inc. (NYSE symbol)
ATAF.......Allied Tactical Air Force
TAFNORNOR..Allied Tactical Air Force Northern Norway (NATO)
ATP........Allied Tactical Publication
ATCC(L).....Allied Tanker Coordinating Committee in London
ATCC(W)....Allied Tanker Coordinating Committee in Washington
ATBI.......Allied Trades of the Baking Industry
ATIS.......Allied Translation and Intelligence Section
AUA........Allied Underwear Association
AWA........Allied Workers' Association (Philippines)
AY.........Allied Youth
AC.........Allis-Chalmers Manufacturing Company
AC-CEF.....Allis-Chalmers Critical Experimental Facility
AH.........Allis-Chalmers Manufacturing Company (NYSE symbol) (Wall Street slang name: "Alice")
ASEA.......Allmanna Svenska Electriska Aktiebolaget (Sweden)
AR.........Allocated Reserve
ACTIONS....Allocation and Control Through Identification of Ongoing Situations (New York City police system)
ABC........Allocations for Budgetary Control
NAVALOT....Allotment Division (Navy)
ASN........Allotment Serial Number
ACL........Allowable Cabin Load (in an aircraft)
ACL........Allowable Cargo Load
AGW........Allowable Gross (takeoff) Weight (for an aircraft)
ASE........Allowable Steering Error
ATOG.......Allowable Takeoff Gross (Weight)
AEL........Allowance Equipage List
APL........Allowance Parts List
AJTR.......Allowance Prescribed in Joint Travel Regulations (Military)
ASC........Allowance Source Code (Military)
AFE........Allowed Failure Effect
AOAT.......Allowed Off Aircraft Time
AAD........Alloxazine Adenine Dinucleotide
ACI........Alloy Casting Institute
AJ.........Alloy Junction
ASPP.......Alloy-Steel Protective Plating
AZS........Alloyed Zinc Sheet
AJ.........Alma & Jonquieres R. R. (AAR code)
AU.........Alma Urbis (Beloved City, Rome)
AWC........Alma White College (New Jersey)
AL.........Almanor R. R. (AAR code)
ALO........Aloha Airlines, Incorporated
AS.........Alongside
ACC........Alpena Community College (Michigan)
AM.........Alpes Maritimes
ACG........Alpha Control Guidance
ACT........Alpha Counter Tube
ACO........Alpha Cut-Off
AD.........Alpha Delta (Society)
ADP........Alpha Delta Phi (Fraternity)
ADP........Alpha Delta Pi (Sorority)
ADE........Alpha Disintegration Energy
AKK........Alpha Kappa Kappa (Fraternity)
AKP........Alpha Kappa Psi (Fraternity)
AHP........Alpha Portland Cement Company (NYSE symbol)
ARS........Alpha Ray Spectrometer
ARSE.......Alpha Ray Spectrometric Equipment
ATO........Alpha Tau Omega
AXD........Alpha Xi Delta (Sorority)
AZO........Alpha Zeta Omega
A..........Alphabetic
ASI........Alphabetical Subject Index
ANTU.......Alphanaphthyl Thiourea (Chemical)
AN.........Alphanumeric
AND........Alphanumeric Display
ADE........Alphanumeric Display Equipment
ANDE.......Alphanumeric Display Equipment
ANK........Alphanumeric Keyboard (Data processing)
ANKB.......Alphanumeric Keyboard (Data processing)
ALMA.......Alphanumeric Language for Music Analysis
ANO........Alphanumeric Output (Data processing)
ANSCR......Alphanumeric System for Classification of Recordings
AC.........Alpine Club (British)
ATC........Alpine Tourist Commission
ASD........Alside, Inc. (NYSE symbol)
AKA........Also Known As
A/C........Alter Course (As used in a navigator's log)
AH.........Alter Heading (Navigation)
ALTID......Alteration Identification
A & I......Alteration and Improvement Program (Navy)

20

ASCID . . . . . . Altered States of Consciousness Induction Device
A . . . . Alternate (Approach and landing charts) (Aviation)
AAR . . . . Alternate Acquisition RADAR
ALTAN . . . . . Alternate Alerting Network (Air Force)
ABLB . . . . Alternate Binaural Loudness Balancing (Audiometry)
ACCC . . . . . . Alternate Command and Control Center (Air Force)
ALCOP . . . . . Alternate Command Post (Military)
ACF . . . . Alternate Communications Facility (Military)
AD . . . . Alternate Days
AFP . . . . Alternate Flight Plan
AIP . . . . Alternate Inspection Policy
AJCC . . . . . . Alternate Joint Communications Center
ALO . . . . Alternate Launch Officer (Air Force)
ALOC . . . . . Alternate Launch Officer Console (Air Force)
AMO . . . . . . Alternate Molecular Orbital
ANMCC . . . . Alternate National Military Command Center
ARV . . . . Alternate Record-Voice
ASD . . . . Alternate Source Development
ASC . . . . Alternate Squadron Commander (Air Force)
ASAS . . . . . . Alternate Stability Augmentation System (Aerospace)
AW . . . . Alternate Weapon
ACW . . . . . . Alternating Continuous Waves (Radio)
AC . . . . Alternating Current
A-C . . . . Alternating Current
ACC . . . . Alternating Current Circuit
ACCW . . . . . Alternating Current Continuous Wave
A-C/D-C . . . . Alternating Current/Direct Current
ACD . . . . Alternating Current Dump
ACG . . . . . . Alternating Current Generator
ACS . . . . Alternating Current Synchronous
VAC . . . . Alternating Current Volts
AF . . . . Alternating Field
AF . . . . Alternating Flow
AGF . . . . . . Alternating Gradient Focusing
AGS . . . . . . Alternating Gradient Synchrotron (AEC)
AGS . . . . Alternating Guidance Section
ASI . . . . Althydusamband Islands (Icelandic Federation of Labor)
A . . . . Altimeter
ACP . . . . Altimeter Check Point (Aviation)
ASI . . . . Altimeter Setting Indicator (Aviation)
H . . . . Altitude
ACI . . . . Altitude Command Indicator
ACK . . . . Altitude Conversion Kit
A . . . . Altitude Difference (Navigation)
ADI . . . . Altitude Direction Indicator
AHRS . . . . . . Altitude Heading Reference System
AMR . . . . Altitude Marking RADAR
AMS . . . . Altitude Measurement System
ARC . . . . Altitude Rate Command
ARR . . . . Altitude Referenced Radiometer
ASS . . . . Altitude Sensing System
ATE . . . . Altitude Transmitting Equipment (FAA)
AVC . . . . Altitude Velocity Chart
AVS . . . . Altitude Vertical Scale
AVVI . . . . . . Altitude-Vertical Velocity Indicator
A . . . . Alto
AC . . . . Altocumulus (Meteorology)
ALCU . . . . . . Altocumulus (Meteorology)
ACC . . . . Altocumulus Castellatus (Meteorology)
ALS . . . . Alton & Southern R. R. (AAR code)
ALT & S . . . . Alton and Southern Railroad
ALST . . . . . . Altostratus (Meteorology)
AS . . . . Altostratus (Meteorology)
ASAC . . . . . . Altostratus and Altocumulus (Meteorology)
ABC . . . . Alum, Blood, and Charcoal (A method of deodorizing by addition of a
            compound of these) (Medicine)
AP . . . . Alum Precipitated
APT . . . . Alum Precipitated Toxoid (Medicine)
ACMA . . . . . . Alumina Ceramic Manufacturers Association
ACT . . . . Alumina Ceramic Test
Al . . . . Aluminum (Chemical element)
ABPCA . . . . . Aluminum Building Products Credit Association
ACSR . . . . . . Aluminum Cable Steel Reinforced
AA . . . . Aluminum Company of America (NYSE symbol) (Wall Street slang names:
            "Ack Ack" or "All American")
ALCOA . . . . . . Aluminum Company of America
ACSR . . . . . . Aluminum Conductor Steel Reinforced
ADEH . . . . . . Aluminum Diethyl Hydride
AEL . . . . Aluminum Electrical Lead
AEJ . . . . Aluminum Extension Jacket
AEC . . . . Aluminum Extruders Council

AFC . . . . Aluminum Field Coil
AFCMA . . . . . Aluminum Foil Container Manufacturers Association
AFFC . . . . . . Aluminum Foil Field Coil
AL . . . . Aluminium Limited (NYSE symbol)
AMCB . . . . . . Aluminum Manufacturers Credit Bureau
ALNICO . . . . . Aluminum, Nickel, Cobalt (Alloy)
ALPETH . . . . . Aluminum and Polyethylene
APM . . . . Aluminum Power Metallurgy
ARI . . . . Aluminum Research Institute
ASA . . . . Aluminum Siding Association
ALSI . . . . Aluminum Silicon (An alloy)
ASRI . . . . Aluminum Smelters Research Institute
AWA . . . . Aluminum Wares Association
AWDMA . . . . Aluminum Window and Door Manufacturers Association
AWMA . . . . . Aluminum Window Manufacturers Association
AWIU . . . . . . Aluminum Workers International Union
AWU . . . . . . Aluminum Workers International Union
AAC . . . . Alumnae Advisory Center
AJC . . . . Alvin Junior College (Texas)
AMC . . . . Amador Central R. R. (AAR code)
ALR . . . . Amagat-Leduc Rule
SERMCE . . . . . Amalgamated Association of Street, Electric Railway and Motor Coach
            Employees of America
AAWWW . . . . . Amalgamated Association of Wistful War Wives (World War II)
ACWA . . . . . . Amalgamated Clothing Workers of America
AEU . . . . Amalgamated Engineering Union (Australia)
AEU . . . . Amalgamated Engineering Union (Rhodesia and Nyasaland)
AFSCA . . . . . Amalgamated Flying Saucers Clubs of America
ALO . . . . Amalgamated Lace Operatives of America
ALOA . . . . . . Amalgamated Lace Operatives of America
ALA . . . . Amalgamated Lithographers of America (Later, Lithographers and
            Photoengravers International Union)
ALOA . . . . . . Amalgamated Lithographers of America
AMCBW . . . . Amalgamated Meat Cutters and Butcher Workmen of North America
MCBW . . . . . Amalgamated Meat Cutters and Butcher Workmen of North America
ANULAE . . . . . Amalgamated National Union of Local Authorities Employees' Federation
            of Malaya
APA . . . . Amalgamated Printers' Association
API . . . . Amalgamated Publishers, Incorporated
ASRS . . . . . . Amalgamated Society of Railway Servants (New Zealand)
AGM . . . . Amalgamated Sugar Company (NYSE symbol)
ATMN . . . . . Amalgamated Tin Mines of Nigeria
ATU . . . . Amalgamated Transit Union
AUPE . . . . . . Amalgamated Union of Public Employees (Singapore)
AGE . . . . Amarillo Grain Exchange
ATTC . . . . . . Amarillo Technical Training Center
A . . . . Amateur
AAA . . . . Amateur Astronomers Association
AAA . . . . Amateur Athletic Association
AAC . . . . Amateur Athletic Club
AAU . . . . Amateur Athletic Union
ABLA . . . . . . Amateur Bicycle League of America
ACMP . . . . . . Amateur Chamber Music Players
ADC . . . . Amateur Dramatic Club (British)
AFLA . . . . . . Amateur Fencers League of America
AFA . . . . Amateur Fencing Association
AFTCA . . . . . Amateur Field Trial Clubs of America
AHAUS . . . . . Amateur Hockey Association of the United States
AREC . . . . . . Amateur Radio Emergency Corps (of ARPSC)
ARM . . . . Amateur Radio Monitor
ARPSC . . . . . . Amateur Radio Public Service Corps
ARA . . . . Amateur Rocketeers of America
ASUUS . . . . . Amateur Skating Union of the United States
ASA . . . . Amateur Softball Association of America
ATA . . . . Amateur Trapshooting Association
AYRS . . . . . . Amateur Yacht Research Society
AMPS . . . . . . Amazing Magic Pivot Swing (Training device for baseball batter's rear
            foot)
AE & P . . . . . Ambassador Extraordinary and Plenipotentiary (Diplomacy)
AMB . . . . Ambient Noise Background
AT . . . . Ambient Temperature
ATR . . . . Ambient Temperature Range
AA of A . . . . Ambulance Association of America
AAOA . . . . . . Ambulance Association of America
ALP . . . . Ambulance Loading Post (Military)
AMA . . . . Ambulance Manufacturers Association
VH . . . . Ambulance Plane (Navy symbol)
ACE . . . . Ambush Communication Equipment (Military)
AEOP . . . . . . Amend Existing Orders Pertaining To
AMRF . . . . . . Amended Route of Flight (Aviation)
ASI . . . . Amended Shipping Instruction

AR . . . . Amendment Request (Navy)
AAE . . . . Amerace Corporation (NYSE symbol)
ARC . . . . Amerada Petroleum Corporation (NYSE symbol)
A . . . . America or American
ABCD . . . . . . America, Britain, China, and Dutch East Indies (The ABCD Powers) (World War II)
AIS . . . . America-Italy Society
AAA . . . . American Abstract Artists
AAA . . . . American Academy of Advertising
AAA . . . . American Academy of Allergy
AAAN . . . . . . American Academy of Applied Nutrition
AAA . . . . American Academy of Art
AAAL . . . . . . American Academy of Arts and Letters
AAAS . . . . . . American Academy of Arts and Sciences
AAAS . . . . . . American Academy of Asian Studies
AACP . . . . . . American Academy for Cerebral Palsy
AACP . . . . . . American Academy of Child Psychiatry
AACM . . . . . . American Academy of Compensation Medicine
AAC . . . . American Academy of Criminalistics
AACBP . . . . . American Academy of Crown and Bridge Prosthodontics
AADM . . . . . . American Academy of Dental Medicine
AADPA . . . . . American Academy of Dental Practice Administration
AAD . . . . American Academy of Dentists
AAD . . . . American Academy of Dermatology
AAFS . . . . . . American Academy of Forensic Sciences
AAGP . . . . . . American Academy of General Practice
AAGFO . . . . . American Academy of Gold Foil Operators
AAHD . . . . . . American Academy of the History of Dentistry
AAH . . . . American Academy of Homiletics
AAID . . . . . . American Academy of Implant Dentures
AAJR . . . . . . American Academy for Jewish Research
AAMP . . . . . . American Academy of Maxillofacial Prosthetics
AAMA . . . . . . American Academy of Medical Administrators
AAMR . . . . . . American Academy on Mental Retardation
AAM . . . . American Academy of Microbiology
AANS . . . . . . American Academy of Neurological Surgery
AAN . . . . American Academy of Neurology
AAN . . . . American Academy of Nutrition
AAOM . . . . . . American Academy of Occupational Medicine
AAOO . . . . . . American Academy of Ophthalmology and Otolaryngology
AAO . . . . American Academy of Optometry
ACO . . . . American Academy of Optometry
AAOM . . . . . . American Academy of Oral Medicine
AAOP . . . . . . American Academy of Oral Pathology
AAOR . . . . . . American Academy of Oral Roentgenology
AOOR . . . . . . American Academy of Oral Roentgenology
AAO . . . . American Academy of Organ
AAOS . . . . . . American Academy of Orthopaedic Surgeons
AAP . . . . American Academy of Pediatrics
AAP . . . . American Academy of Pedodontics
AAP . . . . American Academy of Periodontology
AAPE . . . . . . American Academy of Physical Education
AAPMR . . . . . American Academy of Physical Medicine and Rehabilitation
AAPD . . . . . . American Academy of Physiologic Dentistry
AAPSS . . . . . . American Academy of Political and Social Science
AAP . . . . American Academy of Psychotherapists
AAR . . . . American Academy of Religion
AARD . . . . . . American Academy of Restorative Dentistry
AAR . . . . American Academy in Rome
ACR . . . . American Academy in Rome
AASE . . . . . . American Academy of Safety Education
AATS . . . . . . American Academy of Teachers of Singing
AATP . . . . . . American Academy of Tuberculosis Physicians
AAA . . . . American Accordionists' Association
AAA . . . . American Accounting Association
AAF . . . . American Advertising Federation
AAAEE . . . . . American Afro-Asian Educational Exchange
AHD . . . . American Agricultural Chemical Co. (NYSE symbol) (Delisted)
AAEA . . . . . . American Agricultural Editors' Association
AASWI . . . . . American Aid Society for the West Indies
AAXICO . . . . . American Air Export & Import Company
AAF . . . . American Air Filter Company, Inc.
AAMS . . . . . . American Air Mail Society
AA . . . . American Airlines, Inc.
AMR . . . . American Airlines, Inc. (NYSE symbol)
AAA . . . . American Airship Association
AAA . . . . American Albino Association
AAHC . . . . . . American Albino Horse Club
AAC . . . . American Alpine Club
AAC . . . . American Alumni Council
AAS . . . . American Amaryllis Society

AABC . . . . . . American Amateur Baseball Congress
AAPA . . . . . . American Amateur Press Association
AAGBA . . . . . American Angora Goat Breeders' Association
AAA . . . . American Angus Association
AAHPhA . . . . American Animal Health Pharmaceutical Association
AAHA . . . . . . American Animal Hospital Association
AAA . . . . American Antarctic Association
AAA . . . . American Anthropological Association
AAS . . . . American Antiquarian Society
AAVS . . . . . . American Anti-Vivisection Society
AAMA . . . . . . American Apparel Manufacturers Association
AARA . . . . . . American Arab Relief Agency
AAA . . . . American Arbitration Association
AAC . . . . American Archery Council
AAF . . . . American Architectural Foundation
AAPL . . . . . . American Artists Professional League
AA . . . . American Association (Baseball league)
AAALAC . . . . American Association for Accreditation of Laboratory Animal Care
AAAA . . . . . . American Association for the Advancement of Atheism
AAAC . . . . . . American Association for the Advancement of Criminology
AAAS . . . . . . American Association for the Advancement of Science
AAASS . . . . . American Association for the Advancement of Slavic Studies
AAAA . . . . . . American Association of Advertising Agencies
AAACE . . . . . American Association of Agricultural College Editors
AAAE . . . . . . American Association of Airport Executives
AAAIWD . . . . American Association of Aluminum Importers & Warehouse Distributors (Later, American Metal Importers Association)
AAA . . . . American Association of Anatomists
AAAB . . . . . . American Association of Architectural Bibliographers
AAAA . . . . . . American Association of Audio Analgesia
AABTM . . . . . American Association of Baggage Traffic Managers
AAB . . . . American Association of Bioanalysts
AABB . . . . . . American Association of Blood Banks
AABGA . . . . . American Association of Botanical Gardens and Arboretums
AACE . . . . . . American Association for Cancer Education
AACR . . . . . . American Association for Cancer Research
AACC . . . . . . American Association of Cereal Chemists
AACO . . . . . . American Association of Certified Orthoptists
AACPR . . . . . American Association for Cleft Palate Rehabilitation
AACPS . . . . . American Association of Clinic Physicians and Surgeons
AACC . . . . . . American Association of Clinical Chemists
AACBC . . . . . American Association of College Baseball Coaches
AACUBO . . . . American Association of College and University Business Officers
AACCP . . . . . American Association of Colleges of Chiropody-Podiatry
AACP . . . . . . American Association of Colleges of Pharmacy
AACP . . . . . . American Association of Colleges of Podiatry
AACTE . . . . . American Association of Colleges for Teacher Education
AACRAO . . . . American Association of Collegiate Registrars and Admissions Officers
AACSB . . . . . American Association of Collegiate Schools of Business
AACP . . . . . . American Association of Commerce Publications
AACT . . . . . . American Association of Commodity Traders
AACSL . . . . . American Association for the Comparative Study of Law
AACI . . . . . . American Association for Conservation Information
AACC . . . . . . American Association for Contamination Control
AACP . . . . . . American Association of Convention Planners
AACP . . . . . . American Association of Correctional Psychologists
AACE . . . . . . American Association of Cost Engineers
AACC . . . . . . American Association of Credit Counselors
AAC . . . . American Association of Criminology
AADE . . . . . . American Association of Dental Editors
AADE . . . . . . American Association of Dental Examiners
AADS . . . . . . American Association of Dental Schools
AADN . . . . . . American Association of Doctors' Nurses
AAE . . . . American Association on Emeriti
AAE . . . . American Association of Endodontists
AAE . . . . American Association of Engineers
AAEP . . . . . . American Association of Equine Practitioners
AAES . . . . . . American Association of Evangelical Students
AAFE . . . . . . American Association of Feed Exporters
AAFM . . . . . . American Association of Feed Microscopists
AAFS . . . . . . American Association of Foot Specialists
AAFRC . . . . . American Association of Fund-Raising Counsel
AAGUS . . . . . American Association of Genito-Urinary Surgeons
AAGC . . . . . . American Association for Gifted Children
AAHA . . . . . . American Association of Handwriting Analysts
AAHPER . . . . American Association for Health, Physical Education and Recreation
AAHE . . . . . . American Association for Higher Education
AAHM . . . . . . American Association for the History of Medicine
AAHA . . . . . . American Association of Homes for the Aging
AAHA . . . . . . American Association of Hospital Accountants
AAHC . . . . . . American Association of Hospital Consultants

AAHDC . . . . . . American Association of Hospital Dental Chiefs
AAHP . . . . American Association for Hospital Planning
AAHP . . . . . . American Association of Hospital Podiatrists
AAHPA . . . . . American Association of Hospital Purchasing Agents
AAHE . . . . . . American Association of Housing Educators
AAHP . . . . . . American Association for Humanistic Psychology
AAI . . . . American Association of Immunologists
AAICD . . . . . . American Association of Imported Car Dealers
AAID . . . . . . American Association of Industrial Dentists
AAIE . . . . . . American Association of Industrial Editors
AAIE . . . . . . American Association of Industrial Engineers
AAIM . . . . . . American Association of Industrial Management
AAIN . . . . . . American Association of Industrial Nurses
AAIT . . . . . . American Association of Inhalation Therapists
AAIB . . . . . . American Association of Instructors of the Blind
AAJS . . . . . . American Association of Jesuit Scientists
AAJE . . . . . . American Association for Jewish Education
AAJSA . . . . . . American Association of Journalism School Administrators
AAJC . . . . . . American Association of Junior Colleges
AALS . . . . . . American Association of Language Specialists
AALL . . . . . . American Association of Law Libraries
AALPP . . . . . . American Association for Legal and Political Philosophy
AALT . . . . . . American Association of Library Trustees
AAMI . . . . . . American Association of Machinery Importers
AAMGA . . . . American Association of Managing General Agents
AAMC . . . . . American Association of Marriage Counselors
AAMCH . . . . . American Association for Maternal and Child Health
AAMIH . . . . . . American Association for Maternal and Infant Health
AAMA . . . . . . American Association of Medical Assistants
AAMC . . . . . . American Association of Medical Clinics
AAMMC . . . . . American Association of Medical Milk Commissions
AAMRL . . . . . American Association of Medical Record Librarians
AAMD . . . . . . American Association on Mental Deficiency
AAMES . . . . . . American Association for Middle East Studies
AAMVA . . . . American Association of Motor Vehicle Administrators
AAM . . . . . . American Association of Museums
AAMF . . . . . . American Association of Music Festivals
AAN . . . . American Association of Neuropathologists
AANR . . . . . . American Association of Newspaper Representatives
AANA . . . . . . American Association of Nurse Anesthetists
AANM . . . . . . American Association of Nurse-Midwives
AAN . . . . American Association of Nurserymen
AAOG . . . . . . American Association of Obstetricians and Gynecologists
AAODC . . . . . American Association of Oilwell Drilling Contractors
AAO . . . . . . American Association of Ophthalmology
AAO . . . . . . American Association of Orthodontists
AAOT . . . . . . American Association of Orthoptic Technicians
AAOC . . . . . . American Association of Osteopathic Colleges
AAOME . . . . . American Association of Osteopathic Medical Examiners
AAPRM . . . . . American Association of Passenger Rate Men
AAPTO . . . . . American Association of Passenger Traffic Officers
AAPC . . . . . . American Association of Pastoral Counselors
AAPB . . . . . . American Association of Pathologists and Bacteriologists
AAPG . . . . . . American Association of Petroleum Geologists
AAPL . . . . . . American Association of Petroleum Landmen
AAPA . . . . . . American Association of Physical Anthropologists
AAPM . . . . . . American Association of Physicists in Medicine
AAPT . . . . . . American Association of Physics Teachers
AAPS . . . . . . American Association of Plastic Surgeons
AAPCC . . . . . American Association of Poison Control Centers
AAPA . . . . . . American Association of Port Authorities
AAP . . . . . . American Association of the Professions
AAPSE . . . . . . American Association of Professors in Sanitary Engineering
AAPS . . . . . . American Association for the Promotion of Science
AAPCC . . . . . American Association of Psychiatric Clinics for Children
AAPHD . . . . . American Association of Public Health Dentists
AAPHP . . . . . American Association of Public Health Physicians
AAPOR . . . . . American Association for Public Opinion Research
AARS . . . . . . American Association of Railroad Superintendents
AARTA . . . . . American Association of Railroad Ticket Agents
AARS . . . . . . American Association of Railway Surgeons
AART . . . . . . American Association for Rehabilitation Therapy
AART . . . . . . American Association of Religious Therapists
AARP . . . . . . American Association of Retired Persons
AASA . . . . . . American Association of School Administrators
AASL . . . . . . American Association of School Librarians
AASPA . . . . . American Association of School Personnel Administrators
AASDJ . . . . . American Association of Schools and Departments of Journalism
AASRE . . . . . American Association of Schools of Religious Education
AASR . . . . . . American Association of Securities Representatives
AASPRC . . . . . American Association of Sheriff Posses and Riding Clubs

AASB . . . . . . American Association of Small Business
AAS & GP . . . . American Association of Soap and Glycerin Producers
AASP . . . . . . American Association for Social Psychiatry
AASS . . . . . . American Association for Social Security
AASHO . . . . . American Association of State Highway Officials
AASL . . . . . . American Association of State Libraries
ASL . . . . American Association of State Libraries
AASLH . . . . . American Association for State and Local History
AASP . . . . . . American Association of Stratigraphic Palynologists
AASND . . . . . American Association for Study of Neoplastic Diseases
AASFE . . . . . . American Association of Sunday and Feature Editors
AAST . . . . . . American Association for the Surgery of Trauma
AASACM . . . . American Association of Swiss Alpine Club Members
AATEA . . . . . American Association of Teacher Educators in Agriculture
AATA . . . . . . American Association of Teachers of Arabic
AATCLC . . . . . American Association of Teachers of Chinese Language and Culture
AATESL . . . . . American Association of Teachers of English as a Second Language
AATF . . . . . . American Association of Teachers of French
AATG . . . . . . American Association of Teachers of German
AATI . . . . . . American Association of Teachers of Italian
AATSEEL . . . . American Association of Teachers of Slavic and East European
          Languages
AATSP . . . . . American Association of Teachers of Spanish and Portuguese
AATCC . . . . . American Association of Textile Chemists and Colorists
AATT . . . . . . American Association for Textile Technology
AATS . . . . . . American Association of Theological Schools
AATS . . . . . . American Association for Thoracic Surgery
AATPA . . . . . American Association of Traveling Passenger Agents
AAUN . . . . . . American Association for the United Nations (Later, United Nations
          Association of the United States)
AAUP . . . . . . American Association of University Professors
AAUTI . . . . . American Association of University Teachers of Insurance
AAUW . . . . . American Association of University Women
AAVSO . . . . . American Association of Variable Star Observers
AAVA . . . . . . American Association of Veterinary Anatomists
AAVB . . . . . . American Association of Veterinary Bacteriologists
AAVN . . . . . . American Association of Veterinary Nutritionists
AAVP . . . . . . American Association of Veterinary Parasitologists
AAVRPHS . . . . American Association for Vital Records and Public Health Statistics
AAVSC . . . . . American Association of Volunteer Services Coordinators
AAWM . . . . . American Association of Women Ministers
AAWB . . . . . . American Association of Workers for the Blind
AAYM . . . . . . American Association of Youth Museums
AAZPA . . . . . American Association of Zoological Parks and Aquariums
AAF . . . . American Astronautical Federation
AAS . . . . American Astronautical Society
AAA . . . . American Astronomers Association
AAS . . . . American Astronomical Society
AAI . . . . American Audio Institute
AABC . . . . . . American Austin-Bantam Club
AAA . . . . American Australian Association
AALA . . . . . . American Auto Laundry Association
AARWBA . . . . American Auto Racing Writers and Broadcasters Association
AACC . . . . . . American Automatic Control Council
AAA . . . . American Automobile Association
AATA . . . . . . American Automobile Touring Alliance
AALA . . . . . . American Automotive Leasing Association
AAHS . . . . . . American Aviation Historical Society
ABA . . . . American Badminton Association
ABA . . . . American Bakeries Co. (NYSE symbol)
ABA . . . . American Bakers Association
ABCW . . . . . . American Bakery and Confectionery Workers' International Union
ABA . . . . American Bandmasters Association
ABN . . . . American Bank Note Co. (NYSE symbol)
ABA . . . . American Bankers Association
ABA . . . . American Bantam Association
ABC . . . . American Baptist Convention
ABEA . . . . . . American Baptist Education Association
ABFMS . . . . . American Baptist Foreign Mission Society (Congo--Leopoldville)
ABHS . . . . . . American Baptist Historical Society
ABHMS . . . . . American Baptist Home Mission Societies
ABMU . . . . . . American Baptist Missionary Union
ABW . . . . American Baptist Women
ABA . . . . American Bar Association
ABA/TCP . . . . American Bar Association Traffic Court Program
ABF . . . . American Bar Foundation
ABPRBC . . . . . American Barred Plymouth Rock Bantam Club
ABPRC . . . . . American Barred Plymouth Rock Club
ABA . . . . American Basketball Association (League of professional basketball players)
ABMC . . . . . . American Battle Monuments Commission (Independent government agency)
ABA . . . . American Battleship Association

ABC . . . . American Beagle Club
ABF . . . . American Beekeeping Federation
ABS . . . . American Begonia Society
ABS . . . . American Behavioral Scientist (A periodical)
ABA . . . . American Bell Association
BGA . . . . American Belted Galloway Cattle Breeders' Association
ABA . . . . American Berkshire Association
ABC . . . . American Beveren Club
ABS . . . . American Bible Society
ABES . . . . . . American Biblical Encyclopedia Society
ABC . . . . American Bibliographical Center
ABRDA . . . . . . American Bill of Rights Day Association
ABSMA . . . . . . American Bleached Shellac Manufacturers Association
ABBA . . . . . . American Blind Bowling Association
ABC . . . . American Bloodhound Club
ABAS . . . . . . American Board of Abdominal Surgery
ABA . . . . American Board Association
ABB-A . . . . . . American Board of Bio-Analysis
ABCOP . . . . . American Board for Certification in Orthotics and Prosthetics
ABCH . . . . . . American Board of Clinical Hypnosis
ABCRS . . . . . American Board of Colon and Rectal Surgery
ABCFM . . . . . American Board of Commissioners for Foreign Missions
ABCS . . . . . . American Board on Counseling Services
ABDPH . . . . . American Board of Dental Public Health
ABD . . . . American Board of Dermatology
ABEPP . . . . . . American Board of Examiners in Professional Psychology
ABEPH . . . . . . American Board of Examiners in Psychological Hypnosis
ABFM . . . . . American Board of Foreign Missions
ABHP . . . . . . American Board of Health Physics
ABIM . . . . . . American Board of Internal Medicine
ABIM . . . . . . American Board of International Missions
ABMJ . . . . . . American Board of Missions to the Jews
ABNM . . . . . . American Board of National Missions
ABNS . . . . . . American Board of Neurological Surgery
ABOG . . . . . . American Board of Obstetrics and Gynecology
ABO . . . . American Board of Ophthalmology
ABO . . . . . . American Board of Opticianry
AMBOP . . . . . American Board of Oral Pathology
ABOS . . . . . . American Board of Oral Surgery
ABO . . . . American Board of Orthodontics
ABOS . . . . . . American Board of Orthopaedic Surgery
ABO . . . . . . American Board of Otolaryngology
ABP . . . . American Board of Pathology
ABPD . . . . . . American Board of Pediatric Dermatology
ABP . . . . American Board of Pediatrics
ABP . . . . American Board of Pedodontics
ABP . . . . . . American Board of Periodontology
ABPMR . . . . . American Board of Physical Medicine and Rehabilitation
ABPS . . . . . . American Board of Plastic Surgery
ABPM . . . . . . American Board of Preventive Medicine
ABP . . . . American Board of Prosthodontics
ABPN . . . . . . American Board of Psychiatry and Neurology
ABR . . . . American Board of Radiology
ABS . . . . American Board of Surgery
ABBRA . . . . . American Boat Builders & Repairers Association
ABYC . . . . . . American Boat and Yacht Council
ABMA . . . . . . American Boiler Manufacturers' Association & Affiliated Industries
ABPC . . . . . . American Book Publishers Council (Later, AAP)
BPR . . . . American Book Publishing Record
ABA . . . . American Booksellers Association
AB . . . . American Bosch Arma Corporation (NYSE symbol)
ABWA . . . . . . American Bottled Water Association
ABCB . . . . . . American Bottlers of Carbonated Beverages
ABDFC . . . . . American Bouvier des Flandres Club
ABA . . . . . . American Bowhunters Association
ABC . . . . American Bowling Congress
ABC . . . . American Boxer Club
ABS . . . . American Boxwood Society
ABC . . . . American Brahma Club
ABBA . . . . . . American Brahman Breeders Association
ABK . . . . American Brake Shoe Co. (NYSE symbol)
ABA . . . . . . American Brazilian Association
ABA . . . . . . American Bridge Association
ABTA . . . . . . American Bridge Teachers' Association
ABTTA . . . . . . American Bridge, Tunnel and Turnpike Association
ABC . . . . American, British, and Canadian
ABC-ASP . . . . American-British-Canadian Army Standardization Program
ABCA . . . . . . American, British, Canadian, and Australian
ABCSP . . . . . . American-British-Canadian Standardization Program
ABC . . . . American-British Conversation (as ABC-1, 1941 report that set forth allied worldwide strategy) (World War II)

ABDAIR . . . . . American-British-Dutch-Australian Air Operational Command (1942)
ABDARM . . . . . American-British-Dutch-Australian Army Operational Command
ABDAFLOAT . . . American-British-Dutch-Australian Naval Operational Command (1942)
ABDACOM . . . American-British-Dutch-Australian Supreme Command (1942)
ABC . . . . American Brittany Club
ABC . . . . American Broadcasting Company
ABP . . . . American Broadcasting-Paramount Theatres (Later, American Broadcasting Companies, Incorporated) (NYSE symbol)
ABSIE . . . . . . American Broadcasting Station in Europe (OWI)
ABEA . . . . . . American Broncho-Esophagological Association
ABLC . . . . . . American Brown Leghorn Club
ABMA . . . . . American Brush Manufacturers Association
ABGA . . . . . . American Brussels Griffon Association
ABS . . . . American Bryological Society
ABRA . . . . . . American Buckskin Registry Association
ABA . . . . American Buddhist Association
ABPRC . . . . . American Buff Plymouth Rock Club
ABWC . . . . . . American Buff Wyandotte Club
ABCA . . . . . . American Building Contractors Association
ABL . . . . American Bulgarian League
ABMAC . . . . . American Bureau for Medical Aid to China
ABMS . . . . . . American Bureau of Metal Statistics
AB . . . . American Bureau of Shipping
ABS . . . . American Bureau of Shipping
ABLA . . . . . . American Business Law Association
ABMRF . . . . . American Business Men's Research Foundation
ABP . . . . American Business Press
ABWA . . . . . . American Business Women's Association
ABWA . . . . . . American Business Writing Association
ABI . . . . American Butter Institute
ABCRA . . . . . American-Byelorussian Cultural Relief Association
AC & R . . . . . American Cable & Radio Corporation
ACA . . . . American Cadet Alliance
ACS . . . . American Camellia Society
ACM . . . . American Campaign Medal
ACA . . . . American Camping Association
AC . . . . American Can Company (NYSE symbol)
ACS . . . . American Cancer Society
ACA . . . . American Canoe Association
ACPA . . . . . . American Capon Producers Association
ACF . . . . American Car and Foundry
ACWRRE . . . . . American Cargo War Risk Reinsurance Exchange
ACS . . . . American Carnation Society
ACA . . . . American Carnivals Association
ACI . . . . American Carpet Institute
ACA . . . . American Casting Association
ACA . . . . American Cat Association
ACFA . . . . . . American Cat Fanciers Association
ACCCA . . . . . American Catholic Correctional Chaplains Association
ACHA . . . . . . American Catholic Historical Association
ACPA . . . . . . American Catholic Philosophical Association
ACPA . . . . . . American Catholic Psychological Association
ACSS . . . . . . American Catholic Sociological Society
AAC . . . . American Cement Corp. (NYSE symbol)
ACA . . . . American Cemetery Association
ACS . . . . American Ceramic Society
ACMA . . . . . . American Certified Morticians Association
ACS . . . . American Cetacean Society
ACW . . . . American Chain of Warehouses
ACCE . . . . . . American Chamber of Commerce Executives
ACCRA . . . . . American Chamber of Commerce Researchers Association
AC/IREF . . . . . American Chapter, International Real Estate Federation
ACBA . . . . . . American Charbray Breeders Association
ACF . . . . American Checker Federation (Governing body for sport in US)
ACGC . . . . . . American Checkered Giant Club (Later, American Checkered Giant Rabbit Club)
ACGRC . . . . . American Checkered Giant Rabbit Club
ACS . . . . American Chemical Society
ACC . . . . American Chesapeake Club
ACF . . . . American Chess Foundation
ACSS . . . . . . American Cheviot Sheep Society
ACGF . . . . . . American Child Guidance Foundation
ACA . . . . American Chiropractic Association
ACDA . . . . . . American Choral Directors Association
ACF . . . . American Choral Foundation
ACAI . . . . . . American Christian Association for Israel (Later, American-Israel Cultural Foundation)
ACCR . . . . . . American Christian Committee for Refugees (Post-World War II, Europe)
ACPC . . . . . . American Christian Palestine Committee
ACCS . . . . . . American Christmas Crib Society
ACBFC . . . . . . American Church Building Fund Commission

ACU . . . . American Church Union
ACE . . . . American Cinema Editors
ACMA . . . . . . American Circus Memorial Association
ACA . . . . American Civic Association
ACLU . . . . . . American Civil Liberties Union
ACIIB . . . . . . American Civilian Internee Information Bureau
ACL . . . . American Classical League
ACPA . . . . . . American Cleft Palate Association
ACCA . . . . . American Clinical and Climatological Association
ACSMA . . . . American Cloak and Suit Manufacturers Association
ACPS . . . . American Coalition of Patriotic Societies
ACRI . . . . . . American Cocoa Research Institute
ACCCI . . . . . . American Coke and Coal Chemicals Institute
ACA . . . . American Collectors Association
ACA . . . . American College of Allergists
ACA . . . . American College of Anesthesiologists
ACA . . . . American College of Apothecaries
ACC . . . . American College of Cardiology
ACCP . . . . . . American College of Chest Physicians
ACCA . . . . . . American College of Clinic Administrators
ACCM . . . . . . American College of Clinic Managers
ACD . . . . American College of Dentists
ACFO . . . . . . American College of Foot Orthopedists
ACFR . . . . . . American College of Foot Roentgenologists
ACFS . . . . . . American College of Foot Surgeons
ACG . . . . American College of Gastroenterology
ACGPOMS . . . American College of General Practitioners in Osteopathic Medicine
        and Surgery
ACHA . . . . . . American College Health Association
ACHA . . . . . . American College of Hospital Administrators
ACLAM . . . . . American College of Laboratory Animal Medicine
ACLM . . . . . . American College of Legal Medicine
ACLU . . . . . . American College of Life Underwriters
ACMT . . . . . . American College of Medical Technologists
ACM . . . . American College of Musicians
ACN . . . . American College of Neuropsychiatrists
ACNM . . . . . . American College of Nurse-Midwifery
ACNHA . . . . . American College of Nursing Home Administrators
ACOG . . . . . . American College of Obstetricians and Gynecologists
ACOHA . . . . American College of Osteopathic Hospital Administrators
ACOI . . . . . . American College of Osteopathic Internists
ACOOG . . . . American College of Osteopathic Obstetricians and Gynecologists
ACOP . . . . . . American College of Osteopathic Pediatricians
ACOS . . . . . . American College of Osteopathic Surgeons
ACPA . . . . . . American College Personnel Association
ACP . . . . American College of Pharmacists
ACP . . . . American College of Physicians
ACPM . . . . . . American College of Preventive Medicine
ACPRA . . . . . American College Public Relations Association
ACR . . . . American College of Radiology
ACSM . . . . . American College of Sports Medicine
ACS . . . . American College of Surgeons
ACT . . . . American College Testing (Program)
ACTL . . . . . . American College of Trial Lawyers
ACVP . . . . . . American College of Veterinary Pathologists
ACRA . . . . . . American Collegiate Retailing Association
ACS . . . . American Colonization Society
AOY . . . . American Colortype Company (NYSE symbol)
ACMA . . . . . American Comedy Museum Association
ACBL . . . . . . American Commercial Barge Line Company (AAR code)
ACL . . . . American Commercial Lines, Inc.
ABR . . . . American Commercial Lines, Incorporated (NYSE symbol)
ACMT . . . . . . American Commission on Ministerial Training
ACPSAHMWA . . American Commission for Protection and Salvage of Artistic and
        Historical Monuments in War Areas (World War II)
ACOA . . . . . . American Committee on Africa
ACFN . . . . . . American Committee for Flags of Necessity
ACIWLP . . . . . American Committee for International Wild Life Protection
ACIS . . . . . . American Committee for Irish Studies
ACIM . . . . . . American Committee on Italian Migration
ACJ . . . . American Committee on Japan
ACL . . . . American Committee for Liberation
AMEROSE . . . . American Committee of OSE
ACUE . . . . . . American Committee of United Europe
ACA . . . . American Communications Association
ACTA . . . . . . American Community Theatre Association
ACA . . . . American Commuters Association
ACLA . . . . . . American Comparative Literature Association
ACA . . . . American Composers Alliance
ACC . . . . American Concert Choir
ACCCF . . . . . . American Concert Choir and Choral Foundation

ACAPA . . . . . . American Concrete Agricultural Pipe Association
ACI . . . . American Concrete Institute
ACPA . . . . . . American Concrete Paving Association
ACPA . . . . . American Concrete Pipe Association
ACAD . . . . . American Conference of Academic Deans
ACC . . . . American Conference of Cantors
ACGIH . . . . . American Conference of Governmental Industrial Hygienists
ACJA . . . . . . American Congregation of Jews from Austria
ACA . . . . American Congregational Association
ACU . . . . American Congregational Union
ACPMR . . . . . American Congress of Physical Medicine and Rehabilitation
ACSM . . . . . American Congress on Surveying and Mapping
AOA . . . . American Conservation Association
ACU . . . . American Conservative Union
ACM . . . . American Conservatory of Music
ACT . . . . American Conservatory Theatre
AMCON . . . . . American Consul
AMCONREPO . . American Consular Reporting Officer
ACA . . . . American Consumer Industries, Inc. (NYSE symbol)
ACBL . . . . . . American Contract Bridge League
ACHA . . . . . . American Coon Hunters Association
ACLO . . . . . . American Cooperative Library Association
ACMF . . . . . . American Corn Millers' Federation
ACA . . . . American Correctional Association
ACCA . . . . . . American Correctional Chaplains Association
ACA . . . . American Corriedale Association
ACRA . . . . . . American Cotswold Record Association
ACCI . . . . . . American Cottage Cheese Institute
ACCA . . . . . . American Cotton Cooperative Association
ACLA . . . . . . American Cotton Linter Association
ACMI . . . . . . American Cotton Manufacturers Institute
ACSA . . . . . . American Cotton Shippers Association
ACAP . . . . . . American Council on Alcohol Problems
ACBB . . . . . . American Council for Better Broadcasts
ACCR . . . . . . American Council on Chiropractic Roentgenography (Later,
        Roentgenology)
ACCC . . . . . . American Council of Christian Churches
ACCL . . . . . . American Council of Christian Laymen (Later, Laymen's Commission of
        the American Council of Christian Churches)
ACE . . . . American Council on Education
ACEJ . . . . . . American Council on Education for Journalism
ACESIA . . . . . American Council for Elementary School Industrial Arts
ACEP . . . . . . American Council for Emigres in the Professions
ACG . . . . American Council on Germany
ACHR . . . . . . American Council of Human Rights
ACTION . . . . . American Council to Improve Our Neighborhoods (Defunct)
ACIL . . . . . . American Council of Independent Laboratories
ACIASAO . . . . American Council of Industrial Arts State Association Officers
ACIAS . . . . . . American Council of Industrial Arts Supervisors
ACIATE . . . . . American Council of Industrial Arts Teacher Education
ACJ . . . . American Council for Judaism
ACLS . . . . . . American Council of Learned Societies
ACNS . . . . . . American Council for Nationalities Service
ACN . . . . American Council on NATO
ACPC . . . . . . American Council of Parent Cooperatives
ACPE . . . . . . American Council on Pharmaceutical Education
ACPCC . . . . . American Council of Polish Cultural Clubs
ACRR . . . . . . American Council on Race Relations
ACRW . . . . . . American Council of Railroad Women
ACR . . . . American Council for Romanians
ACSC . . . . . . American Council on Schools and Colleges
ACTFL . . . . . . American Council on the Teaching of Foreign Languages
ACVC . . . . . . American Council of Venture Clubs
ACVAFS . . . . . American Council of Voluntary Agencies for Foreign Service
ACYPL . . . . . . American Council of Young Political Leaders
ACLA . . . . . . American Country Life Association
ACC . . . . American Craftsmen's Council
ACGA . . . . . . American Cranberry Growers' Association
ACDHA . . . . . American Cream Draft Horse Association
ACAC . . . . . . American Croatian Academic Club
ACA . . . . American Cryptogram Association
ACS . . . . American Crystal Sugar Company (NYSE symbol)
ACA . . . . American Crystallographic Association
ACEL . . . . . . American Crystallographic Association
ACF . . . . American Culinary Federation
ACMA . . . . . American Cutlery Manufacturers Association
ACCO . . . . . . American Cyanamid Company
ACY . . . . American Cyanamid Company (NYSE symbol)
ACU . . . . American Cycling Union
ADS . . . . American Daffodil Society
ADS . . . . American Dahlia Society

ADA . . . . American Dairy Association
ADGA . . . . . . American Dairy Goat Association
ADSA . . . . American Dairy Science Association
AMDAG . . . . . American Decartelization Agency (Post-World War II)
ADBC . . . . American Defenders of Bataan and Corregidor
ADSM . . . . . . American Defense Service Medal
ADOGA . . . . . American Dehydrated Onion and Garlic Association
ADA . . . . American Dehydrators Association
ADMRA . . . . . American and Delaine-Merino Record Association
ADAA . . . . . . American Dental Assistants Association
ADA . . . . American Dental Association
ADHA . . . . . . American Dental Hygienists' Association
ADIC . . . . American Dental Interfraternity Council
ADSA . . . . . . American Dental Society of Anesthesiology
ADTA . . . . . . American Dental Trade Association
ADS . . . . American Denture Society
ADR . . . . American Depositary Receipt
ADA . . . . American Dermatological Association
ADCC . . . . . . American Devon Cattle Club
ADA . . . . American Diabetes Association
ADD . . . . American Dialect Dictionary
ADS . . . . American Dialect Society
ADCI . . . . American Die Casting Institute
ADCII . . . . . . American Die Casting Institute, Incorporated
ADA . . . . American Dietetic Association
ADC . . . . American Distilling Company (NYSE symbol)
ADT . . . . American District Telegraph Co. (Alarm systems)
ADI . . . . American Documentation Institute
ADFI . . . . American Dog Feed Institute
ADEA . . . . . . American Driver Education Association
ADTSEA . . . . . American Driver and Traffic Safety Education Association
ADMA . . . . . . American Drug Manufacturers' Association
ADMI . . . . . . American Dry Milk Institute
AEA . . . . American Economic Association
AEF . . . . American Economic Foundation
AEA . . . . American Education Association
AEW . . . . American Education Week
AEPI . . . . American Educational Publishers Institute (Later, AAP)
AERA . . . . . . American Educational Research Association
AESA . . . . . . American Educational Studies Association
AETA . . . . . . American Educational Theatre Association
AEP . . . . American Electric Power System (Group of investor-owned public
          utility companies) (NYSE symbol)
AEMC . . . . . . American Electro Metal Corporation
AES . . . . American Electrochemical Society
AES . . . . American Electroencephalographic Society
AES . . . . American Electromechanical Society
AES . . . . American Electronical Society
AES . . . . American Electroplaters' Society
AMEMB . . . . . American Embassy
AECTR . . . . . . American Emergency Committee for Tibetan Refugees
AEL . . . . American Emigrants' League
AEA . . . . American Engineering Association
AEC . . . . American Engineering Council
AESC . . . . . . American Engineering Standards Committee
ANK . . . . American Enka Corporation (NYSE symbol)
AEA . . . . American Enterprise Association
AEI . . . . American Enterprise Institute for Public Policy Research
AEIPPR . . . . . . American Enterprise Institute for Public Policy Research
AES . . . . American Entomological Society
AES . . . . American Epidemiological Society
AES . . . . American Epilepsy Society
AES . . . . American Equilibration Society
AEU . . . . American Ethical Union
AES . . . . American Ethnological Society
AES . . . . American Eugenics Society
AEF . . . . American European Foundation
AEF . . . . American Expeditionary Forces
AEA . . . . American Export Airlines
AEX . . . . American Export Isbrandtsen Company (NYSE symbol)
AEIL . . . . American Export Isbrandtsen Lines
AMEX . . . . . . American Express Company
AMEXCO . . . . American Express Company
AFTC . . . . . . American Fair Trade Council
AFES . . . . . . American Far Eastern Society
AFB . . . . American Farm Bureau
AFBF . . . . American Farm Bureau Federation
AFEA . . . . . . American Farm Economic Association
AFRA . . . . . . American Farm Research Association
AFA . . . . American Federation of Arts
AFA . . . . American Federation of Astrologers

AFCWB . . . . . American Federation of Catholic Workers for the Blind
AFCR . . . . . . American Federation for Clinical Research
AFFS . . . . . . American Federation of Film Societies
AFGE . . . . . . American Federation of Government Employees
AFGM . . . . . . American Federation of Grain Millers
AFHW . . . . . . American Federation of Hosiery Workers
AFIPS . . . . . . American Federation of Information Processing Societies
AFII . . . . American Federation of International Institutes
AFIE . . . . American Federation of Italian Evangelicals
AFJCE . . . . . . American Federation of Jews from Central Europe
AFL . . . . American Federation of Labor
AFL-CIO . . . . . American Federation of Labor and Congress of Industrial Organizations
AFMS . . . . . . American Federation of Mineralogical Societies
AFM . . . . American Federation of Musicians of the US and Canada
AFPH . . . . . . American Federation of the Physically Handicapped
AFP . . . . American Federation of Police
AFPJ . . . . American Federation for Polish Jews
AFPPA . . . . . . American Federation of Poultry Producers Associations
AFP . . . . American Federation of Priests
AFRKB . . . . . . American Federation of Retail Kosher Butchers
AFSBO . . . . . . American Federation of Small Business Organizations
AFSC . . . . . . American Federation of Soroptimist Clubs
AFSCME . . . . . American Federation of State, County and Municipal Employees
SCME . . . . . . American Federation of State, County and Municipal Employees
AFT . . . . American Federation of Teachers
AFTE . . . . . . American Federation of Technical Engineers
AFTRA . . . . . . American Federation of Television and Radio Artists
AFWC . . . . . . American Federation of World Citizens
AFMA . . . . . . American Feed Manufacturers Association
AFS . . . . American Feline Society
AFS . . . . American Fern Society
AFS . . . . American Fertility Society
AFI . . . . American Fiber Institute
AFS . . . . American Field Service
AFAA . . . . . . American Fighter Aces Association
AFEA . . . . . . American Film Export Association
AFI . . . . American Film Institute
AFA . . . . American Finance Association
AFC . . . . American Finance Conference
AFAS . . . . . . American Fine Arts Society
AFCG . . . . . . American Fine China Guild
AFDCS . . . . . . American First Day Cover Society
AFFF . . . . American Fish Farmers Federation
AFAC . . . . . . American Fisheries Advisory Committee
AFS . . . . American Fisheries Society
AFTMA . . . . . American Fishing Tackle Manufacturers Association
AFA . . . . American Flag Association of the US
AFC . . . . American Flag Committee
AFSA . . . . . . American Flight Strips Association
AFGW . . . . . . American Flint Glass Workers Union of North America
AFGWU . . . . . American Flint Glass Workers Union of North America
AFS . . . . American Folklore Society
AFPC . . . . . . American Food for Peace Council
AFCI . . . . American Foot Care Institute
AFHF . . . . . . American Foot Health Foundation
AFCA . . . . . . American Football Coaches Association
AFL . . . . American Football League
AFGC . . . . . . American Forage and Grassland Council
AFA . . . . American Forces in Action (Military)
AFN . . . . American Forces Network
AFBS . . . . . . American and Foreign Bible Society
AFCU . . . . . . American and Foreign Christian Union
AFIA . . . . American Foreign Insurance Association
AFLA . . . . . . American Foreign Law Association
AF . . . . American & Foreign Power Company, Inc. (NYSE symbol) (Wall Street
          slang name: "Airforce")
A & FP . . . . . American and Foreign Power Company
AFSA . . . . . . American Foreign Service Association
AFSPA . . . . . . American Foreign Service Protective Association
AFA . . . . American Forensic Association
AFPI . . . . American Forest Products Industries
AFA . . . . American Forestry Association
AFFFA . . . . . . American Forged Fitting and Flange Association
AFAE . . . . . . American Foundation on Automation and Employment
AFB . . . . American Foundation for the Blind
AFCE . . . . . . American Foundation for Continuing Education
AFH . . . . American Foundation for Homoeopathy
AFMR . . . . . . American Foundation for Management Research
AFMH . . . . . . American Foundation for Mental Hygiene
AFOB . . . . . . American Foundation for Overseas Blind
AFPE . . . . . . American Foundation for Pharmaceutical Education

AFPE . . . . . . American Foundation for Political Education
AFPPG . . . . . . American Foundation for Psychoanalysis and Psychoanalysis in Groups
AFRAP. . . . . . American Foundation of Religion and Psychiatry
AFRP . . . . . . American Foundation of Religion and Psychiatry
AFTM . . . . . . American Foundation for Tropical Medicine
AFWYU . . . . . American Foundation for World Youth Understanding
AFA . . . . . . American Foundrymen's Association
AFS . . . . . . American Foundrymen's Society
AFTC . . . . . . American Fox Terrier Club
AFC . . . . . . American Foxhound Club
AFA . . . . . . American Fracture Association
AFU . . . . . . American Fraternal Union
AFA . . . . . . American Freedom Association
AFC . . . . . . American Freedom Center
FFH . . . . . . American Freedom from Hunger Foundation
AFRF . . . . . . American Freedom of Residence Fund
AFAIU . . . . . . American Friends of the Alliance Israelite Universelle
AFABBN . . . . . American Friends of the Anti-Bolshevik Bloc of Nations
AFCN . . . . . . American Friends of the Captive Nations
AFG . . . . . . American Friends of Greece
AFHU . . . . . . American Friends of Hebrew University
AFI . . . . American Friends of Israel
AFME . . . . . . American Friends of the Middle East
AFR . . . . American Friends of Refugees
AFRFI . . . . . . American Friends of Religious Freedom in Israel
AFRF . . . . . . American Friends of Russian Freedom (Later, American Friends of Refugees)
AFSC . . . . . . American Friends Service Committee
AFV . . . . American Friends of Vietnam
AFS . . . . American Fuchsia Society
AFCR . . . . . . American Fund for Czechoslovak Refugees
AFDE . . . . . . American Fund for Dental Education
AFFJ . . . . . . American Fund for Free Jurists
AFDEA . . . . . American Funeral Directors and Embalmers Association
AFLCA . . . . . American Fur Liner Contractors Association
AFMA. . . . . . American Fur Merchants' Association
AGD . . . . . . American Gage Design Committee
AGDS . . . . . American Gage Design Standard
AGBA . . . . . American Galloway Breeders' Association
AGA . . . . . . American Gas Association
AG & ES . . . . American Gas & Electric System
AGDA . . . . . American Gasoline Dealers Association
AGA . . . . . . American Gastroenterological Association
AGA . . . . . . American Gastroscopic Society
AGMA . . . . . American Gear Manufacturers Association
AGMSA . . . . . American Gem and Mineral Suppliers Association
AGS. . . . . . American Gem Society
AGA . . . . . . American Genetic Association
AGI . . . . . . American Geographical Institute
AGS. . . . . . American Geographical Society
AGSS . . . . . American Geographical and Statistical Society
AGI . . . . . . American Geological Institute
AGU . . . . . . American Geophysical Union
AGRF . . . . . . American Geriatric Research Foundation
AGS. . . . . . American Geriatrics Society
AGS. . . . . . American Gesneria Society
AGA . . . . . . American Glassware Association
AGS. . . . . . American Gloxinia Society
AGA . . . . . . American Go Association
AGS. . . . . . American Goat Society
AGA . . . . . . American Goiter Association
AGA . . . . . . American Gold Association
AGSM . . . . . American Gold Star Mothers
AGGS . . . . . American Good Government Society
AGS. . . . . . American Graphological Society
AGC . . . . . . American Grassland Council
AGRCO . . . . . American Graves Registration Command
AGRS . . . . . . American Graves Registration Service
AGTOA . . . . . American Greyhound Track Operators Association
AGFSA . . . . . American Ground Flat Stock Association
AGPA. . . . . . American Group Psychotherapy Association
AGCC . . . . . American Guernsey Cattle Club
AGAA . . . . . American Guild of Animal Artists
AGAC . . . . . American Guild of Authors and Composers
AGEHR . . . . . American Guild of English Handbell Ringers
AGM . . . . . . American Guild of Music
AGMA . . . . . American Guild of Musical Artists
AGO . . . . . . American Guild of Organists
AGVA . . . . . American Guild of Variety Artists
AGWI. . . . . . American Gulf West Indies Company
AGDA . . . . . . American Gun Dealers Association

AGA . . . . . . American Guppy Association
AGS. . . . . . . American Gynecological Society
AHHS . . . . . . American Hackney Horse Society
AHSA . . . . . . American Hampshire Sheep Association
AHA. . . . . . . American Hardboard Association
AHC. . . . . . . American Hardware Corporation (NYSE symbol)
AHMA . . . . . American Hardware Manufacturers Association
AHS . . . . American Harp Society
AHS . . . . American Hearing Society
AHA . . . . . . American Heart Association
AHC . . . . . . American Helicopter Company
AHS . . . . . . American Helicopter Society
AHC . . . . . . American Hellenic Congress
AHS . . . . . . American Hemerocallis Society
AHA . . . . . . American Hereford Association
AHF . . . . . . American Heritage Foundation
AHS . . . . . . American Hibiscus Society
AHG . . . . . . American High-Density Gradient
AHCEI . . . . . American Histadrut Cultural Exchange Institute
AHA. . . . . . . American Historical Association
AHPS-CWPS. . . American Historical Philatelic Society - Civil War Philatelic Society
AHF . . . . . . American Hobby Federation
AHCA . . . . . American Hockey Coaches Association
AHL . . . . . . American Hockey League
AHEA . . . . . American Home Economics Association
AHLMA . . . . American Home Laundry Manufacturers Association
AHLI . . . . . . American Home Lighting Institute
AHMS . . . . . American Home Mission Society
HPT . . . . . . American Home Products Corporation (NYSE symbol)
AHI . . . . . . American Honey Institute
AHSA . . . . . American Horse Shows Association
AHC . . . . . . American Horticultural Council
AHS . . . . . . American Horticultural Society
AHA . . . . . . American Hospital Association
AHC . . . . . . American Hospital Corps
AHF . . . . . . American Hospital Formulary (A publication)
AHS . . . . . . American Hospital Society
AHS . . . . . . American Hospital Supply Corporation (NYSE symbol)
AHDGA . . . . American Hot Dip Galvanizers Association
AHRA . . . . . American Hot Rod Association
AHA. . . . . . American Hotel Association
AH & MA . . . . American Hotel and Motel Association
AHIS . . . . . . American Hull Insurance Syndicate
AHA . . . . . . American Humane Association
AHES . . . . . American Humane Education Society
AHS . . . . . . American Humane Society
AHF . . . . . . American Humanics Foundation
AHA . . . . . . American Humanist Association
AHCS . . . . . American Hungarian Catholic Society
AHF. . . . . . . American Hungarian Federation
AHLHS . . . . . American Hungarian Library and Historical Society
AHS . . . . . . American Hypnodontic Society
AHA. . . . . . . American Hypnotherapy Association
AHA. . . . . . . American Hypnotists' Association
AICC . . . . . . American Immigration and Citizenship Conference
AIDES . . . . . American Independent Designers and Engineers Society
AMERIND . . . . American Indian
AMIND . . . . . American Indian
AIECF. . . . . . American Indian and Eskimo Cultural Foundation
AIEC . . . . . . American Indian Ethnohistorical Conference
AIHR . . . . . . American Indian Horse Registry
AIAA . . . . . . American Industrial Arts Association
AIBA . . . . . . American Industrial Bankers Association
AIDC . . . . . . American Industrial Development Council
AIHA . . . . . . American Industrial Hygiene Association
AIMA . . . . . . American Industrial Music Association
AIRXRS . . . . . American Industrial Radium and X-Ray Society
AIR . . . . American Industrial Real Estate Association
AIT . . . . . . American Industrial Transport, Inc.
AIWI . . . . . . American Industrial Writing Institute
AI . . . . American Institute
AIAR . . . . . . American Institute of Aerological Research
AIAA . . . . . . American Institute of Aeronautics and Astronautics
AIA . . . . . . American Institute of Architects
AIAF. . . . . . American Institute of Architects Foundation
AIB . . . . . . American Institute of Baking
AIB . . . . . . American Institute of Banking
AIBS. . . . . . American Institute of Biological Sciences
AICPA . . . . . American Institute of Certified Public Accountants
AIC . . . . . . American Institute of Chefs
AICE . . . . . . American Institute of Chemical Engineers

AIChE . . . . American Institute of Chemical Engineers
AIC . . . . American Institute of Chemists
AICCC . . . . . . American Institute of Child Care Centers
AICA . . . . American Institute of Commemorative Art
AICE . . . . American Institute of Consulting Engineers
AIC . . . . American Institute of Cooperation
AIC . . . . American Institute of Criminology
AICE . . . . American Institute of Crop Ecology
AIDD . . . . American Institute for Design and Drafting
AIER . . . . American Institute for Economic Research
AIEE . . . . American Institute of Electrical Engineers (Later, IEEE)
AIFE . . . . American Institute for Exploration
AIFR . . . . American Institute of Family Relations
AIFB . . . . American Institute of Financial Brokers
AIFRB . . . . . . American Institute of Fishery Research Biologists
AIFD . . . . American Institute of Food Distributors
AIFS . . . . American Institute for Foreign Study
AIFT . . . . American Institute for Foreign Trade
AIF . . . . American Institute of France
AIFLD . . . . . . American Institute for Free Labor Development
AIGA . . . . American Institute of Graphic Arts
AIHP . . . . American Institute of the History of Pharmacy
AIH . . . . American Institute of Homeopathy
AIIS . . . . American Institute for Imported Steel
AIIS . . . . American Institute of Indian Studies
AIIE . . . . American Institute of Industrial Engineers
AIID . . . . American Institute of Interior Designers
AIKD . . . . American Institute of Kitchen Dealers
AILA . . . . American Institute of Landscape Architects
AIL . . . . American Institute of Laundering
AIM . . . . American Institute of Maintenance
AIM . . . . American Institute of Management
AIMU . . . . American Institute of Marine Underwriters
AIMS . . . . American Institute for Marxist Studies
AIMC . . . . American Institute of Medical Climatology
AIMBW . . . . . . American Institute of Men's and Boys' Wear
AIMS . . . . American Institute of Merchant Shipping
AIME . . . . American Institute of Mining, Metallurgical and Petroleum Engineers
AIMMPE . . . . . American Institute of Mining, Metallurgical, and Petroleum Engineers
AIM . . . . American Institute of Musicology
AIN . . . . American Institute of Nutrition
AIPR . . . . American Institute of Pacific Relations (Defunct)
AIP . . . . American Institute of Parliamentarians
AIPE . . . . American Institute of Park Executives
AIP . . . . American Institute of Physics
AIP . . . . American Institute of Planners
AIPE . . . . American Institute of Plant Engineers
AIPG . . . . American Institute of Professional Geologists
AIPLU . . . . . . American Institute for Property and Liability Underwriters
AIREA . . . . . . American Institute of Real Estate Appraisers
AISC . . . . American Institute of Steel Construction
AISA . . . . American Institute of Supply Associations
AITC . . . . American Institute of Timber Construction
AIUM . . . . American Institute of Ultrasonics in Medicine
AIVP . . . . American Institute of Vocal Pedagogy
AIR . . . . American Institutes for Research in the Behavioral Sciences
AID . . . . American Instructors of the Deaf
AIA . . . . American Insurance Association
AIA . . . . American International Academy
AIA . . . . American International Association for Economic and Social Development
AICA . . . . American-International Charolais Association
AIC . . . . American International College (Massachusetts)
AMC . . . . American International Corporation (NYSE symbol)
AIMF . . . . American International Music Fund
AII . . . . American Interprofessional Institute
AIA . . . . American Inventors Association
AIC . . . . American Investment Company of Illinois (NYSE symbol)
AIPA . . . . American Ionospheric Propagation Association
AIS . . . . American Iris Society
AIHS . . . . American-Irish Historical Society
AIOA . . . . American Iron Ore Association
AISI . . . . American Iron and Steel Institute
AIPAC . . . . . . American Israel Public Affairs Committee
AIL . . . . American Israeli Lighthouse
AIC . . . . American Italian Congress
AIHA . . . . American Italian Historical Association
AMITA . . . . . . American-Italian Women of Achievement
AISI . . . . American-Italy Society, Incorporated
AJCC . . . . American Jersey Cattle Club
AJMA . . . . American Jesuit Missionary Association

AJA . . . . American Jewish Archives
AJC . . . . American Jewish Committee
AJC . . . . American Jewish Conference
AJC . . . . American Jewish Congress
AJCCA . . . . . . American Jewish Correctional Chaplains Association
AJHS . . . . American Jewish Historical Society
AJHC . . . . American Jewish History Center
AJI . . . . American Jewish Institute
JDC . . . . American Jewish Joint Distribution Committee
AJLAC . . . . . . American Jewish League Against Communism
AJLI . . . . American Jewish League for Israel
AJPC . . . . American Jewish Periodical Center
AJPC . . . . American Jewish Physicians' Committee
AJPA . . . . American Jewish Press Association
AJPRS . . . . . . American Jewish Public Relations Society
AJSS . . . . American Jewish Society for Service
AJDC . . . . American Joint Distribution Committee
AJS . . . . American Journal of Science
AJS . . . . American Judicature Society
AJBC . . . . American Junior Bowling Congress
AJRC . . . . American Junior Red Cross
AJSA . . . . American Junior Shorthorn Association
AKC . . . . American Kennel Club
AKA . . . . American Kitefliers Association
AKGA . . . . American Knit Glove Association
AKF . . . . American-Korean Foundation
ALES . . . . American Labor Education Service
ALHA . . . . American Labor Health Association
ALP . . . . American Labor Party
ALMA . . . . American Lace Manufacturers Association
ALI . . . . American Ladder Institute
ALC . . . . American Lancia Club
ALTA . . . . American Land Title Association
ALA . . . . American Landrace Association
ALC . . . . American Langshan Club
ALA . . . . American Laryngological Association
ALROS . . . . . . American Laryngological, Rhinological and Otological Society
ALA . . . . American Latvian Association in the United States
AMY . . . . American Laundry Machinery (NYSE symbol)
ALI . . . . American Law Institute
ALR . . . . American Law Reports
ALSA . . . . American Law Student Association
ALBA . . . . American Lawn Bowling Association
ALBA . . . . American Leather Belting Association
ALCA . . . . American Leather Chemists Association
ALSAC . . . . . . American Lebanese Syrian Association Charities
AL . . . . American Legion
ALA . . . . American Legion Auxiliary
AL of H . . . . . . American Legion of Honor
ALPA . . . . American Legion Press Association
AL . . . . American League (Baseball)
ALACP . . . . . . American League to Abolish Capital Punishment
ALPBC . . . . . . American League of Professional Baseball Clubs
ALM . . . . American Leprosy Missions
ALS . . . . American Lessing Society
ALO . . . . American Liaison Office
ALA . . . . American Liberal Association
ALL . . . . American Liberation League
ALA . . . . American Library Association
ALD . . . . American Library Directory
ALERT . . . . . . American Library for Education, Research and Training
ALESCO . . . . . American Library and Educational Service Company
ALTA . . . . American Library Trustee Association
ALC . . . . American Life Convention
ALIA . . . . American Life Insurance Association
ALS . . . . American Liszt Society
ALEAA . . . . . . American Lithuanian Engineers' and Architects' Association
ALPRA . . . . . . American Lithuanian Press and Radio Association
ALRCFA . . . . . American Lithuanian Roman Catholic Federation Ateitis
ALRCOL . . . . . American Lithuanian Roman Catholic Organist Alliance
ALRCWA . . . . . American Lithuanian Roman Catholic Women's Alliance
ALWLA . . . . . . American Lithuanian Workers Literary Association
ALS . . . . American Littoral Society (For underwater study of shore life)
ALF . . . . American Loan Fund
ALCO . . . . American Locomotive Company
ALSC . . . . American Lumber Standards Committee
ALCW . . . . American Lutheran Church Women
ALPB . . . . American Lutheran Publicity Bureau
ALS . . . . American Luxembourg Society
AMF . . . . American Machine & Foundry Company (NYSE symbol)
AMTDA . . . . . . American Machine Tool Distributors Association

AMTEA . . . . . American Machine Tool Export Associates
AMA . . . . . . American Machinery Association
AMS. . . . . . . American Magnolia Society
AML. . . . . . . American Mail Line
AMU . . . . American Malacological Union
AMTC. . . . . . American Manchester Terrier Club
AMPA. . . . . . American Manganese Producers Association
AMA . . . . . . American Management Association
AMQ . . . . American Maracaibo Company (NYSE symbol)
AMICH. . . . . American Marine Insurance Clearing House
AMIF . . . . . . American Marine Insurance Forum
AMISIBR . . . . . American Marine Insurance Syndicate for Insurance of Builder's Risks
AMA . . . . . . American Maritime Association
AMC . . . . American Maritime Cases
AMI . . . . American Maritime Institute (Later, Society for Maritime History)
AMA . . . . . . American Marketing Association
AMTA. . . . . . American Massage and Therapy Association
AMHS. . . . . . American Material Handling Society
AMS. . . . . . . American Mathematical Society
AMA . . . . . . American McAll Association
AMI . . . . American Meat Institute
AMIF . . . . . . American Meat Institute Foundation
AMA . . . . . . American Medical Association
AMA-CIPP. . . . American Medical Association Committee on Insurance and Prepayment Plans
AMA-ERF . . . . American Medical Association Education and Research Foundation
AMCB. . . . . . American Medical Center for Burma
AMPAC. . . . . American Medical Political Action Committee
AMQ . . . . . . American Medical Qualification (British)
AMT. . . . . . . American Medical Technologists
AMTA. . . . . . American Medical Tennis Association
AMWA . . . . . American Medical Women's Association
AMWA . . . . . American Medical Writers' Association
AMP . . . . . . American Melting Point
AMHF . . . . . American Mental Health Foundation
AMMI. . . . . . American Merchant Marine Institute
AMMLA . . . . American Merchant Marine Library Association
AMF. . . . . . . American Messianic Fellowship
AMAX . . . . . American Metal Climax, Inc.
AMM . . . . . . American Metal Climax, Inc. (NYSE symbol)
AMIA . . . . . . American Metal Importers Association
APS . . . . American Metal Products Company (NYSE symbol)
AMRA. . . . . . American Metal Repair Association (Defunct)
AMSA. . . . . . American Metal Stamping Association
AMS. . . . . . . American Meteor Society
AML . . . . . . American Meteorite Laboratory
AMS. . . . . . . American Meteorological Society
AEM. . . . . . . American Meter Company (NYSE symbol)
AMPS . . . . . American Metered Postage Society
AMCC . . . . . American Mexican Claims Commission (Terminated, 1947)
AMS. . . . . . . American Microchemical Society
AMS. . . . . . . American Microscopical Society
AMER . . . . . . American Middle East Relief
MAGIC . . . . . American Military Advisory Group in China (Post-World War II)
AMAS . . . . . American Military Assistance Staff
AMG . . . . . . American Military Government
AMI . . . . American Military Institute
AMMISCA . . . . American Military Mission to China
AMGRA . . . . American Milk Goat Record Association
AMSS . . . . . . American Milking Shorthorn Society
AMMA . . . . . American Millinery Manufacturers Association
AMSCO . . . . American Mineral Spirits Company
AMRCA. . . . . American Miniature Racing Car Association
AMSC. . . . . . American Miniature Schnauzer Club
AMC . . . . . . American Mining Congress
AMA . . . . . . American Ministerial Association
AMSOC . . . . American Miscellaneous Society
AMAG . . . . . American Mission for Aid to Greece
AMAT. . . . . . American Mission for Aid to Turkey
AMC . . . . . . American Mission to the Chinese
AMG . . . . . . American Mission to Greeks
AMOCC . . . . American Mission for Opening Closed Churches
AMA . . . . . . American Missionary Association
AMS. . . . . . . American Mohammedan Society (Later, Moslem Mosque, Inc.)
AMS. . . . . . . American Montessori Society
AMA . . . . . . American Monument Association
AMCA . . . . . American Mosquito Control Association
AMA . . . . . . American Motel Association
AMC . . . . . . American Mothers Committee
AMKO . . . . . American Mothers of Korean Orphans
AMHA . . . . . American Motor Hotel Association

AMA . . . . . . American Motorcycle Association
AMC . . . . . . American Motors Corporation
AMO . . . . American Motors Corporation (NYSE symbol) (Wall Street slang name: "Ammo")
AMC . . . . . . American Movers Conference
AMA . . . . . . American Municipal Association (Later, National League of Cities)
AMI . . . . American Museum of Immigration
AMMA . . . . . American Museum of Marine Archaeology
AMNH . . . . . American Museum of Natural History
AMS. . . . . . . American Museum of Safety
AMI . . . . American Mushroom Institute
AMC . . . . . . American Music Center
AMC . . . . . . American Music Conference
AMS. . . . . . . American Musicological Society
AMA . . . . . . American Mutual Alliance (Insurance association)
AMIA . . . . . . American Mutual Insurance Alliance
ANPC. . . . . . American Nail Producers Council
ANS. . . . . American Name Society
ANA . . . . American Naprapathic Association
ANCA . . . . . American National Cattlemen's Association
ANCHA . . . . American National Committee to Aid Homeless Armenians
ANCHEP . . . . American National Council for Health Education of the Public
ANC . . . . . . American National Cowbelles
ANI . . . . American National Insurance Company
ANRC . . . . . American National Red Cross
ARC . . . . American National Red Cross
ANSI . . . . . . American National Standards Institute (Formerly, ASA and USASI)
ANTA. . . . . . American National Theatre and Academy
ANG . . . . . . American Natural Gas Company (NYSE symbol)
ANHS. . . . . . American Natural Hygiene Society
ANCWA . . . . American Naturalized Citizen Welfare Association
ANA . . . . . . American Nature Association
ANSS . . . . . . American Nature Study Society
ANERA . . . . . American Near East Refugee Aid (An organization)
ANEF . . . . . . American-Nepal Education Foundation
ANA . . . . . . American Neurological Association
ANC . . . . . . American News Company (NYSE symbol)
ANA . . . . . . American Newspaper Association
ANG . . . . . . American Newspaper Guild
ANPA . . . . . American Newspaper Publishers Association
ANWC . . . . . American Newspaper Women's Club
ANSC. . . . . . American Nuclear Science Corporation
ANS. . . . . . . American Nuclear Society
ANA . . . . . . American Numismatic Association
ANS. . . . . . . American Numismatic Society
ANA . . . . . . American Nurses' Association
ANF. . . . . . . American Nurses' Foundation
ANHA . . . . . American Nursing Home Association
ANS. . . . . . . American Nutrition Society
AOTA. . . . . . American Occupational Therapy Association
AOO . . . . American Oceanic Organization
AOSEA . . . . . American Office Supply Exporters Association
AOCS. . . . . . American Oil Chemists' Society
AMOCO . . . . American Oil Company
AOA . . . . . . American Onotoanalytic Association
AOC . . . . . . American Ophthalmological Color (Chart)
AOS. . . . . . . American Ophthalmological Society
AO . . . . American Optical Company
AOC . . . . . . American Optical Company (NYSE symbol)
AOA . . . . . . American Optometric Association
AOF. . . . . . . American Optometric Foundation
AOS. . . . . . . American Orchid Society
AOSE . . . . . . American Order of Stationary Engineers
AOA . . . . . . American Ordnance Association
AOS. . . . . . . American Oriental Society
AOU. . . . . . . American Ornithologists' Union
AOA . . . . . . American Orthopaedic Association
AOA . . . . . . American Orthopsychiatric Association
AOC . . . . . . American Orthoptic Council
AOPA. . . . . . American Orthotics and Prosthetics Association
AOAO . . . . . American Osteopathic Academy of Orthopedics
AOA . . . . . . American Osteopathic Association
AOCA . . . . . American Osteopathic College of Anesthesiologists
AOCD . . . . . American Osteopathic College of Dermatology
AOCP. . . . . . American Osteopathic College of Pathologists
AOCPMR. . . . . American Osteopathic College of Physical Medicine and Rehabilitation
AOCP . . . . . American Osteopathic College of Proctology
AOCR. . . . . . American Osteopathic College of Radiology
AOCR. . . . . . American Osteopathic College of Rheumatology
AOHS . . . . . American Osteopathic Historical Society
AOHA . . . . . American Osteopathic Hospital Association

AOS . . . . American Otological Society
AOSPS . . . . . . American Otorhinologic Society for Plastic Surgery (Later, American Academy of Facial Plastic and Reconstructive Surgery)
AOA . . . . American Overseas Airlines
AOA . . . . American Overseas Association
AODRA . . . . . . American Oxford Down Record Association
API . . . . American Paper Institute
APPA . . . . . . American Paper and Pulp Association
APC . . . . American Parents Committee
APDA . . . . . . American Parkinson Disease Association
APBHR . . . . . . American Part-Blooded Horse Registry
APPRC . . . . . . American Partridge Plymouth Rock Club
APLA . . . . American Patent Law Association
APA . . . . American Patients Association
APA . . . . American Pax Association
APS . . . . American Peace Society
APS . . . . American Pediatric Society
APCS . . . . . . American Pencil Collectors Society
APS . . . . American Penstemon Society
APS . . . . American Peony Society
APM . . . . American People's Mobilization (First called American Peace Mobilization) (World War II)
APRS . . . . American Performing-Rights Society
APGA . . . . . . American Personnel and Guidance Association
APPMA . . . . . . American Pet Products Manufacturers Association
APCA . . . . . . American Petroleum Credit Association
API . . . . American Petroleum Institute
APIR . . . . American Petroleum Institute Research
APRA . . . . . . American Petroleum Refiners Association
APG . . . . American Pewter Guild
APhA . . . . . . American Pharmaceutical Association
APS . . . . American Pheasant Society
APC . . . . American Philatelic Congress
APS . . . . American Philatelic Society
APA . . . . American Philological Association
APA . . . . American Philosophical Association
APS . . . . American Philosophical Society
APY . . . . American Photocopy Equipment Company (NYSE symbol)
APA . . . . American Photoengravers Association
APECO . . . . . . American Photograph Equipment Company
APS . . . . American Physical Society
APTA . . . . . . American Physical Therapy Association
APAA . . . . . . American Physicians Art Association
APF . . . . American Physicians Fellowship for the Israel Medical Association
APS . . . . American Physiological Society
APA . . . . American Physiotherapy Association
APS . . . . American Phytopathological Society
APA . . . . American Pilots' Association
APHA . . . . . . American Pinto Horse Association
APTA . . . . . . American Pioneer Trails Association
APFA . . . . . . American Pipe Fittings Association
APCA . . . . . . American Planning and Civic Association (Later, Urban America, Inc.)
APLS . . . . American Plant Life Society
APS . . . . American Plant Selections
APTA . . . . . . American Platform Tennis Association
APT . . . . American Playwrights Theatre
APA . . . . American Plywood Association
APA . . . . American Podiatry Association
APL . . . . American Poetry League
APS . . . . American Poinsettia Society
APC . . . . American Pointer Club
APS . . . . American Polar Society
APNRP . . . . . . American-Polish National Relief for Poland
APWR . . . . . . American Polish War Relief (Post-World War II)
APIC . . . . American Political Item Collectors (An organization)
APSA . . . . . . American Political Science Association
APHA . . . . . . American Polled Hereford Association
APSS . . . . . . American Polled Shorthorn Society
APA . . . . American Polygraph Association
APC . . . . American Pomeranian Club
APS . . . . American Pomological Society
APCS . . . . . . American Portuguese Cultural Society
APO . . . . American Potash & Chemical Corporation (NYSE symbol)
API . . . . American Potash Institute
APA . . . . American Poultry Association
APHF . . . . . . American Poultry and Hatchery Federation
APHS . . . . . . American Poultry Historical Society
APMI . . . . . . American Powder Metallurgy Institute
APBA . . . . . . American Power Boat Association
APC . . . . American Power Conference
APDA . . . . . . American Power Drinkers Association

APJ . . . . American Power Jet Company
APNA . . . . . . American Power Net Association
APCM . . . . . . American Presbyterian Congo Mission
API . . . . American Press Institute (Columbia University)
APS . . . . American Primrose Society
APFC . . . . . . American Printed Fabrics Council
APH . . . . American Printing House for the Blind
APHB . . . . . . American Printing House for the Blind
APWIB . . . . . . American Prisoner of War Information Bureau
APS . . . . American Proctologic Society
APICS . . . . . . American Production and Inventory Control Society
APPME . . . . . . American Professors for Peace in the Middle East
APB . . . . American Program Bureau (Lectures)
APF . . . . American Progress Foundation
APS . . . . American Prosthodontic Society
APA . . . . American Protective Association (Late-19th-century organization opposed to so-called encroachments of the Catholic Church in the US; initialism was also used by Catholics as an epithet for Protestants)
APA . . . . American Protestant Association
APCCA . . . . . . American Protestant Correctional Chaplains Association
APHA . . . . . . American Protestant Hospital Association
APS . . . . American Protestant Society
APA . . . . American Psychiatric Association
APA . . . . American Psychoanalytic Association
APA . . . . American Psychological Association
APF . . . . American Psychological Foundation
APSA . . . . . . American Psychologists for Social Action
APPA . . . . . . American Psychopathological Association
APS . . . . American Psychosomatic Society
APA . . . . American Psychotherapy Association
APGA . . . . . . American Public Gas Association
APHA . . . . . . American Public Health Association
APPA . . . . . . American Public Power Association
APRA . . . . . . American Public Relations Association
APWA . . . . . . American Public Welfare Association
APWA . . . . . . American Public Works Association
APAL . . . . . . American Puerto-Rican Action League
APA . . . . American Pulpwood Association
APAC . . . . . . American Puppet Arts Council
AQHA . . . . . . American Quarter Horse Association
ARBA . . . . . . American Rabbit Breeders Association
ARDC . . . . . . American Racing Driver's Club
ARPU . . . . . . American Racing Pigeon Union
ARMI . . . . . . American Rack Merchandisers Institute
AMSTAN . . . . American Radiator and Standard Sanitary Corp.
ARSS . . . . . . American Radiator and Standard Sanitary Corporation
AST . . . . American Radiator & Standard Sanitary Corp. (NYSE symbol)
ARA . . . . American Radio Association
ARIA . . . . . . American Radio Importers Association
ARRL . . . . . . American Radio Relay League
ART . . . . American Radiography Technologists (An organization)
ARS . . . . American Radium Society
ARBBA . . . . . American Railway Bridge and Building Association
ARCEA . . . . . American Railway Car Export Association
ARCI . . . . . . American Railway Car Institute
ARC . . . . American Railway Cases (Legal)
ARDA . . . . . . American Railway Development Association
AREA . . . . . . American Railway Engineering Association
ARMEA . . . . . American Railway Magazine Editors Association
ARMMA . . . . . American Railway Master Mechanics' Association
RSA . . . . American Railway Supervisors Association
ARU . . . . American Railway Union
ARSBA . . . . . American Rambouillet Sheep Breeders Association
ARF . . . . American Rationalist Federation
ARI . . . . American Rayon Institute
ARMADA . . . . American Record Merchandisers and Distributors Association
ARS . . . . American Recorder Society
ARMA . . . . . . American Records Management Association
ARS . . . . American Recreation Society
AREA . . . . . . American Recreational Equipment Association
AMCROSS . . . . American Red Cross
ARC . . . . American Red Cross
ARCCF . . . . . . American Red Cross Children's Fund
ARMD . . . . . . American Red Mogen Dovid for Israel
ARIT . . . . American Registry of Inhalation Therapists
ARMA . . . . . . American Registry of Medical Assistants
ARP . . . . American Registry of Pathologists
ARPT . . . . . . American Registry of Physical Therapists
ARRT . . . . . . American Registry of Radiologic Technologists
ARC . . . . American Rehabilitation Committee
ARCA . . . . . . American Rehabilitation Counseling Association

ARF . . . . American Rehabilitation Foundation
ARA . . . . American Relief Administration Association
ARP . . . . American Relief for Poland
ARA . . . . American Reloaders Association
ARA . . . . American Remount Association
ARA . . . . American Rental Association
ARS . . . . American Repair Service
ARA . . . . American Republics Area (State Department)
ARB . . . . American Research Bureau
ARD . . . . American Research & Development Corp. (NYSE symbol)
ARIT . . . . . . American Research Institute in Turkey
ARMI . . . . . . American Research Merchandising Institute
ARCC . . . . . . American Restaurant China Council
ARAE . . . . . . American Retail Association Executives
ARCA . . . . . . American Retail Coal Association
ARF . . . . American Retail Federation
ARA . . . . American Revenue Association
ARV . . . . American Revised Version (of the Bible)
ARBC . . . . . . American Revolution Bicentennial Commission
ARRT . . . . . . American Revolution Round Table
ARA . . . . American Rheumatism Association
ARS . . . . American Rhinologic Society
ARS . . . . American Rhododendron Society
ARGCA . . . . . . American Rice Growers Cooperative Association
ARAB . . . . . . American Riding Association of Berlin (Post-World War II)
ARWA . . . . . . American Right of Way Association
ARIA . . . . . . American Risk and Insurance Association
ARBA . . . . . . American Road Builders' Association
ARRC . . . . . . American Road Race of Champions
ARGS . . . . . . American Rock Garden Society
ARS . . . . American Rocket Society (Later, AIAA)
ARRS . . . . . . American Roentgen Ray Society
AROY . . . . . . American Romanian Orthodox Youth
ARBA . . . . . . American Romney Breeders' Association
ARL . . . . American Roque League
ARF . . . . American Rose Foundation
ARS . . . . American Rose Society
ARA . . . . American Royal Association
ARRHA . . . . . American RSROA Roller Hockey Association
ARDBC . . . . . American Rubberband Duckpin Bowling Congress
ARAA . . . . . . American Russian Aid Association
ASTS . . . . . . American Sabbath Tract Society
ASHBA . . . . . American Saddle Horse Breeders Association
ASDA . . . . . . American Safe Deposit Association
ASC . . . . American Safety Council
ARZ . . . . American Safety Razor Corporation (NYSE symbol)
ASC . . . . American Sailing Council
ASEIB . . . . . . American Sanitary Engineering Intersociety Board
ASRBA . . . . . American Satin Rabbit Breeders' Association
ASLI . . . . American Savings and Loan Institute
ASF . . . . American-Scandinavian Foundation
ASHPS . . . . . American Scenic and Historic Preservation Society
ASBDA . . . . . American School Band Directors' Association
ASCA . . . . . . American School Counselor Association
ASFSA . . . . . . American School Food Service Association
ASHA . . . . . . American School Health Association
ASOR . . . . . . American Schools of Oriental Research
ASFA . . . . . . American Science Film Association
ASII . . . . American Science Information Institute
ASA . . . . American Scientific Affiliation
ASGS . . . . . . American Scientific Glassblowers Society
ASHBA . . . . . American Scotch Highland Breeders' Association
ASGM . . . . . . American Scripture Gift Mission
ASDA . . . . . . American Seafood Distributors Association
AMK . . . . American Seal-Kap Corporation (NYSE symbol)
ASTC . . . . . . American Sealyham Terrier Club
ASFS . . . . . . American Seamen's Friend Society
ASBC . . . . . . American Seat Belt Council
AMZ . . . . American Seating Company (NYSE symbol)
ASSCI . . . . . . American Section of the Societe de Chimie Industrielle
ASC . . . . American Security Council
ASRF . . . . . . American Seed Research Foundation
ASTA . . . . . . American Seed Trade Association
ASP . . . . American Selling Price
ASCA . . . . . . American-Serbian Cultural Association
ASPC . . . . . . American Sheep Producers Council
ASA . . . . American Shellfisheries Association
ASPC . . . . . . American Shetland Pony Club
ASSA . . . . . . American Shetland Sheepdog Association
ASTC . . . . . . American Shih Tzu Club
ABG . . . . American Ship Building Co. (NYSE symbol)

ASHA . . . . . . American Shire Horse Association
ASBPA . . . . . . American Shore and Beach Preservation Association
ASLRRA . . . . . American Short Line Railroad Association
ASA . . . . American Shorthorn Association
ASBA . . . . . . American Shorthorn Breeders Association
ASWLC . . . . . American Shortwave Listeners Club
ASCA . . . . . . American Shrimp Canners Association
ASRA . . . . . . American Shropshire Registry Association
ASL . . . . American Shuffleboard Leagues
ASA . . . . American Sightseeing Association
ASL . . . . American Sign Language (for the deaf)
ASC . . . . American Silk Council
ASSRA . . . . . American Single Shot Rifle Association
ASMA . . . . . . American Ski Manufacturers' Association
ASBA . . . . . . American Skibob Association
KSKJ . . . . American Slovenian Catholic Union of the USA
AR . . . . American Smelting & Refining Company (NYSE symbol)
ASARCO . . . . American Smelting and Refining Company
ASPMA . . . . . American Smoking Pipe Manufacturers Association
ASA . . . . American Snowmobile Association
ASU . . . . American Snowshoe Union
SNU . . . . American Snuff Company (NYSE symbol)
ASHA . . . . . . American Social Health Association
ASHA . . . . . . American Social Hygiene Association
ASAS . . . . . . American Society of Abdominal Surgery
ASA . . . . American Society for Abrasives
ASAP . . . . . . American Society of Adlerian Psychology
ASAGAD . . . . American Society for Advancement of General Anesthesia in Dentistry
ASA . . . . American Society for Aesthetics
AMSAC . . . . . American Society of African Culture
ASAC . . . . . . American Society of Agricultural Consultants
ASAE . . . . . . American Society of Agricultural Engineers
ASA . . . . American Society of Agronomy
ASAI . . . . . . American Society of Ancient Instruments
ASA . . . . American Society of Anesthesiologists
ASAP . . . . . . American Society of Animal Production
ASAS . . . . . . American Society of Animal Science
ASAMN . . . . . American Society of Anthropometric Medicine and Nutrition
ASA . . . . American Society of Appraisers
ASAHC . . . . . American Society of Architectural Hardware Consultants
AS of AC . . . . American Society of Arms Collectors
ASAIO . . . . . . American Society for Artificial Internal Organs
ASAE . . . . . . American Society of Association Executives
ASA . . . . American Society of Auctioneers
ASBE . . . . . . American Society of Bakery Engineers
ASBC . . . . . . American Society of Biological Chemists
ASBE . . . . . . American Society of Body Engineers
ABCD . . . . . . American Society of Bookplate Collectors and Designers
ASBC . . . . . . American Society of Brewing Chemists
ASBPE . . . . . . American Society of Business Press Editors
ASC . . . . American Society of Cartographers
ASCET . . . . . American Society of Certified Engineering Technicians
ASCLU . . . . . American Society of Chartered Life Underwriters
ASCR . . . . . . American Society of Chiropodical Roentgenology
ASCE . . . . . . American Society of Christian Ethics
ASCA . . . . . . American Society for Church Architecture
ASCH . . . . . . American Society of Church History
ASC . . . . American Society of Cinematographers
ASCE . . . . . . American Society of Civil Engineers
ASCH . . . . . . American Society of Clinical Hypnosis
ASCH-ERF . . . American Society of Clinical Hypnosis - Education and Research Foundation
ASCI . . . . . . American Society for Clinical Investigation
ASCN . . . . . . American Society for Clinical Nutrition
ASCP . . . . . . American Society of Clinical Pathologists
ASCAP . . . . . American Society of Composers, Authors and Publishers
ASCC . . . . . . American Society of Concrete Constructors
ASCI . . . . . . American Society of Construction Inspectors
ASCA . . . . . . American Society of Consulting Arborists
ASCA . . . . . . American Society of Contemporary Artists
ASCS . . . . . . American Society of Corporate Secretaries
ASC . . . . American Society of Criminology
ASC . . . . American Society for Cybernetics
ASC . . . . American Society of Cytology
ASDE . . . . . . American Society of Danish Engineers
ASDR . . . . . . American Society of Dental Radiographers
ASDC . . . . . . American Society of Dentistry for Children
ASDJ . . . . . . American Society of Disk Jockeys
ASDM . . . . . . America's Society of Divorced Men (Elgin, Illinois)
ASD . . . . American Society of Dowsers
ASEA . . . . . . American Society for Eastern Arts

ASEP . . . . American Society of Electroplated Plastics
ASEE . . . . American Society for Engineering Education
ASE . . . . American Society of Engineers
ASEA . . . . American Society of Engineers and Architects
ASE . . . . American Society of Enologists
ASEP . . . . American Society for Experimental Pathology
ASFMRA . . . . . American Society of Farm Managers and Rural Appraisers
ASFLH . . . . . . American Society of the French Legion of Honor
ASFS . . . . American Society for Friendship with Switzerland
ASGE . . . . American Society for Gastrointestinal Endoscopy
ASG . . . . American Society of Genealogists
ASGD . . . . . . American Society of Geriatric Dentistry
ASGCA . . . . . . American Society of Golf Course Architects
ASGPP . . . . . . American Society of Group Psychotherapy & Psychodrama
ASHAE . . . . . . American Society of Heating and Air-Conditioning Engineers (Later, ASHRAE)
ASHRAE . . . . . American Society of Heating, Refrigerating and Air-Conditioning Engineers (Formerly, ASHAE)
ASHVE . . . . . . American Society of Heating and Ventilating Engineers
ASH . . . . American Society of Hematology
ASHS . . . . American Society for Horticultural Science
ASHFSA . . . . . . American Society for Hospital Food Service Administrators (of the American Hospital Association)
ASHP . . . . American Society of Hospital Pharmacists
ASHG . . . . . . American Society of Human Genetics
ASIH . . . . American Society of Ichthyologists and Herpetologists
ASI . . . . American Society of Indexers
ASIA . . . . American Society of Industrial Auctioneers
ASID . . . . American Society of Industrial Designers
ASIS . . . . American Society for Industrial Security
ASIS . . . . American Society for Information Science (Formerly, American Documentation Institute)
ASIM . . . . American Society of Insurance Management
ASIM . . . . American Society of Internal Medicine
ASIL . . . . American Society of International Law
ASJSA . . . . . . American Society of Journalism School Administrators
ASLA . . . . American Society of Landscape Architects
ASLH . . . . American Society for Legal History
ASLO . . . . American Society of Limnology and Oceanography
ASLE . . . . American Society of Lubrication Engineers
ASME . . . . American Society of Magazine Editors
ASMP . . . . American Society of Magazine Photographers
ASM . . . . American Society of Mammalogists
ASMS . . . . American Society of Maxillofacial Surgeons
ASME . . . . American Society of Mechanical Engineers
ASMT . . . . American Society of Medical Technologists
ASMHBA . . . . . American Society of Mental Hospital Business Administrators
ASM . . . . American Society for Metals
ASMM . . . . . . American Society for Metals Monographs
ASM . . . . American Society for Microbiology
ASMIC . . . . . . American Society of Military Insignia Collectors
ASMPE . . . . . . American Society of Motion Picture Engineers (Later, ASMPTE)
ASMPTE . . . . . American Society of Motion Picture and Television Engineers (Formerly ASMPE)
ASMA . . . . American Society of Music Arrangers
ASN . . . . American Society of Naturalists
ASNE . . . . American Society of Naval Engineers
ASNE . . . . American Society for Newspaper Editors
ASNT . . . . American Society for Nondestructive Testing (Atomic energy)
ASO . . . . American Society for Oceanography
ASOOA . . . . . . American Society of Ophthalmologic & Otolaryngologic Allergy
ASOS . . . . American Society of Oral Surgeons
ASO . . . . American Society of Orthodontists
ASP . . . . American Society of Papyrologists
ASP . . . . American Society of Parasitologists
ASP . . . . American Society of Perfumers
ASP . . . . American Society of Periodontists
ASPA . . . . American Society for Personnel Administration
ASP . . . . American Society of Pharmacognosy
ASPET . . . . . . American Society for Pharmacology and Experimental Therapeutics
ASP . . . . American Society of Photogrammetry
ASPP . . . . American Society of Picture Professionals
ASPO . . . . American Society of Planning Officials
ASPP . . . . American Society of Plant Physiologists
ASPT . . . . American Society of Plant Taxonomists
ASPRS . . . . . . American Society of Plastic and Reconstructive Surgeons
ASPP . . . . American Society of Polar Philatelists
ASPA . . . . American Society of Practicing Architects
ASPN . . . . American Society of Precision Nailmakers
ASPSPOM . . . American Society for the Preservation of Sacred, Patriotic and Operatic Music

ASPC . . . . American Society for the Prevention of Crime
ASPCA . . . . . . American Society for the Prevention of Cruelty to Animals
ASPB . . . . American Society of Professional Biologists
ASPDA . . . . . . American Society of Professional Draftsmen and Artists
ASPR . . . . American Society for Psychical Research
ASPO . . . . American Society for Psychoprophylaxis in Obstetrics
ASPDM . . . . . . American Society of Psychosomatic Dentistry and Medicine
ASPE . . . . American Society of Psychopathology of Expression
ASPA . . . . American Society for Public Administration
ASQC . . . . American Society for Quality Control
ASQDE . . . . . American Society of Questioned Document Examiners
ASRT . . . . American Society of Radiologic Technologists
ASRM . . . . American Society of Range Management
ASREC . . . . . . American Society of Real Estate Counselors
ASRR . . . . American Society for Reformation Research
ASRE . . . . American Society of Refrigerating Engineers
ASR . . . . American Society of Rocketry
ASRNH . . . . . American Society for Russian Naval History
ASSE . . . . American Society of Safety Engineers
ASSE . . . . American Society of Sanitary Engineering
ASSET . . . . . . American Society of Scientific and Engineering Translators
ASST . . . . American Society for Steel Treating
ASSA . . . . American Society for the Study of Arteriosclerosis
ASSR . . . . American Society for the Study of Religion
ASSS . . . . American Society for the Study of Sterility
ASSBT . . . . . . American Society of Sugar Beet Technologists
ASSH . . . . American Society for Surgery of the Hand
ASSE . . . . American Society of Swedish Engineers
ASTD . . . . American Society of Teachers of Dancing
ASTM . . . . American Society for Testing Materials
ASTR . . . . American Society for Theatre Research
ASTE . . . . American Society of Tool Engineers
ASTME . . . . . . American Society of Tool and Manufacturing Engineers
ASTT . . . . American Society of Traffic and Transportation
ASTD . . . . American Society for Training and Development
ASTD . . . . American Society of Training Directors
ASTA . . . . American Society of Travel Agents
ASTMH . . . . . . American Society of Tropical Medicine and Hygiene
ASUC . . . . American Society of University Composers
ASVO . . . . American Society of Veterinary Ophthalmology
ASVPP . . . . . . American Society of Veterinary Physiologists and Pharmacologists
ASWA . . . . American Society of Women Accountants
ASXT . . . . American Society of X-Ray Technicians
ASZD . . . . American Society for Zero Defects
ASZ . . . . American Society of Zoologists
ASA . . . . American Sociological Association
ASA . . . . American Sociometric Association
ASO . . . . American Sokol Educational and Physical Culture Organization
ASA . . . . American-South African Investment Company Ltd. (NYSE symbol)
ASBA . . . . American Southdown Breeders' Association
ASAC . . . . American-Southern Africa Council
ASA . . . . American Soybean Association
ASC . . . . American Spaniel Club
ASI . . . . American Specification Institute
AS . . . . American Speech (A periodical)
ASHA . . . . American Speech and Hearing Association
ASTA . . . . American Spice Trade Association
ASCMA . . . . . . American Sprocket Chain Manufacturers Association
ASDA . . . . American Stamp Dealers Association
ASCA . . . . American Standard Chinchilla Association
ASCRA . . . . . . American Standard Chinchilla Rabbit Association
ASCII . . . . American Standard Code for Information Interchange (Department of Commerce)
ASEC . . . . American Standard Elevator Codes
ASV . . . . American Standard Version (of the Bible, 1901)
ASA . . . . American Standards Association (Later, USASI; then, ANSI)
ASA . . . . American Statistical Association
ASTEC . . . . . . American Steamship Traffic Executives Committee
ASFA . . . . American Steel Foundrymen's Association
ASWA . . . . American Steel Warehouse Association
ASWG . . . . . . American Steel and Wire Gage
AMEX . . . . American Stock Exchange
ASE . . . . American Stock Exchange
ASYA . . . . American Stock Yards Association
ASA . . . . American Stockyards Association
ASIA . . . . American Stone Importers Association
ASTA . . . . American String Teachers Association
ASU . . . . American Student Union
ASA . . . . American Studies Association
ASA . . . . American Subcontractors Association
ASHA . . . . American Suffolk Horse Association

ASSS . . . . American Suffolk Sheep Society
ASBIPC . . . . . . American Sugar Beet Industry Policy Committee
ASCL . . . . American Sugar Cane League of the USA
ASR . . . . American Sugar Company (NYSE symbol)
ASA . . . . American Sunbathing Association
ASSU . . . . . . American Sunday School Union
ASMMA . . . . . American Supply and Machinery Manufacturers Association
ASA . . . . American Surgical Association
ASTA . . . . . . American Surgical Trade Association
ASHF . . . . . . American Swedish Historical Foundation and Museum
ASI . . . . American Swedish Institute
ASFSE. . . . . . American Swiss Foundation for Scientific Exchange
ASOL . . . . . . American Symphony Orchestra League
ATL . . . . American Tariff League
ATA . . . . American Taxicab Association
ATA . . . . American Taxpayers Association
ATA . . . . American Teachers Association
ATEA . . . . . . American Technical Education Association
ATS . . . . American Technical Society
ATCA . . . . . . American Teilhard de Chardin Association
ATT . . . . American Telephone and Telegraph Company
AT & T . . . . . American Telephone and Telegraph Company
T. . . . . American Telephone & Telegraph Company (NYSE symbol) (Wall Street
            slang name: "Telephone")
ATS . . . . American Temperance Society
AT . . . . American Terms (Grain trade)
A/T . . . . American Terms (Business and trade)
ATMA . . . . . . American Textile Machinery Association
ATMI . . . . . . American Textile Manufacturers Institute
ATPI . . . . . . American Textbook Publishers Institute
ATOE . . . . . . American Theatre Organ Enthusiasts
ATW . . . . American Theatre Wing
ATLA . . . . . . American Theological Library Association
ATS . . . . American Therapeutic Society
ATS . . . . American Thesaurus of Slang
ATS . . . . American Thoracic Society
ATA . . . . American Thyroid Association
ATTS . . . . . . American Time Travel Society
ATTA . . . . . . American Tin Trade Association
ATA . . . . American Title Association
AT . . . . American Tobacco Company (NYSE symbol)
ATA . . . . American Topical Association
ATEA . . . . . . American Toy Export Association
ATRA . . . . . . American Toy Retailers Association
ATS . . . . American Tract Society
ATABW . . . . . American Trade Association for British Woolens
ATAE . . . . . . American Trade Association Executives (now ASAE)
ATID . . . . . . American Trade and Industrial Development
ATUCH . . . . . American Trade Union Council for Histadrut
ATDA . . . . . . American Train Dispatchers Association
TDA . . . . American Train Dispatchers Association
ATSA . . . . . . American Tramp Shipowners Association
ATA . . . . American Transit Association
ATA . . . . American Translators Association
ATA . . . . American Travel Association
ATA . . . . American Tree Association
ATLA . . . . . . American Trial Lawyers Association (Formerly, NACCA)
ATA . . . . American Trucking Associations
ATS . . . . American Trudeau Society
ATA . . . . American Tunaboat Association
ATOA . . . . . . American Tung Oil Association
ATS . . . . American–Turkish Society
ATFAC . . . . . American Turpentine Farmers Association Cooperative
ATCC . . . . . . American Type Culture Collection
AUSS . . . . . . American Union of Swedish Singers
AUA. . . . . . . American Unitarian Association
AUCA . . . . . . American Unitarian Christian Association
AUFS . . . . . . American Universities Field Staff
AU. . . . . American University
AUB . . . . American University of Beirut (Lebanon)
AUA . . . . American Urological Association
AVS . . . . American Vacuum Society
AVA . . . . American Vecturist Association
AVS . . . . American Vegan Society
AVU. . . . . . . American Vegetarian Union
AVPA . . . . . . American Veneer Package Association
AVDA . . . . . . American Venereal Disease Association
AVC . . . . American Veterans Committee
AMVETS . . . . . American Veterans of World War II
AVEA . . . . . . American Veterinary Exhibitors' Association
AVMA . . . . . . American Veterinary Medical Association

AVRS . . . . . . American Veterinary Radiology Society
AV. . . . . American Viewpoint
VIS . . . . American Viscose Corporation (NYSE symbol)
AVA . . . . American Vocational Association
AVERA . . . . . American Vocational Education Research Association
AVG . . . . American Volunteer Group (Flying Tigers) (World War II)
AWAS . . . . . . American Waldensian Aid Society
AWHA . . . . . . American Walking Horse Association
AWMA . . . . . American Walnut Manufacturers Association
AWD . . . . American War Dads
AWDA . . . . . American War Dads Auxiliary
AWM . . . . . . American War Mothers
AWS. . . . . . . American War Standards
AWA . . . . American Warehousemen's Association
AWWI . . . . . . American Wash and Wear Institute
AWA . . . . American Watch Association
AWWU . . . . . American Watch Workers Union
AWI . . . . American Watchmakers Institute
AWRA . . . . . . American Water Resources Association
AWSA . . . . . . American Water Ski Association
AWWA . . . . . American Water Works Association
AWK . . . . American Water Works Company, Inc. (NYSE symbol)
AWS . . . . American Watercolor Society
AWA . . . . American Waterfowl Association
AWC . . . . American Watershed Council
AWO . . . . American Waterways Operators
AMERWAX. . . . American Wax Importers and Refiners Association
AWS . . . . American Welding Society
AWC . . . . American Whippet Club
AWWA . . . . . American White–Water Affiliation
AWHDA . . . . . American Wholesale Horticultural Dealers Association
AWA . . . . American Wine Association
AWG . . . . American Wire Gage (Standard)
AWWPA . . . . . American Wire Weavers Protective Association
AWAG . . . . . . American Wit and Gags (Book title)
AWA . . . . American Woman's Association
AWSCPA . . . . American Woman's Society of Certified Public Accountants
AWBC . . . . . . American Women Buyers Club
AWRT . . . . . . American Women in Radio and Television
AWH . . . . American Women's Hospitals
AWHS . . . . . . American Women's Hospitals Service
AWVS . . . . . . American Women's Voluntary Services (World War II)
AWC . . . . American Wood Council
AWFI . . . . . . American Wood Fabric Institute
AWPA . . . . . . American Wood–Preservers' Association
AWPI . . . . . . American Wood Preservers Institute
AWC . . . . American Wool Council
AWCOA . . . . . American Wrestling Coaches and Officials Association (Later National
            Collegiate Athletic Association of Wrestling Coaches and Officials)
AYA . . . . American Yachtsmen's Association
AYC . . . . American Yorkshire Club
AYC . . . . American Youth Congress
AYD. . . . . . . American Youth for Democracy
AYF. . . . . . . American Youth Foundation
AYH . . . . American Youth Hostels
AYCC . . . . . . American Yugoslav Claims Committee
AZI . . . . American Zellter, Incorporated
AZI . . . . American Zinc Institute
AZII. . . . . . . American Zinc Institute, Incorporated
ZA . . . . American Zinc, Lead & Smelting Company (NYSE symbol)
AZC . . . . American Zionist Council
AZYC . . . . . . American Zionist Youth Commission
AASS . . . . Americanae Antiquarianae Societatis Socius (Fellow of the American
            Antiquarian Society)
AOSS . . . . Americanae Orientalis Societatis Socius (Fellow of the American
            Oriental Society)
ACES . . . . Americans for the Competitive Enterprise System
ACA . . . . Americans for Constitutional Action
ADA . . . . Americans for Democratic Action
AEF . . . . Americans for Economic Freedom
AELE . . . . . . Americans for Effective Law Enforcement
AID . . . . Americans of Italian Descent (An organization)
AMLI . . . . . . Americans for a Music Library in Israel
API . . . . Americans for Progressive Israel
API-HH. . . . . Americans for Progressive Israel – Hashomer Hatzair
AWK . . . . Americans Want to Know (An organization)
AF . . . . America's Future
Am. . . . . Americium (Chemical element)
AS . . . . Amertool Services
AAL . . . . Ames Aeronautical Laboratory (Air Force)
ALRR . . . . . . Ames Laboratory Research Reactor (AEC)

ARC . . . . Ames Research Center (NASA)
AME . . . . Ametek, Inc. (NYSE symbol)
ATM . . . . Amici Thomae Mori
AAN . . . . Amino Acetonitrile
AA . . . . Amino Acid
ABA . . . . Aminobutyric Acid
AE . . . . Aminoethyl
AEEA . . . . Aminoethylethanolamine
AET . . . . Aminoethylisothiuronium (Chemical)
AICA . . . . Aminoimidazole-Carboxylic Acid
ALA . . . . Amino-Levulinic Acid
ALAS . . . . Aminolevulinic Acid Synthetase (Chemical)
AOAA . . . . . . Aminooxyacetic Acid
APT . . . . Aminopropylisothiourea
AMIS . . . . Amistad Recreation Area (National Park Service designation)
ABC . . . . Amities Belgo-Congolaises (Belgian-Congolese Friendship Association)
ADP . . . . Ammonium Dihydrogen Phosphate
AMP . . . . Ammonium Molybdophosphate
AN . . . . Ammonium Nitrate
ANFO . . . . . . Ammonium Nitrate and Fuel Oil (Explosive)
AP . . . . Ammonium Perchlorate
APDC . . . . Ammonium Pyrrolidine Dithiocarbamate
AMMO . . . . . . Ammunition
ACR . . . . Ammunition Condition Report
ACSSR . . . . . . Ammunition Consolidated Stock Status Report
ACP . . . . Ammunition Control Point
AED . . . . Ammunition Engineering Directorate (Army)
AGPA . . . . Ammunition Group - Picatinny Arsenal
AIC . . . . Ammunition Identification Code
ALPEC . . . . . . Ammunition Loading Production Engineering Center (Army)
ALN . . . . Ammunition Lot Number
APE . . . . Ammunition Peculiar Equipment
AP . . . . Ammunition Point
APSA . . . . Ammunition Procurement & Supply Agency (Army)
ARH . . . . Ammunition Railhead
ARP . . . . Ammunition Refilling Point
AE . . . . Ammunition Ship (Navy symbol)
AMSO . . . . . . Ammunition Shipment Order (Army)
ASF . . . . Ammunition Storage Facility (Military)
ASIS . . . . Ammunition Stores Issue Ship
ASO . . . . Ammunition Supply Officer
ASP . . . . Ammunition Supply Point
AO . . . . Among Others
AMP . . . . AMP Incorporated (NYSE symbol)
A . . . . Ampere
A-H . . . . Ampere-Hour
AHM . . . . Ampere-Hour Meter
AT . . . . Ampere-Turn (Technical drawings)
AM . . . . Amperemeter
ASF . . . . Amperes per Square Foot
APX . . . . Ampex Corporation (NYSE symbol)
ABEC . . . . Amphenol-Borg Electronics Corporation
ABE . . . . Amphenol Corporation (NYSE symbol)
A . . . . Amphibian or Amphibious
AMPH . . . . Amphibian
E . . . . Amphibian (Russian aircraft symbol)
ABR . . . . Amphibian Boat Reconnaissance Aircraft
AIF . . . . Amphibian Imperial Forces
AR . . . . Amphibian Reconnaissance (Military)
AMPHIB . . . . . Amphibious
AAFS . . . . Amphibious Assault Fuel System
LHA . . . . Amphibious Assault Ship (Navy symbol)
LPH . . . . Amphibious Assault Ship (Navy symbol)
PHIBSUKAY . . . Amphibious Bases United Kingdom
ACB . . . . Amphibious Construction Battalion
AC . . . . Amphibious Corps (Marine Corps)
PHIBCORPS . . . Amphibious Corps
ACAF . . . . Amphibious Corps, Atlantic Fleet (Marine Corps)
ACPF . . . . Amphibious Corps, Pacific Fleet
PHIBCORPAC . . Amphibious Corps Pacific Fleet
PHIBDET . . . . . Amphibious Detachment
PHIBDETIND . . Amphibious Detachment India
AMPHIBEX . . . . Amphibious Exercise (Navy; Marine Corps)
PHIBFOR . . . . Amphibious Force
AMPHFORLANT . . Amphibious Force, Atlantic
PHIBLANT . . . . Amphibious Force, Atlantic Fleet
AGC . . . . Amphibious Force Flagship (Navy symbol)
AMPHFORMED . . Amphibious Force, Mediterranean
AMPHFORPAC . . Amphibious Force, Pacific
PHIBPAC . . . . Amphibious Force, Pacific Fleet
AMPHIBFOR . . Amphibious Forces

PHIBSLANT . . . Amphibious Forces Atlantic Fleet
AMPHIBFORCENPAC . . Amphibious Forces, Central Pacific
PHIBEU . . . . Amphibious Forces Europe
PHIBSEU . . . . Amphibious Forces Europe
PHIBNAW . . . . Amphibious Forces Northwest African Waters
AF(F)MMIU . . . Amphibious Forces Ordnance Material Mobile Instruction Unit
PHIBSFORPAC . . Amphibious Forces Pacific Fleet
PHIBSPAC . . . . Amphibious Forces Pacific Fleet
PHIBGROUP . . Amphibious Group
AOTE . . . . . . Amphibious Operational Training Element
ARC . . . . Amphibious Research Craft
ARCE . . . . Amphibious River Crossing Equipment (Military)
PHIBRON . . . . Amphibious Squadron
LVK . . . . Amphibious Support Vehicle (Navy symbol)
AMTANK . . . . Amphibious Tank (Military)
AMTK . . . . . . Amphibious Tank
AMTRAC . . . . Amphibious Tractor (Amphibian Tractor)
ATB . . . . Amphibious Training Base (Navy)
PHIBTRABASE . . Amphibious Training Base
PHIBTRBASE . . . Amphibious Training Base
ATCLO . . . . . . Amphibious Training Command Liaison Officer
PHIBTRANS . . . Amphibious Transport
DUKW . . . . . . Amphibious Truck, 2 1/2-ton Cargo
PHIBWARTRACEN . . Amphibious Warfare Training Center
A . . . . Amplification; Amplifier
AF . . . . Amplification Factor
ASER . . . . Amplification by Stimulated Emission of Radiation
AALC . . . . Amplified Automatic Level Control (Air Force)
AMFUR . . . . . . Amplified Failure or Unsatisfactory Report
AD . . . . Amplifier Detector
ADA . . . . Amplifier Detector Assembly
AI . . . . Amplifier Input
AOLR . . . . Amplifier Open Loop Response
AO . . . . Amplifier Output
AOS . . . . Amplifier Output Stage
APS . . . . Amplifier Power Supply
AMPFUR . . . . Amplifying Failure, Unsatisfactory or Removal Report
A . . . . Amplitude (Physics)
AAC . . . . Amplitude Absorption Coefficient
AFD . . . . Amplitude-Frequency Distortion
AK . . . . Amplitude Keyed
ALMIDO . . . . . Amplitude and Latency Measuring Instrument with Digital Output
AMT . . . . Amplitude Modulated Transmitter
AM . . . . Amplitude Modulation (Electronics)
AMDSB . . . . . . Amplitude Modulation, Double Sideband
AMG . . . . Amplitude Modulation Generator
AMLP . . . . Amplitude Modulation Link Program
AMSSB . . . . . . Amplitude Modulation, Single-Sideband
ASK . . . . Amplitude Shift Keying
H . . . . Amplitude of a Tide
AD . . . . Amsted Industries, Inc. (NYSE symbol)
AZKW . . . . . . Amt fuer Zoll und Kontrolle des Warenverkehrs
ALS . . . . Amyotrophic Lateral Sclerosis
A . . . . Anaconda Company (NYSE symbol)
AWC . . . . Anaconda Wire & Cable Company (NYSE symbol)
AP . . . . Anal Pore
AD . . . . Analgesic Dose
AAP . . . . Analog Antenna Positioner
AAS . . . . Analog Alarm Section
ANACOM . . . . Analog Computer
ACSS . . . . Analog Computer Subsystem
ACS . . . . Analog Computer System
ADD . . . . Analog Data Digitizer
ADRT . . . . Analog Data Recorder Transcriber
ADU . . . . Analog Delay Unit
A/D . . . . Analog-to-Digital (Data conversion)
A-to-D . . . . . . Analog-to-Digital (Converter) (Data processing)
ADAPT . . . . . . Analog Digital Automatic Programmable Tester
ADIC . . . . Analog-to-Digital Conversion System
ADC . . . . Analog to Digital Converter
ADCON . . . . . Analog Digital Converter
ADDRESOR . . . . Analog to Digital Data Reduction System for Oceanographic Research
ADIT . . . . Analog Digital Integrating Translator (Data processing)
ADR . . . . Analog-Digital Recorder
ADU . . . . Analog Display Unit
AEC . . . . Analog Electronic Computer
AFC . . . . Analog to Frequency Converter
AFG . . . . Analog Function Generator
APC . . . . Analog to Pressure Converter
APACHE . . . . . Analog Programming and Checking (Data Processing)
APD . . . . Analog-to-Pulse Duration

ARA . . . . Analog RADAR Absorber
ARDA . . . . . . Analog Recording Dynamic Analyzers (Data processing)
ARSC . . . . . . Analog Rotation Speed Control
ASCAT . . . . . . Analog Self-Checking Automatic Tester
ASC . . . . . . Analog Signal Correlator
ASS . . . . Analog Simulation System
ASC . . . . Analog Strip Chart
ASCR . . . . . . Analog Strip Chart Recorder
ASAP . . . . . . Analog System Assembly Pack
ATR . . . . Analog Tape Recorder
AVB . . . . Analog Video Bandwidth
AFCAN . . . . . . Analogue Factor Calibration Network
A/A . . . . Analysis of Accounts
APCOPPLSRF . . Analysis & Program for Calculation of Optimum Propellant Performance for Liquid & Solid Rocket Fuels
ASPC . . . . Analysis Spare Parts Change
AT . . . . Analysis Time
ANOVA . . . . . Analysis of Variance
AC . . . . Analytic Chemist
ALMS . . . . . . Analytic Language Manipulation System
ANSER . . . . . Analytic Services, Inc.
AA . . . . Analytical Abstracts
ACP . . . . Analytical Computer Program
AID . . . . Analytical Instrument Development, Inc.
ALC . . . . Analytical Liquid Chromatograph
APCNY . . . . . . Analytical Psychology Club of New York
AR . . . . Analytical Reagent (Chemistry)
ASSESS . . . . . . Analytical Studies of Surface Effects of Submerged Submarines (Navy)
ARC . . . . . . Analyzer-Recorder-Controller
AC . . . . Anastomosing Cell
AB . . . . Anchor Bolt (Technical drawings)
ARH . . . . . . Anchor Hocking Glass Corporation (NYSE symbol)
APE . . . . Anchor Placement Equipment
AIMP . . . . . . Anchored Interplanetary Monitoring Platform
AASR . . . . . . Ancient Accepted Scottish Rite (Masonic)
AEAONMS . . . Ancient Egyptian Arabic Order Nobles of the Mystic Shrine
NMS . . . . . . Ancient Egyptian Arabic Order Nobles of the Mystic Shrine
AEOS . . . . . . Ancient Egyptian Order of Sciots, Supreme Pyramid
AF & AM . . . . Ancient Free and Accepted Masons
AIOK of M . . . Ancient and Illustrious Order Knights of Malta
AMOB . . . . . . Ancient Mystic Order of Bagmen of Bagdad Imperial Guild
AMOS . . . . . . Ancient Mystic Order of Samaritans
AMORC . . . . . Ancient Mystical Order Rosae Crucis (Rosicrucian Order)
AOD . . . . . . Ancient Order of Druids
AOF . . . . Ancient Order of Foresters
AOFC . . . . . . Ancient Order of Foresters of California
AOH . . . . . . Ancient Order of Hibernians in America
AOS . . . . Ancient Order of Shepherds
AOUW . . . . . Ancient Order United Workmen
AYM . . . . . . Ancient York Mason
AG . . . . And Gate
AO . . . . And Others
AYL . . . . Anderson, Clayton and Company (NYSE symbol)
AP . . . . Andhra Pradesh
ANTS . . . . . . Andover Newton Theological School
AAFB . . . . . . Andrews Air Force Base
A . . . . Androecium (Botany)
AWT . . . . . . Anechoic Water Tank
AWC . . . . . . Angelic Warfare Confraternity
ANR . . . . Angelina & Neches River R. R. (AAR code)
AAI . . . . Angle of Approach Indicator (Aviation)
AOA . . . . . . Angle of Attack (Military)
AAI . . . . Angle of Attack Indicator
AOAI . . . . . . Angle-of-Attack Indicator
AOB . . . . . . Angle of Bank
AOB . . . . Angle of Beam
ABHJ . . . . . . Angle Bulkhead Jack
ABJ . . . . Angle Bulkhead Jack
ADR . . . . Angle Data Recorder
ADJ . . . . Angle Deception Jamming
ADJS . . . . . . Angle Deception Jamming System
AOD . . . . . . Angle of Descent
I . . . . Angle of Incidence
AJS . . . . Angle Jamming System
AL . . . . Angle Lock
AME . . . . . . Angle Measuring Equipment
AME/COTAR . . Angle Measuring Equipment, Correlation Tracking and Ranging
APJ . . . . Angle Panel Jack
AP . . . . Angle Point
API . . . . Angle Position Indicator
AOR . . . . . . Angle of Reflection

AOS . . . . Angle of Site
ASV . . . . Angle Stop Valve (Technical drawings)
AOT . . . . Angle on Target
AT . . . . Angle Template
ATOT . . . . . . Angle Track on Target (Military)
AYI . . . . Angle of Yaw Indicator
A . . . . Anglian
AC . . . . Anglican Communion
AA . . . . Anglo-American
AACR . . . . . . Anglo-American Cataloging Rules
AAHBE . . . . . . Anglo-American-Hellenic Bureau of Education
AAJCS . . . . . Anglo-American Joint Chiefs of Staff
ANB . . . . Anglo-California National Bank (NYSE symbol)
ANDUS . . . . . Anglo-Dutch-United States
AF . . . . Anglo-French
AFVG . . . . . . Anglo-French Variable-Geometry (Combat aircraft)
AI . . . . Anglo-Indian
AI . . . . Anglo-Irish
AI . . . . Anglo-Israelism or Anglo-Israelite
AL . . . . Anglo-Latin
AN . . . . Anglo-Norman
A-N . . . . Anglo-Norman
AS . . . . Anglo-Saxon
A-S . . . . Anglo-Saxon
ASRS . . . . . . Anglo-Soviet Recognition Signals
AV . . . . Anglo-Vernacular
A . . . . Angstrom Unit (of light)
AU . . . . Angstrom Unit (of light)
AAS . . . . Angular Acceleration Susceptibility (Orientation)
AAU . . . . Angular Accelerometer Unit
ADA . . . . Angular Differentiating-Integrating Accelerometer
ADDT . . . . . . Angular Distribution Data Tape
AM . . . . Angular Momentum
AMC . . . . Angular Motion Compensator
APD . . . . Angular Position Digitizer
APS . . . . Angular Position Sensor
ARS . . . . Angular Rate Sensor
AGV . . . . . . Aniline Gentian Violet
AD . . . . Anima Dulcis (Sweet Soul)
AQIC . . . . . . Anima Quiescat in Christo (May His [or Her] Soul Repose in Christ)
ABS . . . . Animal Behavior Society
ACP . . . . Animal Care Panel
ADE . . . . Animal Disease Eradication Division (of ARS, Department of Agriculture)
ADP . . . . Animal Disease and Parasite Research Division (of ARS, Department of Agriculture)
AEL . . . . Animal Education League (Defunct)
AHI . . . . Animal Health Institute
AH . . . . Animal Husbandry Research Division (of ARS, Department of Agriculture)
AIQ . . . . Animal Inspection and Quarantine Division (of ARS, Department of Agriculture)
AMC . . . . Animal Medical Center
ANRC . . . . . . Animal Nutrition Research Council
APO . . . . Animal Procurement Office (Military)
APF . . . . Animal Protein Factor
ARF . . . . Animal Research Facilities
AUM . . . . . . Animal-Unit Month
AWI . . . . . . Animal Welfare Institute
ABBT . . . . . . Animated Backlighted Burtek Trainer
ABT . . . . Animated Burtek Trainer
APA . . . . Animation Producers' Association
ARE . . . . Anion-Responsive Electrode
AKF . . . . Anken Chemical & Film Corporation (NYSE symbol)
AA . . . . Ann Arbor R. R. (AAR code)
ASC . . . . Annapolis Science Center
ACS . . . . Annealed Copper-Covered Steel
AGI . . . . Annee Geophysique Internationale (International Geophysical Year)
AMR . . . . Annee Mondiale du Refugie
ANAD . . . . . Anniston Army Depot
A . . . . Anno or Annus
AAC . . . . Anno Ante Christum (In the Year Before Christ)
AC . . . . Anno Christi (In the Year of Christ)
AD . . . . Anno Domini (In the Year of Our Lord)
AH . . . . Anno Hebraico (In the Hebrew Year) (Latin)
AH . . . . Anno Hegirae (In the Year of the Hegira) (The flight of Mohammed from Mecca)
AHS . . . . Anno Humanae Salutis (In the Year of Human Salvation)
AI . . . . Anno Inventionis (In the Year of the Discovery) (Latin)
AL . . . . Anno Lucis (In the Year of Light)
AM . . . . Anno Mundi (In the Year of the World)
APCN . . . . . . Anno Post Christum Natum (In the Year after Christ Was Born)
AR . . . . Anno Regni (In the Year of the Reign of)

ARR	Anno Regni Regis (or Reginae) (In the Year of the King's [or Queen's] Reign)
ARS	**Anno Reparatæ Salutis (In the Year of Our Redemption)**
AS	**Anno Salvatoris (or Salutis) (In the Year of Salvation)**
AV	Anno Vixit (He Lived [a given number of] Years)
ATC	Annotated Tax Cases
ACB	Annoyance Call Bureau (Pest telephone control)
A	Annual
ANACDUTRA . .	Annual Active Duty for Training (Army)
AARP	Annual Advance Retainer Pay
AAS	Annual Average Score
ABA	Annual Budget Authorization
ACC	Annual Contributions Contract (Public housing development)
AEI	Annual Efficiency Index (Army)
AFP	Annual Funding Program (Army)
AGI	Annual General Inspection (Army)
AL	Annual Leave (US Civil Service)
AMF	Annual Material Forecast (Military)
ANERAC	Annual Northeast Regional Antipollution Conference
APR	Annual Progress Report
AR	Annual Report
ARC	Annual Report Council
ARPC	Annual Report Producers Council
ARTS	Annual Research Task Summary
AR	Annual Return
ARISTOTLE . . .	Annual Review and Information Symposium on the Technology of Training, Learning, and Education (DOD)
ARQ	Annual Review Questionnaire (Military)
ASP	Annual Service Practice (Firings) (Military)
ASR	Annual Summary Report
ATPR	Annual Technical Progress Report
ABEC	Annular Bearing Engineers Committee
AFM	Annular Fire Missile
APC	Annular Primary Combustor
ATC	Annular Turbojet Combustor
ATJC	Annular Turbojet Combustor
ACO	Anodal Closing Odor
ACP	Anodal Closing Picture
ACS	Anodal Closing Sound
AC	Anodal Closure (Medicine)
AC	Anodal Contraction
AD	Anodal Deviation
ADC	Anodal Duration Contraction
AO	Anodal Opening
AOC	Anodal Opening Contraction (Medicine)
AOO	Anodal Opening Odor
AOS	Anodal Opening Sound
A	Anode (Technical drawings)
AR	Anode Reaction
ASV	Anode Supply Voltage
AVD	Anode Voltage Drop
AMM	Anomalous Magnetic Moment
AP	Anomalous Propagation (Electronics)
A	Anonymous
AARS	Anonymous Arts Recovery Society
AKEL	Anorthotion Komma Ergazomenou Laou (Reform Party of the Working People) (Cyprus)
ADEDY	Anotati Diokisis Enosios Demosion Ypallilon (Supreme Council of Civil Servants) (Greece)
AMP	Another Mother for Peace (Antiwar organization)
AM P	Another Mother for Peace (Antiwar organization)
ANSETT	Ansett Airways Pty., Ltd.
AWA	Anstalt zur Wahrung der Auffuehrungsrechte
A	Answer (In transcripts)
AOT	Antarctic Observation Team
ATF	Antarctic Task Force
ASM	Antarctica Service Medal (US)
A	Ante (Before)
AC	Ante Christum (Before Christ)
ACN	Ante Christum Natum (Before the Birth of Christ)
AC	Ante Cibum (Before Meals) (Medicine)
AC	Ante-Communion
AD	Ante Diem (Before the Day)
AM	Ante Meridian (or Meridiem) (Forenoon)
API	Antecedent Precipitation Index
AVJC	Antelope Valley Junior College (California)
ABS	Antenna Base Spring
ACD	Antenna Control Display
ACU	Antenna Control Unit
ACME	Antenna Contour Measuring Equipment
ACCA	Antenna Counterbalance Cylinder Assembly

ACT	Antenna Cross Talk
ADG	Antenna Directive Gain
ADC	Antenna Dish Control
ADL	Antenna Dummy Load
AEH	Antenna Effective Height
AER	Antenna Effective Resistance
AEA	Antenna Elevation Angle
AFH	Antenna Feed Horn
AFS	Antenna Feed System
AFCK	Antenna Field Charge Kit
AFG	Antenna Field Gain
AHS	Antenna Homing System
AI	Antenna Impedance
AIR	Antenna Input Resistance
AL	Antenna Laboratory
ALA	Antenna Lightning Arrester
ALC	Antenna Loading Coil
ANT	Antenna Noise Temperature
AOR	Antenna Ohmic Resistance
APA	Antenna Pattern Analyzer
APEA	Antenna Pattern Error Analysis
API	Antenna Position Indicator
APP	Antenna Position Programmer
APR	Antenna Position Recorder
ANPOD	Antenna Positioning Device
APG	Antenna Power Gain
ARP	Antenna Radiation Pattern
ARR	Antenna Radiation Resistance
ARH	Antenna RADOME Heater
ASG	Antenna Steering Group
ASM	Antenna Switching Matrix
AP	Anteprandial (Before Dinner) (Medicine)
A	Anterior
AA	Anterior Aorta
ACS	Anterior Convex Side
AFT	Anterior Fold from Typhlosole
AF	Anterior (Part of) Foot
AHA	Anterior Hypothalamic Area
ALN	Anterior Lateral Nerve
AK	Anterior (Wall of) Kidney
ALP	Anterior Lobe of Pituitary (Gland)
AP	Anterior Pituitary
APE	Anterior Pituitary Extract
APH	Anterior Pituitary Hormone (Medicine)
APL	Anterior Pituitary-Like Hormone
ASA	Anterior Sorting Area
ASS	Anterior Superior Spine
AVCN	Antero-Ventral Cochlear Nucleus
AIB	Anthracite Information Bureau (Defunct)
AS	Anthranilate Synthetase
ASA	Anthroposophical Society in America
AAO	Anti-Air Output
AAW	Anti-Air Warfare
AAWS	Anti-Air Warfare Systems (Navy)
AA	Antiaircraft (Military)
AAA	Antiaircraft Armament
AAA	Antiaircraft Artillery
AAAC	Antiaircraft Artillery Command
AAIS	Antiaircraft Artillery Intelligence Service
AAAIS	Antiaircraft Artillery Intelligence Service (Army)
AAAOC	Antiaircraft Artillery Operation Center
AAARC	Antiaircraft Artillery Reception Center
AA/B	Anti-Aircraft Balloon
AAC	Antiaircraft Command
AAC	Antiaircraft Common (Projectile)
AADA	Antiaircraft Defense Area
AADC	Antiaircraft Director Center
AAFC	Antiaircraft Fire Control
CLAA	Anti-Aircraft Light Cruiser (Navy symbol)
AALMG	Anti-Aircraft Light Machine-Gun
AAMG	Anti-Aircraft Machine Gun
AAOP	Anti-Aircraft Observation Post
AAOC	Antiaircraft Operations Center (Air Force)
AASL	Antiaircraft Searchlight
AASD	Antiaircraft Self-Destroying
AAT	Antiaircraft Technician
AATC	Anti-Aircraft Training Center (Navy)
AATRACEN . . .	Anti-Aircraft Training Center (Navy)
AAT & TC	Anti-Aircraft Training & Test Center (Navy)
AAV	Antiaircraft Volunteer
AAM	Anti-Antimissile Missile

ABG	Anti-Backlash Gear
ABLG	Anti-Backlash Gear
ABM	Antiballistic Missile (Air Force)
ABMEWS	Antiballistic Missile Early Warning System (Air Force)
ABMM	Antiballistic-Missile Missile
ALS	Anticipated Life Span
ANORS	Anticipated Not Operationally Ready, Supply
ADS	Anti-Coincidence Detection System
ACP	Anti-Comintern Pact
ACLA	Anti-Communist League of America
AC	Anti-Corrosive
ACTER	Anti-Counter-Measures Trainer
ADL	Anti-Defamation League of B'nai B'rith
ADI	Anti-Detonation Injection
ADDL	Anti-Digit Dialing League
ADH	Antidiuretic Hormone (Vasopressin)
ADS	Antidiuretic Substance
ANTI	Antietam National Battlefield Site
AEFS	Anti-Exposure Flight Suit
AVNOJ	Antifasisticko Vece Narodnog Oslobodenja Jugoslavije
AFPFL	Anti-Fascist People's Freedom League (Burma)
AFB	Anti-Friction Bearing
AFBDA	Anti-Friction Bearing Distributors Association
AFBMA	Anti-Friction Bearing Manufacturers Association
AFM	Anti-Friction Metal
AG	Anti-Gas (Military)
ACL	Antigen-Carrier Lipid
G (Suit)	Antigravity Suit (Air Force clothing for supersonic flight)
AHF	Antihemolytic (or Antihemophilic) Factor (Factor VIII – Hematology)
AHG	Antihemophilic Globulin
AI	Anti-Icing (Technical drawings)
AICBM	Anti-Intercontinental Ballistic Missile
AIRBM	Anti-Intermediate Range Ballistic Missile
AIA	Anti-Intrusion Alarm
AIAS	Anti-Intrusion Alarm Set
AJD	Anti-Jam Display
AJF	Anti-Jam Frequency
AJFH	Anti-Jam Frequency Hopper
AJH	Anti-Jam Hopper
AJS	Anti-Jam Synthesizer
AJT	Anti-Jam Technique
AJ	Antijamming (RADAR)
AJAI	Anti-Jamming, Anti-Interference
AID	Antijamming Display
ALBC	Anti-LASER Beam Coating
ANTCOMDUSARCARIB	Antilles Command, United States Army Caribbean
ALRC	Anti-Locust Research Center (British)
ALG	Antilymphocyte Globulin (Used in heart transplants)
ALS	Antilyphocyte Serum
AMC	Anti-Malaria Campaign
AMW	Antimateriel Warhead
AMWH	Antimateriel Warhead
AMSEF	Anti-Mine-Sweeping Explosive Float
AMAR	Antimissile Array RADAR
AMM	Antimissile Missile (Air Force)
AMMSDO	Antimissile Missile and Space Defense Office
AMMTR	Antimissile Missile Test Range (Military)
AMRAC	Anti-Missile Research Advisory Council
AMSAM	Antimissile Surface-to-Air Missile
ANSAM	Anti-Missile Surface to Air Missile
Sb	Antimony (Chemical element)
AMTB	Anti-Motor Torpedo Boat
AME	Anti-Multipath Equipment
ANSW	Anti-Nuclear Submarine Warfare (Navy)
APIE	Antioch Program for Interracial Education (Antioch College)
APAF	Antipernicious Anemia Factor (Hematology)
AP	Antipersonnel
APER	Antipersonnel (Projectile)
APB	Antipersonnel Bomb (Military)
APM	Anti-Personnel Missile
APR	Anti-Plugging Relay
APP	Antipodal Propagation Phenomena
ABAA	Antiquarian Booksellers Association of America
AAA	Antique Airplane Association
AACA	Antique Automobile Club of America
ABYC	Antique Boat and Yacht Club
ABCA	Antique Bottle Collectors Association
AETA	Antique Engine and Thresher Association
ARGA	Antique Radio Guild of America
AWA	Antique Wireless Association
A	Antiquo (I oppose) (Used by Romans to signify a negative vote)

AR	Anti-Racketeering
ARM	Anti-RADAR Missile
ASTAS	Antiradar Surveillance and Target Acquisition System
ARH	Anti-Radiation Homer
ARM	Anti-Radiation Missile
ARR	Anti-Repeat Relay
ACS	Antireticular Cytotoxic Serum
ASI	Anti-Saturation Inverter
ASP	Anti-Ship Phoenix
ASA	Anti-Static Additive
ASC	Anti-Static Compound
ASL	Antistreptolysin
AS	Antisubmarine
A/S	Antisubmarine
S	Antisubmarine (Designation for all US military aircraft)
ASAC	Antisubmarine Air Control (Navy)
ASAP	Antisubmarine Attack Plotter (Navy)
ASATTU	Antisubmarine Attack Teacher Training Unit
ASCAC	Anti-Submarine Classification Analysis Center (Navy)
ASDEFORLANT	Antisubmarine Defense Forces, Atlantic (Navy)
ASDG	Antisubmarine Defense Group
ASDEFORPAC	Antisubmarine Destroyer Forces, Pacific (Navy)
ASDIC	Antisubmarine Detection Investigation Committee (Actually, a device rather than a group of persons) (World War I)
ASDEVLANT	Antisubmarine Development Detachment, Atlantic Fleet
A/SEE	Antisubmarine Experimental Establishment
A/SFDO	Antisubmarine Fixed Defenses Officer
ASLBM	Antisubmarine Launched Ballistic Missile
ASP	Antisubmarine Patrol
ASROC	Antisubmarine Rocket (Navy)
SSK	Anti-Submarine Submarine (Navy symbol)
ASTEC	Antisubmarine Technical Evaluation Center (Military)
ASTER	Antisubmarine Terrier
ASTOR	Antisubmarine Torpedo
ASW	Antisubmarine Warfare
ASWAC	Antisubmarine Warfare Advisory Committee
ASW/AAW	Anti-Submarine Warfare and Anti-Air Warfare
ASWB	Antisubmarine Warfare Barriers (Military)
ASWEPS	Antisubmarine Warfare Environmental Prediction System (Navy)
AWP	Antisubmarine Warfare Programs (Navy)
ASWSPO	Antisubmarine Warfare, Special Projects Office
ASWS	Antisubmarine Warfare Systems (Navy)
ASWL	Antisubmarine Warfare Laboratory (Military)
ASWORG	Antisubmarine Warfare Operational Research Group (World War II)
CVS	ASW (Antisubmarine Warfare) Support Aircraft Carrier (Navy symbol)
ASWSAG	Antisubmarine Warfare Systems Analysis Group (Navy)
ASWTC	Antisubmarine Warfare Training Center (Navy)
ASWTRACEN	Antisubmarine Warfare Training Center
ASWTU	Antisubmarine Warfare Training Unit
ASW/UW	Antisubmarine Warfare/ Underwater Warfare
ASWU	Antisubmarine Warfare Unit (Navy)
ASWEPS	Antisubmarine Weapon Electronic Prediction System
ATBM	Anti-Tactical Ballistic Missile
AT	Antitank
A/T	Anti-Tank
ATAR	Antitank Aircraft Rocket
ATB	Antitank Battery (Military)
ATGAR	Antitank Guided Air Rocket
ATGM	Antitank Guided Missile
ATG	Antitank Gun (Military)
ATM	Antitank Missile (Air Force)
ATR	Antitank Regiment (Military)
ATS	Antitetanic Serum
AT-10	Antitetany Preparation #10
AT	Antitorpedo
A/T	Anti-Torpedo (Nets)
ATORP	Anti-Torpedo
ATP	Anti-Torque Pedal
ATRC	Anti-Tracking Control
ATR	Anti-Transmit-Receive
ATRT	Anti-Transmit-Receive Tube
ATL	Anti-Trust Law
A & M	Antitrust and Monopoly Subcommittee (US Senate)
ATRR	Antitrust & Trade Regulation Report (of Bureau of National Affairs)
AVJ	Anti-Vibration Joint
AVS	Anti-Vivisection Society
AW	Anti-Wear
AKFM	Antokon'ny Kongresin'ny Fahaleovantenan' i Madagasikara (Party for the Congress for the Independence of Madagascar)
ABA	Antoniani Benedictini Armeni (Mechitarists)
A	Anus

ATS . . . . Anxiety Tension State
ABC . . . . Any Boy Can (Program)
AGB . . . . Any Good Brand
AQ . . . . Any Quantity
ADT . . . . Anything That You Desire (Notation in a placebo prescription) (Medicine)
AI . . . . Aortic Insufficiency (Medicine)
AP . . . . Aortic Pressure
AS . . . . Aortic Stenosis (Medicine)
APA . . . . Apache Railway Company (AAR code)
AN . . . . Apalachicola Northern R. R. (AAR code)
AOMA . . . . . Apartment Owners and Managers Association of America
AOL . . . . . . Apco Oil Corporation (NYSE symbol)
APL . . . . Aperture Lip
APCG . . . . . . Aperture Plate Character Generator
AR . . . . Apical Region
AMI . . . . Apogee Motor Igniter
AMT . . . . Apogee Motor Timer
AA . . . . Apollo Applications (NASA program)
AAP . . . . Apollo Applications Program (NASA)
ADC . . . . Apollo Display Console
ADTD . . . . . . Apollo Docking Test Device (Aerospace)
AES . . . . Apollo Earth-Orbiting Station (Aerospace)
AEP . . . . Apollo Experiment Pallet (Aerospace)
AES . . . . Apollo Experiment Support
AES . . . . Apollo Extension System (NASA)
AGC . . . . Apollo Guidance Computer
AGGD . . . . . . Apollo Guidance Ground Display (Aerospace)
AGNIS . . . . . Apollo Guidance & Navigation Industrial Support (Army)
AGANI . . . . . Apollo Guidance and Navigation Information
AIC . . . . Apollo Intermediate Chart (NASA)
ALDS . . . . . . Apollo Launch Data System (NASA)
ALSS . . . . . . Apollo Logistic Support System (Army)
ALEMS . . . . . Apollo Lunar Excursion Module Sensors (Aerospace)
ALEM . . . . . . Apollo Lunar Exploration Mission (NASA)
ALLS . . . . . Apollo Lunar Logistic Support
ALM . . . . Apollo Lunar Module
ALO . . . . Apollo Lunar Orbit (Air Force)
ALSRC . . . . . . Apollo Lunar Sample Return Container (NASA)
ALSCC . . . . . . Apollo Lunar Surface Closeup Camera (Apollo 11) (NASA)
ALSD . . . . . . Apollo Lunar Surface Drill (NASA)
ALSE . . . . . . Apollo Lunar Surface Experiment
ALSEP . . . . . . Apollo Lunar Surface Experiments Package (NASA)
AMS . . . . Apollo Mission Simulator
AORL . . . . . . Apollo Orbital Research Laboratory
AOLM . . . . . . Apollo Orbiting Laboratory Module (NASA)
APPLE . . . . . . Apollo Payload Exploration
ARIA . . . . Apollo Range Instrumentation Aircraft
ARS . . . . Apollo Reentry Ship (Aerospace)
ASCATS . . . . . Apollo Simulation Checkout and Training System
ASPO . . . . . . Apollo Spacecraft Project Office
ATAP . . . . . . Apollo Telemetry Aircraft Project
ATM . . . . Apollo Telescope Mount (NASA)
AWTTP . . . . . Apollo Wind-Tunnel Testing Program (NASA)
A . . . . Apostle (Church calendars)
AE . . . . Apostle and Evangelist (Church calendars)
AC . . . . Apostolic Church
AEL . . . . Appalachia Education Laboratory
AHMI . . . . . . Appalachian Hardwood Manufacturers, Incorporated
ALSCP . . . . . . Appalachian Land Stabilization and Conservation Program
AMC . . . . Appalachian Mountain Club
APC . . . . Appalachian Power Company
ARC . . . . Appalachian Regional Commission
ASTC . . . . . . Appalachian State Teachers College (North Carolina)
ATC . . . . Appalachian Trail Conference
AV . . . . Appalachian Volunteers (Antipoverty agency)
AHC . . . . Appaloosa Horse Club
AMPLAS . . . . Apparatus Mounted in Plastic
AICI . . . . Apparel Industry Committee on Imports
AMEA . . . . . . Apparel Manufacturing Executives Association
ARF . . . . Apparel Research Foundation
AAE . . . . Apparent Activation Energy
ACP . . . . Apparent Candle Power
AMQ . . . . Apparent Molar Quantity
AEO . . . . Appeals Examining Office (CSC)
AD . . . . Appellate Division (Legal)
APDA . . . . . . Appliance Parts Distributors Association
APJA . . . . . . Appliance Parts Jobbers Association
AQT . . . . Applicant Qualification Test (Navy)
AE . . . . Application Engineering
ARMS . . . . . . Application of Remote Manipulators in Space (Robot) (NASA)
ATS . . . . Applications Technology Satellite (NASA)

AVT . . . . Applications Vertical Test Program (Communication Satellite program)
ALPS . . . . . . Applied LASER Projects Staff
AML . . . . Applied Mathematics Laboratory
AMP . . . . Applied Mathematics Panel (of NDRC) (World War II)
AMSL . . . . . . Applied Mathematics and Statistics Laboratory (Stanford University)
App ME . . . . . Applied Mechanics Engineer (An academic degree)
AMR . . . . Applied Mechanics Reviews
ANG . . . . Applied Naturalist Guild
APL . . . . Applied Physics Laboratory (Johns Hopkins University)
APL/JHU . . . . Applied Physics Laboratory, Johns Hopkins University
APP . . . . Applied Psychology Panel (of NDRC) (World War II)
ARL . . . . Applied Research Laboratory (of John Hopkins University)
ARO . . . . Applied Research Objective
ARPO . . . . . . Applied Research Program
AS . . . . Applied Science
ASC . . . . Applied Science Corporation
ASCOP . . . . . Applied Science Corporation of Princeton
ASL . . . . Applied Science Laboratory
ASTI . . . . . . Applied Science and Technology Index
ASDEC . . . . . Applied Systems Development Evaluation Center
APCO . . . . . . Appomattox Court House National Historic Park
AAA . . . . Appraisers Association of America
AS . . . . Apprentice Seaman
AC . . . . Approach Chart
ABC . . . . Approach by Concept (Information retrieval)
A/C . . . . Approach Control (Aviation)
APCON . . . . Approach Control (FAA)
ACR . . . . Approach Control RADAR
ALCH . . . . . . Approach Light Contact Height
ALS . . . . Approach Light System
A/LS . . . . . . Approach Light System (Aviation)
APC . . . . Approach Power Compensator
AA . . . . Appropriate Authority (Office of Censorship) (World War II)
APIPOCC . . . Appropriating Property in Possession of Common Carrier (FBI standardized term)
A & E . . . . . . Appropriation and Expense
APA . . . . Appropriation Purchases Account
ATA . . . . Appropriation Transfer Account
A . . . . Approved
ADE . . . . Approved (or Authorized) Data Element
AFWR . . . . . . Approved Force War Reserves
AML . . . . Approved Materials List (NASA)
AMMP . . . . . Approved Modernization Maintenance Program
APREQS . . . . Approval Requests (Military)
ASTL . . . . . . Approved Supplier Tab List
ATC . . . . Approved Type Certificate (Governmental airworthiness certification for planes)
AVL . . . . Approved Vendors List
AA . . . . Approximate Absolute
AET . . . . Approximate Exposure Time
A . . . . April
AFD . . . . April Fools' Day
APTA . . . . . . Aptitude Area
AI . . . . Aptitude Index
A/I . . . . Aptitude Index
A . . . . Aqua
ACSA . . . . . . Aqua-Cat Catamaran Sailing Association
ASIRC . . . . . . Aquatic Sciences Information Retrieval Center (University of Rhode Island)
AFFF . . . . . . Aqueous Film-Forming Foam (Firefighting chemical for ships)
AHR . . . . Aqueous Homogeneous Reactor (AEC)
AS . . . . Aqueous Solution
AQU . . . . Aquila Airways, Ltd.
AAJ . . . . Arab Airways (Jerusalem) Ltd.
APU . . . . Arab Postal Union
ARA . . . . Arab Relief Agency
ASFEC . . . . . Arab States Fundamental Education Centre
ARAMCO . . . . Arabian-American Oil Company
AHCRA . . . . . Arabian Horse Club Registry of America
ARCRA . . . . . Arabian Horse Club Registry of America
ABF . . . . Arbeiter-und-Bauern-Fakultaet
ABI . . . . Arbeiter-und-Bauern-Inspektion
AE . . . . Arbeitseinheit
AEO . . . . Arbeitsgemeinschaft Ehemaliger Offiziere
AIF . . . . Arbeitsgemeinschaft fuer Industrielle Forschung (Cooperative Group for Industrial Research) (Germany)
ASAT . . . . . . Arbeitsgemeinschaft Satellitentragersystem (Germany)
ADW . . . . Arbeitsgemeinschaft der Waehlerinnen (Association of Women Voters) (Germany)
AK . . . . Arbeitskraft
AMS . . . . Arbetsmarknadsstyrelsen (Labor-Market Agency) (Sweden)

REVERSE ACRONYMS AND INITIALISMS DICTIONARY

ACTH	Arbitrary Correction to Hit (Gunnery term) (Navy)
ACTS	Arc Current Time Simulator
ADU	Arc Detector Unit
ADV	Arc Drop Voltage
AHH	Arc Heater Housing
AHD	Arc Heating Device
AWT	Arc-Jet Wind Tunnel
ALA	Arc Lamp Assembly
ALI	Arc Lamp Igniter
ALL	Arc LASER Light
ALLP	Arc LASER Light Pump
ART	Arc Resistance Tester
ATM	Arc Tangent Mechanism
AVC	Arc Vacuum Cast
AWM	Arc Welding Machine
AXL	Arc Xenon Lamp
ARA	Arcade & Attica Corporation (AAR code)
AMR	Arcata & Mad River R. R. (AAR code)
ALW	Arch-Loop-Whorl (Basis of Galton's System of Fingerprint Classifications)
AIA	Archaeological Institute of America
APA	Archconfraternity of Perpetual Adoration
API	Archconfraternity of Prayer for Israel
ADF	Archdiocesan Development Fund (Catholic)
AD	Archduke
ADM	Archer-Daniels-Midland Company (NYSE symbol)
AMA	Archery Manufacturers Association
AMADA	Archery Manufacturers and Dealers Association
ARCH	Arches National Monument
AC	Architect of the Capitol
AE	Architect-Engineer
AESB	Architect-Engineers -- Spanish Bases
APELSCOR	Architects, Professional Engineers, Land Surveyors Council on Registration
ARCH	Architects Renewal Committee of Harlem
AEC	Architects' Emergency Committee
AAMA	Architectural Aluminum Manufacturers Association
A/B	Architectural Barriers
ABC	Architectural Barriers Committee
Ar E	Architectural Engineer
A & E	Architectural and Engineering
APA	Architectural Photographers Association
APW	Architectural Projected Window (Technical drawings)
AWI	Architectural Woodwork Institute
AAA	Archives of American Art
A	Arctic (Air mass) (Meteorological symbol)
AAML	Arctic Aeromedical Laboratory (Air Force)
AAL	Arctic Aerospace Laboratory (Air Force)
AASRI	Arctic and Antarctic Scientific Research Institute
AAL	Arctic Approach Limitation
AC	Arctic Circle
ACFEL	Arctic Construction & Frost Effects Laboratory (Army)
ADTIC	Arctic-Desert-Tropic Information Center (Air Force)
ADB	Arctic Drift Barge
ADS	Arctic Drift Station
AEEL	Arctic Environmental Engineering Laboratory (University of Alaska)
AHRL	Arctic Health Research Laboratory (HEW)
AI	Arctic Institute
ACNA	Arctic Institute of North America
AINA	Arctic Institute of North America
AMPP	Arctic Meteorology Photographic Probe
AOES	Arctic Ocean Environment Simulator
ARL	Arctic Research Laboratory
ARLIS	Arctic Research Laboratory Island (A floating ice island in the Arctic Ocean) (Navy)
ASNA	Arctic Slope Native Association
ATB	Arctic Test Branch (Army)
ATC	Arctic Test Center (Army)
A	Are (A unit of area in the metric system)
A	Area
ARAC	Area Airports Checked
ACMC	Area Combined Movements Center
ACP	Area Command Post
ACOC	Area Communications Operations Center
ACC	Area Control Center (Aviation)
ACG	Area Coordination Group (Army)
ACT	Area Correlation Tracker (Air Force)
ADCC	Area Damage Control Center (Army)
ADCOC	Area Damage Control Center (Army)
ADCOP	Area Damage Control Party (Army)
ADC	Area Data Center
ADHI	Area Defense Homing Interceptor

ADM	Area Defense Missile
AD	Area Discriminator (SAGE)
ADP	Area Distribution Panel
AD	Area Drain (Technical drawings)
AES	Area Electronic Supervisor
ARFOR	Area Forecast (Aviation)
APO	Area Petroleum Office(r)
APAC	Area Planning-Action Councils
APC	Area Positive Control (FAA)
APD	Area Postal Directory
APME	Area Precipitation Measurement Equipment
APUC	Area Production Urgency Committee
ARA	Area Redevelopment Act (Labor Department)
ARA	Area Redevelopment Administration (Department of Commerce)
ARP	Area Redevelopment Program
AR	Area of Resolution
ARS	Area Re-Supply
ASTD	Area Scale Temperature Display
ASA	Area Scanning Alarm
ASIC	Area Security Information Center
ASCOM	Area Service Command (Army)
ASU	Area Service Unit
ASIGCEN	Area Signal Center (Army)
AST	Area Specialist Team (Army)
ASO	Area Supply Officer (Army)
ASSA	Area Supply Support Activity
AS	Area Surveillance
ATO	Area Traffic Officer
AWCO	Area Wage and Classification Office
AWAR	Area Weighted Average Resolution (Photography)
AIO	Arecibo Ionospheric Observatory (Puerto Rico)
AMA	Arena Managers Association
AMAI	Arena Managers Association, Incorporated
ABC	Argentina, Brazil, Chile
AIA	Argentine Interplanetary Association
Ag	Argentum (Silver) (Chemical element)
AGKO	Arginine, Glutamate, Alpha-Ketoglutorate Oxalacetate
AVP	Arginine Vasopressin
ARG	Argo Oil Company (NYSE symbol)
A	Argon (Chemical element)
Ar	Argon (Chemical element)
ARBOR	Argonne Boiling Reactor (Nuclear power project) (Proposed)
AGL	Argon Gas LASER
AGL	Argon Glow Lamp
AIL	Argon Ion LASER
ALL	Argon LASER Lining
AARR	Argonne Advance Research Reactor (Nuclear energy)
ACRH	Argonne Cancer Research Hospital (Illinois)
AFSR	Argonne Fast Source Reactor
ALPR	Argonne Low Power Reactor (AEC)
ANL	Argonne National Laboratory (AEC)
ANL ID	Argonne National Laboratory, Idaho Division
ARGONAUT	Argonne Nuclear Assembly for University Training
ATSR	Argonne Thermal Source Reactor (AEC)
AUA	Argonne Universities Association
AAID	Arithmetic Array Identification
AAS	Arithmetic Assignment Statement
AA	Arithmetic Average
AC	Arithmetic Computation Test (Military)
ARELEM	Arithmetic Element Program
AFD	Arithmetic Function Designator
AFID	Arithmetic Function Identifier
ALU	Arithmetic and Logical Unit (Data processing)
AP	Arithmetic Progression
ART	Arithmetic Reading Test (Military)
ART	Arithmetic Reasoning Test
ASV	Arithmetic Simple Variable
ASF	Arithmetic Statement Function
AZ	Arizona
APT	Arizona Photopolarimeter Telescope
APSC	Arizona Public Service Company
AZP	Arizona Public Service Company (NYSE symbol)
ASC	Arizona State College
ASTRAC	Arizona Statistical Repetitive Analog Computer
AR	Arkansas
ARKLA	Arkansas-Louisiana Gas Company
ALM	Arkansas & Louisiana Missouri Railway Company (AAR code)
AO	Arkansas & Ozarks Railway (AAR code)
APC	Arkansas Polytechnic College
ARPO	Arkansas Post National Memorial
ARTS	Arkansas Research Test Station

ASC . . . . Arkansas State College
ASTC . . . . . . Arkansas State Teachers College
ARW . . . . . . Arkansas Western Railway Company (AAR code)
AA . . . . Arlington Annex (Navy Department)
AHS . . . . Arlington Hall Station (Army)
AMAC . . . . . . Arlington Memorial Amphitheater Commission
ANC . . . . Arlington National Cemetery
ASC . . . . Arlington State College (Texas)
AL . . . . Arm Length
ALI . . . . Arm Length Index
ALO . . . . Arm Length Order
AW . . . . Arm Width
AWI . . . . Arm Width Index
ANDRO . . . . . Arma Non-Destructive Readout
ABA . . . . Armadillo Breeders Association
ACP . . . . Armament Control Panel
ACS . . . . Armament Control System (Air Force)
ADE . . . . Armament Design Establishment (British)
A & E . . . . . . Armament & Electronics (Air Force)
ARD . . . . Armament Research Development (British)
ASPRL . . . . . Armament Systems Personnel Research Laboratory (Air Force)
AT . . . . Armament Test
ATC . . . . Armament Test Center (Military)
ATD . . . . Armament Test Division
ATPF . . . . . . Armament Test Preparation Facility
ARDE . . . . . . Armaments Research and Development Establishment (British)
AA . . . . Armature Accelerator
AS . . . . Armco Steel Corporation (NYSE symbol)
AFA . . . . Armed Forces Act
AFAITC . . . . . Armed Forces Air Intelligence Training Center
AFAK . . . . . . Armed Forces Assistance to Korea (Military)
AFCA . . . . . . Armed Forces Chemical Association
AFCE . . . . . . Armed Forces Chemical Association
AFCA . . . . . . Armed Forces Communications Association
AFCEA . . . . . Armed Forces Communications & Electronics Association
AFCOS . . . . . Armed Forces Courier Service
ARFCOS . . . . . Armed Forces Courier Service
ARFCQSTA . . . Armed Forces Courier Station
AFDOA . . . . . Armed Forces Dental Officers Association
AFDCB . . . . . Armed Forces Disciplinary Control Board
AFEPBA . . . . . Armed Forces Enlisted Personnel Benefit Association
AFEB . . . . . . Armed Forces Epidemiological Board
AFEES . . . . . . Armed Forces Examining and Entrance Stations
AFES . . . . . . Armed Forces Examining Station
AFEM . . . . . . Armed Forces Expeditionary Medal
AFHA . . . . . . Armed Forces Hostess Association
AFIE . . . . Armed Forces Information and Education
AFIED . . . . . . Armed Forces Information and Education Division
AFIF . . . . Armed Forces Information Film
AFIP . . . . Armed Forces Information Program
AFIS . . . . Armed Forces Information School
AFI . . . . Armed Forces Institute
AFIP . . . . Armed Forces Institute of Pathology
AFLP . . . . . . Armed Forces Language Program
AFM . . . . Armed Forces Management
AFMA . . . . . . Armed Forces Management Association
AFMR . . . . . . Armed Forces Master Records (Solicited phonograph records, and money
      to buy records, for the armed forces) (World War II) (Cf. RFOFM)
AFML . . . . . . Armed Forces Medical Library (Became National Library of Medicine,
      1956)
AFMPA . . . . . Armed Forces Medical Procurement Agency
AFN . . . . Armed Forces Network (Military)
AFNB . . . . . . Armed Forces News Bureau
AFPCB . . . . . . Armed Forces Pest Control Board
AFP . . . . Armed Forces of the Philippines
AFP . . . . Armed Forces Police
AFPD . . . . . . Armed Forces Police Detachment
AFPC . . . . . . Armed Forces Policy Council
AFPS . . . . . . Armed Forces Press Service
AFPR . . . . . . Armed Forces Procurement Regulations
AFQT . . . . . . Armed Forces Qualification Test
AFQTVA . . . . . Armed Forces Qualification Test, Verbal Arithmetic Subtest
AFRS . . . . . . Armed Forces Radio Service (Military)
AFRTS . . . . . . Armed Forces Radio and Television Service
AFRRI . . . . . . Armed Forces Radiobiology Research Institute
AFS . . . . Armed Forces Radiobiology Research Institute
AFRBA . . . . . Armed Forces Relief and Benefit Association
AFRA . . . . . . Armed Forces Reserve Act of 1952, as Amended
AFRC . . . . . . Armed Forces Reserve Center
AFRM . . . . . . Armed Forces Reserve Medal (US)
AFRESM . . . . . Armed Forces Reserve Medal

AFSA . . . . . . Armed Forces Security Agency
AFSAG . . . . . Armed Forces Security Agency
AFSWA . . . . . Armed Forces Special Weapons Agency
AFSWP . . . . . Armed Forces Special Weapons Project
AFSC . . . . . . Armed Forces Staff College
AFSCC . . . . . Armed Forces Supply Control Center (DOD)
AFSSC . . . . . Armed Forces Supply Support Center (Merged with Defense Logistics
      Services Center)
AFSPBRSIO . . . Armed Forces Surplus Property Bidders Registration and Sales Information
      Office (Later, Defense Surplus Bidders Control Office)
AFUS . . . . . . Armed Forces of the United States
AFWST . . . . . Armed Forces Women's Selection Test
AFWL . . . . . . Armed Forces Writers League
AG . . . . Armed Guard
AGC . . . . Armed Guard Center
AGCTS . . . . . . Armed Guard Center Training School
AGIO . . . . . . Armed Guard Inspection Officer
AGIS . . . . . . Armed Guard Inspection Service
AGS . . . . Armed Guard School(s)
XCL . . . . Armed Merchant Cruiser (Navy symbol)
AS . . . . Armed Services Committee (US Senate)
ASDIC . . . . . . Armed Services Documents Intelligence Center
ASESA . . . . . . Armed Services Electro-Standards Agency
ASETC . . . . . . Armed Services Electron Tube Committee
ASESB . . . . . . Armed Services Explosives Safety Board
ASGRO . . . . . Armed Services Graves Registration Office
ASIRC . . . . . . Armed Services Industrial Readiness Council
ASMPA . . . . . Armed Services Medical Procurement Agency
ASMRO . . . . . Armed Services Medical Regulating Office
ASPAB . . . . . Armed Services Patent Advisory Board (DOD)
ASPIC . . . . . . Armed Services Personnel Interrogation Center
ASPA . . . . . . Armed Services Petroleum Agency
ASPB . . . . . . Armed Services Petroleum Board
ASPPA . . . . . Armed Services Petroleum Purchasing Agency
ASPA . . . . . . Armed Services Procurement Act
ASPPO . . . . . Armed Services Procurement Planning Officer
ASPR . . . . . . Armed Services Procurement Regulation
ASPERS . . . . . Armed Services Procurement Regulations
ASRB . . . . . . Armed Services Renegotiation Board
ASTIA . . . . . . Armed Services Technical Information Agency (Later, Defense
      Documentation Center)
ASWBPL . . . . . Armed Services Whole Blood Processing Laboratory
ALN . . . . Armee de la Liberation Nationale (National Liberation Army) (Algeria)
ALNA . . . . . . Armee de Liberation Nationale de l'Angola (Angolan Army of National
      Liberation)
ALNK . . . . . . Armee de Liberation Nationale Kamerounaise (Cameroonese National
      Liberation Army)
ANC . . . . Armee Nationale Congolaise (Congolese National Army)
ACYOA . . . . . Armenian Church Youth Organization of America
AEF . . . . Armenian Educational Foundation
AGBUA . . . . . Armenian General Benevolent Union of America
AMAA . . . . . . Armenian Missionary Association of America
ANCA . . . . . . Armenian National Council of America
APLA . . . . . . Armenian Progressive League of America
ARS . . . . Armenian Relief Society
ARFA . . . . . . Armenian Revolutionary Federation of America
ASA . . . . Armenian Students Association of America
ASAA . . . . . . Armenian Students Association of America
AWWA . . . . . Armenian Women's Welfare Association
AYF . . . . Armenian Youth Federation of America
ADA . . . . Arming Device Assemblies (Army)
A & F . . . . . . Arming and Fuzing
AW . . . . Arming Wire (Bombs)
AA & A . . . . . Armor, Armament and Ammunition
AAC . . . . Armor and Arms Club
AE . . . . Armor, Artillery, and Engineers Aptitude Area (Army)
AB . . . . Armor Board
AG . . . . Armor Grating (Technical drawings)
AHRU . . . . . . Armor Human Research Unit
AP . . . . Armor-Piercing (Army)
APC . . . . Armor-Piercing Capped (Ammunition)
APCI . . . . Armor-Piercing-Capped Incendiary (Ammunition)
APCIT . . . . . . Armor-Piercing-Capped Incendiary with Tracer (Ammunition)
APCT . . . . . . Armor-Piercing-Capped with Tracer (Ammunition)
APHE . . . . . . Armor Piercing High Explosive
API . . . . Armor-Piercing Incendiary (Ammunition)
APIT . . . . Armor Piercing Incendiary Tracer (Ammunition)
APT . . . . Armor Piercing with Tracer (Ammunition)
AC . . . . Armored Cable
ACV . . . . Armored Combat Vehicle
ACRV . . . . . . Armored Command and Reconnaissance Vehicle

ACR . . . . Armored Cruiser (Navy symbol)
AFV . . . . Armored Fighting Vehicle (Marine Corps)
AFV . . . . Armored Force Vehicle
APC . . . . Armored Personnel Carrier
APC/QC . . . . Armored Personnel Carrier/Qualification Course (Army)
AR . . . . Armored Reconnaissance
ARAAV . . . . . . Armored Reconnaissance Airborne Assault Vehicle
ARV . . . . Armored Recovery Vehicle
ARB . . . . Armored Rifle Battalion
ATC . . . . Armored Troop Carrier (Navy)
AUET . . . . . . Armored, Universal Engineer Tractor
AUV . . . . Armored Utility Vehicle
AVLB . . . . . . Armored Vehicle Launched Bridge (Military)
AM . . . . Armour & Company (NYSE symbol)
ARF . . . . Armour Research Foundation
ARR . . . . Armour Research Foundation Reactor
AAD . . . . Arms & Ammunition Division (Army)
ACDA . . . . . . Arms Control and Disarmament Agency
ACOS . . . . . . Arms Control Observation Satellite
AM . . . . Arms Material
ASWAAF . . . . . Arms and Services with the Army Air Forces
ASWAF . . . . . Arms and Services on duty with Air Force
ACK . . . . Armstrong Cork Company (NYSE symbol)
ARM . . . . Armstrong Rubber Company (NYSE symbol)
A . . . . Army
R . . . . Army (Military aircraft identification prefix)
AAMU . . . . . . Army Advanced Marksmanship Unit
AGC . . . . Army Advisory Group, China
ARADMAC . . . . Army Aeronautical Depot Maintenance Center (AMC--ASMC)
AARL . . . . Army Aeronautical Research Center (Ames Research Center) (Army)
AAB . . . . Army Air Base
AAC . . . . Army Air Corps
AAD . . . . Army Air Defense
AADA . . . . . . Army Air Defense Area
AADC . . . . . . Army Air Defense Command(er)
ARADCOM . . . Army Air Defense Command
AADCP . . . . . Army Air Defense Command Post
AADIS . . . . . . Army Air Defense Information Service
AADOO . . . . . Army Air Defense Operations Office(r)
ARADSCH . . . . Army Air Defense School
AADS . . . . . . Army Air Defense System (Formerly, FABMDS)
AAFB . . . . . . Army and Air Force Base
AAFB . . . . . . Army Air Force Board
AAFCFTC . . . . Army Air Force Central Flying Training Command
AAFCTTC . . . . Army Air Force Central Technical Training Command
AAFCWF . . . . Army and Air Force Central Welfare Fund
AAFCWF . . . . Army and Air Force Civilian Welfare Fund
AAFCC . . . . . Army Air Force Classification Center
A-AFCPB . . . . . Army-Air Force Clemency and Parole Board
AAFEFTC . . . . Army Air Force Eastern Flying Training Command
AAFETTC . . . . Army Air Force Eastern Technical Training Command
AAFEMPS . . . . Army and Air Force Exchange and Motion Picture Service
AAFBD . . . . . . Army and Air Force Exchange and Motion Picture Services Board of
                Directors (DOD)
AAFES . . . . . . Army and Air Force Exchange Service
AAFFTD . . . . . Army Air Force Flying Training Detachment
AAFMTO . . . . Army Air Force Headquarters, Mediterranean Theater of Operations
AAFMPS . . . . . Army and Air Force Motion Picture Service
AAFOIC . . . . . Army Air Force Officer in Charge
AAFPS . . . . . . Army and Air Force Postal Service
AAFWB . . . . . . Army and Air Force Wage Board
AAF . . . . Army Air Forces
AAFAS . . . . . . Army Air Forces Aid Society (World War II)
AFSUB . . . . . . Army Air Forces Anti-Submarine Command
AAFBU . . . . . . Army Air Forces Base Unit
AAFBTC . . . . . Army Air Forces Basic Training Center
AAFBS . . . . . . Army Air Forces Bombardier School
AAFC . . . . . . Army Air Forces Center
AAFEC . . . . . . Army Air Forces Engineer Command
AAFGS . . . . . . Army Air Forces Gunnery School
AAFIS . . . . . . Army Air Forces Intelligence School
AAFMC . . . . . . Army Air Forces Materiel Center
AAFNS . . . . . . Army Air Forces Navigation School
AAFPOA . . . . . Army Air Forces, Pacific Ocean Areas
AAFPOA ADMIN . . Army Air Forces, Pacific Ocean Areas (Administrative)
AAFPS . . . . . . Army Air Forces Pilot School
AAFPFS(P) . . . . Army Air Forces Pre-Flight School (Pilot)
AAFSAT . . . . . . Army Air Forces School of Applied Tactics (World War II)
AAFSC . . . . . . Army Air Forces Service Command
AAFTAC . . . . . Army Air Forces Tactical Center (World War II)
AAFTS . . . . . . Army Air Forces Technical School

AAFTTC . . . . . Army Air Forces Technical Training Command (World War II)
AAFTAD . . . . . Army Air Forces Training Aids Division (World War II)
AAFTC . . . . . . Army Air Forces Training Command (World War II)
AAFWFTC . . . . Army Air Forces Western Flying Training Command
AAFWTTC . . . . Army Air Forces Western Technical Training Command
AAGS . . . . Army Air-Ground System
AAMC . . . . . . Army Air Material Command
AAS . . . . Army Air Service
AATCAN . . . . . Army Air Traffic Control and Navigation System
AATRI . . . . Army Air Traffic Regulation and Identification
AATRIS . . . . . . Army Air Traffic Regulation and Identification System
AAESWB . . . . . Army Airborne Electronics & Special Warfare Board (Army)
AAM . . . . Army Aircraft Maintenance
AAMS . . . . Army Aircraft Maintenance Shop
AARRB . . . . . . Army Aircraft Requirements Review Committee
AARS . . . . Army Aircraft Repair Ship
AAF . . . . Army Airfield
AACS . . . . Army Airways Communications System
AACS . . . . Army Alaska Communication System (Air Force)
AARS . . . . Army Amateur Radio System
AAR . . . . Army Area Representative
AASC . . . . Army Area Signal Center
AAMC . . . . . . Army Artillery and Missile Center
AAMS . . . . Army Artillery & Missile School
ARMA . . . . . . Army Attache (Military)
AAS . . . . Army Attache System
AAA . . . . Army Audit Agency
AAAA . . . . Army Aviation Association of America
AAB . . . . Army Aviation Board
AAE . . . . Army Aviation Element
AAE . . . . Army Aviation Engineers
AR Av MO Bad . . Army Aviation Medical Officer's Badge
AAOD . . . . . . Army Aviation Operating Detachment
AVSCOM . . . . Army Aviation Systems Command
AATB . . . . Army Aviation Test Board
AATC . . . . Army Aviation Test Command (ATEC)
AAUTC . . . . . . Army Aviation Unit Training Command
ARAV . . . . Army Aviator
AR Av Bad . . . . Army Aviator Badge
AVBAD . . . . . . Army Aviator Badge
ABMA . . . . . . Army Ballistic Missile Agency
ABL . . . . Army Biological Laboratory
ABWRC . . . . . Army Biological Warfare Research Center
ABCMR . . . . . Army Board for Correction of Military Records
ABRE . . . . Army Board of Review for Eliminations
ABCA . . . . Army Bureau of Current Affairs (To encourage British soldiers to
                think and talk about what they were fighting for) (World War II)
ACS . . . . Army Calibration System
ACGP . . . . . . Army Career Group
ACWF . . . . . . Army Central Welfare Fund
ACC . . . . Army Chemical Center
ACCPA . . . . . . Army Chemical Center Procurement Agency
ACWL . . . . . Army Chemical Warfare Laboratory
ACSS . . . . Army Chief of Support Services
ACSU . . . . Army Civil Services' Union (Singapore)
ACMA . . . . . . Army Class Manager Activity
ACB . . . . Army Classification Battery (of tests)
ACST . . . . Army Clerical Speed Test
ACTMC . . . . . Army Clothing, Textile & Materiel Center
ACCL . . . . Army Coating and Chemical Laboratory
ACDC . . . . . . Army Combat Developments Command
ACAN . . . . . . Army Command and Administrative Network (Domestic and oversea
                integrated system of fixed radio, wire, cable, and associated
                communications facilities)
ACCNET . . . . . Army Command and Control Network
ACMS . . . . . . Army Command Management System
ARCOM . . . . . Army Commendation Medal (US)
ACEC . . . . . . Army Communications & Electronic Command
ACEMIS . . . . . Army Communications and Electronics Management Information System
ACSD . . . . Army Communications - Service Division
ACS . . . . Army Community Service
ACTIV . . . . . . Army Concept Team in Vietnam
ACAB . . . . . . Army Contract Adjustment Board
ACAP . . . . . . Army Contract Appeals Panel
ACPD . . . . . . Army Control Program Directive
ACC . . . . Army Cooperation Command (British)
AC . . . . Army Corps
ACE . . . . Army Corps of Engineers
ACRB . . . . . . Army Council of Review Boards
ADRES . . . . . . Army Data Retrieval Engineering System
ADS . . . . Army Dental Service

ADRB . . . . Army Disability Review Board
ADRB . . . . Army Discharge Review Board
ADF . . . . Army Distaff Foundation
AEC . . . . Army Education Center
AERB . . . . . . Army Education Requirements Board
AEC . . . . Army Educational Corps (British)
AEPG . . . . . . Army Electronic Proving Ground
AEC . . . . Army Electronics Command
AEMSA . . . . . . Army Electronics Material Support Agency
AER . . . . Army Emergency Relief
AEWES . . . . . . Army Engineers Waterways Experiment Station
AEHA . . . . . . Army Environmental Health Agency
AEHL . . . . . . Army Environmental Health Laboratory
AE . . . . Army in Europe
AES . . . . Army Exchange Service (Centralized the control of PX's in US) (World War II)
AEU . . . . Army Exhibit Unit
AECP . . . . . . Army Extension Course Program
AFC . . . . Army Field Commands
AFF . . . . Army Field Forces
AFSCS . . . . . . Army Field Stock Control System
AFW . . . . Army Field Workshop
AFA . . . . Army Finance Association
AFC . . . . Army Finance Center
AFWAB . . . . . . Army Fixed Wing Aptitude Battery
AFA . . . . Army Flight Activity
AF . . . . Army Force
AFDP . . . . Army Force Development Plan
AFFE . . . . Army Forces Far East
AFLL . . . . Army Fuels and Lubricant Laboratory
AGCRSP . . . . . Army Gas-Cooled Reactor Systems Program
AGCT . . . . . . Army General Classification Test
AGEC . . . . . . Army General Equipment Command
AGS . . . . Army General Staff
AGSCPO . . . . Army General Staff Civilian Personnel Office, Office of the Chief of Staff, US Army
AGSCC . . . . . Army General Supplies Commodity Center
AGCMDL . . . . Army Good Conduct Medal
AGF . . . . Army Ground Forces
AGP . . . . Army Ground Pool (for officers)
AGED . . . . . . Army Group Effects Department
AHQ . . . . Army Headquarters
AHP . . . . Army Heliport
AH . . . . Army Hospital
AHC . . . . Army Hospital Corps
AHFRAC . . . . . Army Human Factors Research Advisory Committee
AHFRDC . . . . . Army Human Factors Research and Development Committee
AIIC . . . . Army Imagery Intelligence Corps
AIC . . . . Army Industrial College
AIF . . . . Army Industrial Fund
AIMILO . . . . . Army/Industry Materiel Information Liaison Office
AIDS . . . . Army Information and Data Systems
AIDSCOM . . . Army Information and Data Systems Command
AID . . . . Army Information Digest
AIP . . . . Army Information Program
AMIS . . . . Army Information System
AIM . . . . Army Installation Management
AIAS . . . . Army Institute of Advanced Studies
AIMS . . . . Army Integrated Decision Equipment
AIMS . . . . Army Integrated Meteorological Systems (AEC)
AI . . . . Army Intelligence
AIC . . . . Army Intelligence Center
AID . . . . Army Intelligence Department (British)
AII . . . . Army Intelligence Interpreter
AIR . . . . Army Intelligence Reserve
AIS . . . . Army Intelligence School
AIS . . . . Army Intelligence & Security
AIT . . . . Army Intelligence Translator
AIO . . . . Army Inventory Objective
AJAQ . . . . . . Army Job Activities Questionnaire
AJQ . . . . Army Job Questionnaire
ALANF . . . . . . Army Land Forces
ALAT . . . . . . Army Language Aptitude Test
ALO . . . . Army Liaison Officer
ARLO . . . . . . Army Liaison Officer
ALWL . . . . . . Army Limited War Laboratory
ALDC . . . . . . Army Logistics Data Center
ALMC . . . . . . Army Logistics Management Center (Merged with Defense Logistics Management Center)
ALMC . . . . . . Army Logistics Management Center (Merged with Materiel Management Training Center)

ALMO . . . . . . Army Logistics Manpower Office (Merged with Operations Personnel Office)
ARLD . . . . . . Army Logistics Research & Development
ALRCP . . . . . . Army Long Range Capabilities Plan
ALART . . . . . Army Low-Speed Air Research Tasks
AMB . . . . Army Maintenance Board
AMETA . . . . . Army Management Engineering Training Agency
AMF . . . . . . Army Management Fund
AMS . . . . Army Management Structure
AMS . . . . Army Map Service (Later, Army Topographic Command)
AMU . . . . Army Marksmanship Unit
AMDF . . . . . . Army Master Data File
AMMRC . . . . . Army Materials and Mechanics Research Center
AMRA . . . . . . Army Materials Research Agency
AMC . . . . Army Materiel Command
AMCSA . . . . . Army Materiel Command Support Activity
AMP . . . . Army Materiel Plan
AMSAA . . . . . Army Materiel Systems Analysis Agency
AMC . . . . Army Medical Center
AMC . . . . Army Medical Corps
AMD . . . . Army Medical Department
AML . . . . Army Medical Library (Became Armed Forces Medical Library, 1952; later, NLM)
AMNL . . . . . . Army Medical Nutrition Laboratory
AMRL . . . . . . Army Medical Research Laboratory
AMRNL . . . . . Army Medical Research & Nutrition Laboratory
AMEDS . . . . . . Army Medical Service
AMS . . . . Army Medical Service(s) (British)
AMSGS . . . . . Army Medical Service Graduate School
AMSRDC . . . . Army Medical Service Research and Development Command
AMSS . . . . . . Army Medical Service School
AMSC . . . . . . Army Medical Specialist Corps
AMSCO . . . . . Army Medical Supply Control Officer
AMU . . . . Army Medical Unit
AMP . . . . Army Mine Planter
AMPS . . . . . . Army Mine Planter Service
AMC . . . . Army Missile Command
AMICOM . . . Army Missile Command
AMDC . . . . . . Army Missile Development Center
AMRD . . . . . . Army Missile and Rocket Directorate
AMRD-NASC . . Army Missile and Rockets Directorate -- NATO Supply Center
AMTC . . . . . . Army Missile Test Center
ARMTE . . . . . Army Missile Test and Evaluation
AMMO . . . . . . Army Mobile Missile Operation
AMC . . . . Army Mobility Command
AMOCOM . . . Army Mobility Command
AMRC . . . . . . Army Mobility Research Center
AMSC . . . . . . Army Mobility Support Center
AMCS . . . . . . Army Mobilization Capabilities Study
AMPD . . . . . . Army Mobilization Program Directive
AMPS . . . . . . Army Motion Picture Service
AMUCOM . . . Army Munition Command
AMC . . . . Army Munitions Command
AMUNC . . . . . Army Munitions Command
AMAA . . . . . . Army Mutual Aid Association
ANL . . . . Army Natick Laboratory
ANG . . . . Army National Guard (Military)
ARNG . . . . . . Army National Guard
RNG . . . . Army National Guard
ARNGUS . . . . . Army National Guard of the United States
AN . . . . Army and Navy
ARNA . . . . . . Army with Navy (personnel)
ANA . . . . Army-Navy Aeronautical
ANAF . . . . . . Army-Navy-Air Force
ANAFJ . . . . . . Army-Navy-Air Force Journal (A publication)
ANB . . . . Army-Navy-British
ANC . . . . Army-Navy-Commerce
AND . . . . Army-Navy Design
ANEEG . . . . . . Army, Navy Electronics Evaluation Group
ANIP . . . . Army-Navy Instrumentation Program
ANJSB . . . . . . Army-Navy Joint Specifications Board
AN . . . . Army-Navy Joint Type Ordnance
ANMB . . . . . . Army-Navy Munitions Board (Later, Munitions Board)
ANNA . . . . . . Army, Navy, NASA, Air Force Geodetic Satellite
AN . . . . Army/Navy Number
A 'N . . . . Army/Navy Number
ANPB . . . . . . Army-Navy Petroleum Board
ANPPPC . . . . . Army-Navy Petroleum Pool, Pacific Coast
ANSIA . . . . . . Army-Navy Shipping Information Agency
ANSC . . . . . . Army and Navy Staff College (Redesignated National War College, 1946)
ANSCOL . . . . . Army and Navy Staff College (See ANSC)

ANU	Army and Navy Union, USA
ANF	Army News Features
ANS	Army News Service
ANS	Army Newspaper Service (Military)
ANV	Army of Northern Virginia (Civil War)
ANDL	Army Nuclear Defense Laboratory
ANPP	Army Nuclear Power Program
ANWCG	Army Nuclear Weapon Coordination Group
ANC	Army Nurse Corps
ANS	Army Nursing Service (British)
AOGM	Army of Occupation of Germany Medal
OCCGERMDL . .	Army of Occupation of Germany Medal
AOM	Army of Occupation Medal (Germany–Japan) (US)
OCCMDL	Army of Occupation Medal
AOER	Army Officers' Emergency Reserve (British)
AOAD	Army Operating Availability Data
AOC	Army Operations Center (in the Pentagon)
AOAC	Army Ordnance Ammunition Command (Merged with Munitions Command)
AOCEO	Army Ordnance Combat Equipment Office
AOC	Army Ordnance Corps
ORDC	Army Ordnance Corps
AOD	Army Ordnance Department
AOGMS	Army Ordnance Guided Missile School
AOMC	Army Ordnance Missile Center
AOMC	Army Ordnance Missile Command (Later, Missile Command)
AOMSA	Army Ordnance Missile Support Agency
AOWC	Army Ordnance Weapons Command
APPR	Army Package Power Reactor
APT	Army Parachute Team
APC	Army Pay Corps
APD	Army Pay Department
APL	Army Personnel Letter
APNL	Army Personnel Newsletter
APRO	Army Personnel Research Office
APRS	Army Personnel Research Service
APC	Army Petroleum Center
APIC	Army Photo Interpretation Center
APID	Army Photo Interpretation Detachment
APDA	Army Physical Disability Activity
APDAB	Army Physical Disability Appeal Board
APRC	Army Physical Review Council
APC	Army Pictorial Center
APS	Army Pilot School
APG	Army Planning Group
APC	Army Policy Council
AP & SC	Army Port and Service Command
APO	Army Post Office
APC	Army Postal Clerk
APS	Army Postal Service
APU	Army Postal Unit
APCEC	Army Precommission Extension Course
APSS	Army Printing and Stationery Services (British)
APP	Army Procurement Procedure
APSGD	Army Procurement-Sharpe General Depot
APL	Army Promotion List
APRL	Army Prosthetics Research Laboratory
APG	Army Proving Grounds
APRF	Army Pulse Radiation Facility
APRA	Army Pulsed Experimental Research Assembly
AQB	Army Qualification Battery (of tests)
AQMC	Army Quartermaster Corps (Merged with Supply & Maintenance Command)
ARAC	Army RADAR Approach Control Facility
ARL	Army Radiation Laboratory
ARCT	Army Radio Code Aptitude Test
AREA	Army Reactor Experimental Area (Army)
ARM	Army Ready Materiel
ARB	Army Rearming Base
ARPT	Army Registry of Physical Therapists
ARSEM	Army Registry of Special Educational Materials
AR	Army Regulations
ARS	Army Relief Society
ARD	Army Renegotiation Division (of ASRB)
ARVN	Army of the Republic of Vietnam (South Vietnam)
ARDP	Army Requirements Development Plan
ARDIS	Army Research and Development Management Information System
ARIEM	Army Research Institute of Environment Medicine
ARO	Army Research Office
ARO-D	Army Research Office–Durham
ARO-E	Army Research Office–Europe
ARO-J	Army Research Office–Japan
ARP	Army Research Plan
ARTS	Army Research Task Summary
AR	Army Reserve
ARCOM	Army Reserve Command
ARROTCA	Army Reserve and ROTC Affairs
ARR	Army Retail Requirements
ARB	Army Retiring Board
ARGMA	Army Rocket and Guided Missile Agency
ARWAB	Army Rotary Wing Aptitude Battery
ARO	Army Routine Order (Military)
AST	Army Satellite Tracking Center
ASAP	Army Scientific Advisory Panel
ASA	Army Seal of Approval
AS	Army Security
ASA	Army Security Agency
ASAS	Army Security Agency School (Merged with Defense Security Agency School)
ASRB	Army Security Review Board
ASN	Army Serial Number
ASCOM	Army Service Command
ASC	Army Service Corps
ASF	Army Service Forces
ASFTCU	Army Service Forces Training Center Unit
ASN	Army Service Number
ASSERON	Army Service Squadron (Corresponds to Navy's CASU)
ASBCA	Armed Services Board of Contract Appeals
ASD	Army Shipping Document
ASC	Army Signal Corps
ASMSA	Army Signal Missile Support Agency
ASRPA	Army Signal Radio Propagation Agency
ASRDL	Army Signal Research and Development Laboratory
ASSA	Army Signal Supply Agency
ARSAP	Army Small Arms Program
ASIPRE	Army Snow, Ice and Permafrost Research Establishment
ASS	Army Special Staff
ASWC	Army Special Warfare Center
ASWD	Army Special Weapons Depot
ASC	Army Specialist Corps
AST	Army Specialized Training
ASTP	Army Specialized Training Program (World War II)
ASTU	Army Specialized Training Unit
AS	Army Staff
ASF	Army Stock Fund
ASCP	Army Strategic Capabilities Plan
ASCC	Army Strategic Communications Command
ASOP	Army Strategic Objectives Plan
ASP	Army Strategic Plan (A document)
ARSTRIKE	(US) Army Strike (STRICOM)
ASNP	Army Student Nurse Program
ASAC	Army Study Advisory Committee
ASDIRS	Army Study Documentation and Information Retrieval System
ASC	Army Subsistence Center
ASSC	Army Subsistence Supply Center (Merged with Defense Subsistence Supply Center)
ASMC	Army Supply & Maintenance Command
ASG	Army Surgeon General
ASDSVN	Army Switched Data and Secure Voice Network
ARTOC	Army Tactical Operations Central
ATAC	Army Tank-Automotive Center (or Command)
ATLIS	Army Technical Library Improvement Studies
ATSC	Army Technical Service Corps
ATEC	Army Test and Evaluation Command (AMC)
ATC	Army Topographic Command (Formerly, Army Map Service)
ATC	Army Training Center
ATF	Army Training Film
ATP	Army Training Program
ATT	Army Training Test
ATS	Army Transport Service
ATSQMC	Army Transport Service Quartermaster Corps
ATA	Army Transportation Association
ATB	Army Transportation Board
ATC	Army Transportation Corps
ATP-ASCP	Army Transportation Plan in Support of the Army Strategic Capabilities Plan
ATRC	Army Transportation Research Command
AUS	Army of the United States
AVP	Army Validation Program
AVD	Army Veterinary Department
AVD	Army Victualling Department (British)
AVC	Army Volunteers Corps (British)
ARWC	Army War College
AWC	Army War College

AWR . . . . Army War Room
AWRIS . . . . . Army War Room Information System
AWC . . . . . . Army Weapons Command (AMC)
AWECOM . . . Army Weapons Command
AWMC . . . . . Army Weapons & Mobility Command
AW . . . . Army-Wide
AADC . . . . . . Arnold Air Development Center (Air Force)
AAS . . . . . . Arnold Air Society
ACT . . . . . . Arnold Constable Corporation (NYSE symbol) (Delisted)
AEDC . . . . . . Arnold Engineering Development Center (Air Force)
ATC . . . . . . Arnold Transit Company (AAR code)
ARO . . . . . . Aro Corporation (NYSE symbol)
ASTC . . . . . . Aroostook State Teachers College (Maine)
AVL . . . . . . Aroostook Valley R. R. (AAR code)
APLC . . . . . . Aro-Pneumatic Logic Control
A . . . . Arousal
AES . . . . . . Array Element Study
ARSIP . . . . . Arrears in Pay (Military)
AG . . . . Arresting Gear and Barriers (Navy)
AA . . . . . . Arrival Angle
AN . . . . . . Arrival Notice (Shipping)
ARREP . . . . Arrival Report (Navy)
ARREPISIC . . . Arrival Report Immediate Superior in Command (Navy)
AR . . . . . . Arrival and Return (Shipping)
ARUNK . . . . . Arrival Unknown (Aviation)
ARRUS . . . . . Arrived Within Continental Limits of US (Navy)
As . . . . Arsenic (Chemical element)
AADLA . . . . . Art and Antique Dealers League of America
ACS . . . . . . Art Center School
ACCA . . . . . Art Collectors Club of America
ADAA . . . . . Art Dealers Association of America
AEB . . . . . . Art Exhibitions Bureau
AIC . . . . . . Art Information Center
AIL . . . . . . Art Institute of Light
AMBOT . . . . . Art Material Board of Trade
AMC . . . . . . Art Material Club
ASLNY . . . . . Art Students' League of New York
AWF . . . . . . Art for World Friendship
AJR . . . . . . Artemus-Jellico Railroad Company
ABP . . . . . . Arterial Blood Pressure
AS . . . . Arteriosclerosis (Medicine)
ASCVD . . . . . Arteriosclerotic Cardiovascular Disease (Medicine)
ASHD . . . . . Arteriosclerotic Heart Disease
AF . . . . Arthritis Foundation
ARF . . . . . . Arthritis and Rheumatism Foundation
ARBOR . . . . . Arthropod-Borne (Virology)
ADL . . . . . . Arthur D. Little, Inc.
ALi . . . . . . Arthur Little, Inc.
ARVIDA . . . . Arthur Vining Davis Corporation
AAB . . . . . . Artichoke Advisory Board
A . . . . Article
AID . . . . . . Articles Contributed for Intelligence and Dollars (Education program)
AGN . . . . . . Articles for the Government of the Navy
AOW . . . . . . Articles of War
AW . . . . . . Articles of War (Army)
ARCH . . . . . Articulated Computing Hierarchy (British)
ACN . . . . . . Artificial Cloud Nucleation (Rainmaking)
AES . . . . . . Artificial Earth Satellite (NASA)
AESOP . . . . . Artificial Earth Satellite Observation Program (Navy)
AFMBT . . . . . Artificial Flower Manufacturers Board of Trade
AGS . . . . . . Artificial Gravity Structure
AI . . . . Artificial Insemination (Medicine)
AID . . . . . . Artificial Insemination by Donor (Medicine)
AIH . . . . . . Artificial Insemination by Husband (Medicine)
AIG . . . . . . Artificial Intelligence Group (MIT)
ALC . . . . . . Artificial Luminous Cloud
ARTRON . . . . Artificial Neuron
AR . . . . . . Artificial Respiration
ASTRO . . . . . Artificial Satellite Time and Radio Orbit
ATL . . . . . . Artificial Transmission Line
A . . . . Artillery
AARDL . . . . . Artillery Ammunition and Rocket Development Laboratory (Army)
AFR . . . . . . Artillery Flash Ranging (Army)
AMS . . . . . . Artillery and Missile School (Army)
ASD . . . . . . Artillery Spotting Division
ATB . . . . . . Artillery Test Board (Army)
AV . . . . . . Artillery Volunteers
AOMP . . . . . Artisans Order of Mutual Protection
AGI . . . . . . Artistes Graphiques Internationales
ACRAF . . . . . Artists Civil Rights Assistance Fund (Defunct)
AEA . . . . . . Artists Equity Association

AEF . . . . Artists Equity Fund
AGBI . . . . . . Artists' General Benevolent Institution (British)
AG . . . . Artists Guild
ARA . . . . . . Artists' Representatives Association
ATRI . . . . . . Artists Technical Research Institute
AB . . . . Artium Baccalaureus (Bachelor of Arts)
AED . . . . . . Artium Elegantium Doctor (Doctor of Fine Arts)
ACA . . . . . . Arts Councils of America
ARV . . . . . . Arvin Industries, Inc. (NYSE symbol)
AABY . . . . . . As Amended By (Army)
AGA . . . . . . As Good As
AOD . . . . . . As-Of Date
AP . . . . As Prescribed
AP . . . . As Purchased
AR . . . . As Required
ASAP . . . . . . As Soon As Possible
AS . . . . As Stated
A/S . . . . As Stated
AC . . . . Asbestos Cement (Technical drawings)
ACB . . . . . . Asbestos-Cement Board (Technical drawings)
A-CPA . . . . . Asbestos-Cement Products Association
ACM . . . . . . Asbestos-Covered Metal (Technical drawings)
AIW . . . . . . Asbestos Insulated Wire
AMB . . . . . . Asbestos Mill Board (Technical drawings)
ARS . . . . . . Asbestos Roof Shingles (Technical drawings)
ATI . . . . . . Asbestos Textile Institute
AS . . . . Ascendance-Submission (Psychology)
ARAS . . . . . . Ascending Reticular Activating System
AP . . . . Ascent Phase
APS . . . . . . Ascent Propulsion System (NASA)
AZT . . . . . . Ascheim Zondek Test (Medicine)
ASH . . . . . . Ashland Oil & Refining Company (NYSE symbol)
ADN . . . . . . Ashley, Drew & Northern Railway Company (AAR code)
ACEF . . . . . . Asian Cultural Exchange Foundation
ADB . . . . . . Asian Development Bank
AFLA . . . . . . Asian Federation of Library Associations
ASPAC . . . . . Asian and Pacific Council
APACL . . . . . Asian Peoples' Anti-Communist League
APO . . . . . . Asian Productivity Organization
ARO . . . . . . Asian Regional Organization
ARO-ICFTU . . . Asian Regional Organization - International Federation of
            Free Trade Unions
ASC . . . . . . Asian Socialist Conference
ASIA . . . . . . Asian Studies in America
AF . . . . Asiatic Fleet
APCM . . . . . . Asiatic-Pacific Campaign Medal
APTW . . . . . . Asiatic-Pacific Theater of War
ACTOR . . . . . Askania Cine-Theodolite Optical-Tracking Range
A . . . . Asked
AIH . . . . . . Asociacion Internacional de Hispanistas
ANCI . . . . . . Asociacion Nacional de Comerciantes y Industriales
ALALC . . . . . Asociacion Latino Americana de Libre Comercio (Latin American
            Free Trade Association) (Also uses initials LAFTA)
ARFORA . . . . Asociatiunea Reuniunilor Femeilor Ortodoxe Romane-Americane
AR . . . . Aspect Ratio
AIHS . . . . . . Aspen Institute of Humanistic Studies
ASPHRS . . . . Asphalt Roof Shingles (Technical drawings)
ARIB . . . . . . Asphalt Roofing Industry Bureau
ATB . . . . . . Asphalt-Tile Base (Technical drawings)
ATF . . . . . . Asphalt-Tile Floor (Technical drawings)
AVATI . . . . . Asphalt and Vinyl Asbestos Tile Institute
APC . . . . . . Aspirin, Phenacetin, and Caffeine Compound (Slang translation is,
            "All Purpose Capsules")
ASIS . . . . . . Assateague Island National Seashore (National Park Service designation)
AACO . . . . . Assault Airlift Control Officer
A & B . . . . . Assault and Battery
ABWIK . . . . . Assault and Battery with Intent to Kill
ADW . . . . . . Assault with Deadly Weapon
AFCC . . . . . . Assault Fire Command Console (Army)
AFU . . . . . . Assault Fire Unit (Army)
CVHA . . . . . . Assault Helicopter Aircraft Carrier (Navy symbol)
ALZ . . . . . . Assault Landing Zone
ASH . . . . . . Assault Support Helicopter (Military)
AVRE . . . . . . Assault Vehicle, Royal Engineers (British)
AT . . . . Assay Ton
AEC . . . . . . Assembled Electronic Component
AMJ . . . . . . Assemblee Mondiale de la Jeunesse
ANCE . . . . . . Assemblee des Nations Captives d'Europe
APE . . . . . . Assemblee Parlementaire Europeenne
ABL . . . . . . Assembly Breakdown List
ACEN . . . . . . Assembly of Captive European Nations

ADSL	Assembly Department Shortage List
AD	Assembly-Disassembly
AD	Assembly District
ALA	Assembly of Librarians of the Americas
ALOA	Assembly of Librarians of the Americas
AOR.	Assembly Operations Record
APL	Assembly Part List
A & R	Assembly and Repair
ASCENT	Assembly System for Central Processor (UNIVAC)
ASPER	Assembly System for the Peripheral Processors
ATRS	Assembly Test Recording System
AWSO	Assembly Work Schedule Order
AP	Assessment Paid
AMS.	Assets Management System
ACN	Assignment Control Number (Army)
AIFURC	Assignment Instructions were Furnished your Command
AIRF	Assignment Instructions Remain Firm (Army)
AIMOSACGP . .	Assignment Instructions Will Include MOS (Military Occupational Specialty) within Army Career Group
AM	Assignment Memorandum (Army)
ASD	Assignment Selection Date (Military)
APS	Assimilations Per Second
AQ	Assimulatory Quotient
AWA	Assist Work Authorization
AIDAC	Assistance Information and Data Acquisition Center (Navy)
ATONU	Assistance Technique de l'Organisation des Nations Unies
AAG	Assistant Adjutant-General
AFOAT.	Assistant for Atomic Energy (Air Force)
AC	Assistant Cashier (Banking)
ACNO	Assistant Chief of Naval Operations
ACNOT	Assistant Chief of Naval Operations (Transportation)
ACPI	Assistant Chief Patrol Inspector (Immigration and Naturalization Service)
ACR	Assistant Chief for Research
ACS	Assistant Chief of Staff
AC/SAF	Assistant Chief of Staff, Air Force
AC of S	Assistant Chief of Staff (Army)
ACSC-E	Assistant Chief of Staff for Communications – Electronics
ACSFOR	Assistant Chief of Staff for Force Development (Army)
ACSI	Assistant Chief of Staff for Intelligence (Army)
ACAS(I)	Assistant Chief of Staff (Intelligence) (War Department)
ACSRC	Assistant Chief of Staff for Reserve Components (Army)
ACS/S & A . . .	Assistant Chief of Staff, Studies and Analysis (Air Force)
CA	Assistant Commandant (Coast Guard)
ACG	Assistant Commissary General
ADMG	Assistant Deputy Military Governor (US Military Government, Germany)
AFDAP	Assistant for Development Planning (Air Force)
ADMS	Assistant Director of Medical Services
ADOS	Assistant Director of Ordnance Services (British)
ADA	Assistant District Attorney
ADC	Assistant Division Commander
ADE	Assistant Division Engineer (Army)
ADSO	Assistant Division Supply Officer (Army)
AE	Assistant Engineer
AFDO	Assistant Fighter Director Office (Navy)
AGM	Assistant General Manager (AEC)
AGMA	Assistant General Manager for Administration (AEC)
AGMIA	Assistant General Manager for International Activities (AEC)
AGMO	Assistant General Manager for Operations (AEC)
AGMPP	Assistant General Manager for Plans and Production (AEC)
AGMRD	Assistant General Manager for Research and Development (AEC)
AIG	Assistant Inspector General (Military)
AINO	Assistant Inspector of Naval Ordnance
AINSMAT	Assistant Inspector Naval Material
AINM	Assistant Inspector Navy Materiel
AFMPC	Assistant for Materiel Program Control (Air Force)
AMO	Assistant Medical Officer
ANSO	Assistant Naval Stores Officer
ANMC	Assistant Navy Mail Clerk
AP	Assistant Paymaster
APM.	Assistant Paymaster (Marine Corps)
APE(S)	Assistant Project Engineer(s)
APM.	Assistant Provost Marshal
APWO	Assistant Public Works Officer
AQM	Assistant Quartermaster
AQMG	Assistant Quartermaster General
AS of AF	Assistant Secretary of the Air Force
ASTSECAF	Assistant Secretary of Air Force
SAFMP	Assistant Secretary of Air Force (Manpower & Personnel)
ASAFMA	Assistant Secretary of the Air Force (Materiel)
SAFMA	Assistant Secretary of Air Force (Materiel)

SAFRD	Assistant Secretary of Air Force (Research and Development)
ASA	Assistant Secretary of the Army
AS of A	Assistant Secretary of the Army
ASA (FM)	Assistant Secretary of the Army (Financial Management)
ASA (I & L) . . .	Assistant Secretary of the Army (Installations & Logistics)
ASA (R & D). . .	Assistant Secretary of the Army (Research & Development)
ASD	Assistant Secretary of Defense
ATSD(AE)	Assistant to the Secretary of Defense (Atomic Energy)
ASD (C)	Assistant Secretary of Defense (Comptroller)
ASD/H & M . .	Assistant Secretary of Defense (Health and Medical)
ASD (I & L) . . .	Assistant Secretary of Defense (Installations & Logistics)
ADS (ISA)	Assistant Secretary of Defense (International Security Affairs)
ASD/ISA	Assistant Secretary of Defense (International Security Affairs)
ASD (M)	Assistant Secretary of Defense (Manpower)
ASD/MP & R . .	Assistant Secretary of Defense (Manpower, Personnel, and Reserves)
ASD/P & I . . .	Assistant Secretary of Defense (Properties and Installations)
ASD (PA)	Assistant Secretary of Defense (Public Affairs)
ASD/R & D . . .	Assistant Secretary of Defense (Research and Development)
ASD/R & E . . .	Assistant Secretary of Defense (Research and Engineering)
ASD/S & L . . .	Assistant Secretary of Defense (Supply and Logistics)
ASGAN	Assistant Secretary General for Air Navigation (ICAO)
ASGS	Assistant Secretary General Staff
ASN.	Assistant Secretary of the Navy
ASTSECNAV . .	Assistant Secretary of Navy
ASTSECNAVAIR . .	Assistant Secretary of the Navy for Air
ASN (FM)	Assistant Secretary of the Navy (Financial Management)
ASN(R & D) . . .	Assistant Secretary of the Navy (Research and Development)
ASW	Assistant Secretary of War
AFSWA	Assistant Secretary of War for Air
ASO	Assistant Secretary's Office (Navy)
ASJA	Assistant Staff Judge Advocate (Air Force)
ASOS	Assistant Supervisor of Shipbuilding (Navy)
ATD	Assistant Test Director
AVCS	Assistant Vice Chief of Staff
ATO	Assisted Take-Off (British aviation and rocket term)
ATOS	Assisted Take-Off System
AWC	Assisting Work Center
A	Assists (in putting a man out) (Baseball)
ABI	Associacao Brasileira de Imprensa (Brazilian press association)
ACAR.	Associacao de Credito e Assistencia Rural (Association of Credit and Rural Assistance) (Brazil)
A	Associate (in an academic degree)
AA	Associate in Accounting
A Ae E	Associate in Aeronautical Engineering
AA-C & Ref Tech . .	Associate in Air-Conditioning and Refrigeration Technology
AAGO	Associate of American Guild of Organists
AAA	Associate in Applied Arts
AAS	Associate in Applied Science
AA	Associate in Arts
AA Ag	Associate in Arts in Agriculture
AAA & S	Associate in Arts in Arts and Science
AAHE	Associate in Arts in Home Economics
AA Ter Ed . . .	Associate in Arts in Terminal Education
AB	Associate in Business
ABA	Associate in Business Administration
ABM	Associate in Business Management
ASBM	Associate in Business Management
ABS	Associate in Business Science
ACCO	Associate of the Canadian College of Organists
ACRE	Associate Citizens for Responsible Education (Group opposing sex education in schools)
ACP	Associate of the College of Preceptors (British)
ACV	Associate, College of Violinists
ACP	Associate Collegiate Players
AC	Associate in Commerce
ACA	Associate in Commercial Arts
AC Ed	Associate in Commercial Education
ACS	Associate in Commercial Science
ACAMR	Associate Committee on Aviation Medical Research (Canada)
A Dies Tech . . .	Associate in Diesel Technology
A Dr & Dgn . . .	Associate in Drafting and Design
AE	Associate in Education
AEIS.	Associate of the Educational Institute of Scotland
AET	Associate in Electrical Technology
A El Ed	Associate in Elementary Education
AE	Associate in Engineering
AEE	Associate in Engineering
A Eng	Associate in Engineering
ASE	Associate in Engineering
AEA	Associate in Engineering Administration
A Eng Elect . . .	Associate in Engineering Electronics

A En	Associate in English
AEN	Associate in English
AFA	Associate of the Faculty of Actuaries (British)
AFA	Associate in Fine Arts
AFA Art	Associate in Fine Arts in Art
AFA Dance	Associate in Fine Arts in Dance
AFA Drama	Associate in Fine Arts in Drama
AFA Mus	Associate in Fine Arts in Music
AGE	Associate in General Education
A in G Ed	Associate in General Education
AGS	Associate in General Studies
AHE	Associate in Home Economics
AH Ec	Associate in Home Economics
AI Ed	Associate in Industrial Education
AIM	Associate in Industrial Management
ASIM	Associate in Industrial Management
AIOCC	Associate Infantry Officer Career Course (Army)
AIA	Associate of the Institute of Actuaries (British)
AIAE	Associate Institute of Automobile Engineers
AIC	Associate of the Institute of Chemistry (British)
AICE	Associate of the Institute of Civil Engineers (British)
AIME	Associate of the Institute of Mechanical Engineers
AIME	Associate of the Institute of Mining Engineers
AJ	Associate in Journalism
AJ	Associate Justice (US Supreme Court)
AKC	Associate of King's College (London)
AKCL	Associate of King's College London
ALA	Associate in Liberal Arts
ALS	Associate of the Linnaean Society (British)
AMT	Associate in Mechanical Technology
AMT	Associate in Medical Technology
AM	Associate Member
AMICE	Associate Member of the Institution of Civil Engineers (British)
ANSS	Associate of the Normal School of Science
AN	Associate in Nursing
ASN	Associate in Nursing
ASN	Associate in Nursing Science
A Ph	Associate in Philosophy
AP Ed	Associate in Physical Education
APA	Associate in Public Administration
AQC	Associate of Queen's College (London)
A Rel	Associate in Religion
ARE	Associate in Religious Education
AR	Associate in Retailing
ARA	Associate of the Royal Academy
ARAM	Associate of the Royal Academy of Music (British)
ARHA	Associate of the Royal Hibernian Academy
ARIBA	Associate of the Royal Institute of British Architects
ARIC	Associate of the Royal Institute of Chemistry (British)
ARSA	Associate of the Royal Scottish Academy
ARSL	Associate of the Royal Society of Literature
ARSM	Associate of the Royal Society of Musicians (British)
AS	Associate in Science
ASC	Associate in Science in Commerce
ASMS	Associate in Science in Medical Secretarial
ASSS	Associate in Science in Secretarial Studies
ASTT	Associate in Science in Teacher Training
AAS	Associate in Secretarial Science
A Se S	Associate in Secretarial Science
A Se Sc	Associate in Secretarial Science
ASS	Associate in Secretarial Science
SSA	Associate in Secretarial Science
ASS	Associate in Secretarial Studies
ATA	Associate Technical Aide
ATA	Associate in Technical Arts
ATI	Associate of the Textile Institute (British)
A Th	Associate in Theology
AAA	Associated Actors and Artistes of America
AAAA	Associated Actors and Artistes of America
AAA	Associated Agents of America
ABCD	Associated Baby Carriage Dealers
ABW	Associated Brewing Company (NYSE symbol)
ABP	Associated Business Publications
ABWA	Associated Business Writers of America
ACA	Associated Chiropodists of America
ACP	Associated Church Press
ACM	Associated Colleges of the Midwest
ACUNY	Associated Colleges of Upper New York
ACP	Associated Collegiate Press
ACP	Associated Construction Publications
ACT	Associated Container Transportation

ACIA	Associated Cooperage Industries of America
ACE	Associated Corpuscular Emission
ACNS	Associated Correspondents News Service
ACBM	Associated Corset and Brassiere Manufacturers
ACA	Associated Councils of the Arts
ACWW	Associated Country Women of the World
ACCN	Associated Court and Commercial Newspapers
ACB of A	Associated Credit Bureaus of America
ADCC	Associated Day Care Centers
ADACIOM	Associated Drug and Chemical Industries of Missouri
DG	Associated Dry Goods Corporation (NYSE symbol)
AEI	Associated Electrical Industry, Ltd. (British)
AED	Associated Equipment Distributors
AFMFIC	Associated Factory Mutual Fire Insurance Companies
AFP	Associated Fantasy Publishers
AFDS	Associated Funeral Directors Service
AFM	Associated Fur Manufacturers
AGC	Associated General Contractors of America
AGCA	Associated General Contractors of America
AGA	Associated Geographers of America
AGPM	Associated Glass and Pottery Manufacturers
AGCG	Associated Granite Craftsmens Guild
AIDA	Associated Independent Dairies of America
AIECA	Associated Independent Electrical Contractors of America
AIM	Associated Industries of Massachusetts
ALCA	Associated Landscape Contractors of America
ASX	Associated Laundries of America (NYSE symbol)
ALRA	Associated Legislative Rabbinate of America
ALOA	Associated Locksmiths of America
ALC	Associated Lutheran Charities (Later, Lutheran Social Welfare Conference of America)
AMCA	Associated Male Choruses of America
AMOAP	Associated Marine Officers Association of the Philippines
AMBBA	Associated Master Barbers and Beauticians of America
AME	Associated Memory Equipment
AMU	Associated Midwestern Universities, Inc.
AMM	Associated Millinery Men
AMPA	Associated Motion Picture Advertisers
AMPS	Associated Music Publishers (Musical slang)
AOX	Associated Oil Company (American Stock Exchange symbol)
AOTE	Associated Organizations for Teacher Education
APC	Associated Pimiento Canners
APCO	Associated Police Communications Officers
APKCA	Associated Pot and Kettle Clubs of America
APEI	Associated Poultry and Egg Industries
AP	Associated Press
APME	Associated Press Managing Editors Association
APRTA	Associated Press Radio and Television Association
APSCO	Associated Public-Safety Communications Officers
APSS	Associated Public School Systems
ARP	Associated Reformed Presbyterian
ARBA	Associated Retail Bakers of America
ARC	Associated Retail Confectioners of North America
ARCUS	Associated Retail Confectioners of the US
ASC	Associated Sandblasting Contractors
ASC	Associated Schools of Construction
ASCO	Associated Spring Corporation
ASA	Associated Stenotypists of America
ASUC	Associated Students of the University of California
ATAE	Associated Telephone Answering Exchanges
ATE	Associated Telephone Exchanges
ATV	Associated Television Ltd. (British independent, commercial television company)
ATCMU	Associated Third Class Mail Users
ATM	Associated Tobacco Manufacturers
ATC	Associated Traffic Clubs of America
AUA	Associated Unions of America
AU	Associated Universities
AUI	Associated Universities, Incorporated
AUBBER	Associated University Bureaus of Business and Economic Research
AVL	Associated Veterinary Laboratories
AWU	Associated Western Universities
AWU	Associated Workers' Union (Philippines)
ATS	Associates Investment Company (NYSE symbol)
ARA	Associates for Radio Astronomy
A	Association
ATA	Association for Academic Travel Abroad
AAASUSS	Association of Administrative Assistants and Secretaries to United States Senators
AAEH	Association to Advance Ethical Hypnosis
AALU	Association for Advanced Life Underwriting

AAAR . . . . Association for the Advancement of Aeronautical Research (France)
AABT . . . . Association for Advancement of the Behavioral Therapies
AABC . . . . Association for Advancement of Blind Children
AAFS . . . . Association for the Advancement of Family Stability
AAIAN . . . . . . Association for the Advancement of Instruction about Alcohol and Narcotics
AAMI . . . . Association for the Advancement of Medical Instrumentation
AAP . . . . Association for the Advancement of Psychoanalysis
AAP . . . . Association for the Advancement of Psychotherapy
AAFC . . . . . . Association of Advertising Film Companies
AAMW . . . . . . Association of Advertising Men and Women (Later, Advertising and Marketing Association)
AACC . . . . . . Association for the Aid of Crippled Children
AATU . . . . . . Association of Air Transport Unions
AAMI . . . . . . Association of Allergists for Mycological Investigations
AAPS . . . . . . Association for Ambulatory Pediatric Services
AABM . . . . . . Association of American Battery Manufacturers
AABEVM . . . . Association of American Boards of Examiners in Veterinary Medicine
AACIGO . . . . Association of American and Canadian Importers of Green Olives
AACCLA . . . . Association of American Chambers of Commerce in Latin America
AAC . . . . . . Association of American Choruses
AAC . . . . . . Association of American Colleges
AAD . . . . Association of American Dentists
AAEC . . . . . . Association of American Editorial Cartoonists
AAFCO . . . . . Association of American Feed Control Officials
AAFCO . . . . . Association of American Fertilizer Control Officials
AAFSW . . . . . Association of American Foreign Service Women
AAG . . . . . . Association of American Geographers
AAIA . . . . . . Association of American Indian Affairs
AALS . . . . . . Association of American Law Schools
AALS . . . . . . Association of American Library Schools
AAMBP . . . . . Association of American Medical Book Publishers
AAMC . . . . . Association of American Medical Colleges
AAPCO . . . . . Association of American Pesticide Control Officials
AAP . . . . Association of American Physicians
AAPS . . . . . . Association of American Physicians and Surgeons
AAPCM . . . . . Association of American Playing Card Manufacturers
AAP . . . . Association of American Publishers (Formerly, ABPC and AEPI)
AARDCO . . . . Association of American Railroad Dining Car Officers
AAR . . . . . . Association of American Railroads
AAR . . . . . . Association of American Rhodes Scholars
AARGCE . . . . Association of American Rod and Gun Clubs in Europe
AASCO . . . . . Association of American Seed Control Officials
AASO . . . . . . Association of American Ship Owners
AASG . . . . . . Association of American State Geologists
AASM . . . . . . Association of American Steel Manufacturers
AAU . . . . Association of American Universities
AAUP . . . . . . Association of American University Presses
AAVMC . . . . . Association of American Veterinary Medical Colleges
AAWE . . . . . . Association of American Wives of Europeans
AAWD . . . . . . Association of American Women Dentists
AAWPI . . . . . . Association of American Wood Pulp Importers
ASSANEF. . . . . Association des Anciens Eleves des Ecoles des Freres Chretiennes (Association of Former Students of Catholic Schools)
AAP . . . . Association for Applied Psychoanalysis
AASE . . . . . . Association for Applied Solar Energy
AFASE . . . . . . Association for Applied Solar Energy
AAHM . . . . . . Association of Architectural Hardware Manufacturers
AAMD . . . . . . Association of Art Museum Directors
AAS . . . . Association for Asian Studies
AAPT . . . . . . Association of Asphalt Paving Technologists
AAA . . . . Association of Attenders and Alumni of The Hague Academy of International Law
AAA. . . . . . . Association of Average Adjusters of the United States
AAAUS . . . . . Association of Average Adjusters of the United States
BOP . . . . . . Association for Balance of Political Power
BALUBAKAT. . . Association des Baluba du Katanga (Association of the Baluba of Katanga)
ABHH . . . . . . Association of Baptist Homes and Hospitals
ABPR . . . . . . Association of Baptist Professors of Religion
ABWE . . . . . . Association of Baptists for World Evangelism
ASSOBELA. . . . Association des Batetela de Lodja (Association of Batetelas of Lodja)
ABAG . . . . . . Association of Bay Area Governments (Northern California)
ABFLO . . . . . Association of Bedding and Furniture Law Officials
ABNE . . . . . . Association for the Benefit of Non-contract Employees
ADEA . . . . . . Association Belge pour le Developpement Pacifique de l'Energie Atomique (Belgian Association for the Peaceful Development of Atomic Energy)
ABBB . . . . . . Association of Better Business Bureaus
ABCP . . . . . . Association of Blind Chartered Physiotherapists
ABJS . . . . . . Association of Bone and Joint Surgeons
ABSCM. . . . . . Association of Boys & Students Clothing Manufacturers
ABCC . . . . . . Association of British Chambers of Commerce

ABPR . . . . . . Association of British Picture Restorers
ABS . . . . Association on Broadcasting Standards
ABOPS . . . . . Association of Business Officers of Preparatory Schools
ABO . . . . . . Association of Buying Offices
ACBLF . . . . . Association Canadienne des Bibliothecaires de Langue Francaise
ACB . . . . Association Canadienne des Bibliotheques (Canadian Library Association) (Also known as CLA)
ACA . . . . . . Association Canado-Americaine
ACURIL. . . . . Association of Caribbean University and Research Institute Libraries
ACAS . . . . . Association of Casualty Accountants and Statisticians
ACSC . . . . . . Association of Casualty and Surety Companies
ACT . . . . Association of Catholic Teachers
ACTU . . . . . Association of Catholic Trade Unionists
ACIOPJF . . . . Association Catholique Internationale des Œuvres de Protection de la Jeune Fille
ACOMARS. . . . Association of Centers of Medieval and Renaissance Studies
ACPAE . . . . . Association of Certified Public Accountant Examiners
ACSSAVO . . . . Association of Chief State School Audio-Visual Officers
ACEI . . . . . . Association for Childhood Education International
ACLD . . . . . . Association for Children with Learning Disabilities
A/CRMD . . . . Association for Children with Retarded Mental Development
ACC . . . . . . Association of Choral Conductors
ACTS . . . . . . Association for Christian Training and Service
ACL . . . . . . Association of Cinema Laboratories
ACMAF. . . . . Association des Classes Moyennes Africaines (African Middle Classes Association)
ACP . . . . . . Association of Clinical Pathologists
ACS . . . . . . Association of Clinical Scientists
ACAC . . . . . Association of College Admissions Counselors
ACHS . . . . . Association College Honor Societies
ACRL . . . . . Association of College and Research Libraries
ACU . . . . . . Association of College Unions
ACUCM . . . . Association of College and University Concert Managers
ACUHO . . . . Association of College and University Housing Officers
ACSC . . . . . Association of Colleges and Secondary Schools (Defunct)
ACSSN . . . . . Association of Colleges and Secondary Schools for Negroes
ACSA . . . . . Association of Collegiate Schools of Architecture
ACSN . . . . . Association of Collegiate Schools of Nursing
ACIBU . . . . . Association des Commercants Indigenes du Burundi (Association of Indigenous Merchants of Burundi)
ACICAFE. . . . . Association du Commerce et de l'Industrie du Cafe dans la CEE (Association for the Coffee Trade and Industry in the EEC)
ACFA . . . . . . Association of Commercial Finance Attorneys
ACFC . . . . . Association of Commercial Finance Companies of New York
ACEF . . . . . . Association of Commodity Exchange Firms
ACTC . . . . . Association of Community Travel Clubs
ACA . . . . . . Association of Commuter Airlines
ACE . . . . . . Association for Comparative Economics
ACM . . . . . . Association for Computing Machinery
ACE . . . . . . Association of Conservation Engineers
ACRPP. . . . . . Association pour la Conservation et la Reproduction Photographique de las Presse
ASCOMACE. . . Association des Constructeurs de Machines a Coudre de la CEE (Association of Sewing Machine Manufacturers of the EEC)
ACC & CE . . . Association of Consulting Chemists and Chemical Engineers
ACF . . . . . . Association of Consulting Foresters
ACME. . . . . . Association of Consulting Management Engineers
ACURA . . . . Association for the Coordination of University Religious Affairs
ACG . . . . . . Association for Corporate Growth
ACGD . . . . . Association for Corporate Growth and Diversification
ACES . . . . . . Association Corporative des Etudiants en Sciences (France)
ACA . . . . . . Association of Correctional Administrators
ACP. . . . . . . Association of Correctional Psychologists
ACTM . . . . . Association of Cotton Textile Merchants of New York
ACYD . . . . . Association of Cotton Yarn Distributors
ACS . . . . . . Association of Council Secretaries
ACES . . . . . . Association for Counselor Education and Supervision
ACB . . . . . . Association of Customers' Brokers
ACB . . . . . . Association of the Customs Bar
ADLTDE . . . . Association of Dark Leaf Tobacco Dealers and Exporters
ADAPSO . . . . Association of Data Processing Service Organizations (Includes American and Canadian companies)
ADPSO . . . . . Association of Data Processing Service Organizations
ADE . . . . . . Association of Departments of English
ADDC . . . . . Association of Desk and Derrick Clubs of North America
ADEP . . . . . Association pour le Developpement de l'Exportation des Vins de Bordeaux
ADS . . . . . . Association of Diesel Specialists
AESE . . . . . . Association of Earth Science Editors
AEI . . . . Association des Ecoles Internationales
AEIC . . . . . . Association of Edison Illuminating Companies
AEIB . . . . . . Association for Education in International Business

AEJ . . . . Association for Education in Journalism
AETS . . . . Association for the Education of Teachers in Science
AEDS . . . . Association of Educational Data Systems
AEHHC . . . . . Association of Educators of Homebound and Hospitalized Children
AED . . . . Association of Electronic Distributors
AEM . . . . Association of Electronic Manufacturers
AEM-ED . . . . . Association of Electronic Manufacturers, Eastern Division
AEPEM . . . . . Association of Electronic Parts and Equipment Manufacturers
ASSOFECAM . . Association pour l'Emancipation de la Femme Camerounaise (Association for the Emancipation of Cameroonian Women)
AEG . . . . Association of Engineering Geologists
AESBOW . . . . . Association of Engineers and Scientists of the Bureau of Naval Weapons
AEC . . . . Association of Episcopal Colleges
AEL . . . . Association of Equipment Lessors
ATALA . . . . . Association pour l'Etude et le Developpement de la Traduction Automatique et de la Linguistique Appliquee
AETFAT . . . . . Association pour l'Etude Taxonomique de la Flore d'Afrique Tropicale
AEGF . . . . Association des Etudiants Guineens de France (Association of Guinean Students in France)
AEM . . . . Association des Etudiants Malgaches (Association of Malagasy Students)
AENF . . . . Association des Etudiants Nigeriens en France (Association of Niger Students in France)
AEOM . . . . . . Association des Etudiants d'Origine Malgache (Association of Students of Malagasy Origins Studying in France)
AEJI . . . . . . Association of European Jute Industries
AEC . . . . Association Europeenne de Ceramique
AEDE . . . . . . Association Europeenne des Enseignants
AER . . . . Association Europeenne pour l'Etude du Probleme des Refugies
AEEF . . . . . . Association Europeenne des Exploitations Frigorifiques
AELE . . . . . Association Europeenne de Libre-Echange
AEDT . . . . . . Association Europeenne des Organisations Nationales des Commercants Detaillants en Textiles (European Association of National Organizations of Textile Manufacturers)
EUROPHOT . . . Association Europeenne des Photographes Professionnels
AERTEL . . . . . Association Europeenne Rubans, Tresses, Tissus Elastiques (European Ribbon, Braid and Elastic Material Association)
AERC . . . . . . Association of Executive Recruiting Consultants
ASFALEC . . . . . Association des Fabricants de Laits de Conserve des Pays de la CEE (Association of Powdered Milk Manufacturers of the EEC)
AFHC . . . . . . Association of Fair Housing Committees
AFL . . . . Association for Family Living
AFA . . . . Association of Federal Appraisers
AFA . . . . Association of Federal Architects
AFCCE . . . . . Association of Federal Communications Consulting Engineers
AFI . . . . Association of Federal Investigators
AFP . . . . Association of Federal Photographers
AFSTE . . . . . Association for Field Services in Teacher Education
AFEI . . . . . . Association of Finnish Electric Industries
AFCM . . . . . Association of First Class Mailers
AFAC . . . . . . Association des Fonctionnaires et Agents de la Colonie (Association of Civil Servants and Agents of the Colony) (European civil servants) (East Congo)
AFD . . . . Association of Food Distributors
AFADO . . . . . Association of Food and Drug Officials
AFDOUS . . . . . Association of Food and Drug Officials of the United States
AFD . . . . Association of Footwear Distributors
AFAP . . . . . . Association Francaise pour l'Augmentation de la Productivite (France)
AFCAL . . . . . Association Francaise de Calcul
ADBS . . . . . . Association Francaise des Documentalistes et des Bibliothecaires Specialises
AFITAE . . . . . Association Francaise des Ingenieurs et Techniciens de l'Aeronautique et de l'Espace
AFJA . . . . . . Association Francaise des Journalistes Agricoles
AFFUS . . . . . Association of the Free French in the United States
AFRD . . . . . . Association of Fund-Raising Directors
AFIRE . . . . . Association of Fundamental Institutions of Religious Education
AGLS . . . . . . Association of General and Liberal Studies
AGEFAN . . . . . Association Generale des Etudiants de France en Afrique Noire (General Association of French Students in Black Africa)
AGHTM . . . . Association Generale des Hygienistes et Techniciens Municipaux
AGSPW . . . . . Association of Girl Scout Professional Workers
AGB . . . . Association of Governing Boards of Universities and Colleges
AGS . . . . Association of Graduate Schools (in Association of American Universities)
AGTE . . . . . . Association of Group Travel Executives
AHA . . . . Association of Handicapped Artists
AHE . . . . Association for Higher Education (of the NEA)
AHST . . . . . . Association of Highway Steel Transporters
AHAM . . . . . Association of Home Appliance Manufacturers
AHSS . . . . . . Association of Home Study Schools
AHDME . . . . . Association of Hospital Directors of Medical Education
AHIL . . . . . . Association of Hospital and Institution Libraries (of ALA)

AHMC . . . . . . Association of Hospital Management Committees
AHSA . . . . . . Association of Hospital Security Administrators
AHE . . . . Association for Human Emergence
AHS . . . . Association of Hungarian Students in North America
AHEM . . . . . . Association of Hydraulic Equipment Manufacturers
AINL . . . . . . Association of Immigration and Nationality Lawyers
AICP . . . . . . Association of Independent Composers and Performers
AIOW . . . . . . Association of Independent Optical Wholesalers
AISC . . . . . . Association of Independent Software Companies
AIA . . . . Association of Industrial Advertisers
ASSILEC . . . . . Association de l'Industrie Laitiere de la CEE (Milk Industry Association of the EEC)
AIJE . . . . . . Association des Industries du Jute Europeennes
IMACE . . . . . . Association des Industries Margarinieres des Pays de la CEE
AIPCE . . . . . Association des Industries du Poisson de la CEE
AIM . . . . Association of Innerspring Manufacturers
AID . . . . Association of Institutional Distributors
AIR . . . . Association for Institutional Research
AIEE . . . . . . Association des Instituts d'Etudes Europeennes
AIA . . . . Association of Insurance Advertisers
AIA . . . . Association of Insurance Attorneys
INTERHYBRID . Association Intercontinentale du Mais Hybride
AICB . . . . . . Association des Interets Coloniaux Belges (Merged with AIIB into FEC)
AIIB . . . . Association des Interets Industriels au Congo (Merged with AICB into FEC)
AIAA . . . . . . Association of International Advertising Agencies
AIBA . . . . . . Association of International Border Agencies
AID . . . . Association for International Development
AIAL . . . . . . Association of International Institute of Arts and Letters
AIL . . . . Association of International Libraries
AIRC . . . . . . Association of International Relations Clubs
AIA . . . . Association Internationale d'Allergologie
AIAC . . . . . . Association Internationale d'Archeologie Classique
AIAG . . . . . . Association Internationale des Assureurs Contre la Grele (International Association of Hail Insurers)
INTERASMA . . . Association Internationale d'Asthmologie
AICMR . . . . . . Association Internationale des Constructeurs de Materiel Roulant (International Association of Rolling Stock Builders)
AIBM . . . . . . Association Internationale des Bibliotheques Musicales
AIBA . . . . . . Association Internationale de Boxe Amateur
AICA . . . . . . Association Internationale pour le Calcul Analogique
ASICA . . . . . . Association Internationale pour le Calcul Analogique
AICC . . . . . . Association Internationale de Chimie Cerealiere
ICC . . . . Association Internationale de Chimie Cerealiere
AICS . . . . . . Association Internationale du Cinema Scientifique
AICCF . . . . . . Association Internationale du Congres des Chemins de Fer
AICMA . . . . . . Association Internationale des Constructeurs de Materiel Aeronautique
AICB . . . . . . Association Internationale Contre le Bruit
AICA . . . . . . Association Internationale des Critiques d'Art
AID . . . . Association Internationale pour le Developpement
AIDE . . . . . . Association Internationale des Distributions d'Eau
AIDA . . . . . . Association Internationale de la Distribution des Produits Alimentaires
AIDA . . . . . . Association Internationale du Droit de l'Assurance
AIDP . . . . . . Association Internationale de Droit Penal
AIESEP . . . . . . Association Internationale des Ecoles ou Institut Superieurs d'Education Physique et Sportive (International Association of Schools or Higher Institutes of Physical and Sportive Education)
AIEPE . . . . . Association Internationale des Ecoles Privees Europeennes
AIESS . . . . . . Association Internationale des Ecoles de Service Social
AIEJI . . . . . . Association Internationale des Educateurs de Jeunes Inadaptes
ADPI . . . . . . Association Internationale d'Etudes pour la Protection des Investissements
AIERI . . . . . . Association Internationale des Etudes et Recherches sur l'Information
AIESEE . . . . . . Association Internationale d'Etudes du Sud-Est Europeen (International Association of South-East European Studies)
AIEA . . . . . . Association Internationale des Etudiants en Agriculture
AIED . . . . . . Association Internationale des Etudiants Dentaires
AIESEC . . . . . . Association Internationale des Etudiants en Sciences Economiques et Commerciales
AIEST . . . . . . Association Internationale d'Experts Scientifiques du Tourisme
AIFM . . . . . . Association Internationale des Femmes Medecins
AIG . . . . Association Internationale de Geodesie
AIGA . . . . . . Association Internationale de Geomagnetisme et d'Aeronomie
AIGM . . . . . . Association Internationale de Grands Magasins
AIH . . . . Association Internationale de l'Hotellerie
AIH . . . . Association Internationale d'Hydrologie Scientifique
AIHS . . . . . . Association Internationale d'Hydrologie Scientifique
AIISUP . . . . . . Association Internationale d'Information Scolaire Universitaire et Professionnelle
AIIRM . . . . . . Association Internationale des Interets Radio-Maritimes
AIIC . . . . . . Association Internationale des Interpretes de Conference
AIJP . . . . . . Association Internationale des Journalistes Philateliques (International Association of Philatelic Journalists)

AIJE . . . . Association Internationale des Juges des Enfants
AIJD . . . . Association Internationale de Juristes Democrates (International
          Association of Democratic Lawyers)
AIL . . . . Association Internationale de Limnologie Theorique et Appliquee
AILC . . . . . . Association Internationale de Litterature Comparee
AIMPA . . . . . . Association Internationale de Meteorologie et de Physique de l'Atmosphere
AIMEA . . . . . . Association Internationale des Metiers et Enseignements d'Art
AIM . . . . Association Internationale de la Mutualite
AINP . . . . . . Association Internationale des Numismates Professionnels
AIOP . . . . . . Association Internationale d'Oceanographie Physique
AIOCC . . . . . . Association Internationale d'Organisateurs de Courses Cyclistes
AIOP . . . . . . Association Internationale d'Orientation Professionnelle
AIPC . . . . . . Association Internationale des Palais des Congres
AIPCN . . . . . Association Internationale Permanente des Congres de Navigation
AIPCR . . . . . Association Internationale Permanente des Congres de la Route
AIPC . . . . . Association Internationale des Ponts et Charpentes
AIPEPO . . . . . Association Internationale de Presse pour l'Etude des Problemes
          d'Outre-mer
AIPS . . . . Association Internationale de la Presse Sportive
AIPH . . . . . . Association Internationale des Producteurs de l'Horticulture
AIPS . . . . Association Internationale pour le Progres Social
AIPC . . . . . Association Internationale de Prophylaxie de la Cecite
AIPPI . . . . . . Association Internationale pour la Protection de la Propriete
          Industrielle
AIPA . . . . . . Association Internationale de Psychologie Appliquee
AIRBO . . . . . . Association Internationale pour les Recherches au Bas Fourneau
          d'Ougree
AIRH . . . . . . Association Internationale de Recherches Hydrauliques
AIRBR . . . . . . Association Internationale du Registre des Bateaux du Rhin
AIS . . . . Association Internationale de la Savonnerie et de la Detergence
AISP . . . . . . Association Internationale de Science Politique
AISE . . . . Association Internationale des Sciences Economiques
AISJ . . . . Association Internationale des Sciences Juridiques
AISS . . . . Association Internationale de la Securite Sociale
AISPIT . . . . . Association Internationale de Seismologie et de Physique de l'Interieur
          de la Terre
ASSINSEL . . . Association Internationale des Selectionneurs Professionnels pour la
          protection des Obtentions Vegetales (International Plant Breeders
          Association for the Protection of New Varieties)
AISM . . . . . . Association Internationale de Signalisation Maritime
AISC . . . . . . Association Internationale des Skal Clubs
AISM . . . . . . Association Internationale des Societes de Microbiologie
AIS . . . . Association Internationale de Sociologie
AIS . . . . Association Internationale de la Soie
AITT . . . . . . Association Internationale de la Teinture Textile
AITA . . . . . . Association Internationale du Theatre d'Amateurs
AIT . . . . Association Internationale des Travailleurs (International Association of
          Workers) (France)
AIU . . . . Association Internationale des Universites
AIEP . . . . Association Internationale des Usagers d'Embranchements Particuliers
          (International Association of Users of Private Sidings)
AIUFFAS . . . . Association Internationale des Utilisateurs de Files de Fibres Artificielles
          et Synthetiques
AIVM . . . . . . Association Internationale pour les Voiles Minces (en Beton)
AIV . . . . Association Internationale de Volcanologie
AIDT . . . . . . Association Interparlementaire du Tourisme
AIN . . . . Association of Interpretive Naturalists
AIM . . . . Association of Interracial Marriages
AICCP . . . . . . Association of Interstate Commerce Commission Practitioners
AIB . . . . Association of Investment Brokers
AISE . . . . Association of Iron and Steel Engineers
AJTI . . . . Association on Japanese Textile Imports
AJBA . . . . . . Association de la Jeunesse Bakoko (Association of Bakoko Youth)
AJC . . . . Association de la Jeunesse Camerounaise (Cameroonian Youth Association)
AJM . . . . Association de la Jeunesse Mauritanienne (Mauritanian Youth Association)
AJENAKO . . . . Association des Jeunes Nationalistes du Kongo (Association of
          Nationalist Youth of the Congo) (Leopoldville)
AJBP . . . . . . Association of Jewish Book Publishers
AJCAF . . . . . . Association of Jewish Chaplains of the Armed Forces
AJCRW . . . . . Association of Jewish Community Relations Workers
AJSC . . . . . . Association of Jewish Sponsored Camps
AJLA . . . . . . Association of the Junior Leagues of America
AKFM . . . . . . Association of Knitted Fabrics Manufacturers
ALMA . . . . . . Association of Labor Mediation Agencies
ALGCU . . . . . Association of Land Grant Colleges and Universities
ALAS . . . . . . Association for Latin American Studies (Defunct)
ALIC . . . . . . Association of Life Insurance Counsel
ALIMDA . . . . Association of Life Insurance Medical Directors of America
ALMA . . . . . . Association of Literary Magazines of America
LMSI . . . . . . Association of Lithuanian Foresters in Exile
ALW . . . . Association of Lithuanian Workers

ALAI . . . . Association Litteraire et Artistique Internationale
ALTA . . . . . . Association of Local Transport Airlines
ALPO . . . . . . Association of Lunar and Planetary Observers
ALSS . . . . . . Association of Lutheran Secondary Schools
AMTCL . . . . . Association for Machine Translation and Computational Linguistics
AMTCU . . . . . Association for Machine Translation and Computational Linguistics
AMC . . . . . . Association of Management Consultants
AMPH . . . . . . Association of Management in Public Health
AMCC . . . . . Association of Manufacturers of Confectionery and Chocolate
AMH . . . . . . Association of Marian Helpers
AMES . . . . . . Association of Marine Engineering Schools (British)
AMUUS . . . . . Association of Marine Underwriters of the United States
MST . . . . . . Association of Maximum Service Telecasters
AMEG . . . . . . Association for Measurement and Evaluation in Guidance
AMAA . . . . . . Association of Medical Advertising Agencies
AMGP . . . . . . Association of Medical Group Psychoanalysts
AMI . . . . . . Association of Medical Illustrators
AMRC . . . . . . Association of Medical Record Consultants
AMRDC . . . . . Association of Medical Rehabilitation Directors and Coordinators
AMFA . . . . . . Association Medicale Franco-Americaine
AMM . . . . . . Association Medicale Mondiale
AMHC . . . . . . Association of Mental Hospital Chaplains
AMS . . . . Association of Messenger Services
AMHS . . . . . . Association of Methodist Historical Societies
AMIH . . . . . . Association for Middle Income Housing
AMFGC . . . . . Association of Midwest Fish and Game Commissioners
AMCS . . . . . . Association of Military Colleges and Schools
AMDS . . . . . . Association of Military Dental Surgeons
AMSUS . . . . . Association of Military Surgeons of the United States
AMEMIC . . . . . Association of Mill and Elevator Mutual Insurance Companies
AMRI . . . . . . Association of Missile and Rocket Industries
AMPP . . . . . . Association of Motion Picture Producers
AMV . . . . . . Association Mondiale Veterinaire
ASCOFAM . . . Association Mondiale de Lutte Contre la Faim
AMC . . . . . . Association of Municipal Corporations (British)
AMS . . . . Association of Museum Stores
AMFIE . . . . . Association of Mutual Fire Insurance Engineers
AMFPS . . . . . Association of Mutual Fund Plan Sponsors
AMIE . . . . . . Association of Mutual Insurance Engineers
ANA . . . . Association of National Advertisers
ANRT . . . . . . Association Nationale de la Recherche Technique (France)
ANPP . . . . . . Association of Negro Press Photographers
ANCAM . . . . . Association of Newspaper Classified Advertising Managers
ANADP . . . . . Association of North American Directory Publishers
AOAC . . . . . . Association of Official Analytical Chemists (Formerly, Agricultural)
AORC . . . . . . Association of Official Racing Chemists
AOSA . . . . . . Association of Official Seed Analysts
AOPL . . . . . . Association of Oil Pipe Lines
AOSC . . . . . . Association of Oilwell Servicing Contractors
AORN . . . . . . Association of Operating Room Nurses
AOM . . . . . . Association of Operative Millers
ASSUC . . . . . Association des Organisations Professionnelles du Commerce des Sucres
          pour les Pays de la CEE (Association of Sugar Trade Organizations for
          the EEC Countries)
AOB . . . . Association des Originaires de Bandounga (Association of Natives of
          Bandounga)
AOJS . . . . . . Association of Orthodox Jewish Scientists
AOP . . . . . . Association of Osteopathic Publications
AOLS . . . . . . Association of Our Lady of Salvation
AOE . . . . . . Association of Overseas Educators
APF . . . . Association of Pacific Fisheries
APEA . . . . . . Association Parlementaire Europe-Afrique (Eur-African Parliamentary
          Association)
APA . . . . Association of Paroling Authorities
APANY . . . . . Association of Personnel Agencies of New York
APR . . . . Association of Petroleum Re-Refiners
APW . . . . . . Association of Petroleum Writers
APAW . . . . . . Association of Philippine-American Women
API . . . . Association Phonetique Internationale
APS . . . . Association of Photo Sensitizers
APID . . . . . . Association of Photographic Importers and Distributors
APMR . . . . . . Association for Physical and Mental Rehabilitation
APWUS . . . . . Association of Polish Women of the United States
APA . . . . Association of Port Authorities
APSO . . . . . . Association of Poultry Slaughterhouse Operators
APG . . . . Association for Precision Graphics
APPA . . . . . . Association for the Preservation and Presentation of the Arts
APVA . . . . . . Association for the Preservation of Virginia Antiquities
APA . . . . Associative Principle for Addition (New math)
APM . . . . . . Associative Principle for Multiplication (New math)
APC . . . . Association of Private Camps

APH . . . . Association of Private Hospitals
APOPA . . . . . . Association of Private Office Personnel Agencies
APBPA . . . . . . Association of Professional Ball Players of America
APBE . . . . Association for Professional Broadcasting Education
APP . . . . Association of Professional Photogrammetrists
APAK . . . . Association Professionnelle Apolitique du Katanga (Non-Political Professional Association of Katanga)
APROCOLIN . . Association Professionelle de Colons Individuels (Professional Association of Colonials)
APIM . . . . Association Professionnelle International des Medicins
APM . . . . Association of Professors of Medicine
APM . . . . Association of Professors of Missions
APCK . . . . Association for Promoting Christian Knowledge (Church of Ireland)
APRC . . . . Association for Promoting the Reform of Convocation (British)
APUC . . . . Association for Promoting Unity of Christendom
APROSOMA . . . Association pour la Promotion Sociale de la Masse (Association for the Social Betterment of the People) (Rwanda and Burundi)
APA . . . . Association for the Protection of the Adirondacks
APTO . . . . Association for Psychiatric Treatment of Offenders
APM . . . . Association for Psychoanalytic Medicine
APSS . . . . Association for the Psychophysiological Study of Sleep
APPM . . . . Association of Publication Production Managers
APR . . . . Association of Publishers Representatives
APC . . . . Association of Pulp Consumers
APCI . . . . Association of Pulp Consumers, Incorporated
ARNA . . . . . . Association of Radio-Television News Analysts
ARTNA . . . . . . Association of Radio-Television News Analysts
ARAM . . . . . . Association of Railroad Advertising Managers
ARM . . . . Association of Railway Museums
ARTLF . . . . . . Association of Railway Trainmen and Locomotive Firemen
RTLF . . . . Association of Railway Trainmen and Locomotive Firemen
ARES . . . . Association of Real Estate Syndicators
ARP . . . . Association for Realistic Philosophy
ARPA . . . . Association pour les Recherches sur les Parodontopathies
ARSC . . . . Association for Recorded Sound Collections
AREA . . . . Association of Records Executives and Administrators
ARBHC . . . . . . Association of Registered Bank Holding Companies
ARAS . . . . Association of Regular Army Sergeants
ARC . . . . Association of Rehabilitation Centers
ATRHTRBAA . . . Association to Remind Husbands to Remember Birthdays and Anniversaries (Probably mythical)
ARD . . . . Association of Research Directors
ARE . . . . Association for Research and Enlightenment
ARGR . . . . . . Association for Research in Growth Relationships
ARL . . . . Association of Research Libraries
ARNMD . . . . . Association for Research in Nervous and Mental Disease
ARO . . . . Association for Research in Ophthalmology
ARCB . . . . Association of Reserve City Bankers
ASSORECO . . . Association des Ressortissants du Haut et du Moyen Congo (Association of Natives of the Upper and Middle Congo)
ARIF . . . . Association pour le Retablissment des Institutions et Oeuvres Israelites en France
ARCS . . . . Association of Retail Candy Shops
ARTA . . . . Association of Retail Travel Agents
ARP . . . . Association of Retired Persons International
ARCA . . . . . . Association of Romanian Catholics of America
ARSC . . . . Association Royale Sportive Congolaise (Congolese Royal Sporting Association)
ARINOA . . . . . Association of Russian Imperial Naval Officers in America
ARWI . . . . Association of Russian War Invalids of First World War
ASCE . . . . Association of Safety Council Executives
ASBO . . . . Association of School Business Officials of the United States and Canada
ASCUS . . . . . . Association for School, College, and University Staffing
ASAHP . . . . . . Association of Schools of Allied Health Professions
ASCO . . . . Association of Schools and Colleges of Optometry
ASPH . . . . Association of Schools of Public Health
ASMD . . . . . . Association of Science Museum Directors
ASTMS . . . . . . Association of Scientific, Technical, and Management Staffs (British)
ASEPELT . . . . . Association Scientifique Europeenne pour la Prevision Economique a Moyen et Long Terme (European Scientific Association for Medium and Long-Term Economic Forecasts)
ASPEP . . . . . . Association of Scientists and Professional Engineering Personnel
ASYMCA . . . . Association of Secretaries Young Men's Christian Associations
ASPPF . . . . . . Association of Seminary Professors in the Practical Fields
ASEBS . . . . . . Association of Senior Engineers of the Bureau of Ships
ASBA . . . . Association of Ship Brokers and Agents
ASCA . . . . Association for Sickle Cell Anemia
ASSOSIRACI . . Association des Sinistres et Repatries de Cote d'Ivoire (Association of the Wounded and Repatriates of the Ivory Coast)
ASD . . . . Association for Social Design

ASST . . . . Association of Social Science Teachers
ASNEMGE. . . . Association des Societes Nationales Europeennes et Mediterraneennes de Gastroenterologie
SSP . . . . Association of the Sons of Poland
ASA . . . . Association of Southeast Asia
ASAS . . . . Association of South-East Asian States
ASEAN . . . . . Association of Southeast Asian Nations (Formerly, Association of Southeast Asia)
ASR . . . . Association of Southeastern Railroads
ASLIB . . . . . . Association of Special Libraries and Information Bureaux (Great Britain)
ASLP . . . . Association of Special Libraries of the Philippines
ASID . . . . Association of Sports Information Directors
ASCM . . . . . . Association of Sprocket Chain Manufacturers (Defunct)
ASATOM. . . . . Association pour les Stages et l'Accueil des Techniciens d'Outre-Mer (Association for the Reception and Instruction of Overseas Technicians)
ASE . . . . Association for Stamp Exhibitions
ASL . . . . Association of Standards Laboratories
ASCU . . . . . . Association of State Colleges and Universities
ASCUFRO . . . . Association of State Colleges and Universities Forestry Research Organizations
ASF . . . . Association of State Foresters
ASIWPCA. . . . . Association of State and Interstate Water Pollution Control Administrators
ASLRA . . . . . . Association of State Labor Relations Agencies
ASPDA . . . . . . Association of State Planning and Development Agencies
ASPSC . . . . . . Association of State and Provincial Safety Coordinators
ASPHV . . . . . . Association of State Public Health Veterinarians
ASTCDPD . . . . Association of State and Territorial Chronic Disease Program Directors
ASTDD . . . . . . Association of State and Territorial Dental Directors
ASTDLHS . . . . Association of State and Territorial Directors of Local Health Services
ASTDPHN . . . . Association of State and Territorial Directors of Public Health Nursing
ASTHO . . . . . . Association of State and Territorial Health Officers
ASTND . . . . . . Association of State and Territorial Nutrition Directors
ASTPHLD . . . . Association of State and Territorial Public Health Laboratory Directors
ASTPHND . . . . Association of State and Territorial Public Health Nutrition Directors
ASULGC . . . . Association of State Universities and Land-Grant Colleges
ASARB . . . . . . Association of Statisticians of American Religious Bodies
ASD . . . . Association of Steel Distributors
ASEF. . . . . . . Association of Stock Exchange Firms
ASP . . . . Association-Storing Processor (Data processing)
ASCAIA . . . . . Association of Student Chapters, American Institute of Architects
ASILS . . . . . . Association of Student International Law Societies
AST . . . . Association for Student Teaching
ASA . . . . Association for the Study of Abortion
ASME . . . . . . Association for the Study of Medical Education
ASNLH . . . . . . Association for the Study of Negro Life and History
ASTE . . . . Association for the Study of Soviet-Type Economies
ASPPR . . . . . . Association of Sugar Producers of Puerto Rico
ASSDD . . . . . . Association of Summer Session Deans and Directors
ASCD . . . . Association for Supervision and Curriculum Development
ASST . . . . Association of Supervisory Staff and Technicians (British)
ASL . . . . Association for Symbolic Logic
ASSE . . . . Association Suisse des Syndicats Evangeliques (Swiss Federation of Protestant Trade Unions)
ATESL . . . . . . Association of Teachers of English as a Second Language
ATJ . . . . Association of Teachers of Japanese
ATPM . . . . . . Association of Teachers of Preventive Medicine
ATA . . . . Association of Technical Artists
ATEN . . . . Association Technique pour l'Energie Nucleaire
ATIC . . . . Association Technique de l'Importation Charbonniere
ATIBT . . . . . . Association Technique Internationale des Bois Tropicaux
ATMA . . . . . . Association Technique Maritime et Aeronautique (France)
ATAS . . . . Association of Telephone Answering Services
ATOS . . . . Association of Temporary Office Services
ATPC . . . . Association of Temporary Personnel Contractors
ATDC . . . . Association of Thalidomide-Damaged Children
ATBA . . . . Association of Theatre Benefit Agents
ATSAC . . . . . . Association of Theatre Screen Advertising Companies (Defunct)
ATPAM . . . . . Association of Theatrical Press Agents and Managers
ATSS . . . . Association of Track and Structure Suppliers
ATOCI . . . . . . Association de Traducteurs et Reviseurs des Organisations et Conferences Intergouvernementales
ATB . . . . Association for Tropical Biology
ATCAR . . . . . . Association des Tshokwe de Congo Belge, de l'Angola, et de la Rhodesie (Association of Belgian Congolese, Angolan and Rhodesian Tshokwe)
ATYPI . . . . . . Association Typographique Internationale
AUM . . . . Association of Umbrella Manufacturers and Supplies
AUPA . . . . . . Association of Unclaimed Property Administrators
AUSA . . . . . . Association of the United States Army
AVI . . . . Association Universelle d'Aviculture Scientifique
AUE . . . . Association des Universitaires d'Europe
AUPELF . . . . . Association d'Universites Entierement ou Partiellement de Langue Francaise

AUBC	Association of Universities of the British Commonwealth
AURA	Association of Universities for Research in Astronomy
AUA	Association of University Anesthetists
AUA	Association of University Architects
AUEC	Association of University Evening Colleges
AUPHA	Association of University Programs in Hospital Administration
AUR	Association of University Radiologists
AUSS	Association of University Summer Sessions
AUC	Association of Uptown Converters
AUU	Association of Urban Universities
AVI	Association of Veterinary Inspectors
AVC	Association of Vitamin Chemists
AVS	Association for Voluntary Sterilization
AVBA	Association of Volunteer Bureaus of America
AWTAO	Association of Water Transportation Accounting Officers
AWR	Association of Western Railways
AWA	Association of Women in Architecture
AWB	Association of Women Broadcasters
AWMPA	Association of Women of the Motion Picture Industry
AWARE	Association for Women's Active Return to Education
AWL	Association for a World Language
AWTE	Association for World Travel Exchange
AYD	Association of Yarn Distributors
AYJUSA	Association of Yugoslav Jews in the U.S.A.
ALFRED	Associative Learning from Relative Environmental Data
ALS	Associative List Selection
AMC	Associative Memory Computer
AMOS	Associative Memory Organizing System
ARGUS	Associative Registers for Generalized User Switching (Computer typesetting system)
AIUS	Associazione Internazionale Uomo nello Spazis
AIB	Associazione Italiana Biblioteche
AIRP	Associazione Italiana Relazioni Pubbliche (Italian public relations organization)
ANPI	Associazione Nazionale Partigiani d'Italia
ASLS	Associazione Sindacati Lavoratore della Somalia (Workers' Trade Union Association of Somalia)
ASUS	Associazione Studentesca Universitaria della Somalia (University Students' Association of Somalia)
AL	Assumed Latitude (Navigation)
AP	Assumed Position (Navigation)
ADT	Assured Depot Task
AD	Assured Destruction (Capability) (of missiles)
ADF	Assured Destruction Force (Military)
AFST	Assured Field Shop Task
ABO	Astable Blocking Oscillator
AMV	Astable Multi-Vibrator
At	Astatine (Chemical element)
AD	ASTIA Document
ASL	Astigmatic Spectral Line
ADS	Aston Dark Space
AWN	Aston Whole Number
AWD	Astrogeodetic World Datum
AMT	Astrograph Mean Time (Navigation)
AGA	Astrologers' Guild of America
AI	Astrologers International
AMU	Astronaut Maneuvering Unit (Gemini) (NASA)
ASK	Astronaut Survival Kit
ADOS	Astronautical Defensive-Offensive System
ASC	Astronautical Society of Canada
APG	Astronomiae Professor Greshamii (Professor of Astronomy at Gresham College, London)
AES	Astronomical Explorer Satellite
ACC	Astronomical Great Circle Course
AL	Astronomical League
AO	Astronomical Observatory
ASP	Astronomical Society of the Pacific
ATOM	Astronomical Telescope Orientation Mount (NASA)
AT	Astronomical Time
ATS	Astronomical Time Switch
AU	Astronomical Unit
AMB	Astronomy Missions Board (NASA)
AL	Astronuclear Laboratory (Westinghouse Electric Corporation)
AL	Astropower Laboratory (Douglas Aircraft Corporation)
A	Asymmetric
ASB	Asymmetrical Sideband
ARE	Asymptotic Relative Efficiency (Statistics)
AALUE	Asymptotically Admissible Linear Unbiased Estimator (Statistics)
ABLUE	Asymptotically Best Linear Unbiased Estimator (Statistics)
ADMS	Asynchronous Data Multiplexer Synchronizer
A	At

ATP	At (Time or Place) (Aviation)
AOA	At or Above (Aviation)
AB	At Bat (Baseball)
AOB	At or Below (Aviation)
ALD	At a Later Date
ANEXGOVT	At No Expense to the Government
AST	At Same Time
AS	At Sight
ATTM	At This Time
SFRB	Atchison, Topeka & Santa Fe – DF Loaders (AAR code)
ATSF	Atchison, Topeka & Santa Fe Railway Company (AAR code)
AT & SF	Atchison, Topeka and Santa Fe Railway Company
SF	Atchison, Topeka & Sante Fe Railway Company (NYSE symbol)
SFRD	Atchison, Topeka & Santa Fe – Refrigerator Cars (AAR code)
AALCI	Ateitis Association of Lithuanian Catholic Intellectuals
ACEC	Ateliers de Construction Electriques de Charleroi (Atomic power plant) (Belgium)
AA	Athletic Association
AC	Athletic Club (Usually in combination with proper noun, as, DAC, Detroit Athletic Club)
ACACW	Athletic Conference of American College Women (Became ARFCW)
AGMA	Athletic Goods Manufacturers Association
ARFCW	Athletic and Recreation Federation of College Women
ATAD	Atlanta Army Depot
AB & C	Atlanta, Birmingham and Coast Railroad Company
ATL	Atlanta, Ga. (Airport symbol)
ASAB	Atlanta & Saint Andrews Bay Railway (AAR code)
AWP	Atlanta & West Point R. R. (AAR code)
A & WP	Atlanta and West Point Rail Road Company
LANT	Atlantic (Navy)
AAEW	Atlantic Airborne Early Warning (Military)
AAF	Atlantic Amphibious Force (Navy)
AAI	Atlantic Art Institute
AAYPL	Atlantic Association of Young Political Leaders
ABMR	Atlantic Ballistic Missile Range
BARLANT	Atlantic Barrier Patrol (Eastern seaward extension of the DEW Line)
AC	Atlantic Charter
ACC	Atlantic Christian College (North Carolina)
ATE	Atlantic City Electric Company (NYSE symbol)
ACL	Atlantic Coast Line R. R. (AAR code)
AX	Atlantic Coast Line R.R. Company (NYSE symbol)
ACLRR	Atlantic Coast Line Railroad
LANTCOM	Atlantic Command (Military)
ADELA	Atlantic Community Development Group for Latin America (Joint US – European private investment company)
AC	Atlantic Congress
ACUS	Atlantic Council of the United States
AD	Atlantic & Danville Railway (AAR code)
ADWA	Atlantic Deeper Waterways Association
ATCC	Atlantic Division Transport Control Center (Hq)
AEC	Atlantic & East Carolina Railway (AAR code)
AERS	Atlantic Estuarine Research Society
AES	Atlantic Estuarine Society
AFS	Atlantic Ferry Service (World War II)
LANTFLT	Atlantic Fleet
AFAF	Atlantic Fleet Amphibious Force (Navy)
AFO	Atlantic Fleet Organization
AFWR	Atlantic Fleet Weapons Range (Navy)
AFTA	Atlantic Free Trade Area
AGAFBO	Atlantic & Gulf American Flag Berth Operators
AICT	Atlantic Information Centre for Teachers
AMSI	Atlantic Merchant Shipping Instructions
AMVER	Atlantic Merchant Vessel Report
AMVERS	Atlantic Merchant Vessel Report System
AMR	Atlantic Missile Range (Later, Eastern Test Range)
AMROO	Atlantic Missile Range (Later, Eastern Test Range) Operations Office
ANF	Atlantic Nuclear Force (NATO)
AOA	Atelantic Ocean Area
AOL	Atlantic Oceanographic Laboratories (of Environmental Science Services Administration)
AOML	Atlantic Oceanographic and Meteorological Laboratories
APAG	Atlantic Political Advisory Group (NATO)
ARIS	Atlantic Range Instrumentation Ship
AFI	Atlantic Refining Company (NYSE symbol)
ARC	Atlantic Research Corporation
LANTRESFLT	Atlantic Reserve Fleet
ARCO	Atlantic Richfield Company
ARHCO	Atlantic Richfield Hanford Company
ATRON	Atlantic Squadron
AST	Atlantic Standard Time

AT . . . . Atlantic Standard Time
ATST . . . . Atlantic Standard Time
ASMFC . . . . . . Atlantic States Marine Fisheries Commission
ATTC . . . . . . Atlantic Transportation Terminal Command (Army)
ATA . . . . Atlantic Treaty Association
AUTEC . . . . . . Atlantic Undersea Test and Evaluation Center (Navy) (Acronym also used to refer to device for detection, amplification, and transmission of undersea noise)
AUC . . . . Atlantic Union College (Massachusetts)
A & WI . . . . . . Atlantic and West Indies
ATW . . . . Atlantic & Western R. R. (AAR code)
AC . . . . Atlas Centaur (Missile)
APC . . . . Atlas Chemical Industries, Inc. (NYSE symbol)
AZ . . . . Atlas Corporation (NYSE symbol)
AEC . . . . Atlas Educational Center
ARG . . . . Atlas Reliability Group
AKO . . . . Atlas Tack Corporation (NYSE symbol)
AE-B . . . . . . Atmosphere Explorer B (Satellite)
ALBIS . . . . . . Atmosphere Launched Boost Intercept System
ANI . . . . Atmosphere Normale Internationale (International Normal Atmosphere)
ASP . . . . Atmosphere Sounding Projectile
ACP . . . . Atmospheric Contamination Potential
ATCOS . . . . . Atmospheric Composition Satellite (NASA)
ADMS . . . . . . Atmospheric Diffusion Measuring System
AIRAC . . . . . . Atmospheric Infrared Attenuation Coefficient
AP . . . . Atmospheric Pressure
ARN . . . . Atmospheric Radio Noise
ARW . . . . Atmospheric Radio Wave
ARIES . . . . . . Atmospheric Research Information Exchange Study
ASL . . . . Atmospheric Sciences Laboratory
ASFG . . . . . . Atmospheric Sound-Focusing Gain
ASR . . . . Atmospheric Sound Refraction
AWA . . . . Atmospheric Winds Aloft
ATCOM . . . . . Atoll Commander (In Pacific operations) (World War II)
A . . . . Atom, Atomic, or Atomic Weight
A (Bomb) . . . . . Atom Bomb
ATAD . . . . . . Atomatic Target Designation
ARC . . . . Atomedic Research Center
AMPERE . . . . . Atomes et Molecules par Etudes Radio-Electriques (Switzerland)
AA . . . . Atomic Absorption
AAC . . . . Atomic Absorption Coefficient
AAFS . . . . . . Atomic Absorption Flame Spectrometer
AAS . . . . Atomic Absorption Spectroscopy
ABM . . . . Atomic Beam Method
ABC . . . . Atomic, Biological and Chemical (as, ABC Officer, ABC Warfare)
ABCD . . . . . . Atomic, Biological, Chemical and Damage Control
ABCC . . . . . . Atomic Bomb Casualty Commission
ACBM . . . . . . Atomic Cesium Beam MASER
ACCSIC . . . . . Atomic Collision Cross Sections Information Center (ORNL)
ACO(W) . . . . . Atomic Coordinating Office (Washington, DC) (British Defense Staff)
ACO . . . . Atomic Coordination Office (British)
ADT . . . . Atomic Damage Template (Military drafting)
ATOMDEF . . . . Atomic Defense
ADSG . . . . . . Atomic Defense and Space Group (Westinghouse Electric Corporation)
ADSA . . . . . . Atomic Defense Support Agency
ADM . . . . . . Atomic Demolition Munition
ADA . . . . Atomic Development Authority (Proposed by Bernard Baruch to exercise control over those aspects of atomic energy inimical to global security, never organized)
ATOMDEV . . . . Atomic Device (Military)
AEA . . . . Atomic Energy Act
AEA . . . . Atomic Energy Authority (British)
AEBSTA . . . . . Atomic Energy Bureau of Science and Technics Agency (Japan)
AECL . . . . . . Atomic Energy of Canada, Limited
AEC . . . . Atomic Energy Commission
AECM . . . . . . Atomic Energy Commission Manual
AECB . . . . . . Atomic Energy Control Board (Canada)
AEDS . . . . . . Atomic Energy Detection System (AEC)
AEE . . . . Atomic Energy Establishment
AEEW . . . . . . Atomic Energy Establishment, Winfrith (England)
AEL . . . . Atomic Energy Level
AERE . . . . . . Atomic Energy Research Establishment (of United Kingdom Atomic Energy Authority) (Harwell, England)
ATXPL . . . . . . Atomic Explosion
AFS . . . . Atomic Frequency Standard
AFC . . . . Atomic Fuel Corporation (Japan)
AT/W . . . . . . Atomic Hydrogen Weld
AICP . . . . Atomic Incident Control Plan
AIF . . . . Atomic Industrial Forum
AMN . . . . Atomic Mass Number
AMU . . . . Atomic Mass Unit

AM . . . . Atomic Migration
AMPIC . . . . . . Atomic and Molecular Processes Information Center
AN . . . . Atomic Number
AO . . . . Atomic Orbital (Chemistry)
AOCO . . . . . . Atomic Ordnance Cataloging Office
APE . . . . Atomic Photoelectric Effect
ATPOS . . . . . . Atomic Post-Strike Analysis Report
APC . . . . Atomic Power Construction, Ltd.
APCL . . . . . . Atomic Power Construction, Limited
APDA . . . . . . Atomic Power Development Associates, Inc.
AP . . . . Atomic Powered
ASF . . . . Atomic Scattering Factor
ASA . . . . Atomic Security Agency (Army)
ASD . . . . Atomic Solution Diffusion
ASTREC . . . . . Atomic Strike Evaluation Center
ASN . . . . Atomic Strike Net
ASP . . . . Atomic Strike Plan
ASPCGA . . . . . Atomic Strike Plan Control Group Alternate
ASR . . . . Atomic Strike Recording
ASTREC . . . . . Atomic Strike Recording System (Air Force)
AT . . . . Atomic Time
ATORP . . . . . . Atomic Torpedo (Military)
AW . . . . Atomic Warfare
AWRE . . . . . . Atomic Weapons Research Establishment (British)
AWTG . . . . . . Atomic Weapons Training Group (DASA)
AW . . . . Atomic Weight
AWU . . . . Atomic Weight Unit
AI . . . . Atomics International (of North American Aviation, Inc.)
AST . . . . Atomized Suspension Technique
AF . . . . Atrial Fibrillation (Medicine)
AV . . . . Atrioventricular
A-V . . . . Atrioventricular
ADK . . . . Attach-Detach Kit
AID . . . . Attached Inflatable Decelerator (Aerodynamics)
AOC . . . . Attached to Other Correspondence
A . . . . Attack (Designation for all US military aircraft)
A . . . . Attack (Men's lacrosse position)
CVA . . . . Attack Aircraft Carrier (Navy symbol)
CVA(N) . . . . . Attack Aircraft Carrier (Nuclear propelled)
AKA . . . . Attack Cargo Ship (Navy symbol)
ACSF . . . . . . Attack Carrier Striking Force
ACIP . . . . Attack Center Indicator Panel
ACP . . . . Attack Center Panel
A/T . . . . Attack Teacher
APA . . . . Attack Transport (Navy symbol)
AWS . . . . Attack Warning System (Civil Defense)
AQ . . . . Attainment Quotient
AD . . . . Attention Display (Military communications device)
AIDA . . . . . Attention-Interest-Desire-Action (Formula) (Marketing)
ATR . . . . Attenuated Total Reflectance (Used in field of analytical instruments)
AR . . . . Attenuation Reaction
AAT . . . . Attitude Acquisition Technique
AAT . . . . Attitude Angle Transducer
AAEC . . . . . . Attitude Axis Emergency Control (Aerospace)
ACE . . . . Attitude Control Electronics
ACJ . . . . Attitude Control Jet
ACMES . . . . . . Attitude Control and Maneuver Electronic System
ACME . . . . . . Attitude Control and Maneuvering Electronics
ACPM . . . . . . Attitude Control Propulsion Motors
ACS . . . . Attitude-Control System (Aerospace)
ACTD . . . . . . Attitude Control Torquing Device
ADI . . . . Attitude Director Indicator
AIS . . . . Attitude Indicating System
ARIS . . . . Attitude and Rate Indicating System
ARU . . . . Attitude Reference Unit
ATS . . . . Attitude Thrustor System
ATCU . . . . . . Attitude and Translation Control Unit
a . . . . Atto (Prefix)
AOC . . . . Attock Oil Company (Pakistan)
AG . . . . Attorney General
AGO . . . . Attorney General's Opinion
AULR . . . . . . Attrition, Utilization and Loss Rate
ACC . . . . Auburn Community College (New York)
ACDC . . . . . . Auburn-Cord-Duesenberg Club
AIMO . . . . . . Audibly Instructed Manufacturing Operations (Military)
AIF . . . . Audience Interest Factor
ABF . . . . Audio Bandpass Filter
ABPF . . . . . . Audio Bandpass Filter
AB . . . . Audio Bandwidth
ACS . . . . Audio Communications System
ACC . . . . Audio Control Center

ADO	Audio Decade Oscillator
ADA	Audio Distribution Amplifier
AES	Audio Engineering Society
AFA	Audio Frequency Amplifier
AF	Audio Frequency (Electronics)
AFC	Audio Frequency Coder
AIFT	Audio Input Frequency Tolerance
AIL	Audio Input Level
ALM	Audio Level Meter
AO	Audio Oscillator
APCA	Audio Peak Clipping Amplifier
APU	Audio Playback Unit
AR	Audio Response
ARU	Audio Response Unit (Credit card verification)
AS	Audio Sensitivity
ATD	Audio Tone Decoder
AV	Audio-Visual
AVA	Audio/Visual Annunciator
AVDU	Audio-Visual Display Unit
AVIS	Audio-Visual Information System
AVSEP	Audio Visual Superimposed Electrocardiogram Presentation
AWA	Audio Wave Analyzer
ABC	Audit Bureau of Circulations
AC	Auditor Camerae (Auditor of the Papal Treasury)
AG	Auditor General (Military)
AGD	Auditor General's Department (Air Force)
AGO	Auditor General's Office
AID	Auditory Information Display
AUDIT	Auditory Input Task (Data processing)
ASA	Auditory Sensation Area
ASC	Aughey Spark Chamber
A	Augmentation (Music)
AS	Augmentation System
AAJ	Augmented Air Jet
AMBIT	Augmented Built-In Test
ALM	Augmented Lunar Module
ASI	Augmented Spark Igniter
ASP	Augmented Support Period (or Plan)
ATDA	Augmented Target Docking Adapter (Gemini) (NASA)
ATEP	Augmented Thermally Electric Propulsion
AUGU	Augmenting Unit (Navy)
ATH	August Thyssen Huette (German steel producer)
AUG	Augusta R. R. (AAR code)
AUS	Augusta & Summerville R. R. (AAR code)
ARS	Augustan Reprint Society
AHS	Augustana Historical Society
ALL	Augustana Luther League
ASI	Augustana Swedish Institute
AA	Augustiniani Assumptionis (Assumptionists)
ABG	Aural Bearing Generator
A	Auricle
AV	Auriculo Ventricular
AURBO	Aurora Borealis
AEFR	Aurora, Elgin & Fox River Electric R. R. (AAR code)
AHL	Auroral Hydrogen Line
AHLE	Auroral Hydrogen Line Emission
Au	Aurum (Gold) (Chemical element)
ASAMS	Austere Surface-to-Air Missile System
AHC	Austin Healey Club
AJC	Austin Junior College (Minnesota)
ANO	Austin, Nichols & Company, Inc. (NYSE symbol)
APSC	Austin Peay State College (Tennessee)
AE	Austral English or Australian English
ASE	Australasian Society of Engineers
AD	Australia Day
ANGAU	Australia-New Guinea Administrative Unit (World War II)
ANZAC	Australia-New Zealand Army Corps
ANZUS	Australia, New Zealand, and the United States (The Anzus Pact Nations)
A	Australian
AARDS	Australian Advertising Rate and Data Service
AAWC	Australian Advisory War Council
AAM	Australian Air Mission
AAMC	Australian Army Medical Corps
AABM	Australian Association of British Manufacturers
AAEC	Australian Atomic Energy Commission
ABDA	Australian-British-Dutch-American
ABC	Australian Broadcasting Commission
ABC	Australian Broadcasting Corporation
ACT	Australian Capital Territory
ACMF	Australian Commonwealth Military Forces
ACNB	Australian Commonwealth Naval Board (Navy)
ACA	Australian Council for Aeronautics
ACSPA	Australian Council of Salaried and Professional Associations
ACTU	Australian Council of Trade Unions
AIF	Australian Imperial Forces
AIM	Australian Inland Mission
AINSE	Australian Institute of Nuclear Science and Engineering
AJSS	Australian Joint Staff Service
ALP	Australian Labor Party
AMA	Australian Medical Association
AMDEL	Australian Mineral Development Laboratory
AMP	Australian Mutual Provident Society (Insurance)
ANA	Australian National Airways
ANARE	Australian National Antarctic Research Expeditions
ANZAAS	Australian and New Zealand Association for the Advancement of Science
AS of NY	Australian Society of New York
ATF	Australian Task Force
AWHA	Australian Women's Home Army
AWU	Australian Workers' Union
ARSA	Austrian RADAR Site Analysis
ATUF	Austrian Trade Union Federation
ARIES	Authentic Reproduction of an Independent Earth Satellite
ATM	Authentication Maneuver (Aviation)
A	Author
ADA	Authority Directing Arrest or Confinement (Military)
AUTHGR	Authority Granted
AMS	Authority for Material Substitution
A/P	Authority to Pay or Purchase
ATP	Authority to Proceed
AFP	Authority for Purchase
AFROASI	Authority for Removal of Accepted Spacecraft Installations
ARI	Authority Is Requested to Inter (the remains of) (Army)
AFIO	Authorization for Interceptor Operations
ASSM	Authorization for Sale of Salvage Material
ATTM	Authorization to Transfer Material
AUTHAB	Authorized Abbreviation
ACN	Authorized Code Number
ACM	Authorized Controlled Material Order
ADC	Authorized Data Chain
ADL	Authorized Data List (DOD)
ADSL	Authorized Depot Stockage List (Army)
AOSL	Authorized Organizational Stockage List (Army)
RORET	Authorized Rotational Retention (Navy)
ASL	Authorized Stockage List (Army)
AV	Authorized Version (or King James Version of the Bible, 1611)
AA	Author's Alteration (Printing)
AC	Author's Correction (Printing)
AP	Author's Proof
AGALA	Authors Guild of the Authors League of America
ALA	Authors League of America
AA	Auto Acquisition (RADAR)
ACG	Auto Car Guard
ADTSC	Auto Dealers Traffic Safety Council
AEI	Auto Enthusiasts International
AIHSC	Auto Industries Highway Safety Committee
ALPCA	Auto License Plate Collectors Association
ABW	Autobond Welder
ACCAP	Autocoder to COBOL Conversion Aid Program (Data processing)
ACU	Autocycle Union (British)
AUDAR	Autodyne Detection and Ranging
ACS	Autograph Card Signed
AD	Autograph Document
ADS	Autograph Document Signed
AL	Autograph Letter
ALS	Autograph Letter Signed
ANS	Autograph Note Signal
ANS	Autograph Note Signed
APS	Autograph Postcard Signed
APC	Autographed Presentation Copy
AE	Autoimmune Encephalomyelitis
AIHA	Autoimmune Hemolytic Anemia (Medicine)
ABM	Automated Batch Mixing (Data processing)
ABW	Automated Batch Weighing
ABL	Automated Biological Laboratory (NASA)
ACCESS	Automated Control and Checking of Electrical Systems Support
ACORN	Automated Conversion Routine
ACE	Automated Cost Estimates
AUTOSATE	Automated Data System Analysis Technique
ADW	Automated Data Wiring
ADM	Automated Depot Maintenance
ADMS	Automated Depot Maintenance Study
ADE	Automated Design Engineering

ADCS . . . . Automated Document Control System
AED . . . . Automated Engineering Design
AFD . . . . Automated Flaw Detector
AIMS . . . . Automated Industrial Management System
AIDS . . . . Automated Information and Documentation System
AIRCON . . . . . Automated Information and Reservation Computer Operated Network
AIDA . . . . Automated Inspection of Data
AIS . . . . Automated Instrumentation System
AIDS . . . . Automated Intelligence Data System (Air Force)
ALE . . . . Automated Large Experiment (NASA)
ALP . . . . Automated Learning Process
ALERT . . . . . . Automated Linguistic Extraction and Retrieval Technique
ALPHA . . . . . Automated Literature Processing, Handling, and Analysis
ALDPS . . . . . Automated Logistics Data Processing System
AMD . . . . Automated Maintenance Depot
AMVER . . . . . Automated Merchant Vessel Report (Coast Guard)
AMACUS . . . . Automated Microfilm Aperture Card Updating System (Army)
ANCIF . . . . . Automated Nautical Chart Index File (System) (DOD)
APS . . . . Automated Production System
ARTS . . . . . . Automated RADAR Terminal System
ASL . . . . Automated Soft Lander (Aerospace)
ASAP . . . . . . Automated Statistical Analysis Program
ASB . . . . Automated Status Board
AUTOSCRIPT . . Automated System for Composing, Revising, Illustrating, and Phototypesetting
AUTOSTRAD. . . Automated System for Transportation Data (Military)
AS & SB . . . . . Automated Systems and Services Branch (CFSTI)
ATOMS . . . . . . Automated Technical Order Maintenance Sequences
AWTAS . . . . . Automated Weapons Test Analysis System
AWN . . . . Automated Weather Network (Air Force)
AWDS . . . . . . Automated Wire Data System
AASS . . . . . . Automatic Abort-Sensing System (NASA)
AADS . . . . . . Automatic Aircraft Diagnostic System
AAVCS . . . . . Automatic Aircraft Vectoring Control System (Air Force)
AAVD . . . . . . Automatic Alternate Voice/Data (Data processing)
AATS . . . . . . Automatic Anti-Theft System (Electronic lock)
AAC . . . . Automatic Aperture Control
AACPC . . . . . . Automatic Approach Control Coupler (Aerospace)
AAWS . . . . . . Automatic Attack Warning System
AAC . . . . Automatic Autocollimeter
ABB . . . . Automatic Back Bias (RADAR)
ABC . . . . Automatic Bandwidth Control (Air Force)
ABC . . . . Automatic Bar Checker
ABC . . . . Automatic Bass Compensation (Radio)
ABC . . . . Automatic Bass Control
ABC . . . . Automatic Bias Compensation (Air Force)
ABC . . . . Automatic Bias Control
ABDL . . . . . . Automatic Binary Data Link
ABC . . . . Automatic Blip Counter
ABCS . . . . . . Automatic Blip Counter System
ABSC . . . . . . Automatic Blip-Scan Counter
ABSCS . . . . . Automatic Blip-Scan Counter System
ABC . . . . Automatic Boiling-Column Reactor
ABC . . . . Automatic Brightness Control
ABTD . . . . . . Automatic Bulk Tape Degausser
ACT . . . . Automatic Cable Tester
ACD . . . . Automatic Call Distributor (Telephone system)
ACU . . . . Automatic Calling Unit
AUM . . . . Automatic Canteen Company of America (NYSE symbol)
ACT . . . . Automatic Capacitor Tester
ACI . . . . Automatic Car Identification (Railroads)
ACWA . . . . . . Automatic Car Wash Association International
ACR . . . . Automatic Card Reader
ACLS . . . . . . Automatic Carrier Landing System (Air Force)
ACL . . . . Automatic Carrier Landing System (Navy)
ACN . . . . Automatic Celestial Navigation (Air Force)
ACTA . . . . . . Automatic Centrifugal Tinning Apparatus
ACCS . . . . . . Automatic Checkout & Control System
ACE . . . . Automatic Checkout Equipment
ACOE . . . . . . Automatic Checkout Equipment
ACES . . . . . . Automatic Checkout and Evaluation System (Air Force)
ACRE . . . . . . Automatic Checkout and Readiness Equipment
ACORN . . . . . Automatic Checkout and Recording Equipment
ACBWS . . . . . Automatic Chemical Biological Warning System
ACAP . . . . . . Automatic Circuit Analysis Program
ACA . . . . Automatic Circuit Analyzer
ACBCT . . . . . Automatic Circuit Board Card Tester
ACBT . . . . . . Automatic Circuit Board Tester
ACCEL . . . . . Automatic Circuit Card Etched Layout
ACE . . . . Automatic Circuit Exchange
ACT . . . . Automatic Circuit Tester

ACM . . . . Automatic Clutter Mapping
ACM . . . . Automatic Coating Machine
ACT . . . . Automatic Code Translation (Data processing)
ACAS . . . . . . Automatic Collision Avoidance System (Aviation)
ACC . . . . Automatic Color Control
ACDS . . . . . . Automatic Comprehensive Display System
ACT . . . . Automatic Component Tester
ACR . . . . Automatic Compression - Release
ACRD . . . . . . Automatic Compression - Release Device
AC . . . . Automatic Computer
ACCESS . . . . . Automatic Computer-Controlled Electronic Scanning System (National Bureau of Standards)
ACTS . . . . . . Automatic Computer Telex Services
ACE . . . . Automatic Computing Engine
ACE . . . . Automatic Continuity Equipment
ACE . . . . Automatic Continuous Evaporation
ACFG . . . . . . Automatic Continuous Function Generation (Data processing)
ACC . . . . Automatic Contrast Control
AC . . . . Automatic Control
ACE . . . . Automatic Control Equipment
ACES . . . . . . Automatic Control Evaluation Simulator (Space flight training machine)
ACI . . . . Automatic Control Instrumentation
ACS . . . . Automatic Control System
ACG . . . . Automatic Correlation Guidance
ACS . . . . Automatic Counter System
ACCESS . . . . . Automatic Crane Control Storage System
ADAT . . . . . . Automatic Data Accumulation and Transfer
ADA . . . . Automatic Data Acquisition
ADACC . . . . . Automatic Data Acquisition and Computer Complex (Air Force)
ADDS . . . . . . Automatic Data Digitizing System (Air Force)
ADEM . . . . . . Automatic Data Equalized Modern
ADX . . . . Automatic Data Exchange
ADEPT . . . . . Automatic Data Extractor and Plotting Table
ADFSC . . . . . Automatic Data Field Systems Command (Army)
ADIS . . . . . . Automatic Data Interchange System
ADL . . . . Automatic Data Link (Air Force)
ADP . . . . Automatic Data Processing
ADPC . . . . . . Automatic Data Processing Center
ADPE . . . . . . Automatic Data Processing Equipment
ADPM . . . . . . Automatic Data Processing Machine
ADP . . . . Automatic Data Plotter
ADPP . . . . . . Automatic Data Processing Programs
ADPSC . . . . . Automatic Data Processing Service Center
ADPS . . . . . . Automatic Data Processing Systems
ADRC . . . . . . Automatic Data Rate Changer
ADSC . . . . . . Automatic Data Service Center
ADSAF . . . . . Automatic Data System within the Army in the Field
ADSUP . . . . . Automatic Data Systems Uniform Practices
ADT . . . . Automatic Data Translator
ADRIS . . . . . Automatic Dead Reckoning Instrument Systems (Canadian) (Navigation)
ADOPE . . . . . Automatic Decisions Optimizing Predicted Estimates
ADM . . . . Automatic Degreasing Machine
AD . . . . Automatic Detection (Air Force)
ADMIRE . . . . . Automatic Diagnostic Maintenance Information Retrieval (Data processing)
ADIS . . . . . . Automatic Diffemic Identification of Speakers (University of Bonn)
AUDREY . . . . . Automatic Digit Recognition
ADDAR . . . . . Automatic Digital Data Acquisition and Recording
ADDER . . . . . Automatic Digital-Data-Error Recorder
ADES . . . . . . Automatic Digital Encoding System (Air Force)
AUTODIN . . . . Automatic Digital Information Network (DOD)
ADIOS . . . . . Automatic Digital Input-Output System (Air Force)
ADMS . . . . . . Automatic Digital Message Switch
ADMSC . . . . . Automatic Digital Message Switching Center (AUTODIN)
ADONIS . . . . . Automatic Digital On-Line Instruments System
ADRAC . . . . . Automatic Digital Recording and Control
ADS . . . . Automatic Digital Switch
ADTAC . . . . . Automatic Digital Tracking Analyzer Computer (Data processing)
AUDACIOUS . . Automatic Direct Access to Information with the On-line UDC (Universal Decimal Classification) System
ADF . . . . Automatic Direction Finder (Army)
ADFAP . . . . . Automatic Direction Finding Approach
ADFS . . . . . . Automatic Direction Finding System
ADI . . . . Automatic Direction Indicator
ADSP . . . . . . Automatic Dispatching Stick Repeater
AD . . . . Automatic Display
ADAPS . . . . . Automatic Display and Plotting System
ADSO . . . . . . Automatic Display Switching Oscilloscope
ADAM . . . . . . Automatic Distance and Angle Measurement
ADS . . . . Automatic Door Seal (Technical drawings)
ADMA . . . . . . Automatic Drafting Machine
ADC . . . . Automatic Drift Control

ADEPO ..... Automatic Dynamic Evaluation by Programmed Organizations
ADEPT ...... Automatic Dynamic Evaluation by Programmed Test
AESC ...... Automatic Electronic Switching Center
AEAS ...... Automatic Equalization/Analyzation System
AEA .... Automatic Error Analysis
AEC .... Automatic Exciter Control
AEC .... Automatic Exposure Control
AECT ...... Automatic Exposure Control Technique
AES .... Automatic External Standardization
AEP .... Automatic Extracting Program
AFAR ...... Automatic False Alarm Rate
AFD .... Automatic Fast Demagnetization
AFI .... Automatic Fault Isolation
AFIT ...... Automatic Fault Isolation Test
AFL .... Automatic Fault Location
AFAC ...... Automatic Field Analog Computer
AFA .... Automatic Field Assistant
AFT .... Automatic Fine Tuning
AFAA ...... Automatic Fire Alarm Association
AFTS ...... Automatic Flexible Test Station
AFC .... Automatic Flight Control (Aerospace)
AFCE ...... Automatic Flight Control Equipment
AFCS ...... Automatic Flight Control System (Air Force)
AFT .... Automatic Flight Termination
AF .... Automatic Following (RADAR)
AFC .... Automatic Frequency Control (Electronics)
AFS .... Automatic Frequency Stabilization
AGAA ...... Automatic Gain Adjusting Amplifier
AGC .... Automatic Gain Control (Electronics)
AGS .... Automatic Gain Stabilization
AGAVE ..... Automatic Gimbaled-Antenna Vectoring Equipment (Air Force)
AGACS ..... Automatic Ground/Air/Communications System
AGCA ...... Automatic Ground-Controlled Approach (RADAR)
AGCI ...... Automatic Ground-Controlled Intercept
AGCL ...... Automatic Ground-Controlled Landing
AGE .... Automatic Ground Equipment
AGPI ...... Automatic Ground Position Indicator (Military)
AGE .... Automatic Guidance Electronics
AHC .... Automatic Headway Control
AIOD ...... Automatic Identified Outward Dialing
AII .... Automatic Imagery Interpretation
AIRS ...... Automatic Information Retrieval System
AIT .... Automatic Information Test (Military)
AILAS ...... Automatic Instrument Landing Approach System (RADAR)
AILS ...... Automatic Instrument Landing System (Aviation)
AILAS ...... Automatic Instrument Low Approach System (RADAR)
AIDA ...... Automatic Instrumented Diving Assembly
AID .... Automatic Interaction Detector (Program) (Advertising)
AIC .... Automatic Intercept Center (Bell System)
AIS .... Automatic Intercept System (Bell System)
AICT ...... Automatic Integrated Circuit Tester
AIDAT ..... Automatic Integrated Dynamic Avionics Tester
AIFM ...... Automatic Integrating Fluctuation Meter
AIS .... Automatic Interplanetary Station (USSR)
ALS .... Automatic Landing System
ALDP ...... Automatic Language Data Processing
ALPAC ..... Automatic Language Processing Advisory Committee (National Research Council)
ALF .... Automatic Lead Former
ALF .... Automatic Letter Facer
ALC .... Automatic Level Control
ALR .... Automatic Level Recorder
ALS .... Automatic Level Setting
ALPS ...... Automatic License Plate Scanning
ALARM ..... Automatic Light Aircraft Readiness Monitor
ALIT ...... Automatic Line Insulation Tester
ALTAPE ..... Automatic Line Tracer and Programming Equipment
ALNTS ..... Automatic Liquid Nitrogen Transfer System
ALCAPP ..... Automatic List Classification and Profile Production
ALC .... Automatic Load Control
ALERT ...... Automatic Logging Electronic Reporting and Telemetering System (Maintains surveillance over petroleum wells and pipelines)
ALTARE ..... Automatic Logic Testing and Recording Equipment
ALERT ...... Automatic Logical Equipment Readiness Tester
ALERT ...... Automatic Logician Evaluation Readiness Tester
AUTOLABS ... Automatic Low Altitude Bombing System
ALDRI ...... Automatic Low Date Rate Input
AML .... Automatic Machine Loading
AUTOMAP.... Automatic Machining Program
AML .... Automatic Magazine Loading
AMG .... Automatic Magnetic Guidance

AMPR ...... Automatic Manifold Pressure Regulator (Aircraft)
AMSS ...... Automatic Master Sequence Selector
AUTOMAST ... Automatic Mathematic Analysis and Symbolic Translation (Data processing)
AMTRAN .... Automatic Mathematical Translator (NASA)
AMECOS..... Automatic Measuring Computing and Sorting
AMA .... Automatic Message Accounting
AMC .... Automatic Message Counting
AMX .... Automatic Message Exchange
AMPC...... Automatic Message Processing Center
AMPS ...... Automatic Message Processing System (USAERDL)
AMR .... Automatic Message Registering
AUTOMET.... Automatic Meteorological Correction (A missile guidance technique)
AMOS ...... Automatic Meteorological Observation Station
AMOS ...... Automatic Meteorological Observing System
AMFIS ...... Automatic Microfilm Information System
AMDI ...... Automatic Miss Distance Indicator
AMC .... Automatic Mission Control
AMC .... Automatic Mixture Control
AMT .... Automatic Moon Tracking
AMT .... Automatic Motor Tester
AMSTS ..... Automatic Multiparameter Semiconductor Test Set
ANCLAV..... Automatic Navigation Computer for Land and Amphibious Vehicles
ANS .... Automatic Navigation System
ANA .... Automatic Network Analyzer
ANTS ...... Automatic Nitrogen Transfer System
ANL .... Automatic Noise Limiter (Electronics)
ANI .... Automatic Number Identification (Telephone)
AO .... Automatic Observer
AOSP ...... Automatic Operating and Scheduling Program (Data processing)
ASOP ...... Automatic Operating and Scheduling Program
AUTOPSY .... Automatic Operating System (IBM)
AOC .... Automatic Operation Control
ACOP ...... Automatic Operations Panel
AOC .... Automatic Output Control
AOC .... Automatic Overload Circuit
APH .... Automatic Parts Handler
APR .... Automatic Pattern Recognition
APAS ...... Automatic Performance Analysis System
AUTOPIC .... Automatic Personal Identification Code
APC .... Automatic Phase Control
APL .... Automatic Phase Lock
APMA ...... Automatic Phonograph Manufacturers Association
APT .... Automatic Picture Transmission (NASA)
APTS ...... Automatic Picture Transmission Subsystem (NASA)
APS .... Automatic Pilot System
AUTOP...... Automatic Pistol
APP .... Automatic Plate Processor
APMMRI ..... Automatic Point Marking, Measuring and Recording Instrument
APP .... Automatic Position Planning
APRS ...... Automatic Position Reference System
APE .... Automatic Positioning Equipment
APOTA ...... Automatic Positioning Telemetering Antenna
APIC ...... Automatic Power Input Controller
APPC ...... Automatic Power Plant Checker
APF .... Automatic Press Feed
APC .... Automatic Pressure Conveyor
APL .... Automatic Production Line
APR .... Automatic Production Recording
APLU ...... Automatic Program Loading Unit
APUHS ..... Automatic Program Unit High Speed (Component of ADIS)
APULS ..... Automatic Program Unit Low Speed (Component of ADIS)
APRIL ...... Automatically Programed Remote Indication Logged
APCHE ..... Automatic Programmed Checkout Equipment
APADS ..... Automatic Programmer and Data System (Air Force)
APATS ..... Automatic Programmer and Test System
AUTOPROMT .. Automatic Programming of Machine Tools
APAR ...... Automatic Programming and Recording (Data processing)
APR .... Automatic Programming and Recording
APT .... Automatic Programming for Tools
AQC .... Automatic Quench Correction
ARB .... Automatic RADAR Beacon
ARBS ...... Automatic RADAR Beacon Sequencer
ARCAS ..... Automatic RADAR Chain Acquisition System (Air Force)
ARCADE ..... Automatic RADAR Control and Data Equipment
ARDME ..... Automatic RADAR Data Measuring Equipment
ART .... Automatic Radiating Tester
ARMS ...... Automatic Radiation Monitoring System
ARAT ...... Automatic Random Access Transport
ARC .... Automatic Range Control
ARDME ..... Automatic Range Detector and Measuring Equipment

ART . . . . Automatic Range Tracker
ARTU . . . . . . Automatic Range Tracking Unit (Military)
ARC . . . . Automatic Rate Changer
ARC . . . . Automatic Ratio Control
ARAL . . . . . . Automatic Record Analysis Language
ARE . . . . Automatic Record Evaluation
ARES . . . . . . Automatic Record Evaluation System
ARIS . . . . Automatic Recording Infrared Spectrometer
ARS . . . . Automatic Recording Spectrometer
ARD . . . . Automatic Release Date (Military)
ART . . . . Automatic Reporting Telephone
ARQ . . . . Automatic Request
ARC . . . . Automatic Reset Counter
ARTS . . . . . . Automatic Resistance Test Set
ARLS . . . . . . Automatic Resupply Logistics System
ARA . . . . Automatic Retailers of America Inc. (NYSE symbol)
ARF . . . . Automatic Return Fire (ARPA)
ARIP . . . . . . Automatic Rocket Impact Predictor
ARGUS . . . . . Automatic Routine Generating and Updating System (Data processing)
ASC . . . . Automatic Scan Counter
ASCS . . . . . . Automatic Scan Counter System
ASCU . . . . . . Automatic Scanning Control Unit
AUSCOR . . . . Automatic Scanning Correlator
ASP . . . . Automatic Schedule Procedures
AUTOSEVCOM . . Automatic Secure Voice Communications
ASDEC . . . . . . Automatic Selection of Digital Electronic Computers
ASDI . . . . Automatic Selective Dissemination of Information
ASV . . . . Automatic Self-Verification
ASR . . . . Automatic Send and Receive
AS/R . . . . Automatic Send/Receive (Communications equipment)
ASC . . . . Automatic Sensitivity Control
ASCC . . . . . . Automatic Sequence Controlled Calculator (First all-automatic calculating machine)
ASP . . . . Automatic Services and Products
ASP . . . . Automatic Servo Plotter
ASPDE . . . . . Automatic Shaft-Position Data Encoder
ASDP . . . . . . Automatic Shot Dispensing Pump
ASV . . . . Automatic Shuttle Valve
ASTRA . . . . . Automatic Sorting, Testing, Recording Analysis
ASP . . . . Automatic Specimen Positioning
ASPS . . . . . . Automatic Specimen Positioning System
ASG . . . . Automatic Spray Gun
AS . . . . Automatic Sprinkler (Technical drawings)
ASR . . . . Automatic Sprinkler Riser (Technical drawings)
ASCS . . . . . . Automatic Stabilization & Control System
ASE . . . . Automatic Stabilization Equipment
ASS . . . . Automatic Stabilization System
ASID . . . . . . Automatic Station Identification Device
ASKS . . . . . . Automatic Station Keeping System
ASR . . . . Automatic Step Regulator
ASRA . . . . . . Automatic Stereo Recording Amplifier
ASOS . . . . . . Automatic Storm Observation Service (AFCRL)
AUTO-STATIS . . Automatic Statewide Theft Inquiry System (California Highway Patrol)
ASCA . . . . . . Automatic Subject Citation Alert (Institute for Scientific Information)
ASE . . . . Automatic Support Equipment
ASP . . . . Automatic Switching Panel
ASP . . . . Automatic Synthesis Program
ASC . . . . Automatic System Control
AUTOSPOT . . . Automatic System for Positioning Tools
ASTU . . . . . . Automatic Systems Test Unit
ATC . . . . Automatic Tap Changing
ATD . . . . Automatic Tape Degausser
ATLAS . . . . . Automatic Tape Load Audit System
ATABE . . . . . Automatic Target and Battery Evaluation (Military)
ATC . . . . Automatic Target Counting
ATEWA . . . . . Automatic Target Evaluator and Weapon Assignor
ATF . . . . Automatic Target Follower
ATR . . . . Automatic Target Recognition
AUTRAN . . . . Automatic Target Recognition Analysis
ATRD . . . . . . Automatic Target Recognition Device
ATRID . . . . . . Automatic Target Recognition Identification & Detection
ATD . . . . Automatic Teaching Device
ATSIT . . . . . . Automatic Techniques for Selection and Identification of Targets
ATDS . . . . . . Automatic Telemetry Decommutation System (Air Force)
ATTS . . . . . . Automatic Telemetry Tracking System
TEX . . . . Automatic Teleprinter Exchange Service (of Western Union)
TELEX . . . . . Automatic Teletypewriter Exchange Service (of Western Union)
ATC . . . . Automatic Temperature Compensation
ATC . . . . Automatic Temperature Control
ATIS . . . . Automatic Terminal Information Service (Aviation)

ATF . . . . Automatic Terrain Following (Army)
ATFR . . . . . . Automatic Terrain-Following RADAR
ATRAN . . . . . Automatic Terrain Recognition and Navigation Guidance System
AT . . . . Automatic Test
ATAS . . . . . . Automatic Test Analysis System
ATCE . . . . . . Automatic Test and Checkout Equipment
ATE . . . . Automatic Test Equipment
ATG . . . . Automatic Test Grading
ATOLL . . . . . Automatic Test of Launch Language
ATL . . . . Automatic Test Line
ATS . . . . Automatic Test Scoring
ATER . . . . . . Automatic Testing, Evaluation and Reporting
ATHESA . . . . . Automatic Three-Dimensional Electronic Scanned Array
ATV . . . . Automatic Threshold Variation
AT . . . . Automatic Ticketing
ATWS . . . . . . Automatic Track-While-Scan (RADAR)
ATA . . . . Automatic Tracking Antenna
ATAS . . . . . . Automatic Tracking Antenna System
ATU . . . . Automatic Tracking Unit
ATC . . . . Automatic Train Control
AUTOPOS . . . . Automatic Trains, Protection, Operation and Supervision (Washington, DC, subway monitor)
ATTE . . . . . . Automatic Transistor Test Equipment
AUTOTRAN . . . Automatic Translation
ATMS . . . . . . Automatic Transmission Measuring System
ATRA . . . . . . Automatic Transmission Rebuilders Association
ATC . . . . Automatic Tuning Control
ATL . . . . Automatic Turret Lathe
ATPS . . . . . . Automatic Type Placement System
AUDIT . . . . . . Automatic Unattended Detection Inspection Transmitter (Raytheon)
AUNT . . . . . . Automatic Universal Translator
AUWS . . . . . . Automatic Unmanned Weather Station
AVP . . . . Automatic Variable Perforating
AVM . . . . Automatic Vehicle Monitoring (Antihijack device)
AVERT . . . . . Automatic Verification, Evaluation and Readiness Tester
AVC . . . . Automatic Vibration Control
AVEC . . . . . . Automatic Vibration Exciter Control
AVNL . . . . . . Automatic Video Noise Leveling (Air Force)
AVNL . . . . . . Automatic Video Noise Limited
AVD . . . . Automatic Voice Data
AVOLO . . . . . Automatic Voice Link Observation
AUTOVON . . . Automatic Voice Network (DOD)
AVR . . . . Automatic Voice Relay
AVC . . . . Automatic Voltage Clamp
AVC . . . . Automatic Volume Control (Radio)
AVE . . . . Automatic Volume Expansion
AVM . . . . Automatic Voting Machine
AUR . . . . Automatic Voting Machine Corporation (NYSE symbol)
AWCS . . . . . . Automatic Warning and Control System
AW . . . . Automatic Weapons
AWCS . . . . . . Automatic Weapons Control System
AWBE . . . . . . Automatic Weather Broadcast Equipment
AWS . . . . Automatic Weather Station
AWMA . . . . . Automatic Welding Machinery Association
AWS . . . . Automatic Welding System
AWWM . . . . . Automatic Wire Wrap Machine
AWM . . . . Automatic Writing Machine
AZS . . . . Automatic Zero Set
ACTRUS . . . . . Automatically Controlled Turbine Run-Up System (Navigation)
AEMT . . . . . . Automatically Erectable Modular Torus
AOIV . . . . . . Automatically Operated Inlet Valve
APT . . . . Automatically Programed Tools
AUTOSYN . . . . Automatically Synchronous (Trade name) (Motor)
AEL . . . . Automation Engineering Laboratory
AIDS . . . . Automation Instrument Data Service (Computer-based industrial information system) (British)
APT . . . . Automation Planning and Technology
ASSE . . . . . . Automation System for Scientific Experiments
ATI . . . . Automation Techniques, Incorporated
A . . . . Automobile
AA . . . . Automobile Association (British)
ABCDEFGHIJ . . Automobile Builders' Combination Designed Especially for Getting Hitler including Japan (Suggested name for Automotive Council for War Production) (World War II)
AC . . . . Automobile Club
ACGBI . . . . . Automobile Club of Great Britain and Ireland (Later, Royal Automobile Club)
ACCUS . . . . . Automobile Competition Committee for the United States
ADA . . . . Automobile Dealers Association
AIDA . . . . . . Automobile Information Disclosure Act
ALB . . . . Automobile Labor Board

ALA	Automobile Legal Association
AMA	Automobile Manufacturers Association
ARCA	Automobile Racing Club of America
ASCAA	Automobile Seat Cover Association of America
ASCCA	Automobile Seat Cover Association of America
AUTRA	Automobile Utility Trailer Rental Association
AAC	Automotive Advertisers Council
AAR	Automotive Affiliated Representatives
AACA	Automotive Air Conditioning Association
ABC	Automotive Booster Clubs International
ACAD	Automotive Committee for Air Defense (World War II)
ACEORP	Automotive and Construction Equipment Overhaul and Repair Plant (Navy)
ACEPD	Automotive and Construction Equipment Parts Depot (Navy)
ACIR	Automotive Crash Injury Research
AEA	Automotive Electric Association
AERA	Automotive Engine Rebuilders Association
AERI	Automotive Exhaust Research Institute
AIM	Automotive Industrial Motor
AIT	Automotive Information Test
ALI	Automotive Lift Institute
AMRC	Automotive Market Research Council
AOT	Automotive Old Timers
APRA	Automotive Parts Rebuilders Association
APL	Automotive Pigeon Loft
ASF	Automotive Safety Foundation
ASIA	Automotive Service Industry Association
ATAM	Automotive Trade Association Managers
AWDA	Automotive Warehouse Distributors Association
ABLE	Autonetics Base-Line Equipment
ABACUS	Autonetics Business and Control United Systems, Inc. (Data processing)
AGILE	Autonetics General Information Learning Equipment
AGR	Autonetics Generalized Reset
AMARS	Autonetics Modular Airborne RADAR System
ANS	Autonomic Nervous System (Medicine)
ANS	Autonomous Navigation System
AR	Autonomous Republic
ASSR	Autonomous Soviet Socialist Republic
AP	Autopilot
AMS	Autopilot Mode Selector
ASS	Autopilot Surface Servo
APC	Auto-Pilot Controller
ABS	Aux Bons Soins de (Care of, c/o)
A/S	Aux Soins de (Care of, c/o)
AA	Auxi-Atome (French association)
AAFB	Auxiliary Air Force Base
ACV	Auxiliary Aircraft Carrier (Navy symbol)
AVT	Auxiliary Aircraft Transport (Navy symbol)
AAWF	Auxiliary Aviation Weather Facility (FAA)
ABT	Auxiliary Ballast Tank
ACP	Auxiliary Check Point
ACIC	Auxiliary Combat Information Center
AC	Auxiliary Command
ACPU	Auxiliary Computer Power Unit
ACE	Auxiliary Conversion Equipment
ADAC	Auxiliary Data Annotation Set
ADAS	Auxiliary Data Annotation Set
ADPE	Auxiliary Data Processing Equipment
ADTU	Auxiliary Data Translator Unit
AES	Auxiliary Encoder System
AESP	Auxiliary Engineering Signal Processor
AFSU	Auxiliary Ferry Service Unit
AFDS	Auxiliary Fighter Director Ship
AFS	Auxiliary Fire Service (British)
AFD	Auxiliary, Floating Dock (Navy symbol)
ARD	Auxiliary Floating Dry Dock (Navy symbol)
ARDC	Auxiliary Floating Dry Dock, Concrete (Navy symbol)
AGERS	Auxiliary General Electronics Research Ship (Navy)
AGOR	Auxiliary General Oceanographic Research (Ships) (NOO)
AGE	Auxiliary Ground Equipment
ALF	Auxiliary Landing Field
AM	Auxiliary Memory
AMD	Auxiliary Memory Drum
AMU	Auxiliary Memory Unit
AMBV	Auxiliary Mexican Border Veterans
AMPC	Auxiliary Military Pioneer Corps (British)
ACM	Auxiliary Mine Layer (Navy symbol)
AML	Auxiliary Mine Layer
MMA	Auxiliary Minelayer (Navy symbol)
YMS	Auxiliary Motor Minesweeper (Navy symbol)
ATA	Auxiliary Ocean Tug (Navy symbol)

AUXOPS	Auxiliary Operational Members (Coast Guard)
AOT	Auxiliary Output Tester
APA	Auxiliary Personnel, Attack (Navy designation for combat landing craft) (World War II)
APP	Auxiliary Power Plant
APS	Auxiliary Power Supply
APU	Auxiliary Power Unit (Air Force)
APS	Auxiliary Propulsion System (Apollo) (NASA)
APDA	Auxiliary Pump-Drive Assembly
ARTC	Auxiliary Rescue Team Chief (Air Force)
ARE	Auxiliary Rocket Engine
ARC	Auxiliary Roll Control
XAV	Auxiliary Seaplane Tender (Ship symbol)
ASFTRNTRARONPAC . .	Auxiliary Service Force, Transition Training Squadron, Pacific
AG(SS)	Auxiliary Submarine (Navy symbol)
ASR	Auxiliary Submarine Rescue (Ship) (Navy)
ASCO	Auxiliary Sustainer Cut-Off
ASC	Auxiliary Switch (Breaker) Normally Closed
ASO	Auxiliary Switch (Breaker) Normally Open (Electricity)
ATM	Auxiliary Tape Memory (Spacecraft guidance)
ATS	Auxiliary Territorial Service (British women's service) (World War II)
AT	Auxiliary Timer
ATS	Auxiliary Tug Salvage (Navy)
AC	Availability Code
AVF	Availability Factor
ABNI	Available But Not Installed
AMT	Available Machine Time
AVMH	Available Manhours
APE	Available Power Efficiency
APR	Available Power Response
AVFR	Available for Reassignment
ASR	Available Supply Rate
AVT	Available Time
AID	Avalanche Injection Diode
AMP	Avalanche Mode Photodiode
ATTD	Avalanche Transit Time Diode
AJLO	Avalanching Junction Light Output
AV	Avco Corporation (NYSE symbol)
AERL	Avco-Everett Research Laboratory
AM	Ave Maria
ADA	Average Daily Attendance
ADML	Average Daily Member Load
ADM	Average Daily Membership
ADPL	Average Daily Patient Load
AD	Average Deviation (Statistics)
AEI	Average Efficiency Index
AEC	Average Electrode Current
AER	Averaged Evoked Response
AFN	Average Failure Number
AFC	Average Fixed Cost
AFRA	Average Freight Rate Assessment (Shipping)
AVH	Average Heading
AOT	Average Operation Time
AOQ	Average Outgoing Quality (Quality control term)
AOQL	Average Outgoing Quality Level
AOQL	Average Outgoing Quality Limit (QCR)
APL	Average Picture Level
AQL	Average Quality Level (or Limit)
ARA	Average Response Amplitude
ARAD	Average Response Amplitude Data
ARC	Average Response Computer
ARD	Average Response Data
AR	Average Revenue
ARPM	Average Revenue Per Message
ASN	Average Sample Number (Quality control)
ASL	Average Service Life
ASP	Average Speech Power
ASTHE	Average Straight Time Hourly Earnings
ATT	Average Task Time
ATC	Average Total Cost
ATI	Average Total Inspection (QCR)
ATUC	Average Total Unit Cost
AUL	Average Useful Life
AV	Average Variability
AVC	Average Variable Costs
AWE	Average Weekly Earnings
AVW	Average Width
AWD	Average Working Depth
AS	Aviaeskadra (Russian term for an air squadron)
AVN	AVIANCA (Aerovias Nacionales de Colombia, S.A., Colombian airline)

AP . . . . Aviapolk (Russian term for an air regiment)

ADD. . . . . Aviastiia Dalnego Deistviia (Long-range Aviation) (Strategic bombing force of USSR)

AA. . . . . Aviation Annex (Air Force)

AAL . . . . Aviation Armament Laboratory (Navy) (Later, Naval Air Development Center)

AX. . . . . Aviation ASW (Antisubmarine Warfare) Technician (Navy rating) Center (FAA)

AB . . . . Aviation Battalion (Army)

AVBAT . . . . . . Aviation Battalion (Army)

AB . . . . Aviation Boatswain's Mate

ABM. . . . . . . Aviation Boatswain's Mate (Navy rating)

ABMAG . . . . . Aviation Boatswain's Mate, Arresting Gear and Barriers (Navy rating)

ABMCP. . . . . . Aviation Boatswain's Mate, Catapult (Navy rating)

ABMGA . . . . . Aviation Boatswain's Mate, Gasoline System (Navy rating)

ABMPH . . . . . Aviation Boatswain's Mate, Plane Handler (Navy rating)

AC . . . . Aviation Cadet

A/C . . . . Aviation Cadet (Air Force)

AVCAD . . . . . Aviation Cadet

ACQT. . . . . . Aviation Cadet Qualifying Test

ABCM . . . . . . Aviation Chief Boatswain's Mate

ACBMAG. . . . . Aviation Chief Boatswain's Mate, Arresting Gear and Barriers

ACBMCP . . . . . Aviation Chief Boatswain's Mate, Catapult

ACBMGA . . . . . Aviation Chief Boatswain's Mate, Gasoline System

ACBMPH . . . . . Aviation Chief Boatswain's Mate, Plane Handler

ACEM . . . . . . Aviation Chief Electrician's Mate (Navy)

ACFC . . . . . . Aviation Chief Fire Controlman

ACMM . . . . . . Aviation Chief Machinist's Mate

ACMMC . . . . . Aviation Chief Machinist's Mate, Carburetor Mechanic

ACMMF. . . . . . Aviation Chief Machinist's Mate, Flight Engineer

ACMMT. . . . . . Aviation Chief Machinist's Mate, Gas Turbine Mechanic

ACMMH . . . . . Aviation Chief Machinist's Mate, Hydraulic Mechanic

ACMMI. . . . . . Aviation Chief Machinist's Mate, Instrument Mechanic

ACMMP. . . . . . Aviation Chief Machinist's Mate, Propellor Mechanic

ACM . . . . Aviation Chief Metalsmith

ACOM . . . . . . Aviation Chief Ordnanceman

ACOMT. . . . . . Aviation Chief Ordnanceman, Turret Mechanic

ACRT . . . . . . Aviation Chief Radio Technician

ACRM. . . . . . . Aviation Chief Radioman

ACL . . . . Aviation Circular Letter

ACT . . . . Aviation Classification Test

ACSEB . . . . . . Aviation Clothing and Survival Equipment Bulletin

ACDA. . . . . . Aviation Combat Development Agency (CDC)

AVCOM . . . . . Aviation Command (Army)

ACE . . . . Aviation Construction Engineers (Military)

AVCIR . . . . . Aviation Crash Inquiry Research

AD . . . . Aviation Daily

ADR . . . . Aviation Design Research (Navy)

ADAC. . . . . . Aviation Development Advisory Committee

ADC . . . . Aviation Development Council

ADMA. . . . . . Aviation Distributors and Manufacturers Association

AE . . . . Aviation Electrician's Mate (Navy rating)

AEM . . . . . . Aviation Electrician's Mate

AT . . . . Aviation Electronic Technician (Navy rating)

AETM. . . . . . Aviation Electronic Technician's Mate

AETAC . . . . . Aviation Electronic Technician's Mate, Combat Aircrewman

AVIONICS . . . Aviation Electronics

AL . . . . Aviation Electronicsman (Military)

AVNENGRBN. . Aviation Engineer Battalion (Marine Corps)

AEF . . . . Aviation Engineer Force

AVIEN . . . . . . Aviation Engineering Corporation

AF . . . . Aviation Facilities

AFS . . . . Aviation Facilities Service (of FAA)

AFSI . . . . Aviation Financial Services, Incorporated

AQ . . . . Aviation Fire Control Technician (Navy rating)

AFC . . . . Aviation Fire Controlman

AGAS . . . . . . Aviation Gasoline (Navy)

AVGAS. . . . . . Aviation Gasoline

AGOS . . . . . . Aviation Gunnery Officers School

AHS . . . . Aviation Historical Society

AHRU . . . . . . Aviation Human Research Unit (Army)

AIL . . . . Aviation Instrument Laboratory (Navy)

AVLABS . . . . . Aviation Laboratories (Army)

AVLUB . . . . . . Aviation Lubricant

AD . . . . Aviation Machinist's Mate (Navy rating)

AMM . . . . . . Aviation Machinist's Mate (Navy rating)

AMMC . . . . . Aviation Machinist's Mate, Carburetor Mechanic (Navy rating)

AMMAC . . . . . Aviation Machinist's Mate, Combat Aircrewman (Navy rating)

AMMF . . . . . . Aviation Machinist's Mate, Flight Engineer (Navy rating)

AMMH . . . . . . Aviation Machinist's Mate, Hydraulic Mechanic (Navy rating)

AMMI. . . . . . . Aviation Machinist's Mate, Instrument Mechanic (Navy rating)

AMMP . . . . . . Aviation Machinist's Mate, Propeller Mechanic (Navy rating)

AMMT . . . . . . Aviation Machinist's Mate, Turret Mechanic (Navy rating)

AZ . . . . Aviation Maintenance Administrationman (Navy rating)

AML . . . . Aviation Material Laboratories (Army)

AMMIP . . . . . . Aviation Materiel Management Improvement Program (Army)

AVM . . . . Aviation Medical

AMAL. . . . . . . Aviation Medical Acceleration Laboratory (Air Force)

AME. . . . . Aviation Medical Examiner

AM. . . . . Aviation Medicine

AVT . . . . Aviation Medicine Technician (Navy)

AM . . . . Aviation Metalsmith

AMP . . . . Aviation Modernization Program

AOC . . . . Aviation Officer Candidate (Navy)

AOQ . . . . Aviation Officers' Quarters

AOTC . . . . . . Aviation Officers Training Corps

A OIL . . . . . . Aviation Oil

AVOIL . . . . . . Aviation Oil (Military)

AOO . . . . Aviation Ordnance Officer

AO . . . . Aviation Ordnanceman

AOM . . . . Aviation Ordnanceman (Navy rating)

AOMB . . . . . . Aviation Ordnanceman, Bombsight Mechanic (Navy rating)

AOACB . . . . . Aviation Ordnanceman, Combat Aircrewman, Air Bomber

AOMAC . . . . . Aviation Ordnanceman, Combat Aircrewman (Navy rating)

AOMT . . . . . . Aviation Ordnanceman, Turret Mechanic

AVIA . . . . Aviation Pay (Navy)

APCCLA . . . . . Aviation Petroleum Coordinating Committee, Latin American

APPAC . . . . . . Aviation Petroleum Products Allocation Committee

APPAC-L . . . . . Aviation Petroleum Products Allocation Committee, London

AP . . . . Aviation Pilot (Navy)

APLA . . . . Aviation Pilot, Airship (Navy)

RCM . . . . Aviation Radio and RADAR Countermeasures Technician (Navy)

ART . . . . Aviation Radio Technician

ARM . . . . Aviation Radioman

ARMAC. . . . . . Aviation Radioman, Combat Aircrewman (Navy)

AROU . . . . . . Aviation Repair and Overhaul Unit

ARSD . . . . . . Aviation Repair Supply Depot

ARDS . . . . . . Aviation Research and Development Service (of FAA)

ARMACS . . . . . Aviation Resources Management and Control System

ASDO. . . . . . . Aviation Safety District Office

ASR . . . . Aviation Safety Regulation

ASM. . . . . Aviation School of Medicine

ASI . . . . Aviation Services, Incorporated

A/SWA . . . . . . Aviation/Space Writers Association

AWA . . . . Aviation/Space Writers Association

AK. . . . . Aviation Storekeeper (Navy rating)

AM . . . . Aviation Structural Mechanic (Navy rating)

ASA . . . . Aviation Supply Annex

ASD . . . . Aviation Supply Depot

ASO . . . . Aviation Supply Office (Air Force)

ASOP . . . . . . Aviation Supply Office Philadelphia (Navy)

AVS . . . . Aviation Supply Ship (Navy symbol)

ASMC . . . . . . Aviation Surface Material Command (Army)

AVSCOM . . . . Aviation and Surface Material Command (Air Force)

ASL . . . . Aviation Systems Laboratory

ATDS . . . . . . Aviation Tactical Data System

ATTC . . . . . . Aviation Technical Training Center

ATR . . . . Aviation Training Record

ATF . . . . Aviation Turbine Fuel

AVNU . . . . . . Aviation Unit (Marine Corps)

USMCR(NAV). . Aviation Volunteer Marine Corps Reserve (Naval Aviators)

AWS. . . . . Aviation Weather Service (of Weather Bureau)

AW . . . . Aviation Week

AA . . . . Aviatsionnaya Armiya (Russian – Air Army)

AD . . . . Aviatsionnaya Diviziya (Russian term for an air division)

AVMF. . . . . . . Aviatsiya Voenno Morskikh Flota (Soviet naval aviation) (USSR)

ASOA . . . . . . Avicultural Society of America

AATE . . . . . . Avionics Automatic Transmission Line

AL . . . . Avionics Laboratory (Air Force)

AMS. . . . . Avionics Maintenance Shop

AR . . . . Avionics Requirements

ASM. . . . . Avionics Shop Maintenance

ASSB . . . . Avionics Subsystem for Strategic Bombers

AR. . . . . Avis de Reception (Return receipt)

AVT . . . . Avnet, Incorporated (NYSE symbol)

AVO . . . . Avoid Verbal Orders

AD. . . . . Avoidable Delay

AK. . . . . Avtomat Kalashnikov (Submachine Gun) (USSR)

AADCM . . . . . Awaiting Action Deck Court-Martial

AAGCM . . . . . Awaiting Action General Court-Martial

AAHA . . . . . . Awaiting Action (of) Higher Authority (Army)

AASCM . . . . . Awaiting Action Summary Court-Martial

AAA . . . . Awaiting Aircraft Availability
ABCD . . . . . . Awaiting Bad Conduct Discharge (Military)
AWDISCOM . . Awaiting Disciplinary Action this Command (Army)
AM . . . . Awaiting Maintenance
AWM . . . . Awaiting Maintenance
AOH . . . . Awaiting Office Hours
AP . . . . Awaiting Parts
AWP . . . . Awaiting Parts
ARTL . . . . Awaiting Results of Trial (Military)
AT . . . . Awaiting Transportation
AXFL . . . . Axial Flow
AFC . . . . Axial Flow Compressor
AFW . . . . Axial Flow Wheel
APA . . . . Axial Pressure Angle (Gears)
ATM . . . . Axial Turbo Machine
ASN . . . . Axially Symmetric Nozzle
ABG . . . . Axiobuccogingival
ABL . . . . Axiobuccolingual
AC . . . . Axiocervical
ADC . . . . Axiodistocervical
ADG . . . . Axiodistogingival
ADI . . . . Axiodistoincisal
ADO . . . . Axiodisto-Occlusal
AG . . . . Axiogingival
AI . . . . Axioincisal
AL . . . . Axiolingual
ALC . . . . Axiolinguocervical
ALG . . . . Axiolinguogingival
AM . . . . Axiomesial
ACIM . . . . . . Axis Crossing Interval Meter (SONAR)
AXSIGCOMM . Axis or Axes of Signal Communication
ABB . . . . Axisymmetric Blunt Body
ACF . . . . Axisymmetrical Conical Flow
AFF . . . . Axisymmetrical Flow Field

ACM . . . . Axon Cylinder Membrane
ABA . . . . Ayrshire Breeders' Association
APK . . . . Ayrshire Collieries Company (NYSE symbol)
AHF . . . . Azad Hind Fauj (Indian National Army)
AGIP . . . . Azienda Generale Italiana Petroli (Italian Petroleum Enterprise)
ASST . . . . Azienda de Stato per i Servizi Telefonici (Italy)
AVA . . . . Azimuth vs. Amplitude
Z . . . . Azimuth Angle
AAI . . . . Azimuth Angle Increment
ACP . . . . Azimuth Change Pulse
AC . . . . Azimuth Comparator
ACA . . . . Azimuth Control Amplifier
ACS . . . . Azimuth Control System
ACT . . . . Azimuth Control Torquer
A & E . . . . . Azimuth and Elevation
AZEL . . . . Azimuth Elevation
AEI . . . . Azimuth Error Indicator
AFA . . . . Azimuth Followup Amplifier
AFS . . . . Azimuth Followup System
AI . . . . Azimuth Indicator
ALS . . . . Azimuth Laying Set
AMPA . . . . Azimuth Mark Pulse Amplifier
AZON . . . . . Azimuth Only
AOS . . . . Azimuth Orientation System (Military)
AOU . . . . Azimuth Orientation Unit (Military)
AQGV . . . . . . Azimuth Quantized Gated Video (Air Force)
AZRAN . . . . . Azimuth and Range
ASA . . . . Azimuth Servo Assembly
ASI . . . . Azimuth Speed Indicator
ATA . . . . Azimuth Torquer Amplifier
AQN . . . . Azimuthal Quantum Number
ACI . . . . Azione Cattolica Italiana
AZRU . . . . Aztec Ruins National Monument

B

BFG . . . . B. F. Goodrich Company
BAB . . . . Babbitt (B. T.), Inc. (NYSE symbol)
BAW . . . . Babcock & Wilcox Company (NYSE symbol)
B & W . . . . . . Babcock and Wilcox Company
BWTR . . . . . . Babcock and Wilcox Test Reactor
BRL . . . . Babe Ruth League
BAR . . . . Babinet Absorption Rule
BJC . . . . Babinet Jamin Compensator
BIBA . . . . Babson Institute of Business Administration (Massachusetts)
BHK . . . . Baby Hamster Kidney
B/B . . . . Baby Incendiary Bomb
BIB . . . . Baby Incendiary Bomb
BC . . . . Baccalaureus Chirurgiae (Bachelor of Surgery)
B Ch . . . . Baccalaureus Chirurgiae (Bachelor of Surgery)
B Chir . . . . . . Baccalaureus Chirurgiae (Bachelor of Surgery)
B Ch D . . . . . . Baccalaureus Chirurgiae Dentium (Bachelor of Dental Surgery)
MBCM . . . . . . Baccalaureus Medicinae, Chirurgiae Magister (Bachelor of Medicine, Master of Surgery)
BUJ . . . . Baccalaureus Utriusque Juris (Bachelor of Both Laws; i.e., Canon and Civil Laws)
BONA . . . . . . Bachad Organization of North America
B . . . . Bachelor
B Acc . . . . Bachelor of Accountancy
B Ac . . . . Bachelor of Accounts
B Acc's . . . . . Bachelor of Accounts
B of Adv Art & Des . . Bachelor of Advertising Arts and Design
B of AA . . . . . Bachelor of Aeronautical Administration
BAE . . . . Bachelor of Aeronautical Engineering
B of AE . . . . . Bachelor of Aeronautical Engineering
B Ae E . . . . . . Bachelor of Aeronautical Engineering
B Ae . . . . Bachelor of Aeronautics
BAE . . . . Bachelor of Agricultural Engineering
B Eng A . . . . . Bachelor of Agricultural Engineering
BAS . . . . Bachelor of Agricultural Science
BA Sc . . . . . . Bachelor of Agricultural Science
BA . . . . Bachelor of Agriculture
B Ag . . . . Bachelor of Agriculture
BACE . . . . . . Bachelor of Air Conditioning Engineering
BAC Eng . . . . . Bachelor of Air Conditioning Engineering
BAQ . . . . Bachelor Airmen's Quarters (Air Force)
BAA . . . . Bachelor of Applied Arts
BAM . . . . Bachelor of Applied Mathematics
BAS . . . . Bachelor of Applied Science
BA Sc . . . . . . Bachelor of Applied Science
B Arch Des . . . Bachelor of Architectural Design
BAE . . . . Bachelor of Architectural Engineering
B Ar E . . . . . . Bachelor of Architectural Engineering
B Ar . . . . Bachelor of Architecture
B Arch in City Pl Bachelor of Architecture in City Planning
BAE . . . . Bachelor of Art Education
BA Ed . . . . . . Bachelor of Art Education
BAO . . . . Bachelor of Art of Oratory
BA . . . . Bachelor of Arts
AB (Bible) . . . . Bachelor of Arts in Bible
BA in BA . . . . . Bachelor of Arts in Business Administration
BA in B & E . . . Bachelor of Arts in Business and Economics
BA Class . . . . . Bachelor of Arts - Classical
BA in E & B . . . Bachelor of Arts in Economics and Business
BAE . . . . Bachelor of Arts in Education
BA Ed . . . . . . Bachelor of Arts in Education
BAH Re . . . . . . Bachelor of Arts in Human Relations
BAJ . . . . Bachelor of Arts in Journalism
BA in J . . . . . . Bachelor of Arts in Journalism

ABLS . . . . Bachelor of Arts in Library Science
BAM . . . . Bachelor of Arts in Music
BA in M Ed . . . Bachelor of Arts in Music Education
BA Non-Class . . Bachelor of Arts - Non-Classical
BAPCT . . . . . . Bachelor of Arts in Practical Christian Training
AB (Rel) . . . . . Bachelor of Arts with Religious Major
B Ar Sc . . . . . . Bachelor of Arts and Sciences
BAS . . . . Bachelor of Arts in Speech
BA in Sp . . . . . Bachelor of Arts in Speech
B As S . . . . . . Bachelor of Association Science
B As Sc . . . . . . Bachelor of Association Science
B Au E . . . . . . Bachelor of Automobile Engineering
B Au Eng . . . . . Bachelor of Automobile Engineering
BB . . . . Bachelor of Bacteriology
BBC . . . . Bachelor of Beauty Culture
BBC . . . . Bachelor of Building Construction
B of BC . . . . . Bachelor of Building Construction
BBA . . . . Bachelor of Business Administration
BBM . . . . Bachelor of Business Management
BBS . . . . Bachelor of Business Science
B Can L . . . . . Bachelor of Canon Law
B Ce Eng . . . . . Bachelor of Cement Engineering
BCE . . . . Bachelor of Chemical Engineering
BCS . . . . Bachelor of Chemical Science
BC . . . . Bachelor of Chemistry
B Ch . . . . Bachelor of Chemistry
Ch B . . . . Bachelor of Chemistry
BCE . . . . Bachelor of Christian Education
B Chr Ed . . . . . Bachelor of Christian Education
BSC . . . . Bachelor of Christian Science
CSB . . . . Bachelor of Christian Science
BCT . . . . Bachelor of Christian Training
BCM . . . . Bachelor of Church Music
BCF . . . . Bachelor of City Forestry
BCP . . . . Bachelor of City Planning
BCE . . . . Bachelor of Civil Engineering
BCL . . . . Bachelor of Civil Law
CLB . . . . Bachelor of Civil Law
BC . . . . Bachelor of Classics
BC . . . . Bachelor of Commerce
BCA . . . . Bachelor of Commercial Arts
BCL . . . . Bachelor of Commercial Law
BCS . . . . Bachelor of Commercial Science
BC Sc . . . . . . Bachelor of Commercial Science
BC Se . . . . . . Bachelor of Commercial Service
B Cr . . . . Bachelor of Criminology
BD . . . . Bachelor of Dental Science
BDS . . . . Bachelor of Dental Surgery
B Des . . . . . . Bachelor of Design
B Des A Ed . . . Bachelor of Design in Art Education
BSD . . . . Bachelor of Didactic Science
B Did . . . . . . Bachelor of Didactics
B Di E . . . . . . Bachelor of Diesel Engineering
B Di Eng . . . . . Bachelor of Diesel Engineering
B Dipl . . . . . . Bachelor of Diplomacy
BDL . . . . Bachelor of Divine Literature
BD . . . . Bachelor of Divinity
DB . . . . Bachelor of Divinity
BD in E . . . . . . Bachelor of Divinity in Education
ADB . . . . Bachelor of Domestic Arts
BDA . . . . Bachelor of Domestic Arts
BDA . . . . Bachelor of Dramatic Art
B Dr Art . . . . . Bachelor of Dramatic Art

BE . . . . Bachelor of Education
Ed B . . . . Bachelor of Education
BEE . . . . Bachelor of Electrical Engineering
B of EE (Com Opt) . . Bachelor of Electrical Engineering, Communication Option
B of EE (Power Opt) . . Bachelor of Electrical Engineering, Power Option
BECE . . . . Bachelor of Electro-Chemical Engineering
B Ele . . . . . . Bachelor of Elements
BE . . . . Bachelor of Elocution
B El . . . . Bachelor of Elocution
BE . . . . Bachelor of Engineering
BEC . . . . Bachelor of Engineering Construction
BEM . . . . Bachelor of Engineering of Mines
BEP . . . . Bachelor of Engineering Physics
B of EP . . . . . Bachelor of Engineering Physics
BE Phy . . . . . Bachelor of Engineering Physics
BES . . . . Bachelor of Engineering Sciences
BE . . . . Bachelor of English
B En . . . . Bachelor of English
BED . . . . Bachelor of English Divinity
BEL . . . . Bachelor of English Literature
ELB . . . . Bachelor of English Literature
BEQ . . . . Bachelor Enlisted Quarters
B Ent . . . . . . Bachelor of Entomology
BE . . . . Bachelor of Expression
B Ex . . . . Bachelor of Expression
BFL . . . . Bachelor of Family Life
BF . . . . Bachelor of Finance
BFA . . . . Bachelor of Fine Arts
BFA in DA . . . . Bachelor of Fine Arts in Dramatic Art
BFA in PS . . . . Bachelor of Fine Arts in Painting and Sculpture
BFS . . . . Bachelor of Foreign Service
BFT . . . . Bachelor of Foreign Trade
BFE . . . . Bachelor of Forest Engineering
BF Eng . . . . . Bachelor of Forest Engineering
BF . . . . Bachelor of Forestry
BGS . . . . Bachelor of General Studies
BGE . . . . Bachelor of Geological Engineering
B Ge E . . . . . . Bachelor of Geological Engineering
B Ge Eng . . . . Bachelor of Geological Engineering
BH . . . . Bachelor of Hebrew
BHL . . . . Bachelor of Hebrew Letters
BHL . . . . Bachelor of Hebrew Literature
BH Ec . . . . . . Bachelor of Home Economics
BHS . . . . Bachelor of Home Science
B Hor . . . . . . Bachelor of Horticulture
BHA . . . . Bachelor of Hospital Administration
B Ho Ec . . . . . Bachelor of Household Economy
B Ho Sc . . . . . Bachelor of Household Science
BHL . . . . Bachelor of Humane Letters
LHB . . . . Bachelor of Humane Letters (or Bachelor of Literature, or Bachelor of the More Humane Letters)
BH . . . . Bachelor of Humanics
B Hu . . . . . . Bachelor of Humanities
B Hy . . . . Bachelor of Hygiene
BIA . . . . Bachelor of Industrial Arts
BID . . . . Bachelor of Industrial Design
BIE . . . . Bachelor of Industrial Engineering
BI Eng . . . . . Bachelor of Industrial Engineering
BIM . . . . Bachelor of Industrial Management
B of IM . . . . . Bachelor of Industrial Management
BIT . . . . Bachelor of Industrial Technology
BI Arch E . . . . Bachelor of Interior Architectural Engineering
BI Arch Eng . . . Bachelor of Interior Architectural Engineering
BI Arch . . . . . Bachelor of Interior Architecture
B of ID . . . . . . Bachelor of Interior Design
B Int L . . . . . . Bachelor of International Law
B Ir E . . . . . . Bachelor of Irrigation Engineering
B Ir Eng . . . . . Bachelor of Irrigation Engineering
BJ Ed . . . . . . Bachelor of Jewish Education
BJP . . . . Bachelor of Jewish Pedagogy
BJ . . . . Bachelor of Journalism
JSB . . . . Bachelor of Judicial Science
BLA . . . . Bachelor of Landscape Architecture
BL Arch . . . . . Bachelor of Landscape Architecture
BL Des . . . . . Bachelor of Landscape Design
BL Eng . . . . . Bachelor of Landscape Engineering
BLM . . . . Bachelor of Landscape Management
B La L . . . . . . Bachelor of Latin Letters
BLL . . . . Bachelor of Latin Letters
LB . . . . Bachelor of Law
BL . . . . Bachelor of Laws

BLL . . . . Bachelor of Laws
LLB . . . . Bachelor of Law(s)
BL . . . . Bachelor of Letters
B Lit . . . . . . Bachelor of Letters
B Litt . . . . . . Bachelor of Letters
LB . . . . Bachelor of Letters
BLJ . . . . Bachelor of Letters in Journalism
BLA . . . . Bachelor of Liberal Arts
BLS . . . . Bachelor of Library Science
BL Sc . . . . . . Bachelor of Library Science
BLE . . . . Bachelor of Library Economics
BL Ec . . . . . . Bachelor of Library Economics
LSB . . . . Bachelor of Life Science
BLI . . . . Bachelor of Literary Interpretation
BL . . . . Bachelor of Literature
B Lit . . . . . . Bachelor of Literature
B Litt . . . . . . Bachelor of Literature
B Lt . . . . Bachelor of Literature
LB . . . . Bachelor of Literature
BMS . . . . Bachelor of Marine Science
BM . . . . Bachelor of Mathematics
AMB . . . . Bachelor of Mechanic Arts
BME . . . . Bachelor of Mechanical Engineering
BME (Aero Option) . . Bachelor of Mechanical Engineering (Aeronautical Option)
BMS . . . . Bachelor of Mechanical Science
BM Sc . . . . . . Bachelor of Mechanical Science
B Ms Sc . . . . . Bachelor of Mechanical Sciences
BMT . . . . Bachelor of Medical Technology
BM . . . . Bachelor of Medicine
MB . . . . Bachelor of Medicine
Me B . . . . Bachelor of Metaphysics
BEM . . . . Bachelor of Mining Engineering
BME . . . . Bachelor of Mining Engineering
BMM . . . . Bachelor of Mining and Metallurgy
BML . . . . Bachelor of Modern Languages
BMA . . . . Bachelor of Municipal Administration
BM . . . . Bachelor of Music
MB . . . . Bachelor of Music
BME . . . . Bachelor of Music Education
BME . . . . Bachelor of Music in Education
B Mus Ed . . . . Bachelor of Music in Education
B Mus (PSM) . . . Bachelor of Music in Public School Music
BN Arch . . . . . Bachelor of Naval Architecture
BNE . . . . Bachelor of Naval Engineering
BNS . . . . Bachelor of Naval Science
BNCOQ . . . . . Bachelor Noncommissioned Officers' Quarters
BN . . . . Bachelor of Nursing
BNS . . . . Bachelor of Nursing Science
BAO . . . . Bachelor of Obstetrics
BOQ . . . . Bachelor Officers' Quarters (Army)
B Opt . . . . . . Bachelor of Optometry
BOE . . . . Bachelor of Oral English
BO . . . . Bachelor of Oratory
B Or . . . . Bachelor of Oratory
BOL . . . . Bachelor of Oriental Language
B Orient . . . . . Bachelor of Oriental Studies
BO . . . . Bachelor of Osteopathy
BP . . . . Bachelor of Painting
B Pa . . . . Bachelor of Painting
BPL . . . . Bachelor of Patent Law
B Pd . . . . Bachelor of Pedagogics
B Ped . . . . . . Bachelor of Pedagogics (or Pedagogy)
BP . . . . Bachelor of Pedagogy
B Pd . . . . Bachelor of Pedagogy
B Pe . . . . Bachelor of Pedagogy
B Py . . . . Bachelor of Pedagogy
Pd B . . . . Bachelor of Pedagogy
Py B . . . . Bachelor of Pedagogy
B Pe E . . . . . . Bachelor of Petroleum Engineering
B Ph C . . . . . . Bachelor of Pharmaceutical Chemistry
BP . . . . Bachelor of Pharmacy
B Pharm . . . . . Bachelor of Pharmacy
Ph B . . . . Bachelor of Pharmacy
BP . . . . Bachelor of Philosophy
B Ph . . . . Bachelor of Philosophy
Ph B . . . . Bachelor of Philosophy
Ph B in Arch . . . Bachelor of Philosophy in Architecture
Ph B in Com . . . Bachelor of Philosophy in Commerce
B Pho . . . . . . Bachelor of Photography
BM . . . . Bachelor of Physic
BPB . . . . Bachelor of Physical Biology

Ph B . . . . Bachelor of Physical Culture
BPE . . . . Bachelor of Physical Education
B Ph S . . . . . . Bachelor of Physical Science
BPA . . . . Bachelor of Professional Arts
B Ps Sc . . . . . . Bachelor of Psychic Sciences
B Ps . . . . Bachelor of Psychology
B Ps Th . . . . . . Bachelor of Psychotherapy
BPA . . . . Bachelor of Public Administration
BP Adm . . . . . Bachelor of Public Administration
BPH . . . . Bachelor of Public Health
BPHE . . . . Bachelor of Public Health Engineering
BPHN . . . . . . Bachelor of Public Health Nursing
BPSA . . . . Bachelor of Public School Art
BPSM . . . . Bachelor of Public School Music
B Ra E . . . . . . Bachelor of Radio Engineering
B Ra Eng . . . . . Bachelor of Radio Engineering
BRTE . . . . Bachelor of Radio and Television Engineering
BRT Eng . . . . . Bachelor of Radio and Television Engineering
B Re E . . . . . . Bachelor of Refrigeration Engineering
B Re Eng . . . . . Bachelor of Refrigeration Engineering
B Re . . . . Bachelor of Religion
BRE . . . . Bachelor of Religious Education
BR Ed . . . . . . Bachelor of Religious Education
B Ru E . . . . . . Bachelor of Rural Engineering
BSL . . . . Bachelor of Sacred Literature
BSM . . . . Bachelor of Sacred Music
BS Mu . . . . . . Bachelor of Sacred Music
BS Mus . . . . . . Bachelor of Sacred Music
SMB . . . . Bachelor of Sacred Music
B Sa Sc . . . . . . Bachelor of Sacred Sciences
BST . . . . Bachelor of Sacred Theology
BSE . . . . Bachelor of Sanitary Engineering
BS Eng . . . . . . Bachelor of Sanitary Engineering
BSS . . . . Bachelor of Sanitary Science
BS Sc . . . . . . Bachelor of Sanitary Science
BSM . . . . Bachelor of School Music
BS Mus . . . . . Bachelor of School Music
BS . . . . Bachelor of Science
B Sc . . . . Bachelor of Science
SB . . . . Bachelor of Science
BS in AE . . . . . Bachelor of Science in Administrative Engineering
BSAE . . . . Bachelor of Science in Aeronautical Engineering
BS in AE . . . . . Bachelor of Science in Aeronautical Engineering
BS (AE Elec) . . . Bachelor of Science with Aeronautical Engineering Electives
BSAE–E . . . . . Bachelor of Science in Aeronautical Engineering – Electronics Major
BS in AM . . . . Bachelor of Science in Agricultural Administration
BS in AD . . . . . Bachelor of Science in Agricultural Education
BS in AN . . . . . Bachelor of Science in Agricultural Engineering
BSA . . . . Bachelor of Science in Agriculture
BS in Ag (DM) . . Bachelor of Science in Agriculture in Dairy Manufacturing
BSAT . . . . Bachelor of Science in Air Transportation
BSAME . . . . . . Bachelor of Science in Aircraft Maintenance Engineering
BS (A Math) . . . Bachelor of Science in Applied Mathematics
BS in Math . . . Bachelor of Science in Applied Mathematics
Sc BAM . . . . . Bachelor of Science in Applied Mathematics
BSAE . . . . Bachelor of Science in Architectural Engineering
BS in AE . . . . . Bachelor of Science in Architectural Engineering
BS in Med S . . . Bachelor of Science in Basic Medical Science
BS in BMS . . . . Bachelor of Science in Basic Medical Sciences
BSB . . . . Bachelor of Science in Business
BSBA . . . . Bachelor of Science in Business Administration
BS in BA . . . . . Bachelor of Science in Business Administration
BS (Bus–MR) . . . Bachelor of Science in Business – Medical Records
BS in Cart . . . . Bachelor of Science in Cartography
BS Cr E . . . . . Bachelor of Science in Ceramic Engineering
BS (Ch E Elect) . Bachelor of Science with Chemical Engineering Electives
Sc BC . . . . Bachelor of Science in Chemistry
BS in CE – Music . Bachelor of Science in Christian Education – Music
BSCE . . . . Bachelor of Science in Civil Engineering
BSC . . . . Bachelor of Science in Commerce
BS in C . . . . . . Bachelor of Science in Commerce
BS in C & Ec . . . Bachelor of Science in Commerce and Economics
BS in C & BA . . Bachelor of Science in Commercial and Business Administration
BS Com . . . . . Bachelor of Science in Communications
BS in Comm Rec . . Bachelor of Science in Community Recreation
BSD Hyg . . . . . Bachelor of Science in Dental Hygiene
BS in DH . . . . . Bachelor of Science in Dental Hygiene
BSD . . . . Bachelor of Science in Design
BS Des . . . . . . Bachelor of Science in Design
BS Des (Dec Des) . . Bachelor of Science in Design in Decorative Design
BSE . . . . Bachelor of Science in Education

BS in E . . . . . . Bachelor of Science in Education
BSEE . . . . Bachelor of Science in Electrical Engineering
BS in Elect Eng . Bachelor of Science in Electronic Engineering
BSEE . . . . Bachelor of Science in Elementary Education
BS El Ed . . . . . Bachelor of Science in Elementary Education
BS Elem . . . . . Bachelor of Science in Elementary Education
BES . . . . Bachelor of Science in Engineering
BSE . . . . Bachelor of Science in Engineering
BS in E . . . . . . Bachelor of Science in Engineering
Sc BE . . . . . . Bachelor of Science in Engineering
BSE (Geod & Surv) . . Bachelor of Science in Engineering in Geodesy and Surveying
BSE (Mat E) . . . Bachelor of Science in Engineering in Materials Engineering
BS in E Math . . Bachelor of Science in Engineering Mathematics
BSE (ME) . . . . . Bachelor of Science in Engineering in Mechanical Engineering
BSEM . . . . Bachelor of Science in Engineering of Mines
BS in EM . . . . . Bachelor of Science in Engineering of Mines
BSEP . . . . Bachelor of Science in Engineering Physics
BS in EP . . . . . Bachelor of Science in Engineering Physics
BSES . . . . Bachelor of Science in Engineering Sciences
BS in ES . . . . . Bachelor of Science in Engineering Sciences
BSE Sc . . . . . . Bachelor of Science in Engineering Sciences
BSEL . . . . Bachelor of Science and English Literature
BSF Mgt . . . . . Bachelor of Science in Fisheries Management
BSFS . . . . Bachelor of Science in Foreign Service
BS in FS . . . . . Bachelor of Science in Foreign Service
BSFM . . . . Bachelor of Science in Forest Management
B Sc F . . . . . . Bachelor of Science in Forestry
BSF . . . . Bachelor of Science in Forestry
BS For . . . . . . Bachelor of Science in Forestry
BS in Fy . . . . . Bachelor of Science in Forestry
BSFT . . . . Bachelor of Science in Fuel Technology
BSG Mgt . . . . . Bachelor of Science in Game Management
BS in GE . . . . . Bachelor of Science in General Engineering
BS in GSM . . . Bachelor of Science in General Science and Mathematics
BS in GS . . . . . Bachelor of Science in General Studies
BS in Geod & Surv Bachelor of Science in Geodesy and Surveying
BS Ggr . . . . . . Bachelor of Science in Geography
BS in Ge E . . . Bachelor of Science in Geological Engineering
BS Gl E . . . . . . Bachelor of Science in Geological Engineering
BS Gl . . . . Bachelor of Science in Geology
BS in Gph E . . . Bachelor of Science in Geophysical Engineering
BS Gph . . . . . . Bachelor of Science in Geophysics
BS in GWE . . . Bachelor of Science in Group Work Education
BSHE . . . . Bachelor of Science in Health Education
BS in HPE . . . . Bachelor of Science in Health and Physical Education
BS in H & PE . . Bachelor of Science in Health and Physical Education
B Sc in HE . . . . Bachelor of Science in Home Economics
BSHE . . . . Bachelor of Science in Home Economics
BS (HE) . . . . . . Bachelor of Science in Home Economics
BS in HE . . . . . Bachelor of Science in Home Economics
BS in HD . . . . . Bachelor of Science in Home Economics Education
BSHA . . . . Bachelor of Science in Hospital Administration
BS in H & RA . . Bachelor of Science in Hotel and Restaurant Administration
BS in IA . . . . . Bachelor of Science in Industrial Arts
BSIE . . . . Bachelor of Science in Industrial Education
BS in IE . . . . . Bachelor of Science in Industrial Engineering
BS in IE & M . . . Bachelor of Science in Industrial Engineering and Management
BSIM . . . . Bachelor of Science in Industrial Management
BS in IM . . . . . Bachelor of Science in Industrial Management
BSIR . . . . Bachelor of Science in Industrial Relations
BSIT . . . . Bachelor of Science in Industrial Technology
BSJ . . . . Bachelor of Science in Journalism
BS in J . . . . . . Bachelor of Science in Journalism
BS in LT . . . . . Bachelor of Science in Laboratory Technology
BS in LP . . . . . Bachelor of Science in Land Planning
BSLA . . . . Bachelor of Science in Landscape Architecture
BSL Arch . . . . Bachelor of Science in Landscape Architecture
BSLM . . . . Bachelor of Science in Landscape Management
BSL . . . . Bachelor of Science in Languages
BS in Lat . . . . . Bachelor of Science in Latin
B Sc L . . . . . . Bachelor of the Science of Law
BSL . . . . Bachelor of Science in Law
BS in L & S . . . Bachelor of Science in Letters and Science
BSLS . . . . Bachelor of Science in Library Science
BS in LS . . . . . Bachelor of Science in Library Science
BSL . . . . Bachelor of Science in Linguistics
BS in MA . . . . Bachelor of Science in Mechanical Arts
BSME . . . . Bachelor of Science in Mechanical Engineering
BS (ME) . . . . . . Bachelor of Science in Mechanical Engineering
BS (ME Elect) . . Bachelor of Science with Mechanical Engineering Electives
BS in Mech Ind . Bachelor of Science in Mechanical Industries

REVERSE ACRONYMS AND INITIALISMS DICTIONARY

BS in MRL . . . . Bachelor of Science in Medical Record Library Science
BS in Med Sc . . Bachelor of Science in Medical Secretarial Science
BS in Md . . . . . Bachelor of Science in Medical Technology
BSMT . . . . Bachelor of Science in Medical Technology
BS (MT) . . . . . . Bachelor of Science in Medical Technology
BS in MT . . . . . Bachelor of Science in Medical Technology
BSM . . . . Bachelor of Science in Medicine
BS Mt E . . . . . Bachelor of Science in Metallurgical Engineering
BS in Met . . . . Bachelor of Science in Metallurgy
BS Met . . . . . . Bachelor of Science in Meteorology
BS in Met . . . . Bachelor of Science in Meteorology
BS in MS . . . . . Bachelor of Science in Military Science
BSME . . . . Bachelor of Science in Mining Engineering
BS Mg E . . . . Bachelor of Science in Mining Engineering
BSM . . . . Bachelor of Science in Music
BS Mus . . . . . . Bachelor of Science in Music
BSME . . . . Bachelor of Science in Music Education
BS in Nat G Engin Bachelor of Science in Natural-Gas Engineering
BS in NS . . . . . Bachelor of Science in Natural Science
BS in N Sc . . . Bachelor of Science in Natural Science
BSN . . . . Bachelor of Science in Nursing
BS in N . . . . . Bachelor of Science in Nursing
BS in Nr . . . . . Bachelor of Science in Nursing
BSNA . . . . Bachelor of Science in Nursing Administration
BSNE . . . . Bachelor of Science in Nursing Education
BSOT . . . . Bachelor of Science in Occupational Therapy
BS in OT . . . . . Bachelor of Science in Occupational Therapy
BS in Ocean . . . Bachelor of Science in Oceanography
BS in Opt . . . . Bachelor of Science in Optics
BS in Opt . . . . Bachelor of Science in Optometry
B Sc O . . . . . . Bachelor of the Science of Oratory
BSO . . . . Bachelor of the Science of Oratory
B Or Sc . . . . . Bachelor of the Science of Oratory
BS in OH . . . . . Bachelor of Science in Ornamental Horticulture
BS Orn Hort . . . Bachelor of Science in Ornamental Horticulture
BS in Ortho . . . Bachelor of Science in Orthoptics
BS in PE . . . . . Bachelor of Science in Petroleum Engineering
BSP . . . . Bachelor of Science in Pharmacy
BS Ph . . . . . . Bachelor of Science in Pharmacy
BS in Ph . . . . . Bachelor of Science in Pharmacy
BSPE . . . . Bachelor of Science in Physical Education
BS (PE) . . . . . . Bachelor of Science in Physical Education
BS in PE . . . . . Bachelor of Science in Physical Education
BS in Th . . . . . Bachelor of Science in Physical And Occupational Therapy
BSPT . . . . Bachelor of Science in Physical Therapy
BS (PT) . . . . . . Bachelor of Science in Physical Therapy
BS in PT . . . . . Bachelor of Science in Physical Therapy
BS Phys . . . . . . Bachelor of Science in Physics
Sc BP . . . . Bachelor of Science in Physics
BS in PA . . . . . Bachelor of Science in Practical Arts
BS in Prac Arts . Bachelor of Science in Practical Arts
BS in PAL . . . . Bachelor of Science in Practical Arts and Letters
BS in Pr Ge . . . Bachelor of Science in Professional Geology
BS in Pr Met . . Bachelor of Science in Professional Meteorology
BSPA . . . . Bachelor of Science in Public Administration
BS in PA . . . . . Bachelor of Science in Public Administration
BSPH . . . . Bachelor of Science in Public Health
BSPHN . . . . . . Bachelor of Science in Public Health Nursing
BS in PHN . . . . Bachelor of Science in Public Health Nursing
BS in PHPM . . Bachelor of Science in Public Health and Preventative Medicine
BS in PSM . . . . Bachelor of Science in Public School Music
BS . . . . Bachelor of Science in Pure Science
BSRT . . . . Bachelor of Science in Radiological Technology
BS in RT . . . . . Bachelor of Science in Radiological Technology
BS in RAH . . . . Bachelor of Science in Range Animal Husbandry
BSR . . . . Bachelor of Science in Recreation
BS in Rec Lead . Bachelor of Science in Recreation Leadership
BS in RE . . . . . Bachelor of Science in Religious Education
B Sc in Rest Mgt. Bachelor of Science in Restaurant Management
BSS . . . . Bachelor of Science in Science
BSSE . . . . Bachelor of Science in Secondary Education
BS Sec . . . . . . Bachelor of Science in Secondary Education
BS Sec Ed . . . . Bachelor of Science in Secondary Education
BS (Sec Ed) . . . Bachelor of Science in Secondary Education
BS (Sec Adm) . . Bachelor of Science in Secretarial Administration
BSSA . . . . Bachelor of Science in Secretarial Administration
BSS Sci . . . . . . Bachelor of Science in Secretarial Science
BSSS . . . . Bachelor of Science in Secretarial Studies
BSSS . . . . Bachelor of Science in Social Science
BS (SS) . . . . . . Bachelor of Science in Social Science
BS in SS . . . . . Bachelor of Science in Social Science

BS in Spec Flds . Bachelor of Science in Special Fields
BS Sp . . . . Bachelor of Science in Speech
BS in Stat . . . . Bachelor of Science in Statistics
BST . . . . Bachelor of Science in Teaching
BS in TE . . . . . Bachelor of Science in Textile Engineering
STB . . . . Bachelor of the Science of Theology
BST & IE . . . . . Bachelor of Science in Trade and Industrial Engineering
BS in ZS . . . . . Bachelor of Science in Zoological Sciences
BSA . . . . Bachelor of Scientific Agriculture
BS Di . . . . Bachelor of Scientific Didactics
B Scn . . . . Bachelor of Scientology
B Se A . . . . . . Bachelor of Secretarial Arts
B Sec Sc . . . . . Bachelor of Secretarial Science
BSS . . . . Bachelor of Secretarial Science
B Se St . . . . . . Bachelor of Secretarial Studies
B So Sc . . . . . . Bachelor of Social Science
BSS . . . . Bachelor of Social Science(s)
B So Se . . . . . . Bachelor of Social Service
B So W . . . . . . Bachelor of Social Work
B So . . . . Bachelor of Sociology
B Sp . . . . Bachelor of Speech
B St . . . . Bachelor of Statistics
B St E . . . . . . Bachelor of Structural Engineering
B St Eng . . . . . Bachelor of Structural Engineering
BS . . . . Bachelor of Surgery
B Sy Th . . . . . . Bachelor of Systematic Theology
BT . . . . Bachelor of Teaching
B Sc Tech . . . . Bachelor of Technical Science
B Tech . . . . . . Bachelor of Technology
BTC . . . . Bachelor of Textile Chemistry
B of TC . . . . . . Bachelor of Textile Chemistry
BT Ch . . . . Bachelor of Textile Chemistry
BT Des . . . . . . Bachelor of Textile Design
BTD . . . . Bachelor of Textile Dyeing
BTE . . . . Bachelor of Textile Engineering
B of TE . . . . . . Bachelor of Textile Engineering
BT Eng . . . . . . Bachelor of Textile Engineering
B of TM . . . . . Bachelor of Textile Management
BTT . . . . Bachelor of Textile Technology
BT . . . . Bachelor of Theology
B Th . . . . Bachelor of Theology
Th B . . . . Bachelor of Theology
B Urb Pl . . . . . Bachelor of Urban Planning
BVM . . . . Bachelor of Veterinary Medicine
BVS . . . . Bachelor of Veterinary Science
BVS . . . . Bachelor of Veterinary Surgery
BVA . . . . Bachelor of Vocational Agriculture
BVE . . . . Bachelor of Vocational Education
BWE . . . . Bachelor of Welding Engineering
BZ Sc . . . . Bachelor of Zoological Science
BWD . . . . Bacillary White Diarrhea (Veterinary medicine)
B . . . . Bacillus (Bacteriology)
BCG . . . . Bacillus Calmette-Guerin (TB vaccine)
B . . . . Back
B to B . . . . . Back to Back (Technical drawings)
BC . . . . Back-Connected (Technical drawings)
BC . . . . Back Course (Aviation)
BD . . . . Back Dividends
BDT . . . . Back Door Trot (i.e., a call of nature) (Obsolete slang)
BF . . . . Back-Feed
BFL . . . . Back Focal Length
BG . . . . Back Gear (Technical drawings)
BO . . . . Back Order
BPE . . . . Back Porch Effect
BP . . . . Back Pressure
BPC . . . . Back-Pressure Control
BSL . . . . Back Stage Left (A stage direction)
BSR . . . . Back Stage Right (A stage direction)
BTDL . . . . . . Back Transient Diode Logic (Data processing)
BWV . . . . Back-Water Valve
BII . . . . Background Illumination Intensity
BI . . . . Background Investigation
BLIP . . . . Background-Limited Infrared Photoconductor
BNP . . . . Background Noise Power
BBT . . . . Backlight Burtek Trainer
BEMAR . . . . . . Backlog of Essential Maintenance and Repair
BARS . . . . . . Backup Attitude Reference System
BDC . . . . Back-up Digital Computer
BGS . . . . Backup Gimbal Servo
BUIC . . . . . . Backup Interceptor Control (Air Force emergency system)
BLPC . . . . . . Backward Limit Photocell

BWA . . . . Backward Wave Amplifier
BWC . . . . Backward-Wave Converter
BWO . . . . Backward Wave Oscillator
BWPA . . . . Backward Wave Power Amplifier
BLT . . . . Bacon, Lettuce and Tomato (Sandwich) (Waitress's call to a short order cook)
BAIT . . . . Bacterial Automated Identification Technique
BW . . . . Bacteriological Warfare
BC . . . . Bad Character
BC . . . . Bad Check
BCD . . . . Bad Conduct Discharge (Army)
BDGC . . . . Bad Conduct Discharge, General Court-Martial, After Confinement in Prison (Navy)
BDGP . . . . Bad Conduct Discharge, General Court-Martial, After Violation of Probation (Navy)
BDSP . . . . Bad Conduct Discharge, Summary Court-Martial, After Violation of Probation
BDGI . . . . Bad Conduct Discharge, General Court-Martial, Immediate (Navy)
BDSI . . . . Bad Conduct Discharge, Sentence of Summary Court-Martial, Immediate
BO . . . . Bad Order (i.e., requiring repair)
BKKI . . . . Badan Kongress Kebathinan Indonesia
BAPEKAN . . . . . Badan Pengawas Kegiatan Aparatur Negara (Indonesia)
BPB . . . . Badan Perdjoangan Buruh (Board for the Defense of Labor Interest) (Indonesia)
BASF . . . . Badische, Anilin und Soda Fabrik (Chemical company) (West Germany)
BADL . . . . Badlands National Monument
BHG . . . . Baeuerliche Handelsgesellschaft
B . . . . Bag
BIC . . . . Baha'i International Community
BAPCO . . . . . . Bahrein Petroleum Company
B . . . . Baht (Monetary unit in Siam)
BB . . . . Bail Bond
BGC . . . . Bailiff Grand Cross
BAI . . . . Baird-Associates, Incorporated
BCTN . . . . Baja California – Territorio Norte
BCTS . . . . Baja California – Territorio Sur
BKO . . . . Baker Oil Tools, Inc. (NYSE symbol)
BAK . . . . Baker Raulang Company (NYSE symbol)
BSI . . . . Baker Street Irregulars
BCW . . . . Bakery and Confectionery Workers' International Union of America
BCWIU of A . . Bakery and Confectionery Workers' International Union of America
BEMA . . . . . . Bakery Equipment Manufacturers Association
BISSC . . . . Baking Industry Sanitation Standards Committee
BAWI . . . . . . Balance Agriculture with Industry Program
BCM . . . . Balance Calibration Machine
BMRMO . . . . . Balance Mobilization Reserve Materiel Objective (Army)
BALPA . . . . . . Balance of Payments
BOP . . . . Balance of Payments
BS . . . . Balance Sheet
BALSPACON . . Balance of Space to Space Control Agencies
BOT . . . . Balance of Trade
BALUN . . . . . . Balance-to-Unbalance Network
BES . . . . Balanced Electrolyte Solution (Physiology)
BIBD . . . . Balanced Incomplete Block Designs (Statistics)
BILE . . . . Balanced Inductor Logical Element
BLLE . . . . Balanced Line Logical Element
BLS . . . . Balanced Line System
BMA . . . . Balanced Magnetic Amplifier
BPJ . . . . Balanced Pressure Joint
BPPSJ . . . . . . Balanced Pressure Plane Swivel Joint
BPSJ . . . . Balanced Pressure Swivel Joint
BSS . . . . Balanced Salt Solution
BV . . . . Balanced Voltage
BALUN . . . . . Balancing Unit (Radio)
B . . . . Balboa (Monetary unit in Panama)
5B . . . . Bald man with Bridgework, Bifocals, Baywindow, and Bunions (A humorous unofficial Selective Service Class)
BLH . . . . Baldwin-Lima-Hamilton Company, Inc.
B . . . . Baldwin-Lima-Hamilton Corporation (NYSE symbol)
B . . . . Bale
B/C . . . . Bales of Cotton (Shipping)
BSC . . . . Balkan Supply Center (Navy)
B . . . . Ball
BB . . . . Ball Bearing (Technical drawings)
BBJ . . . . Ball Bearing Joint
BBSJ . . . . . . Ball Bearing Swivel Joint
BBT . . . . Ball Bearing Torque
BBRC . . . . . . Ball Brothers Research Corporation
B & C . . . . . . Ball and Chain (Slang for a wife)
BCV . . . . Ball Check Valve
BJA . . . . Ball Joint Actuator

BJF . . . . Ball Joint Fitting
BLP . . . . Ball Lock Pin
BLSB . . . . . . Ball-Lock Separation Bolt
BMEC . . . . . . Ball Manufacturers Engineers Committee
BRD . . . . Ball Reduction Drive
B . . . . Ballistic
BARS . . . . . . Ballistic Analysis Research System
BAG . . . . Ballistic Attack Game
BC . . . . Ballistic Camera
BALDNY . . . . Ballistic Density
BM . . . . Ballistic Missile
BMAR . . . . . . Ballistic Missile Acquisition RADAR
BAMBI . . . . . . Ballistic Missile Bombardment Interceptor (Military)
BMB . . . . Ballistic Missile Branch
BMC . . . . Ballistic Missile Center, AMC
BMC . . . . Ballistic Missile Checker
OSD-BMC . . . Ballistic Missile Committee (of the OSD)
BMCO . . . . . . Ballistic Missile Construction Office
BMD . . . . Ballistic Missile Defense
BMDC . . . . . . Ballistic Missile Defense Committee
BMDS . . . . . . Ballistic Missile Defense System (Air Force)
BMD . . . . Ballistic Missile Division (Air Research and Development Center)
BMEWS . . . . . Ballistic Missile Early Warning System (Air Force)
BPTO . . . . . . BMEWS (Ballistic Missile Early Warning System) Performance Test Outline
BRCS . . . . . . BMEWS (Ballistic Missile Early Warning System) Rearward Communications System
BSP . . . . BMEWS (Ballistic Missile Early Warning System) Specification
BSPO . . . . . . BMEWS (Ballistic Missile Early Warning System) System Program Office
BTP . . . . BMEWS (Ballistic Missile Early Warning System) Test Procedure
BMI . . . . Ballistic Missile Interceptor (Air Force)
BMO . . . . Ballistic Missile Office(r)
BMORT . . . . . Ballistic Missile Operational Training Readiness
BMOC . . . . . . Ballistic Missile Orientation Course
BAMIRAC . . . . Ballistic Missile Radiation Analysis Center
BMRS . . . . . . Ballistic Missile Reentry Systems
BMS . . . . Ballistic Missile Ship (Navy)
BMSF . . . . . . Ballistic Missile Surface Force
BMTD . . . . . . Ballistic Missile Terminal Defense
BMETO . . . . . Ballistic Missiles European Task Organization (Military)
BMMG . . . . . . Ballistic Missiles Management Group (Air Force)
BMWS . . . . . . Ballistic Missiles Weapon System (Air Force)
BRS . . . . Ballistic Recording System
BROOM . . . . . Ballistic Recovery of Orbiting Man
BRB . . . . Ballistic Reentry Body
BRV . . . . Ballistic Reentry Vehicle
BRLESC . . . . . Ballistic Research Laboratories Electronic Scientific Computer
BRAS . . . . . . Ballistic Rocket Air Suppression
BSD . . . . Ballistic System Division (AFSC)
BSED . . . . . . Ballistic Systems Education Division (Air University) (Air Force)
BATES . . . . . . Ballistic Test Evaluation and Sealing
BALWND . . . . Ballistic Wind
BALLWIN . . . . Ballistic Winds
BLAM . . . . . . Ballistically Launched Aerodynamic Missile
BRL . . . . Ballistics Research Laboratory (Military)
BCG . . . . Ballistocardiogram (Medicine)
BATO . . . . . . Balloon-Assisted Takeoff (Air Force)
BALAST . . . . . Balloon Astronomy
BB . . . . Balloon Barrage
BBN . . . . Balloon-Borne Nephelometer
BBPN . . . . . . Balloon-Borne Polar Nephelometer
BPN . . . . Balloon-borne Polar Nephelometer
BBR . . . . Balloon-Borne Radio
BBRS . . . . . . Balloon-Borne Radio System
B . . . . Balloon Ceiling (Meteorology)
BFA . . . . Balloon Federation of America
BALLUTE . . . . Balloon Parachute
BALUTE . . . . . Balloon Parachute
BPA . . . . Balloon Platoon of America
BRS . . . . Balloon Radio System
BSF . . . . Baltic Student Federation
BWC . . . . . . Baltic Women's Council
BLA . . . . Baltimore & Annapolis R. R. (AAR code)
BCC . . . . Baltimore College of Commerce (Maryland)
BE . . . . Baltimore & Eastern R. R. (AAR code)
BGE . . . . Baltimore Gas & Electric Company (NYSE symbol)
BJC . . . . Baltimore Junior College (Maryland)
B & O RR . . . . Baltimore & Ohio Railroad
BOCT . . . . . . Baltimore & Ohio Chicago Terminal R. R. (AAR code)
B & OCT . . . . Baltimore and Ohio Chicago Terminal Railroad Company
B & O . . . . . . Baltimore and Ohio Railroad Company

BO . . . . Baltimore & Ohio R. R. Company (NYSE symbol)
BSP . . . . Baltimore Steam Packet Company (AAR code)
BDD . . . . Balzac Deflection Door
BPR . . . . Banana Plug Resistor
BIP . . . . Banco Industrial del Peru (Industrial Bank of Peru)
BNDE . . . . Banco Nacional do Desanvolvimento Economico (National Economic
             Development Bank) (Brazil)
B . . . . Bancus (Bench)
B . . . . Band
BAP . . . . Band Amplitude Product
BEE . . . . Band Edge Energy
BE . . . . Band Elimination
BEF . . . . Band Elimination Filter
BFS . . . . Band Filter Set
BIT . . . . Band Ignitor Tube
BLS . . . . Band Limited Signal
B & O . . . . . . Band and Orchestra (Musical slang)
BPC . . . . Band Pass Crystal
BPCF . . . . Band Pass Crystal Filter
BPN . . . . Band Pass Network
BPT . . . . Band Pass Transformer
BPL . . . . Band Pressure Level
BAND . . . . . . Bandelier National Monument
BP . . . . Bandpass
BCF . . . . Bandpass Crystal Filter
BPF . . . . Bandpass Filter
B . . . . Bandwidth
BW . . . . Bandwidth
BCT . . . . Bandwidth Compression Technique
BWR . . . . Bandwidth Ratio
BNK . . . . Bangor & Aroostook Corporation (NYSE symbol)
B & AR . . . . . Bangor and Aroostook Railroad Company
BAR . . . . Bangor & Aroostook R. R. (AAR code)
BAI . . . . Bank Administration Institute (Formerly, National Association for Bank
             Audit, Control and Operation)
BA . . . . Bank Angle
BB . . . . Bank Burglary
BC . . . . Bank for Cooperatives
B/D . . . . Bank Draft
BE . . . . Bank of England
B of E . . . . . Bank of England
BE . . . . Bank Error
BIS . . . . Bank for International Settlements
BL . . . . Bank Larceny
BOG . . . . Bank Officers Guild
BPRMA . . . . . Bank Public Relations and Marketing Association
BR . . . . Bank Rate
BR . . . . Bank Robbery
BR . . . . Bank Roll (Slang)
BSOAL . . . . . Bank-Share Owners Advisory League
BSA . . . . Bank Stationers Association
BUS . . . . Bank of the United States
BWTF . . . . . . Bank Wire Transfer of Funds
BAFT . . . . . . Bankers Association for Foreign Trade
B & C . . . . . . Banking and Currency Committee (US Senate)
BN . . . . Banknote
Q . . . . Bankruptcy or Receivership (Designation used with NYSE symbols)
BBA . . . . Banque Belge d'Afrique (Belgian African Bank)
BEI . . . . Banque Europeenne d'Investissement
BF . . . . Banque de France (Bank of France)
BIRD . . . . . . Banque Internationale pour la Reconstruction et le Developpement
BNB . . . . Banque Nationale de Belgique (National Bank of Belgium)
BNCI . . . . . . Banque Nationale pour le Commerce et l'Industrie (National Bank for
             Commerce and Industry)
BRI . . . . Banque des Reglements Internationaux
B . . . . Baptist
BBFI . . . . Baptist Bible Fellowship International
BJCPA . . . . . . Baptist Joint Committee on Public Affairs
BLA . . . . Baptist Life Association
BMM . . . . Baptist Mid-Missions
BPF . . . . Baptist Peace Fellowship
BPRA . . . . . . Baptist Public Relations Association
BWA . . . . Baptist World Alliance
BYPU . . . . . . Baptist Young People's Union
B . . . . Bar
BCSH . . . . . . Barat College of the Sacred Heart (Illinois)
BATROP . . . . . Baratropic
BOMEX . . . . . Barbados Oceanographic and Meteorological Experiment
BBI . . . . Barbecue Briquet Institute
BBO . . . . Barber Oil Corporation (NYSE symbol)
BRJ . . . . Barco Rotary Joint

BCS . . . . Bardeen-Cooper-Schrieffer (Theory)
BAW . . . . Bare Aluminum Wire
BBCW . . . . . . Bare Beryllium Copper Wire
BBW . . . . Bare Brass Wire
BC . . . . Bare Copper
BCCW . . . . . . Bare Copper Clad Wire
BCW . . . . Bare Copper Wire
BGPW . . . . . . Bare Gold Plated Wire
BMW . . . . Bare Molybdenum Wire
BNCW . . . . . . Bare Nickel Chrome Wire
BPBW . . . . . . Bare Phosphor Bronze Wire
BPW . . . . Bare Platinum Wire
BREN . . . . . . Bare Reactor Experiment at Nevada
B . . . . Barge
BARC . . . . . . Barge, Amphibious, Resupply, Cargo
BDU . . . . Bargraph Display Unit
Ba . . . . Barium (Chemical element)
BFM . . . . Barium Ferrite Magnet
BCF . . . . Barium Oxide Ferrite
BKO . . . . Barkhausen-Kurz Oscillator
BARSTUR . . . . Barking Sands Tactical Underwater Range (Naval Oceanographic Office)
BMI . . . . Barley and Malt Institute
BYDV . . . . . . Barley Yellow Dwarf Virus
B . . . . Barn (Nuclear cross-section)
BCCFSUA . . . . Barn Cleaner, Cattle Feeder and Silo Unloader Association
BEA . . . . Barn Equipment Association
B-G-R . . . . . . Barnes-Gibson-Raymond Division, Associated Spring Corporation
BACLIN . . . . . Baroclinic
BAC . . . . Barometric Altitude Control
B . . . . Barometric pressure correction
B . . . . Baron
B & Q . . . . . . Barracks and Quarters (Army)
APL . . . . Barracks Ship (Nonself-propelled) (Navy symbol)
BRGBLN . . . . Barrage Balloon
ZK . . . . Barrage Balloon (Navy symbol)
BJ . . . . Barrage Jammers (RADAR)
BGA . . . . Barre Granite Association
BC . . . . Barrel Coating
BTR . . . . Barrel-Tile Roof (Technical drawings)
BPCD . . . . . . Barrels Per Calendar Day (Petroleum)
B/D . . . . Barrels Per Day
BPD . . . . Barrels Per Day
BPH . . . . Barrels Per Hour
BPSD . . . . . . Barrels Per Stream Day (Petroleum)
BARCAP . . . . Barrier Combat Air Patrol (Navy)
BFR . . . . Barrier Film Rectifier
BLC . . . . Barrier Layer Cell
BLR . . . . Barrier Layer Rectifier
BPMA . . . . . . Barrier Paper Manufacturers Association
BUISYS . . . . . Barrier Up Indicator System
BCI . . . . Barro Colorado Island (Canal Zone) (Site of Smithsonian Tropical
             Research Institute)
BARZREX . . . . Bartok Archives Z-Symbol Rhythm Extraction (Data processing)
BBT . . . . Basal Body Temperature (Physiology)
BCH . . . . Basal Cell Hyperplasia (Medicine)
BF . . . . Basal Fold
BGR . . . . Basal Granule
BG . . . . Basal Groove
BHR . . . . Basal Heart Rate
BMR . . . . Basal Metabolic Rate
BM . . . . Basal Metabolism
BMR . . . . Basal Metabolism Reading (Medicine)
B . . . . Base
BASO . . . . . . Base Accountable Supply Officer (Air Force)
BAFO . . . . . . Base Accounting and Finance Office (Air Force)
BAN . . . . Base Activation Notice
BADGE . . . . . Base Air Defense Ground Environment (Air Force)
BADA . . . . . . Base Air Depot Area (Air Force)
BA . . . . Base Assembly
BAL . . . . Base Authorization List
BCE . . . . Base Civil Engineer (Military)
BC . . . . Base Collector
BCCO . . . . . . Base Consolidation Control Office
BCDD . . . . . . Base Construction Depot Detachment (Navy)
BDPI . . . . . . Base Data Processing Installation
BDS . . . . Base Data System
BD . . . . Base Detonating
BDF . . . . Base Detonating Fuze
BDSD . . . . . . Base Detonating, Self-Destroying
BD . . . . Base Diameter
BDL . . . . Base of Dorsal Lip

BE . . . . Base Ejection
BEAMS . . . . . . Base Engineer Automated Management System
BEEF . . . . Base Engineer Emergency Force (Air Force)
BRASS . . . . BEEF (Base Engineer Emergency Forces) Reporting, Analysis, and Status System (Air Force)
BEC . . . . Base Equipment Container
BEMO . . . . Base Equipment Management Office (Air Force)
BEC . . . . Base Examination Course
BX . . . . Base Exchange
BEC . . . . Base Extension Course
BFMDS . . . . . . Base Flight Management Data System
BASEFOR . . . . . Base Force
BFSO . . . . Base Fuel Supply Officer
BF . . . . Base Funded
BF . . . . Base Fuze
BHA . . . . Base Helix Angle (NASA)
BH . . . . Base Hospital (Military)
BI . . . . Base Ignition
B & I . . . . Base and Increment (Technical drawings)
BIAR . . . . Base Installation Action Requirements
BLL . . . . Base of Lateral Lip
BLADE . . . . . . Base Level Automation of Data through Electronics
BL . . . . Base Line (Technical drawings)
BLCE . . . . Base Line Calibration Equipment
BLA . . . . Base Loaded Antenna
BALOG . . . . . Base Logistical Command
BMDS . . . . Base Mail Distribution Scheme (Air Force)
BMD . . . . Base Maintenance Division
BMOM . . . . . . Base Maintenance and Operations Model
BMN . . . . Base Manager's Notice
BMSO . . . . Base Medical Supply Office(r) (Air Force)
BMV . . . . Base Mount Valve
BOS . . . . Base Operating Support
BASOPS . . . . . Base Operations Office
BO . . . . Base Order
BOVC . . . . Base of Overcast (Meteorology)
BOF . . . . Base Oxygen Furnace (Steelmaking)
BP . . . . Base Percussion
BPSS . . . . Base Perimeter Security System
BPB . . . . Base Planning Board
BAPE . . . . Base Plate
BP . . . . Base Plate (Technical drawings)
BP . . . . Base Point
BPT . . . . Base Point
BPO . . . . Base Post Office
BPS . . . . Base Postal Section (Air Force)
BPMEL . . . . . . Base Precision Measurement Equipment Laboratory
BP . . . . Base Procured
BP/CP . . . . . . Base Procured/Central Procured
BPO . . . . Base Procurement Office (Air Force)
BPSS . . . . Base Procurement Service Stores (Air Force)
BQM . . . . Base Quartermaster (Marine Corps)
BRC . . . . Base Residence Course
BRT . . . . Base Resistance Transistor
BASEC . . . . . . Base Section
BSC . . . . Base Security Council (Air Force)
BSERBN . . . . . . Base Service Battalion (Marine Corps)
BASESERVUNIT . . Base Service Unit
BSU . . . . Base Service Unit (Navy)
BSAL . . . . Base Spares Allowance List
BSG . . . . Base Spares Group
BSMO . . . . Base Supply Management Office (Air Force)
BSO . . . . Base Supply Officer (Navy)
BSE . . . . Base Support Equipment (Military)
BSGP . . . . . . Base Support Group (Air Force)
BSGS . . . . Base Support Group System (Air Force)
BU . . . . Base Unit (Air Force)
BVRO . . . . . . Base Vehicle Reporting Officer
BWTSDS . . . . . Base Wire and Telephone System Development Schedule (Air Force)
BAU . . . . Baseband Assembly Unit
BGM . . . . Basegram (Navy)
BCA . . . . Basenji Club of America
BB . . . . Bases on Balls (Baseball)
BPSH . . . . Bashkimet Profesionale te Shqiperise (Union of Albanian Trade Unions)
BASD . . . . Basic Active Service Date
BAH . . . . Basic Adaptive Hardware
Bas Adv Tra . . . Basic Advance Training
BAINS . . . . . . Basic Advanced Integrated Navigation System
BA . . . . Basic Agreement
BAS . . . . Basic Airspeed (Flying)
BAQ . . . . Basic Allowance for Quarters

BAS . . . . Basic Allowance for Subsistence
BAS . . . . Basic Angle System
BASIC . . . . Basic Appraisal System for Incoming Components
BAFCOM . . . . Basic Armed Forces Communication Plan
BASE . . . . Basic Army Strategic Estimate (A document)
BAP . . . . Basic Assembler Program
BAL . . . . Basic Assembly Language (Data processing)
BACE . . . . Basic Automatic Checkout Equipment
BBB . . . . Basic Boxed Base
BCT . . . . Basic Combat Training
BCS . . . . Basic Contract Specification
BCF . . . . Basic Control Frequency
BD . . . . Basic Democrats (Pakistan)
BDAM . . . . . . Basic Direct Access Method (Data processing)
BEL . . . . Basic Equipment List
BFM . . . . Basic Field Manual (Military)
BHS . . . . Basic Hole System
BAI . . . . Basic Incorporated (NYSE symbol)
BISAM . . . . . . Basic Indexed Sequential Access Method (Data processing)
BIM . . . . Basic Industrial Materials (Program) (Navy)
BI . . . . Basic Infantry
BIL . . . . Basic Insulation Level
BIIL . . . . Basic Issue Item List (Army)
BILI . . . . Basic Issue List Items (Army)
BJA . . . . Basic Journal Abstracts (A publication of American Chemical Society)
BLI . . . . Basic Learning Institute
BALANCE . . . . Basic and Logically Applied Norms - Civil Engineering
BMS . . . . Basic Meteorological Services
BMR . . . . Basic Military Requirement
BMT . . . . Basic Military Training
BMTS . . . . Basic Military Training School
BMT . . . . Basic Motion-Time Study
BNEP . . . . Basic Naval Establishment Plan
BNU . . . . Basic Notch Unit
BOS . . . . Basic Oblate Spheroid
BOLT . . . . Basic Occupational Language Training
BOS . . . . Basic Operating System
BOP . . . . Basic Operation Plan (Army)
BOTU(FW) . . . . Basic Operational Training Unit (Fixed Wing)
BOTU(RW) . . . . Basic Operational Training Unit (Rotary Wing)
BOA . . . . Basic Ordering Agreement
BASICPAC . . . . Basic Package Computer (Army)
BP . . . . Basic Pay
BPED . . . . Basic Pay Entry Date
BPD . . . . Basic Planning Document (Military)
BPU . . . . Basic Pole Unit
BASICPAC . . . . BASIC Processor and Computer
BPD . . . . Basic Products Corporation (NYSE symbol)
BRER . . . . Basic Radiation Effects Reactor (AEC)
BR . . . . Basic Research
BRD . . . . Basic Retirement Date (Air Force)
BS . . . . Basic Sediment (Petroleum)
BS & W . . . . . Basic Sediment and Water (In crude oil)
BTCA . . . . Basic Tables of Commissioning Allowances (Navy)
BTB . . . . Basic Test Battery (Navy)
BT . . . . Basic Trainer (Air Force)
BTC . . . . Basic Training Center (Military)
BTS . . . . Basic Training School
BUT . . . . Basic Unit Training
BWP . . . . Basic War Plan (Navy)
BS . . . . Basilian Salvatorian Fathers (Roman Catholic religious order)
BOI . . . . Basis of Issue (Army)
BFUSA . . . . . . Basketball Federation of the United States of America
BNA . . . . Basle (Basel) Nomina Anatomica (Basel Anatomical Nomonclature) (Medicine)
B . . . . Bass or Basso (Music)
BC . . . . Bass Clarinet
BHCA . . . . . . Bassett Hound Club of America
BCP . . . . Basutoland Congress Party
BCTU . . . . . . Basutoland Congress of Trade Unions
B . . . . Bat
BF . . . . Batch Fabrication
BFT . . . . Batch Fabrication Technique
B . . . . Bath
BH . . . . Bath & Hammondsport R. R. (AAR code)
BIW . . . . Bath Iron Works Corporation (NYSE symbol)
BC . . . . Bathy-Conductograph
BNE . . . . Bathymetric Navigation Equipment
BOP . . . . Bathyscaphe Oceanographic Program
BT . . . . Bathythermograph
BAT . . . . Battalion Antitank Rifle (Military)

BBH . . . . Battalion Beachhead (Army)
BCT . . . . Battalion Combat Team
BFDC . . . . . . Battalion Fire Distribution Center
BGSS . . . . . . Battalion Ground Surveillance Section (Army)
BNHQ . . . . . . Battalion Headquarters (Marine Corps)
BLT . . . . Battalion Landing Team
BMDCP . . . . . Battalion Mortar and Davy Crockett Platoon (Army)
BSM . . . . Battalion Sergeant-Major (Army)
BNSFCP . . . . . Battalion Shore Fire Control Party
BDIAC . . . . . . Battelle-Defender Information Analysis Center (Battelle Memorial Institute)
BMI . . . . Battelle Memorial Institute
BRR . . . . Battelle Research Reactor (AEC)
BBD & O . . . . Batten, Barton, Durstine and Osborn (Advertising agency)
B . . . . Battery
BAR . . . . Battery Acquisition RADAR
BA . . . . Battery Adjust
BBC . . . . Battery Booster Cable
BC . . . . Battery Chargers (Military)
BCP . . . . Battery Command Post
BC . . . . Battery Commander (Army)
BCI . . . . Battery Condition Indicator
BCA . . . . Battery Control Area
BCC . . . . Battery Control Central (Army)
BCO . . . . Battery Control Officer (Army)
BDL . . . . Battery Data Link (Air Force)
BDLS . . . . . . Battery Data Link System (Air Force)
BDU . . . . Battery Display Unit (Army)
BEOC . . . . . . Battery Echelon Operating Control
BIRDIE . . . . . . Battery Integration and RADAR Display Equipment (Air defense system)
BOC . . . . Battery Operations Center (Air Force)
BP . . . . Battery Package
BPR . . . . Battery Powered Recorder
BSM . . . . Battery Sergeant-Major
BTE . . . . Battery Terminal Equipment
B . . . . Battle
BACU . . . . . . Battle Area Control Unit (Military)
BASIC . . . . . . Battle Area Surveillance and Integrated Communications System (Marine Corps)
BCD . . . . Battle Correlator Display
BC . . . . Battle Cruiser
BCS . . . . Battle Cruiser Squadron
BDA . . . . Battle Damage Assessment
ARB . . . . Battle Damage Repair Ship (Navy symbol)
BD . . . . Battle Dress (Military)
BATFOR . . . . . Battle Force
BG . . . . Battle Group
BGLT . . . . . . Battle Group Landing Team
BS . . . . Battle Squadron (Navy)
BS . . . . Battle Star (Military)
BI . . . . Battlefield Illumination (Army)
BIAS . . . . Battlefield Illumination Airborne System
BIW . . . . Battle Injury or Wound
BATSHIP . . . . Battleship
BB . . . . Battleship (Navy symbol)
BATDIV . . . . . Battleship Division
VO . . . . Battleship Observation Squadron (Navy symbol)
BATRON . . . . Battleship Squadron
BS . . . . Battleship Squadron
BATLANT . . . . Battleships, Atlantic Fleet
BATSHIPSLANT . . Battleships, Atlantic Fleet
BATSHIPSBATFORPAC . . Battleships, Battle Force, Pacific Fleet
BATCRULANT . . Battleships and Cruisers, Atlantic Fleet
BATCRUPAC . . . Battleships and Cruisers, Pacific Fleet
BATPAC . . . . . Battleships, Pacific Fleet
BATSHIPSPAC . . Battleships, Pacific Fleet
BK . . . . Bauernkorrespondent
B . . . . Baume
BOL . . . . Bausch & Lomb, Inc. (NYSE symbol)
BN . . . . Bauxite & Northern Railway Company (AAR code)
BMWCCA . . . . BMW (Bavarian Motor Works) Car Club of America
BBP . . . . Bavarian Border Police (Germany)
BAX . . . . Baxter Laboratories, Inc. (NYSE symbol)
B . . . . Bay (Maps and charts)
BAATC . . . . . Bay Area Army Terminal Center
BART . . . . . . Bay Area Rapid Transit (San Francisco area, California)
BARTD . . . . . Bay Area Rapid Transit District (San Francisco, California)
BCU . . . . Bay Cabinet Unit
BCJC . . . . . . Bay City Junior College (Michigan)
BCDC . . . . . . Bay Conservation and Development Commission (San Francisco)
BPJC . . . . . . Bay Path Junior College (Massachusetts)

BOC . . . . Bayes Operating Characteristic
BAYCANDDC . . Bayonet Candelabra Double Contact
B . . . . Bayou (Maps and charts)
BMW . . . . . . Bayrische Motoren Werke (German automobile manufacturer; initialism used as name of its cars)
BYK . . . . Bayuk Cigars, Inc. (NYSE symbol)
BB . . . . B and Better (Lumber)
BOLO . . . . . . Be On the Lookout For
BA . . . . Beach Abort
BARV . . . . . . Beach Armored Recovery Vehicle
BDL . . . . Beach Discharge Lighter
BEB . . . . Beach Erosion Board (Army)
BG . . . . Beach Group
BJU . . . . Beach Jumper Unit
BMO . . . . Beach Modulator Oscillator
BP . . . . Beach Party
BMU . . . . Beachmaster Unit (Army)
B . . . . Beacon (Aviation)
BAE . . . . Beacon Antenna Equipment
BE-A . . . . Beacon Explorer A (Satellite)
BE-B . . . . Beacon Explorer B (Satellite)
BPS . . . . Beacon Processing System
BRP . . . . Beacon Ranging Pulse
BUPS . . . . . . Beacon, Ultra Portable "S" Band (Navy)
BSIA . . . . Bead and Stone Importers Association
B1S . . . . Beaded One Side (Lumber)
B2S . . . . Beaded Two Sides (Lumber)
BDDI . . . . . . Beading Die
B . . . . Beak
BL . . . . Beak Line
BABS . . . . . . Beam Approach Beacon System (Aviation)
BCP . . . . Beam Candle Power
BCPS . . . . . . Beam Candle Power Seconds
BC . . . . Beam Collimator
BCS . . . . Beam Communications Set
BCC . . . . Beam Coupling Coefficient
BDT . . . . Beam Deflection Tube
BD . . . . Beam Degrader
BJD . . . . Beam (James B.) Distilling Company (NYSE symbol)
BF . . . . Beam Forming
BFE . . . . Beam-Forming Electrode
BOLT . . . . . . Beam of Light Transistor
BM . . . . Beam Monitor
BPA . . . . Beam Plasma Amplification
BPM . . . . Beam Positioning Magnet
BRA . . . . Beam Ride Actuator
BT . . . . Beam Rider - Terrier
BS . . . . Beam Stop
BST . . . . Beam-Switching Tube
B & S . . . . . . Beams and Stringers (Technical drawings)
B . . . . Bearing (angle)
BDI . . . . Bearing Deviation Indicator (Aerospace)
BDH . . . . Bearing, Distance, and Heading
BDHI . . . . . . Bearing, Distance, Heading Indicator
BMC . . . . Bearing Mounted Clutch
BPGC . . . . . . Bearing Per Gyro Compass (Navigation)
BPSC . . . . . . Bearing Per Standard Compass (Navigation)
BPSTGC . . . . . Bearing Per Steering Gyro Compass
BRI . . . . Bearing Range Indicator
BSA . . . . Bearing Specialists Association
BF . . . . Beat-Frequency
BFO . . . . Beat Frequency Oscillator
BO . . . . Beat Oscillator
BM . . . . Beata Maria (The Blessed Virgin)
BMV . . . . Beata Maria Virgo (Blessed Mary the Virgin)
BV . . . . Beata Virgo (Blessed Virgin)
BVM . . . . Beata Virgo Maria (Blessed Virgin Mary)
BM . . . . Beatae Memoriae (Of Blessed Memory)
BP . . . . Beatissime Pater (Most Holy Father)
BV . . . . Beatitudo Vestra (Your Holiness)
BRY . . . . Beatrice Foods Company (NYSE symbol)
BEM . . . . Beaufort & Morehead R. R. (AAR code)
BSL & W . . . . Beaumont, Sour Lake & Western Railway Company
BEM . . . . Beaunit Corporation (NYSE symbol)
BP . . . . Beautiful People (Slang for the wealthy, world-traveling, party-going set)
BBSI . . . . . . Beauty and Barber Supply Institute
BEART . . . . . . Beaver Army Terminal
BME . . . . Beaver, Meade & Englewood R. R. (AAR code)
BDP . . . . Bechuanaland Democratic Party
BPP . . . . Bechuanaland People's Party
BPFP . . . . Bechuanaland Protectorate Federal Party

BEK . . . . Beck (A.S.) Shoe Corporation (American Stock Exchange symbol)
BEC . . . . Beckman Instruments, Inc. (NYSE symbol) (Wall Street slang name: "Becky")
BECKTRAN . . . Beckman Translation (Computer language) (Beckman Instrument, Inc.)
BR . . . . Bedroom Steward (In the first class aboard an ocean liner)
BEDOC . . . . . Beds Occupied
BAPREPT . . . . . Beds and Patients Report
BIA . . . . Bee Industries Association
BKA . . . . Bee Keepers Association
BCX . . . . Beech Aircraft Corporation (NYSE symbol)
BCH . . . . Beech Creek R. R. Co., Gtd. (NYSE symbol)
BEEM . . . . . . Beech Mountain R. R. (AAR code)
BLS . . . . Beech-Nut Life Savers, Inc. (NYSE symbol)
BBU . . . . Beefmaster Breeders Universal
BSDF . . . . . . Beet Sugar Development Foundation
B . . . . Before
B4 . . . . Before
BBC . . . . Before Bottom Center (Valve position)
BBDC . . . . . . Before Bottom Dead Center
BC . . . . Before Christ
BC . . . . Before the Crash (i.e., before the 1929 stock market collapse) (Slang)
BC . . . . Before Croonery (Musical slang)
BIFR . . . . Before Encountering Instrument Flight Rules Conditions
BG . . . . Before Girls (i.e., before women became part of armed forces) (Military)
BM . . . . Before Marriage
BP . . . . Before Present
BPOC . . . . . . Before Proceeding on Course (Aviation)
BQ . . . . Before Queues (Referring to pre-World War II period) (British slang)
BTC . . . . Before Top Center (Valve position)
BSRRO . . . . . Begin Standard RADAR Refuel Orbit (Aviation)
BASIC . . . . . . Beginner's Algebraic Symbolic Interpretive Compiler (Data processing)
BASIC . . . . . . Beginner's All Purpose Symbolic Instruction Code (Data processing)
BOB . . . . Beginning of Business
BC . . . . Beginning Climb (Aviation)
BD . . . . Beginning Descent (Aviation)
BENT . . . . . . Beginning Evening Nautical Twilight
BMCT . . . . . . Beginning Morning Civil Twilight
BMNT . . . . . . Beginning Morning Nautical Twilight (Navigation)
B . . . . Beginning of Precipitation (Meteorology)
BPT . . . . Beginning Procedure Turn (Aviation)
BSHP . . . . . . Beginning Standard Holding Procedure (Aviation)
BSRAP . . . . . . Beginning Standard Range Approach (Aviation)
BSIAP . . . . . . Beginning Straight-In Approach (Aviation)
BMS . . . . Behavior Monitor System
BRAINS . . . . . . Behavior Replication by Analog Instruction of the Nervous System (Data processing)
BD . . . . Behavioral Differential
BEID . . . . Behavioral Effects of Infectious Diseases (Army)
BPS . . . . Behavioral Pharmacology Society
BESRL . . . . . . Behavioral Science Research Laboratory (Army)
BASS . . . . . . Behavioral and Social Sciences
BCD . . . . Behind Completion Date
B/S . . . . Behind Schedule
BDS . . . . Beitrage zur Danziger Statistik (Danzig)
BSRO . . . . . . Beitrage zur Statistik der Republik Osterreich (Austria)
B . . . . Bel (Ten decibels)
BPC . . . . Belco Petroleum Corporation (NYSE symbol)
BHY . . . . Belding Heminway Company, Inc. (NYSE symbol)
BML . . . . Belfast & Moosehead Lake R. R. (AAR code)
B . . . . Belga (Monetary unit in Belgium)
BAEF . . . . . . Belgian American Educational Foundation
BBGA . . . . . . Belgian Begonia Growers Association
BCCUS . . . . . . Belgian Chamber of Commerce in the United States
BDHCA . . . . . . Belgian Draft Horse Corporation of America
BENA . . . . . . Belgian Engineers in North America
BF . . . . Belgian Fourragere
BLA . . . . Belgian Linen Association
BSCA . . . . . . Belgian Sheepdog Club of America
BE . . . . Belgium (NATO)
BLEU . . . . . . Belgium-Luxemburg Economic Union
BENELUX . . . Belgium, Netherlands, Luxemburg (Economic union)
BAC . . . . Bell Aircraft Corporation
B & B . . . . . . Bell and Bell (Technical drawings)
BC . . . . Bell Cord (Technical drawings)
BELCRK . . . . Bell Crank
B & F . . . . . . Bell and Flange (Technical drawings)
BLG . . . . Bell and Gossett Company (NYSE symbol)
BHW . . . . Bell and Howell Company (NYSE symbol)
BLL . . . . Bell Intercontinental Corporation (NYSE symbol)
BLADES . . . . . . Bell Laboratories Automatic Design System
BLADS . . . . . . Bell Laboratories Automatic Design System

BLADE . . . . . . Bell Laboratories Automatic Device
BLIS . . . . Bell Laboratories Interpretive System (Data processing)
BELLREL . . . . Bell Laboratories Library Real-Time Loan System
BLESSED . . . . Bell Little Electrodata Symbolic System for the Electrodata
BLS . . . . Bell Log System
B & S . . . . . . Bell and Spigot (Technical drawings)
BSP . . . . Bell System Practices
BTL . . . . Bell Telephone Laboratories
BFC . . . . Bellefonte Central R. R. (AAR code)
BRD . . . . Bellofram Rolling Diaphragm
BAC . . . . Belmont Abbey College (North Carolina)
BAC . . . . Below All Clouds
BB . . . . Below Bridges (Navigation)
BLD . . . . Below Limit of Detection
BP . . . . Below Proof
BRC . . . . Belt Railway Co. of Chicago (AAR code)
BR of C . . . . . Belt Railway Company of Chicago
BWL . . . . Belt Work Line
BSC . . . . Beltsville Space Center (NASA)
BHLA . . . . . . Ben Hur Life Association
BCC . . . . Benard Convection Cell
BCE . . . . Bench Checkout Equipment
BCOE . . . . . . Bench Checkout Equipment
BM . . . . Bench Mark (In surveying)
BRA . . . . Bench Replaceable Assembly
BD . . . . Bend Down
BDV . . . . Bend-Down Virginia (A picked-up stub of a cigarette)
BR . . . . Bend Radius
BU . . . . Bend Up
BUP . . . . Bend Up (Technical drawings)
BFC . . . . Bending Feedback Control
BAC . . . . Bendix Aviation Corporation
BX . . . . Bendix Corporation (NYSE symbol)
BIDS . . . . Bendix Integrated Data System
BW . . . . Bendix-Westinghouse Automotive Air Brake Company
BMT . . . . Bene Merenti (To the Well-Deserving)
BMF . . . . Bene Merenti Fecit (He Erected This to the Well-Deserving)
BQ . . . . Bene Quiescat (May He or She Rest Well)
BV . . . . Bene Vixit (He Lived a Good Life)
B & B . . . . . . Benedictine and Brandy
BHC . . . . Benedictine Heights College (Oklahoma)
BNL . . . . Beneficial Finance Company (NYSE symbol) (Wall Street slang name: "Big Nose Louie")
BOD . . . . Beneficial Occupancy Date
BGPP . . . . . . Beneficiary Government Production Program
BPOE . . . . . . Benevolent and Protective Order of Elks
BPO-WOW . . . Benevolent Protective Order--Wolves of the World (Limited, not-too-serious order)
BCS . . . . Bengal Civil Service
BNI . . . . Bengal Native Infantry
BSC . . . . Bengal Staff Corps
BE . . . . Benguet Consolidated, Inc. (NYSE symbol)
BFU . . . . Benjamin Franklin University (Washington, DC)
BJC . . . . Bennett Junior College (New York)
BEN . . . . Benrus Watch Company, Inc. (NYSE symbol)
BNU . . . . Benson Needham Univas (International advertising network)
BLPZZ . . . . . . Bent Logarithmically Periodic Zig-Zags
BMM . . . . Benthic Metabolism Measurement
BDC . . . . Bentley Drivers Club
BEOL . . . . . . Bent's Old Fort National Historic Site
BZH . . . . Benzaldehyde
BAC . . . . Benzalkonium Chloride
BHC . . . . Benzene Hexachloride (An insecticide)
BZOH . . . . . . Benzoic Acid
BTDA . . . . Benzophenone Tetracarboxylic Dianhydride
BPO . . . . Benzoyl Peroxide
BD . . . . Benzoylated
BND . . . . Benzoylated-Naphthoylated
BAP . . . . Benzyl-para-aminophenol
BEG . . . . Berghoff Brewing Corporation (NYSE symbol)
BERSEAPAT . . . Bering Sea Patrol (Navy)
B . . . . Bering Standard Time (Aviation)
Bk . . . . Berkelium (Chemical element)
BASC . . . . . . Berlin Air Safety Center
BAD . . . . Berlin Airlift Device
BC . . . . Berlin Command (Allied German Occupation Forces)
BERCOMB . . . . Berlin Commission British (Post-World War II)
BCZ . . . . Berlin Control Zone (Allied German Occupation Forces)
BD . . . . Berlin District (Allied German Occupation Forces)
BDC . . . . Berlin Document Center (Allied German Occupation Forces)
BK . . . . Berlin Kommandatura

BMS . . . . Berlin Mills R. R. (AAR code)
BS . . . . Berlin Sector (Allied German Occupation Forces)
BHZ . . . . Berliner Handelszentrale
BVG . . . . Berliner Verkehrs-Gesellschaft
BMA . . . . Berman Leasing Company (NYSE symbol)
BBA . . . . Bermuda Benevolent Association
BI . . . . Bermuda Islands
BB . . . . Bernard Berenson (American art critic, 1865-1959)
BD . . . . Bernoulli Disk
BT . . . . Berth Terms
Be . . . . Beryllium (Chemical element)
BeO . . . . Beryllium Oxide
BORE . . . . . . Beryllium Oxide Reactor Experiment (Formerly, EBOR) (AEC)
BOW . . . . . . Beryllium Oxide Washer
B & LE . . . . . Bessemer and Lake Erie Railroad Company
BLE . . . . Bessemer & Lake Erie R. R. (AAR code)
BAN . . . . Best Asymptotically Normal (Estimates) (Econometrics)
BATH . . . . . . Best Available True Heading
BBB . . . . Best Berlin Broadcast (Radio program broadcast from Berlin by Robert H. Best, former South Carolina journalist) (World War II)
BST . . . . Best & Company, Inc. (NYSE symbol)
BCA . . . . Best Cruise Altitude
BDL . . . . Best Dressed List
BET . . . . Best-Estimate Trajectory (Apollo) (NASA)
BEB . . . . Best Ever Bottled (Wines and spirits)
BFX . . . . Best Foods, Inc. (American Stock Exchange symbol)
BIG . . . . Best in Group
BLUE . . . . . . Best Linear Unbiased Estimator (Statistics)
BIM . . . . Best in Match
BPE . . . . Best Preliminary Estimate
BIS . . . . Best in Show
BWG . . . . . . Bestwall Gypsum Company (NYSE symbol)
BAG . . . . Beta Absorption Gauge
BDE . . . . Beta Disintegration Energy
BGS . . . . Beta Gamma Sigma
BPL . . . . Beta-Propiolactone (Chemical)
BNC . . . . Bethany Nazarene College (Oklahoma)
BSCO . . . . . . Bethlehem Steel Co. (Form preferred by the company)
BS . . . . Bethlehem Steel Corporation (NYSE symbol) (Wall Street slang name: "Bessie")
BCC . . . . Bethune-Cookman College (Florida)
BKV . . . . Betriebskollektivvertrag
BMF . . . . Betriebsmittelfonds
BPO . . . . Betriebsparteiorganisation
BSG . . . . Betriebssportgemeinschaft
BBB . . . . Better Business Bureau
BEST . . . . . . Better Electronic Service Technicians
BHC . . . . Better Heating-Cooling Council
BHIF . . . . Better Highways Information Foundation (Defunct)
BKI . . . . Better Kitchens Institute
BLTI . . . . . . Better Lawn and Turf Institute
BLBSB . . . . . . Better Light Better Sight Bureau
BOLTOP . . . . Better on Lips Than on Paper (Put at the end of a letter with kisses) (British)
BOAT . . . . . . Better Occupational Awareness Training
BPAC . . . . . . Better Packaging Advisory Council
BPCC . . . . . . Better Postcard Collectors' Club
BVI . . . . Better Vision Institute
BOOST . . . . . Bettering Oregon's Opportunity for Saving Talent (Educational project)
BAPL . . . . . . Bettis Atomic Power Laboratory (AEC)
BOSS . . . . . . Bett's Open Shop System
BC . . . . Between Centers (Technical drawings)
BTL . . . . Between Layers (Aviation)
BP . . . . Between Perpendiculars (Technical drawings)
BWS . . . . Beveled Wood Siding (Technical drawings)
BMMA . . . . . . Beverage Machinery Manufacturers Association
BRC . . . . Beveren Rabbit Club
BVS . . . . Bevier & Southern R. R. (AAR code)
BOC . . . . Bevitron Orbit Code
BDVP . . . . . . Bezirksbehoerde der Deutschen Volkspolizei
BG . . . . Bezirksgericht
BPKK . . . . . . Bezirksparteikontrollkommission
BBWR . . . . . . Bezpartyjny Blok Wspolpracy z Rzadem (Nonpartisan Bloc of Cooperation with the Government) (Poland)
BRSF . . . . . . Biafra Relief Services Foundation
BIC . . . . Bibas In Christo (May You Live in Christ)
B . . . . Bible
BILA . . . . . . Bible Institute of Los Angeles
BML . . . . Bible Meditation League
BMA . . . . Bible Memory Association, International
BPM . . . . Bible Protestant Missions

BSA . . . . . . Bible Sabbath Association
BV . . . . Bible Version (As opposed to the Prayer Book version of the Psalms)
BC . . . . Bibliographic Classification (System of library classification devised by Henry Evelyn Bliss)
BIDAP . . . . . . Bibliographic Data Processing Program (for Keyword Indexing)
BOLD . . . . . . Bibliographic On-Line Library Display (Data processing)
BSS . . . . Bibliographical Services Section (of a library)
BSA . . . . . . Bibliographical Society of America
BIGENA . . . . . Bibliography and Index of Geology Exclusive of North America (American Geological Institute)
BONIS . . . . . . Bibliography of Old Norse-Icelandic Studies
BSS . . . . . . Bibliography of Soil Science (An abstracts journal)
BCG . . . . Bicolor Guaiac (Test)
BFCA . . . . . . Bichon Frise Club of America
BIK . . . . Bickford's, Inc. (American Stock Exchange symbol)
B . . . . Bicuspid (Dentistry)
BIA . . . . Bicycle Institute of America
BMA . . . . Bicycle Manufacturers Association
BTC . . . . Bicycle Touring Club (British)
BWDA . . . . . . Bicycle Wholesale Distributors Association
B . . . . Bid or Buyer (NYSE symbol)
BAWHA . . . . . Bide-A-Wee Home Association
BCG . . . . Bidirectional Categorical Grammar
BCS . . . . Bidirectional Category System
BAFVC . . . . . . Bids Accepted for the Following Vacancies
BSAF . . . . . . Bids Solicited As Follows
BE . . . . Biennial
BIB . . . . Biennale of Illustrations Bratislava
BENREP . . . . . BIG BEN Report (WW II)
BIBE . . . . Big Bend National Park
BBA . . . . Big Brothers of America
BBL . . . . Big Brothers League
BDB . . . . Big Dumb Booster
BFD . . . . Big Fine Deal
BIHO . . . . Big Hole National Battlefield
BMOC . . . . . . Big Machine on Campus (Computer)
BMOC . . . . . . Big Man on Campus (Slang)
BTO . . . . Big-Time Operator (Slang)
BWOC . . . . . . Big Woman on Campus (Slang)
BGS . . . . Bigelow-Sanford, Inc. (NYSE symbol)
BICA . . . . . . Bighorn Canyon National Recreation Area
BPD . . . . Bikini Photo Drone
BITN . . . . . . Bilateral Iterative Network
BZ . . . . Bild Zeitung (Picture newspaper) (Germany)
BB . . . . Bill Book (Shipping)
B/E . . . . Bill of Entry (Business and trade)
BE . . . . Bill of Exchange
B/E . . . . Bill of Exchange (Business and trade)
BL . . . . Bill of Lading
B/L . . . . Bill of Lading
BLADING . . . . Bill of lading (Military)
B/M . . . . Bill of Material
BP . . . . Bill of Parcels
BP . . . . Bill(s) Payable
BR . . . . Bill of Rights
BS . . . . Bill of Sale
B/S . . . . Bill of Sale
BS . . . . Bill of Sight
BS . . . . Bill of Store
BSC . . . . Billet Sequence Code
BAA . . . . Billeting & Accommodations Advisory (Military communications)
B & I . . . . . . Billeting and Inventory (Military)
BBIA . . . . . . Billiard and Bowling Institute of America
BCA . . . . Billiard Congress of America
BPA . . . . Billiard Players Association of America
BEV . . . . Billion Electron Volts
BGD . . . . Billion Gallons per Day
BY . . . . Billion Years
B/D . . . . Bills Discounted
BLA . . . . Bills of Lading Act
BOM . . . . . . Bills of Materials
BR . . . . Bills Receivable
BI-M . . . . . . Bimonthly
BM . . . . Bimonthly
BMPR . . . . . . Bimonthly Progress Report
BPR . . . . Bimonthly Progress Report
BA . . . . Binary Add
BAC . . . . Binary Asymmetric Channel
BADC . . . . . . Binary Asymmetric Dependent Channel
BAIC . . . . . . Binary Asymmetric Independent Channel
BINAC . . . . . . Binary Automatic Computer

BADAS . . . . . . Binary Automatic Data Annotation System
BC . . . . Binary Code
BCB . . . . Binary Code Box
BCFSK . . . . . . Binary Code Frequency Shift Keying (SAGE)
BCD . . . . Binary Coded Decimal (Data processing)
BCDC . . . . Binary Coded Decimal Counter
BCH . . . . Binary Coded Hollerith
BCI . . . . Binary-Coded Information
BCO . . . . Binary-Coded Octal (SAGE)
BCIS . . . . Binary Constitution Information Service
BC . . . . Binary Counter
B/D . . . . Binary to Decimal (Data processing)
BDC . . . . Binary Decimal Counter (Data processing)
BDD . . . . Binary to Decimal Decoder (Data processing)
BDT . . . . Binary Deck to Tape (Data processing)
BDS . . . . Binary Decode Scaler
BD . . . . Binary Decoder (Data processing)
BDM . . . . Binary Delta Modulation
BIT . . . . Binary Digit (Data processing)
BDD . . . . Binary Digital Data (Data processing)
BDD . . . . Binary-to-Digital Decoder (Data processing)
BD . . . . Binary Divide
BESS . . . . . . Binary Electromagnetic Signal Signature
BHD . . . . Binary Homing Device
BIX . . . . Binary Information Exchange
BMC . . . . Binary Magnetic Core
BM . . . . Binary Multiply
BN . . . . Binary Number
BOM . . . . Binary Order of Magnitude (Data processing)
BOP . . . . Binary Output Program
BIPAD . . . . . . Binary Pattern Detector
BSDC . . . . . . Binary Symmetric Dependent Channel
BSC . . . . Binary Synchronous Communication (Data processing)
BIE . . . . Binaural Intensity Effect
BPE . . . . Binaural Phase Effect
BOC . . . . Bingham Oceanographic Collection
BIN . . . . Binks Manufacturing Company (NYSE symbol)
BOSS . . . . . . Bio-astronautic Orbiting Space Station
BOD . . . . Biochemical Oxygen Demand (NASA)
BIC . . . . Biodetermination Information Centre (British)
BDFGA . . . . . Bio-Dynamic Farming and Gardening Association
BEC . . . . Bio-Electro-Chemistry
BIAC . . . . . . Bioinstrumentation Advisory Council
BISS . . . . Bio-Isolator Suit System
BA . . . . Biological Abstracts (A publication)
BASIC . . . . . . Biological Abstracts' Subjects in Context (Documentation)
BADIC . . . . . . Biological Analysis Detection Instrumentation & Control
BAL . . . . Biological Assessment Laboratory
BCWD . . . . . . Biological and Chemical Warfare Division (DOD)
BDI . . . . Biological Damage Indicator
BIODEF . . . . . Biological Defense
BIOLDEF . . . . . Biological Defense (Military)
BDS . . . . Biological Defense System
BDS . . . . Biological Detection System
BEAR . . . . . . Biological Effects of Atomic Radiation
BFP . . . . Biological False Positive
BIO . . . . Biological Information-Processing Organization
BIOS . . . . . . Biological Investigation of Outer Space (NASA)
BIG . . . . Biological Isolation Garment (NASA)
BL . . . . Biological Laboratory
BLBG . . . . . . Biological Laboratory, Brunswick, Georgia (US Bureau of Commercial
Fisheries)
BIOLOP . . . . . Biological Operations (Military)
BOSS . . . . . . Biological Orbiting Space Station (Air Force)
BOD . . . . Biological Oxygen Demand (Water pollution)
BPA . . . . Biological Photographic Association
BRC . . . . Biological Radio Communications
BRI . . . . Biological Research Institute
BIORED . . . . . Biological Resources Development Teams
BIOS . . . . . . Biological Satellite (NASA)
BSCP . . . . . . Biological Sciences Communication Project (American Institute of
Biological Sciences)
BSCS . . . . . . Biological Sciences Curriculum Study
BIOSIS . . . . . . Biological Sciences Information Service (of Biological Abstracts)
BSC . . . . Biological Stain Commission
BIOWAR . . . . Biological Warfare
BW . . . . Biological Warfare
BIOLWPN . . . . Biological Weapons (Military)
BAT . . . . Biomedical Application Teams (NASA)
BME . . . . Bio-Medical Electronics
BIC . . . . Biomedical Instrumentation Consultant

BMS . . . . Biomedical Monitoring System
BSC . . . . Biomedical Sciences Corps (Air Force)
BS . . . . Biometric Society
BAN . . . . Bionics Adaptive Network
BPS . . . . Biophysical Society
BS . . . . Biophysical Society
BSIE . . . . Bio-Sciences Information Exchange (Smithsonian Institution)
BII . . . . Biosophical Institute, Incorporated
BHR . . . . Biotechnology & Human Research
BP . . . . Biotic Potential
BIPD . . . . Biparting Door
BIB . . . . Bipartite Board (Post-World War II, Germany)
BCAP . . . . . . Bipartite Civil Aviation Panel
BICIV . . . . . . Bipartite Civil Service Advisors (Post-World War II, Germany)
BICOM . . . . . . Bipartite Communications Panel (Post-World War II, Germany)
BICO . . . . . . Bipartite Control Office (Post-World War II, Germany)
BIDEC . . . . . . Bipartite Decartelization Commission (Berlin) (Post-World War II, Germany)
BIDESC . . . . . . Bipartite Decartelization Sub-Commission (Minden) (Post-World War II,
Germany)
BIGECO . . . . . Bipartite Economic Control Group (Post-World War II, Germany)
BIECO . . . . . . Bipartite Economic Panel (Post-World War II, Germany)
BIECO/RAIL . . . Bipartite Economic Panel Railway Supplies Committee (Post-World War II,
Germany)
BECG . . . . . . Bipartite Economics Control Group (Post-World War II, Germany)
BIFIN . . . . . . Bipartite Finance Panel (Post-World War II, Germany)
BIF & A . . . . . Bipartite Food and Agriculture Panel (Post-World War II, Germany)
BNO . . . . Bipartite News Office (Post-World War II, Germany)
BISEC . . . . . . Bipartite Secretariat (Post-World War II, Germany)
BTCG . . . . . . Bipartite Transport Control Group (Post-World War II, Germany)
B . . . . Biplane
BAC . . . . Bipolar Active-Plastic Cell
BOA . . . . Bipolar Operational Amplifier
BB . . . . Birmingham Belt R. R. (AAR code)
BR . . . . Birmingham Revision (of BNA) (British medical)
BSA . . . . Birmingham Small Arms, Inc.
BSE . . . . Birmingham & Southeastern R. R. (AAR code)
BS . . . . Birmingham Southern R. R. (AAR code)
BWG . . . . . . Birmingham Wire Gage
BW . . . . Birth Weight
BP . . . . Birthplace
BID . . . . Bis in Die (Twice a day) (Medicine)
BCNU . . . . . . Bis-Chloroethyl-Nitrosourea (Cancer drug)
BBI . . . . Biscuit Bakers Institute
BCDA . . . . . . Biscuit and Cracker Distributors Association
BCMA . . . . . . Biscuit and Cracker Manufacturers' Association
AC-DC . . . . . A Bisexual Person (Pun on electricity's 'AC or DC' -- alternating
current or direct current)
B . . . . Bishop (Chess)
B . . . . Bishop (Ecclesiastical)
BBA . . . . Bishop Baraga Association
BM . . . . Bishop and Martyr (Church calendars)
BS . . . . Bishop Suffragan
BCSS . . . . . . Bishops' Committee for the Spanish Speaking
BJC . . . . Bismarck Junior College (North Dakota)
Bi . . . . Bismuth (Chemical element)
BIP . . . . Bismuth Iodoform Paraffin
BMV . . . . Bistable Multi-Vibrator
BSA . . . . Bistrimethylsilylacetamide
BD . . . . Bit Density
BER . . . . BIT Error Rate (Data processing)
BTC . . . . BIT Time Counter (Data processing)
B . . . . Bitch
BPI . . . . BITS Per Inch (Data processing)
BPS . . . . BITS Per Second (Data processing)
BB . . . . A Bitter and Burton (Drink served in British public houses)
BNML . . . . . . Bitter National Magnet Laboratory
BCI . . . . Bituminous Coal Institute
BCOA . . . . . . Bituminous Coal Operators Association
BCR . . . . Bituminous Coal Research, Inc.
BEMB . . . . . . Bituminous Equipment Manufacturers Bureau
BPI . . . . Bituminous Pipe Institute
BVE . . . . Bivariate Exponential (Distribution) (Statistics)
BI-W . . . . . . Biweekly
BW . . . . Biweekly
BPR . . . . Biweekly Progress Report
BWR . . . . . . Biweekly Report
BDB . . . . Bjerrum Double Band
B . . . . Black (Buoy)
BABC . . . . . . Black American Baptist Churchmen (An organization)
BBT . . . . Black Ball Transport, Inc. (AAR code)
BBR . . . . Black Body Radiator

BLCA . . . . Black Canyon of the Gunnison National Monument
BC . . . . Black Code (Law passed after the Civil War limiting the rights of
            Negroes in the South)
B & D . . . . . . Black and Decker (Commercial firm)
BDK . . . . Black & Decker Mfg. Co. (NYSE symbol)
BESI . . . . Black Educational Services, Incorporated
BGG . . . . Black Granite Gage
BHTC . . . . Black Hills Teachers College (Later, Black Hills State College)
            (South Dakota)
BL . . . . Black Letter (Type)
BOWP . . . . Black Ordinary Working People
BP . . . . Black Powder
BSU . . . . Black Students Union
BUF . . . . Black United Front
BW . . . . Black Watch (British military unit)
B & W . . . . . . Black and White (Photography)
BO . . . . Blackout
BOD . . . . Blackout Door (Military)
BP . . . . Blackout Preparedness
BOW . . . . Blackout Window (Military)
BLDI . . . . Blank Die
BRD . . . . Blank Recording Disc
BPS . . . . Blanked Picture Signal
BO . . . . Blanking Oscillator
BFR . . . . Blast Furnace Research, Inc.
BH . . . . Blasthole
BK . . . . Blaw-Knox Company (NYSE symbol)
B . . . . Blend
B . . . . Blessed
BTS . . . . Blessed Trinity Society
BLIMPRON . . . Blimp Squadron
ZEDRON . . . . . Blimp Squadron (Later separated into BLIPRON and Blimp-HEDRON)
            (Navy)
BA . . . . Blind Approach (Flying)
BABS . . . . Blind Approach Beacon System (for aircraft) (British)
BABS . . . . Blind Approach Beam System (Flying)
BAT . . . . Blind Approach Training (Air Force)
BLEU . . . . Blind Landing Experimental Unit (Aviation)
BL & P . . . . . . Blind Loaded and Plugged
BL & T . . . . . . Blind Loaded and Traced
BRJ . . . . Blind Riveted Joint
BSA . . . . Blind Service Association
BVA . . . . Blinded Veterans Association
BCS . . . . Blip Counter System
BSR . . . . Blip-Scan Ratio
BCA . . . . Bliss Classification Association
EWB . . . . Bliss (E. W.) Company (NYSE symbol)
BLI . . . . Bliss and Laughlin, Incorporated (NYSE symbol)
BAG . . . . Bloc Africain de Guinee (African Bloc of Guinea)
BDG . . . . Bloc Democratique Gabonais (Gabonese Democratic Bloc)
BMS . . . . Bloc des Masses Senegalaises (Bloc of the Senegalese Masses)
BPS . . . . Bloc Polulaire Senegalais (Senegalese People's Bloc)
BLODI . . . . . . Block Diagram Compiler
BFR . . . . Block Format Recording
BLOC . . . . Block Oriented Compiler
BOC . . . . Block-Oriented Computer
BORAM . . . . . . Block Oriented Random Access Memory (Data processing)
BR . . . . Block Replacement
BT . . . . Block Template
BBC . . . . Blockhouse Battery Charger
BO . . . . Blockhouse Operation
BO . . . . Blocking Oscillator
BLK . . . . Blockson Chemical Company (NYSE symbol)
BAB . . . . Blood Agar Base (Chemical)
BB . . . . Blood Bank
BBB . . . . Blood Brain Barrier (Neurology)
BCA . . . . Blood Color Analyzer
BI C . . . . Blood Culture (Bacteriology)
BLS . . . . Blood and Lymphatic System
BP . . . . Blood Pressure
BPG . . . . Blood Pressure Gauge
BPMS . . . . . . Blood Pressure Measuring System
BPR . . . . Blood Pressure Recorder
BRF . . . . Blood Research Foundation
BST . . . . Blood Serological Test (Medicine)
BI S . . . . Blood Sugar (Medicine)
BS . . . . Blood Sugar
BTA . . . . Blood Transfusion Association
BI T . . . . Blood Type (Medicine)
BUN . . . . Blood Urea Nitrogen (Physiology)

BV . . . . Blood Volume
BW . . . . Blood Wassermann (Medicine)
BB . . . . Bloody Bastard
BF . . . . Bloody Fool
BH . . . . Bloody Hell (British)
BN . . . . Bloody Nuisance (British)
BPN . . . . Bloody Public Nuisance (British slang)
BID . . . . Blow in Door
BMS . . . . Blow Molding System
BB . . . . Blowback
BAC . . . . Blower Access Cover
BD . . . . Blowing Dust (Meteorology)
BN . . . . Blowing Sand (Meteorology)
BS . . . . Blowing Snow (Meteorology)
BY . . . . Blowing Spray (Meteorology)
BOC . . . . Blowout Coil
BPS . . . . Blowout Pipe System
B . . . . Blue (Aviation)
BCA . . . . Blue Cross Association
BCP . . . . Blue Cross Plan (Health insurance)
BGDA . . . . . . Blue Grass Depot Activity (Army)
BGA . . . . Blue-Green Algae (Water purification)
BHMO . . . . . . Blue Hill Meteorological Observatory (Harvard University)
BIL . . . . Blue Indicator Light
BLC . . . . Blue Line Copy
BLP . . . . Blue Line Print
BMC . . . . Blue Mountain College (Mississippi)
BMSO . . . . . . Blue Mountain Seismological Observatory
BLRI . . . . . . Blue Ridge Parkway (National Park Service designation)
BSMCP . . . . . Blue Shield Medical Care Plans
BS . . . . Blue Steel (Guns)
BSD . . . . Blue Stellar Object (Astronomy)
BSA . . . . Blue Streak Request (Military)
BJM . . . . Bluejacket's Manual (Navy)
BP . . . . Blueprint
B/P . . . . Blueprint
BCI . . . . Bluff Creek Industries R. R. (AAR code)
BG . . . . Bluish Green
BCM . . . . Blunt Conical Model
BCRV . . . . Blunt Conical Reentry Vehicle
BLE . . . . Blunt Leading Edge
BB . . . . B'nai B'rith
BBHF . . . . B'nai B'rith Hillel Foundation
BBVS . . . . B'nai B'rith Vocational Service
BBW . . . . B'nai B'rith Women
BBYO . . . . B'nai B'rith Youth Organization
BZ . . . . Bnai Zion
BA of NA . . . . Bnei Akiva of North America
BALIC . . . . . . Board of Action on Letter of Intent Conversion (Navy)
BOAR . . . . . . Board of Action on Redetermination (Navy)
BAR . . . . Board of Appeals and Review
BAAR . . . . . . Board for Aviation Accident Research (Army)
BBG . . . . Board of Broadcasting Governors
BCMR . . . . . . Board for Correction of Military Records
BD D & M . . . . Board of Decorations and Medals (Navy)
BEW . . . . Board of Economic Warfare (World War II)
BE . . . . Board of Education
B of E . . . . . . Board of Education
BED . . . . Board of Educational Development (University of California, Berkeley)
BERH . . . . . . Board of Engineers for Rivers and Harbors (Army)
BFUP . . . . . . Board of Fire Underwriters of the Pacific
BFS . . . . Board of Foreign Scholarships (Department of State)
BFE . . . . Board for Fundamental Education
BGN . . . . Board on Geographic Names (Department of the Interior)
BGFRS . . . . . Board of Governors, Federal Reserve System
B of H . . . . . . Board of Health
BHHMC . . . . . Board of Hospitals and Homes of the Methodist Church
BIA . . . . Board of Immigration Appeals (Department of Justice)
BIS . . . . Board of Inspection and Survey (Navy)
INSURV . . . . . Board of Inspection and Survey (Navy)
BM . . . . Board Measure (Lumber)
BOM . . . . Board on Medicine (of the National Academy of Sciences)
BNC . . . . Board of Navy Commissioners
BO . . . . Board of Ordnance
BP . . . . Board of Parole (Department of Justice)
BPI . . . . Board of Patent Interferences (of Patent Office)
B/P . . . . Board President
BPW . . . . Board of Public Works
BOR . . . . Board of Review (Army)
CBD . . . . Board of Review, Discharges and Dismissals (Coast Guard)

BSMT . . . . Board of Schools of Medical Technology
BOSEY . . . . . . Board of Supply, Executive Yuan (Responsible for removing surplus US war material to China from Guam)
BTA . . . . Board of Tax Appeals
BTS . . . . Board of Thoracic Surgery
BT . . . . Board of Trade
B of T . . . . . . Board of Trade
BOT . . . . Board of Trade (British)
B of TCC . . . . Board of Trade of the City of Chicago
B of TKC . . . . Board of Trade of Kansas City
BTU . . . . Board of Trade Unit (British)
BUNY . . . . . . Board of Underwriters of New York
BCSE . . . . Board of US Civil Service Examiners
BVA . . . . Board of Veterans Appeals (VA)
BWC . . . . Board of War Communications (World War II)
BW . . . . Board of Works (British)
BOCES . . . . . . Boards of Cooperative Educational Services
B . . . . Boat
B & ERS . . . . . Boat and Engine Repair Shop (Coast Guard)
BLT . . . . Boat Landing Team
MSB . . . . Boat Minesweeper (Navy symbol)
BORU . . . . . . Boat Operating and Repair Unit (Navy)
BOU . . . . Boat Operating Unit (Navy)
BOAT/US . . . . Boat Owners Association of the United States
BOCA . . . . . . Boat Owners Council of America
BRU . . . . Boat Repair Unit (Navy)
BTMA . . . . . . Boat Trailer Manufacturers Association
BTW . . . . Boat Wave
BIA . . . . Boating Industry Association
B . . . . Boatswain
BM . . . . Boatswain's Mate
BMCBB . . . . . Boatswain's Mate, Construction Battalion, Boatswain
BMCBS . . . . . Boatswain's Mate, Construction Battalion, Stevedore
BM1 . . . . Boatswain's Mate 1st class
BM2 . . . . Boatswain's Mate 2nd class
BMSRS . . . . . Boatswain's Mate, Ship Repair, Canvasman
BMSRC . . . . . Boatswain's Mate, Ship Repair, Crane Operator
BMSRR . . . . . Boatswain's Mate, Ship Repair, Rigger
BJU . . . . Bob Jones University (South Carolina)
BBK . . . . Bobbie Brooks, Inc. (NYSE symbol)
BCW . . . . Bobbin Coil Winder
BI . . . . Bobov in Israel
BBG . . . . Bodenbearbeitungsgerate
BI . . . . Bodily Injury (Insurance)
BCC . . . . Body-Centered Cubic (Metallography)
BCT . . . . Body-Centered Tetragonal (Metallography)
BOC . . . . Body-on-Chassis (Technical drawings)
BMA . . . . Body Mounted Accelerometer
BO . . . . Body Odor (Slang)
BSA . . . . Body Surface Area
BAT . . . . Boeing Air Transport
BAC . . . . Boeing Airplane Company
BACAIC . . . . Boeing Airplane Company Algebraic Interpretive Computing System
BAP . . . . Boeing Associated Products
BA . . . . Boeing Company (NYSE symbol)
BEAC . . . . . . Boeing Electronic Analog Computer
BOMARC . . . . . Boeing-Michigan Aeronautical Research Center
BOSS . . . . . . Boeing Operational Supervisory System
BSRL . . . . . . Boeing Scientific Research Laboratories
BVD . . . . Boeing, Vega, Douglas
BC . . . . Bogus Check
BHK . . . . Bohack (H.C.) Company, Inc. (American Stock Exchange symbol)
BFTSS . . . . . . Bohemian Free Thinking School Society
BHL . . . . Bohn Aluminum and Brass Corporation (NYSE symbol)
BFC . . . . Bohr Frequency Condition
BF . . . . Boiler Feed (Technical drawings)
BFCT . . . . . . Boiler Feed Compound Tank (Technical drawings)
BFP . . . . Boiler Feed Pump (Technical drawings)
BFW . . . . Boiler Feed Water (Technical drawings)
BHP . . . . Boiler Horsepower
BH . . . . Boiler House (Technical drawings)
BP . . . . Boiler Plate
BP . . . . Boiler Pressure
B . . . . Boilermaker (Navy)
BR . . . . Boilermaker (Navy rating)
BSR . . . . Boilermaker, Ship Repair (Navy)
BT . . . . Boilerman (Navy rating)
BHWR . . . . . . Boiling Heavy Water Reactor (AEC)
BONUS . . . . . Boiling Nuclear Superheat Reactor (AEC)
BP . . . . Boiling Point
BPE . . . . Boiling Point Elevation

BORAX . . . . . . Boiling Reactor Experiments (AEC)
BWR . . . . Boiling Water Reactor (AEC)
B . . . . Boils At
BJC . . . . Boise Junior College (Idaho)
BF . . . . Bold Face (Printing term)
B . . . . Bolivar (Monetary unit in Venezuela)
BSUS . . . . Bolivarian Society of the United States
B . . . . Boliviano (Monetary unit in Bolivia)
BWRL . . . . . . Bollweevil Research Laboratory (Department of Agriculture)
BC . . . . Bolt Circle (Technical drawings)
BP . . . . Bolted Plate (Technical drawings)
BAS . . . . Bomb Alarm System (Air Force)
BB . . . . Bomb Bay (of an aircraft)
BDA . . . . Bomb Damage Assessment
BDS . . . . Bomb Damage Survey
BDHSA . . . . . Bomb Director High Speed Aircraft
BDS . . . . Bomb Director System
BD . . . . Bomb Disposal
BDS . . . . Bomb-Disposal Squad
BDU . . . . Bomb, Dummy Unit
BLU . . . . Bomb, Live Unit
BMS . . . . Bomb Maintenance Spares
BNGS . . . . . . Bomb Navigation Guidance System
BNF . . . . Bomb Nose Fuze
BOSS . . . . . . Bomb Orbital Strategic System
BOSS-WEDGE . . Bomb Orbital Strategic System – Weapon Development Glide Entry
BRLG . . . . . . Bomb, Radio, Longitudinal, Generator-Powered
BRL . . . . Bomb Release Line
BSO . . . . Bomb Safety Officer (Navy)
BS . . . . Bomb Service
BTF . . . . Bomb Tail Fuse
BTD . . . . Bomb Testing Device
BIF . . . . Bombardier's Information File
BEER . . . . Bombardment Etch Rate
BIC . . . . Bombardment-Induced Conductivity
BLO . . . . Bombardment Liaison Officer (Navy)
BPTEU . . . . . Bombay Port Trust Employees' Union (India)
BBC . . . . Bombenzyl Cyanide (Tear gas)
AR . . . . Bomber (AR-2, etc.) (Russian aircraft symbol)
B . . . . Bomber (Designation for US military aircraft)
BB . . . . Bomber (BB-1, etc.) (Russian aircraft symbol)
B-SCH . . . . . . Bomber (Russian aircraft symbol)
DB . . . . Bomber (Russian aircraft symbol)
IL . . . . Bomber (Russian aircraft symbol)
SB-RK . . . . . . Bomber (Russian aircraft symbol)
ZKB . . . . Bomber (ZKB-26, etc.) (Russian aircraft symbol)
BC . . . . Bomber Command
BOMCOM . . . . Bomber Command (Army)
BDM . . . . Bomber Defense Missile (Air Force)
B . . . . Bomber Field
VBF . . . . Bomber-Fighter Squadron (Navy symbol)
BR . . . . Bomber Reconnaissance Aircraft
BT . . . . Bomber Transport (Air Force)
BCS . . . . Bombing Computer Set
VBF . . . . Bombing-Fighting Aircraft (Navy symbol)
BGR . . . . Bombing and Gunnery Range
BLP . . . . Bombing Landplane
BANIR . . . . . . Bombing & Navigation Inertial Reference
BNS . . . . Bombing-Navigation System
VB . . . . Bombing Plane (Navy symbol)
BRANE . . . . . . Bombing RADAR Navigation Equipment
BARN . . . . . . Bombing & Reconnaissance Navigation
BOMREP . . . . . Bombing Report
BOMRON . . . . Bombing Squadron
BTO . . . . Bombing Through Overcast (By means of RADAR equipment)
VBT . . . . Bombing, Torpedo Plane (Navy symbol)
BL . . . . Bombline
BF . . . . Bona Fide (In good faith)
BFOQ . . . . . . Bona Fide Occupational Qualification
BFPV . . . . . . Bona Fide Purchaser for Value (of a security, or other negotiable instrument) (Law)
BF . . . . Bonæ Feminæ (To the good woman)
BM . . . . Bonæ Memoriæ (Of happy memory)
BL . . . . Bonanza Air Lines, Incorporated
BAL . . . . Bonanza Airlines, Inc.
B . . . . Bond
BMO . . . . Bond Molecular Orbitals
BND . . . . Bond Stores, Inc. (NYSE symbol)
BTAP . . . . . . Bond Trade Analysis Program (IBM)
B/G . . . . Bonded Goods (Business and trade)
BW . . . . Bonded Warehouse

BWC	Bonded Wine Cellar
BW	Bonded Winery
BC	Bone Conduction
BHS	Bonhomie & Hattiesburg Southern R. R. (AAR code)
BPA	Bonneville Power Administration (Department of the Interior)
BP	Bonum Publicum (The Public Good)
B	Book
BDC	Book Development Council (British)
BMI	Book Manufacturers Institute
BOMC	Book-of-the-Month Club
BOK	Book-of-the-Month Club, Inc. (NYSE symbol)
B/PL	Book-Plate (Bibliography)
BPI	Book Production Industry (A journal)
BRI	Book Review Index (A publication)
BV	Book Value (Business and trade)
B/V	Book Value
BOWA	Booker T. Washington National Monument
BPI	Bookman's Price Index (A reference publication listing rare books and their list prices)
BAS	Books-Across-the-Sea (Project)
BCL	Books for College Libraries (A publication of ALA)
BEE	Books for Equal Education
BIP	Books in Print (A reference publication)
BGB	Booksellers of Great Britain
BA	Boolean Algebra
BAID	Boolean Array Identifier
BAS	Boolean Assignment Statement (Mathematics)
BFD	Boolean Function Designator
BFID	Boolean Function Identifier
BDO	Boom Defense Officer
BJC	Boone Junior College (Iowa)
BGRV	Boost Glide Reentry Vehicle (Air Force)
BIA	Boost, Insertion & Abort
BPI	Boost Phase Intercept (DCD)
BPC	Boost Protective Cover (Apollo) (NASA)
BD	Booster Development
BDA	Booster-Distribution Amplifier
BECO	Booster Engine Cutoff (Rocketry)
BES	Booster Exhaust Stream
BFJ	Booster Fuel Jacket
BIA	Booster Interstage Assembly
BOJ	Booster Jettison
BSW	Boot and Shoe Workers' Union
BAARINC . . .	Booz-Allen Applied Research, Incorporated
BN	Borden Company (NYSE symbol)
BOPAT	Border Patrol
BP	Border Patrol
BPA	Border Patrol Academy
BPSH	Border Patrol Sector Headquarters
BPV	Bordetella Pertussis Vaccine
BH	Borehole
BHC	Bore Hole Capsule
BHS	Bore Hole Seismometer
BSDL	Boresight Datum Line (Military)
BOG	Borg Corporation (NYSE symbol)
BOR	Borg-Warner Corporation (NYSE symbol)
BW	Borg-Warner Corporation
BOBR	Boring Bar
BRF	Borman Food Stores, Inc. (NYSE symbol)
B	Born
BBA	Born Before Arrival (of mother at hospital) (Medicine)
BOA	Born on Arrival (Medicine)
BHC	Born-Haber Cycle
BIT	Born-Infeld Theory
BME	Born-Mayer Equation
BOM	Born-Oppenheimer Method
BYM-AG	Bornu Youth Movement-Action Group Alliance (Nigeria)
BC	Boro-Carbon
B	Boron (Chemical element)
BBF	Boron Based Fuel
BMF	Boron Metal Fiber
BN	Boron Nitride (A fiber)
BNF	Boron Nitride Fiber
BP	Boron Plastic
BPG	Boron Pyrolytic Graphite
BRS	Boron Reinforced Structure
BCOA	Borzoi Club of America
BES	Bose-Einstein Statistics
BA	Boston & Albany R. R. (AAR code)
B & A	Boston and Albany Railroad
B & ARR	Boston & Albany Railroad

BAFGOPI	Boston Area Faculty Group on Public Issues
BCM	Boston Conservatory of Music
BSE	Boston Edison Company (NYSE symbol)
BGFE	Boston Grain and Flour Exchange
BM	Boston & Maine R. R. (AAR code)
BMR	Boston and Maine R. R. (NYSE symbol)
B & M	Boston and Maine Railroad
B & MRR	Boston & Maine Railroad
BMT	Boston & Maine Transportation R. R. (AAR code)
BOS	Boston, Massachusetts (Airport symbol)
BMFA	Boston Museum of Fine Arts
BNHSC	Boston National Historic Sites Commission (Government agency, discontinued 1960)
BNYD	Boston Navy Yard
BOSOX	Boston Red Sox (Baseball team)
BRA	Boston Redevelopment Agency
BTCA	Boston Terrier Club of America
BTI	Boston Theological Institute
BUMP	Boston University Marine Program
BWTA	Boston Wool Trade Association
BSA	Botanical Society of America
BSL	Botanical Society, London
B/B	Both-to-Blame (Shipping)
BF	Both Faces (Technical drawings)
BS	Both Sides (Technical drawings)
BW	Both Ways (Technical drawings)
B/B	Bottled in Bond (Wines and spirits)
BIB	Bottled in Bond (Wines and spirits)
BC	Bottom Center (Valve position)
BC	Bottom Chord
BDC	Bottom Dead Center (Engineering)
BF	Bottom Face (Technical drawings)
BFP	Bottom Finding Pinger
BL	Bottom Layer (Technical drawings)
BMILS	Bottom-Mounted Impact Locations System (Missile technology)
BOSH	Bottom Oriented Shrimp Harvester
BRASS	Bottom Reflection Active SONAR System
BS	Bottom Sediment (Maps and charts)
BS	Bottom Settlings (of crude oil in storage)
BOTOSS	Bottom Topography Survey System (Naval Oceanographic Office)
BOUMAC	Boulder Laboratory Macrosystem (National Bureau of Standards)
BL	Boundary Layer
BLC	Boundary Layer Control
BLS	Boundary Layer Separation
BLZ	Boundary Layer Zone
BOJ	Bourjois, Inc. (American Stock Exchange symbol)
BCA	Bovine Carbonic Anhydrase
BGG	Bovine Gamma Globulin
BPA	Bovine Plasma Albumin
BSA	Bovine Serum Albumin
BTMA	Bow Tie Manufacturers Association
BODN	Bowdon Railway Company (AAR code)
BM	Bowel Movement (Medicine)
BVL	Bowlers' Victory Legion
BEC	Bowles Engineering Corporation
BAM	Bowling Apparel Manufacturers of America
BGCC	Bowling Green College of Commerce (Later, a division of Western Kentucky State College)
BGSU	Bowling Green State University (Ohio)
BPAA	Bowling Proprietors' Association of America
BPAA-DAD . . .	Bowling Proprietors Association of America - Duckpin Activities Department
BWAA	Bowling Writers Association of America
BBA	Box Association of America
BO	Box Office (Theatrical slang)
BRDA	Boxboard Research and Development Association
BWA	Boxing Writers Association
BF	Boy Friend (Slang)
BSYM	Boy Savior Youth Movement
BSA	Boy Scouts of America
BSIB	Boy Scouts International Bureau
BOYC	Boyne City R. R. (AAR code)
BAMA	Boys Apparel and Accessories Manufacturers Association
BABA	Boys' Apparel Buyers Association
BCA	Boys' Clubs of America
BLB	Boy's Life Brigade
BOP	The Boy's Own Paper (Late nineteenth- and early twentieth-century periodical) (British)
BTI	Boy's Towns of Italy
BWSC	Boys of Woodcraft Sportsmen's Clubs
BRK	Brach (E. J.) & Sons (NYSE symbol)

BLA . . . . Bracket and Linkage Assembly
BDCT . . . . Bradford Durfee College of Technology (Later, Southeastern Massachusetts
          Technical Institute)
BJC . . . . Bradford Junior College (Massachusetts)
BAM . . . . Bradley Aberration Method
BRMA . . . . . . Braided Rug Manufacturers Association
BTMA . . . . . . Braided Trimming Manufacturers Association
BIA . . . . Braille Institute of America
BTP . . . . Braille Technical Press
BIS . . . . Brain Information Service (UCLA)
BRAMATEC . . . Brain Mapping Technique
BRF . . . . Brain Research Foundation
BJC . . . . Brainerd Junior College (Minnesota)
BKDI . . . . Brake Die
BHP . . . . Brake Horse-Power
BMEP . . . . . . Brake Mean Effective Pressure
BR . . . . Brake Relay
BA . . . . Braking Action (Aviation)
BRAXP . . . . . . Braking Action Extremely Poor (Aviation)
BRAF . . . . . . Braking Action Fair (Aviation)
BRAG . . . . . . Braking Action Good (Aviation)
BRAN . . . . . . Braking Action Nil (Aviation)
BRAP . . . . . . Braking Action Poor (Aviation)
BRASO . . . . . . Branch Aviation Supply Office (Navy)
BFZ . . . . Branch of Fall Zero
BHO . . . . Branch Hydrographic Office
BI . . . . Branch Immaterial
BIO . . . . Branch Intelligence Officer
BM . . . . Branch Material (Military)
BM . . . . Branch Memorandum
BO . . . . Branch Office
BOMID . . . . . . Branch Office, Military Intelligence Division (Army)
BROI . . . . Branch Operating Instructions (Military)
BPRO . . . . . . Branch Public Relations Office
BR . . . . Branch Report
BTO . . . . Branch Transportation Office(r) (Army)
BRF . . . . Branchial Filament
BNF . . . . Brand Names Foundation
BRI . . . . Brand Rating Index Corporation
B and S . . . . . Brandy and Soda
BNF . . . . Braniff Airways, Inc. (NYSE symbol)
BNC . . . . Brasenose College (Oxford)
BHP . . . . Brashear-Hastings Prism
BBII . . . . . . Brass and Bronze Ingot Institute
BDS . . . . Brass Divider Strip (Technical drawings)
BPL . . . . Brass Pounders League (Unit of American Radio Relay League)
BMI . . . . Bravais-Miller Indices
BRU . . . . Brayton Rotating Unit
BNAF . . . . . . Brazil Nut Advertising Fund
BNA . . . . Brazil Nut Association
BACI . . . . . . Brazilian American Cultural Institute
BCNY . . . . . . Brazilian Center of New York
BCI . . . . Brazilian Coffee Institute
BEF . . . . Brazilian Expeditionary Force
BGTB . . . . . . Brazilian Government Trade Bureau
BN . . . . Brazilian Navy
BTS . . . . Brazilian Thorium Sludge
B of P . . . . . . Breach of Promise
BBK . . . . Bread Board Kit
B & W . . . . . . Bread and Water
B . . . . Breadth or Beam (of a ship)
BL . . . . Breadth-Length
BBM . . . . Break-Before-Make
BOI . . . . Break of Inspection
BOA . . . . Break-Off Altitude
BOH . . . . Break-Off Height (Aviation)
BINOVC . . . . Break in Overcast (Meteorology)
BPI . . . . Break-Point Instruction
BIR . . . . Break-In Relay
BUM . . . . Break-Up Missile
BATCS . . . . . . Breakdown Air Traffic Control Services
BV . . . . Breakdown Voltage
BB . . . . Breaker Block
B & E . . . . . . Breaking & Entering
B & ENT & PL . . Breaking and Entering in Nighttime and Petty Larceny
BRKHIC . . . . . . Breaks in Higher Overcast (Meteorology)
BSE . . . . Breast Self-Examination (for Cancer) (Medicine)
BA . . . . Breathing Apparatus
BL . . . . Breech Loading (Weapon)
BLR . . . . Breech-Loading Rifle
BLRG . . . . . . Breech-Loading Rifled Guns

BM . . . . Breech Mechanism (of a weapon)
BR . . . . Breeder Reactor (AEC)
BRZ . . . . Breeze Corporation (American Stock Exchange symbol)
BPE . . . . Bremen Port of Embarkation (Germany)
BFCF . . . . . . Bremerton Freight Car Ferry, Inc. (AAR code)
BSC . . . . Brethren Service Commission
BAA . . . . Brewers Association of America
BHRI . . . . . . Brewers Hop Research Institute
BYC . . . . Brewers Yeast Council
BIRI . . . . . . Brewing Industries Research Institute
BCC . . . . Briar Cliff College (Iowa)
BCA . . . . Briard Club of America
BRCR . . . . . . Brices Crossroads National Battlefield Site
BMP . . . . Bricklayers, Masons and Plasterers' International Union of America
BBAA . . . . . . Bridal and Bridesmaids Apparel Association
BA . . . . Bridge Amplifier
BBSA . . . . . . Bridge and Building Supply Association
BPR . . . . Bridge Plotting Room (Navy)
BRR . . . . Bridge Receiving Room (Navy)
BEI . . . . Bridgeport Engineering Institute (Connecticut)
BQEP . . . . . . Brief Qualification Evaluation Program
BST . . . . Brief Stimulus Therapy (Psychology)
BR . . . . Briefing Room (Navy)
BAAF . . . . . . Brigade Airborne Alert Force (Military)
BDPS . . . . . . Brigade Data Processing System
BOG . . . . Brigade of Guards
BH . . . . Brigade Headquarters (Army)
BHQ . . . . Brigade Headquarters (Army)
BRIGHED . . . . . Brigade Headquarters (Army)
BM . . . . Brigade Major
BRQM . . . . . . Brigade Quartermaster (Marine Corps)
BG . . . . Brigadier General
BRIGEN . . . . . . Brigadier General
BRIGGEN . . . . . Brigadier General
BGS . . . . Brigadier, General Staff (British Army)
BG . . . . Briggs Manufacturing Company (NYSE symbol)
BGG . . . . Briggs and Stratton Corporation (NYSE symbol)
BYU . . . . Brigham Young University (Utah)
BDE . . . . Bright Display Equipment
BDRI . . . . Bright Display RADAR Indicator
BRITE . . . . . . Bright RADAR Indicator-Equipment
BWGMSB . . . . Bright Wire Goods Manufacturers Service Bureau
BYT . . . . Bright Young Things (The younger set) (British)
B . . . . Brightness
BC . . . . Brightness Contrast
BCV . . . . Brightness Contrast Value
BM . . . . Brightness Merit
BB . . . . Brigitte Bardot (French motion picture star)
BWK . . . . Brillouin-Wentzel-Kramers (Physics)
BRM . . . . Brimstone R. R. (AAR code)
BH . . . . Brinell Hardness
BHN . . . . Brinell Hardness Number
BYO . . . . Bring Your Own (Liquor) (Party invitation notation)
BYOB . . . . . . Bring your Own Booze (or Bottle) (Party invitation notation)
BAC . . . . Bristol Aeroplane Company
BMY . . . . Bristol-Myers Company (NYSE symbol)
BAF . . . . Brith Abraham Foundation
BTA . . . . Brith Trumpeldor of America
B . . . . British
BR . . . . British
BAU . . . . British Absolute Unit
BA . . . . British Academy
BA . . . . British Admiralty
BAD . . . . British Admiralty Delegation (to Washington)
BAE . . . . British Admiralty Establishment
BAMSR . . . . . . British Admiralty Maintenance and Supply Representative
BARM . . . . . . British Admiralty Repair Mission
BATM . . . . . . British Admiralty Technical Mission (World War II)
BACA . . . . . . British Advisory Committee for Aeronautics
BARC . . . . . . British Aeronautical Research Committee
BAC . . . . British Air Commission (Washington)
BAF . . . . British Air Force
BAM . . . . British Air Ministry
BAMCO . . . . British Air Ministry Control Office
BAC . . . . British Aircraft Corporation
BALPA . . . . . . British Airline Pilots Association
BATRS . . . . . . British Amateur Tape Recording Society
BA . . . . British America
BACC . . . . . . British-American Coordinating Committee (Turkey)
BASIC (English) . . British-American Scientific International Commercial English
BAT . . . . British-American Tobacco

BQB . . . . British-American Tobacco Company (American Stock Exchange symbol)
BARB . . . . . . British Angular Rate Bombsight
BAL . . . . British Anti-Lewisite (A drug)
BADA . . . . . . British Antique Dealers' Association
BA . . . . British Army
BAOR . . . . . . British Army of the Rhine (NATO/NORTHAG)
BA . . . . British Association
BAAS . . . . . . British Association for American Studies
BACE . . . . . . British Association of Consulting Engineers
BAA . . . . British Astronomical Association
BAMA . . . . . . British Automobile Manufacturers Association
BB . . . . British Blue (A British sailor)
BBIP . . . . . . British Books in Print
BBC . . . . British Broadcasting Corporation (State-operated radio and television)
BBS . . . . British Bryological Society
BCPSG . . . . . British Caribbean Philatelic Study Group
BCIRA . . . . . . British Cast Iron Research Association
BCN . . . . British Celanese (NYSE symbol)
BCOI . . . . . . British Central Office of Information
BCA . . . . . . British Colonial Airlines, Inc.
BC . . . . British Columbia (A Canadian province)
BCE . . . . . . British Columbia Electric Company, Ltd. (AAR code)
BCN . . . . British Commonwealth of Nations
BCPO . . . . . . British Commonwealth Producers' Organization
BCWVA . . . . . British Commonwealth War Veterans
BCS . . . . British Computer Society
BCAC . . . . . . British Conference on Automation and Computation
BC . . . . British Council
BCC . . . . . . British Crown Colony
BDS . . . . . . British Defence Staff
BDA . . . . British Dental Association
BDE . . . . . . British Destroyer Escort
BDH . . . . British Drug Houses, Ltd.
BEA . . . . British East Africa
BEAMA . . . . . British Electrical and Allied Manufacturers
BEA . . . . . . British Electrical Authority
BEARA . . . . . British Electronic and Applied Research Association
BE . . . . British Element
BE . . . . British Empire
BE & CWLC . . British Empire and Commonwealth Weight-Lifting Council
BEM . . . . . . British Empire Medal
BENA . . . . . . British Empire Naturalist Association
BEU . . . . British Empire Union
BESA . . . . . . British Engineering Standards Association
BEC . . . . . . British Engineers Club
BEACON . . . . British European Airways Computerized Office Network
BEA . . . . British European Airways Corporation
BEF . . . . British Expeditionary Forces
BEPO . . . . . . British Experimental Pile Operation (Atomic energy)
BEMAC . . . . . British Exports Marketing Advisory Committee
BFI . . . . British Film Institute
BFN . . . . British Forces Network
BFBS . . . . . . British and Foreign Bible Society
BG . . . . British Guiana
BGAL . . . . . . British Guiana Airways, Ltd. (A national airline)
BGU . . . . British Guyana
BHC . . . . British High Commissioner
BHRA . . . . . . British Hydromechanics Research Association
BI . . . . British India
BISNC . . . . . British India Steam Navigation Company
BIOT . . . . . . British Indian Ocean Territory
BIATA . . . . . . British Independent Air Transport Association
BICEP . . . . . . British Industrial Collaborative Exponential Program
BIDO . . . . . . British Industrial Development Office (Through foreign branches, encourages investments in Britain from abroad)
BIMCAM . . . . . British Industrial Measuring and Control Apparatus Manufacturers' Association
BITA . . . . . . British Industrial Truck Association
BIF . . . . British Industries Fair
BIF . . . . British Industries Federation
BIS . . . . British Information Services
BIEE . . . . . . British Institute of Electrical Engineers
BIIA . . . . British Institute of Industrial Art
BIRE . . . . . . British Institute of Radio Engineers
BICC . . . . . . British Insulated Collender's Cable
BIA . . . . British Insurance Association
BIOS . . . . . . British Intelligence Objectives Subcommittee
BICEMA . . . . British Internal Combustion Engine Manufacturers' Association
BIS . . . . British Interplanetary Society
BISF . . . . . . British Iron and Steel Federation
BISITS . . . . . . British Iron and Steel Industry Translation Service

BISRA . . . . . . British Iron and Steel Research Association
BJC . . . . British Jewish Cockney
BJCEB . . . . . . British Joint Communications-Electronics Board (Military)
BJS . . . . British Joint Services
BJSM . . . . . . British Joint Services Mission
BJSM . . . . . . British Joint Staff Mission
BLMRA . . . . . British Leather Manufacturers Research Association
BL . . . . British Legion
BLH . . . . British Legion Headquarters
BLV . . . . British Legion Village
BLO . . . . British Liaison Officer
BLC . . . . British Lighting Control
BLESMA . . . . British Limbless Ex-Service Men's Association
BML-BS . . . . . British Matchbox Label and Booklet Society
BMA . . . . British Medical Association
BMJ . . . . British Medical Journal
BMN . . . . British Merchant Navy
BMSM . . . . . . British Merchant Shipping Mission
BMA . . . . British Military Authority
BMS . . . . British Ministry of Supply
BMSRDE . . . . British Ministry of Supply Research and Development Establishment
BMC . . . . British Motor Corporation Ltd.
BMH . . . . British Motor Holdings
BMNH . . . . . . British Museum of Natural History (London)
BNB . . . . British National Bibliography
BNCSR . . . . . British National Committee on Space Research
BNF . . . . British National Formulary (A publication in pharmacy)
BNOC . . . . . . British National Opera Company
BNAS . . . . . . British Naval Air Service
BNAS . . . . . . British Naval Air Staff
BNLUS . . . . . British Naval Liaison (Office) US Navy (London)
BNLO . . . . . . British Naval Liaison Officer
BNFMRA . . . . British Non-Ferrous Metals Research Association
BNMRA . . . . . British Non-Ferrous Metals Research Association
BNA . . . . British North America
BNB . . . . British North Borneo
BNEC . . . . . . British Nuclear Energy Conference
BNES . . . . . . British Nuclear Energy Society
BNX . . . . British Nuclear Export Executives (Group to promote export of nuclear power stations of British design)
BNF . . . . British Nuclear Forum
BOU . . . . British Ornithologists' Union
BOAC . . . . . . British Overseas Airways Corporation
BOADICEA . . . British Overseas Airways Digital Information Computer for Electronic Automation
BPFILO . . . . . British Pacific Fleet Intelligence Liaison Officer
BPFLO . . . . . . British Pacific Fleet Liaison Officer
d . . . . British penny (Derived from Latin "denarius")
BP . . . . British Petroleum Company
BPC . . . . British Pharmaceutical Codex (A publication in pharmacy)
BP . . . . British Pharmacopoeia (A publication in pharmacy)
BPS . . . . British Plain Spirits
BPF . . . . British Plastic Federation
BPO . . . . British Post Office
BPC . . . . British Productivity Council
BP . . . . British Public (Slang)
BPC . . . . British Purchasing Commission
BRM . . . . British Racing Motors
BREMA . . . . . British Radio Equipment Manufacturers Association
BRVMA . . . . . British Radio Valve Manufacturers' Association
BR . . . . British Railways
BRCS . . . . . . British Red Cross Society
BR . . . . British Revision (of BNA) (Medicine)
BRRL . . . . . . British Road Research Laboratory
BRLO . . . . . . British Routing Liaison Officer (World War II)
BRO . . . . British Routing Office
BRPRA . . . . . . British Rubber Products Research Association
BSF . . . . British Salonica Force
BSAS . . . . . . British Ship Adoption Society
BSRA . . . . . . British Ship Research Association
BPD . . . . British Society of Posters Designers
BSI . . . . British Solomon Islands
BSA . . . . British South Africa
BSAA . . . . . . British South American Airways
BS . . . . British Standard
BSCP . . . . . . British Standard Code of Practice
BSF . . . . British Standard Fine Thread
BSS . . . . British Standard Specifications
BSI . . . . British Standards Institution (Promulgates manufacturing standards and specifications)
BSCRA . . . . . British Steel Castings Research Association

BST . . . . British Summer Time
BSC . . . . British Supply Council
BSO . . . . British Supply Office
BTI . . . . British Technology Index
BTHU . . . . . . British Thermal Unit
BTU . . . . British Thermal Unit(s)
BTH . . . . British Thomson-Houston Company
BTA . . . . British Tourist Authority (Formerly, British Travel Association)
BTA . . . . British Travel Association
BTHA . . . . . . British Travel and Holidays Association
BTE . . . . British Troops in Egypt
BUCOP . . . . . . British Union Catalogue of Periodicals
BUP . . . . British United Press
BRUSA . . . . . . British-United States Agreement (Circuits)
BUSCI . . . . . . British-United States Convoy Instructions
BUSRA . . . . . British-United States Routing Agreement (Shipping)
BWC. . . . . . . British War Cabinet
BWRS . . . . . . British War Relief Society (in US)
BWVA . . . . . . British War Veterans of America
BWS . . . . British Water Color Society
BWIA . . . . . . British West Indian Airways, Ltd.
BWI . . . . British West Indies
BYMS . . . . . . British Yard Motor Minesweepers
BZPCA . . . . . British Zone Petroleum Coordinating Authority (Post-World War II, Germany)
BHAD . . . . . . Broach Adapter
BHFX . . . . . . Broach Fixture
BBA . . . . Broad Band Antenna
BBWC . . . . . . Broad Band Waveguide Circulator
BFB . . . . Broad-Flanged Beam
BOA. . . . . . . Broad Ocean Area
BAA . . . . Broadband Active Analyzer
BAK . . . . Broadband Antenna Kit
BKA . . . . Broadband Klystron Amplifier
BLC . . . . Broadband Latching Circulator
BLS . . . . Broadband Latching Switch
BMPA . . . . . . Broadband Microwave Power Amplifier
BAMS . . . . . . Broadcast to Allied Merchant Ships
BCB . . . . Broadcast Band
BB . . . . Broadcast Bureau (of FCC)
BCS . . . . Broadcast Communications System
BC . . . . Broadcast Control
BRECOM . . . . . Broadcast Emergency Communications System
BROFICON . . . Broadcast Fighter Control (Military)
BFA . . . . Broadcasting Foundation of America
BCI . . . . Broadcast Interference (Communications)
BCL . . . . Broadcast Listener (Amateur radio)
BMB . . . . Broadcast Measurement Bureau
BMI . . . . Broadcast Music, Incorporated
BRECOM . . . . . Broadcast Radio Emergency Communication (Air Force)
BRC . . . . Broadcast Rating Council
BTR . . . . Broadcast and Television Receivers
BTS . . . . Broadcast Transmission Systems
BNS . . . . Broadcasters Nonprofit Satellite Service (Ford Foundation)
BPA . . . . Broadcasters' Promotion Association
BC . . . . Broadcasting
BAM. . . . . . . Broadcasting AM
BFC . . . . Broadcasting and Film Commission
BS . . . . Broadcasting Station
BT . . . . Broader Term (Cross-reference) (Indexing)
B . . . . Broken
BO. . . . . Broker's Order (Finance)
Br . . . . Bromine (Chemical element)
BPF . . . . Bromine Pentafluoride
BA . . . . Bromo-Aceton (War gas)
BSP . . . . Bromsulphalein
BTB . . . . Bromthymol Blue
BR . . . . Bronze
BM . . . . Bronze Medal
BSS . . . . Bronze Service Star (Military award)
BSM. . . . . . . Bronze Star Medal
BAMC . . . . . . Brooke Army Medical Center
BDP . . . . Brookes Deflection Potentiometer
BBRR . . . . . . Brookhaven Beam Research Reactor (AEC)
BGRR . . . . . . Brookhaven Graphite Research Reactor (AEC)
BMR . . . . Brookhaven Medical Reactor (AEC)
BMRC . . . . . . Brookhaven Medical Research Center
BNL . . . . Brookhaven National Laboratory (AEC)
BRR . . . . Brookhaven Research Reactor (AEC)
BART . . . . . . Brooklyn Army Terminal
BEDT . . . . . . Brooklyn Eastern District Terminal R. R. (AAR code)
BIAS. . . . . . . Brooklyn Institute of Arts and Sciences

BLS . . . . Brooklyn Law School
BMT . . . . Brooklyn-Manhattan Transit Corporation (A New York City subway line)
BRT . . . . Brooklyn Rapid Transit Company (A New York City subway line) (Became BMT)
BUG. . . . . . . Brooklyn Union Gas (NYSE symbol)
BU . . . . Brooklyn Union Gas Company (NYSE symbol) (Wall Street slang name: "Bug")
B . . . . Brother, Brotherhood
BALC . . . . . . Brotherhood of the American Lutheran Church
BABT . . . . . . Brotherhood of Associated Book Travelers
BHN. . . . . . . Brotherhood of the Holy Name
BHT . . . . Brotherhood of the Holy Trinity
BJC . . . . Brotherhood of the Jungle Cock
BLE . . . . Brotherhood of Locomotive Engineers
BLFE . . . . . . Brotherhood of Locomotive Firemen and Enginemen
LFE . . . . Brotherhood of Locomotive Firemen and Enginemen (AFL-CIO)
BMWE. . . . . . Brotherhood of Maintenance of Way Employees
BOMFOG . . . . The Brotherhood of Man under the Fatherhood of God (Journalistic slang for political platitudes; taken from a speech by Hubert H. Humphrey)
BME . . . . Brotherhood of Marine Engineers (Later merged with MEBA)
BPDP . . . . . . Brotherhood of Painters, Decorators and Paperhangers of America (Also known as B of PDPH of A)
B of PDPH of A . . Brotherhood of Painters, Decorators and Paperhangers of America (Also known as BPDP)
BRS . . . . Brotherhood of Railroad Signalmen
B of RS . . . . . Brotherhood of Railroad Signalmen
BRT . . . . Brotherhood of Railroad Trainmen
BRC of A . . . . Brotherhood Railway Carmen of America
BRSC . . . . . . Brotherhood of Railway and Steamship Clerks, Freight Handlers, Express and Station Employees
BSAC . . . . . . Brotherhood of Shoe and Allied Craftsmen
SCP . . . . Brotherhood of Sleeping Car Porters
UWNE . . . . . . Brotherhood of Utility Workers of New England
BCS . . . . Brothers of Charity of Spokane (Roman Catholic religious order)
BGS . . . . Brothers of Good Shepherd (Roman Catholic religious order)
CSPX . . . . . . Brothers of St. Pius X (Roman Catholic religious order)
BID . . . . Brought In Dead (Medical notation)
B/D . . . . Brought Down (Business and trade)
BF . . . . Brought Forward
B/F . . . . Brought Forward (Business and trade)
B/O . . . . Brought Over (Business and trade)
BGPDC . . . . . Brouwer General Perturbations Differential Correction Program
BR . . . . Brown (Buoy) (Maps and charts)
B & B . . . . . . Brown and Bigelow (Division of Standard Packaging Corporation)
BBC . . . . Brown, Boveri and Company (Germany)
BB/KR . . . . . . Brown, Boveri/Krupp Reaktorbau (Germany)
BOV. . . . . . . Brown Oil of Vitroil
BRN . . . . Brown & Root-Northrop
B & S . . . . . . Brown and Sharpe (Gage)
BWS. . . . . . . Brown Shoe Company, Inc. (NYSE symbol)
BSCBA . . . . . Brown Swiss Cattle Breeders Association of the USA
BAMG . . . . . . Browning Aircraft Machine Gun
BAR . . . . Browning Automatic Rifle
BMG. . . . . . . Browning Machine Gun
BET . . . . Brunauer-Emmett-Teller (Physics equation)
BC . . . . Brunswick Corporation (NYSE symbol)
BBC . . . . Brush Beryllium Company
BRH . . . . Brush Holder
BRO . . . . Brush-Off (Slang)
BSMP . . . . . . Brussels Sprouts Marketing Program
BTN . . . . Brussels Tariff Nomenclature (EEC)
BTO . . . . Brussels Treaty Organization (Became Western European Union)
BRCA . . . . . . Bryce Canyon National Park
BMC. . . . . . . Bryn Mawr College (Pennsylvania)
BC . . . . Bubble Chamber
BCE . . . . Bubble Chamber Experiment
BPP . . . . Bubble Pulse Period
BC . . . . Buccal Cartilage
BC . . . . Buccal Commissure
BM. . . . . Buccal Mass
BA . . . . Buccoaxial
BAC . . . . Buccoaxiocervical
BAG . . . . Buccoaxiogingival
BL . . . . Buccolingual
BBT . . . . Buck-Boost Transformer
BUIS . . . . . . Buck Island Reef National Monument
BKP . . . . Buckeye Pipe Line Company (NYSE symbol)
BCG . . . . Bucking Current Generator
BHM. . . . . . . Buckingham Corporation (NYSE symbol)
BOSOR . . . . . Buckling of Shells of Revolution
BE . . . . Bucyrus-Erie Company

BY . . . . Bucyrus-Erie Company (NYSE symbol)
BF . . . . Budd Company (NYSE symbol)
BCUSA . . . . . . Buddhist Center of the United States of America
BE . . . . Buddhist Era
BA & F . . . . . . Budget, Accounting and Finance
BAO . . . . Budget and Accounting Officer (Military)
BA . . . . Budget Activity (Navy)
BAB . . . . Budget Advisory Board
BAC . . . . Budget Advisory Committee (Army)
BA . . . . Budget Authorization
BAAN . . . . . . Budget Authorization Account Number
BCP . . . . Budget Change Proposal
BEPI . . . . Budget Estimates Presentation Instructions
BEP . . . . Budget Execution Plan
BER . . . . Budget Execution Review (Military)
BEI . . . . Budget Executives Institute
BFC . . . . Budget and Forecast Calendarization
BUD . . . . Budget Office (Army)
BP . . . . Budget Program
BPAC . . . . . . Budget Program Activity Code
BPA . . . . Budget Project Account (Military)
BPSN . . . . . . Budget Project Symbol Number
CBR . . . . Budget and Requirements Division (Coast Guard)
BY . . . . Budget Year
BA . . . . Buenos Aires
BGB . . . . Buergerliches Gesetzbuch
BPWMA . . . . . Buff and Polishing Wheel Manufacturers Association
BCK . . . . Buffalo Creek R. R. (AAR code)
BCG . . . . Buffalo Creek & Gauley R. R. (AAR code)
BFC . . . . Buffalo Forge Company (NYSE symbol)
BR & PRY . . . . Buffalo, Rochester & Pittsburg Railway
BAR . . . . Buffer Address Register
BA . . . . Buffer Amplifier
BI . . . . Buffer Index
BM . . . . Buffer Module
BR . . . . Buffer Register (Data processing)
BEF . . . . Buffered Emitter Follower
BFF . . . . Buffered Flip-Flop
BGM . . . . Buglemaster (Navy)
BUG . . . . Bugler (Navy)
BCCA . . . . . . Buick Collector's Club of America
BUCO . . . . . . Build-Up Control Organization
BU . . . . Builder (Navy rating)
BHMA . . . . . . Builders' Hardware Manufacturers Association
BR . . . . Builder's Risk (Insurance)
BBC . . . . Building Block Concept (Army--ROAD concept)
BBM . . . . Building Block Monochromator
BBP . . . . Building Block Principle
BCTD . . . . . . Building and Construction Trades Department (AFL-CIO)
Bldg E . . . . . . Building Engineer
BL . . . . Building Line (Technical drawings)
B & L . . . . . . Building and Loan (Association)
BMEA . . . . . . Building Maintenance Employers Association
BMEA . . . . . . Building Material Exhibitors Association
BOCA . . . . . . Building Officials Conference of America
BOF . . . . Building Owners Federation of Mutual Fire Insurance Companies
BPEC . . . . . . Building Products Executives Conference
BRA . . . . Building Renovating Association
BRAB . . . . . . Building Research Advisory Board
BRI . . . . Building Research Institute
BRS . . . . Building Research Station (British)
BSE . . . . Building Service Employees' International Union
BSL . . . . Building Service League
BSI . . . . Building Stone Institute
BWA . . . . Building Waterproofers Association
BWIU . . . . . . Building Workers' Industrial Union (Australia)
BIBS . . . . Built-In Breathing System
B . . . . Built for British (As suffix to plane designation)
BILB . . . . Built-In Light Beacon
BOOK . . . . . . Built-in Orderly Organized Knowledge (Learning device)
BIPCO . . . . . . Built-in-Place Component (Electronics)
BIST . . . . Built-In Self Test
BIT . . . . Built-In Test (RADAR)
BITE . . . . Built-In Test Equipment
BAFA . . . . . . Bul Bul Academy of Fine Arts (Dacca, Pakistan)
B . . . . Bulb
BSLF . . . . Bulgarian Socialist Labor Federation (Defunct)
BKP . . . . Bulgarska Komunisticheska Partiia (Bulgarian Communist Party)
BMC . . . . Bulk Molding Compound
BPCI . . . . Bulk Packaging and Containerization Institute
BSF . . . . Bulk Shielding Facility (ORNL)

BCF . . . . Bulked Continuous Fiber (Carpeting)
BC . . . . Bulkhead Connector
BHJ . . . . Bulkhead Jack
BJ . . . . Bulkhead Jack
BHR . . . . Bulkhead Receptacle
BR . . . . Bulkhead Receptacle
BGE . . . . Bull General Electric
BN . . . . Bull Nose
BS . . . . Bull Session (Slang for a random conversation)
BTCA . . . . . . Bull Terrier Club of America
BLD . . . . Bullard Company (NYSE symbol)
BCA . . . . Bulldog Club of America
B . . . . Bulletin
BB . . . . Bulletin Board
BSS . . . . Bulletin de Statistique Suisse (Switzerland)
BUL . . . . Bullock's, Inc. (NYSE symbol)
BAGS . . . . . . Bullpup All-Weather Guidance System (BUWEPS/ASD)
BS . . . . Bullsling(er) (Bowdlerized version)
BVA . . . . Bulova Watch Company, Inc. (NYSE symbol)
BLJ . . . . Bumper Lift Jack
BAO . . . . Bundes-abgabenordnung (Austria)
BFH . . . . Bundesfinanzhof
BRB . . . . Bundesratsbeschluss
BRD . . . . Bundesrepublik Deutschland (Federal Republic of Germany)
BDI . . . . Bundesverband der Deutschen Industrie (Federation of German Industry)
BFB . . . . Bundesverband der Freien Berufe
BV . . . . Bundesvorstand
BCEX . . . . . . Bundle Controlled Expansion
BH . . . . Bung-Hole (i.e., cheese) (British slang)
BU . . . . Buoy Boat
BUSL . . . . . . Buoy Boat, Stern Loading
BPS . . . . Buoy Power Supply
B . . . . Buoyancy
BBIM . . . . . . Buoyant Ballistic Inertial Missile
BUR . . . . Burbank, Calif. (Airport symbol)
BC . . . . Burden Center
BA . . . . Bureau of Accounts (Treasury Department)
BATV . . . . . . Bureau for Adult Thalidomide Victims (West Germany)
BAVE . . . . . . Bureau of Adult and Vocational Education (Office of Education)
BAIR . . . . . . Bureau for the Advancement of Independent Retailing
B/A . . . . Bureau of Aeronautics (Navy)
BUAER . . . . . . Bureau of Aeronautics (Navy) (Functions transferred to Bureau of Naval Weapons, 1959)
BUAIR . . . . . . Bureau of Aeronautics (Navy)
BAGR . . . . . . Bureau of Aeronautics General Representative (Navy)
BAGRED . . . . Bureau of Aeronautics General Representative, Eastern District (Navy)
BAGRWD . . . . Bureau of Aeronautics General Representative, Western District (Navy)
BAIR . . . . . . Bureau of Aeronautics Industrial Reserve
BAMRO . . . . . Bureau of Aeronautics Maintenance Repair Officer
BAMR . . . . . . Bureau of Aeronautics Maintenance Representative (Navy)
BAMRRO . . . . Bureau of Aeronautics Maintenance Resident Representative Office
BAMO . . . . . . Bureau of Aeronautics Material Officer (Navy)
BAR . . . . Bureau of Aeronautics Representative (Navy) (Later, BUWEPS)
BARR . . . . . . Bureau of Aeronautics Resident Representative
BASO . . . . . . Bureau of Aeronautics Shipment Order (Navy)
BAE . . . . Bureau for Africa and Europe (AID)
BAA . . . . Bureau of African Affairs (Department of State)
BAE . . . . Bureau of Agricultural Economics (Department of Agriculture) (Functions dispersed, 1953)
BAIC . . . . . . Bureau of Agricultural and Industrial Chemistry (Department of Agriculture)
BAC . . . . Bureau of Air Commerce
ACTC . . . . . . Bureau of Air Commerce Type Certificate
BATM . . . . . . Bureau of Air Traffic Management
BAE . . . . Bureau of American Ethnology (of the Smithsonian Institution)
BARA . . . . . . Bureau d'Analyse et de Recherche Appliquees (Bureau of Analysis and Applied Research)
BAI . . . . Bureau of Animal Industry (Department of Agriculture)
BA . . . . Bureau of Apprenticeship (Labor Department)
BAT . . . . Bureau of Apprenticeship and Training (Department of Labor)
BAT . . . . Bureau de l'Assistance Technique
BBPS . . . . . . Bureau of Biological and Physical Sciences (of FDA)
BB . . . . Bureau of the Budget (Later, OMB)
BOB . . . . Bureau of the Budget (Later, OMB)
BC . . . . Bureau of the Census
BCC . . . . Bureau Central de Compensation
BCRA . . . . . . Bureau Centrale de Reseignements et d'Action (Free French)
BCF . . . . Bureau of Commercial Fisheries (of USFWS)
BOCF . . . . . . Bureau of Commercial Fisheries (US Department of the Interior)
BUCON . . . . . Bureau of Construction and Repair (Navy)
BUC & R . . . . . Bureau of Construction and Repair (Navy)

C & R ..... Bureau of Construction and Repair (of Navy) (Until 1940)
BC .... Bureau of Consultation (Federal Trade Commission)
BCI .... Bureau of Contract Information
BC .... Bureau of Customs (Department of the Treasury)
BDI .... Bureau of Dairy Industry (Department of Agriculture) (Functions transferred to ARS, 1953)
BDPI....... Bureau de Developpement et de Promotion Industriels (Bureau of Industrial Promotion and Development) (Malagasy Republic)
BDPEC ...... Bureau of Disease Prevention and Environmental Control
BDAC....... Bureau of Drug Abuse Control (Absorbed by Bureau of Narcotics and Dangerous Drugs of Department of Justice)
BEAPA ...... Bureau of East Asian and Pacific Affairs (Department of State) (Formerly, Bureau of Far Eastern Affairs)
BEA .... Bureau of Economic Affairs (Department of State)
BER .... Bureau of Economic Regulation (of CAB)
BE .... Bureau of Economics (Federal Trade Commission)
BEFT....... Bureau of Education for Fair Trade
BEH .... Bureau of Education for the Handicapped (Office of Education)
BEIA....... Bureau d'Education Ibero-Americain
BECA ...... Bureau of Educational and Cultural Affairs (Department of State)
BESE....... Bureau of Elementary and Secondary Education (Office of Education)
BEC .... Bureau of Employees' Compensation (Department of Labor)
BES .... Bureau of Employment Security (Labor)
BOE .... Bureau of Enforcement
BUENG ..... Bureau of Engineering (Navy)
BEP .... Bureau of Engraving and Printing (Treasury Department)
BELC .... Bureau pour l'Enseignement de la Language et de la Civilisation Francaises a l'Etranger (France)
BEPQ ...... Bureau of Entomology and Plant Quarantine (Department of Agriculture) (Functions transferred to ARS, 1953)
BER .... Bureau of Equipment and Recruiting (Navy)
BEEN ...... Bureau d'Etude de l'Energie Nucleaire
BEN .... Bureau d'Etudes Nucleaire (Belgium)
BEPI....... Bureau d'Etudes et des Participations Industries
BEA .... Bureau of European Affairs (Department of State)
BEC .... Bureau Europeen du Cafe
BECEG ..... Bureau Europeen de Controle et d'Etudes Generales
BEEP....... Bureau Europeen de l'Education Populaire
BEJE....... Bureau Europeen de la Jeunesse et de l'Enfance
BEUC ...... Bureau Europeen des Unions Consommateurs
BEM .... Bureau of Executive Manpower (Civil Service Commission)
BFS .... Bureau of Family Services (of SSA)
BFE .... Bureau for Far East (AID)
BFEA ..... Bureau of Far Eastern Affairs (Department of State)
BFCU ...... Bureau of Federal Credit Unions (Social Security Administration)
BFA .... Bureau of Finance and Administration (US Post Office)
BFC .... Bureau of Foreign Commerce (Commerce Department, abolished 1961)
BFDC ...... Bureau of Foreign and Domestic Commerce (In Department of Commerce; functions later dispersed)
BHI .... Bureau of Health Insurance (Social Security Administration)
BHM....... Bureau of Health Manpower
BHS .... Bureau of Health Services (PHS)
BHE .... Bureau of Higher Education (Office of Education)
BHNHE..... Bureau of Human Nutrition and Home Economics (Department of Agriculture) (Functions transferred to ARS, 1953)
BHI .... Bureau Hydrographique International
BIPAD...... Bureau of Independent Publishers and Distributors
BIA .... Bureau of Indian Affairs (Department of the Interior)
BOIA ...... Bureau of Indian Affairs (US Department of the Interior)
BIPE .... Bureau d'Informations et de Previsions Economiques (France)
BIS .... Bureau of Inspection and Survey
BIA .... Bureau of Insular Affairs (Originally, part of War Department; functions transferred to Department of Interior, 1939)
BIR .... Bureau of Intelligence and Research (Department of State)
BIS........ Bureau Interafricain des Sols et de l'Economie Rurale
BIAA ..... Bureau of Inter-American Affairs (Department of State)
BISMRA...... Bureau of Inter-Industrial Statistics & Multiple Regression Analysis
BIR........ Bureau of Internal Revenue (Treasury Department (Later, Internal Revenue Service)
BIAD ...... Bureau International d'Anthropologie Differentielle
BIBO ..... Bureau International Business Operations (Department of Commerce)
BICE....... Bureau International Catholique de l'Enfance
BIC....... Bureau International de la Chaussure et du Cuir
BIC .... Bureau International du Cinema
BIC .... Bureau of International Commerce (Department of Commerce)
BIC .... Bureau International des Containers
BDC .... Bureau International de Documentation des Chemins de Fer (International Office of Railway Documentation)
BIEM ...... Bureau International de l'Edition Mecanique
BIE .... Bureau International d'Education
BIE........ Bureau International des Expositions

BIH .... Bureau International de l'Heure
BIICC....... Bureau International d'Information des Chambres de Commerce
BILA ...... Bureau of International Labor Affairs (Department of Labor)
ILAB....... Bureau of International Labor Affairs (Department of Labor)
BIOA ..... Bureau of International Organization Affairs (Department of State)
BIPCA....... Bureau International Permanent de Chimie Analytique pour les Matieres Destinees a l'Alimentation de l'Homme et des Animaux
BIPM .... Bureau International des Poids et Mesures (International Bureau of Weights and Measures)
BIP .... Bureau of International Programs (Department of Commerce)
BIR........ Bureau International de la Recuperation
BIRISPT ..... Bureau International de Recherche sur les Implications Sociales du Progres Technique
BIS........ Bureau International du Scoutisme
BISFA...... Bureau International pour la Standardisation de la Rayonne et des Fibres Synthetiques (International Bureau for the Standardization of Man-Made Fibres)
BIT .... Bureau International du Travail (International Labour Office)
BIU .... Bureau International des Universites
BI .... Bureau of Investigation (Federal Trade Commission)
BIA .... Bureau Issues Association (Philately)
BJEP .... Bureau on Jewish Employment Problems
BLMR ..... Bureau of Labor-Management Reports (Department of Labor)
BLS .... Bureau of Labor Standards (Department of Labor)
BLS .... Bureau of Labor Statistics (Department of Labor)
BLM....... Bureau of Land Management (Department of the Interior)
BOLM....... Bureau of Land Management (US Department of the Interior)
BLA .... Bureau for Latin America (AID)
BLDCS ...... Bureau of Laundry and Dry Cleaning Standards
BLIC....... Bureau de Liaison des Industries du Caoutchouc de la CEE
BLET....... Bureau of Libraries and Educational Technology (Office of Education)
BL .... Bureau of Litigation (Federal Trade Commission)
BMU....... Bureau of Manpower Utilization (World War II)
BMS .... Bureau of Medical Services (Public Health Service)
BM .... Bureau of Medicine (of FDA)
BMS .... Bureau of Medicine and Surgery (Navy)
BUMED..... Bureau of Medicine and Surgery (Navy)
BUM & S ..... Bureau of Medicine and Surgery (Navy)
M & S ..... Bureau of Medicine & Surgery (Navy)
NMSHC ..... Bureau of Medicine and Surgery Hospital Corps Publication (Later, NAVMED) (Navy)
NM & S ..... Bureau of Medicine and Surgery Publications (Navy)
BM........ Bureau of Mines (Department of the Interior)
BOM .... Bureau of Mines
BMIC ...... Bureau of Mines Information Circular
BMTP ...... Bureau of Mines Technical Paper
BUMIFOM... Bureau Minier de la France d'Outre-Mer (Mining Bureau of Overseas France)
BM........ Bureau of the Mint (Department of the Treasury)
BMC .... Bureau of Motor Carriers (ICC)
BN........ Bureau of Narcotics (Treasury Department) (Absorbed by BNDD of Department of Justice)
BNDD....... Bureau of Narcotics and Dangerous Drugs (Formerly, Bureau of Narcotics and Bureau of Drug Abuse Control) (Department of Justice)
BNA....... Bureau of National Affairs
BNCA ..... Bureau of National Capital Airports (of FAA)
BNKCPA ..... Bureau National Kamerunais pour la Conference des Peuples Africains (Cameroonian National Bureau for African Peoples Conference)
BNG ...... Bureau of Natural Gas (of FPC)
BNP....... Bureau of Naval Personnel
BUPERS ..... Bureau of Naval Personnel
NAVPERS .... Bureau of Naval Personnel
BNPCL ..... Bureau of Naval Personnel Circular Letters
BNP....... Bureau of Naval Personnel Publications
BNS........ Bureau of Naval Ships (Obsolete)
BNW ...... Bureau of Naval Weapons (Obsolete)
BUWEPS ... Bureau of Naval Weapons (Obsolete)
NAVWEPS ... Bureau of Naval Weapons
BWBR ...... Bureau of Naval Weapons [Obsolete] Branch Representative
BUWEPS FR ... Bureau of Naval Weapons [Obsolete], Fleet Readiness
BUWEPSFLEREADREP .. Bureau of Naval Weapons [Obsolete] Fleet Readiness Representative
BWFRR ...... Bureau of Naval Weapons [Obsolete] Fleet Readiness Representative
BUWEPSFLEREADREPLANT.. Bureau of Naval Weapons [Obsolete] Fleet Readiness Representative, Atlantic
BUWEPSFLEREADREPCEN .. Bureau of Naval Weapons [Obsolete] Fleet Readiness Representative, Central
BUWEPSFLEREADREPPAC.. Bureau of Naval Weapons [Obsolete] Fleet Readiness Representative, Pacific
BIMRAB ..... BUWEPS (Bureau of Naval Weapons) [Obsolete] - Industry Material Reliability Advisory Board

BUWEPSINST .. Bureau of Naval Weapons [Obsolete] Instruction
BUWEPSREP ... Bureau of Naval Weapons [Obsolete] Representative
BWR .... Bureau of Naval Weapons [Obsolete] Representative
BUNAV...... Bureau of Navigation (Navy)
BPN .... Bureau of Navigation Publications (Later, NAVPERS) (Navy)
NNAV ...... Bureau of Navigation Publications (Later, BPN; then, NAVPERS) (Navy)
BNYD....... Bureau of Navy Yards and Docks
BNESA ...... Bureau for Near East and South Asia (AID)
BNESAA .... Bureau of Near Eastern and South Asian Affairs (Department of State)
BNM .... Bureau de Normalisation de la Mecanique (France)
BUNO ...... Bureau Number (Aircraft identification) (Navy)
BOASI ...... Bureau of Old-Age and Survivors Insurance (of the Social Security
              Administration)
BOR .... Bureau of Operating Rights
BO........ Bureau of Ordnance (Navy) (Functions transferred to Bureau of Naval
              Weapons, 1960)
BUORD ...... Bureau of Ordnance (Navy)
BODU....... Bureau of Ordnance Design Unit (Navy)
B of TE ..... Bureau of Ordnance Fleet Test Equipment
BOH........ Bureau of Ordnance and Hydrography (Navy)
NORD ...... Bureau of Ordnance Publication (Later, NAVORD) (Navy)
BOSO....... Bureau of Ordnance Shipment Order
BOOR ...... Bureau of Outdoor Recreation (US Department of the Interior)
BOR .... Bureau of Outdoor Recreation (Department of the Interior)
BPITT ...... Bureau Permanent Interafricain de la Tse-Tse et de la Trypanosomiase
BPICA....... Bureau Permanent International des Constructeurs d'Automobiles
BUPERSCONINSTRBIL .. Bureau of Personnel Controlled Instructor Billets (Navy)
BPPG .... Bureau Planned Procurement Guide (Navy)
BPI........ Bureau of Plant Industry (Department of Agriculture)
BPISAE ...... Bureau of Plant Industry, Soils, and Agricultural Engineering
              (Department of Agriculture) (Functions transferred to ARS, 1953)
BPN .... Bureau Politique National (National Political Bureau) (Of the Guinean
              PDG)
BP .... Bureau of Prisons (Department of Justice)
BPC .... Bureau of Provisions and Clothing (Navy)
BPA .... Bureau of Public Assistance (Social Security Administration)
BPD .... Bureau of the Public Debt
BPI........ Bureau of Public Inquiries
BPR ...... Bureau of Public Roads (Department of Transportation)
BP .... Bureau of Power (of FPC)
BRH .... Bureau of Radiological Health (SWRHL)
BRS .... Bureau of Railroad Safety (Department of Transportation)
BORM ...... Bureau of Raw Materials for American Vegetable Oils and Fats
              Industries
BRGM....... Bureau de Recherches Geologiques et Minieres (France)
BRPM ...... Bureau de Recherches et de Participations Minieres
BOR .... Bureau of Reclamation (Department of the Interior)
BR .... Bureau of Reclamation (Department of the Interior)
BRAL .... Bureau de Renseignements et d'Action, Londres (Free French)
BRE .... Bureau of Research and Engineering (Post Office Department)
BSSRS ...... Bureau of Safety and Supply Radio Services
BSNA ...... Bureau of Salesmen's National Associations
BS .... Bureau of Ships (Navy)
BUSHIPS .... Bureau of Ships (Later, ESC) (Navy)
NAVSHIPS.... Bureau of Ships Publications (Navy)
NBS .... Bureau of Ships Publications (Later, NAVSHIPS) (Navy)
BSSR ...... Bureau of Social Sciences Research, Inc.
BSWM ...... Bureau of Solid Waste Management (Environmental Science Services
              Administration)
BOSFW ...... Bureau of Sport Fisheries and Wildlife (US Department of the Interior)
BSFW ...... Bureau of Sport Fisheries and Wildlife (of USFWS)
BS .... Bureau of Standards
B of S ...... Bureau of Standards
BUSTDS ..... Bureau of Standards
BOSS .... Bureau for State Security (South Africa)
BSS .... Bureau of State Services (of Public Health Service)
BSE .... Bureau of Steam Engineering (Navy)
BSA .... Bureau of Supplies and Accounts (Later, NSUPSC) (Navy)
S & A ..... Bureau of Supplies and Accounts (Navy)
NAVSANDA .. Bureau of Supplies and Accounts Publications (Formerly, NSA) (Navy)
SANDASO.... Bureau of Supplies and Accounts (later, NSUPSC) Shipment Order (Navy)
BUSANDA.... Bureau of Supply and Accounts (later, NSUPSC) (Navy)
BTIS....... Bureau of Transportation and International Services (US Post Office)
BUT .... Bureau of University Travel
BVRR ...... Bureau of Veterans Reemployment Rights (Department of Labor)
BVS .... Bureau of Vital Statistics
BV .... Bureau Voucher (Army)
BWRL ...... Bureau of War Risk Litigation
BWC....... Bureau Weather Control
BWP .... Bureau of Work Programs (Department of Labor)
BWTP ...... Bureau of Work-Training Programs (Department of Labor)

BUDOCKS .... Bureau of Yards and Docks (Later, FEC) (Navy)
BUY & D .... Bureau of Yards and Docks (Navy)
BYD ...... Bureau of Yards and Docks (Later, NFEC)
Y & D..... Bureau of Yards and Docks (Navy)
NAVDOCKS ... Bureau of Yards and Docks Publications (Navy)
BIRPI ...... Bureaux Internationaux Reunis pour la Protection de la Propriete
              Intellectuelle (United International Bureau for the Protection of
              Intellectual Property)
BM........ Burgomaster
BJA .... Burlap and Jute Association
BHS .... Burlesque Historical Society
BAWA ..... Burley Auction Warehouse Association
BDLTEA .... Burley and Dark Leaf Tobacco Export Association
BLTDA ..... Burley Leaf Tobacco Dealers Association
BSC ...... Burley Stabilization Corporation
BTGCA ..... Burley Tobacco Growers Cooperative Association
BRC .... Burlingame Research Center
BUR .... Burlington Industries, Inc. (NYSE symbol)
BN........ Burlington Northern (Railroad)
B-RI .... Burlington-Rock Island Railroad Company
BTUC ...... Burma Trade Union Congress
BIAT....... Burn-In/Aging Tester
BOP .... Burn-Out Proof
BIS........ Burn-In Screening
BOV .... Burn-Out Velocity
BDC .... Burndy Corporation (NYSE symbol)
BITO ...... Burnishing Tool
BB .... Burroughs Bibliophiles
BC .... Burroughs Corporation
BGH....... Burroughs Corporation (NYSE symbol)
BEPOC ..... Burrough's Electrographic Printer-Plotter for Ordnance Computing
BEDAC ..... Burst Error Detection and Correlation
BPL .... Burst Position Locator
BC .... Bursting Charge (Military)
BHA .... Bus History Association
BT .... Bus (Electrical Conductor) Tie (Technical drawings)
BHB .... Bush Terminal Buildings (NYSE symbol)
BSH .... Bush Terminal Company (NYSE symbol)
BUSH ...... Bush Terminal R. R. (AAR code)
BAC .... Business Advisory Council
BATS ...... Business Air Transport Service
BCIU ...... Business Council for International Understanding
BCD .... Business Cycle Developments (A publication of Bureau of the Census)
BDPO ...... Business Data Processing Operation
BDSA ...... Business and Defense Services Administration (Department of Commerce)
BEST....... Business EDP Systems Technique
BEAA ...... Business Education Administrators Association
BERF ...... Business Education Research Foundation
BEC .... Business Electronics Computer (Used in training)
BEEF....... Business and Engineering Enriched FORTRAN (UNIVAC)
BEMA ..... Business Equipment Manufacturers Association
BETA ...... Business Equipment Trade Association
BEM .... Business Executives Move for Vietnam Peace
BET .... Business Experience Training (Program) (Chase Manhattan Bank)
BFI........ Business Forms Institute
BFMA ...... Business Forms Management Association
BGLA ...... Business Group for Latin America
BHF .... Business History Foundation
BIE........ Business-Industry-Education (Days) (Usually sponsored by chambers of
              commerce)
BIPAC ...... Business-Industry Political Action Committee
BIS........ Business Information System (Bell Laboratories)
BISCUS ..... Business Information System/Customer Service (Bell System)
BISP ...... Business Information Systems Programs (Bell System)
BIOR ...... Business Input/Output Rerun
BMF .... Business Mail Foundation
BMLUS ..... Business Men's League of the United States
BPW .... Business and Professional Women's Foundation
BPA .... Business Publications Audit of Circulation
BRS .... Business Radio Service
BSC .... Business Service Center
BUSIVISIT .... Business Visit (Program) (United States Travel Service)
BW .... Business Week (A magazine)
BB .... A Bust Bodice
BA .... Busted Aristocrat (A cadet officer reduced to the ranks) (Military slang)
BR .... Butadiene Rubber
B-B .... Butane-Butene Fraction
BEI....... Butanol Extractable Iodine
B......... Butcher (Navy)
BAT ...... Butler Air Transport, Ltd.
BL .... Butt Line (Technical drawings)

BAP . . . . Butte, Anaconda & Pacific Railway (AAR code)
BL . . . . Buttock Line (Technical drawings)
BCB . . . . Button Cell Battery
BGE . . . . Butyl Glycidyl Ether
BHA . . . . Butylated Hydroxyanisole (Chemical)
BHT . . . . Butylated Hydroxytoluene
BOC . . . . Butyloxy Carbonyl
BBI . . . . Buxom Belle, International
BUSH . . . . . . Buy United States Here
B7D . . . . Buyer has 7 Days to Take Up (Securities brokerage)
BO . . . . Buyer's Option (Business and trade)
BPI . . . . Buying Power Index
BBL . . . . Buys Ballot Law

BVD . . . . BVD Company (Initials stand for Bradley, Voorhies, and Day,
　　　　　　　　organizers of the company, and have come to be used as a generic
　　　　　　　　term for underwear)
X . . . . By (As in 9 x 12)
DP . . . . By Direction of the President
BAZA . . . . Byelorussian-American Association in the U.S.A.
BAVA . . . . . . Byelorussian-American Veteran Association
BLF . . . . Byelorussian Liberation Front
BYAA . . . . . . Byelorussian Youth Association of America
ABY . . . . Byers (A.M.) Company (NYSE symbol)
BP . . . . By-Pass
BMS . . . . Bypass Monochrome Signal

C

CMF . . . . C-Band Monopulse Feed
CRT . . . . C-Band RADAR Transponder
CTR . . . . C-Band Tracking RADAR
CBX . . . . C-Band Transponder (Radio)
COE . . . . Cab Over Engine (Type of truck)
CRB . . . . Cab Research Bureau
CAMP . . . . . . Cabin Air Manifold Pressure
CCEP . . . . . . Cabinet Committee for Economic Policy
CPS . . . . Cabinet Pressurization System
C . . . . Cable
CCA . . . . Cable Commuter Airlines
CURV . . . . . . Cable-Controlled Underwater Research Vehicle
CF . . . . Cable, Functional
CJZ . . . . Cable Jacket Zipper
CLS . . . . Cable Laying Ship
CMS . . . . Cable Marking System
CNJC . . . . . . Cable Network Joint Committee
CPE . . . . Cable Pressurization Equipment
ARC . . . . Cable Repairing or Laying Ship (Navy symbol)
CS . . . . Cable Ship (Followed by name of cable-laying ship)
CSK . . . . Cable Splicing Kit
CATV . . . . . . Cable Television
CTN . . . . Cable Termination Network
CT . . . . Cable, Test
CTM . . . . Cable Testing Meter
C/T . . . . Cable Transfer (of funds)
CABR . . . . . . Cabrillo National Monument
CSSA . . . . . . Cactus and Succulent Society of America
CADETRON . . . Cadet Practice Squadron
CLC . . . . Cadillac-LaSalle Club
CAD . . . . Cadiz R. R. (AAR code)
Cd . . . . Cadmium (Chemical element)
CRL . . . . Cadmium Red Line
CdS . . . . Cadmium Sulfide
CSC . . . . Cadmium-Sulfide Cell
CKB . . . . Caequot Kite Balloon
C . . . . Caesar
COBS . . . . . . Caesarean-Originated, Barrier-Sustained (Mice)
CTCA . . . . . . Cairn Terrier Club of America
CCDVT . . . . . Caisse Centrale de Depots et Vriements de Titres
CL . . . . Calamus Length
CLI . . . . Calamus Length Index
CGC . . . . Calavo Growers of California
Ca . . . . Calcium (Chemical element)
CCI . . . . Calcium Chloride Institute
CDC . . . . Calculated Date of Confinement (Medicine)
CMDO . . . . . Calcutta Metropolitan Development Organization
CPSU . . . . . . Calcutta Port Shramik Union (India)
CR . . . . Caledonian Railway
CD . . . . Calendar Day
CRF . . . . Calendar Reform Foundation
CRPAG . . . . . Calendar Reform Political Action Group
CY . . . . Calendar Year
CR . . . . Calendrier Republicain (Republican Calendar)
CYE . . . . Calgary & Edmonton Corporation (NYSE symbol)
CAS . . . . Calibrated Air Speed
CA . . . . Calibrated Altitude (Navigation)
CSD . . . . Calibrated Sweep Delay
CRS . . . . Calibration Requirements Summary
CTB . . . . Calibration Test Box
CVE . . . . Calibration Vibration Exciter
CA . . . . California
CAAA . . . . . . California Agricultural Aircraft Association

CARB . . . . . . California Air Resources Board
CAGE . . . . . . California Almond Growers Exchange
CAAB . . . . . . California Asparagus Advisory Board
CAAB . . . . . . California Avocado Advisory Board
CBR . . . . California Bearing Ratio (Aviation)
CCGA . . . . . California Cactus Growers Association
CCCD . . . . . . California Center for Community Development
CCA . . . . California Central Airlines
CDGA . . . . . California Date Growers Association
CDC . . . . California Debris Commission (Army)
CDO . . . . California Disaster Office
CDFAB . . . . . California Dried Fig Advisory Board
CDFEA . . . . . California Dried Fruit Export Association
CFC . . . . California Fashion Creators
CFI . . . . California Fig Institute
CFI . . . . California Financial Corporation (NYSE symbol)
CFCA . . . . . . California Fish Canners Association
CFA . . . . California Freezers Association
CFE . . . . California Fruit Exchange
CGTFL . . . . . California Grape and Tree Fruit League
CISW . . . . . . California Institute of Social Welfare
CALTECH . . . . California Institute of Technology
CIT . . . . California Institute of Technology
CIW . . . . California Institution for Women
CLETS . . . . . . California Law Enforcement Telecommunications System
CLEAN . . . . . . California League Enlisting Action Now (Antiobscenity group)
CLA . . . . California Library Association
CMA . . . . . . California Maritime Academy
CMT . . . . California Mastitis Test
CMHA . . . . . . California Mental Health Analysis (Testing)
CNFS . . . . . . California National Fuchsia Society
CNGA . . . . . California Natural Gas Association
COA . . . . California Olive Association
COIN . . . . . . California Olive Industry News
CFF . . . . California Packing Corporation (NYSE symbol)
CPGA . . . . . . California Persimmon Growers Association
CPAB . . . . . . California Prune Advisory Board
CPAGA . . . . . . California Prune and Apricot Growers Association
CRAB . . . . . . California Raisin Advisory Board
CRA . . . . California Redwood Association
CRLA . . . . . . California Rural Legal Assistance (Antipoverty program)
CSFA . . . . . . California School of Fine Arts
CSCF . . . . . . California State College at Fresno
CSEA . . . . . . California State Electronics Association
CSPC . . . . . . California State Polytechnical College
CSAB . . . . . . California Strawberry Advisory Board
CT . . . . California Terms (Grain shipping)
CTMM . . . . . California Test of Mental Maturity
CTL . . . . California Testing Laboratory
CUCOSS . . . . . California Universities Council on Space Sciences
CALUTRON . . . California University Cyclotron
CVA . . . . California Vehicle Act
CWR . . . . California Western R. R. (AAR code)
Cf . . . . Californium (Chemical element)
CIT . . . . Call-in Time (Military communications)
CQ . . . . Call to Quarters (General call preceding transmission of radio signals)
CR . . . . Call Request
CCS . . . . Call Seconds (Bell Laboratories)
CS . . . . Call Sign
C/S . . . . Call Sign (or Signal) (Radio)
CTA . . . . Call Time Adjustor (Military communications)
CMN . . . . . . Callahan Mining Corporation (NYSE symbol)
ZM . . . . Callahan Zinc-Lead Company (NYSE symbol)

CW . . . . Calls Waiting (Telephone communication)
C . . . . Calm (i.e., no wind)
C . . . . Calorie
CAH . . . . Calumet & Hecla, Inc. (NYSE symbol)
CLS . . . . Cam Limit Switch
COP . . . . Cam Operated Plunger
CPR . . . . Cam Plate Readout
CTC . . . . Cam Timing Contact
CWC . . . . Cam Wedge Clamp
CWPC . . . . . . Cam Wedge Power Clamp
CSP . . . . Camas Prairie R. R. (AAR code)
CI . . . . Cambria & Indiana Railway (AAR code)
CAS . . . . Cambrian Airways, Ltd.
CBEL . . . . . . The Cambridge Bibliography of English Literature
CBC . . . . Cambridge Bicycle Club (British)
CCC . . . . Cambridge Communication Corporation
CEA . . . . Cambridge Electron Accelerator (AEC)
CERL . . . . . . Cambridge Electronic Research Laboratory
CJC . . . . Cambridge Junior College (Massachusetts)
CLRU . . . . . . Cambridge Language Research Unit
CMH . . . . Cambridge Medieval History (A publication)
CAMROC . . . . Cambridge Radio Observatory Committee
CRC . . . . Cambridge Research Center (Air Force)
CRL . . . . Cambridge Research Laboratory
CUAC . . . . . . Cambridge University Athletic Club
CUBC . . . . . . Cambridge University Boat Club
CUM . . . . Cambridge University Mission
CUMS . . . . . . Cambridge University Musical Society
CUPU . . . . . . Cambridge University Prayer Union
CUPLE . . . . . Cambridge University Press Limited Editions
CCDL . . . . . . Camera Confederale del Lavoro (Confederal Chamber of Labor) (Italy/Trieste)
CCU . . . . Camera Control Unit
CG . . . . Camera Gun
CIWG . . . . . . Camera Industries of West Germany
CR . . . . Camera Repairman (Navy rating)
CTI . . . . Camera Timing Indicator
CSAC . . . . . . Cameron State Agricultural College (Oklahoma)
CAMSTA . . . . . Cameron Station (Army)
CPNC . . . . . . Cameroons People's National Congress
CPLT . . . . Camino, Placerville & Lake Tahoe R. R. (AAR code)
CSV . . . . Cammed-Gear Speed Variator
CD . . . . Camouflage Detection (Often, in regard to a special photographic film, as, "CD film") (Military)
CCSL . . . . . . Camp Coles Signal Laboratory (Army)
CESL . . . . . . Camp Evans Signal Laboratory (Army)
CFCA . . . . . . Camp Fire Club of America
CFG . . . . Camp Fire Girls
CNS . . . . Camp Newspaper Service
CRS . . . . Camp Reception Station (A kind of field hospital) (British)
CND . . . . Campaign for Nuclear Disarmament
CWG . . . . . . Campaign for World Government
C-E . . . . Campbell-Ewald Company (Advertising agency)
CLP . . . . Campbell-Larsen Potentiometer
CRK . . . . Campbell Red Lake Mines, Ltd. (NYSE symbol)
CPB . . . . Campbell Soup Company (NYSE symbol)
CCK . . . . Campbell's Creek R. R. (AAR code)
COPE . . . . . . Campership Outdoor Program of Education (Federal antipoverty program)
CTMA . . . . . . Camping Trailer Manufacturers Association
CADA . . . . . . Campus Americans for Democratic Action
CCC . . . . Campus Crusade for Christ
C . . . . Can (Buoy) (Maps and charts)
CGO . . . . Can Go Over (Newspapers)
CMI . . . . Can Manufacturers Institute
UCM . . . . Can You Come and See Me?
CA . . . . Canada (NATO)
CD . . . . Canada Dry Corporation (NYSE symbol)
CE . . . . Canada East
CGT . . . . Canada & Gulf Terminal Railway (AAR code)
CIR . . . . Canada-India Reactor
CASO . . . . . . Canada Southern R. R. (AAR code)
CNS . . . . Canada Southern Railway Company (NYSE symbol)
CSSL . . . . . . Canada Steamship Lines R. R., Ltd. (AAR code)
CAN-UK . . . . Canada-United Kingdom
CANUKUS . . . . Canada-United Kingdom-United States (Agreement)
CUSRPG . . . . . Canada-United States Regional Planning Group (NATO)
CW . . . . Canada West
C . . . . Canadian
CAI . . . . Canadian Aeronautical Institute
CASI . . . . Canadian Aeronautics and Space Institute
CADIZ . . . . . . Canadian Air Defense Identification Zone

CAD . . . . Canadian Air Division
CANAIRDIV . . . Canadian Air Division Headquarters (Allied Air Forces in Europe)
CAGE . . . . . . Canadian Air-Ground Environment
CANAIRTRAIN . . Canadian Air Training Command Headquarters
CAMSI . . . . . . Canadian, American Merchant Shipping Instructions
CARDE . . . . . Canadian Armament Research and Development Establishment
CAC . . . . Canadian Armoured Corps
CAORE . . . . . Canadian Army Operational Research Establishment
CACL . . . . . . Canadian Association of Children's Librarians
CACUL . . . . . Canadian Association of College and University Libraries
CAHPER . . . . . Canadian Association for Health, Physical Education, and Recreation
CAMSI . . . . . . Canadian Association of Medical Students and Interns
CANLANT . . . . Canadian Atlantic Subarea (Canadian Navy)
CASCO . . . . . Canadian Australian Line
CBPC . . . . . . Canadian Book Publishers' Council
CNB . . . . Canadian Breweries, Ltd. (NYSE symbol)
CBC . . . . Canadian Broadcasting Corporation (State-operated radio and television)
COSC . . . . . . Canadian Chiefs of Staff Committee
CC . . . . Canadian Club (A whiskey)
CCNY . . . . . . Canadian Club of New York
CCZA . . . . . . Canadian Coastal Zone Atlantic
CCZP . . . . . . Canadian Coastal Zone Pacific
CANCON . . . . Canadian Control System (For convoys in Canadian Coastal Zone)
CCURR . . . . . Canadian Council on Urban and Regional Research
CDLS(W) . . . . Canadian Defence Liaison Staff (Washington)
CDA(W) . . . . . Canadian Dental Association
CANDESLANT . . Canadian Destroyers Atlantic
CANDESFE . . . Canadian Destroyers Far East
CANDESPAC . . Canadian Destroyers Pacific
CANDU . . . . . Canadian Deuterium Uranium
CDDA . . . . . . Canadian Diamond Drilling Association
CND . . . . Canadian Dredge & Dock Company, Ltd. (American Stock Exchange symbol)
CESA . . . . . . Canadian Engineering Standards Association (Became Canadian Standards Association)
CEF . . . . Canadian Expeditionary Forces
CAF . . . . Canadian Force
CANAIRPEG . . . Canadian 14th Air Training Group Headquarters, Winnipeg
CGRA . . . . . . Canadian Good Roads Association
CANDU . . . . . Canadian Heavy-Water Reactor
CITL . . . . Canadian Industrial Traffic League
CICA . . . . . . Canadian Institute of Chartered Accountants
CIIA . . . . Canadian Institute of International Affairs
CIMM . . . . . . Canadian Institute of Mining & Metallurgy
C Int C . . . . . Canadian Intelligence Corps
CJS . . . . Canadian Joint Staff
CLC . . . . Canadian Labour Congress
CLA . . . . Canadian Library Association (Also known as ACB)
CLA . . . . Canadian Lumbermen's Association
CMCSA . . . . . Canadian Manufacturers of Chemical Specialties Association
CMA . . . . Canadian Medical Association
CANAVUS . . . . Canadian Member, Canadian Joint Staff, Washington, DC
CAMESA . . . . . Canadian Military Electronics Standards Agency
CMR . . . . Canadian Mounted Rifles
CNE . . . . Canadian National Exhibition (Held annually in Toronto)
CNIB . . . . . . Canadian National Institute for the Blind
CN . . . . Canadian National Railways (AAR code)
CNR . . . . Canadian National Railways
CNSS . . . . . . Canadian National Steamships (AAR code)
CNB . . . . Canadian Naval Board
CANCOMNEW . . Canadian Naval Commander Newfoundland
CNMO . . . . . . Canadian Naval Mission Overseas
CNS . . . . Canadian Naval Service
CNA . . . . Canadian Northwest Atlantic Area
CNA . . . . Canadian Nuclear Association
COEV . . . . . . Canadian Ocean Escort Vessel
CORS . . . . . . Canadian Operational Research Society
COF . . . . Canadian Order of Foresters
COTC . . . . . . Canadian Overseas Telecommunications Corporation
CPAL . . . . . . Canadian Pacific Air Line
CPA . . . . Canadian Pacific Airlines, Ltd.
CPR . . . . Canadian Pacific Railway
CP . . . . Canadian Pacific Railway Company (NYSE symbol)
CPRI . . . . . . Canadian Peace Research Institute
CPSA . . . . . . Canadian Political Science Association
CPC . . . . Canadian Postal Corps (Later, RCPC)
CP . . . . Canadian Press
CPRS . . . . . . Canadian Public Relations Society
CPPA . . . . . . Canadian Pulp and Paper Association
CRDF . . . . . . Canadian Radio-Direction Finding or Finder
CANSAF . . . . . Canadian Sales Finance Long Form Report

CANSERVCOL.. Canadian Services College
CSNY...... Canadian Society of New York
CSA........ Canadian Standards Association
CANAIRTAC .. Canadian Tactical Air Command Headquarters
CTF........ Canadian Teachers Federation
CANTAT..... Canadian Transatlantic Telephone Cable
CUC........ Canadian Union College
CANUKUS JCECS.. Canadian–United Kingdom–United States Joint Communications-
    Electronics Committees
CANUSE..... Canadian–United States Eastern Power Complex
CUSO....... Canadian University Service Overseas
CWB....... Canadian Weekly Bulletin (A publication)
CWA....... Canadian Western Approaches
CWAC...... Canadian Women's Army Corps
CWW....... Canadian Woodmen of the World
CSNYS..... Canal Society of New York State
CZ........ Canal Zone
CZBA ...... Canal Zone Biological Area (A preserve administered by the Smith-
    sonian Institution)
CZG....... Canal Zone Government
CZJC...... Canal Zone Junior College
CCTS...... Canaveral Council of Technical Societies
CTR....... Canaveral Test Report
CCA....... Cancel Corridor Assignment (Aviation)
CIFP....... Cancel IFR (Instrument Flight Rules) Flight Plan
C......... Canceled
CCFRA ..... Cancelled Concurrent with Next Federal Register Amendment
CFO....... Canceling Former Order
CA........ Cancer
CCI....... Cancer Care, Incorporated (of the National Cancer Foundation)
CCNSC..... Cancer Chemotherapy National Service Center
CCF....... Cancer Cytology Foundation of America
CCFA...... Cancer Cytology Foundation of America
CD........ Candela
C Th ...... Candidate of Theology
Th C ...... Candidate of Theology
C......... Candle (Illumination)
CH........ Candle Hours (Illumination)
CMA ...... Candle Manufacturers Association
CP .... Candle Power (Physics)
CBA....... Candy Brokers Association of America
CCCI...... Candy, Chocolate and Confectionery Institute
CN........ Canet Nordenfelt Gun
CEHC...... Canever English History Club
K9........ Canine (K9 Corps - Army Dogs) (World War II)
CD........ Canine Distemper (Veterinary medicine)
CD........ Canine Dose (Pharmacology)
C......... Canine Tooth (Dentistry)
CMa....... Canis Major (IAU)
CMi....... Canis Minor (IAU)
CCSFI..... Canned Chop Suey Foods Industry
CSI .... Canned Salmon Institute
CMSA..... Canning Machinery and Supplies Association
CHOB...... Cannon House Office Building
CHAOS..... Cannon Hunters Association of Seattle
CF........ Cannot Find
CPAO...... Canoga Park Area Office (AEC)
C......... Canon
CLS....... Canon Law Society of America
CRIC ...... Canonici Regulares Immaculate Conceptionis (Canons Regular of the
    Immaculate Conception)
CRL....... Canonici Regulares Lateranenses (Canons Regular of the Lateran)
CMAR...... Can't Manage a Rifle (Formed by reversing the initials of Royal
    Army Medical Corps) (British) (World War I)
CTW....... Can't Tell What (Accounting slang)
CTN....... Canton R. R. (AAR code)
CAA....... Cantors Assembly of America
CF........ Cantus Firmus (Plain Chant)
CAI....... Canvas Awning Institute
CPA....... Canvas Products Association International
CACH...... Canyon de Chelly National Monument
CANY...... Canyonlands National Park
CI .... Capability Inspection (Air Force)
C......... Capacitance
CD........ Capacitor Diode
CDG....... Capacitor Diode Gate
CLI .... Capacitor Leakage Indicator
CQP....... Capacitor Qualification Program
CQT ...... Capacitor Qualification Test
CQTP...... Capacitor Qualification Test Program
CRIG ...... Capacitor Rate-Integrating Gyroscope

CRD....... Capacitor-Resistor Diode
CRF....... Capacitor Resonance Frequency
CTP ...... Capacitor Test Program
CAPSHIPFOR .. Capacity Ships Force
C......... Cape (Maps and charts)
CB........ Cape Breton Island
CCMTA..... Cape Canaveral Missile Test Annex (Later, KSC)
CCMTC..... Cape Canaveral Missile Test Center (Later, KSC)
CCDC...... Cape Cod Direction Center (Air Force)
CACO ..... Cape Cod National Seashore (National Park Service designation)
CCS....... Cape Cod System (Air Force)
CC........ Cape Colony (British Empire)
CF........ Cape Fear Railways, Inc. (AAR code)
CGH....... Cape of Good Hope
CAHA ..... Cape Hatteras National Seashore (National Park Service designation)
CKAFS..... Cape Kennedy Air Force Station
CKSNI..... Cape Kennedy Space Network, Incorporated
CALO...... Cape Lookout National Seashore (National Park Service designation)
CMR....... Cape Mounted Rifles (British)
CMRLW.... Cape Mounted Rifles, Left Wing (British)
CMRRW.... Cape Mounted Rifles, Right Wing (British)
CP........ Cape Province (of South Africa)
CV........ Cape de Verde Island
CVI .... Cape Verde Islands
COP....... Capillary Osmotic Pressure (Physiology)
CP........ Capillary Pressure (Physiology)
C/A........ Capital Account (Business and trade)
CA........ Capital Airlines, Inc.
CAP....... Capital Airlines, Inc.
CA........ Capital Asset
CEP....... Capital Expenditure Proposal
CER....... Capital Expenditure Request
CIP........ Capital Investment Program
CMD....... Capital Military District (Vietnam)
CRF ...... Capital Recovery Factor
CS........ Capital Stock
C & LC .... Capitals and Lower Case (Printing)
C & SC .... Capitals and Small Capitals (Printing)
CHS....... Capitol Historical Society (Washington, DC)
CREI...... Capitol Radio Engineering Institute
CARE...... Capitol Reef National Monument
CAPCOM ... Capsule Communications (or Communicator)
CC........ Capsule Communicator
CITE...... Capsule Integrated Test Equipment
CIP........ Capsule Internal Programmer
CMTM ..... Capsule Mechanical Training Model
COP ...... Capsule Observation Panel
CPM....... Capsule Positioning Mechanism
CSAD ..... Capsule Systems Advanced Development
CST ...... Capsule Systems Test (NASA)
C......... Captain
CCF....... Captain, Coastal Forces
CCFET..... Captain, Coastal Forces, Eastern Theater
CEF....... Captain (Commanding) Escort Forces (Navy)
CG........ Captain-General
CG........ Captain of the Guard
COTP...... Captain of the Port (Coast Guard)
RMC....... Captain of Royal Marines (Military) (British)
COVAM .... Capture Orbit Vehicle Assembly Mode
CAB....... Captured Air Bubble (Surface effect ship)
CABB ..... Captured Air Bubble Boat (Navy)
CEE....... Captured Enemy Equipment (Military)
CEM....... Captured Enemy Material
CESE ..... Captured Enemy Signal Equipment (Military)
CSBN..... Captured Steam Bubble Nuclear
CAMO ..... Capulin Mountain National Monument
C......... Caput (Head)
CDOA ..... Car Department Officers Association
YCF....... Car Float (Navy symbol)
CATRALA ... Car and Truck Renting and Leasing Association
C......... Carat (Signifies a twenty-fourth part; i.e., 24-carat gold is pure
    gold, 12-carat gold is half gold, half other substances)
C......... Carat (Unit of measure for precious stones equal to 200 milligrams;
    see also meaning re gold)
CM .... Carat (Metric)
CEW....... Caravan of East and West
CF........ Carbofuchsin
CMB....... Carbolic Methylene Blue
C......... Carbon (Chemical element)
CBE ...... Carbon Black Export
CC........ Carbon Copy

CBC . . . . Carbon County Railway Company (AAR code)
CFRP. . . . . . . Carbon-Fiber Reinforced Plastic
CFR . . . . Carbon-Film Resistor
CHN . . . . Carbon, Hydrogen, Nitrogen
CMMS . . . . . . Carbon Monoxide Measuring System
CPIRA. . . . . . Carbon Paper and Inked Ribbon Association
CS . . . . Carbon Steel
CT . . . . Carbon Tetrachloride
CTC . . . . Carbon Tetrachloride
CZB . . . . Carbon Zinc Battery
CBCMC . . . . . Carbonated Beverage Can Makers Committee
CBI . . . . Carbonated Beverage Institute
CA . . . . Carbonic Anhydrase (Biochemistry)
CBO. . . . . . . Carborundum Company (NYSE symbol)
CM . . . . Carboxymethyl
CMLE . . . . . . Carboxymuconate Lactonizing Enzyme
CMD . . . . Carboxymuconolactone Decarboxylase
CNR. . . . . . . Carboxy-Nitroso Rubber
CTPB . . . . . . Carboxyl-Terminated Polybutadiene Binder
CAT . . . . Carburetor Air Temperature (Aviation)
CEA . . . . Carcinoembryonic Antigen (Cancerous tumor)
CAP . . . . Card Assembly Program
CARD . . . . . . Card Automated Reproduction and Distribution System (Library of Congress)
CCMA . . . . . . Card Clothing Manufacturers Association
CC . . . . Card Code
CIMCO . . . . . Card Image Correction (Data processing)
CMT . . . . Card Module Tester
CPC . . . . Card Programmed Calculator (Data processing)
CRAM . . . . . Card Random Access Memory (Data processing)
CTT . . . . Card-to-Tape Tape (Data processing)
CARDIAC . . . . Cardboard Illustrative Aid to Computation (Data processing)
CRO. . . . . . . Carded for Record Only
CYA. . . . . . . Carded Yarn Association
CAC . . . . Cardiac Accelerator Center (Physiology)
CIC . . . . Cardiac Inhibition Center (Physiology)
CMO . . . . . . Cardiac Minute Output (Physiology)
CO . . . . Cardiac Output (Physiology)
COR. . . . . . . Cardiac Output Recorder
CWCCA . . . . . Cardigan Welsh Corgi Club of America
CMF . . . . Cardinal Mindszenty Foundation
CSC . . . . Cardinal Stritch College (Wisconsin)
CPR . . . . Cardiopulmonary Resuscitation (Medicine)
CV . . . . Cardiovascular (Medicine)
CRC . . . . Cardiovascular Reflex Conditioning
CRCS . . . . . . Cardiovascular Reflex Conditioning System
CVS . . . . Cardiovascular System
CPM . . . . Cards Per Minute (Data processing)
K . . . . Care; Carus; Cara (Dear One)
C/O. . . . . . . Care Of
C & P. . . . . . Care and Preservation (Army)
CC. . . . . Career Control
CDC . . . . Career Development Center
CDC . . . . Career Development Course
CM . . . . Career Motivation
COY. . . . . . . Career Opportunities for Youth
COPE . . . . . . Career Oriented Preparation for Employment (Federal antipoverty program)
CAY. . . . . . . Carey (The Philip) Mfg. Co. (NYSE symbol)
CDR . . . . Cargo Delivery Receipt
CDI . . . . Cargo Disposition Instructions
CX-HLS . . . . . Cargo Experimental, Heavy Logistic Support (Aircraft) (Air Force)
CG. . . . . Cargo Glider (Military)
CHB . . . . Cargo Handling Battalion (Army)
CHE . . . . Cargo Handling Equipment
CLEM . . . . . . Cargo Lunar Excursion Module
CARA . . . . . . Cargo and Rescue Aircraft
AK . . . . Cargo Ship (of any type)
AKV . . . . Cargo Ship and Aircraft Ferry (Navy symbol)
AKD . . . . Cargo Ship, Dock (Navy symbol)
AK(SS) . . . . . Cargo Submarine (Navy symbol)
ASSA . . . . . . Cargo Submarine (Navy symbol)
SSA . . . . Cargo Submarine (Navy Designation)
C . . . . Cargo/Transport (Designation for all US military aircraft)
CGA . . . . Cargo's Proportion of (General) Average (Business and trade)
CAC . . . . Caribbean Air Command (Air Force)
CAIRC . . . . . Caribbean Air Command (Air Force)
CASCP . . . . . Caribbean Area Small Craft Project
CBA . . . . Caribbean Atlantic Airlines, Inc. (of Puerto Rico)
CARIBCOM . . . Caribbean Command (Military)
CC. . . . . Caribbean Commission (Later, Caribbean Organization)
CCL . . . . Caribbean Congress of Labor
CCC . . . . Caribbean Conservation Corporation

CDC . . . . Caribbean Defense Command(er)
CDB . . . . Caribbean Development Bank (UN)
CES . . . . Caribbean Educational Service
CARIFTA . . . . Caribbean Free Trade Association
CGA . . . . Caribbean Gamefishing Association
CMI . . . . Caribbean Meteorological Institute
CO . . . . Caribbean Organization (An international governmental body, of which the US is a member)
CARIBSEAFRON. . Caribbean Sea Frontier (Navy)
CSF . . . . Caribbean Sea Frontier
CTA . . . . Caribbean Travel (formerly, Tourist) Association
CPT . . . . Caribou Performance Test
CSA . . . . Caricaturists Society of America
K . . . . Carissimus (Dearest)
CSL . . . . Carlisle Corporation (NYSE symbol)
CL . . . . Carload
CL . . . . Carload Lot (Commerce)
CACA . . . . . . Carlsbad Caverns National Park
CBL . . . . Carlyle Barton Laboratory
CMK . . . . . . Carnation Company (NYSE symbol)
CCNY. . . . . . Carnegie Corporation of New York
CEIP. . . . . . . Carnegie Endowment for International Peace
CFAT . . . . . . Carnegie Foundation for the Advancement of Teaching
CIT. . . . . Carnegie Institute of Technology (Pennsylvania)
CIW . . . . Carnegie Institution of Washington
CMU. . . . . . . Carnegie-Mellon University
CCL . . . . Carolina, Clinchfield & Ohio Railway (NYSE symbol)
CRN. . . . . . . Carolina & Northwestern Railway Company (AAR code)
CPL . . . . Carolina Power & Light Company (NYSE symbol)
CRS . . . . Carolina Southern Railway Company (AAR code)
CARW. . . . . . Carolina Western R. R. (AAR code)
CVNPA . . . . . Carolinas-Virginia Nuclear Power Associates, Inc.
CVTR . . . . . . Carolinas-Virginia Tube Reactor
CR . . . . Carolus Rex (King Charles)
CRS . . . . Carpenter Steel Company (NYSE symbol)
CM . . . . Carpenter's Mate
CMCB. . . . . . Carpenter's Mate, Construction Battalion
CMCBB . . . . . Carpenter's Mate, Construction Battalion, Builder
CMCBD . . . . . Carpenter's Mate, Construction Battalion, Draftsman
CMCBE . . . . . Carpenter's Mate, Construction Battalion, Excavation Foreman
CMSR . . . . . . Carpenter's Mate, Ship Repair
CMSRB . . . . . Carpenter's Mate, Ship Repair, Boatbuilder--Wood
CMSRC . . . . . Carpenter's Mate, Ship Repair, Carpenter
CMSRK . . . . . Carpenter's Mate, Ship Repair, Caulker--Boat
CMSRN. . . . . Carpenter's Mate, Ship Repair, Cement Worker--Concrete
CMSRJ . . . . . Carpenter's Mate, Ship Repair, Joiner
CMSRS . . . . . Carpenter's Mate, Ship Repair, Shipwright
CREATE . . . . . Carpet Research, Engineering, Aesthetics, Technological Evaluation (Dow Chemical Company)
CWC . . . . Carpet Wool Council
CPSE . . . . . . Carr-Purcell Spin-Echo
COGSA . . . . . Carriage of Goods by Sea Act
CP. . . . . Carriage Paid
CR . . . . Carriage Return
CRC . . . . Carriage Return Contact
CD. . . . . Carried Down
CF . . . . Carried Forward (Accounting)
CO . . . . Carried Over (Bookkeeping)
CAG . . . . Carrier Air Group (Navy)
CANCARAIRGRP. . Carrier Air Group (Canadian military)
CARAIRGROUP. . Carrier Air Group
CATCC . . . . . . Carrier Air Traffic Control Center (Navy)
CAINS . . . . . . Carrier Aircraft Inertial Navigation System
CASD . . . . . . Carrier Aircraft Service Detachment (Marine Corps)
CASD . . . . . . Carrier Aircraft Service Division (Navy)
CASDIV. . . . . Carrier Aircraft Service Division (Navy)
CASU . . . . . . Carrier Aircraft Service Unit (Navy)
CBALS. . . . . . Carrier Borne Air Liaison Section
CBLS . . . . . . Carrier Borne Air Liaison Section (Navy)
CCA. . . . . . . Carrier Controlled Approach (Aircraft carrier RADAR landing system)
CRR . . . . Carrier Corporation (NYSE symbol)
CARDIV. . . . . Carrier Division (Navy)
CEF . . . . Carrier Elimination Filter
CF . . . . Carrier Frequency (Radio)
CFS . . . . Carrier Frequency Shift
CGF. . . . . . . Carrier Gas Fusion (Chemistry)
CGA . . . . Carrier Group Alarm (Telephone communications)
CNL . . . . Carrier Noise Level
CNR. . . . . . . Carrier-to-Noise Ratio
COD . . . . Carrier-On-Deck (Navy carrier-based aircraft)
COD . . . . Carrier Onboard Delivery (Naval aviation)

CODAN . . . . . Carrier-Operated Device, Antinoise (Radio)
CONS . . . . . . Carrier-Operated Noise Suppression
COR. . . . . . . Carrier-Operated Relay
CARQUALS . . . Carrier Qualification Landings
CQTU . . . . . . Carrier Qualification Training Unit
CRAG. . . . . . Carrier Replacement Air Group
CRAW . . . . . . Carrier Replacement Air Wing (Navy)
CS . . . . Carrier Stability
C-SCAN . . . . . Carrier System for Control Approach of Naval Aircraft
CARTASKFOR. . Carrier Task Force (Navy)
CTR . . . . Carrier Telegraph Receiver
CT . . . . Carrier Telephone Channel
CVR . . . . Carrier Vessel Reactor
CW . . . . Carrier Wave (A form of radio transmission in code) (Navy)
CR . . . . Carrier's Risk (Shipping)
CGR. . . . . . . Carriers & General Corporation (NYSE symbol)
CARPAC . . . . . Carriers, Pacific Fleet (Navy)
CARR . . . . . . Carrollton R. R. (AAR code)
CTT . . . . Carrousel Transfer Tube
CF . . . . Carry Forward
CARBASORD. . Carry Out Unexecuted Portion Basic Orders
CCDW . . . . . . Carrying Concealed Deadly Weapon
CCW . . . . . . Carrying Concealed Weapon
CDW . . . . . . Carrying a Dangerous Weapon (Police term)
CNC . . . . Carson-Newman College (Tennessee)
CDV. . . . . . . Carte-de-Visite (Visiting Card)
C de V. . . . . . Carte de Visite (Visiting Card)
CSC . . . . Cartel des Syndicats Caledoniens (Federation of New Caledonian Trade
           Unions)
CAR . . . . Carter Products, Inc. (NYSE symbol)
CMF. . . . . . . Cartesian Mapping Function
CARPLE . . . . . Cartilla Electoral Para el Plebiscito (Colombia)
C to S . . . . . . Carting to Shipside
CT . . . . Cartographer (Navy rating)
CAST . . . . . . Cartoon Archetypical Slogan Theater (London)
CSGB . . . . . . Cartophilic Society of Great Britain
CAD. . . . . . . Cartridge-Activated Devices (Military)
CSC . . . . Cartridge Storage Case
CEDAM. . . . . Casa Editrice Dott. A. Milani (Italian publisher)
CAGR . . . . . . Casa Grand Ruins National Monument
CIP. . . . . Cascade Improvement Program
C . . . . Case
JI . . . . Case (J. I.) Company (NYSE symbol)
CH. . . . . Case Harden (Metal) (Technical drawings)
CIT. . . . . Case Institute of Technology (Later, Case Western Reserve University)
CN . . . . Case of Need
CWRU. . . . . . Case-Western Reserve University
CIA . . . . Casein Importers Association
CPT . . . . Casement Projected Transom (Technical drawings)
C. . . . . Cash (NYSE symbol)
CAD . . . . Cash Against Documents (Banking)
CBD . . . . Cash Before Delivery
C/B . . . . Cash Book
CCA. . . . . . . Cash Clothing Allowance
CC. . . . . Cash Credit
COD . . . . . . Cash on Delivery
CDS . . . . Cash on Delivery Service
CD. . . . . Cash Discount
C/L . . . . Cash Letter (Banking)
C/O. . . . . . . Cash Order
CWO . . . . . . Cash with Order
CPA . . . . Cash Purchasing Agent
COR. . . . . . . Cash on Receipt
COS. . . . . . . Cash-on-Shipment
CC. . . . . Cashier's Check
CMA . . . . . . Casket Manufacturers Association of America
CJC . . . . Casper Junior College (Wyoming)
CRA . . . . Cassegrain Reflector Antenna
CB . . . . Cast Brass
CBBI. . . . . . . Cast Bronze Bearing Institute
CC. . . . . Cast Copper
CI . . . . Cast Iron
CIP. . . . . Cast-Iron Pipe (Technical drawings)
CIPRA. . . . . . Cast Iron Pipe Research Association
CISPF . . . . . . Cast Iron Soil Pipe Foundation
CISPI . . . . . . Cast Iron Soil Pipe Institute
CMP. . . . . . . Cast Metal Part
CON . . . . Cast-Out-Nines
CS . . . . Cast Steel
CFTMA . . . . . Caster and Floor Truck Manufacturers Association
CT . . . . Casters and Towbar

CASA . . . . . . Castillo de San Marcos National Monument
C . . . . Castle
CACL . . . . . . Castle Clinton National Monument
CCS . . . . Casualty Clearing Station (Military)
CASCOR . . . . Casualty Corrected (Navy)
CEO. . . . . . . Casualty Evacuation Officer
CASREPT . . . . Casualty Reports (Navy)
CSF . . . . Casualty Staging Facility (Military)
CSU . . . . Casualty Staging Unit (Military)
CVN . . . . Casualty Vulnerability Number
CFA . . . . Cat Fanciers' Association
CFF . . . . Cat Fanciers' Federation
C. . . . . Catalog
CANO . . . . . . Catalog Number
CSA . . . . Catalog Services Association
CCS . . . . Cataloging and Classification Section (of RTSD) (Library science)
CIS . . . . Cataloging in Source (Later, CIP)
CCC. . . . . . . Catalytic Construction Company
CAM . . . . . . Catapult Aircraft Merchantship (Used by British RAF to catapult
           Hurricane fighter planes from ships to defend convoys from enemy
           bombers) (World War II)
CAP. . . . . . . Catapult and Arresting-Gear Pool (Navy)
CB . . . . Catapult Bulletin
CB . . . . Catch Basin (Technical drawings)
CP . . . . Catch Phrase
CSA . . . . Catch Society of America
C. . . . . Catcher (Baseball)
COMT . . . . . . Catecholamine-O-Methyl-Transferase
CTR . . . . Caterpillar Tractor Company (NYSE symbol) (Wall Street slang name:
           "Cat")
C . . . . Cathode
CF . . . . Cathode Follower
CFM. . . . . . . Cathode Follower Mixer
COC . . . . Cathode Opening Contraction
COT . . . . Cathode Opening Tetanus
CPS . . . . Cathode Potential Stabilized
CPM. . . . . . . Cathode Pulse Modulation
CR . . . . Cathode Ray
CRDF . . . . . . Cathode-Ray Direction Finding (RADAR)
CRET. . . . . . . Cathode Ray Electron Tube
CRF . . . . Cathode Ray Furnace
CRL . . . . Cathode Ray Lamp
CO . . . . Cathode Ray Oscillator
CRO . . . . Cathode-Ray Oscilloscope or Oscillograph
C-SCOPE . . . . Cathode-Ray Screen (Air Force)
CRT . . . . Cathode-Ray Tube
CRTO . . . . . . Cathode Ray Tube Oscillograph
CRTS . . . . . . Cathode Ray Tube Shield
CRTT. . . . . . . Cathode Ray Tube Tester
CRT . . . . Cathode-Ray Typesetting
CR . . . . Cathode Reaction
CPE . . . . Cathodic Protection Equipment
CPSK . . . . . . Cathodic Protection Survey Kit
CSK . . . . Cathodic Survey Kit
C . . . . Catholic
CAG . . . . Catholic Accountants Guild
CAGA . . . . . . Catholic Actors Guild of America
CAA. . . . . . . Catholic Anthropological Association
CAC. . . . . . . Catholic Anthropological Conference
CAA. . . . . . . Catholic Art Association
CAOF. . . . . . Catholic Association of Foresters
CAIP . . . . Catholic Association for International Peace
CAVE . . . . . . Catholic Audio-Visual Educators Association
CALOLL . . . . . Catholic Aviation League of Our Lady of Loreto
CBSA . . . . . . Catholic Bible Society of America
CBA . . . . Catholic Biblical Association of America
CBB . . . . Catholic Big Brothers
CBW. . . . . . . Catholic Book Week
CBA . . . . Catholic Broadcasters Association
CBEA . . . . . . Catholic Business Education Association
CCU. . . . . . . Catholic Central Union
CCUA. . . . . . Catholic Central Union of America
CCYUA. . . . . . Catholic Central Youth Union of America
CCESUSA . . . . Catholic Church Extension Society of the United States of America
CCCA. . . . . . Catholic Civics Clubs of America (Defunct)
CC. . . . . Catholic Clergyman
CCAIC . . . . . . Catholic College Admissions and Information Center
CCICA . . . . . . Catholic Commission on Intellectual and Cultural Affairs
CCR. . . . . . . Catholic Committee for Refugees
CCS . . . . Catholic Committee on Scouting
CCCL . . . . . . Catholic Council on Civil Liberties

CCWL	Catholic Council on Working Life
CC	Catholic Curate
CDA	Catholic Daughters of America
CEA	Catholic Economic Association
CEEA	Catholic Educational Exhibitors Association
CFLI	Catholic Family Life Insurance
CFAS	Catholic Fine Arts Society
CGS	Catholic Guardian Society
CGFAB	Catholic Guild for All the Blind
CHSAA	Catholic High Schools Athletic Association
CHS	Catholic Homiletic Society
CHA	Catholic Hospital Association of the United States and Canada
CIS	Catholic Information Society
CIFI	Catholic Institute of the Food Industry
CIP	Catholic Institute of the Press
CICOP	Catholic Inter-American Cooperation Program
CIP	Catholic Intercontinental Press
CIEO	Catholic International Education Office
CIUSS	Catholic International Union for Social Service
CIC	Catholic Interracial Council
CICC	Catholic Interracial Council of Chicago
CICNY	Catholic Interracial Council of New York
CKA	Catholic Knights of America
CKSG	Catholic Knights of St. George
CKSA	Catholic Kolping Society of America
CLAS	Catholic Ladies Aid Society
CLC	Catholic Ladies of Columbia
CLMC	Catholic Lay Mission Corps
CLRAP	Catholic League for Religious Assistance to Poland
CLA	Catholic Library Association
CLW	Catholic Library World (Official journal of Catholic Library Association)
CLIU	Catholic Life Insurance Union
CLL	Catholic Listener Library (Later, Maynard Listener Library)
CMMB	Catholic Medical Mission Board
CMC	Catholic Microfilm Center
CNEWA	Catholic Near East Welfare Association
COF	Catholic Order of Foresters
CPS	Catholic Pamphlet Society of the United States
CPSA	Catholic Poetry Society of America
CPA	Catholic Press Association
CRS	Catholic Relief Services
CRS-NCWC	Catholic Relief Services - National Catholic Welfare Conference (Later, Catholic Relief Services - US Catholic Conference)
CRS	Catholic Renascence Society
CSN	Catholic Scholarships for Negroes
CSPA	Catholic School Press Association
CSB	Catholic Slovak Brotherhood
CSMC	Catholic Students' Mission Crusade
CTRI	Catholic Tape Recorders, International
CTC	Catholic Teachers College (Rhode Island)
CTSA	Catholic Theological Society of America
CTAUA	Catholic Total Abstinence Union of America
CTM	Catholic Traditionalist Movement
CUSA	Catholic Union of the Sick in America
CU	Catholic University
CUA	Catholic University of America (Washington, DC)
CUPR	Catholic University of Puerto Rico
CWV	Catholic War Veterans of the USA
CWVA	Catholic War Veterans of the USA Ladies Auxiliary
CWBL	Catholic Women's Benevolent Legion
CWM	Catholic Worker (Movement)
CWGA	Catholic Writers Guild of America
CYMA	Catholic Young Men's Association
CYA	Catholic Youth Adoration Society
CYO	Catholic Youth Organization
CFLA	Catholics for Latin America
CURE	Catholics United for Racial Equality
CRE	Cation-Responsive Electrode
CATO	Catoctin Mountain Park (National Park Service designation)
CAUEOI	Caucasian Except as Otherwise Indicated (Army)
CRE	Cauchy Riemann Equation
C	Caught (by) (In cricket)
CM	Causa Mortis (On Occasion of Death)
C	Cause
CAUFN	Caution Advised Until Further Notice (Aviation)
CB	Cavalry Brigade
CRTC	Cavalry Replacement Training Center
CRA	Cave Research Associates
CE	Caveat Emptor (Let the Buyer Beware)
CTR	Cavitation Tendency Ratio
CTF	Cavity Turnable Filter

CKP	Cayley-Klein Parameter
CJC	Cazenovia Junior College (New York)
CSA	Cebu Stevedores Association (Philippines)
CCA	Cecchetti Council of America
CS	Cechoslovakische Statistik (Czechoslovakia)
CCP	Ceco Steel Products Corporation (NYSE symbol)
CEBR	Cedar Breaks National Monument
CIC	Cedar Rapids & Iowa City Railway Company (AAR code)
CLH	Cedars of Lebanon Hospital
CAVU	Ceiling and Visibility Unlimited (Meteorology)
CZ	Celanese Corporation of America (NYSE symbol)
CMTI	Celestial Moving Target Indicator
CNT	Celestial Navigation Trainer
CELESCOPE	Celestial Telescope (OAO)
CM	Cell Membrane
CW	Cell Wall
CWRM	Cell Water Removal Mechanism
CCA	Cellular Concrete Association
CNR	Cellular Neoprene Rubber
CSV	Cellular Size Volume
CAB	Cellulose Acetate-Butyrate (Chemical)
CPE	Cellulose Polyethylene
CSI	Cellulose Sponge Institute
CLO	Celotex Corporation (NYSE symbol)
C	Celsius (Centigrade) Temperature Scale
CB	Cement Base (Technical drawings)
CF	Cement Floor (Technical drawings)
CPC	Cement-Plaster Ceiling (Technical drawings)
CCPA	Cemented Carbide Producers Association
CNC	Cenco Instruments Corporation (NYSE symbol)
CPB	Censorship Policy Board
CRIME	Censorship Records and Information (Middle East, Military)
CB	Census Bureau (Commerce Department)
CRWP	Census Registration Working Party (US Military Government, Germany)
CENSER	Census Servomechanism and Tape Handler
C	Cent
CA	Centare (Unit of area in metric system)
C	Centavo (Monetary unit in many Spanish-American countries)
CJC	Centenary Junior College (New Jersey)
CCST	Centennial Centre of Science and Technology
C	Center (A position in football, lacrosse, basketball)
ADJUST	Center for the Administration of Justice (American University)
CASBS	Center for Advanced Study in the Behavioral Sciences
CAL	Center for Applied Linguistics
CARA	Center for Applied Research in the Apostolate
CAD	Center Area Discrete (Channel)
CBS	Center Back Stage (A stage direction)
CB	Center of Buoyancy
C to C	Center to Center (Technical drawings)
CCP	Center for Community Planning (HEW)
CCS	Center for Comparative Sociology
CCST	Center for Computer Sciences and Technology (National Bureau of Standards)
CCFMC	Center for the Coordination of Foreign Manuscript Copying (Library of Congress)
CDCR	Center for Documentation and Communication Research (Case-Western Reserve University)
CEAA	Center for Editions of American Authors
CEC	Center for Educational Change (University of California, Berkeley)
CET	Center for Educational Technology
CESB	Center for Experimental Studies in Business (University of Minnesota)
CF	Center Field(er) (Baseball)
CF	Center of Flotation
CF	Center Forward (Soccer position)
CF	Center Frequency
CFM	Center Frequency Modulation
CFS	Center Frequency Stabilization (Radio)
CG	Center of Gravity
C(H & D)	Center (Hospital and Domiciliary) (Veterans Administration)
CI	Center of Impact
CIRAS	Center for Industrial Research and Science
CIOA	Center for Information on America
CIR	Center for Inter-American Relations
CIEG	Center for International Economic Growth
CIS	Center of International Studies (MIT)
CLEAR	Center for Labor Education and Research (University of Colorado)
CL	Center Line
CLA	Center Line Average
CM	Center of Mass
CMC	Center for Mass Communication (Columbia University)
CM	Center Matched (Technical drawings)

CMSE . . . . . . Center for Materials Science and Engineering (MIT)
CNA . . . . Center for Naval Analysis
CNHS . . . . . . Center for Neo-Hellenic Studies
COR . . . . Center for Operations Research (MIT)
COPA . . . . . . Center for Overseas Program Analysis (Department of State)
CPR . . . . Center for Political Research
CP . . . . Center of Pressure
CRR . . . . Center for Radiation Research (National Bureau of Standards)
CRCR . . . . . . Center for Rate Controlled Recordings
C(RO & H) . . . Center (Regional Office and Hospital) (Veterans Administration)
C(RO & INS) . . Center (Regional Office and Insurance) (Veterans Administration)
CRICISAM . . . . Center for Research in College Instruction of Science and Mathematics
CREATE . . . . . Center for Research and Evaluation in Applications of Technology in Education (Palo Alto, California)
CRLLB . . . . . . Center for Research on Language and Language Behavior (University of Michigan)
CRL . . . . Center for Research Libraries
CRMS . . . . . . Center for Research in Management Science (University of California)
CRESS . . . . . . Center for Research in Social Systems (American University)
CR . . . . Center of Resistance
CS . . . . Center Section
CSLP . . . . Center for Short-Lived Phenomena (Miami) (Smithsonian Institution)
CSR . . . . Center for Space Research (MIT)
CS . . . . Center Stage (A stage direction)
CSB . . . . Center Stage Back (A stage direction)
CSF . . . . Center Stage Front (A stage direction)
CSSP . . . . . . Center for Studies of Suicide Prevention (National Institute of Mental Health)
CSDI . . . . Center for the Study of Democratic Institutions
CSI . . . . Center for the Study of Instruction (of NEA)
CSLEA . . . . . . Center for the Study of Liberal Education for Adults
CASR . . . . . . Center Surveillance RADAR
CT . . . . Center Tap (of a winding) (Radio)
CT . . . . Center Tap (Technical drawings)
CUE . . . . Center for Urban Education (New York)
CURS . . . . . . Center for Urban and Regional Studies
CVK . . . . Centerline Vertical Keel
C . . . . Centi (One-hundredth)
C . . . . Centigrade (Celsius)
CHU . . . . Centigrade Heat Unit
CTU . . . . Centigrade Thermal Unit
CGM . . . . . . Centigram(s)
CL . . . . Centiliter
C . . . . Centime (Monetary unit in France)
C . . . . Centimeter
CM . . . . Centimeter
CGS . . . . Centimeter-Gram-Second System
CMPS . . . . . . Centimeters Per Second
CP . . . . Centipoise
CS . . . . Centistere (Metric)
CS . . . . Centistoke
C . . . . Cento (Composition compiled from other works)
CSWV . . . . . . Centraal Sociaal Werkgevers Verbond (Employers' organization) (Netherlands)
CAO . . . . Central Accounting Office (Air Force)
CAP . . . . Central Africa Party (Southern Rhodesia)
CAA . . . . Central African Airways Corporation
CAF . . . . Central African Federation (Disbanded Dec. 31, 1963)
CEG . . . . Central Aguirre Sugar Company (NYSE symbol)
CADC . . . . . . Central Air Data Computer
CADF . . . . . . Central Air Defense Force
CADO . . . . . . Central Air Documents Office
CAMAE . . . . . Central Air Materiel Area, Europe
CEAPD . . . . . . Central Air Procurement District
CATR . . . . . . Central Air Transport
CAMRB . . . . . Central Aircrew Medical Review Board
CEN . . . . Central Airlines, Inc.
CN . . . . Central Airlines, Inc.
CARF . . . . . . Central Altitude Reservation Facility
CA . . . . Central America
CAA . . . . Central American Airways (Kentucky)
CABEI . . . . . . Central American Bank for Economic Integration
CAC . . . . Central American Club of New York
CACM . . . . . . Central American Common Market
CAEA . . . . . . Central American Economics Association
CAFTA . . . . . . Central American Free Trade Area
CAM . . . . . . Central American Mission
CASSP . . . . . . Central Ammunition Supply Status Point
CAMTMTS . . . . Central Area, Military Traffic Management and Terminal Service
CAP . . . . Central Arizona Project (Federal water-and-power project, similar to TVA)

CAPA . . . . . . Central Arizona Project Association
CENTAG . . . . . Central Army Group
CASMT . . . . . . Central Association of Science and Mathematics Teachers
CAREL . . . . . . Central Atlantic Regional Educational Laboratory
CBS . . . . Central Bibliographic System (Library of Congress)
CBJA . . . . Central Bureau for the Jewish Aged
CBS . . . . Central Bureau of Statistics (Netherlands)
CBD . . . . Central Business District
CCT . . . . Central California Traction Company (AAR code)
CCMS . . . . . . Central Cardiac Monitoring System
CCS . . . . Central Certificate Service (NYSE)
CCS . . . . Central Certificate System (Stock exchange automation program)
CCBV . . . . . . Central Circulating Blood Volume (Physiology)
CCPO . . . . . . Central Civilian Personnel Office (Military)
CCC . . . . Central Classification Committee (International Federation for Documentation)
CCD . . . . Central Commissioning Detail (Navy)
CCCO . . . . . . Central Committee for Conscientious Objectors
CCLJ . . . . Central Committee of Lithuanian Jurists
CCR . . . . Central Communication Region (Air Force)
CENCOMMRGN . . Central Communications Region (Military)
CCA . . . . Central Computer Accounting
CCAC . . . . . . Central Computer Accounting Corporation
CC & S . . . . . Central Computer and Sequencer (NASA)
CCF . . . . Central Computing Facility (NASA)
CCAR . . . . . . Central Conference of American Rabbis
CC . . . . Central Console
CCMR . . . . . . Central Contract Management Region (Air Force)
CCU . . . . Central Control Unit
CCS . . . . Central Cooperative Society (United Arab Republic)
CCS-C . . . . . . Central Coordinating Staff, Canada
CCCTU . . . . . . Central Council of Ceylon Trade Unions
CCNRA . . . . . . Central Council of National Retail Associations
CCC . . . . Central Criminal Court (British)
CDAS . . . . . . Central Data Acquisition System
CD & CC . . . . Central Data and Cataloging Center
CDCS . . . . . . Central Data Collection System
CDCE . . . . . . Central Data-Conversion Equipment
CDPC . . . . . . Central Data Processing Computer
CDST . . . . . . Central Daylight Saving Time
CDT . . . . Central Daylight Time
CDL . . . . Central Dental Laboratories (Army)
CDU . . . . Central Display Unit
CDS . . . . Central Distribution System (Publications) (Navy)
CD . . . . Central District
CENDRAFT . . . Central Drafting Officer (Navy)
CEC . . . . Central Economic Committee
CERA . . . . . . Central Electric Railfans' Association
CEGB . . . . . . Central Electricity Generating Board (British)
CEMS . . . . . . Central Electronic Management System
CEPPC . . . . . . Central Europe Pipeline Policy Committee (NATO)
CENEUR . . . . . Central European
CENTAG . . . . . Central European Army Group (NATO)
CEFYM . . . . . . Central European Federal Youth Movement
CEFCTU . . . . . Central European Federation of Christian Trade Unions
CEL . . . . Central European Line (Oil pipeline)
CEOA . . . . . . Central European Operating Agency (NATO)
CEPO . . . . . . Central European Pipeline Office (NATO)
CERD . . . . . . Central Evidence of Research and Development Reports
CX . . . . Central Exchange
CES . . . . Central (Nervous System) Excitatory State
CEPE . . . . . . Central Experimental & Proving Establishment (Canada)
CFE . . . . Central Fighter Establishment (British)
CF . . . . Central Files
CFC . . . . Central Fire Control (Military)
CFSSB . . . . . . Central Flight Status Selection Board (Air Force)
CFS . . . . Central Flying School (Royal Air Force) (British)
CFTC . . . . . . Central Flying Training Command (AAFCFTC)
CFC . . . . Central Forms Committee
FD . . . . Central Foundry Company (NYSE symbol)
CGARY . . . . . Central of Georgia Railway
CG . . . . Central of Georgia Railway Company (AAR code)
C of GA . . . . Central of Georgia Railway Company
GEO . . . . Central of Georgia Railway Company (NYSE symbol)
CADM . . . . . . Central German Administrative Department (Economic) Committee (US Military Government, Germany)
CGM . . . . . . Central Gray Matter (Physiology)
CGRS . . . . . . Central Gyro Reference System
CH . . . . Central Heating
CNH . . . . Central Hudson Gas & Electric Corporation (NYSE symbol)
CER . . . . Central Illinois Light Company (NYSE symbol)

CIP. . . . . Central Illinois Public Service Company (NYSE symbol)
CIF. . . . . Central Index File
CIND. . . . . . Central Indiana Railway Company (AAR code)
CIGTF. . . . . . Central Inertial Guidance Test Facility (Air Force)
CIF. . . . . Central Information File
CIS . . . . Central (Nervous System) Inhibitory State
CID . . . . Central Institute for the Deaf
CINFR . . . . . Central Institute for Nutrition and Food Research (Netherlands)
CIS . . . . Central Instructor School
CIF. . . . . Central Integration Facility
CIA . . . . Central Intelligence Agency (of the US)
CIB . . . . Central Intelligence Board
CIAA . . . . . . Central Intercollegiate Athletic Association
CIU . . . . Central Interpretation Unit (Military)
CI . . . . Central Interval
CIPER . . . . . . Central Inventory of Production Equipment Records (Army)
CJI . . . . Central Juvenile Index
CLRC . . . . . . Central Labor Relations Commission (Japan)
CLRI . . . . . . Central Leather Research Institute (British)
CLT . . . . Central Limit Theorem (Statistics)
CL . . . . Central Line
CLDO. . . . . . Central Load Dispatching Office (US Military Government, Germany)
CLU . . . . Central Logic Unit
CLR . . . . Central London Underground Railway
CMG . . . . . . Central Machine Gun
CMCC . . . . . Central Marine Chamber of Commerce
CMPF . . . . . . Central Meat Processing Facility (Army)
CMEA. . . . . . Central Medical Establishment, Aviation (Air Force)
MEDCENT . . . . Central Mediterranean
CMD. . . . . . . Central Meridian Distance (NASA)
CEMREL . . . . . Central Midwest Regional Educational Laboratory
CMDC . . . . . Central Milk Distributive Committee (British)
CMSC. . . . . . Central Missouri State College
CENO. . . . . . Central Naval Ordnance Management Information System
CNS . . . . Central Nervous System (Physiology)
COB. . . . . . . Central Obrera Boliviana
CO . . . . Central Office
COE. . . . . . . Central Office Equipment
COSVN . . . . . Central Office of South Vietnam (North Vietnamese high command in the South)
CENPAC . . . . . Central Pacific Area (Navy)
CPA . . . . Central Pacific Area (Hawaiian area) (World War II)
CENTPACBACOM. . Central Pacific Base Command (Navy)
CPBC . . . . . . Central Pacific Base Command (Hawaiian Islands) (World War II)
CENCATS . . . . Central Pacific Combat Air Transport Service
CENTCOM . . . Central Pacific Communications Instructions
CENPACFOR . . Central Pacific Forces
CPK . . . . Central Pastry Kitchen (Army)
CPM . . . . Central Path Method (Data processing)
CPAD . . . . . . Central Pay Accounts Division (Navy)
CPTF . . . . . . Central Plains Turfgrass Foundation
CPF . . . . Central Post Fund (Army)
CPD . . . . Central Postal Directory (Army)
CPH . . . . Central Powerhouse
CP . . . . Central Press
CPE . . . . Central Processing Element
CPSS . . . . . . Central Processing Subsystem
CPS . . . . Central Processing System
CPU . . . . Central Processing Unit (Data processing)
CPTC . . . . . . Central Processor Test Console
CPD . . . . Central Procurement Division (Marine Corps)
CPE . . . . Central Programmer and Evaluator
CPO. . . . . . . Central Project Office (of ARS, Department of Agriculture)
CP . . . . Central Provinces (Later, Madhya Pradesh, India)
CRPL . . . . . . Central Radio Propagation Laboratory
CNJ. . . . . . . Central Railroad Company of New Jersey (ARR code)
CRR of NJ . . . . Central Railroad Company of New Jersey
CRP . . . . Central R. R. of Pennsylvania (AAR code)
CRFUSAIC. . . . Central Records Facility, United States Army Intelligence Center
CRO. . . . . . . Central Records Office
CRD . . . . Central Recruiting Division
CRMSS . . . . . Central Registry of Magazine Subscription Solicitors
CROWCASS. . . Central Registry of War Criminals and Security Suspects (Organization which used crime detection methods to ferret out German war criminals) (World War II)
CRC . . . . Central Requirements Committee
CRA . . . . Central Research Agency (Cuc Nghien-Chu Trung-Uong) (North Vietnamese intelligence agency)
CRLT. . . . . . . Central Research Laboratory of Tashiba
CRC. . . . . . . Central Rhine Commission (Post-World War II)
CRRI. . . . . . . Central Rice Research Institute (India)

CSC . . . . Central Security Control (Military)
CSJCA . . . . . Central Sephardic Jewish Community of America
CSP . . . . Central Signal Processor
CSR . . . . Central & South West Corporation (NYSE symbol)
CSY . . . . Central Soya Company, Inc. (NYSE symbol)
C . . . . Central Standard Time (Aviation)
CST . . . . Central Standard Time
CSC . . . . Central State College (Ohio, Oklahoma)
CSCA . . . . . . Central States College Association
CSB . . . . Central Statistical Board (Functions taken over by Bureau of the Budget, 1940)
CSU . . . . Central Statistical Unit (of VLRL)
CSA . . . . Central Supply Association
CSF . . . . Central Switching Facility
CSU . . . . Central Switching Unit
CTF . . . . Central Task Force
CTOCU. . . . . Central Technical Order Control (or Coordination) Unit
CENTREX . . . . Central Terminal Exchange
CTU . . . . Central Terminal Unit
CT . . . . Central Time
CTE . . . . Central Timing Equipment
CTO. . . . . . . Central Torpedo Office
CTB . . . . Central Tracing Bureau (Post-World War II)
CTPB . . . . . . Central Tracing Policy Board (Post-World War II)
CTS . . . . Central Training Section (Air Force)
CTP . . . . Central Transfer Point
CTE . . . . Central Translation Evidence
CENTO. . . . . Central Treaty Organization (Formerly Baghdad Pact)
CTO. . . . . . . Central Treaty Organization
CTT . . . . Central Trunk Terminals
CUSR . . . . . . Central United States Registry (Army)
CVLS . . . . . . Central Vacuum Loading System
CVSSUS . . . . Central Verband der Siebenburger Sachsen of the U.S.
CV. . . . . Central Vermont Railway, Inc. (AAR code)
CVT. . . . . . . Central Vermont Railway, Inc.
CWB. . . . . . . Central Welsh Board
CYCO . . . . . Central Yiddish Culture Organization
CGSLB . . . . . Centrale Generale des Syndicats Liberaux de Belgique (General Federation of Liberal Unions of Belgium)
CNTCCI . . . . Centrale National des Travailleurs Croyants de Cote d'Ivoire (National Union of Believing Workers of the Ivory Coast)
CNTC. . . . . . Centrale National des Travailleurs Croyants de Senegal (National Believing Workers of Senegal)
CNA . . . . . . Centrale Nucleaire des Ardennes
CNI . . . . Centrale Nucleaire Interescaut (A nuclear power station) (Belgium)
CJC. . . . . . . Centralia Junior College (Washington)
CTJC . . . . . . Centralia Township Junior College (Illinois)
COSMOS . . . . Centralization of Supply Management Operations Projects (Army)
CAMPS . . . . . Centralized Automated Military Pay System
CENTCON . . . Centralized Control Facility
CEC . . . . Centralized Electronic Control (Navy)
CIRC . . . . . . Centralized Information Reference and Control
CIB . . . . Centralized Intercept Bureau (Bell System)
CMDS. . . . . . Centralized Message Data System (AT&T)
CRA . . . . Centralized Referral Activity (Military)
CRS . . . . Centralized Referral System
CTC . . . . Centralized Traffic Control (Railroad system)
CF . . . . Centrally Funded
CP . . . . Centrally Procured
CRZZ . . . . . . Centralna Rada Zwiazkow Zawodowych (Central Council of Trade Unions) (Poland)
AEF . . . . Centre d'Action Europeenne Federaliste
CAFRAD . . . . . Centre Africain de Formation et de Recherche Administratives pour la Developpement (African Training and Research Center in Administration for Development)
CARDAN. . . . . Centre d'Analyse et de Recherche Documentaires pour l'Afrique Noire
CEBELCOR. . . . Centre Belge d'Etude de la Corrosion
CORESTA . . . . Centre de Cooperation pour les Recherches Scientifiques Relatives au Tabac
CETO. . . . . . Centre for Educational Television Overseas (British)
CERMA . . . . . Centre d'Enseignement et de Recherches de Medecine Aeronautique (France)
CEEN . . . . . . Centre d'Etude de l'Energie Nucleaire (Belgium) (Also known as NERC)
CELEG . . . . . Centre d'Etude des Litteratures d'Expression Graphique
CEAN. . . . . . Centre d'Etudes pour les Applications de l'Energie Nucleaire (Belgium)
CEDAMEL . . . . Centre d'Etudes et de Distribution des Appareils et du Materiel de l'Enseignement Linguistique
CEN. . . . . . . Centre d'Etudes de l'Energie Nucleaire (Belgium)
CENC. . . . . . Centre d'Etudes Nucleaires de Cadarache (France)
CENS . . . . . . Centre d'Etudes Nucleaires de Saclay (France)
CEPE . . . . . . Centre d'Etudes Phylosociologiques et Ecologiques (France)

CERCHAR . . . . Centre d'Etudes et Recherches des Charbonnages de France
CERDOC . . . . . Centre d'Etudes et Recherches Documentaires (France)
CESP . . . . Centre d'Etudes des Supports de Publicite (France)
CETHEDEC . . . Centre d'Etudes Theoriques de la Detection et des Communications
CEAA . . . . . . Centre Europeen d'Aviation Agricole
CEC . . . . Centre Europeen de la Culture
CEEP . . . . Centre Europeen d'Etudes de Population
CEFIC . . . . . . Centre Europeen des Federations de l'Industrie Chimique (European
    Center of Chemical Manufacturers' Federations)
CESD . . . . . . Centre Europeen de Formation des Statisticiens-Economistes des Pays
    en Voie de Developpement (France)
CET . . . . Centre Europeen de Traduction
CFAE . . . . . . Centre de Formation en Aerodynamique Experimentale
CHEAM . . . . . Centre de Hautes Etudes Administratives sur l'Afrique et l'Asie Modernes
    (Center for Advanced Administrative Study on Modern Africa and Asia)
CICE . . . . . . Centre d'Information des Chemins de Fer Europeens
CIDA . . . . . . Centre d'Information et de Documentation Atlantique (Brussels, Belgium)
CINU . . . . . . Centre d'Information des Nations Unies
CIER . . . . Centre Interamericain d'Education Rurale
CIETB . . . . . . Centre Intercontinental d'Etudes de Techniques Biologiques
CIAFMA . . . . Centre International de l'Actualite Fantastique et Magique
CIA . . . . Centre International des Antiparasitaires
CICG . . . . . . Centre International du Commerce de Gros
CICCA . . . . . Centre International de Coordination pour la Celebration des
    Anniversaires
CICRA . . . . . . Centre International pour la Coordination des Recherches en Agriculture
CIDA . . . . . . Centre International de Developpement de l'Aluminium
CIDESA . . . . . Centre International de Documentation Economique et Sociale Africaine
CIDITVA . . . . Centre International de Documentation de l'Inspection Technique des
    Vehicules Automobiles
CIE . . . . Centre International de l'Enfance
CIEC . . . . Centre International des Engrais Chimiques
CIPEMAT . . . . Centre International pour l'Etude de la Marionnette Traditionnelle
    (International Center for Research on Traditional Marionettes)
CIETA . . . . . . Centre International d'Etudes des Textiles Anciens
CIFJ . . . . Centre International du Film pour la Jeunesse
CIFE . . . . Centre International de Formation Europeenne
CIIM . . . . Centre International d'Information de la Mutualite
CIRF . . . . . . Centre International d'Information et de Recherche sur la Formation
    Professionnelle
CIPC . . . . . . Centre International Provisoire de Calcul
CIRIEC . . . . . Centre International de Recherches et d'Information sur l'Economie
    Collective
CITAM . . . . . Centre International de la Tapisserie Ancienne et Moderne
CLERES . . . . . Centre de Liaison des Etudes et Recherches Economiques et Sociales
    (France)
CLITRAVI . . . Centre de Liaison des Industries Transformatrices de Viandes de la CEE
CLIMMAR . . . Centre de Liaison International des Marchands de Machines Agricoles
    et Reparateurs
CLAA . . . . . . Centre Lyonnais d'Applications Atomiques (France)
CNEEMA . . . . Centre National d'Etudes et d'Experimentation du Machinisme Agricole
CNES . . . . . . Centre National d'Etudes Spatiales (National Center for Space Studies)
    (France)
CNET . . . . . . Centre National d'Etudes des Telecommunications (France)
CNEXO . . . . . Centre National pour l'Exploitation des Oceans (France)
CENECA . . . . Centre National des Expositions et Concours Agricoles
CNOUS . . . . . Centre National des Oeuvres Universitaires et Scolaires (France)
CNRS . . . . . . Centre National de la Recherche Scientifique (National Center of
    Scientific Research) (France)
CNRM . . . . . . Centre National de Recherches Metallurgiques (Belgium)
CPDCET . . . . . Centre de Perfectionnement pour le Developpement et la Cooperation
    Economique et Technique (France)
CERCA . . . . . Centre de Recherches pour Combustibles Atomiques (France)
CREDOC . . . . Centre de Recherches et de Documentation sur la Consommation (France)
CREDIF . . . . . Centre de Recherches et d'Etudes pour la Diffusion du Francais
    (France)
CRI . . . . Centre de Recherches et d'Irradiations (France)
CEREA . . . . . . Centre de Regroupement Africain (Center for African Regroupment)
    (Congo-Leopoldville)
CETIE . . . . . . Centre Technique International de l'Embouteillage
CENTI . . . . . . Centre pour le Traitement de l'Information
CETIS . . . . . . Centre de Traitement de l'Information Scientifique (EURATOM)
CRAP . . . . . . Centres Regionaux d'Action Pedagogique (France)
CF . . . . Centrifugal Force
CS . . . . Centrifugal Spraying
CME . . . . Centrifuge Moisture Equivalent
CAE . . . . Centro Anglo-Espanol
CAMEN . . . . . Centro Automomo Militare Energia Nucleare (Italy)
CBPF . . . . . . Centro Brasileiro de Pesquisas Fisicas (Brazilian Center for Physics Research)
CEASA . . . . . Centro Estadual de Abastecimento SA (State Central Supply Company)
    (Brazil)

CEMLA . . . . . Centro de Estudios Monetarios Latino-Americanos (Center for Latin-
    American Monetary Studies)
CISE . . . . Centro Informazioni Studi Esperienze
CIENES . . . . . Centro Interamericano de Ensenanza de Estadistica
CILA . . . . . . Centro Interamericano de Libros Academicos (Inter-American
    Scholarly Book Center)
CIDEM . . . . . Centro Interamericano de Musica (Inter-American Music Center)
CIDOC . . . . . Centro Intercultural de Documentacion (Cuernavaca, Mexico)
CIMMYT . . . . Centro Internacional de Mejoramiento de Maiz y Trigo (Mexico)
CIRM . . . . . . Centro Internazionale Radio-Medico (International Radio Medical Center;
    gives emergency medical advice to ships at sea)
CIS . . . . Centro de Investigaciones Sociales (Social Research Center) (Colombia)
CELADE . . . . . Centro Latinoamericana de Demografia (Latin American Demographic
    Center)
CUBI . . . . . . Centro Nazionale per il Catalogo Unico delle Biblioteche Italiane (Italy)
CODESA . . . . Centro Operacional del Desarrollo (Operational Center for
    Development) (Colombia)
CPOR . . . . . . Centro de Preparacao de Oficiais de Reserva (Brazil)
CREFAL . . . . . Centro Regional de Education Fundamental para la America Latina
    (Mexico)
CRA . . . . Centro Ricerche Aerospaziali (Italy)
CI . . . . Centromeric Indices (Chromosomes)
C . . . . Centum (Hundred)
CLR . . . . Centurion LASER Range-Finder
C . . . . Century
CTY . . . . Century Industries Company, Inc. (NYSE symbol)
CI . . . . Cephalic Index (Anthropology)
CS . . . . Cephalic Sinus
CPS . . . . Cephalo Pedal Sinus
CERAMAL . . . . Ceramic and Alloy (NASA)
CEC . . . . Ceramic Educational Council
CGSFU . . . . . Ceramic Glazed Structural Facing Units (Technical drawings)
CGSUB . . . . . Ceramic Glazed Structural Unit Base (Technical drawings)
CGU . . . . Ceramic Glazed Units (Technical drawings)
CGIC . . . . . . Ceramic & Graphite Information Center (Air Force)
CIW . . . . Ceramic Insulated Wire
CERMET . . . . . Ceramic and Metal (NASA)
CTMS . . . . . . Ceramic to Metal Seal
COB . . . . Ceramic Oceanographic Buoy
CPT . . . . Ceramic Planar Tube
CRC . . . . Ceramic Refraction Coating
CT . . . . Ceramic Tile (Technical drawings)
CTB . . . . Ceramic-Tile Base (Technical drawings)
CTF . . . . Ceramic-Tile Floor (Technical drawings)
CTF . . . . Ceramic Tube Fabrication
CVR . . . . Ceramic Vacuum Relay
CPC . . . . Ceramic-Wafer Printed Circuit
CGB . . . . Ceramics & Graphite Branch (Air Force)
C & G . . . . . . Ceramics and Graphite Information Center (Air Force)
CBF . . . . Cerebral Blood Flow (Medicine)
CMR . . . . Cerebral Metabolic Rate (Physiology)
CP . . . . Cerebral Palsy (Medicine)
CR . . . . Cerebral Ridge
CPC . . . . Cerebro-Pedal Commissure
CSF . . . . Cerebrospinal Fluid
CSM . . . . Cerebrospinal Meningitis (Medicine)
CVA . . . . Cerebrovascular Accident (Medical term for stroke)
Ce . . . . Cerium (Chemical element)
CRN . . . . Cermet Resistor Network
CMN . . . . . . Cerous Magnesium Nitrate
CDP . . . . Cerro Corporation (NYSE symbol)
CTIO . . . . . . Cerro Tololo Inter-American Observatory (National Science Foundation)
CRT . . . . Certain-teed Products Corporation (NYSE symbol)
CELG . . . . . . Certificat d'Etudes Litteraires Generales (France)
CAGS . . . . . . Certificate of Advanced Graduate Study
CA . . . . Certificate of Airworthiness
C of A . . . . . Certificate of Airworthiness
C/Q . . . . Certificate of Assignment of Quarters (Navy)
COC . . . . . . Certificate of Competency (Small Business Administration)
CDP . . . . Certificate in Data Processing
CD . . . . Certificate of Deposit (Banking)
C/D . . . . Certificate of Deposit
CDS . . . . Certificate of Deposit
CD . . . . Certificate of Destruction
CDD . . . . Certificate of Disability Discharge (Military)
COE . . . . Certificate of Eligibility (Navy)
CI Rel . . . . . Certificate in Industrial Relations
C/I . . . . Certificate of Insurance
CIL . . . . Certificate in Lieu (of)
C of M . . . . . Certificate of Merit
C/O . . . . Certificate of Origin

CPC & N . . . . Certificate of Public Convenience and Necessity
CPH . . . . Certificate in Public Health
CRV . . . . Certificate of Reasonable Value (Veterans Administration)
CS En . . . . . . Certificate in Sales Engineering
CSS . . . . Certificate of Sanitary Science (Cambridge)
CSE . . . . Certificate of Secondary Education (British)
C/S . . . . Certificate of Service (Military)
CWN . . . . Certificate of War Necessity (World War II)
CM . . . . Certificated Master (or Mistress)
CT . . . . Certificated Teacher
COD . . . . Certificates of Deposit (Banking)
CAEM . . . . . . Certified Assistant Export Manager (Designation given by American
　　　　　　　　Society of International Executives)
CBM . . . . Certified Ballast Manufacturers Association
CCE . . . . Certified Chamber Executive (Designation awarded by American
　　　　　　　　Chamber of Commerce Executives)
CCFSA . . . . . Certified Cold Fur Storage Association
CCCE . . . . . . Certified Consumer Credit Executive (Designation awarded by
　　　　　　　　International Consumer Credit Association)
CDM . . . . Certified Decal Manufacturers
CDS . . . . Certified Documentary Specialist (Designation given by American
　　　　　　　　Society of International Executives to persons in international trade)
CFI . . . . Certified Flight Instructor (Aviation)
CGA . . . . Certified General Accountant
CIE-AF . . . . . Certified International Executive - Air Forwarding (Designation given
　　　　　　　　by American Society of International Executives)
CIE-EM . . . . . Certified International Executive - Export Management (Designation
　　　　　　　　given by American Society of International Executives)
CIE-F . . . . . . Certified International Executive - Forwarding (Designation given by
　　　　　　　　American Society of International Executives)
CIE-TM . . . . . Certified International Executive - Traffic Management (Designation
　　　　　　　　given by American Society of International Executives)
CITM . . . . . . Certified International Traffic Manager (Designation given by
　　　　　　　　American Society of International Executives)
CLU . . . . Certified Life Underwriter (Insurance)
CLMA . . . . . . Certified Livestock Markets Association
CMPAA . . . . . Certified Milk Producers Association of America
COGB . . . . . . Certified Official Government Business
CPS . . . . Certified Professional Secretary (Designation given by National
　　　　　　　　Secretaries Association)
CPM . . . . Certified Property Manager (Designation given by Institute of Real
　　　　　　　　Estate Management)
CPA . . . . Certified Public Accountant
CRL . . . . Certified Record Librarian
CSR . . . . Certified Shorthand Reporter
CTD . . . . Certified Test Data
CTC . . . . Certified Travel Counselor (Designation given by Institute of
　　　　　　　　Certified Travel Agents)
CD . . . . Cesarean Delivered (Medicine)
CS . . . . Cesarean Section (Medicine)
Cs . . . . Cesium (Chemical element)
CIPS . . . . Cesium Ion Propulsion System
CIS . . . . Cesium Ion Source
CeO . . . . Cesium Oxide
CTS . . . . Cesium Time Standard
CVC . . . . Cesium Vapor Cathode
CVFS . . . . . . Cesium Vapor Feed System
COS . . . . Ceskoslovenska Obec Sokolska (Czechoslovakia)
CSA . . . . Ceskoslovenske Aerolinie (Czechoslovak Airlines)
CSM . . . . Ceskoslovensky Svaz Mladeze (Czechoslovakia)
CEA . . . . Cessna Aircraft Company (NYSE symbol)
CN . . . . Cetane Number
CTAB . . . . . . Cetyltrimethylammonium Bromide
CFL . . . . Ceylon Federation of Labor
CLU . . . . Ceylon Labor Union
CMU . . . . Ceylon Mercantile Union
CPWU . . . . . . Ceylon Plantation Workers' Union
CRCSU . . . . . Ceylon Railway Clerical Service Union
CTUF . . . . . . Ceylon Trade Union Federation
CWC . . . . Ceylon Workers' Congress
CHCA . . . . . . Chaco Canyon National Monument
CGI . . . . Chadbourn Gotham Incorporated (NYSE symbol)
CHB . . . . Chain Belt Company (NYSE symbol)
CHACOM . . . . Chain of Command
CH . . . . Chain Home (Aviation)
CHB . . . . Chain Home Beamed (Aviation)
CHEL . . . . . . Chain Home Extra Low (Aviation)
CHL . . . . Chain Home Low (Aviation)
CLFMI . . . . . . Chain Link Fence Manufacturers Institute
COEL . . . . . . Chain Overseas Extremely Low (Aviation)
COL . . . . Chain Overseas Low (Aviation)

CRS . . . . Chain RADAR System
CSO . . . . Chained Sequential Operation
C . . . . Chairman
CJCS . . . . . . Chairman, Joint Chiefs of Staff
CRUD . . . . . . Chalk River Unidentified Deposit
CH-P . . . . Challenge Position (Dancing)
CHAL . . . . . . Chalmette National Historical Park
CC . . . . Chamber of Commerce
C of C . . . . . . Chamber of Commerce
CCAI . . . . Chamber of Commerce of the Apparel Industry
CCUS . . . . . . Chamber of Commerce of the United States
CDS . . . . Chamber of Destination of Ships
CP . . . . Chamber Pressure
CCI . . . . Chambre de Commerce Internationale
CHAM . . . . . . Chamizal National Memorial
CPP . . . . Champion Papers, Inc. (NYSE symbol)
CHM . . . . Champion Spark Plug Company (NYSE symbol)
CHI . . . . Champlin Oil & Refining Company (NYSE symbol)
CVA . . . . Chance Vought Aircraft, Inc.
C . . . . Chancellor
CE . . . . Chancellor of the Exchequer (British)
C . . . . Chancery
CD . . . . Chancery Division
CECO . . . . . . Chandler Evans Corporation
C . . . . Change (Army) (Used in combinations only)
COA . . . . Change of Assignment
CTCC . . . . . . Change (or Changing) to Center Control (Aviation)
CCB . . . . Change Control Board
CCS . . . . Change Control System
CC . . . . Change Course
C/C . . . . Change of Course (Aviation)
CID . . . . Change in Design
CF . . . . Change (or Changing) to Frequency (followed by number) (Communications)
CLG . . . . Change to Lower Grade (Army)
CNR . . . . Change(s) to Navy Regulations
CN . . . . Change Notice
CHORD . . . . . Change my Operation Order (Military)
CHOP . . . . . . Change of Operational Control
CO . . . . Change Order
COA . . . . Change Order Account
C/R . . . . Change of Rating
CR . . . . Change Recommendation
CR . . . . Change Release (Military)
CR . . . . Change Request
CSC . . . . Change Schedule Chart
CS . . . . Change Sheet (Marine Corps)
C/S . . . . Change of Status
CTF . . . . Change (or Changing) to Tower Frequency (Aviation)
CWM . . . . Change Weight Manifest (Aviation)
CHOP . . . . . . Changeover Point (Aviation)
CIPAP . . . . . . Changes in Itinerary to Proceed to Additional Places (Military)
CAC . . . . Changing to Approach Control (Aviation)
CPO . . . . Changing Path of Operation
CRAFT . . . . . . Changing Radio Automatic Frequency Transmission
CC . . . . Channel Command (Military) (Refers to English Channel)
CIMA . . . . . . Channel Industries Mutual Aid (Houston, Texas, firefighting group)
CI . . . . Channel Islands
CHIS . . . . . . Channel Islands National Monument
CFO . . . . Channel for Orders (Business and trade)
CS . . . . Channel Status
CTCF . . . . . . Channel and Technical Control Facility (In a tape-relay station in the
　　　　　　　　AIRCOMNET)
CTCA . . . . . . Channel and Traffic Control Agency (of AACS)
CTCU . . . . . . Channel and Traffic Control Unit (Subordinate Unit of the Channel and
　　　　　　　　Traffic Control Agency)
CTEA . . . . . . Channel Transmission and Engineering Activation
CVSG . . . . . . Channel Verification Signal Generator
CTTC . . . . . . Chanute Technical Training Center (Air Force)
CHC . . . . Chaplain Corps
CH of F . . . . . Chaplain of the Fleet (British)
CF . . . . Chaplain to the Forces (British)
CSP . . . . Chaplain Service Personnel (Air Force)
CAA . . . . Chaplains' Aid Association
C . . . . Chapter
COED . . . . . . Char Oil Energy Development (Project of Office of Coal Research)
CHARGUID . . . Character Guidance (Army)
CR . . . . Characteristic Relief
CS . . . . Characteristic Slope
CSV . . . . Characteristic Statistical Value
CPC . . . . Characters Per Column
CPI . . . . Characters Per Inch (Typesetting)

CPM . . . . Characters Per Minute
CHT . . . . Charactron Tube
CRT . . . . Charactron Tube
CABA . . . . . Charge Account Bankers Association
CA . . . . Charge d'Affaires (State Department Foreign Service)
CMAP . . . . . . Charge Material Allocation Processor
CP . . . . Charge Parity
CQ . . . . Charge of Quarters (Army)
CT . . . . Charge-Transfer (or intermolecular electron transfer)
CTP . . . . Charge Transfer Photography
CTS . . . . Charge Transfer Spectrum
CPET . . . . . . Charged Particle Electrostatic Thruster
CPIC . . . . . . Charged Particles Information Center (ORNL)
COS . . . . Charity Organization Society (British)
CCW . . . . . . Charles City Western Railway Company (AAR code)
CRBL . . . . . . Charles River Breeding Laboratories
CHAD . . . . . . Charleston Army Depot
CNSY . . . . . . Charleston Naval Shipyard
CNSYD . . . . . Charleston Naval Shipyard
CNWA . . . . . Charleston Naval Weapons Annex
CWC . . . . . . Charleston & Western Carolina Railway Company (AAR code)
C & WC . . . . Charleston & Western Carolina Railway Company
CCU . . . . . . Chart Comparison Unit
CHUM . . . . . Chart Updating Manual (Air Force)
C/P . . . . Charter Party (Transportation)
CA . . . . Chartered Accountant
CAE . . . . . . Chartered Association Executive (Designation given by American Society of Association Executives)
CFA . . . . . . Chartered Financial Analyst (Designation given by Institute of Chartered Financial Analysts)
CIME . . . . . . Chartered Institute of Marine Engineers
CII . . . . Chartered Insurance Institute
CLU . . . . Chartered Life Underwriter
CPCU . . . . . . Chartered Property and Casualty Underwriter
CSR . . . . Chartered Stenographic Reporter
CPD . . . . Charterers Pay Dues
CMK . . . . . . Chassis Marking Kit
ChON . . . . . . Chasti Osobogo Naznacheniia (Elements of Special Designation) (Political police units attached to the armed forces) (USSR)
CHV . . . . Chattahoochee Valley Railway Company (AAR code)
CLSC . . . . . . Chautauqua Literary and Scientific Circle
CARA . . . . . . Check Area Airports
CP . . . . Check Point
CS . . . . Check Sorter
CV . . . . Check Valve
CHC . . . . Checker Motors Corporation (NYSE symbol)
CDP . . . . Checkout Data Processor (RADAR)
CAM . . . . . . Checkout & Maintenance
COT . . . . Checkout Time
COV . . . . Check-Out Valve
CA . . . . Checks Anonymous
CIAA . . . . . . Cheese Importers Association of America
CDCA . . . . . . Chefs de Cuisine Association of America
CTN . . . . Chemetron Corporation (NYSE symbol)
CA . . . . Chemical Abstracts (A publication)
CAS . . . . Chemical Abstracts Service
CAGNY . . . . . Chemical Advertisers Group of New York
CADIC . . . . . Chemical Analysis Detection Instrumentation Control
CBR . . . . Chemical-Bacteriological-Radiological
CB . . . . Chemical and Biological (Warfare) (Formerly, CBR)
CBAC . . . . . . Chemical-Biological Activities (A publication of Chemical Abstracts Service)
CBM . . . . Chemical-Biological Munitions
CBRA . . . . . . Chemical, Biological, Radiological Agency (Military)
CBRC . . . . . . Chemical, Biological, and Radiological Center
CBRE . . . . . . Chemical, Biological, and Radiological Element (Military)
CBREG . . . . . Chemical-Biological-Radiological Engineering Group (Army)
CBRS . . . . . . Chemical, Biological, and Radiological Section (Military)
CEBAR . . . . . Chemical, Biological, Radiological Warfare
CBR . . . . Chemical, Biological and Radiological Warfare (Later, CB)
CBW . . . . . . Chemical and Biological Warfare
CBW . . . . Chemical and Biological Weapons
CBA . . . . Chemical Bond Approach
CBAS . . . . . . Chemical Bond Approach Study
CMLC . . . . . . Chemical Corps (Army)
CMLCBL . . . . . Chemical Corps Biological Laboratories (Army)
CMLCENCOM . . Chemical Corps Engineering Command
CMLCMATCOM . . Chemical Corps Material Command
CCRC . . . . . . Chemical Corps Research and Development Command (Army)
CMLCRDCOM . . Chemical Corps Research and Development Command
CMLCRECOM . . Chemical Corps Research and Engineering Command

CCTC . . . . . . Chemical Corps Technical Command (Army)
CMLCTNGCOM . . Chemical Corps Training Command
CDRE . . . . . . Chemical Defence Research Establishment (British)
CDEE . . . . . . Chemical Defense Experimental Establishment (British)
CEER . . . . . . Chemical Economy & Engineering Review (A publication)
CEMS . . . . . . Chemical Education Material Study
CHEM . . . . . . Chemical Education Materials (Study)
CE . . . . Chemical Engineer
C & EN . . . . . Chemical and Engineering News (A publication of American Chemical Society)
CEO . . . . Chemical Engineering Operations (MIT)
CIBA . . . . . . Chemical Industry in Basle
CIC . . . . Chemical Industry Council
CIDS . . . . . . Chemical Information Data System (Army)
CIC . . . . Chemical Institute of Canada
LBT . . . . Chemical Laboratory Technician (Navy)
CMRA . . . . . . Chemical Market Research Association
CM & E . . . . . Chemical Marketing and Economics
CMM . . . . . . Chemical Milling Machine
COD . . . . . . Chemical Oxygen Demand
CPIA . . . . . . Chemical Propulsion Information Agency
CPRA . . . . . . Chemical Public Relations Association
CRLR . . . . . . Chemical & Radiological Laboratories (Army)
CR . . . . Chemical Report
CRDL . . . . . . Chemical Research & Development Laboratories (Army)
CRC . . . . Chemical Resistant Coating
CRC . . . . Chemical Rubber Company
CSMA . . . . . . Chemical Specialties Manufacturers Association
CTA . . . . Chemical Toilet Association
CVD . . . . Chemical Vapor Deposition
CVP . . . . Chemical Vapor Plating
CW . . . . Chemical Warfare
CWBW . . . . . Chemical Warfare - Bacteriological Warfare
CWLR . . . . . . Chemical Warfare Laboratories (Army)
CWL . . . . Chemical Warfare Laboratory
CWS . . . . Chemical Warfare Service (Army)
CWT . . . . . . Chemical Warfare Specialist, Medical (Navy rating)
CW . . . . Chemical Warhead
CWU . . . . . . Chemical Workers' Union
CWIK . . . . . . Chemical World Index Key
CLAM . . . . . . Chemically-fueled Low Altitude Missile (Air Force program)
CP . . . . Chemically Pure (Chemistry)
CRSS . . . . . . Chemically Rigidized Space Structure
CSO . . . . Chemically Stable Oxide
CPR . . . . Chemicals, Plastic Research
CRAGS . . . . . Chemistry Records and Grading System (Data processing)
CCNY . . . . . . Chemists' Club (of New York)
CMY . . . . . . Chemway Corporation (NYSE symbol)
CNHS . . . . . . Cherokee National Historical Society
CGIF . . . . . . Cherry Growers and Industries Foundation
CBA . . . . Chesapeake Bay Annex (Navy)
CSK . . . . Chesapeake Corporation of Virginia (NYSE symbol)
CHOH . . . . . . Chesapeake and Ohio Canal National Monument
CO . . . . Chesapeake & Ohio--Chesapeake Dist. R. R. (AAR code)
PM . . . . Chesapeake & Ohio - Pere Marquette Dist. (AAR code)
C & O . . . . . . Chesapeake & Ohio Railway
CO . . . . Chesapeake & Ohio Railway Company (NYSE symbol)
CSPA . . . . . . Chesapeake Seafood Packers Association
CHW . . . . . . Chesapeake Western Railway (AAR code)
CBM . . . . Chesebrough-Pond's Inc. (NYSE symbol)
CC . . . . Chess Club
CWSRA . . . . . Chester White Swine Record Association
CHR . . . . Chestnut Ridge Railway Company (AAR code)
CHH . . . . Cheswick & Harmar R. R. (AAR code)
CFCRFC . . . . . Chewings Fescue and Creeping Red Fescue Commission
CKS . . . . Chiang Kai-shek
CSF . . . . Chi-Squared Function
MDW . . . . . . Chicago (Illinois) (Midway Airport) (Airport symbol)
CAB . . . . Chicago Alliance of Businessmen
C & A . . . . . . Chicago and Alton Railroad Company
CATS . . . . . . Chicago Area Transportation Study
CAE . . . . Chicago Aurora & Elgin Railroad Corporation (AAR code)
CB & I . . . . . . Chicago Bridge & Iron Company
CBQ . . . . Chicago, Burlington & Quincy R. R. (AAR code)
Q . . . . Chicago, Burlington, and Quincy Railroad (Slang)
CB & Q . . . . . Chicago, Burlington & Quincy Railroad Company
CEI . . . . Chicago & Eastern Illinois R. R. (AAR code)
C & EI . . . . . Chicago and Eastern Illinois Railroad Company
CGE . . . . Chicago & Eastern Illinois R. R. Company (NYSE symbol)
CEMA . . . . . . Chicago Envelope Manufacturers Association
C & E . . . . . . Chicago and Erie Railroad Company

CHICAGORILLA.. Chicago Gorilla (Slang for a desperado gunman)
CGW . . . . Chicago Great Western Railway (NYSE symbol)
C & GWRY. . . Chicago & Great Western Railway
CHTT . . . . Chicago Heights Terminal Transfer R. R. (AAR code)
CH. . . . . Chicago Helicopter Airways, Inc. (Also, CHA)
CHA. . . . . Chicago Helicopter Airways, Inc. (Also, CH)
CIM. . . . . Chicago & Illinois Midland Railway Company (AAR code)
C & IM . . . . . Chicago & Illinois Midland Railway Company
CIW. . . . . Chicago & Illinois Western R. R. (AAR code)
CIL . . . . Chicago, Indianapolis & Louisville R. R. (AAR code)
CKS . . . . Chicago, Kalamazoo & Saginaw Railway (AAR code)
CKCL . . . . Chicago-Kent College of Law
CLML . . . . Chicago Linear Music Language
CLE . . . . Chicago Livestock Exchange
CLTS . . . . Chicago Lutheran Theological Seminary
CMS. . . . . Chicago Medical School
CML. . . . . Chicago Midway Laboratory (Army)
CMEMA . . . . . Chicago and Midwest Envelope Manufacturers Association
MILW. . . . . . . Chicago, Milwaukee, St. Paul & Pacific R. R. (AAR code)
CM ST P & P.. . Chicago, Milwaukee, St. Paul and Pacific Railroad Company
CM & STP. . . . Chicago, Milwaukee & St. Paul Railway
CNHM . . . . . . Chicago Natural History Museum
CNSM . . . . . . Chicago North Shore & Milwaukee R. R. (AAR code)
CNW . . . . Chicago & North Western Railway Company (AAR code)
C & NW . . . . . Chicago and North Western Railway Company
NW . . . . Chicago & North Western Railway Company (NYSE symbol)
C & NPRR . . . Chicago & Northern Pacific Railroad
COBT . . . . Chicago Open Board of Trade
COO . . . . Chicago Operations Office (of AEC)
EJE . . . . Chicago Outer Belt R. R. (AAR code)
CP-5 . . . . Chicago Pile-5 (Nuclear heavy-water-research reactor)
CPCC . . . . Chicago Playing Card Collectors
CGG . . . . Chicago Pneumatic Tool Company (NYSE symbol)
CPT . . . . Chicago Produce Terminal Company (AAR code)
CR & I . . . . . . Chicago River and Indiana Railroad Company
CRI & P . . . . . Chicago, Rock Island and Pacific Railway Company
RI . . . . Chicago, Rock Island & Pacific R. R. Company (NYSE symbol and
             AAR code)
CMO . . . . Chicago, St. Paul, Minneapolis & Omaha R. R. (AAR code)
CSTPM & O. . . Chicago, St. Paul, Minneapolis and Omaha Railway Company
CSL . . . . Chicago Short Line Railway Company (AAR code)
CSS . . . . Chicago South Shore & South Bend R. R. (AAR code)
CTC . . . . Chicago Teachers College
CTC . . . . Chicago Technical College
CTSE . . . . Chicago, Terre Haute & Southeastern R. R. (AAR code)
CTS . . . . Chicago Theological Seminary
CTA . . . . Chicago Transit Authority
CTDU . . . . Chicago Truck Drivers Union
CWP. . . . . Chicago, West Pullman & Southern R. R. (AAR code)
CWI . . . . Chicago & Western Indiana R. R. (AAR code)
CHISOX . . . . . Chicago White Sox (Baseball team)
CYC. . . . . Chicago Yellow Cab Company, Inc. (NYSE symbol)
CCA. . . . . Chick Cell Agglutination
CEF . . . . Chick Embryo Fibroblasts
CHCH. . . . . . . Chickamauga and Chattanooga National Military Park
CIK . . . . Chickasha Cotton Oil Company (NYSE symbol)
C . . . . Chief
CA . . . . Chief Accountant
CAO. . . . . Chief Administrative Officer
CAIDO . . . . . . Chief Advisor, International District Office (FAA)
CAIFO . . . . . . Chief Advisor, International Field Office (FAA)
CAER . . . . Chief Aerographer
CHAER . . . . . . Chief Aerographer
CAERM . . . . . Chief Aerographer's Mate
CAC. . . . . Chief of Air Corps
C of AFCH. . . . Chief of Air Force Chaplains
COFAFCH. . . . Chief of Air Force Chaplains
CADO . . . . . . Chief, Airport District Office (FAA)
CAR . . . . Chief Airship Rigger
CATDO. . . . . . Chief Airways Technical District Office
CATFO . . . . . . Chief Airways Technical Field Office
CAAF . . . . Chief, Army Air Forces
CAAA. . . . . . . Chief of Army Audit Agency
CAA. . . . . Chief of Army Aviation
CAR . . . . Chief, Army Reserve
CARROTC . . . . Chief, (US) Army Reserve and Reserve Officers Training Corps Affairs
CAP. . . . . Chief Aviation Pilot (Navy, Coast Guard)
CHBOSN. . . . . Chief Boatswain
CBM. . . . . Chief Boatswain's Mate
CBMM. . . . . . . Chief Boatswain's Mate A (Master-at-Arms)
CBMA. . . . . . . Chief Boatswain's Mate Acting

CBMCBB . . . . . Chief Boatswain's Mate, Construction Battalion, Boatswain
CBMCBS . . . . . Chief Boatswain's Mate, Construction Battalion, Stevedore
CBMSRS . . . . . Chief Boatswain's Mate, Ship Repair, Canvasman
CBMSRC . . . . . Chief Boatswain's Mate, Ship Repair, Crane Operator
CBMSRR . . . . . Chief Boatswain's Mate, Ship Repair, Rigger
CB . . . . Chief Boilermaker (Navy)
CBMKR . . . . . . Chief Boilermaker (Coast Guard)
CBSR . . . . Chief Boilermaker, Ship Repair
CBLO . . . . Chief Bombardment Liaison Officer (Navy)
CHBUAER . . . . Chief of the Bureau of Aeronautics (Navy) (Obsolete)
CHBUMED . . . . Chief of the Bureau of Medicine and Surgery (Navy)
CHBUPERS . . . . Chief of the Bureau of Naval Personnel
CHBUORD . . . . Chief of the Bureau of Ordnance (Navy) (Obsolete)
CHBUSHIPS . . . Chief of the Bureau of Ships (Navy) (Obsolete)
CHBUSANDA . . Chief of the Bureau of Supplies and Accounts (Navy) (Obsolete)
CHBUDOCKS . . Chief of the Bureau of Yards and Docks (Navy) (Obsolete)
CCC . . . . Chief Cable Censor (Navy)
CHCARP . . . . . Chief Carpenter (Navy)
CCM . . . . Chief Carpenter's Mate
CCMCBB . . . . . Chief Carpenter's Mate, Construction Battalion, Builder
CCMCBD . . . . . Chief Carpenter's Mate, Construction Battalion, Draftsman
CCMCBE . . . . . Chief Carpenter's Mate, Construction Battalion, Excavation Foreman
CCMCBS . . . . . Chief Carpenter's Mate, Construction Battalion, Surveyor
CCMSRB . . . . . Chief Carpenter's Mate, Ship Repair, Boatbuilder--Wood
CCMSRJ . . . . . Chief Carpenter's Mate, Ship Repair, Joiner
CC . . . . Chief of Chaplains (Army)
C of CH . . . . . Chief of Chaplains (Army)
COC . . . . Chief of Chaplains (Navy)
COFCH . . . . . . Chief of Chaplains
CCMLO. . . . . . Chief Chemical Officer (Army)
CCO. . . . . Chief Chemical Officer (Army)
CCA. . . . . Chief of Civil Affairs (Army)
CCAO. . . . . . . Chief Civil Affairs Officer (Navy)
CC. . . . . Chief Clerk
CCA. . . . . Chief Clerk of the Admiralty
CCS . . . . Chief Commissary Steward
CCSTD . . . . . . Chief Commissary Steward
CC. . . . . Chief Complaint (Medicine)
CCNT. . . . . . . Chief Controller (Air Force)
CCK. . . . . Chief Cook
CHCK . . . . Chief Cook (Navy)
CCK(B) . . . . . . Chief Cook (Baker)
CCK(C) . . . . . . Chief Cook (Commissary)
CCE. . . . . Chief, Corps of Engineers (Army)
CDM . . . . Chief Decision Makers
CD. . . . . Chief of Division
CHELEC . . . . . Chief Electrician
CEM. . . . . Chief Electrician's Mate
CEMCBC . . . . . Chief Electrician's Mate, Construction Battalion, Communications
CEMCBD . . . . . Chief Electrician's Mate, Construction Battalion, Draftsman
CEMCBG . . . . . Chief Electrician's Mate, Construction Battalion, General
CEMCBL . . . . . Chief Electrician's Mate, Construction Battalion, Line and Station
CEMSRG . . . . . Chief Electrician's Mate, Ship Repair, General Electrician
CEMSRT. . . . . . Chief Electrician's Mate, Ship Repair, IC Repairman
CEMSRS . . . . . Chief Electrician's Mate, Ship Repair, Shop Electrician
CE . . . . Chief Engineer
C of ENGRS . . Chief of Engineers (Army)
COFENGRS . . Chief of Engineers
CEF . . . . Chief Executives Forum
CFA . . . . Chief of Field Artillery
CF . . . . Chief of Finance (Army)
C of F . . . . . . Chief of Finance (Army)
COFF . . . . Chief of Finance
CFO . . . . Chief Financial Officer
CFC . . . . Chief Fire Controlman
CFCO. . . . . . . Chief Fire Controlman, Operator
CFCS . . . . Chief Fire Controlman, Submarines
CFI . . . . Chief Flying Instructor (British Royal Air Force)
CGS. . . . . Chief of the General Staff (in the field) (British military)
CHGUN . . . . . Chief Gunner
CGM . . . . Chief Gunner's Mate
CGMCBG . . . . Chief Gunner's Mate, Construction Battalion, Armorer
CGMCBP. . . . . Chief Gunner's Mate, Construction Battalion, Powderman
CIGS . . . . Chief of the Imperial General Staff (British)
CIP. . . . . Chief Industrial Property
CHINFO . . . . . Chief of Information (Navy)
CI . . . . Chief of Information (Army)
CINFO . . . . . . Chief of Information
CI . . . . Chief Inspector
CIA . . . . Chief Inspector of Armaments
CI . . . . Chief Instructor

CINTC . . . . . . Chief, Intelligence Corps
CIND . . . . Chief Intercept Director
CJ . . . . Chief Judge
CJ . . . . Chief Justice (Various supreme courts)
CLL . . . . Chief of Legislative Liaison (Army)
CHMACH . . . . Chief Machinist (Navy)
CMM . . . . . . Chief Machinist's Mate
CMMCBE . . . . . Chief Machinist's Mate, Construction Battalion, Equipment Operator
CMMG . . . . . Chief Machinist's Mate, Industrial Gas Generating Mechanic
CMMR . . . . . . Chief Machinist's Mate, Refrigeration
CMMSRO . . . . Chief Machinist's Mate, Ship Repair, Outside Machinist C
CMMS . . . . . . Chief Machinist's Mate, Shop
CMAM . . . . . Chief Mailman
CMO . . . . Chief Maintenance Officer
CMG . . . . . . Chief Marine Gunner
CMSGT . . . . . Chief Master Sergeant
CMSAF . . . . . Chief Master Sergeant of the Air Force
CMO . . . . Chief Medical Officer (Military)
CM . . . . Chief Metalsmith
CMSRB . . . . . . Chief Metalsmith, Ship Repair, Blacksmith
CMSRC . . . . . Chief Metalsmith, Ship Repair, Coppersmith
CMSRS . . . . . Chief Metalsmith, Ship Repair, Sheet Metal Worker
CMH . . . . Chief of Military History (Department of the Army)
CMOMM . . . . . Chief Motor Machinist's Mate
CMOMSRD . . . . Chief Motor Machinist's Mate, Ship Repair, Diesel Engineering Mechanic
CMOMSRG . . . Chief Motor Machinist's Mate, Ship Repair, Gasoline Engineering
           Mechanic
CML . . . . Chief Moulder (Navy)
CMUS . . . . . . Chief Musician (Navy rating)
CNGB . . . . . . Chief, National Guard Bureau (Department of the Army)
CNA . . . . Chief of Naval Air
CNAADTRA . . . Chief of Naval Air Advanced Training (Formerly, CNAOPTRA)
CNAVANTRA . . Chief of Naval Air Advanced Training
CNABATRA . . . Chief of Naval Air Basic Training
CNAINTERMTRA . . Chief of Naval Air Intermediate Training (Later, CNABTRA)
CNAIT . . . . . . Chief of Naval Air Intermediate Training
CNAOPTRA . . . Chief of Naval Air Operational Training (Later, CNAADTRA)
CNAOT . . . . . Chief of Naval Air Operational Training
CNAPRIMTRA . . Chief of Naval Air Primary Training (Later, CNARFSTRA)
CNAPT . . . . . Chief of Naval Air Primary Training
CNARFSTRA . . . Chief of Naval Air Primary Training
CNARESTRA . . Chief of Naval Air Reserve Training
CNAS . . . . . . Chief of Naval Air Services (British)
CNATECHTRA . . Chief of Naval Air Technical Training
CNATT . . . . . Chief of Naval Air Technical Training
CNAT . . . . . . Chief of Naval Air Training
CNATRA . . . . Chief of Naval Air Training
CHNAVAIRSHIPTRA . . Chief of Naval Airship Training
CNATE . . . . . . Chief of Naval Airships Training and Experimentation
CNC . . . . Chief Naval Censor
CNC . . . . Chief of Naval Communications (Formerly, DNC)
CND . . . . Chief of Naval Development
CNI . . . . Chief of Naval Intelligence
CNM . . . . . . Chief of Naval Materials
CHNAVMIS . . . Chief, Naval Mission
CNO . . . . Chief of Naval Operations
CNP . . . . Chief of Naval Personnel (The Second Sea Lord) (British)
CNR . . . . Chief of Naval Research
CNTS . . . . . . Chief, Naval Transportation Service
CNDO . . . . . . Chief Navy Disbursing Officer
COPO . . . . . . Chief, Office of Personnel Operations (Army)
CHORI . . . . . . Chief, Office of Research and Inventions
CORC . . . . . . Chief, Office of Reserve Components (Army)
CO . . . . Chief of Ordnance (Army)
COFORD . . . . . Chief of Ordnance
CORD . . . . . . Chief of Ordnance (Army)
C of ORD . . . . Chief of Ordnance (Army)
COO . . . . Chief Ordnance Officer
CPTR . . . . . . Chief Painter (Navy rating)
CPTRV . . . . . Chief Painter, Aircraft (Navy rating)
CP . . . . Chief Patriarch
CPI . . . . Chief Patrol Inspector (Immigration and Naturalization Service)
CPM . . . . Chief Patternmaker (Navy rating)
CHPCLK . . . . Chief Pay Clerk (Navy)
CPC . . . . Chief Pay Clerk (Navy)
CPO . . . . Chief Petty Officer (Navy)
CHPHAR . . . . Chief Pharmacist (Navy)
CPHM . . . . . . Chief Pharmacist's Mate
CPHMDP . . . . . Chief Pharmacist's Mate, Dental Prosthetic Technician
CPHM(RPA) . . . Chief Pharmacist's Mate (Radium Plaque Adaptometer Operator)
CPHO . . . . Chief Photographer (Navy rating)

CHPHOT . . . . . Chief Photographer (Navy)
CPHOM . . . . . Chief Photographer's Mate
CPC . . . . Chief Planning and Control Staff (Coast Guard)
C PRTR . . . . . . Chief Printer (Navy rating)
CPRTRL . . . . . . Chief Printer, Lithographer (Navy rating)
CPRTRM . . . . . Chief Printer, Offset Process (Navy rating)
CPI . . . . Chief of Public Information (Army)
CQM . . . . Chief Quartermaster (Navy)
CHQMCLK . . . Chief Quartermaster Clerk (Coast Guard)
CQMC . . . . . . Chief Quartermaster Clerk (Navy)
CRDM . . . . . . Chief RADARman (Navy rating)
CHRELE . . . . . Chief Radio Electrician (Navy)
CRE . . . . Chief Radio Electrician (Navy rating)
CRT . . . . Chief Radio Technician (Navy rating)
CRM . . . . Chief Radioman (Navy rating)
CR . . . . Chief Ranger
CRD . . . . Chief of Research and Development (Army)
CR & D . . . . . Chief, Research & Development (Army)
CRC . . . . Chief of Reserve Components (Army)
COS . . . . Chief of Section
CS . . . . Chief of Section
C of S . . . . . . Chief of Section
CHSCLK . . . . . Chief Ship's Clerk
CSCLK . . . . . Chief Ship's Clerk
CSSM . . . . . . Chief Ship's Service Man (Navy rating)
CSSMB . . . . . . Chief Ship's Service Man, Barber (Navy rating)
CSSMC . . . . . Chief Ship's Service Man, Cobbler (Navy rating)
CSSML . . . . . . Chief Ship's Service Man, Laundryman (Navy rating)
CSSMT . . . . . Chief Ship's Service Man, Tailor (Navy rating)
CSF . . . . Chief Shipfitter (Navy rating)
CSFCBM . . . . . Chief Shipfitter, Construction Battalion, Mechanical Draftsman (Navy
           rating)
CSFCBP . . . . . . Chief Shipfitter, Construction Battalion, Pipe Fitter and Plumber (Navy
           rating)
CSFCBR . . . . . Chief Shipfitter, Construction Battalion, Rigger (Navy rating)
CSFCBS . . . . . Chief Shipfitter, Construction Battalion, Steel Worker (Navy rating)
CSFCBW . . . . Chief Shipfitter, Construction Battalion, Welder (Navy rating)
CSFSR . . . . . . Chief Shipfitter, Ship Repair (Navy rating)
CSFSRP . . . . . Chief Shipfitter, Ship Repair, Pipe Fitter and Plumber (Navy rating)
CSFSRW . . . . . Chief Shipfitter, Ship Repair, Welder (Navy rating)
CSIGO . . . . . Chief Signal Officer
CSIGC . . . . . . Chief, Signal Corps (Army)
CSO . . . . Chief Signal Officer (Army)
CSM . . . . Chief Signalman (Navy rating)
CSOM . . . . . . Chief SONARman (Navy rating)
CSOMH . . . . . Chief SONARman, Harbor Defense
CSA . . . . Chief Special Artificer (Navy rating)
CSAI . . . . Chief Special Artificer, Instruments (Navy rating)
CSAITR . . . . . . Chief Special Artificer, Instruments, Typewriter and Office Equipment
           Repairman (Navy rating)
CSAIWR . . . . . Chief Special Artificer, Instruments, Watch Repairman (Navy rating)
CSAO . . . . . . Chief Special Artificer, Optical (Navy rating)
CSAD . . . . . . Chief Special Artificer, Synthetic Training Devices (Navy rating)
CSP . . . . Chief Specialist (Navy rating)
CSPX . . . . . . Chief Specialist, All Designators (Navy)
CSPW . . . . . . Chief Specialist, Chaplain's Assistant (Navy rating)
CSPY . . . . . . Chief Specialist, Control Tower Operator (Navy rating)
CSPR . . . . Chief Specialist, Identification (Navy rating)
CSPPLB . . . . . Chief Specialist, Laboratory (Navy rating)
CSPTLT . . . . . . Chief Specialist, Link Trainer Instructor (Navy rating)
CSPMP . . . . . Chief Specialist, Motion Picture Production (Navy rating)
CSPS . . . . Chief Specialist, Personnel Supervisor (Navy rating)
CSPO . . . . . . Chief Specialist, Petroleum Inspector (Navy rating)
CSPPPG . . . . . Chief Specialist, Photogrammetry (Navy rating)
CSPA . . . . Chief Specialist, Physical Training Instructor (Navy rating)
CSPR . . . . Chief Specialist, Recruiter (Navy rating)
CSPS . . . . Chief Specialist, Shore Patrol and Security (Navy rating)
CSPT . . . . Chief Specialist, Teacher (Navy rating)
CSPV . . . . . . Chief Specialist, Transport Airman (Navy rating)
CSPPVM . . . . . Chief Specialist, V-Mail (Navy rating)
COFS . . . . . . Chief of Staff
COS . . . . Chief of Staff
CS . . . . Chief of Staff (Army, Air Force)
C/S . . . . Chief of Staff
C of S . . . . . . Chief of Staff (Army)
CSAFM . . . . . Chief of Staff Air Force Memorandum
C of SA . . . . . Chief of Staff, Army
CSM . . . . Chief of Staff Memorandum (Military)
CSO . . . . Chief Staff Officer
CSR . . . . Chief of Staff Regulations
COSSAC . . . . . Chief of Staff to Supreme Allied Commander (Europe) (World War II)

CSAF . . . . Chief of Staff, United States Air Force
COFSA . . . . . . Chief of Staff, United States Army
CSA . . . . Chief of Staff, United States Army
CST . . . . Chief Steward (Navy rating)
CSK . . . . Chief Storekeeper
CSKV . . . . Chief Storekeeper, Aviation (Navy rating)
CSKCB . . . . . . Chief Storekeeper, Construction Battalion, Stevedore (Navy rating)
CSKD . . . . . . Chief Storekeeper, Disbursing (Navy rating)
CSKT . . . . Chief Storekeeper, Technical (Navy rating)
CSHS . . . . Chief Superintendent of Hydrographic Supplies
CSS . . . . Chief of Support Services (Army)
CTS . . . . Chief(s), Technical Services
CT . . . . Chief Telegrapher (Navy rating)
CHTORP . . . . . Chief Torpedoman
CTORP . . . . . . Chief Torpedoman
CTM . . . . Chief Torpedoman's Mate
CTMV . . . . Chief Torpedoman's Mate, Aviation
CTME . . . . . . Chief Torpedoman's Mate, Electrical
COFT . . . . Chief of Transportation
CT . . . . Chief of Transportation (Army)
C of T . . . . . . Chief of Transportation (Army)
CTC . . . . Chief Turret Captain (Navy)
CUSARROTC . . Chief, United States Army Reserve and Reserve Officers Training Corps Affairs
CV . . . . Chief Value
CWO . . . . Chief Warrant Officer
CWT . . . . Chief Water Tender (Navy rating)
CY . . . . Chief Yeoman (Navy rating)
CCA . . . . Chihuahua Club of America
CHP . . . . Chihuahua Pacific R. R. (AAR code)
CV . . . . Chikungunya Virus
C . . . . Child
CDGM . . . . . . Child Development Group of Mississippi
CDRU . . . . . . Child Development Research Unit (Nigeria)
CEFI . . . . Child Evangelism Fellowship International
CHAP . . . . . . Child Health Associate Program
CSC . . . . Child Safety Council
CSAA . . . . Child Study Association of America
CW . . . . Child Welfare
CWLA . . . . . . Child Welfare League of America
CWS . . . . Child Welfare Service
CAT . . . . Child's Apperception Test (Psychology)
CWPEA . . . . . . Childbirth Without Pain Education Association
CHAP . . . . . . Children Have a Potential (Program for handicapped or disturbed children of Air Force personnel)
CARIH . . . . . . Children's Asthma Research Institute and Hospital (Denver, Colorado)
CBC . . . . Children's Book Council
CB . . . . Children's Bureau (of SSA)
CCFA . . . . Children's Cancer Fund of America
CDCDSCA . . . . Children's Dress, Cotton Dress, and Sportwear Contractors Association
COPB . . . . Children's Organization for Peace and Brotherhood
CPU . . . . Children's Peace Union
CPQ . . . . Children's Personality Questionnaire
CPP . . . . Children's Plea for Peace
CSC . . . . Children's Self-Conceptions Test
CSD . . . . Children's Services Division (of ALA)
CTW . . . . Children's Television Workshop
CTC . . . . Children's Theatre Conference
CWA . . . . Children's Wear Association
CAA . . . . Chile-American Association
CIEB . . . . Chilean Iodine Educational Bureau
CCA . . . . Chimpanzee Coryza Agent
CBI . . . . China-Burma-India Theater (World War II)
CBIVA . . . . . . China-Burma-India Veterans Association
CGGBT . . . . . . China, Glass, Giftware Board of Trade
CGPAA . . . . . . China, Glass and Pottery Association of America
CIM . . . . China Inland Mission
CIM-OMF . . . . China Inland Mission Overseas Missionary Fellowship (Later, Overseas Missionary Fellowship)
CIA . . . . China Institute in America
CIF . . . . China International Foundation
CMFC . . . . China Man-Made Fiber Corporation (Taiwan)
CMBNY . . . . . China Medical Board of New York
CNAC . . . . . . China National Aviation Corps
CPGA . . . . China Pottery and Glassware Association
CHSM . . . . . . China Service Medal
CSA . . . . China Society of America
CT . . . . China Theater, Combat Team
CATF . . . . Chinese Air Task Force
CACA . . . . Chinese American Citizens Alliance
CACW . . . . . . Chinese-American Composite Wing (Air Force)

CARA . . . . Chinese American Restaurant Association
CAI . . . . Chinese Army in India
CASA . . . . Chinese Art Society of America
CHICOM . . . . . Chinese Communist
CCAF . . . . Chinese Communist Air Force
CCF . . . . Chinese Communist Forces
CCP . . . . Chinese Communist Party
CCBA . . . . Chinese Consolidated Benevolent Association
CEA . . . . Chinese Exclusion Act
CEF . . . . Chinese Expeditionary Force
CFL . . . . Chinese Federation of Labor (Nationalist China)
CFMU . . . . . . Chinese Foreign Missionary Union
CHO . . . . Chinese Hamster Ovarian (Tumor)
CHO . . . . Chinese Hamster Ovary (Cells)
CHICODER . . . Chinese Language Encoder
CLA . . . . Chinese Laundry Association
CMA . . . . Chinese Merchants Association
CMTA . . . . Chinese Musical and Theatrical Association
CHINAT . . . . . Chinese Nationalist
CPR . . . . Chinese People's Republic
CPPCC . . . . . . Chinese People's Political Consultative Conference
CRR . . . . Chinese Refugee Relief
CRS . . . . Chinese Restaurant Syndrome (Malady affecting some people while eating in Chinese restaurants)
CWA . . . . Chinese Women's Association
CJC . . . . Chipola Junior College (Florida)
CHIR . . . . Chiricahua National Monument and Fort Bowie National Historic Site
CBRS . . . . Chiropody Bibliographical Research Society
CB . . . . Chirurgiae Baccalaureus (Bachelor of Surgery)
Ch B . . . . Chirurgiae Baccalaureus (Bachelor of Surgery)
Chir Doct . . . . Chirurgiae Doctor (Doctor of Surgery)
D Ch . . . . Chirurgiae Doctor (Doctor of Surgery)
Ch M . . . . Chirurgiae Magister (Master of Surgery)
CM . . . . Chirurgiae Magister (Master of Surgery)
CAP . . . . Chloracetophenone
CHS . . . . Chloracetophenone Solution (Tear gas)
COC . . . . Chlorate Oxygen Candle
CPVC . . . . Chlorinated Polyvinyl Chloride
CI . . . . Chlorine (Chemical element)
CI . . . . Chlorine Institute
CTF . . . . Chlorine Trifluoride
CPIB . . . . Chlorophenoxyisobutyrate (Chemical)
CQ . . . . Chloroquine (Antimalarial drug)
CTFE . . . . Chlorotrifluoroethylene
CPZ . . . . Chlorpromazine
CHF . . . . Chock Full O'Nuts Corporation (NYSE symbol) (Wall Street slang name: "Nuts")
CCT . . . . Chocolate-Colored Tablet (Pharmacy)
CMA . . . . Chocolate Manufacturers Association of the USA
CMF . . . . Chocolate Milk Foundation
CLL . . . . Cholesterol Lowering Lipid (Biochemistry)
ChAc . . . . Choline-Acetylase
ChE . . . . Cholinesterase
CSA . . . . Chopper Stabilized Amplifier
C . . . . Choppy, Short, or Cross Sea
CCG . . . . Choral Conductors Guild
CG . . . . Chorionic Gonadotropin (Endocrinology)
CGH . . . . Chorionic Gonadotropin, Human (Endocrinology)
CCC . . . . Chow Chow Club
CHEKA . . . . . . Chrezvychainaya Komissiya (Extraordinary commission; Soviet secret police organization, 1917-21)
CCN . . . . Chris-Craft Industries, Inc. (NYSE symbol)
CKF . . . . Christ the King Foundation
CAP . . . . Christian Action Party (Puerto Rico)
CAM . . . . Christian Amendment Movement
CANA . . . . . . Christian Anti-Narcotic Association
CAPS . . . . Christian Association for Psychological Studies
CBA . . . . Christian Booksellers Association
CBEA . . . . Christian Brothers Education Association
CBMCI . . . . . . Christian Business Men's Committee International
CCF . . . . Christian Children's Fund
CDUCE . . . . . . Christian Democratic Union of Central Europe
CEU . . . . Christian Endeavor Union
CE . . . . Christian Era
CFM . . . . Christian Family Movement
CFF . . . . Christian Freedom Foundation
CKS . . . . Christian Knowledge Society (Also known as Society for Promoting Christian Knowledge)
CLA . . . . Christian Labor Association of the United States of America
CMC . . . . Christian Medical Council
CMS . . . . Christian Medical Society

CME . . . . Christian Methodist Episcopal (Church)
CM . . . . Christian Mission
CMA . . . . Christian and Missionary Alliance
CMF . . . . Christian Missionary Fellowship
CMML . . . . . . Christian Missions in Many Lands
CSB . . . . Christian Science Teacher
CRBA . . . . . . Christian Record Benevolent Association
CRBF . . . . . . Christian Record Braille Foundation
CRI . . . . Christian Research Institute
CRF . . . . Christian Rural Fellowship
CROP . . . . . . Christian Rural Overseas Program
CS . . . . Christian Science
CSM . . . . Christian Science Monitor (A newspaper)
CSD . . . . Christian Science Teacher (Used only by those teachers who had received instruction directly from Mary Baker Eddy)
CWF . . . . Christian Women's Fellowship
CHRIST . . . . . Christians Heeding Righteousness Instead of Satanic Tyranny (Conservative organization)
CURE . . . . . . Christians United for Responsible Entertainment
CHRI . . . . . . Christiansted National Historic Site
CDU . . . . Christlich-Demokratische Union (Christian Democratic Union) (West German political party)
CNGS . . . . . . Christlich-Nationaler Gewerkschaftsbund der Schweiz (Swiss Federation of National-Christian Trade Unions)
CSU . . . . Christlich-Soziale Union (Political party in Bavaria connected with the CDU) (West Germany)
CGD . . . . Christliche Gewerkschaftsbewegung Deutschlands (Christian Trade Union Movement of Germany) (West Germany)
CVJM . . . . . . Christliche Vereine Junger Manner (Young Men's Christian Associations) (Germany)
CGB . . . . Christlicher Gewerkschaftsbund Deutschlands (Confederation of German Christian Trade Unions) (West Germany)
CNV . . . . Christlijk Nationaal Vakverbond in Nederland (National Federation of Christian Workers) (Protestant) (Netherlands)
CF . . . . Christmas Factor (Physiology)
CTP . . . . Christmas Tree Pattern
X . . . . Christus
XPC . . . . Christus
XS . . . . Christus
CM . . . . Chrom-Moly
CZC . . . . Chromated Zinc Chloride
CASSANDRA . . Chromatogram Automatic Soaking Scanning and Digital Recording Apparatus
CRV . . . . Chrome Vanadium
Cr . . . . Chromium (Chemical element)
CF . . . . Chromosomal Fraction
CBS . . . . Chronic Brain Syndrome (Medicine)
CCI . . . . Chronic Coronary Insufficiency (Medicine)
CHA . . . . Chronic Hemolytic Anemia
CHINA . . . . . . Chronic Infectious Neuropathic Agents
CML . . . . Chronic Myeloid (or Myelogenous) Leukemia
COPD . . . . . . Chronic Obstructive Pulmonary Disease
CPC . . . . Chronic Passive Congestion (Medicine)
CRD . . . . Chronic Respiratory Disease (Medicine)
CA . . . . Chronological Age (Psychology)
CC . . . . Chronometer Correction
CE . . . . Chronometer Error (Navigation)
C . . . . Chronometer Time
C-W . . . . Chronometer Time Minus Watch Time (Navigation)
C . . . . Chrysler Corporation (NYSE symbol)
CC . . . . Chrysler Corporation
COPS . . . . . . Chrysler Optical Processing Scanner
CPRC . . . . . . Chrysler Products Restorers Club
C . . . . Church
CAGA . . . . . . Church Architectural Guild of America
CA . . . . Church Association (British)
CASW . . . . . . Church Association for Seamen's Work
CBS . . . . Church Building Society (British)
CCS . . . . Church of Christ, Scientist
CDI . . . . Church Defence Institution (British)
CE . . . . Church of England
C of E . . . . . . Church of England
CESSI . . . . . . Church of England Sunday School Institute
CETS . . . . . . Church of England Temperance Society
CEWMS . . . . . Church of England Working Men's Society
CEYMS . . . . . Church of England Young Men's Society
CEA . . . . Church Evangelism Association
CEDB . . . . . . Church Executive Development Board
CEA . . . . Church Extension Association (British)
CFMA . . . . . . Church Furniture Manufacturers Association
CGU . . . . Church Guilds Union (British)

CHS . . . . Church Historical Society
CLA . . . . Church League of America
CMJ . . . . Church Mission of Jews
CMS . . . . Church Missionary Society
CMU . . . . Church Missionary Union (British)
CMAA . . . . . . Church Music Association of America
CMPA . . . . . . Church Music Publishers Association
CPAS . . . . . . Church Pastoral Aid Society (British)
CPU . . . . Church Peace Union
CPA . . . . Church Penitentiary Association (British)
CPF . . . . Church Pension Fund
CPC . . . . Church Pensions Conference
CPC . . . . Church Periodical Club
CSCW . . . . . . Church Society for College Work
CSSU . . . . . . Church Sunday School Union (British)
CSLA . . . . . . Church and Synagogue Library Association
CWS . . . . Church World Service (of the National Council of Churches of Christ in the USA)
CWS . . . . Church World Services (Protestant and Eastern Orthodox Church Aid Project)
CRR . . . . Churchill Research Range (Air Force)
CCDP . . . . . . Churchmen's Commission for Decent Publications
CW . . . . Churchwarden
CU . . . . Chymotrypsin Unit
CUI . . . . Chymotrypsin Units Inhibited
CCP . . . . Cibachrome-Print (Color photography)
CBM . . . . Cigar Box Manufacturers
CIA . . . . Cigar Institute of America
CMIU of A . . . Cigar Makers' International Union of America
CMA . . . . Cigar Manufacturers Association of America
CMAA . . . . . . Cigar Manufacturers Association of America
CMAT . . . . . . Cigar Manufacturers Association of Tampa
CSA . . . . Cigar Smokers of America
CAC . . . . Cigarette Advertising Code, Inc.
CLMA . . . . . . Cigarette Lighter Manufacturers Association
CT . . . . Ciguatoxin
CBT . . . . Cincinnati Board of Trade
CVG . . . . Cincinnati (Ohio) - Covington (Ky.) (Airport symbol)
CIN . . . . Cincinnati Gas & Electric Company (NYSE symbol)
CMZ . . . . Cincinnati Milling Machine Company (NYSE symbol)
CNTP . . . . . . Cincinnati, New Orleans & Texas Pacific Railway (AAR code)
CNO & TP . . . Cincinnati, New Orleans and Texas Pacific Railway Company
CNOR . . . . . . Cincinnati Northern R. R. (AAR code)
COTA . . . . . . Cinetheodolite Orientation Target Array
CTTE . . . . . . Cintered Tungsten-Tantalum Emitter
CIPHONY . . . . Cipher and Telephony Equipment (Military)
C . . . . Circa (About)
CA . . . . Circa (About)
CEP . . . . Circle of Equal Probability
C . . . . Circling (Approach and landing charts) (Aviation)
C . . . . Circuit
CB . . . . Circuit Breaker
CC . . . . Circuit Closing
CC . . . . Circuit Court
CCA . . . . Circuit Court of Appeals
CF . . . . Circuit Finder
CI . . . . Circuit Interrupter
CLU . . . . Circuit Line Up
CNL . . . . Circuit Net Loss
CPD . . . . Circuit Protection Device
CQM . . . . Circuit Quality Monitor
CRI . . . . Circuit Reliability Improvement
CSMT . . . . . . Circuit Switching Magnetic Tape
CSN . . . . Circuit Switching Network
CTS . . . . Circuit Test Set
CT . . . . Circuit Theory
C . . . . Circular
CD . . . . Circular Dispersion
CE . . . . Circular Error (Military)
CEA . . . . Circular Error Average (Military)
CEP . . . . Circular Error Probable (Nuclear bombing)
CILET . . . . . . Circular Letter
CIRCLTR . . . . . Circular Letter (Military)
CL . . . . Circular Letter
C/L . . . . Circular Letter
CMW . . . . Circular Magnetic Wave
CM . . . . Circular Measure
CM . . . . Circular Mil (Wire measure)
CMA . . . . Circular Mil Area
CMF . . . . Circular Mil Foot
CN . . . . Circular Note

CP . . . . Circular Pitch (Technical drawings)
CP . . . . Circular Polarization
CPE . . . . . . Circular Probable Error
CVFS . . . . . . Circular Variable Filter Spectrometer
CC . . . . Circulating Copy
CFRE . . . . . . Circulating Fuel Reactor Experiment (AEC)
CWP . . . . . . Circulating Water Pump
CEPI . . . . . . Circulo de Escritores y Poetas Iberoamericanos
C . . . . Circumference
CC . . . . Circumnavigators Club
CFA . . . . . . Circus Fans Association of America
CHS . . . . . . Circus Historical Society
CSSCA . . . . . Circus Saints and Sinners Club of America
CC . . . . Cirrocumulus (Meteorology)
CICU . . . . . . Cirrocumulus (Meteorology)
CS . . . . Cirrostratus (Meteorology)
CI . . . . Cirrus (Meteorology)
CJC . . . . . . Cisco Junior College (Texas)
CLM . . . . . . Cislunar Landing Mission
CLS . . . . . . Cislunar Space
CS . . . . Cities Service Company (NYSE symbol)
CEC . . . . . . Citizen Exchange Corps
CMF . . . . . . Citizen Military Forces (New Guinea)
CACSW . . . . . Citizens' Advisory Council on the Status of Women
CASH . . . . . . Citizens Alliance for Self-Help
CACA . . . . . Citizens Association for the Care of Animals
CB . . . . Citizens Band (A radio frequency band for limited-range, two-way
voice communications by persons without technical training or standard
operator licenses)
CCA . . . . . . Citizens for Clean Air
CCCL . . . . . . Citizens Committee for Constitutional Liberties
CCFLSA . . . . Citizens Committee on the Fair Labor Standards Act
CCFC . . . . . . Citizens Committee for a Free Cuba
CCNR . . . . . . Citizens Committee on Natural Resources
CARP . . . . . . Citizens Concerned About Radiation Pollution (Organization in
Denver, Colorado)
CCSL . . . . . . Citizens Conference on State Legislatures
CCF . . . . . . Citizens' Council Forum
CCA . . . . . . Citizens' Councils of America
CCAP . . . . . . Citizens Crusade Against Poverty
CDL . . . . . . Citizens for Decent Literature
CDC . . . . . . Citizens' Defense Corps
CEAC . . . . . . Citizens Educational Advisory Committee
CEF . . . . . . Citizens for Educational Freedom
CFAC . . . . . . Citizens Foreign Aid Committee
CHEF . . . . . . Citizens Honest Elections Foundation
CLASB . . . . . Citizens League Against the Sonic Boom
CMTC . . . . . . Citizens' (or Civilian) Military Training Camp
CPR . . . . . . Citizens for Parents' Rights (Group opposing sex education in schools)
CPC . . . . . . Citizens for Parental Control (Group opposing sex education in schools)
CQC . . . . . . Citizens for a Quieter City (New York City)
CRF . . . . . . Citizens' Research Foundation
CRASH . . . . . Citizens Responsible Action for Safety on the Highways
CSFA . . . . . . Citizens' Scholarship Foundation of America
CSC . . . . . . Citizens' Service Corps
CSAC . . . . . Citizens Stamp Advisory Committee (Post Office)
CTC . . . . . . Citizens' Training Corps
CCH . . . . . . Citizenship Clearing House
CF . . . . Citrovorum Factor (Physiology)
CJC . . . . . . Citrus Junior College (California)
CCD . . . . . . City (or County) Civil Defense Director
CCCUNY . . . . City College of City University of New York
CCNY . . . . . City College of New York
CC . . . . City Council(lor)
CNV . . . . . . City Investing Company (NYSE symbol)
CLR . . . . . . City of London Rifles (British)
COP . . . . . . City of Prineville Railway (AAR code)
CY . . . . City Products Corporation (NYSE symbol)
CIRE . . . . . . City of Refuge National Historic Park
CSS . . . . . . City Stores Company (NYSE symbol)
CUNY . . . . . City University of New York
CIVIC . . . . . Civic Issues Voluntary Information Council (Michigan)
CAT . . . . . . Civil Action Team
CAC . . . . . . Civil Administration Committee (US Military Government, Germany)
CARI . . . . . . Civil Aeromedical Research Institute (FAA)
CAR . . . . . . Civil Aeronautical Regulation (of FAA)
CAA . . . . . . Civil Aeronautics Administration (Later, part of FAA)
CAA . . . . . . Civil Aeronautics Authority
CHARM . . . . . CAA (Civil Aeronautics Authority) High-Altitude Remote Monitoring
CAB . . . . . . Civil Aeronautics Board (Independent government agency)
CAB . . . . . . Civil Aeronautics Bulletin

CAM . . . . . . Civil Aeronautics Manual
CAMA . . . . . Civil Aerospace Medical Association
CA . . . . Civil Affairs
CAD . . . . . . Civil Affairs Division (Navy)
CAD . . . . . . Civil Affairs Division (US Military Government, Germany)
CA/MG . . . . . Civil Affairs/Military Government
CAO . . . . . . Civil Affairs Officer (Navy)
CAS . . . . . . Civil Affairs Section
G-5 . . . . . . Civil Affairs Section of an Army Division or Brigade General Staff; the
Officer in Charge of this Section
CCSC . . . . . . Civil Affairs Staff Center (Wimbledon, England)
CASUM . . . . . Civil Affairs Summary (Navy)
CATS . . . . . . Civil Affairs Training School (Navy)
CAB . . . . . . Civil Air Branch (Air Force)
CACT . . . . . . Civil Air Carrier Turbojet
CADW . . . . . Civil Air Defense Warning
CAG . . . . . . Civil Air Guard (British)
CAP . . . . . . Civil Air Patrol
CAPCP . . . . . Civil Air Patrol Coastal Patrol (Wartime)
CAPG . . . . . . Civil Air Patrol Guard
CAS . . . . . . Civil Air Surgeon (of FAA)
CAT . . . . . . Civil Air Transport (Free China's International Airline)
CA . . . . Civil Authorities
CAAG . . . . . Civil Aviation Assistance Group
CAA-WTS . . . . Civil Aviation Authority -- War Training Service
CAPC . . . . . . Civil Aviation Planning Committee
CCD . . . . . . Civil Censorship Division (US Military Government, Germany)
CC . . . . Civil Commotion
CDAP . . . . . . Civil Damage Assessment Program (Army)
CD . . . . Civil Defense
CDAC . . . . . . Civil Defense Advisory Council
CDA . . . . . . Civil Defense Agency
CIDERE . . . . . Civil Defense Report
CDRA . . . . . . Civil Defense Research Associates
CEX . . . . . . Civil Effects Experiments (DASA and AEC)
CETG . . . . . . Civil Effects Test Group (DASA and AEC)
CETO . . . . . . Civil Effects Test Operations (DASA and AEC)
CE . . . . Civil Engineer (Navy)
CEC . . . . . . Civil Engineer Corps (Army)
CEMS . . . . . . Civil Engineer Management System
CEPM . . . . . . Civil Engineer Preventive Maintenance (Air Force)
CECL . . . . . . Civil Engineering Computer Laboratory (MIT)
CEREL . . . . . Civil Engineering and Evaluation Laboratory (Navy)
CEL . . . . . . Civil Engineering Laboratory (Navy)
CEMIRT . . . . . Civil Engineering Maintenance, Inspection, Repair, and Training Team
(Air Force)
CEPS . . . . . . Civil Engineering Problems
CER . . . . . . Civil Engineering Report
CERP . . . . . . Civil Engineering Report of Performance
CG . . . . Civil Guard (Air Force)
CIANDE . . . . . Civil Information and Education Section of Allied Headquarters (World
War II)
CL . . . . Civil Law
CLD . . . . . . Civil Liaison Division (Army)
CLO . . . . . . Civil Liaison Officer (Army)
CLB . . . . . . Civil Liberties Bureau (Forerunner of the American Civil Liberties Union)
CLEF . . . . . . Civil Liberties Educational Foundation
CMA . . . . . . Civil-Military Affairs
C & ME . . . . . Civil and Mining Engineer
CNAS . . . . . . Civil Navigation Aids System
CORDS . . . . . Civil Operations and Rural Development Support (South Vietnam
pacification program)
CPTP . . . . . . Civil Pilot Training Program
CP . . . . Civil Power
CP . . . . Civil Procedure (Legal)
CPQ . . . . . . Civil Procedures, Quebec
CRO . . . . . . Civil Readjustment Officer
CRAF . . . . . . Civil Reserve Air Fleet (Department of Commerce)
CR . . . . Civil Rights
CRA . . . . . . Civil Rights Act
CRC . . . . . . Civil Rights Commission
CRD . . . . . . Civil Rights Division (Department of Justice)
CRDP . . . . . . Civil Rights Documentation Project
CSE . . . . . . Civil and Sanitary Engineering
CS . . . . Civil Service
CSAC . . . . . . Civil Service Association of Canada
CSC . . . . . . Civil Service Club (British)
CSC . . . . . . Civil Service Commission
CSCS . . . . . . Civil Service Cooperative Society (British)
CSEA . . . . . . Civil Service Employees Association
CSF . . . . . . Civil Service Forum

CSR . . . . Civil Service Retirement
CSRDF . . . . . . Civil Service Retirement and Disability Fund
CSRV . . . . Civil Service Rifle Volunteers (British)
CSR . . . . Civil Service Rule
CSSA . . . . Civil Service Supply Association (British)
CSWP . . . . . . Civil Service Working Party (US Military Government, Germany)
CWCA . . . . . . Civil War Centennial Association
CWCC . . . . . . Civil War Centennial Commission
CWPS . . . . . . Civil War Philatelic Society
CWPC . . . . . Civil War Press Corps
CWRTNY. . . . Civil War Round Table of New York
CWA . . . . Civil Works Administration (1933-1934)
CWP. . . . . . . Civil Works Program
CAT . . . . Civilian Actress Technician (Term for professional actresses who worked under Army Special Services Division in soldier shows) (World War II)
CBQ . . . . Civilian Bachelor Quarters (Air Force)
CIVCLO . . . . . Civilian Clothing
CCMA . . . . . . Civilian Clothing Maintenance Allowance (Army)
CCC. . . . . Civilian Conservation Corps (Created, 1937; liquidated, 1943)
CDVO. . . . . . . Civilian Defense Volunteer Office
CEHS . . . . Civilian Employee Health Service
CHAMPUS . . . . Civilian Health and Medical Program of the Uniformed Services (Army)
CIMS . . . . Civilian Information Management System (Navy)
CIP. . . . . Civilian Institution Program
CIDG . . . . . . Civilian Irregular Defense Groups (Military)
CLGC. . . . . . Civilian Labor Group Center (Army)
CLGSO. . . . . Civilian Labor Group Special Orders (Army)
CMLC. . . . . . Civilian/Military Liaison Committee
COS. . . . . . . Civilian Occupational Specialty
CPRC . . . . . . Civilian Payroll Circular
CPC . . . . Civilian Personnel Circular (Army)
CPD . . . . Civilian Personnel Division
PC . . . . Civilian Personnel Division (Coast Guard)
CIVPERSINS. . . Civilian Personnel Information System (Army)
CPL . . . . Civilian Personnel Letter
CPL&D . . . . . Civilian Personnel Letters and Dispatches
CPOS . . . . . . Civilian Personnel Occupational Standards (Military)
CPO. . . . . . . Civilian Personnel Office(r)
CPP . . . . Civilian Personnel Pamphlet (Military)
CPPL . . . . . . Civilian Personnel and Payroll Letter (Military)
CPPM . . . . . . Civilian Personnel Procedures Manual (Military)
CPR . . . . Civilian Personnel Regulation (Military)
CPT . . . . Civilian Pilot Training (Became War Training Service) (World War II)
CPA . . . . Civilian Production Administration (Became part of Office of Temporary Controls, 1946)
CPA . . . . . . Civilian Property Agent
CPS . . . . . . Civilian Public Service
CRO. . . . . . . Civilian Repair Organization (Aircraft)
CRIFO . . . . . Civilian Research, Interplanetary Flying Objects
CSC . . . . Civilian Screening Center
CSU . . . . Civilian Service Unit
CSSB . . . . . . Civilian Supervisory Selection Battery
CWD . . . . . . Civilian War Dead
CWF. . . . . . . Civilian Welfare Fund
CIFCO . . . . . Civilians in Foreign Communications Operations (Military)
CI . . . . Civitan International
CA . . . . Claim Agent (Insurance)
CSR . . . . Clamped Speed Regulator
CLCO. . . . . . Claremont & Concord Railway Company (AAR code)
CMC . . . . . . Claremont Men's College (California)
CJC . . . . Clarendon Junior College (Texas)
CL . . . . Clarendon Laboratory (Oxford University)
CLP . . . . Clarendon & Pittsford R. R. (AAR code)
CF . . . . Clarissima Femina (Most Illustrious Woman)
CP . . . . Clarissima Puella (Most Illustrious Maiden)
CLV . . . . Clarissimus Vir (Most Illustrious Man)
CKL . . . . Clark Equipment Company (NYSE symbol)
CMC . . . . . . Clark Memorial College (Mississippi)
CBO. . . . . . . Clarksville Branch Office (AEC)
C . . . . Class (Used with number for Navy rating as: 1c; i.e., first class)
CDF . . . . Class Determination and Finding
CIP. . . . . . . Class Improvement Plan (Navy)
CORAL . . . . . Class-Oriented Ring-Associated Language (Data processing)
CR . . . . Class Rate
CCCA . . . . . . Classic Car Club of America
CJA . . . . Classic Jaguar Association
CTCI . . . . . . Classic Thunderbird Club International
C & A . . . . . . Classification and Audit
CDU. . . . . . . Classification Decimale Universelle (Universal Decimal Classification)
CLASSICS . . . . Classification or Identification of Covert Satellites
C & I. . . . . . . Classification and Index (Air Force)

CI . . . . Classification Inventory (Military)
CR . . . . Classification Research
CRG. . . . . . . Classification Research Group (British)
CRSG . . . . . . Classification Research Study Group
C & T . . . . . . Classification and Testing (Air Force)
CAAAL . . . . . Classified Abstract Archive of the Alcohol Literature
CCC. . . . . . . Classified Control Clerk (Army)
CCO. . . . . . . Classified Control Officer
CDI . . . . Classified Defense Information (Military)
CMA . . . . Classified Mail Address
CSTAR . . . . . Classified Scientific and Technical Aerospace Reports (NASA)
CAP . . . . Classroom Assembly Program
CPPA . . . . . . Classroom Periodical Publishers Association
CRP . . . . Clauson Rolling Platform
CLH . . . . Claussner Hosiery Company (NYSE symbol)
CP . . . . Claw Plate (Technical drawings)
CFLI . . . . Clay Flue Lining Institute
CMS. . . . . . . Clay Minerals Society
CPOC. . . . . . Clay Pigmented Organic Coating
CP . . . . Clay Pipe (Technical drawings)
CPI . . . . Clay Pipe Institute
CPA . . . . Clay Products Association
CSPA . . . . . . Clay Sewer Pipe Association
CAA . . . . Clean Air Act
CIP. . . . . . . Clean in Place
CRK . . . . Clean Room Kit
C and S. . . . . . Clean and Sober (Slang)
CMS. . . . . . . Cleaning Management Station
CLA . . . . Clear and Add
CLAM. . . . . . Clear Air Mass
CAT . . . . Clear Air Turbulence (Aviation)
CCBS . . . . . . Clear Channel Broadcasting Service
CLGSFU . . . . Clear Glazed Structural Facing Units (Technical drawings)
CLGSUB . . . . Clear Glazed Structural Unit Base (Technical drawings)
CS . . . . Clear and Subtract
CLWG . . . . . . Clear Wire Glass (Technical drawings)
CWC . . . . Clear Write Condition
C . . . . Clearance
CFAP . . . . . . Cleared for Approach (Aviation)
CAF . . . . Cleared As Filed
CLRAP. . . . . . Cleared As Planned
CCUS . . . . . . Cleared Customs (Aviation)
F . . . . Cleared to the Fix (Aviation)
L . . . . Cleared to Land (Aviation)
O . . . . Cleared to the Outer Marker (Aviation)
T . . . . Cleared Through (for landing and takeoff) (Aviation)
CH. . . . . Clearing House (Banking)
CHART . . . . . Clearing House for Augmenting Resources for Training (DOD)
CAST . . . . . . Clearinghouse Announcements in Science and Technology (CFSTI)
CFSTI . . . . . . Clearinghouse for Federal Scientific and Technical Information (Later, NTIS) (National Bureau of Standards)
CLIS. . . . . . . Clearinghouse for Library and Information Sciences
CRCL . . . . . . Clearinghouse for Research in Child Life (Federal Security Administration)
CSTI . . . . Clearinghouse for Scientific and Technical Information (National Bureau of Standards)
CCSPP. . . . . . Clergy Counseling Service for Problem Pregnancies
CEEF. . . . . . . Clergy Economic Education Foundation
CALCAV . . . . Clergy and Laymen Concerned about Vietnam
CMAS. . . . . . Clergy Mutual Assurance Society (British)
COC . . . . Clergy Orphan Corporation (British)
CAF . . . . Clerical, Administrative & Fiscal (Used with number, as, CAF-6, to indicate grade of position) (Civil Service)
CAWU. . . . . . Clerical and Administrative Workers Union (British)
CA . . . . Clerical Aptitude (Test)
CAT . . . . Clerical Aptitude Test
CLT . . . . Clerical Technician, Medical (Navy)
CRCS . . . . . . Clerici Regulares Congregationis Somaschæ (Somaschi Fathers)
CRMD. . . . . . Clerici Regulares Matris Dei (Clerks Regular of the Mother of God)
CRMI . . . . . . Clerici Regulares Ministrantes Infirmis (Clerks Regular Attendant on the Sick, Camillini, Camilliani)
CRM. . . . . . . Clerici Regulares Minores (Clerks Regular Minor, Mariani)
CRSP . . . . . . Clerici Regulares Pauperum Matris Dei Scholarum Piarum (Clerks Regular of the Poor Men of the Mother of God for Pious Schools; Piarists)
CRSP . . . . . . Clerici Regulares Sancti Pauli (Barnabites)
CRT . . . . Clerici Regulares Theatini (Theatines)
CSV . . . . Clerici Sancti Viatoris (Clerics of St. Viateur) (Roman Catholic men's religious order)
CRS . . . . Clericorum Regularium Somaschensium (Somascan Fathers) (Roman Catholic religious order)
CC . . . . Clerk of the (Privy) Council (British)
CC . . . . Clerk of the Crown (British)

CP .... Clerk of the Peace
CPC .... Clerk of the Privy Council (British)
CS .... Clerk to the Signet (British)
CLE .... Cleveland (Ohio) (Airport symbol)
CBAA ...... Cleveland Bay Association of America
CCCL .... Cleveland, Cincinnati, Chicago & St. Louis Railway (AAR code)
CLF .... Cleveland-Cliffs Iron Company (NYSE symbol)
CVX .... Cleveland Electric Illum. Company (NYSE symbol)
PTT .... Cleveland & Pittsburgh R. R. Company (NYSE symbol)
CTC .... Cleveland Trust Company
CGH .... Clevite Corporation (NYSE symbol)
CABAL ...... Clifford, Arlington, Buckingham, Ashley, Lauderdale (Ministers of Charles II of England)
CLIF .... Cliffside R. R. (AAR code)
CTC .... Climate Test Chamber
CL .... Climatic Laboratory (Military)
CDS .... Climatological Data Sheet (Air Force)
CXM .... Climax Molybdenum Company (NYSE symbol)
COC .... Climb on Course (Aviation)
CER .... Climb Enroute (Aviation)
CSATC ...... Climb so as to Cross (Aviation)
CSATR ...... Climb so as to Reach (Aviation)
CTAX .... Climb to and Cross (Aviation)
CCRZ .... Climb to and Cruise (Aviation)
CTAM ...... Climb to and Maintain (Aviation)
CWTR ...... Climb Well to Right (Aviation)
CWRC ...... Climb Well to Right of Course (Aviation)
CRM .... Clinch River Mile (AEC)
CRR .... Clinchfield R. R. (AAR code)
CPAB .... Cling Peach Advisory Board
CARE .... Clinical and Administrative Research (System)
CLT .... Clinical Laboratory Technician
LBT .... Clinical Laboratory Technology (Navy)
CLUE .... Clinical Literature Untoward Effects (Service published by International Information Institute)
COS .... Clinical Orthopaedic Society
CP .... Clinical Pathology
CPC .... Clinical Pathology Conference
CR .... Clinical Record (Medicine)
CRCS .... Clinical Record Cover Sheet (Army medical)
CSGUS ..... Clinical Society of Genito-Urinary Surgeons
CU .... Clinical Unit
CLN .... Clipper Negative
CLP .... Clipper Positive
CSTA ...... Cloak and Suit Trucking Association
CAIA ...... Clock Assemblers and Importers Association
CP .... Clock Phase
CP .... Clock Pulse
CPG .... Clock Pulse Generator
CPC .... Clock Pulsed Control
CSC .... Clock Start Command
CT .... Clock Time
CWMAA .... Clock and Watch Manufacturers Association of America
C .... Clockwise
CW .... Clockwise
CPY .... Clopay Corporation (NYSE symbol)
CXC .... Clorox Chemical Company (NYSE symbol)
CAS .... Close Air Support (Military)
CBS .... Close Boundary Sentry (Military)
COB .... Close of Business (With date)
CCB .... Close Control Bombing (Air Force)
CI .... Close-In
CARRS ...... Close-in Automatic Route Restoral System (NORAD)
CIS .... Close-in Support (Military)
CLS .... Close Lunar Satellite
CO .... Close-Open
CPH .... Close-Packed Hexagonal (Metallography)
CPS .... Close Packed Structure
CRZ .... Close Reconnaissance Zone (Army)
CS .... Close Support (Army)
CSARS ...... Close Support Artillery Rocket System
CSM .... Close-Support Mission (Air Force)
CTM .... Close Talking Microphone
CLOTO ..... Close This Office
CT .... Close Tolerance
CU .... Close Up (A photograph or motion picture sequence taken from a short distance)
CBD .... Closed Bladder Drainage (Medicine)
CCCMMM .... Closed Chest Cardiac Massage and Mouth-to-Mouth (Resuscitation)
CCTV ...... Closed Circuit Television
CLAC .... Closed-Loop Approach Control

CLBW ...... Closed Loop Bandwidth
CLG .... Closed Loop Gain
CLT .... Closed Loop Telemetry
CP .... Closed Position (Dancing)
CS .... Closed Shell
CPA .... Closest Position of Approach (Navigation)
CC .... Closing Coil
CLODA ..... Closing Date
CR .... Clot Retraction (Medicine)
CMA .... Clothespin Manufacturers of America
C & E ..... Clothing and Equipage
CH .... Clothing and Housing Research Division (of ARS, Department of Agriculture)
CMA .... Clothing Maintenance Allowance
CMAB ...... Clothing Maintenance (or Monetary) Allowance, Basic (Army)
CMAS ...... Clothing Maintenance Allowance, Standard (Air Force)
CMA .... Clothing Manufacturers Association of the USA
CLMA ...... Clothing Monetary Allowance
CMAIWAC ... Clothing Monetary Allowance Initial (Women's Army Corps)
CMAIISS .... Clothing Monetary Allowance, Initial Issue (Army)
CMAL ...... Clothing Monetary Allowance List (Military)
CMAS ...... Clothing Monetary Allowance, Standard (Army)
C & OM..... Clothing and Organic Materials (Army)
CSSA ...... Clothing and Small Stores Account
CSSF ...... Clothing and Small Stores Fund
C & TM .... Clothing and Textile Materiel (Army)
CRM .... Cloud-Croft Radiation Measurement
C .... Cloudy
CCA .... Clown Club of America
CMAA ...... Club Managers Association of America
CPW .... Club of Printing Women of New York
CLU .... Cluett, Peabody & Company, Inc. (NYSE symbol)
CBU .... Cluster Bomb Unit (Military)
CLAW...... Clustered Atomic Warhead
CRB .... Clutch Release Bearing
CAGC ...... Clutter Automatic Gain Control
CG .... Clutter Gate
CLAMTI .... Clutter-Locked Airborne Moving Target Indicator (Air Force)
CMC .... Clutter Mapper Card
CRR .... Clutter Rejection RADAR
CBA .... Clydesdale Breeders Association of the United States
CS .... Clymer System
CLI .... Coach Lace Institute
CJC .... Coahoma Junior College (Mississippi)
CZ .... Coahuila & Zacatecas AG Railway (AAR code)
CEC .... Coal Experts Committee (Allied German Occupation Forces)
CEA .... Coal Exporters Association of the United States
C & M ..... Coal & Mining
CMIA ...... Coal Mining Institute of America
CMQ .... Coal Mining and Quarrying
COPROD..... Coal Production Committee
CTPEC ..... Coal Tar Pitch Emulsion Council
CS .... Coaling Station (As part of a symbol)
CAPU ...... Coast African People's Union (Kenya)
CA .... Coast Artillery
CAAA ...... Coast Artillery (Antiaircraft)
CA(AA) ..... Coast Artillery (Antiaircraft)
CAC .... Coast Artillery Corps (Army)
CARC ...... Coast Artillery Reserve Corps
CATB ...... Coast Artillery Training Battalion
CD .... Coast Defense(s)
CGMO ...... Coast and Geodetic Magnetic Observatory
CGS .... Coast and Geodetic Survey (Later, National Ocean Survey)
C & GS .... Coast and Geodetic Survey (Later, National Ocean Survey)
CGTS ...... Coast and Geodetic Tide Station
C .... Coast Guard (Military flight identification prefix)
CG .... Coast Guard
COGARD .... Coast Guard
CGA .... Coast Guard Academy
CGACTEUR ... Coast Guard Activities Europe
CGAB ...... Coast Guard Air Base
CGAIRDET.... Coast Guard Air Detachment
CGAS .... Coast Guard Air Station
CGA .... Coast Guard Auxiliary
CGBASE ..... Coast Guard Base
CGC .... Coast Guard Cutter
CGD .... Coast Guard Depot
CGD .... Coast Guard District
CGDIST .... Coast Guard District
CGDO ...... Coast Guard District Office
CGGCM ..... Coast Guard Good Conduct Medal

CGL . . . . Coast Guard League
CGLBSTA . . . . Coast Guard Lifeboat Station
CGLASTA . . . . Coast Guard Light Attendant Station
CGLTSTA . . . . Coast Guard Light Station
CGLS . . . . . . Coast Guard LORAN Station
CGLORSTA . . Coast Guard LORAN Transmitting Station
CGOU . . . . . . Coast Guard Oceanographic Unit
CGOB . . . . . . Coast Guard Operating Base
NCG . . . . Coast Guard Publication (Later, NAVCG)
NAVCG . . . . . Coast Guard Publications
CGRADSTA . . . Coast Guard Radio Station
CGCRUITSTA . . Coast Guard Recruiting Station
CGR . . . . Coast Guard Reserve
CGSTA . . . . . . Coast Guard Station
CGSUPCEN . . . Coast Guard Supply Center
CGTRASTA . . . Coast Guard Training Station
CGTS . . . . . . Coast Guard Training Station
CGYD . . . . . . Coast Guard Yard
RA . . . . Coast RADAR Station (Maps and charts)
CTB . . . . Coast Torpedo Boat (Navy symbol)
CBS . . . . Coastal Base Section (Name changed to Continental Advance Section)
            (World War II)
CC . . . . Coastal Command (British Royal Air Force)
CDU . . . . Coastal Defense RADAR for Detecting U-boats
CERC . . . . . . Coastal Engineering Research Center (Army)
CF . . . . Coastal Frontier (Military)
COFRON . . . . Coastal Frontier (Coast Guard)
CMB . . . . Coastal Motor-Boat
CSQ . . . . Coastal Sentry Quebec
CGP . . . . Coastal States Gas Producing Company (NYSE symbol)
CSC . . . . Coastal Surveillance Center
AGSC . . . . . . Coastal Surveying Ship (Navy symbol)
CGLIHA . . . . . Coastwise-Great Lakes and Inland Hull Association
C/A . . . . Coat of Arms
CAMI . . . . . . Coated Abrasives Manufacturers Institute
CB . . . . Coated on the Back Side (Carbonless paper)
CFB . . . . Coated Front and Back (Carbonless Paper)
CF . . . . Coated on the Front Side (Carbonless paper)
CPPA . . . . . . Coated and Processed Paper Association
CT . . . . Coated Tablet (Pharmacy)
CCL . . . . Coating and Chemical Laboratory
CLA . . . . Coaxial Line Attenuator
CPD . . . . Coaxial Power Divider
CSR . . . . Coaxial Single-Pole Relay
CSL . . . . Coaxial Slotted Line
CSM . . . . Coaxial Switching Matrix
CTV . . . . Coaxial Thermal Voltmeter
CTST . . . . . . Coaxial Triple-Stud Tuner
C . . . . Cobalt
Co . . . . Cobalt (Chemical element)
C (Bomb) . . . . Cobalt Bomb
KNY . . . . Coca-Cola Bottling Company of New York, Inc. (NYSE symbol)
KO . . . . Coca-Cola Company (NYSE symbol)
C . . . . Cocaine (Slang)
CWA . . . . . . Cockcroft-Walton Accelerator
CWE . . . . Cockcroft-Walton Experiment
CPT . . . . Cockpit Procedure Trainer (Air Force)
CVR . . . . Cockpit Voice Recorder
CKP . . . . Cockshutt Farm Equipment (NYSE symbol)
CS . . . . Coco Solo, Canal Zone
CBA . . . . Cocoa Beach Apollo
CMAA . . . . . . Cocoa Merchants' Association of America
CARLA . . . . . Code Actuated Random Load Apparatus
CB . . . . Code Book
COC . . . . Code of Conduct (Military)
CC . . . . Code Control
CDC . . . . Code Directing Character (Data processing)
CFR . . . . Code of Federal Regulations
CMT . . . . Code Matching Technique
CN . . . . Code Napoleon
CNA . . . . Code Not Allocated
CP . . . . Code of Practice
CPO . . . . Code Practice Oscillator
CP . . . . Code of Procedure (Legal)
CP . . . . Code Proficiency (Amateur radio)
CT . . . . Code Telegram
CTDS . . . . . . Code Translation Data System (Air Force)
CAPRI . . . . . . Coded Address Private Radio Intercommunications
CAGC . . . . . . Coded Automatic Gain Control
COBI . . . . . . Coded Biphase
CODORAC . . . Coded Doppler RADAR Command

CODAN . . . . . Coded Weather Analysis (Navy)
CSP . . . . Coder Sequential Pulse
C . . . . Codex
CIC . . . . Codex Iuris Canonici (Code of Canon Law)
CBO . . . . Coding Board Officer
CRWO . . . . . . Coding Room Watch Officer (Navy)
CSCSL . . . . . . Coe's Scrapbook Clipping Service of Laingsburg
C . . . . Coefficient
Q . . . . Coefficient of Association (Statistics)
CC . . . . Coefficient of Correlation (Mathematics)
CI . . . . Coefficient of Intelligence
COP . . . . Coefficient of Performance
CTE . . . . Coefficient of Thermal Expansion
CU . . . . Coefficient of Utilization
COV . . . . Coefficient of Variation
CV . . . . Coefficient of Variation (Mathematics)
CSI . . . . Coelliptic Sequence Initiation (Aerospace)
COA . . . . Coenzyme A
CBC . . . . Coffee Brewing Center
CBI . . . . Coffee Brewing Institute
CGAES . . . . . Coffee Growers' Association of El Salvador
CSM . . . . Coffin Strategic Missile
C . . . . Cognate
CHILD . . . . . . Cognitive Hybrid Intelligent Learning Device
CS . . . . Cognizance Symbol
CFA . . . . Cognizant Field Activity
CTO . . . . Cognizant Transportation Office(r) (Air Force)
CAVORT . . . . Coherent Acceleration & Velocity Observations in Real Time
CODIPHASE . . . Coherent Digital Phased Array System (ARPA)
CODAR . . . . . . Coherent Display Analyzing and Recording
COMET . . . . . Coherent Electromagnetic Energy Transmission
CLI . . . . Coherent LASER Illumination
COLIDAR . . . . Coherent Light Detecting and Ranging (Hughes Aircraft) (RADAR)
COLD . . . . . . Coherent Light Detector
CMF . . . . Coherent Memory Filter
CMM . . . . . . Coherent Microwave Memory
CORE . . . . . . Coherent-On-Receive
CORDS . . . . . Coherent-On Receive Doppler System
COA . . . . Coherent Optical Array
COAT . . . . . . Coherent Optical Array Techniques
COD . . . . Coherent Optical Device
COL . . . . Coherent Optical LASER
COPS . . . . . . Coherent Optical Processing System
COP . . . . Coherent Optical Processor
COR . . . . Coherent Optical Receiver
COHO . . . . . . Coherent Oscillator (RADAR)
CORA . . . . . . Coherent RADAR Array
CSP . . . . Coherent Signal Processor
CSC . . . . Coil Stock Cradle
CWE . . . . Coil Winding Equipment
CWM . . . . . . Coil Winding Machine
CD . . . . Coin Dimple
CLI . . . . Coin Level Indicator (Telephone communications)
COCWA . . . . . Coin-Op Car Wash Association
COSSLOA . . . . Coin Operated Self-Service Laundry Owners' Association
CG . . . . Coincidence Gate
CLIPS . . . . . . Coincident Light Information Photographic Strips
Co-I . . . . Co-Investigator
CB . . . . Col Basso (With the bass)
CO-L . . . . Colatitude (Navigation)
CJCW . . . . . . Colby Junior College for Women (New Hampshire)
C . . . . Cold
CA . . . . Cold Air
CCD . . . . Cold Cathode Discharge
CCIS . . . . Cold-Cathode Ion Source
CDS . . . . Cold-Drawn Steel
CD . . . . Cold-Drawn (Metal)
CFP . . . . Cold Front(al) Passage (Meteorology)
CH and D . . . . Cold, Hungry and Dry (Slang)
CIF . . . . Cold-Insoluble Fibrinogen
CMW . . . . . . Cold Molecular Weld
CP . . . . Cold-Punched (Metal)
CREL . . . . . . Cold Regions Engineering Laboratory
CRRC . . . . . . Cold Regions Research Company
CRREL . . . . . Cold Regions Research and Engineering Laboratory (Army)
CRICKET . . . . Cold Rocket Instrument Carrying Kit
CR . . . . Cold-Rolled (Metal)
CRHH . . . . . . Cold Rolled Half Hard
CRS . . . . Cold Rolled Steel
CSE . . . . Cold Start Entry (Data processing)
CTC . . . . Cold Type Composition (Section of Printing Industries of America)

CWC . . . . Cold War Council
CW . . . . Cold Water (Technical drawings)
CWS . . . . Cold-Water Soluble
L . . . . Cold-weather aircraft with special equipment such as skis or extra insulation (Designation for all US military aircraft)
CWINJ . . . . . . Cold Weather Injury
CWMTU . . . . Cold Weather Materiel Test Unit
CWOP . . . . . . Cold Weather Operations (Military)
CG . . . . Coldstream Guards (British)
CHJ . . . . Colel Hibath Jerusalem
CLM . . . . Coleman Company, Inc. (NYSE symbol)
CSL . . . . Coles Signal Laboratory (Army)
CL . . . . Colgate-Palmolive Company (NYSE symbol)
CRDS . . . . . . Colgate Rochester Divinity School (New York)
CD . . . . Colla Destra (With the Right Hand)
CP . . . . Colla Parte (With the solo part) (Music)
CS . . . . Colla Sinistra (With the Left Hand)
CV . . . . Colla Voce (With the Voice) (Music)
CAMEL . . . . . Collapsible Airborne Military Equipment Lifter
CRAM . . . . . . Collapsible Rollup Antenna Mast
CTMC . . . . . . Collapsible Tube Manufacturers Council
CA . . . . Coll'arco (With the bow) (Music)
CTB . . . . Collateral Trust Bond
CLAD . . . . . . Collect Adapter
COD . . . . Collect on Delivery
C & D . . . . . . Collection and Delivery (Business and trade)
CV . . . . Collection Voucher
CBU . . . . Collective Bargaining Unit
CCS . . . . Collective Call Sign (Radio)
CN . . . . Collective Negotiations
CPL . . . . Collective Pitch Lever
CPE . . . . Collective Protection Equipment
CRU . . . . Collective Reserve Unit (International finance)
CAA . . . . Collectors of American Art
CC . . . . Collectors Club
CONE . . . . . Collectors of Numismatic Errors
COROS . . . . . Collectors of Religion on Stamps
CRSS . . . . . . Collectors of Religion on Stamps Society
C . . . . College
CAT . . . . College Ability Test
CAAC . . . . . . College Admissions Assistance Center
CAC . . . . College Admissions Center
COA . . . . College of Aeronautics (British)
CAP . . . . College of American Pathologists
CAA . . . . College Art Association of America
CAAA . . . . . . College Art Association of America
CABMA . . . . . . College Athletic Business Managers Association
CBDNA . . . . . . College Band Directors National Association
CCI . . . . College Characteristics Index (A questionnaire)
CD . . . . College Discovery (Educational project for disadvantaged youngsters)
CE . . . . College English (A periodical)
CEA . . . . College English Association
CES . . . . College d'Enseignement Secondaire (France)
CEEB . . . . . . College Entrance Examination Board
CFEA . . . . . . College Fraternity Editors Association
CFSOA . . . . . . College Fraternity Scholarship Officers Association
CFSA . . . . . . College Fraternity Secretaries Association
CIP . . . . College International de Podologie
CIRP . . . . . . College Internationale de Recherches pour la Production
CLA . . . . College Language Association
CLEP . . . . . . College-Level Examination Program
CME . . . . College of Medical Evangelists (Los Angeles, California)
CMR . . . . College Militaire Royal (Canada)
CMS . . . . College Music Society
CNR . . . . College of New Rochelle (New York)
COO . . . . College of Optometry of Ontario
COPS . . . . . . College of Osteopathic Physicians and Surgeons
COLE . . . . . . College of Our Lady of the Elms (Massachusetts)
CPS . . . . College Placement Council
CPEA . . . . . . College Physical Education Association
CPS . . . . College of Physicians & Surgeons
CPC . . . . College Placement Council
CPG . . . . College Publishers Group
CRNC . . . . . . College Republican National Committee
CRL . . . . College & Research Libraries (Official journal of ACRL)
CREF . . . . . . College Retirement Equities Fund
CSH . . . . College of the Sacred Heart (Puerto Rico)
CSB . . . . College of Saint Benedict (Minnesota)
CSC . . . . College of Saint Catherine (Minnesota)
CSE . . . . College of Saint Elizabeth (New Jersey)
CSF . . . . College of Saint Francis (Illinois)

CSM . . . . College of Saint Mary (Nebraska)
CSMS . . . . . . College of Saint Mary of the Springs (Ohio)
CSR . . . . College of Saint Rose (New York)
CSS . . . . College of Saint Scholastica (Minnesota)
CST . . . . College of Saint Teresa (Minnesota)
CST . . . . College of Saint Thomas (Minnesota)
CSM . . . . College of San Mateo (California)
COSIP . . . . . . College Science Improvement Program (National Science Foundation)
COSIDA . . . . . College Sports Information Directors of America
CSA . . . . College Stores Association
CSPI . . . . College Student Personnel Institute
CSCAA . . . . . . College Swimming Coaches Association of America
CTD . . . . College Training Detachment
CUES . . . . . . College and University Environment Scales
CUPA . . . . . . College and University Personnel Association
CAUSE . . . . . College and University System Exchange
CWVS . . . . . . College Women's Volunteer Service (World War II)
CWSP . . . . . . College Work-Study Program
CBOB . . . . . . Collegiate Basketball Officials Bureau (Later, Eastern College Basketball Association)
CCUN . . . . . . Collegiate Council for the United Nations
CIA . . . . Collegium Internationale Allergologicum
CCA . . . . Collie Club of America
AC . . . . Collier (Navy symbol)
CMU . . . . Colliery Mazdoor Union (India)
CML . . . . Collimated Monochromatic Light
CK . . . . Collins & Aikman Corporation (NYSE symbol)
CRI . . . . Collins Radio Company (NYSE symbol)
CAS . . . . Collision-Avoidance System (Aviation)
COPAG . . . . . Collision Prevention Advisory Group (US)
CME . . . . Colloid Microthruster Experiment
CST . . . . Colloidal System Test
CMEU . . . . . . Colombo Municipal Employees' Union (Ceylon)
CC . . . . Colon Classification (Library science)
CBF . . . . Colonial Bishoprics' Fund (British)
CCCS . . . . . . Colonial and Continental Church Society (British)
CLA . . . . Colonial Corporation of America (NYSE symbol)
CDC . . . . Colonial Development Corporation
CMD . . . . Colonial Medical Department (British)
COLO . . . . . . Colonial National Historic Park
CO . . . . Colonial Office (British)
C . . . . Color
CAUS . . . . . . Color Association of the United States
CC . . . . Color Code (as, for types of wire) (Technical drawings)
CC . . . . Color Compensation (Photography)
CC . . . . Color Correction (Color Printing)
E . . . . Color Excess (Astronomy)
C . . . . Color Index (Astronomy)
CI . . . . Color Index (Medicine)
CMG . . . . Color Marketing Group (An organization)
CMC . . . . Color Mixture Curve
CMF . . . . Color Mixture Function
CPC . . . . Color Pack Camera
CPA . . . . Color Phase Alternation
CPS . . . . Color Picture Signal
CS . . . . Color Specification
CSS . . . . Color Sync Signal
VC . . . . Color Vision
CWT . . . . Color Word Test
CO . . . . Colorado
CCEI . . . . Colorado Committee for Environmental Information
CF . . . . Colorado Fuel & Iron Corporation (NYSE symbol)
CMA . . . . Colorado Mining Association
COLM . . . . . . Colorado National Monument
CRMWD . . . . . Colorado River Municipal Water District
CRBP . . . . . . Colorado River Basin Project
CRSP . . . . . . Colorado River Storage Project (Department of the Interior)
CSM . . . . Colorado School of Mines
CS . . . . Colorado & Southern Railway Company (AAR code)
C & S . . . . . . Colorado and Southern Railway Company
CSC . . . . Colorado State College
CSU . . . . Colorado State University
CVI . . . . Colorado Video, Incorporated
CWC . . . . Colorado Woman's College
CW . . . . Colorado & Wyoming Railway Company (AAR code)
COMIC . . . . . Colorant Mixture Computer (Du Pont trademark)
CMPS . . . . . . Colosseum of Motion Picture Salesmen
C . . . . Colt
CBS . . . . Columbia Broadcasting System, Inc. (NYSE symbol)
CLC . . . . Columbia & Cowlitz Railway Company (AAR code)
CG . . . . Columbia Gas System, Inc. (NYSE symbol)
COML . . . . . . Columbia & Millstadt R. R. (AAR code)

CNL........ Columbia, Newberry & Laurens R. R. (AAR code)
CPS........ Columbia Pictures Corporation (NYSE symbol)
CRDC....... Columbia Research and Development Corporation
CRSTPA..... Columbia River Salmon and Tuna Packers Association
CSPAA...... Columbia Scholastic Press Advisers Association
CSPA....... Columbia Scholastic Press Association
CSBA....... Columbia Sheep Breeders Association of America
CU........ Columbia University (New York)
CUDWR..... Columbia University Division of War Research
CUHL...... Columbia University Hudson Laboratory
CVA....... Columbia Valley Authority
COLYAHAR... Columbia, Yale, Harvard (Used to refer to a project involving the medical libraries of these universities)
Cb........ Columbium (A chemical element; modern name is niobium)
COAD...... Columbus Army Depot
C & G...... Columbus and Greenville Railway Company
CLG....... Columbus & Greenville Railway Company (AAR code)
COC....... Columbus & Southern Ohio Electric Company (NYSE symbol)
CM........ Columellar Muscle
CDBN...... Column-Digit Binary Network
CPC....... Column Position Counter
CRC....... Column Research Council of Engineering Foundation
CVD....... Column Valve Diaphragm
CPL....... Columns Per Line
C........ Combat (In unit designations and symbols only)
CADD...... Combat Air Delivery Division (Air Force)
CAP....... Combat Air Patrol
CPM....... Combat Air Patrol Mission (Air Force)
CAC....... Combat Air Crew
CASU (F).... Combat Aircraft Service Unit (Navy)
CA........ Combat Aircrew(man)
CATU...... Combat Aircrew Training Unit (Navy)
CALSU..... Combat Airlift Support Unit (Air Force)
CAAC...... Combat Alert Aircrew (Air Force)
CAG....... Combat Arms Group (Army)
CARS...... Combat Arms Regimental System (Army)
CCM....... Combat Cargo Mission (Air Force)
CC........ Combat Center (Military)
CCD....... Combat Center Director
CCR....... Combat Center Remoted (Military)
CC........ Combat Command (Initialism may be followed by a number as, CC2, to indicate a specific, numbered command) (Army)
CCA....... Combat Command A
CCB....... Combat Command B
CCC....... Combat Command C
CCD....... Combat Command D
CCL....... Combat Command L
CCR....... Combat Command R
CCV....... Combat Command V
CC........ Combat Control (Army)
COMCON.... Combat Control (Army)
CCE....... Combat Control Elements (Army)
COMCONSUP .. Combat, Control, Support (Army)
CCT....... Combat Control Team
CC........ Combat Correspondent
CCR....... Combat Crew
CCRC...... Combat Crew Replacement Center (World War II)
CCT....... Combat Crew Training
CCTS...... Combat Crew Training Squadron (TAC)
CD........ Combat Development
CDC....... Combat Development Command (Army)
CDCIA..... Combat Development Command Infantry Agency (Army)
CDC-INTA... Combat Development Command - Intelligence Agency (Army)
CDCEC..... Combat Development Committee Experimentation Center (Army)
CDEC...... Combat Development Experimentation Center (Army)
CDOG...... Combat Development Objective Guide (CDC)
CDP....... Combat Development Project (Army)
CDTEC..... Combat Development Technical Evaluation Center
CDTC-V.... Combat Development and Test Center - Vietnam
CEE....... Combat Emplacement Excavator
CEV....... Combat Engineer Vehicle
CG........ Combat Group
CGOS...... Combat Gunnery Officers School (Army Air Forces)
CIB....... Combat Infantryman's Badge
CIC....... Combat Information Center (Navy)
CBTI...... Combat Intelligence
CIO....... Combat Intelligence Officer (Navy)
CIC....... Combat Intercept Control
CI........ Combat Interviews
CLARK..... Combat Launch and Recovery Kit
COMLOGNET .. Combat Logistics Network (DOD)

COLED-V.... Combat Loss and Expenditure Data - Vietnam
CMB........ Combat Maneuver Battalion(s) (Army)
COMANBAT... Combat Maneuver Battalion(s) (Army)
CMF....... Combat Mission Folder
COC....... Combat Operations Center (Air Force)
COR....... Combat Operations Report
CORG...... Combat Operations Research Group
COSC...... Combat Operations Specialist Course (Air Force)
COP....... Combat Outpost
COPL...... Combat Outpost Line
CPD....... Combat Potential Display (SAGE) (Air Force)
CRT....... Combat Reaction Time
CRAW...... Combat Readiness Air Wing
CRE....... Combat Readiness Evaluation (Army)
CRM....... Combat Readiness Medal
CRT....... Combat Readiness Training or Trainer
CR........ Combat Ready
CRC....... Combat Reporting Center
CR........ Combat Reserve (Military)
CO-STAR... Combat Service to the Army
CSG....... Combat Service Group (Army)
CSSA...... Combat Service Support Area (Military)
CSSS...... Combat Service Support System (ADSAF)
CS3....... Combat Service Support System
CSSG...... Combat Services Support Group (Army)
AFS....... Combat Store Ship (Navy symbol)
CSC....... Combat Support Company (Army)
CST....... Combat Support Training (Military)
COMSUP.... Combat Support Units (Army)
CSU....... Combat Support Units (Army)
CSA....... Combat Surveillance Agency (Signal Corps)
CSL....... Combat Surveillance Laboratory
CSR....... Combat Surveillance RADAR
CSTA...... Combat Surveillance and Target Acquisition
CSTATC.... Combat Surveillance and Target Acquisition Training Command
CT........ Combat Team
CTL....... Combat Training Launch
CTLI...... Combat Training Launch Instrumentation (Minuteman)
CTU....... Combat Training Unit
CUTC...... Combat Unit Training Center (Army)
CUPID..... Combat Using Price Incentives Doctrine
CV........ Combat Vehicle
CVEH...... Combat Vehicle (Army)
CVWS...... Combat Vehicle Weapons System (AWC)
CZ........ Combat Zone
CYSA...... Combed Yarn Spinners Association
CNDI...... Combination Die
CEM....... Combination Export Management (Small Business Administration)
CAT....... Combined Acceptance Trials
CADC...... Combined Administrative Committee
CALA...... Combined Administrative Liquidating Agency (Microfilmed SHAEF documents for each participating country after SHAEF was disbanded) (Post-World War II)
CAFT...... Combined Agencies Field Team (US Military Government, Germany)
CADRC..... Combined Air Documents Research Center
CATOR..... Combined Air Transport Operations Room (Allied office, WW-II)
CAAF...... Combined Allied Air Forces
CALF...... Combined Allied Land Forces
CANF...... Combined Allied Naval Forces
CANFSWPA... Combined Allied Naval Forces, Southwest Pacific Area
CANFSWPAOPPLAN .. Combined Allied Naval Forces Southwest Pacific Ocean Area Operating Plan
CAG....... Combined Army Group
CCF....... Combined Cadet Force (British equivalent of US ROTC)
CC/T...... Combined Center/Tower (Aviation)
CCS....... Combined Chiefs of Staff (DOD)
CCM....... Combined Cipher Machine
CCAC...... Combined Civil Affairs Committee
CCAC/L.... Combined Civil Affairs Committee, London Subcommittee
CCAC/S.... Combined Civil Affairs Committee, Supply Subcommittee
CCM....... Combined Coding Machine
CCATNA.... Combined Committee on Air Training in North America
CCB....... Combined Communications Board
CCBP...... Combined Communications Board Publications
CCC....... Combined Coordinating Committee
CDA....... Combined Development Agency (Anglo-American uranium procurement)
CODAG..... Combined Diesel and Gas (Turbine)
CDF....... Combined Distribution Frame (RADAR)
CEWA...... Combined Economic Warfare Agencies
CFMS...... Combined Field Maintenance Shop (Army)
CFS....... Combined File Search (Data processing)

CFB . . . . Combined Food Board (United States, United Kingdom, and Canada) (World War II)
CIC . . . . Combined Intelligence Committee
CIOS . . . . Combined Intelligence Objectives Subcommittee
CIOS . . . . Combined Intelligence Operations Section (Navy)
CIPC . . . . Combined Intelligence Priorities Committee (US and British) (London, World War II)
CLAC . . . . Combined Liberated Areas Committee
CMC . . . . Combined Meteorological Committee
COMPAS . . . . . Combined Metropolitan Phoenix Arts (Phoenix, Arizona)
CMTC . . . . Combined Military Transportation Committee
COMPAD . . . . Combined Office Material Procurement and Distribution
COIC . . . . Combined Operational Intelligence Center (Navy)
COSC . . . . Combined Operational Service Command
CO . . . . Combined Operations
COHQ . . . . . . Combined Operations Headquarters
COMLO . . . . . Combined Operations Material Liaison Officer
COPP . . . . Combined Operations Pilotage Party
COSU . . . . Combined Operations Scout Unit
COSMD . . . . . Combined Operations Signal Maintenance Depot
COSMO . . . . . Combined Operations Signal Maintenance Officer
COSO . . . . Combined Operations Signal Officer
COSD . . . . Combined Operations Supply Depot
COREP . . . . . . Combined Overload Repair Control
COMPACT . . . . Combined Passive Active Detection (RADAR)
CPIC . . . . Combined Photographic Interpretation Center
CPRB . . . . Combined Production and Resources Board (World War II)
CPL . . . . Combined Programming Language (Data processing)
COMBQUARFOR . . Combined Quarantine Force (US/Venezuela/Dominican Republic/ Argentina)
CRT . . . . Combined Radiation Test
CRMB . . . . Combined Raw Materials Board (US and Britain) (Washington)
CRTU . . . . Combined Receiving and Transmitting Unit
CRESS . . . . . . Combined Reentry Effort in Small Systems
CRPM . . . . . . Combined Registered Publication Memoranda
CRU . . . . Combined Rotating Unit (AEC)
CRC . . . . Combined Rubber Committee
CSDIC . . . . . . Combined Services Detailed Interrogation Center
CSDICNOI . . . . Combined Services Detailed Interrogation Center -- Non-Operational Intelligence
CSU . . . . Combined Shaft Unit
CSC . . . . Combined Shipbuilding Committee (World War II)
CSAB . . . . Combined Shipping Adjustment Board (World War II)
CSP . . . . Combined Staff Planners
CS/C . . . . Combined Station/Center (Aviation)
CS/T . . . . Combined Station/Tower (Aviation)
CSG . . . . Combined Studies Group (Central Intelligence Agency operation in Southeast Asia)
CST . . . . Combined Systems Test
CTA . . . . Combined Target Area
CTG . . . . Combined Test Group
CTC . . . . Combined Training Center
CTB . . . . Combined Travel Board (Allied German Occupation Forces)
CTSB . . . . Combined Travel Security Board (Allied German Occupation Forces)
CWCS . . . . Combined Wheat Control Section (Allied German Occupation Forces)
COREN . . . . . . Combustibili per Reattori Nucleari (A nuclear power company) (Italy)
CE . . . . Combustion Engineering (Navy)
CSP . . . . Combustion Engineering, Inc. (NYSE symbol)
CEND . . . . Combustion Engineering Nuclear Division (AEC)
CI . . . . Combustion Institute
CSM . . . . Combustion Stability Monitor
CLURT . . . . . . Come, Let Us Reason Together (Labor mediators' slogan)
CQD . . . . Come Quick -- Danger
C of E . . . . . . The Comedy of Errors (by Shakespeare)
CI . . . . Comfort Index
CHP . . . . Comhuriyet Halk Partisi (Turkey)
CCA . . . . Comics Code Authority (Regulatory body for comic book and comic magazine publishing industry)
CMAA . . . . . . Comics Magazine Association of America
CIDE . . . . Comision de Inversiones y Desarrollo Economico (Uruguay)
CNEA . . . . Comision Nacional de Energia Atomica (National Commission for Atomic Energy) (Mexico)
CNEN . . . . . . Comision Nacional de Energia Nuclear (National Commission for Nuclear Energy) (Mexico)
CONIE . . . . . . Comision Nacional de Investigacion del Espacio (Spanish space commission)
CNIE . . . . Comision Nacional de Investigaciones Espaciales (Argentina)
CNAE . . . . . . Comissao Nacional de Atividades Espaciais (Brazil)
CLNAI . . . . . . Comitato de Liberazione Nazionale per l'Alta Italia
CNEN . . . . . . Comitato Nazionale per l'Energia Nucleare (National Nuclear Energy Committee) (Italy)
CNRN . . . . . . Comitato Nazionale per le Ricerche Nucleari (Italy) (Now, CNEN)

COMDAC . . . . Comite d'Action en France
CAPISM . . . . . Comite d'Action Politique et Sociale pour l'Independance de Madagascar (Political and Social Committee for Malagasy Independence)
CAUNC . . . . . Comite d'Action de L'Union Nationale des Cabindais (Action Committee for the National Association of the People of Cabinda)
CAC . . . . Comite Administratif de Coordination (des Nations Unies) (Aviation)
CAD . . . . Comite d'Aide au Developpement (OCDE)
CAMEA . . . . . Comite des Applications Militaires de l'Energie Atomique (France)
CAT . . . . Comite de l'Assistance Technique de l'ONU
CCIC . . . . Comite Catholique International de Coordination Aupres de l'Unesco
CCPO . . . . . . Comite Central Permanent de l'Opium
CCPF . . . . . . Comite Central de la Propriete Forestiere de la CEE
COMAF . . . . . Comite des Constructeurs de Materiel Frigorifique de la CEE
CCIC . . . . Comite Consultatif International du Coton
CCIR . . . . Comite Consultatif International des Radiocommunications (International Radio Consultative Committee)
CCITT . . . . . . Comite Consultatif Internationale pour Telegraphie et Telephonie
CCIT . . . . . . Comite Consultatif Internationale Telegraphique (International Telephone Consultative Committee)
CCU . . . . Comite Consultatif des Unites (Advisory Committee on Units)
CCAT . . . . . . Comite de Coordination de l'Assistance Technique (ONU)
COCOCAM . . . Comite de Coordination Camerounaise (Committee for Cameroonese Coordination)
CADEL . . . . . Comite pour la Defense de la Legalite (Committee for Legal Defense) (Dahomey)
CODEMAC . . . Comite des Demenageurs du Marche Commun
CODIA . . . . . Comite pour le Development des Activities Intellectuelles en Afrique (Committee for the Development of Intellectual Activities in Africa)
CES . . . . Comite Economique et Social (of CEE)
CEAP . . . . . . Comite d'Entente et d'Action Politique (Committee for Understanding and Political Action)
COMETEC-GAZ . . Comite d'Etudes Economiques de l'Industrie du Gaz
CEPCEO . . . . Comite d'Etude des Producteurs de Charbon d'Europe Occidentale
CERES . . . . . Comite d'Etudes Regionales Economiques et Sociales
CEA . . . . Comite Europeen des Assurances
CEB . . . . Comite Europeen du Beton
CECT . . . . . . Comite Europeen de la Chaudronnerie et de la Tolerie (European Committee for Boilermaking and Kindred Steel Structures)
CECLB . . . . . Comite Europeen de Controle Laitierbeurrier
CEN . . . . Comite Europeen de Coordination des Normes (European Committee for Coordination of Standards)
CECH . . . . . . Comite Europeen de la Culture du Houblon
CEP . . . . Comite Europeen d'Etudes Phytosanitaires (European Committee for Plant Protection Research)
CEZA . . . . . . Comite Europeen d'Etudes de Zoologie Agricole
CEFACD . . . . . Comite Europeen des Fabricants d'Appareils de Chauffage et de Cuisine Domestiques (European Committee of Manufacturers of Domestic Heating and Cooking Appliances)
CEFS . . . . . . Comite Europeen des Fabricants de Sucre (European Committee of Sugar Manufacturers)
CEMA . . . . . . Comite Europeen des Groupements de Constructeurs de Machines Agricoles
CELIMAC . . . . Comite Europeen de Liaison des Industries de la Machine a Coudre
CELNUCO . . . . Comite Europeen de Liaison des Negociants et Utilisateurs de Combustibles
EUROTOX . . . . Comite Europeen Permanent de Recherches sur la Protection des Populations Contre les Risques de Toxicite a Long Terme
CEPC . . . . . . Comite Europeen pour les Problemes Criminels (Conseil de l'Europe)
CEPES . . . . . Comite Europeen pour le Progres Economique et Social
CERE . . . . . . Comite Europeen pour les Relations Economiques
COFALEC . . . . Comite des Fabricants de Levure de Panification de la CEE
CFLN . . . . . . Comite Francais Liberation Nationale
CIMCEE . . . . . Comite des Industries de la Moutarde de la CEE
CICPE . . . . . . Comite d'Initiative pour le Congres du Peuple Europeen
CIOMR . . . . . Comite Interallie des Officiers Medecins de Reserve
CIAP . . . . Comite Interamericano de la Alianza para el Progreso (Inter-American Committee of the Alliance for Progress)
CIDA . . . . . . Comite Intergouvernemental du Droit d'Auteur
CIME . . . . . . Comite Intergouvernemental pour les Migrations Europeennes
CIAI . . . . Comite International d'Aide aux Intellectuels
CICIAMS . . . . . Comite International Catholique des Infirmieres et Assistantes Medico-Sociales
CIC . . . . Comite International de la Conserve
CICR . . . . Comite International de la Croix-Rouge
CID . . . . Comite International de Dachau
CID . . . . Comite International des Derives Tensio-Actifs
CIDALC . . . . . Comite International pour la Diffusion des Arts et des Lettres par le Cinema
CIDSS . . . . . . Comite International pour la Documentation des Sciences Sociales
CIE . . . . Comite International des Echanges Pres la Chambre de Commerce Internationale

CIEF . . . . Comite International d'Enregistrement des Frequences (International Frequency Registration Board)
CIES . . . . Comite International des Entreprises a Succursales
CITTA . . . . . . Comite International des Fabricants de Tapis et de Tissus d'Ameublement
CIFTA . . . . . . Comite International des Federations Theatrales d'Amateurs de Langue Francaise
CIFE . . . . Comite International du Film Ethnographique
CIFES . . . . . . Comite International du Film Ethnographique et Sociologique (International Committee on Ethnographical and Sociological Films)
CIG . . . . Comite International de Geophysique (International Geophysical Committee)
CIHA . . . . . . Comite International d'Histoire de l'Art
CILOPGO . . . . Comite International de Liaison des Gynecologues et Obstetriciens
CIMPM . . . . . . Comite International de Medecine et de Pharmacie Militaires
CIO . . . . Comite International Olympique
CIOS . . . . Comite International de l'Organisation Scientifique
CIPC . . . . Comite International Permanent de la Conserve
CIPL . . . . Comite International Permanent de Linguistes
CIP . . . . Comite International de Photobiologie
CIPM . . . . Comite International des Poids et Mesures (International Committee on Weights and Measures)
CIPO . . . . Comite International pour la Preservation des Oiseaux
CIRM . . . . . . Comite International Radio-Maritime (International Maritime Radio Committee)
CIRA . . . . Comite International Radioaeronautique
CIRFS . . . . . . Comite International de la Rayonne et des Fibres Synthetiques
CISH . . . . Comite International des Sciences Historiques
CISO . . . . Comite International des Sciences Onomastiques
CISJA . . . . . . Comite International de Solidarite Avec la Jeunesse Algerienne
CISAI . . . . . . Comite International de Soutien aux Antifascistes Iberiques
CISPR . . . . . . Comite International Special des Perturbations Radioelectriques (International Committee on Radio Interference)
CISS . . . . Comite International des Sports Silencieux
CISBH . . . . . . Comite International de Standardisation en Biologie Humaine
CITEN . . . . . . Comite International de la Teinture et du Nettoyage
CIT . . . . Comite International de Television (International Television Committee)
CITCE . . . . . . Comite International de Thermodynamique et de Cinetique Electro-Chimiques
CIT . . . . Comite International des Transports par Chemins de Fer
CIDESCO . . . . Comite Internationale d'Esthetique et de Cosmetologie (International Committee for Aesthetics and Cosmetology)
CITEJA . . . . . . Comite Internationale d'Experts Juridiques Aeriens (International Technical Committee of Aerial Legal Experts)
CJIA . . . . Comite Juridique International de l'Aviation
CLER . . . . Comite de Liaison des Etudiants Revolutionnaires (French student group)
COLIME . . . . . Comite de Liaison des Industries Metalliques Europeennes
CMI . . . . Comite Maritime International
CMI . . . . Comite Meteorologique International
CNLCI . . . . . . Comite National pour la Liberation de la Cote d'Ivoire (National Committee for the Liberation of the Ivory Coast)
COBCCEE . . . . Comite des Organisations de la Boucherie-Charcuterie de la CEE
COCCEE . . . . . Comite des Organisations Commerciales des Pays de la CEE
COPA . . . . . . Comite des Organisations Professionnelles Agricoles de la CEE
COPECIAL . . . . Comite Permanent des Congres Internationaux pour l'Apostolat des Laics
CPCIZ . . . . . . Comite Permanent des Congres Internationaux de Zoologie
CPIUS . . . . . . Comite Permanent International d'Urbanisme Souterrain
CPIV . . . . Comite Permanent International du Vinaigre (Marche Commun)
CLAM . . . . . . Comite Permanent de Liaison de l'Agrumiculture Mediterraneenne
CPE . . . . Comite de Politique Economique (OCDE)
CRACCUS . . . . Comite Regional d'Afrique Centrale pour la Conservation et l'Utilisation du Sol
CROACUS . . . . Comite Regional Ouest-Africain pour la Conservation et l'Utilisation du Sol
CRPB . . . . . . Comite de Relevement du Peuple Bassa (Committee for the Aid of the Bassa People)
CORECA . . . . Comite pour la Reunification du Camaroon (Committee for the Reunification of the Cameroons)
CSEERI . . . . . . Comite Scientifique pour l'Etude des Effets des Radiations Ionisantes
CSIRT . . . . . . Comite Scientifique International de Recherches sur les Trypanosomiases
COSOMA . . . . Comite de Solidarite de Madagascar (Madagascar Solidarity Committee)
CSAGI . . . . . . Comite Special pour l'Annee Geophysique Internationale
CSK . . . . Comite Special du Katanga
CSIT . . . . Comite Sportif International du Travail
CTIF . . . . Comite Technique International de Prevention et d'Extincting du Feu
CUNC . . . . . . Comite d'Union Nationale des Cabindais (Cabindan Committee of National Union)
CUT . . . . Comite d l'Unite Togolaise (Committee for Togolese Unity)
CURAGI . . . . . Comite pour l'Utilisation des Resultats de l'Annee Geophysique Internationale (IGY Completion Committee)
CAFO . . . . Command Accounting and Finance Office

CASS . . . . Command Active Sonobuoy System (Navy)
CAL . . . . Command Authorization List
CBE . . . . Command Budget Estimates (Military)
CC . . . . Command Control (Military)
CCC . . . . Command and Control Center (Air Force)
CC & C . . . . . Command Control and Communications (Air Force)
CC & CP . . . . Command Control and Communications Program (Air Force)
CCDSO . . . . . Command and Control Defense Systems Office
CCDD . . . . . . Command and Control Development Division (Air Force)
CCD . . . . Command and Control Director (Air Force)
CCIS . . . . Command Control Information System
CCN . . . . Command Control Number (Air Force)
CCP . . . . Command Control Panel
CCP . . . . Command Control Post
CCS . . . . Command, Control, Support (Army)
CDA . . . . Command Data Acquisition
CDAS . . . . . . Command and Data Acquisition Station (Aerospace)
CDC . . . . Command and Data-Handling Console (DSIF)
COMDEC . . . . Command Decision & Movement Control Charts
CDR . . . . Command Destruct Receiver (Military)
CDT . . . . Command Destruct Transmitter (Military)
CDO . . . . Command Duty Officer (Navy)
CEO . . . . Command Education Officer (British military)
CEO . . . . Command Entertainments Officer (British military)
CEMO . . . . . . Command Equipment Management Office (Military)
C & GS . . . . . Command and General Staff (Army)
CGSC . . . . . . Command and General Staff College
C & GSC . . . . Command and General Staff College (Military)
C & GSS . . . . Command & General Staff School (Army)
CGTM . . . . . . Command Guided Tactical Missile
CIC . . . . Command Information Center
CIP . . . . Command Information Program (Military)
CIO . . . . Command Issuing Office(r)
CMI . . . . Command Maintenance Inspection (Army)
CMMI . . . . . . Command Maintenance Management Inspection (Military)
CMRI . . . . . . Command Maintenance Readiness Inspection (Military)
CMIA . . . . . . Command Management Inventory Accounting (Army)
COMMAND . . . Command Model for Analysis and Design
CM . . . . Command Module
CEPS . . . . Command Module Electrical Power System (Air Force)
CMP . . . . Command Module Pilot (Apollo) (NASA)
CM-SM . . . . . . Command Module - Service Module (Combined) (NASA)
COP/B . . . . . . Command Operating Program/Budget (DOD)
CO . . . . Command Operations (Army)
COPRL . . . . . . Command Operations Priority Requirements List (Air Force)
CO . . . . Command Orders
C . . . . Command Paper
COMPATPLANEREPRONSPAC . . Command Patrol Plane Replacement Squadrons Pacific
CPS . . . . Command Personnel Summary
CP . . . . Command Pilot
CP . . . . Command Post (Military)
COPAN . . . . . Command Post Alerting Network
CPDD . . . . . . Command Post Digital Display (SAGE) (Air Force)
CPEx . . . . Command Post Exercise
CPX . . . . Command Post Exercise
CPO . . . . Command-Post Officer
CPM . . . . Command Processor Module
CPO . . . . Command Pulse Output
CORAL . . . . . . Command Radio Link
CR . . . . Command Register
CRC . . . . Command Reporting Center
CRIS . . . . Command Retrieval Information System
CS . . . . Command Selector
CSC . . . . Command Selector Control
CSM . . . . Command and Service Module (NASA)
CC . . . . Command Ship (Navy symbol)
CSD . . . . Command Signal Decoder
CSL . . . . Command Signal Limiter
CSC . . . . Command and Staff College (Air Force)
CSDP . . . . . . Command Supply Discipline Program (Army)
CSW . . . . Command Surveillance and Weather
CTI . . . . Command Technical Inspection (Army)
CTB . . . . Command Telemetry Buoy
CTLI . . . . Command Training Launch Instrumentation
CTP . . . . Command Translator and Programmer
CV . . . . Command Vehicle
CVR . . . . Command Voltage Regulator
C . . . . Commandant (Coast Guard)
CA . . . . Commandant Assistant (Coast Guard)
CCG . . . . Commandant of the Coast Guard
CMC . . . . Commandant of the Marine Corps

COMDTNOB .. Commandant, Naval Operating Base
COMDTNY. ... Commandant, Navy Yard
NEARNAVDIST .. Commandant of the Nearest Naval District
COMDTUSCG .. Commandant, United States Coast Guard
COMDTMARCORPS .. Commandant, US Marine Corps
COMDTUSMC .. Commandant, United States Marine Corps
C .... Commander; as: CNAB (Commander Naval Air Bases)
COM .... Commander (Navy)
CAC .... Commander Air Center
COMAIRLANT .. Commander Air Force, Atlantic Fleet
COMAIRPAC .. Commander Air Force, Pacific Fleet
COMAIR ..... Commander Air Forces (Navy)
COMAIRSOLS . Commander Air Forces, Solomons
CAG .... Commander of the Air Group (Navy)
COMAIRTRANS .. Commander Air Transport
COMAIRTRANSRON .. Commander Air Transport Squadron
COMAIR ..... Commander Aircraft (Navy)
COMAIRSOPAC .. Commander Aircraft, South Pacific Force
CASCU ...... Commander Aircraft Support Control Unit (Navy)
COMAIRSHIPGR .. Commander, Airship Group
COMALAMGRU .. Commander Alameda Group
COMALSEC ... Commander Alaskan Sector
CAFAC ...... Commander All Forces, Aruba-Curacao
COMAIRBALTAP .. Commander, Allied Air Forces Baltic Approaches
COMAIRCENT .. Commander, Allied Air Forces Central Europe
COMAIRNORTH .. Commander, Allied Air Forces Northern Europe
COMALAIRNOREUR .. Commander, Allied Air Forces, Northern Europe
COMAIRSOUTH .. Commander, Allied Air Forces Southern Europe
COMLANDCENT .. Commander, Allied Land Forces Central Europe
COMLANDENMARK .. Commander, Allied Land Forces Denmark
COMLANDNORWAY .. Commander, Allied Land Forces Norway
COMLANDSCHLESWIG .. Commander, Allied Land Forces Schleswig-Holstein
COMLANDJUT.. Commander, Allied Land Forces Schleswig-Holstein and Jutland
COMLANDSOUTHEAST .. Commander, Allied Land Forces Southeastern Europe
COMLANDSOUTH .. Commander, Allied Land Forces Southern Europe
COMLANDZEALAND .. Commander, Allied Land Forces Zealand
COMMAIRCHAN .. Commander, Allied Maritime Air Force Channel (NATO)
COMNAVBALTAP .. Commander, Allied Naval Forces Baltic Approaches
COMNAVCENT .. Commander, Allied Naval Forces Central Europe
COMNAVNON .. Commander, Allied Naval Forces North Norway
COMALNAVNOREUR .. Commander, Allied Naval Forces, Northern Europe
COMNAVNORTH.. Commander, Allied Naval Forces, Northern Europe
COMNAVSCAP.. Commander, Allied Naval Forces, Scandinavian Approaches
COMTAFNORNOR .. Commander, Allied Tactical Air Force North Norway
COMTAFSONOR.. Commander, Allied Tactical Air Force, South Norway
COMTASKFORNON .. Commander, Allied Task Forces North Norway
COMPHIB .... Commander, Amphibious Force
COMPHIBFOR .. Commander, Amphibious Force (Navy)
CAFAF ...... Commander, Amphibious Force, Atlantic Fleet
COMPHIBLANT .. Commander, Amphibious Force, Atlantic Fleet
COMPHIBEU .. Commander, Amphibious Force, Europe
COMPHIBNAW.. Commander, (US) Amphibious Force, Northwest African Waters
COMPHIBPAC.. Commander, Amphibious Force, Pacific Fleet
COMPHIBRON .. Commander, Amphibious Squadron
CATCUSAF ... Commander, Amphibious Training Command United States Atlantic Fleet
COMANTDEFCOM .. Commander, Antilles Defense Command
COMFLTBASTILLES.. Commander, (US) Atlantic Fleet Bases, Antilles
COMBATDIV .. Commander, Battleship Division
COMBATLANT.. Commander, Battleships, Atlantic Fleet
COMBATPAC.. Commander, Battleships, Pacific Fleet
COMBISLANT.. Commander, Bay of Biscay Atlantic Subarea (NATO)
COMBENECHAN.. Commander, BENELUX Subarea Channel
COMBOMRON.. Commander, Bombing Squadron
COMBSNGRU.. Commander, Boston Group
COMBREMGRU.. Commander, Bremerton Group
COMBRESTCHAN.. Commander, Brest Subarea Channel
COMCANLANT.. Commander, Canadian Atlantic Subarea (NATO)
CANCOMDESLANT.. Commander, Canadian Destroyers, Atlantic
CANCOMDESFE.. Commander, Canadian Destroyers, Far East
CANCOMDESPAC.. Commander, Canadian Destroyers, Pacific
CCSF ...... Commander, Caribbean Sea Frontier (Navy)
COMCASU .... Commander, Carrier Aircraft Service Unit
COMCARSTRIKFOR.. Commander, Carrier Striking Force
COMCARSTRIKGRUONE .. Commander, Carrier Striking Group One
COMCARSTRIKGRUTWO .. Commander, Carrier Striking Group Two
COMTRAINCARRONPAC .. Commander, Carrier Training Squadron, Pacific Fleet
COMCENTAG.. Commander, Central Army Group, Central Europe
COMCENTLANT.. Commander, Central Atlantic Subarea (NATO)
COMEDCENT.. Commander, Central Mediterranean
COMCENPAC . Commander, Central Pacific
COMCHASNGRU . Commander, Charleston Group

COMCHERCHAN .. Commander, Cherbourg Subarea Channel
C-in-C ...... Commander-in-Chief
CIC .... Commander-in-Chief (Air Force)
CINC ...... Commander-in-Chief
COMINCH ... Commander-in-Chief (US fleet)
CINCAFLANT... Commander-in-Chief, Air Force Atlantic Command
CINCAFSTRIKE.. Commander-in-Chief, Air Force Strike Command
CINCAL ..... Commander-in-Chief, Alaskan Command
CINCALAIRCENEUR.. Commander-in-Chief, Allied Air Forces, Central Europe
CINCAF ..... Commander-in-Chief, Allied Forces
CINCENT .... Commander-in-Chief, Allied Forces Central Europe
CINCAFMED.. Commander-in-Chief, Allied Forces Mediterranean (NATO)
CINCNORTH .. Commander-in-Chief, Allied Forces Northern Europe (NATO)
CINCSOUTH .. Commander-in-Chief, Allied Forces Southern Europe (NATO)
CINCAWI .... Commander-in-Chief, America West Indies Station (British)
CINCARLANT. Commander-in-Chief, (US) Army Forces, Atlantic
CINCAFPAC .. Commander-in-Chief, (US) Army Forces in the Pacific
CINCARPAC .. Commander-in-Chief, (US) Army Forces, Pacific
CINCARSTRIKE.. Commander-in-Chief, Army Strike Command
CINCAF .... Commander-in-Chief, (US) Asiatic Fleet
CINCLANT ... Commander-in-Chief, Atlantic (US Navy and Allies)
CINCLANTFLT.. Commander-in-Chief, Atlantic Fleet
CINCA & WI... Commander-in-Chief, Atlantic and West Indies
CINCBPF.... Commander-in-Chief, British Pacific Fleet
CINCARIB .... Commander-in-Chief, Caribbean
CINCHAN.... Commander-in-Chief Channel and S. North Sea (NATO)
CINCAC.... Commander-in-Chief, Continental Air Command
CINCCONAD. Commander-in-Chief, Continental Air Defense Command
CINCONAD... Commander-in-Chief, Continental Air Defense Command
COMROUTE... Commander-in-Chief, (US Fleet), Convoy and Routing Section
CINCEI...... Commander-in-Chief, East Indies Station (British)
CINCEASTLANT.. Commander-in-Chief, Eastern Atlantic Area (NATO)
CINCEUR .... Commander-in-Chief, Europe
CINCFE ..... Commander-in-Chief, Far East
CINCFESTA ... Commander-in-Chief, Far East Station (British)
CINCMED .... Commander-in-Chief, Mediterranean
CICNMEAFSA.. Commander-in-Chief, Middle East/Southern Asia and Africa
    South of the Sahara (Military)
CINCNAVEASTLANTMED.. Commander-in-Chief, (US) Naval Forces, Eastern Atlantic
    and Mediterranean
CINCNELM ... Commander-in-Chief, Naval Forces, Eastern Atlantic and Medi-
    terranean (Military)
CINCNEDE ... Commander-in-Chief, Netherlands Forces in the East
CINCNORAD. Commander-in-Chief, North American Air Defense
CINCNE .... Commander-in-Chief, (US) Northeast Command
CINCNOREUR.. Commander-in-Chief, Northern Europe
CINCPACAF... Commander-in-Chief, Pacific Air Forces
CINCPAC ... Commander-in-Chief of the Pacific Fleet (World War II)
CINCPACFLT.. Commander-in-Chief, Pacific Fleet
CINCPACHEDPEARL.. Commander-in-Chief, (US) Pacific Fleet Headquarters, Pearl Harbor
CINCPAC-CINCPOA.. Commander-in-Chief, (US) Pacific Fleet and Pacific Ocean Areas
CINCPOA.... Commander-in-Chief, Pacific Ocean Areas (Military)
CINCPOAHEDPEARL.. Commander-in-Chief, Pacific Ocean Areas Headquarters, Pearl
    Harbor
CINCPACREP .. Commander-in-Chief, Pacific Representative
CINCSA ..... Commander-in-Chief, South Atlantic Station (British)
CINCSO .... Commander-in-Chief, (US) Southern Command
CINCSPECOMME.. Commander-in-Chief, Specified Command, Middle East
CINCSAC .... Commander-in-Chief, Strategic Air Command
CINCSTRIKE .. Commander-in-Chief, Strike Forces (Military)
CINCTAC .... Commander-in-Chief, Tactical Air Command
CINCUNC.... Commander-in-Chief, United Nations Command
CINCUSAFE... Commander-in-Chief, United States Air Forces in Europe
CINCUSAREUR.. Commander-in-Chief, United States Army, Europe
CINCUSARPAC.. Commander-in-Chief, United States Army, Pacific
CINCUS ..... Commander-in-Chief, United States Fleet (Obsolete)
CINCUSNAVEUR.. Commander-in-Chief, United States Naval Forces, Europe
CINCWESTLANT.. Commander-in-Chief Western Atlantic Area (NATO)
CCD .... Commander of Coast Defenses
CCGD....... Commander, Coast Guard District
COMCOLUMGRU . Commander, Columbia River Group
COMCOMRON .. Commander, Composite Squadron
COMCRUDESLANT.. Commander, Cruiser-Destroyer Force Atlantic (Navy)
COMCRUDESPAC.. Commander, Cruiser-Destroyer Forces, Pacific
COMCRUDIV .. Commander, Cruiser Division
COMCRULANT.. Commander, Cruiser Forces, Atlantic Fleet
COMCRUSCORON . Commander, Cruiser Scouting Squadron
COMCRUPAC .. Commander, Cruisers, Pacific Fleet
CDDGP...... Commander, Destroyer Development Group, Pacific (Navy)
COMDESDIV .. Commander, Destroyer Division
CDS .... Commander, Destroyer Squadron (Navy)

COMDESRON .. Commander, Destroyer Squadron
COMDES..... Commander, Destroyers
COMDESLANT .. Commander, Destroyers, Atlantic Fleet
COMDESPAC.. Commander, Destroyers, Pacific Fleet
COMYARD ... Commander of the Dockyard at (place)
COMEDEAST .. Commander, Eastern Mediterranean
CESF....... Commander, Eastern Sea Frontier (Navy)
COMEXDIV... Commander, Experimental Division (Navy)
COMFIVEATAF. .Commander, Fifth Allied Tactical Air Force
COMFIGHTRON .. Commander, Fighting Squadron
CANCOMDESFLOT I.. Commander, First Canadian Destroyer Flotilla
COMFAIR .... Commander, Fleet Air
CFAD....... Commander, Fleet Air Detachment
CFAW....... Commander, Fleet Air Wing
COMFAIRWING .. Commander, Fleet Air Wing
COMFAIRWINGNORLANT .. Commander, Fleet Air Wing Northern Atlantic
COMFLOGWING . Commander, Fleet Logistic Air Wing
COTC....... Commander, Fleet Operational Training Command
COTCLANT ... Commander, Fleet Operational Training Command, Atlantic Fleet
COTCPAC ... Commander, Fleet Operational Training Command, Pacific Fleet
COTCPACSUBCOM .. Commander, Fleet Operational Training Command, Pacific Subordinate
    Command
COFT....... Commander, Fleet Train
COMFLAGRU.. Commander, Florida Group
COMFOURATAF .. Commander, Fourth Allied Tactical Air Force, Central Europe
COMGIB..... Commander, Gibraltar (Navy)
COMGIBMED. . Commander, Gibraltar-Mediterranean Command
COMGREPAT .. Commander, Greenland Patrol
COG .... Commander of the Guard (Military)
COMHAWSEAFRON .. Commander, Hawaiian Sea Frontier (Navy)
COMHEDRON .. Commander, Headquarters Squadron
COMICEDEFOR . Commander, Iceland Defense Force
COMJEF..... Commander, Joint Expeditionary Force (Military)
CJTF .... Commander, Joint Task Force
COMLBEACHGRU .. Commander, Long Beach Group
COMAREGRU .. Commander, Mare Island Group
COMMARIANAS .. Commander, Marianas
COMART..... Commander, Marine Air Reserve Training
COMMAIRCENTLANT .. Commander, Maritime Air Central Subarea (NATO)
COMMAIREASTLANT.. Commander, Maritime Air Eastern Atlantic Area (NATO)
COMMAIRNORECHAN .. Commander, Maritime Air Nore Sub-Area Channel
COMMAIRNORLANT.. Commander, Maritime Air Northern Subarea (NATO)
COMMAIRPLYMCHAN.. Commander, Maritime Air Plymouth Sub-Area Channel
COMOROCLANT .. Commander, Maritime Forces, Morocco
COMARCARAREA .. Commander, Marshalls-Carolines Area
COMATS .... Commander, Military Air Transport Service
COMAC ..... Commander, Military Airlift Command
COMSTS .... Commander, Military Sea Transportation Service (Navy)
COMSTSLANTAREA.. Commander, Military Sea Transportation Service, Atlantic Area
COMSTSELMAREA.. Commander, Military Sea Transportation Service, Eastern Atlantic
    and Mediterranean Area
COMSTSGULFSUBAREA .. Commander, Military Sea Transportation Service, Gulf Subarea
COMSTSMIDPACSUBAREA .. Commander, Military Sea Transportation Service,
    Mid-Pacific Subarea
COMSTSNORPACSUBAREA .. Commander, Military Sea Transportation Service, Northern
    Pacific Subarea
COMSTSPACAREA.. Commander, Military Sea Transportation Service, Pacific Area
COMSTSWESTPACAREA .. Commander, Military Sea Transportation Service, West Pacific
    Area
COMINLANT.. Commander, Mine Force, Atlantic Fleet
COMINGRP... Commander, Mine Group
COMINGRPOK .. Commander, Mine Group Okinawa
COMINRON .. Commander, Mine Squadron
COMIN ..... Commander, Minecraft (Navy)
COMINDIV .. Commander, Minecraft Division (Navy)
COMINPAC... Commander, Minecraft, Pacific Fleet
COMORSEAFRON .. Commander, Moroccan Sea Frontier Forces
COMTBFLOT .. Commander, Motor Torpedo Boat Flotilla
COMTBRON .. Commander, Motor Torpedo Boat Squadron
COMTBRONTRACENT .. Commander, Motor Torpedo Boat Squadron Training Center
COMNAVJAP. . Commander, Naval Activities Japan
CNAB....... Commander, Naval Air Bases
COMNAB .... Commander, Naval Air Bases
COMNAVAIR .. Commander, Naval Air Force
COMNAVAIRLANT .. Commander, Naval Air Forces, Atlantic Fleet
COMNAVAIRPAC .. Commander, Naval Air Forces, Pacific Fleet
CNATEC (LTA) .. Commander, Naval Air Technical Training (Lighter Than Air)
CNB........ Commander, Naval Base
CNF........ Commander, Naval Forces
COMNAVZOR.. Commander, (US) Naval Forces, Azores

COMNAVEASTLANTMED.. Commander, (US) Naval Forces, Eastern Atlantic and
    Mediterranean
COMNAVEU .. Commander, (US) Naval Forces in Europe
COMNAVFE .. Commander, (US) Naval Forces, Far East
COMNAVGER.. Commander, (US) Naval Forces, Germany
COMNAVICE.. Commander, Naval Forces Iceland
COMNAVFORJAPAN ..Commander, Naval Forces Japan
COMNAVMARIANA .. Commander, Naval Forces Mariana
CONNORPAC..Commander, (US) Naval Forces, Northern Pacific
COMNAVNAW.. Commander, (US) Naval Forces, Northwest African Waters
CNOB ...... Commander, Naval Operating Base
COMSTRIKFORSOUTH .. Commander, Naval Striking and Support Forces, Southern Europe
COMNAVSUPPACT .. Commander, Naval Support Activity
COMNEWLONGRU.. Commander, New London Group
COMNYKGRU .. Commander, New York Group
COMNORECHAN .. Commander, Nore Subarea Channel
COMNORVAGRU .. Commander, Norfolk Group
COMNORASDEFLANT .. Commander, North American Anti-Submarine Defense Force,
    Atlantic (NATO)
COMNORPAC .. Commander, North Pacific Force
COMEDNOREAST .. Commander, Northeast Mediterranean Area
COMNORTHAG .. Commander, Northern Army Group, Central Europe
COMNORLANT .. Commander, Northern Atlantic Subarea (NATO)
CNG .... Commander, Northern Group
COMOCEANLANT .. Commander, Ocean Atlantic Subarea (NATO)
COMOPDEVFOR. . Commander, Operational Development Force (Navy)
COMOPTEVFOR .. Commander, Operational Test and Evaluation Force (Navy)
COMORTEXGRU .. Commander; Orange, Texas, Group; Inactive Fleet, Atlantic Fleet
CBE .... Commander, Order of the British Empire
CStJ....... Commander, Order of St. John of Jerusalem (British)
COMPASEAFRON .. Commander, Panama Sea Frontier
COMPASU.... Commander, Patrol Aircraft Service Unit
COMPATRON .. Commander, Patrol Squadron
COMPHILAGRU .. Commander, Philadelphia Group
COMPLYMCHAN .. Commander, Plymouth Subarea Channel
COMBASFRANCE.. Commander, (US) Ports and Bases, France
CRASC ...... Commander, Royal Army Service Corps (British)
CRA .... Commander, Royal Artillery (Division level) (British)
CRE .... Commander, Royal Engineers (British)
CVO .... Commander of the Royal Victorian Order
COMDIEGOGRU . Commander, San Diego Group
COMSANFRANGRU .. Commander, San Francisco Group
COMSCORON .. Commander, Scouting Squadron
COMSEAFRON .. Commander, Sea Frontier (Navy)
COMTWOATAF .. Commander, Second Allied Tactical Air Force
COMSERV.... Commander, Service Force
COMSERVLANT .. Commander, Service Force, Atlantic Fleet
COMSERVPAC .. Commander, Service Force, Pacific Fleet
COMSERFORSOPACSUBCOM .. Commander, Service Force, South Pacific Subordinate
    Command
COMSERVSOWESPAC .. Commander, Service Force, Southwest Pacific
COMSERVRON .. Commander, Service Squadron
COMSIXATAF. . Commander, Sixth Allied Tactical Air Force
COMSOLANT. . Commander, South Atlantic Force
COMSOPAC .. Commander, South Pacific
COMEDSOUEAST .. Commander, Southeast Mediterranean
COMSOEASTPAC .. Commander, Southeast Pacific Force
COMSOWESPAC .. Commander, Southwest Pacific Force
COMSTOCKGRU .. Commander, Stockton Group
COMSTRIKEFLTLANT.. Commander, Striking Fleet, Atlantic (NATO)
COMSTRIKFLANT .. Commander, Striking Fleet, Atlantic (Afloat)
COMSUBACLANT .. Commander, Submarine Allied Command, Atlantic
COMSUBASE .. Commander, Submarine Base
COMSUBDIV .. Commander, Submarine Division
COMSUBLANT .. Commander, Submarine Force, Atlantic (Navy)
COMSUBEASTLANT.. Commander, Submarine Force, Eastern Atlantic (NATO)
COMSUBPAC.. Commander, Submarine Force, Pacific (Navy)
COMSUBSPAC .. Commander, Submarine Force, Pacific Fleet
COMSUBWESTLANT .. Commander, Submarine Force, Western Atlantic Area
COMSUBRON .. Commander, Submarine Squadron
COMSUBTRAFAC .. Commander, Submarine Training Facilities
COMSUBS .... Commander, Submarines
COMSUBLANT .. Commander, Submarines, Atlantic Fleet
COMSUBMED.. Commander, Submarines, Mediterranean
COMSUBMEDNOREAST .. Commander, Submarines, Northeast Mediterranean
COMSUBSSOWESPAC .. Commander, Submarines, Southwest Pacific Force
CSFPSC...... Commander, Subordinate Command, Service Force Pacific Fleet (Navy
    rating)
COMSOTFE ... Commander, Support Operations Task Force Europe
COMTACGRU . Commander, Tacoma Group

REVERSE ACRONYMS AND INITIALISMS DICTIONARY

COMTAC .... Commander, Tactical Air Command
CTE .... Commander, Task Element
CTF .... Commander, Task Force
CTG .... Commander, Task Group
CTU .... Commander, Task Unit
COMTEXGRU .. Commander, Texas Group
COMTONGRU .. Commander, Tongue Point Group, Inactive Fleet, Pacific Fleet
COMTORPRON .. Commander, Torpedo Squadron
COMTRANSDIV .. Commander, Transport Division
COMTRANSGR .. Commander, Transport Group
COMTRANSGRSOPAC .. Commander, Transport Group, South Pacific Force
CTD .... Commander, Transportation Division
COMTRANSPHIB .. Commander, Transports, Amphibious Force
COMTRANSPHIBLANT .. Commander, Transports, Amphibious Force, Atlantic Fleet
COMTRANSPHIBPAC .. Commander, Transports, Amphibious Force, Pacific Fleet
COMUKADR .. Commander, United Kingdom Air Defense Region
COMUSAFSO.. Commander, United States Air Forces Southern Command
COMUSARSO.. Commander, United States Army Forces Southern Command
COMUSLANT.. Commander, US Atlantic Subarea
COMUSFAIRWINGMED .. Commander, United States Fleet Air Wing Mediterranean
COMUSFORAZ.. Commander, United States Forces Azores
COMUSJAPAN.. Commander, United States Forces in Japan
COMUSKOREA.. Commander, United States Forces in Korea
COMUSMACTHAI.. Commander, United States Military Assistance Command, Thailand
COMUSMACV.. Commander, United States Military Assistance Command, Vietnam
COMUSMILGP.. Commander, United States Military Group
COUSNAB .... Commander of United States Naval Advanced Base (Weser River, Germany)
COMUSBASFRANCE .. Commander, US Ports and Bases, France
COMUSTDC.. Commander, United States Taiwan Defense Command
COMUTRON .. Commander, Utility Squadron
COMUTWING .. Commander, Utility Wing
COMUTWINGSERVLANT .. Commander, Utility Wing, Service Force, Atlantic
COMUTWINGSERVPAC .. Commander, Utility Wing, Service Force, Pacific
COMEDOC ... Commander, Western Mediterranean
CWSF .... Commander, Western Sea Frontier
CER .... Commanders Evaluation Report (Army)
CIMC .... Commanders' Internal Management Conference (Air Force)
CG. .... Commanding General (Military)
COMDGEN ... Commanding General
COMGEN ... Commanding General
CGAAF..... Commanding General, Army Air Forces
COMGENMED.. Commanding General, (US) Army Forces, Mediterranean Theater of Operations
COMGENPOA.. Commanding General, (US) Army Forces, Pacific Ocean Areas
CGIBT...... Commanding General, India-Burma Theater (World War II)
CGMB ...... Commanding General, Marine Base
CGMTO ..... Commanding General, Mediterranean Theater of Operations (World War II)
COMGENTEN .. Commanding General, Tenth Army
CGUSFET .... Commanding General, United States Forces, European Theater (World War II)
CO .... Commanding Officer
COMDG OF.. Commanding Officer
KO .... Commanding Officer (Military slang)
COAIREVACRON .. Commanding Officer, Air Evacuation Squadron
COAC ...... Commanding Officer, Atlantic Coast
COLANFORASCU .. Commanding Officer, Landing Force Air Support Control Unit
CONAB...... Commanding Officer, Naval Advanced Base
CONAB ..... Commanding Officer, Naval Air Base
CONAS ..... Commanding Officer, Naval Air Station
CONAIR..... Commanding Officer, Naval Air Wing
COND ...... Commanding Officer, Naval Divisions (Canada)
CONSD ..... Commanding Officer, Naval Supply Depot
COOBSRON .. Commanding Officer, Observation Squadron
COPQE...... Commanding Officer, Port of Embarkation
COSECTBASE .. Commanding Officer, Section Base (Navy)
COSCTRACEN .. Commanding Officer, Submarine Chaser Training Center
COUSS ..... Commanding Officer, United States Ship
CONAR ..... Commanding Officer's Narrative Report
CR .... Commendation Ribbon
CRMPT ..... Commendation Ribbon with Metal Pendant
CRWMP ..... Commendation Ribbon with Metal Pendant (US)
CRV .... Comment Recevez-Vous?
CCH....... Commerce Clearing House (A publishing company)
CD........ Commerce Department
C & F ..... Commerce and Finance
CA........ Commercial Agent
CA .... Commercial Air
CAFM ..... Commercial Air Freight Movement
CAM ...... Commercial Air Movement Number
COMAIR .... Commercial Air Service (Pty.) Ltd.
CAWU....... Commercial and Allied Workers' Union (Somali Republic)

CB........ Commercial Bank
CBL .... Commercial Bill of Lading
COMCABCO .. Commercial Cable Company
CCDA ..... Commercial Chemical Development Association
CCWO ..... Commercial Communications Work Order (Air Force)
CCC ...... Commercial Contract Change
CC........ Commercial Credit Company (NYSE symbol)
CD........ Commercial Dock
CERL ...... Commercial Equipment Requirement List
CGWU ..... Commercial and General Workers' Union (Rhodesia and Nyasaland)
CIP........ Commercial Import Program
CLLA ...... Commercial Law League of America
CLIC ...... Commercial Loan Insurance Corporation
CPD .... Commercial Product Development
CPD .... Commercial Program Development
CPW....... Commercial Projected Window (Technical drawings)
CQ .... Commercial Quality
CRMA ..... Commercial Refrigerator Manufacturers Association
CSA .... Commercial Service Area (Military)
CSA .... Commercial-Service Authorization (Military)
CV........ Commercial Solvents Corporation (NYSE symbol)
CSC ...... Commercial Steamship Company
CTU ...... Commercial Telegraphers' Union
CTV....... Commercial Television
CTB .... Commercial Traffic Bulletin
COMTRAN ... Commercial Translator
CTNDS..... Commercial Transport Navigation Display System
CTO....... Commercial Transportation Officer
CT........ Commercial Traveler
CTIF....... Commercial Travelers Insurance Federation
CWM ...... Commercial Water Movement Number
CW .... Commercial Weight
CEA .... Commissariat a l'Energie Atomique (France)
C .... Commissary (Marine Corps)
CG........ Commissary General
COP....... Commissary Operating Program (Air Force)
CS........ Commissary Store (Navy)
CMT....... Commissary Technician, Medical
CS .... Commissaryman (Navy rating)
CARF ...... Commission on Accreditation of Rehabilitation Facilities
CASE ...... Commission on Accreditation of Service Experiences
CAA ...... Commission on Art and Antiquities
CAFEA-ICC ... Commission on Asian and Far Eastern Affairs of the International Chamber of Commerce
CBN....... Commission on Biochemical Nomenclature (IUPAC)
CCR ...... Commission Centrale pour la Navigation du Rhin
CC........ Commission Certified (Bacteriology)
CCIA ...... Commission of the Churches on International Affairs
CCR ...... Commission on Civil Rights
CCP ...... Commission on College Physics
CCIP....... Commission du Commerce International des Produits de Base (Nations Unies)
CCET ...... Commission Consultative des Employes et des Travailleurs Intellectuels (de l'OIT)
CCEP ...... Commission Consultative des Etudes Postales (de l'Union Postale Universelle)
CCUP ..... Commission Consultative Universitaire de Pedagogie (Belgium)
CCTA ...... Commission de Cooperation Technique en Afrique (Commission for Technical Cooperation in Africa)
CCTA ...... Commission de Cooperation Technique en l'Afrique au Sud du Sahara
CD........ Commission du Danube
CDI .... Commission du Droit International (ONU)
CEA .... Commission Economique pour l'Afrique
CEPAL ..... Commission Economique pour l'Amerique Latine (UN)
CEAEO..... Commission Economique pour l'Asie et l'Extreme-Orient
CEE .... Commission Economique pour l'Europe (Nations Unies)
CEBJ ...... Commission of Editors of Biochemical Journals
CEANAR .... Commission on Education in Agriculture and Natural Resources (National Research Council)
CEI .... Commission Electrotechnique Internationale (International Electrotechnical Commission)
CECAL ..... Commission Episcopale de Cooperation Apostolique Canada-Amerique Latine
CEN........ Commission pour l'Etude des Nuages (OMI)
CEAC ...... Commission Europeenne de l'Aviation Civile
CEF .... Commission Europeenne des Forets
CET .... Commission Europeenne du Tourisme
CFA .... Commission of Fine Arts (Independent government agency)
WPFC ..... Commission for Fisheries Research in the West Pacific
CGS....... Commission on Government Security
CIIUAP ...... Commission on Increased Industrial Use of Agricultural Products

CIMO . . . . . . Commission des Instruments et des Methodes d'Observation (OMI)

CIEN . . . . . . Commission Interamericaine d'Energie Nucleaire

CIF . . . . Commission Interamericaine des Femmes

CIR . . . . Commission on Intergovernmental Relations

CICT . . . . . . Commission on International Commodity Trade

CID . . . . Commission for International Development

CIER . . . . . . Commission for International Educational Reconstruction

CIA . . . . Commission Internationale d'Analyses

CICM . . . . . . Commission Internationale Catholique pour les Migrations

CIC . . . . Commission Internationale du Chataignier

CICRC . . . . . Commission Internationale Contre le Regime Concentrationnaire

CIE . . . . Commission Internationale de l'Eclairage (International Commission on Illumination)

CIEC . . . . . . Commission Internationale de l'Etat Civil (International Commission on Civil Status)

CIGR . . . . . . Commission Internationale du Genie Rural

CIGB . . . . . . Commission Internationale des Grands Barrages de la Conference Mondiale de l'Energie

CIIA . . . . Commission Internationale des Industries Agricoles

CIJ . . . . Commission Internationale de Juristes

CILB . . . . . . Commission Internationale de Lutte Biologique Contre les Ennemis des Cultures

CIMAe . . . . . . Commission Internationale de Meteorologie Aeronautique (OMI)

CINA . . . . . . Commission Internationale de Navigation Aerienne

CIN . . . . Commission Internationale de Numismatique (International Numismatic Commission)

CIO . . . . Commission Internationale d'Optique

CIP . . . . Commission Internationale du Peuplier

CIPR . . . . . . Commission Internationale de Protection Contre les Radiations

CIPRA . . . . . . Commission Internationale pour la Protection des Regions Alpines

CITA . . . . . . Commission Internationale de Tourisme Aerien

CIV . . . . Commission Internationale du Verre

CMSER . . . . . Commission on Marine Science, Engineering, and Resources

CMFL . . . . . . Commission on Marriage and Family Life (of NCC)

CME . . . . Commission on Missionary Education (Later, Department of Education for Missions)

CMI . . . . Commission Mixte Internationale pour les Experiences Relatives a la Protection des Lignes de Telecommunication et des Canalisations Souterraines

CMSS . . . . . . Commission on Molecular Structure and Spectroscopy

CNAT . . . . . . Commission Nationale de l'Amenagement du Territoire

CNEUPEN . . . . Commission Nationale pour l'Etude de l'Utilisation Pacifique de l'Energie Nucleaire (Belgium)

CNUIP . . . . . . Commission des Nations Unies pour l'Inde et le Pakistan

CNUURC . . . . Commission des Nations Unies pour l'Unification et le Relevement de la Coree

CON . . . . Commission on the Nomenclature of Organic Chemistry (IUPAC)

COI . . . . Commission Oceanographique Intergouvernementale

COEBG . . . . . . Commission on Organization of the Executive Branch of the Government

CPS . . . . Commission on the Patent System

CPI . . . . Commission Permanente Internationale de l'Acetylene, de la Soudure Autogene et des Industries Qui S'y Rattachent

CPI . . . . Commission Phytosanitaire Interafricaine

CPGAF . . . . . . Commission on Population Growth and the American Future (Presidential commission)

COPERS . . . . . Commission Preparatoire Europeenne de Recherches Spatiales

CPHA . . . . . . Commission on Professional and Hospital Activities

CPRR-NEA . . . . Commission on Professional Rights and Responsibilities of the NEA

CRET . . . . . . Commission Regionale Europeenne du Tourisme

CDR . . . . Commission des Reparations (Reparation Commission)

CSE . . . . Commission on Science Education

CSI . . . . Commission Sericicole Internationale

COMSTAC . . . . Commission on Standards and Accreditation of Services for the Blind

CSOP . . . . . . Commission to Study the Organization of Peace

CSM . . . . Commission for Synoptic Meteorology

CSWI . . . . . . Commission for Synoptic Weather Information (IMO)

CTCA . . . . . . Commission for Technical Cooperation for Africa

CUEBS . . . . . Commission on Undergraduate Education in the Biological Sciences

CWMEWCC . . . Commission on World Mission and Evangelism of the World Council of Churches

CLTE . . . . . . Commissioned Loss to Enlisted Status (Revocation of an officer's appointment)

CORD . . . . . . Commissioned Officer Residency Deferment (Program of Public Health Service)

COSTEP . . . . Commissioned Officer Student Training and Extern Program (Public Health Service)

COM . . . . Commissioned Officers Mess (Navy)

CWO . . . . . . Commissioned Warrant Officer

CWOHC . . . . . Commissioned Warrant Officer Hospital Corps

CO . . . . Commissioner for Oaths

CDC . . . . Commissioners of District of Columbia

CIR . . . . Commissioners of Inland Revenue (British)

COMMDET . . . Commissioning Detail

CASE . . . . . . Committee on Academic Science and Engineering (Federal Council for Science and Technology)

CAEC . . . . . . Committee of the Acta Endocrinologica Countries

CAST . . . . . . Committee Against Student Terrorism (Student group opposed to disruptive campus demonstrations) (Wayne State University, Detroit)

CACWV . . . . . . Committee to Aid Cold War Veterans

COMAP . . . . . Committee for the Alliance for Progress (Commerce Department)

CALROSA . . . . Committee on American Library Resources on South Asia (Later, CALROSEA)

CALROSEA . . . Committee on American Library Resources on Southeast Asia (Formerly, CALROSA)

CASL . . . . . . Committee of American Steamship Lines

CARN . . . . . . Committee for Amnesty and National Recognition (Cameroon)

COAHR . . . . . Committee on Appeal for Human Rights

ABSSOP . . . . Committee for the Application of the Behavioral Sciences to the Strategies of Peace

CAPE . . . . . . Committee on Assessing the Progress of Education

CAPAV . . . . . . Committee on Atmospheric Problems of Aerospace Vehicles (American Meteorological Society)

CAG . . . . Committee on Autonomous Groups

COCEEE . . . . . Committee on Captured Enemy Electronics Equipment

CCS . . . . Committee for Collective Security

COB . . . . Committee of Combined Boards

COC . . . . Committee of Concern

CCPA . . . . . . Committee for Congested Production Areas

CCG . . . . Committee for Constitutional Government

CETEX . . . . . . Committee on Contamination of Extra-Terrestrial Exploration (NASA)

CCESO . . . . . . Committee on Contributions for Elective State Officials

CCIZT . . . . . . Committee of Control of the International Zone of Tangier

CCA . . . . Committee for Conventional Armaments

CCLA . . . . . . Committee on Cooperation in Latin America (of The National Council of Churches of Christ in the USA)

CCSAU . . . . . . Committee for Corporate Support of American Universities

CCH . . . . Committee on Cosmic Humanism

CODATA . . . . Committee on Data for Science and Technology (National Bureau of Standards)

CODCAVE . . . . Committee on Decentralization of Controls after V-E Day (War Production Board)

CDAAA . . . . . . Committee to Defend America by Aiding the Allies (Active prior to US entry into World War II)

CDANC . . . . . Committee for the Development of Art in Negro Colleges

CDRT . . . . . . Committee on Diagnostic Reading Tests

CEAL . . . . . . Committee on East Asian Libraries

CED . . . . Committee for Economic Development

CES . . . . Committee on Economic Security (Terminated as formal agency, 1936, but continued informally for some time thereafter)

CENTAUM . . . . Committee on Education Needs for Teen-Age Unwed Mothers

CEMI . . . . . . Committee on Emergency Medical Identification

CEI . . . . Committee for Environmental Information

CEQ . . . . Committee on Environmental Quality (of Federal Council on Science and Technology)

CEAC . . . . . . Committee on European Airspace Coordination (NATO)

CEEC . . . . . . Committee for European Economic Cooperation (Marshall Plan) (Post-World War II)

CEFSR . . . . . . Committee for Evaluating the Feasibility of Space Rocketry (Navy Bureau of Aeronautics) (Obsolete)

COESA . . . . . . Committee on Extension to the Standard Atmosphere

CFEP . . . . . . Committee on Fair Employment Practices (World War II)

CFE . . . . Committee for a Free Estonia

CFGM . . . . . . Committee for a Free Gold Market

CFL . . . . Committee for a Free Latvia

CFL . . . . Committee for a Free Lithuania

CFAW . . . . . . Committee of French American Wives

CFSS . . . . . . Committee of French Speaking Societies

CFR . . . . Committee on Friendly Relations Among Foreign Students

CHIDE . . . . . . Committee to Halt Indoctrination and Demoralization in Education (Group opposing sex education in schools)

CHABA . . . . . Committee on Hearing, Bio-Acoustics, and Biomechanics (Military)

COINS . . . . . . Committee on Improvement of National Statistics (Inter-American)

CIPA . . . . Committee for Independent Political Action

CID . . . . Committee for Industrial Development (UN)

CIO . . . . Committee of Industrial Organization

COIN . . . . . . Committee on Information Needs

CIC . . . . Committee on Institutional Cooperation (11 midwestern universities) (Language Institute)

CITEL . . . . . . Committee for the Inter-American Telecommunications

CICIREPATO . . . Committee for International Co-operation in Information Retrieval Among Examining Patent Offices

CIEG . . . . Committee for International Economic Growth

CIEP . . . . Committee on International Exchange of Persons
CIMC . . . . . . Committee for International Municipal Cooperation
CIPASH . . . . . . Committee for International Program in Atmospheric Sciences and Hydrology (UN)
CIRA . . . . . . Committee on International Reference Atmosphere
CINWMD . . . . Committee on Interpretation of the Nation-Wide Marine Definition
CICP . . . . Committee to Investigate Copyright Problems
CIH . . . . Committee for Italic Handwriting (Defunct)
CLSF . . . . Committee for Latvian Song Festival in USA
CLWP . . . . . . Committee for Liquidation of German War Potential (Allied German Occupation Forces)
CMU/WA . . . . Committee on Man's Underwater Activities
COMOI . . . . . Committee on Manpower Opportunities in Israel
CMR . . . . Committee on Medical Research (Subdivision of OSRD) (World War II)
CMC . . . . . . Committee for Modern Courts
CNLDP . . . . . Committee for National Land Development Policy
CONLIS . . . . . Committee on National Library Information Systems
CONSCIENCE . . Committee on National Student Citizenship in Every National Case of Emergency
CNTP . . . . . . Committee for a National Trade Policy
CNVA . . . . . . Committee for Nonviolent Action
CNI . . . . Committee for Nuclear Information (Later, Committee for Environmental Information)
COPL . . . . . . Committee for Oil Pipe Lines
COSHD . . . . . Committee for Oil Shale Development
COMPAS . . . . . Committee on Physics & Society (of American Institute of Physics)
CPR . . . . Committee on Polar Research (US)
COPE . . . . . . Committee on Political Education (AFL-CIO)
CPP . . . . Committee on Political Parties
COPSS . . . . . . Committee of Presidents of Statistical Societies
CPVR . . . . . . Committee on Procedure and Valuation of Reparations (Allied German Occupation Forces)
COMPACT . . . . Committee to Promote Action (Poverty program)
CPSAH . . . . . . Committee to Promote the Study of Austrian History
CPURMC . . . . Committee to Promote Uniformity in the Regulation of Motor Carriers
CPCT . . . . Committee to Protect our Children's Teeth
COPEP . . . . . . Committee on Public Engineering Policy (National Academy of Engineering)
CPEP . . . . Committee on Public Engineering Policy
CRWM . . . . . Committee on Radioactive Waste Management
CRD . . . . Committee on Reciprocal Deliveries (Allied German Occupation Forces)
CRI . . . . Committee for Reciprocity Information (A federal government body)
CRAR . . . . . . Committee for the Recovery of Archaeological Remains
CRCP . . . . . . Committee of Religious Concern for Peace
CRIA . . . . Committee to Rescue Italian Art
CORD . . . . . . Committee on Research in Dance
CORE . . . . . . Committee on Research Evaluation (US)
CORMOSEA . . Committee on Research Materials on Southeast Asia
COR . . . . Committee of Responsibility
CROSS . . . . . . Committee to Retain Our Segregated Schools (Group in Arkansas, organized to oppose STOP)
CROCP . . . . . . Committee for Review of our China Policy
CRICO . . . . . . Committee for the Revision of the Criminal Code (Allied German Occupation Forces)
CSB . . . . Committee for Safe Bicycling
CSCNC . . . . . Committee on Scholarly Communications with Mainland China
COSPUP . . . . . Committee on Science and Public Policy (National Academy of Sciences)
COSI . . . . Committee on Scientific Information (Federal Council for Science and Technology)
SATCOM . . . . . Committee on Scientific and Technical Communication
COSATI . . . . . Committee of Scientific and Technical Information (Federal Council for Science and Technology)
COSMEP . . . . Committee of Small Magazine Editors and Publishers
COSPEAR . . . . Committee on Space Programs for Earth Observation (National Academy of Sciences)
CIRA . . . . COSPAR (Committee on Space Programs for Earth Observation) International Reference Atmosphere
COSPAR . . . . . Committee on Space Research (of the International Council of Scientific Unions)
COSEP . . . . . . Committee on Special Educational Projects (Cornell University)
COSRIMS . . . . Committee on Support of Research in the Mathematical Sciences (National Academy of Sciences)
CSS . . . . Committee on State Sovereignty
CTA . . . . Committee on Thrombolytic Agents
CTU . . . . Committee for Time Uniformity
CUPM . . . . . . Committee on the Undergraduate Program in Mathematics (Mathematical Association of America)
CUW . . . . . . Committee on Undersea Warfare
UCR . . . . Committee on Uniform Crime Records
CUSIP . . . . . . Committee on Uniform Security Identification Procedures (Banking)
CUTAS . . . . . . Committee on Uniform Traffic Accident Statistics

CVS . . . . Committee on Valuation of Securities
CVMP . . . . . . Committee on Veterans Medical Problems (US)
CWDWD . . . . Committee for World Development and World Disarmament
WFC . . . . Committee on the World Food Crisis
LIT-LIT . . . . . . Committee on World Literacy and Christian Literature
CCM . . . . Commodity Class Manager
CCG . . . . Commodity Coordination Groups
CCC . . . . Commodity Credit Corporation (Department of Agriculture)
CEA . . . . Commodity Exchange Authority (Department of Agriculture)
CEC . . . . Commodity Exchange Commission
CR . . . . Commodity Rate
CSS . . . . Commodity Stabilization Service (Name changed to Agricultural Stabilization and Conservation Service, 1961)
COMAT . . . . . Commodore Air Train (Navy)
COH . . . . Commodore Hotel, Inc. (NYSE symbol)
COMNAS (EA) . . Commodore, Naval Air Stations, East Africa (British)
COMBRAX . . . . Commodore, Royal Canadian Navy Barracks at (place)
COM(D)WA . . . Commodore, (Destroyers) Western Approaches (British)
CAP . . . . Common Agricultural Policy (Common Market)
CAMAR . . . . . . Common Aperture Multifunction Array RADAR
CAWS . . . . . . Common Aviation Weather Subsystem
CB . . . . Common Battery (Electronics)
CB . . . . Common Battery (Technical drawings)
CBD . . . . Common Bile Duct (Medicine)
COBOL . . . . . Common Business-Oriented Language (Data processing)
CC . . . . Common Carrier
CCB . . . . Common Carrier Bureau (of FCC)
CCF . . . . Common Cold Foundation
CCSA . . . . . . Common Control Switching Arrangement (AT & T)
CC . . . . Common Council(man)
CD . . . . Common Digitizer (FAA)
CE . . . . Common Era
CET . . . . Common External Tariff (for EEC countries)
CXT . . . . Common External Tariff (Common Market)
CIC . . . . Common-Impression Cylinder
CIP . . . . Common Input Processor
CIR . . . . Common IFR (Instrument Flight Rules) Room (Aviation)
CIO . . . . Common Item Order
CL . . . . Common Law
CML . . . . Common Machine Language (Data processing)
CMS . . . . Common Manpower Standards
C . . . . Common Meter
CM . . . . Common Meter (Music)
CMD . . . . Common Meter Double (Music)
CME . . . . Common Mode Error
CMIR . . . . . . Common Mode Input Resistance
CMR . . . . Common Mode Rejection
CMRR . . . . . . Common Mode Rejection Ratio
CMS . . . . Common Mode Signal
CMV . . . . Common Mode Voltage
CMVR . . . . . . Common Mode Voltage Range
CPM . . . . Common Particular Metre (Music)
CP . . . . Common Pleas (Legal)
CPD . . . . Common Pleas Division
CPSG . . . . . . Common Power Supply Group
CP . . . . Common Prayer
CPL . . . . Common Pulse Line
CS . . . . Common Slavic (Language)
CSNF . . . . . . Common Source Noise Figure
CSPG . . . . . . Common Source Power Gain
CSSN . . . . . . Common Source Spot Noise
CSSNF . . . . . . Common Source Spot Noise Figure
CS . . . . Common Steel (Projectile)
CTF . . . . Common Test Facility
C . . . . Common Time
CUDAT . . . . . Common User Data Terminal (Military)
CUG . . . . Common-User Group (SAGE)
CURTS . . . . . . Common User Radio Transmission Sounding System
CV . . . . Common Version (Bible)
CVS . . . . Common Video System
CAB . . . . Commonwealth Agricultural Bureaux
CAC . . . . Commonwealth Aircraft Corporation, Ltd. (Australia)
CDFC . . . . . . Commonwealth Development Finance Company Limited (Joint government and private agency in London established to aid businesses elsewhere in British Commonwealth)
CEC . . . . Commonwealth Economic Committee
CEC . . . . Commonwealth Edison Company (Chicago)
CWE . . . . Commonwealth Edison Company (NYSE symbol)
CELC . . . . . . Commonwealth Education Liaison Committee
CIE . . . . Commonwealth Institute of Entomology (British)
CN . . . . Commonwealth Nation

CPA .... Commonwealth Preference Area
CSC .... Commonwealth Scientific Committee
CSIRO ...... Commonwealth Scientific and Industrial Research Organisation (British Commonwealth)
CSC .... Commonwealth Service Corps
CWC .... Commonwealth of World Citizens
CEE .... Communaute Economique Europeenne
CEGROB ..... Communaute Europeenne des Associations du Commerce de Gros de Biere des Pays Membres de la CEE (European Community of Associations of the Wholesale Beer Trade of the EEC)
CECA ...... Communaute Europeenne du Charbon et de l'Acier
CECC ...... Communaute Europeenne de Credit Communal
CED .... Communaute Europeenne de Defense (European Defense Community)
CEEA ...... Communaute Europeenne de l'Energie Atomique
CEDESE ..... Communaute Europeenne des Etudiants en Sciences Economiques
CEOP ...... Communaute Europeenne des Organisations de Publicitaires
CIAL ...... Communaute Internationale des Associations de la Librairie
CIB .... Communaute Internationale Baha'ie
CBMC ...... Communaute de Travail des Brasseurs du Marche Commun (Working Committee of Common Market Brewers)
CD .... Communicable Disease (or a patient with such a disease) (Medicine)
CDC .... Communicable Disease Center (Atlanta) (Public Health Service)
CAPE ...... Communication Automatic Processing Equipment
CC .... Communication Center
CCF .... Communication Central Facility (Air Force)
CCU .... Communication Control Unit
COMCM .... Communication Countermeasures
C & DSS..... Communication and Data Subsystem
CEI .... Communication Electronic Instructions
CEE .... Communication Electronics Element (Army)
COMMFACMEDME .. Communication Facilities Mediterranean and Middle East
CIN .... Communication Identification Navigation
CI .... Communication Information
CIRES ...... Communication Instructions for Reporting Enemy Sightings (Navy)
CIS .... Communication and Instrumentation System
CLA .... Communication Line Adapters
CLAT ...... Communication Line Adapters for Teletype
COLT ...... Communication Line Terminator
CLSS ...... Communication Link Subsystem
CMA .... Communication Managers Association
CNI .... Communication, Navigation, and Identification
CP .... Communication Personnel (Marine Corps)
CRACC ..... Communication and RADAR Assignment Coordinating Committee
CRPM ...... Communication Registered Publication Memoranda
CSRC ...... Communication Science Research Center (Battelle Memorial Institute)
COMMSECACT. Communication Security Activity
CSPM ...... Communication Security Publication Memorandum (Army)
CSDS ...... Communication Signal Distribution System
CASSIS ...... Communication and Social Science Information Service (Canadian research collection network)
CSO .... Communication Standing Order
CS .... Communication Station
COMMSUPACT. Communication Supplementary Activity
COMMSUPDET . Communication Supplementary Detachment
CT .... Communication Trench (Military)
CVD .... Communication Valve Development (British)
CWO .... Communication Watch Officer
CWA .... Communication Workers Alliance (Philippines)
COMMCEN ... Communications Center
CC .... Communications Central (Military)
CCL .... Communications Circular Letter (Navy)
CCC .... Communications Control Console
CCP .... Communications Control Panel
CCT .... Communications Control Team (Military)
C & D ..... Communications and Data
CADPO...... Communications and Data Processing Operation
CDP .... Communications Data Processor (Electronics)
CDS .... Communications and Data Subsystems
CDCU ...... Communications Digital Control Unit
CDO .... Communications Duty Officer
CE .... Communications-Electronics
C-E .... Communications-Electronics
COMMEL .... Communications Electronics
CEC .... Communications & Electronics Command
CEC .... Communications-Electronics Committee
CECMRL ..... Communications-Electronics Consolidated Mobilization Reserve List
CECS ...... Communications-Electronics Coordinating Section (NATO)
CEDPO...... Communications-Electronics Doctrinal Projects Office (Air Force)
CED .... Communications-Electronics Doctrine (Series of Air Force manuals)
CEIP .... Communications-Electronics Implementation Plan (For major air command requirements within the Communications-Electronics area) (Air Force)

CEIPA....... Communications-Electronics Implementation Plan Amendment
CECMRL ..... Communications-Electronics Materiel Reserve List (List of requirements for Communications-Electronics equipment in support of wartime plans)
CEM....... Communications-Electronics-Meteorological
CEMPAC..... Communications-Electronics-Meteorology Program Aggregate Code
CEO....... Communications-Electronics Officer (Air Force)
CESAC..... Communications-Electronics Scheme Accounting and Control (Air Force)
CESAC..... Communications-Electronics Special Account Code (Air Force)
CEIA ...... Communications Engineering and Installation Agency
CEI .... Communications Engineering and Installation Department (Army)
CE .... Communications Equipment
CIM....... Communications Improvement Memorandum (Military)
COMINST.... Communications Instructions (Navy)
CIMS ..... Communications Instructions for Merchant Ships (Navy)
CIRVIS ..... Communications Instructions for Reporting Visual (or Vital) Intelligence Sightings (Military)
COMINT..... Communications Intelligence (Air Force)
COMJAM.... Communications Jamming (Military)
CJO........ Communications Jamming Operator
CLAS ..... Communications Link Analyzer System
CMTCU..... Communications Message Traffic Control Unit (Air Force)
CMC ...... Communications Mode Control
CMR....... Communications Monitoring Report
CMR....... Communications Moon Relay (System) (NASA)
CM .... Communications Multiplexer
COMNEED ... Communications Need
COMNET .... Communications Network (Military)
CNIPTG ..... Communications, Networks and Information Processing Theory Group (MIT)
CO .... Communications Officer (Navy)
COMO...... Communications Officer
COI .... Communications Operations Instructions (Air Force)
COR ...... Communications Operations Report (Air Force)
COPE ..... Communications Oriented Processing Equipment
COORS..... Communications Outage Restoral Section (ADC)
COMPLAN ... Communications Plan
COMPOOL ... Communications Pool
CP .... Communications Processor
CRC ...... Communications Relay Center (Air Force)
CRI .... Communications Research Institute
CSAR ..... Communications Satellite Advanced Research (AFSC)
COMSAT .... Communications Satellite Corporation (Assignee of operational and developmental responsibilities for Telstar and other international communications space devices)
CSC....... Communications Satellite Corporation
CSPO...... Communications Satellite Project Office
COMSEC .... Communications Security (Air Force)
CSEP....... Communications Security Education Program
CSP .... Communications Security Publication
CRIO ...... COMSEC (Communications Security) Regional Issuing Office (Military)
CSA ...... Communications Service Authorization
COMSOC .... Communications Spacecraft Operation Center
COMSQN.... Communications Squadron (Marine Corps)
CSC....... Communications Sub Committee (Allied German Occupation Forces)
CSS .... Communications Subsystem
CSE .... Communications Support Element (Military)
CST .... Communications Surveillance Transistor
CSC....... Communications Switchboard Console
CS .... Communications System
CSC....... Communications Systems Center
CTOC ..... Communications Technical Operations Center (Air Force)
CT .... Communications Technician
CMTM ..... Communications and Telemetry
CT .... Communications Terminal
CTS .... Communications and Tracking Subsystems
CATS ..... Communications and Tracking System
CUE ...... Communications Unit Executor
CURTS ..... Communications User Radio Transmission Sounding (Navy)
CWA ..... Communications Workers of America
COMZ ..... Communications Zone
CZ .... Communications Zone
COZI ..... Communications Zone Indicator (Air Force)
CTA .... Communiquer a Toutes Adresses (To be circulated to all addresses)
COMINFORM . Communist Information
COMINTERN .. Communist International
CP .... Communist Party
CP (b) ..... Communist Party (Bolsheviks)
CPI .... Communist Party of India
CPL .... Communist Party of Lesotho (Basutoland)
CPP .... Communist Party of the Philippines
CPP/ML ..... Communist Party of the Philippines/Marxist-Leninist
CPSA ...... Communist Party of South Africa

CPSU . . . . Communist Party of the Soviet Union
CPUSA . . . . . . Communist Party, United States of America
COMSYMP . . . Communist Sympathizer
KOMSOMOL . . Communist Youth League (From the Russian)
CAA . . . . Community Action Agencies (Department of Labor)
CAP . . . . Community Action Program
CAP . . . . Community Alert Patrol
CAR . . . . Community Antenna Relay (Service) (FCC)
CARS . . . . . . Community Antenna Relay Service
CATV . . . . . . Community Antenna Television (FCC)
CACI . . . . . . Community Arts Councils, Inc.
CAX . . . . Community Automatic Exchange (Telephone)
CBA . . . . Community Broadcasters Association
CDA . . . . Community Development Agency
CDF . . . . Community Development Foundation
CDO . . . . Community Dial Office
CER . . . . Community Educational Resources
CFA . . . . Community Facilities Administration (of HHFA)
CGS . . . . Community Guidance Service
CHA . . . . Community Health Association
CHILD . . . . . . Community Helps in Life Development
CLUG . . . . . . Community Land Use Game (Urban-planning game)
CMHCA . . . . . Community Mental Health Centers Act
CRW . . . . Community Radio Watch
CRAC . . . . . . Community Relations Advisory Council (Military)
CRS . . . . Community Relations Service (Department of Justice)
CRP . . . . Community Renewal Program
CRA . . . . Community Research Associates
CRWA . . . . . . Community Resources Workshop Association
CR . . . . Community of the Resurrection
CS . . . . Community Service
CSA . . . . Community Service Activities (AFL-CIO)
CSF . . . . Community Systems Foundation
CWS . . . . Community War Services (of FSA) (World War II)
CODES . . . . . Commutating Detection System
CRQ . . . . Commutation of Rations and Quarters (Military)
CPA . . . . Commutative Principle for Addition (New math)
CPM . . . . Commutative Principle for Multiplication (New math)
COMRAT . . . . . Commuted Ration (Military)
CARD . . . . . . Compact Automatic Retrieval Device (or Display) (Data processing)
COG . . . . Compact Orbital Gears, Ltd.
CIGA . . . . . . Compagnia Italiana del Grande Alberghi (Italian hotel chain)
CTIP . . . . Compagnia Tecnica Industrie Petroli (Italy)
CAMECA . . . . . Compagnie d'Applications Mecaniques a l'Electronique au Cinema et a
　　　　　　　　l'Atomistique (French company which invented Scopitone, a coin-
　　　　　　　　operated machine which projects musical movies in places of
　　　　　　　　entertainment)
CARA . . . . . . Compagnie d'Applications et de Recherches Atomiques (France)
CARATOM . . . . Compagnie d'Applications et de Recherches Atomiques (France)
CCCI . . . . Compagnie du Congo pour le Commerce et l'Industrie (Congo Commerce
　　　　　　　　and Industry Company)
CAE . . . . Compagnie Europeenne d'Automatisme (Became part of Compagnie
　　　　　　　　Internationale d'Informatique)
CEJ . . . . Compagnie Europeenne de la Jeunesse
COFINATOME . . Compagnie de Financement de l'Industrie Atomique (France)
CFAO . . . . . . Compagnie Francaise de l'Afrique Occidentale
COFIMPAC . . . Compagnie Francaise Industrielle et Miniere du Pacifique (French
　　　　　　　　commercial firm)
CFMU . . . . . . Compagnie Francaise des Minerais d'Uranium
CFP . . . . Compagnie Francaise des Petroles (France)
CFR . . . . Compagnie Francaise de Raffinage
CFTH . . . . . . Compagnie Francaise Thomson Houston
CGE . . . . Compagnie Generale d'Electricite
CICAF . . . . . . Compagnie Industrielle de Combustibles Atomiques Frittes (France)
CII . . . . Compagnie Internationale d'Informatique (Formed by merger of SEA
　　　　　　　　and CAE)
COMEX . . . . . Compagnie Maritime d' Expertise
COMILOG . . . . Compagnie Miniere de l'Ogooue (Ogooue Mining Company) (Gabon)
CSF . . . . Compagnie de Telegraphie Sans Fil (Electronics concern) (France)
CRS . . . . Compagnies Republicaines de Securite (France)
COMASE . . . . . Companhia Agricola de Sergipe (State of Sergipe, Brazil)
CSN . . . . Companhia Siderurgica Nacional (Steel producer) (Brazil)
CTB . . . . Companhia Telefonica Brasiliera (A telecommunications company) (Brazil)
CAUSA . . . . . . Compania Aeronautics Uruguaya, SA
CDA . . . . Compania Dominicana de Aviacion, SA (Dominican Republic airline)
CINTA . . . . . . Compania Nacional de Turismo Aereo (Chilean airline)
COPA . . . . . . Compania Panamena de Aviacion, SA
CPV . . . . Compania Peruana de Vapores (Peruvian Line)
CSAV . . . . . . Compania Sud America de Vapores (Chilean Line)
CTNE . . . . . . Compania Telefonica Nacionale de Espana
C . . . . Companion

CB . . . . Companion of the Bath (British)
CDS . . . . Companion of the Distinguished Service Order
CD . . . . Companion Dog (Degree of obedience training)
CDX . . . . Companion Dog, Excellent (Degree of obedience training)
CH . . . . Companion of Honour (British)
CC . . . . Companion of the Order of Canada
CIE . . . . Companion of the Order of the Indian Empire (British)
CMG . . . . Companion of the Order of St. Michael and St. George (British)
CSI . . . . Companion of the Star of India
CFA . . . . Companions of the Forest of America
CC . . . . Company Commander
CDP . . . . Company Distributing Point (Army)
CF . . . . Company First (A mealtime whimsicality for use when guests are
　　　　　　　　present)
CMCH . . . . . . Company of Military Collectors & Historians
CMH . . . . Company of Military Historians
COAM . . . . . . Company-Owned and Maintained
CQMS . . . . . . Company Quartermaster-Sergeant
CS . . . . Company of the Savior (Roman Catholic women's religious order)
CSM . . . . Company Sergeant-Major
CSMI . . . . Company Sergeant-Major Instructor (British Army)
CSI . . . . Company Source Inspection
CSFI . . . . Company Standard Form Instruction
CSP . . . . Company Standard Practice
CTDC . . . . . . Company Technical Document Center
CR . . . . Company's Risk (Insurance)
CES . . . . Comparative Education Society
CLA . . . . Comparative Literature Association
CSL . . . . Comparative Systems Laboratory (Case-Western Reserve University)
CRAFT . . . . . . Comparing Reading Approaches in First Grade Teaching
CORAL . . . . . Comparison of Recognition Algorithms (Post Office Department)
C & A . . . . . . Compartment and Access (Technical drawings)
C . . . . Compass
CB . . . . Compass Bearing (Navigation)
CC . . . . Compass Course
CE . . . . Compass Error (Navigation)
CH . . . . Compass Heading
COMLO . . . . . Compass Locator
CN . . . . Compass North
COA . . . . Compass Operation Alarm
CTS . . . . Compass Tilt Signal
CHAMPION . . Compatible Hardware and Milestone Program for Integrating
　　　　　　　　Organizational Needs (AFSC)
CLS . . . . Compatible LASER System
CTC . . . . Compatibility Test Capsule
CTU . . . . Compatibility Test Unit
COMPACT . . . . Compatible Algebraic Compiler and Translator
COBRA . . . . . Compatible on Board Ranging
CDS . . . . Compatible Duplex System
CSSB . . . . . . Compatible Single Sideband
CTSS . . . . . . Compatible Time-Sharing System (Data processing)
CAD . . . . Compensated Avalanche Diode
CA . . . . Compensation Act (Forms)
CRHS . . . . . . Competent Reliability History Survey (Navy)
CR . . . . Competing Risks
CWIC . . . . . . Competition with Industrial Cooperation
CORE . . . . . . Competitive Operational Readiness Evaluation (Air Force)
CSE . . . . Competitive Study Engineer
COLINGO . . . . Compile On-Line and Go (Data processing)
COMPASS . . . . Compiler-Assembler
CAGE . . . . . . Compiler and Assembler by General Electric
CLEAR . . . . . . Compiler, Executive Program, Assembler Routines
CLIP . . . . Compiler Language for Information Processing
COLASL . . . . . Compiler, Los Alamos Scientific Laboratories
CTI . . . . Complaint Type Investigation (Army)
CF . . . . Complement Fixation (Physiology)
CFT . . . . Complement-Fixation Test
CRN . . . . Complement Requiring Neutralizing
COMTECHREP . . Complementary Technical Report (Military)
CTL . . . . Complementary Transistor Logic (Data processing)
CAF . . . . Complete Assembly for Ferry (Air Force)
CAS . . . . Complete Assembly for Strike
CBI . . . . Complete Background Investigation
CBC . . . . Complete Blood Count (Medicine)
CCRU . . . . . . Complete Crew
CER . . . . Complete Engineering Release
COE . . . . Complete Operating Equipment
COIN . . . . . . Complete Operating Information (Data processing)
CPF . . . . Complete Power Failure (Aviation)
CRD . . . . Complete Reaction of Degeneration (Physiology)
CR . . . . Complete Round (Technical drawings)

CRAMSHIP.... Complete Round Ammunition Shipment
CRC........ Complete Round Chart
CUMMFU .... Complete Utter Monumental Military Foul Up
CODIS ...... Completed Discharge
COLOD ..... Completed Loading (Navy)
COPT....... Completed Procedure Turn (Aviation)
CAOS...... Completely Automatic Operational System
CD........ Completely Denatured
CKD........ Completely Knocked Down (i.e., disassembled, as a toy or piece of furniture which must be assembled before use)
CAVD...... Completion, Arithmetic, Vocabulary, Directions (Psychology)
CBOC...... Completion of Bed Occupancy Care (VA)
CMA .... Complex Modulus Apparatus
CRI .... Complex Refraction Index
CSO........ Complex Safety Officer (Air Force)
CUR........ Complex Utility Routine
CWS....... Complex Wiring System
CCS........ Component Control Section
CID .... Component Identification
CIP........ Component Improvement Program
COSMON .... Component Open/Short Monitor
CP .... Component Parts
CPR .... Component Pilot Rework
CQA .... Component Quality Assurance
CQAP....... Component Quality Assurance Program
CRP .... Component Reliability Prediction
CTS .... Component Test Set
CLEAR ..... Components Life Evaluation and Reliability
CML....... Components & Materials Laboratory
CO .... Components Only
CIP........ Compool Interpreter Program
CLUMP ..... Compool Look-Up Memory Print
CAAA ...... Composers, Authors and Artists of America
CAG .... Composers-Authors Guild
CAPAC..... Composers, Authors and Publishers Association of Canada
CCS........ Composers Cooperative Society
CLGA....... Composers and Lyricists Guild of America
CAP........ Composers' Autograph Publications (An organization)
CAPRA ..... Composers' Autograph Publications Records Association
CASF ...... Composite Air Strike Force (Air Force)
VC .... Composite Aircraft Squadron (Navy symbol)
CAM .... Composite Army-Marine
CLASP...... Composite Launch & Spacecraft Program
COMEINDORS . Composite Mechanized Information and Document Retrieval System
CMF....... Composite Medical Facility
CNR....... Composite Noise Rating
CRTV ...... Composite Reentry Test Vehicle
CRA .... Composite Research Aircraft
CSM....... Composite Signal Mixer
COMPORON .. Composite Squadron
CWF....... Composite Wave Filter
CC........ Compound Cathartic (Pills)
FC .... Compound Fracture (Medicine)
CAMPUS .... Comprehensive Analytical Method of Planning in the University Sphere (Cost simulation technique)
CDS .... Comprehensive Display System
CHP .... Comprehensive Health Planning (A requirement for HEW grants to local agencies)
CMS....... Comprehensive Medical Society
CSC .... Comprehensive Self-Check (Computer)
CTBS ...... Comprehensive Tests of Basic Skills
CAAR....... Compressed Air Accumulator Rocket
CAGI...... Compressed Air and Gas Institute
COCODE .... Compressed Coherency Detection (RADAR technique)
CGA .... Compressed Gas Association
CT .... Compressed Tablet (Pharmacy)
CTT .... Compressed Tablet Triturate (Pharmacy)
C......... Compression of Earth
CE .... Compression Engine
CI .... Compression Ignition (Engine)
CITE....... Compression Ignition Turbine Engine
CR .... Compression Ratio
COSAR...... Compression Scanning Array RADAR (Raytheon)
CLC....... Compressive Load Cell
CDP .... Compressor Discharge Pressure
CGCE....... Comptoir Guineen du Commerce Exterieur (Guinean Foreign Trade Agency)
CJC .... Compton Junior College (California)
CRE .... Compton Recoil Electron
CRP .... Compton Recoil Particle
CA .... Comptroller of the Army
COA .... Comptroller of the Army

C-DP .... Comptroller-Directors of Programs (Army)
CG........ Comptroller General
COMPGENDEC .. Comptroller General Decisions (Navy)
CGO .... Comptroller General Opinion
CGD....... Comptroller General's Decision
CAD........ Computation and Analysis Division (NASA)
CC........ Computation Center
CARP ...... Computed Air Release Point
CP........ Computed Point (Navigation)
COMAR .... Computer, Aerial Reconnaissance
CAAS...... Computer Aided Approach Spacing (Aviation)
CAD....... Computer-Aided Design
CAPM...... Computer-Aided Patient Management
CAG .... Computer Applications Group (Air Force)
CAMP...... Computer Applications of Military Problems (Computer users' group)
CAISIM ..... Computer-Assisted Industrial Simulation (Army)
CAI .... Computer-Assisted Instruction
CALOGSIM ... Computer-Assisted Logistics Simulation (Army)
CAMCOS .... Computer-Assisted Maintenance Planning and Control System
CAMSIM ..... Computer-Assisted Maintenance Simulation (Army)
CAMP...... Computer-Assisted Menu Planning
CAPERTSIM ... Computer-Assisted Program Evaluation Review-Technique Simulation (Army)
CATNIP .... Computer-Assisted Technique for Numerical Indexing Purposes
CAT .... Computer of Average Transients
COBESTCO ... Computer-Based Estimating Technique for Contractors
CBI .... Computer-Based Instruction (Education)
CLASS ..... Computer-Based Laboratory for Automated School System
CCS........ Computer Campaign Services (Data processing firm in field of politics)
CCC....... Computer Communications Console
CCSG...... Computer Components & System Group
CCC....... Computer Control Company
CCU....... Computer Control Unit
CACHE ..... Computer-Controlled Automated Cargo Handling Envelope
CCA....... Computer Corporation of America
CODED ..... Computer Design of Electronic Devices
CODIT ..... Computer Direct to Telegraph
CODIC ..... Computer-Directed Communications
CDSE ...... Computer-Driven Simulation Environment (FAA)
CIND ..... Computer Index of Neutron Data
CINDA ..... Computer Index of Neutron Data
CI .... Computer Indicator
COINS ...... Computer and Information Sciences
CITAB...... Computer Instruction and Training Assistance for the Blind
CIC .... Computer Instruments Corporation
CIU .... Computer Interface Unit
CLHU .... Computer Laboratory of Harvard University
CLASSMATE... Computer Language to Aid and Stimulate Scientific, Mathematical, and Technical Education
CLR .... Computer Language Recorder
CLT .... Computer Language Translator
CLO........ Computer Lock-On
CMI .... Computer Managed Instruction
CML .... Computer Managed Laboratory
CMT .... Computer Memory Tester
COMSOAL ... Computer Method of Sequencing Operations for Assembly Lines
CM .... Computer Module
CORD....... Computer with On-Line Remote Devices (National Bureau of Standards)
COED....... Computer-Operated (or -Oriented) Electronic Display
COMET...... Computer-Operated Management Evaluation Technique (AEC-Army)
COUNT ..... Computer-Operated Universal Test
COF........ Computer Operations Facility
COG .... Computer Operations Group
COP........ Computer Optimization Package (or Program)
COL .... Computer-Oriented Language (Data processing)
CORSAIR .... Computer-Oriented Reference System for Automatic Information Retrieval
CORE....... Computer-Oriented Reporting Efficiency
CORRAL .... Computer-Oriented Retrieval of Auto Larcenists
COM ...... Computer Output Microfilmer (or Microfilming)
CPRG ...... Computer Personnel Research Group
CAPAL ..... Computer and Photographic Assisted Learning
CPAWS ..... Computer-Planning and Aircraft-Weighing Scales
CPIP....... Computer Pneumatic Input Panel
CPS .... Computer Power Supply
CPC .... Computer Process Control
COMPAC .... Computer Program for Automatic Control
CPIP....... Computer Program Implementation Process
COMPACT.... Computer Programmed Automatic Checkout & Test System
CPS .... Computer Programming Service
CRAM...... Computer Reliability Analysis Method
CRC....... Computer Response Corporation
CROSSBOW ... Computer Retrieval of Organic Structures Based on Wiswesser

CROC....... Computer Review and Orientation Course
CSL .... Computer Sensitive Language (Data processing)
CSP .... Computer Simulation Program
COSMIC..... Computer Software Management & Information Center (NASA facility
             at University of Georgia)
COM-STAT ... Computer Stock Timing and Analysis Technique
CSST .... Computer System Science Training (IBM)
CSSEC ...... Computer Systems Support and Evaluation Command
CUE .... Computer Update Equipment
CUTS .... Computer Utilized Turning System (Warner & Swasey)
COMPACT.... Computerization of World Facts
CAPRI....... Computerized Advance Personnel Requirements Information (Navy)
CAP .... Computerized Assignment of Personnel (Military)
COMPENDEX.. Computerized Engineering Index (of Engineering Index, Inc.)
COFRS ...... Computerized Freight Remittance System (Pronounced "coffers")
CHART ...... Computerized Hierarchy and Relationship Table
COINS ...... Computerized Information System
CONRAD .... Computerized National Range Documentation
COLT ...... Computerized On-Line Testing
CROSS ...... Computerized Rearrangements of Special Subjects (or Subject Specialties)
CRAFT ...... Computerized Relative Allocation of Facilities Technique (IBM)
COM-STEP ... Computerized Spot Television Evaluation and Processing (Advertising)
CHUM ...... Computers and the Humanities (A periodical)
CW .... Computerworld (A publication)
CR .... Computing Reviews
COMIT ...... Computing System, Massachusetts Institute of Technology
CW .... Concealed Weapons
CFP .... Concentracion de Fuerzas Populares (Concentration of Popular Forces)
             (Political party in Ecuador)
CEP .... Concentrated Employment Program (Department of Labor) (Also known as
             CIEP)
CIEP........ Concentrated Impact Employment Program (Also known as CEP)
COV .... Concentrated Oil of Vitriol
CPEA .... Concentrated Phosphate Export Association
CL .... Concentration Length
CLO........ Concentric Line Oscillator
CSI .... Concentric Sequence Initiation (Aerospace)
CDP .... Concept Definition Proposal
CF .... Concept Formulation (DOD)
CONGA ..... Concept Game (A war game)
COPE .... Concepts of Postal Economics (A series of newsletters of Mail
             Advertising Corporation)
COS........ Conceptual Operational System
CQ .... Conceptual Quotient (Psychology)
CONSTRANS . Conceptual Thought Random Net Simulation
COPES ...... Conceptually Oriented Program in Elementary Science
CCIC .... Concerned Citizens Information Council (Group opposing sex education
             in schools)
CAG .... Concert Artist Guild
CCP .... Conciliation Commission for Palestine (of the UN)
COED....... Concise Oxford English Dictionary
CMT........ Concora Medium Test
CWIT .... Concordance Words in Titles (Indexing)
CHI .... Concordia Historical Institute
CMLA....... Concordia Mutual Life Association
CSC .... Concordia Seminary College (Missouri)
CTC .... Concordia Teachers College (Illinois, Nebraska)
CTS .... Concordia Theological Seminary (Missouri)
CTM........ Concordia Tract Mission
KA......... Concrete Arch (Bridges)
CIC .... Concrete Industries Council
CJI .... Concrete Joint Institute
CP .... Concrete Piercing
CPA .... Concrete Pipe Association
CRSI........ Concrete Reinforcing Steel Institute
CSB .... Concrete Splash Block (Technical drawings)
CP .... Concurrent Planometric (A discrimination task)
CSP .... Concurrent Spare Parts
CS .... Concurrent Stereometric (A discrimination task)
NAS .... Conde Nast Publications, Inc. (NYSE symbol)
C .... Condemned
COS....... Condemned or Suppressed
C .... Condemno (I Condemn) (Used by Romans in criminal trials)
CPS .... Condensation Pressure Spread
CONTRAIL ... Condensation Trail (in the air)
CRC....... Condition Reservation Code (Army)
CONFLEX .... Conditional Reflex
CRAM....... Conditional Relaxation Analysis Method
CRV .... Conditional Release Violator (FBI standardized term)
CAR .... Conditioned Avoidance Response
CER .... Conditioned Emotional Response (Psychology)

COR .... Conditioned Orientation Reflex
CR .... Conditioned Reflex (or Response)
CORA ...... Conditioned Reflex Analogue
CS .... Conditioned Stimulus (Psychology)
CKSO....... Condon, Kinzua & Southern R. R. (AAR code)
CMS........ Condor Missile System
COFT ...... Conduct of Fire Trainer
CP .... Conductive Plastic
CPP .... Conductive Plastic Potentiometer
C .... Conductor
COE....... Cone Mills Corporation (NYSE symbol)
CBL .... Conemaugh & Black Lick R. R. (AAR code)
CS .... Conestoga Society
CLASC ...... Confederacion Latinoamericana de Sindicalistas Cristianos (Latin
             American Federation of Christian Trade Unionists)
CNT........ Confederacion Nacional de Trabajo (National Confederation of Labor)
             (In Exile) (Spain)
COTAL ...... Confederacion de Organizaciones Turisticas de la America Latina
             (Confederation of Tourist Organizations of Latin America)
CTAL ...... Confederacion de Trabahadores de America Latina (Confederation of
             Latin-American Workers)
CTM........ Confederacion de Trabajadores de Mexico (Workers' Confederation
             of Mexico)
CTV .... Confederacion de Trabajadores de Venezuela (Venezuelan Workers'
             Confederation)
CA........ Confederate Army
CHC........ Confederate High Command
CMA .... Confederate Memorial Association
CMLS ...... Confederate Memorial Literary Society
CSA .... Confederate Stamp Alliance
CSA .... Confederate States of America
CSA .... Confederate States Army
CSN........ Confederate States Navy
CSS .... Confederate States Ship
CSS .... Confederated Spanish Societies
CUA....... Confederated Unions of America
CASL-CI ..... Confederation Africaine des Syndicats Libre de Cote d'Ivoire (African
             Confederation of Free Trade Unions of the Ivory Coast)
CASL-FO .... Confederation Africaine des Syndicats Libres-Force Ouvriere (African
             Confederation of Free Trade Unions - Workers' Force) (Cameroon,
             Chad, Gabon)
CASL-FO-RC .. Confederation Africaine des Syndicats Libres - Force Ouvriere -
             Republique Centafricaine (African Confederation of Free Trade Unions -
             Workers' Force - Central African Republic)
CASL-HV..... Confederation Africaine des Syndicats Libres de la Haute Volta (African
             Confederation of Free Trade Unions of the Upper Volta)
CATC ...... Confederation Africaine des Travailleurs Croyants (African Confederation
             of Believing Workers)
CATU ...... Confederation of Arab Trade Unions
CONAKAT ... Confederation des Associations du Katanga (Confederation of Katangan
             Associations)
CAT .... Confederation Autonome de Travail (Autonomous Confederation of Labor)
CBI .... Confederation of British Industry
CCSC ...... Confederation Camerounaise des Syndicats Chretiens (Confederation of
             Believing Workers of the Cameroon)
CCGEU...... Confederation of Central Government Employees' Unions (India)
CCSM....... Confederation Chretienne des Syndicats Malgaches (Christian
             Confederation of Malagasy Unions)
CCLU ...... Confederation of Citizens Labor Union (Philippines)
CCSL ...... Confederation Congolaise des Syndicats Libres (Congolese Confederation
             of Free Unions) (Brazzaville)
CEA .... Confederation des Educateurs Americains
CEA .... Confederation Europeenne de l'Agriculture
CEIBOIS ..... Confederation Europeenne des Industries du Bois
CFCA ...... Confederation Francaise de la Cooperation Agricole
CFSI....... Confederation Francaise des Syndicats Independents (French Confederation
             of Independent Unions)
CFTC ...... Confederation Francaise des Travailleurs Chretiens (French Confederation
             of Christian Workers)
CFTU ...... Confederation of Free Trade Unions (India)
CGAT....... Confederation Generale Africaine du Travail (African General
             Confederation of Labor)
CGA .... Confederation Generale de l'Agriculture (France)
CGC .... Confederation Generale des Cadres (General Confederation of Supervisory
             Employees) (France)
CGCT....... Confederation Generale Camerounaise du Travail (Cameroonian General
             Confederation of Workers)
CGKT....... Confederation Generale Kamerounaise du Travail (Cameroonese General
             Labor Confederation)
CGS........ Confederation Generale des Syndicats (General Confederation of Trade
             Unions) (Congo--Leopoldville)

CGSI . . . . Confederation Generale des Syndicats Independents (General Confederation of Independent Unions) (Algeria)
CGT. . . . . . . Confederation Generale du Travail (General Confederation of Labor)
CGT-FO . . . . . Confederation Generale du Travail-Force Ouvriere (General Confederation of Labor - Workers' Force)
CGT. . . . . . . Confederation Generale des Travailleurs (South Vietnam)
CGTA. . . . . . . Confederation Generale des Travailleurs Africains (General Confederation of African Workers) (Former French Equatorial Africa)
CIEC . . . . Confederation Interamericaine d'Education Catholique
CIA . . . . Confederation Internationale des Accordeonistes
CIAPG . . . . . . Confederation Internationale des Anciens Prisonniers de Guerre
CIDADEC . . . . Confederation Internationale des Associations d'Experts et de Conseils
CIBE. . . . . . . Confederation Internationale des Betteraviers Europeens
CICF. . . . . . . Confederation Internationale des Cadres Fonctionnaires
CICC . . . . Confederation Internationale des Charites Catholiques
CICAE . . . . . . Confederation Internationale des Cinemas d'Art et d'Essai
CIC . . . . Confederation Internationale de la Coiffure
CICA . . . . Confederation Internationale du Credit Agricole
CICP. . . . . . . Confederation Internationale du Credit Populaire
CIITC . . . . . . Confederation Internationale des Industries Techniques du Cinema
CITA . . . . . . Confederation Internationale des Ingenieurs et Techniciens de l'Agriculture
CILPE . . . . . . Confederation Internationale de Liaison Entre Producteurs d'Energie Electrique
CILC . . . . . . Confederation Internationale du Lin et du Chanvre
CINOA. . . . . . Confederation Internationale des Negociants en Oeuvres d'Art
CIRCCE. . . . . . Confederation Internationale de la Representation Commerciale de la Communaute Europeenne
CISF. . . . . . . Confederation Internationale des Sages Femmes
CISAC. . . . . . Confederation Internationale des Societes d'Auteurs et Compositeurs
CISPM . . . . . . Confederation Internationale des Societes Populaires de Musique
CISC . . . . Confederation Internationale des Syndicats Chretiens (International Federation of Christian Trade Unions)
CISL . . . . . . Confederation Internationale des Syndicats Libres
CITI . . . . Confederation Internationale des Travailleurs Intellectuels
CLP . . . . Confederation of Labor in the Philippines
CLL . . . . Confederation of Lebanese Labor
CLSC . . . . . . Confederation Luxembourgeoise des Syndicats Chretiens (Confederation of Christian Trade Unions of Luxembourg)
CMAS. . . . . . Confederation Mondiale des Activities Subaquatiques (World Underwater Federation)
CMOPE. . . . . . Confederation Mondiale des Organisations de la Profession Enseignante (World Confederation of Organizations of the Teaching Profession) (Also known as WCOTP)
CNTU. . . . . . Confederation of National Trade Unions
CNTG . . . . . . Confederation National des Travailleurs de Guinee (National Confederation of Guinean Workers)
CNIT . . . . . . Confederation Nationale Independante des Travailleurs (National Independent Confederation for Workers) (Belgium)
CNIM . . . . . . Confederation Nationale des Instituteurs Malagaches (National Confederation of Malagascan Teachers)
CNSM . . . . . . Confederation Nationale des Syndicats du Mali (National Confederation of Malian Unions)
CNT. . . . . . . Confederation Nationale du Travail (National Confederation of Labor) (France)
CNTC . . . . . . Confederation Nationale des Travailleurs Croyants de Senegal (National Confederation of Believing Workers of Senegal)
CSEU . . . . . . Confederation of Shipbuilding and Engineering Unions (British)
CSA. . . . . . . Confederation Syndicale Africaine (African Trade Union Confederation)
CSC. . . . . . . Confederation des Syndicats Chretiens de Belgique (Confederation of Christian Trade Unions) (Belgium)
CSCC . . . . . . Confederation des Syndicats Chretiens du Congo (Confederation of Christian Syndicates of the Congo) (Leopoldville)
CSLC . . . . . . Confederation des Syndicats Libres du Congo (Leopoldville) (Merger of FGTK, APIC, SNTC) (Congolese Free Trade Union Federation)
CSTV . . . . . . Confederation des Syndicats des Travailleurs du Viet-Nam (Confederation of Workers' Trade Unions of Viet-Nam) (South Vietnam)
CTMC . . . . . . Confederation des Travailleurs des Madagascar et Comores (Confederation of Workers of Madagascar and the Comores)
CUGCO . . . . . Confederation of Unions in Government Corporations and Offices (Philippines)
CVTC . . . . . . Confederation Vietnamienne du Travail Chretien (Vietnamese Confederation of Christian Labor) (South Vietnam)
CGIL . . . . . . Confederazione Generale Italiana del Lavoro (Italian General Confederation of Labor)
CGSL . . . . . . Confederazione Generale Somala dei Lavoratori (Somali General Confederation of Workers)
CISL. . . . . . . Confederazione Italiana Sindacati Lavoratori (Italian Confederation of Labor Unions)
CISL. . . . . . . Confederazione Italiana di Sindacati Liberi (Italian Confederation of Free Workers)

CISNAL . . . . . Confederazione Italiana Sindacati Nazionali Lavoratori (Italian Confederation of National Workers' Unions)
CSL . . . . Confederazione Somala dei Lavoratori (Somali Workers Confederation)
CAPP . . . . . . Conference of Actuaries in Public Practice
CACUCS . . . . . Conference of Administrators of College and University Counseling Services
CASBO . . . . . Conference of American Small Business Organizations
CACEED . . . . . Conference of Americans of Central and Eastern European Descent
CAA . . . . Conference of Asian Affairs
CONTAC . . . . Conference on the Atlantic Community
CBARC . . . . . Conference Board of Associated Research Councils
CBMS . . . . . . Conference Board of the Mathematical Sciences
CBS . . . . Conference on British Studies
CBE . . . . Conference of Business Economists
CCHS . . . . . . Conference of California Historical Societies
CCSN. . . . . . Conference of Catholic Schools of Nursing
CCJ . . . . Conference of Chief Justices
CCL . . . . Conference on Christianity and Literature
CCWAD. . . . . Conference of Church Workers Among the Deaf
CCCC . . . . . . Conference on College Composition and Communication
CCD . . . . Conference of the Committee on Disarmament (Formerly, ENDC)
CCRR . . . . . . Conference Committee for Refugee Rabbis
CODASYL . . . . Conference on Data Systems Languages (Data processing)
CDD . . . . Conference on Dual Distribution
CECL . . . . . . Conference of Eastern College Librarians
CEP . . . . Conference on Economic Progress
CELAM . . . . . Conference de l'Episcopat d'Amerique Latine, ou Conseil Episcopal Latino-Americain
CEPT . . . . . . Conference Europeenne des Administrations des Postes et des Telecommunications
CEEMA . . . . . Conference Europeenne des Experts Meteorologistes de l'Aeronautique
CEERA . . . . . Conference Europeenne des Experts Radiotelegraphistes de l'Aeronautique
CEH . . . . Conference Europeenne des Horaires des Trains de Voyageurs
CEMT . . . . . . Conference Europeenne des Ministres des Transports
CEPL . . . . . . Conference Europeenne des Pouvoirs Locaux
CETS . . . . . . Conference Europeenne des Telecommunications par Satellite
CEASD . . . . . Conference of Executives of American Schools for the Deaf
CFSEB. . . . . . Conference of Funeral Service Examining Boards of the United States
CGPM . . . . . . Conference Generale des Poids et Mesures (General Conference on Weights and Measures)
CHCW . . . . . Conference for Health Council Work
CISS. . . . . . . Conference Interamericaine de Securite Sociale
CIARA . . . . . Conference Internationale Administrative des Radiocommunications Aeronautiques
CIAO . . . . . . Conference Internationale des Africanistes de l'Ouest
CIGRE . . . . . Conference Internationale des Grands Reseaux Electriques
CIMAS . . . . . Conference Internationale de la Mutualite et des Assurances Sociales
CISS. . . . . . . Conference Internationale de Service Social
UT . . . . Conference Internationale pour l'Unite Technique des Chemins de Fer
CIS . . . . Conference of Internationally-Minded Schools
CJSPA . . . . . . Conference of Jesuit Student Personnel Administrators
CJMCAG . . . . Conference on Jewish Material Claims Against Germany
CJSS . . . . . . Conference on Jewish Social Studies
CLAH . . . . . . Conference on Latin American History
CMSW . . . . . Conference of Major Religious Superiors of Women's Institutes of the United States of America
CMSM . . . . . Conference of Major Superiors of Men of the USA
CME. . . . . . . Conference Mondiale de l'Energie
CMERA . . . . . Conference Mondiale des Experts Radiotelegraphistes de l'Aeronautique
CMPHE . . . . . Conference of Municipal Public Health Engineers
CMCC . . . . . . Conference of Mutual Casualty Companies
COASTA . . . . . Conference of Officers of Affiliated States and Territorial Associations
CONCP. . . . . . Conference des Organisations Nationales des Colonies Portugaises (Conference of National Organizations of Portuguese Colonies)
COWLR . . . . . Conference on Oriental-Western Literary Relations
CP . . . . Conference Paper
CPRH . . . . . . Conference on Peace Research in History
EUREMAIL . . . . Conference Permanente de l'Industrie Europeenne de Produits Emailles
CPNU. . . . . . Conference des Plenipotentiaires
CPOSMA . . . . Conference of Presidents and Officers of State Medical Associations
CPLA . . . . . . Conference for Progressive Labor Action
CPPA . . . . . . Conference for Progressive Political Action
CPHV . . . . . . Conference of Public Health Veterinarians
CPS . . . . Conference on the Public Service
CONREC . . . . Conference for Reconciliation, Restitution Fund
CR . . . . Conference Report
CRWAD. . . . . Conference of Research Workers in Animal Diseases
CSR . . . . Conference on Science and Religion
COSOS. . . . . . Conference on Self-Operating Systems (Data processing)
EUSEC . . . . . . Conference des Societes d'Ingenieurs de l'Europe Occidental et des Etats-Unis d'Amerique

CSPAA . . . . . . Conference de Solidarite des Pays Afro-Asiatiques
CSPHA . . . . . . Conference of State and Provincial Health Authorities of North America
CSPPHLD . . . . . Conference of State and Provincial Public Health Laboratory Directors
CSSE . . . . Conference of State Sanitary Engineers
CSS . . . . Conference of State Societies
CSTDPHE . . . . . Conference of State and Territorial Directors of Public Health Education
CSTE . . . . Conference of State and Territorial Epidemiologists
CSTHOPHS . . . Conference of State and Territorial Health Officers with Public Health Service
CSUCE . . . . . . Conference of State Utility Commission Engineers
CTU . . . . Conference on Transportation Unity
CURE . . . . . . Conference for Universal Reason and Ethics (Founded by motion picture actor Lew Ayres)
CURE . . . . . . Conference Upon Research and Education in World Government
CWOIH . . . . . Conference of World Organizations Interested in the Handicapped
COROIPAS . . . Conferences on Research on International Peace and Security (Founded International Peace Research Association)
C . . . . Confessor
CL . . . . Confidence Limits
CTL . . . . Confidence Training Launch
CTLI . . . . Confidence Training Launching Instrumentation
C . . . . Confidential
CAMSI . . . . . . Confidential Admiralty Merchant Shipping Instructions
CB . . . . Confidential Book (British Navy)
CB . . . . Confidential Bulletin
CONFBUL . . . . Confidential Bulletin (Navy)
CD . . . . Confidential Document (Navy)
CELACS . . . . . Confidential Employment Listing (American Chemical Society)
CFRD . . . . . . Confidential, Formerly Restricted Data
CONHYDROLANT . . Confidential Hydrographic Office (Later, Oceanographic Office) Reports (Atlantic) (Navy)
CM . . . . Confidential Memorandum
C-MHA . . . . . Confidential - Modified Handling Authorized (Military)
CONFMOD . . . Confidential - Modified Handling Authorized
CRD . . . . Confidential Restricted Data
CASWO . . . . . . Confidential and Secret Weekly Orders (Naval Air Stations)
CAN . . . . Configuration Accounting Number
CCB . . . . Configuration Control Board (DOD)
CIS . . . . Configuration Information System
CMD . . . . Configuration Management Division
CMO . . . . Configuration Management Office
CSA . . . . Configuration Status Accounting
CC . . . . Confined to Camp (Military)
C to P . . . . . . Confined to Post
CB . . . . Confinement to Barracks (A military punishment)
C of B . . . . . . Confirmation of Balance (Banking)
CEBUS . . . . . . Confirmed Exposure but Unconscious (Advertising)
CMMR . . . . . Confirmed and Made a Matter of Record (Army)
COTA . . . . . . Confirming Telephone (or message) Authority Of
CIQ . . . . Confoederatio Internationalis ad Qualitates Plantarum Edulium Perquirendas (International Association for Quality Research on Food Plants)
CWG . . . . . . Conformal Wire Grating
CBS . . . . Confraternity of the Blessed Sacrament
CCD . . . . Confraternity of Christian Doctrine
CCT . . . . Confrerie des Chevaliers du Tastevin
CRM . . . . Confusion Reflector Material
CHF . . . . Congestive Heart Failure (Medicine)
C . . . . Congius (Apothecaries' gallon)
CPRA . . . . . . Congo Protestant Relief Agency
COG . . . . Congoleum-Nairn, Inc. (NYSE symbol)
MIC . . . . Congregatio Clericorum Regularium Marianorum sub titulo Immaculatae Conceptionis Beatae Mariae Virginis (Marian Fathers) (Roman Catholic religious order)
FSCJ . . . . Congregatio Filiorum Sacratissimi Cordis Jesu (Sons of the Sacred Heart, or Verona Fathers) (Roman Catholic religious order)
FC . . . . Congregatio Fratrum Caritate (Brothers of Charity) (Roman Catholic religious order)
CFA . . . . Congregatio Fratrum Cellitarum seu Alexianorum (Alexian Brothers) (Roman Catholic religious order)
CFP . . . . Congregatio Fratrum Pauperum (Brothers of the Poor of St. Francis) (Roman Catholic religious order)
CFX . . . . Congregatio Fratrum Sancti Francisci Xaverii (Brothers of St. Francis Xavier) (Roman Catholic religious order)
CICM . . . . . . Congregatio Immaculati Cordis Mariae (Congregation of the Immaculate Heart of Mary) (Roman Catholic men's religious order)
CJ . . . . Congregatio Iosephitarum (Josephite Fathers) (Roman Catholic religious order)
CJM . . . . Congregatio Jesu et Mariae (Eudist Fathers)

CM . . . . Congregatio Mariae (Fathers of the Company of Mary)
CMF . . . . Congregatio Missionariorum Filiorum Immaculati Cordis Beatae Maria Virginia (Congregation of Missionary Sons of the Immaculate Heart of the Blessed Virgin Mary, or Claretian Fathers) (Roman Catholic religious order)
CMM . . . . . . Congregatio Missionariorum de Mariannhill (Congregation of Mariannhill Missionaries, or Mariannhill Fathers) (Roman Catholic religious order)
MSF . . . . Congregatio Missionariorum a Sancta Familia (Congregation of the Missionaries of the Holy Family) (Roman Catholic men's religious order)
CS . . . . Congregatio Missionariorum a Sancto Carlo (Congregation of the Missionary Fathers of St. Charles) (Formerly, PSSC) (Roman Catholic religious order)
CM . . . . Congregatio Missionis (Lazarists)
CM . . . . Congregatio Missionis Sancti Vicentii a Paulo (Congregation of the Mission, or Vincentians) (Roman Catholic men's religious order)
CP . . . . Congregatio Passionis (Passionists) (Roman Catholic men's religious order)
CPPS . . . . Congregatio Pretiosissimi Sanguinis (Society of the Most Precious Blood) (Roman Catholic men's religious order)
CRP . . . . Congregatio Reformatorium Præmonstratensium (Premonstratensians)
CR . . . . Congregatio Resurrectionis (Congregation of the Resurrection, or Resurrectionist Fathers) (Roman Catholic religious order)
SCJ . . . . Congregatio Sacerdotum a Corde Jesu (Congregation of the Priests of the Sacred Heart of Jesus) (Roman Catholic religious order)
CSSCC . . . . . . Congregatio Sacratissimorum Cordium (Missionaries of the Sacred Hearts of Jesus and Mary)
CCV . . . . Congregatio a Sacro Corde Jesu (Congregation of the Priests of the Sacred Heart)
SSCC . . . . Congregatio Sacrorum Cordium (Fathers of the Sacred Heart) (Roman Catholic religious order)
CSC . . . . Congregatio a Sancta Cruce (Fathers and Brothers of Holy Cross)
CSB . . . . Congregatio Sancti Basilii (Basilians)
CSJ . . . . Congregatio Sancti Joseph (Congregation of St. Joseph) (Roman Catholic men's religious order)
CSP . . . . Congregatio Sancti Pauli (Paulists) (Roman Catholic men's religious order)
CSSP . . . . Congregatio Sancti Spiritus (Fathers of the Holy Ghost)
CSSR . . . . Congregatio Sanctissimi Redemptoris (Redemptorists)
C . . . . Congregation
CR . . . . Congregation of Clerics Regular (Theatine Fathers) (Roman Catholic religious order)
CDS . . . . Congregation of the Divine Spirit (Roman Catholic women's religious order)
HPB . . . . Congregation of Handmaids of the Precious Blood (Roman Catholic religious order)
CHM . . . . . . Congregation of Humility of Mary (Roman Catholic women's religious order)
IWBS . . . . . . Congregation of the Incarnate Word and Blessed Sacrament (Roman Catholic women's religious order)
COB . . . . Congregation of Oblates of Bethany (Roman Catholic women's religious order)
CO . . . . Congregation of the Oratory (Oratorians) (Roman Catholic men's religious order)
CPM . . . . Congregation of Priests of Mercy (Fathers of Mercy) (Roman Catholic religious order)
CSS . . . . Congregation of the Sacred Stigmata (Stigmatine Fathers and Brothers) (Roman Catholic religious order)
CSB . . . . Congregation of St. Brigid (Roman Catholic women's religious order)
CSSF . . . . Congregation of the Sisters of St. Felix (Felician Sisters) (Roman Catholic religious order)
SSL . . . . Congregation of Sisters of St. Louis (Roman Catholic religious order)
CCHS . . . . . . Congregational Christian Historical Society
CCSC . . . . . . Congregational Christian Service Committee
CPS . . . . Congregational Publishing Society
CIM . . . . Congres International des Fabrications Mecaniques
CIMAC . . . . . Congres International des Machines a Combustion
CIOSTA . . . . . Congres International d'Organisation Scientifique du Travail dans l'Agriculture
CIMTP . . . . . . Congres Internationaux de Medecine Tropicale et de Paludisme (International Congresses on Tropical Medicine and Malaria)
CIM . . . . Congres Islamique Mondial
CJM . . . . Congres Juif Mondial
CPE . . . . Congres du Peuple Europeen
C . . . . Congress
CIU . . . . Congress of Independent Unions
COIU . . . . . . Congress of Independent Unions
CIO . . . . Congress of Industrial Organizations
CIOPAC . . . . . Congress of Industrial Organizations, Political Action Committee
CITI . . . . Congress of the International Theater Institute
CIU . . . . Congress of Irish Unions
CJC . . . . Congress for Jewish Culture
CLP . . . . Congress Liberation Party (Nyasaland)
CNS . . . . Congress of Neurological Surgeons
CORE . . . . . . Congress of Racial Equality

SOS . . . . Congress of Scientists on Survival
CUEPACS . . . . Congress of Unions of Employees in the Public and Civil Services (Malaya)
CUBS . . . . Congress for the Unity of Black Students
COUP . . . . Congress of Unrepresented People
CD . . . . Congressional District
CI . . . . Congressional Interference
CLO . . . . Congressional Liaison Office
CMH . . . . Congressional Medal of Honor
CMHS . . . . Congressional Medal of Honor Society
COST . . . . Congressional Office of Science and Technology
CR . . . . Congressional Record
CSC . . . . Congressional Secretaries Club
CMP . . . . Congruent Melting Point
CMA . . . . Conical Monopole Antenna
CMAK . . . . . . Conical Monopole Antenna Kit
CSA . . . . Conical Scan Antenna
CSV . . . . Conical Shell Vibration
CONFIDAL . . . Conjugate Filter Data Link
COI . . . . Conjugi (To My Husband or Wife)
CO . . . . Conjugi Optimo (To My Excellent Husband)
CAF . . . . Conjunctive Alteration File
CAI . . . . Conjunctive Alteration Indicator
CNF . . . . Conjunctive Normal Formula
CR . . . . Connaught Rangers (British military)
CT . . . . Connecticut
CANEL . . . . . . Connecticut Advanced Nuclear Engine Laboratory (AEC)
CL & P . . . . . . Connecticut Light and Power Company
CC . . . . Connecting Carrier
CL . . . . Connecting Line
CFO . . . . Connection Fitting Out (Navy)
CONARESTRAPROG . . Connection Naval Air Reserve Training Program
CT . . . . Connective Tissue
CP . . . . Connector Panel
CONN . . . . . . Connellan Airways, Ltd.
CD . . . . Conning Director (Navy)
CSAC . . . . Connors State Agricultural College (Oklahoma)
CPJ . . . . Conoseal Pipe Joint
CH . . . . Conquering Hero (British, for returning soldiers)
CO . . . . Conscientious Objector
CONOBJTR . . Conscientious Objector
CNP . . . . Consecutive Number Printer
COT . . . . Consecutive Oversea Tour (Military)
CCE . . . . Conseil des Communes d'Europe
CCC . . . . Conseil de la Cooperation Culturelle (Council for Cultural Cooperation) (of the Council of Europe)
CODEXAL . . . . Conseil Europeen du "Codex Alimentarius"
CECB . . . . Conseil Europeen du Cuir Brut (European Untanned Leather Council)
CERN . . . . Conseil Europeen pour la Recherche Nucleaire (Now Organisation Europeene pour la Recherche Nucleaire)
CFCE . . . . Conseil des Federations Commerciales d'Europe
CFIE . . . . Conseil des Federations Industrielles d'Europe
CGPM . . . . . . Conseil General des Peches pour la Mediterranee
CIPP . . . . Conseil Indo-Pacifique des Peches
CICEP . . . . Conseil Interamericain du Commerce et de la Production
CIA . . . . Conseil International des Archives
CIB . . . . Conseil International du Batiment pour la Recherche, l'Etude et la Documentation (International Council for Building Research, Studies and Documentation)
CIB . . . . Conseil International du Ble
CIC . . . . Conseil International de la Chasse
CICT . . . . Conseil International du Cinema et de la Television
CIC . . . . Conseil International des Compositeurs
CIEPS . . . . Conseil International de l'Education Physique et Sportive
CIEC . . . . Conseil International des Employeurs du Commerce
CIEM . . . . Conseil International pour l'Exploration de la Mer
CIF . . . . Conseil International des Femmes
CIFE . . . . Conseil International du Film d'Enseignement
CII . . . . Conseil International des Infirmieres
CIM . . . . Conseil International de la Musique
CIMP . . . . Conseil International de la Musique Populaire
CIPSH . . . . Conseil International de la Philosophie et des Sciences Humaines
CISS . . . . Conseil International des Sciences Sociales
CISM . . . . Conseil International du Sport Militaire
CIT . . . . Conseil International des Tanneurs
CIUS . . . . Conseil International des Unions Scientifiques
CJ . . . . Conseil de la Jeunesse (Youth Council) (Senegal, Mali, Upper Volta, Niger and Dahomey)
CJA . . . . Conseil de la Jeunesse d'Afrique (African Youth Council) (Senegal)
CJCI . . . . Conseil de la Jeunesse de Cote d'Ivoire (Ivory Coast Youth Council)
CMACP . . . . . . Conseil Mondial pour l'Assemblee Constituante des Peuples

CNR . . . . Conseil National de la Resistance (France)
CNRA . . . . Conseil National de la Revolution Algerienne (National Council of the Algerian Revolution)
CNRG . . . . Conseil National de la Revolution de la Guinee Dite Portugaise (National Revolutionary Council of So-called Portuguese Guinea)
COE . . . . Conseil Oecumenique des Eglises
COSOF . . . . . . Conseil des Organizations Syndicales d'Union Francaise (Council of Labor Unions of the French Union)
CPME . . . . Conseil Parlementaire du Mouvement Europeen
CSA . . . . Conseil Scientifique pour l'Afrique au Sud du Sahara
CSL . . . . Conseil Superieur de Livre (Canada)
CIDEM . . . . . . Consejo Interamericano de Musica (Inter-American Music Council)
CONDESE . . . . Conselho de Desenvolvimento Economico de Sergipe (State of Sergipe, Brazil)
CNPq . . . . Conselho Nacional de Pesquisas (Brazil)
CNT . . . . Conselho Nacional do Trabalho (Brazil)
CAL . . . . Conservation Analytical Laboratory (Smithsonian Institution)
CEA . . . . Conservation Education Association
CF . . . . Conservation Foundation
CLSA . . . . Conservation Law Society of America
CMS . . . . Conservation Materials and Services
CRF . . . . Conservation and Research Foundation
CRP . . . . Conservation Reserve Program
C . . . . Conservative (Politics)
CBAA . . . . Conservative Baptist Association of America
CBFMS . . . . . . Conservative Baptist Foreign Mission Society
CCA . . . . Conservative Clubs of America
CLA . . . . Conservative Library Association
CTP . . . . Conservez Taxe Payee (Retain Charge Paid)
CYK . . . . Consider Yourself Kissed (Correspondence)
CNDR . . . . Consiglio Nazionale delle Ricerche (National Research Council) (Italy)
CNR . . . . Consiglio Nazionale delle Ricerche (National Research Council) (Italy)
CN . . . . Consignment Note
C/N . . . . Consignment Note (Business and trade)
CCS . . . . Consiliul Central al Sindicatelor (Central Council of Trade Unions) (Romania)
CRC . . . . Consistency Recording Controller
CONSO . . . . . Consolan Facility (Aviation)
CMP . . . . Console Message Processor (Data processing)
COPE . . . . Console Operator Proficiency Examination
COMPARE . . . . Console for Optical Measurement and Precise Analysis of Radiation from Electronics
COMB . . . . . . Console Oriented Model Building (Data processing)
COSMOS . . . . Console Oriented Statistical Matrix Operator System (Data processing)
CSG . . . . Console Set Group
CAN DO . . . . . Consolidated Accelerated Navy Documentation Organization
CAMO . . . . . . Consolidated Administrative Management Organization (AID)
CAFT . . . . Consolidated Advance Field Teams
CAEL . . . . Consolidated Aerospace Equipment List
CATMN . . . . . . Consolidated Air Target Material Notices (NOO)
CAM . . . . Consolidated Aircraft Maintenance
CAC . . . . Consolidated Athletic Commission
CBPO . . . . Consolidated Base Personnel Office
CSS . . . . CBPO (Consolidated Base Personnel Office) Strength Summary Card
CDR . . . . Consolidated Cigar Corporation (NYSE symbol)
CCP . . . . Consolidated Cryptologic Program
CDSM . . . . . . Consolidated Defense Supply Material
ED . . . . Consolidated Edison Company of New York, Inc. (NYSE symbol)
CETR . . . . Consolidated Edison Thorium Reactor (AEC)
CEC . . . . Consolidated Electrodynamics Corporation
CEI . . . . Consolidated Electronics Industries Corporation (NYSE symbol)
CFD . . . . Consolidated Foods Corporation (NYSE symbol)
CFC . . . . Consolidated Freight Classification
CIP . . . . Consolidated Intelligence Program
CLUP . . . . Consolidated Labor Union of the Philippines
CL . . . . Consolidated Listing
CMR . . . . Consolidated Mail Room (Air Force)
CMDO . . . . . . Consolidated Material Distribution Objectives (Air Force)
CNG . . . . Consolidated Natural Gas Company (NYSE symbol)
CNSG . . . . Consolidated Nuclear Steam Generator
COAL . . . . . . Consolidated Ordnance Allowance List (Navy)
CPT . . . . Consolidated Pilot Training Program (Air Force)
CPD . . . . Consolidated Programming Document
CPR . . . . Consolidated Progress Report
CRIL . . . . Consolidated Repairable Item List
CR . . . . Consolidated Report
CRPO . . . . Consolidated Reserve Personnel Office (Air Force)
COY . . . . Consolidated Royalty Oil Company (NYSE symbol)
CSSR . . . . Consolidated Stock Status Report
CSSO . . . . Consolidated Surplus Sales Office (Military - Merged with Defense Supply Agency)

CTCS . . . . Consolidated Telemetry Checkout System (Air Force)
CTX . . . . Consolidated Textile Company (NYSE symbol)
CUPS . . . . . . Consolidated Unit Personnel Section
CONVAIR . . . . Consolidated-Vultee Aircraft Corporation
CVAC . . . . . . Consolidated Vultee Aircraft Corporation
CSTA . . . . . . Consolidating Station
CSC . . . . Consolidation Coal Company (NYSE symbol)
CGSBN . . . . . . Consortium for Graduate Study in Business for Negroes
CONPASS . . . . Consortium of Professional Associations to Supervise Studies of
        Special Programs for the Improvement of Instruction in American
        Education
COPE . . . . . . Consortium of Publishers for Employment
CORD . . . . . . Consortium Research Development (Office of Education)
CGM . . . . Conspicuous Gallantry Medal (British)
CSC . . . . Conspicuous Service Cross (British)
C . . . . Constable
COP . . . . Constable on Patrol
C . . . . Constant
CAVT . . . . . . Constant Absolute Vorticity Trajectory
CAPPI . . . . . . Constant Altitude Plan Position Indicator (Aviation)
CAV . . . . Constant Angular Velocity
CBD . . . . Constant Bit Density (Control feature of magnetic tape recorders)
        (Data processing)
CCPM . . . . . . Constant-Choice Perceptual Maze Test
CCG . . . . Constant Current Generator
CCM . . . . . . Constant Current Modulation
CCT . . . . Constant Current Transformer
CDH . . . . Constant Delta Height (Aerospace)
CES . . . . Constant Elasticity of Substitution (Industrial production)
CED . . . . Constant Energy Differences
CFAR . . . . . . Constant False Alarm Rate (Air Force)
CLB . . . . Constant Level Balloon
CLS . . . . Constant Level Speech
COLA . . . . . . Constant Output Level Adapter
CPA . . . . Constant Potential Accelerator
CRTS . . . . . . Constant Returns to Scale (Econometrics)
CSD . . . . Constant-Speed Drives
CTV . . . . Constant Tangential Velocity
CTAS . . . . . . Constant Temperature Anemometer System
CTC . . . . Constant Torque Compensation
CVR . . . . Constant Velocity Recording
CV . . . . Constant-Viscosity (Rubber)
CVR . . . . Constant Voltage Reference
CVU . . . . Constant Voltage Unit
CEL . . . . Constitutional Educational League
CPI . . . . Constitutional Psychopathic Inferior
CPS . . . . Constitutional Psychopathic State
CRF . . . . Constitutional Rights Foundation
CARP . . . . . . Construction of Aircraft and Related Procurement
CB . . . . Construction Battalion (Navy)
SEABEE . . . . . Construction Battalion (CB) (Acronym is a phonetic reference to a
        member of this Naval unit)
VCB . . . . Construction Battalion (USNR classification)
CBBU . . . . . . Construction Battalion Base Unit
CBC . . . . Construction Battalion Center (Navy)
CBD . . . . Construction Battalion Detachment (Navy)
CBMU . . . . . . Construction Battalion Maintenance Unit (Navy)
CBRD . . . . . . Construction Battalion Replacement Depot
CCD . . . . Construction Completion Date
CC . . . . Construction Corps
CDS . . . . Construction-Differential Subsidy (Authorized by Merchant Marine Act
        of 1936)
CE . . . . Construction Electrician (Navy rating)
CERL . . . . . . Construction Engineering Research Laboratory (Army)
C & E . . . . . . Construction and Equipment
CEA . . . . Construction Equipment Advertisers
CIJC . . . . Construction Industry Joint Conference
CIMA . . . . . . Construction Industry Manufacturers Association
CJ . . . . Construction Joint (Technical drawings)
CM . . . . Construction and Machinery
C & M . . . . . . Construction and Machinery
CMS . . . . Construction Maintenance Supervisor
CM . . . . Construction Mechanic (Navy rating)
CP . . . . Construction Permit (FCC)
CANDR . . . . . . Construction and Repair
C and R . . . . . Construction and Repair (Coast Guard)
CONALT . . . . . Construction and Repair, Alteration (Coast Guard)
CSI . . . . Construction Specifications Institute
CSI . . . . Construction Surveyors Institute

CU . . . . Construction Unit (Data processing)
CWA . . . . . . Construction Writers Association
CAI . . . . Constructive Action, Incorporated
CTL . . . . Constructive Total Loss
C . . . . Consul
CG . . . . Consul General
CONGEN . . . . Consul General
CA . . . . Consular Agent
CD . . . . Consular Declaration
CI . . . . Consular Invoice
CLS . . . . Consular Law Society
CONSA . . . . . Consular Shipping Advisor
CSA . . . . Consular Shipping Adviser
CC . . . . Consules (Consuls)
COCU . . . . . . Consultation on Church Union
CCDS . . . . . . Consultative Committee for the Definition of the Second
CCPS . . . . . . Consultative Committee for Postal Studies (UPU)
CCPI . . . . . . Consultative Committee for Public Information (UN)
CCJO . . . . . . Consultative Council of Jewish Organizations
CG . . . . Consultative Group (NATO)
COSPAR . . . . . Consultative Group on Potentially Harmful Effects on Space Research
CEAC . . . . . . Consulting Engineers Association of California
CEC . . . . Consulting Engineers Council
CEVM . . . . . . Consumable Electrode Vacuum Melting
CVM . . . . . . Consumable Vacuum Melt (Steel)
CBA . . . . Consumer Bankers Association
CBE . . . . Consumer Buying Expectations Survey (Bureau of the Census) (Formerly,
        Quarterly Survey of Intentions)
CCC . . . . Consumer Credit Counselors
CCIA . . . . . . Consumer Credit Insurance Association
CCPA . . . . . . Consumer Credit Protection Act (1969)
CEHSA . . . . . . Consumer and Environmental Health Services Administration (HEW)
COLEQUAP . . . Consumer Level Quality Audit Program
CPI . . . . Consumer Price Index (Economics)
CMS . . . . Consumer and Marketing Service (Department of Agriculture)
C & MS . . . . . Consumer and Marketing Service (Department of Agriculture)
CPEHS . . . . . . Consumer Protection and Environmental Health Service (HEW)
CPS . . . . Consumer Purchasing Service
CAC . . . . Consumer's Advisory Council
CAJ . . . . Consumers' Association of Jamaica
CATT . . . . . . Consumers' Association of Trinidad and Tobago
CCA . . . . Consumers Cooperative Association
CMS . . . . Consumers Power Company (NYSE symbol)
CPPD . . . . . . Consumers Public Power District
CRR . . . . Consumer's Reliability Risk
CR . . . . Consumers' Research (Service reporting results of tests on consumers'
        goods)
CU . . . . Consumers Union of United States
C . . . . Contact
CAC . . . . Contact Approach Control (Aviation)
CAC . . . . Contact Area Commander
CTCC . . . . . . Contact Center Control (Aviation)
CFR . . . . Contact Flight Rules (Same as VFR) (Meteorology)
CIT . . . . Contact Ion Thruster
CLAO . . . . . . Contact Lens Association for Optometry
CLMA . . . . . . Contact Lens Manufacturers Association
CL . . . . Contact Lost (RADAR)
CMC . . . . . . Contact-Making Clock
CMVM . . . . . . Contact-Making Voltmeter
CONPY . . . . . Contact Party (Army)
CP . . . . Contact Party
CPD . . . . Contact Potential Difference
CVC . . . . Contactless Vacuum Controller
COR . . . . Contactor, Running
COS . . . . Contactor, Starting
CD . . . . Contagious Diseases
CCA . . . . Container Corporation of America
CNR . . . . Container Corporation of America (NYSE symbol)
CDS . . . . Container Delivery System (Military)
CONEX . . . . . Container Express (Army)
CRB . . . . Container Repair Building
CSE . . . . Containment Systems Experiment (AEC)
CA . . . . Contemporary Authors (A biographical reference book)
CC . . . . Contemporary Civilization (University course)
CMP . . . . Contemporary Music Project
CMS . . . . Contemporary Music Society
COC . . . . Contempt of Court
CAM . . . . Content-Addressable Memory (Data processing)
CONGRESS . . . Contiguous Node Group Restoral Supervision and Switching

C . . . . Continental
CONAD . . . . . Continental Advance Section (Originally called Coastal Base Section) (World War II)
CAAN . . . . . . Continental Advertising Agency Network (Later, Advertising and Marketing International Network)
CAC. . . . . . . Continental Air Command (Air Force)
CONAC . . . . Continental Air Command
CAC & W . . . . Continental Air Control and Warning
CADC. . . . . . Continental Air Defense Command (Air Force)
CONAD . . . . Continental Air Defense Command (Navy, Army, and Air Force)
CADIN . . . . . Continental Air Defense Integration, North (Air Force)
CADS . . . . . . Continental Air Defense System (Air Force)
CAF . . . . Continental Air Forces
CAL. . . . . . . Continental Air Lines, Inc. (NYSE symbol)
CO . . . . Continential Air Lines, Inc.
CAS . . . . Continental Air Services
CACS . . . . . . Continental Airways and Communications Service (Air Force)
CONAR . . . . . Continental Army
CONARC . . . . Continental Army Command (now responsible for induction, processing, training of active duty personnel)
CONALT. . . . . CONARC (Continental Army Command) Alternate Headquarters Plan
COCOAS . . . . CONARC (Continental Army Command) Class One Automated System (Army)
CONREP . . . . . CONARC (Continental Army Command) Emergency Relocation Plan
CARMOCS. . . . Continental Army and Major Overseas Commands Systems
CAFMS . . . . . Continental Association of Funeral and Memorial Societies
CAE . . . . Continental Aviation and Engineering Corporation
CI . . . . Continental Baking Company (NYSE symbol) (Wall Street slang name: "Coney Island")
CBM. . . . . . . Continental Ballistic Missile
CCC. . . . . . . Continental Can Company
CH. . . . . Continental Can Company, Inc. (NYSE symbol)
CCA. . . . . . . Continental Control Area (FAA)
CCX. . . . . . . Continental Copper & Steel Industries, Inc. (NYSE symbol)
CTCC . . . . . . Continental Division, Transport Control Center (Hq)
CDC. . . . . . . Continental Dorset Club
CEC . . . . Continental Entry Charts (Air Force)
CIS . . . . Continental Insurance Company (NYSE symbol) (Wall Street slang name: "Coney Island Sand")
CLUS . . . . . . Continental Limits, United States
CLUSA . . . . . . Continental Limits, United States of America (Navy)
CM . . . . Continental Marines
CMR. . . . . . . Continental Motors Corporation (NYSE symbol)
CLL . . . . Continental Oil Company (NYSE symbol)
CSC . . . . Continental Shelf Crawler
CSM. . . . . . . Continental Shelf Mining
CTL . . . . Continental Steel Corporation (NYSE symbol)
CUSS I . . . . . Continental, Union, Shell, and Superior (Ocean drilling barge; named after oil companies which financed its development)
CONUS . . . . . Continental United States
CUS . . . . Continental United States
CONOPS . . . . Continental United States Operations (Army)
CWS. . . . . . . Continental Wage Schedule (Military)
CA. . . . . Contingencies of the Army
CFM. . . . . . . Contingency for Movement
CONSSTOCS . . . Contingency Support Stocks (Army)
CNV . . . . Contingent Negative Variation
CC . . . . Continuation Clause
CONCA . . . . . Continue Calling Until
CONTH . . . . . Continue to Hold (Aviation)
CONPRESDU . . Continue Present Duty (Military)
CONTREAT . . . Continue Treatment (Navy)
CAMI . . . . . . Continuing Action Maintenance Instruction
CCMCC . . . . . Continuing Committee on Muslim-Christian Cooperation
CLE . . . . Continuing Legal Education
CNDP. . . . . . Continuing Numerical Data Projects
CRA . . . . Continuing Resolution Authority (Military)
COOP . . . . . . Continuity of Operations Plan (Army)
COP. . . . . . . Continuity of Operations Plan
COPDAF . . . . Continuity of Operations Plan, Department of the Air Force
CTC . . . . Continuity Test Current
CAMP. . . . . . Continuous Air Monitoring Program (Public Health Service)
CC. . . . . Continuous Casting (Metalworking)
CCS . . . . Continuous Commercial Service (Equipment specifications)
CCMD. . . . . . Continuous Current-Monitoring Device
CFSTR. . . . . . Continuous Flow Stirred Tank Reactor
CLOPP . . . . . Continuous Level of Production Plan
CLX . . . . Continuous Lightweight Exterior
CLP . . . . Continuous Line Plotter
CM . . . . Continuous Monitor
COMAC . . . . . Continuous Multiple Access Collator (Data processing)

COPAC. . . . . . Continuous Operation Production Allocation and Control (Data processing)
COGS . . . . . . Continuous Orbital Guidance System
CPFR . . . . . . Continuous Page Facsimile Recorder
CPE . . . . Continuous Particle Electrophoresis
CRAFT. . . . . . Continuous Random Analog to Frequency Transmission
CRMR . . . . . . Continuous-Reading Meter Relay
CSC . . . . Continuous Service Certificate (Navy)
CSP . . . . Continuous Stratification Profiler
CSMP . . . . . . Continuous System Modeling Program (Computer)
CSSL . . . . . . Continuous System Simulation Language (Data processing)
CT . . . . Continuous Tone (Color printing)
CTFM . . . . . . Continuous-Transmission Frequency Modulated (SONAR)
CV . . . . Continuous Vulcanization
CW . . . . Continuous Wave (A form of radio transmission)
CWAR. . . . . . Continuous Wave Acquisition RADAR (Military)
CW/FM . . . . . Continuous Wave Frequency Modulated
CWG . . . . . . Continuous Wave Gas
CWIR . . . . . . Continuous Wave Illuminator RADAR (Military)
CWIF . . . . . . Continuous Wave Intermediate Frequency
CWL . . . . Continuous Wave LASER
CWO . . . . . . Continuous Wave Oscillator
CWSD . . . . . . Continuous Wave Space Duplexed
CWV . . . . . . Continuous-Wave Video
CAMAL . . . . . Continuously Airborne Missile Launching and Low-Level (Penetration) (Air Force)
CST . . . . Continuously Stirred Tank
CSTR . . . . . . Continuously Stirred Tank Reactor
CV. . . . . Continuously Variable
CVE. . . . . . . Continuously Variable, for Emergency
CVF . . . . Continuously Variable Filter
CVMAS. . . . . . Continuously Variable Mechanical Advantage Shifter
CT . . . . Contour Template
C . . . . Contra
CC. . . . . Contra Credit (Banking)
CBC . . . . Contraband Control (Navy)
CCB . . . . Contraband Control Base (Navy)
CB . . . . Contrabass
C & A . . . . . . Contract and Administration
CADF . . . . . . Contract Administrative Data File
CA . . . . Contract Administrator
CAB . . . . Contract Appeals Board (VA)
CAM . . . . . . Contract Audit Manual
CA . . . . Contract Authorization
CCE . . . . Contract Change Estimate
CCN . . . . Contract Change Notification
CCO. . . . . . . Contract Change Order
CCP . . . . Contract Change Proposal
CCR . . . . Contract Change Request
CDL . . . . Contract Deficiency Listing
CD. . . . . Contract Definition (Navy)
CDP . . . . Contract Definition Phase (DOD)
CEI . . . . Contract End Item
CFS . . . . Contract Field Service
CFT . . . . Contract Field Technician
CFC . . . . Contract Finance Committee (Military)
CFS . . . . Contract Financial Status
CMA . . . . . . Contract Maintenance Activity
CMR. . . . . . . Contract Management Region
CMP. . . . . . . Contract Monitoring Point
CPS . . . . Contract Pilot School
CPIT . . . . . . Contract Price of Items Terminated
CR. . . . . Contract Report
C/R . . . . Contract Requirement
CRC . . . . Contract Requirement Card
CSN . . . . Contract Serial Number
CSR . . . . Contract Status Report
CSD . . . . Contract Support Detachment
CS . . . . Contract Surgeon (Military)
CSN . . . . Contract Surgeon (Military)
CTCI . . . . . . Contract Technical Compliance Inspection
CTI . . . . Contract Technical Instructor (Army)
CTS . . . . Contract Technical School
CTS . . . . Contract Technical Services (Air Force)
CTSP. . . . . . . Contract Technical Services Personnel
CTS . . . . Contract Termination Settlement
CO . . . . Contracting Officer
COR. . . . . . . Contracting Officer Representatives (Army)
COTR . . . . . . Contracting Officers' Technical Representative (Army)
CPLIA. . . . . . . Contracting Plasterers' and Lathers' International Association
C . . . . Contraction
CAM . . . . . . Contractor-Acquired Materiel

CAP . . . . Contractor-Acquired Property
CETS . . . . Contractor Engineering and Technical Services
CFAE . . . . Contractor-Furnished Aerospace Equipment
CFE . . . . Contractor-Furnished Equipment
CFP . . . . Contractor-Furnished Property (Air Force)
CHAP . . . . . . Contractor Held Air Force Property
CITE . . . . Contractor Independent Technical Effort (DOD)
CODAM . . . . . Contractor-Oriented Data Abstract Modules (Air Force)
COCO . . . . . . Contractor Owned, Contractor Operated (Military)
CPE . . . . Contractor Performance Evaluation
CPES . . . . Contractor Performance Evaluation System
CPS . . . . Contractor Plant Service
CPSR . . . . . . Contractor Procurement System Review (DOD)
CR . . . . Contractor Report
CRSD . . . . . . Contractor Required Shipment Date
CSS . . . . Contractor Storage Site
CDI . . . . Contractor's Demonstration Inspection
CWAS . . . . . . Contractor's Weighted Average Share (in Cost Risk) (Accounting)
CWE . . . . Contractor's Work Estimate (Military)
CPB . . . . Contractors Pump Bureau
CDRL . . . . . . Contractual Data Requirements List
CDSR . . . . . . Contractual Data Status Reporting System
CRAM . . . . . . Contractual Requirements, Recording, Analysis & Management (Air Force)
C . . . . Contralto
CGA . . . . . . Contrast Gate Amplifier
CV . . . . Contrast Value
CV . . . . Contributing Value (Shipping)
CAFSC . . . . . . Control Air Force Specialty Code
CTA . . . . Control Area (Aviation)
CAT . . . . Control and Assessment Team
CAPS . . . . . . Control & Auxiliary Power Supply System
CB . . . . Control Branch (Military)
CC . . . . Control Center
CCG . . . . Control Commission for Germany
CCSB . . . . . . Control Commission Shipping Bureau (Allied German Occupation Forces)
CAC . . . . Control and Coordination (Army)
CODAP . . . . . Control Data Assembly Program
CDA . . . . Control Data Corporation (NYSE symbol)
CDC . . . . Control Data Corporation
CDT . . . . Control Data Terminal
CONELRAD . . . Control of Electromagnetic Radiations (Purpose is to deny the enemy aircraft the use of electromagnetic radiations for navigation, while still providing essential services)
DEC . . . . Control Escort Vessel (Navy symbol)
C & G . . . . . . Control and Guidance
COINS . . . . . . Control in Information Systems
CLI . . . . Control Level Item
CL . . . . Control Logic
CMC . . . . Control Magnetization Curve
CMG . . . . Control Movement Gyro(scope)
CNS . . . . Control Net System (Chiefly British)
COP . . . . Control of Operation Programs
CP . . . . Control Panel
CPS . . . . Control Panel Subassembly
CPAP . . . . . . Control Parameter Assembly Program
CP . . . . Control Point
CP . . . . Control Post (RADAR)
CPS . . . . Control Power Supply
CPP . . . . Control and Protection Panel
CR . . . . Control Relay
CRA . . . . Control Relay Automatic
CRF . . . . Control Relay Forward
CRH . . . . Control Relay, Hand
CRL . . . . Control Relay Latch
CRM . . . . Control Relay Master
CRU . . . . Control Relay Unlatch
CRA . . . . Control Repeater Amplifier
CRC . . . . Control and Reporting Center (Air Force)
CRP . . . . Control and Reporting Post (RADAR) (Air Force)
CRDM . . . . . . Control Rod Drive Mechanism Study
CORPAL . . . . . Control Room Patching and Labeling
CS . . . . Control Scanner
CS . . . . Control Set
CS . . . . Control Signal
CSP . . . . Control Signal Processor (for spacecraft)
CSL . . . . Control and Simulation Language
PCSC . . . . . . Control Submarine Chaser (136 feet) (Navy symbol)
CSTI . . . . Control Surface Tie In
CSE . . . . Control and Switching Equipment (RADAR)
CSN . . . . Control Symbol Number

CSE . . . . Control Systems Engineering
CSL . . . . Control Systems Laboratory (University of Illinois)
CTB . . . . Control Test Bed
CTV . . . . Control Test Vehicles
CT . . . . Control Transformer
CONTRAN . . . Control Translator
CU . . . . Control Unit
CUH . . . . Control Users Handbook
CV . . . . Control Van
CVV . . . . Control Variable Valve
CTZ . . . . Control Zone
C & O . . . . . . Controllability and Observability
CRTS . . . . . . Controllable RADAR Target Simulator
CA . . . . Controlled Atmosphere
CCM . . . . Controlled Carrier Modulation
CCA . . . . Controlled Circulation Audit (Name changed to Business Publications Audit of Circulation)
CCS . . . . Controlled Combustion System (Antipollution device for automobiles)
CCT . . . . Controlled Cord Traction (Medicine)
CCFT . . . . . . Controlled Current Feedback Transformer
CDOS . . . . . . Controlled Date of Separation (Military)
CES . . . . Controlled Environmental System (NASA)
CFC . . . . Controlled Force Circulation (Boilers)
CHIEF . . . . . . Controlled Handling of Internal Executive Functions (UNIVAC)
CMO . . . . Controlled Materials Officer
CMP . . . . Controlled Materials Plan (of War Production Board) (World War II)
CMP . . . . Controlled Materials Production
CM . . . . Controlled Minefield (Navy)
CMAL . . . . . . Controlled Multiple Address Letter
CPO . . . . Controlled Precision Oscillator
CPPO . . . . . . Controlled Production Planning Officer
CPA . . . . Controlled Products Area
CRBR . . . . . . Controlled Recirculation Boiling Water Reactor (AEC)
CR . . . . Controlled Rectifier
CRP . . . . Controlled Referral Plan
CSP . . . . Controlled Surface Process
CTB . . . . Controlled Temperature Bath
CTD . . . . Controlled Thermolytic Dissociation
CTNF . . . . . . Controlled Thermonuclear Fusion
CTR . . . . Controlled Thermonuclear Reaction (AEC)
CTFO . . . . . . Controlled Tuning Fork Oscillator
CURV . . . . . . Controlled Unmanned Recovery Vehicle (Torpedo retrieving device)
CVF . . . . Controlled Visual Flight
CVFR . . . . . . Controlled Visual Flight Rules
CVR . . . . Controlled Visual Rules (FAA)
CA . . . . Controller of Accounts
CODE . . . . . . Controller Decision Evaluation
CDIF . . . . . . Controller/Director Information File
CONE . . . . . . Controller Error
CITE . . . . Controller Input Test Equipment
CIA . . . . Controllers Institute of America
COPCOM . . . . Controllers' Procedures Committee (Aviation)
CTC . . . . Controls Company of America (NYSE symbol)
C & D . . . . . . Controls and Displays
CVC . . . . Convalescent Camp (Military)
CCL . . . . Convective Condensation Level
CHAP . . . . . . Convective Heating and Ablation Program
C of G . . . . . . Convenience of the Government
COG . . . . Convenience of the Government
CA . . . . Convening Authority
CANU . . . . . . Convention African National Union (Nyasaland)
CA . . . . Convention Africaine (African Covenant)
CAID . . . . . . Convention of American Instructors of the Deaf
CIM . . . . Convention Internationale Concernant le Transport des Marchandises par Chemins de Fer
CIV . . . . Convention Internationale Concernant le Transport des Voyageurs et des Bagages par Chemins de Fer
CPP . . . . Convention People's Party (Ghana)
CAIMS . . . . . Conventional Ammunition Integrated Management System
CS . . . . Convergent Stereoscopic (Photography)
CD . . . . Converging-Diverging
CAL . . . . Conversational Algebraic Language (Adaptation of JOSS language) (Data processing)
CPS . . . . Conversational Programming System (Data processing)
CF . . . . Conversion Factor
CL . . . . Conversion Loss
CPCS . . . . . . Conversion Process Controller System
CORTS . . . . . Conversion of Range Telemetry Systems
CGB . . . . Convert Gray to Binary
CMA . . . . . . Convert Makers of America

CONVDD .... Converted Destroyer
XPG .... Converted merchant ships, assigned to antisubmarine patrol or convoy escort (Navy symbol)
CV .... Convertible (NYSE symbol)
CCB .... Convertible Circuit Breaker
CEMA .... Conveyor Equipment Manufacturers Association
CBCC .... Conviction by Civil Court
CONCOMO .. Convoy Commodore
CCO .... Convoy Control Officer (Navy)
CEV .... Convoy Escort Vessel
CANDR ...... Convoy and Routing (Section)
C and R ..... Convoy and Routing
CONROUTE ... Convoy and Routing Section (US Fleet)
C & R .... Convoy and Routing Section
CD .... Convulsive Dose
CST .... Convulsive Shock Therapy
COK .... Cook Paint & Varnish Company (NYSE symbol)
COOK ...... Cook Transit R. R. (AAR code)
CTI .... Cooling Tower Institute
CBE .... Cooper-Bessemer Corporation (NYSE symbol)
COS .... Cooper Ornithological Society
CTB .... Cooper Tire & Rubber Company (NYSE symbol)
CLIC .... Cooperating Libraries in Consortium
CUBE .... Cooperating Users of Burroughs Equipment (Data processing)
CUE .... Cooperating Users' Exchange
CO-TIE ..... Cooperation via Televised Instruction in Education (Colorado State University)
CAPCRA ..... Cooperative Agricole des Producteurs de Cereales de la Region d'Arras
CARE .... Cooperative for American Relief Everywhere (Formerly: Cooperative for American Remittances to Europe; Cooperative for American Remittances to Everywhere)
CAMPS ..... Cooperative Area Manpower Planning System
CBT .... Cooperative Bureau for Teachers
CCDP .... Cooperative College Development Program
CCR .... Cooperative College Registry
CCSS .... Cooperative College-School Science (Program) (National Science Foundation)
CEA .... Cooperative Education Association
CERLI .... Cooperative Educational Research Laboratory, Incorporated
CET .... Cooperative English Test
CES .... Cooperative Extension Service (Department of Agriculture)
CFAA .... Cooperative Finance Association of America
CFDA .... Cooperative Food Distributors of America
CFFP .... Cooperative Forest Fire Prevention (Forest Service, Department of Agriculture)
CFR .... Cooperative Fuels Research (Committee)
CIPPP .... Cooperative International Pupil-to-Pupil Program
CLUSA ...... Cooperative League of the United States of America
CLSA .... Cooperative Logistic Support Arrangement (Military)
CPEA .... Cooperative Program in Educational Administration
COPED ..... Cooperative Project for Educational Development (Office of Education)
CPA .... Cooperative Publication Association
CRS .... Cooperative Recreation Service
CRC .... Cooperative Research Council
CRP .... Cooperative Research Program (Military and US Office of Education)
CS .... Cooperative Society
CSRS .... Cooperative State Research Service (Department of Agriculture)
CWDIC ..... Cooperative Weapons Data Indexing Committee (AEC and DOD)
CWT .... Cooperative Wind Tunnel
CIU .... Coopers' International Union of North America
CIST .... Co-Orbital Interceptor Scoring Technique
COGO ...... Coordinate Geometry (Computer language)
CI .... Coordinate Index
CMM .... Coordinate Measuring Machine
CORDIC .... Coordinate Rotation Digital Computer
CHR .... Coordinated Hungarian Relief
CMC .... Coordinated Manual Control
CSL .... Co-ordinated Science Laboratory (University of Illinois)
CSED .... Coordinated Ship Electronic Design
COSAL ..... Coordinated Shipboard Allowance List (Navy)
CSS .... Coordinated Situation System
CTP .... Coordinated Test Plan
CAPUC ..... Coordinating Area Production Urgency Committee
CBJO .... Co-ordinating Board of Jewish Organizations for Consultation with ECOSOC
COCOM ..... Coordinating Committee
CCIVS .... Coordinating Committee for International Voluntary Service
CCMRD ..... Coordinating Committee on Materials Research and Development (Executive Office of the President)
COCOSEERS .. Coordinating Committee for Slavic and East European Library Resources
CCTA .... Coordinating Committee of Technical Assistance

CCTUO ..... Coordinating Committee of Trade Union Organizations (Ceylon)
CCLM .... Coordinating Council of Literary Magazines
CCSATU .... Coordinating Council of South African Trade Unions
CLR .... Coordinating Lubricant and Equipment Research Committee (Coordinating Research Council)
CRC .... Coordinating Research Council
CRCPI ...... Coordinating Research Council of the Petroleum Industry
CORD .... Coordinating of Research and Development (Navy)
COSEC ...... Coordinating Secretariat of National Unions of Students (in Africa)
CN .... Coordination Number
CODAC ..... Coordination of Operating Data by Automatic Computer
CROSSPATE ... Coordinative Retrieval of Selectively Sorted Permuted Analogue-Title Entries (Data Processing)
CIC .... Coordinator for Industrial Cooperation (Functions ceased, 1937)
CIAA .... Coordinator of Inter-American Affairs
CLMO .... Coordinator and Liaison Maintenance Officer
CBWR .... Coos Bay Wagon Road (Lands) (Department of Interior)
CRF .... Copeland Refrigeration Corporation (NYSE symbol)
CLJC .... Copiah-Lincoln Junior College (Mississippi)
CP .... Co-Pilot
CNS .... Copley News Service
C .... Copper
Cu .... Copper (Chemical element)
CBFC .... Copper & Brass Fabricators Council
CBFFTA ..... Copper and Brass Fabricators Foreign Trade Association (Later, Copper and Brass Fabricators Council)
CABRA ...... Copper and Brass Research Association
CBRA .... Copper and Brass Research Association
CBWA .... Copper and Brass Warehouse Association
CDC .... Copper Data Center (Battelle Memorial Institute)
CDA .... Copper Development Association
CJS .... Copper Jacketed Steel
COM .... Copper Oxide Modulator
COR .... Copper Oxide Rectifier
CPDA .... Copper Products Development Association
CPX .... Copper Range Company (NYSE symbol)
COPR .... Copper Range R. R. (AAR code)
CRC .... Copper Recovery Corporation
CSB .... Copper Shielding Braid
CSR .... Copper Sulfide Rectifier
CW .... Copper Weld
COS .... Copperweld Steel Company (NYSE symbol)
CSTC .... Coppin State Teachers College (Maryland)
COPREX ..... Coprecipitation X-Ray Fluorescence Spectroscopy
CSP .... Coproduction for Security Program (United States and Italy)
C .... Copy
CF .... Copy Furnished (Army)
CRC .... Copy Research Council
C .... Copyright
CO .... Copyright Office (US)
CSUSA ...... Copyright Society of the United States of America
CA .... Cor Anglais (English Horn)
C .... Cord
CI .... Cordage Institute
C .... Cordoba (Monetary unit) (Nicaragua)
COA .... Cordova Airlines, Inc.
CCA .... Corduroy Council of America
CLI .... Core Logic Intervalometer
CLIV .... Core Logic Intervalometer
CM .... Core Memory
CMD .... Core Memory Driver
CS .... Core Shift
CSE .... Core Storage Element
CTF .... Core Test Facility
CTL .... Core Transistor Logic
CTR .... Core Transistor Register
CPK .... Corey-Pauling-Koltun
CRC .... Corinth & Counce R. R. (AAR code)
Z .... Coriolis Correction
CSSI .... Coriolis Sickness Susceptibility Index (Orientation)
CKB .... Cork Base
CIA .... Cork Institute of America
CBLFA ...... Corn Belt Livestock Feeders Association
CFU .... Corn-Equivalent Feed Unit
CIRF .... Corn Industries Research Foundation
CPC .... Corn Products Company (Commercial firm)
CFG .... Corn Products Company (NYSE symbol)
CRA .... Corn Refiners Association
CSM .... Corn, Soybean, and Milk (Products) (Main ingredients of a formulated food)
CSM .... Corn Soybean Mixture

CAL . . . . Cornell Aeronautical Laboratory
CORC . . . . . . Cornell Computing Language
CLARA . . . . . . Cornell Learning and Recognizing Automaton
GLW . . . . Corning Glass Works (NYSE symbol) (Wall Street slang name: "Glow Worm")
CULL . . . . Corning Uniformity Limit Level
CJP . . . . Cornu-Jellet Prism
CWL . . . . Cornwall R. R. (AAR code)
CWF . . . . Cornwell-Weisskoph Formula
CRG . . . . Coro, Inc. (NYSE symbol)
C . . . . Corolla
CrA . . . . Corona Australis (Astronomy)
CrB . . . . Corona Borealis (Astronomy)
CEBM . . . . . . Corona, Eddy Current, Beta Ray, Microwave
CSV . . . . Corona Starting Voltage
CORO . . . . . . Coronado National Memorial
CCU . . . . Coronary Care Unit (Medicine)
CDP . . . . Coronary Drug Project
CHD . . . . Coronary Heart Disease (Medicine)
CSIR . . . . . . Corpo di Spedizione Italiano in Russia
CVL . . . . Corpo Voluntari della Liberta
CC . . . . Corpora Cardiaca (Endocrinology)
CORFO . . . . . . Corporacion de Fomento de la Produccion (Industrial promotion agency) (Chile)
COMIBOL . . . . Corporacion Minera de Bolivia
CVF . . . . Corporacion Venezolana de Fomento (Venezuelan Development Corporation)
CCO . . . . Corporate Contract Officer
CEASD . . . . . . Corporate Engineering and Sales Directive
CIPR . . . . Corporate Industrial Preparedness Representative (Military)
CIC . . . . Corporate Information Center
CMC . . . . Corporate Mountaineers Cult
CTAA . . . . . . Corporate Transfer Agents Association
CEIR . . . . Corporation for Economics and Industrial Research (Subsidiary of Control Data Corporation)
CORNET . . . . . Corporation Network (Telephone communications)
CPEQ . . . . . . Corporation of Professional Engineers of Quebec
CPB . . . . Corporation for Public Broadcasting
C . . . . Corps
C d'A . . . . Corps d'Afrique
CB . . . . Corps Brandenburgia
CD . . . . Corps Diplomatique (Diplomatic Corps)
CE . . . . Corps of Engineers (Army) (Merged with General Equipment Command)
C of E . . . . . . Corps of Engineers
CEBMCA . . . . . Corps of Engineers Ballistic Missile Construction Agency (Army)
CEBMCO . . . . . Corps of Engineers Ballistic Missile Construction Office (COE/BSD)
CE . . . . Corps of Engineers, Construction Electrician's Mate
CETC . . . . . . Corps of Engineers Technical Committee (Army)
CEF . . . . Corps Expeditionaire Francais
CHQ . . . . Corps Headquarters (Army)
CMA . . . . Corps Maintenance Area
CMP . . . . Corps of Military Police (British)
COSA . . . . . . Corps Service Area (Army)
COSCOM . . . . . Corps Support Command (Army)
CTOC . . . . . . Corps Tactical Operations Center
CA . . . . Corpus Allatum
CCC . . . . Corpus Christi College (Cambridge and Oxford)
CJ . . . . Corpus Juris (Body of Law)
CL . . . . Corpus Luteum (Endocrinology)
CSI . . . . Correct Seating Institute
CWPM . . . . . . Correct Words Per Minute (Typewriting, etc.)
CSR . . . . Corrected Sedimentation Rate (Medicine)
C . . . . Correction
CAC . . . . Correction Action Committee
CTF . . . . Correction to Follow
CAA . . . . Correctional Administrators Association of America
CEA . . . . Correctional Education Association
CIA . . . . Correctional Industries Association
CSA . . . . Correctional Service Associates
CSF . . . . Correctional Service Federation - USA
CAR . . . . Corrective Action Request
CM . . . . Corrective Maintenance
CMB . . . . Corrective Maintenance Burden
CT . . . . Corrective Therapist
CBMC . . . . . . Corregidor-Bataan Memorial Commission (Government agency)
CORDPO . . . . Correlated Data Printout (Electronics)
CORDPO-SORD . . Correlated Data Printout - Separation of RADAR Data
CDP . . . . Correlated Data Processor
COTAR . . . . . . Correlated Orientation Tracking and Range system (Satellite and missile tracking term) (RADAR)
CORAL . . . . . . Correlated Radio Link
CAN . . . . Correlation Air Navigation

CODAR . . . . . Correlation Display Analyzing and Recording
CF . . . . Correlation Factor
CORAD . . . . . Correlation RADAR
COTAR-AME . . Correlation Tracking and Ranging Angle Measuring Equipment
COTAR-DAS . . Correlation Tracking and Ranging Data Acquisition System
COTAR-DME . . Correlation Tracking and Ranging Data Measuring Equipment
COTAT . . . . . Correlation Tracking and Triangulation
CCLA . . . . . . Correspondence Chess League of America
CF . . . . Corresponding Fellow
CM . . . . Corresponding Member
CORAS . . . . . Corridor Assignment (Aviation)
CETA . . . . . . Corrosion Evaluation and Test Area (NASA)
CIS . . . . Corrosion Interception Sleeve
CRES . . . . . . Corrosion Resistant Steel
CCI . . . . Corrugated Container Institute
CLOAX . . . . . Corrugated-Laminated Coaxial (Cable)
CMP . . . . Corrugated Metal Pipe (Technical drawings)
CTT . . . . Corrugated TEFLON Tubing
CWG . . . . . . Corrugated Wire Glass (Technical drawings)
CBAA . . . . . . Corset and Brassiere Association of America
CBC . . . . Corset and Brassiere Council
CBWC . . . . . . Corset and Brassiere Women's Club
COEPS . . . . . Cortically Originating Extra-Pyramidal System (Physiology)
CS . . . . Corticosteroid (Endocrinology)
CBG . . . . Corticosteroid-Binding Globulin (Endocrinology)
CRF . . . . Corticotropin Release Factor (Endocrinology)
DDC . . . . Corvette (Navy symbol)
CSC . . . . Cosecant
CSCH . . . . . . Cosecant, Hyperbolic
COSH . . . . . . Cosine, Hyperbolic
CCW . . . . . . Cosmetic Career Women
CIBS . . . . Cosmetic Industry Buyers' and Suppliers' Association
CNA . . . . . . Cosmic Noise Absorption
CRA . . . . Cosmic Ray Altimeter
CRF . . . . Cosmic Ray Flux
CRG . . . . Cosmic Ray Gas
CRP . . . . Cosmic Ray Particle
CRS . . . . Cosmic Ray Shower
CA . . . . Cosmopolitan Associates
C . . . . Cost
CA . . . . Cost Account(ant)
CAIR . . . . . . Cost Analysis Information Report (Air Force)
CC . . . . Cost Center
CEIS . . . . Cost and Economic Information System (DOD)
CER . . . . Cost Estimating Relationship
CAF . . . . Cost and Freight
C & F . . . . . . Cost and Freight (Business and trade)
CFI . . . . Cost, Freight, and Insurance (Business and trade)
CIP . . . . Cost Improvement Program
CIR . . . . Cost Information Reports (DOD)
CIS . . . . Cost Information System
CIS . . . . Cost Inspection Service (Navy)
CI . . . . Cost Inspector
CI . . . . Cost and Insurance (Business and trade)
C & I . . . . . . Cost and Insurance
CIF . . . . Cost, Insurance, and Freight (Business and trade)
CIFC . . . . . . Cost, Insurance, Freight, and Charges
CIFC . . . . . . Cost, Insurance, Freight, and Commission
CIFE . . . . . . Cost, Insurance, Freight, and Exchange
CIFI . . . . Cost, Insurance, Freight, and Interest
CIFLT . . . . . . Cost, Insurance, Freight, London Terms
CLD . . . . Cost Laid Down
COL . . . . . . Cost of Living
COLA . . . . . . Cost of Living Allowance
CLI . . . . Cost-of-Living Index
CMIP . . . . . . Cost Management Improvement Program
CPM . . . . . . Cost Per Thousand (Magazine advertising)
CP . . . . Cost & Performance
CPSR . . . . . . Cost and Performance Summary Report (Army)
CPA . . . . Cost Planning and Appraisal
CPAF . . . . . . Cost Plus Award Fee
CPFF . . . . . . Cost Plus Fixed Fee (Business and trade)
CPIF . . . . . . Cost-Plus-Incentive-Fee
CPPC . . . . . . Cost Plus a Percentage of Cost
CPIC . . . . . . Cost Price of the Items Canceled
CPIT . . . . . . Cost Price of the Items Terminated
CP . . . . Cost Proposal
CRP . . . . Cost Reduction Program
CRR . . . . Cost Reduction Report
CR . . . . Cost Reimbursement
CRC . . . . Cost Reimbursement Contract

CS . . . . Cost Sharing
CHGFA . . . . . . Costs Chargeable to Fund Authorization (Army)
CHGPAA . . . . . Costs Chargeable to Purchase Authorization Advice
CDG . . . . Costume Designers Guild
CJBT . . . . Costume Jewelry Board of Trade of New York
CJSA . . . . . . Costume Jewelry Salesmen's Association
CJTA . . . . . . Costume Jewelry Trade Association
COTH . . . . . . Cotangent, Hyperbolic
CTGH . . . . . . Cotangent, Hyperbolic
CCI . . . . Cotton Council International
CEP . . . . Cotton Equalization Program
CEMAP . . . . . Cotton Export Market Acreage Program
CIA . . . . Cotton Importers Association
CIA . . . . Cotton Insurance Association
CPF . . . . Cotton Plant - Fargo Railway Company (AAR code)
CWIS . . . . . . Cotton Warehouse Inspection Service
COT . . . . Coty, Inc. (NYSE symbol)
CYI . . . . Coty International Corporation (NYSE symbol)
CPA . . . . Coudersport & Port Allegany R. R. (AAR code)
CODA . . . . . Coulee Dam National Recreation Area
C . . . . Coulomb (Quantity of electricity)
CA . . . . Council Accepted (Medicine)
CASE . . . . . . Council of Administrators of Special Education
COAC . . . . . Council on Adoptable Children
CAP . . . . Council on Advanced Programming
CAHR . . . . . . Council for the Advancement of Hospital Recreation
CASW . . . . . . Council for the Advancement of Science Writing
CASE . . . . . . Council for Advancement of Secondary Education
CASC . . . . . . Council for the Advancement of Small Colleges
SPACE . . . . . . Council of AFL-CIO Unions for Scientific, Professional and Cultural
 Employees
CACA . . . . . . Council Against Communist Aggression
CACR . . . . . Council for Agricultural and Chemurgic Research
CACCE . . . . . Council of American Chambers of Commerce in Europe
CAOPT . . . . . Council of American Official Poultry Tests
CAAHA . . . . Council on Arteriosclerosis of the American Heart Association
CBE . . . . Council for Basic Education
CBE . . . . Council of Biology Editors
CBBII . . . . . Council of the Brass and Bronze Ingot Industry
CCAE . . . . . . Council of Canning Association Executives
CCSSO . . . . . Council of Chief State School Officers
CCSA . . . . . . Council for Christian Social Action (United Church of Christ)
CCU . . . . . . Council on Christian Unity
CC . . . . Council of Churches
CCT . . . . Council for Clinical Training
CCS . . . . Council of Communication Societies
CCC . . . . Council of Community Churches
CC . . . . Council of Conservationists
CCI . . . . Council on Consumer Information
CCTE . . . . . . Council on Cooperation in Teacher Education (Defunct)
CCCP . . . . . . Council on Cooperative College Projects
CODSIA . . . . Council of Defense and Space Industry Associations
CDTE . . . . . . Council for Distributive Teacher Education
CDR . . . . Council on Documentation Research (Defunct)
CEA . . . . Council of Economic Advisors (to the President)
CECA . . . . . . Council on Economic and Cultural Affairs (Rockefeller Brothers Fund,
 Ford Foundation activity)
CEGS . . . . . . Council for Economic Growth and Security (Defunct)
CEMA . . . . . . Council for Economic Mutual Assistance (Communist-bloc nations)
 (Also known as COMECON)
CED . . . . Council on Education of the Deaf
CEGS . . . . . . Council on Education in the Geological Sciences
CEPS . . . . . . Council for the Education of the Partially Seeing
CEPR . . . . . . Council on Education in Professional Responsibility
COEPR . . . . . Council on Education in Professional Responsibility (Law)
CESI . . . . Council for Elementary Science International
CEB . . . . Council of Employee Benefits
CEMA . . . . . . Council for the Encouragement of Music and the Arts (Later, Arts Council)
CEL . . . . Council on Engineering Laws
CESS . . . . . . Council of Engineering Society Secretaries
CESO . . . . . . Council of Engineers and Scientists Organizations
CE . . . . Council of Europe
CEAA . . . . . . Council of European-American Associations
CEIF . . . . Council of European Industrial Federations
CEM . . . . Council of European Municipalities
CEC . . . . Council for Exceptional Children
CFDA . . . . . . Council of Fashion Designers of America
CFJO . . . . . . Council of Federated Jewish Organizations
COFO . . . . . . Council of Federated Organizations (in field of civil rights in Mississippi)
CFA . . . . Council on Fertilizer Application
CFAE . . . . . . Council for Financial Aid to Education

CFEP . . . . Council on Foreign Economic Policy (Functions transferred to Secretary
 of State, 1961)
CFM . . . . Council of Foreign Ministers
CFR . . . . Council on Foreign Relations
CGS . . . . Council of Graduate Schools in the United States
CGSUS . . . . . Council of Graduate Schools in the United States
CHEAR . . . . . Council on Higher Education in the American Republics
CHRIE . . . . . . Council on Hotel, Restaurant, and Institutional Education
CHP . . . . Council of Housing Producers
CID . . . . Council for Independent Distribution
CIM . . . . Council for Independent Managers
CISA . . . . . . Council for Independent School Aid
COID . . . . . . Council of Industrial Design (England)
CITE . . . . Council of Institute of Telecommunication Engineers
CIAC . . . . . . Council for Inter-American Cooperation
CIDCOMED . . . Council for Interdisciplinary Communication in Medicine
CII . . . . Council of International Investigators
CILA . . . . . . Council of International Lay Associations
CINE . . . . . . Council on International Nontheatrical Events
CIOMS . . . . . Council for International Organizations of Medical Sciences
CIP . . . . Council of International Programs for Youth Leaders and Social Workers
CIPM . . . . . . Council for International Progress in Management
CIS . . . . Council for Intersocietal Studies
CIA . . . . Council on Islamic Affairs
CJFWF . . . . . Council of Jewish Federations and Welfare Funds
CJO . . . . Council of Jewish Organizations in Civil Service
CLA . . . . Council for Latin America
CLLW . . . . . . Council for Lay Life and Work
CLEO . . . . . . Council for Legal Education Opportunity
CLR . . . . Council on Library Resources
COLT . . . . . . Council on Library Technology
CLW . . . . Council for a Livable World
CLT . . . . Council of the Living Theatre
CLCM . . . . . . Council of Lutheran Church Men
CMRED . . . . . Council on Marine Resources and Engineering Development
CMSCI . . . . . Council of Mechanical Specialty Contracting Industries
CMT . . . . Council on Medical Television
CMC . . . . Council of Mennonite Colleges
CMEA . . . . . . Council for Middle Eastern Affairs
CMAS . . . . . . Council for Military Aircraft Standards
COMPO . . . . . Council of Motion Picture Organizations
COMECON . . . Council for Mutual Economic Assistance (Poland, Russia, East
 Germany, Czechoslovakia, Rumania, Bulgaria, Hungary) (Also known
 as CEMA)
CNAA . . . . . . Council for National Academic Awards (British)
CNCA . . . . . . Council for National Cooperation in Aquatics
CNLA . . . . . . Council of National Library Associations
CNO-AE . . . . . Council of National Organizations for Adult Education
CNOCY . . . . . Council of National Organizations for Children and Youth
COWA . . . . . Council for Old World Archaeology
COAS . . . . . . Council of the Organization of American States (OAS)
COO . . . . Council of Oriental Organizations
CPDA . . . . . . Council for Periodical Distributors Associations
CPL . . . . Council of Planning Librarians
CPRE . . . . . . Council for the Preservation of Rural England
CPEB . . . . . . Council for Professional Education for Business
COPSI . . . . . . Council of Profit Sharing Industries
CPCU . . . . . . Council of Protestant Colleges and Universities
CPP . . . . Council of Psychoanalytic Psychotherapists
CRALOG . . . . Council of Relief Agencies Licensed for Operation in Germany
 (Post-World War II)
CRH . . . . Council on Religion and the Homosexual
CRIS . . . . Council for Religion in Independent Schools
CRIA . . . . . . Council on Religion and International Affairs
CRJWA . . . . . Council of Religious Jewish Workers of America
CORAL . . . . . Council of Research and Academic Libraries
CORST . . . . . Council of Resident Stock Theatres
CRB . . . . Council of Review Board (Army)
CSIR . . . . Council for Scientific and Industrial Research (South Africa)
CSSDA . . . . . Council of Social Science Data Archives
CSWE . . . . . . Council on Social Work Education
CSDH . . . . . . Council of Societies in Dental Hypnosis
CSM . . . . Council of the Southern Mountains
CSCC . . . . . . Council of State Chambers of Commerce
CSG . . . . Council of State Governments
COST . . . . . . Council of Stock Theatres
COSPA . . . . . Council of Student Personnel Associations
CST . . . . Council on Student Travel
CSM . . . . Council for the Study of Mankind
CTA . . . . Council for Technological Advancement
CTD . . . . Council for Television Development

CUTH . . . . Council of University Teaching Hospitals
CUA . . . . Council for Urban Affairs
CURE . . . . . . Council of Urban Rebuilding Enterprises
CVM . . . . Council for a Volunteer Military
CWC . . . . Council of Women Citizens
CWT . . . . Council on World Tensions (Later, Institute on Man and Science)
CSI . . . . Counseling Satisfaction Inventory (Education)
CAI . . . . Counselor Activity Inventory (Guidance)
CAUSE . . . . . . Counselor Advisor University Summer Education (Department of Labor program)
CS . . . . Counselor Structured
CIT . . . . Counselor-in-Training (for summer camps)
C . . . . Count
CDS . . . . Count Dracula Society
CR . . . . Count Reverse
CRAZI . . . . . . Count Routine Applied to Zero Input (Computer program)
CDDT . . . . . . Countdown Demonstration Test (NASA)
CB . . . . Counter Battery
CBO . . . . Counter-Battery Officer
CCM . . . . Counter-Countermeasures (Military)
CDCD . . . . . . Counter-Double-Current Distribution
CEM . . . . Counter Electromotive Cell
CEMF . . . . . . Counter Electromotive Force
CE . . . . Counter-Espionage
COIN . . . . . . Counter-Insurgency (Guerrilla warfare term)
CI . . . . Counter-Intelligence
CIAD . . . . . . Counter-Intelligence Analysis Division (DOD)
CIC . . . . Counter-Intelligence Corps (Military)
CIG . . . . Counter Intelligence Group (Military)
CIWP . . . . . . Counter Intelligence Working Party (US Military Government, Germany)
CM & D . . . . Counter Measures and Deception (RADAR)
CMR . . . . Counter Mortar RADAR
COV . . . . Counter-Operating Voltage
CPD . . . . Counter-Propaganda Directorate (British)
CRM . . . . Counter-RADAR Measures (or Missile)
CRM . . . . Counter Rate Meter
CRT . . . . Counter Recovery Time
CROSS . . . . . Counter Revolutionary Organization on Salvation and Service
CROW . . . . . Counter-Rotating Optical Wedge
CT . . . . Counter Timer
CTC . . . . Counter Timer Control
CV . . . . Counter Voltage
CBIO . . . . . . Counterbattery Intelligence Officer (Army)
CC . . . . Counterclockwise
CCW . . . . . . Counterclockwise
CF . . . . Counterfire
CINFAC . . . . Counterinsurgency Information Analysis Center
CIIC . . . . . . Counterintelligence Interrogation Center (Military)
CM . . . . Countermarked
CM . . . . Countermeasure
CRS . . . . Countermeasures Receiving Set
CMRS . . . . . . Countermeasures Receiving System
CM . . . . Countermortar
CRECON . . . . Counterreconnaissance (Army)
CSCU . . . . . . Countersink Cutter
CSKO . . . . . . Countersink Other Side
CSKH . . . . . . Countersunk Head
CF . . . . Counting Fingers (Psychology)
CS . . . . Counting Switch
CC . . . . Country Club
CC . . . . Country Code
CDSA . . . . . . Country Dance Society of America
CDSHA . . . . . Country Day School Headmasters Association of the US
CMA . . . . Country Music Association
CMDJA . . . . . Country Music Disk Jockeys Association
C & W . . . . . Country and Western (Music)
CWC . . . . Country Women's Council, USA
CPH . . . . Counts Per Hour
C/M . . . . Counts Per Minute
CPM . . . . Counts Per Minute
CA . . . . County Attorney
CB . . . . County Borough
CC . . . . County Circuit
CC . . . . County Commissioner
CC . . . . County Council
CC . . . . County Court
CIUS . . . . . . County and Intermediate Unit Superintendents (of NEA)
CLEAR . . . . . County Law Enforcement Applied Regionally
CLY . . . . County of London Yeomanry (British)
COM . . . . . . County Office Manager
CBSR . . . . . . Coupled Breeding Superheating Reactor

CIS . . . . Coupled Impedance Synthesis
CEU . . . . Coupler Electronics Unit
CCU . . . . Coupling Control Unit
CDU . . . . Coupling Display Unit
C . . . . Coupon
CIJ . . . . Cour Internationale de Justice
CPJI . . . . Cour Permanente de Justice Internationale
CAS . . . . Courier Air Service
CTS . . . . Courier Transfer Station
CTO . . . . Courier Transfer Office(r)
C . . . . Course (Navigation)
C . . . . Course Angle (Navigation)
CDI . . . . Course Deviation Indicator (Aviation)
COI . . . . Course of Instruction (Navy)
CL . . . . Course Line (Aviation)
CLC . . . . Course Line Computer
CPGC . . . . . . Course Per Gyro Compass (Navigation)
CTS . . . . Course Training Standard (Air Force)
C . . . . Court
CA . . . . Court of Appeal
CCLS . . . . . . Court of Claims
CTCLS . . . . . . Court of Claims
CCLSR . . . . . . Court of Claims Reports
CCP . . . . Court of Common Pleas
CCPA . . . . . . Court of Customs and Patent Appeals
CH . . . . Court House
CIR . . . . Court of Industrial Relations (Philippines)
CM . . . . Court-Martial
CMAO . . . . . . Court-Martial Appointing Order
CMF . . . . Court-Martial Forfeiture
CMO . . . . . . Court-Martial Orders (Navy)
CMA . . . . Court of Military Appeals
CP . . . . Court of Probate (Legal)
CS . . . . Court of Session
COU . . . . Courtaulds, Ltd. (American Stock Exchange symbol)
CFLT . . . . Courtesy Flight (Aviation)
C . . . . Cousin
CAF . . . . Cout, Assurance, Fret (Cost, Insurance, Freight)
C . . . . Cove
CYA . . . . Covenant Youth of America
CN . . . . Cover Note (Insurance)
CP . . . . Cover Point (Lacrosse position)
CBANY . . . . . . Covered Button Association of New York
YFN . . . . Covered Lighter (Non-Self-Propelled) (Navy symbol)
YF . . . . Covered Lighter (Self-Propelled) (Navy symbol)
YFRT . . . . . . Covered Lighter (Range Tender) (Navy symbol)
YRL . . . . Covered Lighter (Repair) (Navy symbol)
CTA . . . . Covered Threads Association
CVS . . . . Covert Viewing System
CFA . . . . Cowl-Flap Angle (Air Force)
COWP . . . . . . Cowpens National Battlefield Site
COXCBS . . . . . Coxswain, Construction Battalion, Stevedore
COXSRS . . . . . Coxswain, Ship Repair, Canvasman
COXSRR . . . . . Coxswain, Ship Repair, Rigger
CLVP . . . . Craft, Landing, Vehicle - Personnel
CUD . . . . Craft Union Department (AFL-CIO)
CMT . . . . Craig Mountain Railway (AAR code)
CR . . . . Crane Company (NYSE symbol)
CL . . . . Crane Load
AB . . . . Crane Ship (Navy symbol)
CA . . . . Cranial Academy
CLB . . . . Crash Locator Beacon (Air Force)
CPI . . . . Crash Position Indicator (Air Force)
CWFS . . . . . . Crashworthy Fuel Systems (Aviation)
CRLA . . . . . . Crater Lake National Park
CRMO . . . . . . Craters of the Moon National Monument
CT . . . . Crawler-Transporter
CWCCI . . . . . . Crayon, Water Color and Craft Institute
CTS . . . . Cream of Tartar Substitute
CWH . . . . Cream of Wheat Corporation (NYSE symbol)
C . . . . Created
CP . . . . Creatine Phosphate
CRS . . . . Creation Research Society
CEF . . . . Creative Education Foundation
CPF . . . . Creative Playthings Foundation (Defunct)
CPA . . . . Creative Printers of America
CRP . . . . Creative Protein
CTOA . . . . . . Creative Tour Operators Association
CQ . . . . Creativity Quotient (Testing term)
C/A . . . . Credit Account (Business and trade)
CCP . . . . Credit Card Purchase

CM . . . . Credit Memo
C/N . . . . Credit Note (Shipping)
CR . . . . Credit Requisition
CRF . . . . Credit Research Foundation
CU . . . . Credit Union
CUNA . . . . . . Credit Union National Association
CWBCNA . . . . Credit Women's Breakfast Clubs of North America (Later, Credit Women - International)
CR . . . . Creditable Record
CIS . . . . Credito Industriale Sardo (Sardinia)
CR . . . . Creek (Maps and charts)
CIMA . . . . . . Creek Indian Memorial Association
CRASH . . . . . . Creep in Axisymmetric Shells
CAA . . . . Cremation Association of America
CRC . . . . Crescent Petroleum Corporation (NYSE symbol)
CFCA . . . . . . Crested Fowl Club of America
CFFA . . . . . . Crested Fowl Fanciers' Association
CAO . . . . Cretans' Association Omonia
CB . . . . Crew Boat
CRC . . . . Crew Chief (Military, especially Air Force)
CRCH . . . . . . Crew Chief
CR/M . . . . . . Crew Member
CPS . . . . Crew Procedures Simulator
CPT . . . . Crew Procedures Trainer
CPR . . . . Crew Provisioning Report
CRA . . . . Crew Reception Area (Apollo) (NASA)
CRS . . . . Crew Reserve Status (Military)
CR . . . . Crew Rest (Military)
CSD . . . . Crew Systems Division (NASA)
CTD . . . . Crew Task Demand
CTD . . . . Crew Task Detail
CREWTAF . . . . Crew Training Air Force
CTAF . . . . . . Crew Training Air Force
CTT . . . . Crew Transfer Tunnel (NASA)
CWS . . . . Crew Weapons Sight
CC . . . . Cricket Club
CAA . . . . Crime Aboard Aircraft
CGR . . . . Crime on Government Reservation
CHS . . . . Crime on High Seas
CIR . . . . Crime on Indian Reservation
CIN . . . . Criminal, Immoral, and Narcotic
CIB . . . . Criminal Intelligence Bureau
CI . . . . Criminal Investigation (Military)
CID . . . . Criminal Investigation Department (Often loosely referred to as Scotland Yard) (British)
CID . . . . Criminal Investigation Detachment
CID . . . . Criminal Investigation Division (Army)
CJIS . . . . Criminal Justice Information System
CLP . . . . Criminal Law and Procedure
CRSP . . . . Criminally Receiving Stolen Property
CU & PFC . . . . Criminally Uttering and Publishing False (or Forged) Check
CEC . . . . Criminological Executives Club
CTK . . . . Crimping Tool Kit
CLFT . . . . Crippled Leap-Frog Test
CLT . . . . Crippled Leap-Frog Test
CAMEL . . . . . . Critical Aeronautical Material and Equipment List
CAFEE . . . . . . Critical Assembly Fuel Element Exchange (AEC)
CCP . . . . Critical Compression Pressure
CCR . . . . Critical Compression Ratio
CC . . . . Critical Condition (Medicine)
CDR . . . . Critical Design Review
CET . . . . Critical Experiment Tank
CFF . . . . Critical Flicker Frequency (Psychophysical test)
CRITHOUS . . . . Critical Housing Shortage at (named place) (Army)
CRITICOMM . . Critical Intelligence Communications System (Air Force)
CIRGA . . . . . . Critical Isotope Reactor, General Atomics
CIC . . . . Critical Issues Council
CIL . . . . Critical Item List
CLF . . . . Critical Link Factor
CL . . . . Critical List (Medicine)
CML . . . . Critical Mass Laboratory
CMPL . . . . . . Critical Materials Parts List
CPA . . . . Critical Path Analysis
CPL . . . . Critical Path Length
CPM . . . . Critical Path Method (Management) (Electronics) (PERT)
CPPS . . . . Critical Path Planning and Scheduling
CPS . . . . Critical Path Scheduling
CPT . . . . Critical Path Technique (PERT)
CR . . . . Critical Ratio
CSS . . . . Critical Shear Stress
CT . . . . Critical Temperature

CTS . . . . Critical Tool Service
CAA . . . . Croatian Academy of America
CCU . . . . Croatian Catholic Union of the USA
CFU . . . . Croatian Fraternal Union of America
C de G . . . . . Croix de Guerre (French decoration for gallantry in the field)
CNK . . . . Crompton & Knowles Corporation (NYSE symbol)
CDL . . . . Cronar Dot Litho (Du Pont)
CHL . . . . Cronar Halftone Litho (Du Pont)
CHIAA . . . . . . Crop-Hail Insurance Actuarial Association
CPI . . . . Crop Protection Institute
CQC . . . . Crop Quality Council
CRB . . . . Crop Reporting Board
CSSA . . . . . . Crop Science Society of America
CAP . . . . Cropland Adjustment Program
CCP . . . . Cropland Conversion Program
CR . . . . Crops Research Division (of ARS, Department of Agriculture)
CTS . . . . Crosier Theological Seminary (Minnesota)
X . . . . Cross (As in X-roads)
XCONN . . . . . Cross Connection
XC . . . . Cross Country
XCY . . . . Cross Country
CC . . . . Cross Couple
XFA . . . . Cross Field Acceleration
CLP . . . . Cross Linked Polyethylene
CO . . . . Cross-Over (Genetics)
COV . . . . Cross-Over Value (Genetics)
CPCI . . . . Cross-Pointer Course Indicator
XPD . . . . Cross-Polarization Discrimination
XQ . . . . Cross-Question (Transcripts)
CRM . . . . Cross-Reacting Material
CRAN . . . . . . Cross Scan Terrain-Avoidance Displays
XSECT . . . . . . Cross Section
CSDR . . . . . . Cross Section Data Reduction
CMS . . . . Cross-section Measurement System
CSA . . . . Cross Service Agreement
CSO . . . . Cross Service Order (Military)
CSSS . . . . . . Cross Spin Stabilization Systems
CTE . . . . Cross Track Error
CWF . . . . Cross Wind Force
CPS . . . . Crossfield Plasma Sheath
CR . . . . Crossroads (Maps and charts)
CJTF . . . . Crossroads Joint Task Force (Atomic weapons testing)
CTI . . . . Crossroads Technical Instrumentation (Atomic weapons testing)
CU . . . . Crosstalk Unit
CXI . . . . Crosstell Input
CXO . . . . Crosstell Output
CT . . . . Crosstrail (Military)
CA . . . . Croup-Associated (Virology)
CCM . . . . Crowell-Collier and Macmillan (Publishers)
CRW . . . . Crowell-Collier & Macmillan Inc. (NYSE symbol)
CA . . . . Crown Agent
CC . . . . Crown Colony
CKI . . . . Crown Cork International (NYSE symbol)
CCK . . . . Crown Cork & Seal Company, Inc. (NYSE symbol)
CI . . . . Crown of India
CO . . . . Crown Office (British)
ZB . . . . Crown Zellerbach Corporation (NYSE symbol)
C . . . . Crowned
CMA . . . . Crucible Manufacturers Association
XA . . . . Crucible Steel Company of America (NYSE symbol)
CV . . . . Cruise Vehicle (Military)
CRZWTR . . . . . Cruise Well to Right (Aviation)
C . . . . Cruiser
CRUDESPAC . . Cruiser-Destroyer Force, Pacific Fleet (Navy symbol)
CRUDIV . . . . . Cruiser Division (Navy)
CRULANT . . . . Cruiser Force, Atlantic Fleet (Navy symbol)
CM . . . . Cruiser Minelayer
COA . . . . Cruiser Olympia Association
VCS . . . . Cruiser-Scouting Aircraft Squadron (Navy symbol)
CRU SCO FOR . . Cruiser Scouting Force
CRUSCORON . . Cruiser Scouting Squadron
CS . . . . Cruiser Squadron
SSC . . . . Cruiser Submarine (Navy symbol)
CRULANTFLT . . Cruisers, Atlantic Fleet
CRUBATFOR . . . Cruisers, Battle Force (Navy)
CRUPAC . . . . . Cruisers, Pacific Fleet
CRUPACFLT . . . Cruisers, Pacific Fleet
CCA . . . . Cruising Club of America
CDC . . . . Cryogenic Data Center (National Bureau of Standards)
CEL . . . . Cryogenic Engineering Laboratory (National Bureau of Standards)
CINS . . . . Cryogenic Inertial Navigating System

CIS . . . . Cryogenic Instrumentation System
CPEB . . . . . . Cryogenic Positive Expulsion Bladder
CPT . . . . Cryogenic Pressure Transducer
CRP . . . . Cryogenic Refrigerator Program
CSC . . . . Cryogenic Storage Container
CTS . . . . Cryogenic Temperature Sensor (or Source)
CVC . . . . Cryogenic Vacuum Calorimeter
CEC . . . . Cryogenics Engineering Conference
CCWO . . . . . Cryptocenter Watch Officer
CSQ . . . . Cryptofacility Security Questionnaire (Army)
CR . . . . Cryptographer (Navy rating)
CRF . . . . Cryptographic Repair Facilities
XTAL . . . . . . Crystal
CCO . . . . Crystal-Controlled Oscillator
CCT . . . . Crystal-Controlled Transmitter
CD . . . . Crystal Driver
CK . . . . Crystal Kit
CMO . . . . . . Crystal Marker Oscillator
CO . . . . Crystal Oscillator
XTLO . . . . . . Crystal Oscillator
CP . . . . Crystal Palace, Sydenham (British)
CPT . . . . Crystal Pressure Transducer
CQM . . . . . . Crystal Quartz Modern
CU . . . . Crystal Unit (Piezoelectric)
CUC . . . . Crystal Unit Cell
CST . . . . Crystalline Style
CL . . . . Crystallographic Laboratory (MIT)
CTN . . . . Ctenidial Nerve
CS . . . . Ctenidial Sinus
CTS . . . . CTS Corporation (NYSE symbol)
CUB . . . . Cuban Atlantic Sugar Company (NYSE symbol)
CN . . . . Cuban Navy
C . . . . Cubic
CC . . . . Cubic Centimeter(s)
CUCM . . . . . Cubic Centimeter
CCSTP . . . . . . Cubic Centimeters at Standard Temperature and Pressure (Also CSTP)
CSTP . . . . . . Cubic Centimeters at Standard Temperature and Pressure (Also CCSTP)
CC . . . . Cubic Contents
CF . . . . Cubic Feet
CFH . . . . Cubic Feet per Hour
CFM . . . . Cubic Feet per Minute
CFS . . . . Cubic Feet per Second
CUIN . . . . . . Cubic Inch
CID . . . . Cubic Inch Displacement
CUMU . . . . . Cubic Micron
CUMM . . . . . Cubic Millimeter
CT . . . . Cubic Tonnage (Shipping)
CW . . . . Cubic Weight
CUYD . . . . . . Cubic Yard
CUD . . . . Cudahy Packing Company (NYSE symbol)
CMIA . . . . . . Cultivated Mushroom Institute of America
CAMELOT . . . . Cultural Auction of Many Extraordinary Lots of Treasure (St. Louis, Missouri)
CINFAC . . . . . Cultural Information Analysis Center (American University)
CIF . . . . Cultural Integration Fellowship
CREATION . . . Cultural and Recreational Education Achieved Through Investigations Ordinarily Neglected (University course)
CUE . . . . Culture, Understanding, and Enrichment (New York State Education Department project)
CPAA . . . . . . Cultured Pearl Association of America
CSC . . . . Culver Stockton College (Missouri)
C . . . . Cum
COBQ . . . . . . Cum Omnibus Bonis Quiescat (May He or She Repose with All Good Souls)
CTA . . . . Cum Testamento Annexo (With the Will Annexed)
CUGA . . . . . Cumberland Gap National Historical Park
CPSO . . . . . . Cumberland Plateau Seismological Observatory
CDC . . . . Cumberland Railway & Coal Company (AAR code)
CBI . . . . Cumulative Book Index
CB . . . . Cumulative Bulletin (US Internal Revenue Service)
CDF . . . . Cumulative Distribution Function (Statistics)
CFR . . . . Cumulative Failure Rate
CINL . . . . . . Cumulative Index to the Nursing Literature
CMPF . . . . . . Cumulative Preferred (A class of stock)
CS . . . . Cumulative Sun
CUF . . . . Cumuliform (Meteorology)
CB . . . . Cumulonimbus (Meteorology)
CN . . . . Cumulonimbus (Meteorology)
CM . . . . Cumulonimbus Mammatus (Meteorology)
CU . . . . Cumulus (Meteorology)
CUCB . . . . . . Cumulus and Cumulonimbus (Meteorology)

CUFR . . . . . . Cumulus Fractus (Meteorology)
CUN . . . . Cuneo Press, Inc. (NYSE symbol)
CDD . . . . Cunningham Drug Stores, Inc. (NYSE symbol)
C . . . . Cup(s)
C . . . . Curate, Curacy
CA . . . . Curates' Alliance (British)
CAF . . . . Curates' Augmentation Fund (British)
CURE . . . . . . Curecanti Recreation Area (National Park Service designation)
C . . . . Curie(s) (Unit of measurement of radiation)
C to K . . . . . Curious to Know (An inquisitive customer) (Merchandising slang)
Cm . . . . Curium (Chemical element)
CC . . . . Curling Club
C . . . . Currency
CB . . . . Currency Bond
CR . . . . Currency Regulation
C . . . . Current
CA . . . . Current Account
CAC . . . . Current Actions Center
CATE . . . . . . Current ARDC (Air Research and Development Command) Technical Efforts (DOD program)
CAP . . . . Current Assessment Plan
CA . . . . Current Assets
CC . . . . Current Complaints (Medicine)
CCCS . . . . . . Current Contents Chemical Sciences (A publication)
CC . . . . Current Cost
CDB . . . . Current Data Bit (Data processing)
CD . . . . Current Density
CDR . . . . Current Directional Relay
CFA . . . . Current Files Area
CFY . . . . Current Fiscal Year
CGT . . . . Current Gate Tube
CIJE . . . . Current Index to Journals in Education
CIR . . . . Current Industrial Reports (Census Bureau)
CIS . . . . Current Information Selection (IBM)
CIP . . . . Current Injection Probe
CIR . . . . Current Instruction Register
CLML . . . . . . Current List of Medical Literature
CMDAC . . . . . Current Mode Digital-to-Analog Converter
CML . . . . Current Mode Logic
COA . . . . Current Operating Allowances
CP . . . . Current Paper
CPP . . . . Current Papers in Physics
CPS . . . . Current Population Survey (Census Bureau)
CR . . . . Current Rate
CRQ . . . . Current Requirements
CRDSD . . . . . . Current Research and Development in Scientific Documentation (A publication)
CRIS . . . . Current Research Information System (Department of Agriculture)
CS . . . . Current Series (Army)
CSMP . . . . . . Current Ship's Maintenance Project
CS . . . . Current Source
CSA . . . . Current Source Amplifier
CS . . . . Current Strength
CT . . . . Current Transformer
CVA . . . . Current Variable Attenuator
CVI . . . . Current Variable Inductor
CVD . . . . Current-Voltage Diagram
CWE . . . . Current Working Estimate (Military)
CY . . . . Current Year
C3S . . . . Curriculum Committee on Computer Science (of the Association for Computing Machinery)
CURB . . . . . . Curtis Bay R. R. (AAR code)
CPC . . . . Curtis Publishing Company (NYSE symbol)
CW . . . . Curtiss-Wright Corporation (NYSE symbol)
C-W . . . . Curtiss-Wright Corporation
CWC . . . . Curtiss-Wright Corporation
CWRR . . . . . . Curtiss-Wright Research Reactor
CMC . . . . Curved Motion Cutter
CP . . . . Cushioning Pads
CUST . . . . . . Custer Battlefield National Monument
CPC . . . . Custodial, Protective and Crafts (US government workers)
C of F . . . . . Custodian of Fund
COPE . . . . . . Custodian of Postal Effects (Military)
CPCU . . . . . . Custody Pending Completion of Use
CH . . . . Custom House
COP . . . . Custom of the Port (Shipping)
CSR . . . . Custom Spherical Resins
CTDA . . . . . . Custom Tailors and Designers Association of America
CQD . . . . Customary Quick Dispatch
CEMON . . . . . Customer Engineering Monitor (IBM)
CIC . . . . Customer Identification Code

CMR . . . . Customer Material Return
COP . . . . Customer Owned Property
CRB . . . . Customer Records and Billing (Bell System)
CSDP . . . . . . Customer Service Department Procedure
CCC . . . . Customs Co-operation Council
CEO . . . . Customs Enforcement Officer (Treasury)
CE . . . . Customs and Excise
CUSNO . . . . . Customs Has Been Notified (Aviation)
CIE . . . . Customs Information Exchange (An arm of US Customs Bureau)
CPI . . . . Customs Port Investigator (Treasury)
CPS . . . . Custos Privati Sigilli (Keeper of the Privy Seal) (British)
CR . . . . Custos Rotulorum (Keeper of the Rolls) (British)
CS . . . . Custos Sigilli (Keeper of the Seal) (British)
CHASE . . . . . . Cut Holes and Sink 'em (Navy ammunition disposal project)
CI . . . . Cut In
COFF . . . . Cut Off (Military)
COF . . . . Cut-Off Frequency
COVER . . . . . . Cut-Off Velocity & Range
COV . . . . Cut-Off Voltage
CO . . . . Cut Out
CPR . . . . Cut Paraboloidal Reflector
CP . . . . Cuticular Plate (Biology)
CEH . . . . Cutler-Hammer, Inc. (NYSE symbol)
C-H . . . . Cutler-Hammer, Inc.
COV . . . . Cutout Valve
CDI . . . . Cutting Die Institute
CWIK . . . . Cutting with Intent to Kill
CTMA . . . . Cutting Tool Manufacturers Association
CE . . . . Cuvee Extra
CUVA . . . . Cuyahoga Valley Railway Company (AAR code)
CK . . . . Cyanogen Chloride (Chemical)
CAMS . . . . Cybernetic Anthropomorphous Machine Systems (Robot) (Army)
CYBORG . . . . . Cybernetic Organism (Concept of machine to alter man's bodily
               functions for space environment)
C . . . . Cycle (Electricity)
CEI . . . . Cycle Engineers' Institute
CPA . . . . Cycle Parts and Accessories Association
CS . . . . Cycle Shift

CPM . . . . Cycles Per Minute
CPS . . . . Cycles Per Second
CPC . . . . Cyclic Permutation Code
CPCS . . . . . . Cyclic Pitch Control Stick
CPC . . . . Cyclic Program Control
CC . . . . Cycling Club
CTC . . . . Cyclists' Touring Club
CHA . . . . Cyclohexylamine
CHC . . . . Cyclohexylamine Carbonate (Used in paper preservation)
CPP . . . . Cyclopentenophrenanthrene
CYL . . . . Cyclops Corporation (Formerly, UCS) (NYSE symbol)
CL . . . . Cyclotron Laboratory
CWD . . . . Cyclotron Wave Device
C . . . . Cylinder
CHT . . . . Cylinder-Head Temperature
CSC . . . . Cylinder Stroke Control
CP . . . . Cylindrical Perforated
CVM . . . . Cylindrical Vibration Mount
CSF . . . . Cylindrically Symmetrical Field
CSA . . . . Cymbidium Society of America
CYP . . . . Cyprus Airways, Ltd.
CF . . . . Cystic Fibrosis (Medicine)
CFP . . . . Cystic Fibrosis of the Pancreas
CFS . . . . Cystic Fibrosis Society
CMP . . . . Cystosine Monophosphate
CDP . . . . Cytidine Diphosphate
CPE . . . . Cytopathogenic Effect
C . . . . Cytosine
CTP . . . . Cytosine Triphosphate
CANA . . . . . . Czech American National Alliance
CCU . . . . Czech Catholic Union
CNC . . . . Czechoslovak National Council
CZPS . . . . . . Czechoslovak Philatelic Society
CRFA . . . . . . Czechoslovak Rationalist Federation of America
CRC . . . . Czechoslovak Red Cross
CSA . . . . Czechoslovak Society of America
CSASA . . . . . . Czechoslovak Society of Arts and Sciences in America
CZKR . . . . Czechoslovakian Kronen

D

DC . . . . Da Capo (Return to beginning) (Music)
DCA . . . . . . Dachshund Club of America
DACRYLON . . . Dacron and Nylon
DKT . . . . Dahl-Kirkam Telescope
DAR . . . . Daily Activity Report (Military)
DART . . . . . . Daily Automatic Rescheduling Technique (Data processing)
DB . . . . Daily Bulletin (Military)
DDR . . . . Daily Demand Rate
DESPORT . . . . Daily Equipment Status Report (Army)
DEPSUM . . . . Daily Estimated Position Summary (Navy)
DID . . . . Daily Intelligence Digest
DMR . . . . Daily Mechanical Report
DRO . . . . Daily Receipt of Obligation (Military)
DRN . . . . Daily Reports Notice (Air Force)
DSOT . . . . . . Daily Systems Operability Test (for surface-to-air missiles)
DTR . . . . Daily Transaction Reporting
DWTF . . . . . . Daily and Weekly Till Forbidden (Advertising)
DFISA . . . . . . Dairy and Food Industries Supply Association
DHIA . . . . . . Dairy Herd Improvement Association
DHIR . . . . . . Dairy Herd Improvement Registry
DISA . . . . . . Dairy Industries Supply Association
DIC . . . . . . Dairy Industry Committee
DPII . . . . Dairy Products Improvement Institute
DRF . . . . Dairy Remembrance Fund
DSI . . . . Dairy Society International
DSF . . . . Dairy Suppliers Foundation
DTMI . . . . . . Dairy Training and Merchandising Institute
DLCA . . . . . . Dairymen's League Cooperative Association
DC . . . . "Daisy Cutter" (A type of World War II bomb)
DWU . . . . . . Dakota Wesleyan University (South Dakota)
DS . . . . Dal Segno (Repeat from the mark) (Music)
DAL . . . . . . Dallas (Texas) (Airport symbol)
DCE . . . . . . Dallas Cotton Exchange
DCA . . . . . . Dalmatian Club of America
D . . . . Dam
DACAS . . . . . Damage Assessment and Casualty Report (Military)
DC . . . . Damage Control (Military)
DCS . . . . . . Damage Control School (Navy)
DC . . . . Damage Controlman
DF . . . . Damage Free
DL . . . . Damage Limitation (Strategy) (in a war)
DLP . . . . . . Damage Limiting Program
D . . . . Dame
DBE . . . . . . Dame Commander of the Order of the British Empire
DStJ . . . . . . Dame Order of St. John of Jerusalem (British)
DLL . . . . . . Dames of the Loyal Legion of the United States
D of M . . . . . Dames of Malta
DDS . . . . . . Damien-Dutton Society
D . . . . Damn
DAR . . . . Damned Average Raiser (A diligent student) (Slang)
DB . . . . Damned Bad
DOFAB . . . . . Damned Old Fool About Books (Acronym created by Eugene Field)
DYF . . . . Damned Young Fools (Officers under the age of thirty) (British naval slang)
DRMF . . . . . . Damon Runyon Memorial Fund for Cancer Research
DML . . . . . . Dan River Mills, Inc. (NYSE symbol)
DCN . . . . . . Dana Corporation (NYSE symbol)
DEA . . . . . . Dance Educators of America
DMA . . . . . . Dance Masters of America
DDTCA . . . . . Dandie Dinmont Terrier Club of America
D . . . . Danger Area (Aviation)
DL . . . . Danger List (Medicine)
DG . . . . Dangerous Goods (Shipping)

D & S . . . . . . Dangerous and Suspicious
DW . . . . Dangerous Weapon
DAWA . . . . . . Danish American Women's Association
DAEC . . . . . . Danish Atomic Energy Commission
DBA . . . . Danish Brotherhood in America
DBRI . . . . . . Danish Building Research Institute
DDRB . . . . . . Danish Defense Research Board
DSFU . . . . . . Danish Sailors' and Firemen's Union
DSA . . . . Danish Sisterhood of America
DS . . . . Danmarks Statistik (Denmark)
DAF . . . . Dansk Astronautisk Forening (Danish Astronautical Society)
DMM . . . . . . Dansville & Mount Morris R. R. (AAR code)
DSA . . . . Dante Society of America
DRFO . . . . . . Danube River Field Organization (Allied German Occupation Forces)
DJC . . . . Danville Junior College (Illinois)
DSM . . . . Danziger Statistische Mitteilungen (Danzig)
DR . . . . Dardanelle & Russellville R. R. (AAR code)
DFI . . . . Dark Field Illumination
DI . . . . Dark Ignition
DL . . . . Dark on Light
D . . . . Dart Industries, Inc. (NYSE symbol)
DKW . . . . . . Das Kleine Wunder (Initialism used as name of German automobile, manufactured by Auto Union)
DATE . . . . . . Dash Automatic Test Equipment
DP . . . . Dash Pot (Relay)
DDD . . . . Dat, Dicat, Dedicat (He Gives, Devotes, and Dedicates)
DAC . . . . Data Acquisition Center (NASA)
DAC . . . . Data Acquisition Computer
DAC . . . . Data Acquisition Controller
DAF . . . . Data Acquisition Facility (of STADAN)
DAISY . . . . . . Data Acquisition and Interpretation System
DAMPS . . . . . Data Acquisition Multiprogramming System (Data processing)
DAR . . . . Data Acquisition Recorder
DARS . . . . . . Data Acquisition Recording System
DARS . . . . . . Data Acquisition and Reduction System
DASR . . . . . . Data Acquisition Statistical Recorder
DAS . . . . Data Acquisition System
DASCOTAR . . . Data Acquisition System, Correlation Tracking and Ranging (Air Force)
DAU . . . . Data Acquisition Unit
DAEMON . . . . Data Adaptive Evaluator and Monitor
DAM . . . . . . Data Addressed Memory (Data processing)
DATE . . . . . . Data for Allotments Transmitted Electronically
DATAC . . . . . Data Analog Computer
DA . . . . Data Analysis
DAC . . . . Data Analysis Console
DAMIT . . . . . Data Analysis (Program) of Massachusetts Institute of Technology
DART . . . . . . Data Analysis Recording Tape
DARES . . . . . Data Analysis and Reduction System
DASY . . . . . . Data Analysis System
DATDC . . . . . Data Analysis and Technique Development Center
DAM . . . . . . Data Association Message
DAA . . . . Data Automation Activity
DADO . . . . . . Data Automation Design Office (Air Force)
DAP . . . . Data Automation Proposal
DAR . . . . Data Automation Requirement
DAS . . . . Data Automation System (NASA)
DA . . . . Data Available
DBK . . . . Data Bank
DBF . . . . Data Base File (Military)
DBIL . . . . Data Base Input Languages (Data processing)
DBL . . . . Data Base Load (Data processing)
DBUT . . . . . . Data Base Update Time
DBM . . . . Data Buffer Memory (Data processing)

DATACOL .... Data Collection
DC .... Data Collection
DCAS ...... Data Collection and Analysis System (NASA)
DCDU ...... Data Collection and Distribution Units (Military)
DCMH ...... Data Collection Module, High Speed
DCML ...... Data Collection Module, Low Speed
DCRS ...... Data Collection and Reduction System
DCU .... Data Collection Unit
DCIB ...... Data Communication Input Buffer
DATACOM ... Data Communications
DCC .... Data Communications Channel
DCCU ...... Data Communications Control Unit
DCS .... Data Communications Subsystem
DCPS ...... Data Compression Processing System
DCC .... Data Condition Code
DCS .... Data Conditioning System (NASA)
DC .... Data Control
DCMS ...... Data Control Multiplex System
DCPS ...... Data Control Panel Submodule
DCU .... Data Control Unit
DACON ..... Data Controller
DCR ...... Data Conversion Receiver
DCS .... Data Conversion System
DCT .... Data Conversion Transmitter
DACOR ..... Data Correction (IBM)
DCA .... Data Correction Amplifier
DCS .... Data Correction System
DCF .... Data Correlation Facility
DACOR ..... Data Correlator
DACPO ..... Data Count Printout (Data processing)
DADIC ..... Data Dictionary
DDB .... Data Display Board
DDC .... Data Display Central
DDG .... Data Display Generator
DDI .... Data Display Indicator
DDS .... Data Display System
DDC .... Data Distribution Center
DDS .... Data Distribution System
DEC .... Data Equipment Company
DXC .... Data Exchange Control
DEP .... Data Exchange Program
DEU .... Data Exchange Unit
DF .... Data Folder
DGP .... Data Generating Program
DHE .... Data Handling Equipment
DHS .... Data Handling System
DIN .... Data Identification Number
DISC ...... Data Information System for Management Control (Military)
DIC .... Data Input Clerk
DID .... Data Input Display (Data processing)
DIDC ...... Data Input Display Console (Data processing)
DIC .... Data Insertion Converter
DLFDU ..... Data Line Flight Direction Unit
DL .... Data Link
DLA .... Data Link Address
DLE .... Data Link Escape
DLS .... Data Link Set
DLS .... Data Link Simulator
DLT .... Data Link Terminal
DLTM ...... Data Link Test Message
DALTS ..... Data Link Test Set
DLT .... Data Link Translator
DLF .... Data List File
DLS .... Data Logging System
DMA .... Data Management Analysis
DMC .... Data Management Channel
DMO .... Data Management Office(r) (Air Force)
DMS .... Data Measuring System
DMS .... Data Monitoring System
DMX .... Data Multiplex (Computer)
DMSS ...... Data Multiplex Subsystem (Data processing)
DMS .... Data Multiplexing System
DOTC ...... Data Observing Testing Console
DOC .... Data, Operations, and Control
DOC .... Data Optimizing Computer
DPB .... Data Plotting Board
DPS .... Data Present Signal
DP .... Data Printer
DPOP ...... Data Printout Program
DP .... Data Processing
DPA .... Data Processing Activities

DPC .... Data Processing Centrals
DPC .... Data Processing Control
DPD .... Data Processing Department
DPE .... Data Processing Equipment
DPF .... Data Processing Facility
DPG .... Data Processing Group
DPI .... Data Processing Installation
DPMA ...... Data Processing Management Association
DPO .... Data Processing Operation
DPPC ...... Data Processing Products Contract
DPR .... Data Processing Request
DPSS ...... Data Processing Subsystem
DPS ...... Data–Processing System (SAGE)
DPU .... Data Processing Unit
DPCTE ..... Data Processor and Computer Test Equipment
DPD .... Data Project Directive
DQC .... Data Quality Control
DQCM ...... Data Quality Control Monitor
DQM .... Data Quality Monitors
DRC .... Data Rate Changer
DR .... Data Recorder
DRC .... Data Recording Camera
DRAPE ..... Data Recording and Processing Equipment
DRS .... Data Recording Set
DRV .... Data Recovery Vehicle
DR & A .... Data Reduction and Analysis
DRANS ..... Data Reduction and Analysis System
DRAT ...... Data Reduction and Analysis Tape
DRC .... Data Reduction Center
DRC .... Data Reduction Compiler
DRC .... Data Reduction Complex
DRE .... Data Reduction Equipment
DRIP ...... Data Reduction Input Program (Data processing)
DRI .... Data Reduction Interpreter
DRL .... Data Reduction Laboratory
DRP .... Data Reduction Procedure
DRP .... Data Reduction Program
DRS .... Data Reduction System (Data processing)
DART ...... Data Reduction Translator
DRN .... Data Reference Number
DRS .... Data Relay Satellite
DRSS ...... Data Relay Satellite System (NASA)
DR .... Data Report
DR & A .... Data Reporting and Accounting
DRF .... Data Reporting Form
DRC .... Data Return Capsule
DRED ...... Data Routing and Error Detecting
DSAR ...... Data Sampling Automatic Receiver
DSF .... Data Scanning and Formatting
DSR .... Data Scanning and Routing
DSR .... Data Specification Request
DSW .... Data Status Word
DSD .... Data Storage Device
DSE .... Data Storage Equipment
DSS .... Data Storage System
DATCOM .... Data Support Command (Army)
DS & DH ... Data Switching and Data Handling
DSU .... Data Synchronization (or Synchronizer) Unit
DSC .... Data Synchronizer Channel
DSAP ...... Data Systems Automation Program
DSD .... Data Systems Designator
DSE .... Data Systems Engineering
DSO .... Data Systems Office
DS & S .... Data Systems and Statistics
DASSO ..... Data Systems Support Office
DS .... Data Systems Technician (Navy rating)
DTO .... Data Takeoff (Air Force)
DTR .... Data Telemetering Register
DTE .... Data Terminal Equipment
DTS .... Data Test Station
DTR .... Data Transfer Rate
DTU .... Data Transformation Unit
DT .... Data Transmission
DTF .... Data Transmission Feature (or Factor or Function)
DT/RSS .... Data Transmission/Recording Subsystem
DTSG ...... Data Transmission Study Group
DTAS ...... Data Transmission and Switching
DATS ...... Data Transmission System
DTS .... Data Transmission System (Air Force)
DTE .... Data Transmitting Equipment
DUC .... Data Utilization Console

DACOM . . . . . Datascope Computer Output Microfilmer
DAS . . . . Dataton Assembly System
DUO . . . . Datatron Users' Organization
D . . . . Date
DAS . . . . Date Arrived Station (Military)
DOA . . . . Date of Availability (Military)
DOB . . . . Date of Birth
DOC . . . . Date of Change
DOCA . . . . . . Date of Change of Accountability (Military)
DOCA . . . . . . Date of Current Appointment (Military)
DOCE . . . . . . Date of Current Enlistment
DDCONUS . . . Date Departed Continental United States (Military)
DDLDS . . . . . . Date Departed Last Duty Station (Military)
DDUS . . . . . . Date Departed United States (Army)
DEROS . . . . . . Date Eligible for Return from Overseas
DOE . . . . Date of Enlistment
DE . . . . Date of Entry (Military)
EOD . . . . Date of Entering Office
DE . . . . Date of Extension (Military)
DGI . . . . Date Growers' Institute
DIA . . . . Date of Initial Appointment
DMR . . . . Date Material Required
DN . . . . Date Number
DPG . . . . Date of Permanent Grade
DPOB . . . . . . Date and Place of Birth
DOR . . . . Date of Rank
DR . . . . Date of Rank
DOCG . . . . . . Date of Rank in Current Grade (Military)
DORCG . . . . . Date of Rank, Current Grade (Air Force)
DORPG . . . . . Date of Rank, Permanent Grade (Air Force)
DOR . . . . Date of Request
DROS . . . . . . Date Returned from Overseas
DOS . . . . Date of Separation (Military)
DS . . . . Date of Service (Military)
DTG . . . . Date-Time Group (Group of figures at head of radio or teletype message
    indicating filing time)
D . . . . Datum
DOM . . . . Datur Omnibus Mori (It is Allotted unto All to Die)
D . . . . Daughter
D of A . . . . . . Daughters of America
DAR . . . . Daughters of the American Revolution
DC . . . . Daughters of the Cincinnati
DC . . . . Daughters of Charity of St. Vincent de Paul (Roman Catholic religious
    order)
D of C . . . . . . Daughters of the Confederacy
DC . . . . Daughters of the Cross (Roman Catholic religious order)
DDR . . . . Daughters of the Defenders of the Republic, USA
DDR . . . . Daughters of the Divine Redeemer (Roman Catholic religious order)
IHM . . . . Daughters of the Immaculate Heart of Mary (Roman Catholic religious
    order)
DMJ . . . . Daughters of Mary and Joseph (Roman Catholic religious order)
DMHR . . . . . . Daughters of the Most Holy Redeemer (Roman Catholic religious order)
DNST . . . . Daughters of the Nile, Supreme Temple
DRT . . . . Daughters of the Republic of Texas
DSF . . . . Daughters of St. Francis of Assisi (Roman Catholic religious order)
DSMP . . . . . . Daughters of St. Mary of Providence (Roman Catholic religious order)
DSR . . . . Daughters of St. Rita of the Immaculate Heart (Roman Catholic religious
    order)
D of S . . . . . . Daughters of Scotia
DUVCW . . . . . Daughters of Union Veterans of the Civil War
DW . . . . Daughters of Wisdom (Montfort Sisters) (Roman Catholic religious order)
SBD . . . . "Dauntless" single-engine scout-bomber (Navy symbol)
DVG . . . . Davega Stores Corporation (NYSE symbol)
DVY . . . . Davenport Hosiery Mills, Inc. (NYSE symbol)
DRI . . . . Davenport, Rock Island & North Western Railway (AAR code)
DLC . . . . David Lipscomb College (Tennessee)
DSRC . . . . . . David Sarnoff Research Center (RCA)
DTAL . . . . David Taylor Aerodynamics Laboratory
DTMB . . . . . . David Taylor Model Basin (Military)
TMB . . . . David W. Taylor Model Basin
DEC . . . . Davis and Elkins College (West Virginia)
DUSAA . . . . . . Davison United States Army Airfield
DGE . . . . Davisson-Gernier Experiment
DC . . . . Davy Crockett (A tactical atomic weapon) (Army)
DADCAP . . . . . Dawn and Dusk Combat Air Patrol
DCJC . . . . . . Dawson County Junior College (Montana)
D . . . . Day (Approach and landing charts) (Aviation)
DB . . . . Day Book
DL . . . . Day Letter (Telegraphy)
DN . . . . Day and Night (Approach and landing charts) (Aviation)
DRO . . . . Day Room Orderly (Army)

K (Day) . . . . . Day Set for Strike or Assault by a Carrier's Aircraft; Corresponds to
    D-Day (Navy)
D of S . . . . . . Day of Supply (Military)
DAY . . . . Dayco Corporation (NYSE symbol)
DST . . . . Daylight Saving Time
DT . . . . Daylight Time
D/A . . . . Days after Acceptance (Business and trade)
DD . . . . Days after Date
D/D . . . . Days after Date (Business and trade)
DD . . . . Days after Delivery
D/S . . . . Days after Sight (Business and trade)
DD . . . . Day's Date
DDALV . . . . . . Day's Delay Enroute Authorized Chargeable as Leave (Military)
DL . . . . Days Lost (Military)
DS . . . . Day's Sight
DADIT . . . . . . Daystrom Analog-to-Digital Integrating Translator
DYM . . . . Daystrom, Inc. (NYSE symbol)
DBA . . . . Daytime Broadcasters Association
DAFD . . . . . . Dayton Air Force Depot
DH . . . . Dayton-Hudson Corporation (NYSE symbol)
DPL . . . . Dayton Power & Light Company (NYSE symbol)
DBV . . . . De Badande Vannerna (Sweden)
DBN . . . . De Bonis Non (Of the goods not yet administered)
DD in D . . . . . De Die in Diem (From Day to Day)
DACC . . . . . . DeHavilland Aircraft Company, Canada
DKWT . . . . . . De Kalb & Western Transportation R. R. (AAR code)
DP . . . . De Profundis
D . . . . Deacon
DM . . . . Deacon and Martyr (Church calendars)
DAN . . . . Deacon and Nike (Research rocket)
D . . . . Dead or Deceased
DOA . . . . Dead on Arrival (Medicine)
DB . . . . Dead Band
DF . . . . Dead Freight (Shipping)
DI . . . . Dead Indian (Careless man) (Army slang)
DLO . . . . Dead Letter Office (US Post Office)
DL . . . . Dead Load
DR . . . . Dead Reckoning
D/R . . . . Dead Reckoning
DRAI . . . . Dead Reckoning Analog Indicator
DRA . . . . Dead Reckoning Analyzer
DRAI . . . . Dead Reckoning Analyzer Indicator
DRP . . . . Dead Reckoning Plotter
DRT . . . . Dead Reckoning Tracer (RADAR)
DRTR . . . . Dead Reckoning Trainer
DS . . . . Dead Space
DT . . . . Dead Time
DTC . . . . Dead Time Correction
DTL . . . . Dead Time Log
DW . . . . Dead Weight
DWC . . . . Dead Weight Capacity
DWG . . . . Dead Weight Gage
DH . . . . Deadhead (Freight)
DD . . . . Deadline Date
DLD . . . . Deadline Date (Air Force)
DDD . . . . Deadline Delivery Date
DWA . . . . Deadly Weapon Act
DWT . . . . Deadweight
DWT . . . . Deadweight Tester
DWT . . . . Deadweight Tons
DFT . . . . Deaerating Feed Tank
DESOMS . . . . Deaf Sons of Master Masons
DRF . . . . Deafness Research Foundation
DPI . . . . Deal Proneness Index (Marketing)
D . . . . Dean
DF . . . . Dean of the Faculty
DAI . . . . Death from Accidental Injuries (Military)
DEVA . . . . . . Death Valley National Monument
DN . . . . Debit Note
DR . . . . Debit Request
DLS . . . . Debt Liquidation Schedule
DM . . . . Debugging Mode
D . . . . Debye
DDT . . . . Debye Dipole Theory
DFE . . . . Debye-Falkenhagen Effect
DHE . . . . Debye-Huckel Equation
DSC . . . . Debye-Sears Cell
DSE . . . . Debye-Sears Effect
DC . . . . Decade Counter
DCU . . . . Decade Counting Unit
DRT . . . . Decade Ratio Transformer

DRB . . . . Decade Resolver Bridge
DSB . . . . Decade Synchro Bridge
DECAL . . . . . . Decalcomania
DSL . . . . Decalogue Society of Lawyers
DM . . . . Decameter
DM . . . . Decamired
DS . . . . Decanning Scuttle
DR . . . . Decanus Ruralis (Rural Dean)
DF . . . . Decapacitation Factor
DBC . . . . Decatur Baptist College (Iowa)
DRM . . . . Decay Rate Meter
DMF . . . . Decayed, Missing, Filled (Dentistry)
DIAN . . . . . . Decca Integrated Airborne Navigator
DKA . . . . Decca Records, Inc. (NYSE symbol)
DECELERON . . Decelerator and Aileron (NASA)
DSC . . . . Decent Suit of Civvies (British slang military decoration) (World War I)
DPP . . . . Decentralized Printing Program (Army)
DJS . . . . Deception Jamming System
D. . . . . Decessit (Died)
DSP . . . . Decessit Sine Prole (Died without Issue)
DVP . . . . Decessit Vita Patris (He, or She, Died during His, or Her, Father's Lifetime)
d . . . . Deci (Prefix)
db . . . . Decibel (Unit of sound)
DB . . . . Decibel Meter (Radio equipment)
DBV . . . . Decibel Referred to 1 Volt
DBW . . . . Decibel Referred to 1 Watt
DBM . . . . Decibels (Referred to 1 Milliwatt in 600 Ohms)
DBA . . . . Decibels, Adjusted (Communications)
DBRN . . . . Decibels Above Reference Noise (Communications)
D . . . . Deciduous
DG . . . . Decigram
DL . . . . Deciliter
DA . . . . Decimal Add
DC . . . . Decimal Classification
DCT . . . . Decimal Code Translator
DCU . . . . Decimal Counting Unit
DDDA . . . . . . Decimal Digital Differential Analyzer
DD . . . . Decimal Divide
DKB . . . . Decimal Keyboard (Data processing)
DM . . . . Decimal Multiply
DN . . . . Decimal Number
DOC . . . . Decimal to Octal Conversion
DRB . . . . Decimal Register Binary
DS . . . . Decimal Subtract
DVO . . . . Decimal Voltage Output
DM . . . . Decimeter (Metric)
DCR . . . . Decision Circuit Reception
DE . . . . Decision Element
DEAL . . . . . . Decision Evaluation and Logic
DIDS . . . . . . Decision Information Distribution System
DLT . . . . Decision Logic Table (DOD)
DM . . . . Decision Maker
DEMON . . . . . Decision Mapping via Optimum Go-No Networks
DS . . . . Decision and Switching
DETAB . . . . . . Decision Tables
DTC . . . . Decision Threshold Computer
DCG . . . . Decisions of the Comptroller General
LD . . . . Decisions Lost (Boxing)
WD . . . . Decisions Won (Boxing)
DC . . . . Deck Cargo
DC . . . . Deck Court
DDC . . . . Deck Decompression Chamber (Undersea technology)
DDV . . . . Deck Drain Valve
DEO . . . . Deck Edge Outlet (Navy)
DE . . . . Deck and Engineering Duties, General Service (USNR officer designation)
DLT . . . . Deck Landing Training
DLTS . . . . . . Deck Landing Training School
DP . . . . Deck Piercing
DW . . . . Deck Watch (A small chronometer) (Navy)
WD . . . . (Qualified for) Deck Watch (USNR officer classification)
DWT . . . . Deck Watch Time (Navigation)
DWS . . . . Deck Working Space
DE . . . . Deckle Edged (Paper)
DAU . . . . Declaration of Atlantic Unity
D . . . . Declination
DER . . . . Declining Error Rate
DSU . . . . Decoder Switching Unit
DARS . . . . . . Decommutation and Readout System (Data processing)
DECOMP . . . . . Decomposition Mathematical Programming System

DF . . . . Decontamination Factor
DDSM . . . . . . Decontrolled Defense Supply Material
DECS . . . . . . Decoration for Exceptional Civilian Service (Army civilian employee award)
DFI . . . . Decorative Fabrics Institute
DFM . . . . . . Decorative Furniture Manufacturers Association
DDR . . . . . . Decoy Discrimination RADAR
DEM . . . . Decoy Ejection Mechanism
DFR . . . . Decreasing Failure Rate
DD . . . . Dedit, Dedicavit (Gave, Dedicated)
DAC . . . . Deductible Average Clause (Insurance)
DAXBT . . . . . . Deep Airborne Expendable Bathythermograph (NOO)
DCH . . . . Deep Case Hardened
DRV . . . . Deep-Diving Research Vehicles
DDS . . . . Deep-Diving System
DDV . . . . Deep-Diving Vehicle
DD . . . . Deep-Drawn (Metals)
DDMP . . . . . . Deep-Drawn Metal Part
DERI . . . . Deep Electric Research Investigation (Navy)
DE . . . . Deep Etch (Lithography term)
DOE . . . . Deep Ocean Environment
DOF . . . . Deep Ocean Floor
DOI . . . . Deep Ocean Installation
DOOLAR . . . . . . Deep Ocean Object Location and Recovery
DOT . . . . Deep-Ocean Technology
DOT . . . . Deep Ocean Transponder
DOWB . . . . . . Deep Ocean Work Boat
DOSV . . . . . . Deep Oceanographic Survey Vehicle (Naval Oceanographic Office)
DOWB . . . . . . Deep Operating Work Boat
DP . . . . Deep Penetration (Air Force)
DP . . . . Deep Pulse (Medicine)
DQ . . . . Deep Quest
DRZ . . . . Deep Reconnaissance Zone (Army)
DRV . . . . Deep Research Vehicle (NOO)
DRV . . . . Deep Research Vessel
DSL . . . . Deep Scattering Layer (Undersea plankton)
DSDP . . . . . . Deep Sea Drilling Project (National Science Foundation)
DSW . . . . Deep Sea Winch
DSIF . . . . . . Deep Space Instrumentation Facility
DSN . . . . Deep Space Network (NASA)
DSP . . . . Deep Space Probe
DSS . . . . Deep-Space Station
DSG . . . . Deep Submergence Group
DSRV . . . . . . Deep Submergence Rescue Vehicle (Navy)
DSSV . . . . . . Deep Submergence Search Vehicle (Research submarine) (Navy)
DSS . . . . Deep Submergence System (Navy)
DSSP . . . . . . Deep Submergence Systems Project (Navy)
DSSPO . . . . . . Deep Submergence Systems Project Office
DSSPTO . . . . . . Deep Submergence Systems Project Technical Office (Navy)
DSSRG . . . . . . Deep Submergence Systems Review Group (Navy)
DTR . . . . Deep Tendon Reflex (Physiology)
DUCS . . . . . . Deep Underground Communications System
DUSC . . . . . . Deep Underground Support Center (Air Force)
DUSS . . . . . . Deep Underground Support System
DUNC . . . . . . Deep Underwater Nuclear Counting
DWICA . . . . . . Deep Water Isotopic Current Analyzer (TVA)
DXR . . . . Deep X-Ray
DXRT . . . . . . Deep X-Ray Therapy
DWD . . . . . . Deepest Working Depth
DMPS . . . . . . Deepwater Motion Picture System
DE . . . . Deere & Company (NYSE symbol)
D . . . . Defeated
DMR . . . . Defective Materiel Report (Air Force)
DPC . . . . Defence Production Chief (British)
DORA . . . . . . Defence of the Realm Act (British) (World War I)
DRCL . . . . . . Defence Research Chemical Laboratories (Canada)
DRET . . . . . . Defence Research Establishment, Toronto (Canada)
DRKL . . . . . . Defence Research Kingston Laboratory (Canada)
DRML . . . . . . Defence Research Medical Laboratory (Canada)
DRNL . . . . . . Defence Research Northern Laboratory (Canada)
DRTE . . . . . . Defence Research Telecommunication Establishment (Canada)
DSAG . . . . . . Defence Systems Analysis Group (Canada)
DTRE . . . . . . Defence Telecommunications Research Establishment
DF . . . . Defender of the Faith
DAC . . . . Defenders of the American Constitution
DOF . . . . Defenders of Furbearers
D. . . . . Defense (Men's lacrosse position)
DAR . . . . Defense Acquisition RADAR
DACOWITS . . . Defense Advisory Committee on Women in the Services
DAME . . . . . . Defense Against Methods of Entry (Military intelligence)
DAMS . . . . Defense Against Missiles Systems

DASE . . . . Defense Against Sound Equipment (Military intelligence)
DA . . . . Defense Aid (Lend-Lease) (World War II)
DAAE . . . . Defense Aid (Lend-Lease) Administration Expenses (World War II)
DAAI & OC . . . Defense Aid (Lend-Lease) Agricultural, Industrial and Other Commodities (World War II)
DAA & AM . . . Defense Aid (Lend-Lease) Aircraft and Aeronautical Material (World War II)
DAF & E . . . . . Defense Aid (Lend-Lease) Facilities and Equipment (World War II)
DAO & OS . . . Defense Aid Ordnance and Ordnance Stores (Lend-Lease)
DAS & E . . . . . Defense Aid (Lend-Lease) Services and Expenses (World War II)
DASF . . . . Defense Aid (Lend-Lease) Special Fund (World War II)
DAT & OV . . . Defense Aid (Lend-Lease) Tanks and Other Vehicles (World War II)
DATRDA . . . . . Defense Aid (Lend-Lease) Testing, Reconditioning, etc., of Defense Articles (World War II)
DAV & OW . . . Defense Aid (Lend-Lease) Vessels and Other Watercraft (World War II)
DATA . . . . Defense Air Transportation Administration
DAVID . . . . . . Defense of Airborne Vehicles in Depth
DACCC . . . . . . Defense Area Communications Control Center
DASA . . . . Defense Atomic Support Agency
DASA-DC . . . . Defense Atomic Support Agency Data Center
DATT . . . . Defense Attaché
DALO . . . . Defense Attaché Liaison Officer
DAO . . . . Defense Attaché Office
DAS . . . . Defense Attaché System (Department of State)
DAIS . . . . Defense Automatic Integrated Switch (Army communications system)
DASC . . . . Defense Automotive Supply Center
DCII . . . . Defense Central Index of Investigations
DCIC . . . . Defense Ceramic Information Center (Battelle Memorial Institute)
DCTSC . . . . . . Defense Clothing and Textile Supply Center (DOD)
DC & TSC . . . Defense Clothing and Textile Supply Center (DOD)
DECCO . . . . . . Defense Commercial Communications Office (Military)
DCCS . . . . Defense Communication Control System (Air Force)
DECEA . . . . . . Defense Communication Engineering Agency
DECEO . . . . . . Defense Communication Engineering Office
DCA . . . . Defense Communications Agency (Military)
DCAC . . . . . . Defense Communications Agency Circular
DCAI . . . . Defense Communications Agency Instruction
DCAN . . . . . . Defense Communications Agency Notice
DCAOC . . . . . . Defense Communications Agency Operations Center
DOCC . . . . . . Defense Communications Agency Operations Center Complex
DCB . . . . Defense Communications Board
DCCC . . . . Defense Communications Control Center
DCEO . . . . . . Defense Communications Engineering Office
DCSP . . . . Defense Communications Satellite Project
DCS . . . . Defense Communications System
DCSTTYNET . . Defense Communications System Teletype Network
DCSAIROPNET . Defense Communications Systems Air Operational Network
DCI . . . . Defense Computer Institute
DCC . . . . Defense Concessions Committee
DCSC . . . . . . Defense Construction Supply Center
DCAS . . . . . . Defense Contract Administration Services (DOD)
DCASD . . . . . . Defense Contract Administration Services District
DCASO . . . . . . Defense Contract Administration Services Office
DCASPRO . . . . . Defense Contract Administration Services Plant Representative Office
DCASR . . . . . . Defense Contract Administrative Services Region
DCAA . . . . Defense Contract Audit Agency (DOD)
DCMA . . . . . . Defense Contract Management Agency
DCSAR . . . . . . Defense Contract Services Administration Region
DCPR . . . . Defense Contractor Planning Report
DCA . . . . Defense Contre Avion (French)
DCC . . . . Defense Control Center
DC . . . . Defense Counsel
DDEL . . . . Defense Development and Engineering Laboratories (Military)
DDEP . . . . . . Defense Development Exchange Program
DDR & E . . . . . Defense Development Research and Engineering
DDC . . . . Defense Documentation Center for Scientific and Technical Information (DOD)
DEPA . . . . . . Defense Electric Power Administration (Department of the Interior)
DECM . . . . . . Defense Electronic Countermeasures
DEP . . . . Defense Electronic Products
DESC . . . . Defense Electronic Supply Center (DSA)
DEI . . . . Defense Electronics, Incorporated
DFA . . . . Defense Fisheries Administration (Abolished, 1953)
DFSB . . . . Defense Force Section Base (Navy)
DFSC . . . . Defense Fuel Supply Center (DOD)
DGSC . . . . . . Defense General Supply Center
DHC . . . . Defense Homes Corporation (World War II)
DIZ . . . . Defense Identification Zone
DIPEC . . . . . . Defense Industrial Plant Equipment Center
DISCO . . . . . . Defense Industrial Security Clearance Office
DISTO . . . . . . Defense Industrial Security Education and Training Office

DISC . . . . Defense Industrial Supply Center
DIAC . . . . Defense Industry Advisory Council
DIAGE . . . . . . Defense Industry Advisory Group Europe
DI . . . . Defense Information
DINFOS . . . . . Defense Information School
DIDS . . . . Defense Integrated Data System
DIMES . . . . . . Defense Integrated Management Engineering System
DIA . . . . Defense Intelligence Agency (Formerly JJ-2)
DIAI . . . . Defense Intelligence Agency Instruction
DIRM . . . . . . Defense Intelligence Requirement Manual
DIS . . . . Defense Intelligence School
DICBM . . . . . . Defense Intercontinental Ballistic Missile
DLI . . . . Defense Language Institute
DLIEC . . . . . . Defense Language Institute, East Coast Branch (Military)
DLISC-EP . . . . Defense Language Institute Support Command - El Paso
DLIWC . . . . . . Defense Language Institute, West Coast Branch (Military)
DLPT . . . . Defense Language Proficiency Tests
DLP . . . . Defense Language Program
DEFLOWH . . . . Defense Liaison Officer to the White House
DLMTB . . . . . . Defense Logistics Management Training Board
DLSC . . . . Defense Logistics Services Center (Military)
DLSIE . . . . . . Defense Logistics Studies Information Exchange (DOD)
DMET . . . . . . Defense Management Educating and Training
DMA . . . . Defense Manpower Administration (Department of Labor) (Superseded by Office of Manpower Administration, 1953)
DMP . . . . Defense Manpower Policy
DMG . . . . Defense Marketing Group (AMA)
DMS . . . . Defense Marketing Survey
DMPA . . . . . . Defense Materials Procurement Agency
DMS . . . . Defense Materials Service (of GSA)
DMS . . . . Defense Materials System
DMIP . . . . . . Defense Materiel Interservicing Program (Department of Defense)
DMUP . . . . . . Defense Materiel Utilization Program (DOD)
DMMB . . . . . . Defense Medical Material Board
DMSC . . . . . . Defense Medical Supply Center
DMIC . . . . . . Defense Metals Information Center
DMEA . . . . . . Defense Minerals Exploration Administration (Interior Department)
DMB . . . . Defense Mobilization Board (Terminated, 1958)
DMO . . . . Defense Mobilization Order
DNCCC . . . . . Defense National Communications Control Center
DO . . . . Defense Order
DOES . . . . . . Defense Organization Entity Standards
DOES . . . . . . Defense Organization Entity System (DOD)
DOCA . . . . . . Defense Orientation Conference Association
DPSC . . . . . . Defense Personnel Support Center
DPSC . . . . . . Defense Petroleum Supply Center
DPC . . . . Defense Plant Corporation (Subsidiary of Reconstruction Finance Corporation)
DPS . . . . Defense Printing Service
DPC . . . . Defense Procurement Circular
DPP . . . . Defense Procurement Program (DOD)
DPA . . . . Defense Production Administration
DPSO . . . . . . Defense Projects Support Office (NASA)
DRADS . . . . . . Defense RADAR Degradation System
DEFCON . . . . . Defense Readiness Condition
DRCCC . . . . . Defense Regional Communications Control Center
DRA . . . . Defense Reorganization Act
DEFREPNAMA . . Defense Representative, North Atlantic Mediterranean Area
DRB . . . . Defense Research Board (Canada)
DRC . . . . Defense Research Corporation
DRE . . . . Defense Research Establishment (Israel)
DRI . . . . Defense Research Institute
DRL . . . . Defense Research Laboratory
DSCS . . . . . . Defense Satellite Communications System (DOD)
DSB . . . . Defense Science Board (DOD)
DSBS . . . . . . Defense Science Board Subcommittee
DEFSIP . . . . . . Defense Scientists Immigration Program
DEFSEC . . . . . Defense Sector (Navy)
DSIATP . . . . . . Defense Sensor Interpretation and Application Training Program
DSA . . . . Defense Shipping Authority
DSFA . . . . . . Defense Solid Fuels Administration (Abolished, 1954)
DEFSCAP . . . . Defense Standard Contract Administration Procedure
DSP . . . . Defense Standardization Program (DOD)
DSSC . . . . . . Defense Subsistence Supply Center
DSA . . . . Defense Supply Agency (DOD)
DSAH . . . . . . Defense Supply Agency Handbook
DSAM . . . . . . Defense Supply Agency Manual
DSAR . . . . . . Defense Supply Agency Regulation
DSA . . . . Defense Supply Association
DSC . . . . Defense Supply Center
DSC . . . . Defense Supply Corporation (World War II)

REVERSE ACRONYMS AND INITIALISMS DICTIONARY

DSMA . . . . Defense Supply Management Agency
DSPR . . . . . . Defense Supply Procurement Regulation (Military)
DSS-W . . . . . . Defense Supply Service – Washington
DSM . . . . Defense Suppression Missile
DSR . . . . Defense Suppression Rocket
DSBCO . . . . . . Defense Surplus Bidders Control Office
DSSO . . . . . . Defense Surplus Sales Office
DSO . . . . Defense System Operator (ECM operator)
DSA . . . . Defense Systems Analysis (DOD)
DATAC . . . . . . Defense & Tactical Armament Control
DTC . . . . Defense Technical Center
DTS-W . . . . . . Defense Telephone Service – Washington
DTMS . . . . . . Defense Traffic Management Service
DTA . . . . Defense Transport Administration
DVFR . . . . . . Defense Visual Flight Rules
DWS . . . . Defense Weapons System
DWSMC . . . . . Defense Weapons System Management Center
DF . . . . Defensive Fire
DEMS . . . . . . Defensively Equipped Merchant Ships
DD . . . . Deferred Delivery (Especially, of securities)
DAS . . . . Deficiency Analysis Summary
DCAP . . . . . . Deficiency Corrective Action Program (Surface Missile Systems)
DFRP . . . . . . Deficiency and Replacement
DR . . . . Deficiency Report (Air Force)
DA . . . . Define Area
DCW . . . . . . Define Constant with Wordmark
DS . . . . Define Symbol
DQ . . . . Definite Quantity
DAM . . . . . . Definition, Analysis, and Mechanization
DC . . . . Definitive Contract
DPM . . . . Deflectable Photomultiplier
DJE . . . . Deflected Jet Exhaust
DCA . . . . Deflection Coil Amplifier
DCD . . . . Deflection Coil Drive
DE . . . . Deflection Error (Military)
DEP . . . . Deflection Error Probable (Military)
DP . . . . Deflection Plate (Technical drawings)
V . . . . Deflection of the Vertical
DY . . . . Deflection Yoke
DYA . . . . Deflection Yoke Amplifier
DG . . . . Degaussing
DEG and DEP . . Degaussing and Deperming (Navy)
DGO . . . . . . Degaussing Officer
DGRO . . . . . . Degaussing Range Officer
DGTO . . . . . . Degaussing Technical Officer
ADG . . . . Degaussing Vessel (Navy symbol)
YDG . . . . Degaussing Vessel (Navy symbol)
DGWO . . . . . Degaussing Wiping Officer
DEG . . . . Degenerate Electron Gas
DOS . . . . Degenerate Oscillating System
DR . . . . Degeneration Reaction
DDRF . . . . . . Degenerative Diseases Research Foundation
DJD . . . . Degenerative Joint Disease
DRDS . . . . . . Degradation RADAR Defense System
DRADS . . . . . Degradation of RADAR Defense Systems
DMA . . . . Degraded Mission Assessment
DMC . . . . Degraded Mission Capability
D . . . . Degree
DOF . . . . Degree of Freedom
DHPA . . . . . . Degree of Honor Protective Association
D of P . . . . . . Degree of Pocahontas
DP . . . . Degree of Polymerization
DS . . . . Degree of Substitution
DF . . . . Degrees of Freedom
DFIC . . . . . . Dehydrated Foods Industry Council
DH . . . . Dehydrogenase (Biochemistry)
DG . . . . Dei Gratia (By the Grace of God)
DI . . . . De-Icing
DKG . . . . Dekagram
DKL . . . . Dekaliter
DKM . . . . . . Dekameter
DE . . . . Delaware
DH . . . . Delaware & Hudson Company (NYSE symbol)
D & HCO . . . . Delaware & Hudson Company
D & H . . . . . Delaware and Hudson Railroad
DLW . . . . . . Delaware, Lackawanna & Western R. R. (AAR code)
DL & WRR . . . Delaware, Lackawanna & Western Railroad
DL & W . . . . . Delaware, Lackawanna and Western Railroad Company
DELMARVA . . . Delaware, Maryland, Virginia
DEW . . . . Delaware Power & Light Company (NYSE symbol)
DRILL . . . . . . Delaware Rapid Interlibrary Loan and Reference Service

DELRIBACO . . . Delaware River Basin Commission (Successor to INCODEL)
DRPA . . . . . . Delaware River Port Authority
DSC . . . . Delaware State College
DEWA . . . . . . Delaware Water Gap National Recreation Area
DALVP . . . . . Delay Enroute Authorized as Ordinary Leave Provided It Does not Interfere with Reporting Date
DF . . . . Delay Fuse
DI . . . . Delay Indefinite (Aviation)
DKO . . . . . . Delay Key On
DL . . . . Delay Line
DLA . . . . Delay Line Assembly
DLC . . . . Delay Line Case
DLM . . . . . . Delay Line Memory
DLR . . . . Delay Line Register
DELTIC . . . . . Delay Line Time Compression
DOPI . . . . . . Delay-On-Pull-In
DA . . . . Delayed Action (Bomb or shell fuze)
DA . . . . Delayed Action (Pharmacy)
DAT . . . . Delayed Action Tablet (Pharmacy)
DAP . . . . Delayed Alpha Particle
DA . . . . Delayed Arming (of explosive device)
DAGC . . . . . . Delayed Automatic Gain Control
DAVC . . . . . . Delayed Automatic Volume Control
DLC . . . . Delayed Clearance (Aviation)
DCS . . . . Delayed Coincidence Spectroscopy
DCC . . . . Delayed Contact Closure
DD . . . . Delayed Delivery
DERM . . . . . . Delayed Echo RADAR Marker
DJOT . . . . . . Delayed Jam on Target
DN . . . . Delayed Neutron
DOC . . . . Delayed Opening Chaff
DOLLS . . . . . Delayed Opening Leaflet System (Military propaganda)
DLO . . . . Delayed Output (Data processing)
DPS . . . . Delayed Printer Simulator
DROT . . . . . . Delayed Range on Target (Air Force)
DROD . . . . . . Delayed Readout Detector (Satellite instrument)
DSR . . . . Delayed Sound Reinforcement
DOT . . . . Delayed on Target
DVOT . . . . . . Delayed Voltage (or Velocity) on Target
DW . . . . Delayed Weather
DGRST . . . . . Delegation Generale a la Recherche Scientifique et Technique (France)
DMA . . . . Delegation Ministerielle a l'Armement (France)
D . . . . Deleted
DMCEUF . . . . Delhi Municipal Corporation Employees' Unions' Federation (India)
DELACCT . . . . Delinquent Account
DT's . . . . Delirium Tremens (Hallucinatory condition of advanced alcoholism)
DELPHO . . . . . Deliver by Telephone (Message handling)
DD . . . . Delivered at Docks
DAS . . . . Delivered Alongside Ship
DOF . . . . Delivery on Field
DO . . . . Delivery Order
DP . . . . Delivery Point
DS . . . . Delphian Society
DC . . . . Delray Connecting R. R. (AAR code)
DAL . . . . Delta Air Lines, Inc. (NYSE symbol)
DL . . . . Delta Air Lines, Inc.
DKE . . . . Delta Kappa Epsilon (Society)
DMS . . . . Delta Milliohm Sensor
DM . . . . Delta Modulation
DMS . . . . Delta Modulation System
DPK . . . . Delta Psi Kappa (Society)
DSG . . . . Delta Smelta Guefelta
DVS . . . . Delta Valley & Southern Railway Company (AAR code)
DVD . . . . Delta Velocity Display
DVL . . . . Delta Velocity Launch
DVP . . . . Delta Velocity Planet
D/D . . . . Demand Draft
D/L . . . . Demand Loan
DM . . . . Demand Meter
DP . . . . Dementia Praecox (or a patient with this condition) (Medical slang)
DMZ . . . . . . Demilitarized Zone
DMW . . . . . . De-Mineralized Water
D . . . . Democrat
DFL . . . . Democrat-Farmer-Labor (Party) (Minnesota)
DAP . . . . Democratic Action Party (Malaysia)
DCA . . . . Democratic Congress Alliance - Gambia
DLA . . . . Democratic Labor Association (Philippines)
DLP . . . . Democratic Labor Party (Australia)
DNC . . . . Democratic National Committee
DP . . . . Democratic Party (Uganda)
DPNC . . . . . . Democratic Party of Nigeria and the Cameroons

DPC . . . . Democratic Policy Committee
DRV . . . . Democratic Republic of Vietnam (North Vietnam)
DRVN . . . . . . Democratic Republic of Viet-Nam (Communist North Vietnam)
DSCC . . . . Democratic Senatorial Campaign Committee
DSG . . . . Democratic Study Group
DWC . . . . Democratic Workers' Congress (Ceylon)
DNRC . . . . Democritus Nuclear Research Center (Greece)
D/M . . . . Demodulate/Modulate
DND . . . . Demodulator Neon Driver
DBD . . . . Demokratische Bauernpartei Deutschlands (Democratic Peasants' Party) (East Germany)
DFD . . . . Demokratischer Frauenbund Deutschlands
DML . . . . Demolition
DFD . . . . Demolition Firing Device
DRU . . . . Demolition Research Unit
DAF . . . . Demonstration Air Force
DOF . . . . Demonstration of Operational Feasibility
DPA . . . . Demonstration Programs Administration (HUD)
DRAT . . . . Demonstration Reliability Acceptance Test
DASOP . . . . . Demonstration and Shakedown Operation Piggyback (Kit)
DASO . . . . Demonstration and Shakedown Operations (Military)
DSOTS . . . . . Demonstration Site Operational Test Series
D . . . . Denarius, Denarii (Silver coin in Ancient Rome; gold coin in Roman Empire)
DENDRAL . . . . Dendritic Algorithm (Organic molecules)
DHF . . . . Dengue Hemorrhagic Fever
DPS . . . . Denison & Pacific Suburban Railway Company (AAR code)
DA . . . . Denmark (NATO)
DCH . . . . Denote Chassis
DEP . . . . Dense Electronic Population
DUC . . . . Dense Upper Cloud
D . . . . Density
DA . . . . Density Altitude (Navigation)
DENALT . . . . . Density-Altitude (Computer)
DDI . . . . Density Dependent Inhibition (of cell growth)
DEDE . . . . Density-Depth
DOW . . . . Density of Water
DA . . . . Dental Apprentice
DC . . . . Dental Corps (Navy)
DENTCORPS . . Dental Corps (Air Force)
DCR . . . . Dental Corps, General Service (USNR officer designation)
DDA . . . . Dental Dealers of America
DDF . . . . Dental Documentary Foundation
DEB . . . . Dental Examining Board
DMA . . . . Dental Manufacturers of America
DO . . . . Dental Officer
DENPAY . . . . Dental Pay
DP . . . . Dental Prosthetic Technician
DR . . . . Dental Recruit
DRM . . . . Dental Repair Technician (Navy)
DT . . . . Dental Technician
DN . . . . Dentalman (Nonrated enlisted man) (Navy)
DSP . . . . Dentists' Supply Company of N.Y. (NYSE symbol)
DEN . . . . Denver (Colo.) (Airport symbol)
DRI . . . . Denver Research Institute
DRGW . . . . . . Denver & Rio Grande Western R. R. (AAR code)
DGR . . . . Denver & Rio Grande Western R. R. Company (NYSE symbol)
D & RGW . . . . Denver & Rio Grande Western Railroad Company
DSL . . . . Denver & Salt Lake R. R. (AAR code)
D & SL . . . . . . Denver and Salt Lake Railway Company
DD . . . . Deo Dedit (He Gave to God)
DG . . . . Deo Gratias (Thanks Be to God; or God Be Thanked)
DOM . . . . Deo Optimo Maximo (To God, the Best and Greatest)
DV . . . . Deo Volente (God Willing)
DOC . . . . Deoxycorticosterone (Endocrinology)
DOCA . . . . . . Deoxycorticosterone Acetate (Endocrinology)
DNA . . . . Deoxyribonucleic Acid (Biochemistry, genetics)
D . . . . Depart or Departure
DASP . . . . Departamento Administrativo do Servico Publico (Administrative Department of Public Service) (Brazil)
DIP . . . . Departamento de Imprensa e Propaganda (Brazil)
DNC . . . . Departamento Nacional do Cafe (Brazil)
DNSP . . . . . . Departamento Nacional de Saude Publica (Brazil)
D . . . . Department
DAA . . . . Department of Aeronautics and Astronautics (MIT)
DA . . . . Department of Agriculture
D of A . . . . . Department of Agriculture
DOA . . . . Department of Agriculture
DAF . . . . Department of Agriculture and Fisheries (Scotland)
DAF . . . . Department of the Air Force

DAFICCS . . . . . Department of the Air Force Integrated Command and Control Systems
DA . . . . Department of the Army
DOA . . . . Department of the Army
DAAA . . . . Department of the Army Administrative Area
DAATCO . . . . . Department of the Army Air Traffic Coordinating Officer
DACE . . . . Department of the Army Alternate Command and Control Element
DACA . . . . Department of Army Certificate of Achievement
DAC . . . . Department of the Army Civilian
DACCS . . . . . . Department of the Army Command and Control System
DACC . . . . Department of the Army Communications Center
DADMCS . . . . . Department of Army Decoration for Meritorious Civilian Service
DADAC . . . . . . Department of the Army Distribution/Allocation Committee
DAFD . . . . Department of the Army Forward Depot
DAIP . . . . Department of the Army Intelligence Plan
DAMA . . . . . . Department of the Army Materiel Annex
DAMP . . . . . . Department of the Army Materiel Program
DAMWO . . . . Department of the Army Modification Work Order
DAPEP . . . . . Department of Army Panel on Environmental Physiology
DADCMI . . . . Department of the Army Policy for Disclosure of Classified Military Information (to foreign government)
DA-AHEW . . . . Department of the Army Plan for Assistance in Department of Health, Education, and Welfare
DARRIS . . . . . Department of Army Requisitioning, Receipt, and Issue System
DARS . . . . . . Department of the Army Relocation Sites
DASD . . . . . . Department of the Army Shipping Document
DASO . . . . Department of the Army Special Order
DASPO . . . . . Department of the Army Special Photographic Office
DASL . . . . . . Department of the Army Strategic Logistics (Study)
DASEB . . . . . . Department of the Army Suitability Evaluation Board
DASSO . . . . . Department of the Army Systems Staff Officer
DAVI . . . . . . Department of Audiovisual Instruction (of NEA)
BAD . . . . Department of Bantu Administration and Development (An agency of South African government)
DCRP . . . . . . Department of City and Regional Planning (MIT)
DCT . . . . Department of Classroom Teachers (of NEA)
DC . . . . Department of Commerce
D of C . . . . . Department of Commerce
DOC . . . . Department of Commerce
DCE . . . . Department of Conservation and Environment (Proposed name for US Department of the Interior)
DDM . . . . Department of Data Management (VA)
DD . . . . Department of Defense
DOD . . . . Department of Defense
DODAAD . . . . Department of Defense Activity Address Directory
DODAC . . . . . Department of Defense Ammunition Code
DODCAPS . . . . Department of Defense Central Automated Personnel System
DODCLPMI . . . Department of Defense Consolidated List of Principal Military Items
DODDAC . . . . Department of Defense Damage Assessment Center
DODD . . . . . . Department of Defense Directive
DODEP . . . . . Department of Defense Emergency Plans
DODEP . . . . . . Department of Defense Exercise Planning
DODFDCO . . . Department of Defense Foreign Disclosure Coordinating Office
DODGE . . . . . Department of Defense Gravity Experiment (Satellite)
DODGE-M . . . Department of Defense Gravity Experiment, Multipurpose
DODHSNS . . . . Department of Defense High School Newspaper Service
DODHGCSO . . . Department of Defense Household Goods Commercial Storage Office
DODHGFO . . . Department of Defense Household Goods Field Office
DODIC . . . . . . Department of Defense Identification Code
DODISS . . . . . Department of Defense Index of Specifications and Standards
DODIER . . . . . Department of Defense Industrial Equipment Reserve
DISP . . . . DOD (Department of Defense) Industrial Security Program
DODI . . . . Department of Defense Instruction
DODIC . . . . . . Department of Defense Item Code
DOD/MIS . . . . Department of Defense Management Information System
DDMS . . . . . . Department of Defense Manned Space Flight
DODMUL . . . . Department of Defense Master Urgency List
DODMPAC . . . Department of Defense Military Pay and Allowance Committee
DODMPRC . . . Department of Defense Military Personnel Records Center
DODNACC . . . Department of Defense National Agency Check Center
DORE . . . . DOD (Department of Defense) Officer Record Examination
DDP . . . . Department of Defense Production
DODRE . . . . . . Department of Defense Research and Engineering
DTS . . . . Department of Defense Transportation System
DEA . . . . Department of Economic Affairs (British)
ECA . . . . Department of Economic Affairs of the United Nations
ESA (UN) . . . . Department of Economic and Social Affairs (of United Nations) (Later, Department of Social Affairs)
DESS . . . . . . Department of Economics and Social Science (MIT)
DE . . . . Department of Education
EKNE . . . . Department of Elementary, Kindergarten, and Nursery Education (NEA)

DESP . . . . Department of Elementary School Principals (of NEA)
DFL . . . . Department of Family Life (Later, Commission on Marriage and Family Life) (of NCC)
DGG . . . . . . Department of Geology and Geophysics (MIT)
DHEW . . . . . Department of Health, Education, and Welfare
HEW . . . . Department of Health, Education, and Welfare
DHE . . . . Department of Home Economics (of NEA)
DHUD . . . . . . Department of Housing and Urban Development
HUD . . . . . . Department of Housing and Urban Development
DIED . . . . . . Department of Industrial and Economic Development (of Ohio) (Now defunct)
DIR . . . . **Department of Industrial Research**
DIB . . . . **Department of Information and Broadcasting (India)**
DIB . . . . **Department Information Bulletin**
D of I . . . . . . **Department of Interior**
DOI . . . . Department of the Interior
IBCA . . . . . . Department of Interior Board of Contract Appeals
D of J . . . . . Department of Justice
DOJ . . . . Department of Justice
DL . . . . Department of Labor
D of L . . . . . . Department of Labor
DOLITAC . . . . Department of Labor International Technical Assistance Corps
LEG (UN) . . . . Department of Legal Affairs of the United Nations
DMS . . . . Department of Medicine and Surgery (VA)
DMTS . . . . . . Department of Mines and Technical Survey (Canada)
DMV . . . . . . Department of Motor Vehicles
DND . . . . . . Department of National Defense (Canadian)
DNAME . . . . . Department of Naval Architecture and Marine Engineering (MIT)
DN . . . . . . Department of the Navy
DON . . . . Department of the Navy
DNFYP . . . . . Department of the Navy Five-Year Program
DONMICS . . . . Department of the Navy Management Information Control System
DNE . . . . . . Department of Nuclear Engineering (MIT)
DNFST . . . . . Department of Nutrition, Food Science and Technology (MIT)
DOI . . . . Department Operating Instruction
DOT . . . . Department of Overseas Trade (British)
DP . . . . Department of the Pacific (Marine Corps)
DPR . . . . Department Performance Rating
DPM . . . . Department Personnel Manual
DPR . . . . Department of Physical Research (British)
DPH . . . . Department of Public Health
DPI . . . . Department of Public Information (of United Nations)
DPSS . . . . . . Department of Public Social Services
DRE . . . . Department of Rural Education (of NEA)
DSIR . . . . Department of Scientific and Industrial Research (of the Privy Council for Scientific and Industrial Research) (Great Britain)
SCA(UN) . . . . . Department of Security Council Affairs of the United Nations
DEPSO . . . . . Department Standardization Office (Navy)
DS . . . . Department of State
D of S . . . . . . Department of State
DOS . . . . Department of State
DSCA . . . . . . Department of State Correspondents Association
DTD . . . . Department of Tank Design (British)
DOT . . . . Department of Transport (Canada)
DOTC . . . . . . Department of Transport (Canada)
DOT . . . . Department of Transportation (US)
D of T . . . . . . Department of the Treasury (Commonly TD, Treasury Department)
DOT . . . . Department of the Treasury
TRIUN . . . . . . Department of Trusteeship and Information from Non-Self-Governing Territories of the United Nations
DVB . . . . **Department of Veterans Benefits (VA)**
DCPB . . . . . . **Departmental Civilian Personnel Branch**
DIPR . . . . **Departmental Industrial Plant Reserve (Department of the Army)**
DIRS . . . . . . **Departmental Industrial Reserve System**
P . . . . Departure
DAF . . . . Departure Airfield
DAFC . . . . . . Departure Airfield Control
DAFCG . . . . . Departure Airfield Control Group
DNB . . . . Departure from Nuclear Boiling
DP . . . . Departure Point
DEPU . . . . . . De Paul University (Illinois)
DIC . . . . Dependency and Indemnity Compensation (Military)
DD . . . . Dependent Drainage (Medicine)
DHA . . . . Dependent Housing Area (Army)
DMO . . . . . . Dependent Meteorological Office
DOT . . . . Dependent Overseas Territory
DV . . . . Dependent Variable
DAA . . . . Dependents Assistance Act
DMCA . . . . . . Dependents' Medical Care Act (HEW)
DR . . . . Dependents Rate (Air Force)
DEPERMSTA . . . Deperming and Flashing Station (Navy)

DSP . . . . Deployable Solar Panel
DPR . . . . Depolymerized Rubber
DA . . . . Deposit Account (Banking)
D/A . . . . Deposit Account (Banking)
D/B . . . . Deposit Book
DLB . . . . Deposit Liquidation Board
DPB . . . . Deposit Passbook (Banking)
DR . . . . Deposit Receipt
DC . . . . Deposited Carbon
D . . . . Depositus (Laid to Rest)
DAP . . . . Depot Acceptance Procedures
DEPACTV . . . . . Depot Activity
DART . . . . . . Depot Automatic Rescheduling Technique
DCMS . . . . . . Depot Command Management System
DCN . . . . Depot Control Number
DIR . . . . Depot Inspection and Repair
DIMATE . . . . . Depot-Installed Maintenance Automatic Equipment
DLM . . . . Depot Level Maintenance (Air Force)
DMCC . . . . . . Depot Maintenance Control Center (Army)
DMSP . . . . . . Depot Maintenance Support Plan (Air Force)
DPO . . . . Depot Property Officer
DQM . . . . . . Depot Quartermaster (Marine Corps)
DQN . . . . Depot Quartermaster, Norfolk, Virginia (Marine Corps)
DQPH . . . . . . Depot Quartermaster, Pearl Harbor, Hawaii (Marine Corps)
DQP . . . . Depot Quartermaster, Philadelphia, Pennsylvania (Marine Corps)
DQQ . . . . Depot Quartermaster, Quantico, Virginia (Marine Corps)
DQR . . . . Depot Quartermaster, Richmond, Virginia (Marine Corps)
DQSF . . . . . . Depot Quartermaster, San Francisco, California (Marine Corps)
D of S . . . . . . Depot of Supplies (Marine Corps)
DSC . . . . Depot Supply Center
DTC . . . . Depot Training Center
DEVAT . . . . . . Depot Vehicle Automatic Tester
DDI . . . . Depression Deviation Indicator
DPF . . . . Depression Position-Finder
D . . . . Depth
DB . . . . Depth Bomb (Military)
DOB . . . . Depth of Burial (of explosives)
DC . . . . Depth Charge (Aerial)
DCP . . . . Depth Charge Projector
DCT . . . . Depth-Charge Thrower
DCT . . . . Depth Charges Track
DDI . . . . Depth Deviation Indicator
DDA . . . . Depth-Duration-Area
DFOLS . . . . . . Depth of Flash Optical Landing System (Navy)
DEGA . . . . . . Depth Gage
DOM . . . . Depth of Modulation
D . . . . Depth of Ship
DS . . . . Depth Sounder
DTP . . . . Depth Telemetering Pinger
D . . . . Deputy
DAG . . . . Deputy Adjutant-General
DA . . . . Deputy Administrator
DAAG . . . . . . Deputy Assistant Adjutant-General
DAD . . . . Deputy Assistant Director
DADOS . . . . . . Deputy Assistant Director of Ordnance Stores (Military)
DAQMG . . . . . Deputy Assistant Quartermaster General
DBC . . . . Deputy Brigade Commander (Army)
DC . . . . Deputy Chief
DCAS . . . . . . Deputy Chief of the Air Staff (British)
DCCAO . . . . . Deputy Chief Civil Affairs Officer (US and Britain)
DCGS . . . . . . Deputy Chief of the General Staff in the Field (British military)
DCIGS . . . . . . Deputy Chief of the Imperial General Staff (British military)
DCM . . . . Deputy Chief of Mission (Diplomatic corps)
DCNM(D) . . . . Deputy Chief of Naval Material, Development
DCNM(M & O) . . Deputy Chief of Naval Material (Management and Organization)
DCNM(M & F) . . Deputy Chief of Naval Material, Material and Facilities
DCNM(P & FM) . . Deputy Chief of Naval Material, Programs and Financial Management
DCNO . . . . . . Deputy Chief of Naval Operations
DCNOA . . . . Deputy Chief of Naval Operations, Administration
DCNO(AIR) . . . Deputy Chief of Naval Operations (Air)
DCNO(D) . . . . Deputy Chief of Naval Operations (Development)
DCNO(L) . . . . Deputy Chief of Naval Operations (Logistics)
DCNO(P & P) . . Deputy Chief of Naval Operations (Plans and Policies)
DCNOFOR . . . Deputy Chief of Naval Operations, Fleet Operations and Readiness
DCNO(M & NR) . . Deputy Chief of Naval Operations for Manpower and Naval Reserve
DCNO(P & R) . . Deputy Chief of Naval Operations, Personnel and Naval Reserve
DCNS . . . . . . Deputy Chief of Naval Staff (Marine Corps)
DCPI . . . . . . Deputy Chief Patrol Inspector (Immigration and Naturalization Service)
DCOFS . . . . . Deputy Chief of Staff
DCS . . . . Deputy Chief of Staff
DCA . . . . Deputy Chief of Staff for Administration

DC/SAF . . . . . Deputy Chief of Staff, Air Force
DC of SA . . . . Deputy Chief of Staff, Army
DCS/C . . . . . . Deputy Chief of Staff, Comptroller
AFDDC . . . . . . Deputy Chief of Staff, Development (Air Force)
DCS/D . . . . . . Deputy Chief of Staff, Development
DCS/I . . . . . . Deputy Chief of Staff, Intelligence (Army)
DCS/INT . . . . . Deputy Chief of Staff, Intelligence (Air Force)
DC/SL . . . . . . Deputy Chief of Staff, Logistics (Army)
DCSLOG . . . . Deputy Chief of Staff, Logistics (Army)
DDPC . . . . DCSLOG (Deputy Chief of Staff for Logistics) Data Processing Center
      (Military)
DCSM . . . . . . Deputy Chief of Staff, Materiel
DC/SMO . . . . . Deputy Chief of Staff, Military Operations (Army)
DCSOPS . . . . . Deputy Chief of Staff for Military Operations (Army)
AFODC . . . . . Deputy Chief of Staff, Operations (Air Force)
DCSO . . . . . . Deputy Chief of Staff, Operations
DCSOA . . . . . Deputy Chief of Staff, Operations and Administration
AFPDC . . . . . . Deputy Chief of Staff Personnel (Air Force)
DCS/P . . . . . . Deputy Chief of Staff, Personnel
DCSPER . . . . . Deputy Chief of Staff for Personnel (Army)
DCS/P & O . . . Deputy Chief of Staff for Plans and Operations
DCS/P & P . . . Deputy Chief of Staff, Plans and Programs
DCPR . . . . . . Deputy Chief of Staff for Plans and Research
DCSPR . . . . . . Deputy Chief of Staff for Plans and Research (Army)
DCS/P & R . . . Deputy Chief of Staff for Programs and Resources
DCS/R & D . . . Deputy Chief of Staff, Research & Development (Army)
DCS/R & T . . . Deputy Chief of Staff, Research and Technology
DCS/RC . . . . . Deputy Chief of Staff, Reserve Components (Army)
DCS/S & L . . . Deputy Chief of Staff, Systems and Logistics
DCRE . . . . Deputy Commandant Royal Engineers (British)
DCAS . . . . . . Deputy Commander Aerospace System (Air Force)
DCG . . . . Deputy Commanding General
DCG/CONARC . . Deputy Commanding General, Continental Army Command (Later,
      Deputy Commanding General, Training)
DCG/T . . . . . . Deputy Commanding General, Training (CONARC) (Army)
DCO . . . . Deputy Commanding Officer
DCG . . . . Deputy Commissary-General
DC . . . . Deputy Consul
DCF . . . . Deputy for Contract Financing (Air Force)
DD . . . . Deputy Director
DDAS (ET) . . . . Deputy Director of Armament Supply (Eastern Theater)
DDCO (I) . . . . Deputy Director of Combined Operations (India)
DDMS . . . . . . Deputy Director of Medical Services (British)
DDMI . . . . . . Deputy Director of Military Intelligence
DDMOI . . . . . . Deputy Director of Military Operations and Intelligence (British)
DDMT . . . . . . Deputy Director of Military Training (British)
DDO . . . . Deputy Director of Operations (Air Force)
DEPDIRPACDOCKS . . Deputy Director Pacific Division, Bureau of Yards and Docks
      (Navy)
DDST . . . . . . Deputy Director of Supply and Transport (British)
DEAN . . . . . . Deputy Educators Against Narcotics
DGM . . . . . . Deputy General Manager (AEC)
DGM . . . . . . Deputy Grand Master (Masonry)
DIG . . . . Deputy Inspector-General
DIGS . . . . . . Deputy Inspector General for Safety (Air Force)
DINO . . . . . . Deputy Inspector of Naval Ordnance
DJAG . . . . . . Deputy Judge Advocate General
DL . . . . Deputy Lieutenant
DLNC . . . . . . Deputy Local Naval Commander
DMG . . . . . . Deputy Military Governor (US Military Government, Germany)
DMCCC . . . . . Deputy Missile Combat Crew Commander
DQMG . . . . . . Deputy Quarter-Master-General
DQMG . . . . . . Deputy Quartermaster General
DSDAR . . . . . . Deputy and Scientific Director of Army Research
DEPSECDEF . . . Deputy Secretary of Defense
DSS . . . . Deputy of Space Systems (Air Force)
DSAC . . . . . . Deputy Supreme Allied Commander (Military)
DUSA . . . . . . Deputy Under Secretary of the Army
DQE . . . . De Queen & Eastern R. R. (AAR code)
DYO . . . . Derby Oil Company (Kansas) (NYSE symbol)
DDHP . . . . . . Deringer Duell Head Process
DDM . . . . . . Derived Delta Modulation
DF . . . . Dermatology Foundation
DST . . . . Dermatology and Syphilology Technician (Navy)
D . . . . Descend(ing) (Aviation)
DSATC . . . . . Descend so as to Cross (Aviation)
DTAX . . . . . . Descend to and Cross (Aviation)
DTAM . . . . . Descend to and Maintain (Aviation)
DSATR . . . . . Descend so as to Reach (Aviation)
DWTR . . . . . . Descend Well to Right (Aviation)
DWRC . . . . . . Descend Well to Right of Course (Aviation)

DMLF . . . . . . Descending Medial Longitudinal Fasciculus
DOI . . . . Descent Orbit Insertion (Aerospace)
DPS . . . . Descent Propulsion System (NASA)
DRR . . . . Descent Rate RADAR
DF . . . . Describing Function
DP . . . . Description Pattern
DOUCHE . . . . . Description of Underwater Contacts Hastily and Exactly (Navy slang)
DAM . . . . Descriptor Attribute Matrix
DWI . . . . Descriptor Word Index
DST . . . . Desensitization Test (Allergy)
DBC . . . . Desert Bighorn Council
DPC . . . . Desert Protective Council
DRI . . . . Desert Research Institute (University of Nevada)
DTC . . . . Desert Test Center (Army)
D. . . . . Deserter
DESEFF . . . . . . Deserter's Effects (Military)
DESILU . . . . . . Desi-Lucille Arnaz Company
DAT . . . . Design Approval Test
DATR . . . . Design Approval Test Report
DAC . . . . Design Augmented by Computer
DA . . . . Design Authorization
DBW . . . . Design Bandwidth
DCB . . . . Design Certificate Board
DCC . . . . Design Change Control
DCN . . . . Design Change Notice
DCP . . . . Design Change Proposal
DCR . . . . Design Change Request
DCREO . . . . . . Design Change Request Engineering Order
DCS . . . . Design Change Schedule
DCWO . . . . . . Design Change Work Order
DDB . . . . Design Data Book
DDP . . . . Design Data Package
DDF . . . . Design Discharge Format
DDRI . . . . Design Drafting Reference Information
DDT . . . . Design and Drafting Techniques
DEI . . . . Design Engine Inspection
DET . . . . Design Evaluation Test
DES . . . . Design Expansion System
DFA . . . . Design Fabrication Assembly
DH . . . . Design Handbook
DIP . . . . Design Improvement Program
DIS . . . . Design Improvement Study
DIB . . . . Design Information Bulletin
DIW . . . . Design Information Worksheet
DM . . . . Design Manual
DM . . . . Design Memorandum
DOR . . . . Design Objective Reliability
DPV . . . . Design Point Vehicle
DPT . . . . Design Proof Tests
DP . . . . Design Proposal
DR . . . . Design Requirement
DRB . . . . Design Review Board
DSF . . . . Design Safety Factor
DSA . . . . Design Schedule Analysis
DESSIM . . . . . Design Simulator
DS . . . . Design Standards
DETAB-X . . . . . Design Table, Experimental (Computer language)
DVD . . . . Design Verification Demonstration
DVT . . . . Design Verification Test
DER . . . . Designated Engineer Representative (FAA title)
DESIGNAP . . . Designated as Naval Aviation Pilot (Marine Corps)
DOP . . . . Designated Overhaul Point
DPM . . . . Designated Project Manager
DPM . . . . Designated for Prompt Mobilization
DSP . . . . Designated Stock Point
DSMG . . . . . . Designated Systems Management Group (Air Force)
DWL . . . . Designed Water Line (Technical drawings)
DCL . . . . Designer Choice Logic
DSG . . . . Designer Shoe Guild
DOM . . . . Designing Out Maintenance
DDD . . . . Desired Delivery Date
DGZ . . . . Desired Ground Zero (Bombing)
DIDOC . . . . . . Desired Image Distribution Using Orthogonal Constraints
      (Illinois Institute of Technology)
DMPI . . . . Desired Mean Point of Impact (Military)
DPI . . . . Desired Point of Impact
FT & TW . . . . . Desk, Combination Flat Top and Typewriter
D & D . . . . . . Desk and Derrick (Oil industry)
DPFT . . . . Desk, Double-Pedestal Flat-Top
DPTW . . . . . . Desk, Double-Pedestal Typewriter
DTC . . . . Desk Top Computer

DAT . . . . Desktop Analysis Tool (A publication)
DMI . . . . Desmethylimipramine (Chemical)
DCI . . . . Des Moines & Central Iowa R. R. (AAR code)
DMU . . . . Des Moines Union Railway Company (AAR code)
DSO . . . . De Soto Chemical Coatings, Inc. (NYSE symbol)
DESO . . . . . . DeSoto National Memorial
DCA . . . . Desoxycorticosterone Acetate
DR . . . . Despatch Rider (British military)
DRLS . . . . . . Despatch-Rider Letter-Service (British military)
DBS . . . . Despeciated Bovine Serum
DATS . . . . . . Despun Antenna Test Satellite (Air Force)
DHS . . . . Despun Heat Shield
DM . . . . Destra Mano (Right Hand)
DIU . . . . Destratification Impeller Unit
DMI . . . . Destratification Motor Impeller
DMIU . . . . . . Destratification Motor Impeller Unit
DMU . . . . Destratification Motor Unit
D . . . . Destroyed
DD . . . . Destroyer (Navy symbol)
DAB . . . . Destroyer Advisory Board
DASH . . . . . . Destroyer Antisubmarine Helicopter
DASTARD . . . . Destroyer Antisubmarine Transportable Array Detector
DESBATFOR . . . Destroyer Battle Force (Navy)
DESDIV . . . . . Destroyer Division (Navy)
DE . . . . Destroyer Escort
DE's . . . . Destroyer Escorts (Navy)
DESFLOT . . . . Destroyer Flotilla (Navy)
DF . . . . Destroyer Flotilla
DESLANT . . . . Destroyer Force, Atlantic Fleet (Navy symbol)
DL . . . . Destroyer Leader
DM . . . . Destroyer Minelayer (Light minelayer)
DMS . . . . Destroyer Minesweeper (Navy symbol)
DESREP . . . . . Destroyer Repair (Navy)
DESREP . . . . . . Destroyer Representative (Navy)
DESCOFOR . . . Destroyer Scouting Force (Navy)
DESRON . . . . Destroyer Squadron (Navy)
DTB . . . . Destroyer Tactical Bulletin
AD . . . . Destroyer Tender (Navy symbol)
DESAF . . . . . Destroyers, Asiatic Fleet (Navy)
DESCRUPAC . . . Destroyers/Cruisers, Pacific Fleet (Navy)
DDO . . . . Destroyers, Disbursing Office (Navy)
DESPAC . . . . . Destroyers, Pacific Fleet
DESSOWESPAC . . Destroyers, Southwest Pacific Fleet
DC . . . . Destruct Charge
DSAD . . . . . . Destruct Safe Arm Device
DAMV . . . . . . Destruction of Aircraft or Motor Vehicles
DGP . . . . Destruction of Government Property
DIP . . . . Destruction of Interstate Property
DRO . . . . Destructive Readout
DDL . . . . Det Danske Luftfartselskab A/S (Danish Airlines)
DNL . . . . Det Norske Luftfartselkap (Norwegian Airlines)
DETALL . . . . . Detached from Duty Indicated and from all Other Duty Assigned
DEML . . . . . . Detached Enlisted Men's List (Army)
DOL . . . . Detached Officer's List (Army)
DS . . . . Detached Service (Army)
DAALPS . . . . . Detachment d'Armee des Alpes
DAATL . . . . . . Detachment d'Armee de l'Atlantique
DEAL . . . . . . Detachment Equipment Authorization List (Military)
DOP . . . . Detachment of Patients
DLIC . . . . . . Detachments Left in Contact (Military)
DAT . . . . . . Detail Assembly Template
DCR . . . . Detail Condition Register
DS . . . . Detail Specification
DBD . . . . Detailed Budget Decision
DCL . . . . Detailed Check List
DDD . . . . Detailed Data Display
DHEP . . . . . . Detailed Human Engineering Plan
DIC . . . . Detailed Interrogation Center (Navy)
DELTA . . . . . . Detailed Labor and Time Analysis (PERT)
DPP . . . . Detailed Project Plan
DR . . . . Detailed Report
DSFR . . . . . . Detailed System Functional Requirements
DST . . . . Detailed System Test
DTO . . . . Detailed Test Objective
DOB . . . . Detained on Board (Referring to seamen)
D/P . . . . Detained Pay
DYN . . . . Detectability of Yes-No
DR . . . . Detection RADAR
DRDTO . . . . . Detection RADAR Data Takeoff (Air Force)
DREC . . . . . . Detection RADAR Electronic Component

DRED . . . . Detection RADAR Environmental Display (Air Force)
DERAX . . . . . Detection and Range (Early name for RADAR)
DBB . . . . Detector Back Bias
DBB . . . . Detector Balanced Bias
DM . . . . Detector Mosaic
DTS . . . . Detector Tracker Switch
DC . . . . Deterioration Control
D & F . . . . Determination and Finding
DFA . . . . Deterministic Finite Automaton
DIG . . . . Detonator Inspection Gage
DEADS . . . . . Detroit Air Defense Sector (ADS)
DA . . . . Detroit Arsenal (Army)
DCL . . . . Detroit College of Law
DTE . . . . Detroit Edison Company (NYSE symbol)
DGY . . . . Detroit Gray Iron Foundry (NYSE symbol)
DHM . . . . . . Detroit Hardware Manufacturing Company (NYSE symbol)
DIMA . . . . . . Detroit Institute of Musical Arts
DIT . . . . Detroit Institute of Technology
DM . . . . Detroit & Mackinac Railway Company (AAR code)
D & M . . . . . Detroit and Mackinac Railway Company
DOD . . . . . . Detroit Ordnance District
DSL . . . . Detroit Signal Laboratory (Army)
DES . . . . Detroit Steel Corporation (NYSE symbol)
DT . . . . Detroit Terminal R. R. (AAR code)
DTI . . . . Detroit, Toledo & Ironton R. R. (AAR code)
DT & I . . . . . Detroit, Toledo and Ironton Railroad Company
DTS . . . . Detroit & Toledo Shore Line R. R. (AAR code)
D & TSL . . . . Detroit and Toledo Shore Line Railroad Company
DTA . . . . Detroit Tooling Association
DETW . . . . . . Detroit & Western R. R. (AAR code)
DP . . . . Detrucking Point
D . . . . Deus (God)
D . . . . Deuterium
H2 . . . . Deuterium
DIMPLE . . . . . Deuterium Moderated Pile Low Energy (Reactor)
D-T . . . . Deuterium-Tritium Reaction (Fusion program)
DAPG . . . . Deutsch-Amerikanische Petroleum Gesellschaft (German-American Petroleum Society)
DLG . . . . Deutsch-Lateinamerikanische Gesellschaft
DAL . . . . Deutsche Akademie der Landwirtschaftswissenschaften
DANA . . . . . . Deutsche Allgemeine Nachrichten Agentur (German general news agency, sponsored by US newspapermen as a successor to the NAZI-controlled DNB) (Post-World War II)
DAZ . . . . Deutsche Allgemeine Zeitung (German newspaper)
DAG . . . . Deutsche Angestellten Gewerkschaft (German Salaried Employees' Union) (West Germany)
DARA . . . . . . Deutsche Arbeitgemeinschaft fuer Rechen-Anlagen (A data processing association)
DAF . . . . Deutsche Arbeitsfront (German Workers Front) (Post-World War II)
DBW . . . . . . Deutsche Babcock Wilcox Werke
DBB . . . . Deutsche Bauernbank
DBG . . . . Deutsche Beamtengesetz (Germany)
DBP . . . . Deutsche Bundespost
DDR . . . . Deutsche Demokratische Republik (German Democratic Republic) (East Germany)
DFL . . . . Deutsche Forschungsanstalt fuer Luftfahrt
DFG . . . . Deutsche Forschungsgemeinschaft (German Research Association)
DFG . . . . Deutsche Friedensgesellschaft
DGON . . . . . . Deutsche Gesellschaft fuer Ortung und Navigation (West Germany)
DGPH . . . . . . Deutsche Gesellschaft fuer Photographie (West Germany)
DGRR . . . . . . Deutsche Gesellschaft Raketentecknik und Raumfahrt (German Society for Rocket Research and Space Flight)
DGG . . . . Deutsche Grammophon Gesellschaft (Phonograph recording company)
DHZ . . . . Deutsche Handelszentrale
DHFK . . . . . . Deutsche Hochschule fuer Koerperkultur
DHZ . . . . Deutsche Hydrographische Zeitschrift
DIN . . . . Deutsche Industrie-Normen (German industry standards)
DIB . . . . Deutsche Investitionsbank
DLT . . . . Deutsche Landmaschinen und Traktorenindustrie
DLG . . . . Deutsche Landwirtschafts-Gesellschaft
DM . . . . Deutsche Mark (German money)
DPA . . . . Deutsche Presse-Agentur (West German news agency)
DSP . . . . Deutsche Sex Partei (Political party) (Germany)
DVL . . . . Deutsche Versuchsanstalt fuer Luftfahrt
DVP . . . . Deutsche Volkspolizei
DWStK . . . . . Deutsche Waffen Stillstandkommission (German Armistice Commission, in France) (World War II)
DEWAG . . . . . Deutsche Werbe-Anzeigen-Gesellschaft
DBB . . . . Deutscher Beamtenbund (Federation of German Civil Service Officials) (West Germany)

DFF . . . . Deutscher Fernsehfunk
DGB . . . . Deutscher Gewerkschaftsbund fuer das Gebiet der Bundesrepublik
         Deutschland und Berlin (German Trade Union Federation for the Area
         of the Federal Republic and Berlin) (West Germany)
DHV . . . . Deutscher Handels-und Industrieangestellten-Verband (Association of
         Clerical Employees of Germany) (West Germany)
DJR . . . . Deutscher Jugendring
DOH . . . . Deutscher Orden der Harugari (German Order of Harugari)
DPA . . . . Deutscher Personalausweis
DTSB . . . . . . Deutscher Turn und Sportbund
DVD . . . . Deutscher Veranstaltungsdienst
DAMW . . . . . . Deutsches Amt fuer Material und Warenpruefung
DESY . . . . . . Deutsches Elektron-Synchrotron
DIM . . . . Deutsches Institut fuer Marktforschung
DNB . . . . Deutsches Nachrichtenburo (German news agency)
DRP . . . . Deutsches Reichs-Patent (German patent)
DRK . . . . Deutsches Rotes Kreuz
DNVP . . . . . . Deutschnationale Volkspartei (German National People's Party)
DHY . . . . Develet Hava Yollari (Airline)
DHP . . . . Developed Horsepower
DLR . . . . Developing Learning Readiness
DNT . . . . Developing Nations Tractor (Ford Motor Company)
DOP . . . . Developing-Out Paper
D & P . . . . . . Developing and Printing
DP . . . . Developing Proboscis
DART . . . . . . Development of Advanced Rate Techniques
DAT . . . . Development Assist Test
DAC . . . . Development Assistance Committee (OECD)
DAG . . . . Development Assistance Group
DCN . . . . Development Change Notice
DC . . . . Development Characteristic
DCP . . . . Development Concept Paper
DCC . . . . Development Control Center
DD . . . . Development Directive
DE . . . . Development Engineering
DEI . . . . Development Engineering Inspection
DEMS . . . . . . Development Engineering Management System (Air Force)
AFDFO . . . . . Development Field Office (Air Force)
DFCK . . . . . . Development Finance Company of Kenya
DIMES . . . . . Development of Improved Management Engineering Systems
DIPS . . . . Development Information Processing System
DEIMOS . . . . . Development Investigation in Military Orbiting Systems
DLC . . . . Development Loan Committee (Department of State)
DLF . . . . Development Loan Fund
DPM . . . . Development Planning Memo
DPO . . . . Development Planning Objective
DPR . . . . Development Planning Reports
DPP . . . . Development Program Plan
DPS . . . . Development and Proof Services
DQ . . . . Development Quotient
DRM . . . . Development Reactor Mockup
DR . . . . Development Report
DSM . . . . Development of Substitute Materials
DATA . . . . . . Development and Technical Assistance International
DTA . . . . Development Test Article
DT & E . . . . . Development, Test and Evaluation
DWO . . . . Development Work Order
DBOI . . . . . . Developmental Basis of Issue (Military)
DEEP . . . . . . Developmental Economic Education Program
DFP . . . . Deviant Flight Plan
DO . . . . Deviating Oscillator
D . . . . Deviation
DC . . . . Deviation Clause
DFL . . . . Deviation for Failure Location
DI . . . . Deviation Indicator
DR . . . . Deviation Range
DRT . . . . Deviation for Replacement Time
DTB . . . . Deviation Test Bridge
DC . . . . Device Control
DMNI . . . . . . Device Multiplexing Nonsynchronized Inputs (Data processing)
DS . . . . Device Selector
DSU . . . . Device-Switching Unit
DUT . . . . Device Under Test
DEV . . . . De Vilbiss Company (NYSE symbol)
DEPO . . . . . . Devils Postpile National Monument
DETO . . . . . . Devils Tower National Monument
DVO . . . . Devon Leduc Oils, Ltd. (NYSE symbol)
DP . . . . Dew Point
DPSD . . . . . . Dew Point Sensing Device
DPT . . . . Dew Point Tester

DPS . . . . Dewan Pengurus Sementara (Provisional Management Board Section)
         (Indonesia)
PPBI . . . . Dewan Pimpinan Pusat Persatuan Pengendara Betja Indonesia (Central Board
         of Indonesian Betja Drivers' Association)
DC . . . . Dewey Decimal Classification
DDC . . . . Dewey Decimal Classification
D . . . . Dexter (Right)
D . . . . Dextrorotary (Pharmacology)
D : N . . . . . . Dextrose : Nitrogen Ratio
DK . . . . Dezimal-Klassifikation
DFI . . . . Diabetes Foundation, Incorporated
DIAPAS . . . . . Diabetes Personalized Alerting Service
DREGE . . . . . Diabetes Retrieval Element Generator & Executor
DU . . . . Diagnosis Unknown (Medicine)
DC . . . . Diagnostic Center
DRT . . . . Diagnostic Rhyme Test
DPL . . . . Diagonal Proof Line (Technical drawings)
DAIRS . . . . . . Dial Access Information Retrieval System
DDG . . . . Dial Depth Gage
DDB . . . . Dial Drive Belt
DMK . . . . Dial Marking Kit
DP . . . . Dial Pulsing
DTWX . . . . . . Dial Teletypewriter Exchange
DS . . . . Dial System
DAS . . . . Dialdehyde Starch
DIALGOL . . . Dialect of Algorithmic Language
DN . . . . Dialect Notes (A periodical)
DIAMAT . . . . . Dialektischer Materialismus
DAP . . . . Diallylphthalate
D . . . . Diameter
DBC . . . . Diameter Bolt Circle (Technical drawings)
DBH . . . . Diameter at Breast Height
DP . . . . Diametrical Pitch
DAB . . . . Diaminobenzidine
DDS . . . . Diaminodiphenylsulfone (Antimalaria drug)
DAP . . . . Diammonium Phosphate (Fertilizer)
DIA . . . . Diamond Alkali Company (NYSE symbol)
DCDMA . . . . . Diamond Core Drill Manufacturers Association
DCA . . . . Diamond Council of America
DDC . . . . Diamond Dealers Club
DN . . . . Diamond International Corporation (NYSE symbol)
DLK . . . . Diamond Locking Knurl
DORF . . . . . . Diamond Ordnance Radiation Facility (AEC)
DMIAA . . . . . . Diamond Manufacturers and Importers Association of America
DOFL . . . . . . Diamond Ordnance Fuze Laboratory (AMC) (Later, Harry Diamond
         Laboratories)
DRF . . . . Diamond Radiation Facility
DTE . . . . Diamond Tool Engineering Company
DTAA . . . . . . Diamond Trade Association of America
DWG . . . . Diamond Walnut Growers
DWMI . . . . . . Diamond Wheel Manufacturers Institute
DAAP . . . . . . Diamylamyephosphonate
DIN . . . . Diana Stores Corporation (NYSE symbol)
DSIA . . . . Diaper Service Industry Association
DNS . . . . Diaphragm Nerve Stimulation
DOV . . . . Diaphragm Operated Valve
DP . . . . Diastatic Power
DM . . . . Diastolic Murmur (Medicine)
DDNP . . . . . . Diazonitrophenol
DBA . . . . Dibenzanthracene (Chemical)
DBCP . . . . . . Dibromochloropropane (Chemical)
DBS . . . . Dibutyl Sebacate
DCP . . . . Dicetyl Phosphate
DCA . . . . Dichloroaniline
DD . . . . Dichloropropene-Dichloropropane (Chemical)
DDT . . . . Dichlorodiphenyltrichloroethane (Chemistry)
DCPA . . . . . . Dichloropropionanilide
DSL . . . . Dickinson School of Law (Carlisle, Pennsylvania)
DMT . . . . Dictaphone Machine Transcriber
DA . . . . Dictionary of Americanisms
DAB . . . . Dictionary of American Biography
DAE . . . . Dictionary of American English
DAH . . . . Dictionary of American History
DCB . . . . Dictionary of Canadian Biography (More correctly, DCB/DBC)
DCB/DBC . . . . Dictionary of Canadian Biography/Dictionnaire Biographique du Canada
DFS . . . . A Dictionary of Forces' Slang
DNB . . . . Dictionary of National Biography
DOT . . . . Dictionary of Occupational Titles
DSUE . . . . . . A Dictionary of Slang and Unconventional English
DU . . . . A Dictionary of the Underworld

DBC . . . . Dictionnaire Biographique du Canada (More correctly, DCB/DBC)
DNRQ . . . . . . Did Not Receive Questionnaire
DAPHNE . . . . . Dido and Pluto Handmaiden for Nuclear Experiments (Nuclear reactor at Harwell, England)
DCRF . . . . . . Die Casting Research Foundation
DFA . . . . Die Forged Aluminum
DSC . . . . Die Sinkers Conference
D . . . . Died
DOD . . . . . . Died of Disease
DOW . . . . . . Died of Wounds
DWA . . . . . . Died of Wounds Resulting from Action with Enemy
DCI . . . . Dielectric Constant Indicator
DDF . . . . Dielectric Dissipation Factor
DHE . . . . Dielectric Heating Equipment
DIB . . . . Dielectric Infrared Beamsplitter
DRA . . . . Dielectric Rod Antenna
DST . . . . Dielectric Strength Test
D . . . . Dies (Day)
DDD . . . . . . Diesel Direct Drive (Navy)
DE . . . . Diesel-Electric
DIEL . . . . . . Diesel Electric
DEDD . . . . . Diesel Electric Direct Drive (Navy)
DERD . . . . . Diesel Electric Reduction Drive
DEMA . . . . . . Diesel Engine Manufacturers Association
DIFR . . . . . . Diesel Fruit Vessel
DGD . . . . . . Diesel Geared Drive (Navy)
DG-MG . . . . Diesel Geared-Motor Geared (Navy)
DM . . . . Diesel-Mechanical
DESOIL . . . . . Diesel Oil
DO . . . . Diesel Oil
DR . . . . Diesel Radial (Aircraft engine)
DRD . . . . . . Diesel Reduction Drive
DITA . . . . . . Diesel Tank Vessel
DEA . . . . Diethanolamine
DEHP . . . . . . Diethyl Hydrogen Phosphite
DEAE . . . . . . Diethylaminoethyl
DEGS . . . . . . Diethylene Glycol Succinate
DETA . . . . . . Diethylenetriamine
DTPA . . . . . . Diethylenetriaminepentaacetic Acid (Chemical)
DEN . . . . Di-Ethylnitrosamine (Carcinogen)
DES . . . . Diethylstilbestrol
DETC . . . . . . Diethylthiacarbocyanine (Chemical)
DTTC . . . . . . Diethylthiatricarbocyanine
DET . . . . Diethyltryptamine (Hallucinogenic drug)
D . . . . Difference
DA . . . . Difference Amplifier
DDM . . . . . . Difference in Depth Modulation
DL . . . . Difference Limen (Physiology, psychology)
L . . . . Difference of Latitude
DLO . . . . . . Difference of Longitude (Navigation)
DP . . . . Difference in Pressure
DPCS . . . . . . Difference Pressure Control Switch
DS . . . . Difference Sensation (Psychology)
D . . . . Differential of
DA . . . . Differential Amplifier
DAT . . . . Differential Aptitude Test (Psychology)
DBW . . . . . . Differential Ballistic Wind
DBWC . . . . . Differential Ballistic Wind Computer
DBWO . . . . . Differential Ballistic Wind Offset
DBCD . . . . . . Differential Base Current Drift
DBI . . . . Differential Bearing Indicator
DD . . . . Differential Diagnosis (Medicine)
DELTA . . . . . . Differential Electronically Locking Test Accessory
DES . . . . Differential Equation Solver
DEPI . . . . Differential Equations Pseudocode Interpreter
DG . . . . Differential Generator
DLSC . . . . . . Differential Logistics Services Center (AEC)
DOI . . . . Differential Orbit Improvement
DP . . . . Differential Pressure
DPC . . . . Differential Pressure Control
DPSW . . . . . . Differential Pressure Sea Water
DR . . . . Differential Rate
DRCPR . . . . . Differential Reactive Current Project Relay
DSC . . . . Differential Scanning Calorimeter
DSC . . . . Differential Signal Control
DTMD . . . . . . Differential Temperature Measuring Device
DTA . . . . Differential Thermal Analyzer (or Analysis)
DTVM . . . . . . Differential Thermocouple Voltmeter
DTC . . . . Differential Throttle Control
DVE . . . . Differential Vector Equation
DVA . . . . Differential Voltage Amplifier

DV . . . . Differential Voltmeter
DPSK . . . . . . Differentially Phase Shift Keying
D . . . . Differentiation (Calculus)
DLF . . . . Diffraction Limited Focusing
DLRL . . . . . . Diffraction Limited Raman LASER
DAP . . . . Diffused Alloy Power
DB . . . . Diffused Base
DJ . . . . Diffused Junction
DM . . . . Diffused Mesa
DP . . . . Diffused Planar
DFC . . . . Diffusion Formed Coating
DPD . . . . Diffusion Pressure Deficit
DFDT . . . . . . Difluorodiphenyltrichloroethane (Insecticide)
DIA . . . . Dig-In Angle
DA . . . . Digestive Anlage
DG . . . . Digestive Gland
DIG . . . . Di Giorgio Fruit Corporation (NYSE symbol)
DP . . . . Digit Present
DARS . . . . . . Digital Adaptive Recording System (Data processing)
DATEC . . . . . Digital Adaptive Technique for Efficient Communications
DADC . . . . . . Digital Air Data Computer
DA . . . . Digital Alternator
DAS . . . . Digital Altimeter Scanner
D-to-A . . . . . Digital-to-Analog (Converter) (Data processing)
DAC . . . . Digital-to-Analog Converter
DACON . . . . . Digital-to-Analog Converter
DADAC . . . . . Digital-to-Analog Deck Angle Converter (Navy)
DAFT . . . . . . Digital/Analog Function Table (Data processing)
DAIU . . . . . . Digital to Analog Interface Unit
DAS . . . . Digital Analog Simulator
DAD . . . . Digital Angle Data
DADR . . . . . . Digital Angle Data Recorder
DAR . . . . Digital Angle Recorder
DATE . . . . . . Digital Angular Torquing Equipment
DAC . . . . Digital Arithmetic Center
DAS . . . . Digital Attenuator System
DAFC . . . . . . Digital Automatic Frequency Control
DATICO . . . . . Digital Automatic Tape Intelligence Check-Out
DATAC . . . . . Digital Automatic Tester and Classifier
DATAR . . . . . Digital Automatic Tracking and Ranging (or Remoting) (Air Force)
DAWN . . . . . Digital Automatic Weather Network
DARTS . . . . . Digital Azimuth Range Tracking System
DBD . . . . Digital Bargraph Display
DBDU . . . . . . Digital Bargraph Display Unit
DBC . . . . Digital-to-Binary Converter
DB . . . . Digital Block (Data processing)
DBCO . . . . . . Digital Block Clock Oscillator (Data processing)
DBFF . . . . . . Digital Block Flip-Flop (Data processing)
DBIA . . . . . . Digital Block Inverter Amplifier (Data processing)
DBMV . . . . . . Digital Block Multivibrator (Data processing)
DBNA . . . . . . Digital Block Noninverting Amplifier (Data processing)
DBST . . . . . . Digital Block Schmitt Trigger
DBSC . . . . . . Digital Block Slave Clock
DCCS . . . . . . Digital Camera Control System
DCAO . . . . . . Digital Card And-Or Gate (Data processing)
DCCO . . . . . . Digital Card Clock Oscillator
DCFF . . . . . . Digital Card Flip-Flop (Data processing)
DCIA . . . . . . Digital Card Inverting Amplifier (Data processing)
DCMV . . . . . . Digital Card Multivibrator
DCNA . . . . . . Digital Card Noninverting Amplifier
DCST . . . . . . Digital Card Schmitt Trigger
DCSC . . . . . . Digital Card Slave Clock
DCM . . . . . . Digital Circuit Module (Data processing)
DCQM . . . . . . Digital Circuit Quality Monitor
DC . . . . Digital Clock
DCI . . . . Digital Clock Indicator
DCP . . . . Digital Clock Pulse
DCPG . . . . . . Digital Clock Pulse Generator
DCTV . . . . . . Digital Color Television
DCS . . . . Digital Command System
DICON . . . . . . Digital Communication through Orbiting Needles
DIGICOM . . . . Digital Communications
DC . . . . Digital Comparator
DC . . . . Digital Computer
DCCP . . . . . . Digital Computer Control Panel
DCL . . . . Digital Computer Laboratory (MIT)
DCA . . . . Digital Computers Association
DCR . . . . Digital Concentration Readout (Data processing)
DCC . . . . Digital Control Computer
DCS . . . . Digital Control System
DCR . . . . Digital Conversion Receiver

DICODE . . . . . Digital Correlation Demonstrator
DCD . . . . Digital Countdown Display (Data processing)
DCDS . . . . . . Digital Countdown Display System (Data processing)
DCS . . . . Digital Countdown System (Data processing)
DCU . . . . Digital Counting Unit
DDAS . . . . . . Digital Data Acquisition System
DDAS . . . . . . Digital Data Archives System
DATOR . . . . . Digital Data, Auxiliary Storage, Track Display, Outputs, and RADAR
　　　　　　　　　Display
DDB . . . . Digital Data Buffer (Data processing)
DIDAC . . . . . Digital Data Computer
DDCE . . . . . . Digital Data Conversion Equipment
DDC . . . . Digital Data Converter
DDDS . . . . . . Digital Data Display System
DDG . . . . Digital Data Group
DDH . . . . Digital Data Handling
DDL . . . . Digital Data Link
DDL . . . . Digital Data Logger
DDMS . . . . . . Digital Data Measuring System
DDOCE . . . . . Digital Data Output Conversion Element
DDPE . . . . . . Digital Data Processing Equipment
DDPS . . . . . . Digital Data Processing System
DDP . . . . Digital Data Processor
DIDAP . . . . . Digital Data Processor
DDR . . . . Digital Data Receiver
DDR . . . . Digital Data Recorder
DDRH . . . . . . Digital Data Recording Head
DDRS . . . . . . Digital Data Recording System
DDSU . . . . . . Digital Data Storage Unit (Data processing)
DDTE . . . . . . Digital Data Terminal Equipment
DDTESM . . . . Digital Data Terminal Equipment Service Module
DDS . . . . Digital Data Servo
DDS . . . . Digital Data System
DDT . . . . Digital Data Transmitter
DDT . . . . Digital Debugging Tape
DDG . . . . Digital Delay Generator
DDR . . . . Digital Demand Recorder
DDA . . . . Digital Differential Analyzer
D-to-D . . . . . Digital-to-Digital
DD . . . . Digital Display (SAGE)
DDG . . . . Digital Display Generator (SAGE)
DDGE . . . . . . Digital Display Generator Element
DDM . . . . Digital Display Makeup
DDM . . . . Digital Display Machine
DDS . . . . Digital Display Scope
DDU . . . . Digital Display Unit
DDU . . . . Digital Distributing Unit
DDS . . . . Digital Drafting System
DEMON . . . . . Digital Electric Monitor
DETS . . . . . . Digital Element Test Set
DE . . . . Digital Encoder
DEH . . . . Digital Encoder Handbook
DEHB . . . . . . Digital Encoder Handbook
DECUS . . . . . Digital Equipment Computer Users Society
DEC . . . . Digital Equipment Corporation
DECAL . . . . . Digital Equipment Corporation's Adaptation of Algorithmic Language
　　　　　　　　　(Data processing)
DEE . . . . Digital Evaluation Equipment
DEE . . . . Digital Event Evaluator
DECOR . . . . . Digital Electronic Continuous Ranging
DEUCE . . . . . Digital Electronic Universal Calculating Engine
DES . . . . Digital Expansion System
DEXAN . . . . . Digital Experimental Airborne Navigator
DFIS . . . . Digital Facsimile Interface System
DFPS . . . . . . Digital Ferrite Phase Shifter
DFS . . . . Digital Field System
DFT . . . . Digital Filtering Technique
DFD . . . . Digital Flight Display
DFBPT . . . . . Digital Force Balance Pressure Transducer
DFA . . . . Digital Frequency Analyzer
DFD . . . . Digital Frequency Display
DFM . . . . Digital Frequency Meter (or Monitor)
DFS . . . . Digital Frequency Synthesizer
DFG . . . . Digital Function Generator
DGBC . . . . . . Digital Geoballistic Computer
DGC . . . . Digital Geoballistic Computer
DGS . . . . Digital Ground System
DIGACC . . . . Digital Guidance and Control Computer
DIP . . . . Digital Incremental Plotter
DID . . . . Digital Information Display (SAGE)
DIDS . . . . . . Digital Information Display System (Data processing)

DIOB . . . . . . Digital Input/Output Buffer (Data processing)
DIVA . . . . . . Digital Inquiry - Voice Answer
DIU . . . . Digital Insertion Unit
DIANE . . . . . Digital Integrated Attack and Navigation Equipment
DICE . . . . . . Digital Integrated Circuit Element
DLC . . . . Digital Logic Circuit
DLM . . . . Digital Logic Module
DLS . . . . Digital Logic System
DMTPS . . . . . Digital Magnetic Tape Plotting System
DMED . . . . . . Digital Message Entry Device (Police and military communications)
DMC . . . . Digital Micro-Circuit
DMAT . . . . . . Digital Module Automatic Tester
DMTS . . . . . . Digital Module Test Set
DIMUS . . . . . Digital (or Directional) Multibeam Steering (SONAR)
DMSS . . . . . . Digital Multibeam Steering System
DMM . . . . . . Digital Multimeter
DMMC . . . . . Digital Multi-Meter Control
DMS . . . . Digital Multiplexing Synchronizer (Data processing)
DINA . . . . . . Digital Network Analyzer
DNCG . . . . . . Digital Null Command Generator
DOLARS . . . . Digital Off-Line Automatic Recording System
DOM . . . . Digital Ohmmeter
DO . . . . Digital Output (Data processing)
DO/IT . . . . . . Digital Output/Input Translator
DOT . . . . Digital Output Timer (Data processing)
DPG . . . . Digital Pattern Generator
DPC . . . . Digital Phase Comparator
DPD . . . . Digital Phase Difference
DPS . . . . Digital Phase Shifter
DPS . . . . Digital Plotter System
DPC . . . . Digital Pressure Converter
DPC . . . . Digital Process Controller
DPCU . . . . . . Digital Processing and Control Unit
DPU . . . . Digital Processing Unit
DQM . . . . Digital Quality Monitor
DRR . . . . Digital RADAR Relay
DRRL . . . . . . Digital RADAR Relay Link
DRS . . . . Digital RADAR Simulator
DRM . . . . Digital Radiometer
DRM . . . . Digital Range Machine
DRU . . . . Digital Range Unit
DRISS . . . . . . Digital Read-In Subsystem (Data processing)
DRH . . . . Digital Readout Head (Data processing)
DRL . . . . Digital Readout Light (Data processing)
DRO . . . . Digital Readout Oscilloscope (Data processing)
DROO . . . . . . Digital Readout Oscilloscope (Data processing)
DRS . . . . Digital Readout System (Data processing)
DRT . . . . Digital Readout Timer (Data processing)
DRS . . . . Digital Receiver Station (Data processing)
DRA . . . . Digital Recorder Analyzer
DRSG . . . . . . Digital Recorder Signal Generator (Data processing)
DRAMS . . . . . Digital Recording and Measuring System
DRAPE . . . . . Digital Recording and Playback Equipment
DRP . . . . Digital Recording Process
DR . . . . Digital Resolver
DRT . . . . Digital Rotary Transducer
DISCOM . . . . Digital Selective Communications
DSR . . . . Digital Shift Register
DSG . . . . Digital Signal Generator
DSPS . . . . . . Digital Signal Processing System
DSS . . . . Digital Signal Synchronizer
DYSAC . . . . . Digital Simulated Analog Computer
DSL . . . . Digital Simulation Language (Data processing)
DSCS . . . . . . Digital Simulator Computer System
DSS . . . . Digital Simulator System
DISTRAM . . . . Digital Space Trajectory Measurement System (Raytheon)
DSR . . . . Digital Stepping Recorder
DSR . . . . Digit Storage Relay
DSS . . . . Digital Storage System
DSP . . . . Digital Strip Printer
DST . . . . Digital Subscriber Terminal
DSTE . . . . . . Digital Subscriber Terminal Equipment
DSS . . . . Digital Subset
DSS . . . . Digital Subsystem
DIGITAC . . . . Digital Tactical Airborne Computer
DTCS . . . . . . Digital Tank Control (or Command) System
DTC . . . . Digital Tape Conversion
DT . . . . Digital Technique
DTR . . . . Digital Telemetering Register
DTS . . . . Digital Telemetry System
DTU . . . . Digital Telemetry Unit

DTV . . . . Digital Television
DTC . . . . Digital Television Camera
DTDS . . . . . . Digital Television Display System
DTE . . . . Digital Television Encoder
DTM . . . . Digital Television Monitor
DTMS . . . . . . Digital Test Monitor System
DTU . . . . Digital Test Unit
DTC . . . . Digital to Tone Converter
DTAS . . . . . . Digital Transmission and Switching
DIVIC . . . . . . Digital Variable Increment Computer
DVB . . . . Digital Video Bandwidth
DIVOT . . . . . . Digital-to-Voice Translator
DVOM . . . . . . Digital Volt-Ohmmeter
DVM . . . . Digital Voltmeter
DWR . . . . Digital Wired Recorder
DIFAD . . . . . . Digitally Integrated Fleet Air Defense
DAM . . . . Digitized Analog Magnetogram
DML . . . . Digitized Message Link
DHA . . . . Dihydroanthracene (Chemical)
DST . . . . Dihydrostreptomycin
DAP . . . . Dihydroxy Acetone Phosphate
DHG . . . . Dihydroxyethylglycinate (Chemical)
DOPA . . . . . . Dihydroxyphenylalanine (Biochemistry)
DIAC . . . . . . Di-Iodothyroacetic Acid (Endocrinology)
DIT . . . . Di-Iodotyrosine (Endocrinology)
DM . . . . Diis Manibus (To the Manes [Departed Souls])
DMS . . . . Diis Manibus Sacrum (Sacred to the Manes [Departed Souls])
DFP . . . . Diisopropylfluorophosphate (A drug)
D and C . . . . Dilation and Curettage (Of the uterus) (Obstetrics)
DS . . . . Dilute Strength (Chemistry)
DV . . . . Dilute Volume (Chemistry)
D . . . . Dime
D . . . . Dimensional
DDQ . . . . . . Dimensions Description Questionnaire
DMPEA . . . . . Dimethoxyphenylethylamine
DMSO . . . . . . Dimethyl Sulfoxide (Chemical)
DMAC . . . . . . Dimethylacetamide
DMAM . . . . . . Dimethylaminoethylmethacrylate
DIMAPA . . . . Dimethylaminopropylamine
DMF . . . . Dimethylformamide (Chemical)
DMT . . . . Dimethyltriptamine (A drug)
DKMS . . . . . . Dimitrovski Komunisticheski Mladezhki Suiuz (Bulgaria)
DSNM . . . . . . Dimitrovski Suiuz na Narodnata Mladesh (Bulgaria)
DPDI . . . . . . Dimple Die
DCL . . . . Diners' Club, Inc. (NYSE symbol)
DP . . . . Dining Permit (Slang)
DR . . . . Dining Room
DNB . . . . Dinitrobenzene
DNC . . . . Dinitro-Cellulose
DNFB . . . . . . Dinitrofluorobenzene
DNOC . . . . . . Dinitro-Ortho-Cresol (Insecticide and herbicide)
DNP . . . . Dinitrophenyl
DNT . . . . Dinitrotoluene (An explosive)
DINO . . . . . . Dinosaur National Monument
DHM . . . . Diocesan Home Missionary
DOP . . . . Dioctyl Phthalate
DOS . . . . Dioctyl Sebacates
DCD . . . . Diode-Capacitor-Diode
DCDG . . . . . . Diode-Capacitor-Diode Gate (Data processing)
DCG . . . . Diode Capacitor Gate
DCT . . . . Diode Curve Tracer
DFP . . . . Diode Flat Pack
DFG . . . . Diode Function Generator
DG . . . . Diode Gate (Data processing)
DII . . . . Diode Ion Injector
DISI . . . . . . Diode Ion Source Injector
DL . . . . Diode Logic
DMO . . . . . . Diode Microwave Oscillator
DPS . . . . Diode Phase Shifter
DPSM . . . . . . Diode Phase Shifter Module
DQP . . . . Diode Qualification Program
DQT . . . . Diode Qualification Test
DQTP . . . . . . Diode Qualification Test Program
DRT . . . . Diode Recovery Tester
DSD . . . . Diode Semiconductor Device
DS . . . . Diode Switch
DTP . . . . Diode Test Program
DTL . . . . Diode-Transistor Logic
DUT . . . . Diode Under Test
D . . . . Diopter
DS . . . . Dioptric Strength

D . . . . Dip
DC . . . . Dip Coating
DPO . . . . Diphenyl Oxide
DC . . . . Diphenylarsine Cyanide
DPG . . . . Diphenylguanidine
DPH . . . . Diphenylhydantoin
DPPH . . . . . . Diphenylpicrylhydrazyl
DP . . . . Diphosgene
DPG . . . . Diphosphoglyceric Acid (or Diphosphoglycerate)
DPN . . . . . . Diphosphopyridine Nucleotide (Biochemistry)
DT . . . . Diphtheria-Tetanus
DTP . . . . Diphtheria, Tetanus, Pertussis (Medicine)
DTT . . . . Diphtheria-Tetanus Toxoid
DTN . . . . Diphtheria Toxin Normal (Medicine)
2N . . . . Diploid Number
DA . . . . Diploma in Anesthetics
DAP & E . . . . . Diploma in Applied Parasitology and Entomology (British)
DCH . . . . Diploma in Child Health
DCMT . . . . . . Diploma in Clinical Medicine of the Tropics (British)
DCP . . . . Diploma in Clinical Pathology
DDO . . . . . . Diploma in Dental Orthopaedics (British)
DDM . . . . . . Diploma in Dermatological Medicine (British)
DDR . . . . Diploma in Diagnostic Radiology (British)
D El Ed . . . . . Diploma in Elementary Education
D Ed AS . . . . . Diploma in Education Administration and Supervision
DGO . . . . . . Diploma in Gynecology and Obstetrics
DIH . . . . Diploma in Industrial Health (British)
DLO . . . . Diploma in Laryngology and Otolaryngology (British)
DMRT . . . . . . Diploma in Medical Radio-Therapy (British)
DMR . . . . . . Diploma in Medical Radiology
DMRE . . . . . . Diploma in Medical Radiology and Electrolysis (British)
DMSA . . . . . . Diploma in Medical Services Administration (British)
DOMS . . . . . Diploma in Ophthalmic Medicine and Surgery
DO . . . . Diploma in Ophthalmology
DPM . . . . Diploma in Psychological Medicine
DPA . . . . Diploma in Public Administration (British)
DPD . . . . Diploma in Public Dentistry (British)
DPH . . . . Diploma in Public Health
DR . . . . Diploma in Radiology
DTM . . . . Diploma in Tropical Medicine
DTM & H . . . . Diploma in Tropical Medicine and Hygiene (British)
DTPH . . . . . . Diploma in Tropical Public Health (British)
DTVM . . . . . . Diploma in Tropical Veterinary Medicine
DVH . . . . Diploma in Veterinary Hygiene
DVSM . . . . . . Diploma in Veterinary State Medicine
DACOR . . . . . . Diplomatic and Consular Officers, Retired
DTS . . . . Diplomatic Telecommunications Service
DAS . . . . Dipole Antenna System
DFP . . . . Dipole Flat Plate
DACC . . . . . . Direct Access Communications Channels
DAPS . . . . . . Direct Access Programming System (Data processing)
DATRIX . . . . . . Direct Access to Reference Information (Xerox)
DA . . . . Direct Action (Bomb or shell fuze)
DACI . . . . . . Direct Adjacent Channel Interference
DAC . . . . Direct Air Cycle
DAS . . . . Direct Air Support (Military)
DASC . . . . . . Direct Air Support Center
DASF . . . . . . Direct Air Support Flight (Military)
DAIRE . . . . . . Direct Altitude and Identification Readout Equipment (Aviation)
DAIR . . . . . . Direct Altitude and Identity Readout (FAA)
DAS . . . . Direct Automotive Support
DCT . . . . Direct Carbon Transfer
DCF . . . . Direct Centrifugal Flotation (Parasitology)
DC . . . . Direct Command
DCR . . . . Direct Conversion Reactor
DCR . . . . Direct Cortical Response
DCTL . . . . . . Direct-Coupled Transistor Logic
DCUTL . . . . . . Direct Coupled Unipolar Transistor Logic
DC . . . . Direct Current
DCA . . . . Direct Current Amplifier
DCA . . . . Direct Current Arc
DCDT . . . . . . Direct-Current Differential Transformer
DCD . . . . Direct Current Dump
DCX . . . . Direct Current Experiments (ORNL)
DCFG . . . . . . Direct Current Free Gyro
DCG . . . . Direct Current Generator
DCPT . . . . . . Direct Current Plasma Torch
DCR . . . . Direct-Current Restorer
DCS . . . . Direct Current Sensor
DCSA . . . . . . Direct Current Servo Amplifier
VDCT . . . . . . Direct-Current Test Volts

DCTM . . . . Direct Current Torque Motor
DCVR . . . . Direct Current Voltage Reference (or Regulator)
DCV . . . . Direct Current, Volts
VDC . . . . Direct-Current Volts
DCWV . . . . . . Direct Current Working Volts
VDCW . . . . . . Direct-Current Working Volts
DC . . . . Direct Cycle
DCDR . . . . Direct Cycle Diphenyl Reactor
DDTS . . . . Direct Dial Telephone System
DDC . . . . Direct Digital Control
DDCS . . . . Direct Digital Control System
DDE . . . . Direct Digital Encoder
DDD . . . . Direct Distance Dialing (Of telephone numbers for toll calls)
DEC . . . . Direct Energy Conversion
DECO . . . . . . Direct Energy Conversion Operation
DEW . . . . Direct Energy Weapon
DEACON . . . . Direct English Access and Control (Data processing)
DX . . . . Direct Exchange (Army)
DXI . . . . Direct Exchange Item (Army)
DFAW . . . . . . Direct Fire Anti-Tank Weapon
DFS . . . . Direct Fire Simulator
DFS . . . . Direct Fire System
DF . . . . Direct Flight
DFM . . . . Direct Flight Mode
DFS . . . . Direct Forces Support (Military)
DIHEST . . . . . Direct Induced High Explosive Simulation
DI . . . . Direct Investor
DID . . . . Direct Inward Dial (Method of bypassing central switchboards in
                   telephoning extensions from outside)
DL . . . . Direct Labor
DLS . . . . Direct Least Squares (Econometrics)
DLC . . . . Direct Lift Control
DMAA . . . . . . Direct Mail Advertising Association
DMH . . . . Direct Manhours
DME . . . . Direct Measurements Explorer (Satellite)
DME-A . . . . . . Direct Measurements Explorer A (Satellite)
DMA . . . . Direct Memory Address
DMT . . . . Direct Modulation Technique
DINA . . . . Direct Noise Amplifier (Airborne RADAR Transmitter)
DO . . . . Direct Obligation
DOC . . . . Direct Operating Cost
DO . . . . Direct Order
DORIS . . . . . . Direct Order Recording and Invoicing System (A computer-based system
                   of British petroleum companies)
DOD . . . . Direct Outward Dialing
DP . . . . Direct Port (Transportation)
DQ . . . . Direct Question (Legal testimony)
DRSC . . . . . . Direct RADAR Scope Camera
DRSR . . . . . . Direct RADAR Scope Recorder
DRC . . . . Direct-Reaction Calculation
DRE . . . . Direct Reading Encoder
DRR . . . . Direct Reading Receiver
DRT . . . . Direct Reading Totalizer
DREWS . . . . . Direct Readout Equatorial Satellite
DRIR . . . . Direct Readout Infrared
DROMDI . . . . . Direct Readout Miss Distance Indicator (Data processing)
DROS . . . . . . Direct Readout Satellite
DROWS . . . . . Direct Readout Weather Satellite
DRO . . . . Direct Recording Oscillograph
DRET . . . . . . Direct Reentry Telecommunications
DRET . . . . . . Direct Reentry Telemetry (Air Force)
DRETS . . . . . . Direct Reentry Telemetry System (Air Force)
DRF . . . . Direct Relief Foundation
D/R . . . . Direct/Reverse
DR . . . . Direct Route
DSRS . . . . . . Direct Scope Recording System
DSR . . . . Direct Stage Recorder
DSS . . . . Direct Station Selection
DSUH . . . . . . Direct Suggestion Under Hypnosis
DSSD . . . . . . Direct Supply Support Depot (Military)
DSSP . . . . . . Direct Supply Support Point (DOD)
DS . . . . Direct Support (Army)
D/S . . . . Direct Support (Military)
DSAS . . . . . . Direct Support Aviation Section
DSG . . . . Direct Support Group (Army)
DSU . . . . Direct Support Unit
DVST . . . . . . Direct-Viewing Storage Tube
DWO . . . . . . Direct Writing Oscillograph
DAP . . . . Directed Audit Program
DDI . . . . Directed Drawing Instrument
DDA . . . . Directed Duty Assignment (Military)

DP . . . . Directing Point
DS . . . . Directing Staff
DC . . . . Direction Center (SAGE) (RADAR)
DCA . . . . Direction Center Active (SAGE) (RADAR)
DCS . . . . Direction Center Standby (SAGE)
DIRCOL . . . . . Direction Cosine Linkage
DF . . . . Direction-Finder (or Finding) (Radio aid to navigation)
DIF . . . . Direction Finder (Radio)
DFA . . . . Direction Finding Antenna
DFE . . . . Direction Finding Equipment
DFR . . . . Direction Finding Receiver
DFS . . . . Direction Finding Set
DFSTN . . . . . . Direction Finding Station (Aviation)
DFS . . . . Direction Finding System
DRME . . . . . . Direction des Recherces et Moyens d'Essais (France)
DRM . . . . Direction of Relative Movement (Navigation)
DSM . . . . Direction de Service de Securite Militaire (France)
DSM . . . . Direction of Systems Management
DAD . . . . Directional Aerial Disposal (Insecticide spray)
DAPN . . . . . . Directional Antenna Phasing Network
DAL . . . . Directional Arm Lock
DCV . . . . Directional Control Valve
DC . . . . Directional Coupler
DDRR . . . . . . Directional Discontinuity Ring Radiator
DEER . . . . . . Directional Explosive Echo Ranging
DG . . . . Directional Gyro
DGM . . . . Directional Gyro Mode
DGO . . . . Directional Gyro Operation
DHI . . . . Directional Horizon Indicator
D/R . . . . Directional Radio
DRL . . . . Directional Reference Locator
DVM . . . . Directional Variable Microphone
DWF . . . . Directional Warhead Fuze
DR . . . . Directive Antenna
DICAB . . . . . . Directive Coordinated and Approved by Budget Director (Air Force)
DI . . . . Directivity Index
D . . . . Director aircraft capable of controlling drones or missiles (Designation
                   for all US military aircraft)
DAS . . . . Director of Administrative Services (US Military Government, Germany)
DABLC . . . . . . Director, Advanced Base Logistics Control (Navy)
DABOA . . . . . Director, Advanced Base Office, Atlantic (Navy)
DABOP . . . . . Director, Advanced Base Office, Pacific (Navy)
DASM . . . . . . Director of Advanced Systems Management
DASP . . . . . . Director of Advanced Systems Planning
DAT . . . . Director(ate) of Advanced Technology (Air Force)
DAMR(W) . . . . Director of Aircraft Maintenance and Repair (Washington) (Navy)
DARME . . . . . Director, Armament Engineering (Military) (Canada)
DAE . . . . Director of Army Education (British)
DAP . . . . Director of Army Programs
DAR . . . . Director of Army Research
DATI . . . . Director of Army Technical Information
DIRLANTDOCKS . . Director Atlantic Division, Bureau of Yards and Docks
DBMS . . . . . . Director of Base Medical Services
DB . . . . Director Bomber (Air Force)
DCE . . . . Director(ate) of Civil Engineering (Air Force)
DCM . . . . Director of Civilian Marksmanship (Army)
DCP . . . . Director of Civilian Personnel (Navy)
DCO(I) . . . . . . Director of Combined Operations (India)
DCO(ME) . . . . Director of Combined Operations (Middle East)
DDRE . . . . . . Director of Defense Research and Engineering (Army)
DDP . . . . Director(ate) of Development Planning (Air Force)
DED . . . . Director of the Education Department (British Navy)
DES . . . . Director of Engineer Stores Service (British)
DE . . . . Director Error (Military)
DIRFM . . . . . . Director Field Maintenance (Army)
DFT . . . . Director, Fleet Training
DFS . . . . Director of Flight Safety (Air Force)
DFSR . . . . . . Director(ate) of Flight Safety Research (Air Force)
DFW . . . . Director of Fortifications and Works (British)
DG . . . . Director General
DGAMS . . . . . Director-General of Army Medical Services (British)
DGAV . . . . . . Director-General of Armoured Vehicles (British)
DGCA . . . . . . Director-General of Civil Aviation (British)
DGCC . . . . . . Director-General of Civilian Clothing (British)
DGFG . . . . . . Director General of the Foreign Service (Department of State)
DGMS . . . . . . Director-General of Medical Services (British)
DGP . . . . Director-General of Production (British Air Ministry)
DGRD . . . . . . Director-General of the Research Department (British)
DG Tn . . . . . . Director-General of Transportation Services (British)
DGR . . . . Director of Graves Registration (British)
DGS . . . . Director of Ground Safety (Air Force)

REVERSE ACRONYMS AND INITIALISMS DICTIONARY

DIWT . . . . Director of Inland Water Transport Service (British)
DI . . . . Director(ate) of Installations (Air Force)
DJS . . . . Director Joint Staff (Military)
DMO . . . . . . Director of Manpower and Organization (Air Force)
DMCR . . . . . . Director, Marine Corps Reserve
DMR . . . . Director of Materiel Readiness (Army)
DME . . . . Director of Medical Education
DMHS . . . . . . Director of Medical and Health Services
DMS . . . . Director of Medical Services
DMSS . . . . . . Director of Medical and Sanitary Services (British)
DMA . . . . Director of Military Assistance
DMI . . . . Director of Military Intelligence (US, British)
DMO . . . . . . Director of Military Operations
DMOI . . . . . . Director of Military Operations and Intelligence
DMP . . . . Director of Military Personnel (Air Force)
DMT . . . . Director of Military Training
DMSR . . . . . . Director of Missile Safety Research (Air Force)
DMQ . . . . . . Director of Movements and Quartering (British)
DMS . . . . Director for Mutual Security
DIRNSA . . . . . Director, National Security Agency
DNA . . . . Director of Naval Accounts
DNAD . . . . . . Director of Naval Air Division
DNC . . . . Director of Naval Communications
DNCINST . . . . Director, Naval Communications Instruction
DNCNOTE . . . Director, Naval Communications Notice
DNE . . . . Director of Naval Equipment
DIRNAVHIST . . Director of Naval History
DNI . . . . Director of Naval Intelligence (US, British)
DNMS . . . . . Director of Naval Medical Services (Royal Australian Navy)
DNOP . . . . . Director of Naval Officer Procurement
DNO . . . . Director of Naval Operations
DOTM . . . . . . Director of Naval Ordnance, Torpedoes, and Mines (Royal Australian Navy)
DNRH . . . . . . Director of Naval Records and History
DNR . . . . Director of Naval Recruiting (British)
DNTS . . . . . . Director, Naval Transportation Service (Now CNTS)
DNPP . . . . . . Director, Navy Program Planning
DNS . . . . Director of Nuclear Safety (Air Force)
DNSR . . . . . . Director of Nuclear Safety Research (Air Force)
DNE . . . . Director of Nursing Education
DIROCD . . . . . Director, Office of Civil Defense
DOO . . . . Director, Office of Oceanography (UNESCO)
DO . . . . Director of Operations
DOD . . . . Director of Operations Division (British Navy)
DOS . . . . Director of Ordnance Services (British military)
DIRPACALDOCKS . . Director, Pacific and Alaskan Divisions, Bureau of Yards and Docks
DIRPACDOCKS . . Director, Pacific Division, Bureau of Yards and Docks
DPS . . . . Director of Personal Services (British Navy)
DPMC . . . . . . Director of Personnel, Marine Corps
AFPDP . . . . . . Director of Personnel Planning (Air Force)
DPP . . . . Director of Personnel Planning (Air Force)
DPPT . . . . . . Director of Personnel Procurement and Training (Air Force)
DPT . . . . Director of Personnel and Training (Army)
DPTS . . . . . . Director of Physical Training and Sports (British Navy)
DPD . . . . Director of Plans Division (British Navy)
DPSS . . . . . . Director of Printing and Stationery Services (British military)
DPW . . . . Director of Prisoners of War (British) (World War II)
DPP . . . . Director of Procurement and Production (Army)
DP . . . . Director of Programs (Air Force, Army)
DPI . . . . Director of Public Instruction
DPP . . . . Director of Public Prosecutions (British)
DPR . . . . Director of Public Relations
DRO . . . . Director of Recruiting and Organization (British military)
DRE . . . . Director of Religious Education
AFDRQ . . . . . Director of Requirements (Air Force)
AFDRD . . . . . Director of Research and Development (Air Force)
DRD . . . . Director(ate) of Research and Development (Air Force)
DRE . . . . Director(ate) of Research and Engineering (Military)
DS . . . . Director of Services (Air Force)
DSW . . . . Director of Special Weapons (Army)
DSS . . . . Director(ate) of Statistical Services (Air Force)
D of S (W) . . . . Director of Stores (Washington) (Navy)
DSTP . . . . . . Director of Strategic Target Planning (Military)
DST . . . . Director of Supplies and Transport (British)
DSM . . . . Director of Supply and Maintenance (Army)
DSR . . . . Director of Surveillance and Reconnaissance (Army)
DTM . . . . Director of Telecommunications Management (Air Force)
DTSD . . . . . . Director of Training and Staff Duties Division (British Navy)
DUW . . . . Director of Underwater Weapons (British)
DVFE . . . . . . Director, Vehicle and Field Engineering (Military) (Canada)

DVS . . . . Director of Veterinary Services (British military)
DIRW . . . . . . Director of Women Marines
DWAC . . . . . . Director, Women's Army Corps (United States)
DOWB . . . . . . Director of Works and Buildings (British)
DWD . . . . Director of Wreck Disposal
DAST . . . . . . Directorate of Advanced Systems Technology
DAMMO . . . . . Directorate of Ammunition (Military) (Canada)
DAD . . . . Directorate of Armament Development
DAFIE . . . . . . Directorate for Armed Forces Information and Education (Military)
DAW . . . . Directorate of Atomic Warfare
DBO . . . . Directorate of Biological Operations
DCM . . . . Directorate for Classification Management (DOD)
DCE . . . . Directorate of Communications – Electronics (ADC)
DFMSR . . . . . . Directorate of Flight & Missile Safety Research (Air Force)
DIAC . . . . . . Directorate of Internal Affairs & Communications (Allied German Occupation Forces)
DMR . . . . Directorate of Medical Research (Army)
DMO . . . . . . Directorate of Military Operations
DMI . . . . Directorate of Missile Intelligence (Army)
DOI . . . . Directorate Office Instruction
DSIS . . . . . . Directorate of Scientific Information Service (Canada)
DWET . . . . . . Directorate of Weapons Effect Tests
DRIL . . . . . . Directorio Revolucionario Iberico de Liberta (Revolutionary Directorate for Iberian Liberation)
DO . . . . Director's Office
DGA . . . . . . Directors Guild of America
D & O . . . . . . Directors' and Officers' (Liability insurance)
DDS . . . . Directory Development Study
DTP . . . . Directory Tape Processor
DB . . . . Dirty Book
DOM . . . . . . Dirty Old Man (Slang)
DITC . . . . . . Disability Insurance Training Council
DPB . . . . Disability Policy Board (VA)
DSABLSEVP . . . Disability Severance Pay
DAV . . . . . . Disabled American Veterans
DAVA . . . . . . Disabled American Veterans Auxiliary
DOA . . . . . . Disabled Officers Association
DRU . . . . . . Disaccharide Repeating Unit
DF . . . . Disaccommodation Factor
DC . . . . Disarmament Commission (Also known as UNDC)
DC (UN) . . . . . Disarmament Commission of the United Nations
DMP . . . . Disarmed Military Personnel
DA . . . . Disassemble
DIR . . . . Disassembly and Inspection Report
DCP . . . . Disaster Control Plan
DCRP . . . . . . Disaster Control Recovery Plan
DCT . . . . Disaster Control Team
DLC . . . . Disaster Loan Corporation
DPPB . . . . . . Disaster Preparedness Planning Board
DV . . . . Disbursement Voucher
DK . . . . Disbursing Clerk (Navy rating)
DO . . . . Disbursing Officer
D/O . . . . Disbursing Officer
DOSN . . . . . . Disbursing Office Serial Number
DOLO . . . . . . Disbursing Officers Liaison Office
DOV . . . . Disbursing Officer's Voucher
DSSN . . . . . . Disbursing Station Symbol Number (Military)
DATO . . . . . . Disbursing and Transportation Office
DDU . . . . Disc Data Unit
DG . . . . Disc Grind (Technical drawings)
DJ . . . . Disc Jockey
DS . . . . Discarding Sabot
DA . . . . Discharge Afloat
HCCG . . . . . . Discharge (from Military Service) under Honorable Conditions, Convenience of Government
HCCM . . . . . . Discharge (from Military Service) under Honorable Conditions, Convenience of Man
HCDP . . . . . . Discharge (from Military Service) under Honorable Conditions, Dependency Existing Prior to Enlistment
HCEE . . . . . . Discharge (from Military Service) under Honorable Conditions, Expiration of Enlistment
HCMS . . . . . . Discharge (from Military Service) under Honorable Conditions, Medical Survey
HCMW . . . . . . Discharge (from Military Service) under Honorable Conditions, Minor Enlisted Without Consent, under 18 at Time of Discharge
HCMU . . . . . . Discharge (from Military Service) under Honorable Conditions, under Age of Authorized Enlistment
DRF . . . . Discharge Ringing Frequency
D . . . . Discharged
DD . . . . Discharged Dead (On a serviceman's papers)
DPAS . . . . . . Discharged Prisoners' Aid Society (British)

REVERSE ACRONYMS AND INITIALISMS DICTIONARY

DSQ	Discharged to Sick Quarters
DC	Disciples of Christ
DCHS	Disciples of Christ Historical Society
DPF	Disciples Peace Fellowship
DB	Disciplinary Barracks
DTC	Disciplinary Training Center
DCMI	Disclosure of Classified Military Information (to foreign governments)
DI	Discomfiture Index (Weather)
DSC	Discone Antenna
DCF	Discounted Cash Flow
DATO	Discover America Travel Organizations, Inc. (Formerly, National Association of Travel Organizations, and Discover America, Inc.)
DRC	Discoverer Recovery Capsule (NASA)
DICO	Discovery (or Dissemination) of Information through Co-operative Organization
DCAR	Discrepancy and Corrective Action Report
DISCREP	Discrepancy Report
DA	Discrete Address
DACS	Discrete Address Communications System
DDPS	Discrete Depth Plankton Sampler
DFG	Discrete Frequency Generator
DNS	Discrete Network Simulation
DNWS	Discrete Network Simulation
DOS	Discrete Orthonormal Sequence
DSDT	Discrete Space and Discrete Time
DSC	Discrete System Concept
DR	Discrimination RADAR
DP	Discussion Paper
DD	Dishonorable Discharge
DDGC	Dishonorable Discharge, General Court-Martial, after Confinement in Prison (Navy)
DDGI	Dishonorable Discharge, General Court-Martial, Immediate (Navy)
DDGP	Dishonorable Discharge, General Court-Martial, after Violation of Probation (Navy)
DPH	Disintegrations Per Hour
D/M	Disintegrations Per Minute
DPM	Disintegrations Per Minute
DNF	Disjunctive Normal Formula
DL	Disjunctively Linear
DBR	Disk, Balls, and Roller
DOS	Disk Operating System (Data processing)
DTA	Disk Turbine Assembly
DA	Dislocation Allowance (Military)
DLA	Dislocation Allowance
DIS	Disney (Walt) Productions (NYSE symbol) (Wall Street slang name: "Mickey Mouse")
DAH	Disordered Action of the Heart (Medicine)
DC	Disorderly Conduct
DH	Disorderly House
DP	Disorderly Person
DLO	Dispatch Loading Only
D/R	Dispatch Rider (Marine Corps)
DB	Dispersal Base (Military)
DOB	Dispersed Operating Base (Air Force)
DO	Dispersing Officer
DDL	Dispersive Delay Line
DP	Displaced Person (Post-World War II)
DPC	Displaced Persons Commission (Terminated, 1952)
DG	Displacement Gyro
DMMG	Displacement Method Matrix Generator
DAC	Display Analysis Console
DAB	Display Attention Bits (Data processing)
DB	Display Buffer (Data processing)
DC	Display Computer
DCP	Display Control Panel
DEI	Display Evaluation Index
DGS	Display Generation System
DH	Display Hold
DIP	Display Information Processor (Air Force)
DIU	Display Interface Unit
DSKY	Display and Keyboard (Data processing)
DLU	Display Logic Unit
DMP	Display Maintenance Program
DOCUS	Display Oriented Compiler Usage System
DP	Display Panel
DPCA	Displaced Phase Center Antenna
DPC	Display Power Control
DPS	Display Power Supply
DSP	Display Simulation Program
DSO	Display Switching Oscilloscope
DISYNDA	Display of Synoptic Data

DTC	Display Test Chamber
DTG	Display Transmission Generator
DUPC	Displayed Under Program Control
DBCATA	Disposable Barrel Cartridge Area Target Ammunition (Weapon launcher)
DPI	Disposable Personal Income
DF	Disposition Form (Army)
DIP	Disposition of Inactive Parts List
DPAIAI	Disregard Previous Assignment Instructions and Assign as Indicated (Army)
DCT	Dissector Camera Tube
DLE	Disseminated Lupus Erythematosus (Medicine)
DIS	Dissertation Inquiry Service (Xerox)
DF	Dissipation Factor
DA	Dissolved Acetylene
DO	Dissolved Oxygen
DTP	Distal Tingling on Percussion (Medicine)
D	Distance
DIE	Distance in Error
DFS	Distance Finding Station
DIANE	Distance Indicating Automatic Navigation Equipment
DME	Distance Measuring Equipment (Aeronautics)
DME	Distance Measuring Equipment (Navigation)
DECAN	Distance-Measuring Equipment Command and Navigation
DME/COTAR	Distance Measuring Equipment/Correlation Tracking and Ranging
DMET	Distance Measuring Equipment TACAN
DMI	Distance Measuring Instrument
DMS	Distance Measuring System
DME	Distance Monitoring Equipment (Military)
DT	Distance Test
DVL	Distance Velocity Laboratory
DCOT	Distant Central Office Transceivers
DCB	Distant-Control Boat
DEW	Distant Early Warning (RADAR picket line) (Obsolete)
DEWIZ	Distant Early Warning Identification Zone (Obsolete)
DEW LINE	Distant Early Warning Line (North American RADAR system) (Obsolete)
DV	Distemper Virus
DBMA	Distillate Burner Manufacturers Association
D & L	Distillate plus Loss
DDS	Distillation Desalination System
DOV	Distilled Oil of Vitriol
DSI	Distilled Spirits Institute
DSP	Distilled Spirits Plant
DW	Distilled Water
D & R	Distiller and Rectifier
DCL	Distillers Company Limited
DCS	Distillers Corporation-Seagrams Ltd. (NYSE symbol)
DFRC	Distillers Feed Research Council
DRWAW	Distillery, Rectifying, Wine & Allied Workers International Union of America
AW	Distilling Ship (Navy symbol)
DI	Distinctive Insignia (Military)
DCM	Distinguished Conduct Medal (British)
DFC	Distinguished Flying Cross (US and British)
DFM	Distinguished Flying Medal (British)
DG	Distinguished Graduate (Military)
DG	Distinguished Guest (Hotel term)
DMB	Distinguished Marksmanship Badge
DMG	Distinguished Military Graduate
DMS	Distinguished Military Students
DNG	Distinguished Naval Graduate
DPB	Distinguished Pistol Badge
DSC	Distinguished Service Cross (US and British)
DSM	Distinguished Service Medal (US and British)
DSO	Distinguished Service Order (British)
DUC	Distinguished Unit Citation (Military)
DUCE	Distinguished Unit Citation Emblem
DUE	Distinguished Unit Emblem
DV	Distinguished Visitor
DWBA	Distorted-Wave Born Approximation
DEVR	Distortion-Eliminating Voltage Regulator
DTI	Distortion Transmission Impairment
QRRR	Distress call for emergency use only by amateur radio stations in an emergency situation
DAJS	Distributed Area Jamming System (Air Force)
DEMATRON	Distributed Emission Magnetron Amplifier
DRAC	Distributed Read Address Counter
DSR	Distributed State Response
DWAC	Distributed Write Address Counter
DPO	Distributing Post Office
DTA	Distributing Terminal Assembly (Electronics)
DA	Distribution Amplifier
DISTRA	Distribution Authority (Army)

DAL . . . . Distribution Authority List
DB . . . . Distribution Box (Technical drawings)
DCF . . . . Distribution Chart File
DCA . . . . Distribution Contractors Association
DODIS . . . . . . Distribution of Oceanographic Data at Isentropic Levels
DPL . . . . Distribution Plot List
DP . . . . Distribution Point
DSP . . . . Distribution Point
DE . . . . Distributive Education
DECA . . . . Distributive Education Clubs of America
DPMA . . . . Distributive Principle of Multiplication over Addition (New math)
DPOWA . . . . . Distributive, Processing and Office Workers Union of America
DGDG . . . . . . Distributor-to-Group Display Generator
DMR . . . . Distributor-Manufacturer-Representative
DPE . . . . Distributor-to-Printer Electronics
DAO . . . . District Accounting Office(r) (Navy)
DAE . . . . District Airport Engineer
DA . . . . District Attorney
DAGO . . . . . . District Aviation Gas Office (Navy)
DAO . . . . District Aviation Office(r) (Navy)
YFP . . . . District Barge, Floating Power (Navy symbol)
DBSO . . . . . . District Base Service Office
DCO . . . . District Camouflage Office(r)
DCH . . . . District Chaplain (Navy)
DCR . . . . District Chief Ranger (Ancient Order of Foresters)
DCRO . . . . . . District Civil Readjustment Office(r)
DCPO . . . . . . District Civilian Personnel Office(r)
DCO . . . . District Clothing Office(r)
DCGO . . . . . . District Coast Guard Officer
DC . . . . District of Columbia
DCMD . . . . . . District of Columbia Military District
DCNG . . . . . . District of Columbia National Guard
DNG . . . . District of Columbia National Guard
DCTC . . . . . . District of Columbia Teachers College
DCO . . . . District Communication Officer
DCC . . . . District Communications Center (Navy)
DC . . . . District Court
DCM . . . . District Court-Martial
DDO . . . . District Dental Office(r) (Navy)
DD . . . . District Director
DDIR . . . . . . District Directors of Internal Revenue (IRS)
DDTO . . . . . . District Domestic Transportation Office(r)
DESO . . . . . . District Educational Services Officer (Navy)
DE . . . . District Engineer (Army)
DEO . . . . District Engineer Officer (Army)
DJ . . . . District Judge
DHIRS . . . . . District Headquarters Induction and Recruiting Station (Marine Corps)
DHO . . . . District Historical Office(r) (Navy)
DIIO . . . . . . District Industrial Incentive Office(r) (Navy)
DIM . . . . District Industrial Manager (Navy)
DIRO . . . . . . District Industrial Relations Officer (Navy)
DI . . . . District Inspector (Navy)
DIO . . . . District Intelligence Officer
DLRO . . . . . . District Labor Relations Office(r) (Navy)
DLO . . . . District Legal Office(r) (Navy)
DMO . . . . District Management Office
DMO . . . . District Marine Officer (Navy)
DMO . . . . District Material Officer (Navy)
DMO . . . . District Medical Officer (Navy)
DNMO . . . . . District Naval Material Office
DO . . . . District Office (or Officer)
DORCSA . . . . District Officer for Reserve Communication Supplementary Activities
DOO . . . . District Operations Office(r) (Navy)
DOO . . . . District Ordnance Office(r) (Navy)
DPO . . . . District Personnel Office(r) (Navy)
DPD . . . . District Port Director (Navy)
DPLO . . . . . . District Postal Liaison Officer (Navy)
DPO . . . . District Postal Office(r) (Navy)
DPR . . . . District Probate Registry
DPTO . . . . . . District Property Transportation Office(r) (Navy)
DPIO . . . . . . District Public Information Office(r) (Navy)
DPRO . . . . . . District Public Relations Office(r) (Navy)
DPWO . . . . . District Public Works Office
DPPO . . . . . . District Publications and Printing Office
DR . . . . District Railway (London)
DRMO . . . . . District Records Management Office
DR . . . . District Registry
DREPO . . . . . District Reserve Electronics Program Officer
DRE . . . . District Reserve Equipment (Army)
DSO . . . . District Sales Office
DSO . . . . District Security Office(r) (Navy)

DSO . . . . District Service Office(r) (Navy)
DSSO . . . . . . District Ships Service Office(r) (Navy)
DSCR . . . . . . District Sub-Chief Ranger (Ancient Order of Foresters)
DSO . . . . District Supply Officer
DTO . . . . District Training Office(r) (Navy)
DTO . . . . District Transportation Officer
DWBO . . . . . District War Bond Office(r) (Navy)
DWPO . . . . . District War Plans Officer
DF . . . . Distrito Federal (Mexico City)
DTBP . . . . . . Di-Tert-Butyl Peroxide
DBPC . . . . . . Ditertiary-Butyl-Para-Cresol
DIRC . . . . . . Dithered Infrared Configuration
DTT . . . . Dithiothreitol
DO . . . . Ditto
DCO . . . . Divco-Wayne Corporation (NYSE symbol)
DB . . . . Dive Bomb
DB . . . . Dive Bomber Aircraft
VB . . . . Dive Bomber Squadron (Navy symbol)
DRD . . . . Diver Restraint Device
DS . . . . Diver, Salvage (Navy)
DT . . . . Diver, Second Class (Navy rating)
DIV . . . . Diversey Corporation (NYSE symbol)
DCS . . . . Diversity Combiner System
DRIFT . . . . . . Diversity Receiving Instrumentation for Telemetry
DRR . . . . Diversity Reception Receiver
DRIFT . . . . . . Diversity Reliability Instantaneous Forecasting Technique
DALC . . . . . . Divided Access Line Circuit
D . . . . Dividend
DSB . . . . Divine Science Bachelor
DSD . . . . Divine Science Doctor
DVDY . . . . . . Diving Duty (Military)
DS . . . . Diving Saucer
YDT . . . . Diving Tender (Navy symbol)
DETA . . . . . . Divisao de Exploracao dos Transportes Aereos
DTA . . . . Divisao de Exploracao dos Transportes Aereos (Angola Airline)
D . . . . Division
DAES . . . . . . Division of Adult Education Service (of NEA)
DAVR . . . . . . Division of Adult and Vocational Research (US Office of Education)
DAST . . . . . . Division for Advanced Systems Technology
DAO . . . . Division Air Officer
DAP . . . . Division of Air Pollution (Public Health Service)
DAO . . . . Division Ammunition Office (Army)
DA . . . . Division Artillery (Army)
DIVART . . . . . Division Artillery (Army)
DB . . . . Division Base (Army)
DIVBASE . . . . Division Base (Army)
DBH . . . . Division Beachhead (Army)
DBS . . . . Division of Biologics Standards (of National Institutes of Health)
DBPH . . . . . . Division for the Blind and Physically Handicapped (Library of Congress)
DCC . . . . Division of Cataloging and Classification (Became CCS)
DCL . . . . Division of Chemical Literature (ACS)
DCO . . . . Division Classification Officer
DCUA . . . . . . Division of College and University Assistance (HEW)
DIVCOM . . . . Division Commander (Navy)
DCC . . . . Division of Consumer Credit (FTC)
DC . . . . Division of Contracts
DCB . . . . Division Crime Buffer
DEAP . . . . . . Division of Engineering and Applied Physics (Harvard University)
DFF . . . . Division Final Fade
DFLC . . . . . . Division of Foreign Labor Conditions (Department of Labor)
DFCP . . . . . . Division Funding Control Point
DGMS . . . . . . Division of General Medical Sciences (of National Institutes of Health)
DGES . . . . . . Division of Graduate Education in Science (National Science Foundation)
DHCY . . . . . . Division of Handicapped Children and Youth (HEW)
DHQ . . . . Division Headquarters (Army)
DIVHED . . . . . Division Headquarters (Army)
DIC . . . . Division of Industrial Cooperation (MIT)
DIP . . . . Division of Industrial Participation (AEC)
DIF . . . . Division of International Finance (of FRS)
DID . . . . Division of Isotopes Development (of AEC)
DJDS . . . . . . Division of Juvenile Delinquency Service (of SSA)
DLSEF . . . . . . Division of Library Services and Educational Facilities (US Office of Education)
DLOC . . . . . . Division Logistical Operation Center
DLCC . . . . . . Division Logistics Control Center
DLST/SEACAPS . . Division Logistics System Test/Seventh Army Card Processor System
DMA . . . . Division of Military Application (AEC)
DNI . . . . Division of Naval Intelligence
DNET . . . . . . Division of Nuclear Education and Training (of AEC)
DNMM . . . . . Division of Nuclear Materials Management (of AEC)
DOS . . . . Division of Operational Safety (AEC)

DIVOO . . . . . Division Ordnance Officer
DOO . . . . Division Ordnance Officer
DOM . . . . Division of Overseas Ministries (National Council of Churches)
DPNE . . . . . . Division of Peaceful Nuclear Explosives (of AEC)
DRRF . . . . Division Rapid Reaction Force (Army)
DRD . . . . Division of Reactor Development (AEC)
DRL . . . . Division of Reactor Licensing (AEC)
DRF . . . . Division Ready Force (Army)
DRC . . . . Division of Rehabilitation Counseling (of the APGA)
DR . . . . Division of Research (Navy)
DRFR . . . . Division of Research Facilities and Resources (of National Institutes of Health)
DRG . . . . Division of Research Grants (of National Institutes of Health)
DRS . . . . Division of Research Services (of National Institutes of Health)
DSPE . . . . Division of Scientific Personnel and Education (National Science Foundation)
DSA . . . . Division Service Area (Army)
DSO . . . . Division Signal Officer
DSR . . . . Division of Sponsored Research (MIT)
DSCP . . . . Division Supply Control Point
DISCOM . . . . . Division Support Command (Army)
DSCC . . . . . . Division Support Control Center (Army)
DTA . . . . Division Tactical Area (Army)
DTOC . . . . . . Division Tactical Operations Center
DTR . . . . Division of Tax Research
DTI . . . . Division of Technical Information (AEC)
DTIE . . . . Division of Technical Information Extension (AEC)
DIVTAG . . . . . Division Through Army Group
DVR . . . . Division of Vocational Rehabilitation (D.C.)
DEO . . . . Divisional Education Officer (British)
DEO . . . . Divisional Entertainments Officer (British)
DO . . . . Divisional Orders
DRO . . . . Divisional Routine Order(s)
DJC . . . . Dixie Junior College (Utah)
DZ . . . . Dizygotic
DAP . . . . Do All Possible
DIY . . . . Do-It-Yourself
DNL . . . . Do Not Load (Instruction re a freight car)
DBK . . . . Dobeckman Company (NYSE symbol)
DPCA . . . . . . Doberman Pinscher Club of America
DOSAAF . . . . . Dobrovol'noe Obshchestvo Sodeistviia Armii, Aviatsii, i Flotu (Voluntary Society for Cooperation with the Army, Aviation, and the Fleet) (USSR)
LSD . . . . Dock Landing Ship (Navy symbol)
DR . . . . Dock Receipt
DW . . . . Dock Warrant
DY . . . . Dockyard
D . . . . Doctor
D Ac . . . . Doctor of Accounts
DACE . . . . Doctor of Air Conditioning Engineering
DAC Eng . . . . . Doctor of Air Conditioning Engineering
DAA . . . . Doctor of Applied Arts
DA Chem . . . . Doctor of Applied Chemistry
DAS . . . . Doctor of Applied Science
DA Sc . . . . . . Doctor of Applied Science
D Ark . . . . . . Doctor of Archaeology
DAE . . . . Doctor of Art Education
DAO . . . . Doctor of Art of Oratory
AD . . . . Doctor of Arts
Art D . . . . Doctor of Arts
DA . . . . Doctor of Arts
D Ar Sc . . . . . Doctor of Arts and Sciences
D As S . . . . . . Doctor of Association Science
D As Sc . . . . . Doctor of Association Science
D As . . . . Doctor of Astronomy
D Au E . . . . . . Doctor of Automobile Engineering
Dr Ae . . . . Doctor of Aviation
DBC . . . . Doctor of Beauty Culture
Ph BD . . . . . . Doctor of Bible Philosophy
Dr Bi Phy . . . . Doctor of Biophysics
BPD . . . . Doctor of Bio-Psychology
DBA . . . . . . Doctor of Business Administration
DBM . . . . . . Doctor of Business Management
DBS . . . . Doctor of Business Science
DCL . . . . Doctor of Canon Law
D Can L . . . . Doctor of Canon Law
D Cn L . . . . . Doctor of Canon Law
DLC . . . . Doctor of Celtic Literature
D Ce Eng . . . . Doctor of Cement Engineering
Ch D . . . . Doctor of Chemistry
Cp D . . . . Doctor of Chiropody

DC . . . . Doctor of Chiropractic
DCPT . . . . Doctor of Chiropractic and Physiological Therapeutics
DC . . . . Doctor of Chiropraxis
CSD . . . . Doctor of Christian Science
DCS . . . . Doctor of Christian Science
DSC . . . . Doctor of Christian Science
DCS . . . . Doctor of Christian Service
DCT . . . . Doctor of Christian Theology
DCT . . . . Doctor of Christian Training
DCF . . . . Doctor of City Forestry
DCP . . . . Doctor of City Planning
DCE . . . . Doctor of Civil Engineering
CLD . . . . Doctor of Civil Law
DCL . . . . Doctor of Civil Law(s)
DCL . . . . Doctor of Classical Literature
D Com . . . . . . Doctor of Commerce
DCA . . . . Doctor of Commercial Arts
DC Ed . . . . . . Doctor of Commercial Education
DCL . . . . Doctor of Commercial Law
DCS . . . . Doctor of Commercial Science
DC Sc . . . . . . Doctor of Commercial Science
Dr CS . . . . . . Doctor of Commercial Science
DSC . . . . Doctor of Commercial Science
SCD . . . . Doctor of Commercial Science
DC Se . . . . . . Doctor of Commercial Service
D Comp L . . . . Doctor of Comparative Law
DCM . . . . Doctor of Comparative Medicine
MCD . . . . Doctor of Comparative Medicine
DCR . . . . Doctor of Comparative Religion
D Co . . . . Doctor of Cosmology
CJD . . . . Doctor of Criminal Jurisprudence
DCJ . . . . Doctor of Criminal Jurisprudence
Dr Cr Jus . . . . Doctor of Criminal Jurisprudence
D Cr . . . . Doctor of Criminology
Dr Cul S . . . . . Doctor of Cultural Science
DDM . . . . Doctor of Dental Medicine
DMD . . . . Doctor of Dental Medicine
MDD . . . . Doctor of Dental Medicine
DD Sc . . . . . . Doctor of Dental Science
DDS . . . . Doctor of Dental Surgery
DD Sc . . . . . . Doctor of Dental Surgery
DD Sur . . . . . Doctor of Dental Surgery
D Des . . . . . . Doctor of Design
D Dn . . . . Doctor of Design
D Did . . . . . . Doctor of Didactics
D Di E . . . . . . Doctor of Diesel Engineering
D Di Eng . . . . Doctor of Diesel Engineering
D Dipl . . . . . . Doctor of Diplomacy
DDL . . . . Doctor of Divine Literature
DD . . . . Doctor of Divinity
Dr D . . . . Doctor of Divinity
DD . . . . Doctor of Divinity in Metaphysics
DDA . . . . Doctor of Dramatic Art
DDT . . . . Doctor of Drugless Therapy
Ed D . . . . Doctor of Education
DEE . . . . Doctor of Electrical Engineering
DE Ch E . . . . . Doctor of Electro-Chemical Engineering
DE Ch Eng . . . . Doctor of Electro-Chemical Engineering
DEL . . . . Doctor of Elements
D Elo . . . . Doctor of Elocution
D Eng . . . . . . Doctor of Engineering
ED . . . . Doctor of Engineering
DE Phy . . . . . . Doctor of Engineering Physics
DES . . . . Doctor of Engineering Science
DE Sc . . . . . . Doctor of Engineering Science
D En . . . . Doctor of English
Dr En . . . . Doctor of English
DED . . . . Doctor of English Divinity
DEL . . . . Doctor of English Literature
DE . . . . Doctor of Entomology
D Ent . . . . . . Doctor of Entomology
D Ex . . . . Doctor of Expression
DFL . . . . Doctor of Family Life
Dr Fi . . . . Doctor of Finance
DFA . . . . Doctor of Fine Arts
DFS . . . . Doctor of Foreign Science
DFS . . . . Doctor of Foreign Service
DFE . . . . Doctor of Forest Engineering
DF Eng . . . . . . Doctor of Forest Engineering
DFS . . . . Doctor of Forest Science
DF . . . . Doctor of Forestry

Dr F . . . . Doctor of Forestry
Dr Geo . . . . . . Doctor of Geography
D Ge E . . . . . . Doctor of Geological Engineering
D Ge Eng . . . . Doctor of Geological Engineering
Dr Ge . . . . . . Doctor of Geology
Dr GP. . . . . . . Doctor of Geopolitics
DHL. . . . . Doctor of Hebrew Letters
DH Litt . . . . . . Doctor of Hebrew Letters
DHL . . . . Doctor of Hebrew Literature
DH Lit . . . . . . Doctor of Hebrew Literature
DH Litt . . . . . . Doctor of Hebrew Literature
DH Ec. . . . . . . Doctor of Home Economics
DHH . . . . Doctor of Honorary Humanities
HHD . . . . Doctor of Honorary Humanities
DHA . . . . Doctor of Hospital Administration
DH Adm . . . . . Doctor of Hospital Administration
DH Ec. . . . . . . Doctor of Household Economy
D Ho Sc . . . . . Doctor of Household Science
DHL. . . . . Doctor of Humane Letters
LHD . . . . Doctor of Humane Letters (or Doctor of Humanities; Doctor of Letters;
          Doctor of Letters of Humanity; Doctor of Polite Literature; Doctor of
          the More Humane Letters)
DH . . . . Doctor of Humanics
DHS. . . . . Doctor of Humanitarian Service
Dr HS . . . . . . Doctor of Humanitarian Service
DH . . . . Doctor of Humanities
Dr HL . . . . . . Doctor of Humanities of Learning
HHD . . . . Doctor of Humanities
D Hyg. . . . . . Doctor of Hygiene
DIA . . . . Doctor of Industrial Arts
DIE . . . . Doctor of Industrial Engineering
SID . . . . Doctor of Industrial Science
DI Arch E . . . . Doctor of Interior Architectural Engineering
DI Arch . . . . . Doctor of Interior Architecture
DIL . . . . Doctor of International Law
DJP . . . . Doctor of Jewish Pedagogy
DJT . . . . Doctor of Jewish Theology
DJ Th . . . . . . Doctor of Jewish Theology
DJS . . . . Doctor of Judicial Science
DJ Sc . . . . . . Doctor of Judicial Science
Jur Sc D . . . . Doctor of Judicial Science (or Doctor of Science of Jurisprudence)
J Sc D . . . . . . Doctor of Juridical Science
JSD . . . . Doctor of Juridical (or Judicial) Science (or Doctor of the Science
          of Law)
SJD . . . . Doctor of Juridical Science (or Doctor of the Science of Jurisprudence
          or Doctor of the Science of Law)
DJ . . . . Doctor Juris (Doctor of Law)
DL Arch . . . . . Doctor of Landscape Architecture
DL Des . . . . . Doctor of Landscape Design
DL Eng . . . . . Doctor of Landscape Engineering
DLM . . . . Doctor of Landscape Management
DLL . . . . Doctor of Late Laws
D La L . . . . . . Doctor of Latin Letters
DL . . . . Doctor of Law
Dr LL . . . . . . Doctor of Laws
LLD . . . . Doctor of Law(s)
DL . . . . Doctor of Letters
Dr Litt . . . . . . Doctor of Letters
LD . . . . Doctor of Letters
LJD . . . . Doctor of Letters of Journalism
DLA . . . . Doctor of Liberal Arts
DL Ec . . . . . . Doctor of Library Economics
DLS . . . . Doctor of Library Science
Dr LS . . . . . . Doctor of Library Science
DL Sc . . . . . . Doctor of Library Science
LSD . . . . Doctor of Library Science
LSD . . . . Doctor of Life Science
DLI . . . . Doctor of Literary Interpretation
DL . . . . Doctor of Literature
Phil LD . . . . . Doctor of Lithuanian Philology
DM . . . . Doctor of Mathematics
DMD . . . . Doctor of Mathematics and Didactics
DME . . . . Doctor of Mechanical Engineering
DMS . . . . Doctor of Mechanical Science
Dr MT. . . . . . . Doctor of Mechanotherapy
DMD . . . . Doctor of Medical Dentistry
DMJ . . . . Doctor of Medical Jurisprudence
MJD . . . . Doctor of Medical Jurisprudence
DMS . . . . Doctor of Medical Science(s)
M Sc D . . . . . . Doctor of Medical Science

MSD . . . . Doctor of Medical Science
DMT . . . . Doctor of Medical Technology
DM . . . . Doctor of Medicine
MD . . . . Doctor of Medicine
D Me . . . . Doctor of Metaphysics
Ms D . . . . Doctor of Metaphysics
D Mic . . . . . . Doctor of Microbiology
Mic D . . . . . . Doctor of Microbiology
DMS . . . . Doctor of Military Science
DML . . . . Doctor of Modern Languages
DMA . . . . Doctor of Municipal Administration
DM Adm . . . . . Doctor of Municipal Administration
DM . . . . Doctor of Music
DMA . . . . Doctor of Musical Arts
Mus AD . . . . . Doctor of Musical Arts
Dr N Ph . . . . . Doctor of Natural Philosophy
Dr Phil Nat . . . Doctor of Natural Philosophy
Dr N Sc . . . . . Doctor of the Natural Sciences
Dr Sci Nat . . . . Doctor of Natural Sciences
D Nat . . . . . . Doctor of Naturopathy
ND . . . . Doctor of Naturopathy
DNE . . . . Doctor of Naval Engineering
D Na S . . . . . . Doctor of Naval Science
D Na Sc . . . . . Doctor of Naval Science
D Na . . . . Doctor of Navigation
DN . . . . Doctor of Nursing
DNS . . . . Doctor of Nursing Science
D Oc S . . . . . . Doctor of Ocular Science
D Oc Sc . . . . . Doctor of Ocular Science
DOS . . . . Doctor of Ocular Science
D Oec . . . . . . Doctor Oeconomiae (Doctor of Economics)
DOS . . . . Doctor of Optical Science
DOS . . . . Doctor of Optometric Science
DO Sc . . . . . . Doctor of Optometric Science
DO . . . . Doctor of Optometry
OD . . . . Doctor of Optometry
DOE . . . . Doctor of Oral English
DO . . . . Doctor of Oratory
D Or . . . . Doctor of Oratory
DOL . . . . Doctor of Oriental Languages
DO . . . . Doctor of Osteopathic Medicine and Surgery
DO . . . . Doctor of Osteopathy
D Pa . . . . Doctor of Painting
Dr Pa . . . . . . Doctor of Painting
DPL . . . . Doctor of Patent Law
D Pd . . . . Doctor of Pedagogy
PD . . . . Doctor of Pedagogy
Pd D . . . . Doctor of Pedagogy
DOC . . . . Dr. Pepper Company (NYSE symbol)
D Pe E . . . . . . Doctor of Petroleum Engineering
D Phar C . . . . . Doctor of Pharmaceutical Chemistry
D Ph C . . . . . . Doctor of Pharmaceutical Chemistry
D Phc . . . . . . Doctor of Pharmacology
PD . . . . Doctor of Pharmacy
Ph D . . . . Doctor of Pharmacy
Dr Phi . . . . . . Doctor of Philanthropy
D Phil. . . . . . . Doctor of Philanthropy
DP . . . . Doctor of Philosophy
D Phil. . . . . . . Doctor of Philosophy
PD . . . . Doctor of Philosophy
Ph D . . . . Doctor of Philosophy
D Ph M . . . . . . Doctor of Philosophy in Metaphysics
D Pho . . . . . . Doctor of Photography
Dr Pho . . . . . . Doctor of Photography
DPB . . . . Doctor of Physical Biology
DPE . . . . Doctor of Physical Education
Dr of PE . . . . . Doctor of Physical Education
DPM . . . . Doctor of Physical Medicine
D Ph S . . . . . . Doctor of Physical Science
Dr P Sc . . . . . Doctor of Physical Science
D Phy. . . . . . . Doctor of Physics
Dr Phy . . . . . . Doctor of Physics
Pod D . . . . . . Doctor of Podiatry
DPS . . . . Doctor of Political Science
PSD . . . . Doctor of Political Science
SPD . . . . Doctor of Political Science
Dr Pr M . . . . . Doctor of Preventative Medicine
D Ps . . . . Doctor of Psychology
Ps D . . . . Doctor of Psychology
Ps D . . . . Doctor of Psychology in Metaphysics
D Ps Th . . . . . . Doctor of Psycho-Therapy

REVERSE ACRONYMS AND INITIALISMS DICTIONARY

DPA . . . . Doctor of Public Administration	DTT . . . . Doctor of Textile Technology
Dr PA . . . . . . Doctor of Public Administration	D Th . . . . Doctor of Theology
DPH . . . . Doctor of Public Health	DT . . . . Doctor of Theology
Dr PH . . . . . . Doctor of Public Health	Th D . . . . Doctor of Theology
DPH Ed . . . . . . Doctor of Public Health Education	Dr T Med . . . . Doctor of Tropical Medicine
DPHE . . . . . . Doctor of Public Health Engineering	DTM . . . . Doctor of Tropical Medicine
DPH Eng . . . . . Doctor of Public Health Engineering	DVM . . . . Doctor of Veterinary Medicine
Dr PH Hy . . . . Doctor of Public Health and Hygiene	MDV . . . . Doctor of Veterinary Medicine
DPHN . . . . . . Doctor of Public Health Nursing	MVD . . . . Doctor of Veterinary Medicine
DPH . . . . Doctor of Public Hygiene	VMD . . . . Doctor of Veterinary Medicine
Dr PH . . . . . . Doctor of Public Hygiene	DVMS . . . . . . Doctor of Veterinary Medicine and Surgery
DP Sc . . . . Doctor of Political Science	DVS . . . . Doctor of Veterinary Science
DPSA . . . . . . Doctor of Public School Art	DVS . . . . Doctor of Veterinary Surgery
DPSM . . . . . . Doctor of Public School Music	DV Ed . . . . . . Doctor of Vocational Education
DPS . . . . Doctor of Public Service	DZ. . . . . Doctor of Zoology
PSD . . . . Doctor of Public Service	DIR . . . . Doctrine of Incremental Reduction
DRTE . . . . . . Doctor of Radio and Television Engineering	D. . . . . Document
DRT Eng . . . . Doctor of Radio and Television Engineering	DCN . . . . Document Control Number
DRP . . . . Doctor of Regional Planning	DDIS . . . . Document Data Indexing Set
D Re . . . . Doctor of Religion	DD & RB . . . . Document Distribution and Reproduction Branch (CFSTI)
DRE . . . . Doctor of Religious Education	DER . . . . Document Error Report
DR Ed . . . . . . Doctor of Religious Education	DOCGEN . . . . Document Generator
Ed RD . . . . . . Doctor of Religious Education	DI . . . . Document Identifier (Military)
D Ru E . . . . . . Doctor of Rural Engineering	DPB . . . . Document Processing Branch (CFSTI)
DSS . . . . Doctor Sacrae Scripturae (Doctor of Holy Scripture)	DPS . . . . Document Processing System (Data processing)
DSL . . . . Doctor of Sacred Literature	DR . . . . Document Report
DSM . . . . Doctor of Sacred Music	DSC . . . . Document Service Center
SMD . . . . Doctor of Sacred Music	DS . . . . Document Signed
D Sa Sc . . . . . . Doctor of Sacred Sciences	DSR . . . . Document Status Report (Military)
SSD . . . . Doctor of Sacred Scripture	DA . . . . Documentary Bill for Acceptance
DST . . . . Doctor of Sacred Theology	DRD . . . . Documentary Research Division (Air Force)
DSE . . . . Doctor of Sanitary Engineering	DA . . . . Documentation Abstracts (A journal)
DS Eng . . . . . Doctor of Sanitary Engineering	DARE . . . . . . Documentation Automated Retrieval Equipment
DSS . . . . Doctor of Sanitary Science	DIA . . . . Documentation et Information Africaines (African Documentation and Information (Catholic News Agency)
DS Sc . . . . . . Doctor of Sanitary Science	DMS. . . . . . . Documentation of Molecular Spectroscopy
DS. . . . . Doctor of Science	DPC . . . . Documentation Processing Center (British)
D Sc . . . . Doctor of Science	DRP . . . . Documentation Research Project (American Institute of Physics)
Sc D. . . . . . . Doctor of Science	DRTC . . . . . . Documentation Research and Training Centre (India)
SD . . . . Doctor of Science	DRN. . . . . . . Documentation Revision Notice
DS in BA . . . . Doctor of Science in Business Administration	DMP. . . . . . . Documented Material Processed
DSEL . . . . . . Doctor of Science and English Literature	DA. . . . . Documents against Acceptance, or Documents for Acceptance
DSF . . . . Doctor of the Science of Forestry	D/P . . . . Documents against Payment (Banking)
DS in Gp Engr . Doctor of Science in Geophysical Engineering	DA. . . . . Documents Attached
D Sci H . . . . . Doctor of Science and Hygiene	D/A . . . . Documents upon Acceptance of Draft
DSIM . . . . . . Doctor of Science in Industrial Medicine	D/P . . . . Documents upon Payment of Draft
DSJ . . . . Doctor of the Science of Jurisprudence	DCC. . . . . . . Dodge City College (Kansas)
L Sc D . . . . . . Doctor of the Science of Law	DBS . . . . Dodecylbenzene Sulfonate (Chemical)
M Sc D . . . . . . Doctor of the Science of Medicine	DJC . . . . Doehler-Jarvis Corporation (NYSE symbol)
D Or Sc . . . . . Doctor of the Science of Oratory	D . . . . Dog
Dr O Sc . . . . . Doctor of the Science of Oratory	DKTC . . . . . . Dog Kidney Tissue Culture
D Sc O . . . . . . Doctor of the Science of Oratory	DAL. . . . . . . Dog at Large (Humorous notation put on letters that cannot be delivered) (British postmen's slang)
DSO . . . . Doctor of the Science of Oratory	DOLA . . . . . . Dog Owners League of America
D Sc Os . . . . . Doctor of the Science of Osteopathy	DOLOA . . . . . Dog Owners League of America
DS in PE . . . . . Doctor of Science in Petroleum Engineering	DU. . . . . Dog Unit (Veterinary medicine)
DS in PRE . . . . Doctor of Science in Petroleum Refining Engineering	DVOT. . . . . . Dog Vomit On Toast (Creamed beef or tuna on toast) (Military slang)
DSS . . . . Doctor of Science in Surgery	DFD . . . . Dogs for Defense (Organization which trained dogs for armed services) (World War II)
STD . . . . Doctor of Science of Theology	DBA . . . . Doing Business As (Followed by company name)
D Sc in VM . . . Doctor of Science in Veterinary Medicine	DBA . . . . Doing Business At
DS Di . . . . . . Doctor of Scientific Didactics	DCT . . . . Doklady Chemical Technology
D Scn . . . . . . Doctor of Scientology	DPC . . . . Doklady Physical Chemistry
D Se A . . . . . . Doctor of Secretarial Arts	DATUM. . . . . Dokumentations–und Ausbildungszentrum fuer Theorie und Methode der Regionalforschung (Documentation and Training Center for Theory and Methods of Regional Research) (Germany)
D Se Sc . . . . . . Doctor of Secretarial Science	DISZ . . . . Dolgozo Ifjusay Szovetsege
DSS . . . . Doctor of Secretarial Science	DSMA. . . . . . Doll Supply Manufacturers Association
D Se St . . . . . . Doctor of Secretarial Studies	D. . . . . Dollar
Dr So Sc . . . . Doctor of Social Science	DTO. . . . . . . Dollar Tradeoff
DS Sc . . . . . . Doctor of Social Science	DTP . . . . Dolph-Tchebyscheff Pattern
Sc SD . . . . . . Doctor of Social Sciences	DTPL . . . . . . Domain Tip Propagation Logic
DSS . . . . Doctor of Social Service	DALTO . . . . . Doman Approach Landing Take-Off
DSW . . . . Doctor of Social Welfare	DM . . . . Dome Mines, Limited (NYSE symbol)
DSW . . . . Doctor of Social Work	DRT . . . . Dome Removal Tool
Dr So . . . . . . Doctor of Sociology	DFMS . . . . . . Domestic and Foreign Missionary Society (British)
D Sp . . . . Doctor of Speech	DIB . . . . Domestic and International Business (Department of Commerce)
D St . . . . Doctor of Statistics	DISC . . . . . . Domestic International Sales Corporations (Proposed)
DSC . . . . Doctor of Surgical Chiropody	DP . . . . Domestic Prelate
D Sy Th . . . . . Doctor of Systematic Theology	DS . . . . Domestic Service (Equipment specification)
DT Ch . . . . . . Doctor of Textile Chemistry	D . . . . Dominant (Applied to a species)
DTC. . . . . . . Doctor of Textile Chemistry	
DT Des . . . . . Doctor of Textile Design	
DTD . . . . Doctor of Textile Dyeing	
DTE . . . . Doctor of Textile Engineering	
DTS . . . . Doctor of Textile Science	

DFA . . . . Dominant Feature Analysis
DL . . . . Dominical Letter
DCM . . . . Dominican Campaign Medal
DCSR . . . . Dominican College of San Rafael (California)
DJCB . . . . Dominican Junior College of Blauvelt (New York)
DOMREP . . . . . Dominican Republic
DMK . . . . Dominick Fund, Inc. (NYSE symbol)
DTX . . . . Dominion Textile (NYSE symbol)
DA . . . . Dominion Atlantic Railway (AAR code)
DBS . . . . Dominion Bureau of Statistics (Canada)
DO . . . . Dominions Office (British)
DDNN . . . . . . Dominis Nostris (To Our Lords)
DN . . . . Domino Nostro (To Our Lord)
D . . . . Dominus (The Lord)
DN . . . . Dominus (Lord)
DN . . . . Dominus Noster (Our Lord)
DNJC . . . . . . Dominus Noster Jesus Christus (Our Lord Jesus Christ)
DOM . . . . Dominus Omnium Magister (God the Master, or Lord, of All)
              (Motto of the Benedictine Order)
DBC . . . . Don Bosco College (New Jersey)
D/D . . . . Donation on Discharge
DKS . . . . Doniphan, Kensett & Searcy Railway (AAR code)
DNY . . . . Donnelley (R. R.) & Sons Company (NYSE symbol)
DD . . . . Dono Dedit (He or She Gave as a Gift)
DDD . . . . Dono Dedit Dedicavit (He Gave and Dedicated as a Gift)
DEL . . . . Donor Energy Level
DSO . . . . Donora Southern R. R. (AAR code)
DC . . . . Donor's Cells
DP . . . . Donor's Plasma (Medicine)
DS . . . . Donor's Serum (Physiology)
DA . . . . Don't Answer
DCD . . . . Don't-Care-a-Damn (British naval slang term for torpedo-boat destroyer)
              (World War I)
DK . . . . Don't Know
DD . . . . Donum Dedit; Dedicavit (Gave, Dedicated)
DMJP . . . . . . Door Mounted Junction Panel
DORCMA . . . . Door Operator and Remote Controls Manufacturers Association
DSW . . . . Door Switch
DBO . . . . Dopamine-Beta-Oxidase (Chemical)
DEO . . . . Doped Erbium Oxide
DGL . . . . Doped Glass LASER
DDT . . . . Doppler Data Translator
DDS . . . . Doppler Detection Station (Detection station on the Mid-Canada Line)
DDS . . . . Doppler Detection System
DOPDF . . . . . . Doppler Direction-Finding Equipment
DI . . . . Doppler Inertial
DIL . . . . Doppler-Inertial-LORAN
DILS . . . . Doppler Inertial LORAN System
DLR . . . . Doppler LASER RADAR
DOLARS . . . . . Doppler Location and Ranging System
DMS . . . . Doppler Measurement System
DNS . . . . Doppler Navigation System
DON . . . . Doppler Optical Navigation
DOPLOC . . . . Doppler Phase Lock
DRA . . . . Doppler RADAR
DARE . . . . . . Doppler and Range Evaluation
DORAN . . . . . Doppler Range and Navigation (Electronics)
DSA . . . . Doppler Spectrum Analyzer
DSP . . . . Doppler Spectrum Processor
DTS . . . . Doppler Tracking Station
DTC . . . . Doppler Translation Channel
DTP . . . . Doppler Techniques Proposal
DOUSER . . . . Doppler Unbeamed Search RADAR
DOVAP . . . . . Doppler, Velocity and Position (NASA)
DVS . . . . Doppler Velocity Sensor
DVOR . . . . . . Doppler VHF Omnirange
DWS . . . . Dorcas Welfare Society
DIP . . . . Dormit In Pace (Sleeps in Peace)
D . . . . Dorsal
DK . . . . Dorsal (Kidney)
DNG . . . . Dorsal (Nephridial Gland)
DF . . . . Dorsal Fold
DFO . . . . Dorsal Fold (Oesophagus)
DL . . . . Dorsal Lip
DMN . . . . Dorsal Motor Nucleus (of the vagus)
DPCF . . . . . . Dorsal Peristomial Collar Fold
DP . . . . Dorsal Pit
DVL . . . . Dorsal Velar Lobe
D . . . . Dose (in prescriptions)
DDS . . . . Dose Detector System
DRI . . . . Dose Rate Instrumentation

DOSAR . . . . . . Dosimetry Applications Research Facility (AEC)
DV . . . . Douay Version (Bible)
D . . . . Double
DA . . . . Double Acting
DAD . . . . Double-Acting Door (Technical drawings)
DALS . . . . . . Double-Acting Limit Switch
DAC . . . . Double Action Cylinder
DAMV . . . . . . Double-Air Movement Valve
DAZD . . . . . . Double Anode Zener Diode
DBM . . . . Double Balanced Mixer
DBD . . . . Double-Base Diode
DBT . . . . Double Base Transistor
DBD . . . . Double Beta Decay
DB . . . . Double Biased (Relay)
DB's . . . . Double Bottoms (Naval)
DBCP . . . . . . Double Bounce, Circularly Polarized
DB . . . . Double Break
DOG . . . . Double Chain Branch-Oblong Master Link-Grab Hook
DCD . . . . Double Channel Duplex
DCS . . . . Double Channel Simplex
DCV . . . . Double Check Valve
DCFT . . . . . . Double Coated Foam Tape
DC . . . . Double Column
DCM . . . . Double Common Meter (Music)
DCS . . . . Double Compton Scattering
DHFA . . . . . . Double-Conductor, Heat and Flame-Resistant, Armor (Cable)
DC . . . . Double Contact (Switch)
DCA . . . . Double Conversion Adapter
D Cx . . . . . . Double Convex
DCC . . . . Double Cotton Covered (Insulation for certain types of magnet wire)
DCDS . . . . . . Double Cotton Double Solk (Insulation)
DC . . . . Double Crochet
DCG . . . . Double Current Generator
DDB . . . . Double Declining Balance (Statistics)
DDM . . . . Double Diffused Mesa
DD . . . . Double Drift (As used in a navigator's log)
DDC . . . . Double Doped Crystal
DE . . . . Double End (Technical drawings)
DE . . . . Double-ended, Cylindrical Boiler
DEP . . . . Double Ended Pivot
DE . . . . Double Entry (Bookkeeping)
DF . . . . Double Feeder (Line) (Technical drawings)
DFSK . . . . . . Double Frequency Shift Keying (Radio)
DG . . . . Double Groove (Insulators)
DGDP . . . . . . Double Groove, Double Petticoat (Insulators)
DGW . . . . Double Gypsy Winch
DHD . . . . Double Heat-Sink Diode
DHA . . . . Double Heave Amplitude
DHW . . . . Double-Hung Windows (Technical drawings)
DI . . . . Double Injection
DIE . . . . Double Injection Effect
DIL . . . . Double Injection Luminescence
DLEA . . . . . . Double Leg Elbow Amplifier
DLL . . . . Double Length Line
DLN . . . . Double Length Number
DLO . . . . Double Local Oscillator
DLM . . . . Double Long Meter (Music)
DOPI . . . . . . Double O (Zero) Pass One (System in game of bridge)
DOPE . . . . . . Double Odd Pass Even (System in game of bridge)
DOV . . . . Double Oil of Vitriol
DOHC . . . . . . Double Overhead Camshaft (Automotive term)
DPDC . . . . . . Double Paper, Double Cotton (Insulation)
DP . . . . Double Petticoat
DP . . . . Double Play (Baseball)
DP . . . . Double Pole (Switch)
DPBC . . . . . . Double Pole, Both Connected (Switch)
DPDT . . . . . . Double Pole, Double Throw (Switch)
DPFC . . . . . . Double Pole, Front Connected (Switch)
DPST . . . . . . Double Pole, Single Throw (Switch)
DPTT . . . . . . Double Pole, Triple Throw
DAISY . . . . . . Double Precision Automatic Interpretive System
DPQ . . . . Double Precision Quantity
DPL . . . . Double Propellant Loading
DPO . . . . Double Pulse Operation
DPPA . . . . . . Double Pumped Parametric Amplifier
DP . . . . Double Purpose Gun
DRN . . . . Double-Round Nose
DSBV . . . . . . Double-Seated Ball Valve
DSM . . . . Double Short Meter (Music)
DSB . . . . Double Sideband
DSBSC . . . . . . Double-Sideband Suppressed Carrier

DSBTC . . . . Double-Sideband Transmitted Carrier
DSC . . . . Double Silk Covered (Wire)
DSP . . . . Double Silver Plate
DSS . . . . Double Spot System
DST . . . . Double Spot Tuning
DS . . . . Double Stitch (Bookbinding)
DST . . . . Double Summer Time (Daylight Saving Time two hours ahead of
          Standard Time) (British)
DTA . . . . Double Tape Armored (Heavy duty telephone buried cable)
DTP . . . . Double Test Position
DT . . . . Double Throw (Switch)
DTS . . . . Double Throw Switch
DT . . . . Double Time
DT . . . . Double Tube
DU . . . . Double Uptake (Boilers)
DV . . . . Double Vibration (Cycles)
VD . . . . Double Vibrations (Cycles)
DW . . . . Double Weight
DWSS . . . . . . Double Wipe Slide Switch
DWA . . . . Double-Wire Armor
DZR . . . . Double Zigzag Rectifier
Y . . . . Doublecross (i.e., to betray) (Criminal slang)
D . . . . Doublet
DAC . . . . Douglas Aircraft Company
D . . . . Douglas Aircraft Company, Inc. (NYSE symbol)
DACO . . . . . . Douglas Aircraft Corporation Overseas
DFEC . . . . . . Douglas Fir Export Company
DFPA . . . . . . Douglas Fir Plywood Association
DERE . . . . . . Dounreay Experimental Reactor Establishment (British)
DFR . . . . Dounreay Fast Reactor (British)
DMTR . . . . . Dounreay Materials Testing Reactor (British)
DOV . . . . . . Dover Corporation (NYSE symbol)
DCC . . . . Dow Chemical Company
DOW . . . . . . Dow Chemical Company (NYSE symbol)
DEN . . . . Dow Epoxy Novolac
D-J . . . . Dow Jones & Co. (Also, the stock market averages compiled by this
          company)
DJI . . . . Dow-Jones Index
DJIA . . . . . . Dow-Jones Industrial Average
D . . . . Dowager
DFS . . . . Down Feeding Spindle
DL . . . . Down Left (The front left portion of a stage) (A stage direction)
D/R . . . . Down Range
DR . . . . Down Right (The front right portion of a stage) (A stage direction)
DS . . . . Down Stage (Toward audience) (A stage direction)
DSC . . . . Down Stage Center (Toward audience) (A stage direction)
DSL . . . . Down Stage Left (Toward audience) (A stage direction)
DSR . . . . Down Stage Right (Toward audience) (A stage direction)
DAMP . . . . . . Downrange Antimissile Measurement Program (RADAR)
DAM . . . . Downrange Antimissile Program (Army)
DDR . . . . Downrange Data Report
DRAB . . . . . . Downriver Residents Against Bowling
DNT . . . . Downtime
DLIR . . . . . . Downward Looking Infrared (Air Force)
DDB . . . . Doyle Dane Bernbach, Inc. (Advertising agency)
D . . . . Drachma (Monetary unit in Greece)
DPM . . . . Draft Presidential Memorandum (DOD)
DS . . . . Draft Stop (Technical drawings)
DPM . . . . Drafting Practice Manual
DRM . . . . . . Drafting Room Manual
DM . . . . Draftsman (Navy rating)
DF . . . . Drag Friction
DA . . . . Dragon Airways, Ltd.
DRG . . . . Dragon Cement Company (NYSE symbol)
DG . . . . Dragoon Guards (British)
D . . . . Dragoons (Military) (British)
DCOC . . . . . . Drain Cut-Off Current
DSC . . . . Drain Saturation Current
DT . . . . Drain Tile (Technical drawings)
DWV . . . . . . Drain, Waste, and Vent (System)
DRAP . . . . . . Dram, Apothecary
DRAV . . . . . . Dram Avoirdupois
DBS . . . . Drama Book Specialists
DAS . . . . Dramatic Authors' Society (British)
DOKK . . . . . Dramatic Order Knights of Khorassan
DGALA . . . . . Dramatists Guild of the Authors League of America
DHMA . . . . . . Drapery Hardware Manufacturers Association
DMK . . . . Dravida Munnetra Kazhagam (Political party in India seeking
          independent socialist state of Dravidanad)
DBHP . . . . . . Drawbar Horsepower
DBP . . . . Drawbar Pull

DAL . . . . Drawing Assembly List
DCN . . . . Drawing Change Notice
DCR . . . . Drawing Change Request
DCR . . . . Drawing Copy Request
DL . . . . Drawing List (Engineering)
DCRB . . . . . Drawn Cup Roller Bearing
YM . . . . Dredge (Navy symbol)
D & H . . . . . . Dressed and Headed (Lumber)
D & M . . . . . . Dressed and Matched (Technical drawings)
DI . . . . Dresser Industries, Inc. (NYSE symbol)
DRE . . . . Drewrys Limited USA, Inc. (NYSE symbol)
DIT . . . . Drexel Institute of Technology (Pennsylvania)
DFA . . . . Dried Fruit Association of California
DFAC . . . . . . Dried Fruit Association of California
DA . . . . Drift Angle (Navigation)
DAI . . . . Drift Angle Indicator
DCA . . . . Drift Correction Angle
DARMS . . . . . . Drifting Automatic Radiometeorological Station
DRAD . . . . . . Drill Adapter
DRBG . . . . . . Drill Bushing
DRFX . . . . . . Drill Fixture
DRHD . . . . . . Drill Head
DI . . . . Drill Instructor (Marine Corps)
DRJG . . . . . . Drill Jig
DJB . . . . Drill Jig Bushing
DNP . . . . Drill Non-Pay Status (Naval Reserve)
DRPL . . . . . . Drill Plate
DPF . . . . Drill Press Feed
DR . . . . Drill Regulations
DR . . . . Drill Rod
DS . . . . Drill Sergeant (Army)
DRSH . . . . . . Drill Shell
DRTP . . . . . . Drill Template
DRVS . . . . . . Drill Vise
DBS . . . . Drinking Behavior Scale (Test)
DSI . . . . Drinking Straw Institute
DCE . . . . Drive Control Equipment
DF . . . . Drive Fit (Technical drawings)
DGHP . . . . . . Drive-Gearhead Package
DGP . . . . Drive-Gearhead Package
DS . . . . Drive System
DEFT . . . . . . Driven Equilibrium Fourier Transform
DAIR . . . . . . Driver Aid, Information and Routing (Data processing)
DAR . . . . Driver Augmented Readout (Data processing)
DM . . . . Driver, Master
DPU . . . . Driver Propulsion Unit
DSST . . . . . . Driver Stage Silicon Transistor
DUS . . . . Driver Units Speaker
D . . . . Driving
DCI . . . . Driving Car Intoxicated
DIVEAR . . . . . . Driving Instrumentation Vehicle for Environmental and Acoustic Research
DPA . . . . Driving Point Admittance
DP . . . . Driving Power
DWD . . . . . . Driving While Drunk
DWI . . . . Driving While Intoxicated (Police term)
L . . . . Drizzle (Weather reports)
D . . . . Drizzling
Q . . . . Drone (Designation for all US military aircraft)
YV . . . . Drone Aircraft Catapult Control Craft (Navy symbol)
DASH . . . . . . Drone Antisubmarine Helicopter (Air Force, Navy)
DAT . . . . Drone Assisted Torpedo
DCS . . . . Drone Control System
D . . . . Drone Plane (Navy symbol)
DTF . . . . Drone Test Facility
DALT . . . . . . Drop Altitude
DF . . . . Drop Forge
DFC . . . . Drop Forged Clamp
DFA . . . . Drop Forging Association
DLZ . . . . Drop Landing Zone (Air Force)
DMH . . . . . . Drop Manhole (Technical drawings)
DP . . . . Drop Point (Air Force)
DS . . . . Drop Siding
DT . . . . Drop Test Report
DWTT . . . . . . Drop-Weight Tear Test
DW . . . . Drop Wire
DWS . . . . . . Drop Wood Siding (Technical drawings)
DZ . . . . Drop(ping) Zone (For parachute troops and gliders)
DZA . . . . Drop Zone Area (Military)
DZCO . . . . . . Drop Zone Control Officer (Air Force)
DZSO . . . . . . Drop Zone Safety Officer (Army)
DHDI . . . . . . Drophammer Die

D	Droppable Fuel Tank (Suffix to plane designation)
DFR	Dropped from Rolls
DARE	Drug Addiction Rehabilitation Enterprise
DAPG	Drug & Allied Products Guild
DCAT	Drug, Chemical and Allied Trades Association
D & C	Drug and Cosmetic Colors
DEC	Drug Evaluation Center
DIA	Drug Information Association
DS	Drug Store (US maps)
DSB	Drug Supervisory Body
DSB (UN)	Drug Supervisory Body of the United Nations
DTI	Drug and Therapeutic Information
DGSJ	Druggist's Guild of St. James
D	Druids (Freemasonry)
DD	Drum Demand
DIAD	Drum Information Assembler and Dispatcher
DID	Drum Information Display
DRMAJ	Drum Major (Marine Corps)
DMA	Drum Memory Assembly (Data processing)
DMS	Drum Memory System (Data processing)
D-PAT	Drum Programmed Automatic Tester
DRD	Drum Read Driver (Data processing)
DSA	Drum Seiners Association
DSS	Drum Storage System
DSU	Drum Storage Unit
DS	Drum Switch
DSW	Drum Switch
DTP	Drum Timing Pulse
DW	Drum Write
DWD	Drum Write Drive
DLC	Drummond Lighterage R. R. (AAR code)
D & D	Drunk and Dirty (Military)
D & D	Drunk and Disorderly
D & DC	Drunk and Disorderly Conduct
DB	Dry Bulb (Thermometer, of a psychrometer) (Meteorology)
DBT	Dry Bulb Temperature
DBM	Dry Bulk Material
DCMA	Dry Color Manufacturers Association
DDP	Dry Discharge Pump
DDTV	Dry Diver Transport Vehicle (Navy)
DEC	Dry Electrolytic Capacitor
DFC	Dry-Filled Capsules (Pharmacy)
DFL	Dry Film Lubricant
DFP	Dry Film Processor
DFP	Dry Filter Processing
DGP	Dry Gas Pump
DHM	Dry Honing Machine
DPP	Dry Photo Process
DPV	Dry Pipe Valve
DP	Dry Point
DRPS	Dry Reed Pushbutton Switch
DRS	Dry Reed Switch
DSD	Dry Sterile Dressing (Medicine)
DTW	Dry Tank Weight
DVPDF	Dry Vacuum Pump Discharge Filter
DVPF	Dry Vacuum Pump Filter
DD	Drydock
YFND	Drydock Companion Craft (Navy symbol)
DLF	Drydock Launch Facility
DART	Dual Axis Rate Transducer (A gyroscope)
DBO	Dual Beam Oscilloscope
DBF	Dual Bowl Feeder
DBVF	Dual Bowl Vibratory Feeder
DCC	Dual Cam Clutch
DCDS	Dual Channel Dual Speed
DDC	Dual Diversity Comparator
DDU	Dual Diversity Unit
DUET	Dual Emitter Transistor
DES	Dual Exciter System
DFCA	Dual Fault Correction Actuator
DFH	Dual Filter Hybrid
DGE	Dual Gage Expander
DIP	Dual In-Line Package
DIDF	Dual Input Describing Function (Data processing)
DINN	Dual Input Null Network
DMU	Dual Maneuvering Unit (A spacecraft)
DMD	Dual Mode Display
DMH	Dual Mode Hydrazine
DML	Dual Mode LASER
DLRV	Dual Mode Lunar Roving Vehicle
DOETS	Dual-Object Electronic Tracking System
DUPPA	Dual Path Protection Arrangement (AT & T)
DPR	Dual Pen Recorder
DPS	Dual Porosity Sinter
DPLM	Dual Pulse LASER Microwelder
DRMI	Dual Radio Magnetic Indicator
DRI	Dual Roll Idler
DRTI	Dual Roll Trough Idler
DSD	Dual Speed Drive
DSMT	Dual-Speed Magnetic Transducer
DTRM	Dual Thrust Rocket Motor
DT	Dual Tires
DTA	Dual Trace Amplifier
DTE	Dual Track Etcher
DTG	Dual Track Geneva
DVF	Dualbowl Vibratory Feeder
PD	Dublin Pharmacopoeia
DUBC	Dublin University Boat Club
DUM	Dublin University Mission
DURC	Dublin University Rowing Club
DU	Du Bois Chemicals, Inc. (NYSE symbol) (Delisted)
DOSC	Dubois Oleic Serum Complex (Bacteriology)
D	Duchess
DVE	Duck Virus Enteritis (Duck plague)
DU	Ducks Unlimited
DES	Ducosyn Excitation Switch
DBA	Duct Burner Augmentation
DBTT	Ductile to Brittle Transition Temperature
DIS	Ductile Iron Society
DRA	Dude Ranchers' Association
DD	Due Date
DUDAT	Due Date
DI	Due In
DIFM	Due in from Maintenance (Air Force)
DO	Due Out (Army)
DOC	Due-Out Cancellation (Military)
DWML	Due West Motor Line R. R. (AAR code)
DPG	Dugway Proving Ground (Army)
DPGR	Dugway Proving Ground (Army)
D	Duke
DCO	Duke of Cambridge's Own (Military unit) (British)
DCO	Duke of Connaught's Own (Military unit) (British)
DCLI	Duke of Cornwall's Light Infantry (British)
DEO	Duke of Edinburgh's Own (Military unit) (British)
DUK	Duke Power Company (NYSE symbol)
DWR	Duke of Wellington's Regiment (British Army)
D	Dulcis (Dear One)
DIA	Dulles International Airport (FAA)
DMIR	Duluth, Missabe & Iron Range Railway (AAR code)
DM & IR	Duluth, Missabe and Iron Range Railway
DNE	Duluth & Northeastern R. R. (AAR code)
DSA	Duluth, South Shore & Atlantic R. R. (AAR code)
DSS & A	Duluth, South Shore and Atlantic Railway Company
DUWCAL	Duluth Weapons Calibration System
DWP	Duluth, Winnipeg & Pacific Railway Company (AAR code)
DW & P	Duluth, Winnipeg and Pacific Railway Company
DAO	Duly Authorized Officer
DA	Dummy Antenna
DDS	Dummy Director Set
DGM	Dummy Guided Missile
DSR	Dummy Stowage Receptacle
D & B	Dun & Bradstreet, Inc.
DBCO	Dunbar Brothers Company, Division of Associated Spring Corporation
DCHC	Dunbarton College of Holy Cross (Washington, DC)
DHI	Dunhill International, Incorporated (NYSE symbol)
DA	Dunlap and Associates, Inc.
DSC	Duns Scotus College (Michigan)
DSA	Duodecimal Society of America
D	Duodecimo
DPI	Duo-Plasmation Ion
DPIS	Duo-Plasmation Ion Source
DUP	Duplan Corporation (NYSE symbol)
DD	Duplex-Drive (Tank)
DOT	Duplex One-Tape System
DX	Duplex Repeater (Teletypewriter designation for quality of reception)
DDD	Duplexed Display Distributor
DEU	Duplicates Exchange Union (Library)
DR	Duplicating Requisition
DUT	Duplication Technician, Photolithography (Navy rating)
DD	du Pont de Nemours (E.I.) & Company (NYSE symbol)
DQU	Duquesne Light Company (NYSE symbol)
DWI	Durable Woods Institute

DLY . . . . Duraloy Company (NYSE symbol)
DAT . . . . Duration Adjusting Type
DPE . . . . Duration of the Present Emergency (British) (World War II)
DVA . . . . Duration of Voluntary Apnea (Physiology)
DOW . . . . Duration of War
DB . . . . Durchfuehrungsbestimmung
DAA . . . . Durene Association of America
DAC . . . . Durex Abrasives Corporation
DS . . . . Durham & Southern Railway Company (AAR code)
DTAO. . . . . . During the Temporary Absence of (Military)
DUR . . . . Duro-Test Corporation (NYSE symbol)
DGA . . . . Durum Growers Association of the United States
DWI . . . . Durum Wheat Institute
D . . . . Dust (Meteorology)
DFC . . . . Dust Free Chamber
DFR . . . . Dust Free Room
DJ . . . . Dust Jacket (Paper cover for a hard-bound book)
DTREM . . . . . . Dust, Thermal, and Radiation Engineering Measurements Package (NASA)
DW . . . . Dust Wrapper
D . . . . Dutch
DBCAA . . . . . Dutch Belted Cattle Association of America
DD . . . . Dutch Door (Technical drawings)
DEI . . . . Dutch East Indies
D . . . . Duty (Navy)
DAFS . . . . Duty Air Force Specialty
DAFSC . . . . . . Duty Air Force Specialty Code
DUCON . . . . Duty Connection
DCMA . . . . . . Duty Cycle Modulation Alternator
DPUO . . . . . . Duty Directed is Being Performed for Unit Issuing Order
DOPF . . . . . . Duty Directed in Order is Being Performed For
DFCO . . . . . . Duty Flying Control Officer (Navy)
DIFOT . . . . . . Duty in a Flying Status Involving Operational or Training Flights
DIO . . . . Duty Intelligence Officer (Air Force)
DIF . . . . Duty Involving Flying (Navy)
DUFLY . . . . . . Duty Involving Flying (Military)
DUFLYTECH. . . Duty Involving Flying as a Technical Observer (Military)
DIFOTINS . . . . Duty Involving Operational or Training Flights under Instruction (Air Force)
DIFOTECH. . . . Duty Involving Operational or Training Flights as a Technical Observer (Air Force)
DMOS . . . . . . Duty Military Occupational Specialty
DO . . . . Duty Officer (Military)
DUTOUT . . . . (For) Duty Outside the Continental Limits of the United States
DP . . . . Duty Paid
DP . . . . Duty Pay
DS . . . . Duty Section (Air Force)
DSSO . . . . . . Duty Space Surveillance Officer (Air Force)
DUSTA . . . . . . Duty Station (Navy)
DS . . . . Duty Status (Air Force)
DUINS . . . . . . Duty Under Instruction
DIS . . . . Dwarf Iris Society
DWG . . . . . . Dwarf Iris Society
DWG . . . . . . DWG Cigar Corporation (NYSE symbol)
DATS . . . . . . Dynamic Accuracy Test Set
DYNAMO . . . . Dynamic Action Management Operations (BSD)
DAWG . . . . . . Dynamic Air War Game (Military)
DADEE . . . . . Dynamic Analog Differential Equation Equalizer
DACL . . . . . . Dynamic Analysis and Control Laboratory (MIT)
DYANA . . . . . Dynamic Analyzer
DAVI . . . . . . Dynamic Antiresonant Vibration Isolator

DALC . . . . . . Dynamic Asynchronous Logic Circuit
DBE . . . . Dynamic Balancing Equipment
DB . . . . Dynamic Braking
DYB . . . . Dynamic Braking
DCL . . . . Dynamic Characteristic Load
DCF . . . . Dynamic Coercive Force
DYCOP. . . . . Dynamic Console for Operations Planners
DYCON . . . . . Dynamic Control
DCPS . . . . . . Dynamic Crew Procedures Simulator
DCFEM. . . . . Dynamic Crossed-Field Electron Multiplication
DCFEM . . . . . Dynamic Crossed Fields, Electric and Magnetic
DDT . . . . Dynamic Display Tester
DEM. . . . . . . Dynamic Effect Model
DEMS . . . . . . Dynamic Effectiveness Model Study
DES . . . . Dynamic Electro-Speaker
DEC . . . . Dynamic Energy Conversion
DE . . . . Dynamic Engineer
DEFT . . . . . . Dynamic Error-Free Transmission
DGD . . . . Dynamic Gravity Detector
DGG . . . . Dynamic Gravity Generator
DIV . . . . Dynamic Imagery Viewer
DIM . . . . Dynamic Impedance Measurement
DIDA . . . . . . Dynamic Instrumentation Digital Analyzer
DIDD . . . . . . Dynamic Integrated Data Display
DIDDS . . . . . . Dynamic Integrated Data Display System
DIAS . . . . . . Dynamic Inventory Analysis System (Data processing)
DLR . . . . Dynamic Line (or Load) Regulation
DLC . . . . Dynamic Load Characteristics
DLCA . . . . . . Dynamic Logic Chassis Analyzer
DMOS . . . . . . Dynamic Model Operations Section
DOL. . . . . . . Dynamic Octal Load
DORA. . . . . . Dynamic Operator Response Apparatus
DORS . . . . . . Dynamic Operator Response System
DOC . . . . Dynamic Overload Controls
Q . . . . Dynamic Pressure (NASA)
DPF . . . . Dynamic Pressure Feedback
DP . . . . Dynamic Programming
DQC . . . . Dynamic Quality Control
DRAM . . . . . . Dynamic Random Access Mechanization
DR . . . . Dynamic Range
DRS . . . . Dynamic Reflectance Spectroscopy
DRIFT . . . . . . Dynamic Reliability Instantaneous Forecasting Technique
DSR . . . . Dynamic Sideband Regulator
DSA . . . . Dynamic Signal Analyzer
DYNA-SOAR . . Dynamic Soaring (Space flight)
DSS . . . . Dynamic Steady State
DYSTAL . . . . . Dynamic Storage Allocation Language (in FORTRAN) (Data processing)
DYSTAC . . . . . Dynamic Storage Analog Computer
DSE . . . . Dynamic System Electronics
DTS . . . . Dynamic Test System
DTV . . . . Dynamic Test Vehicle
DVS . . . . Dynamic Vacuum Seal
DCA. . . . . . . Dynamics Corporation of America (NYSE symbol)
DRC . . . . Dynamics Research Corporation
DEA . . . . Dynamo Electric Amplifier
DDY . . . . Dynayoke Deflection Yoke
D. . . . . Dyne (Unit of force)
Dy . . . . Dysprosium (Chemical element)

E

EF . . . . Each Face (Technical drawings)
EL . . . . Each Layer (Technical drawings)
ETFL. . . . . . . Each Thousand-Foot Level (Aviation)
EGJC . . . . . . Eagle Grove Junior College (Iowa)
EGP . . . . Eagle-Picher Company (NYSE symbol)
E . . . . Earl
EM . . . . Earl Marshal (British)
EAT . . . . Earliest Arrival Time
EFD . . . . Earliest Finish Date
EPD . . . . Earliest Possible (or Practicable) Date
EARLPRADATE . . (At) Earliest Practicable Date
ESD . . . . Earliest Start Date
EAIA . . . . Early American Industries Association
EAL . . . . Early American Life Insurance Association
EASEP . . . . . . Early Apollo Scientific Experiments Payload (or Package) (NASA)
EBA . . . . Early Birds of Aviation
EBM . . . . Early-Break-Make (Data Processing)
EB . . . . Early Burst (Premature explosion of a warhead)
ECOMS . . . . . . Early Capability Orbital Manned Station
ECA . . . . Early Closing Association (British)
EDA . . . . Early Departure Authorized
EE . . . . Early English (Language, etc.)
EETS . . . . Early English Text Society
EFD . . . . Early Failure Detection
EFT . . . . Early Finish Time
ELF . . . . Early Lunar Flare
EMB . . . . Early-Make-Break (Data processing)
EMPIRE . . . . . . Early Manned Planetary-Interplanetary Round Trip Experiment
EMPIRE . . . . . . Early Manned Planetary Interruptionless Reconnaissance Expedition
EMT . . . . Early Missile Test
ERP . . . . Early Receptor Potential (of the eye)
ESAWR . . . . . . Early Settlers Association of the Western Reserve
EST . . . . Early Start Time
EW . . . . Early Warning (Air Force)
EW/CRP . . . . . Early Warning/Control and Reporting Post
EWF . . . . Early Warning Fighter
EWR . . . . Early Warning RADAR (Air Force)
EWS . . . . Early Warning System
EWTAD . . . . . Early Warning Threat Analysis Display
ER . . . . Earned Run (Baseball)
ERA . . . . Earned Run Average (of a baseball pitcher)
EPS . . . . Earnings Per Share (Finance)
EPSI . . . . Earnings Per Share Issued (Finance)
ENT . . . . Ears, Nose, and Throat
E . . . . Earth (Wind triangle problems and relative movement problems)
EAS . . . . Earth Aspect Sensor
EDW . . . . Earth Departure Window
EEP . . . . Earth Equatorial Plane
EHS . . . . Earth Horizon Scanner
EIC . . . . Earth Inductor Compass
EIC . . . . Earth-Ionosphere Cavity
ELS . . . . Earth Landing System
ELV . . . . Earth Launch Vehicle
EHS . . . . Earth-Lunar Horizon Sensor
EME . . . . Earth-Mars-Earth
EMOS . . . . . . Earth Mean Orbital Speed (Aerospace)
ESES . . . . Earth-Moon Space Exploration Study
END . . . . Earth Net Dial
EOED . . . . . . Earth Orbit Escape Device
EOE . . . . Earth Orbit Equipment
EOM . . . . Earth Orbit Mission
EOR . . . . Earth Orbit Rendezvous (NASA)
EORBS . . . . . . Earth Orbiting Recoverable Biological Satellite

EPI . . . . Earth Path Indicator
EROS . . . . Earth Resources Observation Satellite (Environmental Science Services Administration)
EPIC . . . . Earth-Pointing Instrument Carrier (A satellite)
EPM . . . . Earth-Probe-Mars (NASA)
ERC . . . . Earth Rate Compensation
ERDR . . . . Earth Rate Directional Reference
ERM . . . . Earth Reentry Module
ERS . . . . Earth Resources Satellite
ERSP . . . . Earth Resources Survey Program
ERTS . . . . Earth Resources Technology Satellite (NASA)
ERM . . . . Earth Return Module
ESV . . . . Earth Satellite Vehicle (Air Force)
ESWS . . . . Earth Satellite Weapon Systems
ESCP . . . . Earth Science Curriculum Project (Education)
ESS . . . . Earth-Sighting Simulator (NASA)
ESA . . . . Earth Station - Arabia
ESB . . . . Earth Station - Brazil
ESCH . . . . . . Earth Station - Chile
ESCO . . . . . . Earth Station - Columbia
ESC . . . . Earth Station - Congo
ESEC . . . . . . Earth Station - Ecuador
ESEG . . . . . . Earth Station - Egypt
ESG . . . . Earth Station - Greece
ESHK . . . . . . Earth Station - Hong Kong
ESI . . . . Earth Station - Iran
ESIS . . . . Earth Station - Israel
ESIC . . . . Earth Station - Ivory Coast
ESJ . . . . Earth Station - Jordan
ESK . . . . Earth Station - Kenya
ESL . . . . Earth Station - Libya
ESM . . . . Earth Station - Mexico
ESMO . . . . . . Earth Station - Morocco
ESSC . . . . . . Earth Station - Scandinavia
ESSE . . . . Earth Station - Senegal
ESSA . . . . . . Earth Station - South Africa
ESS . . . . Earth Station - Sudan
ESSY . . . . . . Earth Station - Syria
EST . . . . Earth Station - Turkey
ESV . . . . Earth Station - Venezuela
ESY . . . . Earth Station - Yugoslavia
EERI . . . . Earthquake Engineering Research Institute
E . . . . Easily
E . . . . East
EA . . . . East Africa
EAA . . . . East African Airways
EACSO . . . . . East African Common Services Organization
EAEC . . . . . . East African Economic Community
EARCCUS . . . . East African Regional Committee for Conservation and Utilisation of Soil
EACC . . . . East Asia Christian Conference
EAROPH . . . . . East Asia Regional Organization for Planning and Housing
ECC . . . . East Carolina College (North Carolina)
EC . . . . East Carolina Railway (AAR code)
EC . . . . East Central (Refers especially to London postal district)
ECJC . . . . East Central Junior College (Mississippi)
ECNG . . . . . . East Central Nuclear Group
ECSC . . . . . . East Central State College (Oklahoma)
EASTCO . . . . . East Coast
ECA . . . . East Coast Aeronautics, Inc.
EASTCOBASE . . East Coast Base
ECCANE . . . . . East Coast Conference on Aerospace and Navigational Electronics
ECJS . . . . East Coast Joint-Stock (British railroad)

ECL . . . . East Coast Laboratory (Environmental Science Services Administration)
EEC . . . . East Erie Commercial R. R. (AAR code)
EIC . . . . East India Company
EICS . . . . . . East India Company's Service
EID . . . . East India Dock
EIR . . . . East Indian Railway
EI . . . . East Indies
EJR . . . . East Jersey R. R. & Terminal Company (AAR code)
EJS . . . . East Jordan & Southern R. R. (AAR code)
EKR . . . . East Kent Regiment
ELD . . . . East Longitude Date
EMEB . . . . . . East Midlands Electricity Board (British)
EMJC . . . . . . East Mississippi Junior College
ENE . . . . East–Northeast
EASTOMP . . . . East–Ocean Meeting Point
EPFL . . . . . . East Pakistan Federation of Labor
ERDC . . . . . . East Region Development Corporation
ESLJ . . . . . . East St. Louis Junction R. R. (AAR code)
ESE . . . . East–Southeast
ESR . . . . East Surrey Regiment (British Army)
ETSC . . . . . . East Tennessee State College
ETWN . . . . . . East Tennessee & Western North Carolina R. R. (AAR code)
ETBC . . . . . . East Texas Baptist College
ETSC . . . . . . East Texas State College
EW . . . . East Washington Railway Company (AAR code)
EW . . . . East–West
EWA . . . . East–West Acceleration
EWA . . . . East–West Airlines, Ltd.
EWFH . . . . . . East–West Fine, Hundreds
EWFT . . . . . . East–West Fine, Tens
EWFU . . . . . . East–West Fine, Units
EWS . . . . East–West Speed
EB . . . . Eastbound
E . . . . Easter
EO . . . . Easter Offerings (to a church)
ET . . . . Easter Term
E . . . . Eastern
EAC . . . . Eastern Air Command (CBI Theater)
EADF . . . . . . Eastern Air Defense Force
EA . . . . Eastern Air Lines, Inc.
EAL . . . . Eastern Air Lines, Inc. (NYSE symbol)
EAPD . . . . . . Eastern Air Procurement District
EAS . . . . Eastern Apicultural Society of North America
EAMTMTS . . . . Eastern Area, Military Traffic Management and Terminal Service
EAJC . . . . . . Eastern Arizona Junior College
EARC . . . . . . Eastern Association of Rowing Colleges
EASTLANT . . . . Eastern Atlantic Area
ELM . . . . Eastern Atlantic and Mediterranean (Military)
EAMC . . . . . . Eastern Atlantic & Mediterranean Command (DOD)
EASTLANTMEDCOM . . Eastern Atlantic and Mediterranean Command (Military)
EBC . . . . Eastern Baptist College (Pennsylvania)
EBBA . . . . . . Eastern Bird Banding Association
ECAC . . . . . . Eastern College Athletic Conference
ECBA . . . . . . Eastern College Basketball Association
ECSOB . . . . . Eastern College Soccer Officials Bureau
EC . . . . Eastern Command (British)
ECCDA . . . . . Eastern Connecticut Clam Diggers Association
ECMR . . . . . . Eastern Contract Management Region (Air Force)
ECMA . . . . . . Eastern Cosmetic Manufacturers Association
EDFTGA . . . . . Eastern Dark–Fired Tobacco Growers Association
EDST . . . . . . Eastern Daylight Saving Time
EDT . . . . Eastern Daylight Time
EDC . . . . Eastern Defense Command (Army)
EDD . . . . Eastern Development Division (Air Force)
ED . . . . Eastern District (ATSC)
EDCLMDA . . . . Eastern Dry Cleaning and Laundry Machinery Distributors Association
EEB . . . . Eastern Electricity Board (British)
EEE . . . . Eastern Equine Encephalitis
EE . . . . Eastern Establishment (Politics)
EEM . . . . Eastern European Mission
EFU . . . . Eastern Gas & Fuel Associates (NYSE symbol)
EISC . . . . . . Eastern Illinois State College
EIGL . . . . . . Eastern Inter–Collegiate Gymnastic League
EJCC . . . . . . Eastern Joint Computer Conference
EKSC . . . . . . Eastern Kentucky State College
EL . . . . Eastern League (Baseball)
EMC . . . . Eastern Mennonite College (Virginia)
EMU . . . . Eastern Michigan University
EMR . . . . Eastern and Midlands Railway (British)
EMCE . . . . . . Eastern Montana College of Education
ENC . . . . Eastern Nazarene College (Massachusetts)

ENMU . . . . . . Eastern New Mexico University
EOC . . . . Eastern Oregon College
EPOC . . . . . . Eastern Pacific Oceanic Conference
EPPI . . . . . . Eastern Pennsylvania Psychiatric Institute
EPC . . . . Eastern Pilgrim College (Pennsylvania)
EPSL . . . . . . Eastern Primary Standards Laboratory
EPD . . . . Eastern Procurement Division (Navy)
EPD . . . . Eastern Production District (Navy)
EPA . . . . Eastern Psychological Association
ERPC . . . . . . Eastern Railroad Presidents Conference
ERD . . . . Eastern Recruiting Division
ERIE . . . . . . Eastern Regional Institute for Education
EROPA . . . . . Eastern Regional Organization for Public Administration
EASTSEAFRON . . Eastern Sea Frontier
ESF . . . . Eastern Sea Frontier
EASTCON . . . . Eastern Sea Frontier Control Local of Shipping in Gulf of Maine
ESSL . . . . . . Eastern Secondary Standards Laboratory
ESC . . . . Eastern Simulation Council
ESAOA . . . . . Eastern Ski Area Operators Association
ESOB . . . . . . Eastern Soccer Officials Bureau (Later, Eastern College Soccer Officials Bureau)
ES . . . . Eastern Stainless Steel Corporation (NYSE symbol)
E . . . . Eastern Standard Time
EST . . . . Eastern Standard Time
ETF . . . . Eastern Task Force
ETN . . . . Eastern Technical Net (Air Force)
ETR . . . . Eastern Test Range (Formerly, Atlantic Missile Range)
ET . . . . Eastern Time
EASTAF . . . . . Eastern Transport Air Force
EUA . . . . Eastern Underwriters Association
EUS . . . . Eastern United States
EWT . . . . Eastern War Time (World War II)
EWHA . . . . . . Eastern Women's Headwear Association
EZ . . . . Eastern Zone
EK . . . . Eastman Kodak Company (NYSE symbol)
EKC . . . . Eastman Kodak Company
EP . . . . Eastward Position
EPC . . . . Easy Processing Channel
ENX . . . . Eaton Manufacturing Company (NYSE symbol)
ODV . . . . Eau–de–Vie (Taken from the French pronunciation and used to refer to brandy)
EGO . . . . Eccentric Geophysical Observatory (NASA)
EOGO . . . . . . Eccentric Orbiting Geophysical Laboratory (NASA)
ESCS . . . . . . Eccentrically Stiffened Cylindrical Shell
E . . . . Eccentricity
EJC . . . . Eccles–Jordan Circuit (Electronics)
EJT . . . . Eccles–Jordan Trigger (Electronics)
ECH . . . . Echlin Manufacturing Company (NYSE symbol)
EDS . . . . Echo Depth Sounder
EFR . . . . Echo Free Room
ERE . . . . Echo Range Equipment
ER . . . . Echo Ranging
ES . . . . Echo Sounding
ESD . . . . Echo Sounding Device (Navigation)
ENA . . . . Ecole Nationale d'Administration (France)
ENJC . . . . . . Ecole Normale Jacques Cartier
ENS . . . . Ecole Normale Superieure (French teacher–training institution)
ESA . . . . Ecole Superieure d'Agriculture
ESA . . . . Ecological Society of America
EASE . . . . . . Econolite Automatic Sensing Equipment
ES . . . . Econometric Society
EA . . . . Economic Adviser
EBF . . . . Economic and Business Foundation
ECA . . . . Economic Commission for Africa (of UN)
ECAFE . . . . . Economic Commission for Asia and the Far East (of UN)
ECE . . . . Economic Commission for Europe (of UN)
ECLA . . . . . . Economic Commission for Latin America (of UN)
ECME (UN) . . . Economic Commission for the Middle East (Proposed) of the United Nations
ECRS . . . . . . Economic and Contingency Reserve Stock (Military)
ECA . . . . Economic Control Agency (Allied German Occupation Forces)
ECA . . . . Economic Cooperation Act (of 1948)
ECA . . . . Economic Cooperation Administration (Administered aid under Marshall Plan; abolished, 1951)
ECO . . . . Economic Cooperation Organization
ECE . . . . Economic Coverage Endorsement
EDB . . . . Economic Defense Board (Later, Board of Economic Warfare) (World War II)
EDA . . . . Economic Development Administration (Formerly, Office of Appalachian Assistance) (Department of Commerce)
EDD . . . . Economic Development District (EDA)
EDFO . . . . . . Economic Development Financing Organization (Greece)

EDI . . . . Economic Development Institute (of the International Bank for Reconstruction and Development)
EDP . . . . . . Economic Development Program
EHA . . . . . . Economic History Association
EIB . . . . Economic Impact Budget
EIP . . . . Economic Inventory Procedures (Army)
EOA . . . . . . Economic Opportunity Act
EOL . . . . . . Economic Opportunity Act Loan
EOQ . . . . . . Economic Order Quantity
EOSP . . . . . . Economic Order and Stockage Procedure
EPC . . . . Economic Policy Committee (OECD)
EPDC . . . . . . Economic Power Dispatch Computer
EPT . . . . Economic Power Transmission
ERRT . . . . . . Economic Research Round Table
ERS . . . . Economic Research Service (Department of Agriculture)
ESC . . . . Economic and Social Council (of UN)
ECOSOC . . . . Economic and Social Council of the United Nations
ESA . . . . Economic Stabilization Agency (Terminated, 1953)
ESB . . . . Economic Stabilization Board (World War II)
EWAS . . . . . . Economic Warfare Analysis Section
EWD . . . . . . Economic Warfare Division (US) (London)
EYOA . . . . . . Economic and Youth Opportunity Agency
ECSTASY . . . . Economical Storage and Access System (Data processing)
EDF . . . . Economics of Distribution Foundation
ED . . . . Economics Division (US Military Government, Germany)
ETIL . . . . Economisch Technologisch Instituut in Limburg (Germany)
ENCMP . . . . . Economists' National Committee on Monetary Policy
EAA . . . . Ecuadorean American Association
ECLOF . . . . . . Ecumenical Church Loan Fund
EVS . . . . Ecumenical Voluntary Service
EAHF . . . . . . Eczema, Asthma, Hay Fever
ECB . . . . Eddy Current Brake
ECC . . . . Eddy Current Clutch
ECE . . . . Eddy Current Energy
ECL . . . . Eddy Current Loss
ECTI . . . . Eddy Current Testing Instrument
ERB . . . . Edgar Rice Burroughs (1875-1950) (Author of Tarzan books)
E . . . . Edge (Lumber)
E & CB1S . . . . Edge and Center Bead on One Side
E & CB2S . . . . Edge and Center Bead on Two Sides
E & CV1S . . . . Edge and Center V on One Side
E & CV2S . . . . Edge and Center V on Two Sides
EC . . . . Edge Connector
ED . . . . Edge Distance
EG . . . . Edge Grain
EGS . . . . Edge Guide System
ELD . . . . Edge-Lighted Display
ELSB . . . . . . Edge Lighted Status Board (Navy)
EMTI . . . . Edge Mounted Threaded Inserts
ERC . . . . Edge Reading Controller
ERM . . . . Edge Reading Meter
ET . . . . Edge Thickness (Technical drawings)
EWM . . . . . . Edge-Wise Meter
EDM . . . . Edgmoor & Manetta Railway (AAR code)
EA . . . . Edgewood Arsenal (Army)
EANDC . . . . . Edgewood Arsenal Nuclear Defense Center (Army)
EASP . . . . . . Edgewood Arsenal Special Publication
EATM . . . . . . Edgewood Arsenal Technical Memorandum
EATR . . . . . . Edgewood Arsenal Technical Report
ECSH . . . . . . Edgewood College of the Sacred Heart (Wisconsin)
ESM . . . . Edible Structure Material
ETH . . . . Edigenossische Technische Hochschule
EOS . . . . Edison Brothers Stores, Inc. (NYSE symbol)
EEI . . . . Edison Electric Institute
EDIS . . . . Edison National Historic Site
ERE . . . . Edison Responsive Environment (Automated learning system)
EBNY . . . . . . Edition Bookbinders of New York
EDL . . . . Edition Deluxe
EDCOM . . . . . Editor and Compiler
EPE . . . . Editorial Projects for Education
EPC . . . . Editor's Presentation Copy
ESM . . . . Edmund S. Muskie (Candidate for US vice president, 1968)
EMH . . . . Educable Mentally Handicapped
E . . . . Educated
ECS . . . . Education Commission of the States
ECGAI . . . . . . Education Council of the Graphic Arts Industry
EDC . . . . Education Development Center (Formerly, ESI and IEI)
EET . . . . Education Equivalency Test
EFL . . . . Education Facilities Laboratories
EWI . . . . Education with Industry
EL . . . . Education Level

EM . . . . Education Manual (Military)
EMC . . . . Education Media Council
ENABLE . . . . . Education and Neighborhood Action for Better Living Environment
EO . . . . Education Officer (Military)
EPDA . . . . . . Education Professions Development Act
ERA . . . . Education & Religious Affairs (US Military Government, Germany)
Ed Sp . . . . . . Education Specialist
EWA . . . . Education and World Affairs (An organization)
EWA . . . . Education Writers Association
EAC . . . . Educational Advisory Committee (AIAA)
EA . . . . Educational Age
EAS . . . . Educational Analog Simulator
EAP . . . . Educational Awareness Project
EDUCOM . . . . Educational Communications (Inter-University Communications Council)
ECOX . . . . . . Educational Communications on Exhibit (Commercial firm)
EC . . . . Educational Coordinates (Business firm)
ECFMG . . . . . Educational Council For Foreign Medical Graduates
ECFMS . . . . . . Educational Council for Foreign Medical Students
EDOMP . . . . . . Educational Development of Military Personnel
EDL . . . . Educational Developmental Libraries, Inc.
EFLA . . . . Educational Film Library Association
EFAI . . . . Educational Foundation for the Apparel Industry
EFJG . . . . Educational Foundation for Jewish Girls
EFNS . . . . Educational Foundation for Nuclear Science
EIS . . . . Educational Institute of Scotland
EJMA . . . . . . Educational Jewelry Manufacturers Association
EMIS . . . . Educational Management Information System
EMPC . . . . . . Educational Materials Producers Council (National Audio-Visual Association)
EMIE . . . . Educational Media Institutes Evaluation (Project)
EMRIC . . . . . . Educational Media Research Information Center
EOB . . . . Educational Opportunity Bank
EOG . . . . Educational Opportunity Grant
EPC . . . . Educational Policies Commission
EPAA . . . . . . Educational Press Association of America
EPIE . . . . Educational Products Information Exchange
EQ . . . . Educational Quotient (Psychology)
ERN . . . . Educational Radio Network
ER . . . . Educational Ratio
ERB . . . . Educational Records Bureau
ERT . . . . Educational Requirements Test
ERCA . . . . . . Educational Research Council of America
ERIC . . . . Educational Resources (formerly, Research) Information Center (Office of Education)
ERIC/CLIS . . . . Educational Resources Information Center/Clearinghouse for Library Information Sciences
EDRS . . . . . . ERIC (Educational Resources Information Center) Document Reproduction Service
ESI . . . . Educational Services Incorporated (Became Education Development Center)
ESO . . . . Educational Services Office(r) (Navy)
ESS . . . . Educational Services Section (Navy)
Ed S . . . . Educational Specialist, or Specialist in Education
ES . . . . Educational Specialist
ESC . . . . Educational Systems Corporation
ETS . . . . Educational Talent Search
ETV . . . . Educational Television
ETMA . . . . . . Educational Television for the Metropolitan Area
ETS . . . . Educational Testing Service
ET . . . . Educational Therapy
ET . . . . Educational Training
ETI . . . . Educational Travel, Incorporated
EFMC . . . . . . Educators Fund Management Corporation (of NEA)
EKM . . . . Edwald-Kornfeld Method
EMK . . . . Edward Moore Kennedy
EWC . . . . Edward Walters College (Florida)
EAFB . . . . . . Edwards Air Force Base
EFRC . . . . . . Edwards Flight Research Center (NASA)
EPPS . . . . . . Edwards Personal Preference Schedule (Marketing)
ETS . . . . Edwards Test Station
ER . . . . Edwardus Rex (King Edward)
EVC . . . . Eenheidsvakcentrale (United Dutch Trade Union Central)
EKP . . . . Eestimaa Kommunistlik Partei
EOG . . . . Effect on Guarantees
EAC . . . . Effective Acoustic Center
EAV . . . . Effective Angular Velocity
EAC . . . . Effective Atomic Charge
EAN . . . . Effective Atomic Number
EBW . . . . Effective Band Width
ECO . . . . Effective Citizens Organization
ECONOMAN . . Effective Control of Manpower
ECF . . . . Effective Cutoff Frequency

EDOC . . . . Effective Date of Change
EDCMR . . . . . . Effective Date of Change of Morning Report
EDSA . . . . Effective Date of Change in Station Assignment (Military)
EDCSA . . . . . . Effective Date of Change of Strength Accountability
EDFR . . . . Effective Date of Federal Recognition
EDRT . . . . Effective Date of Release from Training
EDT . . . . Effective Date of Training
EDO . . . . Effective Diameter of Objective (Optics)
ED . . . . Effective Dose
EEM . . . . Effective Engineering Management
EFP . . . . Effective Filtration Pressure (Physiology)
EFR . . . . Effective Filtration Rate (Physiology)
EFL . . . . Effective Focal Length (Optics)
EHL . . . . Effective Halflife (Nuclear science)
EHP . . . . Effective Horsepower
EIV . . . . Effective Initial Value
EIRP . . . . Effective Isotropically Radiated Power
EOA . . . . Effective On or About
EPNL . . . . Effective Perceived Noise Level
EPP . . . . Effective Program Projections
ERP . . . . Effective Radiated Power
ERPF . . . . Effective Renal Plasma Flow (Physiology)
ESR . . . . Effective Signal Radiated
ET . . . . Effective Temperature
ETD . . . . Effective Transfer Date (Military)
ETAS . . . . Effective True Airspeed
EWL . . . . Effective Wave Length
EES . . . . Effectiveness Evaluation System
ER . . . . Effectiveness Report (Military)
ESM . . . . Effectiveness Simulation Model
ENW . . . . Effects of Nuclear Weapons (AEC-DOD book)
EBV . . . . Efferent Branchial Vein
ERV . . . . Efferent Renal Vein
EVNG . . . . . . Efferent Vein from Nephridial Gland
EV . . . . Efferent Vessel
EASY . . . . . . Efficient Assembly System
E . . . . Efficiency or Efficient
ED . . . . Efficiency Decoration (British)
EM . . . . Efficiency Modulation
EFMO . . . . . . Effigy Mounds National Monument
EFEC . . . . Efforts from Ex-Convicts (Organization in Washington, DC)
EY . . . . Eger's Yellow
EL . . . . Egg Length
ESL . . . . Egg Stalk Length
EW . . . . Egg Width
EPG . . . . Eggs Per Gram (Parasitology)
EAFB . . . . . . Eglin Air Force Base
EGMTR . . . . . Eglin Gulf Missile Test Range
EGTR . . . . . . Eglin Gulf Test Range
EMV . . . . Egress Maintenance Vehicle
E . . . . Egyptian
EA . . . . Egyptian Army
ECL . . . . Egyptian Confederation of Labor (United Arab Republic)
EEF . . . . Egyptian Expeditionary Force (British military)
EFL-UAR . . . . Egyptian Federation of Labor (United Arab Republic)
EAL . . . . Ehrenfest Adiabatic Law
EAC . . . . Ehrlich Ascites Carcinoma (Cells)
ECA . . . . Eigenvaule Change Analysis
ENDC . . . . . . Eighteen-Nation Committee on Disarmament (Convened March 14, 1962;
 . . . . actually attended by 17 nations, with France absent) (Later, CCD)
ELA . . . . Eighth Lively Art (Advertising award)
EUSA . . . . . . Eighth United States Army
EUSAR . . . . . Eighth United States Army Rear
ES . . . . Einheitliche Systematik (Library science)
EVE . . . . Einstein Viscosity Equation
E . . . . Einsteinium (Radioactive element) (See also Es)
Es . . . . Einsteinium (Chemical element)
EPA . . . . Eire Philatelic Association
EVO . . . . Eisenbahn-Verkehrsordnung (Germany)
EEF . . . . Eisenhower Exchange Fellowships
EKO . . . . Eisenhuettenkombinat Ost
ERC . . . . Eject Rocket Container
ELF . . . . Ejected Lunar Flare
EGLMT . . . . . Ejector-Launcher, Guided Missile, Transporter
EPO . . . . Ekco Products Company (NYSE symbol)
L . . . . An El or elevated railway
ELAL . . . . . . El Al Israel Airlines, Ltd.
ECC . . . . El Camino College (California)
EDW . . . . . . El Dorado & Wesson Railway (AAR code)
ELMO . . . . . . El Morro National Monument
ELG . . . . El Paso Natural Gas Company (NYSE symbol)

EPS . . . . El Paso Southern Railway Company (AAR code)
ERC . . . . El Reno College (Oklahoma)
ETIYRA . . . . . El Toro International Yacht Racing Association
EMT . . . . Elapsed Maintenance Time
ET . . . . Elapsed Time (Automobile racing)
ETCG . . . . . . Elapsed-Time Code Generator
ETI . . . . Elapsed Time Indicator
ETM . . . . Elapsed Time Meter
EBMA . . . . . . Elastic Braid Manufacturers Association
EFMI . . . . Elastic Fabric Manufacturers Institute
EHC . . . . Elastic Hysteresis Constant
EL . . . . Elastic Limit
EPM . . . . Elastic Plastic Membrane
ESV . . . . Elastic Space Vehicle
ESN . . . . Elastic Stop Nut Corporation of America (NYSE symbol)
ESNA . . . . . . Elastic Stop Nut Corporation of America
ETB's . . . . . . Elastic Top and Bottom (British naval slang for WREN's knickers)
E . . . . Elasticity
EVT . . . . Elasticity, Viscosity and Tixotropy
EHL . . . . Elasto-Hydrodynamic Lubrication
EIM . . . . Elastomeric Insulation Material
EJ . . . . Elbow Jerk (Medicine)
E . . . . Eldest
ES . . . . Eldest Son
ERICR . . . . . . Eleanor Roosevelt Institute for Cancer Research
ED . . . . Election District
EL . . . . Election Laws
EAMU . . . . . . Electric Accounting Machine Unit
EAM . . . . Electric (or Electronic) Accounting Machines
EAMG . . . . . . Electric Arc Metallizing Gun
EAW . . . . Electric Arc Weld
EBP . . . . Electric Bilge Pump
EB . . . . Electric Boat
EBS . . . . Electric Bond & Share Company (NYSE symbol)
ECRA . . . . . . Electric Car Racing Association
ECTS . . . . . . Electric Circuit Test Set
ECV . . . . Electric Clock Valve
ECM . . . . Electric Coding (or Cipher) Machine
EC . . . . Electric Coding (Cipher) Machine Repairman (Navy rating)
ECAP . . . . . . Electric Companies' Advertising Program
ECPIP . . . . . . Electric Companies' Public Information Program
ECIC . . . . Electric Consumers Information Committee
ECD . . . . Electric Control Drive
EDL . . . . Electric Delay Line
EDF . . . . Electric Depth Finder
EDST . . . . . . Electric Diaphragm Switch Technique (IBM)
EDD . . . . Electric Displacement Density
EDL . . . . Electric Double Layer
ED . . . . Electric Dynamic (Motors)
EFB . . . . Electric Feedback
EFM . . . . Electric Field Meter
EFS . . . . Electric Field Strength
EFV . . . . Electric Field Vector
EFF . . . . Electric Flow Field
EFD . . . . Electric Flux Density
EFMG . . . . . . Electric Fuse Manufacturers Guild
EGG . . . . Electric Glue Gun
EHA . . . . Electric Heating Association
EHU . . . . Electric Heating Unit
EHFA . . . . . . Electric Home and Farm Authority (Terminated, 1947)
EHP . . . . Electric Horsepower
EIO . . . . Electric Induction Oven
EJE . . . . Electric Junction Equation
ELPG . . . . . . Electric Light and Power Group
ELS . . . . Electric Limit Switch
EMD . . . . Electric-Motor-Driven
EMI . . . . Electric & Musical Industries, Inc. (NYSE symbol)
EMI . . . . Electric & Musical Industries Limited (Group of phonograph recording
 . . . . companies in Great Britain)
EMIDEC . . . . . EMI (Electric and Musical Industries, Ltd.) Data Electronic Computer
 . . . . (Made by EMI Industries – Great Britain)
EOCI . . . . . . Electric Overhead Crane Institute
EPV . . . . Electric Polarization Vector
EPD . . . . Electric Power Distribution
EPW . . . . Electric Pressure Wave
EP . . . . Electric Primer
EPEC . . . . . . Electric Programmer Evaluator Controller
EPIC . . . . Electric Properties Information Center
EPS . . . . Electric Propulsion System
ERA . . . . Electric Railroaders Association
ERC . . . . Electric Regulation Company

ESB . . . . Electric Storage Battery Company (NYSE symbol)
ESC . . . . Electric Surface Current
ET . . . . Electric Telegraph
ETI . . . . Electric Test Installation
ETI . . . . Electric Tool Institute
EUP . . . . Electric Utility Pump
EVG . . . . Electric Vacuum Gyro
EWC . . . . Electric Water Cooler
EWSC . . . . . . Electric Water Systems Council
EWSF . . . . . . Electric Wave Section Filter
EASA . . . . . . Electrical Apparatus Service Association
EASE . . . . . . Electrical Automatic Support Equipment
ECTS . . . . . . Electrical Cable Test Set
EC . . . . Electrical Conductivity
ECS . . . . Electrical Connector Subassembly
ECP . . . . Electrical Contact Plate
ECU . . . . Electrical Conversion Unit
ED . . . . Electrical Differential
EEPM . . . . . . Electrical and Electronic Properties of Materials
EE . . . . Electrical Engineer(ing)
EEA . . . . Electrical Engineering Abstracts
EEE . . . . Electrical Engineering Exposition
EERA . . . . . . Electrical Equipment Representatives Association
EES . . . . Electrical Equipment Shelter
EET . . . . Electrical Equipment Trailer
EEC . . . . Electrical Export Corporation (Defunct)
EFC . . . . Electrical Field Current
EFICO . . . . . . Electrical Fitting Inventory Control Branch
EGSE . . . . . . Electrical Ground Support Equipment
EHP . . . . Electrical Hull Penetration
EIT . . . . Electrical Information Test
EI . . . . Electrical Insulation
EIT . . . . Electrical Insulation Tape
EKW . . . . Electrical Kilowatts
EMT . . . . Electrical Mechanical Tubing
EMW . . . . Electrical Megawatt
EMT . . . . Electrical Metallic Tubing
EMK . . . . Electrical Meter Kit
EPRD . . . . . . Electrical Power Requirements Data
EPS . . . . Electrical Power Subsystem
EPS . . . . Electrical Power Supply
EPU . . . . Electrical Power Unit
ERMA . . . . . . Electrical Reproduction Method of Accounting
ERA . . . . Electrical Research Association (British)
ERM . . . . Electrical Research Memorandum
R . . . . Electrical Resistance
ERW . . . . Electrical Resistance Weld
ESI . . . . Electrical Specialties, Incorporated
ESB . . . . Electrical Stimulation of the Brain
ESA . . . . Electrical Stress Analysis
ESE . . . . Electrical Support Equipment
ELS . . . . Electrical System
ESDR . . . . . . Electrical System Design Report
ETM . . . . Electrical Tactical Map
ETMB . . . . . . Electrical Techniques in Medicine and Biology
ETN . . . . Electrical Terminal Nut
ETL . . . . Electrical Testing Laboratories, Inc.
ET . . . . Electrical Time
ETM . . . . Electrical Time Measurement
ETSQ . . . . . . Electrical Time, Superquick
ETP . . . . Electrical Tough Pitch
ET . . . . Electrical Transcription (A phonograph recording) (Musical slang)
EWM . . . . . . Electrical Welding Machine
EWRT . . . . . . Electrical Women's Round Table
EZ . . . . Electrical Zero
EAROS . . . . . . Electrically Alterable Read Only Store (Data processing)
ECP . . . . Electrically Compensated Pyrometer
EIC . . . . Electrically Insulated Coating
EOV . . . . Electrically Operated Valve
EP . . . . Electrically Polarized (Relay)
ESA . . . . Electrically Supported (or Suspended) Accelerometer
ESGA . . . . . . Electrically Supported (or Suspended) Gyro Accelerometer
ESG . . . . Electrically Suspended Gyro
ETAC . . . . . . Electrically Tuned Antenna Coupler
EM . . . . Electrician's Mate
EMCB . . . . . . Electrician's Mate, Construction Battalion (Navy rating)
EMCBC . . . . . Electrician's Mate, Construction Battalion, Communications (Navy rating)
EMCBD . . . . . Electrician's Mate, Construction Battalion, Draftsman (Navy rating)
EMCBG . . . . . Electrician's Mate, Construction Battalion, General (Navy rating)
EMCBL . . . . . . Electrician's Mate, Construction Battalion, Line and Station (Navy rating)

EMSR . . . . Electrician's Mate, Ship Repair (Navy rating)
EMSRG . . . . . Electrician's Mate, Ship Repair, General Electrician (Navy rating)
EMSRT . . . . . Electrician's Mate, Ship Repair, I.C. Repairman (Navy rating)
EMSRS . . . . . Electrician's Mate, Ship Repair, Shop Electrician (Navy rating)
EMT . . . . Electrician's Mate, Telephone (Coast Guard rating)
EDF . . . . Electricite de France (National electric company)
EC . . . . Electrification Council
EASL . . . . . . Electroacoustic Systems Laboratory
EAG . . . . Electroantennogram
ECC . . . . Electrocardiocorder
ECG . . . . Electrocardiogram (Medicine)
EKG . . . . Electrocardiogram (Medicine)
EKS . . . . Electrocardiogram Simulator
ELT . . . . Electrocardiography and Basal Metabolism Technician (Navy)
ECS . . . . Electrocardioscanner
ECD . . . . Electrochemical Debarring
ECDC . . . . . . Electrochemical Diffused-Collector Transistor
EFC . . . . Electrochemical Fuel Cell
ECM . . . . Electrochemical Machining
ECR . . . . Electrochemical Reaction
ECS . . . . Electrochemical Society
ES . . . . Electrochemical Society
EC . . . . Electrocoating
ECS . . . . Electroconvulsive Shock
ECT . . . . Electroconvulsive Therapy (Medicine)
ECOG . . . . . . Electrocorticogram
ESD . . . . Electrocular Symbol Display
EDC . . . . Electrode Dark Current
EEP . . . . Electrode Electrostatic Precipitator
EHK . . . . Electrode Heater Kit
E . . . . Electrode Potential
EDTS . . . . . . Electro-Depositer Technology Society
EM . . . . Electrodeposition Memo
EDR . . . . Electrodermal Response
EDC . . . . Electro Development Corporation
EDM . . . . Electrodischarge Machine (or Machining)
EEG . . . . Electroencephalogram or Electroencephalography (Medicine)
ENC . . . . Electroencephalography Technician (Navy)
EED . . . . Electro-Explosive Device
EFD . . . . Electrofluid Dynamic (Process)
EGD . . . . Electrogasdynamic (Generator)
EHA . . . . Electro-Hydraulic Actuator
EHF . . . . Electrohydraulic Forming
EHM . . . . Electrohydraulic Motor
EHPM . . . . . . Electrohydraulic Pulse Motor
EHD . . . . Electro-Hydrodynamics
EKY . . . . Electrokymogram
ENP . . . . Electroless Nickel Plating
EL . . . . Electro Luminescence
ELD . . . . Electroluminescent Diode
ELF . . . . Electroluminescent Ferroelectric
ELFC . . . . . . Electro-Luminescent Ferroelectric Cell
ELPE . . . . . . Electroluminescent-Photoelectric
ELQC . . . . . . Electroluminescent Quantum Counter
ELVIS . . . . . . Electroluminescent Vertical Indication System
ESA . . . . Electrolysis Society of America
EPG . . . . Electrolytic Plunge Grinder
ETP . . . . Electrolytic Tough Pitch (Copper)
EM . . . . Electromagnetic
EAL . . . . Electromagnetic Amplifying Lens
EMC . . . . Electromagnetic Compatibility
ECAC . . . . . . Electromagnetic Compatibility Analysis Center (AFSC)
ECP . . . . Electromagnetic Compatibility Program (Air Force)
EMCP . . . . . . Electromagnetic Compatibility Program
ECAC . . . . . . Electromagnetic Computer Analysis Center
EME . . . . Electromagnetic Environment
EEA . . . . Electromagnetic Environment Analysis
EMEG . . . . . . Electromagnetic Environment Generator
EETF . . . . . . Electromagnetic Environmental Test Facility (Military)
EMFM . . . . . . Electromagnetic Flowmeter
EMG . . . . Electromagnetic Gyro
ELINT . . . . . . Electromagnetic Intelligence
ELMINT . . . . . Electromagnetic Intelligence
EICS . . . . . . Electromagnetic Intelligence Collection System
EIS . . . . Electromagnetic Intelligence System (Air Force)
EMIS . . . . . . Electromagnetic Intelligence Systems
EI . . . . Electromagnetic Interference
EMI . . . . Electromagnetic Interference
EIT . . . . Electromagnetic Interference Testing
EMIT . . . . . . Electromagnetic Interference Testing
EMQ . . . . Electromagnetic Quiet

EMR . . . . Electromagnetic Radiation
EMRG . . . . . . Electromagnetic Radiation Generator
ERG . . . . Electromagnetic Radiation Generator
ES . . . . Electromagnetic Storage
EMS . . . . Electromagnetic Submarine (Navy)
EMS . . . . Electromagnetic Surveillance (Air Force)
EMTECH . . . . . Electromagnetic Technology
ETEDS . . . . . . Electromagnetic Test Environment Data System
EMU . . . . Electro-Magnetic Unit(s)
EVF . . . . Electromagnetic Vibrating Feeder
EWCL . . . . . . Electromagnetic Warfare and Communications Laboratory
EMW . . . . Electromagnetic Wave
EWASER . . . . . Electromagnetic Wave Amplification by Simulated Emission of Radiation
EMWF . . . . . . Electromagnetic Wave Form
EMW . . . . Electromagnetic Window
EM . . . . Electromechanical
EMAC . . . . . . Electromechanical Averaging Circuit
EMDS . . . . . . Electromechanical Development Section
EMLA . . . . . . Electromechanical Linear Actuator
EMP . . . . Electromechanical Power (or Pulse)
EMR . . . . Electro-Mechanical Research, Inc.
EMSC . . . . . . Electromechanical Stop Clock
ESC . . . . Electromechanical Stop Clock
EM . . . . Electromicroscopic
EMISS . . . . . . Electromolecular Instrument Space Simulator
EM . . . . Electro-Motive Corporation
EMDP . . . . . . Electromotive Difference of Potential
EMD . . . . Electro-Motive Division (General Motors Corporation)
E . . . . Electromotive Force
EMF . . . . Electromotive Force
EMK . . . . Electro-Motorische Kraft (Electromotive Force) (German)
EMG . . . . Electromyogram
EMG . . . . Electromyographic
E . . . . Electron
EB . . . . Electron Beam
EBC . . . . Electron Beam Cutting (Engraving)
EBEE . . . . . . Electron Beam Evaporation Equipment
EBE . . . . Electron Beam Evaporator
EBG . . . . Electron Beam Generator
EBG . . . . Electron Beam Gun
EBM . . . . Electron Beam Melted
EBM . . . . Electron Beam Method
EBMD . . . . . . Electron Beam Mode Discharge
EBPA . . . . . . Electron Beam Parametric Amplifier
EBR . . . . Electron Beam Readout
EBR . . . . Electron Beam Recorder
EBR . . . . Electron Beam Regulator
EBS . . . . Electron Beam System
EBE . . . . Electron Binding Energy
EBIC . . . . Electron-Bombardment-Induced Conductivity (NASA)
EBICON . . . . . Electron Bombardment Induced Conductivity
EIT . . . . Electron-Bombardment Ion Thrustor
EBV . . . . Electron Bombardment Vehicle
EC . . . . Electron Capture
ECO . . . . Electron Coupled Oscillator
ED . . . . Electron Devices
EDI . . . . Electron Diffraction Instrument
EIL . . . . Electron Injection LASER
ELA . . . . Electron Linear Accelerator
EM . . . . Electron Microprobe
EMP . . . . Electron Microprobe
EMX . . . . Electron Microprobe X-Ray Analyzer (ARL)
EMSA . . . . . . Electron Microscope Society of America
EMS . . . . Electron Multiplex Switch
ENDOR . . . . . Electron-Nuclear Double Resonance
EPR . . . . Electron Paramagnetic Resonance
EPA . . . . Electron Probe Analyzer
EPM . . . . Electron Probe Microanalysis
ERC . . . . Electron Reflection Coefficient
ESCA . . . . . . Electron Spectroscopic Chemical Analysis
ESR . . . . Electron Spin Resonance
ESSFL . . . . . . Electron Steady State Fermi Level
ES . . . . Electron Synchrotron (AEC)
ETF . . . . Electron-Transfering Flavoprotein (Biochemistry)
ETP . . . . Electron Transport Particle
ET . . . . Electron Tube
ETIC . . . . Electron Tube Information Council
ETK . . . . Electron Tube Klystron
ETMG . . . . . . Electron Tube Management Group
ETR . . . . Electron Tube Rectifier
ETT . . . . Electron Tube, Triode

EV . . . . Electron Volts
EY . . . . Electron Yield
EYM . . . . Electron Yield Measurement
EYMS . . . . . . Electron Yield Measurement System
EGAD . . . . . . Electronegative Gas Detector
EASB . . . . . . Electronic Area Support Base (Air Force)
EACC . . . . . . Electronic Asset Control Center
EA . . . . Electronic Associates, Inc. (NYSE symbol)
EAI . . . . Electronic Associates, Incorporated
EADI . . . . . . Electronic Attitude Direction Indicator
EAR . . . . Electronic Audio Recognition
EAGER . . . . . Electronic Audit Gager
EAX . . . . Electronic Automatic Exchange
EBS . . . . Electronic Band Spectra
EBC . . . . Electronic Batch Control
EBW . . . . Electronic Beam Welding
ECU . . . . Electronic Cabling Unit
ECP . . . . Electronic Calculating Punch
ECC . . . . Electronic Calibration Center (National Bureau of Standards)
ECO . . . . Electronic Central Office
ECO . . . . Electronic Check-Out
ECAP . . . . . . Electronic Circuit Analysis Program
ECME . . . . . . Electronic Circuit-Making Equipment (Data processing)
ECP . . . . Electronic Circuit Protector
ECOM . . . . . . Electronic Command (Army)
ECD . . . . Electronic Communications Division (Air Force)
ECI . . . . Electronic Communications, Incorporated
ECG . . . . Electronic Component Group
ECRDC . . . . . Electronic Component Research and Development Grant (Canada)
ECL . . . . Electronic Components Laboratory
ECRC . . . . . . Electronic Components Research Center
ECPI . . . . Electronic Computer Programming Institute
EC . . . . Electronic Computers
ELECOM . . . . Electronic Computing
EC . . . . Electronic Conductivity
ECA . . . . Electronic Confusion Area
ECSG . . . . . . Electronic Connector Study Group
ECO . . . . Electronic Contact Operate
EC . . . . Electronic & Control
ECI . . . . Electronic Control Instrumentation
ECARS . . . . . . Electronic Coordinatograph Readout System
EC . . . . Electronic Counter
ECCM . . . . . . Electronic Counter-Countermeasures
ECM . . . . Electronic Counter Measure
ECMSN . . . . . Electronic Countermeasures Mission
ECMob . . . . . Electronic Countermeasures Observer
ECMP . . . . . . Electronic Countermeasures Program
ECS . . . . Electronic Countermeasures System
EDGE . . . . . . Electronic Data Gathering Equipment
EDLCC . . . . . Electronic Data Local Communications Central
EDP . . . . Electronic Data Processing
EDPC . . . . . . Electronic Data Processing Center
EDPE . . . . . . Electronic Data Processing Equipment
EDPM . . . . . . Electronic Data Processing Machine (Also translated by some users of such equipment as "Every Damn Problem Multiplied")
EDPS . . . . . . Electronic Data Processing System
EDPT . . . . . . Electronic Data Processing Test
EDRCC . . . . . Electronic Data Remote Communications Complex
EDSAC . . . . . Electronic Data Storage Automatic Computer
EDTCC . . . . . Electronic Data Traffic Control Center
EDTCC . . . . . Electronic Data Transmission Communications Central
EDR . . . . Electronic Decoy Rocket
EDL . . . . Electronic Defense Laboratory (Sylvania, Inc.)
EDSD . . . . . . Electronic Defense Systems Division
EDD . . . . Electronic Dehydration Dryer
EDQA . . . . . . Electronic Devices Quality Assurance
EDPS . . . . . . Electronic Dew Point Sensor
EDA . . . . Electronic Differential Analyzer
EDA . . . . Electronic Digital Analyzer
EDC . . . . Electronic Digital Computer
EDITAR . . . . . Electronic Digital Tracking and Ranging
EDVAC . . . . . Electronic Digital-Vernier Analog Computer
EDM . . . . Electrical Discharge Machining
EDVAC . . . . . Electronic Discrete Variable Automatic Computer
EDP . . . . Electronic Display Panel
EDU . . . . Electronic Display Unit
EDRI . . . . Electronic Distributors' Research Institute
EDAC . . . . . . Electronic Dive Angle Control
EDM . . . . Electronic Drafting Machine
EE . . . . Electronic Engineering
EEA . . . . Electronic Engineering Association (British)

EEFT . . . . Electronic Environmental Test Facility
EEE . . . . Electronic Equipment Engineering (A publication)
EEES . . . . Electronic Equipment Environment Survey
EEMK . . . . Electronic Equipment Maintenance Kit
EEM . . . . Electronic Equipment Modification
EFR . . . . Electronic Failure Report
EFFI . . . . Electronic Fiber Fineness Indicator
EFICON . . . . Electronic Financial Control
EFAS . . . . Electronic Flash Approach System
EFFI . . . . Electronic Forum for Industry (British)
EFC . . . . Electronic Frequency Control
EGECON . . . . Electronic Geographic Coordinate Navigation System
EGAD . . . . Electronic Ground Automatic Destruct
EGADS . . . . . Electronic Ground Automatic Destruct Sequencer (Air Force)
EGC . . . . Electronic Gyro Compass
EIA . . . . Electronic Industries Association
EIAC . . . . Electronic Industries Association of Canada
EIA-J . . . . Electronic Industries Association – Japan
EIB . . . . Electronic Information Bulletin (Navy)
EI . . . . Electronic Installation
EIT . . . . Electronic Installation Technician
EID . . . . Electronic Instrusion Detection
ELINT . . . . . Electronic Intelligence (Air Force)
EI . . . . Electronic Interface
EIMO . . . . . . Electronic Interface Management Office
EI . . . . Electronic Interference
EJ . . . . Electronic Jamming
EKB . . . . Electronic Key Board
EKBS . . . . Electronic Keyboard System
EKS . . . . Electronic Keyboard System
EKB . . . . Electronic Knowledge Bank
ELE . . . . Electronic Launching Equipment
ELSIE . . . . Electronic Letter Sorting and Indicator Equipment
ELD . . . . Electronic Lie Detector
EMA . . . . Electronic Maintenance Assembly
EMEA . . . . . . Electronic Maintenance Engineering Association
EMI . . . . Electronic Maintenance Inspector
EMPT . . . . . . Electronic Maintenance Proficiency Test
EMT . . . . Electronic Maintenance Technician (FAA)
EMS . . . . Electronic Management System
EMB . . . . Electronic Material Bulletin (Army)
EMC . . . . Electronic Material Change
EMSL . . . . . . Electronic Material Sciences Laboratory
EMSR . . . . . . Electronic Material Shipment Request (Navy)
ELMT . . . . . . Electronic Mechanic Technician
EMS . . . . Electronic Medical System
EMI . . . . Electronic Memories, Incorporated
EMSO . . . . . . Electronic Memory Systems Organization (Burroughs Corporation)
EMT . . . . Electronic Mind Tester
EMA . . . . Electronic Missile Acquisition
EMC . . . . Electronic Modules Corporation
EMR . . . . Electronic Moisture Recorder
E . . . . Electronic Night Bombing Capability (When a plane designation)
ENIG . . . . . . Electronic Nuclear Instrumentation Group
END . . . . Electronic Null Detector
ENIAC . . . . . Electronic Numerical Integrator and Calculator
EOC . . . . Electronic Operations Center (Military)
EOB . . . . Electronic Order of Battle
EOEM . . . . . . Electronic Original Equipment Market
EOP . . . . Electronic Overload Protection
EP . . . . Electronic Package
EPH . . . . Electronic Package Housing
EPDS . . . . . . Electronic Parts Distributors' Show
EPEM . . . . . . Electronic Parts and Equipment Manufacturers Association
EPM . . . . Electronic Parts Manual
EPMA . . . . . . Electronic Parts Manufacturers Association
EPR . . . . Electronic Parts Reliability
EPIC . . . . Electronic Photochromic Integrating Cathode-Ray (Tube)
EPI . . . . Electronic Position Indicator
EPBX . . . . . . Electronic Private Branch Exchange
EPRA . . . . . . Electronic Production Resources Agency (Military)
EPD . . . . Electronic Products Department
EPC . . . . Electronic Program Control
EPG . . . . Electronic Proving Ground (Army)
ERAC . . . . . . Electronic Random Action Control
ERNIE . . . . . Electronic Random Number Indicating Equipment (Used for selecting winning premium savings bond numbers) (British)
ERA . . . . Electronic Reading Automation (Information retrieval)
ER . . . . Electronic Reconnaissance
ERAS . . . . . . Electronic Reconnaissance Access Set

ELRAC . . . . . . Electronic Reconnaissance Accessory Set
ERPD . . . . . . Electronic Reconnaissance Procurement Division
ERS . . . . Electronic Reconnaissance Set
ERMA . . . . . . Electronic Recording Machine Accounting
ERIC . . . . Electronic Remote and Independent Control
ERX . . . . Electronic Remote Switching
ERPAL . . . . . . Electronic Repair Parts Allowance List (Navy)
ERA . . . . Electronic Representatives Association
ERP . . . . Electronic Requirement Plan (Navy)
ERA . . . . Electronic Research Association (British)
ERDL . . . . . . Electronic Research and Development Laboratory (Army)
ERD . . . . Electronic Research Directorate (Air Force)
ERSA . . . . . . Electronic Research Supply Agency
ERDA . . . . . . Electronic Resources Development Agency
ERGS . . . . . . Electronic Route Guidance System (Road sign aid)
ESMA . . . . . . Electronic Sales-Marketing Association
ESC . . . . Electronic Scan Converter
ESR . . . . Electronic Scanning RADAR
ESRS . . . . Electronic Scanning RADAR System
ESSA . . . . . . Electronic Scanning and Stabilizing Antenna
ES . . . . Electronic Section (Weather bureau)
ELSEC . . . . . . Electronic Security (Air Force)
ESS . . . . Electronic Security System
ESP . . . . Electronic Seismic Photography
ESSU . . . . . . Electronic Selective Switching Unit
ESS . . . . Electronic Sequence Switching
EST . . . . Electronic Sequencer Timer
ESC . . . . Electronic Shop Computer
ES . . . . Electronic Shop Major (Coast Guard)
EST . . . . Electronic Shop Major Telephone and Teletype (Coast Guard)
ESM . . . . Electronic Shop Minor (Coast Guard)
ESMT . . . . . . Electronic Shop Minor Telephone and Teletype (Coast Guard)
ELSSE . . . . . . Electronic Sky Screen Equipment (Air Force)
ECSP . . . . . . Electronic Specialist
ELS . . . . Electronic Specialty Company (NYSE symbol)
ESBR . . . . Electronic Stacked Beam RADAR
ES . . . . Electronic Standard
ESP . . . . Electronic Standard Procedure
ESO . . . . Electronic Standards Office (Navy)
ESE . . . . Electronic Stock Evaluator Corporation
ESSNSS . . . . . Electronic Supply Segment of the Navy Supply System
ESSB . . . . Electronic Supply Support Base (Air Force)
ESE . . . . Electronic Support Equipment
ESL . . . . Electronic Support Laboratory
ESSPO . . . . . . Electronic Support Systems Project Office (Air Force)
ESA . . . . Electronic Surge Arrester
ESS . . . . Electronic Surveillance System
ESG . . . . Electronic Sweep Generator
ESM . . . . Electronic Switch Module
ES . . . . Electronic Switching
ESS . . . . Electronic Switching System
ESSFLO . . . . . Electronic Switching System Flow Chart
ESE . . . . Electronic System Evaluator
ESTU . . . . . . Electronic System Test Unit
ESC . . . . Electronic Systems Center (Air Force)
ESC . . . . Electronic Systems Command (Formerly, Bureau of Ships) (Navy)
ESD . . . . Electronic Systems Division (AFSC)
ESL . . . . Electronic Systems Laboratory
ECTAR . . . . . . Electronic Tactical Action Report
ETM . . . . Electronic Technician's Mate (Navy rating)
ETMSR . . . . . . Electronic Technician's Mate, Ship Repair (Navy rating)
ETL . . . . Electronic Technology Laboratory (Air Force)
ETS . . . . Electronic Telegraph System
ETC . . . . Electronic Temperature Control
ETO . . . . Electronic Temperature Offset
ETT . . . . Electronic Tensile Tester
ETSAL . . . . . . Electronic Terms for Space Age Language
ET . . . . Electronic Test(s)
ETS . . . . Electronic Test Set
ETS . . . . Electronic Test Stand
ETS . . . . Electronic Test Station
ETS . . . . Electronic Timing Set
ETMWG . . . . . Electronic Trajectory Measurements Working Group (IRIG)
ETS . . . . Electronic Translator System (Bell System)
ETR . . . . Electronic Trouble Report
ET . . . . Electronic Tube
ETF . . . . Electronic Tuning Fork
ETG . . . . Electronic Turbine Governor
EUDS . . . . . . Electronic Unit Design Section
EVS . . . . Electronic Valve Specification

EVA . . . . Electronic Velocity Analyzer
EVR . . . . Electronic Video Recording (CBS Laboratories' brand name for tape
       cartridges of TV programs)
EVATA . . . . . . Electronic-Visual-Auditory Training Aid
EVS . . . . Electronic Voice Switching
EVA . . . . Electronic Vote Analysis (Election poll)
ELWAR . . . . . . Electronic Warfare
EW. . . . . Electronic Warfare
EWF . . . . Electronic Warfare
EWD . . . . Electronic Warfare Department
EWES . . . . . . Electronic Warfare Evaluation Simulator
EWL . . . . Electronic Warfare Laboratory
EWO . . . . Electronic Warfare Office(r)
EWOT . . . . . . Electronic Warfare Officer Training
EWTT . . . . . . Electronic Warfare Tactics Trainer
EWT . . . . Electronic Warfare Trainer
EWDI . . . . . . Electronic Wind Direction Indicator
EWSI . . . . . . Electronic Wind Speed Indicator
EWI . . . . Electronic Wiring Intercommunication
ESPAR. . . . . . Electronically Phased Array RADAR
ESAR . . . . . . Electronically Scanned Array RADAR
ESSBR . . . . . . Electronically Scanned Stacked Beam RADAR (Program)
ESAIRA . . . . . Electronically Scanning Airborne Intercept RADAR Antenna
ESAR . . . . . . Electronically Steerable Array RADAR
ESPAR . . . . . . Electronically Steerable Phased Array RADAR (SPADATS)
ETF . . . . Electronically Tunable Filter
ETPA . . . . . . Electronically Tunable Parametric Amplifier
ETR . . . . Electronically Tuned Receiver
ETRT . . . . . . Electronically Tuned Receiver Tuner
ETT . . . . Electronically Tuned Tuner
EC . . . . Electronics Chassis
ECA . . . . Electronics Corporation of America
ECME . . . . . . Electronics Countermeasures Environment
EE . . . . Electronics Engineering Division (Coast Guard)
EEE . . . . Electronics Engineering Division (Coast Guard)
EIB . . . . Electronics Information Branch (Navy)
ELIT . . . . Electronics Information Test
EIMB . . . . . . Electronics Installation and Maintenance Bulletin
EL . . . . Electronics Laboratory
EMEC . . . . . . Electronics Maintenance Engineering Center (Navy)
EMA . . . . Electronics Manufacturers Association
EMA. . . . . . . Electronics Materiel Agency (Army)
EMSA . . . . . . Electronics Materiel Support Agency (Army)
EN . . . . Electronics News
EPLA . . . . . . Electronics Precedence List Agency
ERC . . . . Electronics Research Center (NASA)
ERDA . . . . . . Electronics Research and Development Activity (Army)
ELRDL . . . . . . Electronics Research and Development Laboratory
ERL . . . . Electronics Research Laboratory (MIT)
ESBC . . . . . . Electronics Small Business Council
ESO . . . . Electronics Supply Office(r)
ETFO . . . . . . Electronics Technical Field Office
ET . . . . Electronics Technician
ETECG . . . . . . Electronics Test Equipment Coordination Group (Military)
EU . . . . Electronics Unit
ENG . . . . Electronystagmography
EOG . . . . Electro-Oculogram
EOG . . . . Electro-Oculographic
EOG . . . . Electroolfactogram
EOD . . . . Electro-Optic Display
EODTC . . . . . . Electro-Optic Display Test Chamber
EOF . . . . Electro-Optic Force
EOP . . . . Electro-Optic Projector
EOTC . . . . . . Electro-Optic Test Chamber
EOGS . . . . . . Electro-Optical Guidance Section
EOLM . . . . . . Electro-Optical Light Modulator
EOM . . . . Electro-Optical Modulator
EOR . . . . Electro-Optical Research
EOS . . . . Electro-Optical Systems, Inc. (Subsidiary of Xerox Corporation)
EOTD . . . . . . Electro-Optical Tracking Device
EOTS . . . . . . Electro-Optical Tracking System
EVS . . . . Electro-Optical Viewing System (Air Force)
EOWS . . . . . . Electro-Optical Weapons System
EPR . . . . Electrophrenic Respiration (Medicine)
EP . . . . Electroplate
EPNS . . . . . . Electroplated Nickel Silver
EP . . . . Electro-Pneumatic
EPV . . . . Electro-Pneumatic Valve
ERG . . . . . . Electroretinogram (Medicine)
ESP . . . . Electrosensitive Programming
ECS . . . . Electroshock Therapy

EST . . . . Electroshock Therapy
ESTA . . . . . . Electroshock Therapy Apparatus
ESR . . . . Electroslag Refining
ESR . . . . Electroslag Remelting (Steel alloy)
ESP . . . . Electrosonic Profiler
ES . . . . Electrostatic
EEM . . . . Electrostatic Electron Microscope
ESF . . . . Electrostatic Focusing (Electronics)
ESG . . . . Electrostatic Gyroscope
ESK . . . . Electrostatic Klystron
EPSA . . . . . . Electrostatic Particle Size Analyzer
EPO . . . . Electrostatic Plasma Oscillator
EP . . . . Electrostatic Powder
EPG . . . . Electrostatic Power Generator
EPT . . . . Electrostatic Printing Tube
EPE . . . . Electrostatic Probe Experiment
ES . . . . Electrostatic Spraying
ES . . . . Electrostatic Storage
ESD . . . . Electrostatic Storage Deflection
EST . . . . Electrostatic Storage Tube
ETVM . . . . . . Electrostatic Transistorized Voltmeter
ESU . . . . Electrostatic Unit(s)
EVM . . . . Electrostatic Voltmeter
EFT . . . . Electrostatically Focused Tube
ESG . . . . Electrostatically Suspended Gyro
EVD . . . . Electro-Vacuum Drive
EVM . . . . Elektronno-Vychislitel'naya Mashina (Electronic Calculating Machine)
       (Russia)
ECE . . . . Element Characteristics Equation
EEIC . . . . Element of Expense/Investment Code
ELM . . . . Element Load Model
EMT . . . . Elemental Method of Training
EB . . . . Elementary Body
EE & RM . . . . . Elementary Electrical and Radio Material (Training School) (Navy)
EFTC . . . . . . Elementary Flying Training School (British)
EFTS . . . . . . Elementary Flying Training School (Navy)
EPAM . . . . . . Elementary Perceiver and Memorizer
EPDCC . . . . . . Elementary Potential Digital Computing Component
EPC . . . . Elementary Processing Centers
ERT . . . . Elementary Renewal Theorem
ESASC . . . . . . Elementary School Administrative Supervisory Certificate
ESSP . . . . . . Elementary School Science Project
ESS . . . . Elementary Science Study (National Science Foundation)
ESEA . . . . . . Elementary and Secondary Education Act (of 1965)
EGE . . . . Elevated Glandular Epidermis
ERASER . . . . . Elevated Radiation Seeking Rocket
ERS . . . . Elevated Radio System
ETSG . . . . . . Elevated Temperature Strain Gage
EAGLE . . . . . . Elevation Angle Guidance Landing Equipment
EF . . . . Elevation Finder (Military)
EGAL . . . . . . Elevation Guidance for Approach and Landing
EPI . . . . Elevation Position Indicator (Aviation)
EVIL. . . . . . . Elevation Versus Integrated Log
ECC . . . . Elgin Community College (Illinois)
EJE . . . . Elgin, Joliet & Eastern Railway Company (AAR code)
ENW . . . . Elgin National Watch Company (NYSE symbol)
EWMC . . . . . . Eli Whitney Metrology Center
EOS . . . . Eligible for Overseas Service
ES . . . . Eligible for Separation
ELCO . . . . . . Eliminate and Count (Coding) (Data processing)
EROS . . . . . . Eliminate Range Zero System (Aviation)
El . . . . Eline
ER . . . . Elizabetha Regina (Queen Elizabeth)
ERR . . . . Elk River Reactor (AEC)
E . . . . Ell
ELAS . . . . . . Ellenikos Laikos Apeleutherotikos Stratos (Hellenic Peoples Army of
       Liberation) (Military arm of EAM) (Greece)
ELF . . . . Ellipsometry, Low Field (Microscopy)
EFFORPA. . . . . Elliptic Function First Order Ripple Phase Approximation
EFSORPA. . . . . Elliptic Function Second Order Ripple Phase Approximation
ECP . . . . Elliptical Cavity Pump
EGP . . . . Elliptical Gear Planetary
EOGO . . . . . . Elliptical Orbiting Geological Observatory
EPL . . . . Elliptically Polarized Light
EPW . . . . Elliptically Polarized Wave
ES . . . . Ellis Air Lines
EJC . . . . Ellsworth Junior College (Iowa)
ERI . . . . Elm Research Institute
EU . . . . Elms Unlimited (Later, Elm Research Institute)
EDB . . . . Elongated Die Bushing
EP . . . . Elongated Punch

ESD . . . . Elongated Single Domain
EL2 . . . . Elongation in 2 Inches
EG . . . . Else Good (In good condition except for defects mentioned) (Antiquarian book trade)
EQF . . . . Elswick Quick-Firing Gun
ET . . . . Eltra Corporation (NYSE symbol)
EJC . . . . Ely Junior College (Minnesota)
EMBA . . . . . . Emba Mink Breeders Association
EMT . . . . Embalmer (Navy rating)
ECMA . . . . . . Embalming Chemical Manufacturers Association (Defunct)
EMO . . . . Embarkation Medical Official (British)
ESO . . . . Embarkation Staff Officer (British)
ESSA . . . . . . Embassy Social Secretaries Association
EST . . . . Embedded Sensor Technique
EGP . . . . Embezzlement of Government Property
EGR . . . . Embossed Groove Recording
EPS . . . . Embossing Press Station
ERSA . . . . . . Embry-Riddle School of Aviation
EE . . . . Embryo Extract
E . . . . Emergency (Symbol placed in neighborhood windows to indicate that resident will aid passing schoolchildren in the event of an emergency)
EAF . . . . Emergency Action File (Air Force)
EARFLAP . . . . Emergency Action Reporting for Logistics Action Programming
EASA . . . . . . Emergency Air Staff Actions
EA . . . . Emergency Area
EMBERS . . . . . . Emergency Bed Request System (Data processing)
EBA . . . . Emergency Breathing Apparatus
EBS . . . . Emergency Broadcast System (Formerly CONELRAD)
EC . . . . Emergency Capability
ECLC . . . . . . Emergency Civil Liberties Committee
ECC . . . . Emergency Combat Capability
ECBMD . . . . . . Emergency Committee to Boycott Mother's Day
ECK . . . . Emergency Communications Key
ECC . . . . Emergency Conservation Committee
ECM . . . . Emergency Conservation Measures
ECW . . . . Emergency Conservation Work (Succeeded by CCC, 1937, now obsolete)
EDDS . . . . . . Emergency Detection and Decision System
EDS . . . . Emergency Detection System
EDC . . . . Emergency Digital Computer
EECE . . . . . . Emergency Economic Committee for Europe (A "Western Nation" organization) (Post-World War II)
EED . . . . Emergency Escape Device
EEP . . . . Emergency Essential Personnel
EEL . . . . Emergency Exposure Limits
EFAG . . . . . . Emergency Field Arresting Gear
EFC . . . . Emergency Fleet Corporation
EFT . . . . Emergency Flight Termination
EGAA . . . . . . Emergency General Account of Advances
EGRESS . . . . . . Emergency Global Rescue, Escape and Survival System (NASA)
EHC . . . . Emergency Housing Corporation
ELG . . . . Emergency Landing Ground
EL/G . . . . Emergency Landing Ground
ELZC . . . . . . Emergency Lead-Zinc Committee
ELOI . . . . . . Emergency Letter of Instructions
ELSS . . . . Emergency Life Support System
ELE . . . . Emergency Lighting Equipment
EMIC . . . . . . Emergency Maternity and Infant Care
EMO . . . . Emergency Measures Organization (Canada)
EMCCS . . . . . . Emergency Medical Command and Communications System
EMS . . . . Emergency Medical Service
EMT . . . . Emergency Medical Tag
EMT . . . . Emergency Medical Treatment (Military)
EMATS . . . . . . Emergency Message Automatic Transmission System (Air Force)
EMS . . . . Emergency Mission Support (Air Force)
EMSS . . . . . . Emergency Mission Support System
EMA . . . . Emergency Movements Atomic (Military)
ENT . . . . Emergency Negative Thrust
EORL . . . . . . Emergency Officers' Retired List (Army)
EORC . . . . . . Emergency Operations Research Center
EOS . . . . Emergency Operations System
EPE . . . . Emergency Passenger Exit
EPGA . . . . . . Emergency Petroleum and Gas Administration (Department of the Interior)
EPSC . . . . . . Emergency Petroleum Supply Committee
EPRD . . . . . . Emergency Plans and Readiness Division (of OEP)
EPF . . . . Emergency Plant Facilities
EPCCS . . . . . . Emergency Positive Control Communications System
EPG . . . . Emergency Power Generator
EPS . . . . Emergency Power Supply
EPU . . . . Emergency Power Unit
EPA . . . . Emergency Powers Act (British) (World War II)

EPDA . . . . Emergency Powers Defence Act (British) (World War II)
EPS . . . . Emergency Pressurization System
EPS . . . . Emergency Procurement Service
EPVS . . . . . . Emergency Propellant Venting System
EPPVS . . . . . . Emergency Propulsive Propellant Venting System
ERM . . . . Emergency Radiation Monitor
ERA . . . . Emergency Relief Administration
ERS . . . . Emergency Relocation Site (Military)
ERO . . . . Emergency Repair Overseer (Navy)
ER . . . . Emergency Request
ER . . . . Emergency Rescue
ERTC . . . . . . Emergency Rescue Team Chief (Air Force)
ERD . . . . Emergency Reserve Decoration (British)
ERD . . . . Emergency Return Device (Aerospace)
ERCS . . . . . . Emergency Rocket Communications System
ER . . . . Emergency Room (Medicine)
ESCAT . . . . . . Emergency Security Control of Air Traffic
ESO . . . . Emergency Security Operations
ES . . . . Emergency Service
ESHU . . . . . . Emergency Ship Handling Unit
ESRP . . . . Emergency Substitute in a Regular Position (Education)
ETL . . . . Emergency Time Limit
ETCO . . . . . . Emergency Traffic Coordinating Officer (Army)
ETDP . . . . . . Emergency Traffic Disposition Plan (Military)
ETC . . . . Emergency Training Centre (British)
ETE . . . . Emergency Transceiver Equipment
EUR . . . . Emergency Unsatisfactory Report (Military)
EUO . . . . Emergency Use Only
EVS . . . . Emergency Venting System
EVT . . . . Emergency Veterinary Tag
EVIF . . . . Emergency Virus Isolation Facility (National Cancer Institute)
EWO . . . . Emergency War Operations
EWO . . . . Emergency War Order (Air Force)
EWP . . . . Emergency War Plan
EWS . . . . Emergency Water Supply
EWS . . . . Emergency Welfare Service (Civil Defense)
EEC . . . . Emerson Electric Company
EMR . . . . Emerson Electric Manufacturing Company (NYSE symbol)
EPEC . . . . . . Emerson Programmer – Evaluator – Controller
ERP . . . . Emerson Radio & Phonograph Corporation (NYSE symbol)
ERPC . . . . . . Emerson Radio and Phonograph Corporation
EAF . . . . Emery Air Freight Corporation (NYSE symbol)
EMM . . . . Emhart Manufacturing Company (NYSE symbol)
ECM . . . . Emission Characteristics Monitor
EMCON . . . . . Emission Control Orders
EMISEC . . . . . . Emission Security
EMS . . . . Emission Spectrograph
ECR . . . . Emitted Coherent Radiation
ECL . . . . Emitter-Coupled Logic
ECLO . . . . . . Emitter-Coupled Logic Operator
ECTL . . . . . . Emitter-Coupled Transistor Logic (Data processing)
EF . . . . Emitter Follower
EIDAP . . . . . . Emitter Isolated Difference Amplifier Paralleling (Bell System)
ELME . . . . . . Emitter Location Method
EHC . . . . Emory & Henry College (Virginia)
EDE . . . . Empire District Electric Company (NYSE symbol)
EML . . . . Empire Lines, Inc.
ESADA . . . . . . Empire State Atomic Development Associates, Inc.
EVESR . . . . . . ESADA (Empire State Atomic Development Associates, Inc.) Vallecitos Experimental Superheat Reactor
ESHP . . . . . . Empire State Historical Publications (Series)
EIC . . . . Emplaced Instrument Complex
ELSS . . . . Emplaced Lunar Scientific Station
ESS . . . . Emplaced Scientific Station (NASA)
EDO . . . . Employee Development Officer
EHME . . . . . . Employee Health Maintenance Examination
EPA . . . . Employee Plan Administrators
ERCN . . . . . . Employee Record Change Notice
ERI . . . . Employee Relations Index
ERREAC . . . . . . Employee Relocation Real Estate Advisory Council
ECAB . . . . . . Employees' Compensation Appeals Board (Department of Labor)
ECC . . . . Employees' Compensation Commission
EICM . . . . . . Employer's Inventory of Critical Manpower
ELRIC . . . . . . Employers Labor Relations Information Committee
EPEAA . . . . . . Employing Photo-Engravers Association of America
EPAA . . . . . . Employing Printers Association of America
EAPAUS . . . . . . Employment Agencies Protective Association of the United States
EMSKED . . . . . . Employment Schedule
ESS . . . . Employment Security System (Department of Labor)
AVIATECA . . . Empresa Guatemalteca de Aviacion

GU . . . . Empresa Guatemalteca de Aviacion (Aviateca) (Guatemalan Airlines)
ENMISA . . . . . Empresa Nacional Mineral del Sahara (Corporation owned by the Spanish government)
VARIG . . . . . . Empresa de Viacao Aerea Rio Grandense
ECBC . . . . Empress Chinchilla Breeders Cooperative
E . . . . Empty
MT . . . . Empty (Slang)
ELP . . . . Emulsified Liquid Propellant
EBR . . . . Emulsion Butadiene Rubber
EP . . . . En Passant (In passing) (Chess)
ENRT . . . . . . En Route
E/R . . . . En Route
EP . . . . En Route Penetration (Aviation)
ERAD . . . . . . En Route Radial (Aviation)
EST . . . . En-Route Support Team (Military)
ENRFOSCOMD . . En Route This Station from Oversea Command
ECS . . . . Enable Control System
EBDC . . . . . . Enamel Bonded Double Cotton (Insulation)
EBDP . . . . . . Enamel Bonded Double Paper (Insulation)
EBDS . . . . . . Enamel Bonded Double Silk (Insulation)
EC . . . . Enamel Covered
EDCV . . . . . . Enamel Double Cotton Varnish (Insulation)
EDSV . . . . . . Enamel Double Silk Varnish
EIW . . . . Enamel Insulated Wire
EIC . . . . Enamel Insulating Compound
ETI . . . . Encapsulated Toroidal Inductor
EVI . . . . Encapsulated Variable Inductor
EEC . . . . Encased Elastic Cylinder
EMC . . . . Encephalomyocarditis
CIFAX . . . . . . Enciphered Facsimile Communications
ETC . . . . Enclosed Track Conveyor
EAT . . . . Encoder Address Translator
EPS . . . . Encoder Power Supply
EFTO . . . . . . Encrypt for Transmission Only (Military)
EAA . . . . Encyclopedia of American Associations (Later, Encyclopedia of Associations)
EA . . . . Encyclopedia of Associations (Formerly, Encyclopedia of American Associations)
EB . . . . Encyclopaedia Britannica
EBIS . . . . Encyclopedia of Business Information Sources (A publication) (Formerly, EGIS)
ECT . . . . Encyclopedia of Chemical Technology
EPST . . . . Encyclopedia of Polymer Science & Technology
ESS . . . . Encyclopedia of the Social Sciences
E . . . . End (Football position)
EOA . . . . End of Address
EAC . . . . End-Around Carry
EAS . . . . End-Around Shift
EOB . . . . End of Block
EOB . . . . End of Bombardment
EOC . . . . End of Course
EOD . . . . End of Date
EOD . . . . End of Day
E to E . . . . . . End to End (Technical drawings)
EECT . . . . . . End, Evening Civil Twilight (Navigation)
EENT . . . . . . End, Evening Nautical Twilight (Navigation)
EOF . . . . End of File (Data processing)
EFY . . . . End of Fiscal Year
EFP . . . . End Forming Press
EIS . . . . End Interruption Sequence
EI . . . . End Item
EID . . . . End Item Designators
EOJ . . . . End of Job
EOL . . . . End of Life
EOL . . . . End of Line (Communications)
EOLT . . . . . . End of Logic Tape
EM . . . . End Matched
EOM . . . . . . End of Message
ENML . . . . . . End Mill
EOM . . . . End of Month
EMP . . . . End of Month Payment
E/P . . . . End-Paper (Bibliography)
EPR/G . . . . . . End-Paper Rubbed, Else Good (Condition) (Antiquarian book trade)
EPOE . . . . . . End Piece of Equipment
EP . . . . End Point (Distilling)
EPIC . . . . . . End Poverty in California (Slogan used by Upton Sinclair during campaign as Democratic candidate for governor of California, 1934)
EOPF . . . . . . End of Powered Flight
EPC . . . . End Products Committee (of WPB) (World War II)
EP . . . . End of Program

EOQ . . . . End of Quarter
EOR . . . . End of Reel
EOT . . . . End of Tape
ETT . . . . End of Tape Test
EOT . . . . End-of-Transmission
EVT . . . . End Viewing Tube
EJN . . . . Endicott Johnson Corporation (NYSE symbol)
EJC . . . . Endicott Junior College (Massachusetts)
E . . . . Ending of Precipitation (Meteorology)
ELM . . . . Endings (of nerves) to Lip Muscle
EAD . . . . Endo-Atmospheric Decoy
ES . . . . Endocrine Society
ER . . . . Endoplasmic Reticulum (Cytology)
E/I . . . . Endorsement Irregular (Banking)
ECM . . . . Ends Matched, Center (Lumber)
EA . . . . Enemy Aircraft
E/A . . . . Enemy Aircraft
ECIIB . . . . . . Enemy Civilian Internee Information Bureau (Military)
ECIIB(Br) . . . . Enemy Civilian Internee Information Bureau (Branch) (Military)
ED . . . . Enemy Dead
EFD . . . . Enemy Forward Disposition (Military)
EF & LTC . . . . Enemy Fuels and Lubricants Technical Committee
EOU . . . . Enemy Objective Unit (of US) (in London)
EOE . . . . Enemy Occupied Europe (World War II)
EOC . . . . Enemy Oil Committee (US)
EOB . . . . Enemy Order of Battle
EPWIB . . . . . . Enemy Prisoner of War Information Bureau
EPWIB(Br) . . . . Enemy Prisoner of War Information Bureau (Branch)
EPE . . . . Energetic Particles Explorer (Satellite) (NASA)
ESP . . . . Energetic Storm Particle
ENSI . . . . Energia Nucleare Sud Italia (Italian nuclear power plant project)
E . . . . Energy
ENCO . . . . . . Energy Company (Slogan and brand name used by Humble Oil & Refining Company)
ECD . . . . Energy Conversion Devices
ECL . . . . Energy Conversion Laboratory (MIT)
EDS . . . . Energy Depot Systems
EFD . . . . Energy Flux Density
ELD . . . . Energy Level Diagram
EMDI . . . . . . Energy Management Display Indicator
EREF . . . . . . Energy Research and Education Foundation
ESM . . . . Energy Storage Modulator
ESS . . . . Energy Storage System
EDM . . . . Enforced Dipole Moment
EHY . . . . Engage High Yield
ENG . . . . Engelhard Industries, Inc. (NYSE symbol)
ENTAC . . . . . . Engin Teleguide Anti-char (Antitank missile) (French)
E . . . . Engine, Engineer, or Engineering
EASY . . . . . . Engine Analyzer Systems (Air Force)
EAV . . . . Engine Assembly Vehicle
EBMA . . . . . . Engine, Booster Maintenance Area
EBS . . . . Engine Breather Separator
EB . . . . Engine Bulletin
ECS . . . . Engine Control System
EDN . . . . Engine Deflector Nozzle
E/G . . . . Engine-Generator
EGSMA . . . . . Engine Generator Set Manufacturers' Association
EIV . . . . Engine Installation Vehicle
ELF . . . . Engine Lube Filter
ELP . . . . Engine Lube and Purge (System)
EM . . . . Engine Maintenance
E-MAD . . . . . . Engine Maintenance and Disassembly (Building)
EMS . . . . Engine Management System (Army)
EO . . . . Engine Oil
EOCP . . . . . . Engine Out of Commission for Parts
EPCO . . . . . . Engine Parts Coordinating Office (Navy)
EPR . . . . Engine-Pressure Ratio
ER . . . . Engine Room (Force)
ERT . . . . Engine Rotor Tester
ES . . . . Engine-Sized
ESP . . . . Engine Start Panel
ESS . . . . Engine Start Signal
ETF . . . . Engine Test Facility
ETI . . . . Engine Test Information
ETS . . . . Engine Test Stands (NERVA program)
ETV . . . . Engine Test Vehicle
E/VTS . . . . . . Engine/Vehicle Test Stand
EVS . . . . Engine Vertical Scale
EVDP . . . . . . Engine Vibration Diagnostic Program
EAA . . . . Engineer in Aeronautics and Astronautics

EAC . . . . Engineer Amphibian Command (Had logistical rather than engineering mission, namely, to load, carry, and unload a complete infantry division) (World War II)
EABN . . . . . . Engineer Aviation Battalion (Military)
EAUTC . . . . . . Engineer Aviation Unit Training Center (Military)
EB . . . . Engineer Battalion (Army)
ENGBAT . . . . Engineer Battalion (Army)
EC . . . . Engineer Captain (British Navy)
EIC . . . . Engineer-in-Charge
E in C . . . . . . Engineer-in-Chief
ENGCOMDC . . Engineer Commissioner, District of Columbia (Military)
ECAD . . . . . . Engineer Control and Advisory Detachment (Air Force)
E in EE . . . . . Engineer in Electrical Engineering
EFCS . . . . . . Engineer Functional Components System
EF & I . . . . . . Engineer, Furnish, and Install
EIN . . . . Engineer Intelligence Note
EL . . . . Engineer Lieutenant (British Navy)
E-MAD . . . . . Engineer-Maintenance Assembly-Disassembly (NERVA program)
EMC . . . . . . Engineer Maintenance Center
EMC . . . . . . Engineer Maintenance Control (Army)
EM . . . . Engineer Manager
E in ME . . . . Engineer in Mechanical Engineering
E Met . . . . . . Engineer of Metallurgy
EM . . . . Engineer of Mines (or Mining)
EPTO . . . . . . Engineer Packaging Technical Office (Merged with General Equipment Command)
EP . . . . Engineer Personnel (Marine Corps)
EPR . . . . Engineer Photographic and Reproduction (Marine Corps)
EPCO . . . . . . Engineer Procurement Office (Army)
ERG . . . . . . Engineer Reactors Group (Army)
EA . . . . Engineer Rear Admiral (British)
ERPPO . . . . . Engineer Repair Parts Packaging Office (Merged with General Equipment Command)
ERTC . . . . . . Engineer Replacement Training Center
ESTO . . . . . . Engineer/Service Test Office
ESS . . . . Engineer Specialized Services
EIT . . . . Engineer-in-Training
ET . . . . Engineer Training
EVA . . . . Engineer Vice-Admiral (British)
EVC . . . . Engineer Volunteer Corps (British)
EFD . . . . Engineered Fasteners Division (Townsend Company)
EMC . . . . . . Engineered Military Circuit (Leased long lines established in continental US) (Military)
EA . . . . Engineering Aide (Navy rating)
EASL . . . . . . Engineering Analysis and Simulation Language (Data processing)
EAA . . . . Engineering and Architects Association
EAMHD . . . . . Engineering Aspects of Magnetohydrodynamics
EAPL . . . . . . Engineering Assembly Parts List
EASE . . . . . . Engineering Automatic System for Solving Equations
ECF . . . . Engineering Central Files
ECA . . . . Engineering Change Analysis
ECI . . . . Engineering Change Information
ECM-D . . . . . Engineering Change Management-Development
ECN . . . . Engineering Change Notice
ECO . . . . . . Engineering Change Order
ECP . . . . Engineering Change Package
ECP . . . . Engineering Change Proposals
ECR/A . . . . . . Engineering Change Request/Authorization
ECR . . . . Engineering Change Requirement (NASA)
ECS . . . . Engineering Change Summary
EC . . . . Engineering Changes
ECAC . . . . . . Engineering College Administrative Council
ECMA . . . . . . Engineering College Magazines Associated
ECRC . . . . . . Engineering College Research Council
ECCP . . . . . . Engineering Concepts Curriculum Project
EC . . . . Engineering Construction
ECRC . . . . . . Engineering Contracts Requirement Committee
EC . . . . Engineering Corps
ED . . . . Engineering Data
EDF . . . . Engineering Data File
EDIS . . . . . . Engineering Data & Information System (Army)
EDM . . . . . . Engineering Data Management
EDMS . . . . . . Engineering Data Management System
EDMS . . . . . . Engineering Data Micro-Reproduction System (DOD)
EDRS . . . . . . Engineering Data Retrieval System (Military)
EDSC . . . . . . Engineering Data Service Center (Air Force)
EDS & R . . . . . Engineering Data Storage and Retrieval (Army)
EDS . . . . Engineering Data Systems (DOD)
EDIAC . . . . . . Engineering Decision Integrator and Communicator
EDR . . . . Engineering Department Report
EDICT . . . . . . Engineering Departmental Interface Control Technique

ED . . . . Engineering Depot
ED . . . . Engineering Design
EDALHAB . . . . Engineering Design and Analysis Laboratory Habitat
EDCP . . . . . . Engineering Design Change Proposal
EDCS . . . . . . Engineering Design Change Schedule
ED & I . . . . . Engineering, Design, and Inspection
EDM . . . . . . Engineering Design Machine
EDM . . . . Engineering Design Memorandum
EDP . . . . Engineering Design Plan
EDT . . . . Engineering Design Test
EDIT . . . . . . Engineering Development Integration Test
EDL . . . . Engineering Development Laboratory
EDM . . . . Engineering Development Model
ED . . . . Engineering Division
EDR . . . . Engineering Division Report
EDICT . . . . . . Engineering Document Information Collection Task (or Technique)
EDM . . . . Engineering Drafting Machine
ED . . . . Engineering Draftsman
EDL . . . . Engineering Drawing List
EDRA . . . . . . Engineering Drawing Release Authorization
ED . . . . Engineering Duty (Navy)
EDO . . . . Engineering Duty Officer (Military)
EDO . . . . Engineering Duty Only (Aeronautical)
EEL . . . . Engineering Electronics Laboratory
EEUA . . . . . . Engineering Equipment Users Association
EETP . . . . . . Engineering Evaluation Test Program
EES . . . . Engineering Experiment Station
EEM . . . . Engineering Experimental Memo
EFTI . . . . Engineering Flight Test Inspector
EFTR . . . . Engineering Flight Test Report
EG . . . . Engineering Geologist
EI . . . . Engineering Index
EIC . . . . Engineering Information Center
E-I . . . . Engineering-Installation
EIC . . . . Engineering Institute of Canada
EIMO . . . . . . Engineering Interface Management Office
EIR . . . . Engineering Investigation Request
EJS . . . . Engineering Job Sheet
EJT . . . . Engineering Job Ticket
ELR . . . . Engineering Laboratory Report
ELD . . . . Engineering Logic Diagram
ELMS . . . . . . Engineering Lunar Model Surface
EMR . . . . Engineering Malfunction Report
EM . . . . Engineering Management
EMIT . . . . . . Engineering Management Information Technique
EMM . . . . . . Engineering Management Manual
EMC . . . . . . Engineering Manpower Commission
EM . . . . Engineering Manual
EMDI . . . . . . Engineering Manufacturing Division Instruction
EMS . . . . Engineering Master Schedule
EML . . . . Engineering Materials List (AEC)
EMB . . . . Engineering in Medicine and Biology
EM . . . . Engineering Memorandum
EMJ . . . . Engineering & Mining Journal
EN . . . . Engineering Note
E/O . . . . Engineering Opportunities (A journal)
EO . . . . Engineering Order
EODP . . . . . . Engineering Order Delayed for Parts
EOW . . . . . . Engineering Order Worksheet
EP . . . . Engineering Paper
EPC . . . . Engineering Part Card
EPS . . . . Engineering Performance Standards
EPM . . . . Engineering Procedures Manual
EPB . . . . Engineering Process Bulletin
EP . . . . Engineering Project
EPS . . . . Engineering Purchase Specification
ER . . . . Engineering Release
ERA . . . . Engineering Release Authorization
ERP . . . . Engineering Release Package
E & R . . . . . . Engineering and Repair (Department) (Navy)
ER . . . . Engineering Report
ERA . . . . Engineering Research Associates
ERDL . . . . . . Engineering Research and Development Laboratory (AMC)
ERR . . . . Engineering Research Report
ESM . . . . Engineering Schedule Memo
ESP . . . . Engineering Schedule Plan
ESMWT . . . . . Engineering, Science and Management War Training
ESP . . . . Engineering Signal Processor
ESL . . . . Engineering Society Library
ENSP . . . . . . Engineering Specification (Air Force)
ESF . . . . Engineering Specification Files

ES . . . . Engineering Study
ESR . . . . Engineering Summary Report
ETA . . . . Engineering Task Assignment
ETS . . . . Engineering and Technical Service
ET . . . . Engineering Test
ETD . . . . Engineering Test Directive
ETR . . . . Engineering Test Reactor (AEC)
ETRC . . . . . . Engineering Test Reactor Critical Facility (AEC)
ETU . . . . Engineering Test Unit
WM . . . . (Qualified for) Engineering Watch (USNR officer classification)
EWES . . . . . . Engineering Waterways Experiment Station (Army)
EWA . . . . Engineering Work Assignment
EWO. . . . . . . Engineering Work Order
EWS . . . . Engineering Work Schedule
EWS . . . . Engineering Writing and Speech
EYD . . . . Engineering Youth Day
ECPD . . . . . . Engineers Council for Professional Development
EJC . . . . Engineers Joint Council
EPOC . . . . . . Engineers Procurement Office, Chicago
EPIC. . . . . . . Engineers Public Information Council
ESA . . . . Engineers and Scientists of America
ESCO . . . . . . Engineers Supply Control Office (Army)
ELATE . . . . . . Engineers' Language for Automatic Test Equipment
ESG . . . . Engineers' and Scientists' Guild
ESWP . . . . . . Engineers' Society of Western Pennsylvania
EN . . . . Engineman (Navy rating)
E . . . . English
EIA . . . . English in Action
ECC . . . . English Ceramic Circle
ECU . . . . English Church Union
ECSCA . . . . . English Cocker Spaniel Club of America
EDD . . . . English Dialect Dictionary
EDS . . . . English Dialect Society
EEC . . . . English Electric Company, Ltd.
EF . . . . English Finish (Paper)
EFL . . . . English as a Foreign Language
EFF . . . . English for Foreigners
EAGS . . . . . . English and Germanic Studies
EIMC . . . . . . English Institute Materials Center
EJ . . . . English Journal (A periodical)
EM . . . . English Market
ENA. . . . . . . English Newspaper Association
ERU . . . . English Rugby Union
ESL . . . . English as a Second Language
ESAA . . . . . . English Setter Association of America
ESN . . . . English-Speaking Nations (of NATO)
ESU . . . . English-Speaking Union of the United States
ESSFTA . . . . . English Springer Spaniel Field Trial Association
ET . . . . English Translation
EV . . . . English Version
EVV . . . . English Versions
ESMA . . . . . . Engraved Stationery Manufacturers Association
ESMRI . . . . . . Engraved Stationery Manufacturers Research Institute
EPG . . . . Eniwetok Proving Ground (AEC)
EAS . . . . Enlisted Assignment System
EEC . . . . Enlisted Evaluation Center (Army)
EES . . . . Enlisted Evaluation System
ELTC . . . . . . Enlisted Loss to Commissioned Status (Military)
ELTW . . . . . . Enlisted Loss to Warrant Status (Military)
EM . . . . Enlisted Man (or Men)
EMR . . . . Enlisted Manning Report (Air Force)
EMTR . . . . . . Enlisted Master Tape Record (Army)
DEML(CIC). . . . Enlisted Men on Duty with the Counter Intelligence Corps (Army)
DEML(NG). . . . Enlisted Men on Duty with the National Guard (Army)
DEML(OR) . . . . Enlisted Men on Duty with the Organized Reserves (Army)
DEML(ROTC) . . Enlisted Men on Duty with the Reserve Officers' Training Corps (Army)
EPD . . . . Enlisted Personnel Directorate (Army)
EPDO . . . . . . Enlisted Personnel Distribution Office (Navy)
ERC . . . . Enlisted Reserve Corps
EW. . . . . Enlisted Woman or Women
EA . . . . Enlistment Allowance
ENC. . . . . . . Enlistment Cancelled
EST . . . . Enlistment Screening Test
ELH . . . . Enol-Lactone Hydrolase
EFFBR . . . . . . Enrico Fermi Fast Breeder Power Reactor (AEC)
EFINS. . . . . . Enrico Fermi Institute for Nuclear Studies (University of Chicago)
EMS . . . . Ente Minerario Siciliano
ENAL . . . . . . Ente Nazionale Assistenza Lavoratori (Italy)
ENI . . . . Ente Nazionale Idrocarburi (State-owned oil agency) (Italy)
ENIT . . . . . . Ente Nazionale per le Industrie Turistiche (Italy)
ETFAS . . . . . . Ente per la Trasformazione Fondiaria e Agraria in Sardegna (Italy)

ECA . . . . Enter Control Area (Aviation)
EWI . . . . Entered without Inspection (Usually applies to aliens who enter at other than a port of entry)
EC . . . . Enteric Coated (Pharmacy)
ECT . . . . Enteric Coated Tablet (Pharmacy)
EADIZ . . . . . . Entering Air Defense Identification Zone
EC . . . . Entering Complaint (Medicine)
ECHO. . . . . . Entero-Cytopathogenic Human Orphan (Virology)
ENSA . . . . . . Entertainments National Service Association (For British military forces)
EO . . . . Entertainments Officer (British military)
ESHH . . . . . . Enthronement of the Sacred Heart in the Home
EFA . . . . Entire Field Available (Aviation)
ETSP . . . . . . Entitled to Severance Pay
ESA . . . . Entomological Society of America
E . . . . Entrance
EOD. . . . . . . Entrance on Duty (Military)
ENTAC . . . . . Entrance National Agency Check
ERAP . . . . . . Entreprise de Recherches et d'Activites Petrolieres (State-owned petroleum agency) (France)
EU . . . . Entropy Unit
EP . . . . Entrucking Point (Military)
EAD . . . . Entry on Active Duty
EMS . . . . Entry Monitor System (NASA)
EQCC . . . . . . Entry Query Control Console
ERNO . . . . . . Entwicklungsring Nord (Germany)
EA . . . . Enumeration Area (Statistics)
ED . . . . Enumeration District (Census)
EDD . . . . Envelope Delay Distortion
EER . . . . Envelope Elimination and Restoration
EIA . . . . Envelope Institute of America
EMA . . . . Envelope Manufacturers Association
EG. . . . . Environment Generator
ENACT . . . . . Environmental Action (An organization)
EARS . . . . . . Environmental Analog Recording System
ENVANAL. . . . Environmental Analysis (Program)
ECS . . . . Environmental Chamber Shroud
ECA . . . . Environmental Control Administration (US Government)
ECE . . . . Environmental Control Equipment
EC/LS . . . . . . Environmental Control/Life Support (NASA)
ECO. . . . . . . Environmental Control Organization (Proposed in 1970 by Walter J. Hickel, Secretary of the Interior)
ECS . . . . Environmental Control System (NASA)
ECU . . . . Environmental Control Unit
ECO. . . . . . . Environmental Crisis Operation (University of British Columbia)
EDS . . . . Environmental Data Service
EDF . . . . Environmental Defense Fund
EEIB . . . . Environmental Engineering Intersociety Board
EES . . . . Environmental Engineering Section
EEI . . . . Environmental Equipment Institute
EHS . . . . Environmental Health Service (US Government)
EHA . . . . Environmental Hygiene Agency (Army)
EIC . . . . Environmental Improvement Commission (Maine)
EME . . . . Environmental Measurements Experiment
EMO . . . . Environmental Medicine Officer (Military)
EQT . . . . Environmental Qualification Test
ERS . . . . Environmental Research Satellite (NASA)
ER . . . . Environmental Resistance (Ecology)
ERIE . . . . Environmental Resistance Inherent in Equipment
ESSA . . . . . . Environmental Science Services Administration
ERL . . . . ESSA (Environmental Science Services Administration) Research Laboratories
EWWS. . . . . . ESSA (Environmental Science Services Administration) Weather Wire Service
ESE . . . . Environmental Simulation Equipment
ESC . . . . Environmental Stress Crack
ESSA . . . . . . Environmental Survey Satellite
ET . . . . Environmental Test
ETC . . . . Environmental Test Chamber
ETD . . . . Environments and Threats Directorate (Army)
EE . . . . Envoy-Extraordinary
EE & MP . . . . Envoy Extraordinary and Minister Plenipotentiary (State Department)
EC . . . . Enzyme Commission (of the International Union of Biochemistry)
ES . . . . Enzyme Substrate (Biochemistry)
EMB . . . . Eosin-Methylene Blue (Chemical)
ET . . . . Ephemeris Time
EL . . . . Epidemiological Laboratory (Air Force)
EPIREPT. . . . . Epidemiological Report
EST . . . . Epidemiology and Sanitation Technician (Navy)
EC . . . . Epidermal Cell
E . . . . Epidermis
EKP . . . . Epikeraprosthesis (Ophthalmology)

EAA	Epilepsy Association of America
EAC	Epiphany Apostolic College (New York)
ESA	Epiphyllum Society of America
ESOA	Epiphyllum Society of America
EAGA	Episcopal Actors' Guild of America
EC	Episcopal Church
ECW	Episcopal Church Women
ECSA	Episcopal Churchmen for South Africa
ECFSOV	Episcopal Council for Foreign Students and Other Visitors, Inc.
EGB	Episcopal Guild for the Blind
EPF	Episcopal Pacifist Fellowship
ESY	Episcopal Service for Youth
ESCRU	Episcopal Society for Cultural and Racial Unity
ETS	Episcopal Theological School
EM	Episcopus et Martyr (Bishop and Martyr)
E	Epistle
EM	Epitaxial Mesa
EPIC	Epitaxial Passivated Integrated Circuits
ETV	Epitaxial Tuning Varactor
EHD	Epizootic Hemorrhagic Disease (Veterinary medicine)
EBR	Epoxy Bridge Rectifier
ECA	Epoxy Curing Agent
EET	Epoxy-Encapsulated Transistor
EEK	Epoxy Experimental Kit
EFET	Epoxy Field Effect Transistor
ESC	Epoxy Spray Coater
EEP	Epsilon Eta Phi (Society)
EBV	Epstein-Barr Virus
EEO	Equal Employment Opportunity
EEOC	Equal Employment Opportunity Commission
ES	Equal Section (Technical drawings)
ETS	Equal Time Spacing
ETGT	Equal To or Greater Than
ETLT	Equal To or Less-Than
ESA	Equalized Sidelobe Antenna
EOS	Equation of State
EQT	Equation of Time (Navigation)
EET	Equator Earth Terminal
E	Equatorial (Air mass)
EQS	Equatorial Scatter
EATR	Equilibrium Air Total Radiation
ERS	Equilibrium Radiation Spectra
EE	Equine Encephalitis
EMSI	Equipes Medico-Sociales Itinerantes
EATS	Equipment Accuracy Test Station
EAG	Equipment Advisory Group
EAD	Equipment Allowance Document (Military)
EARP	Equipment Allowance Revision Program
EAA	Equipment Approval Authority
EAID	Equipment Authorization Inventory Data (Air Force)
EAIDL	Equipment Authorization Inventory Data Listing (Air Force)
ECAT	Equipment Category
ECL	Equipment Component List
ECO	Equipment Control Officer (Air Force)
EDM	Equipment Deadlined for Maintenance (Army)
EDP	Equipment Deadlined for Parts
EDAC	Equipment Distribution and Condition (Military)
EDT	Equipment Downtime
EFR	Equipment Failure Rate
EIC	Equipment Identification Code
EIR	Equipment Improvement Recommendations (Military)
EIR	Equipment Improvement Report (DOD)
EIDS	Equipment Integration Design Section
EIA	Equipment Interchange Association
EIC	Equipment Interstage Container
EMR	Equipment Maintenance Record (Army)
EMSD	Equipment Major Subdivision
EMG	Equipment Management Group
EML	Equipment Modification List
EOC	Equipment Operational Control
EO	Equipment Operator (Navy rating)
EPS	Equipment Policy Statement (Army)
EPP	Equipment Procurement Program
EQA	Equipment Quality Analysis
ERSR	Equipment Reliability Status Report
ERP	Equipment Repair Parts
ERPL	Equipment Repair Parts List
ERT	Equipment Repair Time
ER	Equipment Requirement
ERAA	Equipment Review and Authorization Activity (Military)
ERB	Equipment Review Board

ES	Equipment Section
ESC	Equipment Section Container
ESLT	Equipment Section Leakage Test
ESS	Equipment Section Shell
ESC	Equipment Serviceability Criteria (Military)
ESDC	Equipment Sliding Drawer Cabinet
E & SP	Equipment and Spare Parts
ES	Equipment Specification
ETN	Equipment Table Nomenclature
ETT	Equipment Task Time
ET	Equipment Time
EATI	Equipment and Tool Institute
ETI	Equipment and Tool Institute
ETC	Equipment Trust Certificate
EUT	Equipment Under Test
EUR	Equipment Unsatisfactory Report
EWG	Equipment Working Group
ERP	Equipments Requirement Program
EPC	Equipotential Cathode
EPK	Equipotential Kathode
EPR	Equipotential Region
EPS	Equipotential Surface
L	Equipped with Search Light (Suffix to plane designation) (Navy)
EQT	Equitable Gas Company (NYSE symbol)
ELI	Equitable Life Interpreter (Computer)
ERA	Equitable Reserve Association
EM	Equitum Magister (Master of the Horse) (British)
EQU	Equity Corporation (NYSE symbol)
EAP	Equivalent Air Pressure
EAS	Equivalent Airspeed
EAN	Equivalent Atomic Number
EBI	Equivalent Background Input
EBD	Equivalent Binary Digit
EDR	Equivalent Direct Radiation
EF	Equivalent Focal Length (Optics)
EFC	Equivalent Full Discharge
EFPH	Equivalent Full-Power-Hour (FCC)
EGT	Equivalent Gear Train
EIOC	Equivalent Input Offset Current
EIOV	Equivalent Input Offset Voltage
EIOD	Equivalent Instruction or Duty
ELL	Equivalent Loudness Level
EMTTF	Equivalent Mean Time to Failure
ENL	Equivalent Noise Level
ENR	Equivalent Noise Ratio
ENSI	Equivalent-Noise-Sideband Input
ENT	Equivalent Noise Temperature
ENV	Equivalent Noise Voltage
EPS	Equivalent Prior Sample (Information) (Statistics)
ERD	Equivalent Residual Dose
ER	Equivalent Roentgen
ESR	Equivalent Series Resistance
ESR	Equivalent Service Rounds (A standard for indicating gun erosion)
ESHP	Equivalent Shaft Horsepower (Air Force)
ETSPL	Equivalent Threshold Sound Pressure Level
ETP	Equivalent Top Product
EWF	Equivalent-Weight Factor
Er	Erbium (Chemical element)
EOC	Erbium Oxide Crystal
ENV	Erdbeernekrosevirus
EIR	Erdgenoessisches Institut fuer Reaktorforschung (Switzerland)
E & M	Erection and Maintenance
EMMCC	Erection Mechanism Motor Control Center
ELGMT	Erector-Launcher, Guided Missile, Transportable
EKI	Eregli Komurleri Isletmesi
ER CAM	Eremitarum Camaldulensium (Monk Hermits of Camaldoli) (Roman Catholic religious order)
E	Erg
EEF	Erickson Educational Foundation
ECTI	Erie County Technical Institute (New York)
EL	Erie-Lackawanna R. R. (AAR code)
E	Erie-Lackawanna R. R. Company (NYSE symbol)
EPB	Erie & Pittsburgh R. R. Company (NYSE symbol)
ERIE	Erie R. R. (AAR code)
EAS	Error Analysis Study
ECI	Error Cause Identification (Military)
ECR	Error Cause Removal (Management)
EOC	Error of Closure
ECT	Error Control Translator (or Transmitter)
EC	Error Correcting (Data processing)
EDIT	Error Deletion by Iterative Transmission

ED .... Error Detecting (Data processing)
EDC .... Error Detecting Code
EDCG ...... Error Detection Code Generator
EDAC .... Error Detection and Correction
EDDF .... Error Detection and Decision Feedback
EDA .... Error Detector Assembly
EFP .... Error Free Performance
ERFC .... Error Function Complementary
ER .... Error Relay
ERRDEP ...... Error Variance Dependent on Level (Statistical test)
E .... Errors (Baseball)
EE .... Errors Excepted (Business and commerce)
EO........ Errors and Omissions
EOE .... Errors and Omissions Excepted
E and OE .... Errors and Omissions Excepted
ED .... Erythema Dose
EMF .... Erythrocyte Maturation Factor (Physiology)
ESR .... Erythrocyte Sedimentation Rate (Physiology)
ESF .... Erythropoietic Stimulating Factor (Physiology)
ELS .... Escanaba & Lake Superior R. R. (AAR code)
EAR .... Escape and Rescue
EFP .... Escaped Federal Prisoner
CVE .... Escort Aircraft Carrier (Navy symbol)
ESCARFOR.... Escort Carrier Force
DDE .... Escort Destroyer (Navy symbol)
CORTDIV..... Escort Division
ESCORTDIV ... Escort Division
ESCORTFIGHTRON .. Escort Fighter Squadron
VGF........ Escort-Fighting Squadron (Navy symbol)
EG .... Escort Group
ESCRG ...... Escort Guard
CVHE .... Escort Helicopter Aircraft Carrier (Navy symbol)
ESM........ Escort Mission (Military)
EOSO....... Escort Oilers Supervising Officer
AG .... Escort Research (Navy ship symbol)
AGDE....... Escort Research Ship (Navy symbol)
ESCORON.... Escort Scouting Squadron
VGS........ Escort-Scouting Squadron (Navy symbol)
BDE .... Escort Vessel (Lend-Lease to Great Britain)
DE .... Escort Vessel (Navy symbol)
PCE .... Escort Vessel (180 foot) (Navy symbol)
EVA .... Escort Vessel Administration (World War II)
EV .... Escort Vessels (Enemy)
E .... Escudo (Monetary unit of Portugal and its territories)
ESAN .... Escuela de Administracion de Negocios para Graduados (A graduate
       school of business administration) (Lima, Peru)
ESAPAC ..... Escuela Superior de Administracion Publica America Central (Costa Rica)
ESV .... Esophagal Valve
E .... Esophagus
EANA ...... Esperanto Association of North America
ELNA....... Esperanto League for North America
EJC .... Espoir de la Jeunesse Camerounaise (Hope of the Cameroonese Youth)
EN........ Esquimalt & Nanaimo Railway (AAR code)
EEA .... Essential Elements of Analysis
EEI........ Essential Elements of Information (Military)
EFA .... Essential Fatty Acids (Biochemistry)
EOA .... Essential Oil Association
ESAUS ...... Essential Oil Association of the United States
ETL .... Essex Terminal Railway (AAR code)
ESSOBA ..... Essor Social des Bashi (Social Development of the Bashi)
EC .... Established Church
EUB .... Estados Unidos do Brasil
E-B .... Estate-Bottling (Wine)
EJC .... Estherville Junior College (Iowa)
E .... Estimate or Estimated
EAT .... Estimated (or Estimating) Approach Time (Aviation)
ESTAR....... Estimated Arrival Date
EAD .... Estimated Availability Date (Military)
ECD........ Estimated Completion Date
ECT .... Estimated Completion Time
EDC .... Estimated Date of Completion
EDDFEC ..... Estimated Date of Departure Far East Command (Military)
EDS .... Estimated Date of Separation
EDD........ Estimated Delivery Date
EDT .... Estimated Delivery Times
EET .... Estimated Elapsed Time (Aviation)
ETI........ Estimated Information (Aviation)
EMTF .... Estimated Mean Time to Failure
EP .... Estimated Position (Navigation)
ESD .... Estimated Shipping Date
ETA .... Estimated Target Assurance

ETA .... Estimated Time of Arrival
ETB .... Estimated Time of Berthing (Navigation)
ETIC .... Estimated Time in Commission (Army)
ETOC .... Estimated Time out of Commission
ETC .... Estimated Time of Completion
ETD .... Estimated Time of Departure
ETE .... Estimated Time En Route
ETI........ Estimated Time of Interception
ETO .... Estimated Time Off
ETO .... Estimated Time Over (Aviation)
ETP .... Estimated Time of Penetration (Aviation)
ETDP .... Estimated Time and Point of DEWIZ (Distant Early Warning Identification
       Zone) Penetration
ETRA .... Estimated Time to Reach Altitude
ETR .... Estimated Time of Return
ETRO .... Estimated Time of Return to Operation (Military)
ETS .... Estimated Time of Sailing (Navigation)
ETP .... Estimated Turnaround Point
EPP .... Estimating Price Policy
EES .... Estonian Educational Society
ERC .... Estonian Relief Committee
ESAUSA ..... Estonian Student Association in the United States of America
ET AL....... Et Alibi (And Elsewhere)
ET AL....... Et Alii (And Others)
ETC .... Et Cetera (And So Forth)
EKN........ Eta Kappa Nu (Fraternity)
E-M........ Etat-Major (Headquarters) (French military)
E-U........ Etats-Unis (United States)
ECB .... Etched Circuit Board
ECS .... Etched Circuit Society
EMC........ Etched Metal Circuit
EP .... Etched Plate
ETL .... Etching by Transmitted Light
EQ......... Ethnic Quotient
EOKA....... Ethnike Organosis Kypriakou Agonos (Greece)
EAM........ Ethnikon Apeleutherotikon Metopon (National Liberation Front) (Greece)
EDES .... Ethnikos Demokratikos Ellenikos Stratos (Hellenic National Democratic
       Army) (Greek)
EBA .... Ethoxybenzoic Acid (Dental cement)
EMA........ Ethyl Methacrylate
EAA........ Ethylene Acrylic Acid
EDT .... Ethylene Diamine Tartrate
EB .... Ethylene Dibromide
EDB .... Ethylene Dibromide (Chemical)
EDC .... Ethylene Dichloride (Chemical)
EG......... Ethylene Glycol
EDMA....... Ethylene Glycol Dimethacrylate
EGDN .... Ethylene Glycol Dinitrate
EGME....... Ethylene Glycol Monomethyl Ether
EO......... Ethylene Oxide
ETO .... Ethylene Oxide
EOC........ Ethylene Oxide Cycle
EOD........ Ethylene Oxide Decontamination
EPDM....... Ethylene-Propylene Diene Monomer
EPR .... Ethylene Propylene Rubber
EPT .... Ethylene Propylene Terpolymer
EVA .... Ethylene Vinyl Acetate (Copolymer)
EDTA .... Ethylenediamine-Tetraacetate
EHPA .... Ethylhexyl Phosphoric Acid (Chemical)
EM......... Etna & Montrose R. R. (AAR code)
EGNA .... Eucharistic Guard for Nocturnal Adoration
EUC .... Euclid R. R. (AAR code)
EVDF .... Eugene V. Debs Foundation
ERP .... Euler-Rodrigues Parameter
EIN .... Eulerian Iterative Nonsteady (Method)
EKA .... Eureka Corporation, Ltd. (NYSE symbol)
EKU .... Eureka Pipe Line Company (American Stock Exchange symbol)
EFD .... Eurofund, Inc. (NYSE symbol)
ESU .... Europa Study Unit (An organization)
EVG........ Europaeische Verteidigungsgemeinschaft
EWG........ Europaeische Wirtschaftsgemeinschaft (European Economic Community)
EAME....... Europe-Africa-Middle East
EAC........ European Advisory Commission
EAC........ European Advisory Committee (Allied German Occupation Forces)
EAMECM..... European-African-Middle Eastern Campaign Medal
EAAC...... European Agricultural Aviation Centre
EAGGF...... European Agricultural Guidance and Guarantee Fund
EURAL...... European Air Lines
EATS .... European Air Transport Service
EARB .... European Airlines Research Bureau
EANA....... European Alliance of News Agencies

EACRP . . . . . . European-American Committee on Reactor Physics
EANDC . . . . . . European-American Nuclear Data Committee (OECD)
EACP . . . . European Area Communications Plan (Military)
EAAA . . . . European Association of Advertising Agencies
EAAS . . . . European Association for American Studies
EAMTC . . . . . . European Association of Management Training Centres
EAPR . . . . European Association for Potato Research
EURATOM . . . European Atomic Energy Community
EAES . . . . European Atomic Energy Society
EBC . . . . European Billiards Confederation
EBL . . . . European Bridge League
EBU . . . . European Broadcasting Union
EBYC . . . . European Bureau for Youth and Childhood
ECL . . . . European Calibration Line
ECIMOT . . . . . European Central Inland Movements of Transport
ECITO . . . . . . European Central Inland Transport Organization
ECMRA . . . . . . European Chemical Market Research Association
ECA . . . . European Civil Affairs
ECAD . . . . European Civil Affairs Division (US Military Government, Germany)
ECAR . . . . European Civil Affairs Regiment
ECAC . . . . European Civil Aviation Conference
ECO . . . . European Coal Organization
ECSC . . . . European Coal and Steel Community (France, West Germany, Italy, Benelux)
EUCOM . . . . . European Command (Military)
ECCC . . . . European Command Coordination Committee (Military)
ECCP . . . . European Committee on Crime Problems
ECP . . . . European Committee of Crop Protection
ECFA . . . . European Committee on Future Accelerators (Nuclear energy)
ECMBR . . . . . . European Committee on Milk-Butter-fat Recording
ECM . . . . European Common Market
EUROMART . . . European Common Market
ECSA . . . . European Communication Security Agency
ECIS . . . . European Community Information Service
ECMA . . . . European Computer Manufacturers' Association
ECA . . . . European Confederation of Agriculture
ECMEA . . . . . . European Conference of Meteorological Experts for Aeronautics
ECMT . . . . European Conference of Ministers of Transport
ECREA . . . . . . European Conference of Radiotelegraphy Experts for Aeronautics
ECC . . . . European Coordinating Committee
ECC . . . . European Cultural Centre
EDC . . . . European Defence Community (NATO)
EEC . . . . European Economic Community
EED . . . . European Enterprises Development Company (Luxembourg)
EES . . . . European Exchange System
EFPW . . . . European Federation for the Protection of Waters
TBE . . . . European Federation of Tile and Brick Manufacturers
EFC . . . . European Forestry Commission
EFF . . . . European Furniture Federation
EFTA . . . . European Free Trade Association (Known as the "Outer Seven" as opposed to the "Inner Six" Common Market nations)
EGM . . . . European Glass Container Manufacturers' Committee
EIRMA . . . . . . European Industrial Research Management Association
EUROSPACE . . . European Industrial Space Study Group
EIB . . . . European Investments Bank
ELF . . . . European Landworkers Federation
ELOISE . . . . . . European Large Orbiting Instrumentation for Solar Experiments
ELDO . . . . European Launch Development Organization
ELEC . . . . European League for Economic Cooperation
ELLA . . . . European Long Lines Agency (NATO)
EMD . . . . European Market Development
EUM . . . . European-Mediterranean (Military)
EPPO . . . . European and Mediterranean Plant Protection Organization
EMCCC . . . . . . European Military Communications Co-ordinating Committee (NATO)
EMU . . . . European Mineworkers' Union (Zambia)
EMBO . . . . . . European Molecular Biology Organization
EMA . . . . European Monetary Agreement
EMF . . . . European Motel Federation
EM . . . . European Movement
EMCC . . . . . . European Municipal Credit Community
ENCA . . . . European Naval Communications Agency (NATO)
ENDS . . . . European Nuclear Documentation System
ENEA . . . . European Nuclear Energy Agency
EOAR . . . . European Office of Aerospace Research (Air Force)
EOARDC . . . . . European Office Air Research and Development Command
EUROCAE . . . . European Organization for Civil Aviation Electronics
EOQC . . . . European Organization for Quality Control
EUROCONTROL . . European Organization for the Safety of Air Navigation
EPU . . . . European Payments Union
EPG . . . . European Press Group
EPA . . . . European Productivity Agency

ERFA . . . . European Radio Frequency Agency (NATO)
EURAILPASS . . . European Railway Passenger (Ticket)
ERP . . . . European Recovery Program
ERO . . . . European Regional Organization of the ICFTU
ERL . . . . European Requirements List (Military)
ERA . . . . European Research Associates
ERO . . . . European Research Office
ESOMAR . . . . . European Society for Opinion Surveys and Market Research
ESRS . . . . European Society for Rural Sociology
ESO . . . . European Southern Observatory (La Silla Mountain, Chile)
ESDAC . . . . . . European Space Data Center
ESLO . . . . European Space Launcher Organization
ESOC . . . . European Space Operations Center
ESRANGE . . . . European Space Range (Sweden)
ESRIN . . . . European Space Research Institute
ESRO . . . . European Space Research Organization
ESTEC . . . . European Space Technology Center
ESTRACK . . . . . European Space Tracking and Telemetry Network
EUR/SV/LDO . . European Space Vehicle Launcher Development Organization
ETOG . . . . European Technical Operations Group
EUROVISION . . European Television
ET . . . . European Theater
ETO . . . . European Theater of Operations (World War II)
ETOUSA . . . . . European Theater of Operations, United States Army (World War II)
ETC . . . . European Translations Center
ETO . . . . European Transport Organization (ECE)
ETC . . . . European Travel Commission
ETA . . . . European Tropospheric – Army
EUF . . . . European Union of Federalists
EUW . . . . European Union of Women
EVW . . . . European Voluntary Worker
EWRC . . . . European Weed Research Council
EWCS . . . . European Wideband Communications System (Army)
EYC . . . . European Youth Campaign
Eu . . . . Europium (Chemical element)
ESA . . . . Euthanasia Society of America
ETA . . . . Euzkadi Ta Azkatasuna (Long Live Basque Freedom) (An organization in Spain)
E & E . . . . Evacuation and Evasion
AHP . . . . Evacuation Hospital Ship (Navy symbol)
EVM . . . . Evacuation Mission (Air Force)
EU . . . . Evacuation Unit (Army)
EAG . . . . Evaluation and Analysis Group (Navy)
EAS . . . . Evaluation and Analysis Staff (Navy)
EGRESS . . . . . . Evaluation of Glide Reentry Structural Systems
ER . . . . Evaluation Report
ESAWC . . . . . . Evaluation Staff, War College (Air Force)
ETS . . . . Evaluation Trainers
EPIC . . . . Evaluator Programmer Integrated Circuit (NASA)
EES . . . . Evangelical Education Society of the Protestant Episcopal Church
EFMA . . . . Evangelical Foreign Missions Association
ELO . . . . Evangelical Literature Overseas
EPA . . . . Evangelical Press Association
ERHS . . . . Evangelical & Reformed Historical Society
ETTA . . . . Evangelical Teacher Training Association
ETS . . . . Evangelical Theological Society
EU . . . . Evangelical Union (British)
EUB . . . . Evangelical United Brethren (Church)
EVNG . . . . . . Evangeline Railway Company (AAR code)
EKD . . . . Evangelische Kirche Deutschlands
E . . . . Evangelist (Church calendars)
EM . . . . Evangelist and Martyr (Church calendars)
ECF . . . . "Evangelize China" Fellowship
EVY . . . . Evans Products Company (NYSE symbol)
ESL . . . . Evans Signal Laboratory (Army)
EMA . . . . Evaporated Milk Association
ECP . . . . Evaporative Cooling Processor
ECT . . . . Evaporative Cooling Techniques
EEC . . . . Evaporative Emission Control (Antipollution device for automobiles)
ELCD . . . . Evaporative Loss Control Device (Motor exhaust control)
E & E . . . . Evasion and Escape (Military)
EJC . . . . Eveleth Junior College (Minnesota)
ESF . . . . Even Side Flat
EP . . . . Evening Prayer
ESPA . . . . Evening Student Personnel Association
E . . . . Evensong
ERL . . . . Event Record Log
ESDU . . . . Event Storage and Distribution Unit
ETD . . . . Event Time Digitizer
EPUT . . . . Events Per Unit Time
EJC . . . . Everett Junior College (Washington)

EV . . . . Everett R. R. (AAR code)
EVER . . . . Everglades National Park
EVR . . . . Eversharp, Inc. (NYSE symbol)
Q4H . . . . Every Fourth Hour (Medicine)
EMF . . . . Every Morning Fixum (An old car) (Slang)
EOD . . . . Every Other Day (Advertising)
Q2H . . . . Every Second Hour (Medicine)
Q3H . . . . Every Third Hour (Medicine)
E . . . . Evidence (Law)
ERD . . . . Evoked Response Detector
ECHO . . . . . . Evolution of Competing Hierarchical Organizations
EVOP . . . . . . Evolutionary Operation
EKO . . . . Evreiskoe Kolonizatsionnoe Obshchestvo (Jewish Colonization Association)
X-C . . . . Ex-Coupon (Without the right to coupons, as of a bond) (Finance)
XDIS . . . . Ex-Distribution (NYSE symbol)
ED . . . . Ex-Dividend
X-D . . . . Ex-Dividend (Without the right to dividend) (NYSE symbol)
X-I . . . . Ex-Interest (Without the right to interest) (Finance)
XIN . . . . Ex (Without) Interest (Stock brokerage)
XN . . . . Ex-New (NYSE symbol)
EO . . . . Ex Officio
XPR . . . . Ex (Without) Privileges (Stock brokerage)
XRT . . . . Ex-Rights (NYSE symbol)
EXTM . . . . . . Ex Testamento (In Accordance with the Testament Of)
EV . . . . Ex Voto (In Fulfillment of a Vow)
EDE . . . . Exact Differential Equation
XYL . . . . Ex-Young-Lady (i.e., a former sweetheart) (Slang)
END . . . . Exaltation Newcastle Disease
X . . . . An Examination (Slang)
EOA . . . . Examination, Opinion, and Advice (Medicine)
EPO . . . . Examination Procedure Outline (Weighing equipment)
ERAN . . . . . . Examine and Repair As Necessary
E . . . . Excellence; Excellency; Excellent
ECB-P . . . . . . Excellence-in-Competition Badge (Pistol) (Army)
ECB-R . . . . . . Excellence-in-Competition Badge (Rifle) (Army)
E . . . . "Excellence in Production" (Army-Navy "E" awarded manufactures) (World War II)
XLO . . . . Ex-Cell-O Corporation (NYSE symbol)
EOHP . . . . . . Except as Otherwise Herein Provided
EAON . . . . . . Except as Otherwise Noted
EN . . . . Exception Noted
ETA . . . . Exception Time Accounting
EWQ . . . . . . Exceptionally Well Qualified
EMF . . . . Excerpta Medica Foundation
ECRA . . . . . . Excess and Casualty Reinsurance Association
XL . . . . Excess Lactate
ENR . . . . Excess Noise Ratio
EP . . . . Excess Profits
EPD . . . . Excess Profits Duty
EPL . . . . Excess Profits Levy (British)
EPT . . . . Excess Profits Tax
ETC . . . . Excess Three Code
X . . . . Exchange
EIVR . . . . Exchange of Information, Visits and Reports
ERILCO . . . . . . Exchange of Ready for Issue in Lieu of Concurrent Overhaul
EPSP . . . . . . Excitatory Post-Synaptic Potential (Physiology)
X . . . . Exclusive (Concession in a circus or carnival)
EXDIS . . . . . . Exclusive Distribution
EC . . . . Excretory Cell
ED . . . . Excused from Duty
EFD . . . . Excused from Duty
XIO . . . . Execute Input/Output
EXAGT . . . . . . Executive Agent
EBT . . . . Executive Business Transport (Aircraft)
ECA . . . . Executive Chef Association
ECCAA . . . . . Executive Chefs de Cuisine Association of America
ECCP . . . . . . Executive Committee on Commercial Policy (Abolished, 1944)
ECP . . . . Executive Control Program
ECS . . . . Executive Control System
EG . . . . Executive Generator
EGIS . . . . . . Executive Guide to Information Sources (A publication) (Later, EBIS)
EJA . . . . Executive Jet Aviation, Inc.
ELJ . . . . Executive-Legislative-Judicial
EMR . . . . Executive Management Responsibility (Military)
EMG . . . . Executive Mansion and Grounds (i.e., the White House and its grounds) (Executive Office of the President)
EOB . . . . Executive Office Building (Washington, DC)
EOP . . . . Executive Office of the President
EXOS . . . . . . Executive Office of the Secretary (Navy)
NAVEXOS . . . . Executive Office of the Secretary Publications (Navy)

EO . . . . Executive Officer
EXO . . . . Executive Officer
XO . . . . Executive Officer (Military)
EOC . . . . Executive Officers Council
EO . . . . Executive Order (Rule or regulation having the force of law, issued by the President with congressional authorization)
ES . . . . Executive Secretary
ESC . . . . Executive Seminar Center (Civil Service Commission)
ESCA . . . . . . Executive Stewards' and Caterers' Association
XVP . . . . Executive Vice President
EVC . . . . Executive Volunteer Corps
ESI . . . . Executives' Secretaries, Incorporated
ESS . . . . Executive's Shopping Service
EC . . . . Exempli Causa (For the Sake of Example)
EG . . . . Exempli Gratia (For Example)
ECO . . . . Exempted by Commanding Officer
EH . . . . Exercise Head
EC . . . . Exhaust Closes (Valve position)
EDA . . . . Exhaust Deflection Angle
EGT . . . . Exhaust-Gas Temperature
EO . . . . Exhaust Opens (Valve position)
EPR . . . . Exhaust Pressure Ratio
EDPA . . . . . . Exhibit Designers and Producers Association
EPDA . . . . . . Exhibit Producers and Designers Association
EAC . . . . Exhibitors Advisory Council
ESPWO . . . . . Exigencies of the Service Having Been Such as to Preclude the Issuance of Competent Written Orders in Advance
EPTE . . . . . . Existed Prior to Enlistment (Especially, dependency)
EPTE . . . . . . Existed Prior to Entry
EPTS . . . . . . Existed Prior to Entry Service
EPTI . . . . . . Existed Prior to Induction (Especially, dependency or physical defect)
ED . . . . Existence Doubtful (Navigation charts)
EGV . . . . Exit Guide Vane
EPA . . . . Exoatmospheric Penetration Aid
EPF . . . . Exophthalmos-Producing Factor (Endocrinology)
EPS . . . . Exophthalmos-Producing Substance (Endocrinology)
ESP . . . . Expandable Stored Program
EWT . . . . Expandable Wing Tank
EWTS . . . . . . Expandable Wing Tank Structure
EBI . . . . Expanded Background Investigation
EXBEDCAP . . . . Expanded Bed Capacity
ECSA . . . . . . Expanded Clay and Shale Association
EXCELS . . . . . . Expanded Communications - Electronics System (DOD)
EDDD . . . . . . Expanded Direct Distance Dialing (Telephone)
ED . . . . Expanded Display
XFLT . . . . Expanded Flight Line Tester
EM . . . . Expanded Metal
EPI . . . . Expanded Position Indicator
EXPERT . . . . . . Expanded Program Evaluation and Review Technique
EPTA . . . . . . Expanded Program of Technical Assistance (UN)
ERS . . . . Expanded RADAR Service
ERSER . . . . . . Expanded Reactance Series Resonator
ESV . . . . Expanded Service Volume
ESCS . . . . . . Expanded Shale Clay and Slate Institute
ESCSI . . . . . . Expanded Shale Clay and Slate Institute
ETAP . . . . . . Expanded Technical Assist Program (of UN)
ETAB . . . . . . Expanded Technical Assistance Board (UN)
ET . . . . Expander Tube
ESPPI . . . . . . Expanding and Specialty Paper Products Institute
EJI . . . . Expansion Joint Institute
EJMA . . . . . . Expansion Joint Manufacturers Association
ERMA . . . . . . Expansion Rate Measuring Apparatus
ESCAPE . . . . . . Expansion Symbolic Compiling Assembly Program for Engineers
EC . . . . Expansive Classification
EACNL . . . . . . Expect Approach Clearance Not Later Than (Aviation)
ETA . . . . Expect to Arrive
EDC . . . . Expect Departure Clearance (Aviation)
EDR . . . . Expect Departure Release (Aviation)
EFC . . . . Expect Further Clearance (Aviation)
EHA . . . . Expect Higher Altitude (Aviation)
EVT . . . . Expect Vector To (Aviation)
EAC . . . . Expected Approach Clearance (Aviation)
EAT . . . . Expected Approach Time
EAL . . . . Expected Average Life
EDC . . . . Expected Date of Confinement (Obstetrics)
EDD . . . . Expected Date of Delivery (Obstetrics)
EOF . . . . Expected Operations Forecast (Aviation)
EQL . . . . Expected Quality Level
EXPHO . . . . . . Expedite Delivery by Telephone
EXREP . . . . . . Expedite Mail Reply

EF . . . . Expeditionary Force
EFM . . . . Expeditionary Force Message (Low-rate cable or radio message selected from a list of standard wordings)
XFM . . . . Expeditionary Force Message (Usually, EFM)
ERRC . . . . Expendability, Recoverability, Reparability Cost
XBT . . . . Expendable Bathythermograph (Naval Oceanographic Office)
EER . . . . Expendable-Expendable-Reusable
EIS . . . . Expendable Instrument System
EXACCT . . . . . Expenditure Account
EAN . . . . Expenditure Account Number
EOB . . . . Expense Operating Budget
EU . . . . Experience Unit
EEM . . . . Experienced Export Manager (Designation given by American Society of International Executives)
EP . . . . An Experienced Playgoer (Theatrical)
X & D . . . . . . Experiment and Development (Flotilla) (Landing Craft)
EIS . . . . Experiment Information System
EIL . . . . Experiment in International Living
E . . . . Experimental, when precedes vessel classification (Navy)
XN . . . . Experimental (Navy)
XAAM . . . . . . Experimental Air-to-Air Missile (Air Force, NASA)
XASM . . . . . . Experimental Air-to-Surface Missile (Air Force, NASA)
EAA . . . . Experimental Aircraft Association
EAE . . . . Experimental Allergic Encephalomyelitis
EAST . . . . Experimental Army Satellite, Tactical
EASTT . . . . . . Experimental Army Satellite Tactical Terminals
EASL . . . . Experimental Assembly and Sterilization Laboratory (NASA)
EBA . . . . Experimental Behavioral Analyzer
EBOR . . . . . . Experimental Beryllium Oxide Reactor (Later, BORE) (AEC)
EBWR . . . . . . Experimental Boiling Water Reactor (Nuclear reactor)
XB . . . . Experimental Bomber
EBR . . . . Experimental Breeder Reactor (AEC)
XBR . . . . Experimental Breeder Reactor
XC . . . . Experimental Cargo Aircraft
XCG . . . . Experimental Cargo Glider
ECC . . . . Experimental Computer Complex
ECHO . . . . . . Experimental Contract Highlight Operation (NASA)
EDHE . . . . . . Experimental Data Handling Equipment
EDTR . . . . . . Experimental, Developmental, Test and Research
EDGE . . . . . . Experimental Display Generator
EDU . . . . Experimental Diving Unit
EXPDIVUNIT . . Experimental Diving Unit
EXDIV . . . . . . Experimental Division
EDU . . . . Experimental Drive Unit
EEP . . . . Experimental Education Program
XE . . . . Experimental Engine (NASA)
EFCR . . . . Experimental Fast Ceramic Reactor
XF . . . . Experimental Fighter
EAG . . . . Experimental Firing Ship (Navy symbol)
EF . . . . Experimental Flight
EFT . . . . Experimental Flight Test
EGCR . . . . . . Experimental Gas-Cooled Reactor (AEC)
XGAM . . . . . . Experimental Guided Air Missiles
XH . . . . Experimental Helicopter
EXAMETNET . . Experimental Inter-American Meteorological Rocket Network (NASA)
XLR . . . . Experimental Liquid Rocket (Air Force, NASA)
ELPHR . . . . . . Experimental Low Temperature Process Heat Reactor
EMSS . . . . Experimental Manned Space Station (Air Force)
EM . . . . Experimental Memo
EMAR . . . . . . Experimental Memory - Address Register
ZMC . . . . Experimental Metal-Clad Airship (Navy)
XM . . . . Experimental Missile (Air Force, NASA)
EMB . . . . Experimental Model Basin (Navy)
EOC . . . . Experimental Operations Center
EOCR . . . . . . Experimental Organic Cooled Reactor (AEC)
EPS . . . . Experimental Procurement Service
EPCOT . . . . . . Experimental Prototype Community of Tomorrow
EPGCR . . . . . . Experimental Prototype Gas-Cooled Reactor
EPE . . . . Experimental and Proving Establishment (Canada)
EROS . . . . Experimental Reflector Orbital Shot (NASA project)
ERMU . . . . . . Experimental Remote Maneuvering Unit
ERGS . . . . Experimental Route Guidance System (US Bureau of Public Roads)
ERK . . . . Experimental Research Kit
ERS . . . . Experimental Research Society
ESS . . . . Experimental SAGE (Semi-Automatic Ground Environment) Sector
XSPV . . . . Experimental Solid Propellant Vehicle
ESSEX . . . . . . Experimental Solid State Exchange
XSL . . . . Experimental Space Laboratory
XSS . . . . Experimental Space Station (NASA)
ES . . . . Experimental Station
EXSTA . . . . . . Experimental Station

XSM . . . . Experimental Strategic Missile
XSM . . . . Experimental Surface Missile
ETDE . . . . Experimental Target Designation Equipment
XQ . . . . Experimental Target Drone (Air Force, NASA)
EUCLID . . . . . . Experimental Use Computer, London Integrated Display
XW . . . . Experimental Warhead
XWS . . . . Experimental Weapon System (or Specification)
EC . . . . Experimentation Command (Army)
EAT . . . . Experiments in Art and Technology, Inc.
EDAM . . . . . . Experiments, Drill and Maintenance
EG . . . . Expert Gunner (Army)
EIB . . . . Expert Infantryman's Badge
EIBAD . . . . . . Expert Infantryman Badge
ER . . . . Expert Rifleman
EAOS . . . . Expiration of Active Obligated Service
EE . . . . Expiration of Enlistment
E of E . . . . . . Expiration of Enlistment
E of S . . . . . . Expiration of Service
ETS . . . . Expiration Term of Service
EC . . . . Expiratory Center (Physiology)
ERV . . . . Expiratory Reserve Volume (Physiology)
EBW . . . . Exploding Bridge Wire
XB . . . . Exploding Bridgewire
EWP . . . . Exploding Wire Phenomena
ECAPE . . . . . . Exploratory Committee on Assessing the Progress of Education
EDG . . . . Exploratory Development Goal (DOD)
EDM . . . . Exploratory Development Model
EDR . . . . Exploratory Development Request (DOD)
EDR . . . . Exploratory Development Requirement (Navy)
EC . . . . Explorers Club
EP . . . . Explosion-Proof
EPE . . . . Explosion-Proof Enclosure
EPH . . . . Explosion-Proof Housing
EPR . . . . Explosion-Proof Relay
EAV . . . . Explosive Actuated Valve
EER . . . . Explosive Echo Ranging
EET . . . . Explosive-to-Electric Transducer
EGI . . . . Explosive Gas Indicator
ELF . . . . Explosive Lens Flashbinder
EMF . . . . Explosive Metal Forming
EO . . . . Explosive Ordnance
EOD . . . . Explosive, Ordnance, and Demolition
EOD . . . . Explosive Ordnance Disposal
EODB . . . . Explosive Ordnance Disposal Bulletin
EODC . . . . . . Explosive Ordnance Disposal Control (Army)
EOR . . . . Explosive Ordnance Reconnaissance
EORA . . . . . . Explosive Ordnance Reconnaissance Agent (Army)
EPOMA . . . . . . Explosive and Pyrotechnic Ordnance Manufacturing Association
ERDE . . . . . . Explosive Research and Development Establishment (British)
ESA . . . . Explosive Safe Area (NASA)
ECA . . . . Explosives Corporation of America
EXCOA . . . . . . Explosives Corporation of America
EIL . . . . Explosives Investigation Laboratory
EIM . . . . Explosives Investigation Memorandum (Navy)
ER . . . . Explosives Report
ERM . . . . Explosives Research Memorandum
ERN . . . . Explosives Research Note
EHF . . . . Exponential Hazard Function
ERF . . . . Exponential Reliability Function
ERD . . . . Exponentially Retrograded Diode
E . . . . Export
ECRB . . . . . . Export Control Review Board
EGA . . . . Export Guarantees Act
E-IB . . . . Export-Import Bank
EXIM . . . . . . Export-Import Bank
EIB(W) . . . . . . Export-Import Bank (of Washington)
EPANY . . . . . . Export Packers Association of New York
EPA . . . . Export Pound Account (Special type of currency) (United Arab Republic)
ETR . . . . Export Traffic Release
ECGD . . . . . . Exports Credit Guarantee Department
EMA . . . . Exposition Management Association
E . . . . Exposure
ECT . . . . Exposure Control Technique
EGC . . . . Exposure Growth Curve
EI . . . . Exposure Index (Photography)
XP . . . . Express Paid
XPT . . . . Express Paid Telegraph
ETO . . . . Express Transportation Order (Army)
A-OK . . . . Expression meaning in perfect working order (Popularized during early development of NASA's space program)
EAD . . . . Extended Active Duty

EASCOMINT . . Extended Air Surveillance Communications Intercept (Air Force)
EAS . . . . Extended Area Service (Telephone communications)
EBCDIC. . . . . . Extended Binary-Coded Decimal Interchange Code (Data processing)
EC . . . . Extended Coverage (Insurance)
ECE . . . . Extended Coverage Endorsement (Insurance)
ELM . . . . Extended Lunar Module
EMA. . . . . Extended Mission Apollo (Aerospace)
ENS . . . . Extended Nylon Shaft
EPIC . . . . Extended Performance & Increased Capability
EP . . . . Extended Play
ER . . . . Extended Range
ERBM . . . . Extended-Range Ballistic Missile
EXTRADOP . . . Extended Range Doppler
ERFPI . . . . Extended Range Floating Point Interpretive System
XRL . . . . Extended Range Lance (Missile)
ERSC . . . . Extended Range and Space Communication
ERZ . . . . Extended Reconnaissance Zone (Army)
ER . . . . Extended Release (Pharmacy)
ESQT . . . . Extended Sterilization Qualification Test
ETT . . . . Extended Time Tests
EUVT . . . . Extended Ultraviolet Transmission
EWW . . . . Extended Work Week
ECOP . . . . Extension Committee on Organization and Policy
EC . . . . Extension and Conversion (Public buildings)
EC . . . . Extension Course
ECI . . . . Extension Course Institute (Air Force)
EGS . . . . Extension of the Gastric Shield
ELV . . . . Extension Lay Volunteers
EXTLV . . . . . . Extension of Leave (Army)
EMIS . . . . Extension Management Information System (Department of Agriculture)
ESV . . . . Extension Society Volunteers
EAS . . . . Extensive Air Shower
EW. . . . . Extensive Wound
ES . . . . Exterior Surface
ECDC . . . . External Count-Down Clock
ED . . . . External Device
EDCW. . . . . . . External-Device Control Word
EE . . . . External Environment
EFE . . . . External Field Emission
EXGA. . . . . . . External Gage
ELM . . . . External Limiting Membrane
EM. . . . . External Memorandum
EMSN. . . . . . . External-Mix Spray Nut
EPT . . . . External Pipe Thread (Technical drawings)
EP . . . . External Pressure
EPV . . . . External Pressure Vessel
EPB . . . . External Proton Beam
EP . . . . External Publication
ERJ . . . . External Ramjet
ERP . . . . External Ramjet Program
ER . . . . External Report
ER . . . . External Resistance (Physics)
ESR . . . . External Standard Ratio
ETM. . . . . External Technical Memorandum
ETR . . . . External Technical Report
ETG . . . . External Thermal Garment
ETR . . . . External Timing Register
EVDE . . . . External Visual Display Equipment (Used in Apollo mission)
ECF . . . . Externally Caused Failure
EQC. . . . . Externally-Quenched Counter
ESI. . . . . Externally Specified Indexing
X . . . . Extra (As in x-hvy, or extra-heavy)
EBB . . . . Extra Best Best (Steel wire)
ED . . . . Extra Duty (Marine Corps)
XXS . . . . Extra Extra Strong
EF . . . . Extra Fine (Threads)
XF . . . . Extra Fine
EHR . . . . Extra High Reliability
XHR. . . . . Extra High Reliability

EI . . . . Extra-Illustrated
EHT . . . . Extra High Tension
EHV . . . . Extra-High Voltage (FPC)
XL . . . . Extra Large
ELD . . . . Extra-Long Distance
ELS . . . . Extra-Long Staple (Cotton)
XLWB . . . . Extra Long Wheel Base
ELC . . . . Extra Low Carbon
ELI. . . . . Extra Low Impurity (Metals)
ELI. . . . . Extra-Low-Interstitial (Alloy)
XLI . . . . Extra Low Interstitial
EOM . . . . Extra-Ocular Movements
XOS. . . . . Extra Outside (Clothing)
EPD . . . . Extra Police Duty (Extra cleaning chores) (Military)
ES . . . . Extra Series
XS . . . . Extra Strong
EXTAL . . . . . . Extra Time Allowance
EVEA . . . . Extra Vehicular Engineering Activity
ECF . . . . Extracellular Fluid (Physiology)
ECI . . . . Extracorporeal Irradiation
EXREQ . . . . . . Extract of Requisition
ETI. . . . . Extraction Tool Insert
EZ . . . . Extraction Zone (Military)
EZCO. . . . . . . Extraction Zone Control Officer (Military)
ETTO . . . . Extractor Tool
EHBF . . . . Extrahepatic Blood Flow (Medicine)
EARC . . . . Extraordinary Administrative Radio Conference (ITU)
EEW . . . . Extraordinary Electromagnetic Wave
E & P. . . . . . . Extraordinary and Plenipotentiary
ESP . . . . Extrasensory Perception
ETH . . . . Extraterrestrial Hypothesis
ETI. . . . . Extraterrestrial Intelligence
EVA . . . . Extravehicular Activity (Aerospace)
ELSS. . . . . EVA (Extravehicular Activity) Life-Support System
EMU . . . . Extravehicular Mobility Unit (Spacesuit)
EVO. . . . . Extravehicular Operation (Aerospace)
EVSTC . . . . . . Extravehicular Suit Telemetry and Communication
ESP . . . . Extravehicular Support Pack (NASA)
EVS . . . . Extravehicular System (Aerospace)
E-I. . . . . Extraversion-Introversion (Jungian psychology)
XHV . . . . Extreme High Vacuum
EHW . . . . Extreme High Water
ELW . . . . Extreme Low Water
E-P . . . . Extreme Pressure
EUV . . . . Extreme Ultraviolet (NASA)
XUV. . . . . Extreme Ultraviolet
EUVT . . . . Extreme Ultraviolet Telescope
EF . . . . Extremely Fine
EHF . . . . Extremely High Frequency (Electronics, radio wave)
ELF . . . . Extremely Low Frequency
ESI. . . . . Extremely Sensitive Information (Army)
EBS . . . . Extruded Bar Solder
EVB . . . . Extruded Vinyl Bumper
EVCS . . . . Extruded Vinyl Chamfer Strip
E . . . . Eye
EBI. . . . . Eye Ball In
EBO. . . . . Eye Ball Out
EBSR. . . . . Eye-Bank for Sight Restoration
EE . . . . Eye and Ear
EMC. . . . . Eye-Motion Camera
EMG . . . . Eye Movement Gauge
EMMA . . . . . . Eye-Movement Measuring Apparatus
EPS . . . . Eye Protection Shutter
ES . . . . Eye Stalk
EIM . . . . Eyelet Installing Machine
EB . . . . Eyepiece Box
EENT . . . . Eyes, Ears, Nose, and Throat (Medicine)
ERI . . . . Eyes Right
EIS. . . . . Eyes in the Sky

F

FLJ . . . . F. L. Jacobs Company (NYSE symbol)
Z . . . . F. W. Woolworth Company (NYSE symbol) (Wall Street slang name:
     "Five & Dime")
FIAT . . . . Fabbrica Italiana Automobile, Torino (Italian automobile manufacturer;
     acronym used as name of its cars)
FIM . . . . Fabric Insulation Material
FLA . . . . Fabric Laminators Association
FUNSA . . . . . Fabrica Uruguaya de Neumaticos, SA (A tire manufacturer)
FIRST . . . . . . Fabrication of Inflatable Reentry Structures for Test (Air Force)
FIT . . . . Fabrication, Integration, and Test
FMG . . . . . . Fabricated Metal Goods
FN . . . . Fabrique Nationale (d'Armes de Guerre, Societe Anonyme)
FSS . . . . Fabrique Suisse d'Explosifs
FPI . . . . Fabry-Perot Interferometer
FSO . . . . Fabryka Samochodow Osbowych (Poland)
FCC . . . . Face-Centered Cubic (Metallography)
FCT . . . . Face-Centered Tetragonal (Metallography)
F to F . . . . . . Face to Face (Technical drawings)
FM . . . . Face Measurement
FACTS . . . . . . Facilities Action Control Target System (Post Office Department)
FACTS . . . . . . Facilities Administration Control and Time Schedule
FAP . . . . Facilities Assistance Program
FC . . . . Facilities Contract
FCRU . . . . . . Facilities Control Relay Unit (Army)
FEC . . . . Facilities Engineering Command (Navy) (Formerly, Bureau of Yards
     and Docks)
FIS . . . . Facilities Inventory Study
FMC . . . . Facilities Management Contract
FRS . . . . Facilities Requirements Study
FSE . . . . Facilities System Engineer
FAST . . . . . . Facility for Automatic Sorting and Testing
FCR . . . . Facility Capability Report (Military)
FCR . . . . Facility Capability Review
FCIR . . . . Facility Change Initiation Request
FCR . . . . Facility Change Request
FCF SE . . . . . . Facility Checking Flight - Service Evaluation (Air Force)
FCB . . . . Facility Clearance Board (WPB)
FCEI . . . . Facility Contract End Item
FDR . . . . Facility Data Report (AEC)
FGC . . . . Facility Group Control (Military)
FRC . . . . Facility Review Committee
FSP . . . . Facility Security Program (World War II)
FUB . . . . Facility Utilization Board
FUP . . . . Facility Utilization Plan
FWG . . . . . . Facility Working Group
FTI . . . . Facing Tile Institute
FCS . . . . Facsimile Communications System
INTRAFAX . . . Facsimile System (Western Union trade name)
FTS . . . . Facsimile Text Society
FACTS . . . . . Facsimile Transmission System
FAC . . . . Factor & Company (Max) (NYSE symbol)
FS . . . . Factor of Safety
FAT . . . . Factory Acceptance Test
FACO . . . . . . Factory Assembly and Check-Out
FACE . . . . . . Factory Automatic Checkout Equipment
FETO . . . . . . Factory Equipment Transfer Order
FIMATE . . . . . . Factory-Installed Maintenance Automatic Test Equipment
FIA . . . . Factory Insurance Association
FMA . . . . Factory Materials Association
FO . . . . Factory Order
FT . . . . Factory Test
FTE . . . . Factory Test Equipment
FTEM . . . . . . Factory Test Equipment Manufacturing

FTS . . . . Factory Test Set
FTS . . . . Factory Training School
FWG . . . . . . Factory Work Group
FLACSO . . . . Facultad Latinoamericana de Ciencias Sociales (Santiago, Chile)
FPI . . . . Faded Prior to Interception (RADAR)
FTF . . . . Faellesraadet for Danske Tjenestemands-og Funktionaerorganisationer
     (Federation of Civil Servants' and Salaried Employees' Organizations)
     (Denmark)
FAF . . . . Faellesrepraesentationen for Danske Arbejdsleder- og Tekniske
     Funktinaerforeninger (Council of Danish Supervisors' and Technical
     Employees' Associations)
FDB . . . . Faelliesforeningen for Danmarks Brugsforeninger (Denmark)
FAF . . . . Fafnir Bearing Company (NYSE symbol)
F . . . . Fahrenheit
FEDAL . . . . . . Failed Element Detection and Location
F . . . . Failure
FAC . . . . Failure Analysis Coordinator
FAR . . . . Failure Analysis Report
FAS . . . . Failure Analysis Section
FCDR . . . . . . Failure Cause Data Report
FC . . . . Failure Count
FDF . . . . Failure Density Function
FEA . . . . Failure Effect Analysis
FE . . . . Failure Equation
FEQ . . . . Failure Equation
FIF . . . . Failure Indicating Fuse
FIM . . . . Failure Indication Modules
FMA . . . . Failure Mode Analysis
FMEA . . . . . . Failure Mode and Effect Analysis
FR . . . . Failure Rate
FARADA . . . . Failure Rate Data Program (Navy)
FARR . . . . . . Failure and Rejection Report
FRR . . . . Failure and Replacement Report
FR . . . . Failure Report
FUR . . . . Failure, Unsatisfactory or Removal
FUR . . . . Failure or Unsatisfactory Report
FURS . . . . . . Failure or Unsatisfactory Report System
FWAS . . . . . . Failure Warning and Analysis System
F . . . . Fair
FAIR . . . . . . Fair Access to Insurance Requirements
FAQ . . . . Fair Average Quality
FCPC . . . . . . Fair Campaign Practices Committee
FEPA . . . . . . Fair Educational Practice Act (New York, New Jersey, Massachusetts)
FEB . . . . Fair Employment Board (of Civil Service Commission) (Abolished, 1955)
FEP . . . . Fair Employment Practice
FEPC . . . . . . Fair Employment Practice Committee (or Commission)
FEPA . . . . . . Fair Employment Practices Act
FHI . . . . Fair Housing, Incorporated
FAIR . . . . Fair and Impartial Random Selection (System) (Military draft)
FLSA . . . . . . Fair Labor Standards Act
FMV . . . . Fair Market Value
FPLA . . . . . . Fair Packaging and Labeling Act
FWT . . . . Fair Wear and Tear
FWC . . . . Fair Weather Current
FAS . . . . Fairbanks Air Service (Alaska)
FKM . . . . Fairbanks Morse & Company (NYSE symbol) (Later, Colt Industries)
FW . . . . Fairbanks Whitney Corporation (NYSE symbol) (Wall Street slang name:
     "Fuzzy Wuzzy") (Later, Colt Industries, Inc.)
FJC . . . . Fairbury Junior College (Nebraska)
FA . . . . Fairchild Aircraft
FACT . . . . . . Fairchild Assured Component Test
FCI . . . . Fairchild Camera & Instrument Corporation (NYSE symbol)
FCIC . . . . . . Fairchild Camera and Instrument Corporation

FEAC . . . . Fairchild Engine and Airplane Corporation
FCS . . . . Fairchild Semiconductor
FEN . . . . Fairchild Stratos Corporation (NYSE symbol)
FS . . . . Faire Suivre (Please Forward)
FDU . . . . Fairleigh Dickinson University (New Jersey)
FIP. . . . . Fairly Important Person
FMF . . . . Fairmont Foods Company (NYSE symbol)
FSC . . . . Fairmont State College (West Virginia)
FPE . . . . Fairport, Painesville & Eastern R. R. (AAR code)
FTS . . . . Faith Theological Seminary
FSB . . . . Falange Socialista Boliviana (Bolivian Socialist Falange)
FIP. . . . . Falcon Improvement Program
FLSS. . . . . . . Falcon Launching Saber System
FJCC . . . . Fall Joint Computer Conference
FBC . . . . Fallen Building Clause
FMH. . . . . . . Falling Mass Hazard
FIDO . . . . . . Fallout Intensity Detector Oscillator
FPHS . . . . . . Fallout Protection in Houses
FSB . . . . Fallout Studies Branch (AEC)
FAR . . . . False Alarm Rate
FC's . . . . False Calves (Padding worn under tights by actors, to improve shape
    of their legs)
FERIC . . . . . . False Entries in Records ~f Interstate Carriers (FBI standardized term)
FP . . . . False Pretenses
FCC . . . . Falsely Claiming (US) Citizenship
FL . . . . Falso Lectio (False reading, in a text)
FAL . . . . Falstaff Brewing Corporation (NYSE symbol)
FMF . . . . Familial Mediterranean Fever
FFLT. . . . . . . Familiarization Flight (Aviation)
FGB . . . . Familiengesetzbuch
F . . . . Family
FA . . . . Family Allowance
FAA . . . . Family Allowance Class A
FAAB . . . . . . Family Allowance, Class A and B
FAB . . . . Family Allowance, Class B
FCF . . . . Family Camping Federation
FCC . . . . Family Communion Crusade
FCIU . . . . Family Crisis Intervention Unit (New York Police Department)
FAM. . . . . . . Family Finance Corporation (NYSE symbol)
FHO. . . . . . . Family Hands Off, or Family Hold Off (Indicates that a certain dish
    is not to be eaten by members of the family at a meal where
    guests are present)
FHB . . . . Family Hold Back (i.e., take small portions) (A mealtime whimsicality
    for use when guests are present)
FLB . . . . Family Life Bureau
FLS . . . . Family Location Service
FMPM. . . . . . Family Manned Planetary Mission
FAMECE . . . . Family of Military Engineer Construction Equipment
FPI. . . . . Family Pitch In (i.e., eat freely of a given food) (A mealtime
    whimsicality for use when guests are present)
FPL . . . . Family Protection League of USA
FSA . . . . Family Separation Allowance (Military)
FSAA . . . . . . Family Service Association of America
FSC . . . . Family Services Center (Military)
FSP . . . . Family Services Program (Military)
FOSWAC . . . . Family of Special Weapons Atomic Contractors
FSE . . . . Family Stop Eating (A table signal) (Slang)
FSL . . . . Family Strike Light (i.e., take small portions) (A mealtime whimsicality
    for use when guests are present)
FM . . . . Fan Marker (Aviation)
FM. . . . . Fan Marker Approach (Aviation)
FMAP . . . . . . Fan Marker Approach (Aviation)
FO. . . . . Fan Out
FPR . . . . Fan Pressure Ratio
FTR . . . . Fan Thrust Reverser
FTM . . . . Fan Type Marker
FBA . . . . Fanned Beam Antenna
FFY . . . . Fanny Farmer Candy Shops (NYSE symbol)
FNL. . . . . . . Fansteel Metallurgical Corporation (NYSE symbol)
FAPA . . . . . . Fantasy Amateur Press Association
FE . . . . Far East
FEAF . . . . . . Far East Air Force
FEALOGFOR . . Far East Air Logistical Force
FEAMCOM . . . Far East Air Materiel Command
FEACCI . . . . . Far-East-America Council of Commerce and Industry
FECB . . . . . . Far East Combined Bureau (Singapore, 1940) (Military)
FEC . . . . Far East Command
FECOM. . . . . Far East Command (Military)
FECR . . . . . . Far East Communications Region (Air Force)
FEC . . . . Far East Conference
FEMAS . . . . . Far East Merchants Association

FEN . . . . Far East Network
FERO . . . . . . Far East Research Office
FEAC . . . . . . Far Eastern Advisory Council
FEC . . . . Far Eastern Commission
FEPA . . . . . . Far-Eastern Prehistory Association
FFP . . . . Far Field Pressure
FIR. . . . . Far Infrared
FID . . . . Far Infrared Detector
FIRD. . . . . . . Far Infrared Detector
FIM . . . . Far Infrared MASER
FIO . . . . Far Infrared Observation
FIRO . . . . . . Far Infrared Observation
FIP. . . . . Far Infrared Pointer
FIRP . . . . Far Infrared Pointer
FIPP . . . . Far Infrared Pointer Package
FIRPP . . . . . . Far Infrared Pointer Package
FIR. . . . . Far Infrared Radiometer
FIS. . . . . Far Infrared Search
FIRST . . . . . . Far Infrared Search and Track
FIS. . . . . Far Infrared Spectrometer
FITD. . . . . . . Far Infrared Target Detector
FITI . . . . Far Infrared Target Indicator
FIT. . . . . Far Infrared Track
FS . . . . Far Side
F. . . . . Farad
F . . . . Faraday Constant
FDS . . . . Faraday Dark Space
FDM. . . . . . . Faraday Disc Machine
FLZO . . . . . . Farband Labor Zionist Order
FCA . . . . Farm Credit Administration (Independent government agency)
FCS . . . . Farm Credit System (of FCA)
FE . . . . Farm Economics Research Division (of ARS, Department of Agriculture)
FEC . . . . Farm Electrification Council
FEPC . . . . . . Farm Employment Practices Committee
FEI . . . . Farm Equipment Institute
FEMA . . . . . . Farm Equipment Manufacturers Association
FEWA . . . . . . Farm Equipment Wholesalers Association
FFF . . . . Farm Film Foundation
FF . . . . Farm Foundation
FLS . . . . Farm Labor Service (of USES)
FPR . . . . Farm Publications Reports
FSA . . . . Farm Security Administration (Succeeded by Farmers Home Administration,
    1946)
FSFLP . . . . . . Farm Storage Facility Loan Program
FUA . . . . Farm Underwriters Association
FCS . . . . Farmer Cooperative Service (Department of Agriculture)
FCCA . . . . . . Farmers Chinchilla Cooperative of America
FECUA . . . . . Farmers' Educational & Cooperative Union of America
FFC . . . . Farmers Federation Cooperative
FHA . . . . Farmers Home Administration (Department of Agriculture)
FAMBSA . . . . Farmers and Manufacturers Beet Sugar Association
FMBSA . . . . . Farmers and Manufacturers Beet Sugar Association
FWA . . . . Farmers and World Affairs
FSTC . . . . . . Farmington State Teachers College (Maine)
F . . . . Farthing (British monetary unit)
FCI . . . . Fashion Coordination Institute
FG . . . . Fashion Group
FIT. . . . . Fashion Institute of Technology (New York)
FOGA . . . . . . Fashion Originators Guild of America
FRANY . . . . . Fashion Reporters Award – New York
F . . . . Fast
FAIR. . . . . . . Fast Access Information Retrieval
FASTI . . . . . . Fast Access to Systems Technical Information
FAF . . . . Fast Acting Fuse
FAS . . . . Fast Announcement Service (CFSTI publication)
FACS . . . . . . Fast Attack Class Submarine
FAGC. . . . . . Fast Automatic Gain Control
FAST . . . . . . Fast Automatic Shuttle Transfer
FAT . . . . Fast Automatic Transfer
FBR . . . . Fast Breeder Reactor (AEC)
FBR . . . . Fast Burn Rate
FBRF. . . . . . . Fast Burst Reactor Facility
FBR . . . . Fast Burst Reactor
FCB . . . . Fast Capacitor Bank
FCR . . . . Fast Ceramic Reactor (Program)
AOE . . . . Fast Combat Support Ship (Navy symbol)
FDLS . . . . . . Fast Deployment Logistic Ship (Navy)
FDL . . . . Fast Deployment Logistics (Ships) (Navy)
FDS . . . . Fast Diode Switch
FES . . . . Fast Erect System
FEF . . . . Fast Extrusion Furnace

FFF . . . . Fast Fission Factor
FFTF . . . . Fast Flux Text Facility (AEC)
FFV . . . . Fast Flying Vestibule (Old railroad term for a deluxe coach)
FFOT . . . . Fast Frequency on Target
FMO . . . . Fast Moving Object
FND . . . . Fast Neutron Dose
FO . . . . Fast Operating (Relay)
FOREST . . . . . . Fast Order Radiation Effects Sampling Technique
PTF . . . . Fast Patrol Boat (Navy symbol)
FRISCO . . . . . . Fast Reaction Integrated Submarine Control
FRCTF . . . . Fast Reactor Core Test Facility (AEC)
FARET . . . . Fast Reactor Experiment Test
FARET . . . . Fast Reactor Test Facility (AEC)
FR . . . . Fast Release (Relay)
FRS . . . . Fast Retrieval Storage (Data processing)
FRB . . . . Fast Rise Balloon
FRRRB . . . . Fast Rise RADAR Reflective Balloon
FRRB . . . . Fast Rise Reflective Balloon
FSM . . . . Fast Settle Mode
FSO . . . . Fast Settle Operation
FSR . . . . Fast Slew Rate
FSPPR . . . . Fast Supercritical Pressure Power Reactor
FTR . . . . Fast Test Reactor
FTC . . . . Fast Time Constant (RADAR)
FRC . . . . Fasteners Research Council
FBS . . . . Fasting Blood Sugar (Physiology)
FCM . . . . Fat Corrected Milk
FF . . . . Fat Free (Biochemistry)
FMS . . . . Fat Mobilizing Substance
FD . . . . Fatal Dose
F . . . . Father
F@L . . . . Fathers-At-Large
F . . . . Fathom
FDS . . . . Fathometer Depth Sounder
FCT . . . . Fatigue Cracking Test
FL . . . . Fatigue Limit
FPRF . . . . Fats and Proteins Research Foundation
FA . . . . Fatty Acid (Biochemistry)
FAPC . . . . Fatty Acid Producers' Council
FDT . . . . Fault Detection Tester
FICS . . . . Fault Isolation Checkout System
FIC . . . . Fault Isolation Code
FIM . . . . Fault Isolation Meter
FIR . . . . Fault Isolation Routine
FIST . . . . Fault Isolation by Semiautomatic Techniques (National Bureau of Standards)
FIT . . . . Fault Isolation Test
FLT . . . . Fault Locating Test
FLI . . . . Fault Location Indicator
FLC . . . . Fault Locator Cable
FAW . . . . Fawick Corporation (NYSE symbol)
FSTC . . . . Fayetteville State Teachers College (North Carolina)
FDP . . . . Feasibility Demonstration Program
FS . . . . Feasibility Study
FVP . . . . Feasibility Validation Program
F . . . . Feast
FR . . . . Feather River R. R. (AAR code)
FC . . . . Feature Count (Data processing)
FP . . . . Fecal Pellet
F . . . . Fecit (Did)
FJQ . . . . Fedders Corporation (NYSE symbol)
FEDECAME . . . Federacion Cafetalera de America (Central American Coffee Growers' Federation)
FEUE . . . . Federacion de Estudiantes Universitaries de Ecuador
FEV . . . . Federacion de Estudiantes de Venezuela
FNV . . . . Federacion Nacional Velasquista (Political party in Ecuador)
FOITAF . . . . . . Federacion Obrera de la Industria Tabaquera de Filipinas (Workers' Federation of the Tobacco Industry of the Philippines)
FOR . . . . Federacion Obrera Revolucionaria (Mexican political party)
FOCAP . . . . . . Federacion Odontologica Centro America Panama (Odontological Federation of Central America and Panama)
FPAA . . . . Federacion Panamericana de Asociaciones de Arquitectos (Panamerican Federation of Architects' Associations)
FSH . . . . Federacion de Sociedades Hispanas
FUDE . . . . Federacion Universitaria Democratica Espanola (Spanish union of students)
FAC . . . . Federal Advisory Council
FACMTA . . . . Federal Advisory Council on Medical Training Aids
FACSI . . . . . . Federal Advisory Council on Scientific Information
FAAP . . . . Federal-Aid Airport Program (FAA)
FACA . . . . Federal Alcohol Control Administration (Established, 1933; abolished, 1935)
FAP . . . . Federal Art Project

FAST . . . . Federal Assistance for Staff Training (Education)
FAST . . . . Federal Assistance Streamlining Taskforce (HEW)
FAMA . . . . Federal Association of Management Analysts
FAA . . . . Federal Aviation Administration (Formerly, Agency) (Independent government agency)
FAA/CAS . . . . Federal Aviation Administration – Canadian Air Services Committee
FAC . . . . Federal Aviation Commission
FAR . . . . Federal Aviation Regulations (FAA)
FBA . . . . Federal Bar Association
FBL . . . . Federal Barge Lines R. R., Inc. (AAR code)
FBH . . . . Federal Board of Hospitalization (Coordinated hospitalization activities of Army, Navy, and various government agencies; terminated, 1948)
FBI . . . . Federal Bureau of Investigation
FC . . . . Federal Cabinet (Australia)
FCP . . . . Federal Catalog Program
FCS . . . . Federal Catalog System (of GSA)
FCDA . . . . Federal Civil Defense Administration (Transferred to Office of Defense and Civilian Mobilization, 1958)
FCMSBR . . . . Federal Coal Mine Safety Board of Review (Independent government agency)
FCA . . . . Federal Committee on Apprenticeship
FCPC . . . . Federal Committee on Pest Control
FCA . . . . Federal Communications Act
FCBA . . . . Federal Communications Bar Association
FCC . . . . Federal Communications Commission (Independent government agency)
FCCN . . . . Federal Communications Commission Network
FECL . . . . Federal Constitutional Law
FCC . . . . Federal Construction Council
FCC . . . . Federal Consultative Council of South African Railways and Harbors Staff Association
FCRC . . . . Federal Contract Research Center
FCA . . . . Federal Council on Aging (Succeeded by President's Council on Aging, 1962)
FCC . . . . Federal Council of Churches
FCST . . . . Federal Council for Science and Technology (Executive Office of President)
FCI . . . . Federal Crop Insurance
FCIC . . . . Federal Crop Insurance Corporation (Department of Agriculture)
FDIC . . . . Federal Deposit Insurance Corporation (Independent government agency)
DF . . . . Federal District (Mexico)
FD . . . . Federal Document
FEA . . . . Federal Editors Association
FEAPW . . . . . . Federal Emergency Administration of Public Works (Consolidated into Federal Works Agency and administered as PWA, 1939)
FERA . . . . Federal Emergency Relief Administration (Liquidated, 1937)
FECA . . . . Federal Employees Compensation Act
FEGLI . . . . Federal Employees' Group Life Insurance
FEHB . . . . Federal Employees Health Benefits
FEHBA . . . . . . Federal Employees Health Benefits Act
FEHBP . . . . . . Federal Employees Health Benefit Program
FESO . . . . Federal Employment Stabilization Office (Functions transferred to National Resources Planning Board, 1939)
FET . . . . Federal Excise Tax
FETC . . . . Federal Excise Tax Council
FEB . . . . Federal Executive Board (Civil Service Commission)
FEI . . . . Federal Executive Institute
FES . . . . Federal Extension Service (Department of Agriculture)
FFC . . . . Federal Facilities Corporation (Dissolved, 1961)
FFB . . . . Federal Farm Board (Name changed to Farm Credit Administration, 1933)
FFCB . . . . Federal Farm Credit Board (of FCA)
FFMC . . . . Federal Farm Mortgage Corporation (Established, 1934; assets transferred to Secretary of the Treasury, 1961)
FFC . . . . Federal Fire Council
FFA . . . . Federal Firearms Act
FGAA . . . . Federal Government Accountants Association
FEHA . . . . Federal Hall National Memorial
FHSA . . . . Federal Hazardous Substances Act
FHWA . . . . Federal Highway Administration (Department of Transportation)
FHLB . . . . Federal Home Loan Bank
FHLBB . . . . . . Federal Home Loan Bank Board (Independent government agency)
FHA . . . . Federal Housing Administration (of HHFA)
FHC . . . . Federal Housing Corporation
FHR . . . . Federal Housing Representative (Australia)
FIT . . . . Federal Income Tax
FITW . . . . Federal Income Tax Withholding
FIC . . . . Federal Information Center
FIPS . . . . Federal Information Processing Standards
FIRR . . . . Federal Institute for Reactor Research (Switzerland)
FICA . . . . Federal Insurance Contributions Act (Under which collections are made from employers and employees for OASDI benefits)
FICE . . . . Federal Interagency Committee on Education
FICB . . . . Federal Intermediate Credit Bank

FII . . . . Federal Item Identification
FIIG . . . . Federal Item Identification Guides
FIIN . . . . Federal Item Identification Number
FIIG . . . . Federal Item Inventory Group
FJC . . . . Federal Judicial Center
FLB . . . . Federal Land Bank
FLBA . . . . . . Federal Land Bank Association
FLDA . . . . . . Federal Land Development Authority (Malaysia)
FLC . . . . Federal Library Committee (Library of Congress)
FLOA . . . . . . Federal Licensed Officers Association
FLA . . . . Federal Loan Administration
FLA . . . . Federal Loan Agency
FMB . . . . Federal Maritime Board (1950-1961; functions transferred to FMC)
FMC . . . . Federal Maritime Commission (Independent government agency)
FMCS . . . . . . Federal Mediation and Conciliation Service (Independent government agency)
FMRS . . . . . . Federal Mediation and Reconciliation Service
FMPP . . . . . . Federal Merit Promotion Program
FMO . . . . Federal-Mogul Corporation (NYSE symbol)
FNMA . . . . . . Federal National Mortgage Association (Nickname: Fannie Mae)
FOB . . . . Federal Office Building
FOMC . . . . . . Federal Open Market Committee (of FRS)
FPC . . . . Federal Pacific Electric Company (NYSE symbol)
FBO . . . . Federal Paper Board Company, Inc. (NYSE symbol)
FPG . . . . Federal Pecan Growers
FPC . . . . Federal Personnel Council (Civil Service Commission) (Abolished, 1954)
FPI . . . . Federal Personnel Intern (Program) (Civil Service Commission)
FPM . . . . Federal Personnel Manual
FPB . . . . Federal Petroleum Board (Department of the Interior)
FPQINA . . . . . Federal Plant Quarantine Inspectors National Association
FPC . . . . Federal Power Commission (Independent government agency)
FPI . . . . Federal Prison Industries
FPS . . . . Federal Prison System
FPR . . . . Federal Procurement Regulations
FPA . . . . Federal Professional Association
FPMR . . . . . . Federal Property Management Regulations
FPHA . . . . . . Federal Public Housing Authority (Functions transferred to Public Housing Administration, 1947)
FRC . . . . Federal Radiation Council
FRC . . . . Federal Radio Commission (Functions transferred to FCC, 1934)
FREC . . . . . . Federal Radio Education Committee
FREB . . . . . . Federal Real Estate Board (Abolished, 1951)
FRC . . . . Federal Records Center, GSA
FRC . . . . Federal Records Council
FR . . . . Federal Register
FRA . . . . Federal Regular Army (Federation of South Arabia)
FRLA . . . . . . Federal Regulation of Lobbying Act
FRG . . . . Federal Republic of Germany
GE . . . . Federal Republic of Germany (NATO)
FR . . . . Federal Reserve
FRA . . . . Federal Reserve Act
FRB . . . . Federal Reserve Banks (of FRS)
FRB . . . . Federal Reserve Board
FRD . . . . Federal Reserve District
FRS . . . . Federal Reserve System (Independent government agency)
FSC . . . . Federal Safety Council
FSLIC . . . . . . Federal Savings and Loan Insurance Corporation (of FHLBB)
FSA . . . . Federal Security Administration
FSA . . . . Federal Security Agency (Functions and units transferred to HEW, 1953)
FSCNHA . . . . Federal Service Campaign for National Health Agencies
FSEE . . . . Federal Service Entrance Examination (Civil Service)
FSRA . . . . . . Federal Sewage Research Association
FSIP . . . . Federal Shelter Incentive Program
FS . . . . Federal Specification
FSB . . . . Federal Specifications Board
FSEC . . . . . . Federal Specifications Executive Committee
FS . . . . Federal Standard
FEDSTRIP . . . . . Federal Standard Requisitioning & Issue Procedure
FSUC . . . . . . Federal Statistics Users' Conference
FSC . . . . Federal Stock Class
FSI . . . . Federal Stock Item
FSL . . . . Federal Stock Listings
FSN . . . . Federal Stock Number
FSC . . . . Federal Supply Classification
FSCG . . . . . . Federal Supply Classification Group
FSC . . . . Federal Supply Code
FSCM . . . . . . Federal Supply Code for Manufacturers
FSG . . . . Federal Supply Group
FSS . . . . Federal Supply Schedule
FSS . . . . Federal Supply Service (of GSA)
FSCC . . . . . . Federal Surplus Commodities Corporation

FTI . . . . Federal Tax Included
FTL . . . . Federal Telecommunications Laboratory (Air Force)
FTS . . . . Federal Telecommunications System (of GSA)
FTR . . . . Federal Telephone and Radio
FTP . . . . Federal Theater Project
FTCA . . . . . . Federal Tort Claims Act
FTC . . . . Federal Trade Commission (Independent government agency)
FTUC . . . . . . Federal Trade Union Congress (European)
FTZ . . . . Federal Trade Zone
FTWS . . . . . . Federal Train Wreck Statute
FTEC . . . . . . Federal Trial Examiners Conference
FT . . . . Federal Triangle (Washington, DC)
FUTA . . . . . . Federal Unemployment Tax Act
FUEN . . . . . . Federal Union of European Nationalities
FWPCA . . . . . Federal Water Pollution Control Administration (Department of the Interior)
FWRC . . . . . . Federal Water Resources Council
FWDA . . . . . . Federal Wholesale Druggists Association
FWA . . . . Federal Works Agency (Abolished, 1949)
FWP . . . . Federal Writers' Project
FFRDC . . . . . Federally Funded Research and Development Centers
FCUA . . . . . . Federated Clerks' Union of Australia
FCII . . . . Federated Council of Israel Institutions
FDS . . . . Federated Department Stores, Inc. (NYSE symbol)
FEU . . . . Federated Engineering Union
FFD of A . . . . Federated Funeral Directors of America
FIA . . . . Federated Ironworkers' Association of Australia
FMS . . . . Federated Malay States
FPGAUS . . . . . Federated Pecan Growers' Associations of the United States
FROC . . . . . . Federated Russian Orthodox Clubs
FSSU . . . . . . Federated Superannuation Scheme for Universities (British)
FAI . . . . Federation Abolitionniste Internationale
FAI . . . . Federation Aeronautique Internationale
FAOLU . . . . . Federation of All Okinawan Labor Unions
FAOMELU . . . . Federation of All Okinawan Military Employees' Labor Unions
FACGD . . . . . Federation of American Citizens of German Descent
FAH . . . . Federation of American Hospitals
FAS . . . . Federation of American Scientists
FASEB . . . . . . Federation of American Societies for Experimental Biology
FAWCO . . . . . Federation of American Women's Clubs Overseas
FAWA . . . . . . Federation of Asian Women's Associations
FAIB . . . . Federation des Associations Internationales Etablies en Belgique
FATIPEC . . . . . Federation d'Associations de Techniciens des Industries des Peintures, Vernis, Emaux et Encres d'Imprimerie de l'Europe Continentale
FEDEKA . . . . . Federation des Associations Tribales des Originaires du Kasai (Federation of Associations of Kasai Tribes)
FAGS . . . . . . Federation of Astronomical and Geophysical Services
FBI . . . . Federation of British Industries
FCA . . . . Federation of Canadian Artists
FCGCMA . . . . Federation of Cash Grain Commission Merchants Assns.
FCPG . . . . . . Federation of Catholic Physicians' Guilds
CUF . . . . Federation of Catholic Universities
FCSPASTU . . . Federation of Civil Service and Primary Aided School Teachers' Unions (Mauritius)
FCSUM . . . . . Federation of Civil Service Unions of Mauritius
FCG . . . . Federation for Constitutional Government
FDTU . . . . . . Federation of Danish Trade Unions
FDIF . . . . Federation Democratique Internationale des Femmes
FDI . . . . Federation Dentaire Internationale
FEN . . . . Federation de l'Education Nationale (Federation of National Education) (Malagasy)
FECB . . . . . . Federation des Employes Congolais des Banques (Federation of Congolese Bank Clerks)
FEGS . . . . . . Federation Employment and Guidance Service
FEAN . . . . . . Federation des Enseignants d'Afrique Noire (Federation of Teachers of Black Africa)
FEC . . . . Federation des Entreprises au Congo (Merger of AIIB and AICB)
FEI . . . . Federation Equestre Internationale
FEANF . . . . . . Federation des Etudiants d'Afrique Noire en France (Federation of Students of Black Africa in France)
FEAO . . . . . . Federation of European American Organizations
FEBS . . . . Federation of European Biochemical Societies
FEIEA . . . . . . Federation of European Industrial Editors' Associations
FEPEM . . . . . Federation of European Petroleum Equipment Manufacturers
FEACO . . . . . Federation Europeenne des Associations de Conseils en Organisation
FEAICS . . . . . Federation Europeenne des Associations d'Ingenieurs de Securite et de Chefs de Service de Securite
FEANI . . . . . . Federation Europeenne d'Associations Nationales d'Ingenieurs
FECEP . . . . . . Federation Europeenne des Constructeurs d'Equipement Petrolier
FEFAC . . . . . . Federation Europeenne des Fabricants d'Aliments Composes pour Animaux

FEFCO . . . . . . Federation Europeenne des Fabricants de Carton Ondule
FECS . . . . Federation Europeenne des Fabricants de Ceramiques Sanitaires
EUROSAC . . . . Federation Europeenne des Fabricants de Sacs en Papier a Grande Contenance
FRUCOM. . . . . Federation Europeenne des Importateurs de Fruits Secs, Conserves, Epices et Miels
FEITC . . . . . . Federation Europeenne des Industries Techniques du Cinema
FEM. . . . . . . Federation Europeenne de la Manutention
FEMK . . . . . . Federation Europeenne des Masseurskinesitherapeutes Praticiens en Physiotherapie
FEM. . . . . . . Federation Europeenne des Motels
FEPE. . . . . . . Federation Europeenne de la Publicite Exterieure
FESFP . . . . . . Federation Europeenne des Syndicats de Fabricants de Parquets
FETAP. . . . . . Federation Europeenne des Transports Aeriens Prives
FEZ . . . . Federation Europeenne de Zootechnie
FFCAA . . . . . . Federation Francaise des Cooperatives Agricoles d'Approvisionnement
FFCAC . . . . . . Federation Francaise des Cooperatives Agricoles de Cereales
FOFATUSA . . . Federation of Free African Trade Unions of South Africa
FFF . . . . Federation of Free Farmers (Philippines)
FFL . . . . Federation of Free Labor (Philippines)
FFW . . . . Federation of Free Workers (Philippines)
FFAUS . . . . . . Federation of French Alliances in the United States
FFWV . . . . . . Federation of French War Veterans
FGC . . . . Federation Generale du Congo (Congolese General Federation)
FGTB . . . . . . Federation Generale du Travail de Belgique (Belgian General Federation of Labor)
FGTK . . . . . . Federation Generale du Travail du Kongo (General Federation of Labor of the Congo) (Leopoldville)
FETRIKAT . . . . Federation Generale des Tribes du Haut Katanga (General Federation of Tribes of North Katanga)
FGI . . . . Federation Graphique Internationale
FHAS . . . . . . Federation of Hellenic American Societies of Greater New York
FITU . . . . Federation of Independent Trade Unions (Lebanon)
FIBAT . . . . . . Federation Independente des Batetelas (Independent Federation of Batetelas)
FIDE. . . . . . . Federation de l'Industrie Dentaire en Europe
FITCE . . . . . . Federation des Ingenieurs des Telecommunications de la Communaute Europeenne
FIIG. . . . . Federation des Institutions Internationales Semi-Officielles et Privees Etablies a Geneve
FIC . . . . Federation of Insurance Counsel
FIDEGEP . . . . . Federation Interalliee des Evades de Guerre et des Passeurs
FIAC . . . . Federation Interamericaine des Automobile Clubs
FICSA . . . . . . Federation of International Civil Servants' Associations
FIA . . . . Federation Internationale des Acteurs
FIABCI . . . . . . Federation Internationale des Administrateurs de Biens Conseils Immobiliers
FIAV . . . . Federation Internationale des Agences de Voyages
FIAJF . . . . . . Federation Internationale des Amies de la Jeune Fille
FIAF . . . . Federation Internationale des Archives du Film
FIAP. . . . . . . Federation Internationale de l'Art Photographique
FIAB. . . . . . . Federation Internationale des Associations de Bibliothecaires
FIAD . . . . Federation Internationale des Associations des Distributeurs de Films
FIEC . . . . Federation Internationale des Associations d'Etudes Classiques
FIAEM . . . . . . Federation Internationale des Associations des Etudiants en Medecine
FIAI . . . . Federation Internationale des Associations d'Instituteurs
FIAMC . . . . . . Federation Internationale des Associations des Medecins Catholiques
FIANEI . . . . . . Federation Internationale d'Associations Nationales d'Eleves Ingenieurs
FIAPL . . . . . . Federation Internationale des Associations de Pilotes de Ligne
FIAPF . . . . . . Federation Internationale des Associations de Producteurs de Films
FIDAQ . . . . . . Federation Internationale des Associations de Quincailliers et Marchands de Fer
FIATE . . . . . . Federation Internationale des Associations de Travailleurs Evangeliques
FIATC . . . . . . Federation Internationale des Associations Touristiques de Cheminots
FIATA. . . . . . Federation Internationale des Associations de Transitaires et Assimiles
FIAA . . . . Federation Internationale Athletique d'Amateur
FIAJ. . . . . . . Federation Internationale des Auberges de la Jeunesse
FIA . . . . Federation Internationale de l'Automobile
FIBA. . . . . . . Federation Internationale de Basketball Amateur
FIBTP . . . . . . Federation Internationale du Batiment et des Travaux Publics
FIBT . . . . Federation Internationale de Bobsleigh et de Tobogganing
FIB . . . . Federation Internationale de Boules
FIBEP . . . . . . Federation Internationale des Bureaux d'Extraits de Presse
FICCIA . . . . . . Federation International des Cadres de la Chimie et des Industries Annexes
FICM . . . . . . Federation Internationale des Cadres des Mines
FICC . . . . Federation Internationale de Camping et de Caravanning
FICEP . . . . . . Federation Internationale Catholique d'Education Physique
FIS . . . . Federation Internationale des Centres Sociaux et Communautaires (International Federation of Settlements and Neighborhood Centers)
FICT. . . . . . . Federation Internationale de Centres Touristiques
FICS. . . . . . . Federation Internationale des Chasseurs de Sons

FICA . . . . Federation Internationale des Cheminots Antialcooliques (International Railway Temperance Union)
FICC . . . . Federation Internationale des Cine-Clubs
FICP. . . . . . . Federation Internationale des Clubs de Publicite
FICIC . . . . Federation Internationale du Commerce et des Industries du Camping
FIS . . . . Federation Internationale du Commerce des Semences
FICE . . . . Federation Internationale des Communautes d'Enfants
FICJF . . . . . . Federation Internationale des Conseils Juridiques et Fiscaux
FIDI . . . . Federation Internationale des Demenageurs Internationaux
FID . . . . Federation Internationale du Diabete
FIDJC. . . . . . . Federation Internationale des Directeurs de Journaux Catholiques
DISTRIPRESS. . . Federation Internationale des Distributeurs de Presse
FID . . . . Federation Internationale de Documentation (International Federation for Documentation)
FIDE. . . . . . . Federation Internationale pour le Droit Europeen (International Federation for European Law)
FIDE. . . . . . . Federation Internationale des Echecs
FIEJ . . . . Federation Internationale des Editeurs de Journaux et Publications
FIDEM . . . . . . Federation Internationale des Editeurs de Medailles
FEA . . . . Federation Internationale pour l'Education Artistique
FIEP. . . . . . . Federation Internationale d'Education Physique
FIET . . . . Federation Internationale des Employes et des Techniciens
FIEM . . . . . . Federation Internationale de l'Enseignement Menager
FIE. . . . . Federation Internationale d'Escrime
FIEP. . . . . . . Federation Internationale des Etudiants en Pharmacie
FIESP . . . . . . Federation Internationale des Etudiants en Sciences Politiques
FIPAGO . . . . . Federation Internationale des Fabricants de Papiers Gommes
FINAT . . . . . . Federation Internationale des Fabricants et Transformateurs d'Adhesifs et Thermo-Collants sur Papiers et Autres Supports
FIFCLC . . . . . . Federation Internationale des Femmes de Carrieres Liberales et Commerciales
FIFDU . . . . . . Federation Internationale des Femmes Diplomees des Universites
FIFA. . . . . . . Federation Internationale du Film sur d'Art
FIFSP . . . . . . Federation Internationale des Fonctionnaires Superieurs de Police
FIFA. . . . . . . Federation Internationale de Football Association
FIG . . . . Federation Internationale des Geometres
FIGED . . . . . . Federation Internationale des Grandes Entreprises de Distribution
FIG . . . . Federation Internationale de Gymnastique
FIGO . . . . Federation Internationale de Gynecologie et d'Obstetrique
FIHU . . . . Federation Internationale de l'Habitation et de l'Urbanisme
FIHC . . . . Federation Internationale Halterophile et Culturiste
FIH . . . . Federation Internationale de Handball
FIH . . . . Federation Internationale de Hockey
FIH . . . . Federation Internationale des Hopitaux
FIIP . . . . Federation Internationale de l'Industrie Phonographique
FIDIC . . . . . . Federation Internationale des Ingenieurs-Conseils
FIICPI . . . . . . Federation Internationale des Ingenieurs-Conseils en Propriete Industrielle
FERES . . . . . . Federation Internationale des Instituts Catholiques de Recherches Socio-Religieuses
FIDIA . . . . . . Federation Internationale des Intellectuels Aveugles
FIJC. . . . . . . Federation Internationale de la Jeunesse Catholique
FIJM . . . . Federation Internationale des Jeunesses Musicales
FIJ . . . . Federation Internationale des Journalistes
FIJET . . . . . . Federation Internationale des Journalistes et Ecrivains du Tourisme
FIJL . . . . Federation Internationale des Journalistes Libres de l'Europe Centrale et Orientale et des Pays Baltes et Balkaniques
FIJPA . . . . . . Federation Internationale des Journalistes Professionnels de l'Aeronautique
FIJ . . . . Federation Internationale de Judo
FIL. . . . . Federation Internationale de Laiterie
FILDIR . . . . . . Federation Internationale Libre des Deportes et Internes de la Resistance
FIL. . . . . Federation Internationale de Luge
FIMP . . . . . . Federation Internationale de Medecine Physique
FIMS . . . . . . Federation Internationale Medecine Sportive
FIM . . . . Federation Internationale Motocycliste
FIMEM . . . . . . Federation Internationale des Mouvements d'Ecole Moderne
FIMOC . . . . . . Federation Internationale des Mouvements Ouvriers Chretiens
FIM . . . . Federation Internationale des Musiciens
FIMITIC . . . . . Federation Internationale des Mutiles et Invalides du Travail et des Invalides Civils
FINA . . . . Federation Internationale de Natation Amateur (International Amateur Swimming Federation)
FIO . . . . Federation Internationale d'Oleiculture
FIORH . . . . . . Federation Internationale pour l'Organisation de Rencontres de Handicapes
FIOCES. . . . . . Federation Internationale des Organisations de Correspondances et d'Echanges Scolaires
FIOCC . . . . . . Federation Internationale des Ouvriers de la Chaussure et du Cuir
FIOM . . . . . . Federation Internationale des Ouvriers sur Metaux
FIP. . . . . Federation Internationale Pharmaceutique
FIP. . . . . Federation Internationale de Philatelie
FIP. . . . . Federation Internationale de la Precontrainte

FIPRA . . . . Federation Internationale de la Presse Agricole
FIPRESCI . . . . . Federation Internationale de la Presse Cinematographique
FIPP . . . . Federation Internationale de la Presse Periodique
FIPA . . . . . . Federation Internationale des Producteurs Agricoles
FIPACE . . . . . . Federation Internationale des Producteurs Auto-Consommateurs Industriels d'Electricite
FIJU . . . . Federation Internationale des Producteurs de Jus de Fruits
FIPJF . . . . . . Federation Internationale des Producteurs de Jus de Fruits
FIPESO . . . . . . Federation Internationale des Professeurs de l'Enseignement Secondaire Officiel
FIPP . . . . Federation Internationale pour la Protection des Populations
FIPM . . . . . . Federation Internationale de Psychotherapie Medicale
FIREC . . . . . . Federation Internationale des Redacteurs en Chef
FIR . . . . Federation Internationale des Resistants
FIRS . . . . Federation Internationale de Roller-Skating
FIRA . . . . Federation Internationale de Rugby Amateur
FIS . . . . Federation Internationale de Sauvetage
FISA . . . . Federation Internationale des Semaines d'Art
FIS . . . . Federation Internationale de Ski (International Ski Association)
FISA . . . . Federation Internationale des Societes Aerophilateliques
FISAIC . . . . . . Federation Internationale des Societes Artistiques et Intellectuelles de Cheminots
FISA . . . . Federation Internationale des Societes d'Avion
FISEM . . . . . . Federation Internationale des Societes d'Ecrivains-Medecins
FISITA . . . . . . Federation Internationale des Societes d'Ingenieurs des Techniques de l'Automobile
FISP . . . . Federation Internationale des Societes de Philosophie
FISU . . . . Federation Internationale du Sport Universitaire
FISEC . . . . . . Federation Internationale Sportive de l'Enseignement Catholique
FISD . . . . Federation Internationale de Stenographie et de Dactylographie
FISEMA . . . . . . Federation Internationale et Syndicale des Employes de Madagascar (International Federation and Union of Malagasy Employees) (WFTU affiliate)
FISE . . . . Federation Internationale Syndicale de l'Enseignement
FISCETCV . . . . Federation Internationale des Syndicats Chretiens d'Employes, Techniciens, Cadres et Voyageurs de Commerce
FISCM . . . . . . Federation Internationale des Syndicats Chretiens de la Metalurgie
FISCOA . . . . . . Federation Internationale des Syndicats Chretiens d'Ouvriers Agricoles
FISCOBB . . . . . Federation Internationale des Syndicats Chretiens d'Ouvriers du Batiment et du Bois
FISCTTH . . . . . Federation Internationale des Syndicats Chretiens des Travailleurs du Textile et de l'Habillement
FITT . . . . Federation Internationale de Tennis de Table
FITEC . . . . . . Federation Internationale du Thermalisme et du Climatisme
FITA . . . . Federation Internationale de Tir a l'Arc
FIT . . . . Federation Internationale des Traducteurs (International Federation of Translators)
FITAP . . . . . . Federation Internationale des Transports Aeriens Prives
FITBB . . . . . . Federation Internationale des Travailleurs du Batiment et du Bois
FITH . . . . Federation Internationale des Travailleurs de l'Habillement
FITP . . . . Federation Internationale des Travailleurs du Petrole
FITP . . . . Federation Internationale des Travailleurs des Plantations
FITPASC . . . . . Federation Internationale des Travailleurs des Plantations, de l'Agriculture et des Secteurs Connexes
FITT . . . . Federation Internationale des Travailleurs de la Terre
FIVZ . . . . Federation Internationale Veterinaire de Zootechnie
FIVB . . . . Federation Internationale de Volleyball
FJCEE . . . . . . Federation des Jeunes Chefs d'Entreprises d'Europe
FJP . . . . Federation of Jewish Philanthropies of New York
FJSTO . . . . . . Federation of Jewish Student Organizations
FJWO . . . . . . Federation of Jewish Women's Organizations
FKTU . . . . . . Federation of Korean Trade Unions (South Korea)
FLU . . . . Federation of Labor Unions (Lebanon)
FLUL . . . . Federation of Labor Unions in Lebanon
FLI . . . . Federation Lainiere Internationale
FLLU . . . . Federation of Libyan Labor Unions
FLIA . . . . Federation Life Insurance of America
FLC . . . . Federation of Lutheran Clubs
FLM . . . . Federation Lutherienne Mondiale
FMHC . . . . . . Federation of Mental Health Centers
FMAC . . . . . . Federation Mondiale des Anciens Combattants
FMANU . . . . . Federation Mondiale des Associations pour les Nations Unies
FMJD . . . . . . Federation Mondiale de la Jeunesse Democratique
FMJFC . . . . . . Federation Mondiale des Jeunesses Feminines Catholiques
FMPA . . . . . . Federation Mondiale pour la Protection des Animaux (World Federation for the Protection of Animals) (Also known as WFPA and WTB)
FMSM . . . . . . Federation Mondiale pour la Sante Mentale (World Federation for Mental Health)
FMS . . . . Federation Mondiale des Sourds
FMTS . . . . . . Federation Mondiale des Travailleurs Scientifiques (World Federation of Scientific Workers)

FMDJ . . . . . . Federation Mondiale des Villes Jumelees (United Towns Organization)
FMPC . . . . . . Federation of Motion Picture Councils
FMFIC . . . . . . Federation of Mutual Fire Insurance Companies
FNPOR . . . . . . Federation of National Professional Organizations for Recreation
FNCETA . . . . . Federation Nationale des Centres d'Etudes Techniques Agricoles
FNCC . . . . . . Federation Nationale des Cooperatives de Cereales
FNCUMA . . . . Federation Nationale des Cooperatives d'Utilisation de Materiel Agricole
FNGAA . . . . . Federation Nationale des Groupements Agricoles d'Approvisionnement
FNIE . . . . Federation Nationale des Industries Electroniques Francaises (National Federation of French Electronics Manufacturers)
FNOSS . . . . . . Federation Nationale des Organismes de Securite Sociale (France)
FNRS . . . . . . Federation Nationale Research Scientifique (Belgium)
FENASYCOA . . Federation Nationale des Syndicats du Commerce Ouest Africain (National Federation of Commerce Unions – West Africa)
FNTAPSCM . . . Federation Nationale des Travailleurs de l'Agriculture, des Plantations, et Secteurs Connexes de Madagascar (National Federation of Workers of Agriculture, Plantations and Related Sectors of Madagascar)
FNI . . . . Federation Naturiste Internationale
FON . . . . Federation of Ontario Naturalists
FPVPC . . . . . . Federation of Paint and Varnish Production Clubs
FAPAP . . . . . . Federation des Personnels Africains de Police (Federation of African Police)
FPTU . . . . . . Federation of Progressive Trade Unions (Zanzibar)
FPI . . . . Federation Prohibitionniste Internationale
FPO . . . . Federation of Prosthodontic Organizations
FPWA . . . . . . Federation of Protestant Welfare Agencies
FRCF . . . . . . Federation of Reconstructionist Congregations and Fellowships
FRACHE . . . . . Federation of Regional Accrediting Commissions of Higher Education
FABI . . . . Federation Royale des Association Belges d'Ingenieurs (Belgium)
FRCOUSA . . . . Federation of Russian Charitable Organizations of the United States of America
FSSP . . . . Federation des Salaries du Secteur Prive (South Vietnam)
FEBOSCO . . . . Federation des Scouts du Congo
FSFMJC . . . . . Federation Senegalaise des Foyers et Maisons des Jeunes et de la Culture (Senegalese Federation of Hearth and Homes of Youth and Culture)
FSIWA . . . . . . Federation of Sewage and Industrial Wastes Association
FSPT . . . . . . Federation of Societies for Paint Technology
FSSE . . . . Federation des Societes Suisses d'Employes (Federation of Swiss Employees' Societies)
FSI . . . . Federation Spirite Internationale
FSMBUS . . . . . Federation of State Medical Boards of the United States
FSSCN . . . . . . Federation Suisse des Syndicats Chretiens-Nationaux (Swiss Federation of National-Christian Trade Unions)
FSES . . . . Federation of Swiss Employees' Societies
FSM . . . . Federation Syndicale Mondiale (World Federation of Trade Unions)
FSEC . . . . Federation des Syndicats de l'Enseignement du Cameroon (Federation of Teachers' Unions of the Cameroons)
FSL . . . . Federation des Syndicats Libres des Travailleurs Luxembourgeois (Free Luxembourg Workers' Federation)
FTA . . . . Federation of Tax Administrators
FTW . . . . Federation of Telephone Workers
FTAS . . . . . . Federation of Turkish-American Societies (Later, Turkish-American Associations)
FUSE . . . . Federation for Unified Science
FUNL . . . . . . Federation of Unions of Workers and Employees of North Lebanon
FUACE . . . . . . Federation Universelle des Associations Chretiennes d'Etudiants (Universal Federation of Christian Students Associations)
FUW . . . . Federation of University Women
FWI . . . . Federation of West Indies
FWOC . . . . . . Federation of Western Outdoor Clubs
FOWSAB . . . . . Federation of Women Shareholders in American Business
FWSAB . . . . . Federation of Women Shareholders in American Business
FWGIP . . . . . . Federation of Workers of Government of India Presses
FWSSUSA . . . . Federation of Workers' Singing Societies of the United States of America
FNRJ . . . . . . Federationa Narodna Republika Jugoslavija (Yugoslavia)
FAPI . . . . Federazione Artisti e Professionisti Italiani (Italian Federation of the Arts and Professions)
FANUS . . . . . . Federazione fra le Associazioni Nazionali Ufficiali e Sottufficiali in Congedo Provenienti dal Servizio Effettivo (Federation of National Associations for Discharged Career Officers and Petty Officers) (Italy)
FAI . . . . Federazione Autonoma Indossatrici (Autonomous Federation of Models) (Italy)
FCP . . . . Federazione dei Chimici e Petrolieri (Federation of Chemical and Petroleum Workers) (Italy)
FEGEMARE . . . Federazione della Gente del Mare (Federation of Seamen) (Italy)
FGS . . . . Federazione Giovanile Socialista (Italy)
FIOM . . . . . . Federazione Impiegati e Operai Metallurgici (Federation of Metal Workers and Employees) (Italy)
FIOT . . . . Federazione Impiegati Operai Tessili (Federation of Textile Workers) (Italy)

FIAIZA . . . . . . Federazione Italiana Addetti Industrie Zucchero e Alcole (Italian
Federation of Workers in the Sugar and Alcohol Industry)

FIARVEP . . . . . Federazione Italiana Agenti Rappresentanti Viaggiatorie e Paizzisti
(Italian Federation of Commercial Agents and Travelers)

FIAI . . . . Federazione Italiana Autoferrotramvieri e Internavigators (National
Federation of Busdrivers, Streetcar Conductors) (Italy)

FIALS . . . . . . Federazione Italiana Autonoma Lavoratori dello Spettacolo (Italian
Autonomous Federation of Entertainment Workers)

FIB . . . . Federazione Italiana Bancari (Italian Federation of Bank Employees)

FIDAC . . . . . . Federazione Italiana Dipendenti da Aziende di Credito (Italian Federatio
of Credit Institution Employees)

FIDAE . . . . . . Federazione Italiana Dipendenti Aziende Elettriche (Italian Federation of
Electrical Workers)

FIDAG . . . . . . Federazione Italiana Dipendenti Aziende Gas (Italian Federation of Gas
Workers)

FIDAT . . . . . . Federazione Italiana Dipendenti Aziende Telecomunicazioni (Italian
Federation of Communications Workers)

FIDEL . . . . . . Federazione Italiana Dipendenti Enti Local (Italian Federation of Local
Government Employees)

FIDEP . . . . . . Federazione Italiana Dipendenti da Enti Parastatali e di Diritto Pubblico
(Italian Federation of Employees of Quasi-Governmental and State-
Controlled Agencies)

FIDGA . . . . . . Federazione Italiana della Gente dell'Aria (Italian Federation of Airline
Workers)

FILA . . . . Federazione Italiana Lavoratori Abbigliamento (Italian Federation of
Garment Workers)

FILDA . . . . . . Federazione Italiana Lavoratori degli Acquedotti (Italian Federation of
Aqueduct Workers)

FILAM . . . . . . Federazione Italiana Lavoratori Albergo Mensa e Termali (National
Union of Hotel and Restaurant Workers) (Italy)

FILAI . . . . . . Federazione Italiana Lavoratori Ausiliari dell' Impiego (Italian Federation
of Auxiliary Services)

FILC . . . . Federazione Italiana Lavoratori Chimici (Italian Federation of Chemical
Workers)

FILCEA . . . . . Federazione Italiana Lavoratori Commercio e Aggregati (Italian Federation of Commercial and Associated Workers)

FILCA . . . . . . Federazione Italiana Lavoratori Costruzioni e Affini (Italian Federation
of Construction and Related Workers)

FILIA . . . . . . Federazione Italiana Lavoratori Industrie Alimentari (Italian Federation of
Food Processing Workers)

FILIE . . . . . . Federazione Italiana Lavoratori Industrie Estrattive (Italian Federation of
Workers in Mining Industries)

FILLBAV . . . . . Federazione Italiana Lavoratori Legno-Boschivi -- Artistiche e Varie
(National Federation of Carpenters, Lumbermen, Cabinetmakers) (Italy)

FILLEA . . . . . . Federazione Italiana Lavoratori del Legno, dell'Edilizia e Industrie
Affini (Italian Federation of Construction and Allied Workers)

FILM . . . . Federazione Italiana Lavoratori del Mare (Italian Federation of Merchant
Seamen)

FILPC . . . . . . Federazione Italiana Lavoratori Poligrafici e Cartai (Italian Federation
of Printers and Paperworkers)

FILP . . . . Federazione Italiana Lavoratori dei Porti (Italian Federation of Longshoremen)

FENALPORTI . . Federazione Nazionale dei Lavoratori Portuali (National Federation of
Port Workers) (Italy)

FILSA . . . . . . Federazione Italiana Lavoratori Sanatoriali (Italian Federation of Public
Health Workers - Hospital and Sanatorium Employees)

FILSTA . . . . . . Federazione Italiana Lavoratori Servizi Tributari e Assicuratori (Italian
Federation of Tax Workers)

FILS . . . . Federazione Italiana Lavoratori dello Spettacolo (Italian Federation of
Entertainment Workers)

FILS . . . . Federazione Italiana Lavoratori Statali (Italian Federation of Government
Employees)

FIL . . . . Federazione Italiana del Lavoro (Italian Federation of Labor)

FIM . . . . Federazione Italiana Metal-Meccanici (Italian Metal Mechanic Workers'
Federation)

FIP . . . . Federazione Italiana Pensionati (Italian Federation of Pensioners)

FIP . . . . Federazione Italiana Postelegrafonici (Italian Federation of Postal,
Telegraph, and Telephone Workers)

FISBA . . . . . . Federazione Italiana Salariati Braccianti Agricoli e Maestranze
Specializzate Agricole e Forestali (Italian Federation of Permanent
Unskilled and Skilled Agricultural Workers)

FISBTA . . . . . . Federazione Italiana Salariati, Braccianti e Tecnici Agricoli (Italian
Federation of Permanent, Daily and Technical Agricultural Workers)

FISP . . . . Federazione Italiana Servizi Pubblici (Italian Federation of Public
Services)

FISASCA . . . . Federazione Italiana Sindacati Addetti Servizi Commerciali ed Affini
(Italian Federation of Commercial and Related Workers' Unions)

FISO . . . . Federazione Italiana Sindacato Ospedalieri (Italian Federation of Hospital
Workers' Union)

FILTAT . . . . . . Federazione Italiana Trasporti ed Ausiliari del Traffico (Italian Federation of Transportation and Auxiliary Services)

FIVAG . . . . . . Federazione Italiana Venditori Ambulanti e Giornalai (Italian **Federation**
of Street Vendors and Newspaper Sellers)

FIVF . . . . Federazione Italiana Vigili del Fuoco (Italian Federation of Firemen)

FLAEI . . . . . . Federazione Laboratori Aziende Elettriche Italiane (Federation of Workers
for Italian Electrical Firms)

FLS . . . . Federazione Lavoratori Somali (Somali Labor Federation)

FNDEL . . . . . . Federazione Nazionale Dipendenti Enti locali (National Federation of
Local Government) (Italy)

FENEAL . . . . . Federazione Nazionale Edili, Affini e del Legno (National Federation
of Building and Construction Workers) (Italy)

FNDS . . . . Federazione Nazionale delgi Statali (Italian Federation of Government
Employees)

FNVCA . . . . . . Federazione Nazionale Vetro e Ceramica (National Federation of Glass
and Pottery Workers) (Italy)

FSLUS . . . . . . Federazione dei Sindacati Lavoratori Uniti della Somalia (Somali
Federation of United Trade Unions)

FSSC . . . . Federazione Svizzera dei Sindacati Cristiani (Swiss Federation of
National-Christian Trade Unions)

FUILA . . . . . . Federazione Unitaria Italiana Lavoratori Abbigliamento (Italian
Amalgamated Federation of Garment Workers)

FULPIA . . . . . . Federazione Unitaria Lavoratori Prodotti Industrie Alimentari e dello
Zucchero e dell 'Alcool (Amalgamated Federation of Food Processing,
Sugar and Liquor Industries' Workers) (Italy)

FULS . . . . Federazione Unitaria Lavoratori dello Spettacolo (Amalgamated Federation of Entertainment Workers) (Italy)

FBN . . . . Feed Back Network

FMPC . . . . . . Feed Materials Production Center (AEC)

FWHMA . . . . . Feed Water Heater Manufacturers Association

F . . . . Feedback

FCS . . . . Feedback Control System

FBFM . . . . . . Feedback Frequency Modulation

FM . . . . Feedback Mechanism

FML . . . . Feedback, Multiple Loop

FP . . . . Feedback Positive

FP . . . . Feedback Potentiometer

FSR . . . . Feedback Shift Register

FS . . . . Feedback, Stabilized

FHM . . . . Feedwater Heater Management

FITCAL . . . . . . Feel, Inspect, Tighten, Clean, Adjust, Lubricate (A keyword
representing operations in preventive maintenance of communications
equipment) (Military)

FRI . . . . Feeling Rough Inside (Slang)

F . . . . Feet or Foot

FBM . . . . Feet Board Measure

FPM . . . . Feet Per Minute

FPS . . . . Feet Per Second

FS . . . . Feet Per Second (Ordnance)

FE . . . . Feliciana Eastern R. R. (AAR code)

F . . . . Feliciter (Happily)

FELV . . . . Feline Leukemia Virus

F . . . . Fellow

FAAS . . . . . . Fellow of the Academy of Arts and Sciences

FAAAS . . . . . Fellow of the American Association for the Advancement of Science

FAAC . . . . . . Fellow of the American Association of Criminology

FACA . . . . . . Fellow of the American College of Anesthesiologists

FACC . . . . . . Fellow of the American College of Cardiologists

FCCP . . . . . . Fellow of the American College of Chest Physicians

FACD . . . . . . Fellow of the American College of Dentists

FACOG . . . . . Fellow of the American College of Obstetricians and Gynecologists

FACP . . . . . . Fellow of the American College of Physicians

FACR . . . . . . Fellow of the American College of Radiologists

FACS . . . . . . Fellow of the American College of Surgeons

FAGS . . . . . . Fellow of the American Geographical Society

FAIA . . . . . . Fellow of the American Institute of Architects

FAIC . . . . . . Fellow of the American Institute of Criminology

FAMA . . . . . Fellow of the American Medical Association

FAPS . . . . . . Fellow of the American Physical Society

FAPHA . . . . . Fellow of the American Public Health Association

FAS . . . . Fellow of the Antiquarian Society (British)

FASE . . . . . . Fellow of the Antiquarian Society of Edinburgh

FANZCP . . . . Fellow of the Australian and New Zealand College of Psychiatrists

FBS . . . . Fellow of the Botanical Society (British)

FBA . . . . Fellow of the British Academy

FBOA . . . . . . Fellow of the British Optical Association

FBPsS . . . . . . Fellow of the British Psychological Society

FCCO . . . . . . Fellow of the Canadian College of Organists

FCIS . . . . . . Fellow of the Chartered Institute of Secretaries

FCS . . . . Fellow of the Chemical Society (British)

FCAP . . . . . . Fellow of the College of American Pathologists

FCGP . . . . . . Fellow of the College of General Practitioners

FCO . . . . Fellow of the College of Organists (British)

FCPS . . . . Fellow of the College of Physicians and Surgeons
FCP . . . . Fellow of the College of Preceptors (British)
FDS . . . . Fellow of Dental Surgery
FEIS . . . . Fellow of the Educational Institute of Scotland
FES . . . . Fellow of the Ethnological Society (British)
FFA . . . . Fellow of the Faculty of Actuaries (British)
FFPS . . . . . . Fellow of the Faculty of Physicians and Surgeons
FFR . . . . Fellow of the Faculty of Radiologists (British)
FGS . . . . Fellow of the Geological Society (British)
FGSA . . . . Fellow of the Geological Society of America
FIA . . . . Fellow of the Institute of Actuaries (British)
FIC . . . . Fellow of the Institute of Chemistry (British)
FIF . . . . Fellow of the Institute of Fuels
FICD . . . . . . Fellow of the International College of Dentists
FICS . . . . Fellow of the International College of Surgeons
FKC . . . . Fellow of King's College (London)
FKCL . . . . Fellow of King's College, London
FKQCP . . . . . . Fellow of the King's and Queen's College of Physicians, Ireland
FLA . . . . Fellow of the Library Association (British)
FLS . . . . Fellow of the Linnaean Society
FMS . . . . Fellow of the Meteorological Society (British)
FPS . . . . Fellow of the Pharmaceutical Society
FPS . . . . Fellow of the Philological Society (British)
FPS . . . . Fellow of the Physical Society (British)
FRAI . . . . Fellow of the Royal Anthropological Institute (British)
FR and ASS . . . Fellow of the Royal and Antiquarian Societies (British)
FRAS . . . . Fellow of the Royal Asiatic Society
FRAS . . . . . Fellow of the Royal Astronomical Society (British)
FRACP . . . . . . Fellow of the Royal Australasian College of Physicians
FRACS . . . . . . Fellow of the Royal Australasian College of Surgeons
FRBS . . . . Fellow of the Royal Botanic Society (British)
FRCM . . . . . . Fellow of the Royal College of Music
FRCOG . . . . . . Fellow of the Royal College of Obstetricians and Gynaecologists (British)
FRCO . . . . Fellow of the Royal College of Organists
FRCP . . . . Fellow of the Royal College of Physicians (British)
FRCS . . . . Fellow of the Royal College of Surgeons (British)
FRCSL . . . . . . Fellow of the Royal College of Surgeons of London
FRCVS . . . . . . Fellow of the Royal College of Veterinary Surgeons (British)
FRCI . . . . Fellow of the Royal Colonial Institute (British)
FRES . . . . Fellow of the Royal Entomological Society (British)
FRFPS . . . . . . Fellow of the Royal Faculty of Physicians and Surgeons (British)
FRGS . . . . Fellow of the Royal Geographical Society (British)
FRHS . . . . Fellow of the Royal Historical Society (British)
FRHS . . . . Fellow of the Royal Horticultural Society (British)
FRIBA . . . . . . Fellow of the Royal Institute of British Architects
FRIC . . . . Fellow of the Royal Institute of Chemistry (British)
FRIPHH . . . . . Fellow of the Royal Institute of Public Health and Hygiene (British)
FRMS . . . . Fellow of the Royal Microscopical Society (British)
FRS . . . . Fellow of the Royal Society
FRSE . . . . Fellow of the Royal Society of Edinburgh
FRSH . . . . Fellow of the Royal Society of Health (British)
FRSL . . . . Fellow of the Royal Society of Literature (British)
FRSS . . . . Fellow of the Royal Statistical Society
FSA . . . . Fellow of the Society of Actuaries
FSA . . . . Fellow of the Society of Antiquaries (British)
FSAS . . . . Fellow of the Society of Antiquaries of Scotland
FSSA . . . . Fellow of the Society of Science and Art (British)
FSS . . . . Fellow of the Statistical Society (British)
FSI . . . . Fellow of the Surveyors' Institute (British)
FTPS . . . . . . Fellow of the Technical Publishing Society
FTI . . . . Fellow of the Textile Institute (British)
FTCD . . . . . . Fellow of Trinity College, Dublin
FZA . . . . Fellow of the Zoological Academy
FZS . . . . Fellow of the Zoological Society (British)
FAS . . . . Fellows in American Studies
FCA . . . . Fellowship of Christian Athletes
FOR . . . . Fellowship of Reconciliation
FRH . . . . Fellowship of Religious Humanists
FORJ . . . . Fellowship of Religious Journalists
FSC . . . . Fellowship of Southern Churchmen
FA . . . . Felonious Assault
FMC . . . . Felt Manufacturers Council
FEL . . . . Felt & Tarrant Manufacturing Company (NYSE symbol)
FREL . . . . . . Feltman Research & Engineering Laboratory (Army)
FRL . . . . Feltman Research Laboratory (Army)
F . . . . Female
FG . . . . Female Groove
F . . . . Feminine
FDS . . . . Feminine Deodorant Spray (Initialism used as brand name)
f . . . . Femto (Prefix)
FAST . . . . Fence Against Satellite Threats

FNT . . . . Fenestra Incorporated (NYSE symbol)
FB . . . . Fenian Brotherhood (Irish)
FRDN . . . . . . Ferdinand R. R. (AAR code)
F . . . . Fermi
FDG . . . . Fermi-Dirac Gas
FDS . . . . Fermi-Dirac Statistics
FSR . . . . Fermi Selection Rules
Fm . . . . Fermium (Chemical element)
FCG . . . . Fernwood, Columbia & Gulf R. R. (AAR code)
FLD . . . . Ferret LASER Detector
FGD . . . . Ferri-Gas Duplexer
FAD . . . . Ferrite Array Demonstration (RADAR)
FCA . . . . Ferrite Control Amplifier
FC . . . . Ferrite Core
FDA . . . . Ferrite Driver Amplifier
FMA . . . . Ferrite Manufacturers Association
FMC . . . . Ferrite Memory Core
FM . . . . Ferrite Metal
FPD . . . . Ferrite Phase Driver
FPS . . . . Ferrite Phase Shifter
FOE . . . . Ferro Corporation (NYSE symbol)
CHP . . . . Ferrocarril de Chihuahua al Pacifico, SA (AAR code)
FCM . . . . Ferrocarril Mexicano (AAR code)
MDP . . . . . . Ferrocarril Mexicano del Pacifico (AAR code)
FDMA . . . . . . Ferrocarril de Minatitlan al Carmen (AAR code)
NDT . . . . . . Ferrocarril Nacional de Tehuantepec (AAR code)
FCDN . . . . . . Ferrocarril de Nacozari (AAR code)
NODM . . . . . . Ferrocarril Nor-Oeste de Mexico (Mexico North Western R. R.) (AAR code)
FCP . . . . Ferrocarril del Pacifico (AAR code)
SCOP . . . . . . Ferrocarril del Sureste (AAR code)
FNM . . . . . . Ferrocarriles Nacionales des Mexico (National Railroad of Mexico)
MGRS . . . . . . Ferrocarriles Nacionales de Mexico (AAR code)
NDM . . . . . . Ferrocarriles Nacionales de Mexico (AAR code)
FPCP . . . . . . Ferrocene Polymer Cure Process
FE . . . . Ferroelectric
FEC . . . . Ferroelectric Ceramic
FE-EL . . . . . . Ferroelectric-Electroluminescent
FEVAC . . . . . . Ferroelectric Variable Capacitor
FMM . . . . . . Ferromagnetic Material
FMD . . . . . . Ferrous Metal Detector
FMP . . . . . . Ferrous Metal Powder
FJC . . . . Ferrum Junior College (Virginia)
FC . . . . Ferry Command (British Royal Air Force)
FPL . . . . Ferry-Potter Law
FSU . . . . Ferry Service Unit
YFB . . . . Ferryboat (Navy symbol)
FGAN . . . . . . Fertilizer Grade Ammonium Nitrate
FIRT . . . . Fertilizer Industry Round Table
FHS . . . . Fetal Heart Sounds
HbF . . . . Fetal Hemoglobin (Physiology)
FTT . . . . Fever Therapy Technician (Navy)
FUO . . . . Fever of Undetermined Origin (Medicine)
F . . . . Fiat (Let There Be Made)
FSA . . . . Fiat Secundum Artem (Let It Be Done According to Art) (Old medical term)
FCM . . . . Fiber Composite Material
FGB . . . . Fiber Glass Brush
FGCB . . . . . . Fiber Glass Cone Brush
FGC . . . . Fiber Glass Curtain
FGH . . . . Fiber Glass Hull
FOBS . . . . . . Fiber Optic Borescope
FOPP . . . . . . Fiber Optic Photo Pickup
FOPT . . . . . . Fiber Optic Photo Transfer
FOB . . . . Fiber Optics Bundle
FOL . . . . Fiber Optics LASER
FOL . . . . Fiber Optics Light
FOP . . . . Fiber Optics Probe
FPCA . . . . . . Fiber Producers Credit Association
FRC . . . . Fiber Reinforced Composite
FRCJ . . . . Fiber Reinforced Composite Junction
FIW . . . . Fiberglass Insulated Wire
FRP . . . . Fiberglass-Reinforced Plastic
FRTP . . . . . . Fiberglass Reinforced Thermoplastic
FBA . . . . Fibre Box Association
FDMA . . . . . . Fibre Drum Manufacturers Association (Defunct)
FPP . . . . Fibreboard Paper Products Corporation (NYSE symbol)
FSF . . . . Fibrinstabilizing Factor
FTA . . . . Fiches Typologiques Africaines
FDL . . . . Fick Diffusion Law
F . . . . Fiction

FD . . . . Fidei Defensor (Defender of the Faith)
FC . . . . Fideicommissum (Bequeathed in Trust)
FPX . . . . Fidelity-Phoenix Fire Insurance Company (NYSE symbol)
F . . . . Field
FAC . . . . Field Accelerator
F/A . . . . Field Activities
FAWESP . . . . . Field Activity War and Emergency Support Plan
FA . . . . Field Ambulance (Military)
FA . . . . Field Army
FABMDS . . . . . Field Army Ballistic Missile Defense System
FABMIDS . . . . Field Army Ballistic Missile Defense System (anti-missile missile)
FACTS . . . . . . Field Army Calibration Team Support
FACS . . . . Field Army Communication System
FAIO . . . . Field Army Issuing Office
FAMS . . . . Field Army Messenger Service
FAPO . . . . Field Army Petroleum Office
FARS . . . . Field Army Replacement System
FASA . . . . Field Army Service Area
FASCOM . . . . . Field Army Strategic Command
FASCOM . . . . . Field Army Support Command
FATOC . . . . . . Field Army Tactical Operation Center
FATRACS . . . . . Field Army Tactical Random Access Communications System
FA . . . . Field Artillery
FAA . . . . Field Artillery Airborne
FACE . . . . Field Artillery Computer Equipment
FADAC . . . . . . Field Artillery Data Computer (Military)
FALT . . . . FADAC (Field Artillery Data Computer) Automatic Logic Tester (Military)
FADAC . . . . . . Field Artillery Digital Automatic Computer (Army)
FAGMS . . . . . . Field Artillery Guided Missile (Air Force)
FALT . . . . Field Artillery Logic Tester (Army)
FAM . . . . Field Artillery Missile
FARC . . . . Field Artillery Replacement Center
FATAB . . . . . . Field Artillery Target Acquisition Battalion (Army)
FATAG . . . . . . Field Artillery Target Acquisition Group (Army)
FACT . . . . Field Audit and Completion Test (Market research)
FAO . . . . Field Audit Office
FAIF . . . . Field Automated Intelligence File
FCIP . . . . Field Cable Installation Platoon (Army)
FC . . . . Field Camera
FCC . . . . Field Camera Control
FCLP . . . . Field Carrier Landing Passes
FCLP . . . . Field Carrier Landing Practice
FCA . . . . Field Change Authorization
FCK . . . . Field Change Kit
FCE . . . . Field Checkout Equipment
FC/DASA . . . . Field Command, Defense Atomic Support Agency
FCP . . . . Field Command Post
FCAD . . . . . . Field Contract Administration Division (of ONM)
FCC . . . . Field Control Center
FLDCK . . . . . . Field Cook (Marine Corps)
FLDCK(B) . . . . Field Cook (Baker) (Marine Corps)
FLDCK(C) . . . . Field Cook (Commissary) (Marine Corps)
FAST . . . . Field Data Applications, Systems, and Techniques
FDC . . . . Field Data Computer
FIELDATA . . . . Field Data Computers (Army)
FDE . . . . Field Decelerator
FDAS . . . . Field Depot Aviation Squadron (Air Force)
FDN . . . . Field Designator Number (Air Force)
FDI . . . . Field Discharge
FDI . . . . Field Displacement Isolator
FDB . . . . Field Dynamic Braking
FEA . . . . Field Effect Amplifier
FED . . . . Field Effect Device
FET . . . . Field Effect Transistor
FETS . . . . Field Effect Transistors
FEM . . . . Field-Electron Microscopy
FEMS . . . . Field Electronic Maintenance Section (Weather bureau)
FEM . . . . Field Emission Microscope
FES . . . . Field Emitting Surface
FE . . . . Field Engineer(ing)
FES . . . . Field Engineering Service
FESE . . . . Field-Enhanced Secondary Emission
FEA . . . . Field Evaluation Agency (Army)
FEM . . . . Field Evaluation Model
F of F . . . . . . Field of Fire (Military)
FFD . . . . Field Forcing (Decreasing)
FFI . . . . Field Forcing (Increasing)
FFEC . . . . Field-Free Emission Current
FGCM . . . . . . Field General Court-Martial
FHDO . . . . . . Field Handling Design Objective

FHAA . . . . Field Hockey Association of America
FIAT . . . . Field Information Agency, Technical (Under G-2, SHAEF)
FIS . . . . Field Infrared Spectrometer
FIS . . . . Field Installation Simulator
FIC . . . . Field Installed Connector
FID . . . . Field Intelligence Department
FI . . . . Field Intensity
FIMS . . . . Field Intensity Measuring System
FIM . . . . Field Intensity Meter
FIR . . . . Field Intensity Receiver
FOIR . . . . Field-of-Interest Register (DOD)
FIM . . . . Field Ion Microscope
FLT . . . . Field Level Training
FLR . . . . Field Loss Relay
FM . . . . Field Maintenance
FMP . . . . Field Maintenance Party (Aviation)
FLDMS . . . . . . Field Maintenance Shop (Army)
FMTS . . . . Field Maintenance Test Station (Army)
FM . . . . Field Manual
FM . . . . Field Marshal
FMLP . . . . Field Mirror Landing Practice
FM . . . . Field Music (Marine Corps)
FMCORP . . . . Field Music Corporal (Marine Corps)
FMCPL . . . . . . Field Music Corporal (Marine Corps)
FMS . . . . Field Music School (Marine Corps)
FMSGT . . . . . . Field Music Sergeant (Marine Corps)
FOF . . . . Field Observing Facility (of National Center for Atmospheric Research)
FO . . . . Field Office
FLDO . . . . Field Officer
FO . . . . Field Officer
FOD . . . . Field Officer of the Day (Army)
FOD . . . . Field Operations Department
FOG . . . . Field Operations Group
FOI . . . . Field Operations Intelligence
FO . . . . Field Order
FPR . . . . Field Personnel Record
FPO . . . . Field Post Office (British military)
FPS . . . . Field Power Supply
FPA . . . . Field Profit Analysis
FPO . . . . Field Project Officer
FP . . . . Field Punishment (Military)
FR . . . . Field Report
FRE . . . . Field Representative Europe
FRFE . . . . Field Representative Far East
FRL . . . . Field Requirements List
FS . . . . Field Security (British Army detective police – a branch of Intelligence)
FSO . . . . Field Security Officer (Military)
FSB . . . . Field Selection Board (Military)
FS . . . . Field Service
FSMWO . . . . . Field Service Modification Work Order
FSR . . . . Field Service Regulations (Army)
FSR . . . . Field Service Representative
FSS . . . . Field Service Section (Military)
FSU . . . . Field Storage Unit (Military)
FSM . . . . Field Strength Meter
FSR . . . . Field Strength Radio
FST . . . . Field Suitability Test
FSE . . . . Field Support Engineer
FSE . . . . Field Support Equipment (Military)
FTDC . . . . . . Field Testing and Development Center
FTU . . . . Field Torpedo Unit
FT . . . . Field Training (AFROTC)
FTD . . . . Field Training Detachment
FTECS . . . . . . Field Training Equipment Concentration Site (Army)
FTX . . . . Field Training Exercise
FOV . . . . Field of View (or Vision)
FW . . . . Field Weakening
FW . . . . Field Worship (British Army)
FRED . . . . Fiendishly Rapid Electronic Device
FC . . . . Fieri Curavit (Caused to Be Made)
FF . . . . Fieri Fecit (Caused to Be Made)
FCL . . . . Fifth Avenue Coach Lines, Inc. (NYSE symbol)
FOT . . . . Fifth Order Theory
FADD . . . . . . Fight Against Dictating Designers (Group opposing below-the-knee fashions introduced in 1970)
DI . . . . Fighter (Russian aircraft symbol)
F . . . . Fighter (Aircraft)
I . . . . Fighter (Russian aircraft symbol)
JP . . . . Fighter (Russian aircraft symbol)
LA . . . . Fighter (Russian aircraft symbol)
LAGG . . . . . . Fighter (Russian aircraft symbol)

LF	Fighter Aircraft Fitted with Engine Rated for Low Altitude Performance
FANTAC	Fighter Analysis Tactical Air Combat
F/B	Fighter Bomber
FB	Fighter Bomber Aircraft
FBP	Fighter Bomber Program
VFB	Fighter Bombing Plane (Navy symbol)
FC	Fighter Command (Air Force)
FCS	Fighter Command School (Air Force)
FCA	Fighter Control Area (Military)
FDP	Fighter Development Program
FD	Fighter Direction
FDNET	Fighter Direction Net (Navy)
FDCS	Fighter Director Control Schools (Navy)
FDO	Fighter Director Officer (Navy)
FDS	Fighter Director Ship (Navy)
FDT	Fighter Director Tender (Navy)
FDB	Fighter Dive-Bomber
FE	Fighter Escort
FIS	Fighter Identification System
FINE	Fighter Inertial Navigation System
FI	Fighter Interceptor
FIS	Fighter-Interceptor Squadron (Air Force)
FIW	Fighter Interceptor Wing
FMS	Fighter Missile System
FOI	Fighter Officer for Interceptors (Member of the SAGE Command Post staff)
FOM	Fighter Officer for Missiles (Member of the SAGE Command Post staff)
VF	Fighter Plane (Navy symbol)
VF(M)	Fighter Plane (Two-engine) (Navy symbol)
FR	Fighter Reconnaissance
F/R	Fighter Reconnaissance (Air Force)
VF	Fighter Squadron (Navy symbol)
VF AW	Fighter Squadron – All Weather
VFP	Fighter Squadron, Photo
FLP	Fighting Landplane
FIGHTRON	Fighting Squadron
FBA	Figural Bottle Association
FM	Figure of Merit
FOM	Figure of Merit
FRED	Figure Reading Electronic Device (Information retrieval)
FFL	Fiji Federation of Labor
FIWC	Fiji Industrial Workers' Congress
FIMMEMA	Fikambanan' Ny Mpanoratra Sy Mpamoron-Kira Ary Editora Malagasy (Malagasy Republic)
FCT	Filament Center Tap
FCM	Filament Composite Material
FM	Filament Midtop
FGF	Filament-Wound Glass Fiber
FWS	Filament Wound Structure
FC	File Copy
FMA	File Manufacturers Association
FRINGE	File and Report Information Processing Generators (Data processing)
FIBI	Filed but Impracticable (to transmit)
FABB	Filene's (Boston) Automatic Bargain Basement
FCO	Files Control Office
FDP	Filii Divinae Providentiae (Sons of Divine Providence) (Roman Catholic religious order)
FMSI	Filii Mariae Salutis Infirmorum (Sons of Mary, Health of the Sick) (Roman Catholic religious order)
FLT	Filing Time
FT	Filing Time (Time a message is presented for transmission)
FRC	Filipino Rehabilitation Commission (Post-World War II)
F	Filius (Son)
FEE	Fill Exit Entry (Data processing)
FPA	Fill Producers' Association
FSE	Fill Start Entry (Data processing)
FQH	Filled Quartz Helix
FSN	Filler Sensor Nozzle
FWA	Filler Wire Addition
F	Filly
FB	Film Bulletin
F & EE	Film and Equipment Exchange (Army)
FIDAC	Film Input to Digital Automatic Computer
FIDACSYS	Film Input to Digital Automatic Computer System
FLIC	Film Library Information Council
FLIP	Film Library Instantaneous Presentation (Data processing)
FOSDIC	Film Optical Sensing Device for Input to Computers (of the National Bureau of Standards)
FPANY	Film Producers Association of New York
FRM	Film Reading Machine
FR	Film Report

FATCAT	Film and Television Correlation Assessment Technique
FTI	Film Thickness Indicator
FTM	Film Thickness Monitor
FTR	Film Tracing Reproduction
FTA	Film Training Aid
FS	Filmstrip
FFW	Filoil Free Workers (Philippines)
F	Filter
FAC	Filter Address Correction
FBSA	Filter Band Suppressor Assembly
FC	Filter Center
FILCEN	Filter Center
FCK	Filter Change Kit
FA	Filterable Agent (Virology)
FF	Filtration Fraction (Physiology)
FLT	Filtrol Corporation (NYSE symbol) (Wall Street slang name: "Flit")
FS	Fin Stabilized (Rocketry)
FSR	Fin Stabilized Rockets
F	Final Approach (Aviation)
FAP	Final Approach (Aviation)
FAE	Final Approach Equipment
FAF	Final Approach Fix (Aviation)
FAT	Final Assembly Test
FBP	Final Boiling Point
FBRL	Final Bomb Release Line
FCP	Final Common Pathway (Neurology)
FCL	Final Coordination Line (Military)
FDR	Final Data Report
FDC(M)	Final Design Criteria
FER	Final Engineering Report
FLDO	Final Limit, Down
FLF	Final Limit, Forward
FLH	Final Limit, Hoist
FLL	Final Limit, Lower
FLR	Final Limit, Reverse
FLU	Final Limit, Up
FMR	Final Meteorological Radiation
FMRT	Final Meteorological Radiation Tape
FOC	Final Operational Capability (Military)
FPA	Final Power Amplifier
FPC	Final Processing Center
FPBG	Final Program and Budget Guidance
FPR	Final Progress Report
FPF	Final Protective Fire (Artillery term)
FPL	Final Protective Line (Military)
FR	Final Report
FSTDY	Final Semester Temporary Duty (Air Force)
FS	Final Settlement
FSV	Final Stage Vehicle
F/S	Final Statement (Army)
FSV	Final Storage Vehicle
F	Final Target
FTR	Final Technical Report
FYTDY	Final Year Temporary Duty (Air Force)
F	Finance or Financial
FAAO	Finance and Accounts Office (Army)
FAO	Finance and Accounts Office(r) (Military)
FAOUSA	Finance and Accounts Office(r), United States Army
FCUSA	Finance Center, United States Army
FC	Finance Charge
FC	Finance Corps
FD	Finance Department
FDS	Finance Disbursing Section (Army)
FGO	Finance Group Office
FIRE	Finance, Insurance, and Real Estate (Insurance)
FINO	Finance Officer (Army)
FO	Finance Officer
FOUSA	Finance Officer, United States Army
FSUSA	Finance School, United States Army
FSA	Finance Service, Army
FINSUPSCOL	Finance and Supply School (Coast Guard)
FAC	Financial Administrative Control
FA	Financial Adviser
FINAL	Financial Analysis Language
FAME	Financial Analysis of Management Effectiveness (Department of Agriculture)
FAP	Financial Analysis Program (IBM)
FAF	Financial Analysts Federation
FAP	Financial Assistance Program
FAST RIPSAW	Financial Automation Systems Team for Writing Programs for Standardized Army-Wide Applications

FDRF . . . . Financial Data Records Folder
FEI . . . . Financial Executives Institute
FERF . . . . Financial Executives Research Foundation
FEP . . . . Financial Evaluation Program (IBM)
FFI . . . . Financial Federation, Inc. (NYSE symbol)
FIRM . . . . Financial Information for Resources Management
FIA . . . . Financial Inventory Accounting
FIC . . . . Financial Inventory Control
FICR . . . . Financial Inventory Control Report
FAMIS . . . . . . Financial and Management Information System (Naval Oceanographic Office)
FIMIS . . . . . . Financial Management Information System (Army)
FMP . . . . Financial Management Plan
FMPEC . . . . . Financial Management Plan for Emergency Conditions
FMS . . . . Financial Management System
FOP . . . . Financial Operating Plan
FP . . . . Financial Plan
FPRA . . . . . . Financial Public Relations Association
FS . . . . Financial Secretary
FIASA . . . . . . Financiera Industrial y Agropecuaria, SA (Guatemala)
F & D . . . . . . Findings and Determination
F . . . . Fine (Condition) (Antiquarian book trade)
FAF . . . . Fine Arts Foundation
FAP . . . . Fine Arts Philatelists
FACS . . . . . . Fine Attitude Control System (Aerospace)
FBS . . . . Fine Bearing Servo
FB . . . . Fine Business (i.e., excellent) (Amateur radio)
FC . . . . Fine Champagne
FC . . . . Fine Cognac
FDW . . . . Fine (Condition) in Dust Wrapper (Antiquarian book trade)
FG . . . . Fine Grain
FGD . . . . Fine Grain Data (Equipment) (RADAR)
FHA . . . . Fine Hardwoods Association
FM . . . . Fine Measurement
FO . . . . Fine Old
FOB . . . . Fine Old Blend (Wines and spirits)
FOES . . . . . . Fine Old Extra Special
FP . . . . Fine Paper
FSWMA . . . . . Fine and Specialty Wire Manufacturers Association
FR . . . . Fineness Ratio
FIRE . . . . Fingerprint Reader
F . . . . Finish
FAO . . . . Finish All Over (Technical drawings)
F 1S . . . . Finish One Side (Technical drawings)
FS . . . . Finish Specification
F 2S . . . . Finish Two Sides (Technical drawings)
FWE . . . . Finished with Engines
FGC . . . . Finished Goods Control
FA . . . . Finite Automaton
FAL . . . . Finite Automaton Language
FEM . . . . Finite Element Method
FSG . . . . Finite State Grammar
FSL . . . . Finite State Language
FAHA . . . . . . Finnish-American Historical Archives
FAHSM . . . . . Finnish American Historical Society of Michigan
FALD . . . . . . Finnish American League for Democracy
FAS . . . . Finnish-American Society
FRIA . . . . Finnish Radio Industries Association
FWVA . . . . . . Finnish War Veterans in America
FWEA . . . . . . Finnish Workers' Educational Association
FHDA . . . . . . Fir and Hemlock Door Association
FISEMA . . . . . Firaisan'ny Sendika eran'i Madagaskara (Confederation of All Unions in Madagascar)
F . . . . Fire
FABL . . . . Fire Alarm Bell
FABX . . . . Fire Alarm Box
FAMA . . . . . . Fire Apparatus Manufacturers Association
F & B . . . . . . Fire and Bilge
FB . . . . Fire Brigade
FBH . . . . Fire Brigade Hydrant
FBU . . . . Fire Brigade Union
FACILE . . . . . . Fire and Casualty Insurance Library Edition
FC . . . . Fire Clay
FC . . . . Fire Control (Of guns)
FCA . . . . Fire Control Area (Army)
FCC . . . . Fire Control Code
FCE . . . . Fire Control Equipment
FCG . . . . Fire Control Group
FCO . . . . Fire Control Operator (Army)
FCOI . . . . Fire Control Optical Instrument
FCP . . . . Fire Control Personnel (Marine Corps)

FCP . . . . Fire Control Platoon (Army)
FCR . . . . Fire Control RADAR
FCSG . . . . Fire Control Sensor Group
FCS . . . . Fire Control Simulator
FCSU . . . . Fire Control Switching Unit
FCS . . . . Fire Control System
FCSL . . . . Fire Control System Laboratory
FCT . . . . Fire Control Technician (Navy)
FT . . . . Fire Control Technician
FCTP . . . . Fire Control Test Package
FCT . . . . Fire Control Trainer
FCU . . . . Fire Control Unit
FC . . . . Fire Controlman
FCR . . . . Fire Controlman, Range-Finder Operator (Navy rating)
FCS . . . . Fire Controlman, Submarine (Navy)
FCL . . . . Fire Coordination Line (Military)
FD . . . . Fire Department
FDC . . . . Fire-Department Connection (Technical drawings)
FDIC . . . . Fire Department Instructors Conference
FDC . . . . Fire Detection Center
FDS . . . . Fire Detection System
FD . . . . Fire Direction
FDC . . . . Fire Direction Center (Military)
FDO . . . . Fire Direction Officer (Army)
FDS . . . . Fire Distribution System
FEMA . . . . . . Fire Equipment Manufacturers Association
F & F . . . . . . Fire and Flushing
FG . . . . Fire Guardsman (British) (World War II)
FITH . . . . Fire-in-the-Hole (Burn) (NASA)
FHR . . . . Fire Hose Rack
FHY . . . . Fire Hydrant
FIRAA . . . . . . Fire Insurance Research and Actuarial Association
FMANA . . . . . Fire Marshals Association of North America
FP . . . . Fire Plug
FRES . . . . Fire Resistant
FR . . . . Fire (or Flame) Retardant (or Resistant)
FROF . . . . . . Fire Risk on Freight (Insurance)
FSI . . . . Fire Service Instructors
FS . . . . Fire Station (Maps and charts)
FS . . . . Fire Support
FAS . . . . Fire Support Aerial System
FSA . . . . Fire Support Area (Military)
FSCC . . . . . . Fire Support Coordination Center (Military)
FSCL . . . . . . Fire Support Coordination Line (Military)
FSCS . . . . . . Fire Support Coordination Section
FSCOORD . . . . Fire Support Coordinator (Military)
FSE . . . . Fire Support Element (Military)
FSS . . . . Fire Support Ship
FT . . . . Fire-Tube (Scotch-Type) Boiler
FU . . . . Fire Unit (Military)
FUA . . . . Fire Unit Analyzer (Military)
FUIF . . . . Fire Unit Integration Facility (Military)
FUD . . . . Fire Up Decoder
FW . . . . Fire Wall (Technical drawings)
FWWMR . . . . . Fire, Water, Weather, Mildew Resistant
FBR . . . . Fireball Radius (Military)
F . . . . Fireman (Navy rating)
FN . . . . Fireman (Nonrated enlisted man) (Navy)
FA . . . . Fireman Apprentice
FR . . . . Fireman Recruit
FP . . . . Fireplace
FAA . . . . Fireplace Association of America
FIR . . . . Firestone Tire & Rubber Company (NYSE symbol)
FEI . . . . Firing Error Indicator
FIRETRAC . . . . Firing Error Trajectory Recorder and Computer
FT . . . . Firing Tables (Military)
F . . . . Firm
FFP . . . . Firm-Fixed Price (Government contracting)
FFPC . . . . Firm-Fixed Price Contract
FO . . . . Firm Offer (Business and trade)
FAAG . . . . . . First Advertising Agency Group
FAAN . . . . . . First Advertising Agency Network
FA . . . . First Aid (Medicine)
FANY . . . . . . First Aid Nursing Yeomanry (British women's organization formed to do medical transport work for the army; later did general transport work)
FAP . . . . First-Aid Post
FAR . . . . First Alarm Register
FAAA . . . . . . First Allied Airborne Army (World War II)
FACI . . . . First Article Configuration Inspection (Gemini) (NASA)
FAD . . . . First Article Demonstration
FAPIG . . . . . . First Atomic Power Industry Group (Japan)

FAST . . . . First Atomic Ship Transport, Inc.
FA . . . . First Attack (Men's lacrosse position)
FIRAV . . . . . . First Available (Military)
FAIRTRANS . . . First Available Air Transportation
FAGAIRTRANS . . First Available Government Air Transportation (Navy)
FAGTRANS . . . First Available Government Surface Transportation
FAGT . . . . . . First Available Government Transportation
FATRANS . . . . (Via) First Available Transportation
CANDESFLOT 1 . . 1st Canadian Destroyer Flotilla
FCSLU . . . . . . First Catholic Slovak Ladies Union
FCSU . . . . . . First Catholic Slovak Union of the USA
FCF . . . . First Charter Financial Corporation (NYSE symbol)
A1 . . . . First Class or First Quality
FCC . . . . First-Class Certificate
FCPO . . . . . . First Class Post Office
FD . . . . First Day (Philately)
FDC . . . . First-Day Cover (Philately)
FD . . . . First Defense (Men's lacrosse position)
FDT . . . . First Destination Transportation (Military)
FD . . . . First Down (Football)
FF . . . . First Families (i.e., the aristocracy) (Slang)
FF's . . . . First Families (Supposedly elite society) (Slang)
FFV's . . . . . . First Families of Virginia (Supposedly elite society) (Slang)
FFNC . . . . . . First Fix Not Converted
FIRFLT . . . . . . First Fleet (Pacific) (Navy)
FHLS . . . . . . First Hungarian Literary Society
FIFO . . . . . . First In, First Out (Inventory)
FIT . . . . First Indication of Trouble
FLIRT . . . . . . First Ladies' International Racing Team (Group of women racing at
Le Mans, France)
FLAP . . . . . . First Level Adaptive Program
FMW . . . . . . First Main Watch
FMAW . . . . . . First Marine Aircraft Wing
FNCB . . . . . . First National City Bank (New York City)
FST . . . . First National Stores, Inc. (NYSE symbol)
FOW . . . . . . First Open Water (Shipping)
FOPI . . . . . . First Order Polynomial Interpolator
FOPP . . . . . . First Order Polynomial Predictor
FCB . . . . First Overtone Band
FPU . . . . First Production Unit
FROKA . . . . . First Republic of Korea Army
FSWW . . . . . First Society of Whale Watchers
FSR . . . . First Soviet Reactor
FS . . . . First Stage
FSC . . . . First Stage Conduit
FSCC . . . . . . First Stage Conduit Container
FSH . . . . First Stage Hydraulics
FSM . . . . First Stage Motor
FSMC . . . . . . First Stage Motor Container
FSRM . . . . . . First Stage Rocket Motor
FSSD . . . . . . First Stage Separation Device (Aerospace)
FSM . . . . First Surface Mirror
FIRSTASKFLT . . First Task Fleet
FTU . . . . First Training Unit
FUSA . . . . . . First United States Army
FUSAG . . . . . First United States Army Group
FYK . . . . First York Corporation (American Stock Exchange symbol)
FZIA . . . . . . First Zen Institute of America
FAS . . . . Firsts and Seconds
FTH . . . . Firth Carpet Company (NYSE symbol)
FQ . . . . Fiscal Quarter
FSN . . . . Fiscal Station Number (Military)
FY . . . . Fiscal Year
FYDP . . . . . . Fiscal Year Development Plan
FIS . . . . Fischbach & Moore, Inc. (NYSE symbol)
FGS . . . . Fischerei-Geraete-Station
FPC . . . . Fish Protein Concentrate (For use in antistarvation programs)
F & WS . . . . . Fish and Wildlife Service (Department of the Interior)
FJC . . . . Fisher Junior College (Massachusetts)
FAC . . . . Fisheries Advisory Committee
FRI . . . . Fisheries Research Institute
FOM . . . . . . Fishers of Men
FB . . . . Fishery Board
FC . . . . Fishery Council
FPV . . . . Fishery Protection Vessel
FRC . . . . Fishery Research Craft
FRV . . . . Fishing Research Vessel
FPCE . . . . . . Fission Products Conversion and Encapsulation Plant (AEC)
FPDL . . . . . . Fission Products Development Laboratory (ORNL)
FYC . . . . Fission Yield Curve
FFI . . . . Fit for Issue (Navy)

F . . . . Fitted as Flagship (Suffix to plane designation)
FZA . . . . Fitzsimmons Stores, Ltd. (NYSE symbol)
FZ . . . . Fitz Simon & Connell (NYSE symbol)
V . . . . Five dollars (Slang)
FYDP . . . . . . Five Year Defense Program
FYFS & FP . . . Five Year Force Structure and Financial Program (DOD)
FYMP . . . . . . Five Year Materiel Program (Military)
FYP . . . . Five Year Plan
V . . . . Five-year sentence (Criminal slang)
FMM . . . . . . Fivondronamben'ny Mpiasa Malagasy (Confederation of Malagasy Workers)
FUOP . . . . . . Fix Up On Printer (Have technician add or change an effect by means
of optical printing) (Motion-picture production)
F . . . . Fixed (A continuous steady light) (Navigation)
FAC . . . . Fixed Air Capacitor
FAV . . . . Fixed-Angle Variable
FASA . . . . . . Fixed Area Scanning Alarm
FAR . . . . Fixed Array RADAR
FAT . . . . Fixed Asset Transfer
FBO . . . . Fixed Base Operator (Provider of aviation [non-airline] services to users
of airports)
FBC . . . . Fixed Bathtub Capacitor
FCD . . . . Fixed Center Drive
FCC . . . . Fixed Ceramic Capacitor
FCDC . . . . . . Fixed Ceramic Disc Capacitor
FCA . . . . Fixed Coaxial Attenuator
FCO . . . . Fixed Cycle Operation
FDC . . . . Fixed Decade Capacitor
FDL . . . . Fixed Delay Line
FEC . . . . Fixed Electrolytic Capacitor
FFMN . . . . . . Fixed Federal Monitoring Network (Aviation)
FFTC . . . . . . Fixed Feed Through Capacitor
FFAG . . . . . . Fixed-Field Alternating Gradient (Accelerator) (Nuclear energy)
FFC . . . . Fixed Film Capacitor
FFL . . . . Fixed and Flashing (Signal Light) (Navigation charts)
FF . . . . Fixed Focus (Photography)
FFR . . . . Fixed Frequency Receiver
FGC . . . . Fixed Gain Control
FGFC . . . . . . Fixed Gas-Filled Capacitor
FGC . . . . Fixed Glass Capacitor
FGPFL . . . . . . Fixed and Group Flashing (Signal Light) (Navigation charts)
FHTC . . . . . . Fixed High Temperature Capacitor
FHVC . . . . . . Fixed High Volt Capacitor
FI . . . . Fixed Interval
FIT . . . . Fixed Interval Timer
FLSC . . . . . . Fixed Laboratory Standard Capacitor
FLCR . . . . . . Fixed Length Cavity Resonance
FMC . . . . Fixed Mica Capacitor
FMRC . . . . . . Fixed Motor Run Capacitor
FMSC . . . . . . Fixed Motor Starting Capacitor
FMC . . . . Fixed Mylar Capacitor
FMMC . . . . . . Fixed Mylar Metallized Capacitor
FNC . . . . Fixed Niobium Capacitor
FOC . . . . Fixed Oil Capacitor
FPC . . . . Fixed Paper Capacitor
FPMC . . . . . . Fixed Paper Metallized Capacitor
FPO . . . . Fixed Path of Operation
FPC . . . . Fixed Photoflash Capacitor
FPFC . . . . . . Fixed Photoflash Capacitor
FPS . . . . Fixed Plasma Sheath
FPC . . . . Fixed Point Calculation
FPO . . . . Fixed Point Operation
FPR . . . . Fixed Point Representation
FPS . . . . Fixed Point System
FPC . . . . Fixed Polycarbonate Capacitor
FPCC . . . . . . Fixed Polycarbonate Capacitor
FPEC . . . . . . Fixed Porcelain Enamel Capacitor
FPK . . . . Fixed Position Keyboard
FPC . . . . Fixed Precision Capacitor
FP . . . . Fixed Price
FPB . . . . Fixed Price Basis
FPC . . . . Fixed Price Call
FPC . . . . Fixed Price Contracts
FPE . . . . Fixed Price with Escalation
FPF . . . . Fixed Price Firm
FPI . . . . Fixed Price Incentive
FPIC . . . . . . Fixed Price Incentive Contract
FPIF . . . . . . Fixed Price Incentive Fee
FPIF . . . . . . Fixed Price Incentive Firm (Award) (Government contracting)
FPIF . . . . . . Fixed Price Incentive Force(s)
FPIS . . . . . . Fixed Price Incentive Successive
FPO . . . . Fixed Price Open

FPR . . . . Fixed Price Redeterminable
FPRA . . . . . . Fixed Price Redetermination Article
FPS . . . . Fixed-Price Supply
FPCC . . . . Fixed Printed Circuit Capacitor
FPC . . . . Fixed Program Computer
FPN . . . . Fixed Pulse RADAR Navigation Aid
FPS . . . . Fixed Pulse RADAR Search Equipment
FRC . . . . Fixed Radio Communication
FRTF . . . . Fixed Radio Transmission Facility
FR . . . . Fixed Ratio
FSP . . . . Fixed Sample-Size Procedure
FSF . . . . Fixed Sequence Format
FST . . . . Fixed Service Tower
FSC . . . . Fixed Silicon Capacitor
FSMC . . . . Fixed Silver Mica Capacitor
FSOC . . . . Fixed Stand-Off Capacitor
FTC . . . . Fixed Tantalum Capacitor
FTCC . . . . Fixed Temperature Compensating Capacitor
FT . . . . Fixed Tone
FVC . . . . Fixed Vacuum Capacitor
FW . . . . **Fixed Wing** (Aircraft)
V . . . . Fixed-wing aircraft (Navy designation)
FWL . . . . Fixed Word Length
FF . . . . Fixing Fluid (Histology)
FMD . . . . **Fixtures Manufacturers and Dealers**
FTW . . . . Fizean Toothed Wheel
FAU . . . . Flag Administrative Unit
FCO . . . . Flag Communications Officer (Navy)
FEO . . . . Flag Engineering Officer (British)
FGO . . . . Flag Gunnery Officer
FH . . . . Flag Hoist
FL . . . . Flag Lieutenant (Naval)
FO . . . . Flag Officer (Navy)
CANFLAGLANT . . Flag Officer, Atlantic Coast (Canadian Navy)
FOBAA . . . . . . Flag Officer British Assault Area
FLAGCENT . . . Flag Officer Central Europe
FOIC . . . . Flag Officer-in-Charge (British-controlled port)
FOCWA . . . . . Flag Officer Commanding West Africa (British)
FONAP . . . . . . Flag Officer, Naval Air, Pacific (British)
FONF . . . . Flag Officer Newfoundland (British)
CANFLAGPAC . . Flag Officer, Pacific Coast (Canadian Navy)
FOTALI . . . . . . Flag Officer Taranto and Adriatic and for Liaison
FOWABPF . . . . Flag Officer Western Area, British Pacific Fleet
FRP . . . . Flag Register Processing
FTR . . . . Flag Tower (Maps and charts)
FP . . . . Flagpole
FLAG . . . . Flagstaff National Park Service Group
FRAK . . . . Flak RADAR Automatic Kanon
FMG . . . . Flakmessgerat (Antiaircraft, gun-laying RADAR) (German)
FCS . . . . Flame Control System
FDF . . . . Flame Deflector Firex
FIAD . . . . Flame Ionization Analyzer and Detector
FID . . . . Flame-Ionization Detector
FS . . . . Flame Shielding
FT . . . . Flame Tight
FGH . . . . Flameless Gas Heater
FS . . . . Flameless, Smokeless (Gunpowder)
FFA . . . . Flammability Fabrics Act
FACT . . . . . . Flanagan Aptitude Classification Test (Psychology)
FTT . . . . Flanged Tongue Terminal
FLDI . . . . Flare Die
FDP . . . . Flare Dispenser Pod
FSA . . . . Flared Slot Antenna
FILS . . . . Flarescan Instrument Landing System
FEP . . . . Flash Evaporator Plant
FLASH . . . . . Flash Lights and Send Help (Aid to drivers in distress)
FPS . . . . Flash Photolysis System
FP . . . . Flash Point
FLRNG . . . . . . Flash Ranging
FR . . . . Flash Ranging
FTR . . . . Flash Triangulation Reduction
FXD . . . . Flash X-Ray Device
FXF . . . . Flash X-Ray Facility
FOD . . . . Flashblindness Orientation Device
FL . . . . Flashing (Signal Light) (Navigation)
FNH . . . . Flashless Nonhygroscopic (Gunpowder)
F . . . . Flat
FBK . . . . Flat Back
FB . . . . Flat Bar (Technical drawings)
FCST . . . . Flat Cable Stripping Tool
FCPC . . . . Flat Computer Programming Center

FCC . . . . Flat Conductor Cables
FF . . . . Flat Face (Diamonds)
FGJA . . . . Flat Glass Jobbers Association
FG . . . . Flat Grain (Lumber)
FH . . . . Flat Head (Screw)
FK . . . . Flat Keel (Shipbuilding)
FLC . . . . Flat Load Cell
FN . . . . Flat Nose (Projectile)
FO . . . . Flat Oval (Technical drawings)
FPD . . . . Flat Pack Diode
FPW . . . . Flat Pack Welder
FPWS . . . . . . Flat Pack Welder System
F/P . . . . Flat Pattern
FPA . . . . Flat Plate Antenna
FPAA . . . . Flat Plate Array Antenna
FP . . . . Flat Point (Technical drawings)
FT . . . . Flat Template
FVPA . . . . . . Flat Veneer Products Association
FIA . . . . Flatware Importers Association
FAD . . . . Flavin-Adenine Dinucleotide (Biochemistry)
FMN . . . . Flavin Mononucleotide
FP . . . . Flavin Phosphate
FP . . . . Flavo Protein
FEMA . . . . . . Flavoring Extract Manufacturers Association of the US
FDE . . . . Flaw Detection Equipment
FIUS . . . . . . Flax Institute of the United States
FANG . . . . . . Flechette Area Neutralizing Gun
F . . . . Fleet
FAO . . . . Fleet Accountant Officer (British)
FLEACT . . . . . Fleet Activities
FLTACT . . . . . Fleet Activities
FAC . . . . Fleet Activities Command (Navy)
FAO . . . . Fleet Administration Office
FADM . . . . . . Fleet Admiral
FAIR . . . . . . Fleet Air (Wing)
FAA . . . . Fleet Air Arm (British)
FAB . . . . Fleet Air Base
FABU . . . . . . Fleet Air Base Unit
FAD . . . . Fleet Air Defense
FAD . . . . Fleet Air Detachment
FAETUPAC . . . . Fleet Air Electronics Training Unit, Pacific (Navy)
FAGU . . . . . . Fleet Air Gunnery Unit
FAMOS . . . . . . Fleet Air Meteorological Observation Satellite
FAPRON . . . . Fleet Air Photo Squadron
FAPG . . . . . . Fleet Air Photographic Group
FASRON . . . . Fleet Air (craft) Service Squadron
FATU . . . . . . Fleet Air Tactical Unit
FAIRWING . . . Fleet Air Wing
FAW . . . . Fleet Air Wing
FAIRWESTPAC . . Fleet Air Wing, Western Pacific Area
FAWAF . . . . . . Fleet Air Wings Atlantic Fleet (Navy)
FAETU . . . . . . Fleet Airborne Electronic Training Unit
FAETUA . . . . . Fleet Airborne Electronics Unit, Atlantic
FAMU . . . . . . Fleet Aircraft Maintenance Unit
FAIRSHIPWING . Fleet Airship Wing
FAIRSHIPS . . . . Fleet Airships
FASA . . . . . . Fleet Airships, Atlantic
FASP . . . . . . Fleet Airships, Pacific
FAWTU . . . . . . Fleet All-Weather Training Unit
FAWTULANT . . Fleet All Weather Training Unit, Atlantic
FAWTUPAC . . . Fleet All Weather Training Unit, Pacific
FASTULANT . . . Fleet Ammunition Ship Training Unit, Atlantic
FASTUPAC . . . . Fleet Ammunition Ship Training Unit, Pacific
FAAWTC . . . . . Fleet Anti-Air Warfare Training Center
FADAP . . . . . . Fleet Antisubmarine Data Analysis Program
FAGLANT . . . . Fleet Assistance Group, Atlantic
FAGPAC . . . . . Fleet Assistance Group, Pacific
FAAO . . . . . . Fleet Aviation Accounting Office
FAVO . . . . . . Fleet Aviation Officer (British)
FBM . . . . Fleet Ballistic Missile
FBMP . . . . . . Fleet Ballistic Missile Program (Navy)
SSBN . . . . . . Fleet Ballistic Missile Submarine (Nuclear powered) (Navy symbol)
FBMS . . . . . . Fleet Ballistic Missile System
FBMWS . . . . . Fleet Ballistic Missile Weapon System
SSB . . . . Fleet Ballistic Submarine (Navy symbol)
FBP . . . . Fleet Boat Pool
FCE . . . . Fleet Civil Engineer
FCPCP . . . . . . Fleet Computer Programming Center, Pacific
FDO . . . . Fleet Dental Officer
FEO . . . . Fleet Engineer Officer (British)
FEX . . . . Fleet Exercise (Navy, Marine Corps)

FXP . . . . Fleet Exercise Publication (Navy)
FF . . . . Fleet Fighter (Air Force)
FFR . . . . Fleet Fighter Reconnaissance
FF . . . . Fleet Flagship
FFP . . . . Fleet Frequency Plans
FGO . . . . Fleet Gunnery Officer
FLTGUNSCH . . Fleet Gunnery School
FIP . . . . Fleet Improvement Program (Navy)
FIB . . . . Fleet Installation Budget (Navy)
FIO . . . . Fleet Intelligence Officer
FIP . . . . Fleet Introduction Program
FIRM . . . . Fleet Introduction of Replacement Models (Military)
FILL . . . . Fleet Issue Load List (Navy)
FLTLOSCAP . . . Fleet Liaison Officer, Supreme Commander Allied Powers (World War II)
FLAW . . . . Fleet Logistic Air Wing
FLSW . . . . . . Fleet Logistic Support Wing (Navy)
FLOG . . . . Fleet Logistics
FLOGWING . . Fleet Logistics Air Wing (Military)
FMO . . . . Fleet Maintenance Office(r)
FMCR . . . . . . Fleet Marine Corps Reserve
FMF . . . . Fleet Marine Force (Military)
FMFLANT . . . . Fleet Marine Force, Atlantic
FMFPAC . . . . Fleet Marine Force, Pacific Fleet (Navy, Marine Corps)
FMSO . . . . . Fleet Material Support Office (Navy)
FMO . . . . Fleet Medical Officer
MMF . . . . Fleet Minelayer (Navy symbol)
MFS . . . . Fleet Minesweeper (Steel-hulled) (Navy symbol)
FMSAEG . . . . . Fleet Missile Systems Analysis and Evaluation Group (Navy)
FMP . . . . Fleet Modernization Plan (Navy)
FNOIO . . . . . . Fleet Naval Ordnance Inspecting Officer
FNWC . . . . . . Fleet Numerical Weather Central (Navy)
FNWF . . . . . . Fleet Numerical Weather Facility
FLOOD . . . . . . Fleet Observation of Oceanographic Data (Navy)
ATF . . . . Fleet Ocean Tug (Navy symbol)
FOI . . . . Fleet Operational Investigation (NOO)
FORACS . . . . . Fleet Operational Readiness Accuracy Check Sites (Navy)
OTCLANT . . . . Fleet Operational Training Command, Atlantic (usually, COTCLANT)
OTCPAC . . . . Fleet Operational Training Command, Pacific (usually, COTCPAC)
FOCSL . . . . . . Fleet Oriented Consolidated Stock List (Navy)
FPO . . . . Fleet Post Office
FRU . . . . Fleet Radio Unit
FRUPAC . . . . . Fleet Radio Unit, Pacific
FRAN . . . . . . Fleet Readiness Analysis (NORRS)
FRAP . . . . . . Fleet Readiness Assistance Program
FRIP . . . . Fleet Readiness Improvement Plan
FLTREADREP . . Fleet Readiness Representative
FRO . . . . Fleet Records Office
FRAM . . . . . . Fleet Rehabilitation and Modernization (Navy)
FRU . . . . Fleet Requirements Units (Aircraft)
FR . . . . Fleet Reserve (Navy)
FRA . . . . Fleet Reserve Association
FRAA . . . . . . Fleet Reserve Association Auxiliary
FSC . . . . Fleet Satellite Communications
FLTSERVSCOL . . Fleet Service School
FSS . . . . Fleet Service School
FSO . . . . Fleet Signals Officer (Naval)
FLTSOUNDSCOL . . Fleet Sound School
SF . . . . Fleet Submarine (Navy symbol)
FSO . . . . Fleet Supply Officer
FS . . . . Fleet Surgeon
FTB . . . . Fleet Torpedo Bomber
FTO . . . . Fleet Torpedo Officer (British)
FLETRABASE . . . Fleet Training Base
FLTTRACEN . . . Fleet Training Center
TRALANT . . . . . Fleet Training Command, Atlantic (Navy)
TRAPAC . . . . . Fleet Training Command, Pacific (Navy)
FLETRAGRUWATE . . Fleet Training Group and Underway Training Element
FTP . . . . Fleet Training Publication
FUT . . . . Fleet Utility
FWC . . . . Fleet Weather Central
FWO . . . . Fleet Wireless Officer (British)
FWSG . . . . . . Fleet Work Study Group (Navy)
FAC . . . . Flettner Aircraft Corporation
FF . . . . Flexi-Filament
FAST . . . . . . Flexible Algebraic Scientific Translator
FACT . . . . . . Flexible Automatic Circuit Tester
FAD . . . . Flexible Automatic Depot
FCE . . . . Flexible Critical Experiment
FDS . . . . Flexible Display System
FDS . . . . Flexible Drive Shaft
FFOB . . . . . . Flexible Fiber Optic Borescope

FGH . . . . Flexible Gyro Header
FGHA . . . . . . Flexible Gyro Header Assembly
FHA . . . . Flexible Header Assembly
FISCA . . . . . . Flexible Integrated Solar Cell Assembly
FLSC . . . . . . Flexible Linear Shaped Charge
FMS . . . . Flexible Measuring System
FMSWR . . . . . Flexible Mild Steel Wire Rope
FMC . . . . Flexible Monte Carlo
FMC . . . . Flexible Motor Coupling
FNC . . . . Flexible Nylon Coupling
FPA . . . . Flexible Packaging Association
FPF . . . . Flexible Polyurethane Foam
FPC . . . . Flexible Printed Circuit
FSC . . . . Flexible Shielded Cable
FSG . . . . Flexible Space Garment
FSW . . . . Flexible Steel Wire
FSWR . . . . . . Flexible Steel Wire Rope
FTS . . . . Flexible Test Station
FTM . . . . Flexible Theatre Missile
FWG . . . . Flexible Wave Guide
FMA . . . . Flexicore Manufacturers Association
FTA . . . . Flexographic Technical Association
FMMF . . . . . . Flexure Monitor Mounting Fixture
FFT . . . . Flicker Fusion Threshold
FLAK . . . . . . Fliegerabwehrkanone, Flugzeugabwehrkanone, or Fugabwehrkanone (German word for antiaircraft gun; acronym used for antiaircraft fire)
FACT . . . . . . Flight Acceptance Composite Test (NASA)
FAT . . . . Flight Acceptance Test
FAPA . . . . . . Flight Accrual Payment Action (Air Force)
FAS . . . . Flight Advisory Service (FAA)
FAST . . . . . . Flight Advisory Service Test
FAWS . . . . . . Flight Advisory Weather Service
FAS . . . . Flight Analysis Section
FAR . . . . Flight Aptitude Rating
FAS . . . . Flight Assistance Service
FACS . . . . . . Flight Augmentation Control System (Aviation)
F/C . . . . Flight Certificate
FLTCERT . . . . . Flight Certificate
FCCO . . . . . . Flight Change Control Order
FC . . . . Flight Charts
FCC . . . . Flight Communications Center
FCAT . . . . . . Flight Composite Acceptance Test
FCMT . . . . . . Flight Configuration Mode Test (Gemini) (NASA)
FC . . . . Flight Control
FLICON . . . . . Flight Control(ler)
FCA . . . . Flight Control Assemblies
FCC . . . . Flight Control Container
FCGC . . . . . . Flight Control Gyro Container
FCL . . . . Flight Control Laboratory
FCRL . . . . . . Flight Control Ready Light (System)
FCS . . . . Flight Control System
FCSS . . . . . . Flight Control Systems Section
FCU . . . . Flight Control Unit
FCH . . . . Flight Controllers Handbook
FCC . . . . Flight Coordination Center
FCCC . . . . . . Flight Coordination Control Central
FCIF . . . . . . Flight Crew Information File
FLIDEN . . . . . Flight Data Entry (Device) (SAGE)
FLIDAP . . . . . Flight Data Position
FDR . . . . Flight Data Recorder
FDSIS . . . . . . Flight Deck System Integration Simulator
FDLH . . . . . . Flight Determination Laboratory, Holloman Air Force Base
FDAI . . . . . . Flight Director Attitude Indicator
FDC . . . . Flight Director Computer
FDI . . . . Flight Director Indicator
FDO . . . . Flight Duty Officer (Air Force)
FDL . . . . Flight Dynamic Laboratory (Air Force)
FIDO . . . . . . Flight Dynamics Officer (NASA)
FETF . . . . . . Flight Engine Test Facility
FE . . . . Flight Engineer(ing)
FEIA . . . . . . Flight Engineers' International Association
FEB . . . . Flight Evaluation Board
FESS . . . . . . Flight Experiment Shielding Satellite
FFS . . . . Flight Following Service (FAA)
FIFOR . . . . . . Flight Forecast
FH . . . . Flight Hour
FLIFO . . . . . . Flight Information
FIA . . . . Flight Information Area
FIC . . . . Flight Information Center
FIM . . . . Flight Information Manual
FLIP . . . . Flight Information Plan

FLIP . . . . Flight Information Publication (Air Force)	FTCP . . . . . . Flight Test Change Proposal
FLIPs . . . . . . Flight Information Publications (Air Force, Navy)	FTCC . . . . . . Flight Test Coordinating Committee (Air Force)
FIR . . . . Flight Information Region (FAA)	FTD . . . . Flight Test Division
FIRB . . . . Flight Information Region Boundary	FTDIP . . . . . . Flight Test Division, Internal Project (Navy)
FIS . . . . Flight Information Service	FTE . . . . Flight Test Evaluation
FIDO . . . . Flight Inspection District Office	FTO . . . . Flight Test Operations
FIFO-H . . . . . . Flight Inspection Field Office, High Altitude	FTP . . . . Flight Test Program
FI/P . . . . Flight Inspection (Permanent)	FTR . . . . Flight Test Report
FI/T . . . . Flight Inspection (Temporary)	FTS . . . . Flight Test Support
FIIC . . . . Flight Inspector In Charge	FTV . . . . Flight Test Vehicle (Air Force)
FIP . . . . Flight Instruction Program (Air Force)	FTWG . . . . . . Flight Test Working Group
FIT . . . . Flight Instrument Trainer	FVPB . . . . Flight Vehicle Power Branch
FIRE . . . . Flight Investigation Reentry Environment	FVS . . . . Flight Vehicle Structure
FLIP . . . . Flight Launched Infrared Probe	FWAS . . . . . . Flight Warning and Analysis System
FLI . . . . Flight Leader Identity (RADAR)	FWP . . . . Flight Watch Point
FL . . . . Flight Level	FJC . . . . Flint Junior College (Michigan)
FL . . . . Flight Lieutenant	FO . . . . Flintkote Company (NYSE symbol)
FLTL . . . . Flight Line	F/F . . . . Flip-Flop (Electronics)
FLIDIT . . . . . . Flight Line Detection and Isolation Techniques	FLIP . . . . Floated Lightweight Inertial Platform
FLM . . . . Flight Line Maintenance	FAMF . . . . . . Floating Aircraft Maintenance Facility
FLP . . . . Flight Line Printer	FCR . . . . Floating Control Regulator
FLT . . . . Flight Line Taxi	FACS . . . . . . Floating Decimal Abstract Coding System
FLT . . . . Flight Line Tester	YD . . . . Floating Derrick (Navy symbol)
FM . . . . Flight Manual	FDD . . . . Floating Digital Drive
FM . . . . Flight Mechanic	FDH . . . . Floating Divide or Halt
FMO . . . . . . Flight Medical Officer (Air Force)	FDTK . . . . . . Floating Drift Tube Klystron
FMS . . . . Flight Motion Simulator	FDD . . . . Floating Drydock (Navy)
FN . . . . Flight Nurse	YRDH . . . . . . Floating Dry Dock Workshop (Hull) (Navy symbol)
FO . . . . Flight Officer (Air Force)	YRDM . . . . . Floating Dry Dock Workshop (Machinery) (Navy symbol)
FOC . . . . Flight Operations Center	FLIP . . . . Floating Indexed Point Arithmetic (Data processing)
FOF . . . . Flight Operations Facility	FLIMBAL . . . . . Floated Inertial Measurement Ball
FLIOP . . . . . . Flight Operations Planner	FIFO . . . . . . Floating Input – Floating Output
FO . . . . Flight Order	FITGO . . . . . Floating Input to Ground Output
FPA . . . . Flight Path Analysis	FLINT . . . . . . Floating Interpretive Language (Princeton University)
FPAC . . . . . . Flight Path Analysis and Command (Team) (NASA)	FLIP . . . . Floating Laboratory Instrument Platform (Movable oceanographic
DI . . . . Flight Path Deviation Indicator (Navigation)	research station)
FPDI . . . . . . Flight Path Deviation Indicator	FMS . . . . Floating Machine Shop
FP . . . . Flight Pay	FORDS . . . . . Floating Ocean Research & Development Station
FP . . . . Flight Plan (Aviation)	FLOP . . . . . . Floating Octal Point (IBM)
FPA . . . . Flight Plan Approval	YPD . . . . Floating Pile Driver (Navy symbol)
FPGL . . . . . . Flight Plan Gas Load (Air Force)	FPA . . . . Floating Point Arithmetic
FPNO . . . . . . Flight Plan Not Received	FAP . . . . Floating-Point Arithmetic Package
FPPS . . . . . . Flight Plan Processing System (British)	FLBIN . . . . . . Floating-Point Binary
FPR . . . . Flight Planned Route	FPC . . . . Floating Point Calculation
FPS . . . . Flight Preparation Sheet	FLDEC . . . . . Floating-Point Decimal
FPC . . . . Flight Programmer Computer	FLIP . . . . Floating Point Interpretive Program (Data processing)
FPB . . . . Flight Progress Board (Aviation)	FMEVA . . . . . Floating Point Means and Variance
FPL . . . . Flight Propulsion Laboratory	FPR . . . . Floating Point Routine
FQ . . . . Flight Qualification	FPS . . . . Floating Point System
FQPA . . . . . . Flight Quality Photomultiplier Assembly	FP . . . . Floating Policy (Insurance)
FIRE . . . . Flight in a Radiation Environment	YFP . . . . Floating Power Barge (Navy symbol)
FRO . . . . Flight Radio Officer (Aviation)	FRN . . . . Floating Round
FREDI . . . . . . Flight Range and Endurance Data Indicator	FS . . . . Floating Sign
FRB . . . . Flight Rated Bioinstrumentation	OFU . . . . Floating Units Division (Coast Guard)
FRT . . . . Flight Rating Test	YR . . . . Floating Workshop (Navy symbol)
FRD . . . . Flight Readiness Demonstration	FZM . . . . Floating Zone Melting
FRF . . . . Flight Readiness Firing	FR . . . . Flocculation Reaction (Medicine)
FRT . . . . Flight Readiness Test	FC . . . . Flood Control
FRI . . . . Flight Refueling, Incorporated	FCD . . . . Flood Control District (Florida)
FRC . . . . Flight Research Center (of NASA)	FR . . . . Flood Relief Punt (Coast Guard)
FS . . . . Flight Safety	FLWIS . . . . . . Flood Warnings Issued
FSF . . . . Flight Safety Foundation	FAR . . . . Floor Area Ratio (in office buildings)
FSR . . . . Flight Safety Research	FD . . . . Floor Drain (Technical drawings)
FSRB . . . . . . Flight Safety Review Board	FMMA . . . . . Floor Machine Manufacturers Association
FS . . . . Flight Sergeant (British Royal Air Force)	FVMMA . . . . Floor and Vacuum Machinery Manufacturers' Association
FS . . . . Flight Service	FDRMA . . . . Flooring Division, Rubber Manufacturers Association
FSC . . . . Flight Service Center	FCAA . . . . . . Florence Crittenton Association of America
FSCS . . . . . . Flight Service Communications System	FLAP . . . . . . Flores Assembly Program (Data processing)
FSS . . . . Flight Service Station (FAA)	FL . . . . Florida
FSR . . . . Flight Simulation Report	FAME . . . . . . Florida Association of Marine Explorers
FSTD . . . . . . Flight Simulation Test Data	FAU . . . . Florida Atlantic University
FS . . . . Flight Simulator	FLAC . . . . . . Florida Automatic Computer (Air Force)
FSR . . . . Flight Solar Reflectometer	FCC . . . . Florida Christian College
FS . . . . Flight Standards Service (FAA)	FCC . . . . Florida Citrus Commission
FSS . . . . Flight Standards Service	FCM . . . . . . Florida Citrus Mutual
FLTST . . . . . . Flight Steward	FCNA . . . . . . Florida Citrus Nurserymen's Association
FSM . . . . Flight System Mockup	FCFA . . . . . . Florida Commercial Fisheries Association
FTS . . . . Flight Termination System	FEC . . . . Florida East Coast R. R. (AAR code)
FT . . . . Flight Test (Report)	FLA . . . . Florida East Coast Railway Company (NYSE symbol)
FTB . . . . Flight (or Flying) Test Bed	FFCSA . . . . . Florida Fresh Citrus Shippers Association
FTC . . . . Flight Test Center	FFVA . . . . . . Florida Fruit and Vegetable Association

FGFSA .... Florida Gift Fruit Shippers Association
FLAGRP ..... Florida Group (Navy)
FIE .... Florida Industries Exposition
FIO .... Florida Institute of Oceanography
FIT .... Florida Institute of Technology
FLGA .... Florida Lychee Growers Association
FMF .... Florida Mango Forum
FMAS .... Florida Marine Aquarium Society
FDP .... Florida Power Corporation (NYSE symbol)
FPL .... Florida Power & Light Company (NYSE symbol)
FSC .... Florida Southern College
FSBC .... Florida State Board of Conservation
FSU .... Florida State University
FTFI .... Florida Tropical Fish Industries
FUN .... Florida United Numismatists
FWCNG ..... Florida West Coast Nuclear Group
F .... Florin (Same as gulden, monetary unit in Netherlands)
FTDA .... Florists' Telegraph Delivery Association
FLO .... Florsheim Shoe Company (NYSE symbol)
LSFF .... Flotilla Flagship Landing Ship (Navy symbol)
FMEA .... Flour Millers Export Association
FC .... Flow Coating
FCV .... Flow Control Valve
FG .... Flow Gauge
FI .... Flow Indicator
FL .... Flow Line (Technical drawings)
FMS .... Flow Measuring System
FR .... Flow Recorder
FRC .... Flow Recorder Controller
FRT .... Flow Recording Transmitter
FLS .... Flow Switch
FS .... Flow Switch
F .... Flower
FDT .... Flowing Gas Detonation Tube
FGS .... Flowing Gas Stream
FCS .... Flowmeter Calibration Stand
FOIU .... Flowmeter Ordering and Indicating Unit
FSCT .... Floyd Satellite Communications Terminal
FCTCSC ..... Flue-Cured Tobacco Cooperative Stabilization Corporation
FCTGA ..... Flue-Cured Tobacco Growers Association
FLUG .... Flugfelag Islands H. F. (Iceland Airways, Ltd.)
F .... Fluid
FACET ...... Fluid Amplifier Control Engine Test
FACS .... Fluid Amplifier Control System
FCC .... Fluid Catalytic Cracking
FCI .... Fluid Conductivity Indicator
FCI .... Fluid Controls Institute
FDC .... Fluid Digital Computer
FLDR .... Fluid Dram
FDRG .... Fluid Dynamics Research Group (MIT)
FDRL .... Fluid Dynamics Research Laboratory (MIT)
FES .... Fluid to Electric Switch
FFB .... Fluid Film Bearing
FFI .... Fluid Flow Indicator
FLICR ...... Fluid Logic Industrial Control Relay
FMP .... Fluid Motion Panel (of the British Aeronautical Research Council)
FLODAC ..... Fluid-Operated Digital Automatic Computer
F .... Fluid Ounce
FLOZ .... Fluid Ounce
FPS .... Fluid Power Society
FPS .... Fluid Power System
FPS .... Fluid Purification System
FRD .... Fluid Rate Damper
FSE .... Fluid Shaft Encoder
FS .... Fluid Switch
FSC .... Fluid Storage Container
FVM .... Fluid Vacancy Model
FVP .... Fluid Velocity Potential
FLM .... Fluidic Logic Module
FVO .... Fluidic Valve Operator
FB .... Fluidized Bed
FBP .... Fluidized Bed Process
FLR .... Fluor Corporation, Ltd. (NYSE symbol)
FLSP .... Fluorescein Labeled Serum Protein (Chemical)
FAST .... Fluorescent Antibody Staining Technique
FIA .... Fluorescent Indicated Analysis
FP .... Fluorescent Particle
FLORL ..... Fluorescent Runway Lighting
FT .... Fluorescent Target
FTA .... Fluorescent Treponemal Antibody (Test)
FDPC .... Fluorimetric Determination of Plasma Cortisol

FEP .... Fluorinated Ethylene-Propylene Copolymer
F .... Fluorine (Chemical element)
FLOX .... Fluorine–Liquid Oxygen
FEP .... Fluorocarbon Ethylene Propylene
FUDR .... Fluorodeoxyuridine
FLR .... Fluoroleucine Resistant (Mutant)
FDF .... Flush Door Fastener
FJ .... Flush Joint (Diamond drilling)
FMT .... Flush Metal Threshold (Technical drawings)
FT .... Flush Threshold (Technical drawings)
FV .... Flush Valve (Technical drawings)
FCL .... Flux Current Loop
FLEA .... Flux Logic Element Array
FSR .... Flux Sensitive Resistor
FSA .... Flux Switch Alternator
FV .... Flux Valve
FBW .... Fly by Wire
FAF .... Flyaway Factory
FAK .... Fly-Away Kit
FCW .... Flyer Coil Winder
FB .... Flying Boat
GST .... Flying Boat (Russian aircraft symbol)
N .... Flying Boat (Russian aircraft symbol)
FCO .... Flying Control Officer (Navy)
CF .... Flying-Deck Cruiser (Navy symbol)
FDA .... Flying Dentists Association
FDATC ..... Flying Division Air Training Command
FFDA .... Flying Funeral Directors of America
FLEEP ...... Flying Lunar Excursion Experimental Platform (NASA)
FO .... Flying Officer (British)
FPRC .... Flying Personnel Research Committee (British)
FPA .... Flying Physicians Association
FRS .... Flying Relay Station
FSO .... Flying Safety Officer (Air Force)
FSD .... Flying Spot Digitizer
FSS .... Flying Spot Scanner
FS .... Flying Status
FSC .... Flying Status Code
FLY .... Flying Tiger Line, Inc. (NYSE symbol)
FTL .... Flying Tiger Line, Inc.
FLYTAF ..... Flying Training Air Force
FTAF .... Flying Training Air Force
FTC .... Flying Training Command (Air Force)
FTS .... Flying Training School
FVA .... Flying Veterinarians Association
FMC .... FMC Corporation (NYSE symbol)
FLA .... Foam Laminators Association
FIS .... Foam in System
FT .... Foam Tape
FD .... Focal Distance
F .... Focal length
FL .... Focal Length
FW .... Focke-Wulf (A German fighter plane)
FAIR .... Focus on Arms Information & Reassurance
FPS .... Focus Projection and Scanning
FUS .... Focused Ultrasonic Surgery
FAS .... Focusing Array Study
F .... Fog (Weather)
FB .... Fog Bell (Navigation charts)
FD .... Fog Diaphone (Navigation charts)
FG .... Fog Gong (Navigation charts)
FG .... Fog Gun (Navigation charts)
FH .... Fog Horn (Navigation charts)
FIDO .... Fog, Intense, Dispersal of (NASA)
FIDO .... Fog Investigation and Dispersal Operation (System used on airfield landing strips) (World War II)
FN .... Fog Nautophone (Navigation charts)
FOGSIG .... Fog Signal (Station)
FS .... Fog Signal Station (Maps and charts)
FSS .... Fog Signal Station (Coast Guard)
FS .... Fog Siren (Maps and charts)
FT .... Fog Trumpet (Navigation charts)
FW .... Fog Whistle (Navigation charts)
FRESH ...... Foil Research Supercavitating Hydrofoil
FWC .... Foil Wound Coil
FDA .... Folded Dipole Antenna
FF .... Folded Flat
FFR .... Folded Flow Reactor (AEC)
F & G ...... Folded and Gathered (Printing)
FSM .... Folded Sideband Modulation
FCRAA ..... Folding Chair Rental Association of America

REVERSE ACRONYMS AND INITIALISMS DICTIONARY

FFAR . . . . Folding-Fin Air Rocket
FPBAA . . . . . . Folding Paper Box Association of America
FOPEN . . . . . . Foliage Penetration (RADAR)
FPR . . . . Foliage Penetration RADAR
FA . . . . Folic Acid (Biochemistry)
F . . . . Folio (Book 30 centimeters and over in height)
FV . . . . Folio Verso (On the back of the page)
FF . . . . Folios (Leaves)
FA . . . . Folklore Americas
FBE . . . . Follansbee Steel Corporation (NYSE symbol)
FSH . . . . Follicle-Stimulating Hormone (Endocrinology)
FC . . . . Follow Copy (Printing)
F . . . . Following
FF . . . . Following (Pages)
FAMAE . . . . . . Following Amendment Authorized Effective (followed by date)
FIRTS . . . . . . Following Individual Reported This Station (Army)
FOLIS . . . . . . Following Information Is Submitted (Army)
FINA . . . . . . Following Items Not Available
FOLNOAVAL . . Following Items Not Available
FNA . . . . Following Named Airmen
FNERAS . . . . . Following Named Enlisted Men Are Relieved Assignment
FNEORID . . . . Following Named Enlisted Men Organization Indicated
FNE . . . . Following Named Enlisted Personnel
FNI . . . . Following Named Individuals
FNO . . . . Following Named Officers
FNOA . . . . . . Following Named Officers and Airmen
FTAR . . . . . . Following Transmitted As Received
FOC . . . . Follow-On Contract
FOOT . . . . . . Follow-On Operational Test
FOT . . . . Follow-on Operational Test
FU . . . . Follow-Up
FAS . . . . Followup Alarm System
FUA . . . . Follow-Up Amplifier
FEA . . . . Followup Error Alarm
FUPOSAT . . . Followup on Supply Action Taken
FJG . . . . Fonda, Johnstown & Gloversville R. R. (AAR code)
FAMA . . . . . . Fondation pour l'Assistance Mutuelle en Afrique au Sud du Sahara (Foundation for Mutual Assistance in Africa South of the Sahara)
FDD . . . . Fondation Documentaire Dentaire
FEC . . . . Fondation Europeenne de la Culture
FIPP . . . . Fondation Internationale Penale et Penitentiaire
FUH . . . . Fondazione Universale Hallesint (Italy)
FLAK . . . . . . Fondest Love and Kisses (Correspondence)
FAC . . . . Fonds d'Aide et de Cooperation (Aid and Cooperation Fund) (France)
FEDOM . . . . . Fonds Europeen de Developpement pour les Pays et Territoires d'Outre-Mer (European Development Fund for Overseas Countries and Territories)
FIDES . . . . . . Fonds d'Investissement pour le Developpement Economique et Social (UN)
FMI . . . . Fonds Monetaire International (International Monetary Fund)
FNUR . . . . . . Fonds des Nations Unies pour les Refugies (United Nations Funds for Refugees)
FORMA . . . . . Fonds d'Orientation et de Regularisation des Marches Agricoles (French government food agency)
FOREAMI . . . . Fonds Reine Elisabeth d'Assistance Medicale aux Indigenes (Queen Elisabeth Funds for Medical Assistance to the Natives)
FE . . . . Fonetic English (for spelling words the way they sound)
FESA . . . . . . Fonetic English Spelling Association
FAP . . . . Food Additive Petition
F & ABR . . . . . Food and Agriculture Branch (US Military Government, Germany)
FAO . . . . Food and Agriculture Organization (of the United Nations)
F & CI . . . . . . Food and Container Institute
FC . . . . Food Controller (British) (World War II)
FDA . . . . Food Distribution Administration
FD . . . . Food Distribution Division (of AMS, Department of Agriculture)
FDO . . . . Food Distribution Order
FDA . . . . Food and Drug Administration (of HEW)
FDC . . . . Food, Drug and Cosmetic (Act)
FDLI . . . . Food and Drug Law Institute
FEAST . . . . . . Food Education and Service Training
FFES . . . . . . Food Facilities Engineering Society
FFS . . . . Food Fair Stores, Inc. (NYSE symbol)
FGT . . . . Food Giant Markets, Inc. (NYSE symbol)
FIAE . . . . . . Food Industry Association Executives
FIR . . . . Food Irradiation Reactor (AEC)
FLI . . . . Food Law Institute
FMC . . . . . . Food Machinery Corporation (Later, FMC Corporation)
FMR . . . . Food Mart, Inc. (NYSE symbol)
FMA . . . . Food Merchandisers of America
FNB . . . . Food and Nutrition Board
FPC . . . . Food Packaging Council
FPDI . . . . Food Processing Development Irradiator

FPA . . . . Food Production Administration (World War II)
FROST . . . . . Food Reserves on Space Trips
FSEI . . . . Food Service Equipment Industry
FSEA . . . . . . Food Service Executives' Association
FSP . . . . Food Stamp Program
FSC . . . . Food Storage Cell
FSCC . . . . . . Food Surplus Commodities Corporation
FTA . . . . Food Tray Association
FTBA . . . . . . Food Tray and Board Association
FAST . . . . . . Foolproof Auditing and Sale of Tickets (in motion picture theaters)
FC . . . . Foot-Candle
FT-C . . . . Foot-Candle (Illumination)
FG . . . . Foot Groove
FG . . . . Foot Guards (British)
FL . . . . Foot-Lambert
FT-L . . . . Foot-Lambert
FMD . . . . . . Foot-and-Mouth Disease (Veterinary medicine)
FMDV . . . . . . Foot-and-Mouth Disease Virus
FP . . . . Foot Patrol
FP . . . . Foot-Pound
FPS . . . . Foot-Pound-Second (System)
FTGDV . . . . . Footage Dives (Military)
FA . . . . Football Association (Controlling body of British soccer)
FC . . . . Football Club
FOA . . . . Football Officials Association
FWAA . . . . . . Football Writers Association of America
FTE . . . . Foote Mineral Company (NYSE symbol)
FN . . . . Footnote
F . . . . For
FORAC . . . . . For Action
FAA . . . . For an Approach To (Aviation)
FFA . . . . For Further Assignment
FFC . . . . For Further Clearance (Aviation)
FFT . . . . For Further Transfer (to) (Military)
FOUO . . . . . . For Official Use Only
FO . . . . For Orders
FPRC . . . . . . For Possible Reclearance (Aviation)
FPC . . . . For Private Circulation
FPUR . . . . . . For the Purpose Of
FORTSK . . . . . For Task Force (Military)
FYA . . . . For Your Attention
FYI . . . . For Your Information
FYIG . . . . . . For Your Information and Guidance
FA . . . . Forage Acre
FCC . . . . Forbidden Combination Check
FAB . . . . Forca Aerea Brasileira (Brazilian Air Force)
FEB . . . . Forca Expedicionaria Brasileira (Brazilian Expeditionary Force, 1944-1955)
F . . . . Force
FAD . . . . Force/Activity Designator (Military)
F/AD . . . . Force/Activity Designator
FAIS . . . . . . Force Air Intelligence Study (Air Force)
FACC . . . . . . Force Associated Control Communications (Military)
FBHDL . . . . . Force Beachhead Line
FCU . . . . Force Control Unit
FDMIS . . . . . Force Development Management Information System (Army)
FF . . . . Force Field
FFDO . . . . . . Force Fighter Director Officer
F & FP . . . . . . Force and Financial Program
FF . . . . Force Flagship
FLNK . . . . . . Force de Liberation Nationale Kamerunaise (National Cameroonian Liberation Force)
FMP . . . . Force Modernization Program
FO . . . . Force Ouvriere
FRM . . . . Force Reaction Motor
FRP . . . . Force Rendezvous Point (Military)
F & R . . . . . . Force and Rhythm (of Pulse) (Medicine)
FSP . . . . Force Sensing Probe
FSD . . . . Force Spectral Density
FSC . . . . Force Structure Committee
FUNC . . . . . . Force de l'Union National Cambodge (Cambodia)
FUNU . . . . . . Force d'Urgence des Nations Unies
FD . . . . Forced Draft
FDB . . . . Forced-Draft Blower
FEV . . . . Forced Expiratory Volume (Physiology)
FFE . . . . Forced Fault Entry (Data processing)
FOI . . . . Forced Oil Injection
FR . . . . Forced Removal
FVC . . . . Forced Vital Capacities
FARK . . . . . . Forces Armee Kmer
FAL . . . . Forces Armee Lao

185

FENDRE . . . . . Forces to Eliminate No-Deposit/No-Return
FFA . . . . Forces Francaises en Allemagne (French Forces in Germany)
FFI . . . . Forces Francaises de l'Interieur (France) (World War II)
FFL . . . . Forces Francaises Libres (Free French Forces)
FFO . . . . Forces Francaises de l'Ouest
FNU . . . . Forces des Nations Unies (United Nations Forces)
FF . . . . Ford Foundation
F . . . . Ford Motor Company (NYSE symbol) (Wall Street slang names: "Tin Lizzy" or "Flivver")
FOMOCO . . . . Ford Motor Company
FNR . . . . Ford Nuclear Reactor
FSP . . . . Ford Satellite Plan (Communications)
FP . . . . Fordyce & Princeton R. R. (AAR code)
F & A . . . . . . Fore and Aft
FEP . . . . Fore Edges Painted (Paper)
FOR . . . . Fore River Corporation (AAR code)
FSD . . . . Forecast Support Date
FICS . . . . Forecasting for Inventory Control System
FAME . . . . . . Forecasts, Appraisals, and Management Evaluations
FAIME . . . . . . Foreign Affairs Information Management Effort (Computer) (Department of State)
FAR . . . . Foreign Agricultural Relations Office
FAS . . . . Foreign Agricultural Service (Department of Agriculture)
FASC . . . . . . Foreign Agricultural Service Club
FAS . . . . Foreign Aid Society (British)
FAM . . . . Foreign Air Mail
FAP . . . . Foreign Air Program
FACD . . . . . . Foreign Area Consumer Dialing
FAFP . . . . . . Foreign Area Fellowship Program
FALS . . . . . . Foreign Area and Language Study
FAR . . . . Foreign Area Research Coordination Group (Department of State)
FAS . . . . Foreign Area Specialist (Military)
FAST . . . . . . Foreign Area Specialist Training (Military)
FASTP . . . . . . Foreign Area Specialist Training Program
FB . . . . Foreign Body (Medicine)
FBPC . . . . . . Foreign Bondholders Protective Council
FBIS . . . . Foreign Broadcast Intelligence Service (of FCC) (World War II)
FBO . . . . Foreign Building Office (of Department of State)
FCSC . . . . . . Foreign Claims Settlement Commission
FCG . . . . Foreign Clearance Guide
FCC . . . . Foreign Commerce Club of New York
FCIA . . . . . . Foreign Credit Insurance Association (Export-Import Bank)
FCIB . . . . Foreign Credit Interchange Bureau
FC . . . . Foreign Currency
FDD . . . . Foreign Document Division (of CIA)
FDP . . . . Foreign Duty Pay
FEA . . . . Foreign Economic Administration
FEC . . . . Foreign Economic Coordination (Office of)
FEPP . . . . . . Foreign Excess Personal Property
FX . . . . Foreign Exchange (Business and trade)
FEBNYC . . . . . Foreign Exchange Brokers of New York City
FEC . . . . Foreign Exchange Cost
FEOF . . . . . . Foreign Exchange Operations Fund
FFC . . . . Foreign Funds Control
FGA . . . . Foreign General Agent
FGA . . . . Foreign General Average (Insurance)
FL . . . . Foreign Language
FLB . . . . Foreign Language Bulletin
FLPA . . . . . . Foreign Language Press of America
FLP . . . . Foreign Language Program
FLTP . . . . . . Foreign Language Training Program (Air Force)
FLES . . . . . . Foreign Languages in Elementary Schools
FLC . . . . Foreign Liquidation Commission
FMB . . . . Foreign Materiel Branch (Military)
FOMCAT . . . . Foreign Material Catalog
FMRA . . . . . . Foreign Media Representatives Association
FMACC . . . . . Foreign Military Assistance Coordinating Committee
FMASC . . . . . Foreign Military Assistance Steering Committee
FMS . . . . Foreign Military Sales
FM . . . . Foreign Mission
FOD . . . . Foreign Object Damage
FO . . . . Foreign Office
FONOFF . . . . Foreign Office
FORD . . . . . . Foreign Office Research Department (British)
FOA . . . . Foreign Operations Administration
FOEU . . . . . . Foreign Organizations' Employees Union
FOKEU . . . . . Foreign Organizations Korean Employees' Union (South Korea)
FPSC . . . . . . Foreign Petroleum Supply Committee
FPA . . . . Foreign Policy Association
FPCH . . . . . . Foreign Policy Clearing House
FPA . . . . Foreign Press Association

FR . . . . Foreign Relations Committee (US Senate)
FSTC . . . . . . Foreign Science and Technology Center (Army)
FSD . . . . Foreign Sea Duty
FS . . . . Foreign Service (State Department)
FSA . . . . Foreign Service Availability (Military)
FSC . . . . Foreign Service Credits (Military)
FSIC . . . . Foreign Service Inspection Corps (Department of State)
FSI . . . . Foreign Service Institute (Department of State)
FSO . . . . Foreign Service Officer (Department of State)
FSOTS . . . . . Foreign Service Officers' Training School
FSP . . . . Foreign Service Pay
FSSE . . . . . . Foreign Service Sales Expense
FSSD . . . . . . Foreign Service Selection Date
FST . . . . Foreign Service Tour (Military)
FSS . . . . Foreign Shore Service
FSSC . . . . . . Foreign Student Service Council
FTAO . . . . . . Foreign Technology Activity Office(r)
FTD . . . . Foreign Technology Division (AFSC)
FTZB . . . . . . Foreign Trade Zone Board
FT . . . . Foreign Transaction
FAA . . . . Foreman's Association of America
FF . . . . Foremanship Foundation
FOR . . . . Foremost Dairies, Inc. (NYSE symbol)
FDL . . . . Foremost (or Forward) Defended Localities (or Locations) (British)
FCSA . . . . . . Forest Conservation Society of America
FE . . . . Forest Engineer
F Eng . . . . . . Forest Engineer
FFAC . . . . . . Forest Farmers Association Cooperative
FGRF . . . . . . Forest Genetics Research Foundation
FHS . . . . Forest History Society
FIC . . . . Forest Industries Council
FIRC . . . . . . Forest Industries Radio Communications
FP . . . . Forest Patrol (Activity of Civil Air Patrol)
FPL . . . . Forest Products Laboratory (Department of Agriculture)
FPRS . . . . . . Forest Products Radio Service
FPRS . . . . . . Forest Products Research Society
FPSC . . . . . . Forest Products Safety Conference
FS . . . . Forest Service (Department of Agriculture)
FOA . . . . Foresters of America
FCCA . . . . . . Forestry, Conservation Communications Association
FEY . . . . Forever Yours
FCS . . . . Forged Carbon Steel
FCM . . . . Forged Chrom-Moly
FS . . . . Forged Steel
FST . . . . Forged Steel (Technical drawings)
FIA . . . . Forging Industry Association
FIERF . . . . . . Forging Industry Educational and Research Foundation
FMA . . . . Forging Manufacturers Association
FBI's . . . . Forgotten Boys of Iceland (Nickname for US soldiers in Iceland) (World War II)
FG . . . . Forgotten Generation
FLT . . . . Fork Lift Truck
FMCU . . . . . . Form Cutter
FMDI . . . . . . Form Die
FF . . . . Form Feed
FOREMAN . . . . Form Retrieval and Manipulation Language
FMRL . . . . . . Form Roll
FMTO . . . . . . Form Tool
F . . . . Forma
FDR . . . . Formal Design Review
FDI . . . . Formal Documents Issued (Federal Power Commission)
FSL . . . . Formal Semantic Language
FTD . . . . Formal Technical Documents
FTL . . . . Formal Technical Literature
FT . . . . Formal Training (Military)
FAA . . . . Formalin, Acetic Acid, Alcohol (Solution)
F . . . . Formality
FCB . . . . Format Control Buffer
FE . . . . Format Effector
FFD . . . . Formation Flight Display
FFO . . . . Formation Flight Operation
F . . . . Formed
FSTI . . . . Formed Steel Tube Institute
FP . . . . Former Priest
XYL . . . . Former Young Lady (Wife) (Ham radio slang)
FM . . . . Formerly Married
FORESDAT . . . . Formerly Restricted Data (Military)
FRD . . . . Formerly Restricted Data (Military)
FORMPATPAC . . Formosa Patrol Force, US Pacific Fleet
F . . . . Formula
FORAST . . . . . Formula Assembler Translator

REVERSE ACRONYMS AND INITIALISMS DICTIONARY

FORC . . . . Formula Coder
FORMAC . . . . . Formula Manipulation Compiler (Data processing)
FAST . . . . Formula and Statement Translator
FORTRAN . . . . Formula Translation (Data processing)
FAP . . . . FORTRAN (Formula Translation) Assembly Program
FRUGAL . . . . . FORTRAN (Formula Translation) Rules Used as a General Applications Language
FORTRUNCIBLE. . FORTRAN (Formula Translation) Style Runcible (Data processing)
FW . . . . Formula Weight
FGVT . . . . Forschungs-Gesellschaft Verfahrens-Technik (West Germany)
FKH . . . . Forschungs Kommission fuer Hochspannungsfragen (Swiss)
FRB . . . . Forschungs-Reaktor Berlin
FSDH . . . . Forsyth School for Dental Hygienists
FOBO . . . . Fort Bowie National Historic Site
FOCA . . . . Fort Caroline National Memorial
FOCL . . . . Fort Clatsop National Memorial
FODA . . . . Fort Davis National Historic Site
FDDM . . . . Fort Dodge, Des Moines & Southern Railway Company (AAR code)
FODO . . . . . . Fort Donelson National Military Park
FOFR . . . . Fort Frederica National Monument
FOJE . . . . Fort Jefferson National Monument
FOLA . . . . Fort Laramie National Historic Site
FOLS . . . . Fort Larned National Historic Site
FOMA . . . . Fort Matanzas National Monument
FOMC . . . . Fort McHenry National Monument
FMPD . . . . Fort Monmouth Procurement Division
FMPO . . . . Fort Monmouth Procurement Office
FMSL . . . . Fort Monmouth Signal Laboratory (Army)
FMS . . . . Fort Myers Southern R. R. (AAR code)
FONE . . . . Fort Necessity National Battlefield
FOPU . . . . Fort Pulaski National Monument
FORA . . . . Fort Raleigh National Historic Site
FSHPC . . . . . . Fort Sam Houston Purchasing and Contracting Office
FSJC . . . . Fort Scott Junior College (Kansas)
FSJC . . . . Fort Smith Junior College (Arkansas)
FOSM . . . . Fort Smith National Historic Site
FSVB . . . . Fort Smith & Van Buren R. R. (AAR code)
FOSU . . . . Fort Sumter National Monument
FOUN . . . . Fort Union National Monument
FOUS . . . . Fort Union Trading Post National Historic Site
FVSC . . . . Fort Valley State College (Georgia)
FOVA . . . . Fort Vancouver National Historic Site
FWBC . . . . Fort Wayne Bible College (Indiana)
FWU . . . . Fort Wayne Union R. R. (AAR code)
FWAD . . . . Fort Wingate Army Depot
FWB . . . . Fort Worth Belt Railway Company (AAR code)
FW & DC . . . . Fort Worth and Denver City Railway Company
FWD . . . . Fort Worth & Denver Railway Company (AAR code)
F . . . . Forte (Loud) (Music)
FP . . . . Forte Piano (Loud, then soft) (Music)
FA . . . . Fortified Aqueous (Pharmacy)
FF . . . . Fortissimo (Very loud) (Music)
FORATOM. . . . Forum Atomique Europeen
FIEN . . . . Forum Italiano dell'Energia Nucleare
F . . . . Forward
FAR . . . . Forward Acquisition RADAR
FAC . . . . Forward Air Control(ler) (Air Force)
FACP . . . . Forward Air Control Post
FAST-VAL . . . . Forward Air Strike Evaluation
FASO . . . . Forward Airfield Supply Organization
FAAD . . . . Forward Area Air Defense
FAADS . . . . . . Forward Area Air Defense System
FAADW . . . . . . Forward Area Air Defense Weapon
FAAR . . . . Forward Area Alerting RADAR
FASOR . . . . . . Forward Area SONAR Research
FAW . . . . Forward Area Weapons (Military)
FB . . . . Forward Body
FWDBL . . . . . . Forward Bomb Line
FDC . . . . Forward Direction Center (Air Force)
FDP . . . . Forward Distribution Point (Military)
FEBA . . . . Forward Edge of the Battle Area
FEC . . . . Forward End Cap
FER . . . . Forward Engine Room
FEDAC . . . . . . Forward Error Detection and Correction
FFAR . . . . Forward-Fighting Aerial Rocket
FFOB . . . . Forward Fighting Operating Base (Military)
FFD . . . . Forward Floating Depot (Army)
FG . . . . Forward Gate
FHL . . . . Forward Half-Line (Feed)
FIT . . . . Forward Inspection Team (Military)
FIU . . . . Forward Interpretation Unit (Military)

FLAM . . . . Forward Launched Aerodynamic Missiles
FLAR . . . . Forward Looking Airborne RADAR
FLI . . . . Forward Looking Infrared
FLIRAS . . . . . . Forward Looking Infrared Attack Set
FLIR . . . . Forward Looking Infrared RADAR
FLR . . . . Forward Looking RADAR
FMC . . . . Forward Motion Compensation
FO . . . . Forward Observer
FOB . . . . Foward Observer Bombardment
FCC . . . . Forward Observer Colidar
FOLR . . . . Forward Observer LASER Range-Finder
FOBTSU . . . . . Forward Observer Target Survey Unit
FOO . . . . Forward Observation Officer (Military)
FOP . . . . Forward Observation Post (Military)
FOB . . . . Forward Operating Base (Air Force)
FP . . . . Forward Perpendicular
FPIS . . . . Forward Propagation by Ionospheric Scatter (Radio communication technique)
FPTS . . . . Forward Propagation by Tropospheric Scatter (Radio communications technique)
FS . . . . Forward Scatter
FSP . . . . Forward Supply Point (Military)
FS . . . . Forward Support
FTA . . . . Forward Transfer Admittance
FV . . . . Forward Visibility
FWA . . . . Forward Wave Amplifier
FWT . . . . Forward Wave Tube
FLT . . . . Foss Launch & Tug (AAR code)
FF . . . . Foster Father
FPP . . . . Foster Parents' Plan (An organization)
FSD . . . . Foster-Seeley Discriminator
FWC . . . . Foster Wheeler Corporation (NYSE symbol)
FRM . . . . Foucault Rotating Mirror
F . . . . Foul
FU . . . . Foul(ed) Up (To describe a confused, mixed-up situation, person, or action) (Bowdlerized version)
FUBAR . . . . . . Fouled Up Beyond All Recognition (Slang) (See FU)
FUBB . . . . Fouled Up Beyond Belief (Slang) (See FU)
FUMTU . . . . . . Fouled Up More Than Usual (See FU)
FACE . . . . Foundation for Accredited Chiropractic Education
FAA . . . . Foundation for American Agriculture
ARC . . . . Foundation for the Arts, Religion and Culture
FBL . . . . Foundation for Better Living
FCE . . . . Foundation for Character Education
FCB . . . . Foundation for Commercial Banks
FCH . . . . Foundation for Cooperative Housing
FCRE . . . . Foundation for Cotton Research and Education
FEE . . . . Foundation for Economic Education
FFA . . . . Foundation for Foreign Affairs
FIER . . . . Foundation for Instrumentation Education and Research
FIE . . . . Foundation for Integrative Education
FIC . . . . Foundation for International Cooperation
FIPR . . . . Foundation for International Potash Research
FITR . . . . Foundation for International Trade Research
FJNF . . . . Foundation for the Jewish National Fund
FM . . . . Foundation Member
FFM . . . . Foundation for Microbiology
FMPP . . . . Foundation of the Motion Picture Pioneers
FORE . . . . Foundation for Oceanographic Research and Education
FRASCO . . . . . Foundation for Religious Action in the Social and Civil Order
FRHB . . . . Foundation for Research on Human Behavior
FRNM . . . . Foundation for Research on the Nature of Man
FSR . . . . Foundation for Scientific Relaxation
FSU . . . . Foundation for Spiritual Understanding
FSC . . . . Foundation for the Study of Cycles
FSPC . . . . Foundation for the Study of Primitive Culture
FWL . . . . Foundation for World Literacy
FYSA . . . . Foundation for Youth and Student Affairs
FEF . . . . Foundry Educational Foundation
FEMA . . . . Foundry Equipment Manufacturers Association
FFMG . . . . Foundry Facings Manufacturers Group
FCD . . . . Four-Bar Cutter Device
FCDT . . . . Four Coil Differential Transformer
4/C . . . . Four-Conductor (Wire or cable)
FHFA . . . . Four-Conductor, Heat- and Flame-Resistant, Armor (Cable)
FCCA . . . . Four Cylinder Club of America
4P . . . . Four-Pole (Switch)
FQM . . . . Four Quadrant Multiplier
QUADRADAR . . Four-Way RADAR Surveillance
FWB . . . . Four-Wheel Brake
FWD . . . . Four-Wheel Drive

FSGA . . . . Four-Wire, Shipboard, General Use, Armored (Cable)
FKBI . . . . Fourdrinier Kraft Board Institute
FWC. . . . . . . Fourdrinier Wire Council
FCCOHANA . . Fourier Coefficient Harmonic Analyzer
FT . . . . Fourier Transform
FTO . . . . Fourier Transform Operator
FARGO. . . . . . Fourteen-o-one Automatic Report Generating Operation
FOURATAF . . . Fourth Allied Tactical Air Force, Central Europe
FD . . . . Fourth Day (NYSE symbol)
F of JR . . . . . . Fourth of July Road
FSAC . . . . Fourth Stowage Adapter Container
FPV . . . . Fowl Plague Virus
FOX . . . . Foxboro Company (NYSE symbol)
FRD . . . . Fraction Reliability Deviation
FCT . . . . Fraction Thereof
FDG. . . . . . . Fractional Doppler Gate
FOB . . . . Fractional Orbital Bombardment
FOBS . . . . . . Fractional Orbital Bombardment System
FRAC . . . . . . Fractionator Reflux Analog Computer
FC . . . . Fractocumulus (Meteorology)
FRCU . . . . . . Fractocumulus (Meteorology)
FGE. . . . . . . Fracto-Graphic Examination
FS . . . . Fractostratus (Meteorology)
FATT . . . . . . Fracture Appearance Transition Temperature
FS . . . . Fracture, Simple
FTP . . . . Fracture Toughness Parameter
F . . . . Fragile
F . . . . Fragmentation
FRAGBOMB . . . Fragmentation Bomb
FF . . . . Fragrance Foundation
FRC . . . . Fram Corporation (NYSE symbol)
FD . . . . Frame Difference
FDS . . . . Frame Difference Signal
FSI. . . . . Frame Sync Indication
FPS . . . . Frames Per Second
F . . . . Franc(s) (French monetary unit)
FDD . . . . Franc de Droits (Free of charge)
FR . . . . France (NATO)
FINEBEL . . . . . France, Italy, Netherland, Belgium & Luxembourg (economic agreement)
FIT. . . . . Franchise Industry Training (High school dropout program) (Department of Labor)
FAWC . . . . . . Franciscan Apostolate of the Way of the Cross
FEC . . . . Franciscan Educational Conference
FHIC . . . . Franciscan Hospitaller Sisters of the Immaculate Conception (Roman Catholic religious order)
FMDM . . . . . . Franciscan Missionaries of the Divine Motherhood (Roman Catholic women's religious order)
FMM . . . . Franciscan Missionaries of Mary (Roman Catholic women's religious order)
FMSJ . . . . Franciscan Missionaries of St. Joseph (Patricroft Sisters) (Roman Catholic religious order)
FMDC. . . . . . . Franciscan Missionary Sisters of the Divine Child (Roman Catholic religious order)
FPS . . . . Franciscan Preparatory Seminary
SA . . . . Franciscan Sisters of the Atonement, Third Order Regular of St. Francis (Graymoor Sisters) (Roman Catholic religious order)
FSSE . . . . Franciscan Sisters of St. Elizabeth (Roman Catholic religious order)
FSSJ . . . . Franciscan Sisters of St. Joseph (Roman Catholic religious order)
FSIC. . . . . Franciscan Sisters of the Third Order of the Immaculate Conception (Roman Catholic religious order)
TFSC . . . . (From the Latin for) Franciscan Tertiaries of the Holy Cross
FRA . . . . Francisco Sugar Company (NYSE symbol)
Fr . . . . Francium (Chemical element)
FTPF. . . . . . . Francs-Tireurs et Partisans Francais (France)
FJSRL . . . . . . Frank J. Seiler Research Laboratory (Air Force)
FPC . . . . Frank Phillip College (Texas)
FA . . . . Frankford Arsenal (Army)
FCIN . . . . . . Frankfort & Cincinnati R. R. (AAR code)
HHFC. . . . . . Franklin (H.H.) Club
FCI . . . . Franklin College of Indiana
FDR . . . . Franklin Delano Roosevelt
FDRPS. . . . . . Franklin D. Roosevelt Philatelic Society
FIRL . . . . Franklin Institute Research Laboratories
FMC . . . . Franklin and Marshall College (Pennsylvania)
FPA . . . . Franklin Pierce Adams (1881-1960) (American newspaper columnist)
FKS . . . . Franklin Simon & Company (NYSE symbol)
FSC . . . . Franklin Stores Corporation (NYSE symbol)
FRS . . . . Franz Rosenzweig Society
F . . . . Frater (Brother)
FAA . . . . Fraternal Actuarial Association
FFMA . . . . . . Fraternal Field Managers' Association
FICA . . . . Fraternal Insurance Counsellors Association

FIC . . . . Fraternal Insurance Counselor (Designation given by Fraternal Field Managers' Association)
FMCMA . . . . . Fraternal and Military Club Managers Association
FOE . . . . Fraternal Order of Eagles
FOO . . . . Fraternal Order of Orioles
FOP . . . . Fraternal Order of Police, Grand Lodge
FM . . . . Fratemite Mondiale
FSA . . . . Fraternity Scholarship Association (Late , College Fraternity Scholarship Officers Association)
FWL . . . . Fraternity of the Wooden Leg
FMS . . . . Fratres Maristae a Scholis (Marist Brothers) (Roman Catholic religious order)
FSJ . . . . Fratres Sancti Joseph (Brothers of St. Joseph) (Roman Catholic religious order)
FSC . . . . Fratres Scholarum Christianarum (Brothers of the Christian Schools, or Christian Brothers) (Roman Catholic religious order)
FIC . . . . Fratrum Instructionis Christianae (Brothers of Christian Instruction, or La Mennais Brothers) (Roman Catholic religious order)
FAG. . . . . . . Fraud Against the Government
F/E . . . . Fraudulent Enlistment
FLD . . . . Fraunhofer Line Discriminator
FRSP. . . . . . . Fredericksburg and Spotsylvania County Battlefield Memorial National Military Park
F & AM . . . . Free and Accepted Masons
FAD . . . . Free Air Delivered
FATF . . . . . . Free Air Test Facility
FAO . . . . Free Albania Organization
FA . . . . Free of All Average (Insurance)
FAA . . . . Free of All Average (Insurance)
FA . . . . Free Alongside
FAS . . . . Free Alongside Ship (Business and trade)
FA . . . . Free Aperture (Technical drawings)
FA . . . . Free Astray
ZF . . . . Free Balloon (Navy symbol)
FB . . . . Free Baptist
FIB. . . . . Free into Barge
FBD . . . . Free Board
FOB . . . . Free on Board
FBD . . . . Free Body Diagram
FIB. . . . . Free into Bunker
FCS . . . . Free of Capture and Seizure (Insurance)
FC & S . . . . . Free of Capture and Seizure (Insurance)
FOC. . . . . . . Free on Car
FOC . . . . Free of Charge (Business and trade)
FCA . . . . Free China Assistance
FCF . . . . Free China Fund for Medical and Refugee Aid
FC . . . . Free Church (of Scotland)
FCB . . . . Free Cutting Brass
FOD . . . . Free of Damage (Business and trade)
FD . . . . Free Delivery
FD . . . . Free Discharge
FD . . . . Free Dispatch
FD . . . . Free Dock
FD . . . . Free Drop
FEC . . . . Free Energy Change
FEF . . . . Free Energy Function
FEAA . . . . . . Free Enterprise Awards Association
FEP . . . . Free Enterprise Personnel
FEAR . . . . . . Free Expression of Appreciation or Revenge (Customer opinion campaign operated by Bekins Van and Storage Company)
FEC . . . . Free Europe Committee
FEI. . . . . Free Europe, Incorporated
FFA . . . . Free Fatty Acid (Biochemistry)
FFR . . . . Free Field Room
FFAS . . . . . . Free Flight Analysis Section
FFD . . . . Free Flight Data
FFTV . . . . . . Free Flight Test Vehicle
FFSD . . . . . . Free Foil Switching Device
FFA . . . . Free Foreign Agency (or Agent) (Business and trade)
FF . . . . Free French
FRF . . . . Free French (World War II)
FFA . . . . Free from Alongside
FFA . . . . Free from Average (Insurance)
FFC . . . . Free from Chlorine
FFI. . . . . Free from Infection
FGA. . . . . . . Free of General Average
FIH . . . . Free in Harbor (Navigation)
FHA . . . . Free-Heave Amplitude
FHT . . . . Free-Heave Test
FIO . . . . Free In and Out
FIT. . . . . Free of Income Tax

FIP	Free Instrument Package
FJE	Free Jet Expansion
FOK	Free of Knots
FMS	**Free-Machining Steel**
FMI	Free Motion Impedance
FOIF	Free Oceanographic Instrument Float
FOCA	Free and Open Church Association (British)
FO	Free Overside
FPA	Free of Particular Average (Insurance)
FPAAC	Free of Particular Average, American Conditions (Insurance)
FPAEC	Free of Particular Average, English Conditions (Insurance)
FPCS	Free Polar Corticosteroids (Chemical)
FPW	Free Progressive Wave
FAQ	Free at Quay
FOQ	Free on Quay (Business and trade)
FRP	Free Radical Photography
FOR	Free on Rail (Business and trade)
FR & CC	Free of Riot and Civil Commotion
FOR	Free on Road (Business and trade)
FRF	Free Running Frequency
FSI	Free Sons of Israel
FST	Free Southern Theater
FSMWI	Free Space Microwave Interferometer
FSM	Free Speech Movement (University of California, Berkeley)
FOS	Free on Station
FOS	Free on Steamer (Business and trade)
FSWT	Free Surface Water Tunnel
FTT	Free Territory of Trieste
FTA	Free Trade Association (European)
FTUB	Free Trade Unions of Burma
FTUP	Free Trade Unions of the Philippines
FTW	Free Trade Wharf
FIT	Free in Truck
FOT	Free on Truck (Business and trade)
FUNY	Free University of New York
FVWU	Free Visayan Workers' Union (Philippines)
FIW	Free in Wagon
FOW	Free on Wagon
FWR	Free Wheel Rectifier
FWB	**Free-Will Baptists**
FWTUC	Free Workers' Trade Union Congress (Aden)
FWMAF	Free World Military Assistance Forces (Vietnam)
FWMAO	Free World Military Assistance Organization
FHC	Freed-Hardeman College (Tennessee)
FDP	**Freedom Democratic Party (in Mississippi)**
FHI	Freedom House, Incorporated
FFHC	Freedom from Hunger Campaign
FIA	Freedom of Information Act
FIS	Freedom Information Service
FIGHT	Freedom, Integration, God, Honor, Today (Organization in Rochester, New York)
FFVF	Freedoms Foundation at Valley Forge
FLJTC	Freeland League for Jewish Territorial Colonization
FMHS	Freely Moving Human Subject
FJC	Freeman Junior College (South Dakota)
FTU	Freeman Time Unit (Psychology)
FU	Freeman (Time) Unit (Psychology)
FT	Freeport Sulphur Company (NYSE symbol)
FDP	Freeze Desalination Plant
ZL	Freezing Drizzle (Meteorology)
FGJ	Freezing Gas Jet
FP	**Freezing Point**
FPCS	Freezing Point Calibration Standard
ZR	Freezing Rain (Meteorology)
FDP	**Freie Demokratische Partei (Free Democratic Party) (West Germany)**
FDJ	Freie Deutsche Jugend (Free German Youth)
FLA	Freie Letzeburger Arbechterverband (Free Luxembourg Workers' Federation)
FA	Freight Agent
FAK	Freight, All Kinds (Railroad)
FB	Freight Bill
F & D	Freight and Demurrage (Shipping)
FF	Freight Forwarder
FFI	Freight Forwarders Institute
FROF	Freight Office
FP	Freight and Passenger Vessels (Army)
FRRU	Freight Receiving and Redistribution Unit
FR	Freight Release
FS	Freight Supply Vessel
FTD	**Freight Traffic Division**
FDGB	Freier Deutscher Gewerkschaftsbund (Trade union confedeation, Russian Zone of Germany)

F	French
FAF	French Air Force
FAUSST	French-Anglo-United States Supersonic Transport
FBDCA	French Bulldog Club of America
FCCUS	French Chamber of Commerce of the United States
FCNL	French Committee of National Liberation (World War II)
FCA	French Computing Association
FEUS	French Engineers in the United States
FEC	French Expeditionary Force
FF	French Fourragere (Military)
FF	French Fried
FIUS	French Institute in the United States
FSN	French-Speaking Nations (NATO)
FRTO	French Togoland
FWI	French West Indies
FRAP	Frente de Accion Popular (Popular Action Front) (Chile)
FADN	Frente Anti-Communista de Defensa Nacional (Anti-Communist Front for National Defense) (Ecuador)
FUA	Frente Unita Angolana (Angolan United Front)
FTC	Freon Tank Container
F	Frequency
FAR	Frequency Adjusting Rheostat
FA	Frequency Agility
FAC	Frequency Allocation Committee (CCB)
FACSC	Frequency Allocation Coordinating Subcommittee (Canada)
FAL	Frequency Allocation List
FAP	Frequency Allocation Panel
FAPUSMCEB . . .	Frequency Allocation Panel, United States Military Communications Electronics Board
FAU	Frequency Allocation and Uses
FAS	Frequency Allocations Subcommittee
FAC	Frequency Analysis and Control
FASTAR	Frequency Angle Scanning, Tracking and Ranging
FABRIC	Frequency Assignment by Reference to Interference Charts
FAS	Frequency Assignment Subcommittee
FAI	Frequency-Azimuth Intensity (RADAR)
FCAS	Frequency Coded Armaments System
FCD	Frequency Compression Demodulator
FCF	Frequency Compressive Feedback
FCA	Frequency Control and Analysis
FCAF	Frequency Control Analysis Facility
FCWG	Frequency Control Working Group
FC	Frequency Converter
FCE	Frequency Converter Excitation
FCU	Frequency Converter Unit
FCWG	Frequency Coordination Working Group
FDU	Frequency Determining Unit
FDM	Frequency Deviation Meter
FDA	Frequency Distortion Analyzer
FDAS	Frequency Distribution Analysis Sheet
FD	Frequency Diversity (Radio)
FDR	Frequency Diversity RADAR
FD	Frequency Divider
FDDL	Frequency Division Data Link (Radio)
FDMVC	Frequency Division Multiplex Voice Communication
FDM	Frequency Division Multiplexing (Radio)
FDC	Frequency Domain Coding
FDCT	Frequency Domain Coding Technique
FDL	Frequency Double LASER
FD	Frequency Doublers
FDLD	Frequency Doubling LASER Device
FD	Frequency Drift
FEAT	Frequency of Every Allowable Term
FIC	Frequency Interference Control
FICC	Frequency Interference Control Center (Air Force)
FJI	Frequency Jumper Identification
FREJID	Frequency Jumper Identification
FLC	Frequency and Load Controller
FMST	Frequency Mass Spectrometer Tube
FME	Frequency-Measuring Equipment
FM	Frequency Meter
FRM	Frequency Meter
FMD	Frequency of Minimum Delay
FMS	Frequency Mixer Stage
FM/CW	Frequency-Modulated/Continuous-Wave (RADAR)
FMC	Frequency Modulated Cyclotron (AEC)
FMQ	Frequency Modulated Quartz
FMR	Frequency Modulated RADAR
FMR	Frequency Modulated Receiver
FMT	Frequency Modulated Transmitter
FM	Frequency Modulation (Radio)

FMB . . . . Frequency Modulation Broadcasters
FMDA . . . . . . Frequency Modulation Development Association
FMDM . . . . . . Frequency Modulation Deviation Meter
FMFB . . . . Frequency Modulation with Feedback
FM-FM . . . . . Frequency Modulation-Frequency Modulation
FMG . . . . Frequency Modulation Generator
FMI . . . . Frequency Modulation Intercity Relay Broadcasting
FM-PM . . . . . Frequency Modulation - Phase Modulation (RADAR)
FMIC . . . . Frequency Monitoring and Interference Control (Radio)
FM. . . . . Frequency Multiplex
FMS . . . . Frequency Multiplier Storer
FNA. . . . . Frequency Network Analyzer
FOG . . . . Frequency Offset Generator
FOT . . . . Frequency Optimum Traffic
FPL . . . . Frequency Phase Lock
FR . . . . Frequency Range
FR . . . . Frequency Response
FRP . . . . Frequency Response Plotter
FRT . . . . Frequency Response Tracer
FRESCANNAR . . Frequency Scan RADAR
FSR . . . . Frequency Scan RADAR
FRESCAN . . . . Frequency Scanning
FSR . . . . Frequency Selective Relay
FSVM . . . . . . Frequency Selective Voltmeter
FSCS . . . . Frequency Shift Communications System
FSC . . . . Frequency Shift Converter
FSK . . . . Frequency Shift Keying (Radio)
FSM . . . . Frequency Shift Modulation
FSP . . . . Frequency Shift Pulsing
FSR . . . . Frequency Shift Receiver
FSR . . . . Frequency Shift Reflector
FST . . . . Frequency Shift Transmission
FSCI. . . . . . . Frequency Space Characteristic Impedance
FS . . . . Frequency Stability
FSA . . . . Frequency Stability Analyzer
FSP . . . . Frequency Standard, Primary
FSO . . . . Frequency Sweep Oscillator
FOT . . . . Frequency on Target
FTC . . . . Frequency Time Control
FATDL . . . . . . Frequency and Time-Division Data Link
FTI . . . . Frequency Time Indicator (or Intensity) (RADAR)
FTMC . . . . . . Frequency and Time Measurement Counter
FTS . . . . Frequency Time Standard
FT . . . . Frequency Tolerance
FTU . . . . Frequency Transfer Unit
FTD . . . . Frequency Translation Distortion
FTBF . . . . Frequency Tuned Bandpass Filter
F . . . . Frequent (In mention of occurrence of species)
FHIF. . . . . . . Frequenting House of Ill Fame
F . . . . Fresh Water (Load line mark)
FW . . . . Fresh Water (Technical drawings)
FW. . . . . Fresh Water (Vessel load line mark)
FWD . . . . Fresh Water Damage
FWDCT . . . . . . Fresh Water Drain Collecting Tank
FWFWA. . . . . . Fresh Water Fish Wholesalers Association
FLOLS . . . . . Fresnel Lens Optical Landing System
FAT . . . . Fresno Air Terminal (California)
FSC . . . . Fresno State College (California)
FRC . . . . Fresuel Reflection Coefficient
FIGA . . . . Fretted Instrument Guild of America
FA . . . . Freund's Adjuvant
F . . . . Friar
FAST . . . . Friction Assessment Screening Test (for brake linings)
FG. . . . . Friction Glaze
FHP . . . . Friction Horsepower
FMSI . . . . Friction Materials Standards Institute
FMT . . . . Friction Measurement Test
F & HE. . . . . . Fridays and Holidays Excepted (Mohammedan)
FR . . . . Friden, Inc. (NYSE symbol)
FDV . . . . Friend Disease Virus
FLV . . . . Friend Leukemia Virus
FIND . . . . Friendless, Isolated, Needy, Disabled (Project of National Council on the Aging)
FA . . . . Friendly Aircraft
FFD . . . . Friendly Forward Disposition
FSES . . . . Friendly Society of Engravers and Sketchmakers
FAA . . . . Friends of Africa in America
FAW . . . . Friends of American Writers
FOA . . . . Friends of Animals
FBC . . . . Friends Bible College (Kansas)
FCNL . . . . Friends Committee on National Legislation

FCE . . . . Friends Council on Education
FOFA . . . . . . Friends of Free Asia
FGC . . . . Friends General Conference
FGS . . . . Friends of the Golden State
FHA . . . . Friends Historical Association
FHP . . . . Friends of Historical Pharmacy
FOL . . . . Friends of the Land
FPC . . . . Friends Peace Committee
FUSLA . . . . . . Friends of the United States of Latin America
FOW . . . . Friends of the Wilderness (An organization)
FWCC . . . . . . Friends World Committee for Consultation (Quakers)
FH . . . . Friendship House
FJC . . . . Friendship Junior College (South Carolina)
FLAME . . . . . . Friendship Loans to Latin American Endeavors, Inc.
DL . . . . Frigate (Navy symbol)
F . . . . From
FPP . . . . From Present Position (Aviation)
FC . . . . Front-Connected
FD . . . . Front of Dash (Technical drawings)
FF . . . . Front Focal Length (Optics)
FFL . . . . Front Focal Length
FJN . . . . Front Jednosci Narodowej (Polish Front of National Unity)
FJNA . . . . Front des Jeunes Nationalistes Africains (National African Youth Front)
FLN . . . . Front de Liberation Nationale (National Liberation Front) (Algeria)
FLOSY . . . . . Front for the Liberation of Occupied South Yemen
FLG . . . . Front de Libertacao de Guine (Guinean Liberation Front) (Portuguese Guinea)
FLID. . . . . . . Front de la Lutte pour l'Independence du Dahomey (Battle Front for the Independence of Dahomey)
FLING . . . . . . Front de Lutte pour l'Independence de la Guinee (Battle Front for the National Independence of Portuguese Guinea)
FML . . . . Front Mounting Light
FPC . . . . Front Panel Control
FPS . . . . Front Populaire Soudanais (Sudanese Popular Front)
FQF . . . . Front du Quebec Francais
FRAIN . . . . . . Front Revolutionnaire Africain pour l'Independance Nationale des Colonies Portugaises (African Revolutionary Front for the National Independence of Portuguese Colonies)
FSA . . . . Front Suspension Arm
FUL . . . . Front Uni Liberateur de la Guinee Portuguesa et des Isles du Cap Vert (United Liberation Front of Portuguese Guinea and Cape Verde)
FUNA. . . . . . . Front d'Union Nationale de l'Angola (National Union Front of Angola)
FUB . . . . Front de l'Unite Bangala (Bangala United Front)
FGP . . . . Frontal Groove of Pinnule
FND . . . . Frontal National Democratic (Rumania)
FNLA . . . . Fronte Nacional de Libertacao da Angola (Angolan National Liberation Front)
FAL . . . . Frontier Airlines, Inc.
FL . . . . Frontier Airlines, Inc.
FNS . . . . Frontier Nursing Service (An organization)
FI . . . . Frontiers International
FDA . . . . Fronto-Dextra Anterior
FDP . . . . Fronto-Dextra Posterior
FDT . . . . Fronto-Dextra Transversa
X. . . . . Frost
FFTA . . . . Frozen Fish Trades Association
FFI . . . . Frozen Food Institute
FPC . . . . Frozen Pea Council
FPPI . . . . Frozen Potato Products Institute
FTR . . . . Fruehauf Corporation (NYSE symbol)
FSME . . . . . . Fruhsommer-Meninzoencephalitis
FV . . . . Fruit and Vegetable Division (of AMS, Department of Agriculture)
FMIR . . . . Frustrated Multiple Internal Reflectance
F . . . . Fuel
FABU . . . . Fuel Additive Blender Unit
FAMU . . . . . . Fuel Additive Mixture Unit
F/A . . . . Fuel-Air (Ratio)
FAX . . . . Fuel Air Explosive
FOB . . . . Fuel on Board (Aviation)
FBP . . . . Fuel Booster Pump
FCB . . . . Fuel Cell Battery
FCC . . . . Fuel Cell Catalyst
FCM. . . . . . . Fuel Cell Module
FCK . . . . Fuel Charge Kit
FCMV . . . . . . Fuel Consuming Motor Vehicle
FCDA . . . . . . Fuel Control Diaphragm Assembly
FCF . . . . Fuel Cycle Facility (AEC)
FDI . . . . Fuel Desulphurization, Incorporated
FFI . . . . Fuel Flow Indicator
FG. . . . . Fuel Gas
FIR. . . . . Fuel Indicator Reading

FQI . . . . Fuel Quantity Indicator
FO . . . . Fuel Oil
YON . . . . Fuel Oil Barge (Non-Self-Propelled) (Navy symbol)
YO . . . . Fuel Oil Barge (Self-Propelled) (Navy symbol)
FOC . . . . Fuel Oil Cooler
FORDACS . . . Fuel-Oil Route Delivery and Control System (Computer-based system)
FOT . . . . Fuel-Oil Transfer
FOWHM . . . . . Fuel Oil and Water Heater Manufacturers Association
FPI . . . . Fuel Pressure Indicator
FPO . . . . Fuel Pressure Out
FR . . . . Fuel Remaining (Aviation)
FSD . . . . Fuel Supply Depot (Military)
FSO . . . . Fuel Supply Office (Military)
FTT . . . . Fuel Transfer Tool
FANDT . . . . . Fuel and Transportation (Navy)
F & T . . . . . Fuel and Transportation
FTA . . . . Fuel Treatment Apparatus
FVD . . . . Fuel Vapor Detector
F . . . . Fueler (Aircraft designation)
YCD . . . . Fueling Barge (Navy symbol)
FRC . . . . Fuels Research Council
FRL . . . . Fuels Research Laboratory (MIT)
F . . . . Fugacity
FOA . . . . Fugitive Other Authorities (FBI standardized term)
FOF . . . . Fukuoka Occupation Force
F . . . . Full
FA . . . . Full Action
FA . . . . Full Adder (Data processing)
FA . . . . Full Automatic
FTB . . . . Full to Bursting (Reply to question, "Have you had enough to eat?")
FD . . . . Full Dress (Colloquial reference to formal dress)
FD . . . . Full Dress (Military)
FD . . . . Full Duplex
FDX . . . . Full Duplex
FDT . . . . Full Duplex Teletype
FDV . . . . Full Duplex Vocoder
FEL . . . . Full Employment League
FF . . . . Full-Fashioned
FF . . . . Full Field
FFRR . . . . . . Full Frequency Range Recording
FUFO . . . . . . Full Fuzing Option
FGBMFI . . . . . Full Gospel Business Men's Fellowship International
FIR . . . . Full Indicator Reading
FIML . . . . Full-Information Maximum Likelihood (Econometrics)
FIA . . . . Full Interest Admitted
FLFT . . . . . . Full Load Frame Time (Term used in SAGE operations)
FMX . . . . . . Full Mouth Radiograph (Dentistry)
FUNOP . . . . . Full Normal Plot (Data processing)
FOF . . . . Full Octave Filter
FOS . . . . Full Operational Status
FO . . . . Full Organ (Music)
FO . . . . Full Out (Flush left) (Typesetting)
FOPR . . . . . . Full Out-Patient Rate
FPD . . . . Full Paid (NYSE symbol)
FP . . . . Full Period
FPF . . . . Full Power Frequency
FPR . . . . Full Power Response
FPT . . . . Full Power Trial
FRJM . . . . . . Full Range Joint Movement (Occupational therapy)
FROM . . . . . . Full Range of Movement (Occupational therapy)
FR . . . . Full-Rate (Telegrams and cables)
FRR . . . . Full Reimbursement Rate
FRRS . . . . . . Full Remaining Radiation Service (Unit) (Military)
FRN . . . . Full-Round Nose (Diamond drilling)
FS . . . . Full Scale
FSO . . . . Full Scale Output
FSTV . . . . . . Full-Scale Test Vehicle (NASA)
FST . . . . Full Scale Tunnel (Aerospace)
FS . . . . Full and Soft (Dietetics)
FSL . . . . Full Stop Landing (Aviation)
FT . . . . Full Terms
FTE . . . . Full-Time Equivalent (Employees)
FTR . . . . Full Time Regular (Civil Service employee category)
FTT . . . . Full Time Temporary (Civil Service employee category)
FTRAC . . . . . Full-Tracked Vehicle
FURPO . . . . . Full Utilization of Rural Program Opportunities
FW . . . . Full Wave
FWAC . . . . . . Full Wave Alternating Current
FWA . . . . Full Wave Amplifier
FWBA . . . . . . Full Wave Balanced Amplifier
FWBR . . . . . . Full Wave Bridge Rectifier

FWDC . . . . . . Full Wave Direct Current
FWRU . . . . . . Full Wave Rectified Unfiltered
FWR . . . . Full-Wave Rectifier
FWHM . . . . . . Full Width at Half Maximum
FB . . . . Fullback (Football position)
FJC . . . . Fullerton Junior College (California)
FS . . . . Fullrack System
FACT . . . . . . Fully Automatic Compiler-Translator
FACS . . . . . . Fully Automatic Compiling System
FACT . . . . . . Fully Automatic Compiling Technique
FAHQT . . . . . . Fully Automatic, High Quality Translation
FATAL . . . . . Fully Automatic Test Algebraic Language
FBC . . . . Fully Buffered Channel
FG . . . . Fully Good
FISH . . . . Fully Instrumented Submersible Housing (An oceanographic instrument)
FP . . . . Fully Paid
FT . . . . Fume-Tight (Technical drawings)
FB . . . . Fumigation and Bath (Military)
F . . . . Function
FB . . . . Function Button (Data processing)
FS . . . . Function Set
FAB . . . . Functional Adhesive Bonding
FA . . . . Functional Analysis
FAST . . . . . . Functional Analysis System Technique
FCF . . . . Functional Check Flight (Air Force)
FCO . . . . Functional Check Out
FC . . . . Functional Code
FEA . . . . Functional Economic Area
FEB . . . . Functional Electronic Block
FEBS . . . . . . Functional Electronic Blocks
FFB . . . . Functional Flow Block
FFBD . . . . . . Functional Flow Block Diagram
FFD . . . . Functional Flow Diagram
FIR . . . . Functional Item Replacement
FLO . . . . Functional Line Organization
FNS . . . . Functional Nomenclature Signal
FPT . . . . Functional Performance Time
FPV . . . . Functional Proofing Vehicle
FRC . . . . Functional Residual Capacity (of the Lungs) (Medicine)
FS . . . . Functional Selector
FT . . . . Functional Test
FTCR . . . . . . Functional Test Change Request
FTE . . . . Functional Test Equipment
FTF . . . . Functional Test Flight
FTP . . . . Functional Test Procedure
FTR . . . . Functional Test Report
FVR . . . . Functional Vestibular Reserve (Orientation)
F & R . . . . . . Functions and Responsibilities
FAE . . . . Fund for the Advancement of Education
FEWO . . . . . . Fund for Education in World Order
FOF . . . . Fund of Funds
FMIC . . . . . . Fund Management Identification Code (Military)
FPAD . . . . . . Fund for Peaceful Atomic Development
LITFUND . . . . . Fund for the Relief of Russian Writers and Scientists in Exile
FIRO . . . . . . Fundamental Interpersonal Relations Orientation
FASE . . . . . . Fundamentally Analyzable Simplified English (Data processing)
FPA . . . . Funding Program Advice (Military)
FMAL . . . . . . Funds Management Audit List (Military)
FMR . . . . Funds Management Record (Military)
FWNEOFAP . . Funds Will Not Be Entrusted to Others for Any Purpose (Army)
FTS . . . . Funeral Telegraph Service
FSO . . . . Funksjonaerenes Sentralorganisasjoh (Central Organization of Salaried Employees) (Norway)
FSN . . . . Funksjonaersambandet i Norge (Employees Federation of Norway)
FL . . . . Funnel Length
FLI . . . . Funnel Length Index
FBAA . . . . . . Fur Brokers Association of America
FBACSI . . . . . Fur Buyers Association, Coat and Suit Industry
FDG . . . . Fur Dressers Guild
FGTSA . . . . . Fur Garment Traveling Salesmen's Association
FIFC . . . . Fur Information and Fashion Council
FMEC . . . . . . Fur Merchants Employers Council
F . . . . Furlong
FR . . . . Furlough Rations (Army)
FWOP . . . . . . Furloughed Without Pay
FR . . . . Furness Railway (British)
FAWOD . . . . . Furnish Assignment Instructions Without Delay
FCOAC . . . . . Furnish Copies of Orders to Appropriate Commanders
FBSI . . . . Furniture and Bedding Spring Institute
F & F . . . . . Furniture and Fixtures
FF & E . . . . . Furniture, Fixtures, and Equipment (Insurance)

FJCNY . . . . . . Furriers Joint Council of New York
FPWA . . . . . . Further Particulars When Available
FUREPT . . . . . . (And) Further Report To (Army)
FCR . . . . Fuse Current Rating
FVR . . . . Fuse Voltage Rating
FJ . . . . Fused Junction
FQT . . . . Fused Quartz Tubing
FS . . . . Fuselage Station
FNP . . . . Fusion Point
FUP . . . . Fusion Point
FBY . . . . Future Budget Year
FBLA . . . . Future Business Leaders of America
FEA . . . . Future Engineers of America
FFA . . . . Future Farmers of America

FHA . . . . Future Horsemen of America
FJA . . . . Future Journalists of America
FPO . . . . Future Projects Office
FSA . . . . Future Scientists of America
FSAF . . . . Future Scientists of America Foundation
FTA . . . . Future Teachers of America
FWA . . . . Future Weapons Agency (Army)
FATE . . . . Fuze Arming Test Experiment
FC . . . . Fuze Committee (Military)
FD . . . . Fuze Delay
FA . . . . Fuzed Alloy
FQIL . . . . Fuzed Quartz Incandescent Lamp
FST . . . . Fuzed Silica Tube
FATE . . . . Fuzing and Arming Test and Evaluation (Space vehicle)

G

GOBSII . . . . . Gabungan Organisasi Buruh Serikat Islam Indonesia (Federation of Indonesian Moslem Trade and Labor Unions)
GASERBUN . . . Gabungan SB2 Non-Vakcentral (Federation of Non-Affiliated Trade Unions) (Indonesia)
GSBI . . . . Gabungan Serikat Buruh Indonesia (Federation of Indonesian Trade Unions)
GASBIINDO. . . Gabungan Serikat Buruh Islam Indonesia (Federation of Indonesian Islamic Trade Unions)
Gd . . . . Gadolinium (Chemical element)
GO . . . . Gadolinium
GDLG . . . . . . Gadolinium Iron Garnet
GDP. . . . . . . Gaede Diffusion Pump
GPG . . . . Gaertnerische Produktionsgenossenschaft
GAF. . . . . . . G/A/F Corporation (Formerly, General Aniline & Film Corporation)
GCN . . . . Gage Code Number
GL . . . . Gage Length
GAA . . . . Gain Adjuster Adapter
GBM . . . . Gain Band Merit
GBP . . . . Gain-Bandwidth Product
GC . . . . Gain Control
GCA . . . . Gain Control Amplifier
GCD . . . . Gain Control Driver
GCR . . . . Gain Control Range
GTC . . . . Gain Time Control
GJC . . . . Gainesville Junior College (Later, Cooke County Junior College) (Texas)
GM . . . . Gainesville Midland R. R. (AAR code)
GIM. . . . . Gaining Inventory Managers
GMAJCOM . . . Gaining Major Command (Military)
GCR . . . . Galactic Cosmic Ray
GCRP . . . . . . Galactic Cosmic Ray Particle
GREB . . . . . . Galactic Radiation Experiment Background Satellite (Navy transit satellite)
GRC . . . . Gale Research Company
GB . . . . Gall Bladder (or a patient with an affliction of this organ) (Medicine)
GBS . . . . Gall Bladder Series (Radiography)
GLCA . . . . . . Gallery of Living Catholic Authors
GSUSA . . . . . . Gallipoli Society in the United States of America
Ga . . . . Gallium (Chemical element)
GaAs . . . . Gallium Arsenide
GAD . . . . Gallium Arsenide Diode
GAL . . . . Gallium Arsenide LASER
GaAsP. . . . . . . Gallium Arsenide-Phosphide
GaP . . . . Gallium Phosphide
GAYIG. . . . . . Gallium Substituted Yttrium Iron Garnet
GPAD . . . . . . Gallons Per Acre (per) Day (Irrigation)
GPC . . . . Gallons Per Capita
GPCD . . . . . . Gallons Per Capita (per) Day
GPD. . . . . . . Gallons Per Day
GPH. . . . . . . Gallons Per Hour
GPM . . . . Gallons Per Mile
GPM . . . . Gallons Per Minute
GPS . . . . Gallons Per Second
GCSA . . . . . . Galloway Cattle Society of America
GSR . . . . Galvanic Skin Response (Physiology)
GSR . . . . Galvanic Stimulation Rate
GAC . . . . Galvanized Aircraft
GIP . . . . Galvanized Improved Plow (Steel)
GI . . . . Galvanized Iron
GS . . . . Galvanized Steel
GSWR . . . . . . Galvanized Steel Wire Rope
GWMC . . . . . . Galvanized Ware Manufacturers Council
GCR . . . . Galvanocutaneous Reaction
GML . . . . Galvanometer-Mirror Lightbeam

GHH . . . . Galveston, Houston & Henderson R. R. (AAR code)
GWF . . . . Galveston Wharves R. R. (AAR code)
GDA . . . . Galvo-Drive Amplifier
GLU. . . . . Gambia Labour Union
GWU . . . . Gambia Workers' Union
GSK. . . . . Gamble-Skogmo, Inc. (NYSE symbol)
GA . . . . Gamblers Anonymous
G . . . . Game
GT. . . . . Game Theory
GB . . . . Games Behind
GAH . . . . Games at Home (Baseball)
G . . . . Games Played (Sports statistics)
GABA. . . . . . . Gamma-Aminobutyric Acid
GARD. . . . . . . Gamma Atomic Radiation Detector
GBH. . . . . Gamma Benzene Hydrochloride
GDDS. . . . . . . Gamma Dose Detector System
GEG . . . . Gamma Eta Gamma (Fraternity)
GG . . . . Gamma Globulin (Medicine)
GIGI . . . . Gamma Inspection of Grain Integrity
GLI . . . . Gamma Linac Instrumentation
GRS . . . . Gamma Radiation Source
GRS . . . . Gamma Radiation Spectrometer
GR . . . . Gamma Ray
GRA . . . . Gamma Ray Amplification
GRASER . . . . . Gamma Ray Amplification by Stimulated Emission of Radiation
GRAPE . . . . . . Gamma Ray Attenuation Porosity Evaluator
GRE . . . . Gamma Ray Experiment
GRP . . . . Gamma Ray Projector
GRSE . . . . Gamma Ray Spectrometric Equipment
GRS . . . . Gamma Ray Spectrum
GRT . . . . Gamma Ray Telescope
GRT . . . . Gamma Ray Tube
GSHR . . . . Gandhi Society for Human Rights
GNF . . . . Gannett Newspaper Foundation
GIP . . . . Ganssian Image Point
GF. . . . . Gap Filler (RADAR)
GFD. . . . . Gap-Filler Data (RADAR)
GFI . . . . Gap-Filler Input (RADAR)
GFO . . . . Gap-Filler Output
GFR . . . . Gap-Filler RADAR
GF/RP . . . . . . Gap Filler/Reporting Post (RADAR)
GS. . . . . Gap Separation
G . . . . Garage
GIGO . . . . . . Garbage In, Garbage Out (Data processing)
YG. . . . . Garbage Lighter (Self-Propelled) (Navy symbol)
YGN . . . . Garbage Lighter (Non-Self-Propelled) (Navy symbol)
GRF . . . . Garbell Research Foundation
GCW . . . . Garden City Western Railway Company (AAR code)
GCA . . . . Garden Club of America
GSA. . . . . Garden Seed Association
GSDN . . . . . . Garden Supply Dealers National
GWAA . . . . . . Garden Writers Association of America
GDC . . . . Gardner-Denver Company (NYSE symbol)
GWJC . . . . . . Gardner Webb Junior College (North Carolina)
GAK . . . . Garlock, Inc. (NYSE symbol)
GDGA . . . . . . Garment Dyers Guild of America
GSG . . . . Garment Salesmen's Guild of New York
GAR . . . . . Garrett Corporation (NYSE symbol)
GA . . . . Garrison Adjutant (British military)
GMP. . . . . Garrison Military Police (British)
GKA . . . . Garter King of Arms
GIA . . . . Garuda Indonesian Airways, Ltd.
GA . . . . Gas Amplification

GASP . . . . Gas Annulus Sizing Program
GAES . . . . Gas Appliance Engineers Society
GAMA . . . . . . Gas Appliance Manufacturers Association
GBP . . . . Gas Bearing Part
GC . . . . Gas Chromatograph (or Chromatography)
GC-MS . . . . . Gas Chromatography - Mass Spectrometry
GCFR . . . . . . Gas-Cooled Fast Reactor (for commercial atomic power)
GCR . . . . . . Gas-Cooled Reactor
GCRE . . . . . . Gas-Cooled Reactor, Experimental (AEC)
GDG . . . . . . Gas Discharge Gauge
GDF . . . . Gas Dynamic Facility (Air Force)
GDS . . . . Gas Dynamic System
GDL . . . . Gas Dynamics Laboratory
GE . . . . Gas Ejection (Opening) (Technical drawings)
GFC . . . . Gas Filled Counter
GFR . . . . Gas-Filled Rectifier
GFRT . . . . . . Gas-Filled Rectifying Tube
GFO . . . . Gas-Fired Oven
GFPM . . . . . . Gas Fission Products Monitor
GGAR . . . . . . Gas-Guided Aircraft Rocket
GHP . . . . Gas High Pressure
GIO . . . . Gas Identification Officer
GL . . . . Gas LASER
GLDT . . . . . . Gas LASER Discharge Tube
GLT . . . . Gas LASER Tube
GLD . . . . Gas Leak Detector
GLC . . . . Gas-Liquid Chromatography (NASA)
GLB . . . . Gas (or Grease) Lubricated Bearing
GMS . . . . . . Gas Measurement System
GMT . . . . . . Gas Missile Tube
GNP . . . . Gas, Nonpersistent
GOC . . . . Gas Operated Core
GOE . . . . Gas, Oxygen, Ether (Anesthesiology)
GP . . . . Gas, Persistent
GPE . . . . Gas Power Exchange
GPBS . . . . . . Gas Pressure Bending System
GPF . . . . Gas Proof
GR . . . . Gas Ratio
GASSP . . . . . . Gas Source Seismic Section Profiler
GSH . . . . Gas Space Heater
GT . . . . Gas Tight
GTV . . . . Gas Toggle Valve
GTL . . . . . . Gas Transport LASER
GTAW . . . . . . Gas Tungsten Arc Weld
GT . . . . Gas Turbine
GTC . . . . Gas Turbine Compressor
GTG . . . . Gas Turbine Generator
GTGS . . . . . . Gas Turbine Generator Set
GTL . . . . Gas Turbine Laboratory (MIT)
GTPS . . . . . . Gas Turbine Power System
GTSS . . . . . . Gas Turbine Selfcontained Starter
GTS . . . . Gas Turbine Ship
GTTF . . . . . . Gas Turbine Test Facility
GUP . . . . Gas Under Pressure
GVI . . . . Gas Vent Institute
GAJ . . . . Gaseous Axisymmetric Jet
GDP . . . . Gaseous Discharge Principle
GFMS . . . . . . Gaseous Flow Measuring System
GFCS . . . . . . Gaseous Flowmeter Calibration Stand
GIL . . . . Gaseous Ion LASER
GNFMS . . . . . Gaseous Nitrogen Flow Measuring System
GNMS . . . . . Gaseous Nitrogen Measuring System
GNR . . . . . . Gaseous Nuclear Rocket
GOX . . . . Gaseous Oxygen
YOG . . . . . . Gasoline Barge (Self-Propelled) (Navy symbol)
YOGN . . . . . . Gasoline Barge (Non-Self-Propelled) (Navy symbol)
GED . . . . . . Gasoline Engine Driven
GPMA . . . . . . Gasoline Pump Manufacturers Association
GA . . . . Gasoline Stowage and Fuel System Man (Navy)
AOG . . . . . . Gasoline Tanker (Navy symbol)
GA . . . . Gastric Analysis
GS . . . . Gastric Shield
GU . . . . Gastric Ulcer
GE . . . . Gastroenterology (Medicine)
GRG . . . . . . Gastroenterology Research Group
GI . . . . Gastrointestinal (Medicine)
GIS . . . . Gastrointestinal Series (Radiology)
GAI . . . . Gate Alarm Indicator (RADAR)
GBDV . . . . . . Gate Breakdown Voltage
GBV . . . . Gate Breakdown Voltage
GCS . . . . Gate Controlled Switch

GD . . . . Gate Driver
GLC . . . . Gate Leakage Current
GTO . . . . Gate Turn Off (Data processing)
YNG . . . . Gate Vessel (Navy symbol)
GA . . . . Gated Attenuation (Data processing)
GIIV . . . . Gated Image Intensifier Viewer
GOCR . . . . . . Gated-Off Controlled Rectifier
GVT . . . . Gated Video Tracker
GARDAE . . . . . Gathers Alarms, Reports, Displays and Evaluates
GHC . . . . Gating Half-Cycle (Data processing)
GWF . . . . Gating Wave Form
G . . . . Gauche (Left)
G . . . . Gauge
GCA . . . . Gauge Control Analyzer
GA . . . . Gauge Man (Navy)
GPC . . . . Gauge Pressure Control
G . . . . Gauss
GEF . . . . Gauss Error Function
GHE . . . . Gauss Hypergeometric Equation
GHF . . . . Gauss Hypergeometric Function
GLF . . . . Gaussian Lens Formula
GNG . . . . Gaussian Noise Generator
GRP . . . . Gaussian Random Process
GWG . . . . Gaussian Wave Group
GADNA . . . . . Gduei Noar (Youth Battalions) (Israel)
GA . . . . Gear Assembly
GTD . . . . Gear Test Data
GTA . . . . Gear Train Analyzer
GR . . . . Geared Radial (Aircraft engine)
GRTM . . . . . . Geared Roller Test Machine
GESTAPO . . . . Geheime Staats Polizei (Secret State Police) (German)
GI . . . . Geheimer Informant
GM . . . . Geheimer Mitarbeiter
GM . . . . Geiger-Mueller (Counter)
GMT . . . . Geiger Muller Tube
GTE . . . . Geipipari Tudomanyos Egyesulet
GEF . . . . Gel Electrofocusing
GPC . . . . Gel Permeation Chromatography
GMIA . . . . . . Gelatin Manufacturers Institute of America
GMS . . . . . . Gelatin Matrix System
GRF . . . . Gelatin, Resorcinol, and Formaldehyde
GRP . . . . Gelatin Rigidized Panel
GMVL . . . . . . Geldersche Maatschappij van Landbouw (Netherlands)
G . . . . Gelding
GLP . . . . Gelled Liquid Propellant
GEL . . . . Gellman Manufacturing Company (NYSE symbol)
GUBI . . . . . . Gemeinschaft Unabhangiger Beratender Ingenieurbueros (Association of German Consulting Engineers)
GAT . . . . Gemini-Agena Target
GATV . . . . . . Gemini Agena Target Vehicle (NASA)
GAATV . . . . . Gemini Atlas/Agena Target Vehicle
GLV . . . . Gemini Launch Vehicle (NASA)
GMS . . . . . . Gemini Mission Simulator
GRIP . . . . . . Gemini Reentry Integration Program (Aerospace)
GEST . . . . . . Gemini Slowscan Television
GT . . . . Gemini-Titan
GIA . . . . Gemological Institute of America
G . . . . Gender
GSP . . . . Genealogical Society of Pennsylvania
GREMAS . . . . . Genealogische Recherche mit Magnetband-Speicherung (Organic chemistry coding system)
GVP . . . . Geneeskundige Versorging Polittie (Netherlands)
G . . . . General
GASP . . . . . . General Academic Simulation Program (Data processing)
GAC . . . . General Acceptance Corporation (NYSE symbol)
GAA . . . . . . General Account of Advances
GAI . . . . General Accounting Instructions
GAO . . . . . . General Accounting Office (of the US government)
GAOW . . . . . General Accounting Office, Washington
GASL . . . . . . General Activity Simulation Language
GAS . . . . . . General Adaptation Syndrome (Medicine)
GAB . . . . . . General Adjustment Bureau (Insurance)
G & A . . . . . . General and Administrative
GAE . . . . . . General Administrative Expense (A budget appropriation title)
GAO . . . . . . General Administrative Order
GAC . . . . . . General Advisory Committee (to the AEC)
GAM . . . . . . General Aeronautical Material
GAA . . . . . . General Agency Agreement (Navy)
GAC . . . . . . General Agency Check
GA . . . . General Agent (Business and trade, especially insurance)
GAMC . . . . . . General Agents and Managers Conference of Nalu

GATT ...... General Agreement on Tariffs and Trade (Organizations, and the concept it represents, concerned with adjustment of tariffs between 73 member nations)
GAWU ..... General Agricultural Workers' Union (Kenya)
GNY .... General Alloys Company (NYSE symbol)
GAM .... General American Investors Company, Inc. (NYSE symbol)
GAO .... General American Oil Company of Texas (NYSE symbol)
GARD ...... General American Research Division
GATX ...... General American Transportation Corporation
GMT .... General American Transportation Corporation (NYSE symbol)
GAT....... General Analysis Technique
GASL ...... General Applied Science Laboratory
GATB....... General Aptitude Test Battery
GATBY...... General Aptitude Test Battery
GACTI ..... General Arbitration Council of the Textile Industry
GA .... General of the Army
GA .... General Assembly
GAP....... General Assembly Program
GA (UN) .... General Assembly of the United Nations
GA .... General Assistance (A form of public charity)
G .... General Audiences (All Ages Admitted) (Movie rating)
GAS....... General Automotive Support
GA .... General Average (Insurance)
GADO ...... General Aviation District Office (FAA)
GAFPG ..... General Aviation Facilities Planning Group
GAPE....... General Aviation Pilot Education (Safety project)
GARMI ..... General Aviation Radio Magnetic Indicator
GAT .... General Aviation Transponder
GB........ General Background
GBG ...... General Baking Company (NYSE symbol)
GBS....... General Bancshares Corporation (NYSE symbol)
GEBCO...... General Bathymetric Chart of the Oceans (International Hydrographic Bureau)
GB........ General Board (Military judicial or investigative body)
GBCSCMC ... General Board of Christian Social Concerns of the Methodist Church
GBX ...... General Box Company (NYSE symbol)
GB........ General Bronze Corporation
GLZ....... General Bronze Corporation (NYSE symbol)
GBD....... General Builders Supply (NYSE symbol)
GK .... General Cable Corporation (NYSE symbol)
GCE .... General Certificate of Education (British)
GCR....... General Cigar Company, Inc. (NYSE symbol)
GC .... General Circular
GCA ...... General Claim Agent
GCT....... General Classification Test (Military)
GCC ...... General Commission on Chaplains & Armed Forces Personnel
GECOM .... General Compiler (Data processing)
GCD ...... General and Complete Disarmament
GECOS..... General Comprehensive Operating System
GCF....... General Contract Finance Corporation (NYSE symbol)
GC .... General Counsel
GCM ..... General Counsel's Memorandum (US Internal Revenue Service)
GCM...... General Court-Martial
GCMO ..... General Court-Martial Order
GCMP ..... General Court-Martial Prisoner
GC .... General Cueing
GD .... General Delivery
GENDEP..... General Depot (Military)
GENDET .... General Detail (Coast Guard)
GD .... General Diagram
GDC ...... General (Purpose) Digital Computer
GD .... General Discharge
GD .... General Dispensary
GENDISP .... General Dispensary (Military)
GDB ...... General Duties Branch (RAF)
GDMO ..... General Duties Medical Officer
GD .... General Duty
GENDYN .... General Dynamics
GD/A ..... General Dynamics/Astronautics
GD .... General Dynamics Corporation (NYSE symbol)
GDC ...... General Dynamics Corporation
GDY ...... General Dynamics Corporation (NYSE symbol)
GD/T...... General Dynamics/Telecommunications
GED....... General Educational Development (Test)
GEDT...... General Educational Development Test
GEAP ..... General Electric Atomic Power
GE........ General Electric Company (NYSE symbol)
GEC....... General Electric Company
GELAP ..... General Electric Computer Analysis Program
GEEP ..... General Electric Electronic Processor
GEL ...... General Electric Laboratory

GEMAGS .... General Electric Magnetically Anchored Gravity System
GE/MAC .... General Electric Measurement and Control
GEPEXS .... General Electric Parts Explosion System
GEPAC ..... General Electric Programmable Automatic Comparator
GERSIS ..... General Electric Range Safety Instrumentation System
GERTS ..... General Electric Range Tracking System (Aerospace)
GESOC .... General Electric Satellite Orbit Control
GESAC .... General Electric Self-Adaptive Control System
GES........ General Electric Semiconductor
GESCO...... General Electric Supply Corporation
GETR ...... General Electric Test Reactor
GEVIC ..... General Electric Variable Increment Computer
GEESE ..... General Electric's Electronic System Evaluator
GEC ...... General Electrodynamics Company
GER .... General Engineering Research
GEC ...... General Equipment Command (Army - Equipment and support of Engineers and Quartermaster)
GEPL ...... General Equipment and Packaging Laboratory (Army)
GETA ...... General Equipment Test Activity (Army)
GEE .... General Evaluation Equipment
GFLU ..... General Federation of Labor Unions (Syria)
GFTU ..... General Federation of Trade Unions (Various countries)
GFWC ..... General Federation of Women's Clubs
GFN ...... General Finance Corporation of Delaware (NYSE symbol)
GFCM ..... General Fisheries Council for the Mediterranean
GF........ General Foods Corporation (NYSE symbol)
GFMVT...... General Foods Moisture Vapor Transmission
GFA ...... General Freight Agent
GEGR ...... General Grant National Memorial
GHQ ...... General Headquarters (Military)
GH .... General Hospital
GIC .... General Improvement Contractors Association
GIRD ...... General Incentive for Research and Development (Canada)
GI......... General Index
GIER ..... General Industrial Equipment Reserve
GIAC ...... General Industry Advisory Committee
GIRSS ..... General Information Retrieval System Simulation
GIT .... General Information Test
GID....... General Installation Dolly
GIRO ...... General Instructions for Routing and Reporting Officers
GRL .... General Instrument Corporation (NYSE symbol)
G .... General Intelligence
GIU....... General Intelligence Unit (US, London)
GISMO...... General Interpretative System for Matrix Operations (Data processing system used in engineering) (Navy)
GI .... General Issue
GKI........ General Kinetics, Incorporated
GLA ...... General Laboratory Associates
GLO ...... General Land Office (Became part of Bureau of Land Management, 1946)
GENLED .... General Ledger
GL .... General Ledger
GLA ...... General Ledger Account
GLIC ...... General Ledger Identification Code
GLSA ...... General Ledger Subsidiary Account
GLS ...... General Lighting Service
GM .... General Maintenance (Army)
GM .... General Manager
GMSU ..... General Maritime Stevedores' Union (Philippines)
GMS ...... General Material Services
GMPR..... General Maximum Price Regulation (World War II)
GMC ...... General Medical Council (British)
GeMSAEC .... General Medical Sciences and Atomic Energy Commission
GMS ..... General Medical Services
GM .... General Medicine
GM & S ..... General Medicine and Surgery
GMA ...... General Mental Ability
GM .... General Merchandise
GME ...... General Micro-Electronics
GMC ...... General Military Course
GMS ...... General Military Science
GMST...... General Military Subjects Test
D (Day) ..... General military term designating the day on which a specific action is planned to commence; by extension, the beginning of any activity of importance
GMT ...... General Military Training
GMTRB ..... General Military Training Review Board
GMS ...... General Milk Sales
GIS .... General Mills, Inc. (NYSE symbol)
GMRMR .... General Mobilization Reserve Materiel Requirement
GMRS...... General Mobilization Reserve Stock
GMRSO ..... General Mobilization Reserve Stockage Objective

GMR .... General Mobilization Reserves
GMC .... General Monte Carlo Code (Data processing)
GM .... General Mortgage (Bonds)
GMB .... General Mortgage Bond
GMAC ...... General Motors Acceptance Corporation
GMAD ...... General Motors, Allison Division
GM .... General Motors Corporation (NYSE symbol)
GMC .... General Motors Corporation
GMI .... General Motors Institute (Company-financed engineering school)
GNRP ...... General Neighborhood Renewal Plan
GENOT ..... General Notice
GNEC ...... General Nuclear Engineering Corporation
GNC .... General Nursing Council
GOR .... General Ocean Research (Navy ship symbol)
GO .... General Office(r)
GOC .... General Officer Commanding
GOB .... General Officers Branch (Air Force)
GOA .... General Operating Agency
GOR .... General Operating Room
GOP .... General Operational Plot
GOR .... General Operational Requirement
GO .... General Order(s)
GOU .... General Outdoor Advertising Company, Inc. (NYSE symbol)
GOP .... General Outpost (Army)
GOPL ...... General Outpost Line
GPI .... General Paralysis of the Insane is literal meaning, but is also medical slang for eccentricity
GP .... General Paresis (or Paralysis) (Medicine)
GPA .... General Passenger Agent
GPC-ERR.... General Passenger Committee-Eastern Railroads
GP .... General Pause (Music)
GPN .... General Performance Number
GPG .... General Planning Group
GPER ...... General Plant Equipment Requirements
GPP .... General Plant Projects
GPY .... General Plywood Corporation (NYSE symbol)
GPT .... General Portland Cement Company (NYSE symbol)
GPO .... General Post Office (British)
GP .... General Practice (or Practitioner) (of medicine)
GPE .... General Precision Equipment Corporation (NYSE symbol)
GPI .... General Precision, Incorporated
GENPRL .... General Precision Laboratory
GPL .... General Precision Laboratory
GPS .... General Problem Solver (Data processing)
GPSS ...... General Process Simulation Studies
GP .... General Provision
GP .... General Public (Merchandising slang)
GPA .... General Public Assistance (A form of public charity)
GPV .... General Public Service Corporation (NYSE symbol)
GUY .... General Public Utilities Corporation (NYSE symbol)
GPA .... General Purchasing Agency (Allied German Occupation Forces)
GP .... General Purpose (Military)
GPAS ...... General-Purpose Airborne Simulator
GPA .... General-Purpose Amplifier
GPAT ...... General Purpose Automatic Test
GPATS ..... General Purpose Automatic Test System (Air Force)
GPB .... General Purpose Buffer
GPC .... General-Purpose Computer
GPDC ...... General-Purpose Digital Computer
GPE .... General Purpose Equipment
GPF .... General-Purpose Forces
GPI .... General-Purpose Interface
JEEP ...... General Purpose 1/4-ton Military Utility Vehicle
GPM .... General Purpose Missile
GPO .... General Purpose Oscilloscope
GPRR ...... General Purpose Radio Receiver
GPRT ...... General Purpose Radio Transmitter
GPR .... General Purpose Radiometer
GPR .... General Purpose Receiver
GPR .... General Purpose Relay
GPSDIC .... General Purpose Scientific Document Image Code (System) (National Bureau of Standards)
GPSDW ..... General Purpose Scientific Document Writer (National Bureau of Standards)
GPS .... General Purpose Simulation
GPSSM ..... General Purpose Surface-to-Surface Missile (Army)
GPSS ...... General Purpose Systems Simulator (Data processing)
GPVEH ..... General Purpose Vehicle
GPVB ...... General Purpose Video Buffer
GQ .... General Quarters (General Alert) (Navy)
GR .... General Radio

GRS .... General Radio Service (Canada)
GRW .... General Railway Warrants (US Military Government, Germany)
GR .... General Reconnaissance (Marine Corps)
GRX .... General Refractories Company (NYSE symbol)
GR .... General Research
GR .... General Reserve
GRIPHOS .... General Retrieval and Information Processor for Humanities Oriented Studies
GRO .... General Routine Order(s)
GSDO ...... General (Aviation) Safety District Office
GSI .... General Safety Inspector (Aviation)
GS .... General Schedule (Federal employee job classification GS-1 to GS-18)
GS .... General Secretary
GS .... General Semantics
GENSV ..... General Service (Military)
GSI .... General Service Infantry
GS .... General Service is literal translation, but used in sense of "excessively keen," or "overly acute" (British Army)
GSR .... General Service Recruit
GSS .... General Service School (Army)
GSU .... General Service Unit (Marine Corps)
GSA .... General Services Administration
GS .... General Sessions
GENESCO .... General Shoe Corporation (Acronym now official name of firm)
GSH .... General Shoe Corporation (NYSE symbol)
GSX .... General Signal Corporation (NYSE symbol)
GSCW ...... General Society of Colonial Wars
GSMD ...... General Society of Mayflower Descendants
SR .... General Society, Sons of the Revolution
GSW 1812 ... General Society of the War of 1812
GS .... General Staff (Military)
GSCARNGARP .. General Staff Committees on Army National Guard and Army Reserve Policy
GSC .... General Staff Corps (Military)
GSO .... General Staff Officer
GSOR ...... General Staff Operational Requirements (Army)
GST .... General Staff with Troops
GSWT ...... General Staff with Troops
GSUSA ..... General Staff, United States Army
GSNC ...... General Steam Navigation Company (British)
GSCC ...... General Steel Casting Corporation
GSI .... General Steel Industries, Inc. (NYSE symbol)
GSK .... General Storekeeper (Navy)
AKS .... General Stores Issue Ship (Navy symbol)
GSM .... General Stores Material (Navy)
GSSO ...... General Stores Supply Office
GSP .... General Strike for Peace
GS .... General Superintendent
GSD .... General Supply Depot
GSS .... General Supply Schedule
GENSUP .... General Support (Army)
GS .... General Support (Army)
G/S .... General Support (Military)
GSG .... General Support Group (Army)
GSR .... General Support Reinforcing (Army)
GENSURG ... General Surgery
GSETD ..... General Systems Engineering and Technical Direction
GT .... General Technical Aptitude Area
GLF .... General Telephone Company of Florida (NYSE symbol)
GEN .... General Telephone & Electronics Corporation (NYSE symbol) (Wall Street slang name: "Jennie")
GENTEL .... General Telephone & Electronics Corporation
GT & E .... General Telephone & Electronics Corporation
GLI .... General Time Corporation (NYSE symbol)
GY .... General Tire & Rubber Company (NYSE symbol)
GTM .... General Traffic Manager
GTAV ...... General Transport Administrative Vehicle
GTS .... General Trouble Shooting
GULP ...... General Utility Library Program
GVA .... General Visceral Afferent (Neurology)
GVE .... General Visceral Efferent (Neurology)
GW .... General Warning
GW .... General Will (Collectivist theory of government)
GWU .... General Workers Union (Malta)
GYM .... General Yardmaster (Railroading)
GAMD ...... Generale Aeronautique Marcel Dassault (Switzerland)
GECOMIN ... Generale Congolaise des Minerais (Congo)
GPS .... Generality and Problem Solving
GAT .... Generalized Algebraic Translator (Data processing)
GCP .... Generalized Computer Program
GENDARME ... Generalized Data Reduction, Manipulation, Evaluation

GEREP . . . . . . Generalized Equipment Reliability Evaluation Procedure
GGE . . . . Generalized Glandular Enlargement (Medicine)
GHC . . . . Generalized Hyperbolic Class
GIRLS . . . . . . Generalized Information Retrieval and Listing System
GPF . . . . Generalized Production Function (Industrial economics)
GP . . . . Generalized Programming
GPX . . . . Generalized Programming Extended
GRASP . . . . . . Generalized Retrieval and Storage Program
GSQ . . . . Generalized Sinusoidal Quantity
GTF . . . . Generalized Transformation Function
GAAP . . . . . . Generally Accepted Accounting Principles
GRAS . . . . . . Generally Recognized As Safe (FDA term)
GTT . . . . Generated Target Tracking
GPU . . . . Generating Power Unit
GMS . . . . Generation Management Station
GCB . . . . Generator Control Breaker
GF . . . . Generator Field
GOV . . . . Generator Output Voltage
GC . . . . Generic Code
GF . . . . Generic Failure
GCO . . . . Genesco, Inc. (NYSE symbol)
GNW . . . . Genesee & Wyoming R. R. (AAR code)
GSA . . . . Genetics Society of America
GRR . . . . Geneva Radio Regulations
GSEE . . . . Geniki Synomospondia Ergaton Hellados (General Confederation of
 Greek Labor)
GV . . . . Genital Vein
G . . . . Genitive (case) (Grammar)
GU . . . . Genitourinary
GV . . . . Gentian Violet (Bacteriology)
GAFS . . . . Gentile Air Force Station
GC . . . . Gentleman Cadet (British)
GPC . . . . Geocentric Pendulum Control
GS . . . . Geochemical Society
GIMRADA . . . . Geodesy, Intelligence & Mapping Research & Development Agency
 (Army)
GDR . . . . Geodetic Data Reduction
GDM . . . . Geodetic Distance Measurement
GEOS . . . . . . Geodetic Earth-Orbiting Satellite (NASA)
GDAP . . . . . . GEOS (Geodetic Earth-Orbiting Satellite) Data Adjustment Program
GOS . . . . Geodetic Optical System
GSP . . . . Geodetic Satellite Program
GASSER . . . . . Geographic Aerospace Search RADAR
GEOIS . . . . . . Geographic Information System (Data processing)
GEOREF . . . . . Geographic Reference System (Civil Defense)
GEOLOC . . . . . Geographical Location (Military)
GP . . . . Geographical Position
GSGS . . . . Geographical Section General Staff (British)
GSU . . . . Geographically Separated Units (Military)
GA . . . . Geological Abstracts
GSA . . . . Geological Society of America
GS . . . . Geological Survey (Department of the Interior)
GEEK . . . . . . Geomagnetic Electrokinetograph (Equipment for exploring ocean depths)
GEK . . . . Geomagnetic Electrokinetograph (Equipment for exploring ocean depths)
GMT . . . . Geo-Marine Technology
GDOP . . . . . . Geometric Dilution of Precision
GM . . . . Geometric Mean
GMD . . . . Geometric Mean Distance
GMR . . . . Geometric Mean Radii
GPT . . . . Geometric and Positional Tolerance (Drafting symbol)
GP . . . . Geometric Progression
GA . . . . Geometrical Acoustics
GMD . . . . Geometrodynamics
GPB . . . . Geon Process Butadiene
GAI . . . . Geophysical Associates International
GATU . . . . . . Geophysical Automatic Tracker Unit
GDC . . . . Geophysical Data Center
Gp E . . . . Geophysical Engineer (An academic degree)
GSI . . . . Geophysical Service, Incorporated
GEOSS . . . . . . Geophysical Survey System (Naval Oceanographic Office)
GCA . . . . Geophysics Corporation of America
GRB . . . . Geophysics Research Board
GRD . . . . Geophysics Research Directorate (US)
GSDB . . . . Geophysics & Space Data Bulletin (Air Force)
GPM . . . . Geopotential Meter
GAFB . . . . George Air Force Base
GBS . . . . George Bernard Shaw
GCMSC . . . . . George C. Marshall Space Flight Center (Also known as MSFC)
GFC . . . . George Fox College (Oregon)
GM . . . . George Medal (British)
GPCT . . . . George Peabody College for Teachers (Tennessee)

GERO . . . . . . George Rogers Clark National Historical Park
GEWA . . . . . . George Washington Birthplace National Monument
GWCA . . . . . . George Washington Carver National Monument
GEWP . . . . . . George Washington Memorial Parkway (National Park Service designation)
GWU . . . . George Washington University
GWC . . . . George Williams College (Illinois)
GAT . . . . Georgetown Automatic Translation (Data processing)
GCRI . . . . Georgetown Clinical Research Institute (FAA)
GCO . . . . Georgetown College Observatory
GRR . . . . Georgetown R. R. (AAR code)
GA . . . . Georgia
GASC . . . . . . Georgia, Ashburn, Sylvester & Camilla R. R. (AAR code)
GELAC . . . . . Georgia Division, Lockheed Aircraft Corporation
GF . . . . Georgia & Florida R. R. (AAR code)
G & F . . . . . . Georgia & Florida Railroad
GIT . . . . Georgia Institute of Technology
GTRR . . . . . . Georgia Institute of Technology Research Reactor
GMC . . . . Georgia Military College
GANO . . . . . . Georgia Northern Railway Company (AAR code)
GNL . . . . Georgia Nuclear Laboratory (AEC)
GP . . . . Georgia-Pacific Corporation (NYSE symbol)
GXP . . . . Georgia-Pacific Plywood Company (NYSE symbol)
GOW . . . . Georgia Power Company (NYSE symbol)
GA . . . . Georgia R. R. (AAR code)
GSF . . . . Georgia Southern & Florida R. R. (AAR code)
GS & F . . . . . Georgia Southern and Florida Railway Company
GSCW . . . . . . Georgia State College for Women
GTC . . . . Georgia Teachers College
GWSF . . . . . . Georgia Warm Springs Foundation
GCC . . . . Georgian Court College (New Jersey)
GR . . . . Georgius Rex (King George of England)
GR et I . . . . . Georgius Rex et Imperator (George, King and Emperor) (British)
GE . . . . Geoscience Electronics
GIS . . . . Geoscience Information Society
GOES . . . . . . Geostationary Orbit Environmental Satellite
GSS . . . . Geo-Stationary Satellite
GOAT . . . . . . Gerber Oscillogram Amplitude Translator
GEB . . . . Gerber Products Company (NYSE symbol)
GUV . . . . Gerecht und Volkommen (Correct and Complete) (German)
GPV . . . . Gereformeerd Politiek Verbond
GOOD EGGS . . Geriatric Order of Old Dolls Who Encourage the Generation Gap
 Singlemindedly (Tongue-in-cheek teachers' organization)
GER . . . . Gerity-Michigan Corporation (NYSE symbol)
G . . . . German
GAF . . . . German Air Force (German Luftwaffe)
GAFSC . . . . . German Air Force Southern Command
GAFA . . . . . . German-American Football Association
DANK . . . . . . German-American National Congress
GDR . . . . German Democratic Republic (East Germany)
GEPC . . . . . . German External Property Control Commission (Minden) (Allied German
 Occupation Forces)
GFR . . . . German Federal Republic (West Germany)
GMDS . . . . . . German Military Documents Section (of AGO, Army) (World War II)
GMSO . . . . . . German Mine Supplies Organization (Allied German Occupation Forces)
GMSA . . . . . . German Minesweeping Administration (Allied German Occupation Forces)
GME . . . . German Minimum Economy (Allied German Occupation Forces)
GERMDF . . . . German Ministry of Defense
GOH . . . . German Order of Harugari
GRS . . . . German Research Satellite (NASA)
GRCD . . . . . . German Rhine Coordinating Directorate (Allied German Occupation Forces)
GSDCA . . . . . German Shepherd Dog Club of America
GSPCA . . . . . German Shorthaired Pointer Club of America
GS . . . . German Silver
GTSA . . . . . . German Telecommunications Statistics Agency
GT . . . . German Translation
GSA . . . . Germanistic Society of America
Ge . . . . Germanium (Chemical element)
GR . . . . Germanium Rectifier
GSR . . . . Germanium Stack Rectifier
GPS . . . . Germany Philatelic Society
GS . . . . Gerontological Society
GRC . . . . Gerontology Research Center (HEW)
GB/BHE . . . . . Gesamtdeutscher Block/Bund der Heimatvertrievenen und Entrechteten
 (All-German Bloc/Union of Expellees)
GAMM . . . . . . Gesellschaft fuer Angewante Mathematik und Mechanik (German
 Association for Applied Mathematics and Mechanics)
GmbH . . . . . . Gesellschaft mit Beschraenkter Hoftung (Company with limited liability)
GDSF . . . . . . Gesellschaft fuer Deutsch-Sowjetische Freundschaft
GEFFA . . . . . . Gesellschaft fuer Forstliche Arbeitswissenschaft
GKSS . . . . Gesellschaft fuer Kernenergieverwertung in Schiffbau und Schiffahrt
 (Atomic power) (Germany)

REVERSE ACRONYMS AND INITIALISMS DICTIONARY

GEMA . . . . . . Gesellschaft fuer Musikalische Auffuhrungs
GNV . . . . Gesellschaft fuer Nukleare Verfshrenstechnik (Commercial firm)
GST . . . . Gesellschaft fuer Sport und Technik
GFW . . . . Gesellschaft fuer Weltraumforschung (Society for Space Research) (Germany)
GOO . . . . Get Oil Out (An organization in Santa Barbara, California)
GQA . . . . Get Quick Answer
GET . . . . Getty Oil Company (NYSE symbol)
GBPA . . . . . . Gettysburg Battlefield Preservation Association
GETT . . . . . . Gettysburg National Military Park
GPF . . . . Geuder, Paeschke & Frey Company
GASP . . . . . . Gevic Arithmetic Simulation Program
GLOP . . . . . . Gevic Logic Operation Program
GERE . . . . . . Gewerkschaft Erdoel-Raffinerie Emsland (West Germany)
GTUC . . . . . . Ghana Trades Union Congress
GYP . . . . Ghana Young Pioneers
GAP . . . . Ghetto Arts Program
G . . . . Ghost
GAS . . . . Giant Air Shower
GAS . . . . Giant Attribute Survey
GCRA . . . . . Giant Chinchilla Rabbit Association
GDR . . . . Giant Dipole Resonance
GIQ . . . . Giant Imperial Quart (of beer)
GPO . . . . Giant Portland Cement Company (NYSE symbol)
GP . . . . Giant Pulse
GPL . . . . Giant Pulse LASER
GPLS . . . . . . Giant Pulse LASER System
GYK . . . . Giant Yellow Knife Gold Mines (NYSE symbol)
GAE . . . . Gibbs Absorption Equation
GAI . . . . Gibbs Absorption Isotherm
GDE . . . . Gibbs-Duhem Equation
GFE . . . . Gibbs Free Energy
G . . . . Gibbs Function
GHE . . . . Gibbs-Helmholtz Equation
GIBAIR . . . . . Gibraltar Airways, Ltd.
GFC . . . . Gibraltar Financial Corporation of California (NYSE symbol)
GIB . . . . Gibson Greeting Cards, Inc. (NYSE symbol)
GI . . . . Gideons International
GDIS . . . . . . Gier-Dunkle Integrating Sphere
GDAAA . . . . . Gift and Decorative Accessories Association of America
GWTA . . . . . . Gift Wrappings and Tyings Association
G . . . . Giga
GeV . . . . Giga Electron Volt
GC . . . . Gigacycle (Measurement)
GHz . . . . Gigahertz
GWh . . . . Gigawatt-Hour
GICL . . . . . . Gila Cliff Dwellings National Monument
G . . . . Gilbert (A unit of magnetomotive force)
GKC . . . . Gilbert Keith Chesterton (British journalist and author)
GSS . . . . Gilbert and Sullivan Society
GMO . . . . . . Gill-Morrell Oscillator
GS . . . . Gillette Company (NYSE symbol)
G . . . . Gilt (Bibliography)
GBE . . . . Gilt Bevelled Edges
GE . . . . Gilt Edges (Bookbinding)
GME . . . . Gilt Marbled Edges (Paper)
GT . . . . Gilt Top (Bibliography)
GTE . . . . Gilt Top Edge (Bibliography)
GAC . . . . Gimbal Angle Change
GAIF . . . . . . Gimbal Angle Information Failure
GAL . . . . Gimbal Angle Loss
GAR . . . . Gimbal Angle Rate
GAR . . . . Gimbal Angle Readout
GE . . . . Gimbal Electronics
GP . . . . Gimbal Package
GPL . . . . Gimbal Pickoff Loop
GIN . . . . Gimbaled Integral Nozzle
GAINS . . . . . . Gimballess Analytic Inertial Navigation System
GIMU . . . . . . Gimballess Inertial Measuring Unit
GIRS . . . . . . Gimballess Inertial Reference System
GI . . . . Gimbel Brothers, Inc. (NYSE symbol)
GPI . . . . Gingival-Periodontal Index (Dentistry)
GNN . . . . Ginn & Company (NYSE symbol)
G . . . . Girder (Technical drawings)
GF . . . . Girl Friend (Slang)
GSA . . . . Girl Scouts of America
GSP . . . . Girl Scouts of the Philippines
GS . . . . Girl Scouts of the USA
GWS-A & L . . Girl Watchers Society - Ankle & Leg Division
GAMS . . . . . . Girls Against More Skirt (Group opposing below-the-knee fashions introduced in 1970)

GCA . . . . . . Girls Clubs of America
GFS . . . . Girls' Friendly Society of the USA
GNTC . . . . . . Girls' Naval Training Corps (British)
GSL . . . . Girls' Service League
GBA . . . . Give Better Address (Communications)
GBR . . . . Give Better Reference
GLBA . . . . . . Glacier Bay National Monument
GLAC . . . . . . Glacier National Park
GDL . . . . Gladstone-Dale Law
GA . . . . Gland Anlage
GBV . . . . Glass (or Globe) Ball Valve
GBJ . . . . Glass Bell Jar
GBM . . . . Glass Bonded Mica
GBBA . . . . . . Glass Bottle Blowers Association of the United States and Canada
GB . . . . Glass Bowl
GCT . . . . Glass Cloth Tape
GCMI . . . . . . Glass Container Manufacturers Institute
GCA . . . . . . Glass Crafts of America
GDL . . . . Glass Delay Line
GFT . . . . Glass Fabric Tape
GF . . . . Glass Fiber
GFIT . . . . . . Glass Fiber Insulation Tubing
GFM . . . . Glass Fiber Material
GFR . . . . Glass-Fiber Reinforced
GFRP . . . . . . Glass-Fiber-Reinforced Plastic
GIW . . . . Glass Insulated Wire
GIM . . . . Glass Insulation Material
GLR . . . . Glass LASER Rod
GMF . . . . Glass Manufacturers Federation
GOB . . . . Glass Oceanographic Buoy
GPN . . . . Glass Plate Negative
GPT . . . . Glass Precision Tubing
GPT . . . . Glass Probe Thermistor
GRP . . . . Glass-Reinforced Plastic
GRPJ . . . . . . Glass Reinforced Plastic Joint
GRSP . . . . . . Glass Reinforced Structural Plastic
GTA . . . . Glass Tempering Association
GGMA . . . . . . Glassine and Greaseproof Manufacturers Association
G & SWR . . . . Glasgow and South-Western Railway
GRU . . . . Glavnoe Razvedivatel noe Upravlenie (Chief Administration for Intelligence) (Division of the General Staff of the Soviet Army); (USSR)
GUKR . . . . . . Glavnoe Upravlenie Kontrrazvedkoi (Chief Administration for Counter-intelligence) (of the Ministry of War) (USSR) (World War II)
GICG . . . . . . Glaze Icing (Aviation)
GFU . . . . Glazed Facing Units (Technical drawings)
GSFU . . . . . . Glazed Structural Facing Units (Technical drawings)
GSU . . . . Glazed Structural Unit (Technical drawings)
GSUB . . . . . . Glazed Structural Unit Base (Technical drawings)
GWT . . . . Glazed Wall Tile (Technical drawings)
GWTB . . . . . . Glazed Wall Tile Base (Technical drawings)
GLWB . . . . . . Glazed Wallboard (Technical drawings)
GHV . . . . Gleaner Harvester Corporation (NYSE symbol)
GLIS . . . . . . Gleaner Life Insurance Society
GA . . . . Glen Alden Corporation (NYSE symbol)
GLCA . . . . . . Glen Canyon National Recreation Area
GSC . . . . Glenville State College (West Virginia)
GLN . . . . Glidden Company (NYSE symbol)
GA . . . . Glide Angle (Aviation)
GB . . . . Glide Bomb (Air Force)
GLOMB . . . . . Glide Bomb (Air Force)
GP . . . . Glide Path
GPIP . . . . . . Glide Path Intercept Point
GS . . . . Glide Slope (Aviation)
GSA . . . . Glide Slope Antenna
GSR . . . . Glide Slope Receiver
G . . . . Glider
VLB . . . . Glider (Special) (Navy symbol)
L . . . . Glider Aircraft (When first letter in Navy aircraft designation)
GLIBAD . . . . . Glider Badge
GFCES . . . . . . Glider Flight Control Electronics Subsystem
GAMP . . . . . . Global Atmospheric Measurements Program (National Science Foundation)
GARP . . . . . . Global Atmospheric Research Program (National Academy of Sciences)
GCW . . . . Global Chart of the World (Air Force)
GCSS . . . . . . Global Communications Satellite System
GLOBECOM . . Global Communications System (Air Force)
GLOCOM . . . . Global Communications System
GDA . . . . Global Data Area
GHOST . . . . . . Global Horizontal Sounding Technique (Meteorology)
GIRLS . . . . . . Global Interrogation Recording and Location System
GLU . . . . Global Land Use (NASA)

GLANCE .... Global Lightweight Airborne Navigation Computer Equipment
GLC .... Global Loran Navigation Charts (Air Force)
GLOMEX .... Global Meteorological Experiment (Also known as GARP)
GNC ...... Global Navigation and Planning Chart (Air Force)
GOFAR ..... Global Ocean Floor Analysis and Research (Navy)
GRBM....... Global Range Ballistic Missile (Air Force)
GRM .... Global Range Missile
GSS........ Global Satellite System
GSS........ Global Surveillance System (Air Force)
GLOTRAC .... Global Tracking (RADAR)
GLAD .... GLOTRAC (Global Tracking) Adjustment
GWC .... Global Weather Central
GSV .... Globe Stop Valve (Technical drawings)
GLB........ Globe-Union, Inc. (NYSE symbol)
GW........ Globe-Wernicke Industries, Inc. (NYSE symbol)
GI .... Globin Insulin
GF........ Globular-Fibrous (Biochemistry)
GBM ...... Glomerular Basement Membrane
GF .... Glomerular Filtrate (Physiology)
GFR....... Glomerular Filtration Rate (Physiology)
GTN ...... Glomerulo-Tubulo Nephritis (Medicine)
G .... Gloom
GP........ Gloria Patri (Glory to the Father)
GFA ...... Gloucester Fisheries Association
GMMA..... Gloucester Master Mariners Association
GDT....... Glow Discharge Tube
GC .... Glucocorticoid (Endocrinology)
GITT ...... Glucose Insulin Tolerance Test (Medicine)
G : N ..... Glucose : Nitrogen (Ratio)
GP .... Glucose Phosphate
GTT ...... Glucose Tolerance Test (Medicine)
GLH....... Glue Line Heating
GWJ ...... Glue Weld Joint
GMTC ..... Glutamate Manufacturers Technical Committee
GAD ...... Glutamic Acid
GOT ...... Glutamic Oxalo-acetic Transaminase
GPT....... Glutamic Pyruvic Transaminase
GBM ...... Glycerine Ball Memory
GPA ...... Glycerine Producers Association
GTA ...... Glycerol Triacetate (Chemical)
GP........ Glycerophosphate
GMA ...... Glycol Methacrylate
GA .... Go Ahead (or resume sending) (Communications)
G .... Goal (A position in lacrosse, soccer, hockey, etc.)
GOMALCO ... Gobel O'Malley Company (Entertainer George Gobel's firm; O'Malley is business manager)
GD .... God Damn
GDI .... God Damned Independent (College slang for student not affiliated with a fraternity or sorority)
GOK ...... God Only Knows (Facetious diagnosis for a puzzling medical case)
GEP....... Goddard Experiment Package (NASA)
GISS ...... Goddard Institute for Space Studies
GLO ...... Goddard Launch Operations (NASA)
GRARR ..... Goddard Range and Range Rate (Tracking system) (NASA)
GRRR ...... Goddard Range and Range Rate
GREMEX .... Goddard Research Engineering Management Exercise (NASA)
GSFC ...... Goddard Space Flight Center (NASA)
GOM ...... God's Medicine; also, God's Own Medicine (Morphine) (Slang)
GOAT ..... Goes Over All Terrain (Vehicle)
GCC ...... Gogebic Community College (Michigan)
GPC ...... Golay Pneumatic Cell
G .... Gold
GB........ Gold Bond (Bond payable in gold coin)
GCD ...... Gold Coupling Dendrite
GF........ Gold Field
GFMA ..... Gold-Filled Manufacturers Association
GLSM...... Gold Life Saving Medal
GM ...... Gold Medal
GMAA ..... Gold Mining Association of America
GS........ Gold Standards
GSM ...... Gold Star Mothers
GSWA ..... Gold Star Wives of America
GSB....... Gold Surface Barrier
GOL ...... Goldblatt Brothers, Inc. (NYSE symbol)
GGC ...... Golden Gate College (California)
GHT....... Golden Hour Tango
GN ...... Golden Number (Number used to fix the date of Easter)
GRCA...... Golden Retriever Club of America
GRF ...... Golden Rule Foundation
GOSP ..... Golden Spike National Historic Site
GF........ Goldflow

GSDS ...... Goldstone Duplicate Standard
AuH2O ..... Goldwater, Barry (Chemical symbols for gold and water; used to refer to the 1964 Republican presidential candidate)
GBMA ...... Golf Ball Manufacturers Association
GC .... Golf Club
GCSAA ..... Golf Course Superintendents Association of America
GWAA ..... Golf Writers Association of America
GTH....... Gonadotrophic Hormone (Endocrinology)
GWTW ..... "Gone with the Wind," a novel by Margaret Mitchell; also, a motion picture
GC .... Gonorrhea Case (Medical slang)
GCFT ..... Gonorrhea Complement Fixation Test
G .... Good (condition) (Antiquarian book trade)
GB....... Good-bye (Amateur radio)
GCM ...... Good Conduct Medal
GCMC ..... Good Conduct Medal Clasp
GCC ...... Good Counsel College (New York)
GD .... Good Delivery (Business and trade)
GE........ Good Evening (Amateur radio)
GFA....... Good Fair Average (Insurance)
GMP...... Good Manufacturing Practices
GMQ...... Good Marketable Quality
GMB ...... Good Merchantable Brand
GM ...... Good Morning (Amateur radio)
GN ...... Good Night (Amateur radio)
GOF ...... Good Old Friday (Slang)
GOMA ..... Good Outdoor Manners Association
GSP....... Good-Service Pension (British Navy)
GT........ Good Templar
GTM ...... Good This Month
GTW ...... Good This Week
GTC ...... Good Till Canceled (as in a brokerage order)
GTC ...... Good Till Countermanded
GWIGWO.... Good Will In, Good Will Out (Data processing)
GMF ...... Goodman Manufacturers (NYSE symbol)
BFG ...... Goodrich (B. F.) Company
GR........ Goodrich (B. F.) Company (NYSE symbol)
GBO ...... Goods in Bad Order
GIA .... Goodwill Industries of America
GAC ...... Goodyear Aircraft Corporation
GER ...... Goodyear Engineering Report
GT........ Goodyear Tire & Rubber Company (NYSE symbol)
GADS..... Goose Air Defense Sector
GMC ...... Gordon Military College (Georgia)
GSCA ..... Gordon Setter Club of America
GSTC ..... Gorham State Teachers College (Maine)
GRI .... Gospel Recordings, Incorporated
GPU....... Gosudarstvennoe Politicheskoe Upravlenie (Government Political Administration) (Soviet secret service organization, also known as OGPU)
GOSSTRAKH . Gosudarstvennoe Strakhovanie (State insurance) (USSR)
GKO ...... Gosudarstvennyi Komitet Oborony (State Defense Committee) (USSR) (World War II)
GEI .... Gosudorstvenuse Energeticheskoe Izdatel'stvo
GHM ...... Gotham Hosiery Company, Inc. (NYSE symbol)
GL .... Gothic Letter
GNB ...... Gould National Batteries, Inc. (NYSE symbol)
GSA ...... Gourd Society of America
G .... Gourde (Monetary unit in Haiti)
GRAE ...... Gouvernement de la Republique de l'Angola en Exile (Government of the Republic of Angola in Exile)
G .... Government
GAY ...... Government Accumulation Yard
GAD ...... Government Actuary's Department
GAF ...... Government Affairs Foundation
GAP....... Government Aircraft Plant
GBL....... Government Bill of Lading
G/B ...... Government Boat
GCSU ..... Government Clerical Services' Union (Ceylon)
GCC ...... Government Contract Committee (Government agency)
GCMA ... Government Contract Management Association of America
GC .... Government Contribution
GEC....... Government Employees Council
GEICO ..... Government Employees Insurance Company
GETA ..... Government Employees Training Act
GEBA ..... Government Excess Baggage Authorization
GFB ...... Government Facilities Brochure
GFI .... Government Free Issue
GFP ...... Government Full Period
GFAE ..... Government-Furnished Aeronautical Equipment
GFAEL ..... Government-Furnished Aeronautical Equipment List
GFAE ...... Government-Furnished Aerospace Equipment

GFAE . . . . Government-Furnished Aircraft Equipment
GFCE . . . . Government-Furnished Capital Equipment
GFE . . . . Government Furnished Equipment
GFERR . . . . . . Government-Furnished Equipment Requirements Request
GFM . . . . Government-Furnished Material
GFP . . . . Government-Furnished Parts
GFP . . . . Government-Furnished Property
GG . . . . Government Girl
GGMA . . . . . . Government Gold Mining Areas
GI . . . . Government of India
GOI . . . . Government of Indonesia
GICORP . . . . . Government Industry Cooperative Oyster Research Program
GAIT . . . . Government and Industry Team
GI . . . . Government Issue (Army)
GLM . . . . Government-Loaned Material
GOMAC . . . . . Government Microcircuit Applications Conference
GNMA . . . . . . Government National Mortgage Association
GO . . . . Government Operations Committee (US Senate)
GOA . . . . Government-Owned Aircraft
GOCO . . . . . . Government-Owned, Contractor-Operated
GOD . . . . Government-Owned Depot
GOF . . . . Government-Owned Facility
GOGO . . . . . Government-Owned, Government-Operated
GOI . . . . Government-Owned Installation
GOM . . . . . . Government-Owned Material
GOP . . . . Government-Owned Property
GPB . . . . Government Patents Board (Functions transferred to Secretary of Commerce, 1961)
GPO . . . . Government Printing Office
GP . . . . Government Property
GPLD . . . . . . Government Property Lost or Destroyed (or Damaged)
GPRA . . . . . . Gouvernement Provisionnel de la Republique Algerienne (Provisional Government of the Algerian Republic)
GPRA . . . . . . Government Public Relations Association
GARIOA . . . . Government and Relief in Occupied Areas (Post-World War II)
GRC . . . . Government of the Republic of China
GRB . . . . Government Reservation Bureau
GR-I . . . . Government Rubber-Isobutylene
GRS . . . . Government Rubber Styrene (A plastic substitute for rubber) (World War II)
GRI . . . . Government of the Ryukyu Islands
GS . . . . Government Service
GSISEA . . . . . Government Service Insurance System Employees' Association (Philippines)
GSI . . . . Government Source Inspection
GTF . . . . Government Test Facility
GTR . . . . Government Transportation Request
GUB . . . . Government Union of Burma
GVN . . . . Government of Vietnam
GWP . . . . Government White Paper
GWI . . . . Government-Wide Index (Later, USGRDR)
GWTUF . . . . . . Government Workers' Trade Union Federation (Ceylon)
GAI . . . . Governmental Affairs Institute
GDC . . . . Governmental Defence Council (British)
GRA . . . . Governmental Research Association
GG . . . . Governor General
GOVMAR . . . . Governor, Marshall Islands
GC . . . . Governors' Conference
GFG . . . . Governor's Foot Guard
GHG . . . . Governor's Horse Guard
GBI . . . . Grace Bible Institute (Nebraska)
GRA . . . . Grace (W. R.) & Company (NYSE symbol)
GLE . . . . Grade Level Equivalent (Educational testing)
GL . . . . Grade Line
GPA . . . . Grade-Point Average (Education)
GBT . . . . Graded Base Transistor
GP . . . . Graded Program
GEF . . . . Gradient Elution Fractionation
GGE . . . . Gradient Gel Electrophoresis
GAM . . . . Graduate Aerospace Mechanical Engineering
GA . . . . Graduate in Agriculture
AB . . . . Graduate in Arts (An academic degree)
BA . . . . Graduate in Arts
USMCR(NAVO) . . Graduate Aviation Cadets, Volunteer Marine Corps Reserve
GCSW . . . . . . Graduate Certificate of Social Work
GENESYS . . . . Graduate Engineering Education System
GGPA . . . . . . Graduate Grade-Point Average (Higher education)
GL . . . . Graduate in Law
BL . . . . Graduate in Letters
LB . . . . Graduate in Letters
BLA . . . . Graduate in Liberal Arts
GLS . . . . Graduate Library School
Mid G . . . . . . Graduate Midwife

G in N . . . . . Graduate in Nursing
G Ph . . . . . . Graduate in Pharmacy
Ph G . . . . . . Graduate in Pharmacy
GRE . . . . Graduate Record Examination (Higher education)
GRE . . . . Graduate Reliability Engineering
GRCSW . . . . . Graduate Research Center of the Southwest
GRAD . . . . . . Graduate Resume Accumulation and Distribution (Data processing)
BS . . . . Graduate in Science
B Sc . . . . . . Graduate in Science
GRIT . . . . . . Graduated Reduction in Tensions (Cold War term)
GVH . . . . Graft Versus Host (Disease)
GU . . . . Grafton & Upton R. R. (AAR code)
GC . . . . Graham County R. R. (AAR code)
GISC . . . . . . Grail International Student Center
G . . . . Grain
GBR . . . . Grain Boundary Relaxation
GEAPS . . . . . Grain Elevator and Processing Superintendents
GFDNA . . . . . Grain and Feed Dealers National Association
GFA . . . . Grain Futures Administration (Superseded by Commodity Exchange Administration, 1936)
GNS . . . . Grain Neutral Spirits (Alcohol)
GPMMA . . . . . Grain Processing Machinery Manufacturers Association
GPI . . . . Grain Products Irradiator (AEC)
GSPA . . . . . . Grain Sorghum Producers Association
GPG . . . . Grains Per Gallon (Unit of measure for water hardness)
G . . . . Gram (Metric)
GAW . . . . . . Gram Atomic Weight
GCAL . . . . . . Gram Calorie
GMV . . . . . . Gram-Molecular Volume
GMW . . . . . . Gram Molecular Weight
GRN . . . . Gram-Negative (Bacteriology)
GRP . . . . Gram-Positive (Bacteriology)
GS . . . . Grammar School
GRQU . . . . . . Gran Quivira National Monument
GTX . . . . Gran Tourisimo Experimental
GT . . . . Gran Turismo (Grand Touring) (Automotive term)
GB . . . . Granby Mining Company, Ltd. (NYSE symbol)
G . . . . Grand (Slang term for $1,000)
GASP . . . . . . Grand Accelerated Space Platform
GAR . . . . Grand Army of the Republic
GB . . . . Grand Bounce (Suspension or dismissal) (Slang)
GCC . . . . Grand Canyon College (Arizona)
GRCA . . . . . . Grand Canyon National Park
GC . . . . Grand Chancellor
GC . . . . Grand Chaplain
GC . . . . Grand Chapter
GC . . . . Grand Commander
GC . . . . Grand Cross
GD . . . . Grand Deacon (Masonry)
GDC . . . . Grand Director of Ceremonies (Masonry)
GD . . . . Grand Division
GD . . . . Grand Duchess
GD . . . . Grand Duchy
GD . . . . Grand Duke
GFC . . . . Grand Falls Central R. R. (AAR code)
GJC . . . . Grand Junction Canal
GJ(O) . . . . . . Grand Junction Office (AEC)
GJD . . . . Grand Junior Deacon (Masonry)
GJW . . . . Grand Junior Warden (Masonry)
GL . . . . Grand Larceny
GL . . . . Grand Lodge (Masonry)
FOP . . . . Grand Lodge, Ladies Auxiliary, Fraternal Order of Police
OSHT . . . . . . Grand Lodge Order of the Sons of Hermann in Texas
GL . . . . Grand Lot
GM . . . . Grand Master (Masonry)
GMB . . . . Grand Master of the Bath (British)
GMIE . . . . . . Grand Master of the Order of the Indian Empire (British)
GMMG . . . . . . Grand Master of the Order of St. Michael and St. George
GMP . . . . Grand Master of the Order of St. Patrick
GMSI . . . . . . Grand Master of the Order of the Star of India (British)
GN . . . . Grand National (Automobile racing)
GNCCA . . . . . Grand National Curling Club of America
GNH . . . . Grand National Hunt (British)
GOM . . . . Grand Old Man (A venerated man, especially in a specific field)
GOP . . . . Grand Old Party (The Republican Party)
GPM . . . . Grand Past Master (Masonry)
GQG . . . . Grand Quartier-General (French GHQ)
GRFMA . . . . . Grand Rapids Furniture Market Association
GRJC . . . . . . Grand Rapids Junior College (Michigan)
GRV . . . . Grand Rapids Varnish Corporation (NYSE symbol)
GR . . . . Grand Recorder

GRNR ...... Grand River Railway Company (AAR code)
GS .... Grand Secretary
GSD .... Grand Senior Deacon (Masonry)
GS .... Grand Steward (Masonry)
GS of W .... Grand Superintendent of Works (Masonry)
GSB .... Grand Sword-Bearer (Masonry)
GRTE ...... Grand Teton National Park
GT .... Grand Theft
GT .... Grand Tiler (Masonry)
GT .... Grand Treasurer (Masonry)
GTRY ...... Grand Trunk Railway
GTW ...... Grand Trunk Western R. R. (AAR code)
GTI .... Grand Turk Island
GUX .... Grand Union Company (NYSE symbol)
GVC .... Grand View College (Iowa)
GD .... Granddaughter
GV .... Grande Vitesse (Fast train) (France)
GAWS ...... Grandmothers of America in War Service (World War II)
GS .... Grandson
GCAD ...... Granite City Army Depot
GRC .... Granite City Steel Company (NYSE symbol)
GCIA ...... Granite Cutters' International Association of America
GGIA ...... Granite Grit Institute of America
GVL .... Graniteville Company (NYSE symbol) (Wall Street slang name: "Grannie")
GFF .... Granolithic Finish Floor (Technical drawings)
GA .... Grant Aid
GRA ...... Grant Aid (Military)
GTY .... Grant (W. T.) Company (NYSE symbol)
GIT .... Graph Isomorphism Tester
GARD ...... Graphic Analyzer of Resistance Defects
GAAC ...... Graphic Arts Advertisers Council
GAAE ...... Graphic Arts Association Executives
GRACE ..... Graphic Arts Composing Equipment
GAMIS ..... Graphic Arts Marketing Information Service (Printing Industries of America)
GARC ...... Graphic Arts Research Center (Rochester Institute of Technology)
GARF ...... Graphic Arts Research Foundation
GASM ..... Graphic Arts Spray Manufacturers
GATF ...... Graphic Arts Technical Foundation
GATAE ..... Graphic Arts Trade Association Executives
GCS .... Graphic Communications Section
GDR ...... Graphic Depth Recorder
GIS .... Graphic Input System
GLEAM ..... Graphic Layout and Engineering Aid Method
GLR .... Graphic Level Recorder
GOCAP ..... Graphic Output Circuit Analysis Program
GRID ...... Graphic Remote Integrated Display
GRID ...... Graphic Reproduction by Integrated Design
GTA .... Graphic Training Aid
GAPT ...... Graphical Automatically Programmed Tools
GVC .... Graphics Vendor Control
GLEEP ..... Graphite Low Energy Experimental Pile (Nuclear reactor) (British)
GBSR ...... Graphite-Moderated Boiling and Superheating Reactor (AEC)
GORX ..... Graphite Oxidation from Reactor Excursion (Engineering computer code)
GO .... Graphitic Oxide
GRIN ...... Grapline Input (Data processing)
GALOVAL ... Grappling and Lock-On Validation
GRS .... Grass (Maps and charts)
GMP .... Grass Model Polygraph
GRA ...... Grass Roots Association
GR .... Grasse River R. R. Corporation (AAR code)
GRF .... Grassland Research Foundation
GP .... Gratitude Patient (A nonpaying patient) (Medical slang)
G .... Gravel (Maps and charts)
GSBR ...... Gravel-Surface Built-Up Roof (Technical drawings)
GR .... Graves Registration (Military)
GRREG ..... Graves Registration (Military)
GRS .... Graves Registration Service (Military)
GD .... Gravimetric Density
GV .... Gravimetric Volume
GGT .... Gravitational Gradiant Torque
GMS .... Gravitational Mass Sensor
GIF .... Gravito-Inertial Force
G .... Gravity (or the force or acceleration produced by it)
GAUSS ..... Gravity Association for Universal Scientific Study
GCG .... Gravity-Controlled Gyro
GCGS ...... Gravity-Controlled Gyro System
GGS .... Gravity Gradient Satellite
GGS .... Gravity Gradient Sensor
GGSE ...... Gravity Gradient Stabilization Experiment
GGTS ...... Gravity Gradient Test Satellite (NASA)

GIPSE ...... Gravity Independent Photo-Synthetic Gas Exchanger
GMS .... Gravity Measuring System
GOTS ...... Gravity-Oriented Test Satellite (NASA)
GRS .... Gravity Reference Signal (or System)
GRF .... Gravity Research Foundation
GVT .... Gravity Vacuum Transit
GVT .... Gravity Vacuum Tube System (High-speed ground transportation)
GEA ...... Gravure Engravers Association
GRI .... Gravure Research Institute
GTA .... Gravure Technical Association
GY .... Gray (Buoy) (Maps and charts)
GCI .... Gray Cast Iron
GRACO ..... Gray Company, Inc.
GDIFS ..... Gray and Ductile Iron Founders' Society
GIFS ...... Gray Iron Founders Society
GHC .... Grays Harbor College (Washington)
QGRB ...... Grayson Robinson Stores, Inc. (NYSE symbol) (Delisted)
GNA .... Graysonia, Nashville & Ashdown R. R. (AAR code)
GVF .... Grazhdanskii Vozdushnyi Flot (Civil Air Fleet) (USSR)
G .... Great
GAWAM .... Great American Wife and Mother (Slang)
GASS ...... Great Analog Signal Saver
A & P ...... Great Atlantic & Pacific Tea Company
GAP ...... Great Atlantic & Pacific Tea Company, Inc. (NYSE symbol)
GBF .... Great Books Foundation
GB .... Great Britain
GB & I ..... Great Britain and Ireland
GBMA ..... Great Britain Ministry of Aviation
GC .... Great Circle
GCD ...... Great Circle Distance
GCT .... Great Circle Track
GDCA ..... Great Dane Club of America
GER .... Great Eastern Railway (British)
GE .... Great Exuma (Bahama Islands)
GGD ...... Great Granddaughter
GG .... Great Gross
GIP .... Great Indian Peninsular R. R.
GL .... Great Lakes (Vessel load line mark)
GLBC ...... Great Lakes Basin Commission
GLCA ...... Great Lakes Colleges Association
GLC .... Great Lakes Commission
GLHA ...... Great Lakes Harbor Association
GLHS ...... Great Lakes Historical Society
GLMI ...... Great Lakes Maritime Institute
GLMA ..... Great Lakes Mink Association
GLNTC ..... Great Lakes Naval Training Center
GLK .... Great Lakes Oil & Chemical (NYSE symbol)
GLPA ...... Great Lakes Pilotage Administration (Department of Transportation)
GLASLA .... Great Lakes - St. Lawrence Association
GLS .... Great Lakes Screw
GLSA ...... Great Lakes Seaplane Association
GNSR ...... Great North of Scotland Railway
GNI .... Great Northern Iron Ore Properties (NYSE symbol)
GPP .... Great Northern Paper Company (NYSE symbol)
GNR .... Great Northern Railway (British)
GNRY ...... Great Northern Railway
GN .... Great Northern Railway Company (NYSE symbol)
GPCP ...... Great Plains Conservation Program
GPHA ...... Great Plains Historical Association
GPNITL .... Great Plains National Instructional Television Library
GPW .... Great Plains Wheat, Inc.
GP .... Great Primer
GPCA ...... Great Pyrenees Club of America
GRSA ...... Great Sand Dunes National Monument
GRSM ...... Great Smoky Mountains National Park
GSL .... Great Somalia League
GSW .... Great Southwest R. R., Inc. (AAR code)
GWF .... Great Western Financial Corporation (NYSE symbol)
GWR .... Great Western Railway (Prior to nationalization) (AAR code)
GSW ...... Great Western Sugar Company (NYSE symbol)
GASP ...... Greater (name of city) Alliance to Stop Pollution
GBSCA ..... Greater Blouse, and Skirt Contractors Association
GCCA ...... Greater Clothing Contractors Association
GEA .... Greater East Asia (Used by Japanese in such terms as War of Greater East Asia and Greater East Asia Co-Prosperity Sphere) (World War II)
GLC .... Greater London Council
GLQ ...... Greater than Lot Quantities
GNYCFS .... Greater New York Council for Foreign Students
GRASP ..... Greater Rensselaer Alcoholic Service Project
GUPPY ..... Greater Underwater Propulsive Power (Type of submarine)
GWETA ..... Greater Washington Educational Television Association

GCD . . . . Greatest Common Denominator
GCD . . . . Greatest Common Divisor
GCF . . . . Greatest Common Factor
GCM . . . . Greatest Common Measure
GRAP . . . . Greatest Response Amplitude Probability
GRAPD . . . . . . Greatest Response Amplitude Probability Data
GRD . . . . Greatest Response Data
GRP . . . . Greatest Response Probability
GIS . . . . Greatness is Simplicity (Also see SIG)
GR . . . . Greece (NATO)
GAPA . . . . . Greek-American Progressive Association
GAEC . . . . . . Greek Atomic Energy Commission
GCUUSA . . . . Greek Catholic Union of the United States of America
GOYA . . . . . . Greek Orthodox Youth of America
GRR . . . . Greek Research Reactor
G . . . . Green (light or buoy) (Navigation charts)
GN . . . . Green (Maps and charts)
GARB . . . . . . Green, Amber, Red, Blue (Priority of the airways)
GBW . . . . Green Bay & Western R. R. (AAR code)
GB & W . . . . . Green Bay and Western Railroad Company
GCA . . . . Green Coffee Association (of New Orleans or of New York City)
GIL . . . . Green Indicating Lamp
GLS . . . . Green LASER System
GMJC . . . . . . Green Mountain Junior College (Vermont)
GMTOA . . . . . Green Mountain Textile Overseers Association
GRTC . . . . . . Green River Test Complex
GSR . . . . Green Shoe Manufacturing Company (NYSE symbol)
GB . . . . Greenish Blue
GY . . . . Greenish Yellow
GBC . . . . Greenland Base Command
GC . . . . Greenland Cruiser
GIUK . . . . Greenland, Iceland, United Kingdom
GREPAT . . . . . Greenland Patrol (Navy)
GAT . . . . Greenwich Apparent Time
GCN . . . . Greenwich Civil Noon
GCT . . . . Greenwich Civil Time
GCT . . . . Greenwich Conservatory Time
GHA . . . . Greenwich Hour Angle
GJ . . . . Greenwich & Johnsonville Railway (AAR code)
GMAT . . . . . . Greenwich Mean Astronomical Time
GMT . . . . Greenwich Mean Time
Z . . . . Greenwich Mean Time (Aviation)
g . . . . Greenwich Meridian (Lower branch)
GM . . . . Greenwich Meridian
G . . . . Greenwich Meridian (Upper branch)
GST . . . . Greenwich Sidereal Time
G . . . . Greenwich Time
GZT . . . . Greenwich Zone Time
GRN . . . . Greenville & Northern R. R. (AAR code)
GRH . . . . Greer Hydraulics, Inc. (NYSE symbol)
GCA . . . . Greeting Card Association
GIA . . . . Gregorian Institute of America
GL . . . . Grenade Launcher
GSF . . . . Grenade Safety Fuze
GG . . . . Grenadier Guards (British military)
GAA . . . . Grenfell Association of America
GNSH . . . . . . Grey Nuns of the Sacred Heart (Roman Catholic religious order)
GCA . . . . Greyhound Club of America
G . . . . Greyhound Corporation (NYSE symbol)
GPX . . . . Greyhound Package Express
G . . . . Grid (Electronics)
GB . . . . Grid Bearing (Navigation)
GCK . . . . Grid Controlled Klystron
GC . . . . Grid Course (Navigation)
GDM . . . . Grid Dip Modulator
GDO . . . . Grid-Dip Oscillator
GDP . . . . Grid Driving Power
GH . . . . Grid Heading (Navigation)
GL . . . . Grid Leak
GM . . . . Grid Modulation
GPT . . . . Grid Pool Tank
GR . . . . Grid Resistor
GR . . . . Grid Return
GSR . . . . Grid Space Relay
GV . . . . Grid Variation (Navigation)
GEPB . . . . . . Grievance and Employment Policy Board (Army)
GAFB . . . . . . Griffis Air Force Base
GCR . . . . Grignards Chemical Reaction
GAC . . . . . . Grilled American Cheese (Sandwich) (Waitress's call to a short order cook)
GRAR . . . . . . Grinding Arbor

GRFX . . . . . . Grinding Fixture
GWD . . . . Grinding Wheel Dresser
GWI . . . . Grinding Wheel Institute
GMA . . . . Grocery Manufacturers of America
GRUB . . . . . . Grocery Update and Billing
GC . . . . Grolier Club
GG . . . . Groove Gauge
GPF . . . . Groove between Parallel Folds
GR . . . . Grooved Roofing (Lumber)
G . . . . Groschen (Monetary unit in Austria)
G . . . . Gross
GCV . . . . Gross Caloric Value
GDO . . . . Gross Domestic Output (Economics)
GDP . . . . Gross Domestic Product (Economics)
GI . . . . Gross Investment
GLA . . . . Gross Leasable Area
GLV . . . . Gross Leukemia Virus
GLD . . . . Gross Logical Design
GNI . . . . Gross National Income (Economics)
GNP . . . . Gross National Product (Economics)
GRT . . . . Gross Register Tons (Navigation)
GTOW . . . . . . Gross Take-Off Weight (of an aircraft)
GTW . . . . Gross Take-Off Weight
G-T . . . . Gross Ton
GT . . . . Gross Tonnage
GRWT . . . . . . Gross Weight
GWT . . . . Gross Weight
GOC . . . . Grosseinkaufsgesellschaft Osterreichischer Consumvereine
G/A . . . . . Ground-to-Air (Communications, weapons)
GTAC . . . . . . Ground-to-Air Cycle
GADL . . . . . . Ground-to-Air Data Link
G/A/G . . . . . Ground-to-Air-to-Ground
GAGDT . . . . . Ground-to-Air-to-Ground Data Terminal (Air Force)
GAPA . . . . . . Ground-to-Air Pilotless Aircraft (Early US test missiles)
GRASS . . . . . Ground-to-Air Scanner Surveillance
GAT . . . . Ground-to-Air Transmitter
GATT . . . . . . Ground-to-Air Transmitter Terminal
GATR . . . . . . Ground-to-Air Transmitting-Receiving (Station)
GAPE . . . . . . Ground Anchor Placement Equipment
GAA . . . . Ground Area Attainable
GA . . . . Ground Attacker Aircraft
GBC . . . . Ground Based Computer
GEOSCAN . . . Ground-Based Electronic Omnidirectional Satellite Communications Antenna
GBF . . . . Ground Based Field
GBII . . . . Ground Based Infrared Instrumentation
GBIIS . . . . . . Ground Based Infrared Instrumentation System
GBR . . . . Ground Based Radiometer
GBS . . . . Ground-Based Scanner
GBT . . . . Ground-Based Telemetry
GCT . . . . Ground Checkout and Test
GCU . . . . Ground Checkout Unit
GCTS . . . . . . Ground Communication Tracking Systems
GCE . . . . Ground Communications Equipment
GCS . . . . Ground Communications System
GCSM . . . . . . Ground Composite Signal Mixer
GC . . . . Ground Control
GCC . . . . Ground Control Center (Aviation)
GCE . . . . Ground Control Equipment
GCI . . . . Ground Control Intercept (RADAR)
GCIS . . . . . . Ground Control Intercept Squadron
GCL . . . . Ground Control Landing (Aviation)
GCA . . . . Ground-Controlled Aircraft
GCA . . . . Ground-Controlled Approach (for lateral and vertical guidance of landing aircraft through use of ground RADAR and radio communications)
GCR . . . . Ground Controlled RADAR
GCSS . . . . . . Ground-Controlled Space System
GCO . . . . Ground Cutout
GDAS . . . . . . Ground Data Acquisition System
GDE . . . . Ground Data Equipment (Electronics)
GDF . . . . Ground Decommutation Facility
GRD . . . . Ground Detector
GDI . . . . Ground Detector Indicator
GDS . . . . Ground Display System
GEM . . . . Ground Effect Machine
GERM . . . . . . Ground Effect Research Machine
GETOL . . . . . Ground-Effect Take-Off and Landing
GEV . . . . Ground Effect Vehicle
GEP . . . . Ground Effects Phenomenon
GET . . . . Ground-Elapsed Time (Aerospace)
GEEIA . . . . . . Ground Electronics Engineering Installation Agency (Air Force)

GWS . . . . GEEIA (Ground Electronics Engineering Installation Agency) Workload
Schedule
GETIS. . . . . . Ground Environment Team of the International Staff (NATO)
GE . . . . Ground Equipment
GEF. . . . . . . Ground Equipment Failure (Air Force)
GES. . . . . . . Ground Equipment System
GETS . . . . . . Ground Equipment Test Set
GFLS . . . . . . Ground Fire Locating System
GFL . . . . Ground Fire Locator
GF . . . . Ground Fog (Meteorology)
GFRS . . . . . . Ground Forces Replacement Service
GGL . . . . . . Ground Glass
G/G . . . . Ground-to-Ground (Communications, weapons, etc.)
GTG . . . . . . Ground-to-Ground
GGM. . . . . . Ground-to-Ground Missile
GGC . . . . . . Ground Guidance Computer
GGE . . . . . . Ground Guidance Equipment
GGR . . . . . . Ground Gunnery Range
GH . . . . Ground Handling
GHE. . . . . . . Ground Handling Equipment
GHX . . . . . . Ground Heat Exchanger
GIMS . . . . . . Ground Identification of Missions in Space
GISAT . . . . . . Ground Identification of Satellites
GIPS . . . . . . Ground Information Processing System
GIE . . . . Ground Instrumentation Equipment
GL . . . . Ground Level
GLO . . . . . . Ground Liaison Officer (Military)
GLOC . . . . . . Ground Line of Communications
GMS . . . . . . Ground Maintenance Support
GM . . . . Ground Malfunction
GMR . . . . . . Ground Mapping RADAR
GMS . . . . . . Ground Mapping System
GMS . . . . . . Ground Marking System
GMC . . . . . . Ground Mobile Cenetheodolite
GMR . . . . . . Ground Mobile RADAR
GMR . . . . . . Ground Movement RADAR
GMTI . . . . . . Ground Moving Target Indicator
GOBC . . . . . . Ground Observer Corps (Canada)
GOC . . . . . . Ground Observer Corps
GOP . . . . . . Ground Observer Post
GOE . . . . . . Ground Operation Equipment
GOE/RPIE . . . . Ground Operational Equipment/Real Property Installed Equipment
GOSS. . . . . . Ground Operational Support System (MSFC)
GORID . . . . . Ground Optical Recorder for Intercept Determination
GOB . . . . . . Ground Order of Battle
GPERF . . . . . Ground Passive Electronic Reconnaissance Facility
GPA . . . . . . Ground Plane Antenna
GPI . . . . Ground Point of Intercept
GPI . . . . Ground Position Indicator (Dead-reckoning computer)
GPC . . . . . . Ground Power Contactor
GPP . . . . Ground Power Panel
GPU. . . . . . . Ground Power Unit
GPES . . . . . . Ground Proximity Extraction System
GR . . . . Ground Range
GRE. . . . . . . Ground Reconstruction Electronics (Used in photographing moon) (NASA)
GRF . . . . Ground Repetition Frequency
GRT. . . . . . . Ground Resistance Tester
GRD. . . . . . . Ground Resolved Distance (Satellite camera)
GSO . . . . . . Ground Safety Office(r) (Air Force)
GSDF . . . . . . Ground Self-Defense Force (Japan)
GSDFJ . . . . . Ground Self Defense Force Japan
GSE . . . . . . Ground Service Equipment (Air Force)
GSM . . . . . . Ground Signal Mixer
GSSF . . . . . . Ground Special Security Forces
GS . . . . Ground Speed (Aviation)
GSI . . . . Ground Speed Indicator
GSO . . . . . . Ground Speed Oscillator
GSE . . . . . . Ground Support Equipment (Air Force)
GSES . . . . . . Ground Support Equipment Section
GSME . . . . . . Ground Support Maintenance Equipment
GSO . . . . . . Ground Support Operations
GSQC . . . . . . Ground Surveillance Qualification Course (Army)
GSR. . . . . . . Ground Surveillance RADAR
G . . . . Ground Swell
GSG . . . . . . Ground Systems Group
GSL. . . . . . . Ground Systems Laboratory
GSPO. . . . . . Ground Systems Project Office
GTD. . . . . . . Ground Target Detection
GTMS. . . . . . Ground Target Marking System
GTS . . . . Ground Telemetry Subsystem
GTS . . . . Ground Terminal System

GTM . . . . Ground Test Missile
GTR . . . . Ground Test Reactor (Air Force)
GTU. . . . . . . Ground Test Unit
GTIP . . . . . . Ground Tilt Isolation Platform
GT. . . . . Ground Track
GT. . . . . Ground Transmit
GTX . . . . . . Ground Transport Express (Airport baggage computer)
GTV. . . . . . . Ground Transport Vehicle
GVS. . . . . . . Ground Vibration Survey
GV . . . . Ground Visibility
GWI . . . . Ground Water Institute
GWRI . . . . . . Ground Water Resources Institute
GZ . . . . Ground Zero (Atomic detonation)
GB . . . . Grounded Base
GCA . . . . . . Grounded Cathode Amplifier
GC . . . . Grounded Collector
GE . . . . Grounded Emitter
GGA . . . . . . Grounded Grid Amplifier
GKA . . . . . . Grounded Kathode Amplifier
GPA . . . . . . Grounded Plate Amplifier
G . . . . Group
GARL . . . . . . Group Action Request Lists
GAP . . . . . . Group for the Advancement of Psychiatry
GOAD . . . . . Group of Ancient Drama
GAPL . . . . . . Group Assembly Parts List
GAP . . . . . . Group Attainment Program
GC . . . . Group Captain
GCC . . . . . . Group Change Control
GDG . . . . . . Group Display Generator
GDF. . . . . . . Group Distributing Frames
GED. . . . . . . Group on Electronic Devices
GE. . . . . Group Engineer
GEE . . . . . . Group for Environmental Education
GFD. . . . . . . Group Finance Department
GPFL . . . . . . Group Flashing (Navigation signal lights)
GHAA . . . . . . Group Health Association of America
GIT . . . . Group Inclusive Tour (Travel)
GLEP . . . . . . Group for Lunar Exploration and Planning
GRNC . . . . . Group Number No Count (Military communication)
GPOCC . . . . . Group Occulting (Navigation signal lights)
GROPAC . . . . Group Pacific
GR. . . . . Group Report
GRACE . . . . . Group Routing and Charging Equipment (British)
GSR . . . . . . Group Selective Register
GS. . . . . Group Structured (Counseling Group)
GSC . . . . . . Group Study Course
GTM . . . . . . Group Talk Microphone
GTEA . . . . . . Group Test Equipment Assembly
GpTh . . . . . . Group Therapy
GANC . . . . . . Groupe d'Action Nationale Comerounaise (Cameroonian National Action
Group)
GDC . . . . . . Groupe des Democrates Camerounais (Cameroonian Democratic Group)
GEERS . . . . . Groupe d'Etudes Europeen des Recherches Spatiales
GEMPPS . . . . Groupe d'Etudes Mathematiques de Problemes Politiques et Strategiques
(France)
GERS . . . . . . Groupe d'Etude et Recherches Sous-Marin
GIRT. . . . . . . Groupe des Independants et Ruraux Tchadiens (Chadian Independent and
Rural Group)
GRETI . . . . . . Groupe Romand pou l'Etude des Techniques d'Instruction (Switzerland)
GUC . . . . . . Groupe d'Union Comerounaise (Group for Cameroonian Union)
GAA . . . . . . Groupement Atomique Alsacienne Atlantique (French)
GEFAP . . . . . Groupement Europeen des Associations Nationales de Fabricants de
Pesticides
GIA . . . . . . Groupement des Independants Africains (Independent Africans Group)
GIIP. . . . . . . Groupement International de l'Industrie Pharmaceutique des Pays de la
CEE
GMMTA . . . . . Groupement des Moyens Militaires de Transport Aerien (France)
GOMAC . . . . Groupement des Opticiens du Marche Commun
GPIN . . . . . . Groupement Professionnel de l'Industrie Nucleaire (Belgium) (Also known
as NIC)
GPM . . . . . . Groups (of code transmitted) Per Minute (or Message) (Communications)
GCC . . . . . . Grove City College (Pennsylvania)
GD . . . . Grown Diffused
GAF. . . . . . . Growth of the American Family (A study)
GAR . . . . . . Growth Analysis and Review
GDH . . . . . . Growth and Differentiation Hormone (Endocrinology)
GF . . . . Growth Fraction (Endocrinology)
GH . . . . Growth Hormone (Endocrinology)
GAC . . . . . . Grumman Aircraft Corporation
GAEC . . . . . . Grumman Aircraft Engineering Corporation
GQ . . . . Grumman Aircraft Engineering Corporation (NYSE symbol)

GARD . . . . Grumman–Alderson Research Dummy (Aircraft ejection seats)
GSV . . . . Grumman Submersible Vehicle
GHS . . . . Grunberg Hydrofoil System
GBA . . . . Grupo Buenos Aires
GOU . . . . Grupo de Oficiales Unidos (Group of United Officers) (Argentine)
GU . . . . Guam
GASH . . . . . . Guanidine Aluminum Sulfate Herahydrate
GE . . . . Guanidoethyl
GED . . . . Guanidoethyl Disulfide
G . . . . Guanine
GC . . . . Guanine, Cystine (Biochemistry)
GMP . . . . Guanine Monophosphate
GDP . . . . Guanosine Diphosphate (Biochemistry)
GTP . . . . Guanosine Triphosphate (Biochemistry)
GTMO . . . . . . Guantanamo Bay, Cuba
GTD . . . . Guaranteed (NYSE symbol)
GAI . . . . Guaranteed Annual Income
GAM . . . . Guaranteed Annual Minimum
GAW . . . . Guaranteed Annual Wage
GHM . . . . Guaranteed Hourly Minimum
GHW . . . . Guaranteed Hourly Wage
GMV . . . . Guaranteed Minimum Value
GRI . . . . Guaranteed Retirement Income
GVB . . . . Guaranteed Voltage Breakdown
GWM . . . . Guaranteed Weekly Minimum
GWW . . . . Guaranteed Weekly Wage
G . . . . Guard (Position in football, basketball, etc.)
GHL . . . . Guard House Lawyer (Military slang)
GM . . . . Guard Mail
GRC . . . . Guard Ring Capacitor
GWC . . . . Guard Well Capacitor
GERA . . . . . . Guard's Expense in Returning Absentee
GRM . . . . Guarded Relay Multiplexer
GH . . . . Guardhouse
G . . . . Guardian
GS . . . . Guardship
GD . . . . Gudermannian Amplitude
GW . . . . Guerrilla Warfare
GWOA . . . . . . Guerrilla Warfare Operational Area (Army)
GAM . . . . Guest Aerovias Mexico, SA
GAL . . . . Guggenheim Aeronautical Laboratory
GALCIT . . . . . . Guggenheim Aeronautical Laboratory (at California Institute of Technology)
GCH . . . . Guidance Capsule Handling
GCC . . . . Guidance Checkout Computer
GCJB . . . . . . Guidance Checkout Junction Box
GC . . . . Guidance Computer
GCJB . . . . . . Guidance Computer Junction Box
GC . . . . Guidance Control
G & C . . . . . . Guidance and Control
GC & A . . . . . . Guidance, Control and Airframe
GCFAP . . . . . . Guidance & Control Flight Analysis Program
GCG . . . . Guidance Control Group (Military)
GCU . . . . Guidance Coupler Unit
GEAV . . . . . . Guidance Error Analysis Vehicles (Air Force)
GEM . . . . Guidance Evaluation Missile
G & N . . . . . . Guidance and Navigation (System) (Apollo) (NASA)
GNE . . . . Guidance and Navigation Equipment
GUIDO . . . . . . Guidance and Navigation Officer (NASA)
GPA . . . . Guidance Platform Assembly (Military)
GRM . . . . Guidance Rate Measurement
GSC . . . . Guidance Shipping Container
GTF . . . . Guidance Test Fixture
GTV . . . . Guidance Test Vehicle
GTC . . . . Guidance Transfer Container
GU . . . . Guidance Unit (Military)
GUA . . . . Guidance Unit Assembly
GUIDE . . . . . . Guidance for Users of Integrated Data Processing Equipment
GUSTO . . . . . . Guidance Using Stable Tuning Oscillations
G . . . . Guide
GISPA . . . . . . Guide to International Scientific Publications and Associations
GLIPAR . . . . . . Guide Line Identification Program for Antimissile Research (ARPA)
GLIPAR . . . . . . Guide Lines for Investigations, Planning and Research
GB . . . . Guidebook
GADR . . . . . . Guided Air Defense Rocket
GAR . . . . Guided Airborne (or Aircraft) Rocket
GAM . . . . Guided Aircraft Missile
GAW . . . . Guided Atomic Warhead
GFV . . . . Guided Flight Vehicle
GFFAR . . . . . . Guided Folding Fin Aircraft Rocket
GM . . . . Guided Missile

GMAIC . . . . . . Guided Missile and Aerospace Intelligence Committee
GMA . . . . Guided Missile Ammunition
GMB . . . . Guided Missile Brigade (Army)
BBG . . . . Guided Missile Capital Ship (Navy symbol)
GMC . . . . Guided Missile Committee
GMCM . . . . . . Guided Missile Counter–Measures
CG . . . . Guided Missile Cruiser (Navy symbol)
CG(N) . . . . . . Guided Missile Cruiser (Nuclear-propelled) (Naval ship designation)
GMDEP . . . . . . Guided Missile Data Exchange Program (Navy)
DDG . . . . Guided Missile Destroyer (Navy symbol)
DEG . . . . Guided Missile Destroyer Escort (Navy symbol)
GMD . . . . Guided Missile Division
GME . . . . Guided Missile Evaluator
GMFC . . . . . . Guided Missile Fire Control
DLG . . . . Guided Missile Frigate (Navy symbol)
DLG(N) . . . . . . Guided Missile Frigate (Nuclear propelled) (Navy symbol)
CAG . . . . Guided Missile Heavy Cruiser (Navy symbol)
CAG(N) . . . . . . Guided Missile Heavy Cruiser (Nuclear propelled) (Navy symbol)
GML . . . . Guided Missile Laboratory
GMLS . . . . . . Guided Missile Launching System
CLG . . . . Guided Missile Light Cruiser (Navy symbol)
CLGN . . . . . . Guided Missile Light Cruiser (Nuclear powered) (Navy symbol)
GMRWG . . . . . . Guided Missile Relay Working Group (Navy)
GMS . . . . Guided Missile School
GMSR . . . . . . Guided Missile Service Record
GMSU . . . . . . Guided Missile Service Unit (Air Force)
AVM . . . . Guided Missile Ship (Navy symbol)
SSG . . . . Guided Missile Submarine (Navy symbol)
SSGN . . . . . . Guided Missile Submarine (Nuclear powered) (Navy symbol)
GMS . . . . Guided Missile System
GMTS . . . . . . Guided Missile Test Set
GMU . . . . Guided Missile Unit
GSV . . . . Guided Space Vehicle (Air Force)
GTV . . . . Guided Test Vehicle
GW . . . . Guided Weapon (Air Force)
GEB . . . . Guiding Eyes for the Blind
GAJ . . . . Guild of Agricultural Journalists
GAPAN . . . . . . Guild of Air Pilots and Air Navigators
GAS . . . . Guild of All Souls (British)
GAFD . . . . . . Guild of American Funeral Directors
GBSM . . . . . . Guild of Better Shoe Manufacturers
GBW . . . . Guild of Book Workers
GCL . . . . Guild of Catholic Lawyers
GCP . . . . Guild of Catholic Psychiatrists
GEFP . . . . . . Guild of Ethical Funeral Practice
GIS . . . . Guild for Infant Survival
GPOA . . . . . . Guild of Prescription Opticians of America
GRA . . . . Guild for Religious Architecture
GREEN . . . . . . Guild to Revive Exhausted Nurses
GSA . . . . Guild of Saint Alban
GSM . . . . Guild of Saint Matthew
GVC . . . . Guild Vector Colorimeter
GWIBIT . . . . . . Guild of Washington Incompetent Bureaucratic Idea Throatcutters (An organization rumored to have been active in World War II)
GIC . . . . Guilde Internationale des Cooperatrices
G . . . . Guilder (Dutch monetary unit) (Modification of Gulden)
GUCO . . . . . . Guilford Courthouse National Military Park
GZTS . . . . . . Guilford–Zimmerman Temperament Survey
G . . . . Guinea (Coin or sum of money) (British)
GAL . . . . Guinea Airways, Limited
GP . . . . Guinea Pig
GAMA . . . . . . Guitar and Accessory Manufacturers Association of America (Formerly, NAMMM)
G . . . . Gulden (Monetary unit in the Netherlands)
G . . . . Gulf (Maps and charts)
GCFI . . . . . . Gulf and Caribbean Fisheries Institute
GULFCOBASESERVUNIT . . Gulf Coast Base Service Unit
GCSF . . . . . . Gulf, Colorado & Santa Fe Railway Company (AAR code)
GC & SF . . . . Gulf, Colorado and Sante Fe Railway Company
GULFCON . . . Gulf Control
GEFA . . . . . . Gulf-European Freight Association
GIW . . . . Gulf Intracoastal Waterway
GIWW . . . . . . Gulf Intracoastal Waterway
GIF . . . . Gulf It to FORTRAN (Translator)
GMO . . . . Gulf, Mobile & Ohio R. R. (AAR code)
GFO . . . . Gulf, Mobile & Ohio R. R. Company (NYSE symbol)
GM & O . . . . Gulf, Mobile & Ohio Railroad Company
GOC . . . . Gulf Oil Company
GO . . . . Gulf Oil Corporation (NYSE symbol)
GUPAC . . . . . . Gulf Permanent Assistance Committee (Persian Gulf)
GSY . . . . Gulf Science Year (1970)

GSF . . . . Gulf Sea Frontier
GULFSEAFRON . . Gulf Sea Frontier
G & SI . . . . . . Gulf and Ship Island Railroad Company
GSMFC . . . . . Gulf States Marine Fisheries Commission
GTU. . . . . . . Gulf States Utilities Company (NYSE symbol)
GTC. . . . . . . Gulf Transport R. R. (AAR code)
GTTC . . . . . . Gulf Transportation Terminal Command
GURC . . . . . . Gulf University Research Corporation
G & W. . . . . . Gulf and Western Industries, Inc.
G & WI . . . . . Gulf and Western Industries, Inc.
GIA . . . . Gummed Industries Association
G . . . . Gun
GBR . . . . Gun, Bomb and Rocket
GC . . . . Gun Captain
GC . . . . Gun Control
GCO . . . . . . Gun Control Officer (Navy)
GDA . . . . . . Gun Defended Area
GDC . . . . . . Gun Direction Computer
GDP . . . . . . Gun Director Pointer (Naval gunnery)
GDP(CL) . . . . . Gun Director Pointer (Cross Leveler) (Naval gunnery)
GDP(L) . . . . . Gun Director Pointer (Leveler) (Naval gunnery)
GDP(P) . . . . . Gun Director Pointer (Pointer) (Naval gunnery)
GDP(SS) . . . . Gun Director Pointer (Sight Setter) (Naval gunnery)
GDP(T) . . . . . Gun Director Pointer (Trainer) (Naval gunnery)
GFA . . . . . . Gun Fire Area
GFCS . . . . . Gun Fire Control System
GFDD. . . . . . Gun Fire Detection Device
GL . . . . Gun Lay(er)(ing)
GMC . . . . . . Gun Motor Carriage
GP . . . . Gun Pointer (Naval gunnery)
GRFO. . . . . . Gun Range Finder Operator
GSAP. . . . . . Gun Sight Aiming Point
GB. . . . . Gunboat (Naval)
GFSS . . . . . . Gunfire Support Ship
GM . . . . Gunmetal
GED. . . . . . . Gunn Effect Device
GEM . . . . . . Gunn Effect Material
GI . . . . Gunner Instructor (British Navy)
GM . . . . Gunner's Mate
GMCB . . . . . Gunner's Mate, Construction Battalion (Navy rating)
GMCBG . . . . . Gunner's Mate, Construction Battalion, Armorer (Navy rating)
GMCBP. . . . . Gunner's Mate, Construction Battalion, Powderman (Navy rating)
GMSR . . . . . Gunner's Mate, Ship Repair (Navy rating)
GMSRP . . . . . Gunner's Mate, Ship Repair, Powderman (Navy rating)

GLO . . . . Gunnery Liaison Officer (Navy)
GOC . . . . . . Gunnery Officer's Console (Army)
GOOS . . . . . . Gunnery Officers Ordnance School
GR . . . . Gunnery Range
GS. . . . . Gunnery School (Air Force)
GS. . . . . Gunnery Sergeant
GUNSGT . . . . Gunnery Sergeant
GYSGT. . . . . Gunnery Sergeant
GSW . . . . . . Gunshot Wound (Medicine)
GASDSAS . . . . Gust Alleviation and Structural Dynamic Stability
GAC . . . . . . Gustavus Adolphus College (Minnesota)
GBA . . . . . . Gustin-Bacon Manufacturing Company (NYSE symbol)
G . . . . Gusts (Meteorology)
GT. . . . . Gutta (Drop of liquid)
GTT. . . . . . . Guttae (Drops of liquid)
GIBS . . . . . . Guy-In-The-Back-Seat (Copilot) (Air Force slang)
GYN . . . . . . Gynecology
G . . . . Gynoecium (Botany)
GA . . . . Gypsum Association
GDCI . . . . . . Gypsum Drywall Contractors International
GPC . . . . . . Gypsum-Plaster Ceiling (Technical drawings)
GPW . . . . . . Gypsum-Plaster Wall (Technical drawings)
GRDF . . . . . . Gypsum Roof Deck Foundation (Technical drawings)
GSB . . . . . . Gypsum Sheathing Board (Technical drawings)
GWB . . . . . . Gypsum Wallboard (Technical drawings)
GLS. . . . . . . Gypsy Lore Society
GDRC. . . . . . Gyro Drift Rate Compensation
GEON . . . . . . Gyro Erected Optical Navigation
GE. . . . . Gyro Error (Navigation)
GHA . . . . . . Gyro Header Assembly
GP. . . . . Gyro Package
GPP. . . . . . . Gyro Pitch Position
GRA . . . . . . Gyro Reference Assembly
GSO . . . . . . Gyro Storage Oven
GTS . . . . Gyro Tilt Signal
GTTS . . . . . . Gyro Transfer Table System
GYP. . . . . . . Gyro Yaw Position
GCS. . . . . . . Gyroless Control System
GMK . . . . . . Gyromagnetic Kompass
G . . . . Gyromagnetic Ratio
GPS . . . . . . Gyroscope Parameter Shift
GPV. . . . . . . Gyroscope Pickoff Voltage
GVA . . . . . . Gyroscope Vibration Absorber
GLOPAC . . . . Gyroscopic Low-Power Attitude Control

H

BHK . . . . H. C. Bohack Company, Inc. (American Stock Exchange symbol)
HHFC . . . . . . H. H. Franklin Club
HTJ . . . . H-Plane Tee Junction
HC . . . . Habitual Criminal
HBSAA . . . . . Hack and Band Saw Manufacturers Association of America
HWA . . . . Hackensack Water Company (NYSE symbol)
HVO . . . . Hackfleisch Verordnung
HMRA . . . . . . Hadassah Medical Relief Association
Hf . . . . Hafnium (Chemical element)
HfC . . . . Hafnium Carbide
Hf(C,N) . . . . . Hafnium Carbonitride
HAL . . . . Haftarbeitslager
HF . . . . Hageman Factor (in blood plasma)
HJC . . . . Hagerstown Junior College (Maryland)
A . . . . Hail (Meteorological symbol)
H . . . . Hail
HIARA . . . . . . Hail Insurance Adjustment and Research Association
HR . . . . Hair Space Between Letters (Proofreader's mark)
HTB . . . . Hair Tuning Bar
HAC . . . . Haitian Air Corps
HAA . . . . Haitian-American Association
HASCO . . . . . Haitian-American Sugar Company
HCM . . . . Haitian Campaign Medal
HBWR . . . . . . Halden Boiling Heavy Water Reactor
HPR . . . . Halden Reaktor Prosjekt (Norway)
HO . . . . Hale Observatories (Formerly, Mount Palomar and Mount Wilson Observatories)
HALE . . . . . . Haleakala National Park
H . . . . Haler (Monetary unit in Czechoslovakia)
H . . . . Half
HA . . . . Half Add
HBS . . . . Half Bar Symbology
HB . . . . Half Bound (Bibliography)
HC . . . . Half Calf
HC . . . . Half Chest
HDX . . . . Half Duplex
HFO . . . . Half Fare Order (Aviation)
HH . . . . Half Hard (Metallurgy)
HL . . . . Half-Life (of radioactive elements)
HM . . . . Half Morocco
HOB . . . . Half Octave Bandwidth
HPP . . . . Half Page Printer
HP . . . . Half Pay
HSP . . . . Half-Shade Plate
HS . . . . Half Strength
HS . . . . Half Subtractor
HT . . . . Half-Time (Survey) (Shipping)
HTRK . . . . . . Half-Track (A type of military vehicle)
HVL . . . . Half-Value Layer
HVP . . . . Half Value Period
HW . . . . Half Wave
HWBR . . . . . . Half Wave Bridge Rectifier
HWP . . . . Half-Wave Plate
HWR . . . . Half-Wave Rectifier
HB . . . . Halfback (Football position)
HT . . . . Halftone (Photoengraving)
HANA . . . . . . Halibut Association of North America
HCM . . . . Halifax Conservatory of Music
HOMP . . . . . Halifax Ocean Meeting Point
H . . . . Hall
HED . . . . Hall Effect Device
HEFG . . . . . . Hall Effect Function Generator
HEG . . . . Hall Effect Generator

HEM . . . . Hall Effect Multiplier
HEP . . . . Hall Effect Probe
HPG . . . . Hall (W. F.) Printing Company (NYSE symbol)
HNPF . . . . . . Hallam Nuclear Power Facility (AEC)
HAL . . . . Halliburton Company (NYSE symbol)
HLF . . . . Hallicrafters Company (NYSE symbol)
HIPSA . . . . . . Hallicrafters Incremental Power Spectrum Analyzer
HM . . . . Hallmark
HQT . . . . Halogen Quenched Tube
HSSG . . . . . . Halograph Stress Strain Gauge
HARP . . . . . . Halpern's AntiRADAR Point
HT . . . . Halt and Transfer
HTR . . . . Halt and Transfer
HALPRO . . . . Halverson Project (World War II plan to bomb Japan from China)
HAL . . . . Hamburg-Amerika Linie (Hamburg-America Steamship Company)
HAWIK . . . . . Hamburg-Wechsler-Intelligenztest fuer Kinder (Intelligence test for children)
HAGR . . . . . . Hamilton Grange National Memorial
HNS . . . . Hamilton Normal School
HMW . . . . Hamilton Watch Company (NYSE symbol)
H . . . . Hamiltonian Function
HES . . . . Hamlet Evaluation Survey (South Vietnam)
HML . . . . Hammermill Paper Company (NYSE symbol)
HML . . . . Hammond Metallurgical Laboratory (Yale)
HMD . . . . Hammond Organ Company (NYSE symbol)
HSC . . . . Hampden-Sydney College (Virginia)
HSR . . . . Hampshire Swine Registry
HB . . . . Hampton & Branchville R. R. (AAR code)
HAMP . . . . . . Hampton National Historic Site
HRAT . . . . . . Hampton Roads Army Terminal
HCK . . . . Hancock Oil Company (NYSE symbol)
HC . . . . Hand Control (Technical drawings)
HD . . . . Hand Drawn
HG . . . . Hand Generator
HHMU . . . . . . Hand-Held Maneuvering Unit (NASA)
HJP . . . . Hand Jewel Pusher
HOT . . . . Hand Over Transmitter
HPB . . . . Hand-Printed Books
HDR . . . . Hand Rail
HTD . . . . Hand Target Designator
HTI . . . . Hand Tool Institute
HT . . . . Hand Translation
HSSA . . . . . . Handbag Supply Salesmen's Association
HELPR . . . . . Handbook of Electronic Parts Reliability
HIMR . . . . . . Handbook of Inspection Maintenance Requirements
HIR . . . . Handbook of Inspection Requirements (Navy)
HIAPSD . . . . . Handbook of Instructions for Aerospace Personnel Subsystem Designers
HIASD . . . . . Handbook of Instructions for Aerospace Systems Design
HIAFSB . . . . . Handbook of Instructions for Air Force Subsystem Designers
HIAD . . . . . . Handbook of Instructions for Aircraft Designers
HIAGSED . . . . Handbook of Instructions for Aircraft Ground Support Equipment Designers
HIGED . . . . . Handbook of Instructions for Ground Equipment Designers
HIMD . . . . . . Handbook of Instructions for Missile Designers
HMI . . . . Handbook of Maintenance Instructions
HOPI . . . . . . Handbook of Operating Instructions (Navy)
HOHI . . . . . . Handbook of Overhaul Instructions
HOI . . . . Handbook of Overhaul Instructions (Navy)
HOVI . . . . . . Handbook of Overhaul Instructions
HOSI . . . . . . Handbook of Service Instructions
HSI . . . . Handbook of Service Instructions
HA . . . . Handelsabgabe
HO . . . . Handelsorganisation
HCHS . . . . . . Handicapped Children's Home Service

H	Handily
HIA	Handkerchief Industry Association
HDF	Handle Door Fastener
H-P	Handley-Page Ltd.
HE	Handling Equipment
HGE	Handling Ground Equipment
HQC	Handling Quality Criteria
HR	Handling Room
HT	Handling Time
HM	Handmade
HMP	Handmade Paper
HP	Handmade Paper
HATRAC	Handover Transfer and Receiver Accept Change (SAGE)
HS	Handset
HWB	Handwarterbuch
HAI	Handwriting Analysts, Incorporated
HF	Handwriting Foundation
HAPO	Hanford Atomic Products Operations (General Electric Company)
HEW	Hanford Engineering Works
HIP	Hanford Isotopes Plant
HOO	Hanford Operations Office (AEC)
HCO	Hangar Control Officer (Navy)
HCP	Hangar Control Position (Navy)
HNA	Hanna (M. A.) Company (NYSE symbol)
HC	Hannibal Connecting R. R. (AAR code)
HD	Hansen's Disease (Leprosy) (Medicine)
HF	Harassing Fire (Military)
HKM	Harbison-Walker Refractories Company (NYSE symbol)
H	Harbor (Maps and charts)
HBS	Harbor Boat Service (Military)
HCPNY	Harbor Carriers of the Port of New York
HARCFT	Harbor Craft
HD	Harbor Defense (Military)
HDC	Harbor Defense Command (Army)
HERALDS	Harbor Echo Ranging and Listening Devices
HECP	Harbor Entrance Control Post
HECVES	Harbor Entrance Control Vessel
HM	Harbor Master
HPF	Harbor Patrol Fleet
HARSAP	Harbor Survey Assistance Program (Naval Oceanographic Office)
YT	Harbor Tug (Navy symbol)
YFU	Harbor Utility Craft (Navy symbol)
HBW	Harcourt, Brace & World, Inc. (NYSE symbol)
HJC	Harcum Junior College (Pennsylvania)
H	Hard(ness) (Of pencil leads)
HB	Hard Black (Of pencil leads)
HDCR	Hard Chromium
HC	Hard Copy
HCP	Hard Copy Printer
HD	Hard-Drawn (Metallurgy)
HFA	Hard Fibres Association
HFC	Hard Filled Capsules (Pharmacy)
HF	Hard Firm (Of pencil leads)
HH	Hard of Hearing
HP	Hard Point
HAPDEC	Hard Point Decoys
HPD	Hard Point Defense
HPDI	Hard Point Defense Interceptor
HPDS	Hard Point Defense System
HAPDAR	Hard Point Demonstration Array RADAR
HSM	Hard Structure Munition
HTM	Hard Tube Modulator (Electronics)
HXQ	Hard X-Ray Quanta
H & G	Harden & Grind (Technical drawings)
HART	Hardened Amplifier for Radiation Transients
H & D	Hardened and Dispersed
HFA	Hardened Flexible Array
HPS	Hardened Power System
HSM	Hardened Silo Missile
HSU	Hardin-Simmons University (Texas)
HS	Hardstand
HMSA	Hardware Manufacturers Statistical Association
HDMA	Hardwood Dimension Manufacturers Association
HPI	Hardwood Plywood Institute
HPMA	Hardwood Plywood Manufacturers Association
HRC	Hardwood Research Council
HCC	Harlem Cultural Council
HARYOU-ACT	Harlem Youth Opportunities Unlimited - Associated Community Teams (A kind of Peace Corps for Harlem area of New York City)
HFG	Harmonic Frequency Generator
HG	Harmonic Generator
HM	Harmonic Mean (Music)
HMS	Harmonic Multiplier Source
HST	Harmonic and Spurious Totalizer
HVF	Harmonically Varying Field
HCA	Harness and Cable Assembly
HHI	Harness Horsemen International
HTA	Harness Tracks of America
HTS	Harness Tracks Security (An organization)
HAFE	Harpers Ferry National Historical Park
HNE	Harriman & Northeastern R. R. (AAR code)
HI	Harris-Intertype Corporation (NYSE symbol)
HTC	Harris Teachers College (Missouri)
HTC	Harris Transducer Corporation
HNA	Harrison Narcotic Act
HDL	Harry Diamond Laboratory (Military) (Formerly, DOFL)
HST	Harry S Truman
HSC	Harsco Corporation (NYSE symbol)
HCM	Harshaw Chemical Company (NYSE symbol)
HSM	Hart, Schaffner & Marx (NYSE symbol)
HEL	Hartford Electric Light Company (NYSE symbol)
HSF	Hartford Seminary Foundation
HS	Hartford & Slocomb R. R. (AAR code)
HDF	Hartmann Dispersion Formula
HRT	Hartwell R. R. (AAR code)
HBS	Harvard Business School
HCO	Harvard College Observatory
HER	Harvard Educational Review
HPP	Harvard Project Physics
HU	Harvard University
HYP	Harvard, Yale, and Princeton Universities
HAR	Harvey Aluminum, Inc. (NYSE symbol)
HCS	Harvey Cushing Society
HUB	Harvey Hubbell, Inc. (NYSE symbol)
HAEE	Harwell Atomic Energy Establishment
HBD	Has Been Drinking (Medical notation)
HH	Hashomer Hatzair
HZYO	Hashomer Hatzair Zionist Youth Organization
HICO	Hastings Instrument Company
HBDMA	Hat Block and Die Makers Association
HAT	Hat Corporation of America (NYSE symbol)
HI	Hat Institute
HLA	Hat Leather Association
H	Hatch (Technical drawings)
HA	Hatch Act
HBK	Hathaway Bakeries, Inc. (NYSE symbol)
HFCAA	Hatters' Fur Cutters Association of America (Formerly, HFCAUS)
HFCAUS	Hatters Fur Cutters Association of the United States (Later, HFCAA)
HMEA	Hatters Machinery and Equipment Association
HDZ	Haubarkeitsdurchschnittszuwachs
H	Hauch (Film)
HV	Hauptverwaltung
HVA	Hauptverwaltung Aufklaerung (Main Administration for Intelligence) (East Germany)
HGL	Hausgemeinschaftsleitung
HCR	Haut-Commissaire des Nations Unies pour les Refugies
HED	Haut-Einheits-Dosis (Unit Skin Dose)
HP	Haut Parleur (Loudspeaker)
HOTBUN	Have Not Yet Begun to Fight (Simulated war game)
HAYSTAQ	Have You Stored Answers to Questions? (Data processing)
HVG	Haveg Industries, Inc. (NYSE symbol)
HBAT	Having Been Assigned to This Organization (or Headquarters)
HI	Hawaii
HAC	Hawaii Aeronautics Commission
HAD	Hawaii Air Defense
HADS	Hawaii Air Defense System
HFAF	Hawaii Foundation for American Freedoms
HAVO	Hawaii Volcanoes National Park
HADD	Hawaiian Air Defense Division
HADIZ	Hawaiian Air Defense Identification Zone
HANG	Hawaiian Air National Guard
HAL	Hawaiian Airlines, Limited
HAT	Hawaiian Archives for Tsunamis
HAAFE	Hawaiian Army and Air Force Exchange (Military)
HADA	Hawaiian Defense Area
HIADS	Hawaiian Integrated Air Defense System
HAWSEAFRON	Hawaiian Sea Frontier
HSF	Hawaiian Sea Frontier
HST	Hawaiian Standard Time
HSPA	Hawaiian Sugar Planters' Association
HT	Hawaiian Telephone Company (NYSE symbol)
HT	Hawaiian Territory

HT	Hawaiian Theater (Military)
HT	Hawaiian Time
HTS	Hawaiian Tracking Station
HMSA	Hawk Mountain Sanctuary Association
HSD	Hawker Siddeley Dynamics
HSNP	Hawker-Siddeley Nuclear Power Company, Ltd. (British)
HFPS	Hay Fever Prevention Society
HAY	Hayes Industries, Inc. (NYSE symbol)
HYB	Hayes Manufacturing Corporation (NYSE symbol)
HAKASH	Hayl Kashish (Elderly Army) (Israel)
HAOC	Haynes-Apperson Owners Club
HBN	Hazard Beacon
HF	Hazard Function
HWN	Hazard Warning Network
HAB	Hazards Analysis Board (Air Force)
HERO	Hazards of Electromagnetic Radiation to Ordnance
H	Haze (Weather reports)
HF	Haze Filter (Photography)
HZT	Hazel-Atlas Glass Company (NYSE symbol)
HZ	Hazeltine Corporation (NYSE symbol)
HEC	Hazeltine Electronics Corporation
HEENT	Head, Ears, Eyes, Nose, Throat
HES	Head End Steering
4H	Head, Heart, Hands, and Health (as in 4H organizations)
HHHH	Head, Heart, Hands, and Health (as in 4H organizations)
HN	Head Nurse
HO	Head Office
HPM	Head Positioning Mechanism
HPA	Head Post Assembly
HPA	Head of a Procuring Activity (Army)
HUG	Head of Units Group (American Library Association)
HW	Head Width
HWI	Head Width Index
HW	Head Wind (Navigation)
HID	Headache, Insomnia, Depression (Syndrome)
HT	Headed Type
HPGC	Heading Per Gyro Compass (Navigation)
HPSC	Heading Per Standard Compass (Navigation)
HPSTGC	Heading Per Steering Compass (Navigation)
HM	Headmaster or Headmistress
H	Headquarters
HQ	Headquarters
HA	Headquarters Administration Division (Coast Guard)
HAF	Headquarters Air Force
HASC	Headquarters Air Service Command (Air Force)
HAFMED	Headquarters, Allied Forces Mediterranean
HALFSEE	Headquarters, Allied Land Forces Southeastern Europe
HACOM	Headquarters Area Command
HQBA	Headquarters Base Area
BETFOR	Headquarters British Element Trieste Forces
HQ-CAP	Headquarters, Civil Air Patrol
HC	Headquarters Command (Military)
HEADCOM	Headquarters Command (Military)
HEDCOM	Headquarters Command
HQC	Headquarters Command (Air Force)
HQCOMDUSAF	Headquarters Command, United States Air Force
HDA	Headquarters, Department of the Army
HQDP	Headquarters, Department of the Pacific (Marine Corps)
MARPAC	Headquarters, Department of the Pacific (Marine Corps)
HHB	Headquarters and Headquarters Battery
HHC	Headquarters and Headquarters Company
HHD	Headquarters and Headquarters Detachment (Army)
HHT	Headquarters and Headquarters Troop (Army)
LIB (UN)	Headquarters Library of the United Nations
HAMS	Headquarters and Maintenance Squad
HQMC	Headquarters, Marine Corps
HOI	Headquarters Office Instruction
HOI	Headquarters Operating Instructions (Air Force)
HQ & SERV	Headquarters and Service (Marine Corps)
H & S	Headquarters and Service (Battery) (Army)
HS & SS	Headquarters and Service Squadron
HEDRON	Headquarters Squadron
HQSQ	Headquarters Squadron
HEDRONFAIRWING	Headquarters Squadron Fleet Air Wing
HDNPRSGR	Headquarters Squadron Personnel Group
HEDSUPPACT	Headquarters Support Activities
HQ USAF	Headquarters United States Air Force
HUSAFICPA	Headquarters, United States Army Forces in Central Pacific Area
HUD	Heads-Up Display (Air Force)
HW	Headwaiter
H & A	Health and Accident (Insurance)
HCBI	Health Conference for Business and Industry
HIA	Health Industries Association
HIF	Health Information Foundation
HIAA	Health Insurance Association of America
HIC	Health Insurance Council
HII	Health Insurance Institute
HIP	Health Insurance Plan (of Greater New York)
HMAC	Health Manpower Advisory Council
HMWC	Health of Munition Workers Committee (British) (World War I)
HNI	Health News Institute (Defunct)
HOPE	Health Opportunity for People Everywhere (Philanthropic project operating hospital ship)
HPER	Health, Physical Education, and Recreation
HPRR	Health Physics Research Reactor (ORNL)
HPS	Health Physics Society
HELREC	Health Record(s)
HREC	Health Record
HASL	Health and Safety Laboratory (of AEC)
HSAA	Health Sciences Advancement Award (National Institutes of Health)
HSMHA	Health Services and Mental Health Administration (Department of Health, Education, and Welfare)
HAA	Hearing Aid Amplifier
HAB	Hearing Aid Battery
HAIC	Hearing Aid Industry Conference
HAM	Hearing Aid Microphone
HD	Hearing Distance (Medicine)
HEAR	Hearing Education through Audiotory Research (Foundation)
HE	Hearing Examiner
HRN	Hearn Department Stores (NYSE symbol)
HB	Heart Block (Medicine)
HIA	Heart Infusion Agar
HLF	Heart and Lung Foundation
HMO	Heart Minute Output (Physiology)
HPR	Heart Profile Recorder
HR	Heart Rate
HVP	Heart Valve Prostheses
HEF	Hearth Electric Furnace
H	Heat
HAD	Heat Actuated Device
HAZ	Heat-Affected Zone
HCF	Heat Control Filter
HEF	Heat-Curing Epoxy Film
HOD	Heat of Detonation
HDT	Heat Distortion Temperature
HE	Heat Engine
HEI	Heat Exchange Institute
HFE	Heat Flow Experiment
HFSU	Heat Flux Sensing Unit
HJPP	Heat Jacketed Proportioning Pump
HJP	Heat Jacketed Pump
HLCS	Heat Limiter Control Switch
HPS	Heat Protection System
HRA	Heat Rate Acceleration
HRV	Heat Rate Variability
HRR	Heat Rejection Radiator
HRP	Heat-Resistant Phenolic
HR	Heat Resisting (Technical drawings)
HRP	Heat Resisting Plastic
HSB	Heat Shield Boost
HST	Heat Shrinkable Tubing
HSK	Heat Sink Kit
HSPC	Heat Sterilizable Potting Compound
HSC	Heat Sterilization Compound
HSTP	Heat Sterilization Test Program
HTF	Heat Transfer Fluid
HTFMI	Heat Transfer and Fluid Mechanics Institute
HTL	Heat Transfer Laboratory (MIT)
HTM	Heat Transfer Meter
HTRE	Heat Transfer Reactor Experiment
HTS	Heat Transfer Section
HTS	Heat Transfer System
HTU	Heat Transfer Unit
HT	Heat Treat
HTTR	Heat Treat
HTFX	Heat Treat Fixture
HTS	Heat-Treated Steel
HWCU	Heated Window Control Unit
HAA	Heater Amplifier Assembly
HCT	Heater Center Top
HC	Heater Cord
HK	Heater Kit

YHT . . . . Heating Scow (Navy ship designation)
HVAC . . . . . . Heating, Ventilating, and Air Conditioning (Building construction)
HVRA . . . . . . Heating and Ventilating Research Association (British)
HTA . . . . Heavier Than Air (Aircraft)
V . . . . Heavier-than-air aircraft or personnel with duties related thereto (Navy designation)
VFAX . . . . . . Heavier-Than-Air Fighter/Attack/Experimental (Aircraft)
HAV . . . . Heavily Armed Vessels
HCB . . . . Heaviside-Campbell Bridge (Electronics)
HATU . . . . . . Heavy Air Training Unit
CVA . . . . Heavy Aircraft Carrier (65,000 tons) (Navy ship designation)
HAA . . . . . . Heavy Antiaircraft
HAW . . . . . . Heavy Antiarmor Weapon
HAAW . . . . . . Heavy Antitank/Assault Weapon (Army)
HA . . . . Heavy Artillery
HAW . . . . . . Heavy Assault Weapon
HAM . . . . . . Heavy Atom Method
HADM . . . . . . Heavy Atomic Demolition Munition (Military)
VAX . . . . . . Heavy Attack Aircraft, Experimental
HATU . . . . . . Heavy Attack Training Unit
HATWING . . . Heavy Attack Wing
HAM . . . . . . Heavy Automotive Maintenance
HBM . . . . . . Heavy Ballistic Missile
HB . . . . Heavy Barrel (In reference to a rifle)
HB . . . . Heavy Bombardment (or Bomber)
CA . . . . Heavy Cruiser (Navy symbol)
HVDP . . . . . . Heavy Drop (Military)
HD . . . . Heavy-Duty
HDY . . . . . . Heavy Duty
HDAC . . . . . . Heavy Duty Air Cylinder
HDA . . . . . . Heavy Duty Amplifier
HDAP . . . . . . Heavy Duty Automatic Press
HDIF. . . . . . . Heavy Duty Industrial Filter
HDIR . . . . . . Heavy Duty Industrial Relay
HERMES . . . . . Heavy Element and Radioactive Material Electromagnetic Separator (British)
HEBC . . . . . . Heavy Enamel Bonded Cotton (Insulation)
HEBP . . . . . . Heavy Enamel Bonded Paper (Insulation)
HEBS . . . . . . Heavy Enamel Bonded Silk (Insulation)
HECV . . . . . . Heavy Enamel Cotton Varnish (Insulation)
HEDC . . . . . . Heavy Enamel Double Cotton (Insulation)
HEDS . . . . . . Heavy Enamel Double Silk (Insulation)
HESV . . . . . . Heavy Enamel Silk Varnish (Insulation)
HEAF . . . . . . Heavy End Aviation Fuel
HEST . . . . . . HEAF (Heavy End Aviation Fuel) Emergency Service Tanks
HE . . . . Heavy Equipment
HET . . . . Heavy Equipment Transporter
HFA . . . . Heavy Field Artillery
HFS . . . . Heavy Flushing Spray
ARH . . . . Heavy-Hull Repair Ship (Navy symbol)
HH . . . . Heavy Hydrogen
HILAC . . . . . . Heavy-Ion Linear Accelerator (AEC)
HIS . . . . Heavy Ion Source
HLH . . . . Heavy-Lift Helicopter
HLHS . . . . . . Heavy-Lift Helicopter System
HLS . . . . Heavy Lift System
HLS . . . . Heavy Logistics System
HMG . . . . . . Heavy Machine Gun
ARM . . . . Heavy Machinery Repair Ship (Navy symbol)
HM . . . . Heavy Maintenance (Ordnance)
HMED . . . . . . Heavy Military Electronics Department
HM . . . . Heavy Mobile
HOA . . . . Heavy Observation Aircraft
HORSE . . . . . . Heavy Operational Repair Squadron Engineer (Air Force)
HPI . . . . Heavy Positive Ion
HPN . . . . Heavy Primary Nuclei
HRA . . . . Heavy Replaceable (or Replacement) Assembly
H. . . . . Heavy Sea (Weather reports)
HSCC . . . . . . Heavy Specialized Carriers Conference
HTT . . . . Heavy Tactical Transport
HT . . . . Heavy Tank
HW . . . . Heavy Wall
HW . . . . Heavy Water
HWCTR . . . . . Heavy-Water Components Test Reactor
HWGCR . . . . . Heavy Water-Moderated Gas-Cooled Reactor
HWOCR . . . . . Heavy Water-Moderated Organic-Cooled Reactor (AEC)
HWP . . . . Heavy Water Plant (AEC)
HAU. . . . . . . Hebrew Actors Union
HAF . . . . . . Hebrew Arts Foundation
HCAA . . . . . . Hebrew Christian Alliance of America
HFBA . . . . . . Hebrew Free Burial Association

HMBA . . . . . . Hebrew Master Bakers Association
HOD . . . . Hebrew Order of David
HRPA . . . . . . Hebrew Religious Protection Association of Greater New York
HTC . . . . Hebrew Teachers College (Massachusetts)
HUC . . . . Hebrew Union College (California, New York, Ohio)
HVWS . . . . . . Hebrew Veterans of the War with Spain
HYMA . . . . . . Hebrew Young Men's Association
HOA . . . . Hechalutz Organization of America
HCH. . . . . . . Hecht Company (NYSE symbol)
h . . . . Hecto (Prefix)
HA. . . . . Hectocotylized Arm
HG . . . . Hectogram(s)
HL . . . . Hectoliter
HM . . . . Hectometer (100 meters)
H to H . . . . . . Heel to Heel
HPI . . . . Heifer Project, Incorporated
H. . . . . Height
HAA . . . . Height Above Airport
HOB. . . . . . . Height (Depth) of Burst
HETP . . . . . . Height Equivalent to a Theoretical Plate
HETS . . . . . . Height Equivalent to a Theoretical Stage
HE . . . . Height of Eye
HF . . . . Height Finding (RADAR)
HIE . . . . Height Integration Equipment
HL . . . . Height-Length
HOC . . . . Height Overlap Coverage (RADAR)
HR . . . . Height Range (RADAR)
HRI . . . . Height-Range Indicator (Electronics)
HRIO . . . . . . Height-Range Indicator Operator
HRF . . . . Height Ranger Finder
HSD . . . . Height Sensing Device
HTSUP . . . . . . Height Supervisor (RADAR)
HT . . . . Height of Target
HT . . . . Height Technician (Air Force)
HT . . . . Height Telling (RADAR)
HTS . . . . Height-Telling Surveillance
HTU . . . . Height of Transfer
HVD. . . . . . . Height Velocity Diagram
HNW . . . . . . Hein Werner Corporation (NYSE symbol)
HNZ . . . . Heinz (H. J.) Company (NYSE symbol)
HIA . . . . Held in Abeyance
HC . . . . Held Covered or Hold Covered
HSW . . . . Helena Southwestern R. R. (AAR code)
HC . . . . Helene Curtis Industries, Inc. (NYSE symbol)
HCC . . . . Heliax Coaxial Cable
HAS. . . . . . . Helical Antenna System
HFP . . . . Helical Flight Path
HSLWI . . . . . . Helical Spring Lock Washer Institute
HWI . . . . Helical Washer Institute
H. . . . . Helicopter (Navy symbol) (Obsolete)
H . . . . Helicopter (When the second letter or only letter) (Designation for all US military aircraft)
HAS. . . . . . . Helicopter Air Service
HAMD . . . . . . Helicopter Ambulance Medical Detachment
HELASRON . . . . Helicopter Antisubmarine Squadron
HAX . . . . Helicopter Armored Experiment
HAA . . . . Helicopter Association of America
HATS . . . . . . Helicopter Attack System
HAS . . . . Helicopter Avionics System (Air Force)
HBS . . . . Helicopter Blade Slap
HC . . . . Helicopter Council
HDC. . . . . . . Helicopter Direction Center
HELP . . . . . . Helicopter Electronic Landing Path (Army)
HXBT . . . . . . Helicopter Expendable Bathythermograph (NOO)
HEAP . . . . . . Helicopter Extended Area Platform
HGMS . . . . . . Helicopter Gravity-Measuring System (Naval Oceanographic Office)
HIR . . . . Helicopter Instrument Rules
HLZ . . . . Helicopter Landing Zone
HLR . . . . Helicopter LASER Range-Finder
HOP. . . . . . . Helicopter Operations
HOTAC . . . . . Helicopter Optical Tracking and Control
HEPCAT . . . . . Helicopter Pilot Control and Training
HELIPATH . . . . Helicopter Position and Terrain Height
HELITEAM. . . . Helicopter Team
HUP . . . . Helicopter Utility (Piasecki)
HUS. . . . . . . Helicopter Utility Squadron
HUTRON . . . . Helicopter Utility Squadron
HVR . . . . Helicopter Visual Rules
HOR . . . . Heliocentric Orbit Rendezvous
HG . . . . Heliogram

HPOT	Helipotentiometer
He	Helium (Chemical element)
HC	Helium Circulation (System)
HFL	Helium Fill Line
HLD	Helium Leak Detector
HL	Helium Level
HNGL	Helium Neon Gas LASER
HNL	Helium Neon LASER
HPV	Helium Pressure Vessel
HR	Helium Rebottled (System)
HRC	Helium Research Center
HUSTLE	Helium Underwater Speech Translating Equipment
HPSA	Hellenic Philatelic Society of America
HLR	Heller (Walter E.) and Company (NYSE symbol)
GHH	Helme (George W.) Company (NYSE symbol)
HP	Helmerich & Payne, Inc. (NYSE symbol)
HMD	Helmet-Mounted Display
HOPS	Helmet-Mounted Optical Projection System
HELPS	Helmet-Position Sensing System
HFE	Helmholtz Free Energy
HRT	Helmholtz Reciprocal Theorem
HAF	Helms Athletic Foundation
HELP	Help Establish Lasting Peace
HHS	Helpers of the Holy Souls (Roman Catholic women's religious order)
HANA	Helvetia Association of North America
HCT	Hematocrit (Medicine)
HRA	Hemispherical Reflective Antenna
HB	Hemoglobin
HGB	Hemoglobin
HDN	Hemolytic Disease of Newborn
H & E	Hemotoxylin and Eosin (Histology)
HS	Hemstitched
H	Hence
HCJC	Henderson County Junior College (Texas)
HSTC	Henderson State Teachers College (Arkansas)
H	Henry (Unit of measurement) (Electricity)
HFCC	Henry Ford Community College (Michigan)
HTY	Henry Holt & Company (NYSE symbol)
H/M	Henry per Meter
HGO	Hepatic Glucose Output (Physiology)
HCP	Hepatocatalase Peroxidase
HGA	Heptagonal Games Association
HMN	Heptamethyl Nonane (Fuel)
HMTS	Her Majesty's Telegraph Ship
HQCS	Heraldic Quality Control System
HC	Heralds' College (British)
HSA	Herb Society of America
HEHO	Herbert Hoover National Historic Site
HPC	Hercules Powder Company (NYSE symbol)
HT	Herd Test
HERDET	Hereby Detached from Duty Assigned (Military)
H & E	Heredity and Environment
HAP	Heredopathia Atactica Polyneuritiformis
HOH	Hereford Otter Hounds
H	Heres (Heir)
HW	Herewith (Enclosures)
HCG	Hermanas Catequistas Guadalupanas (Roman Catholic women's religious order)
HPS	Hermetic Pivoting Seal
HSB	Hermetically Sealed Bushing
HIG	Hermetically Sealed, Integrating Gyros
HSZD	Hermetically Sealed Zener Diode
HNP	Herniated Nucleus Pulposus (Medicine)
H	Heroin (Slang)
HMC	Heroin, Morphine and Cocaine (Mixture) (Slang)
HTV	Herpes-Type Virus
HL	Herpetologists' League
HHE	Herringer-Hulster Effect
HSY	Hershey Chocolate Corporation (NYSE symbol)
HRZ	Hertz Corporation (NYSE symbol)
HES	Hess Oil & Chemical Corporation (NYSE symbol)
HAIC	Hetero-Atom-In-Context
HTN	Heterodyne
HMD	Heterodyne Matrix Detector
HJD	Heterojunction Device
HBL	Heublein, Inc. (NYSE symbol)
HEW	Hewitt-Robins, Inc. (NYSE symbol)
HP	Hewlett-Packard Company
HWP	Hewlett-Packard Company (NYSE symbol)
HAN	Hex Aluminum Nut
HHES	Hex Head Electrical Squib

HHS	Hex Head Squib
HC	Hexachlorethane
AT-7	Hexachlorophene
HETP	Hexaethyltetraphosphate (Chemical)
HFIP	Hexafluoroisopropanol (Chemistry)
HFPO	Hexafluoropropylene Oxide
HTH	Hexagon Tungsten Honeycomb
HCP	Hexagonal Close-Packed (Crystal structure)
HEXHD	Hexagonal Head
HMTA	Hexamethanetetramine
HMTT	Hexamethyl Trithione
HPT	Hexamethylphosphorsauretrimide
HMT	Hexamethyltetramine
HNM	Hexanitro Mannite
HNS	Hexanitrostilbene (High explosive)
HDP	Hexose Diphosphate
HMP	Hexosemonophosphate
HDN	Heyden Newport Chemical Corporation (NYSE symbol)
HMS	Hiarachial Memory Storage (Data processing)
HJC	Hibbing Junior College (Minnesota)
HIE	Hibernation Information Exchange (Navy)
Hi	Hiburnium
H	Hic (Here)
HIS	Hic Iacet Sepulters (Here Lies Buried)
HJ	Hic Jacet (Here Lies)
HJS	Hic Jacet Sepultus (Here Lies Buried)
HRIP	Hic Requiescit in Pace (Here Rests in Peace)
HSE	Hic Sepultus Est (Here Lies Buried)
HS	Hic Situs (Laid Here)
HHA	Hickory Handle Association
HCI	Hierarchically Classified Index
H	High
HIDE	High-Absorption Integrated Defense Electromagnetic Warfare System
HIAC	High Accuracy (RADAR)
HARDTS	High-Accuracy RADAR Transmission System
HATS	High-Accuracy Targeting Subsystem
HAV	High-Accuracy Voltmeter
HA	High Altitude
HAATC	High Altitude Air Traffic Control
HIBAL	High Altitude Balloon
HAB	High Altitude Bombing (Military)
HICAT	High Altitude Clear Air Turbulence (Aviation)
HADOPAD	High-Altitude Delayed Opening Parachute Actuation Device
HAD	High-Altitude Density (Sounding rocket)
HAD	High-Altitude Diagnostic (Unit) (Rocket launcher)
HALCON	High-Altitude Long-Focus Convergent Mapping System
HALO	High Altitude, Low Opening (Parachute)
HAMP	High-Altitude Measurement Probe
HANDS	High-Altitude Nuclear Detection Studies (National Bureau of Standards)
HANE	High-Altitude Nuclear Explosion
HAO	High Altitude Observatory (Boulder, Colorado) (National Bureau of Standards)
HAPPE	High-Altitude Particle Experiment (NASA)
HAP	High-Altitude Platform
HARA	High-Altitude RADAR Altimeter Antenna
HARC	High-Altitude RADAR Controller
HARIS	High-Altitude Radiological Instrumentation System
HARP	High-Altitude Relay Point
HARP	High-Altitude Research Project (Military)
HARP	High-Altitude Rocket Probe (Army)
HAS	High-Altitude Sampler
HASP	High-Altitude Sampling Plane
HASP	High-Altitude Sounding Program (Navy)
HASP	High-Altitude Sounding Projectile
HASTI	High-Altitude Strike Indicator
HAT	High-Altitude Target
HATS	High-Altitude Terrain Contour Data Sensor
HAIRS	High-Altitude Test and Evaluation of Infrared Sources
HATS	High-Altitude Test Stand
HATV	High-Altitude Test Vehicle
HAT	High-Altitude Testing (Sounding rocket)
HAT	High-Altitude Transmitter
HA	High-Angle
HBP	High Blood Pressure (Medicine)
HB	High Boilers
HC	High Capacity
HICAPCOM	High Capacity Communication system
HC	High Carbon (Steel)
HCHC	High Carbon, High Chrome
HCS	High Carbon Steel
HCSHT	High Carbon Steel, Heat-Treated

HCR	High Chief Ranger (Ancient Order of Foresters)
HC	High Church
HICOM	High Command
HC	High Commissioner
HICOG	High Commissioner for Germany
HICOM	High Commissioner, Germany
HICOMRY	High Commissioner of Ryukyu Islands
HICOMTERPACIS	High Commissioner Trust Territory, Pacific Islands
HC	High-Compression
HCL	High Cost of Living (Slang)
HCJB	High Court Junior Beadle (Ancient Order of Foresters)
HCJW	High Court Junior Woodward (Ancient Order of Foresters)
HCJ	High Court of Justice
HCS	High Court Secretary (Ancient Order of Foresters)
HCSB	High Court Senior Beadle (Ancient Order of Foresters)
HCSW	High Court Senior Woodward (Ancient Order of Foresters)
HCT	High Court Treasurer (Ancient Order of Foresters)
HCD	High Current Density
HCD	High Current Diode
HCI	High Current Inductor
HDR	High Definition RADAR
HD	High Density
HIDAN	High Density Air Navigation
HDATZ	High Density Air Traffic Zone
HDDS	High-Density Data System
HDDR	High-Density Digital Recording
HDEP	High-Density Electronic Packaging
HDL	High-Density Lipoproteins (Medicine)
HDMS	High-Density Memory System
HDPS	High-Density Power Supply
HDP	High Detonation Pressure
HDIP	High Dose Immune Paralysis
HE	High Efficiency
HEA	High-Efficiency Antireflection (Coating)
HEPA	High Efficiency Particulate Air
HEC	High Emission Cathode
HEBS	High Energy Battery System
HEC	High-Energy Chemistry
HEEB	High-Energy Electrolyte Battery
HEED	High-Energy Electron Diffraction
HEF	High Energy Forming
HEF	High Energy Fuel (Air Force)
HEGR	High Energy Gamma Ray
HELB	High Energy LASER Beam
HELS	High Energy LASER System
HELP	High Energy Lightweight Propellant
HELO	High Energy Liquid Oxidizer
HENRE	High Energy Neutron Reactions Experiment (AEC)
HEOB	High Energy Organic Battery
HEOEBS	High Energy Organic Electrolyte Battery System
HEP	High Energy Particle
HEP	High Energy Phosphate (Biochemistry)
HEP	High Energy Physics
HEPL	High Energy Physics Laboratory (Stanford University)
HEPDEX	High Energy Proton Detection Experiment
HERF	High Energy Rate Forging (Metalworking)
HERF	High Energy Rate Forming
HER	High Energy Ray
HESO	High Energy Solid Oxidizer
HETS	High Energy Transfer Stage
HEUS	High Energy Upper Stage (NASA)
HEAT	High Enthalpy Arc Tunnel
HETS	High Environment Test System (Air Force)
HE	High Explosive
HEAA	High Explosive, Antiaircraft (Shell)
HEAT	High Explosive Antitank (Projectile)
HEAP	High Explosive Armor-Piercing (Projectile)
HEDS	High Explosive, Discarding Sabot
HEI	High Explosive Incendiary
HEIT	High Explosive Incendiary (Shell) Traced (i.e., fitted with tracer)
HEP	High Explosive Plastic
HEP-T	High Explosive Plastic Tracer (Military)
HERJ	High Explosive Ramjet (Rocketry)
HERA	High Explosive Rocket Assisted
HES	High Explosive Spotting
HET	High Explosive (Shell) Traced (i.e., fitted with tracer)
HEWH	High Explosive Warhead
HI-FI	High-Fidelity (Usually, in reference to home sound-reproducing equipment)
HFI	High Fidelity Institute
HFSV	High Flow Shutoff Valve

HFBR	High Flux Beam Reactor (AEC)
HFIR	High Flux Isotope Reactor (AEC)
HFR	High Flux Reactor (Netherlands)
HF	High Frequency (Electronics)
HFAA	High-Frequency Airborne Antenna
HFC	High-Frequency Choke
HFC	High-Frequency Correction
HFC	High-Frequency Current
HFDF	High-Frequency Direction Finder
HUFF-DUFF	High-Frequency Direction Finder
HDF	High-Frequency Direction Finding
HF/DF	High-Frequency Direction Finding (Electronics)
HIFAR	High-Frequency Fixed Array RADAR
HFF	High-Frequency Furnace
HFJ	High-Frequency Jammer
HFO	High-Frequency Oscillator
HFRT	High-Frequency Radio Transmitter
HFR	High-Frequency Resistor
HFT	High-Frequency Transceiver
HFX	High-Frequency Transceiver
HFWA	High-Frequency Wave Analyzer
HGA	High Gain Antenna
HGL	High Gain Link
HIGH GASSER	High Geographic Aero-Space Search RADAR
HG	High German (language, speech, etc.)
HGL	High Go Low Test
HGPS	High Grade Plow Steel
HGR	High Group Receiving
HGT	High Group Transmitting
HHV	High Heat Value
HI-HICAT	High, High Altitude Clear Air Turbulence (Aviation)
HI	High Impact
HIB	High Impedance Bridge
HIF	High Impedance Follower
HIBEX	High Impulse Booster Experiments
HIRS	High-Impulse Retrorocket System
HII	High Input Impedance
HIST	High Input Shock Test
HI	High Intensity
HIALS	High-Intensity Approach Lighting System (Airport runways)
HIFI	High-Intensity Food Irradiator
HIL	High Intensity Light
HIM	High Intensity Microphone
HIN	High Intensity Noise
HING	High Intensity Noise Generator
HIRDL	High-Intensity Radiation Development Laboratory
HIRD	High-Intensity Radiation Device
HIRF	High-Intensity Reciprocity Failure
HIRL	High-Intensity Runway Lights (Aviation)
HISS	High Intensity Sound Simulator (or System)
HISE	High Interference Signalling Environment
HIPR	High Internal Phase Ratio
HLM	High Latitude Mode
HLO	High Latitude Operation
HL	High Level
HLFM	High Level Flux Monitor
HIFOR	High-Level Forecast (Meteorology)
HLL	High Level Language
HLM	High Level Mixer
HLRM	High Level Radio Modulator
HLSE	High Level, Single Ended
HLTL	High-Level Transistor Logic
HLTTL	High-Level Transistor Translator Logic
HLF	High Loss Ferrite
HMF	High Magnetic Field
HMP	High Melting Point
HMGF	High Modulus Glass Fiber
HMW	High Molecular Weight
HNA	High Nickel Alloy
HO	High Oblique (Aerospace)
HOBS	High Orbital Bombardment System
HOC	High Output Current
HOP	High Oxygen Pressure
HP	High Pass (Electronics)
HPF	High Pass Filter
HPN	High Pass Network
HP	High Performance
HPAS	High Performance Adhesive System
HPAG	High Performance Air-to-Ground
HPD	High Performance Drone

HIPEG	High Performance External Gun
HPIS	High Performance Insulation System
HPI	High Performance Interceptor
HIPERNAS	High Performance Navigation System
HPC	High Point College (North Carolina)
HPTD	High Point, Thomasville & Denton R. R. (AAR code)
HPR	High Polymer Rheology
HPT	High Pot Tester
HP	High Potency
HP	High Power
HIPAR	High Power Acquisition RADAR
HPA	High Power Amplifier
HPDLRL	High Power Diffraction Limited Raman LASER
HPF	High Power Field (Microscopy)
HPG	High Power Generator
HPIR	High Power Illuminator RADAR
HPJ	High Power Jammer
HPK	High Power Klystron
HPKA	High Power Klystron Amplifier
HPL	High Power LASER
HPSD	High Power Switching Device
HPV	High Power Veractor
HH	High-Powered, Nondirectional Radio Homing Beacon (Navigation)
RA	High-Powered Radio Range (Adcock)
RL	High-Powered Radio Range (Loop radiators)
HIRAN	High Precision Short Range Navigation
HP	High Pressure (Turbines)
HPA	High Pressure Air
HPAA	High Pressure Air Accumulator
HP	High Pressure Cylinder (Especially, a locomotive cylinder)
HPHD	High Pressure High Density
HPH	High Pressure Hose
HPIP	High Pressure Intensifier Pump
HPJ	High Pressure Jet
HPLJ	High-Pressure Liquid Jet
HPLF	High-Pressure Low-Flow
HPMV	High Pressure Mercury Vapor
HPO	High Pressure Oxygen
HPOX	High Pressure Oxygen
HPS	High Pressure Steam (Technical drawings)
HPT	High Pressure Test
HPV	High Pressure Valve
HP	High Priest
HPS	High Protein Supplement
H-P	High-Purity
HQC	High "Q" Circuit
HQC	High "Q" Coil
HQTC	High "Q" Tuned Circuit
HQES	High Quality Exitaxial Silicon
HQS	High Quality Silicon
HIRAC	High Random Access
HRPC	High Range Pressure Control
HRH	High Rate Heat
HRT	High-Rate Telemetry (NASA)
HRL	High Refraction Layer
HRR	High Reliability Relay
HRIS	High Repetition Illuminator System
HRL	High Repetition LASER
HRLIS	High Repetition LASER Illuminating System
HRLI	High Repetition LASER Illuminator
HRLS	High Repetition LASER System
HR	High Resistance
HRD	High Resolution Display
HRES	High Resolution Electronic System
HIHAT	High Resolution Hemispherical Reflector Antenna Technique
HRIR	High-Resolution Infrared-Radiometer
HRR	High Resolution RADAR
HRS	High Resolution System
HRT	High Resolution Tracker
HRTS	High Risk Test Site
HR	High Run
HS	High School
HEP	High-School Equivalency Program
HSEF	High School Evangelism Fellowship
HSGP	High School Geography Project
HSR	High School Percentile Rank
HSPT	High School Placement Test
HSI	High Solar Intensity
HS	High Speed
HAM	High-Speed Automatic Monitor
HSBP	High-Speed Bench Press

HSBR	High-Speed Bombing RADAR
HSB	High-Speed Bus
HSC	High-Speed Carry
HSDA	High-Speed Data Acquisition
HS-DARS	High-Speed - Data Acquisition and Reduction System
HSDL	High-Speed Data Link
HSDM	High-Speed Die Mounter
HSDT	High-Speed Distributor Transmitter
HSFS	High-Speed Flight Station (National Aeronautics and Space Administration)
HSFF	High-Speed Force Feed
HSGT	High-Speed Ground Transportation
HISTEP	High-Speed Integrated Space Transportation Evaluation Program
HITS	High-Speed Integrated Test System
HSL	High-Speed Launch
HSL	High-Speed Logic
HSMS	High-Speed Microwave Switch
HSPA	High-Speed Parallel Adder
HSP	High-Speed Printer (Data processing)
HSP	High-Speed Pulse
HSR	High-Speed Reader (Data processing)
HSR	High-Speed Relay
HSRO	High-Speed Repetitive Operation
HSRP	High-Speed Rotary Prism
HSS	High-Speed Steel
HSSG	High-Speed Symbol Generator
AGSS	High-Speed Target Submarine (Navy symbol)
HST	High-Speed Telemetry
HSTT	High-Speed Test Track
APD	High-Speed Transport (Navy symbol)
HSS	High Spread Shears
HSI	High Strand Intensity
HSA	High Strength Adhesive
HSLA	High-Strength Low-Alloy (Steel)
HSTRA	High Strength Thermal Resistant Alloy
HSCR	High Sub-Chief Ranger (Ancient Order of Foresters)
HT	High Temperature
HTA	High Temperature Adhesive
HTA	High Temperature Alloy
HTC	High Temperature Coil
HTGR	High-Temperature Gas-Cooled Reactor (AEC)
HTGR-CX	High-Temperature Gas Reactor Critical Experiment
HTH	High Temperature Heater
HTL	High Temperature Lacquer
HTLTR	High-Temperature Lattice Test Reactor
HTM	High Temperature Materials
HTRDA	High Temperature Reactor Development Associates
HTR	High Temperature Resistor
HTW	High-Temperature Water
HTW	High Temperature Wire
HTCI	High Tensile Cast Iron
HTS	High Tensile Steel
HTS	High Tensile Strength
HT	High Tension
HTP	High Test Hydrogen-Peroxide
HTH	High-Test Hypochlorite
HTL	High Threshold Logic
HT	High Tide
HTL	High Turbulence Level
HVE	High Vacuum Environment
HVES	High Vacuum Evaporation System
HVE	High Vacuum Evaporator
HIVOS	High Vacuum Orbital Simulator
HVP	High Vacuum Pump
HVR	High-Vacuum Rectifier
HIVAC	High Value Asset Control
HV	High Velocity
HVAR	High Velocity Aircraft Rocket
HVAT	High Velocity Antitank (Projectile)
HVAP	High Velocity, Armor-Piercing (Projectile)
HVAPDS	High Velocity, Armor-Piercing, Discarding Sabot (Projectile)
HVTP	High Velocity, Target Practice (Projectile)
HVTPDS	High Velocity, Target Practice Discarding Sabot (Projectile)
HVDF	High and Very-High-Frequency Direction Finding
HV	High Voltage
HVB	High Voltage Bias
HVC	High Voltage Connector
HVDC	High Voltage Direct Current
HVE	High Voltage Engineering Corporation (NYSE symbol)
HVG	High Voltage Gradient
HVL	High Voltage Laboratory (MIT)

HVMVI	High Voltage Mercury Vapor Isolator
HVPS	High Voltage Power Supply
HVP	High Voltage Pump
HVR	High Voltage Rectifier
HVR	High Voltage Relay
HVRL	High Voltage Research Laboratory (MIT)
HVR	High Voltage Resistor
HVSCR	High-Voltage Selenium Cartridge Rectifier
HVS	High Voltage Switch
HVST	High Voltage Switching Transistor
HVT	High Voltage Termination
HVT	High Voltage Tester
HVT	High Voltage Transformer
HVW	High Voltage Waveform
HVW	High Voltage Wire
HV	High Volume
HW	High Water
HWF & C	High Water Full and Change
HWQ	High Water Inequality
HWI	High Water Interval
HWL	High Water Line (Technical drawings)
HWM	High Water Mark (Maps and charts)
HWOST	High Water Ordinary Spring Tides (Maps and charts)
HWQ	High Water Quadrature
HDD	Higher Dental Diploma (British)
HEA	Higher Education Act
HEFA	Higher Education Facilities Act
HEGIS	Higher Education General Information Survey (US Office of Education)
HEOC	Higher Education Opportunities Committee
HEO	Higher Executive Order
HHW	Higher High Water
HHWI	Higher High Water Interval
HLW	Higher Low Water
HLWI	Higher Low Water Interval
HNC	Higher National Certificate (British)
HND	Higher National Diploma (British)
HSC	Higher School Certificate (British)
HCF	Highest Common Factor (Mathematics)
HPF	Highest Possible Frequency (Electronics)
HPF	Highest Probable Frequency
HRA	Highest Rank Aboard
HIEAT	Highest Temperature Equaled for All Time (Meteorology)
HIEFM	Highest Temperature Equaled for the Month (Meteorology)
HIESE	Highest Temperature Equaled So Early (Meteorology)
HIESL	Highest Temperature Equaled So Late (Meteorology)
HIXAT	Highest Temperature Exceeded for All Time (Meteorology)
HIXFM	Highest Temperature Exceeded for the Month (Meteorology)
HIXSE	Highest Temperature Exceeded So Early (Meteorology)
HIXSL	Highest Temperature Exceeded So Late (Meteorology)
HUCR	Highest Useful Compression Ratio (Aerospace)
HJC	Highland Junior College (Kansas)
HLI	Highland Light Infantry (British)
HPJC	Highland Park Junior College (Later, Highland Park College) (Michigan)
HR	Highland Railway (British)
HEOS	Highly Eccentric Orbit Satellite
HOPE	Highly-Instrumented Orbiting Primate Experiment
HIP	Highly Ionized Plasma
HP	Highly Purified
HQ	Highly Qualified
HUGO	Highly Unusual Geophysical Operation (A meteorological research vehicle)
H/W	Highway
HY-COM	Highway Communications
HELP	Highway Emergency Locating Plan
HEEP	Highway Engineering Exchange Program (IBM)
HRB	Highway Research Board
HRIS	Highway Research Information Service (of Highway Research Board)
HSRC	Highway Safety Research Center (University of Michigan)
HSRI	Highway Safety Research Institute (University of Michigan)
HTC	Highway Traffic Control
HWTC	Highway Traffic Control
HTSC	Highway Traffic Safety Center (Michigan State University)
HTO	Highway Transportation Officer (Army)
HD	Hilda Doolittle (Pen name of American poet, 1886-1961)
HLL	Hill Corporation (NYSE symbol)
HLNE	Hillsboro & Northeastern Railway Company (AAR code)
HLT	Hilton Hotels Corporation (NYSE symbol)
HMS	Hind Mazdoor Sabha (India)
HOKS	Hind Oil Kamger Sabha (India)
HJC	Hinds Junior College (Mississippi)
HBI	Hindustan Bible Institute
HAC	Hines Administrative Center (VA)
HL	Hinge Line (Technical drawings)
HPLR	Hinge Pillar (Technical drawings)
HPB	Hinged Plotting Board
HDT	Hi-Pot Dwell Time
HC	Hippocampal
HIR	Hiram Walker-Gooderham & Worts, Ltd. (NYSE symbol)
HP	Hire Purchase
HFWF	Hired Farm Working Force
HRT	Hiring, Retention, and Tenure (of college professors)
HPCA	Hiroshima Peace Center Associates
HB	His Beatitude or His Blessedness
HBM	His (or Her) Britannic Majesty
HBMS	His (or Her) Britannic Majesty's Service
HCM	His (or Her) Catholic Majesty
HE	His Eminence
HEH	His (or Her) Exalted Highness (Term applied only to personages of British India)
HE	His Excellency
HG	His (or Her) Grace
HGDH	His (or Her) Grand Ducal Highness
HHMS	His Hellenic Majesty's Ship
HH	His (or Her) Highness
HH	His Holiness
HIH	His (Her) Imperial Highness
HIJMS	His Imperial Japanese Majesty's Ship
HIM	His (Her) Imperial Majesty
HM	His (or Her) Majesty
HMA	His (or Her) Majesty's Airship (British)
HMAS	His (or Her) Majesty's Australian Ship
HMBS	His Majesty's British Ship
HMCS	His (or Her) Majesty's Canadian Ship
HMCS	His (or Her) Majesty's Civil Service
HMC	His (or Her) Majesty's Customs
HMF	His (or Her) Majesty's Forces
HMG	His (or Her) Majesty's Government
HMGB	His (or Her) Majesty's Gun-Boat
HMH	His (or Her) Majesty's Household
HMIMF	His (or Her) Majesty's Indian Military Forces
HMIN	His (or Her) Majesty's Indian Navy
HMI	His (or Her) Majesty's Inspector
HML	His (or Her) Majesty's Lieutenant
HMS	His (or Her) Majesty's Service
HMS	His (or Her) Majesty's Ship
HMSO	His (or Her) Majesty's Stationery Office
HMS	His (or Her) Majesty's Steamer
HMT	His (or Her) Majesty's Trawler
HMV	His Master's Voice (Phonograph records)
HRH	His (or Her) Royal Highness
HSH	His (or Her) Serene Highness (Used for certain Continental European princes or princesses)
HSM	His (or Her) Serene Majesty
HIUS	Hispanic Institute in the United States
HSA	Hispanic Society of America
HISSBI	Hispunan Serikat Buruh Indonesia (Federation of Indonesian Trade Unions)
HIA	Histadruth Ivrith of America
HL	Histocompatibility Locus
HAVOC	Histogram Average Ogive Calculator
HABS	Historic American Buildings Survey (Library of Congress)
HC	Historical Commission
HCSBC	Historical Commission, Southern Baptist Convention
HD	Historical Development
HD	Historical Division (Air Force)
HERO	Historical Evaluation and Research Organization
HMC	Historical Manuscripts Commission (British)
HMPMA	Historical Motion Picture Milestones Association
HSEAD	Historical Society of Early American Decoration
HSERC	Historical Society of the Evangelical & Reformed Church
HSEUBC	Historical Society of the Evangelical United Brethren Church
HS	Historical Survey
HES	History of Education Society
H & P	History and Physical (Examination) (Medicine)
HPI	History of Present Illness
HSS	History of Science Society
HIS	Hit Indicator System
HSD	Hit Scoring Device
HW	Hit Wicket
HIPAC	Hitachi Parametron Automatic Computer
HTR	Hitachi Training Reactor (Japan)
H	Hits (Baseball)
HDMS	Hizb Dastur Mustaghil Somalia (Somali Independent Constitution Party)

HDM .... Hizbia Dighill e Mirifle (Somali Political Party)
HSL'S ...... Hlinkova Slovenska L'udova Strana
HCA .... Hobby Clubs of America
HGA .... Hobby Guild of America
HHBLG ..... Hobby Horse Brigade of the Legion of Guardsmen
HIAA ...... Hobby Industry Association of America
HBS .... Hoboken Shore R. R. (AAR code)
HA .... Hoc Anno (This Year)
HL .... Hoc Loco (In This Place)
HLS .... Hoc Loco Situs (Laid in This Place)
HM .... Hoc Mense (In This Month)
HMFF ..... Hoc Monumentum Fieri Fecit (Caused This Monument to Be Made)
HMP .... Hoc Monumentum Posuit (He Erected This Monument)
HQ .... Hoc Quaere (Look for This; See This)
HS .... Hoc Sensu (In This Sense)
HT .... Hoc Tempore (At This Time)
HT .... Hoc Titulo (In, or Under, This Title)
HC .... Hockey Club
HCD .... Hoffman Core Driver
HEC .... Hoffman Electronics Corporation (NYSE symbol)
HEPP ...... Hoffman Evaluation Program and Procedure (Hoffman Electronics
            Corporation)
HIFC ...... Hog Intrinsic Factor Concentrate
HMA ...... Hoist Manufacturers Association
HMI .... Hoist Manufacturers Institute
HAG ...... Hold for Arrival of Goods
HF .... Hold Fire (Military)
HFM ...... Hold for Money (Business and trade)
HON ...... Hold Off Normal
HFR .... Hold for Release
HDC .... Holder in Due Course (Owner or holder of a negotiable instrument at
            some future time)
HAPI ...... Holding As Previously Instructed (Aviation)
H .... Holding Instructions Issued (Aviation)
HP .... Holding Pattern (Aviation)
H & R ..... Holding and Reconsignment (Military)
H & RP .... Holding and Reconsignment Point (Army)
HO .... Holdover (Theater)
HEP .... Hole-Electron Pair
HAL .... Holland-America Lines
HCEA ...... Holland Cheese Exporters Association
HLN .... Holland Furnace Company (NYSE symbol)
HSNY ...... Holland Society of New York
HEC .... Hollerith Electronic Computer
HE .... Hollis & Eastern R. R. (AAR code)
HADC ..... Holloman Air Development Center
HAFB ..... Holloman Air Force Base
HCT ...... Hollow Cathode Tube
HCC ...... Hollow Copper Conductor
HEB ...... Hollow Electron Beam
HKT ...... Hollow Kathode Tube
HM .... Hollow Metal (Technical drawings)
HMDBA ..... Hollow Metal Door and Buck Association
HMDF ...... Hollow Metal Door and Frame (Technical drawings)
HSRA ...... Hollow Shaft Rotary Actuator
HT .... Hollow Tile (Technical drawings)
HLO ...... Holly Oil Company (NYSE symbol)
HSA ...... Holly Society of America
HLY .... Holly Sugar Corporation (NYSE symbol)
HCC ...... Hollywood Comedy Club
HJC ...... Holmes Junior College (Mississippi)
HNI .... Holmes and Narver, Incorporated
Ho .... Holmium (Chemical element)
HLI .... Holmium LASER Illuninator
HAS ...... Holograph Assessment System
HLS ...... Holograph Letter Signed
HFAA ..... Holstein-Friesian Association of America
HDC ...... Holston Defense Corporation
HRW ...... Holt, Rinehart & Winston, Inc. (NYSE symbol)
HI .... Holton Inter-Urban R. R. (AAR code)
H .... Holy
HC .... Holy Communion
HC .... Holy Cross
HO .... Holy Day of Obligation
HFC ...... Holy Family College (California, Pennsylvania, Wisconsin)
HFS ...... Holy Family Seminary (Connecticut)
HG .... Holy Ghost
HNS ...... Holy Name Society
HRE ...... Holy Roman Emperor (or Empire)
HSG ...... Holy Shroud Guild
HJC ...... Holyoke Junior College (Massachusetts)

H .... Home
HAFO ..... Home Accounting and Finance Office
HA .... Home Address
HBDC ..... Home Base Development Committee (Navy)
HC .... Home Care
HCS ...... Home Civil Service (British)
HCSS ..... Home and Colonial School Society (British)
HD .... Home Defence (British)
HDR ...... Home Dockyard Regulations (Navy)
HEIB ..... Home Economists in Business
HF .... Home Fleet (British)
HF .... Home Forces (British Military)
HOFR ..... Home of Franklin D. Roosevelt and Vanderbilt Mansion National
            Historic Sites
HFIC ..... Home Furnishings Industry Committee
HG .... Home Guard (British)
HIDA ..... Home Improvement Dealers Association of America
HIPA ..... Home Improvement Products Association
HOJ ...... Home on Jamming
HLBB ..... Home Loan Bank Board
HMA ...... Home Manufacturers Association
HM .... Home Mission
HO .... Home Office (British)
HOLUA .... Home Office Life Underwriters Association
HOLC ..... Home Owners' Loan Corporation
HSC ...... Home Products Safety Council
HOR ...... Home of Record
HRS ...... Home Reunion Society (British)
HR .... Home Rule
HR .... Home Run (Baseball)
HS .... Home Secretary (British)
HOSTWOY ... Home of Selection and Completion of Travel Within One Year is
             Authorized (Military)
HVI ...... Home Ventilating Institute
HOMOCO.... Homemakers and Mothers Cooperatives, Inc.
HRO ...... Homes Registration Office
HM .... Homestake Mining Company (NYSE symbol)
HOME ..... Homestead National Monument
HAWK ..... Homing All the Way Killer (Small missile)
HB .... Homing Beacon (Aviation)
HCU ...... Homing Comparator Unit
HLG ...... Homing Level Gage
HOB ...... Homing on Offset Beacon
HOG ...... Homing Optical Guidance
HOGS ..... Homing Optical Guidance System
HOSS ..... Homing Optical System Survey
HT .... Homing Terrier
HAZEL .... Homogeneous Assembly Zero Energy (AERE)
HBC ...... Homogeneous Boundary Condition
HDE ...... Homogeneous Differential Equation
HRE ...... Homogeneous Reactor Equipment
HRT ...... Homogeneous Reactor Test
HTR ...... Homogeneous Thorium Reactor
HDD ...... Homopolar Disk Dynamo
HVA ...... Homovanillic Acid
HAA ...... Honduran-American Association
HFMF ..... Hone-Finish Monolithic Floor (Technical drawings)
HBA ...... Honest Ballot Association
HJ .... Honest John (A type of short range, unguided Army rocket)
HJL ...... Honest John Launcher
HJR ...... Honest John Rocket
HAP ...... Honeycomb Aluminum Panel
HCC ...... Honeycomb Corrugated Construction
HSAP ..... Honeycomb Sandwich Aluminum Panel
HSS ...... Honeycomb Supported Screen
HSJ ...... Honey-Combed Sandwich Joint
HARP ..... Honeywell Acoustic Research Project
HBC ...... Honeywell Business Computer
HON ...... Honeywell, Inc. (NYSE symbol) (Formerly, M-H)
HIG ...... Honeywell Integrating Gyro
HASHS .... Honeywell's Anti-Square Hat Society
HKA ...... Hong Kong Airways, Ltd.
HKSU ..... Hong Kong Seamen's Union
HMSO ..... Honolulu Magnetic and Seismological Observatory
HNU ...... Honolulu Oil Corporation (NYSE symbol)
H .... Honor
HD .... Honorable Discharge
HDCG ..... Honorable Discharge, Convenience of Government (Military)
HDCM ..... Honorable Discharge, Convenience of Man (Military)
HDDS ..... Honorable Discharge, Dependency Arising Since Enlistment (Military)
HDDP ..... Honorable Discharge, Dependency Existing Prior to Enlistment (Military)

HDEE .... Honorable Discharge, Expiration of Enlistment (Military)
HDMW ...... Honorable Discharge, Minors Enlisted w/o Consent, Under 18 at Discharge
HAR .... Honorary Air Reserve (Air Force)
HFRA .... Honorary Fellow of the Royal Academy
HRS .... Honorary Reserve Section
HRA .... Honorary Royal Academician (British)
HS .... Honorary Secretary
HSK .... Honorary Surgeon of the King
HC .... Honoris Causa (For the Sake of Honor)
HAC .... Honourable Artillery Company (British)
HEIC .... Honourable East India Company
HEICS ...... Honourable East India Company's Service (British)
HTT .... Hook Tongue Terminal
HKR .... Hooker Chemical Corporation (NYSE symbol)
HECC .... Hooker Electro-Chemical Company
HCB .... Hoopes Conductivity Bridge (Electronics)
HTW .... Hoosac Tunnel & Wilmington R. R. (AAR code)
HBB .... Hoover Ball & Bearing Company (NYSE symbol)
HGA .... Hop Growers of America
HOVI .... Hopewell Village National Historic Site
O .... Hora (Hour)
HHLR .... Horace Hardy Lestor Reactor
HML .... Horace Mann League of the USA
HS .... Horizon Scanner
HS .... Horizon Sensor
H .... Horizontal
HAD .... Horizontal Array Dipole
HAB .... Horizontal Axis Bearing
HAEH .... Horizontal Axis Electrical Hairspring
HAP .... Horizontal Axis Pivot
HB .... Horizontal Bands (on buoys, beacons)
HB .... Horizontal Bomber
HBM .... Horizontal Boring Mill
HCP .... Horizontal Candle Power
HCPS .... Horizontal Candle Power Seconds
HCL .... Horizontal Center Line
HCO .... Horizontal Control Operator (Military)
HCD .... Horizontal Correlation Distance
HDA .... Horizontal Danger Angle (Navigation)
HDP .... Horizontal Data Processing
HDF .... Horizontal Distributing Frame
HD .... Horizontal Drive
HDB .... Horizontal Dynamic Balancing
HDBA .... Horizontal Dynamic Balancing Adjustment
HER .... Horizontal Earth Rate
HE .... Horizontal Equivalent
HFV .... Horizontal Flight Vector
HIP .... Horizontal Injection Press
HL .... Horizontal Line
HLF .... Horizontal Line Frequency
HCG .... Horizontal Location of Center of Gravity
O .... Horizontal Opposed (Aircraft engine)
HOT .... Horizontal Output Transformer
HOT .... Horizontal Output Tube
HPM .... Horizontal Panel Mount
HP .... Horizontal Parallax (Navigation)
HPT .... Horizontal Plot Table
HP .... Horizontal Polarization
HORAD ...... Horizontal RADAR Display
HRL .... Horizontal Reference Line (Technical drawings)
HS .... Horizontal Shear
HSD .... Horizontal Situation Display
HSI .... Horizontal Situation Indicator
HSTS .... Horizontal Stabilizer Trim Setting
HSBA .... Horizontal Static Balancing Adjustment
HS .... Horizontal Stripes (as on buoys, beacons)
HSCA .... Horizontal Sweep Circuit Analyzer
HT .... Horizontal Tabulation
HTDU .... Horizontal Tactical Display Unit
HTD .... Horizontal Tactics Display
HTI .... Horizontal Tactics Indicator
HTO .... Horizontal Take-Off
HVSS .... Horizontal Volute Spring Suspension (Projectile)
H .... Horn
HGSW .... Horn Gap Switch
HNB .... Horn & Hardart Baking Company of New Jersey (American Stock Exchange symbol)
HIA .... Horological Institute of America
HC .... Hors Concours (Not Competing)
H .... Horse
HA .... Horse Artillery

HD .... Horse-Drawn
HDV .... Horse Drawn Vehicle
HG .... Horse Guards (British)
HP .... Horse Power
HT .... Horsed Transport (Military)
HCCA .... Horseless Carriage Club of America
HBPA .... Horsemen's Benevolent and Protective Association
HPH .... Horsepower-Hour
HP-HR ...... Horsepower-Hour
HPN .... Horsepower Nominal
HOBE .... Horseshoe Bend National Military Park
HA .... Horticultural Abstracts
HRI .... Horticultural Research Institute
HWNA .... Hosiery Wholesalers National Association
HOM .... Hoskins Manufacturing Company (NYSE symbol)
HAD .... Hospital Administrator (or Administration)
HA .... Hospital Apprentice (Navy rating)
HBSS .... Hospital Bureau of Standards and Supplies
HC .... Hospital Corps(man) (Navy rating)
HM .... Hospital Corpsman (Navy rating)
HESO .... Hospital Educational Services Officer
HEF .... Hospital Employees' Federation of Australia
HFDA .... Hospital Food Directors Association
HIPO .... Hospital Indicator for Physicians' Orders
HIA .... Hospital Industries' Association
H .... Hospital Plane (When suffixed to Navy plane designation)
HOSPRATS ... Hospital Rations (Navy)
HRS .... Hospital Reading Society
HR .... Hospital Recruit
HRET .... Hospital Research and Educational Trust
HSA .... Hospital Savings Association
AH .... Hospital Ship (Navy symbol)
HS .... Hospital Ship
HT .... Hospital Train
HTO .... Hospital Transfer Order
HCUND ...... Hospitality Committee for United Nations Delegations
HN .... Hospitalman (Nonrated enlisted man) (Navy)
HN .... Host Nation
HI .... Hostesses Internationales (French date service)
H .... Hostile (Military)
HUKP .... Hostile, Unknown, Faker, and Pending (Used in SAGE to designate certain tracks and raids)
HO .... Hostilities Only (Applied to men who joined for duration of war only) (British Navy) (World War II)
H .... Hot
HA .... Hot Air
HAV .... Hot Air Vulcanization
HBS .... Hot Blade Stripper
HCQ .... Hot Carrier Quad
HCT .... Hot Cathode Tube
HC .... Hot and Cold
HOTCE ...... Hot Critical Experiments (AEC)
HDG .... Hot Dip Galvinization
HEA .... Hot Electron Amplifier
HECTOR ..... Hot Enriched Carbon-Moderated Thermal Oscillator Reactor (British)
HERO .... Hot Experimental Reaction of O Power
HGB .... Hot Gas Bonder
HGG .... Hot Gas Generator
HGRF .... Hot Gas Radiating Facility
HGSE .... Hot Gas Soldering Equipment
HGTVC ...... Hot Gas Thrust Vector Control
HHN .... Hot Hydrogen Nozzle
HIP .... Hot Isostatic Pressure (Metals)
HKT .... Hot Kathode Tube
HLAS .... Hot Line Alert System
HMA .... Hot Melt Applicator
HP .... Hot Pack or Pad (Physical therapy)
HP .... Hot Pilot (An egotistic flying cadet) (Air Force slang)
HP .... Hot-Pressed (Paper)
HRS .... Hot Rolled Steel
HST .... Hot Shot Tunnel
HS .... Hot Spraying
HOSP .... Hot Springs National Park
HSP .... Hot Stamping Press
HS .... Hot Stuff (Slang)
HW .... Hot Water
HWC .... Hot Water Circulating (Technical drawings)
HWR .... Hot Water Return
HWS .... Hot Water Soluble
HWA .... Hot Wire Anemometer
HWEP .... Hot Wire Emissive Probe

HAA	Hotel Accountants Association of New York City
HCA	Hotel Corporation of America (NYSE symbol)
HCMA	Hotel Credit Managers Association
HGA	Hotel Greeters of America
HMGI	Hotel-Motel Greeters International
HREBIU	Hotel and Restaurant Employees and Bartenders International Union
HREU	Hotel and Restaurant Employees and Bartenders International Union
HSMA	Hotel Sales Management Association
HSF	Hotel Sundry Fund (Air Force)
HWO	Hotel Waldorf Astoria (American Stock Exchange symbol)
HH	Houdaille Industries, Inc. (NYSE symbol)
HA	Hour Angle (Navigation)
HAMS	Hour Angle of the Mean Sun (Navigation)
HATS	Hour Angle of the True Sun (Navigation)
HC	Hour Circle
HGD	Hourglass Device (Military decoration)
HD	Hourly Difference
H.	Hours
H	House
YHB	House Boat (Navy symbol)
HCIS	House Committee on Internal Security (Formerly, HUAC)
HC	House of Commons (British)
HCB	House of Commons Bill (British)
HC	House of Correction
HDI	House Dress Institute
H of IF	House of Ill Fame
HJR	House Joint Resolution
HJ Res	House Joint Resolution
HK	House of Keys (Isle of Man)
HL	House of Lords (British)
HOL	House of Lords (British)
HLC	House of Lords Cases (Law) (British)
HMI	House Magazine Institute
HMMFC	House Merchant Marine and Fisheries Committee
HO	House Officer
HP	House Physician
HR	House of Representatives
H Res	House Resolution, United States House of Representatives
HS	House Surgeon
HT	House Trailer
HUAC	House Un-American Activities Committee (Later, HCIS)
HB	Housebreaking
HHE	Household Economics Research Division (of ARS, Department of Agriculture)
HHE	Household Effects
HFC	Household Finance Corporation (NYSE symbol)
HHF	Household Furniture (Insurance)
HHG	Household Goods
HGCB	Household Goods Carriers' Bureau
HHGFAA	Household Goods Forwarders Association of America
HGWA	Household Goods for Warders Association
HPCGS	(Frank-Massy) Household Purchasing Characteristics Generating System (Marketing)
HP	Houses of Parliament (British)
HAA	Housing Assistance Administration (HUD)
HHFA	Housing and Home Finance Agency
HOPE	Housing Our People Economically
HASP	Houston Automatic Spooling Priority System (Data processing)
HB & T	Houston Belt & Terminal Railway Company
HBT	Houston Belt & Terminal Railway Company (AAR code)
HCEBT	Houston Cotton Exchange and Board of Trade
HOU	Houston Lighting & Power Company (NYSE symbol)
HOVE	Hovenweep National Monument
HOTRAN	Hover and Transition (Simulator)
HHC	Hovercraft-Helicopter Carrier
HRS	Hovering Rocket System
HCJC	Howard County Junior College (Texas)
HOJO	Howard Johnson (Restaurant chain) (Slang)
HJ	Howard Johnson Company (NYSE symbol)
HPC	Howard Payne College (Texas)
HRC	Howard Research Corporation
HOS	Howard Stores Corporation (NYSE symbol)
HOWT	Howard Terminal R. R. (AAR code)
HW	Howe Sound Company (NYSE symbol)
HMC	Howitzer Motor Carriage
HRSS	Hrvatska Republikanska Seljacka Stranka
HUTR	Hubbell Trading Post National Historic Site
HHH	Hubert Horatio Humphrey
HD	Hudson Bay Mining & Smelting Co., Ltd. (NYSE symbol)
HUBA	Hudson Bay R. R. (AAR code)
HETOC	Hudson-Essex-Terraplane Owners Club

HI	Hudson Institute
HDM	Hudson & Manhattan R. R. (AAR code)
HXR	Hudson & Manhattan R.R. (NYSE symbol)
HRDL	Hudson River Day Line R. R. (AAR code)
HBC	Hudson's Bay Company
HMO	Hueckel Molecular Orbitals
HARAS	Hughes Active RADAR Augmentation System
HACI	Hughes Aircraft Company, International Division
HAC	Hughes Aircraft Corporation
HCI	Hughes Communications International (Hughes Aircraft Company)
HDIV	Hughes Dynamic Imagery Viewer
HES	Hughes Earth Station
HELP	Hughes Emergency Locator Pack
HHEFG	Hughes Hall Effect Function Generator
HHEG	Hughes Hall Effect Generator
HIT	Hughes, Induced Turbulence
HUCO	Hughes NADGE Consortium
HPR	Hughes Photoelectric Reader
HPPS	Hughes Post Processor, Surveyor
HSCT	Hughes Satellite Communications Terminal
HSES	Hughes Satellite Earth Station
HTC	Hughes Tool Company
HTLT	Hughes Transportable Link Terminal
HUMID	Hughes Unit Malfunction Isolation Detector
HCV	Hull Check Valve
HCT	Hull Collector Tank
HF	Hull Filter
HG	Hull Gage
HM & E	Hull – Mechanical and Electrical
HPS	Hull Pressure Switch
HSS	Hull Seal Section
HSV	Hull Solenoid Valve
HA	Human Adaptability
HB	Human Being (Slang)
HBAVS	Human Betterment Association for Voluntary Sterilization
HCE	Human Caused Error
HCG	Human Chorionic Gonadotrophin (Endocrinology)
HCA	Human Component Analysis
HDD	Human Disorientation Device
HEF	Human Ecology Fund
HE	Human Engineering
HED	Human Engineering Data
HEI	Human Engineering Institute
HEL	Human Engineering Laboratory (Army)
HEP	Human Engineering Plan
HE	Human Enteric (Virology)
HER	Human Error Rate
HERAP	Human Error Research and Analysis Program
HEAT	Human Erythrocyte Agglutination Test
HF	Human Factors
HFE	Human Factors in Electronics
HFG	Human Factors Group
HFMS	Human Factors Measurement System
HFORL	Human Factors Operation Research Laboratory (Air Force)
HF & OR	Human Factors and Operations Research (Army)
HFR	Human Factors Research
HFS	Human Factors Society
HGH	Human Growth Hormone (Endocrinology)
HIF	Human Initiated Failure
HUMINT	Human Intelligence
HLH	Human Luteinizing Hormone
HL-A	Human Lymphocyte – Antigen (System for recognizing foreign tissue)
HK	Human Kidney
HMG	Human Menopausal Gonadotropin (Hormone)
HN	Human Nutrition Research Division (of ARS, Department of Agriculture)
HOT	Human Old Tuberculin
HPG	Human Pituitary Gonadotrophin
HPL	Human Placental Lactogen
HRAF	Human Relations Area Files
HR	Human Reliability
HRP	Human Reliability Program
HRA	Human Resources Administration (New York City)
HRD	Human Resources Development (An affiliate of International Correspondence Schools)
HRRC	Human Resources Research Center
HRRI	Human Resources Research Institute
HRRL	Human Resources Research Laboratory (Air Force)
HUMRRO	Human Resources Research Office (CONARC)
HSA	Human Serum Albumin
HSUS	Humane Society of the United States
HSUNA	Humanist Student Union of North America

HUMS	Humanitarian Reasons
HR	Humanitarian Reassignment (Military)
HCLE	Humanities Center for Liberal Education
HH	Humbert Humbert (Character in Vladimir Nabokov's "Lolita")
HSC	Humboldt State College (California)
H	Humidity
HEI	Humidity-Electronic Indicator
HI	Humidity Index
HMP	Humidity Monitoring Panel
HR	Humidity, Relative
HTP	Humidity Test Procedure
H	Hundred
HMC	Hundred Million Club
CWT	Hundredweight
HBUA	Hungarian Baptist Union of America
HCLA	Hungarian Catholic League of America
HCSLP	Hungarian Committee of Socialist Labor Party
HFFF	Hungarian Freedom Fighters Federation
HNSF	Hungarian National Sports Federation
HRFA	Hungarian Reformed Federation of America
HFD	Hunt Foods, Inc. (NYSE symbol)
HFI	Hunt Foods and Industries, Inc. (NYSE symbol)
HUK	Hunter-Killer (Operations against submarines)
DDK	Hunter Killer Destroyer (Navy ship symbol)
HUKFORLANT . .	Hunter-Killer Forces, Atlantic (Navy)
HUK	Hunter-Killer Groups (Navy)
CLK	Hunter-Killer Ship (Navy symbol)
HUKS	Hunter-Killer Submarine (Navy)
HCA	Hunting-Clan Air Transport Ltd.
H	Hupp Corporation (NYSE symbol)
HUR	Hurd Lock & Manufacturing Company (NYSE symbol)
HD	Hurricane Deck
H	Hurricane Evacuation - General (Military aircraft identification prefix)
HMRP	Hurricane Microseismic Research Problem (Aerology)
HOC	Hurricane Operations Center
HUREP	Hurricane Report
HSRS	Hurricane Supersonic Research Site
H	Husband
HAESZ	Husipari Allatorvosi Ellenorzo Szolgalat
H	Hussars
HRF	Hussmann Refrigerator Company (NYSE symbol)
HTC	Huston Tillotson College (Texas)
HJC	Hutchinson Junior College (Kansas)
HN	Hutchinson & Northern Railway Company (AAR code)
HUT	Huttig Sash & Door Company (NYSE symbol)
HMD	Hyaline Membrane Disease
HA	Hyaluronic Acid
HGS	Hyberbolic Grid System
HYACS	Hybrid Analog-Switching Attitude Control System for Space Vehicles
HYCOL	Hybrid Computer Link
HYCOTRAN . . .	Hybrid Computer Translator
HYDAC	Hybrid Digital-Analog Computing (System) (Satellite)
HYDAPT	Hybrid Digital-Analog Pulse Time
HEM	Hybrid Electromagnetic (Wave)
HYLA	Hybrid Language Assembler
HPS	Hybrid Propulsion System
HRC	Hybrid Receiver Circuit
HSS	Hybrid Simulation System
HTS	Hybrid Test Set
H	Hydrant
Hg	Hydrargyrum (Mercury) (Chemical element)
HAAC	Hydraulic Actuator Assembly Container
HATF	Hydraulic Actuator Test Fixture
HAS	Hydraulic Adjustable Speed
HBP	Hydraulic Bench Press
HCT	Hydraulic Components Test
HCV	Hydraulic Control Valve
HCU	Hydraulic Cycling Unit
HC	Hydraulic Cylinder
HFF	Hydraulic Fluid Filter
HFRE	Hydraulic Fluid Replenishment Equipment
HHP	Hydraulic Hand Pump
HMD	Hydraulic Mean Depth
HMU	Hydraulic Mock-Up
HPC	Hydraulic Package Container
HPPTS	Hydraulic Package Pressure Test Set
HPSA	Hydraulic Package Servovalve Actuator
HPSC	Hydraulic Package Storage Container
HPCRB	Hydraulic Power Control Relay Box
HPS	Hydraulic Power Supply
HPTP	Hydraulic Power Transfer Panel

HPU	Hydraulic Power Unit
HPI	Hydraulic Pressure Indicator
HPU	Hydraulic Pumping Unit
HPM	Hydraulic Punching Machine
HQC	Hydraulic Quick Coupler
HRD	Hydraulic Rate Damper
HRV	Hydraulic Relief Valve
HRA	Hydraulic Rotary Actuator
HSV	Hydraulic Selector Valve
HS	Hydraulic Supply
HSU	Hydraulic Supply Unit
HS	Hydraulic System
HYTAC	Hydraulic Tachometer
HTE	Hydraulic Test Equipment
HTS	Hydraulic Test Set (or Station)
HVM	Hydraulic Valve Motor
HOE	Hydraulically Operated Equipment
HE	Hydraulics Engineer
HCP	Hydrazine Catalytic Plenum
HEP	Hydrazine Electrolysis Plenum
HHHMU	Hydrazine Hand-Held Maneuvering Unit
HMT	Hydrazine Monopropellant Thruster
HRE	Hydrazine Rocket Engine
HI	Hydriodic Acid
HAC	Hydroballistic Advisory Committee
HC	Hydrocortisone (Endocrinology)
HCN	Hydrocyanic Acid (Fumigant)
HPT	Hydrocylic Pressure Testing
H	Hydrodynamic Head
HJB	Hydrodynamic Journal Bearing
HDW	Hydrodynamic Welding
HL	Hydrodynamics Laboratory (MIT)
HEP	Hydroelectric Plant
HEP	Hydroelectric Power
HEPC	Hydro-Electric Power Commission (Ontario, Canada)
HEU	Hydroelectric Unit
HF	Hydrofluoric Acid
HARPY	Hydrofoil Advanced Research Study Program
AGEH	Hydrofoil Research Ship (Navy symbol)
HS	Hydrofoil Ship
HYSTAD	Hydrofoil Stabilization Device
HTDS	Hydrofoil Tactical Data System
HTC	Hydrofoil Test Craft
H	Hydrogen (Chemical element)
H (Bomb)	Hydrogen Bomb
HBC	Hydrogen Bubble Chamber
HCZ	Hydrogen Convection Zone
HCS	Hydrogen Cyanide
HDS	Hydrogen Detection System
HEP	Hydrogen Embrittlement Proof
HF	Hydrogen Fluoride
HG	Hydrogen Generator
HLE	Hydrogen Line Emission
HOFS	Hydrogen-Oxygen Fuel System
HOPE	Hydrogen-Oxygen Primary Extraterrestrial (Fuel cell) (NASA)
HELEN	Hydrogenous Exponential Liquid Experiment
HYDRA	Hydrographic Digital Positioning and Depth Recording (System) (NOO)
HO	Hydrographic Office (Terminated 1963; later, NOO) (Navy)
HYDRO	Hydrographic Office (Later, NOO) (Navy)
HOS	Hydrographic Office Scale
HYSURCH	Hydrographic Surveying and Charting (System) (NOO)
MOH	Hydrological and Meteorological Mobile Station (ITU designation)
H	Hydrolysis
HLB	Hydrophile-Lipophile Balance (Biochemistry)
HSD	Hydropneumatic Suspension Device
HSG	Hydro-Shift Gun
HYTREC	Hydrospace Target Recognition, Evaluation and Control
HMD	Hydrostatic Motor Driven
HP	Hydrostatic Pressure
HT	Hydrotherapy
HEEDTA	Hydroxy Ethylenediaminetetraacetic Acid (Chemical)
HEMA	Hydroxyethyl Methacrylate
HIOMT	Hydroxyindole-O-Methyltransferase
HAP	Hydroxylammonium Perchlorate
HPMA	Hydroxypropyl Methacrylate
HT	Hydroxytryptamine
HTP	Hydroxytryptophan
HU	Hydroxyurea
HARE	Hydrozine Auxiliary Rocket Engine
HL	Hygienic Laboratory (US)
HSA	Hymn Society of America

HAM . . . . Hymns Ancient and Modern
HYPERDOP. . . . Hyperbolic Doppler
HU . . . . Hyperemia Unit
HER . . . . Hyper-Environmental RADAR
HETS . . . . . . Hyperenvironmental Test System (Air Force)
HGF . . . . Hyperglycemic-Glycogenolytic Factor (Endocrinology)
HIPS . . . . . . Hyper-Intense Proximal Scanning
HLN . . . . Hyperplastic Liver Nodules
HPG . . . . Hyper-Pure Germanium
HYPREM . . . . . Hyper-Response Electric Motor
HS . . . . Hypersonic
HAF . . . . Hypersonic Aerothermaldynamic Facility
HADES . . . . . . Hypersonic Air Data Entry System
HBGM . . . . . . Hypersonic Boost-Glide Missile
HYFES . . . . . . Hypersonic Flight Environmental Simulator
HIRES . . . . . . Hypersonic In-Flight Refueling System
HIT . . . . Hypersonic Interference Technique
HLP . . . . Hypersonic Local Pressure
HRF . . . . Hypersonic Rarefied Flow
HRE . . . . Hypersonic Research Engine (NASA)
HRV . . . . Hypersonic Research Vehicle
HTV . . . . Hypersonic Test Vehicle (Air Force)
HST . . . . Hypersonic Transport (Aircraft)
HVS . . . . Hypersonic Vehicle Shield
HWT . . . . Hypersonic Wind Tunnel
HP . . . . Hypertension and Proteinuria

HCVD . . . . . . Hypertensive Cardiovascular Disease (Medicine)
HVD. . . . . Hypertensive Vascular Disease
HP . . . . Hypertransfused Polycythemic
HSAS . . . . . . Hypertrophic Subaortic Stenosis (Medicine)
HT . . . . Hypertropia
HV . . . . Hypervelocity
HART . . . . . . Hypervelocity Aircraft Rocket, Tactical
HVAP-T . . . . . Hypervelocity Armor Piercing - Tracer (Military)
HCP . . . . Hypervelocity Countermeasures Program
HFF . . . . Hypervelocity Flow Field
HFFF . . . . . . Hypervelocity Free Flight Facility
HIT . . . . Hypervelocity Impulse Tunnel
HIG . . . . Hypervelocity Intercept Guidance
HIGSS . . . . . . Hypervelocity Intercept Guidance Simulator Study
HYVIA . . . . . . Hyper-Velocity Interceptor Armament
HIGS . . . . . . Hypervelocity Interceptor Guidance Simulation
HVTP-T . . . . . Hypervelocity Target Practice - Tracer (Military)
HY . . . . Hypobranchial (Gland)
HG . . . . Hypobranchial Gland
HT . . . . Hypodermic Tablet
HPGC . . . . . . Hypopressure Gas Chromatography
HSF . . . . Hypothalamic Secretory Factor
HFS . . . . Hypothetical Future Samples (Statistics)
HGPRT . . . . . Hypoxanthine-Guanine Phosphoribosyl Transferase
HC . . . . Hysteresis Comparator
HYTRESS . . . . Hyway Test Recorder and Simulator System

I . . . . I-Beam (Structural metal shape)
IOU . . . . I Owe You (Business and trade slang)
IQ . . . . I Quit (Smoking)
IB . . . . Iberia-Lineas Aereas Espanalos (Air Lines of Spain)
IRIS . . . . IBM Recruitment Information System
IBIT . . . . ICBM Blast Interference Test
ICC . . . . Ice Crystal Cloud
IC . . . . Ice Crystals
IF . . . . Ice Fog
IP . . . . Ice Point
IR . . . . Ice on Runways (Aviation)
ISIA . . . . Ice Skating Institute of America
IASOR . . . . . . Ice and Snow on Runway (Aviation)
AGB. . . . . Icebreaker (Navy ship symbol)
IC . . . . Iceland (NATO)
ICOMP. . . . . . Iceland Ocean Meeting Point (Navy)
ICEPAT . . . . . Iceland Patrol (Navy)
IFL . . . . Icelandic Federation of Labor
ICGICIP . . . . . Icing in Clouds and in Precipitation (Meteorology)
ICGIP. . . . . . . Icing in Precipitation (Meteorology)
I . . . . Id (That)
IE . . . . Id Est (That Is)
IQED . . . . Id Quod Erat Demonstrandum (That Which Was to Be Proved)
ID . . . . Idaho
ICPP. . . . . . . Idaho Chemical Processing Plant (AEC)
IDO . . . . Idaho Operations Office (AEC)
IDA . . . . Idaho Power Company (NYSE symbol)
IPCO . . . . . . Idaho Power Company
ISC . . . . Idaho State College
ID . . . . Idea (Slang)
IDL . . . . Ideal Cement Company (NYSE symbol)
INIC . . . . Ideal Current Negative Immittance Converter
IGL . . . . Ideal Gas Law
ILPF . . . . Ideal Low Pass Filter
IMHEP . . . . . . Ideal Man Helicopter Engineering Project
IFD . . . . Idealization to Frustration to Demoralization
IQ . . . . Idem Quod (The Same As)
ILAF. . . . . . . Identically Located Acceleration and Force (Aerospace)
ID . . . . Identification
INDAIR. . . . . . Identification of Aircraft
IBN . . . . Identification Beacon
ID(Card) . . . . . Identification Card
IFF. . . . . Identification, Friend or Foe (Military)
IFF/SIF . . . . . Identification, Friend or Foe/Selective Identification Feature
IFS. . . . . Identification, Friend or Foe, Switching Circuit
IDLT. . . . . . . Identification Light
IDO . . . . Identification Officer (Military)
IP . . . . Identification Peculiarity
IP . . . . Identification Point
IP . . . . Identification of Position
IDS . . . . Identification Section
IFO . . . . Identified Flying Object (Air Force)
IDFR. . . . . . . Identified Friendly (Military)
IPI . . . . Identified Friendly Prior to Interception (Military)
IPL. . . . . Identified Parts List
IP . . . . Identity Preserved (Wheat) (US Department of Agriculture)
ITP . . . . Idiopathic Thrombocytopenic Purpura (Medicine)
ILN . . . . Idle Line Network
IDREA. . . . . . Idle Other Reasons (Vessel status) (Navy)
IDSTO . . . . . . Idle Used for Storage (Shipping)
IDFOR . . . . . . Idle Waiting Convoy Forward (Vessel status) (Navy)
IDLOD . . . . . . Idle Waiting to Load (Shipping)
IDU . . . . Idoxuridine (A drug)

IC . . . . Iesus Christus (Jesus Christ)
IHS . . . . Iesus Hominum Salvator (Jesus, Savior of Men)
INRI. . . . . . . Iesus Nazarenus Rex Iudaeorum (Jesus of Nazareth, King of the Jews)
IFAMP . . . . . . If Approach Missed Proceed (Aviation)
IAATCD . . . . . If Authorized by Air Traffic Control, DME (Distance Measuring
            Equipment) May Be Used (Aviation)
IFC . . . . If Clause
IFVLS . . . . . . If Flight Visibility Becomes Less Than
IIA . . . . If Incorrect Advise
IISD . . . . If Incorrect Service Direct (Aviation)
IISO. . . . . . . If Incorrect Service Originator (Aviation)
IFINS . . . . . . If Instrument Conditions Encountered (Aviation)
INOAVNOT . . If Not Available Notify this Office at Once
INP . . . . If Not Possible
IFUN . . . . . . If Unable
IFVR. . . . . . . If Visibility Remains (Aviation)
IBA . . . . Igniter Booster Assembly (Aerospace)
IIC . . . . Igniter Initiator Cartridge (or Container)
IITS . . . . Igniter Initiator Test Set
INC . . . . Igniter Nozzle Closure
IMI . . . . Ignition Manufacturers Institute
ISA . . . . Ignition Separation Assembly
ISS. . . . . Ignition Shielding System
ITS. . . . . Ignition Test Simulator
IBA . . . . Ignorant Bloody Aircrafthand (British Royal Air Force slang)
IKH . . . . Ihre Kongliche (His Royal Highness) (German)
IBKB . . . . . . Ikatan Buruh Kendaaran Bermotor (Motor Transport Workers' Union)
            (Indonesia)
IBKA . . . . . . Ikatan Buruh Kereta Api (Railroad Workers' Union) (Indonesia)
IBU . . . . Ikatan Buruh Umum (General Workers' Union)
II. . . . . Ikebana International
IPGP . . . . . . Illegal Possession of Government Property
IWU . . . . Illegal Wearing of Uniform
IDB . . . . Illicit Diamond Buyer (or Buying)
IL . . . . Illinois
ILLIAC . . . . . Illinois Automatic Computer
IL . . . . Illinois Central Industries (NYSE symbol)
IC . . . . Illinois Central R. R. (AAR code)
ICO . . . . Illinois College of Optometry
IIT . . . . Illinois Institute of Technology
IITRI . . . . . . Illinois Institute of Technology Research Institute
IN . . . . Illinois Northern Railway (AAR code)
IPC . . . . Illinois Power Company (NYSE symbol)
IRM . . . . Illinois Railway Museum
ISNU . . . . . . Illinois State Normal University
ISCPET . . . . . Illinois State-Wide Curriculum Study Center in the Preparation of
            Secondary School English Teachers
ITC . . . . Illinois Terminal R. R. (AAR code)
ILLT . . . . Illinois Terminal Railroad Company
ITPA. . . . . . . Illinois Test of Psycholinguistic Abilities
IWU . . . . Illinois Wesleyan University
ILZ . . . . Illinois Zinc Company (American Stock Exchange symbol)
IIG . . . . Illuminated Internal Graticule
IAGMA. . . . . . Illuminating and Allied Glassware Manufacturers Association
IERI . . . . Illuminating Engineering Research Institute
IES. . . . . Illuminating Engineering Society
IPM . . . . Illuminations Per Minute
IMPL . . . . . . Illustrated Maintenance Parts List
IPB. . . . . Illustrated Parts Breakdown
IJ . . . . Im Jahre (In the Year) (German)
ICC . . . . Image Converter Camera
ICT . . . . Image Converter Tube
IDS . . . . Image Display System

IDC . . . . Image Dissector Camera
IDCS . . . . . . Image Dissector Camera System
IDPT . . . . . . Image Dissector Photomultiplier Tube
IDT . . . . Image Dissector Tube
IFE . . . . Image Feature Extraction
IFR . . . . Image to Frame Ratio
IMITAC . . . . . Image Input to Automatic Computers
II . . . . Image Intensifier
IIA . . . . Image Intensifier Assembly
IID . . . . Image Intensifier Device
IINS . . . . Image Intensifier Night Sight
IIO . . . . Image Intensifier Orthicon
IIT . . . . Image Intensifier Tube
IIV . . . . Image Intensifier Viewer
IIVD . . . . Image Intensifier Viewing Device
IIC . . . . Image Interpretation Cell
IIR . . . . Image Interpreter Response
IMC . . . . Image Motion Compensation
IMS . . . . Image Motion Simulator
IOS . . . . Image Optical Scanner
IO . . . . Image Orthicon
IOC . . . . Image Orthicon Camera
IOC . . . . Image Orthicon Control
IOS . . . . Image Orthicon System
IPC . . . . Image Products Company
IQI . . . . Image Quality Indicator
IR . . . . Image Rejection
ISS . . . . Image Sensor System
ISTAR . . . . . . Image Storage Translation and Reproduction
IVD . . . . Image Velocity Detector
IMPRINT . . . . . Imbricated Program for Information Transfer (Data processing)
ICJC . . . . . . Immaculate Conception Junior College (New Jersey)
IHC . . . . Immaculate Heart College (California)
IBF . . . . Immature Brown-Fat (Cells)
IAS . . . . Immediate Access Storage
IAD . . . . Immediate Action Directive
ICO . . . . Immediate Commanding Officer
IC . . . . Immediate Constituent
IDA . . . . Immediate Damage Assessment
IKOR . . . . . . Immediate Knowledge of Results
IOU . . . . Immediate Operation Use
IPM . . . . Immediate Past Master (Masonry)
IPIR . . . . Immediate Photograph Intelligence Report (Military)
IRF . . . . Immediate Reaction Force (Military)
IRE . . . . Immediate Ready Element (Military)
IRF . . . . Immediate Ready Force (Army)
IRR . . . . Immediate (or Individual) Ready Reserve (Army)
ISIC . . . . Immediate Superior in Command (Military)
ISINC . . . . . . Immediate Superior in Command (Military)
IT . . . . Immediate Transportation
IMAP . . . . . . Immediately After Passing (Aviation)
IA . . . . Immediately Available
IMREP . . . . . . Immediately Report
II . . . . Immigrant Inspector (Immigration and Naturalization Service)
I & N . . . . . . Immigration and Naturalization (Service)
INS . . . . Immigration and Naturalization Service (Department of Justice)
IPI . . . . Immigration Patrol Inspector (Immigration and Naturalization Service)
IDA . . . . Immortalis Dei Auspicio (With the Help of God)
ISG . . . . Immune Serum Globulin
IT . . . . Immunity Test
IR . . . . Immunization Rate
IU . . . . Immunizing Unit (Medicine)
IEA . . . . Immunoelectro Adsorption
IMPATT . . . . . Impact Avalanche and Transit Time
IET . . . . Impact Excited Transmitter
IHT . . . . Impact Hand Tool
IP . . . . Impact Point
IP . . . . Impact Prediction
IPD . . . . Impact Prediction Data
IPP . . . . Impact Prediction Point (NASA)
IP . . . . Impact Predictor (NASA)
IPS . . . . Impact Predictor System
Z . . . . Impedance (Symbol)
IA . . . . Impedance Angle
IMA . . . . Impedance Matching Attenuator
IHO . . . . Impeded Harmonic Operation
I . . . . Imperator or Imperatrix (Emperor; Empress)
I . . . . Imperial
ICI . . . . Imperial Chemical Industries
AAONMS . . . . Imperial Council of the Ancient Arabic Order of the Nobles of the Mystic Shrine for North America

ICDI . . . . . . Imperial Court, Daughters of Isis
IDC . . . . Imperial Defence College (British)
IEAF . . . . Imperial Ethiopian Air Force
IG . . . . Imperial Gallon
IGS . . . . Imperial General Staff
IIAF . . . . Imperial Iranian Air Force
IJN . . . . Imperial Japanese Navy
IM . . . . Imperial Measure
IMI . . . . Imperial Metal Industries, Ltd. (British)
IMNS . . . . . . Imperial Military Nursing Service (British)
IOD . . . . Imperial Order of the Dragon
ISC . . . . Imperial Service College (British)
ISO . . . . Imperial Service Order (British)
ISTD . . . . . . Imperial Society of Teachers of Dancing
ISG . . . . Imperial Standard Gallon
ISWG . . . . . . Imperial Standard Wire Gauge
ITC . . . . Imperial Tobacco Company (of Great Britain and Ireland) Limited
IVC . . . . Imperial Valley College (California)
IVDBA . . . . . . Imperial Valley Dune Buggy Association
IWGC . . . . . . Imperial War Graves Commission (British)
IY . . . . Imperial Yeomanry (British)
IDT . . . . Implantation Doping Technique
IET . . . . Implanted Electrode Technique
IMPACT . . . . . Implementation Planning and Control Technique (Data processing)
IA . . . . Implementing Agency
IEA . . . . Import Entitlement Agreement (Special type of currency) (United Arab Republic)
IF . . . . Importance Factor (Statistics)
IHPA . . . . . . Imported Hardwood Plywood Association
IMF . . . . Impossible Mission Force (Fictitious group of undercover agents in TV series, "Mission: Impossible")
IMO . . . . Improper Order
IAMW . . . . . . Improved Antimateriel Warhead
IAMWH . . . . . Improved Antimateriel Warhead
IAW . . . . Improved Antimateriel Warhead
IAWH . . . . . . Improved Antimateriel Warhead
IBPOEW . . . . . Improved Benevolent Protective Order of Elks of the World
ICM . . . . Improved Capability Minuteman (or Missile) (Air Force)
IMCO . . . . . . Improved Combustion
ICBWR . . . . . . Improved Cycle Boiling Water Reactor
IDI . . . . Improved Data Interchange
IFO . . . . Improved Fiber Optics
IFOB . . . . . . Improved Fiber Optics Bundle
IFC . . . . Improved Flotation Chamber
IGS . . . . Improved Gray Scale
IHSBR . . . . . . Improved High-Speed Bombing RADAR
ILBB . . . . . . Improved Life Blower Bearing
IMP . . . . Improved Maintenance Program (Air Force)
IMI . . . . Improved Manned Interceptor (Proposed plane) (Air Force)
IMPACT . . . . . Improved Manpower Production and Controller Technique (Navy)
IMTS . . . . . . Improved Mobile Telephone Service
INH . . . . Improved Nike Hercules (Missile)
IORM . . . . . . Improved Order of Red Men
IPD . . . . Improved Point Defense
IPDSMS . . . . . Improved Point Defense Surface Missile System
IRAM . . . . . . Improved Reliability and Maintainability
IRM . . . . Improved Risk Mutuals
ISLF . . . . Improved Saturn Launch Facility
ISOPAR . . . . . Improved Symbolic Optimizing Assembly Routine
IT . . . . Improved Tartar
ITOS . . . . . . Improved TIROS Operational Satellite (ESSA)
IP . . . . Improvement Program
IBS . . . . Impulse Balance System
ICS . . . . Impulse Conducting System (Physiology)
IMP . . . . Impulse Generator
IM . . . . Impulse Modulation
IRB . . . . Impulse Resistance Bridge
IRAR . . . . . . Impulse Response Area Ratio
ISR . . . . Impulse Sequencing Relay
IPM . . . . Impulses Per Minute
IA . . . . In Absentia
IAW . . . . In Accordance With
IAOD . . . . . . In Addition to Other Duties (Military)
IATOD . . . . . . In Addition To Other Duties (Military)
IB . . . . In Bond (Wines and spirits)
INB . . . . In Bono (In Good Order)
ICO . . . . In Case Of
IC . . . . In Charge Of
I/C . . . . In Charge Of
ICN . . . . In Christi Nomine (In the Name of Christ)
IX . . . . In Christo (In Christ)

INC . . . . In Cloud (Aviation)
ICIR . . . . In Commission, In Reserve (Navy vessel status)
ICR . . . . In-Commission Rate
ICW . . . . In Connection With
IDN . . . . In Dei Nomine (In God's Name)
IFD . . . . In Flagrante Delicto (Caught in the Act)
IFEP . . . . In-Flight Experiments Panel
IFH . . . . In-Flight Helium
IFM . . . . In-Flight Maintenance
IFMS . . . . In-Flight Management System
IMS . . . . In-Flight Management System
INFOES . . . . . In-Flight Operational Evaluation of a Space System
IFPM . . . . In-Flight Performance Monitor
IFR . . . . In-Flight Refueling
IFS . . . . In-Flight Safety
IFTS . . . . In-Flight Test System
IFT . . . . In-Flight Text (Air Force)
IFTA . . . . In-Flight Thrust Augmentation
IF . . . . In Full
IHCA . . . . In Hands of Civil Authorities (Military)
IHN . . . . In His Name
IHS . . . . In Hoc Salus (In This Cross Is Salvation)
IHS . . . . In Hoc Signo, Vinces (In This Sign, Thou Shalt Conquer)
IH . . . . In Home (Men's lacrosse position)
ILIR . . . . In-House Laboratory Independent Research Program (Army)
ILO . . . . In Lieu Of
INLO . . . . In Lieu Of
ILT . . . . In Lieu Thereof (Military)
ILOUE . . . . . . In Lieu of Until Exhausted (Military)
ILIC . . . . In-Line Integrated Circuit
INV . . . . In-Line Needle Valve
ILP . . . . In-Line Printer
ILR . . . . In-Line Reciprocator
ILRV . . . . In-Line Relief Valve
IM . . . . In Maintenance
IAO . . . . In and Out (of clouds) (Aviation)
INC . . . . In Nomine Christi (In the Name of Christ)
IND . . . . In Nomine Dei (In God's Name)
INI . . . . In Nomine Iesu (In the Name of Jesus)
INJ . . . . In Nomine Jesu (In the Name of Jesus)
INST . . . . In Nomine Sanctae Trinitatis (In the Name of the Holy Trinity)
IO . . . . In Order
IOW . . . . In Other Words
IOC . . . . In Our Culture
IOC . . . . In-Out Converter
I & OP . . . . . . In and Out Processing
IOVC . . . . In the Overcast (Aviation)
INP . . . . In Pace (In Peace)
IPI . . . . In Partibus Infidelium (In the countries, lands, or regions of unbelievers)
IP . . . . In Place (Dancing)
IPRA . . . . In-Place Repairable Assembly
IPPMA . . . . . . In-Plant Powder Metallurgy Association
IPMA . . . . In-Plant Printing Management Association
IPD . . . . In Praesentia Dominorum (In the presence of the Lords of Session)
IPF . . . . In-Process Factor
IPQC . . . . In-Process Quality Control
ISIR . . . . In Service, In Reserve (Vessel status) (Navy)
INTNS . . . . . . In Transit
ITR . . . . In Transit Rendezvous
IT . . . . In Transitu (In Transit)
IV . . . . In Verbo (Under the Word)
INVOF . . . . . . In the Vicinity Of
IVFRC . . . . . . In Visual Flight Rules Conditions
IAR . . . . Inactive Air Reserve
INACDUTRA . . Inactive Duty Training (Air Force)
INACTLANT . . Inactive Fleet, Atlantic Fleet
INACTFLTPAC . . Inactive Fleet, Pacific Fleet
INACTPAC . . . Inactive Fleet, Pacific Fleet
INA/IC . . . . . . Inactive-In Commission, In Reserve (Vessel status)
INA/IS . . . . . . Inactive-In Service, In Reserve (Vessel status)
ING . . . . Inactive National Guard
INA/OC . . . . . Inactive-Out of Commission, In Reserve (Vessel status)
INA/OS . . . . . Inactive-Out of Service, In Reserve (Vessel status)
IRS . . . . Inactive Reserve Section (Military)
ISLRS . . . . Inactive Status List Reserve Section
ISDS . . . . Inadvertent Separation and Destruct System (Aerospace)
IECO . . . . Inboard Engine Cutoff
IRS . . . . Inboard Rotating Shield
IB . . . . Inbound
IRAD . . . . Inbound Radial (Aviation)
ILRA . . . . Inbred Livestock Registry Association

ILMA . . . . Incandescent Lamp Manufacturers Association
IWC . . . . Incarnate Word College (Texas)
I . . . . Incendiary (Bomb)
IB . . . . Incendiary Bomb
IBEN . . . . Incendiary Bomb with Explosive Nose
IAP . . . . Incentive Awards Program (of the federal government, administered by CSC)
ICPFF . . . . Incentive Cost Plus Fixed Fee
IP . . . . Incentive Pay
IPE . . . . Incentive PERT Events
ITD . . . . Inception-to-Date
IPM . . . . Inches Per Minute
IPR . . . . Inches Per Revolution
IPS . . . . Inches Per Second
IPY . . . . Inches Per Year
IPM . . . . Incidental Phase Modulation
IIA . . . . Incinerator Institute of America
INI . . . . Incipient Nonequilibrium Index
I & D . . . . Incision and Drainage (Medicine)
IP . . . . Incisoproximal
I . . . . Incisor (Dentistry)
IIT . . . . Inclinable Indexing Table
IPEE . . . . Inclination of a Plane to the Plane of the Earth's Equator (Aerospace)
ICBC . . . . Inclined Cleated Belt Conveyor
IHIA . . . . Include This Headquarters Information Addressee (Army)
INCAIR . . . . . . Including Air
IL . . . . Including Loading
IPA . . . . Including Particular Average (Insurance)
IncB . . . . Inclusion Body (Cytology)
IB . . . . Inclusion Body (Cytology)
ITC . . . . Inclusive Tour Charter
IEO . . . . Incoherent Electronic Oscillator
ITU . . . . Income Tax Unit
IT . . . . Income Tax Unit Rulings (US Internal Revenue Service)
IL . . . . Incoming Letter
ICL . . . . Incoming Line
IO . . . . Incoming Orders
IPAD . . . . Incoming Procurement Authorization Document (Air Force)
INREPL . . . . . . Incoming Replacement (Army)
ITT . . . . Incoming Teletype
ITL . . . . Incoming Transaction Listing
I . . . . Incomplete
ITBL . . . . Incompressible Turbulent Boundary Layer
IA . . . . Incorporated Accountant
ICBS . . . . Incorporated Church Building Society (British)
ILS . . . . Incorporated Law Society (British)
ISLFD . . . . Incorporated Society of London Fashion Designers
IROS . . . . Increase Reliability of Operational System
IRAA & A . . . . Increase and Replacement of Armor, Armament and Ammunition (Naval budget appropriation title)
IRC & M . . . . Increase and Replacement of Construction and Machinery (Naval budget appropriation title)
IREC . . . . Increase and Replacement of Emergency Construction (Ships) (Naval budget appropriation title)
IRNV . . . . Increase and Replacement of Naval Vessels (Naval budget appropriation title)
ICE . . . . Increased Combat Effectiveness
IHR . . . . Increased Hazard Rate
IMK . . . . Increased Maneuverability Kit
IV . . . . Increased Value
IFR . . . . Increasing Failure Rate
IHRA . . . . Increasing Hazard Rate Average
IA . . . . Incremental Analysis (Statistics)
ICEM . . . . Incremental Cost Effectiveness Model
IDR . . . . Incremental Digital Recorder
IFC . . . . Incremental Frequency Control
ILSO . . . . Incremental Life Support Operations
IVI . . . . Incremental Velocity Indicator (NASA)
ICH . . . . Incumbent Come Home (Political humor) (Pronounced "itch")
IQ . . . . Indefinite Quantity
ISTMH . . . . . . Indefinite Substitute Temporary Mail Handler (US Post Office employee classification)
IPAS . . . . Independants, et Paysans d'Action Sociale (Right wing political party of independents and peasants) (France)
ICC . . . . Independence Community College (Kansas)
INDE . . . . Independence National Historical Park
I . . . . Independent
IADA . . . . Independent Aeronautical Dealers Association
IACA . . . . Independent Air Carriers Association
IAA . . . . Independent Airlines Association
IAWA . . . . Independent American Whiskey Association

IASM ...... Independent Association of Stocking Manufacturers
IBA .... Independent Bankers Association
IBAA ...... Independent Bankers Association of America
IBA ...... Independent Bar Association
IBMA ...... Independent Battery Manufacturers of America
ICDMA ..... Independent Carbon-Dioxide Manufacturers Association
ICRDA ..... Independent Cash Register Dealers Association
ICFA ...... Independent College Funds of America
ICTOC ..... Independent Corps Tactical Operations Center
IDSB........ Independent Double Side Band
IEMC ...... Independent Electronic Music Center
IFIDA ...... Independent Film Importers and Distributors of America
IFPEC ...... Independent Film Producers Export Corporation
IFY .... Independent Fission Yield
IFPA ...... Independent Fluorspar Producers Association
IFOMA ..... Independent Fuel Oil Marketers of America
IGOA....... Independent Garage Owners of America
IGA .... Independent Grocers Alliance Distributing Company
ILC .... Independent Labor Congress (Nigeria)
ILP........ Independent Labour Party (British)
ILM .... Independent Landing Monitor (RADAR – TV landing guidance)
IMP .... Independent Motion Picture Company
IMPDAA .... Independent Motion Picture Distributors Association of America
IMPPA ..... Independent Motion Picture Producers Association
INGAA..... Independent Natural Gas Association of America
INA .... Independent Newsletter Association
IOCA ...... Independent Oil Compounders Association
IOBB ...... Independent Order of B'nai B'rith
IOF .... Independent Order of Foresters
IOLV ...... Independent Order Ladies of Vikings
IOOF ...... Independent Order of Odd Fellows
IOR .... Independent Order of Rechabites
IOSL ...... Independent Order of St. Luke
IOSM ..... Independent Order of Sons of Malta
IOS .... Independent Order of Svithiod
IOV........ Independent Order of Vikings
IOMA...... Independent Oxygen Manufacturers Association
IPAA ...... Independent Petroleum Association of America
IPSA........ Independent Postal System of America (Proposed name for public postal
            delivery)
IPEA....... Independent Poster Exchanges of America
IPET ...... Independent Professional Electronic Technicians
IRAA ...... Independent Refiners Association of America
IRAD ...... Independent Research & Development
IRS........ Independent Research Service
IRLDA ..... Independent Retail Lumber Dealers Association
IRTA ...... Independent Retail Tobacconists Association of America
ISTSP ...... Independent Schools Talent Search Program
ISMDA ..... Independent Sewing Machine Dealers of America (Defunct)
IS .... Independent Shoemen of America
ISA .... Independent Shoemen of America
ISB........ Independent Sideband
ISP........ Independent Studies Project (Navy)
ISS........ Independent Sweep System
ITPA ...... Independent Telephone Pioneer Association
ITA .... Independent Television Authority (British)
ITC .... Independent Television Corporation
ITN .... Independent Television News (British)
ITVSDA..... Independent Television Service Dealers' Association
ITUA ...... Independent Trade Union Association (Turkey)
ITS........ Independent Triggering System
IUPPE ...... Independent Union of Plant Protection Employees
PPE .... Independent Union of Plant Protection Employees in the Electrical and
            Machine Industry
IULC ...... Independent United Labor Congress (Nigeria)
IVDS ...... Independent Variable Depth SONAR
IVS .... Independent Vertical System
IVA .... Independent Voters Association (Political organization in North Dakota,
            1918-1932)
IVI........ Independent Voters of Illinois
IWA .... Independent Watchmen's Association
WA .... Independent Watchmen's Association
IWDA ...... Independent Wire Drawers Association
IWRC ...... Independent Wire Rope Center (or Core)
IWRMA ..... Independent Wire Rope Manufacturers Association
IEI .... Indeterminate Engineering Items
IB .... Index of Body Build (Anatomy)
ICRS........ Index Chemicus Registry System (A publication of Institute for Scientific
            Information)
ICRD ...... Index of Codes for Research Drugs (A publication)
ICN........ Index of Community Noise

IC .... Index Correction (on a sextant)
IDEA ...... Index for Design Engineering Applications (Data retrieval service)
            (Product engineering)
IE .... Index of Enrichment
IE .... Index Error (Navigation)
IIP .... Index of Industrial Production
IM .... Index Medicus
IP .... Index of Performance
ISC .... Index of Status Characteristics
IT .... Index Translationum (UNESCO)
I & P ...... Indexed and Paged
IPT........ Indexed, Paged, and Titled
IST........ Indexing Slide Table
IS .... Indexing in Source
IAS .... India-America Society
IATC ...... India America Trade Council
IBT........ India-Burma Theater
ICW........ India-China Wing (World War II)
EEPC ...... India Engineering Export Promotion Council
IO........ India Office
IP .... India Paper
IPP........ India Paper Proofs
IAF........ Indian Air Force
IAC........ Indian Airlines Corporation
IACB ...... Indian Arts and Crafts Board (Department of the Interior)
IA .... Indian Army
IAMC ...... Indian Army Medical Corps
IARO ...... Indian Army Reserve of Officers
IAA .... Indian Association of America
IASLIC ..... Indian Association of Special Libraries and Information Centres
IAS .... Indian Astronautical Society
ICM ...... Indian Campaign Medal
ICS .... Indian Civil Service
ICC .... Indian Claims Commission
ICP .... Indian Communications Project
ICC .... Indian Cultural Center
IDR .... Indian Defense Rules
IE .... (Order of the) Indian Empire
IFWJ ...... Indian Federation of Working Journalists
IHS .... Indian Health Service
ILF........ Indian Local Forces (Military) (British)
IMD ...... Indian Medical Department
IMS ...... Indian Medical Service
IMA ...... Indian Military Academy
INA ...... Indian National Army
INCWF ..... Indian National Cement Workers' Federation
INEWF ..... Indian National Electricity Workers' Federation
INISWF ..... Indian National Iron and Steel Workers' Federation
INMWF...... Indian National Mine Workers' Federation
INSDOC..... Indian National Scientific Documentation Center (New Delhi)
INTWF ..... Indian National Textile Workers' Federation
INTUC ..... Indian National Trades Union Congress
IN .... Indian Navy
IO .... Indian Ocean
IOS .... Indian Ocean Ship
IOS .... Indian Ocean Site
IOSS ...... Indian Ocean Station Support
IOM....... Indian Order of Merit
IOCP ...... Indian Overseas Communication Project
IRA .... Indian Rights Association
ISLW....... Indian Spring Low Water
ISC .... Indian Staff Corps
ISI .... Indian Standards Institution
ISI .... Indian Statistical Institute
INSTEP...... Indian Steel Training and Education Program (India)
IT .... Indian Territory (in United States)
IN .... Indiana
ICC .... Indiana Central College
IGC....... Indiana General Corporation (NYSE symbol)
IHB .... Indiana Harbor Belt R. R. (AAR code)
ILI........ Indiana Limestone Institute
ISTC....... Indiana State Teachers College
ITC .... Indiana Technical College
IND .... Indianapolis (Indiana) (Airport symbol)
IPL........ Indianapolis Power and Light Company (NYSE symbol)
IU .... Indianapolis Union Railway Company (AAR code)
I .... Indicated (or Indicative)
IAS .... Indicated Air Speed
IAT .... Indicated Air Temperature
IA .... Indicated Altitude (Navigation)
IHP .... Indicated Horsepower

IHPH . . . . Indicated Horsepower Hour
IMN . . . . Indicated Mach Number
IMEP . . . . Indicated Mean Effective Pressure (Aerospace)
ITAS . . . . Indicated True Air Speed (Aviation)
ID . . . . Indicating Device
IL . . . . Indicating Light
ILR . . . . Indicating Light Relay
IWP . . . . Indicative World Plan
I . . . . Indicator
IC . . . . Indicator and Control
ICU . . . . Indicator Control Unit
IDS . . . . Indicator Drive Screw
IGS . . . . Indicator Group Speed
IK . . . . Indicator Kit
IA . . . . Indirect Addressing
IBPMS . . . . . . Indirect Blood Pressure Measuring System
IBDA . . . . . . Indirect Bomb-Damage Assessment
IMS . . . . Indirect Measuring System
IOC . . . . Indirect Operating Costs
IW . . . . Indirect Waste
IHC . . . . Indirectly Heated Cathode
In . . . . Indium (Chemical element)
IAV . . . . Indium Antimode Veractor
InAs . . . . Indium Arsenide
IAF . . . . Indium Arsenide Filter
IAT . . . . Individual Acceptance Tests
IAR . . . . Individual Action Report
ICA . . . . Individual Combat Actions (Army)
IDQA . . . . . . Individual Documented Quality Assurance
IDG . . . . Individual Drop Glider
IFPFP . . . . . . Individual Flight Plans from This Point
IKET . . . . Individual Knowledge Evaluation Test
IMR . . . . Individual Medical Record
IOT . . . . Individual Operation Test
IPD . . . . Individual Package Delivery
IPR . . . . Individual Pay Record (Military)
IPANY . . . . . . Individual Psychology Association of New York
IRT . . . . Individual Reliability Test
IRR . . . . Individual Retirement Record (Air Force)
ISE . . . . Individual Ship Exercises
ISO . . . . Individual System Operation
ITA . . . . Individual Task Authorization
ITT . . . . Individual Technical Training (Military)
IPI . . . . Individually Planned (or Prescribed) Instruction (Education)
IPI/MIS . . . . . . Individually Planned Instruction/Management and Information System
IASA . . . . . . Indo-American Sports Association
IE . . . . Indo-European
IG . . . . Indo-Germanic (Language, etc.)
IPCCIOS . . . . . Indo-Pacific Council of the International Committee of Scientific
            Management
IPFC . . . . Indo-Pacific Fisheries Council
IAA . . . . Indole-3-Acetic Acid
IBA . . . . Indolebutyric Acid
InGPS . . . . . . Indoleglycerolphosphate Synthetase
InGP . . . . . . Indolglycerophosphate
ISAUS . . . . . . Indonesian Students Association in the United States
ISC . . . . Indoor Sports Club
IMMS . . . . . . Indore Mill Mazdoor Sangh (Indore Textile Labour Association) (India)
I/I . . . . Indorsement Irregular (Banking)
IDM . . . . Induced Dipole Moment
ID . . . . Induced Draft
IEE . . . . Induced Electrical Effect
IEE . . . . Induced Electron Emission
IND . . . . Induced Nuclear Disintegration
IRF . . . . Induced Radiation Flux
L . . . . Inductance (Symbol)
ICR . . . . Inductance-Capacitance-Resistance
IDB . . . . Inductance Decade Box
ISA . . . . Inductee Special Assignment
ICS . . . . Induction Communications System
ICH . . . . Induction-Conduction Heating
IIL . . . . Induction Ion LASER
ILCS . . . . . . Induction Loop Communications System
IOT . . . . Induction Output Tube
IPG . . . . Induction Plasma Gun
IPT . . . . Induction Plasma Torch
IRS . . . . Induction and Recruiting Station (Marine Corps)
ISD . . . . Induction System Deposit
ITM . . . . Induction Tube Modulation
IES . . . . Inductive Energy Storage
IESM . . . . . . Inductive Energy Storage Modulator

INV . . . . Inductive Null Voltage
ISS . . . . Inductive Storage Switch
IRB . . . . Inducto-Ratio Bridge
ILCK . . . . . . Inductosyn Linearity Checkout Kit
ICOMI . . . . . Industria e Commercio de Mineros, SA
IEX . . . . Industria Electrica de Mexico, SA (NYSE symbol)
I/H . . . . Industria del Hierro (Part of a large Mexican industrial complex)
ILTE . . . . Industria Libraria Tipografica Editrice
IME . . . . Industria Machine Electroniche
I . . . . Industrial
IAPO . . . . . . Industrial Accountable Property Officer (Air Force)
IARI . . . . Industrial Advertising Research Institute
IAB . . . . Industrial Advisory Board (World War II)
IACC . . . . . . Industrial Analysis and Control Council
IAF . . . . Industrial Areas Foundation
IAJAM . . . . . Industrial Association of Juvenile Apparel Manufacturers
IAVA . . . . . . Industrial Audio-Visual Association
IBJ . . . . Industrial Bank of Japan
ICAF . . . . . . Industrial College of the Armed Forces
ICDC . . . . . . Industrial and Commercial Development Corporation (Kenya)
ICFC . . . . . . Industrial and Commercial Finance Corporation (British)
ICC . . . . Industrial Communication Council
ICA . . . . Industrial Communications Association
ICS . . . . Industrial Control System
ICD . . . . Industrial Cooperation Division
IDP . . . . Industrial Data Processing
IDA . . . . Industrial Design Award
IDI . . . . Industrial Designers' Institute
IDSA . . . . . . Industrial Designers' Society of America
ID . . . . Industrial Development
IDC . . . . Industrial Development Corporation
IDI . . . . Industrial Development Institute (France)
IDQ . . . . Industrial Development Quotient
IDRC . . . . . . Industrial Development Research Council
IDA . . . . Industrial Diamond Association of America
ID . . . . Industrial Dynamics (Management analysis)
IEA . . . . Industrial Editors Association
IEI . . . . Industrial Education Institute
IEC . . . . Industrial Electrification Council
INDELSEC . . . . Industrial Electronic Security
IE . . . . Industrial Electronics
IECI . . . . Industrial Electronics and Control Instrumentation
IE . . . . Industrial Engineer
I & EC . . . . . . Industrial and Engineering Chemistry (A publication of American
            Chemical Society)
IEI . . . . Industrial Engineering Institute
IES . . . . Industrial Engineering Services
IEMC . . . . . . Industrial Equipment Manufacturers Council
IER . . . . Industrial Equipment Reserve
IEB . . . . Industrial Evaluation Board (BDSA)
IFI . . . . Industrial Fasteners Institute
IFEMA . . . . . . Industrial Finishing Equipment Manufacturers Association
IFA . . . . Industrial Forestry Association
IFC . . . . Industrial Frequency Changer
IF . . . . Industrial Fund
IGCI . . . . . . Industrial Gas Cleaning Institute
IHEA . . . . . . Industrial Heating Equipment Association
IHF . . . . Industrial Hygiene Foundation of America
IIS . . . . Industrial Information Service
ILLRI . . . . . . Industrial Lift and Loading Ramp Institute
IMAS . . . . . . Industrial Management Assistance Survey (Air Force)
IMP . . . . Industrial Management Program
IMS . . . . Industrial Management Society
INDMAN . . . . Industrial Manager
INDMGR . . . . Industrial Manager
IMA . . . . Industrial Marketing Association
IMS . . . . Industrial Mathematics Society
IMA . . . . Industrial Medical Association
IMS . . . . Industrial Methylated Spirit
IMIMI . . . . . . Industrial Mineral Insulation Manufacturers Institute
IMP . . . . Industrial Mobilization Planning
IMTP . . . . . . Industrial Mobilization Training Program
IO . . . . Industrial Operations
IPA . . . . Industrial Perforators Association
IPAA . . . . . . Industrial Photographers Association of America
IP . . . . Industrial Planning
IPS . . . . Industrial Planning Specification
IPE . . . . Industrial Plant Equipment
IP . . . . Industrial Police
IPT . . . . Industrial Power Tube
IPM . . . . Industrial Preparedness Measures

IPC . . . . Industrial Process Control (by computers)
IP . . . . Industrial Production
IPC . . . . Industrial Property Committee (US Military Government, Germany)
IPA . . . . Industrial Publicity Association
IQC . . . . Industrial Quality Control
IRL . . . . Industrial Reactor Laboratories (New Jersey)
IRPP . . . . Industrial Readiness Planning Program
IRB . . . . Industrial Readjustment Branch
IRC . . . . Industrial Reconstruction Corporation
IRU . . . . Industrial Rehabilitation Units (British)
IR . . . . Industrial Relations
IRAC . . . . Industrial Relations Advisory Committee
IRB . . . . Industrial Relations Board
IRCPPFI . . . . . Industrial Relations Council for the Plumbing and Pipe Fitting Industry
IRC . . . . Industrial Relations Counselors, Inc.
IRO . . . . Industrial Relations Office
IRRA . . . . Industrial Relations Research Association
IRG . . . . Industrial Reprocessing Group
IRAP . . . . Industrial Research Assistance Program (Canada)
IRI . . . . Industrial Research Institute
IRR . . . . Industrial Retaining Ring Company
ISEA . . . . Industrial Safety Equipment Association
ISM . . . . Industrial, Scientific, and Medical
ISC . . . . Industrial Security Committee
ISM . . . . Industrial Security Manual
ISP . . . . Industrial Security Program (Air Force, Army)
ISR . . . . Industrial Security Regulations (DOD)
IS . . . . Industrial Service (Equipment specifications)
ISI . . . . Industrial Static Inverter
ISD . . . . Industrial Systems Division
ITG . . . . Industrial Tachometer Generator
ITV . . . . Industrial Television
ITL . . . . Industrial Test Laboratory (Navy)
ITC . . . . Industrial Training Council
ITVAC . . . . Industrial Transistor Value Automatic Computer
ITA . . . . Industrial Truck Association
IUD . . . . Industrial Union Department (of AFL-CIO)
IUMSWA . . . . . Industrial Union of Marine and Shipbuilding Workers of America
IVC . . . . Industrial View Camera
IWS . . . . Industrial Water Supply
IWCI . . . . Industrial Wire Cloth Institute
IWW . . . . Industrial Workers of the World ("Wobblies")
IXF . . . . Industrial X-Ray Film
IHK . . . . Industrie und Handelskammer
IG . . . . Industriegewerkschaft (Industrial Trade Union) (West Germany)
INA . . . . Industrija Nafta (State-owned company) (Yugoslavia)
IAC . . . . Industry Advisory Committee (World War II)
IAGAL . . . . . . Industry Advisory Group for Air Logistics
ICD . . . . Industry Cooperation Division (Navy)
ICESC . . . . . . Industry Crew Escape Systems Committee
IDEP . . . . Industry Data Exchange Program
IFPA . . . . Industry Film Producers Association
IGA . . . . Industry and General Applications
IMSC . . . . Industry Missile and Space Conference
IOGA . . . . Industry-Organized Government-Approved
IRS . . . . Ineligible Reserve Section
ICPB . . . . Inert Components Processing Building
IOW . . . . Inert Ordnance Warehouse
IPB . . . . Inert Processing Building
ICB . . . . Inertia Compensated Balance
IACS . . . . Inertial Attitude Control System (Aerospace)
ICOSS . . . . . . Inertial-Command Off-Set System
IC . . . . Inertial Component
ICTE . . . . Inertial Component Test Equipment
IDSM . . . . Inertial Dampened Servomotor
IDS . . . . Inertial Data System
IDS . . . . Inertial Doppler System
IG . . . . Inertial Guidance
IGCG . . . . Inertial Guidance & Calibration Group (Air Force)
IGP . . . . Inertial Guidance Package (or Platform)
IGS . . . . Inertial Guidance System (NASA)
IHSD . . . . Inertial Height Sensing Device
IMU . . . . Inertial Measurement Unit
INE . . . . Inertial Navigation Element
ING . . . . Inertial Navigation Gyro
INS . . . . Inertial Navigation System
IP . . . . Inertial Platform
IQA . . . . Inertial Quality Attitude
IRIG . . . . Inertial Reference Integrating Gyro
IRSS . . . . Inertial Reference Stabilization System
IRU . . . . Inertial Reference Unit

ISC . . . . Inertial Start Command
IUA . . . . Inertial Unit Assembly
INSTAR . . . . . . Inertialess Scanning, Tracking and Ranging
ISCAN . . . . . . Inertialess Steerable Communications Antenna
IJMA . . . . Infant and Juvenile Manufacturers Association
IAFI . . . . Infantile Amaurotic Family Idiocy (Medicine)
I . . . . Infantry
IB . . . . Infantry Battalion (Army)
INFBAT . . . . . . Infantry Battalion (Army)
ICDA . . . . . . Infantry Combat Developments Agency (Army) (Pronounced Ick-da)
IDR . . . . Infantry Drill Regulations
LSIL . . . . Infantry Landing Ship (Large)
IOBC . . . . Infantry Officer Basic Course
IOCC . . . . Infantry Officer Career Course (Army)
IOTC . . . . Infantry Officers Training Camp
IRTC . . . . Infantry Replacement Training Center
IRUS . . . . Infantry Rifle Unit Study (Army)
IS . . . . Infantry School (Army)
ITC . . . . Infantry Training Center (Army)
ITR . . . . Infantry Training Replacement
ICCA . . . . . . Infants' and Children's Coat Association
ICNA . . . . . . Infants' and Children's Novelties Association
ICTBA . . . . . . Infants', Children's and Teens' Wear Buyers Association
ICWSG . . . . . Infants' and Children's Wear Salesmen's Guild
IA . . . . Infected Area
IBK . . . . Infectious Bovine Kerato-Conjunctivitis (Veterinary medicine)
IB . . . . Infectious Bronchitis (Veterinary medicine)
ICH . . . . Infectious Canine Hepatitis (Veterinary medicine)
ID . . . . Infectious Disease (Medicine)
IH . . . . Infectious Hepatitis
IM . . . . Infectious Mononucleosis
IPN . . . . Infectious Pancreatic Necrosis (Disease)
IPV . . . . Infectious Pustular Vulvovaginitis (Veterinary medicine)
ID . . . . Infective Dose
ID/50 . . . . . . Infective Dose, Median
INFEREX . . . . . Inference Execution Language
IVC . . . . Inferior Vena Cava (Anatomy)
I . . . . Infield
IRT . . . . Infinite-Resolution Trimmer
ITS . . . . Infinite Time Span
ICT . . . . Inflammation of Connective Tissue (Medicine)
IMP . . . . Inflatable Micrometeoroid Paraglide
IC . . . . Informal Communication
IM . . . . Informal Memo
IMR . . . . Informal Memorandum Report
IPCOG . . . . . Informal Policy Committee for Germany
IPR . . . . Informal Progress Report
IR . . . . Informal Report
IAO . . . . Information Activities Office(r) (Military)
IAC . . . . Information Analysis Center (DOD)
INFORMAL . . . Information for Avionics Laboratory
IB . . . . Information Bulletin
IC . . . . Information Center (Army)
INFOCEN . . . . Information Center
ICER . . . . . . Information Centre of the European Railways
IC . . . . Information Circular
IDEEA . . . . . . Information and Data Exchange Experimental Activities
IDC . . . . Information and Direction Center
IDIIOM . . . . . . Information Displays, Incorporated, Input-Output Machine
ID . . . . Information Distributor
IE . . . . Information and Education (Army)
IEG . . . . Information Exchange Group (National Institutes of Health)
IEL . . . . Information Exchange List (Military)
IHS . . . . Information Handling Services
III . . . . Information International, Incorporated
IMD . . . . Information Media Department
IO . . . . Information Officer
INFOL . . . . . . Information Oriented Language (Computer program)
IOTA . . . . . . Information Overload Testing Aid
IOTA . . . . . . Information Overload Testing Apparatus
IPC . . . . Information Processing Center
INPRONS . . . . Information Processing in the Central Nervous System
IPCCS . . . . . . Information Processing in Command and Control Systems
IPE . . . . Information Processing Equipment
IPL . . . . Information Processing Language (Data processing)
IPS . . . . Information Processing System
IRC . . . . Information Recovery Capsule
IR . . . . Information Report
INFOREQ . . . . Information Requested
INREQ . . . . . . Information Requested
IRRM . . . . . . Information Requested in Above Referenced Message (Army)

INREQS . . . . . Information Requests (Army)
IRIS . . . . Information Resources Information System (Library of Congress)
IR . . . . Information Retrieval
INFRAL. . . . . Information Retrieval Automatic Language (Data processing)
IRI . . . . Information Retrieval, Incorporated
IRL . . . . Information Retrieval Language (Data processing)
IRS. . . . . Information Retrieval System
ISAD . . . . . . Information Science and Automation Division (of ALA)
ISL . . . . Information Search Language
IS . . . . Information Series
IS . . . . Information Service
INSPEC. . . . . Information Service for Physics, Electrotechnology and Control (IEE)
ISR. . . . . Information Service Representative (Veterans Administration)
ISO . . . . . . Information Services Officer
ISAP. . . . . . . Information Sort and Predict
ISR. . . . . Information Storage and Retrieval (Data processing)
IS & R . . . . . . Information Storage and Retrieval
INSTARS . . . . Information Storage and Retrieval System
ISD . . . . Information Systems Division (National Library of Medicine)
ISO . . . . Information Systems Office (Library of Congress)
ISP. . . . . Information Systems Program (National Science Foundation)
IT . . . . Information Theory
INTREX . . . . . Information Transfer Experiments (MIT)
ITS. . . . . Information Transmission System
IVD . . . . Information Viewing Device
IAI . . . . Informational Acquisition and Interpretation
IMG. . . . . . . Informational Media Guaranty
INBEL. . . . . . Informations Belges (Belgian Information Agency)
IA . . . . Infra-Audible (Sound)
IBR. . . . . Infra-Black Region
IF . . . . Infrared
IR . . . . Infrared
IRACQ . . . . . Infrared Acquisition RADAR
IRAC . . . . . . Infrared Advisory Center
IRADDS. . . . . Infrared Air Defense Detection System
IRAH . . . . . . Infrared Alternate Head
IRASER . . . . . Infrared Amplification by Stimulated Emission of Radiation
IRAS. . . . . . . Infrared Attack System
IAE . . . . Infrared Auroral Emission
ICS . . . . Infrared Calibration System
ICS . . . . Infrared Camera System
ICER. . . . . . . Infrared Cell, Electronically Refrigerated
ICU . . . . Infrared Command Unit
ICS . . . . Infrared Communications System
IRCS. . . . . . . Infrared Communications System
IRCCM . . . . . . Infrared Counter-Countermeasures (Military electronics)
IRCM . . . . . . Infrared Counter-Countermeasures (Military electronics)
IRC . . . . Infrared Countermeasures (Military electronics)
ICS . . . . Infrared Countermeasures System
IDE . . . . Infrared Decoy Evaluator
IRDS . . . . . . Infrared Detecting Set
IDS . . . . Infrared Detection System
IDU . . . . Infrared Detection Unit
IRDU . . . . . . Infrared Detection Unit
IFD . . . . Infrared Detector
IRD . . . . Infrared Detector
IDC . . . . Infrared Detector Cryostat
IDO . . . . Infrared Drying Oven
IRDO . . . . . . Infrared Drying Oven
IE . . . . Infrared Emission
IRE. . . . . Infrared Engineering
IR . . . . Infrared Equipment (Navy)
IF . . . . Infrared Filter
IFR. . . . . Infrared Filter Radiometer
IFC . . . . Infrared Fire Control
IFCS. . . . . . . Infrared Fire Control System
IRGAR . . . . . Infrared Gas Radiation
IRG . . . . Infrared Generator
IGL . . . . Infrared Gunfire Locator
IRGL . . . . . . Infrared Gunfire Locator
IRH . . . . Infrared Heater
IHS . . . . Infrared Horizon Sensor
IRIC . . . . . . Infrared Image Converter
IRIS . . . . Infrared Image Scanner
IRI . . . . Infrared Imagery
IIS . . . . Infrared Imaging System
IRIA . . . . . . Infrared Information and Analysis
IIAC. . . . . . . Infrared Information and Analysis Center (University of Michigan)
IRIS . . . . Infrared Information Symposia (Navy)
IRI . . . . Infrared Instrumentation
IIS . . . . Infrared Instrumentation System

IRIS . . . . Infrared Interferometer Spectrometer
IRK . . . . Infrared Kit
IRL. . . . . Infrared Lamp
IRLAS . . . . . . Infrared LASER
IRL. . . . . Infrared Lens
ILS. . . . . Infrared Live Scanner
IRM . . . . Infrared Mapper
IRMS . . . . . . Infrared Mapping System
IRM . . . . Infrared Measurement
IMI . . . . Infrared Measurement Instrument
IRMP . . . . . . Infrared Measurement Program
IMS . . . . Infrared Measuring System
IMJ . . . . Infrared Miniaturized Jammer
IRMJ . . . . . . Infrared Miniaturized Jammer
IRMA . . . . . . Infrared Miss-Distance Approximator
IMRA . . . . . . Infrared Monochromatic Radiation
INT . . . . Infrared Nondestructive Testing
IRPM . . . . . . Infrared Physical Measurement
IPP. . . . . Infrared Pointer Package
IRPP . . . . . . Infrared Pointer Package
IRP. . . . . Infrared Preamplifier
IRQC . . . . . . Infrared Quantum Counter
IRRMP. . . . . . Infrared RADAR Measurement Program
IR . . . . Infrared Radiation
IRP. . . . . Infrared Radiation Profile
IR . . . . Infrared Radiometer
IRR . . . . Infrared Radiometer
IRRAD . . . . . . Infrared Range and Detection
IRR . . . . Infrared Receiver
IRS. . . . . Infrared Reconnaissance Set
IRS. . . . . Infrared Reflective Spectra
IRP. . . . . Infrared Responsive Phosphor
IRSS . . . . . . Infrared Search Set
IRSSO. . . . . . Infrared Search Set Operator
IRST . . . . . . Infrared Search and Track
IRSTS . . . . . . Infrared Search-Track System
ISEEP . . . . . . Infrared Sensitive Element Evaluation Program
IRSS . . . . . . Infrared Sensor System
ISS. . . . . Infrared Sensor System
ISC . . . . Infrared Sightline Control
IRSO . . . . . . Infrared Solder Oven
ISR. . . . . Infrared Spectral Radiometer
IRSP . . . . . . Infrared Spectrometer
ISP. . . . . Infrared Spectrophotometer
IRS. . . . . Infrared Spectroscopy
ISD . . . . Infrared Suppression Device
ISS. . . . . Infrared Surveillance Set
IRSE . . . . . . Infrared Systems Engineering
IRSGHL. . . . . . Infrared Systems and Guidance Heads Laboratory
IRSM . . . . . . Infrared Systems Manufacturing
ISM . . . . Infrared Systems Manufacturing
IRCT . . . . . . Infrared on Target
IRTD. . . . . . . Infrared Target Detector
ITD . . . . Infrared Target Detector
ITEC. . . . . . . Infrared Techniques for Electronics Committee
IRT. . . . . Infrared Thermometer
IRT. . . . . Infrared Tracker
ITDU . . . . . . Infrared Tracking Display Unit
ITS. . . . . Infrared Tracking System
IRTRAN . . . . . Infrared Transmitting
IRT. . . . . Infrared Tube
IRICON . . . . . Infrared Vidicon Tube
IVS . . . . Infrared Viewing Set
IRW . . . . Infrared Window
IS . . . . Infrasonic
ICA . . . . Ingenieros Civiles Asociados (Mexican construction company)
Ing B . . . . . . Ingenium Baccalaureus (Bachelor of Engineering)
Ing D . . . . . . Ingenium Doctor (Doctor of Engineering)
Ing M . . . . . . Ingenium Magister (Master of Engineering)
IR . . . . Ingersoll-Rand Company (NYSE symbol)
II. . . . . Ingot Iron
IGA . . . . Inhaled Gas Analyzer
ICMW. . . . . . Inherent Corrective Maintenance Workload
IER. . . . . Inherent Equipment Reliability
IHF . . . . Inhibit Halt Flip-Flop (Data processing)
INTO . . . . . . Inhibited Nitrogen Tetroxide
IRFNA . . . . . . Inhibited Red Fuming Nitric Acid
I . . . . Inhibitory
IPSP . . . . Inhibitory Postsynaptic Potential (Physiology)
I . . . . Initial
IAP . . . . Initial Aiming Point (Gunnery)

IA . . . . Initial Appearance (RADAR)
I . . . . Initial Approach (Aviation)
IAP . . . . Initial Approach (Aviation)
INA . . . . Initial Approach (Aviation)
IAF . . . . Initial Approach Fix (Aviation)
IA . . . . Initial Authorization
IBH . . . . Initial Beachhead (Military)
IBHD . . . . . . Initial Beachhead (Military)
IBP . . . . Initial Boiling Point
IBRL . . . . Initial Bomb Release Line
ICI . . . . Initial Capabilities Inspection (Military)
ICCA . . . . . . Initial Cash Clothing Allowance (Military)
IC . . . . Initial Conditions
IC . . . . Initial Course (Navigation)
IDCS . . . . Initial Defense Communication Satellite (NASA)
IDCSP . . . . . . Initial (or Interim) Defense Communication Satellite Program (or Project)
IDP . . . . Initial Delay Position (Military)
IDR . . . . Initial Design Review
IET . . . . Initial Engine Test
IETF . . . . Initial Engine Test Facility
IE . . . . Initial Equipment (Navy aircraft)
IIE . . . . Initial Ion Event
II . . . . Initial Issue
ILC . . . . Initial Launch Capability (Aerospace)
IOCD . . . . . . Initial Operation Capability Date (Military)
IOC . . . . Initial Operational Capability (Air Force)
IOT . . . . Initial Orbit Time (Aerospace)
IOL . . . . Initial Outfitting List (for advanced naval bases)
IP . . . . Initial Point (Military)
IPE . . . . Initial Portable Equipment
IPF . . . . Initial Protective Force
IRP . . . . Initial Receiving Point
ISACC . . . . . . Initial Satellite Command and Control
ISD . . . . Initial Search Depth
ISM . . . . Initial Segment Membrane
IS . . . . Initial Shortage
ISSL . . . . Initial Spares Support List
IST . . . . Initial Support Team (Military)
ISCO . . . . Initial Systems Check-Out
i/t/a . . . . Initial Teaching Alphabet (A 44-symbol alphabet planned to simplify beginning reading by representing sounds more precisely)
ITA . . . . Initial Teaching Alphabet (See i/t/a)
ITP . . . . Initial Test Phase
IVP . . . . Initial Vapor Pressure
IV . . . . Initial Velocity (Ballistics)
IVI . . . . Initial Ventricular Impulse
IRT . . . . Initialize Reset Tape
IAD . . . . Initiation Area Discriminator (RADAR)
IS . . . . Initiation Supervisor
I & R . . . . . . Initiative and Referendum
ICM . . . . Initiator Command Module
ILI . . . . Injection LASER Illuminator
IMK . . . . Injection Molding Kit
IO . . . . Injector Orifice
IBBA . . . . . . Inland Bird Banding Association
IDPA . . . . . . Inland Daily Press Association
IMIB . . . . . . Inland Marine Insurance Bureau
IMUA . . . . . . Inland Marine Underwriters Association
ILX . . . . Inland Molasses Company (American Stock Exchange symbol)
IR . . . . Inland Revenue (British)
IRC . . . . Inland Revenue Commissioners (British)
IRO . . . . Inland Revenue Office(r) (British)
IAD . . . . Inland Steel Company (NYSE symbol)
ITC . . . . Inland Transport Committee (UN)
IWS . . . . Inland Waterway Service
IWT . . . . Inland Waterway Transport
IWCCA . . . . . . Inland Waterways Common Carriers Association
IWC . . . . Inland Waterways Corporation
IAP . . . . Inlet Absolute Pressure
IC . . . . Inlet Contact
IGV . . . . Inlet Guide Vane
IMH . . . . Inlet Manhole (Technical drawings)
ITR . . . . Inlet Temperature Rise
IVA . . . . Inlet Vane Actuator
IRM . . . . Innate Release Mechanism (Endocrinology)
I . . . . Inner
IAZ . . . . Inner Artillery Zone
IBP . . . . Inner (Edge of) Basal Piece
IB . . . . Inner Bottom (Technical drawings)
IDZ . . . . Inner Defense Zone
IEE . . . . Inner Enamel Epithelium (Dentistry)

IG . . . . Inner Gimbal
IGA . . . . Inner Gimbal Axis
IGI . . . . Inner Gird Injection
IG . . . . Inner Guard (Masonry)
IK . . . . Inner Keel
ILEA . . . . Inner London Education Authority (British)
IM . . . . Inner Marker (Part of an instrument landing system) (Aviation)
IMKR . . . . . . Inner Marker, Instrument Landing System (Aviation)
IPM . . . . Inner Peace Movement
IPV . . . . Inner Pilot Valve
IQN . . . . Inner Quantum Number
IRB . . . . Inner Radiation Belt
IRZ . . . . Inner Radiation Zone
IT . . . . Inner Temple
IP . . . . Innings Pitched
ID . . . . Inniskilling Dragoons (Military) (British)
ISA . . . . Innkeepers Society of America
IOM . . . . Innovator of the Month
IAIP . . . . Inorganic Ablative Insulative Plastic
IAP . . . . Inorganic Ablative Plastic
IIP . . . . Inorganic Insulative Plastic
IDP . . . . Inosine Diphosphate
IMP . . . . Inosine Monophosphate
ITP . . . . Inosine Triphosphate
IHP . . . . Inositol Hexaphosphate
IMPS . . . . Inpatient Multidimensional Psychiatric Scale
I . . . . Input
IBC . . . . Input Bias Current
ICE . . . . Input-Checking Equipment
IC . . . . Input Circuit
ICR . . . . Input and Compare Register
INC . . . . Input Control System (Military)
IC . . . . Input Current
ICO . . . . Input Current Offset (Data processing)
IDA . . . . Input Data Assembler
IDC . . . . Input Display Console (Data processing)
IFT . . . . Input Frequency Tolerance (Data processing)
II . . . . Input Impedance
ILL . . . . Input Logic Level
IMCD . . . . . . Input Marginal Checking and Distribution
IMB . . . . Input Memory Buffer (Data processing)
IMP . . . . Input Message Processor
IOC . . . . Input Offset Current
IOV . . . . Input Offset Voltage
IO . . . . Input-Output (Electronics)
I/O . . . . Input/Output (Data processing)
IOB . . . . Input-Output Buffer (Data processing)
IOCC . . . . . . Input-Output Control Center (Data processing)
IOCC . . . . . . Input/Output Control Command (Data processing)
IOCS . . . . . . Input-Output Control System (Data processing)
IOC . . . . Input/Output Controller (Data processing)
IODC . . . . . . Input Output Data Channel (Data processing)
IODC . . . . . . Input Output Delay Counter (Data processing)
I/OM . . . . . . Input/Output Multiplexer (Data processing)
IOP . . . . Input/Output Processor (Data processing)
IOPS . . . . . . Input-Output Programming System (Data processing)
IOR . . . . Input-Output Register (SAGE)
IOS . . . . Input-Output Skip (Data processing)
IOT . . . . Input-Output Termination (Data processing)
IP . . . . Input Power
IRS . . . . Input Read Submodule
ISV . . . . Input Signal Voltage
IS . . . . Input Simulator
ITE . . . . Input Test Equipment
INTRAN . . . . . Input Translator (Data processing)
IT . . . . Input Translator
IV . . . . Input Voltage
IVO . . . . Input Voltage Offset
IVS . . . . Input Voltage Supply
ICT . . . . Insect Carrier Toxicant
IWSB . . . . . . Insect Wire Screening Bureau
ICS . . . . Insert Card Section
IPD . . . . Insertion Phase Delay
IVAR . . . . . . Insertion Velocity Adjust Routine (NASA)
IFS . . . . Inshore Fire Support Ship (Navy symbol)
MSI . . . . Inshore Minesweeper (Navy symbol)
INSHOREPAT . . Inshore Patrol
INSPAT . . . . . Inshore Patrol
IUW . . . . Inshore Underwater Warfare
I . . . . Inside
IAT . . . . Inside Air Temperature

ICUS . . . . Inside Continental United States (Military)
ID . . . . Inside Diameter
ID . . . . Inside Dimensions
IE . . . . Inside Edge
IH . . . . Inside Height
IL . . . . Inside Layer (Technical drawings)
IL . . . . Inside Left (Soccer position)
IL . . . . Inside Length (Technical drawings)
IML . . . . Inside Mold Line (Technical drawings)
IR . . . . Inside Radius (Technical drawings)
IR . . . . Inside Right (Soccer position)
INUS . . . . Inside the United States
IW . . . . Inside Width
IR . . . . Insoluble Residue
IRAN . . . . Inspect(ion) and Repair as Necessary (Aviation)
IROAN . . . . . Inspect and Repair Only as Necessary (Military)
IC . . . . Inspected and Condemned (Military)
IVP . . . . Inspected Variety Purity (Agriculture)
I/O . . . . Inspecting Order
IOO . . . . Inspecting Ordnance Officer
ITO . . . . Inspecting Torpedo Officer (Navy)
IA . . . . Inspection Administration (Navy)
IBA . . . . Inspection by Attribute
INS . . . . Inspection Division (Coast Guard)
INFX . . . . . . Inspection Fixture
INGA . . . . . . Inspection Gage
IIS . . . . Inspection Instruction Sheet
ILS . . . . Inspection Lot Size
I & M . . . . . . Inspection and Maintenance
IM . . . . Inspection Manual
IM . . . . Inspection Memorandum
IPPA . . . . . . Inspection, Palpation, Percussion, Auscultation (Medicine)
IPN . . . . Inspection Progress Notifications
IQA . . . . Inspection Quality Assurance
IR . . . . Inspection Rejection
IR . . . . Inspection Release
IROR . . . . . . Inspection, Repair, Overhaul and Rebuild
I & S . . . . . . Inspection and Security
INSH . . . . . . Inspection Shell
I & S . . . . . . (Board of) Inspection and Survey
IT . . . . Inspection Tag
ITP . . . . Inspection Test Procedure
ITR . . . . Inspection Test Report
IBV . . . . Inspection by Variables
I . . . . Inspector
IDG . . . . Inspector of Degaussing (Navy)
INSDEN . . . . . Inspector of Dental Activities
IG . . . . Inspector General (Air Force, Army, Marine Corps)
INSGEN . . . . Inspector General (Navy)
IGT . . . . Inspector-General to the Forces for Training (British)
IGFA . . . . . . Inspector General, Foreign Assistance (Department of State)
IGF . . . . Inspector-General of Fortifications (British)
INSGENPAC . . Inspector General, Pacific Fleet and Pacific Ocean Areas
IGD . . . . Inspector General's Department
INSP-INSTR . . Inspector-Instruction (Marine Corps)
INSINSTR . . . Inspector-Instructor, Naval Reserve
I/K . . . . Inspector/Killer
IM . . . . Inspector of Machinery
INA . . . . Inspector of Naval Aircraft
INSAIR . . . . . Inspector of Naval Aircraft
INSENG . . . . Inspector Naval Engineering Material
INM . . . . Inspector of Naval Machinery
INSMACH . . . . Inspector of Naval Machinery
INM . . . . Inspector of Naval Material
INSMAT . . . . Inspector of Naval Material
INSNAVMAT . . Inspector of Navigational Material
INSCRUIT . . . Inspector of Navy Recruiting and Naval Officer Procurement
INSORD . . . . Inspector of Ordnance
INSORDINC . . Inspector of Ordnance in Charge
INSPETRES . . . Inspector of Petroleum Reserves
INSRADMAT . . Inspector Radio Material
ITM . . . . Inspector of Torpedoes and Mines (Navy)
IW . . . . Inspector of Works
IC . . . . Inspiration Consolidated Copper Company (NYSE symbol)
IC . . . . Inspiratory Capacity (Physiology)
IC . . . . Inspiratory Center (Physiology)
IRV . . . . Inspiratory Reserve Volume
IPP . . . . Inspired Partial Pressure
I & C . . . . . . Installation and Check (Military)
I & C . . . . . . Installation and Construction (Military)
IIPR . . . . . . Installation Inspection Procedure Report

IMDO . . . . Installation and Materiel District Office (FAA)
IPO . . . . Installation Planning Order
IPO . . . . Installation Production Order
IPB . . . . Installation Property Book (Military)
ISSS . . . . Installation Service Supply Support
ITO . . . . Installation Transportation Office(r) (Air Force)
IFK . . . . Installations Fragenkommission (CEE)
I & L . . . . . . Installations and Logistics
ILI . . . . Instant Lunar Ionosphere
IOCS . . . . . . Instant Ocean Culture System
IPPA . . . . Instant Potato Products Association
IRF . . . . Instant Ready Force (Military)
I . . . . Instantaneous
IAMS . . . . . . Instantaneous Audience Measurement System
IAFC . . . . . . Instantaneous Automatic Frequency Control
IAGC . . . . . . Instantaneous Automatic Gain Control (RADAR)
IAVC . . . . . . Instantaneous Automatic Volume Control (Electronics)
ICM . . . . Instantaneous Center of Motion
ICR . . . . Instantaneous Center of Rotation
ICPAC . . . . . Instantaneous Compressor Performance Analysis Computer
IFC . . . . Instantaneous Frequency Correlation
IFM . . . . Instantaneous Frequency Measurement
IIP . . . . Instantaneous Impact Point
IOL . . . . Instantaneous Overload
IPO . . . . Instantaneous Power Output
IROD . . . . . . Instantaneous Readout Detector (Satellite instrument)
IR . . . . Instantaneous Relay
ISP . . . . Instantaneous Sound Pressure
IVV . . . . Instantaneous Vertical Velocity
IVVI . . . . Instantaneous Vertical Velocity Indicator
ITAL . . . . . . Instituut voor de Toepassing van Atoomenergie in de Landboury
           (Netherlands)
IDI . . . . Institut de Droit International
IEREGEM . . . . Institut Equatorial de Recherches et d'Etudes Geologiques et Minieres
IEDES . . . . . . Institut d'Etude du Developpement Economique et Social (France)
IMEDE . . . . . Institut pour l'Etude des Methodes de Direction de l'Enterprise
           (A management development institute) (Lausanne, Switzerland)
IEC . . . . Institut d'Etudes Congolaises (Congolese Institute of Studies)
IFOCAP . . . . Institut de Formation pour les Cadres Paysans
IFFA . . . . Institut fuer Forstliche Arbeitswissenschaft
IFAN . . . . . . Institut Francais d'Afrique Noire (French Institute of Black Africa)
IFOP . . . . . . Institut Francais d'Opinion Publique (French Institute of Public Opinion)
IDHEC . . . . . Institut des Hautes Etudes Cinematographiques (French institute for the
           study of the motion picture)
IIT . . . . Institut Interafricain du Travail
IIB . . . . Institut International de Bibliographie
IIB . . . . Institut International des Brevets
ICARES . . . . . Institut International Catholique de Recherches Sociales
INCIDI . . . . . Institut International des Civilisations Differentes
IIE . . . . Institut International de l'Epargne
IIEL . . . . Institut International d'Etudes Ligures
IIF . . . . Institut International du Froid
IIP . . . . Institut International de la Presse
IIRB . . . . Institut International de Recherches Betteravieres
IIRG . . . . Institut International de Recherches Graphologiques
IISA . . . . Institut International des Sciences Administratives
IIS . . . . Institut International de la Soudure
IIS . . . . Institut International de Statistique
IIT . . . . Institut International du Theatre
UNIDROIT . . . . Institut International pour l'Unification du Droit Prive
INEAC . . . . . . Institut National pour l'Etude Agronomique du Congo (National Institute
           for the Study of Agronomy in the Congo)
INR . . . . Institut National de Radiodiffusion (Belgium)
INRA . . . . . . Institut National de la Recherche Agronomique (France)
INSERM . . . . Institut National de la Sante et de la Recherche Medicale (France)
INSTN . . . . . . Institut National des Sciences et Techniques Nucleaires (France)
INSEE . . . . . . Institut National de la Statistique et des Etudes Economiques
           (National Institute of Statistics and Economic Research) (France)
IOSTA . . . . . Institut d'Organisation Scientifique du Travail en Agriculture
IPC . . . . Institut Politique Congolais (Congolese Political Institute)
IRAM . . . . . . Institut de Recherche et Application des Methodes de Developpement
IRFED . . . . . . Institut de Recherche et de Formation en vue du Developpement
           Harmonise (France)
IRIA . . . . . . Institut de Recherche d'Informatique et d'Automatique (France)
IRSAC . . . . . . Institut pour le Recherche Scientifique en Afrique Centrale (Brussels)
IRAT . . . . . . Institut de Recherches d'Agronomie Tropicale et de Culture Vivrieres
           (Food and agricultural research foundation supported by France and
           several African states)
IRHO . . . . . . Institut de Recherches pour les Huiles et Oleagineux
IRSAC . . . . . . Institut de Recherches Scientifiques au Congo
ISEA . . . . Institut de Science Economique Appliquee (France)

ISPH........ Institut Superieur de Pedagogie du Hainaut (Belgium)
ITF........ Institut Textile de France
ITA........ Institut du Transport Aerien (Institute of Air Transport)
IURN ...... Institut Unifie de Recherches Nucleaires
IUT .... Institut Universitaire de Technologie
I .... Institute (or Institution)
IOA........ Institute of Actuaries
IAIES ...... Institute for Advanced Interdisciplinary Engineering Studies (Purdue University)
IAMM & D ... Institute for Advanced Materials, Mechanics, and Design (Army Materiel Command)
IASTA...... Institute for Advanced Studies in the Theatre
IAS .... Institute for Advanced Study
IAMC ...... Institute for Advancement of Medical Communication
IAS .... Institute of Aeronautical Sciences
IAS .... Institute of Aerospace Sciences (Later, AIAA)
IARSEP ...... Institute Africain de Recherches Sociales et Economiques pour l'Education Populaire (African Institute of Social and Economic Research for Popular Education)
IAWR ...... Institute of Air Weapons Research (Air Force)
IAD .... Institute for American Democracy
IAF .... Institute on American Freedoms
IAPI .... Institute of American Poultry Industries
IAS .... Institute of American Strategy
IAS .... Institute of Andean Studies
IAM .... Institute of Appliance Manufacturers
IAT .... Institute for Applied Technology (National Bureau of Standards)
IAMR ...... Institute of Arctic Mineral Resources (University of Alaska)
IAS .... Institute of Atmospheric Sciences (Environmental Science Services Administration)
IAE .... Institute of Atomic Energy (Academy of Sciences, USSR)
IASA ...... Institute for Atomic Sciences in Agriculture
IAE .... Institute of Automobile Engineers
IBR........ Institute for Basic Research (National Bureau of Standards)
IBS........ Institute for Basic Standards (National Bureau of Standards)
IBN .... Institute Belge de Normalisation (Brussels, Belgium)
IBP .... Institute for Better Packaging
IBA .... Institute of Bioenergetic Analysis
IBVM ...... Institute of the Blessed Virgin Mary (Sisters of Loretto) (Roman Catholic religious order)
IBR .... Institute of Boiler and Radiator Manufacturers
IBRM ...... Institute of Boiler and Radiator Manufacturers
IBA .... Institute of British Architects
IBIA .... Institute of British Industrial Art
IBFM ...... Institute of Broadcasting Financial Management
IBD .... Institute of Business Designers
ICR .... Institute for Cancer Research
ICER ...... Institute for Central European Research
ICET....... Institute for the Certification of Engineering Technicians
ICTA ...... Institute of Certified Travel Agents
IC .... Institute of Charity (Rosminians)
ICC .... Institute of Chinese Culture
ICUA ...... Institute for College and University Administrators
ICM .... Institute of Composite Materials
ICT .... Institute of Computer Technology
ICRS....... Institute of Contemporary Russian Studies (Fordham University)
ICR .... Institute for Cooperative Research
ICR .... Institute for Creative Research
ICD .... Institute for the Crippled and Disabled
ICWA ...... Institute of Current World Affairs
IDA .... Institute of Defense Analyses
IDE .... Institute for Democratic Education (Absorbed by Anti-Defamation League of B'nai B'rith)
I/D/E/A ..... Institute for Development of Educational Activities (of Charles F. Kettering Foundation)
ID .... Institute of Distribution
IEAHC ...... Institute of Early American History and Culture
IES........ Institute for Earth Sciences (Environmental Science Services Administration)
IED .... Institute for Educational Development
IEI .... Institute for Educational Innovation (Became Education Development Center)
IER .... Institute of Educational Research
IEEE .... Institute of Electrical and Electronics Engineers
IECEJ .... Institute of Electronic Communications Engineers of Japan
IER........ Institute of Engineering Research (University of California)
IEE .... Institute of Environmental Engineers
IER........ Institute for Environmental Research (Environmental Science Services Administration)
IES .... Institute of Environmental Sciences
IES .... Institute of European Studies
IER........ Institute of Exploratory Research (Army)

IFE........ Institute of Fire Engineers
IFEM ...... Institute of Fireplace Equipment Manufacturers
IFPE ...... Institute of Fiscal and Political Education
IFT .... Institute of Food Technologists
IGT .... Institute of Gas Technology
IGS .... Institute of General Semantics
IG .... Institute of Geophysics (University of California)
IGIP....... Institute of Geophysics and Interplanetary Physics
IGSP ...... Institute for Gravitational Strain Pathology
IHT .... Institute of Heat Technology
IOH .... Institute of Heraldry (DOD)
IHF .... Institute of High Fidelity
IHFM ...... Institute of High Fidelity Manufacturers
ICH .... Institute of Hispanic Culture
IHE .... Institute of Home Economics (of ARS, Department of Agriculture)
IHOU....... Institute of Home Office Underwriters
IHP .... Institute for Human Progress
IIL........ Institute of Industrial Launderers
IIRR .... Institute of Industrial Race Relations
IIAA .... Institute of Inter-American Affairs (UN)
IIS .... Institute for Intercultural Studies
IIA........ Institute of Internal Affairs
IIA........ Institute of Internal Auditors
IICE .... Institute for Internal Combustion Engines
IIE .... Institute of International Education
IILR .... Institute of International Labor Research
IIO .... Institute for International Order
IIYA .... Institute for International Youth Affairs
IJS .... Institute of Jazz Studies
IJA .... Institute of Jewish Affairs
IJA .... Institute of Judicial Administration
ILAR...... Institute of Laboratory Animal Resources
ILM .... Institute of Labour Management
ILC .... Institute of Land Combat (Army)
ILI .... Institute of Life Insurance
ILL........ Institute of Lifetime Learning
IME .... Institute of Makers of Explosives
IMS .... Institute on Man and Science (Formerly, Council on World Tensions)
IMS .... Institute of Management Sciences
IMS .... Institute of Marine Science
IMST ...... Institute of Marine Sciences and Technology
IMR .... Institute of Masonry Research
IMR .... Institute for Materials Research (National Bureau of Standards)
IMS .... Institute of Mathematical Statistics
IMA........ Institute for Mediterranean Affairs
IOM....... Institute of Metals (British)
IMB .... Institute of Microbiology
IMD....... Institute for Muscle Disease
INSA ...... Institute National de Science Applique (France)
INS .... Institute for Naval Studies
ION....... Institute of Navigation
INCFO ...... Institute of Newspaper Controllers and Finance Officers
INMM ..... Institute of Nuclear Materials Management
INS .... Institute for Nuclear Study (Japan)
INCAP ..... Institute of Nutrition of Central America and Panama
IO .... Institute for Oceanography (Environmental Science Services Administration)
IOS .... Institute of Optimization and Systems Theory (Stockholm)
IOA .... Institute of Outdoor Advertising
IPR .... Institute of Pacific Relations
IPC .... Institute of Paper Chemistry
IPC .... Institute of Pastoral Care
IP .... Institute of Petroleum (British)
IP .... Institute of Physics (USSR)
IPSS ...... Institute of Planetary and Space Science
IPS........ Institute for Policy Studies
IPI .... Institute of Poultry Industries
IPC .... Institute of Printed Circuits
IPTAR...... Institute for Psychoanalytic Training and Research
IPA .... Institute of Public Administration
IPA .... Institute of Public Affairs
IPR........ Institute of Public Relations (British)
IOP .... Institute of Pyramidology
IOQ....... Institute of Quarrying
IRE .... Institute of Radio Engineers (Later, IEEE)
IRT........ Institute for Rapid Transit
IRL........ Institute for Rational Living
IRR........ Institute for Reactor Research (Switzerland)
IREM ...... Institute of Real Estate Management
IRAS...... Institute on Religion in an Age of Science
IRHR....... Institute for Research in Human Relations
IRH........ Institute for Research in Hypnosis

IRR . . . . Institute of Rubber Research
ISS . . . . Institute of Salesian Studies
ISM . . . . Institute of Sanitation Management
ISI . . . . Institute for Scientific Information
ISIS . . . . Institute of Scrap Iron and Steel
ISR . . . . Institute of Semiconductor Research (USSR)
ISEO . . . . Institute of Shortening and Edible Oils
SSD . . . . Institute of the Sisters of St. Dorothy (Roman Catholic religious order)
ISOSJ . . . . . . Institute of Social Order of the Society of Jesus
ISR . . . . Institute for Social Research
ISAS . . . . Institute of Space and Aeronautical Science
ISL . . . . Institute of Space Law
ISP . . . . Institute of Store Planners
ISS . . . . Institute for Strategic Studies
ISNV . . . . . . Institute for the Study of Nonviolence
ISD . . . . Institute of Surplus Dealers
ITG . . . . Institute Technical Group
IT . . . . Institute of Technology (Air Force)
ITE . . . . Institute of Telecommunications Engineers
ITSA . . . . Institute for Telecommunications Science and Aeronomy (Environmental
 Science Services Administration)
ITS . . . . Institute of Temporary Services
ITT . . . . Institute of Textile Technology
ITM . . . . Institute of Thread Machiners
ITE . . . . Institute of Traffic Engineers
ITMA . . . . . . Institute for Training in Municipal Administration
ITTE . . . . Institute of Transportation & Traffic Engineering (UCLA)
ITF . . . . Institute of Tropical Forestry (Department of Agriculture)
ITFCS . . . . . . Institute for Twenty-First Century Studies
IUSTFI . . . . . . Institute on United States Taxation of Foreign Income
IUD . . . . Institute for Urban Development
IUL . . . . Institute of Urban Life
IWE . . . . Institute of Water Engineers (British)
IWA . . . . Institute of World Affairs
ICE . . . . Institution of Civil Engineers (British)
IEE . . . . Institution of Electrical Engineers (British)
IME . . . . Institution of Mechanical Engineers (British)
IMM . . . . Institution of Mining and Metallurgy
INA . . . . Institution of Naval Architects (British)
IRI . . . . Institution of the Rubber Industry (British)
IFDA . . . . . . Institutional Food Distributors of America
IFMA . . . . . . Institutional Food Manufacturers Association
IRC . . . . Institutional Research Council
ISTDA . . . . . . Institutional and Service Textile Distributors Association
IAPC . . . . Instituto de Aposentadoria e Pensoes dos Comerciarios (Brazil)
IAN . . . . Instituto de Asuntos Nucleares (Colombia)
ICAITI . . . . . . Instituto Centroamericano de Investigacion y Technologia Industrial
 (Central American Research Institute for Industry)
ICIT . . . . Instituto Cubano de Investigacione Technologicas
IEA . . . . Instituto de Energia Atomica (Brazil)
IDEN . . . . . . Instituto de Engerharia Nuclear (Brazil)
IESA . . . . Instituto de Estudios Superiores de Administracion (Institute of Higher
 Studies of Administration) (Venezuela)
INFONAC . . . . Instituto de Fomento Nacional (Industrial promotion agency) (Nicaragua)
IFSC . . . . Instituto de Formacao Social e Corporativa (Portugal)
INTAL . . . . . . Instituto para la Integracion de America Latina
II . . . . Instituto Interamericano
IICA . . . . Instituto Interamericano de Ciencias Agricolas (Inter-American Institute
 of Agricultural Sciences)
IIN . . . . Instituto Interamericano del Nino (Inter-American Children's Institute)
 (Uruguay)
IILI . . . . Instituto Internacional de Literatura Iberoamericana (International
 Institute of Iberoamerican Literature)
INDE . . . . . . Instituto Nacional de Electricidad (Guatemala)
INPI . . . . Instituto Nacional de Promocion (National Institute of Industrial
 Promotion) (Peru)
INPI . . . . Instituto Nacional de Proteccion a la Infancia (Mexico)
INRA . . . . . . Instituto Nacional de Reforma Agraria (Cuba)
INTA . . . . . . Instituto Nacional de Tecnica Aerospacial (Spain)
INTA . . . . . . Instituto Nacional de Tecnologia Agropecuaria (Argentina)
INPS . . . . Instituto Nazionale della Prevedenza Sociale (Italy)
INSORA . . . . . Instituto de Organizacion Racional (Universidad de Chile)
IPEE . . . . Instituto de Pesquisas e Estudos Economicos (Brazil)
INPRODE . . . . Instituto Profesional para el Desarrollo (Professional Development
 Institute) (Colombia)
INPIBOL . . . . . Instituto Promotor de Inversiones en Bolivia
IPASE . . . . . . Instituto de Providencia e Assistencia dos Servidores do Estado (Brazil)
INSAFI . . . . . . Instituto Salvadoreno de Fomento Industrial (Industrial promotion agency)
 (El Salvador)

ISAV . . . . Instituto de Sistemas Audio-Visuales (Institute of Audio-Visual Media)
 (Colombia)
IVIC . . . . Instituto Venezolano de Investigaciones Cientificas
IFA . . . . Institutt for Atomenergi (Norway)
IB . . . . Instruction Book
ICU . . . . Instruction Control Unit
IC . . . . Instruction Counter (Data processing)
IR . . . . Instruction Register (Data processing)
IMC . . . . Instructional Materials Center
ITV . . . . Instructional Television
ITFS . . . . Instructional Television Fixed Service
ICOC . . . . . . Instructions for Commodores of Convoys (Navy)
ICP . . . . Instructor Control Panel
IDP . . . . Instructor Display Panel
IN . . . . Instructor Navigator
IP . . . . Instructor Pilot
IPS . . . . Instructor Power Supply
ITC . . . . Instructor Training Course
IBTU . . . . . . Instructors Basic Training Unit
IM . . . . Instructor's Manual
IA . . . . Instrument Abstracts
IAF . . . . Instrument Air Filter
IALC . . . . . . Instrument Approach and Landing Chart (Aviation)
IAP . . . . Instrument Approach Procedure (Aviation)
IAS . . . . Instrument Approach System
IAC . . . . Instrument Array Cable
IBJ . . . . Instrument Bearing Jewel
ICL . . . . Instrument Calibration Laboratory
ICMR . . . . . . Instrument Calibration and Maintenance Record
I . . . . Instrument Correction
IC . . . . Instrument Correction
IDL . . . . Instrument Development Laboratories
IDS . . . . Instrument Development Section
IEP . . . . Instrument for Evaluation of Photographs
IFM . . . . Instrument Flag Motor
IFIS . . . . Instrument Flight Instructors School (Navy)
IFR . . . . Instrument Flight Recovery (NASA)
IFR . . . . Instrument Flight Rules (Aviation)
IGOR . . . . . . Instrument Ground Optical Recording
ILA . . . . Instrument Landing Approach
ILAS . . . . Instrument Landing Approach System
ILG . . . . Instrument Landing Guidance
ILS . . . . Instrument Landing System (Aviation)
ILSAP . . . . . . Instrument Landing System Approach
ILSTAC . . . . . Instrument Landing System and TACAN
ILA . . . . Instrument Low Approach (Aircraft landing method)
ILAS . . . . Instrument Low-Approach System (Aircraft landing method)
IM . . . . Instrument Man (Air Force)
IMK . . . . Instrument Marking Kit
IMB . . . . Instrument Material Bulletin
IMC . . . . Instrument (Flight) Meteorological Conditions (Aviation)
IN . . . . Instrument Note
IPIS . . . . Instrument Pilot Instructor School (Air Force)
IPN . . . . Instrument Plan Number
IR . . . . Instrument Reading
ISS . . . . Instrument Servo System
ISA . . . . Instrument Society of America
ITSO . . . . . . Instrument Technician Service Organization
IU . . . . Instrument Unit (NASA)
I . . . . Instrumental (or Instrumentation)
IAA . . . . Instrumental Activation Analysis
IED . . . . Instrumental Engineering Division (Weather Bureau)
INAA . . . . . . Instrumental Neutron Activation Analysis
INSCAIRS . . . . Instrumentation Calibration Incident Repair Service
ICP . . . . Instrumentation Calibration Procedure
ICM . . . . Instrumentation and Communications Monitor
ICS . . . . Instrumentation and Control Subsystem
IDTS . . . . . . Instrumentation Data Test Station
IDTS . . . . . . Instrumentation Data Transmission System
IDTSC . . . . . . Instrumentation Data Transmission System Controller
IDIOT . . . . . . Instrumentation Digital On-Line Transcriber
IESD . . . . Instrumentation and Electronic Systems Division (NASA)
IL . . . . Instrumentation Laboratory
IM . . . . Instrumentation and Measurement
IPC . . . . Instrumentation Package Container
IPS . . . . Instrumentation Power Supply
IPS . . . . Instrumentation Power System
IRACQ . . . . . Instrumentation RADAR and Acquisition Panel
IRS . . . . Instrumentation RADAR Set
IR . . . . Instrumentation Report

ISPO .... Instrumentation Ships Project Office (Navy)
ISCO ...... Instrumentation Specialties Company
ISS........ Instrumentation Support Service
ITR........ Instrumentation Tape Recorder
IBT........ Instrumented Bend Test
IMS .... Instrumented Measuring System
IMP .... Instrumented Monkey Pod
IVMS ...... Instrumented Vibration Measuring System
IEA .... Instruments, Electronics, and Automation (Exhibit)
IBP........ Insulated Binding Post
ICT .... Insulated (or Insulating) Core Transformer
IGFET...... Insulated Gate Field Effect Transistor
IPCEA...... Insulated Power Cable Engineers Association
ISA .... Insulating Siding Association
ISCBA...... Insulating Siding Core Board Association
IS .... Insulating Sleeve
IBI........ Insulation Board Institute
IBDT....... Insulation Breakdown Tester
IBT........ Insulation Breakdown Tester
IDCNA ..... Insulation Distributor Contractors National Association
ICT .... Insulin Coma Therapy
ILA .... Insulin-Like Activity
IST .... Insulin Shock Therapy (Psychiatry)
ITT .... Insulin Tolerance Test (Physiology)
IZS .... Insulin Zinc Suspension
IAA .... Insurance Accountants Association
IASA ...... Insurance Accounting and Statistical Association
IAC .... Insurance Advertising Conference
IAIU....... Insurance Agents International Union
ICBPA ..... Insurance Company and Bank Purchasing Agents Association
ICEDS...... Insurance Company Education Directors Society
INA .... Insurance Company of North America
ISU .... Insurance Company of North America (NYSE symbol)
IESA....... Insurance Economics Society of America
III .... Insurance Information Institute
IIA........ Insurance Institute of America
IIHS....... Insurance Institute for Highway Safety
IPFA....... Insurance Premium Finance Association
ISA .... Insurance Service Associates
ISAA ...... Insurance Service Association of America
ISNY ...... Insurance Society of New York
IWA .... Insurance Workers of America
IWIU ...... Insurance Workers International Union
IC .... Intake Closes (Valve position)
IO .... Intake Opens (Valve position)
I & O ...... Intake and Output
IAE .... Integral of Absolute Error
IBR........ Integral Boiling Reactor
IBSHR...... Integral Boiling and Superheat Reactor
ICR........ Integral Cesium Reservoir
ICP .... Integral Circuit Package
IFSAL...... Integral Frequency Scan Approach and Landing
IRHF....... Integral Radiative Heat Flux
ISE........ Integral Squared Error
ISR........ Integral Superheat Reactor
ITB........ Integral Terminal Block
ITD .... Integral Trap Door (Technical drawings)
IMI .... Integrally Molded Insulation
IS .... Integrally Stiffened
ITL........ Integrate-Transfer-Launch (Complex) (at Cape Kennedy) (Aerospace)
IAE .... Integrated Absolute Error
IAAA ...... Integrated Advance Avionics for Aircraft
IAD .... Integrated Airbase Defense
IAADS ..... Integrated Anti-Airborne Defense System
IAD .... Integrated Automatic Documentation (System)
IAS .... Integrated Avionics System
INCA ...... Integrated Catalog Algorithm
ICC .... Integrated Chip Circuit
INCH....... Integrated Chopper
IC .... Integrated Circuit (Electronics)
ICA .... Integrated Circuit Array
ICM .... Integrated Circuit Mask
ICT .... Integrated Circuit Tester
ICE .... Integrated Circuits Engineering Corporation
ICES....... Integrated Civil Engineering System (Data processing)
ICG .... Integrated Combat Group (Air Force)
ICS .... Integrated Combat Ship
ICS .... Integrated Combat System
ICST....... Integrated Combined System Test
ICAR ...... Integrated Command Accounting and Reporting
ICS .... Integrated Command System

ICNI ...... Integrated Communication, Navigation, Identification (System)
INCA ...... Integrated Communications Agency (Air Force)
ICSAL...... Integrated Communications System, Alaska (Air Force, FAA)
ICT .... Integrated Computer Telemetry
ICA .... Integrated Conformal Array
ICON...... Integrated Control
ICAD ...... Integrated Control and Display
ICE .... Integrated Cooling for Electronics
ICICLE ..... Integrated Cryogenic Isotope Cooling Equipment
IDDS ...... Integrated Data Display System
IDF .... Integrated Data File
IDGIT...... Integrated Data Generation Implementation Technique
IDP .... Integrated Data Presentation
IDP .... Integrated Data Processing
IDPC ...... Integrated Data Processing Center
IDPS ...... Integrated Data Processing System
IDS .... Integrated Data Store
IDES....... Integrated Defense System
IDACS ..... Integrated Detection and Classification Station
IDLC ...... Integrated Digital Logic Circuit
IDS .... Integrated Display Situation
IEC .... Integrated Electronic Central
IEP........ Integrated Engineering Program
IEC .... Integrated Equipment Component
IFMIS ...... Integrated Facilities Management Information System
IFS........ Integrated Facilities System (Army)
IFA .... Integrated Feed Antenna
IFC .... Integrated Fire Control (RADAR)
IFCS ...... Integrated Flight Control System
IFIS ...... Integrated Flight Instrument System
IFS........ Integrated Flight System
IGLOSS ..... Integrated Global Ocean Station System (Ocean information and forecasting service)
IGOSS ..... Integrated Global Ocean Station System (Also see IGLOSS)
IGACS ..... Integrated Guidance and Control System
IHF .... Integrated Hazard Function
IHAS ...... Integrated Helicopter Avionics System (Navy)
IHI........ Integrated Hit Indicator
IHIS ...... Integrated Hit Indicator System
INTIP ...... Integrated Information Processing
INTIPS ..... Integrated Information Processing System
IID........ Integrated Instrument Development
IIDP ...... Integrated Instrument Development Program
IIR........ Integrated Instrumentation RADAR
IIS .... Integrated Insulation System
IKS .... Integrated Key Set (Data processing)
ILOSS...... Integrated LASER Optical Sight Set
ILCCS...... Integrated Launch Control & Checkout System
ILSS ...... Integrated Life Support System (NASA)
ILAAS...... Integrated Light Aircraft Attack System
ILC .... Integrated Logic Circuit
ILS .... Integrated Logistic Support (DOD)
ILSMP...... Integrated Logistic Support Management Plan
ILSMT...... Integrated Logistic Support Management Team
ILSP ...... Integrated Logistics Support Plan (or Program)
ILS .... Integrated Logistics System
ILLLTV ..... Integrated Low Light Level Television
IMC .... Integrated Maintenance Chart (or Concept)
IMM....... Integrated Maintenance Management
IMMP ...... Integrated Maintenance Management Plan
IMMT ...... Integrated Maintenance Management Team
IMM....... Integrated Maintenance Manual
IMP .... Integrated Maintenance Plan
IMS .... Integrated Maintenance System
IMIS ...... Integrated Management Information System (Air Force)
IMPACT ..... Integrated Managerial Programming Analysis Control Technique (Air Force)
IMS .... Integrated Mapping System
IMPS ...... Integrated Master Programming and Scheduling
IMM....... Integrated Materiel Management
IMP .... Integrated Memory Processor
IMC .... Integrated Microwave Circuit
IMCC...... Integrated Missile Control Center (NASA)
IMFSS...... Integrated Missile Flight Safety System
IMGCN ..... Integrated Missile Ground Control Network
IMAT ...... Integrated, Modification and Trial
IMP .... Integrated Monitoring Panel
IMC .... Integrated Monolithic Circuit
INCA ...... Integrated Navigation and Communications, Automatic
INS .... Integrated Navigation System
IOTA ...... Integrated Online Text Arrangement

IOGE . . . . . . Integrated Operational Ground Equipment
IOIC . . . . . . Integrated Operational Intelligence Center
IOIS . . . . . . Integrated Operational Intelligence System
IOOSF . . . . . Integrated Orbital Operations Simulation Facility
IPADAE . . . . . Integrated Passive Action Detection Acquisition Equipment
IPD . . . . Integrated Pin Diode
IPECS . . . . . . Integrated Power and Environmental Control System
IPS . . . . Integrated Power System
IPC . . . . Integrated Process Control
IRA . . . . Integrated RADOME Antenna
IRAS . . . . . . Integrated RADOME Antenna Structure
IRI . . . . Integrated Range Instrumentation
IRM . . . . Integrated Range Mission (Military)
IRG . . . . Integrated Rate Gyro
IRS . . . . Integrated Rate System
IS . . . . Integrated Satellite (Military spacecraft)
ISVS . . . . . . Integrated Secure Voice System
INSITE . . . . . Integrated Sensor Interpretation Techniques
ISIS . . . . . . Integrated Strike and Interceptor System
ISSAC . . . . . . Integrated Surface Search and Attack Coordinate
ISAM . . . . . . Integrated Switching and Multiplexing (IBM)
ISSEP . . . . . . Integrated System Safety Engineering Plan
ITIS . . . . . . Integrated Tank Insulation System
ITC . . . . Integrated Telemetry Complex
ITOP . . . . . . Integrated Test Operate Panel
ITP . . . . Integrated Test Program
ITPB . . . . . . Integrated Test Program Board
ITMG . . . . . . Integrated Thermal Micrometeoroid Garment (Spacesuit)
ITAE . . . . . . Integrated Time and Absolute Error
ITS . . . . Integrated Trajectory System
ITMIS . . . . . . Integrated Transportation Management Information System (Army)
ITDA . . . . . . Integrated Tunnel Diode Amplifier
IVALA . . . . . . Integrated Visual Approach and Landing Aid (System) (RADAR)
IWSM . . . . . . Integrated Weapon Support Management
IWST . . . . . . Integrated Weapon System Training (Air Force)
IWCS . . . . . . Integrated Weapons Control System
IWCS . . . . . . Integrated Wideband Communications System (Military)
IXR . . . . Integrated X-Ray Reflection
IACC . . . . . . Integrating Assembly and Checkout Contractor
IAC . . . . Integrating Assembly Contractor
IDV . . . . Integrating Digital Voltmeter
IFM . . . . Integrating Fluctuation Meter
IMP . . . . Integrating Motor Pneumotachograph
IS . . . . Integrating Support
IAC . . . . Integration, Assembly, and Checkout
ISS . . . . Integration Support Service
ITL . . . . Integration, Test, and Launch
ICO . . . . Integrator Cut-Off
IDA . . . . Integro-Differential Analyzer
I . . . . Intelligence
IBW . . . . Intelligence Bandwidth
IB . . . . Intelligence Branch
ICDP . . . . . . Intelligence Career Development Program
INTELCEN . . . Intelligence Center
ICPOA . . . . . . Intelligence Center, Pacific Ocean Areas
INTELCENPAC . . Intelligence Center Pacific Ocean Areas
INTC . . . . . . Intelligence Corps
IDHS . . . . . . Intelligence Data Handling System
ID . . . . Intelligence Department (Army)
INDIGO . . . . . Intelligence Division Gaming Operations
ID . . . . Intelligence Duties
IFU . . . . Intelligence Field Unit (Navy)
INT . . . . Intelligence and Law Enforcement Division (Coast Guard)
IM . . . . Intelligence Memorandum
IO . . . . Intelligence Office(r)
INTO . . . . . . Intelligence Officer (Army)
IQ . . . . Intelligence Quotient (Psychological and educational testing)
IRR . . . . Intelligence RADAR Reporting
IR . . . . Intelligence Ratio
I & R . . . . . . Intelligence and Reconnaissance
INTREPT . . . . Intelligence Report
IR . . . . Intelligence Report
IR . . . . Intelligence Review
ISUSAIC . . . . Intelligence School, United States Army Intelligence Center
A-2 . . . . Intelligence Section of an Air Staff; also, officer in charge of this section (Air Force)
J-2 . . . . Intelligence Section of a Joint Military Staff; the Officer in Charge of this Section
S-2 . . . . Intelligence Section in Army brigades or smaller units, and in Marine Corps units smaller than a brigade; the officer in charge of this section
ISC . . . . Intelligence Subject Code

INTSUM . . . . . Intelligence Summary
ISUM . . . . . . Intelligence Summary
IA . . . . Intemperate to Alcohol (An alcoholic) (Slang)
IG . . . . Intendant-General
IIF . . . . Intense Irregular Field
IMF . . . . Intense Magnetic Field
ING . . . . Intense Neutron Generator
ITR . . . . Intense Thermal Radiation
ICTP . . . . . . Intensified Combat Training Program
U . . . . Intensity Unknown (Meteorology)
IJAJ . . . . . . Intentional Jitter Antijam (Military)
IJJU . . . . . . Intentional Jitter Jamming Unit (Military)
IAM . . . . Interactive Algebraic Manipulation (Data processing)
IDA . . . . Interactive Differential Analyzer
IACED . . . . . . Inter-African Advisory Committee on Epizootic Diseases
IBAHP . . . . . Inter-African Bureau for Animal Health and Protection
IBED . . . . . . Inter-African Bureau for Epizootic Diseases
ILI . . . . Inter-African Labour Institute
IAPSC . . . . . . Inter-African Phytosanitary Commission
IPC . . . . Inter-African Phytosanitary Commission
IAPG . . . . . . Interagency Advanced Power Group
IAG . . . . Interagency Advisory Group (Civil Service Commission)
IAB . . . . Interagency Board of Examiners (Civil Service Commission)
IACC . . . . . . Inter-Agency Cartographic Committee
ICBC . . . . . . Interagency Committee on Back Contamination (Aerospace)
ICIAP . . . . . . Interagency Committee on International Aviation Policy (State Department)
ICO . . . . Interagency Committee on Oceanography
ICRA . . . . . . Interagency Committee on Radiological Assistance
ICTRM . . . . . Interagency Committee on the Transportation of Radioactive Materials
ICWR . . . . . . Interagency Committee on Water Resources
ICS . . . . Interagency Communications System
IADPC . . . . . . Inter-Agency Data Processing Committee
IGIA . . . . . . Interagency Group on International Aviation
IGIPAS . . . . . Interagency Group on International Programs in Atmospheric Science
ILSE . . . . Interagency Life Sciences Supporting Space Research and Technology Exchange
IRAP . . . . . . Interagency Radiological Assistance Plan (AEC)
IAR . . . . Interagency Rate
ITAC . . . . . . Interagency Textile Administrative Committee
IA . . . . Inter Alia (Among Other Things)
IANF . . . . . . Inter-Allied Nuclear Force
IAPB . . . . . . Inter-Allied Personnel Board (World War II)
IPRB . . . . . . Inter-Allied Postwar Requirements Bureau (World War II)
IARA . . . . . . Inter-Allied Reparations Agency (Brussels)
ISCB . . . . . . Interallied Staff Communications Board (World War II)
IAAB . . . . . . Inter-American Association of Broadcasters
IAADF . . . . . . Inter-American Association for Democracy and Freedom
IADF . . . . . . Inter-American Association for Democracy and Freedom
IAASE . . . . . . Inter-American Association of Sanitary Engineering
IABA . . . . . . Inter-American Bar Association
IABF . . . . . . Inter-American Bar Foundation
IABLA . . . . . . Inter-American Bibliographical and Library Association
IBLA . . . . . . Inter-American Bibliographical and Library Association
IACID . . . . . . Inter-American Center for Integral Development (OAS)
IACI . . . . . . Inter-American Children's Institute (OAS)
IACA . . . . . . Inter-American College Association
I-ACAC . . . . . Inter-American Commercial Arbitration Commission
IACHR . . . . . Inter-American Commission on Human Rights (OAS)
IACW . . . . . . Inter-American Commission of Women (OAS)
ICW . . . . Inter-American Commission of Women
ICAP . . . . . . Inter-American Committee for the Alliance for Progress
ICI . . . . Inter-American Cooperative Institute
IACCP . . . . . . Inter-American Council of Commerce and Production
IACA . . . . . . Inter-American Cultural Association
IACC . . . . . . Inter-American Cultural Council
IADB . . . . . . Inter-American Defense Board
IADC . . . . . . Inter-American Defense College (Washington)
IADB . . . . . . Inter-American Development Bank
IDB . . . . Inter-American Development Bank
IADC . . . . . . Inter-American Development Commission
IAESC . . . . . . Inter-American Economic and Social Council
IAECOSOC . . . Inter-American Economic and Social Council (UN)
IAEACPD . . . . Inter-American Emergency Advisory Committee for Political Defense
IFPRA . . . . . . Interamerican Federation of Public Relations Associations
IAFWNO . . . . Inter-American Federation of Working Newspapermen's Organizations
IAFA . . . . . . Inter-American Foundation for the Arts
IAFC . . . . . . Inter-American Freight Conference
IAGS . . . . . . Inter-American Geodetic Survey
IAHA . . . . . . Inter-American Hospital Association
IAHA . . . . . . Inter-American Hotel Association

IAII . . . . Inter-American Indian Institute (OAS)
III . . . . Inter-American Indian Institute
IAIAS . . . . . . Inter-American Institute of Agricultural Sciences (OAS)
IAJC . . . . Inter-American Juridical Committee
ILI . . . . Interamerican Labour Institute
IALF . . . . Inter-American Literacy Foundation
IMO . . . . Inter-American Municipal Organization
IANEC . . . . . . Inter-American Nuclear Energy Commission (OAS)
IAPC . . . . Inter-American Peace Committee (OAS)
IAPF . . . . Inter-American Peacekeeping Force
IAPA . . . . . . Inter-American Police Academy
IAPA . . . . . . Inter-American Press Association
IAPSP . . . . . . Inter-American Program for Social Progress (AID)
IASC . . . . . . Inter-American Safety Council
ISC . . . . Interamerican Society of Cardiology
ISP . . . . Interamerican Society of Psychology
IASI . . . . Inter-American Statistical Institute (OAS)
ITAS . . . . Interamerican Travel Agents Society
IATC . . . . . . Inter-American Travel Congress
IATTC . . . . . . Inter-American Tropical Tuna Commission
IAUF . . . . . . Interamerican Underwater Festival
IUF . . . . Interamerican Underwater Festival
IACH . . . . . . Inter-Association Committee on Health
IAG . . . . Inter-Association Group
IASD . . . . . . Interatrial Septal Defect (Medicine)
IBC . . . . Interboard Committee for Christian Work in Japan
IRT . . . . Interboro Rapid Transit (A New York City subway line)
ICF . . . . Inter-Bureau Citation of Funds (Navy)
ICLM . . . . . . Inter-California Line in Mexico R. R. (AAR code)
IND . . . . Intercept Director (Military)
IDB . . . . Intercept During Boost
IGOR . . . . . . Intercept Ground Optical Recorder (NASA)
IGORTT . . . . . Intercept Ground Optical Recorder Tracking Telescope
IMD . . . . Intercept Monitoring Display
IO . . . . Intercept Officer
IP . . . . Intercept Point (Air Force)
ITOR . . . . . . Intercept Target Optical Reader
INTAC . . . . . Intercept Tracking and Control Group
INM . . . . Interception Mission (Air Force)
INSATRAC . . . . Interception with Satellite Tracking
I . . . . Interceptor
IC . . . . Interceptor Command
IDC . . . . Interceptor Distance Computer
IIC . . . . Interceptor Identification Capability
IIP . . . . Interceptor Improvement Program
IM . . . . Interceptor Missile
IMDC . . . . . . Interceptor Missile Direction Center
IMIR . . . . . . Interceptor Missile Interrogation RADAR
IMSOC . . . . . Interceptor Missile Squadron Operations Center (Air Force)
IMSSCE . . . . . Interceptor Missile Squadron and Supervisory Control Equipment
IMSSS . . . . . Interceptor Missile Squadron Supervisory Station
IPS . . . . Interceptor Pilot Simulator (SSTM)
ITM . . . . Interceptor Tactical Missile (Air Force)
IWCS . . . . . . Interceptor Weapon Control System
I/C . . . . Interchange
IC . . . . Interchange Center
ISTIM . . . . . . Interchange of Scientific and Technical Information in Machine Language
I & S . . . . . . Interchangeability and Substitute
IP . . . . Interchangeable Solid and Screen Panels (Technical drawings)
ICMP . . . . . . Interchannel Master Pulse
ITD . . . . Interchannel Time Displacement
ICTD . . . . . . Inter-Channel Time Displacement
ITDE . . . . . . Interchannel (or Intertrack) Time Displacement Error
IKN . . . . Interchemical Corporation (NYSE symbol)
IPI . . . . Interchemical Printing Inks
IMA . . . . Interchurch Medical Assistance
ITC . . . . Interchurch Transportation Council
ISFA . . . . . . Intercoastal Steamship Freight Association
IAAAA . . . . . Intercollegiate Association of Amateur Athletes of America
ICAAAA . . . . Intercollegiate Association of Amateur Athletes of America
IC4A . . . . . . Intercollegiate Association of Amateur Athletes of America
IASAP . . . . . Intercollegiate Association for Study of the Alcohol Problem
IAWS . . . . . . Intercollegiate Association of Women Students
IBS . . . . Intercollegiate Broadcasting System
IDA . . . . Intercollegiate Dramatic Association
IFA . . . . Intercollegiate Fencing Association
IIHA . . . . . . Intercollegiate Ice Hockey Association
IMC . . . . Intercollegiate Musical Council
IOG . . . . Intercollegiate Opera Group

IPGS . . . . . . Intercollegiate Program of Graduate Studies
IRA . . . . Intercollegiate Rowing Association
ISI . . . . Intercollegiate Society of Individualists
IWFA . . . . . . Intercollegiate Women's Fencing Association
ICF . . . . Intercommunication Flip-Flop (Data processing)
IC . . . . Intercommunications
ICS . . . . Intercommunications System
ICBS . . . . . . Interconnected Business System
IPL . . . . Interconnected Porosity Level
ISG . . . . Interconnected Systems Group
ICARUS . . . . . Inter-Continental Aerospacecraft-Range Unlimited System
IBM . . . . Intercontinental Ballistic Missile
ICBM . . . . . . Intercontinental Ballistic Missile
ICBMS . . . . . Intercontinental Ballistic Missile System
ICBT . . . . . . Intercontinental Ballistic Transport
ICCA . . . . . . Intercontinental Corrugated Case Association
ICJUB . . . . . Intercontinental Jet Unmanned Bomber
ICM . . . . Intercostal Margin (Anatomy)
ICS . . . . Intercostal Space (Anatomy)
IS . . . . Intercostal Space
ICUA . . . . . . Interdenominational Church Ushers Association
IFMA . . . . . . Interdenominational Foreign Mission Association of North America
IDC . . . . Inter-Department Correspondence
IRAC . . . . . . Interdepartment Radio Advisory Committee (Aviation)
IATCB . . . . . . Interdepartmental Air Traffic Control Board
IDC . . . . Interdepartmental Committee
INDEC . . . . . Interdepartmental Committee
ICAS . . . . . . Interdepartmental Committee for Atmospheric Sciences (US)
ICIS . . . . Interdepartmental Committee on Internal Security
ICNND . . . . . Interdepartmental Committee on Nutrition for National Defense
ICSW . . . . . . Interdepartmental Committee on the Status of Women
ICWM . . . . . Interdepartmental Committee on Weather Modification (Military)
IDC . . . . Interdepartmental Communication
IPCOG . . . . . Interdepartmental Planning Committee on Germany (US)
ISBC . . . . . . Interdepartmental Savings Bond Committee (Military)
IDM . . . . Interdiction Mission (Air Force)
ICIC . . . . . . Interdisciplinary Committee on Institutes and Conferences
IREP . . . . . . Interdisciplinary Research Equipment Program
IDB . . . . Inter-Dynamic Balance
IG . . . . Interessen Gemeinschaft
IDC . . . . Interest During Construction
IET . . . . Interest Equalization Tax
IA . . . . Interface Amplifier
ICD . . . . Interface Control Drawing
IDD . . . . Interface Design Document
INI . . . . Interface Noise Inverter
IPU . . . . Interface and Priority Unit
ISC . . . . Interface Signal Chart
ITWG . . . . . . Interface Technical Working Group
ITD . . . . Interface Timing Diagram
IFT . . . . Interfacial Test
IZ . . . . Interfacial Zone
IFCN . . . . . . Interfacility Communication Network
IC . . . . Interfaith Compassionists
IFC . . . . Inter-Faith Compassionists
INTERDICT . . . Interference Detection and Interdiction Countermeasures Team (Electromagnetic compatibility programs)
IFRU . . . . . . Interference Frequency Rejection Unit (Military)
IGB . . . . Interference Guard Bands
IPM . . . . Interference Prediction Model
IU . . . . Interference Unit (Military)
ID . . . . Interferometer and Doppler
ILS . . . . Interferometric LASER Source
IFD . . . . Inter-Fighter Director
IRAC . . . . . . Interfraternity Research and Advisory Council
ICEM . . . . . . Intergovernmental Committee for European Migration
IGCR . . . . . . Intergovernmental Committee on Refugees (Post-World War II)
ICOR . . . . . . Intergovernmental Conference on Oceanic Research
IGCC . . . . . . Intergovernmental Copyright Committee
IMCO . . . . . . Intergovernmental Maritime Consultative Organization
IOC . . . . Intergovernmental Oceanographic Commission (UNESCO)
IGO . . . . Intergovernmental Organization (Generic term)
IAA . . . . Interim Access Authorization
ICM . . . . Interim Catalog Module (MEDLARS)
IC . . . . Interim Change
ICN . . . . Interim Change Notice
IC . . . . Interim Commission
ICIRO . . . . . . Interim Commission of the International Refugee Organization
ICITO . . . . . . Interim Commission for the International Trade Organization
IC . . . . Interim Committee

REVERSE ACRONYMS AND INITIALISMS DICTIONARY

ICSC . . . . Interim Communications Satellite Committee
ICCICA . . . . . . Interim Co-ordinating Committee for International Commodity Arrangements
IDCCC . . . . . . Interim Data Communications Collection Center
IDR . . . . Interim Development Report
IER . . . . Interim Engineering Report
IHA . . . . Interim Housing Allowance (Military)
IIAILS . . . . . . Interim Integrated Aircraft Instrumentation & Letdown System
IIIS . . . . Interim International Information Service (World War II)
ILAADS . . . . . Interim Low Altitude Air Defense System
IM . . . . Interim Memorandum
IMS . . . . Interim Meteorological Satellite
INSSCC . . . . . Interim National Space Surveillance Control Center
IOI . . . . Interim Operating Instructions
IOMS . . . . . . Interim Operation Meteorological System
IPL . . . . Interim Parts List (Navy)
IPR . . . . Interim Progress Report
IRATE . . . . . . Interim Remote Area Terminal Equipment (Air Force)
IR . . . . Interim Report
IRM . . . . Interim Research Memo
ISR . . . . Interim Scientific Report
ISS . . . . Interim Standard Set
ITEWS . . . . . . Interim Tactical Electronic Warfare System
ITM . . . . Interim Technical Memorandum
ITN . . . . Interim Technical Note
ITO . . . . Interim Technical Order
ITOFCN . . . . . Interim Technical Order Field Change Notice (Air Force)
ITR . . . . Interim Technical Report
ITR . . . . Interim Test Report
IIEC . . . . Inter-Industry Emissions Control (Program)
IIHSC . . . . . . Inter-Industry Highway Safety Committee
IAT . . . . Interionic Attraction Theory
ICRD . . . . . . Interior Committee on Research and Development
IC . . . . Interior Communication
IC . . . . Interior Communications Electrician (Navy rating)
ICB . . . . Interior Control Board
ID . . . . Interior Department
IDEC . . . . . . Interior Design Educators Council
I & IA . . . . . . Interior and Insular Affairs
IS . . . . Interior Surface
ILCEP . . . . . . Inter-Laboratory Committee on Editing and Publishing (Navy)
ILCF . . . . Inter-Laboratory Committee on Facilities (Navy)
IK . . . . Interlake Iron Corporation (NYSE symbol)
I-L YA . . . . . . Inter-Lake Yachting Association
ILL . . . . Interlibrary Loan
IL . . . . Interline
IDSS . . . . Interlingua Division of Science Service
IU . . . . Interlingue Union
I . . . . Interlocked Metallic Armor (Technical drawings)
I . . . . Intermediate (Vessel load line mark)
IAC . . . . Intermediate Air Command (Air Force)
ICU . . . . Intermediate Care Unit
IDF . . . . Intermediate Distributing Frame
IFLOT . . . . . . Intermediate Focal Length Optical Tracker
IF . . . . Intermediate Frequency (Electronics)
I-F . . . . Intermediate Frequency (Electronics)
IFA . . . . Intermediate Frequency Amplifier (or Attenuator)
IFS . . . . Intermediate Frequency Strip
IFT . . . . Intermediate Frequency Transformer
IHE . . . . Intermediate Heat Exchanger
IIR . . . . Intermediate Infrared
IICBM . . . . . . Intermediate Intercontinental Ballistic Missile
ILMT . . . . . . Intermediate-Level Maintenance Training
ILRIS . . . . . . Intermediate Long Range Interceptor System
IMA . . . . Intermediate Maintenance Activity
IMF . . . . Intermediate Maintenance Facility
IM . . . . Intermediate Modulation
INDO . . . . . . Intermediate Neglect of Differential Overlap (X-ray diffraction)
IOL . . . . Intermediate Objective Lens
IPLV . . . . Intermediate Payload Launch Vehicle
IPA . . . . Intermediate Power Amplifier (Electronics)
IP . . . . Intermediate Pressure
IPC . . . . Intermediate Processing Centers
IQL . . . . Intermediate Query Language
IRBM . . . . . . Intermediate Range Ballistic Missile
IRTF . . . . Intermediate Range Task Force
ISHR . . . . Intermediate Scale Homogeneous Reactor
ISW . . . . Intermediate Scale Warfare
IS . . . . Intermediate School
ISCS . . . . Intermediate Science Curriculum Study
ISS . . . . Intermediate Service School (Military)

ISAF . . . . Intermediate Super-Abrasion Furnace
ITA . . . . Intermediate Thrust Arc
INTERMTRA . . . Intermediate Training (Naval Air)
IAA . . . . Interment Association of America
IAR . . . . Interment is Authorized for the Remains of (Military)
IEA . . . . Interment Exchange of America
IAO . . . . Intermittent Aortic Occlusion (Medicine)
IBI . . . . Intermittent Bladder Irrigation (Medicine)
ICAS . . . . . . Intermittent Commercial and Amateur Service (Radio)
IDU . . . . Intermittent Drive Unit
IDR . . . . Intermittent-Duty Rating
IF . . . . Intermittent Frequency
IMD . . . . Intermittent Motion Driver
IPPB . . . . Intermittent Positive Pressure Breathing
IPPR . . . . Intermittent Positive Pressure Respiration
IM . . . . Intermodulation
ID . . . . Intermodulation Distortion
IDP . . . . Intermodulation Distortion Percentage
ICA . . . . Intermuseum Conservation Association
IKUE . . . . . . Internacia Katolica Unuigo Esperantista (International Catholic Esperanto Union)
ISAE . . . . Internacia Science Asocio Esperantista (International Esperantist Scientific Association)
IAJE . . . . Internacia Socio de Juristoj-Esperantistoj (International Association of Esperantist Lawyers)
IAD . . . . Internal Absorbed Dose
IAO . . . . Internal Automation Operation
IC . . . . Internal Combustion
ICE . . . . Internal Combustion Engine
ICEI . . . . Internal Combustion Engine Institute
ARG . . . . . . Internal Combustion Engine Repair Ship (Navy symbol)
IC . . . . Internal Connection (Electronics)
ICV . . . . Internal Correction Voltage
IDAP . . . . . . Internal Development and Assistance Program
IDR . . . . Internal Development Report
IDP . . . . Internal Distribution Publication (Navy)
IDIC . . . . Internal Dose Information Center (ORNL)
IE . . . . Internal Environment
IFRO . . . . . . Internal Feed Rate Override
IFE . . . . Internal Field Emission
IFR . . . . Internal Function Register
IGFM . . . . . . Internal Gamma Flux Monitor
IMRO . . . . . . Internal Macedonian Revolutionary Organization (World War II)
IMF . . . . Internal Magnetic Focus
INTMED . . . . . Internal Medicine
IM . . . . Internal Memorandum
IMN . . . . Internal Mix Nozzle
IMSN . . . . . . Internal-Mix Spray Nozzle
IN . . . . Internal Note
IPT . . . . Internal Pipe Thread
IPR . . . . Internal Progress Report
IQ . . . . Internal Quality
IRR . . . . Internal Rate of Return (Finance)
IRN . . . . Internal Reference Number
IR . . . . Internal Reliability
IR . . . . Internal Report
IR . . . . Internal Resistance
IR . . . . Internal Revenue
IRA . . . . Internal Revenue Act
IRO . . . . Internal Revenue Office(r)
IRC . . . . Internal Revenue Code
IRS . . . . Internal Revenue Service (Treasury Department)
IRSC . . . . Internal Revenue Service Centers
IRASI . . . . . . Internal Review and System Improvement
ISR . . . . Internal Scientific Report
INSEC . . . . . . Internal Security
ISD . . . . Internal Security Division (Department of Justice)
IS . . . . Internal Shield (Electronics)
ISG . . . . Internal Shutter Grid
ISL . . . . Internal Standard Line
ITM . . . . Internal Technical Memorandum
ITR . . . . Internal Technical Report
IT . . . . Internal Thread
IT . . . . Internal Translator
ITHL . . . . Internal Triangular Hinge Ligament (of scallops)
IVI . . . . Internal Vibration Isolator
IWP . . . . Internal Working Paper
ISI . . . . Internally Specified Index
I-NS . . . . Inter-Nation Simulation (Simulation of international relations)
I . . . . International
IAF . . . . International Abolitionist Federation

IABS . . . . International Abstracts of Biological Sciences
IAOR . . . . International Abstracts in Operations Research
IAA . . . . International Academy of Astronautics
IAO . . . . International Academy of Orthodontics
IAP . . . . International Academy of Pathology
IAP . . . . International Academy of Proctology
IATL . . . . International Academy of Trial Lawyers
IAS . . . . International Accountants Society
IAA . . . . International Acetylene Association
IASY . . . . International Active Sun Years
IAARC . . . . . . International Administrative Aeronautical Radio Conference
IAA . . . . International Advertising Association
IAC . . . . International Advisory Committee (ANSI)
IACOMS . . . . . International Advisory Committee on Marine Sciences
IAF . . . . International Aeronautics Federation
IAA . . . . International Aerospace Abstracts
IAI . . . . International African Institute
IALA . . . . International African Law Association
IARC . . . . International Agency for Research on Cancer
IADS . . . . . . International Agricultural Development Service (Department of Agriculture)
IABA . . . . International Air Brokers Association
IACE . . . . International Air Cadet Exchange
IAC . . . . International Air Convention
IAFF . . . . International Air Freight Forwarder
ALPA . . . . International Air Line Pilots Association
ALSS . . . . International Air Line Stewards and Stewardesses Association
IALSSA . . . . . . International Air Line Stewards and Stewardesses Association
IASA . . . . International Air Safety Association
IATC . . . . International Air Traffic Communications
IATCR . . . . . . International Air Traffic Communications Receiver Station
IATCS . . . . . . International Air Traffic Communications Station
IATCT . . . . . . International Air Traffic Communications Transmitter Station
IATA . . . . International Air Transport Association
IANC . . . . International Airline Navigators Council
IAP . . . . International Airport
IAC . . . . International Algebraic Compiler
IAL . . . . International Algebraic Language (Replaced by ALGOL)
IAL . . . . International Algorithmic Language
IAA . . . . International Allergy Association
IABPBD . . . . . . International Alliance of Bill Posters, Billers and Distributors
BPBD . . . . International Alliance of Bill Posters, Billers and Distributors of US and Canada
IAFP . . . . International Alliance of Film Producers
IATSE . . . . . . International Alliance of Theatrical Stage Employees and Moving Picture Machine Operators of the United States and Canada
IAW . . . . International Alliance of Women - Equal Rights, Equal Responsibilities
IAPTA . . . . . . International Allied Printing Trades Association
IAAF . . . . International Amateur Athletic Federation
IABBS . . . . . . International Amateur Boat Building Society
IARU . . . . International Amateur Radio Union
IATA . . . . International Amateur Theatre Association
IAC . . . . International Analysis Code (Meteorology)
IARS . . . . International Anesthesia Research Society
IA . . . . International Angstrom
IACS . . . . International Annealed Copper Standard
IAA . . . . . . International Apple Association
IAHA . . . . International Arabian Horse Association
IACS . . . . International Arms-Control Symposium
IASRA . . . . . . International Arthur Schnitzler Research Association
IAAHU . . . . . . International Association of Accident and Health Underwriters
IAAE . . . . International Association of Agricultural Economists
IAALD . . . . . . International Association of Agricultural Librarians and Documentalists
IAA . . . . International Association of Allergology
IAAP . . . . International Association of Amusement Parks
IAAC . . . . International Association for Analog Computing
IAAP . . . . International Association of Applied Psychology
IAABO . . . . . . International Association of Approved Basketball Officials
IAAI . . . . International Association of Arson Investigators
IAAC . . . . International Association of Art Critics
IAAO . . . . International Association of Assessing Officers
IAAM . . . . International Association of Auditorium Managers
IAATI . . . . . . International Association of Auto Theft Investigators
IAAM . . . . International Association of Automotive Modelers
IABPAI . . . . . . International Association of Blue Print and Allied Industries
IABG . . . . International Association of Botanic Gardens
IABSE . . . . . . International Association for Bridge and Structural Engineering
BSOIW . . . . . . International Association of Bridge, Structural and Ornamental Iron Workers
IABSOIW . . . . International Association of Bridge, Structural and Ornamental Iron Workers
IACP . . . . International Association of Chiefs of Police

IACP . . . . International Association for Child Psychiatry and Allied Professions
CDHW . . . . . . International Association of Cleaning and Dye House Workers
IACD . . . . International Association of Clothing Designers
IACM . . . . International Association of Concert Managers
IACB . . . . International Association of Convention Bureaus
IACME . . . . . . International Association of Crafts and Small and Medium-sized Enterprises
IADL . . . . International Association of Democratic Lawyers
IADR . . . . International Association for Dental Research
IADS . . . . International Association of Dental Students
IADS . . . . International Association of Department Stores
IAEI . . . . International Association of Electrical Inspectors
IAEL . . . . International Association of Electrical Leagues
IAES . . . . International Association of Electrotypers and Stereotypers
IAESC . . . . . . International Association of Evening Student Councils
IAESTE . . . . . . International Association for the Exchange of Students for Technical Experience
IAFE . . . . International Association of Fairs and Expositions
IAFC . . . . International Association of Fire Chiefs
IAFF . . . . International Association of Fire Fighters
IAFD . . . . International Association on Food Distribution
IAGFCC . . . . . International Association of Game, Fish and Conservation Commissioners
IAGM . . . . . . International Association of Garment Manufacturers (Absorbed by NOSA)
IAG . . . . International Association of Geodesy
IAGA . . . . International Association of Geomagnetism and Aeronomy
IAG . . . . International Association of Gerontology
IAGFA . . . . . . International Association of Governmental Fair Agencies
IAGLO . . . . . . International Association of Governmental Labor Officials
IAGLP . . . . . . International Association of Great Lakes Ports
IAHU . . . . International Association of Health Underwriters
HFIAW . . . . . . International Association of Heat and Frost Insulators and Asbestos Workers
IAHFIAW . . . . International Association of Heat and Frost Insulators and Asbestos Workers
IAHR . . . . International Association for the History of Religions
IAHP . . . . International Association of Horticultural Producers
IAHR . . . . International Association for Hydraulic Research
IAH . . . . International Association of Hydrology
IAICM . . . . . . International Association of Ice Cream Manufacturers
IAIAA . . . . . . International Association for Iranian Art and Archaeology
IAI . . . . International Association for Identification
IAIP . . . . International Association of Independent Producers
IAIP . . . . International Association of Individual Psychology
IAIABC . . . . . . International Association of Industrial Accident Boards and Commissions
IAIC . . . . International Association of Insurance Counsel
IAL . . . . International Association of Laryngectomees
IALL . . . . International Association of Law Libraries
IALS . . . . International Association of Legal Science
IARF . . . . International Association for Liberal Christianity and Religious Freedom
IALA . . . . International Association of Lighthouse Authorities
IAL . . . . International Association of Limnology
IALC . . . . International Association of Lions Clubs
IALP . . . . International Association of Logopedics and Phoniatrics
IAM . . . . International Association of Machinists (Later, International Association of Machinists and Aerospace Workers)
IAMAW . . . . . International Association of Machinists and Aerospace Workers
MSSP . . . . International Association of Marble, Slate and Stone Polishers, Rubbers and Sawyers, Tile and Marble Setters' Helpers and Marble Mosaic and Terrazzo Workers' Helpers
IAMCR . . . . . . International Association for Mass Communication Research
IAMPTH . . . . . International Association of Master-Penmen and Teachers of Handwriting
IAMAT . . . . . . International Association for Medical Assistance to Travelers
IAMAP . . . . . . International Association of Meteorology and Atmospheric Physics
INTAMEL . . . . International Association of Metropolitan City Libraries
IAMS . . . . International Association of Microbiological Societies
IAMCA . . . . . . International Association of Milk Control Agencies
IAMFES . . . . . International Association of Milk, Food and Environmental Sanitarians
IAMFS . . . . . . International Association of Milk and Food Sanitarians
IAMFPA . . . . . International Association of Mouth and Foot Painting Artists
IAML . . . . International Association of Music Libraries
IPH . . . . International Association of Paper Historians
IAPES . . . . . . International Association of Personnel in Employment Security
IAPW . . . . International Association of Personnel Women
IAPESGW . . . . International Association of Physical Education and Sports for Girls and Women
IAPO . . . . International Association of Physical Oceanography
IAPS . . . . International Association of Pipe Smokers Clubs
IAPT . . . . International Association for Plant Taxonomy
IAPMO . . . . . . International Association of Plumbing and Mechanical Officials
IAPP . . . . International Association of Police Professors

IAPH	International Association of Ports and Harbors
IAPB	International Association for the Prevention of Blindness
IAPHC	International Association of Printing House Craftsmen
IAPN	International Association of Professional Numismatists
APPI	International Association for the Promotion and Protection of Private Foreign Investments
IAPIP	International Association for the Protection of Industrial Property
INTAPUC	International Association of Public Cleansing
IAPPW	International Association of Pupil Personnel Workers
IAQ	International Association for Quality
INQUA	International Association for Quaternary Research
IARE	International Association of Railway Employees
IRE	International Association of Railway Employees
IARMI	International Association of Rattan Manufacturers and Importers
IARA	International Association of Rebekah Assemblies (IOOF)
IARSC	International Association of Religious Science Churches
IARIW	International Association for Research into Income and Wealth
IARIGAI	International Association of Research Institutes for the Graphic Arts Industry
IASSW	International Association of Schools of Social Work
IASH	International Association of Scientific Hydrology
IASSMD	International Association for the Scientific Study of Mental Deficiency
IASC	International Association of Seed Crushers
IASPEI	International Association of Seismology and Physics of the Earth's Interior
IASS	International Association for Shell Structures
IAS	International Association of Siderographers
IASP	International Association for Social Progress
IASA	International Association of Sound Archives
IASP	International Association for Suicide Prevention
IATUL	International Association of Technical University Libraries
IATE	International Association for Temperance Education
IAL	International Association of Theoretical and Applied Limnology
IATC	International Association of Tool Craftsmen
IATC	International Association of Torch Clubs
IAU	International Association of Universities
IAUPL	International Association of University Professors and Lecturers
IAVFH	International Association of Veterinary Food Hygienists
IAVCM	International Association of Visual Communications Management (Formerly, SRE)
IAVG	International Association for Vocational Guidance
IAW	International Association of Wholesalers
WOMPI	International Association of the Women of the Motion Picture Industry
IAWP	International Association of Women Police
IAWA	International Association of Wood Anatomists
IAWMC	International Association of Workers for Maladjusted Children
IAYM	International Association of Youth Magistrates
IAC	International Astronautical Congress
IAF	International Astronautical Federation
IAU	International Astronomical Union
IAD	International Astrophysical Decade
IADA	International Atomic-Development Authority (Proposed by Bernard M. Baruch, 1946, but never created)
IAEA	International Atomic Energy Agency
IAEC	International Atomic Energy Committee
IALA	International Auxiliary Language Association
INTAVA	International Aviation Association
IAS	International Aviation Service (of FAA)
IBF	International Badminton Federation
IBP	International Balance of Payments
IBRD	International Bank for Reconstruction and Development (Also known as World Bank)
IBA	International Bar Association
IBSA	International Barber Schools Association
IBEC	International Basic Economy Corporation
IBTS	International Beer Tasting Society
IBFS	International Benjamin Franklin Society
IBS	International Bible Students
IBID	International Bibliographical Description
IBBRIS	International Biodeterioration Bulletin Reference Index (A publication) (British)
IBP	International Biological Program (National Research Council)
IBY	International Biological Year
IBBY	International Board on Books for Young People
IBEG	International Book Export Group
IBG	International Boxing Guild
IBCA	International Braille Chess Association
IBRO	International Brain Research Organization
IBBA	International Brangus Breeders Association
IBA	International Bridge Academy
IBT	International Bridge & Terminal Company (AAR code)
IBTTA	International Bridge, Tunnel and Turnpike Association
IBC	International Brightness Coefficient
IBA	International Briquetting Association
IBI	International Broadcast Institute
IB	International Broadcasting
IBO	International Broadcasting Organization
BWM	International Broom and Whisk Makers' Union of America
BBF	International Brotherhood of Boilermakers, Iron Shipbuilders, Blacksmiths, Forgers and Helpers
IBB	International Brotherhood of Bookbinders
IBEW	International Brotherhood of Electrical Workers
IBFO	International Brotherhood of Firemen and Oilers
IBL	International Brotherhood of Longshoremen
IBM	International Brotherhood of Magicians
IBOP	International Brotherhood of Operative Potters
IBPM	International Brotherhood of Paper Makers
PSPMW	International Brotherhood of Pulp, Sulphite and Paper Mill Workers
IBT	International Brotherhood of Teamsters, Chauffeurs, Warehousemen and Helpers of America
IBEE	International Builders Exchange Executives
IBE	International Bureau of Education
IBFMP	International Bureau of the Federations of Master Printers
IBWM	International Bureau of Weights and Measures
IBC	International Business Corporation
IBM	International Business Machines Corporation (NYSE symbol)
INTOP	International Business Operations Game (Developed at University of Chicago)
ICF	International Canoe Federation
ICWI	International Car Wash Institute
ICHCA	International Cargo Handling Coordination Association
ICF	International Casting Federation
ICI	International Castles Institute
ICOA	International Castor Oil Association
ICA	International Catholic Auxiliaries
ICCB	International Catholic Child Bureau
ICDA	International Catholic Deaf Association
ICGS	International Catholic Girls' Society
ICMC	International Catholic Migration Commission
ICMICA	International Catholic Movement for Intellectual and Cultural Affairs
ICPU	International Catholic Press Union
ICTS	International Catholic Truth Society
ICYF	International Catholic Youth Federation
ICAME	International Center for the Advancement of Management Education (Stanford University)
ICCAS	International Center for Communication Arts and Sciences
ICFTUE	International Center of Free Trade Unionists in Exile
ICSISP	International Center for Science Information Services in Phytovirology
ICTA	International Center for the Typographic Arts
ICFC	International Centre of Films for Children
ICRICE	International Centre of Research and Information on Collective Economy
ICC	International Chamber of Commerce
ICS	International Chamber of Shipping
ICA	International Chefs' Association
ICN	International Chemical and Nuclear Corporation
ICW	International Chemical Workers Union
ICWU	International Chemical Workers Union
ICC	International Children's Centre
ICPTO	International China Painting Teachers Organization
ICA	International Chiropractors Association
ICL	International Christian Leadership
ICLM	International Christian Leprosy Mission
ICYE	International Christian Youth Exchange
ICU	International Christian University (Tokyo)
ICBS	International Cigar Band Society
ICD	International Circulation Distributors, Inc.
ICMA	International Circulation Managers Association
ICMA	International City Managers' Association
ICAO	International Civil Aviation Organization
ICDO	International Civil Defence Organization
ICSAB	International Civil Service Advisory Board
ICA	International Claim Association
ICCUS	International Claims Commission of the United States (Department of State) (Abolished, 1954)
ICD	International Classification of Diseases
ICDA	International Classification of Diseases Adapted
INTCO	International Code of Signals
ICO	International Coffee Organization
ICAN	International College of Applied Nutrition
ICD	International College of Dentists
ICS	International College of Surgeons
ICAE	International Commission of Agricultural Engineering

ICAI........ International Commission for Agricultural Industries
ICAN....... International Commission for Air Navigation
ICG........ International Commission on Glass
ICI........ International Commission on Illumination
ICID .... International Commission on Irrigation and Drainage
ICJ........ International Commission of Jurists (of the United Nations)
ICOLD ...... International Commission on Large Dams of the World Power Conference
ICMI .... International Commission on Mathematical Instruction
ICNP .... International Commission on National Parks
ICNAF ...... International Commission for the Northwest Atlantic Fisheries
ICO .... International Commission for Optics
ICPA .... International Commission for the Prevention of Alcoholism
ICRP .... International Commission on Radiological Protection
ICRU .... International Commission on Radiological Units and Measurements
CEE .... International Commission on Rules for the Approval of Electrical Equipment
ICSEMS...... International Commission for the Scientific Exploration of the Mediterranean Sea
ICSS........ International Commission on Signs and Symbols
ICUMSA ..... International Commission for Uniform Methods of Sugar Analysis
ICZN .... International Commission on Zoological Nomenclature
ICAC .... International Committee for Accounting Co-operation
ICAF .... International Committee of Aeronautical Fatigue
ICAD .... International Committee for Automobile Documentation
ICBLB .... International Committee for Breaking the Language Barrier
ICOBLA ..... International Committee for Breaking the Language Barrier
ICEL........ International Committee on English in the Liturgy
ICHS .... International Committee of Historical Sciences
ICHC .... International Committee for Horticultural Congresses
ICIREPAT..... International Committee on Information Retrieval Among Examining Patent Offices
ICLA .... International Committee on Laboratory Animals
ICMMP...... International Committee of Military Medicine and Pharmacy
ICOS .... International Committee of Onomastic Sciences
ICRC ...... International Committee of the Red Cross
ICSSD....... International Committee for Social Sciences Documentation
ICSHB....... International Committee for Standardization in Human Biology
ICWM....... International Committee on Weights and Measures
ICSC .... International Communications Satellite Consortium
ICBA .... International Community of Booksellers' Associations
ICLA .... International Comparative Literature Association
ICC .... International Computation Center (Rome, Italy) (Sponsored by UNESCO)
ICCPC ...... International Computation Center's Preparatory Committee
ICB .... International Computer Bibliography (A publication of National Computing Center)
INCOMEX.... International Computer Exhibition
ICT .... International Computers and Tabulators, Ltd.
ICOHH...... International Concatenated Order of Hoo-Hoo
ICALU ...... International Confederation of Arab Labour Unions
ICATU....... International Confederation of Arab Trade Unions
ICDP .... International Confederation for Disarmament and Peace
ICFPW....... International Confederation of Former Prisoners of War
ICFTU ...... International Confederation of Free Trade Unions
IPS .... International Confederation for Plastic Surgery
IC .... International Conference
ICAE .... International Conference of Agricultural Economists
ICBO .... International Conference of Building Officials
ICCP .... International Conference on Cataloging Principles
ICCC .... International Conference of Catholic Charities
ICCC .... International Conference of Coordination Chemistry
ICIP........ International Conference on Information Processing (Paris, 1959)
ICMST ...... International Conference on Machine Searching and Translation
INTERMAG ... International Conference on Magnetics
ICME .... International Conference on Medical Electronics
ICPUAE...... International Conference on the Peaceful Uses of Atomic Energy
ICOPA ...... International Conference of Police Associations
ICPS .... International Conference on the Properties of Steam
ICSW .... International Conference of Social Work
ICSPFT ...... International Conference on the Standardization of Physical Fitness Tests
ICC .... International Congregational Council
ICG .... International Congress of Genetics
ICM .... International Congress of Mathematicians
ICMLT....... International Congress of Medical Laboratory Technologists
ICOH .... International Congress on Occupational Health
ICR .... International Congress of Radiology
ICTMM...... International Congresses on Tropical Medicine and Malaria
ICCTA ...... International Consultative Council of Travel Agents
ICCA .... International Consumer Credit Association
ICB .... International Container Bureau
IC .... International Control

ICC .... International Control Commission (Composed of representatives of Canada, India, and Poland, and charged with supervising the cease-fire in Laos established at Geneva Conference of 1962)
ICTASD...... International Convention on Transistors and Associated Semiconductor Devices
ICA .... International Cooperation Administration (Later, Agency for International Development)
ICC .... International Cooperation Council
ICREPAT .... International Cooperation in Information Retrieval Among Examining Patent Offices
ICY .... International Cooperation Year (1965) (20th Anniversary of UN)
ICA .... International Co-operative Alliance
ICDA .... International Cooperative Development Association
ICHDA ...... International Cooperative Housing Development Association
ICITA .... International Cooperative Investigations of the Tropical Atlantic (Navy)
ICPA .... International Cooperative Petroleum Association
ICWG...... International Co-operative Women's Guild
INCRA ...... International Copper Research Association
INCINC ..... International Copyrights Information Center
ICBBA....... International Cornish Bantam Breeders' Association
ICCF .... International Correspondence Chess Federation
ICS .... International Correspondence School
ICSA .... International Correspondence Society of Allergists
ICAC .... International Cotton Advisory Committee
ICAS .... International Council of the Aeronautical Sciences
ICAS .... International Council of Aerospace Sciences
ICA .... International Council on Archives (UNESCO)
ICBD .... International Council of Ballroom Dancing
ICBP .... International Council for Bird Preservation
ICCP .... International Council for Children's Play
ICCC .... International Council of Christian Churches
ICL .... International Council for Christian Leadership
ICCE .... International Council of Commerce Employers
ICEF .... International Council for Educational Films
ICEC .... International Council for Exceptional Children
ICES .... International Council for the Exploration of the Sea
ICOGRADA ... International Council on Graphic Design Associations
ICHPER...... International Council on Health, Physical Education and Recreation
ICIE .... International Council of Industrial Editors
ICIE .... International Council of Industrial Engineers
ICJW .... International Council of Jewish Women
ICOM ...... International Council of Museums
ICN........ International Council of Nurses
ICPHS....... International Council for Philosophy and Humanistic Studies
ICP .... International Council of Psychologists
ICRSC....... International Council for Research in the Sociology of Co-operation
ICSU .... International Council of Scientific Unions
ICSC .... International Council of Shopping Centers
ICSID .... International Council of Societies of Industrial Design
ICSPE .... International Council of Sport and Physical Education
ICT .... International Council of Tanners
ICW .... International Council of Women
ICWP .... International Council of Women Psychologists
ICJ .... International Court of Justice
ICIA .... International Credit Insurance Association
ICPO .... International Criminal Police Organization
INTERPOL .... International Criminal Police Organization
ICT .... International Critical Tables
ICIA .... International Crop Improvement Association
ICCY .... International Cultural Centers for Youth
ICE .... International Cultural Exchange
ICES........ International Cultural Exchange Service
IDF .... International Dairy Federation
IDL & RS .... International Data Library and Reference Service
IDL .... International Date Line
IDOE .... International Decade of Ocean Exploration (1970's)
IDDRG ..... International Deep Drawing Research Group
IDA .... International Defenders of Animals (An organization)
IDF .... International Democratic Fellowship
IDU .... International Dendrology Union
IDLIS .... International Desert Locust Information Service
IDRA .... International Desert Racing Association (Automobile racing)
IDA .... International Development Association (An agency of the International Bank for Reconstruction and Development)
IDC .... International Development Conference
IDEAS....... International Development - Economics Awareness System
IDS .... International Development Services
IDF .... International Diabetes Federation
IDSO .... International Diamond Security Organization
IDO .... International Disarmament Organization (Proposed)
DSC .... International Die Sinkers' Conference

IDSC . . . . International Die Sinkers' Conference
IDO . . . . International District Office
IDOC . . . . . . International Documentation on the Contemporary Church (A publication)
IDS . . . . International Documents Service
IDEA . . . . . . International Downtown Executives Association
IDA . . . . International Dredging Association
IEA . . . . International Economic Association
IEPA . . . . . . International Economic Policy Association
IEA . . . . International Education Act
IEA . . . . International Education Association
IEES . . . . . . International Education Exchange Service (State Department)
IEC . . . . International Electric Corporation
IERC . . . . . . International Electronic Research Corporation
IEC . . . . International Electrotechnical Commission
IEFC . . . . . . International Emergency Food Council (Post-World War II)
IESS . . . . . . International Encyclopedia of the Social Sciences
IEO . . . . International Exchange Office
IES . . . . International Exchange Service (For publications) (Smithsonian Institution)
IESC . . . . . . International Executive Service Corps
IEA . . . . International Executives Association
IEB . . . . International Exhibitions Bureau
IEF . . . . International Eye Foundation
IFM . . . . International Falcon Movement
IFA . . . . International Federation of Actors
IFAP . . . . . . International Federation of Agricultural Producers
IFALPA . . . . . International Federation of Air Line Pilots Associations
IFATCA . . . . . International Federation of Air Traffic Controller Associations
IF . . . . International Federation of American Homing Pigeon Fanciers
IFAS . . . . . . International Federation of Aquarium Societies
IFATCC . . . . . International Federation of Associations of Textile Chemists and
            Colourists
IFAC . . . . . . International Federation of Automatic Control
IFBWW . . . . . International Federation of Building and Wood Workers
IFBPW . . . . . . International Federation of Business and Professional Women
BPWC . . . . . . International Federation of Business and Professional Women Clubs
IFCC . . . . . . International Federation of Camping and Caravanning
IFCA . . . . . . International Federation of Catholic Alumnae
IFCJ . . . . . . International Federation of Catholic Journalists
IFCP . . . . . . International Federation of Catholic Pharmacists
IFCC . . . . . . International Federation of Children's Communities
IFCM . . . . . . International Federation of Christian Metalworkers Unions
IFCMU . . . . . International Federation of Christian Miners' Unions
IFCTU . . . . . . International Federation of Christian Trade Unions (Often uses initialism
            CISC, based on name in French, to avoid confusion with ICFTU)
IFCTUBWW . . . International Federation of Christian Trade Unions of Building and Wood
            Workers
IFCUAW . . . . International Federation of Christian Unions of Agricultural Workers
IFCCTE . . . . . International Federation of Commercial, Clerical and Technical
            Employees
IFCTIO . . . . . International Federation of Commercial Travelers Insurance
            Organizations
IFCCA . . . . . International Federation of Community Centre Associations
IFCS . . . . . . International Federation of Computer Sciences
IFCATI . . . . . International Federation of Cotton and Allied Textile Industries
IFEMS . . . . . International Federation of Electron Microscope Societies
IFFA . . . . . . International Federation of Film Archives
IFFPA . . . . . . International Federation of Film Producers' Associations
IFFS . . . . . . International Federation of Film Societies
IFFJ . . . . . . International Federation of Free Journalists of Central and Eastern
            Europe and Baltic and Balkan Countries
IFFTU . . . . . . International Federation of Free Teachers' Unions
IFFJP . . . . . . International Federation of Fruit Juice Producers
IFJU . . . . . . International Federation of Fruit Juice Producers
IFGA . . . . . . International Federation of Grocers' Associations
IFGO . . . . . . International Federation of Gynecology and Obstetrics
IFHE . . . . . . International Federation of Home Economics
IFHP . . . . . . International Federation for Housing and Planning
IFHTP . . . . . . International Federation for Housing and Town Planning
IFIAT . . . . . . International Federation of Independent Air Transport
IFIF . . . . . . International Federation of Industrial Organizations and General
            Workers' Unions
IFIP . . . . . . International Federation for Information Processing
IFIPS . . . . . . International Federation of Information Processing Societies
IFIF . . . . . . International Federation for Internal Freedom (Later, Castalia Foundation)
IFIA . . . . . . International Federation of Ironmongers and Iron Merchants Associations
IFJ . . . . International Federation of Journalists
IFLA . . . . . . International Federation of Landscape Architects
IFLA . . . . . . International Federation of Library Associations
IFME . . . . . . International Federation for Medical Electronics
IFMP . . . . . . International Federation for Medical Psychotherapy
IFMSA . . . . . International Federation of Medical Student Associations

IFNE . . . . . . International Federation for Narcotic Education
IFORS . . . . . . International Federation of Operational Research Societies
IFOS . . . . . . International Federation of Ophthalmological Societies
IFPW . . . . . . International Federation of Petroleum Workers
IFPI . . . . . . International Federation of the Phonographic Industry
IFPM . . . . . . International Federation of Physical Medicine
IFPAAW . . . . . International Federation of Plantation, Agricultural and Allied Workers
IFPWA . . . . . International Federation of Protestant Workers' Associations
IFSO . . . . . . International Federation of Sanitarians Organizations
IFSPO . . . . . . International Federation of Senior Police Officers
IFS . . . . International Federation of Settlements and Neighbourhood Centres
IFSNC . . . . . . International Federation of Settlements and Neighbourhood Centres
IFST . . . . . . International Federation of Shorthand and Typewriting
IFSW . . . . . . International Federation of Social Workers
IFSCC . . . . . . International Federation of Societies of Cosmetic Chemists
IFSP . . . . . . International Federation of Societies of Philosophy
IFSDA . . . . . . International Federation of Stamp Dealers' Associations
IFS . . . . International Federation of Surveyors
IFTA . . . . . . International Federation of Teachers' Associations
IFTWA . . . . . International Federation of Textile Workers' Associations
IFTW . . . . . . International Federation of Tobacco Workers
IFTU . . . . . . International Federation of Trade Unions
IFT . . . . International Federation of Translators
IFPCS . . . . . . International Federation of Unions of Employees in Public and Civil
            Services
IFUW . . . . . . International Federation of University Women
IFWA . . . . . . International Federation for Weeks of Art
IFWL . . . . . . International Federation of Women Lawyers
IFWHA . . . . . International Federation of Women's Hockey Associations
IFWEA . . . . . International Federation of Workers Educational Associations
IFYC . . . . . . International Federation of Young Cooperators
IFES . . . . . . International Fellowship of Evangelical Students
IFOFSAG . . . . International Fellowship of Former Scouts and Guides
IFOR . . . . . . International Fellowship of Reconciliation
IFO . . . . International Field Office (FAA)
IFA . . . . International Fertility Association
IFA . . . . International Festivals Association
IFSWA . . . . . International Figure Skating Writers Association
IFF . . . . International Film Foundation
IFS . . . . International Film Seminars
IFTC . . . . . . International Film and Television Council
IFC . . . . International Finance Corporation (Affiliate of International Bank for
            Reconstruction and Development)
IFBA . . . . . . International Fire Buff Associates
IFSTA . . . . . . International Fire Service Training Association
IFA . . . . International Fiscal Association
IFC . . . . International Fisheries Commission (US and Canada)
IFP . . . . International Fixed Public
IFRF . . . . . . International Flame Research Foundation
IFIM . . . . . . International Flight Information Manual
IFSR . . . . . . International Flight Service Receiver Site
IFSS . . . . . . International Flight Service Station (FAA)
IFST . . . . . . International Flight Service Transmitter Site
IFF . . . . International Flying Farmers
IFMC . . . . . . International Folk Music Council
IFA . . . . International Footprint Association
INFO . . . . . . International Fortean Organization
IFA . . . . International Franchise Association
IFTA . . . . . . International Free Trade Area
IFLC . . . . . . International Frequency List Committee
IFRB . . . . . . International Frequency Registration Board (of the ITU)
IFT . . . . International Frequency Tables
IFL . . . . International Friendship League
IFM . . . . International Fund for Monuments
IFRA . . . . . . International Fund-Raising Association
IFRI . . . . . . International Fund-Raising Institute
FLW . . . . International Fur and Leather Workers Union of United States and
            Canada
IGFA . . . . . . International Game Fish Association
IGC . . . . International Garden Club
IGWF . . . . . . International Garment Workers' Federation
IGU . . . . International Gas Union
IGAS . . . . . . International General Assembly of Spiritualists
IGA . . . . International Geneva Association
IGA . . . . International Geographical Association (Esperantist)
IGU . . . . International Geographical Union
IGC . . . . International Geophysical Cooperation
IGE . . . . International Geophysical Extension
IGY . . . . International Geophysical Year
IGY-WDC . . . . International Geophysical Year, World Data Center
IGS . . . . International Geranium Society

GWU . . . . International Glove Workers' Union of America
IGWU . . . . . . International Glove Workers' Union of America
IGA . . . . International Golf Association
IGSA . . . . International Golf Sponsors' Association
IGA . . . . International Graduate Achievement
IGM. . . . . International Grail Movement
IGAEA . . . . . . International Graphic Arts Education Association
IGAS . . . . International Graphic Arts Society
IGF . . . . International Graphical Federation
IGAS . . . . International Graphoanalysis Society
IGC . . . . International Grassland Congress
IGN. . . . . International-Great Northern R. R. (AAR code)
I-GN . . . . . . International-Great Northern Railroad Company
IGESUCO . . . . International Ground Environment Sub-Committee (NATO)
GUA . . . . International Guards Union of America
IGE . . . . International Guiding Eyes
IGF . . . . International Gymnastic Federation
IHA . . . . International Hahnemannian Association
HR . . . . International Harvester Company (NYSE symbol)
IH . . . . International Harvester Company
IHCA . . . . International Hebrew Christian Alliance
IHC . . . . International Help for Children
IHJ . . . . International Heroines of Jericho (Later, General Conference of Grand
                    Courts Heroines of Jericho, Prince Hall Affiliation, USA)
IHATIS . . . . . . International Hide and Allied Trades Improvement Society
IHF . . . . International Hockey Federation
IHL . . . . International Hockey League
HCL . . . . International Hod Carriers', Building and Common Laborers' Union of
                    America (Later, Laborers' International Union of North America)
IHL . . . . International Homeopathic League
IHF . . . . International Hospital Federation
IHA . . . . International Hotel Association
IHA . . . . International House Association
IHEU . . . . International Humanist and Ethical Union
IHB . . . . International Hydrographic Bureau
IHO . . . . International Hydrographic Organization
IHP . . . . International Hydrographic Program
IHD . . . . International Hydrological Decade (UNESCO)
IIP . . . . International Ice Patrol
IIOE . . . . International Indian Ocean Expedition (Navy)
IIA. . . . . International Information Administration (Department of State)
                    (Transferred to USIS, 1953)
IPKO . . . . International Information on Peace-Keeping Operations
IIAS . . . . International Institute of Administrative Sciences
IIA. . . . . International Institute of Agriculture
IIAI . . . . International Institute of American Ideals
IIC . . . . International Institute for Conservation of Historic and Artistic Works
IIC . . . . International Institute for the Conservation of Museum Objects
IIEP . . . . International Institute for Educational Planning
IIE . . . . International Institute of Embryology
IIFA . . . . International Institute of Films on Art
IIIC (LN) . . . . International Institute of Intellectual Cooperation of the League of
                    Nations
IIMC . . . . International Institute of Municipal Clerks
IINSE . . . . International Institute of Nuclear Science and Engineering
IIP . . . . International Institute of Philosophy
IIR . . . . International Institute of Refrigeration
IIRR . . . . International Institute of Rural Reconstruction
IISL . . . . International Institute of Space Law
IICC . . . . International Institute for Study and Research in the Field of Commercial
                    Competition
IISRP . . . . International Institute of Synthetic Rubber Producers
IITA . . . . International Institute for Tropical Agriculture (Ibadan, Nigeria)
IIW . . . . International Institute of Welding
INTERFILM . . . International Inter-Church Film Centre
IICP . . . . International Intersociety Committee on Pathology
IJWU . . . . International Jewelry Workers Union
JWU . . . . International Jewelry Workers' Union
IJLB . . . . International Jewish Labor Bund
IJRCS . . . . International Joint Rules Committee on Softball
IJA . . . . International Jugglers Association
IKF . . . . International Kart Federation
IKA . . . . International Kitefliers Association
IKFC . . . . International Knife and Fork Clubs
IKF . . . . International Kraft Federation
ILC . . . . International Labor Conference (A section of the International Labor
                    Organization)
ILD . . . . International Labor Defense (An organization)
ILO . . . . International Labor Office (A section of the International Labor
                    Organization) (UN)
ILO . . . . International Labor Organization

ILPA . . . . International Labor Press Association
ILGB . . . . International Laboratory of Genetics and Biophysics
ILFI . . . . International Labour Film Institute
ILGWU . . . . . . International Ladies' Garment Workers' Union
ILF . . . . International Landworkers' Federation
ILA . . . . International Language for Aviation
ILC . . . . International Latex Corporation
ILS . . . . International Latitude Service
ILA . . . . International Laundry Association
ILA . . . . International Law Association
ILC . . . . International Law Commission (UN)
ILC (UN) . . . . . International Law Commission of the United Nations
ILTF . . . . International Lawn Tennis Federation
ILZRO . . . . . . International Lead Zinc Research Organization
IL . . . . International League (Baseball)
ILAB . . . . International League of Antiquarian Booksellers
ILBA . . . . International League for Bolivarian Action
ILEI . . . . International League of Esperantist Teachers
ILNY . . . . International League of New York
ILPBC . . . . . . International League of Professional Baseball Clubs
ILRM . . . . International League for the Rights of Man
ILGPNWU . . . . International Leather Goods, Plastic and Novelty Workers' Union
LGPN . . . . International Leather Goods, Plastic and Novelty Workers' Union
ILC . . . . International Legal Center (Formerly, SAILER)
ILA . . . . International Leprosy Association
ILOST . . . . . . International Liaison Center of Schools of Cinema and Television
ILCOP . . . . . . International Liaison Committee of Organizations for Peace
ILIC . . . . International Library Information Center
ILTTA . . . . . . International Light Tackle Tournament Association
ILCA . . . . International Lightning Class Association
ILRA . . . . International Log Rolling Association
ILN . . . . International Logistics Negotiations (Military export sales)
ILP . . . . International Logistics Program
ILA . . . . International Longshoremen's Association
ILWU . . . . International Longshoremen's and Warehousemen's Union
ILW . . . . International Low Water
ILS . . . . International Lunar Society
IMDA . . . . International Mail Dealers Association
IMC . . . . International Mailbag Club
IMU . . . . International Mailers Union
IMI . . . . International Maintenance Institute
IMA . . . . International Management Association
IMW. . . . . International Map of the World
IMC . . . . International Maritime Committee
IMRAN . . . . . . International Marine Radio Aids to Navigation
IMF . . . . International Marketing Federation
IMI . . . . International Marketing Institute
IMEM . . . . International Mass Education Movement
IMP . . . . International Match Point (Game of bridge)
IMMS . . . . International Material Management Society
IMU . . . . International Mathematical Union
IMEKO . . . . . . International Measurement Confederation (Hungary)
IMBA . . . . International Media Buyers Association
IMR . . . . International Medical Research
IMBEX . . . . . . International Men's and Boys' Wear Exhibition
IMS . . . . International Metallographic Society
IMF . . . . International Metalworkers' Federation
IMC . . . . International Meteorological Committee
IMO . . . . International Meteorological Organization (Later, World Meteorological
                    Organization)
IMCO . . . . International Metered Communications
IMC . . . . International Micrographic Congress
IMPI . . . . International Microwave Power Institute
INTERMILPOL . . International Military Police (NATO)
IMT . . . . International Military Tribunal (Post-World War II)
IMTE . . . . International Military Tribunal for Europe
IMTFJ . . . . . . International Military Tribunal for Japan
IMA . . . . International Mineralogical Association
IGL . . . . International Minerals & Chemical Corporation (NYSE symbol)
IMC . . . . International Minerals and Chemical Corporation
IMC . . . . International Mining Corporation (NYSE symbol)
IMF . . . . International Ministerial Federation
IMRA . . . . International Mission Radio Association
IMC . . . . International Missionary Council
IMPBA . . . . . . International Model Power Boat Association
IM & AWU . . . International Molders' & Allied Workers' Union (AFL-CIO)
IMFWUNA . . . . International Molders and Foundry Workers Union of North America
                    (Later, IM & AWU)
IMF . . . . International Monetary Fund
IMF/IBRD . . . . International Monetary Fund and International Bank for Reconstruction
                    and Development

IMCA .... International Motor Contest Association
IMPA .... International Motor Press Association
IMF .... International Motorcycle Federation
IMAU .... International Movement for Atlantic Union
IMCS .... International Movement of Catholic Students
IMSA .... International Municipal Signal Association
IMC .... International Music Council
IMS .... International Musicological Society
INCB .... International Narcotics Control Board
INF .... International Naturist Federation
INS .... International Navigation System
INTA .... International New Thought Alliance
INP .... International News Photos
INS .... International News Service (Merged with United Press to form UPI)
INCC .... International Newspaper Collectors' Club
INCA .... International Newspaper Colour Association
INA .... International Newsreel Association
INCO .... International Nickel Company
N .... International Nickel Company of Canada, Ltd. (NYSE symbol)
INGO ...... International Non-Governmental Organization
INA .... International Normal Atmosphere
INPFC-US .... International North Pacific Fisheries Commission, United States Section
INPFC ...... International North Pacific Fisheries Convention
INIS .... International Nuclear Information System
INC .... International Numismatic Commission
INRF .... International Nutrition Research Foundation
IOF .... International Oceanographic Foundation
IOCU .... International Office of Consumers' Unions
IOE .... International Office of Epizootics
IOMTR ...... International Office for Motor Trades and Repairs
IOSA .... International Oil Scouts Association
IOA .... International Olympic Academy
IOC .... International Olympic Committee
IOGT .... International Order of Good Templars
IOJD .... International Order of Job's Daughters
IOKDS ...... International Order of the King's Daughters and Sons
IOR .... International Order of Runeberg
IOAT .... International Organization Against Trachoma
IOCV .... International Organization of Citrus Virologists
IOE .... International Organization of Employers
IOJ .... International Organization of Journalists
MMP .... International Organization of Masters, Mates and Pilots of America
IOOTS ...... International Organization of Old Testament Scholars
IOPB .... International Organization of Plant Biosystematists
IOPAB ...... International Organization for Pure and Applied Biophysics
IOS .... International Organization for Standardization
IOVST ...... International Organization for Vacuum Science and Technology
IPHC .... International Pacific Halibut Commission
IPSFC ...... International Pacific Salmon Fisheries Commission
IPK .... International Packers, Limited (NYSE symbol)
IPRA .... International Paddle Racket Association
IPA .... International Paddleball Association
IP .... International Paper Company (NYSE symbol)
IPO .... International Parents' Organization
IPRO .... International Patent Research Office
IPB .... International Peace Bureau
IPRA .... International Peace Research Association
IPU .... International Peasant Union
PEN .... International PEN (Official name; PEN, never spelled out in use, is said, however, to stand for poets, playwrights, editors, essayists, novelists)
IPPF .... International Penal and Penitentiary Foundation
IPI .... International Pesticide Institute
IPC .... International Petroleum Company
IPSF .... International Pharmaceutical Students' Federation
IP .... International Pharmacopoeia
PhI .... International Pharmacopoeia
IPS .... International Phenomenological Society
IPA .... International Phonetic Alphabet
IPA .... International Phonetic Association
IPEU .... International Photo-Engravers Union of North America (Later, Lithographers and Photoengravers International Union)
IPTA .... International Piano Teachers Association
INP .... International Pipe & Ceramics Corporation (NYSE symbol)
IPS .... International Pipe Standard
IPPF .... International Planned Parenthood Federation
IPG .... International Planning Group
IPIx .... International Plant Index (A publication)
IPPS .... International Plant Propagators' Society
IPMS/USA .... International Plastic Modelers Society/US Branch

IPPDSEU ..... International Plate Printers, Die Stampers & Engravers' Union of North America
PPDSE .... International Plate Printers', Die Stampers' and Engravers' Union of North America
IPA .... International Platform Association
IPY .... International Polar Year
IPA .... International Police Academy (Formerly, Inter-American Police Academy)
IPA .... International Police Association
IPC .... International Poliomyelitis Congress
IPSA .... International Political Science Association
IPC .... International Poplar Commission
IPOR .... International Population Research Center (University of California)
IKI .... International Potash Institute
IPTS .... International Practical Temperature Scale (National Bureau of Standards)
IPI .... International Press Institute
IPSSG ...... International Printers Supply Salesmen's Guild
IPPA .... International Printing Pressmen and Assistants' Union of North America
IPPAU ...... International Printing Pressmen & Assistants' Union of North America
IPAA .... International Prisoners' Aid Association
IPSRA ...... International Professional Ski Racers Association
IEA .... International Project for Evaluation of Educational Achievement
PI .... International Protocol
IPK .... International Prototype Kilogram
IPM .... International Prototype Meter
IPA .... International Psychoanalytical Association
INPRA ...... International Public Relations Association
IPRA .... International Public Relations Association
IPA .... International Publishers Association
IQS .... International "Q" Signal
IQC .... International Quality Centre
IRPA .... International Radiation Protection Association
IRASA ...... International Radio Air Safety Association
IRCA .... International Radio Club of America
IRCC .... International Radio Consultative Committee
IRFB .... International Radio Frequency Board
IRS .... International Radio Silence
IRTS .... International Radio and Television Society
IRU .... International Radium Unit
IRCA .... International Railway Congress Association
IRTU .... International Railway Temperance Union
IRC .... International Railways of Central America (NYSE symbol)
IRC .... International Rainwear Council
IRSFC ...... International Rayon and Synthetic Fibers Committee
IRA .... International Reading Association
IRA .... International Recreation Association
IRF .... International Rectifier Corporation (NYSE symbol)
IRC .... International Red Cross
IRLCS ...... International Red Locust Control Service
IRF .... International Reform Federation
IRO .... International Refugee Organization
IRWC .... International Registry of World Citizens
IRRT .... International Relations Round Table (American Library Association)
IRO .... International Relief Organization (Post-World War II)
IRRC .... International Relief and Rescue Committee (Post-World War II)
IRU .... International Relief Union
IRLA .... International Religious Liberty Association
IRC .... International Reply Coupon
IRC .... International Rescue Committee
IRFAA ...... International Rescue and First Aid Association
IRCDP ...... International Research Career Development Program (Public Health Service)
IRCT .... International Research on Communist Techniques
IREX .... International Research and Exchanges Board
IRGRD ...... International Research Group on Refuse Disposal
INT .... International Resistance Company (NYSE symbol)
IRC .... International Resistor Center
IRC .... International Rice Commission
IRRI .... International Rice Research Institute (Philippines)
IRF .... International Road Federation
IRW .... International Rocket Week
IRA .... International Rodeo Association
IRA .... International Roleo Association (Later, International Log Rolling Association)
IRS .... International Rorschach Society
IRF .... International Rowing Federation
IRDC .... International Rubber Development Committee
IRRB .... International Rubber Research Board
IRSG .... International Rubber Study Group
ISI .... International Safety Institute
ILS .... International Salt Company (NYSE symbol)

ISCAN . . . . . . International Sanitary Convention for Air Navigation
ISIS . . . . International Satellite for Ionospheric Studies (NASA-Canada)
ISAP . . . . International School Art Program
ISA . . . . International Schools Association
ISS . . . . International Schools Service
ISF . . . . International Science Foundation
ISIS . . . . International Science Information Services (Earth sciences data center in Dallas, Texas)
ISO . . . . International Science Organization
ISFA . . . . International Scientific Film Association
ISRU . . . . International Scientific Radio Union (Also, URSI)
ISU . . . . International Scientific Union
ISV . . . . International Scientific Vocabulary
ISPA . . . . . . International Screen Publicity Association
ISU . . . . International Seaman's Union
ISUSE . . . . . . International Secretariat for the University Study of Education
ISVS . . . . International Secretariat for Volunteer Service
ISA . . . . International Security Affairs (DOD)
ISAC . . . . . . International Security Affairs Committee
ISA . . . . International Security Agency
ISTA . . . . . . International Seed Testing Association
ISC . . . . International Sericultural Commission
ISTC . . . . International Shade Tree Conference
ISA . . . . International Shipmasters Association of the Great Lakes
ISAGL . . . . . . International Shipmasters Association of the Great Lakes
ISMA . . . . . . International Shipmasters Association of the Great Lakes
ISF . . . . International Shipping Federation, Ltd.
ISS . . . . International Shoe Company (NYSE symbol)
ISLWF . . . . . . International Shoe and Leather Workers' Federation
ISHC . . . . . . International Siberian Husky Club
ISSE . . . . International Sight and Sound Exposition
ISA . . . . International Sign Association
ISA . . . . International Silk Association
INR . . . . International Silver Company (NYSE symbol)
ISU . . . . International Skating Union
ISA . . . . International Skeeter Association
ISIA . . . . International Snowmobile Industry Association
ISL . . . . International Soccer League
ISSC . . . . International Social Science Council
ISSI . . . . International Social Science Institute
ISSA . . . . International Social Security Association
ISS . . . . International Social Service
ISADPM . . . . . International Society for the Abolition of Data Processing Machines
ISAW . . . . . . International Society of Aviation Writers
ISBC . . . . International Society of Bible Collectors
ISBE . . . . International Society for Business Education
ISC . . . . International Society of Cardiology
ISCB . . . . International Society for Cell Biology
ISCE . . . . International Society of Christian Endeavor
ISCEH . . . . . . International Society for Clinical and Experimental Hypnosis
ISCLT . . . . . . International Society of Clinical Laboratory Technologists
ISCP . . . . . . International Society of Clinical Pathology
ISCD . . . . . . International Society for Community Development
ISCM . . . . . . International Society for Contemporary Music
INSEA . . . . . . International Society for Education through Art
ISEK . . . . International Society of Electromyographic Kinesiology
ISE . . . . International Society of Endocrinology
ISF . . . . International Society for Fat Research
FSI . . . . International Society of Fire Service Instructors
ISFNR . . . . . . International Society for Folk-Narrative Research
ISFSC . . . . . . International Society of Food Service Consultants
ISGE . . . . International Society of Gastroenterology
ISGS . . . . International Society for General Semantics
ISGC . . . . International Society of Guatemala Collectors
ISH . . . . International Society of Hematology
ISHI . . . . International Society for the History of Ideas
ISHS . . . . International Society for Horticultural Science
ISHAM . . . . . . International Society for Human and Animal Mycology
ISIM . . . . International Society of Internal Medicine
ISLLSL . . . . . . International Society for Labor Law and Social Legislation
ISMH . . . . . . International Society of Medical Hydrology
ISME . . . . International Society for Musical Education
ISNP . . . . International Society of Naturopathic Physicians
ISPP . . . . International Society for Portuguese Philately
ISPMB . . . . . . International Society for the Protection of Mustangs and Burros
ISR . . . . International Society of Radiology
ISRD . . . . International Society for Rehabilitation of the Disabled
RCC . . . . International Society of Reply Coupon Collectors
ISSCB . . . . . . International Society for Sandwich Construction and Bonding
ISST . . . . International Society of Skilled Trades
ISSS . . . . International Society for Socialist Studies

ISSMFE . . . . . . International Society of Soil Mechanics and Foundation Engineering
ISSS . . . . International Society of Soil Science
ISSS . . . . International Society for the Study of Symbols
ISSCT . . . . . . International Society of Sugar Cane Technologists
ISTM . . . . . . International Society for Testing Materials
ISTC . . . . International Society for Training and Culture
ISTF . . . . International Society of Tropical Foresters
ISWC . . . . . . International Society for the Welfare of Cripples
ISA . . . . International Sociological Association
ISC . . . . International Softball Congress
ISF . . . . International Softball Federation
ISCAY . . . . . . International Solidarity Committee with Algerian Youth
ISC . . . . International Space Congress
ISF . . . . International Spiritualist Federation
ISPA . . . . . . International Sporting Press Association
ISGA . . . . . . International Stained Glass Association
ISA . . . . International Standard Atmosphere
ISO . . . . International Standardization Organization
ISA . . . . International Standards Association
ISCYRA . . . . . International Star Class Yacht Racing Association
ISC . . . . International Statistical Classification
ISI . . . . International Statistical Institute
ISEU . . . . International Stereotypers-Electrotypers Union of North America
ISC . . . . International Student Conference
ISIS . . . . International Student Information Service
ISMUN . . . . . . International Student Movement for the United Nations
ISI . . . . International Students, Incorporated
ISS . . . . International Students Society
ISA . . . . International Studies Association
ISGA . . . . . . International Study Group for Aerogrammes
ISC . . . . International Sugar Council
ISS . . . . International Sunshine Society
ISMA . . . . . . International Superphosphate Manufacturers' Association
ISC . . . . International Supreme Council of World Masons
ISASNP . . . . . International Symposium on Aerospace Nuclear Populsion
ISRSM . . . . . . International Symposium on Rocket and Satellite Meteorology
ISSET . . . . . . International Symposium on Space Electronics
ISR . . . . International Synthetic Rubber Company (United Kingdom)
ITTF . . . . International Table Tennis Federation
ITI . . . . International Technical Institute of Flight Engineers
ITTTA . . . . . . International Technical Tropical Timber Association
ITS . . . . International Technogeographical Society
ITU . . . . International Telecommunication Union (A specialized agency of the United Nations)
INTELSAT . . . . International Telecommunications Satellite
ITTAC . . . . . . International Telegraph and Telephonic Advisory Committee
ITT . . . . International Telephone and Telegraph (NYSE symbol) (Wall Street slang name: "It Girl," the sobriquet for early movie star Clara Bow)
IT and T . . . . . International Telephone and Telegraph Company
ITTF . . . . International Telephone and Telegraph, Federal
ITTFL . . . . . . International Telephone & Telegraph Federal Laboratories
ITTCOM . . . . . International Telephone & Telegraph World Communications, Inc.
ITVB . . . . International Television Broadcasting
ITA . . . . International Temperance Association
ITU . . . . International Temperance Union
ITGWF . . . . . . International Textile and Garment Workers' Federation
ITI . . . . International Theatre Institute
ITI . . . . International Thrift Institute
ITC . . . . International Tin Council
ITC . . . . International Toastmistress Clubs
IT . . . . International Tolerance
ITA . . . . International Touring Alliance
ITY . . . . International Tourist Year
ITTC . . . . International Towing Tank Conference
ITFO . . . . International Trade Fairs Office (Commerce Department)
ITO . . . . International Trade Organization
ITS . . . . International Trade Secretariat(s)
ITC . . . . International Traders Club
INTRATA . . . . . International Trading and Credit Company of Tanzania (Formerly, Tanganyika)
ITB . . . . International Training Branch (US Office of Education)
ITAA . . . . . . International Transactional Analysis Association
ITF . . . . International Transport Workers' Federation
ITWF . . . . . . International Transport Workers' Federation
ITMRC . . . . . . International Travel Market Research Council
INTREDIS . . . . International Tree Disease Register System for Literature Retrieval in Forest Pathology (National Agricultural Library)
IT & TS . . . . . International Turtle and Tortoise Society
ITA . . . . International Twins Association
ITCA . . . . . . International Typographic Composition Association
ITU . . . . International Typographical Union

IUC .... International Underwater Contractors, Inc.
IURC .... International Underwater Research Corporation
IUSA .... International Underwater Spearfishing Association
IUAA .... International Union of Advertisers Associations
IUAT .... International Union Against Tuberculosis
IUVDT ...... International Union Against the Venereal Diseases and the Trepone-
             matoses
IUAJ. ...... International Union of Agricultural Journalists
AIW........ International Union, Allied Industrial Workers of America
IUAA .... International Union of Alpine Associations
IUAES ...... International Union of Anthropological and Ethnological Sciences
IUAO .... International Union for Applied Ornithology
IUADM...... International Union of Associations of Doctor-Motorists
IUAI........ International Union of Aviation Insurers
IUB .... International Union of Biochemistry
IUBS .... International Union of Biological Sciences
IUCW ...... International Union for Child Welfare
IUCN .... International Union for Conservation of Nature and Natural Resources
IU Cr ...... International Union of Crystallography
IUDZG ..... International Union of Directors of Zoological Gardens
IDTW .... International Union of Doll and Toy Workers of the US and Canada
             (Later, International Union of Dolls, Toys, Playthings, Novelties and
             Allied Products of the US and Canada)
IUE .... International Union of Electrical, Radio and Machine Workers
IUEW ...... International Union of Electrical Workers
IUE .... International Union for Electroheat
IUEC .... International Union of Elevator Constructors
IUFO .... International Union of Family Organizations
IUFDT...... International Union of Food, Drink and Tobacco Workers' Associations
IUF .... International Union of Food-Workers
IUFRO ...... International Union of Forest Research Organizations
IUGG .... International Union of Geodesy and Geophysics
IUGS .... International Union of Geological Sciences
IUGM....... International Union of Gospel Missions
IUHPS ...... International Union of the History and Philosophy of Science
IUHR .... International Union of Hotel, Restaurant and Bar Workers
IUJHUSC .... International Union of Journeymen Horseshoers of the United States and
             Canada
UJH........ International Union of Journeymen Horseshoers of the United States
             and Canada
IULCS....... International Union of Leather Chemists Societies
IULCW ...... International Union of Liberal Christian Women
IULIA .... International Union of Life Insurance Agents
LIA .... International Union of Life Insurance Agents
IULA .... International Union of Local Authorities
IUMI .... International Union of Marine Insurance
IUMMSW .... International Union of Mine, Mill and Smelter Workers
MMSW ..... International Union of Mine, Mill and Smelter Workers
HORECA .... International Union of National Associations of Hotel, Restaurant and
             Cafe Keepers
IUNS .... International Union of Nutritional Sciences
IUOTO ..... International Union of Official Travel Organizations
IUOE .... International Union of Operating Engineers
IUPW ...... International Union of Petroleum Workers
IUPS .... International Union of Physiological Sciences
IUPA .... International Union of Practitioners in Advertising
IUPM ...... International Union for Protecting Public Morality
IUPAC ...... International Union of Pure and Applied Chemistry
IUPAP...... International Union of Pure and Applied Physics
IUR .... International Union of Railways
IUSDT ...... International Union of Social Democratic Teachers
IUSY. ...... International Union of Socialist Youth
IUS .... International Union of Speleology
IUS .... International Union of Students
IUSSI .... International Union for the Study of Social Insects
IUTAM ..... International Union of Theoretical and Applied Mechanics
UAW .... International Union, United Automobile, Aerospace and Agricultural
             Implement Workers of America
BFCSD ...... International Union of United Brewery, Flour, Cereal, Soft Drink and
             Distillery Workers of America
UMWA ..... International Union, United Mine Workers of America
IUUW....... International Union, United Welders
IU .... International Units (Vitamins)
IUB .... International Universities Bureau
IUC .... International University Contact for Management Education
XXX........ International Urgency Signal
IUWDS ..... International Ursigram and World Days Service
IU .... International Utilities Corporation (NYSE symbol)
IVU .... International Vegetarian Union
IVFZ .... International Veterinary Federation of Zootechnics
IVSU .... International Veterinary Students Union

IWO .... International Vine and Wine Office
IVIS .... International Visitors Information Service
IVBA .... International Volleyball Association
IVS .... International Voluntary Services
IWL .... International Walther League
IWCT .... International War Crimes Tribunal
IWVA ...... International War Veterans' Alliance
IWSA .... International Water Supply Association
IW .... International Wattier (Process) (A method of making transparencies for
             rotogravure plates)
IWC .... International Whaling Commission
IWA .... International Wheat Agreement
IWC .... International Wheat Council
IWWA ...... International Wild Waterfowl Association
IWOC ...... International Wizard of Oz Club
IWA .... International Women's Auxiliary to the Veterinary Profession
IWFA .... International Women's Fishing Association
IWCS .... International Wood Collectors Society
IWA .... International Woodworkers of America
IWS .... International Wool Secretariat (Australia, New Zealand, South Africa)
IWSG .... International Wool Study Group
IWTO ...... International Wool Textile Organization
IWSA .... International Workers Sport Association
IWCA .... International World Calendar Association
IWDS ...... International World Day Service
IYRU. ...... International Yacht Racing Union
IQSY ...... International Year of the Quiet Sun (1964-65)
IYC .... International Youth Congress
IYHF. ...... International Youth Hostel Federation
IZY .... International Zoo Yearbook
INTERATOM .. Internationale Atomreactorbau (Germany)
ICPIGP...... Internationale Chretienne Professionelle pour les Industries Graphiques et
             Papetieres
IDFF........ Internationale Demokratische Frauenfoerderation
IGA .... Internationale Gartenbauansstellung
IGM........ Internationale Gesellschaft fuer Moorforschung (International Society for
             Research on Moors)
IGMG ...... Internationale Gustav Mahler Gesellschaft (International Gustav Mahler
             Society)
IL .... L'Internationale Liberale
IPTT .... Internationale du Personnel des Postes, Telegraphes et Telephones
IRG .... Internationale des Resistants a la Guerre
ISP .... Internationale des Services Publics
IVMB .... Internationale Vereinigung der Musikbibliotheken (International
             Association of Music Libraries)
IVT .... Internationale Vereinigung der Textileinkaufsverbande (International
             Association of Textile Purchasing Societies)
IAK .... Internationales Auschwitz-Komitee (International Auschwitz Committee)
IGB .... Internationales Gewerkschafts Buro (International Trades Union Office)
             (Germany)
IC .... Internment Camp
ISN .... Internment Serial Number
INSTA ...... Inter-Nordic Standardization
IC .... Internuclear Company
INDOR ..... Internuclear Double Resonance
IOM........ Inter-Office Memorandum
ISV .... Interorbital Space Vehicle
IVAM ...... Interorbital Vehicle Assembly Mode
IPU .... Inter-Parliamentary Union
IBI .... Interpersonal Behavior Inventory (VA)
IP .... Interphalangeal (Anatomy)
ICV .... Interphase Chromosome Volume
ICS .... Interphone Control Station
IPBM .... Interplanetary Ballistic Missile (Air Force)
IMF .... Interplanetary Magnetic Field
IMP .... Interplanetary Magnetometer Probe
IMP .... Interplanetary Measurement Probe
IMPS .... Interplanetary Measurement Probes
IMS .... Interplanetary Mission Support
IMSR .... Interplanetary Mission Support Requirements
IMP .... Interplanetary Monitoring Platform (Aerospace)
IMP .... Interplanetary Monitoring Probe (A spacecraft)
IMRO .... Interplant Material Requisition Order
ISA .... Inter-Plant Shipping Authority
ISN .... Inter-Plant Shipping Notice
ISO .... Interplant Shipping Order
IDAST....... Interpolated Data and Speech Transmission (Data processing)
IPJP .... Interpost Junction Panel
IPE........ Interpret Parity Error
ISE........ Interpret Sign Error
IR .... Interpretation Report

IPS . . . . Interpretative Programming System
IO . . . . Interpretive Operation
ICED . . . . Interprofessional Commission on Environmental Design
IRCOPPS . . . . . Interprofessional Research Commission on Pupil Personnel Services
IPG . . . . Interproject Group
PD . . . . Interpupillary Distance
IQR . . . . Interquartile Range
ICBO . . . . Interracial Council for Business Opportunity
ICPC . . . . Interrange Communications Planning Committee
IRIG . . . . Inter-Range Instrumentation Group
IRMFSG . . . . . Inter-Range Missile Flight Safety Group
IRTWG . . . . . Interrange Telemetry Working Group
IRIC . . . . Inter-Regional Insurance Conference
IFS . . . . Interrelated Flow Simulation
ILAS . . . . Interrelated Logic Accumulating Scanner
IFCO . . . . Interreligious Foundation for Community Organization
IRL . . . . Interrogation and Locating
IPW . . . . Interrogation Prisoner of War
IRLS . . . . Interrogation, Recording, and Locating System (Naval Oceanographic Office)
IR . . . . Interrogation Report
ISLS . . . . Interrogation Side Lobe Suppression
IR . . . . Interrogator-Responder
IRT . . . . Interrogator-Responser-Transponder (Military)
ICR . . . . Interrupt Control Register
IJS . . . . Interrupt Jet Sensor
ILSW . . . . Interrupt Level Status Word
ICW . . . . Interrupted Continuous Waves (Electronics)
IPM . . . . Interruptions Per Minute
IPS . . . . Interruptions Per Second
ITFMSG . . . . . Interscience Technological Forecasting Methodology Study Group
X . . . . Intersect, Intersection
ISR . . . . Intersecting Storage Rings
IAR . . . . Intersection of Air Routes
ITS . . . . Intersectional Transportation Service
IS . . . . Interservice
ISBIC . . . . Interservice Balkan Intelligence Committee (World War II)
IDEP . . . . Interservice Data Exchange Program (DOD)
ISG . . . . Interservice Group
IHTU . . . . Interservice Hovercraft Trials Unit
IMUA . . . . Interservice Materiel Utilization Agency (Military)
ISMET . . . . Inter-Service Metallurgical Research Council (British)
IRMP . . . . Interservice Radiation Measurement Program
IRPL . . . . Interservice Radio Propagation Laboratory
ISRB . . . . Inter-Service Research Bureau (British)
ISSB . . . . Inter-Service Security Board (British)
ISC . . . . Inter-Service Sports Council (Military)
ISSC . . . . Interservice Sports Council
ISS . . . . Interservice Supply Support (Military)
ISSC . . . . Interservice Supply Support Committee
ISSP . . . . Interservice Supply Support Program (Military)
ISSRO . . . . Interservice Supply Support Records Office (Military)
ISSA . . . . Interservice Support Agreements (Military)
ISTD . . . . Inter-Service Topographical Department (British)
IWGCSFIPERM . . Inter-Service Working Group for Cooperation & Standardization of Foto Interpretation Procedures, Equipment & Related Matters
ISCC . . . . Intersociety Color Council
ICPI . . . . Intersociety Committee on Pathology Information
ISCC . . . . Intersociety Cytology Council
IECEC . . . . . . Intersociety Energy Conversion Engineering Conference
IS . . . . Interstage Section
ISC . . . . Interstage Section Container
ISS . . . . Interstage Section Shell
I . . . . Interstate (Highway)
IS . . . . Interstate
INSACS . . . . . Interstate Airways Communication System
INACS . . . . . . Interstate Airways Communications Station
ICHMH . . . . . . Interstate Clearing House on Mental Health
ISC . . . . Interstate Commerce
ICC . . . . Interstate Commerce Commission (Independent government agency)
INCODEL . . . . Interstate Commission on the Delaware River Basin
ICPRB . . . . . . Interstate Commission on Potomac River Basin
ICESA . . . . Interstate Conference of Employment Security Agencies
ICSBC . . . . . . Interstate Council of State Boards of Cosmetology
ISD . . . . Interstate Department Stores, Inc. (NYSE symbol)
IEC . . . . Interstate Electronics Corporation
IGA . . . . Interstate Gambling Activities
ISMA . . . . Inter-State Manufacturers Association
IMF . . . . Interstate Motor Freight System (NYSE symbol)
IOC . . . . Interstate Oil Compact
IOCC . . . . Interstate Oil Compact Commission

IPMANA . . . . . Interstate Postgraduate Medical Association of North America
IPW . . . . Interstate Power Company (NYSE symbol)
INT . . . . Interstate R. R. (AAR code)
IT . . . . Interstate Theft
ITWI . . . . Interstate Transmission of Wagering Information
ITAR . . . . Interstate Transportation in Aid of Racketeering
ITF . . . . Interstate Transportation of Fireworks
ITGD . . . . Interstate Transportation of Gambling Devices
ITLT . . . . Interstate Transportation of Lottery Tickets
ITOM . . . . Interstate Transportation of Obscene Matter
ITPMG . . . . . . Interstate Transportation of Prison-Made Goods
ITPFF . . . . Interstate Transportation of Prize Fight Films
ITSA . . . . Interstate Transportation of Stolen Aircraft
ITSC . . . . Interstate Transportation of Stolen Cattle
ITSMV . . . . . . Interstate Transportation of Stolen Motor Vehicle
ITSP . . . . Interstate Transportation of Stolen Property
ITSB . . . . Interstate Transportation of Strikebreakers
ITUR . . . . Interstate Transportation of Unsafe Refrigerators
ITWP . . . . Interstate Transportation of Wagering Paraphernalia
INS . . . . Interstation Noise Suppression
ISTRACON . . . Interstation Supersonic Track Conferences
ICSH . . . . Interstitial Cell-Stimulating Hormone
IC . . . . Interstitial Cells (Histology)
IF . . . . Interstitial Fluid
ISF . . . . Interstitial Fluid (Physiology)
ISI . . . . Intersymbol Interference
ISIC . . . . Intersymbol Interference Corrector
ITT . . . . Inter-Theater Transfer (Army)
ITh . . . . Interthecal (Anesthesiology)
ITIC . . . . Inter-Tribal Indian Ceremonial Association
ITC . . . . Inter-Tropic Zone of Conveyence
ICZ . . . . Intertropical Convergence Zone
ITZ . . . . Inter-Tropical Convergence Zone
IRY . . . . Intertype Corporation (NYSE symbol)
IUCSTP . . . . . Inter-Union Commission on Solar-Terrestrial Physics
ICP . . . . Inter-University Case Program
IUC . . . . Inter-University Committee for Debate on Foreign Policy
IUCI . . . . Inter-University Committee on Israel (Later, America-Israel Cultural Foundation)
IUCRCB . . . . . Inter-University Committee for Research on Consumer Behavior
ICSS . . . . Inter-University Committee on the Superior Student
IUCTG . . . . . . Inter-University Committee on Travel Grants
ICPR . . . . Inter-University Consortium for Political Research
IUC . . . . Interuniversity Council
IULEC . . . . . . Inter-University Labor Education Committee
ISAC . . . . Interuniversity Southeast Asia Committee (of the Association for Asia Studies)
IUR . . . . Inter-User Reliability
IA . . . . Interval Availability
IET . . . . Interval Embossed Tube
ISC . . . . Interval Selection Circuit
IS . . . . Interval Signal
IT . . . . Interval Timer
IU . . . . Interval of Uncertainty (Psychology)
IBASF . . . . . . Intervals Between Aircraft in Stream Type Formation
IPDP . . . . Intervals of Pulsations of Diminishing Period
IVCF . . . . Inter-Varsity Christian Fellowship of the United States of America
IV . . . . Interventricular
IVSD . . . . Interventricular Septal Defect (Pathology)
IV . . . . Intervertebral
IVJC . . . . Intervertebral Joint Complex
IAC . . . . Interview-After-Combat
ICG . . . . Interviewer's Classification Guide
IG . . . . Intestinal Groove
I . . . . Intestine
IAA . . . . Intimate Apparel Associates
IA . . . . Intra-Arterial (Physiology)
IA . . . . Intra-Articular (Orthopedics)
IBCC . . . . Intra-Bureau Change Committee
ICF . . . . Intracellular Fluid (Physiology)
IC . . . . Intracerebral (Medicine)
IWW . . . . Intracoastal Waterway
IC . . . . Intracutaneous (Medicine)
ID . . . . Intradermal
IDWA . . . . Intra-Divisional Work Authorization
IEC . . . . Intra-Epithelial Carcinoma
IMP . . . . Intra-Industry Management Program (Small Business Administration)
IM . . . . Intramuscular (Medicine)
IDC . . . . Intransit Data Card
II . . . . Intransit Inventory
INI . . . . Intranuclear Inclusion

IO . . . . Intraocular
IOP . . . . Intraocular Pressure
ITR . . . . Intra-Ocular Tension Recorder
IPI . . . . Intrapair Interval
IP . . . . Intraperitoneal (Medicine)
IPDA . . . . . . Intra-Pulse Demodulation Analysis
IUCD . . . . . . Intrauterine Contraception (or Contraceptive) Device
IUD . . . . Intrauterine Device (A contraceptive)
IEA . . . . Intravascular Erythrocyte Aggregation
IVA . . . . Intravehicular Activity
IV . . . . Intravenous (Medicine)
IVP . . . . Intravenous Pyelogram (Radiology)
IVT . . . . Intravenous Transfusion (Medicine)
IVCD . . . . . . Intraventricular Conduction Defect (Pathology)
ICF . . . . Intrinsic Coercive Force
U . . . . Intrinsic Energy (Physics symbol)
IID . . . . Intrinsic Infrared Detector
IPV . . . . Intrinsic Payload Value
IPS . . . . Introductory Physical Science (Project) (Education)
ICN . . . . Intromogenous Computer Network
IAS . . . . Intrusion Alarm System
IS . . . . Invalided from Service (Medical) (Navy)
IIA . . . . Invention Industry Association of America
IR . . . . Invention Report
IAR . . . . Inventory Adjustment Report (Military)
IAV . . . . Inventory Adjustment Voucher
ICC . . . . Inventory Control Center (of Field Army Support Command)
ICPE . . . . . . Inventory Control Point Europe
ICP . . . . Inventory Control Points
IC & RR . . . . . Inventory Control and Requirements Review Board (CNO)
IER . . . . Inventory Equipment Requirement
IERS . . . . . . Inventory Equipment Requirement Specification
II . . . . Inventory and Inspection Report
I/I . . . . Inventory and Inspection Report (Army)
I & MA . . . . . Inventory and Management Analysis
IMPACT . . . . . Inventory Management Program and Control Technique (Data processing)
IMR . . . . Inventory Management Record (Military)
IM . . . . Inventory Manager (Military)
IMSC & D . . . . Inventory Manager Stock Control and Distribution (Military)
IO . . . . Inventory Objective
IPI . . . . Inventory, Print, and Index (System)
IS . . . . Inventory Schedule
ISCP . . . . Inventory Stock Cataloging Program
ITIU . . . . Inventory Temporarily in Use (Army)
IT . . . . Inventory Transfer
IT/R . . . . Inventory Transfer Receipt
ITAL . . . . Inventory Trial Allowance List
IVA . . . . Inventory Valuation Adjustments
IEC . . . . Inverse Electrode Current
IHF . . . . Inverse Hyperbolic Function
IJE . . . . Inverse Joule Effect
IPE . . . . Inverse Photoelectric Effect
IPP . . . . Inverse Polarity Protection
ISP . . . . Inverse Sampling Procedure
ITL . . . . Inverse Taper Lens
ITF . . . . Inverse Trigonometric Function
IBC . . . . Inverted Bowl Centrifuge
IEP . . . . Inverted Energy Population
IV . . . . Inverted Vertical (Aircraft engine)
I . . . . Inverter
IANC . . . . . . Invest-in-America National Council, Inc.
INVSTAR . . . . . Investigate and Report
IR . . . . Investigation Record
I & SSFR . . . . . Investigation and Security Service Field Representative (Veterans Administration)
IND . . . . Investigational New Drug (Application) (FDA)
IBA . . . . Investing Builders Association
IBA . . . . Investment Bankers Association of America
ICI . . . . Investment Casting Institute
ICI . . . . Investment Company Institute
ICAA . . . . . . Investment Counsel Association of America
IGP . . . . Investment Guaranty Program (AID)
IDS . . . . Investor Diversified Services, Inc. (Mutual fund)
IOS . . . . Investors Overseas Services, Ltd. (Firm which sells mutual funds in foreign countries)
IPC . . . . Investors Planning Corporation
IFB . . . . Invitation for Bid (Military)
ITO . . . . Invitational Travel Order (Army)
IB . . . . Invoice Book
IBI . . . . Invoice Book Inbound (Business and trade)
IBO . . . . Invoice Book Outbound (Business and trade)

IDR . . . . Invoice Discrepancy Report
IV . . . . Invoice Value
ISS . . . . Involuntary Servitude and Slavery
IHSA . . . . . . Iodinated Human Serum Albumin
I . . . . Iodine (Chemical element)
IDC . . . . Iodine Dextrin Color
IV . . . . Iodine Value
IAA . . . . Iodoacetic Acid
INT . . . . Iodonitro Tetrazolium Violet
IBP . . . . Ion Beam Projector
IBS . . . . Ion Beam Scanning
IBW . . . . Ion Beam Weapon
ICR . . . . Ion Cyclotron Resonance
IDEP . . . . . . Ion Density Electronics Package
IDI . . . . Ion Dipole Interaction
IDT . . . . Ion Doping Technique
IDS . . . . Ion Drift Semiconductor
IES . . . . Ion Energy Selector
IES . . . . Ion Engine Simulator
IES . . . . Ion Engine System
IESS . . . . Ion Engine System Section
IED . . . . Ion Exchange Desalination
IEM . . . . Ion Exchange Membrane
IFT . . . . Ion Focusing Technique
IGA . . . . Ion Gun Assembly
IGC . . . . Ion Gun Collector
IID . . . . Ion Implantation Doping
IIDT . . . . Ion Implantation Doping Technique
IIMS . . . . Ion Implantation Manufacturing System
IIS . . . . Ion Implantation Study
IPY . . . . Ion Pair Yield
IPS . . . . Ion Plating Supply
IPVS . . . . Ion Pump Vacuum System
IRC . . . . Ion Recombination Chamber
ISI . . . . Ion Source Injector
ISK . . . . Ion Source Kit
ITS . . . . Ion Thrust System
ITB . . . . Ion Thruster Beam
IVP . . . . Ion Vacuum Pump
IZ . . . . Ion, Zwitter
IHC . . . . Ionic Heated Cathode
IHK . . . . Ionic Heated Kathode
I . . . . Ionic Strength
IO . . . . Ionium
IGT . . . . Ionization Gauge Tube
ITA . . . . Ionization Test Apparatus
IFF . . . . Ionized Flow Field
IGL . . . . Ionized Gas LASER
ISF . . . . Ionizer, Slab Fabrication
IPP . . . . Ionospheric Propagation Path
IRS . . . . Ionospheric Radio Signal
ICF . . . . Iota-Cam Fiberscope
ICFS . . . . Iota-Cam Fiberscope
ICFI . . . . Iota-Cam Fiberscope Instrument
IA . . . . Iowa
IEL . . . . Iowa Electric Light & Power Company (NYSE symbol)
IWG . . . . Iowa-Illinois Gas & Electric Company (NYSE symbol)
IIHR . . . . Iowa Institute of Hydraulic Research
IOP . . . . Iowa Power & Light Company (NYSE symbol)
IQ . . . . Iowa Quality (of pigs)
ISU . . . . Iowa Southern Utilities (Southern Iowa Railway) (AAR code)
ISC . . . . Iowa State College
ISCP . . . . Iowa State College Press
ISTC . . . . Iowa State Teachers College
ISU . . . . Iowa State University
ITBS . . . . Iowa Test of Basic Skills
ITED . . . . Iowa Tests of Educational Development
IWC . . . . Iowa Wesleyan College
IF . . . . Ipse Fecit (He Did It Himself)
IF . . . . Ipso Facto (By the Fact Itself)
IRA . . . . Iranian Airways Company
ISA . . . . Iranian Students Association
ISAUS . . . . . . Iranian Students Association in the United States
IFTU . . . . . . Iraq Federation of Trade Unions
I . . . . Iraqi
IA . . . . Iraqi Airways
ICTU . . . . . . Iraqi Confederation of Trade Unions
INOC . . . . . . Iraqi National Oil Company (Government company)
IPC . . . . Iraqi Petroleum Company
Ir . . . . Iridium (Chemical element)
IACI . . . . Irish American Cultural Institute

ICTU . . . . Irish Congress of Trade Unions
IES . . . . Irish Emigrant Society
IFS. . . . . Irish Free State
IG . . . . Irish Guards (Military unit)
II. . . . . Irish Institute
ILG . . . . Irish Linen Guild
IMA . . . . Irish Medical Association
IO . . . . Irish Office
IRA . . . . Irish Republican Army
IRB . . . . Irish Republican Brotherhood
ISCA . . . . . . Irish Setter Club of America
IS . . . . Irish Society
ITCA . . . . . . Irish Terrier Club of America
ITUC . . . . . . Irish Trade Union Congress
IUP . . . . Irish University Press
IWSCA . . . . . . Irish Water Spaniel Club of America
IWCA . . . . . . Irish Wolfhound Club of America
Fe . . . . Iron (Chemical element)
I . . . . Iron
IBBM . . . . . . Iron Body Brass Mounted
IBBM . . . . . . Iron Body Bronze-Mounted
IMBT . . . . . . Iron Masters Board of Trade
INA . . . . Iron Nickel Alloy
INS . . . . Iron Nickel System
IP . . . . Iron Pipe
IPS. . . . . Iron Pipe Size
ISWU . . . . . . Iron and Steel Workers' Union (India)
IRN . . . . Ironton R. R. (AAR code)
IMS . . . . Irradiance Measuring System
IML . . . . Irradiated Materials Laboratory
J . . . . Irradiation Correction
ICNF . . . . . . Irredundant Conjunctive Normal Formula
IDNF . . . . . . Irredundant Disjunctive Normal Formula
INF . . . . Irredundant Normal Formula
IRC . . . . Irregular Route Carrier
IHV . . . . Irving Air Chute Company, Inc. (NYSE symbol)
IATA . . . . . . Is Amended to Add
IATD . . . . . . Is Amended to Delete
IATR. . . . . . . Is Amended to Read
ICFATCMUTAI . . Is Cleared for Access to Classified Material Up to and Including
IKL . . . . Isanmaallinen Kansanluke (National Patriotic Movement) (Finland)
IHD . . . . Ischemic Heart Disease
ISZ . . . . Iskustvennyi Sputnik Zemil (USSR)
IC . . . . Islamic Congress
IMA . . . . Islamic Mission of America
I . . . . Island (Maps and charts)
IBS. . . . . Island Base Section
ISCOM . . . . . . Island Commander (Navy)
ISCOMAZORES . . Island Commander Azores
ISCOMBERMUDA . . Island Commander Bermuda
ISCOMFAROES . . Island Commander Faroes
ISCOMGREENLAND . . Island Commander Greenland
ISCOMICELAND . . Island Commander Iceland
ISCOMADEIRA . . Island Commander Madeira
ITB . . . . Island Tug and Barge R. R. (AAR code)
IRF. . . . . Islands Research Foundation
IM . . . . Isle of Man
IOM. . . . . Isle of Man
ISRO . . . . . . Isle Royale National Park
IOW . . . . Isle of Wight
IW . . . . Isle of Wight
IWR . . . . Isle of Wight Railway (British)
IBVE . . . . . . Isobutyl Vinyl Ether
IDT . . . . Isodensitracer
IEF. . . . . Isoelectric Focusing
IP . . . . Iso-electric Point
IA . . . . Isolation Amplifier
IT . . . . Isomeric Transition
INA . . . . Isonicotinic Acid
INH . . . . Isonicotinic Acid Hydrazide ("Wonder drug" for treatment of tuberculosis)
ISONIAZID . . . Isonicotinic Acid Hydrazide ("Wonder drug" for treatment of tuberculosis)
IPA . . . . Isopentenyl Adenosine
IPC . . . . Isopropyl N-Phenylcarbamate (Crystalline herbicide)
IGC . . . . Isothermal Gas Chromatography
IPP. . . . . Isothermal Pressure Profile
IRM . . . . Isothermal Remanent Magnetization
IDL . . . . Isotope Development, Limited
IDP . . . . Isotope Development Program (AEC)
IELS . . . . . . Isotope Exciter Light Source

IPG . . . . Isotope Power Generator
IPD. . . . . Isotope Powered Device
IRS. . . . . Isotope Radiography System
ISP. . . . . Isotope Separation Power
IIC. . . . . Isotopes Information Center (ORNL)
IRD . . . . Isotopes and Radiation Division (American Nuclear Society)
IAW . . . . Isotopic Atomic Weight
IDA . . . . Isotopic Dilution Analysis
IW . . . . Isotopic Weight
IFOA . . . . . . Isotta Fraschini Owners' Association
IAI. . . . . Israel Aircraft Industries, Ltd.
IEF. . . . . Israel Education Fund
IMF . . . . Israel Music Foundation
IPPSA . . . . . . Israel-Palestine Philatelic Society of America
IPST . . . . Israel Program for Scientific Translations (an agency of the Government of Israel)
I . . . . Israeli
IRR. . . . . Israeli Research Reactor
INO. . . . . Issue Necessary Orders
IPD . . . . Issue Priority Designator
IWISTK . . . . . . Issue While in Stock
IA . . . . Issuing Agency
IO . . . . Issuing Office
ICZ . . . . Isthmian Canal Zone
IAI. . . . . Istituto Affairi Internazionali (Institute for International Affairs) (Italy)
IENGF . . . . . . Istituto Electrotecnico Nazionale Gallileo Ferraris
IMI . . . . Istituto Mobiliare Italiano (Italy)
IPR. . . . . Istituto per le Pubbliche Relazioni (Italian public relations institute)
IRI . . . . Istituto per la Ricostruzione Industriale (Government holding company)
ISRT . . . . Istituto Storico della Resistenza in Toscana (Italy)
ISVE . . . . Istituto di Studi per lo Sviluppo Economico (Institute for the Study of Economic Development) (Italy)
IAU . . . . Italian Actors Union
IAF. . . . . Italian Air Force (Regia Aeronautica Italiana) (World War II)
ITAMVETS . . . Italian American War Veterans of the United States
IBAA . . . . . . Italian Baptist Association of America
ICF . . . . Italian Catholic Federation Central Council
ICA . . . . Italian Charities of America
ICI . . . . Italian Cultural Institute
ICC . . . . Italian Culture Council
IEF. . . . . Italian Expeditionary Force
IGCA . . . . . . Italian Greyhound Club of America
IHS . . . . Italian Historical Society of America
IRCS. . . . . . . Italian Red Cross Society
ISU . . . . Italian Service Unit (Italian prisoners of war who became volunteers in the Allied war effort)
ISP. . . . . Italian Society of Physics
ISC . . . . Italian Space Commission
IWL . . . . Italian Welfare League
IANU . . . . . . Italo-American National Union
IT . . . . Italy (NATO)
IJC . . . . Itasca Junior College (Minnesota)
IJC . . . . Itawamba Junior College (Mississippi)
ITE. . . . . I-T-E Circuit Breaker Company (NYSE symbol)
ICP . . . . Item Control Point
ID . . . . Item Description
IDC . . . . Item Detail Card (Military)
IEC . . . . Item Entry Control
IOH . . . . Item(s) on Hand
IIN . . . . Item Identification Number
IMCP . . . . . . Item Management Coding Program
IMC . . . . Item Master Card (Military)
INC . . . . Item Name Code (Military)
INLR . . . . . . Item No Longer Required
IP . . . . Item Processing
IRC . . . . Item Responsibility Code
ISL . . . . Item Study Listings
IT . . . . Item Transfer
ICFLPRMFS . . . Item . . . . through Cannibalization, Fabrication, or Local Procurement or Replacement from Maintenance Float Stock
IFI . . . . Iterated Fission Expectation
IDACON . . . . . Iterative Differential Analyzer Control
IDAP . . . . . . Iterative Differential Analyzer Pinboard
IDAS . . . . . . Iterative Differential Analyzer Slave
IO . . . . Iterative Operation
IOC . . . . Iterative Orbit Calculator
ISUDS . . . . . . Iterative Scheme Using a Direct Solution
ITOS . . . . . . Iterative Time Optimal System
IRD . . . . Itinerant Recruiting Detail
ISCT . . . . Ito System Color Television (Japan)
IMF . . . . Iuliu Maniu American Romanian Relief Foundation
IWLA . . . . . . Izaak Walton League of America

J

JCP . . . . J. C. Penney Company (NYSE symbol)
JI . . . . J. I. Case Company (NYSE symbol)
JJN . . . . J. J. Newberry Company (NYSE symbol)
MJW . . . . J. W. Mays, Inc. (NYSE symbol) (Wall Street slang name: "Say Hey," derived from nickname of baseball star Willie Mays, "The Say Hey Kid")
JWT . . . . J. Walter Thompson Company (An advertising agency)
J . . . . Jack (Technical drawings)
JW . . . . Jacket Water
JMI . . . . Jackson and Moreland, Incorporated
JAX . . . . Jacksonville, Fla. (Airport symbol)
FLJ . . . . Jacobs (F. L.) Company (NYSE symbol)
JAE . . . . Jaeger Machine Company (NYSE symbol)
JLP . . . . Jamaica Labour Party
JFRC . . . . James Forrestal Research Center (Princeton University)
JGS . . . . James Griffiths & Sons R. R. (AAR code)
JJS . . . . James Joyce Society
JMMF . . . . James Monroe Memorial Foundation
TLC . . . . James Talcott, Inc. (NYSE symbol)
JAPCO . . . . . Jamestown Paint and Varnish Company
JWYCC . . . . . . Jamestown-Williamsburg-Yorktown Celebration Committee
JAI . . . . Jami'at Al Islan
JAMTRAC . . . . Jammers Tracked by Azimuth Crossings (RADAR)
J/S . . . . Jamming to Signal
JMU . . . . Jamshedpur Mazdoor Union (India)
JAPA . . . . Jane Addams Peace Association
J . . . . January
JADF . . . . Japan Air Defense Force
JAL . . . . Japan Air Lines
JASSC . . . . . . Japan-America Society of Southern California
JASW . . . . . . Japan-America Society of Washington
JAPA . . . . Japan Area
JARRP . . . . . . Japan Association for Radiation Research on Polymers
JAEC . . . . Japan Atomic Energy Commission
JAEIP . . . . Japan Atomic Energy Insurance Pool
JAFC . . . . Japan Atomic Fuel Corporation
JAIF . . . . Japan Atomic Industrial Forum
JAPCO . . . . . Japan Atomic Power Company
JAPIA . . . . Japan Auto Parts Industries Association
JEOL . . . . Japan Electron Optics Laboratory Company
JEOLCO . . . . . Japan Electron Optics Laboratory Company
JEPIA . . . . Japan Electronic Parts Industry Association
JETR . . . . Japan Engineering Test Reactor
JETRO . . . . . . Japan External Trade Organization
JFEA . . . . Japan Federation of Employers Association
JICST . . . . Japan Information Center of Science and Technology
JICUF . . . . Japan International Christian University Foundation
JLMIC . . . . Japan Light Machinery Information Center
JMA . . . . Japan Meteorological Agency
JMA . . . . Japan Microphotography Association
JNR . . . . Japan National Railways
JP . . . . Japan Paper
JPP . . . . Japan Paper Proofs
JPDR . . . . Japan Power Demonstration Reactor
JPA . . . . Japan Procurement Agency
JSF . . . . Japan Scholarship Foundation
JSR . . . . Japan Science Review
JSA . . . . Japan Silk Association
JSP . . . . Japan Socialist Party
JSPS . . . . Japan Society for the Promotion of Science
JASDF . . . . . . Japanese Air Self-Defense Force
JACL . . . . Japanese-American Citizens League
JAPS . . . . Japanese American Philatelic Society

JARE . . . . Japanese Antarctic Research Expedition
JAAF . . . . Japanese Army Air Force
JAERI . . . . Japanese Atomic Energy Research Institute
JCP . . . . Japanese Communist Party
JEIPAC . . . . . . Japanese Electronic Information Processing Automatic Computer
JGSDF . . . . . . Japanese Ground Self-Defense Forces
JIS . . . . Japanese Industrial Standard
JAKIS . . . . . . Japanese Keyword Indexing Simulator
JMSDF . . . . . . Japanese Maritime Self-Defense Force
JMA . . . . Japanese Military Administration
JRR . . . . Japanese Research Reactor
JSCA . . . . Japanese Spaniel Club of America
JV . . . . Japanese Vellum
JVP . . . . Japanese Vellum Proofs
JAS . . . . Jazz Arts Society
JI . . . . Jazz International
JATP . . . . Jazz at the Philharmonic
JDA . . . . Jefferson Davis Association
JFL . . . . Jefferson Lake Petrochemicals (American Stock Exchange symbol)
JEF . . . . Jefferson Lake Sulphur Company (NYSE symbol) (Later, JFL)
JEFF . . . . Jefferson National Expansion Memorial National Historic Site
JPG . . . . Jefferson Proving Ground (Military)
INA . . . . Jena Nomina Anatomica (Anatomy)
JNA . . . . Jena Nomina Anatomica (Anatomy)
JSY . . . . Jersey Airlines
JI . . . . Jersey Institute
JE . . . . Jerseyville & Eastern R. R. (AAR code)
KEREN-OR . . . Jerusalem Institutions for the Blind
JEA . . . . Jesuit Educational Association
JPA . . . . Jesuit Philosophical Association of the United States and Canada
JSA . . . . Jesuit Seismological Association
IC . . . . Jesus (First and third letters of His name in Greek)
IHS . . . . Jesus (Contraction of the Greek word)
JC . . . . Jesus Christ (Jesus Christus)
JMJ . . . . Jesus, Maria, Joseph (Jesus, Mary, Joseph)
ISM . . . . Jesus Salvator Mundi (Jesus, Savior of the World)
JAC . . . . Jet Age Conference
JASU . . . . Jet Aircraft Starting Unit
JAL . . . . Jet Approach and Landing Chart
JALC . . . . Jet Approach and Landing Chart
JATO . . . . . . Jet-Assisted Take Off (Aviation)
JB . . . . Jet Bomb
JEFM . . . . Jet Engine Field Maintenance
JFI . . . . Jet Flight Information
JN . . . . Jet Navigation Charts (Air Force)
JP . . . . Jet Penetration
JPAP . . . . Jet Penetration Approach
JP . . . . Jet Petroleum
JP . . . . Jet Pilot
JP . . . . Jet Power
JP . . . . Jet Propellant (or Propelled; Propulsion)
JETP . . . . Jet Propelled
JPL . . . . Jet Propulsion Laboratory (NASA)
JRL . . . . Jet Research Laboratory
J-BAR . . . . . . Jet Runway Barrier
JTSTR . . . . . . Jet Stream
JTU . . . . Jet Training Unit
JUT . . . . Jet Utility Transport
JBP . . . . Jettison Booster Package (NASA)
J & WO . . . . . Jettison and Washing Overboard
JAC . . . . Jeunesse Acricole Catholique (Catholic Farm Youth) (Congo--Brazzaville)
JAC . . . . Jeunesse Anarchiste Communiste (French student group)
JCM . . . . Jeunesse Chretienne Malgache (Malagasy Christian Youth)

JCR . . . . Jeunesse Communiste Revolutionnaire (French student group)
JDC . . . . Jeunesse Democratique Camerounaise (Cameroonian Democratic Youth)
JECI . . . . Jeunesse Etudiante Catholique Internationale
JKKB . . . . Jeunesse du Kwilu-Kwango-Bateke (Kwilu-Kwango-Bateke Youth)
JMNCL . . . . . . Jeunesse du Mouvement National Congolaise - Lumumba (Youth of the Lumumba Wing of the Congolese National Movement)
JENAKAT . . . . Jeunesse Nationale Katangaise (Katangan National Youth)
JOC . . . . Jeunesse Ouvriere Chretienne Internationale
JOM . . . . Jeunesse Ouvriere Marocaine (Moroccan Working Youth)
JOS . . . . Jeunesse Ouvriere du Senegal (Senegalese Working Youth)
JPS . . . . Jeunesse Populaire Senegalaise (Senegalese People's Youth)
JPC . . . . Jeunesse Progressiste Casamancaise (Casamance Progressive Youth) (Senegal)
JPD . . . . Jeunesse Progressiste Dahomeenne (Dahomey Progressive Youth)
JEPUNA . . . . . Jeunesse du Puna
JRDA . . . . Jeunesse du Rassemblement Democratique Africain (Youth of the African Democratic Rally)
JRDACI . . . . . . Jeunesse du Rassemblement Democratique Africain de Cote d'Ivoire (Youth of the African Democratic Rally of the Ivory Coast)
JSD . . . . Jeunesse Social Democrate (Social Democratic Youth) (Malagasy)
JSK . . . . Jeunesse du Sud-Kasai
JTO . . . . Jeunesse Travailleuse Oubanguienne (Ubangi Working Youth)
JUD . . . . Jeunesse d'Union Dahomeene (Dahomean Youth Union)
JUNC . . . . Jeunesse d'Union Nationale Congolaise (Congolese National Union Youth)
JUT . . . . Jeunesse de l'Unite Togolaise (Togolese Unity Youth)
JU . . . . Jeunesse Universelle
JEF . . . . Jeunesses Europeennes Federalistes
JEL . . . . Jeunesses Europeennes Liberales
JFM . . . . Jeunesses Federalistes Mondiales
JECA . . . . . . Jewel Cave National Monument
JWT . . . . Jewel Tea Company, Inc. (NYSE symbol)
JBT . . . . Jewelers Board of Trade
JMB . . . . Jewelers Memorandum Bureau
JSA . . . . Jewelers Security Alliance of the US
JSA . . . . Jewelers Shipping Association
JVC . . . . Jewelers Vigilance Committee
JCA . . . . Jewelry Crafts Association
JIC . . . . Jewelry Industry Council
JITC . . . . Jewelry Industry Tax Committee
JMA . . . . Jewelry Manufacturers Association
JAAS . . . . Jewish Academy of Arts and Sciences
JAI . . . . Jewish Agency for Israel (Later, United Israel Appeal)
JAFP . . . . Jewish Agency for Palestine
JAP . . . . Jewish Agency for Palestine
JAS . . . . Jewish Agricultural Society
JASA . . . . Jewish Association for Services for the Aged (New York City)
JBG . . . . Jewish Board of Guardians
JBC . . . . Jewish Book Council of America
JBIA . . . . Jewish Braille Institute of America
JCS . . . . Jewish Chautauqua Society
JCA . . . . Jewish Colonization Association
JCRA . . . . Jewish Committee for Relief Abroad
JCBA . . . . Jewish Conciliation Board of America
JDL . . . . Jewish Defense League
JFS . . . . Jewish Family Service
JFSNY . . . . . . Jewish Folk Schools of New York
JFLA . . . . Jewish Free Loan Association
JFS . . . . Jewish Friends Society
JFDA . . . . Jewish Funeral Directors of America
JGB . . . . Jewish Guild for the Blind
JIB . . . . Jewish Information Bureau
JIS . . . . Jewish Information Society of America
JLB . . . . Jewish Labor Bund
JLC . . . . Jewish Labor Committee
JLA . . . . Jewish Librarians Association
JLMSA . . . . . . Jewish Liturgical Music Society of America
JMCA . . . . Jewish Ministers Cantors Association of America
JMA . . . . Jewish Music Alliance
JMF . . . . Jewish Music Forum
JNF . . . . Jewish National Fund
JNHAC . . . . . . Jewish National Home for Asthmatic Children
JNVOA . . . . . Jewish Nazi Victims Organization of America
JOC . . . . Jewish Occupational Council
JPF . . . . Jewish Peace Fellowship
JPSA . . . . Jewish Pharmaceutical Society of America
JPF . . . . Jewish Philanthropic Fund of 1933
JPS . . . . Jewish Publication Society of America
JRF . . . . Jewish Reconstructionist Foundation
JRSO . . . . Jewish Restitution Successor Organization
JSVA . . . . Jewish Socialist Verband of America
JSA . . . . Jewish Society of Americanists
JSB . . . . Jewish Society for the Blind

JSD . . . . Jewish Society for the Deaf
JSB . . . . Jewish Statistical Bureau
JVA . . . . Jewish Vacation Association (Superseded by Association of Jewish Sponsored Camps)
JWV . . . . Jewish War Veterans of the USA
JAS . . . . Job Analysis Schedule (Department of Labor)
JAM . . . . Job Assignment Memo
JCN . . . . Job Control Number
JD . . . . Job Description (Department of Labor)
JET . . . . Job Element Text
JIT . . . . Job Information Test (Military)
JI . . . . Job Instruction
JIT . . . . Job Instruction Training
JKT . . . . Job Knowledge Test (Military)
JMT . . . . Job Methods Training
JOBS . . . . Job Opportunities for Better Skills
JOBS . . . . Job Opportunities in the Business Sector (Program)
JOY . . . . Job Opportunity for Youth (NASA employment program)
JO . . . . Job Order
JOS . . . . Job Order Supplement
JOIN . . . . Job Orientation in the Neighborhoods
JOTS . . . . Job Oriented Training Standards
JPW . . . . Job Processing Word
JPG . . . . Job Proficiency Guide
JRT . . . . Job Relations Training
JSI . . . . Job Satisfaction Inventory (Guidance)
JSCR . . . . Job Schedule Change Request
JSN . . . . Job Sequence Number
JS . . . . Job Specification (Department of Labor)
JTS . . . . Job Training Standard
JET . . . . Jobs-Education-Training (Organization in Buffalo, New York)
JC . . . . Jockey Club
JA . . . . Jockey's Association
JG . . . . Jockeys' Guild
JBES . . . . Jodrell Bank Experimental Station (British)
JAACS . . . . . . John A. Andrew Clinical Society
JBS . . . . John Birch Society
JB . . . . John Bull (The typical Englishman)
JBMA . . . . John Burroughs Memorial Association
JDS . . . . John Dewey Society
JES . . . . John Ericsson Society
JFK . . . . John Fitzgerald Kennedy
JFKC . . . . John F. Kennedy Center for the Performing Arts
JOKI . . . . John F. Kennedy National Historic Site
JFKSC . . . . . . John F. Kennedy Spaceflight Center (Also known as KSC)
JHCNHS . . . . . John Henry Cardinal Newman Honorary Society
JHA . . . . John Howard Association
JMS . . . . John Milton Society
JOMU . . . . . . John Muir National Historic Site
THM . . . . John R. Thompson Company (NYSE symbol)
JHU . . . . Johns Hopkins University (Maryland)
JOHNNIAC . . Johns (Von Neumann) Integrator and Automatic Computer
JOSS . . . . JOHNNIAC (Johns [Von Neumann] Integrator and Automatic Computer) Open Shop System (Data processing)
JM . . . . Johns-Manville Corporation (NYSE symbol) (Wall Street slang name: "Jump")
JNJ . . . . Johnson & Johnson (NYSE symbol)
JOFL . . . . Johnstown Flood National Memorial
JHSC . . . . Johnstown & Stony Creek R. R. (AAR code)
J . . . . Join
JAWYS . . . . . . Join Airways
JDENL . . . . . . Joined by Enlistment (Military)
JDFR . . . . Joined From (Military)
JDIND . . . . . . Joined by Induction (Military)
JDREENL . . . . . Joined by Reenlistment (Military)
J . . . . Joiner (Machinery)
JPFT . . . . Joiner Pilaster Fumetight (Technical drawings)
JPNT . . . . Joiner Pilaster Nontight (Technical drawings)
J/A . . . . Joint Account
JAAF . . . . Joint Action Armed Forces
JACS . . . . Joint Action in Community Service
JACO . . . . Joint Actions Control Office
JAB . . . . Joint Activity Briefing (Military)
JASG . . . . Joint Advanced Study Group
JA . . . . Joint Agent
JACSPAC . . . . . Joint Air Communications of the Pacific
JADB . . . . Joint Air Defense Board
JADOC . . . . . . Joint Air Defense Operation Center
JAFNA . . . . . . Joint Air Force-NASA
JAOC . . . . Joint Air Operations Center
JASASA . . . . . Joint Air-Surface Antisubmarine Action

JATP . . . . Joint Air Transportation Plan
JATS . . . . Joint Air Transportation Service
JAGOS . . . . . Joint Air-Ground Operations System (Military)
JAAP . . . . . . Joint Airborne Advance Party (Military)
JACC/CP . . . . Joint Airborne Communications Center/Command Post
JAC . . . . Joint Aircraft Committee (World War II)
JAMTO . . . . . . Joint Airlines Military Traffic Office
JACE . . . . Joint Allied Communications Element
JAMPO . . . . . Joint Allied Military Petroleum Office (NATO)
JACCI . . . . . . Joint Allocation Committee Civil Intelligence (of US and Great Britain)
    (World War II)
JACE . . . . Joint Alternate Command Element
JACFU . . . . . . Joint American-Chinese Foul Up (World War II slang)
JAMAG . . . . . Joint American Military Advisory Group
JAB . . . . Joint Amphibious Board (Military)
JAAFU . . . . . . Joint Anglo-American Foul Up (Armed services slang) (World War II)
JAAOC . . . . . . Joint Antiaircraft Artillery Operations Center (Military)
JASA . . . . Joint Antisubmarine Action
JAC . . . . Joint Apprenticeship Council
JAWS . . . . Joint Arctic Weather Stations (Canada-US)
JAPO . . . . Joint Area Petroleum Office
JAAF . . . . Joint Army and Air Force
JAAFAR . . . . . Joint Army-Air Force Adjustment Regulations
JAAFCTB . . . . Joint Army-Air Force Commercial Traffic Bulletin
JAAFPC . . . . . Joint Army-Air Force Procurement Circular
JAFPUB . . . . . Joint Army-Air Force Publication
JAN . . . . Joint Army and Navy
JANAF . . . . . . Joint Army-Navy-Air Force
JANAP . . . . . . Joint Army-Navy-Air Force Publication
JANAST . . . . . Joint Army-Navy-Air Force Sea Transportation Message
JANAIR . . . . . Joint Army-Navy Aircraft Instrument Research
JB . . . . Joint Army-Navy Board
JANCOM . . . . Joint Army-Navy Communications
JANET . . . . . . Joint Army-Navy Experimental and Testing Board
JANFU . . . . . . Joint Army-Navy Foul Up (Military slang) (Bowdlerized version)
JANGRID . . . . Joint Army-Navy Grid
JANIC . . . . . . Joint Army-Navy Information Center
JANIS . . . . . . Joint Army-Navy Intelligence Studies
JANMAT . . . . . Joint Army-Navy Material
JANMB . . . . . . Joint Army and Navy Munitions Board (Terminated, 1947)
JANOT . . . . . Joint Army-Navy Ocean Terminal
JANPPA . . . . . Joint Army-Navy Petroleum Purchase Agency
JANP . . . . Joint Army-Navy Publication
JANTAB . . . . . Joint Army and Navy Technical Aeronautical Board
JANWSA . . . . Joint Army-Navy War Shipping Administration
JASCO . . . . . . Joint Assault Signal Company (Small unit in Pacific amphibious warfare)
    (World War II)
JAIEG . . . . . . Joint Atomic Information Exchange Group (DOD)
JAWPM . . . . . Joint Atomic Weapon Planning Manual
JAWPS . . . . . . Joint Atomic Weapons Publication System
JAWPB . . . . . Joint Atomic Weapons Publications Board
JALPG . . . . . . Joint Automatic Language Processing Group
JBC . . . . Joint Blood Council
JBDAAFES . . . Joint Board of Directors, Army-Air Force Exchange Service
JBFSAW . . . . . Joint Board on Future Storage of Atomic Weapons
JB . . . . Joint Bond
JBUSDC . . . . . Joint Brazil-United States Defense Commission
BMC . . . . Joint Brazil-United States Military Commission
JBUSMC . . . . . Joint Brazil-United States Military Commission
JBMTO . . . . . . Joint Bus Military Traffic Office
JCSLHG . . . . . Joint Center for the Study of Law and Human Genetics
JCUS . . . . Joint Center for Urban Studies
JCS . . . . Joint Chiefs of Staff (United States)
JCSAN . . . . . . Joint Chiefs of Staff Alerting Network
JCSO . . . . Joint Chiefs of Staff Organization
JCA . . . . Joint Church Aid (Biafra relief program in late 1960's)
JCA-USA . . . . Joint Church Aid - United States of America (Also see JCA)
JCAC . . . . Joint Civil Affairs Committee
JCCDG . . . . . . Joint Command and Control Development Group (DOD)
JCCRG . . . . . . Joint Command and Control Requirements Group (Joint Chiefs
    of Staff) (DOD)
JCCSC . . . . . . Joint Command and Control Standards Committee
JCAH . . . . Joint Commission for Accreditation of Hospitals
JCA . . . . Joint Commission on Accreditation of Universities (Military)
JCK . . . . Joint Commission on Korea
JCMIH . . . . . . Joint Commission on Mental Illness and Health
JCRR . . . . Joint Commission on Rural Reconstruction
JCAE . . . . . . Joint Committee on Atomic Energy (of the US Congress)
JCAFU . . . . . . Joint Committee of the Autonomous Federations and Unions (Comite
    d'Entente des Federations et Syndicats Autonomes d'Algerie) (Algeria)
JCBC . . . . Joint Committee on Building Codes

JCCLE . . . . . . Joint Committee on Continuing Legal Education
JCLC . . . . Joint Committee (of Congress) on the Library of Congress
JCLE . . . . Joint Committee on Library Education
JNW . . . . Joint Committee on New Weapons and Equipment
JCP . . . . Joint (Congressional) Committee on Printing
CMTT . . . . Joint Committee on Television Transmission
JCULS . . . . . . Joint Committee on the Union List of Serials
JCA . . . . Joint Communication Activity
JCA . . . . Joint Communications Agency (Military)
JCB . . . . Joint Communications Board
JCC . . . . Joint Communications Center
JCEC . . . . Joint Communications-Electronics Committee
JCEG . . . . Joint Communications-Electronics Group
JCI . . . . Joint Communications Instruction
JC . . . . Joint Compound (Plumbing)
JCA . . . . Joint Construction Agency
JCCA . . . . Joint CONEX (Container Express) Control Agency
JCDSIPS . . . . . Joint Continental Defense Systems Integration Planning Staff (Air Force)
JCCOMNET . . . Joint Coordination Center Communications Network
JCEE . . . . Joint Council on Economic Education
JCEB . . . . Joint Council on Educational Broadcasting
JCET . . . . Joint Council on Educational Television
JCIHCA . . . . . Joint Council to Improve Health Care of the Aged
JCPOA . . . . . . Joint Council of Post Office Associations (South Africa)
JCR . . . . Joint Council for Repatriation
JDA . . . . Joint Defense Appeal
JDPC . . . . Joint Defense Production Committee (Later, Joint War Production
    Committee) (World War II)
JDCS . . . . Joint Deputy Chiefs of Staff
JD . . . . Joint Determination
JD . . . . Joint Dictionary (Dictionary of US Military Terms for Joint Usage)
JDC . . . . Joint Distribution Committee (Short form of American Jewish Joint
    Distribution Committee)
JEC . . . . Joint Economic Committee (of Congress)
JECC . . . . Joint Economic Committee of Congress
JET . . . . Joint Economic Team(s)
JEB . . . . Joint Economy Board (Army-Navy)
JELC . . . . Joint Effort against Lefthanded Complications
JEEP . . . . Joint Effort Evaluation Program (Military)
JEDEC . . . . . . Joint Electron Device Engineering Council
JETEC . . . . . . Joint Electron Tube Engineering Council
JEIA . . . . Joint Electronics Information Agency
JETDS . . . . . . Joint Electronics Type Designation System (Military)
JETD . . . . Joint Electronics Type Designator
JEEP . . . . Joint Emergency Evacuation Plan (Military)
JEEP . . . . Joint Environmental Effects Program (Military)
JEEP . . . . Joint Establishment Experimental Pile (Atomic energy)
JENER . . . . . . Joint Establishment for Nuclear Energy Research
JEOCN . . . . . Joint European Operations Communications Network
JEA . . . . Joint Export Agent
JEIA . . . . Joint Export-Import Agency (Munich) (Allied German Occupation Forces)
JFSG . . . . Joint Feasibility Study Group (Air Force)
J-FACT . . . . . Joint Flight Acceptance Composite Test (Gemini) (NASA)
JFEA . . . . Joint Foreign Exchange Agency (Berlin) (Post-World War II, Germany)
JFIAP . . . . . . Joint Foreign Intelligence Assistance Program
JFAP . . . . Joint Frequency Allocation Panel
JFL . . . . Joint Frequency List
JFP . . . . Joint Frequency Panel
JHGSOWA . . . Joint Household Goods Shipping Office, Washington Area (Military)
JIC . . . . Joint Industrial Council
JIBEI . . . . Joint Industry Board of the Electrical Industry
JIC . . . . Joint Industry Conference
JIGTSC . . . . . Joint Industry-Government Tall Structures Committee
JILA . . . . Joint Institute for Laboratory Astrophysics (located at
    University of Colorado)
JINR . . . . Joint Institute for Nuclear Research
JIB . . . . Joint Intelligence Bureau (British)
JIC . . . . Joint Intelligence Center
JICA . . . . Joint Intelligence Center, Africa
JICPOA . . . . . Joint Intelligence Center, Pacific Ocean Areas
JICA . . . . Joint Intelligence Collecting Agency
JICACBI . . . . . Joint Intelligence Collecting Agency, China, Burma, India (World
    War II)
JICAME . . . . . Joint Intelligence Collecting Agency, Middle East (World War II)
JICANA . . . . . Joint Intelligence Collecting Agency, North Africa (World War II)
JICARC . . . . . Joint Intelligence Collecting Agency, Reception Committee (Navy
    Department)
JIC . . . . Joint Intelligence Committee
JICS . . . . Joint Intelligence Coordination Staff (Central Intelligence Agency)
JIEP . . . . Joint Intelligence Estimate for Planning
JIG . . . . Joint Intelligence Group (Military)

JIOA . . . . Joint Intelligence Objectives Agency
JIS . . . . Joint Intelligence Staff
JISPB . . . . Joint Intelligence Studies Publishing Board
JLFB . . . . Joint Landing Force Board
JLC . . . . Joint Logistics Committee
JLPPG . . . . . . Joint Logistics and Personnel Policy Guidance (Military)
JLPC . . . . . . Joint Logistics Plans Committee
JLPG . . . . Joint Logistics Plans Group (Military)
JLRSE . . . . Joint Long-Range Strategic Estimates (Military)
JLRSS . . . . Joint Long-Range Strategic Study (Military)
JMDC . . . . . . Joint Manual Direction Center (Air Force)
JMC . . . . . . Joint Maritime Commission
JMRO . . . . Joint Medical Regulating Office
JMVB . . . . Joint Merchant Vessels Board (World War II)
JMC . . . . Joint Meteorological Committee
JMG . . . . Joint Meteorological Group (DOD)
JMRP . . . . Joint Meteorological Radio Propagation Committee (British)
JMSAC . . . . Joint Meteorological Satellite Advisory Committee
JMSPO . . . . . . Joint Meteorological Satellite Program Office
JMUSDC . . . . . Joint Mexican–United States Defense Commission
JMAHEP . . . . . Joint Military Aircraft Hurricane Evacuation Plan
JAMMAT . . . . . Joint Military Mission for Aid to Turkey
JMPTC . . . . . . Joint Military Packaging Training Center
JMRO . . . . Joint Military Regulating Office
JMTG . . . . Joint Military Terminology Group
JMTB . . . . . . Joint Military Transportation Board
JMTC . . . . . . Joint Military Transportation Committee
JMAC . . . . . . Joint Munitions Allocation Committee
JMEM . . . . . . Joint Munitions Effectiveness Manual (Military)
JNSC . . . . Joint Navigation Satellite Committee
JNACC . . . . . . Joint Nuclear Accident Coordinating Center
JNRI . . . . Joint Nuclear Research Institute (USSR)
JOD . . . . Joint Occupancy Data (Military)
JOSPRO . . . . . Joint Ocean (or Overseas) Shipping Procedure
JOIDES . . . . . Joint Oceanographic Institutions for Deep Earth Sampling
JOPREP . . . . . . Joint Operational Report (Military)
JOC . . . . Joint Operations Center
JOEG . . . . Joint Operations Evaluation Group
JOEG-V . . . . . Joint Operations Evaluation Group, Vietnam (Air Force)
JOG . . . . Joint Operations Graphic (Military)
JOG . . . . Joint Operations Group (DOD)
JOR . . . . Joint Operations Requirements (Military)
JO . . . . Joint Organization
JOTU . . . . . . Joint Organization of Trade Unions (Finland)
JOSCO . . . . . Joint Overseas Shipping Control Office
JPTF . . . . Joint Parachute Test Facility (DOD)
JPA . . . . Joint Passover Association of the City of New York
JPPL . . . . Joint Personnel Priority List
JPO . . . . Joint Petroleum Office
JPA . . . . Joint Planning Activity (DOD)
JPB . . . . Joint Planning Board
JPC . . . . Joint Planning Committee
JPS . . . . Joint Planning Staff (US and Great Britain) (World War II)
JPWC . . . . . . Joint Postwar Committee
JPR . . . . Joint Procurement Regulations (of Army and Air Force)
JPB . . . . Joint Production Board (US and British)
JPSC . . . . Joint Production Survey Committee
JPO . . . . Joint Project Office(r)
JPRS . . . . Joint Publications Research Service (Department of Commerce)
JPB . . . . Joint Purchasing Board
JRMTO . . . . . . Joint Rail Military Traffic Office
JRC . . . . Joint Reconnaissance Center (Military)
JRPM . . . . Joint Registered Publications Memorandum
JRCC . . . . Joint Rescue Coordination Center (Military)
JRDB . . . . Joint Research and Development Board
JRATA . . . . . . Joint Research and Test Activity
JR . . . . Joint Resolution (Usually, of the US Senate and House of Representatives)
JSMA . . . . Joint Sealer Manufacturers Association
JSC . . . . Joint Security Control
JSAG . . . . . . Joint Service Advisory Group
JSCM . . . . Joint Service Commendation Medal (Military)
JSC . . . . Joint Service Committee (Military)
JIFDATS . . . . . Joint Service in Flight Data Transmission System
JSIA . . . . Joint Service Induction Area
JSO . . . . Joint Service Office
JSOC . . . . Joint Ship Operations Committee
JSRC . . . . Joint Ship Repair Committee
JSWPB . . . . . . Joint Special Weapons Publications Board
JSP . . . . Joint Staff Planners (Joint Chiefs of Staff)
JSAP . . . . Joint Statement of Agreed Principles (US–USSR)
JSC . . . . Joint-Stock Company

JSCP . . . . Joint Strategic Capabilities Plan (Military)
JSC . . . . Joint Strategic Committee
JSPC . . . . Joint Strategic Plans Committee (Military)
JSPG . . . . . . Joint Strategic Plans Group (Military)
JSSC . . . . Joint Strategic Survey Council (DOD)
JSTPS . . . . . . Joint Strategic Target Planning Staff (DOD)
JSOP . . . . . . Joint Strategy Objective Plan (Military)
JSGOMRAM . . Joint Study Group on Military Resources Allocation Methodology
JS . . . . Joint Support (Military)
JSL . . . . Joint Support List (Military)
JSESPO . . . . . Joint (Maritime Administration - Navy) Surface Effect Ship Program Office
JTA . . . . Joint Table of Allowance
JTD . . . . Joint Table of Distribution (Military)
JTF . . . . Joint Task Forces (Military)
JTG . . . . Joint Task Groups (Military)
JTAC . . . . . . Joint Technical Advisory Committee (Electronics)
JTC . . . . Joint Telecommunications Committee (Military)
JTA . . . . Joint Tenancy Agreement (Military)
JTR . . . . Joint Termination Regulation
JTETF . . . . . . Joint Test Evaluation Task Force (Air Force)
JTDS . . . . . . Joint Track Data Storage
JTUAC . . . . . . Joint Trade Union Advisory Committee
JTR . . . . Joint Travel Regulation
JUWTF . . . . . . Joint Unconventional Warfare Task Force
JUWTFA . . . . . Joint Unconventional Warfare Task Force, Atlantic
JUMPS . . . . . . Joint Uniform Military Pay System
JUSMAG . . . . Joint United States Military Advisory Group
JUSMAP . . . . . Joint United States Military Advisory and Planning Group
JUSMAGG . . . Joint United States Military Aid Group, Greece
JUSMG . . . Joint United States Military Group
JUSMMAT . . . . Joint United States Military Mission for Aid to Turkey
JUSPAO . . . . . Joint United States Public Affairs Office (Vietnam)
JUSSC . . . . . . Joint United States Strategic Committee
JUG . . . . Joint Users Group
JVB . . . . Joint Vulnerability Board
JWGA . . . . . . Joint War Games Agency (JCS) (DOD)
JWPC . . . . . . Joint War Plans Committee
JWPC . . . . . . Joint War Production Committee
JWPS . . . . . . Joint War Production Staff
JOWOG . . . . . Joint Working Group
JWG . . . . Joint Working Groups (Military)
JET . . . . Jointly Endorsed Training (Union-management)
J . . . . Joist (Technical drawings)
J & P . . . . . . Joists and Planks (Technical drawings)
JOL . . . . Jonathan Logan, Inc. (NYSE symbol)
JL . . . . Jones & Laughlin Steel Corporation (NYSE symbol)
J & L . . . . . . Jones & Laughlin Steel Corp.
JLC & E . . . . Jonesboro, Lake City and Eastern Railroad
JFTU . . . . . . Jordan Federation of Trade Unions
JOR . . . . Jorgensen (Earle M.) Company (NYSE symbol)
JOTR . . . . . . Joshua Tree National Monument
J . . . . Joule
J/K . . . . Joule per Kelvin
JOVIAL . . . . . Joules Own Version of the International Algorithmic Language (Data processing)
J . . . . Journal, Journalism
JAS . . . . Journal of Aerospace Science
JAMA . . . . . . Journal of the American Medical Association (A periodical)
JASIS . . . . . . Journal of the American Society for Information Science
JAC . . . . Journal of Applied Chemistry (Refers to either USSR or British publication)
JASB . . . . . . Journal of the Asiatic Society of Bengal
JACM . . . . . . Journal of the Association for Computing Machinery
JEGP . . . . . . Journal of English and Germanic Philology
JETP . . . . Journal of Experimental and Theoretical Physics
JGC . . . . Journal of General Chemistry
JGE . . . . Journal of General Education
JGR . . . . Journal of Geophysical Research
JOHPER . . . . . Journal of Health, Physical Education, Recreation
JOLA . . . . . . Journal of Library Automation
JLH . . . . Journal of Library History (A publication)
JOC . . . . Journal of Organic Chemistry (Refers either to US or USSR publication)
JPS . . . . Journal of Polymer Science
JRAS . . . . . . Journal of the Royal Asiatic Society
JSFA . . . . . . Journal of the Science of Food and Agriculture
JSC . . . . Journal of Structural Chemistry
JSL . . . . Journal of Symbol Logic (A publication)
JUSNC . . . . . . Journal of the United States National Committee
JV . . . . Journal Voucher (Accounting)
JAJC . . . . Journalism Association of Junior Colleges

JEA . . . . Journalism Education Association
JO . . . . Journalist (Navy rating)
BHC . . . . Journeymen Barbers, Hairdressers, Cosmetologists and Proprietors'
International Union of America
JBHCPIUA . . . Journeymen Barbers, Hairdressers, Cosmetologists and Proprietors'
International Union of America
JSA . . . . Journeymen Stone Cutters Association of North America
JSCA . . . . Journeymen Stone Cutters Association of North America
JOY . . . . Joy Manufacturing Company (NYSE symbol)
JHPS . . . . Judaica Historical Philatelic Society
J . . . . Judean or Yahwistic (Used in biblical criticism to designate Yahwistic
material)
J . . . . Judge
JA . . . . Judge Advocate
JAG . . . . Judge Advocate General (Air Force, Army, Navy)
JAGAR . . . . . Judge Advocate General Area Representatives
JAGC . . . . . . Judge Advocate General's Corps
JAGD . . . . . . Judge Advocate General's Department (Air Force, Army)
NAVJAG . . . . Judge Advocate General's Office Publications (Navy)
JAA . . . . Judge Advocates Association
JJ . . . . Judges
JMCA . . . . . . Judges, Marshals and Constables Association
JRF . . . . Judicial Research Foundation
JAGO . . . . . . Jugendarrestgeschaeftsordnung (Germany)
JAT . . . . Jugoslovenski Aerotransport (Yugoslav Air Transport)
JD . . . . Julian Date (or Day)
JC . . . . Julius Caesar
J . . . . July
JA . . . . Jump Address
JB . . . . Junction Box (Technical drawings)
JFET . . . . Junction Field-Effect Transistor
JGN . . . . Junction Gate Number
J . . . . June
JP . . . . Junge Pioniero
JGWTC . . . . . Jungle and Guerrilla Warfare Training Center (Army)
JWTC . . . . . . Jungle Warfare Training Center
J . . . . Junior
JA . . . . Junior Achievement (A youth organization)
JADE . . . . Junior Administrator Development Examination
JANGO . . . . . Junior Army-Navy Guild Organization (Organization of teenage
daughters of military officers, who helped out in war work) (World
War II)
JB . . . . Junior Beadle (Ancient Order of Foresters)
JBA . . . . Junior Bluejackets of America
JCDA . . . . . . Junior Catholic Daughters of America
JAYCEES . . . . . (United States) Junior Chamber of Commerce
JC of C . . . . . Junior Chamber of Commerce
JCI . . . . Junior Chamber International
JCL . . . . Junior Classical League
JC . . . . Junior College
JCP . . . . Junior Collegiate Players (Later, Associate Collegiate Players)
JCR . . . . Junior Common Room (in British colleges and public schools)
JD . . . . Junior Deacon
JD . . . . Junior Dean
JETS . . . . Junior Engineering Technical Society
JESSI . . . . Junior Engineers' and Scientists' Summer Institute
JGTC . . . . Junior Girls' Training Corps (British) (World War II)
JG . . . . Junior Grade
JGW . . . . Junior Grand Warden (Masonry)
JHMO . . . . . . Junior Hospital Medical Officer
JMRT . . . . Junior Members Round Table
JMA . . . . Junior Military Aviator
JOOMS . . . . . Junior Observers of Meteorology (Trainees for government service to re-
place Weather Bureau men who had gone to war) (World War II)
JOOD . . . . . . Junior Officer of the Deck (Navy)
JOOW . . . . . . Junior Officer of the Watch

JO . . . . Junior Officers
JOPA . . . . Junior Officers and Professional Association
JOUAM . . . . . Junior Order United American Mechanics
JPOAA . . . . . . Junior Panel Outdoor Advertising Association
JP . . . . Junior Partner (i.e., a husband) (Slang)
JPSA . . . . Junior Philatelic Society of America
JRC . . . . Junior Red Cross
JSHS . . . . Junior Science and Humanities Symposium
JSCS . . . . Junior Slovak Catholic Sokol
JSA . . . . Junior Statesmen of America
JSF . . . . Junior Statesmen Foundation
JTML . . . . Junior Town Meeting League
JTC . . . . Junior Training Corps (British)
JV . . . . Junior Varsity
JVA . . . . Junior Victory Army (World War II)
JW . . . . Junior Warden (Masonry)
JW . . . . Junior Wolf (A young philanderer) (Slang)
JW . . . . Junior Woodward (Ancient Order of Foresters)
JEN . . . . Junta de Energia Nuclear (Spanish nuclear agency)
J . . . . Jupiter
JB . . . . Juris Baccalaureus (Bachelor of Laws)
J Can B . . . . . Juris Canna Baccalaureus (Bachelor of Canon Law)
JCB . . . . Juris Canna Baccalaureus (Bachelor of Canon Law)
J Can D . . . . . Juris Canna Doctor (Doctor of Canon Law)
J Can M . . . . . Juris Canna Magister (Master of Canon Law)
JCD . . . . Juris Canonici Doctor (Doctor of Canon Law)
JCL . . . . Juris Canonici Licentiatus (Licentiate in Canon Law)
JCB . . . . Juris Civilis Baccalaureus (Bachelor of Civil Law)
JCD . . . . Juris Civilis Doctor (Doctor of Civil Law)
JCL . . . . Juris Civilis Licentiatus (Licentiate of Civil Law)
JCM . . . . Juris Civilis Magister (Master of Civil Law)
JD . . . . Juris Doctor (Doctor of Jurisprudence)
JM . . . . Juris Magister (Master of Laws)
DUJ . . . . Juris Utriusque Doctor (Doctor of Both Laws; i.e., Canon and Civil
Law)
JUD . . . . Juris Utriusque Doctor (Doctor of Both Laws; i.e., Canon and
Civil Law)
JUL . . . . Juris Utriusque Licentiatus (Licentiate in Both Laws; i.e., Canon
and Civil Law)
JC . . . . Jurisconsult
JD . . . . Jurum Doctor (Doctor of Laws)
J . . . . Jus (Law)
ILH . . . . Jus Liberorum Habens (Possessing the Right of Children)
JL . . . . Just Looking (A browser) (Retail slang)
JND . . . . Just Noticeable Difference (Psychology)
JADITBHKNYC . . Just a Drop in the Basket Helps Keep New York Clean
(Antilitter campaign)
JOB . . . . Just One Break (An organization devoted to securing employment for
physically handicapped workers)
J & B . . . . . . Justerini & Brooks (Scotch)
J . . . . Justice (i.e., a judge; plural is JJ)
JC . . . . Justice Clerk
JD . . . . Justice Department
JP . . . . Justice of the Peace
JJ . . . . Justices
JCBC . . . . Jute Carpet Backing Council
J . . . . Juvenile
JAI . . . . Juvenile Amaurotic Idiocy (Medicine)
JC . . . . Juvenile Court
JD . . . . Juvenile Delinquency (or Delinquent)
JDA . . . . Juvenile Delinquency Act
JDEP . . . . Juvenile Delinquency Evaluation Project
JH . . . . Juvenile Hormone (Endocrinology)
JPMA . . . . Juvenile Products Manufacturers Association
JGA . . . . Juxtaglomerular Apparatus (Histology)
JGC . . . . Juxtaglomerular Cells

K

KK . . . . Kabushiki Kaishi (Joint stock company) (Japan)
KTL . . . . Kai Ta Loipa (Et cetera)
KILLS . . . . . . Ka-Inertial Launch & Leave System
KLU . . . . Kaiser Aluminum & Chemical Corporation (NYSE symbol)
KFOC . . . . . . Kaiser-Frazier Owners Clubs of America
KK . . . . Kaiser Koenigliche
KDF . . . . Kalamein Door and Frame
K . . . . Kalendas (Calends)
K . . . . Kalium (Potassium) (Chemical element)
KAC . . . . Kaman Aircraft Corporation
KNC . . . . Kamerun National Congress
KNDP . . . . . . Kamerun National Democratic Party
KDT . . . . Kammer der Technik
KG . . . . Kampfgruppen
KC . . . . Kanawha Central Railway Company (AAR code)
KRR . . . . Kansai Research Reactor (Japan)
KS . . . . Kansas
KCA . . . . Kansas City Area Office (AEC)
KCCC . . . . . . Kansas City Computer Center (Phillips Petroleum Company)
KCC . . . . Kansas City Connecting R. R. (AAR code)
KVW . . . . Kansas City, Kaw Valley R. R., Inc. (AAR code)
KCMO . . . . . . Kansas City, Mexico & Orient Railway (AAR code)
KAYSEE . . . . . Kansas City, Missouri (Slang)
MKC . . . . Kansas City, Missouri (Airport symbol)
KC . . . . Kansas City, Missouri (Slang)
KLT . . . . Kansas City Power and Light Company (NYSE symbol)
KCPS . . . . . . Kansas City Public Service Company (AAR code)
KSU . . . . Kansas City Southern Industries, Inc. (NYSE symbol)
KCS . . . . Kansas City Southern Railway Company (AAR code)
KCT . . . . Kansas City Terminal Railway Company (AAR code)
KGE . . . . Kansas Gas & Electric Company (NYSE symbol)
KMRT . . . . . . Kansas & Missouri Railway & Terminal Company (AAR code)
KOG . . . . Kansas, Oklahoma & Gulf Railway Company (AAR code)
KO & G . . . . . Kansas, Oklahoma & Gulf Railway Company
KAN . . . . Kansas Power & Light Company (NYSE symbol)
KEPZ . . . . . . Kaohsiung Export Processing Zone (Reexport manufacturing complex) (Taiwan)
KMSMRR . . . . Kapisanan ng mga Manggagawa Sa MRR (Manila Railroad Workers' Union) (Philippines)
KFSR . . . . . . Karakul Fur Sheep Registry
K . . . . Karat (Variant of "carat," C, q.v.)
KBM . . . . Karissimo Bene Merenti (To the Most Dear and Well-Deserving)
KVP . . . . Kasernierte Volkspolizei
KVPD . . . . . . Kasernierte Volkspolizei-Dienststelle
K . . . . Kathode (Cathode)
KAB . . . . Katholieke Arbeidersbewegung (Netherlands)
KFC . . . . Katholieke Film-Centrale
KDA . . . . Katholischer Deutscher Akademikerinnen (Bund) (Union of German Catholic University Women) (Germany)
KMP . . . . Katipunang Manggagawang Pilipino (Confederation of Trade Unions of the Philippines)
KATM . . . . . . Katmai National Monument
KSM . . . . Katubsanan sa Mamumio (Philippine United Labor Congress)
K . . . . Kayser
KYR . . . . Kayser-Roth Corporation (NYSE symbol)
KSAA . . . . . . Keats-Shelley Association of America
K . . . . Keel
KCP . . . . Keene's Cement Plaster (Technical drawings)
KCPC . . . . . . Keene's Cement Plaster Ceiling (Technical drawings)
KAB . . . . Keep America Beautiful
KD . . . . Keep It Dark (Say Nothing About It) (Slang)
KISMIF . . . . . Keep It Simple, Make It Fun
KISS . . . . Keep It Simple, Sir (Data processing)

KO . . . . Keep Off (i.e., avoid assuming the risk on an application, pending further investigation) (Insurance)
KOPS . . . . . . Keep Off Pounds Sensibly (Club)
KEPOA . . . . . Keep This Office Advised
KS . . . . Keep Type Standing (Printing)
KHIF . . . . . Keeping House of Ill Fame
KCA . . . . Keeshond Club of America
K . . . . Keg
K . . . . Kellogg Company (NYSE symbol)
KCNW . . . . . Kelly's Creek & Northwestern R. R. (AAR code)
KEC . . . . Kelly's Creek R. R. (AAR code)
KW . . . . Kelsey-Hayes Company (NYSE symbol)
K . . . . Kelvin (The absolute scale of temperature in which zero equals -273.1 degrees Centigrade)
KSTR . . . . . . Kema Suspension Test Reactor (Netherlands)
KEN . . . . Kendall Company (NYSE symbol)
KN . . . . Kennecott Copper Corporation (NYSE symbol)
KSC . . . . Kennedy Space Center (NASA)
KC . . . . Kennel Club
KEMO . . . . . . Kennesaw Mountain National Battlefield Park
KSU . . . . Kent State University (Ohio)
K . . . . Kentish
KY . . . . Kentucky
KIT . . . . Kentucky & Indiana Terminal R. R. (AAR code)
KT . . . . Kentucky & Tennessee Railway (AAR code)
KADU . . . . . . Kenya African Democratic Union (A political party)
KAM . . . . Kenya African Movement
KANU . . . . . . Kenya African National Union (A political party)
KFL . . . . Kenya Federation of Labour
KPU . . . . Kenya People's Union
KPOWU . . . . . Kenya Petroleum and Oil Workers' Union
KTUC . . . . . . Kenya Trades Union Congress
KMEF . . . . . . Keratin, Myosin, Epidermin, Fibrin (Biochemistry)
KP . . . . Keratitis Precipitates (Medicine)
KCL . . . . Kern County Land Company (NYSE symbol) (Wall Street slang name: "Casey")
KFK . . . . Kernforschungszentrum Karlsruhe (West Germany)
KBWP . . . . . . Kernkraftwerk Baden-Wuerttemberg Planungsgesellschaft
KMG . . . . Kerr-McGee Oil Industries, Inc. (NYSE symbol)
KERUK-NASI . . Kerukunan Nasional (Compaign for National Harmony) (Indonesia)
KBKI . . . . Kesatuan Buruh Kerakjatan Indonesia (Indonesian Democratic Workers' Federation)
KPGMPTM . . . Kesatuan Persekutuan Guru Melayu, Persekutuan Tanah Melayu (Federation of Malay Teachers' Unions, Federation of Malaya)
KGS . . . . Ketogenic Steroid (Endocrinology)
KS . . . . Ketosteroid
KGB . . . . Kewaunee, Green Bay & Western R. R. (AAR code)
K . . . . Key
KCI . . . . Key Club International
KFL . . . . Key Facilities List (AEC)
KIP . . . . Key Intelligence Position
KP . . . . Key Personnel
KP . . . . Key Pulsing
KP . . . . Key Punch
KTU . . . . Key Telephone Unit
KWOC . . . . . Key Word Out of Context (Indexing)
KB . . . . Keyboard Button (Data processing)
KCB . . . . Keyboard Change Button (Data processing)
KCC . . . . Keyboard Common Contact (Data processing)
KSR . . . . Keyboard Send and Receive
KTR . . . . Keyboard Typing Reperforator (Data processing)
KLIC . . . . . . Keyletter-in-Context (Data processing)
KPO . . . . Keypunch Operator

KES	Keystone Steel & Wire Company (NYSE symbol)
KWIC	Keyword in Context (A punched-card or computer-based indexing system)
KWIT	Keyword in Title
KTZ	Khar'kovskii Traktornyi Zavod
KTIBF	Kibris Turk Ischi Birlikleri Federasyonu (Cyprus Turkish Trade Unions Federation)
KRA	Kickback Racket Act
KOP	Kickoff Point (Diamond drilling)
KUB	Kidney, Ureter, Bladder (Medicine)
KALDAS	Kidsgrove ALGOL (Algorithmic Language) Digital Analogue Simulation (Data processing) (British)
KP	Kill Probability
KBA	Killed by Air (Military)
KIA	Killed in Action
KNA	Killed; Not Enemy Action
KFO	Killing Federal Officer
KFRST	Killing Frost (Meteorology)
KD	Kiln-Dried (Lumber)
K	Kilo
KB	Kilobar
kB	Kilobit(s)
kBS	Kilobits per Second
KCAL	Kilocalorie
KC.	Kilocycle (Radio)
KCS	Kilocycles Per Second
KEV	Kiloelectron Volt
kG	Kilogauss
K	Kilogram
KG	Kilogram(s)
KGCAL	Kilogram Calorie
KG-M	Kilogram-Meter
KG/CUM	Kilograms Per Cubic Meter
KGPS	Kilograms Per Second
KG/S	Kilograms Per Second
kHz	Kilohertz (Electronics)
K.	Kilohm
kJ	Kilojoule
KL	Kiloliter(s)
KM	Kilo-Mega
KMC	Kilo-Megacycles
KM	Kilometer(s)
KWOT	Kilometer-Wave Orbiting Telescope (NASA)
KMH	Kilometers Per Hour
KPH	Kilometers Per Hour
KMPS	Kilometers Per Second
KM/S	Kilometers Per Second
kN	Kilonewton
kOe	Kilo-Oersted
KR	Kiloroentgen(s)
KT	Kiloton
KVAR	Kilovar
KV	Kilovolt(s)
KV(s)	Kilovolt(s)
KV-A	Kilovolt-Ampere
KVAH	Kilovolt-Ampere Hour
KVAR	Kilovolt-Ampere Reactive
KVCP	Kilovolt Constant Potential
KVP	Kilovolts Peak
KW	Kilowatt(s)
KWH	Kilowatt-Hour
KWE	Kilowatts of Electric Energy
KWR	Kilowatts Reactive
KMB.	Kimberly-Clark Corporation (NYSE symbol)
KSMMP.	Kin Seeking Missing Military Personnel (Organization of parents with sons missing in action with purpose of supplementing US government search for missing personnel) (Post-World War II)
KELP	Kindergarten Evaluation for Learning Potential (McGraw-Hill)
KE	Kinetic Energy
KEWB	Kinetic Experiment on Water Boiler (AEC)
L	Kinetic Potential (Symbol)
KAC	Kinetics and Catalysis
K.	King
K.	King (Chess)
KA	King of Arms
KJV	King James Version (or Authorized Version of the Bible, 1611)
KM	King and Martyr (Church calendars)
KP	King Post
KST	King-Seeley Thermos Company (NYSE symbol)
KNC	Kingcome Navigation R. R. (AAR code)
KBART	Kings Bay Army Terminal
KB	King's Bench (of law courts) (British)

KCL	King's College, London
KC	King's Counsel (British)
KDG	The King's Dragoon Guards (British)
KHB	King's Hard Bargain (British military slang for undesirable sailor or soldier)
KH	King's Hussars (Military) (British)
KKT	King's Knight (Chess)
KLI	King's Light Infantry (Military) (British)
KIMO.	Kings Mountain National Military Park
KO	King's Own (Military unit) (British)
KOLI	King's Own Light Infantry (Military) (British)
KOR	King's Own Royal (Military unit) (British)
KORR	The King's Own Royal Regiment (British)
KOSB	The King's Own Scottish Borderers (British)
KOYLI	The King's Own Yorkshire Light Infantry (British)
KP	King's Proctor
KQCP.	King's and Queen's College of Physicians (Ireland)
KR	The King's Regiment (British)
KR	The King's Regulations for the Army and the Army Reserves (British)
KR	King's Rook (Chess)
KRI	King's Royal Irish (Military unit) (British)
KRRC	The King's Royal Rifle Corps (British)
KRR	The King's Royal Rifles (British Army Regiment)
KS	King's Scholar (British)
KSLI	The King's Shropshire Light Infantry (British)
K.	Kip (1000 lb)
KS	Kipling Society
KSF	Kips per Square Foot
KAFB	Kirtland Air Force Base
KMPP	Kisan Mazdoor Praja Party (India)
KKK	Kissel Kar Klub
K	Kitchen
KB	Kitchen and Bathroom
KB	Kitchen Biddy (Female kitchen worker) (Restaurant slang)
KM	Kitchen Mechanic (Restaurant slang)
KP	Kitchen Police (Kitchen helpers) (Military)
KB	Kite Balloon (Air Force)
KYTOON	Kite Balloon
KBO.	Kite and Balloon Officer (Navy)
KBP	Kite Balloon Pilot
KPNO	Kitt Peak National Observatory
KI	Kiwanis International
KN.	Klamath Northern R. R. (AAR code)
KL	Klebs-Loeffler (Bacteriology)
KKHL	Klung Kidney-Heart-Lung (Machine)
K	Klystron
KLA	Klystron Amplifier
KLO.	Klystron Oscillator
KPA	Klystron Power Amplifier
KPSM	Klystron Power Supply Modulator
KTMS	Knapp Time Metaphor Scale
KB	Knee Brace (Technical drawings)
KJ	Knee Jerk (Medicine)
KNSW	Knife Switch
K	Knight (Chess)
KT	Knight (Chess)
KB	Knight Bachelor or Knight Companion of the Bath (British)
KC.	Knight(s) of Columbus
K of C	Knight(s) of Columbus
KC	Knight Commander
KCB	Knight Commander of the Bath
KBE	Knight Commander of the British Empire
KCCH	Knight Commander of Court of Honor
KCH	Knight Commander of the Guelphic Order of Hanover (British)
KCIE	Knight Commander of the Indian Empire (British)
KStJ	Knight Commander, Order of St. John of Jerusalem (British)
KCVO	Knight Commander of the Royal Victorian Order (British)
KCMG	Knight Commander of St. Michael and St. George (British)
KCSI	Knight Commander of the Star of India (British)
KG	Knight of the Garter (British)
KGC	Knight Grand Commander
GCIE	Knight Grand Commander of the Indian Empire (British)
GCSI	Knight Grand Commander of the Order of the Star of India (British)
KGC	Knight Grand Cross
GCB	Knight Grand Cross of the Bath (British)
GCH	Knight Grand Cross of the Guelphic Order of Hanover
GBE	Knight Grand Cross, Order of the British Empire
GCStJ	Knight Grand Cross, Order of St. John of Jerusalem (British)
GCVO	Knight Grand Cross of the Royal Victorian Order (British)
GCMG	Knight Grand Cross of St. Michael and St. George (British)
KH.	Knight of the Guelphic Order of Hanover (British)

KHS . . . . Knight of the Holy Sepulchre
KM . . . . Knight of Malta
KMJ . . . . Knight of Maximilian Joseph (Bavaria)
KP . . . . Knight of Pius IX
KSG . . . . Knight of St. Gregory
KP . . . . Knight of St. Patrick
KSS . . . . Knight of St. Sylvester
NOST . . . . . . Knights of the Square Table
KT . . . . Knight(s) Templar
KT . . . . Knight of the Thistle (British)
KGE . . . . Knights of the Golden Eagle
KKA . . . . Knights of King Arthur
K of L . . . . . . Knights of Labor
KL . . . . Knights of Lithuania
K of L . . . . . . Knights of Lithuania
KPC . . . . Knights of Peter Claver
KP . . . . Knights of Pythias
KV . . . . Knights of Vartan
KYCH . . . . . . Knights York Cross of Honour
K . . . . Knit
KOF . . . . Knitted Outerwear Foundation
KMMA . . . . . . Knitting Machine Manufacturers Association
KMRA . . . . . . Knitwear Mill Representatives Association
KD . . . . Knock(ed) Down (i.e., disassembled)
KDCL . . . . . . Knocked Down, in Carloads
KDF . . . . Knocked Down Flat
KDLCL . . . . . . Knocked Down, in Less than Carloads
KO . . . . Knockout (Boxing)
KO . . . . Knockout (Partly cut out or loosened area which can be easily removed,
          as in a junction box) (Technical drawings)
KO's . . . . Knockout Drops (A drug producing unconsciousness) (Slang)
KAPL . . . . . . Knolls Atomic Power Laboratory (AEC)
KN(s) . . . . . . Knot(s)
K . . . . Knots (Nautical speed unit)
KCAS . . . . . . Knots Calibrated Airspeed
KIAS . . . . . . Knots Indicated Airspeed
KP . . . . Knotty Pine
KYERI . . . . . . Know Your Endorsers - Require Identification (Advice to businessmen
          and others who cash checks for the public)
KISC . . . . . . Knowledge Industry Systems Concept (Publishing and education)
          (Pronounced "Kiss")
KDP . . . . Known Datum Point
KG . . . . Known Gambler (Police slang)
KUED . . . . . . Kodak Unitized Engineering Data (Eastman Kodak)
KDD . . . . Kokusai Denshin Denwa (Telegraph and telephone corporation) (Japan)
KGST . . . . . . Kolcsonos Gazdasag Segitseg Tanacs
K . . . . Kollsman (When followed by altimeter setting) (Also see KOL) (Aviation)
KOL . . . . Kollsman (Also see K) (Aviation)
KGB . . . . Komitet Gossudarstvennoi Bezopastnosti (Committee of State Security)
          (Russian Secret Police)
KISZ . . . . . . Kommunista Ifjusagi Szovetseg (Communist Youth Organization) (Hungary)
KPSS . . . . . . Kommunisticheskaia Partiia Sovetskogo Soiuza
KPU . . . . Kommunisticheskaia Partiia Ukrainy
KPUZ . . . . . . Kommunisticheskaia Partiia Uzbekistana
KKE . . . . Kommunistikon Komma Ellada (Communist Party of Greece)
KP . . . . Kommunistische Partei (Communist Party) (German)
KPD . . . . Kommunistische Partei Deutschlands
KPO . . . . Kommunistische Partei Oesterreichs
KPDSU . . . . . . Kommunistische Partei der Sowjetunion
KBR . . . . Komplementbindungsreaktion
KPJ . . . . Komunisticka Partija Jugoslavije
KSC . . . . Komunisticka Strana Ceskoslovenska
KPH . . . . Komunisticke Partija Hrvatske
KSMU . . . . . . Komunistycha Spilka Molodi Ukrainy
KPP . . . . Komunistyczna Partia Polski (Communist Party of Poland)
KSSBI . . . . . . Konfederasi Serikat Serikat Buruh Islam (Confederation of Islamic Trade
          Unions of Indonesia)
KBIM . . . . . . Kongres Buruh Islam Merdeka (Free Islamic Trade Union Congress)
          (Indonesia)
KBKA . . . . . . Kongres Buruh Karata Api (Congress of Railway Workers) (Indonesia)
KBSI . . . . . . Kongres Buruh Seluruh Indonesia (All Indonesia Congress of Workers)
KJCPL . . . . . . Koninklijke Java-China-Paketvaart Lijnen
KLM . . . . Koninklijke Luchtvaart Maatschappij (Royal Dutch Airlines)

KZO . . . . Koninklijke Zout-Organon, NV (Netherlands)
KG . . . . Konsumgenossenschaften
KZ . . . . Konzentrationslager
K . . . . Kopeck (Monetary unit in Russia)
KOP . . . . Koppers Company, Inc. (NYSE symbol)
KACIA . . . . . Korea-American Commerce and Industry Association
KDFC . . . . . . Korea Development Finance Corporation
KOCO . . . . . . Korea Oil Corporation
KPA . . . . Korea Procurement Agency
KSS . . . . Korea Stamp Society
KOTRA . . . . . Korea Trade Promotion Corporation
KAI . . . . Korean Affairs Institute
KACC . . . . . . Korean-American Chamber of Commerce
KACF . . . . . . Korean-American Cultural Foundation
KATUSA . . . . . Korean Augmentation to the United States Army (Military)
KCRF . . . . . . Korean Conflict Research Foundation
KCLU . . . . . . Korean Council of Organization (South Korea)
KDH . . . . Korean Direct Hire
KFEA . . . . . . Korean Federation of Education Associations
KFTU . . . . . . Korean Federation of Trade Unions (North Korea)
KNA . . . . Korean National Airlines
KNA . . . . Korean National Association
KSC . . . . Korean Service Corps
KSM . . . . Korean Service Medal
KSFUS . . . . . . Korean Student Federation of the United States
KW . . . . Korean War
K . . . . Koruna (Monetary unit in Czechoslovakia)
KC . . . . Koruna Ceskoslovensky (Czechoslovakian monetary unit)
KOR . . . . . . Korvette (E. J.), Inc. (NYSE symbol)
KF . . . . Kosciuszko Foundation
KF . . . . Kossuth Foundation
KMF . . . . Koussevitzky Music Foundation
KMP . . . . Koyala Mazdoor Panchayat (India)
KDF . . . . Kraft durch Freude (Strength through Joy Movement) (Pre-World War II,
          Germany)
KPA . . . . Kraft Paper Association
KPKK . . . . . . Kraisparteikontrollkommission
KVAB . . . . . . Krankenversicherungsanstalt Berlin
KG . . . . Kresge (S. S.) Company (NYSE symbol)
KSC . . . . Kress (S. H.) & Company (NYSE symbol)
KTB . . . . Kriegstagebuch (War Diary) (German)
KELU . . . . . . Kristana Esperantista Ligo Usona
KFUK . . . . . . Kristelig Forening for Unge Kvinder (Young Women's Christian
          Associations) (Denmark)
KFUM . . . . . Kristelig Forening for Unge Maend (Young Men's Christian
          Associations) (Denmark)
KAS . . . . Kroeber Anthropological Society
KFM . . . . Kroehler Manufacturing Company (NYSE symbol)
KR . . . . Kroger Company (NYSE symbol)
K . . . . Krona (Monetary unit in Sweden)
K . . . . Krone (Monetary unit in Denmark, Norway)
K . . . . Kroon (Monetary unit in Estonia)
KQF . . . . Krupp Quick-Firing Gun
Kr . . . . Krypton (Chemical element)
KKK . . . . Ku Klux Klan
KELU . . . . . . Kuching Employees and Labourers' Union (Sarawak)
KAS . . . . Kulanka Afka Somalyed
KB . . . . Kulturbund
KAK . . . . Kungliga Automobil Klubben
KMT . . . . Kuo Ming Tang (Nationalist Party of China)
KTL . . . . Kuratorium fuer Technik in der Landwirtschaft
Ku . . . . Kurchatovium (Chemical element)
KDPS . . . . . . Kurdish Democratic Party of Syria
K . . . . Kurus (Monetary unit in Turkey)
KA . . . . Kuwait Airways
KFAED . . . . . Kuwait Fund for Arab Economic Development
KOC . . . . Kuwait Oil Company
KMA . . . . Kvindelige Missions Arbejdere
KSP . . . . KVP Sutherland Paper Company (NYSE symbol)
KTS . . . . Kwajalein Test Site
KEEP . . . . . . Kyosato Education Experiment Project (Self-help program for Japanese
          farmers established by Americans in 1948)

L

LAG . . . . L' Aiglon Apparel, Inc. (NYSE symbol)
LDPS . . . . L–Band Digital Phase Shifter
LEFC . . . . L–Band Electronic Frequency Converter
LFC . . . . L–Band Frequency Converter
LPS . . . . L–Band Phase Shifter
LBT . . . . L–Band Tetrode
LBT . . . . L–Band Transmitter
LCN . . . . La Cosa Nostra (Our Thing)
LACBWR . . . . . LaCrosse Boiling Water Reactor (AEC)
LCBWR . . . . . . La Crosse Boiling Water Reactor (AEC)
LGA . . . . La Guardia Airport (New York) (Airport symbol)
LLI . . . . La Leche League International
LPA . . . . La Posada Airways (Texas)
LSBC . . . . . . LaSalle & Bureau County R. R. (AAR code)
LRSM . . . . . . Lab for Research on the Structure of Matter
LC . . . . Label Clause
LMNA . . . . . . Label Manufacturers National Association
LCL . . . . Labor Congress of Liberia, Incorporated
LCI . . . . Labor Cost Index
LD . . . . Labor Department
LEAP . . . . . . Labor Education Advance Program
LE . . . . Labor Exchange
LMMC . . . . . . Labor–Management Maritime Committee
LMRA . . . . . . Labor–Management Relations Act
LMRDA . . . . . . Labor–Management Reporting and Disclosure Act
LMSA . . . . . . Labor–Management Services Administration (Department of Labor)
LMWP . . . . . . Labor–Management Welfare-Pension (Reports) (Department
 of Labor)
LPA . . . . Labor Policy Association
LRRC . . . . . . Labor Relations and Research Center (University of Massachusetts)
LRA . . . . Labor Research Associates (An organization)
LRA . . . . Labor Research Association
LS . . . . Labor Service (Military)
LSU . . . . Labor Service Unit
LSA . . . . Labor Surplus Area
LZOA . . . . . . Labor Zionist Organization of America-Poale Zion
LASLA . . . . . Laboratoire d'Analyse Statistique des Langues Anciennes
 (Laboratory for the Statistical Analysis of Ancient Languages)
 (University of Liege, Belgium)
LCIE . . . . . . Laboratoire Central des Industries Electriques (France)
LCT . . . . Laboratoire Central de Telecommunications
LEP . . . . Laboratoire d'Electronique de Physique (France)
LRBA . . . . . . Laboratoire de Recherches Balistiques et Aerodynamiques
LAPB . . . . . . Laboratories' Applied Physiology Branch (Army)
LAS . . . . Laboratories of Applied Sciences (University of Chicago)
LASR . . . . . . Laboratories for Astrophysics and Space Research (University of Chicago)
LCSS . . . . . . Laboratorio Central del Servicio de Sismologia
LABA . . . . . . Laboratory Animal Breeders Association
LAB . . . . Laboratory for Applied Biophysics (MIT)
LAS . . . . Laboratory of Atmospheric Sciences (National Science Foundation)
LBBP . . . . . . Laboratory of Blood and Blood Products (Public Health Service)
LB . . . . Laboratory Bulletin
LCSSP . . . . . . Laboratory of Chemistry and Solid-State Physics (MIT)
LACONIQ . . . Laboratory Computer On-Line Inquiry
LDP . . . . Laboratory Distribution Panel
LET . . . . Laboratory of Electromagnetic Theory
LEM . . . . Laboratory of Electro-Modeling (USSR)
LFE . . . . Laboratory for Electronics, Inc. (NYSE symbol)
LID . . . . Laboratory of Infectious Diseases (NIAID) (Became Laboratory of Viral
 Diseases)
LINC . . . . . . Laboratory Instrument Computer (Medical analyzer)
LIR . . . . Laboratory for Insulation Research (MIT)
LNS . . . . Laboratory for Nuclear Science (MIT)

LPSO . . . . . . Laboratory Procurement Supply Office
LPC . . . . Laboratory Pulse Compression
LPCL . . . . . . Laboratory Pulse Compression Loop
LR . . . . Laboratory Reagent
LR . . . . Laboratory Report
LABROC . . . . Laboratory Rocket
LSR . . . . Laboratory for Space Research (Netherlands)
LSS . . . . Laboratory Support Service
LLPE . . . . . . Labor's League for Political Education (AFL) (Later merged into
 Committee on Political Education [COPE] of AFL-CIO)
LRC . . . . Labrador Retriever Club
LWV . . . . Lackawanna & Wyoming Valley R. R. (AAR code)
LEAA . . . . . . Lace and Embroidery Association of America
LW . . . . Lacerated Wound
LCY . . . . Laclede-Christy Company (NYSE symbol)
LG . . . . Laclede Gas Company (NYSE symbol)
LIC . . . . Lacquer Insulating Compound
LAD . . . . Lactic Acid Dehydrogenase
LDH . . . . Lactic Dehydrogenase (Medicine)
LBF . . . . Lactobacillus Bulgaricus Factor (Bacteriology)
LLD . . . . Lactobacillus Lactis Dorner
LS . . . . Lactose Synthetase
LFT . . . . Ladd-Franklin Theory
LGU . . . . Ladies Golf Union
LGAR . . . . . . Ladies of the Grand Army of the Republic
LHA . . . . Ladies Hermitage Association
LHJ . . . . Ladies' Home Journal (A publication)
LKAA . . . . . . Ladies Kennel Association of America
LOS of NA . . . Ladies Oriental Shrine of North America
LPGA . . . . . . Ladies Professional Golf Association
L . . . . Lady
LBJ . . . . Lady Bird Johnson (Mrs. Lyndon Baines Johnson)
LD . . . . Lady Day (In old books)
LLA . . . . Lady Licentiate of Arts (Scotland)
LMBC . . . . . . Lady Margaret Boat Club (of St. John's College, Cambridge) (British)
CI . . . . Lady of the Order of the Crown of India
L . . . . Laevorotary (Pharmacology)
LTC . . . . Lafferty Transportation Company (AAR code)
LA . . . . Lag Amplifier
LDE . . . . Lagrange Differential Equation
LHE . . . . Lagrange-Helmholtz Equation
L . . . . Lake (Maps and charts)
LCA . . . . Lake Carriers' Association
LC . . . . Lake Central Airlines
LCA . . . . Lake Central Airlines
LCM . . . . Lake Champlain & Moriah Rail Road Company (AAR code)
LEC . . . . Lake Erie College (Ohio)
LEE . . . . Lake Erie & Eastern R. R. (AAR code)
LEFW . . . . . . Lake Erie & Fort Wayne R. R. (AAR code)
LEF . . . . Lake Erie, Franklin & Clarion R. R. (AAR code)
LEN . . . . Lake Erie & Northern Railway Company (AAR code)
LESA . . . . . . Lake Erie Steam Association
LEM . . . . Lake Exploration Module (University of Wisconsin)
LFC . . . . Lake Forest College (Illinois)
LAME . . . . . . Lake Mead National Recreation Area
LOOW . . . . . . Lake Ontario Ordnance Works
LPTW . . . . . . Lake Providence, Texarkana & Western R. R. (AAR code)
L & R . . . . . . Lake and Rail
LRS . . . . Lake Reporting Service
LKK . . . . Lake Shore Mines, Ltd. (NYSE symbol)
LSI . . . . Lake Superior & Ishpeming R. R. (AAR code)
LS & I . . . . . . Lake Superior & Ishpeming Railroad Company
LSTT . . . . . . Lake Superior Terminal & Transfer Railway Company (AAR code)

LT . . . . Lake Terminal R. R. (AAR code)
LAVERS . . . . . Lake Vessel Reporting System
LDT . . . . Lakefront Dock & R. R. Terminal (AAR code)
LSM . . . . Lakeside & Marblehead R. R. (AAR code)
LKY . . . . Lakey Foundry Corporation (NYSE symbol)
LJC . . . . Lamar Junior College (Colorado)
LSCT . . . . Lamar State College of Technology (Texas)
LRS . . . . Lamb-Rutherford Shift
LEX . . . . Lambda Epsilon Chi (Acronym is taken from the Greek letters, but also
       represents Latin word for law, area of interest for the society's members)
LGD . . . . Lambda Gamma Delta (Society)
LLP . . . . Lambda Limiting Process
L . . . . Lambert (Unit of brightness)
LCL . . . . Lambert Cosine Law
LANAC . . . . . . Laminar Air Navigation and Anticollision (Air Force)
LBL . . . . Laminar Boundary Layer
LBLS . . . . Laminar Boundary-Layer Separation
LBS . . . . Laminar Boundary-Layer Separation
LFC . . . . Laminar Flow Control (Military)
LFZ . . . . Laminar Flow Zone
LAM . . . . Laminate
LFMA . . . . Laminated Foil Manufacturers' Association
LMP . . . . Laminated Metal Part
LSHV . . . . . . Laminated Synthetic High Voltage
LT . . . . Laminated TEFLON
LDGO . . . . . . Lamont-Doherty Geological Observatory (Formerly, LGO) (Columbia
       University)
LGO . . . . Lamont Geological Observatory (Later, Lamont-Doherty) (Columbia
       University)
LD . . . . Lamp Driver
LSIA . . . . Lamp and Shade Institute of America
LF . . . . The Lancashire Fusiliers (British military)
LYR . . . . Lancashire and Yorkshire Railway (British)
LC . . . . Lancaster & Chester Railway Company (AAR code)
LC . . . . Lance Corporal
L . . . . Lancers
L . . . . Land(ing)
LAMS . . . . . . Land Acoustical Monitoring System (NASA)
LBC . . . . Land Bank Commission
LCM . . . . Land Combat Missile
LCSS . . . . . . Land Combat Support Systems
LCS . . . . Land Combat System
LEX . . . . Land Exercise (Marine Corps)
LFDA . . . . Land and Facilities Development Administration (HUD)
LICA . . . . Land Improvement Contractors of America
LICOF . . . . . Land Lines Communications Facilities (Aviation)
LLL . . . . Land Locomotion Laboratory
LMS . . . . Land Mass Simulator
LM . . . . Land Mine (Military)
LNS . . . . Land Navigation System
LP . . . . Land Plane
LASAIL . . . . . Land-Sea-Air Interaction Laboratory
LASIL . . . . . . Land and Sea Interaction Laboratory (Environmental Science Services
       Administration)
LS . . . . Land Service
LUAP . . . . . . Land Use Adjustment Program
LSF . . . . Lande Splitting Factor
LT . . . . Landed Terms
LFSA . . . . Landesverband Freier Schweizer Arbeiter (Swiss Association of Autonomous
       Unions)
LTS . . . . Landfall Technique School (Navy)
L/A . . . . Landing Account (Shipping)
LAS . . . . Landing Approach Simulator
LASSO . . . . . Landing and Approach System, Spiral-Oriented
LB . . . . Landing Barge(s)
LBE . . . . Landing Barge, Emergency Repair
LBK . . . . Landing Barge, Kitchen
LBS . . . . Landing Barge, Support
LBV . . . . Landing Barge, Vehicle
LCC . . . . Landing Control Center
LANCRA . . . . . Landing Craft (Navy)
LC . . . . Landing Craft
L/C . . . . Landing Craft
LCAVAT . . . . . Landing Craft and Amphibious Vehicle Assignment Table
LCA . . . . Landing Craft, Assault
LANCRAB . . . . Landing Craft and Bases (Navy)
LANDCRAB . . . Landing Craft and Bases (Military)
LANCRABEU . . Landing Craft and Bases, Europe (Navy)
LANCRABNAW . . Landing Craft and Bases, Northwest African Waters (World War II)
       (Navy)
LCC . . . . Landing Craft, Control

LCE . . . . Landing Craft, Emergency Repair
LCEOP . . . . . Landing Craft, Engine Overhaul Parties
LCF . . . . Landing Craft, Flak
LC(FF) . . . . . Landing Craft, Flotilla Flagship
LCFLOTSPAC . . Landing Craft, Flotilla, Pacific Fleet
LCGP . . . . . . Landing Craft, Group
LCG (L) . . . . Landing Craft, Gun (Large)
LCG . . . . Landing Craft, Gunboat (Navy)
LCGM . . . . . Landing Craft, Gunboat
LVHX . . . . . . Landing Craft, Hydrofoil, Experimental (Navy symbol)
LCI . . . . Landing Craft, Infantry
LCIDIV . . . . . Landing Craft, Infantry, Division
LCIFLOT . . . . Landing Craft, Infantry, Flotilla
LC(FF) . . . . . Landing Craft, Infantry (Flotilla Flagship) (Navy symbol)
LCIGRP . . . . . Landing Craft, Infantry, Group
LSIG . . . . . . Landing Craft, Infantry (Gunboat) (Navy symbol)
LCI(G) . . . . . Landing Craft, Infantry Gunboat
LCIL . . . . . . Landing Craft Infantry, Large
LCILFLOT . . . . Landing Craft Infantry, Large, Flotilla
LSIM . . . . . . Landing Craft, Infantry, Large, Flotilla
LCI(M) . . . . . Landing Craft, Infantry (Mortar) (Navy symbol)
LSIR . . . . . . Landing Craft, Infantry (Mortar Ship)
LCI(R) . . . . . Landing Craft, Infantry (Rocket) (Navy symbol)
LCSL . . . . . . Landing Craft, Infantry (Rocket Ship)
LCK . . . . Landing Craft Infantry (Support)
LCMSO . . . . . Landing Craft, Kitchen
LCM . . . . . . Landing Craft Material Supply Officer
LCM6 . . . . . Landing Craft, Mechanized
LCM8 . . . . . Landing Craft, Mechanized, MKVI (Navy symbol)
LCN . . . . Landing Craft, Mechanized, MKVIII (Navy symbol)
LCOCU . . . . . Landing Craft, Navigation
LCP . . . . Landing Craft, Obstruction Clearance Unit
LCPL . . . . . . Landing Craft, Personnel
LCP(L) . . . . . Landing Craft, Personnel (Navy symbol)
LCPL . . . . . . Landing Craft, Personnel (Large)
LCP(M) . . . . . Landing Craft - Personnel/Logistics
LCP(N) . . . . . Landing Craft, Personnel (Medium)
LCP(P) . . . . . Landing Craft, Personnel (Nested)
LCP(R) . . . . . Landing Craft, Personnel (Plastic)
LCP(SY) . . . . Landing Craft, Personnel (Ramp)
LCRU . . . . . . Landing Craft, Personnel (Survey)
ARL . . . . Landing Craft, Recovery Unit
LCR . . . . Landing Craft Repair Ship (Navy symbol)
LCR(L) . . . . . Landing Craft, Rubber
LCR(R) . . . . . Landing Craft, Rubber (Large)
LCR(S) . . . . . Landing Craft, Rubber (Rocket)
LCS . . . . Landing Craft, Rubber (Small)
LCS(L) . . . . . Landing Craft, Support
LCS(M) . . . . . Landing Craft, Support (Large)
LCS(R) . . . . . Landing Craft, Support (Medium)
LCS(S) . . . . . Landing Craft, Support (Rocket)
LCSR . . . . . . Landing Craft, Support (Small)
LCT . . . . Landing Craft, Swimmer Reconnaissance (Navy symbol)
LCT(A) . . . . . Landing Craft, Tank
LCV . . . . Landing Craft, Tank (Armored)
LCVP . . . . . . Landing Craft, Vehicle
LDI . . . . Landing Craft, Vehicle and Personnel (Navy symbol)
LANDFOR . . . . Landing Direction Indicator (Aviation)
LANFORASCU . . Landing Force
LFM . . . . Landing Force Air Support Control Unit (Navy)
LFNGFT . . . . . Landing Force Manual (Navy)
LFSS . . . . . . Landing Force Naval Gunfire Team
LFSW . . . . . . Landing Force Support Ship (Navy)
LFTU . . . . . . Landing Force Support Weapon
LG . . . . Landing Force Training Unit (Marine Corps)
LG . . . . Landing Gear (Aircraft)
LHA . . . . Landing Ground (Navy)
LNDIS . . . . . Landing Helicopter Assault (Ship) (Navy)
LOSSYS . . . . . Landing Intermediate Station (Aviation)
LPD . . . . Landing Observer's Signal System
LPD . . . . Landing, Personnel, and Dock (Navy)
LPH . . . . Landing Platform, Dock (Navy symbol)
LRD . . . . Landing Platform, Helicopter (Navy symbol)
LS . . . . Landing and Recovery Division (NASA)
LSB . . . . Landing Ship (Navy)
LSX . . . . Landing Ship, Bombardment
LSH . . . . Landing Ship Experimental (Navy)
LSH(L) . . . . . Landing Ship, Headquarters
LSH(S) . . . . . Landing Ship, Headquarters (Large)
LSMSO . . . . . Landing Ship, Headquarters (Small)
LSM . . . . Landing Ship, Material Supply Officer (Navy)
       Landing Ship, Medium (Navy)

LST	Landing Ship, Tank
LST(H)	Landing Ship, Tank (Casualty evacuation)
LSU	Landing Ship, Utility (Navy symbol)
LSV	Landing Ship, Vehicle
LSE	Landing Signal Enlisted (Military)
LSO	Landing Signal Officer
LT	Landing Team
LV	Landing Vehicle
LVH	Landing Vehicle, Hydrofoil
LVTP	Landing Vehicle, Track, Personnel (Military)
LVT (A) (1) . . .	Landing Vehicle, Tracked (Armored) (Mark I) ("Water Buffalo," Turret Type)
LV (A) (2)	Landing Vehicle, Tracked (Armored) (Mark II) ("Water Buffalo," Canopy Type)
LVT (A) (4) . . .	Landing Vehicle, Tracked (Armored) (Mark IV)
LVT (A) (5) . . .	Landing Vehicle, Tracked (Armored) (Mark V)
LVT (A)	Landing Vehicle, Tracked (Armored) (Turret Type)
LVTE	Landing Vehicle, Tracked, Engineer (Model 1)
LVTH	Landing Vehicle, Tracked, Howitzer (Model 6)
LVT (3)	Landing Vehicle, Tracked (Mark III)
LVT	Landing Vehicle, Tracked (Unarmored)
LVTU	Landing Vehicle, Tracked, Unarmored (Navy)
LVT (1)	Landing Vehicle, Tracked (Unarmored) (Mark I) ("Alligator")
LVT (2)	Landing Vehicle, Tracked (Unarmored) (Mark II) ("Water Buffalo")
LVT (4)	Landing Vehicle, Tracked (Unarmored) (Mark IV)
LVW	Landing Vehicle, Wheeled
LZ	Landing Zone
LZCO	Landing Zone Control Officer (Air Force)
LL	Landline (Aviation)
LLTT	Landline Teletype
LLTTY	Landline Teletype (Military)
LTT	Landline Teletypewriter
LPC	Landmarks Preservation Commission (New York City)
L	Landplane
L/P	Landplane
LNC	Landscape Nursery Council
LO	Landsorganisasjonen i Norge (Norwegian Federation of Trade Unions)
LO	Landsorganisationen i Sverige (General Federation of Swedish Trade Unions)
LW	Landsteiner-Wiener (Serum)
L-W	Landsverk-Wollan (Radiation survey meter)
LN	Landwirtschaftliche Nutzflaeche
LPG	Landwirtschaftliche Produktionsgenossenschaft
LWV	Landwirtschaftsversorgungsamt (German Land Economic Supply Office) (Post-World War II)
LNY	Lane Bryant, Inc. (NYSE symbol)
LPM	Lane Photograph Method
LAL	Langley Aeronautical Laboratory (Air Force)
LARC	Langley Research Center (NASA)
LRC	Langley Research Center (NASA)
LDS	Langmuir Dark Space (Electronics)
LDP	Langmuir Diffussion Pump (Electronics)
LA	Language Age (Score)
LAT	Language Aptitude Test (Military)
LDP	Language Data Processing
LIFE	Language Improvement to Facilitate Education of Hearing-Impaired Children (A project of NEA)
LINCS	Language Information Network and Clearinghouse System
LLBA	Language and Language Behavior Abstracts
LPT	Language Proficiency Test (Military)
LTS	Language Teaching System
LT	Language Translation (Data processing)
LTS	Language Translation System
LUCID	Language Used to Communicate Information System Design
LUCID	Language for Utility Checkout and Instrumentation Development
LEWU	Lanka Estate Workers' Union (Ceylon)
LJEWU	Lanka Jatika Estate Workers' Union (Ceylon National Estate Workers' Union)
LPP	Lanka Prajatantrawadi Party (Ceylon)
LSSP	Lanka Sama Samaja Party (Ceylon)
La	Lanthanum (Chemical element)
LF	Lanthanum Fluoride
LNV	Lanvin-Parfums, Inc. (NYSE symbol)
LRS	Lanyard Release Switch
LCSU	Lao Civil Servants' Union
LNO	Laona & Northern Railway (AAR code)
L & R	Larceny and Receiving
LJC	Laredo Junior College (Texas)
L	Large (Size designation for clothing, etc.)
CVB	Large Aircraft Carrier (Navy symbol)
LASA	Large Aperture Seismic Array (Nuclear detection device)
LAD	Large Area Display

LAED	Large Area Electronic Display
LAEDP	Large Area Electronic Display Panel
LAEP	Large Area Electronic Panel
LAP	Large Area Panel
LASCA	Large Area Solar Cell Array
LANNET	Large Artificial Nerve Net
LAS	Large Astronomical Satellite (ESRO)
LARC	Large Automatic Research Computer
AFDB	Large Auxiliary Floating Dry Dock (Navy symbol)
LBS	Large Bulb Ship
AVC	Large Catapult Lighter (Navy symbol)
YFNB	Large Covered Lighter (Navy symbol)
CB	Large Cruiser (Navy symbol)
LED	Large Electronic Display
LEDP	Large Electronic Display Panel
LEP	Large Electronic Panel
LFA	Large Families of America
LG	Large Grain
YTB	Large Harbor Tug (Navy symbol)
LLVPG	Large Launch Vehicle Planning Group (NASA)
LL	Large Letter
LOSS	Large Object Salvage System (Navy)
LOR	Large Optical Reflector
LOTAS	Large Optical Tracker - Aerospace
LORL	Large Orbital Research Laboratory (NASA)
LP	Large Paper
LPP	Large Paper Proofs
LP	Large Particle
LPTV	Large Payload Test Vehicle
LP	Large Post
LR	Large Ring
LSC	Large-Scale Computer
LSHI	Large-Scale Hybrid Integration
LSI	Large-Scale Integration (of circuits) (Electronics)
LSD	Large Screen Display
LSDS	Large Screen Display System
LSRI	Large Screen RADAR Indicator
LSR	Large Ship Reactor
LSA	Large Spherical Array
LST-G	Large Steam Turbine-Generator
LSD	Large Steel Desk (Position given to ex-astronauts)
LTE	Large Thrust per Element
LTA	Large Transport Airplane
LT	Large Tug (Army)
LWD	Larger Word (Data processing)
LFST	Largest Feasible Steerable Telescope
LSI	Largest Single Item
LH	Larval Heart
LO	Larval Operculum
LJC	Lasell Junior College (Massachusetts)
LAVO	Lassen Volcanic National Park
LAD	LASER Acoustic Delay
LAGS	LASER-Activated Geodetic Satellite (AFCRL)
LARGOS	LASER-Activated Reflecting Geodetic Optical Satellite
LACE	LASER Aerospace Communications Experiment
LAD	LASER Air Defense
LADS	LASER Air Defense System
LAC	LASER Amplifier Chain
LARS	LASER Angular Rate Sensor
LAS	LASER Anti-Flash System
LASH	LASER Antitank Semiactive Homing
LATT	LASER Atmospheric Transmission Test
LAA	LASER Attenuator Assembly
LBS	LASER Beam Surgery
LBS	LASER Bombing System
LCTS	LASER Coherence Techniques Section
LCSE	LASER Communication Satellite Experiment (NASA)
LCS	LASER Communications System
LDS	LASER Deep Space
LADAR	LASER Detection and Ranging
LDD	LASER Detector Diode
LDT	LASER Discharge Tube
LDRS	LASER Discrimination RADAR System
LDMI	LASER Distance Measuring Instrument
LDMS	LASER Distance Measuring System
LADAR	LASER Doppler RADAR
LDM	LASER Drilling Machine
LDS	LASER Drilling System
LEED	LASER-Energized Explosive Device
LEM	LASER Energy Monitor
LEK	LASER Experimental Package

REVERSE ACRONYMS AND INITIALISMS DICTIONARY

LERK . . . . LASER Experimental Research Kit	L . . . . Late
LFL . . . . LASER Flash Lamp	LC . . . . Late Commitment (Reason for missed intercept) (Military)
LFT . . . . LASER Flash Tube	LFT . . . . Late Finish Time
LGM . . . . . . LASER Ground Mapper	LFP . . . . Late Flight Plan
LGMS . . . . . . LASER Ground Mapping System	LL . . . . Late Latin (Language)
LHDS . . . . . . LASER Hole Drilling System	LPR . . . . Late Position Report (Report of a flight which is off flight plan)
LIS . . . . LASER Illuminator System	LPR . . . . Late Procurement Request (Air Force)
LIC . . . . LASER Image Converter	LS . . . . Late Scramble (Reason for missed interception) (Military)
LIODD . . . . . LASER In-Flight Obstacle Detection Device	LST . . . . Late Start Time
LIMIRIS . . . . . LASER-Induced Modulation of Infrared In Silicon	LR . . . . Latency Relaxation
LIA . . . . LASER Industry Association	L . . . . Latent Heat
LIED . . . . LASER Initiating Explosive Device	LP . . . . Latent Period (Physiology)
LIF . . . . LASER Interference Filter	LPI . . . . Latent Photographic Image
LIS . . . . LASER Interferometer System	LD . . . . Lateral Drift
LID . . . . LASER Intrusion Detector	LGB . . . . Lateral Geniculate Body
LLD . . . . LASER Light Detector	LHDC . . . . . . Lateral Homing Depth Charge
LLP . . . . LASER Light Pump	LHA . . . . Lateral Hypothalamic Area
LLS . . . . LASER Light Source	LL . . . . Lateral Lip
LLSS . . . . . . LASER Light Source Station	LS . . . . Lateral Septum
LLS . . . . LASER Line Scanner	LSA . . . . Lateral Spherical Abberation
LMS . . . . LASER Mapping System	LT . . . . Lateral Tooth
LAMP . . . . . . LASER and MASER Patents	LCFLOLS . . . . Laterally Compounded Fresnel Lens Optical Landing System
LMS . . . . LASER Mass Spectrometer	LCT . . . . Latest Closing Time
LMO . . . . LASER Master Oscillator	LFD . . . . Latest Finish Date
LMD . . . . LASER Microwave Division (Army)	LSD . . . . Latest Start Date
LMW . . . . . . LASER Micro-Welder	LTIOV . . . . . . Latest Time Information of Value (Military)
LMG . . . . LASER Milling Gauge	LTOT . . . . . . Latest Time Over Target
LMC . . . . LASER Mirror Coating	LFRC . . . . . . Latex Foam Rubber Council
LNS . . . . LASER Night Sensor	LCS . . . . Lathe Control System
LOM . . . . . . LASER Optical Modulator	L . . . . Latin
LPM . . . . . . LASER Phase Macroscope	LA . . . . Latin America
LPD . . . . LASER Polarization Detector	LAAD . . . . . . Latin American Agribusiness Development Corporation
LPS . . . . LASER Power Supply	LABP . . . . . . Latin American Book Programs (Defunct)
LPP . . . . LASER Produced Plasma	LACAP . . . . . Latin American Cooperative Acquisitions Project
LAPS . . . . . . LASER Profile System	LAFC . . . . . . Latin-American Forestry Commission
LPL . . . . LASER-Pumped-LASER	LAFTA . . . . . Latin-American Free Trade Association
LARIAT . . . . . LASER RADAR Intelligence Acquisition Technology	LAMCS . . . . . Latin American Military Communications System
LRF . . . . LASER Range-Finder	LAM . . . . Latin-American Mission (Air Force)
LRT . . . . LASER Rangefinder Theodolite	LAOAR . . . . . Latin American Office of Aerospace Research (Air Force)
LRTS . . . . . . LASER Range-Finder Theodolite System	LASPAU . . . . . Latin American Scholarship Program of American Universities
LRBS . . . . . . LASER Ranging Bombing System	LASCO . . . . . Latin American Science Cooperation Office
LRRR . . . . . . LASER Ranging Retroreflection (Apollo II experiment) (NASA)	LASAS . . . . . Latin American Secretariat for Academic Services
LRS . . . . LASER Ranging System	LASA . . . . . . Latin American Studies Association
LRK . . . . LASER Research Kit	L . . . . Latitude
LRP . . . . LASER Retinal Photocoagulator	LDC . . . . Latitude Data Computer
LRS . . . . LASER Roster Scanner	LLI . . . . Latitude and Longitude Indicator
LASAM . . . . . LASER Semi-Active Missile	LDS . . . . Latter-Day Saints
LSIS . . . . . . LASER Shutterable Image Sensor	LTR . . . . Lattice Test Reactor
LSD . . . . LASER Signal Device	LSDSP . . . . . . Latvijas Socialdemokratiska Stradnieku Partija
LSM . . . . LASER Slicing Machine	LLF . . . . Laubach Literacy Fund
LSC . . . . LASER Spectral Control	L . . . . Launch
LSCT . . . . . . LASER Spectral Control Technique	YFB . . . . Launch (Navy symbol)
LSW . . . . . . LASER Spot Welder	LACE . . . . . . Launch Angle Condition Evaluator
LSRF . . . . . . LASER Submarine Range Finder	LAS . . . . Launch Area Supervisor
LSI . . . . LASER Surface Interaction	LAS . . . . Launch Auxiliary System
LS . . . . LASER System	LCC . . . . Launch Command and Control
LTR . . . . LASER Tank Range-Finder	LC . . . . Launch Complex
LTRF . . . . . . LASER Tank Range-Finder	LCX . . . . Launch Complex
LTD . . . . LASER Target Designator	LCE . . . . Launch Complex Equipment
LTDR . . . . . . LASER Target Designator Receiver	LCB . . . . Launch Control Building (NASA)
LTRS . . . . . . LASER Target Recognition System	LCC . . . . Launch Control Center
LTF . . . . LASER Terrain Follower	LCC . . . . Launch Control Console
LTFS . . . . . . LASER Terrain Following System	LCEB . . . . . . Launch Control Equipment Building
LXD . . . . LASER Transceiver Device	LCF . . . . Launch Control Facility
LWU . . . . . . LASER Welder Unit	LCP . . . . Launch Control Panel
LC . . . . Last Card	LCSS . . . . . . Launch Control and Sequencer System
LDM . . . . . . Last Day of the Month	LCS . . . . Launch Control System
LFAR . . . . . . Last Frame Address Register	LCT . . . . Launch Control Trailer
LIFO . . . . . . Last In, First Out (Inventories last purchased are first sold) (Accounting)	LC . . . . Launch Cost
LMA . . . . Last Manufacturers Association	LCE . . . . Launch Countdown Exercise
LMF . . . . Last Meal Furnished	LCQ . . . . Launch Crew Quarters
LMP . . . . . . Last Menstrual Period (Medicine)	LTE . . . . Launch to Eject
LNMP . . . . . Last Normal Menstrual Period	LELU . . . . . . Launch Enable Logic Unit
LP . . . . Last Paid (Military)	LEU . . . . Launch Enable Unit
LARCT . . . . . . Last Radio Contact (Aviation)	LES . . . . Launch Enabling System
LRT . . . . Last Resort Target (Military)	LEPS . . . . . . Launch Escape Propulsion System
LRTGT . . . . . Last Resort Target (Military)	LES . . . . Launch Escape System (Apollo) (NASA)
LY . . . . Last Year's Model (Merchandising slang)	LF . . . . Launch Facility
L . . . . Lat (Monetary unit in Latvia)	LFS . . . . Launch Facility Simulator
LRM . . . . . . Latching Relay Matrix	LFT . . . . Launch Facility Trainer
LSD . . . . Latching Semiconductor Diode	LFM . . . . Launch First Motion

L & I . . . . Launch and Impact
LIEF . . . . Launch Information Exchange Facility (NASA)
LMT . . . . Launch Motor Test
LM . . . . Launch Mount
LNT . . . . Launch Network Test
LO . . . . Launch Operations (NASA)
LOB . . . . Launch Operations Branch (NASA)
LOB . . . . Launch Operations Building (NASA)
LOC . . . . Launch Operations Center (NASA)
LOC . . . . Launch Operations Complex (AMR/PMR)
LOCC . . . . . . Launch Operations Control Center
LOD . . . . Launch Operations Department
LOD . . . . Launch Operations Directorate (NASA)
LOP . . . . Launch Operation Panel
LOSM . . . . . . Launch Operations Simulation Model
LOTS . . . . . . Launch Operations Television System
LP . . . . Launch Platform
LPD . . . . Launch Point Determination
LPG . . . . Launch Preparations Group (NASA)
LRF . . . . Launch Rate Factor
LSO . . . . Launch Safety Officer (NASA)
LSCE . . . . . . Launch Sequence and Control Equipment
LSE . . . . Launch Sequencer Equipment
LSS . . . . Launch Sequency Simulator
LS . . . . Launch Service
LSB . . . . Launch Service Building
LS . . . . Launch Site
LSS . . . . Launch Status Summarizer
LSS . . . . Launch Support Section
LSD . . . . Launch Systems Data
LTS . . . . Launch Telemetry Stations
LTV . . . . Launch Test Vehicles
LTS . . . . Launch Tracking System
LTDS . . . . . . Launch Trajectory Data System
LUT . . . . Launch Umbilical Tower
LV . . . . Launch Vehicle
LVA . . . . Launch Vehicle Availability (Aerospace)
LVDA . . . . . . Launch Vehicle Data Adapter (NASA)
LVDC . . . . . . Launch Vehicle Digital Computer (NASA)
LVFC . . . . . . Launch Vehicle Flight Control
LVFCS . . . . . . Launch Vehicle Flight Control System
LVM . . . . Launch Vehicle Monitor
LVO . . . . Launch Vehicle Operation
LVOD . . . . . . Launch Vehicles Operations Division
LWW . . . . . . Launch Window Width
LZD . . . . Launch Zone Display
LZDF . . . . . . Launch Zone Display Flag
LZF . . . . Launch Zone Flag
LZO . . . . Launch Zone Override
LAMTS . . . . . Launcher Adapter Missile Test Set
LBU . . . . Launcher Booster Unit
LCA . . . . Launcher Control Area (Missile)
LCI . . . . Launcher Control Indicator (Military)
LHP . . . . Launcher Handling Procedure
LLD . . . . Launcher Load Dolly
LMTC . . . . . . Launcher Maintenance Trainer Course
LSM . . . . Launcher Status Multiplexer
LSB . . . . Launcher Support Building
LCH . . . . Launching Charging Header
LC . . . . Launching Control (Military)
LCO . . . . Launching Control Office(r)
LE . . . . Launching Equipment
LECS . . . . . . Launching Equipment Checkout Set
LP . . . . Launching Platoon (Army)
LACATA . . . . . Laundry and Cleaners Allied Trades Association
LCATA . . . . . . Laundry and Cleaners Allied Trades Association
LCDHWIU . . . . Laundry, Cleaning and Dye House Workers International Union
LWIU . . . . . . Laundry, Dry Cleaning and Dye House Workers International Union
LDC . . . . Laundry and Dry Cleaning International Union
LDCO . . . . . . Laundry and Dry Cleaning Operations (Military)
AL . . . . Laureate of Arts
LA . . . . Laureate in Arts
LC . . . . Laureate of Arts
LC . . . . Laureate of Letters
LP . . . . Laureate of Philosophy
L Sc . . . . Laureate of Science
LRS . . . . Laurinburg & Southern R. R. (AAR code)
LD . . . . Laus Deo (Praise Be to God)
LDS . . . . Laus Deo Semper (Praise to God Always)
LVI . . . . Laus Verbo Incarnato (Praise to the Incarnate Word)
LA . . . . Lava (Maps and charts)

LABE . . . . Lava Beds National Monument
L . . . . Law
LA . . . . Law Agent
LAWASIA . . . . Law Association for Asia and the Western Pacific
LLC . . . . Law Certificate
LC . . . . Law Courts
LE . . . . Law Enforcement
LEAA . . . . . . Law Enforcement Assistance Act
LEAA . . . . . . Law Enforcement Assistance Administration (Justice Department)
LEA . . . . Law Enforcement Assistance Program
LETS . . . . . . Law Enforcement Teletypewriter Service
LO . . . . Law Officer
LSAT . . . . . . Law School Admission Test
LSA . . . . Law and Society Association
LSCRRC . . . . . Law Students Civil Rights Research Council
LMI . . . . Lawn Mower Institute
LT . . . . Lawn Tennis
LTC . . . . Lawn Tennis Club (British)
LTWA . . . . . . Lawn Tennis Writers' Association of America
LRI . . . . Lawndale Railway & Industrial Company (AAR code)
LIT . . . . Lawrence Institute of Technology (Michigan)
LLAT . . . . . . Lawrence Lowery Apperception Test
LRL . . . . Lawrence Radiation Laboratory (AEC)
Lr . . . . Lawrencium (Chemical element)
LRNA . . . . . . Laws Relating to the Navy Annotated (Military law)
LHA . . . . Lay Helpers' Association (British)
LTF . . . . Layman Tithing Foundation
LL . . . . Laymen's League
LNC . . . . Laymen's National Committee
LAOS . . . . . . Laymen's Overseas Service
LO . . . . Layout (Graphic arts)
LSA . . . . Layton School of Art (Wisconsin)
LTU . . . . Le Tourneau, Inc. (NYSE symbol)
Pb . . . . Lead (Chemical element)
LAB . . . . Lead Acid Battery
LAMA . . . . . . Lead Air Materiel Area (Air Force)
LA . . . . Lead Amplifier
LAE . . . . Lead Angle Error
LCM . . . . Lead Coated Metal (Technical drawings)
LCGS . . . . . . Lead Computing Gun Sight
LCOSS . . . . . . Lead Computing Optical Sighting System
LC . . . . Lead Covered
LFG . . . . Lead Free Glass
LTF . . . . Lead the Force
LIL . . . . Lead-In-Light-System (Airport runway lighting)
LDIN . . . . . . Lead-In Lighting (or Lights) (Aviation)
LIA . . . . Lead Industries Association
LJR . . . . Lead Joint Runner
LPMA . . . . . . Lead Pencil Manufacturers Association
LRC . . . . Lead Resistance Compensator
LSPPO . . . . . . Lead Screw Position Pickoff
LS . . . . Lead Sheet (Military)
LSA . . . . Lead Spring Assembly
LSTF . . . . . . Lead Sulfide Thin Film
LTC . . . . Lead Telluride Crystal
LPC . . . . Leader Preparation Course
LPP . . . . Leader Preparation Program
LCCR . . . . . . Leadership Conference on Civil Rights
LEAP . . . . . . Leadership and Education for Advancement of Phoenix (Arizona)
LPR . . . . Leadership Potential Rating (Army)
LAWS . . . . . . Leadership and World Society (An organization)
LA . . . . Leading Aircraftsman
LAC . . . . Leading Aircraftman (Great Britain, Canada)
LACW . . . . . . Leading Aircraftswoman
LCL . . . . Leading Catholic Layman
LE . . . . Leading Edge (Aerospace)
LEAP . . . . . . Leading Edge Airborne PANAR
LEMAC . . . . . . Leading Edge Mean Aerodynamic Chord
LET . . . . Leading Edge Tracker
LETS . . . . . . Leading Edge Tracker Seeker
LS . . . . Leading Seaman
LID . . . . Leadless Inverted Device
L . . . . Leaf (Bibliography)
LTEA . . . . . . Leaf Tobacco Exporters Association
LDP . . . . Leaflet Dispensing Pod
L . . . . League
LAA . . . . League of Advertising Agencies
LAW . . . . League of American Wheelmen
LAUD . . . . . . League of Americans of Ukrainian Descent
LDSR . . . . . . League of Distilled Spirits Rectifiers (Defunct)
LEDC . . . . . . League for Emotionally Disturbed Children

LFRA . . . . League of Federal Recreation Associations
LID . . . . League for Industrial Democracy
LICROSS . . . . . League of International Red Cross Societies
LLN . . . . League for Less Noise
LFL . . . . League for Liberty
LMA . . . . League for Mutual Aid
LNLI . . . . League for National Labor in Israel
LN . . . . League of Nations
L of N . . . . . . League of Nations
LNU . . . . League of Nations Union
LNYT . . . . League of New York Theatres
LNAH . . . . League of Night Adoration in the Home
LPU . . . . League of Prayer for Unity
LRCS . . . . League of Red Cross Societies
LRFI . . . . League for Religious Freedom in Israel (Later, American Friends of Religious Freedom in Israel)
LRLEI . . . . League for Religious Labor in Eretz Israel
LRS . . . . League of Religious Settlements
LSIS . . . . League of Shut-In Sodalists
LTSH . . . . League of Tarcisians of the Sacred Heart
LULAC . . . . . . League of United Latin American Citizens
LWV . . . . League of Women Voters of the United States
LWVUS . . . . . . League of Women Voters of the United States
LRL . . . . Leakage Resistance Limit
LPA . . . . Leaky Pipe Antenna
LFT . . . . Leap-Frog Test
LIFE . . . . Lear Integrated Flight Equipment
LSI . . . . Lear-Siegler, Incorporated (NYSE symbol)
LDL . . . . Learned Doctor of Laws
L . . . . Learner
LAT . . . . Learning Ability Test (Military)
LINC . . . . Learning Institute of North Carolina
LRDC . . . . Learning Research and Development Center (University of Pittsburgh)
LRI . . . . Learning Resources Institute
LACT . . . . Lease Automatic Custody Transfer
LL . . . . Lease-Lend (Bill) (World War II)
LL . . . . Leased Line (Private telephone or teletype line)
TWL . . . . Leased Teletypewriter Service
LCD . . . . Least (or Lowest) Common Denominator
LCF . . . . Least Common Factor
LCM . . . . Least Common Multiple (Mathematics)
LESS . . . . Least Cost Estimating and Scheduling
LC . . . . Least Count
LEP . . . . Least Energy Principle
LFD . . . . Least Fatal Dose
LPD . . . . Least Perceptible Difference (Psychology)
LSB . . . . Least Significant Bit
LSD . . . . Least Significant Difference
LSF . . . . Least Square Fit
LVCD . . . . Least Voltage Coincidence Detector
L . . . . Leather
LIA . . . . Leather Industries of America
LPC . . . . Leather Personnel Carriers (i.e., boots) (Army slang)
LWIU . . . . Leather Workers International Union of America
LWU . . . . Leather Workers International Union of America
L . . . . Leave
LOA . . . . Leave of Absence
LAB . . . . Leave Authorization Balance (Air Force)
LOP . . . . Leave on Pass
LEAVERATS . . . Leave Rations
LR . . . . Leave Rations (Military)
L/R . . . . Leave Rations (Military)
LTA . . . . Leave Travel Allowance
LWOP . . . . Leave Without Pay (Civil Service)
LLMA . . . . Leavers Lace Manufacturers of America
LL . . . . Leaves (Bibliography)
LADIZ . . . . . . Leaving Air Defense Identification Zone
LAS . . . . Lebanese-American Society of Greater New York
LVC . . . . Lebanon Valley College (Pennsylvania)
LOF . . . . Lecherous Old Fool
LF . . . . Ledger Folio
LCCE . . . . Lee County Central Electric R. R. (AAR code)
LR . . . . Lee Rubber & Tire Corporation (NYSE symbol)
LJC . . . . Lees Junior College (Kentucky)
LSO . . . . Leesona Corporation (NYSE symbol)
LML . . . . Leesona Moos Laboratory
L . . . . Left (Direction)
L . . . . Left (side of a stage) (A stage direction)
LA . . . . Left Angle
LAD . . . . Left Anterior Descending (Artery)
LAD . . . . Left Anterior Digestive (Gland)

LAE . . . . Left Arithmetic Element
LA . . . . Left Ascension
LA . . . . Left Atrium (Anatomy)
LAW . . . . Left Attack Wing (Women's lacrosse position)
LA . . . . Left Auricle (Anatomy)
LB . . . . Left on Base (Baseball)
LBCD . . . . Left Border Cardiac Dullness (Cardiology)
LBD . . . . Left Border of Dullness (Cardiology)
LBG . . . . Left Buccal Ganglion
LBBSB . . . . . . Left Bundle Branch System Block (Cardiology)
LC . . . . Left Center (Stage direction)
LCG . . . . Left Cerebral Ganglion
LCM . . . . Left Costal Margin
LD . . . . Left Defense
LDW . . . . Left Defense Wing (Women's lacrosse position)
LDG . . . . Left Digestive Gland
LE . . . . Left End
LE . . . . Left Extremity
LE . . . . Left Eye
LF . . . . Left Field(er) (Baseball)
LF . . . . Left Foot
LF . . . . Left Forward (Football)
LF . . . . Left Front
LFA . . . . Left Fronto-Anterior (Anatomy)
LFP . . . . Left Fronto-Posterior (Anatomy)
LF . . . . Left Fullback (Soccer position)
LFB . . . . Left Fullback (Football)
LG . . . . Left Guard (Football)
LHW . . . . Left Half Word
LH . . . . Left Halfback (Soccer and football position)
LHB . . . . Left Halfback (Football)
LH . . . . Left Hand
LHCP . . . . Left Hand Circularly Polarized
LHDR . . . . Left Hand Drive
LHH . . . . Left Hand Head
LHR . . . . Left Hand Rule
LHS . . . . Left Hand Side
LHTH . . . . Left Hand Thread
LAW . . . . Left-Handers Against the World
LIF . . . . Left Iliac Fossa (Medicine)
LICM . . . . Left Intercostal Margin (Anatomy)
LLBCD . . . . . . Left Lower Border of Cardiac Dullness (Cardiology)
LLE . . . . Left Lower Extremity (Medicine)
LLL . . . . Left Lower Lobe (of lung) (Medicine)
LLQ . . . . Left Lower Quadrant (of abdomen) (Medicine)
LOT . . . . Left Occipitotransverse (Anatomy)
LOA . . . . Left Occiput Anterior (A fetal position) (Obstetrics)
LOP . . . . Left Occiput Posterior (A fetal position) (Obstetrics)
LOP . . . . Left Outside Position (Dancing)
LPLG . . . . Left Pleural Ganglion
LR . . . . Left Rear
L/R . . . . Left Right
LRI . . . . Left-Right Indicator
LSA . . . . Left Sacro-Anterior (Anatomy)
LSP . . . . Left Sacroposterior (A fetal position, the breech position) (Obstetrics)
LSAL . . . . Left Salivary (Gland)
LS . . . . Left Side
LSC . . . . Left Stage Center (A stage direction)
LSB . . . . Left Sternal Border
LT . . . . Left Tackle (Football)
LP . . . . Left Traffic Pattern (Aviation)
LUE . . . . Left Upper Extremity
LUL . . . . Left Upper Lobe (of lung) (Medicine)
LUQ . . . . Left Upper Quadrant (of abdomen) (Medicine)
LVB . . . . Left Ventricular Bypass (Artificial heart booster)
LVH . . . . Left Ventricular Hypertrophy (Medicine)
LVP . . . . Left Ventricular Pump (Heart pump)
LVG . . . . Left Visceral Ganglion
LW . . . . Left Wing
LBW . . . . Leg Before Wicket (Cricket)
LB . . . . Leg Bye (Cricket)
LGS . . . . Lega dei Giovani Somali (Somali Youth League)
L . . . . Legal Division (Coast Guard)
LITE . . . . Legal Information Through Electronics (Air Force)
LS . . . . Legal Scroll
LT . . . . Legal Tender (Currency)
LV . . . . Legal Volt
LEMAR . . . . . . Legalize Marijuana (Acronym is used for name of an organization)
LQ . . . . Lege Quaeso (Please Read)
LCK . . . . Legion of Christ the King
LOG . . . . Legion of Guardsmen

L d'H . . . . . . Legion d'Honneur (French decoration)
LH . . . . Legion of Honour
LM . . . . Legion of Merit
LOM . . . . . . Legion of Merit (Military award)
LVUSA . . . . . Legion of Valor of the United States of America
LVF . . . . Legion des Volontaires Francais Contre le Bolchevism
LTA . . . . Legionarios Del Trabajo in America
LASH . . . . . . Legislative Action on Smoking and Health
LA . . . . Legislative Assembly
LCP . . . . Legislative Council for Photogrammetry
LL . . . . Legislative Liaison
LRS . . . . Legislative Reference Service (Library of Congress)
L . . . . Legitimate
LC . . . . Legitimate Child
LHR . . . . Lehigh & Hudson River Railway Company (AAR code)
L & HR . . . . . Lehigh and Hudson River Railway Company
LNE . . . . Lehigh & New England R. R. (AAR code)
L & NE . . . . . Lehigh and New England Railroad Company
LPT . . . . Lehigh Portland Cement Company (NYSE symbol)
LVEA . . . . . . Lehigh Valley Electronic Association
LEH . . . . Lehigh Valley Industries, Inc. (NYSE symbol)
LV . . . . Lehigh Valley R. R. (AAR code)
LVRR . . . . . . Lehigh Valley Railroad
LECA . . . . . . Lehman Caves National Monument
LEM . . . . Lehman Corporation (NYSE symbol)
LNP . . . . Lehn & Fink Products Corporation (NYSE symbol)
LVG . . . . Lehr-und-Versuchgut
LTA . . . . Leisure Time Activity
L . . . . Lempira (Monetary unit in Honduras)
LLA . . . . Lend-Lease Administration
LLLO . . . . . . Lend-Lease Liaison Office
LL . . . . Lending Library
LLU . . . . Lending Library Unit
L . . . . Length
LBP . . . . Length Between Perpendiculars (Technical drawings)
LBH . . . . Length, Breadth, Height
L/D . . . . Length-Diameter
LOL . . . . Length of Lead (Actual) (Technical drawings)
LMT . . . . Length, Mass, Time (Physics)
LOA . . . . . . Length Over-All (Technical drawings)
LOPS . . . . . . Length of Patient Stay
LWL . . . . Length at Waterline
LMZ . . . . . . Leningradskii Metallicheskii Zavod
LKSMB . . . . . Leninski Komunistychny Saiuz Moladzi Belarusi
LRC . . . . Lenoir Rhyne College (North Carolina)
L . . . . Lens
LEL . . . . Lens-End-Lamp
LMO . . . . . . Lens-Modulated Oscillator
LSC . . . . Lens Sign Convention
LBI . . . . Leo Baeck Institute
LNR . . . . Leonard Refineries, Inc. (NYSE symbol)
LWMEL . . . . . Leonard Wood Memorial for the Eradication of Leprosy
LS . . . . Lepidopterists' Society
LER . . . . Lerner Stores Corporation (NYSE symbol)
LA . . . . Leschetizky Association
LCL . . . . Less than Carload Lots
LDC . . . . Less Developed Countries
LS and MS . . . Less Sleep and More Speed (Hobo slang)
LTL . . . . Less than Truckload
LUV . . . . Let Us Vote (Organization dedicated to lowering voting age to 18)
LC . . . . Lethal Concentration
LD . . . . Lethal Dose (Pharmacology)
LD/50 . . . . . . Lethal Dose, Median (Lethal for 50% of inoculated group)
L . . . . Letter
LA . . . . Letter of Activation (Military)
POINTMAIL . . Letter Appointment in Mail
L/A . . . . Letter of Authority
LB . . . . Letter Box
LC . . . . Letter Contract
LC . . . . Letter of Credit
L/C . . . . Letter of Credit
LDD . . . . Letter of Determination of Dependency
LOI . . . . Letter of Instruction
L/I . . . . Letter of Intent
LO . . . . Letter Orders
LOP . . . . Letter of Proposal (Military)
LR . . . . Letter Report
LR-QR . . . . . Letter Requirement - Quick Reaction (Army)
LS . . . . Letter Service
LS . . . . Letter Signed (Manuscript descriptions)
LSM . . . . Letter Sorting Machine (US Post Office)

LT . . . . Letter Telegram
LF . . . . Lettering Faded
LEAD . . . . . . Letterkenny Army Depot
LAIR . . . . . . Letterman Army Institute of Research
LTP . . . . Let's Tax Plutocrats (Humorous interpretation of LTP - Limit on Tax Preferences)
LCGB . . . . . . Letzeburger Chreschtliche Gewerkschaftsbond (Confederation of Christian Trade Unions of Luxembourg)
L . . . . Leu (Monetary unit in Romania)
LAP . . . . Leucine Aminopeptidase (Biochemistry)
LS . . . . Leukemia Society
LSI . . . . Leukemia Society, Incorporated
LAPA . . . . . . Leukocyte Alkaline Phosphatase Activity
LPF . . . . Leukocytosis-Promoting Factor
L . . . . Lev (Monetary unit in Bulgaria)
LAT . . . . Level Above Threshold
LC . . . . Level Control
LC . . . . Level Crossing
LDT . . . . Level Delay Time
LD . . . . Level Discriminator
LDR . . . . Level Distribution Recorder
LFC . . . . Level of Free Convection
LG . . . . Level Gage
LOGIC . . . . . Level of Greatest Item Control (DOD)
LI . . . . Level Indicator
LR . . . . Level Recorder
LRC . . . . Level Recording Controller
LSA . . . . Level Shift Amplifier
LS . . . . Level Switch
LT . . . . Level Trigger
LCA . . . . Leveling Control Amplifier
LCS . . . . Leveling Control System
LTA . . . . Leveling Torquer Amplifier
L & L . . . . . . Lewd and Lascivious
LCSA . . . . . . Lewis and Clark Society of America
LFPL . . . . . . Lewis Flight Propulsion Laboratory (NASA)
LG . . . . Lewis Gun
LRC . . . . Lewis Research Center (NASA)
LZGF . . . . . . Lewis Zero Gravity Facility
L . . . . Lewisite (Chemical warfare)
LGCP . . . . . . Lexical-Graphical Composer Printer (Photocomposition)
LBAD . . . . . . Lexington-Blue Grass Army Depot
L . . . . Liaison (Airplane designation)
LCS . . . . Liaison Call Sheet
LC . . . . Liaison-Cargo (Air Force)
LIDIA . . . . . . Liaison Internationale des Industries de l'Alimentation
LO . . . . Liaison Office(r)
LOS . . . . Liaison Office Support
LOC . . . . Liaison Officer Coordinator (Air Force)
LOF . . . . Libbey-Owens-Ford Glass Company (NYSE symbol)
LJ . . . . Libby, McNeill & Libby (NYSE symbol)
L . . . . Liber (Book)
LCGIL . . . . . Libera Confederazione Generale Italiana dei Lavoratori (Free Italian General Confederation of Workers)
LFILIE . . . . . . Libera Federazione Italiana Lavoratori Industrie Estrattive (Free Italian Federation of Workers in Mining Industries)
L . . . . Liberal
LC . . . . Liberal Conservative
LDP . . . . Liberal Democratic Party (Japan)
LDPD . . . . . . Liberal-Demokratische Partei Deutschlands (Liberal Democratic Party of Germany) (East Germany)
LEY . . . . Liberal European Youth
LI . . . . Liberal Internationale (World Liberal Union)
LREDA . . . . . Liberal Religious Education Directors Association
LRPF . . . . . . Liberal Religious Peace Fellowship
LRY . . . . Liberal Religious Youth
LAMCO . . . . . Liberian American-Swedish Minerals Company
LIAC . . . . . . Liberian International American Corporation (New York)
LAC . . . . Liberty Amendment Committee of the USA
LBY . . . . Liberty Fabrics of New York (NYSE symbol)
LIBCO . . . . . Liberty Investors Benefit Insurance Company
LMIC . . . . . . Liberty Mutual Insurance Company
L . . . . Libra (Pound)
LSD . . . . Librae, Solidi, Denarii (Pounds, Shillings, Pence)
LC . . . . Librarian of Congress
LAMP . . . . . . Library Addition and Maintenance Program
LAD . . . . Library Administration Division (of ALA)
LA . . . . Library Association (British)
LAA . . . . Library Association of Australia
LACUNY . . . . Library Association of the City University of New York
LAUK . . . . . . Library Association of the United Kingdom

LARC . . . . Library Automation Research and Consulting
LBI . . . . Library Binding Institute
LB . . . . Library Bulletin
LB . . . . Library Bureau (of Sperry Rand Corporation)
LCA . . . . Library Club of America
LC . . . . Library of Congress
LOC . . . . . . Library of Congress
LOCATE . . . . . Library of Congress Automation Techniques Exchange
LCC . . . . Library of Congress Classification
LDT . . . . Library Development Team
LED . . . . Library Education Division (of American Library Association)
LEEP . . . . Library Education Experimental Project (Syracuse University)
LFVO . . . . . . Library Foundation for Voluntary Organizations
LISST . . . . . . Library and Information Scholarship Today (A publication)
LISTS . . . . . . Library Information System Time-Sharing
LICET . . . . . . Library of Industrial and Commercial Education and Training
LJ . . . . Library Journal (Professional periodical)
L/L . . . . Library Labels (Antiquarian book trade)
LL . . . . Library Literature (A serial index)
LIBMAS . . . . . Library Master File (FORTRAN program)
LMP . . . . Library Material Processed
LIBNAT . . . . . . Library Network Analysis Theory
LPRC . . . . . . Library Public Relations Council
L/R/S . . . . . . Library Rubber Stamps (Antiquarian book trade)
LS . . . . Library Science
LSA . . . . Library Science Abstracts
LSSO . . . . . . Library Science Student Organization
LSA . . . . Library Services Act (1956)
LSCA . . . . . . Library Services and Construction Act (1963)
LISA . . . . . . Library Systems Analysis
LTP . . . . Library Technology Program (Formerly, Project) (ALA)
LOCS . . . . . . Librascope Operations Control System
LEO . . . . Librating Equidistant Observer
LARC . . . . Libyan-American Reconstruction Commission
LFLPU . . . . . . Libyan Federation of Labor and Professional Unions
LGWF . . . . . . Libyan General Workers' Federation
LBI . . . . Licensed Beverage Industries
LO . . . . Licensed Officer (US Merchant Marine)
LPN . . . . Licensed Practical Nurse
LV . . . . Licensed Victualer
LAO . . . . Licensing Authorities Office
LES . . . . Licensing Executives Society
L . . . . Licentiate
LAH . . . . Licentiate of the Apothecaries' Hall (Dublin)
LA . . . . Licentiate in Arts
LCL . . . . Licentiate of Civil Law
LCPS . . . . . . Licentiate of the College of Physicians and Surgeons (British)
LCP . . . . Licentiate of the College of Preceptors (British)
LDM . . . . Licentiate of Dental Medicine
LDSc . . . . . . Licentiate in Dental Science (British)
LDS . . . . Licentiate in Dental Surgery
LDSI . . . . . . Licentiate in Dental Surgery (Ireland)
LDSRCS . . . . . Licentiate in Dental Surgery in the Royal College of Surgeons (British)
L Div . . . . . . Licentiate in Divinity
LFPS . . . . Licentiate of the Faculty of Physicians and Surgeons (Glasgow)
LI . . . . Licentiate of Instruction (or Licentiate Instructor)
LKQCP . . . . . Licentiate of the King's and Queen's College of Physicians (Ireland)
LLL . . . . Licentiate in Laws
LLCO . . . . . . Licentiate of the London College of Osteopathy
LM . . . . Licentiate in Medicine
ML . . . . Licentiate in Medicine
LMS . . . . Licentiate in Medicine and Surgery (British)
LM . . . . Licentiate in Midwifery
ML . . . . Licentiate in Midwifery
Ph L . . . . Licentiate of Pharmacy
Ph L . . . . Licentiate in Philosophy
LRCS . . . . . . Licentiate of the Royal College of Surgeons (British)
LRCSE . . . . . . Licentiate of the Royal College of Surgeons (Edinburgh)
LRCP . . . . . . Licentiate in the Royal College of Physicians (British)
LRCPE . . . . . . Licentiate of the Royal College of Physicians (Edinburgh)
LRFPS . . . . . . Licentiate of the Royal Faculty of Physicians and Surgeons (British)
LRIBA . . . . . . Licentiate of the Royal Institute of British Architecture
SSL . . . . Licentiate of Sacred Scripture
LS . . . . Licentiate in Science
LSA . . . . Licentiate of the Society of Apothecaries (British)
LS . . . . Licentiate in Surgery
LT . . . . Licentiate in Theology
L Th . . . . Licentiate in Theology
Th L . . . . Licentiate in Theology
L Ch . . . . Licentiatus Chirurgiae (Licentiate in Surgery)
LT . . . . Lid Tank

LKP . . . . Lietuvos Komunistu Partija
LA . . . . Lieutenant-at-Arms
LTC . . . . Lieutenant Colonel (Army)
LTG . . . . Lieutenant General (Army)
LTJG . . . . . . Lieutenant Junior Grade (Navy)
LACA . . . . . . Life Agency Cashiers Association of the United States and Canada
LBB . . . . Life Blower Bearing
LCT . . . . Life Component Tester
LDI . . . . Life Detection Instrument
LEF . . . . Life Extension Foundation
LF . . . . Life Float
LG . . . . Life Guards
LIAB . . . . Life Insurance Adjustment Bureau
LAA . . . . Life Insurance Advertisers Association
LIAMA . . . . . Life Insurance Agency Management Association
LIAA . . . . . . Life Insurance Association of America
LIMRF . . . . . Life Insurance Medical Research Fund
LIP . . . . Life Insurance Policy
LISA . . . . . . Life Insurance Society of America
LIC . . . . Life Insurers Conference
LJ . . . . Life Jacket
LOMA . . . . . Life Office Management Association
LPU . . . . Life Preserver Unit
LPF . . . . Life Probability Function
LOP . . . . Life of Program
LSS . . . . Life Saving Service
LSS . . . . Life Support System
LUTC . . . . . . Life Underwriter Training Council
LD . . . . Lifeboat Deck
LIFESTA . . . . Lifeboat Station (Coast Guard)
LS . . . . Lifesaving Service (Coast Guard)
LSS . . . . Lifesaving Station (Maps and charts)
LSEP . . . . . . Lifetime Sports Education Project (of Lifetime Sports Foundation)
L . . . . Lift
L/D . . . . Lift-Drag (Ratio)
LAV . . . . Lifting Ascent Vehicle
LBD . . . . Lifting Body Development
LCL . . . . Lifting Condensation Level (Air Force)
LEV . . . . Lifting Entry Vehicle
LE . . . . Lifting Eye
L/O . . . . Lift-Off
LOAS . . . . . . Liftoff Acquisition System
LEAP . . . . . . Lift-off Elevation and Azimuth Programmer
LUD . . . . Lift-Up Door (Technical drawings)
L . . . . Ligament(um)
LM . . . . Liggett & Myers Tobacco Company (NYSE symbol)
L . . . . Light
L & A . . . . . . Light and Accommodation (Optometry)
LASCR . . . . . Light-Activated Silicon-Controlled Rectifier
LASS . . . . . . Light Activated Silicon Switch
LAS . . . . Light-Activated Switch
LAD . . . . Light Aid Detachment (British military)
LADA . . . . . . Light Air Defense Artillery
LAD . . . . Light Air Detachment
LAAV . . . . . . Light Airborne ASW (Antisubmarine Warfare) Vehicle
LAMPS . . . . . Light Airborne Multiple Package System
LAMPS . . . . . Light Airborne Multi-Purpose System (Navy)
LABIL . . . . . . Light Aircraft Binary Information Link
LASER . . . . . Light Amplification by Stimulated Emission of Radiation
LAAM . . . . . Light Anti-Air Missile
LAA . . . . Light Antiaircraft (Guns)
LAW . . . . . . Light Antiarmor Weapon
LAW . . . . . . Light Antitank Weapon (Military)
LAW . . . . . . Light Area Weapon
LARA . . . . . . Light Armed Reconnaissance Aircraft (Air Force)
LAA . . . . Light Army Aircraft
LAAW . . . . . Light Assault Anti-Tank Weapon
LAW . . . . . . Light Assault Weapon
LASTA . . . . . Light Attendant Station (Coast Guard)
LASSO . . . . . Light Aviation Special Support Operations
LBC . . . . Light Barrier Control
LBP . . . . Light Beam Pickup
LB . . . . Light Bombardment (Air Force)
LB . . . . Light Bomber (Air Force)
L/B . . . . Light Bomber
AKL . . . . Light Cargo Ship (Navy symbol)
LCL . . . . Light Center Length
LCR . . . . Light Chopping Reticle
CL . . . . Light Cruiser (Navy symbol)
LD . . . . Light-Dark (Cycles)
LD . . . . Light on Dark

LDR . . . . Light Dependent Resistor
LIDAR . . . . . . Light Detection and Ranging
LD . . . . Light Difference (Difference between amounts of light perceptible to
         the two eyes) (Ophthalmology)
LDC . . . . Light Direction Center (Military)
LDLE . . . . . . Light Duty Lathe Engine
LED . . . . Light-Emitting Diode
LE . . . . Light Equipment
LFF . . . . Light Filter Factor
LFQ . . . . . . Light Foot Quantizer
LGAF . . . . . . Light Ground Attack Fighter
LG . . . . Light Gun
LGA . . . . . . Light-Gun Amplifier
LGG . . . . . . Light Gun-Pulse Generator
LH . . . . Light Horse (Cavalry)
LI . . . . Light Infantry
LIT . . . . Light Intratheater Transport (Air Force)
LL . . . . Light Line (Military)
LL . . . . Light Lock
LILOC . . . . . . Light Lyne Optical Correlation
LMG . . . . . . Light Machine Gun
LMH . . . . . . Light Metal Hydride
LMP . . . . Light Metal Products
LM . . . . Light Metals
LMED . . . . . . Light Military Electronics Department
LMEE . . . . . . Light Military Electronics Equipment
LMR . . . . Light Modulation Recording
LOA . . . . . . Light Observation Aircraft
LOH . . . . . . Light Observation Helicopter (Air Force)
LOLA . . . . . . Light Observation Light-Armored Aircraft
LP . . . . Light Perception
LPA . . . . Light Pulser Array
LPM . . . . Light Pulser Matrix
LRS . . . . Light Radiation Sensor
LRA . . . . Light Replaceable Assemblies
LSR . . . . Light Sensitive Relay
LSR . . . . Light Sensitive Resistor
LST . . . . Light Sensitive Tube
LS . . . . Light Ship or Vessel
LS . . . . Light Source
LSS . . . . Light Spot Scanner
LTSTA . . . . . . Light Station (Coast Guard)
LSR . . . . Light Stopping Reticle
LTT . . . . Light Tactical Transport
LT . . . . Light Tank
LTI . . . . Light Transmission Index
VG . . . . Light Transport Plane (Single-engine) (Navy symbol)
LT . . . . Light Trap
LUG . . . . Light Utility Glider
LUME . . . . . . Light Utilization More Efficient
LVP . . . . Light Valve Projector
LV . . . . Light Vessel
LW . . . . Light Wall
LW . . . . Light Warning
LW(STA) . . . . Light Warning (Station)
LWBR . . . . . . Light Water Breeder Reactor (AEC)
LWR . . . . Light-Water Reactor (AEC)
LWA . . . . . . Light Weight Armor
LIOC . . . . . Lighted Independent of Computer
LUPC . . . . . Lighted Under Program Control
LTGH . . . . . . Lightening Hole (Engineering)
YFNX . . . . . . Lighter (Special Purpose) (Navy symbol)
LASH . . . . . . Lighter Aboard Ship (Barge-carrying ship)
YH . . . . Lighter, Ambulance (Navy symbol)
YE . . . . Lighter, Ammunition (Navy symbol)
LARC . . . . . . Lighter, Amphibious, Resupply Cargo (Vessel)
LA . . . . Lighter than Air (Aircraft)
LTA . . . . Lighter than Air (Aircraft)
Z . . . . Lighter-than-air aircraft (Airship)
LASS . . . . . . Lighter than Air Submarine Simulator
LSD . . . . Lightermen, Stevedores, and Dockers
LF . . . . Lightface (Type)
LH . . . . Lighthouse (Maps and charts)
LS . . . . Lighthouse Service (Coast Guard)
AGL . . . . Lighthouse Tender (Navy symbol)
LHT . . . . Lighthouse Tender (Navy symbol)
LC . . . . Lightly Canceled
LWA . . . . . . Lightly Wounded in Action
L . . . . Lightning
LA . . . . Lightning Arrester
LTGCC . . . . . . Lightning Cloud-to-Cloud (Meteorology)

LTGCCCG . . . . Lightning Cloud-to-Cloud, Cloud-to-Ground (Meteorology)
LTGCG . . . . . Lightning Cloud-to-Ground (Meteorology)
LTGCW . . . . . Lightning Cloud-to-Water (Meteorology)
LTGIC . . . . . Lightning in Clouds (Meteorology)
LICOR . . . . . Lightning Correlation
LPI . . . . Lightning Protection Institute
LTRI . . . . . . Lightning and Transients Research Institute
LPL . . . . Lightproof Louver (Technical drawings)
LPS . . . . Lightproof Shade (Technical drawings)
LPV . . . . Lightproof Vent (Technical drawings)
AL . . . . Lightship (Navy symbol)
LAPA . . . . . . Lightweight Aggregate Producers Association
LWASV . . . . . Lightweight Aircraft-to-Surface Vessel (Military)
LAK . . . . Lightweight Antenna Kit
LATS . . . . . . Lightweight Antenna Terminal Seeker
LBAK . . . . . . Lightweight Broadband Antenna Kit
LCD . . . . Lightweight Ceramic Dome
LWC . . . . . . Lightweight Concrete (Technical drawings)
LELTS . . . . . . Lightweight Electronic Locating and Tracking System
LWHVR . . . . . Lightweight High Velocity Rifle
LINS . . . . . . Lightweight Inertial Navigation System
LWIC . . . . . Lightweight Insulating Concrete (Technical drawings)
LRS . . . . Lightweight RADAR Set
LWS . . . . Lightweight Sight
LSF . . . . Lightweight Strike Fighter (NATO Air Forces)
LWSF . . . . . . Lightweight Strike Fighter
LWS . . . . Lightweight System
LWT . . . . Lightweight Transponder
LWT . . . . Lightweight Type (Anchor gear)
LWW . . . . Lightweight Weapon
LWWS . . . . . . Lightweight Weapons Sight
LWRS . . . . . . Lightweight Weather RADAR Set
LECE . . . . . . Ligue Europeenne de Cooperation Economique
LGTA . . . . . . Ligue Generale des Travailleurs Angolais (General League of Angolan
         Workers in Exile)
LHI . . . . Ligue Homeopathique Internationale
LICCD . . . . . Ligue Internationale Contre la Concurrence Deloyale
LIDH . . . . . . Ligue Internationale des Droits de l'Homme
LIEN . . . . . . Ligue Internationale pour l'Education Nouvelle
LIFPL . . . . . . Ligue Internationale de Femmes pour la Paix et la Liberte
LIHG . . . . . . Ligue Internationale de Hockey sur Glace
LILA . . . . Ligue Internationale de la Librairie Ancienne
LI . . . . Ligue Internationale de la Representation Commerciale
LOCI . . . . . . Ligue des Originaires de Cote d'Ivoire (League of Ivory Coast Natives)
LSCR . . . . . . Ligue des Societes de la Croix-Rouge
LU . . . . Ligue Universelle (Esperantiste)
LLI . . . . Ligula Length Index
LES . . . . Lilliput Edison Screw
LIL . . . . Lily-Tulip Cup Corporation (NYSE symbol)
LBAB . . . . . . Lima Bean Advisory Board
LMC . . . . Lime-Magnesium Carbonate
L . . . . Limen or Threshold (Psychology)
LS . . . . Liminal (or Least) Sensation (Psychology)
LAR . . . . Limit Address Register
LF . . . . Limit of Flocculation
LSC . . . . Limit Signaling Comparator
LS . . . . Limit Switch (Electronics)
LSW . . . . Limit Switch
LTP . . . . Limit on Tax Preferences
LV . . . . Limit Value
LOV . . . . Limit of Visibility
LOM . . . . Limitation of Movement
LAF . . . . Limited Amplifier Filter
LADS . . . . . . Limited Attack Defense System
LAWRS . . . . . Limited Aviation Weather Reporting Station
LIMDIS . . . . . Limited Distribution (Military)
LIMDU . . . . . Limited Duty (Navy)
LD . . . . Limited Duty Officer (Navy)
LDO . . . . Limited Duty Officer
LEDT . . . . . . Limited Entry Decision Table
LFB . . . . Limited Frequency Band
LIFEL . . . . . . Limited Functional English Literacy
LIE . . . . Limited Information Estimation
LIML . . . . . . Limited-Information Maximum Likelihood (Econometrics)
LL . . . . Limited Liability (Finance)
LNAC . . . . . Limited National Agency Check
LP . . . . Limited Production
LRL . . . . Limited Raman LASER
LRM . . . . Limited Register Machine
LRRS . . . . . . Limited Remaining Radiation Service (Unit) (Military)
LRCO . . . . . . Limited Remote Communication Outlets (ATCS)

LRS	Limited Resources Specialty
LSPS	Limited Serial Project Slip
LSSF	Limited Service Storage Facility
LSA	Limited Space-Charge Accumulation (Electronics)
LSS	Limited Storage Site
LW	Limited War
LWCS	Limited War Capabilities Study
LWL	Limited War Laboratory (Army)
LWO	Limited War Office (Air Force)
LWP	Limited War Plan(s)
LWIRC	Limited Warfare Intelligence Reduction Complex
LWO	Limited Warning Operation
LIMDAT	Limiting Date
LIA	Limiting Interval Availability
LIR	Limiting Interval Reliability
LL	Limiting Level
LND	Limiting Nose Dive (Aerospace)
LIBO	Lincoln Boyhood National Memorial
LCS	Lincoln Calibration Sphere
LCPA	Lincoln Center for the Performing Arts
LCOC	Lincoln Continental Owners Club
LEF	Lincoln Educational Foundation
LES	Lincoln Experimental Satellites (Lincoln Laboratory, MIT)
LET	Lincoln Experimental Terminal (NASA)
LL	Lincoln Laboratory (MIT)
LMU	Lincoln Memorial University (Tennessee)
LOC	Lincoln Owners Club
LSC	Lincoln Sesquicentennial Committee (Government agency)
LSP	Lincoln Society of Philately
LZOC	Lincoln Zephyr Owner's Club
LWC	Lindsey Wilson College (Kentucky)
L	Line
LASS	Line Amplifier and Super Sync Mixer
LOB	Line of Balance
LBC	Line Balance Converter
LB	Line Buffer (Data processing)
LBS	Line Buffer System (Data processing)
LBO	Line Building Out
LC	Line-Carrying
LCA	Line Clearance Airdrome (Air Force)
LCS	Line Coding Storage
LC	Line Collector
LC	Line of Communication
L of C	Line of Communication (Military)
LOCCOZO . . .	Line of Communications Combat Zone (Military)
LC	Line Connection
LC	Line of Contact (Military)
LOD	Line of Dance
LD	Line of Departure (Military)
LOD	Line of Departure
LD is FFD	Line of Departure is Friendly Forward Disposition (Army)
LD is PPOS . . .	Line of Departure is Present Positions (Army)
LOD	Line of Direction
LDC	Line Directional Coupler
LD	Line Driver
LDA	Line Driving Amplifier
LD	Line of Duty (Military)
LOD	Line of Duty
LEA	Line Equalizing Amplifier
LF	Line Finder (Teletype)
LOF	Line of Fire
LOF	Line of Force
LGN	Line Gate Number (Data processing)
LISN	Line Impedance Stabilization Network
LOI	Line of Induction
LIR	Line Integral Refractometer
LIDF	Line Intermediate Distributing Frame
LIE	Line Islands Experiment (National Science Foundation)
LIN	Line Item Number (Army)
LLR	Line of Least Resistance
LTL	Line-to-Line
LLP	Line Link Pulsing
LMU	Line Monitor Unit
LON	Line of Nodes
LOP	Line of Position (Electronics)
LRC	Line Rectifier Circuit
LR	Line Relay
LRU	Line Removable (or Replaceable) Unit
LST	Line Scan Tube
LSS	Line Scanner System
LOS	Line of Sight (Military)

LSQ	Line Squall (Meteorology)
LSN	Line Stabilization Network
LSO	Line Stabilized Oscillator
LS	Line Stretcher
LSP	Line Synchronizing Pulse
L/T	Line Telecommunications
LT	Line Telegraphy
LTM	Line Type Modulation (Radio)
LVM	Line Voltage Monitor
LVR	Line Voltage Regulator
LBAF	Line Width, Black-to-White-Ratio, Area, Fixation Point
LAN	Linea Aerea Nacional de Chile (Chilean airline)
TACAV	Linea Aerea TACA de Venezuela
LAV	Linea Aeropostal Venezolana (Venezuelan airline)
LET	Lineal Energy Transfer
LF	Lineal Feet
LAC	Linear Absorption Coefficient
LINAC	Linear (Electron) Accelerator
LAT	Linear Accelerator Tube
LAS	Linear Alkylate Sulfonate (Liquid detergent)
LA	Linear Assembly
LBB	Linear Ball Bushing
LBT	Linear Beam Tube
LCAO	Linear Combination of Atomic Orbitals
LD	Linear Decision
LDE	Linear Differential Equations
LDT	Linear Differential Transformer
LDV	Linear Differential Vector
LDVE	Linear Differential Vector Equation
LDO	Linear Diophantine Object
LDG	Linear Displacement Gauge
LDI	Linear Displacement Indicator
LDR	Linear Dynamic Range
LDS	Linear Dynamic System
LAMAR	Linear Elastic Matrix Analysis Routine
LEN	Linear Electrical Network
LEF	Linear-Energy Spectrophotofluorometry
LETS	Linear Energy Transfer System
LFM	Linear Feet Per Minute
LFL	Linear Field Line
LFT	Linear Flash Tube
LINFT	Linear Foot
LFI	Linear Function Interpolator
LIM	Linear Induction Motor (Magnetic rapid-transit car)
LIC	Linear Integrated Circuit
LKF	Linear Kalman Filter
LLFPB	Linear, Lumped, Finite, Passive, Bilateral
LMO	Linear Master Oscillator
LMS	Linear Measuring System
LMB	Linear Motion Bearing
LPW	Linear Polarized Wave
LPA	Linear Power Amplifier
LPC	Linear Power Controller
LP	Linear Programming
LPUU	Linear Programming Under Uncertainty
LSP	Linear Selenium Photocell
LSPC	Linear Selenium Photocell
LSM	Linear Sequential Machine
LSN	Linear Sequential Network
LSA	Linear Servo Actuator
LSC	Linear Shaped Charge
LSIT	Linear Strip Ion Thruster
LISA	Linear Systems Analysis
LTBO	Linear Time Base Oscillator
LTN	Linear Time-Varying Network
LTC	Linear Transmission Channel
LUE	Linear Unbiased Estimator (Statistics)
LVDT	Linear Variable (or Voltage) Differential (or Displacement) Transformer
LVT	Linear Variable Transformer
LVE	Linear Vector Equation
LVF	Linear Vector Function
LV	Linear Velocity
LVT	Linear Velocity Transducer
LXFT	Linear Xenon Flash Tube
LXT	Linear Xenon Tube
LY	Linear Yard
LET	Linearer Energiegtransfer
LTS	Linearity Test Set
LIFMOP	Linearly Frequency-Modulated Pulse
LACSA	Lineas Aereas Costarricenses, SA (Costa Rican airline)
LADE	Lineas Aereas del Estada (Argentine Air Force airline)

LANSA . . . . . Lineas Aereas Nacionales Consolidadas, SA
LANICA . . . . . Lineas Aereas de Nicaragua, SA (Nicaraguan airline)
LAI . . . . Linee Aeree Italiane (Italian airline)
LHC . . . . Lined Hollow Charge
LF . . . . Linefeed
LLPI . . . . Linen and Lace Paper Institute
LSAA . . . . . . Linen Supply Association of America
LTA . . . . Linen Trade Association
L . . . . Liner (Nautical)
LSR . . . . Liner Seal Ring
LL . . . . Lines (as in a book)
LOC . . . . Lines of Communication
LPM . . . . Lines Per Minute (Data processing)
LTV . . . . Ling-Temco-Vought, Inc. (NYSE symbol)
LMA . . . . Lingerie Manufacturers Association
LINCOS . . . . . Lingua Cosmica (Artificial language consisting of radio signals
              of varying lengths and frequencies)
LASCODOCS . . Linguistic Analysis of Spanish Colonial Documents
LP . . . . Linguistic Problems
LSA . . . . Linguistic Society of America
LRS . . . . Linguistics Research System
LA . . . . Linguoaxial
LG . . . . Linguogingival
LI . . . . Linguoincisal
LO . . . . Linguoocclusal
LP . . . . Linguopulpal
L . . . . Link
LA . . . . Link Allotter
LKB . . . . Link-Belt Company (NYSE symbol)
LCNT . . . . . . Link Celestial Navigation Trainer
LC . . . . Link Circuit
LIFT . . . . Link Intellectual Functions Tester
LTS . . . . Link Terminal Simulator
LT . . . . Link Trainer Instructor
LSS . . . . Linking Segment Subprogram
L . . . . Linnaean
LS . . . . Linnaean Society
LSNY . . . . . . Linnaean Society of New York
LB . . . . Linoleum Base (Technical drawings)
LF . . . . Linoleum Floor (Technical drawings)
LAT . . . . Linseed Association Terms (Shipping)
LD . . . . Linz and Donawitz (Furnace) (Metallurgy) (Named after two plant
              sites in Austria)
LIO . . . . Lionel Corporation (NYSE symbol)
LI . . . . Lions International
LNS . . . . Lioville-Neumann Series
L . . . . Lip
LN . . . . Lip Nerve
LMH . . . . Lipid Mobilizing Hormone (Endocrinology)
LTPP . . . . Lipothiamide Pyrophosphate
LTF . . . . Lipotropic Factor
LNG . . . . Liquefied Natural Gas
LP . . . . Liquefied Petroleum (Gas)
LPG . . . . Liquefied Petroleum Gas
L . . . . Liquid
LAAR . . . . . . Liquid Air Accumulator Rocket
LAAR . . . . . . Liquid Air Augmented Rocket
LACE . . . . . . Liquid Air Collection Engine
LACE . . . . . . Liquid Air Cycle Engine (Aerospace plane engine concept)
LAR . . . . Liquid Air Rocket
LQT . . . . Liquid Carbonic Corporation (NYSE symbol)
LC . . . . Liquid Chromatography
LCNR . . . . . . Liquid Core Nuclear Rocket
LCM . . . . Liquid Curing Medium
LCP . . . . Liquid Cyclone Process (for making high-protein edible cottonseed flour)
LDL . . . . Liquid Delay Line
LDS . . . . Liquid, Diesel-Cycle, Supercharged
LEF . . . . Liquid Expanded Film
LFS . . . . Liquid Flow System
LFBR . . . . . . Liquid Fluidized Bed Reactor
LFBR-CX . . . . Liquid Fluidized Bed Reactor Critical Experiment
LG . . . . Liquid Gas
LGT . . . . Liquid Gas Tank
LHE . . . . Liquid Helium
LH . . . . Liquid Hydrogen
LH2 . . . . Liquid Hydrogen
LHC . . . . Liquid Hydrogen Container
LHV . . . . Liquid Hydrogen Vessel
LITVC . . . . . . Liquid Injection Thrust Vector Control
LJP . . . . Liquid Junction Potential
LLC . . . . Liquid Level Control

LLCS . . . . . . Liquid Level Control Switch
LLI . . . . Liquid Level Indicator
LLS . . . . Liquid Level Sensor
LLE . . . . Liquid Liquid Extraction
LME . . . . Liquid Mercury Engine
LMI . . . . Liquid Mercury Isolator
LIMB . . . . . . Liquid Metal Breeder (Reactor)
LMCR . . . . . . Liquid Metal Cooled Reactor
LMC . . . . Liquid Metal Cycle
LMD . . . . Liquid Metal Detector
LMFBR . . . . . Liquid Metal Fast Breeder Reactor (AEC)
LMFR . . . . . . Liquid Metal Fueled Reactor
LMFRE . . . . . Liquid Metal Fueled Reactor Experiment
LMS . . . . Liquid Metal System
LMTBR . . . . . Liquid Metal Thorium Breeder Reactor
LM . . . . Liquid Metals
LMSC . . . . . . Liquid Metals Safety Committee (AEC)
LMG . . . . Liquid Methane Gas
LMP . . . . Liquid Monopropellant
LIN . . . . Liquid Nitrogen
LN . . . . Liquid Nitrogen
LNE . . . . Liquid Nitrogen Evaporater
LNP . . . . Liquid Nitrogen Processing
LNTS . . . . . . Liquid Nitrogen Transfer System
LOX . . . . Liquid Oxygen
LOP-GAP . . . . Liquid Oxygen Petrol, Guided Aircraft Projectile
LOZ . . . . Liquid Ozone
LPF . . . . Liquid Pressure Filter
LPG . . . . Liquid Propane Gas
LP . . . . Liquid Propellant
LPA . . . . Liquid Propellant Analysis
LPARM . . . . . Liquid Propellant Applied Research Motor
LPGG . . . . . . Liquid Propellant Gas Generator
LPIA . . . . . . Liquid Propellant Information Agency (Johns Hopkins University)
LP . . . . Liquid Propellant Missile
LPR . . . . Liquid Propellant Rocket (Air Force)
LPRE . . . . . . Liquid Propellant Rocket Engine
LR . . . . Liquid Rocket
LRE . . . . Liquid Rocket Engine
LSK . . . . Liquid Sample Kit
LSC . . . . Liquid Scintillation Counter
LSS . . . . Liquid Scintillation Spectrometer
LTF . . . . Liquid Thermal Flowmeter
LVDS . . . . . . Liquid, Vee, Diesel-Cycle, Supercharged
LWC . . . . Liquid Water Content
LVVS . . . . . . Liquidatie Vermogens Verwaltung Sarphatistraat (Amsterdam, Holland)
LL . . . . Liquor Law
L . . . . Lira(s) (Italian monetary unit)
LOAP . . . . . . List of Applicable Publications (Air Force)
LAP . . . . List Assembly Programing (Data processing)
LOB . . . . List of Bidders
LD . . . . List of Drawings
LOI . . . . List of Items
LOM . . . . List of Modifications
LISP . . . . List Processor (Data processing)
L . . . . Listed (on a securities exchange)
LS . . . . Listed Securities
L . . . . Listening Post (in symbol only)
L . . . . Lit
L . . . . Litas (Monetary unit in Lithuania)
LM . . . . Litchfield & Madison Railway Company (AAR code)
L . . . . Liter (Metric measure of volume)
LSF . . . . Literary Society Foundation
LA . . . . Literate in Arts
LS . . . . Literature Search
LPM . . . . Liters Per Minute
Li . . . . Lithium (Chemical element)
LCRE . . . . . . Lithium Cooled Reactor Experiment (AEC)
LIDS . . . . . . Lithium Ion Drift Semiconductor
LNA . . . . Lithium Nitrate Ammoniate
LPA . . . . Lithium Perchlorate Ammoniate
LI . . . . Lithographer (Navy rating)
LNA . . . . Lithographers National Association
LPIU . . . . . . Lithographers and Photoengravers International Union
LPNA . . . . . . Lithographers and Printers National Association
LEPMA . . . . . Lithographic Engravers and Plate Makers Association
LAA . . . . Lithuanian Alliance of America
LAC . . . . Lithuanian American Council
LAIC . . . . . . Lithuanian-American Information Center
LANA . . . . . . Lithuanian American National Alliance
LARCF . . . . . Lithuanian American Roman Catholic Federation

LCPS .... Lithuanian Catholic Press Society
MAS .... Lithuanian Catholic Youth Association Ateitis
LCS .... Lithuanian Cultural Society
LNLA .... Lithuanian National League of America
LPSNY ...... Lithuanian Philatelic Society of New York
LRA .... Lithuanian Regeneration Association
LRCA .... Lithuanian Roman Catholic Alliance of America
LSSA .... Lithuanian Student Scout Association (Later, Lithuanian Scouts
              Association College Division)
LSA .... Lithuanian Students Association
LVAR .... Lithuanian Veterans Association Ramove
LP .... Litter Patient
LCRVR ...... Little Change in River Stage
LCTMP ...... Little Change in Temperature (Meteorology)
LDSJ .... Little Daughters of St. Joseph (Roman Catholic religious order)
LFML .... Little Flower Mission League
LGM .... Little Green Men (British term for space signals)
LJ .... Little Joe (Spacecraft) (NASA)
LJLV .... Little Joe Launch Vehicle (Missile)
LJL .... Little John Launcher (Missile)
LJR .... Little John Rocket
LLB .... Little League Baseball
LOL .... Little Old Lady (Slang)
LPA .... Little People of America (An organization)
LRCE .... Little Rock Cotton Exchange
LRU .... Little Rock University (Arkansas)
LSA .... Little Sisters of the Assumption (Roman Catholic religious order)
LIT .... Litton Industries, Inc. (NYSE symbol)
LIPS .... Litton Industries Privacy System
LAS .... Liturgical Arts Society
LET .... Live Environment Testing
LL .... Live Load
LLP .... Live Load Punch
LOPG .... Live Oak, Perry & Gulf R. R. (AAR code)
LP .... Livens Projector (Military)
LKS .... Liver, Kidney, Spleen (Medicine)
LRF .... Liver Residue Factor
LSK .... Liver, Spleen, Kidney (Medicine)
LARC .... Livermore Atomic Research Computer
LPTR .... Livermore Pool Type Reactor
LRL .... Livermore Research Laboratory (AEC)
LIWB .... Livermore Water Boiler
LUA .... Liverpool Underwriters Association
LAMA .... Livestock Auction Markets Association
LCI .... Livestock Conservation, Incorporated
LEC .... Livestock Equipment Council
LFP .... Livestock Feed Program
LAF .... Living Arts Foundation
LQA .... Living Quarters Allowance (Air Force)
LR .... Living Room
L & W ...... Living and Well
LAB .... Lloyd Aereo Boliviano (Bolivian airline)
L/A .... Lloyd's Agent
LGM .... Lloyd's Gold Medal
LR .... Lloyd's Register (of Shipping)
LAC .... Load Accumulator
LAM .... Load Accumulator With Magnitude
LAMS .... Load Alleviation and Mode Stabilization (Air Force)
LANS .... Load Alleviation and Stabilization
LAP .... Load, Assemble, Pack (Army)
LBM .... Load Buffer Memory (Data processing)
LC .... Load Carrier
LC .... Load Cell
LCE .... Load Circuit Efficiency
LCN .... Load Classification Number
LCDTL ...... Load-Compensated Diode Transistor Logic (Data processing)
LCCA .... Load Current Contacting Aiding
LDB .... Load Determining Bolt
LF .... Load Factor
LHD .... Load, Haul, Dump (Mining)
LXA .... Load Index from Address
LXD .... Load Index from Decrement
LDI .... Load Indicator
LLR .... Load Limiting Resistor
LLM .... Load Line Method
LMN .... Load Matching Network
LMS .... Load Matching Switch
LMLR .... Load Memory Lockout Register
LPPC .... Load Point Photocell
LR .... Load Ratio
LRCS .... Load Relief Control System

LSN .... Load Sharing Network
LTC .... Load Tap Changing
LTS .... Load Transfer Switch
LU .... Load Unit
LUS .... Load, Update, Subset
LWL .... Load Water Line
LWP .... Load Water Plane
LWI .... Load Wear Index
LAI .... Loaded Applicator Impedance
LMI .... Loaded Motional Impedance
LODOR ...... Loaded, Waiting Orders or Assignment (Navy)
LPB .... Loan Policy Board (of SBA)
L & D ...... Loans and Discounts (Banking)
LORO .... Lobe on Receive Only
LAR .... Local Acquisition RADAR
LAC .... Local Agency Check
LA .... Local Agent
LAW .... Local Air Warning
LAN .... Local Apparent Noon (Navigation)
LAT .... Local Apparent Time
LA .... Local Authority
LACE .... Local Automatic Circuit Exchange (Communications)
LAMA .... Local Automatic Message Accounting (Telephone)
LBR .... Local Base Rescue (Air Force)
LB .... Local Battery (Radio)
LB .... Local Board
LBH .... Local Board of Health (British)
LCNC .... Local Cartage National Conference
LCT .... Local Civil Time
LCC .... Local Communications Complex
LCC .... Local Communications Console
LCSO .... Local Communications Service Order
LDT .... Local Daylight Saving Time
LDC .... Local Defense Center
LODC .... Local Defense District Craft
LDF .... Local Defense Forces
LDV .... Local Defense Volunteers (Later called Home Guards) (British) (World
          War II)
LD .... Local Delivery
LEAS .... Local Education Agencies
LEA .... Local Education Authority (British)
LES .... Local Excitatory State
LFA .... Local Freight Agent
LGB .... Local Government Board
LHA .... Local Hour Angle
LHA .... Local Housing Authority
LLRC .... Local Labor Relations Board (Japan)
LMMF .... Local Maintenance and Management of Facilities (Military)
LMT .... Local Mean Time
LN .... Local National(s)
LNC .... Local Naval Commander
LOP .... Local Operating Procedures
LOP .... Local Operational Plot
LO .... Local Oscillator (Electronics)
LOF .... Local Oscillator Filter
LOF .... Local Oscillator Frequency
LP .... Local Procurement (Military)
LPD .... Local Procurement Direct (Military)
LPA .... Local Public Agency
LP .... Local Purchase
LOCPURO .... Local Purchase Order
LPO .... Local Purchase Order
LRB .... Local Reference Beam (Holography)
LSSM .... Local Scientific Survey Module
LSHCNC ..... Local and Short Haul Carriers National Conference
LST .... Local Sidereal Time
LST .... Local Standard Time
LSR .... Local Sunrise
LS .... Local Sunset
LTE .... Local Thermodynamic Equilibrium
LT .... Local Time
LTF .... Local Training Flight
LWR .... Local Wage Rate
LZT .... Local Zone Time
LTDA .... Localizer Type Directional Aid (Aviation)
LF .... Locally Funded
LMPRT ...... Locally Most Powerful Rank Test (Statistics)
L .... Locator (Aviation)
LM .... Locator, Middle (Aviation)
LMM .... Locator at Middle Marker (Aviation)
LO .... Locator, Outer (Aviation)

REVERSE ACRONYMS AND INITIALISMS DICTIONARY

LOM . . . . Locator at Outer Marker (Aviation)
L . . . . Loch
LNPIB . . . . . Loch Ness Phenomena Investigation Bureau
LO . . . . Lock-On
LR . . . . Lock Rail
LOT . . . . Lock on Track
LC . . . . Locked Closed
LORBI . . . . . . Locked-On RADAR Bearing Indicator
LO . . . . Locked Open (Technical drawings)
LO . . . . Locked Oscillator
LO-QG . . . . . Locked Oscillator-Quadrature Grid (Data processing)
LAT . . . . Lockheed Air Terminal
LAC . . . . Lockheed Aircraft Corporation
LK . . . . Lockheed Aircraft Corporation (NYSE symbol)
LAWSO . . . . . Lockheed Antisubmarine Warfare Systems Organization
LCC . . . . Lockheed California Company
LEC . . . . Lockheed Electronic Company
LEAP . . . . . . Lockheed Electronics Assembly Program
LEND . . . . . . Lockheed Engineers for National Deployment
LMRS . . . . . . Lockheed Maintenance Recording System
LMSD . . . . . . Lockheed Missile System Division (Lockheed Aircraft Corporation)
LMSC . . . . . . Lockheed Missiles Space Company
LOCATS . . . . . Lockheed Optical Communications & Tracking System
LOCTRACS . . . Lockheed Tracking and Control System
LTR . . . . Lockheed Training Reactor
LC . . . . Loco Citato (At the Place Already Cited)
LL . . . . Loco Laudato (In the Place Cited)
LSC . . . . Loco Supra Citato (In the Place Cited Above)
LEML & AIA . . . Locomotive Engineers Mutual Life and Accident Insurance Association
LMOA . . . . . . Locomotive Maintenance Officers' Association
LT . . . . Locum Tenens (In the Place Of; a substitute)
L . . . . Locus (Place)
LM . . . . Locus Monumenti (Place of the Monument)
L/R . . . . Locus of Radius
LS . . . . Locus Sepulchri (Place of the Sepulchre)
LS . . . . Locus Sigilli (Place of the Seal) (Legal)
L . . . . Lodge
LTR . . . . Loew's Theatres, Inc. (NYSE symbol)
LBRC . . . . . . Loft Bomb Release Computer
LL . . . . Loftleidir H. F. (Icelandic Airlines)
LCVM . . . . . . Log Conversion Voltmeter
LMT . . . . Log Mean Temperature
LPA . . . . Log Periodic Antenna
LPAA . . . . . . Log Periodic Array Antenna
LPBBA . . . . . Log Periodic Broad Band Antenna
LPD . . . . Log Periodic Dipole
LPDA . . . . . . Log Periodic Dipole Array
LPV . . . . Log Periodic V (Antenna)
LR . . . . Log Run (Lumber)
LVC . . . . Log Voltmeter Converter
L . . . . Logair (Air Force contract aircraft identification prefix)
L . . . . Logarithm, Logarithmic
LN . . . . Logarithm (Natural)
LA . . . . Logarithmic Amplifier
LOCI . . . . . . Logarithmic Computing Instrument
LOGFTC . . . . Logarithmic Fast Time Constant
LFE . . . . Logarithmic Feedback Element (Data processing)
LMTD . . . . . . Logarithmic Mean Temperature Difference
LRM . . . . Logarithmic Ratio Module
LSD . . . . Logarithmic Series Distribution (Statistics)
LUT . . . . Loge Unie des Theosophes
LCPG . . . . . . Logic Clock Pulse Generator
LC . . . . Logic Corporation
LD . . . . Logic Driver
LFS . . . . Logic Fault Simulator
LFC . . . . Logic Flow Chart
LGE . . . . Logic Gate Expander
LOGEL . . . . . Logic Generating Language (Data processing)
LT . . . . Logic Theory (Computers)
LOGALGOL . . Logical Algorithmic Language
LOGANDS . . . Logical Commands
LEM . . . . Logical End of Media
IET . . . . Logical Equipment Table
LOGIT . . . . . Logical Inference Tester (NASA)
LOGAN . . . . Logical Language
LOGLAN . . . Logical Language
LOGIPAC . . . Logical Processor and Computer
LOGRAM . . . . Logical Program
LIFT . . . . . . Logically Integrated FORTRAN Translator (UNIVAC)
LODESTAR . . . Logically Organized Data, Entry, Storage, and Recording
LPF . . . . Logically Passive Function

LPSD . . . . . . Logically Passive Self-Dual
LCR . . . . Logistic Change Report (Military)
LOC . . . . Logistic Operation Center (Military)
LSCP . . . . . . Logistic Support Control Point (Military)
LSM . . . . Logistic Support Manager
LBC . . . . Logistical Base Command (Korea)
LOGCOMD . . . Logistical Command
LOGEX . . . . . Logistical Exercise (Army)
LEG . . . . Logistical Expediting Group
LOGR . . . . . . Logistical Ratio
LOGSUP . . . . Logistical Support (Army)
LS . . . . Logistical Support (Army)
LSOC . . . . . . Logistical Support Operations Center
LATAF . . . . . Logistics Activation Task Force (Air Force)
LOGAIRNET . . Logistics Air Network (Air Force)
LOGBALNET . . Logistics Ballistic Missile Network (Air Force)
LCMS . . . . . . Logistics Command Management System
LDSA . . . . . . Logistics Doctrine and Systems Agency (Army)
LEV . . . . Logistics Entry Vehicle
LEG . . . . Logistics Evaluation Group
LEAR . . . . . . Logistics Evaluation and Review
LEDC . . . . . . Logistics Executive Development Course (Army)
LFS . . . . Logistics/Ferry Station
LIIG . . . . Logistics Item Identification Guide (Military)
LMC . . . . Logistics Management Center (Army)
LOGMIS . . . . Logistics Management Information System (Army)
LMI . . . . Logistics Management Institute
LOPU . . . . . . Logistics Organization Planning Unit
LOTS . . . . . . Logistics Over the Shore (Military)
LRC . . . . Logistics Readiness Center (Air Force)
LRP/GWU . . . . Logistics Research Project, George Washington University
S-4 . . . . Logistics Section in Army Brigades or smaller units, and in Marine Corps units smaller than a brigade; the officer in charge of this section
G-4 . . . . Logistics Section of an Army or Marine Corps Division (or Marine brigade or aircraft wing) General Staff; the Officer in Charge of this Section
J-4 . . . . Logistics Section of a Joint Military Staff; the Officer in Charge of this Section
LOGLAND . . . Logistics Support for Land Operations (DOD)
LSP . . . . Logistics Support Plan
LSD . . . . Logistics Systems Division (Air Force)
LSL . . . . Logistics Systems Laboratory
LOGAIR . . . . . Logistics Transport by Air (Military)
LOGLAND . . . Logistics Transport by Land (Military)
LOGSEA . . . . Logistics Transport by Sea (Military)
LAP . . . . Loide Aereo Nacional, SA (Brazilian airline)
LRT . . . . Loki Ranging Transponder
LMC . . . . Lon Morris College (Texas)
LAM . . . . London Academy of Music
LBC . . . . London Bankruptcy Court
LBSCR . . . . . London, Brighton, and South Coast Railway
LCDR . . . . . . London, Chatham, and Dover Railway
LCCA . . . . . . London Church Choir Association
LCM . . . . London City Mission
LCC . . . . London Communications Committee (World War II)
LCTA . . . . . . London Corn Trade Association
LCC . . . . London County Council(or)
LDBE . . . . . . London Diocesan Board of Education
LDHM . . . . . . London Diocesan Home Mission (or Missionary)
LDT . . . . London Dipole Theory
LD . . . . London Docks
LER . . . . London Electric Railway
LEB . . . . London Electricity Board
LGOC . . . . . . London General Omnibus Company
LGCA . . . . . . London Gregorian Choral Association
LME . . . . London Metal Exchange
LMS . . . . London Missionary Society
LNS . . . . London Normal School
LNER . . . . . . London and North-Eastern Railway
LNWR . . . . . . London and North-Western Railway
LO . . . . London Office
LPDC . . . . . . London Parcels Delivery Company
LPS . . . . London & Port Stanley Railway Company (AAR code)
LPFO . . . . . . London Procurement Field Office
LRB . . . . London Rifle Brigade (British)
LRC . . . . London Rowing Club
LSB . . . . London School Board
LSE . . . . London School of Economics
LS . . . . London Scottish (Army regiment)
LSAC . . . . . . London Small Arms Company (Military)
LSWR . . . . . . London and South-Western Railway

265

LSE	London Stock Exchange
LSO	London Symphony Orchestra
LTB	London Transport Board
LUR	London Underground Railway
LIF	Lone Indian Fellowship
LCE	Lone Star Cement Corporation (NYSE symbol) (Delisted)
LSG	Lone Star Gas Company (NYSE symbol)
L	Long
LA	Long-Acting (Pharmacy)
LATS	Long Acting Thyroid Stimulator
LOBAR	Long Baseline RADAR
LBCC	Long Beach City College (California)
LBWSYD	Long Beach Naval Shipyard
LBSC	Long Beach State College (California)
LCT	Long Calcined Ton (Bauxite, etc.)
LOCO	Long Core
LD	Long Delay
LD	Long Distance
LDC	Long Distance Communications
LDNA	Long Distance Navigation Aid
NAVAGLOBE	Long Distance Navigation System, Global (Air Force)
LDX	Long Distance Xerography (Communications facsimile system)
LD	Long Duration
LEA	Long Endurance Aircraft
LEPT	Long-Endurance Patrolling Torpedo
LIBA	Long Island Biological Association
LIEFC	Long Island Early Fliers Club
LLT	Long Island Lighting Company (NYSE symbol)
LI	Long Island R. R. (AAR code)
LIRR	Long Island Railroad
LIU	Long Island University
LLIL	Long Lead Item List
LLP	Long Lead Part
LLRP	Long Lead Repair Part
LLT	Long Lead Time
LLYP	Long Leaf Yellow Pine (Lumber)
LLE	Long Line Effect
LM	Long Metre (Music)
LMD	Long Metre Double (Music)
LOPAIR	Long Path Infrared
LPM	Long Peculiar Metre (Music)
LPP	Long Periodic Perturbation
LP	Long Persistence
LP	Long Picot
LP	Long Play(ing) (Phonograph record)
LPTD	Long Play Talkdown
LPR	Long-Playing Rocket (Aerospace)
LP	Long Primer
LPL	Long Pulse LASER
LR	Long Range
LORAC	Long-Range Accuracy
LORAD	Long-Range Active Detection
LORADAC	Long-Range Active Detection and Communications System
LRADP	Long-Range Active Duty Program (Army)
LORAN	Long-Range Aid to Navigation
LRAF	Long-Range Air Force
LRBM	Long-Range Ballistic Missile
LRBR	Long-Range Ballistic Rocket
LRD	Long-Range Data (RADAR)
LOREC	Long-Range Earth Current Communications
LORA-HOJ	Long Range - Home on Jam
LRIM	Long-Range Input Monitor (RADAR)
LRI	Long-Range Interceptor
LRLG	Long-Range Logistics Guidance (Air Force)
LRM	Long-Range Missile Launcher
LRO	Long-Range Objectives (Navy)
LROG	Long-Range Objectives Group (Navy)
LOROP	Long-Range Oblique Photography
LRO	Long-Range Order
LORAPH	Long-Range Passive Homing System
LRP	Long-Range Patrol (Army)
LRP	Long-Range Penetration
LRPG	Long-Range Penetration Group (Military) (World War II)
LRPPD	Long-Range Planning Purpose Document
LRP	Long-Range Plans
LRPG	Long-Range Proving Ground
LRPGD	Long-Range Proving Ground Division (Air Force)
LRRP	Long-Range Reconnaissance Patrol (Army)
LRR	Long-Range RADAR
LRI	Long-Range RADAR Input
LRR	Long-Range Requirements (Navy)
LRS	Long-Range Search
LRSM	Long-Range Seismic Measurement
LORS	Long-Range SONAR
LORSU	Long-Range Special Unit (Military)
LRSS	Long-Range Survey System (Military)
LORTAN	Long-Range & Tactical Navigation System
LRTM	Long-Range Training Mission (Military)
LRWE	Long-Range Weapons Establishment (Australia)
LRS	Long Right Shift
LRT	Long Ring Timer
L	Long, Rolling Sea (Weather charts)
LRAC	Long-Run Average Costs
LRDE	Long-Run Deal Effect (Marketing)
LRPE	Long-Run Price Effect (Marketing)
LS	Long Shot (A photograph or motion picture sequence taken from a distance)
LTD	Long Tank Delta
LTTAT	Long Tank Thrust Augmented Thor
LTA	Long-Term Arrangements (Department of State)
LTD	Long Term Disability (Military)
LT/FM	Long Term/Frequency Modulation
LTHA	Long Term Heat Aging
LTM	Long Term Memory
LTS	Long Term Stability
LTTR	Long Term Tape Recorder
LTV	Long Term Vibration
LT	Long Ton (2240 pounds)
LTON	Long Ton
LOTON	Long Tons Discharged or Loaded
LTV	Long Tube Vertical
LVL	Long Vertical Left
LVR	Long Vertical Right
LW	Long Wave (Radio)
LWIR	Long Wavelength Infrared
LWII	Long Wavelength Infrared Illuminator
LWB	Long Wheelbase
LWA	Long Wire Antenna
LGW	Longines-Wittnauer Watch Company (NYSE symbol)
L	Longitude
LIR	Longitude Independent Reset
LAC	Longitudinal Aerodynamic Characteristics
LAS	Longitudinal Air Spring
LCA	Longitudinal Chromatic Aberration
LCGF	Longitudinal Ciliated Groove of Filament
LEPW	Longitudinal Electric Pressure Wave
LEJ	Longitudinal Expansion Joint (Technical drawings)
LM	Longitudinal Muscle (Anatomy)
LMP	Longitudinal Muscles of Pinnule
LCB	Longitudinal Position of Center of Buoyancy
LCF	Longitudinal Position of Center of Flotation
LCG	Longitudinal Position of Center of Gravity
LPW	Longitudinal Pressure Wave
LRC	Longitudinal Redundancy Check
LRBF	Longitudinal Ridge of Basal Fold
LRDL	Longitudinal Ridge of Dorsal Lip
LRLL	Longitudinal Ridge of Lateral Lip
LS	Longitudinal Section
LSA	Longitudinal Spherical Aberration
LSS	Longitudinal Static Stability
LTC	Longitudinal Time Constant
LVST	Longitudinal Velocity Sorting Tube
LWUI	Longshoremen's and Warehousemen's Union International
LPN	Longview, Portland & Northern Railway Company (AAR code)
LHOB	Longworth House Office Building
LMAFS	Lookout Mountain Air Force Station
LWD	Loomis-Woods Diagram
LES	Loop Error Signal
LEA	Loop Extension Amplifier
LFS	Loop Feedback Signal
LG	Loop Gain
LIS	Loop Input Signal
LI	Loop of Intestine
LPR	Looper Position Regulator
LL	Loose Leaf
LLBBMA	Loose Leaf and Blank Book Manufacturers Association
LSR	Loose Snow on Runway (Aviation)
LAWV	Lorain & West Virginia Railway Company (AAR code)
LOR	Loral Corporation (NYSE symbol)
LINS	LORAN Inertial System
LIEP	LORAN Integrated Engineering Program
LIEPS	LORAN Integrated Engineering Program, Shed Light

LORMONSTA...LORAN Monitor Station
LOTS .... LORAN Operational Training School
LORSTA ..... LORAN Transmitting Station
L .... Lord
LC .... Lord Chamberlain (British)
LC .... Lord Chancellor (British)
LCB .... Lord Chief Baron (British)
LCJ .... Lord Chief Justice (of England)
LOC .... Lord of Creation
LHA .... Lord High Admiral (British)
LHC .... Lord High Chancellor (British)
LHT .... Lord High Treasurer (British)
LJ .... Lord Justice
LJA .... Lord Justice of Appeal
LL .... Lord Lieutenant
LLI .... Lord-Lieutenant of Ireland
LM .... Lord Mayor
LPS .... Lord Privy Seal (British)
LP .... Lord Provost (British)
LDA .... Lord's Day Alliance of the United States
LQ .... Lordosis Quotients
LJJ .... Lords Justices
LLJJ .... Lords Justices
LDP .... Lorentz Doppler Profile (Electronics)
LDR .... Lorentz Double Refraction
L .... Lorentz Unit
LHC .... Loretto Heights College (Colorado)
LJC .... Loretto Junior College (Kentucky)
LL .... Lorillard (P.) Company (NYSE symbol)
LASL .... Los Alamos (New Mexico) Scientific Laboratory
LAA .... Los Alamos Area Office (AEC)
LAMPF ...... Los Alamos Meson Physics Faculty
LAMPRE ..... Los Alamos Molten Plutonium Reactor Experiment (AEC)
LAPRE ...... Los Alamos Power Reactor Experiment
LA .... Los Alamos Scientific Laboratory (AEC)
LA .... Los Angeles (California) (Slang)
LAX .... Los Angeles (California) (International airport symbol)
LAADS ...... Los Angeles Air Defense Sector (ADC)
LAAFS ...... Los Angeles Air Force Station
LAAPD ...... Los Angeles Air Procurement District
LAPD .... Los Angeles Air Procurement District
LAAS .... Los Angeles Air Service, Incorporated
LAA .... Los Angeles Airways
LX .... Los Angeles Airways, Inc.
LAB .... Los Angeles Branch (AEC)
LACC .... Los Angeles City College
LAC .... Los Angeles College
LACO .... Los Angeles College of Optometry
LACS .... Los Angeles Copyright Society
LACES ...... Los Angeles Council for Engineering Societies
LACM .... Los Angeles County Museum
LACSD ...... Los Angeles County Sanitation District
LAEC .... Los Angeles Electronic Club
LAFO .... Los Angeles Foundation of Otology
LAGE .... Los Angeles Grain Exchange
LAJ .... Los Angeles Junction Railway Company (AAR code)
LAPC .... Los Angeles Pacific College
LAPFO ...... Los Angeles Procurement Field Office
L & D ...... Loss and Damage
LEA .... Loss Executives Association
LOFT .... Loss of Flow Test Facility (AEC)
LOFT .... Loss of Fluid Test (Reactor)
LP .... Loss of Pay (Court-martial sentence) (Marine Corps)
LOS .... Loss of Signal
LIW .... Loss in Weight
L .... Lost (RADAR)
L .... Lost (Sports statistics)
LF .... Lost on Foul (Boxing)
LHB .... Lost Heart Beat (An attractive girl) (Slang)
LIR .... Lost Item Replacement
LCL .... Lot-Car Load
LFRD .... Lot Fraction Reliability Deviation (Quality control)
LI .... Lot Indices
LRR .... Lot Rejection Report
LTO .... Lot Time Order
LTFRD ...... Lot Tolerance Fraction Reliability Deviation (Quality control)
LTPO .... Lot Tolerance Percent Defective
LTL .... Lot Truck Load
LC .... Loud and Clear
LCS .... Loudness Contour Selector
LL .... Loudness Level

LS .... Loudspeaker
LAL .... Loudspeaker Acoustical Labyrinth
LAP .... Loudspeaker Acoustical Phase-Inverter
LBF .... Louis Braille Foundation for Blind Musicians
LLK .... Louis Leakey - Korongo (Anthropological skull)
LA .... Louisiana
LA .... Louisiana & Arkansas Railway Company (AAR code)
L & A ..... Louisiana & Arkansas Railway Company
LOE .... Louisiana Eastern R. R. (AAR code)
LLX .... Louisiana Land and Exploration (NYSE symbol)
LMD .... Louisiana Midland Railway Company (AAR code)
LMT .... Louisiana Midland Transport R. R. (AAR code)
LNW .... Louisiana & North West R. R. (AAR code)
LPGA ...... Louisiana Pecan Growers' Association
LPB .... Louisiana & Pine Bluff Railway Company (AAR code)
LPI .... Louisiana Polytechnical Institute
LPTS ...... Louisiana Presbyterian Theological Seminary
LSO .... Louisiana Southern Railway Company (AAR code)
LSU .... Louisiana State University
LSUNO ..... Louisiana State University in New Orleans
LSF .... Louisiana Sugar Exchange
LSPC ...... Louisiana Sweet Potato Commission
LOU .... Louisville Gas & Electric Company (Kentucky) (NYSE symbol)
LMC .... Louisville Municipal College (Kentucky)
L & NRR ... Louisville & Nashville Railroad
LN .... Louisville & Nashville R. R. Company (NYSE symbol, AAR code)
L & N ..... Louisville and Nashville Railroad Company
LNAC ...... Louisville, New Albany & Corydon R. R. (AAR code)
SDF .... Louisville (Kentucky) Standiford Airport (Airport symbol)
LW .... Louisville & Wadley R. R. (AAR code)
LLL .... Love's Labour's Lost (Shakespeare)
LFMER ..... Lovelace Foundation for Medical Education and Research
L .... Low
LOAC ...... Low Accuracy
LARDS ..... Low Accuracy RADAR Data Transmission System
LAS .... Low-Alloy Steel
LA .... Low Altitude
LAADS ..... Low Altitude Air Defense (or Delivery) System
LAA .... Low Altitude Attack
LAB .... Low Altitude Bombing (Military)
LABPIE .... Low Altitude Bombing Position Indicator Equipment
LABS ...... Low Altitude Bombing System (Air Force)
LACAS ..... Low-Altitude Close Air Support (Military)
LACA ...... Low Altitude Control Area
LACR ...... Low Altitude Coverage RADAR
LADS ...... Low Altitude Detection System (Air Force)
LADD ...... Low Altitude Drogue Delivery
LAHS ...... Low-Altitude, High-Speed
LAHIVE .... Low Altitude/High Velocity Experiment
LAI .... Low Altitude Indicator
LAINS ..... Low Altitude Inertial Navigation System (Air Force)
LALLL ..... Low Altitude Low Light Level
LAMP ...... Low Altitude Manned Penetrator
LALO ...... Low Altitude Observation
LAPES ..... Low Altitude Parachute Extraction System (Military)
LAP .... Low Altitude Penetration
LAP .... Low Altitude Performance
LAR .... Low Altitude Release
LARVA ..... Low Altitude Research Vehicular Advancements
LASO ...... Low Altitude Search Option (Search mode of the BOMARC guidance system)
LASRM ..... Low Altitude Short Range Missile
LASP ...... Low Altitude Space Platform
LASV ...... Low-Altitude Supersonic Vehicle (Air Force)
LAVM ...... Low Altitude Vulnerability Model (Aerospace)
LAR .... Low Angle Reentry (Aerospace)
LA .... Low Approach (Aviation)
LAR .... Low Aspect Ratio
LBP .... Low Back Pain
LBT .... Low Bandpass Transformer
LBP .... Low Blood Pressure
LC .... Low Carbon (content, as low carbon steel)
LCG .... Low Cost Generator
LCI .... Low Cost Inertial
LDR .... Low Data Rate (RADAR)
LDRA ...... Low Data Rate Auxiliary
LDRI ...... Low Data Rate Input (RADAR)
LDDS ...... Low-Density Data System
LD .... Low Drag
LDB .... Low Drag Bomb
LDBLC ..... Low Drag Boundary Layer Control (Military)

LD . . . . Low Dutch (Philology)
LE . . . . Low Efficiency
LED . . . . Low-Energy Diffraction
LEED . . . . . . Low-Energy Electron Diffraction
LEGM . . . . . . Low-Energy Gamma Monitor
LEID . . . . Low-Energy Ion Detector
LES . . . . Low-Energy Sputter
LE . . . . Low Explosive (Military)
LFR . . . . Low Flux Reactor
LF . . . . Low Frequency (Electronics)
LOFAR . . . . . . Low-Frequency Acquisition and Ranging
LOFAR . . . . . . Low-Frequency Analysis and Recording
LFB . . . . Low-Frequency Beacon
LFC . . . . Low-Frequency Correction
LFC . . . . Low-Frequency Current
LFD . . . . Low-Frequency Decoy
LFD . . . . Low-Frequency Disturbance
LFG . . . . Low-Frequency Generator
LFI . . . . Low-Frequency Inductor
LFINT . . . . . . Low-Frequency Intersection
LFJ . . . . Low-Frequency Jammer
LF/MF . . . . . . Low Frequency, Medium Frequency
LFM . . . . Low-Frequency Modulation
LFO . . . . Low-Frequency Oscillator
LOM . . . . Low-Frequency Outer Marker
LOFTI . . . . . . Low-Frequency Trans-Ionospheric Satellite
LFV . . . . Low-Frequency Vibration
LG . . . . Low German (Language, etc.)
LGO . . . . Low Gravity Orbit
LGR . . . . Low Greek
LGR . . . . Low Group Receiving Unit
LGT . . . . Low Group Transmitting Unit
LHR . . . . Low Hybrid Resonance
LIT . . . . Low Impedance Transmission
LX . . . . Low Index (Aviation)
LIC . . . . Low Inertia Clutch
LIVCR . . . . . . Low Input Voltage Conversion and Regulation
LIVC . . . . . . Low Input Voltage Converter
LIVR . . . . . . Low Input Voltage Regulation
LI . . . . Low Intensity
LITR . . . . Low Intensity Test Reactor (ORNL)
LIMEA . . . . . . Low Iron Content Monoethanolamine
LL . . . . Low Latin (Language)
LL . . . . Low Level
LLAMA . . . . . . Low-Level Acceleration Measurement Apparatus
LOLEX . . . . . . Low-Level Extraction (Military aviation)
LLL . . . . Low-Level Logic
LPB . . . . Low-Level Penetration Bomb
LLRM . . . . . . Low-Level Radio Modulator
LLL . . . . Low Light Level
LLLTV . . . . . . Low Light-Level Television (Air Force)
LLTV . . . . . . Low Light-Level Television
LLC . . . . Low Liquid Cutoff
LMSG . . . . . . Low Magnetic Saturation Garnet
LMF . . . . Low and Medium Frequency
LFR . . . . Low/Medium Frequency Radio Range
LMP . . . . Low Melting Point
LMC . . . . Low Middling Clause (Business and trade)
LMW . . . . Low Molecular Weight
LONO . . . . . . Low Noise
LNA . . . . Low Noise Antenna
LNC . . . . Low Noise Cable
LNR . . . . Low Noise Receiver
LNTWA . . . . . Low Noise Traveling Wave Amplifier
LO . . . . Low Oblique (Aerospace)
LORV . . . . . . Low Observable Reentry Vehicle
LP . . . . Low Pass (Electronics)
LPF . . . . Low Pass Filter
LPN . . . . Low Pass Network
LPD . . . . Low Performance Drone
LP . . . . Low Point
LP . . . . Low Power (Microscopy)
LOPAR . . . . . . Low-Power Acquisition RADAR
LPF . . . . Low Power Field (Microscopy)
LPTF . . . . . . Low Power Test Facility (AEC)
LFM . . . . Low-Powered Fan Marker
LVOR . . . . . . Low-Powered, Very High Frequency Omnirange
LP . . . . Low Pressure
LPC . . . . Low-Pressure Chamber Technician (Navy)
LP . . . . Low-Pressure Cylinder (Especially, a locomotive cylinder)
LPHB . . . . . . Low-Pressure Heating Boiler

LPOX . . . . . . Low-Pressure Oxygen
LPT . . . . Low-Pressure Test
LPT . . . . Low-Pressure Transducer
LRFG . . . . . . Low Range Force Gauge
LRF . . . . Low Refraction Layer
LRO . . . . Low Resistance Ohmmeter
LRIR . . . . Low Resolution Infrared Radiometer
LSL . . . . Low Sight Lobe
LS . . . . Low Speed
LSD . . . . Low Speed Data
LSP . . . . Low Speed Printer
LT . . . . Low Temperature
LTC . . . . Low Temperature Coefficient
LTC . . . . Low Temperature Cooling
LTOF . . . . . . Low Temperature Optical Facility
LT . . . . Low Tension
LTB . . . . Low Tension Battery
LTE . . . . Low Thrust Engine
LT . . . . Low Torque
LVD . . . . Low Velocity Drop
LVS . . . . Low Velocity Scanning
LVTR . . . . . . Low VHF Transmitter-Receiver
LVZ . . . . Low-Viscosity Zone
LV . . . . Low Voltage
LVB . . . . Low-Voltage Bias
LVC . . . . Low-Voltage Capacitor
LVDC . . . . . . Low-Voltage Direct Current
LVF . . . . Low-Voltage Fast (Electronics)
LVN . . . . Low-Voltage Neon
LVP . . . . Low-Voltage Plate
LVPS . . . . . . Low-Voltage Power Supply
LVP . . . . Low-Voltage Protection (Electronics)
LVR . . . . Low-Voltage Release (Electronics)
LVT . . . . Low-Voltage Tubular
LVRJ . . . . . . Low Volume Ramjet
LVRIS . . . . . . Low Volume Ramjet Inlet System
LW . . . . Low Water (Maps and charts)
LWD . . . . . . Low Water Datum (Data)
LWF & C . . . . . Low Water Full and Change
LWI . . . . Low Water Interval
LWL . . . . Low Water Line
LWM . . . . . . Low Water Mark
LWOST . . . . . . Low Water Ordinary Spring Tides
LWOS . . . . . . Low Water Ordinary Springs
LWQ . . . . . . Low Water Quadrature
LTI . . . . Lowell Technological Institute (Massachusetts)
LTIRF . . . . . . Lowell Technological Institute Research Foundation
LST . . . . Lowenstein (M.) & Sons, Inc. (NYSE symbol)
LAL . . . . Lower Acceptance Level
LAL . . . . Lower Acceptance Limit
LB . . . . Lower Bearing
LBNP . . . . . . Lower Body Negative Pressure (Boots) (Space flight equipment)
LBRF . . . . Lower Branchial Filament
LC . . . . Lower Canada
LC . . . . Lower Case (i.e., small letters) (Typesetting)
LCRA . . . . . . Lower Colorado River Authority
LCJC . . . . . . Lower Columbia Junior College (Washington)
LCL . . . . Lower Control Limit (QCR)
LCM . . . . Lower of Cost or Market
LC . . . . Lower Cylinder
LDC . . . . Lower Dead Center
LD . . . . Lower Deck
LDK . . . . Lower Deck
LEAS . . . . . . Lower Echelon Automatic Switchboard
LEL . . . . Lower Explosive Limit
LFM . . . . Lower Figure of Merit
LH . . . . Lower Half
LHA . . . . Lower Half Assembly
LHW . . . . Lower High Water
LHWI . . . . . . Lower High Water Interval
LH . . . . Lower Hold (Shipping)
LL . . . . Lower Left
LL . . . . Lower Lid (Ophthalmology)
LL . . . . Lower Limb (Lower edge of sun, moon, etc.) (Navigation)
LL . . . . Lower Limen (Psychology)
LL . . . . Lower Limit
LLW . . . . Lower Low Water
LLWI . . . . . . Lower Low Water Interval
LMVD . . . . . . Lower Mississippi Division (Army Engineers)
LM . . . . Lower Motor (Neurology)
LOT . . . . Lower Outer Tube

LP . . . . Lower Peninsula (Michigan)
LRM . . . . Lower Reject Limit Median
LR . . . . Lower Right
LSB . . . . Lower Sideband
LS . . . . Lower Structure
LTP . . . . Lower Trip Point
LCM . . . . Lowest Common Multiple
LDA . . . . Lowest Designated Assembly
LEP . . . . Lowest Effective Power
LMR . . . . Lowest Maximum Range
LOF . . . . Lowest Observed Frequency
LQ . . . . Lowest Quadrile
LRRP . . . . Lowest Required Radiated Power
LOEAT . . . . . Lowest Temperature Exceeded for All Time (Meteorology)
LOESE . . . . . Lowest Temperature Exceeded So Early (Meteorology)
LOXSL . . . . . Lowest Temperature Exceeded So Late (Meteorology)
LOEFM . . . . Lowest Temperature Exceeded for the Month (Meteorology)
LUF . . . . Lowest Usable (or Useful) Frequency (Radio)
LUHF . . . . . . Lowest Usable (or Useful) High-Frequency (Radio)
LTTC . . . . . . Lowry Technical Training Center
LBR . . . . Lowville & Beaver River R. R. (AAR code)
LCBA . . . . . . Loyal Christian Benefit Association (Formerly, Ladies' Catholic Benevolent Association)
LKRT . . . . . . Loyal Knights of the Round Table
LOIUSA . . . . . Loyal Orange Institution of United States of America
LOLI . . . . . . Loyal Orange Ladies Institution
LOB . . . . Loyal Order of the Boar
LOM . . . . . . Loyal Order of Moose
LOOM . . . . . Loyal Order of Moose
LRB . . . . Loyalty Review Board (Civil Service Commission) (Abolished, 1953)
LULA . . . . . . Loyola University of Los Angeles
LO . . . . Lubricating Oil
LO . . . . Lubrication Order
LLDB . . . . . . Luc-Luong Dac-Biet (Vietnamese Special Forces)
LS/MFT . . . . . Lucky Strike Means Fine Tobacco (Advertising slogan)
LUN . . . . Ludington & Northern Railway (AAR code)
LH . . . . Lues Hereditaria (Medicine)
LT . . . . Lug Terminal
LLGMA . . . . . Luggage and Leather Goods Manufacturers of America
LLG . . . . Luggage and Leather Goods Salesmen's Association of America
LUC . . . . Lukens Steel Company (NYSE symbol)
LP . . . . Lumbar Puncture
LDRC . . . . . . Lumber Dealers Research Council
LWNA . . . . . . Lumber (Timber), Winter, North Atlantic (Vessel load line mark)
L-S . . . . Lumbo-Sacral
L . . . . Lumen (Unit of light)
LM . . . . Lumen
LUH . . . . Lumen Hour
LPW . . . . Lumens Per Watt
LBC . . . . Lummer-Brodhun Cube
LGP . . . . Lummer-Gehrcke Plate
LS . . . . Lump Sum
LSLP . . . . . . Lump Sum Leave Payment (Air Force)
LSPAFRO . . . . Lump Sum Payment to Air Force Reserve Officers
LCD . . . . Lumped Constant Dispersion
LEC . . . . Lumped Element Circulator
LLPN . . . . . . Lumped, Linear, Parametric Network
LSAM . . . . . . Lumped Shell Analysis Method
LAC . . . . Lunar Aeronautical Chart (Air Force)
LAMP . . . . . . Lunar Analysis and Mapping Program
LIMP . . . . . . Lunar-Anchored Interplanetary Monitoring Platform (Aerospace)
LASS . . . . . . Lunar Applications of a Spent Stage (Aerospace)
LASSO . . . . . Lunar Applications of a Spent Stage in Orbit (Aerospace)
LAC . . . . Lunar Astronautical
LAD . . . . Lunar Atmosphere Detector
LAS . . . . Lunar Attitude System
LUCOM . . . . . Lunar Communication (System)
LDSS . . . . . . Lunar Deep Seismic Sounding (Aerospace)
LDMS . . . . . . Lunar Distance Measuring System
LDS . . . . Lunar Drill System
LET . . . . Lunar Energy Transfer
LE . . . . Lunar Ephemeris
LEZ . . . . Lunar Equatorial Zone (Army Map Service)
LEC . . . . Lunar Equipment Conveyor (Aerospace)
LEAP . . . . . . Lunar Escape Ambulance Pack
LEM . . . . Lunar Excursion Module (Also, LM) (NASA)
LMS . . . . LEM (Lunar Excursion Module) Mission Simulator
LTA . . . . LEM (Lunar Excursion Module) Test Articles
LEV . . . . Lunar Excursion Vehicle
LETS . . . . . . Lunar Experiment Telemetry System
LESA . . . . . . Lunar Exploration System for Apollo

LESA . . . . . . Lunar Extended Stay, Apollo (NASA)
LEVA . . . . . . Lunar Extravehicular Visor Assembly (Aerospace)
LFC . . . . Lunar Farside Chart (Air Force)
LFU . . . . Lunar Flying Unit (NASA)
LFV . . . . Lunar Flying Vehicle (NASA)
LGC . . . . Lunar Gas Chromatograph
LGE . . . . Lunar Geological Equipment (NASA)
LGS . . . . Lunar Geophysical Surface
LGS . . . . Lunar Gravity Simulator
LHT . . . . Lunar Hand Tool (NASA)
LHS . . . . Lunar Horizon Sensor (Aerospace)
LIP . . . . Lunar Impact Probe
LIL . . . . Lunar International Laboratory
LIV . . . . Lunar and Interplanetary Vehicle
LLP . . . . Lunar Landing Program
LLRF . . . . . . Lunar Landing Research Facility
LLRV . . . . . . Lunar Landing Research Vehicle
LLTV . . . . . . Lunar Landing Training Vehicle
LLV . . . . Lunar Landing Vehicle (NASA)
LLRF . . . . . . Lunar LASER Range Finder
LULS . . . . . . Lunar Logistic System
LLS . . . . Lunar Logistics System (OMSF)
LLSV . . . . . . Lunar Logistics System Vehicle (OMSF)
LLV . . . . Lunar Logistics Vehicle (NASA)
LUMAS . . . . . Lunar Mapping System
LMS . . . . Lunar Measuring System
LMA . . . . Lunar Meteoroid Analyzer
LMD . . . . Lunar Meteoroid Detector (NASA)
LMDA . . . . . . Lunar Meteoroid Detector-Analyzer (NASA)
LM . . . . Lunar Module (Also, LEM) (NASA)
LMDE . . . . . . Lunar Module Descent Engine (NASA)
LGC . . . . Lunar Module Guidance Computer (NASA)
LMP . . . . Lunar Module Pilot (Apollo) (NASA)
LORS . . . . . . Lunar Optical Rendezvous System
LOI . . . . Lunar Orbit Insertion (Aerospace)
LOLA . . . . . . Lunar Orbit and Landing Approach (Simulator)
LOM . . . . . . Lunar Orbital Map (Air Force)
LOR . . . . Lunar Orbital Rendezvous (NASA)
LO . . . . Lunar Orbiter (Aerospace)
LODCS . . . . . Lunar Orbiter Data Conversion System
LODP . . . . . . Lunar Orbiter Data Printer
LOPP . . . . . . Lunar Orbiter Photographic Project
LOPS . . . . . . Lunar Orbiting Photographic System
LORS . . . . . . Lunar Orbiting Reconnaissance System
LOS . . . . Lunar Orbiting Satellite
LPM . . . . Lunar Payload Module (Aerospace)
LPS . . . . Lunar Penetrometer System
LPS . . . . Lunar Pilotage System
LPP . . . . Lunar Precepts Positioner
LPL . . . . Lunar Projects Laboratory
LRL . . . . Lunar Receiving Laboratory (NASA)
LRM . . . . Lunar Reconnaissance Mission
LRM . . . . Lunar Reconnaissance Module
LRV . . . . Lunar Rover (or Roving) Vehicle (NASA)
LSAPT . . . . . Lunar Sample Analysis Planning Team (NASA)
LSPET . . . . . Lunar Sample Preliminary Examination Team (NASA)
LSSM . . . . . . Lunar Scientific Survey Module (NASA)
LSP . . . . Lunar Spectral Photometrics
LSE . . . . Lunar Support Equipment
LSD . . . . Lunar Surface Drill
LSE . . . . Lunar Surface Experiment
LSEP . . . . . . Lunar Surface Experiment Package (NASA)
LSEV . . . . . . Lunar Surface Exploration Vehicle
LUSI . . . . . . Lunar Surface Inspection
LSI . . . . Lunar Surface Instrument
LSP . . . . Lunar Surface Probe
LSRV . . . . . . Lunar Surface Roving Vehicle
LSSD . . . . . . Lunar Surface Sampling Device
LST . . . . Lunar Surface Transponder
LSV . . . . Lunar Surface Vehicle
LSVC . . . . . . Lunar Surface Vehicle Communications
LSV . . . . Lunar Survey Viewfinder
LSS . . . . Lunar Surveying System
LSSP . . . . . . Lunar Surveying System Program
LTMS . . . . . . Lunar Terrain Measuring System
LTT . . . . Lunar Test Table
LUVO . . . . . . Lunar Ultraviolet Observatory (NASA)
LLC . . . . Luneberg Lens Commutator
LLRC . . . . . . Luneberg Lens Rapid Commutator
LRC . . . . Luneberg Rapid Commutator
LCR . . . . Lung Configuration Recorder

LRC . . . . Lung Rate Counter
LTSPC . . . . . . L'Union Territoriale des Syndicats Professionelles Caledoniens (Territorial Federation of New Caledonian Unions of Private Employees)
LKAB . . . . Luossavaara-Kiirunavaara Aktiebolag
LE . . . . Lupus Erythematosus
LH . . . . Luteinizing Hormone (Endocrinology)
LTH . . . . Luteotrophic Hormone (Endocrinology)
Lu . . . . Lutetium
LLA . . . . Luther League of America
LAS . . . . Lutheran Academy for Scholarship
LBA . . . . Lutheran Benevolent Association
LBEA . . . . . . Lutheran Braille Evangelism Association
LCAF . . . . . . Lutheran Church in America Foundation
LCMA . . . . . . Lutheran Church Men of America
LCW . . . . Lutheran Church Women
LCA . . . . Lutheran Collegiate Association
LDA . . . . Lutheran Deaconess Association
LEA . . . . Lutheran Education Association
LFD . . . . Lutheran Foundation for Religious Drama
LFA . . . . Lutheran Fraternities of America
LHC . . . . Lutheran Historical Conference
LH & HS . . . . Lutheran Hospitals and Homes Society
LHRAA . . . . . . Lutheran Human Relations Association of America
LIS . . . . Lutheran Immigration Service
LLL . . . . Lutheran Laymen's League

LMMA . . . . . . Lutheran Medical Mission Association
LMS . . . . Lutheran Mission Societies
LPF . . . . Lutheran Peace Fellowship
LSWMA . . . . . Lutheran Society for Worship, Music and the Arts
LWML . . . . Lutheran Women's Missionary League
LWF . . . . Lutheran World Federation
LWR . . . . Lutheran World Relief, Inc.
LU . . . . Luxembourg (NATO)
LBA . . . . Luxembourg Brotherhood of America
LPSC . . . . Luxembourg Philatelic Study Club
LYK . . . . Lykes Brothers Steamship Company, Inc. (NYSE symbol)
LLP . . . . Lyman Laboratory of Physics (Harvard)
LN . . . . Lymph Node
LCM . . . . Lymphocytic Choriomeningitis (Pathology)
LGV . . . . Lymphogranuloma Venereum (Medicine)
LGL . . . . Lynch Corporation (NYSE symbol)
LPR . . . . Lynchburg Pool Reactor
LSR . . . . Lynchburg Source Reactor
LBJ . . . . Lyndon Baines Johnson
LEO . . . . Lyon's Electronic Office
LTJC . . . . Lyons Township Junior College (Illinois)
LAP . . . . Lyophilized Anterior Pituitary (Endocrinology)
LSM . . . . Lysergic Acid Morpholide
LSD 25 . . . . . . Lysergsaeure Diethyamid (Lysergic Acid Diethylamine Tartrate) (Hallucinogenic drug)

M

MDFMR . . . . . M-Day Force Materiel Requirement
MDMR . . . . . . M-Day Mobilization Requirement
MAF. . . . . MacAndrews & Forbes Company (NYSE symbol)
MACNIMAATZ . . . MacArthur, Nimitz, and Spaatz (Nickname for tripartite
                command in the Pacific of General of the Army Douglas MacArthur,
                Fleet Admiral Chester W. Nimitz, and Strategic Air Commander
                General Carl A. Spaatz) (World War II)
MFTU . . . . . . Macau Federation of Trade Unions
MTUC. . . . . . Macau Trade Union Council
MPO . . . . Macedonian Patriotic Organization of US and Canada
M . . . . Mach Number
MA . . . . Machine Accountant
MAC . . . . . . Machine-Aided Cognition (Computer project) (DOD)
MACE . . . . . Machine Aided Composition and Editing
MAIDS . . . . . Machine-Aided Information and Dissemination Systems
MAMI . . . . . Machine-Aided Manufacturing Information (Data processing)
MAPED . . . . Machine-Aided Program for Preparation of Electrical Programs
MAPID . . . . Machine-Aided Program for Preparation of Instruction Data
MAD . . . . . . Machine Analysis Display
MATICO . . . . Machine Applications to Technical Information Center Operations
MAPS . . . . . Machine Automated Parts System
MARS . . . . . Machine Automated Realty Service
MAGIC . . . . Machine for Automatic Graphics Interface to a Computer
MCMA . . . . . Machine Chain Manufacturers Association
MF . . . . Machine Finish (Paper)
MG . . . . Machine-Glazed
MACHGR . . . . Machine Group
MG . . . . Machine Gun
MGC . . . . . . Machine-Gun Company or Machine-Gun Corps
MKA . . . . . . Machine Knife Association
ML . . . . Machine Language (Data processing)
MLP . . . . . . Machine Language Program
MO . . . . Machine Operation
MOL . . . . . . Machine Oriented Language (Data processing)
MPBA . . . . . Machine Printers' Beneficial Association of the United States
MPEA . . . . . Machine Printers and Engravers Association of the United States
MARC . . . . . Machine-Readable Catalog (Library of Congress)
MR . . . . Machine Records
MRA . . . . . . Machine Records Activity
MRI . . . . . . Machine Records Installation (Military)
MRU . . . . . . Machine Records Unit
MARCO . . . . Machine Referenced and Coordinated Outline
MR . . . . Machine Rifle
MS. . . . . Machine Screw
MS . . . . Machine Steel
MTBA . . . . . Machine Tool Builders' Association
MTS . . . . . . Machine-Tractor Stations
MT . . . . Machine Translation (Data processing)
MU . . . . Machine Unit
MAPI . . . . . . Machinery and Allied Products Institute
MC . . . . Machinery Certificate (Shipping)
MDNA . . . . . Machinery Dealers' National Association
MMEC . . . . . Machinery-Metals Export Club
M & O . . . . . Machinery and Optics
MR . . . . Machinery Repairman (Military)
MARS . . . . . Machinery Retrieval System
MS. . . . . Machinery Survey (Shipping)
MM . . . . . . Machinist's Mate
MMCBE. . . . . Machinist's Mate, Construction Battalion, Equipment Operator
MME . . . . . . Machinist's Mate, Engineman (Navy rating)
MMG . . . . . . Machinist's Mate, Industrial Gas Generating Mechanic (Navy rating)
MMR . . . . . . Machinist's Mate, Refrigeration (Navy rating)
MMSR. . . . . . Machinist's Mate, Ship Repair (Navy rating)

MMSRE . . . . . Machinist's Mate, Ship Repair, Engine Operator (Navy rating)
MMSRS . . . . . Machinist's Mate, Ship Repair, Inside Machinist (Navy rating)
MMSRI . . . . . Machinist's Mate, Ship Repair, Instrument Maker (Navy rating)
MMSRO . . . . . Machinist's Mate, Ship Repair, Outside Machinist (Navy rating)
MMS . . . . . . Machinist's Mate, Shop Mechanic (Navy rating)
MVA . . . . . . Machinists Vise Association
MQ . . . . Mack Trucks, Inc. (NYSE symbol)
MRTC . . . . . . Mackay Radio and Telegraph Company
MK . . . . Mackey Airlines, Inc.
MCTR . . . . . . Mackinac Transportation Company (AAR code)
MICA . . . . . . Macro Instruction Compiler Assembler (Data processing)
MMA . . . . . . MacRobertson-Miller Airlines, Ltd.
MADDAM . . . . Macromodule and Digital Differential Analyzer Machine
MOBL . . . . . . Macro-Oriented Business Language
MR . . . . Macrophage Rich
MAV . . . . . . Macrosiphum Avenae Virus
MZ . . . . Macy (R. H.) & Company, Inc. (NYSE symbol)
MOMA . . . . . Madagasikara Otronin'ny Malagasy (Madagascar Led by Malagasy)
                (Formerly MONIMA)
MBK . . . . . . Madchen-Bibel-Kreise (Bible Reading Circles) (Germany)
MM . . . . Made Merchantable
MDCK . . . . . . Madin-Darby Canine Kidney
MAD . . . . . . Madison Fund, Inc. (NYSE symbol)
MSG . . . . . . Madison Square Garden Corporation (NYSE symbol)
MIPI . . . . . . Madjelis Ilmu Pengetahuan Indonesia (Council for Sciences of Indonesia)
MPRS . . . . . . Madjelis Permusjawaratan Rakjat Sementara
MCS . . . . . . Madras Civil Service (British)
MI . . . . Madras Infantry (British)
MKOWU . . . . . Madras Kerosene Oil Workers' Union (India)
MNI . . . . . . Madras Native Infantry (British)
MSC . . . . . . Madras Staff Corps (British)
MM . . . . Maelzel's Metronome (Music)
MAB. . . . . . . Magazine Advertising Bureau (of MPA)
MASC . . . . . . Magazine Advertising Sales Club
MF & S . . . . . Magazine Flooding and Sprinkling
MPG . . . . . . Magazine Promotion Group
MPA. . . . . . . Magazine Publishers Association
MSA . . . . . . Magazine Shippers Association
MF. . . . . Magazines for Friendship
MAP. . . . . . . Maghreb-Arabe Presse (Maghreb Arab Press Agency)
MDA . . . . . . Magic Dealers Association
MAI . . . . . . Magister in Arte Ingeniaria (Master of Engineering Art)
MC . . . . Magister Chirurgiae (Master of Surgery)
M Ch . . . . . . Magister Chirurgiae (Master of Surgery)
M . . . . Magistrate
MA. . . . . Magma Arizona R. R. (AAR code)
MMX . . . . . . Magma Copper Company (NYSE symbol)
MCD . . . . . . Magna Carta Dames, National Society
M . . . . Magnaflux
MGL . . . . . . Magnanimous Green Leprechaun
MAG . . . . . . Magnavox Company (NYSE symbol) (Wall Street slang name: "Maggie")
MEDIA . . . . . Magnavox Electronic Data Image Apparatus
Mg . . . . Magnesium (Chemical element)
MAALOX . . . . Magnesium-Aluminum Hydroxide (Commercial antacid)
MA . . . . Magnesium Association
MgO . . . . . . Magnesium Oxide
MgPe . . . . . . Magnesium Pemoline
M . . . . Magnetic
MAD . . . . . . Magnetic Airborne Detector (Navy)
MARS . . . . . Magnetic Airborne Recording System
MAGAMP . . . . Magnetic Amplifier
MAGTRAC . . . Magnetic Amplifier, Transistorized, Automatic Target Tracker
MAST . . . . . . Magnetic Annular Shock Tube

MAD. . . . . Magnetic Anomaly Detection
MB. . . . . Magnetic Bearing (Navigation)
MCD . . . . . . Magnetic Circular Dichroism
MC . . . . Magnetic Core
MCM . . . . . . Magnetic Core Memory (Data processing)
MC . . . . Magnetic Course (Navigation)
MADE . . . . . . Magnetic Device Evaluator (Data processing)
MDI . . . . Magnetic Direction Indicator
MD . . . . Magnetic Drum
MADDIDA . . . Magnetic Drum Digital Differential Analyzer
MADRE . . . . . . Magnetic Drum Receiving Equipment
MFTRS . . . . . . Magnetic Flight Test Recording System
MFU . . . . Magnetic Force Upset (Metals)
MFD . . . . Magnetic Frequency Detector
MH . . . . Magnetic Heading
MIPE . . . . Magnetic Induction Plasma Engine
MICR . . . . . . Magnetic Ink Character Recognition (or Reader) (Data processing technique used for automatic sorting of bank checks and in other applications)
MIX . . . . Magnetic Ionization Experiment
MLI . . . . Magnetic Level Indicator
MAGLOC . . . . Magnetic Logic Computer
MAGMOD . . . Magnetic Modulator
MN . . . . Magnetic North
MOC . . . . . . Magnetic Optic Converter
MPI . . . . Magnetic Particle Inspection
MPCA . . . . . . Magnetic Powder Core Association
MRB . . . . . . Magnetic Recording Borescope
MRIA . . . . . . Magnetic Recording Industry Association
MRC . . . . . . Magnetic Research Corporation
S . . . . Magnetic Solar Daily Variation
MS . . . . Magnetic Storage
MT . . . . Magnetic Tape
MTCU . . . . . Magnetic Tape Control Unit
MFC . . . . Magnetic-Tape Field Scan
MTH . . . . . . Magnetic Tape Handler
MT/MF . . . . . Magnetic Tape to Microfilm
MTR . . . . . . Magnetic Tape Recorder
MTRE . . . . . Magnetic Tape Recorder End
MTRS . . . . . Magnetic Tape Recorder Start
MTSC . . . . . . Magnetic Tape Selectric Composer
MT/ST . . . . . Magnetic Tape "Selectric" Typewriter (IBM)
MTS . . . . . . Magnetic Tape System
MTT . . . . . . Magnetic Tape Terminal
MTU . . . . . . Magnetic Tape Unit
MT . . . . Magnetic Tube
MVS . . . . . . Magnetic Voltage Stabilizer
MGD . . . . . . Magnetogasdynamic
ML . . . . Magnetogasdynamics Laboratory (MIT)
MHD . . . . . . Magnetohydrodynamic (Generator) (Electric power)
MMF . . . . . . Magnetomotive Force
MPD . . . . . . Magnetoplasmadynamic
M/S . . . . Magnetostruction
MBS . . . . . . Magnetron Beam Switching
MAV . . . . . . Magyar Allamvasutak
MDP . . . . . . Magyar Dolgozok Partja
MNOT . . . . . Magyar Nok Orszagos (National Council of Hungarian Women)
MSK . . . . . . Magyar Statisztikai Kozlemenyek (Hungary)
MEP . . . . . . Mahajana Eksath Peramuna Party (Ceylon)
MA . . . . Mahogany Association
M . . . . Maiden
MA . . . . Maids of Athens (An organization)
M . . . . Mail
MASA . . . . . . Mail Advertising Service Association International
MASAI . . . . . Mail Advertising Service Association International
MDS . . . . . . Mail Distribution Schedule (Air Force)
MDS. . . . . . . Mail Distribution Scheme (Army)
MO . . . . Mail Order (Business and trade)
MOAA . . . . . Mail Order Association of America
MOD . . . . . . Mail-Order Department
M/P . . . . Mail Payment (Banking)
MS . . . . Mail Steamer
MT . . . . Mail Transfer
MWBAS . . . . Mail Will Be Addressed to Show
MAO . . . . . . Mailing Address Only (Military)
M . . . . Main (Hand)
MADP. . . . . . Main Air Display Plot
MBS . . . . . . Main "Bang" Suppressor
MB . . . . Main Battery (Guns)
MBT . . . . . . Main Battle Tank (Army)
MBC . . . . . . Main Beam Clutter
MCO . . . . . . Main Civilian Occupation

MC . . . . Main Cock
MCC . . . . . . Main Communications Center
MDC . . . . . . Main Display Console
MDF. . . . . . . Main Distributing Frame
MDS. . . . . . . Main Dressing Station
MD . . . . Main Droite or Mano Destra (Right Hand)
MECO . . . . . Main Engine Cut-Off (Aerospace)
MF . . . . Main Feed (Technical drawings)
MLG . . . . . . Main Landing Gear
MLR . . . . . . Main Line of Resistance
MMNIC . . . . . Main Mediterranean Naval Intelligence Center (Navy)
MM . . . . Main Memory
MMO . . . . . . Main Meteorological Office
MOI . . . . . . Main d'Oeuvre Indigene (Indigenous Manpower) (Congo – Leopoldville)
MOB . . . . . . Main Operating Base
MSR . . . . . . Main Supply Road (or Route)
MSB . . . . . . Main Support Base (Air Force)
MS . . . . Main Switch
ME . . . . Maine
MEC . . . . . . Maine Central Railroad Company
MLFA . . . . . . Maine Lobster Fishermen's Association
MLA . . . . . . Maine Lobstermen's Association
MSC . . . . . . Maine Sardine Council
MSPA . . . . . . Maine Sardine Packers Association
MWLDA . . . . Maine Wholesale Lobster Dealers Association
MP . . . . Mains Propres (Personal Delivery)
MFL. . . . . . . Maintain Flight Level (Aviation)
MAL . . . . . . Maintain at Least (followed by altitude) (Aviation)
MPVA . . . . . Maintain a Position VFR (Visual Flight Rules) and Advise (Aviation)
MAPROS . . . . . Maintain Production Schedules
MRHV . . . . . Maintain Runway Heading for Vector (Aviation)
MVFR . . . . . Maintain Visual Flight Rules (Aviation)
MVSP . . . . . . Maintain Visual Separation (Aviation)
MDA . . . . . . Maintainability Design Approach
MAF . . . . . . Maintenance Action Form
MAR . . . . . . Maintenance Action Report
MAC . . . . . . Maintenance Advisory Committee (NSIA)
MAN . . . . . . Maintenance Alert Network (RCA)
MAC . . . . . . Maintenance Allocation Chart
MAPS . . . . . Maintenance Analysis and Procedures System (Data processing)
MART . . . . . Maintenance Analysis Review Technique
MAJAC . . . . . Maintenance Anti-Jam Console (Air Force)
MAD . . . . . . Maintenance, Assembly, and Disassembly
MAID . . . . . . Maintenance Automatic Integration Director (Data processing)
MBY & D . . . . Maintenance, Bureau of Yards and Docks (Budget category) (Navy) (Obsolete; see FEC)
MCK . . . . . . Maintenance Check
MCC . . . . . . Maintenance of Close Contact
MACMIS . . . . Maintenance and Construction Management Information System (Data processing)
MCC . . . . . . Maintenance Control Center (Military)
MCN . . . . . . Maintenance Control Number
MCR . . . . . . Maintenance Control Report
MCS. . . . . . . Maintenance Control Section (DCE)
MDC . . . . . . Maintenance Data Collection (Military)
MDCS . . . . . Maintenance Data Collection System
MDS . . . . . . Maintenance Data System
MDA . . . . . . Maintenance Depot Assistance (Air Force)
MDS . . . . . . Maintenance Documentation System (Bell System)
MES. . . . . . . Maintenance Electrolyte Solution (Physiology)
MEA . . . . . . Maintenance Engineering Analysis
MEAB . . . . . Maintenance Engineering Analysis Board
MEADS . . . . . Maintenance Engineering Analysis Data System
MEAR. . . . . . Maintenance Engineering Analysis Record (Navy)
MEARS . . . . . Maintenance Engineering Analysis Records
MECR . . . . . Maintenance Engineering Change Request
MENEX . . . . . Maintenance Engineering Exchange
MF . . . . Maintenance Factor
MGE . . . . . . Maintenance Ground Equipment
MIP . . . . Maintenance Index Page
MMIS . . . . . . Maintenance Management Information System (Military)
MM . . . . Maintenance Manual
3M . . . . Maintenance and Material Management (Navy)
MMM . . . . . Maintenance and Material Management (Navy)
MMMIS . . . . . Maintenance & Material Management Information System
MMMPC . . . . Maintenance and Material Management Project Center (Navy)
M of M . . . . . Maintenance of Membership (Labor unions)
M & O . . . . . Maintenance and Operations
MOC . . . . . . Maintenance Operations Center (Military)
MPL . . . . . . Maintenance Parts Lists
MP . . . . Maintenance Point

REVERSE ACRONYMS AND INITIALISMS DICTIONARY

MRPF . . . . Maintenance of Real Property Facilities
M & RDET . . . Maintenance and Repair Detachment
MRO . . . . Maintenance, Repair, and Operation
M & R . . . . Maintenance and Repairs
MRR . . . . Maintenance, Repairs and Replacements (Military)
MRC . . . . Maintenance Requirement Card
MS . . . . Maintenance and Service
MANDS . . . . . Maintenance and Supply
M & S . . . . . . Maintenance and Supply
MSL . . . . Maintenance Supply Liaison (Air Force)
MSO . . . . Maintenance Support Office (Navy)
MSS . . . . Maintenance Support Schedule (Air Force)
MTB . . . . Maintenance of True Bearing
MU . . . . Maintenance Unit (Military)
M of W . . . . . Maintenance of Way (Railroading)
MOLB . . . . . . Majestic Circle, Military Order of Lady Bugs of USA
MM . . . . Majesties
M . . . . Majesty
MAF . . . . Major Academic Field
MAC . . . . Major Air Command (Later, MAJCOM)
MAJCON . . . . Major Air Command Controlled (units)
MAR . . . . Major Assembly Release (Military)
MAJCOM . . . Major Command (Military) (Formerly, Major Air Command)
MCOP . . . . . . Major Command Orientation Program (Air Force)
MCOPR . . . . . Major Command of Primary Responsibility (Air Force)
AGMR . . . . . . Major Communication Relay Ship (Navy symbol)
MC . . . . Major Component
MEO . . . . Major Engine Overhaul
MFOI . . . . . . Major Force Oriented Issue (Military)
MFCT . . . . . . Major Fraction Thereof
MFT . . . . Major Fraction Thereof
MG . . . . Major General
M/G . . . . Major General
MGC . . . . Major General Commandant
MGGS . . . . . . Major General, General Staff
MGRA . . . . . . Major-General, Royal Artillery (British)
MIEETAT . . . . Major Improvements in Electronics Through Advanced Technology
MISR . . . . Major Item Status Report
MISMA . . . . . Major Item Supply Management Agency
MIDA . . . . . . Major Items Data Agency (Military)
MLC . . . . Major Landing Craft
MLBPA . . . . . . Major League Baseball Players Association
ML . . . . Major Lobe
MRC . . . . Major Retail Center
MS . . . . Major Subject (Military)
MSMA . . . . . . Major Symphony Managers Association
MWARA . . . . . Major World Air Route Area
M . . . . Make
MACVFR . . . . Make Altitude Changes Visual Flight Rules (Aviation)
MBB . . . . Make-Before-Break
M-B . . . . Make-Break
MDFR . . . . . . Make Descent From (Aviation)
MG . . . . Make Good
MGMT . . . . . Make Good a Magnetic Track Of (followed by degrees) (Aviation)
MGAT . . . . . . Make Good a Track Of (followed by degrees) (Aviation)
MO . . . . Make Offer
MAPS . . . . . . Make-a-Picture Story (Psychological testing)
MAKSUTSUB . . Make Suitable Substitution
MSS . . . . Make Suitable Substitution
MKE . . . . Makina ve Kimya Endustrisi Kurumu (Mechanical and Chemical Industrial Establishment) (Turkey)
MAL . . . . Malariology Technician (Navy)
MDH . . . . Malate Dehydrogenase
MCP . . . . Malawi Congress Party (Nyasaland)
MWL . . . . Malawi Women's League
MAPHILINDO . . Malaya-Philippines-Indonesia
MAL . . . . Malayan Airways, Limited
MCA . . . . Malayan Chinese Association
MCS . . . . Malayan Civil Service
MEWU . . . . . . Malayan Estates Workers' Union
MIC . . . . Malayan Indian Congress
MTSU . . . . . . Malayan Technical Services' Union
MTB . . . . Malayan Tin Bureau
MTUC . . . . . . Malayan Trades Union Congress
MACC . . . . . . Malaysian-American Chamber of Commerce
M . . . . Male
MF . . . . Male to Female (ratio)
M & F . . . . . Male and Female (components, as of connecting devices)
MH . . . . Maleic Hydrazide (Plant-growth retardant)
MADAR . . . . . Malfunction Analysis Detection and Recording (Data processing)
MDS . . . . Malfunction Detection System (Gemini) (NASA)

MIU . . . . Malfunction Insertion Unit
MRP . . . . Malfunction Reporting Program (Navy)
MIHS . . . . . . Malian Institute of Human Sciences
MDP . . . . Malicious Destruction of Property
MAC . . . . Malignancy-Associated Changes (Cancer)
MCI . . . . Malleable Cast Iron
MCMI . . . . . . Malleable Chain Manufacturers Institute
MFS . . . . Malleable Founders' Society
MI . . . . Malleable Iron
MIP . . . . Malleable Iron Pipe
MRDF . . . . . . Malleable Research and Development Foundation
MCW . . . . . . Mallinckrodt Chemical Works
MRY . . . . Mallory (P. R.) & Company, Inc. (NYSE symbol)
MH . . . . Malt House
MRI . . . . Malt Research Institute
MFA . . . . Malta Fencible Artillery (British)
MABS . . . . . . Maltese-American Benevolent Society
MBIA . . . . . . Malting Barley Improvement Association
MTV . . . . Mammary Tumor Virus
M . . . . Mammato
MACA . . . . . . Mammoth Cave National Park
MCMG . . . . . . Man-Carrying Motion Generator (Space-flight simulation)
M/D . . . . Man Day
M/H . . . . Man-Hours
MIMO . . . . . . Man In, Machine Out (Data processing)
MISS . . . . . . Man In Space Soonest
MITS . . . . . . Man-in-the-Sea Program (Navy)
MITS . . . . . . Man In The Street (The average man) (Usually "Mr. Mits")
MMFPA . . . . . Man-Made Fiber Producers Association
MM . . . . Man-Month
M/M . . . . Man-Month
MOPS . . . . . . Man-Operated Propulsion System
MOOSE . . . . . Man (or Manual) Orbital Operations Safety Equipment (Space life-raft) (NASA)
MOOSE . . . . . Man Out of Space Easiest
M/W . . . . Man-Week
MY . . . . Man-Years
M & A . . . . . Management and Administration
MAS . . . . Management Advisory Services
MAD . . . . Management Analysis Division (NASA)
MAR . . . . Management Analysis Report (DOD)
MARS . . . . . . Management Analysis Reporting System (Data processing)
MAP . . . . Management Assistance for Profits
MCSL . . . . . . Management Control Systems List (DOD)
MDL . . . . Management Data List
MDSC . . . . . . Management Data Service Center
MD . . . . Management Directive
MEP . . . . Management Engineering Program (Air Force)
MET . . . . Management Engineering Team (Air Force)
MICR . . . . . . Management Improvement and Cost Reduction Project Reporting System
MIP . . . . Management Improvement Program (Air Force)
MIP . . . . Management Incentive Program
MIC . . . . Management Information Center
MIDAC . . . . . . Management Information for Decision-Making and Control (Data processing)
MIO . . . . Management Information Office(r) (Air Force)
MIS . . . . Management Information Service
MIS . . . . Management Information Specialist
MISI . . . . . . Management Information System Directorate
MISP . . . . . . Management Information System Plan
MIS . . . . Management Information Systems
MI . . . . Management Intern
MISTR . . . . . . Management of Items Subject to Repair (Air Force)
MLPC . . . . . . Management-Labor Policy Committee
MODE . . . . . . Management of Objectives with Dollars through Employees (Department of Agriculture)
MO . . . . Management Office
MOO C of S . . Management Office, Office, Chief of Staff
MOLDS . . . . . Management On-Line Data System
MOS . . . . Management Operating System
MPACS . . . . . Management Planning and Control System (IBM)
MPS . . . . Management Policy Statement
MRM . . . . Management Responsibility Matrix
MRO . . . . Management Review Officer
MASIS . . . . . . Management and Scientific Information System
MSDO . . . . . . Management Systems Development Office
MANTRAP . . . Management Training Program (of Center for Research in Business and Economics, University of Houston)
MATRIX . . . . . Management Trial Exercise (Career orientation simulation)
MD . . . . Managing Director
ME . . . . Managing Editor

MANA ..... Manassas National Battlefield Park
MAFA ...... Manchester Academy of Fine Arts
MG .... Manchester Guardian (A newspaper)
MSLR ...... Manchester, Sheffield, and Lincolnshire Railway (British)
MT .... Mandated Territory
MAC ...... Maneuver Area Command (Army)
MDH ...... Maneuver Director Headquarters (Military)
MBRV ..... Maneuverable Ballistic Reentry Vehicle
MRSV ..... Maneuverable Recoverable Space Vehicle
MRV ...... Maneuverable Reentry Vehicle (Air Force)
MARV ..... Maneuvering Anti-RADAR Vehicle
MANDEC ... Maneuvering Decoy
MEL ...... Maneuvering Element (Military)
MRVLP .... Maneuvering Reentry Vehicle for Low Level Penetration
M .... Maneuvering Ship (In speed triangle of relative movement problems)
MWP ...... Maneuvering Work Platform (NASA)
Mn .... Manganese (Chemical element)
MDDC ..... Manhattan District Declassified Code (AEC)
MED....... Manhattan Engineer District (Developed atomic bomb; dissolved, 1946)
MSH....... Manhattan Shirt Company (NYSE symbol)
MH .... Manhours
MAP....... Manifold Absolute Pressure (Air Force)
MAP ...... Manifold Air Pressure
M .... Manila (Rope)
M .... Manipulus (Handful)
MAR....... Manistee & Repton R. R. (AAR code)
MLS....... Manistique & Lake Superior R. R. (AAR code)
MM .... Manmade (Diamonds)
MARS ..... Manned Aerodynamic Reusable Spaceship
MASH ..... Manned Antisubmarine Helicopter
MARS ..... Manned Astronautical Research Station (Space laboratory)
MCC ...... Manned Control Car (AEC)
MER ...... Manned Earth Reconnaissance (Navy Bureau of Aeronautics project)
MESA ..... Manned Environmental Systems Assessment (A project of NASA)
MES ...... Manned Exploration Site
MEMU ..... Manned Extravehicular Manipulating Unit
MFOD ..... Manned Flight Operations Division
MFS ...... Manned Flying System
MHV ...... Manned Hypersonic Vehicle
MISER .... Manned Interceptor SAGE Evaluation Routine
MLEV ..... Manned Lifting Entry Vehicle
MLL ...... Manned Lunar Landing (NASA)
MLLP ..... Manned Lunar Landing Program
MALLAR ... Manned Lunar Landing & Return
MLO ...... Manned Lunar Orbiter (NASA)
MLS ...... Manned Lunar Surface (NASA)
MMM ...... Manned Mars Mission (NASA)
MAVES .... Manned Mars & Venus Exploration Studies
MODM ..... Manned One-Day Mission (NASA)
MOD ...... Manned Orbital Development (Station)
MODS ..... Manned Orbital Development System (NASA/Air Force)
MORDS .... Manned Orbital Research and Development System
MORL ..... Manned Orbital (or Orbiting) Research Laboratory (NASA)
MOST ..... Manned Orbital Solar Telescope
MOSS ..... Manned Orbital Space Station
MOSS...... Manned Orbital Space System (NASA/Air Force)
MOT ...... Manned Orbital Telescope (NASA)
MOWS ..... Manned Orbital Weapon System (or Station)
MODS ..... Manned Orbiting Development Station (Air Force)
MOL ...... Manned Orbiting Laboratory (NASA)
MES ...... MOL (Manned Orbiting Laboratory) Environmental Shelter
MOV ...... Manned Orbiting Vehicle (NASA)
MRS ...... Manned Reconnaissance Satellite (Air Force)
MSIS ..... Manned Satellite Inspection System
MSI ...... Manned Satellite Inspector
MSCC ..... Manned Space-Flight Control Center (Air Force)
MSFH ..... Manned Space Flight Headquarters
MSFN ..... Manned Space Flight Network
MSSCS .... Manned Space Station Communications System
MSC....... Manned Spacecraft Center, Houston, Texas (NASA)
MCABM .... Manner Common Among Business Men
MOP ...... Manner of Performance (Officer rating)
MOPR ..... Manner of Performing Rating
MXR ...... Manning, Maxwell & Moore, Inc. (NYSE symbol) (Delisted)
MUG ...... Manning Unit Group (Air Force)
M .... Mano (Hand)
MA .... Manpower Administration (Department of Labor)
MAAS ..... Manpower Allocation and Accounting Subsystem (Air Force)
MAF....... Manpower Authorization File
MARC ..... Manpower Authorization Request for Change (Air Force)
MAV ...... Manpower Authorization Voucher

MCDA ..... Manpower and Career Development Agency
MDP ...... Manpower Development Program (Department of Labor)
MDTA ..... Manpower Development and Training Act (Labor)
MEAT ..... Manpower Employment Assistance Training (Act) (Pennsylvania)
MID ...... Manpower Information Division (Navy)
M & O .... Manpower and Organization (Military)
MOD ...... Manpower & Organization Division (Air Force)
MPAD ..... Manpower Personnel Assignment Document
MPC....... Manpower and Personnel Council (DOD)
MPC....... Manpower Priorities Committee
MUST ..... Manpower Utilization System and Techniques (Department of State)
MV .... Manpower Voucher (Army)
MD .... Manu Dextra (With the Right Hand) (Music)
M .... Manual
MANAM .... Manual Amendment
MANTRAC ... Manual Angle Tracking Capability
MAT....... Manual Arts Therapist
MCC ...... Manual Combat Center (Air Force)
MCC ...... Manual Control Center (Air Force)
MCM ...... Manual for Courts-Martial
MD .... Manual Data
MDI ...... Manual Data Input (SAGE)
MDIF ..... Manual Data Input Function (Data processing)
MDIS ..... Manual Data Input Section
MDIU ..... Manual Data Input Unit (Data processing)
MDR ...... Manual Data Room
MDC ...... Manual Direction Center (Air Force)
MDF ...... Manual Direction Finder (Radio)
MEI ...... Manual of Engineering Instructions
MFC ...... Manual Frequency Control
MGC ...... Manual Gain Control
MIP ...... Manual Index Page (SNMMMS)
MANIP ..... Manual Input
MI .... Manual Input (Electronics)
MIP ...... Manual Input Processing (or Program)
MMDC ..... Manual Master Direction Center
MANMED .... Manual of Medical Department (Navy)
MANMEDDEPT .. Manual of the Medical Department (Navy)
MMD ...... Manual of the Medical Department (Navy)
MANOP ..... Manual of Operation(s)
MO .... Manual Output
MP .... Manual Proportional (Attitude control system of Mercury spacecraft)
MSDC ..... Manual Slave Direction Center (RADAR site)
MVC ...... Manual Volume Control
MW .... Manual Word
MO .... Manually Operated
MOPB ..... Manually Operated Plotting Board
MEP ...... Manuals of Engineering Practice (ASCE)
MAFSI ..... Manufacturers' Agents for Food Service Industry
MANA ..... Manufacturers' Agents National Association
MAA ...... Manufacturers Aircraft Association
MARLSR .... Manufacturers Association of Robes, Leisurewear, Shirts and Rainwear
MIP ...... Manufacturers of Illumination Products
MJ .... Manufacturers' Junction Railway Company (AAR code)
MRS ...... Manufacturers Railway Company (AAR code)
MR .... Manufacturer's Representative
MSS....... Manufacturers Standardization Society (Valves and fittings)
MSSVFI .... Manufacturers Standardization Society of the Valve and Fittings Industry
MSTA ..... Manufacturers Surgical Trade Association
MA .... Manufacturing Assembly
MAD ...... Manufacturing Assembly Drawing
MAPL...... Manufacturing Assembly Parts List
MCN ...... Manufacturing Change Notice
MCP ...... Manufacturing Change Point
MCR ...... Manufacturing Change Request
MCA ...... Manufacturing Chemists Association
MACCS .... Manufacturing Cost Collection System
MACCS .... Manufacturing and Cost-Control System (Data processing)
MEC ...... Manufacturing Engineering Council
MI .... Manufacturing Inspector
MJSA ..... Manufacturing Jewelers Sales Association
MJSA ..... Manufacturing Jewelers and Silversmiths of America
MJ & SA ... Manufacturing Jewelers & Silversmiths of America
MMC ...... Manufacturing Methods Committee
MOS ...... Manufacturing Operating System (IBM)
MPC ...... Manufacturing Plan Change
MRL ...... Manufacturing Reference Line
MRO ...... Manufacturing Rework Order
MSM ...... Manufacturing Standards Manual
MTD ...... Manufacturing Technology Division (Air Force)
MS .... Manuscript

MOP	Manuscript on Paper
MS	Manuscript Society
MOV	Manuscript on Vellum
MSS	Manuscripts
MN	Manx Airlines, Ltd.
MEL	Many-Element LASER
MA	Map Analysis
MCC	Map Collectors' Circle
MIO	Map Information Office (US Geological Survey)
MR	Map Reference
MVD	Map and Visual Display
MFMA	Maple Flooring Manufacturers Association
MSC	Maple Syrup Council
MSG	Mapper Sweep Generator
MC & G	Mapping, Charting, and Geodesy
MCRL	Mapping and Charting Research Laboratory (Ohio State University)
MARKAR	Mapping & Reconnaissance Ku-Band Airborne RADAR
MAB	Maracaibo Oil Exploration Corporation (NYSE symbol) (Delisted)
MRO	Marathon Oil Company (NYSE symbol)
MIA	Marble Institute of America
ME	Marbled Edges
MPS	Marbled Paper Sides
M	March
MB	March-Bender Factor (Physiology)
MOT	"The March of Time" (Radio and motion picture series)
M	Mare
MI	Mare Island, California (Site of naval base)
MINS	Mare Island Naval Shipyard (Navy)
MINSY	Mare Island Naval Shipyard
MAR.	Maremont Corporation (NYSE symbol)
MSRB	Margaret Sanger Research Bureau
MS.	Margin of Safety (Engineering)
MC	Marginal Check (Computer)
MCE	Marginal Cost Efficiency (Marketing)
M/C	Marginal Credit (Business and trade)
MPC	Marginal Propensity to Consume (Econometrics)
M	Maria (Mary)
MARBO	Mariana-Bonins Command
MABO	Marianas-Bonins Group
MBT	Marianna & Blountstown R. R. (AAR code)
MM	Marilyn Monroe (Deceased American motion picture star)
MAFIA	Marimba and Fife Inspectors Association (Women's tongue-in-cheek organization) (Defunct)
MARS	Marine Account Reconciliation Service
MAB.	Marine Air Base
MABDW	Marine Air Base Defense Wing
MABRON	Marine Air Base Squadron
MABS	Marine Air Base Squadron (Marine Corps)
MACG	Marine Air Control Group
MACS	Marine Air Control Squadron (Air Force)
MAIRMAR	Marine Air Depot, Miramar, California
MADEPSQ. . . .	Marine Air Depot Squadron
MAD	Marine Air (or Aviation) Detachment
MAF.	Marine Air Facility
MAGTAF	Marine Air Ground Task Force
MAREQSQ . . .	Marine Air Regulating Squadron
MARTC	Marine Air Reserve Training Command
MASCU.	Marine Air Support Control Unit
MASG	Marine Air Support Group
MASRU	Marine Air Support RADAR Unit (DOD)
MASS	Marine Air Support Squadron
MATCU	Marine Air Tactical Control Unit (Marine Corps)
MAWS	Marine Air Warning Squadron
MAWC	Marine Air West Coast
MAW	Marine Air Wing (Marine Corps)
MAWP	Marine Air Wing Pacific
MABDG.	Marine Aircraft Base Defense Group
MAEE	Marine Aircraft Experimental Establishment
MAG	Marine Aircraft (or Aviation) Group
MAMRON . . .	Marine Aircraft Maintenance Squadron
MARAIRWING . .	Marine Aircraft Wing
MARALLWEAFITRARON . .	Marine All Weather Fighter Training Squadron
MAC	Marine Amphibious Corps
MAMOS	Marine Automatic Meteorological Observing Station (Automatic system)
MARBKS	Marine Barracks
MB.	Marine Barracks
MBNAS.	Marine Barracks, Naval Air Station
MBNAD	Marine Barracks, Naval Ammunition Depot
MBNMD	Marine Barracks, Naval Mine Depot
MBNOB	Marine Barracks, Naval Operating Base
MBNS.	Marine Barracks, Naval Station

MBNYD	Marine Barracks, Navy Yard
MBSB	Marine Barracks, Submarine Base
MB	Marine Base
MBAWS	Marine Base Air Warning System
MBDG	Marine Base Defense Group
MBL	Marine Biological Laboratory
MARBRIG	Marine Brigade
MCS.	Marine Cooks and Stewards Union
M	Marine Corps (When used as prefix with plane designation)
MARCOR.	Marine Corps
MARCORPS . . .	Marine Corps
MC	Marine Corps
MCAB.	Marine Corps Air Base
MCAD	Marine Corps Air Depot
MCAF	Marine Corps Air Facility
MCAF.	Marine Corps Air Field
SERVon	Marine Corps Air Service Squadron
MCAS.	Marine Corps Air Station (Navy)
MCA	Marine Corps Association
MCAAF	Marine Corps Auxiliary Air Facility
MCAAS	Marine Corps Auxiliary Air Station
MARCAD.	Marine Corps Aviation Cadet(s)
MCB.	Marine Corps Base
MARBASSCOL . .	Marine Corps Basic School
MCBM	Marine Corps Brevet Medal
MCCD	Marine Corps Clothing Depot
MCCCA	Marine Corps Combat Correspondents Association
MCC	Marine Corps Commandant
MARCORDISBOF . .	Marine Corps Disbursing Office
MCEC.	Marine Corps Education Center
MCEAC.	Marine Corps Emergency Actions Center
MCEB	Marine Corps Equipment Board
MCGCM	Marine Corps Good Conduct Medal
MCI	Marine Corps Institute
MCLFDC	Marine Corps Landing Force Development Center
MCL	Marine Corps League
MCLA.	Marine Corps League Auxiliary
MLRP	Marine Corps Long Range Plans
MARCORMAN . .	Marine Corps Manual
MCM	Marine Corps Manual
MCMC	Marine Corps Memorial Commission
MCO	Marine Corps Order
MCPD.	Marine Corps Procurement District
NAVMC	Marine Corps Publications
NMC	Marine Corps Publications (Later, NAVMC)
MCRD.	Marine Corps Recruit Depot
MCR.	Marine Corps Reserve
MCROA	Marine Corps Reserve Officers Association
MCRR	Marine Corps Reserve Ribbon
MCS	Marine Corps Schools
MCS	Marine Corps Station
MCS	Marine Corps Supply Activity
MCSC.	Marine Corps Supply Center
MARCORSUPDEP . .	Marine Corps Supply Depot
MTDS	Marine Corps Tactical Data System
MUMMS	Marine Corps Unified Materiel Management System
MCWR	Marine Corps Women's Reserve
MD	Marine Detachment
MARDIV	Marine Division
ME	Marine Engineer
MEL	Marine Engineering Laboratory (Navy)
MEB.	Marine Expeditionary Brigade (Air Force)
MEF.	Marine Expeditionary Force (Military)
MEU	Marine Expeditionary Unit
MARINEX . . .	Marine Express
VMBF	Marine Fighter Bomber Squadrons (Navy symbol)
VMF.	Marine Fighter Squadrons (Navy symbol)
MARFAIR	Marine Fleet Air
MARFAIRWEST . .	Marine Fleet Air, West Coast
MFAIRWEST . . .	Marine Fleet Air, West Coast
MFWC	Marine Fleet Air, West Coast
MARGARFOR . .	Marine Garrison Force
MGS	Marine Geophysical Survey (NOO)
VML.	Marine Glider Squadron (Navy symbol)
MG	Marine Gunner
MGUN	Marine Gunner
MHA	Marine Historical Association
MIO	Marine Inspection Office (Coast Guard)
MARINTRARON . .	Marine Instrument Training Squadron
MIP	Marine Insurance Policy
MJ.	Marine Jet

SEA . . . . Marine Manufacturers Safety Equipment Association
VMB. . . . . Marine Medium and Heavy Patrol Bomber Squadron (Land-based and seaplane) (Navy symbol)
MM . . . . Marine Midland Corporation (NYSE symbol)
VMF(N) . . . . . Marine Night Fighter Squadrons (Navy symbol)
VMO . . . . Marine Observation Squadron (Navy symbol)
VMO(AS) . . . . Marine Observation Squadron (Artillery Spotting) (Navy symbol)
MOA . . . . Marine Office of America (Insurance company)
MOT. . . . . Marine Oil Transportation R. R. (AAR code)
MOTG . . . . . . Marine Operational Training Group
VMD . . . . Marine Photographic Squadrons (Navy symbol)
MPDI . . . . Marine Products Development Irradiator
MRC . . . . Marine Resources Council
VMSB . . . . Marine Scout Bombing Squadron (Navy symbol)
SMS . . . . Marine Service Squadron
MSCNY . . . . . Marine Society of the City of New York
MTS . . . . Marine Technology Society
MTB . . . . Marine Test Boat
VMTB . . . . Marine Torpedo Bomber Squadron (Navy symbol)
MTTEA . . . . . . Marine Towing and Transportation Employers Association
MARTRA & REPLCOMS . . Marine Training and Replacement Commands
VMR. . . . . Marine Transport Squadron (Navy symbol)
VMJ. . . . . Marine Utility Squadron (Navy symbol)
MWB . . . . Marine (or Motor) Whaleboat
MWSG . . . . . . Marine Wing Service Group (Marine Corps)
MTW. . . . . Marinette, Tomahawk & Western R. R. (AAR code)
MSA . . . . Mariological Society of America
MH . . . . Marital History
MARSTA . . . . Marital Status (Army)
M . . . . Maritime (Air mass)
MA . . . . Maritime Administration (Department of Commerce)
MARAD . . . . . Maritime Administration (Department of Commerce)
MAIRAIRMED . . Maritime Air Forces, Mediterranean (NATO)
MAPNY . . . . . Maritime Association of the Port of New York
MAPONY . . . Maritime Association of the Port of New York
MCTC . . . . . . Maritime Cargo Transportation Conference (of MTRB)
MAR . . . . Maritime Central Airways
MCRP . . . . . . Maritime Coal, Railway & Power Company, Limited (AAR code)
MARITCOM . . . Maritime Commission
MC . . . . Maritime Commission (of Department of Commerce) (Merged with Federal Maritime Commission)
MCV . . . . Maritime Commission, Victory Ship
MCA . . . . Maritime Control Area
MGCR . . . . . . Maritime Gas-Cooled Reactor
MGCR-CX . . . . Maritime Gas-Cooled Reactor Critical Experiment
CANAIRFAX . . . Maritime Group Headquarters, Halifax, Nova Scotia, Canada
MLB. . . . . Maritime Labor Board (Terminated, 1942)
MLA . . . . Maritime Law Association of the US
MPS . . . . Maritime Postmark Society
MSC . . . . Maritime Service Committee
MSP. . . . . Maritime Shore Patrol
MARISP. . . . . . Maritime Strike Plan
MSB . . . . Maritime Subsidy Board (Maritime Administration) (Department of Commerce)
MTD . . . . Maritime Trades Department (AFL-CIO)
MTRB . . . . . . Maritime Transportation Research Board (National Research Council)
MUI . . . . Maritime Union of India
M . . . . Mark (Coin)
MDN . . . . . . Mark der Deutschen Notenbank (East German currency)
MTRF . . . . . . Mark Twain Research Foundation
MC . . . . Marked Capacity (Freight cars)
M/F . . . . Marked For
MBR . . . . Marker Beacon Receiver
MLI . . . . Marker Light Indicator
MKR . . . . Marker Radio Beacon
MRC . . . . Market Research Council
MV. . . . . Market Value
MC . . . . Marketing Center (Veterans Administration)
MCRC . . . . . . Marketing Communications Research Center
MIS . . . . Marketing Information System
MQ . . . . Marketing Quota
MR. . . . . Marketing Research Division (of AMS, Department of Agriculture)
MRTA . . . . . . Marketing Research Trade Association
MSI . . . . Marketing Science Institute
MPCA. . . . . . . Markham Prayer Card Apostolate
MDA . . . . Marking Device Association
MOS . . . . Marking of Overseas Shipments
M . . . . Markka (Monetary unit in Finland)
MQO . . . . . . Marksmanship Qualification Order (Marine Corps)
MU . . . . Markup
MRC . . . . Marlin-Rockwell Corporation (NYSE symbol) (Delisted)

MRQ . . . . Marquardt Corporation (NYSE symbol) (Wall Street slang name: "Mr. Q.")
MARNAF . . . . Marquardt Navair Fuel (A boron slurry propellant for spacecraft)
MQC . . . . . . Marquette Cement Manufacturing Company (NYSE symbol)
MLCIM . . . . . Marquette League for Catholic Indian Missions
M . . . . Marquis
MCD . . . . Marr, Cahalan, and Dunn
MLDU . . . . . . Marriage Law Defence Union (British)
MLRA . . . . . . Marriage Law Reform Association (British)
M . . . . Married
MEMQ . . . . . . Married Enlisted Men's Quarters
MOQ . . . . Married Officer Quarters
MWA . . . . . . Married Women's Association (British group fighting for economic equality for wives)
M . . . . Mars
MEM . . . . Mars Excursion Module
MMM . . . . . . Mars Mission Module
MOI . . . . Mars-Orbital Insertion (Aerospace)
MOR . . . . . . Mars Orbital Rendezvous
MSSR . . . . . . Mars Soil Sample Return
M . . . . Marshal
MRAF . . . . . . Marshal of the Royal Air Force (British)
M/Y. . . . . Marshaling Yards (Military)
MF. . . . . Marshall Field & Company (NYSE symbol)
M & I . . . . . . Marshall & Ilsley Bank
MI . . . . Marshall Islands
MSFC . . . . . . Marshall Space Flight Center (Also known as GCMSC)
MA . . . . Marshalling Area (Military)
MACG . . . . . . Marshalling Area Control Group (Military)
MACO . . . . . . Marshalling Area Control Officer (Military)
MARGILSAREA . . Marshalls-Gilberts Area
MERGV . . . . . Martian Exploratory Rocket Glide Vehicle
MADRE . . . . . Martin Automatic Data-Reduction Equipment
ML . . . . Martin Marietta Corporation (NYSE symbol)
MND . . . . Martin Nuclear Division (AEC)
MARTEC . . . . . Martin Thin-Film Electronic Circuit
M . . . . Martyr
MM . . . . Martyres (Martyrs)
MMC . . . . Mary Morston's Companions
MM . . . . Maryknoll Missioners (Catholic Foreign Mission Society) (Roman Catholic religious order)
MD . . . . Maryland
MNCPPC . . . . . Maryland-National Capital Park and Planning Commission
MPA. . . . . Maryland & Pennsylvania R. R. (AAR code)
MCC . . . . Marylebone Cricket Club (Governing body for cricket)
MAS . . . . Maschinen-Ausleih-Station
MTS . . . . Maschinen-Traktoren-Station (Machine-Tractor-Stations) (Germany)
MAN . . . . . . Maschinenfabrik Augsburg-Neurnberg (Germany)
MG . . . . Maschinengewehr
M . . . . Masculine
MTS . . . . Mashinno-Traktornye Stantsii (Machine-Tractor-Stations) (USSR)
MXR . . . . Mask Index Register
MCCL. . . . . . . Mason City & Clear Lake R. R. (AAR code)
MCAA . . . . . . Mason Contractors Association of America
MRA . . . . Masonic Relief Association of USA and Canada
MSA . . . . Masonic Service Association of the United States
MNC . . . . Masonite Corporation (NYSE symbol)
MO . . . . Masonry Opening (Technical drawings)
MT . . . . Masoretic Text (Hebrew tradition)
M . . . . Mass
MASSCAL . . . . Mass Casualties (Military)
MASCON . . . Mass Concentration (of gravitational pull)
MMD . . . . . . Mass Median Diameter
MO . . . . Mass Observation
MRAD . . . . . . Mass Random Access Disk
MRI . . . . Mass Retailing Institute (Formerly, Mass Merchandising Research Institute)
MSID . . . . . . Mass Spectrometric Isotope Dilution
MS . . . . Mass Spectrometry
MU . . . . Mass Units
MA . . . . Massachusetts
MBTA . . . . . . Massachusetts Bay Transit Authority
MCAD . . . . . . Massachusetts Commission Against Discrimination
MCH . . . . Massachusetts Council for the Humanities
MIT . . . . Massachusetts Institute of Technology
MITRE . . . . . . Massachusetts Institute of Technology – RAND Corporation Engineering
MITR . . . . . . Massachusetts Institute of Technology Reactor
MIT . . . . Massachusetts Investors Trust
MMHC . . . . . Massachusetts Mental Health Center
MMA . . . . . . Massachusetts Military Academy
MSTR . . . . . . Massena Terminal R. R. (AAR code)
MHL. . . . . Mast Hull Loop

M . . . . Master
MAS . . . . Master of Accounting Science
MAE . . . . Master of Aeronautical Engineering
MACE . . . . . . Master of Air Conditioning Engineering
MAC Eng . . . . Master of Air Conditioning Engineering
MAA . . . . Master of Applied Arts
MA Mech . . . . Master of Applied Mechanics
MAS . . . . Master of Applied Science
M Ar . . . . Master of Architecture
M Arch in CP . . Master of Architecture in City Planning
MAA. . . . . . . Master-at-Arms (Navy)
MAA . . . . Master of Arms (Head of a ship's police) (British)
MAA . . . . Master Army Aviator
MASTARAV . . Master Army Aviator
Mast AR Av Bad . . Master Army Aviator Badge (Army)
MAE . . . . Master of Art Education
MAO . . . . Master of Art of Oratory
AM . . . . Master of Arts
MA . . . . Master of Arts
MA in Comm . . Master of Arts in Communications
MAE . . . . Master of Arts in Education
MALD . . . . . . Master of Arts in Law and Diplomacy
MALS. . . . . . . Master of Arts in Liberal Studies
MA in LS . . . . Master of Arts in Liberal Studies
AMLS. . . . . . . Master of Arts in Library Science
MA in LS . . . . Master of Arts in Library Science
MAR . . . . Master of Arts in Religion
AM(R) . . . . . . Master of Arts in Research
M Ar Sc . . . . . Master of Arts and Sciences
MASW . . . . . . Master of Arts in Social Work
AMT . . . . Master of Arts for Teachers
AMT . . . . Master of Arts in Teaching
AM(T) . . . . . . Master of Arts in Teaching
AM in T . . . . . Master of Arts in Teaching
MAT . . . . Master of Arts in Teaching
MA in T . . . . . Master of Arts in Teaching
MATE . . . . . . Master of Arts in the Teaching of English
STM. . . . . Master of Arts in Theology
M As S . . . . . . Master of Association Science
M As Sc . . . . . Master of Association Science
Ms B . . . . Master of Bacteriology
MBS . . . . Master of Basic Science
MBC . . . . Master of Beauty Culture
M Biorad . . . . Master of Bioradiology
MBAA. . . . . . . Master Brewers Association of America
MBA . . . . Master of Business Administration
MB Adm . . . . . Master of Business Administration
MBAAS . . . . . . Master of Business Administration in Actuarial Science
MBM . . . . Master of Business Management
MCCS . . . . . . Master Calendar Control System (New York City courts' speedup system)
M Can L . . . . . Master of Canon Law
MCBA . . . . . . Master Car Builders' Association
MCTS . . . . . . Master Central Timing System (NASA)
EMCEE . . . . . . Master of Ceremonies (Slang)
MC . . . . Master of Ceremonies
MCR . . . . Master Change Record
MC . . . . Master of Chemistry
M Cp . . . . Master of Chiropody
MCE . . . . Master of Christian Education
CSM . . . . Master of Christian Science
MCT . . . . Master of Christian Training
MCM . . . . Master of Church Music
MCP . . . . Master of City Planning
MCE . . . . Master of Civil Engineering
MCL . . . . Master of Civil Law
MC . . . . Master of Classics
MCD . . . . Master Clerical Data (Management system)
MC . . . . Master Commandant
M Com . . . . . . Master of Commerce
MCA . . . . Master of Commercial Arts
MC Ed . . . . . . Master of Commercial Education
MCS . . . . Master of Commercial Science
MC Sc . . . . . . Master of Commercial Science
MC Se . . . . . . Master of Commercial Service
MCJ . . . . Master of Comparative Jurisprudence
MCL . . . . Master of Comparative Law
MCR . . . . Master of Comparative Religion
MCL . . . . Master Configuration List
MC . . . . Master Control
MCP . . . . Master Control Program (Data processing)
MCR . . . . Master Control Routine

MCS . . . . Master Control Station
MCK . . . . Master Cook (Navy)
M Co . . . . Master of Cosmology
M Cr . . . . Master of Criminology
MCRL . . . . . . Master Cross Reference Listing
MDCC . . . . . . Master Data Control Console
MDL . . . . Master Data Library (NASA)
DDM . . . . Master of Dental Medicine
MD Sc . . . . . . Master of Dental Science
MDS . . . . Master of Dental Surgery
M Des . . . . . . Master of Design
M Did . . . . . . Master of Didactics
M Di E . . . . . . Master of Diesel Engineering
MDCS . . . . . . Master Digital Command System
M Dip . . . . . . Master of Diplomacy
MDC . . . . Master Direction Center (Air Force)
MDI . . . . Master Direction Indicator
DM . . . . Master Diver (Navy)
Mast Div Bad . . Master Diver Badge (Army)
MDL . . . . Master of Divine Literature
DM . . . . Master of Divinity
M Div . . . . . . Master of Divinity
MDA . . . . Master of Dramatic Art
MDS . . . . Master Drum Sender
MDA . . . . Master Dyers Association
ME . . . . Master of Education
Ed M in BT Ed. . Master of Education in Business Teacher Education
M Ed LS . . . . . Master of Education in Library Science
MEE . . . . Master of Electrical Engineering
MECE . . . . . . Master of Electro-Chemical Engineering
ME Ch E . . . . . Master of Electro-Chemical Engineering
MED. . . . . Master of Elementary Didactics
ME . . . . Master of Elements
M El . . . . Master of Elements
M Elo . . . . . . Master of Elocution
ME . . . . Master of Engineering
M Eng . . . . . . Master of Engineering
MEA . . . . Master of Engineering Administration
MEC . . . . Master of Engineering Chemistry
MEP . . . . Master of Engineering Physics
ME Phy . . . . . . Master of Engineering Physics
MEPA . . . . . . Master in Engineering and Public Administration
MES . . . . Master of Engineering Sciences
M En . . . . Master of English
M Eng . . . . . . Master of English
MED . . . . Master of English Divinity
MEL . . . . Master of English Literature
MEAL . . . . . . Master Equipment Allowance List (Air Force)
MEAL . . . . . . Master Equipment Authorization List
MEMI . . . . . . Master Equipment Management Index (Air Force)
MEML . . . . . . Master Equipment Management List (Air Force)
M Ex . . . . Master of Expression
MFR . . . . Master Facility Register (AEC)
MFL . . . . Master of Family Life
MFA . . . . Master of Fine Arts
MFS. . . . . Master of Food Science
MFS. . . . . Master of Foreign Service
MFS. . . . . Master of Foreign Study
MFT . . . . Master of Foreign Trade
MFE . . . . Master of Forest Engineering
MF . . . . Master of Forestry
MFH . . . . Master of Fox Hounds
MFGA . . . . . . Master Furriers Guild of America
MGO. . . . . Master General of Ordnance (British)
M Ge E . . . . . Master of Geological Engineering
MGYSGT . . . . Master Gunnery Sergeant (Marine Corps)
MH PE & R . . Master of Health, Physical Education, and Recreation
MHL . . . . Master of Hebrew Literature
M Hi E . . . . . . Master of Highway Engineering
MHE . . . . Master of Home Economics
MHB. . . . . Master Horizontal Bomber
MH . . . . Master of Horticulture
MHA . . . . Master of Hospital Administration
MH . . . . Master Hosts
M Ho Ec . . . . . Master of Household Economy
LHM . . . . Master of Humane Letters (or Master of the More Humane Letters)
MHL . . . . Master of Humane Letters
MH . . . . Master of Humanics
MH . . . . Master of Hygiene
MIF . . . . Master Index File
MIA . . . . Master of Industrial Arts

MID . . . . Master of Industrial Design
MIE . . . . Master of Industrial Engineering
MI Eng . . . . . Master of Industrial Engineering
MILR . . . . . . Master of Industrial and Labor Relations
MIT . . . . Master Instruction Tape (Data processing)
M I Arch Eng . . Master of Interior Architectural Engineering
M I Arch . . . . Master of Interior Architecture
MIA . . . . Master of International Affairs
MIFL . . . . . . Master International Frequency List
MIFR . . . . . . Master International Frequency Register
MIS . . . . Master of International Service
MIE . . . . Master of Irrigation Engineering
MJP . . . . Master of Jewish Pedagogy
MJ . . . . Master of Journalism
JSM . . . . Master of Judicial Science
Jur M . . . . . . Master of Jurisprudence
MLA . . . . . . Master of Landscape Architecture
MLD . . . . . . Master of Landscape Design
MLM . . . . . . Master of Landscape Management
MLL . . . . Master of Latin Literature
LLM . . . . Master of Law(s)
ML . . . . Master of Law(s)
MLT . . . . Master of Law and Taxation
LLM (CL) . . . . Master of Laws in Comparative Law
LLM (Int L) . . Master of Laws in International Law
ML . . . . Master of Letters
LAM . . . . . . Master of Liberal Arts
MLS . . . . . . Master of Librarianship
LSM . . . . Master of Life Science
MALIMET . . . . Master List of Medical Indexing Terms
MLI . . . . Master of Literary Interpretation
ML . . . . Master of Literature
M Ma E . . . . . Master of Marine Engineering
MM . . . . Master Mason (Freemasonry)
MM . . . . . . Master Mechanic
AMM . . . . . . Master of Mechanic Arts
MME . . . . . . Master of Mechanical Engineering
MMS . . . . . . Master of Mechanical Science
MM Sc . . . . . Master of Mechanical Science
MM Sc . . . . . Master of Medical Science
MSM . . . . . . Master of Medical Science
MMT . . . . . . Master of Medical Technology
MMB . . . . . . Master Menu Board (Military)
Me M . . . . . . Master of Metaphysics
M Me . . . . . . Master of Metaphysics
MME . . . . . . Master of Mining Engineering
MML . . . . . . Master of Modern Languages
MM . . . . . . Master Monitor
Mor M . . . . . Master Mortician
MMA . . . . . . Master of Municipal Administration
MM Adm . . . . Master of Municipal Administration
MM . . . . Master of Music
MME . . . . . . Master of Music Education
M Mus (PSM) . Master of Music in Public School Music
M Mus (W Inst) . Master of Music in Wind Instruments
MMA . . . . . . Master of Musical Arts
MNE . . . . . . Master of Naval Engineering
M Na . . . . . . Master of Navigation
MNE . . . . . . Master of Nuclear Engineering
MN . . . . Master of Nursing
MNA . . . . . . Master of Nursing Administration
MN Ed . . . . . Master of Nursing Education
MNS . . . . . . Master of Nursing Science
MNS . . . . . . Master of Nutritional Science
MAO . . . . . . Master of Obstetric Art
MO . . . . Master of Obstetrics
OMV . . . . . . Master of Obstetrics
MO & G . . . . Master Obstetrics and Gynaecology (British)
MOIG . . . . . Master of Occupational Information and Guidance
MORT . . . . . . Master Operational Recording Tape (SAGE)
MOC . . . . . . Master Operations Console
MOC . . . . . . Master Operations Control
MOE . . . . . . Master of Oral English
MO . . . . Master of Oratory
M Or . . . . . . Master of Oratory
MOC . . . . . . Master Ordnance Configuration File (Navy)
MOSP . . . . . . Master Ordnance Systems Pattern File (Navy)
MOL . . . . . . Master of Oriental Languages
MO . . . . Master Oscillator (Radio)
MOPA . . . . . . Master Oscillator Power Amplifier (Radio)
MOPAR . . . . . Master Oscillator - Power Amplifier RADAR

MO . . . . Master of Osteopathy
MOH . . . . . . Master of Otter Hounds
MP . . . . Master of Painting
MRPARABAD . . Master Parachutist Badge
MPL . . . . . . Master of Patent Law
MPERR . . . . . Master Personnel Record
MPS . . . . . . Master of Personnel Services
M Ph C . . . . . Master of Pharmaceutical Chemistry
Ph M . . . . . . Master in Pharmacy
M Ph . . . . . . Master of Philosophy
Ph M . . . . . . Master of Philosophy
MPDFA . . . . . Master Photo Dealers' and Finishers' Association
MPB . . . . . . Master of Physical Biology
MPE . . . . . . Master of Physical Education
MPH . . . . . . Master of Physical Education and Health
M Ps Sc . . . . . Master of Physic Sciences
MPL . . . . . . Master of Polite Literature
M Pr M . . . . . Master of Preventive Medicine
MPA . . . . . . Master Printers of America (Division of Printing Industries of America)
MPA . . . . . . Master of Professional Accountancy
MPA . . . . . . Master of Professional Arts
M Pr Gph . . . . Master in Professional Geophysics
M Ps . . . . . . Master of Psychology
M Ps Th . . . . Master of Psycho-Therapy
MPA . . . . . . Master of Public Administration
MPA . . . . . . Master of Public Affairs
MPH . . . . . . Master of Public Health
MPHE . . . . . . Master of Public Health Engineering
MPHN . . . . . . Master of Public Health Nursing
MPHTM . . . . . Master of Public Health and Tropical Medicine
MPSA . . . . . . Master of Public School Art
MPSM . . . . . . Master of Public School Music
M Ra E . . . . . Master of Radio Engineering
MRTE . . . . . . Master of Radio and Television Engineering
MRT Eng . . . . Master of Radio and Television Engineering
M Re E . . . . . Master of Refrigeration Engineering
MRP . . . . . . Master of Regional Planning
MRC . . . . . . Master of Rehabilitation Counseling
M Re . . . . . . Master of Religion
MRE . . . . . . Master of Religious Education
MRG . . . . . . Master of Religious Guidance
MRS . . . . . . Master Repair Schedule (Air Force)
MRL . . . . . . Master Report List
MRD . . . . . . Master Requirements Directory (Military)
M Ret . . . . . . Master of Retailing
Roent M . . . . . Master of Roentgenology
MR . . . . Master of the Rolls (British)
M Ru E . . . . . Master of Rural Engineering
MRH . . . . . . Master of Russian History
MSL . . . . Master of Sacred Literature
MSM . . . . . . Master of Sacred Music
SMM . . . . . . Master of Sacred Music
M Sa Sc . . . . . Master of Sacred Sciences
MST . . . . Master of Sacred Theology
MSE . . . . Master of Sanitary Engineering
MSS . . . . . . Master of Sanitary Science
M San . . . . . . Master of Sanitation
MSL . . . . . . Master Scheduling Letter
MSM . . . . . . Master Scheduling Manager
MS . . . . Master of Science
MSc . . . . Master of Science
SM . . . . Master of Science
MSAE . . . . . . Master of Science in Aeronautical Engineering
MS in AE . . . . . Master of Science in Aeronautical Engineering
MS in AN . . . . Master of Science in Agricultural Engineering
MSA . . . . . . Master of Science in Agriculture
MSAM . . . . . . Master of Science in Applied Mechanics
MSA . . . . . . Master of Science and Arts
MS in Aud & Sp . . Master of Science in Audiology and Speech
MS in BI Sc . . . Master of Science in Biological Sciences
MSBC . . . . . . Master of Science in Building Construction
MSBA . . . . . . Master of Science in Business Administration
MS in BA . . . . Master of Science in Business Administration
M Sc CE . . . . . Master of Science in Chromo-Electronic Science
MS in CRP . . . Master of Science in City and Regional Planning
MSCE . . . . . . Master of Science in Civil Engineering
MS in CE . . . . Master of Science in Civil Engineering
MS in C . . . . . Master of Science in Commerce
MS in C & BA . . Master of Science in Commercial and Business Administration
MSCP . . . . . . Master of Science in Community Planning
MS Cons . . . . . Master of Science in Conservation

SM Dendrol . . . Master of Science in Dendrology
MSD . . . . Master of Science in Dentistry
MS Des . . . . . Master of Science in Design
MS in Dt . . . . . Master of Science in Dietetics
MSE . . . . Master of Science in Education
MS in E . . . . . Master of Science in Education
MSEE . . . . . . Master of Science in Electrical Engineering
MS in EE . . . . Master of Science in Electrical Engineering
MSE . . . . Master of Science in Engineering
MS in E . . . . . Master of Science in Engineering
MSEM . . . . . . Master of Science in Engineering Mechanics
MS in EM . . . . Master of Science in Engineering Mechanics
MS in EM . . . . Master of Science in Engineering of Mines
MS in EP . . . . Master of Science in Engineering Physics
MS in ES . . . . Master of Science in Engineering Science(s)
MSEL . . . . . . Master of Science and English Literature
MS Ent . . . . . Master of Science in Entomology
MSFM . . . . . . Master of Science in Forest Management
MSF . . . . Master of the Science of Forestry
MSG Mgt . . . . Master of Science in Game Management
MS in GE . . . . Master of Science in General Engineering
MS in GSM . . . Master of Science in General Science and Mathematics
MS in Gp Engr . Master of Science in Geophysical Engineering
MSGM . . . . . . Master of Science in Government Management
MSH & Ph Ed . . Master of Science in Health and Physical Education
MSHE . . . . . . Master of Science in Home Economics
MS in HE . . . . Master of Science in Home Economics
MSHA . . . . . . Master of Science in Hospital Administration
MS in HR . . . . Master of Science in Human Relations
MS in ID . . . . Master of Science in Industrial Design
MSIE . . . . . . Master of Science in Industrial Engineering
MS in IE . . . . Master of Science in Industrial Engineering
MS in IM . . . . Master of Science in Industrial Management
MSJ . . . . Master of Science in Journalism
MSL . . . . Master of Science in Language
MS (LS) . . . . . Master of Science in Library Science
MS in LS . . . . Master of Science in Library Science
MSL . . . . Master of Science in Linguistics
M Sc in ME . . . Master of Science in Mechanical Engineering
MSME . . . . . . Master of Science in Mechanical Engineering
MS in ME . . . . Master of Science in Mechanical Engineering
M Sc M . . . . . Master of the Science of Medicine
MSM . . . . Master of Science in Music
MS in NT . . . . Master of Science in Nuclear Technology
MSN . . . . Master of Science in Nursing
MS in N . . . . . Master of Science in Nursing
MS in NE . . . . Master of Science in Nursing Education
MS in Nr Ed . . Master of Science in Nursing Education
M Or Sc . . . . . Master of the Science of Oratory
M Sc O . . . . . Master of the Science of Oratory
MSO . . . . Master of the Science of Oratory
MS Orn Hort . . Master of Science in Ornamental Horticulture
MS in PE . . . . . Master of Science in Petroleum Engineering
MS in PRE . . . . Master of Science in Petroleum Refining Engineering
MSP . . . . Master of Science in Pharmacy
MSPE . . . . . . Master of Science in Physical Education
MS in PE . . . . . Master of Science in Physical Education
MS in Phy . . . . Master of Science in Physics
MSPH . . . . . . Master of Science in Poultry Husbandry
MS in Py Sc . . . Master of Science in Poultry Science
MS in PA . . . . Master of Science in Public Administration
MSPH . . . . . . Master of Science in Public Health
MS in PH . . . . Master of Science in Public Health
MSPH Ed . . . . Master of Science in Public Health Education
MSPHE . . . . . Master of Science in Public Health Engineering
MS in PSM . . . Master of Science in Public School Music
MS (R) . . . . . . Master of Science in Research
MSSE . . . . . . Master of Science in Sanitary Engineering
MS in SS . . . . Master of Science in Sanitary Science
MSST . . . . . . Master of Science in Science Teaching
MSSS . . . . . . Master of Science in Social Science
MS in SS . . . . . Master of Science in Social Service
MSSW . . . . . . Master of Science in Social Work
MS in SW . . . . Master of Science in Social Work
MS in Sp . . . . . Master of Science in Speech
MSS & H . . . . . Master of Science in Speech and Hearing
MS (T) . . . . . . Master of Science in Teaching
MST . . . . Master of Science in Teaching
STM . . . . Master of the Science of Theology
MS in T & I . . . Master of Science in Trade and Industrial Education
MSA . . . . Master of Scientific Agriculture

MSD . . . . Master of Scientific Didactics
MS Di . . . . . . Master of Scientific Didactics
M Se A . . . . . . Master of Secretarial Arts
M Se Sc . . . . . Master of Secretarial Science
M Se St . . . . . Master of Secretarial Studies
MS . . . . Master Sergeant
MSG . . . . Master Sergeant (Army)
MSGT . . . . . . Master Sergeant
MSAMP . . . . . Master Ship Acquisition Milestone Plan
MSIR . . . . Master of Social and Industrial Relations
M So Sc . . . . . Master of Social Science
M So Se . . . . . Master of Social Service
MSS . . . . Master of Social Service
MSS . . . . Master of Social Studies
MSW . . . . Master of Social Welfare
M So W . . . . . Master of Social Work
MSW . . . . Master of Social Work
M So . . . . Master of Sociology
MSPR . . . . . . Master Spares Positioning Resolver (Data processing)
M Sp . . . . Master of Speech
MSH . . . . Master of Staghounds
M St . . . . Master of Statistics
MSTD . . . . . . Master Steward (Marine Corps)
M St E . . . . . . Master of Structural Engineering
MS . . . . Master of Surgery
MSS . . . . Master Surveillance Station (Air Force)
MS . . . . Master Switch
M Sy Th . . . . . Master of Systematic Theology
MTC . . . . Master Tape Control
MTL . . . . Master Tape Loading
MTLP . . . . . . Master Tape Loading Program
MTVAL . . . . . Master Tape Validation
MST . . . . Master of Teaching
MT . . . . Master of Teaching
MTSGT . . . . . . Master Technical Sergeant (Marine Corps)
MTSGT(C) . . . . Master Technical Sergeant (Commissary) (Marine Corps)
MTC . . . . Master of Textile Chemistry
MT Ch . . . . . . Master of Textile Chemistry
MT Des . . . . . Master of Textile Design
MTD . . . . Master of Textile Dyeing
MTE . . . . Master of Textile Engineering
MT Eng . . . . . Master of Textile Engineering
MTT . . . . Master of Textile Technology
Th M . . . . Master of Theology
MT . . . . Master Timer
MTCC . . . . . . Master Timing and Control Circuit
MUP . . . . Master of Urban Planning
MDV . . . . Master of Veterinary Medicine
MVM . . . . Master of Veterinary Medicine
MWI . . . . Master Weavers Institute
MWT . . . . Master of Wood Technology
MM . . . . Masters
MFAA . . . . . . Masters of Foxhounds Association of America
MF . . . . Mastic Floor (Technical drawings)
MJ . . . . Mastic Joint (Technical drawings)
MCA . . . . Mastiff Club of America
MI . . . . Match Institute
M & B . . . . . Matched and Beaded
MASTER . . . . . Matching Available Student Time to Educational Resources (Data processing)
M . . . . Mate (of a ship)
M . . . . Mater (Latin)
MARC . . . . . . Material Accountability Recoverability Code
MALI . . . . . . Material Annex Line Item
MCA . . . . Material Control Adjustment
MCA . . . . Material Coordinating Agency
MDA . . . . Material Disposal Authority
MERM . . . . . . Material Evaluation Rocket Motor
MHEDA . . . . . Material Handling Equipment Distributors Association
MHI . . . . Material Handling Institute
MIAC . . . . . . Material Identification and Accounting Code
MIP . . . . Material Improvement Program (Aviation)
MIFD . . . . . . Material Information Flow Device (Military)
MIFS . . . . . . Material Information Flow System (Military)
MI . . . . Material Inspection
MIR . . . . Material Inspection Report
MIS . . . . Material Inspection Service (Navy)
MIR . . . . Material Investigators Reactor (NASA)
MME . . . . Material Military Establishment (Formerly, OSRD)
MATNO . . . . . Material (Requested) is Not Available
MOG . . . . Material Ordering Guide

MOS . . . . Material Ordering Schedule
MPB . . . . Material Performance Branch (Air Force)
MPSC . . . . . . Material Planning Schedule and Control (Division of Inspection Offices, Navy)
M & P. . . . . . Material and Process
MRU. . . . . . . Material Recovery Unit
MRC. . . . . . . Material Redistribution Center
MR & D. . . . . Material Redistribution & Disposal
MR & DA. . . . Material Redistribution and Disposal Administration
MRR . . . . Material Rejection Report
MRR . . . . Material Reliability Report
MATRE . . . . . Material Requested
MATSO . . . . . Material Requested Being Supplied (Military)
MRES . . . . . . Material Requirements Estimation System (Navy)
MRPL . . . . . . Material Requirements Planning List
MR . . . . Material Requisition
MRB . . . . Material Review Board
MRR . . . . Material Review Record (or Reports)
MSO . . . . Material Sales Order
MSU. . . . . . . Material Salvage Unit
MSC . . . . Material Source Code
MS. . . . . Material Specifications
MTD . . . . Material Test Directorate (Army)
MURF . . . . . . Material Utilization Reference File (Military)
MATCH . . . . . Materials and Activities for Teachers and Children
MAB. . . . . . . Materials Advisory Board (National Research Council)
MDC . . . . Materials Dissemination Center (Institute for Development of Educational Activities)
MHE . . . . Materials Handling Equipment (Military)
MHSS . . . . . . Materials Handling Support System (Military)
MMRC . . . . . . Materials and Mechanics Research Center (Army)
MPD . . . . Materials Physics Division (Air Force)
MPR . . . . Materials & Process Requirement (Navy)
MTR. . . . . . . Materials Testing Reactor (AEC)
MTR. . . . . . . Materials Testing Report
MAL . . . . Materiel Allowance List
MC . . . . Materiel Command (Air Force)
MDLC . . . . . . Materiel Development and Logistic Command (Army – replaced Ordnance, Engineer, Signal, Chemical and Quartermaster Overall Commands)
METRO . . . . . Materiel Essential to Reconstitution Operations (Air Force)
MINT. . . . . . . Materiel Identification and New Item Control Technique (AFLC)
MIP . . . . Materiel Improvement Project
MIRR . . . . . . Materiel Inspection and Receiving Report
MMC . . . . Materiel Management Code (Military)
MMD . . . . . . Materiel Management Division (Army)
MMTC . . . . . . Materiel Management Training Center (Military)
MPP . . . . Materiel Performance Package (Military)
MPS . . . . Materiel Planning Study
MPC . . . . Materiel Program Code (Air Force)
MRAL . . . . . . Materiel Readiness Authorization List
MRD . . . . Materiel Redistribution Division
MRO . . . . Materiel Release Order
MRS . . . . Materiel Repair System (Air Force)
MRL . . . . Materiel Requirements List
MRRC . . . . . . Materiel Requirements Review Committee
A-4 . . . . Materiel and Supply Section of an Air Staff; also, officer in charge of this section (Air Force)
MTC. . . . . . . Materiel Testing Command (Army) (Merged with Weapons & Mobility Command)
MCH . . . . Maternal and Child Health (Service)
MCA . . . . Maternity Center Association
MR . . . . Mate's Receipt
MAPP . . . . . . Mathematical Analysis of a Perception and Preference
MAP . . . . Mathematical Analysis without Programming (Data processing)
MANIAC. . . . . Mathematical Analyzer, Numerical Integrator and Computer
MAGI . . . . . . Mathematical Applications Group, Incorporated
MAA . . . . Mathematical Association of America
MOS . . . . Mathematical Off-print Service (American Mathematical Society)
MP . . . . Mathematical Programming
MR . . . . Mathematical Review (A publication)
MTAC . . . . . . Mathematical Tables and Other Aids to Computation
MCB . . . . Matheson, Coleman and Bell (Commercial firm)
M . . . . Matins (Early morning prayers)
MFSFU . . . . . Matt-Finish Structural Facing Units (Technical drawings)
M . . . . Mature Audiences (Movie rating) (Replaced by GP)
MLO . . . . Mauna Loa Observatory (Hawaii) (Weather Bureau)
MFL. . . . . . . Mauritius Federation of Labor
MTUC . . . . . . Mauritius Trades' Union Congress
MTUF . . . . . . Mauritius Trades' Union Federation
MN . . . . Maxim Nordenfelt Gun

MEF . . . . Maximal Expiratory Flow
MEMP . . . . . . Maximization of Expected Maximum Profit (Econometrics)
MAC . . . . Maximum Allowable Concentration
MAF . . . . Maximum Amplitude Filter
MAA . . . . Maximum Authorized Altitude (Aviation)
MAP . . . . Maximum Average Price
MBC . . . . Maximum Breathing Capacity
MCE . . . . Maximum Capability Envelope
MCT . . . . Maximum Continuous Thrust (Aviation)
MDFNA . . . . . Maximum Density Fuming Nitric Acid
MD . . . . Maximum Design Meter
MEJ . . . . Maximum Economic Justification
MER . . . . Maximum Efficient Rate (Oil)
ME . . . . Maximum Effort
METO. . . . . . Maximum Except Takeoff (Power) (Air Force)
MEOV . . . . . . Maximum Expected Operating Value (FCC)
METOP . . . . . Maximum Expected Takeoff Power
MFED . . . . . . Maximum Flat Envelope Delay
MHB . . . . Maximum Hospital Benefit(s)
MEETAT. . . . . Maximum Improvement in Electronics Effectiveness Through Advanced Techniques
ML . . . . Maximum Likelihood (Statistics)
MLE . . . . Maximum Likelihood Estimate (Statistics)
MME . . . . Maximum Maintenance Effort (Military)
MMC . . . . Maximum Material Condition
MMD . . . . Maximum Mixing Depths (Meteorology)
MAXMAR . . . . Maximum Mobile Army
MOF . . . . Maximum Observed Frequency (Radio)
MPC . . . . Maximum Permissible Concentration (Radiation)
MPD . . . . Maximum Permissible Dose (Radiation)
MPE . . . . Maximum Permissible Exposure (AEC)
MPO . . . . Maximum Power Output
MST . . . . Maximum Service Telecasters
MS . . . . Maximum Stress
MT . . . . Maximum Torque
MTE . . . . Maximum Tracking Error
MUA . . . . Maximum Usable Altitude (Aviation)
MUF . . . . Maximum Usable Frequency (Aviation)
MUST . . . . . . Maximum Utilization of Skills and Training (Civil Service Commission)
MVV . . . . Maximum Voluntary Ventilation
MWP . . . . Maximum Working Pressure
MWV . . . . Maximum Working Voltage
M . . . . May
MBI . . . . May Be Issued
MBRUU . . . . . May Be Retained Until Unserviceable
MA . . . . May Department Stores Company (NYSE symbol)
MLL . . . . Maynard Listener Library
MSDI . . . . . . Mayonnaise and Salad Dressings Institute
MJW . . . . Mays (J.W.), Inc.
MYG . . . . Maytag Company (NYSE symbol)
MMS . . . . Mazdoor Mahajan Sangh (Textile Labor Association) (India)
MCA . . . . MCA Incorporated (NYSE symbol)
MLL. . . . . . . McCall Corporation (NYSE symbol)
MISCO . . . . . McCall Information Systems Company
MR. . . . . McCloud River R. R. (AAR code)
MCAFB . . . . . McConnell Air Force Base
MCR . . . . McCord Corporation (NYSE symbol)
MS. . . . . McCrory Corporation (NYSE symbol)
MDE. . . . . . . McDermott (J. Ray) & Company, Inc. (NYSE symbol)
MAE . . . . McDonnell Airborne Evaluator (McDonnell Aircraft Corporation)
MASE . . . . . . McDonnell Airborne Sidewinder Evaluator (McDonnell Aircraft Corporation)
MATE . . . . . . McDonnell Airborne Trainer and Evaluator (McDonnell Aircraft Corporation)
MAC . . . . McDonnell Aircraft Corporation (NYSE symbol)
MCAIR . . . . . McDonnell Aircraft Corporation
MAAT . . . . . . MAC (McDonnell Aircraft Corporation) Acquisition and Attack Trainer
MCASTRO . . . McDonnell Astronautics Company
MCAUTO . . . . McDonnell Automation Company
MDAC/E . . . . McDonnell Douglas Astronautics Company/East
MDAC/W . . . . McDonnell Douglas Astronautics Company/West
MLV . . . . McDonnell Launch Vehicle
MSR . . . . McDonnell Simulator Recorder (McDonnell Aircraft Corporation)
MUSRP . . . . . McGill University Savanna Research Project
MGR . . . . McGraw-Edison Company (NYSE symbol)
MHP . . . . McGraw-Hill, Inc. (NYSE symbol)
MGD . . . . McGregor-Doniger, Inc. (NYSE symbol)
MP. . . . . McIntyre Porcupine Mines, Ltd. (NYSE symbol)
MKE. . . . . . . McKee (Arthur G.) & Company (NYSE symbol)
MKC . . . . McKeesport Connecting R. R. (AAR code)
MCK . . . . McKesson & Robbins, Inc. (NYSE symbol)
MLN . . . . McLean Trucking Company (NYSE symbol)

MNR . . . . McMaster Nuclear Reactor (Canada)
MME . . . . McNeil Machine & Engineering Company (Later, McNeil Corporation) (NYSE symbol)
MFG . . . . McQuay-Norris Manufacturing Company (NYSE symbol)
MEA. . . . . Mead Corporation (NYSE symbol)
MTAI . . . . . . Meal Tickets Authorized and Issued (Army)
MMF . . . . Meals for Millions Foundation
M . . . . Mean (Arithmetic average)
MAC . . . . Mean Aerodynamic Chord (Aerospace)
MABP. . . . . . . Mean Arterial Blood Pressure (Physiology)
B. . . . . Mean barometric pressure
MBP . . . . Mean Blood Pressure (Physiology)
MCD . . . . Mean Corpuscular Diameter
MCH . . . . Mean Corpuscular Hemoglobin
MCHC . . . . . . Mean Corpuscular Hemoglobin Concentration
MCV . . . . Mean Corpuscular Volume
MD . . . . Mean Deviation
DHQ . . . . Mean Diurnal High Water Inequality
DLQ . . . . Mean Diurnal Low Water Inequality
MDT. . . . . Mean Down Time
MEP . . . . Mean Effective Pressure
MHSCP . . . . . Mean Hemispherical Candlepower
MHT. . . . . Mean High Tide
MHW . . . . Mean High Water
MHWI. . . . . . . Mean High Water Lunitidal Interval
MHWN . . . . . . Mean High Water Neap (Tides)
MHWS . . . . . . Mean High Water Springs
MHHW . . . . . . Mean Higher High Water
MHLW . . . . . . Mean Higher Low Water (Navigation)
MHCP . . . . . . Mean Horizontal Candlepower
MIP . . . . Mean Indicated Pressure
ML . . . . Mean Level
MLT. . . . . Mean Low Tide
MLW . . . . Mean Low Water
MLWI . . . . . . Mean Low Water Lunitidal Interval
MLWN . . . . . . Mean Low Water Neap (Tides)
MLWS. . . . . . . Mean Low Water Springs
MLHW . . . . . . Mean Lower High Water (Navigation)
MLLW . . . . . . Mean Lower Low Water
MNR . . . . Mean Neap (Tide) Rise
MPI . . . . Mean Point of Impact (Air Force)
MRI . . . . Mean Rise Interval
MSL. . . . . Mean Sea Level
MSD . . . . Mean Solar Day
MST . . . . Mean Solar Time
MSCP . . . . . . Mean Spherical Candlepower
MSR . . . . Mean Spring Rise
MS . . . . Mean Square
MSE . . . . Mean Square Error (Statistics)
MSEE . . . . . . Mean Square Error Efficiency (Statistics)
MSEI . . . . Mean Square Error Inefficiency (Statistics)
MST . . . . Mean Survival Time (Bacteriology)
MTD . . . . Mean Temperature Difference
MT . . . . Mean Tide
MTL. . . . . Mean Tide Level
MT . . . . Mean Time
MTBE . . . . . . Mean Time Between Events
MTBF . . . . . . Mean Time Between Failures
MTBM . . . . . . Mean Time Between Maintenance
MTBMA . . . . . Mean Time Between Maintenance Action
MTBR . . . . . . Mean Time Between Repair
MTCF . . . . . . Mean Time to Catastrophic Failure
MTTF . . . . . . Mean Time to Failure (Quality control)
MTTFF . . . . . . Mean Time to First Failure (Quality control)
MTR . . . . Mean Time to Repair
MTR . . . . Mean Time to Restore (Air Force)
MTTR . . . . . . Mean Time to Restore (or Repair)
MTT. . . . . Mean Transit Time
MV . . . . Mean Variation
MWL . . . . Mean Water Level
MWR . . . . Mean Width Ratio
M . . . . Measure(s) (Music)
MOE . . . . Measure of Effectiveness
M . . . . Measured Ceiling (Aviation)
MD . . . . Measured Depth (Diamonds)
MD . . . . Measured Drilling (Diamonds)
METON . . . . . Measured Tons Discharged or Loaded (Shipping)
MV . . . . Measured Value
MRC . . . . Measurement Research Center (University of Iowa)
MTON . . . . . . Measurement Ton
M/T. . . . . Measurement Tons

MIC . . . . Meat Importers' Council
MI . . . . Meat Inspection Division (of ARS, Department of Agriculture)
MMMA . . . . . . Meat Machinery Manufacturers Association
MMMI . . . . . . Meat Machinery Manufacturers Institute
MPEA . . . . . . Meat and Poultry Export Association
M and V . . . . Meat-and-Vegetable (A canned ration) (Military) (World War I)
M . . . . Mechanical
MAIS . . . . . . Mechanical Aids for the Individual Soldier (Army)
MAT . . . . Mechanical Aptitude Test
MCT. . . . . Mechanical Comprehension Test
MCA . . . . Mechanical Contractors Association of America
MCAA . . . . . . Mechanical Contractors Association of America
ME . . . . Mechanical Efficiency
ME. . . . . Mechanical Engineer
M Eng. . . . . . . Mechanical Engineer
J . . . . Mechanical Equivalent of Heat (Symbol)
MIS . . . . Mechanical Interruption Summary (FAA)
MLA . . . . Mechanical Lubricator Association
MPA . . . . Mechanical Packing Association
MP . . . . Mechanical Part
MPTA . . . . . . Mechanical Power Transmission Association
MPTEDA . . . . Mechanical Power Transmission Equipment Distributors Association (Later, Power Transmission Distributors Association)
MPDC. . . . . . . Mechanical Properties Data Center (Air Force)
MRH . . . . Mechanical Recording Head
MRR . . . . Mechanical Reliability Report(s) (FAA)
MRR . . . . Mechanical Research Report
MT . . . . Mechanical Time
MTF . . . . Mechanical Time Fuze
MTSQ . . . . . Mechanical Time, Superquick
MT . . . . Mechanical Translation (Data processing)
MT. . . . . Mechanical Transport
MTC . . . . Mechanical Transport Corps
MVSMA . . . . . Mechanical Vibrating Screen Manufacturers Association
MASS . . . . . . Mechanically Accelerated Sabot System (Generation of high-density molecular beams)
MESA . . . . . . Mechanics Educational Society of America
MTI . . . . Mechanics Technology, Incorporated
MUJE . . . . . . Mechanics' Unions' Joint Executives (South Africa)
MDDA. . . . . . . Mechanicsburg Defense Depot Activity (AEC)
MOWASP . . . . Mechanization of Warehousing and Shipment Processing
MARRS . . . . . Mechanized Ammunition Recording and Reporting System
APM. . . . . Mechanized Artillery Transport (Navy symbol)
MB. . . . . Mechanized Battalion (Army)
MECHBAT . . . . Mechanized Battalion (Army)
MEDDA. . . . . . Mechanized Defense Decision Anticipation (AFSC)
MFT . . . . Mechanized Flame Thrower
MECHINF . . . . Mechanized Infantry (Army)
MICV . . . . . . Mechanized Infantry Combat Vehicle (Army)
MISPC . . . . . . Mechanized Infantry Squad Proficiency Course (Army)
MIFAS . . . . . . Mechanized Integrated Financial Accounting System (Department of State)
MMI . . . . Mechanized Manufacturing Information
MERGE . . . . . Mechanized Retrieval for Greater Efficiency (Data processing)
MSR . . . . Mechanized Storage and Retrieval (Data processing)
MCPP . . . . . . Mecoprop (Weed-control chemical)
CM . . . . Medal of Courage of the Order of Canada
MFS. . . . . Medal Field Service (Canada)
MF . . . . Medal of Freedom
MH . . . . Medal of Honor (Often erroneously called Congressional Medal of Honor)
MFHA. . . . . . . Medal for Humane Action (Military – Berlin Airlift, 1948-9)
MHA . . . . Medal for Humane Action
MM . . . . Medal of Merit
SM. . . . . Medal of Service of the Order of Canada
MISER . . . . . . Media Insertion Schedule Evaluation Report (Advertising)
MIID . . . . Media Institutes for Institute Directors
MRDA. . . . . . . Media Research Directors Association
MAA . . . . Mediaeval Academy of America
MFB . . . . Medial Forebrain Bundle
MLF . . . . Medial Longitudinal Fasciculus
CD/50 . . . . . . Median Curative Dose
MED . . . . Median Erythrocyte Diameter
MIS . . . . Median Iris Society
MLD . . . . Median Lethal Dose
MLT. . . . . Median Lethal Time (Radiation)
MAFI . . . . . . Medic-Alert Foundation International
MEDAC . . . . . Medical Accounting (and Billing Process)
MAB . . . . Medical Advisory Board
MEDICAID . . . Medical Aid (Federal program providing financial assistance for medical expenses of individual needy citizens)
MAP. . . . . Medical Aid Post
MAE . . . . Medical Air Evacuation

MAA . . . . Medical Assistance for the Aged
MAIN . . . . Medical Automation Intelligence (System)
MBAD . . . . Medical Badge
MB . . . . Medical Board
MEDICARE . . . Medical Care (Federal program providing financial assistance for medical expenses of individual senior citizens)
MC . . . . Medical Center
MEDCAP . . . . Medical Civic Action Programs (Army)
MEDCAT . . . . Medical Civic Action Teams
MCCR . . . . . . Medical Committee for Civil Rights
MCHR . . . . . . Medical Committee for Human Rights
MCLO . . . . . . Medical Construction Liaison Office(r) (Air Force)
MC . . . . Medical Corps (Navy)
MEDCORPS . . . Medical Corps (Air Force)
MCR . . . . Medical Corps, General Service (USNR officer designation)
MC-M . . . . . . Medical Corps, Merchant Marine (USNR officer designation)
MCM . . . . Medical Corps, Merchant Marine, General Service (USNR officer designation)
MCMR . . . . . . Medical Corps, Merchant Marine, General Service (USNR officer designation)
MCMS . . . . . . Medical Corps, Merchant Marine, Special Service (USNR officer designation)
MCS . . . . Medical Corps, Special Service (USNR officer designation)
MCW . . . . Medical Corps, Women's Reserve (USNR officer designation)
MCA . . . . Medical Correctional Association
MHBA . . . . . . Medical-Dental-Hospital Bureaus of America
MD . . . . Medical Department
MDG . . . . Medical Director General (British Navy)
MD . . . . Medical Discharge (from military service)
MEND . . . . . . Medical Education for National Defense
MERCY . . . . . Medical Emergency Relief Care for Youth
MEMO . . . . . Medical Equipment Management Office (Air Force)
MEDEVAC . . . Medical Evacuation Team (Army)
MEDEVAL . . . Medical Evaluation (Military)
ME . . . . Medical Examiner
MEBD . . . . . . Medical Examining Board
MEA . . . . Medical Exhibitors Association
MFSS . . . . . . Medical Field Service School
MFT . . . . Medical Field Service Technician (Navy)
MGMA . . . . . . Medical Group Management Association
MHD . . . . Medical Holding Detachment
M & HDA . . . . Medical and Hospital Department, Army
MI . . . . Medical Illustrator
MIIA . . . . Medical Information and Intelligence Agency (DOD)
MIMS . . . . . . Medical Information Management System
MIST . . . . Medical Information Service by Telephone
MI . . . . Medical Inspection
MIC . . . . Medical Inter-Fraternity Conference
MEDICO . . . . . Medical International Cooperation
MLCR . . . . . . Medical Laboratory Contract Reports (Army)
MLA . . . . Medical Library Association
MEDLARS . . . . Medical Literature Analysis and Retrieval System
MEDMIS . . . . Medical Management Information System (Army)
MMMR . . . . . Medical Material Mission Reserve (Military)
MMAC . . . . . . Medical Materiel Advice Code (Military)
MMPNC . . . . Medical Materiel Program for Nuclear Casualties
MMM . . . . . . Medical Missionaries of Mary (Roman Catholic women's religious order)
MNL . . . . Medical Nutrition Laboratory (Army)
MO . . . . Medical Officer
MOIC . . . . . . Medical Officer in Charge or Command
MEDOFCOM . . Medical Officer-in-Command (Military)
MOD . . . . Medical Officer of the Day (Military)
MOH . . . . Medical Officer of Health
MC-V(G) . . . . Medical Officers (Qualified for General Detail) (USNR designation)
MC-V(S) . . . . Medical Officers (Qualified for Specialist Duties) (USNR designation)
MORC . . . . . . Medical Officers' Reserve Corps
MPF . . . . Medical Passport Foundation
PMT . . . . Medical Photography Technician (Navy)
MPA . . . . Medical Procurement Agency
MRS . . . . Medical Receiving Station
MRL . . . . Medical Record Librarian
MRO . . . . Medical Regulating Office(r) (Army)
MRM . . . . . . Medical Repair Technician (Navy)
MRC . . . . Medical Research Council (Formerly, Committee) (British)
MRDC . . . . . . Medical Research & Development Committee (Army)
MRI . . . . Medical Research Institute (Navy)
MRL . . . . Medical Research Laboratory (Navy and Air Force)
MRNL . . . . . . Medical Research and Nutrition Laboratory (Army)
MRR . . . . Medical Research Reactor
MRC . . . . Medical Reserve Corps
MEDSERVC . . . Medical Service Corps (Military)

MSC . . . . Medical Service Corps (Navy)
MSS . . . . Medical Service School (Air Force)
MSU . . . . Medical Service Unit (Air Force)
MSA . . . . Medical Services Account
MSAO . . . . . . Medical Services Accountable Officer
MSEA . . . . . . Medical Society Executives Association
MEDSPECC . . . Medical Specialist Corps (Military)
MSC . . . . Medical Specialist Corps (Military)
MSPC . . . . . . Medical Specialist Corps
MESH . . . . . . Medical Subject Headings (MEDLARS)
MEDSUPDEP . . . Medical Supply Depot
MSMA . . . . . . Medical-Surgical Manufacturers Association
MSRC . . . . . . Medical and Surgical Relief Committee
MS . . . . Medical Survey (Navy)
MTA . . . . Medical and Technical Assistant
MT . . . . Medical Technologist
MTC . . . . Medical Training Center
MTO . . . . Medical Transport Officer
MUST . . . . . . Medical Unit Self-Contained Transportable (Army)
MUSE . . . . . . Medical Use of Simulation Electronics
MWIA . . . . . . Medical Women's International Association
MEDOL . . . . . Medically Oriented Language
M . . . . Medicine or Medical
MCMC . . . . . . Medicine Cabinet Manufacturers Council
M & D . . . . . Medicine and Duty
MC . . . . Medico-Chirurgical
M-C . . . . Medico-Chirurgical
MV . . . . Medicus Veterinarius (Veterinary Physician)
M . . . . Medieval
MGR . . . . Medieval Greek or Middle Greek
ML . . . . Medieval Latin (Language)
MAC . . . . Mediterranean Air Command (Military)
MATS . . . . . . Mediterranean Air Transport Service
MAAF . . . . . . Mediterranean Allied Air Force
MACAF . . . . . . Mediterranean Allied Coastal Air Forces
MAPRC . . . . . Mediterranean Allied Photographic Reconnaissance Command
MASAF . . . . . . Mediterranean Allied Strategic Air Force
MATAF . . . . . . Mediterranean Allied Tactical Air Force
MA . . . . Mediterranean Area
MAACP . . . . . Mediterranean Area Airlift Command Post
MAFOG . . . . . Mediterranean Area Fighter Operations Grid
MAAF . . . . . . Mediterranean Army Air Forces
MBC . . . . Mediterranean Bombardment Code
MCAF . . . . . . Mediterranean Coastal Air Force Headquarters
MCR . . . . Mediterranean Communication Region (Air Force)
MEDCOM . . . Mediterranean Communications (Military)
MED . . . . Mediterranean Engineer Division (Army Engineers)
MEDFLY . . . . Mediterranean Fruit Fly
MEDICOS . . . . Mediterranean Instructions to Convoys (World War II)
MJAO . . . . . . Mediterranean Joint Air Orders
MSCI . . . . . . Mediterranean Secret Convoy Instructions (World War II)
MSGO . . . . . . Mediterranean Secret General Orders
MSC . . . . Mediterranean Sub-Commission (Silva Mediterranea) (FAO)
MTAF . . . . . . Mediterranean Tactical Air Force Headquarters
MTO . . . . Mediterranean Theater of Operations, United States Army (Shortened form of MTOUSA) (World War II)
MTOUSA . . . . Mediterranean Theater of Operations, United States Army (Sometimes shortened to MTO) (World War II)
M . . . . Medium (Size designation for clothing, etc.)
MACS . . . . . . Medium-Altitude Communications Satellite
MACSS . . . . . . Medium-Altitude Communications Satellite System
MAW . . . . . . Medium Antiarmor (or Antitank) Weapon
MAAW . . . . . Medium Antitank Assault Weapon
MA . . . . Medium Artillery
MAW . . . . . . Medium Assault Weapon
MADM . . . . . . Medium Atomic Demolition Munition (Military)
MAM . . . . Medium Automotive Maintenance
AFDM . . . . . . Medium Auxiliary Floating Dry Dock (Navy symbol)
ARDM . . . . . . Medium Auxiliary Repair Dry Dock (Navy symbol)
MB . . . . Medium Bomber
MB . . . . Medium Bomber
MCT . . . . Medium Chain Triglyceride
MCU . . . . Medium Close Up (A photograph or motion picture sequence taken from a relatively short distance)
MCF . . . . Medium Corpuscular Fragility
MF . . . . Medium Frequency (Radio electronics)
MDF . . . . Medium-Frequency Direction Finding
YTM . . . . Medium Harbor Tug (Navy symbol)
VPB . . . . Medium and Heavy Patrol Bomber Squadron (Land based and seaplane) (Navy symbol)
MHF . . . . Medium High Frequency

MHDF ...... Medium and High Frequency Direction-Finding Station
MHVDF ..... Medium, High, and Very High Frequency Direction-Finding Station
LSM .... Medium Landing Ship (Navy symbol)
LSMR ...... Medium Landing Ship (Rocket)
MLS .... Medium Long Shot (A photograph or motion picture sequence taken from a relatively great distance)
MMG ...... Medium Machinegun
MOA ...... Medium Observation Aircraft
MORL ..... Medium Orbital Research Laboratory
M .... Medium (or 2-engine) Plane
MEDP ...... Medium Port
MPRE ...... Medium Power Reactor Experiment
MRA ...... Medium-Powered Radio Range (Adcock)
MRL .... Medium-Powered Radio Range (Loop radiators)
MP .... Medium Pressure
MR .... Medium Range
MRG ...... Medium Range
MRBM ..... Medium Range Ballistic Missile
MRI .... Medium Range Interceptor
MRM ...... Medium Range Missile
MR .... Medium Range Planes (Navy)
MRIR ...... Medium-Resolution Infrared Radiometer (NASA)
MRN ...... Medium-Round Nose (Diamond drilling)
MSI .... Medium-Scale Integration (Circuit packaging)
MS .... Medium Shot
MS .... Medium Steel
MTK .... Medium Tank
MTB .... Medium Tank Battalion
MVDF ..... Medium and Very High Frequency Direction-Finding Station
MV .... Medium Voltage
MW .... Medium Wave
MPD .... Medusa Portland Cement Company (NYSE symbol)
MSK .... Medvedev, Sponheuer, Karnick (Earthquake intensity scale)
MIND ..... Meeting Individual Needs Daily (Program of District of Columbia School Board)
MOON ..... Meeting Our Operational Needs
MP .... Meeting Point (Military)
M .... Mega
MB .... Megabar
MB .... Megabit
MB/S ...... Megabit Per Second
MC .... Megacycles
MCS .... Megacycles per Second
ME .... Megacycles Per Second
MHz ...... Megahertz
MM .... Megameter
MT .... Megaton
MV .... Megavolt
MEGW ..... Megawatt (Also, MW)
MW .... Megawatt
MAGIS ..... Megawatt Air-to-Ground Illumination System
MEGWH ..... Megawatt-Hour
MTR .... Meinicke Turbidity Reaction
MC .... Melamine Council
MSH .... Melanocyte-Stimulating Hormone (Endocrinology)
MH .... Melanophore Hormone (Endocrinology)
MSH .... Melanophore-Stimulating Hormone (Endocrinology)
MB .... Melbourne Bitter (Brand of beer) (Initialism used by Australians as slang for "inebriated")
MUDPAC .... Melbourne University Dual-Package Analog Computer (Australia)
MBP .... Melitensis Antigen Brucellosis Bovine, Porcine (Bacteriology)
MLANA ..... Melkite Laymen's Association of North America
MP .... Melting Point
M .... Melts at
MES .... Melville Shoe Corporation (NYSE symbol)
M .... Member
MACR ..... Member of the American College of Radiology
MAI ...... Member of the Anthropological Institute (British)
MAI ...... Member, Appraisal Institute (Designation awarded to appraisers of real property)
MAS ...... Member of the Arundel Society (British)
MAPUC ..... Member of the Association for Promoting the Unity of Christendom (British)
MANZCP .... Member of the Australian and New Zealand College of Psychiatrists
MCD ...... Member of the College of Dentists (British)
MCGP ..... Member of the College of General Practitioners (British)
MCM ...... Member of the College of Musicians (British)
MCPA ..... Member of the College of Pathologists Australasia
MCPS ..... Member of the College of Physicians and Surgeons (British)
MCP ...... Member of the College of Preceptors (British)
MCRA ..... Member of the College of Radiologists Australasia

MC .... Member of Congress
MC .... Member of Council
MEIC ...... Member of the Engineering Institute of Canada
MECU ..... Member of the English Church Union
MFPS ..... Member of the Faculty of Physicians and Surgeons (Glasgow)
MGI ...... Member of the Gas Institute (British)
MHK ...... Member of the House of Keys (Isle of Man)
MHR .... Member of the House of Representatives
MILS ...... Member of the Incorporated Law Society (British)
MIME ..... Member of the Institute of Mining Engineers
MICE ..... Member of the Institution of Civil Engineers (British)
MIME ..... Member of the Institution of Mechanical Engineers (British)
MINA ..... Member of the Institution of Naval Architects (British)
MKQCP ..... Member of the King's and Queen's College of Physicians (Ireland)
MLA ...... Member of the Legislative Assembly
MLC ...... Member of the Legislative Council
MLMS ..... Member of the London Mathematical Society
MLSB ..... Member of the London School Board
MMF ...... Member of the Medical Faculty
MNAS ..... Member of the National Academy of Sciences
MNS ...... Member of the Numismatical Society (British)
MBE ...... Member of the Order of the British Empire
MP .... Member of Parliament (British)
MPC ...... Member of Parliament of Canada
MPS ...... Member of the Pharmaceutical Society (British)
MPS ...... Member of the Philological Society (British)
MPS ...... Member of the Physical Society (British)
MPP .... Member of Provincial Parliament (British)
MRAM ..... Member of the Royal Academy of Music (British)
MRAC ..... Member of the Royal Agricultural College (British)
MRASE ..... Member of the Royal Agricultural Society of England
MRAS ..... Member of the Royal Asiatic Society (British)
MRASB ..... Member of the Royal Asiatic Society of Bengal
MRCOG .... Member of the Royal College of Obstetricians and Gynaecologists (British)
MRCP ..... Member of the Royal College of Physicians (British)
MRCS ..... Member of the Royal College of Surgeons (British)
MRSH ..... Member of the Royal Society of Health (British)
MRSPWC .... Member of the Royal Society of Painters in Water-Colours (British)
MRVC ..... Member of the Royal Veterinary College (British)
MVO ...... Member of the Royal Victorian Order (British)
MSA ...... Member of the Society of Apothecaries (British)
MSA ...... Member of the Society of Arts (British)
MSE ...... Member of the Society of Engineers (British)
MTS ...... Members of the Technical Staff (A generic term)
M .... Membrana (Membrane) (Anatomy)
MWP .... Membrane Waterproofing
MRS .... Memo Routing Slip
M .... Memorandum
M/D .... Memorandum of Deposits (Business and trade)
M/P .... Memorandum of Partnership (Business and trade)
M/R .... Memorandum Receipt (Military)
MFR .... Memorandum for Record (Military)
MR .... Memorandum for Record
MR .... Memorandum Report
MOU ...... Memorandum of Understanding
M .... Memoria (Memory)
MS .... Memoriae Sacrum (Sacred to the Memory Of)
MC .... Memorial Commission (Federal body)
MI .... Memorial Inscription
MA .... Memory Address (Data processing)
MAR .... Memory Address Register
MARS ..... Memory-Address Register Storage
MB .... Memory Buffer
MBR ...... Memory Buffer Register (Data processing)
MBRE ..... Memory Buffer Register, Even (Data processing)
MBRO ..... Memory Buffer Register, Odd (Data processing)
MCP ...... Memory-Centered Processing (or Processor) (System)
MC .... Memory Control (Unit) (Data processing)
MDR ...... Memory-Data Register
MGG ...... Memory Gate Generator (Data processing)
MIR .... Memory-Information Register
MLU ...... Memory Loading Unit (of FADAC) (Military)
MLR ...... Memory Lockout Register
MR .... Memory Register
MS .... Memory System
MTC ...... Memory Test Computer (SAGE)
MEAD ..... Memphis Army Depot
MCE .... Memphis Cotton Exchange
MFMI ...... Men for Missions International
MOM ..... Men Our Masters (Anti-feminist women's group)

MBE	Mennonite Board of Education
MCC	Mennonite Central Committee
MDS	Mennonite Disaster Service
MVS	Mennonite Voluntary Service
MA	Menorah Association
MGCA	Men's Garden Clubs of America
MHLTA	Men's Hat Linings and Trimmings Association
MNMANY	Men's Neckwear Manufacturers Association of New York
MNMIA	Men's Neckwear Manufacturers Institute of America
MTF	Men's Tie Foundation
MA	Menstrual Age
MH	Menstrual History
MRA	Menswear Retailers of America
MA	Mental Age (Psychology)
MH	Mental Health
MHA	Mental Health Administration
MHFB	Mental Health Film Board
MHMC	Mental Health Materials Center
MHRI	Mental Health Research Institute (University of Michigan)
MHCS	Mental Hygiene Consultation Service
MRI	Mental Research Institute
MD	Mentally Deficient
MDA	Mento-Dextra Anterior
MDP	Mento-Dextra Posterior
MDT	Mento-Dextra Transversa
MACRI	Mercantile Atlantic Coastal Routing Instructions
MARI	Mercantile Atlantic Routing Instructions
MERCO	Mercantile Communications (Shipping)
MFA	Mercantile Fleet Auxiliary (British)
MM	Mercantile Marine or Merchant Marine
MMSA	Mercantile Marine Service Association (British)
MPCRI	Mercantile Pacific Coastal Routing Instructions
MST	Mercantile Stores Company, Inc. (NYSE symbol)
MBT	Mercaptobenzothiazole
MMB	Mercedarian Missionaries of Berriz (Roman Catholic women's religious order)
MBCA	Mercedes-Benz Club of America
MMAA	Merchandise Mart Apparel Association
MOR	Merchandising and Operating Results
XAPC	Merchant Coastal Transport, Small (Ship symbol)
MERCOS	Merchant Codes (Shipping)
MMC	Merchant Marine Council (Coast Guard)
MMD	Merchant Marine Detail
MMOG	Merchant Marine Officers Guild
MMP	Merchant Marine Personnel Division (Coast Guard)
MMS	Merchant Marine Safety
MMT	Merchant Marine Technical Division (Coast Guard)
MN	Merchant Navy
MPRI	Merchant Pacific Routing Instructions (Shipping)
MERCAST	Merchant Ship Broadcast
MERCO	Merchant Ship Control
MSCS	Merchant Ship Control Service
XAM	Merchant Ship Converted to a Minesweeper (Navy symbol) (Obsolete)
MS	Merchant Shipping
MERSIGS	Merchant Signals (Shipping)
XAP	Merchant Transport (Ship symbol)
M of V	The Merchant of Venice (by Shakespeare)
M/V	Merchant Vessel
MVI	Merchant Vessel Inspection Division (Coast Guard)
MRK	Merck & Company, Inc. (NYSE symbol)
MSD	Merck, Sharp and Dohme (Commercial firm)
MA	Mercury-Atlas (Spacecraft) (NASA)
MCC	Mercury Control Center
MRPC	Mercury Rankine Power Conversion (AEC)
MR	Mercury-Redstone (NASA)
MR-BD	Mercury-Redstone Booster Development (Spacecraft) (NASA)
MS	Mercury-Scout (Spacecraft) (NASA)
MAFR	Merged Accountability and Fund Reporting (Air Force)
MAID	Merger Acquisition Improved Decision (Data processing)
m	Meridian (Lower branch)
M	Meridian (Upper branch)
T	Meridian Angle
MB	Meridian & Bigbee R. R. (AAR code)
MHF	Meridian House Foundation
M	Meridies (Noon)
M	Meridional Parts
MBA	Merion Bluegrass Association
MQ	Merit Quotient
MCSA	Meritorious Civilian Service Award
MUC	Meritorious Unit Citation (Army award)
MUC	Meritorious Unit Commendation (Air Force award)
MUE	Meritorious Unit Emblem
MCS	Merritt-Chapman & Scott Corporation (NYSE symbol)
MILA	Merritt Island Launch Area (NASA)
MLPFS	Merrill Lynch, Pierce, Fenner & Smith (Stockbrokers) (Wall Street slang name: "Thundering Herd")
MMA	Merrill's Marauders Association
MEVE	Mesa Verde National Park
MSB	Mesabi Trust, Units of Beneficial Interest (NYSE symbol)
MOD	Mesial, Occlusal, and Distal (Describes location of openings in a carious tooth) (Dentistry)
MO	Mesio-Occlusal
MP	Mesiopulpal
MEF	Mesopotamian Expeditionary Force (British)
M/A	Mess Attendant
MESCPL	Mess Corporal (Marine Corps)
MD	Mess Deck (Naval)
MESSSGT	Mess Sergeant (Marine Corps)
MAP	Message Acceptance Pulse (Aerospace communications)
MA	Message Assembler
MFB	Message from Base
MTB	Message to Base
MB	Message Business
MSGCEN	Message Center
MC	Message Composer (Communications)
MC	Message Composer (Computer)
MCU	Message Construction Unit
MD	Message Data
MDU	Message Decoder Unit
MD	Message-Dropping (Military)
MG	Message Generator
MIU	Message Injection Unit
MPIC	Message Processing Interrupt Count
MRO	Message Releasing Officer
MR	Message Repeat
MRU	Message Retransmission Unit
MSU	Message Switching Unit
MTS	Message Traffic Study
MWI	Message-Waiting Indicator
MM	Messageries Maritimes (Forwarding agents)
MD	Messages per Day
MRNA	Messenger Ribonucleic Acid
M-RNA	Messenger Ribonucleic Acid
MBB	Messerschmitt-Boelkow-Blohm (West German aircraft company)
MM	Messieurs (Plural of Mister) (French)
MBAA	Messinian Benevolent Association "Aristomenis"
MCC	Mesta Machine Company (NYSE symbol)
MPVO	Mestnaia Protivovozdushnaia Oborona (Local Anti-Air Defense) (USSR)
MABA	Meta-Aminobenzoic Acid
MI	Metabolic Index
MR	Metabolic Rate
ME	Metabolizable Energy
MCPH	Metacarpal-Phalangeal
M	Metacenter
MLD	Metachromatic Leukodystrophy (Medicine)
M	Metal
MAS	Metal Anchor Slots (Technical drawings)
MBDA	Metal Building Dealers Association
MBMA	Metal Building Manufacturers Association
MCW	Metal Casement Window (Technical drawings)
MCMA	Metal Cookware Manufacturers Association
MCB	Metal Corner Bead (Technical drawings)
MCD	Metal-Covered Door (Technical drawings)
MCKA	Metal Cutting Knife Association
MCTI	Metal Cutting Tool Institute
MEFA	Metal Etching and Fabricating Association
MFMA	Metal Findings Manufacturers Association
MFSA	Metal Finishing Suppliers' Association
MGI	Metal Grating Institute
MGS	Metal Gravel Stop
MIG	Metal-Inert-Gas (Underwater welding)
MLMA	Metal Ladder Manufacturers Association
MLA	Metal Lath Association
MLMA	Metal Lath Manufacturers Association
MLP	Metal Lath and Plaster (Technical drawings)
MOS	Metal-Oxide Semiconductor
MOST	Metal Oxide Semiconductor Transistor
MOS	Metal-Oxide-Silicon (Integrated circuit) (Electronics)
MOSFET	Metal-Oxide-Silicon Field-Effect Transistor
MPTS	Metal Parts
MPBP	Metal Polishers, Buffers, Platers and Helpers International Union
MPA	Metal Powder Association

MPI	Metal Powder Industries Federation
MPIF	Metal Powder Industries Federation
MPPA	Metal Powder Producers Association
MRD	Metal Rolling Door (Technical drawings)
MRDTI	Metal Roof Deck Technical Institute
MTNS	Metal-Thick Oxide-Nitride-Silicon
MTOS	Metal-Thick Oxide-Silicon
MTWF	Metal Thru-Wall Flashing (Technical drawings)
MTD	Metal Trades Department (AFL-CIO)
MTI	Metal Treating Institute
MVI	Metal Ventilator Institute
MC	Metaling Clause (Marine insurance)
MLB	Metallic Link Belt
MYI	Metallic Yarns Institute (Defunct)
MMN	Metallurgic et Mechanique Nucleaires (Belgium)
MS	Metallurgical Society (of AIME)
MCD	Metals & Ceramics Division (Air Force)
MEI	Metals Engineering Institute
MPL	Metals Processing Laboratory (MIT)
MRC	Metals Reserve Company
M	Metalsmith (Navy)
ME	Metalsmith (Navy)
MSMTH	Metalsmith (Navy)
MSR	Metalsmith, Ship Repair (Navy)
MSRB	Metalsmith, Ship Repair, Blacksmith (Navy)
MSRC	Metalsmith, Ship Repair, Coppersmith (Navy)
MSRF	Metalsmith, Ship Repair, Forger-Anglesmith (Navy)
MSRS	Metalsmith, Ship Repair, Sheet Metal Worker (Navy)
MZ	Metalurgichen Zavod
MNS	Meta-Nitride Semiconductor
MSA	Metaphysical Society of America
MS	Meteoritical Society
MDS	Meteoroid Detection Satellite (NASA)
MTS	Meteoroid Technology Satellite
METLO	Meteorological Electronic Technical Liaison Office (Navy)
MGA	Meteorological and Geoastrophysical Abstracts (American Meteorological Society)
MGT	Meteorological and Geoastrophysical Titles
METO	Meteorological Officer (Air Force)
MRC	Meteorological Research Committee (British)
METROC	Meteorological Rocket
MRN	Meteorological Rocket Network (NASA)
MSL	Meteorological Satellite Laboratory
MWO	Meteorological Watch Office
MD	Meteorology Department (Navy)
M	Meter(s)
MA	Meter Angle
MC	Meter-Candle
MKS	Meter Kilogram Second (Physics)
MKSA	Meter, Kilogram, Second, and Ampere (System)
MPM	Meters Per Minute
MPS	Meters Per Second
M/S	Meters Per Second
MSA	Methanesulfonic Acid
MSO	Methionine Sulfoximine
MO	Method of Operation
MOPE	Method of Personnel Evaluation
M	Methodist
MCOR	Methodist Committee for Overseas Relief
ME	Methodist Episcopal
MEC	Methodist Episcopal Church
MECH	Methodist Episcopal Church
ME(S)	Methodist Episcopal, South
MFSA	Methodist Federation for Social Action
MPF	Methodist Peace Fellowship
MP	Methodist Protestant
MPCH	Methodist Protestant Church
MYF	Methodist Youth Fellowship
MCR	Methodists for Church Renewal
MIP	Methods Improvement Program (IBM)
MOI	Methods of Instruction
MIND	Methods of Intellectual Development (National Association of Manufacturers)
MPTO	Methods and Procedures Technical Orders
MTM	Methods-Time Measurement (Management)
MTM	Methods Time Measurement Association for Standards and Research
MB	Methyl Bromide
MCH	Methyl Cyclohexane (Chemical)
MEK	Methyl Ethyl Ketone (Solvent)
MIBK	Methyl Isobutyl Ketone
MIK	Methyl Isobutyl Ketone (Chemical)

MM	Methyl Methacrylate
MR	Methyl Red (An indicator)
MRVP	Methyl-Red, Voges-Proskauer (Medium) (Bacteriology)
MV	Methyl Violet
MAK	Methylated Albumin Kieselguhr (Chromatography)
MBSA	Methylated Bovine Serum Albumin
MCA	Methylcholanthrene (Chemical)
MD	Methyldichloroarsine
MB	Methylene Blue
MDI	Methylene Di-p-phenyl Diisocyanate (Chemistry)
MU	Methylene Unit
MPA	Methylphosphonic Acid
MP	Methylpurine
MTU	Methylthiouracil
MA	Metric Association
MC	Metric Carat (200 milligrams)
MS	Metric System
MT	Metric Ton (1,000 kilograms)
MTU	Metric Units
MGM	Metro-Goldwyn-Mayer (Motion picture production corporation) (NYSE symbol)
MEASURE	Metrology Automated System for Uniform Recall and Reporting (Navy)
MEC	Metrology Engineering Center (Navy)
MET	Metromedia, Inc. (NYSE symbol)
M	Metropolitan
MAHA	Metropolitan Association of Handwriting Analysts
MAB	Metropolitan Asylums Board (British)
MBPDA	Metropolitan Bag and Paper Distributors Association
MBW	Metropolitan Board of Works (British)
MCDAS	Metropolitan Cities Drug Association Secretaries
MCA	Metropolitan Club of America
MCTA	Metropolitan Commuter Transportation Authority (Greater New York City) (Later, Metropolitan Transportation Authority)
MCA	Metropolitan Cycle Association (New York)
MDR	Metropolitan District Railway (London)
MEA	Metropolitan Economic Area
MTT	Metropolitan Edison Company (NYSE symbol)
MECAR	Metropolitan Engineers Council on Air Resources
MFB	Metropolitan Fire Brigade (British)
MELSA	Metropolitan Library Service Agency
MMA	Metropolitan Magazine Association
MOG	Metropolitan Opera Guild
MP	Metropolitan Police
MPO	Metropolitan Police Office (British) (Familiarly called "Scotland Yard" from its site at New Scotland Yard)
MR	Metropolitan Railway (London)
MSMA	Metropolitan Symphony Managers Association
MTA	Metropolitan Transportation Authority (Greater New York City)
MVRA	Metropolitan Visiting and Relief Association (British)
MVA	Mevalonic Acid
MAAU	Mexican-American Affairs Unit (US Office of Education)
MAPA	Mexican-American Political Association
MAYO	Mexican-American Youth Organization
MBSM	Mexican Border Service Medal
MBV	Mexican Border Veterans
MCCM	Mexican Chamber of Commerce of US
MCI	Mexican Coffee Institute
ML	Mexican League (Baseball)
MEXSVM	Mexican Service Medal
MWV	Mexican War Veteran
MPF	Mexico Pilgrims Foundation
METE	Mezogazdasagi es Elelmiszeripari Tudomanyos Egyesulet
M	Mezzo (Half)
MF	Mezzo Forte (Moderately loud) (Music)
MP	Mezzo Piano (Moderately soft) (Music)
MIA	Miami (Florida) (International airport, symbol)
MIA	Mica Industry Association
MI	Michigan
MAD	Michigan Algorithmic Decoder (IBM)
MACU	Michigan Association of Colleges and Universities
MC	Michigan Central R. R. (AAR code)
MCSA	Michigan Council for the Study of Abortion
MIDAC	Michigan (University of) Digital Automatic Computer
MERIT	Michigan Educational Research Information Triad, Inc.
MOREL	Michigan-Ohio Regional Educational Laboratory
MOMP	Michigan Ordnance Missile Plant (Army)
MSU	Michigan State University
MAF	Michoud Assembly Facility (NASA)
MP	Michoud Plant (NASA)
MADT	Microalloy Diffused Base Transistor
MAT	Microalloy Transistor

MAR . . . . Microanalytical Reagent
MIKER . . . . . . Microbalance Inverted Knudsen Effusion Recoil
MC'F . . . . Micro-Complement Fixation (Quantitative immunochemistry)
MED . . . . Microelectronic Device
MIRAGE . . . . . Microelectronic Indicator for RADAR Ground Equipment
MITE . . . . Microlectronic Integrated Test Equipment
MMF . . . . Microelectronics Manufacturing Facility (Philco Corporation)
MF . . . . Microfarad
MFD . . . . Microfarad
MF . . . . Microfiche (Sheet microfilm)
MF . . . . Microfilm
MM . . . . Microfilm
MIRACODE . . . Microfilm Information Retrieval Access Code
FILMSORT . . . . Microfilm Sorter (Electronics)
MFC . . . . Microfunctional Circuit
MCR . . . . Micrographic Catalog Retrieval
MIDAS . . . . . Micro-Imaged Data Addition System
MEDAL . . . . . Micromechanized Engineering Data for Automated Logistics
ME . . . . Micrometeoroid Explorer (Satellite)
MIC . . . . Micrometer (A "mike")
MMFD . . . . . . Micromicrofarad
MR . . . . Microminiature Relay
MAUTEL . . . . Microminiaturized Autonetics Telemetry
MA . . . . Microphone and Amplifier (Television)
MCDP . . . . . . Micro-Programmed Data Processor
MW . . . . Microwave
MAN . . . . . . Microwave Aerospace Navigation
MATCON . . . . Microwave Aerospace Terminal Control (Air Force)
MASER . . . . . Microwave Amplification by Stimulated Emission of Radiation
MCS . . . . Microwave Carrier Supply
MCG . . . . . . Microwave Command Guidance
MCGS . . . . . Microwave Command Guidance System (RADC)
MIDAR . . . . . Microwave Detection and Ranging
MEW . . . . Microwave Early Warning (Radio) (Air Force)
MELABS . . . . . Microwave Engineering Laboratories, Inc.
ML . . . . Microwave Laboratory (Stanford University)
MLS . . . . Microwave Landing System
MOGA . . . . . Microwave and Optical Generation and Amplification
MOD . . . . . . Microwave Oscillating Diode
MPG . . . . . . Microwave Pulse Generator
MRU . . . . Microwave Relay Unit
MRI . . . . Microwave Research Institute (Polytechnic Institute of Brooklyn)
MISRE . . . . . . Microwave Space Relay (Electronics)
MWS . . . . . . Microwave Station
MTT . . . . Microwave Theory and Technique
MAA . . . . Mid America Airlines
MAECON . . . . Mid-America Electronics Conference
MARPDA . . . . Mid-America Periodical Distributors Association
MASUA . . . . . Mid-America State Universities Association
MB . . . . Midbody
MBP . . . . Mid-Boiling Point
MIDIZ . . . . . . Mid-Canada Identification Zone
MCL . . . . Mid-Canada Line (RADAR warning chain of fence across Canada; sometimes called the McGill Fence)
MIAPD . . . . . . Mid-Central Air Procurement District
MCD . . . . Mid-Central District (ATSC)
MCL . . . . Midclavicular Line
MAPP . . . . . . Mid-Continent Area Power Planners Committee (Electric power)
MCAPI . . . . . . Mid-Continent Association of the Pet Industry
MCOGA . . . . Mid-Continent Oil and Gas Association
MAS . . . . Midcourse Active System
MCC . . . . Midcourse Correction
MMC . . . . . . Midcourse Measurement Correction
M . . . . Middle
MA . . . . Middle Ages
MARU . . . . . . Middle America Research Unit
MAC . . . . Middle Atlantic Conference
MAFA . . . . . . Middle Atlantic Fisheries Association
MAPS . . . . . . Middle Atlantic Planetarium Society
MARM . . . . . Middle Atlantic Regional Meeting (of American Chemical Society)
MBMU . . . . . Middle Belt Mineworkers' Union (Nigeria)
MING . . . . . . Middle Class, Intelligent, Nice Girls
MD . . . . Middle Dutch (Language, etc.)
ME . . . . Middle East(ern)
MEA . . . . Middle East Airlines Company
MECAS . . . . . Middle East Center for Arab Studies
MECOM . . . . Middle East Command (Military)
MIDEASTFOR . . Middle East Force (Navy)
MEF . . . . Middle East Forces (British)
MEI . . . . Middle East Institute
MEIU . . . . . . Middle East Interpretation Unit (British)

MELG . . . . . . Middle East Liaison Group (Military)
MENA . . . . . . Middle East News Agency
ME/SA . . . . . . Middle East/South Asia
MEAFSA . . . . . Middle East/Southern Asia and Africa South of the Sahara (Military)
MESA . . . . . . Middle East Studies Association of North America
MESC . . . . Middle East Supply Center
METU . . . . . . Middle East Technical University (Ankara, Turkey)
METO . . . . . . Middle East Treaty Organization
ME . . . . Middle English (Language, etc.)
MF . . . . Middle Fork R. R. (AAR code)
MFP . . . . Middle Free Path
MFR . . . . Middle French (Language, etc.)
MHG . . . . Middle High German (Language, etc.)
MI . . . . Middle Initial
ML . . . . Middle Latin (Language, etc.)
LM . . . . Middle Latitude (Navigation)
MLG . . . . Middle Low German (Language)
MM . . . . Middle Marker (in an instrument landing system)
MMKR . . . . . Middle Marker (in a instrument landing system)
MOM . . . . . . Middle of the Month
MSU . . . . Middle South Utilities, Inc. (NYSE symbol)
MSRA . . . . . . Middle States Regatta Association
MW . . . . Middle Welsh
MR . . . . The Middlesex Regiment (British)
MAMA . . . . . Middletown Air Materiel Area
MASC . . . . . . Middletown Air Service Command (Air Force)
MATSC . . . . . Middletown Air Technical Service Command (Air Force)
MNJ . . . . Middletown & New Jersey Railway Company (AAR code)
MELP . . . . . . Mid-European Law Project
M . . . . Midfield (Men's lacrosse position)
MORC . . . . . Midget Ocean Racing Club (or Class)
MICO . . . . . . Midland Continental R. R. (AAR code)
MR . . . . Midland Railway (British)
MLR . . . . Midland-Ross Corporation (NYSE symbol)
MLD . . . . Midland Valley R. R. (AAR code)
MV . . . . Midland Valley R. R. (AAR code)
MLN . . . . Mid-Lateral Nerve
MAST . . . . . . Midlevel Positions in Administrative, Staff and Technical Services (Civil Service Commission)
MOMP . . . . . Mid-Ocean Meeting Place
MRBM . . . . . . Mid-Range Ballistic Missile
MRE . . . . Mid-Range Estimate
MRO . . . . Mid-Range Objectives
MSL . . . . Midsternal Line
MSU . . . . Mid-Stream Urine Specimen
MND . . . . . . Midsummer Night's Dream (Shakespeare)
MAUSED . . . . Midwest Association of University Student Employment Directors
MWA . . . . . . Midwest Aviation, Inc.
MCPA . . . . . . Midwest College Placement Association
MCA . . . . Midwest Commuter Airlines
MCA . . . . Mid-West Compensation Association
MCA . . . . Midwest Curling Association
MFMA . . . . . . Midwest Feed Manufacturers Association
MILC . . . . . . Midwest Inter-Library Center (Formerly, Center for Research Libraries)
MJGA . . . . . . Midwest Job Galvanizers Association
MWO . . . . . . Midwest Oil Corporation (NYSE symbol)
MOSTA . . . . . Midwest Old Settlers and Threshers Association
MOLA . . . . . . Midwest Open Land Association
MPATI . . . . . . Midwest Program for Airborne Television Instruction
MRI . . . . Midwest Research Institute
MRA . . . . Midwest Resources Association (Defunct)
MSE . . . . Midwest Stock Exchange
MPA . . . . Midwestern Psychological Association
MURA . . . . . . Midwestern Universities Research Association
MCF . . . . Migrant Children's Fund
MBA . . . . Migratory Bird Act
MBCC . . . . . . Migratory Bird Conservation Commission (A federal government body)
MIG . . . . Mikoyan and Gurevich (Acronym used as designation for a Russian aircraft and is formed from the names of the aircraft's designers)
MEBD . . . . . . Milcherzeugerberatungsdienst
MDF . . . . Mild Detonating Fuse
MS . . . . Mild Steel
MRT . . . . Mildew-Resistant Thread
MSC . . . . Mile of Standard Cable
MAD . . . . Mileage Accumulation Dynamometer
MRB . . . . Mileage Rationing Board (World War II)
MP . . . . Mile-Post
M . . . . Miles
MC . . . . Miles on Course
MIH . . . . Miles in the Hour
MIL . . . . Miles Laboratories, Inc. (NYSE symbol)

M/G. . . . . Miles Per Gallon
MPG . . . . . . Miles Per Gallon
M/H. . . . . . . Miles Per Hour
MPH. . . . . . . Miles Per Hour
M/H/S . . . . . Miles Per Hour Per Second
MPHPS . . . . . Miles Per Hour Per Second
MPM . . . . Miles Per Minute
MPS . . . . . . Miles Per Second
MRM . . . . Miles of Relative Movement (Navigation)
M . . . . Military
MA . . . . Military Academy
MARSA . . . . . Military Accepts Responsibility for Separation of Aircraft
MILADGOVT . . Military Advisory Government
MAG . . . . . . Military Advisory Group
MILADGRU . . . Military Advisory Group
MAMB . . . . . . Military Advisory Mission, Brazil
MARS . . . . . . Military Affiliated Radio System (Amateur-operated radio stations)
MAS . . . . . . Military Agency for Standardization (NATO)
MILSTAN . . . . Military Agency for Standardization
MAP . . . . Military Aid (or Assistance) Program
MADW . . . . . Military Air Defense Warning Net
MAM . . . . . . Military Air Movement Number
MATCO . . . . . Military Air Traffic Coordinating Office(r) (Air Force)
MAT. . . . . . . Military Air Transport
MATB . . . . . . Military Air Transport Board
MATS . . . . . . Military Air Transport Service (Later, Military Air Command)
MTCC . . . . . . Military Air Transport Service Transport Control Center
MASDC . . . . . Military Aircraft Storage and Disposition Center
MAT. . . . . . . Military Aircraft Types
MAC . . . . Military Airlift Command (Formerly, Military Air Transport Service)
MACOPS . . . . Military Airlift Command Operational Phone System
MACTELNET . . MAC (Military Airlift Command) Teletype Network
MTA . . . . MAC (Military Airlift Command) Transportation Authorization
MAW . . . . . . Military Airlift Wing (Air Force)
MAS . . . . . . Military Alert System
MADAEC . . . . Military Application Division of the Atomic Energy Commission
MAC(K) . . . . . Military Armistice Commission (Korea)
MAAG . . . . . Military Assistance Advisory Group (Merged with US Military Assistance Command)
MASL . . . . . . Military Assistance Articles and Services List
MACV . . . . . . Military Assistance Command, Vietnam
MAI. . . . . . . Military Assistance Institute
MAM . . . . . . Military Assistance Manual
MAOT . . . . . . Military Assistance Observer Team
MAPAG . . . . . Military Assistance Program Advisory Group
MAPCC . . . . . Military Assistance Program Country Code
MAPLA . . . . . Military Assistance Program Logistics Agency (Merged with Defense Supply Agency)
MAPOM . . . . Military Assistance Program Owned Materiel
MAPT. . . . . . Military Assistance Program Training
MAPSAD . . . . Military Assistance Property Sales and Disposal
MAS . . . . . . Military Assistance Sales
MATP . . . . . . Military Assistance Training Program
MA . . . . Military Assistant (Air Force)
MAP . . . . Military Association of Podiatrists
MA . . . . Military Attaché (Diplomacy)
MAIN . . . . . . Military Authorization Identification Number
MASA . . . . . . Military Automotive Supply Agency
MASC . . . . . . Military Automotive Supply Center
MAN . . . . . . Military Aviation Notice (Air Force)
MAN's . . . . . Military Aviation Notices (Air Force)
MA . . . . Military Aviator
MBF . . . . Military Banking Facility
MBA . . . . . . Military Benefit Association
MBPA . . . . . . Military Blood Program Agency
MCA . . . . . . Military Chaplains Association of the USA
MC . . . . Military Characteristics
MCE . . . . . . Military Characteristics Equipment
MCM . . . . . . Military Characteristics Motor Vehicles
MCAA . . . . . Military Civil Affairs Administration (The Netherlands) (World War II)
MCTSA . . . . . Military Clothing and Textile Supply Agency (Army – Merged with Defense Supply Agency)
MC . . . . Military Committee (NATO)
MCREP . . . . . Military Committee Representative (to the North Atlantic Council)
MCEB . . . . . . Military Communications-Electronics Board
MILCOMSAT. . . Military Communications Satellite
MCSS . . . . . . Military Communications Satellite System
MCS . . . . . . Military Communications Stations
MCOHM . . . . . Military Community Oral Health Managers (Army)
MCR . . . . . . Military Compact Reactor (AEC)
MCUG . . . . . . Military Computers Users Group

MC . . . . Military Construction
MILCON . . . . Military Construction (Navy)
MCAF . . . . . Military Construction, Air Force
MCA . . . . . . Military Construction Appropriation (or Authorization)
MCA . . . . . . Military Construction, Army (Appropriation)
MCARNG . . . . Military Construction, Army National Guard
MCAR . . . . . . Military Construction, Army Reserve
MCAP. . . . . . Military Construction Authorized Program
MCNRF . . . . . Military Construction, Naval Reserve Facilities
MCON . . . . . Military Construction, Navy
MCP . . . . . . Military Construction Program
MCPAC . . . . . Military Construction Programs Advisory Committee
MCSA . . . . . Military Construction Supply Agency (Later, Defense Construction Supply Center)
MCAD . . . . . Military Contracts Administration Department
MCD . . . . . . Military Contracts Department
MCC . . . . . . Military Coordinating Committee
MC . . . . Military Cross
MDW . . . . . . Military Defence Works (British)
MDW . . . . . . Military District of Washington (DC)
MELVA . . . . . Military Electronic Light Valve
ME . . . . Military Engineer
MEXE . . . . . . Military Engineering Experimental Establishment (British)
MEDT . . . . . . Military Equipment Delivery Team
MEC . . . . . . Military Essentiality Code
METRI . . . . . Military Essentiality Through Readiness Indices
MEGA . . . . . Military Evaluation of Geographic Areas
MEX . . . . . . Military Exchange
MFH . . . . . . Military Family Housing
MFIC . . . . . . Military Flight Information Center
MFS. . . . . . . Military Flight Service
MFO . . . . . . Military Forwarding Officer
MFA . . . . . . Military Functions Appropriation
MGSA . . . . . Military General Supply Agency (Merged with Defense General Supply Center)
MGST . . . . . Military Geography Specialist Team
MG . . . . Military Government or Governor
MGA . . . . . . Military Government Association
MGO . . . . . . Military Government Officer
MGU . . . . . . Military Government Unit
MGRS . . . . . Military Grid Reference System
MHFR . . . . . . Military Height-Finder RADAR Equipment
MHS . . . . . . Military Historical Society
MIP . . . . . . Military Improvement Program
MILDDU . . . . Military Inductory Logistics Data Division Unit
M-IC . . . . . . Military-Industrial Complex
MISA . . . . . . Military Industrial Supply Agency
MILDIP . . . . . Military Industry Logistics Data Interchange Procedures
MITM . . . . . . Military Industry Technical Manual
MITMS . . . . . Military/Industry Technical Manual Specifications (NPPO)
MI . . . . Military Intelligence (Army)
MIBARS . . . . . Military Intelligence Battalion (Aerial Reconnaissance and Surveillance) (Army)
MID . . . . . . Military Intelligence Detachment
MID. . . . . . . Military Intelligence Division (War Department) (World War II)
MII . . . . Military Intelligence Interpreter
MII . . . . Military Intelligence Interrogation
MIRS . . . . . . Military Intelligence Research Section (Navy)
G-2 . . . . Military Intelligence Section of an Army or Marine Corps Division (or Marine brigade or aircraft wing) General Staff; the Officer in Charge of this Section
MIS . . . . . . Military Intelligence Services (Army)
MIT . . . . Military Intelligence Translator
MIUTC . . . . . Military Intelligence Unit Training Center
MIPR . . . . . . Military Interdepartmental Procurement Request
MIS . . . . . . Military Interim Specification (Army)
MI . . . . Military Internee
MJC . . . . . . Military Junior College
MLC. . . . . . . Military Landing Craft
MLO . . . . . . Military Landing Officer
ML . . . . Military Liaison
MLC . . . . . . Military Liaison Committee
MLCAEC . . . . Military Liaison Committee to the Atomic Energy Commission
MM . . . . Military Medal
MMSA . . . . . Military Medical Supply Agency (Later, Defense Medical Supply Center)
MM . . . . Military Medicine
PMM . . . . . . Military Morale Division (Coast Guard)
MMP . . . . . . Military Mounted Police
MINEC . . . . . Military Necessity
MNM . . . . . . Military Necessity Modification
MOS . . . . . . Military Occupational Specialty Specification Serial Number

MOTBA	Military Ocean Terminal, Bay Area
MOTBY	Military Ocean Terminal, Bayonne
MOTKI	Military Ocean Terminal, King's Bay
MOTSU	Military Ocean Terminal, Sunny Point
MOSC	Military Oil Subcommittee (of North African Economic Board) (World War II)
MOPS	Military Operation Phone System
MOI	Military Operations and Intelligence
MORD	Military Operations Research Department
MORS	Military Operations Research Society
MOC	Military Order of the Carabao
DDF	Military Order, Devil Dog Fleas
MODDF	Military Order, Devil Dog Fleas
MODD	Military Order of Devil Dogs
MOFW	Military Order of Foreign Wars of the United States
MOLLUS	Military Order of the Loyal Legion of the United States
MOPH	Military Order of the Purple Heart of the USA
MOWW	Military Order of the World Wars
MOM	Military Ordinary Mail
MOVP	Military–Owned Vehicle Plan
MP	Military Pay
MPAC	Military Pay and Allowance Committee
MPA	Military Pay Area
MPD	Military Pay Division, Finance Center, US Army
MPO	Military Pay Order
MPR	Military Pay Record
MPV	Military Pay Voucher
MPVSCS	Military Pay Voucher Summary and Certification Sheet
MPC	Military Payment Certificate
ML	Military Payroll Money List
MPO	Military Permit Office(r)
MPA	Military Personnel Appropriation
MPA	Military Personnel, Army
MPC	Military Personnel Center
MILPERSINS	Military Personnel Information System
MPN	Military Personnel, Navy
MPO	Military Personnel Office
MPR	Military Personnel Record
MPRJ	Military Personnel Records Jacket (Army)
MPSC	Military Personnel Security Committee
MPSP	Military Personnel Security Program
MPAB	Military Petroleum Advisory Board
MPSA	Military Petroleum Supply Agency (Later, Defense Petroleum Supply Center)
MPC	Military Pioneer Corps (British)
MP	Military Police (Army)
MPA	Military Police Association
MPCO	Military Police Company
MPC	Military Police Corps
MPCI	Military Police Criminal Investigation
MPCID	Military Police Criminal Investigation Detachment
MPEG	Military Police Escort Guard
MPMIS	Military Police Management Information System
MP(TSWG)	Military Police Tripartite Standing Working Group
MPO	Military Post Office
MPI	Military Procurement Instruction
MPMUL	Military Production Master Urgency List
MPS	Military Production Specifications
MPUS	Military Production Urgencies System
MP	Military Prohibitionist (Slang)
MPSC	Military Provost Staff Corps (British)
MRS	Military Railway Service (Army)
MRSV	Military Railway Service Veterans
MR	Military Readiness
MRDC	Military Research and Development Center (US–Thailand)
MSD	Military Sales Department
MILSAT	Military Satellite
MS	Military Science
MST	Military Science Training
MSTS	Military Sea Transportation Service (Navy)
MSTSO	Military Sea Transportation Service Office
MSN	Military Serial Number
MS	Military Service Act (British)
MSO	Military Service Obligation
MSOD	Military Service Obligation Date
MILSPEC	Military Specification
MSC(UN)	Military Staff Committee of the United Nations
MILSTD	Military Standard
MS	Military Standard
MILSTAAD	Military Standard Activity Address Dictionary
MILSCAP	Military Standard Contract Administration Procedures (DOD)
MILSTEP	Military Standard Evaluation Procedure

MILSTICCS	Military Standard Item Characteristics Coding Structure
MILSTRAP	Military Standard Requisition and Accounting Procedures
MILSTRIP	Military Standard Requisitioning and Issue Procedure
MRI	MILSTRIP (Military Standard Requisitioning and Issue Procedure) Routing Identifier
MILSTRAMP	Military Standard Transportation and Movement Procedure
MILSTAMP	Military Standard Transportation and Movement Procedures
MSBR	Military Strength Balance Report
MSA	Military Subsistence Agency (Merged with Defense Supply Agency)
MSSA	Military Subsistence Supply Agency (Later, Defense Subsistence Supply Center)
MSO	Military Supply Officer
MSS	Military Supply Standards (DOD)
MILSTEP	Military Supply and Transportation Evaluation Procedures
MS	Military Survivors
MILTAG	Military Technical Assistance Group
MTSS	Military Test Space Station
MITMA	Military Traffic Management Agency
MTMA	Military Traffic Management Agency (Later, Defense Traffic Management Service)
MTMR	Military Traffic Management Regulation
MTMTS	Military Traffic Management and Terminal Service (Army)
MT	Military Training
MTC	Military Training Cadets (A boys' World War II organization)
MTI	Military Training Instructor
MTSD	Military Transmission Systems Department (NORAD)
MT	Military Transport
MUTT	Military Utility Tactical Truck
MVSN	Milizia Voluntaria per la Sicurezza Nazionale (Italy)
MBCMC	Milk Bottle Crate Manufacturers Council
MBF	Milk Bottlers Federation
MCI	Milk Can Institute
MCQP	Milk Carton Quality Performing Council
MIPP	Milk Indemnity Payment Program
MIF	Milk Industry Foundation
MMB	Milk Marketing Board for England and Wales
MPAMA	Milk Products Advertising–Merchandising Association
M	Mill(s)
MA	Mill Annealed
MCO	Mill Culls Out (Lumber)
MF	Mill Finish
MG	Mill Glazed
MHM	Mill Hill Missionaries
MMFPB	Mill Mutual Fire Prevention Bureau
MR	Mill Run (Unselected lot of a manufactured product)
M	Mille (Thousand, in roman numerals)
MIT	Milled in Transit (Commodities)
MAL	Miller Airlines (Michigan)
MI	Miller Integrator
MNF	Millers' National Federation
M	Milli– (A thousandth, in metric system)
MA	Milliampere(s)
MAM	Milliampere Minutes
MaS	Milliampere–Second
MAS	Milliampere Second
MB	Millibars
MC	Millicurie(s)
mCi	Millicurie
MEQ	Milliequivalent(s)
MF	Millifarad
MG	Milligram(s)
ME	Milligram Equivalent or Milliequivalent (Also, MEQ)
MDD	Milligrams per square Decimeter per Day
MH	Millihenry
ML	Millilambert
ML	Milliliter(s)
MM	Millimeter (Metric)
MSM	Millimeter and Submillimeter Conference
MCA	Millinery Credit Association
MIA	Millinery Institute of America
M	Million
M̄CF	Million Cubic Feet (M̄ with bar)
MMCF	Million Cubic Feet
MDRT	Million Dollar Round Table (of the NALU)
MEV	Million Electron Volts
MGD	Million Gallons Per Day
M–GPD	Million US Gallons Per Day (AEC, OSW)
MEGV	Million Volts
MV	Million Volts
MY	Million Years
MYBP	Million Years Before Present (Geology)

MC . . . . Millipere Corporation (Bedford, Massachusetts)
MR . . . . Milliroentgen
MR/HR . . . . . . Milliroentgens Per Hour
MS. . . . . Millisecond
MSEC . . . . . Millisecond
mS . . . . Millisiemens
MV. . . . . Millivolt
MADIS . . . . . Millivolt Analog-Digital Instrumentation System
MW . . . . . . Milliwatt
MWL . . . . . . Milliwatt Logic
MD . . . . Millwall Dock (British)
MCB . . . . . . Millwork Cost Bureau
MLST . . . . . . Milstead R. R. (AAR code)
MSA . . . . . . Milton Society of America
MERT . . . . . . Milwaukee Electric Railway & Transport Company (AAR code)
MGE . . . . . . Milwaukee Grain Exchange
MYOB . . . . . Mind Your Own Business (Slang)
MFL . . . . Mindanao Federation of Labor (Philippines)
M . . . . Mine
MAC . . . . Mine Advisory Committee (NAS-NRC)
MAD . . . . . . Mine Assembly Depot (Navy)
MINECTRMEASSTA . . Mine Counter-Measure Station
MCS . . . . . . Mine Countermeasure Support (Military)
MCS. . . . . . . Mine Countermeasures Ship (Navy symbol)
MDL . . . . . . Mine Defense Laboratory (Panama City, Florida) (Navy)
MD . . . . Mine Depot (Naval)
MD . . . . Mine Disposal
MDU . . . . . . Mine Disposal Unit
MINDIV . . . . Mine Division (Navy)
MIIA . . . . . . Mine Inspectors' Institute of America
MIS . . . . Mine Issuing Ship
CM . . . . Mine Layer (Navy symbol)
APS . . . . . . Mine Laying Submarine (Navy symbol)
MPR . . . . . . Mine Production Report
MR . . . . Mine-Run
MSA . . . . . . Mine Safety Appliance
MSAR . . . . . Mine Safety Appliances Research
MINRON . . . . Mine Squadron
LSB . . . . . . Mine Sweeping Boat (Navy symbol)
MATD . . . . . . Mine and Torpedo Detector (SONAR) (Navy)
AM . . . . Mine Vessel (Navy symbol)
MINEVDET . . . Mine Warfare Evaluation Detachment
MINLANT. . . . Mine Warfare Forces, Atlantic (Navy)
MINPAC. . . . . Mine Warfare Forces, Pacific (Navy)
MINBATFOR . . Minecraft Battle Force, Pacific Fleet
MLCC . . . . . . Mined Land Conservation Conference
MHA . . . . . . Minehunter, Auxiliary (Navy symbol)
MHC . . . . . . Minehunter, Coastal (Navy symbol)
ML . . . . Minelayer
M/L . . . . Minelayer (British)
MMC . . . . . . Minelayer, Coastal (Navy symbol)
MM . . . . . . Minelayer Fleet (Navy symbol)
MN . . . . Mineman (Navy rating)
MFPB . . . . . . Mineral Fiber Products Bureau
MR . . . . Mineral Rubber
MSR . . . . Mineral-Surface Roof (Technical drawings)
M-C. . . . . . . Mineralo-Corticoid (Endocrinology)
MSA . . . . . . Mineralogical Society of America
MIC . . . . . . Minerals & Chemicals Philipp Corporation (NYSE symbol)
MRL . . . . . . Minerals Research Laboratory
MIF . . . . Miners' International Federation
MASA. . . . . . Mines' African Staff Association
MACTU. . . . . Mines and Countermeasures Technical Unit (Navy)
MIFERMA . . . . Mines de Fer de Mauritanie (Iron Mining Company of Mauritania)
M . . . . Minesweeper (Navy)
MS . . . . Minesweeper (or Minesweeping)
MSA . . . . . . Minesweeper, Auxiliary (Navy symbol)
MSC . . . . . . Minesweeper, Coastal (Navy symbol)
MSC(O) . . . . . Minesweeper, Coastal (Old) (Navy symbol)
MSF . . . . . . Minesweeper, Fleet (Navy symbol)
MSI . . . . Minesweeper, Inshore (Navy symbol)
MSO . . . . . . Minesweeper Ocean
MSB . . . . . . Minesweeping Boat
MATRS . . . . . Miniature Airborne Telemetry Receiving Station
MINEAC . . . . Miniature Electronic Auto-Collimator
MESA . . . . . . Miniature Electrostatic Accelerometer
MFCA. . . . . . Miniature Figure Collectors of America
MFM . . . . . . Miniature Fluxgate Magnetometer
MINS . . . . . . Miniature Inertial Navigation System
MINRA . . . . . Miniature International Racing Association
MPCA . . . . . . Miniature Pinscher Club of America

MINI-SUBLAB. . Miniature Submarine Laboratory
MITE . . . . Miniaturized Integrated Telephone Equipment
MASTER . . . . . Miniaturized Sink-Rate Telemetering RADAR
M . . . . Minim(s)
MAR. . . . . . . Minimal Angle Resolution
MED . . . . . . Minimal Effective Dose
MED . . . . . . Minimal Erythema Dose
MEM . . . . . . Minimal Essential Medium
MFC. . . . . . . Minimal Flight Forecasting Charts (Air Force)
MFP . . . . Minimal Flight Path
MPC. . . . . . . Minimal Flight Planning Charts (Air Force)
MIO . . . . . . Minimal Identifiable Odor
MID . . . . . . Minimal Inhibiting Dose
MIC . . . . Minimal Inhibitory Concentration
MRU. . . . . . . Minimal Reproductive Units (Bacteriology)
MINIAPS . . . . Minimum Accessory Power Supply
MAFD . . . . . . Minimum Acquisition Flux Density
MADE . . . . . . Minimum Airborne Digital Equipment
MAFAP . . . . . Minimum Altitude over Facility on Final Approach Course (Aviation)
MAGSI . . . . . Minimum Altitude at Glide Slope Intersection Inbound (Aviation)
MAF. . . . . . . Minimum Audible Field
MAP. . . . . . . Minimum Audible Pressure
MAMIE. . . . . . Minimum Automatic Machine for Interpolation and Extrapolation
MBA . . . . . . Minimum Burst Altitude
MINICOM . . . . Minimum Communications
MCD . . . . . . Minimum Cost Design
MCX . . . . . . Minimum-Cost Expediting
MCA . . . . . . Minimum Crossing Altitude (Aviation)
MDAR . . . . . Minimum Daily Adult Requirement
MDR. . . . . . . Minimum Daily Requirement (of a vitamin, etc.) (Drug and food
           advertising)
MDA . . . . . . Minimum Descent Altitude (Aviation)
MDL . . . . . . Minimum Detectable Limit
MDS. . . . . . . Minimum Discernible Signal (Radio)
MER . . . . . . Minimum Energy Requirements
MEA . . . . . . Minimum Enroute IFR Altitude
MEE . . . . . . Minimum Essential Equipment
MFD . . . . . . Minimum Fatal Dose
MFOB . . . . . . Minimum Fuel on Board (Aviation)
MHL . . . . . . Minimum Helium Loss (System)
MHD . . . . . . Minimum Hemolytic Dose
MHA . . . . . . Minimum Holding Altitude (Aviation)
MIE . . . . Minimum Ignition Energy
MIP . . . . Minimum Impulse Pulse
MIT . . . . Minimum Individual Training
MID. . . . . . . Minimum Infective Dose (Bacteriology)
MIA . . . . Minimum Instrument Altitude (Aviation)
MITO . . . . . . Minimum Interval Take Off
MLD . . . . . . Minimum Lethal Dose (Biology)
MLD . . . . . . Minimum Line of Detection (Air Force)
MLI . . . . Minimum Line of Interception (Air Force)
MND . . . . . . Minimum Necrosing Dose
MNBA . . . . . Minimum Normal Burst Altitude
MOCA . . . . . Minimum Obstruction Clearance Altitude (Aviation)
MOUSE . . . . . Minimum Orbital Unmanned Satellite of the Earth
MRD. . . . . . . Minimum Reacting Dose
MRA. . . . . . . Minimum Reception Altitude (Aviation)
MIREQ . . . . . Minimum Requirements Specified
MIRAK . . . . . Minimum Rocket (from the German)
MSD . . . . . . Minimum Safe Distance
MSHB . . . . . . Minimum Safe Height of Burst (Military)
MSA . . . . . . Minimum Section Altitudes (Aviation)
MTCA . . . . . . Minimum Terrain Clearance Altitude (Aviation)
MVU . . . . . . Minimum Variance Unbiased (Statistics)
MVUE . . . . . . Minimum Variance Unbiased Estimate (Statistics)
MVULE . . . . . Minimum Variance Unbiased Linear Estimator (Statistics)
MVS . . . . . . Minimum Visual Signal
MCZE . . . . . . Minimum When Control Zone Effective (Aviation)
MCZNE . . . . . Minimum When Control Zone Not Effective (Aviation)
ME. . . . . Mining Engineer
EM in Geol . . . Mining Engineer in Geology
MMSA . . . . . . Mining and Metallurgical Society of America
MUJCSA. . . . . Mining Unions' Joint Committee of South Africa
MM . . . . Minister of Munitions (British) (World War II)
MND . . . . Minister of National Defence (Canada)
MP. . . . . Minister Plenipotentiary
MPS. . . . . . . Minister of Public Security (British)
MR. . . . . Minister-Residentiary (Diplomacy)
MWC . . . . . . Minister for (or Ministry of) War Communications (British) (World War II)
MTIC . . . . . . Ministerio do Trabalho, Industria e Comercio
MGB . . . . . . Ministerstvo Gosudarstvennoi Bezopasnosti (Russia)

MO . . . . Ministerstvo Oborony (Ministry of Defense) (USSR)
MVD . . . . Ministerstvo Vnutrennykh Del (Ministry of Internal Affairs) (Political
    police and security organization) (USSR)
MVMF . . . . . . Ministerstvo Voenno-Morskogo Flota (Ministry of the Navy) (1950-53;
    merged into the MO) (USSR)
MVS . . . . Ministerstvo Vooruzhennykh Sil (Ministry of the Armed Forces) (1946-50;
    superseded by VM and MVMF) (USSR)
MAP . . . . Ministry of Aircraft Production (British)
MOA . . . . Ministry of Aviation (British)
MOD . . . . Ministry of Defense
MEW . . . . Ministry of Economic Warfare (British)
MF . . . . Ministry (or Minister) of Food (British)
MOF . . . . Ministry of Food (British)
MOFAP . . . . . . Ministry of Fuel and Power (British)
MH . . . . Ministry of Health (British)
MOH . . . . Ministry of Health (British)
MHS . . . . Ministry (or Minister) of Home Security (British)
MI . . . . Ministry of Information (British) (Acronym used in World War I;
    MOI used in World War II)
MOI . . . . Ministry of Information (British) (World War II)
MIME . . . . . . Ministry of Information Middle East (British) (World War II)
MITI . . . . . . Ministry of International Trade and Industry (Japan)
MLNS . . . . . . Ministry of Labour and National Service (British) (World War II)
MNS . . . . Ministry of National Service (British) (World War I)
MR . . . . Ministry of Reconstruction (British) (World War I)
MS . . . . Ministry of Shipping (British)
MOS . . . . Ministry of State (British)
MOS . . . . Ministry of Supply (British)
MS . . . . Ministry of Supply (Also MOS) (British)
MOT . . . . Ministry of Transport (British)
MT . . . . Ministry of Transport (British)
MWTC . . . . . . Ministry of War Time Communications (British) (World War II)
MOWT . . . . . . Ministry of War Transport (British)
MWT . . . . Ministry of War Transport (British)
MOW . . . . Ministry of Work (British)
MOTS . . . . . . Minitrack Optical Tracking System (or Station) (NASA)
MSP . . . . Minneapolis (Minnesota) (Airport symbol)
MACR . . . . . . Minneapolis, Anoka & Cuyuna Range R. R. (AAR code)
MINE . . . . . . Minneapolis Eastern Railway (AAR code)
MGE . . . . Minneapolis Grain Exchange
M-H . . . . Minneapolis-Honeywell Regulator Company (Later, HON)
MIR . . . . Minneapolis Industrial Railway Company (AAR code)
MNS . . . . Minneapolis, Northfield & Southern Railway (AAR code)
MSTL . . . . . . Minneapolis & St. Louis Railway Company (AAR code)
MSTP & SSM . . Minneapolis, St. Paul & Sault Ste. Marie Railway Company
MN . . . . Minnesota
MDW . . . . . . Minnesota, Dakota & Western Railway Company (AAR code)
MEI . . . . Minnesota Enterprises, Incorporated (NYSE symbol)
MINITEX . . . . Minnesota Interlibrary Teletex Experiment
MINNEMAST . . Minnesota Mathematics and Science Teaching Project
3M . . . . Minnesota Mining & Manufacturing Company
MMM . . . . . . Minnesota Mining & Manufacturing Company (NYSE symbol)
MMPI . . . . . . Minnesota Multiphasic Personality Inventory (Psychology)
MNL . . . . Minnesota National Laboratory
MNT . . . . Minnesota & Ontario Paper Company (NYSE symbol) (Delisted)
MPL . . . . Minnesota Power & Light Company (NYSE symbol)
MSAT . . . . . . Minnesota Scholastic Aptitude Test
MTFR . . . . . . Minnesota Transfer Railway (AAR code)
M . . . . Minor
MIRD . . . . . . Minor Irregularities and Deficiencies
MESBIC . . . . . Minority Enterprise Small Business Investment Company
MIADS . . . . . . Minot Air Defense Sector (ADC)
MS . . . . Mint State
MIMA . . . . . . Minute Man National Historical Park
MRV . . . . Minute Respiratory Volume
MWUSA . . . . . Minute Women of the United States of America
MEP . . . . Minuteman Education Program (Air Force)
MISS-D . . . . . Minuteman Integrated Schedules Status and Data Systems
M . . . . Minutes
MIT . . . . Miracidal Immobilization Test (Parasitology)
MYCI . . . . . . Mirrer Yeshiva Central Institute
MLP . . . . Mirror Landing Procedures
MMA . . . . . . Mirror Manufacturers Association
M . . . . Misce (Mix)
M . . . . Miscellaneous
AG . . . . Miscellaneous (Navy ship symbol)
YAG . . . . Miscellaneous Auxiliary (Navy ship symbol)
MD . . . . Miscellaneous Document
MIEU . . . . . . Miscellaneous Industries Employees' Union (Aden)
MLU . . . . Miscellaneous Live Unit (Military)
MOD . . . . Miscellaneous Obligation Document

MP . . . . Miscellaneous Paper or Publication
MRI . . . . Miscellaneous RADAR Input
MR . . . . Miscellaneous Report
MSG . . . . Miscellaneous Simulation Generator
MSP . . . . Miscellaneous Small Parts
MM . . . . Mis-Mated (Merchandising slang)
MS . . . . Misrair, SAE (Egyptian Airlines)
MDI . . . . Miss-Distance Indicator (Air Force)
MA . . . . Missed Approach (Aviation)
MAP . . . . Missed Approach Point (Aviation)
MAP . . . . Missed Approach Procedure (Aviation)
MI . . . . Missed Interception (Military)
MIAEF . . . . . . Missed Interception Due to Airborne Equipment Failure (Air Force)
M . . . . Missile (Air Force)
MAET . . . . . . Missile Accident Emergency Team
MARTEL . . . . . Missile Anti-RADAR and Television (Anglo-French missile)
MAB . . . . Missile Assembly Building
MAST . . . . . . Missile Automatic Supply Technique
MASG . . . . . . Missile Auxiliary Signal Generator
MAZH . . . . . . Missile Azimuth Heading (Air Force)
MB . . . . Missile Bomber
M . . . . Missile carrier aircraft (Designation for all US military aircraft)
MCCC . . . . . . Missile Combat Crew Commander
MC . . . . Missile Command (Army)
MICOM . . . . . Missile Command (Army)
MSLCOMD . . . Missile Command
MC . . . . Missile Control
MCC . . . . Missile Control Center (Air Force)
MACE . . . . . . Missile and Control Equipment Division, North American Aviation
MCO . . . . Missile Control Officer
MCS . . . . Missile Control System
MIDAS . . . . . Missile Defense Alarm Satellite
MIDAS . . . . . . Missile Defense Alarm System (Air Force)
MIDES . . . . . . Missile Detection System
MDC . . . . Missile Development Center (Air Force)
MDE . . . . Missile Display Equipment
MIDOP . . . . . Missile Doppler
MEWS . . . . . . Missile Early Warning Station
MEWS . . . . . . Missile Electronic Warfare System (Army)
MEDIA . . . . . . Missile Era Data Integration Analysis
MEDIUM . . . . Missile Era Data Integration - Ultimate Method
MET . . . . Missile Escort Team (Air Force)
MFS . . . . Missile Firing Station
MFCC . . . . . . Missile Flight Caution Corridor
MFHC . . . . . . Missile Flight Hazard Corridor
MIFI . . . . Missile Flight Indicator
MGC . . . . Missile Guidance and Control
MGCC . . . . . . Missile Guidance and Control Computer
MGS . . . . Missile Guidance Set
MHR . . . . Missile Hazard Report
MHS . . . . Missile Hazard Space
MILS . . . . . . Missile Impact Location System
MIP . . . . Missile Impact Predictor (Air Force)
MITOC . . . . . Missile Instrumentation Technical Operations Communications
MITE . . . . . . Missile Integration Terminal Equipment
MIDAS . . . . . Missile Intercept Data Acquisition System
MISS . . . . . . Missile Intercept Simulation System
MLCB . . . . . . Missile Launch Control Blockhouse
ML . . . . Missile Launcher
MMC . . . . Missile Maintenance Crew
MMT . . . . Missile Maintenance Technician
MM . . . . Missile Master (Fire direction and coordination system)
MMS . . . . Missile Monitor System (Army)
MNORM . . . . . Missile Not Operationally Ready - Maintenance (Air Force)
MNORP . . . . . Missile Not Operationally Ready - Parts (Air Force)
MNPD . . . . . . Missile and Nuclear Programming Data
MOC . . . . Missile Operation Center (Air Force)
MOR . . . . Missile Operationally Ready (Air Force)
MOPS . . . . . . Missile Operations
MODEST . . . . Missile Optical Destruction Technique
MOB . . . . Missile Order of Battle
MOCP . . . . . . Missile Out of Commission for Parts
MIPIR . . . . . . Missile Precision Instrumentation RADAR
MPT . . . . Missile Procedure Trainer
MPD . . . . Missile Purchase Description (Army)
AGM . . . . Missile Range Instrumentation Ship (Navy symbol)
MIRAN . . . . . Missile Ranging
MRICC . . . . . . Missile & Rockets Inventory Control Center (Army)
MSO . . . . Missile Safety Officer
MSCA . . . . . . Missile Site Construction Agency (Army)
MSR . . . . Missile Site RADAR (Army)

MSLC ...... Missile Sites Labor Commission (A federal government body)
M & SC .... Missile and Space Council (Defunct)
MSRP ...... Missile, Space and Range Pioneers, Inc.
MSTS ...... Missile Static Test Site (Air Force)
MSS ...... Missile Station Select
MSD ...... Missile Systems Division (Lockheed)
MT .... Missile Technician (Navy rating)
MT......... Missile Test
MTC ...... Missile Test Center
MTS....... Missile Test Station
MTR ...... Missile-Track RADAR (Air Force)
MTU....... Missile Training Unit (Air Force)
MISTRAM .... Missile Trajectory Measurement (Air Force)
MISHAP .... Missiles High-Speed Assembly Program
M/R ...... Missiles & Rockets Magazine
M .... Missing
MIA ...... Missing in Action (Military)
MACR ...... Missing Air Crew Report
MPB ...... Missing Persons Bureau
MNA ...... Missing, Not Enemy Action
MA .... Mission Accomplished (Air Force)
MSNA ..... Mission Accomplished (Military)
MC .... Mission Control (NASA)
MCC ...... Mission Control Center (NASA)
MCC-H .... Mission Control Center – Houston (NASA)
MSS....... Mission Corporation (NYSE symbol)
MDR ...... Mission Data Reduction
MDS ...... Mission Design and Series (Military)
MDV ...... Mission Development Company (NYSE symbol)
MEP ...... Mission Effects Projector (Lunar exploration)
MEEL ..... Mission Equipment Essentiality List
MHSH ..... Mission Helpers of the Sacred Heart (Roman Catholic women's religious
           order)
ML .... Mission Load
MIMOSA .... Mission Modes and Systems Analysis
MOC ...... Mission Operation Computer
MOCR ..... Mission Operations Control Room
MOS ...... Mission Operations System (NASA)
MPS ...... Mission Parcels Society (British)
MPAS ...... Mission Planning and Analysis Division (Aerospace)
MPS ...... Mission Preparation Sheet
MISREP ..... Mission Report (Air Force)
MS .... Mission Sisters of the Holy Ghost (Roman Catholic religious order)
MSS ...... Mission Support Site (Army)
MTO ...... Mission, Task, Objective
MTC ...... Mission and Traffic Control
MSpS ..... Missionaries of the Holy Ghost (Roman Catholic men's religious order)
MS......... Missionaries of La Salette (France)
MSC ...... Missionarii Sacratissimi Cordis (Missionaries of the Most Sacred Heart)
           (Roman Catholic men's religious order)
MSC ...... Missionarii Sancti Caroli (Missionaries of St. Charles) (Roman Catholic
           men's religious order)
ST .... Missionarii Servi Sanctissimae Trinitatis (Missionary Servants of the
           Most Holy Trinity) (Roman Catholic men's religious order)
MA .... Missionarius Apostolicus (Missionary Apostolic)
MR......... Missionarius Rector (Missionary Rector)
MACW ..... Missionary Association of Catholic Women
MAF ...... Missionary Aviation Fellowship
MCDP ..... Missionary Catechists of Divine Providence (Roman Catholic women's
           religious order)
MFTF ...... Missionary Flight Training Foundation
MPA ...... Missionary Pilots Association
MRL ...... Missionary Research Library
MSSA ..... Missionary Servants of St. Anthony (Roman Catholic women's religious
           order)
MSSJ ..... Missionary Servants of St. Joseph (Roman Catholic women's religious
           order)
MSA ...... Missionary Sisters of the Assumption (Roman Catholic religious order)
MIC ...... Missionary Sisters of the Immaculate Conception (Roman Catholic religious
           order)
MSMG ..... Missionary Sisters of the Mother of God (Roman Catholic religious order)
MNDA ..... Missionary Sisters of Notre Dame des Anges (Roman Catholic religious
           order)
SSC ...... Missionary Sisters of St. Columban (Roman Catholic religious order)
SSPC ..... Missionary Sisters of St. Peter Claver (Roman Catholic religious order)
MS .... Missionary Society (British)
MUCUSA .... Missionary Union of the Clergy in the United States of America
MZSH ...... Missionary Zelatrices of the Sacred Heart (Roman Catholic women's
           religious order)
MS .... Mississippi
MSC....... Mississippi Central R. R. (AAR code)

MSE .... Mississippi Export R. R. (AAR code)
MFDP...... Mississippi Freedom Democratic Party
MRC....... Mississippi River Commission (Army)
MIS .... Mississippi River Fuel Corporation (NYSE symbol)
MRD ...... Mississippi River Division (Army Engineers)
MSV....... Mississippi & Skuna Valley R. R. (AAR code)
MTF ...... Mississippi Test Facility (NASA)
MTO ...... Mississippi Test Operations (NASA)
MISS ...... Mississippian Railway (AAR code)
MO .... Missouri
M & A ..... Missouri and Arkansas Railway Company
MAMOS .... Missouri Associated Migrant Opportunities Services
MIBB ...... Missouri & Illinois Bridge & Belt R. R. (AAR code)
MI .... Missouri-Illinois R. R. (AAR code)
M-I .... Missouri-Illinois Railroad Company
KATY ..... Missouri-Kansas-Texas Lines (Railroad)
MKT....... Missouri-Kansas-Texas R. R. (AAR code)
KT .... Missouri-Kansas-Texas R. R. Company (NYSE symbol) (Wall Street slang
           name: "Katy")
MKTT ...... Missouri-Kansas-Texas of Texas R. R. (AAR code)
MP......... Missouri Pacific R. R. (AAR code)
MOP....... Missouri Pacific R. R. Company (NYSE symbol)
MOPAC .... Missouri Pacific Railroad Company
MRP....... Missouri Portland Cement Company (NYSE symbol)
MPV....... Missouri Public Service Company (NYSE symbol)
MSMR ..... Missouri School of Mines Reactor
MVA ...... Missouri Valley Authority
MVC ...... Missouri Valley Conference (Sports)
M .... Mist
X .... Mistake or Error
AM .... Mistress of Arts
ME .... Mistress of English
MEL....... Mistress of English Literature
MLA ...... Mistress of Liberal Arts
MLL ...... Mistress of Liberal Learning
Mis Mus .... Mistress of Music
MM .... Mistress of Music
MP .... Mistress of Philosophy
M Ph ..... Mistress of Philosophy
MPL ...... Mistress of Polite Literature
B Sc ..... Mistress of Science
ME .... Miter End (Technical drawings)
MDB ...... Mitglied des Deutschen Bundestages (German Federal Parliament)
MD .... Mitral Disease (Pathology)
MI .... Mitral Insufficiency
MS .... Mitral Stenosis (Medicine)
MELISS .... Mitsubishi Electric Corporation Literature and Information Search Service
MEMOCS .... Mitsubishi Electric Corporation Multiterm Out of Context System
MER....... Mitteleuropaisches Reisebuero (Middle European Travel Bureau)
MAF ...... Mixed Amine Fuel
MFP ...... Mixed Fission Products
MFPG ..... Mixed Fission Products Generator (AEC)
MG .... Mixed Grain
MHF ...... Mixed Hydrazine Fuel
ML .... Mixed Lengths
MLC ...... Mixed Leukocyte Culture
MLR ...... Mixed Leukocyte Reactions
MRV ...... Mixed Respiratory Vaccine
MSCA ..... Mixed Spectrum Critical Assembly
MSS ...... Mixed Spectrum Superheater
MSSCE .... Mixed Spectrum Superheater Critical Experiment
MSSR ..... Mixed Spectrum Superheat Reactor
MVRI ..... Mixed Vaccine, Respiratory Infections
MW .... Mixed Widths
MMB ...... Mixer Manufacturers Bureau
M .... Mixture
MFLU...... Miyako Federation of Labor Unions (Ryukyu Islands)
MPF ...... Mizrachi Palestine Fund
MWOA ..... Mizrachi Women's Organization of America
MOAMA .... Mobile Air Materiel Area
MASD ..... Mobile Air & Space Defense (Air Force)
MAWCS .... Mobile Air Weapons Control System (ESD)
MAIRU .... Mobile Aircraft Instrument Repair Unit
MATMU .... Mobile Aircraft Torpedo Maintenance Unit
MAERU..... Mobile Ammunition Evaluation and Reconditioning Unit
MAATC..... Mobile Antiaircraft Training Center
MASWT .... Mobile Antisubmarine Warfare Target
MASH ..... Mobile Army Surgical Hospital (Acronym also used as title of a satirical
           film, 1970)
MOREST .... Mobile Arresting Gear (Navy)
MARS ...... Mobile Atlantic Range Ships (Tracking ships)

MAPCHE . . . . Mobile Automatic Programed Checkout Equipment
MART . . . . . . Mobile Automatic Radiation Tester
MBMU . . . . . . Mobile Base Maintenance Unit
MBDET . . . . . Mobile Boarding Detachment (Coast Guard)
MBT . . . . Mobile Boarding Team
MCG . . . . Mobile Command Guidance
MCB . . . . Mobile Construction Battalion
MOBIDAC . . . Mobile Data Acquisition System
MDENDET . . . Mobile Dental Detachment (Coast Guard)
MDA . . . . Mobile Depot Activities (Air Force)
MDM . . . . . . Mobile Depot Maintenance (Air Force)
MDU . . . . Mobile Development Unit (Thailand)
MOBIDIC . . . . Mobile Digital Computer (Army)
MDLP . . . . . . Mobile Dryer Loan Program
MOBED . . . . . Mobile Education Demonstration
METU . . . . . . Mobile Electronics Technical Unit
MEEF . . . . . . Mobile Equipment Employment File (Air Force)
MEIF . . . . . . Mobile Equipment Information File (Air Force)
MEL . . . . Mobile Erector Launcher (Military)
MOBEX . . . . . Mobile Excursion
MOBEX . . . . . Mobile Exploration (NASA)
MEIU . . . . . . Mobile Explosives Investigation Unit
MFTD . . . . . . Mobile Field Training Detachment (Military)
MFAB-F . . . . . Mobile Floating Assault Bridge-Ferry (Military)
MGI . . . . Mobile Gamma Irradiator (AEC)
MGU . . . . . . Mobile & Gulf R. R. (AAR code)
MHDNA . . . . Mobile Home Dealers National Association
MHMA . . . . . Mobile Home Manufacturers Association
MOBS . . . . . . Mobile Hospitals (Military slang)
MHCC . . . . . . Mobile Housing Carriers Conference
MICA . . . . . . Mobile Industrial Caterers' Association
MIT . . . . Mobile Information Team (Thailand)
MIU . . . . Mobile Inspection Unit (Military)
MINU . . . . . . Mobile Instrument Investigation Unit
MISS . . . . . . Mobile Integrated Support System
MIO . . . . Mobile Issuing Office (Navy)
MOLAB . . . . . Mobile Laboratory (NASA)
MLCP . . . . . . Mobile Land Command Post
MLU . . . . Mobile Laundry Unit
MLU . . . . Mobile Living Unit (Mobile home)
MLSF . . . . . . Mobile Logistic Support Forces
MLPNPP . . . . Mobile Low-Power Nuclear Power Plant
MMMOS . . . . Mobile Micrometeorological Observation System
MMRBM . . . . Mobile Mid-Range Ballistic Missile (Air Force)
MNECP . . . . . Mobile National Emergency Command Post (Air Force)
MONAB . . . . . Mobile Naval Air Base
MNAO . . . . . . Mobile Naval Airfield Organization
MNAU . . . . . . Mobile Naval Airfield Unit
MONOB . . . . . Mobile Noise Barge
M & O . . . . . . Mobile and Ohio Railroad Company
MOTU . . . . . . Mobile Optical Tracking Unit
MOTOR . . . . . Mobile Oriented Triangulation of Reentry
MPTS . . . . . . Mobile Photographic Tracking Station
MPTR . . . . . . Mobile Position Tracking RADAR
MPOS . . . . . . Mobile Post Office Society
MPA . . . . Mobile Press Association
MPN . . . . Mobile Pulse RADAR Navigational Aid
MQF . . . . Mobile Quarantine Facility (NASA)
MRAPCON . . . Mobile RADAR Approach Control
MRCP . . . . . . Mobile RADAR Control Post
MRT . . . . Mobile RADAR Target
MRU . . . . Mobile Radio Unit (Air Force)
MRMU . . . . . . Mobile Radiological Measuring Unit
MOBOT . . . . . Mobile Remote-Controlled Robot
MRH . . . . Mobile Remote Handler
MRMU . . . . . . Mobile Remote Manipulating Unit (Air Force)
MST . . . . Mobile Service Tower (Aerospace)
MO . . . . Mobile Station (Air Force)
MSF . . . . Mobile Striking Force (Military)
MSGP . . . . . . Mobile Support Group (Military)
MSGR . . . . . . Mobile Support Group
MOSAIC . . . . Mobile System for Accurate ICBM Control
MOTARDIV . . . Mobile Target Division (Navy)
MTD . . . . Mobile Target Division (Mine Force)
MTS . . . . Mobile Telephone Service
MTS . . . . Mobile Tracking Station (NASA)
MTS . . . . Mobile Training Set
MTT . . . . Mobile Training Team
MTU . . . . Mobile Training Unit
MTUOP . . . . . Mobile Training Units Out for Parts
MTW . . . . . . Mobile Training Wing (Air Force)

MUST . . . . . . Mobile Underwater Surveillance Teams
MU . . . . Mobile Unit
MDNA . . . . . . Mobilehome Dealers National Association
MOCOM . . . . Mobility Command (AMC)
ME . . . . Mobility Equipment (Military)
MEC . . . . Mobility Equipment Command (Army)
MECOM . . . . Mobility Equipment Command (Army)
MERDC . . . . . Mobility Equipment Research and Development Center (Army)
MOP . . . . Mobility Operating Procedure (Military)
MSK . . . . Mobility Support Kit
MTA . . . . Mobility Test Article (Lunar-surface rover) (NASA)
MOBEX . . . . . Mobility Test Exercise (Military)
M . . . . Mobilization (as in M-Day) (Military)
MAFS . . . . . . Mobilization Air Force Specialty
MAFSC . . . . . Mobilization Air Force Specialty Code
MOARS . . . . . Mobilization Assignment Reserve Section (Military)
MA . . . . Mobilization Augmentee (Military)
MOBU . . . . . . Mobilization Base Units
MOBCON . . . . Mobilization Construction Plan
MDI . . . . Mobilization Day Increment (Military)
MDRS . . . . . . Mobilization Designation Reserve Section
MOBDES . . . . Mobilization Designee
MMPC . . . . . . Mobilization Material Procurement Capability
MMR . . . . . . Mobilization Materiel Requirement
MR . . . . Mobilization Regulation (Army)
MRS . . . . Mobilization Requirement Study
MRSI . . . . . . Mobilization Requirements, Secondary Items
MOBRASOP . . . Mobilization Requirements in Support of the Army Strategic Objectives Plan
MRCPA . . . . . Mobilization Reserve Components Program of the Army
MRMO . . . . . . Mobilization Reserve Materiel Objective
MRMPO . . . . . Mobilization Reserve Materiel Procurement Objective
MRMR . . . . . . Mobilization Reserve Materiel Requirement
MRSO . . . . . . Mobilization Reserve Stockage Objective
MRS . . . . Mobilization Reserve Stocks
MTP . . . . Mobilization Training Program (Military)
MOBTB . . . . . Mobilization Troop Basis (Army)
MTP . . . . Mobilization Troop Program
MFY . . . . Mobilization for Youth
M⁄U . . . . Mockup
MUPL . . . . . . Mockup Planning
MUR . . . . Mock-Up Reactor (NASA)
MURL . . . . . . Mockup Release
MS . . . . Modal Sensation (Psychology)
MS . . . . Modal Sensitivity
M . . . . Mode
MC . . . . Mode Counter
MT . . . . Mode Transducer
M . . . . Model (in military nomenclature)
MAFCA . . . . . Model A Ford Club of America
MARC . . . . . . Model "A" Restorers Club
MAC . . . . Model Airplane Club
MCA . . . . Model Cities Administration (HUD)
MCS . . . . Model-Controlled System (NASA)
MEDICO . . . . Model Experiment in Drug Indexing by Computer
MFR . . . . Model Form and Record
MICCO . . . . . Model Inner City Community Organization (Washington, DC)
MRA . . . . Model Reporting Area (for Blindness Statistics) (HEW)
MSPR . . . . . . Model State Packaging Regulation (National Bureau of Standards)
MTFCI . . . . . . Model T Ford Club International
MYRAA . . . . . Model Yacht Racing Association of America
MAA . . . . Modeling Association of America
MOGR . . . . . . Moderate or Greater
M . . . . Moderate Sea or Swell (Weather charts)
MADAM . . . . Moderately Advanced Data Management (Data processing)
MAU . . . . Modern American Usage (A publication)
MAMS . . . . . . Modern Army Maintenance System
MASS . . . . . . Modern Army Supply System
MNE . . . . Modern English
MFC . . . . Modern Foods Council
MFL . . . . Modern Foreign Language
MHRA . . . . . . Modern Humanities Research Association
MLAT . . . . . . Modern Language Aptitude Test (Military)
MLA . . . . Modern Language Association of America
MLAA . . . . . . Modern Language Association of America
MLN . . . . Modern Language Notes (A periodical)
MOMAR . . . . . Modern Mobile Army (Military)
MMM . . . . Modern Music Masters Society
MNT . . . . Modern Network Theory (Electrical engineering computer)
MPA . . . . Modern Poetry Association
MULL . . . . . . Modern Uses of Logic in Law

MWA . . . . Modern Woodmen of America
METC . . . . . . Modesto & Empire Traction Company (AAR code)
MR . . . . Modification Requirement
MRB . . . . . . Modification Review Board
MWO . . . . . . Modification Work Order
MAGIC . . . . . Modified Action Generated Input Control
MODAP . . . . . Modified Apollo (NASA)
MAPUC. . . . . Modified Area Production Urgency Committee (World War II)
MCC . . . . . . Modified Close Control (Air Force)
MG . . . . Modified Guaranteed (Securities trading)
MHA . . . . . . Modified Handling Authorized (Air Force)
MIDAS . . . . . Modified Integration Digital Analog Simulator (Air Force)
MMPVS . . . . . Modified Military Pay Voucher System
MNBLE . . . . . Modified Nearly Best Linear Estimator (Statistics)
K. . . . . Modified for use as target aircraft (Suffix to Navy plane designation)
MACC . . . . . . Modular Alter and Compose Console (Data Processing)
MASSDAR . . Modular Analysis, Speedup, Sampling, and Data Reduction
MATE . . . . . . Modular Automatic Test Equipment
MBSA . . . . . . Modular Building Standards Association
MDE . . . . Modular Design of Electronics
MODICON . . Modular-Dispersed-Control
MFS . . . . Modular Flexible Scheduling (Education)
MIPE . . . . . . Modular Information Processing Equipment
MMU . . . . . . Modular Maneuvering Unit (Aerospace)
MXQ . . . . . . Modular X-Ray Quantometer
MESA . . . . . Modularized Equipment Storage (or Stowage) Assembly (Apollo) (NASA)
METS . . . . . Modularized Equipment Transport System (NASA)
MBAG . . . . . Modulated Bayard-Alpert Gauge
MCW . . . . . . Modulated Continuous Wave (Radio)
MIP . . . . Modulated Interframe Plan
MAVAR . . . . . Modulating Amplifier Using Variable Reactance
M-D . . . . Modulation-Demodulation
MDTA . . . . . . Modulation, Demodulation, Terminal and Associated (Equipment)
ME . . . . Modulation Efficiency
MIRROS . . Modulation Inducing Reactive Retrodirective Optical System (NASA)
MIROS . . . . . Modulation Inducing Retro-Directive Optical System
MOSAR . . . . . Modulation Scan Array Receiver
MTF . . . . Modulation Transfer Function
MODEM . . . . . Modulator-Demodulator (Data-processing term)
MOTS . . . . . . Module Test Set
M . . . . Modulus
E . . . . Modulus of Elasticity
MO . . . . Modus Operandi (Police term for distinctive techniques used by criminals)
MOPA . . . . . . Modus Operandi – Personal Appearance (FBI computer procedure)
MOH . . . . . . Mohasco Industries, Inc. (NYSE symbol)
MO . . . . Mohawk Airlines, Inc.
MOH . . . . . . Mohawk Airlines, Inc.
MOHO . . . . . Mohorovicic Discontinuity
MVTR . . . . . . Moisture Vapor Transmission Rate
MAS . . . . . . Moksleiviu Ateitininku Sajunga
M . . . . Molar (Dentistry)
MS . . . . Molar Solution (Chemistry)
MR . . . . Molasses Residuum
ML . . . . Mold Line (Technical drawings)
ML . . . . Molder (Navy)
MLSR . . . . . . Molder, Ship Repair (Navy)
MLSRC . . . . . Molder, Ship Repair, Cupola Tender (Navy)
MLSRF . . . . . Molder, Ship Repair, Foundryman (Navy)
MLSRM . . . . . Molder, Ship Repair, Molder (Navy)
M . . . . Mole
MAN . . . . . . Molecular Anatomy
ME . . . . Molecular Electronics
MOLETRONICS. Molecular Electronics
MERA . . . . . Molecular Electronics RADAR Arrays
MEML . . . . . . Molecular Engineering and Material Laboratory (MIT)
MO . . . . Molecular Orbital (Chemistry)
MPI . . . . Molecular Parameter Index
MRR . . . . . . Molecular Rotational Resonance
MOLSINK . . . Molecular Sink of Outer Space (Vacuum testing chamber for spacecraft systems)
M . . . . Molecular Weight
MW . . . . Molecular Weight
MOLECOM . . Molecularized Digital Computer
MSBR . . . . . . Molten-Salt Breeder Reactor (AEC)
MSR . . . . Molten-Salt Reactor (AEC)
MSRE . . . . . . Molten-Salt Reactor Experiment (AEC)
Mo . . . . Molybdenum (Chemical element)
M . . . . Moment
MOI . . . . Moment of Inertia
MC . . . . Momentary Contact (Electronics)
MOI . . . . Monaco Oceanographic Institute

MMO . . . . . . Monarch Machine Tool Company (NYSE symbol)
M . . . . Monday
M/A. . . . . Monetary Allowance
MAQ . . . . . . Monetary Allowance in Lieu of Quarters
MAS. . . . . . . Monetary Allowance in Lieu of Subsistence
MRCAS . . . . . Monetary Ration Credit Allowance System (Military)
MRMS . . . . . Monetary Ration Management System (Military)
ML. . . . . Money List
MO . . . . Money Order
MOB . . . . . . Money-Order Business
MOD . . . . . . Money-Order Department
MOO . . . . . . Money-Order Office
MCCTU. . . . . Mongolian Central Council of Trade Unions
MDC . . . . . . Mongoloid Development Council
BM . . . . Monitor (Navy symbol)
MAJAC . . . . . Monitor, Antijam, and Control
MI . . . . Monitor Inspection
MONOS . . . . . Monitor Out of Service (Aviation communications)
MR . . . . Monitor Recorder
MONOK. . . . . Monitor Resumed Normal Operation (Aviation communications)
MOREPS . . . . Monitor Station Reports
MIC . . . . Monitoring, Identification, and Correlation
MC . . . . Monkey Cells
MK . . . . Monkey Kidney
MAO . . . . . . Monoamine Oxidase
MAOI . . . . . . Monoamine Oxidase Inhibitor
MPM . . . . . . Monocycle Position Modulation
MWC . . . . . . Monod-Wyman-Changeux (Mathematics)
MEA . . . . . . Monoethanolamine
MFP . . . . Monofluorophosphate (Colgate toothpaste ingredient)
MIT . . . . Mono-Iodotyrosine
MIC . . . . Monolithic Integrated Circuit
MMH . . . . . . Monomethylhydrazine (Chemical)
MON . . . . . . Monon R. R. (AAR code and NYSE symbol)
MGAC . . . . . Monongahela Connecting R. R. (AAR code)
MGA . . . . . . Monongahela Railway (AAR code)
MNT . . . . . . Mononitrotoluene
M . . . . Monoplane
MRI . . . . Monopulse Resolution Improvement
MMA . . . . . . Monorail Manufacturers Association
MSG . . . . . . Monosodium Glutamate
MSMV . . . . . Monostable Multi-Vibrator
MZ . . . . Monozygotic
MAID . . . . . . Monrobot Automatic Internal Diagnosis (Data processing)
MTC . . . . Monsanto Company (NYSE symbol)
MRC . . . . . . Monsanto Research Corporation
M . . . . Monsieur (Mister) (French)
M . . . . Monsoon
M . . . . Mont, Monte, etc. (Italy and Sicily only)
MSB . . . . Montadale Sheep Breeders Association
MT . . . . Montana
MDK . . . . . . Montana-Dakota Utilities Company (NYSE symbol)
MOGA . . . . . Montana Outfitters and Guides Association
MTP. . . . . . . Montana Power Company (NYSE symbol)
MSC . . . . . . Montana State College
MOW . . . . . . Montana Western Railway (AAR code)
MDS . . . . . . Montant de Soutien (A trade negotiating plan of EEC) (French expression means amount of support)
MCM . . . . . . Monte Carlo Method (Data processing)
MC . . . . Montecatini Mining & Chemical Company (NYSE symbol)
MOCA . . . . . Montezuma Castle National Monument
MPMA . . . . . Montford Point Marine Association
MCE . . . . . . Montgomery Cotton Exchange
M . . . . Montgomery Ward & Company, Inc. (NYSE symbol) (Wall Street slang name: "Monkey")
M . . . . Month
MOT . . . . . . Month of Travel (Military)
M . . . . Monthly
MB . . . . Monthly Breakdown (Used in atmospheric studies)
MBPAS . . . . . Monthly Bulk Petroleum Accounting Summary (Army)
MDSOR. . . . . Monthly Depot Space and Operating Report
MIRA . . . . . . Monthly Index of Russian Accessions (Library of Congress)
MIPR . . . . . . Monthly Interim Progress Report
MIP . . . . Monthly Investment Plan (NY Stock Exchange)
MLR . . . . Monthly Letter Report
MO . . . . Monthly Order (Navy)
MPR . . . . . . Monthly Progress Report
MPE . . . . Monthly Project Evaluation
MPR . . . . Monthly Project Report
MR. . . . . Monthly Report
MRP . . . . . . Monthly Report of Progress

MR. . . . . Monthly Review
MRR . . . . Monthly Review Report
MSR . . . . Monthly Status Report (Navy)
MTS . . . . Monthly Treasury Statement (Government)
MD . . . . Months after Date or Month's Date
MS . . . . Month's Sight (Banking and commerce)
MTR . . . . Montour R. R. (AAR code)
MPB . . . . Montpelier & Barre R. R. (AAR code)
MOTC . . . . . Montreal Tramways (AAR code)
MBA. . . . . Monument Builders of America
MBNA . . . . . . Monument Builders of North America
MFA & A. . . . . Monuments, Fine Arts and Archives (SHAEF) (World War II)
M . . . . Monumentum (Monument)
MP . . . . Monumentum Posuit (Erected a Monument)
M . . . . Moon
MSRE . . . . . . Moon Signal Rejection Equipment
MPCL . . . . . . Mooney Problem Check List (Education)
MCL . . . . Moore and McCormack Lines, Inc. (NYSE symbol)
MSISL . . . . . Moore School Information Systems Laboratory
MOCR . . . . . Moores Creek National Military Park
MRA. . . . . Moral Re-Armament
MRW . . . . Morale, Recreation and Welfare (Military)
MHS . . . . Moravian Historical Society
MMS . . . . Moravian Missionary Society
MMF . . . . Moravian Music Foundation
MORBREPT . . . Morbidity Report
MORBTGREPT. . Morbidity Telegraphic Report
MES . . . . More Effective Schools (Program)
MIK . . . . More in the Kitchen (Family dinner-table expression)
MNF . . . . Morehead & North Fork R. R. (AAR code)
MHC . . . . Morgan Horse Club
MHA . . . . Mormon History Association
M . . . . Morning
MR . . . . Morning Report
M/R . . . . Morning Report (Army)
MLU . . . . Moroccan Labor Union
MORSEAFRON. . Moroccan Sea Frontier (Navy) (World War II)
MSF . . . . Moroccan Sea Frontier (Navy)
MSHAA . . . . . Morocco Spotted Horse Association of America
MUSLO . . . . . Morocco United States Liaison Office
M . . . . Morphine (Slang)
MS . . . . Morphine Sulphate (Chemistry)
MOL . . . . Morrell (John) & Company (NYSE symbol)
MG . . . . Morris Garage (British automobile manufacturer; initialism used as name
                    of sports car it produces)
MPI . . . . Morris Pratt Institute Association
MFM . . . . Morrissey, Fernie & Michel Railway (AAR code)
MOED . . . . . . Morristown-Edison National Park Service Group
ME. . . . . Morristown & Erie R. R. (AAR code)
MORR . . . . . . Morristown National Historical Park
MAUDE . . . . . Morse Automatic Decoder
MTC . . . . Morse Telegraph Club
M . . . . Mortar
MORTREP . . . . Mortar Bombing Report
MMC . . . . Mortar Motor Carrier
MAFIA . . . . . Morte Alla Francia Italia Anelo (Death to the French is Italy's
                    Cry), or Movimento Anti Francesi Italiano Azione (Italian Action
                    Movement Against the French)
M . . . . Mortgage
MBA . . . . Mortgage Bankers Association of America
MIP . . . . Mortgage Insurance Premium
M . . . . Mortis (Of Death)
MOS . . . . Morton Air Services, Ltd.
MAT . . . . Moscow Art Theater
MCSA . . . . . . Moscow, Camden & San Augustine R. R. (AAR code)
MOV . . . . Moshassuck Valley R. R. (AAR code)
MOLMI . . . . . Moskovskii Ordena Lenina Meditsinskii Institut
ME. . . . . Most Excellent (In titles)
MFN . . . . Most-Favored-Nation (Tariff)
MH . . . . Most Honorable
MIP . . . . Most Important Person
MPN . . . . Most Probable Number
MPP. . . . . Most Probable Position (Navigation)
MSB . . . . Most Significant BIT (Data processing)
MVP . . . . Most Valuable Player (Athletics)
MW . . . . Most Worshipful
MW . . . . Most Worthy
MWGM. . . . . . Most Worthy (or Worshipful) Grand Master (Masonry)
MWP . . . . Most Worthy Patriarch
MAA . . . . Motel Association of America
M . . . . Mother

MOP . . . . Mother-of-Pearl
MAW . . . . . . Mothers for Adequate Welfare
MDA . . . . Mothers for Decency in Action (Group opposing sex education in schools)
MOMS . . . . . . Mothers of Men in Service (World War II)
MOMS . . . . Mothers for Moral Stability (Group opposing sex education
                    in schools)
MOSS. . . . . . Mothers of Sons in Service (World War II)
MWWII. . . . . . Mothers of World War II
MOTPICT . . . . Motion Picture
MPA . . . . Motion Picture Alliance for the Preservation of American Ideals
MPAA . . . . . . Motion Picture Association of America
MPEA . . . . . . Motion Picture Export Association
MPEAA . . . . . Motion Picture Export Association of America
MPFE . . . . . . Motion Picture Film Editors
MPIC . . . . Motion Picture Industry Controllers
MPIC . . . . Motion Picture Industry Council
MP & MTD. . . . Motion Picture & Medical Television Department (of AMA)
MPO . . . . Motion Picture Operator
MPP . . . . Motion Picture Pioneers
MP. . . . . Motion Picture Production (Navy)
MPRF . . . . . . Motion Picture Relief Fund
MPRC . . . . . . Motion Picture Research Council
MPS . . . . Motion Picture Service (Department of Agriculture)
MPSE . . . . . . Motion Picture Sound Editors
MPTCMA . . . . Motion Picture and Television Credit Managers Association
M . . . . Motor
MAC . . . . Motor Ambulance Convoy
MA/SB . . . . . . Motor Antisubmarine Boat
MAD . . . . Motor Assembly and Disassembly
MB. . . . . Motor Boat
MBS . . . . Motor Bus Society
MCB . . . . Motor Cargo Boat
MCC . . . . Motor Carrier Cases (ICC)
MDA . . . . Motor Discriminative Acuity (Psychology)
MD . . . . Motor Drive
MEP . . . . Motor End Plate
MEMA . . . . . . Motor and Equipment Manufacturers Association
MEWA . . . . . . Motor and Equipment Wholesalers Association
MF . . . . Motor Field
MF . . . . Motor Freight
MOGAS . . . . . Motor Gasoline
MOTOGAS . . . Motor Gasoline (Military)
MG . . . . Motor Generator
MGB . . . . Motor Gunboat (British)
MHCOA . . . . . Motor, Hearse and Car Owners Association
MOTEL. . . . . . Motor Hotel
ML. . . . . Motor Launch
MLC . . . . Motor Launch, Cabin
MLDS . . . . . . Motor Launch, Double Shelter
MLB . . . . Motor Lifeboat
MOMM . . . . . Motor Machinist's Mate (Navy rating)
MOMMSR . . . . Motor Machinist's Mate, Ship Repair (Navy rating)
MOSRD. . . . . . Motor Machinist's Mate, Ship Repair, Diesel Engineering Mechanic
                    (Navy rating)
MOSRG . . . . . Motor Machinist's Mate, Ship Repair, Gasoline Engine Mechanic
                    (Navy rating)
MM . . . . Motor Maintenance (Army)
MM . . . . Motor Maintenance Aptitude Area
YMP . . . . Motor Mine Planter (Navy symbol)
AMS. . . . . Motor Minesweeper (Navy symbol)
MMS . . . . Motor Minesweeper
MON . . . . Motor Octane Number
MOIL. . . . . . . Motor Oil
MTS . . . . Motor-Operated Transfer Switch
SP . . . . Motor Patrol Boat (Navy symbol)
MRB . . . . Motor Rescue Boat
MRO . . . . Motor Route Order Number
MS . . . . Motor Ship
MSB . . . . Motor Surfboat
MT . . . . Motor Tanker
MTB. . . . . Motor Torpedo Boat
PT . . . . Motor Torpedo Boat (Navy symbol)
MTBRON. . . . . Motor Torpedo Boat Squadron
MTBSTC . . . . . Motor Torpedo Boat Squadrons Training Center (Melville, Rhode Island)
AGP . . . . Motor Torpedo Boat Tender (Navy symbol)
MT. . . . . Motor Transport
MTC . . . . Motor Transport Corps
YMT. . . . . Motor Tug (Navy symbol)
MU . . . . Motor Union
MVD . . . . Motor Vehicle Driver Selection Battery (Army)
MVI . . . . Motor Vehicle Inspection

MVMC . . . . . Motor Vehicle Maintenance Conference
MVPCB . . . . . Motor Vehicle Pollution Control Board (California)
MVSB . . . . . . Motor Vehicle Storage Building (Army)
MVSS . . . . . . Motor Vehicle Storage Shed (Army)
MV . . . . Motor Vessel
MRW . . . . Motor Wheel Corporation (NYSE symbol) (Delisted)
MY . . . . Motor Yacht
MC . . . . Motorcycle
MATA . . . . . . Motorcycle and Allied Trades Association
MSATA . . . . . Motorcycle, Scooter and Allied Trades Association
MASCOT . . . . . Motorola Automatic Sequential Computer Operated Tester
MOT . . . . Motorola, Inc. (NYSE symbol)
MOCI . . . . . . Mound City Group National Monument
MTH . . . . Mount Hood R. R. (AAR code)
MHM . . . . . . Mount Hope Mineral R. R. (AAR code)
MOMC . . . . . Mount McKinley National Park
MORA . . . . . . Mount Ranier National Park
MORU . . . . . . Mount Rushmore National Memorial
MVLA . . . . . . Mount Vernon Ladies' Association of the Union
MVT . . . . Mt. Vernon Terminal R. R. (AAR code)
M . . . . Mountain
MA . . . . Mountain Artillery
MDT . . . . Mountain Daylight Time
MFS . . . . Mountain Fuel Supply Company (NYSE symbol)
MRA . . . . Mountain Rescue Association
M . . . . Mountain Standard Time (Aviation)
MST . . . . Mountain Standard Time
MODAC . . . . . Mountain System Digital Automatic Computer
MT . . . . Mountain Time
MTW . . . . Mountain Waves (Aviation)
MI . . . . Mounted Infantry
MP . . . . Mounted Police
MIA . . . . "Mouse in Able" Program
MU . . . . Mouse Unit (With reference to radium emanations)
MALN . . . . . . Mouvement Africain de Liberation Nationale (African Movement for
National Liberation)
MDIA . . . . . . Mouvement pour la Defense des Interets de l'Angola (Movement for the
Defense of Angolan Interests)
MDD . . . . . . Mouvement Democratique Dahomeen (Dahomean Democratic Movement)
MDRM . . . . . Mouvement Democratique de Renovation Malgache (Democratic Movement
Malagasy Restoration)
MDV . . . . . . Mouvement Democratique Voltaique (Upper Volta Democratic Movement)
ME . . . . Mouvement Europeen
MEDAC . . . . . Mouvement de l'Evolution Democratique de L'Afrique Centrale (Central
African Democratic Evolution Movement)
MEDERCO . . . . Mouvement de l'Evolution et de Developpement Rural - Congo (Movement
for the Evolution and Rural Development - Congo) (Leopoldville)
MESAN . . . . . Mouvement de l'Evolution Sociale de l'Afrique Noire (Black African
Social Evolution Movement)
MFC . . . . Mouvement Familial Chretien (Christian Family Movement)
MFR . . . . Mouvement Familial Rural (Rural Family Movement)
MFE . . . . Mouvement Federaliste Europeen (European Federalist Movement)
MIIC . . . . . . Mouvement International des Intellectuels Catholiques (International
Movement of Catholic Students) (Pax Romana)
MIJARC . . . . . Mouvement International de la Jeunesse Agricole et Rurale Catholique
UFER . . . . . . Mouvement International pour l'Union Fraternelle Entre les Races et
les Peuples
MJUPS . . . . . . Mouvement des Jeunes de l'Union Progressiste Senegalaise (Youth
Movement of the Senegalese Progressive Movement)
MJPS . . . . . . Mouvement des Jeunesses Progressistes Soudanaises (Sudanese Progressive
Youth Movement) (Mali)
MJSA . . . . . . Mouvement des Jeunesses Socialistes Africaines (African Socialist Youth
Movement)
MLEC . . . . . . Mouvement pour la Liberation de l'Enclave de Cabinda (Movement for
the Liberation of the Cabinda Enclave)
MLN . . . . Mouvement de Liberation Nationale (National Liberation Movement)
(Dahomey)
MOLINA . . . . . Mouvement pour la Liberation Nationale (Movement for National
Liberation)
MMM . . . . . . Mouvement Mondial des Meres
MNA . . . . Mouvement National Algerien (National Algerian Movement)
MNC . . . . Mouvement National Congolais (Congolese National Movement)
MNC-K . . . . . Mouvement National Congolais (Congolese National Movement) (Kalonji
Wing)
MNC-L . . . . . . Mouvement National Congolais - Lumumba (Congolese National Movement)
(Lumumba Wing)
MONIMA . . . . Mouvement National pour l'Independance Malgache (National Movement
for the Independence of Madagascar) (Became MOMA)
MNJTS . . . . . Mouvement National des Jeunes Travailleurs du Senegal (National
Movement of Young Workers of Senegal)
MPJ . . . . Mouvement Panafricain de la Jeunesse (Pan-African Youth Movement)

MPL . . . . Mouvement Politique Lulua (Lulua Political Movement)
MPEA . . . . . . Mouvement Populaire d'Evolution Africaine (African People's Evolution
Movement)
MPA . . . . Mouvement Populaire de Liberation de l'Angola
MPS . . . . Mouvement Populaire Senegalais (Senegal Popular Movement)
MPT . . . . Mouvement Populaire Tchadien (Chadian Popular Movement)
MPT . . . . Mouvement Populaire Togolais (Togolese Popular Movement)
MPNC . . . . . . Mouvement pour le Progres National Congolais (Movement for National
Congolese Progress)
MPB . . . . Mouvement Progressiste de Burundi (Progressive Movement of Burundi)
MRLPC . . . . . Mouvement de Regroupement et de Liberation du Peuple Congolais
(Movement for the Regroupment and Liberation of the Congolese People)
(Leopoldville)
MRPC . . . . . . Mouvement de Regroupement des Populations Congolaises (Movement for
the Regroupment of the Congolese People)
MRV . . . . Mouvement de Regroupement Voltaique (Upper Volta Regroupment
Movement)
MRP . . . . Mouvement Republicain Populaire (Popular Republican Movement) (France)
MSM . . . . Mouvement Social Mohutu (Mohutu Social Movement)
MSA . . . . Mouvement Socialiste Africain (African Socialist Movement) (Congo--
Brazzaville)
MSEUE . . . . . Mouvement Socialiste pour les Etats Unis d'Europe
MSUS . . . . . . Mouvement Socialiste d'Union Senegalaise (Senegalese Socialist Movement)
MSM . . . . Mouvement Solidaire Muluba (Muluba Solidarity Movement)
MTC . . . . Mouvement Traditionaliste Congolais (Congolese Traditionalist Movement)
MTLD . . . . . . Mouvement pour le Triomphe des Libertes Democratiques (Movement for
the Triumph of Democratic Liberties) (Algeria)
MSC . . . . Moved, Seconded, and Carried
MBW . . . . Movement for a Better World
MC . . . . Movement Control (of troops)
MCC . . . . Movement Control Center
MCO . . . . Movement Control Officer
MCT . . . . Movement Control Team (Air Force)
MDC . . . . Movement Designator Code
MD . . . . Movement Directive
MFA . . . . Movement for Federation of the Americas
MIDS . . . . . . Movement Information Distribution Station
MLGCV . . . . . Movement for the Liberation of Portuguese Guinea and the Cape Verde
Islands
MO . . . . Movement Orders
MRC . . . . Movement Report Center
MRCC . . . . . . Movement Report Control Center
MRO . . . . Movement Report Office
MRS . . . . Movement Report Sheet
MOTOREDE . . Movement to Restore Decency (Group opposing sex education in schools)
MI . . . . Movements Identification (Military)
M & I . . . . . . Movements and Identification (Military)
MIO . . . . Movements Identification Officer (Air Force)
MCA . . . . Movers Conference of America
MWAA . . . . . Movers' and Warehousemen's Association of America
ME . . . . Movie Editor
GP . . . . Movie Rating for "Parental Guidance Suggested (All Ages Admitted)"
X . . . . Movie Rating for "Persons under 18 (16 in some localities) Not
Admitted"
MAC . . . . Movimento Anti-Colonialista (Anti-Colonialist Movement)
MLGP . . . . . . Movimento de Liberacao da Guine Portuguesa (Portuguese Guinea
Liberation Movement)
MPLA . . . . . . Movimento Popular de Libertacao de Angola (Popular Movement for the
Liberation of Angola)
MRL . . . . Movimento Revolucionario Liberal (Colombian political party)
MSI . . . . Movimento Sociale Italiano
MDM . . . . . . Movimiento Democratico de Mozambique (Democratic Movement of
Mozambique)
MDN . . . . . . Movimiento Democratico Nacionalista (Political party in Guatemala)
MDP . . . . Movimiento Democratico Peruano (Peruvian Democratic Movement)
MPI . . . . Movimiento pro Independencia de Puerto Rico
MIP . . . . Movimiento Independiente Peruano (Peruvian Independent Movement)
MIR . . . . Movimiento de Izquierda Revolucionario (Venezuelan political party)
MJUPG . . . . . Movimiento da Juventude da Uniao Popular da Guine (Youth Movement
of Guinean People's Union)
MLN . . . . Movimiento de Liberacion Nacional (Movement for National Liberation)
(Guatemala, Mexico)
MNR . . . . Movimiento Nacional Reformista (National Reformist Movement)
(Honduras)
MNR . . . . Movimiento Nacionalista Revolucionario (National Revolutionary
Movement) (Bolivia)
MNPS . . . . . . Movimiento Nazionale Pan-Somalo (Pan-Somali National Movement)
MPD . . . . Movimiento Popular Dominicano (Dominican Popular Movement)
MRP . . . . Movimiento Republicano Progresista (Progressive Republican Movement)
(Venezuela)
MBO . . . . Moving Base Operator

MMD	Moving Map Display
MPE	Moving Paper Electrophoresis
MTI	Moving Target Indicator (RADAR) (Air Force)
MTR	Moving Target Reactor
MANU	Mozambique African National Union
MSL	MSL Industries, Inc. (NYSE symbol)
MM	Much Married (Slang)
MRU	Much Regret, I Am Unable
M	Mucoid
MM	Mucous Membrane
M	Mud
MUB	Mueller Brass Company (NYSE symbol)
MAO	Muhammadan Anglo-Oriental
ME	Muhammadan Era
MUWO	Muir Woods National Monument
MAC	Multiaction Computer
MAD	Multi-Aperture Device (Data processing)
MARS	Multi-Aperture Reluctance Switch (Data storage unit)
MAGI	Multiarray Gamma Irradiator
MARLIS	Multiaspect Relevance Linkage Information System
MBR	Multibomb Rack
MADE	Multichannel Analog-to-Digital Data Encoder
MDR	Multichannel Data Recorder
MCRT	Multi-Channel Rotary Transformer (Electronics)
MCC	Multicomponent Circuits
MSRPP	Multidimensional Scale for Rating Psychiatric Patients
METRIC	Multi-Echelon Technique for Recoverable Item Control
MET	Multiemitter Transistor
ME	Multi-Engine
M-ENG	Multi-Engined
MFKP	Multifrequency Key Pulsing
MFR	Multifrequency Receiver
MAR	Multifunction Array RADAR
MFS	Multifunction Sensor
MG	Multi-Gage
MLF	Multilateral Missile Fleet (NATO)
MLF	Multilateral Force
MNF	Multilateral Nuclear Force
MLCB	Multilayer Circuit Board
MMM	Multi-Mission Module
MNA	Multi-Network Area (Term used in TV ratings)
MD	Multinomial Distribution (Statistics)
MOPTAR	Multi-Object Phase Tracking and Ranging
MRF	Multipath Reduction Factor (Electronics)
MPI	Multiphasic Personality Inventory
MAC	Multiple Access Computer
MAD	Multiple Access Device
MASTER	Multiple Access Shared Time Executive Routine (Data processing)
MAPU	Multiple Address Processing Unit (Military)
MARSAM	Multiple Airborne Reconnaissance Sensors Assessment Model
MATTS	Multiple Airborne Target Trajectory System
MAP	Multiple Allocation Procedure (PERT)
MATIC	Multiple Area Technical Information Center
MARS	Multiple Artillery Rocket System (Army)
MAMI	Multiple Association Management Institute
MAD	Multiple Audio Distribution (Communications)
MASTIF	Multiple Axis Space Test Inertia Facility (Training device for astronauts)
MUBIS	Multiple Beam Interval Scanner
MBK	Multiple Beam Klystron
MBS	Multiple Business System
MCCU	Multiple Communications Control Unit (Data processing)
MCT	Multiple Compressed Tablet (Pharmacy)
MCC	Multiple Computer Complex
MC	Multiple Contact
MC	Multiple Copy
MCIS	Multiple Corridor Identification System (Air Force)
MDA	Multiple Docking Adapter (NASA)
MEF	Multiple Effect Flash (Evaporator) (Seawater conversion system)
MER	Multiple Ejector Rack
MEN	Multiple Event Network
MFSK	Multiple Frequency Shift Keying
MGMC	Multiple Gun Motor Carriage
MIRV	Multiple Independent(ly) (Targeted) Reentry Vehicle (Military)
MIRPS	Multiple Information Retrieval by Parallel Selection
MITE	Multiple Input Terminal Equipment
MIRF	Multiple Instantaneous Response File
MIDOT	Multiple Interferometer Determination of Trajectories
MMA	Multiple Module Access
MOBS	Multiple-Orbit Bombardment System
MOMS	Multiple Orbit - Multiple Satellite
MPC	Multiple-Purpose Communications
MRV	Multiple Reentry Vehicles
MRL	Multiple Rocket Launcher
MS	Multiple Sclerosis (Medicine)
MTD	Multiple Target Detection
MTR	Multiple Track RADAR
MTR	Multiple Tracking Range
MT	Multiple Transfer
MTG	Multiple-Trigger Generator
MU	Multiple Unit
MUSA	Multiple Unit Steerable Antenna (Electronics)
MUTA	Multiple Unit Training Assembly (Army)
MUPS	Multiple Utility Peripheral System (Data processing)
MW	Multiple Wounds
MPX	Multiplex
MX	Multiplex
MIFS	Multiplex Interferometric Fourier Spectroscopy
MRP	Multiplex Recording Photography
MULTICS	Multiplexed Information and Computing Service
MMP	Multiplexed Message Processor
MTU	Multiplexer and Terminal Unit
MUX	Multiplexing Equipment
MP	Multiplier Phototube
MQ	Multiplier Quotient Register (Data processing)
MAD	Multiply and Add
MLR	Multiply and Round
MF	Multiplying Factor (Microscopy)
MP	Multipole
MVT	Multiprogramming with a Variable Number of Tasks (Data processing)
MACS	Multiproject Automated Control System
MADAM	Multipurpose Automatic Data Analysis Machine
MAIDS	Multipurpose Automatic Inspection and Diagnostic Systems (Army)
MPC	Multi-Purpose Center
MPCSW	Multipurpose Close Support Weapon (Military)
MCS	Multipurpose Communications and Signaling
MPF	Multi-Purpose Food (Refers to a specific combination of ingredients used in a food relief program)
MPLE	Multi-Purpose Long Endurance (Aircraft)
MPM	Multipurpose Meal
MPPL	Multi-Purpose Programming Language
MPSS	Multi-Purpose Sampling System
MRCA	Multirole Combat Aircraft
MUSAP	Multi-Satellite Augmentation Program
MSC	Multi-Service Center
MSF	Multistage Flash (Desalination method)
M-STEP	Multi-State Teacher Education Project
MSTPHC	Multistop Time-to-Pulse Height Converter (NASA)
MSTS	Multi-Subscriber Time-Shared (Computer system)
MTE	Multisystem Test Equipment (Military)
MAPS	Multivariate Analysis and Prediction of Schedules
MANOVA	Multivariate Analysis of Variance (Statistics)
MVE	Multivariate Exponential Distribution (Statistics)
MVB	Multivesicular Body
MVB	Multi-Vibrator
MGKU	Mumbai Girni Kamgar Union (Bombay Mill Workers' Union) (India)
MWR	Muncie & Western R. R. (AAR code)
MB	Municipal Borough
MD	Municipal Docks (AAR code)
MFOA	Municipal Finance Officers Association of US and Canada
MMU	Municipal Mazdoor Union (India)
MP	Municipal Police
MR	Municipal Reform(er)
METW	Municipality of East Troy, Wisconsin R. R. (AAR code)
MAB	Munitions Assignment Board (Anglo-American) (World War II)
MBW	Munitions Assignment Board (Washington)
MAC (Air)	Munitions Assignment Committee (Air) (Washington)
MB	Munitions Board
MBCA	Munitions Board Cataloging Agency
MBPC	Munitions Board Petroleum Committee
MBSA	Munitions Board Standards Agency
MUNBG	Munitions Building (Washington, DC)
MCC	Munitions Carriers Conference
MC	Munitions Command (Army)
MUCOM	Munitions Command (Army)
MUNC	Munitions Command (Army)
MMS	Munitions Maintenance Squadron (Air Force)
MWA	Munitions of War Act (British)
MUN	Munsingwear, Inc. (NYSE symbol)
MH	Murine Hepatitis
MHV	Murine Hepatitis Virus
MPH	Murphy (G. C.) Company (NYSE symbol)

MUR . . . . Murphy Oil Corporation (NYSE symbol)
MUY . . . . Murray Corporation of America (NYSE symbol)
MVE. . . . . Murray Valley Encephalitis
MAP . . . . Muscle Action Potential
MFT . . . . Muscle Function Test
MSF . . . . Muscle Shock Factor
MS . . . . Muscle Strength
MD . . . . Muscular Dystrophy (Medicine)
MDAA . . . . . . Muscular Dystrophy Associations of America
M . . . . Musculus (Muscle) (Anatomy)
MCZ . . . . Museum of Comparative Zoology (Harvard University)
MHT . . . . Museum of History and Technology (Smithsonian Institution)
MOMA . . . . . . Museum of Modern Art (New York)
MNH . . . . . . Museum of Natural History (Smithsonian Institution)
MCL . . . . Mushroom Canners League
MGA . . . . Mushroom Growers Cooperative Association
MGCA . . . . . . Mushroom Growers Cooperative Association
MB. . . . . Music for the Blind
MCOA . . . . . . Music Center Opera Association (Los Angeles)
MUSICOMP . . Music Composition
MCA . . . . Music Critics Association
MEA . . . . Music Editors Association
MEL . . . . Music Education League
MERC. . . . . . Music Education Research Council
MENC . . . . . . Music Educators National Conference
MIC . . . . Music Industry Council
MIR . . . . Music Information Retrieval (Data processing)
MLA . . . . Music Library Association
MOA . . . . Music Operators of America
MPCE . . . . . . Music Publishers Contact Employees
MPA . . . . Music Publishers' Association of the United States
MPPA . . . . . . Music Publishers' Protective Association
MRF . . . . Music Research Foundation
MTNA . . . . . . Music Teachers National Association
MUW . . . . Music Wire
MW . . . . Music Wire
MWG . . . . . . Music Wire Gauge
MAP . . . . Musical Aptitude Profile
MATA . . . . . . Musical Arena Theatres Association (Later, Musical Theatres Association)
MBSI . . . . . . Musical Box Society International
MD . . . . Musical Director
MTA . . . . Musical Theatres Association
MU . . . . Musician (Navy rating)
MCA . . . . Musicians Club of America
MEF . . . . Musicians Emergency Fund
M . . . . Mustard Gas
M . . . . Muster
MO . . . . Mustered Out (of military service)
MOP. . . . . . . Mustering-Out Pay (Military)
MM . . . . Mutatis Mutandis (With the Necessary Changes)
MTV . . . . Mutatur Terminatio Versiculi (The Termination of the Little Verse Is Changed)
MABCGT . . . . Mutual Adjustment Bureau of Cloth and Garment Trades, Inc.
MAAN . . . . . . Mutual Advertising Agency Network
MAP. . . . . . . Mutual African Press Agency
MAANPI . . . . . Mutual Aid Association of the New Polish Immigration
MAAC . . . . . . Mutual Assistance Advisory Committee
MAD . . . . Mutual Assured Destruction
MAELU . . . . . . Mutual Atomic Energy Liability Underwriters
MAERP . . . . . Mutual Atomic Energy Reassurance Pool
MBAS . . . . Mutual Benefit and Aid Society
MBS . . . . Mutual Broadcasting System

MDA . . . . Mutual Defense Assistance
MDAA . . . . . . Mutual Defense Assistance Act
MDAC . . . . . . Mutual Defense Assistance, General Area of China
MDAGT . . . . . Mutual Defense Assistance, Greece and Turkey
MDAIKP . . . . . Mutual Defense Assistance, Iran, Republic of Korea, and Philippines
MDANAA . . . . Mutual Defense Assistance, North Atlantic Area
MDAP . . . . . . Mutual Defense Assistance Program
MDCS . . . . . . Mutual Defense Control Staff (Department of State)
MDT. . . . . Mutual Defense Treaty
MFIC . . . . . . Mutual Federation of Independent Cooperatives (Later, Northeast Dairy Cooperative Federation)
MI . . . . Mutual Inductance
MIAA . . . . . . Mutual Insurance Advisory Association
MICOFT . . . . Mutual Insurance Committee on Federal Taxation
MICE . . . . . . Mutual Insurance Council of Editors
MIRB . . . . . . Mutual Insurance Rating Bureau
MLRB . . . . . . Mutual Loss Research Bureau
MONY . . . . . Mutual of New York (Insurance company)
MRB . . . . Mutual Reinsurance Bureau
MR. . . . . Mutual Responsibility (Movement within Anglican Communion to make its mission more efficacious)
MSA . . . . . . Mutual Security Act
MSA . . . . . . Mutual Security Agency (Functions transferred to Foreign Operations Administration, 1953)
MSMS . . . . . . Mutual Security Military Sales
MSP. . . . . Mutual Security Program
MSMDA . . . . . Mutual Sewing Machine Dealers Association
MSFC. . . . . . . Mutual Society of the French Community
MWDDEA . . . . Mutual Weapons Development Data Exchange Agreement (NATO)
MWDP . . . . . . Mutual Weapons Development Program (NATO)
MWDT . . . . . . Mutual Weapons Development Team (Military)
MOSS . . . . . . Mutually Owned Society for Songwriters
MUTACI . . . . . Mutuelle des Autochtones de la Cote d'Ivoire (Mutual Association of the Natives of the Ivory Coast)
ME . . . . Muzzle Energy
ML. . . . . Muzzle-Loading
MLR . . . . Muzzle-Loading Rifle
MLRG. . . . . . . Muzzle-Loading Rifled Gun
MV . . . . Muzzle Velocity (Ballistics)
MA . . . . My Account
MYDIS . . . . . . My Dispatch (Military)
MYLTR . . . . . (Reference) My Letter (Military)
MYMGM. . . . . My Mailgram (Military)
MYMSG . . . . . My Message (Military)
MP. . . . . My Pal (Slang)
MYRAD. . . . . . My Radio (Military)
MYSER . . . . . (Reference) My Serial (Military)
MYTEL . . . . . My Telegram (Military)
MG . . . . Myasthenia Gravis Foundation
MGF . . . . Myasthenia Gravis Foundation
MSA . . . . Mycological Society of America
M:E . . . . Myeloid:Erythocryte (Ratio)
MBTI . . . . Myers-Briggs Type Indicator (A personality test)
MUO . . . . Myocardiopathy of Unknown Origin
MHb. . . . . Myohemoglobin
M . . . . Myopia
MRF . . . . Myopia Research Foundation
MYG . . . . . . Myriagram
MYL . . . . Myrialiter
MYM . . . . . . Myriameter
MWA . . . . Mystery Writers of America
MTC. . . . . Mystic Terminal R. R. (AAR code)

N

NMIA . . . . N-Methyl Indoxyl Acetate
LDF . . . . NAACP Legal Defense and Educational Fund
NV . . . . Naamloze Vennootschap (Limited company) (Netherlands)
NDF. . . . . Nacelle Drag Efficiency (Factor) (Aerospace)
NAM . . . . an-Nahdah al-Wataniyyah al-Mauritaniyyah (The Call of Nationalism of
     Mauritania)
N . . . . Nail
NPCP . . . . Nairobi Peoples' Convention Party
NW . . . . Naked Weight
N . . . . Name
N/EP . . . . Name on End-Paper (Antiquarian book trade)
N/O . . . . (In the) Name Of (Business and trade)
NARANO . . . . Name, Rate and Service Number
NARANEXOS . . Name, Rate, Service Number, and Expiration of Obligated Service
     (Navy)
NREP . . . . Name Removed from End-Paper (Antiquarian book trade)
NU . . . . Name Unknown
NN . . . . Names
n . . . . Nano (Prefix)
nA . . . . Nanoampere
Nf . . . . Nanofarad
NM . . . . Nanometer
NS . . . . Nanosecond (100 billionth of a second)
NSEC. . . . . . . Nanosecond (100 billionth of a second)
nW. . . . . Nanowatt
E . . . . Naperian logarithm base (2.7182818)
NAA. . . . . . . Naphthaleneacetic Acid (Chemical)
NAA . . . . Naphthylacetic Acid
NAJ. . . . . Napierville Junction Railway Company (AAR code)
NARA. . . . . . . Narcotic Addict Rehabilitation Act
NACC . . . . . . Narcotic Addiction Control Commission (New York)
NDSB. . . . . . . Narcotic Drugs Supervisory Body (UN)
NA . . . . Narcotics Anonymous
NARCO . . . . . Narcotics Commission (UN)
NFM . . . . Narodni Front Makedonije
NTS . . . . Narodno-Trudovoi Soyuz (National-Labor Federation) (Anti-Soviet
     organization in Western Europe)
NKO . . . . Narodnyi Komissariat Oborony (People's Commissariat of Defense)
     (Existed until 1946) (USSR)
NARKOMVNUDEL . . Narodnyi Komissariat Vnutrennikh Del (People's Commissariat
     of Internal Affairs) (Soviet secret police organization) (Also known as
     NKVD)
NKVD. . . . . . . Narodnyi Komissariat Vnutrennikh Del (People's Commissariat of
     Internal Affairs) (Soviet secret police organization) (Also known as
     NARKOMVNUDEL)
ND . . . . Narodowa Demokracja
NPR . . . . Narodowa Partia Robotnicza (National Workers Party) (Poland)
NBP. . . . . Narodowy Bank Polski
NAP. . . . . Narragansett Pier R. R. (AAR code)
NARCOM . . . . Narration, Commentary (Motion pictures)
NOVEL . . . . . Narrative Output Vocabulary Editing Language (Psychiatric test)
NAMG . . . . . . Narrow-Angle Mars Gate (NASA)
NB. . . . . Narrow Band (Electronics)
NBT . . . . Narrow-Beam Transducer (Coast and Geodetic Survey)
NFI . . . . Narrow Fabrics Institute
NG . . . . Narrow Gage
NBA. . . . . Narrowband Allocation
NBDL. . . . . . . Narrowband Data Line
NBFM. . . . . . . Narrowband Frequency Modulation
NFM . . . . Narrowband Frequency Modulation (Radio)
NT . . . . Narrower Term (Cross-reference) (Indexing)
NASCOP. . . . . NASA Communications Operating Procedures
NEBA. . . . . . . NASA Employees Benefit Association

NLVP . . . . NASA Launch Vehicle Planning Project
NPC . . . . NASA Procurement Circular
NASA-TR . . . . NASA Tank Reactor
NULO . . . . . . NASA Unmanned Launch Operations
NASCOM . . . . NASA Worldwide Communications Network
N . . . . Nasal
NC . . . . Nashville, Chattanooga & St. Louis R. R. (AAR code)
NC & ST L . . . Nashville, Chattanooga & St. Louis Railway
NASO . . . . . . Natchez & Southern Railway Company (AAR code)
NATR . . . . Natchez Trace Parkway (National Park Service designation)
NUR . . . . Natchez, Urania & Ruston Railway Company (AAR code)
NCP. . . . . Natco Corporation (NYSE symbol)
NBI . . . . Nathaniel Branden Institute
N . . . . National (American) form of screw threads
NA . . . . National Academy or Academician
NAAJS . . . . . . National Academy for Adult Jewish Studies
NAA . . . . National Academy of Arbitrators
NAD . . . . National Academy of Design
NAEPS . . . . . . National Academy of Economics and Political Science
NAE. . . . . National Academy of Education
NAE. . . . . National Academy of Engineering
NARAS . . . . . . National Academy of Recording Arts and Sciences
NAS. . . . . National Academy of Sciences
NASCO . . . . . National Academy of Sciences Committee on Oceanography
NAS-NRC . . . . National Academy of Sciences - National Research Council
NATAS . . . . . . National Academy of Television Arts and Sciences
NATVAS . . . . . National Academy of Television Arts and Sciences
NAL. . . . . National Accelerator Laboratory (AEC)
NAM . . . . National Account Management (Bell System)
NAC . . . . National Achievement Clubs
NCM . . . . National Acme Company (NYSE symbol)
NACA . . . . . . National Acoustical Contractors Association
NASA. . . . . . . National Acoustical Suppliers Association
NATMC . . . . . National Advanced Technology Management Conference
NAAN . . . . . . National Advertising Agency Network
NABS . . . . National Advertising Benevolent Society (British)
NANA . . . . . . National Advertising Newspaper Association
NACC . . . . . . National Advisory Cancer Council
NACL . . . . . . National Advisory Commission on Libraries
NACOL . . . . . National Advisory Commission on Libraries
NAC . . . . National Advisory Committee (or Council)
NACA . . . . . . National Advisory Committee for Aeronautics (Functions transferred to
     NASA, 1958)
NACFL . . . . . . National Advisory Committee on Farm Labor
NACOR . . . . . National Advisory Committee on Radiation
NAC . . . . National Advisory Council on Education of Disadvantaged Children
NACECE. . . . . National Advisory Council on Extension and Continuing Education
NACRCD. . . . . National Advisory Council on Rural Civil Defense
NACTEFL . . . . National Advisory Council on the Teaching of English as a Foreign
     Language
NAS . . . . National Advocates Society
NAC . . . . National Aero Club
NAA . . . . National Aeronautic Association
NARCO . . . . . National Aeronautical Corporation
NAE . . . . National Aeronautical Establishment (Canada)
NAL . . . . National Aeronautical Laboratory
NASA . . . . . . National Aeronautics and Space Administration
NASC . . . . . . National Aeronautics and Space Council
NAEC . . . . . . National Aerospace (formerly, Aviation) Education Council
NAECON . . . . National Aerospace Electronics Conference (IEEE)
NASSA . . . . . . National Aerospace Services Association
NAS . . . . National Aerospace Standards
NAS . . . . National Aerospace System (FAA)

NAC . . . . National Agency Check (of security clearance)
NACC . . . . . . National Agency Check Center
NACI . . . . National Agency Check and Written Inquiries
NAAMA . . . . . National Agricultural Advertising and Marketing Association
NACA . . . . . . National Agricultural Chemicals Association
NAL . . . . National Agricultural Library (Department of Agriculture)
NALA . . . . . . National Agricultural Limestone Association (Later, National Limestone Institute)
NALI . . . . National Agricultural Limestone Institute (Later, National Limestone Institute)
NATL . . . . . . National Agricultural Transportation League
NAW . . . . . . National Agricultural Workers Union
NAWU . . . . . National Agricultural Workers Union
NAVH . . . . . . National Aid to Visually Handicapped (An organization)
NACA . . . . . . National Air Carrier Association
NAM . . . . . . National Air Museum (of the Smithsonian Institution)
NAPCA . . . . . National Air Pollution Control Administration
NASM . . . . . . National Air and Space Museum (of the Smithsonian Institution) (Formerly, National Air Museum)
NATC . . . . . . National Air Taxi Conference
NATCC . . . . . National Air Transport Coordinating Committee
NAAIS . . . . . . National Aircraft Accident Investigation School (FAA)
NAB . . . . National Aircraft Beacon
NANAC . . . . . National Aircraft Noise Abatement Council
NAS . . . . National Aircraft Standards
NASC . . . . . . National Aircraft Standards Committee
NAWPC . . . . . National Aircraft War Production Council (World War II)
NA . . . . National Airlines, Inc.
NAL . . . . National Airlines, Inc. (NYSE symbol)
NAS . . . . National Airspace or Aviation System (FAA)
NASPO . . . . . . National Airspace System Program Office (FAA)
NABCA . . . . . National Alcoholic Beverage Control Association
NAAA . . . . . . National Alliance of Athletic Associations
NAB . . . . National Alliance of Businessmen
NACC . . . . . . National Alliance of Czech Catholics
NAPE . . . . . . National Alliance of Postal Employees
NATESA . . . . . National Alliance of Television and Electronic Service Associations
NAA . . . . National Alumni Association
NABF . . . . . . National Amateur Baseball Federation
NAMAC . . . . . National Amateur Missile Analysis Center
NAPA . . . . . . National Amateur Press Association
NAWGA . . . . . National-American Wholesale Grocers' Association
NAWLA . . . . . National-American Wholesale Lumber Association
NAF . . . . National Amputation Foundation
NAGA . . . . . . National Amputee Golf Association
NASA . . . . . . National Animal Speech Agency (Humorous)
NASR . . . . National Annual Symposium on Reliability (IEEE)
NADC . . . . . . National Anti-Dumping Committee
NAVS . . . . National Anti-Vivisection Society
NAOA . . . . . . National Apartment Owners Association
NAPI . . . . National Appaloosa Pony, Incorporated
NAI . . . . National Apple Institute
NAWA . . . . . . National Apple Week Association
NARDA . . . . . . National Appliance and Radio-TV Dealers Association
NASA . . . . National Appliance Service Association
NAML . . . . . . National Applied Mathematics Laboratory (National Bureau of Standards)
NAS . . . . National Aquarium Society
NAA . . . . National Arborist Association
NAA . . . . National Archery Association of the United States
NAAB . . . . . . National Architectural Accrediting Board
NA . . . . National Archives (of the United States)
NARS . . . . . . National Archives and Records Service (of GSA)
NATFB . . . . . . National Archives Trust Fund Board
NAFMAB . . . . National Armed Forces Museum Advisory Board (Smithsonian Institution)
NACA . . . . . . National Armored Car Association
NA . . . . National Army
NAEA . . . . . . National Art Education Association
NAMTA . . . . . National Art Materials Trade Association
NAMOS . . . . . National Art Museum of Sport
NAC . . . . National Arts Club
NAF . . . . National Arts Foundation
NAPA . . . . . . National Asphalt Pavement Association
NACLSO . . . . . National Assembly of Chief Livestock Sanitary Officials
NAEP . . . . . . National Assessment of Educational Progress (Sponsored by Carnegie Corporation)
NAL . . . . National Assistance League
NAB . . . . National Associated Businessmen
NATSA . . . . . National Associated Truck Stops and Associates
NA . . . . National Association
NAAW . . . . . National Association of Accordion Wholesalers
NAA . . . . National Association of Accountants

NAACP . . . . . National Association for the Advancement of Colored People
NAANACM . . . National Association for the Advancement of Native American Composers and Musicians
NAAOP . . . . . National Association for the Advancement of Older People
NAAP . . . . . . National Association of Advertising Publishers
NAAE . . . . . . National Association of Afro-American Educators
NAAFW . . . . . National Association of Air Forces Women
NAATTFO . . . . National Association of Alcohol & Tobacco Tax Field Officers
NAAABI . . . . . . National Association of Alcoholic Beverage Importers
NAAD . . . . . . National Association of Aluminum Distributors
NAAO . . . . . . National Association of Amateur Oarsmen
NAABCV . . . . . National Association American Balloon Corps Veterans
AMBUC . . . . . National Association American Business Clubs
NAABC . . . . . National Association American Business Clubs
NAACC . . . . . National Association for American Composers and Conductors
NAAPPB . . . . . National Association of Amusement Parks, Pools and Beaches
NAACC . . . . . National Association of Angling and Casting Clubs
NAAB . . . . . . National Association of Animal Breeders
NAAMM . . . . National Association of Architectural Metal Manufacturers
NAASR . . . . . National Association for Armenian Studies and Research
NAAS . . . . . . National Association of Art Services
NAAB . . . . . . National Association of Artificial Breeders
NAAO . . . . . . National Association of Assessing Officers
NAAG . . . . . . National Association of Attorneys General
NAATS . . . . . National Association of Auto Trim Shops
NAAMIC . . . . National Association of Automotive Mutual Insurance Companies
NABCM . . . . . National Association of Baby Carriage Manufacturers
NABR . . . . . . National Association of Baby Sitter Registries
NABIM . . . . . National Association of Band Instrument Manufacturers
NABAC . . . . . National Association for Bank Auditors and Comptrollers (Later, BAI)
NABW . . . . . National Association of Bank-Women
NABE . . . . . . National Association of Bar Executives (Formerly, NCBE)
NABS . . . . . . National Association of Barber Schools
NABC . . . . . . National Association of Basketball Coaches of the United States
NABM . . . . . National Association of Bedding Manufacturers
NAFBRAT . . . . National Association for Better Radio and Television
NABI . . . . National Association of Biblical Instructors (Later, American Academy of Religion)
NABT . . . . . . National Association of Biology Teachers
NABM . . . . . National Association of Blouse Manufacturers
NABSP . . . . . National Association of Blue Shield Plans
NABDC . . . . . National Association of Blueprint and Diazotype Coaters
NABE . . . . . . National Association of Book Editors
NABET . . . . . National Association Broadcast Employees and Technicians
NABUG . . . . . National Association of Broadcast Unions and Guilds
NAB . . . . National Association of Broadcasters
NABP . . . . . . National Association of Boards of Pharmacy
NABM . . . . . National Association of Boating Magazines
NABCM . . . . . National Association of Brattice Cloth Manufacturers
NABM . . . . . National Association of British Manufacturers
NABOM . . . . . National Association of Building Owners and Managers
NABSC . . . . . National Association of Building Service Contractors
NABE . . . . . . National Association of Business Economists
NABER . . . . . National Association of Business and Educational Radio
NABTE . . . . . National Association for Business Teacher Education
NABTTI . . . . . National Association of Business Teacher-Training Institutions
NACRO . . . . . National Association for the Care and Resettlement of Offenders (British)
NACS . . . . . . National Association of Carpet Specialists
NACSA . . . . . National Association of Casualty and Surety Agents
NACSE . . . . . National Association of Casualty and Surety Executives
NACAC . . . . . National Association of Catholic Alumni Clubs
NACC . . . . . . National Association of Catholic Chaplains
NACPDCG . . . National Association of Catholic Publishers and Dealers in Church Goods
NAC . . . . National Association of Cemeteries
NACDS . . . . . National Association of Chain Drug Stores
NACM . . . . . National Association of Chain Manufacturers
NACGM . . . . . National Association of Chewing Gum Manufacturers
NACS . . . . . . National Association of Christian Schools
NACBA . . . . . National Association of Church Business Administrators
NACIFO . . . . . National Association of Church and Institutional Financing Organizations
NACCC . . . . . National Association of Citizens' Crime Commissions
NACS . . . . . . National Association of Civic Secretaries
NACCA . . . . . National Association of Claimants' Counsel of America (Also known as NACCA Bar Association) (Later, American Trial Lawyers Association)
NACLEO . . . . . National Association of Coin Laundry Equipment Operators
NACDR . . . . . National Association of College Deans and Registrars
NACGC . . . . . National Association of College Gymnastic Coaches
NACS . . . . . . National Association of College Stores
NACUA . . . . . National Association of College and University Attorneys

NACUBO .... National Association of College and University Business Officers
NACUCDRL ... National Association of College & University Chaplains and Directors of Religious Life
NACUFS ..... National Association of College and University Food Services
NACUSS ..... National Association of College and University Summer Sessions
NACUTSO .... National Association of College and University Traffic and Security Officers
NACWPI ..... National Association of College Wind and Percussion Instructors
NACW ...... National Association of College Women
NACTA ..... National Association of Colleges and Teachers of Agriculture
NACU ...... National Association of Colleges and Universities
NACC ...... National Association of Collegiate Commissioners (Later, Collegiate Commissioners Association)
NACDA ..... National Association of Collegiate Directors of Athletics
NACGC ..... National Association of Colored Girls Clubs
NACWC ..... National Association of Colored Women's Clubs
NACLS ..... National Association of Commission Lumber Salesmen
NACSDA .... National Association of Commissioners, Secretaries and Directors of Agriculture (Later, NASDA)
NACD ...... National Association for Community Development
NAC .... National Association of Concessionaires
NACCA ..... National Association of Consumer Credit Administrators
NACO ...... National Association of Consumer Organizations
NACD ...... National Association of Container Distributors
NACS ...... National Association of Convenience Stores
NACSPMR .... National Association of Coordinators of State Programs for the Mentally Retarded
NAC .... National Association of Coroners
NACE ...... National Association of Corrosion Engineers
NACS ...... National Association of Cosmetology Schools
NACA ...... National Association of Cost Accountants
NACJ ...... National Association of Costume Jewelers
NACBS ..... National Association and Council of Business Schools
NACO ...... National Association of Counties
NACA ...... National Association of County Administrators
NACAA ..... National Association County Agricultural Agents
NACE ...... National Association of County Engineers
NACCA ..... National Association of County 4-H Club Agents
NACPRO .... National Association of County Park and Recreation Officials
NACPA ..... National Association of County and Prosecuting Attorneys
NACRC ..... National Association of County Recorders and Clerks
NACTFO ..... National Association of County Treasurers and Finance Officers
NACP .... National Association of Creamery Proprietors (British)
NACM ...... National Association of Credit Management
NADEM ..... National Association of Dairy Equipment Manufacturers
NADDM ..... National Association of Daytime Dress Manufacturers
NAD .... National Association of the Deaf
NADA ...... National Association of Dealers in Antiques
NADWAGNS .. National Association of Deans of Women and Advisers to Girls in Negro Schools
NADAF...... National Association of Decorative Architectural Finishes
NADLCC..... National Association of Defense Lawyers in Criminal Cases
NADL ...... National Association of Dental Laboratories
NADUSM .... National Association of Deputy United States Marshals
NADAG ..... National Association of Diocesan Altar Guilds of the Protestant Episcopal Church
NADMW ..... National Association of Direct Mail Writers
NADSC ..... National Association of Direct Selling Companies
NADM ...... National Association of Discount Merchants
NADI .... National Association of Display Industries
NADET...... National Association of Distributive Education Teachers
NADD ...... National Association of Distributors & Dealers of Structural Clay Products
NADUS ..... National Association of Doctors in the United States
NADM ...... National Association of Doll Manufacturers
NADFPM .... National Association of Domestic and Farm Pump Manufacturers
NADSA ..... National Association of Dramatic and Speech Arts
NADASO .... National Association of Drug and Allied Sales Organizations
NADMR ..... National Association of Drug Manufacturers Representatives
NAEYC ..... National Association for the Education of Young Children
NAEB ...... National Association of Educational Broadcasters
NAEB ...... National Association of Educational Buyers
NAES ...... National Association of Educational Secretaries
NAEC ...... National Association of Electric Companies
NAED ...... National Association of Electrical Distributors
NAEOM ..... National Association of Electronic Organ Manufacturers
NAEC ...... National Association of Elevator Contractors
NAEBM ..... National Association of Engine and Boat Manufacturers
NAEC ...... National Association of Engineering Companies
NAEFTA ..... National Association of Enrolled Federal Tax Accountants
NAES ...... National Association of Episcopal Schools

NAE........ National Association of Evangelicals
NAEM ...... National Association of Exhibit Managers
NEXCO ..... National Association of Export Management Companies
NAEHE ..... National Association of Extension Home Economists
NAFM ...... National Association of Fan Manufacturers
NAFB....... National Association of Farm Broadcasters
NAFAD...... National Association of Fashion and Accessory Designers
NAFCE...... National Association of Federal Career Employees
NAFV....... National Association of Federal Veterinarians
NAFSLAC .... National Association of Federations of Syrian & Lebanese American Clubs
NAFTF ...... National Association of Finishers of Textile Fabrics
NAFED ...... National Association of Fire Distributors
NAFI .... National Association of Fire Investigators
NAFM ...... National Association of Flag Manufacturers
NAFA ...... National Association of Fleet Administrators
NAFI .... National Association of Flight Instructors
NAFCI ...... National Association of Floor Covering Installers
NAFD....... National Association of Flour Distributors
NAFMB...... National Association of FM Broadcasters
NAFC ...... National Association of Food Chains
NAFEM...... National Association of Food Equipment Manufacturers
NAFMG ..... National Association of Foreign Medical Graduates
NAFSA ..... National Association of Foreign Student Advisors
NAFIC ...... National Association of Fraternal Insurance Counsellors
NAFLU...... National Association of Free Labor Unions (Philippines)
NAFFP ..... National Association of Frozen Food Packers
NAFM ...... National Association of Furniture Manufacturers
NAG .... National Association of Gagwriters
NAG .... National Association of Gardeners
NAGT ...... National Association of Geology Teachers
NAGC ...... National Association for Gifted Children
NAGCD ..... National Association of Glass Container Distributors
NAGM...... National Association of Glove Manufacturers
NAGM...... National Association of Glue Manufacturers
NAGCM..... National Association of Golf Club Manufacturers
NAGE ...... National Association of Government Employees
NAGE ...... National Association of Government Engineers
NAGI....... National Association of Government Inspectors
NAGS ...... National Association of Government Secretaries
NAGVG ..... National Association Greenhouse Vegetable Growers
NAGSCT .... National Association of Guidance Supervisors and Counselor Trainers
NAHA ...... National Association of Handwriting Analysts
NAHW ..... National Association of Hardwood Wholesalers
NAHSA ..... National Association of Hearing and Speech Agencies
NAHDSA .... National Association of Hebrew Day School Administrators
NAHD ..... National Association of Hillel Directors
NAHB....... National Association of Home Builders of the United States
NAHES...... National Association of Home Economics Supervisors
NAHB ...... National Association of Homes for Boys
NAHS....... National Association of Horological Schools
NAHP ..... National Association of Horseradish Packers
NAHM ..... National Association of Hosiery Manufacturers
NAHCSP..... National Association of Hospital Central Service Personnel
NAHPA..... National Association of Hospital Purchasing Agents
NAHA ...... National Association of Hotel Accountants (Later, NAHMA)
NAHMA .... National Association of Hotel and Motel Accountants (Formerly, NAHA)
NAHRMP..... National Association of Hotel and Restaurant Meat Purveyors
NAHDDM .... National Association of House and Daytime Dress Manufacturers
NAHHIC..... National Association of House to House Installment Companies
NAHC ...... National Association of Housing Cooperatives
NAHRO ..... National Association of Housing and Redevelopment Officials
NAII .... National Association of Ice Industries
NAIEHS ..... National Association of Importers and Exporters of Hides and Skins
NAIB .... National Association of Independent Business
NAIFR ...... National Association of Independent Food Retailers
NAIIA ...... National Association of Independent Insurance Adjusters
NAII .... National Association of Independent Insurers
NAIS .... National Association of Independent Schools
NAIA ...... National Association of Industrial Artists
NAIP .... National Association of Industrial Parks
NAITE ...... National Association of Industrial Teacher Educators
NAIEC ...... National Association for Industry-Education Cooperation
NAIEM...... National Association of Insect Electrocutor Manufacturers
NAILM...... National Association of Institutional Laundry Managers
NAIA ...... National Association of Insurance Agents
NAIB .... National Association of Insurance Brokers
NAIC....... National Association of Insurance Commissioners
NAIW....... National Association of Insurance Women
NAIA ...... National Association of Intercollegiate Athletics
NAIRO ...... National Association of Intergroup Relations Officials
NAIRE ...... National Association of Internal Revenue Employees

NAIC . . . . . . National Association of Investment Clubs
NAJCW . . . . . National Association of Jewish Center Workers
NAJD . . . . National Association of Journalism Directors (Later, JEA)
NALCM . . . . . National Association of Lace Curtain Manufacturers
NALLD . . . . . . National Association of Language Laboratory Directors
NALUS . . . . . . National Association of Leagues, Umpires and Scorers
NALGM . . . . . National Association of Leather Glove Manufacturers
NALS . . . . . . National Association of Legal Secretaries
NALOH . . . . . National Association Legions of Honor
NALT . . . . National Association of the Legitimate Theatre
NALC . . . . National Association of Letter Carriers of the United States of America
NALLO . . . . . National Association of License Law Officials
NALC . . . . . . National Association of Life Companies
NALU . . . . . . National Association of Life Underwriters
NALMC . . . . . National Association of Lighting Maintenance Contractors
NALC . . . . . . National Association of Litho Clubs
NALAM . . . . . National Association of Livestock Auction Markets
NALS . . . . National Association of Lumber Salesmen
NAMP . . . . . . National Association of Magazine Publishers
NAM . . . . . . National Association of Manufacturers
NAMPBG . . . . National Association of Manufacturers of Pressed and Blown Glassware
NAMD . . . . . National Association of Marble Dealers
NAMP . . . . . National Association of Marble Producers
NAMM . . . . . National Association of Margarine Manufacturers
NAMMD . . . . . National Association of Marinas and Marine Dealers
NAMD . . . . . National Association of Marine Dealers
NAMS . . . . . National Associated Marine Suppliers
NAMD . . . . . . National Association of Market Developers
NAMO . . . . . . National Association of Marketing Officials
NAMM . . . . . . National Association of Mass Merchandisers
MMF . . . . National Association of Master Mechanics and Foremen of Naval
         Shore Establishments
NAMPW . . . . . National Association of Meat Processors and Wholesalers
NAMP . . . . . National Association of Meat Purveyors
NAMDB . . . . . National Association of Medical-Dental Bureaus
NAMAC . . . . National Association of Men's Apparel Clubs
NAMBAC . . . . National Association Men's and Boys' Apparel Clubs
NAMSB . . . . . . National Association of Men's Sportswear Buyers
NAMH . . . . . . National Association for Mental Health
NAMB . . . . . . National Association of Merchandise Brokers
NAMF . . . . . . National Association of Metal Finishers
NAMHH . . . . . National Association of Methodist Hospitals and Homes
NAMG . . . . . . National Association of Mining Groups
NAMW . . . . . . National Association of Ministers' Wives
NAMM . . . . . . National Association of Mirror Manufacturers
NAMBO . . . . . National Association of Motor Bus Owners
NAMO . . . . . . National Association of Multifamily Owners
NAMESU . . . . . National Association of Music Executives in State Universities
NAMM . . . . . . National Association of Music Merchants
NAMT . . . . . National Association for Music Therapy
NAMIM . . . . . National Association of Musical Instrument Mechanics
NAMMM . . . National Association of Musical Merchandise Manufacturers (Later,
         GAMA)
NAMMW . . . . . National Association of Musical Merchandise Wholesalers
NAMCC . . . . . National Association of Mutual Casualty Companies
NAMIA . . . . . . National Association of Mutual Insurance Agents
NAMIC . . . . . . National Association of Mutual Insurance Companies
NAMSB . . . . . . National Association of Mutual Savings Banks
NANP . . . . . . National Association of Naturopathic Physicians
NANTS . . . . . . National Association of Naval Technical Supervisors
NANBPWC . . . . National Association of Negro Business and Professional Women's Clubs
NANM . . . . . . National Association of Negro Musicians
NANTDDDC . . National Association of Negro Tailors, Designers, Dressmakers and
         Dry Cleaners
NANPE . . . . . National Association of Newspaper Purchasing Executives
NANE . . . . . National Association for Nursery Education
NAOEJ . . . . . . National Association of Oil Equipment Jobbers
NAOP . . . . . . National Association of Operative Plasterers
NAO . . . . . . National Association of Optometrists
NAOO . . . . . National Association of Optometrists and Opticians
NAOT . . . . . National Association of Organ Teachers
NAPFM . . . . . . National Association of Packaged Fuel Manufacturers
NAP . . . . National Association of Parliamentarians
NAPA . . . . . . National Association of the Partners of the Alliance
NAPPC . . . . . . National Association of Party Plan Companies
NAPR . . . . National Association for Pastoral Renewal
NAPM . . . . . National Association of Pattern Manufacturers
NAPA . . . . . . National Association of Performing Artists
NAPI . . . . . . National Association of the Pet Industry
NAPET . . . . . National Association of Photo Equipment Technicians
NAPL . . . . National Association of Photo-Lithographers

NAPM . . . . . . National Association of Photographic Manufacturers
NAPECW . . . . . National Association for Physical Education of College Women
NAPPA . . . . . . National Association of Physical Plant Administrators of Universities &
        Colleges
NAPT . . . . . . National Association of Physical Therapists
NAPH . . . . . . National Association of the Physically Handicapped
NAPCA . . . . . National Association of Pipe Coating Applicators
NAPNM . . . . . National Association of Pipe Nipple Manufacturers
NAPEP . . . . . National Association of Planners, Estimators & Progressmen
NAPPO . . . . . . National Association of Plant Patent Owners
NAPF . . . . . . National Association of Plastic Fabricators
NAPP . . . . . . National Association of Play Publishers
NAPC . . . . . . National Association of Plumbing Contractors
NAPHCC . . . . . National Association of Plumbing-Heating-Cooling Contractors
NAPA . . . . . National Association of Polish Americans
POSM . . . . . . National Association of Post Office and General Services Maintenance
        Employees
NAPOMHWMGL . . National Association of Post Office Mail Handlers, Watchmen,
        Messengers and Group Leaders
POMH . . . . . . National Association of Post Office and Postal Transportation Service
        Mail Handlers, Watchmen and Messengers
NAPS . . . . . . National Association of Postal Supervisors
NAP . . . . National Association of Postmasters
NAPUS . . . . . . National Association of Postmasters of the United States
NAPE . . . . . . National Association of Power Engineers
NAPNE . . . . . . National Association for Practical Nurse Education
NAPNES . . . . . National Association for Practical Nurse Education and Service
NAPRE . . . . . . National Association Practical Refrigerating Engineers
NAPC . . . . . . National Association of Precancel Collectors
NAPAN . . . . . National Association for the Prevention of Addiction to Narcotics
NAPP . . . . . . National Association Priest Pilots
NAPSG . . . . . . National Association of Principals of Schools for Girls
NAPIM . . . . . National Association of Printing Ink Makers
NAPPH . . . . . National Association of Private Psychiatric Hospitals
NAPMM . . . . . National Association of Produce Market Managers
NAPBL . . . . . National Association of Professional Baseball Leagues
NATAPROBU . . National Association of Professional Bureaucrats
NAPCA . . . . . National Association of Professional Contracts Administrators
NAPH . . . . . . National Association of Professors of Hebrew
NAPEM . . . . . National Association of Public Exposition Managers
NAPIA . . . . . . National Association of Public Insurance Adjusters
NAPSAA . . . . National Association of Public School Adult Administrators (Later,
        NAPSAE)
NAPSAE . . . . . National Association of Public School Adult Educators
NAP . . . . National Association of Publishers
NAPCR . . . . . National Association for Puerto Rican Civil Rights
NAPM . . . . . National Association of Punch Manufacturers
NAPA . . . . . . National Association of Purchasing Agents
NARTB . . . . . . National Association of Radio & Television Broadcasters
NARP . . . . . . National Association of Railroad Passengers
NARTC . . . . . . National Association of Railroad Trial Counsel
NARUC . . . . . . National Association of Railroad and Utilities Commissioners
NARBW . . . . . National Association of Railway Business Women
NAREB . . . . . . National Association of Real Estate Boards
NAREB . . . . . . National Association of Real Estate Brokers
NAREE . . . . . National Association of Real Estate Editors
NAREIF . . . . . . National Association of Real Estate Investment Funds
NARM . . . . . National Association of Record Merchandisers
NARRD . . . . . National Association of Record Retailer Dealers
NART . . . . . . National Association Recreational Therapists
NARB . . . . . . National Association of Referees in Bankruptcy
NARW . . . . . . National Association of Refrigerated Warehouses
NARM . . . . . National Association of Relay Manufacturers
NARAL . . . . . . National Association for Repeal of Abortion Laws
NARST . . . . . National Association for Research in Science Teaching
NARI . . . . . . National Association of Residents and Interns
NARCF . . . . . National Association of Retail Clothiers and Furnishers
NARD . . . . . . National Association of Retail Druggists
NARGUS . . . . . National Association of Retail Grocers of the United States
NARICM . . . . . National Association of Retail Ice Cream Manufacturers
NARMFD . . . . . National Association of Retail Meat and Food Dealers
NARC . . . . . . National Association for Retarded Children
NARCE . . . . . National Association of Retired Civil Employees
NARVRE . . . . . National Association of Retired and Veteran Railroad Employees
NARHC . . . . . National Association of River and Harbor Contractors
NAR . . . . National Association of Rocketry
NARD . . . . . . National Association of Rudimental Drummers
NAS . . . . National Association of Sanitarians
NASMBCM . . . . National Association of Sanitary Milk Bottle Closure Manufacturers
NASMD . . . . National Association of School Music Dealers
NASA . . . . . . National Association of Schools of Art

NASD . . . . . . National Association of Schools of Design
NASM . . . . . . National Association of Schools of Music
NASW . . . . . . National Association of Science Writers
NASMI . . . . . . National Association of Secondary Material Industries
NASSP . . . . . . National Association of Secondary-School Principals
NASS . . . . . . National Association of Secretaries of State
NASSTA . . . . . National Association of Secretaries of State Teachers Associations
NASA . . . . . . National Association of Securities Administrators
NASD . . . . . . National Association of Securities Dealers
NASDAQ . . . . National Association of Securities Dealers Automated Quotations (Over-the-counter stock quotations)
NASM . . . . . . National Association of Service Managers
NASUP . . . . . . National Association on Service to Unmarried Parents
NASDAD . . . . National Association of Seventh-Day Adventist Dentists
NASMD . . . . . National Association of Sewing Machine Dealers
NASMD . . . . . National Association of Sewing Machine Distributors
NASMD . . . . . National Association of Sheet Metal Distributors
NASMD . . . . . National Association of Sheet Music Dealers
NASWHP . . . . . National Association of Sheltered Workshops and Homebound Programs
NASAB . . . . . National Association of Shippers Advisory Boards
NASPSM . . . . National Association of Shirt, Pajama and Sportswear Manufacturers
NASCS . . . . . . National Association of Shoe Chain Stores
NASDA . . . . . National Association of Sign and Display Advertisers
NASPM . . . . . National Association of Slipper and Playshoe Manufacturers
NASBIC . . . . . National Association of Small Business Investment Companies
NASLS . . . . . . National Association of Small Loan Supervisors
NASW . . . . . . National Association of Social Workers
NASWSO . . . . National Association of Soft Water Service Operators
NASCD . . . . . National Association of Soil Conservation Districts
NACD . . . . . . National Association of Soil and Water Conservation Districts
NASDM . . . . . National Association of Special Delivery Messengers
SDM . . . . National Association of Special Delivery Messengers
NASRP . . . . . National Association of Special and Reserve Police
NASC . . . . . . National Association of Specialized Carriers
NASFT . . . . . National Association for the Specialty Food Trade
NASGW . . . . . National Association of Sporting Goods Wholesalers
NASASP . . . . . National Association State Agencies for Surplus Property
NASACT . . . . . National Association of State Auditors, Comptrollers and Treasurers
NASAO . . . . . National Association of State Aviation Officials
NASBO . . . . . . National Association of State Budget Officers
NASCDD . . . . . National Association of State Civil Defense Directors
NASDA . . . . . National Association of State Departments of Agriculture (Formerly, NACSDA)
NASDSE . . . . . National Association of State Directors of Special Education
NASDSSE . . . . National Association of State Directors and Supervisors of Secondary Education
NASDTEC . . . . National Association of State Directors of Teacher Education and Certification
NASDVA . . . . . National Association of State Directors of Veterans Affairs
NASDVE . . . . . National Association of State Directors of Vocational Education
NASEAN . . . . . National Association for State Enrolled Assistant Nurses
NASF . . . . National Association of State Foresters
NASMHPD . . . National Association of State Mental Health Program Directors
NASM . . . . . . National Association of State Militia
NASORLO . . . . National Association of State Outdoor Recreation Liaison Officers
NASPO . . . . . . National Association of State Purchasing Officials
NASRC . . . . . . National Association of State Racing Commissioners
NASRA . . . . . National Association of State Retirement Administrators
NASSSA . . . . . National Association of State Social Security Administrators
NASSDSE . . . . National Association of State Supervisors and Directors of Secondary Education
NASSDE . . . . . National Association of State Supervisors of Distributive Education
NASSHE . . . . National Association of State Supervisors of Home Economics
NASSTIE . . . . National Association of State Supervisors of Trade and Industrial Education
NASTBD . . . . National Association of State Text Book Directors
NASU . . . . National Association of State Universities (Defunct)
NASULGC . . . National Association of State Universities and Land Grant Colleges
NASHAW . . . . National Association for Statewide Health and Welfare
NASE . . . . . . National Association of Steel Exporters
NAS . . . . National Association of Stevedores
NASCAR . . . . . National Association for Stock Car Auto Racing
NASFM . . . . . . National Association of Store Fixture Manufacturers
NASC . . . . National Association of Student Councils
NASPA . . . . . National Association of Student Personnel Administrators
NASS . . . . . . National Association of Suggestion Systems
NASBP . . . . . National Association of Surety Bond Producers
NAS . . . . National Association of Supervisors
NASAE . . . . . National Association of Supervisors of Agricultural Education
NASBOE . . . . . National Association of Supervisors of Business and Office Education
NASSB . . . . . National Association of Supervisors of State Banks

NASR . . . . . . National Association of Swine Records
NASA . . . . . . National Association of Synagogue Administrators
NATC . . . . . . National Association of Taurine Clubs
NATA . . . . . . National Association of Tax Accountants
NATA . . . . . . National Association of Tax Administrators
NATO . . . . . . National Association of Taxicab Owners
NATE . . . . . . National Association of Teachers of English
NATS . . . . . . National Association of Teachers of Singing
NATA . . . . . . National Association of Teachers' Agencies
NATPE . . . . . National Association of Television Program Executives
NATRFD . . . . . National Association of Television-Radio Farm Directors
NATA . . . . . . National Association of Temple Administrators
NATE . . . . . . National Association of Temple Educators
NATAW . . . . . National Association of Textile and Apparel Wholesalers
NATO . . . . . . National Association of Theatre Owners
NATD . . . . . . National Association of Tobacco Distributors
NATTS . . . . . National Association of Trade and Technical Schools
NATU . . . . . . National Association of Trade Unions (Philippines)
NATO . . . . . . National Association of Trailer Owners
NATSC . . . . . National Association of Training School Chaplains
NATSJA . . . . . National Association of Training Schools and Juvenile Agencies
NATA . . . . . . National Association of Transportation Advertising
NATSC . . . . . National Association of Trap and Skeet Clubs
NATO . . . . . . National Association of Travel Organizations (Later, DATO)
NATSO . . . . . National Association of Truck Stop Operators
NAUI . . . . . . National Association of Underwater Instructors
NAUM . . . . . . National Association of Uniform Manufacturers
NAVS . . . . . . National Association of Variety Stores
NAVHT . . . . . National Association of Vocational Homemaking Teachers
NAWMD . . . . National Association of Waste Material Dealers
NAWMP . . . . . National Association of Waste Material Producers
NAWCC . . . . National Association of Watch and Clock Collectors
NAWG . . . . . National Association of Wheat Growers
NAWFC . . . . . National Association of Wholesale Fur Cleaners
NAWPB . . . . . National Association of Wholesale Pie Bakers
NAW . . . . . . National Association of Wholesalers
NAWB . . . . . National Association of Wine Bottlers
NAWCM . . . . National Association of Wiping Cloth Manufacturers
NAWA . . . . . National Association of Women Artists
NAWIC . . . . . National Association of Women in Construction
NAWDC . . . . National Association of Women Deans and Counselors
NAWL . . . . . National Association of Women Lawyers
NAWCAS . . . . National Association of Women's and Children's Apparel Salesmen
NAWM . . . . . National Association of Wool Manufacturers
NAWWO . . . . National Association of Woolen and Worsted Overseers
NAWTS . . . . . National Association of World Trade Secretaries
NAL . . . . National Astronomical League
NASO . . . . . . National Astronomy (or Astronomical) Space Observatory (NASA)
NATA . . . . . . National Athletic Trainers Association
NAA . . . . National Auctioneers Association
NAVA . . . . . National Audio-Visual Association
NAS . . . . National Audubon Society
NALHI . . . . . National Authority for the Ladies Handbag Industry
NAAA . . . . . National Auto Auction Association
NAFGDA . . . . National Auto and Flat Glass Dealers Association
NATWA . . . . . National Auto and Truck Wreckers Association
NACC . . . . . . National Automatic Controls Conference
NAPALM . . . . National ADP (Automatic Data Processing) Program for AMC (Army Materiel Command) Logistics Management
NALCC . . . . . . National Automatic Laundry and Cleaning Council
NAMA . . . . . . National Automatic Merchandising Association
NASFCA . . . . National Automatic Sprinkler and Fire Control Association
NAVTA . . . . . National Automatic Vendors' Trade Association
NADA . . . . . National Automobile Dealers Association
NASA . . . . . . National Automobile Salesmen's Association
NATB . . . . . . National Automobile Theft Bureau
NATA . . . . . . National Automobile Transporters Association
NAUA . . . . . National Automobile Underwriters Association
NAMA . . . . . . National Automotive Muffler Association
NAPA . . . . . . National Automotive Parts Association
NARSA . . . . . National Automotive Radiator Service Association
NAC . . . . National Aviation Club
NAC . . . . National Aviation Corporation
NTA . . . . National Aviation Corporation (NYSE symbol)
NAFEC . . . . . National Aviation Facilities Experimental Center (of FAA) (Atlantic City, NJ)
NATA . . . . . . National Aviation Trades Association
NBCC . . . . . . National Baby Care Council
NBSA . . . . . . National Bakery Suppliers Association
NBOA . . . . . National Ballroom Operators Association
NBA . . . . National Band Association

NBG .... National Bank of Greece
NBNA ...... National Bank of North America (New York)
BANDES .... National Bank for Social and Economical Development (Cuba)
NBA........ National Bankers Association
NBA .... National Banking Association
NBA .... National Bankruptcy Act
NBA........ National Bar Association
NBMC ...... National Bar Mitzvah Club
NBADA...... National Barrel and Drum Association
NBDA ...... National Barrel and Drum Association
NBC .... National Baseball Congress of America (Semiprofessional baseball)
NBA........ National Basketball Association (Professional basketball league)
NBC........ National Beagle Club
NBBMA...... National Beauty and Barber Manufacturers Association
NBCL ...... National Beauty Culturists' League
NBC .... National Beef Council
NBWA ...... National Beer Wholesalers' Association of America
NBHCA...... National Belgian Hare Club of America
NBRSA ..... National Bench Rest Shooters Association
NBBB ...... National Better Business Bureau
NBDA ...... National Bicycle Dealers Association
NBCC ..... National Bidders Control Center
NBRF ...... National Biochemical Research Foundation
BI .... National Biscuit Company (NYSE symbol)
NABISCO .... National Biscuit Company
NBCC....... National Bituminous Coal Commission (Functions transferred to Department
.... of the Interior, 1939)
NBCA....... National Bituminous Concrete Association
NBAWADU ... National Black Anti-War Anti-Draft Union
NBEDC ..... National Black Economic Development Conference
NBSC...... National Black Sisters' Conference
B & B ...... National Block and Bridle Club
NBTS ...... National Blood Transfusion Service
NBCSI ..... National Board of the Coat and Suit Industry
NBEOPS .... National Board of Examiners for Osteopathic Physicians and Surgeons
NBFU ...... National Board of Fire Underwriters
NBFFO ..... National Board of Fur Farm Organizations
NBME...... National Board of Medical Examiners
NBPE ...... National Board of Podiatry Examiners
NBPE ...... National Board of Polygraph Examiners
NBPRP ..... National Board for the Promotion of Rifle Practice (Army)
NBR .... National Board of Review of Motion Pictures
NBRMP ..... National Board of Review of Motion Pictures
NBA........ National Boat Association
NBA .... National Book Awards
NBC .... National Book Committee
NBC .... National Book Council (Great Britain)
NBS........ National Bookkeepers' Society
NBA .... National Bowling Association
NBC........ National Bowling Council
NBA .... National Boxing Association of America
NBA .... National Braille Association
NBC........ National Braille Club
NBP .... National Braille Press
NBSDI ..... National Brands Soft Drinks Institute
NBC....... National Broadcasting Company
NBS........ National Broadcasting Service (of New Zealand)
NBC....... National Broiler Council
NBCSDA .... National Broom Corn and Supply Dealers Association
NBMAIA .... National Broom Manufacturers and Allied Industries Association
NBPDW...... National Brotherhood of Packinghouse and Dairy Workers
NBPW....... National Brotherhood of Packinghouse Workers
NBCC ...... National Budget and Consultation Committee
NBHA....... National Builders' Hardware Association
NBGQA ..... National Building Granite Quarries Association
NBMDA ..... National Building Material Distributors Association
NBPA ...... National Building Products Association
NBCU...... National Bureau of Casualty Underwriters
NBCC ..... National Bureau for Co-operation in Child Care (British)
NBER ...... National Bureau of Economic Research
NBLP ...... National Bureau for Lathing and Plastering
NBS........ National Bureau of Standards (Department of Commerce)
NBSR ...... National Bureau of Standards Reactor
NBFAA ..... National Burglar and Fire Alarm Association
NBBDA ..... National Burlap Bag Dealers Association
NBC .... National Bus Company (British)
NBMB ..... National Bus Military Bureau
NBTA ...... National Bus Traffic Association
NBAA...... National Business Aircraft Association
NBEA ...... National Business Education Association
NBFA ...... National Business Forms Associates
NBL .... National Business League

NBP .... National Business Publications
NBMC ...... National Businessmen's Council
NBA........ National Button Association
NBS........ National Button Society
NCTA ...... National Cable (formerly, Community) Television Association
NCBW ..... National Cage Bird Week Association
NCHA ..... National Campers and Hikers Association
NCA .... National Camping Association
NAC .... National Can Corporation (NYSE symbol)
NCI........ National Cancer Institute (of National Institutes of Health)
NCWA ..... National Candy Wholesalers Association
NCA .... National Canners Association
NCCHI ..... National Cap and Cloth Hat Institute
NCA .... National Capital Award
NCHA ..... National Capital Housing Authority
NCPPC..... National Capital Park and Planning Commission
NCPC ..... National Capital Planning Commission
NCRPC..... National Capital Regional Planning Council
NCTA ..... National Capital Transportation Agency
NONC...... National Captive Nations Committee
NCC .... National Carbon Company
NCB .... National Cargo Bureau
NCSA ..... National Carl Schurz Association
NCS .... National Cartoonists Society
NC .... National Cash Register Company (NYSE symbol)
NCR .... National Cash Register Company
NEAT....... National Cash Register Electronic Autocoding Technique (Data
.... processing)
NCA .... National Cashmere Association
NML .... National Castings Company (NYSE symbol)
NCC .... National Castings Council
NCFA ..... National Cat Fanciers' Association
NCA .... National Cathedral Association
NCBA ..... National Catholic Bandmasters' Association
NCCA ..... National Catholic Camping Association
NCCC ..... National Catholic Cemetery Conference
NCCS...... National Catholic Community Service
NCCFL ..... National Catholic Conference on Family Life
NCCIJ ..... National Catholic Conference for Interracial Justice
NCDC ..... National Catholic Development Conference
NCEA...... National Catholic Educational Association
NCEE ..... National Catholic Educational Exhibitors
NCFL...... National Catholic Forensic League
NCGC ..... National Catholic Guidance Conference
NCLC ..... National Catholic Liturgical Conference
NCMEA ..... National Catholic Music Educators Association
NCORT...... National Catholic Office for Radio and Television
NCRC...... National Catholic Resettlement Council
NCRLC..... National Catholic Rural Life Conference
NCSAC ..... National Catholic Social Action Conference
NCSAW ..... National Catholic Society for Animal Welfare
NCTC ..... National Catholic Theatre Conference
NCWC ..... National Catholic Welfare Conference (Later, USCC)
NCWU ..... National Catholic Women's Union
NCTA ..... National Cattle Theft Act
NCCA ..... National Cedar Chest Association
NCIMA...... National Cellulose Insulation Manufacturers Association
NCS........ National Cemetery System
NCAPC ..... National Center for Air Pollution Control (of Public Health
.... Service)
NCEP....... National Center for Education in Politics
NCAR ...... National Center for Atmospheric Research (National Science Foundation)
NCCD ..... National Center for Chronic Disease Control (Public Health Service)
NCCE ..... National Center for Citizens in Education
NCCCD ..... National Center Confraternity of Christian Doctrine
NCES ..... National Center for Educational Statistics (US Office of Education)
NCHS ..... National Center for Health Statistics (of OSG)
NCRH...... National Center for Radiological Health (Public Health Service)
NCSCT..... National Center for School and College Television
NCUI...... National Center for Urban and Industrial Health (Public Health Service)
NCVA ..... National Center for Voluntary Action
NCL .... National Central Library (British)
NCA .... National Ceramic Association
NCMA ..... National Ceramic Manufacturers Association
NCPWB ..... National Certified Pipe Welding Bureau
NCAYR ..... National Chaplains Association for Youth Rehabilitation
NCA .... National Charcoal Association
NCA .... National Cheerleaders Association
NCI .... National Cheese Institute
NCCA ..... National Chemical Credit Association
NCL........ National Chemical Laboratory

NCRL . . . . National Chemical Research Laboratory (South Africa)
NCLC . . . . . . National Child Labor Committee
NCPTO . . . . . . National China Painting Teachers Organization
NCBA . . . . National Chinchilla Breeders of America
NCA . . . . National Chiropractic Association (Later, American Chiropractic
        Association)
NCCS . . . . . . National Christ Child Society
NCTGA . . . . . . National Christmas Tree Growers Association
NCS . . . . National Chrysanthemum Society
NCMF . . . . National Church Music Fellowship
NCLTA . . . . . . National Cigar Leaf Tobacco Association
NCCPA . . . . . . National Cinder Concrete Products Association
NCCB . . . . National Citizens Committee for Broadcasting
NCCCR . . . . . . National Citizens Committee for Community Relations
SELF . . . . National Citizens Committee to Save Education and Library Funds
NCCWHO . . . . National Citizens Committee for the World Health Organization
NTL . . . . National City Lines, Inc. (NYSE symbol)
NCA . . . . National Civic Association
NCDAC . . . . . National Civil Defense Advisory Council
NCLCH . . . . . National Civil Liberties Clearing House
NCSL . . . . National Civil Service League
NCB . . . . National Classification Board (American Trucking Association)
NCMS . . . . . National Classification Management Society
NCPI . . . . . . National Clay Pipe Institute
NCPM . . . . . . National Clay Pot Manufacturers
CU-PU-FU . . . National Clean Up - Paint Up - Fix Up Bureau
NCH . . . . National Clearing House (Public Health Service)
NCMHI . . . . . . National Clearinghouse for Mental Health Information (HEW)
NCPTWA . . . . National Clearinghouse for Periodical Title Word Abbreviations (ANSI)
NCSH . . . . National Clearinghouse for Smoking and Health (Public Health Service)
NCCA . . . . . . National Clergy Conference on Alcoholism
NCA . . . . National Club Association
NCA . . . . National Coal Association
NCB . . . . National Coal Board (British)
NCPC . . . . . . National Coal Policy Conference
NC . . . . National Coarse (Thread)
NCA . . . . National Coffee Association of United States of America
NCCA . . . . . . National Coil Coaters Association
NCMDA . . . . . National Coin Machine Distributors Association
NCAWA . . . . . National Coinamatic Auto Wash Association
NCFA . . . . . . National Collection of Fine Arts (Smithsonian Institution)
NCTC . . . . National Collection of Type Cultures (Bacteriology)
NCFS . . . . National College of Foot Surgeons
NCPEA . . . . . . National College Physical Education Association
NCPEAM . . . . . National College Physical Education Association for Men
NCSF . . . . National College Student Foundation
NCAA . . . . . . National Collegiate Athletic Association
NCAB . . . . . . National Collegiate Athletic Bureau
NCCCCA . . . . National Collegiate Cross Country Coaches Association
NCPL . . . . National Collegiate Parachuting League
NCP . . . . National Collegiate Players
NCPC . . . . . . National Collegiate Poultry Club
NCTCA . . . . . National Collegiate Track Coaches Association
NCSWDI . . . . . National Combination Storm Window and Door Institute
NCA . . . . National Command Authorities
NCCS . . . . . . National Command and Control System
NCS . . . . National Commemorative Society
NCFC . . . . . . National Commercial Finance Conference
NCRSA . . . . . . National Commercial Refrigerator Sales Association
NCA . . . . National Commission on Accrediting
NCFM . . . . . . National Commission on Food Marketing
NCLIS . . . . . . National Commission on Libraries and Information Science
NCPS . . . . . . National Commission on Product Safety
NCSE . . . . . . National Commission on Safety Education
NCTEPS . . . . . National Commission on Teacher Education and Professional Standards
TEPS . . . . National Commission on Teacher Education and Professional Standards
NCAHUAC . . . National Committee to Abolish the House Un-American Activities
        Committee
NCADH . . . . . National Committee Against Discrimination in Housing
NCDH . . . . . National Committee Against Discrimination in Housing
NCAF . . . . . . National Committee Against Fluoridation
NCAMI . . . . . . National Committee Against Mental Illness
NCAB . . . . . . National Committee for Amateur Baseball
NCCMT . . . . . National Committee for Careers in Medical Technology
NCCY . . . . . . National Committee for Children and Youth
CWC . . . . National Committee for a Confrontation with Congress
NCDC . . . . . . National Committee for the Day Care of Children
NCEFF . . . . . . National Committee for Education in Family Finance
NCEMC . . . . . National Committee on the Education of Migrant Children
NCEC . . . . . . National Committee for an Effective Congress
NCEDL . . . . . . National Committee for Effective Design Legislation

NCEEF . . . . . . National Committee for Electrical Engineering Films
NCE . . . . National Committee on the Emeriti
NCEY . . . . . . National Committee on Employment of Youth
NCEHAI . . . . . National Committee on Ethics of the Hearing Aid Industry
NCFS . . . . National Committee on Films for Safety
NCFNP . . . . . . National Committee for a Freedom Now Party
NCGA . . . . . . National Committee on Governmental Accounting
NCHS . . . . National Committee on Homemaker Service
NCHE . . . . . . National Committee on Household Employment
NCIT . . . . . . National Committee for Insurance Taxation
NCITD . . . . . . National Committee on International Trade Documentation
NCLI . . . . National Committee for Labor Israel
NCLS . . . . . . National Committee for Liberation of Slovakia
NCMH . . . . . . National Committee on Maternal Health
NCMFST . . . . National Committee for Motor Fleet Supervisor Training
NCOMD . . . . National Committee on the Observance of Mothers' Day
NCPA . . . . . . National Committee for the Prevention of Alcoholism
NCRPM . . . . . National Committee on Radiation Protection and Measurements (Later,
        NCRP)
NCRLS . . . . . . National Committee of Religious Leaders of Safety
NCRC . . . . . . National Committee for a Representative Congress
NCRND . . . . . National Committee for Research in Neurological Disorders
NCRP . . . . . . National Committee for Responsible Patriotism
NCRS . . . . . . National Committee for Rural Schools
SANE . . . . . . National Committee for a Sane Nuclear Policy
NCSE . . . . . . National Committee on Secondary Education (of NASSP)
NCSPS . . . . . . National Committee for Support of the Public Schools
NCUTLO . . . . National Committee on Uniform Traffic Laws and Ordinances
NCDC . . . . . . National Communicable Disease Center (Public Health Service)
NCSI . . . . National Communication System Instructions
NCSM . . . . . . National Communication System Memoranda
NACOM . . . . . National Communications (System)
NATCOM . . . . National Communications Center (FAA)
NACOS . . . . . National Communications Schedule
NATCOM . . . . National Communications Symposium (IEEE)
NCS . . . . National Communications System (GSA)
NCSC . . . . . . National Communications System Circulars
NCRAC . . . . . National Community Relations Advisory Council
NCC . . . . National Company of Crossbowmen
NCC . . . . National Computer Center (of Internal Revenue Service)
NCC . . . . National Computing Center (England)
NCBVA . . . . . National Concrete Burial Vault Association
NCCA . . . . . . National Concrete Contractors Association
NCMA . . . . . . National Concrete Masonry Association
NCA . . . . National Confectioners Association of the United States
NCSAA . . . . . National Confectionery Salesmen's Association of America
NCAEG . . . . . National Confederation of American Ethnic Groups
NCAR . . . . . . National Conference on the Administration of Research
NCAE . . . . . . National Conference on Airborne Electronics
NCBE . . . . . . National Conference of Bar Examiners
NCBE . . . . . . National Conference of Bar Executives (Later, NABE)
NCBP . . . . . . National Conference of Bar Presidents
NCCC . . . . . . National Conference of Catholic Charities
NCCYSA . . . . National Conference of Catholics in Youth Serving Agencies
NCCJ . . . . National Conference of Christians and Jews
NCC . . . . National Conference on Citizenship
NCCUSL . . . . . National Conference of Commissioners on Uniform State Laws
NCEW . . . . . . National Conference of Editorial Writers
NCEHELP . . . . National Conference of Executives of Higher Education Loan Plans
NCHWPPTA . . . National Conference of Health, Welfare and Pension Plans, Trustees
        and Administrators
NCIR . . . . National Conference on Industrial Research
NCIESD . . . . . National Conference on International Economic and Social Development
NCIMS . . . . . . National Conference on Interstate Milk Shipments
NCJCS . . . . . . National Conference of Jewish Communal Service
NCJC . . . . . . National Conference of Judicial Councils
NCLP . . . . . . National Conference on Law and Poverty
NCL & SW . . . National Conference of Lawyers and Social Workers
NCNPSA . . . . National Conference of Non-Profit Shipping Associations
NCOPA . . . . . National Conference of Police Associations
NCPEA . . . . . . National Conference of Professors of Educational Administration
NCPER . . . . . . National Conference on Public Employee Retirement Systems
NCPYA . . . . . National Conference of Public Youth Agencies
NCSS . . . . . . National Conference of Shomrim Societies
NCSW . . . . . . National Conference on Social Welfare
NCS . . . . National Conference on Solicitations
NCSL . . . . . . National Conference of Standards Laboratories
NCSLL . . . . . . National Conference of State Legislative Leaders
NCSLA . . . . . . National Conference of State Liquor Administrators
NCSP . . . . . . National Conference on State Parks
NCSPAS . . . . . National Conference of State Pharmaceutical Association Secretaries

NCSRA . . . . . . National Conference of State Retail Associations
NCSSSA . . . . . National Conference of State Social Security Administrators
NCSTS . . . . . National Conference of State Transportation Specialists
NCSTSR . . . . . National Conference of Superintendents of Training Schools & Reformatories
NCSY . . . . . . National Conference of Synagogue Youth
NCTW . . . . . . National Conference of Tuberculosis Workers
NCWM . . . . . National Conference on Weights and Measures
NCYP . . . . . . National Conference of Yeshiva Principals
NCAI . . . . . . National Congress of American Indians
NCJD . . . . . . National Congress of the Jewish Deaf
NCPT . . . . . . National Congress of Parents and Teachers
NCPR . . . . . . National Congress of Petroleum Retailers
NCB . . . . National Conservation Bureau
NCA . . . . National Constructors Association
NCFA . . . . . . National Consumer Finance Association
NCCRE . . . . . National Consumers Committee for Research & Education
NCL . . . . National Consumers League
NCC . . . . National Container Committee
NCA . . . . National Contesters Association
NCMA . . . . . . National Contract Management Association
NCGCC . . . . . National Convention of Gospel Choirs and Choruses
NCHRP . . . . . National Cooperative Highway Research Program
NCSS . . . . . National Cooperative Soil Survey
NC . . . . National Cooperatives (Association)
NACCAM . . . . National Coordinating Committee for Aviation Meteorology
NCCBI . . . . . National Coordinating Committee of the Beverage Industry
NCCEWV . . . . National Coordinating Committee to End the War in Vietnam
NCGA . . . . . . National Corn Growers Association
NCHP . . . . . . National Corporation for Housing Partnerships
NCMPA . . . . . National Corrugated Metal Pipe Association
NCSPA . . . . . National Corrugated Steel Pipe Association
NCA . . . . National Costumers Association
NCBI . . . . . . National Cotton Batting Institute
NCCCWA . . . . National Cotton Compress and Cotton Warehouse Association
NCC . . . . National Cotton Council of America
NCGA . . . . . . National Cotton Ginners Association
NCPA . . . . . . National Cottonseed Products Association
NCATE . . . . . National Council for Accreditation of Teacher Education
NCAC . . . . . . National Council of Acoustical Consultants
NCAWE . . . . . National Council of Administrative Women in Education
NCAPO . . . . . National Council of Adoptive Parents Organizations
NCAC . . . . . . National Council Against Conscription
NCOA . . . . . . National Council on the Aging
NCAE . . . . . . National Council of Agricultural Employers
NCALL . . . . . . National Council on Agricultural Life and Labor
NCA . . . . National Council on Alcoholism
NCAI . . . . . . National Council of American Importers
NCARB . . . . . National Council of Architectural Registration Boards
NCA . . . . National Council on the Arts
NCAG . . . . . . National Council on the Arts and Government
NCBJS . . . . . National Council of Beth Jacob Schools
NCBM . . . . . . National Council on Business Mail
NCCEM . . . . . National Council of Catholic Employers and Managers
NCCM . . . . . . National Council of Catholic Men
NCCN . . . . . . National Council of Catholic Nurses
NCCW . . . . . . National Council of Catholic Women
NCCY . . . . . . National Council of Catholic Youth
NCC . . . . National Council of Churches of Christ in the USA
NCCL . . . . . . National Council of Coal Lessors
NCCPA . . . . . National Council of College Publications Advisers
NCCB . . . . . . National Council to Combat Blindness
NCCPB . . . . . National Council of Commercial Plant Breeders
NCCF . . . . . . National Council on Community Foundations
COSERV . . . . . National Council for Community Services to International Visitors
NCCS . . . . . . National Council for Community Services to International Visitors
NCCI . . . . . . National Council on Compensation Insurance
NCCC . . . . . . National Council of Corvette Clubs
NCCD . . . . . . National Council on Crime and Delinquency
DA . . . . National Council, Daughters of America
NCERT . . . . . National Council of Educational Research and Training (India)
NCFR . . . . . . National Council on Family Relations
NCFC . . . . . . National Council of Farm Cooperatives
NCFAE . . . . . National Council of Forestry Association Executives
NCGE . . . . . . National Council for Geographic Education
NCG . . . . National Council for the Gifted
NCH . . . . National Council on the Humanities
NCIMC . . . . . National Council of Industrial Management Clubs
NCIP . . . . . . National Council for Industrial Peace
NCJAVM . . . . National Council on Jewish Audio-Visual Materials
NCJCC . . . . . National Council of Jewish Correctional Chaplains

NCJE . . . . . . National Council for Jewish Education
NCJW . . . . . National Council of Jewish Women
NCJO . . . . . . National Council of Junior Outdoorsmen
NCJCJ . . . . . National Council of Juvenile Court Judges
NCLC . . . . . National Council of Labour Colleges
NCLC . . . . . National Council on Legal Clinics
NCLA . . . . . National Council of Local Administrators of Vocational Education and Practical Arts
NCMLB . . . . . National Council of Mailing List Brokers
NCMRED . . . . . National Council on Marine Resources and Engineering Development
NCMS . . . . . . National Council of Marine Sciences
NCMTA . . . . . National Council of Marine Trade Associations
NCME . . . . . . National Council on Measurement in Education
NCMTE . . . . . National Council on Medical Technology Education
NCMA . . . . . National Council of Millinery Associations
NCMI . . . . . . National Council of Music Importers
NCNASEO . . . National Council of Naval Air Stations Employee Organizations
NCNW . . . . . . National Council of Negro Women
NCNC . . . . . . National Council of Nigeria and the Cameroons
NCNC . . . . . . National Council of Nigerian Citizens
NCOSTA . . . . National Council of Officers of State Teachers Associations
NCPLA . . . . . National Council of Patent Law Associations
NCP . . . . National Council on Philanthropy
NCPDM . . . . . National Council of Physical Distribution Management
NCPAD . . . . . National Council on Psychological Aspects of Disability
NCRP . . . . . . National Council (formerly, Committee) on Radiation Protection and Measurements
NCRA . . . . . . National Council of Research Administrators
NCSO . . . . . . National Council of Salesmen's Organizations
NCSN . . . . . . National Council for School Nurses (AAHPER)
NCSC . . . . . . National Council on Schoolhouse Construction
NCSA . . . . . . National Council of Seamen's Agencies
NCSC . . . . . . National Council of Senior Citizens
NCSS . . . . . . National Council for the Social Studies
SDL . . . . National Council, Sons and Daughters of Liberty
NCSAB . . . . . National Council of State Agencies for the Blind
NCSBEE . . . . National Council of State Boards of Engineering Examiners
NCSCCY . . . . National Council of State Committees for Children and Youth
NCSCEE . . . . National Council of State Consultants in Elementary Education
NCSEA . . . . . National Council of State Education Associations
NCSGC . . . . . National Council of State Garden Clubs
NCSSIA . . . . . National Council of State Self-Insurers Associations
NCSI . . . . . . National Council for Stream Improvement
NCTR . . . . . . National Council on Teacher Retirement
NCTE . . . . . . National Council of Teachers of English
NCTM . . . . . . National Council of Teachers of Mathematics
NCTS . . . . . . National Council of Technical Schools
NCTSI . . . . . National Council of Technical Service Industries
NCTE . . . . . . National Council for Torah Education
NCUPM . . . . . National Council of United Presbyterian Men
NCURA . . . . . National Council of University Research Administrators
NCWC . . . . . National Council of Women Chiropractors
NCWFC . . . . . National Council of Women of Free Czechoslovakia
NCW . . . . . . National Council of Women of the United States
NCYC . . . . . . National Council of Yacht Clubs
NCYI . . . . . . National Council of Young Israel
NCICA . . . . . National Counter Intelligence Corps Association
NCA . . . . National Coursing Association
NCA . . . . National Cranberry Association
NCA . . . . National Creameries Association
NCC . . . . National Crime Commission
NCIC . . . . . . National Crime Information Center (FBI)
NCJSC . . . . . National Criminal Justice Statistics Center
NCIC . . . . . . National Crop Insurance Council
NCYF . . . . . . National Crusaders Youth Federation
NCSA . . . . . . National Crushed Stone Association
NCC . . . . National Cultural Center (Smithsonian Institution)
NCBFAA . . . . National Customs Brokers and Forwarders Association of America
NCSA . . . . . . National Customs Service Association
NCHA . . . . . . National Cutting Horse Association
NCFRF . . . . . National Cystic Fibrosis Research Foundation
NDC . . . . National Dairy Council
ND . . . . National Dairy Products Corporation (NYSE symbol)
NADAC . . . . . National Damage Assessment Center
NDG . . . . National Dance Guild
ND . . . . National Debt
NDPA . . . . . . National Decorated Packaging Association
NDC . . . . National Defence Contribution (British)
NDC . . . . National Defence Corps (British)
NDA . . . . National Defense Act
NDAC . . . . . . National Defense Advisory Commission (World War II)

NDCC . . . . . . National Defense Cadet Corps
NDC . . . . National Defense Council (Netherlands)
NDE. . . . . National Defense Education
NDEA . . . . National Defense Education Act
NDEI . . . . National Defense Education Institute
NDERR . . . . . National Defense Executive Reserve Roster (of the CSC)
NDHQ . . . . . . National Defense Headquarters (Canadian)
NDMB . . . . . . National Defense Mediation Board (World War II)
NDOS . . . . . . National Defense Operations Section (FCC)
NDPRP . . . . . . National Defense Project Rating Plan
NDRC . . . . . . National Defense Research Committee (of Office of Scientific Research and Development) (World War II)
NDRF . . . . . . National Defense Reserve Fleet (Maritime Administration, Department of Commerce)
NDTA . . . . . . National Defense Transportation Association
NATDEFSM . . . National Defense Service Medal
NDSM . . . . . . National Defense Service Medal
NDC . . . . National Democratic Club
NDP. . . . . National Democratic Party (Rhodesia and Nyasaland)
NDPD. . . . . . . National–Demokratische Partei Deutschlands (National Democratic Party) (East Germany)
NDA . . . . National Dental Association
NDC . . . . National Development Corporation (Philippines)
NDFA . . . . National Dietary Foods Association
NDP . . . . National Diocesan Press
NDA . . . . National Diploma in Agriculture
NDP. . . . . National Disclosure Policy
NDSA . . . . National Disposal Services Association
DR . . . . National Distillers & Chemical Corporation (NYSE symbol)
NDAAF . . . . . National District Attorneys Association Foundation
NDHA . . . . . . National District Heating Association
NDLB. . . . . . . National Dock Labour Board (British)
NDR . . . . National Dog Registry
NDA . . . . National Door Association (Defunct)
NDMA . . . . . . National Door Manufacturers Association
NDTMA . . . . . National Drain Tile Manufacturers Association
NDMA . . . . . . National Dress Manufacturers Association
NDBC . . . . . . National Dried Bean Council
NDAPTA . . . . . National Drivers Association for the Prevention of Traffic Accidents
NDCD . . . . . . National Drug Code Directory (FDA)
NDTC . . . . . . National Drug Trade Conference
NDPBC. . . . . . National Duck Pin Bowling Congress
NEAGC . . . . . National Early American Glass Club
NEIC . . . . National Earthquake Information Center
NEMA . . . . . . National Eclectic Medical Association
NEC . . . . National Economic Council
NEDC. . . . . . . National Economic Development Council (British)
NEDO . . . . . . National Economic Development Office
NEGRO . . . . . National Economic and Growth Reconstruction Organization (Negro entrepreneurial organization)
NEA . . . . National Editorial Association
NEA . . . . National Education Association
NEFSA . . . . . . National Education Field Service Association
NER . . . . National Educational Radio
NET . . . . National Educational Television
NETRC . . . . . National Educational Television and Radio Center
NEF. . . . . National Educators Fellowship
NEC . . . . National Egg Council
NEC. . . . . National Electric(al) Code
NELA . . . . . . National Electric Light Association
NERC. . . . . . . National Electric Reliability Council
NESC. . . . . . . National Electric Safety Code
NESA . . . . . . National Electric Sign Association
NEMA . . . . . . National Electrical Manufacturers Association
NECS . . . . . . National Electrical Code Standards
NECA . . . . . . National Electrical Contractors Association
NEWA . . . . . . National Electrical Wholesalers Association
NEA . . . . National Electronic Associations
NEDA . . . . . . National Electronic Distributors Association
NEC . . . . National Electronics Conference
NEFO. . . . . . . National Electronics Facilities Organization
NERC. . . . . . . National Electronics Research Council
NETS . . . . . . National Electronics Teachers' Service
NEMI . . . . . . National Elevator Manufacturing Industry
NEL . . . . National Emancipation League (Nigeria)
NE. . . . . National Emergency
NEACP . . . . . National Emergency Airborne Command Post (DOD)
NEAR . . . . . . National Emergency Alarm Repeater (Civil defense warning system for homes)
NECPA . . . . . National Emergency Command Post Afloat
NEC. . . . . National Emergency Council (Abolished, 1939)

NEDA . . . . . . National Emergency Defense Airlift
NERA . . . . . . National Emergency Relief Administration
NESS . . . . . . National Emergency Steel Specification (World War II)
NEST . . . . . . National Emergency Survivable Tropo System
NEU. . . . . National Employees' Union (Ceylon)
NEA . . . . National Employment Association
NECH. . . . . . . National Employment Clearing House (American Chemical Society)
NECA. . . . . . . National Employment Counselors Association
NEA . . . . National Endowment for the Arts
NEH . . . . National Endowment for the Humanities
NEUC . . . . . . National Engine Use Council
NEL. . . . . National Engineering Laboratory (British)
NESCO. . . . . . National Engineering Science Company
NEED. . . . . . . National Environmental Education Development (Program of National Park Service)
NESC . . . . . . National Environmental Satellite Center (Formerly, National Weather Satellite Center) (Environmental Science Services Administration)
NEL . . . . National Epilepsy League
NERSICA . . . . National Established Repair, Service and Improvement Contractors Association
NEC . . . . National Exchange Club
NEHA . . . . . . National Executive Housekeepers Association
NEEC . . . . . . National Export Expansion Council (Department of Commerce)
NETL . . . . . . National Export Traffic League
NEHC . . . . . . National Extension Homemakers Council
NEF . . . . National Extra Fine (Thread)
NEI . . . . National Eye Institute
NERF . . . . . . National Eye Research Foundation
NFA . . . . National Faculty Association of Community and Junior Colleges
NFACJC . . . . National Faculty Association of Community and Junior Colleges
NFCDA . . . . . National Family Council on Drug Addiction
NFLF . . . . . . National Family Life Foundation
NFO . . . . National Family Opinion
NFCC . . . . . . National Farm-City Committee
NFHEA . . . . . National Farm Home Editors Association
NFPEDA . . . . National Farm and Power Equipment Dealers Association
NFWA . . . . . . National Farm Workers Association
NFO . . . . National Farmers Organization
NFU . . . . National Farmers' Union
NFFF . . . . . . National Fantasy Fan Federation
NFDC. . . . . . . National Father's Day Committee
NFOBA . . . . . National Fats and Oils Brokers Association
NFAA . . . . . . National Federation of Advertising Agencies
NFB. . . . . National Federation of the Blind
NFBPWC . . . . National Federation of Business and Professional Women's Clubs
NFCCS . . . . . National Federation of Catholic College Students
NFCPG. . . . . . National Federation of Catholic Physicians' Guilds
NFCGC . . . . . National Federation of Coffee Growers of Colombia
NFFE . . . . . . National Federation of Federal Employees
NFFGB . . . . . National Federation of Flemish Giant Breeders
NFFGRB . . . . National Federation of Flemish Giant Rabbit Breeders
NFGC . . . . . . National Federation of Grain Cooperatives
NFGCA . . . . . National Federation of Grandmother Clubs of America
NFGMIC. . . . . National Federation of Grange Mutual Insurance Companies
NFHTP . . . . . National Federation of Hebrew Teachers and Principals
NFIB . . . . . . National Federation of Independent Business
NFISYD . . . . National Federation of Independent Scrap Yard Dealers
NFIU . . . . . . National Federation of Independent Unions
NFIR . . . . . . National Federation of Indian Railwaymen
NFJMC . . . . . National Federation of Jewish Men's Clubs
NFLU . . . . . . National Federation of Labor Unions (Philippines)
NFLPN . . . . . National Federation of Licensed Practical Nurses
NFMLTA . . . . National Federation of Modern Language Teachers Associations
NFMC . . . . . . National Federation of Music Clubs
NFPW. . . . . . . National Federation of Petroleum Workers (India)
NFPOC . . . . . National Federation of Post Office Clerks (Later, UFPC)
POMV. . . . . . . National Federation Post Office Motor Vehicle Employees
NFPTE . . . . . National Federation of Posts' and Telegraphs' Employees (India)
NFPW . . . . . . National Federation of Press Women
NFPC. . . . . . . National Federation of Priests' Councils
NFRW . . . . . . National Federation of Republican Women
NFSE . . . . . . National Federation of Sales Executives
NFSAIS . . . . National Federation of Science Abstracting and Indexing Services
NFS. . . . . National Federation of Settlements
NFS & NC . . . National Federation of Settlements and Neighborhood Centers
NFSC . . . . . . National Federation of Stamp Clubs
NFSHSAA . . . . National Federation of State High School Athletic Associations
NFSPS . . . . . National Federation of State Poetry Societies
NFTW. . . . . . . National Federation of Telephone Workers

NFTB . . . . . . National Federation of Temple Brotherhoods
NFTS . . . . . . National Federation of Temple Sisterhoods
NFTY . . . . . . National Federation of Temple Youth
NFWE . . . . . . National Federation of Woman's Exchanges
NFIA . . . . . . National Feed Ingredients Association
NFMM . . . . . . National Fellowship of Methodist Musicians
NFCAA . . . . . National Fencing Coaches Association of America
NFSA . . . . . . National Fertilizer Solutions Association
NFCTA . . . . . National Fibre Can and Tube Association
NFAA . . . . . . National Field Archery Association
NFBC . . . . . . National Film Board of Canada
NFC . . . . . . National Film Carriers
NFFC . . . . . . National Film Finance Corporation (British)
NFMC . . . . . . National Film Music Council (Defunct)
NFRC . . . . . . National Finals Rodeo Commission
NF . . . . . . National Fine (Thread)
NFPA . . . . . . National Fire Protection Association
NFA . . . . . . National Firearms Act
NFH . . . . . . National Fish Hatchery
NFI . . . . National Fisheries Institute
NFPA . . . . . . National Flaxseed Processors Association
NFPA . . . . . . National Flexible Packaging Association
NFDC . . . . . . National Flight Data Center (FAA)
NFPA . . . . . . National Fluid Power Association
NFFA . . . . . . National Folk Festival Association
NFA . . . . National Food Administration
NFBA . . . . . . National Food Brokers Association
NFC . . . . . . National Food Conference Association
NFDA . . . . . . National Food Distributors Association
NFDCAMD . . . National Food, Drug & Cosmetic Association of Manufacturers and
                Distributors
NFSA . . . . . . National Food Service Association
NFHC . . . . . . National Foot Health Council
NFF . . . . The National Football Foundation and Hall of Fame
NFL . . . . National Football League
NFLPA . . . . . . National Football League Players Association
NFMA . . . . . . National Footwear Manufacturers Association
NAFTRAC . . . . National Foreign Trade Council
NFTC . . . . . . National Foreign Trade Council
NFL . . . . National Forensic League
NFPA . . . . . . National Forest Products Association
NFRA . . . . . . National Forest Recreation Association
NF . . . . National Formulary (A publication listing standard drugs)
NF . . . . National Foundation
NFAH . . . . . National Foundation on Arts and Humanities
NFAC . . . . . . National Foundation for Asthmatic Children at Tucson
NFCC . . . . . . National Foundation for Consumer Credit
NFEAC . . . . . National Foundation for Education in American Citizenship
NFER . . . . . . National Foundation for Educational Research (British)
NFER . . . . . . National Foundation for Eye Research
NFFS . . . . . . National Foundation of Funeral Service
NFGND . . . . . National Foundation for Genetics and Neuromuscular Disease
NFHPER . . . . . National Foundation for Health, Physical Education, and Recreation
NFIP . . . . . . National Foundation for Infantile Paralysis
NFJC . . . . . . National Foundation for Jewish Culture
NFJM . . . . . . National Foundation for Junior Museums
NFMR . . . . . . National Foundation for Metabolic Research
NFMD . . . . . . National Foundation for Muscular Dystrophy
NFND . . . . . . National Foundation for Neuromuscular Diseases
NFRM . . . . . . National Foundation for Research in Medicine
NFA . . . . National Foundry Association
NFHA . . . . . . National Fox Hunters Association
NFCA . . . . . . National Fraternal Congress of America
NFFDF . . . . . National Fraternal Flag Day Foundation
NFSD . . . . . . National Fraternal Society of the Deaf
NFSM . . . . . . National Fraternity of Student Musicians
NFLPA . . . . . . National Free Lance Photographers Association
NFA . . . . . . National Freedom Academy
NFSF . . . . . . National Freedom Shrine Foundation
NFC . . . . . . National Freight Corporation (British)
NFTA . . . . . . National Freight Traffic Association
NFLSV . . . . . National Front for the Liberation of South Vietnam
NFFA . . . . . . National Frozen Food Association
NFFDA . . . . . National Frozen Food Distributors Association
NFSMA . . . . . National Fruit and Syrup Manufacturers Association
NFCA . . . . . . National Fuel Credit Association
NFG . . . . . . National Fuel Gas Company (NYSE symbol)
NFGNE . . . . . National Fund for Graduate Nursing Education
NFME . . . . . . National Fund for Medical Education
NFDA . . . . . . National Funeral Directors Association
NFDMA . . . . . National Funeral Directors and Morticians Association

NFTC . . . . . . National Furniture Traffic Conference
NFWA . . . . . . National Furniture Warehousemen's Association
NGMA . . . . . . National Gadget Manufacturers Association
NGA . . . . . . National Gallery of Art
NGB . . . . . . National Garden Bureau
NGMA . . . . . . National Gas Measurement Association
NGO . . . . . . National Gas Outlet
NGTE . . . . . . National Gas Turbine Establishment (British)
NGS . . . . . . National Genealogical Society
NTR . . . . National General Corporation (NYSE symbol)
NGSP . . . . . . National Geodetic Satellite Program (NASA)
NGS . . . . . . National Geographic Society
NGS . . . . . . National Geriatrics Society
NGAA . . . . . . National Gift and Art Association
NGAA . . . . . . National Girls Athletic Association
NGS . . . . . . National Gladiolus Society
NGDA . . . . . . National Glass Dealers Association
NGSM . . . . . . National Gold Star Mothers
NGS . . . . . . National Goldfish Society
NGF . . . . . . National Golf Foundation
NGRC . . . . . . National Government of the Republic of China
NGTC . . . . . . National Grain Trade Council
NGLIOGT . . . . National Grand Lodge, International Order of Good Templars
NGD . . . . National Grassland Demonstration (British)
NG . . . . National Guard(man)
NGARP . . . . . National Guard and Army Reserve Policy
NGAUS . . . . . National Guard Association of the United States
NGB . . . . . . National Guard Bureau (Army)
NGCC . . . . . . National Guard Computer Center
NGFT . . . . . . National Guard on Field Training Exercises
NGNF . . . . . . National Guard not in Federal Service
NGOCS . . . . . National Guard Officer Candidate School
NGR . . . . . . National Guard Regulations
NGUS . . . . . . National Guard of the United States
NGC . . . . . . National Guild of Churchmen
NGCMS . . . . . National Guild of Community Music Schools
NGPT . . . . . . National Guild of Piano Teachers
NGC . . . . . . National Guinea Club
NG . . . . National Gypsum Company (NYSE symbol)
NHCA . . . . . . National Hairdressers and Cosmetologists Association
NHP . . . . National Hamiltonian Party
NHENMA . . . . National Hand Embroidery and Novelty Manufacturers Association
NHKYA . . . . . National Hand Knitting Yarn Association
NHASA . . . . . National Handbag & Accessories Salesmen's Association
NHA . . . . National Handbag Association
NHMA . . . . . . National Handle Manufacturers Association
NHLA . . . . . . National Hardwood Lumber Association
NHA . . . . National Hay Association
NHFRA . . . . . National Hay Fever Relief Association
NHA . . . . . . National Health Association
NHC . . . . . . National Health Council
NHF . . . . National Health Federation
NHI . . . . National Health Insurance (British)
NHS . . . . National Health Service (British)
NHS . . . . National Health Survey
NHSD . . . . . . National Health Survey Division (of OSG)
NHWRA . . . . . National Health and Welfare Retirement Association
NHI . . . . . . National Heart Institute (Later, NHLI) (of NIH)
NHLI . . . . National Heart and Lung Institute (Formerly, NHI)
NHAS . . . . . . National Hearing Aid Society
NHCC . . . . . . National Hebrew Culture Council
NHF . . . . National Hemophilia Foundation
NHSS . . . . . . National Herb Study Society
NHHRA . . . . . National Hereford Hog Record Association
NHA . . . . National Hide Association
NHSACA . . . . National High School Athletic Coaches Association
NHSRA . . . . . National High School Rodeo Association
NHSB . . . . . . National Highway Safety Bureau
NHUC . . . . . . National Highway Users Conference
NHPC . . . . . . National Historical Publications Committee
NHI . . . . National Hobby Institute
NHA . . . . National Hockey Association (to 1917)
NHL . . . . National Hockey League
NHLPA . . . . . National Hockey League Players' Association
NHA . . . . National Holiness Association
NHDAA . . . . . National Home Demonstration Agents' Association
NHDC . . . . . . National Home Demonstration Council
NHFL . . . . . . National Home Fashions League
NHIC . . . . . . National Home Improvement Council
NHSA . . . . . . National Home Service Association
NHSC . . . . . . National Home Study Council

NHPDA . . . . . National Honey Packers and Dealers Association
NHS . . . . National Honor Society
NHSA . . . . . . National Horse Show Association of America
NHPAA. . . . . . National Horseshoe Pitchers Association of America
NHAM . . . . . National Hose Assemblies Manufacturers Association
NHSR . . . . . . National Hospital Service Reserve
NHRA . . . . . . National Hot Rod Association
NHMA . . . . . . National Housewares Manufacturers Association
NHLA . . . . . . National Housewives' League of America
NHA . . . . National Housing Act
NHA . . . . National Housing Administration
NHA . . . . National Housing Agency (Superseded by HHFA, 1947)
NHB. . . . . . . National Housing Bank (Brazil)
NHC . . . . National Housing Center
NHC . . . . National Housing Conference
NHC . . . . National Housing Council (of the HHFA)
NHP. . . . . . . National Housing Partnership (HUD)
NHS . . . . National Huguenot Society
NHF. . . . . . . National Humanities Faculty
NHR . . . . National Hunt Rules (British)
NHRP . . . . . . National Hurricane Research Project
NIA . . . . National Ice Association
NICMA . . . . . National Ice Cream Mix Association
NICRA . . . . . National Ice Cream Retailers Association
NIA . . . . National Iceboat Authority
NICDA . . . . . National Imported Car Dealers Association
NIA . . . . National Income Accounts
NIADA . . . . . National Independent Automobile Dealers Association
NICOA . . . . . National Independent Coal Operators Association
NIDA . . . . . . National Independent Dairies Association
NIMPA . . . . . National Independent Meat Packers Association
NIUC. . . . . . . National Independent Union Council
NIVA . . . . . . National Independent Vendors Association
NIYC . . . . . . National Indian Youth Council
NIC. . . . . National Indications Center (DOD)
NITMDA . . . . . National Indoor Track Meet Directors Association
NIAA . . . . . . National Industrial Advertisers Association
NIBL . . . . National Industrial Basketball League
NICMA . . . . . National Industrial Cafeteria Managers Association
NICB . . . . . . National Industrial Conference Board
NIC. . . . . National Industrial Council
NIDA . . . . . . National Industrial Distributors Association
NIEM . . . . . . National Industrial Engineering Mission
NIER . . . . . . National Industrial Equipment Reserve (of DMS)
NILA . . . . . . National Industrial Leather Association
NIPR . . . . . . National Industrial Plant Reserve
NIRA . . . . . . National Industrial Recovery Act
NIRB . . . . . . National Industrial Recovery Board (Terminated 1935)
NIRA . . . . . . National Industrial Recreation Association
NISA . . . . . . National Industrial Sand Association
NISA . . . . . . National Industrial Service Association
NISA . . . . . . National Industrial Stores Association
NITL . . . . National Industrial Traffic League
NIW . . . . National Industrial Workers Union
NIWU . . . . . . National Industrial Workers Union
NIZC . . . . . . National Industrial Zoning Committee
NIB . . . . National Industries for the Blind
NIAC . . . . . . National Industry Advisory Committee (FCC)
NIAC . . . . . . National Information & Analysis Center
NIB . . . . National Information Bureau
NIBJL. . . . . . National Information Bureau for Jewish Life
NICEM . . . . . National Information Center for Educational Media
NIDOC . . . . . National Information and Documentation Center
NIN. . . . . National Information Network (ASTIA)
NISARC . . . . . National Information Storage and Retrieval Center
NIAM. . . . . . . National Institute of Advertising Management
NIAID . . . . . . National Institute of Allergy and Infectious Diseases (of National
              Institutes of Health)
NIADA . . . . . National Institute of American Doll Artists
NIAA . . . . . . National Institute of Animal Agriculture
NIAE . . . . . . National Institute for Architectural Education
NIAMD. . . . . . National Institute of Arthritis and Metabolic Diseases (of National
              Institutes of Health)
NIAL . . . . . . National Institute of Arts and Letters
NIAR . . . . . . National Institute of Atmospheric Research
NIB . . . . National Institute for the Blind
NICE . . . . . . National Institute of Ceramic Engineers
NICHHD . . . . . National Institute of Child Health and Human Development
NIC. . . . . National Institute of Credit
NICD . . . . . . National Institute on Crime and Delinquency
NIDR . . . . . . National Institute of Dental Research (of National Institutes of Health)

NIDS . . . . . . National Institute of Diaper Services
NIDM . . . . . . National Institute for Disaster Mobilization
NID. . . . . National Institute of Drycleaning
NIESR . . . . . . National Institute of Economic and Social Research (British)
NIEHS . . . . . . National Institute of Environmental Health Sciences
NIFB . . . . . . National Institute of Farm Brokers
NIGMS. . . . . . National Institute of General Medical Sciences
NIGP. . . . . . . National Institute of Governmental Purchasing
NIIP. . . . . . . National Institute of Industrial Psychology
NILE . . . . . . National Institute of Labor Education
NILECJ . . . . . National Institute for Law Enforcement and Criminal Justice (National
              Institutes of Health)
NILFP . . . . . . National Institute of Locker and Freezer Provisioners
NIMC . . . . . . National Institute of Management Counsellors
NIMMP. . . . . . National Institute of Marine Medicine and Pharmacology (Proposed) (NIH)
NIMR . . . . . . National Institute for Medical Research
NIMH. . . . . . . National Institute of Mental Health (of National Institutes of Health)
NIMC. . . . . . . National Institute of Municipal Clerks
NIMLO. . . . . . National Institute of Municipal Law Officers
NINDB. . . . . . National Institute of Neurological Diseases and Blindness (of
              National Institutes of Health)
NINDS. . . . . . National Institute of Neurological Diseases and Stroke
NIO . . . . National Institute of Oceanography (British)
NIOP. . . . . . . National Institute of Oilseed Products
NIPHLE . . . . . National Institute of Packaging, Handling and Logistic Engineers
NIRS . . . . . . National Institute for Radiological Science (Japan)
NIREB . . . . . . National Institute of Real Estate Brokers
NIRNS . . . . . . National Institute for Research in Nuclear Science (British)
NIRC . . . . . . National Institute of Rug Cleaning
NIS . . . . National Institute of Science
NISBS . . . . . . National Institute of Social and Behavioral Science
NISS . . . . . . National Institute of Social Sciences
NISEC . . . . . . National Institute for the Study of Educational Change
NISA . . . . . . National Institute of Supply Associations
NITPICKERS . . National Institute of Technical Processors, Information Consultants,
              Keyword Experts, and Retrieval Specialists (Fictitious organization)
NIWKC . . . . . National Institute of Wood Kitchen Cabinets
NIWS . . . . . . National Institute on Workshop Standards
NIH. . . . . National Institutes of Health (of Public Health Service)
NIFDA . . . . . . National Institutional Food Distributor Associates
NITPA . . . . . . National Institutional Teacher Placement Association
NIT . . . . National Instructional Television Center
NIMA . . . . . . National Insulation Manufacturers Association
NIASO . . . . . National Insurance Actuarial and Statistical Association
NIA. . . . . National Insurance Association
NIE . . . . National Intelligence Estimate
NIPP . . . . . . National Intelligence Projection for Planning
NIS . . . . National Intelligence Survey
NIT . . . . National Intelligence Test (Psychology)
NIC . . . . National Interagency Council
NIBCA . . . . . National Intercollegiate Boxing Coaches Association
NIFA . . . . . . National Intercollegiate Flying Association
NIRA . . . . . . National Intercollegiate Rodeo Association
NISOA . . . . . National Intercollegiate Soccer Officials Association
NISRA . . . . . National Intercollegiate Squash Racquets Association
NIC . . . . National Interfraternity Conference
NIF . . . . National Interfraternity Foundation
NIMP . . . . . . National Intern Matching Program
NIDCC . . . . . National Internal Defense Coordination Center
NIRA . . . . . . National Inter-Racial Association
NIMAC . . . . . National Interscholastic Music Activities Commission
NIC. . . . . National Interstate Council of State Boards of Cosmetology
NISC . . . . . . National Intramural Sports Council
NIC. . . . . National Inventors Council (Department of Commerce)
NICP . . . . . . National Inventory Control Point (Military)
NICAP . . . . . National Investigations Committee on Aerial Phenomena
NIBID . . . . . . National Investment Bank for Industrial Development (Greece)
NIT . . . . National Invitation Tournament (Basketball)
NIOC. . . . . . . National Iranian Oil Company
NJA . . . . National Jail Association
NAJAFRA . . . . National Jazz Fraternity
NJCSE . . . . . National Jewish Civil Service Employees
NJCS . . . . . . National Jewish Committee on Scouting
NJIS . . . . . . National Jewish Information Service (for the Propagation of Judaism)
NJMC . . . . . . National Jewish Music Council
JWB . . . . National Jewish Welfare Board
NJWB . . . . . . National Jewish Welfare Board
NJAC. . . . . . . National Joint Advisory Council (on labor-management relations)
              (British)
NJCC . . . . . . National Joint Computer Committee (of ACM, AIEE, IRE) (Superseded by
              AFIPS)

NJBBF . . . . . . National Judo Black Belt Federation of the USA
NJCAA . . . . . National Junior College Athletic Association
NJHS . . . . . . National Junior Honor Society
NJHA . . . . . . National Junior Horitcultural Association
NJVGA . . . . . National Junior Vegetable Growers Association
NJCF . . . . . . National Juvenile Court Foundation
NKDF . . . . . . National Kidney Disease Foundation
NKF . . . . National Kidney Foundation
NKA . . . . National Kindergarten Association
NKCA . . . . . . National Kitchen Cabinet Association
NKOA . . . . . . National Knitted Outerwear Association
NKPA . . . . . . National Kraut Packers Association
NLMF . . . . . . National Labor-Management Foundation
NLRA . . . . . . National Labor Relations Act
NLRB . . . . . . National Labor Relations Board
NLU . . . . National Labor Union (Philippines)
JWVA . . . . . . National Ladies Auxiliary, Jewish War Veterans of the USA
NLFA . . . . . . National Lamb Feeders Association
NLNA . . . . . . National Landscape Nurserymen's Association
NLM . . . . National Language Mediator
NLG . . . . National Lawyers Guild
NLBA . . . . . . National Lead Burning Association
LT . . . . National Lead Company (NYSE symbol)
NL . . . . National Lead Company
NLAPW . . . . . National League of American Pen Women
NLC . . . . National League of Cities (Formerly, American Municipal Association)
NLISA . . . . . . National League of Insured Savings Associations
NLMC . . . . . . National League of Masonic Clubs
NLN . . . . National League for Nursing
NLP . . . . National League of Postmasters of the United States
NL . . . . National League of Professional Baseball Clubs
NLTA . . . . . . National League of Teachers' Associations
NLAA . . . . . . National Legal Aid Association
NLADA . . . . . National Legal Aid and Defender Association
NLD . . . . National Legion of Decency (Later, National Catholic Office for Motion Pictures)
NLC . . . . National Legislative Conference
NLC . . . . National Legislative Council
NLL . . . . National Lending Library for Science and Technology
NL . . . . National Liberal (British politics)
NLC . . . . National Liberal Club (British)
NLF . . . . National Liberal Federation (British)
NLL . . . . National Liberal League (Later, National League for Separation of Church and State)
NLC . . . . National Liberation Committee (South Africa)
NLF . . . . National Liberation Front (Aden)
NLM . . . . National Library of Medicine (of National Institutes of Health)
NLP . . . . National Library of Peiping
NLW . . . . National Library Week
NLBA . . . . . . National Licensed Beverage Association
NLB . . . . National Lighting Bureau
NLA . . . . National Lime Association
NLI . . . . National Limestone Institute
NLSBA . . . . . . National Lincoln Sheep Breeders' Association
NLS . . . . National Linen Service Corporation (Later, National Service Industries, Inc.) (NYSE symbol)
NLSA . . . . . . National Liquor Stores Association
ALTS . . . . . . National Lithuanian Society of America
NLSMB . . . . . National Live Stock and Meat Board
NLSPA . . . . . National Live Stock Producers Association
NLBC . . . . . . National Livestock Brand Conference
NLDA . . . . . . National Livestock Dealers Association
NLE . . . . National Livestock Exchange
NLFA . . . . . . National Livestock Feeders Association
NLTC . . . . . . National Livestock Tax Committee
NLA . . . . National Locksmiths Association
NLSA . . . . . . National Locksmith Suppliers Association
NLSMA . . . . . National Longitudinal Study of Mathematical Abilities
NLPGA . . . . . National LP-Gas Association
NLGI . . . . . . National Lubricating Grease Institute
NLDA . . . . . . National Luggage Dealers Association
NLBMDA . . . . National Lumber and Building Material Dealers Association
NLEA . . . . . . National Lumber Exporters Association
NLMA . . . . . . National Lumber Manufacturers Association
NLCS . . . . . . National Lutheran Commission (formerly, Committee) on Scouting
NLC . . . . National Lutheran Council
NLEMA . . . . . National Lutheran Editors and Managers Association
NLEC . . . . . . National Lutheran Educational Conference
NLPTL . . . . . . National Lutheran Parent-Teacher League
NMI . . . . National Macaroni Institute
NMMA . . . . . . National Macaroni Manufacturers Association

NMAA . . . . . . National Machine Accountants Association
NMTBA . . . . . National Machine Tool Builders' Association
NML . . . . National Magnet Laboratory
NMJL . . . . . . National Mah Jongg League
NMONA . . . . . National Mail Order Nurserymen's Association
NMP . . . . National Maintenance Point
NMA . . . . National Management Association
NMC . . . . National Manpower Council
NMTA . . . . . . National Manpower Training Association
NMBF . . . . . . National Manufacturers of Beverage Flavors
NMSC . . . . . . National Maple Syrup Council
NMB . . . . National Marine Board (British) (World War I)
MEBA . . . . . . National Marine Engineers' Beneficial Association
NMEBA . . . . . National Marine Engineers' Beneficial Association
NMRA . . . . . . National Marine Representatives Association
NMU . . . . National Maritime Union of America
NAMARCO . . . National Marketing Corporation (Philippines)
NMFHG . . . . . National Master Farm Homemakers Guild
NM . . . . National Match
NMS . . . . National Measurement System (National Bureau of Standards)
NMCA . . . . . . National Meat Canners Association
NMIC . . . . . . National Meat Industry Council
NMB . . . . National Mediation Board
NMA . . . . National Medical Association
NMAC . . . . . . National Medical Audiovisual Center (of the National Library of Medicine)
NMDA . . . . . . National Medical and Dental Association
NMF . . . . National Medical Fellowships
NMFEC . . . . . National Medical Foundation for Eye Care
NMUC . . . . . . National Medical Utilization Committee (HEW)
NMDCEF . . . . . National Medico-Dental Conference for the Evaluation of Fluoridation
NMSC . . . . . . National Merit Scholarship Corporation
NMSQT . . . . . National Merit Scholarship Qualifying Test
NMAA . . . . . . National Metal Awning Association
NMDA . . . . . . National Metal Decorators Association
NMSA . . . . . . National Metal Spinners Association
NMTA . . . . . . National Metal Trades Association
NMC . . . . National Meteorological Center (Weather Bureau)
NMRN . . . . . . National Meteorological Rocket Network
NMA . . . . National Microfilm Association
NMCC . . . . . . National Military Command Center (DOD)
NMCS . . . . . . National Military Command System
NMCSS . . . . . National Military Command System Standards
NMCSSC . . . . National Military Command System Support Center
NME . . . . National Military Establishment (Designated Department of Defense, 1949)
NMGA . . . . . . National Military Guidance Association
NMR . . . . National Military Representatives with SHAPE (NATO)
NMPF . . . . . . National Milk Producers Federation
NMTS . . . . . . National Milk Testing Service
NMPB . . . . . . National Millinery Planning Board
NMRA . . . . . . National Mine Rescue Association
NMWA . . . . . . National Mineral Wool Association
NMWIA . . . . . National Mineral Wool Insulation Association
NMWU . . . . . National Mining Workers' Union of Malaya
NMRS . . . . . . National Mobile Radio System
NMRA . . . . . . National Model Railroad Association
NMFC . . . . . . National Motor Freight Classification
NMFTA . . . . . National Motor Freight Traffic Association
NMVSAC . . . . National Motor Vehicle Safety Advisory Council
NMVTA . . . . . National Motor Vehicle Theft Act
NMSS . . . . . . National Multiple Sclerosis Society
NMSS . . . . . . National Multipurpose Space Station
NML . . . . National Municipal League
NMCB . . . . . . National Munitions Control Board (World War II)
NMR . . . . National Museum of Racing
NMT . . . . National Museum of Transport
NMC . . . . National Music Camp (Interlochen, Michigan)
NMC . . . . National Music Council
NML . . . . National Music League
NMPATA . . . . National Music Printers and Allied Trades Association
NMPA . . . . . . National Music Publishers Association
NMB . . . . National Mutual Benefit
NMLRA . . . . . National Muzzle Loading Rifle Association
NNMC . . . . . . National Naval Medical Center (Bethesda, Maryland)
NATNAVMEDCEN . . National Naval Medical Center (Bethesda, Maryland)
NNA . . . . National Neckwear Association
NNB . . . . National Needlecraft Bureau
NNBL . . . . . . National Negro Business League
NNCAA . . . . . National Negro County Agents Association
NNEA . . . . . . National Negro Evangelical Association
NNPA . . . . . . National Negro Press Association

NNRA . . . . . . National Negro Republican Assembly
NNF . . . . National Nephrosis Foundation
NNRF . . . . . . National Neurological Research Foundation
NNCSDC . . . . National Neutron Cross Section Data Center
NNAA . . . . . . National Newman Alumni Association
NNA . . . . National Newman Apostolate
NNAFS . . . . . National Newman Association of Faculty and Staff
NNCA . . . . . . National Newman Chaplains Association
NNCF . . . . . . National Newman Club Federation
NNF . . . . National Newman Foundation
NNPA . . . . . . National Newspaper Promotion Association
NNPA . . . . . . National Newspaper Publishers Association
NNAC . . . . . . National Noise Abatement Council
NNA . . . . National Notary Association
NNA . . . . National Notion Association
NNEC . . . . . . National Nuclear Energy Commission (Brazil)
NNES . . . . . . National Nuclear Energy Series (of AEC-sponsored books)
NNRDC . . . . . National Nuclear Rocket Development Center (Also known as NRDS)
NNC . . . . National Nudist Council
NNEB . . . . . . National Nursery Examination Board
NOFMA . . . . . National Oak Flooring Manufacturers Association
NOSTA . . . . . National Ocean Science and Technology Agency
NOAA . . . . . . National Oceanic and Atmospheric Agency
NOA . . . . National Oceanographic Association
NODC . . . . . National Oceanographic Data Center (Navy)
NOP . . . . National Oceanographic Program
NORC . . . . . . National Oceanographic Records Center
NOSE . . . . . National Odd Shoe Exchange
NORRA . . . . . National Off Road Racing Association
NODL . . . . . . National Office for Decent Literature
NOFA . . . . . . National Office Furniture Association
NOMDA . . . . . National Office Machine Dealers Association
NOMA . . . . . . National Office Management Association
NORI . . . . . . National Office for the Rights of the Indigent
NOVS . . . . . . National Office of Vital Statistics
NOFI . . . . . . National Oil Fuel Institute
NOJC . . . . . . Nation Oil Jobbers Council
NOMA . . . . . . National Oil Marketers Association
NOSLA . . . . . National Oil Scouts and Landmen's Association
NOL . . . . National Old Lacers
NOA . . . . National Onion Association
NOA . . . . National Opera Association
NOMSS . . . . . National Operational Meteorological Satellite System
NOS . . . . National Operational Satellite
NOTB . . . . . . National Ophthalmic Treatment Board
NOP . . . . National Opinion Poll
NORC . . . . . . National Opinion Research Center (University of Chicago)
NOA . . . . National Optical Association
NOF . . . . National Optical Font (Typography)
NOSS . . . . . . National Orbiting Space Station
NOA . . . . National Orchestral Association
NOTR . . . . . . National Order of Trench Rats
OWL . . . . National Order of Women Legislators
NOTC . . . . . . National Ordnance Traffic Committee
NOBC . . . . . . National Organization of Bar Counsel
NOHSN . . . . . National Organization of Hospital Schools of Nursing
NOLPE . . . . . National Organization of Legal Problems of Education
NOMOTC . . . . National Organization of Mothers of Twins Clubs
NOR . . . . National Organization for Rehabilitation (Ireland)
NOW . . . . National Organization for Women
NOWWN . . . . National Organization of World War Nurses
NOMMA . . . . . National Ornamental Metal Manufacturers Association
NOF . . . . National Osteopathic Foundation
NOGA . . . . . . National Osteopathic Guild Association
NOIC . . . . . . National Osteopathic Interfraternity Council
NOAB . . . . . . National Outdoor Advertising Bureau
NOSA . . . . . . National Outerwear and Sportswear Association
NOTC . . . . . National Over the Counter Clearance Corporation
NPA . . . . National Paddleball Association
NPSA . . . . . . National Paint Salesmen's Association
NPVLA . . . . . National Paint, Varnish and Lacquer Association
NPBA . . . . . . National Palomino Breeders Association
NPACOE . . . . . National Panhellenic Association of Central Office Executives
NPC . . . . . National Panhellenic Conference
NPEC . . . . . . National Panhellenic Editors' Conference
NPBMA . . . . . National Paper Box Manufacturers Association
NPBSA . . . . . National Paper Box Supplies Association
NPTA . . . . . . National Paper Trade Association
NPA . . . . National Paperboard Association
NPF . . . . National Paraplegia Foundation
NPF . . . . National Park Foundation (Formerly, National Park Trust Fund Board)

NPS . . . . National Park Service (Department of the Interior)
NPTFB . . . . . . National Park Trust Fund Board
NPA . . . . National Parking Association
NPF . . . . National Parkinson Foundation
NPI . . . . National Parkinson Institute
NPA . . . . National Parks Association
NPA . . . . National Particleboard Association
NPC . . . . National Patent Council
NPA . . . . National Patrolmen's Association
NPC . . . . National Peach Council
NPC . . . . National Peanut Council
NPSPA . . . . . National Pecan Shellers and Processors Association
NPC . . . . National People's Congress (Nigerian political party)
NPA . . . . National Personnel Associates
NPC . . . . National Personnel Consultants
NPRC . . . . . . National Personnel Records Center (National Archives and Records
                 Service)
NPCA . . . . . . National Pest Control Association
NPA . . . . National Pet Association
NPA . . . . National Petroleum Association
NPC . . . . National Petroleum Council
NPN . . . . National Petroleum News (A periodical)
NPRA . . . . . . National Petroleum Refiners Association
NPF . . . . National Piano Foundation
NPMA . . . . . . National Piano Manufacturers Association of America
NPTA . . . . . . National Piano Travelers Association
NPPA . . . . . . National Pickle Packers Association
NPA . . . . National Pigeon Association
NPA . . . . National Pilots Association
NP . . . . National Pipe
NPA . . . . National Pituitary Agency
NPA . . . . National Pharmaceutical Association
NPC . . . . National Pharmaceutical Council
NPDAA . . . . . National Pharmaceutical Direct Advertising Association
NPS . . . . National Philatelic Society
NPL . . . . National Physical Laboratory (British)
NPL . . . . National Physics Laboratory
NPA . . . . National Planning Association
NPB . . . . National Plant Board
NPFFG . . . . . National Plant, Flower and Fruit Guild
NPFI . . . . . . National Plant Food Institute
NPDA . . . . . . National Plywood Distributors Association
NPDC . . . . . . National Poetry Day Committee
NPLEI . . . . . National Police Law Enforcement Institute
NAPA . . . . . . National Police Officers' Association
NPOAA . . . . . National Police Officers' Association of America
NPTL . . . . . . National Police Testing Laboratories
NPBE . . . . . . National Political Button Exchange (An organization)
NAPOLI . . . . . National Politics (Behavioral science game)
NPCF . . . . . . National Pollution Control Foundation
NPPC . . . . . . National Pork Producers Council
NPG . . . . National Portrait Gallery (Smithsonian Institution)
NPTA . . . . . . National Postal Transport Association
PTA . . . . National Postal Transport Association
NPTCO . . . . . National Postal and Travelers Censorship Organization
NPU . . . . National Postal Union
NPCI . . . . . . National Potato Chip Institute
NPC . . . . National Potato Council
NPBEA . . . . . National Poultry, Butter & Egg Association
NPIP . . . . . . National Poultry Improvement Plan
NPPF . . . . . . National Poultry Producers Federation
NPPC . . . . . . National Power Policy Committee (World War II)
NPGTC . . . . . National Prairie Grouse Technical Council
NPMR . . . . . . National Premium Manufacturers Representatives
NPSE . . . . . . National Premium Sales Executives
NPFFPA . . . . . National Prepared Frozen Food Processors Association
NPHWA . . . . National Presbyterian Health and Welfare Association
NPC . . . . National Press Club
NPPA . . . . . . National Press Photographers Association
NPA . . . . National Preservers Association
NPBI . . . . . . National Pretzel Bakers Institute
NPEA . . . . . . National Printing Equipment Association
NPIRI . . . . . . National Printing Ink Research Institute
NPPA . . . . . . National Probation and Parole Association
NPA . . . . National Proctologic Association
NPACI . . . . . National Production Advisory Council on Industry (British)
NPA . . . . National Production Authority (Functions merged into BDSA, 1953)
NPC . . . . National Productivity Council (India)
NPDEA . . . . . National Professional Driver Education Association
NPSL . . . . . . National Professional Soccer League
NPSRA . . . . . National Professional Squash Racquets Association

NPAC . . . . National Program for Acquisitions and Cataloging (Library of Congress)
NPA . . . . National Prohibition Act
NPP . . . . National Prohibition Party
NPITI . . . . National Project for the Improvement of Televised Instruction (National
         Association of Educational Broadcasters)
NPP . . . . National Promotion Plan
NPJPA . . . . . National Prune Juice Packers Association
NPRI . . . . National Psychiatric Reform Institute
NPAP . . . . . . National Psychological Association for Psychoanalysis
NPPTA . . . . . National Public Parks Tennis Association
NPC . . . . National Public Relations Council of Health and Welfare Services
NPRR . . . . . . National Public Relations Roundtable
NPC . . . . National Publicity Council for Health and Welfare Services
NP . . . . National Publishing Company (Philadelphia)
NPL . . . . National Puzzlers' League
NQHR . . . . . . National Quarter Horse Registry
NQPC . . . . . . National Quartz Producers Council
NQB . . . . National Quotation Bureau (Stock market)
NRAO . . . . . . National Radio Astronomy Observatory
NRAB . . . . . . National Railroad Adjustment Board
NRPF . . . . . . National Railroad Pension Forum
NRAA . . . . . National Railway Appliances Association
NRHS . . . . . . National Railway Historical Society
NRLP . . . . . . National Railway Labor Panel (World War II)
NRC . . . . National Ramah Commission
NRD . . . . National Range Division (Air Force)
NRBC . . . . . . National Rare Blood Club
NRTS . . . . National Reactor Testing Station
NRMCA . . . . . National Ready Mixed Concrete Association
NREFA . . . . . National Real Estate Fliers Association
NRA . . . . National Reclamation Association
NRC . . . . National Records Center
NRMC . . . . . National Records Management Council
NR . . . . National Recovery Act (or Administration)
NRA . . . . National Recovery Act
NRA . . . . National Recovery Administration
         (Voided by Supreme Court, 1935)
NRA . . . . National Recreation Association
NRPA . . . . . National Recreation and Park Association
NRCI . . . . . . National Red Cherry Institute
NRS . . . . National Reemployment Service
NRLSI . . . . . . National Reference Library of Science and Invention (British)
NRC . . . . National Referral Center (of Library of Congress)
NRA . . . . National Reform Association
NRA . . . . National Register of Archives (Historical Manuscripts Commission)
         (British)
NRMM . . . . . National Register of Microform Masters (Library of Congress)
NRMS . . . . . National Registry of Medical Secretaries
NRW-KA . . . National Registry of Willys-Knight Automobile
NRA . . . . National Rehabilitation Association
NRB . . . . National Religious Broadcasters
NRA . . . . National Renderers Association
NRT . . . . National Repertory Theatre Foundation
NRC . . . . . . National Republican Club
NRC . . . . . . National Research Corporation
NRC . . . . . . National Research Council
NRCPS . . . . . National Research Council on Peace Strategy
NRDC . . . . . . National Research Development Corporation (British)
NRFF . . . . . . National Research Foundation for Fertility
NRL . . . . National Research Laboratory
NRPB . . . . . . National Research Planning Board
NROTCBA . . . . National Reserve Officers' Training Corps Band Association
NRC . . . . National Resources Committee (Functions transferred to National
         Resources Planning Board)
NRCA . . . . . . National Resources Council of America
NREC . . . . . . National Resources Evaluation Center (of OEP) (Nuclear effects)
NRPB . . . . . . National Resources Planning Board (Abolished, 1943)
NRA . . . . National Restaurant Association
NRCA . . . . . . National Retail Credit Association
NRFEA . . . . . National Retail Farm Equipment Association
NRFA . . . . . . National Retail Florists Association (Defunct)
NRFA . . . . . . National Retail Furniture Association
NRHA . . . . . . National Retail Hardware Association
NRLDA . . . . . National Retail Lumber Dealers Association
NRMA . . . . . National Retail Merchants Association
NRPSA . . . . . National Retail Pet Supply Association
NRT&CMA . . . . National Retail Tea and Coffee Merchants Association
NRTA . . . . . . National Retired Teachers Association
NARIC . . . . . National Rice and Corn Board (Philippines)
NRA . . . . National Rifle Association of America
NRWC . . . . . . National Right to Work Committee

NR & HC . . . . National Rivers and Harbors Congress
NRCA . . . . . . National Roofing Contractors Association
NRF . . . . National Rowing Foundation
NRECA . . . . . National Rural Electric Cooperative Association
NRLCA . . . . . National Rural Letter Carriers' Association
RLCA . . . . . . National Rural Letter Carriers' Association
NSBA . . . . . . National Safe Boating Association
NSBWC . . . . . National Safe Boating Week Committee
NSC . . . . National Safety Council
NSE . . . . National Sales Executives
NSGA . . . . . National Sand and Gravel Association
NSSA . . . . . . National Sanitary Supply Association
NSF . . . . National Sanitation Foundation
NSMA . . . . . . National Scale Men's Association
NSSFNS . . . . . National Scholarship Service and Fund for Negro Students
NSTF . . . . . . National Scholarship Trust Fund (An affiliate of the Graphic Arts
         Technical Foundation)
NSPA . . . . . . National Scholastic Press Association
NSBA . . . . . . National School Boards Association
NSCSC . . . . . . National School Calendar Study Committee
NSOA . . . . . . National School Orchestra Association
NSPRA . . . . . National School Public Relations Association
NSSEA . . . . . National School Supply and Equipment Association
NSVP . . . . . . National School Volunteer Program
NSYA . . . . . . National School Yearbook Association
NSB . . . . National Science Board (of the National Science Foundation)
NSDB . . . . . . National Science Development Board
NSF . . . . National Science Foundation
NSFA . . . . . . National Science Foundation Act
NSSA . . . . . . National Science Supervisors Association
NSTA . . . . . . National Science Teachers Association
NSL . . . . National Scientific Laboratory, Inc.
NSR . . . . National Scientific Register
NSMPA . . . . . National Screw Machine Products Association
NSS . . . . National Sculpture Society
NSTS . . . . . . National Sea Training Schools (British)
NSRP . . . . . . National Search and Rescue Plan
NSA . . . . National Secretaries Association (International)
NSA . . . . National Security Agency (DOD)
NSC . . . . National Security Council
NSCID . . . . . . National Security Council Intelligence Directive
NSIA . . . . . . National Security Industrial Association
NATSECM . . . . National Security Medal
NSM . . . . National Security Medal
NSPC . . . . . . National Security Planning Commission
NSRB . . . . . . National Security Resources Board
         (Functions transferred to ODM, 1953)
NSTA . . . . . . National Security Traders Association
NSTC . . . . . . National Security Training Commission (Expired, 1957)
NSM . . . . National Selected Morticians
NSSAB . . . . . National Selective Service Appeal Board (of SSS)
NSGC . . . . . . National Self Government Committee
NSOGA . . . . National Seniors' Open Golf Association
NSS . . . . National Serigraph Society
NSA . . . . National Service Acts (British)
NSAFC . . . . . National Service Armed Forces Act (British)
NSBRO . . . . . National Service Board for Religious Objectors
NSEC . . . . . . National Service Entertainments Council (British)
NSI . . . . National Service (Life) Insurance
NSLI . . . . . . National Service Life Insurance
NSSL . . . . . . National Service Star Legion
NSSP . . . . . . National Severe Storms Project (Weather Bureau)
NSTC . . . . . . National Shade Tree Conference
NSF . . . . National Sharecroppers Fund
NSMS . . . . . National Sheet Music Society
NSA . . . . National Shellfisheries Association
NSA . . . . National Sheriffs' Association
NSA . . . . National Shipping Authority (Department of Commerce)
NSI . . . . National Shoe Institute
NSMA . . . . . National Shoe Manufacturers Association
NSRA . . . . . . National Shoe Retailers Association
NSTA . . . . . . National Shoe Traveler's Association
NSBC . . . . . . National Shoeboard Conference
NSSF . . . . . . National Shooting Sports Foundation
NSRA . . . . . . National Shorthand Reporters Association
NSA . . . . National Showmen's Association
NSBA . . . . . . National Shrimp Breaders Association
NSCA . . . . . . National Shrimp Canners Association
NSA . . . . National Shuffleboard Association
NSCC . . . . . . National Siamese Cat Club
NSD . . . . National Silage Demonstration (British)

NSA . . . . National Silo Association
NSSA . . . . . . National Skeet Shooting Association
NSAA . . . . . National Ski Areas Association
NSA . . . . National Ski Association of America (Later, United States Ski Association)
NSPS . . . . . . National Ski Patrol System
NSSG . . . . . . National Ski Study Group
NSSA . . . . . . National Skirt and Sportswear Association
NSA . . . . National Slag Association
NSA . . . . National Slate Association
NSS . . . . National Slovak Society of the USA
NSBA . . . . . . National Small Business Association
NSBMA . . . . . National Small Business Men's Association
NSSTC . . . . . National Small Shipments Traffic Conference
NSS . . . . National Snapdragon Society
NSCA . . . . . . National Soccer Coaches Association of America
NSSF . . . . . . National Social Science Foundation (Proposed in 1966)
NSWA . . . . . . National Social Welfare Assembly
NSWPP . . . . . National Socialist White People's Party (Formerly, American NAZI Party)
NS . . . . National Society
NSAC . . . . . . National Society of Accountants of Cooperatives
NSAD . . . . . . National Society of Art Directors
NSA . . . . National Society of Auctioneers
NSBB . . . . . . National Society for Business Budgeting
NSCAR . . . . . National Society of the Children of the American Revolution
NSCTE . . . . . National Society of College Teachers of Education
CDA . . . . National Society of Colonial Dames of America
NSCDA . . . . National Society of Colonial Dames of America
NSCP . . . . . . National Society for Corporate Planning
NSCCA . . . . . National Society for Crippled Children and Adults
NSC . . . . National Society of Cwens
DAC . . . . National Society, Daughters of the American Colonists
NSDAR . . . . . National Society, Daughters of the American Revolution
DBR . . . . National Society, Daughters of the Barons of Runnemede
NSDBR . . . . . National Society, Daughters of the Barons of Runnemede
NSDBE . . . . . National Society, Daughters of the British Empire
DCW . . . . National Society, Daughters of Colonial Wars
DFPA . . . . . . National Society, Daughters of Founders and Patriots of America
DUP . . . . National Society, Daughters of Utah Pioneers
NSDUP . . . . . National Society, Daughters of Utah Pioneers
NSDP . . . . . . National Society of Dental Prosthetists
NSFC . . . . . . National Society of Film Critics
NSFR . . . . . . National Society of Fund Raisers
NSID . . . . . . National Society of Interior Designers
NSLSRA . . . . National Society of Live Stock Record Associations
NSMR . . . . . National Society for Medical Research
NSMT . . . . . . National Society of Medical Technologists
NSMP . . . . . . National Society of Mural Painters
NSNEW . . . . . National Society of New England Women
NATSOPA . . . . National Society of Operative Printers and Assistants (British)
NSPC . . . . . . National Society of Painters in Casein
NSPWA . . . . . National Society Patriotic Women of America
NSPR . . . . . . National Society of Pershing Rifles
NSPCB . . . . . National Society for the Preservation of Covered Bridges
NSPB . . . . . . National Society for the Prevention of Blindness
NSPCA . . . . . National Society for the Prevention of Cruelty to Animals
NSPCC . . . . . National Society for the Prevention of Cruelty to Children
NSPE . . . . . . National Society of Professional Engineers
NSPI . . . . . . National Society for Programmed Instruction
NSPIE . . . . . National Society for the Promotion of Industrial Education
NSPA . . . . . . National Society of Public Accountants
NSSTE . . . . . National Society of Sales Training Executives
NSSB . . . . . . National Society of Scabbard and Blade
SAR . . . . National Society, Sons of the American Revolution
NSSDP . . . . . National Society, Sons and Daughters of the Pilgrims
SDP . . . . National Society, Sons and Daughters of the Pilgrims
NSSL . . . . . . National Society of State Legislators
NSSO . . . . . . National Society of Student Organists
NSSC . . . . . . National Society for the Study of Communication
NSSE . . . . . . National Society for the Study of Education
NSWDAHAC . . National Society Women Descendants of the Ancient and Honorable Artillery Company
WDAHAC . . . . National Society Women Descendants of the Ancient and Honorable Artillery Company
NSWMA . . . . . National Soft Wheat Millers Association
NSSO . . . . . . National Solar Space Observatory (NASA)
NSBEO . . . . . National Sonic Boom Evaluation Office (Air Force)
NSMA . . . . . . National Soup Mix Association
NSCIC . . . . . National Soybean Crop Improvement Council
NSPA . . . . . . National Soybean Processors Association
NSC . . . . National Space Club

NSC . . . . National Space Council
NSSDC . . . . . National Space Science Data Center (NASA)
NSSCC . . . . . National Space Surveillance Control Center
NSSS . . . . . . National Space Surveillance System
NS . . . . National Special (Thread)
NSS . . . . National Speleological Society
NSA-US . . . . . National Spiritual Assembly of the Baha'is of the United States
NSAC . . . . . . National Spiritualist Association of Churches
NSPA . . . . . . National Split Pea Association
NSGA . . . . . . National Sporting Goods Association
NSCCA . . . . . National Sports Car Club of America
NSPFEA . . . . . National Spray Painting and Finishing Equipment Association
NSDA . . . . . . National Sprayer and Duster Association
NSDC . . . . . . National Square Dance Convention
NSTA . . . . . . National Squash Tennis Association
NSCSCC . . . . National Standard for Common System Component Characteristics
NSD . . . . National Standard Company (NYSE symbol)
NSPA . . . . . . National Standard Parts Association
NSRDS . . . . . National Standard Reference Data System (National Bureau of Standards)
NSA . . . . National Standards Association
NSRMCA . . . . National Star Route Mail Carriers Association
NSC . . . . National Starch & Chemical Corporation (NYSE symbol)
NSRP . . . . . . National States Rights Party
NSOEA . . . . . National Stationery and Office Equipment Association
NS . . . . National Steel Corporation (NYSE symbol)
NSHA . . . . . . National Steeplechase and Hunt Association
NSCRC . . . . . National Stock Car Racing Commission
NSC & MP . . . National Stock Control and Maintenance Point
NATEX . . . . . National Stock Exchange
NSE . . . . National Stock Exchange
NSS . . . . National Stockpile Site
NSP . . . . National Stolen Property
NSL . . . . National Story League
NSTL . . . . . . National Strategic Target Line (or List)
NSWA . . . . . . National Stripper Well Association
NSCF . . . . . . National Student Christian Federation (Later, UCM)
NSFAC . . . . . National Student Financial Aid Council
NSMC . . . . . . National Student Marketing Corporation
NSNA . . . . . . National Student Nurses' Association
NSMRSE . . . . National Study of Mathematics Requirements for Scientists and Engineers
NSSSE . . . . . National Study of Secondary School Evaluation
NSSA . . . . . . National Suffolk Sheep Association
NSBA . . . . . . National Sugar Brokers Association
NSU . . . . National Sugar Refining Company (NYSE symbol)
NSSA . . . . . . National Sunday School Association
NSAA . . . . . . National Supply Association of America
NSDA . . . . . . National Surplus Dealers Association
NSPI . . . . . . National Swimming Pool Institute
NSGC . . . . . . National Swine Growers Council
NSQCRE . . . . National Symposium on Quality Control and Reliability in Electronics (IEEE)
NSRQCE . . . . National Symposium on Reliability and Quality Control in Electronics
NSSET . . . . . National Symposium on Space Electronics and Telemetry (IEEE)
NST . . . . National Symposium on Telemetering
NTMA . . . . . . National Tank Manufacturers Association
NTTC . . . . . . National Tank Truck Carriers
NTR . . . . National Tape Repository
NPT . . . . National Taper Pipe Thread
NTA . . . . National Tax Association
NTEA . . . . . . National Tax Equality Association
NTSAD . . . . . National Tay-Sachs and Allied Diseases Association (Formerly, NTSA)
NTSA . . . . . . National Tay-Sachs Association (Later, NTSAD)
NTY . . . . National Tea Company (NYSE symbol)
NTC . . . . National Teachers Corps
NTA . . . . National Technical Association
NTPC . . . . . . National Technical Processing Center
NTSA . . . . . . National Technical Services Association
NTTCIW . . . . National Technical Task Committee on Industrial Wastes
NTC . . . . National Telemetering Conference (IEEE)
NTCA . . . . . . National Telephone Cooperative Association
NTX . . . . National Teletypewriter Exchange
NTFC . . . . . . National Television Film Council
NTSC . . . . . . National Television System Committee
NTL . . . . National Temperance League
NTPC . . . . . . National Temperance and Prohibition Council
NTEF . . . . . . National Tennis Educational Foundation
NTMA . . . . . . National Terrazzo and Mosaic Association
NTPG . . . . . . National Textile Processors Guild
NTC . . . . National Theatre Conference
NTS . . . . National Thespian Society
NTC . . . . National Thrift Committee

NTDRA . . . . . . National Tire Dealers and Retreaders Association
NTTA . . . . . . National Tobacco Tax Association
NTDPMA . . . . National Tool, Die and Precision Machining Association
NTSEA . . . . . National Trade Show Exhibitors Association
NTUC . . . . . . National Trade Union Congress (Singapore)
NTUC . . . . . . National Trade Union Council (Hungary)
NTUC . . . . . . National Trade Union Council for Human Rights
NTSB . . . . . . National Traffic Safety Bureau
NTS . . . . National Traffic System (Amateur radio)
NTRA . . . . . . National Trailer Rental Association
NTL . . . . National Training Laboratories
NTC . . . . National Translations Center
NTSB . . . . . . National Transportation Safety Board (Department of Transportation)
NTA . . . . National Trappers Association of America
NTAA . . . . . . National Travelers Aid Association
NTPA . . . . . . National Trotting Pony Association
NTLS . . . . . . National Truck Leasing Service (of National Truck Leasing Association)
NTTTTI . . . . . National Truck Tank and Trailer Tank Institute
NT . . . . National Trust for Historic Preservation
NTHP . . . . . . National Trust for Historic Preservation
NTA . . . . National Tuberculosis Association
NTS . . . . National Tulip Society
NTOMC . . . . . National Tung Oil Marketing Cooperative
NTSR . . . . . . National Tunis Sheep Registry
NTWA . . . . . . National Turf Writers Association
NTF . . . . National Turkey Federation
NTIP . . . . . . National Turkey Improvement Plan
NU . . . . National Union
NUBE . . . . . . National Union of Bank Employees (Malaya)
NUC . . . . National Union Catalog (of American libraries)
NUCAL . . . . . National Union Catalog Author List
NUCMC . . . . . National Union Catalog of Manuscript Collections (Library of Congress)
NUCS . . . . . . National Union of Christian Schools
NUCW . . . . . . National Union of Commercial Workers (Malaya)
NUCP . . . . . . National Union of Czechoslovak Protestants in America and Canada
NUCSE . . . . . National Union of Czechoslovak Students in Exile
NUET . . . . . . National Union of Elementary Teachers (British)
NUES . . . . . . National Union of Ethiopian Students
NUPAAWP . . . . National Union of Plantation, Agricultural and Allied Workers of the Philippines
NUPW . . . . . . National Union of Plantation Workers (Uganda)
NUPW . . . . . . National Union of Plantation Workers in Malaya
NUPTE . . . . . National Union of Port Trust Employees (India)
NUS . . . . National Union of Seamen (British)
NUSI . . . . . . National Union of Seamen of India
NUSAS . . . . . National Union of South African Students
NUS . . . . National Union of Students (British)
NUT . . . . National Union of Teachers (Federation of Malaya)
NUUSFE . . . . . National Union of United States Forces Employees (South Korea)
NUIA . . . . . . National United Italian Associations
NUEA . . . . . . National University Extension Association
NUI . . . . National University of Ireland
NUL . . . . National Urban League
NUCA . . . . . . National Utility Contractors' Association
NUS . . . . National Utility Service, Inc.
NVA . . . . National Variety Artists
NVPA . . . . . . National Visual Presentation Association
NVSD . . . . . . National Vital Statistics Division (of OSG)
NVDA . . . . . . National Vitamin Distributors Association
NVF . . . . National Vitamin Foundation
NVATA . . . . . National Vocational Agricultural Teachers' Association
NVGA . . . . . . National Vocational Guidance Association
NVGI . . . . . . National Voluntary Groups Institute
NVB . . . . National Volunteer Brigade (South African equivalent of the British Home Guard)
NLV . . . . National Vulcanized Fibre Company (NYSE symbol)
NWSB . . . . . . National Wage Stabilization Board (Superseded NWLB, 1945; terminated, 1947)
NWC . . . . National War College (DOD)
NWCAA . . . . National War College Alumni Association
NWF . . . . National War Formulary
NWF . . . . National War Fund
NWLB . . . . . . National War Labor Board (World War II)
WLB . . . . National War Labor Board (World War II)
NWAHACA . . . National Warm Air Heating and Air Conditioning Association
NAWAS . . . . National Warning System (Civil Defense)
NWCA . . . . . National Water Carriers Association
NWC . . . . National Water Commission
NWL . . . . National Water Lift Company
NWPF . . . . . . National Water Purification Foundation
NWSC . . . . . . National Water Safety Congress

NWWA . . . . . National Water Well Association
NWC . . . . National Waterfowl Council
NWC . . . . National Waterways Conference
NAWAC . . . . National Weather Analysis Center
NWAC . . . . . National Weather Analysis Center (Air Force - Navy)
NWRC . . . . . National Weather Records Center (Weather Bureau)
NWSC . . . . . National Weather Satellite Center (Weather Bureau)
NWSA . . . . . National Welding Supply Association
NWRO . . . . . National Welfare Rights Organization
NWRA . . . . . National Wheel and Rim Association
NWAA . . . . . National Wheelchair Athletic Association
NWAC . . . . . National Wheelchair Athletic Committee
NWWC . . . . . National White Wyandotte Club
NWDA . . . . . National Wholesale Druggists Association
NWDGA . . . . National Wholesale Dry Goods Association
NWFA . . . . . National Wholesale Furniture Association
NWHA . . . . . National Wholesale Hardware Association
NWJA . . . . . National Wholesale Jewelers Association
NWLDYA . . . . National Wholesale Lumber Distributing Yard Association
NWF . . . . National Wildlife Federation
NWA . . . . National Wine Association
NWCME . . . . . National Winter Convention on Military Electronics (IEEE)
NWS . . . . National Winter Sports
NWSA . . . . . National Winter Sports Association
NWG . . . . National Wire Gauge
NWB . . . . National Wiring Bureau
NWF . . . . National Woman's Forum
NWP . . . . National Woman's Party
WAABI . . . . . National Women's Association of Allied Beverage Industries
NWL . . . . National Women's League of the United Synagogue of America
NWNSA . . . . National Women's Neckwear and Scarf Association
NWTI . . . . . . National Wood Tank Institute
NWCA . . . . . National Woodcarvers Association
NWBC . . . . . National Wooden Box Council
NWPCA . . . . . National Wooden Pallet and Container Association (Formerly, NWPMA)
NWPMA . . . . . National Wooden Pallet Manufacturers Association (Later, NWPCA)
NWMA . . . . . National Woodwork Manufacturers Association
NWGA . . . . . National Wool Growers Association
NWMC . . . . . National Wool Marketing Corporation
NWTA . . . . . National Wool Trade Association
NWC . . . . National Writers Club
F . . . . National Yeomen
NYBA . . . . . . National Young Buddhist Association
NYJ . . . . National Young Judaea
NYA . . . . National Youth Administration (Terminated, 1943)
NYA . . . . National Youth Alliance
YCCA . . . . . . National Youth Council on Civic Affairs
NYAL . . . . . . National Yugoslav Army of Liberation (World War II)
NZP . . . . National Zoological Park (Smithsonian Institution)
NF . . . . Nationale Front
NAW . . . . . . Nationales Aufbauwerk
NOK . . . . Nationales Olympisches Komitee
NKFD . . . . . . Nationalkomitee Freies Deutschland
NDAP . . . . . . Nationalsozialistische Deutsche Arbeiter-Partei
NAZI . . . . . . Nationalsozialistische Deutsche Arbeiterpartei (National Socialist German Workers' Party, 1919-45)
NSDAP . . . . . Nationalsozialistische Deutsche Arbeiterpartei (National Socialist German Workers', or NAZI, Party, 1919-45)
NWCIEP . . . . Nation-Wide Committee on Import-Export Policy
NHA . . . . Nationwide Hotel Association
NIMS . . . . . . Nationwide Improved Mail Service (Post Office)
NIPS . . . . . . Nationwide Integrated Postal Service (Post Office)
NTRS . . . . . . Nationwide Trailer Rental System
NDGW . . . . . Native Daughters of the Golden West
NI . . . . Native Infantry
NSGW . . . . . Native Sons of the Golden West
DNJC . . . . . . Nativitas Domini Nostri Jesu Christi (Nativity of Our Lord Jesus Christ)
NVM . . . . . . Nativity of the Virgin Mary
NAGARD . . . . NATO Advisory Group for Aeronautical Research and Development
NATO-AGARD . . NATO-Advisory Group for Aeronautical Research and Development
NADGE . . . . . NATO Air Defense Ground Environment
NADGECO . . . NATO Air Defense Ground Environment Consortium
NADGEMO . . . NATO Air Defense Ground Environment Management Office
NBMR . . . . . NATO Basic Military Requirements
NADEFCOL . . . NATO Defense College
NDDP . . . . . . NATO Defense Data Program
NEPR . . . . . . NATO Electronic Parts Recommendations
NATOELLA . . . NATO-European Long Lines Agency
NIAG . . . . . . NATO Industrial Advisory Group
NATO-LRSS . . . NATO-Long-Range Scientific Studies

NAMSO . . . . . NATO Maintenance and Supply Organization (Formerly, NATO Maintenance Supply Services Agency)
NMSSA . . . . . . NATO Maintenance Supply Service Agency
NMSSS . . . . . NATO Maintenance Supply Service System
NMSO . . . . . . NATO Maintenance and Support Operation
NAMFI . . . . . . NATO Missile Firing Installation
NATO-RDPP . . NATO-Multilateral Research and Development Production Program
NPC . . . . NATO Parliamentarians' Conference
NPC . . . . NATO Pipeline Committee
NATO-SC . . . . NATO Science Committee
NASC . . . . . . NATO Supply Center
NOM . . . . Natomas Company (NYSE symbol)
NTS . . . . Natsional'no-Trudovoi Soiuz
NABR . . . . . . Natural Bridges National Monument
NCI . . . . Natural Casing Institute
NDH . . . . Natural Disaster Hospitals (Public Health Service)
NADWARN . . . Natural Disaster Warning
NFPA . . . . . . Natural Family Planning Association of Connecticut
NAFLI . . . . . . Natural Flight Instrument System
NGL . . . . Natural Gas Liquids
NGPA . . . . . . Natural Gas Processors Association
NGPSA . . . . . Natural Gas Processors Suppliers Association
NGAA . . . . . . Natural Gasoline Association of America
NGSMA . . . . . Natural Gasoline Supply Men's Association
NO . . . . Natural Order (Botany)
NRC . . . . Natural Resources Council of America
NR . . . . Natural Rubber
NRB . . . . Natural Rubber Bureau
NATSYN . . . . Natural and Synthetic (Type of long-wearing rubber, which is actually wholly synthetic)
NOA . . . . Nature of Action (Military)
N . . . . Natus (Born)
NAU . . . . Nautec Corporation (NYSE symbol)
N . . . . Nautical
NA . . . . Nautical Almanac
NM . . . . Nautical Mile(s)
NMI . . . . Nautical Mile(s)
NML . . . . Nautical Mile(s)
NMR . . . . Nautical Mile Radius Of
NMH . . . . Nautical Miles per Hour
NMPS . . . . . . Nautical Miles Per Second
NRG . . . . Nautical Research Guild
NAAD . . . . . . Navajo Army Depot
NAVA . . . . . . Navajo National Monument
NA . . . . Naval Academy
NAC . . . . Naval Academy
NAPS . . . . . . Naval Academy Preparatory School
NADM . . . . . . Naval Administration
NAVADCOM . . Naval Administrative Command
NAVADUNIT . . Naval Administrative Unit
NAVAD . . . . . Naval Administrator at (place)
NAB . . . . Naval Advanced Base
NABD . . . . . . Naval Advanced Base Depot
NABU . . . . . . Naval Advanced Base Unit
NAUWS . . . . . Naval Advanced Undersea Weapons School
NAG . . . . Naval Advisory Group
NAL . . . . Naval Aeronautical Laboratory
NATL . . . . . . Naval Aeronautical Turbine Laboratory
NARTS . . . . . Naval Aeronautics Test Station
NAMC . . . . . . Naval Aerospace Medical Center
NAMI . . . . . . Naval Aerospace Medical Institute
NAATC . . . . . Naval Air Advanced Training Command
NAVANTRACOM . . Naval Air Advanced Training Command
NAAWFS . . . . Naval Air All Weather Flight Squadron
NAB . . . . Naval Air Base
NAC . . . . Naval Air Center (Military)
NACIO . . . . . . Naval Air Combat Information Office(r)
NACIS . . . . . . Naval Air Combat Information School
NAD . . . . Naval Air Depot
NAD . . . . Naval Air Detail
NADC . . . . . . Naval Air Development Center (BUWEPS)
NADEVCEN . . . Naval Air Development Center
NADMC . . . . . Naval Air Development & Material Center
NADS . . . . . . Naval Air Development Station
NAD . . . . Naval Air Division (British)
NAELSI . . . . . Naval Air Electronics Shipboard Installation
NAEC . . . . . . Naval Air Engineering Center
NAEF . . . . . . Naval Air Engineering Facility
NAES . . . . . . Naval Air Experimental Station
NAXSTA . . . . . Naval Air Experimental Station
NAF . . . . Naval Air Facility

NAVAIRFAC . . Naval Air Facility
NAFC . . . . Naval Air Ferry Command (World War II)
NAFS . . . . Naval Air Fighter School
NAFI . . . . Naval Air Fighting Instructions
NAVAIRLANT . . Naval Air Force, Atlantic Fleet
NAVAIRPAC . . Naval Air Force, Pacific Fleet
NAGCO . . . . . Naval Air Ground Center
NAGS . . . . . . Naval Air Gunners School
NAIRU . . . . . . Naval Air Intelligence Reserve Units
NAIT . . . . Naval Air Intermediate Training
NAIT(C) . . . . . Naval Air Intermediate Training (Command)
NALO . . . . . . Naval Air Liaison Officer
NALCOLANT . . Naval Air Logistic Control Office Atlantic
NALCOPACREP . . Naval Air Logistic Control Office Pacific Representative
NAMATCEN . . Naval Air Material Center
NAMC . . . . . . Naval Air Materiel Center (BUWEPS)
NAMC . . . . . . Naval Air Materiel Command
NAMISTESTCEN . . Naval Air Missile Test Center
NAMTC . . . . . Naval Air Missile Test Center
NANFAC . . . . . Naval Air Navigation Facility Advisory Committee
NANS . . . . . . Naval Air Navigation School
NAOT . . . . . . Naval Air Operational Training
NAOTC . . . . . Naval Air Operational Training Command
NAPT . . . . . . Naval Air Primary Training
NAPT(C) . . . . . Naval Air Primary Training (Command)
NAPTCRO . . . . Naval Air Primary Training Command Regional Office
NAP . . . . Naval Air Priorities
NAPO . . . . . . Naval Air Priorities Office
NARSTC . . . . . Naval Air Rescue Training Command
NARTC . . . . . . Naval Air Research Training Command
NAVAIRRES . . . Naval Air Reserve
NARDIV . . . . . Naval Air Reserve Divisions
NARMU . . . . . Naval Air Reserve Maintenance Units
NARTU . . . . . . Naval Air Reserve Training Unit
NARF . . . . . . Naval Air Rework Facility
NAROCTESTSTA . . Naval Air Rocket Test Station
NARTS . . . . . . Naval Air Rocket Test Station
NASS . . . . . . Naval Air Signal School
NASWF . . . . . Naval Air Special Weapons Facility
CANAS . . . . . . Naval Air Station (Canadian Navy)
NAS . . . . Naval Air Station
NASBERM . . . . Naval Air Station Bermuda
NASCRIST . . . . Naval Air Station Corpus Christi
NASGTMO . . . Naval Air Station Guantanamo
NASJAX . . . . . Naval Air Station Jacksonville
NASLAKE . . . . Naval Air Station Lakehurst
NASPENSA . . . Naval Air Station Pensacola
NASQUON . . . Naval Air Station Quonset Point
NASDIEGO . . . Naval Air Station San Diego
NASD . . . . . . Naval Air Supply Depot
NASC . . . . Naval Air Systems Command
NASCOM . . . . Naval Air Systems Command
NAVAIRSYSCO . . Naval Air Systems Command
NATSF . . . . . . Naval Air Technical Services Facility
NATT . . . . Naval Air Technical Training
NATECHTRACEN . . Naval Air Technical Training Center
NAVTECHTRACEN . . Naval Air Technical Training Center
NATTC . . . . . . Naval Air Technical Training Center or Command
NATECHTRAU . . Naval Air Technical Training Unit
NATTU . . . . . . Naval Air Technical Training Unit
NATESTCEN . . Naval Air Test Center
NATF . . . . Naval Air Test Facility
NATC . . . . Naval Air Testing Center
NAT . . . . Naval Air Training
NATB . . . . Naval Air Training Base
NATBASES . . . . Naval Air Training Bases
NATC . . . . . . Naval Air Training Center (or Command)
NAVAIRTRACEN . . Naval Air Training Center
NATEC . . . . . . Naval Air Training and Experimental Command
NATOPS . . . . . Naval Air Training and Operating Procedures Standardization
NATS . . . . Naval Air Transport Service
NATSLANT . . . Naval Air Transport Service, Atlantic Wing
NATSFERRY . . . Naval Air Transport Service, Ferry Command (World War II)
NATSPAC . . . . Naval Air Transport Service, Pacific Wing
NATWP . . . . . Naval Air Transport Wing, Pacific
NATTS . . . . . . Naval Air Turbine Test Station
NATURBTESTSTA . . Naval Air Turbine Test Station
NADU . . . . . . Naval Aircraft Delivery Unit
NAF . . . . Naval Aircraft Factory
NAMO . . . . . . Naval Aircraft Maintenance Orders
NAMP . . . . . . Naval Aircraft Maintenance Program

NAMU . . . . . . Naval Aircraft Material (Utility)
NAMT . . . . . . Naval Aircraft Mobile Trainer
NAM . . . . . . Naval Aircraft Modification
NAMU . . . . . . Naval Aircraft Modification Unit
NATU . . . . . . Naval Aircraft Torpedo Unit
NAC . . . . . . Naval Aircraftman (British)
NATECOM . . . Naval Airship Training and Experimentation Command
NAWTPD . . . . Naval All Weather Testing Program Detachment
NAD . . . . . Naval Ammunition Depot
NAMD . . . . . . Naval Ammunition Depot
NAVAMDEP . . . Naval Ammunition Depot
NAND . . . . . Naval Ammunition and Net Depot
NAB . . . . Naval Amphibious Base
NAMB . . . . . . Naval Amphibious Base
NABA . . . . . . Naval Amphibious Base Annex
NAG . . . . . . Naval Analysis Group
NAG . . . . Naval Applications Group
NASL . . . . . . Naval Applied Science Laboratory
NA . . . . Naval Architect(s)
NARL . . . . . . Naval Arctic Research Laboratory
NAVAREAAUDSVC . . Naval Area Audit Service
NAGC . . . . . . Naval Armed Guard Center
CANAVAT . . . . Naval Attaché (Canadian Navy)
NA . . . . Naval Attaché (Diplomacy)
NAA . . . . Naval Attaché for Air
NAVAUTH . . . . Naval Authority
NA . . . . Naval Auxiliary
NAAF . . . . . . Naval Auxiliary Air Facility
NAAS . . . . . . Naval Auxiliary Air Station
NAVC . . . . . Naval Aviation Cadet
NAVCAD . . . . Naval Aviation Cadet
NACSB . . . . . Naval Aviation Cadet Selection Board
NAESU . . . . . Naval Aviation Electronic Service Unit
NAMTRAGRU . . Naval Aviation Maintenance Training Group
NANEWS . . . . Naval Aviation News
NAO . . . . . . Naval Aviation Observer
NAOC . . . . . Naval Aviation Officer Candidate
NAOTS . . . . . Naval Aviation Ordnance Test Station
NAP . . . . Naval Aviation Pilot
NAP(G) . . . . . Naval Aviation Pilot (Glider)
NAPP . . . . . . Naval Aviation Preparatory Program
NAPTC . . . . . Naval Aviation Primary Training Command
NAPF . . . . . . Naval Aviation Publication Facility
NASC . . . . . . Naval Aviation Safety Center
NASO . . . . . . Naval Aviation Supply Office
NA . . . . Naval Aviator
NAF . . . . Naval Avionics Facility
NAFI . . . . . . Naval Avionics Facility, Indianapolis
NAVBASE . . . . Naval Base
NB . . . . Naval Base
NBLU . . . . . . Naval Base Labour Union (Singapore)
NBAD . . . . . . Naval Bases Air Defense
NBSS . . . . . . Naval Beach Signal Section
NBL . . . . Naval Biological Laboratory (Oakland, California)
NBTL . . . . . . Naval Boiler and Turbine Laboratory
NCP . . . . Naval Capabilities Plan
NCEL . . . . . . Naval Civil Engineering Laboratory (FEC)
NCAA . . . . . Naval Civilian Administrators Association
NAVCLODEP . . Naval Clothing Depot
NCSL . . . . . . Naval Code and Signal Laboratory
NCDT & EBASE . . Naval Combat Demolition Training and Experimental Base (Maui, Hawaii)
NCDU . . . . . . Naval Combat Demolition Unit
NCA . . . . . . Naval Command Assistant
NAVCOSSACT . Naval Command Systems Support Activity (Military)
NCSSA . . . . . Naval Command Systems Support Activity
NCSSC . . . . . Naval Command Systems Support Center
NCWTF . . . . . Naval Commander Western Task Force
NAVCOMMSTA . . Naval Communication Station
NAVCOM . . . . Naval Communications
NAVCOMMU . . Naval Communication Unit
NAVCOMM . . . Naval Communications (System)
NCA . . . . . . Naval Communications Annex
NCB . . . . Naval Communications Board
NCS . . . . . . Naval Communications Station (or System)
NCBC . . . . . . Naval Construction Battalion Centers
NAVCONTRACEN . . Naval Construction Training Center
NCTC . . . . . . Naval Construction Training Center
NCDC . . . . . . Naval Contract Distribution Center
NCSO . . . . . Naval Control Service Office (World War II British Routing Service)
NCSO . . . . . . Naval Control of Shipping Officer

NCSORG . . . . Naval Control of Shipping Organization
NAVCONVHOSP . . Naval Convalescent Hospital
NC . . . . Naval Correspondence
NCI . . . . Naval Cost Inspector
NCISC . . . . . . Naval Counterintelligence Support Center
NC & B . . . . . Naval Courts & Boards
NDF . . . . Naval Dairy Farm
NDBS . . . . . . Naval Despatch Boat Service
NAVDET . . . . Naval Detachment
NAVDISCBAR . . Naval Disciplinary Barracks
NDB . . . . Naval Disciplinary Barracks
NAVDISP . . . . Naval Dispensary
ND . . . . Naval Dispensary
NAVDIS . . . . . Naval District
NAVDIST . . . . Naval District
ND . . . . Naval District
NDW . . . . . . Naval District Washington
NDD & RF . . . . Naval Dry Dock and Repair Facility
NESC . . . . . . Naval Electronic Systems Command
NEWS . . . . . . Naval Electronic Warfare Simulator
NEL . . . . Naval Electronics Laboratory
NELIAC . . . . . Naval Electronics Laboratory International Algebraic Compiler
NAVELEXSYSCOM . . Naval Electronics Systems Command
WESTNAVELEX . . Naval Electronics Systems Command; Western Division; Mare Island; Vallejo, Calif.
NEF . . . . Naval Emergency Fund (A budget category)
NE . . . . Naval Engineer
NEES . . . . . . Naval Engineering Experiment Station
NAVEXAM . . . Naval Examining Board
NEMO . . . . . . Naval Experimental Manned Observatory
NES . . . . Naval Experimenting Station
NFEC . . . . . . Naval Facilities Engineering Command (Formerly, Bureau of Yards and Docks)
NAVFACENSYSCOM . . Naval Facilities Engineering Systems Command
NAVFAC . . . . Naval Facility
NFIS . . . . . . Naval Fighting Instruction School
NFMSAEG . . . Naval Fleet Missile System Analysis & Evaluation Group
NFTB . . . . . . Naval Fleet Training Base
NFO . . . . Naval Flight Officer
NAVFLIGHTPREPSCOL . . Naval Flight Preparatory School
NFPS . . . . . . Naval Flight Preparatory School
NFTS . . . . . . Naval Flight Training School
NELM . . . . . . Naval Forces Eastern Atlantic and Mediterranean
NAVFE . . . . . Naval Forces Far East
NAVFORJAP . . Naval Forces, Japan
NAVFORKOR . . Naval Forces, Korea
NAVMAR . . . . Naval Forces, Marianas
NAVNZ . . . . . Naval Forces, New Zealand (World War II)
NAVNORSOLS . . Naval Forces, Northern Solomons (World War II)
NAVPHIL . . . . Naval Forces, Philippines
NAVRYUKYUS . . Naval Forces, Ryukyus (World War II)
NFB . . . . Naval Frontier Base
NFA . . . . Naval Fuel Annex
NAVFUELDEP . . Naval Fuel Depot
NFD . . . . Naval Fuel Depot
NAVGUN . . . . Naval Gun Factory
NGF . . . . Naval Gun Factory (Later, NWF)
NGF . . . . Naval Gunfire
NGFLO . . . . . Naval Gunfire Liaison Officer
NGLO . . . . . . Naval Gunfire Liaison Officer
NGFLT . . . . . Naval Gunfire Liaison Team
NGFO . . . . . . Naval Gunfire Officer
NGS . . . . Naval Gunfire Support
CANAVHED . . . Naval Headquarters, Ottawa, Ontario, Canada
NHF . . . . Naval Historical Foundation
NH . . . . Naval Home
NH . . . . Naval Hospital
NHOS . . . . . . Naval Hospital
NAVINSGEN . . Naval Inspector General
NIG . . . . Naval Inspector General
NIM . . . . Naval Inspector of Machinery
NIO . . . . Naval Inspector Ordnance
NI . . . . Naval Instructor (British)
NAVINTEL . . . Naval Intelligence
NI . . . . Naval Intelligence
NIPSSA . . . . . Naval Intelligence Processing Systems Support Activity
NIS . . . . Naval Intelligence School
SIS . . . . Naval Intelligence Service (Italian)
NIU . . . . Naval Intelligence Unit
NIS . . . . Naval Investigative Service
NLFED . . . . . . Naval Landing Force Equipment Depot

NAVLO . . . . . Naval Liaison Officer
NLO. . . . . . . Naval Liaison Officer
NL . . . . Naval Lighter
NLD. . . . . . . Naval Lighter (Pontoon) Dock
NLDF. . . . . . Naval Local Defense Forces
NM . . . . Naval Magazine
NMAG . . . . . . Naval Magazine
NMND . . . . . . Naval Magazine and Net Depot
NMP . . . . Naval Management Program
NMIS. . . . . . . Naval Manpower Information System
NMES . . . . . . Naval Marine Engineering Station
NAVMAT . . . . Naval Material
NMC . . . . Naval Material Command
NMCOM . . . . Naval Material Command (Formerly, NMSE)
NMR & DO . . . Naval Material Redistribution and Disposal Office(r)
NMSE . . . Naval Material Support Establishment (Later, NMCOM)
NMC . . . . Naval Medical Center
NMFRL . . . . . . Naval Medical Field Research Laboratory
NMNRU . . . . . Naval Medical Neuropsychiatric Research Unit
NMRI . . . . . . Naval Medical Research Institute
NMRL . . . . . . Naval Medical Research Laboratory
NMRU . . . . . . Naval Medical Research Unit
NMS . . . . Naval Medical School
NMSD. . . . . . Naval Medical Supply Depot
NAVMED . . . . Naval Medicine
NMCJS. . . . . . Naval Member, Canadian Joint Staff
CANAVBRIT. . . Naval Member, Canadian Joint Staff, London, England
NMS . . . . Naval Meteorological Service
NMOSAW . . . . Naval and Military Order of the Spanish-American War
NAVMINDEP . . Naval Mine Depot
NMD . . . . Naval Mine Depot
NMDS . . . . . . Naval Mine Disposal School
NMEF. . . . . . . Naval Mine Engineering Facility
NMTF. . . . . . . Naval Mine Test Facility
NMTC . . . . . . Naval Mine Testing Center
NMWS . . . . . . Naval Mine Warfare School
NMWTS . . . . . Naval Mine Warfare Test Station
NMWTS . . . . . Naval Mine Warfare Training School
NMB . . . . Naval Minecraft Base
NMC . . . . Naval Missile Center
NMF . . . . Naval Missile Facility
NMFPA . . . . . Naval Missile Facility, Point Arguello
NMTC . . . . . . Naval Missile Testing Center
NAVMIS . . . . . Naval Mission
NMB . . . . Naval Model Basin
NAVNETDEP . . Naval Net Depot
NND . . . . Naval Net Depot
NAVOBSY. . . . Naval Observatory
NO . . . . Naval Observatory
NOBSY . . . . . Naval Observatory
NAVOCEANO . . Naval Oceanographic Office (Also known as NOO)
NOO . . . . Naval Oceanographic Office (Formerly, NHO or HO)
OO . . . . Naval Oceanographic Office (Also known as NOO; formerly, Hydrographic Office)
NO . . . . Naval Officer
NAVOCS . . . . Naval Officer Candidate School
NOIC. . . . . . . Naval Officer-in-Charge
NOPCL. . . . . . Naval Officer Personnel Circular Letter
NOP . . . . Naval Officer Procurement
NOB . . . . Naval Operating Base
NOBSOLO . . . Naval Operating Base, Coco Solo, Canal Zone
NOBDUCHAR . . Naval Operating Base, Dutch Harbor, Aleutians
NOBNEWT . . . Naval Operating Base, Newport, Rhode Island
NOBFRAN. . . . Naval Operating Base, San Francisco, California
NOBTRIN . . . . Naval Operating Base, Trinidad
NODC . . . . . . Naval Operating Development Center
NOF . . . . Naval Operating Facility
NAVOPFAC . . Naval Operation Facility
NORRS . . . . . . Naval Operational Readiness Reporting Systems
NOTU . . . . . . Naval Operational Training Unit
NOUS . . . . . . Naval Order of the United States
NORD . . . . . . Naval Ordnance
NODAC . . . . . Naval Ordnance Data Automation Center
NOD . . . . Naval Ordnance Department (British)
NOEU . . . . . . Naval Ordnance Experimental Unit
NOGL . . . . . . Naval Ordnance Gage Laboratory
NOIO . . . . . . Naval Ordnance Inspecting Officer
NOL . . . . Naval Ordnance Laboratory (BUWEPS)
NOLC . . . . . . Naval Ordnance Laboratory Corona
NOL-MDI . . . . Naval Ordnance Laboratory Miss Distance Indicator
NOMIS . . . . . Naval Ordnance Management Information System

NOMTF . . . . . Naval Ordnance Missile Test Facility
NOP . . . . Naval Ordnance Plant
NOPI . . . . Naval Ordnance Plant Institute
NOPL . . . . . . Naval Ordnance Plant, Louisville
NAVORD . . . . Naval Ordnance Publications
NORC . . . . . . Naval Ordnance Research Computer (Naval Ordnance Proving Grounds)
NOS . . . . Naval Ordnance Station
NAVORDSYSCO . . Naval Ordnance Systems Command
NOSC . . . . . . Naval Ordnance Systems Command
NAVORDSYSSUPPO . . Naval Ordnance Systems Support Office
NOSSOLANT. . . Naval Ordnance Systems Support Office, Atlantic
NOSSOPAC . . . Naval Ordnance Systems Support Office, Pacific
NOTS. . . . . . . Naval Ordnance Test Station (BUWEPS)
NOU . . . . Naval Ordnance Unit
NOACT . . . . . Naval Overseas Air Cargo Terminal
NOFT . . . . . . Naval Overseas Freight Terminal
NPF . . . . Naval Parachute Facility
NPU . . . . Naval Parachute Unit
NAVPERS . . . . Naval Personnel
NPSC . . . . . . Naval Personnel Separation Center
NP & OSR . . . Naval Petroleum and Oil Shale Reserve
NPR. . . . . Naval Petroleum Reserve
NAVPHOTOCEN . . Naval Photographic Center
NPC . . . . Naval Photographic Center
NPIC . . . . Naval Photographic Interpretation Center
NPSD. . . . . . . Naval Photographic Services Depot (Hollywood)
NAVPORCO . . Naval Port Control Office
NAVPORCOF. . Naval Port Control Officer
NPO . . . . Naval Port Officer
NPS . . . . Naval Postgraduate School
NPANX . . . . . Naval Potomac Annex
NAVPOWFAC. . Naval Powder Factory
NPF . . . . Naval Powder Factory
NAVPREFLIGHTSCOL . . Naval Preflight School
NPFS . . . . Naval Pre-Flight School
NAVPRIS . . . . . Naval Prison
NP . . . . Naval Prison
NPF & PP . . . . Naval Prison Farms and Prison Personnel (Budget appropriation title)
NPA. . . . . Naval Procurement Account
NPF . . . . Naval Procurement Fund (Budget appropriation title)
NAVPECO. . . . Naval Production Equipment Control Office
NPP . . . . Naval Propellant Plant
NAVPROV. . . . Naval Proving Ground (Dahlgren, Virginia)
NPG . . . . Naval Proving Ground
NRA. . . . . Naval Radio Activity
NRDFS . . . . . . Naval Radio Direction Finder Service
NRRS . . . . Naval Radio Research Station
NAVRADSTA . . Naval Radio Station
NRS . . . . Naval Radio Station
NRDL . . . . . . Naval Radiological Defense Laboratory
NRES . . . . Naval Receiving Station
NRS . . . . Naval Receiving Station
NAVRECONTECHSUPPCEN . . Naval Reconnaissance & Technical Support Center
NRTSC . . . . . Naval Reconnaissance & Technical Support Center
NRC . . . . Naval Records Club
NRMC . . . . . . Naval Records Management Center
NRMCEN . . . . Naval Records Management Center
NRS . . . . Naval Recruiting Station
NRPIO . . . . . . Naval Registered Publications Issuing Office
NRB. . . . . Naval Repair Base
NRAC. . . . . . . Naval Research Advisory Committee
NARAD. . . . . . Naval Research and Development
NAREC. . . . . . Naval Research Electronic Computer
NAVRESLAB. . . Naval Research Laboratory
NRL. . . . . Naval Research Laboratory (ONR)
NRR . . . . Naval Research Reactor
NRR . . . . Naval Research Requirement
NRRC. . . . . . . Naval Research Reserve Company
NRS . . . . Naval Research Section (Library of Congress)
NAVRES . . . . . Naval Reserve
NR. . . . . Naval Reserve
NRAB . . . . . . Naval Reserve Air Base
NRA . . . . Naval Reserve Association
NRAF . . . . . . Naval Reserve Auxiliary Field
NRAB . . . . . . Naval Reserve Aviation Base
NRMC . . . . . . Naval Reserve Manpower Center
NRM . . . . Naval Reserve Medal
NAVRESMIDSCOL. . Naval Reserve Midshipmen's School
NRMS. . . . . . . Naval Reserve Midshipmen's School
NROS . . . . . . Naval Reserve Officer School
NROTC . . . . . Naval Reserve Officers' Training Corps

NRTC . . . . Naval Reserve Training Center
NAVRETRAINCOM . . Naval Retraining Command
NRC. . . . . Naval Retraining Command
NSAM . . . . . . Naval School of Aviation Medicine
NSMG . . . . . . Naval School of Military Government
NSMG & A . . . Naval School of Military Government and Administration
NSM. . . . . . . Naval School of Music
NS & T . . . . . Naval Science and Tactics
NSTIC . . . . . . Naval Science Technical Information Center (British)
NSU. . . . . Naval Scout Unit
NAVSECGRU . . Naval Security Group
NSG . . . . Naval Security Group
NSGA . . . . . . Naval Security Group Activity
NAVSECGRUDET . . Naval Security Group Detachment
NSHO . . . . . . Naval Service Headquarters, Ottawa, Canada
NSEC . . . . . . Naval Ship Engineering Center
NSMSES . . . . . Naval Ship Missile Systems Engineering Station
NSRDC. . . . . . Naval Ship Research and Development Center
NAVSHIPSYSCOM . . Naval Ship Systems Command
NSSC . . . . . . Naval Ship Systems Command
NAVSHIPYD . . Naval Shipyard
NS . . . . Naval Shipyard
NSY . . . . Naval Shipyard
NSYD . . . . . . Naval Shipyard
NSEEC . . . . . Naval Shore Electronics Engineering Center
NSPD . . . . . . Naval Shore Patrol Detachment
NSCF . . . . . . Naval Small Craft Facilities
NAVSPASUR . . Naval Space Surveillance System
NSO . . . . Naval Staff Officer
NSB . . . . Naval Standardization Board
NAVSTA . . . . Naval Station
NS . . . . Naval Station
NSA. . . . . . . Naval Stock Account
NSF . . . . Naval Stock Fund
NSCP . . . . . . Naval Stores Conservation Program
CANAVSTORES. . Naval Stores Officer (Canadian Navy)
NSS . . . . Naval Strategic Study
NSB . . . . Naval Submarine Base
NSF . . . . Naval Supersonic Facility
NSL . . . . Naval Supersonic Laboratory
NSA. . . . . . . Naval Supply Account
NSAF . . . . . . Naval Supply Account Fund
NSC . . . . Naval Supply Center
NSD. . . . . . . Naval Supply Depot
NSDA . . . . . . Naval Supply Depot Annex
NSF . . . . Naval Supply Force
NAVSO . . . . . Naval Supply Office
NSRS . . . . . . Naval Supply Radio Station
NSRDF . . . . . Naval Supply Research and Development Facility
NAVSUPSYSCOM . . Naval Supply Systems Command
NSSC . . . . . . Naval Supply Systems Command
NSUPSC . . . . Naval Supply Systems Command (Formerly, Bureau of Supplies and Accounts)
NAVSUPFORANT . . Naval Support Forces, Antarctica
NTS . . . . Naval Target Subdivision (G-2, SHAEF)
NTA. . . . . . . Naval Technical Assistants
NAVTECMISEU . . Naval Technical Mission in Europe
NTME . . . . . . Naval Technical Missions in Europe
NAVTECHJAP . . Naval Technical Mission to Japan
NTMJ . . . . . . Naval Technical Missions in Japan
NTTC . . . . . . Naval Technical Training Center
NAVTORPSTA . . Naval Torpedo Station
NTORS . . . . . Naval Torpedo Station
NTS . . . . Naval Torpedo Station (BUWEPS)
NTTR . . . . . . Naval Torpedo Testing Range
NT. . . . . Naval Training
NTC. . . . . . . Naval Training Center
NAVTRADEVCEN . . Naval Training Device Center
NTDC . . . . . . Naval Training Devices Center
NAVTRADISTCEN . . Naval Training and Distribution Center
NT & DC. . . . Naval Training and Distribution Center
NAVTRASCOL . . Naval Training School
NTS . . . . Naval Training School (or Station)
NTSCH . . . . . Naval Training School
NAVTRASTA . . Naval Training Station
NTU. . . . . . . Naval Training Unit
NAVTRANSAIR. . (For) Naval Transport Aircraft Class Travel, Priority is Hereby Certified
NTO . . . . . . Naval Transport Officer
NTS . . . . Naval Transport Service
NAVTRANSCO. . Naval Transportation Control Office
NTS . . . . Naval Transportation Service

NTI . . . . Naval Travel Instructions
NURDC . . . . . Naval Undersea Research and Development Center (Formerly, NUWC)
NUWC . . . . . . Naval Undersea Warfare Center (Later, NURDC)
NUOS . . . . . . Naval Underwater Ordnance Station (BUWEPS)
NUSL. . . . . . . Naval Underwater Sound Laboratory
NUWRES . . . . Naval Underwater Weapons Research and Engineering Station (Newport, Rhode Island)
NUWS . . . . . . Naval Underwater Weapons Station
NUWSEC . . . . Naval Underwater Weapons Systems Engineering Center
NAVWARCOL . . Naval War College
NAWC . . . . . . Naval War College
NWC . . . . Naval War College
NWA . . . . Naval Warfare Analysis
NAVWAG . . . . Naval Warfare Analysis Group
NWAG . . . . . . Naval Warfare Analysis Group
NWIP . . . . . . Naval Warfare Information Publication
NWP . . . . Naval Warfare Publications
NWA . . . . Naval Weapons Annex
NWEF. . . . . . . Naval Weapons Evaluation Facility
NWF . . . . Naval Weapons Factory (Formerly, NGF)
NWIRP . . . . . . Naval Weapons Industrial Reserve Plant
NWL . . . . Naval Weapons Laboratory (BUWEPS)
NWP . . . . Naval Weapons Publications
NAVWPNQUALASSURO. . Naval Weapons Quality Assurance Office
NAVWPNSERVO. . Naval Weapons Services Office (Also known as WEPSO or NWSO)
NWSO . . . . . . Naval Weapons Services Office
WEPSO . . . . . . Naval Weapons Services Office (Also known as NWSO and NAVWPNSERVO)
NWS . . . . Naval Weapons Station
NWRF . . . . . . Naval Weather Research Facility
NWSD . . . . . . Naval Weather Service Division
NWSO . . . . . . Naval Weather Service Office
NWF. . . . . . . Naval Working Fund (Navy, Coast Guard)
N . . . . Navigate, Navigating, or Navigation
NLS . . . . Navigating Light System
NAVAID . . . . . Navigation Aid
NATCAS . . . . . Navigation, Air Traffic Control and Collision Avoidance System
NAB . . . . Navigation-Avoidance System
NAVICERT . . . Navigation Certificate (Paper issued by British government to merchant vessel, certifying that cargo was noncontraband; that is, not consigned to Germany) (World War II)
NAVCM . . . . . Navigation Countermeasures and Deception
NAVDAC . . . . Navigation Data Assimilation Computer
NIDS . . . . Navigation Instrument Development Unit
NLF . . . . Navigation Light Flasher
NMC . . . . Navigation Map Computer
NO . . . . Navigation Officer
NOCC . . . . . . Navigation Operational Checkout Console
NAVAR . . . . . Navigation RADAR
NAVASCREEN. . Navigation RADAR Screen (Air Force)
NAVARHO . . . Navigation and Radio Homing (Aviation)
NAVS . . . . . . Navigation System
NAB . . . . Navigational Aid to Bombing (Air Force)
NAFIS . . . . . . Navigational Aid Flight Inspection System
NAIOP. . . . . . Navigational Aid Inoperative for Parts
NIO. . . . . . . Navigational Information Office
NMP . . . . Navigational Microfilm Projector
NR. . . . . Navigational RADAR
NAVSAT . . . . . Navigational Satellite
NBT . . . . Navigator Bombardier Training (Air Force)
NTS . . . . Navigator Training Squadrons (Air Force)
N . . . . Navy
NADO . . . . . . Navy Accounts Disbursing Office
NAVAER . . . . Navy Aeronautics
NACEL . . . . . Navy Air Crew Equipment Laboratory (Philadelphia, Pennsylvania)
NAWAF . . . . . Navy with Air Force
NANEP . . . . . Navy Air Navigation Electronic Project
NALC . . . . . . Navy Ammunition Logistics Code
NAR . . . . Navy Ammunition Reclassification
NAVARA . . . . Navy Appellate Review Activity
NAAO . . . . . . Navy Area Audit Office (London)
NAWAR . . . . . Navy with Army
NAAFI . . . . . . Navy, Army and Air Force Institutes (Responsible for clubs, canteens, and provision of some items for messing of British armed forces)
NAVAUD . . . . Navy Auditor
NARDIS . . . . . Navy Automated Research and Development Information System
NBC . . . . Navy Beach Commando
NBPA . . . . . . Navy Board for Production Awards
NAVBOILAB . . Navy Boiler Laboratory
NCL . . . . Navy Calibration Laboratory
NCDO . . . . . . Navy Central Disbursing Office

REVERSE ACRONYMS AND INITIALISMS DICTIONARY

NAVCENFRACO .. Navy Central Freight Control Office	NMPO ...... Navy Motion Picture Office
NCPI .... Navy Civilian Personnel Instructions	NAVMUTAID .. Navy Mutual Aid
NCTO ...... Navy Clothing and Textile Supply Office	NMA ...... Navy Mutual Aid Association
NCUSA...... Navy Club of the United States of America	NMAA ...... Navy Mutual Aid Association
COMNAV.... Navy Command (Part of North American Air Defense Command)	NNSS ..... Navy Navigational Satellite System
NCA ...... Navy Contract Administrator	NANWEP..... Navy Numerical Weather Prediction
NCSLO...... Navy Control of Shipping Liaison Officer	NNC ...... Navy Nurse Corps
NACO ...... Navy Cool (Gunpowder)	NOP .... Navy Objectives Plan
NCIS .... Navy Cost Information System	NOSM ...... Navy Occupation Service Medal
NC .... Navy Cross	NOMAD ..... Navy Oceanographic Meteorological Automatic Device (Navy)
ND .... Navy Department	NOCT ...... Navy Overseas Cargo Terminals
NDBCA...... Navy Department Board of Contract Appeals	NPO .... Navy Post Office
NDB....... Navy Department Bulletin	NPA....... Navy Postal Affairs Section Publication
NDBULCUMED .. Navy Department Bulletins, Cumulative Editions	NPE .... Navy Preliminary Evaluation
NDGO...... Navy Department General Order	NPAB ...... Navy Price Adjustment Board
NDP....... Navy Department Personnel	NPAC ...... Navy Procurement Assignment Committee
NDPIC ...... Navy Department Program Information Center	NPD....... Navy Procurement Directives
NAVPUBSCONBD .. Navy Department Publications Control Board	NPR....... Navy Procurement Regulation
NDO....... Navy Disbursing Office	NPPO....... Navy Program and Planning Office
NEW ...... Navy Early Warning	NPPO....... Navy Publications and Printing Office
NELM ...... Navy Elements Atlantic and Mediterranean	NPPS ...... Navy Publications and Printing Service
NEC .... Navy Enlisted Code	NPPSO...... Navy Publications and Printing Services Office
NESEP ...... Navy Enlisted Scientific Education Program	NAVPUR ..... Navy Purchasing Office
NEDU...... Navy Experimental Diving Unit	NPO .... Navy Purchasing Office
NFCU...... Navy Federal Credit Union	NARATE ..... Navy RADAR Automatic Test Equipment
NFSA ...... Navy Field Safety Association	NRFSA ..... Navy Radio Frequency Spectrum Activity
NFC .... Navy Finance Center	NRB....... Navy Recruiting Bureau
NFO .... Navy Finance Office	NRAO...... Navy Regional Accounts Office
NFMS ...... Navy Fleet Material Support	NRFO...... Navy Regional Finance Office
NAVFROF .... Navy Freight Office	NAVREGS .... Navy Regulations
NFSO....... Navy Fuel Supply Office	NR......... Navy Regulations
NG .... Navy General (MCD files)	NAVREL ..... Navy Relief Society
NAVGEN .... Navy General Publications	NRS....... Navy Relief Society
NGCM...... Navy Good Conduct Medal	NRDU-V ..... Navy Research and Development Unit – Vietnam
NHO....... Navy Hydrographic Office (Later, NOO)	NRB....... Navy Reservation Bureau
NIA .... Navy Industrial Association	NRT....... Navy Reserve Training
NIF .... Navy Industrial Fund	NAVROUTE ... Navy Routing Office
NICOP...... Navy Industry Cooperation Plan	NSEF ...... Navy Security Engineering Facility
NAVIC...... Navy Information Center	NSC....... Navy Service Center
NIS .... Navy Inspection Service	NSSO....... Navy Ships' Store Office (PX)
NAICOM/MIS .. Navy-Integrated Command Management Information System	NSFO...... Navy Special Fuel Oil
NICRISP ..... Navy Integrated Comprehensible Repairable Item Scheduling Program	NSP....... Navy Standard Part
NICO....... Navy Inventory Control Office	NAVSTRIP .... Navy Standard Requisitioning and Issuing Procedure
NJPMB ..... Navy Jet Propelled Missile Board	NSCS....... Navy Supply Corps School
NJC....... Navy Job Classification Manual	NTDS ...... Navy Tactical Data System (Computer system)
NL .... Navy League	NTDO ...... Navy Technical Data Office (of the Office of Naval Material)
NLUS ...... Navy League of the United States	NTE........ Navy Teletypewriter Exchange (Later, NTX)
NLOGM..... Navy Liaison Office for Guided Missiles	NTLDO...... Navy Terminal Leave Disbursing Office
NLSC...... Navy Lockheed Service Center	NATRI ...... Navy Training Requirements Information
NLCP...... Navy Logistics Capabilities Plan	NUSRL ...... Navy Underwater Sound Reference Laboratory
NAVLIS ..... Navy Logistics Information System	NUMIS...... Navy Uniform Management Information System
NLRG ...... Navy Long-Range Guidance	NUC .... Navy Unit Commendation
NLRSS ...... Navy Long-Range Strategic Study	NWCRB ..... Navy War Contracts Relief Board
NMC ...... Navy Mail Clerk	NWCA ...... Navy Wives Clubs of America
NMCLK ..... Navy Mail Clerk	NY .... Navy Yard
NMMFO ..... Navy Maintenance Management Field Office	NYD .... Navy Yard
NMMMS..... Navy Maintenance and Material Management System (Also known as MMM and 3M)	NYBOS...... Navy Yard, Boston, Massachusetts
NMO....... Navy Management Office	NYCHARL .... Navy Yard, Charleston, South Carolina
NMSB...... Navy Manpower Survey Board	NYMI....... Navy Yard, Mare Island, California
N & MC .... Navy and Marine Corps (Medal)	NYNYK ..... Navy Yard, New York, New York
NMCM..... Navy and Marine Corps Medal	NYNOR .... Navy Yard, Norfolk, Virginia
N & MCM.... Navy and Marine Corps Medal	NYPH....... Navy Yard, Pearl Harbor, Hawaii
NMRTC...... Navy and Marine Corps Reserve Training Center	NYPHIL ..... Navy Yard, Philadelphia, Pennsylvania
NMCSA ..... Navy Material Command Support Activity	NYPORT .... Navy Yard, Portsmouth, New Hampshire
NAVMATMOCON ..Navy Material Movement Control Plan	NYPS ...... Navy Yard, Puget Sound (Bremerton), Washington
NMRC ...... Navy Material Redistribution Center	NYWASH ..... Navy Yard, Washington, DC (Obsolete)
NMR & DA ... Navy Material Redistribution and Disposition Administration	NWMS ...... Nazarene World Missionary Society
NMTO ...... Navy Material Transportation Office	NPU........ Ne Plus Ultra (No Further; i.e., the pinnacle of attainment)
NAMRU ..... Navy Medical Research Unit (World War II)	NERO....... Near Earth Rescue Operation (NASA)
NMC .... Navy Memorandum Correction	NEADS ...... Near East and African Development Service
NMRG ...... Navy Mid-Range Guidance	NECA ...... Near East College Association
NMRO ...... Navy Mid-Range Objectives	NEED ...... Near East Emergency Donations
NMS ...... Navy Mid-Range Study	NEFC ...... Near East Forestry Commission
NMAP ...... Navy Military Assistance Programs	NEF .... Near East Foundation
NMG ...... Navy Military Government	NESA ...... Near East and South Asia (State Department)
NAVMINCOMEASTA.. Navy Mine Countermeasures Station	NEXT .... Near-End Crosstalk Loss
NAVMINDEFLAB .. Navy Mine Defense Laboratory	NF .... Near Face (Technical drawings)
NMDL ...... Navy Mine Defense Laboratory (BUWEPS)	NLTS .... Near Launch Tracking System
NMCA ...... Navy Mothers' Clubs of America	NP .... Near Point
NMPX ...... Navy Motion Picture Exchange	NPC .... Near Point of Convergence
	NS .... Near Side (Technical drawings)

NSRT . . . . Near-Surface Radiation Thermometer
NV . . . . Near Vertical (Aerospace)
NLF . . . . Nearest Landing Field
NBLE . . . . . . Nearly Best Linear Estimator (Statistics)
NB . . . . Nebraska
NU . . . . Nebraska University
NN . . . . Necessary Nuisance (i.e., a husband) (Slang)
NSU. . . . . . . Neckarsulm (Location in Wuerttemberg, Germany, of NSU Werke, automobile manufacturer; initialism used as name of its cars)
NWAB . . . . . . Necks With Any Boy (Slang)
NVV . . . . Nederlands Verbond van Vakverenigingen (Netherlands Federation of Trade Unions)
NBT . . . . Nederlandse Bond van Middelbare en Hogare Technici (Netherlands Union of Professional Engineers)
NTB . . . . Nederlandse Toonkunstenaarsbond (Netherlands Musicians' Union)
NVC . . . . Nederlandse Vakcentrale (Netherlands Trade Union Central)
NNP . . . . Needle Nosed Probe
NGA . . . . Needlework Guild of America
NBD . . . . Negative Binomial Distribution (Statistics)
NEMAG . . . . . Negative Effective Mass Amplifiers and Generators
NIB . . . . Negative Impedance Booster
NIC. . . . . Negative Impedance Converter
NIT . . . . Negative Income Tax
NIPO . . . . . . Negative Input, Positive Output
NLS . . . . Negative Lens Systems
NLL. . . . . Negative Logic Level
NNP . . . . Negative Node Point
NPN . . . . Negative-Positive-Negative (Transistor)
NONEG . . . . Negative Replies Neither Required nor Desired
NR. . . . . Negative Resistance
NRD . . . . Negative Resistance Diode
NTC. . . . . Negative Temperature Coefficient
NVA . . . . Negative Vorticity Advection (Aviation)
NMA . . . . Negligee Manufacturers Association
NSF . . . . Negotiated Search Facility (Information retrieval)
N . . . . Negro, Negroid
NAG . . . . Negro Actors Guild of America
NAGA . . . . . . Negro Actors Guild of America
NALC. . . . . . . Negro American Labor Council
NEED . . . . . . Negro Education Emergency Drive
NEC . . . . Negro Ensemble Company (A theater group)
NHSA. . . . . . . Negro Historical Society of America
NIEU . . . . Negro Industrial and Economic Union
NLC . . . . Negro Labor Committee
NEWS . . . . . . Neighborhood Environmental Workshops (Program of Full Circle Associates, group serving the urban poor)
NF. . . . . Neighborhood Final Fade
NLSP . . . . Neighborhood Legal Services Program
NYC. . . . . Neighborhood Youth Corps (Department of Labor)
NOW . . . . Neighbors of Woodcraft
NRT . . . . Neighbours of the Roundtable
NPD. . . . . Neimann-Pick's disease
NEB . . . . Neisner Brothers, Inc. (NYSE symbol)
NEA . . . . Nelson & Albermarle Railway (AAR code)
NECOLIM. . . . Neocolonialist, Colonialist, and Imperialist
Nd . . . . Neodymium (Chemical element)
NLI . . . . Neodymium LASER Illuminator
NLS . . . . Neodymium LASER System
Ne . . . . Neon (Chemical element)
Np. . . . . Neper
N . . . . Nephew
NPM . . . . Neptune Meter Company (NYSE symbol)
Np . . . . Neptunium (Chemical element)
NGF . . . . Nerve Growth Factor
NS . . . . Nervous System
NS & SO . . . . Nervous System and Sense Organs
N . . . . Nervus (Nerve) (Anatomy)
N . . . . Net
NETAPPS . . . . Net Ad-Produced Purchases (Advertising)
AKN . . . . . Net Cargo Ship (Navy symbol)
NCS . . . . Net Control Station (Communications) (Amateur radio)
NET . . . . Net Equivalent Temperature
NESCNSC. . . . Net Evaluation Subcommittee, National Security Council
NEW . . . . Net Explosive Weight
AN . . . . Net Laying Ship (Navy symbol)
NLT. . . . . Net Long Ton
NMP . . . . Net Material Product (Economics)
NNP . . . . Net National Product (Economics)
NPSH . . . . . . Net Positive Suction Head (Pumps)
NP. . . . . Net Proceeds
NR. . . . . Net Register (Shipping)

NRT . . . . Net Register Ton
NRR . . . . Net Retail Requirements
YN . . . . Net Tender (Navy symbol)
YNT. . . . . Net Tender (Tug Class) (Navy symbol)
NTM . . . . Net Ton Mile (Shipping)
NT. . . . . Net Tons (Shipping)
NUR. . . . . Net Unduplicated Research
NW . . . . Net Weight
NAF. . . . . Netherland-America Foundation
NAUL . . . . . . Netherland-America University League
NBS . . . . Netherland Benevolent Society of New York
NL . . . . Netherlands (NATO)
NCP. . . . . Netherlands and Colonial Philately
NEI . . . . Netherlands East Indies
NM . . . . Netherlands Museum
NRC. . . . . Netherlands Red Cross
NUFFIC . . . . . Netherlands Universities Foundation for International Co-operation
NWI . . . . Netherlands West Indies
NAFT . . . . . . Network for Analysis of Fireball Trajectories
NASAP. . . . . . Network Analysis for Systems Applications Program (Computer program) (NASA)
NCG . . . . Network Control Group
NC. . . . . Network Controller
NDR. . . . . Network Data Reduction
NIS . . . . Network Information System (AT & T)
NOF. . . . . Network Operations and Facilities
NRA . . . . Network Resolution Area
NSD. . . . . Network Status Display
NETS . . . . . . Network Techniques
NF . . . . Neue Folge (New Series) (Bibliography)
NNS . . . . Neural Network Simulator
NCA . . . . Neurocirculatory Asthenia (Medicine)
NM . . . . Neuromuscular
NP. . . . . Neuropsychiatric or Neuropsychiatry
NPI . . . . Neuro-Psychiatric Institute
NRU . . . . Neuropsychiatric Research Unit (Navy)
NPC. . . . . Neuropsychiatry Clerical Procedure (Navy)
NP-CLT . . . . . Neuropsychiatry Clerical Procedure Technician (Navy)
NPC. . . . . Neuropsychiatry Clerical Technician (Navy)
NPT . . . . Neuropsychiatry Technician (Navy)
NSC . . . . Neurosecretory Cells
NSM . . . . Neurosecretory Material
NS . . . . Neurosurgery, Neurosurgeon
NSA . . . . Neurosurgical Society of America
NSQ . . . . Neuroticism Scale Questionnaire
NAIL . . . . Neurotics Anonymous International Liaison
N . . . . Neuter
N . . . . Neutral
NF . . . . Neutral Fraction
NGS . . . . Neutral Grain Spirits
NNSC . . . . . . Neutral Nations Supervisory Commission
NPH. . . . . Neutral Protamine Hegedorn (Insulin)
NSSC . . . . . . Neutral Sulfite Semichemical (Pulp)
N . . . . Neutron (as in N-Ray)
NAA. . . . . Neutron Activation Analysis
NIGA . . . . . . Neutron-Induced Gamma Activity
NMM . . . . Neutron Magnetic Moment
NSR . . . . Neutron Source Reactor
NV . . . . Nevada
NN . . . . Nevada Northern Railway Company (AAR code)
NVP. . . . . Nevada Power Company (NYSE symbol)
NTS . . . . Nevada Test Site (AEC)
NH . . . . Never Hinged
NW . . . . Neville and Winther's Acid
N . . . . Nevins (NYSE symbol)
NAI . . . . New Acronyms and Initialisms (A publication)
NAL . . . . New American Library (Publisher)
NA . . . . New Associations (A publication) (Later, NAP)
NAP. . . . . New Associations and Projects (A publication) (Formerly, NA)
NBS. . . . . New British Standard (Imperial wire gage)
NB. . . . . New Brunswick (Canadian province)
NBAO. . . . . . . New Brunswick Area Office (AEC)
NBL. . . . . New Brunswick Laboratory (AEC)
NC . . . . New Caledonia
NCE . . . . New Catholic Edition (Bible)
NCE. . . . . New Catholic Encyclopedia
N/C. . . . . New Charter (Navigation)
NCCV . . . . . . New Construction and Conversion
NCCR . . . . . . New Construction/Conversion Requirements System
NC . . . . New Crop
NCAD . . . . . . New Cumberland Army Depot

NDP . . . . New Democratic Party (Canadian)
NDRB . . . . New Developments Research Branch (Navy)
NDC . . . . New Dramatists Committee
NDA . . . . New Drug Application
NDUSTA . . . . . New Duty Station (Navy)
NEP . . . . New Economic Policy (Program of USSR, 1921-28)
NE . . . . New Edition
NEF . . . . New Education Fellowship
NE . . . . New England
NEABFGP . . . . New England Advisory Board for Fish and Game Problems
NEBHE . . . . . . New England Board of Higher Education
NECNVA . . . . . New England Committee for Nonviolent Action
NECDC . . . . . New England Consumer Development Council
NEC . . . . New England Council
NEDL . . . . New England Deposit Library
NED . . . . New England Division (Army Engineers)
NEEDS . . . . . . New England Educational Data Systems
NEES . . . . . . New England Electric System
NES . . . . New England Electric System (NYSE symbol)
NEFCO . . . . . . New England Fish Company
NEFE . . . . . . New England Fish Exchange
NEGRO . . . . . New England Grass Roots Organization
NEHGS . . . . . New England Historic Genealogical Society
NEKOA . . . . . New England Knitted Outerwear Association
NELA . . . . . . New England Library Association
NELINET . . . . New England Library Information Network
NEMRIP . . . . . New England Marine Resources Information Program
NEMEA . . . . . New England Media Evaluators Association
NEMCH . . . . . New England Medical Center Hospitals
NEOP . . . . . . New England Order of Protection
NEPEA . . . . . . New England Project on Education of the Aging
NERMLS . . . . . New England Regional Medical Library Service
NERAC . . . . . New England Research Application Center (University of Connecticut)
NESDEC . . . . . New England School Development Council
NESLA . . . . . . New England Shoe and Leather Association
NTT . . . . New England Telephone & Telegraph Company (NYSE symbol)
NEAC . . . . . . New English Art Club
NEB . . . . New English Bible
NED . . . . New English Dictionary (i.e., the Oxford English Dictionary)
NEFOS . . . . . New Emerging Forces
NEI . . . . New Equipment Introduction (Army)
NEIT . . . . New Equipment Introductory Team (Army)
NEPRS . . . . . New Equipment Personnel Requirements Summary (Army)
NEXT . . . . . . New/Experimental Techniques
NEN . . . . New Eyes for the Needy
NFA . . . . New Farmers of America
NF . . . . New Franc (French currency)
NG . . . . New Genus
NG . . . . New Guinea
NGVR . . . . . New Guinea Volunteer Reserve
NH . . . . New Hampshire
NHG . . . . New High German
NHA . . . . New Homemakers of America
NICCO . . . . . . New Inner City Community Organization (Washington, DC)
NIRTS . . . . . . New Integrated Range Timing System
NID . . . . New International Dictionary (Webster's)
NJ . . . . New Jersey
NJII . . . . New Jersey, Indiana & Illinois R. R. (AAR code)
NJNY . . . . . . New Jersey & New York R. R. (AAR code)
NJP . . . . New Jersey Power & Light Company (NYSE symbol)
NL . . . . New Latin
NLL . . . . New Life League
NL . . . . New Line
NLC . . . . New Location Code (Military)
NEWLON . . . . New London, Connecticut
NL . . . . New London, Connecticut
NLONTEVDET . . New London Test and Evaluation Detachment
NMST . . . . . . New Materials System Test
NM . . . . New Mexico
NMEX . . . . . . New Mexico
NMHU . . . . . . New Mexico Highlands University
NMMI . . . . . . New Mexico Military Institute
NMPG . . . . . . New Mexico Proving Ground
NMSU . . . . . . New Mexico State University
NMWC . . . . . . New Mexico Western College
NND . . . . New and Non-official Drugs (Pharmacy)
NNR . . . . New and Non-official Remedies (Publication)
NOA . . . . New Obligational Authority
NOELS . . . . . . New Office Education Learning Systems
NO . . . . New Orleans (Louisiana)
NOART . . . . . New Orleans Army Terminal

NOJC . . . . . . New Orleans Jazz Club
NLC . . . . New Orleans & Lower Coast R. R. (AAR code)
NONE . . . . . . New Orleans & Northeastern R. R. (AAR code)
NOPE . . . . . . New Orleans Port of Embarkation
NOPB . . . . . . New Orleans Public Belt R. R. (AAR code)
NOT . . . . New Orleans Terminal R. R. (AAR code)
NOTM . . . . . . New Orleans, Texas & Mexico Railway Company (AAR code)
NOTP . . . . . . New Orleans Times Picayune (A newspaper)
NODEX . . . . . New Over the Beach Discharge Exercise
NP . . . . New Paragraph
NOZ . . . . New Process Company (NYSE symbol)
NPEF . . . . . . New Product Evaluation Form
NPR . . . . New Production Reactor (Electronic)
NP . . . . New Providence
NS . . . . New School
NSOB . . . . . . New Senate Office Building
NST . . . . New Serial Titles (A publication of Library of Congress)
NS . . . . New Series (Bibliography)
NS . . . . New Side
NSP . . . . New Species
NSW . . . . New South Wales
NS . . . . New Style
NT . . . . New Testament (of the Bible)
NT . . . . New Translation
NTM . . . . New Tribes Mission
NUC . . . . New University Conference
NV . . . . New Version (of the Bible)
NWB . . . . New War Department Building
NWC . . . . New World Club
NWF . . . . New World Foundation
NY . . . . New Year
NY . . . . New York (City or State)
NYK . . . . New York (City)
NY . . . . New York (Naval Shipyard)
NYAS . . . . . . New York Academy of Sciences
NYAMP . . . . . New York Advertising Media Planners
NRB . . . . New York Air Brake Company (NYSE symbol)
NYAB . . . . . . New York Air Brake Company
NYPFO . . . . . New York Air Force Procurement Field Office
NY . . . . New York Airways, Inc.
NYA . . . . New York Airways, Inc.
NYAP . . . . . . New York Assembly Program (Data processing)
NYABIC . . . . . New York Association for Brain Injured Children
NYAIC . . . . . New York Association of Industrial Communicators
NYANA . . . . . New York Association for New Americans
NYBT . . . . . . New York Board of Trade
NYCC . . . . . . New York Candy Club
NYCBAN . . . . New York Center Beacon Alphanumerics (FAA)
NYC . . . . New York Central R. R. (AAR code)
CN . . . . New York Central R. R. Company (Later, Penn Central) (NYSE symbol)
NKP . . . . New York, Chicago & St. Louis R. R. Company (NYSE symbol) (Wall Street slang name: "Nickel Plate")
NYC & STL . . . New York, Chicago and St. Louis Railroad Company
NYC . . . . New York City
NYCCC . . . . . New York City Community College
NYMA . . . . . New York City Metropolitan Area
NEYO . . . . . . New York City National Park Service Group
NYCHA . . . . . New York Clearing House Association
NYCME . . . . . New York Clothing Manufacturers Exchange
NYCSA . . . . . New York Coat & Suit Association
NYCE . . . . . . New York Cocoa Exchange
NYCSE . . . . . New York Coffee and Sugar Exchange
NYCTCG . . . . New York Cold Type Composition Group
NYCSA . . . . . New York College Stores Association
NYCER . . . . . New York Conference on Electronic Reliability
NYCN . . . . . . New York Connecting R. R. (AAR code)
NYCSG . . . . . New York Constitution Study Group
NYCE . . . . . . New York Cotton Exchange
NYCFMA . . . . New York Credit and Financial Management Association
NYCDC . . . . . New York Curtain and Drapery Club
NYD . . . . New York Dock Railway (AAR code)
NYDCC . . . . . New York Drama Critics Circle
NYEWW . . . . New York Exchange for Woman's Work
NYFD . . . . . . New York Fashion Designers
NYFBT . . . . . New York Film Board of Trade
NYFC . . . . . . New York Film Critics
NYFWA . . . . . New York Financial Writers Association
NYFFFBA . . . . New York Foreign Freight Forwarders and Brokers Association
NYGBS . . . . . New York Genealogical and Biographical Society
NYKGRP . . . . New York Group (Navy)
NYGJB . . . . . New York Guild for Jewish Blind

NYHS . . . . . . New York Historical Society
NYIDA . . . . . New York Importers and Distillers Association
NYIT . . . . . . New York Institute of Technology
NYLSMA . . . . New York Lamp and Shade Manufacturers Association
NYLB . . . . . . New York & Long Branch R. R. (AAR code)
NYMC . . . . . . New York Medical College
NYME . . . . . . New York Mercantile Exchange
NYMA . . . . . . New York Mounters Association
NYNS . . . . . . New York Naval Shipyards
NH . . . . New York, New Haven & Hartford R. R. (AAR code)
NYNH & H . . New York, New Haven and Hartford Railroad Company
NYO & W . . . . New York, Ontario and Western Railway Company
NYO . . . . . . New York Operations (AEC)
NYPC . . . . . . New York Pigment Club
NYPE . . . . . . New York Port of Embarkation
NYPE . . . . . . New York Produce Exchange
NYPL . . . . . New York Public Library
NYRMA . . . . . New York Raincoat Manufacturers Association
NYSDA . . . . . New York Security Dealers Association
NYS . . . . . . New York Shavians
NYS . . . . . . New York Shipbuilding Company
NSB . . . . New York Shipbuilding Corporation (NYSE symbol)
NYSA . . . . . New York Shipping Association
NYSSA . . . . . New York Society of Security Analysts
NYSCS . . . . . New York State Colonization Society
NGE . . . . . . New York State Electric & Gas Corporation (NYSE symbol)
NYSIIS . . . . . New York State Identification and Intelligence System
NYSE . . . . . . New York Stock Exchange
NYSW . . . . . . New York, Susquehanna & Western R. R. (AAR code)
NYTCL . . . . . New York Temperance Civic League
NYT . . . . . . The New York Times
NYU . . . . . . New York University
NZ . . . . New Zealand
NZEF . . . . . . New Zealand Expeditionary Force
NZFL . . . . . . New Zealand Federation of Labor
NZLO . . . . . . New Zealand Liaison Officer
NZ . . . . New Zealand National Airways Corporation
NZNB . . . . . New Zealand Naval Board (Wellington)
NZSEAFRON . . New Zealand Sea Frontier
EWR . . . . . . Newark (New Jersey) (Municipal airport symbol)
NCUP . . . . . . Newark Community Union Project (New Jersey)
NTCD . . . . . Newark Transportation Control Depot
JJN . . . . Newberry (J. J.) Company (NYSE symbol)
NSS . . . . Newburgh & South Shore Railway Company (AAR code)
NDV . . . . . . Newcastle Disease Virus
NSNA . . . . . . Newcomen Society in North America
NF . . . . Newfoundland (with Labrador, a Canadian province)
NFLD . . . . . . Newfoundland (Canadian province)
NFBC . . . . . . Newfoundland Base Command (Military)
NCA . . . . . . Newfoundland Club of America
N . . . . Newfoundland Standard Time (Aviation)
NEM . . . . . . Newmont Mining Corporation (NYSE symbol)
NP . . . . Newport (Rhode Island)
NND . . . . . . Newport News Shipbuilding & Dry Dock Company (NYSE symbol)
NNSB & DDCO . . Newport News Shipbuilding and Dry Dock Company
NPSB . . . . . . News Print Service Bureau
N . . . . Newspaper
NAEA . . . . . . Newspaper Advertising Executives Association
NAM . . . . . . Newspaper Association Managers
NCC . . . . . . Newspaper Comics Council
NCMA . . . . . Newspaper Credit Managers' Association
NEA . . . . Newspaper Enterprise Association (A syndicate)
NFEA . . . . . . Newspaper Farm Editors' Association
NFEC . . . . . . Newspaper Food Editors Conference
NIC . . . . Newspaper Indexing Center (Flint, Michigan)
NMDU . . . . . Newspaper & Mail Deliverers Union of New York and Vicinity
NPRA . . . . . . Newspaper Personnel Relations Association
NOM . . . . . . Newspapers on Microfilm
NIC . . . . Newsprint Information Committee
NSB . . . . Newsprint Service Bureau
N . . . . Newton (Unit of force)
N/M . . . . . . Newton per Meter
NSC . . . . . . Newtex Steamship Company (AAR code)
N/A . . . . . . Next Assembly
ND . . . . Next Day (NYSE symbol)
ND . . . . Next Day's Delivery
NHA . . . . . . Next Higher Assembly (Engineering)
NIR . . . . Next Inferior Rank
NK . . . . Next of Kin
NOK . . . . . . Next of Kin (Military)
NEPE . . . . . . Nez Perce National Historical Park

NEZP . . . . . . Nezperce R. R. Company (AAR code)
NJ . . . . Niagara Junction Railway (AAR code)
NMPC . . . . . . Niagara Mohawk Power Company
NMK . . . . . . Niagara Mohawk Power Corporation (NYSE symbol)
NSCT . . . . . . Niagara, St. Catherines & Toronto R. R. (AAR code)
NGS . . . . Niagara Share Corporation (NYSE symbol)
NCM . . . . . . Nicaraguan Campaign Medal
Ni . . . . Nickel (Chemical element)
NICHROME . . Nickel-Chromium (Alloy)
NE . . . . Nickel Equivalent (Coinage)
NP . . . . Nickel Plated (Guns)
NS . . . . Nickel Steel
NAD . . . . . . Nicotinamide-Adenine Dinucleotide
NADP . . . . . . Nicotinamide Adenine Dinucleotide Phosphate
NADPH . . . . . Nicotinamide Adenine Dinucleotide Phosphate
NMN . . . . . . Nicotinamide Mononucleotide
NA . . . . Nicotinic Acid (Biochemistry)
NAMU . . . . . Nigerian African Mine Workers' Union
NESCO . . . . . Nigerian Electricity Supply Corporation African Workers' Union
NPA . . . . Nigerian Ports Authority Clerical Workers' Union
NSUA . . . . . Nigerian Students Union in the Americas
NTUC . . . . . Nigerian Trade Union Congress
N . . . . Night (Approach & landing charts) (Aviation)
NAPS . . . . . . Night Aerial Photographic System
NACTU . . . . . Night Attack Combat Training Unit (Navy)
NBL . . . . Night Bombardment-Long Distance (Air Force)
NBS . . . . Night Bombardment-Short Distance (Air Force)
NCAP . . . . . . Night Combat Air Patrol
NITEDEVRON . . Night Development Squadron
N . . . . Night Fighter (When suffix to plane designation) (Navy)
NF . . . . Night Fighter Aircraft
N/F . . . . Night Fighter Aircraft
NFA . . . . Night Fighter Association
VF(N) . . . . . . Night Fighter Squadrons (Navy symbol)
NFQ . . . . Night Frequency (Aviation)
NIM . . . . Night Intruder Mission (Air Force)
NL . . . . Night Letter
NLT . . . . Night Letter (Telegraphic communications)
NTX . . . . "Night Letter" (Navy communications class)
NM . . . . Night Message
N & M . . . . . Night and Morning
NOD . . . . . . Night Observation Device
NOTIP . . . . . Night Observation Television in a Pod
VT(N) . . . . . . Night Torpedo Bomber Squadron (Navy symbol)
NIRO . . . . . . Nike-Iroquois (Rockets)
NOPS . . . . . Nike Operator Proficiency Scale (Army)
NS . . . . Nimbostratus (Meteorology)
NB . . . . Nimbus (Meteorology)
NAIREC . . . . . Nimbus Arctic Ice Reconnaissance (Canadian project)
NMRT . . . . . . Nimbus Meteorological Radiation Tape (NASA)
NOSS . . . . . . Nimbus Operational Satellite System (GSFC/USWB)
NOS . . . . . . Nimbus Operational System
Nb . . . . Niobium (Chemical element)
NAIG . . . . . . Nippon Atomic Industry Group (Japan)
NC . . . . Nippon Club
NDC . . . . . . Nippon Decimal Classification (Library science)
NET . . . . Nippon Educational Television (Japan)
NYK . . . . Nippon Yusen Kaisha (Japanese steamship company)
NAN . . . . Nisi Aliter Notetur (Unless Otherwise Noted)
NP . . . . Nisi Prius (Unless Before) (Law)
NO . . . . Nitric Oxide
NTA . . . . Nitrilotriacetic Acid (Chemical)
N . . . . Nitrogen (Chemical element)
NMS . . . . . . Nitrogen Measuring System
NM . . . . Nitrogen Mustards
NOR . . . . . . Nitrogen Oxide Reduction (Research in automotive air pollution)
NOX . . . . . . Nitrogen-Oxygen
NG . . . . Nitroglycerin
NA . . . . No Account (Banking)
N/A . . . . . . No Account (Business and trade, banking)
N/A . . . . No Action
NOAC . . . . . No Action Necessary
NAT . . . . . . No Action Taken
NATR . . . . . No Additional Traffic Reported (Aviation)
NAI . . . . No Airborne Intercept (Fighter aircraft lacking airborne intercept RADAR)
NAIF . . . . . . No AI-Equipped Fighters (Air Force)
NAR . . . . . . No Answer (Action) Required
NAD . . . . . . No Apparent Defect (Shipping)
NAD . . . . . . No Appreciable Disease (Medicine)
NB . . . . No Ball

NB . . . . No Bias (Relay) (Electronics)
NB . . . . No Bid(ders)
NBG . . . . No Blasted Good (Slang)
NBG . . . . No Bloody Good (British slang)
NCD . . . . No Can Do (From pidgin English)
NC . . . . No Change
NCDD . . . . . . No Change in the Due Date
NCE . . . . No Change in Estimates
NCWX . . . . . . No Change in Weather (Aviation)
NC . . . . No Charge
NC. . . . . No Circuits
NCV . . . . No Commercial Value (Business and trade)
NCUP . . . . . . No Commission Until Paid
NC . . . . No Connection (Technical drawings) (Radio)
NC . . . . No Contest (Sports)
ND . . . . No Date (of publication)
NDC . . . . No Date Club (Brooklyn girls – no dates for the duration) (World War II)
NDG . . . . No Date Given
ND . . . . No Decision (Sports)
NDE . . . . No Delay Expected
ND. . . . . No Detect
NODIS . . . . . . No Distribution
ND . . . . No Drawing (Engineering)
NDC-PS . . . . No Drawing Change Project Slip
NETR . . . . . . No Essential Traffic Reported (Aviation)
NFT . . . . No Filing Time (Aviation)
NFL . . . . No Fire Line (Military)
NFD . . . . No Fixed Date
NF . . . . No Fool
NF. . . . . No Funds (Banking)
N/F . . . . No Funds (Banking)
NFA. . . . . . . No Further Action (Shipping)
NOFIN . . . . . No Further Information
NFR . . . . No Further Requirement
NG . . . . No Go (i.e., an unacceptable arrangement)
NG . . . . No Good (Similar to IC-- Inspected and Condemned)
NHM . . . . . . No Hot Metal (Photocomposition)
NIICP . . . . . . No Increase in Contract Price
NIBMAR . . . . . No Independence Before Majority African Rule (British policy in regard to Rhodesia)
NOIFN . . . . . . No Information Available
NINA . . . . . . No Irish Need Apply (Classified advertising)
NL . . . . No Layers (Aviation)
NLFT . . . . . . No Load Frame Time
NLS . . . . No-Load Speed
NLS . . . . No Load Start
NM . . . . No Mark
NM . . . . No Message
NMI . . . . No Middle Initial
NMN . . . . . . No Middle Name
NMB . . . . . . No Military Branch
NNM . . . . . . No Neutral Mode
N/O . . . . No Orders (Business and trade)
NP . . . . No Paging
NPV . . . . No Par Value
NP or D . . . . No Place or Date
NP . . . . No Place of Publication (Bibliography)
NOPOL . . . . . No Pollution
NPSR . . . . . . No Primary Staff Responsibility (Army)
NPFS . . . . . . No Prior or Current Federal Service
NPS . . . . No Prior Service
NP . . . . No Protest (Banking)
NPNA . . . . . . No Protest Non-Acceptance (Banking)
NQB . . . . . . No Qualified Bidders
NORDO . . . . . No Radio
RADNOS . . . . . No Radio (Military)
NORAC . . . . . No Radio Contact (Aviation)
NOREC . . . . . . No Record
NRD . . . . No Record of Destination (Aviation)
NRF . . . . No Reflight
NRRS . . . . . . No Remaining Radiation Service (Unit) (Military)
NRA. . . . . . . No Repair Action (Military)
NOREP . . . . . No Reply Received
NORR . . . . . . No Reply Received
NR . . . . No Risk (Business and trade)
NRAD . . . . . . No Risk After Discharge (Shipping)
NSCSWD . . . . No Small Craft or Storm Warnings are Being Displayed (Weather)
NSR . . . . No Staff Responsibility (Army)
NSN . . . . No Stock Number
N/T . . . . No Terms (Shipping)

NTL . . . . No Time Lost (Military)
NTP . . . . No Title Page (Bibliography)
NTR . . . . No Traffic Reported (Aviation)
NT . . . . No Transmission
NTI . . . . No Travel Involved (Military)
NTIOC . . . . . . No Travel Involved for Officer Concerned (Military)
NTO . . . . No Try On (Purchaser did not have a fitting) (Merchandising slang)
NVR. . . . . . . No Voltage Release (Electronics)
NW . . . . No Wind (Air) Position (Navigation)
X. . . . . No-wind distance between pressure pattern observations
NW-NW . . . . No Work – No Woo (Slogan adopted by women war workers in Albina shipyards in Portland, Oregon, who agreed not to date men who were absent from work) (World War II)
NY. . . . . No Year
NWDS . . . . . . Noah Worcester Dermatological Society
NAHAL . . . . . Noar Halutzi Lohem (Pioneering Fighting Youth) (Israel)
No . . . . Nobelium (Chemical element)
N . . . . Nocte (At Night)
NM . . . . Nocte et Mane (Night and Morning)
NLC . . . . Noctilucent Clouds
NAS. . . . . . . Nocturnal Adoration Society
NOCO . . . . . . Noise Correlation
NC. . . . . Noise Criterion
NEB . . . . Noise Equivalent Bandwidth
NEFD . . . . . . Noise-Equivalent Flux Density
NEP . . . . Noise Equivalent Power
NEPD . . . . . . Noise Equivalent Power Density
NET . . . . Noise Equivalent Temperature
NF. . . . . Noise Factor
NF. . . . . Noise Figure
NI . . . . Noise Index
NOISE . . . . . . Noise Information Service
NLC . . . . Noise Level Cable
NLM . . . . Noise-Level Monitor (SONAR)
NLI . . . . Noise Limit Indicator
NLR . . . . Noise Load Ratio
NMB . . . . Noise, Measurement Buoy
NMTS . . . . . . Noise Measurement Test Set
NME. . . . . . . Noise-Measuring Equipment
NNI. . . . . Noise and Number Index
NOALA . . . . . . Noise-Operated Automatic Level Adjustment
NOGAD . . . . . Noise-Operated Gain-Adjusting Device
NOD . . . . Noise Output Device
NPR . . . . Noise Power Ratio
NR. . . . . Noise Ratio
NTI . . . . Noise Transmission Impairment (Telephone)
NK . . . . Nomenklatur Kommission (German) (Commission on Nomenclature) (Anatomy)
NAP. . . . . . . Nomina Anatomica Parisiensia
NHP . . . . Nominal Horsepower
NLW . . . . Nominal Line Width
N . . . . Nominative
NEI . . . . Non Est Inventus (It Has Not Been Found or Discovered)
NL . . . . Non Licet (It Is Not Permitted)
NL . . . . Non Liquet (It Is Not Clear)
NL . . . . Non Longe (Not Far)
NR . . . . Non Repetatur (Not to Be Repeated)
N/A . . . . Non-Acceptance (Business and trade)
NAMP . . . . . . Non-Accounting Majors Program
NONADD . . . Nonadditivity (Statistics)
NABU . . . . . . Non-Adjusting Ball-Up (A hopeless state of confusion) (Military slang)
NARS . . . . . . Non-Affiliated Reserve Section
NAP. . . . . . . Nonagency Purchase
NAC . . . . . . Non-Airline Carrier (Aerospace)
NAF . . . . . . Nonappropriated Fund(s)
NAFSONW . . . Nonappropriated Fund Statement of Operations and Net Worth
NC . . . . Non-Callable (A type of bond)
NCVP. . . . . . . Noncapsid Viral Protein
NOPS . . . . . . Noncoherent Optical Processing System
NOP . . . . . . Noncoherent Optical Processor
NC . . . . Noncollectible
NEO . . . . . . Noncombatant Evacuation Order (Army)
NCO . . . . . . Noncommissioned Officer (Military)
NONCOM . . . Noncommissioned Officer (Military)
NCOA . . . . . . Noncommissioned Officer Association
NCOBQ . . . . Noncommissioned Officer Bachelor Quarters
NCOIC . . . . . . Noncommissioned Officer-in-Charge (Military)
NCOLP. . . . . . Noncommissioned Officer Logistics Program (Army)
NCOOM . . . . Noncommissioned Officers' Open Mess
NONCOMECM . . Noncommunications Electronics Countermeasures (Military)
NONCOMJAM . . Noncommunications Jamming (Military)

NCM	Noncorrosive Metal
NCM	Non-Crew Member
ND	Non-Delay (Military)
NDI	Nondestructive Inspection (Military)
NDRO.	Nondestructive Readout
NDT.	Non-Destructive Testing (QCR)
NDB	Nondirectional Beacon
H	Nondirectional Radio Homing Beacon (Navigation charts)
N	None
NESTS	Non-Electric Stimulus Transfer System
NSA	Nonenyl Succinic Acid (Chemical)
NE	Nonessential
NEFA	Non-Esterified Fatty Acid (Biochemistry)
NEUM	Non-European Unity Movement
NF.	Nonferrous
NFFS	Non-Ferrous Founders Society
NF	Nonfundable
NGQ	Non-Government Quarters
NGO	Non-Governmental Organization (Generic term)
NH	Nonhygroscopic
NIPP	Non-Impact Printing Process
NIB	Non-Interference Basis
NJP	Nonjudicial Punishment (Military)
NQT.	Nonlanguage Qualification Test
NDE	Nonlinear Differential Equations
NLE	Nonlinear Element
NLKF	Nonlinear Kalmán Filter
NLR	Nonlinear Resistive
NLS	Nonlinear Smoothing
NLS	Nonlinear Systems
NLTE	Non-Local Thermodynamic Equilibrium
APN	Nonmechanized Artillery Transport (Navy symbol)
NM	Nonmetallic
NNWH	Non-Normal Working Hours
NO	Nonofficial
NOI.	Non-Operational Intelligence
NOS	Non-Oriented Satellite
NO	Non-Original
NP.	Nonparticipating (Insurance or finance)
NPL	Nonpartisan League (Political party in North Dakota opposed by the IVA)
NPDI	Non-Performance of Duty because Imprisoned (Navy)
NPL	Nonpersonal Liability
NPPR	Non-Productive Procurement Directive
NPT	Nonproliferation Treaty (to halt the spread of nuclear weapons)
NPN	Nonprotein Nitrogen (Physiology)
NRT	Nonradiating Target
NR	Nonrated
NR	Nonreactive (Relay)
NRA.	Nonregistered Accountable (Military)
NRP	Non-Registered Publication
NRPM.	Non-Registered Publications Memoranda
NRCP	Nonreinforced Concrete Pipe (Technical drawings)
NRIPMVLIC . . .	Non-Resident Inter-Province Motor Vehicle Liability Insurance Card (for travel in Canada)
NMA	Nonresonant Magnetic Amplifier
NMDA	Nonresonant Magnetic Deflection Amplifier
NMDY	Nonresonant Magnetic Deflection Yoke
NMY	Nonresonant Magnetic Yoke
NRZ.	Nonreturn to Zero
NRZC.	Nonreturn to Zero Change
NRZL.	Nonreturn to Zero Level
NRZM.	Nonreturn to Zero Mark
NRV.	Non-Revenue (Passengers or cargo) (Transportation)
ZNO	Non-rigid observation airship (Navy)
ZNP	Non-rigid patrol airship (Navy)
ZNS.	Non-rigid scouting airship (Navy)
ZNN	Non-rigid training airship (Navy)
NSI	Nonsatellite Identification
NSANL	Non-Sectarian Anti-NAZI League
NSD.	Non-Self-Destroying
NSGT	Non-Self-Governing Territories
NSC.	Non-Service Connected
NST	Nonslip Tread (Technical drawings)
NEL	Nonspecific Excitability Level (Animal behavior)
NSU.	Non-Specific Urethritis
NSP	Nonstandard Holding Pattern (Aviation)
NSI	Non-Standard Item
NSME	Nonstandard Measuring Equipment (Aviation)
NNE	Nonstandard Negro English
NSF	Nonstock Fund
NME	Nonsupervisory Manufacturing Engineer

NTB	Nontariff Barrier (Kennedy Round)
NTS	Nontariff Size
NTIR	Nontechnical Intelligence Report
NTWS.	Nontrack While Scan
NMF	Nonuniform Magnetic Field
NVOCC	Non-Vessel Owning Common Carrier (Transportation)
NV	Nonvintage (Wine)
NVM	Nonvolatile Matter
NV	Nonvoting (Business and trade) (Finance)
NWB	Non-Weight-Bearing
NF.	Nonwhite Female
NM	Nonwhite Male
NWFI	Non-Woven Fabrics Institute
N	Noon
NN	Noon
NOP	Nopco Chemical Company (NYSE symbol)
NCMC	NORAD Cheyenne Mountain Complex
NORADCOC . .	NORAD Combat Operations Center
NCC	NORAD Control Center
NDC.	NORAD Direction Center
NJMDC	NORAD Joint Manual Direction Center (Military)
NRCC	NORAD Region Combat Center (Military)
NSDC	NORAD Section Direction Center (Military)
NSDCM	NORAD Section Direction Center Manual (Military)
NA	Noradrenaline
NNO	Nord-Nord-Ouest (North-North-West) (French)
NDL	Norddeutscher Lloyd (German steamship company)
NLC	Norden Laboratories Corporation
NOSMO	Norden Optics Setting, Mechanized Operation (Air Force bombsight)
NDGA	Nordihydroguaiaretic Acid
NE.	Norepinephrine (Chemical)
NF.	Norfolk (Virginia) (Navy Yard)
NNSY	Norfolk Naval Shipyard
NNYD	Norfolk Navy Yard (Virginia)
NPB.	Norfolk & Portsmouth Belt Line R. R. (AAR code)
NSDP	Norfolk Sample Drug Program
NS	Norfolk Southern Railway Company (AAR code)
NORVA	Norfolk, Virginia (Navy)
NORVAGRP . .	Norfolk, Virginia Group (Navy)
NFK	Norfolk & Western Railway (NYSE symbol)
NW	Norfolk & Western Railway Company (AAR code)
N & W	Norfolk and Western Railway Company
NKF	Norges Kjott og Fleskesentral
NOS	Norges Offisielle Statistikk (Norway)
NTH	Norges Tekniske Hogskole
N	Normal
NBP	Normal Boiling Point
NDR	Normal Daily Requirement (Military)
NED	Normal Equivalent Deviation
NG	Normal Graduate
NHS	Normal Human Serum
NHE	Normal Hydrogen Electrode
NI	Normal Impurity (Metals)
NICE	Normal Input-Output Control Executive (Data processing)
NMPF.	Normal Magnitude Probability Function
NMO	Normal Mode Operation
NMR	Normal Mode Rejection
NPS	Normal Pipe Size
NP	Normal Pressure
NPT	Normal Pressure and Temperature
NRS	Normal Rabbit Serum
NRP	Normal Rated Power
NRC	Normal Retinal Correspondence
NS	Normal Saline
NSS	Normal Saline Solution
NS	Normal Serum
NSR	Normal Sinus Rhythm (Physiology)
N	Normal Solution
NSFTD	Normal, Spontaneous, Full Term, Delivery (Medicine)
NTP.	Normal Temperature and Pressure
NT.	Normal Tour
NTC.	Normal Tour of Duty Completed
NORMSHOR . .	Normal Tour of Shore Duty
NWH	Normal Working Hours
NVA	Normalized Volt-Ampere
NC	Normally Closed (Switch)
NO	Normally Open (Switch)
NF	Norman French
NORM	Normetal R. R. (AAR code)
NMN	Normetanephrine (Chemical)
NT.	Norris-Thermador Corporation (NYSE symbol)

N . . . . Norse (Philology)
NUH . . . . Norske Ungdomsherberger
N . . . . North, Northerly, Northern
NAEB . . . . North African Economic Board (World War II)
NAT . . . . North African Theater (World War II)
NATO . . . . North African Theater of Operations (World War II)
NATOUSA . . . . North African Theater of Operations United States Army (World War II)
NA . . . . North America(n)
NAM . . . . North America
NAAE . . . . North American Academy of Ecumenists
NORAD . . . . . . North American Air Defense (Integrated United States-Canada command)
NAAAP . . . . . North American Association of Alcoholism Programs
NAA . . . . North American Aviation
NAVION . . . . North American Aviation, Inc. (Also used to refer to light aircraft of World War II)
NV . . . . North American Aviation, Inc. (NYSE symbol) (Wall Street slang name: "Navy")
NABA . . . . . . North American Ballet Association
NABDCC . . . . North American Band Directors Coordinating Committee
NABA . . . . . . North American Benefit Association
NABC . . . . . . North American Blueberry Council
NOA . . . . North American Car Corporation (NYSE symbol)
NACATS . . . . North American Clear Air Turbulence Tracking System (Aviation)
NCO . . . . North American Coal Corporation (NYSE symbol)
NACGG . . . . . North American Commercial Gladiolus Growers
NADAR . . . . . North American Data Recorder Airborne
NADOP . . . . . North American Defense Operational Plan (NORAD)
NAEGA . . . . . North American Export Grain Association
NAGPORT . . . . North American Export Grain Association
NAGBSPA . . . North American Game Breeders and Shooting Preserve Association
NAGTC . . . . . North American Gasoline Tax Conference
NAGC . . . . . . North American Gladiolus Council
NAHA . . . . . . North American Highway Association
NAIA . . . . North American Indian Association
NAJA . . . . . . North American Judges Association
NALS . . . . . . North American Lily Society
NAMRC . . . . . North American Marten Rabbit Club
NAMSA . . . . . North American Multi-Hull Sailing Association
NANA . . . . . . North American Newspaper Alliance
NAPSIC . . . . . North American Power Systems Interconnection Committee (US and Canada) (Electric power)
NAPS . . . . North American Precis Syndicate
NAR . . . . North American Rockwell Corporation
NARC . . . . . . North American Rockwell Corporation
NARTRANS . . . North American Rockwell Training and Services
NASARR . . . . North American Search and Ranging RADAR (Navy)
NASA . . . . . . North American Securities Administrators
NASU . . . . . . North American Singers Union
NASPSPA . . . . North American Society for the Psychology of Sport and Physical Activity
NASCL . . . . . . North American Student Cooperative League
NTS . . . . North American Sugar Industries, Inc. (NYSE symbol)
NASC . . . . . . North America Supply Council
NASA . . . . North American Swiss Alliance
NATIV . . . . . . North American Test Instrument Vehicle (Air Force test rocket)
NATAS . . . . . . North American Thermal Analysis Society
NAULAS . . . . North American Union Life Assurance Society
NAWAPA . . . . North American Water and Power Alliance
NAWPA . . . . . . North American Water and Power Alliance
NAWF . . . . . . North American Wildlife Foundation
NAYRU . . . . . North American Yacht Racing Union
NAYGTA . . . . North American Youth Glider Training Association
NAC . . . . North Atlantic Council
NAD . . . . North Atlantic Division (Army Engineers)
NAFTA . . . . . . North Atlantic Free Trade Area
NALI . . . . North Atlantic Lobster Institute
NAMC . . . . . . North Atlantic Military Committee
NAMILCOM . . North Atlantic Military Committee
NANCF . . . . . . North Atlantic Naval Coastal Frontier
NARS . . . . North Atlantic Radio System
NARTEL . . . . North Atlantic Radiotelephone
NAT . . . . North Atlantic Treaty
NATA . . . . . . North Atlantic Treaty Alliance
NATO . . . . . . North Atlantic Treaty Organization
PLANAT . . . . . North Atlantic Treaty Regional Planning Group
NB . . . . North Britain (i.e., Scotland)
NBR . . . . North British Railway
NC . . . . North Carolina
NCLPGA . . . . North Carolina Liquefied Petroleum Gas Association
NCSC . . . . . . North Carolina State College
NCSCR . . . . . . North Carolina State College Reactor

NCSU . . . . North Carolina State University
NOCA . . . . . . North Cascades National Park
NO . . . . North Central Airlines, Inc.
NOR . . . . North Central Airlines, Inc.
NCA . . . . North Central Association of Colleges and Secondary Schools
NCD . . . . North Central Division (Army Engineers)
NCNA . . . . . North China News Agency
ND . . . . North Dakota
NORTHAG . . . . North European Army Group (NATO)
NGCC . . . . . . North German Coal Control (Post-World War II)
NGCDO . . . . . North German Coal Distribution Organization (Post-World War II)
NGOC . . . . . . North German Oil Control (Post-World War II)
NL . . . . North Latitude
NLR . . . . North London Railway
NLG . . . . North Louisiana & Gulf R. R. (AAR code)
NNE . . . . North-Northeast
NNW . . . . North-Northwest
NORPAC . . . . North Pacific Area; North Pacific Force
NPD . . . . North Polar Distance
PN . . . . North Pole
NSMFA . . . . . North Sea Mine Force Association
NSSA . . . . North-South Skirmish Association
NVN . . . . North Vietnam
NVA . . . . North Vietnamese Army
NVAS . . . . . . North Vietnamese Army Suspect
NW . . . . North Wales
NB . . . . Northampton & Bath R. R. (AAR code)
NHAW . . . . . . Northamerican Heating and Airconditioning Wholesalers Association
NB . . . . Northbound
NE . . . . Northeast, Northeastern, Northeasterly
NASAF . . . . . Northeast African Strategic Air Force
NAC . . . . Northeast Air Command
NEAC . . . . . . Northeast Air Command
NE . . . . Northeast Airlines, Inc.
NEA . . . . Northeast Airlines, Inc.
NCTS . . . . . . Northeast Corridor Transportation System (Boston to Washington high-speed transportation)
NEREM . . . . . . Northeast Electronics Research and Engineering Meeting
NEFA . . . . . . North-East Frontier Agency (India)
NEIULS . . . . . Northeast Iowa Union List of Serials
NENYIAC . . . . Northeast-New York Inter-Agency Committee
NEO . . . . Northeast Oklahoma R. R. (AAR code)
NEPA . . . . . . Northeast Pacific Area
NEROC . . . . . Northeast Radio Observatory Corporation
NEAPD . . . . . Northeastern Air Procurement District
NBBA . . . . . . Northeastern Bird Banding Association
NIDA . . . . . . Northeastern Industrial Developers Association
NLSC . . . . . . Northeastern Louisiana State College
NEMDA . . . . . Northeastern Minnesota Development Association
NMJC . . . . . . Northeastern Mississippi Junior College
NEO . . . . Northeastern Operations Office (NASA)
NEPPCO . . . . . Northeastern Poultry Producers Council
NERHL . . . . . Northeastern Radiological Health Laboratory
NEWCC . . . . . Northeastern Weed Control Conference
NAMAE . . . . . Northern Air Materiel Area, Europe
NAMAP . . . . . Northern Air Materiel Area, Pacific
NAR . . . . Northern Alberta Railways Company (AAR code)
NACOM . . . . Northern Area Command
NAA . . . . Northern Attack Area
NAF . . . . Northern Attack Force
NAFC . . . . . . Northern Attack Force Commander (Navy)
NORBS . . . . . . Northern Base Section (Corsica)
NORCALSEC . . Northern California Section, Western Sea Frontier
NNX . . . . Northern Central Railway Company (NYSE symbol)
NCAC . . . . . . Northern Combat Area Command (Burma)
NC . . . . Northern Command
NCA . . . . Northern Consolidated Airlines
NC . . . . Northern Consolidated Airlines, Inc.
NEPU . . . . . . Northern Elements Progressive Union (Nigeria)
NFVOA . . . . . Northern Fishing Vessel Owners Association
NFP . . . . Northern Frontier Province (Kenya)
NHPMA . . . . . Northern Hardwood and Pine Manufacturers Association
NIU . . . . Northern Illinois University
NIBCO . . . . . . Northern Indiana Brass Company
NIMCGA . . . . Northern Indiana Muck Crop Growers Association
NI . . . . Northern Indiana Public Service Company (NYSE symbol)
NI . . . . Northern Ireland
NMC . . . . Northern Michigan College
NMC . . . . Northern Montana College
NNG . . . . Northern Natural Gas Company (NYSE symbol)
NNC . . . . Northern Navigation Company, Limited (AAR code)

NNF. . . . . Northern Nurses Federation
NNGA . . . . . . Northern Nut Growers Association
NOJC . . . . . . Northern Oklahoma Junior College
NORTH. . . . . Northern Operations of Rail Transportation and Highways (Alaska)
NORPAC. . . . Northern Pacific Railroad
NPM . . . . Northern Pacific Railway (AAR code)
NPRB . . . . . . Northern Pacific Railway (AAR code)
NP . . . . Northern Pacific Railway Company (NYSE symbol) (Wall Street slang name: "Nipper")
NPT . . . . Northern Pacific Terminal R. R. (AAR code)
NPC . . . . Northern Peoples Congress
NR. . . . . Northern Range (Navigation)
NRRL . . . . . . Northern Regional Research Laboratory
NRMU . . . . . Northern Rhodesia European Mineworkers' Union
MOSSA. . . . . Northern Rhodesia Mine Officials and Salaried Staff Association
NRUTUC . . . . Northern Rhodesia United Trades Union Congress
NRATUC . . . . Northern Rhodesian African Trades Union Congress
NRRTUC . . . . . Northern Rhodesian Reformed Trades Union Congress
NRM . . . . Northern Rocky Mountains
NSDJA . . . . . . Northern Sash and Door Jobbers Association
NORSOLS. . . . Northern Solomons Area
NSP. . . . . Northern States Power Company (NYSE symbol)
NSM . . . . Northern Student Movement
NT . . . . Northern Territory (Australia)
NTA . . . . Northern Textile Association
NOTIP . . . . . . Northern Tier Integration Project
NTLF . . . . Northern Troops and Landing Force
NVCC . . . . . . Northern Virginia Community College
NAI . . . . Northrop Aircraft, Incorporated
NOC . . . . Northrop Corporation (NYSE symbol)
NPRF . . . . . . Northrop Pulse Radiation Facility
NW . . . . Northwest, Northwesterly, Northwestern
NAAF. . . . . . . Northwest African Air Force
NWAAF . . . . . Northwest African Air Forces
NACAF. . . . . . Northwest African Coastal Air Force (World War II)
NAPRW. . . . . . Northwest African Photographic Reconnaissance Wing
NATAF. . . . . . Northwest African Tactical Air Force (World War II)
NAW . . . . Northwest African Waters
CANAIRNORWEST. . North-West Air Command Headquarters, Edmonton, Alberta, Canada
NW . . . . Northwest Airlines, Inc.
NWA . . . . Northwest Airlines, Inc. (NYSE symbol)
NANA . . . . . . Northwest Alaska Native Association
HEPP . . . . Northwest Association of Horticulturists, Entomologists and Plant Pathologists
NAPCU . . . . . . Northwest Association of Private Colleges and Universities
NOB . . . . Northwest Bancorporation (NYSE symbol)
NWCA . . . . . . Northwest Cherry Briners Association
NDFEA . . . . . . Northwest Dried Fruit Export Association
NFMA. . . . . . . Northwest Farm Managers Association
NWFMA . . . . . Northwest Farm Managers Association
NFA . . . . Northwest Fisheries Association
NWGA . . . . . . Northwest Guides Association
NHA . . . . Northwest Hardwood Association
NMC . . . . Northwest Michigan College
NMA . . . . Northwest Mining Association
NMJC . . . . . . Northwest Mississippi Junior College
NMSC . . . . . . Northwest Missouri State College
NWMP . . . . . . North-West Mounted Police (now the RCMP) (Canada)
NNC . . . . Northwest Nazarene College (Idaho)
NWP . . . . North-West Provinces
NWREL . . . . . . Northwest Regional Educational Laboratory
NSCA . . . . . . Northwest Salmon Canners Association
NWSF. . . . . . . Northwest Sea Frontier
NWT . . . . Northwest Territories, Canada
NORAP. . . . . . Northwestern Alumni Players
NLA . . . . Northwestern Lumbermen's Association
NWP. . . . . Northwestern Pacific R. R. (AAR code)
NORWESSEAFRON . . Northwestern Sea Frontier
NORWESSEC . . Northwestern Sector, Western Sea Frontier
NSW . . . . Northwestern Steel & Wire Company (NYSE symbol)
NWT. . . . . Northwestern Terminal R. R. (AAR code)
NAFB . . . . . . Norton Air Force Base
NRT . . . . Norton Company (NYSE symbol)
NATEL . . . . . . Nortronics Automatic Test Equipment Language
NO . . . . Norway (NATO)
NORDEK . . . . Norway-Denmark (and Finland) (Trade bloc)
NACC . . . . . . Norwegian American Chamber of Commerce
NAHA . . . . . . Norwegian-American Historical Association
NDRE . . . . . . Norwegian Defense Research Establishment
NEAA . . . . . . Norwegian Elkhound Association of America

NSA . . . . Norwegian Seamen's Association
NSAA . . . . . . Norwegian Singers Association of America
NOR . . . . Norwich Pharmacal Company (NYSE symbol)
NTC . . . . Norwich Terrier Club
NSL . . . . Norwood & St. Lawrence R. R. (AAR code)
NC . . . . Nose Cone
NF . . . . Nose Fuse
NLG . . . . Nose Landing Gear
NSP . . . . Nose Shipping Plug
NTW . . . . Nose, Tail, Waist (Aviation)
NSIC . . . . Noster Salvator Iesus Christus (Our Saviour Jesus Christ)
NSJC . . . . Noster Salvator Jesus Christus (Our Savior Jesus Christ)
ND . . . . Nostra Domina, Notre Dame (Our Lady)
NS. . . . . Nostro Signore (Our Lord)
N/A. . . . . Not Above
NAB. . . . . Not Above
NAR. . . . . Not According to Routine
NAD . . . . Not on Active Duty
NOTAL . . . . . Not at All
NAA . . . . Not Always Afloat (Shipping)
NA . . . . Not Applicable
N/A . . . . Not Applicable
NA . . . . Not Appropriated
NA. . . . . Not Assigned
NA . . . . Not Authorized
NAIIU . . . . . . Not Authorized If Issued Under
NA . . . . Not Available
NVAL . . . . . . Not Available
NBL. . . . . Not Bloody Likely (British slang)
NC . . . . Not Carried
NCW . . . . Not Complied With (Military)
NCD . . . . Not Considered Disqualifying
NIC . . . . Not in Contract (Technical drawings)
ND . . . . Not Dated (Banking, bibliography)
NODEL . . . . . Not to Delay
NDBLO . . . . . Not to Descend Below (Aviation)
NET . . . . Not Earlier Than
NEC . . . . Not Elsewhere Classified
NEI . . . . Not Elsewhere Indicated
NEM . . . . Not Elsewhere Mentioned
NES . . . . Not Elsewhere Specified
NTE . . . . Not to Exceed (Aviation)
N/E . . . . Not Exceeding (Business and trade)
NX . . . . Not Exceeding
NFC . . . . Not Favorably Considered
NFFI . . . . Not Fit for Issue (Navy)
NFS. . . . . Not on Flying Status
NFS. . . . . Not For Sale
NFU. . . . . Not For Us (Communications)
NF . . . . Not Fordable (Maps and charts)
NHD . . . . Not Heard (Communications)
NOHOL . . . . . Not Holding (a given course or altitude) (Aviation)
NAH . . . . Not at Home
NONTSDSL . . . Not Included in Technical Service Demand Stockage Lists (Army)
NI . . . . Not Interested
NK . . . . Not Known
NLT . . . . Not Later Than
NLT . . . . Not Less Than
NLD. . . . . Not in Line of Duty (as, of an injury) (Military)
NL . . . . Not Listed
NL. . . . . Not Located
N/M . . . . Not Marked (Business and trade)
NM . . . . Not Measured
NMB . . . . Not Member of a Branch
NMT . . . . Not More Than
NOTAL . . . . . Not to, nor Needed by, All
N/N . . . . Not To Be Noted (Business and trade)
NO . . . . Not Operational
NOR . . . . Not Operationally Ready
NORM . . . . . . Not Operationally Ready - Maintenance
NORO . . . . . . Not Operationally Ready - Other
NORS. . . . . . . Not Operationally Ready - Supply
NORSAIR . . . . Not Operationally Ready Supply Aeronautical Items Report (Navy)
N/O . . . . Not Otherwise
NOA . . . . Not Otherwise Authorized
NOE . . . . Not Otherwise Enumerated
NOHP . . . . . . Not Otherwise Herein Provided
NOIBN. . . . . . Not Otherwise Indexed by Name (Tariffs)
NOIBN. . . . . . Not Otherwise Indicated (or Identified) by Name (Military)
NOP . . . . Not Otherwise Provided
NOS . . . . Not Otherwise Specified

NOS . . . . Not Otherwise Stated
NOP . . . . Not Our Publication
NO . . . . Not Out
NOY . . . . Not Out Yet
NPOPR . . . . . . Not Paid on Prior Rolls
NAP . . . . Not at Present
NPF . . . . Not Provided For
NIPD . . . . Not in the Public Domain
NRFI . . . . Not Ready for Issue
NOFORN . . . . Not Releasable to Foreign Nationals
NRTS . . . . Not Reparable This Station
NR . . . . Not Required
N/R . . . . Not Responsible For
NTBR . . . . Not To Be Resuscitated
NTS . . . . Not to Scale (Drafting)
NSBT . . . . Not Series By Title
NS . . . . Not Significant
NSPF . . . . Not Specifically Provided for
NS . . . . Not Specified
NSG . . . . Not So Good
NSH . . . . Not So Hot (Slang)
NSMAPMAWOL . . Not So Much a Programme, More a Way of Life (British television
            program)
NST . . . . Not Sooner Than
NIS . . . . Not in Stock
NS . . . . Not Sufficient
NSF . . . . Not Sufficient Funds (Banking)
NTO . . . . Not Taken Out (Insurance)
NYA . . . . Not Yet Answered
NYD . . . . Not Yet Dead (Humorous variant of Not Yet Diagnosed)
NYD . . . . Not Yet Diagnosed (Medicine)
NYP . . . . Not Yet Published
NYR . . . . Not Yet Reported (Air Force)
NYR . . . . Not Yet Returned (Military)
NB . . . . Nota Bene (Note Well)
NP . . . . Notary Public
NOC . . . . Notation of Content (Aerospace)
N . . . . Note
NN . . . . Notes (Finance)
N/P . . . . Notes Payable
N/R . . . . Notes Receivable
NAD . . . . Nothing Abnormal Detected
ND . . . . Nothing Doing (Amateur radio slang)
NTR . . . . Nothing To Report
NOTAM . . . . . Notice to Airmen (Air Force)
NOTAD . . . . . Notice to Airmen Address
NOTOF . . . . . . Notice to Airmen Office
NOSUM . . . . . Notice to Airmen Summary
NOTAS . . . . . Notice to Airmen Summary
NTCAVAL . . . . Notice of Availability
NAWD . . . . . . Notice of Award
NOC . . . . Notice of Contents (Indexing)
NCD . . . . Notice of Credit Due
NODI . . . . . . Notice of Delayed Items
NOE . . . . Notice of Exception
NIP . . . . Notice of Intelligence Potential (Military)
NONA . . . . . . Notice of Nonavailability
NOO . . . . Notice of Obligation (Military)
NOR . . . . Notice of Readiness (Shipping)
N/R . . . . Notice of Readiness (Shipping)
NRP . . . . Notice of Research Project
NSFD . . . . . . Notice of Structural or Functional Deficiency
NOFT . . . . . . Notification of Foreign Travel
NRT . . . . Notion Round Table
NS . . . . Nôtre Seigneur (Our Lord)
NSJC . . . . . . Notre Seigneur Jesus Christ (Our Lord Jesus Christ)
N . . . . Noun
NP . . . . Noun Phrase (Grammar)
NN . . . . Nouns
NHKG . . . . . . Nova Hut' Klementa Gottwalda
NS . . . . Nova Scotia (A Canadian province)
NOG . . . . Novadel Agene Corporation (NYSE symbol)
NF . . . . Nouveau Franc (New Franc) (French monetary unit, introduced in 1960)
NRF . . . . Nouvelle Revue Francaise (French periodical; initials also used on books
            published by Gallimard)
NEI . . . . Nouvelles Equipes Internationales
N . . . . November
NT . . . . Novum Testamentum (New Testament)
NOSI . . . . Now Simultaneous
NAD . . . . Nuclear Accident Dosimetry
NAICC . . . . . . Nuclear Accident Incident Control Center

NAICP . . . . . . Nuclear Accident and Incident Control Plan
NARF . . . . Nuclear Aerospace Research Facility (Air Force)
NARI . . . . Nuclear Aerospace Research Institute (Air Force)
NAB . . . . Nuclear Assembly Building
NAHICUS . . . . Nuclear Attack Hazards in the Continental United States
NAPU . . . . Nuclear Auxiliary Power Unit
NAPUS . . . . . . Nuclear Auxiliary Power Unit System
NBC . . . . Nuclear, Biological, and Chemical (Warfare)
NC . . . . Nuclear Capability
NCUC . . . . . Nuclear Chemistry Users Committee
NCS . . . . Nuclear–Chicago Solubilizer
NUPLEX . . . . . Nuclear Complex
NC . . . . Nuclear Congress
NCSAG . . . . . Nuclear Cross Section Advisory Group
NUCREP . . . . . Nuclear Damage Report
NDIC . . . . . . Nuclear Data Information Center (ORNL)
NUCDEF . . . . . Nuclear Defense
NDAC . . . . . . Nuclear Defense Affairs Committee (NATO)
NDV . . . . Nuclear Delivery Vehicle
NDS . . . . Nuclear Detection Satellite
NUDETS . . . . . Nuclear Detection System (NORAD/ESD)
NUDET . . . . . . Nuclear Detonation
NUCDETS . . . . Nuclear Detonation Detection Reporting System
NUDETS . . . . . Nuclear Detonation Reporting System (Air Force)
NDCA . . . . . . Nuclear Development Corporation of America
NEEP . . . . Nuclear Electronics Effects Program
NETOPS . . . . . Nuclear Emergency Team Operations
NET . . . . Nuclear Emergency Teams (DASA)
NERV . . . . . . Nuclear Emulsion Recovery Vehicle (NASA, Air Force)
NELIA . . . . . . Nuclear Energy Liability Insurance Association
NEPA . . . . . . Nuclear Energy Powered Aircraft
NEPIA . . . . . . Nuclear Energy Property Insurance Association
NERC . . . . . . Nuclear Energy Research Center (Belgium) (Also known as CEEN)
NETF . . . . Nuclear Energy Test Facility
NETAC . . . . . . Nuclear Energy Trade Associations' Conference
NEWA . . . . . . Nuclear Energy Writers Association (Defunct)
NERVA . . . . . . Nuclear Engine for Rocket Vehicle Application (NASA)
NRX . . . . NERVA (Nuclear Engine for Rocket Vehicle Application) Reactor
            Experiment (AEC)
NE . . . . Nuclear Engineer
NET . . . . Nuclear Engineer Trainees (AEC)
NED . . . . Nuclear Engineering Directorate (Army)
NESC . . . . . . Nuclear Engineering and Scientific Congress
NETR . . . . . . Nuclear Engineering Test Reactor (Air Force)
NEEC . . . . . . Nuclear Explosion Effects Center
NEWRADS . . . . Nuclear Explosion Warning and Radiological Data System
NFZ . . . . Nuclear Free Zone
NFS . . . . Nuclear Fuel Services, Inc.
NICP . . . . Nuclear Incident Control Plan
NI . . . . Nuclear Industries, Inc.
NIC . . . . Nuclear Industry Consortium (Belgium) (Also known as GPIN)
NIF . . . . Nuclear Information File
NIM . . . . Nuclear Instrument Module
NIAC . . . . Nuclear Insurance Association of Canada
NIRB . . . . Nuclear Insurance Rating Bureau
NIMPHE . . . . . Nuclear Isotope Monopropellant Hydrazine Engine
NULACE . . . . . Nuclear Liquid Air Cycle Engine
NMDR . . . . . . Nuclear Magnetic Double Resonance
NMR . . . . Nuclear Magnetic Relaxation
NMR . . . . Nuclear Magnetic Resonance (Spectrum)
NMRP . . . . . . Nuclear Magnetic Resonance Program
NUMEC . . . . . Nuclear Materials and Equipment Company
NMC . . . . Nuclear Measurements Corporation
NMC . . . . Nuclear Metal Conference
NMI . . . . Nuclear Metals, Incorporated
NMSO . . . . . . Nuclear Missile Safety Office(r)
NNFP . . . . . . Nuclear Nitrogen Fixation Plant
NOB . . . . Nuclear Order of Battle
NOCM . . . . . . Nuclear Ordnance Commodity Manager
NOG . . . . Nuclear Ordnance Group (Air Force)
NPG . . . . Nuclear Planning Group (NATO)
NPD . . . . Nuclear Power Demonstration (Reactor) (Canada)
NPPC . . . . . . Nuclear Power Plant Company, Ltd.
NUPAD . . . . . . Nuclear-Powered Active Detection System
NPSRA . . . . . . Nuclear-Powered Ship Research Association (Japan)
N . . . . Nuclear Propelled, when follows vessel classification, as CAG(N) (Navy)
NQR . . . . Nuclear Quadrupole Resonance (Frequencies)
NQAA . . . . . . Nuclear Quality Assurance Agency
NR . . . . Nuclear Reactor
NRSSG . . . . . . Nuclear Reactor Systems Safety Group (Air Force)
NRTS . . . . Nuclear Reactor Testing Station (AEC)

NRB . . . . Nuclear Reactors Branch (AEC)
NRC . . . . Nuclear Research Council
NRDS . . . . Nuclear Rocket Detection System (NASA)
NRDS . . . . . . Nuclear Rocket Development Station (AEC)
NSF . . . . Nuclear Safety Facility
NSIC . . . . Nuclear Safety Information Center (AEC)
NSI . . . . Nuclear Safety Institute
NSL . . . . Nuclear Safety Line
NSPP . . . . . . Nuclear Safety Pilot Plant (ORNL)
NS . . . . Nuclear Science
NSA . . . . Nuclear Science Abstracts (AEC)
NSCR . . . . . . Nuclear Science Center Reactor
NSE . . . . Nuclear Science and Engineering
NSEC . . . . . . Nuclear Science and Engineering Corporation (Pittsburgh)
NSV . . . . Nuclear Service Vessel
NSI . . . . Nuclear Services International
NS . . . . Nuclear Ship
NSIC . . . . . . Nuclear Strike Information Center
NS . . . . Nuclear Submarine
NS . . . . Nuclear Systems
NTL . . . . Nuclear Technology Laboratory (Stanford University)
NTA . . . . Nuclear Test Aircraft
NTD . . . . Nuclear Test Directorate (Air Force)
NTF . . . . Nuclear Test Facility
NTP . . . . Nuclear Test Plant
NTR . . . . Nuclear Test Reactor (Also known as GETR)
NUS . . . . Nuclear Utility Services
NVPO . . . . . . Nuclear Vehicle Projects Office (NASA)
NUCWAR . . . . Nuclear War
NUCWPN . . . . Nuclear Weapon(s)
NWAIB . . . . . . Nuclear Weapon Accident Investigation Board
NWEO . . . . . . Nuclear Weapon Employment Officer
NWSG . . . . . . Nuclear Weapon Systems Surety Group (Army)
NWCG . . . . . . Nuclear Weapons Coordinating Group
NWSA . . . . . . Nuclear Weapons Supply Annex
NWSSG . . . . . Nuclear Weapons System Safety Group
NCS . . . . Nucleolar Channel System
NA . . . . Nucleic Acid (Biochemistry)
NP . . . . Nucleoplasmic Index (Cytology)
NP . . . . Nucleoprotein (Biochemistry)
NLMF . . . . Nucleus of Longitudinal Muscle Fiber
NNC . . . . Nudist National Committee
NL . . . . Nuevo Leon (Mexican province)
NC . . . . "Nuff Ced" (Enough Said) (Slang)
NIJS . . . . Nuklearni Institut (Jozef Stefan Nuclear Institute) (Yugoslavia)

NLG . . . . Null Line Gap
N . . . . Number
NOB . . . . Number of Bursts
N . . . . Number of cases in sample studied (Statistics)
NMT . . . . Number of Module Types
NRIP . . . . Number of Rejected Initial Pickups
NTP . . . . Number of Theoretical Plates
NTU . . . . Number of Transfer Units
NU . . . . Number Unobtainable
N . . . . Number of variables involved (Statistics)
NWDS . . . . . . Number of Words
NWDSEN . . . . . Number of Words Per Entry
NAF . . . . Numbered Air Force
NOTO . . . . . . Numbered Tool
NT . . . . Numbering Transmitter
N . . . . Numeric
NAL . . . . Numerical Analysis Laboratory
NAR . . . . Numerical Analysis Research
NA . . . . Numerical Aperture (Microscopy)
NCS . . . . Numerical Control Society
NC . . . . Numerical Controls (Space)
NI & RT . . . . Numerical Index and Requirement Table
NIOBE . . . . . . Numerical Integration of the Boltzmann Transport Equation
NSC . . . . Numerical Sequence Code
NUSUM . . . . . Numerical Summary Report (Military)
NWP . . . . Numerical Weather Prediction
NIDA . . . . Numerically Integrated Differential Analyzer (Data processing)
NS . . . . Numismatic Society
N . . . . Nun (Buoy)
NCCdL . . . . . Nuova Camero Confederale del Lavoro (New Confederated Chamber of Labor) (Italy - Trieste)
NC . . . . Nurse Corps (Military)
NA . . . . Nurse's Aide
NAS . . . . Nursery Association Secretaries
NAMS . . . . . . Nurses and Army Medical Specialists
NA . . . . Nursing Auxiliary
NAS . . . . Nursing Auxiliary Service (British)
NP . . . . Nursing Procedure
NECAP . . . . . . Nutmeg Electric Companies Atomic Project
NF . . . . Nutrition Foundation
NOC . . . . Nuttall Ornithological Club
NVF . . . . NVF Company (Formerly, National Vulcanized Fibre Company)
NRAWU . . . . . Nyasaland Railways African Workers' Union
NRAU . . . . Nyasaland Railways Asian Workers' Union
NTUC . . . . Nyasaland Trade Union Congress

O

OEN. . . . . Oak Electro-Netics Corporation
WI. . . . . Oak Harbor, Whidbey Island, Washington (Naval base)
ORAU . . . . . . Oak Ridge Associated Universities (AEC)
ORACLE . . . . . Oak Ridge Automatic Computer and Logical Engine
ORBIT . . . . . . Oak Ridge Binary Internal-Translator
ORELA . . . . . . Oak Ridge Electron Linear Accelerator
ORGDP. . . . . . Oak Ridge Gaseous Diffusion Plant (AEC)
ORINS . . . . . . Oak Ridge Institute of Nuclear Studies
ORIC . . . . Oak Ridge Isochronous Cyclotron
ORMI . . . . Oak Ridge Military Institute
ORNL . . . . . . Oak Ridge National Laboratory
OGR . . . . ORNL (Oak Ridge National Laboratory) Graphite Reactor
ORO . . . . Oak Ridge Operations Office (AEC)
ORR . . . . Oak Ridge Reactor
ORSORT . . . . . Oak Ridge School of Reactor Technology (AEC)
OAK . . . . Oakland (California) (Airport symbol)
OARB. . . . . . . Oakland Army Base
OART . . . . . . Oakland Army Terminal
OKT . . . . Oakland Terminal Railway (AAR code)
OLC. . . . . Oakleaf Cluster
O & A (Date) . . Oath and Acceptance Date (Date from which a military officer's
　　　　　　　　commissioned service runs)
OKH . . . . Oberkommando des Heeres (Army High Command, German) (World
　　　　　　　　War II)
OKM . . . . Oberkommando der Kriegsmarine (Navy High Command, German)
　　　　　　　　(World War II)
OKL. . . . . Oberkommando der Luftwaffe (Air Force High Command, German)
　　　　　　　　(World War II)
OKW . . . . Oberkommando der Wehrmacht (Armed Forces High Command, German)
　　　　　　　　(World War II)
O . . . . Obiit (Died)
OBINXTO . . . . Obiit in Christo (Died in Christ)
OBSP . . . . Obiit sine Prole (Died without Issue)
OSP . . . . Obiit sine Prole (Died without Issue)
O . . . . Object
OOA . . . . Object of Affections (Slang)
OC . . . . Object Class (Military)
OCC . . . . Object Class Code
OIT . . . . Object Identification Test
OET . . . . Objective End Time
ORP . . . . Objective Rallying Point (Military)
OST . . . . Objective Start Time
OT . . . . Objective Test (Psychology)
OTC . . . . Objective, Time, and Cost
OVNI. . . . . . . Objectos Volantes No Identicados (Unidentified Flying Objects)
O . . . . Oblast (Governmental subdivision in USSR corresponding to a
　　　　　　　　province or state)
OJS . . . . Las Oblatas de Jesus Sacerdote (Oblates of Jesus the Priest) (Roman
　　　　　　　　Catholic women's religious order)
OEA . . . . Oblate Education Association
OA . . . . Oblate Sisters of the Assumption (Roman Catholic religious order)
OSBS . . . . Oblate Sisters of the Blessed Sacrement (Roman Catholic religious order)
OSP . . . . Oblate Sisters of Providence (Roman Catholic religious order)
OSHJ . . . . Oblate Sisters of the Sacred Heart of Jesus (Roman Catholic religious
　　　　　　　　order)
OSC . . . . Oblate Spherical Coordinates
OSJ . . . . Oblates of St. Joseph (Roman Catholic religious order)
OMI . . . . Oblati Mariae Immaculate (Oblate Fathers of Mary Immaculate) (Roman
　　　　　　　　Catholic religious order)
OSSC . . . . Oblati Sacratissimi Cordis (Oblate Fathers of the Sacred Heart) (Roman
　　　　　　　　Catholic religious order)
OSC . . . . Oblati Sancti Caroli (Oblate Fathers of St. Charles) (Roman Catholic
　　　　　　　　religious order)

OSFS . . . . Oblati Sancti Francisci Salesii (Oblate Fathers of St. Francis of Sales)
　　　　　　　　(Roman Catholic religious order)
OBI . . . . Obligated Involuntary Officer (Military)
ORS . . . . Obligated Reserve Section (Air Force)
OBV. . . . . Obligated Volunteer Officer (Military)
OA . . . . Obligation Authority (Military)
OBLAUTH . . . . Obligation Authority (Army)
OIT . . . . Oblique-Incidence Transmission
OPS. . . . . Oblique Photo Sketcher
OSW . . . . Oblique Shock Wave
OWGL . . . . . . Obscure Wire Glass
OEGT. . . . . . . Observable Evidences of Good Teaching
O . . . . Observation Aircraft (Designation for all US military aircraft)
OAP. . . . . Observation Amphibian Plane (Coast Guard)
ZKO . . . . Observation Balloon (Navy symbol)
VOF. . . . . Observation Fighter Squadron (Navy symbol)
HO . . . . Observation Helicopter
OLP. . . . . Observation Landplane (Coast Guard)
OMBI . . . . Observation-Measurement-Balancing and Installation (Production
　　　　　　　　analysis)
OO . . . . Observation Officer (Military)
OP. . . . . Observation Plane
VO . . . . Observation Plane (Navy symbol)
VOG . . . . Observation Plane Squadron (Navy symbol)
OP . . . . Observation Post
ORCON . . . . . Observation Report Conversion (Program)
VOS. . . . . Observation Scout Plane (Navy symbol)
OS . . . . Observation-Scouting Plane (When first two letters in Navy designation)
VOC . . . . Observation Spotter Squadron (Navy symbol)
OBSRON . . . . Observation Squadron
OBW . . . . Observation Window
OBOE . . . . . . Observed Bombing of Enemy
OD . . . . Observed Drift
OQL . . . . Observed Quality Level
ORL. . . . . Observed Range Limit
OTR . . . . Observed Temperature Rise
OZD . . . . Observed Zenith Distance (Navigation)
O . . . . Observer; Observation
OC . . . . Observer Corps (Became ROC, 1941) (British)
OLOS. . . . . . . Observer Line of Sight
OT. . . . . Observer-Target
OTNG . . . . . . Observer Training (Army)
OGS . . . . Obsolete General Supplies (Military)
OCS . . . . Obstacle Clearance Surface (Aviation)
ODD . . . . Obstacle Detection Device
OB . . . . Obstetrician, Obstetrics (Medicine)
OB-GYN . . . . Obstetrics-Gynecology (Medicine)
OC . . . . Obstruction Chart
OCL . . . . Obstruction Clearance Limit (Aviation)
OOJ . . . . Obstruction of Justice
GETMA. . . . . . Obtain by Local Manufacture (Military)
GETLO. . . . . . Obtain by Local Purchase (Military)
ORE . . . . Obtained Radiation Emittance
OGFP. . . . . . . Obtaining Goods by False Pretense
OMFP. . . . . . . Obtaining Money by False Pretense
O . . . . Occasional (Concerning occurrence of species)
O . . . . Occident or Occidental
OAF. . . . . Occidentale Afrique Francaise (French West Africa)
OM . . . . Occupation Medal (as used with special reference to Germany or Japan)
OEP . . . . Occupational Education Project
OHI . . . . Occupational Health Institute
OIS . . . . Occupational Interest Survey (Aptitude test)
OL. . . . . Occupational Level

OCCMED . . . . Occupational Medicine (Army)
OTR . . . . Occupational Therapist, Registered
OT . . . . Occupational Therapy or Therapist
OT . . . . Occupational Therapy Technician (Navy)
OVT . . . . Occupational-Vocational-Technical Training
OAS . . . . Occupied Areas Section (Military government)
O . . . . Ocean (Maps and charts)
OASIS . . . . . . Ocean All-Source Information System
OARS . . . . . . Ocean Area Reconnaissance Satellite (Antisubmarine warfare)
OBV . . . . Ocean Boarding Vessel
OB . . . . Ocean Bottom
OBSS . . . . . . Ocean Bottom Scanning SONAR
OBS . . . . Ocean Bottom Station
OCP . . . . Ocean Culture Product
OCS . . . . Ocean Culture System
ODESSA . . . . . Ocean Data Environmental Science Services Acquisition (Buoy)
ODSB . . . . . . Ocean Data Station Buoy
ODT . . . . Ocean Data Transmitter
OESD . . . . Ocean Engineering System Development
OFD . . . . Ocean Floor Drilling
OGI . . . . Ocean General, Incorporated
OIA . . . . Ocean Industries Association
O & LS . . . . . Ocean and Lake Surveys (Navy) (Budget appropriation title)
OL . . . . Ocean Letter
MSO . . . . Ocean Minesweeper (Nonmagnetic)
OMD . . . . Ocean Movement Designator
OPBMA . . . . . Ocean Pearl Button Manufacturers Association
OPL . . . . Ocean Pressure Laboratory
O & R . . . . . . Ocean and Rail (Shipping)
ORV . . . . Ocean Range Vessel (Air Force)
ORE . . . . Ocean Research Equipment, Inc.
OSE . . . . Ocean Science & Engineering, Inc.
OSN . . . . Ocean Science News
OSTAC . . . . . . Ocean Science and Technology Advisory Committee
OSTG . . . . . . Ocean Science and Technology Group (Navy)
OSI . . . . Ocean Search, Incorporated
OSPRO . . . . . . Ocean Shipping Procedures
OS . . . . Ocean Station (Maps and charts)
OSV . . . . Ocean Station Vessel
OSP . . . . Ocean Survey Program (Navy)
OSI . . . . Ocean Systems, Incorporated
OSO . . . . Ocean Systems Operations
OT . . . . Ocean (Oversea) Transportation (Military)
ATO . . . . Ocean Tug, Old (Navy symbol)
OATC . . . . . . Oceanic Air Traffic Center
OCAC . . . . . . Oceanic Air Traffic Control
OAC . . . . Oceanic Area Control (Aviation)
OCA . . . . Oceanic Control Area (ICAO)
OIH . . . . Oceanic Institute of Hawaii
AGOR . . . . . . Oceanic Research Ship (Navy symbol)
ORB . . . . Oceanic Ridge Basalts
OCEAN . . . . . . Oceanographic Coordination, Evaluation and Analysis Network
ODDS . . . . . . Oceanographic Digital Data System (Navy)
OF . . . . Oceanographic Facility
OOP . . . . Oceanographic Observations of the Pacific
OO . . . . Oceanographic Office
ORE . . . . Oceanographic Research Equipment
ORS . . . . Oceanographic Research Ship
OSI . . . . Oceanographic Services, Incorporated
OM . . . . Oceanography and Meteorology
OW . . . . Ocellus Width
OCMU . . . . . . Ocmulgee National Monument
ODA-HCL . . . . Octadecylamine Hydrochloride
ORS . . . . Octahedral Research Satellite (NASA)
OPP . . . . Octal Print Punch
OTN . . . . Octal Track Number
OMPA . . . . . . Octamethyl Pyrophosphoramide (Insecticide)
ON . . . . Octane Number
OBA . . . . Octave Band Analyzer
OBADRS . . . . . Octave Band Automatic Data Reduction System
OBF . . . . Octave Band Filter
OBFS . . . . Octave Band Filter Set
OFS . . . . Octave Filter Set
O . . . . Octavo (Book from 20 to 25 centimeters in height)
O . . . . October
T . . . . Octodecimo (Book from 12 1/2 to 15 centimeters in height) (Bibliography)
OHI . . . . Ocular Hypertension Indicator
OU . . . . Oculi Unitas (Both Eyes Together)
OGI . . . . Oculogyral Illusion (NASA)
O . . . . Oculus (Eye)
OD . . . . Oculus Dexter (Right Eye) (Medical)

OL . . . . Oculus Laevus (Left Eye) (Medical)
OS . . . . Oculus Sinister (Left Eye)
OEC . . . . Odd-Even Check
OEN . . . . Odd-Even Nuclei
OER . . . . Odd-Even Rule
OF . . . . Odd Fellows
OLD . . . . Odd Lot Dealer
OON . . . . Odd-Odd Nuclei
OSF . . . . Odd Side Flat
OS . . . . Odd Symmetric
ODB . . . . Odontoblast
OC . . . . Odor Control
OLB . . . . Oertliche Landwirtschaftsbetriebe
OMS . . . . Oesterreichische Mineraloel und Stickstoffwerke AG (Formed by merger of OMV and OSW)
OMV . . . . Oesterreichische Mineraloelverwaltung AG (Later, OMS)
OSW . . . . Oesterreichische Stickstoffwerke AG (Later, OMS)
OCTAP . . . . . Of Concern to Air Passengers (Group affiliated with PATCO)
OC . . . . Of Course
O . . . . Off
OOPS . . . . . . Off-Line Operating Simulator
ON . . . . Off Normal
ONS . . . . Off-Normal Switch
OOB . . . . Off-Off Broadway (Theater)
ORM . . . . Off Road Mobility
OMEGA . . . . . Off-Road Mobility Evaluation and Generalized Analysis (Army)
OTS . . . . Off the Shelf
OS . . . . Off Stage
O . . . . Offered (NYSE symbol)
O . . . . Office(r)
OAG . . . . Office of the Adjutant General
OAD . . . . Office of Administration
OAASA . . . . . Office of the Administrative Assistant to the Secretary of the Army
OAASN . . . . . Office of the Administrative Assistant to the Secretary of the Navy
OARP . . . . . . Office of Advanced Research Programs (NASA) (Now, Office of Advanced Research and Technology)
OART . . . . . . Office of Advanced Research and Technology (NASA)
OAT . . . . Office for Advanced Technology (Air Force)
OAP . . . . Office of Aerial Phenomena (Air Force)
OAI . . . . Office of Aeronautical Intelligence
OASR . . . . . . Office of Aeronautical and Space Research (NASA) (Now, Office of Advanced Research and Technology)
OAR . . . . Office of Aerospace Research (Air Force)
OACD . . . . . . Office of Agricultural and Chemical Development (of TVA)
OAFC . . . . . . Office of Air Force Chaplains
OARAC . . . . . Office of Air Research Automatic Computer
OARC . . . . . . Office of Air Research Calculator
OAP . . . . Office of Aircraft Production (World War II)
OAPC . . . . . . Office of Alien Property Custodian (World War II)
OAR . . . . Office of Analysis and Review (Army, Navy)
OAP . . . . Office of Antarctic Programs (National Science Foundation)
OABETA . . . . . Office Appliance and Business Equipment Trades Association
OA . . . . Office of Applications (NASA)
OAFIE . . . . . . Office of Armed Forces Information and Education
OCSA . . . . . . Office of the Army Chief of Staff
OACSC-E . . . . Office of the Assistant Chief of Staff for Communications-Electronics
OACSFOR . . . Office of the Assistant Chief of Staff for Force Development (Army)
OACSI . . . . . . Office of the Assistant Chief of Staff for Intelligence (Army)
OASD . . . . . . Office of the Assistant Secretary of Defense (Comptroller)
OASN . . . . . . Office of the Assistant Secretary of the Navy
OASN(FM) . . . Office of the Assistant Secretary of the Navy for Financial Management
OASN(I & L) . . Office of the Assistant Secretary of the Navy for Installations and Logistics
OASN(P & RF) . Office of the Assistant Secretary of the Navy for Personnel and Reserve Force
OASN(R & D) . . Office of the Assistant Secretary of the Navy for Research and Development
OAP . . . . Office of Atomic Programs (DOD)
OAM . . . . Office of Automation and Manpower (Labor Department) (Also see OMAT)
OAA . . . . Office of Aviation Affairs (Army)
OBI . . . . Office of Basic Instrumentation (National Bureau of Standards)
OBN . . . . Office of Biochemical Nomenclature (NAS - NRC)
OBR . . . . Office of Budgets and Reports
OBA . . . . Office of Business Administration (NASA) (Later, Office of Administration)
OBE . . . . Office of Business Economics (Department of Commerce)
OCAS . . . . . . Office of Carrier Accounts and Statistics (of CAB)
OCIC . . . . Office Catholique International du Cinema (International Catholic Film Office)
OC . . . . Office of Censorship
OOC . . . . Office of Censorship
OCP . . . . Office Cherifien des Phosphates

OCAC . . . . Office, Chief of Air Corps
OCAFF . . . . . . Office, Chief of Army Field Forces
OCAR . . . . . . Office of the Chief, Army Reserve
OCCMLC . . . . Office, Chief, Chemical Corps (Army)
OCCMLO . . . . Office, Chief Chemical Officer (Army)
OCCWS . . . . . Office of the Chief of Chemical Warfare Service
OCCA . . . . . . Office, Chief of Civil Affairs
OCCWC . . . . . Office of Chief of Counsel, War Crimes (Allied German Occupation Forces)
OCE . . . . Office, Chief of Engineers (Army)
OCF . . . . Office, Chief of Finance (Military)
OC of F . . . . . Office of the Chief of Finance (Army)
OCOFF . . . . . . Office of the Chief of Finance
OCINFO . . . . Office of the Chief of Information (Military)
OCLL . . . . . . Office, Chief of Legislative Liaison
OCMH . . . . . . Office of the Chief of Military History
OCNO . . . . . . Office, Chief of Naval Operations
OPNAV . . . . . Office of the Chief of Naval Operations
OCO . . . . Office, Chief of Ordnance (Army)
OCORD . . . . Office, Chief of Ordnance (Army)
OC of ORD . . . Office, Chief of Ordnance (Army)
OCQM . . . . . . Office of Chief Quartermaster (Military)
OCRD . . . . . . Office, Chief of Research & Development (Army)
OCSIGO . . . . . Office of the Chief Signal Officer
OCSO . . . . . . Office of the Chief Signal Officer
OSIGO . . . . . . Office of Chief Signal Officer
OCSPWAR . . . . Office of the Chief of Special Warfare (Army)
OC/S . . . . . . Office, Chief of Staff (Army)
OCSS . . . . Office of the Chief of Support Services
OCOFT . . . . . Office of the Chief of Transportation (Army)
OCOT . . . . . . Office, Chief of Transportation (Military)
OCT . . . . Office, Chief of Transportation (Army)
OCD . . . . Office of Child Development (HEW)
OCDM . . . . . . Office of Civil and Defense Mobilization (Merged with Office of Emergency Planning)
OCR . . . . Office of Civil Rights (HEW)
OCD . . . . Office of Civilian Defense (Within Office of Emergency Management) (World War II)
OCMM . . . . . . Office of Civilian Manpower Management (Navy)
OCO . . . . Office of Civilian Operations (Vietnam)
OCP . . . . Office of Civilian Personnel
OCR . . . . Office of Civilian Requirements (Division of War Production Board) (World War II)
OCS . . . . Office of Civilian Supply (Division under the War Production Board) (World War II)
OCR . . . . Office of Coal Research (Department of the Interior)
OCDR . . . . . . Office of Collateral Development Responsibility
OCPR . . . . . . Office of Collateral Policy Responsibility
OCR . . . . Office of Collateral Responsibility
OCCM . . . . . . Office of Commercial Communications Management
OCFP . . . . . . Office of Commercial and Financial Policy (Department of Commerce)
OCS . . . . Office of Commercial Services (Department of Commerce)
OCA . . . . Office de Commercialisation Agricole (Senegal)
OCS . . . . Office of Communication Systems (Air Force)
OCD . . . . Office of Community Development (HUD)
OCOMS . . . . . Office of Community Services
OCA . . . . Office, Comptroller of the Army
OCC . . . . . . Office of the Comptroller of the Currency (Department of the Treasury)
NAVCOMPT . . Office of the Comptroller of the Navy
OC-N . . . . . . Office of the Comptroller, Navy
OCS . . . . Office of Contract Settlement (Functions transferred to GSA, 1949; now obsolete)
OCSAB . . . . . . Office of Contract Settlement Appeal Board (Abolished, 1952)
OCAU . . . . . Office de Cooperation et d'Accueil Universitaire (France)
OCR . . . . Office of Coordinating Responsibility (Air Force)
OCIAA . . . . . . Office of Coordinator of Inter-American Affairs (World War II)
OC . . . . Office Copy
OCT . . . . Office of Critical Tables (NAS-NRC)
OCE . . . . Office of Cultural Exchange (Department of State)
ODCSO . . . . . Office of Data Collection and Survey Operations (Bureau of Labor Statistics)
ODA . . . . Office of Debt Analysis (Department of the Treasury)
ODHWS . . . . . Office of Defense Health and Welfare Services (World War II)
ODL . . . . Office of Defense Lending (Department of the Treasury)
ODMO . . . . . . Office of Defense Management and Organization (Military)
ODM . . . . Office of Defense Manpower
ODM . . . . Office of Defense Mobilization (Transferred to Office of Defense and Civilian Mobilization, 1958)
ODP . . . . Office of Defense Planning (of FRS)
ODRE . . . . . . Office of Defense Research and Engineering

ODT . . . . Office of Defense Transportation (Within Office for Emergency Management) (World War II)
ODB . . . . Office of Dependency Benefits
ODAA . . . . . . Office of Dependent Area Affairs (Department of State)
ODMC . . . . . . Office for Dependents' Medical Care (Army)
ODCSOPS . . . . Office of the Deputy Chief of Staff for Military Operations (Army)
ODCSPER . . . . Office of the Deputy Chief of Staff for Personnel (Army)
ODCM . . . . . . Office of the Director of Civilian Marksmanship
ODDRE . . . . . . Office of Director of Defense Research and Engineering
ODDP . . . . . . Office, Director of Development Planning (Air Force)
ODI . . . . Office of Director of Intelligence (Military)
ODMA . . . . . . Office of the Director of Military Assistance
ODPI . . . . Office of Director Public Information (Military)
ODI . . . . Office Document Index
ODGSO . . . . Office of Domestic Gold and Silver Operations (Department of the Treasury)
OEA . . . . Office of Economic Adjustment
OEO . . . . Office of Economic Opportunity
OEP . . . . Office of Economic Programs (of BDSA)
OER . . . . Office of Economic Research (Department of Commerce)
OES . . . . Office of Economic Stabilization (World War II)
OEW . . . . Office of Economic Warfare (World War II)
OE . . . . Office of Education (HEW)
OEA . . . . Office Education Association
OEE . . . . Office of Educational Exchange (Department of State)
OEX . . . . Office of Educational Exchange
OEPS . . . . Office of Educational Programs and Services
OEM . . . . Office of Emergency Management (World War II)
OEP . . . . Office of Emergency Preparedness (Formerly, Office of Emergency Planning)
OET . . . . Office of Emergency Transportation (FAA)
OEIU . . . . Office Employes International Union
OEEO . . . . Office of Equal Educational Opportunities (US Office of Education)
OEM . . . . Office Equipment Maintenance
OEMI . . . . Office Equipment Manufacturers Institute
OEC . . . . Office of Export Control (World War II)
OFCC . . . . Office of Federal Contract Compliance (Department of Labor)
OFR . . . . Office of the Federal Register
OFDAP . . . . . . Office of the Field Directorate of Ammunition Plants
OFS . . . . Office of Field Service (OSRD) (World War II)
OFS . . . . Office of Field Services (Department of Commerce)
OFA . . . . Office of Financial Analysis (Department of the Treasury)
OFMS . . . . Office of Financial and Management Services (Department of Labor)
OFC . . . . Office of Fishery Coordination (World War II)
OFO . . . . Office of Flight Operations
OFTDA . . . . . . Office of Flight Tracking and Data Acquisition (NASA)
OFAR . . . . Office of Foreign Agricultural Relations (Department of Agriculture)
OFCS . . . . Office of Foreign Commercial Services (Department of Commerce)
OFDI . . . . Office of Foreign Direct Investments (Department of Commerce)
OFEA . . . . Office of Foreign Economic Administration (Lend-Lease) (World War II)
OFEC . . . . Office of Foreign Economic Coordination (World War II)
OFERRA . . . . . Office of Foreign Economic Relief and Rehabilitation Administration
OFRR . . . . Office of Foreign Relief and Rehabilitation
OFRRO . . . . . . Office of Foreign Relief and Rehabilitation Operations
OFE . . . . Office Francais d'Edition
OGC . . . . Office of General Counsel
OGC-N . . . . Office of General Counsel, Navy
OG . . . . Office of Geography (Department of the Interior)
OGLA . . . . . . Office Grade Limitations Act
OGM . . . . Office of Grants Management (Public Health Service)
OGRC . . . . . . Office of Grants and Research Contracts (NASA)
OGM . . . . Office of Guided Missiles
OHSGT . . . . . . Office of High Speed Ground Transportation (Department of Transportation)
OHS . . . . Office of Highway Safety (of BPR)
OH . . . . Office Hours
OHE . . . . Office of the Housing Expediter (Terminated, 1951)
OIGR . . . . . . Office of Industrial Growth and Research (of BDSA)
OIM . . . . Office of Industrial Managers (Navy)
OIM . . . . Office of Industrial Mobilization (of BDSA)
OIPAAR . . . . . Office of Industrial Personnel Access Authorization Review (Army)
OIR . . . . Office of Industrial Relations (Navy)
OIR-N . . . . . . Office of Industrial Relations, Navy
OIS . . . . Office of Industrial Survey (Navy)
OI . . . . Office of Information
OI-N . . . . Office of Information, Navy
OIS . . . . Office of Information Services
OIG . . . . Office of the Inspector General (Army)
OTIG . . . . Office, the Inspector General
OIR . . . . Office of Institutional Research
OI . . . . Office Instruction

OICO....... Office of Integration and Checkout
OIAA....... Office of Inter-American Affairs (Later, BIAA)
OIA........ Office of International Administration (Department of State)
OICRF...... Office International du Cadastre et Regime Foncier
OIC........ Office of International Conferences (Department of State)
OIC........ Office of International Cooperation (in CAA)
OIESA...... Office of International Economic and Social Affairs (Department of State)
OIEC....... Office International de l'Enseignement Catholique
OIE........ Office International des Epizooties
OIF........ Office of International Finance (Department of the Treasury)
OII........ Office of International Investment (Department of Commerce)
OILA....... Office of International Labor Affairs (Labor Department)
OIO........ Office of International Operations (of IRS)
OISA....... Office of International Science Activities (National Science Foundation)
OITA....... Office of International Tax Affairs (Department of the Treasury)
OIT........ Office of International Trade (Department of Commerce)
OITF....... Office of International Trade Fairs (Department of Commerce)
OITF....... Office of International Trade and Finance (Department of State)
OIV........ Office International de la Vigne et du Vin
OI & I..... Office of Invention and Innovation (National Bureau of Standards)
OJPR....... Office for Jewish Population Research
OJCS....... Office of the Joint Chiefs of Staff
OTJAG...... Office, the Judge Advocate General
OJDYD...... Office of Juvenile Delinquency and Youth Development (HEW)
OLP........ Office of Labor Production (WPB) (World War II)
OLM........ Office for Laboratory Management (DOD)
OLUC....... Office of Land Use Coordination (Department of Agriculture) (Abolished, 1944)
OLVP....... Office of Launch Vehicle Programs (NASA) (No longer in existence)
OLEA....... Office of Law Enforcement Assistance
OLC........ Office of Legal Counsel (Department of Justice)
OLA........ Office of Legislative Affairs
OLR........ Office of Legislative Reference (Bureau of the Budget; later, OMB)
OLLA....... Office of Lend-Lease Administration (World War II)
OLE........ Office for Library Education (American Library Association)
OLSP....... Office of Life Science Programs (NASA) (No longer in existence)
OMB........ Office of Management and Budget (Formerly, Bureau of the Budget)
OME........ Office of Management Engineer
OMI........ Office of Management Improvement (Department of Agriculture)
MS......... Office of Management Services (FAA)
OMS........ Office of Management Services (Department of Agriculture)
OM......... Office Manager
OMSF....... Office of Manned Space Flight (NASA)
OMAT....... Office of Manpower, Automation, and Training (Department of Labor) (Also see OAM)
OMPER..... Office of Manpower Policy, Evaluation and Research (Department of Labor)
OMS........ Office of Marketing Services (of BDSA)
OMMS....... Office of Merchant Marine Safety (Coast Guard)
OMA........ Office of Military Assistance
OMG........ Office of Military Government
OMGB....... Office of Military Government for Bavaria (US Military Government, Germany)
OMGBS..... Office of Military Government for Berlin Sector (US Military Government, Germany)
OMGH...... Office of Military Government for Hesse (US Military Government, Germany)
OMGUS..... Office of Military Government, United States
OCEA....... OMGUS (Office of Military Government, United States) Civilian Employees Association (Post-World War II, Germany)
OMGWB.... Office of Military Government for Wuerttemberg-Baden (US Military Government, Germany)
OME....... Office of Minerals Exploration (Department of the Interior)
OMM....... Office of Minerals Mobilization (Later, OMSF) (Department of the Interior)
OMSF....... Office of Minerals and Solid Fuels (Formerly, OMM) (Department of the Interior)
OMBE...... Office of Minority Business Enterprise (Department of Commerce)
OMVTO.... Office Motor Vehicle Transportation Officer (Army)
OMC....... Office of Munitions Control (Department of State)
ONERA..... Office National d'Etudes et de Recherches Aerospatiales (France)
OFFNAVHIST.. Office of Naval History
ONH....... Office of Naval History
ONIO...... Office of Naval Inspectors of Ordnance
ONI....... Office of Naval Intelligence
NNI....... Office of Naval Intelligence Publications
ONM....... Office of Naval Material (Later, NMCOM)
ONOP...... Office of Naval Officer Procurement
ONO....... Office of Naval Operations

ONPOSR..... Office of Naval Petroleum and Oil Shale Reserves
ONR....... Office of Naval Research
NRD....... Office of Naval Research and Development
ONRL...... Office of Naval Research, London
ONW....... Office of Naval Weapons
ONWS..... Office of Naval Weather Service
ONC....... Office of New Careers (HEW)
NA........ Office of Noise Abatement (FAA)
OOL....... Office of Oceanography and Limnology (Smithsonian Institution)
OOG...... Office of Oil and Gas (Department of the Interior)
O........ Office of Operations (Coast Guard)
OOD....... Office Operations Department
OOR...... Office of Ordnance Research (Later, Army Research Office)
OOP....... Office of Organization Planning
O/O....... Office of Origin
OPA....... Office of the Pardon Attorney (Department of Justice)
OP & I..... Office of Patents and Inventions
OP........ Office of Personnel
P........ Office of Personnel (Coast Guard)
OPO....... Office of Personnel Operations (Army)
OP........ Office of Pesticides (Public Health Service)
OPSC...... Office of Planning Standards and Coordination (HUD)
OPG....... Office of the Postmaster General
OPA....... Office of Price Administration (World War II)
OPACS..... Office of Price Administration and Civilian Supply (Name changed to Office of Price Administration) (World War II)
OPC....... Office of Price Control (World War II)
OPS....... Office of Price Stabilization (Terminated 1953)
OPDR...... Office of Primary Development Responsibility
OPI....... Office of Primary Interest
OPR....... Office of Primary Responsibility (Air Force)
OPR....... Office of Private Resources (Department of State)
OPM....... Office of Procurement and Material
OPDL...... Office of Production and Defense Lending (Treasury Department)
OPM....... Office of Production Management (Superseded by WPB, 1942)
OPRD...... Office of Production Research and Development
OPEIU..... Office & Professional Employees' International Union
OPA....... Office of Program Appraisal
OPD....... Office of Program Development (NASA)
OPRM..... Office of Program Review and Resources Management
OPPE...... Office of Programming, Planning, and Evaluation
OPMG..... Office of Provost Marshal General (Also, PMGO)
PMGO..... Office of Provost Marshal General
OTPMG.... Office, the Provost Marshal General
OPEI..... Office of Public Education and Information (NASA)
OPI...... Office of Public Information
PUBINFO.... Office of Public Information (Formerly, Office of Public Relations) (Navy)
OPR........ Office of Public Relations
OPRRE...... Office of Public Roads and Rural Engineering (Later, Bureau of Public Roads)
OPB....... Office of the Publication Board (Department of Commerce)
OP & I...... Office of Publications and Information (Department of Commerce)
OQMG...... Office, Quartermaster General (Army)
ORS....... Office of Radiation Standards (AEC)
ORTF...... Office de Radiodiffusion Television Francaise (State-owned radio and television network) (France)
O/R....... Office of Record
ORMA..... Office of Refugee and Migration Affairs (Department of State)
ORE....... Office of Regional Economics (Department of Commerce)
ORMOA.... Office for Relations with Military and Occupation Authorities
ORQA..... Office of Reliability and Quality Assurance
ORS....... Office of Rent Stabilization (Functions transferred to Office of Defense Mobilization, 1953)
ORA...... Office of Research Analysis (Air Force)
ORD....... Office of Research and Development (Various federal government agencies, etc.)
ORI....... Office of Research and Inventions
ORC....... Office of Reserve Components (Army)
ORI....... Office of Road Inquiry (Later, Bureau of Public Roads)
ORD....... Office of Rubber Director (WPB) (World War II)
ORAD..... Office of Rural Areas Development (Department of Agriculture)
OSW....... Office of Saline Water (Department of the Interior)
OSIS...... Office of Science Information Service (National Science Foundation)
OST....... Office of Science and Technology (Executive Office of the President)
OSI....... Office of Scientific Information (National Science Foundation)
OSP....... Office of Scientific Personnel (NAS-NRC)
OSR....... Office of Scientific Research (AFSC)
OSRD...... Office of Scientific Research and Development (World War II)
OSRMD..... Office of Scientific Research, Mechanics Division
OSTI...... Office of Scientific and Technical Information (NASA)

OSAF ...... Office of the Secretary of the Air Force
OSA .... Office of the Secretary of the Army
OSD .... Office of the Secretary of Defense
OSD/ISA .... Office of the Secretary of Defense for International Security Affairs
OSG .... Office of the Secretary General (UN)
OSN .... Office of the Secretary of the Navy
OSW .... Office of Secretary of War
OSR .... Office of Security Review (DOD)
OSSR .... Office of Selective Service Records
OSIA .... Office, Services and Information Agency (Military)
OSG .... Office of the Solicitor General (Department of Justice)
OSFCW ...... Office of Solid Fuels Coordinator for War (World War II)
OSW .... Office of Solid Wastes (Public Health Service)
OSFD .... Office of Space Flight Development (NASA) (No longer in existence)
OSFP .... Office of Space Flight Programs (NASA) (No longer in existence)
OSSA ...... Office of Space Science and Applications (NASA)
OSS .... Office of Space Sciences (NASA)
OSS .... Office of Space Systems (Air Force)
OSFM .... Office of Spacecraft and Flight Missions
OSALSTC .... Office, Special Assistant for Logistical Support of Tactical
            Communications
OSHA .... Office of Special Housing Assistance (HUD)
OSI .... Office of Special Investigation (Air Force)
OSWD .... Office of Special Weapons Development (Army)
OSRD .... Office of Standard Reference Data (National Bureau of Standards)
OSTS .... Office of State Technical Services (Department of Commerce)
STS .... Office of State Technical Services (Department of Commerce) (Also see
            OSTS)
OSS .... Office of Statistical Standards (Bureau of the Budget; later, OMB)
OSI .... Office of Strategic Information
OSS .... Office of Strategic Services (World War II)
OSD .... Office of Student Detachment (Navy)
OSS .... Office of Support Services (Army)
OSG .... Office of the Surgeon General (of Public Health Service)
OTSG .... Office of the Surgeon General
OSP .... Office of Surplus Property (Superseded by War Assets Corporation)
            (World War II)
OTA .... Office of Tax Analysis (Department of the Treasury)
OTCR .... Office of Technical Cooperation and Research (Department of State)
OTIA .... Office of Technical Information Agency (Army)
OTIEP .... Office of Technical Information and Educational Programs (NASA) (No
            longer in existence)
OTS .... Office of Technical Services (Later, Clearinghouse for Scientific and
            Technical Information) (National Bureau of Standards)
OTA .... Office of Technology Assessment (Proposed name for Government
            technology agency)
OTU .... Office of Technology Utilization (NASA)
OTC .... Office of Temporary Controls
OT .... Office of Territories (Department of the Interior)
OTADA ..... Office of Tracking and Data Acquisition
OTDA ...... Office of Tracking and Data Acquisition (NASA)
OTP .... Office of Trade Promotion (Department of Commerce)
OTT .... Office of Traffic and Transportation
OTRACO ..... Office des Transports du Congo (Office for Congo Transports)
OTUS .... Office of the Treasurer of the United States
OTAD ...... Office of Tributary Area Development (of TVA)
OUSAF ...... Office, Under Secretary of Air Force
OUSA ...... Office, Under Secretary of Army
OUSOFA .... Office of the Under Secretary of the Army
OUSN ...... Office, Under Secretary of Navy
OUSW ...... Office of the Under Secretary of War
OUNC ...... Office for the United Nations' Conference (NASA) (Ad hoc office)
OUNPSA .... Office of United Nations Political and Security Affairs (Department of
            State)
OUSARMA ... Office of the United States Army Attache
ODRI .... Office of United States Defense Representative, India
OUNS ...... Office of Urban Neighborhood Services (HUD)
OUSCS ...... Office of Urban Studies and Clearinghouse Services (HUD)
OVSR .... Office of Vehicle Systems Research (National Bureau of Standards)
OVA .... Office of Veterans' Affairs
OVR .... Office of Vocational Rehabilitation
OWI .... Office of War Information (World War II)
OWM ...... Office of War Mobilization (Succeeded by OWMR, 1944)
OWMR ...... Office of War Mobilization and Reconversion (Succeeded OWM, 1944;
            became part of Office of Temporary Controls, 1946)
OWU .... Office of War Utilities (WPB)
OWRR ...... Office of Water Resources Research (of Department of the Interior)
OWPP ...... Office of Welfare and Pension Plans (Department of Labor)
OWLS ...... Office Workers Link Shift (After-hours production workers) (World War II)
OAF .... Officer Assignment Folder (Military)
OBE .... Officer (of the Order) of the British Empire

OC .... Officer Candidate (Army)
OCS .... Officer Candidate School (Military)
OCT .... Officer Candidate Test (Military)
O/C .... Officer-in-Charge (Army)
O in C ...... Officer-in-Charge
OIC .... Officer in Charge
OINC .... Officer-in-Charge (Navy)
OINCABCCTC .. Officer-in-Charge, Advanced Base Combat Communication Training
            Center (Pearl Harbor) (Navy)
OCAS ...... Officer-in-Charge of Armament Supply
OCCA ...... Officer(s) in Charge of Civilian Affairs (in newly occupied countries)
            (Army) (World War II)
OICC ...... Officer in Charge of Construction (Navy)
OCNGA .... Officer in Charge of National Guard Affairs
OCMI ...... Officer in Charge, United States Coast Guard Marine Inspection Office
OC .... Officer Commanding (Marine Corps)
OCE .... Officer Conducting the Exercise (Navy, Coast Guard)
OCE .... Officer Corps Engineers
OD .... Officer of the Day (or Deck) (Navy)
OOD .... Officer of the Deck (Navy)
OERL ...... Officer Education Research Laboratory (Air Force)
OER .... Officer Effectiveness Report (Air Force)
OER .... Officer Efficiency Report (Army)
OG .... Officer of the Guard
OMR .... Officer Master Record (Air Force)
OMTR ...... Officer Master Tape Record (Army)
OM .... Officer Messenger
OMM ...... Officer Messenger Mail
OMMC ..... Officer Messenger Mail Center
OMM(S)C .... Officer Messenger Mail (Sub) Center
OStJ .... Officer of the Order of St. John of Jerusalem (British)
OPA .... Officer Personnel Act
OPD .... Officer Personnel Directorate (Army)
PO .... Officer Personnel Division (Coast Guard)
OPRRB ...... Officer Personnel Record Review Board (Air Force)
OOQ .... Officer of the Quarters
OR .... Officer Records (Military)
OSB .... Officer Selection Board
OTC .... Officer in Tactical Command (Air Force)
OOW .... Officer of the Watch (Navigation)
OAD .... Officers' Accounts Division (Navy)
OAD .... Officers' Assignment Division, The Adjutant General's Office (Army)
OBMC ...... Officers' Basic Military Corps (Air Force)
OCC .... Officers' Chief Cook
OCS .... Officers' Chief Steward (Navy)
OC .... Officers' Cook
OER .... Officers' Emergency Reserve (British)
OFF .... Officer's Family Fund
OOM .... Officers' Open Mess
OQR .... Officer's Qualification Record (Military)
ORC .... Officers' Reserve Corps
OTC .... Officers' Training Camp (World War I)
OTC .... Officers' Training Corps
OTS .... Officers' Training School
OWC .... Officers' Wives Club (Military)
O .... Official
OAG .... Official Airline Guide (Publication)
OBS .... Official Bulletin Station (Amateur radio)
OBO .... Official Business Only
OC .... Official Classification
OES .... Official Experimental Station (Amateur radio)
OIB .... Official Information Base
OMC .... Official Mail Center (Air Force)
OMPF ...... Official Military Personnel File
OMPUS ...... Official Munitions Production United States
OPF .... Official Personnel Folder (Military)
OPS .... Official Phone Station (Amateur radio)
OR .... Official Receiver
ORUS .... Official Register of the United States
ORS .... Official Relay Station (Amateur radio)
OSA .... Official Secrets Act (British)
OS .... Official Station
OTD .... Official Table of Distances
OTI .... Official Test Insecticide
OUO .... Official Use Only
OAP .... Offset Aiming Point
ODOP ...... Offset Doppler
ODP .... Offshore Drilling Platform
OECON ..... Offshore Engineering Conference
OSP .... Offshore Procurement
OSST .... Offshore Storage Tank

OSS	Offshore Surveillance System
OTB	Offtrack Betting
OEI	Oficina de Educacion Iberoamericana (Ibero-American Bureau of Education)
OIR	Oficina Interamericana de Radio (Inter-American Radio Office)
ONRAP	Oficina Nacional de Racionalizacion y Capacitacion de la Administracion Publica (Peru)
OAMA	Ogden Air Material Area
OOAMA	Ogden Air Materiel Area (AFLC)
OURD	Ogden Union Railway & Depot (AAR code)
OG	Oh, Gee! (Slang)
O	Ohio
OH	Ohio
OAES	Ohio Agricultural Experimental Station
OCC	Ohio College of Chiropody
OEC	Ohio Edison Company (NYSE symbol)
OIC	Ohio Improved Chesters (Initialism itself now used as name of breed of swine)
OMI	Ohio Mechanics Institute
OMLP	Ohio Midland Light & Power Company (AAR code)
ONU	Ohio Northern University
OHO	Ohio Oil Company (NYSE symbol)
OPRA	Ohio Penal Racing Association
OHP	Ohio Power (NYSE symbol)
ORSANCO . . .	Ohio River Water Sanitation Commission
OSU	Ohio State University
OSURO	Ohio State University Radio Observatory
OSUR	Ohio State University Reactor
OSURF	Ohio State University Research Foundation
OWU	Ohio Wesleyan University
O	Ohm (Electricity)
OH	Ohmic Heating
OPV	Ohms Per Volt (British)
OJ	Ohne Jahr (Without Date of Publication) (Bibliography)
OO	Ohne Ort (Without Place of Publication) (Bibliography)
O	Oil
OBH	Oil Bath Heater
OBP	Oil Breather Pressure
OBNREN	Oil Burner Entry Point (Aviation)
OBNREX	Oil Burner Exit Point (Aviation)
OBNR	Oil Burner Route (Aviation)
OCV	Oil Check Valve
OCAW	Oil, Chemical and Atomic Workers International Union
OCB	Oil Circuit Breaker
OCCA	Oil and Colour Chemists' Association
OC	Oil Cooler
OD	Oil Desurger
OFHA	Oil Field Haulers Association
OFR	Oil-Filled Resistor
OFP	Oil Filter Pack
OFC	Oil Free Compressor
OG	Oil Gage
OHTS	Oil Hardened Tool Steel
OHI	Oil-Heat Institute of America
OHIA	Oil Heat Institute of America
OHS	Oil Hydraulic Assembly
OHPS	Oil Hydraulic Power Switch
OI	Oil Immersed
OIA	Oil Import Administration (Department of the Interior)
OI	Oil-Insulated
OIFC	Oil-Insulated, Fan-Cooled
OISC	Oil-Insulated, Self-Cooling
OIWC	Oil-Insulated, Water-Cooled
OIA	Oil Insurance Association
OMMMSA . . .	Oil Mill Machinery Manufacturers and Supply Association
OOT	Oil Out Temperature
OP	Oil Pressure
OPI	Oil Pressure Indicator
OPO	Oil Pressure Out
OPS	Oil Pressure Switch
OPT	Oil Pressure Transmitter
OP	Oil Pump
OQI	Oil Quantity Indicator
OS	Oil Solenoid
YOS	Oil Storage Barge (Navy symbol)
OS	Oil Switch
OTO	Oil Temperature Out
OT	Oil-Tight
OTL	Oil Tight Light
OTA	Oil Trades Association of New York
OTANY	Oil Trades Association of New York

OVP	Oil-Vapor Pump
OV	Oil of Vitriol
O/W	Oil in Water
OWG	Oil, Water, Gas
OWIU	Oil Workers International Union
AO	Oiler (Navy ship symbol)
OPEMA	Oilfield Production Equipment Manufacturers Association
OTMA	Oilfield Tank Manufacturers Association
OKA	Okalta Oils, Ltd. (NYSE symbol)
OIC	Okinawa Interboard Committee
OK	Oklahoma
OBU	Oklahoma Baptist University
OCAA	Oklahoma City-Ada-Atoka Railway Company (AAR code)
OCAMA	Oklahoma City Air Materiel Area
OCU	Oklahoma City University
OCW	Oklahoma College for Women
OGE	Oklahoma Gas & Electric Company (NYSE symbol)
OMRF	Oklahoma Medical Research Foundation
OMRI	Oklahoma Medical Research Institute
OMA	Oklahoma Military Academy
ONG	Oklahoma Natural Gas Company (NYSE symbol)
OTIS	Oklahoma Teletype Interlibrary System
OU	Oklahoma University
OURI	Oklahoma University Research Institute
OIO	Oklahomans for Indian Opportunity
OKN	Okmulgee Northern Railway Company (AAR code)
OKO	Okonite Company (NYSE symbol)
OSV	Okulierschnellverschluss
O	Old
OAA	Old-Age Assistance (HEW)
OAB	Old-Age Benefits
OAP	Old Age Pension(s)
OAS	Old Age Security
	Security Act)
OASDI	Old-Age and Survivors Disability Insurance Program (of the Social
OASI	Old Age and Survivors Insurance
OCV	Old Aircraft Carrier (Navy symbol)
OAE	Old Antarctic Explorer
OB	The Old Bailey (London court)
OBB	Old Battleship (Navy)
OBH	Old Berkeley Hunt
OBH	Old Berkshire Hounds
OB	Old Boy (Communications operators' colloquialism)
OC	Old Carthusian
OC	Old Catholic
O/C	Old Charter (Business and trade)
OCS	Old Church Slavonic
OC	Old Crop
ODD	Old Destroyer (Navy symbol)
OD	Old Dutch
OE	Old English (Language) (i.e., before 1150 or 1200)
OEGCA	Old English Game Club of America
OESCA	Old English Sheepdog Club of America
OE	Old Etonian (British)
OF	Old Face (Typography)
OFA	Old Farmer's Almanac
OF	Old French
OFR	Old French (Language, etc.)
OG	Old Girl (A wife) (Slang)
OHG	Old High German (Language)
OL	Old Latin
OCL	Old Light Cruiser (Navy symbol)
OLF	Old Low Franconian
OLG	Old Low German (Language)
OM	Old Man (Communications operators' colloquialism)
OM	Old Measurement
ONF	Old Norman French (Language, etc.)
ON	Old Norse (Language, speech, grammar)
ONF	Old Northern French (Language, etc.)
OOTC	Old Old Timers Club
OPH	Old Parliamentary Hand (Political) (British)
OPB	Old Picked Bumpers (Choice cigarette butts) (Australian slang)
OPR	Old Prussian
ORS	Old Red Sandstone
OS	Old Saxon (Language)
OS	Old School
OS	Old Series
OS	Old Side
OS	Old Style
OSS	Old Submarine (Navy symbol)
OT	Old Term

OT .... Old Terminology
O/T .... Old Terms (Business and trade)
OT .... Old Testament (of the Bible)
OT .... Old Timer (Communications operators' colloquialism)
OTACS ..... Old Timer Assay Commissioners Society
OTC .... Old Timers' Club
OT .... Old Top (Communications operators' colloquialism)
OLD .... Old Town Corporation (NYSE symbol)
OT .... Old Tuberculin
OW .... Old Welsh
OW .... Old Woman (A wife) (Slang)
OWL .... Older Women's Liberation (Feminist group)
OT .... Olfactory Threshold
OLN .... Olin Corporation (Formerly, OLM) (NYSE symbol)
OLM .... Olin Mathieson Chemical Corporation (Later, OLN) (NYSE symbol)
OMCC ...... Olin Mathieson Chemical Corporation (Also see OLN)
OAB .... Olive Advisory Board
OD .... Olive Drab (Color often used for military clothing and equipment)
OOAA ...... Olive Oil Association of America
OWHA ...... Oliver Wendell Holmes Association
ONC .... Olivet Nazarene College (Illinois)
OAS .... Olley Air Service, Ltd.
OG .... Olympic Games
OLYM ...... Olympic National Park
OLBR ...... Omaha, Lincoln & Beatrice Railway Company (AAR code)
OMR .... Omar, Inc. (NYSE symbol)
OHGS ...... Omega Hyberbolic Grid System
OPLE ...... Omega Position Location Equipment (NASA)
OWR .... Omega West Reactor (AEC)
ODK .... Omicron Delta Kappa (Fraternity)
OKU .... Omicron Kappa Upsilon (Fraternity)
OE .... Omissions Excepted
OA. .... Omniantenna
OBD .... Omnibearing-Distance
OBI .... Omnibearing Indicator (Radio)
OBS .... Omnibearing Selector (Radio)
OPI .... Omnibus Personality Inventory (Guidance in education)
OSA .... Omnibus Society of America
ODA .... Omnidirectional Antenna
ORB .... Omnidirectional Radio Beacon
OR .... Omnidirectional Radio Range
ODR .... Omni-Directional Range
OTA .... Omnidirectional Transmitter Antenna
OINT ...... Omni-Intersection (Aviation)
OMNITENNA. Omnirange Antenna
ORDIR ..... Omnirange Digital RADAR
ORZ .... Omnirange Zone
OHF. ...... Omsk Hemorrhagic Fever
OA .... On or About (Military)
OA .... On Account (Business and trade)
O/A. ...... On Account
OA .... On Account of
OAS .... On Active Service
OB .... On Board
OCS .... On-Board Checkout System
ODCC ...... On-Board Digital Computer Control
OBIFCO .... On-Board In-Flight Checkout
OBP .... On Board Processor
OC .... On Center (Technical drawings)
OC .... On Course (Navigation)
OTD. ...... On the Deck
OD .... On Demand (Business and trade)
O/D .... On Demand
OD .... On Duty
OEM .... On Equipment Materiel (Army)
OFP .... On-the-Fly Printer
OG .... On Ground (Aviation)
OH .... On Hand
OHBMS ..... On His (or Her) Britannic Majesty's Service
OHMS ...... On His (or Her) Majesty's Service
OI .... On Instruments (Aviation)
OTJ .... On the Job
OJT .... On-the-Job Training
OLCA ...... On-Line Circuit Analysis (System)
OLHMIS .... On-Line Hospital Management Information System
OLM .... On-Line Monitor
OLO .... On-Line Operation
OLPARS .... On-Line Pattern Analysis and Recognition System (Data processing)
OPS .... On-Line Process Synthesis (Data processing)
OLRT ...... On-Line Real Time
ORBIT ..... On-Line, Real-Time, Branch Information (IBM)

OLSC ...... On-Line Scientific Computer (Data processing)
OLTEP ..... On-Line Test Executive Program
OAOI ...... On and Off Instruments (Aviation)
OTQ .... On the Quarter
O/R .... On Request
OS .... On Sale
OS .... On Sample
OS .... On Schedule
OS .... On Side
ONSIDIV ... On-Sight Surveys Division
OSDP ...... On-Site Data Processor (NASA)
OS .... On Station (Military)
OSM .... On Station Mode
OS .... On Switch
OT .... On Time
OLDR ...... On-Time Data Reduction
OT .... On Truck
OVE .... On Vehicle Equipment
OVM .... On Vehicle Materiel (Military)
ONW .... On Watch
OWF .... On Weight of Fiber
OVB .... Onafhankelijk Verbond van Bedrijfsorganisaties (Independent Federation of Industrial Organizations) (Netherlands)
OO .... Once Over (To examine cursorily) (Slang)
OTSR ...... Once-Through Superheat Reactor (AEC)
C. .... One Hundred Dollar Bill (C Note) (Slang)
OMPRA ..... One-Man Propulsion Research Apparatus (NASA)
OAO .... One and Only (A favorite girl or boy friend)
OS .... One Shot
OS .... One Side
OT .... One-Time
OTT .... One Time Tape
OW .... One Way (Fare)
OWP .... One-Way Polar (Telegraph)
O .... Only
OC .... Only Child
OS .... Only Son
O & C ..... Onset and Course (of a disease) (Medicine)
OACETT .... Ontario Association of Certified Engineering Technicians and Technologists
OCA .... Ontario College of Agriculture
OCA .... Ontario College of Art
OCE .... Ontario College of Education
OCP .... Ontario College of Pharmacy
OHR .... Ontario Hydro-Research
OISE ...... Ontario Institute for Studies in Education
OLC .... Ontario Ladies College
ONULP ..... Ontario New Universities Library Project
ONT .... Ontario Northland Railway (AAR code)
OVC .... Ontario Veterinary College
OPIL ...... Opalescent Indicating Light
OPK .... Opelika Manufacturing Corporation (NYSE symbol)
O .... Open (Dancing position)
OA .... Open Account
OBP .... Open Break Position (Dancing)
OTB .... Open to Buy
YCK .... Open Cargo Lighter (Navy ship symbol)
OCF .... Open Channel Flow
O/C .... Open Charter (Business and trade)
OC. .... Open Circuit
OCS .... Open-Circuit-Stable
OCTV ...... Open-Circuit Television
OCTL ...... Open Circuited Transmission Line
OCO .... Open-Close-Open (Technical drawings)
OC .... Open Contract
OC .... Open Cover
ODFI ...... Open Die Forging Institute
ODI .... Open Door International, for the Economic Emancipation of the Woman Worker
OEW .... Open End Wrench
OH .... Open Hearth
OHS .... Open Hearth Steel
OJ .... Open-Joisted (Technical drawings)
YLA .... Open Landing Lighter (Navy symbol)
YC .... Open Lighter (Navy symbol)
OL. .... Open Loop
OLB .... Open Loop Bandwidth
OLBW ...... Open Loop Bandwidth
OLD .... Open Loop Damping
OLG .... Open Loop Gain
OLR .... Open Loop Response

REVERSE ACRONYMS AND INITIALISMS DICTIONARY

OLVG ...... Open Loop Voltage Gain
OMC ...... Open Market Committee (Federal Reserve System)
OOM ...... Open Ocean Mining
OP .... Open Policy
OPF .... Open Pore Foam
OP .... Open Position (Dancing)
ORCCA ..... Open Road Camper Clubs of America
OSL .... Open/Short Locator
OSAC ...... Open Space Action Committee
OSFI .... Open Steel Flooring Institute
O .... Opening
OAD ...... Opening of Anterior Digestive (Gland)
OB .... Opening of Books
OI .... Opening of Intestine
OOE .... Opening of Oesophagus
OPD ...... Opening of Posterior Digestive (Gland)
OSAL ...... Opening of Salivary (Gland)
OSS .... Opening of the Style Sac
ONIG....... Opera Nazionale Invalidi di Guerra (Italy)
OAT ...... Operating Acceptance Test
OAC ...... Operating Agency Code
OAT ...... Operating Ambient Temperature
OB .... Operating Base (Navy)
OB .... Operating Budget
OPBU...... Operating Budget
OC .... Operating Characteristic
OCP .... Operating Control Procedure (Military)
OCMODL .... Operating Cost Model
ODS .... Operating-Differential Subsidy (Authorized by Merchant Marine Act
             of 1936)
OEW ...... Operating Empty Weight
OPFAC...... Operating Facilities (Coast Guard publication)
OFSD ...... Operating Flight Strength Diagram
OFP .... Operating Force Plan
OF .... Operating Forces (Navy)
OGE .... Operating (or Operational) Ground Equipment
OGE/RPIE .. Operating Ground Equipment/Real Property Installed Equipment
OGSE ...... Operating Ground Support Equipment
OHIR ...... Operating House of Ill Repute
OL .... Operating Location
OL .... Operating Log
OMVWI ..... Operating Motor Vehicle While Intoxicated
ONP ...... Operating Nursing Procedure
OPCO ...... Operating Plan Change Orders (Coast Guard publication)
OPPR ...... Operating Program
OR .... Operating Resources
OR .... Operating Room (Medicine)
ORT .... Operating Room Technician (Navy)
OS .... Operating System
OT .... Operating Temperature
OTL .... Operating Temperature Limit
OTR .... Operating Temperature Range
OT .... Operating Time
OVWD ..... Operating Vehicle While Drunk
OPW ...... Operating Weight (Air Force)
O .... Operation
OBJ........ Operation Buster-Jangle (Atomic weapons testing)
O & C...... Operation and Checkout
OCNPR...... Operation and Conservation of Naval Petroleum Reserves (Budget
             appropriation title)
OPCON ..... Operation and Control
OC .... Operation Crossroads (Atomic weapons testing)
OCA ...... Operation Crossroads Africa
OG .... Operation Greenhouse (Atomic weapons testing)
O & M ..... Operation and Maintenance
OMA ...... Operation and Maintenance (Army)
OMARNG ... Operation and Maintenance, Army National Guard
OMF....... Operation and Maintenance of Facilities
OMFBAA .... Operation and Maintenance of Facilities Budget Activity Account (Army)
OMFCA .... Operation and Maintenance of Facilities Cost Account (Army)
OMFSCA .... Operation and Maintenance of Facilities Summary Cost Account (Army)
O & MN .... Operation and Maintenance, Navy
OMA ...... Operation Medicare Alert
OMEGA ..... Operation Model Evaluation Group, Air Force
OO .... Operation Order (Military)
OPLAN...... Operation Plan
OP .... Operation Plans
OANDR ..... Operation and Regulation
OS .... Operation Sandstone (Atomic weapons testing)
OS .... Operation Snapper (Atomic weapons testing)
OSE........ Operation Status Equipment

OTA ...... Operation Town Affiliations
OUK ...... Operation Upshot-Knothole (Atomic weapons testing)
OAV ...... Operational Aerospace Vehicle
OAIDE ...... Operational Assistance and Instructive Data Equipment
OAD ...... Operational Availability Data (Military)
OB .... Operational Base (Navy)
OBF .... Operational Base Facility
OCO ...... Operational Capability Objectives (Army)
OCCB ...... Operational Configuration Control Board
OPC ...... Operational Control (Aviation)
OCA ...... Operational Control Authority
OCL ...... Operational Control Level
OCU ...... Operational Control Unit
ODA ...... Operational Data Analysis
ODG ...... Operational Design Group
ODP....... Operational Development Program
ODS....... Operational Display System
OEP ...... Operational Employment Plan (Military)
OET & E .... Operational Employment Testing and Evaluation
OED....... Operational Engineering Detachment
OPENAH .... Operational Evaluation of Armed Helicopters
OPEX ...... Operational and Executive (UN)
OF........ Operational Fixed
OFMC ...... Operational Fixed Microwave Council
OFC ...... Operational Flight Control
OFT .... Operational Flight Trainer
OGES ...... Operational Ground Equipment Section
OHR ...... Operational Hazard Report (Air Force)
OIP .... Operational Improvement Plan
OIS .... Operational Instrumentation System
OPINTEL..... Operational Intelligence
OMIS ...... Operational Management Information System (Data processing)
OMRV ...... Operational Maneuvering Reentry Vehicle
OMS ...... Operational Meteorological Satellite (NASA)
OMU ...... Operational Mock-Up
ONC ...... Operational Navigation Charts (Air Force)
OPDD ...... Operational Plan Data Document (Military)
OPS........ Operational Power Supply
OP........ Operational Priority
OP........ Operational Procedure
OPR....... Operational Project Requirements
OR .... Operational Readiness
ORC ...... Operational Readiness Check
ORE ...... Operational Readiness Evaluation (Military)
ORI .... Operational Readiness Inspection
ORIT ...... Operational Readiness Inspection Test
ORT ...... Operational Readiness Test
ORT ...... Operational Readiness Training (Air Force)
ORD....... Operational Ready Date
OR .... Operational Reliability (Army)
ORC ...... Operational Reports Control (Military)
OR........ Operational (or Operations) Requirement
ORH ...... Operational Requirements Handbook
ORB .... Operational Research Branch (Canada)
OSIP ...... Operational Safety Improvement Program
OSR ...... Operational Scanning Recognition
OS .... Operational Sheets
OSTF ...... Operational Silo Test Facility
OSS........ Operational Storage Site (Military)
OST .... Operational Suitability Test (Air Force)
OSTF ...... Operational Suitability Test Facility
OS .... Operational Supplements (Air Force)
OSD....... Operational Support Directive (Military)
OSE ...... Operational Support Equipment
OSR ...... Operational Support Requirement (Military)
OSTV ...... Operational Support Television (Military)
OSD....... Operational System Diagram
OSTF ...... Operational System Test Facility (Air Force)
OTN ...... Operational Teletype Network
OT .... Operational Test
OPTEV ..... Operational Test and Evaluation
OT & E ..... Operational Test and Evaluation (Military)
OPTEVFOR ... Operational Test and Evaluation Force (Navy)
OTEP ...... Operational Test and Evaluation Plan (Military)
OTIS ...... Operational Test Instrumentation Ship (Navy)
OTC ...... Operational Training Capability (Air Force)
OTU........ Operational Training Unit
OUD ...... Operational Use Data
OVCS ...... Operational Voice Communication Subsystem
OWS ...... Operational Weather Support
OR .... Operationally Ready

OA .... Operations Analysis
OAC .... Operations Analysis Center
OAC .... Operations Analysis Chief (Air Force)
OAD .... Operations Analysis Division
OAR....... Operations Analysis Report
OC .... Operations Center (Military)
OPCODE .... Operations Code (Army)
OC & R ..... Operations, Commitments and Requirements (Military)
OP-COM .... Operations-Communications
OC .... Operations Control
OCC........ Operations Control Center
OCC .... Operations Control Console
OCS .... Operations Control System
OCB .... Operations Coordination Board (National Security Council)
OPDEVFOR ... Operations Development Forces
OD .... Operations Directive
ODH .... Operations Directive Handbook
OPD........ Operations Division (War Department General Staff) (World War II)
OEG .... Operations Evaluation Group (Military)
OI .... Operations Instruction
O/L .... Operations/Logistics
OM .... Operations Maintenance
OMC .... Operations Monitoring Computer
OO .... Operations Office (AEC)
OPORD ..... Operations Order (Military)
OPM .... Operations Per Minute
OPU .... Operations Priority Unit
ORD........ Operations Requirement Document
OR .... Operations Research (Data processing)
ORG .... Operations Research Group (Navy)
ORI .... Operations Research, Incorporated
ORO .... Operations Research Office
ORS........ Operations Research Society (British)
ORSA ...... Operations Research Society of America
OR/SA ..... Operations Research/Systems Analysis
OR/SAEC .... Operations Research/Systems Analysis Executive Course (Army)
OR........ Operations Room
OSCAR...... Operations, Scheduling, Control, and Reporting
A-3 .... Operations and Training Section of an Air Staff; also, officer in charge of this section (Air Force)
S-3 .... Operations and Training Section in Army Brigades or smaller units, and in Marine Corps units smaller than a brigade; the officer in charge of this section
G-3........ Operations and Training Section of an Army or Marine Corps Division (or Marine brigade or aircraft wing) General Staff; the Officer in Charge of this Section
J-3 .... Operations and Training Section of a Joint Military Staff; the Officer in Charge of this Section
OPCM ...... Operative Plasterers' and Cement Masons International Association of the United States and Canada
ODD........ Operator Distance Dialing
OIST .... Operator Integration Shakedown Test
ONI........ Operator Number Identification (Bell System)
OOL ...... Operator Oriented Language (Data processing)
OPM .... Operator Programming Method
OQC .... Operator Quality Control (RADAR)
OS .... Operator's Set
OPN .... Opercular Nerve
OR .... Operculum Ridge
OC .... Opere Citato (In the Work Cited)
OPCIT ...... Opere Citato (In the Work Cited)
OND .... Ophthalmic Nursing Diploma
OF........ Ophthalmological Foundation
OOLR ...... Ophthalmology, Otology, Laryngology, Rhinology
ODB........ Opiate-Directed Behavior
OP(S)ARMYJAG .. Opinion(s) of the Army Judge Advocate General
OAIS .... Opinion, Attitude, and Interest Survey (Testing)
OPATTYGEN .. Opinion of the Attorney General
ORC .... Opinion Research Center
ORC .... Opinion Research Corporation
O .... Opium (Slang)
O-P .... Oppenheimer-Phillips (Process)
OICW....... Opportunities Industrial Center West
OIC........ Opportunities Industrialization Center (Washington, DC)
OP........ Opposite Prompt (i.e., the left side) (A stage direction)
ODTC ...... Optic Display Test Chamber
OG .... Optic Ganglion
OAT .... Optical Adaptive Technique
OAE .... Optical Alignment Equipment
OAL .... Optical Alignment Equipment
OAMP ...... Optical Analog Matrix Processing

OAR .... Optical Angle Readout
OAR .... Optical Automatic Ranging
OPTAR ..... Optical Automatic Ranging
OBS........ Optical Beam Scanner
OBS........ Optical Beam Steering
OBSD .... Optical Beam Steering Device
OCR .... Optical Character Reader (or Recognition) (Data processing)
OCS........ Optical Character Scanner
OCCS ...... Optical Contrast Contour Seeker
ODT .... Optical Data Transmission
ODTS....... Optical Data Transmission System
OD .... Optical Density
OPDAR...... Optical Detection and Ranging
ODM .... Optical Display Memory
ODS .... Optical Docking System
OFE .... Optical Flight Evaluation
OF........ Optical Frequency
OFG .... Optical Frequency Generator
OFS........ Optical Fuzing System
OGS .... Optical Guidance System
OIP .... Optical Image Processor
OIE .... Optical Incremental Encoder
OIE .... Optical Infrared Equipment
OIRE .... Optical Infrared Equipment
OLS........ Optical Landing System
OLRS .... Optical LASER Ranging System
OMA .... Optical Manufacturers Association
OMS .... Optical MASER System
OMF .... Optical Matched Filter
OMFT ...... Optical Matched Filter Technique
OMR .... Optical Meter Relay
OPADEC ..... Optical Particle Decoy
OPD .... Optical Particle Detector (for evaluating film quality)
OPAL....... Optical Platform Alignment Linkage
OPT .... Optical Point Transfer
OPM .... Optical Power Meter
OPTIC ...... Optical Procedural Task Instruction Compiler
OPS........ Optical Processing System
OPF .... Optical Propagation Facility
OPS........ Optical Propagation Study
OPTEC ...... Optical Properties Technical Evaluation Center
OPD........ Optical Proximity Detector
OPTUL ..... Optical Pulse Transmitter Using Leaser
ORR........ Optical Ratio Reflector
ORU .... Optical Reference Unit
ORD .... Optical Rotary Dispersion
ORP .... Optical Rotary Power
ORT .... Optical Rotary Table
OS .... Optical Scanning (Data processing)
OSD........ Optical Scanning Device
OSR........ Optical Scanning Recognition
OST .... Optical Sensing Trigger
OSS .... Optical Sight System
OSA .... Optical Society of America
OSR........ Optical Sound Recorder
OPTICON ... Optical Tactical Converter (Electronic reader for the blind)
OTES ...... Optical Technology Experiment System
OTS........ Optical Technology Satellite
OTFE .... Optical Terminal Flight Evaluation
OTD........ Optical Tracking Device
OTE .... Optical Tracking Electronics
OTS........ Optical Tracking System
OTF .... Optical Transfer Function
OVS .... Optical Viewing System
OWA .... Optical Wholesalers Association
OPW .... Optical Window
OVL .... Optically Void Liquid
OM .... Opticalman (Navy rating)
OKN .... Opticokinetic Nystagmus (Eye condition)
OTI .... Optics Technology, Incorporated
OAPM ...... Optimal Amplitude and Phase Modulation
OAC .... Optimal Automatic Control
ODF .... Optimal Decision Function
OI .... Optimist International
OSIC .... Optimization of Subcarrier Information Capacity
OMEC ...... Optimized Microminiature Electronic Circuit
OPCON ..... Optimizing Control (Military)
OATS....... Optimum Aerial Target Sensor
OBIS .... Optimum Burn-In Screening
OCR .... Optimum Charge Regulator
OERC....... Optimum Earth Reentry Corridor (Aerospace)

OGM . . . . Optimum Gradient Method
OMSRADS . . . . Optimum Mix of Short Range Air Defense Systems
OOP . . . . Optimum Optical Pump
OQP . . . . Optimum Qualification Procedure
ORT . . . . Optimum Resolution Technique
OSR . . . . Optimum Ship Routing
OTOCTA . . . . Optimum Technical Operational Concept to Accomplish
OTF . . . . Optimum Traffic Frequency (Radio)
OWE . . . . Optimum Working Efficiency
OWF . . . . Optimum Working Frequency (Communications)
O . . . . Optimus (Best)
OF . . . . Optional Form
OEI . . . . Optoelectronic Isolator
OPA . . . . Optoelectronic Pulse Amplifier
OPK . . . . Optokinetic
OMDM . . . . . . Opto-Mechanical Display Module
OG . . . . Or Gate (Data processing)
OO . . . . Or Order
ORBIT . . . . . . Oracle Binary Internal Translator (Algebraic programming system)
ORAL . . . . . . Oral Access to Library
OHA . . . . Oral History Association
ORS . . . . Oral Surgeon
OTT . . . . Oral Trade Tests (Department of Labor)
O . . . . Orange (Maps and charts)
OCC . . . . Orange Coast College (California) (Now OCJC)
OCJC . . . . . . Orange Coast Junior College (California)
OFS . . . . Orange Free State
OJ . . . . Orange Juice
OLT . . . . Orange Light
OPC . . . . Orange Pigment Cell
ORC . . . . Orange River Colony (Became Orange Free State)
ORU . . . . Orange and Rockland Utilities, Inc. (NYSE symbol)
OY . . . . Orange Yellow
OURS . . . . . . Orangutan Recovery Service
OAMS . . . . . . Orbit Attitude and Maneuvering System (NASA)
ODVAR . . . . . Orbit Determination and Vehicle Attitude Reference
OSC . . . . Orbit Shift Coil
OST . . . . Orbit Stay Time
OASV . . . . . . Orbital Assembly Support Vehicle
OAME . . . . . . Orbital Attitude and Maneuvering Electronics
OBGS . . . . . . Orbital Bombardment Guidance System
OBS . . . . Orbital Bombardment System
OCT . . . . Orbital Circularization Technique
ODC . . . . Orbital Data Collector
ODM . . . . Orbital Determination Module
OEC . . . . Orbital Electron Capture
OES . . . . Orbital-Escape System (NASA)
OLF . . . . Orbital Launch Facility
OLO . . . . Orbital Launch Operation
OLV . . . . Orbital-Launch Vehicle
OMS . . . . Orbital Multifunction Satellite
OPEP . . . . . . Orbital-Plane Experiment Package (NASA)
OPI . . . . Orbital Position Indicator
ORMU . . . . . . Orbital Remote Maneuvering Unit
ORBS . . . . . . Orbital Rendezvous Base System
ORPICS . . . . . Orbital Rendezvous Positioning, Indexing and Coupling System
OSS . . . . Orbital Space Station
OSSS . . . . . . Orbital Space Station Study
OSSS . . . . . . Orbital Space Station System (of NASA)
OSV . . . . Orbital Support Vehicle
OTV . . . . Orbital Transfer Vehicle
OUL . . . . Orbital Utility Light
OVAM . . . . . . Orbital Vehicle Assembly Mode
OVERS . . . . . Orbital Vehicle Reentry Simulator (NASA)
OAO . . . . Orbiting Astronomical Observatory (NASA)
OASF . . . . . . Orbiting Astronomical Support Facility
ODRN . . . . . Orbiting Data Relay Network
ODRS . . . . . . Orbiting Data Relay System
OED . . . . Orbiting Energy Depot
OEC . . . . Orbiting Experimental Capsule
OGO . . . . Orbiting Geophysical Observatory (NASA)
OLAFS . . . . . Orbiting and Launch Approach Flight Simulator
OPO . . . . Orbiting Planetary Observatory
ORBIS . . . . . . Orbiting Radio Beacon Ionospheric Satellite (NASA)
OREO . . . . . . Orbiting Radio Emission Observatory (Satellite)
ORL . . . . Orbiting Research Laboratory (NASA)
OSCAR . . . . . Orbiting Satellite Carrying Amateur Radio (Aerospace)
OSO . . . . Orbiting Solar Observatory (A satellite)
OSL . . . . Orbiting Space Laboratory
OV . . . . Orbiting Vehicle (Aerospace)
OVM . . . . Orbiting Velocity Meter

OXO . . . . Orbiting X-Ray Observatory (NASA)
OZO . . . . Orbiting Zoological Observatory to Track Animals
OF . . . . Orbitofrontal
ORBA . . . . . Orde Baru (New Order) (Indonesia)
ORLA . . . . . Orde Lama (Old Order) (Indonesia)
O . . . . Order
OA . . . . Order of the Alhambra
O of A . . . . . Order of Amaranth
OA . . . . Order of the Arrow
OB . . . . Order of Battle
OBL . . . . Order Bill of Lading (Shipping)
OBO . . . . Order By Order
OC . . . . Order Canceled
OCSO . . . . . Order of Cistercian Nuns of the Strict Observance (Roman Catholic religious order)
OC . . . . Order of Cistercians (Roman Catholic religious order)
OCSO . . . . . Order of Cistercians of the Strict Observance (Trappists) (Roman Catholic men's religious order)
OCR . . . . Order of Corporate Reunion (British)
O/D . . . . Order of Deportation
OES . . . . Order of the Eastern Star
OFPA . . . . . . Order of the Founders and Patriots of America
OFM Cap . . . . Order of Friars Minor Capuchin (Capuchins) (Roman Catholic religious order)
OFM Conv . . . Order of Friars Minor Conventual (Conventuals) (Roman Catholic religious order)
OGC . . . . Order of the Golden Chain
OHC . . . . Order of the Holy Cross (Episcopalian religious order)
OID . . . . Order Initiated Distribution
OJD . . . . Order of Job's Daughters
ODM . . . . Order of Mercy (Mercedarians) (Roman Catholic religious order)
OM . . . . Order of Merit
O/N . . . . Order Notify (Bill of lading) (Shipping)
O/O . . . . Order Of (Business and trade)
OOO . . . . Order of Owls
OPIM . . . . . . Order Processing and Inventory Monitoring (Data processing)
ORT . . . . Order of Railroad Telegraphers (Later, Transportation-Communication Employees Union)
ORC . . . . Order of Railway Conductors
ORCB . . . . . . Order of Railway Conductors and Brakemen
ORSA . . . . . . Order of Recollects of St. Augustine
ORC . . . . Order of the Red Cross
OS Cam . . . . Order of St. Camillus (Camillians) (Roman Catholic religious order)
OSD . . . . Order of St. Dominic
OSF . . . . Order of St. Francis (Franciscans) (Roman Catholic religious order)
OSL . . . . Order of Saint Luke the Physician
OSP . . . . Order of St. Paul the First Hermit (Pauline Fathers) (Roman Catholic religious order)
OSU . . . . Order of St. Ursula
OS . . . . Order of Servites
OS . . . . Order Sheet
OSB . . . . Order of Shepherds of Bethlehem
OST . . . . Order Shipping Time
OSC . . . . Order to Show Cause
OSB . . . . Order of the Stars and Bars
OTC . . . . Order of Three Crusades
OUAM . . . . . . Order of United American Mechanics
OUA . . . . Order of United Americans
OUCTA . . . . . Order of United Commercial Travelers of America
OWSJ . . . . . . Order of the White Shrine of Jerusalem
WSJ . . . . Order of the White Shrine of Jerusalem
OW . . . . Order Wire (Military)
OB . . . . Ordered Back
OCCULT . . . . . Ordered Computer Collation of Unprepared Literary Texts
ORATE . . . . . Ordered Random Access Talking Equipment
OR . . . . Ordered Recorded
ORBIS . . . . . . Ordering and Billing System
OFR . . . . Ordering Function Register
ORDCAN . . . . Orders Cancelled (Air Force)
ORDCONCAN . . Orders Considered Cancelled (Air Force)
ORDCOR . . . . Orders Corrected (Air Force)
OMSA . . . . . Orders and Medals Society of America
ORDMOD . . . . Orders Modified (Navy)
O . . . . Ordinary
OARC . . . . . . Ordinary Administrative Radio Conference
ORDDIS . . . . . Ordinary Discharge (Military)
OEW . . . . Ordinary Electromagnetic Wave
OHD . . . . Ordinary Hydrodynamic
OLS . . . . Ordinary Least Squares (Statistics)
OLSE . . . . . . Ordinary Least-Squares Estimators (Statistics)
OL . . . . Ordinary Leave (Military)

OLD ECC .... Ordinary Linear Differential Equations with Constant Coefficients (Mathematics)

OMO .... Ordinary Money Order

ONC .... Ordinary National Certificate (British)

OND .... Ordinary National Diploma (British)

OS .... Ordinary Seaman

OST .... Ordinary Spring Tides

OW .... Ordinary Warfare

OWC .... Ordinary Wave Component

O .... Ordinis (By the Order of)

OSFC ...... Ordinis Sancti Francisci Capuccini (Franciscan Capuchins) (Roman Catholic men's religious order)

O .... Ordnance

OAR .... Ordnance Accomplishment Requirement (Navy)

OAL .... Ordnance Aerophysics Laboratory

OAR .... Ordnance Allowance Report (Navy)

ORDIP ..... Ordnance Alteration Installation Plan (Navy)

ORDALT .... Ordnance Alterations

OAC .... Ordnance Ammunition Command (Army) (Merged with Munitions Command)

OASMS ..... Ordnance Ammunition Surveillance and Maintenance School

OB .... Ordnance Battalion (Navy)

OB .... Ordnance Board (Navy)

OCL .... Ordnance Circular Letter

OCD .... Ordnance Classification Defect (Navy)

OCMS ...... Ordnance Command Management System

OCAS ...... Ordnance Configuration Accounting System (Navy)

ORDCORPS ... Ordnance Corps (Army)

ORDP ...... Ordnance Corps Pamphlet (Army)

OCTI ...... Ordnance Corps Technical Instruction

OD .... Ordnance Data (Inspection and test data)

OD .... Ordnance Department or Division

ORDRAT .... Ordnance Dial Reader and Translator

OD .... Ordnance Document (Navy)

ORDENG .... Ordnance Engineering

OEC .... Ordnance Equipment Chart

O & FN .... Ordnance and Facilities - Navy

OFSB ...... Ordnance Field Service Bulletin (Military)

OFSC ...... Ordnance Field Service Circular (Military)

OGMS ...... Ordnance Guided Missile School

OGR .... Ordnance, Gunnery and Readiness Division (Coast Guard)

OHI .... Ordnance Handling Instructions

OIDA ...... Ordnance Industrial Data Agency

OIL .... Ordnance Investigation Laboratory

ORDLIS .... Ordnance Logistics Information System (Navy)

OMS .... Ordnance Machine Shop

OMB .... Ordnance Maintenance Bulletin

OMMIC ..... Ordnance Maintenance Management Information Center (Navy)

OMETA ..... Ordnance Management Engineering Training Agency (Army)

OMRR ...... Ordnance Material Research Reactor

OMRO ...... Ordnance Materials Research Office (Army)

OMC .... Ordnance Missile Command (Later, Missile Command)

OMI .... Ordnance Modifications Instructions

OO .... Ordnance Office(r)

OANDOS .... Ordnance and Ordnance Stores (Coast Guard)

O & OS .... Ordnance and Ordnance Stores (Navy)

OP .... Ordnance Pamphlets

OP .... Ordnance Personnel

OPC .... Ordnance Procurement Center (Army)

OPI .... Ordnance Procurement Instructions

OP .... Ordnance Publications (Navy)

OPSI ...... Ordnance Publications for Supply Index (Military)

OPERA ..... Ordnance Pulses Experimental Research Assembly (Nuclear reactor)

OR .... Ordnance Report

ORDC ...... Ordnance Research and Development Center (Aberdeen Proving Ground, Maryland) (Navy)

ORL .... Ordnance Research Laboratory (Pennsylvania State University)

OSM .... Ordnance Safety Manual (Military)

OS .... Ordnance School (Army)

OSWAC ..... Ordnance Special and Ammo Weapons Command (Later, Weapons Command)

OSWC ...... Ordnance Special Weapons Command (Army) (Merged with Missile Command)

OS .... Ordnance Specifications (Navy)

OSTD ...... Ordnance Standards

OSSC ...... Ordnance Storage and Shipment Chart (Army)

OSB .... Ordnance Supply Bulletin

OSD .... Ordnance Supply Depot

OSO .... Ordnance Supply Office

OSC .... Ordnance Systems Command (Navy) (Formerly, Bureau of Naval Weapons)

OTAC ...... Ordnance Tank-Automotive Command (Army) (Merged with Weapons and Mobility Command)

OTCM ...... Ordnance Technical Committee Minutes (Military)

OTI .... Ordnance Technical Instructions (Navy)

OTIS ...... Ordnance Telemetry Instrumentation Station (Army)

OTB .... Ordnance and Terminal Ballistics

OTC .... Ordnance Training Command (Army)

OUTC ...... Ordnance Unit Training Center (Military)

ORDVAC .... Ordnance Variable Automatic Computer (AEC)

OWS .... Ordnance Weapon Systems (Army)

OWC .... Ordnance Weapons Command (Later, Weapons Command)

OCC .... Ordo Carmelitarum Calceatorum (Carmelites)

OCD .... Ordo Carmelitarum Discalceatorum (Discalced, or barefoot, Carmelites) (Roman Catholic religious order)

OC .... Ordo Charitatis (Fathers of the Order of Charity) (Roman Catholic religious order)

SchP ...... Ordo Clericorum Regularium Pauperum Matris Dei Scholarum Piarum (Piarist Fathers) (Roman Catholic religious order)

OCM .... Ordo Constantini Magni (International Constantinian Order)

OM .... Ordo (Fratrum) Minimorum (Minims of St. Francis of Paul) (Roman Catholic men's religious order)

OMC .... Ordo Minorum Cappucinorum (Capuchins) (Roman Catholic men's religious order)

OMC .... Ordo Minorum Conventualium (Conventual Franciscans) (Roman Catholic men's religious order)

OP .... Ordo Praedicatorum (Order of Preachers) (Dominicans) (Roman Catholic religious order)

OCR .... Ordo Reformatorum Cisterciensium (Cistercians, Trappists) (Roman Catholic men's religious order)

OSA .... Ordo (Eremitarum) Sancti Augustini (Augustinians) (Roman Catholic religious order)

OSBM ...... Ordo Sancti Basil Magni (Order of St. Basil the Great) (Roman Catholic men's religious order)

OSB .... Ordo Sancti Benedicti (Order of Saint Benedict) (Benedictines) (Roman Catholic religious order)

OSH .... Ordo Sancti Hieronymi (Hieronymites)

OSsT ...... Ordo Sanctissimae Trinitatis Redemptionis Captivorum (Order of the Most Holy Trinity) (Trinitarians) (Roman Catholic religious order)

OSM .... Ordo Servorum Mariae (Order of Servants of Mary) (Servites) (Roman Catholic religious order)

OBO .... Ore-Bulk-Oil (Supertanker)

OR .... Oregon

OCE .... Oregon, California & Eastern Railway Company (AAR code)

ORCA ...... Oregon Caves National Monument

OCE .... Oregon College of Education

OE .... Oregon Electric Railway (AAR code)

ONW .... Oregon & Northwestern R. R. (AAR code)

OPE .... Oregon, Pacific & Eastern Railway Company (AAR code)

UP .... Oregon Short Line R. R. (AAR code)

OSC .... Oregon State College

OSU .... Oregon State University

OTI .... Oregon Technical Institute

OT .... Oregon Trunk Railway (AAR code)

UP .... Oregon-Washington R. R. & Navigation (AAR code)

OHS .... Organ Historical Society

ORPI ...... Organ Pipe Cactus National Monument

OTD .... Organ Tolerance Dose

OCS .... Organe de Controle des Stupefiants

OAIP ...... Organic Ablative Insulative Plastic

OAP .... Organic Ablative Plastic

OASP ...... Organic Acid Soluble Phosphorus

OCC .... Organic Carbon Cycle

OCDRE ..... Organic-Cooled Deuterium Reactor Experiment

ORCON ..... Organic Control

OEB .... Organic Electrolyte Battery

OEBS ...... Organic Electrolyte Battery System

OGG .... Organic Geochemistry Group

OHD .... Organic Heart Disease (Medicine)

OIM .... Organic Insulating Material

OIP .... Organic Insulative Plastic

OLL .... Organic Liquid LASER

OLMR ...... Organic Liquid Moderated Reactor

OMR .... Organic Magnetic Resonance

OMS .... Organic Mass Spectroscopy

OM .... Organic Matter

OMCR ...... Organic-Moderated Cooled Reactor

OMFBR ..... Organic-Moderated Fluidized Bed Reactor

OMRCA ..... Organic-Moderated Reactor Critical Assembly

OMRE ...... Organic-Moderated Reactor Experiment (AEC)

OMC .... Organic Molecular Crystal

OPHIR ..... Organic Power and Heat Industrial Reactor (AEC)

ORACLE . . . . . Organic Rankine Cycle
OTR . . . . Organic Test Reactor
OTCC . . . . . . Organic Thermal Control Coating
OBPI . . . . Organisasi Buruh Perkebunan Indonesia (Estate Workers' Union of
      Indonesia)
OBSI . . . . Organisasi Buruh Seluruh Indonesia (Plantation Workers' Union of
      Indonesia)
OAS . . . . Organisation de l'Armee Secrete (Secret Army Organization) (Algeria and
      metropolitan France)
OACI . . . . Organisation de l'Aviation Civile Internationale
OCM . . . . Organisation Civile et Militaire
OCAM . . . . . . Organisation Commune Africaine et Malgache (Common Organization
      of African and Malagasy States)
OCLALAV . . . . Organisation Commune de Lutte Antiaviaire (Formerly, OCLAV)
OCLAV . . . . . Organisation Commune de Lutte Antiaviaire (Later, OCLALAV)
OCRS . . . . Organisation Commune des Regions Sahariennes (Common Organization of
      the Saharan Regions)
OCDE . . . . Organisation de Cooperation et de Developpement Economiques
ODECA . . . . . . Organisation de Estados Centroamericanos
OEA . . . . Organisation des Etats Americains
OECQ . . . . . Organisation Europeenne pour le Controle de la Qualite
OECE . . . . . . Organisation Europeenne de Cooperation Economique
OEPP . . . . . . Organisation Europeenne et Mediterraneenne pour la Protection
      des Plantes
ONG . . . . Organisation non Gouvernementale
OIG . . . . Organisation Intergouvernementale
OMCI . . . . Organisation Intergouvernementale Consultative de la Navigation
      Maritime
OIC . . . . Organisation Internationale Catholique
OIC . . . . Organisation Internationale du Commerce
OIE . . . . Organisation Internationale des Employeurs
OING . . . . Organisation Internationale non Gouvernementale
OIJ . . . . Organisation Internationale des Journalistes
OIML . . . . Organisation Internationale de Metrologie Legale
OIPC . . . . Organisation Internationale de Police Criminelle
OIPC . . . . Organisation Internationale de Protection Civile
OIR . . . . Organisation Internationale de Radiodiffusion
OIRT . . . . Organisation Internationale de Radiodiffusion et Television (International
      Radio and Television Organization)
OISTV . . . . . . Organisation Internationale pour la Science et la Technique du Vide
OIT . . . . Organisation Internationale du Travail
OLR . . . . Organisation Pour la Liberation du Rwanda (Organization for the
      Liberation of Rwanda)
OMI . . . . . . Organisation Meteorologique Internationale
OMM . . . . . . Organisation Meteorologique Mondiale
OMAI . . . . . . Organisation Mondiale Agudas Israel
OMEP . . . . . . Organisation Mondiale pour l'Education Prescolaire
OMGE . . . . . . Organisation Mondiale de Gastro-Enterologie
OMPSA . . . . . Organisation Mondiale pour la Protection Sociale des Aveugles
OMS . . . . . . Organisation Mondiale de la Sante
OTA . . . . Organisation Mondiale du Tourisme et de l'Automobile (World
      Touring and Automobile Organization)
ONU . . . . . . Organisation des Nations Unies (United Nations Organization)
OAA . . . . Organisation des Nations Unies pour l'Alimentation et l'Agriculture
ONUC . . . . . Organisation des Nations Unies au Congo
ORAF . . . . . . Organisation Regionale Africaine de la CISL
OREAP . . . . . Organisation Regionale de l'Est pour l'Administration Publique
ORE . . . . Organisation Regionale Europeenne de la CISL
OSPA . . . . . . Organisation Sanitaire Panamericaine
OSTIV . . . . . . Organisation Scientifique et Technique Internationale du Vol a Voile
      (International Technical and Scientific Organization for Soaring Flight)
OTAN . . . . . . Organisation du Traite de l'Atlantique Nord (French equivalent of NATO)
OTASE . . . . . . Organisation du Traite de Defense Collective pour l'Asie du Sud-Est
      (French equivalent of Southeast Asia Treaty Organization)
ORCA . . . . Organisme Europeen de Coordination des Reserches sur le Fluor et la
      Prophylaxie de la Carie Dentaire (European Organization for Research
      on Fluorine and Dental Caries Prevention)
ORGALIME . . . Organisme de Liaison des Industries Metalliques Europeennes
OIRSA . . . . . . Organismo Internacional Regional de Sanidad Agropecuaria (Central
      American Phytosanitary Organization)
OEA . . . . Organizacion de los Estados Americanos (Organization of American
      States)
OISS . . . . Organizacion Iberoamericana de Seguridad Social (Ibero-American
      Social Security Organization)
ORIT . . . . Organizacion Regional Interamericana de Trabajadores (Inter-
      American Regional Organization of Workers of the ICFTU)
OSM . . . . Organizacion Submarina Mexicana, SA
OAU . . . . . . Organization of African Unity
OAMCE . . . . . Organization Africaine et Malgache de Cooperation Economique (Afro-
      Malagasy Organization for Economic Cooperation) (Later, Common
      Afro-Malagasy Organization)

OAH . . . . Organization of American Historians
OAS . . . . Organization of American States
OAS . . . . Organization of Arab Students in the USA & Canada
OCAS . . . . Organization of Central American States
OCN . . . . Organization Change Notice
OCR . . . . Organization Change Request
OCA . . . . Organization of the Cooperatives in the Americas
ODFFU . . . . . . Organization for Defense of Four Freedoms for Ukraine
OD . . . . Organization Development
ODC . . . . Organization Development Council
OECD . . . . Organization for Economic Co-operation and Development (Formerly,
      OEEC)
OEG . . . . Organization and Equipment Guide (Army)
OEEC . . . . . . Organization for European Economic Cooperation (Later, OECD)
OENR . . . . . . Organization for European Nuclear Research
OFSC . . . . Organization and Finance Sub-Committee
OFN . . . . Organization for Flora Neotropica
OGLE . . . . . . Organization for Getting Legs Exposed (Group opposing below-the-
      knee fashions introduced in 1970)
OHPO . . . . . . Organization Health Program Officer
OLAS . . . . Organization of Latin American Solidarity (Cuba)
O & M . . . . . Organization and Management
O & M . . . . . Organization and Methods
ONIT . . . . Organization Nationale Independante des Travailleurs (National Inde-
      pendent Organization for Workers) (Belgium)
OPET . . . . . . Organization, Personnel Equipment and Training (Group)
OPEC . . . . . . Organization of Petroleum Exporting Countries
OPEDA . . . . . Organization of Professional Employees of the Department of Agriculture
ORGY . . . . . . Organization for the Rational Guidance of Youth (Fictitious
      organization in film, "The Man from ORGY")
ORU . . . . Organization for Rebirth of Ukraine
ORT . . . . Organization for Rehabilitation through Training (Acronym is used in
      names of several Jewish social welfare organizations)
ORA . . . . Organization de Resistance de l'Armee (France)
OSTI . . . . Organization for Social and Technical Innovation
OT . . . . Organization Table
OTC . . . . Organization for Trade Cooperation (GATT)
OTS . . . . Organization of Tropical Studies
OWAEC . . . . . Organization for West African Economic Co-operation
OEL . . . . Organizational Equipment List
OEA . . . . Organizational Expense Accounts
OMS . . . . Organizational Maintenance Shop
OMTS . . . . . . Organizational Maintenance Test Station (Army)
OSPE . . . . . . Organizational Spare Parts and Equipment
OSC . . . . Organizational Supply Code (Army)
ORVAT . . . . . Organizational Vehicle Automatic Tester
OUN . . . . Organizatsiia Ukrains' kykh Natsionalistiv
OGSS . . . . . . Organizazione Generale degli Studenti Somali (Organization of Somali
      Students)
OAR . . . . Organized Air Reserve
OCRS . . . . Organized Crime and Racketeering Section (Department of Justice)
OMICA . . . . . Organized Migrants in Community Action (Florida)
O . . . . Organized Naval Reserve
O2 . . . . Organized Naval Reserve Aviation
O1 . . . . Organized Naval Reserve Seagoing
OOC . . . . Organized Occupational Curricula
ORPHIC . . . . Organized Projected Hypotheses for Innovations in Curriculum
      (Educational planning)
ORC . . . . Organized Reserve Corps
ORPSU . . . . . Organized Reserve Port Security Unit
ORTC . . . . Organized Reserve Training Center
ORTU . . . . . . Organized Reserve Training Unit
ORTUAM . . . . Organized Reserve Training Unit, Administration of Mobilization
ORTUAV . . . . . Organized Reserve Training Unit, Aviation Support (Military)
ORTUF . . . . . Organized Reserve Training Unit, Coastal Force
ORTUEL . . . . . Organized Reserve Training Unit, Electronics (Coast Guard)
ORTUPS . . . . . Organized Reserve Training Unit, Port Security (Coast Guard)
ORTUPS(O) . . . Organized Reserve Training Unit, Port Security (Operational)
ORTUR . . . . . Organized Reserve Training Unit, Rescue Coordination Center (Military)
ORTUAG . . . . . Organized Reserve Training Unit, Vessel Augmentation (Military)
ODP . . . . Organized Reservists in Drill Pay Status
OMM . . . . Organo-Metallic Material
OSNC . . . . . . Orient Steam Navigation Company (British)
O . . . . Oriental
ORAMCO . . . . Oriental American Trade Development Corporation
OBM . . . . Oriental Boat Mission
OMS . . . . Oriental Missionary Society
OMP . . . . . . Oriental Music-Tape & Publishers
ORIA . . . . . . Oriental Rug Importers Association
OLSCA . . . . . . Orientation Linkage for a Solar Cell Array
OPAL . . . . Orientation Program in American Law (of AALS)

OCS . . . . Oriented Cellular Structure
OSV. . . . . . . Oriented Space Vehicle
OCM . . . . Origin of Columellar Muscle
O & D . . . . . Origin and Destination (Airlines)
O . . . . Original
OATS . . . . Original Article Tear Sheets (A publication)
OC . . . . Original Cover
OD . . . . Original Design
ODJB . . . . . . Original Dixieland Jazz Band
OE . . . . Original Equipment (Automobile industry)
OEM . . . . . . Original Equipment Manufacturer
OFP. . . . . . . Original Flight Plan
OG . . . . Original Gum
OLS . . . . Original Line of Sight
OS. . . . . Original Series
ORS . . . . Originating Register Sender
OJC . . . . . . Orlando Junior College (Florida)
OGA . . . . . . Ornamental Growers Association
OCT . . . . . . Ornithinecarbamoyl Phosphate Transferase
OFA . . . . . . Oronite Fuel Additive
OT. . . . . Orotracheal
OMMI . . . . . . Orszagos Mezogazdasagi Minosegvizsgalo Intezet
O . . . . Ortho (Chemistry)
OYA . . . . . . Orthodox Youth of America
ORR. . . . . . . Orthographic RADAR Restitutor
OJ. . . . . Orthomode Junction
OMJ . . . . . . Orthomode Junction (Electronics)
OJSA . . . . . . Orthomode Junction and Switching Assembly
OBES . . . . . . Orthonormal Basis of an Error Space (Statistics)
ORS . . . . Orthopaedic Research Society
OALMA . . . . . Orthopedic Appliance and Limb Manufacturers Association
OAM . . . . . Orthopedic Appliance Mechanic (Navy)
ON . . . . Orthopedic Nurse
ONC . . . . . . Orthopedic Nursing Certificate
OMT . . . . . . Orthotropic Multicell Tank
O . . . . Os (Bone)
OSK . . . . . . Osaka Syosen Karsha (Japanese steamship company)
OA . . . . Osborne Association
OWI. . . . . . . Oscellus Width Index
OCE . . . . . . Oscillating Current Element
ODA . . . . . . Oscillating Doublet Antenna
OOG . . . . . . Oscillating Output Geneva
OPM . . . . . . Oscillating Pressure Method
OHA . . . . . . Oscillator Housing Assembly
OMF . . . . . . Oscillatory Magnetic Field
ON-OFF. . . . . Oscillatory, Non-Oscillatory Flip-Flop (Data processing)
OTRAC . . . . . Oscillogram Trace Reader (Data processing)
ORS . . . . Oscillographic Recording System
OFP . . . . Oscilloscope Face Plane
Os . . . . Osmium (Chemical element)
OER . . . . Osmotic Erythrocyte Resistance
OO . . . . Osobyi Otdel (Counterintelligence surveillance unit in military
           formation until 1943) (USSR)
OSG . . . . Osphradial Ganglion
OSN . . . . Osphradial Nerve
O . . . . Osphradium
OCOO . . . . . Osteopathic College of Ophthalmology and Otorhinolaryngology
OCA . . . . . . Osteopathic Cranial Association
OF. . . . . Osteopathic Foundation
OLA . . . . . . Osteopathic Libraries Association
OGB . . . . . . Osterreichischer Gewerkschaftsbund (Austrian Trade Union Federation)
ODL . . . . . . Ostwald Dilution Law
OGPU . . . . . . Otdelenie Gosudarstvenni Politcheskoi Upravi (Special Government
           Political Administration) (Former Soviet secret service organization, also
           known as GPU)
OLEYIS. . . . . . Otel, Lokanta ve Eglence Yerleri Iscileri Sendikasi (Istanbul Hotel,
           Restaurant and Amusement Places Workers' Union) (Turkey)
OJC . . . . Otero Junior College (Colorado)
OA & S . . . . . Other Arms and Services (Military)
ODC . . . . Other Direct Costs
OP. . . . . Other People's (Borrowed money, cigarettes, etc.) (Slang)
OPB . . . . Other People's Butts (Cigarette butts garnered from ash trays) (Slang)
OPT . . . . Other People's Tobacco (Slang)
OPN . . . . . . Other Procurement, Navy
OR . . . . Other Ranks (Ranks other than officers) (Military)
OSSN. . . . . . . Other Specialty Serial Numbers (Air Force)
OTRA . . . . . . Other Than Regular Army
OTRAR . . . . . Other Than Regular Army
O/TSC . . . . . Other Than Special Consultants (Military)
OKA . . . . . . Otherwise Known As
OT. . . . . Otis Elevator Company (NYSE symbol)

OHC . . . . Ottumwa Heights College (Iowa)
OBC . . . . . . Ouachita Baptist College (Arkansas)
OZIN. . . . . . Ounce Inch
OZT . . . . . . Ounces Troy
O/A . . . . Our Account (Business and trade)
OLCC . . . . . . Our Lady of Cincinnati College (Ohio)
OLLC . . . . . . Our Lady of the Lake College (Texas)
OM . . . . Our Message
ONT . . . . . . Our New Thread (Clark thread designation)
OCP. . . . . . . Out of Commission for Parts
OCTLA . . . . . Out of Control Area (Aviation)
OGE . . . . . . Out-of-Ground Effect
OH . . . . Out Home (Men's lacrosse position)
O to O. . . . . . Out to Out (Technical drawings)
OOP . . . . . . Out of Plane
OP. . . . . Out of Print (Publishing)
OPP . . . . Out of Print at Present
OR. . . . . Out of Range
OSC . . . . Out, See Copy (Proofreader's note)
O/S . . . . Out of Service
OTS . . . . Out of Service
O/S . . . . Out of Stock (Business and trade)
OB. . . . . Outboard
OBMA . . . . . Outboard Boat Manufacturers Association
OBC . . . . . . Outboard Boating Club of America
OECO . . . . . . Outboard Engine Cutoff
OIA . . . . . . Outboard Industry Associations
OM . . . . . . Outboard Marine Corporation (NYSE symbol)
OMMA . . . . Outboard Motor Manufacturers Association
OMB . . . . . . Outboard Motorboat
ORS . . . . Outboard Rotating Shield
ORAD . . . . . . Outbound Radial (Aviation)
OAAA . . . . . Outdoor Advertising Association of America
OEA . . . . . . Outdoor Education Association
OMS . . . . . . Outdoor Microphone System
OPEI . . . . . . Outdoor Power Equipment Institute
ORI . . . . . . Outdoor Recreation Institute
ORRRC . . . . . Outdoor Recreation Resources Review Commission (Department of the
           Interior)
OWAA . . . . . Outdoor Writers Association of America
O/A. . . . . . . Outer Anchorage (Navigation)
OBP . . . . Outer (Edge of) Basal Piece
ODZ . . . . . . Outer Defense Zone
OG . . . . Outer Gimbal
OGA . . . . . . Outer Gimbal Axis
OGI. . . . . . . Outer Grid Injection
OJ . . . . Outer Jacket
OK . . . . Outer Keel
OM . . . . Outer Marker
OMB . . . . . . Outer Marker Beacon (Aviation)
OMKR . . . . . Outer Marker, Instrument Landing System (Aviation)
OPFAD . . . . . Outer-Perimeter Fleet Air Defense
ORZ . . . . . . Outer Radiation Zone
OSSP . . . . . . Outer Solar System Probe
OTE. . . . . . . Outer Tube Equipment
OW . . . . Outer Wing
OWP . . . . . . Outer Wing Panel
O . . . . Outfield (Baseball)
OSP . . . . Outfitting Stock Point
OL . . . . Outgoing Letter
OGL . . . . . . Outgoing Line
OLC . . . . . . Outgoing Line Circuit
OQL . . . . . . Outgoing Quality Level
OQL . . . . . . Outgoing Quality Limit
OGR . . . . . . Outgoing Repeater
OTT . . . . . . Outgoing Teletype
OGT . . . . . . Outgoing Trunk
OGU . . . . . . Outgoing Unit
OC . . . . Outing Club
O . . . . Outlet
OAP. . . . . . . Outlet Absolute Pressure
OTU. . . . . . . Outlet Company (NYSE symbol)
OC. . . . . Outlet Contact
OGV . . . . . . Outlet Guide Vane
OSBA . . . . . . Outlet and Switch Box Association
OLF . . . . . . Outlying Field
OPC. . . . . . . Out-Patient Clinic (Medicine)
OCH . . . . . . Outpatient Clinic (Hospital) (Veterans Administration)
OCI. . . . . . . Outpatient Clinic (Independent) (Veterans Administration)
OCS . . . . . . Outpatient Clinic Substation (Veterans Administration)
OPD. . . . . . . Out-Patient Department

OPD........	Out-Patient Dispensary
OPR........	Outpatient Rate
OPL........	Out-of-Phase Loading
OP.........	Outpost
OPL........	Outpost Line
OPLR.......	Outpost Line of Resistance
OITT.......	Outpulser, Identifier, Trunk Test
OA.........	Output Amplitude
OAS.......	Output Amplitude Stability
OA.........	Output Axis
OB........	Output Buffer (Air Force)
OC........	Output Computer
OCB.......	Output Current Booster
ODB.......	Output to Display Buffer (Data processing)
ODU.......	Output Display Unit
OFTMS......	Output Format Table Modification Submodule
OI.........	Output Impedance
OLL........	Output Logic Level
OMP.......	Output Makeup
OMS.......	Output per Man Shift
OMS.......	Output Multiplex Synchronizer
OP.........	Output Power
ORA.......	Output Register Address
OS........	Output Secondary (Electronics)
OSV.......	Output Serving Voltage
OSR.......	Output Shift Register
OSR.......	Output Signal Range
OUTRAN....	Output Translator (IBM)
OV........	Output Voltage
OS.........	Outside
OAT.......	Outside Air Temperature (Aviation)
OCLUS......	Outside Continental Limits of United States
OCONUS....	Outside Continental United States
OD........	Outside Diameter
OD........	Outside Dimension
OF........	Outside Face (Technical drawings)
OG........	Outside Guard
OHA.......	Outside Helix Angle
OL........	Outside Left (Soccer position)
OLP.......	Outside Left Position (Dancing)
OML.......	Outside Mold Line (Technical drawings)
OP........	Outside Production
OPCO......	Outside Production Consignment Order
OPG.......	Outside Production Group
OPMSO.....	Outside Production Material Sales Order
OPOS......	Outside Production Operation Sheet
OR........	Outside Radius (Technical drawings)
OR........	Outside Right (Soccer position)
ORP.......	Outside Right Position (Dancing)
OS & Y.....	Outside Screw and Yoke
OS........	Outside Sentinel
OUTUS.....	Outside the United States
OVP.......	Outside Vendor Personnel
OS........	Outsize (Of clothes)
O/S........	Outstanding
OCSA......	Outstanding Civilian Service Award
ORAAP.....	Outstanding Reserve Airman Appointment Program
OB.........	Outward Bound
OVHD......	Oval Head
ORS.......	Oval Ring Seal
O..........	Over
OA........	Over-All (Technical drawings)
O/C........	Over-the-Counter (Also, OTC)
OTC.......	Over the Counter (Stock)
OTC.......	Over-the-Counter (Pharmacy)
OFR.......	Over Frequency Relay
OTH.......	Over-the-Horizon (RADAR)
OHDETS....	Over-Horizon Detection System
OHD.......	Over-the-Horizon Detector
OHR.......	Over-the-Horizon RADAR
OTHR......	Over-the-Horizon RADAR
O/H........	Over-the-Horizon Transmission
OTN.......	Over the Nose
OOC.......	Over-Ocean Communications
ORS.......	Over Range Station (Aviation)
ORC.......	Over Run Clutch
OS/D.......	Over, Short, and Damaged (Report) (Shipping)
OS & DR....	Over, Short and Damaged Report (Shipping)
OST.......	Over Stress Testing
OV.........	Over Voltage
OVV.......	Over Voltage
OVLP......	Over Voltage Load Protection
OVP.......	Over Voltage Protection
OVR.......	Over Voltage Relay
OEDP......	Overall Economic Development Program (Bureau of Indian Affairs)
OEI........	Overall Efficiency Index
OR........	Overall Report
OASPL.....	Overall Sound Pressure Level
OAT.......	Overall Test
OATS......	Overall Test Set
OTFR......	Overall Transfer Function Response
O..........	Overcast (Nautical)
OC........	Overcharge (Merchandising slang)
O/C........	Overcharge
OC........	Overcurrent
OD........	Overdraft, Overdrawn (Banking)
O/D........	Overdraft (Banking)
OF.........	Overflow
OL........	Overflow Level
OSF.......	Overgrowth Stimulating Factor (Cancer cause)
OH........	Overhaul
O/H........	Overhaul
OCL.......	Overhaul Cycle Limit
OAR.......	Overhaul and Repair
OR........	Overhaul and Repair
O & R......	Overhaul and Repair (Navy)
OH........	Overhead
OAH.......	Overhead Air Hoist
OA........	Overhead Approach (Aviation)
OHC.......	Overhead Camshaft (Automotive term)
OER.......	Overhead Expenditure Request
OL........	Overhead Line
OPS.......	Overhead Positioning System (AEC)
OHV.......	Overhead Valve
ORT.......	Overland RADAR Technology
OL........	Overlap
OT........	Overlap Technician
OL........	Overload (Electricity)
OLR.......	Overload Relay
OVT.......	Overnite Transportation Company (NYSE symbol)
OPL.......	Overpaid Last Account
OP........	Overprint
OP........	Overproof (Distilling)
OCB.......	Override Control Bits
OCV.......	Overriding Cam Valve
ORCV.....	Overriding Cam Valve
ORL.......	Overrun Lights (Aviation)
OS........	Oversea (Military)
ODSD.....	Oversea Duty Selection Data (Air Force)
OEO.......	Oversea Employment Office(r) (Air Force)
OIDPS......	Oversea Intelligence Data Processing System
OSREPL.....	Oversea Replacement (Military)
OSR.......	Oversea Returnee
OSRET.....	Oversea Returnee (Military)
OTAD......	Oversea Terminal Arrival Date (Army)
OTRA.....	Oversea Theater Requisitioning Authority (Military)
OAB.......	Overseas Affairs Branch (Department of the Army)
OATC.....	Overseas Air Traffic Control
OAC.......	Overseas Automotive Club
OBR.......	Overseas Business Reports (Department of Commerce)
OC........	Overseas Commands (Air Force)
OCP.......	Overseas Communication Project
OCCA.....	Overseas Communications Cooperation Association
ODI........	Overseas Development Institute (British)
OD & RD....	Overseas Discharge and Replacement Depot
OEA.......	Overseas Education Association
OEF.......	Overseas Education Fund of the League of Women Voters
OES.......	Overseas Educational Service
OERP......	Overseas Expenditure Reduction Program (Military)
OFAS......	Overseas Flight Assistance Service
OFACS.....	Overseas Foreign Aeronautical Communications Statistician
OFARS.....	Overseas-Foreign Aeronautical Receiver Station
OFATS.....	Overseas-Foreign Aeronautical Transmitter Station
OISP......	Overseas Internal Security Program
OLC.......	Overseas Liaison Committee (of the American Council on Education)
OLSS......	Overseas Limited Storage Site (Military)
OMS.......	Overseas Mission Society
OMF.......	Overseas Missionary Fellowship
ONA.......	Overseas National Airways, Inc.
ONA.......	Overseas News Agency
OOSS.....	Overseas Operational Storage Site
OPU.......	Overseas Plexiglas Unit

OPC . . . . Overseas Press Club of America
OPEDC . . . . . . Overseas Private Enterprise Development Corporation (Proposed
         successor to Agency for International Development)
OPIC . . . . Overseas Private Investment Corporation (US)
ORCEN . . . . . . Overseas Records Center (Military)
OR . . . . Overseas Replacement
ORPL . . . . Overseas Replacement
ORD . . . . Overseas Replacement Depot (Military)
OVU . . . . Overseas Securities Company (NYSE symbol)
OSSF . . . . Overseas Services Storage Facility
OSC . . . . Overseas Settlement Committee (British) (World War I)
OSD . . . . Overseas Settlement Department (British) (World War I)
OSA . . . . Overseas Supply Agency
OTCA . . . . . . Overseas Technical Cooperation Agency (Japan)
OTC . . . . Overseas Trade Corporation (British)
OVUREP . . . . Overseas Unit Replacement (System)
OVAC . . . . . Overseas Visual Aids Centre (British)
OW . . . . Overseas Writers (Association)
OT . . . . Overtime (Business and trade)
O/T . . . . Overtime (Business and trade)
OAR . . . . Overtime Authorization Request
ORE . . . . Overtraining Reversal Effect
OTS . . . . Ovonic Threshold Switch
OIH . . . . Ovulation-Inducing Hormone (Endocrinology)
OR . . . . Owasco River Railway (AAR code)
OCF . . . . Owens-Corning Fiberglas Corporation (NYSE symbol)
OI . . . . Owens-Illinois Glass Company (NYSE symbol)
OVRO . . . . . Owens Valley Radio Observatory
ODN . . . . Own Doppler Nullifier
OSC . . . . Own Ship's Course
OSH . . . . Own Ship's Heading
OSS . . . . Own Ship's Speed
OSSR . . . . Own Ship's Speed Repeater
O & O . . . . . . Owned and Operated (Radio and TV stations)
O . . . . Owner
OR . . . . Owner's Risk (Shipping)
ORW . . . . . . Owner's Risk of Becoming Wet
ORB . . . . Owner's Risk of Breaking
ORC . . . . Owner's Risk of Chafing
ORD . . . . Owner's Risk of Damage
ORF . . . . Owner's Risk of Fire
ORF . . . . Owner's Risk of Freezing
ORL . . . . Owner's Risk of Leakage
ORR . . . . . . Owner's Risk Rates (Shipping)
ORS . . . . Owner's Risk of Shifting
OL & T . . . . . Owners, Landlords, and Tenants
O/P . . . . Ownership Purpose Code (Military)

OXA . . . . . . Oxalic Acid
OXFAM . . . . . Oxford Committee for Famine Relief (British)
OCAL . . . . The Oxford Companion to American Literature
OED . . . . Oxford English Dictionary
OXP . . . . . . Oxford Paper Company (NYSE symbol)
OUBC . . . . . . Oxford University Boat Club
OUDS . . . . . . Oxford University Dramatic Society
OUEL . . . . Oxford University Engineering Laboratory
OUM . . . . . . Oxford University Mission
OUP . . . . . . Oxford University Press
O/F . . . . Oxidant/Fuel
O-R . . . . Oxidation-Reduction
ORP . . . . Oxidation Reduction Potential
ORC . . . . Oxidation Resistant Coating
OBC . . . . Oxide-Coated Brush Cathode
OLIS . . . . . . Oxide Layer Isolation Structure
OSR . . . . Oxide Stable Resin
OTI . . . . Oxide Throat Insert
OPS . . . . Oxidizer Particle Size
OVC . . . . Oxidizer Vent Control
OF . . . . Oxidizing Flame
OCA . . . . Oxychloride Cement Association
ODA . . . . Oxydianiline (Chemical)
O . . . . Oxygen (Chemical element)
OAF . . . . Oxygen Alternate Fill
OBA . . . . Oxygen Breathing Apparatus
OC . . . . Oxygen Consumed
OCG . . . . . . Oxygen Consumption Gauge
OFTD . . . . . . Oxygen Furnace Tilt Drive
OOI . . . . Oxygen/Ozone Indicator
OOR . . . . Oxygen/Ozone Recorder
OPP . . . . Oxygen Partial Pressure
OPPS . . . . . . Oxygen Partial Pressure Sensor
OPS . . . . Oxygen Purge System (NASA)
ORP . . . . Oxygen Reduction Potential
OSM . . . . Oxygen Steel Making
OTC . . . . Oxygen Transfer Compressor
OUF . . . . Oxygen Utilization Factor
OVF . . . . Oxygen Vent Fill
OGDA . . . . . . Oyster Growers and Dealers Association
OINA . . . . . . Oyster Institute of North America
OSI . . . . Oyster Shell Institute
OAL . . . . Ozark Air Lines, Inc.
OZA . . . . Ozark Air Lines, Inc.
OZAR . . . . . . Ozark National Scenic Riverways (National Park Service designation)
O3 . . . . Ozone
OZ . . . . Ozone

P

PCPA . . . . P-chlorophenylalanine
PIN . . . . P-type Intrinsic-N-type
PBR . . . . Pabst Blue Ribbon (Beer) (Used by barmaids)
P . . . . Pacer
PAC . . . . Pacific Air Command (Air Force)
PACUSA . . . . . Pacific Air Command, United States Army
PAF . . . . Pacific Air Forces
PACAF . . . . . . Pacific Air Forces (Air Force)
PACAFBASECOM . . Pacific Air Forces Base Command
PJSS . . . . PACAF (Pacific Air Forces) Jungle Survival School
PAL . . . . Pacific Air Lines
PAC . . . . Pacific Airmotive Corporation
PCF . . . . Pacific American Corporation (NYSE symbol)
PATA . . . . Pacific American Tankship Association
PASA . . . . Pacific American Steamship Association
PASSA . . . . . . Pacific American Steamship Association
PACOM . . . . . Pacific Area Command (Military)
PATA . . . . . . Pacific Area Travel Association
PAAC . . . . Pacific and Asian Affairs Council
PAC . . . . Pacific Automotive Corporation
BARPAC . . . . . Pacific Barrier Patrol (Military)
PAG . . . . Pacific Cement & Aggregates, Inc. (NYSE symbol)
PCCP . . . . Pacific Coast Canned Pear Service
PACORNALOG . . Pacific Coast Coordinator of Naval Logistics
PCCNL . . . . . . Pacific Coast Coordinator of Naval Logistics
PCGM . . . . . . Pacific Coast Garment Manufacturers
PCHL . . . . Pacific Coast Hockey League (Later, Western Hockey League)
PCL . . . . Pacific Coast League (Baseball)
MFOW . . . . . . Pacific Coast Marine Firemen, Oilers, Watertenders and Wipers
Association
PCOGA . . . . . Pacific Coast Oyster Growers Association
PC . . . . Pacific Coast R. R. (AAR code)
PCSE . . . . Pacific Coast Stock Exchange
POLO . . . . . . Pacific Command Operations Liaison Office
PCA . . . . Pacific Communications Area (Air Force)
PN . . . . Pacific Communications Net (Air Force)
PDT . . . . Pacific Daylight Time
PACD . . . . Pacific Division (Military)
PTCC . . . . Pacific Division Transport Control Center
PE . . . . Pacific Electric Railway (AAR code)
PETS . . . . Pacific Electronics Trade Show
PACEX . . . . . . Pacific Exchange (System) (Military)
PFC . . . . Pacific Finance Corporation
PACFLT . . . . . . Pacific Fleet
PACADV . . . . . Pacific Fleet Advance Headquarters (Guam)
PACCALL . . . . Pacific Fleet Calls (Radio call signs)
PACCOM . . . . Pacific Fleet Communications Instructions
PFI . . . . Pacific Forest Industries
PCG . . . . Pacific Gas & Electric Company (NYSE symbol)
PG & E . . . . . Pacific Gas and Electric Company
PGE . . . . Pacific Great Eastern Railway Company (AAR code)
PACHEDPEARL . . Pacific Headquarters, Pearl Harbor, Hawaii (Navy)
PHPA . . . . Pacific Herring Packers Association
PIE . . . . Pacific Intermountain Express (NYSE symbol) (Wall Street slang name:
"Pizza")
PITA . . . . . . Pacific International Trapshooting Association
PLO . . . . Pacific Launch Operations (NASA)
PLOO . . . . . . Pacific Launch Operations Office (NASA)
PLT . . . . Pacific Lighting Corporation (NYSE symbol)
PLC . . . . Pacific Logging Congress
PLEA . . . . . . Pacific Lumber Exporters Association
PLIB . . . . Pacific Lumber Inspection Bureau
PMA . . . . Pacific Maritime Association

PMR . . . . Pacific Missile Range (Later, WTR)
PNL . . . . Pacific Naval Laboratory (British)
PN . . . . Pacific Northern Airlines, Inc.
PNA . . . . Pacific Northern Airlines, Inc.
PNNCF . . . . . Pacific Northern Naval Coastal Frontier
PNB . . . . Pacific Northwest Bell (AT & T)
PNBMS . . . . . . Pacific Northwest Bird and Mammal Society
PNL . . . . Pacific Northwest Laboratory (AEC)
PNLA . . . . Pacific Northwest Library Association
PNLA . . . . Pacific Northwest Loggers Association
PNRBC . . . . . . Pacific Northwest River Basins Commission
PNTA . . . . . Pacific Northwest Trade Association
POA . . . . Pacific Ocean Area (World War II)
POAHEDPEARL . . Pacific Ocean Areas Headquarters Pearl Harbor
POS . . . . Pacific Orchid Society of Hawaii
POATSC . . . . . Pacific Overseas Air Technical Service Command
PP . . . . Pacific Petroleums, Ltd. (NYSE symbol)
PPL . . . . Pacific Power and Light Company
PPG . . . . Pacific Proving Ground (AEC)
PRESS . . . . Pacific Range Electromagnetic Signature Studies (Military)
PRCO . . . . . . Pacific Requisition Control Office (Navy)
PACRESFLT . . . Pacific Reserve Fleet
PRS . . . . Pacific Rocket Society
PSA . . . . Pacific Science Association
PSC . . . . Pacific Science Council
PSI . . . . Pacific Semiconductors, Incorporated
PSNCF . . . . . . Pacific Southern Naval Coastal Frontier
P . . . . Pacific Standard Time (Aviation)
PST . . . . Pacific Standard Time
PAC . . . . Pacific Telephone & Telegraph Company (NYSE symbol)
PTT . . . . Pacific Telephone and Telegraph Company
PTO . . . . Pacific Theater of Operations (World War II)
PT . . . . Pacific Time
PTC . . . . Pacific Tin Consolidated Corporation (NYSE symbol)
PTTC . . . . . . Pacific Transportation Terminal Command (Army)
PWC . . . . Pacific War Council (World War II)
PWA . . . . Pacific Western Airlines
PCF . . . . Pacificulture Foundation
PKDOM . . . . . Pack for Domestic Use
PKHOW . . . . . Pack Howitzer (Marine Corps)
PKSEA . . . . . . Pack for Overseas
PDC . . . . Package Designers Council
PSP . . . . Package Size Proneness (Marketing)
PAC . . . . Packaged Assembly Circuit
PACE . . . . . . Packaged Cram Executive (Data processing)
PDH . . . . Packaged Disaster Hospital (Public Health Service)
PLAAR . . . . . Packaged Liquid Air-Augmented Rocket
PKG . . . . Packaging Corporation of America (NYSE symbol)
PEDS . . . . Packaging Engineering Data System
PI . . . . Packaging Institute
PMMI . . . . . . Packaging Machinery Manufacturers Institute
PAC . . . . Packard Automobile Classics
PKB . . . . Packard-Bell Electronics Corporation (NYSE symbol)
PCV . . . . Packed Cell Volume
PSR . . . . Packed Snow on Runway (Aviation)
PW . . . . Packed Weight
P & S . . . . . . Packers and Stockyards
P & SA . . . . . Packers and Stockyards Administration (Department of Agriculture)
PC & H . . . . . Packing, Crating, and Handling
PHP . . . . Packing-House Products (Food Industry)
PPI . . . . Packing, Postage, and Insurance
P & P . . . . . . Packing and Preservation
PS . . . . Packing Sheet

343

PTCR .... Pad Terminal Connection Room
PSPS .... Paddle Steamer Preservation Society
PAIS .... Padre Island National Seashore (National Park Service designation)
PI .... Paducah & Illinois R. R. (AAR code)
P .... Page
PCE .... Page Communications Engineers, Inc. (Canada)
PCC .... Paid Circulation Council
PDS .... Paid-During-Service (Magazine subscriptions)
PWJC .... Paine, Webber, Jackson & Curtis (Stockbrokers)
PRI .... Paint Research Institute
PWAA .... Paint and Wallpaper Association of America
PDCA .... Painting and Decorating Contractors of America
P & O .... Paints and Oil
PST .... Paired Selected Ternary (Data processing)
PJ's .... Pajamas (Slang)
PAMC .... Pakistan Army Medical Corps
PARR .... Pakistan Atomic Research Reactor
PFUJ .... Pakistan Federal Union of Journalists
PICIC .... Pakistan Industrial Credit Investment Corporation
PITAC .... Pakistan Industrial Technical Assistance Centre
PIA .... Pakistan International Airlines
PMF .... Pakistan Mazdoor Federation
PML .... Pakistan Muslim League (Political party)
PPWF .... Pakistan Petroleum Workers' Federation
PSAA .... Pakistan Students' Association of America
PTWF .... Pakistan Transport Workers' Federation
PRI .... Paleontological Research Institution
PS .... Paleontological Society
PAD .... Palestine Arab Delegation
PEC .... Palestine Economic Commission
PEF .... Palestine Endowment Funds
PEF .... Palestine Exploration Fund
PLO .... Palestine Liberation Organization
PPF .... Palestine Pioneer Foundation
PSCP .... Palestine Symphonic Choir Project
Pd .... Palladium (Chemical element)
PS .... Palm Society
PPL .... Palmer Physical Laboratory (Princeton University)
PHA .... Palomino Horse Association
PHBA .... Palomino Horse Breeders of America
PPR .... Palomino Pony Registry
P .... Pamphlet
PAFMECSA .... Pan-African Freedom Movement of East, Central and South Africa
PASU .... Pan-African Socialist Union (Southern Rhodesia)
PAC .... Pan-Africanist Congress (South Africa)
PA .... Pan-American Airways
PANAMAC ..... Pan-American Airways Communications System
PAAO .... Pan-American Association of Ophthalmology
PACCS .... Pan American Cancer Cytology Society
PACB .... Pan-American Coffee Bureau
PACT .... Pan American Commission of Tampa
PAC .... Pan-American Congress
PACCIOS ..... Pan American Council of International Committee of Scientific Management
PAF .... Pan American Foundation
PANAGRA ..... Pan American-Grace Airways, Inc.
PAGTU .... Pan-American Ground Training Unit
PAHO .... Pan American Health Organization (OAS)
PAIGH .... Pan American Institute of Geography and History (OAS)
PAIMEG ...... Pan American Institute of Mining, Engineering and Geology (Defunct)
PALCO .... Pan American Liaison Committee of Women's Organizations
PAMA .... Pan American Medical Association
PAMWA .... Pan American Medical Women's Alliance
PAOA .... Pan American Odontological Association
PPBF .... Pan-American Pharmaceutical and Biochemical Federation
PARCA .... Pan American Railway Congress Association
PART .... Pan American Round Tables in the USA
PASB .... Pan American Sanitary Bureau (Executive organ of PAHO)
PASO .... Pan American Sanitary Organization
PASUS .... Pan American Society of the United States
PASC .... Pan American Standards Committee
PAS .... Pan American Sulphur Company (NYSE symbol)
PATRDL ...... Pan American Tung Research and Development League
PAU .... Pan American Union (Central organ and permanent secretariat of the OAS)
PAWA .... Pan American Women's Association
PAA .... Pan American World Airways, Inc. (Also see PAN-AM and PN)
PAN-AM ...... Pan-American World Airways, Inc. (Also see PN and PAA)
PN .... Pan American World Airways, Inc. (NYSE symbol)
PAZA .... Pan American Zebu Association
PIOSA .... Pan Indian Ocean Science Association

PMIP .... Pan Malayan Islamic Party
PPPRF .... Pan Pacific Public Relations Federation
PPSAWA ...... Pan Pacific and Southeast Asia Women's Association of the USA
PPSA .... Pan-Pacific Surgical Association
PNM .... Pan-Somali Nationalist Movement
PAB .... Panair do Brasil, SA
PANAIR ...... Panama Air Lines
PATCA .... Panama Air Traffic Control Area
PC .... The Panama Canal
PCC .... Panama Canal Company
PCD .... Panama Canal Department
PANHONLIB ... Panama, Honduras, and Liberia (Acronym used to refer to merchant ships operating under "flags of convenience")
PANLIBHONCO . Panama-Liberia-Honduras-Costa Rica
PANSEAFRON .. Panama Sea Frontier
PSF .... Panama Sea Frontier
PCAA .... Pancretan Association of America
POA .... Panel of Americans
PCPA .... Panel of Consultants for the Performing Arts (of CFC)
POE .... Panel on the Environment (of President's Science Advisory Committee)
POISE .... Panel on Inflight Scientific Experiments (NASA)
POMS .... Panel on Operational Meteorological Satellites
PP .... Panel Point (Technical drawings)
PEL .... Panhandle Eastern Pipe Line Company (NYSE symbol)
PSF .... Panhandle & Santa Fe Railway Company (AAR code)
P & SF ...... Panhandle and Santa Fe Railway Company
PEO .... Pankypria Ergatiki Omospondia (Pancyprian Federation of Labour) (The "Old Trade Unions") (Cyprus)
POAS .... Pankypria Omospondia Anexartiton Syntechnion (Pancyprian Federation of Independent Trade Unions) (Cyprus)
PANAR .... Panoramic RADAR
PMS .... Pantone Matching System (Printing)
PAK .... Panzer Abwehr Kanone (Means, "Cannon Against Armor") (German anti-tank gun)
PP .... Papa (Pope)
PAVLA .... Papal Volunteers for Latin America
PBI .... Paper Bag Institute
PC .... Paper Copy
PCCI .... Paper Cup and Container Institute
PFT .... Paper, Flat Tape
PIMA .... Paper Industry Management Association
PI .... Paper Insulated
PMAA .... Paper Makers Advertising Association
PMFWCMA ..... Paper Mill Fourdrinier Wire Cloth Manufacturers Association
PNA .... Paper Napkin Association
PPA .... Paper Pail Association
PPA .... Paper Plate Association
PPS .... Paper Publications Society
PSSMA .... Paper Shipping Sack Manufacturers' Association
PSTMA .... Paper Stationery and Tablet Manufacturers Association
PSIA .... Paper Stock Institute of America
PT .... Paper Tape
PT .... Paper Trooper (One who salvaged paper for war effort) (World War II)
PTA .... Paper and Twine Association
PBCA .... Paperboard Butter Chip Association
PPC .... Paperboard Packaging Council
PCT .... Papercraft Corporation (NYSE symbol)
PL .... Paperleg (A favored student) (Teen slang)
PFA .... Papermakers Felt Association
PELL .... Papers on English Language and Literature (A journal)
PCA .... Paperweight Collectors' Association
PCA .... Papillon Club of America
PNGWA .... Papua and New Guinea Workers' Association (Australian New Guinea)
PIB .... Papuan Infantry Battalion
PV .... Par Value (Finance)
PABA .... Para-Aminobenzoic Acid
PAB .... Para-Aminobenzyl
PAH .... Para-Aminohippuric Acid (Physiology)
PAS .... Paraaminosalicylic (Acid)
PASA .... Para-Aminosalicylic Acid
P & S .... Paracentesis and Suction (Medicine)
POP .... Para-Chlorophenylalanine
PARABAT ..... Parachute Battalion (Army)
PCA .... Parachute Club of America
FRP .... Parachute Fragmentation Bomb
PARAFRAG .... Parachute Fragmentation Bomb (Air Force)
PARATROOPS .. Parachute Infantry (Military)
PIB .... Parachute Infantry Battalion (Army)
PLF .... Parachute Landing Fall (Military)
PLAD .... Parachute Low-Altitude Delivery (Air Force)
PLADS .... Parachute Low-Altitude Delivery System

PR . . . . Parachute Rigger
PTV . . . . Parachute Test Vehicle
Prcht Bad . . . . Parachutist Badge (Army)
PDB . . . . Paradichlorobenzene (Moth balls)
PS . . . . Paradoxical Sleep
PCRC . . . . . . Paraffined Carton Research Council
PONA . . . . . . Paraffins, Olefins, Naphthenes, Aromatics
PARASEV. . . . . Paraglider Research Vehicle (NASA)
X. . . . . Parallactic angle
P . . . . Parallax
P in A . . . . . . Parallax in Altitude (Navigation)
PINA . . . . . . Parallax in Altitude (Navigation)
PARSEC. . . . . Parallax Second (Unit of interstellar-space measure)
PC . . . . PARSEC (Parallax Second)
PMAC. . . . . . . Parallel Memory Address Counter (Data processing)
PA . . . . Paralysis Agitans
PVA . . . . Paralyzed Veterans of America
PD . . . . Paralyzing Dose
PAT . . . . Parametric Artificial Talker
PARASYN . . . . Parametric Synthesis (Data processing)
PARSYN . . . . Parametric Synthesis (Data processing)
PXN. . . . . . . Paramount Pictures Corporation (NYSE symbol)
PA . . . . Parapsychological Association
PARSQ . . . . . Pararescue
PNS . . . . Parasympathetic Nervous System
PNI . . . . Paratai Nasionalis Indonesia (Nationalist Party of Indonesia)
PTE . . . . Parathyroid Extract (Medicine)
PTH . . . . Parathyroid Hormone
PV . . . . Paravane (Anti-moored-mine device) (Naval)
PP . . . . Parcel Post
PPA . . . . Parcel Post Association
PPI . . . . Parcel Post, Insured
PG. . . . . Paregoric (Slang)
PARI . . . . . . Parent Attitude Research Instrument (A questionnaire)
PC . . . . Parent Cells
PCC . . . . . . Parent and Child Center (Project Head Start)
PCPI . . . . . . Parent Cooperative Preschools International
PDA . . . . Parenteral Drug Association
PTA . . . . Parent-Teacher Association
PARAN . . . . . Parents Assume Responsibility, Act Now (Group opposing sex education in schools)
POL . . . . Parents of Large Families
POSE . . . . . . Parents Opposed to Sex Education (An organization)
POSSE . . . . . Parents Opposed to Sex and Sensitivity Education (An organization)
POPE . . . . . . Parents for Orthodoxy in Parochial Education (Group opposing sex education in schools)
PWP . . . . Parents Without Partners (An organization)
PG. . . . . Paris Granite
PPFO . . . . . . Paris Procurement Field Office
PL . . . . Parish Line R. R. (AAR code)
PP . . . . Parish Priest
PVMI . . . . . . Parish Visitors of Mary Immaculate (Roman Catholic women's religious order)
PS . . . . Parity Switch
P. . . . . Park
PDC . . . . Parke, Davis & Company (NYSE symbol)
PAC . . . . Parker Aircraft Corporation
PO. . . . . Parking Orbit
POI . . . . Parking Orbit Injection
PDF . . . . Parkinson's Disease Foundation
PRCA . . . . . . Parks, Recreation and Cultural Affairs Administration (New York City)
PARGS . . . . . Parks and Recreation Girls Service
PCEM. . . . . . Parliamentary Council of the European Movement
PGWG . . . . . Parliamentary Group for World Government
PLP . . . . Parliamentary Labour Party (British)
PPS . . . . Parliamentary Private Secretary (British)
PR . . . . Parliamentary Report
PUS . . . . Parliamentary Under-Secretary
PM. . . . . Parlor Maid
PS . . . . Parlor Snake (Slang for "to escort visitors around post")
PTE . . . . Parmelee Transportation Company (NYSE symbol)
PPCAA . . . . . Parole and Probation Compact Administrators Association
PATC . . . . . . Paroxysmal Atrial Tachycardia (Medicine)
PCH . . . . Paroxysmal Cold Hemoglobinuria
PDE . . . . Paroxysmal Dyspnea on Exertion
PND . . . . Paroxysmal Nocturnal Dyspnea
PNH . . . . Paroxysmal Nocturnal Hemoglobinuria
PRT . . . . Parr Terminal (AAR code)
PARAMI . . . . Parsons Active Ring-Around Miss Indicator
PLS . . . . Parsons Language Sample
P. . . . . Part

PTCLD . . . . . . Part Called (NYSE symbol)
PFR . . . . Part Failure Rate
PN . . . . Part Number
P/N . . . . Part Number
PP . . . . Part Paid (Business and trade)
PTPD . . . . . . Part Paid (NYSE symbol)
PTRD . . . . . . Part Redeemed (NYSE symbol)
PRD . . . . Part Reference Designator
PRC . . . . Part Requirement Card
PKI . . . . Partai Komunis Indonesia (Communist party) (Indonesia)
PSI. . . . . Partai Socialis Indonesia
PAE . . . . Partes Aequales (Equal parts)
PAP . . . . Parti d'Action Paysanne (Farmers Actions Party) (Upper Volta)
PAI . . . . Parti Africain de l'Independance (African Independence Party) (Senegal and Upper Volta)
PADI . . . . . . Parti pour l'Avancement de la Democratie en Ituri (Party for Democratic Advancement in Ituri)
PCA . . . . Parti Communiste Algerien (Algerian Communist Party)
PCF . . . . Parti Communiste Francaise (French Communist Party)
PCM . . . . Parti Communiste Marocain (Moroccan Communist Party)
PCT . . . . Parti Communiste Tunisien (Tunisian Communist Party)
PCIM . . . . . . Parti du Congres de l'Independance de Madagascar (Party of the Congress for Malagasy Independence)
PDU . . . . Parti Dahomeen de l'Unite (Dahomean Unity Party)
PDC. . . . . . . Parti Democrate Chretien (Christian Democratic Party) (Burundi)
PDU . . . . Parti Democratie Unifie (Unified Democratic Party) (Name replaced by Section Voltaique de Rassemblement)
PDA . . . . Parti Democratico da Angola (Democratic Party of Angola)
PDCI . . . . . . Parti Democratique de la Cote d'Ivoire (Democratic Party of the Ivory Coast)
PRD . . . . Parti Democratique Dahomeen (Dahomey Democratic Party)
PDG. . . . . . . Parti Democratique de Guinee (Democratic Party of Guinea)
PDHV-RDA . . . Parti Democratique de la Haute Volta-Rassemblement Democratique Africain (Democratic Party of Upper Volta-African Democratic Rally)
PDI . . . . Parti Democratique de l'Independance (Democratic Independence Party) (Morocco)
PDM . . . . Parti Democratique Malgache (Malagasy Democratic Party)
PDPT . . . . . . Parti Democratique des Populations Togolaises (Togolese Democratic People's Party)
PADESM . . . . . Parti des Desherites de Madagascar (Party of the Deprived of Madagascar)
PFA . . . . Parti de la Federation Africaine (African Federation Party)
PIL. . . . . Parti de l'Independance et de la Liberte (Party for Independence and Liberty) (Congo - Leopoldville)
PARTICO. . . . . Parti d'Interets Congolais (Party for Congolese Interests)
PLP . . . . Parti de la Liberte et du Progres (Freedom and Progress Party) (Belgium)
PMP . . . . Parti du Mouvement Populaire de la Cote Francaise des Somalis (Popular Movement Party of French Somaliland)
PANALU . . . . . Parti National Lumumba (Lumumba National Party)
PNP . . . . Parti National du Progres (National Progress Parties) (Congo - Leopoldville)
PNTC . . . . . . Parti National Travailliste Camerounais (Cameroonese National Workers' Party)
PNV. . . . . . . Parti National Voltaique (Voltaic National Party)
PNA. . . . . . . Parti Nationale Africain (African National Party) (Chad)
PND . . . . Parti des Nationalistes du Dahomey (Dahomean Nationalists Party)
POC. . . . . . . Parti d'Opposition Congolais (Congolese Opposition Party)
POI . . . . Parti Oubanguien de l'Independance (Ubangi Independence Party)
PP . . . . Parti du Peuple (People's Party) (Burundi)
PPF . . . . Parti Populaire Francais
PPU . . . . Parti Populaire des Ueles (Ueles Peoples Party)
PESIC . . . . . . Parti du Progres Economique et Social des Independants Congolais Luluabourg (Party for Economic and Social Progress of the Congolese Independents in Luluabourg)
PPD . . . . Parti Progressiste Dahomeen (Dahomey Progressive Party)
PPK . . . . Parti Progressiste Katangais
PPN . . . . Parti Progressiste Nigerien (Nigerian Progressive Party)
PPS . . . . Parti Progressiste Soudanais (Sudanese Progressive Party)
PPT . . . . Parti Progressiste Tchadien (Progressive Party of Chad)
PRA . . . . Parti du Regroupement Africain (African Regroupment Party)
PRM . . . . Parti de Regroupement Mauritanien (Mauritanian Regroupment Party)
PRL . . . . Parti Republicain de la Liberte (Republican Party for Liberty) (Upper Volta)
PRESS . . . . . . Parti Republicain Social du Senegal (Social Republican Party of Senegal)
PRD . . . . Partido Revolucionario Dominicano (Dominican Revolutionary Party)
PRS . . . . Parti de la Revolution Socialiste (Party of Socialist Revolution) (Benin - Senegal)
PSC . . . . Parti Social Chretien (Christian Social Party) (Belgium)
PSD . . . . Parti Social Democrate de Madagascar et des Comores (Social Democratic Party of Madagascar and Comores)
PSEMA . . . . . Parti Social d'Education des Masses Africaines (African Party for Social Education of the Masses) (Upper Volta)
PSF . . . . Parti Social Francais

PSB . . . . Parti Socialiste Belge (Belgian Socialist Party)
PSC . . . . Parti Socialiste Camerounais (Cameroonese Socialist Party)
PSU . . . . Parti Socialiste Unifie (United Socialist Party) (France)
PSA . . . . Parti Solidaire Africain (African Solidarity Party) (Congo – Leopoldville)
PSS . . . . Parti de Solidarite Senegalaise (Senegalese Solidarity Party)
PSP . . . . Parti Soudanais Progressiste (Sudanese Progressive Party) (Mali)
PTP . . . . Parti Togolais du Progres (Party for Togolese Progress)
PTC . . . . Parti Travailliste Congolais (Congolese Labor Party)
PUSMM. . . . . . Parti d'Union Socialiste des Musulmans Mauritaniens (Party for Socialist Unity of Moslems of Mauritania)
UCBC . . . . Parti de l'Unite et da la Communaute Belgo-Congolaise
PUC . . . . Parti de l'Unite Congolaise (Congolese Unity Party)
PUK . . . . Parti d'Unite Katangaise (Katanga Unity Party)
PUNA . . . . Parti de l'Unite Nationale (National Unity Party) (Congo)
PUNGA . . . . . . Parti de l'Unite Nationale Gabonaise (Party for Gabonese National Unity)
PBI . . . . Partial Background Investigation
PL . . . . Partial Loss (Insurance)
P/P . . . . Partial Pay (Air Force)
PPC . . . . Partial Pay Card
PRD . . . . Partial Reaction of Degeneration
PTT . . . . Partial Thromboplastin Time
PUG . . . . Partially Underground (Military)
PC . . . . Participation Certificate
PESO . . . . Participation Enriches Science, Music and Art Organizations (Orlando, Florida)
PA . . . . Participial Adjective
P . . . . Participle
POINTER. . . . . Particle Orientation Interferometer (ASD)
PA . . . . Particular Average
PAN . . . . Partido Accion Nacional (Mexican political party)
PAP . . . . Partido Accion Popular (Popular Action Party) (Ecuador, Peru)
PAR . . . . Partido Accion Renovadora (Political party in El Salvador)
PAIGC . . . . . . Partido Africano da Independencia da Guine e Cabo Verde (African Party for Independence of Guinea and Cape Verde)
PAC . . . . Partido Autentico Constitucional (Authentic Constitutional Party) (El Salvador)
PARM . . . . . . Partido Autentico de la Revolucion de Mexicana (Mexican political party)
PCB . . . . Partido Comunista de Bolivia (Communist Party of Bolivia)
PCN. . . . . Partido de Conciliacion Nacional (Party of National Conciliation) (El Salvador)
PCN. . . . . Partido Conservador Nicaraguense (Nicaraguan Conservative Party)
PCT . . . . Partido Conservador Tradicional (Traditionalist Conservative Party) (Nicaragua)
PCU . . . . Partido Conservador Unido (Chilean Catholic political party)
PDCG. . . . . . . Partido Democracia Cristiana Guatemalteca (Political party in Guatemala)
PD . . . . Partido Democrata (Democratic Party) (Chile)
PDC . . . . Partido Democrata Cristiano (Democratic Christian Party) (Bolivia, Chile, El Salvador)
PDC . . . . Partido Democratico Cristao (Christian Democratic Party) (Brazil)
PDN. . . . . Partido Democratico Nacional (National Democratic Party) (Chile)
PER . . . . Partido Estadista Republicano (Political party) (Puerto Rico)
PIP . . . . Partido Independencia de Puerto Rico (Political party) (Puerto Rico)
PI . . . . Partido Independente (Independent Party) (Costa Rica)
PIR . . . . Partido de la Izquierda Revolucionaria (Revolutionary Party of the Left) (Bolivia)
PLN . . . . Partido Liberacion Nacional (National Liberation Party) (Costa Rica)
PL . . . . Partido Liberal (Liberal Party) (Bolivia, Chile)
PLI . . . . Partido Liberal Independiente (Independent Liberal Party) (Nicaragua)
PLN . . . . Partido Liberal Nacionalista (Nationalist Liberal Party) (Nicaragua)
PND. . . . . Partido Nacional Democratico (National Democratic Party) (Dominican Republic)
PNH. . . . . Partido Nacional Hondureno (Honduran National Party)
PNM . . . . Partido Nacionalista de Mexicano (Nationalist Party of Mexico)
POCM . . . . . . Partido Obrero y Campesino de Mexico (Mexican political party)
POR . . . . Partido Obrero Revolucionario (Revolutionary Workers' Party) (Bolivia)
PPD . . . . Partido Popular Democratico (Political party) (Puerto Rico)
PPS . . . . Partido Popular Socialista (Popular Socialist Party) (Mexico)
PR . . . . Partido Radical (Radical Party) (Chile)
PRDN . . . . . . Partido de Reconciliacion Democratica Nacional (Party of National Democratic Reconciliation) (Guatemala)
PR . . . . Partido Republicano (Republican Party) (Brazil)
PRN . . . . Partido Republicano Nacional (National Republican Party) (Costa Rica)
PRS . . . . Partido de la Revolucion Socialista (Party of the Socialist Revolution) (Cuba)
PR . . . . Partido Revolucionario (Revolutionary Party) (Guatemala)
PRA . . . . Partido Revolucionario Autentico (Authentic Revolutionary Party) (Bolivia)
PRI . . . . Partido Revolucionario Institucional (Mexican political party)
PRUD . . . . . . Partido Revolucionario de Unificacion Democratica (Revolutionary Party of Democratic Unification) (El Salvador)

PRUC . . . . Partido Revolucionario de Union Civico (Revolutionary Party for Civic Union) (Costa Rica)
PSC . . . . Partido Social Cristiano (Social Christian Party) (Bolivia)
PSD . . . . Partido Social Democratico (Social Democratic Party) (Brazil, El Salvador)
PSP. . . . . Partido Social Progresista (Social Progressive Party) (Brazil)
PS . . . . Partido Socialista (Socialist Party) (Chile)
PSA . . . . Partido Socialista Argentino (Moderate socialist political party) (Argentina)
PTB . . . . Partido Trabalhista Brasileiro (Brazilian Workers' Party)
PTN . . . . Partido Trabhista Nacional (National Workers' Party) (Brazil)
PUR . . . . Partido de Unificacion Revolucionaria (Party of Revolutionary Unification) (Guatemala)
PUD . . . . Partido Union Democratica (Political party in Guatemala)
PUN . . . . Partido Union Nacional (National Union Party) (Costa Rica)
PURS . . . . . . Partido de la Union Republicana Socialista (Socialist Republican Union Party) (Bolivia)
PCR . . . . Partidul Comunist din Rominia
PMR . . . . Partidul Muncitoresc Romin
PSR . . . . Partiia Sotsialistov-Revoliutsionerov
P . . . . Partim (In Part)
PLGS . . . . . . Partita Liberale Giovani Somali (Somali Liberal Youth Party)
PCI . . . . Partito Comunista Italiano (Italian Communist Party)
DC. . . . . Partito Democrazia Cristiana (Christian Democrats) (Italy)
PLI . . . . Partito Liberale Italiano (Liberal Party of Italy)
PNF . . . . Partito Nazionale Fascista (National Fascist Party) (Italy)
PNUA. . . . . . . Partito Nazionale Unito Africa (National Party of United Africans) (Somalia)
PPS . . . . Partito Populare Somalo (Somali People's Party)
PRI . . . . Partito Repubblicano Italiano (Republican Party of Italy)
PSDI. . . . . . . Partito Socialista Democratico Italiano (Italian Social Democratic Party)
PSI . . . . Partito Socialista Italiano (Italian Socialist Party)
PSS . . . . Partito Socialista Somalo (Somali Socialist Party)
PIP. . . . . Partners in Progress (Government) (Civil rights)
PART . . . . . . Parts Allocation Requirements Technique
PCN . . . . Parts Change Notice
PDPS . . . . . . Parts Data Processing System
PDL . . . . Parts Difference List
PL . . . . Parts List
PLAO . . . . . . Parts List Assembly Order
PAMAC . . . . . Parts and Materials Accountability Control
PMP . . . . Parts, Materials and Packaging
PP . . . . Parts Per
PPB . . . . Parts Per Billion
PPM . . . . Parts Per Million (Chemistry)
PPD . . . . Parts Provisioning Document
PRINCE . . . . . Parts Reliability Information Center (of NASA)
PS . . . . Parts Shipper
PSMR . . . . . . Parts Specification Management for Reliability
PT . . . . Paschale Tempore (Easter Time)
PADRA . . . . . Pass to Air Defense RADAR
PSSO . . . . . . Pass Slip Stitch Over (Knitting)
PFN . . . . Passamaquoddy Ferry & Navigation Company (AAR code)
PB . . . . Passbook (Banking)
PAS . . . . Passed to the Adjacent Sector
PB . . . . Passed Ball
PFC . . . . Passed Flying College (British)
PASEP . . . . . Passed for Separate Action
PASEP. . . . . . Passed Separately (Military)
PSC . . . . Passed Staff College (British)
PA . . . . Passenger Agent
PS . . . . Passenger Service
PS . . . . Passenger Steamer
PTA . . . . Passenger Transport Authorities (British)
PS . . . . Passing Scuttle
PAT . . . . Passive Acoustic Torpedo
PADS . . . . . . Passive-Active Data Simulation
PADLOC . . . . Passive Active Detection and Location
PARADE . . . . . Passive-Active Ranging and Determination
PACE . . . . . . Passive Attitude Control Experimental (Satellite)
PACOR . . . . . Passive Correlation and Ranging
PCM . . . . Passive Countermeasure
PCA . . . . Passive Cutaneous Anaphylaxis
PDH . . . . Passive Defense Handbook (Navy)
PD . . . . Passive Detection (Electronics)
PADLOC . . . . . Passive Detection and Location of Countermeasures (Air Force)
PADAR . . . . . Passive Detection and Ranging
PAGEOS . . . . . Passive Geodetic Earth-Orbiting Satellite (NASA)
PITS . . . . . . Passive Intercept Tracking System
POSS . . . . . . Passive Optical Satellite Surveillance
PP . . . . Passive Participle

PARDOP . . . . . Passive Ranging Doppler
PSEP. . . . . . . Passive Seismic Experiments Package (NASA)
PTC . . . . Passive Thermal Control (NASA)
PUFFS . . . . . . Passive Underwater Fire Control Feasibility Study
PO . . . . Passport Office (Department of State)
P . . . . Past
PC . . . . Past Commander
PDH . . . . Past Dental History
PDPGM. . . . . . Past Deputy Provincial Grand Master (Masonry)
PDD . . . . Past Due Date
PGCh . . . . . . Past Grand Chaplain (Masonry)
PGD . . . . Past Grand Deacon (Masonry)
PGM . . . . Past Grand Master (Masonry)
PGSD . . . . . . Past Grand Senior Deacon (Masonry)
PGW . . . . Past Grand Warden (Masonry)
PM . . . . Past Master (Masonry)
PMH. . . . . . . Past Medical History
PMI . . . . Past (or Previous) Medical Illness
PP . . . . Past Participle
PP . . . . Past President
PPGM. . . . . . . Past Provincial Grand Master (Masonry)
PPGSW . . . . . . Past Provincial Grand Senior Warden (Masonry)
PSGW . . . . Past Senior Grand Warden (Masonry)
PSD . . . . Past Start Date
PT . . . . Past Tense
PWP . . . . Past Worthy Patriarch
P . . . . Paste
P . . . . Pastor
PARDON . . . . . Pastors' Anonymous Recovery-Directed Order for Newness (Rehabilitation program for troubled clergymen)
PBR . . . . Patapsco & Back Rivers R. R. (AAR code)
PATCENT . . . . Patching Central (Army)
P . . . . Patchy (Decelerometer readings) (Aviation)
PCT . . . . Patent Cooperation Treaty (Proposed international treaty, Sweden, 1967)
PDA . . . . Patent Ductus Arteriosus (Medicine)
PO. . . . . Patent Office
POCS . . . . . . Patent Office Classification System
POPA . . . . . . Patent Office Professional Association
P . . . . Pater (Father)
PP . . . . Pater Patriae (The Father of His Country)
PFF . . . . Pathfinder Force (British RADAR designation which became over-all synonym for RADAR) (Military)
PAL . . . . Pathology Laboratory (Test)
PEPSU. . . . . . Patiala and East Punjab States Union
PA . . . . Patient (Medical slang)
PACENS . . . . . Patient Census
PNTCENS . . . . Patient Census Report
PLF . . . . Patient Load Factor
PS . . . . Patient's Serum (Medicine)
PAS . . . . Patients' Aid Society
PPAA . . . . . . Patres Amplissimi (Cardinals)
PC . . . . Patres Conscripti (The Roman Senate in early days of Rome)
PAFB . . . . . . Patrick Air Force Base
PAYS . . . . . . Patriotic American Youth Society
POSA . . . . . . Patriotic Order Sons of America
P . . . . Patrol (Designation for all US military aircraft)
PACV . . . . . . Patrol Air Cushion Vehicle (Also called Hovercraft) (Navy)
PASU . . . . . . Patrol Aircraft Service Unit
PATSU . . . . . Patrol Aircraft Service Unit
PAP . . . . Patrol Amphibian Plane
PB . . . . Patrol Boat
PB . . . . Patrol Bomber
PBY . . . . Patrol Bomber (Navy designation for Catalina aircraft)
VPB(HL) . . . . Patrol Bomber, 4-engine, Landplane (Navy symbol)
VPB(ML) . . . . Patrol Bomber, 2-engine, Landplane (Navy symbol)
VPB(HS). . . . . Patrol Bomber, 4-engine, Seaplane (Navy symbol)
VPB(MS) . . . . Patrol Bomber, 2-engine, Seaplane (Navy symbol)
VPB . . . . Patrol-Bombing Plane (Navy symbol)
PATBOMRON. . Patrol Bombing Squadron
PC . . . . Patrol Craft
PCE . . . . Patrol Craft Escort
PCE(R) . . . . . Patrol Craft, Escort (Rescue) (180 feet) (Navy symbol)
PCS . . . . Patrol Craft Sweeper
PATFOR . . . . Patrol Force
PGH. . . . . . . Patrol Gunboat, Hydrofoil (Navy)
PI . . . . Patrol Inspector (Immigration and Naturalization Service)
VP . . . . Patrol Plane (Navy symbol)
PPC . . . . Patrol Plane Commander
PSP . . . . Patrol Seaplane
PBM. . . . . . . Patrol Search Plane (Navy designation for Mariner aircraft)

PATRON . . . . Patrol Squadron
VP . . . . Patrol Squadron (Navy symbol)
ZPRON. . . . . . Patrol (Lighter-Than-Air) Squadron (Navy symbol)
PT . . . . Patrol Torpedo Boat (Navy)
VPT . . . . Patrol-Torpedo Plane (Navy symbol)
PV . . . . Patrol Vessel
YP . . . . Patrol Vessel (Navy symbol)
PE . . . . Patrol Vessel, Eagle (Eagle boat) (Navy symbol)
PCE(C) . . . . . Patrol Vessel, Escort (Control) (180 feet) (Navy symbol)
PF . . . . Patrol Vessel, Frigate (Navy symbol)
PG . . . . Patrol Vessel, Gunboat
PGM . . . . . . Patrol Vessel, Motor Gunboat (Navy symbol)
PTC . . . . Patrol Vessel, Motor Torpedo Boat, Submarine Chaser (Navy symbol)
PR . . . . Patrol Vessel, River Gunboat (Navy symbol)
PC . . . . Patrol Vessel, Submarine Chaser (Navy)
PCS . . . . Patrol Vessel, Submarine Chaser (Control) (136 feet) (Navy symbol)
PY . . . . Patrol Vessel, Yacht
PYC . . . . Patrol Vessel, Yacht, Coastal (Navy symbol)
PATWING . . . . Patrol Wing (Later, Fleet Air Wing)
PATWINGLANTFLT . . Patrol Wing Atlantic Fleet
PATWINGSCOFOR . . Patrol Wings Scouting Force
PBA . . . . Patrolmen's Benevolent Association
PONCHO . . . . Patrons of Northwest Culture Organizations (Seattle, Washington)
PA . . . . Pattern Analysis (Test)
PADAL . . . . . Pattern for Analysis, Decision, Action, and Learning
PAT . . . . Pattern Analysis Test
PCI . . . . Pattern Correspondence Index
PM. . . . . Pattern Maker
PMANY . . . . . Pattern Makers Association of New York
PML . . . . Pattern Makers' League of North America
PATRIC . . . . . Pattern Recognition Interpretation and Correlation
PRS . . . . Pattern Recognition Society
PRS. . . . . Pattern Recognition System
PRT. . . . . Pattern Recognition Technique
PMSR . . . . . . Patternmaker, Ship Repair (Navy)
PTR . . . . Patuxent River (Navy)
PBI . . . . Paving Brick Institute
PLATR. . . . . . Pawling Lattice Test Rig (United Nuclear Company)
PRR . . . . Pawling Research Reactor (AEC)
P . . . . Pawn (Chess)
P . . . . Pax (Peace)
MIEC . . . . Pax Romana, Mouvement International des Etudiants Catholiques
PTCS . . . . . . Pax Tibi Cum Sanctis (Peace to Thee with the Saints)
PADOC . . . . . Pay Adjustment Document
PAV . . . . Pay Adjustment Voucher (Military)
PALCRU . . . . Pay and Allowances Accrue From (Air Force)
PAYE . . . . . . Pay As You Earn
PAYE . . . . . . Pay As You Enter
PC . . . . Pay Clerk
PCLK . . . . . . Pay Clerk
POD . . . . Pay on Delivery (Business and trade)
PEBD . . . . . . Pay Entry Base Date
PG. . . . . Pay Group
POP . . . . Pay One Price
PP . . . . Pay Period
PRA . . . . Pay Readjustment Act (1942)
PAREC . . . . . Pay Record(s)
PAHEL . . . . . Pay Record(s) and Health Record(s)
POR . . . . Pay on Return (Business and trade)
P & SNP . . . . Pay and Subsistence of Naval Personnel (Budget appropriation title)
PSANDT . . . . Pay, Subsistence, and Transportation (Military)
PS & T . . . . . Pay, Subsistence, and Transportation (Military)
PS & TN . . . . Pay, Subsistence and Transportation, Navy
PANDS. . . . . . Pay and Supply (Coast Guard)
P & S . . . . . . Pay and Supply (Coast Guard)
P & SI . . . . . Pay and Supply Instruction (Coast Guard)
PYC . . . . Pay Your Cash (Australian slang)
POD . . . . Payable on Death
POR . . . . Payable on Receipt (Business and trade)
P & CA . . . . . Paying and Collecting Area
PG . . . . Paying Guest
PM . . . . Paymaster
PMG . . . . Paymaster General (Navy)
PAYMARCORPS . . Paymaster, Marine Corps
PS . . . . Paymaster Sergeant
PMSGT . . . . . Paymaster Sergeant (Marine Corps)
PIK . . . . Payment in Kind
PILOT . . . . . Payment in Lieu of Taxes
PR . . . . Payroll
PAPERMAN . . . Payroll and Accounting, Personnel Management, Manpower Utilization (Air Force)

PADA . . . . Payroll Automation for Department of Agriculture
PDA . . . . Payroll Deduction Authorization
PERK . . . . . . Payroll Earnings Record Keeping
PRSEC . . . . . . Payroll Section
PERI . . . . Pea Ridge National Military Park
PDY . . . . Peabody Coal Company (NYSE symbol)
PPVT . . . . . . Peabody Picture Vocabulary Test
PSL . . . . Peabody Short Line R. R. (AAR code)
PAC . . . . Peace Action Center
PCF . . . . Peace Centers Foundation
PC . . . . Peace Corps
PCV . . . . Peace Corps Volunteer
PERC . . . . . . Peace on Earth Research Center
PME . . . . Peace Movement of Ethiopia
POST . . . . . . Peace Officer Standards and Training
PORAC . . . . . Peace Officers Research Association of California
PREP . . . . . . Peace Research and Education Project
PRI . . . . Peace Research Institute
PRIO . . . . . . Peace Research Institute, Oslo (Norway)
PROF . . . . . . Peace Research Organization Fund
PAAP . . . . . . Peaceful Alternatives to the Atlantic Pact
PNE . . . . Peaceful Nuclear Explosives (Division of AEC)
PUMF . . . . . . Peaceful Uses of Military Forces
PAR . . . . Peacetime Airborne Reconnaissance
PTFMO . . . . . Peacetime Force Materiel Objective
PTFMPO . . . . Peacetime Force Materiel Procurement Objective
PTFMR . . . . . Peacetime Force Materiel Requirements
PTOS . . . . . . Peacetime Operating Stock (Military)
PPF . . . . Peacetime Planning Factors
PSC . . . . Peacetime Subcontract
PB-HTGR . . . . . Peach Bottom High-Temperature Gas-Cooled Reactor
PAR . . . . Peak-to-Average Ratio (Communications)
PEP . . . . Peak Envelope Power
PEFR . . . . . . Peak Expiratory Flow Rate
PIV . . . . Peak Inverse Voltage (RADAR)
PkV . . . . Peak Kilovolts
POV . . . . Peak Operating Voltage
PP . . . . Peak to Peak
PPHA . . . . . . Peak Pulse Height Analysis
PPP . . . . Peak Pulse Power
PRV . . . . Peak Reverse Voltage
P/V . . . . Peak-to-Valley
PBMA . . . . . . Peanut Butter Manufacturers Association
PBSCMA . . . . Peanut Butter Sandwich and Cookie Manufacturers Association (Later, PBMA)
PNSA . . . . . . Peanut and Nut Salters Association
PEDIN . . . . . . Peapod Dinghy
PH . . . . Pearl Harbor, Hawaii
PHNY . . . . . . Pearl Harbor Navy Yard
PHSA . . . . . . Pearl Harbor Survivors Association
PRV . . . . Pearl River Valley R. R. (AAR code)
PMA . . . . . . Peat Moss Association
PPAUS . . . . . . Peat Producers Association of the United States
PBR . . . . Pebble-Bed Reactor (AEC)
PBRE . . . . . . Pebble-Bed Reactor Experiment
P . . . . Pebbles
PECO . . . . . . Pecos National Monument
PVS . . . . Pecos Valley Southern Railway Company (AAR code)
PM . . . . Peculiar Meter
PTE . . . . Peculiar Test Equipment
PLA . . . . Pedestrian League of America
PX . . . . Pedro Ximenez (A blending sherry)
PXV . . . . Pedro Ximenez Viejo (A blending sherry)
PDB . . . . Pee Dee Belemnite
PCA . . . . Pekingese Club of America
PG . . . . Pelham Grenville Wodehouse (British humorist)
PP . . . . Pellagra Preventive (Factor)
PPF . . . . Pellagra-Preventive Factor (Niacinamide)
PID . . . . Pelvic Inflammatory Disease (Medicine)
PWCC of A . . . Pembroke Welsh Corgi Club of America
PBC . . . . Pen and Brush Club
PS . . . . Penal Servitude
PIEA . . . . Pencil Industry Export Association
PMA . . . . . . Pencil Makers Association
PT . . . . Pencil Tube
PA . . . . Pending Availability
PDT . . . . Pendleton Tool Industries, Inc. (NYSE symbol) (Delisted)
PIG . . . . Pendulous Integrating Gyro
PIGA . . . . . . Pendulous Integrating Gyro Accelerometers
PENAID . . . . . Penetration Aid (Air Force)
PENRAD . . . . . Penetration RADAR

PENSAM . . . . . Penetration Survivability Assessment Model
PENTAC . . . . . Penetration for Tactical Aircraft (Air Force)
PTV . . . . Penetration Test Vehicle (Aerospace)
PENW . . . . . . Penetrating Wound
P . . . . Pengo (Monetary unit in Hungary until 1946)
PFK . . . . Penick & Ford, Ltd., Inc. (NYSE symbol) (Delisted)
PAT . . . . Peninsula Air Transport Company (Michigan)
PDMA . . . . . . Peninsula Drafting Management Association
PT . . . . Peninsula Terminal (AAR code)
PAT . . . . Peninsular Air Transport
PBS . . . . Peninsular Base Section
PCR . . . . Peninsular Chemresearch (Calgon Corporation)
P & O . . . . . . Peninsular and Oriental Steam Navigation Company (Steamship line)
DXC . . . . Penn-Dixie Cement Corporation (NYSE symbol)
PFR . . . . Penn Fruit Company, Inc. (NYSE symbol)
PENNSTAC . . . Penn State University Automatic Digital Computer
JCP . . . . Penney (J. C.) Company (NYSE symbol)
PSM . . . . Pennsalt Chemicals Corporation (NYSE symbol)
PA . . . . Pennsylvania
PAR . . . . Pennsylvania Advanced Reactor (AEC)
PAN . . . . Pennsylvania Association of Notaries
PAA . . . . Pennsylvania & Atlantic R. R. (AAR code)
PBMR . . . . . . Pennsylvania Bureau of Municipal Research
PGS . . . . Pennsylvania German Society
PGS . . . . Pennsylvania Glass Sand Corporation (NYSE symbol)
PGCOA . . . . . Pennsylvania Grade Crude Oil Association
PJM . . . . Pennsylvania-Jersey-Maryland
P & LERR . . . . Pennsylvania and Lake Erie Railroad
POT . . . . Pennsylvania-Ontario Transportation Company (AAR code)
PPL . . . . Pennsylvania Power & Light Company (NYSE symbol)
PRR . . . . Pennsylvania R. R. (AAR code)
PA . . . . Pennsylvania Railroad Company (NYSE symbol)
PRS . . . . Pennsylvania-Reading Seashore Lines (AAR code)
PRSL . . . . . . Pennsylvania-Reading Seashore Lines
PSU . . . . Pennsylvania State University
PSUR . . . . . . Pennsylvania State University Reactor
PENNTAP . . . . Pennsylvania Technical Assistance Program
D . . . . Penny (Nail size)
P . . . . Penny
DWT . . . . Pennyweight
PZL . . . . Pennzoil Company (NYSE symbol)
PMM . . . . . . Penobscot Marine Museum
PRC . . . . Pension Research Council
PRAS . . . . . . Pension and Retirement Annuity System
PB . . . . Pentaborane
PCNB . . . . . . Pentachloronitrobenzene
PETN . . . . . . Pentaerythritol Tetranitrate (Explosive)
PENTENG . . . . Pentagon English (Pseudotechnical language)
PA of W . . . . . Pentecostal Assemblies of the World
PFNA . . . . . . Pentecostal Fellowship of North America
PNA . . . . Pentose Nucleic Acid
P . . . . People
PAR . . . . People Against Racism (Civil rights organization)
PAUSE . . . . . . People Against Unconstitutional Sex Education
PEEK . . . . People for the Enjoyment of Eyeballing Knees (Group opposing below-the-knee fashions introduced in 1970)
POPS . . . . **People Opposed to Pornography in Schools** (Group opposing sex education in schools)
PTP . . . . **People-to-People**
PAP . . . . People's Action Party (Malaya)
PAT . . . . People's Action Team (South Vietnam)
PAVN . . . . . . People's Army of Vietnam
PCCL . . . . People's Community Civic League
PDG . . . . People's Drug Stores, Inc. (NYSE symbol)
PGL . . . . People's Gas Light & Coke Company (NYSE symbol)
PLA . . . . People's Liberation Army (Communist China)
PMC . . . . People's Mandate Committee
PNP . . . . People's National Party (Jamaica)
PRE-ARM . . . . . People's Rights Enforced Against Riots and Murder (Vigilante group in New Jersey)
PUP . . . . **People's United Party (British Honduras)**
PAE . . . . Peoria & Eastern Railway (AAR code)
PPU . . . . Peoria & Pekin Union Railway Company (AAR code)
PTC . . . . Peoria Terminal Company (AAR code)
DOC . . . . Pepper (Dr.) Company (NYSE symbol)
PD . . . . Pepper Dust (An adulterating element)
PEP . . . . Pepsi-Cola Company (NYSE symbol)
P . . . . Per
PA . . . . Per Annum (By the Year)
PC . . . . Per Cent; Percentage
PD . . . . Per Diem

PDC . . . . Per Diem, Travel and Transportation Allowance Committee for Departments of the Army, Navy, and Air Force
PGT . . . . Per Gross Ton (Shipping)
PGC . . . . Per Gyro Compass (Navigation)
PM . . . . Per Month
PO . . . . Per Os (By Mouth) (Medicine)
PPA . . . . Per Power of Attorney (Business and trade)
PP . . . . Per Procurationem (By Proxy)
PPC . . . . Per Pupil Cost
PPL . . . . Per Pupil Limitation
PS . . . . Per Ship
PSC . . . . Per Standard Compass (Navigation)
PSTGC . . . . . . Per Steering Compass (Navigation)
PNB . . . . Perceived Noise Decibel (Sonic boom)
PNDB . . . . Perceived Noise Decibels
PNL . . . . Perceived Noise Level
PCT . . . . Percent
PRW . . . . Percent Rated Wattage
PETI . . . . Percent of Travel Involved
PIL . . . . Percentage Increase in Loss (Statistics)
PR . . . . Percentile Rank
PL . . . . Perception of Light
P . . . . Perch
PHAA . . . . . . Percheron Horse Association of America
PCA . . . . Perchloric Acid
P & A . . . . . . Percussion and Auscultation (Medicine)
PA & F . . . . . . Percussion, Auscultation, and Fremitus (Medicine)
PN . . . . Percussion Note (Physiology)
PAS . . . . Percussive Arts Society
P . . . . Pere (Father)
PM . . . . Pere Marquette Railway Company (AAR code)
PERFW . . . . . . Perforating Wound
P . . . . Perforation
PA . . . . Performance Analysis
PAR . . . . Performance Analysis & Review
PERCOS . . . . . Performance Coding System
PACE . . . . . . Performance and Cost Evaluation
PEARL . . . . . . Performance Evaluation of Amplifiers from a Remote Location
PEP . . . . Performance Evaluation Program
PET . . . . Performance Evaluation Test
PF . . . . Performance Factor
PH . . . . Performance History
PI . . . . Performance Index
PN . . . . Performance Number
PRI . . . . Performance Registry International
PR . . . . Performance Report
PR . . . . Performance Requirement
PROBE . . . . . . Performance Review of Base Supply Effectiveness (Air Force)
PSP . . . . Performance Standards Program
PT . . . . Performance Test
PVS . . . . Performance Verification System
PRS . . . . Performing Right Society
PIA . . . . Perfumery Importers Association
P . . . . Perianth
P . . . . Perimeter
PAR . . . . Perimeter Acquisition RADAR (Air Force)
P . . . . Period
POS . . . . Period of Service
PAS . . . . Periodic–Acid–Schiff (Stain)
PEIC . . . . . . Periodic Error Integrating Controller
PI . . . . Periodic Inspection (Military)
PERINTREPT . . Periodic Intelligence Report
PM . . . . Periodic Maintenance
PMRM . . . . . . Periodic Maintenance Requirements Manual (Navy)
PPM . . . . Periodic Permanent Magnet
PPSR . . . . Periodic Personnel Strength Report (Army)
PPT . . . . Periodic Programs Termination (Data processing)
PST . . . . Periodic Self-Test (Data processing)
PPG . . . . Periodical Press Gallery (US Senate)
PPA . . . . Periodical Publishers Association
PB . . . . Peripheral Buffer
PCI . . . . Peripheral Command Indicator
PERCOM . . . . . Peripheral Communications
PIP . . . . Peripheral Interchange Program (Data processing)
PIT . . . . Peripheral Input Tape (Data processing)
PR . . . . Peripheral Resistance
PUP . . . . Peripheral Unit Processor (Data processing)
PVD . . . . Peripheral Vascular Disease
PDR . . . . Periscope Depth Range (SONAR)
P . . . . Perishable
PEC . . . . Perkin-Elmer Corporation

PKN . . . . Perkin-Elmer Corporation (NYSE symbol)
PI . . . . Perlite Institute, Inc.
PR . . . . Permanens Rector (Permanent Rector)
PA . . . . Permanent Appointment
PBM . . . . Permanent Bench Mark
PBA . . . . Permanent Budget Account
PB . . . . Permanent Bunkers
PCOB(UN) . . . . Permanent Central Opium Board of the United Nations
PCA . . . . Permanent Change of Assignment
PCS . . . . Permanent Change of Station (Military)
PCCEMRSP . . . . Permanent Commission for the Conservation and Exploitation of the Maritime Resources of the South Pacific
PCIFC . . . . . . Permanent Commission of the International Fisheries Convention
PCGN . . . . . . Permanent Committee of Geographical Names
IVC . . . . Permanent Committee for the International Veterinary Congresses
PCNB . . . . . . Permanent Control Narcotics Board
PCA . . . . Permanent Court of Arbitration
PCIJ . . . . Permanent Court of International Justice
PDRL . . . . . . Permanent Disability Retired List
PDA . . . . Permanent Duty Assignment (Air Force)
PDS . . . . Permanent Duty Station (Air Force)
PE . . . . Permanent Echo (RADAR)
PERMAFROST . . Permanent Frost
PG . . . . Permanent Grade
PIT . . . . Permanent Income Theory (Econometrics)
IOC . . . . Permanent Intergovernmental Oceanographic Commission
PIANC . . . . . . Permanent International Association of Navigation Congresses
PIARC . . . . . . Permanent International Association of Road Congresses
PIBAC . . . . . . Permanent International Bureau of Analytical Chemistry of Human and Animal Food
PICGC . . . . . . Permanent International Committee for Genetic Congresses
PICM . . . . . . Permanent International Committee of Mothers
PICUTP . . . . . Permanent and International Committee of Underground Town Planning
PJBD . . . . . . Permanent Joint Board on Defense
PM . . . . Permanent-Magnet (Loudspeaker)
PMMC . . . . . . Permanent Magnetic Movable Coil
PMPA . . . . . . Permanent Magnet Producers Association
PMT . . . . Permanent-Magnet Twistor (Memory) (Bell Laboratories)
PERMU . . . . . . Permanent Magnet Users Association
POOD . . . . . . Permanent Officer of the Deck (Day) (Navy)
PP . . . . Permanent Party
PPR . . . . Permanent Pay Record
PERMR . . . . . . Permanent Residence
PS . . . . Permanent Secretary
PSF . . . . Permanent Signal Finder
PSBLS . . . . . . Permanent Space Based Logistics System
P & T . . . . . . Permanent and Total (Disability)
PWI . . . . Permanent Ware Institute
PNC . . . . Permanente Cement Company (NYSE symbol)
PSDS . . . . . . Permanently Separated from Duty Station (Military)
PF . . . . Permeability Factor
PERMINVAR . . . Permeability Invariant
PQ . . . . Permeability Quotient
PERGRA . . . . . Permission Granted (Military)
PERNOGRA . . . Permission Not Granted (Military)
PAL . . . . Permissive Action Link
PALS . . . . . . Permissive Action Link Systems
PR . . . . Permissive Reassignment (Air Force)
PA . . . . Pernicious Anemia
PO . . . . Peroral or Per Os (By Mouth) (Medicine)
PAN . . . . Peroxyacetyl Nitrate (Chemical)
PPN . . . . Peroxypropionyl Nitrate (Chemical)
POP . . . . Perpendicular Ocean Platform (Oceanography)
PC . . . . Perpetual Curate (or Curacy)
PICS . . . . . . Perpetual Inventory Control System
PMPM . . . . . . Perpetual Motion Poetry Machine
PLC . . . . Perry-Link Cubmarine (A submersible vehicle)
PEVI . . . . . . Perry's Victory and International Peace Memorial National Monument
PBKB . . . . . . Persatuan Buruh Kendaraan Bermotor (Motorized Vehicle Workers' Union) (Indonesia)
PBKA . . . . . . Persatuan Buruh Kereta Api (National Railway Workers' Union) (Indonesia)
PERBUM . . . . . Persatuan Buruh Minjak (Federation of Oil Workers) (Indonesia)
PPBDT . . . . . . Persatuan Buruh Pengendara Betja Dokar dan Tjikar (Dogcart and Bullock-cart Drivers' Union) (Indonesia)
PERBUPRI . . . . Persatuan Buruh Perkebunan Republik Indonesia (Plantation Workers' Union) (Indonesia)
PERBUTI . . . . Persatuan Buruh Textiel Indonesia (Textile Workers' Union) (Indonesia)
PGKI . . . . . . Persatuan Guru Katholik Indonesia (Indonesian Catholic Teachers' Union)
PGRI . . . . . . Persatuan Guru Republik Indonesia (Union of Teachers of the Republic of Indonesia)
PGTI . . . . . . Persatuan Guruh Teknik Indonesia (Technical Teachers' Union of Indonesia)

PKF . . . . Persatuan Karyawan Fadjarbhakti (Fadjar Bhakti State Trading Enterprise Workers' Union) (Indonesia)

PKP . . . . Persatuan Karyawan Permorin (Permorin Company Workers' Union) (Indonesia)

PERKAPPEN . . Persatuan Karyawan Perusahaan Perkebunan Negara (State Estate Enterprise Workers' Union) (Indonesia)

PDKI . . . . Persatuan Pegawai Departemen Kesehatan Indonesia (Union of Health Department Employees) (Indonesia)

PPTT . . . . . . Persatuan Pegawai Tambang Timah (Tin Mine Employees' Union) (Indonesia)

PR . . . . Pershing Rifles (Honorary military organization)

PGC . . . . Persian Gulf Command (World War II)

PGSC . . . . . . Persian Gulf Service Command

GP (Gas) . . . . . Persistent Chemical Agent Gas

PT . . . . Persistent Tease (Slang) (Bowdlerized version)

PTI . . . . Persistent Tolerant Infection

PNG . . . . Persona Non Grata

PAM . . . . Personal Accounting Management

PA . . . . Personal Affairs

PAC . . . . Personal Analog Computer

PA . . . . Personal Appearance

PCA . . . . Personal Cash Allowance

PC . . . . Personal Correction

PEREF . . . . . . Personal Effects

PEDC . . . . . . Personal Effects Distribution Center

PERSEXP . . . . . Personal Expense Money

PIP . . . . Personal Identification Project (Data processing)

PI . . . . Personal Income

PLB . . . . Personal Locator Beacon (Military)

PP . . . . Personal Property

PPSIA . . . . . . "Personal Property Shipping Information" (Pamphlet) Is Applicable (Military)

PRM . . . . Personal Radiation Monitor (Military)

PR & D . . . . . . Personal Rest and Delay (Air Force)

PSQ . . . . Personal Security Questionnaire

PSS . . . . Personal Signaling System

PT . . . . Personal Trade (In some retail establishments, customers are assigned to salesmen in rotation. A customer who is the "PT" or personal client of a salesman is not counted as part of the salesman's share of customers)

PERSTRAN . . . . Personal Transportation (Navy)

PQ . . . . Personality Quotient

PAID . . . . Personnel and Accounting Integrated Data (System) (Veterans Administration)

PAL . . . . Personnel Accounting Level (Air Force)

PAMI . . . . . . Personnel Accounting Machine Installation

PAS . . . . Personnel Accounting Symbol (Air Force)

PERAM . . . . . Personnel Action Memorandum

PAM . . . . Personnel Actions Memorandum (Military)

P & A . . . . Personnel and Administration (Army)

PAP . . . . Personnel Allocation Plan (Navy)

PAV . . . . Personnel Allotment Voucher

PAL . . . . Personnel Augmentation List (Military)

PAT . . . . Personnel Authorization Table (Air Force)

PADS . . . . . . Personnel Automated Data System (TIMMS)

PATS . . . . . . Personnel in an Awaiting Training Status (Air Force)

PC . . . . Personnel Carrier (A vehicle)

PERSCON . . . . Personnel Control (Military)

PCC . . . . Personnel Control Center (Air Force)

PDS . . . . Personnel Daily Summary (Army)

PDS . . . . Personnel Data Summary

PDS . . . . Personnel Data System

PDS-A . . . . . . Personnel Data System for Airmen (Air Force)

PDS-A(I) . . . . . Personnel Data System – Airmen (Interim) (Air Force)

PDS-O . . . . . . Personnel Data System – Officers (Air Force)

PDSP . . . . Personnel Data System Planning (Air Force)

PERSD . . . . . . Personnel Department (Marine Corps)

PDC . . . . Personnel Distribution Command

PE . . . . Personnel, Enlisted or Enlisted Personnel Division (Coast Guard)

PE . . . . Personnel Equipment (Air Force)

PED . . . . Personnel Equipment Data

P & EML . . . . . Personnel and Equipment Modification List (Air Force)

PHASR . . . . . Personnel Hazards Associated with Space Radiation (Satellite)

PICS . . . . Personnel Information Communication System (Data processing)

PERSINS . . . . . Personnel Information System (Army)

LBP . . . . Personnel Landing Boat (Navy symbol)

PERMACAP . . . Personnel Management and Accounting Card Processor

PMA . . . . Personnel Management Assistance

PMIC . . . . . . Personnel Management Information Center

PMIS . . . . . . Personnel Management Information System (NASA)

PMS . . . . Personnel Management System (Air Force)

PERSOF . . . . . Personnel Officer (Navy)

PO . . . . Personnel Officer

PORDA . . . . . . Personnel Officers of Research and Development Agencies

PPD . . . . Personnel Priority Designator (Military)

PERSPROC . . . . Personnel Processing

PPG . . . . Personnel Processing Group

PRO . . . . Personnel Relations Officer (for Shore Stations) (Navy)

PRBA(AG) . . . . Personnel Research Board of the Army, Adjutant General

PRB . . . . Personnel Research Branch (Army)

PRD . . . . Personnel Research Division (Navy)

PRL . . . . Personnel Research Laboratory (DOD)

PRT . . . . Personnel Research Test

A-1 . . . . Personnel Section of an Air Staff; also, officer in charge of this section (Air Force)

S-1 . . . . Personnel Section in Army Brigades or smaller units, and in Marine Corps units smaller than a brigade; the officer in charge of this section; also refers to adjutant (1st staff section, brigades and lower units)

G-1 . . . . Personnel Section of an Army or Marine Corps Division (or Marine brigade or aircraft wing) General Staff; the Officer in Charge of this Section

J-1 . . . . Personnel Section of a Joint Military Staff; the Officer in Charge of this Section

PERSSEPCENT . . Personnel Separation Center

PSD . . . . Personnel Services Division (Army)

PSNCO . . . . . Personnel Staff Noncommissioned Officer (Military)

PSS . . . . Personnel Subsystem (Air Force)

PS & M . . . . . Personnel Supervision and Management Division of ASTSECNAV's Office (Absorbed into SECP, 1944)

PSS . . . . Personnel Support System (Army)

PSM . . . . Personnel Systems Management (Air Force)

PERS & TRACOMD . . Personnel and Training Command

PTRC . . . . . . Personnel & Training Research Center (Air Force)

PTI . . . . Personnel Transaction Identifier (Air Force)

PTC . . . . Personnel Transfer Capsule (Undersea technology)

PN . . . . Personnelman (Navy rating)

PAA . . . . Peruvian–American Association

PGII . . . . Pesatawan Guruh Islam Indonesia (Islamic Teachers' Union) (Indonesia)

P . . . . Peseta (Spanish and Latin American monetary unit)

P . . . . Peso (Spanish and Latin American monetary unit)

PCO . . . . Pest Control Operator

PFV . . . . Pestalozzi–Froebel–Verband (Pestalozzi–Froebel Association)

PIC . . . . Pesticides Information Center (National Agricultural Library)

PFI . . . . Pet Food Institute

PET . . . . Pet Milk Company (NYSE symbol)

PSR . . . . Petaluma & Santa Rosa R. R. (AAR code)

PETE . . . . . . Petersburg National Battlefield

PEFO . . . . . . Petrified Forest National Park

PWS . . . . Petrified Wood Society

PTO . . . . Petrolane Gas Service, Inc. (NYSE symbol)

PEMEX . . . . . Petroleos Mexicanos (Mexican government petroleum operating company)

PAD . . . . Petroleum Administration for Defense (Abolished, 1954)

PAW . . . . Petroleum Administration for War (World War II)

PAB . . . . Petroleum Administrative Board (Terminated, 1936)

PEO . . . . Petroleum Corporation of America (NYSE symbol)

PEPA . . . . . . Petroleum Electric Power Association

PESA . . . . . . Petroleum Electric Supply Association

PE . . . . Petroleum Engineer

PECA . . . . . . Petroleum Equipment Contractors Association

PESA . . . . . . Petroleum Equipment Suppliers Association

PAGICEP . . . . . Petroleum and Gas Industry Communications Emergency Plan (FCC)

PGWU . . . . . . Petroleum and General Workers' Union (Aden)

PIEA . . . . . . Petroleum Industry Electrical Association

PIRINC . . . . . . Petroleum Industry Research Foundation, Incorporated

PIWC . . . . . . Petroleum Industry War Council

POLIC . . . . . . Petroleum Intersectional Command

POLIS . . . . . . Petroleum Intersectional Service

PLPB . . . . Petroleum Labor Policy Board (Abolished, 1936)

POL . . . . Petroleum Oil Lubricants (Military)

PPPC . . . . . . Petroleum Pool Pacific Coast

PRE . . . . Petroleum Refining Engineer

PRL . . . . Petroleum Refining Laboratory (Pennsylvania State University)

PRF . . . . Petroleum Research Fund

PETRES . . . . . Petroleum Reserves (Navy)

PRC . . . . Petroleum Reserves Corporation

PETSEC . . . . . Petroleum Section (Allied Force Headquarters)

PSCLA . . . . . . Petroleum Supply Committee for Latin America

PIR . . . . Petrolite Irradiation Reactor (AEC)

PP . . . . Petticoat Peeping (From one girl to another, in reference to dress disarrangement)

PC . . . . Petty Cash

PCB . . . . Petty Cash Book (Business and trade)

PCV . . . . Petty Cash Voucher

PL . . . . Petty Larceny

PO .... Petty Officer (Navy)
PT .... Petty Theft
PCCA .... Pewter Collectors Club of America
PPM .... Pfaudler Permutit, Inc. (NYSE symbol)
PFE .... Pfizer (Chas.) & Company, Inc. (NYSE symbol)
PAC .... Pharmaceutical Advertising Club
Ph C .... Pharmaceutical Chemist
PMA........ Pharmaceutical Manufacturers Association
PWA .... Pharmaceutical Wholesalers Association
PHM .... Pharmacist's Mate (Navy rating)
PHMDP..... Pharmacist's Mate, Dental Prosthetic Technician (Navy rating)
P.......... Pharmacopoeia
PB .... Pharmacopoeia Britannica (British Pharmacopoeia)
PG........ Pharmacopoeia Germanica
PI .... Pharmacopoeia Internationalis
PUS .... Pharmacopeia of the United States
PCT .... Pharmacy and Chemistry Technician (Navy)
PC .... Pharmacy Corps (Army)
PAS .... Phase Address System
PAL .... Phase Alternating Line (German color television system)
PAV .... Phase Angle Voltmeter
PCM .... Phase–Change Materials
PC .... Phase Coherent
PER .... Phase Engineering Report
PL .... Phase Line
PHLODOT .... Phase Lock Doppler Tracking
PLO .... Phase-Locked Oscillator
PHM........ Phase Meter
PM .... Phase Modulation (Radio)
PPP .... Phase Program Planning (NASA)
PSD .... Phase Sensitive Demodulator
PS .... Phase Shift
PSK .... Phase-Shift Key
PLE .... Phased Loading Entry (Data processing)
PD .... Phelps Dodge Corporation (NYSE symbol)
PAC .... Phenacetin (Acetophenetidin), Aspirin, Caffeine
PAD .... Phenacetin, Aspirin, Desoxyephedrine
PF .... Phenol Formaldehyde
PHO........ Phenolic Heavy Oil
PSP .... Phenolsulfonphthalein Test (for kidney disease)
POM .... Phenomenon of Man (Project)
PPT........ Phenylalanine-Pyruvate Transaminase
PBD .... Phenylbiphenyloxadiazole (Chemistry)
PKU .... Phenylketonuria (Congenital metabolism disorder) (Medicine)
PMC .... Phenylmercuric Chloride
POPOP ...... Phenyl-Oxazolyl-Phenyloxazolyl-Phenyl
PPA .... Phenylpyruvic Acid (Chemical)
PTC .... Phenylthiocarbamide
PTU .... Phenylthiourea (Medicine)
PTA .... Phenyltrimethylammonium
PBK .... Phi Beta Kappa
PDK .... Phi Delta Kappa (Fraternity in field of education)
PHL .... Philadelphia (Airport symbol)
PBL .... Philadelphia Belt Line R. R. (AAR code)
PBNE .... Philadelphia, Bethlehem & New England R. R. (AAR code)
PE .... Philadelphia Electric Company (NYSE symbol)
PIDC .... Philadelphia Industrial Development Corporation
PNS .... Philadelphia & Norfolk Steamship (AAR code)
PQMC ...... Philadelphia Quartermaster Center (Merged with Defense Clothing and Textile Supply Center)
PRG .... Philadelphia & Reading Corporation (NYSE symbol)
P & R ...... Philadelphia & Reading Railway
PW........ Philadelphia & Western R. R. (AAR code)
PAGE...... Philatelic Association of Government Employees
PLA .... Philatelic Literature Association
PNC .... Philatelic-Numismatic Combination
PPC .... Philatelic Press Club
PRS .... Philatelic Research Society
PEM .... Philco Electronic Module
MO .... Philip Morris, Inc. (NYSE symbol)
PAL .... Philippine Air Lines
PALEA ...... Philippine Air Lines Employees' Association
PALSA ...... Philippine Air Lines Supervisors' Association
PAPA .... Philippine Alien Property Administration (Post-World War II)
PA .... Philippine Army
PA .... Philippine Association
PAFLU ...... Philippine Association of Free Labor Unions
PCM........ Philippine Campaign Medal
PCAU ...... Philippine Civil Affairs Unit (Army unit which supplied emergency subsistence after end of Japanese dominance) (World War II)
PHILCAG ... Philippine Civil Assistance Group

PCWF .... Philippine Communications Workers' Federation
PC .... Philippine Constabulary
PDR .... Philippine Defense Ribbon
PIR .... Philippine Independence Ribbon
PI .... Philippine Islands
PLF .... Philippine Labor Federation
PLO .... Philippine Labor Organization
PLUM ...... Philippine Labor Unity Movement (of Federation of Industrial and Agrarian Workers)
PLR .... Philippine Liberation Ribbon
PMA .... Philippine Mahogany Association
PMOG ...... Philippine Marine Officers' Guild
PNG .... Philippine Newspaperworkers' Guild
PHILPUC .... Philippine Presidential Unit Citation Badge
PRPUC ...... Philippine Republic Presidential Unit Citation (Military award)
PRPUCE..... Philippine Republic Presidential Unit Citation Emblem
PRRM ...... Philippine Rural Reconstruction Movement
PS .... Philippine Scouts
PHILSEAFRON .. Philippine Sea Frontier
PSF .... Philippine Sea Frontier
PSA .... Philippine Sugar Association
PTUC .... Philippine Trade Union Council
PTGWO ..... Philippine Transport and General Workers' Organization
PVTAEA ..... Philippine Virginia Tobacco Administration Employees' Association
PWDC ...... Philippine War Damage Commission (Post-World War II)
PAEC .... Philippines Atomic Energy Commission
PASCAL ..... Philips Automatic Sequence Calculator
PHLH ...... Phillips Head (Screw)
P.......... Phillips Petroleum Company (NYSE symbol)
PPC .... Phillips Petroleum Company
PHLAG ..... Phillips Petroleum Load and Go (System)
PVH .... Phillips-Van Heusen Corporation (NYSE symbol)
Ph C .... Philosopher of Chiropractic
PES .... Philosophy of Education Society
PSA .... Philosophy of Science Association
PCMI .... Phochromic Microimage (Data processing)
PPI .... Phoenix Precision Instrument Company
PB .... Phonetically Balanced (With reference to word lists)
PCG .... Phonocardiogram
PMA .... Phonograph Manufacturers Association
POETS ...... Phooey on Everything, Tomorrow's Saturday (Bowdlerized version)
P-BS........ Phosphate-Buffered Saline
PCC .... Phosphate Carrier Compound
PRI .... Phosphate Rock Institute
PA .... Phosphoarginine
PC .... Phosphocreatine (Creatine phosphate, phosphagen)
PEP .... Phosphoenolpyruvate
PGUT .... Phospho-Galactose-Uridyl Transferase
PGAL .... Phosphoglyceraldehyde
PGA .... Phosphoglyceric Acid
PHI .... Phosphohexose Isomerase
PHBRZ ..... Phosphor Bronze
PRAI .... Phosphoribosyl Anthranilate Isomerase
PRT........ Phosphoribosyl Transferase
P.......... Phosphorus (Chemical element)
PTA .... Phosphotungstic Acid
PTAH .... Phosphotungstic Acid Hematoxylin
PFI .... Photo Finishing Institute
PIB........ Photo Intelligence Brief
PIC .... Photo Interpretation Center
PID .... Photo Interpretation Department (Military)
INTERPRON .. Photo Interpretation Squadron
PORT .... Photo-Optical Recorder Tracker
POSS .... Photo-Optical Surveillance Subsystem
PPR .... Photo-Plastic-Recording
PRI........ Photo RADAR Intelligence
F .... Photo-Reconnaissance (Aircraft designation)
PHOTRIPART .. Photo Triangulation Party (Military)
PC .... Photocell
PCMI .... Photochromic Microimage (Film miniature)
PE .... Photoelectric
PEC .... Photoelectric Cell
PEP .... Photoelectric Potential
PES .... Photoelectric Scanner
PEM .... Photoelectromagnetic
PERI .... Photoengravers Research Institute
PH .... Photographer's Mate (Navy rating)
PHOM ...... Photographer's Mate (Navy rating)
PHOAC..... Photographer's Mate, Combat Aircrewman (Navy rating)
PTA .... Photographers' Telegraph Association
PAI .... Photographic Administrators, Incorporated

PCI . . . . Photographic Credit Institute
PT . . . . Photographic Intelligenceman (Navy rating)
PIU . . . . Photographic Interpretation Unit (Marine Corps)
LB . . . . Photographic Laboratory Specialist(s) (Navy)
PMDA . . . . . . Photographic Manufacturers and Distributors Association
PPC . . . . Photographic Processing Cells
PR . . . . Photographic Reconnaissance Aircraft
P . . . . Photographic Reconnaissance Capability (When suffix to Navy aircraft designation)
PRISIC . . . . . . Photographic Reconnaissance Interpretation Section (Squadron) Intelligence Center (JICPOA)
PRU . . . . Photographic Reconnaissance Unit (Aircraft) (Marine Corps)
PARU . . . . . . Photographic and Reproduction Unit
PSL . . . . Photographic Science Laboratory (Navy)
PS . . . . Photographic Service
PSA . . . . Photographic Society of America
PICS . . . . Photography in Community Self-Development (Program of Master Photo Dealers and Finishers Association)
PI . . . . Photointerpreter (or Photointerpretation)
PME . . . . Photomagnetoelectric
PHODEC . . . . . Photometric Determination of Equilibrium Constants (Data processing)
PMT . . . . Photomultiplier Tube
PRL . . . . Photoreactivating Light
PR . . . . Photoreconnaissance (Air Force)
POISE . . . . . . Photosynthetic Oxygenation Illuminated by Solar Energy
PHT . . . . Phototube
PHP . . . . PHP Company (Formerly, Pacific Hawaiian Products Company)
PSA . . . . Phycological Society of America
PAE . . . . Physical Aptitude Examination
PCPT . . . . . . Physical Combat Proficiency Test (Army)
PCTR . . . . . . Physical Constant Test Reactor (AEC)
PDD . . . . Physical Damage Division (Navy)
PDD . . . . Physical Defense Division (Army)
PDAB . . . . . . Physical Disability Appeals Board (Military)
PE Dir . . . . . . Physical Education Director
PEP . . . . Physical Education Program
PEF . . . . Physical Electronics Facility
PEPAG . . . . . Physical Electronics and Physical Acoustics Group (MIT)
P & ESI . . . . . Physical and Engineering Sciences Division (Army Research Office)
PET . . . . Physical Equipment Table
PEB . . . . Physical Evaluation Board (Military)
PEBLO . . . . . Physical Evaluation Board Liaison Officer (Air Force)
PHYSEXAM . . . Physical Examination
PX . . . . Physical Examination (Medicine)
PER . . . . Physical Examination Rate (Military)
PFI . . . . Physical Fitness Index
PM . . . . Physical Medicine
PM & R . . . . . Physical Medicine and Rehabilitation
PMRS . . . . . . Physical Medicine and Rehabilitation Service
PMSR . . . . . . Physical, Mental, Social, Religious ("Fourfold Life" symbol of American Youth Foundation)
PMB . . . . Physical Metallurgy Branch
PP . . . . Physical Profile
PPSC . . . . . . Physical Profile Serial Code
PP . . . . Physical Properties
PRC . . . . Physical Review Council (DOD)
PSNS . . . . . . Physical Science for Nonscience Students
PSSG . . . . . . Physical Science Study Group
PSL . . . . Physical Sciences Laboratory
PSSC . . . . . . Physical Sciences Study Committee (India)
PSEA . . . . . . Physical Security Equipment Agency
PTI . . . . Physical-Technical Institute (USSR)
PTT . . . . Physical Therapist Technician
PT . . . . Physical Therapy
PHT . . . . Physical Therapy Technician (Navy)
PT . . . . Physical Training
PVD . . . . Physical Vulnerability Division (Air Force)
PRS . . . . Physically Restricted Status (Military)
PDR . . . . Physicians' Desk Reference
PF . . . . Physicians Forum
PSR . . . . Physicians for Social Responsibility
PA . . . . Physics Abstracts
PAT . . . . Physics Achievement Test
PD . . . . Physics Department
PTR . . . . Physikalisch-Technische Reichsanstalt (Germany)
PEP . . . . Physiological Evaluation of Primates
PSS . . . . Physiological Saline Solution (Physiology)
PHYSBE . . . . . Physiological Simulation Benchmark Experiment
PHA . . . . Phytohemagglutinin (Chemical)
PSM . . . . Pia Societas Missionum (Fathers of the Pious Society of Missions, Pallottini) (Roman Catholic religious order)

SX . . . . Pia Societas Sancti Francisci Xaverii pro Exteris Missionibus (St. Francis Xavier Foreign Mission Society, or Xaverian Missionary Fathers) (Roman Catholic religious order)
PM . . . . Piae Memoriae (Of Pious Memory)
PP . . . . Pianissimo (Very softly) (Music)
P . . . . Piano (Softly) (Music)
PTG . . . . Piano Technicians Guild
PF . . . . Pianoforte (Soft, then loud) (Music)
P . . . . Piaster (Monetary unit in Spain, Republic of Vietnam, and some Middle Eastern countries)
PA . . . . Picatinny Arsenal (Army)
PIC . . . . Pickens R. R. (AAR code)
PB . . . . Picket Boat (Navy)
PS . . . . Picket Ships (Navy)
PPI . . . . Pickle Packers International
P & O . . . . . . Pickled and Oiled
PP . . . . Pickpocket
PU . . . . Pick-Up (Business and trade)
PC . . . . Pickup Cargo
P & D . . . . . . Pickup and Delivery
PUD . . . . Pick-Up and Delivery (Business and trade)
PZ . . . . Pickup Zone
p . . . . Pico (Prefix: one-trillionth part of)
pA . . . . Picoampere
pCi . . . . Picocurie
pF . . . . Picofarad
pm . . . . Picometer
PSEC . . . . . . Picosecond
pW . . . . Picowatt (A trillionth of a watt)
PAT . . . . Picture Arrangement Test
PFI . . . . Picture and Frame Institute
PPC . . . . Picture Postcard
PIRO . . . . . . Pictured Rocks National Lakeshore (National Park Service designation)
PPI . . . . Pictorial Position Indicator
P . . . . Pie
PFI . . . . Pie Filling Institute
PZ . . . . Pie Zeses (May You Live Piously)
PB . . . . Piebald
PGBA . . . . . . Piece Goods Buyers Association
PI . . . . Piedmont Airlines
PN . . . . Piedmont & Northern Railway Company (AAR code)
PAS . . . . Pierce Arrow Society
PAP . . . . Pierced Aluminum Plank (Technical drawings)
PSP . . . . Pierced Steel Planking (Military)
PFA . . . . Pierre Fauchard Academy
PP . . . . Piers Plowman (Middle English poem)
PI . . . . Pigeon Trainer (Navy)
PBT . . . . Piggyback Twistor (Computer)
PVC . . . . Pigment Volume Concentration
P . . . . Pilaster (Technical drawings)
PH D . . . . . . Piled Higher and Deeper (Humorous interpretation of the Ph D degree)
PSY . . . . Pillsbury Company (NYSE symbol)
P . . . . Pilot
PARD . . . . . . Pilot Airborne Recovery Device (A balloon-parachute)
PIBOL . . . . . . Pilot Back Up Control
PIBAL . . . . . . Pilot Balloon
PCK . . . . Pilot Check
PCI . . . . Pilot Club International
PDI . . . . Pilot Direction Indicator (Electronic communications)
PFSV . . . . . . Pilot-to-Forecaster Service
PGDF . . . . . . Pilot Guide Dog Foundation
PIO . . . . Pilot-Induced Oscillation
PIF . . . . Pilot Information File
PLAT . . . . . . Pilot Landing Aid Television
PO . . . . Pilot Officer
PPMI . . . . . . Pilot Plant Meat Irradiator (AEC)
PP . . . . Pilot Punch
PIRFC . . . . . . Pilot Requests Forecast
PSO . . . . Pilot Systems Operator
PV . . . . Pilot Vessel
PWB . . . . Pilot Weather Briefing
PIREPS . . . . . Pilot Weather Reports (FAA)
PC . . . . Pilotage Charts (Air Force)
PILOT . . . . . . Piloted Low-Speed Test (Aerospace)
KD . . . . Pilotless Aerial Target (Navy)
P/A . . . . Pilotless Aircraft
PADL . . . . . . Pilotless Aircraft Development Laboratory (Navy)
PAD . . . . Pilotless Aircraft Division (Navy)
PARD . . . . . . Pilotless Aircraft Research Division (Langley Research Center) (Later, Applied Materials and Physics Division)
PARS . . . . . . Pilotless Aircraft Research Station (NASA)

PAU . . . . Pilotless Aircraft Unit
PB . . . . Pilotless Bomber (Air Force)
V-1 . . . . Pilotless flying bomb employed by the Germans (World War II)
PI . . . . Pilotless Intercepter (Air Force)
PAS . . . . Pilots Advisory Service
PATWAS . . . . Pilots Automatic Telephone Weather Answering Service
PRM . . . . Pilots Radio Manual
PUSS . . . . Pilots Universal Sighting System
PIREP . . . . . . Pilots' Report (Air Force)
SBE . . . . Pimpinan Pusat Serikat Buruh Es (Ice Workers' Union) (Indonesia)
PCFA . . . . Pin, Clip and Fastener Association
PBCE . . . . Pine Bluff Cotton Exchange
PGAH . . . . . . Pineapple Growers Association of Hawaii
PRI . . . . Pineapple Research Institute of Hawaii
PA . . . . Pinellas Area Office (AEC)
PE . . . . Pinion End
PINN . . . . . . Pinnacles National Monument
P . . . . Pint
PAS . . . . Pioneer Aerodynamic Systems, Inc.
P & A . . . . . . Pioneer and Ammunition
P & D . . . . . . Pioneer and Demolition Section
P & DSEC . . . . Pioneer and Demolition Section (Army)
PF . . . . Pioneer & Fayette R. R. (AAR code)
PFA . . . . Pioneer Fraternal Association
PTETS . . . . . . Pioneer Television and Electronic Technicians Society
PYA . . . . Pioneer Youth of America
PYA . . . . Pioneer Youth Authority (Ghana)
PRL . . . . Pioneering Research Laboratory (Massachusetts) (Army)
PSSC . . . . Pious Society of Missionaries of St. Charles (Later, CS) (Roman Catholic
              men's religious order)
PUSJDS . . . . . Pious Union of St. Joseph for Dying Sinners
P . . . . Pipe
PFI . . . . Pipe Fabrication Institute
PFMA . . . . . . Pipe Fittings Manufacturers Association
PLCA . . . . . . Pipe Line Contractors Association
PLUTO . . . . . Pipe Line Under the Ocean (British project) (World War II)
PPPC . . . . . . Pipe Plug Producers Council
PISP . . . . Pipe Springs National Monument
PTC . . . . Pipe and Tobacco Council
PV . . . . Pipe Ventilated
FP . . . . Pipefitter (Navy)
PL . . . . Pipeline
PLT . . . . Pipeline Time
PPA . . . . Piper Aircraft Corporation (NYSE symbol)
PIPE . . . . Pipestone National Monument
PNPF . . . . . . Piqua Nuclear Power Facility (AEC)
PSA . . . . Pisces Society of America
PE . . . . Pistol Expert
PS . . . . Pistol Sharpshooter (Army)
PPSG . . . . . . Piston and Pin Standardization Group
PRMG . . . . . . Piston Ring Manufacturers Group
P . . . . Pitch (Technical drawings)
P . . . . Pitch or Pitcher (Baseball)
PBI . . . . Pitch Boundary Indicator
PC . . . . Pitch Circle (Technical drawings)
PCM . . . . . . Pitch Control Motor
PCS . . . . Pitch Control System
PD . . . . Pitch Diameter
PR . . . . Pitch Ratio
PBI . . . . Pitney-Bowes, Incorporated (NYSE symbol)
PS & N . . . . . Pittsburg, Shawmut & Northern Railroad Company
PS . . . . Pittsburg & Shawmut R. R. (AAR code)
P & S . . . . . . Pittsburg & Shawmut Railroad Company
PIT . . . . Pittsburgh (Airport symbol)
PAM . . . . Pittsburgh, Allegheny & McKees Rocks R. R. (AAR code)
PCY . . . . Pittsburgh, Chartiers & Youghiogheny Railway (AAR code)
PCK . . . . Pittsburgh Coke & Chemical Company (NYSE symbol)
PC . . . . Pittsburgh Commerce Institute
PFG . . . . Pittsburgh Forgings Company (NYSE symbol)
PLE . . . . Pittsburgh & Lake Erie R. R. (AAR code)
PMKY . . . . . . Pittsburgh, McKeesport & Youghiogheny R. R. (AAR code)
PNR . . . . Pittsburgh Naval Reactors Office (AEC)
POV . . . . Pittsburgh & Ohio Valley Railway Company (AAR code)
PPG . . . . Pittsburgh Plate Glass Company (NYSE symbol)
PSC . . . . Pittsburgh Steel Company (NYSE symbol)
PW . . . . Pittsburgh & West Virginia Railway (NYSE symbol)
PWV . . . . Pittsburgh & West Virginia Railway (AAR code)
P & WV . . . . Pittsburgh & West Virginia Railway
PYA . . . . Pittsburgh, Youngs. & Ash. Railway (NYSE symbol)
PCO . . . . Pittston Company (NYSE symbol)
PATH . . . . . . Pituitary Adrenotrophic Hormone

PF . . . . Piu Forte (A little louder) (Music)
PP . . . . Piu Piano (More softly) (Music)
P . . . . Pius (Dutiful)
PAFE . . . . . . Place Accepted for Enlistment
PLOB . . . . . . Place of Birth
POB . . . . Place of Birth
POD . . . . Place of Discharge
PIF . . . . Place in Inactive File
PFWOAD . . . . Place from Which Ordered to Active Duty (Military)
PCO . . . . Placement Contracting Officer (Army)
POP . . . . Placing Older People (North Carolina)
PL . . . . Plain Language (As opposed to coded message) (Military)
POTS . . . . . . Plain Old Telephone Service
PCG . . . . Plains Cotton Growers
PMMS . . . . . . Plainsong and Mediaeval Music Society
PACT . . . . . . Plan of Action for Challenging Times (Educational program for low-
              income students)
PACE . . . . . . Plan for Action by Citizens in Education
PTC . . . . Plan to Clear (Aviation)
PTJA . . . . . . Plan to Join Airways
PPDD . . . . . . Plan Position Data Display
PPI . . . . Plan-Position Indicator (RADAR)
PSI . . . . Plan Speed Indicator
PC . . . . Plane Commander
PH . . . . Plane Handler (Navy)
P . . . . Planed
PMSFN . . . . . Planetary Manned Space Flight Network
PO . . . . Planetary Orbit
PROP . . . . . . Planetary Rocket Ocean Platform
PANIC . . . . . Planned Attack on Nine Inner Cities (to build education parks)
YTX . . . . Planned District Craft (Navy symbol)
PEER . . . . . . Planned Experience for Effective Relating
PIIM . . . . Planned Interdependency Incentive Method
PMS . . . . Planned Maintenance System (SNMMS)
PPFA . . . . . . Planned Parenthood Federation of America
PP-WP . . . . . . Planned Parenthood-World Population
PPG . . . . Planned Procurement Guide
PSP . . . . Planned Standard Programming (Data processing)
PVD . . . . Planned View Display (RADAR)
PAM . . . . Planning, Activation, Modification (Army reorganization)
PBEIST . . . . . . Planning Board European Inland Surface Transport (Army)
PCG . . . . Planning & Control Guide
PCS . . . . Planning Control Sheet
PCT . . . . Planning & Control Techniques
PERA . . . . . . Planning and Engineering for Repair and Alteration (Navy)
PLANNET . . . . Planning Network
PO . . . . Planning Objectives
PPB . . . . Planning-Programming-Budgeting (System)
PPBS . . . . Planning-Programming-Budgeting System
PRC . . . . Planning Research Corporation
PRIME . . . . . . Planning through Retrieval of Information for Management Extrapolation
PS . . . . Planning and Scheduling
PD . . . . Plans Directive
PLENAPS . . . . Plans for the Employment of Naval and Air Forces of the Associated
              Powers in the Eastern Theater in the Event of War with Japan
PBA . . . . Plant Breeding Abstracts
PCO . . . . Plant Clearance Order
PEC . . . . Plant Equipment Codes (DOD)
P & F . . . . . . Plant and Facilities
PLANN . . . . . Plant Location Assistance Nationwide Network
PPC . . . . Plant Pest Control Division (of ARS, Department of Agriculture)
PIP . . . . Plant-in-Place
PIPR . . . . Plant-in-Place Records
PQ . . . . Plant Quarantine Division (of ARS, Department of Agriculture)
PR . . . . Plant Report
PSS . . . . Plant Science Seminar
PTAC . . . . . . Plant Transportation Advisory Committee
PU . . . . Plant Unit(s)
PWIF . . . . . . Plantation Workers' International Federation
PFC . . . . Plaque-Forming Cells
PFU . . . . Plaque Forming Unit
PDGDL . . . . . Plasma Dynamics and Gaseous Discharge Laboratory (MIT)
PITR . . . . Plasma Iron Turnover Rate
PPL . . . . Plasma Physics Laboratory (Also known as PPPL)
PPL . . . . Plasma Propulsion Laboratory
PPCAA . . . . . Plasma Prothrombin Conversion Accelerator (Physiology)
PPCF . . . . . . Plasma Prothrombin Conversion Factor (Physiology)
PTA . . . . Plasma Thromboplastin Antecedent (Factor X)
PTC . . . . Plasma Thromboplastin Component
PTF . . . . Plasma Thromboplastin Factor (Physiology)
PV . . . . Plasma Volume (Medicine)

PP . . . . Plaster of Paris
PCMI . . . . . . Plastic Container Manufacturers Institute
PFCA . . . . . . Plastic Food Container Association (Defunct)
PHMA. . . . . . Plastic Houseware Manufacturers Association
PIC . . . . Plastic Insulated Conductor
PL . . . . Plastic Laboratory (Princeton University)
PPMA . . . . . . Plastic Products Manufacturers Association
PSMMA. . . . . . Plastic Soft Materials Manufacturers Association
PS . . . . Plastic Surgery (Medicine)
PSurg . . . . . . Plastic Surgery (Medicine)
PWP . . . . Plasticized White Phosphorus
PEF . . . . Plastics Education Foundation
PEA . . . . Plastics Engineers Association
PIA . . . . Plastics Institute of America
PPI. . . . . Plastics Pipe Institute
PRL . . . . Plastics Research Laboratory (MIT)
PLASTEC . . . . . Plastics Technical Evaluation Center (DOD)
PTEC . . . . Plastics Technical Evaluation Center (Army)
P. . . . . Plate (Electron tube) (Technical drawings)
PTH . . . . Plated Through Hole
PEP . . . . Platform Electronic Package
Pt . . . . Platinum (Chemical element)
PANY . . . . . Platinumsmiths Association of New York
PLC . . . . Platoon Leader's Class
PLU . . . . Platoon Leaders Unit (Marine Corps)
PSG . . . . Platoon Sergeant (Army)
PLAT . . . . . . Platt National Park
PCS . . . . Plausible Conflict Situations (Army)
PSA . . . . Play Schools Association
PCCA . . . . . . Playing Card Collectors' Association
P. . . . . Pleasant
PSA . . . . Pleasant Sunday Afternoon(s)
PX . . . . Please Exchange (Merchandising slang)
PMYOB. . . . . Please Mind Your Own Business
PN. . . . . Please Note
PTO . . . . Please Turn Over (the page)
PSEA . . . . . . Pleaters, Stitchers and Embroiderers Association
PT . . . . Plenty Tough (Slang)
PT . . . . Plenty Trouble (Slang)
PAT . . . . Plenum Air Tread (Army amphibian vehicle)
PPO . . . . Pleuropneumonia Organisms (Bacteriology)
PPLO . . . . . Pleuropneumonia-like Organisms (Bacteriology)
PLENCH . . . . Pliers & Wrench (combination)
PLO . . . . Plough, Inc. (NYSE symbol)
PSR . . . . Plow-Steel Rope
PAC . . . . Plowshare Advisory Committee (AEC)
P. . . . . Plug
PB . . . . Plugboard
PIE . . . . Plug-In Electronics
PIU . . . . Plug-In Unit
PIUMP . . . . . . Plug-In Unit Mounting Panel
PBR . . . . Plum Brook Reactor (AEC)
PBRF. . . . . . . Plum Brook Reactor Facility (Lewis Research Center)
PIADL . . . . . . Plum Island Animal Disease Laboratory (of ARS, Department of Agriculture)
PBI . . . . Plumbing Brass Institute
PDI . . . . Plumbing and Drainage Institute
PFMA . . . . . . Plumbing Fixture Manufacturers Association
PHCIB. . . . . . Plumbing-Heating-Cooling Information Bureau
PIFS . . . . Plume-Induced Flow Separation
P. . . . . Plus (More)
PEH . . . . Plus Each Hour (Aviation)
PM . . . . Plus Minus (More or less)
Pu . . . . Plutonium (Chemical element)
PLUCON. . . . . Plutonium Decontamination Emergency Teams
PRCF . . . . . . Plutonium Recycle Critical Facility (AEC)
PRTR . . . . . . Plutonium Recycle Test Reactor (AEC)
PRF . . . . Plywood Research Foundation
PETE . . . . . . Pneumatic End to End
PEDRO . . . . . Pneumatic Energy Detector with Remote Optics
PEG . . . . Pneumatic Explosion Generator
PF . . . . Pneumatic Float
PFBRG . . . . . Pneumatic Float Bridge
PTS . . . . Pneumatic Test Set
PT . . . . Pneumatic Tube (Technical drawings)
POV. . . . . . . Pneumatically Operated Valve
PVM. . . . . . . Pneumonia Virus of Mice
PAI . . . . Poale Agudat Israel of America
PB . . . . Pocket Book
PTL . . . . Pocket Testament League
PBS . . . . Podiatry Bibliographical Society

PL . . . . Poet Laureate
PSA . . . . Poetry Society of America
P. . . . . Point (Lacrosse position)
PAT . . . . Point After Touchdown (Football)
PA . . . . Point of Aim (Military)
PBC . . . . Point of Basal Convergence
PCA . . . . Point of Closest Approach
PCN. . . . . . . Point Comfort & Northern Railway Company (AAR code)
PC . . . . Point of Curve (Technical drawings)
PDSMS . . . . . Point-Defense Surface Missile System
PD . . . . Point Detonating (Projectile)
PDF . . . . Point Detonating Fuze
PDSD . . . . . . Point Detonating Self-Destroying (Projectile)
PET . . . . Point of Equal Time (Aviation)
PI . . . . Point of Impact
PI . . . . Point Initiating
PIBD . . . . . . Point Initiating, Base Detonating (Projectile)
PI . . . . Point Insulating
PIM . . . . Point of Intended Movement (Military)
PI . . . . Point of Interception (Navigation)
PI . . . . Point of Intersection
PMI . . . . Point of Maximal Impulse
PMI . . . . Point of Maximum Intensity
PNR . . . . Point of No Return (Aviation)
P/P . . . . Point-to-Point (Air Force)
PTP. . . . . Point-to-Point
POP . . . . Point of Purchase (Advertising)
POPAI. . . . . . Point-of-Purchase Advertising Institute
PORE . . . . . . Point Reyes National Seashore (National Park Service designation)
P/S. . . . . Point of Shipment
PSF . . . . Point Spread Function
PSE . . . . Point of Subjective Equality (Psychology)
PS . . . . Point of Switch
PS . . . . Point of Symmetry
PT . . . . Point of Tangency
PT . . . . Point of Turn (Navigation)
PCS . . . . Pointing-Control System
P . . . . Poise
PDA . . . . Poise Distribution Amplifier
PCC . . . . Poison Control Center
PI . . . . Poison Ivy (Campers' slang)
PWM . . . . . . Pokeweed Mitogen
PCRA . . . . . . Poland China Record Association
P . . . . Polar (Air mass)
PA . . . . Polar Atlantic (American air mass)
PBA . . . . . . Polar Bear Association
PBRESD . . . . . Polar Branch, Research Environmental Science Division (Army)
PCA . . . . Polar Cap Absorption
POCIBO . . . . . Polar Circling Balloon Observatory
PC. . . . . Polar Continental (American air mass)
P. . . . . Polar distance
PD . . . . Polar Distance (Navigation)
PIB. . . . . Polar Ionosphere Beacon
PIBS . . . . . . Polar Ionospheric Beacon Satellite (NASA)
POGO . . . . . . Polar Orbiting Geophysical Observatory
POSSUM . . . . . Polar Orbiting Satellite System – University of Michigan (Designed by engineering students)
PP . . . . Polar Pacific (American air mass)
B . . . . Polar radius of earth
PRDC . . . . . . Polar Research and Development Center (Army)
Q . . . . Polaris Correction
PRD . . . . Polaroid Corporation (NYSE symbol)
PSC . . . . Polaroid Stereoscopic Chroncyclegraph
P. . . . . Pole
PK . . . . Pole Cat (Slang)
PAL . . . . Police Athletic League (New York)
PC . . . . Police-Constable (British)
PD . . . . Police Department
PFIA . . . . . . Police and Firemen's Insurance Association
PIN . . . . Police Information Network (San Francisco Bay area, California)
PJP . . . . Police Judiciaire des Parquets (Investigatory Police of the Public Prosecutor) (Belgium)
PJ . . . . Police Justice
PM. . . . . Police Magistrate
PS . . . . Police Sergeant
PTF . . . . Police Training Foundation
PIDE. . . . . . . Policia Internacional e de Defesa do Estado (Police for the Control of Foreigners and Defense of the State) (Portugal and Portuguese Africa)
PPI . . . . Policy Proof of Interest
PAS . . . . Polish Academy of Sciences
PAMA . . . . . . Polish Alma Mater of America

PAGS . . . . . . Polish-American Guardian Society
PAHA . . . . . . Polish American Historical Association
PAIRC . . . . . . Polish American Immigration and Relief Committee
PAIB . . . . . . Polish-American Information Bureau
PAWAF . . . . . . Polish American Workmen's Aid Fund
PAVA . . . . . . Polish Army Veterans Association of America
PAA . . . . Polish Association of America
PBA . . . . Polish Beneficial Association
PFA . . . . Polish Falcons of America
PIASA . . . . . . Polish Institute of Arts and Sciences in America
PLAV . . . . . . Polish Legion of American Veterans
PNA . . . . . . Polish National Alliance of the United States of North America
PNUA . . . . . . Polish National Union of America
PPRC . . . . . . Polish Peace Research Committee
PRCS . . . . . Polish Red Cross Society
PRCUA . . . . . Polish Roman Catholic Union of America
PSLA . . . . . . Polish Sea League of America
PSAA . . . . . . Polish Singers Alliance of America
PSAUSA . . . . . Polish Socialist Alliance of the United States of America
PUA . . . . . . Polish Union of America
PUPA . . . . . . Polish Union Printers Association (Chicago)
PUUSNA . . . . . Polish Union of the United States of North America
PWAA . . . . . . Polish Women's Alliance of America
PWP . . . . . . Polish Workers' Party
PAC . . . . Political Action Committee (of the CIO) (Now COPE)
POLAD . . . . . . Political Adviser (Military)
POLITBUREAU . . Political Bureau (of USSR)
DPOL . . . . . . Political Directorate (Allied German Occupation Forces)
PEP . . . . Political and Economic Planning
PID . . . . Political Intelligence Department (British)
PSO . . . . Political Survey Officers (Navy)
P-M-C . . . . . . Pollen-Mother-Cell
Po . . . . Polonium (Chemical element)
PPS . . . . Polonus Philatelic Society
PPR . . . . Polska Partia Robotnicza (Polish Workers' Party)
PPSD . . . . . . Polska Partia Socjaino-Demokratycana (Polish Social-Democrat Party)
PPS . . . . Polska Partia Socjalistyczna (Polish Socialist Party)
PZPR . . . . . . Polska Zjednoczona Partia Robotnicza (Polish United Workers' Party)
PKWN . . . . . . Polski Komitet Wyzwolenia Narodowego
PBI . . . . Polybenzimidazole (Plastics)
PBAA . . . . . . Polybutadiene Acrylic Acid
PBIC . . . . . . Polybutylisocyanate
PLC . . . . Polycaprolactone (Polymer)
PCB . . . . Polychlorinated Biphenyls (Chemical)
PCTFE . . . . . . Polychlorotrifluoroethylene
PCA . . . . Polycrystalline Alumina
PE . . . . Polyethylene
PAP . . . . Polyethylene Aluminum Polyethylene
PG . . . . Polyethylene Glycol
PIC . . . . Polyethylene Insulated Conductor
PETF . . . . . . Polyethylene Terephthalate
PEI . . . . Polyethyleneimine
PMM . . . . Polymethyl Methacrylate (Chemical)
PMMA . . . . . . Polymethyl Methacrylate
PPA . . . . Polymer Permeation Analyzer
POST . . . . . . Polymer Science and Technology (A publication of American Chemical Society)
POST-J . . . . . . Polymer Science and Technology - Journals (Chemical abstracts)
POST-P . . . . . . Polymer Science and Technology - Patents (Chemical abstr
PMB . . . . Polymorphonuclear Basophilic (Leucocytes)
PME . . . . Polymorphonuclear Eosinophile
PMN . . . . Polymorphonuclear Neutrophiles
PV . . . . Polyoma Virus
PFBA . . . . . . Polyperfluorobutyl Acrylate
PPO . . . . Polyphenoloxidase
PPO . . . . Polyphenylene Oxide (A thermoplastic)
PP . . . . Polypropylene
PIB . . . . Polytechnic Institute of Brooklyn
PTFE . . . . . . Polytetrafluoroethylene
TFE . . . . Polytetrafluoroethylene (TEFLON)
PUFA . . . . . . Polyunsaturated Fats (Dietetics)
PVAC . . . . . . Polyvinyl Acetate
PVA . . . . Polyvinyl Alcohol (Fixative)
PVC . . . . Polyvinyl Chloride (Chemical)
PVDC . . . . . . Polyvinyl Dichloride (A plastic)
PVF . . . . Polyvinyl Fluoride
PVME . . . . . . Polyvinyl Methyl Ether
PVP . . . . Polyvinylpyrrolidone (A plasma extender)
P . . . . Pond
PPW . . . . Ponderosa Pine Woodwork
PPWA . . . . . . Ponderosa Pine Woodwork Association

P . . . . Ponendum (To Be Placed)
PC . . . . Poni Curavit (Caused to Be Placed)
PI . . . . Poni Iussit (Ordered to Be Placed)
PM . . . . Pontifex Maximus
PAHC . . . . . . Pontifical Association of the Holy Childhood
PIME . . . . . . Pontifical Institute for Mission Extension
PMP . . . . . . Pontifical Mission for Palestine
PP . . . . Pontificum (Of the Popes)
PGO . . . . . . Ponto-Geniculate-Occipital (Cortex)
PAD . . . . Pontoon Assembly Detachment
YSP . . . . Pontoon Salvage Vessel (Navy ship designation)
YPK . . . . Pontoon Stowage Barge (Navy symbol)
POAC . . . . . . Pony of the Americas Club
PCA . . . . . . Poodle Club of America
PCA . . . . . . Pool Critical Assembly (AEC)
PTR . . . . . . Pool Training Reactor
PBI . . . . Poor Bloody Infantry (British military slang)
PCHE . . . . . . Poor Clare Nuns of the Holy Eucharist (Roman Catholic religious order)
PC . . . . Poor Clares of Ireland (Roman Catholic women's religious order)
PCRS . . . . . . Poor Clergy Relief Society (British)
POR . . . . Poor & Company (NYSE symbol)
PHJC . . . . . . Poor Handmaids of Jesus Christ (Ancilla Domini Sisters) (Roman Catholic religious order)
PLC . . . . Poor Law Commissioners (British)
PLG . . . . Poor Law Guardian (British)
PI . . . . Popcorn Institute
PPA . . . . . . Popcorn Processors Association
P . . . . Pope
PTA . . . . Pope & Talbot Line (AAR code)
POGR . . . . . . Poplar Grove National Cemetery
PDAS . . . . . . A Popular Dictionary of Australian Slang
PF . . . . Popular Force (ARVN)
PFLP . . . . . . Popular Front for the Liberation of Palestine
PPDMG . . . . . . Popular Priced Dress Manufacturers Group, Inc.
PRA . . . . . . Popular Rotocraft Association
PSDF . . . . . . Popular Self-Defense Force (Local armed units protecting Vietnamese hamlets)
P . . . . Population
PAA . . . . . . Population Association of America
PCC . . . . . . Population Crisis Committee
PGE . . . . . . Population Growth Estimation
PRB . . . . . . Population Reference Bureau
PR . . . . Populus Romanus (The Roman People)
PEI . . . . . . Porcelain Enamel Institute
PSC . . . . Porcelain on Steel Council
PCT . . . . . . Porphyria Cutanea Tarda (Drug)
PCA . . . . . . Porsche Club of America
P . . . . Port
PACREP . . . . . . Port Activities Report (Navy)
PAD . . . . Port of Aerial Debarkation (Air Force)
PAE . . . . Port of Aerial Embarkation (Air Force)
POAE . . . . . . Port of Aerial Embarkation (Air Force)
PA . . . . Port Agency (Army)
PAMO . . . . . . Port Air Materiel Office
PA/SO . . . . . . Port Anti-Submarine Officer (Navy)
PANY . . . . . . Port Authority of New York
PATH . . . . . . Port Authority Trans-Hudson (New York)
PC . . . . Port Call
POC . . . . Port of Call
PCWU . . . . . . Port Commissioners Workers' Union (India)
PD . . . . Port of Debarkation
POD . . . . Port of Debarkation (Military)
POD . . . . Port of Delivery (Shipping)
PD . . . . Port Director
PORDIR . . . . . . Port Director
POD . . . . Port of Discharge (Navy)
PD . . . . Port Dues
PE . . . . Port of Embarkation
POE . . . . Port of Embarkation (Military)
POE . . . . Port of Entry
PEBL . . . . . . Port Everglades Belt Line Railway (AAR code)
PHO . . . . . . Port Health Officer
PHB . . . . . . Port Huron & Detroit R. R. (AAR code)
PLA . . . . Port of London Authority
PNYA . . . . . . Port of New York Authority
PONYA . . . . . Port of New York Authority
PO . . . . Port Officer
POSH . . . . . . Port Outward-bound, Starboard Homeward-bound
PPBD . . . . . . Port of Palm Beach District (AAR code)
PPO . . . . Port Postal Office
PS . . . . Port Security

PSSTA . . . . Port Security Station (Coast Guard)
P & S . . . . . . Port and Starboard
PTS . . . . Port Townsend R. R. (AAR code)
PTO . . . . Port Transportation Officer
PUR . . . . Port Utilities (AAR code)
PUC . . . . Port Utilization Committee
PADRE . . . . . . Portable Automatic Data Recording Equipment
PCT . . . . Portable Camera-Transmitter
PCI . . . . Portable Cesium Irradiator (AEC)
PET . . . . Portable Electronic Telephone
PECS . . . . . . Portable Environmental Control System (NASA)
PET. . . . . Portable Executive Telephone
PFT . . . . Portable Flame Thrower
PINS . . . . Portable Inertial Navigation System
PINSAC . . . . . PINS (Portable Inertial Navigation System) Alignment Console
PKB . . . . Portable Keyboard
PLSS. . . . . . . Portable Life Support System (NASA)
PMU . . . . Portable Memory Unit
PVTR . . . . . . Portable Video Tape Recorder
P of E . . . . . . Portal of Entry (Bacteriology)
PHK . . . . Porter (H. K.) Company, Inc. (NYSE symbol)
PCA . . . . Portland Cement Association
PGE . . . . Portland Grain Exchange
PTM . . . . Portland Terminal Company (AAR code)
PRTD . . . . . . Portland Traction Company (AAR code)
PNS . . . . Portsmouth (NH) Naval Shipyard
PO. . . . . Portugal (NATO)
PAPCNY . . . . . Portuguese American Progressive Club of New York
PCU . . . . Portuguese Continental Union of the United States of America
P. . . . . Position
PA . . . . Position Approximate (Navigation)
PCFO . . . . . . Position Classification Field Office
PCS . . . . Position Classification Standard (Civil Service)
PCN. . . . . . . Position Control Number
PCS . . . . Position, Course, and Speed
PD . . . . Position Description
PDPC . . . . . . Position Display Parallax Corrected
PD . . . . Position Doubtful (On a chart) (Nautical)
PET. . . . . Position-Event-Time
PFCO . . . . . . Position Field Classification Officer
PFNS . . . . . . Position Fixing Navigation System
PHI . . . . Position Homing Indicator
PHIN . . . . . . Position and Homing Inertial Navigator
PI . . . . Position Indicator
PIN . . . . Position Indicator
PIDL. . . . . . . Position Involves Intermittent Duty at Isolated Locations
PIO . . . . Position Iterative Operation
PL . . . . Position Line (Navigation)
POMAR. . . . . . Position Operational, Meteorological Aircraft Report
POREP . . . . . Position Report (Air Force)
PR . . . . Position Report (Air Force)
PSRI . . . . Position Subject Return of Incumbent
PSRS. . . . . . . Position Subject to Rotating Shifts
PTR. . . . . Position Track RADAR
PV . . . . Position Value
PAV . . . . Position and Velocity
PVC . . . . Position and Velocity Computer
PAVE . . . . . . Position and Velocity Extraction
PAVT . . . . . . Position and Velocity Tracking
PAN. . . . . . . Positional Alcohol Nystagmus (NASA)
PT . . . . Positional Tolerancing
PCCS . . . . . . Positive Control Communications System
PCV . . . . Positive Crankcase Ventilation (For automotive antipollution systems)
POSITRON . . . Positive Electron
PHAA . . . . . . Positive High Angle of Attack
PINO . . . . Positive Input – Negative Output (Data processing)
PIA . . . . Positive Ion Accelerator
PLAA . . . . . . Positive Low Angle of Attack
PN. . . . . Positive – Negative
PNAvQ . . . . . Positive-Negative Ambivalent Quotient (Psychology)
PNP. . . . . . . Positive-Negative-Positive (Transistor)
PNPR . . . . . . Positive-Negative Pressure Respiration
PTC . . . . Positive Target Control
PTC . . . . Positive Temperature Coefficient
POVORTAD . . . Positive Vorticity Advection (Meteorology)
PVA . . . . Positive Vorticity Advection (Meteorology)
P . . . . Post
PA . . . . Post Adjutant
PACCS . . . . . Post Attack Command and Control System (Military)
PAMUSA . . . . . Post-Attack Mobilization of the United States Army
PARM . . . . . . Post-Attack Resource Management System

PBCS . . . . . . Post Boost Control System (Missile technology)
PBPS. . . . . . . Post Boost Propulsion System (Aerospace)
PBV . . . . Post Boost Vehicle (Aerospace)
PCS . . . . Post, Camp, or Station (Military)
PCMA . . . . . Post Card Manufacturers Association
PC . . . . Post Cibum (After Meals) (Medicine)
PC . . . . Post Commander (Military)
PC . . . . Post Consulatum (After the Consulate)
PE . . . . Post Engineer (Army)
PER . . . . Post Engineer Request
PE . . . . Post Exchange (Marine Corps)
PX . . . . Post Exchange (Military)
PHPC . . . . . Post-Hostilities Planning Committee (Navy) (World War II)
PIV . . . . Post Indicator Valve
PL . . . . Post Laundry (Army)
PMDL. . . . . . Post M-Day Deployment List (Military)
PMS. . . . . . . Post-Menopausal Syndrome (Medicine)
PM. . . . . Post Meridiem (After noon)
PM . . . . Post Mortem (After Death) (Examination)
PMD. . . . . . . Post Mortem Dump (Data processing)
PO. . . . . Post Office
POB . . . . Post Office Box
PO & CS . . . . Post Office and Civil Service Committee (US Senate)
POD. . . . . . . Post Office Department (Later, United States Postal Service)
POD. . . . . . . Post Office Directory
POMSIP . . . . . Post Office Management and Service Improvement Program (Post Office)
POO . . . . Post Office Order
POPI . . . . Post Office Position Indicator (A form of long-range position indicator) (Great Britain)
POREA . . . . . Post Office Regional Employees' Association
POSB . . . . . . Post Office Savings Bank
PP . . . . Post Paid
PP . . . . Post Partum (Medicine)
PPH . . . . Post-Partum Hemorrhage
PPS . . . . Post-Postscriptum (Further postscript)
PQM . . . . . . Post Quartermaster (Marine Corps)
PR . . . . Post Request
PRC . . . . Post Roman Conditam (After the Founding of Rome)
PS . . . . Post Scriptum (Written Afterwards; a postscript)
PSA . . . . Post Shakedown Availability
PST . . . . Post-Stimulus Time
POSTER. . . . . . Post Strike Emergency Reporting
PT . . . . Post Town
PTA . . . . Post-Traumatic Amnesia (Medicine)
PV . . . . Post Village
PW . . . . Post War
PWWC . . . . . . Post War World Council
P . . . . Postage
PD . . . . Postage Due
PP . . . . Postage Paid
PC . . . . Postal Clerk (Navy rating)
PCC . . . . Postal Concentration Center
PD . . . . Postal District
PFO. . . . . . . Postal Finance Officer
PHS of A . . . . Postal History Society of the Americas
PIS. . . . . Postal Inspection Service
PL & R . . . . . Postal Laws and Regulations
PO. . . . . Postal Order
PRD . . . . Postal Regulating Detachment (Military)
PSS . . . . Postal Savings System
PTC . . . . Postal Telegraph Cable
PT . . . . Postal Telegraph Company (Terminated)
PTTI. . . . . . . Postal, Telegraph and Telephone International
PUAS . . . . . . Postal Union of the Americas and Spain
PAR . . . . Postanesthetic Recovery Room (Medicine)
PARU . . . . . . Postanesthetic Recovery Unit (Medicine)
PC . . . . Postcard
PCCA . . . . . . Postcard Collector's Club of America
PD . . . . Postdated
PAV . . . . Poste-Avion (Airmail)
PR . . . . Poste Recommandee (Registered Post)
P . . . . Posterior
PAL . . . . Posterior Axillary Line
POSTP . . . . . . Posterior Probability (Computations)
PSC . . . . Posterior Subcapsular Cataracts
PTT . . . . Postes, Telegraphes, et Telephones (Post, Telephone, and Telegraph) (General Post Office) (France)
PG. . . . . Postgraduate (Refers to courses or students) (Slang)
PCP . . . . Postgraduate Center for Psychotherapy
PDT . . . . Posting Data Transfer (Air Force)
PJM . . . . Postjunctional Membrane

PMCC .... Postmark Collectors' Club
PM .... Postmaster
PMG .... Postmaster General
PND .... Postnasal Drip
PO .... Postoperative
PTIWU ...... Posts and Telegraphs Industrial Workers' Union (India)
P & T .... Posts and Timbers (Technical drawings)
PSS. .... Postscripts
PSP .... Postsynaptic Potential
PWP .... Postwar Planning (World War II)
PEA .... Potash Export Association
PEC .... Potasse et Engrais Chimiques
K .... Potassium (Chemical element)
KDP .... Potassium Dihydrogen Phosphate (Chemical)
KHb .... Potassium Hemoglobinate
PAA .... Potato Association of America
PCI .... Potato Chip Institute, International
PSTV ...... Potato Spindle Tuber Virus
PCF .... Potential Conflict Forecasts (Army)
PD .... Potential Difference (Electricity)
V .... Potential Difference (Symbol)
PE .... Potential Energy
PT .... Potential Transformer
PS .... Potentiometer Synchro
POTANN .... Potomac Annex (Navy Department)
PEPCO ..... Potomac Electric Power Company
POM .... Potomac Electric Power Company (NYSE symbol)
PRNC ...... Potomac River Naval Command (Washington, DC)
PBA .... Poultry Breeders of America
PENB ...... Poultry and Egg National Board
PIMCO ..... Poultry Industry Manufacturers Council
PPA .... Poultry Publishers Association
PSA .... Poultry Science Association
PCU .... Pound Centigrade Unit
PBHP ...... Pounds Per Brake Horsepower
PCF .... Pounds per Cubic Foot
PHP .... Pounds per Horsepower
PM .... Pounds per Minute
PP .... Pounds Pressure
PSF .... Pounds per Square Foot
PSI........ Pounds per Square Inch
PSIA....... Pounds per Square Inch Absolute
PSIG ...... Pounds per Square Inch Gage
PC .... Pour Condoler (To Offer Sympathy)
PDA .... Pour Dire Adieu (To Say Farewell) (On visiting cards)
PF .... Pour Feliciter (To Congratulate)
PPC .... Pour Prendre Conge (To Take Leave)
PP .... Pour Presenter (To Present)
PR .... Pour Remercier (To Express Thanks)
PDL .... Poverty Datum Line
PHRA ...... Poverty and Human Resources Abstracts
PATMI ..... Powder Actuated Tool Manufacturers' Institute
PMEA ...... Powder Metallurgy Equipment Association
PMPMA ..... Powder Metallurgy Parts Manufacturers Association
P .... Power (Mechanics)
PA .... Power Amplifier
PAD .... Power Amplifier Device
PAS .... Power Apparatus and Systems
PA .... Power Approach (Aerospace)
P/A .... Power of Attorney
PBF .... Power Burst Facility (AEC)
PCF .... Power Cathode Follower
PCCA ...... Power and Communication Contractors Association
PCSC ...... Power Conditioning, Switching, & Control
PCD .... Power Control and Distribution
PCU .... Power Control Unit
PCETF...... Power Conversion Equipment Test Facility
PCS .... Power Conversion System
PCSA ...... Power Crane and Shovel Association
PDRP ...... Power Demonstration Reactor Program (AEC)
PDR .... Power Directional Relay
PD .... Power Distribution
PDS .... Power Distribution System
PF .... Power Factor (Radio)
PFM .... Power Factor Meter
PGS .... Power Generation System
PH .... Power House
PIC .... Power Information Center
PJM .... Power Jets Memorandum
PJR .... Power Jets Report
PLF .... Power for Level Flight (Aeronautics)

PLC .... Power-Line Carrier
PO .... Power-Operated
POGT ...... Power-Operated Gun Turret
PO .... Power Oscillator (Electronics)
PP .... Power Package
PP .... Power Plant
PRDC ...... Power Reactor Development Company
PRT .... Power Recovery Turbine
PSMA ...... Power Saw Manufacturers Association
PSA .... Power and Servo Assembly
PSD .... Power Spectral Density
PS .... Power Supply
PTO .... Power Take-Off
PTC .... Power Testing Code
PTC .... Power Transmission Council
PTDA ...... Power Transmission Distributors Association
PU .... Power Unit
PAW .... Powered All the Way
PDI .... Powered Descent Initiation (Aerospace)
PURV ...... Powered Underwater Research Vehicle (Navy)
PAMPER .... Practical Application of Mid-Points for Exponential Regression
PACIR ..... Practical Approach to Chemical Information Retrieval
PEP. ...... Practical Engineering Paperwork
P .... Practical Intelligence
PN .... Practical Nurse
PNE .... Practical Nurse's Education
PUNC...... Practical, Unpretentious, Nomographic Computer
PDC .... Practice Depth Charge
PLA .... Practice Low Approach (Aviation)
PLI........ Practicing Law Institute
PCF .... Prairie Chicken Foundation
PFRA ...... Prairie Farm Rehabilitation Act (Canada)
PPM .... Prairie Print Makers
Pr .... Praseodymium (Chemical element)
P & W...... Pratt & Whitney (Aircraft engine manufacturer)
PRC .... Prattsburgh Railway Corporation (AAR code)
PK .... Prausnitz-Kustner (Reaction)
PB .... Prayer Book
PFC .... Praying for Corporal (Private First Class desirous of promotion, or female in wartime desirous of a boy friend)
PG .... Preacher General
PATS ...... Preacademic Training Student (Military)
PIEA ...... Pre-Arrangement Interment Exchange of America
PSS .... Precancel Stamp Society
P .... Precipitation Ceiling (Aviation weather reports)
P-E .... Precipitation-Evaporation
PH .... Precipitation Hardening
POPSI...... Precipitation and Off-Path Scattered Interference (Report) (FCC)
PTTI ...... Precise Time and Time Interval
PADS ...... Precision Aerial Deliver (or Display) System
PATS ...... Precision Altimeter Techniques Study
PACE ...... Precision Analog Computing Equipment
PARD ...... Precision Annotated Retrieval Display (System) (Data processing)
PAR .... Precision Approach RADAR (Aviation)
PARTAC .... Precision Askania Range Target Acquisition
PBR .... Precision Bombing Range
PDGS ...... Precision Delivery Glides System
PDR .... Precision Depth Recorder
PDG .... Precision Drop Glider (Military)
PEPR ...... Precision Encoding and Pattern Recognition Device (Data processing)
PGP .... Precision Gas Products (Commercial firm)
PGR .... Precision Graphic Recorder
PIRT ...... Precision Infrared Tracking
PIRT ...... Precision Infrared Triangulation
PRELORT.... Precision Long-Range Tracking RADAR
PMA .... Precision Measurements Association
PME .... Precision Measuring Equipment
PMEL ...... Precision Measuring Equipment Laboratory
PPPI ...... Precision Plan Position Indicator
PPMA ...... Precision Potentiometer Manufacturers Association
PROOF ..... Precision Recording (Optical) of Fingerprints
PRIME ..... Precision Recovery Including Maneuvering Entry (Air Force)
PRL .... Precision Reduction Laboratory
PVOR...... Precision VHF Omnirange
PVR .... Precision Voltage Reference
PRECOMMDET .. Pre-Commissioning Detail (Navy)
PRECOMMSCOL .. Pre-Commissioning School (Navy)
PCC .... Pre-Compressor Cooling
PDA .... Predelivery Acceptance Test (NASA)
P .... Predicate
PDA .... Predicted Drift Angle (Navigation)

PGS . . . . Predicted Ground Speed (Navigation)
PAT . . . . Prediction Analysis Techniques
PMG . . . . . . Prediction Marker Generator
PREDICT . . . . . Prediction of Radiation Effects by Digital Computer Techniques
PSAD . . . . . . Prediction, Simulation, Adaptation, Decision (Data processing)
PRINT. . . . . . . Pre-Edited Interpretive System (Data processing)
PBS . . . . Prefabricated Bituminous Surfacing
PA . . . . Prefect Apostolic
PPL . . . . Preferential Planning List
PAD . . . . Preferred Arrival Date
PDD . . . . Preferred Delivery Date
PPL . . . . . . Preferred Parts List
PF . . . . Pre-Flight
PACE/LV . . . . Preflight Acceptance Checkout Equipment–Launch Vehicle
PACE-S/C . . . . Preflight Acceptance Checkout Equipment for Spacecraft
POD . . . . Preflight Operations Division
PFS . . . . Preflight School (Military)
PFT . . . . Preflight Team (Air Force)
PFB . . . . Pre-Formed Beams (SONAR)
PU . . . . Pregnancy Urine (Medicine)
PG . . . . Pregnant
PMS . . . . Pregnant Mare's Serum (Endocrinology)
PMSG . . . . . . Pregnant Mare's Serum Gonadotrophin (Endocrinology)
PKP . . . . Pre-Knock Pulse
PACE . . . . . . Prelaunch Automatic Checkout Equipment
PLSS . . . . . . Prelaunch Status Simulator
PDR . . . . Preliminary Data Report
PD . . . . Preliminary Design
PDR . . . . Preliminary Design Review
PDC . . . . Preliminary Diagnostic Clinic
PECI . . . . Preliminary Equipment Component Inventory
PE . . . . Preliminary Evaluation
PET . . . . Preliminary Examination Team (NASA)
PFRT . . . . Preliminary Flight Rating Test (Air Force)
PFTM . . . . . . Preliminary Flight Test Memo
PETR . . . . . . Preliminary Flight Test Report
PL . . . . Preliminary Leaf (Bibliography)
PLDC . . . . . . Preliminary List of Design Changes
PML . . . . Preliminary Materials List (NASA)
PNR . . . . Preliminary Negotiation Reports
POMM . . . . . Preliminary Operating and Maintenance Manual (Military)
PPBG . . . . . . Preliminary Program and Budget Guidance
PPDP . . . . . . Preliminary Project Development Plan (NASA)
PR . . . . Preliminary Report
PRM . . . . . . Preliminary Requirements Model (NASA)
PRI . . . . . . Preliminary Rifle Instruction
PSAT . . . . . . Preliminary Scholastic Aptitude Test
PS . . . . Preliminary Study
PTDP . . . . . . Preliminary (or Proposed) Technical Development Plan
PTR . . . . . . Preliminary Technical Report
PVC . . . . Premature Ventricular Contraction (Medicine)
PMT . . . . . . Premenstrual Tension (Medicine)
PMS . . . . . . Pre-Midshipmen School
PAAA . . . . . . Premium Advertising Association of America
PIC . . . . Premium Industry Club
PMC . . . . . . Premium Merchandising Club of New York
PPE . . . . Premodulation Processing Equipment
PMP . . . . Premodulation Processor
PDD . . . . Premodulation Processor – Deep Space – Data
PDV . . . . . . Premodulation Processor – Deep Space – Voice
P . . . . Premolar (Dentistry)
PM . . . . Premolar (Dentistry)
PEJ . . . . Premolded Expansion Joint (Technical drawings)
PP . . . . Prepaid
POM . . . . . . Preparation for Overseas Movement
POR . . . . Preparation of Replacements for Oversea Movement (Military)
PC . . . . Preparatory Commission
PCIRO . . . . . Preparatory Commission for International Refugee Organization
PRECO . . . . . Preparatory Commission of the United Nations Organization
PC . . . . Preparatory Committee
PHS . . . . Prepared Hessian Surfacing (Air Force)
PIP . . . . Preparedness and Industrial Planning
PH D . . . . . . Pre-Pearl Harbor Dad (A humorous wartime degree)
PWRS . . . . . . Prepositioned War Reserve Stock
PPWR . . . . . . Prepositioned War Reserves
PP . . . . Preprocessor
PR . . . . Pre-Raphaelite
PRB . . . . Pre-Raphaelite Brotherhood
PO. . . . . Presbyteri Oratorii (Oratorians)
PSS . . . . Presbyteri Sancti Sulpicii (Sulpicians) (Roman Catholic men's religious order)

P . . . . Presbyterian
PEAS . . . . . . Presbyterian Educational Association of the South
PHA . . . . Presbyterian Historical Society
PIC . . . . Presbyterian Interracial Council
PLC . . . . Presbyterian Lay Committee
PNW. . . . . . . Prescott & Northwestern R. R. (AAR code)
PAL . . . . Prescribed Action Link (DOD)
PLL . . . . Prescribed Load List
P . . . . Present
PAU . . . . Present Address Unknown
PFD . . . . Present for Duty
PI . . . . Present Illness
PRIND . . . . . . Present Indications Are
PNFD . . . . . . Present Not For Duty (Military)
PPR . . . . Present Participle
PP . . . . Present Position (Military)
PPI. . . . . Present Position Indicator
PV . . . . Present Value
PWAFRR . . . . . Present Worth of All Future Revenue Requirements
PBVM . . . . . . Presentation of the Blessed Virgin Mary (Roman Catholic women's religious order)
PRESSAR . . . . . Presentation Equipment for Slow Scan RADAR
POOFF . . . . . . Preservation of Our Femininity and Finances (Women's group opposing below-the-knee fashions introduced in 1970)
UPSTEP . . . . . . Pre-Service Teacher Education Program
P . . . . President
PCC . . . . President of the Canteen Committee (Military) (British)
PGS . . . . President of the Geological Society (British)
PLS . . . . President of the Linnaean Society (British)
PMS . . . . President of the Meteorological Society (British)
PRA . . . . President of the Royal Academy (British)
PRCP . . . . . . President of the Royal College of Physicians (British)
PRCS . . . . . . President of the Royal College of Surgeons (British)
PRES . . . . President of the Royal Entomological Society (British)
PRGS . . . . . . President of the Royal Geographical Society (British)
PRHA . . . . . . President of the Royal Hibernian Academy
PRI . . . . President of the Royal Institution (British)
PRSA . . . . . . President of the Royal Scottish Academy
PRS . . . . President of the Royal Society (British)
PSA . . . . President of the Society of Antiquaries (British)
POTUS . . . . . . President of the United States
PZS . . . . President of the Zoological Society (British)
PD . . . . Presidential Determination
PRESPROC . . . . Presidential Proclamation
PUC . . . . Presidential Unit Citation
PACGO . . . . . President's Advisory Committee on Government Organization
PASSIM . . . . . President's Advisory Staff on Scientific Information Management
PARC . . . . . . President's Appalachian Regional Commission
PCM . . . . President's Certificate of Merit (Military award)
PCSW . . . . . . President's Commission on the Status of Women
PCCI . . . . President's Committee on Consumer Interests
PCEH . . . . . . President's Committee on Employment of the Handicapped
PCEEO . . . . . . President's Committee on Equal Employment Opportunity
PCMR . . . . . . President's Committee on Mental Retardation
PCML . . . . . . President's Committee on Migratory Labor
PCSE . . . . . . President's Committee on Scientists and Engineers
PCTS . . . . President's Committee for Traffic Safety
PCA . . . . President's Council on Aging
PCPF . . . . . . President's Council on Physical Fitness (Formerly, PCYF)
PCYF . . . . . . President's Council on Youth Fitness (Later, PCPF)
PCOYO . . . . . President's Council on Youth Opportunity
PDNC . . . . . . Presidents' Day National Committee
PFIAB . . . . . . President's Foreign Intelligence Advisory Board
PPA . . . . Presidents' Professional Association
PSAC . . . . . . President's Science Advisory Committee (Executive Office of the President)
PSRAAALAA . . President's Special Representative and Adviser on African, Asian, and Latin American Affairs (Department of State)
PWRCB . . . . . President's War Relief Control Board (World War II)
PB . . . . Presiding Bishop (Episcopal Church)
PE . . . . Presiding Elder
PJ . . . . Presiding Judge
PA . . . . Press Agent
PA . . . . Press Association
PG. . . . . Press Gallery (US Senate)
PR . . . . Press Release
PREWI . . . . . . Press Wireless (A radio service for the transmission of news)
PMI . . . . Pressed Metal Institute
P. . . . . Pressure (Mechanics)
PA . . . . Pressure Altitude (Aviation)
PAV . . . . Pressure Altitude Variation

PB . . . . Pressure Breathing
PRESFR . . . . . . Pressure Falling Rapidly (Meteorology)
PLOP . . . . Pressure Line of Position (Air Force)
PP . . . . Pressure-Proof (Technical drawings)
PR . . . . Pressure Ratio
PRV . . . . Pressure Reducing Valve
PRESRR . . . . . . Pressure Rising Rapidly (Meteorology)
P-S. . . . . Pressure-Sensitive
PSTC . . . . . . Pressure Sensitive Tape Council
PTR . . . . Pressure-Tube Reactor (AEC)
PTSR. . . . . . . Pressure Tube Superheat Reactor (AEC)
PVT . . . . Pressure, Volume, Temperature
PDR . . . . Pressurized Deuterium Reactor (AEC)
PHWR . . . . . . Pressurized Heavy Water Reactor
PSE . . . . Pressurized Subcritical Experiment
PWR . . . . Pressurized Water Reactor (AEC)
PRES. . . . . . . Preston R. R. (AAR code)
PCI . . . . Prestressed Concrete Institute
PM . . . . Presystolic Murmur
PDQ . . . . Pretty Damn Quick
PDC . . . . Prevention of Deterioration Center
PRI . . . . La Prevention Routiere Internationale (International Prevention of Road Accidents) (An organization)
PM. . . . . Preventive Maintenance
PMD . . . . . . Preventive Maintenance Division (Air Force)
PMI . . . . Preventive Maintenance Inspection
PM. . . . . Preventive Medicine
PVNTMED . . . . Preventive Medicine
PEC . . . . Previous Element Coding
PH . . . . Previous History (Medicine)
PMP . . . . Previous Menstrual Period
PO . . . . Previous Orders
PQ . . . . Previous Question (Parliamentary law)
PNVAL . . . . . . Previously Not Available (Army)
PAB . . . . Price Adjustment Board
PA . . . . Price Analyst
PDB . . . . Price Decontrol Board (Post-World War II)
P/E . . . . Price/Earnings Ratio (Relation between price of a company's stock and its annual net income)
PL . . . . Price List
PAMD . . . . . . Price and Management Data
PRISCO. . . . . . Price Stabilization Corporation
PC . . . . Prices Current
PEAT . . . . . . Pricing Evaluation for Audit Technique (Finance)
P . . . . Pridie (The Day Before)
PK . . . . Pridie Kalendas (The Day Before the Calends)
PRK . . . . Pridie Kalendas (The Day Before the Calends)
PRN . . . . . . Pridie Nonas (The Day Before the Nones)
P . . . . Priest
PM . . . . Priest and Martyr (Church calendars)
PV . . . . Priest Vicar
PEL . . . . Priests Eucharistic League
P. . . . . Primary
PAC . . . . Primary Address Code
PAFS . . . . . . Primary Air Force Specialty
PAFSC . . . . . . Primary Air Force Specialty Code
PAS . . . . Primary Alerting System
PCW. . . . . . . Primary Cooling Water (Reactor)
PEA . . . . Primary Expense Account
PRI-FLY . . . . . Primary Flight Control (on an aircraft carrier) (Navy)
PMA . . . . Primary Mental Abilities (Test)
PMOS. . . . . . . Primary Military Occupational Specialty
PMD. . . . . . . Primary Myocardial Disease
POA. . . . . . . Primary Optic Atrophy
PPS . . . . Primary Propulsion System (Spacecraft)
PSU . . . . Primary Sampling Unit (Statistics)
PSO . . . . Primary Standardization Office
PSP . . . . Primary Supply Point (Military)
PSP . . . . Primary Support Point (Military)
PT . . . . Primary Target (Army)
PTGT . . . . . . Primary Target
PTA . . . . Primary Target Area
PTL . . . . Primary Target Line (Military)
PT . . . . Primary Trainer (Aircraft)
PD . . . . Prime Driver
PLC . . . . Prime Level Code
PM. . . . . Prime Minister
PMVR . . . . . . Prime Mover (Technical drawings)
P and Q . . . . . Prime Quality (Slang)
PV . . . . Prime Vertical
PAINT . . . . . . Primera Asociacion Internacional de Noticieros y Television

PLUNA . . . . . . Primeras Lineas Uruguayas de Navegacion Aerea
PGC. . . . . Primordial Germ Cell
P. . . . . Primus (First)
PA . . . . Prince Albert Coat (Slang)
PALI. . . . . Prince Albert's Light Infantry (Military) (British)
PAO. . . . . Prince Albert's Own (Military unit) (British)
PCO. . . . . Prince Consort's Own (Military unit) (British)
PEI . . . . Prince Edward Island (A Canadian province)
PW . . . . Prince of Wales' (Military unit) (British)
PWO . . . . Prince of Wales' Own (Military unit) (British)
PWOR. . . . . . . Prince of Wales' Own Royal (Military unit) (British)
PWR. . . . . Prince of Wales' Royal (Military unit) (British)
PWV. . . . . Prince of Wales' Volunteers (Military) (British)
PRWI . . . . . . Prince William Forest Park (National Park Service designation)
P. . . . . Princeps (Prince)
PCW. . . . . Princess Charlotte of Wales (Military unit) (British)
PR . . . . Princess Royal's (Military unit) (British)
PAVFC . . . . . . Princeton Azimuthally-Varying-Field Cyclotron
PPA . . . . Princeton-Pennsylvania Accelerator (AEC)
PPPL. . . . . . . Princeton Plasma Physics Laboratory (Also known as PPL)
P. . . . . Principal
PCS . . . . Principal Clerk of Session
PDA . . . . Principal Development Activities (Navy)
PDF . . . . Principal Direction of Fire (Military)
PDY . . . . Principal Duty (Military)
PITI . . . . Principal, Interest, Taxes, Insurance (on house payments)
PI . . . . Principal Investigator
PK . . . . Principal Keeper (Slang for a warden)
PMO . . . . Principal Medical Officer
PMLO . . . . . . Principal Military Landing Offices (British)
PRINMUS . . . . Principal Musician (Marine Corps)
PP . . . . Principal Point
PSTO . . . . . . Principal Sea Transport Officer
PSO . . . . Principal Scientific Officer
PVS . . . . Principal Veterinary Surgeon (British)
PA . . . . Principle of Adding (New math)
PM . . . . Principle of Multiplying (New math)
PORACC . . . . . Principles of Radiation and Contamination Control
PAA . . . . Print Advertising Association
PCA . . . . Print Council of America
PC . . . . Printed Circuit
PCB . . . . Printed Circuit Board
PCBA . . . . . . Printed Circuit Board Assembly
PCL . . . . Printed Circuit Lamp
PPMI . . . . . . Printed Paper Mat Institute
PWM . . . . . . Printed Wiring Master
PRD . . . . Printer Dump
PRTRL . . . . . . Printer, Lithographer (Navy)
PRLTRL & M. . . Printer, Lithographer and Multilith Operator (Navy)
PRTRM . . . . . Printer, Offset Process (Navy)
PE . . . . Printer's Error
PAC . . . . Printing Accountants Club
PCO. . . . . Printing Control Officer (Air Force)
PEPMC . . . . . . Printing Estimators and Production Men's Club
PHS . . . . Printing Historical Society
PIA . . . . Printing Industries (formerly, Industry) of America
PIMNY . . . . . Printing Industries of Metropolitan New York
PICA . . . . . . Printing Industry Computer Associates, Inc.
PII . . . . Printing Industry Institute (A graphic arts training school)
PMIS . . . . . . Printing Management Information Systems
PATRA . . . . . Printing, Packaging and Allied Trades Research Association
PR . . . . Printing Request
PTA . . . . Prior to Admission
PETS . . . . . . Prior to Expiration of Term of Service (Military)
PN. . . . . Prior Notice Required
PNR. . . . . Prior Notice Required
PPO . . . . Prior Permission Only
PPR . . . . Prior Permission Required
PS . . . . Prior Service
PY . . . . Prior Year
PAM. . . . . Priorities and Allocations Manual (Army)
PAB . . . . Priorities Allotment Board
PA . . . . Priority Aggregate
PDR . . . . Priority Data Reduction
PDW. . . . . Priority Delayed Weather (Aviation)
PDD . . . . Priority Delivery Date
PDD/RDD . . . . Priority Delivery Date/Required Delivery Date
PD . . . . Priority Directive
PDS . . . . Priority Distribution System (Military)
PRIME . . . . . . Priority Management Efforts (Army)
PRIME. . . . . . Priority Management Evaluation (Navy)

PPC . . . . Priority Placement Certificate (Military)
PR . . . . Priority Regulation
PRI . . . . Priority Requirement for Information
PROL . . . . Priority Requirement Objective List
PROVOST . . . . Priority Research Objectives for Vietnam Operations
PROCTOT . . . . Priority Routine Organizer for Computer Transfers and Operations and Transfers
PD . . . . Prism Diopter
PIRA . . . . Prison Industries Reorganization Administration (Terminated 1940)
PAL . . . . Prisoner-at-Large
POW . . . . Prisoner(s) of War
PW . . . . Prisoner(s) of War
PWC . . . . Prisoner of War Cage, Camp, Command, or Compound
PWE . . . . Prisoner of War Enclosure
PWIB . . . . Prisoner of War Information Bureau (Post-World War II)
POC . . . . Prisoners of Conscience (File of persons imprisoned for political or religious beliefs kept by Amnesty International)
DPOW . . . . . . Prisoners of War and Displaced Persons Directorate (Allied German Occupation Forces)
PG . . . . Prisonnier de Guerre (Prisoner of War, POW)
PA . . . . Private Account
P/A . . . . Private Account (Banking)
PABX . . . . Private Automatic Branch Exchange (or dial PBX) (Communications)
PAX . . . . Private Automatic Exchange (Telephone)
PBX . . . . Private Branch Telephone Exchange
PBP . . . . Private Brand Proneness (Marketing)
PCC . . . . Private Carrier Conference (of ATA)
PCA . . . . Private Communications Association
PDCP . . . . Private Development Corporation of the Philippines
PDC . . . . Private Diagnostic Clinic
PEFCO . . . . . . Private Export Finance Corporation
PFC . . . . Private, First Class (Army)
PI . . . . Private Investigator
PICA . . . . Private Investment Company for Asia, SA
PLA . . . . Private Libraries Association
PL . . . . Private Line
PLS . . . . Private Line Service
PLF . . . . Private Line Telephone
PLT . . . . Private Line Teletypewriter
PP & NA . . . . Private Plants and Naval Activities
PP . . . . Private Property (Military)
PS . . . . Private Secretary
PT . . . . Private Terms
PTCA . . . . Private Truck Council of America
PWS . . . . Private Wire Service
PB . . . . Privately Bonded
PO . . . . Privately Owned
POC . . . . Privately Owned Conveyance
POV . . . . Privately Owned Vehicle
PP . . . . Privately Printed
PC . . . . Privileged Character (A favored student) (Teen slang)
P & E . . . . . . Privileges and Elections Subcommittee (US Senate)
PC . . . . Privy Council(lor) (British)
PS . . . . Privy Seal (British)
PM . . . . Prize Money
PR . . . . Prize Ring (Boxing)
P . . . . Pro (For)
PM . . . . Pro Mille (Per Thousand)
PR . . . . Pro Rata
PRN . . . . Pro Re Nata (Whenever Necessary) (Medicine)
PT . . . . Pro Tempore (For the Time Being)
PROBCOST . . . Probabilistic Budgeting and Forward Costing
PIP . . . . Probabilistic Information Processing
P . . . . Probability (Statistics)
PDF . . . . Probability Density Function (Statistics)
PD . . . . Probability of Detection
PDC . . . . Probability of Detection and Conversion
PDA . . . . Probability Distribution Analyzer
PDF . . . . Probability Distribution Function
P . . . . Probability Ratio
PE . . . . Probable Error (Statistics)
PLD . . . . Probable Line of Deployment (Army)
PUNC . . . . . . Probable Ultimate Net Cost
PJ . . . . Probate Judge
PO . . . . Probation Officer
PRA . . . . Probation and Rehabilitation of Airmen (Air Force)
PIQSY . . . . . . Probes for the International Quiet Solar Year (OSS)
PD/S . . . . Problem Definition/Solution
POL . . . . Problem Oriented Language (Data processing)
PSI . . . . Problem Solving Information (Apparatus)
POL . . . . Procedure-Oriented Language

PRESIGN . . . . Procedure Sign
PROSI . . . . . . Procedure Sign (Aviation)
PROSIGN . . . . Procedure Sign (Army)
PROSINE . . . . Procedure Sign
PROSIG . . . . . Procedure Signal (Navy)
PROTN . . . . . . Procedure Turn (Aviation)
PT . . . . Procedure Turn (Aviation)
PTN . . . . Procedure Turn (Aviation)
PROWORD . . . . Procedure Word
PANS . . . . Procedures for Air Navigation Services (ICAO)
PICA . . . . Procedures for Inventory Control Afloat (Navy)
POC . . . . Proceed(ing) on Course (Aviation)
PDOC . . . . Proceed Directly on Course (Aviation)
PRODUTAS . . . Proceed on Duty Assigned (Military)
PBI . . . . Process Branch Indicator
PCL . . . . Process Capability Laboratory
PDP . . . . Process Development Pile (AEC)
PEMA . . . . Process Equipment Manufacturers Association
PHR . . . . Process Heat Reactor (Program) (AEC)
PIR . . . . Process and Indoctrinate Recruits
PISW . . . . Process Interrupt Status Word
POC . . . . Process Operator Console
PS . . . . Process Specification
PAI . . . . Processed Apples Institute
PDR . . . . Processed Data Recorder
PROLAN . . . . . Processed Language (Data processing)
PIT . . . . Processing of Indexing Terms
PIL . . . . Processing Information List (Data processing)
PSR . . . . Processor State Register
PTR . . . . Processor Tape Read
P . . . . Proconsul
PG . . . . Procter & Gamble Company (NYSE symbol)
P & G . . . . . . Procter and Gamble Company
PF . . . . Procurator Fiscal
P & A . . . . Procurement and Assignment
PA . . . . Procurement Authorization
PC . . . . Procurement Command (Army)
PC & OR . . . . Procurement, Commitment and Obligation Record (Navy)
PROCOM . . . . Procurement Committee
P & C . . . . . . Procurement and Contracting
PCO . . . . Procurement Contracting Officer
PCD . . . . Procurement and Contracts Division (NASA)
PCN . . . . Procurement Control Number
PDP . . . . Procurement Data Package
PDS . . . . Procurement Data Sheet
PD . . . . Procurement Directive
PEMA . . . . Procurement of Equipment and Missiles, Army
P & E . . . . Procurement & Expedition
PFO . . . . Procurement Field Office(s)
PIC . . . . Procurement Information for Contracts (AFSC)
PID . . . . Procurement Information Digest
PJ . . . . Procurement Justification (Navy)
PLT . . . . Procurement Lead Time
PROLT . . . . . . Procurement Lead Time
PLD . . . . Procurement Legal Division (Later, Office of General Counsel) (Navy)
PM . . . . Procurement and Material
PMA . . . . Procurement Methods Analyst
PROVER . . . . . Procurement for Minimum Total Cost Through Value Engineering and Reliability
POMAS . . . . . . Procurement Office for Military Automotive Supplies
POAN . . . . Procurement of Ordnance and Ammunition - Navy
PPSMEC . . . . . Procurement, Precedence of Supplies, Material and Equipment Committee (Joint Communications Board)
PPN . . . . Procurement Program Number (Military)
PRN . . . . Procurement Reallocation Notice
PR . . . . Procurement Regulations
PR . . . . Procurement Request
PRB . . . . Procurement Review Board
PSC . . . . Procurement Source Code
PSD . . . . Procurement Surveys Division (NASA)
PROVER . . . . . Procurement, Value, Economy, Reliability
PCO . . . . Procuring Contrast Offer
PPA . . . . Produce Packaging Association
PCA . . . . Producers Commission Association
PC . . . . Producers' Council
PLMA . . . . Producers Livestock Marketing Association
PCN . . . . Product Control Number
PEP . . . . Product Engineering and Production
PIB . . . . Product Improvement Bulletin
PICO . . . . Product Improvement Control Office
PIP . . . . Product Improvement Plan

R . . . . Product Moment Coefficient of Correlation (Statistics)
PPT . . . . Product Positioning Time
PQEP . . . . . . Product Quality Evaluation Plan (Military)
PAC . . . . Production Acceleration Capacity
PAIP . . . . . . Production Acceleration Insurance Program
PA . . . . Production Adjustment
PAP . . . . Production Allocation Program
PACT . . . . . . Production Analysis Control Technique (Navy)
PAR . . . . Production Automated Riveting
PCP . . . . Production Change Point
PRODC . . . . . . Production Command (Army)
PCC . . . . Production Compression Capability
PCA . . . . Production Credit Association
PD . . . . Production Department
PERG . . . . . . Production Emergency Redistribution Group
PE . . . . Production Engineering
PEM . . . . Production Engineering Measures (Army)
PEO . . . . Production Engineering Order
PERA . . . . . . Production Engineering Research Association (British)
PES . . . . Production Engineering Service
PET . . . . Production Environmental Tests
PEQUA . . . . . . Production Equipment Agency
PEC . . . . Production Equipment Code
PEMA . . . . . . Production-Equipment-Missile Agency (Army)
PERG . . . . . . Production Equipment Redistribution Group
PERI . . . . . . Production Equipment Redistribution Inventory
PET . . . . Production Evaluation Test
PEC . . . . Production Executive Committee
PIR . . . . Production Inspection Record
PI . . . . Production Interval
PLM . . . . Production-Line Maintenance (Air Force)
PMA . . . . Production and Marketing Administration (Department of Agriculture)
(Functions dispersed, 1953)
PMGDINYC . . Production Men's Guild of the Dress Industry of New York City
POC . . . . . . Production Operational Capability
PPB . . . . Production Parts Breakdown
PMH . . . . Production per Man-Hour
PP . . . . Production Processes
P & P . . . . . Production and Procurement (Military)
PRC . . . . Production Readjustments Committee (WPB)
PRP . . . . Production Requirements Plan
PRP . . . . . . Production Reserve Policy
PT . . . . Production Techniques
PT . . . . Production Test
PTE . . . . Production Test Equipment
PUC . . . . Production Urgency Committee (WPB)
PWO . . . . . . Production Work Order
PTAD . . . . . . Productivity and Technical Assistance Division (Mutual Security Agency)
(Abolished, 1953)
PACC . . . . . . Products Administration & Contract Control
PLC . . . . Products List Circular (Patents)
PDA . . . . Produktions und Dienstleistungsabgabe
PG . . . . Produktionsgenossenschaft
PGH . . . . Produktionsgenossenschaft des Handwerks
P . . . . Professional (Civil Service employees designation)
PAS . . . . Professional Activities Study
PATCO . . . . . . Professional Air Traffic Controllers Organization
PAA . . . . Professional Archers Association
PAVE . . . . . . Professional Audiovisual Education Study
PBA . . . . Professional Bookmen of America
PBA . . . . Professional Bowlers Association of America
PCMA . . . . . . Professional Convention Management Association
PDP . . . . Professional Development Document
PDA . . . . Professional Drivers Association
PDG . . . . Professional Dyers Guild
PE . . . . Professional Education
PEMS . . . . . . Professional Education of the Media Specialist
PE . . . . Professional Engineer
PECBI . . . . . . Professional Engineers Conference Board for Industry
PEPP . . . . . . Professional Engineers in Private Practice
PES . . . . Professional Examining Service
PGA . . . . Professional Golfers' Association of America
PGANE . . . . . Professional Group on Aeronautical and Navigational Electronics
PGEC . . . . . . Professional Group on Electronic Computers (of IRE)
PGEWS . . . . . . Professional Group on Engineering Writing and Speech (Institute of Radio
Engineers)
PHA . . . . Professional Horsemen's Association
PIC . . . . Professional Interfraternity Conference
PLS . . . . Professional Legal Secretary (Designation awarded by National
Association of Legal Secretaries)
PMF . . . . Professional Medical Film

PME . . . . Professional Military Education
PMM . . . . Professional Music Men, Inc.
PNG . . . . Professional Numismatic Guild
POC . . . . Professional Officer Course (AFROTC)
POOFF . . . . . Professional Oglers of Female Figures (Men's group opposing below-the-
knee fashions introduced in 1970)
PPA . . . . Professional Panhellenic Association
PP . . . . Professional Paper
PPA . . . . Professional Photographers of America
PPA . . . . Professional Programmers Association
PPA . . . . Professional Putters Association
PRPA . . . . . . Professional Race Pilots Association
PRC . . . . Professional Relations Council (American Chemical Society)
PSIA . . . . Professional Ski Instructors of America
PTGEC . . . . . . Professional Technical Group on Electronic Computers (Affiliated with IEEE)
PTGEWS . . . . . Professional Technical Group on Engineering Writing and Speech (of the
IEEE)
PWBA . . . . . . Professional Woman Bowlers Association
POWER . . . . . . Professionals Organized for Women's Equal Rights (Feminist group)
PAS . . . . Professor of Air Science (Air Force)
PAST . . . . . . Professor of Air Science and Tactics
PMS . . . . Professor of Military Science
PMS & T . . . . Professor of Military Science and Tactics
PMP . . . . Professor of Moral Philosophy
PNS . . . . Professor of Naval Science
PNS & T . . . . Professor of Naval Science and Tactics (Naval ROTC)
P . . . . Proficiency
PDC . . . . Proficiency Data Card
PROFP . . . . . . Proficiency Pay
PRD . . . . Proficiency Rating Designator
PAR . . . . Profile of Average Reflectivity
PT . . . . Profile Template
P . . . . Profit
P/L . . . . Profit and Loss (Accounting)
PM . . . . Profit Motivated (Housing)
PSRF . . . . . . Profit Sharing Research Foundation
PAD . . . . Program Action Directive
PACER . . . . . . Program of Active Cooling Effects & Requirements
PAC . . . . Program Adjustment Committee
PAIT . . . . Program for Advancement of Industrial Technology (Canada)
PAC . . . . Program Advisory Committee
PAAC . . . . . . Program Analysis Adaptable Control
PAR . . . . Program Appraisal and Review
PADAR . . . . . . Program Approval Disposal and Redistribution (Army)
PARSECS . . . . Program for Astronomical Research and Scientific Experiments Concerning
Space
PA . . . . Program Authorization
PACT . . . . . . Program for Automatic Coding Techniques (Data processing)
PBAC . . . . . . Program Budget Advisory Committee
PBG . . . . Program and Budget Guidance
PCA . . . . Program Change Analysis (DOD)
PCCS . . . . . . Program Change Control System
PCD . . . . Program Change Decision (Military)
PCP . . . . Program Change Proposal (DOD)
PCR . . . . Program Change Request (DOD)
PCN . . . . Program Control Number
PCR . . . . Program Control Register
PCE . . . . Program Cost Estimate
PC . . . . Program Counter
PCS . . . . Program Counter Store
PDP . . . . Program (or Project) Definition Phase (DOD)
PDPS . . . . . . Program Definition Phase Studies (Navy)
PDI . . . . Program Design, Incorporated (Commercial firm)
PWDI . . . . . . Program with Developing Institutions
PDP . . . . Program Development Plan (NASA)
PDR . . . . Program Drum Recording
PE . . . . Program Element
PEC . . . . Program Element Code
PEM . . . . Program Element Monitor
PESD . . . . . . Program Element Summary Data
PEF . . . . Program Estimating Factor
PEBCO . . . . . Program Evaluation and Budget Committee (American Library Association)
PEGE . . . . . . Program for Evaluation of Ground Environment
PEO . . . . Program Evaluation Office
PEP . . . . Program Evaluation Procedure (Air Force)
PERT . . . . . . Program Evaluation and Review Technique (Data processing)
PERTCO . . . . . Program Evaluation Review Technique with Cost
POTC . . . . . . PERT (Program Evaluation and Review Technique) Orientation &
Training Center
PESD . . . . . . Program Execution Sub-Directive (Army)
PROFIT . . . . . . Program for Financed Insurance Techniques

PFT	Program Flying Training (Air Force)
PG	Program Guidance
PRIME	Program Independence, Modularity, Economy
POI	Program of Instruction
PIRD	Program Instrumentation Requirements Document (NASA)
PRISE	Program for Integrated Shipboard Electronics
PIM	Program Integration Manual
PIC	Program Interrupt Control (Data processing)
PIE	Program Interrupt Entry (Data processing)
PI	Program Interrupter
PLO	Program Line Organization
PMB	Program Management Board
PMP	Program Management Plan
PMS	Program Management Support
PMS	Program Management System (Data processing)
PMC	Program Marginal Checking
PMT	Program Master Tape
PRONTO	Program for Numeric Tool Operation (Data processing)
PO	Program Objective
POED	Program Organization for Evaluation and Decision
PO	Program Originator
PPBES	Program Planning-Budgeting-Evaluation System Project
PRESTO	Program for Rapid Earth-to-Space Trajectory Optimization (NASA)
PRA	Program Reader Assembly (Data processing)
PRT	Program Reference Table
PRISM	Program Reliability Information System for Management (Polaris)
PRESTO	Program Reporting and Evaluation System for Total Operations (AFSC)
PRD	Program Requirement Document (Air Force)
PROM	Program, Resources, Objectives, Management (Air Force Systems Command technique)
PRC	Program Review Committee
PSW	Program Status Word
PSC	Program Structure Code
PTT	Program Technical Training
PTM	Program Timing and Miscellaneous (Electronics)
PURS	Program Usage Replenishment System
PWR	Program Work Requirement
PY	Program Year
PAC	Programmable Automatic Comparator
PDS	Programmable Data Station
PEAT	Programme Elargi d'Assistance Technique (Expanded Program of Technical Assistance) (UN)
PAREX	Programmed Accounts Receivable Extra Service (Data processing)
PAL	Programmed Application Library (Data processing)
PACT	Programmed Automatic Circuit Tester
PACE	Programmed Automatic Communications Equipment
PATE	Programmed Automatic Test Equipment
PAWS	Programmed Automatic Welding System
PCSP	Programmed Communications Support Program (Air Force)
PDP	Programmed Data Processor
PDQ	Programmed Data Quantizer
PRODAC	Programmed Digital Automatic Control (Data processing)
PREP	Programmed Educational Package
PFR	Programmed Film Reader (System)
PICOE	Programmed Initiations, Commitments, Obligations and Expenditures (AFSC)
PI	Programmed Instruction
PRIME	Programmed Instruction for Management Education (American Management Association)
PLANIT	Programmed Language for Interaction Teaching (Data processing)
PLATO	Programmed Logic for Automatic Teaching Operations
PMCV	Programmed Multichannel Valve (Chromatography)
PRINCE	Programmed Reinforced Instruction Necessary to Continuing Education
PRIDE	Programmed Reliability in Design Engineering
PROSAM	Programmed Single Axis Mount (Military camera)
PTGC	Programmed Temperature Gas Chromatography
PAT	Programmer Aptitude Tester
PROC	Programming Computer
PL	Programming Language (Data processing)
PLACE	Programming Language for Automatic Checkout Equipment
PP	Programming Plan
PRM	Programming and Resources Management (NASA)
PRORA	Programs for Research on Romance Authors
PPSEI	Progres Politique, Social et Economique de l'Itasy (Political, Social and Economic Progress of the Itasy)
PAG	Progress Analysis Group (Navy)
PP	Progress Payments (Military procurement)
PR	Progress Report
PSR	Progress Summary Report
PT & E	Progress Tests and Examinations
PARC	Progressive Aircraft Repair Cycle
PABA	Progressive Angus Breeders Association

PCA	Progressive Citizens of America
PCP	Progressive Constitutional Party (Malta)
PEA	Progressive Education Association (Became defunct in 1955)
PLP	Progressive Labor Party
PMF	Progressive Massive Fibrosis
PMP	Progressive Merger Procedure (Econometrics)
PMW	Progressive Mine Workers of America
PMD	Progressive Muscular Dystrophy
POW	Progressive Order of the West
PPC	Progressive Patient Care
PRISM	Progressive Refinement of Integrated Supply Management
PRL	Progressive Republican League
PR	Progressive Resistance
PRE	Progressive Resistive Exercise
PSMA	Progressive Spinal Muscular Atrophy (Medicine)
PWT	Progressive Wave Tube
PZL	Progressive Zionist League-Hashomer Hatzair
PNC	Prohibition National Committee
PACT	Project for the Advancement of Coding Techniques
PAG	Project Advisory Group
PAR	Project Audit Report
PBS	Project Breakdown Structure
PDM	Project Design Memo
PE	Project Engineer
PEM	Project Engineering Memorandum
PLO	Project Line Organization
PROMPT	Project Management and Production Team Technique (Data processing)
PMTO	Project Manager Test Offices (Military)
PMAP	Project Master Plans (Navy)
PMTHP	Project Mercury Technical History Program (NASA)
PNDM	Project Non-Design Memo
P/O	Project Office
POCL	Project Office Change Letter
POM	Project Office Memo
POIR	Project Officers Interim Report (Air Force)
POR	Project Officers Report
PR	Project Report
PROMPT	Project Reporting Organization & Management Planning Technique
PREPARE	Project for Retraining of Employable Persons as Relates to EDP
PSIEP	Project in Scientific Information Exchange in Psychology
PS	Project Slip
PSR	Project Summary Report
PWW	Project West Wing
PBI	Projected Books, Incorporated
PD	Projected Display
PPPI	Projection Plan Position Indicator
PTOA	Projective Tests of Attitudes
PC	Projector Charge
PIAT	Projector Infantry, Anti-Tank (British shoulder-controlled weapon)
PACE	Projects to Advance Creativity in Education (HEW)
PP	Proletarian Party
PA	Prolonged Action
Pm	Promethium (Chemical symbol)
PM	Promethium (Chemical element)
PN	Promissory Note (Business and trade)
PEP	Promoting Enduring Peace
PED	Promotion Eligibility Date (Military)
PLSD	Promotion List Service Date (Air Force)
PQS	Promotion Qualification Score (Military)
PSD	Promotion Service Date
P	Prompt (i.e., the right side) (A stage direction)
PMW	Prompt Mobilization Designation Withdrawn
POP	Prompt Ordering Plan
PS	Prompt Side (of a stage) (i.e., the right side) (A stage direction)
PARTNER	Proof of Analog Results Through a Numerical Equivalent Routine (Data processing)
PG	Proof Gallon (Wines and spirits)
PIP	Proof in Print
PS	Proof Shot (Ammunition)
PTM	Proof Test Model (NASA)
PTR	Proof Test Reactor (AEC)
PCNY	Proofreaders Club of New York
PAD	Propellant-Actuated Devices
POBATO	Propellant on Board at Take-Off
PEREF	Propellant Engine Research Environmental Facility
PLPS	Propellant Loading & Pressurization System
PLS	Propellant Loading System
PMC	Propellant Monitor and Control
PT	Propellant Transfer
PTO	Propellant Transfer Operation
PTS	Propellant Transfer System

PU . . . . Propellant Utilization (Air Force)
PUTT . . . . Propellant Utilization Time Trace (Computer)
P & E . . . . Propellants and Explosives (Military)
PCUS . . . . Propeller Club of the United States
PHP . . . . Propeller Horsepower
PT . . . . Propeller Torpedo (Boat)
P & I . . . . Properties and Installations
PAT . . . . Property and Accounting Technician (Navy)
PBO . . . . Property Book Officer (Army)
PD . . . . Property Damage
PDA . . . . Property Disposal Agent
PDCO . . . . Property Disposal Contracting Officer (Military)
PDD . . . . Property Disposal Division
PDO . . . . Property Disposal Officer (Military)
PMDS . . . . Property Management and Disposal Service (General Services Administration)
POAA . . . . Property Owners Association of America
POPA . . . . Property Owners' Protection Association
P . . . . Proportion in a Specific Class
Q . . . . The Proportion Not in a Specific Class
PL . . . . Proportional Limit
PR . . . . Proportional Representation (in legislatures, etc.)
PO . . . . Proposals Outstanding
P . . . . Proposed Departure (Aviation)
PDA . . . . Proposed Development Approach (Navy)
PSPP . . . . . Proposed System Package Plan
PTA . . . . Proposed Technical Approach
PPP . . . . Propria Pecunia Posuit (Erected at His Own Expense)
PA . . . . Proprietary Association
PCW . . . . Proprietor of copyright on a Composite Work
PCB . . . . Proprietor of copyright on a work by a Corporate Body
PWH . . . . Proprietor of copyright on a Work made for Hire
POA . . . . Proptic Area
PM . . . . Propulsion Memorandum
PPG . . . . . . Propulsion & Power Generation
PRC . . . . Propulsion Research Corporation
PREF . . . . Propulsion Research Environmental Facility
PRL . . . . Propulsion Research Laboratory
PTVA . . . . . . Propulsion Test Vehicle Assembly (NASA)
PTV . . . . Propulsion Test Vehicles
P & VE . . . . . . Propulsion and Vehicle Engineering (A Marshall Space Flight Center laboratory)
PWT . . . . Propulsion Wind Tunnel (Air Force)
PC . . . . Propulsive Coefficient
PROFAC . . . . Propulsive Fluid Accumulator
PA . . . . Prosecuting Attorney
PCO . . . . Prospective Commanding Officer
PEO . . . . Prospective Engineer Officer
PXO . . . . Prospective Executive Officer
PC . . . . Prospectors Club
PMOA . . . . . . Prospectors and Mine Owners Association
PG . . . . Prostaglandin
PDC . . . . Prosthetic Distribution Center (Veterans Administration)
PC . . . . Prosthetics Center (Veterans Administration)
Pa . . . . Protactinium (Chemical element)
PI . . . . Protamine Insulin
PZI . . . . Protamine Zinc Insulin
PONY . . . . . . Protect Our Nation's Youth (Baseball league) (Name usually written Pony)
PYE . . . . Protect Your Environment (Groups)
PMRMO . . . . . Protectable Mobilization Reserve Materiel Objective (Army)
C . . . . Protected Cruiser
PHCLIS . . . . . . Protected Home Circle Life Insurance Society
PMRMR . . . . . Protectible Mobilization Reserve Materiel Requirements
P & I . . . . Protection and Indemnity (Business and trade)
PAG . . . . Protective Action Guide (Federal Radiation Council)
PMP . . . . Protective Mobilization Plan
PBI . . . . Protein-Bound Iodine (Medicine)
PG . . . . Protein Granule
P . . . . Protestant
PBS . . . . Protestant Big Sisters
PCPA . . . . . . Protestant Church-Owned Publishers Association
PCCG . . . . . . Protestant Cinema Critics Guild (Later, PCG)
PCG . . . . Protestant Cinema Guild (Formerly, PCCG)
PE . . . . Protestant Episcopal
PTA . . . . Protestant Teachers Association
POAU . . . . . . Protestants and Other Americans United (for Separation of Church and State)
PCF . . . . Prothrombin Conversion Factor
PT . . . . Prothrombin Time (Medicine)

PKHO . . . . Protivo-Khimicheskaia Oborona (Antichemical defense) (USSR)
PTO . . . . Protivo-Tankovaia Oborona (Antitank Defense) (in USSR field forces)
PVO . . . . Protivo-Voxdushnaia Oborona (Antiaircraft defense) (USSR)
PI . . . . Protocol Internationale
P . . . . Proton
PBE . . . . Proton Balance Equation
PBTS . . . . Proton Beam Transport System
PESTF . . . . . . Proton Event Start Forecast (Solar weather information)
PMR . . . . Proton Magnetic Resonance
PRR . . . . Proton Relaxation Rate
PS . . . . Proton Synchrotron (AEC)
PTA . . . . Proton Target Area
Y . . . . Prototype (Designation for all US military aircraft)
POSS . . . . Prototype Optical Surveillance System
POPR . . . . Prototype Organic Power Reactor
PRTOT . . . . . Prototype Real-Time Optical Tracker (Data processing)
PID . . . . Protruded Intervertebral Disc (Medicine) (British)
PCMC . . . . Provided Chief of Mission Concurs
PNMO . . . . Provided No Military Objection Exists
POQ . . . . Provided Otherwise Qualified (Military)
PUC . . . . Provided You Concur
PAUCA . . . . . . Providence Association of Ukrainian Catholics in America
PO . . . . Province of Ontario (Canada)
PQ . . . . Province of Quebec, Canada
PT . . . . Provincetown-Boston Airline, Inc.
PCC . . . . Provincial Congress Committee
PGDC . . . . Provincial Grand Director of Ceremonies (Masonry)
PGS . . . . Provincial Grand Secretary (Masonry)
PGSB . . . . Provincial Grand Sword-Bearer (Masonry)
PG . . . . Proving Ground
PGC . . . . Proving Ground Command (Air Force)
PPF . . . . Provision of Production Facilities (Military)
YF . . . . Provision Store Lighter (Navy symbol)
PAAP . . . . . . Provisional Algal Assay Procedure (Test measuring impact of chemicals on algal growth)
PA . . . . Provisional Allowance
PC . . . . Provisional Costs
PFB . . . . Provisional Frequency Board (ITU)
PGAR . . . . Provisional Government of the Algerian Republic
PICAO . . . . . . Provisional International Civil Aviation Organization (Later, ICAO)
PICC . . . . Provisional International Computation Center
PPB . . . . Provisional Parts Breakdown
PRSN . . . . Provisional Relative Sunspot Number (NASA)
PTCAD . . . . . . Provisional Troop Carrier Airborne Division
PO . . . . Provisioning Order
POOD . . . . . . Provisioning Order Obligating Document
PPS . . . . Provisioning Performance Schedule
PRAP . . . . Provisions of Following Reference Apply (Army)
PSO . . . . Provisions Supply Office
PM . . . . Provost Marshal
PMG . . . . Provost Marshal General (Army)
PMGS . . . . . . Provost Marshal General's School, United States Army
PCT . . . . Proximal Convoluted Tubule (of a nephron)
PIP . . . . Proximal Interphalangeal (Joint)
PF . . . . Proximity Fuze (Bomb, rocket or shell)
PWI . . . . Proximity Warning Indicator (or Instrument)
PMI . . . . Pseudo Matrix Isolation
PN . . . . Pseudo-Noise
PRN . . . . Pseudo-Random Noise
PRP . . . . Pseudo-Random Pulse
P-LGV . . . . . . Psittacosis-Lymphogranuloma Venereum
PRA . . . . Psoriasis Research Association
POCA . . . . . . Psychiatric Outpatient Centers of America
PRF . . . . Psychiatric Research Foundation
PSW . . . . Psychiatric Social Worker
PN . . . . Psychiatry-Neurology
PAL . . . . Psycho-Acoustic Laboratory (Harvard University)
PA . . . . Psychoanalyst
PGR . . . . Psychogalvanic Reflex (or Response) (Psychology)
PK . . . . Psychokinesis
PARRS . . . . . . Psychological Abstracts Reference Retrieval System (Syracuse University)
PSYOP . . . . . Psychological Operations (Military)
PRA . . . . Psychological Research Associates
PSYWAR . . . . Psychological Warfare
PW . . . . Psychological Warfare
PWB . . . . Psychological Warfare Branch (Allied Forces) (World War II)
PWD . . . . Psychological Warfare Division (Military)
PWS . . . . Psychological Warfare Service (Allied Forces) (World War II)
PIAP . . . . Psychologists Interested in the Advancement of Psychotherapy
PN . . . . Psychoneurotic (Cases, patients, etc.)

PS	Psychonomic Society
PIAPACS	Psychophysiological Information Acquisition, Processing, and Control System
PRF	Psychosynthesis Research Foundation
PDGA	Pteroyldiglutamic Acid
PGA	Pteroylglutamic Acid (Folic acid)
PS	Pubblica Sicurezza
PA	Public Act
PA	Public Address (Amplification equipment) (Communications)
PA	Public Administration
PACH	Public Administration Clearing House (1931-1956)
PAS	Public Administration Service
PA	Public Affairs
PAC	Public Affairs Committee
PAD	Public Affairs Division (Military)
PAIS	Public Affairs Information Service
PAI	Public Affairs Institute
PAO	Public Affairs Officer (Embassies)
PA	Public Assistance
PAD	Public Assistance Division (District of Columbia)
PBL	Public Broadcast Laboratory
PBA	Public Buildings Administration (Functions transferred to GSA, 1949)
PBC	Public Buildings Commission (Functions transferred to PBA, 1939)
PBS	Public Buildings Service (of GSA)
PC	Public Contracts
PDA	Public Display of Affection (Slang)
PD	Public Domain
PG	Public Gaol
PH	Public Health
PHCAA	Public Health Cancer Association of America
PHL	Public Health Law
PHS	Public Health Service (HEW)
PHB	Public Health Service Building
PHA	Public Housing Administration (of HHFA)
PIA	Public Information Act
CPI	Public Information Division (Coast Guard symbol)
PID	Public Information Division (Military)
PILO	Public Information Liaison Officer (Military)
PIO	Public Information Office(r)
PLO	Public Land Order (Interior)
PL	Public Law (An act of Congress)
PLR	Public Lending Right (Royalty for books borrowed from public libraries) (British)
PL	Public Liability (Business and trade)
PL & PD	Public Liability and Property Damage (Insurance)
PL	Public Library
PLA	Public Library Association
PUBLINX	Public Links (Amateur golf)
PPA	Public Personnel Association
PP	Public Property
PRO	Public Record Office (British)
PR	Public Relations
PRAC	Public Relations Advisory Committee
PRD	Public Relations Division
PRF	Public Relations Foundation
PRO	Public Relations Officer (Usually military)
PRP	Public Relations Personnel (Navy)
PRSA	Public Relations Society of America
PRSSA	Public Relations Student Society of America
PRA	Public Resources Association
PREC	Public Revenue Education Council
PRA	Public Roads Administration
PS	Public Sale
PS	Public School
PSC	Public Service Commission (Usually, of a specific state)
PSR	Public Service Company of Colorado (NYSE symbol)
PIN	Public Service Company of Indiana, Inc. (NYSE symbol)
PEG	Public Service Electric & Gas Company (NYSE symbol)
PSWTUF	Public Service Workers' Trade Union Federation (Ceylon)
PSI	Public Services International
PS	Public Stenographer
PTV	Public Television
PULSE	Public Urban Locator Service
PUAA	Public Utilities Advertising Association
PUC	Public Utilities Commission
PUP	Public Utilities Panel (EECE)
PUD	Public Utility District
PV	Public Voucher
PW	Public Works
PWA	Public Works Administration (All functions transferred to office of Federal Works Agency, 1943)

PWC	Public Works Center (Navy)
PWCEN	Public Works Center
PWD	Public Works Department (Navy)
PWDEPT	Public Works Department
PWO	Public Works Officer (Navy)
P	Publication
PA	Publication Announcement
PCR	Publication Contract Requirements
PWR	Publication Work Request
PADS	Publications of the American Dialect Society
PB	Publications Board (Later, CFSTI)
PB	Publications Bulletin
PC	Publications in Climatology
PDC	Publications Distribution Center (Military)
PDM	Publications Distribution Manager (Military)
PDO	Publications Distribution Officer
PMLA	Publications of the Modern Language Association of America
POS	Publications de l'Office de Statistique (Luxembourg)
PPO	Publications and Printing Office (Military)
PSH	Publications Statistiques Hongroises (Hungary)
PM	Publicity Man (Slang)
P & PW	Publicity and Psychological Warfare
PSO	Publicity Security Officer (Navy)
PUL	Publicker Industries, Inc. (NYSE symbol)
PIB	Publishers Information Bureau
PLPG	Publishers' Library Promotion Group
PPA	Publishers' Publicity Association
PTLA	Publishers' Trade List Annual
PW	Publishers' Weekly (Trade periodical)
PWA	Publishers' Weekly Announcements (Now called Forthcoming Books)
PUAD	Pueblo Army Depot
PRN	Puerto Rican Cement Company, Inc. (NYSE symbol)
PRF	Puerto Rican Forum
PRWRA	Puerto Rican Water Resources Authority
PR	Puerto Rico
PRANG	Puerto Rico Air National Guard
PRA	Puerto Rico Area Office (AEC)
PRCA	Puerto Rico Communications Authority
PRIDCO	Puerto Rico Industrial Development Company
PRNC	Puerto Rico Nuclear Center
PRRA	Puerto Rico Reconstruction Administration (Terminated, 1955)
PRRI	Puerto Rico Rum Institute
PRRPA	Puerto Rico Rum Producers Association
PDA	Pug Dog of America
PSFL	Puget Sound Freight Lines (AAR code)
PSNS	Puget Sound Naval Shipyard
PSNSY	Puget Sound Naval Shipyard
PSD	Puget Sound Power & Light Company (NYSE symbol)
PS	Puget Sound, Washington, and Puget Sound Naval Shipyard
P & PP	Pull and Push Plate
PS	Pull Switch
PE	Pulley End
PWB	Pulling Whaleboat
PU	Pullman Inc. (NYSE symbol)
PAVS	Pulmonary Arterial Vasoconstrictor Substance
PAP	Pulmonary Artery Pressure
PS	Pulmonary Stenosis
PCA	Pulp Chemicals Association
PMRL	Pulp Manufacturers' Research League
PPMA	Pulp and Paper Machinery Association
PPPEA	Pulp, Paper and Paperboard Export Association of the United States
PPPI	Pulp, Paper & Paperboard Institute (USA), Inc.
PAPPA	Pulp and Paper Prepackaging Association
PPPA	Pulp and Paper Prepackaging Association
PPTL	Pulp and Paper Traffic League
PREMA	Pulp Refining Equipment Manufacturers Association
PD	Pulpodistal
PL	Pulpolingual
PLA	Pulpolinguoaxial
PM	Pulpomesial
PC	Pulsating Current
PULSAR	Pulsating Star
PAR	Pulse Acquisition RADAR (Military)
PAMA	Pulse-Address Multiple Access (Satellite communications)
PA	Pulse Amplifier
PACM	Pulse Amplitude Code Modulation
PAM	Pulse Amplitude Modulation (Radio)
PAM-FM	Pulse Amplitude Modulation-Frequency Modulation
PARIS	Pulse Analysis-Recording Information System
PCM	Pulse Code Modulation (Electronics)
PCMD	Pulse Code Modulation Digital

PCME . . . . Pulse Code Modulation Event
PCM-FM . . . . . Pulse Code Modulation - Frequency Modulation
PCP . . . . Pulse Comparator
PC . . . . Pulse Compression
PC . . . . Pulse Controller
PCM . . . . Pulse-Count Modulation
PCF . . . . Pulse-to-Cycle Fraction
PD . . . . Pulse Driver
PD . . . . Pulse Duration
PDM . . . . Pulse-Duration Modulation (Radio)
PDMFM . . . . . Pulse Duration Modulation - Frequency Modulation
PE . . . . Pulse Encoding (Data processing)
PECAN . . . . . Pulse Envelop Correlation Air Navigation
PFN . . . . Pulse Forming Network
PF . . . . Pulse Frequency
PFM . . . . Pulse-Frequency Modulation (RADAR)
PG . . . . Pulse Generator
PGRF . . . . . . Pulse Group Repetition Frequency
PHA . . . . Pulse Height Analysis
PIB . . . . Pulse Interference Blanker (Radio)
PIE . . . . Pulse Interference Eliminator (RADAR)
PISAB . . . . . . Pulse Interference Separation and Blanking (RADAR)
PIM . . . . Pulse Interval Modulation
PLM . . . . Pulse-Length Modulation
PMM . . . . Pulse Mode Multiplex
PMCS . . . . . . Pulse-Modulated Communications System
PM . . . . Pulse Modulation
PNM . . . . Pulse Number Modulation
POD . . . . Pulse Omission Detector
PPM . . . . Pulse Position Modulation (Radio)
PRN . . . . Pulse Ranging Navigation
PR . . . . Pulse Rate
PRI . . . . Pulse Rate Indicator
PRM . . . . Pulse Rate Modulation
PRF . . . . Pulse Recurrence Frequency (Radio)
PRF . . . . Pulse Repetition Frequency (RADAR)
PRADOR . . . . . PRF (Pulse Repetition Frequency) Ranging Doppler RADAR
PRP . . . . Pulse Repetition Period (RADAR)
PRR . . . . Pulse Repetition Rate (RADAR)
PRT . . . . Pulse-Repetition Time
PSE . . . . Pulse Sense
PSD . . . . Pulse Shape Discriminator
PS . . . . Pulse Shaper
PS . . . . Pulse Stretcher
PTC . . . . Pulse Time Code
PTM . . . . Pulse Time Modulation (Radio)
PTM . . . . Pulse Time Multiplex
PT . . . . Pulse Timer
PW . . . . Pulse Width (RADAR)
PWC . . . . Pulse-Width Coded
PWD . . . . Pulse-Width Discriminator (RADAR)
PWE . . . . Pulse-Width Encoder
PWM . . . . Pulse-Width Modulation (RADAR)
PWM-FM . . . . . Pulse-Width Modulation - Frequency Modulation (RADAR)
PGC . . . . Pulsed Gas Crymotography
PIP . . . . Pulsed Integrating Pendulum
PIPA . . . . Pulsed Integrating Pendulum Accelerometer
PIPS . . . . Pulsed Integrating Pendulums
PIPER . . . . . . Pulsed Intense Plasma for Exploratory Research
PJ . . . . Pulsejet
PPH . . . . Pulses Per Hour
PPM . . . . Pulses Per Minute
PPS . . . . Pulses Per Second (RADAR)
PLA . . . . Pulverized Limestone Association
PIA . . . . Pumice Institute of America
PDA . . . . Pump Drive Assembly
PHP . . . . Pump Horsepower
P . . . . Punch
PCE . . . . Punch Card Equipment
PCM . . . . Punch-Card Machine (Data processing)
PCAM . . . . . . Punched-Card Accounting Machines
PCMS . . . . . . Punched Card Machine System
PCS . . . . Punched Card System
PC . . . . Punched Cards

PPT. . . . . Punched Paper Tape
PT . . . . Punched Tape
PTBR. . . . . . . Punched Tape Block Reader (Data processing)
PP . . . . Punctum Proximum (Near Point)
PR . . . . Punctum Remotum (Far Point)
PNI . . . . Punjab Native Infantry (India)
P. . . . . Pupil
PROF . . . . . . Pupil Registering and Operational Filing (Data processing)
PT . . . . Pupil Teacher
PA . . . . Puppeteers of America
PCO . . . . Purchase Change Order
PD . . . . Purchase Description
PM . . . . Purchase Memo
PM . . . . Purchase Money
PO . . . . Purchase Order
POCN . . . . . . Purchase Order Change Notice
POR . . . . Purchase Order Request
PORR . . . . . . Purchase Order Revision Request
PPR . . . . Purchase Parts Request
PR . . . . Purchase Requests
PE . . . . Purchased Equipment
PPSN . . . . . . Purchased Part Shortage Notice
PP . . . . Purchased Parts
PA . . . . Purchasing Agent
PAEI . . . . . . Purchasing Agents of the Electronic Industry
PARTEI . . . . . Purchasing Agents of the Radio, TV, and Electronics Industries
PC . . . . Purchasing and Contracting
P & C . . . . . . Purchasing and Contracting
PPE . . . . Purchasing Power Equivalent
PRF . . . . Purdue Research Foundation
PUFFT. . . . . . Purdue University Fast FORTRAN Translator (Data processing)
PUR . . . . Purdue University Reactor
PUR . . . . Purdue University Research
PAC . . . . Pure and Applied Chemistry (IUPAC)
PY . . . . Pure Oil Company (NYSE symbol)
PDCA . . . . . . Purebred Dairy Cattle Association
PC . . . . Purified Concentrate
PEBA . . . . . . Purified Extract of Brucella Abortus
PPD . . . . Purified Protein Derivative (Tuberculin)
PPD-S . . . . . . Purified Protein Derivative-Standard
P . . . . Purl (Knitting)
PPD . . . . Purolator Products, Inc. (NYSE symbol)
P . . . . Purple
PH . . . . Purple Heart (Decoration given to personnel wounded in military service)
PPA . . . . Purple Plum Association
PB . . . . Purplish Blue
PR . . . . Purplish Red
PONY . . . . . . Purpose of Neighborhood Youth (Foundation)
PSVOA. . . . . . Purse Seine Vessel Owners Association
PSVOMA . . . . Purse Seine Vessel Owners Marketing Association
PAC . . . . Pursuant to Authority Contained in
PIC . . . . Pursuant to Instructions Contained in (Military)
P. . . . . Pursuit (Airplane designation)
PB . . . . Push Button
PBP. . . . . Push-Button Panel
POPO . . . . . . Push-On, Pull-Off (Data processing)
PP . . . . Push-Pull (Technical drawings)
PTT. . . . . Push to Talk
PAC . . . . Put and Call (Stock market)
PCBDA . . . . . Put and Call Brokers and Dealers Association
PO . . . . Put Outs (Baseball)
P & C . . . . . . Puts and Calls (Securities trading)
PED . . . . Pyramid Element Designator
PUO . . . . Pyrexia (fever) of Unknown Origin (Commonly called Trench Fever)
PMDA . . . . . . Pyromellitic Dianhydride (Chemical)
PCE . . . . Pyrometric Cone Equivalent (Refractory industry)
PCA . . . . Pyrotechnic Control Assembly (NASA)
PAS . . . . Pyrotechnics Arming Switch
PX . . . . Pyroxene (Also PYX)
PYX . . . . Pyroxene (Also PX)
PCA . . . . Pyrrolidone Carboxylic Acid
PMCG . . . . . . Pyrrolidyl Methyl Cyclopentylphenyl Glycolate (Chemical)
POF . . . . Pyruvate Oxidation Factor (Biochemistry)

Q

QEA .... QANTAS Empire Airways, Ltd.
QPC....... Qatar Petroleum Company
Q .... Quadrans (Farthing)
QCW ...... Quadrant Continuous Wave
QEM ...... Quadrant Electrometer
QE .... Quadrant Elevation
QES .... Quadrant Eleventh-Gram Second
QTA .... Quadrant Transformer Assembly
QG .... Quadrature Grid
QM .... Quadrature Modulation
QRF .... Quadrature Rejection Frequency
QRR .... Quadrature Rejection Ratio
QASC...... Quadripartite Armaments Standardization Committee (Military)
QCSC...... Quadripartite Chemical, Biological, Radiological Standardization Committee (Military)
QNMC ..... Quadripartite Nonmateriel Committee (Military)
QQSC ..... Quadripartite Quartermaster Standardization Committee (Military)
QRCC...... Quadripartite Research Coordination Committee (Military)
QTPC ...... Quadripartite Technical Procedures Committee (Military)
CT & C ...... Quadripartite Trade & Commerce Committee (Allied German Occupation Forces)
QWMP ...... Quadruped Walking Machine Program (Army)
QFF .... Quadrupole Flip-Flop (Data processing)
QRG .... Quadrupole Residual Gas
QRGA ..... Quadrupole Residual Gas Analyzer
QRGAS..... Quadrupole Residual Gas Analyzer System
QRR .... Quadrupole Resonance Response
QSS .... Quadrupole Screw Ship
Q .... Quaere (Inquire)
QO .... Quaker Oats (Trade name)
OAT....... Quaker Oats Company (NYSE symbol)
KSF .... Quaker State Oil Refining Corporation (NYSE symbol)
QCC ...... Qualification Correlation Certification
QC .... Qualification Course
QMI .... Qualification Maintainability Inspection
QP........ Qualification Proposal
QT........ Qualification Test
QTP .... Qualification Test Program (or Procedure)
QTR .... Qualification Test Report
QTS .... Qualification Test Specification
QB........ Qualified Bidders
QEM ...... Qualified Export Manager (Designation given by American Society of International Executives)
QFI .... Qualified Flight Instructor
QIE-AF...... Qualified International Executive – Air Forwarding (Designation given by American Society of International Executives)
QIE-EM ..... Qualified International Executive – Export Management (Designation given by American Society of International Executives)
QIE-TM ..... Qualified International Executive – Traffic Management (Designation given by American Society of International Executives)
QMAO ...... Qualified for Mobilization Ashore Only (Navy)
QO .... Qualified in Ordnance (Navy)
QPS .... Qualified Processing Source
QPL ...... Qualified Products List (Navy)
QRPAO...... Qualified Radium Plaque Adaptometer Operator (Navy)
QSE .... Qualified Scientists and Engineers
QDRI ...... Qualitative Development Requirement Information
QER .... Qualitative Equipment Requirements (Army)
QMDO...... Qualitative Materiel Development Objective (Army)
QMR ...... Qualitative Materiel Requirement (Army)
QOR ...... Qualitative Operational Requirement (Military)
QPRI ...... Qualitative Personnel Requirements Information
QRRI ...... Qualitative Research Requirements Information (Army)

QA .... Quality Assurance
QAC ...... Quality Assurance Code
QADS...... Quality Assurance Data System
QAD ...... Quality Assurance Directive
QAD ...... Quality Assurance Division
QAE....... Quality Assurance Engineering
QAFO ..... Quality Assurance Field Operations
QAF....... Quality Assurance Function
QAIP ...... Quality Assurance Inspection Procedure
QAI .... Quality Assurance Instruction
QAL....... Quality Assurance Laboratory
QALTR ..... Quality Assurance Laboratory Test Request
QAM ...... Quality Assurance Manual
QAO ...... Quality Assurance Office (Navy)
QAO ...... Quality Assurance Operation
QAP....... Quality Assurance Procedures
QAP....... Quality Assurance Program
QUART ..... Quality Assurance and Reliability Team
QAR....... Quality Assurance Representative
QBAC...... Quality Bakers of America Cooperative
QBACI ..... Quality Bakers of America Cooperative, Incorporated
QBA....... Quality Brands Associates of America
QOC ...... Quality of Conformance
QC .... Quality Control
QCCARS..... Quality Control Collection Analysis and Reporting System
QCD ...... Quality Control Data
QCDR...... Quality Control Deficiency Report
QCE....... Quality Control Engineers
QCI .... Quality Control Information
QCL....... Quality Control Level
QCM ...... Quality Control Manager
QCM ...... Quality Control Manual
QCOP ..... Quality Control Operating Procedure
QCO ...... Quality Control Organization
QCP....... Quality Control Procedure
QCR....... Quality Control/Reliability
QCR....... Quality Control Report
QCR....... Quality Control Representative
QCR....... Quality Control Review
QCR....... Quality Control Room
QCS....... Quality Control System
QCTR ..... Quality Control Test Report
QCS....... Quality Cost System
QCM ...... Quality Courts Motels
QCU ...... Quality Courts United
QOD ...... Quality of Design
QUEST ..... Quality Electrical Systems Test (Interpreter)
QE........ Quality Engineering
QEO ...... Quality Engineering Operations
QEL....... Quality Evaluation Laboratory
QEP....... Quality Examination Program
Q .... Quality Factor
QF........ Quality Factor
QI........ Quality Index
QIC....... Quality Information Center
QIT .... Quality Information and Test (System)
QIC .... Quality Inspection Criteria
QM .... Quality Memorandum
QM .... Quality of Merit
QPP....... Quality Program Provision
Q & R ..... Quality and Reliability
QRAC...... Quality and Reliability Assessment Council
QRA....... Quality Reliability Assurance

Q & RA . . . . . Quality and Reliability Assurance
QRCR . . . . . . Quality Reliability Consumption Reports
QRY . . . . Quality and Reliability Year
QR . . . . Quality Review
QSI . . . . Quality Salary Increase
QSIC . . . . . . Quality Standard Inspection Criteria
QSD . . . . Quality Surveillance Division (Navy)
QVT . . . . Quality Verification Test
QAP . . . . Quanah, Acme & Pacific Railway (AAR code)
QC . . . . Quantitative Command
QDTA . . . . . . Quantitative Differential Thermal Analysis
QFC . . . . Quantitative Flight Characteristics
QFCC . . . . . . Quantitative Flight Characteristics Criteria
QLT . . . . Quantitative Leak Test
QOD . . . . Quantitative Oceanographic Data
QPS . . . . Quantitative Physical Science
QQPRI . . . . . Quantitative and Qualitative Personnel Requirements Information
QQC . . . . Quantitative Quality Characteristics
QR . . . . Quantitative Restrictions (International trade)
Q . . . . Quantity
QTYDESREQ . . Quantity Desired as Requested
QDA . . . . Quantity Discount Agreement
QNS . . . . Quantity Not Sufficient (Pharmacy)
QUP . . . . Quantity per Unit Pack
QR . . . . Quantity Required
QDD . . . . Quantized Decision Detection
QFT . . . . Quantized Field Theory
QFM . . . . Quantized Frequency Modulation
QGV . . . . Quantized Gate Video (RADAR)
QPM . . . . Quantized Pulse Modulation
QPP . . . . Quantized Pulse Position
QPAM . . . . . . Quantized Pulsed Amplitude Modulation
QUASER . . . . . Quantum Amplification by Stimulated Emission of Radiation
QC . . . . Quantum Counter
QEC . . . . Quantum Electronics Council
QL . . . . Quantum Libet (As Much as Is Desired) (In medical prescriptions)
QM . . . . Quantum Mechanics
QN . . . . Quantum Number
QP . . . . Quantum Placet (As Much as Is Desired)
QS . . . . Quantum Satis or Sufficit (A Sufficient Quantity) (Prescription term)
QTP . . . . Quantum Theory of Paramagnetism
QV . . . . Quantum Vis (As Much as You Wish) (Pharmacy)
QY . . . . Quantum Yield
QD . . . . Quaque Die (Everyday) (Pharmacy)
QH . . . . Quaque Hora (Every Hour) (Pharmacy)
QQH . . . . . . Quaque Hora (Every Hour) (Pharmacy)
QM . . . . Quaque Matin (Every Morning) (Pharmacy)
QN . . . . Quaque Nocte (Every Night) (Pharmacy)
QTB . . . . Quarry-Tile Base (Technical drawings)
QTF . . . . Quarry-Tile Floor (Technical drawings)
QTR . . . . Quarry-Tile Roof (Technical drawings)
Q . . . . Quart
Q . . . . Quarter; Quarterly
QCWA . . . . . Quarter Century Wireless Association
QD . . . . Quarter Die (Four Times a Day)
QID . . . . Quarter in Die (Four Times Daily) (Pharmacy)
QON . . . . Quarter Ocean Net
QOMAC . . . . . Quarter Orbit Magnetic Attitude Control
QS . . . . Quarter Section
QIS . . . . Quarter Sessions
QSM . . . . Quarter Square Multiplier
QW . . . . Quarter Wave
QWA . . . . . . Quarter-Wave Antenna
QWP . . . . . . Quarter Wave Plate
QB . . . . Quarterback (Football position)
QD . . . . Quarterdeck
QAL . . . . Quarterly Accession List
QCIM . . . . . . Quarterly Cumulative Index Medicus
QI . . . . Quarterly Index
QM . . . . Quarterly Memorandum
QPR . . . . Quarterly Progress Report
QRR . . . . Quarterly Research Review
QSR . . . . Quarterly Status Report
QSSR . . . . . . Quarterly Stock Status Report
QSR . . . . Quarterly Summary Report
QSI . . . . Quarterly Survey of Intentions (Bureau of the Census) (Became Consumer Buying Expectations Survey)
QTPR . . . . . . Quarterly Technical Progress Report
QTR . . . . Quarterly Technical Report
QWD . . . . . . Quarterly World Day
Q . . . . Quartermaster

QM . . . . Quartermaster
QMC & SO . . . Quartermaster Cataloging and Standardization Office
QMC . . . . . . Quartermaster Clerk (Marine Corps)
QMCLK . . . . . Quartermaster Clerk (Coast Guard)
QMC . . . . . . Quartermaster Corps (Army)
QMCR . . . . . . Quartermaster Corps Regulations
QMCTC . . . . . Quartermaster Corps Technical Committee
QMDPC . . . . . Quartermaster Data Processing Center
QMDEP . . . . . Quartermaster Depot
QEOP . . . . . . Quartermaster Emergency Operation Plan
QMEPCC . . . . Quartermaster Equipment and Parts Commodity Center
QFCI . . . . . . Quartermaster Food and Container Institute (Army)
QMFCI . . . . . Quartermaster Food and Container Institute
QMFCIAF . . . . Quartermaster Food and Container Institute for the Armed Forces
QG . . . . Quartermaster General (Military)
QMG . . . . . . Quartermaster General (Army)
QMGMC . . . . . Quartermaster General of the Marine Corps
QMIMSO . . . . Quartermaster Industrial Mobilization Services Offices
QMIA . . . . . . Quartermaster Intelligence Agency (Merged with Defense Intelligence Agency)
QMORC . . . . . Quartermaster Officers' Reserve Corps
QO . . . . Quartermaster Operation
QMPCUSA . . . . Quartermaster Petroleum Center, United States Army
QMPA . . . . . . Quartermaster Purchasing Agency
QMRL . . . . . . Quartermaster Radiation Laboratory (Army)
QMRPA . . . . . Quartermaster Radiation Planning Agency
QRDC . . . . . . Quartermaster Research and Development Command (Army)
QRDEA . . . . . Quartermaster Research and Development Evaluation Agency (Army)
QMREC . . . . . Quartermaster Research & Engineering Command (Army)
QREC . . . . . . Quartermaster Research and Engineering Command
QMREFEA . . . . Quartermaster Research & Engineering Field Evaluation Agency (Merged with Troop Evaluation Test)
QMRC . . . . . . Quartermaster Reserve Corps
QMS . . . . Quartermaster School (Army)
QMS . . . . Quartermaster Sergeant
QMSGT . . . . . Quartermaster Sergeant (Marine Corps)
QS . . . . Quartermaster Sergeant
QMSO . . . . . . Quartermaster Supply Officer (Army)
QMTOE . . . . . Quartermaster Table of Organization and Equipment (Units) (Military)
QUARPEL . . . . Quartermaster Water-Repellent Clothing (Military)
QMA . . . . . . Quartermasters Association
QA . . . . Quarters Allowance
QS & L . . . . . Quarters, Subsistence, and Laundry (Military)
Q . . . . Quarto (From 25 to 30 centimeters) (Bibliography)
QZ . . . . Quartz
QAL . . . . Quartz Aircraft Lamp
QALL . . . . . . Quartz Aircraft Landing Lamp
QC . . . . Quartz Crystal
QCF . . . . Quartz Crystal Filter
QCFO . . . . . . Quartz Crystal Frequency Oscillator
QCM . . . . . . Quartz Crystal Monitor
QCO . . . . Quartz Crystal Oscillator
QCU . . . . Quartz Crystal Unit
QCUS . . . . . . Quartz Crystal Unit Set
QFP . . . . Quartz Fiber Product
QFO . . . . Quartz Frequency Oscillator
QH . . . . Quartz Helix
QIL . . . . Quartz Incandescent Lamp
QIP . . . . Quartz Insulation Part
QIC . . . . Quartz-Iodine Crystal
QIL . . . . Quartz Iodine Lamp
QLL . . . . Quartz Landing Lamp (Aviation)
QMSW . . . . . Quartz Metal Sealed Window
QMW . . . . . . Quartz Metal Window
QTS . . . . Quartz Thermometer Sensor
Q . . . . Quasi
QD . . . . Quasi Dicat (As If, or, as Though, One Should Say)
QD . . . . Quasi Dictum (As If Said; as Though It Had Been Said)
QD . . . . Quasi Dixisset (As If One Had Said)
QFL . . . . Quasi-Fermi Level
QLM . . . . . . Quasi-Linear Machine
QLSM . . . . . . Quasi-Linear Sequential Machine
QSM . . . . Quasi-Linear Sequential Machine
QORGS . . . . . Quasi Optimal (or Optimum) Rendezvous Guidance System
QP . . . . Quasi-Peak
QRBM . . . . . . Quasi-Random Band Model
QSSP . . . . . . Quasi-Solid State Panel
QSF . . . . Quasi-Static Field
QSF . . . . Quasi-Stationary Front
QSG . . . . Quasi-Stellar Galaxy
QSO . . . . Quasi-Stellar Object

QUASAR . . . . . Quasi-Stellar Radio Source (Astronomy)
QSS . . . . Quasi-Stellar Source
QAL . . . . Quebec Airways, Limited
QC . . . . Quebec Central Railway Company (AAR code)
QLR . . . . Quebec Law Reports
QBA . . . . Quebecair, Inc.
Q . . . . Queen
Q . . . . Queen (Chess)
QAB . . . . Queen Anne's Bounty
QCA . . . . Queen Charlotte Airlines, Ltd.
QE 2 . . . . Queen Elizabeth 2 (Luxury liner)
QG . . . . Queen Groupie
QMAAC . . . . Queen Mary's Army Auxiliary Corps (The WAAC) (British)
QP . . . . Queen Post
QVR . . . . Queen Victoria's Rifles (British)
QADC . . . . . . Queen's Aid-de-Camp (British)
QB . . . . Queen's Bays (Military) (British)
QB . . . . Queen's Bench (in Law Courts) (British)
QBD . . . . Queen's Bench Division (Military) (British)
QB . . . . Queen's Bishop (Chess)
QC . . . . Queen's Counsel (Only in a Queen's reign) (British)
QHC . . . . Queen's Honorary Chaplain (British)
QHP . . . . Queen's Honorary Physician (British)
QHS . . . . Queen's Honorary Surgeon (British)
QK . . . . Queen's Knight (Chess)
QKT . . . . Queen's Knight (Chess)
QL . . . . Queen's Lancers (Military) (British)
QM . . . . Queen's Messenger(s) (British)
QO . . . . Queen's Own (Military unit) (British)
QOCH . . . . . . The Queen's Own Cameron Highlanders (British)
QOR . . . . Queen's Own Royal (Military unit) (British)
RWK . . . . The Queen's Own Royal West Kent Regiment (British)
QRS . . . . Queen's Row Spare
QRU . . . . Queen's Row Unit
QRUS . . . . . . Queen's Row Unit Spare
QR . . . . Queen's Royal (Military unit) (British)
QU . . . . Queen's University (Canada)
QUB . . . . Queen's University, Belfast (Ireland)
QUI . . . . Queen's University, Ireland
QAPL . . . . Queensland Airlines Party Limited
QANTAS . . . . Queensland and Northern Territories Air Service (Now QANTAS Airways) (Australian airline)
QC . . . . Quench Correction
Q . . . . Query
QRCC . . . . . . Query Response Communications Console
Q . . . . Question
QUANTRAS . . . Question Analysis Transformation and Search (Data processing)
QCT . . . . Questionable Corrective Task
QQ . . . . Questionable Questionnaires
Q . . . . Quetzal (Monetary unit in Guatemala)
QT . . . . Queuing Theory
QBAN . . . . . . Qui Bixit Annos (Who Lived —— Years)
QV . . . . Qui Vixit (Who Lived)
Q . . . . Quick
QAR . . . . Quick Access Recording
QA . . . . Quick-Acting
QAS . . . . Quick Action Shuttle
QAD . . . . Quick Attach-Detach
QADK . . . . . . Quick Attach-Detach Kit
QAK . . . . Quick Attach Kit
QCR . . . . Quick Change Response (System)
QCU . . . . Quick Change Unit
QC . . . . Quick Connect
QCC . . . . Quick Connect Coupling
QCH . . . . Quick Connect Handle
QCK . . . . Quick Connect Kit
QCR . . . . Quick Connect Relay
QCVC . . . . . . Quick Connect Valve Coupler
QDC . . . . Quick Dependable Communications

QDK . . . . Quick Detach Kit
QD . . . . Quick Disconnect
QDC . . . . Quick Disconnect Cap
QDCC . . . . . . Quick Disconnect Circular Connector
QDC . . . . Quick Disconnect Connector
QDC . . . . Quick Disconnect Coupling
QDH . . . . Quick Disconnect Handle
QDK . . . . Quick Disconnect Kit
QDL . . . . Quick Disconnect, Large
QDM . . . . Quick Disconnect, Miniature
QDN . . . . Quick Disconnect Nipple
QDP . . . . Quick Disconnect Pivot
QDS . . . . Quick Disconnect Series
QDS . . . . Quick Disconnect, Small
QDS . . . . Quick Disconnect Swivel
QDV . . . . Quick Disconnect Valve
QUESTER . . . . . Quick and Effective System to Enhance Retrieval (Data processing)
QEC . . . . Quick Engine Change
QECU . . . . . . Quick Engine Change Unit
QED . . . . Quick Erection Dome
QEAV . . . . . . Quick Exhaust Air Valve
QEV . . . . Quick Exhaust Valve
QF . . . . Quick-Firer (Gun)
QFIRC . . . . . . Quick Fix Interference Reduction Capability
QFP . . . . Quick Fix Program
QF . . . . Quick Freeze
QLAP . . . . Quick Look Analysis Program
QLIT . . . . Quick Look Intermediate Tape
QMQB . . . . . . Quick-Make, Quick-Break
QMDK . . . . . . Quick Mechanical Disconnect Kit
QOD . . . . Quick-Opening Device
QQP . . . . Quick Query Program
QR . . . . Quick Reaction
QRA . . . . Quick Reaction Alert
QRC . . . . Quick Reaction Capability (Electronics)
QRP . . . . Quick Reaction Program
QRV . . . . Quick Release Valve
QED . . . . Quick Text Editor
QWL . . . . Quick Weight Loss
Q4V . . . . Quicker for Victory (World War II)
QIP . . . . Quiescat In Pace (May He or She Rest in Peace)
QA . . . . Quiescent Aerial
QPS . . . . Quiescent Power Supply
QPSC . . . . . . Quiescent Power Supply Current
Q . . . . Quiescit (He Rests)
QT . . . . Quiet (or Sub Rosa, as, "On the QT")
QAVC . . . . . . Quiet Automatic Volume Control
QB . . . . Quiet Birdmen (An organization)
QEL . . . . Quiet Extended Life
QSY . . . . Quiet Sun Year
QUI . . . . Quincy R. R. (AAR code)
QAP . . . . Quinine, Atebrin, Plasmoquine (Treatment for malaria)
Q . . . . Quintal (Unit of weight)
Q . . . . Quire (Measure of paper)
QBI . . . . Quite Bloody Impossible (British slang, applied particularly to flying conditions)
QM . . . . Quo Modo (In What Manner)
QED . . . . Quod Erat Demonstrandum (Which Was the Thing to Be Proved)
QEF . . . . Quod Erat Faciendum (Which Was to Be Made, or Done)
QEI . . . . Quod Erat Inveniendum (Which Was to Be Found Out)
QE . . . . Quod Est (Which Is)
QV . . . . Quod Vide or Quod Videte (Which See)
QUP . . . . Quonset Point (Navy)
QH . . . . Quorn Hounds
QCI . . . . Quota Club International
QI . . . . Quota International
QS . . . . Quota Source
QR . . . . Quotation Request

R

R . . . . Rabbi
RAA . . . . Rabbinical Alliance of America
RA . . . . Rabbinical Assembly
RCA . . . . Rabbinical Council of America
RAS . . . . Rabbonim Aid Society
RKKA . . . . . . Raboche-Krest'ianskaia Krasnaia Armiia (Workers' and Peasants' Red
              Army) (Redesignated Soviety Army) (USSR)
RRF . . . . Racing Research Fund
RAM . . . . RADAR Absorbing Material
RAVE . . . . . . RADAR Acquisition Visual-Tracking Equipment
RAMPART . . . . RADAR Advanced Measurements Program for Analysis of Reentry
              Techniques (ARPA - Raytheon)
RARAD . . . . . RADAR Advisory
RAS . . . . RADAR Advisory Service
RAP . . . . RADAR Aim Point
RATCC . . . . . RADAR Air Traffic Control Center
RADVS . . . . . RADAR Altimeter Doppler Velocity Sensor
RAWS . . . . . . RADAR Altimeter Warning Set
RATAC . . . . . RADAR Analog Target Acquisition Computer
RADU . . . . . . RADAR Analysis and Detection Unit (Weather Bureau)
RAPCON . . . . . RADAR Approach Control
RATCC . . . . . RADAR Approach Control Center (Navy)
RADATA . . . . RADAR Automatic Data Transmission Assembly
RACON . . . . . RADAR Beacon
RADON . . . . . RADAR Beacon
RB . . . . RADAR Beacon
YH . . . . RADAR Beacon (Maps and charts)
YK . . . . RADAR Beacon (Maps and charts)
RBA . . . . RADAR Beacon Antenna
RBS . . . . RADAR Bomb Scoring
RBS . . . . RADAR Bombsight
RBDE . . . . . . RADAR Bright Display Equipment (FAA)
RCD . . . . RADAR Cloud Detection Report (Aviation)
RCDNE . . . . . RADAR Cloud Detection Report No Echoes Observed (Meteorology)
RCDNA . . . . RADAR Cloud Detection Report Not Available (Meteorology)
R . . . . RADAR Contact (A diagonal line through R indicates RADAR service
              terminated. A cross through R indicates RADAR contact lost.)
              (Aviation)
RCO . . . . RADAR Control Officer
RCS . . . . RADAR Control Ship
RCT . . . . RADAR Control Trailer
RADCM . . . . . RADAR Countermeasures and Deception (Military)
RCDC . . . . . . RADAR Course-Directing Center
RCI . . . . RADAR Coverage Indicator
RCS . . . . RADAR Cross Section
RD . . . . RADAR Data
RADCON . . . . RADAR Data Converter
RDPC . . . . . . RADAR Data Processing Center
RDPE . . . . . . RADAR Data Processing Equipment
RADAT . . . . . RADAR Data Transmission
RDB . . . . RADAR Decoy Balloon (Air Force)
RADEP . . . . . RADAR Departure
RD . . . . RADAR Display
RADIST . . . . . RADAR Distance Indicator
RADOME . . . . RADAR Dome (NASA)
RADAN . . . . . RADAR Doppler Automatic Navigator
READ . . . . . . RADAR Echo Augmentation Device
RESS . . . . . . RADAR Echo Simulation Study (or Subsystem)
REST . . . . . . RADAR Electronic Scan Technique
REB . . . . RADAR Evaluation Branch (ADC)
REP . . . . RADAR Evaluation Pod (Spacecraft)
RAFAX . . . . . RADAR Facsimile Transmission
RGS . . . . RADAR Ground Stabilization

YJ . . . . RADAR Homing Beacon (Maps and charts)
RHB . . . . RADAR Homing Bomb (Air Force)
RHAW . . . . . . RADAR Homing and Warning System
RIP . . . . RADAR Identification Point
RIC . . . . RADAR Indicating Console (FAA)
RINAL . . . . . RADAR Inertial Altimeter
RI . . . . RADAR Input
RIC . . . . RADAR Input Control
RICMO . . . . . RADAR Input Countermeasures Officer (Air Force)
RID . . . . RADAR Input Drum
RICMT . . . . . RADAR Inputs Countermeasures Technician
RIT . . . . RADAR Inputs Test
RADINT . . . . RADAR Intelligence
RIO . . . . RADAR-Intercept Officer (Navy)
RLD . . . . RADAR Laydown Delivery
RLS . . . . RADAR Line of Sight
RLADD . . . . . RADAR Low Angle Drogue Delivery
RMM . . . . . . RADAR Map Matching
RM . . . . RADAR Mapper
RML . . . . . . RADAR Mapper, Long Range
RAMP . . . . . . RADAR Mapping of Panama
RAMARK . . . . RADAR Marker (Military)
RML . . . . . . RADAR Microlink
RADAN . . . . . RADAR Navigation
RNS . . . . RADAR Netting Station
RNU . . . . RADAR Netting Unit
RNFP . . . . . . RADAR Not Functioning Properly
ROFT . . . . . . RADAR Off Target
ROBEPS . . . . . RADAR Operating Below Prescribed Standards
RO . . . . RADAR Operator
RADOP . . . . . RADAR/Optical Weapons (Military)
ROB . . . . RADAR Order of Battle
ROCP . . . . . . RADAR Out of Commission for Parts (ADC)
RPA . . . . RADAR Performance Analyzer
DDR . . . . RADAR Picket Destroyer (Navy symbol)
DER . . . . RADAR Picket Escort Vessel (Navy symbol)
AGR . . . . RADAR Picket Ship (Navy symbol)
SSR . . . . RADAR Picket Submarine (Navy symbol)
SSRN . . . . . . RADAR Picket Submarine (Nuclear powered) (Navy symbol)
RPC . . . . RADAR Planning Chart
RPD . . . . RADAR Planning Device
RPP . . . . RADAR Power Programmer
RPI . . . . RADAR Precipitation Integrator (USWB)
RPC . . . . RADAR Processing Center
RQC . . . . RADAR Quality Control
RRIC . . . . . . RADAR Repeater Indicator Console
RAREP . . . . . . RADAR Report
RRE . . . . RADAR Research Establishment (British)
RSBS . . . . . . RADAR Safety Beacon System
RSC . . . . RADAR Set Control
RSA . . . . RADAR Signature Analysis (Air Force)
RADRON . . . . RADAR Squadron (Air Force)
RSH . . . . RADAR Status History
ROT . . . . RADAR on Target
RTIP . . . . RADAR Target Identification Point
RTM . . . . RADAR Target Materiel
RTMS . . . . . . RADAR Target Measuring System
RATSCAT . . . . RADAR Target Scatter Site (RADAR program)
RTS . . . . RADAR Target Simulator
RATAN . . . . . RADAR and Television Aid to Navigation
RTC . . . . RADAR Tracking Center (or Control)
RTEM . . . . . . RADAR Tracking Error Measurement
RTS . . . . RADAR Tracking Station (Military)

RAVEC . . . . . . RADAR Vector
RAWARC . . . . . RADAR and Warning Coordination (Teletypewriter circuit)
RAWIN . . . . . . RADAR Wind Sounding
RD . . . . RADARman (Navy rating)
RDM . . . . RADARman (Navy)
R . . . . Radial
RTN . . . . Radial, Tangential, Normal
RTB . . . . Radial Time Base
REC . . . . Radiant Energy Conversion
RHCI . . . . . . Radiant Heating and Cooling Institute
J . . . . Radiant Intensity (Symbol)
RADFAC . . . . . Radiating Facility
RAD . . . . Radiation Absorbed Dose (Unit of measurement of radiation energy)
RAMP . . . . . . Radiation Airborne Measurement Program
RAI . . . . Radiation Applications, Incorporated
RBL . . . . Radiation Biology Laboratory (Smithsonian Institution)
RACC . . . . . . Radiation and Contamination Control
RCL . . . . Radiation Counter Laboratories, Inc.
RD . . . . Radiation Detection
RADOSE . . . . . Radiation Dosimeter Satellite (NASA)
REIC . . . . . . Radiation Effects Information Center (Battelle Memorial Institute)
RER . . . . Radiation Effects Reactor (Air Force)
REMAB . . . . . Radiation Equivalent Manikin Absorption
REMCAL . . . . . Radiation Equivalent Manikin Calibration
RADEX . . . . . Radiation Exclusion Plot (Chart of actual or predicted fallout)
RADHAZ . . . . . Radiation Hazards
RIDL . . . . . . Radiation Instrument Development Laboratory
RL . . . . Radiation Laboratory
RMC . . . . Radiation Material Corporation
RM . . . . Radiation Measurement
RPL . . . . Radiation Physics Laboratory (National Bureau of Standards)
RPG . . . . Radiation Protection Guide (AEC)
RRS . . . . Radiation Research Society
RR . . . . Radiation Response
RSIC . . . . . . Radiation Shielding Information Center (ORNL)
RSN . . . . Radiation Surveillance Network (Public Health Service)
RTT . . . . Radiation Tracking Transducer
R . . . . Radical
REP . . . . Radical Education Project
RSIS . . . . Radical Science Information Service (News service attempting to interrelate radical politics and scientific issues)
R . . . . Radio
RAR . . . . Radio Acoustic Ranging
RAB . . . . Radio Advertising Bureau
RAMSA . . . . . Radio Aeronautics Mexicana, SA
RAMNAC . . . . . Radio Aids to Marine Navigation Committee (British)
RACES . . . . . . Radio Amateur Civil Emergency Service (Civil Defense)
RASER . . . . . . Radio Amplification by Stimulated Emission of Radiation
RAO . . . . Radio Astronomical Observatory
RAE . . . . Radio Astronomy Explorer (Satellite)
RAM . . . . Radio Attenuation Measurement (Spacecraft for testing communications)
RAFAR . . . . . . Radio Automated Facsimile and Reproduction
R/B . . . . Radio Beacon
RCK . . . . Radio Check (Aviation)
RCC . . . . Radio-Chemical Center
RCA . . . . Radio Club of America
RC . . . . Radio Code Aptitude Area
RCTSR . . . . . . Radio Code Test, Speed of Response
RCS . . . . Radio Command System
RCC . . . . Radio Common Channels
RACFI . . . . . . Radio and Communication Facilities Inoperative
RC . . . . Radio Compass
RCAT . . . . . . Radio Controlled Aerial Target
RCM . . . . Radio-Controlled Mine (Military)
RCA . . . . Radio Corporation of America (NYSE symbol)
RCAC . . . . . . Radio Corporation of America Communications
RCM . . . . Radio (or RADAR) Countermeasures
RADAL . . . . . Radio Detection and Location
RADAR . . . . . Radio Detection and Ranging
RDF . . . . Radio Direction Finder (or Finding)
RDFSTA . . . . . Radio Direction Finder Station
DFING . . . . . . Radio Direction-Finding (Military)
RDI . . . . Radio Doppler Inertial
RS . . . . Radio Duties – Special
RE . . . . Radio Electrician
RELE . . . . . . Radio Electrician
RETMA . . . . . Radio-Electronics-Television Manufacturers Association (Later, Electronic Industries Association)
REACT . . . . . . Radio Emergency Associated Citizens Team (Citizen ham radio volunteers in law enforcement)
RESCU . . . . . . Radio Emergency Search Communications Unit

REINS . . . . . . Radio-Equipped Inertial Navigation System
RFC . . . . Radio Facility Charts
RFP . . . . Radio Finger Printing (Identification of wireless radio operators by individual keying characteristics)
RFE . . . . Radio Free Europe
RF . . . . Radio Frequency
RFA . . . . Radio Frequency Amplifier
RFA . . . . Radio Frequency Attenuator
RFA . . . . Radio Frequency Authorizations (Air Force)
RFC . . . . Radio Frequency Chart
RFC . . . . Radio-Frequency Choke (Electronics)
RFCP . . . . . . Radio Frequency Compatibility Program
RFI . . . . Radio Frequency Interference
RFL . . . . Radio-Frequency Laboratories
RFTS . . . . . . Radio Frequency Test Set
RGS . . . . Radio Guidance System
RI . . . . Radio Inertial
RIGS . . . . . . Radio Inertial Guidance System
RI . . . . Radio Influence
RIV . . . . Radio-Influence Voltage
RIT . . . . Radio Information Test
RI . . . . Radio Inspector
RID . . . . Radio Intelligence Division (of the Federal Communications Commission)
RI . . . . Radio Interference
RIFI . . . . . . Radio Interference Field Intensity
RIFI . . . . . . Radio-Interference-Free Instrument
RIL . . . . Radio Interference Level
RIPS . . . . . . Radio Isotope Power System
RKO . . . . Radio-Keith-Orpheum (Motion picture production and exhibition firm, also active in broadcasting)
RLCS . . . . . . Radio Launch Control System
RLC . . . . Radio Liberty Committee
RLTS . . . . . . Radio Linked Telemetry System
RMI . . . . Radio Magnetic Indicator
RMA . . . . Radio Manufacturers Association
RMO . . . . Radio (or RADAR) Material Office (Navy)
RM . . . . Radio Monitor
RN . . . . Radio Navigation
RIT . . . . Radio Network for Inter-American Telecommunications
RNTWPA . . . . . Radio-Newsreel-Television Working Press Association
RNIT . . . . . . Radio Noise Interference Test
RNV . . . . Radio Noise Voltage
RADNOTE . . . . Radio Note (Military)
RADOP . . . . . . Radio Operator (Navy)
RO . . . . Radio Operator
ROA . . . . Radio Operator's Aptitude Test (Military)
ROAT . . . . . . Radio Operator's Aptitude Test
ROI . . . . Radio, Optical, Inertial
R & P SEC . . . Radio and Panel Section (Navy)
RPU . . . . Radio Phone Unit (Navy)
RADPLANBD . . Radio Planning Board (Navy)
RADPROPCAST . Radio Propagation Forecast
RPU . . . . Radio Propagation Unit (Army)
RADIQUAD . . . Radio Quadrangle (Military)
RARU . . . . . . Radio Range Station Reported Unreliable (Message abbreviation)
RDO . . . . Radio Readout
RR . . . . Radio Regulations
RADREL . . . . . Radio Relay
RRL . . . . Radio Research Laboratories (Japan)
RRS . . . . Radio Research Station (British)
RS . . . . Radio Simulator
RSGB . . . . . . Radio Society of Great Britain
RSL . . . . Radio Standards Laboratory (National Bureau of Standards)
RADSTA . . . . . Radio Station
RASTA . . . . . . Radio Station (Coast Guard)
RS . . . . Radio Station (Maps and charts)
RSP . . . . Radio Switch Panel
RTCA . . . . . . Radio Technical Commission for Aeronautics
RT . . . . Radio Technician
RTST . . . . . . Radio Technician Selection Test
RT . . . . Radio Telegraphy
RTRC . . . . . . Radio Telemetry and Remote Control
RT . . . . Radio Telephone or Telephony
R/T . . . . Radio Telephony
RATT . . . . . . Radio Teletype(writer)
RTTY . . . . . . Radio Teletype
RTCA . . . . . . Radio & Television Correspondents Association
RTDG . . . . . . Radio and Television Directors Guild
RTMA . . . . . . Radio and Television Manufacturers Association
RTNDA . . . . . Radio-Television News Directors Association
RTRC . . . . . . Radio and Television Research Council

RAWIND . . . . . Radio Wind (Coast Guard)
RWI . . . . Radio Wire Integration (Military)
RWP . . . . Radio Working Party
RA . . . . Radioactive
RADA . . . . . . Radioactive
C^{14} . . . . Radioactive Carbon (Key substance for determination of age of objects by measurement of radioactivity)
$CO.^{60}$ . . . . . . Radioactive Cobalt
RFSP . . . . Radioactive Fallout Study Program (Canada)
RHD . . . . Radioactive Health Data
RAI . . . . Radioactive Interference (NASA)
RISA . . . . . . Radioactive Iodinated Serum Albumin (Medicine)
I^{131} . . . . Radioactive Iodine
FE^{59} . . . . Radioactive Iron
P^{32} . . . . Radioactive Phosphorus
NA^{24} . . . . Radioactive Sodium
S^{35} . . . . Radioactive Sulphur
RCG . . . . Radioactivity Concentrate Guide (Formerly MPC - Maximum Permissible Concentration) (AEC)
RADIAC . . . . . Radioactivity Detection, Indication, and Computation (Radiological measuring instruments)
RBN . . . . Radiobeacon (Maps and charts)
RKG . . . . Radiocardiogram
RGAA . . . . . . Radiochemical Gamma Activation Analysis
RNAA . . . . . . Radiochemical Neutron Activation Analysis
RTF . . . . Radiodiffusion-Television Francaise (French radio and television)
REG . . . . Radioencephalogram
RIFS . . . . Radioisotope Field Support
RIM . . . . Radioisotope Medicine
RPDL . . . . . . Radioisotope Process Development Laboratory (ORNL)
RTG . . . . Radioisotope Thermoelectric Generator
RL . . . . Radiolocation
RAIC . . . . . . Radiological Accident and Incident Control
RAP . . . . Radiological Assistance Plan (AEC)
RADLCEN . . . . Radiological Center
RCBW . . . . . . Radiological Chemical Biological Warfare
RCC . . . . Radiological Control Center (Army)
RADDEF . . . . . Radiological Defense (Army)
RADLDEF . . . . Radiological Defense (Military)
RDL . . . . Radiological Defense Laboratory (Navy)
RADLO . . . . . Radiological Defense Officer
REAT . . . . . . Radiological Emergency Assistance Team (AEC)
REMT . . . . . . Radiological Emergency Medical Teams
RADFO . . . . . Radiological Fallout
RHL . . . . Radiological Health Laboratory
RADLMON . . . Radiological Monitor(ing)
RAMONT . . . . Radiological Monitoring
RADLOP . . . . Radiological Operations
YRR . . . . Radiological Repair Barge (Navy symbol)
RADLSAFE . . . Radiological Safety (Military)
RSNA . . . . . . Radiological Society of North America
RADLSV . . . . Radiological Survey
RADLSO . . . . Radiological Survey Officer
RADLWAR . . . Radiological Warfare (Military)
RADWAR . . . . Radiological Warfare
RW . . . . Radiological Warfare
RM . . . . Radioman (Navy)
RPF . . . . Radiometer Performance Factor
RP . . . . Radioplane Company
RAVU . . . . . . Radiosonde Analysis and Verification Unit
RABAR . . . . . Radiosonde Balloon Release
RABAL . . . . . Radiosonde Balloon Wind Data
RAOB . . . . . . Radiosonde Observation
RADAT . . . . . Radiosonde Observation Data
RAWINSONDE . . Radiosonde and RADAR Wind Sounding (Upper air observation)
RATG . . . . . . Radiotelegraph
RTG . . . . Radiotelegraph
RATEL . . . . . . Radiotelephone
RTF . . . . Radiotelephone
RATELO . . . . Radiotelephone Operator
RTT . . . . Radioteletypewriter
RAI . . . . Radiotelevisione Italiana (Italian government-controlled radio and television company)
Ra . . . . Radium (Chemical element)
RE . . . . Radium Emanation
RPA . . . . Radium Plaque Adaptometer (Navy)
RPAO . . . . . . Radium Plaque Adaptometer Operator (Navy)
R . . . . Radius
R/A . . . . Radius of Action (Air Force)
Rn . . . . Radon (Chemical element)
RCC . . . . Rag Chewers' Club (Amateur radio)

RV . . . . Rahway Valley R. R. (AAR code)
RP . . . . Raid Plotter
R & C . . . . . . Rail and Canal
RDC . . . . Rail Diesel Car
R & L . . . . . . Rail and Lake
RL & R . . . . . Rail, Lake, and Rail
R & O . . . . . . Rail and Ocean
RSBA . . . . . . Rail Steel Bar Association
RTO . . . . Rail Transportation Officer(r) (Military)
RTA . . . . Rail Travel Authorization (Military)
RTPA . . . . . . Rail Travel Promotion Agency
RHO . . . . Railhead Officer (Military)
R . . . . Railroad (or Railway)
RR . . . . Railroad
RAWB . . . . . . Railroad and Airline Wage Board (Terminated, 1953)
RED . . . . Railroad Employees' Department (of AFL-CIO)
RRE . . . . Railroad Enthusiasts
REA . . . . Railroad Evangelistic Association
RIU . . . . Railroad Insurance Underwriters
RPRA . . . . . . Railroad Public Relations Association
RRB . . . . Railroad Retirement Board
RTU . . . . Railroad Telegraphers Union
RYA . . . . Railroad Yardmasters of America
RYNA . . . . . . Railroad Yardmasters of North America
RROA . . . . . . Railroadians of America
RW . . . . Rail-Water (Shipping)
RWR . . . . Rail-Water-Rail (Shipping)
RAWU . . . . . . Railway African Mineworkers Trade Union (Southern Rhodesia)
RAU . . . . Railway African Union
RESMA . . . . . Railway Electric Supply Manufacturers Association
REMSA . . . . . Railway Engineering Maintenance Suppliers Association
REA . . . . Railway Express Agency (Later, REA Express)
RF & OOA . . . Railway Fuel & Operating Officers Association
RYGD . . . . . . Railway Grand Division
RISA . . . . Railway and Industrial Spring Association
RIRB . . . . Railway Insurance Rating Bureau
RLEA . . . . . . Railway Labor Executives Association
RLPL . . . . . . Railway Labor's Political League
RLHS . . . . . . Railway and Locomotive Historical Society
RMS . . . . Railway Mail Service
RPU . . . . Railway Patrolmen's International Union
RPO . . . . Railway Post Office
RPI . . . . Railway Progress Institute
RSCSA . . . . . Railway Signal and Communications Suppliers Association
RSO . . . . Railway Sorting Office
RSO . . . . Railway Suboffice
RSA . . . . Railway Supply Association
RSMA . . . . . . Railway Supply Manufacturers Association
RSMA . . . . . . Railway Systems and Management Association
RSPA . . . . . . Railway Systems and Procedures Association
RTTAA . . . . . Railway Telegraph and Telephone Appliance Association
RTA . . . . Railway Tie Association
RTO . . . . Railway Traffic Officer
RTM . . . . Railway Transfer of Minneapolis (AAR code)
RWA . . . . Railway Wheel Association
RUM . . . . Railwaymen's Union of Malaya
R . . . . Rain (Weather reports)
RA . . . . Rain (Meteorology)
RHIB . . . . Rain and Hail Insurance Bureau
RW . . . . Rain Showers (Meteorology)
RABR . . . . . . Rainbow Bridge National Monument
RRR . . . . Raleigh Research Reactor
RP . . . . Rally Point (Air Force)
RVW . . . . Ralph Vaughn Williams (British composer, 1872-1958)
RAL . . . . Ralston Purina Company (NYSE symbol)
RARE . . . . . . Ram Air Rocket Engine
RAT . . . . Ram Air Turbine
RJ . . . . Ramjet
RCK . . . . Ramp Check (Aviation)
RCL . . . . Ramped Cargo Lighter
RDB . . . . Ramped Dump Barge
RNI . . . . Ranco Incorporated (NYSE symbol)
RAFB . . . . . . Randolph Air Force Base
RACE . . . . . . Random Access Computer Equipment
RAX . . . . Random Access Computing System (Data processing)
RACEP . . . . . Random Access and Correlation for Extended Performance
RADEM . . . . . Random Access Delta Modulation
RADA . . . . . . Random Access Discrete Address (Army division-level battlefield radio communications system)
RADAS . . . . . Random Access Discrete Address System
RADIR . . . . . Random Access Document Indexing and Retrieval

RAI . . . . Random Access and Inquiry
RAM . . . . Random Access Memory (Data processing)
RAMAC. . . . . . Random Access or Memory Accounting
RAMAC . . . . Random Access Method of Accounting and Control (Data processing)
RANDAM . . . . Random-Access Nondestructive Advanced Memory
RAPPI . . . . . . Random Access Plan-Position Indicator (Air Force)
RAPCOE . . . . Random Access Programming and Checkout Equipment
RASTAC . . . . . Random Access Storage and Control (Data processing)
RASTAD . . . . . Random Access Storage and Display (Data processing)
RAMD. . . . . . . Random Accessory Memory Device
RBS . . . . Random Barrage System
RANCOM . . . . Random Communication Satellite
RCSS . . . . Random Communication Satellite System
RD . . . . Random Drift
RH . . . . Random House, Inc. (NYSE symbol)
RHD . . . . Random House Dictionary
RL . . . . Random Lengths (Lumber)
RW . . . . Random Widths (Lumber)
ROCKET . . . . . Rand's Omnibus Calculator of the Kinetics of Earth Trajectories
R . . . . Range
RAZEL . . . . . . Range, Azimuth and Elevation
RAET . . . . . . Range, Azimuth, Elevation, and Time
RAZON . . . . . Range and Azimuth Only
RCC . . . . Range Control Center
RC . . . . Range Correction
RDMU. . . . . . . Range-Drift Measuring Unit
REGAL . . . . . . Range and Elevation Guidance for Approach and Landing (Aviation)
REEP . . . . . . Range Estimating and Evaluation Procedure (Data processing)
RF . . . . Range-Finder (Gunnery)
RHI . . . . Range-Height Indicator (RADAR)
RHINO . . . . . . Range Height Indicator Not Operating (Aviation)
RI . . . . Range Instrumentation
RICS. . . . . Range Instrumentation Control System
RIDD . . . . Range Instrumentation Development Division
RIPS . . . . Range Instrumentation Planning Study (AFSC)
RIS . . . . Range Instrumentation Ship
RISS . . . . Range Instrumentation and Support Systems
ROJ . . . . Range on Jamming
RKO. . . . . Range Keeper Operator (Navy)
RM. . . . . Range Marks
RMAX. . . . . . Range, Maximum
ROM . . . . Range of Movement
ROMOTAR. . . . Range-Only Measurement of Trajectory and Recording
ROR . . . . Range Only RADAR
ROPS . . . . . . Range Operation Performance Summary
ROMACC . . . . Range Operational Monitoring and Control Center
ROO . . . . Range Operations Officer
REP . . . . Range Probable Error (Formerly, Range Error Probable) (Air Force)
RRI . . . . Range Rate Indicator
RSDS . . . . . . Range Safety Destruct System
RSLA . . . . Range Safety Launch Approval
RSO . . . . Range Safety Officer
RSS . . . . Range Safety System
RS . . . . Range Selector
RSSP . . . . Range Single Shot Probability (Military)
R/S . . . . Range Surveillance
ROTS . . . . . . Range on Target Signal
RTAG . . . . . . Range Technical Advisory Group
RTC . . . . Range Telemetry Central (Aerospace)
YF . . . . Range Tender (Navy Symbol)
RTD . . . . Range Time Decoder
RTS . . . . Range Time Signal
RTOT . . . . . . Range Track on Target (Air Force)
RT . . . . Range Tracking
RU . . . . Range User
RBA . . . . Ranger Battalions Association
RT . . . . Ranger Tab (Army)
RAVEN . . . . . Ranging and Velocity Navigation
R . . . . Rank
RHIP. . . . . . . Rank Has Its Privileges (Military slang)
RHIR . . . . Rank Has Its Responsibilities (Military slang)
R. . . . . Rankine (Temperature)
RATA . . . . . . Rankine Cycle Air Turboaccelerator
REO. . . . . . . Ransom E. Olds Co. (Automobile)
RAD . . . . Rapid Access Disk
RANDID . . . . Rapid Alphanumeric Digital Indicating Device
RAM . . . . Rapid Area Maintenance (Air Force)
RASS . . . . . . Rapid Area Supply Support (Military)
RATS . . . . . . Rapid Area Transportation Support (Air Force)
RACE . . . . . . Rapid Automatic Checkout Equipment
RAMIS . . . . . . Rapid Automatic Malfunction Isolation System

RACOMS . . . . Rapid Combat Mapping System (Military)
RADAC. . . . . . Rapid Digital Automatic Computing
RED HORSE . . Rapid Engineer Development, Heavy Operational Repair Squadron, Engineering (Air Force)
REM . . . . Rapid Eye Movement
REMS . . . . Rapid Eye Movement State
RF . . . . Rapid-Fire
RFG . . . . Rapid-Fire Gun
RITE . . . . Rapid Information Technique for Evaluation
RIPFCOMTF . . . Rapid Item Processor to Facilitate Complex Operations on Magnetic Tape Files (Data processing)
RPR . . . . Rapid Plasma Reagin (Card test) (for venereal disease)
RR . . . . Rapid Rectilinear
RAPTUS. . . . . . Rapid Thorium-Uranium-Sodium (Nuclear reactor)
RTX . . . . Rapid Transit Experimental (Gas-turbine bus)
RTM. . . . . Rapid Tuning Magnetron
R. . . . . Rare (When applied to species)
RBPCA. . . . . . Rare Breeds Poultry Club of America
RE . . . . Rare Earth
REE . . . . Rare-Earth Elements
REO . . . . Rare Earth Oxide
RR . . . . Rarely Reversed (Decisions in law)
RR . . . . Raritan River R. R. (AAR code)
RCM. . . . . . . Rassemblement Chretien de Madagascar (Christian Rally of Madagascar)
RC . . . . Rassemblement Congolais (Congolese Rally) (Buakvu)
RDA . . . . Rassemblement Democratique Africain (African Democratic Rally)
RDD . . . . Rassemblement Democratique Dahomeen (Dahomean Democratic Rally)
RADER . . . . . Rassemblement Democratique du Ruanda (Democratic Rally of Ruanda)
RGR . . . . Rassemblement de Gauche Republicain (Assembly of the Republican Left) (French political party)
RGDU. . . . . . Rassemblement General pour le Desarmement Universel
RJT . . . . Rassemblement des Jeunes Togolais (Togolese Youth Rally)
RJDA . . . . . . Rassemblement des Jeunesses Democratiques Africaines (Rally of African Democratic Youth)
RK . . . . Rassemblement Katangais (Katanga Rally) (Elisabethville)
RNM . . . . . . Rassemblement National Malagache (National Malagasy Rally)
RNP . . . . Rassemblement National Populaire (France)
RAPECA . . . . Rassemblement du Peuple Camerounais (Camerounese People's Rally)
RPF . . . . Rassemblement du Peuple Francais (Rally of the French People)
RGW . . . . . . Rat fuer Gegenseitige Wirtschaftshilfe
RIFC. . . . . . . Rat Intrinsic Factor Concentrate
RU . . . . Rat Unit
RATC . . . . . . Rate-Aided Tracking Computer
RA . . . . Rate of Application
RC . . . . Rate of Change
R/C . . . . Rate of Climb
REL . . . . Rate of Energy Loss
RE . . . . Rate of Exchange
RGP . . . . Rate Gyro Package
RPM . . . . Rate Per Minute
RQS . . . . Rate Quoting System
R & R . . . . . . Rate and Rhythm (of pulse)
RSCS . . . . . . Rate Stabilization and Control System
RATS . . . . . . Rate and Track Subsystem
ROT . . . . Rate of Turn
RHP . . . . Rated Horsepower
RV . . . . Rated Voltage
RMS. . . . . . . Rathkamp Matchcover Society
R . . . . Ratio
RCC. . . . . . . Ratio of Charges to Costs
RT . . . . Ratio Transformer
RDP . . . . Ration Distributing Point (Military)
R-EP . . . . . . Rational-Emotive Psychotherapy (Also known as R-ET and RT)
R-ET. . . . . . . Rational-Emotive Psychotherapy (Also known as R-EP and RT)
RT . . . . Rational Therapy (Short form for rational-emotive psychotherapy) (Also known as R-ET and R-EP)
RMIA . . . . . . Rattan Manufacturers and Importers Association
RS . . . . Rauwolfia Serpentina
RM . . . . Raw Material
RME . . . . Raw Materials
RW . . . . Raw Water (Technical drawings)
RAY. . . . . . . Raybestos-Manhattan, Inc. (NYSE symbol)
RII . . . . Raymond International, Incorporated (NYSE symbol)
RMCO . . . . . . Raymond Manufacturing Company
RNR. . . . . . . Rayonier Inc. (NYSE symbol)
R. . . . . Rays
RABAR . . . . . Raytheon Advanced Battery Acquisition RADAR
RAM . . . . Raytheon Airborne Microwave
RAMP. . . . . . Raytheon Airborne Microwave Platform (Sky station)
RAY-COM. . . . Raytheon Communications Equipment (Citizens band radiotelephone)
RTN. . . . . . . Raytheon Company (NYSE symbol)

RAYCI	Raytheon Controlled Inventory (Data processing)
RMC	Raytheon Manufacturing Company
RAYSISTOR	Raytheon Resistor (Electro-optical control device)
RAYSPAN	Raytheon Spectrum Analyzer
RAY-TEL	Raytheon Telephone (Citizens band radio)
RCA	Reach Cruising Altitude (Aviation)
RCALT	Reach(ed) Cruising Altitude (Aviation)
RSS	Reactant Service System
RCS	Reaction Control System (Apollo) (NASA)
De R	Reaction of Degeneration (Neurology)
DR	Reaction of Degeneration (Physiology)
RD	Reaction of Degeneration
RMI	Reaction Motors, Incorporated
RRS	Reaction Research Society
RT	Reaction Time
RFM	Reactive Factor Meter
RKVA	Reactive Kilovolt-Ampere
VAR	Reactive Volt-Ampere
RVA	Reactive Volt-Ampere Meter
RVM	Reactive Voltmeter
RMF	Reactivity Measurement Facility (AEC)
RCN	Reactor Centrum Nederland (Atomic power) (Netherlands)
RDD	Reactor Development Division (of AEC)
RIFT	Reactor-in-Flight Test (NASA)
R-MAD	Reactor Maintenance, Assembly, and Disassembly (AEC)
RPCC	Reactor Physics Constants Center (Argonne National Laboratory)
RA	Read Amplifier
RB	Read Back (Communications)
RB	Read Buffer
RCC	Read Channel Continue
RCI	Read Channel Initialize
RC	Read and Compute
R & D	Read and Destroy
RF	Read Forward
ROM	Read-Only Memory (Data processing)
ROS	Read-Only Store (Data processing)
RPR	Read Printer
RTD	Read Tape Decimal
RWC	Read, Write, and Compute
RWC	Read-Write-Continue
RWI	Read-Write-Initialize
RST	Readability, Strength, Tone
RC	Reader Code
RCC	Reader Common Contact
RCR	Reader Control Relay
REA	Reader R. R. (AAR code)
RTC	Reader Tape Contact
3R	Readin', Ritin', and Rithmetic
RRR	Readin', Ritin', and Rithmetic
REDCAPE	Readiness Capability (Military)
REDCON	Readiness Condition (Military)
RD	Readiness Date
RFAED	Readiness Forecast Authorization Equipment Data (Air Force)
REIS	Readiness Information System (Army)
REDCAT	Readiness Requirement (Military)
RDG	Reading Company (NYSE symbol and AAR code)
RE	Reading-Ease (Score) (Advertising)
RL	Reading List
RdQ	Reading Quotient
RRF	Reading Reform Foundation
RS	Reading of Standard
RT	Reading Test
RU	Reading of Unknown
RV	Reading and Vocabulary Test (Also, RVT) (Military)
RVT	Reading and Vocabulary Test (Also, RV) (Military)
READJP	Readjustment Pay
RR	Readout and Relay
RC	Ready Calendar
RFI	Ready for Issue
RMD	Ready Money Down (Means immediate payment)
RQS	Ready Qualified for Standby
RRPS	Ready Reinforcement Personnel Section (Air Force)
RRAF	Ready Reserve of the Armed Forces
RRMRP	Ready Reserve Mobilization Reinforcement Pool (Army)
RRMRS	Ready Reserve Mobilization Reinforcement System
RRSTRAF	Ready Reserve Strategic Army Forces
RFS	Ready for Sea (Navy)
RFTO	Ready for Takeoff (Aviation)
RAW	Ready and Waiting (Slang)
RG	Reagent Grade
R	Real

BIA	Real-Aerovias Brasil (Airline)
ABR	Real-Aerovias Brasil, SA (Brazilian international airline)
RE	Real Estate
REC	Real Estate Council
REIT	Real Estate Investment Trust (Generic term)
REO	Real Estate Owned (Banking)
REPR	Real Estate Planning Report (Military)
RP	Real Property
RPIE	Real Property Installed Equipment (Air Force)
RT	Real Time
RADOT	Real-Time Automatic Digital Optical Tracker (NASA)
RTC	Real-Time Command (Data processing)
REALCOM	Real-Time Communications (RCA)
RCC	Real-Time Computer Complex
RTCC	Real-Time Computer Complex
RTCU	Real-Time Control Unit
RTDD	Real-Time Data Distribution
RTDHS	Real-Time Data Handling System
RTD	Real-Time Display
READ	Real-Time Electronic Access and Display (System)
REX	Real Time Executive Routine (Data processing)
RIOT	Real-Time Input-Output Transducer (Translator)
RTTDS	Real-Time Telemetry Data System
RTTV	Real-Time Television
RSVP	Really Sexy Vamp Pants (Slacks for evening wear by women)
R	Rear
RA	Rear Admiral
RADM	Rear Admiral
RAACEF	Rear Admiral Aircraft Carriers, Eastern Fleet (British)
RAL	Rear Admiral Alexandria (British)
RAC	Rear Admiral Commanding (British)
RACOB(WA)	Rear Admiral Commanding Combined Operational Bases (Western Approaches) (Britain)
RAD(BPF)	Rear Admiral Commanding Destroyers (British Pacific Fleet)
RA(A)EF	Rear Admiral (Administration) Eastern Fleet (British)
RAFT	Rear Admiral Fleet Train (British Pacific Fleet)
RASO	Rear Airfield Supply Organization
RADCC	Rear Area Damage Control Center
RASC/DC	Rear Area Security and Area Damage Control (Military)
RASCC	Rear Area Security Control Center
RASC	Rear Area Security Controller
RA	Rear Artillery
REMCO	Rear Echelon Maintenance Combined Operation (Military)
RV	Rear View (Technical drawings)
RCS	Rearward Communications System
RLBM	Rearward Launched Ballistic Missiles
R	Reaumur (Thermometric scale)
RCF	Recall Finder
REACK	Receipt Acknowledged
RECAU	Receipt Acknowledged and Understood
RCN	Receipt of Change Notice
RDU	Receipt and Despatch Unit (Aircraft)
ROG	Receipt of Goods
RIM	Receipt, Inspection, and Maintenance (Air Force)
RSI	Receipt, Storage, and Issue (Army)
RFG	Receive Format Generator
RO	Receive Only
R/OC	Receive Only Center
ROPP	Receive-Only Page Printer
ROTR	Receive-Only Tape Reperforator
RPCRAAIO	Receive and Process Complaints and Requests for Assistance, Advice, or Information Only (Army)
RT	Receive-Transmit (Radio)
R	Received
RBDNRQ	Received But Did Not Return Questionnaire
RNB	Received, Not Billed
R	Received Solid (Amateur radio)
RIT	Receiver Incremental Tuning
RM	Receiver, Mobile
RNF	Receiver Noise Figure
ROTCC	Receiver-Off-Hook Tone Connecting Circuit
RONLY	Receiver Only (Radio)
ROC	Receiver Operating Characteristics
RS	Receiver Station
RTM	Receiver-Transmitter-Modulator
Q	Receivership or Bankruptcy (Designation used with NYSE symbols)
RAMD	Receiving Agency Materiel Division (Military)
RAMIS	Receiving, Assembly Maintenance, Inspection, Storage (Military)
RBOF	Receiving Basins for Off-Site Fuels (AEC)
RM	Receiving Memo
RO	Receiving Office(r)

RON . . . . Receiving Only
ROMON . . . . . Receiving-Only Monitor
RPROP . . . . . . Receiving Proficiency Pay (Military)
RS . . . . Receiving Ship or Station
RECSTA. . . . . . Receiving Station
RSG . . . . Receiving Stolen Goods
RSP. . . . . Receiving Stolen Property
RC . . . . Reception Center (Army)
RF . . . . Reception Fair (Radio logs)
RG . . . . Reception Good (Radio logs)
RN . . . . Reception Nil (Radio logs)
RP . . . . Reception Poor (Radio logs)
RS . . . . Reception Station
RDE . . . . Receptor-Destroying Enzyme
RRO . . . . Rechnungslegungsordnung fuer das Reich (Germany)
R . . . . Recipe
RTA . . . . Reciprocal Trade Agreement
RMJM . . . . . . Recluse Missionaries of Jesus and Mary (Roman Catholic women's religious order)
RECOMP . . . . . Recommended Completion
RDA . . . . Recommended Dietary Allowance
RDA . . . . Recommended Duty Assignment
RGZ . . . . Recommended Ground Zero
RMOC . . . . . Recommended Maintenance Operation Chart (Army)
RP . . . . Recommended Practice
RAFT . . . . Recomp Algebraic Formula Translator (Data processing)
RECIPE . . . . . . Recomp Computer Interpretive Program Expediter
RUG . . . . Recomp Users Group (Data processing)
RAPP . . . . Reconciliation and Purification Program (Air Force)
R . . . . Reconnaissance (Designation for all US military aircraft)
RAN. . . . . Reconnaissance/Attack Navigator
RECONCO . . . Reconnaissance Company (Military)
REWSON. . . . . Reconnaissance Electronic Warfare Special Operations and Naval Intelligence Processing Systems
RCNLR . . . . . . Reconnaissance Long Range (Army)
RENMR . . . . . . Reconnaissance Medium Range (Army)
RO. . . . . Reconnaissance Officer
ROSIE. . . . . . Reconnaissance by Orbiting Ship-Identification Equipment
ARK . . . . Reconnaissance Seaplane (Russian symbol)
RSL . . . . Reconnaissance and Security Line
RSP . . . . Reconnaissance and Security Positions
RSOP . . . . Reconnaissance, Selection, and Occupation of Position (Military)
RECSQUAD . . . Reconnaissance Squadron (Army)
RS . . . . Reconnaissance Squadron (Army)
RSM . . . . Reconnaissance Strategic Missile
RS . . . . Reconnaissance-Strike (Military)
RS . . . . Reconnaissance Strip (Military)
RESTA . . . . . . Reconnaissance, Surveillance and Target Acquisition
RSO . . . . Reconnaissance and Survey Officer
RTM . . . . Reconnaissance Tactical Missile
RATS . . . . Reconnaissance and Tactical Security (Teams) (Military)
RTF . . . . Reconnaissance Task Force
RC . . . . Reconstruction Committee (British) (World War I)
RFC . . . . Reconstruction Finance Corporation (Abolished, 1957)
RFCA . . . . Reconstruction Finance Corporation Act (Obsolete)
RFCMC . . . . . . Reconstruction Finance Corporation Mortgage Company
RCN. . . . . Record Control Number
RIC . . . . Record Identification Code (Navy)
RIN . . . . Record Identification Number
RIAA . . . . . . Record Industry Association of America
ROSA . . . . Record One Stop Association
ROP. . . . . Record of Performance or Record of Production
RAIR . . . . Recordak Automated Information Retrieval (System)
RGM . . . . Recorder Group Monitor
RFB . . . . Recording for the Blind
RDM. . . . . Recording Demand Meter
RIMPTF . . . . . . Recording Industries Music Performance Trust Funds
RIRTI . . . . Recording Infrared Tracking Instrument
ROTI. . . . . Recording Optical Tracking Instruments (Missiles)
RS . . . . Recording Secretary
RC . . . . Records Check
RHA . . . . Records Holding Area
RMO . . . . Records Management Office(r) (Military)
RO. . . . . Records Office(r) (Air Force)
RFOFM . . . . . . Records for Our Fighting Men (Collected phonograph records during World War II)
RPC . . . . Records Processing Center (Veterans Administration)
RR & C . . . . . Records, Reports and Control
RWBH . . . . . . Records Will Be Handcarried (Army)
RWNBH . . . . . Records Will Not Be Handcarried (Army)
RBSS . . . . Recoverable Booster Support System

RIP. . . . . Recoverable Item Program (Marine Corps)
ROLS . . . . . . Recoverable Orbital Launch System
RAMP . . . . . . Recovered Allied Military Personnel
REBE. . . . . . . Recovery Beacon Evaluation
RCC . . . . Recovery Control Center
REP . . . . Recovery and Evacuation Program (Marine Corps)
RECGP . . . . . . Recovery Group (Air Force)
RI . . . . Recovery, Incorporated
RQ. . . . . Recovery Quotient
RR . . . . Recovery Room
RUBSG . . . . . Recovery Unit and Base Support Group (Air Force)
RECSYS . . . . . Recreation Systems Analysis (Data processing)
RW . . . . Recreation and Welfare (Navy)
RCEA . . . . . . Recreational Coach and Equipment Association
RT . . . . Recreational Therapy
RVI . . . . Recreational Vehicle Institute
RV . . . . Recreational Vehicles
RDEP . . . . . . Recruit Depot (Navy)
RI . . . . Recruit Instruction (Navy)
RRC . . . . Recruit Reception Center
RR . . . . Recruit Roll (Navy)
RC . . . . Recruiting Center
RMS. . . . . . . Recruiting Main Station (Military)
RO. . . . . Recruiting Officer (Military)
RPC . . . . Recruiting Publicity Center (Military)
RS . . . . Recruiting Service
CRUITSTA . . . . Recruiting Station
RS . . . . Recruiting Station
CRUITNOP. . . . Recruiting Station and Office of Naval Officer Procurement
RW . . . . Recruiting Warrant
RMO . . . . Recruitment and Manning Organization (WSA)
RAS . . . . Rectified Air Speed (Navigation)
RAC . . . . Rectified Alternating Current (Radio)
R . . . . Recto (Bibliography)
R . . . . Rector, Rectory
RT . . . . Recueillis Temporaires (Temporarily Taken In) (of unadoptable children) (France)
RR . . . . Recurrence Rate
R . . . . Red (Light, buoy, beacon)
RAAA . . . . . . Red Angus Association of America
RBSRA . . . . . . Red Berkshire Swine Record Association
RBC . . . . Red Blood Corpuscle or Cell (Medicine)
RBC . . . . Red Blood Count (Medicine)
RCSHSB . . . . . Red Cedar Shingle and Handsplit Shake Bureau
RC . . . . Red Cell or Corpuscle (Medicine)
RC . . . . Red China
RC . . . . Red Cross
RCA . . . . Red Cross Act
RCC . . . . Red Cross of Constantine
RCIC . . . . . . Red Cross International Committee
RE . . . . Red Edges
RFNA . . . . . . Red Fuming Nitric Acid
RG. . . . . Red-Green
ROS . . . . Red Owl Stores, Inc. (NYSE symbol)
RPCCA . . . . . . Red Poll Cattle Club of America
RRAD . . . . . . Red River Army Depot
RO. . . . . Reddish Orange
RP . . . . Reddish Purple
R . . . . Redetermination
RLA . . . . Redevelopment Land Agency (Washington, DC)
R & M . . . . . Redistribution and Marketing
RDO. . . . . . . Redistribution Order (Military)
RA . . . . Redstone Arsenal (Army)
RAIC . . . . . . Redstone Arsenal Information Center (Army)
RSIC . . . . . . Redstone Scientific Information Center (Army)
REDAS . . . . . Reduced to Apprentice Seaman (Navy)
RAR . . . . . . Reduced Aspect Ratio
REX . . . . Reduced Exoatmospheric Cross-Section
HHb . . . . Reduced Hemoglobin
RL . . . . Reduced Level
ROS . . . . Reduced Operational Status
YEH . . . . Reduced Yellow Enzyme
RF . . . . Reducing Flame
RA . . . . Reduction of Area
RIF . . . . Reduction in Force (Civil service)
RG. . . . . Reduction Gear
RNIR . . . . . . Reduction to Next Inferior Rank
REDOX . . . . . Reduction and Oxydization
RIR . . . . Reduction in Requirement (Air Force)
RT . . . . Reduction Tables
REDW . . . . . . Redwood National Park

RBI	Reed Roller Bit Company (NYSE symbol)
RAL	Reenlistment Allowance (Military)
REENLA	Reenlistment Allowance (Military)
REENLB	Reenlistment Bonus (Military)
RLTA	Reenlistment Leave Travel Allowance (Military)
R & S	Reenlistment and Separation (Military)
REDAP	Reentrant Data Processing
REA	Reentry Angle
RCS	Reentry Control System (Aerospace)
REST	Reentry Environment & Systems Technology
RFD	Reentry Flight Demonstration
RMV	Reentry Measurement Vehicle
RMIP	Reentry Measurements Instrumentation Package
REP	Reentry Physics Program
RS	Reentry System
REST	Reentry System Test Program
RESER	Reentry Systems Evaluation RADAR (Aerospace)
RTV	Reentry Test Vehicle (Air Force)
REV	Reentry Vehicle
RV	Reentry Vehicle
RVS	Reeves Brothers, Inc. (NYSE symbol)
REAC	Reeves Electronic Analog Computer
RA	Refer to Acceptor
R/A	Refer to Accepter (as, a check or draft) (Banking)
R/D	Refer to Drawer (Banking)
REURAD	Refer to Your Message (Military)
RN	Reference Noise
ROMEMO	Reference Our Memorandum
RP	Reference Pulse
RSD	Reference Services Division (of ALA)
REFURDIS	Reference Your Dispatch (Military)
REFURLTR	Reference Your Letter (Military)
RYM	Reference Your Message (Army)
RP	Refilling Point
ROV	Refined Oil of Vitriol
RIT	Refining in Transit
RSI	Reflected Signal Indication (Air Force)
RESCAN	Reflecting Satellite Communication Antenna
RDFL	Reflection Direction Finding, Low Angle
RI	Reflective Insulation (Technical drawings)
ROE	Reflector Orbital Equipment
RF	Re-Flight
RJA	Reform Jewish Appeal
RC	Reformed Church
RE	Reformed Episcopal (Church)
RECH	Reformed Episcopal Church
ROF	Reformed Ogboni Fraternity (Nigeria)
RP	Reformed Presbyterian
RPCH	Reformed Presbyterian Church
RPE	Reformed Protestant Episcopal
RS	Reformed Spelling
R	Refraction
N	Refractive Index
RI	Refractive Index
RI	Refractories Institute
AKF	Refrigerated Cargo Ship (World War II)
YFR	Refrigerated Covered Lighter (Self-Propelled) (Navy symbol)
YFRN	Refrigerated Covered Lighter (Non-Self-Propelled) (Navy symbol)
RETA	Refrigerating Engineers and Technicians Association
RACCA	Refrigeration and Air Conditioning Contractors Association-National
RRF	Refrigeration Research Foundation
RSES	Refrigeration Service Engineers Society
RTA	Refrigeration Trade Association of America
R	Refrigerator
REEFER	Refrigerator, Refrigerated or Cold Storage (Airplane, railway car, truck)
RFM	Refueling Mission (Air Force)
R & R	Refueling and Rearming (Air Force)
RF	Refunding
RFS	Regardless of Feature Size
REO	Regenerated Electrical Output
RTE	Regenerative Turboprop Engines
RCD	Regent's Canal Dock (British)
RSS	Regiae Societatis Sodalis (Fellow of the Royal Society)
RATP	Regie Autonome des Transports Parisiens
R	Regiment
RAP	Regimental Aid Post
RBH	Regimental Beachhead (Army)
RCT	Regimental Combat Team
RCM	Regimental Court-Martial
RHQ	Regimental Headquarters
RLT	Regimental Landing Team (Military)
RMO	Regimental Munitions Officer (Army)
RO	Regimental Orders (Army)
RQMS	Regimental Quartermaster-Sergeant (British)
RRL	Regimental Reserve Line
RSM	Regimental Sergeant Major (Army)
RSB	Regimental Stretcher-Bearer
RSO	Regimental Supply Officer (Army)
RTL	Regimental Training Line (Army)
R	Regina (Queen)
R et I	Regina et Imperatrix (Queen and Empress)
RAD	Regional Accountable Depot (Military)
RAFT	Regional Accounting and Finance Test (Military)
RACNE	Regional Advisory Committee on Nuclear Energy
RACC	Regional Agricultural Credit Corporation
RAN	Regional Air Navigation (ICAO)
RAAG	Regional Aviation Assistance Group (FAA)
RC	Regional Center
RCDCB	Regional Civil Defense Coordination Boards
RCDMB	Regional Civil and Defense Mobilization Boards
RCP	Regional Conservation Program
RCD	Regional Cooperation for Development (Iran, Pakistan, Turkey)
RCIUA	Regional Council of the Independent Unions of Algeria (Union Regionale des Syndicats Independants d'Algerie)
RCIE	Regional Council for International Education (University of Pittsburgh)
RDL	Regional Development Laboratory (Philadelphia, Pennsylvania)
RD	Regional Director
RDC	Regional Dissemination Center (NASA)
RDARA	Regional and Domestic Air Route Area
REL	Regional Education Laboratory
RELCV	Regional Educational Laboratory for the Carolinas and Virginia
RESC	Regional Educational Service Center
REEC	Regional Export Expansion Council (Department of Commerce)
RF	Regional Force (ARVN)
RHB	Regional Hospital Board
RHCSA	Regional Hospitals Consultants' and Specialists' Association
RIDC	Regional Industrial Development Corporation (Southwest Pennsylvania)
RICE	Regional Information and Communication Exchange
RLO	Regional Liaison Office (Military)
RMR	Regional Maintenance Representative
RMO	Regional Medical Officer
RO	Regional Office
ROCAP	Regional Office, Central America and Panama (AID)
RPA	Regional Plan Association
RPC	Regional Planning Commission
RPEA	Regional Planning and Evaluation Agency (California State Board of Education)
RPB	Regional Preparedness Board (Military)
RSA	Regional Science Association
RSEC	Regional Science Experience Center
RSG	Regional Seat of Government
RTAC	Regional Technical Aid Center (Agency for International Development)
RTRC	Regional Technical Report Centers (Department of Commerce)
RTS	Regional Technical Support (Military)
RUDI	Regional Urban Defense Intercept
RVO	Regional Veterinary Officer
RWLB	Regional War Labor Board
RBMU	Regions Beyond Missionary Union
RC	Register of Copyrights (US)
REACT	Register Enforced Automated Control Technique (Cash register-computing system)
RPEP	Register of Planned Emergency Producers
RT	Register Ton
R	Registered
RAPP	Registered Air Parcel Post
RC	Registered Criminologist
REMS	Registered Equipment Management System (Air Force)
RFN	Registered Fever Nurse
RGN	Registered General Nurse
L Hy	Registered Hypnotist
RMCB	Registered Mail Central Bureau
MT(ASCP)	Registered Medical Technologist (American Society of Clinical Pathologists)
RMN	Registered Mental Nurse
RN	Registered Nurse
RNMD	Registered Nurse for Mental Defectives
RODATA	Registered Organization Data Bank
RG PH	Registered Pharmacist
RPH	Registered Pharmacist
RPT	Registered Physical Therapist
RPC	Registered Publication Clerk (Navy)
RPIO	Registered Publication Issuing Office

RPMIO . . . . . . Registered Publication Mobile Issuing Office(r)
RPSM . . . . . . Registered Publication Shipment Memorandum
RPU . . . . Registered Publication Unit
RPM . . . . Registered Publications Manual (Navy)
RPS-DL . . . . . Registered Publications Section - District Library (Navy)
RPS-PL . . . . . Registered Publications Section - Personnel Library (Navy)
RPS . . . . Registered Publications System
RRL . . . . Registered Record Librarian (Medicine)
RSNP . . . . . . Registered Student Nurse Program
RT . . . . Registered Technician (American Registry of X-ray Technicians)
RTN . . . . Registered Trade Name
RA . . . . Registration Act
RICM . . . . . . Registre International des Citoyens du Monde
RMT . . . . . . Registry of Medical Technologists
RP . . . . Regius Professor
RSITA . . . . . . Reglement du Service international des Telecommunications de l'Aeronautique
RTG . . . . Reglement Telegraphique (Telegraph Regulations)
RIV . . . . Regolamento Internazionale Veicoli (Italian generic term meaning "International Regulation of Vehicles") (Initialism also refers to International Railway Wagon Union)
RUUR . . . . . . Regrade Unclassified Upon Receipt (Air Force)
REC . . . . Regroupement des Etudiants Camerounais (Regrouping of Cameroonese Students)
RIPC . . . . Regroupement des Independants et Paysans Camerounais (Regrouping of Independents and Farmers of the Cameroons)
RENEC . . . . . Regroupement National des Etudiants Camerounais (National Regrouping of Cameroonese Students)
RPCI . . . . Regroupement des Partis de la Cote d'Ivoire (Regroupment of the Parties of the Ivory Coast)
RAF . . . . Regular Air Force
REGAF . . . . . Regular Air Force
RA . . . . Regular Army
RAR . . . . Regular Army Reserve
RCCC . . . . . . Regular Common Carrier Conference
RIN . . . . Regular Inertial Navigator
RRC . . . . Regular Route Carrier
RSR . . . . Regular Sinus Rhythm (Physiology)
RSC . . . . Regular, Slotted, Corrugated (Container)
RS . . . . Regular Station (Military)
RVA . . . . Regular Veterans Association of the United States
RESP . . . . Regulated Electrical Supply Package
R . . . . Regulating
RS . . . . Regulating Station
RS . . . . Regulation Station (Air Force)
RC . . . . Regulatory Council (FAA)
RC . . . . Rehabilitation Center
RSS . . . . Rehabilitation Support Schedule
RCRF . . . . Rei Cretariae Romanae Fautores (Society of Roman Ceramic Archeologists)
RMI . . . . Reich Ministry of Interior
RCI . . . . Reichhold Chemicals, Incorporated (NYSE symbol)
RAT . . . . Reichsangestellten-Tarifuertrag (Germany)
RAD . . . . Reichsarbeitsdienst
RHO . . . . Reichshaushaltsordnung (Germany)
RKO . . . . Reichskassenordnung (Germany)
RKFDV . . . . . . Reichskommissar fuer die Festigung Deutschen Volkstums
RM . . . . Reichsmark (German currency) (Later, DM)
RSHA . . . . . . Reichssicherheitshauptampt (Central Security Office of the Reich) (NAZI Germany)
RSG . . . . Reichssiedlungsgesetz
RVO . . . . Reichsversicherungsordnung (German insurance laws)
RVG . . . . Reichsversorgungsgesetz (Germany)
RVP . . . . Reid Vapor Pressure
R . . . . Reigned
RA . . . . Reimbursement Authorization
RC . . . . Reinforced Concrete (Technical drawings)
RCCP . . . . . . Reinforced Concrete Culvert Pipe (Technical drawings)
RCP . . . . Reinforced Concrete Pipe (Technical drawings)
RCRC . . . . . . Reinforced Concrete Research Council
RP . . . . Reinforced Plastic
RTL . . . . Reinforced Tile Lintel (Technical drawings)
RCD . . . . Reinforcement Control Depot (Air Force)
RD . . . . Reinforcement Designee (Air Force)
RST . . . . Reinforcing Steel (Technical drawings)
RS . . . . Reinforcing Stimulus
RI . . . . Reinsurance
R . . . . Reiz (Stimulus)
RL . . . . Reiz Stimulus Limen (Psychology)
RFR . . . . Reject Failure Rate
RPE . . . . Related Payroll Expense
RT . . . . Related Terms (Indexing)

RLT . . . . Relating To
RAPID . . . . Relative Address Programming Implementation Device (Data processing)
RB . . . . Relative Bearing (Navigation)
RBE . . . . Relative Biological Effectiveness (of stated types of radiation)
RBW . . . . Relative Biologische Wirkungsweise
RCD . . . . Relative Cardiac Dullness (Medicine)
RCF . . . . Relative Centrifugal Force
RCP . . . . Relative Competitive Preference (Marketing)
RF . . . . Relative Flow (Rate)
RHD . . . . Relative Hepatic Dullness (Medicine)
RH . . . . Relative Humidity
RIOMETER . . . . Relative Ionospheric Opacity Meter
RQY . . . . Relative Quantum Yield
RSA . . . . Relative Specific Activity
RVC . . . . Relative Velocity Computer
RVD . . . . Relative Vertebral Density
RVA . . . . Relative Volt-Ampere
RWR . . . . Relative Weight Response
ROOT . . . . Relaxation Oscillator Optically Tuned
RPF . . . . Relaxed Pelvic Floor
RVO . . . . Relaxed Vaginal Outlet (Physiology)
RL . . . . Relay Logic
REFRAD . . . . . Release from Active Duty (Military)
RC . . . . Release Clause
REF . . . . Release of Excess Funds
RP . . . . Release Point (Ground traffic)
RSIUFL . . . . . . Release Suspension for Issue and Use of Following Lots
RAD . . . . Released from Active Duty (Navy)
RFAD . . . . . . Released from Active Duty not Result of Demobilization
ROR . . . . Released on Own Recognizance (Law)
RT . . . . Released Time
RF . . . . Releasing Factor
R . . . . Reliability
RATR . . . . Reliability Abstracts and Technical Reviews (NASA)
RAC . . . . Reliability Analysis Center (Air Force)
RAT . . . . Reliability Assurance Test
RECON . . . . . . Reliability and Configuration Accountability System
RIF . . . . Reliability Improvement Factor
RI . . . . Reliability Index
R & M . . . . . . Reliability and Maintainability (Navy)
RMI . . . . Reliability Maturity Index (Polaris)
RPM . . . . Reliability Performance Measure (QCR)
R & QA . . . . . Reliability & Quality Assurance
RTA . . . . Reliability Test Assembly
RVA . . . . Reliability Variation Analysis
RAP . . . . Reliable Acoustic Path
RES . . . . Reliable Stores Corporation (NYSE symbol)
REE . . . . Reliance Electric & Engineering Company (NYSE symbol)
RMC . . . . Reliance Manufacturing Company (NYSE symbol)
RC . . . . Relief Claim
REMT . . . . Relief Electronic Maintenance Technician
RES . . . . Relief Electronics Specialist
RV . . . . Relief Valve
RFA . . . . Relieved from Assigned (Military)
RFAA . . . . . . Relieved from Attached and Assigned
RIAL . . . . Religion in American Life
RLCA . . . . Religion and Labor Council of America
RLF . . . . Religion and Labor Foundation
RCE . . . . Religious of Christian Education (Roman Catholic women's religious order)
RCM . . . . Religious Conceptionist Missionaries (Roman Catholic women's religious order)
REA . . . . Religious Education Association
RHA . . . . Religious Heritage of America, Inc.
RHSJ . . . . Religious Hospitallers of St. Joseph (Roman Catholic women's religious order)
RIA . . . . Religious Instruction Association
RJM . . . . Religious of Jesus-Mary (Roman Catholic women's religious order)
RMWR . . . . . . Religious, Morale, Welfare and Recreation (Military)
RNS . . . . Religious News Service
RNA . . . . Religious Newswriters Association
RPRC . . . . Religious Public Relations Council
RPG . . . . Religious Publishers Group
RRA . . . . Religious Research Association
RSHM . . . . Religious of the Sacred Heart of Mary (Roman Catholic women's religious order)
RTS . . . . Religious Tract Society (British)
RZA . . . . Religious Zionists of America
RCF . . . . Remain on Company Frequency (Aviation)
RWRC . . . . Remain Well to Right of Course (Aviation)
ROB . . . . Remaining on Board
ROVNITE . . . . Remaining Over Night

RON . . . . Remaining Overnight (Aviation)
READ . . . . Remedial Education for Adults
RM . . . . Remedial Maintenance
ROT . . . . Remedial Occupation Therapy
REM-RAND . . . Remington Rand (Later, a division of Sperry-Rand)
6R . . . . Remedial Readin', Remedial Ritin', and Remedial Rithmetic (Humorous interpretation of the three R's)
RRRRRR . . . . . . Remedial Readin', Remedial Ritin', and Remedial Rithmetic (Humorous interpretation of the three R's)
RACS . . . . Remote Access Computing System
RAPID . . . . . . Remote Access Procedure for Interactive Design (General Motors)
RAGF . . . . Remote Air-Ground Facility (Aviation)
RACIC . . . . . . Remote Area Conflict Information Center (Battelle Memorial Institute)
RAILS . . . . Remote Area Instrument Landing Sensor
RAILS . . . . Remote Area Instrument Landing System (Army)
RATE . . . . Remote Automatic Telemetry Equipment (Data processing)
RCO. . . . . . . Remote Communication Outlet (ATCS)
RCC . . . . Remote Communications Central
RCC . . . . Remote Communications Complex
RCC . . . . Remote Communications Console
RC . . . . Remote Control
RCO. . . . . . . Remote Control Office
RCO . . . . Remote Control Oscillator
RCS . . . . Remote Control System
RUM . . . . Remote-Control Underwater Manipulator (Oceanography)
RCAG. . . . . . . Remote Controlled (or Center) Air-Ground Facility
RDC . . . . Remote Data Collection (Data processing)
RDT . . . . Remote Data Transmitter
RESCUE. . . . . . Remote Emergency Salvage and Clean Up Equipment
RFMS . . . . Remote File Management System
RGM . . . . Remote Geophysical Monitor
RISC . . . . Remote Information Systems Center
REMAD . . . . . . Remote Magnetic Anomaly Detection
RMU . . . . Remote Maneuvering Unit (NASA)
ROTL . . . . Remote Office Test Line (Bell Laboratories)
RPMC. . . . . . . Remote Performance Monitoring and Control
RPPI . . . . Remote Plan Position Indicator (Navy)
RPC . . . . Remote Position Control
RRIS . . . . Remote RADAR Integration Station
RSEU . . . . Remote Scanner-Encoder Unit (Bell Laboratories)
RSDP . . . . Remote Site Data Processor
RSL . . . . Remote Sprint Launching
RS . . . . Remote Station
RSA . . . . Remote Station Alarm
RSCIE . . . . Remote Station Communication Interface Equipment
RTS. . . . . Remote Targeting System
RETAIN . . . . Remote Technical Assistance and Information Network (Data processing)
RTU . . . . Remote Terminal Unit
RTP. . . . . Remote Transfer Point
RUFAS . . . . . . Remote Underwater Fisheries Assessment System
RUSH . . . . . . Remote Use of Shared Hardware (Data processing)
REVOCON . . . Remote Volume Control
ROSE . . . . Remotely Operated Special Equipment (AEC)
RETS . . . . Renaissance English Text Society
RIY . . . . Renaissance of Italian Youth
RSA . . . . Renaissance Society of America
RBF . . . . Renal Blood Flow (Physiology)
RD . . . . Renal Disease
RPF . . . . Renal Plasma Flow (Physiology)
RPS . . . . Renal Pressor Substance
RSP . . . . Render Safe Procedure
RV . . . . Rendezvous
REP . . . . Rendezvous Exercise Pod (NASA)
RR . . . . Rendezvous RADAR
RRT. . . . . Rendezvous RADAR Transponder
RB . . . . Renegotiation Board
RBR . . . . Renegotiation Board Regulation
RRO . . . . Renegotiation Regional Office
RR . . . . Renegotiation Regulations
RAA . . . . Renewal Assistance Administration (HUD)
RPA . . . . Renewal Projects Administration (HUD)
READS . . . . . . Reno Air Defense Sector (ADC)
RPI . . . . Rensselaer Polytechnic Institute (New York)
RA . . . . Rental Agreement
RSA . . . . Rental Service Association
ROCID . . . . . Reorganization of Combat Infantry Division (Army)
ROAD . . . . . . Reorganization Objective, Army Division (Military)
RODAC . . . . . Reorganization Objectives Army Division, Army and Corps
RAAN. . . . . . . Repair Activity Accounting Number (Navy)
RAN. . . . . . . Repair Activity Accounting Number (Navy)
RCF . . . . Repair Cost Factor (Navy)

RPL . . . . Repair Parts List (Army)
R & S SQ . . . . Repair and Salvage Squadron (Military)
AR . . . . Repair Ship (Navy symbol)
RIC . . . . Repairable Item Code
RP/H . . . . Repairs, Heavy
RLO. . . . . . . Repairs Liaison Officer (Landing craft and barges) (Navy)
RP/L . . . . Repairs, Light
R & U . . . . . . Repairs and Upkeep (Military)
R & U . . . . Repairs and Utilities
RAC . . . . Reparable Assets Control
RPC . . . . Reparable Processing Centers
RR & D. . . . . . Reparations, Removal, and Demolition (Section) (Industry Branch, US Military Government, Germany)
RAMPS . . . . . . Repatriated American Military Personnel (World War II)
RE . . . . Repayable to Either
RAT . . . . Repeat Action Tablet (Pharmacy)
RB . . . . Repeated Back (Communications)
RT . . . . Reperforator-Transmitter
RILM . . . . Repertoire International de la Litterature Musicale (International Repertory of Music Literature)
RISM . . . . Repertoire International des Sources Musicales
RR . . . . Repetition Rate
REPPAC. . . . . Repetitively Pulsed Plasma Accelerator
RCVG . . . . . . Replacement Carrier Fighter Group (V is Navy code for Fighter)
RF . . . . Replacement Factor
RNV . . . . Replacement Naval Vessels
RSI . . . . Replacement Stream Input (Military)
RTC . . . . Replacement Training Center
RTU . . . . Replacement Training Unit (Military)
RDIS . . . . Replenishment Demand Inventory System
AOR . . . . Replenishment Fleet Tanker (Navy symbol)
RF . . . . Replicate Form
RC . . . . Reply Coupon
REPIN . . . . . . Reply if Negative
RP . . . . Reply Paid (Communications)
RPP . . . . Reply Paid Postcard
RPC . . . . Reply Post Card
RAOMP. . . . . Report of Accrued Obligations, Military Pay
RB . . . . Report Bibliography
ROB . . . . Report on Board (Navy)
RPC . . . . Report(ing) to Commander (Military)
REPCAT . . . . Report Corrective Action Taken
RX . . . . Report Crossing (Aviation)
REPDU . . . . . Report(ing) for Duty (Military)
RIPOM . . . . . Report (command indicated) If Present, Otherwise by Message (Navy)
REPISIC . . . . . Report Immediate Superior in Command (Navy)
RI . . . . Report of Investigation
ROI . . . . Report of Investigation
RLETFL . . . . . Report Leaving Each Thousand-Foot Level (Aviation)
PX Me . . . . . Report My Arrival or Departure (Aviation slang)
RPOC. . . . . . Report Proceeding on Course (Aviation)
RPG . . . . Report Program Generator
REPSNO . . . . Report(ing) through Senior Naval Officer
RS . . . . Report of Survey
R/S . . . . Report of Survey (Army)
RTN . . . . Report Test Number (NASA)
RTX . . . . Report Time Crossing (Aviation)
RTO . . . . Report Time Over (Aviation)
RUDAEE . . . . Report of Unsatisfactory or Defective Airborne Electronic Equipment
RUDAOE . . . . Report of Unsatisfactory or Defective Aviation Ordnance Equipment (Navy)
RUDI . . . . . . Report of Unsatisfactory or Defective Instrumentation
RUDM . . . . . . Report of Unsatisfactory or Defective Material (Aircraft) (Navy)
RUAT . . . . . . Report Upon Arrival Threat (Army)
REOC . . . . . . Report When Established on Course (Aviation)
REWRC . . . . Report When Established Well to Right of Course (Aviation)
RICC . . . . . . Reportable Item Control Code (Army)
RIMC . . . . . . Reportable Items of Major Combinations (Army)
RAD . . . . Reported for Active Duty (Navy)
RPFOD . . . . . Reported for Duty
R of D . . . . . Reporter of Debate (US Senate)
RACC. . . . . . Reporting Activity Control Card (Army)
RFD . . . . Reporting for Duty
RIO . . . . Reporting In and Out (Military)
REPO . . . . . . Reporting Officer (Navy)
ROF . . . . Reporting Organizational File (Military)
REP . . . . Reporting Point (Aviation)
RP . . . . Reporting Post (RADAR)
RP/CL . . . . . Reporting Post, Coastal Low (RADAR)
RP/CM . . . . . Reporting Post, Coastal Medium (RADAR)
R & R . . . . . Reporting and Requisitioning (Air Force)
RARI. . . . . . . Reporting and Routing Instructions

R . . . . Reports
RCLO . . . . . . Reports Control Liaison Officer (Army)
RCO . . . . Reports Control Officer (Army)
RCS . . . . Reports Control Symbol (Military)
REPSHIPS . . . . . Reports of Shipments
R & S . . . . . . Reports and Statistics Branch (US Military Government, Germany)
RECE . . . . . . Representacion Cubana del Exilio
RCO . . . . Representative Calculating Operation
REPCOMDESPAC . . Representative of Commander Destroyers, Pacific Fleet
RCS . . . . Representative Conflict Situations (Army)
RF . . . . Representative Fraction
REPFORMAINT . . Representative of Maintenance Force
RTM . . . . Representative Town Meeting
REHVA . . . . . . Representatives of European Heating and Ventilating Associations
R . . . . Reprint
RP . . . . Reprint
RES . . . . Reprint Expediting Service
RU . . . . Reproducing Unit
R . . . . Republic(an)
RA . . . . Republic Aviation Corporation (NYSE symbol)
RAC . . . . Republic Aviation Corporation
REP . . . . Republic Corporation (NYSE symbol)
ROK . . . . Republic of (South) Korea
ROKAF . . . . . . Republic of Korea Air Force
ROKA . . . . . . Republic of Korea Army
ROKPUCE . . . . Republic of Korea Presidential Unit Citation
ROKPUC . . . . Republic of Korea Presidential Unit Citation Badge
RNA . . . . Republic of New Africa (Black separatist group)
RP . . . . Republic of Panama
RSA . . . . Republic of South Africa
RSARR . . . . . . Republic of South Africa Research Reactor
RS . . . . Republic Steel Corporation (NYSE symbol)
RVN . . . . Republic of Vietnam
RVNAF . . . . . . Republic of Vietnam Air Force
RVNAF . . . . . . Republic of Vietnam Armed Forces
RVCM . . . . . . Republic of Vietnam Campaign Medal (Military award)
RCCUS . . . . . . Republican Citizens Committee of the United States
RGA . . . . Republican Governors Association
RNC . . . . Republican National Committee
ROC . . . . Republican Organizing Committee (Political organization in opposition to the NPL of North Dakota)
RPC . . . . Republican Policy Committee
RPPA . . . . . . Republican Postwar Policy Association (Encouraged Republican party to drop its isolationist viewpoint and take a stand for an American share in international collaboration after the war) (World War II)
RSCC . . . . . . Republican Senatorial Campaign Committee
RFP . . . . Republicans for Progress
RI . . . . Republik Indonesia
RCM . . . . La Republique des Citoyens du Monde (Commonwealth of World Citizens)
RF . . . . Republique Francaise (French Republic)
REQAFA . . . . . Request Advise as to Further Action (Army)
RAC . . . . Request Altitude Change (Aviation)
RACE . . . . . . Request Altitude Changes En Route (Aviation)
RFA . . . . Request for Analysis
REQANS . . . . . Request Answer By (Date)
RAN . . . . Request for Authority to Negotiate
REQAURQN . . . Request Authority to Requisition
RFB . . . . Request for Bid
R/C . . . . Request for Checkage (Navy)
RQDCZ . . . . . . Request Clearance to Depart Control Zone (Aviation)
RQECZ . . . . . . Request Clearance to Enter Control Zone (Aviation)
RCTDPOVALCAN . . Request Concurrent Travel of Dependents by Privately Owned Vehicle (ALCAN Highway or via Route Required) (Army)
REQDI . . . . . . Request Disposition Instructions (Army)
REC . . . . Request for Engineering Change
RTE . . . . Request to Expedite
RFO . . . . Request for Factory Order
RFA . . . . Request Further Airways (Aviation)
REQID . . . . . . Request If Desired
RFI . . . . Request for Information
REQINT . . . . . Request Interim Reply by (Date) (Military)
RFI . . . . Request for Investigation
RFI . . . . Request for Issue
REQIBO . . . . . Request Item be Placed on Back Order
RLIEVDP . . . . . Request Line Items Be Expedited for Vehicles (or Equipment) Deadlined for Parts (Army)
RLE . . . . Request Loading Entry (Data processing)
REQMAD . . . . . Request Mailing Address
RME . . . . Request Monitor Entry (Data processing)
RPA . . . . Request Present Altitude (Aviation)

RPP . . . . Request Present Position (Aviation)
RPQ . . . . Request for Price Quotation
RPT . . . . Request Programs Termination (Data processing)
RFP . . . . Request for Proposal
RTP . . . . Request to Purchase
RQDP . . . . . . Request, Quandary and Deferment Plan
RFQ . . . . Request for Quotation
RSE . . . . Request Select Entry (Data processing)
REQSI . . . . . . Request Shipping Instructions
REQSSD . . . . . Request Supply Status and Expected Delivery Date (Army)
REQSUPSTAFOL . . Request Supply Status of Following (Army)
RQTAO . . . . . . Request Time and Altitude Over (Aviation)
REQTRAC . . . . Request Tracer Be Initiated
RFP . . . . Requests for Purchases
R . . . . Requiescat (He Rests)
RIP . . . . Requiescat in Pace (May He, or She, Rest in Peace)
RI . . . . Require Identification
RD . . . . Required Date
RDD . . . . Required Delivery Date
ROC . . . . Required Operational Capability
ROD . . . . Required Operational Data
ROD . . . . Required Operational Date
RSR . . . . Required Supply Rate
RCS . . . . Requirement Clearance Symbol (Military)
RTP . . . . Requirement & Test Procedures
RAD . . . . Requirements Action Directive
RAG . . . . Requirements Advisory Group (Air Force)
R & D . . . . . . Requirements and Distribution
RIAR . . . . . . Requirements Inventory Analysis Report
RRC . . . . Requirements Review Committee (Navy)
RAC . . . . Requisition Advice Care
RCU . . . . Requisition Control Unit
RPP . . . . Requisition Processing Point
RO . . . . Requisitioning Objective (Military)
RPD . . . . Rerum Politicarum Doctor (Doctor of Political Science)
RP . . . . Res Publica
RB . . . . Rescue Boat
RBA . . . . Rescue Breathing Apparatus
RESCAP . . . . . Rescue Combat Air Patrol
RCC . . . . Rescue Control Center
RCC . . . . Rescue Coordination Center (Coast Guard)
RCC . . . . Rescue Crew Commander
RI . . . . Rescue, Incorporated
PARARESCUE . . Rescue by Individuals Parachuted to Distressed Person(s) (Air Force)
RML . . . . Rescue Motor Launch (Air/sea rescue) (Navy)
ATR . . . . Rescue Ocean Tug (Navy symbol)
VH . . . . Rescue Squadrons (Navy symbol)
RSC . . . . Rescue Sub-Centre (Aviation)
APR . . . . Rescue Transport (Navy symbol)
R . . . . Research
X . . . . Research (or Experimental) (Designation for all US military aircraft)
RAC . . . . Research Advisory Council
RAC . . . . Research Analysis Corporation
RAC . . . . Research Analysis Corps (Army)
RAPID . . . . . . Research in Automatic Photocomposition and Information Dissemination
RAM . . . . Research Aviation Medicine (Navy program of research into aerospace medical techniques)
RBS . . . . Research for Better Schools, Inc.
RB . . . . Research Bulletin
RCUEP . . . . . . Research Center for Urban and Environmental Planning (Princeton University)
RCD . . . . Research Centers Directory
ROCAPPI . . . . . Research on Computer Applications for the Printing and Publishing Industries
RCRBSJ . . . . . . Research Council on Riveted & Bolted Structural Joints
RDP . . . . Research Data Publication (Center)
RDS . . . . Research Defence Society (British)
RDX . . . . Research Department Explosive
RD . . . . Research and Development
R & D . . . . . . Research and Development
RAND . . . . . . Research and Development (Origin of name of RAND Corporation, a non-profit national defense research organization)
RDA . . . . Research and Development, Army
RDAFCI . . . . . . Research and Development Associates, Food and Container Institute
RDB . . . . Research and Development Board
RDC . . . . Research and Development Command (Military)
RDD . . . . Research and Development Division
R & DELSEC . . Research and Development Electronic Security
RD & E . . . . . Research, Development, and Engineering
RDFU-V . . . . . Research and Development Field Unit – Vietnam
RADIC . . . . . . Research and Development Information Center

RDO........ Research and Development Objectives (Military)
RDO........ Research, Development, and Operation (Military appropriation)
RDR........ Research and Development Report
RDS........ Research and Development Service (Army-Ordnance)
RD & S..... Research, Development, and Studies (Marine Corps)
RDS........ Research and Development Survey
RDT & E..... Research, Development, Testing, and Evaluation Programs (Military)
RDR........ Research Division Report
RDTR....... Research Division Technical Report
RIE........ Research in Education (Monthly publication of ERIC)
REFCD...... Research and Education Foundation for Chest Disease
RE......... Research and Engineering
RECGA...... Research and Engineering Council of Graphic Arts Industry
REPC....... Research and Engineering Policy Council (DOD)
RESG....... Research Engineering Standing Group (DOD)
REP........ Research Expenditure Proposal
REPAS...... Research, Evaluation, and Planning Assistance Staff (AID)
RFED....... Research Facilities and Equipment Division (NASA)
RFF........ Research Flight Facility (Air Force)
REMP....... Research Group for European Migration Problems
RIAC....... Research Information Analysis Corporation
RICASIP..... Research Information Center and Advisory Service on Information
            Processing (National Bureau of Standards - National Science
            Foundation)
RIAS....... Research Institute for Advanced Studies (Martin Marietta Corporation)
RIA........ Research Institute of America
RIEM....... Research Institute for Environmental Medicine (Army)
RIND....... Research Institute of National Defense
RINS....... Research Institute for the Natural Sciences
RIRJ....... Research Institute of Religious Jewry
RISSB...... Research Institute on the Sino-Soviet Bloc
RISM....... Research Institute for the Study of Man (Army)
RIEDAC..... Research in International Economics of Disarmament and Arms Control
            (A program of Columbia University School of International Affairs)
RESLAB..... Research Laboratory
RL......... Research Laboratory
RILAMAC.... Research in Laboratory Animal Medicine and Care
RLE........ Research Laboratory for Electronics
RLHTE...... Research Laboratory of Heat Transfer in Electronics (MIT)
RLMM...... Research Laboratory for Mechanics of Materials
RMIC....... Research Materials Information Center (ORNL)
RM......... Research Memorandum
RN......... Research Note
RON....... Research Octane Number
RP......... Research Paper
RPHST...... Research Participation for High School Teachers (National Science
            Foundation)
RPRD...... Research Policy and Review Division (of OEP)
RPB........ Research to Prevent Blindness, Inc.
RPDES...... Research Program Development and Evaluation Staff (Department of
            Agriculture)
RPPE....... Research, Program, Planning, and Evaluation
RR......... Research Report
RSA........ Research Security Administrators
RSVP....... Research Selected Vote Profile (Election poll)
RSO........ Research Ship of Opportunity
RSVP....... Research Society for Victorian Periodicals
RSI........ Research Studies Institute
RST........ Research Study Team
RS......... Research Summary
RISE....... Research in Supersonic Environment
RTM........ Research Technical Memorandum
RTS........ Research and Technical Services (Military)
RT......... Research and Technology
R & T...... Research and Technology
RTD........ Research and Technology Division (Air Force)
RTV........ Research Test Vehicle
RTI........ Research Triangle Institute
RGK........ Reserv Glavnogo Komandovaniia (Reserve of the High Command) (USSR)
R.......... Reserve
ROB........ Reserve on Board
RCTP....... Reserve Component Troop Program
RCCF....... Reserve Components Contingency Force
RCMIS...... Reserve Components Management Information System (Army)
RCPA....... Reserve Components Program of the Army
RCTB....... Reserve Components Troop Basis (Army)
RD......... Reserve Decoration (British)
RESDIST..... Reserve District
RDT........ Reserve Duty Training (Military)
REP........ Reserve Enlisted Program (Military)
REC........ Reserve Equalization Committee (Military)

READ....... Reserve on Extended Active Duty (Military)
RFW........ Reserve Feed Water (Technical drawings)
RESV...... Reserve Fleet (Navy)
RF......... Reserve Force
RFA........ Reserve Forces Act
RFASIX...... Reserve Forces Act of 1955, Six Months Trainee
RFATHREE.... Reserve Forces Act of 1955, Three Months Trainee
RFPB....... Reserve Forces Policy Board (DOD)
RG......... Reserve Grade (Military)
RES/IC...... Reserve - In Commission (Vessel status)
RES/IS...... Reserve - In Service (Vessel status)
RMN....... Reserve Material (Account) Navy
ROC........ Reserve Officer Candidate
RORA...... Reserve Officer Recording Activity
ROA....... Reserve Officers Association of the United States
RONAG..... Reserve Officers Naval Architecture Group
RONS...... Reserve Officers of the Naval Service
ROPA...... Reserve Officers Personnel Act
ROPB...... Reserve Officers Promotion Board (Air Force)
ROSC...... Reserve Officers Sanitary Corps
ROTC...... Reserve Officers Training Corps (Separate units for Army, Navy, Air
            Force)
ROTCM...... Reserve Officers Training Corps Manual
RO........ Reserve Order
RES/OC..... Reserve - Out of Commission (Vessel status)
RES/OS..... Reserve - Out of Service (Vessel status)
RP........ Reserve Personnel (Air Force)
RPA....... Reserve Personnel, Army
R & ROTC... Reserve & Reserve Officers' Training Corps (Army)
RRL....... Reserve Retired List (Military)
RSC....... Reserve Service Control (Navy)
RSCR...... Reserve Special Commendation Ribbon
RT........ Reserve Training
RESTRACEN... Reserve Training Center
RTC....... Reserve Training Corps
RTU....... Reserve Training Unit
RU........ Reserve Unit (Equal to one US dollar) (International finance)
RAD....... Reservists on Active Duty (Navy)
RG........ Reset Gate
RID........ Reset Inhibit Drum
R......... Reside, Residence, or Resident
RA........ Resident Agent
RA........ Resident Auditor
RCI....... Resident Cost Inspector
RINA...... Resident Inspector of Naval Aircraft
RINM..... Resident Inspector of Naval Material
RIO....... Resident Inspector Office (Coast Guard)
RM........ Resident Magistrate
RINSORD.... Resident Naval Inspector of Ordnance
RNIO...... Resident Naval Inspector of Ordnance
RINSPOW.... Resident Naval Inspector of Powder
RO in C.... Resident Officer-in-Charge (Navy)
ROIC...... Resident Officer-in-Charge
ROICC..... Resident Officer in Charge of Construction
RSG....... Resident Study Group (Army)
RUSNO..... Resident United States Naval Officer
RERL...... Residual Equivalent Return Loss
RGA....... Residual Gas Analyzer
RSS....... Residual Sum of Squares (Statistics)
RV........ Residual Volume
REMC...... Resin-Encapsulated Mica Capacitor
RITA...... Resist Inside the Army (Peace-movement slang)
R......... Resistance
RBT........ Resistance Bulb Thermometer
RC........ Resistance Capacitance (or Resistor-Capacitor)
RCCPLD.... Resistance-Capacitance Coupled
RWMA..... Resistance Welder Manufacturers Association
R......... Resistor
RCTL...... Resistor-Capacitor Transistor Logic
RTL....... Resistor-Transistor Logic
RC........ Resolver Control
RCT....... Resolver Control Transformer
RDG....... Resolver Differential Generator
RX........ Resolver-Transmitter
RGT....... Resonant Gate Transistor
RESOJET.... Resonant Pulse Jet
RAL....... Resorcylic Acid Lactone (Chemical)
RAL....... Resort Airlines, Inc.
REACT..... Resource Allocation and Control Technique (Management)
RAMPS..... Resources Allocation and Multi-Project Scheduling
RMS....... Resources Management System (Army)

REVERSE ACRONYMS AND INITIALISMS DICTIONARY

RPMD ...... Resources Planning and Mobilization Division (of OEP)
RPSM .... Resources Planning and Scheduling Method
RPB .... Resources Protection Board
RTSD .... Resources and Technical Services Division (of ALA)
R .... Respiration
RC .... Respiratory Center (Medicine)
RI .... Respiratory Illness (Medicine)
RMV .... Respiratory Minute Volume (Physiology)
RM .... Respiratory Movement
RQ .... Respiratory Quotient (Physiology)
RR .... Respiratory Rate (Medicine)
RSV .... Respiratory Syncytial Virus
R .... Respond; Response
RSP .... Responder Beacon
RVSVP ...... Respondez Vite, s'il Vous Plait (Please Reply at Once)
RSVP .... Respondez, s'il Vous Plait (The Favor of an Answer is Requested)
REASON ..... Responding to Elderlies' Abilities and Sicknesses Otherwise
                 Neglected (Baltimore, Maryland)
RATER ...... Response Analysis Tester (NASA)
R-A .... Response Errors (Statistics)
RF .... Response Factor
RFS .... Response Feedback System (NASA)
RS .... Response-Stimulus
RC .... Responsibility Center (Air Force)
RESPO ..... Responsible Property Officer (Army)
RR .... Responsible Receiver
RAMMS ...... Responsive Automated Materiel Management (Army)
R .... Responsorium (Responsory)
R & R ...... Rest and Recuperation (Military)
RSVP .... Restartable Solid Variable Pulse (Motor)
RL .... Restaurant Liquor (License)
RW .... Restaurant Wine (License)
RACE ...... Restoration of Aircraft to Combat Effectivity
R .... Restricted (Military document classification)
R .... Restricted (Persons under 18 [16 in some localities] not admitted
                 unless accompanied by parent or adult guardian) (Movie rating)
RA/MCC ..... Restricted Area/Military Climb Corridor (Aviation)
RB .... Restricted Bulletin
RD .... Restricted Data
RESDAT ..... Restricted Data (Atomic Energy Act of 1954)
RCIA ...... Retail Clerks International Association
RCIA ...... Retail Credit Institute of America
RJA .... Retail Jewelers of America
RLD .... Retail Liquor Dealer
RPWDA ..... Retail Paint and Wallpaper Distributors of America
RTDA ...... Retail Tobacco Dealers of America
RWDSU ..... Retail, Wholesale and Department Store Union
RUA .... Retailer's Uniform Agency
RCB .... Retailers Credit Bureau, Inc. (New York metropolitan area)
RP .... Retained Personnel
RIS .... Retarded Infants Service
R .... Retarder (Slow) (On clock-regulators)
RPU .... Retention Pending Use (Air Force)
RT .... Retention Time
RSB .... Reticulocyte Standard Buffer
RES .... Reticulo-Endothelial System (Physiology)
RE .... Reticulo-Endothelium (Medicine)
RD .... Retinal Detachment
R .... Retired, Retiree
RPRC ...... Retired and Pioneer Rural Carriers of US
RRS .... Retired Reserve Section
RSFPP ...... Retired Servicemen's Family Protection Plan
RFCSEUSG ... Retirement Federation of Civil Service Employees of the United States
                 Government
RIP .... Retirement Improvement Program (Air Force)
RIE .... Retirement Income Endowment (Insurance)
RYE .... Retirement Year Ending (Army)
R & RA ..... Retraining and Reemployment Administration (Terminated 1947)
RRPB ...... Retraining and Reemployment Policy Board
RETA ...... Retrieval of Enriched Textual Abstracts
RIDT ...... Retrieval of Information via Online Terminal (Data processing)
ROSE ...... Retrieval by On-Line Search (Data processing)
RI .... Retroactive Inhibition (Psychology)
RA .... Retrograde Amnesia
REP .... Retrograde Pyelogram (Medicine)
RRS .... Retrograde Rocket System
RLF .... Retrolental Fibroplasia (Eye disease in premature babies)
RMD .... Retromanubrial Dullness (Medicine)
RECON ..... Retrospective Conversion of Bibliographic Records (Library of Congress)
RV .... Retroversion
RAD .... Return to Active Duty (Military)

ROAM ..... Return on Assets Managed (Finance)
RTB .... Return to Base (Military)
RBV .... Return Beam Vidicon (Satellite camera)
RB .... Return to Bias
RTD .... Return to Duty (Military)
ROE .... Return on Equity (Finance)
ROI .... Return on Investment
RL .... Return Loss
ROM .... Return on Market Value (Finance)
RMCM ..... Return Material Credit Memo
ROS .... Return from Overseas (Military)
RP .... Return of Post
RP .... Return Premium
RPSCTDY .... Return to Proper Station Upon Completion of Temporary Duty
RTS .... Return(ed) to Service (Aviation)
RTSM ..... Return to Stock Memo
RTS .... Return to Stores
RT .... Return Ticket
RTZ .... Return-to-Zero
RZ .... Return-to-Zero
RZL .... Return-to-Zero Level
RZM .... Return-to-Zero Mark
RTDA ...... Returned Absentees
RAWX ...... Returned Account Weather (Aviation)
RLO .... Returned Letter Office
R .... Returning
RTR .... Returning to Ramp (Aviation)
RILEM ...... Reunion Internationale des Laboratoires d'Essais et de Recherches sur
                 les Materiaux et les Constructions
RITA .... Reusable Interplanetary Transport Approach Vehicle
ROOST ..... Reusable One-Stage Orbital Space Truck
ROC .... Reusable Orbital Carrier
ROMBUS ..... Reusable Orbital Module Booster & Utility Shuttle
ROT .... Reusable Orbital Transport
RCS .... Revenue Cutter Service (Coast Guard)
RCG .... Reverberation Control of Gain
REVEL ...... Reverberation Elimination
RS .... Reverberation Strength
RVB .... Revere Copper & Brass, Inc. (NYSE symbol)
RA .... Reverendus Admodum (Very Reverend)
RP .... Reverendus Pater (Reverend Father)
R .... Reverse
RC .... Reverse Course (Aviation)
RCADV ..... Reverse Course and Advise (Aviation)
RC .... Reverse Current
RF .... Reverse Free
RG .... Reverse Gate
RHL .... Reverse Half-Line (Feed)
RO .... Reverse Osmosis (Desalination)
RPC .... Reversed Phase Column
RHE .... Reversible Hydrogen Electrode
RML .... Review of Metal Literature (American Society for Metals abstracting
                 journal)
RC .... Revised Code
RMPR ...... Revised Maximum Price Regulation (World War II)
RPBG ...... Revised Program and Budget Guidance
RRI .... Revised Ring Index (A reference book)
RSV .... Revised Standard Version (of the Bible, 1952)
RS .... Revised Statutes
RSC .... Revised Statutes of Canada
RSR .... Revised Supplementary Regulation
RUNCIBLE .... Revised Unified New Compiler with Its Basic Language Extended
                 (Data processing)
RV .... Revised Version (of the Bible, 1881)
RIDEQ ...... Revista Iberoamericana de Educacion Quimica (A publication)
REV .... Revlon, Inc. (NYSE symbol)
RARC ...... Revoked Appointment and Returned to Civilian Status (Navy)
RCRC ...... Revoked Commission, Returned to Civilian Status (Navy)
ROH .... Revolucni Odborove Hnutf
RPO .... Revolution Per Orbit
RAM .... Revolutionary Action Movement
RD .... Revolutionary Development (South Vietnam)
RGUB ...... Revolutionary Government of the Union of Burma
RYM-I ...... Revolutionary Youth Movement I (Also known as "Weatherman") (A
                 faction of Students for a Democratic Society)
RYM-II ...... Revolutionary Youth Movement II (A faction of Students for a
                 Democratic Society)
R/M .... Revolutions Per Minute
RPM .... Revolutions Per Minute (e.g., in reference to phonograph records)
RPMI ...... Revolutions-Per-Minute Indicator
RPS .... Revolutions Per Second

R/S . . . . Revolutions per Second
RDS . . . . Revolving Discussion Sequence
RO. . . . . Rework Order
R . . . . Rex (King)
R et I . . . . Rex et Imperator (King and Emperor)
REX . . . . Rexall Drug & Chemical Company (NYSE symbol)
RLM . . . . Reynolds Metals Company (NYSE symbol)
R . . . . Reynolds Number
RN. . . . . Reynolds Number
RJR . . . . Reynolds (R. J.) Tobacco Company (NYSE symbol)
RHE . . . . Rheem Manufacturing Company (NYSE symbol)
ROW . . . . Rheinische Olefinwerke
RWE . . . . Rheinische-Westfallishes Electricitaet
Re . . . . Rhenium (Chemical element)
REG . . . . Rhenoencephalography (Medicine)
Rh . . . . Rhesus (Blood factor)
RF . . . . Rheumatic Fever
RHD . . . . Rheumatic Heart Disease (Medicine)
RF . . . . Rheumatoid Factor (Medicine)
RRFO . . . . . Rhine River Field Organization (Post-World War II)
RI . . . . Rhode Island
RIAEC . . . . . . Rhode Island Atomic Energy Commission
RIOPR . . . . . . Rhode Island Open Pool Reactor (AEC)
RIRCA . . . . . . Rhode Island Red Club of America
RRWU . . . . . . Rhodesia Railway Workers' Union
RLTA . . . . . . Rhodesian Lawn Tennis Association
RHO. . . . . . . Rhodesian Selection Trust Limited (NYSE symbol) (Later, RNO)
Rh . . . . Rhodium (Chemical element)
RPV . . . . Rhopalosiphum Padi Virus
RL . . . . Rhumb Line
R & B . . . . . . Rhythm and Blues (Music)
R . . . . Rial (Monetary unit in Iran)
RNA. . . . . . . Ribonucleic Acid (Genetics)
RCMD. . . . . . Rice Council for Market Development
REA . . . . Rice Export Association
RMA . . . . Rice Millers' Association
RXM. . . . . . . Richardson-Merrell, Inc. (NYSE symbol)
RL . . . . Richfield Oil Corporation (NYSE symbol)
RFP . . . . Richmond, Fredericksburg & Potomac R. R. (AAR code)
RICH . . . . . . Richmond National Battlefield Park
RQMD . . . . . . Richmond Quartermaster Depot (Merged with Defense General Supply Center)
RIO . . . . Ride-It-Out
RIDL . . . . Ridge Instrument Development Laboratory (Navy)
RM . . . . Riding Master (British)
RGP. . . . . . . Riegel Paper Company (NYSE symbol)
R . . . . Rifle
RB . . . . Rifle Brigade
RE . . . . Rifle Expert
RMM . . . . . . Rifle Marksman
R & PT . . . . . . Rifle and Pistol Team (Navy)
RR . . . . Rifle Range
RSS . . . . Rifle Sharpshooter
RUQ. . . . . . . Rifle Unqualified (Military)
RVC . . . . Rifle Volunteer Corps (Military) (British)
RV . . . . Rifle Volunteers
RWP . . . . Rifle and Weapons Platoon (Army)
R . . . . Right (side of a stage) (A stage direction)
RA . . . . Right Arch (Masonry)
RA . . . . Right Ascension (Astronomy)
RAMS . . . . . . Right Ascension Mean Sun (Navigation)
RAM . . . . . . Right Ascension of the Meridian (Navigation)
RAW. . . . . . . Right Attack Wing (Women's lacrosse position)
RBD . . . . Right Border of Dullness
RBBSB . . . . . Right Bundle-Branch System Block (Physiology)
RC. . . . . Right Center (Theatrical)
RCM. . . . . . . Right Costal Margin (Medicine)
RD . . . . Right Defense
RDW. . . . . . . Right Defense Wing (Women's lacrosse position)
RE . . . . Right End
RE . . . . Right Excellent
RE . . . . Right Eye
RF . . . . Right Field(er) (Baseball)
RF . . . . Right Foot
RF . . . . Right Forward
RF . . . . Right Front
RFA . . . . Right Fronto-Anterior
RFP. . . . . Right Frontoposterior
RFT . . . . Right Frontotransverse
RB . . . . Right Fullback (Football)
RF . . . . Right Fullback (Soccer position)

RG. . . . . Right Guard (Football)
RH . . . . Right Halfback (Soccer position)
RHB . . . . Right Halfback (Football)
RH . . . . Right Hand
RHS . . . . Right-Hand Side
RHF . . . . Right Heart Failure (Medicine)
RICM . . . . . . Right Intercostal Margin (Anatomy)
RL . . . . Right Line
RIF. . . . . Right Iliac Fossa (Anatomy)
RLBCD . . . . . Right Lower Border of Cardiac Dullness (Medicine)
RLL. . . . . Right Lower Lobe (Lungs)
RLQ . . . . Right Lower Quadrant (of abdomen) (Medicine)
RMA . . . . Right Mento-Anterior
RMP . . . . Right Mentoposterior
RMT . . . . Right Mentotransverse
RML . . . . Right Middle Lobe (Lungs)
ROA . . . . Right Occiput Anterior (A normal position of fetus at delivery) (Obstetrics)
ROP. . . . . . . Right Occiput Posterior (A normal position of fetus before delivery) (Obstetrics)
ROT . . . . Right Occipitotransverse
ROP . . . . Right Outside Position (Dancing)
RR . . . . Right Rear
RR . . . . Right Reverend
RSA . . . . Right Sacro-Anterior
RSP . . . . Right Sacroposterior
RST. . . . . Right Sacrotransverse
RS . . . . Right Side
RSWC . . . . . . Right Side Up with Care
RSC . . . . Right Stage Center (A stage direction)
RT . . . . Right Tackle (Football)
RP . . . . Right Traffic Pattern (Aviation)
RT . . . . Right Turn After Takeoff (Aviation)
RUE . . . . Right Upper Entrance (Theatrical)
RUE . . . . Right Upper Extremity (Medicine)
RUL . . . . Right Upper Lobe (of lung) (Medicine)
RUQ. . . . . . . Right Upper Quadrant (of abdomen) (Medicine)
RV . . . . Right Ventricle (of heart)
RVH . . . . Right Ventricular Hypertrophy (Medicine)
ROW . . . . . . Right(s)-of-Way
R/W . . . . Right-of-Way
RW. . . . . Right Wing
RTW . . . . Right to Work
RW. . . . . Right Worshipful
RWGM . . . . . Right Worshipful Grand Master (Masonry)
RWSGW . . . . . Right Worshipful Senior Grand Warden (Masonry)
RW. . . . . Right Worthy
RWGS. . . . . . Right Worthy Grand Secretary (Masonry)
RWGT. . . . . . Right Worthy Grand Templar (Masonry)
RWGW . . . . . Right Worthy Grand Warden (Masonry)
RR . . . . Rights Reserved
RB . . . . Rigid Boat
ZRP . . . . Rigid patrol airship (Navy symbol)
ZRS . . . . Rigid scouting airship (Navy symbol)
ZRN . . . . Rigid training airship (Navy symbol)
RL . . . . Rinderleistungbuch
R . . . . Ring (Technical drawings)
RGA . . . . Ring Guild of America
RI . . . . Ring Index (A reference book)
RS . . . . Ringer's Solution
R & CC . . . . . . Riot and Civil Commotion
R . . . . Riser (Technical drawings)
R . . . . Rises
RAPS . . . . . . Risk Appraisal of Programs System
ROW . . . . Risk of War
RDL . . . . Ritter Company, Inc. (NYSE symbol)
R . . . . River
RAG. . . . . . . River Assault Group (Military)
PR . . . . River Gunboat (Navy symbol)
RGB. . . . . . . River Gunboat
RL . . . . River Lines, Inc. (AAR code)
RT . . . . River Terminal Railway (AAR code)
RUC . . . . Riverine Utility Craft (Vehicle for transporting through shallow water and snow)
RD . . . . Rix Dollar
R . . . . Road
RB . . . . Road Bend
RJ . . . . Road Junction (Maps and charts)
RMICBM . . . . . Road Mobile Intercontinental Ballistic Missile
RRC . . . . Road Runners Club of America
RS . . . . Road Space

RMWAA . . . . . Roadmasters and Maintenance of Way Association of America
RBA . . . . Roadside Business Association
RNO . . . . Roan Selection Trust, Ltd. (Formerly, RHO) (NYSE symbol)
RA . . . . Robbery Armed
RNA . . . . Robbery Not Armed
RATSEC . . . . . Robert A. Taft Sanitary Engineering Center
RFK . . . . Robert Francis Kennedy
RMA . . . . Robert Morris Associates (National Association of Bank Loan Officers
          and Credit Men)
ROF . . . . Robertshaw Controls Company (NYSE symbol)
RS . . . . Roberval & Saguenay Railway Company (AAR code)
ROBOMB . . . . . Robot Bomb (Air Force)
RGS . . . . Rochester Gas & Electric Corporation (NYSE symbol)
RIT . . . . Rochester Institute of Technology
ROS . . . . Rochester Subway Company (AAR code)
RTC . . . . Rochester Telephone Corporation (NYSE symbol)
RIA . . . . Rock Island Arsenal (Illinois) (Army)
R & R . . . . . . Rock and Roll (Music)
R & R . . . . . . Rock and Rye
RSS . . . . Rockdale, Sandow & Southern R. R. (AAR code)
RIMR . . . . . . Rockefeller Institute for Medical Research
RAPEC . . . . . . Rocket-Assisted Personnel Ejection Catapult
RAP . . . . Rocket-Assisted Projectiles
RATO . . . . . . Rocket-Assisted Takeoff (Flying)
RAT . . . . Rocket-Assisted Torpedo (Anti-submarine warfare)
ROCKOON . . . . Rocket Balloon (Navy)
V-2 . . . . Rocket bomb employed by the Germans (World War II)
RCAA . . . . . . Rocket City Astronomical Association
RCU . . . . Rocket Countermeasure Unit
RCA . . . . Rocket Cruising Association
RDL . . . . Rocket Development Laboratory (Air Force)
RESCU . . . . . . Rocket-Ejection Seat Catapult Upward (Aviation)
READI . . . . . . Rocket Engine Analyzer & Decision Instrumentation
RENE . . . . . . Rocket Engine/Nozzle Ejector
RETL . . . . Rocket Engine Test Laboratory (Air Force)
RL . . . . Rocket Launcher (Air Force)
RMROCK . . . . Rocket Motors Records Office Center (Navy)
ROBO . . . . Rocket Orbital Bomber
RP . . . . Rocket Projectile
RP . . . . Rocket Propellant (Air Force)
RPIA . . . . Rocket Propellant Information Agency
RPG . . . . Rocket-Propelled Grenade
RPL . . . . Rocket Propulsion Laboratory (Air Force)
RPT . . . . Rocket Propulsion Technician (Air Force)
RRC . . . . Rocket Research Corporation
RRI . . . . Rocket Research Institute
RKTSTA . . . . . . Rocket Station
RT . . . . Rocket Target
RTV . . . . Rocket Test Vehicle
RTT . . . . Rocket-Thrown Torpedo
RAPID . . . . Rocketdyne Automatic Processing of Integrated Data (Data processing)
RKG . . . . Rockingham R. R. (AAR code)
ROR . . . . Rockton & Rion Railway (AAR code)
RH . . . . Rockwell Hardness
RKS . . . . Rockwell-Standard Corporation (NYSE symbol)
RFA . . . . Rocky Flats Area Office (AEC)
RMCMI . . . . . . Rocky Mountain Coal Mining Institute
RML . . . . Rocky Mountain Laboratory (National Institutes of Health)
ROMO . . . . . . Rocky Mountain National Park
RMPA . . . . . . Rocky Mountain Psychological Association
R . . . . Rod (Measurement)
RMC . . . . Rod Memory Computer
RCA . . . . Rodeo Cowboys Association
RF . . . . Rodeo Foundation
RIC . . . . Rodeo Information Commission
R . . . . Roentgen
RAD . . . . Roentgen Administered Dose
REM . . . . Roentgen Equivalent Man (AEC)
REP . . . . Roentgen Equivalent Physical
RHM . . . . Roentgen per Hour at one Meter
RKY . . . . Roentgen Kymography
RU . . . . Roentgen Unit
R . . . . Roger (All right or OK) (Communications slang)
ROH . . . . Rohm & Haas Company (NYSE symbol)
RHR . . . . Rohr Corporation (NYSE symbol)
RLMA . . . . . . Roll Label Manufacturers Association
RMI . . . . Roll Manufacturers Institute
RPY . . . . Roll, Pitch, and Yaw
RG . . . . Rolled Gold
RSJ . . . . Rolled-Steel Joist

RZMA . . . . Rolled Zinc Manufacturers Association
RBC . . . . Roller Bearing Corporation
RBEC . . . . Roller Bearing Engineers Committee
RSFA . . . . Roller Skating Foundation of America
RSROA . . . . . . Roller Skating Rink Operators Association of America
RMMEA . . . . . . Rolling Mill Machinery and Equipment Association
RSD . . . . Rolling Steel Door (Technical drawings)
RVTOL . . . . . . Rolling Vertical Take-Off and Landing
RO/RO . . . . . . Rollon/Rolloff
RROC . . . . Rolls-Royce Owners' Club
R . . . . Roma(n)
RC . . . . Roman Catholic
RCC . . . . Roman Catholic Church (British)
RCCH . . . . . . Roman Catholic Church
RBAUS . . . . . . Romanian Baptist Association of United States
RADC . . . . Rome Air Development Center (ESD)
RAMA . . . . . . Rome Air Materiel Area (Air Force) (Deactivated)
ROAMA . . . . . . Rome Air Materiel Area (Air Force) (Deactivated)
RASC . . . . Rome Air Service Command (Air Force)
RATSC . . . . . . Rome Air Technical Service Command (Air Force)
RDA . . . . Rome Daily American (An English-language newspaper in Italy)
R & J . . . . Romeo and Juliet (by Shakespeare)
RP . . . . Ron Pair!
RPE . . . . Ron Pair Enterprises (Division of Wilson, Inc.)
RONCOM . . . . Ronald Como, Inc. (Perry Como's production firm; Ronald is his son)
RON . . . . Ronson Corporation (NYSE symbol)
R . . . . Rood
RDMI . . . . Roof Drainage Manufacturers Institute
R . . . . Rook (Chess)
RT . . . . Room Temperature
RTV . . . . Room Temperature Vulcanizing
RBI . . . . Root Beer Institute
RMS . . . . Root Mean Square
RMSE . . . . Root Mean Square Error
RSS . . . . Root-Sum-Square
ROP . . . . Roper (George D.) Corporation (NYSE symbol)
RCT . . . . Rorschach Content Test (Psychology)
RSP . . . . Roscoe, Snyder & Pacific Railway Company (AAR code)
RKV . . . . Rose Knot Victor (Gemini tracking ship)
ROGOPAG . . . Rossellini, Jr.; Godard, Pasolini, Gregoretti (Title of episodic motion
          picture formed from surnames of its directors)
RFS . . . . Rossendorfer Forschungs-Reaktor
RSDRP . . . . . . Rossiiskaia Sotsial-Demokraticheskaia Rabochaia Partiia
RC . . . . Rosslyn Connecting R. R. (AAR code)
RUR . . . . Rossum's Universal Robots (Acronym is title of play by Karel
          Capek)
RPMI . . . . Roswell Park Memorial Institute (Buffalo, New York)
RI . . . . Rotary International
RVDT . . . . Rotary Variable Differential Transformer
R . . . . Rotary Wing (Aircraft designation)
RW . . . . Rotary Wing (Aircraft)
RBCNO . . . . . . Rotating Beam Ceilometer Inoperative (Aviation)
RPS . . . . Rotating Passing Scuttle
RCP . . . . Rotation Combat Personnel
RPM . . . . Rotation Per Minute
RFB . . . . Roter Frontkaempferbund
RA . . . . Rotogravure Association
R . . . . Rotor
REVS . . . . Rotor-Entry Vehicle System (Aerospace)
RINS . . . . Rotorace Inertial Navigation System
RRP . . . . Rotterdam-Rhine Pipeline (Oil)
R . . . . Rough (Appearance of bacterial colony)
RF . . . . Rough Finish
RNA . . . . Rough, Noncapsulated, Avirulent (with reference to bacteria)
RO . . . . Rough Opening (Technical drawings)
R . . . . Rough Sea
RH . . . . Round Head
RHFS . . . . Round Hill Field Station (MIT)
RH . . . . Round House (Maps and charts)
RR & E . . . . . . Round, Regular and Equal (with reference to pupils of eyes)
RT . . . . Round Table
RTI . . . . Round Table International
RT . . . . Round Trip
RGM . . . . Rounds per Gun per Minute
RPGPM . . . . . . Rounds Per Gun Per Minute
RDS/M . . . . . . Rounds Per Minute (Gunnery)
RSV . . . . Rous Sarcoma Virus
R . . . . Route
ROFOR . . . . . . Route Forecast (Aviation)
RO . . . . Route Order (Military)
RT . . . . Router Template

ROCALDIS ... Routine Calls May Be Dispensed With
RI .... Routing Identifier
RO .... Routing Office(r) (Navy)
R & R ...... Routing and Record Sheet (Air Force)
R/S .... Routing Slip (Air Force)
RO........ Routine Order(s)
RFS .... Rover Flight Safety
R .... Royal
RA .... Royal Academy (or Academician) (British)
RADA ...... Royal Academy of Dramatic Art (British)
RAM ...... Royal Academy of Music (British)
RAS .... Royal Aeronautical Society (British)
RAC .... Royal Agricultural College (British)
RASE ...... Royal Agricultural Society of England
RAF .... Royal Air Force (British)
RAFSC ..... Royal Air Force Staff College (British)
RAFS ...... Royal Air Force Station (British)
RAFVR ..... Royal Air Force Volunteer Reserve (British)
RAFA ...... Royal Air Forces Association
RAFTC ..... Royal Air Forces Transport Command
RAE .... Royal Aircraft Establishment (Great Britain)
RAF .... Royal Aircraft Factory (British) (World War I)
RAD .... Royal Albert Dock (British)
RAMSS ..... Royal Alfred Merchant Seamen's Society (British)
RAOB ...... Royal Antediluvian Order of Buffaloes
RAC .... Royal Arch Chapter (Masonry)
RAM ...... Royal Arch Mason
RARDE ..... Royal Armament Research & Development Establishment (British)
RAC .... Royal Armoured Corps (British)
RADC ...... Royal Army Dental Corps (British)
RAMC ..... Royal Army Medical Corps (British)
RAOC ...... Royal Army Ordnance Corps (British)
RAPC ...... Royal Army Pay Corps (British)
RAR .... Royal Army Reserve (British)
RASC ...... Royal Army Service Corps (British)
RAVC ...... Royal Army Veterinary Corps (British)
RA .... Royal Artillery (British)
RAS .... Royal Asiatic Society (British)
RAS .... Royal Astronomical Society (British)
RAAF ...... Royal Australian Air Force
RAN(V)R..... Royal Australian Naval (Volunteer) Reserve
RAN....... Royal Australian Navy
RAR .... Royal Australian Regiment
RAC .... Royal Automobile Club (Controlling body of motor racing in Britain)
RCA........ Royal Cambrian Academy (British)
RCA........ Royal Canadian Academy (or Academician)
RCAF ...... Royal Canadian Air Force
RCAF(WD) .... Royal Canadian Air Force, Women's Division
RCAC ...... Royal Canadian Armoured Corps
RCAMC ..... Royal Canadian Army Medical Corps
RCAPC ..... Royal Canadian Army Pay Corps
RCASC ..... Royal Canadian Army Service Corps
RCA .... Royal Canadian Artillery
RCCS ...... Royal Canadian Corps of Signals
RCDC ...... Royal Canadian Dental Corps
RCEME ..... Royal Canadian Electrical and Mechanical Engineers
RCE .... Royal Canadian Engineers
RCFR ...... Royal Canadian Fleet Reserve
RCIC ...... Royal Canadian Infantry Corps
RCL .... Royal Canadian Legion
RCMP ...... Royal Canadian Mounted Police (Formerly, RNWMP)
RCNAS..... Royal Canadian Naval Air Station
RCNC ..... Royal Canadian Naval College (1943-1948)
RCNR ..... Royal Canadian Naval Reserve
RCN(V)R.... Royal Canadian Naval (Volunteer) Reserve
RCN....... Royal Canadian Navy
CANDEP ..... Royal Canadian Navy Depot
RCOC ...... Royal Canadian Ordnance Corps
RCPC ...... Royal Canadian Postal Corps (Formerly, CPC)
OSC .... Royal Clan, Order of Scottish Clans
RCM .... Royal College of Music (British)
RCP........ Royal College of Physicians (British)
RCPE ...... Royal College of Physicians, Edinburgh
RCS .... Royal College of Surgeons
RCVS ...... Royal College of Veterinary Surgeons (British)
RCI .... Royal Colonial Institute (British)
RCNC ...... Royal Corps of Naval Constructors
RCT .... Royal Corps of Transport (British Army)
RCJ .... Royal Courts of Justice (British)
RCC .... Royal Crown Cola Company (NYSE symbol)
RCCC....... Royal Curling Club of Canada

RDC .... Royal Defence Corps (British)
RDI .... Royal Designer for Industry
RDY........ Royal Dockyard
RD .... Royal Dragoons (British)
RDF .... Royal Dublin Fusiliers (British)
RD .... Royal Dutch Petroleum Company (NYSE symbol)
REME ...... Royal Electrical and Mechanical Engineers (British)
RE .... Royal Engineers (Military) (British)
RES .... Royal Entomological Society (British)
RE .... Royal Exchange (British)
RFA .... Royal Field Artillery (British)
RFA .... Royal Fleet Auxiliary (British)
RFR .... Royal Fleet Reserve (British)
RFC .... Royal Flying Corps (British)
RFDS ...... Royal Flying Doctor Service (Australia)
RF .... Royal Fusiliers (British)
RGA........ Royal Garrison Artillery (British)
RGS .... Royal Geographical Society (British)
RGG .... Royal Grenadier Guards (British)
RHAF ...... Royal Hellenic Air Force
RHA .... Royal Hibernian Academy
RHMS..... Royal Hibernian Military School (Dublin)
RH .... Royal Highlanders (British)
RH .... Royal Highness
RHS .... Royal Historical Society (British)
RHA .... Royal Horse Artillery (British)
RHG....... Royal Horse Guards (British)
RHS .... Royal Horticultural Society (British)
RHS .... Royal Humane Society (British)
RIAF....... Royal Indian Air Force
RIEC ...... Royal Indian Engineering College (British)
RIM .... Royal Indian Marine
RIN .... Royal Indian Navy
RIBA ...... Royal Institute of British Architects
RIC........ Royal Institute of Chemistry (British)
RIE........ Royal Institute of Engineers (British)
RIIA ...... Royal Institute of International Affairs (British)
RIPWC ..... Royal Institute of Painters in Water-Colours (British)
RI .... Royal Institution (British)
RINA ...... Royal Institution of Naval Architects (British)
RI .... Royal Irish (Military unit) (British)
RIA .... Royal Irish Academy
RIC .... Royal Irish Constabulary
RIF .... Royal Irish Fusiliers
RLG .... Royal Lao Government
RLF .... Royal Literary Fund (British)
RLM .... Royal London Militia
RM .... Royal Mail
RMS .... Royal Mail Steamship (or Service) (British)
RM .... Royal Marine(s) (British)
RMA .... Royal Marine Artillery (British)
RMLI ...... Royal Marine Light Infantry (British)
RMO .... Royal Marine Office (British)
RMB........ Royal McBee Corporation (NYSE symbol) (Wall Street slang name: "Rhumba") (Delisted)
RMS .... Royal Microscopical Society (British)
RMA........ Royal Military Academy (For cadets of Royal Engineers and Royal Artillery; frequently referred to as Woolwich) (British)
RMA .... Royal Military Asylum
RMC........ Royal Military College (For army cadets; often referred to as Sandhurst) (British)
RMF........ Royal Munster Fusiliers (British)
RNLBI ...... Royal National Life-Boat Institution (British)
RNLI ...... Royal National Life-Boat Institution (British)
RNAF ...... Royal Naval Air Force (British)
RNAS....... Royal Naval Air Service (Precursor of Fleet Air Arm) (British)
RNAS ...... Royal Naval Air Station
RNATE ..... Royal Naval Air Training Establishment (British)
RNAMY ..... Royal Naval Aircraft Maintenance Yard (British)
RNBC ...... Royal Naval Beach Commando (British)
RNCVR..... Royal Naval Canadian Volunteer Reserve (World War I)
RNC........ Royal Naval College (For future officers; often spoken of as Dartmouth) (British)
RNCC ...... Royal Naval College of Canada (1911-1922)
RND........ Royal Naval Division
RNLO ..... Royal Naval Liaison Officer (British)
RNOC ...... Royal Naval Officers Club
RNPS ...... Royal Naval Patrol Service (British)
RNR .... Royal Naval Reserve (British)
RN(V)R..... Royal Naval (Volunteer) Reserve (British)
RNS .... Royal Naval School (British)

RNSC . . . . Royal Naval Staff College (British)
RNVSR . . . . . . Royal Naval Volunteer Supplementary Reserve (World War II) (British)
RN . . . . Royal Navy (British)
RNGHQ . . . . . Royal Navy General Headquarters (British)
RNA . . . . Royal Neighbors of America
RNEIAF . . . . . . Royal Netherlands East Indies Air Force
RNEIN . . . . . . Royal Netherlands East Indies Navy
RNN . . . . Royal Netherlands Navy
RNZAF . . . . . . Royal New Zealand Air Force
RNZN(V)R . . . Royal New Zealand Naval (Volunteer) Reserve
RNZN . . . . . . Royal New Zealand Navy
RNWMP . . . . . Royal North West Mounted Police (Later, RCMP)
NF . . . . The Royal Northumberland Fusiliers (British)
RNOAF . . . . . . Royal Norwegian Air Force
RO . . . . Royal Observatory (British)
ROC . . . . Royal Observer Corps (British civilian aircraft observers) (World War II)
RORC . . . . Royal Ocean Racing Club (British)
RO . . . . Royal Octavo
ROAR . . . . Royal Optimizing Assembly Routine (Data processing)
ROS . . . . Royal Order of Scotland
ROC . . . . . . Royal Ordnance Corps (British)
RRE . . . . Royal RADAR Establishment (British)
RRC . . . . Royal Red Cross (British)
RS . . . . Royal Scots (Military)
RSG . . . . Royal Scots Greys (Military unit) (British)
RSA . . . . Royal Scottish Academy (or Academician)
RS . . . . Royal Society
RBA . . . . Royal Society of British Artists
RBS . . . . Royal Society of British Sculptors
RSD . . . . Royal Society, Dublin
RSE . . . . Royal Society of Edinburgh
RSL . . . . Royal Society of Literature (British)
RSL . . . . Royal Society, London
RSM . . . . Royal Society of Musicians (British)
RSPWC . . . . . . Royal Society of Painters in Water-Colours (British)
RSPCA . . . . . . Royal Society for the Prevention of Cruelty to Animals
RSAAF . . . . . . Royal South African Air Force
RSAF . . . . Royal Swedish Air Force
RTAF . . . . Royal Thai Air Force
RTA . . . . Royal Thai Army
RTS . . . . Royal Toxophilite Society (British)
RUC . . . . Royal Ulster Constabulary
RUI . . . . Royal University of Ireland
RVC . . . . Royal Veterinary College (British)
RWF . . . . Royal Welch Fusiliers (British)
RWS . . . . Royal West Surrey (Regiment) (British)
RYS . . . . Royal Yacht Squadron (British)
R . . . . Rubber
RAL . . . . Rubber-Air-Lead (Tile)
RAC . . . . Rubber Allocation Committee
RB . . . . Rubber Base (Technical drawings)
RCB . . . . Rubber Control Board
RDC . . . . Rubber Development Corporation
REA . . . . Rubber Export Association
RHSI . . . . Rubber Heel and Sole Institute
RHC . . . . Rubber Hydrocarbon
RI . . . . Rubber Insulation (Technical drawings)
RMA . . . . Rubber Manufacturers Association
RPA . . . . Rubber Peptizing Agent
RPASMC . . . . . Rubber & Plastic Adhesive & Sealant Manufacturers Council (Later, Adhesive and Sealant Council)
RRA . . . . Rubber Reclaimers Association
RRC . . . . Rubber Reserve Committee (Navy)
RRC . . . . Rubber Reserve Company
RSA . . . . Rubber Shippers Association
RTF . . . . Rubber-Tile Floor (Technical drawings)
RTA . . . . Rubber Trade Association of New York
RER . . . . Rubberized Equipment Repair
RBD . . . . Rubbermaid, Inc. (NYSE symbol)
RVIMI . . . . . . Rubella Virus-Induced Mitotic Inhibitor
RBR . . . . Ruberoid Company (NYSE symbol)
Rb . . . . Rubidium (Chemical element)
R . . . . Ruble (Monetary unit in Russia)
RDP . . . . Rubulosediphosphate
RPD . . . . Ruchnoi Pulemet Degtyarev (Light Machine Gun) (USSR)
RGSA . . . . . . Ruffed Grouse Society of America
RFC . . . . Rugby Football Club
RU . . . . Rugby Union (Controlling body of British Rugby football)
RRPA . . . . . . Ruhr Regional Planning Authority (Post-World War II)
R . . . . Rule
R & A . . . . . . Rules and Administration Committee (US Senate)

ROA . . . . . . Rules of the Air
RAC . . . . Rules of the Air and Air Traffic Control (ICAO Air Navigation Commission)
RP . . . . Rules of Procedure
RS & I . . . . . Rules, Standards, and Instructions
RCL . . . . Ruling Case Law
RNC . . . . Rumanian National Committee
R . . . . Run(s) (Cricket)
RK . . . . Run of Kiln
ROM . . . . . . Run of Mine
ROP . . . . Run of Paper (Advertising which is to appear on no specified page)
ROP . . . . Run of Press (i.e., on an unspecified page or plate in web press set-up) (Printing)
RIAS . . . . Rundfunk Im Amerikanischen Sektor Berlins (Radio in American Sector) (West Berlin, Germany)
R . . . . Runic
RD . . . . Running Days
RPL . . . . Running Program Language
RR . . . . Running Reverse
RSALT . . . . . . Running, Signal and Anchor Lights
RT . . . . Running Title
R . . . . Runs (scored) (Baseball)
RBI . . . . Runs Batted In (Baseball)
RT . . . . Runup and Taxi (Air Force)
RW . . . . Runway
RAIL . . . . Runway Alignment Indicator Light (or Lighting) (FAA)
RCLS . . . . Runway Centerline Lights System (Aviation)
RCR . . . . Runway Condition Reading (or Report) (Aviation)
REIL . . . . Runway End Identification Lights (FAA)
RUNEL . . . . . Runway-End Lighting
RIGS . . . . Runway Identifiers with Glide Slope
RV . . . . Runway Visibility
RVO . . . . Runway Visibility Observer (Aviation)
RVR . . . . Runway Visual Range (Aviation)
R . . . . Rupee (Monetary unit in India)
RAP . . . . Rupees, Annas, Pies (Denominations of Indian money)
RUP . . . . Ruppert (Jacob) (NYSE symbol)
RAD . . . . Rural Areas Development
RCDS . . . . . . Rural Community Development Service (Department of Agriculture)
RCPA . . . . . . Rural Cooperative Power Association
RD . . . . Rural Dean
RD . . . . Rural Delivery
RD . . . . Rural District
RDC . . . . Rural District Council
RE . . . . Rural Electrification
REA . . . . Rural Electrification Administration (Department of Agriculture)
RFD . . . . Rural Free Delivery (of mail)
RHA . . . . Rural Housing Alliance
RITA . . . . . . Rural Industrial Technical Assistance (Latin American building program)
RIP . . . . Rural Industrialization Program (Department of Agriculture)
RR . . . . Rural Route
RSA . . . . Rural Sanitary Authority (British)
RSS . . . . Rural Sociological Society
RYC . . . . Rural Youth Corps (Maine)
RN . . . . Ruritan National
RX . . . . "Rush" (on teletype messages)
RR . . . . Rush Release
RUCA . . . . . . Russell Cave National Monument
RBOUSA . . . . . Russian Brotherhood Organization of the United States of America
RCWS . . . . . . Russian Children's Welfare Society
RCP(b) . . . . . Russian Communist Party (Bolsheviks)
RCMASA . . . . Russian Consolidated Mutual Aid Society of America
RCC . . . . Russian Corps Combatants
RUSDIC . . . . . Russian Dictionary
RHGSA . . . . . Russian Historical and Genealogical Society in America
RIRAA . . . . . Russian Immigrants' Representative Association in America
RIMAS . . . . . Russian Independent Mutual Aid Society
RNAA . . . . . . Russian Nobility Association in America
ROCMAS . . . . Russian Orthodox Catholic Mutual Aid Society of USA
ROCWMAS . . . Russian Orthodox Catholic Women's Mutual Aid Society
ROFL . . . . Russian Orthodox Fraternity Lubov
RPC . . . . Russian People's Center
RSDLP . . . . . . Russian Social-Democratic Labor Party
RSDLP(b) . . . . . Russian Social-Democratic Labor Party (Bolsheviks)
RSDWP . . . . . Russian Social Democratic Workers Party
RSFSR . . . . . . Russian Soviet Federated Socialist Republic
RSF . . . . Russian Student Fund
RPA . . . . Rust Prevention Association
RP . . . . Rust Preventive
RANSA . . . . . . Rutas Aereas Nacionales, SA (Venezuelan cargo airline)
Ru . . . . Ruthenium (Chemical element)

RUT . . . . Rutland Railway Corporation (AAR code)
RYC . . . . Ryan Aeronautical Company (NYSE symbol)
RN & CR . . . . Ryde, Newport, and Cowes Railway (British)

RDR . . . . Ryder System, Inc. (NYSE symbol)
RADS . . . . Ryukyu Air Defense System
RAFP . . . . Ryukyuan Armed Forces Police

S

WDM . . . . S.S. White Dental Mfg. Company (NYSE symbol)
SHIRAN . . . . . S-Band High-Accuracy Ranging and Navigation
SPA . . . . S-Band Power Amplifier
SBX . . . . S-Band Transponder
SM . . . . Sa Majeste (His Majesty)
S . . . . Sabbath
SO Cist . . . . . Sacer Ordo Cisterciensis (Cistercian Order of the Common
             Observance, or Cistercian Fathers) (Roman Catholic religious order)
SC . . . . Sacra Congregatio (Sacred Congregation)
SCC . . . . Sacra Congregatio Concilii (Sacred Congregation of the Council)
SCEERR . . . . . Sacra Congregatio Episcoporum et Regularium (Sacred Congregation
             of Bishops and Regulars)
SCI . . . . Sacra Congregatio Indicis (Sacred Congregation of the Index)
SCPF . . . . . . Sacra Congregatio de Propaganda Fide (Sacred Congregation for the
             Propagation of the Faith)
SRC . . . . Sacra Rituum Congregatio (Sacred Congregation of Rites)
SV . . . . Sacra Virgo (Holy Virgin)
STB . . . . Sacrae Theologiae Baccalaureus (Bachelor of Sacred Theology)
STD . . . . Sacrae Theologiae Doctor (Doctor of Sacred Theology)
STL . . . . Sacrae Theologiae Lector (Reader in Sacred Theology)
STL . . . . Sacrae Theologiae Licentiatus (Licentiate of Sacred Theology)
STM . . . . Sacrae Theologiae Magister (Master of Sacred Theology)
S . . . . Sacral
SMAMA . . . . . Sacramento Air Material Area
SAAD . . . . . . Sacramento Army Depot
SN . . . . Sacramento Northern Railway (AAR code)
SPO . . . . Sacramento Peak Observatory
S . . . . Sacred
SS . . . . Sacred Scripture
SH . . . . Sacrifice Hit (Baseball)
SDA . . . . Sacro-Dextra Anterior
SDP . . . . Sacro-Dextra Posterior
SDT . . . . Sacro-Dextra Transversa
SORS . . . . . . Sacro Occipital Research Society
STP . . . . Sacrosanctae (or Sacrae) Theologiae Professor (Professor of Sacred
             Theology)
SPA . . . . Sacrum Palatium Apostolicum (Sacred Apostolic Palace, Vatican,
             Quirinal)
SRI . . . . Sacrum Romanum Imperium (The Holy Roman Empire)
SC . . . . Sad Case (An unpopular person) (Teen slang)
SHMI . . . . . . Saddlery Hardware Manufacturers Institute
S & M . . . . . . Sadism and Masochism (Generic term)
S . . . . Saeculum
V . . . . A safe (Criminal slang)
S & A . . . . . . Safe (or Safety) and Arm (or Arming) Device
SAT . . . . Safe Arming Time
SCEI . . . . Safe Car Educational Institute
SLAG . . . . . . Safe Launch Angle Gate
SMA . . . . Safe Manufacturers' Association
SMNA . . . . . . Safe Manufacturers' National Association
SWDL . . . . . . Safe Winter Driving League
SWL . . . . Safe Working Load (Shipping)
SWP . . . . Safe Working Pressure
SAFSM . . . . . . Safeguard System Manager
SAD . . . . Safety, Arming and Destruct
SAD . . . . Safety and Arming Device
SEA . . . . Safety Engineering Analysis
SF . . . . Safety Factor
SFR . . . . Safety of Flight Requirements
SHCA . . . . . . Safety Helmet Council of America
SOLAS . . . . . Safety of Life at Sea (Convention) (International sea rules)
SOP . . . . Safety Operating Plan
SSRSB . . . . . . Safety and Special Radio Services Bureau (of FCC)

SS . . . . Safety Supplements (Air Force)
STEP . . . . Safety Test Engineering Program (AEC)
STEEP . . . . . . Safety Training for the Execution of Emergency Procedures (NASA)
SA . . . . Safeway Stores, Inc. (NYSE symbol)
SAHI . . . . . . Sagamore Hill National Historic Site
SAGU . . . . . . Saguaro National Monument
SOOM . . . . . . Saigon Officers Open Mess (Vietnam)
SA . . . . Sail Area
SV . . . . Sailing Vessel
SUP . . . . Sailors' Union of the Pacific
S . . . . Saint
SART . . . . . . St. Alban's Repertory Theater
SAG . . . . St. Apollonia Guild
SBCA . . . . . . Saint Bernard Club of America
SAGA . . . . . . Saint-Gaudens National Historic Site
SJBC . . . . . . Saint John the Baptist, Clewer
SJRT . . . . St. Johns River Terminal Company (AAR code)
SJLC . . . . . . St. Johnsbury & Lamoille County R. R. (AAR code)
SJB . . . . St. Joseph Belt Railway (AAR code)
SJO . . . . St. Joseph Lead Company (NYSE symbol)
SAJ . . . . St. Joseph Light & Power Company (NYSE symbol)
SJT . . . . St. Joseph Terminal R. R. (AAR code)
SJL . . . . St. Jude's League
SLSAC . . . . . Saint Lawrence Seaway Authority of Canada
SLSDC . . . . . Saint Lawrence Seaway Development Corporation (Independent government
             agency)
STL . . . . St. Louis (Missouri) (Airport symbol)
SBM . . . . St. Louis, Brownsville & Mexico Railway Company (AAR code)
STLB & M . . . . St. Louis, Brownsville and Mexico Railway Company
SLE . . . . Saint Louis Encephalitis (Medicine)
SLPC . . . . . . St. Louis Production Center
FN . . . . St. Louis-San Francisco Railway Company (NYSE symbol)
SLSF . . . . St. Louis-San Francisco Railway Company (AAR code)
STL-SF . . . . . St. Louis-San Francisco Railway Company
SLST . . . . . . St. Louis, San Francisco & Texas Railway Company (AAR code)
STL-SF & T . . . St. Louis, San Francisco and Texas Railway Company
STLSW of T . . . St. Louis Southwestern Railway Company of Texas
SSW . . . . St. Louis Southwestern Railway Lines (AAR code)
SM . . . . St. Marys R. R. (AAR code)
SPS . . . . St. Patrick's Missionary Society
SPG . . . . Saint Paul Guild
SPUD . . . . . . St. Paul Union Depot Company (AAR code)
SPSP . . . . . . St. Peter and St. Paul (The Papal seal)
SRT . . . . St. Regis Paper Company (NYSE symbol)
SATH . . . . . . St. Thomas National Historic Site
SI . . . . Saintpaulia International
SS . . . . Saints (as in "SS Peter and Paul")
S/D . . . . Salaried Direct (Ratio)
S & E . . . . . . Salaries and Expenses
SAMA . . . . . . Salem Maritime National Historic Site
SB . . . . Sales Book
SC . . . . Sales Costs
SL . . . . Sales Letter
SLR . . . . Sales Letter Report
SMF . . . . Sales Manpower Foundation
SME . . . . Sales and Marketing Executives-International
SME-I . . . . . . Sales and Marketing Executives-International
SPACE . . . . . . Sales Profitability and Contribution Evaluator (Data processing)
SPEA . . . . . . Sales Promotion Executives Association
SLTX . . . . Sales Tax
SC . . . . Salesianorum Congregatio (Congregation of St. Francis of Sales)
             (Salesian Fathers) (Roman Catholic religious order)
SDB . . . . Salesians of Don Bosco

SAACI . . . . . . Salesmen's Association of the American Chemical Industry
SAPAI . . . . . . Salesmen's Association of Paper and Allied Industries
SAPI . . . . Salesmen's Association of the Paper Industry
SATDPI . . . . . Salesmen's Association of the Textile Dyeing and Printing Industry
SPC . . . . Salicylamide, Phenacetin (Acetophenetidin) and Caffeine (Pharmacy)
SS . . . . Saline Soak
SWC . . . . Saline Water Conversion
SWCP . . . . . . Saline Water Conversion Program (Department of the Interior)
SI . . . . Salinity Indicator
STD . . . . Salinity/Temperature/Depth
SC . . . . Salmagundi Club
SRF . . . . Salmonellosis-Resistance Factor
SIMA . . . . . . Salon International de la Machine Agricole
SLAD . . . . . . Salon Litteraire, Artistique et Diplomatique
SA . . . . Salt Added
SDAA . . . . . . Salt Distributors Association of America
SGSFU . . . . . Salt-Glazed Structural Facing Units (Technical drawings)
SLGW . . . . . . Salt Lake, Garfield & Western Railway Company (AAR code)
SPA . . . . Salt Producers Association
SW . . . . Salt Water
SMART . . . . . Salton's Magical Automatic Retriever of Texts (Data processing)
SML . . . . Saluda Motor Lines (AAR code)
SCA . . . . Saluki Club of America
SC . . . . Salvage Charges
ARST . . . . . . Salvage Craft Tender (Navy ship symbol)
Salv Div Bad . . Salvage Diver Badge (Army)
SALVDV . . . . Salvage Dives
ARSD . . . . . . Salvage Lifting Vessel (Navy symbol)
SL . . . . Salvage Loss
SM . . . . Salvage Mechanic (Navy)
SOCC . . . . . . Salvage Operational Control Center (On submarine rescue ship during salvage operation)
ARS . . . . Salvage Ship (Navy symbol)
SA . . . . Salvation Army
SRF . . . . Sam Rayburn Foundation
Sm . . . . Samarium (Chemical element)
SC . . . . Same Case (Law)
SD . . . . Same Day
SOS . . . . Same Old Slum (Sailor slang for food) (Bowdlerized version)
SOS . . . . Same Old Stew (Military slang) (Bowdlerized version)
SOS . . . . Same Only Softer (Band leader's signal) (Slang)
SS . . . . Same Size
SBSK . . . . . . Samodzielna Brygada Strzelcow Karpackich (Poland)
SMOG . . . . . . Samoye Molodoye Obyedinenie Geniev (Youngest Federation of Geniuses) (Clandestine group of writers in Moscow, USSR; initials may also stand for "Smelost'..." - see separate entry)
SC of A . . . . . Samoyed Club of America
SD . . . . Sample Delay
SDS . . . . Sample Display Service (Department of Commerce)
SI . . . . Sample Interval
SRC . . . . Sample Rock Container (NASA)
SADSAC . . . . . Sampled Data Simulator and Computer
SPS . . . . Samples Per Second
SFAL . . . . . . Samuel Feltman Ammunition Laboratory (Army)
SAAD . . . . . . San Antonio Air Depot (Air Force)
SAAMA . . . . . San Antonio Air Material Area
SAASC . . . . . San Antonio Air Service Command (Air Force)
SAATSC . . . . . San Antonio Air Technical Service Command (Air Force)
SAU & G . . . . San Antonio, Uvalde & Gulf Railroad Company
SBAMA . . . . . San Bernardino Air Materiel Area
SCI . . . . San Clemente Island
SDAE . . . . . . San Diego & Arizona Eastern Railway Company (AAR code)
SDO . . . . San Diego Gas & Electric Company (NYSE symbol)
SND . . . . San Diego Imperial Corporation (NYSE symbol)
SANDOCC . . . San Diego Oceanic Coordinating Committee
SF . . . . San Francisco (California)
SFO . . . . San Francisco (California) (Airport symbol)
S and FRAN . . San Francisco (California) (Navy)
SFADS . . . . . San Francisco Air Defense Sector (ADC)
SFBNS . . . . . San Francisco Bay Naval Shipyard
SFGE . . . . . . San Francisco Grain Exchange
SFIC . . . . . . San Francisco Information Center (Army Air Warning Service)
SFNSY . . . . . San Francisco Naval Shipyard
SFPE . . . . . . San Francisco Port of Embarkation
SFPOE . . . . . San Francisco Port of Embarkation
SJART . . . . . . San Jacinto Army Terminal
SJ . . . . San Juan (Puerto Rico)
SAJH . . . . . . San Juan Island National Historic Park
SLC . . . . San Luis Central R. R. (AAR code)
SL . . . . San Luis Obispo (Mexican state; city and county in California)
SMA . . . . San Manuel Arizona R. R. (AAR code)

SP . . . . San Pedro (California)
SQQ . . . . . . San Quentin Quail (A minor female) (Slang)
SMM . . . . . . Sancta Mater Maria (Holy Mother Mary)
SRE . . . . Sancta Romana Ecclesia (Most Holy Roman Church)
SCM . . . . Sanctae Memoriae (Of Holy Memory)
SM . . . . Sanctae Memoriae (Of Holy Memory)
SRE . . . . Sanctae Romanae Ecclesiae (of the Most Holy Roman Church)
SS . . . . Sancti (Saints)
SP . . . . Sanctissime Pater (Most Holy Father)
SSD . . . . Sanctissimus Dominus (Most Holy Lord) (The Pope)
SSDN . . . . . . Sanctissimus Dominus Noster (Our Most Holy Lord, Jesus Christ)
SV . . . . Sanctitas Vestra (Your Holiness)
S . . . . Sand
SLIGO . . . . . . Sand Lake Irish Gatherings Organization
SL . . . . Sand-Loaded (Technical drawings)
SS . . . . Sand Springs Railway Company (AAR code)
SNDL . . . . . . Sandale R. R. (AAR code)
SAN . . . . Sandersville R. R. (AAR code)
SI . . . . Sandwich Islands
SGM . . . . . . Sangamo Electric Company (NYSE symbol)
SA . . . . Sandia Area Office (AEC)
SC . . . . Sandia Corporation
SCLL . . . . . . Sandia Corporation, Livermore Laboratory
SER . . . . Sandia Engineering Reactor
SERF . . . . . . Sandia Engineering Reactor Facility
SNARE . . . . . Sandia Nuclear Assembly for Reactor Experiments
SPRF . . . . . . Sandia Pulsed Reactor Facility
SE . . . . Sanford & Eastern R. R. (AAR code)
SANF . . . . . . Sanford Recreation Area
SC . . . . Sanitary Corps
SE . . . . Sanitary Engineer
SEC . . . . Sanitary Engineering Center
SED . . . . Sanitary Engineering Division (MIT)
SERL . . . . . . Sanitary Engineering Research Laboratory (University of California)
SIA . . . . Sanitary Institute of America
SOS . . . . Sanity on Sex (Group opposing sex education in schools)
SBCED . . . . . Santa Barbara (California) Citizens for Environment Defense
SBRC . . . . . . Santa Barbara Research Center (Hughes Aircraft Company)
SCARF . . . . . Santa Cruz Acoustic Range Facility
SGBI . . . . . . Santa Gertrudis Breeders International
SMV . . . . Santa Maria Valley R. R. (AAR code)
SND . . . . Sap No Defect
SMSRL . . . . . Sarah Mellon Scaife Radiation Laboratory (University of Pittsburgh)
SARA . . . . . . Saratoga National Historical Park
STUC . . . . . . Sarawak Trade Union Congress
SUPP . . . . . . Sarawak United People's Party
SR . . . . Sarcoplasmic Reticulum
SD . . . . Sash Door
S . . . . Satang (Monetary unit of Thailand)
SATAN . . . . . Satellite Active Nullifier (Antisatellite weapon)
SATAR . . . . . Satellite for Aerospace Research (NASA)
SATRAC . . . . Satellite Automatic Terminal Rendezvous and Coupling
SATAN . . . . . Satellite Automatic Tracking Antenna
SAMS . . . . . . Satellite Automonitor System
SCAR . . . . . . Satellite Capture and Retrieval
SCOMO . . . . . Satellite Collection of Meteorological Observations
SCA . . . . Satellite Committee Agency (Army)
SATCOM . . . . Satellite Communications Agency (Army)
SATCOMA . . . Satellite Communications Agency (AEC/DCA)
SCTOC . . . . . Satellite Communications Test Operations Center
SCORE . . . . . Satellite Computer-Operated Readiness Equipment (SSD)
SCC . . . . Satellite Control Center
SCD . . . . Satellite Control Department
SCF . . . . Satellite Control Facility (Sunnyvale, California) (NASA)
SCN . . . . Satellite Control Network
SDAD . . . . . . Satellite Digital and Analog Display
SDADS . . . . . Satellite Digital and Display System
SEIT . . . . . . Satellite Educational and Informational Television
SIPOP . . . . . Satellite Information Processor Operational Program
SIRS . . . . . . Satellite Infrared Spectrometer (Environmental Science Services Administration)
SINAP . . . . . Satellite Input to Numerical Analysis and Prediction (Weather Bureau)
SAINT . . . . . Satellite Inspector and Satellite Interceptor (Air Force spacecraft program)
SIS . . . . Satellite Interceptor System
SIB . . . . Satellite Ionospheric Beacons (Military)
SKILL . . . . . . Satellite Kill
AGSL . . . . . . Satellite Launching Ship (Navy symbol)
SLV . . . . Satellite Launching Vehicle (Air Force)
SL . . . . Satellite-Like (Virus)
SMART . . . . . Satellite Maintenance and Repair Techniques (Air Force)
SAMOS . . . . . Satellite-Missile Observation System

SOC......... Satellite Operations Center (Cape Kennedy)
SORTI....... Satellite Orbital Track and Intercept (ARPA)
SPEARS..... Satellite Photo-Electric Analog Rectification System
SPAD....... Satellite Position Prediction and Display
SP .... Satellite Processor (Data transmission)
SPAD....... Satellite Protection for Area Defense (ARPA)
SATELCO .... Satellite Telecommunications Company (Japanese-American firm)
STARS...... Satellite Telemetry Automatic Reduction System (NASA)
STC .... Satellite Test Center (Air Force)
STROBE...... Satellite Tracking of Balloons and Emergencies
STC .... Satellite Tracking Committee (Military)
STADAD ..... Satellite Tracking and Data Acquisition Department
STADAN .... Satellite Tracking and Data Acquisition Network
STF. .... Satellite Tracking Facility (Air Force)
STP .... Satellite Tracking Program (of the Smithsonian Institution's Astrophysical
            Observatory)
STS .... Satellite Tracking Station
SV .... Satellite Virus
SERTH..... Satisfactory Evidence Received This Headquarters
SR .... Saturable Reactor
SD .... Saturation Deficit
S.......... Saturday
SEP ...... Saturday Evening Post
SI .... Saturday Inspection (Slang)
SR .... Saturday Review (A magazine)
S.......... Saturn
SAAP ...... Saturn/Apollo Applications Program (NASA)
SAUCERS..... Saucer and Unexplained Celestial Events Research Society
SDI .... Saudi Arabian Airlines
SAIR....... Saugus Ironworks National Historic Site
SPO....... Sausages, Potatoes and Onions (Meaning a cheap restaurant which
            specializes in these) (British slang)
SVAD...... Savannah Army Depot
SA .... Savannah & Atlanta Railway Company (AAR code)
SRL .... Savannah River Laboratory (AEC)
SRO .... Savannah River Operation (AEC)
SRP .... Savannah River Plant (AEC)
SSDK ...... Savannah State Docks (AAR code)
SCL .... Save a Cat League
SCF .... Save the Children Federation
SRL .... Save-the-Redwoods League
SOS........ Save Our Schools
SOS .... Save Our Ship (or Souls) (Improper popular explanation of three wireless
            letters with meaning sent as code-signal for extreme distress)
SSJ .... Savez Sindikata Jugoslavije (Yugoslavia Federation of Trade Unions)
SB .... Savings Bank
SIMSA ...... Savings Institutions Marketing Society of America
SL .... Savings and Loan
S & L ..... Savings and Loan (Association)
SLF .... Savings and Loan Foundation
SU .... Savings Unit
SG......... Sawtooth Generator
S.......... Saxon
SNEC....... Saxton Nuclear Engineering Corporation
SFS ...... Saybolt Furol Second
SSF .... Saybolt Seconds Furol (Oil viscosity)
SSU .... Saybolt Seconds Universal (Oil viscosity)
SF .... Scale Factor
SMA .... Scale Manufacturers Association
SCODA...... Scan Coherent Doppler Attachment
SCE .... Scan Conversion Equipment (TV)
SGN .... Scan Gate Number
SPG .... Scan Pattern Generator
NJF .... Scandinavian Agricultural Research Workers' Association
SAS ...... Scandinavian Airlines System
SAF .... Scandinavian American Fraternity
SCC .... Scandinavian Collectors Club
SCAR...... Scandinavian Council for Applied Research
SCANDOC ... Scandinavian Documentation Center (Washington, DC)
SFA .... Scandinavian Fraternity of America
STC .... Scandinavian Travel Commission (Later, Scandinavian National Travel
            Offices)
Sc .... Scandium (Chemical element)
SCU ...... Scanner Control Unit
SADIE...... Scanning Analog-to-Digital Input Equipment (National Bureau of
            Standards)
SCADS ...... Scanning Celestial Attitude Determination System
SCR ...... Scanning Control Register
SEM ...... Scanning Electron Microscope (or Microscopy)
SG......... Scanning Gate
SCIP....... Scanning for Information Parameters

SCADAR ..... Scatter Detection and Ranging
SCE .... Schedule Compliance-Evaluation (Polaris)
SOC........ Schedule of Organizational Change (Air Force)
SPERT ...... Schedule Performance Evaluation and Review Technique
SARP ...... Schedule and Report Procedure (NASA)
SPEED ...... Scheduled Procurement of Essential Equipment Deliveries (Post Office
            Department)
STOT ...... Scheduled Time Over Target
SCANS..... Scheduling and Control by Automated Network System
SMD........ Scheduling Management Display
SPECTROL ... Scheduling, Planning, Evaluation and Cost Control (Air Force)
SCAD ...... Schenectady Army Depot
SNR .... Schenectady Naval Reactors Office (AEC)
SO......... Schenectady Operation (AEC)
SOO .... Schenectady Operations Office (AEC)
SH .... Schenley Industries, Inc. (NYSE symbol)
SIMR ...... Schenley Instant Market Reports
SRG .... Schering Corporation (NYSE symbol)
SHK .... Schick Electric, Inc. (NYSE symbol)
SLEMA ..... Schiffli Lace and Embroidery Manufacturers Association
S.......... Schilling (Monetary unit in Austria)
SCA .... Schipperke Club of America
SA .... Schizophrenics Anonymous
SAI .... Schizophrenics Anonymous International
SLB .... Schlumberger, Limited (NYSE symbol)
ST .... Schmitt Trigger
SEDFRE ..... Scholarship, Education and Defense Fund for Racial Equality
SAT .... Scholastic Aptitude Test
S .... School
SAT .... School Ability Test (Psychology)
SAM....... School of Aerospace Medicine (Formerly, School of Aviation Medicine)
            (Air Force)
SAMCTT ..... School of Aerospace Medicine Color Threshold Test
SAT .... School of Applied Tactics (AAFSAT)
SAFA ...... School Assistance in Federally Affected Areas
SCHAVMED ... School of Aviation Medicine (Later, School of Aerospace Medicine)
            (Navy)
SCOLAVNMED.. School of Aviation Medicine (Later, School of Aerospace Medicine)
SBMI ...... School Bus Manufacturers Institute
SC .... School Certificate
SCA .... School and College Ability (Test)
SCAT ...... School and College Ability Test (of ETS)
SCCE ...... School and College Conference on English
SCOPP ..... School-College Orientation Program of Pittsburgh
SCSD ...... School Construction Systems Development (Project) (of Educational
            Facilities Laboratories)
SE .... School of Engineering
SFC .... School Facilities Council of Architecture, Education and Industry
SHARP ..... School Health Additional Referral Program (Public Health Service)
SIM .... School of Industrial Management (MIT)
SCHLA ..... School for Latin America (Military)
SLM .... School for Latin America (Air Force)
SMSG...... School Mathematics Study Group
SONA ...... School of Naval Administration, Leland Stanford University
SQL........ School Quota Letter
SQN ...... School Quota Number
SSCP ...... School Science Curriculum Project
SSND ...... School Sisters of Notre Dame (Roman Catholic religious order)
STS .... School Television Service
SRAA ...... Schoolboy Rowing Association of America
SH .... Schoolhouse
ST .... Schuler Tuning
SG......... Schutzgemeinschaft Gegen Meinungsterror (Guard Society Against
            Opinion Terror) (Germany)
SS .... Schutzstaffel (Elite Guard) (NAZI Germany)
SC .... Schwann Cell (Biology)
SGB....... Schweizerischer Gewerkschaftsbund (Swiss Federation of Trade Unions)
SKVV ...... Schweizerischer Katholischer Volksverein
SVEAA ..... Schweizerischer Verband Evangelischer Arbeiter und Angestellter (Swiss
            Federation of Protestant Trade Unions)
SAAS ...... Science Achievement Awards for Students
SAC........ Science Advisory Committee (Air Force)
S & AD ..... Science and Applications Directorate (NASA)
SCI .... Science Citation Index
SCA ...... Science Clubs of America
SCI .... Science Curriculum Improvement (Study) (Education)
SCIS ...... Science Curriculum Improvement Study
SEIAC ..... Science Education Information Analysis Center (ERIC)
SF .... Science Fiction
SFWA ...... Science Fiction Writers of America
SIC .... Science Information Council (National Science Foundation)

SIE . . . . Science Information Exchange (Smithsonian Institution)
SMFL . . . . Science, Mathematics, Foreign Languages
SN . . . . Science News (A publication)
SODB . . . . . . Science Organization Development Board (National Academy of Sciences)
SPRD . . . . Science Policy Research Division (of Legislative Reference Service, Library of Congress)
SRA . . . . Science Research Associates
SRPO . . . . Science Resources Planning Office (National Science Foundation)
SS . . . . Science Service
STS . . . . Science Talent Search
STAR . . . . Science Teaching Achievement Recognition
STRC . . . . Science and Technology Research Center
SAB . . . . Scientific Advisory Board (Air Force)
SAT . . . . Scientific Advisory Team (Navy)
SAMA . . . . Scientific Apparatus Makers Association
SCRIPT . . . . . . Scientific and Commercial Subroutine Interpreter and Program Translator
SCAR . . . . Scientific Committee on Antarctic Research
SCEAR . . . . . . Scientific Committee on the Effects of Atomic Radiation
SCOR . . . . Scientific Committee on Oceanic Research
SCOOP . . . . . . Scientific Computation of Optimum Procurement (Air Force)
SDC . . . . Scientific Data Center
SDS . . . . Scientific Data System (Later, XDS)
SEP . . . . Scientific and Engineering Personnel
SEC . . . . Scientific Estimates Committee
SEAMAP . . . . . Scientific Exploration and Mapping Program
SEARCH . . . . . Scientific Exploration and Research (Seventh-Day Adventist foundation)
SIC . . . . Scientific Information Center
SIN . . . . Scientific Information Notes (Publication of the Natural Science Foundation)
SIPE . . . . Scientific Information Program on Eutrophication (University of Wisconsin)
SIMA . . . . Scientific Instrument Manufacturers' Association (British)
SIMAJ . . . . . . Scientific Instrument Manufacturers' Association of Japan
SIM . . . . Scientific Instrument Module (NASA)
SIMCON . . . . . Scientific Inventory Management and Control
SMY . . . . Scientific Man-Year
SMC . . . . Scientific Manpower Commission
SMF . . . . Scientific Marriage Foundation
SM . . . . Scientific Memorandum
SN . . . . Scientific Note
SP . . . . Scientific Paper
SPD . . . . Scientific Passenger Pod
SPS . . . . Scientific Power Switching
SR . . . . Scientific Report
SR . . . . Scientific Research
SRIAER . . . . . . Scientific Research Institute for Atomic Energy Reactors (USSR)
RESA . . . . Scientific Research Society of America
SRSA . . . . Scientific Research Society of America
STAR . . . . Scientific and Technical Aerospace Reports (NASA)
STAF . . . . Scientific and Technical Application Forecasts
STEP . . . . Scientific and Technical Exploitation Program
STINFO . . . . . Scientific and Technical Information (Project) (DOD)
STID . . . . Scientific and Technical Information Dissemination (NASA)
SATIF . . . . Scientific and Technical Information Facility (NASA)
STIC . . . . Scientific and Technical Intelligence Center (DOD)
STIR . . . . Scientific and Technical Intelligence Register
STLO . . . . Scientific Technical Liaison Office (AFSC)
STR . . . . Scientific Technical Report
STP . . . . Scientifically Treated Petroleum (A motor fuel oil additive) (Initials reported, by extension of meaning, also to stand for a hallucinogenic drug, DOM)
SOS . . . . Scientists on Survival
SCPI . . . . Scientists' Committee for Public Information
SCRI . . . . Scientists' Committee for Radiation Information
SIPI . . . . Scientists' Institute for Public Information
SSMIMA . . . . . Scissor, Shear and Manicure Implement Manufacturers Association
SH . . . . Scleroscope Hardness
SCM . . . . SCM Corporation (Formerly, Smith, Corona, Marchant) (NYSE symbol)
STAR . . . . Score, Teach and Record (Teaching machine)
SCORAN . . . . . Scorer and Analyzer (Computerized educational testing)
SISUSA . . . . . . Scotch-Irish Society of the United States of America
SG . . . . Scots Guards
SPP . . . . Scott Paper Company (NYSE symbol)
SPRI . . . . Scott Polar Research Institute (Cambridge, England)
SANCAD . . . . . Scottish Association for National Certificates and Diplomas
SCU . . . . Scottish Church Union
SED . . . . Scottish Education Department
SNP . . . . Scottish National Party
SCOTNATS . . . Scottish Nationalists
SR . . . . Scottish Rifles (British military unit)
STCA . . . . Scottish Terrier Club of America
STUC . . . . Scottish Trades Union Congress

SWVA . . . . . . Scottish War Veterans of America
SCBL . . . . Scotts Bluff and Agate Fossil Beds National Monuments
VSB . . . . Scout-Bombing Plane (Navy symbol)
SCQC . . . . . . Scout Crew Qualification Course (Army)
CS . . . . Scout Cruiser (Navy symbol)
SEL . . . . Scout Esperanto League
SEV . . . . Scout Evaluation Vehicle
VSO . . . . Scout Observation Plane (Navy symbol)
SOSU . . . . . . Scout Observation Service Unit (Navy)
VSN . . . . Scout-Training Plane (Navy symbol)
S . . . . Scouting (Naval aircraft designation)
SAP . . . . Scouting Amphibian Plan (Coast Guard)
SB . . . . Scouting-Bombing Plane (When prefixed to Navy aircraft designation)
SCOFOR . . . . . Scouting Force (Navy)
SF . . . . Scouting Force (Navy)
SLP . . . . Scouting Landplane
SO . . . . Scouting-Observation Plane (When prefixed to Navy aircraft designation)
VS . . . . Scouting Plane (Navy symbol)
SSP . . . . Scouting Seaplane
SCORON . . . . Scouting Squadron
SCOTRACEN . . Scouting Training Center (Navy)
SOSSI . . . . . . Scouts on Stamps Society International
SCO . . . . Scovill Manufacturing Company (NYSE symbol)
SRPI . . . . Scrap Rubber and Plastics Institute
SSD . . . . Scrap Salvage Division (Navy)
SAG . . . . Screen Actors Guild
SCG . . . . Screen Cartoonists Guild
SCA . . . . Screen Composers' Association
SDG . . . . Screen Directors' Guild of America, Inc.
SDIG . . . . Screen Directors International Guild (Absorbed by Directors Guild of America)
SEG . . . . Screen Extras Guild
SG . . . . Screen Grid (Electrode or vacuum tube)
SMA . . . . Screen Manufacturers Association
SPPA . . . . Screen Process Printing Association, International
SPG . . . . Screen Producers Guild
HC . . . . Screening Smoke (Mixture)
SCW . . . . Screw & Bolt Corporation of America (NYSE symbol)
SRA . . . . Screw Research Association
SS . . . . Screw Steamer
SB . . . . Scrieve Board
SRM . . . . Scrim-Reinforced Material (Nonwoven sheets)
SIO . . . . Scripps Institutions of Oceanography
SSE . . . . Scuola de Sviluppo Economico (Italy)
S . . . . Scuttle
SAIL . . . . Sea-Air Interaction Laboratory (Oceanography)
SEAL . . . . Sea, Air and Land
SEAL . . . . Sea, Air, and Land Capability (Refers to Navy personnel trained in unconventional warfare)
SALUT . . . . . . Sea, Air, Land and Underwater Targets (Navy)
S . . . . Sea-air temperature difference correction
SD . . . . Sea Damaged (Grain trade)
SDP . . . . Sea Duty Pay (Navy)
SF . . . . Sea Flood
S & FSD . . . . . Sea and Foreign Service Duty (A Navy pay status)
S & FSD(A) . . . . Sea and Foreign Service Duty (Aviation) (A Navy pay status)
S & FSD(S) . . . . Sea and Foreign Service Duty (Submarine) (A Navy pay status)
SEAFRON . . . . Sea Frontier
SFF . . . . Sea Frontier Force (Navy)
SLS . . . . Sea-Land Service (AAR code)
SLBM . . . . Sea-Launched Ballistic Missile (DOD)
SLM . . . . Sea-Launched Missile
SL . . . . Sea Level
SLP . . . . Sea-Level Pressure
SLPL . . . . Sea Loading Pipe Line (Technical drawings)
SPO . . . . Sea Post Office
SEAS . . . . Sea School (Marine Corps)
SST . . . . Sea Surface Temperature
STO . . . . Sea Transport Officer
STAT . . . . SEABEE Technical Assistance Team
SVA . . . . SEABEE Veterans of America
SAL . . . . Seaboard Air Line R. R. (AAR code)
SBD . . . . Seaboard Air Line R. R. Company (NYSE symbol)
SCL . . . . Seaboard Coast Line Railroad
SEF . . . . Seaboard Finance Company (NYSE symbol)
SBW . . . . Seaboard and Western Airlines, Inc. (Later, Seaboard World Airlines, Inc.) (American Stock Exchange Symbol)
SABMIS . . . . . Seaborne Anti-Ballistic Missile Intercept System (Navy)
SES . . . . Seafarers Education Service (British)
SIU . . . . Seafarers' International Union of North America
SIUNA . . . . . . Seafarers' International Union of North America

SUNA . . . . . . Seafarers' International Union of North America
SIU-AGLI . . . . Seafarers' International Union of North America (AFL-CIO); Atlantic, Gulf, Lakes and Inland Waters District
SIU-IUP . . . . . Seafarers' International Union of North America (AFL-CIO); Inland-boatmen's Union of the Pacific
SIU-MCS . . . . Seafarers' International Union of North America (AFL-CIO); Marine Cooks and Stewards' Union
SIU-MFOW . . . Seafarers' International Union of North America (AFL-CIO); Pacific Coast Marine Firemen, Oilers, Watertenders and Wipers Association
SIU-SUP . . . . Seafarers' International Union of North America (AFL-CIO); Sailors' Union of the Pacific
AGD . . . . Seagoing Dredge (Navy symbol)
SPAR . . . . Seagoing Platform for Acoustic Research (NOL)
SVE . . . . Seagrave Corporation (NYSE symbol)
SEADAC . . . . . Seakeeping Data Analysis Center (Navy)
SLI . . . . Seal and Label Institute
SIGMA . . . . . . Sealed Insulating Glass Manufacturers Association
SWAK . . . . . . Sealed With a Kiss (Correspondence)
SWALK . . . . . . Sealed With a Loving Kiss (Correspondence)
SLR . . . . Sealright-Oswego Falls Corporation (NYSE symbol) (Delisted)
S . . . . Seaman, as S1 (Seaman 1st class) (Navy)
SN . . . . Seaman (Navy rating)
SA . . . . Seaman Apprentice
SR . . . . Seaman Recruit
ST . . . . Seaman Torpedoman
SC . . . . Seamen's Center
SCI . . . . Seamen's Church Institute of New York
SSTU . . . . Seamless Steel Tubing
KOR . . . . Seaplane (Russian symbol)
S . . . . Seaplane (Navy)
S/P . . . . Seaplane
MTB . . . . Seaplane Bomber (Russian symbol)
SPD . . . . Seaplane Depot Ship
SR . . . . Seaplane Reconnaissance Aircraft
SRU . . . . Seaplane Reconnaissance Unit
SRB . . . . Seaplane Repair Base
AV . . . . Seaplane Tender (Navy symbol)
AVD . . . . Seaplane Tender, Destroyer (Navy symbol)
YSD . . . . Seaplane Wrecking Derrick (Navy symbol)
SENA . . . . . . Seaport Navigation Company (AAR code)
S . . . . Search
SAU . . . . Search Attack Unit
SDR . . . . Search Decision Rule (Data processing)
SEEK . . . . . . Search for Education, Elevation and Knowledge (Program)
SITE . . . . Search Information Tape Equipment
SRT . . . . Search RADAR Terminal
H . . . . Search/Rescue (When the first letter of a pair) (Designation for all US military aircraft)
SAR . . . . Search and Rescue
SARLANT . . . . . Search and Rescue, Atlantic (Coast Guard)
SARCAP . . . . . Search and Rescue – Civil Air Patrol
SARCC . . . . . . Search and Rescue Coordination Center (Air Force)
SARAH . . . . . . Search and Rescue and Homing
SARTEL . . . . . . Search and Rescue, Telephone (Coast Guard)
SSG . . . . Search Signal Generator
S/T . . . . Search/Track
SPIN . . . . Searchable Physics Information Notices (Computer tapes)
SL . . . . Searchlight
S/L . . . . Searchlight
SLT . . . . Searchlight
SLC . . . . Searchlight Control (Military)
SLT & SDL . . . . Searchlight and Sound Locator (Navy)
S . . . . Sears, Roebuck & Company (NYSE symbol)
SEA . . . . Seasonal Employees in Agriculture
STL . . . . Seatrain Lines, Inc. (AAR code)
SART . . . . Seattle Army Terminal
SATD . . . . Seattle Army Terminal Detachment
SEPE . . . . Seattle Port of Embarkation
SW . . . . Seawater
SPAD . . . . Seaway Port Authority of Duluth
S . . . . Second(ary)
TWOATAF . . . . Second Allied Tactical Air Force Central Europe
SA . . . . Second Attack (Men's lacrosse position)
SC Div Bad . . . Second Class Diver Badge (Army)
SD . . . . Second Defense (Men's lacrosse position)
SDD . . . . Second Development Decade (UN)
SE . . . . Second Entrance (Theatrical slang)
SECFLT . . . . . . Second Fleet (Atlantic) (Navy)
SHG . . . . Second-Harmonic Generation (LASER)
SLEP . . . . Second Large ESRO Project
SMAW . . . . . . Second Marine Aircraft Wing

SNCM . . . . . . Second Nicaraguan Campaign Medal
SROKA . . . . . . Second Republic of Korea Army
SSGDFB . . . . . Second Sight-Guide Dog Foundation for the Blind
SECTASKFLT . . Second Task Fleet
STAE . . . . Second Time Around Echo
SAFS . . . . Secondary Air Force Specialty
SB . . . . Secondary Battery (Navy)
SCSC . . . . Secondary Curriculum Study Center (of NASSP)
SEB . . . . Secondary Education Board
SECON . . . . . . Secondary Electron Conduction (Television camera system)
SEC . . . . Secondary Emission and Conduction
SGP . . . . Secondary Gun Pointer (Navy)
SITVC . . . . Secondary Injection Thrust Vector Control
SMO . . . . Secondary Market Operation
SMI . . . . Secondary Metal Institute
SMOS . . . . Secondary Military Occupational Specialty
SPS . . . . Secondary Propulsion System (NASA)
SECRA . . . . . . Secondary RADAR (RADAR beacon)
SSAT . . . . Secondary School Admission Test Board
SSAC . . . . Secondary School Admissions Center
SSTC . . . . Secondary School Theatre Conference
SSR . . . . Secondary Surveillance RADAR
STGT . . . . Secondary Target
S . . . . Secret
SAO . . . . Secret Army Organization (English initialism for OAS, terrorist group in Algeria and metropolitan France)
S-C . . . . Secret and Confidential Files (Navy)
SFRD . . . . Secret Formerly Restricted
SIS . . . . Secret Intelligence Service (British)
SOE . . . . Secret Operations Executive (British research unit corresponding to OSS) (World War II)
SRD . . . . Secret Restricted Data
SS . . . . Secret Service
SWIP . . . . Secret Work in Process
SIAC . . . . Secretariat International des Artistes Catholiques
SIEUSE . . . . . . Secretariat International de l'Enseignement Universitaire des Sciences de l'Education
SIIC . . . . Secretariat International des Groupements Professionnels des Industries Chimiques des Pays de la CEE
SIIAEC . . . . . . Secretariat International des Ingenieurs, des Agronomes et des Cadres Economiques Catholiques
SPIE . . . . Secretariat Professionnel International de l'Enseignement
SSDMIC . . . . . Secretariat State-Defense Military Information Control Committee
SEC(UN) . . . . . Secretariat of the United Nations
SPI . . . . Secretariats Professionnels Internationaux
S . . . . Secretary
SAF . . . . Secretary of the Air Force
SAFAA . . . . . . Secretary of the Air Force, Administrative Assistant
SAFGC . . . . . . Secretary of Air Force General Counsel
SAFOI . . . . . . Secretary of the Air Force, Office of Information
SAFIS . . . . Secretary of Air Force, Office of Information Services
SAFLL . . . . Secretary of the Air Force, Office of Legislative Liaison
SAFO . . . . Secretary of the Air Force Order
SAFPC . . . . . . Secretary of Air Force Personnel Council
SAFIE . . . . Secretary of Air Force, Special Assistant for Installations
SAFIN . . . . Secretary of Air Force, Special Assistant for Intelligence
SA . . . . Secretary of the Army
SARS . . . . Secretary of the Army Research and Study (Fellowship)
SD . . . . Secretary of Defense
SECDEF . . . . . . Secretary of Defense
SG . . . . Secretary-General (UN)
SGS . . . . Secretary of the General Staff (Army)
S-G(UN) . . . . . Secretary-General of the United Nations
SECNAV . . . . . Secretary of the Navy
SN . . . . Secretary of the Navy
SS . . . . Secretary for Scotland
SS . . . . Secretary of State
S of S . . . . Secretary of State
SSA . . . . Secretary of State for Air (British)
SSW . . . . Secretary of State for War (British)
SECWAR . . . . . Secretary of War
SW . . . . Secretary of War (Obsolete)
SCOROR . . . . Secretary's Committee on Research on Reorganization (Navy)
SO . . . . Secretary's Office (Navy)
SOME . . . . . . Secretary's Office, Management Engineer (Navy)
SOND . . . . . . Secretary's Office, Navy Department
SONRD . . . . . . Secretary's Office, Office of Research and Development (Navy)
SORA . . . . Secretary's Office, Records Administration (Navy)
SOSED . . . . . . Secretary's Office, Shore Establishments Division (Incorporated into SECP, 1944)
SOTB . . . . Secretary's Office, Transportation Branch (Navy)

S . . . . Section
SB . . . . Section Base (Military)
SECTBASE . . . . Section Base (Navy)
SCS . . . . Section Control Station (RADAR)
SES . . . . Section d'Eclaireurs-Skieurs (of Chasseurs Alpins, French Army)
SFID. . . . . Section Francaise de l'Internationale Ouvriere (French Section of the
　　　　　　　　Workers International)
SECOFF . . . . . Section Office
SP . . . . Section Patrol (Navy)
SR . . . . Section Report
SECAC . . . . . . Sectional Aeronautical Chart
SCAMP . . . . . . Sectionalized Carrier and Multipurpose Vehicle (Military)
SAS . . . . Sections Administratives Specialisees (Frency Army)
SCP . . . . Sector Command Post (Military)
SOC . . . . Sector Operations Center (Air Force)
SSI . . . . Sector Scan Indicator
SS of A . . . . . Secular Society of America (Defunct)
SA . . . . Secundum Artem (According to Art)
SL . . . . Secundum Legem (According to Law)
SN . . . . Secundum Naturam (Naturally)
SABRE. . . . . . Secure Airborne Bombing RADAR Equipment
SESE. . . . . . . Secure Echo-Sounding Equipment (SONAR) (Navy)
SESCO . . . . . Secure Submarine Communications
SEVOCOM . . . Secure Voice Communications
SEC . . . . Securities and Exchange Commission
SRC . . . . Securities Research Company
SAT . . . . Security Alert Team (Military)
SCCO. . . . . . . Security Classification Control Officer
SCG . . . . Security Classification Guide
SCP . . . . Security Classification Procedure
SCAT . . . . . . Security Control of Air Traffic
SCATANA . . . Security Control of Air Traffic and Air Navigation Aids (FAA)
SCATER. . . . . Security Control of Air Traffic and Electromagnetic Radiations (during
　　　　　　　　an air defense emergency)
SCPT . . . . . . Security Control Point
SC . . . . Security Council of the United Nations
SC(UN). . . . . Security Council of the United Nations
SF . . . . Security Forces (Japanese army)
SIZ . . . . Security Identification Zone
SIC . . . . Security Intelligence Corps
SILO . . . . . . Security Intelligence Liaison Office (Central Mediterranean Forces)
　　　　　　　　(Navy)
SIME . . . . . . Security Intelligence, Middle East (Navy)
SID . . . . Security and Intelligence Service (Army)
SP . . . . Security Police (Air Force)
SP . . . . Security Publication (Navy)
SSB . . . . Security Screening Board (Army)
SSR . . . . Security Survey Report (AEC)
STS . . . . Security Termination Statement (Military)
STC . . . . Security Time Control
STANY . . . . . Security Traders Association of New York
STAQ . . . . . . Security Traders Automated Quotation (System)
SVP . . . . Security Vehicle Patrol (Air Force)
SW . . . . Security Watch
SWSG. . . . . . Security Window Screen and Guard
SPM . . . . Sedimentary Phosphate Method
SR . . . . Sedimentation Rate
SRT . . . . Sedimentation Rate Test
ST . . . . Sedimentation Time
SL . . . . Seditious Libeler
S . . . . See
SC . . . . See Copy
SOM . . . . . . See Our Message
SYH . . . . See You Home (Teen slang)
CUL . . . . See You Later (Telegrapher's slang)
SPG . . . . Seed Pea Group
SAZO . . . . . . Seeker Azimuth Orientation (Air Force)
SRL . . . . Seeler Research Laboratory (Air Force)
SRU . . . . Seiberling Rubber Company (NYSE symbol)
SADSAC . . . . Seiler ALGOL Digitally Simulated Analog Computer
SLASH . . . . . Seiler Laboratory ALGOL Simulated Hybrid (Data processing)
SA . . . . Seiners Association
SID. . . . . Seismic Intrusion Detector (Army)
SSWWS . . . . . Seismic Sea-Wave Warning System
SMG . . . . . . Seismocardiogram
SSA . . . . Seismological Society of America
SACO . . . . . . Select Address and Contract Operate
SLRN . . . . . . Select Read Numerically
SV . . . . Selecta Vision (RCA brand name for tape cartridges of TV programs)
SAIMS . . . . . Selected Acquisitions, Information and Management System
SECAL . . . . . . Selected Calling System (Military)

SCAN . . . . . . Selected Current Aerospace Notices (NASA)
SDI . . . . Selected Descriptive Item
SEPOS . . . . . Selected Enlisted Personnel for Overseas Service
SIM . . . . Selected Item Management
SMEADO. . . . . Selected Major Exploratory Advanced Development Objective
SNPRI . . . . . . Selected Nonpriority List Item(s)
SRF . . . . Selected Reserve Force (Units) (of Army National Guard) (Discontinued,
　　　　　　　　1969)
SWRA . . . . . . Selected Water Resources Abstracts (Service of WRSIC)
SWIFT. . . . . . Selected Words in Full Title (Data processing)
SB . . . . Selection Board
S/B . . . . Selection Board (Military)
SACMAP . . . . . Selective Automatic Computational Matching & Positioning System
SB . . . . Selective Bibliography
SELCAL . . . . . Selective Calling (Radio)
SCRAM . . . . . Selective Combat Range Artillery Missile
SCO . . . . Selective Conscientious Objection
SCORE . . . . . Selective Conversion and Retention (Navy)
SCRAP . . . . . Selective Curtailment of Reports and Paperwork (Navy)
SDI . . . . Selective Dissemination of Information (System) (Data processing)
SDM . . . . Selective Dissemination of Microfiche
SET . . . . Selective Employment Tax (British)
SIF . . . . Selective Identification Feature (Military decoder modification)
SIF/IFF . . . . . Selective Identification Feature/Identification Friend or Foe (Military)
SIPU . . . . . . Selective Inactivation Photo-Dynamic Unit
SIR . . . . Selective Information Retrieval
SOLO. . . . . . Selective Optical Lock-On (Sighting device)
SPINDEX . . . . Selective Permutation Indexing (Library of Congress)
SPRINT . . . . . Selective Printing (Data processing term)
SPIT . . . . . . Selective Printing of Items From Tape (Data processing)
SR . . . . Selective Ringing
SSEC . . . . . . Selective Sequence Electronic Calculator (Data processing)
SS . . . . Selective Service
SSVC . . . . . . Selective Service
SSA . . . . Selective Service Act
SSB . . . . Selective Service Board
1A . . . . Selective Service Class (for Man Available for Military Service)
1A-O . . . . . . Selective Service Class (for a Conscientious Objector Available for
　　　　　　　　Noncombatant Military Service)
2A . . . . Selective Service Class (for Man Deferred or Deferrable from
　　　　　　　　Military Service Because of Essential Civilian Activity [supporting
　　　　　　　　the national health, safety, or interest])
2A-F . . . . . . Selective Service Class (for Man Physically Disqualified for
　　　　　　　　Military Service but Engaged in Work in the National Health,
　　　　　　　　Safety, or Interest)
3A . . . . Selective Service Class (for Man Deferred or Deferrable from
　　　　　　　　Military Service Because of Extreme Hardship [such as familial
　　　　　　　　responsiblity] or Because of Child Support)
4A . . . . Selective Service Class (for Man 38 Years of Age or Over Who is
　　　　　　　　Deferred from Military Service by Reason of Age)
2B . . . . Selective Service Class (for Man Deferred or Deferrable from
　　　　　　　　Military Service Because of His Necessity to War Production)
2B-F. . . . . . . Selective Service Class (for Man Physically Disqualified for Military
　　　　　　　　Service but Necessary to War Production)
4B . . . . Selective Service Class (for Public Officials Deferred by Law from
　　　　　　　　Military Service; Men Interned by the Enemy)
1C . . . . Selective Service Class (for a Member or Former Member of
　　　　　　　　US Land or Naval Forces Who Has an Honorable Discharge)
2C . . . . Selective Service Class (for Man Deferred from Military Service by
　　　　　　　　Reason of His Agricultural Occupation or Endeavor)
4C . . . . Selective Service Class (for Neutral Aliens Requesting Relief
　　　　　　　　from Military Liability and Aliens not Acceptable for the Armed Forces)
3D . . . . Selective Service Class (for Man Deferred from Military Service
　　　　　　　　because Induction Would Cause Extreme Hardship and Privation to
　　　　　　　　a Wife, Child, or Parent)
4D . . . . Selective Service Class (for a Minister of Religion or Divinity Student)
4E . . . . Selective Service Class (for a Conscientious Objector Available for,
　　　　　　　　Assigned to, or Released from Work of National Importance)
4F . . . . Selective Service Class (for Man Physically, Mentally or Morally
　　　　　　　　Unfit for Military Service)
SSCQT . . . . . . Selective Service College Qualifying Test
SSS . . . . Selective Service System
STP . . . . Selective Tape Print
STAR . . . . . . Selective Training and Retention (Navy)
SV . . . . Selective Volunteer (Navy)
SCA . . . . Selectivity Clear Accumulator
Se . . . . Selenium (Chemical element)
SD . . . . Selenium Diode
SRS . . . . Selenium Rectifier Stack
SADT . . . . . . Self-Accelerating Decomposition Temperature
SAE . . . . Self-Addressed Envelope

SABU . . . . Self-Adjusting Ball-Up (A state of confusion which may, or may not, clear up of itself) (Military slang)
SAMFU . . . . . . Self-Adjusting Military Foul Up (Slang)
SASSIF . . . . . . Self-Adjusting System of Scientific Information Flow
SABRE . . . . Self-Aligning Boost and Reentry (Air Force)
SADSACT. . . . . Self-Assigned Descriptors from Self and Cited Titles (Automatic indexing)
SCOR . . . . Self-Calibrating Omni-Range
SC . . . . Self-Closing
SCF . . . . Self-Consistent Fields
SC . . . . Self-Contained
SCAPE . . . . . . Self-Contained Atmospheric Personnel (or Protective) Ensemble (Suit) (Aerospace)
SCBA . . . . Self-Contained Breathing Apparatus
SCNS . . . . Self-Contained Navigation System (NASA)
SCUBA . . . . . . Self-Contained Underwater Breathing Apparatus
SCAN. . . . . . . Self-Correcting Automatic Navigator
SDC . . . . Self Defense Corps (Vietnam)
SDSS . . . . Self-Deploying Space Station
SD . . . . Self-Destroying (Projectile)
SECA . . . . . . Self-Employment Contributions Act (under which self-employed persons contribute to OASDI coverage for themselves)
STORC . . . . . . Self-ferrying Trans-Ocean Rotary-wing Crane (Helicopter)
SGSUB . . . . . . Self-Glazed Structural Unit Base (Technical drawings)
SIW . . . . Self-Inflicted Wound (Military)
SIA . . . . Self-Insurers Association
SLT . . . . Self-Loading Tape
SMU . . . . Self-Maneuvering Unit (Air Force)
SOAP . . . . Self-Optimizing Automatic Pilot
SOBLIN . . . . . Self-Organizing Binary Logical Network (OTS)
SOFCS . . . . . . Self-Organizing Flight Control System
SPEED . . . . Self-Programmed Electronic Equation Delineator
SPACE . . . . . . Self-Programming Automatic Circuit Evaluator
SP . . . . Self-Propelled (Military)
APB . . . . Self-Propelled Barracks Ship (Navy symbol)
SPM . . . . Self-Propelled Mount
SRF . . . . Self-Realization Fellowship
SR . . . . Self-Rectifying
SECO . . . . . . Self-Regulating Error-Correct Coder-Decoder
SRFCMP . . . . . Self-Rising Flour and Corn Meal Program
SRFI . . . . Self-Rising Flour Institute
SSS. . . . . Self-Service Store
SSSC . . . . Self-Service Supply Centers
SSU . . . . Self-Service Unit
SELSYN . . . . . Self-Synchronous (Trade name) (Motor)
STAR . . . . . . Self-Testing and Repairing (Computer self-repair)
SV . . . . Self-Verification
SECE . . . . Selfhelp of Emigres from Central Europe
SAAU . . . . . . Selfreliance Association of American Ukrainians
SO. . . . . Seller's Option (Business and trade)
SOD . . . . Seller's Option to Double
SP . . . . Selling Price
SIP . . . . Selma (Alabama) Inter-Religious Project
SEMCOR . . . . . Semantic Correlation (Machine-aided indexing)
SR . . . . Semantic Reaction
SH . . . . Semester Hour
SAGS . . . . Semiactive Gravity Gradient System (NASA)
SAH . . . . Semi-Active Homer (Missiles)
SA . . . . Semiannual
SAIR. . . . . . . Semiannual Inventory Report (Air Force)
SAPR . . . . . . Semi-Annual Progress Report
SAR . . . . Semi-Annual Report
STPR . . . . Semiannual Technical Progress Report
SAP . . . . Semi-Armor-Piercing (Projectile)
SA . . . . Semiautomatic
SABIR . . . . . . Semi-Automatic Bibliographic Information Retrieval
SAC . . . . Semiautomatic Coding
SADIE. . . . . . Semi-Automatic Decentralized Intercept Environment
SADIE . . . . . . Semiautomatic Defense Intercept Environment (Air Force)
SAFTAC . . . . . Semiautomatic Facility for Terminal Area Control
SAFI . . . . Semiautomatic Flight Inspection (FAA)
SAGE . . . . Semi-Automatic Ground Environment (US defense system)
SATIN. . . . . . SAGE (Semi-Automatic Ground Environment) Air Traffic Integration
SABRE . . . . . . SAGE (Semi-Automatic Ground Environment) Battery Routing Equipment
SITS . . . . SAGE (Semi-Automatic Ground Environment) Intercept Target Simulation
SMDF . . . . . . SAGE (Semi-Automatic Ground Environment) Main Distributing Frame
SMC . . . . SAGE (Semi-Automatic Ground Environment) Maintenance Control (RADAR)
SMCO. . . . . . . SAGE (Semi-Automatic Ground Environment) Maintenance Control Office (ADC)
SSSR . . . . SAGE (Semi-Automatic Ground Environment) System Status Report (ADC)

SSTM . . . . SAGE (Semi-Automatic Ground Environment) System Training Mission (ADC)
STP. . . . . SAGE (Semi-Automatic Ground Environment) System Training Program
SSTU . . . . . . SAGE (Semi-Automatic Ground Environment) System Training Unit (ADC)
STRANGE . . . . SAGE (Semi-Automatic Ground Environment) Tracking and Guidance Evaluation System
SAHF . . . . Semiautomatic Height Finder
SARAH . . . . . . Semiautomatic Range Azimuth and Height (Subsystem)
SAR . . . . Semi-Automatic Rifle (Army)
SATIRE . . . . . Semiautomatic Technical Information Retrieval
SAT . . . . Semiautomatic Test Equipment (NASA)
SAW . . . . Semiautomatic Weapons
SCIC . . . . Semiconductor Integrated Circuit
SIC. . . . . Semiconductor Integrated Circuit
SEMLAM . . . . . Semiconductor LASER Amplifier
SEMLAT . . . . . Semiconductor LASER Array Techniques
SD . . . . Semidiameter
SEALF. . . . . . . Semi-Empirical Absorption Loss Formula (Radio)
SEM . . . . Semi-Enriched Minimal (Agar)
SF . . . . Semifinished (Steel or other material)
SHE . . . . Semi-Homogeneous Experiment
Q . . . . Semi-Interquartile Range or Quartile Deviation (Statistics)
SM. . . . . Semimonthly
S-MPR . . . . . . Semi-Monthly Progress Reports (Navy)
SALALM . . . . . Seminars on the Acquisition of Latin American Library Materials
SPARK . . . . . . Seminars on Practical Applications of Research Knowledge (Advertising Research Foundation)
SOP . . . . Semi-Open Position (Dancing)
SP . . . . Semipostal
SS . . . . Semi-Steel
STLR . . . . Semitrailer
SW . . . . Semiweekly
SFV . . . . Semliki Forest Virus
SPAR . . . . Semper Paratus (Always Ready) (Coast Guard motto)
SPARS. . . . . . . Semper Paratus (US Coast Guard Women's Auxiliary; name taken from Coast Guard motto)
S. . . . . Sen (Japanese monetary unit)
S . . . . Senate
S . . . . Senate Bill (with number)
SOB . . . . Senate Office Building
SPO . . . . Senate Post Office
SR . . . . Senate Resolution
SC . . . . Senatus Consulto (By the Decree of the Senate)
SPQR . . . . . . Senatus Populusque Romanus (The Senate and People of Rome)
SO. . . . . Send Only
SR . . . . Send and Receive
S/RC . . . . Send/Receive Center
SCM . . . . Sender's Composition Message (Cable)
SEAD . . . . . . Seneca Army Depot
SAFI. . . . . . . Senior Air Force Instructor
SAFO . . . . Senior Air Force Officer (present)
SAFR . . . . . . Senior Air Force Representative
SASO . . . . Senior Air Staff Officer (British)
SAA . . . . Senior Army Advisor
SRARAV . . . . . Senior Army Aviator
Sr AR Av Bad . . Senior Army Aviator Badge
SAI . . . . Senior Army Instructor
SB . . . . Senior Beadle (Ancient Order of Foresters)
SBNO. . . . . . . Senior British Naval Officer
SBNOWA. . . . . Senior British Naval Officer, Western Atlantic
SCA . . . . Senior Citizens of America
SCL . . . . Senior Citizens League
SCOPE . . . . . . Senior Citizens' Opportunities for Personal Enrichment (Federal anti-poverty program)
SCAO . . . . . . Senior Civil Affairs Officer
SCR . . . . Senior Common Room (in British colleges and public schools)
SRCC . . . . . . Senior Control Center (Air Force)
SD . . . . Senior Deacon (Masonry)
SF . . . . Senior Fellow
SG . . . . Senior Grade
SGW . . . . Senior Grand Warden (Masonry)
SHMO. . . . . . . Senior Hospital Medical Officer
SHO . . . . Senior House Officer
SIG . . . . Senior Interdepartmental Group (Department of State)
SM. . . . . Senior Magistrate
SMSGT . . . . . . Senior Master Sergeant
SMO . . . . Senior Medical Officer (Military)
SMA . . . . Senior Military Attache
SMLO . . . . . . Senior Military Liaison Officer
SENAVAV . . . . Senior Naval Aviator (Navy)

SNAP . . . . Senior Naval Aviator Present
SNM . . . . Senior Naval Member
SNO . . . . Senior Naval Officer
SNOAD. . . . . . Senior Naval Officer Adriatic (British)
SNOL . . . . . . Senior Naval Officer, Landings (British)
SNOP . . . . . . Senior Naval Officer Present
SNTFC . . . . . . Senior Naval Task Force Commander
SNO . . . . Senior Navigation Officer
CANAVCHARGE. . Senior Officer (or Officer in Charge) at (Canadian Navy)
SO. . . . . Senior Officer (Military)
CANCOMFLT. . Senior Officer Afloat (Canadian Navy)
CANCOMFLTLANT. . Senior Officer Afloat Atlantic (Canadian Navy)
CANCOMFLTPAC. . Senior Officer Afloat Pacific (Canadian Navy)
SOASC(I) . . . . Senior Officer Assault Ships and Craft (India) (British)
SOP . . . . Senior Officer Present
SOPA . . . . . . Senior Officer Present Afloat
SOP(A) . . . . . Senior Officer Present (Ashore) (Navy)
SOPUS . . . . . Senior Officer Present, US Navy
CANRESLANT. . Senior Officer Reserve Fleet East Coast (Canadian Navy)
CANRESPAC . . Senior Officer Reserve Fleet West Coast (Canadian Navy)
SORNE(I). . . . . Senior Officer, Royal Naval Establishment (India) (British) (World War II)
SRPARABAD . . Senior Parachutist Badge
Sr Prcht Bad . . Senior Parachutist Badge (Army)
SPI . . . . Senior Patrol Inspector (Immigration and Naturalization Service)
SPGCPS . . . . . Senior Policy Group for Canadian Production Sharing
SR . . . . Senior Registrar
SRA . . . . Senior Residential Appraiser (Designation given by Society of Real Estate Appraisers)
SR . . . . Senior Reviewer
CANAIRNEW. . Senior Royal Canadian Air Force Liaison Officer, St. Johns Newfoundland, Canada
SSS . . . . Senior Service School (Military)
SUSMOP . . . . Senior United States Military Observer Palestine
SUSNO. . . . . Senior United States Naval Officer
SW. . . . . Senior Warden (Masonry)
SWD . . . . . . Senior Weapon Director (Air Force)
SW. . . . . Senior Wolf (An accomplished philanderer) (Slang)
SW. . . . . Senior Woodward (Ancient Order of Foresters)
SWAP . . . . . . Senior Worker Action Program
SAT . . . . Sennacieca Asocio Tutmonde (Nationless Worldwide Association) (Promotes use of Esperanto)
S . . . . Sensation (Psychology)
S-I. . . . . Sensation-Intuition (Jungian psychology)
SL . . . . Sensation Level (Audiometry)
SU . . . . Sensation Units
SA . . . . Sense Amplifier
SABO . . . . . . Sense Amplifier Blocking Oscillator
SPR . . . . Sense Printer
SCN . . . . Sensitive Command Network
SIN . . . . Sensitive Information Network
STC . . . . Sensitivity-Time Control (RADAR)
ST . . . . Sensitivity Training
SR . . . . Sensitization Response
STT . . . . Sensitization Test
SATAN . . . . . Sensor for Airborne Terrain Analysis
SOR . . . . Sensor Operation Room
SSC . . . . Sensor Signal Conditioner
SET . . . . Sensory Evaluation Test (Army)
S . . . . Sent (Communications)
SW . . . . Sent Wrong (i.e., misdirected)
SCT . . . . Sentence Completion Technique
SS . . . . Sentence Suspended
SENLOG. . . . . Sentinel Logistics Command
SENPO . . . . . Sentinel Project Office (Army)
SSS . . . . Sentinel-Spartan System
SENSEA . . . . Sentinel System Evaluation Agency
SSEA . . . . . . Sentinel System Evaluation Agency (DOD)
SENSCOM. . . . Sentinel Systems Command (Army)
SOBP . . . . . . Sentral Organisasi Buruh Pantjasila (Central Organization of Pantjasila Labor) (Indonesia)
SOBRI. . . . . . Sentral Organisasi Buruh Republik Indonesia (Central Labor Organization of the Republic of Indonesia)
SOKSI . . . . . Sentral Organisasi Karyawan Sosialis Indonesia (Central Organization of Indonesian Socialist Workers)
SDP . . . . Sentry Dog Patrol
S . . . . Senza (Without)
SS . . . . Senza Sordini (Played without mutes) (Music)
ST . . . . Senza Tempo (Without regard to time)
SC. . . . . Separate Cover
SR . . . . Separate Rations
SSR . . . . Separate Superheater Reactor (AEC)

SCE . . . . Separated Career Employee
SWORD. . . . . Separated, Widowed, or Divorced (New York City organization)
SB . . . . Separately Binned
S. . . . . Separation
SEPCEN . . . . Separation Center (Navy)
SDN . . . . Separation Designation Number
SIT. . . . . Separation-Initiated Timer
SEPROS. . . . . Separation Processing
SPN . . . . Separation Program Number (Military)
SJBA . . . . . . Sephardic Jewish Brotherhood of America
S . . . . September
S . . . . Sepulchrum (Sepulchre)
S. . . . . Sepultus (Buried)
SECAM . . . . . Sequence de Couleurs avec Memoire (Color Sequence with Memory) (French color television system)
SFL . . . . Sequence Flash Lights (FAA)
SEFLO . . . . . Sequence Flow (Tracing technique)
SMS . . . . Sequence Milestone System
SNI . . . . Sequence Number Indicator
SFR . . . . Sequenced Flashing Lights
SECO . . . . . . Sequential Coding and Decoding
SECOR . . . . . Sequential Collation of Range (Army program)
SCF . . . . Sequential Compatibility Firing
SECO . . . . . . Sequential Control (Computer; teletype)
SCOPE . . . . . Sequential Customer Order Processing Electronically
SMART . . . . . Sequential Mechanism for Automatic Recording and Testing
SMA . . . . Sequential Multiple Analyzer
SP . . . . Sequential Phase
SPRT. . . . . . . Sequential Probability Ratio Test (Statistics)
STEP. . . . . . . Sequential Tests of Educational Progress (of ETS; given in 10th and 12th grades)
SCATS . . . . . Sequentially-Controlled Automatic Transmitter Start
SEQU . . . . . . Sequoia and Kings Canyon National Parks
SSV . . . . Seraphic Society for Vocations
SNF . . . . Serb National Federation
SNDC. . . . . . Serbian National Defense Council
SFC . . . . Sergeant First Class
SIM . . . . Sergeant Instructor of Musketry
SL . . . . Sergeant-at-Law
SGM . . . . . . Sergeant Major (Army)
SM . . . . Sergeant-Major
SMAC. . . . . . Serial Memory Address Counter (Computer)
SN. . . . . Serial Number
S/N . . . . Serial Number
SSC . . . . Serial Shift Counter (Data processing)
SMACS . . . . . Serialized Missile Accounting and Control System
SWIMS . . . . . Serialized Weapons Information Management System (Navy)
SERDES . . . . . Serializer, Deserializer
SBS . . . . Serially Balanced Sequence (Statistics)
SRT . . . . Serials Round Table (of ALA)
S . . . . Series
SCRAP . . . . . Series Computation of Reliability and Probability (Data processing)
SRE . . . . Series Relay (Electronics)
SERBAUD. . . . Serikat Buruh Angkutan Udara (Airways' Union) (Indonesia)
SBB . . . . Serikat Buruh Batik (Batik Workers' Union) (Indonesia)
SEBBETSI . . . . Serikat Buruh Beras dan Tapioca Seluruh Indonesia (Rice and Tapioca Workers' Union) (Indonesia)
SARBUBSI . . . . Serikat Buruh Betjak Seluruh Indonesia (Pedicab Workers' Union) (Indonesia)
SEBDA . . . . . Serikat Buruh Daerah Autonoom (Civil Servants' Union) (Indonesia)
SBDPU . . . . . Serikat Buruh Djawantan Pekerdjaan Umun (Public Works' Union) (Indonesia)
SBDP . . . . . . Serikat Buruh Djawatan Perindustrian (Department of Industry Workers' Union) (Indonesia)
SARBUFIS . . . . Serikat Buruh Film Senidrama Indonesia (Union of Film Artists of Indonesia)
SBGSN. . . . . . Serikat Buruh Garam dan Soda Negeri (Salt Workers' Association) (Indonesia)
SBGI . . . . . . Serikat Buruh Gelas Indonesia (Glass Workers' Union) (Indonesia)
SBGP . . . . . . Serikat Buruh Gula Proklamasi (Sugar Workers' Union) (Indonesia)
SERBUHI . . . . Serikat Buruh Harian Indonesia (Newspaper Employees' Union) (Indonesia)
SBHRT . . . . . Serikat Buruh Hotel, Rumah-Makan dan Toko (Hotel, Restaurant and Shops' Workers' Union) (Indonesia)
SBI. . . . . Serikat Buruh Industri (Industrial Workers' Union) (Indonesia)
SARBIM . . . . Serikat Buruh Industri Bahan Makanan Rakjat (People's Food Processors' Union) (Indonesia)
SBIM . . . . . . Serikat Buruh Industri Metal (Metal Industries Workers' Union) (Indonesia)
SBIR . . . . . . Serikat Buruh Industri Ringan (Small Industry Workers' Union) (Indonesia)
SERBIUM . . . . Serikat Buruh Industri dan Umum (Industrial and General Workers' Union) (Indonesia)
SBIL . . . . . . Serikat Buruh Islam Indonesia (Central Islamic Labor Union of Indonesia)
SBJ . . . . Serikat Buruh Jodium (Iodine Factory Workers' Union) (Indonesia)

SBK . . . . Serikat Buruh Kehutanan (Indonesian National Forestry Workers' Union)
SARBUKSI . . . . Serikat Buruh Kehutanan Seluruh Indonesia (Forestry Workers' Union of Indonesia)
SBKP. . . . . . . Serikat Buruh Kementerian Pertahanan (Defense Ministry Union) (Indonesia)
SBKB . . . . Serikat Buruh Kendaraan Bermotor (Union of Motorized Transport Workers) (Indonesia)
SBK . . . . Serikat Buruh Kependjaraan (Prisons Workers' Unions) (Indonesia)
SBKA . . . . Serikat Buruh Kereta Api (Railway Labor Union) (Indonesia)
SARBUKRI . . . . Serikat Buruh Kristen Indonesia (Union of Christian Workers of Indonesia)
SBLGI. . . . . . . Serikat Buruh Listrik dan Gas Indonesia (Union of Electrical and Gas Workers) (Indonesia)
SBL . . . . Serikat Buruh Logam (Metal Workers' Union) (Indonesia)
SBMW . . . . . . Serikat Buruh Maclaine, Watson (Maclaine Watson Company Workers' Union) (Indonesia)
SERBUMAMI. . . Serikat Buruh Makanan dan Minuman (Food Workers' Union) (Indonesia)
SARBUMRI . . . . Serikat Buruh Metaal Republik Indonesia
SERBUMIKSI. . . Serikat Buruh Minjak Kelapa Seluruh (Coconut Oil Workers' Union) (Indonesia)
SBMSI. . . . . . . Serikat Buruh Minjak Shell Indonesia (Union of Oil Workers for Shell Indonesia)
SEBUMI. . . . . . Serikat Buruh Minjak, Stanvac (Oil Workers' Union, Stanvac) (Indonesia)
SERBUMIT . . . . Serikat Buruh Minjak dan Tambang (Oil and Minerals Workers' Union) (Indonesia)
SERBUMUSI . . . Serikat Buruh Muslimin Indonesia (Moslem Workers' Union of Indonesia)
SBOSI. . . . . . . Serikat Buruh Obat Seluruh Indonesia (All Indonesian Medicinal Factory Workers' Union)
SBP . . . . Serikat Buruh Pegadaian (Pawnshop Workers' Union) (Indonesia)
SESPENDO . . . Serikat Buruh Pegawai Negeri dan Daeran Otonom (Civil Servants Workers' Union) (Indonesia)
SBPU . . . . Serikat Buruh Pekerdjaan Umum (Public Workers' Ministry Union) (Indonesia)
SBPI. . . . . Serikat Buruh Pelabuhan Indonesia (Dockworkers' Union) (Indonesia)
SBPP . . . . Serikat Buruh Pelebuhan dan Pelajaran (Dockworkers' Union) (Indonesia)
SBPPK . . . . . . Serikat Buruh Pendidikan, Pengadjaran dan Kebudjaan (Department of Education Workers' Union) (Indonesia)
SBPI . . . . Serikat Buruh Pendjahit Indonesia (Tailors' Union) (Indonesia)
SBP . . . . Serikat Buruh Penerbangan (Airways' Unions) (Indonesia)
SBPT. . . . . Serikat Buruh Perhubungan dan Transport (Communications and Transportation Workers' Union) (Indonesia)
SERBUPI . . . . . Serikat Buruh Perkebunan Indo (Plantation Workers' Union of Indonesia)
SARBUPRI . . . . Serikat Buruh Perkebunan Republik Indonesia (Plantation Workers' Union of the Republic of Indonesia)
SBPKB. . . . . . . Serikat Buruh Persuahaan Kaju dan Bangunan (Indonesian Building, Road and Irrigation Workers' Union)
SERBUPRI. . . . . Serikat Buruh Pertambangan Indonesia (Mining Workers' Union) (Indonesia)
SBPT. . . . . Serikat Buruh Pertambangan Timah (Tin Mine Labor Union) (Indonesia)
SPBI . . . . Serikat Buruh Pertjetakan Indonesia (Printing Workers' Union) (Indonesia)
SBPG . . . . Serikat Buruh Perusahaan Gula (Sugar Workers' Union) (Indonesia)
SBQ . . . . Serikat Buruh Qantas (Qantas Labor Union) (Indonesia)
SBRRI . . . . Serikat Buruh Radio Republik Indonesia (Indonesian Broadcasting Workers' Association)
SABRI . . . . Serikat Buruh Rokok Indonesia (Cigarette Workers' Union) (Indonesia)
SBRI . . . . Serikat Buruh Rokok Indonesia (Cigarette Factory Workers' Union) (Indonesia)
SBSI . . . . Serikat Buruh Seluruh Indonesia (All Indonesian Laborers' Union)
SBSKK . . . . . . Serikat Buruh Sepatu Keradjinan Kulit Karet (Shoe Workers' Union) (Indonesia)
SBT . . . . Serikat Buruh Tambang (Mine Workers' Union) (Indonesia)
SBTT. . . . . Serikat Buruh Tambang Timah (Tin Mine Laborers' Union) (Indonesia)
SBT . . . . Serikat Buruh Teknik (Technicians' Union) (Indonesia)
SBTP. . . . . Serikat Buruh Teknik dan Pelabuhan (Technical and Harbour Workers' Union) (Indonesia)
SBTU . . . . Serikat Buruh Teknik Umum (Indonesia)
SBT . . . . Serikat Buruh Tekstil (Textile Workers' Union) (Indonesia)
SARBUTRI . . . . Serikat Buruh Textil Republik Indonesia (Textile Workers' Union) (Indonesia)
SERBU . . . . . . Serikat Buruh Umum (General Workers' Union) (Indonesia)
SERBUNI . . . . . Serikat Buruh Unilever Indonesia (Unilever Employees' Union) (Indonesia)
SKBM . . . . Serikat Kaum Buruh Minjak (Federation of Oil Unions of Indonesia)
SARNI . . . . . . Serikat Nelajan Indonesia (Sailors' Union) (Indonesia)
SOBSI. . . . . . . Serikat Organisasi Buruh Seluruh Indonesia (All Indonesia Central Labor Organization)
SARIPADI . . . . Serikat Pamong Desa Indonesia (Village Officials' Union)
SPSI . . . . Serikat Pelajaran Seluruh Indonesia (Sailors' Union) (Indonesia)
SSBPT . . . . Serikat Sekerdja Balai Penelitian Tekstil (Textile Research Institute Workers' Union) (Indonesia)
SSBKTN . . . . . Serikat Sekerdja Bank Koporasi, Tani dan Nelajan Disingkat (Cooperative, Farmers and Fishers Bank Employees' Union) (Indonesia)
SSBPI . . . . Serikat Sekerdja Bank Pembangunan Indonesia (Indonesian Development Bank Employees' Union)

SSB/DPUT . . . . Serikat Sekerdja Biro/Dinas Pembangunan Usaha Tani (Agricultural Development Service Workers' Union) (Indonesia)
SSBKD . . . . . . Serikat Sekerdja/Buruh Ketapradja Djakarta Raja (General Union of Government Officials of Greater Djakarta) (Indonesia)
SESDA . . . . . . Serikat Sekerdja Departemen Agama (Brotherhood of Employees of Department of Religious Affairs) (Indonesia)
SSDP . . . . Serikat Sekerdja Djawalan Padjak (Brotherhood of Tax Office Employees) (Indonesia)
SSKDN . . . . . . Serikat Sekerdja Kementerian Dalam Negeri (Union of Workers in the Department of Interior) (Indonesia)
SSKP . . . . Serikat Sekerdja Kementerian Pertaganan (Ministry of Defense Workers' Unions) (Indonesia)
SSPSM . . . . . . Serikat Sekerdja Pabrik Sendjata dan Mesiu (Armaments' Union) (Indonesia)
SSPP. . . . . Serikat Sekerdja Pamong Pradja (Public Officials' Union) (Indonesia)
SSPTT . . . . Serikat Sekerdja Pos, Telegrap dan Telepon (National Postal, Telegraph and Telephone Employees' Union) (Indonesia)
SSTI . . . . Serikat Sekerdja Topografi Indonesia (Indonesian Topography Employees' Union)
SIR . . . . Serious Incident Report (Military)
SIL . . . . Seriously Ill List
SWA . . . . Seriously Wounded in Action (Military)
STS . . . . Serological Test for Syphilis (Medicine)
SI . . . . Serra International
SI . . . . Sertoma International
SALD . . . . Serum Aldolase (Enzyme)
SGO-T . . . . . . Serum Glutamic Oxaloacetic-acid Transaminase
SGP-T . . . . . . Serum Glutamic Pyruvic Transaminase
SH . . . . Serum Hepatitis (Medicine)
SHBD . . . . Serum Hydroxy Butyrate Dehydrogenase (Enzyme)
SLD . . . . Serum Lactate Dehydrogenase (Medicine)
SLDH . . . . Serum Lactic Dehydrogenase (Enzyme)
SLPP. . . . . Serum Lipophosphoprotein
SMD . . . . Serum Malic Dehydrogenase (Enzyme)
SPI . . . . Serum Precipitable Iodine (Medicine)
SPCA . . . . Serum Prothrombin Conversion Accelerator (Factor VII)
SPGT . . . . Serum Pyruvic Glutamic Transaminase
STA . . . . Serum Thrombotic Accelerator
STI. . . . . Serum-Trypsin-Inhibitor (Medicine)
SWR . . . . Serum Wassermann Reaction (Medicine)
SP . . . . Servants of the Paraclete
SSHJP. . . . . Servants of the Sacred Heart of Jesus and of the Poor (Roman Catholic women's religious order)
SE . . . . Servel, Inc. (NYSE symbol)
SEMS . . . . Severe Environment Memory Series (Data processing)
SAM . . . . Service Attitude Measurement (Bell System)
SB . . . . Service Bulletin
S/C . . . . Service Ceiling
SCOPE . . . . . . Service Center of Private Enterprise
SCTH . . . . Service Center for Teachers of History
SCA . . . . Service Cinematographique des Armees (France)
SCI . . . . Service Civil International (International Voluntary Service)
SC . . . . Service Club (Military enlisted men's club)
SC . . . . Service Command (Marine Corps)
SVC . . . . Service Command (Army)
SCAT . . . . Service Command Air Transportation
SERVCOMFMFPAC . . Service Command, Fleet Marine Force, Pacific
SCU . . . . Service Command Unit
SCD . . . . Service Computation Date (Military)
SCORE . . . . . . Service Corps of Retired Executives (Small Business Administration)
SERVDIV . . . . Service Division (Navy)
SDECE . . . . . . Service de Documentation Exterieure et Contre Espionage (Intelligence organization) (France)
SDIT. . . . . Service de Documentation et d'Information Techniques de l'Aeronautique
SD . . . . Service Dress
SEA . . . . Service Educational Activities (Military)
SER . . . . Service, Employment, Redevelopment (Operation for Mexican-Americans)
SEDR . . . . Service Engineering Department Report
SEMH . . . . . . Service Engineering Man-Hours
SERVFOR . . . . Service Force (Navy)
SERVLANT. . . . Service Force, Atlantic Fleet
SERVLANTSUBORDCOMD. . Service Force, Atlantic Fleet, Subordinate Command
SERVPAC. . . . . Service Force, Pacific Fleet
SERFORSOPACSUBCOM . . Service Force South Pacific Subordinate Command
SERVSOWESPAC . . Service Force, Southwest Pacific Fleet
SERLANT. . . . . Service Forces, Atlantic (Navy)
SERPAC . . . . . Service Forces, Pacific (Navy)
SFO . . . . Service Fuel Oil
SIL . . . . Service Information Letter
SI . . . . Service Instruction
SIR(CICR). . . . . Service International de Recherches (du Comite International de la Croix-Rouge)

REVERSE ACRONYMS AND INITIALISMS DICTIONARY

SK	Service Kit
S & M	Service and Maintenance
SERTOMA	Service to Mankind (Meaning of name of Sertoma International Organization)
SMC	Service Men's Center (World War II)
SMA	Service Merchandisers of America
SM	Service Module (NASA)
SERVNO	Service Number (Navy)
SN	Service Number (Military)
SOAI	Service des Organisations Aeronautiques Internationales (France)
SPI	Service Pedalogique Interafricain
SPD	Service Project Drawing
SPS	Service Propulsion System (NASA)
SERVHEL	Service Record(s) and Health Record(s)
SERVPA	Service Record(s) and Pay Record(s)
SERVPAHEL	Service Record(s), Pay Record(s) and Health Record(s)
SERVREC	Service Record(s)
SR	Service Record
SRAP	Service Record and Allied Papers
SRB	Service Record Book (Military)
SR	Service Report
SVS	Service School (Military)
SSI	Service Social International
SESAME	Service, Sort and Merge (Data processing term)
SERON	Service Squadron (Navy)
SERRON	Service Squadron (Navy)
SERVON	Service Squadron (Navy)
Svc Strs	Service Stars (Army)
SSF	Service Storage Facility
SOS	Service of Supply
SOSSPA	Service of Supply, South Pacific Area (Navy) (World War II)
ST	Service Test
STI	Service Tools Institute
STU	Service Trials Unit
SU	Service Unit (Military)
SVM	Service Volontaire Mennonite
SDAA	Servicemen's Dependents Allowance Act
SGLI	Servicemen's Group Life Insurance
SRA	Servicemen's Readjustment Act
SERL	Services Electronics Research Laboratory (British)
SNLR	Services No Longer Required
SVLTE	Services Valve Life Test Establishment (British)
SAHSA	Servicio Aereo de Honduras, SA
SALA	Servicios Aeronauticos Latina America
SEGBA	Servicios Electricos del Gran Buenos Aires, SA (Electrical utility) (Argentina)
SAPS	Servico de Alimentacao da Providencia Social (Brazil)
SENAC	Servico Nacional de Aprendizagem Comercial (Brazil)
SENAI	Servico Nacional de Aprendizagem Industrial (Brazil)
SPES	Servico de Propaganda e Educacao Sanitaria (Brazil)
CRUZEIRO . . .	Servicos Aereos Cruzeiro do Sul
SBStJ	Serving Brother, Order of St. John of Jerusalem (British)
SIS	Serving the Indigent Sick
SSStJ	Serving Sister, Order of St. John of Jerusalem (British)
SID	Servizio Informazione Difesa (Defense intelligence service) (Italy)
SIE	Servizio Informazioni Esercito (Italy)
SIM	Servizio Informazioni Militare (Italian)
SPA	Servo Power Assembly
SPA	Servo Preamplifier
SDPL	Servomechanisms and Data Processing Laboratory (MIT)
SL	Servomechanisms Laboratory (MIT)
SD	Servus Dei (Servant of God)
S	Sesquiplane (Navy)
S	Set
SG	Set Gate
SS	Set Screw (Technical drawings)
SU	Set Up (Freight)
SUCL	Set Up, in Carloads (Business and trade)
SULCL	Set Up in Less than Carloads
SDA	Seventh-Day Adventist
SDBHS	Seventh Day Baptist Historical Society
SEVFLT	Seventh Fleet (Pacific) (Navy)
SEFIC	Seventh Fleet Intelligence Center (Navy)
SD	Several Dates
SEVP	Severance Pay (Military)
SELS	Severe Local Storm
SNRC	Severn Naval River Command
S & P RES DIS . .	Severn and Potomac Reserve District (Marine Corps)
SRNC	Severn River Naval Command
SMTA	Sewing Machine Trade Association
SA	Sex Appeal (Slang)
SIECUS	Sex Information and Education Council of the United States
SO	Sex Offender
SR	Sex Ratio
SF	Sexagesimo-quarto (Book up to 7 1/2 centimeters in height) (Bibliography)
SFR	SFC Financial Corporation (NYSE symbol)
SCORDES	Sferics Correlation Detection System
SPARSA	Sferics, Pulse, Azimuth, Rate, and Spectrum Analyzer
SF	Sforzando (Indicates sudden emphasis on single note or chord) (Music)
SFZ	Sforzando (Indicates sudden emphasis on single note or chord) (Music)
STGAA	Shade Tobacco Growers Agricultural Association
SHMO	Shadow Mountain National Recreation Area
SA	Shaft Alley (Technical drawings)
SHP	Shaft Horsepower (Nautical)
SES	Shahmoon Industries, Inc. (NYSE symbol)
SAA	Shakespeare Association of America
SWORD	Shallow Water Oceanographic Research Data (System) (Naval Ordnance Laboratory and Naval Oceanographic Office)
SHM	Shamrock Oil & Gas Corporation (NYSE symbol)
SADTC	Shape Air Defense Technology Center (Netherlands)
SC	Shaped Charge (of explosive)
SAP	Share Assembly Program (Data processing)
SCAT	Share Compiler-Assembler, Translator
SHARE	Share Happily and Reap Endlessly (Hollywood women's charity organization)
SIFT	Share Interval for FORTRAN Translator
SNACS	Share News on Automatic Coding Systems (Data processing)
SOS	Share Operating System (Data processing)
SHIEF	Shared Information Elicitation Facility (Data processing)
SSH	Sharon Steel Corporation (NYSE symbol)
S	Sharp
SC	Sharp Cash
Sp S	Sharp Shooter (Army)
SHAD	Sharpe Army Depot
SS	Sharpshooter (Marine Corps)
FHK	Shattuck (Frank G.) Company (NYSE symbol)
SSA	Shaw Society of America
SP	Shear Plate (Technical drawings)
SCAT	Sheep Cell Agglutination Test
SEA	Sheep Erythrocyte Agglutination (Test)
SM	Sheet Metal
SMACNA	Sheet Metal & Air Conditioning Contractors' National Association
SMIPP	Sheet Metal Industry Promotion Plan
SMW	Sheet Metal Workers' International Association
SMWIA	Sheet Metal Workers' International Association
SLI	Shelf Life Item (Military)
SS	Shelf Stock
SD	Shell Destroying (Device)
SDT	Shell Destroying Tracer (Ammunition)
SUO	Shell Oil Company (NYSE symbol)
SC	Shell Transport & Trading Company, Ltd. (NYSE symbol)
SHL	Sheller Manufacturing Corporation (NYSE symbol)
SHELREP	Shelling Report
SW	Shelter Warden (British Home Defence) (World War II)
SHEN	Shenandoah National Park
SHR	Sheraton Corporation of America (NYSE symbol)
SFTC	Sherman Fairchild Technology Center
SWP	Sherwin-Williams Paints
SF	Sherwood Foresters (Military unit) (British)
SPIB	Shetland Pony Identification Bureau
SSS	Shevchenko Scientific Society
SMR	Shield Mock-Up Reactor
STAR	Shield Test Air Facility Reactor
STIR	Shield Test and Irradiation Reactor (AEC)
STPF	Shield Test Pool Facility
SEFR	Shielding Experiment Facility Reactor (AEC)
SCR	Shift Count Register
SF	Shift Forward
SP	Shift Pulses
SR	Shift Register
SR	Shift Reverse
SWS	Shift Word, Substituting
S	Shilling(s) (British monetary unit)
SHIL	Shiloh National Military Park
SS	Shimmy Showing (From one girl to another, in reference to dress disarrangement)
S	Ship
SAN	Ship Account Number (Navy)
SAM & R	Ship Activation, Maintenance and Repair
SALES	Ship Aircraft Locating Equipment
SHIPALT	Ship Alteration
SAMID	Ship Anti-Missile Integrated Defense (Program) (Navy)

SHIPREQ	Ship to Apply on Requisition
SHPTARBY	Ship to Arrive By
SCDL	Ship Configuration Detail List (Navy)
SCI	Ship Controlled Intercept (RADAR) (Navy)
SHIPDTO	Ship on Depot Transfer Order
SHM	Ship Heading Marker (Navigation)
SHIPIM	Ship Immediately
SIG	Ship Improvement Guide
SINS	Ship Inertial Navigational System
SINEWS	Ship Integrated Electronic Warfare System(s)
SLT	Ship Letter Telegram
S-of-L	Ship-of-the-Line
SOSM	Ship Overhaul Schedule Milestone (Navy)
SPS	Ship Planning System
SHRF	Ship Regular Freight
SR	Ship Repair Ratings
SRTU	Ship Repair Training Unit
SRU	Ship Repair Unit
SS	Ship Service
SSC	Ship Structure Committee
SSV	Ship-to-Surface Vessel
SSC	Ship Systems Command (Formerly, Bureau of Ships) (Navy)
STAR	Ship-Tended Acoustic Relay (Military)
STD	Ship Training Detachment
SASAT	Shipboard Anti-Submarine Attack Teacher (Navy)
SXBT	Shipboard Expendable Bathythermograph (System) (Naval Oceanographic Office)
SILS	Shipboard Impact Locator System
SORCS	Shipboard Ordnance Requirement Computer System (Navy)
SWM	Shipboard Wave Meter
SCA	Shipbuilders Council of America
SB	Shipbuilding (Navy)
SAC	Shipbuilding Advisory Council (British)
SBCO	Shipbuilding Company
SCN	Shipbuilding and Conversion, Navy
SBCORP	Shipbuilding Corporation
SBDC	Shipbuilding and Drydock Company
SSC	Shipbuilding Stabilization Committee
SF	Shipfitter (Navy)
SFCB	Shipfitter, Construction Battalion (Navy)
SFCBB	Shipfitter, Construction Battalion, Blacksmith (Navy)
SFCBM	Shipfitter, Construction Battalion, Mechanical Draftsman (Navy)
SFCBP	Shipfitter, Construction Battalion, Pipe Fitter and Plumber (Navy)
SFCBR	Shipfitter, Construction Battalion, Rigger (Navy)
SFCBS	Shipfitter, Construction Battalion, Steelworker (Navy)
SFCBW	Shipfitter, Construction Battalion, Welder (Navy)
SFSR	Shipfitter, Ship Repair (Navy)
SFSRC	Shipfitter, Ship Repair, Chipper-Caulker (Navy)
SFSRD	Shipfitter, Ship Repair, Diver (Navy)
SFSRL	Shipfitter, Ship Repair, Driller-Reamer (Navy)
SFSRP	Shipfitter, Ship Repair, Pipe Fitter-Plumber (Navy)
SFSRR	Shipfitter, Ship Repair, Riveter (Navy)
SFSRS	Shipfitter, Ship Repair, Shipfitter (Navy)
SFSRF	Shipfitter, Ship Repair, Steelworker-Anglesmith (Navy)
SFSRW	Shipfitter, Ship Repair, Welder (Navy)
SCONS	Shipment Control System (Military)
SDC	Shipment Detail Card
SM	Shipment Memorandum (Navy)
SO	Shipment (or Shipping) Order (Business and trade)
SHIPS	Shipment Planning System (Military)
SR	Shipment (or Shipping) Request
SAPC	Shipowners Association of the Pacific Coast
SCB	Shipowners Claims Bureau
SL	Shipowner's Liability (Business and trade)
SOL	Shipowner's Liability (Business and trade)
S & C	Shipper and Carrier (Business and trade)
SPT	Shipper Pays Taxes
SL & C	Shipper's Load and Count (Bills of lading)
SL & T	Shipper's Load and Tally (Bills of lading)
SOFTA	Shippers Oil Field Traffic Association
SW	Shipper's Weights (Bills of lading)
SA	Shipping Authority
SB	Shipping Board
SCI	Shipping Container Institute
SCAJAP	Shipping Control Administrator Japan
SCOFA	Shipping Control Office, Forward Area (Navy)
SCOMA	Shipping Control Office, Marianas (Navy)
WPSC	Shipping Control War Plan (Navy)
SHIPDA	Shipping Data
SHIPDAFOL . . .	Shipping Data Follows
S & FA	Shipping and Forwarding Agent

SI	Shipping Instructions
S/N	Shipping Note (Business and trade)
S/N	Shipping Number
SHIPGO	Shipping Order
SR	Shipping Receipt (Business and trade)
ST	Shipping Ticket (Military)
S/T	Shipping Ticket (Army)
SAISAC	Ship's Aircraft Inertial System Alignment Console
SAMS	Ship's Alteration Management System (Navy)
SHARP	Ships Analysis and Retrieval Project (Navy)
SAIL	Ship's Armament Inventory List (Navy)
SCI	Ship's Capability Impaired (Navy)
SCIP	Ship's Capability Impaired for Lack of Parts
SCB	Ships Characteristics Board
SCLK	Ship's Clerk
SC	Ship's Cook (Navy)
SCB	Ship's Cook, Butcher (Navy)
SEA	Ships Editorial Association (Navy)
SH	Ship's Head (Heading) (Navigation)
SIO	Ship's Information Officer (Navy)
SI	Ship's Installation (Navy)
SMA	Ship's Material Account
SMT	Ship's Mean Time (Navigation)
SMS	Ship's Missile System
SO	Ship's Option
SPCC	Ship's Parts Control Center
SQAT	Ship's Qualification Assistance Team (Navy)
SSCNS	Ship's Self-Contained Navigation System
SSF	Ship's Service Force (Navy)
SH	Ship's Service-Man (Navy rating)
SSMB	Ship's Service Man, Barber (Navy)
SSMC	Ship's Service Man, Cobbler (Navy)
SSML	Ship's Service Man, Laundryman (Navy)
SSMT	Ship's Service Man, Tailor (Navy)
SSS	Ship's Service Stores
SSA	Ship's Stores Ashore (Navy)
SS & CS	Ship's Stores and Commissary Stores
SSP	Ship's Stores Profit (Navy)
SSPN	Ship's Stores and Profit, Navy
SW	Ship's Warrant (Marine Corps)
SS	Shipside
SY	Shipyard
SOA	Shoe Corporation of America (NYSE symbol)
SLMA	Shoe Lace Manufacturers Association
SPMA	Shoe Pattern Manufacturers Association
SSIA	Shoe Service Institute of America
SAFI	Sholem Aleichem Folk Institute
SCA	Shooters Club of America
SMT	Shop Mechanic's Test
SO	Shop Order
AIRFORWARD . .	Shore-Based Air Force, Forward Area, Central Pacific
VS	Shore-Based Scouting Squadron (Navy symbol)
SHORDU	Shore Duty (Navy)
SHORVEY	Shore Duty Survey
SEE ACT	Shore Electronic Engineering Activity (Navy)
SEEO	Shore Electronic Engineering Office (Navy)
SECP	(Division of) Shore Establishment and Civilian Personnel (Navy)
SED	Shore Establishments Division (Navy)
SFCP	Shore Fire Control Party (Air Force)
SP	Shore Party (Navy)
SP	Shore Patrol(man)
SPO	Shore Patrol Officer (Navy)
SP	Shore Police (Navy)
SSDB	Shore Station Development Board
SATS	Short Airfield for Tactical Support (Marine Corps)
SAL	Short Approach Light (FAA)
SB	Short Bill
SC	Short Circuit
SCC	Short-Circuit Current
SCS	Short-Circuit-Stable
SCTL	Short-Circuited Transmission Line
SD	Short Delay
SD	Short Delivery
SD	Short Duration
SFA	Short Field Aircraft
SI	Short Interest (Brokerage)
SIP	Short Irregular Pulses
SLYP	Short Leaf Yellow Pine (Lumber)
S-L	Short-Long (as, of a signal light's flash cycle)
SOL	Short of Luck (Bowdlerized version)
SMLE	Short Magazine Lee-Enfield Rifle

SM . . . . Short Metre (Music)
SMD . . . . Short Metre Double (Music)
SNAP . . . . . . Short Notice Annual Practice (Military)
SP . . . . Short Page
SPM . . . . Short Particular Metre (Music)
SP . . . . Short Period
SP . . . . Short Persistence
SR . . . . Short Range
SRG . . . . Short Range
SRAM . . . . . . Short-Range Attack Missile (Navy)
SRBM . . . . . . Short-Range Ballistic Missile
SHODOP . . . . Short-Range Doppler
SRGR . . . . . . Short Range Guided Rocket
SHORAN . . . . Short-Range Navigation
SHANICLE . . . Short Range Navigation Vehicle (System) (Air Force)
SR . . . . Short Rate
STOL . . . . . . Short Takeoff and Landing (Air Force)
STA . . . . Short-Term Arrangements (Department of State)
STA . . . . Short-Terms Abroad
STC . . . . Short Time Constant
STC . . . . Short Title Catalog
ST . . . . Short Ton (2000 lbs.)
STON . . . . . . Short Ton
SW . . . . Short Wave (Electronics)
SWB . . . . Short Wheel Base
SOB . . . . Shortness of Breath (Medicine)
SS . . . . Shortstop
SWF . . . . Shortwave Fadeouts
SWL . . . . Shortwave Listener (Radio)
SW . . . . Shotgun Wedding (Forced marriage) (Slang)
S/B . . . . Should Be
SSI . . . . Shoulder Sleeve Insignia (Military)
SCN . . . . Show Cause Notice
SFA . . . . Show Folks of America
SNUB . . . . . . Show Nothing Unless Bad
SLA . . . . Showmen's League of America
SNDT . . . . . . Shreemati Nathibai Domodar Thackersey Women's University (India)
SAOTA . . . . . Shrimp Association of the Americas
SRANA . . . . . Shrine Recorders Association of North America
ST . . . . Shrink Template
SFP . . . . Shungwayah Freedom Party (Kenya)
SIS . . . . Shut-In Society
SOV . . . . Shut-Off Valve
SOS . . . . Si Opus Sit (If Occasion Require)
SCSA . . . . . . Siamese Cat Society of America
SCJ . . . . Siberian Chemistry Journal
SHCA . . . . . . Siberian Husky Club of America
SD . . . . Sicherheitsdienst (Police system) (NAZI Germany)
SBA . . . . Sick Bay Attendant (Navy)
SH . . . . Sick in Hospital
SL . . . . Sick Leave
SOQ . . . . . . Sick Officer Quarters
S . . . . Side
SLB . . . . Side-Lobe Blanking (RADAR)
SLC . . . . Side-Lobe Cancellation (RADAR)
SLC . . . . Side Lobe Clutter
SLS . . . . Side Lobe Suppression
SLAR . . . . . . Side-Looking Aerial (or Airborne) RADAR
SCARF . . . . . . Side-Looking Coherent All-Range Focused
SLR . . . . Side-Looking RADAR
SLS . . . . Side-Looking SONAR
SN . . . . Side Note
SS . . . . Side Seam
STOW . . . . . . Side Transfer Optimum Warehousing
SWD . . . . Side Water Depth
SHA . . . . Sidereal Hour Angle
SPACE . . . . . Sidereal Polar Axis Celestial Equipment
SIDOR . . . . . . Siderurgica del Orinoco (Government steel company) (Venezuela)
SW . . . . Sidewinder
SU . . . . Siedlungsunternehmen
S . . . . Siemens
SSW . . . . Siemens-Schuckert Werke (Germany)
SU . . . . Siemens Unit
SIAD . . . . . . Sierra Army Depot
SLCL . . . . . . Sierra Leone Council of Labour
SLOS . . . . . . Sierra Leone Organization Society
SLPP . . . . . . Sierra Leone People's Party
SaLSUA . . . . . Sierra Leone Students Union of the Americas
SERA . . . . . . Sierra R. R. (AAR code)
SIFTOR . . . . . Sifting of Information for Technology of Reactors (MIT-AEC study)
SD . . . . Sight Draft (Business and trade)

S/D . . . . Sight Draft (Banking)
SDBL . . . . . . Sight Draft Bill of Lading Attached (Business and trade)
SRS . . . . Sight Restoration Society
SCISRS . . . . . Sigma Center Information Storage and Retrieval System
SPD . . . . Sigma Phi Delta
SR . . . . Sigma Reaction
S . . . . Sign(ed)
SOBIGM . . . . Sign Off Brother, I've Got Mine (Remark used by seamen who avoided risky assignments during World War II) (Also used as hoax by National Maritime Union for name of organization issuing pamphlet about low state of merchant marine service)
S . . . . Signa (Mark a prescription)
SAA . . . . Signal Appliance Association
SATCO . . . . . Signal Automatic Air Traffic Control System
SATSA . . . . . Signal Aviation Test and Support Activity
SB . . . . Signal Battalion (Army)
SIGBAT . . . . . . Signal Battalion (Army)
SB . . . . Signal Boatswain
SIGCEN . . . . . Signal Center (Military)
SCMS . . . . . . Signal Command Management System
SCORE . . . . . . Signal Communication by Orbiting Relay Equipment (Radio)
SCS . . . . Signal Communications System (Air Force)
SCE . . . . Signal Conditioning Equipment
SC . . . . Signal Corps (Army)
SIGC . . . . Signal Corps (Army)
SCEL . . . . . . Signal Corps Engineering Laboratories
SCIA . . . . . . Signal Corps Intelligence Agency (Army) (Obsolete)
SCL . . . . Signal Corps Laboratory (Army) (Obsolete)
SCR . . . . Signal Corps Radio (Followed by model number) (Army)
SDC . . . . Signal Data Converter
SDP . . . . Signal Data Processor
SEAL . . . . . . Signal Evaluation Airborne Laboratory (FAA)
SF . . . . Signal-Frequency
SIAM . . . . . . Signal Information and Monitoring Service (American radio monitoring service)
SIGINT . . . . . Signal Intelligence (Military)
SI . . . . Signal to Intermodulation Ratio
SN . . . . Signal-to-Noise Ratio
S/N . . . . Signal-to-Noise Ratio
SNR . . . . Signal-to-Noise Ratio (Electronics)
SIGO . . . . . . Signal Officer
SO . . . . Signal Officer
SORC . . . . . . Signal Officers' Reserve Corps
SOI . . . . Signal Operation Instructions
SINAD . . . . . Signal Plus Noise and Distortion
SPEED . . . . . . Signal Processing in Evacuated Electronic Devices
SPO . . . . Signal Property Office
SRC . . . . Signal Reserve Corps
SIGSEC . . . . . . Signal Security (Military)
SSA . . . . Signal Security Agency (Navy)
SS/CF . . . . . . Signal Strength, Center Frequency
STIT . . . . Signal Technical Intelligence Team (Army)
SM . . . . Signalman (Navy)
ZFB . . . . Signals Fading Badly
SRDE . . . . . . Signals Research and Development Establishment (British)
SRDL . . . . . . Signals Research & Development Laboratory (Army) (British)
S . . . . Signature
SAMMI . . . . . Signature Analysis Methods for Mission Identification
/S/ . . . . Signed (Before signature on typed copy of a document, original of which was signed)
SMSA . . . . . . Signed Missile Support Agency (Air Force)
SOS . . . . Signed-Off Sick
SCIB . . . . Significant Counterintelligence Briefs
SIDASE . . . . . Significant Data Selection
SIGMET . . . . . Significant Meteorological Information (Aviation)
SMILE . . . . . . Significant Milestone Integration Lateral Evaluation (Data processing)
SGS . . . . Signode Corporation (NYSE symbol)
S . . . . Signor
SVP . . . . S'il Vous Plait (If You Please)
SCAP . . . . . . Silent Compact Auxiliary Power
S . . . . Silicate
SMS . . . . Silico-Manganese Steel
Si . . . . Silicon (Chemical element)
SI . . . . Silicon
SiC . . . . Silicon Carbide
SCR . . . . Silicon-Controlled Rectifier (Electronics)
SCS . . . . Silicon-Controlled Switch
SPR . . . . Silicon Power Rectifier
SPAT . . . . . . Silicon Precision Alloy Transistor
SOS . . . . Silicon on Sapphire
SSMD . . . . . . Silicon Stud-Mounted Diode

SZVR . . . . Silicon Zener Voltage Regulator
SRMA . . . . Silk and Rayon Manufacturers Association
SRPI . . . . Silk and Rayon Print Institute
SRPDAA . . . . . Silk and Rayon Printers and Dyers Association of America
STCA . . . . Silky Terrier Club of America
SOB's . . . . Silly Old Buggers (Wardroom officers over the "advanced" age of 39)
            (British naval slang)
S . . . . Silver
SCAL . . . . Silver City Airways, Limited
SLSM . . . . Silver Life Saving Medal
SM . . . . Silver Medalist
SILS . . . . Silver Solder
SS . . . . Silver Star (Military award)
SSC . . . . Silver Star Citation
SSM . . . . Silver Star Medal
SUA . . . . Silver Users Association
SWCA . . . . . . Silver Wyandotte Club of America
S . . . . Silversmith
SSA . . . . Simian Society of America
SV . . . . Simian Virus (Medicine)
SIM . . . . Simmons Company (NYSE symbol)
SDS . . . . Simonds Saw and Steel Company (NYSE symbol)
SALE . . . . Simple Algebraic Language for Engineers
SCRAP . . . . . . Simple Complex Reaction-Time Apparatus
FS . . . . Simple Fracture (Medicine)
SHM . . . . Simple Harmonic Motion
SP . . . . Simple Printing
STEP . . . . Simple Transition to Electronic Processing
SSA . . . . Simpler Spelling Association
S . . . . Simplex
SPX . . . . Simplex Instrument (Telegraphy)
SRCC . . . . . . Simplex Remote Communications Central
SIG . . . . Simplicity is Greatness (Also see GIS)
SYP . . . . Simplicity Pattern Company, Inc. (NYSE symbol)
SANS . . . . . . Simplified Account-Numbering System
SAILS . . . . Simplified Aircraft Instrument Landing System
SADAP . . . . . . Simplified Automatic Data Plotter
SBLP . . . . Simplified Bank Loan Participation Plan (Small Business Administration)
SEMP . . . . . . Simplified Early Maturities Participation Plan (Small Business Administration)
SETA . . . . Simplified Electronic Tracking Apparatus (Air Force)
SIFT . . . . Simplified Input for Toss (Data processing)
SNAP . . . . Simplified Numerical Automatic Programmer (Data processing)
SPR . . . . Simplified Practice Recommendation
SPERT . . . . . . Simplified Program Evaluation and Review Technique (Trademark)
SRWS . . . . . . Simplified and Regularized Writing System
SSAL . . . . Simplified Short Approach Light (FAA)
SS . . . . Simplified Spelling
SUIAP . . . . . Simplified Unit Invoice Accounting Plan
SARD . . . . Simulated Aircraft RADAR Data
SDG . . . . Simulated Data Generator
SDT . . . . Simulated Data Tape
SFO . . . . Simulated Flame Out (Aviation)
SLC . . . . Simulated Linguistic Computer
SMACS . . . . . Simulated Message Analysis and Conversion Subsystem
SMIT . . . . . . Simulated Midcourse Instruction Test (NASA)
SIMOC . . . . . Simulated Occupant (People Machine) (Office of Civil Defense)
SOPE . . . . Simulated Off-the-Pad Ejection (NASA)
SRS . . . . Simulated Remote Station
SRSCC . . . . . . Simulated Remote Station Control Center
SIMSOC . . . . . Simulated Society
STAGE . . . . . . Simulated Total Atomic Global Exchange (DOD)
SV . . . . Simulated Video
SWET . . . . . . Simulated Water Entry Test
SLEDGE . . . . . Simulating Large Explosive Detonable Gas Experiment
SAHYB . . . . . . Simulation of Analog and Hybrid Computers
SAM . . . . Simulation of Analogue Methods (Data processing) (British)
SIMBAD . . . . . Simulation as a Basis for Social Agents' Decisions (Data processing)
SCATS . . . . . . Simulation, Checkout and Training System
SCUL . . . . . . Simulation of the Columbia University Libraries (Data processing
            research)
SIMCOM . . . . . Simulation and Computer (Data processing)
SIMCON . . . . . Simulation Controller
SMI . . . . Simulation of Machine Indexing
SMITE . . . . . . Simulation Model of Interceptor Terminal Effectiveness
SOL . . . . Simulation Oriented Language (Data processing)
SIMPAC . . . . . Simulation Package (Data processing)
SR . . . . Simulation Report
SMOTE . . . . . . Simulation of Turbofan Engine
SIMCOM . . . . . Simulator Compiler (Computer)
SERAPE . . . . . Simulator Equipment Requirements for Accelerating Procedural Evolution
SIMILE . . . . . . Simulator of Immediate Memory in Learning Experiments

SLANT . . . . . . Simulator Landing Attachment for Night Landing Training
SANOVA . . . . Simultaneous Analysis of Variance
SABH . . . . . . Simultaneous Automatic Broadcast Homer
SBMPL . . . . . Simultaneous Binaural Mid-Plane Localization (Audiometry)
SB . . . . Simultaneous Broadcast(ing)
SLMM . . . . . . Simultaneous Compass Locator at Middle Marker (Aviation)
SLOM . . . . . . Simultaneous Compass Locator at Outer Marker (Aviation)
SIR . . . . Simultaneous Impact Rate
SIMICOR . . . . . Simultaneous Multiple Image Correlation
SOLOMON . . . Simultaneous Operation Linked Ordinal Modular Network
SIPROS . . . . . . Simultaneous Processing Operation System (Data processing)
SRA . . . . Simultaneous Range Adcock Antenna (Military RADAR)
STRAW . . . . . Simultaneous Tape Read and Write
STP . . . . Simultaneous Test Procedure (Statistics)
STP . . . . Simultaneous Track Processor
S . . . . Simultaneous transmission of range signals and voice
SK . . . . Sinclair-Koppers Company
L . . . . Sinclair Oil Company (NYSE symbol)
SIABA . . . . . . Sindacato Italiano Artisti Belle Arti (Italian Union of Fine Arts)
SAUFI . . . . . . Sindacato Autonomo Unificato Ferrovieri Italiani (Autonomous Union of
            Italian Railroad Workers)
SFI . . . . Sindacato Ferrovieri Italiani (Union of Italian Railroad Workers)
SILAF . . . . . . Sindacato Italiano Lavoratori Appalti Ferroviari (Italian Union of Rail-
            road Contract Workers)
SILCA . . . . . . Sindacato Italiano Lavoratori Cappellai ed Affini (Italian Federation of
            Hat and Allied Workers)
SILP . . . . Sindacato Italiano Lavoratori del Petrolio (Oil Workers' Union) (Italy)
SILP . . . . Sindicato Italiano Lavoratori Postelegrafonici (Italian Union of Postal
            and Telegraph Workers)
SILTE . . . . . . Sindacato Italiano Lavoratori Telecomuniczioni (Italian Union of
            Telecommunications' Workers)
SILTS . . . . . . Sindacato Italiano Lavoratori Telefoni di Stato (Italian Union of
            Government Telephone Workers)
SILULAP . . . . . Sindacato Italiano Lavoratori Uffici Locali ed Agenzie Postelegrafonici
            (Italian Union of Local Post and Telegraph Office Workers)
SIOD . . . . . . Sindacato Italiano Odonototecnici Diplomati (Italian Union of
            Odontotechnicians)
SIO . . . . Sindacato Italiano Ostetriche (Italian Union of Midwives)
SIP . . . . Sindacato Italiano Pescatori (National Union of Fishermen) (Italy)
SNAV . . . . . . Sindacato Nazionale Attrazionisti Viaggianti (National Union of
            Traveling Entertainers) (Italy)
SINDAF . . . . . Sindacato Nazionale Dipendenti Amministrazioni Finanziarie (National
            Union of Financial Administration Employees) (Italy)
SINACMA . . . . Sindacato Nazionale Dipendenti Corte dei Conti e Magistrature
            Amministrative (National Union of General Accounting Office
            Employees) (Italy)
SINAMN . . . . Sindacato Nazionale Dipendenti Marina Mercantile (National Union of
            Merchant Marine Workers) (Italy)
SINCOE . . . . . Sindacato Nazionale Dipendenti Ministeri Industria e Commercio Estero
            (National Union of Ministry of Industry and Foreign Commerce
            Employees) (Italy)
SINAMAI . . . . Sindacato Nazionale e Dipendenti Ministero Africa Italiana (National
            Union of Former Italian Employees of African Ministry) (Italy)
SINAF . . . . . . Sindacato Nazionale Dipendenti Ministero Agricoltura e Foreste (National
            Union of Ministry of Agriculture and Forestry Employees) (Italy)
SILAP . . . . . . Sindacato Nazionale Dipendenti Ministero Dei Lavori Pubblici (National
            Union of Employees in the Ministry of Public Welfare) (Italy)
SINADIMID . . . Sindacato Nazionale Dipendenti Ministero Difesa (National Union of
            Ministry of Defense Employees) (Italy)
SNADIGC . . . . Sindacato Nazionale Dipendenti Ministero Grazia e Giustizia (National
            Union of Ministry of Justice Employees) (Italy)
SINAMIL . . . . . Sindacato Nazionale Dipendenti Ministero del Lavoro e Previdenza
            Sociale (National Union of Ministry of Labor and Social Security
            Employees) (Italy)
SNELPIF . . . . . Sindacato Nazionale Esperti Laureati Propagandisti Industrie
            Farmaceutiche (National Union of University Graduated Experts for
            Propaganda in Pharmaceutical Industries) (Italy)
SNIE . . . . Sindacato Nazionale Insegnanti Elementari (National Union of Elementary
            Teachers) (Italy)
SILI . . . . Sindacato Nazionale Lavoratori Italcable (National Union of Italian
            Cable Workers)
SLAVCA . . . . . Sindacato Nazionale Lavoratori Vetro e Ceramica (National Union of
            Glass and Ceramics' Workers) (Italy)
SINAPI . . . . . . Sindacato Nazionale Ministero Pubblica Istruzione (National Union of
            Ministry of Public Instructors) (Italy)
SINASCEL . . . . Sindacato Nazionale Scuola Elementare (National Union of Elementary
            School Teachers) (Italy)
SNSM . . . . . . Sindacato Nazionale Scuola Media (National Union of Intermediate
            Schoolteachers) (Italy)
SNT . . . . Sindacato Nazionale Tabacchine (National Union of Women Tobacco
            Workers) (Italy)

SNTS . . . . Sindacato Nazionale Telefonici di Stato (National Union of State Telephone Workers) (Italy)

SPEM . . . . Sindacato Petrolieri e Methanieri (Union of Oil and Methane Gas Workers) (Italy)

SINS . . . . Sindacato Scuola non Statale (Italian Union of Private Schools' Employees)

SLAT . . . . Sindicato Lavoratori Amministrativi e Technichi (Union of Administation and Technical Workers) (Somalia)

SLS . . . . Sindicato Lavoratori della Somalia (Workers Union of Somali)

SNECIPA . . . . Sindicato Nacional dos Empregados do Comercio e da Industria da Provincia de Angola (National Syndicate of Workers of Commerce and Industry of the Province of Angola)

SNECI . . . . . . Sindicato Nacional dos Empregados do Comercio e da Industria da Provincia de Mocambique (National Union of Commercial and Industrial Workers of Mozambique)

STML . . . . Sindicato de Trabajadores Mineros de Llallagua

SU . . . . Sindicato Unico (Confederation of Labor) (Italy -- Trieste)

SUTRASFCO . . . Sindicato Unificado de Trabajadores de la Standard Fruit Company (Honduras)

S . . . . Sine (Without)

SAT . . . . Sine Acido Thymonucleico (Without Thymonucleic Acid)

SA . . . . Sine Anno (Without date of publication)

SC . . . . Sine-Cosine

SD . . . . Sine Dato (Undated book)

SD . . . . Sine Die (Without Day)

SINH . . . . Sine, Hyperbolic

SLP . . . . Sine Legitima Prole (Without Lawful Issue)

SL . . . . Sine Loco (Without Indication of Place)

SLAN . . . . . . Sine Loco, Anno, vel Nomine (Without Place, Year, or Name)

SLND . . . . . . Sine Loco Nec Data (Without Indication of Place or Date of Printing)

SMP . . . . Sine Mascula Prole (Without Male Issue)

SN . . . . Sine Nomine (Without Name)

SP . . . . Sine Prole (Without Bodily Issue) (Law)

SPL . . . . Sine Prole Legitima (Without Legitimate Issue)

SPM . . . . Sine Prole Mascula (Without Male Issue)

SPS . . . . Sine Prole Superstite (Without Surviving Issue) (Law)

SWR . . . . Sine Wave Response

SALSU . . . . . . Singapore Admiralty Local Staff Union

SATU . . . . . . Singapore Association of Trade Unions

SBEU . . . . . . Singapore Bank Employees' Union

SBWU . . . . . . Singapore Bus Workers' Union

SBHEU . . . . . . Singapore Business Houses Employees' Union

SCAWU . . . . . Singapore Clerical and Administrative Workers' Union

SFSU . . . . . . Singapore Federation of Services' Unions

SFUGE . . . . . . Singapore Federation of Unions of Government Employees

SGEU . . . . . . Singapore General Employees' Union

GACSU . . . . . Singapore Government Administrative and Clerical Services' Union

SNUJ . . . . . . Singapore National Union of Journalists

SPA . . . . Singapore People's Alliance

SSWU . . . . . . Singapore Sawmill Workers' Union

STUC . . . . . . Singapore Trade Union Congress

SWWU . . . . . Singapore Wood Workers' Union

SMF . . . . Singer Company (NYSE symbol)

S . . . . Single

SA . . . . Single-Action (Firearm)

SAVOR . . . . Single-Actuated Voice Recorder

SAQS . . . . . . Single Agency Qualification Standards (Aviation)

SARS . . . . . . Single-Axis Reference System

SB . . . . Single Braid

SBS . . . . Single-Business Service

SC . . . . Single Case

SCP . . . . Single-Cell Protein

SCS . . . . Single Channel Simplex

SC . . . . Single Circuit (Electricity)

SC . . . . Single Column

SC . . . . Single Comb

SCU . . . . Single Conditioning Unit

1/C . . . . Single Conductor

SC . . . . Single Contact (Switch)

SCOP . . . . . . Single Copy Order Plan (Bookselling)

SCC . . . . Single-Cotton Covered (To identify single-strand cotton-covered magnet wire)

SC . . . . Single Counter

SC . . . . Single Crochet

SCE . . . . . . Single Cycle Execute

SD . . . . Single Deck (Navigation)

SDGA . . . . . . Single Degaussing Cable

SDF . . . . Single Degree of Freedom

SDP . . . . Single Department Purchasing (Agency)

S & D . . . . . Single and Double (Reduction gears)

SDC . . . . Single Drift Correction

SE . . . . Single End

SE . . . . Single-Ended, Cylindrical Boiler (Navy)

SE . . . . Single Engine

SEFT . . . . . . Single Engine Flight Training

SE . . . . Single Entry (Bookkeeping)

SF . . . . Single Feeder

SFA . . . . Single Frequency Approach (Aviation)

SG . . . . Single Groove (Insulators)

SGSP . . . . . . Single Groove, Single Petticoat (Insulators)

SHP . . . . Single Highest Peak (Aerospace)

SIE . . . . Single Instruction Execute

SIAT . . . . Single Integrated Attack Team

SIOP . . . . . . Single Integrated Operations Plan (Military)

STOP . . . . . . Single Integrated Operations Plan (Not strictly an acronym, but STOP is correct; it is a master list of Communist targets for attack in event of war, drawn up by Department of Defense)

SIWL . . . . . . Single Isolated Wheel Load (Aviation)

SLR . . . . Single-Lens Reflex (Camera)

SL . . . . Single Line

SLA . . . . Single Line Approach

SM . . . . Single Manager (Defense)

SMOA . . . . . . Single Manager Operating Agency

SNACS . . . . . . Single Nuclear Attack Case Study (DOD)

SOC . . . . Single Orbit Computation

SPFP . . . . Single Pass Fit Program

SPFT . . . . Single-Pedestal Flat-Top (Desk)

SPTW . . . . . . Single-Pedestal Typewriter (Desk)

1PH . . . . Single-Phase

SP . . . . Single Phase

SPOC . . . . . . Single Point Orbit Calculator

SP . . . . Single Pole (Switch)

SPDT . . . . . . Single Pole, Double Throw (Switch)

SPST . . . . Single-Pole, Single-Throw (Switch)

SPSTNODM . . . Single-Pole, Single-Throw, Normally Open, Double-Make (Electronics relay)

SP . . . . Single Programmer

SPL . . . . Single Propellant Loading

SP . . . . Single Purpose Gun

SIRIN . . . . . . Single Readiness Information System (NORRS)

SRO . . . . Single-Room Occupancy (New York housing term)

SS . . . . Single Scan

SS . . . . Single-Seated

SSF . . . . Single-Seated Fighter

SSKP . . . . . . Single-Shot Kill Probability

SSHP . . . . . . Single Shot Probability

SSP . . . . Single-Shot Probability

SS . . . . Single Sideband

SSB . . . . Single Sideband (Communications)

SSFM . . . . . . Single Sideband Frequency Modulation

SSM . . . . Single Sideband Modulation

SS . . . . Single Signal

SS . . . . Single Stranded

SS . . . . Single Strength (Citrus juices)

ST . . . . Single Throw (Switch)

ST . . . . Single Tire

STC . . . . Single-Trip Container

SU . . . . Single Uptake (Boilers)

SV . . . . Single Vibrations (Half cycles)

VS . . . . Single Vibrations (Half cycles)

SW . . . . Single Weight

S . . . . Singular

SMD . . . . Singular Multinomial Distribution (Statistics)

S . . . . Sinister (Left)

SM . . . . Sinistra Mano (Left Hand)

S . . . . Sink

SF . . . . Sinking Fund (Finance)

SAAF . . . . . . Sino-American Amity Fund

SACO . . . . . . Sino-American Cooperative Organization (Guerrilla and intelligence agency) (World War II)

SAP . . . . Sintered Aluminum Power

SA . . . . Sinu-Atrial (Physiology)

SR . . . . Sinus Rhythm (Medicine)

SV . . . . Sinus Venosus (Anatomy)

SIDF . . . . . . Sinusoidal Input Describing Function (Data processing)

SCADS . . . . . Sioux City Air Defense Sector (ADC)

SNBL . . . . . . Sioux City & New Orleans Barge Line (AAR code)

SCT . . . . Sioux City Terminal Railway (AAR code)

S . . . . Sire

Ar S . . . . . . Sister of Arts

AS . . . . Sister of Arts

SA . . . . Sister of Arts

SEKF . . . . Sister Elizabeth Kenny Foundation
SSCK . . . . Sister Servants of Christ the King (Roman Catholic religious order)
SSMI . . . . Sister Servants of Mary Immaculate of Mariowka (Roman Catholic religious order)
APB . . . . Sisters Adorers of the Precious Blood (Roman Catholic religious order)
SALT . . . . Sisters All Learning Together (Feminist group)
AA . . . . Sisters Auxiliaries of the Apostolate (Roman Catholic religious order)
SBS . . . . Sisters of the Blessed Sacrament (Roman Catholic religious order)
SC . . . . Sisters of Charity (Roman Catholic religious order)
SCSJA . . . . . Sisters of Charity of St. Joan Antida (Roman Catholic religious order)
SCL . . . . Sisters of Charity (of Leavenworth) (Roman Catholic religious order)
SCSL . . . . . . Sisters of Charity (of St. Louis) (Roman Catholic religious order)
SCN . . . . Sisters of Charity (of Nazareth) (Roman Catholic religious order)
OLM . . . . Sisters of Charity of Our Lady of Mercy (Roman Catholic religious order)
SCMM . . . . . Sisters of Charity of Our Lady, Mother of Mercy (Roman Catholic religious order)
SCQ . . . . Sisters of Charity of Quebec (Grey Nuns) (Roman Catholic religious order)
CSVP . . . . Sisters of Charity of St. Vincent de Paul (Roman Catholic religious order)
SCC . . . . Sisters of Christian Charity (Roman Catholic religious order)
CSA . . . . Sisters of the Congregation of St. Agnes (Roman Catholic religious order)
CND . . . . Sisters of the Congregation of Notre Dame (Roman Catholic religious order)
SDS . . . . Sisters of the Divine Saviour (Roman Catholic religious order)
SHF . . . . Sisters of the Holy Faith (Roman Catholic religious order)
SHF . . . . Sisters of the Holy Family (Roman Catholic religious order)
HHM . . . . Sisters of the Holy Humility of Mary (Roman Catholic religious order)
HIJ . . . . Sisters of the Holy Infant Jesus (Roman Catholic religious order)
SNJM . . . . . . Sisters of the Holy Names of Jesus and Mary (Roman Catholic religious order)
HVM . . . . Sisters, Home Visitors of Mary (Roman Catholic religious order)
IHM . . . . Sisters of the Immaculate Heart of Mary (California Institute of the Most Holy and Immaculate Heart of the BVM) (Roman Catholic religious order)
SIW . . . . Sisters of the Incarnate Word and the Blessed Sacrament (Roman Catholic religious order)
SL . . . . Sisters of Loretto at the Foot of the Cross (Roman Catholic religious order)
SM . . . . Sisters of Mercy (Roman Catholic religious order)
MHS . . . . Sisters of the Most Holy Sacrament (Roman Catholic religious order)
SND . . . . Sisters of Notre Dame (Roman Catholic religious order)
OLCR . . . . Sisters of Our Lady of Charity of Refuge (Roman Catholic religious order)
OLP . . . . Sisters of Our Lady of Providence (Roman Catholic religious order)
OLS . . . . Sisters of Our Lady of Sorrows (Roman Catholic religious order)
PM . . . . Sisters of the Presentation of Mary (Roman Catholic religious order)
SP . . . . Sisters of Providence (Roman Catholic religious order)
SPIC . . . . Sisters of Providence and of the Immaculate Conception (Roman Catholic religious order)
SSHJM . . . . . . Sisters of the Sacred Hearts of Jesus and Mary (Roman Catholic religious order)
SSA . . . . Sisters of St. Ann of Providence (Roman Catholic religious order)
SSA . . . . Sisters of St. Anne (Roman Catholic religious order)
SSC . . . . Sisters of St. Casimir (Roman Catholic religious order)
SSE . . . . Sisters of St. Elizabeth (Roman Catholic religious order)
SSJ . . . . Sisters of St. Joseph (Roman Catholic religious order)
SJC . . . . Sisters of St. Joseph of Cluny (Roman Catholic religious order)
SSJSM . . . . . . Sisters of St. Joseph of St. Mark (Roman Catholic religious order)
SSJ . . . . Sisters of St. Joseph of the Third Order of St. Francis (Roman Catholic religious order)
SSMN . . . . . . Sisters of St. Mary of Namur (Roman Catholic religious order)
SSMO . . . . . . Sisters of St. Mary of Oregon (Roman Catholic religious order)
SSM . . . . Sisters of St. Mary of the Third Order of St. Francis (Roman Catholic religious order)
SSCH . . . . Sisters of Ste. Chretienne (Roman Catholic religious order)
SMSH . . . . Sisters of Sainte Marthe (of St. Hyacinthe) (Roman Catholic religious order)
SSCM . . . . Sisters of Saints Cyril and Methodius (Roman Catholic religious order)
IHM . . . . Sisters, Servants of the Immaculate Heart of Mary (Roman Catholic religious order)
SSMI . . . . Sisters Servants of Mary Immaculate (Roman Catholic religious order)
SOS . . . . Sisters of Service (Roman Catholic religious order)
SSS . . . . Sisters of Social Service (Roman Catholic religious order)
SSM . . . . Sisters of the Sorrowful Mother (Third Order of St. Francis) (Roman Catholic religious order)
SAD . . . . Site Activation Division
SATAF . . . . . . Site Alteration Task Force (Air Force)
SCL . . . . Site Concurrence Letter
SDP . . . . Site Data Processors
SSS . . . . Site Security Supervisor
SSSM . . . . Site Space Surveillance Monitor

SITK . . . . Sitka National Monument
SAD . . . . Situation Attention Display
SD . . . . Situation Display
SID . . . . Situation Display (RADAR)
SDC . . . . Situation Display Converter
SDG . . . . Situation Display Generator
SNAFU . . . . . . Situation Normal, All Fouled Up (Military)
SNRAFU . . . . . Situation Normal – Really All Fouled Up (Military slang)
SPD . . . . Situation Projected Display
SITREP . . . . . . Situation Report
STK . . . . Situation Track Display
SUSFU . . . . . . Situation Unchanged, Still Fouled Up
S . . . . Situs (Placed)
SB . . . . Sitzungsberichte (Used in German journals)
SADR . . . . . . Six Hundred Megacycle Air Defense RADAR
S . . . . Sixteenmo (Book from 15 to 17 1/2 centimeters in height) (Bibliography)
SIXFLT . . . . . . Sixth Fleet (Atlantic) (Navy)
SC . . . . Sized and Calendered (Paper)
S & C . . . . . Sized and Calendered (Paper)
S and SC . . . . Sized and Supercalendered
SLF . . . . Skandinaviska Lackteknikers Forbund (Federation of Scandinavian Paint and Varnish Technicians)
SKSL . . . . Skaneateles Short Line R. R. (AAR code)
SSAA . . . . Skate Sailing Association of America
SDAA . . . . . . Skein Dyers Association of America
SYE . . . . Skelly Oil Company (NYSE symbol)
SCA . . . . Ski Council of America
SIA . . . . Ski Industries America
SCRL . . . . . . Skill Components Research Laboratory (Air Force)
SEED . . . . . . Skill Escalation Employment Development
SUWU . . . . . . Skilled and Unskilled Workers' Union – Somali Republic
SD . . . . Skin Dose
SED . . . . Skin Erythema Dose (Medicine)
ST . . . . Skin Test
STD . . . . Skin Test Dose
STU . . . . Skin Test Unit
SKYCAV . . . . Sky Cavalry
SKC . . . . Sky Clear (Meteorology)
STCA . . . . . . Skye Terrier Club of America
SMA . . . . Skymark Airlines
SSLORAN . . . . Skywave Synchronized Long-Range Aid to Navigation
SLAR . . . . . . Slant Range
S/R . . . . Slant Range
SSR . . . . Slate-Shingle Roof (Technical drawings)
SBOST . . . . . . Slavonic Benevolent Order of the State of Texas
SLURBS . . . . . Sleazy Suburbs
SOP . . . . Sleeping-Out Pass (British armed forces)
E . . . . Sleet (Weather reports)
EW . . . . Sleet Showers (Meteorology)
SLI . . . . Slick Airways, Incorporated
SFA . . . . Slide Fastener Association
SEJ . . . . Sliding Expansion Joint (Technical drawings)
SWD . . . . Sliding Watertight Door
ST . . . . Slight Trace
S . . . . Slip
SJ . . . . Slip Joint (Technical drawings)
SKI . . . . Sloan-Kettering Institute
SPL . . . . Sloane Physics Laboratory (Yale)
SS . . . . Slop Sink
S . . . . Slope (Technical drawings)
SCFA . . . . . . Slovak Catholic Federation of America
SCS . . . . Slovak Catholic Sokol
SGUS . . . . . . Slovak Gymnastic Union Sokol of the USA
SLA . . . . Slovak League of America
SRF . . . . Slovak Relief Fund
SWAA . . . . . . Slovak Writers and Artists Association
SNPJ . . . . . . Slovene National Benefit Society
SMBA . . . . . . Slovenian Mutual Benefit Association
SWU . . . . . . Slovenian Women's Union
S . . . . Slow
SF . . . . Slow Fire (Military)
SMV . . . . Slow Moving Vehicle (Emblem to prevent rear-end collisions)
SO . . . . Slow Operate (Relay)
SRS . . . . Slow Reacting Substance
SR . . . . Slow Release (Electronics)
SRR . . . . Slow Rotation Room (NASA)
SDV . . . . Slowed Down Video (RADAR)
YSR . . . . Sludge Removal Barge (Navy symbol)
SOS . . . . Slum on a Shingle (Army breakfast dish) (Bowdlerized version)
SLR . . . . Slush on Runway (Aviation)
S . . . . Small (Size designation for clothing, etc.)

CVL .... Small Aircraft Carrier (Navy symbol)
SATS .... Small Airfield (for) Tactical Support (Air Force)
SA .... Small Arms (All firearms other than cannon)
SAA .... Small-Arms Ammunition
SAAD .... Small-Arms Ammunition Depot
SAEMR ...... Small Arms Expert Marksmanship Ribbon (Military decoration)
SAIC .... Small Arms Interpost Competition (Military)
SAPC ...... Small Arms Post Competition
SARDC ...... Small-Arms Research and Development Center (Army)
SATP .... Small Arms Target Practice (Navy)
SAWS ...... Small Arms Weapons System
SAS .... Small Astronomy Satellite
AFDL ...... Small Auxiliary Floating Dry Dock (Navy symbol)
SBT .... Small Boat
SB .... Small Bonds
SB .... Small Business
SBA ...... Small Business Administration
SBAAM...... Small Business Association of Apparel Manufacturers
SBDC ...... Small Business Development Center
SBDC ...... Small Business Development Corporation
SBETC ...... Small Business Export Trade Corporation
SBIC ...... Small Business Investment Company (Generic term)
SBLSA...... Small Business and Labor Surplus Advisor
SC .... Small Caps (Printing term)
SCAT ...... Small Car Automatic Transit (System)
APC ...... Small Coastal Transport (Navy symbol)
SCID ...... Small Column Insulated Delays
SCTC ...... Small Craft Training Center
SMACRATRACEN .. Small Craft Training Center
SDPA ...... Small Defense Plants Administration (Terminated, 1953)
SDR .... Small Development Requirement (Military)
AP .... Small Hail (Meteorology)
YTL .... Small Harbor Tug (Navy symbol)
SLATE ...... Small, Lightweight Altitude-Transmission Equipment (FAA)
SMO ...... Small Magnetospheric Observatory (Satellite)
SMS .... Small Magnetospheric Satellite (NASA)
SMR .... Small Missile Range
SMRVS ...... Small Modular Recovery Vehicle System (AEC)
SOD....... Small Object Detector
SP .... Small Packet
SP .... Small Paper (Printing)
SM........ Small Pica
SPWR ...... Small Pressurized Water Reactor
SPQR ...... Small Profits, Quick Returns
SR .... Small Ring
SRLD ...... Small Rocket Lift Device
SSS........ Small Scientific Satellite (NASA)
AVP ...... Small Seaplane Tender (Navy symbol)
SSNPP ..... Small Size Nuclear Power Plant
SSPWR ..... Small Size Pressurized Water Reactor (AEC)
SSS........ Small Solar Satellite (NASA)
STO....... Small-Time Operator (Slang)
SB of A...... Smaller Business of America
SBANE ..... Smaller Business Association of New England
SPM .... Smaller Profit Margin
SWPC ...... Smaller War Plants Corporation (World War II)
SWPD ...... Smaller War Plants Division
SWD........ Smaller Word
SSI........ Smart Set International (Program to discourage drug abuse)
SOCCER ..... Smart's Own Concordance Constructor, Extremely Rapid (Data processing)
SMOG ...... Smelost', Mysl', Obraz, Glubina (Boldness, Thought, Image, Depth) (Clandestine group of writers in Moscow, USSR; initials may also stand for "Samoye..." - see separate entry)
SMC....... Smith (A. O.) Corporation (NYSE symbol)
SDG....... Smith-Douglass Company, Inc. (NYSE symbol) (Delisted)
SKL .... Smith Kline & French Laboratories (NYSE symbol)
SA .... Smithsonian Associates
SAO....... Smithsonian Astrophysical Observatory
SI .... Smithsonian Institution
SOA....... Smithsonian Office of Anthropology
SPOT ...... Smithsonian Precision Optical Tracking
STRI ...... Smithsonian Tropical Research Institute
K.......... Smoke (Weather charts)
SMOG ...... Smoke and Fog
SG........ Smoke Generator
SP .... Smokeless Powder
SMTN...... Smoky Mountain R. R. (AAR code)
S......... Smooth (Appearance of bacterial colony)
SB .... Smooth Bore (Ballistics)
SCV .... Smooth, Capsulated, Virulent (Bacteriology)
SC .... Smooth Contour (Technical drawings)

SFSCT ...... Smooth-Face Structural Clay Tile (Technical drawings)
S .... Smooth Sea
SSBR....... Smooth-Surface Built-Up Roof (Technical drawings)
SCIRA ...... Snipe Class International Racing Association
SOS........ The Sniping, Observation and Scouting (Course) (British military) (World War I)
S .... Snow
SG......... Snow Grains (Meteorology)
SIPRE ...... Snow, Ice and Permafrost Research Establishment
SIR........ Snow and Ice on Runways (Aviation)
SP .... Snow Pellets (Meteorology)
SW........ Snow Showers (Meteorology)
SATR ...... So As To Reach (Aviation)
SMO ...... So Much Of
SMOP....... So Much of Paragraph
SDA .... Soap and Detergent Association
SS .... Soap Suds
SSA .... Soaring Society of America
SAUS ...... Soccer Association of the United States
SAC .... Social and Athletic Club
SCP .... Social Credit Party (Canadian)
SOCRED .... Social Credit Party (Canadian)
SDF .... Social Democratic Federation (Political coalition)
SEAC ...... Social and Economic Archive Centre (British)
SEC .... Social Economic Council (Sociaal Economische Raad) (Netherlands)
SERD ...... Social, Educational Research & Development, Inc.
SH .... Social History
SLIS........ Social Legislation Information Service
SMP .... Social Marginal Productivity
SR .... Social Register
SRS .... Social and Rehabilitation Service (HEW)
SS .... Social Science
SSRC ...... Social Science Research Council
SS .... Social Security
SSAN ...... Social Security Account Number
SSA .... Social Security Act
SSACT ..... Social Security Act
SSA .... Social Security Administration (of HEW)
SSB .... Social Security Board (Abolished, 1946)
SS .... Social Service
SWHG ...... Social Welfare History Group
SW........ Social Work
SWVB ...... Social Work Vocational Bureau
S.......... Socialist
SLP .... Socialist Labor Party
SMUSE ..... Socialist Movement for the United States of Europe
SP .... Socialist Party
SP-SDF ..... Socialist Party - Social Democratic Federation (Later, Socialist Party, USA)
SR .... Socialist Revolutionary (Russia)
SSC .... Socialist Scholars Conference
SUCEE ..... Socialist Union of Central-Eastern Europe
SWP .... Socialist Workers Party
CCF .... Socialistic Co-operative Commonwealth Federation (Former Canadian political party; later, NDP)
SA .... Sociedad Anonima (Stock company) (Spanish)
S en C ..... Sociedad en Comandita (Limited partnership company) (Spain)
SHH .... Sociedad Honoraria Hispanica
SIAP....... Sociedad Interamericana de Planificacion (Inter-American Planning Society)
SIP .... Sociedad Interamericana de Psicologia (Inter-American Society of Psychology)
SOMISA ..... Sociedad Mixta Siderurgia Argentina (Steel producer in Argentina)
SMU ...... Sociedadas Mexicanas Unedas
SATA ...... Sociedade Acoriana de Transportes Aereos, Ltda.
SAM....... Sociedade Africana de Mocambique (African Society of Mozambique)
SAIS....... Societa Agricola Italo-Somala (Italo-Somali Agricultural Society)
S/A .... Societa Anonima (Italy)
SAI .... Societa Anonima Italiana (An incorporated company) (Italian)
SPA .... Societa per Azioni (Appears after the name of a company) (Italian)
SELNI...... Societa Electtronuclear Italiana (Power reactor) (Italy)
SENN....... Societa Ellettronucleare Nazionale (Italy)
SIMCA ..... Societa Industrielle de Mecanique et Carrosserie Automobile (French)
SIMEA ..... Societa Italiana Meriadionale per l'Energia Atomica (Italy)
SIPRA ...... Societa Italiana Pubblicita Per Azioni (Italian radio and television advertising company)
SIR........ Societa Italiana Resine
SIUCB...... Societa Italiana della Union Chimique Belge
SOMIREN .... Societa Minerali Radiaettini Energia Nucleare
SNI .... Societa Nazionale Italiana
SORIN ...... Societa Ricerche Impianti Nucleari (Italy)

401

SA . . . . Societas Adunationis (Franciscan Friars of the Atonement) (Roman
Catholic religious order)

SDS . . . . Societas Divini Salvatoris (Society of the Divine Saviour) (Roman
Catholic men's religious order)

SC . . . . Societas Fratrum Sacris Cordis (Brothers of the Sacred Heart) (Roman
Catholic religious order)

SMM . . . . Societas Mariae Montfortana (Missionaries of the Company of Mary,
or Montfort Fathers) (Roman Catholic religious order)

SJ . . . . Societas Jesu (Society of Jesus) (Jesuits) (Roman Catholic men's religious
order)

SM . . . . Societas Mariæ (Marists)

SMB . . . . Societas Missionaria Bethlehem

SPM . . . . Societas Patrum Misericordiae (Fathers of Mercy) (Roman Catholic
religious order)

SSJ . . . . Societas Sancti Joseph Sanctissimi Cordis (St. Joseph's Society of the
Sacred Heart, or Josephites) (Roman Catholic men's religious order)

SSS . . . . Societas Sanctissimi Sacramenti (Fathers of the Blessed Sacrament)
(Roman Catholic religious order)

SVD . . . . Societas Verbi Divini (Society of the Divine Word) (Roman Catholic
men's religious order)

SRS . . . . Societatis Regiae Socius (Fellow of the Royal Society)

SATGA . . . . . . Societe Aerienne de Transport Guyane Antilles (French Guiana Air
Transport)

SAC . . . . Societe Africaine de Culture (African Society of Culture)

SATEC . . . . . . Societe d'Aide Technique et de Cooperation (An independent French
company)

SAM . . . . Societe des Americanistes

SA . . . . Societe Anonyme (Limited company) (French)

SAB . . . . Societe Anonyme Belge d'Exploitation de la Navigation Aerienne
(Sabena Belgian World Airlines)

SABENA . . . . . Societe Anonyme Belge d'Exploitation de la Navigation Aerienne
(Sabena Belgian World Airlines)

SPAD . . . . Societe pour Aviation et ses Derives (French) (World War I airplane)

SCUMRA . . . . . Societe Central de l'Uranium et des Minerals et Metaux Radioactifs
(France)

SCOA . . . . Societe Commerciale de l'Ouest Africain (West African Commercial
Society)

SCP . . . . Societe Culinaire Philanthropique

SODEPALM . . . Societe pour le Developpement et l'Exploitation du Palmier a Huile
(Ivory Coast)

SELF . . . . Societe des Ecrivains Luxembourgeois de Langue Francaise

SEA . . . . Societe d'Electronique et d'Automatique (Became part of Compagnie
Internationale d'Informatique)

SENA . . . . . . Societe d'Energie Nucleaire Franco-Belge Ardennes (Belgian-French power
consortium)

SEPR . . . . Societe d'Etude de la Propulsion Par Reaction

SEREB . . . . . . Societe pour l'Etude et la Realisation d'Engins Balistiques (France)

SEDES . . . . . . Societe d'Etudes pour le Developpement Economique et Social (France)

SEDEIS . . . . . Societe d'Etudes et de Documentation Economiques Industrielles et
Sociales (France)

SEPEMIAG. . . . Societe d'Etudes pour l'Equipement Miniere, Agricole et Industrial du
Gabon (Gabon Society for Study of Mining Agricultural and Industrial
Equipment)

SEMA . . . . . . Societe d'Etudes de Mathematiques Appliquees (France)

SENTA . . . . . . Societe d'Etudes Nucleaires et de Techniques Advances (France)

SODERN . . . . . Societe d'Etudes et Realisations Nucleaires

SETU . . . . . . Societe d'Etudes et de Travaux pour l'Uranium (France)

SEC . . . . Societe Europeenne de Culture

SEEA . . . . . . Societe Europeenne d'Energie Atomique

SETIS . . . . Societe Europeenne pour l'Etude et l'Integration des Systemes Spatiaux

SEH . . . . Societe Europeenne d'Hematologie

SESR . . . . Societe Europeenne de Sociologie Rurale

SFI . . . . Societe Financiere Internationale

SFU . . . . Societe de Fluoration de l'Uranium (An international nuclear fuel
company)

SFE . . . . Societe Francaise des Electriciens (France)

SFERMA . . . . . Societe Francaise d'Entretien et de Reparation de Materiel
Aeronautique (France)

SFENA . . . . . . Societe Francaise d'Equipements pour la Navigation Aerienne

SFIO . . . . . . Societe Francaise de l'Internationale Ouvriere (French Socialist Party)

SAIP . . . . . . Societe d'France Applications Industrielle de la Physique

SGTM . . . . . . Societe Generale des Transports Maritimes (France)

SIAN . . . . Societe Industrielle et Agriculturelle du Niari (Industrial and Agricultural
Society of Niari)

SICN . . . . Societe Industrielle de Combustibles Nucleaires (France)

SIMO . . . . Societe Industrielle des Minerais de l'Ouest

SIA . . . . Societe Internationale d'Acupuncture

SIA . . . . Societe Internationale Arthurienne (International Arthurian Society)

AUDI . . . . Societe Internationale d'Audiologie

SIBC . . . . Societe Internationale de Biologie Clinique

SIC . . . . Societe Internationale de Cardiologie

SIC . . . . Societe Internationale de Chirurgie

SICOT . . . . . . Societe Internationale de Chirurgie Orthopedique et de Traumatologie

SIDS. . . . . . . Societe Internationale de Defense Sociale

SIDS. . . . . . . Societe Internationale de Droit Sociale

SIEC . . . . Societe Internationale pour l'Enseignement Commercial

SIEPM. . . . . . . Societe Internationale pour l'Etude de la Philosophie Medievale

SIH . . . . Societe Internationale d'Hematologie

SIL . . . . Societe Internationale de la Lepre

SIM . . . . Societe Internationale de la Moselle

SIM . . . . Societe Internationale de Musicologie

SIMC . . . . Societe Internationale pour la Musique Contemporaine

SIMHA . . . . . . Societe Internationale de Mycologie Humaine et Animale

SIPG . . . . Societe Internationale de Pathologie Geographique

SIPE . . . . Societe Internationale de Psychopathologie de l'Expression

SIRI . . . . Societe Internationale pour la Readaptation des Invalides

SISS . . . . Societe Internationale de la Science du Sol

SITA . . . . Societe Internationale des Telecommunications Aeronautiques

SITS . . . . Societe Internationale de Transfusion Sanguine

SIU . . . . Societe Internationale d'Urologie

SICOVAM . . . . Societe Interprofessionnelle pour la Compensation des Valeurs Mobilieres

SOMIEX . . . . . Societe Malienne d'Importation et d'Exportation (Malian Import Export
Company)

SMPC . . . . Societe des Mines et Produits Chimiques (France)

SNCF . . . . Societe Nationale des Chemins de Fer Francais

SNPA . . . . Societe Nationale des Petroles d'Aquitaine (France)

SDN. . . . . Societe des Nations (League of Nations)

SPAEF. . . . . . . Societe des Petroles d'Afrique Equatoriale Francaise (French Equatorial
African Petroleum Company)

SPFA . . . . Societe des Professeurs Francais en Amerique

SORAFOM. . . . Societe de Radiodiffusion de la France d'Outre-Mer (Society for Radio
Broadcasting of Overseas France)

SRU . . . . Societe de Raffinage d'Uranium (France)

SIR . . . . Societe Rorschach Internationale (International Rorschach Society)
(Originally, Societe Internationale du Test de Rorschach et Autres
Methodes Projectives)

ST . . . . Societe Theosophique

TU . . . . Societe Tunisienne de l'Air

S . . . . Society

SAA . . . . Society for Academic Achievement

SA . . . . Society of Actuaries

SAP . . . . Society for Adolescent Psychiatry

SACEM . . . . . . Society for the Advancement of Continuing Education for Ministry

SAE . . . . Society for the Advancement of Education

SAFSR . . . . . . Society for the Advancement of Food Service Research

SAJ . . . . Society for the Advancement of Judaism

SAM . . . . Society for Advancement of Management

SASS . . . . Society for the Advancement of Scandinavian Study

SAST . . . . Society for the Advancement of Space Travel

SAWE . . . . Society of Aeronautical Weight Engineers

SAMPE . . . . . . Society of Aerospace Material and Process Engineers

SAAS . . . . Society of African and Afro-American Students

SAM . . . . Society of African Missions

SALM . . . . Society of Air Line Meteorologists

SASI . . . . Society of Air Safety Investigators

SOAP . . . . Society of Airway Pioneers

SAA . . . . Society for American Archaeology

SAA . . . . Society of American Archivists

SAB . . . . Society of American Bacteriologists

SABW . . . . Society of American Business Writers

SAF . . . . Society of American Florists

SAFOH . . . . . . Society of American Florists and Ornamental Horticulturists

SAF . . . . Society of American Foresters

SAGA . . . . Society of American Graphic Artists

SAH . . . . Society of American Historians

SAM . . . . Society of American Magicians

SAME . . . . Society of American Military Engineers

SAP . . . . Society for American Philosophy

ARA . . . . Society of American Registered Architects

SATW . . . . Society of American Travel Writers

SAVE . . . . Society of American Value Engineers

SAGP . . . . Society for Ancient Greek Philosophy

SAA . . . . Society of Animal Artists

SAPL . . . . Society for Animal Protective Legislation

SA . . . . Society of Antiquaries (British)

SAA . . . . Society for Applied Anthropology

SAS . . . . Society for Applied Spectroscopy

SAH . . . . Society of Architectural Historians

SABCO . . . . . . Society for the Area of Biological and Chemical Overlap

SA . . . . Society of Arts (British)

SAA . . . . Society for Asian Art

SAM . . . . Society for Asian Music

SAFE . . . . Society of Associated Financial Executives
SAS . . . . Society of Australasian Specialists
SAR . . . . Society of Authors Representatives
SABE . . . . Society for Automation in Business Education
SAEH . . . . Society for Automation in English and the Humanities
SAFA . . . . Society for Automation in the Fine Arts
SAPE . . . . Society for Automation in Professional Education
SASM . . . . Society for Automation in Science and Mathematics
SASS . . . . Society for Automation in the Social Sciences
SAE . . . . Society of Automotive Engineers
SBL . . . . Society of Biblical Literature (Formerly, SBLE)
SBLE . . . . Society of Biblical Literature and Exegesis (Later, SBL)
SBP . . . . Society of Biological Psychiatry
SBR . . . . Society for Biological Rhythm
SBAC . . . . Society of British Aerospace Companies
SBAC . . . . Society of British Aircraft Constructors
SBAP . . . . Society of Business Advisory Professions
SBME . . . . Society of Business Magazine Editors
SBPD . . . . Society of Business Publication Designers
SCP . . . . Society of California Pioneers
SCE . . . . Society of Carbide Engineers
SCGC . . . . Society of Carnival Glass Collectors
SAC . . . . Society of the Catholic Apostolate (Pallottines)
SCCTSD . . . . . Society of Catholic College Teachers of Sacred Doctrine
SCMM . . . . . . Society of Catholic Medical Missionaries, Incorporated (Medical Mission Sisters) (Roman Catholic religious order)
SCPCU . . . . . . Society of Chartered Property and Casualty Underwriters
SCI . . . . Society of Chemical Industry
SCCH . . . . Society of Cinema Collectors and Historians
SOC . . . . Society of Cinematologists
SCEWA . . . . . Society for Citizen Education in World Affairs
SCG . . . . Society of the Classic Guitar
SCEH . . . . Society for Clinical and Experimental Hypnosis
SCS . . . . Society of Clinical Surgery
SCUP . . . . Society for College and University Planning
SCH . . . . Society for Colonial History
SCW . . . . Society of Colonial Wars
SCARP . . . . . . Society for Comic Art Research and Preservation
SCST . . . . Society of Commercial Seed Technologists
SCO . . . . Society of Commissioned Officers
SCEA . . . . Society of Communications Engineers and Analysts
SCRAP . . . . . . Society for Completely Removing All Parking Meters
SCSBM . . . . . . Society for Computer Science in Biology and Medicine
SOCIM . . . . . . Society of Connoisseurs in Murder
SCS . . . . Society for Conservative Studies
SCS . . . . Society of Construction Superintendents
SCC . . . . Society of Cosmetic Chemists
SCE . . . . Society for Creative Ethics
SCUM . . . . Society for Cutting Up Men
SDC . . . . Society of Daily Communicants
SDE . . . . Society of Data Educators
DPMOAP . . . . Society of Data Processing Machine Operators and Programmers
SDHD . . . . Society of Daughters of Holland Dames
SDB . . . . Society for Developmental Biology
SDSH . . . . Society Devoted to the Sacred Heart (Roman Catholic women's religious order)
CHJ . . . . Society of the Devotees of Jerusalem
SDCE . . . . Society of Die Casting Engineers
SDUK . . . . Society for the Diffusion of Useful Knowledge
SDC . . . . Society of the Divine Compassion
SDV . . . . Society of Divine Vocations (Vocationist Fathers) (Roman Catholic religious order)
SERM . . . . Society of Early Recorded Music
SEB . . . . Society for Economic Botany
SEG . . . . Society of Economic Geologists
SEPM . . . . Society of Economic Paleontologists and Mineralogists
SEAC . . . . Society for Economic, Social, Cultural Study and Expansion in Central Africa
SEDS . . . . Society for Educational Data Systems
SEAM . . . . Society for the Emancipation of the American Male
SEI . . . . Society of Engineering Illustrators
SEP . . . . Society of Engineering Psychologists
SES . . . . Society of Engineering Science
SEM . . . . Society for Ethnomusicology
SEC . . . . Society of Exchange Counselors
SEBM . . . . Society for Experimental Biology and Medicine
SEP . . . . Society of Experimental Psychologists
SESP . . . . Society of Experimental Social Psychology
SESA . . . . Society for Experimental Stress Analysis
SETP . . . . Society of Experimental Test Pilots

SEG . . . . Society of Exploration Geophysicists
STENCH . . . . . Society to Exterminate Neo-Communist Harbingers
SFL . . . . Society of Federal Linguists
SFE . . . . Society of Fire Engineers
SFPE . . . . Society of Fire Protection Engineers
SFSAFBI . . . . . Society of Former Special Agents of the Federal Bureau of Investigation
SFS . . . . Society for Freedom in Science
FACSEA . . . . . Society for French American Cultural Services & Educational Aids
SFHS . . . . Society for French Historical Studies
FOPR . . . . Society of Friends of Puerto Rico
SGL . . . . Society of Gas Lighting
SGM . . . . Society for General Microbiology (British)
SGP . . . . Society of General Physiologists
SGSR . . . . Society for General Systems Research
SGP . . . . Society of Ghana Philatelists
SGES . . . . Society of Grain Elevator Superintendents
SGA . . . . Society of Graphic Art (British)
SOGAT . . . . . . Society of Graphical and Allied Trades (British)
SGI . . . . Society for Gynecologic Investigation
SHNS . . . . . . Society of Head and Neck Surgeons
SHAA . . . . Society of Hearing Aid Audiologists
SHARE . . . . . . Society to Help Avoid Redundant Effort (in data processing)
SHAFR . . . . . . Society for Historians of American Foreign Relations
SHA . . . . Society for Historical Archaeology
SHGM . . . . . . Society for the History of the Germans in Maryland
SHOT . . . . Society for the History of Technology
SHT . . . . Society for the History of Technology
SHCJ . . . . Society of the Holy Child Jesus (Roman Catholic women's religious order)
SI . . . . Society of Illustrators
SINA . . . . Society for Indecency to Naked Animals (A hoax organization)
SIGMA . . . . . . Society of Independent Gasoline Marketers of America
SIMPP . . . . . . Society of Independent Motion Picture Producers
SIPES . . . . . . Society of Independent Professional Earth Scientists
SIR . . . . Society for Individual Responsibility
SIAM . . . . Society for Industrial and Applied Mathematics
SICA . . . . Society of Industrial and Cost Accountants of Canada
SIE . . . . Society of Industrial Engineers
SIM . . . . Society of Industrial Microbiology
SIR . . . . Society of Industrial Realtors
SID . . . . Society for Information Display
SIA . . . . Society of Insurance Accountants
SID . . . . Society for International Development
SIGE . . . . Societe Internationale de Gastro-Enterologie
SIRE . . . . Society for the Investigation of Recurring Events
SID . . . . Society for Investigative Dermatology
SIHS . . . . Society for Italian Historical Studies
SIH . . . . Society for Italic Handwriting
SJB . . . . Society of Jewish Bibliophiles
SJCPS . . . . . . Society of Jewish Composers, Publishers and Songwriters
SJS . . . . Society of Jewish Science
SKO . . . . Society of Kastorians "Omonia"
SLF . . . . Society of the Little Flower
SOLE . . . . Society of Logistics Engineers
SLI . . . . Society for Louisiana Irises
SMW . . . . Society of Magazine Writers
SMF . . . . Society for the Maintenance of the Faith (British)
SMACK . . . . . . Society of Males Who Appreciate Cute Knees (Group opposing below-the-knee fashions introduced in 1970)
SMIS . . . . Society for Management Information Systems
SMA . . . . Society of Manufacturer's Agents
SMPE . . . . Society of Marine Port Engineers
SMA . . . . Society of Maritime Abitrators
SMH . . . . Society for Maritime History (Formerly, American Maritime Institute)
SM . . . . Society of Mary (Marianists)
SMR . . . . Society of Mary Reparatrix (Roman Catholic women's religious order)
SM . . . . Society of Medalists
SMCAF . . . . . . Society of Medical Consultants to the Armed Forces
SMJ . . . . Society of Medical Jurisprudence
SMCC . . . . Society of Memorial Cancer Center
SME of AIME . . Society of Mining Engineers of American Institute of Mining, Metallurgical, and Petroleum Engineers
SMPAD . . . . . . Society of Motion Picture Art Directors
SMPTE . . . . . . Society of Motion Picture and Television Engineers
SMMT . . . . . . Society of Motor Manufacturers and Traders
SMEP . . . . Society for Multivariate Experimental Psychology
SNAP . . . . Society of National Association Publications
SNAME . . . . . Society of Naval Architects & Marine Engineers
SON . . . . Society of Nematologists
SNS . . . . Society of Neurological Surgeons
SNT . . . . Society for Nondestructive Testing

SONS . . . . . . Society of Non-Smokers
SNOBS . . . . . . Society of the Nourishment of Body and Soul (Gourmet club in North Carolina)
SNM . . . . Society of Nuclear Medicine
SNSE . . . . Society of Nuclear Scientists and Engineers (Defunct)
SOPO . . . . . . Society of Oral Physiology and Occlusion
SPHE . . . . . . Society of Packaging and Handling Engineers
SOPMC . . . . . Society of Paper Money Collectors
SPR . . . . Society for Pediatric Research
SPS . . . . Society of Pelvic Surgeons
SPA . . . . Society for Personnel Administration
SPE . . . . Society of Petroleum Engineers (of AIME)
SPE of AIME . . Society of Petroleum Engineers of American Institute of Mining, Metallurgical and Petroleum Engineers
SPEP . . . . Society for Phenomenology and Existential Philosophy
SPA . . . . Society of Philatelic Americans
SPAN . . . . . . Society of Philatelists and Numismatists
SPSDM . . . . . . Society for the Philosophical Study of Dialectical Materialism
SPC . . . . Society for Philosophy of Creativity
SPAR . . . . . . Society of Photographer and Artist Representatives
SPI . . . . Society of Photographic Illustrators
SPSE . . . . . . Society of Photographic Scientists & Engineers
SPIE . . . . Society of Photo-Optical Instrumentation Engineers
SPT . . . . Society of Photo-Technologists
SPE . . . . Society of Plastics Engineers
SPI . . . . Society of the Plastics Industry
SPEBSQSA . . . . Society for the Preservation and Encouragement of Barber Shop Quartet Singing in America
SPECA . . . . . . Society for the Preservation and Enjoyment of Carriages in America
SPNEA . . . . . . Society for the Preservation of New England Antiquities
SPC . . . . Society for the Prevention of Crime
SPCA . . . . . . Society for the Prevention of Cruelty to Animals
SPCC . . . . . . Society for the Prevention of Cruelty to Children
SPCTYS . . . . . Society for Prevention of Cruelty to Young Singers
SPDRAB . . . . . Society for the Prevention of Disparaging Remarks About Brooklyn
SFPOMMPAB . . Society for the Prevention of Married Men Posing as Bachelors
SPWWIII . . . . . Society for the Prevention of World War III
SPFM . . . . . . Society of Priests for a Free Ministry
SPP . . . . Society of Private Printers
SPA . . . . Society of Professional Assessors
SPBC . . . . . . Society of Professional Business Consultants
SPEC . . . . . . Society for Professional Engineering Checkers
SPI . . . . Society of Professional Investigators
SPMC . . . . . . Society of Professional Management Consultants
SPWLA . . . . . Society of Professional Well Log Analysts
SPT . . . . Society for Projective Techniques
SPT & PA . . . . Society for Projective Techniques and Personality Assessment
SPCK . . . . . . Society for Promoting Christian Knowledge (Publisher) (British)
SPEE . . . . . . Society for the Promotion of Engineering Education
SPMM . . . . . . Society for the Promotion of Mohammedan Missions
SPSI . . . . Society for the Promotion of Scientific Industry (British)
SPF . . . . Society for the Propagation of the Faith
SPG . . . . Society for the Propagation of the Gospel (British)
SPGJ . . . . Society for the Propagation of the Gospel among the Jews (British)
SP . . . . Society of Protozoologists
SPR . . . . Society for Psychical Research
SPSSI . . . . . . Society for the Psychological Study of Social Issues
SPA . . . . Society for Public Administration
SOPHE . . . . . . Society of Public Health Educators
SPRC . . . . . . Society of Public Relations Counsellors
SPAM . . . . . . Society for the Publication of American Music
SPD . . . . Society of Publication Designers
SPWC . . . . . . Society for the Punishment of War Criminals
SPE . . . . Society for Pure English
SREA . . . . . . Society of Real Estate Appraisers
SORD . . . . . . Society of Record Dealers of America
SRFD . . . . . . Society for the Rehabilitation of the Facially Disfigured
SRD . . . . Society for the Relief of Distress (British)
SRHE . . . . . . Society for Religion in Higher Education
SRE . . . . Society of Reproduction Engineers (Later, IAVCM)
SRA . . . . Society of Research Administrators
SRCD . . . . . . Society for Research in Child Development
SRA . . . . Society of Residential Appraisers
SOR . . . . Society of Rheology
SR . . . . Society of Rheology
SRSTA . . . . . . Society of Roller Skating Teachers of America
SRV . . . . Society of Russian Veterans
SSM . . . . Society of the Sacred Mission
SSE . . . . Society of St. Edmund
SSGA . . . . . . Society of St. Gregory of America
SSJE . . . . Society of St. John the Evangelist

SSP . . . . Society of St. Paul for the Apostolate of Communications (Pauline Fathers) (Roman Catholic religious order)
SS . . . . Society of St. Sulpice (Sulpicians) (Roman Catholic men's religious order)
STJ . . . . Society of St. Teresa of Jesus (Roman Catholic women's religious order)
SSLC . . . . . . Society of Savings and Loan Controllers
SSSR . . . . . . Society for the Scientific Study of Religion
SSSS . . . . . . Society for the Scientific Study of Sex
SSI . . . . Society of Scribes and Illuminators
SSA . . . . Society of Security Analysts
SSC . . . . Society of Silver Collectors
FCJ . . . . Society of the Sisters, Faithful Companions of Jesus (Roman Catholic religious order)
SSCD . . . . . . Society of Small Craft Designers
SSRS . . . . . . Society for Social Responsibility in Science
SSDT . . . . . . Society of Soft Drink Technologists
SSUSN . . . . . . Society of Sponsors of the United States Navy
SSTDC . . . . . . Society of Stage Directors and Choreographers
SSDHPER . . . . Society of State Directors of Health, Physical Education and Recreation
SSB . . . . Society for the Study of Blood
SSDG . . . . . . Society for the Study of Development and Growth
SSE . . . . Society for the Study of Evolution
SSSP . . . . . . Society for the Study of Social Problems
SSS . . . . Society for the Suppression of Speculative Stamps (Now defunct)
SSZ . . . . Society of Systematic Zoology
STWE . . . . . . Society of Technical Writers and Editors (Later, STWP)
STWP . . . . . . Society of Technical Writers and Publishers (Formerly, STWE)
STEL . . . . Society of Telegraphic Engineers (British)
STD . . . . Society for Theological Discussion
STE . . . . Society of Tractor Engineers
STA . . . . Society of Typographic Arts
SUCKER . . . . . Society for Understanding Cats, Kangaroos, Elks and Reptiles (Slang)
SUS . . . . Society of University Surgeons
SVC . . . . Society of Vacuum Coaters
SSV . . . . Society for Vascular Surgery
SVP . . . . Society of Vertebrate Paleontology
SWCP . . . . . . Society of the War of 1812 in the Commonwealth of Pennsylvania
SWG . . . . Society of Woman Geographers
SWE . . . . Society of Women Engineers
SWST . . . . . . Society of Wood Science and Technology
SWSF . . . . . . Society for a World Service Federation
SES . . . . Socioeconomic Status
SP . . . . Sociolinguistics Program
SRA . . . . Sociological Research Association
SRSS . . . . . . Sociological Resources for Secondary Schools
SRSS . . . . . . Sociological Resources for Social Studies (Project of American Sociological Association)
S . . . . Socius or Sodalis (Fellow)
SDKPIL . . . . . Socjaldemokracja Krolestwa Polskiego i Litwy
SSPB . . . . . . Socket Screw Products Bureau
SOM . . . . Socony Mobil Oil Company, Inc. (NYSE symbol)
SHSN . . . . . . Sod House Society of Nebraska
SFMA . . . . . . Soda Fountain Manufacturers Association
SPMA . . . . . . Soda Pulp Manufacturers Association
Na . . . . Sodium (Chemical element)
SAS . . . . Sodium Alkane Sulfonate (A detergent)
SAS . . . . Sodium Aluminum Sulfate
SCTI . . . . Sodium Components Test Installation
SCGA . . . . . . Sodium-Cooled Graphite Assembly (AEC)
SDS . . . . Sodium Dodecyl Sulfate
SGR . . . . Sodium Graphite Reactor (AEC)
SMDC . . . . . . Sodium Methyl Dithiocarbamate (Chemical)
SRE . . . . Sodium Reactor Experiment (AEC)
S . . . . Soft
SD . . . . Soft Drawn
SEC . . . . Soft Elastic Capsule (Pharmacy)
SFMI . . . . . . Soft Fibre Manufacturers' Institute
SLV . . . . Soft Landing Vehicle (NASA)
SSDPA . . . . . . Soft-Serv Dairy Products Association
STA . . . . Softening Temperature of Ash
SCD . . . . Soil Conservation District (Agriculture)
SCS . . . . Soil Conservation Service (Department of Agriculture)
SCSA . . . . . . Soil Conservation Society of America
SES . . . . Soil Erosion Service (Became Soil Conservation Service, 1935)
SM . . . . Soil Mechanics
SP . . . . Soil Pipe
SSSA . . . . . . Soil Science Society of America
SWC . . . . Soil and Water Conservation Research Division (of ARS, Department of Agriculture)
SF . . . . Soils and Fertilisers (An abstracts journal)
STK . . . . Soiuz Trudovogo Krest'ianstva (Union of Working Peasantry) (Russia)
S . . . . Sol (Monetary unit in Peru)

SBE . . . . Solar Beam Experiment(s)
SC . . . . Solar Cell
SOCOM . . . . . Solar Communications
SCR . . . . Solar Cosmic Ray
SEPS . . . . Solar Electric-Propelled Spacecraft
SES . . . . Solar Energy Society
SETS . . . . . . Solar Energy Thermionic Conversion System (NASA)
SET . . . . Solar Energy Thermionic Program (NASA)
SFF . . . . Solar Forecast Facility (Air Force)
SHEP . . . . . . Solar High-Energy Particles
SOHR . . . . . . Solar Hydrogen Rocket Engine
SMF . . . . Solar Magnetic Field
SOFNET . . . . . Solar Observing and Forecasting Network (Air Force)
SOEP . . . . . . Solar-Oriented Experimental Package (NASA)
SPAN . . . . . . Solar Particle Alert Network (NASA)
SPADES . . . . . Solar Perturbation and Atmospheric Density Measurement Satellite
SPARCS . . . . . Solar Pointing Aerobee Rocket Control System
SPS . . . . Solar Probe Spacecraft (Pioneer satellite)
SOLRAD . . . . . Solar Radiation (NASA)
STEPS . . . . . Solar Thermionic Electrical Power System
SWC . . . . Solar Wind Compensator (or Composition) (Apollo 11) (NASA)
GI . . . . Soldier (Wartime slang)
SOL . . . . Soldier Out of Luck (Military slang)
SMRLH . . . . . . Soldier's Mail, Rush Like Hell (On correspondence)
SM . . . . Soldier's Medal
SH . . . . Soldiers' Home (Government agency)
SAPE . . . . . . Solenoid Array Pattern Evaluator
SG . . . . Solicitor General
SL . . . . Solicitor-at-Law
SSC . . . . Solicitor, Supreme Court
S . . . . Solid
SB . . . . Solid Body (Technical drawings)
SCTI . . . . Solid Carbide Tool Institute
SD . . . . Solid Drawn
SFAW . . . . . . Solid Fuel Administration for War (World War II) (Terminated 1947)
SFA . . . . Solid Fuels Administration (Terminated 1954)
SHA . . . . Solid Homogeneous Assembly
SLT . . . . Solid Logic Technology (IBM)
SMR . . . . Solid Moderated Reactor
SN . . . . Solid Neutral
SOX . . . . Solid Oxygen
SPET . . . . . . Solid Propellant Electric Thruster (Aerospace)
SPIA . . . . . . Solid Propellant Information Agency (Air Force)
SP . . . . Solid Propellant Missile
SPR . . . . Solid Propellant Rocket
SPRINT . . . . . . Solid Propellant Rocket Intercept Missile (ARPA/AMC)
SPSTP . . . . . . Solid Propellant Rocket Static Test Panel (Military)
SPSP . . . . Solid Propellant Surveillance Panel (Military)
SP . . . . Solid Propellants
SRM . . . . Solid Rocket Motor
SS . . . . Solid State
SSA . . . . Solid State Abstracts
SALS . . . . . . Solid-State Acoustoelectric Light Scanner
SADIC . . . . . . Solid-State Analog-to-Digital Computer
SSC . . . . Solid-State Circuit
SC . . . . Solid-State Circuits
SSD . . . . Solid-State Detector
SSE . . . . Solid-State Electronics
SSEL . . . . Solid-State Electronics Laboratory (Stanford University)
SMTG . . . . . . Solid-State and Molecular Theory Group (MIT)
SSMTG . . . . . . Solid State and Molecular Theory Group (MIT)
SPEDAC . . . . . Solid-State, Parallel, Expandable, Differential Analyzer Computer
STV . . . . Solidaridad de Trabajadores Vascos (Solidarity of Basque Workers) (In exile) (Spain)
SNF . . . . Solids Not Fat
S . . . . Solo (Music)
S . . . . Solubility
SA . . . . Soluble in Alkaline Solution
SG . . . . Soluble Gelatin (Pharmacy)
SI . . . . Soluble Insulin
SNP . . . . Soluble Nucleoprotein
SR . . . . Soluble, Repository (With reference to penicillin)
SRNA . . . . . . Soluble Ribonucleic Acid
SDR . . . . Solution Development Record
SOLION . . . . . Solution of Ions (Office of Naval Research)
STA . . . . Solution Treat and Age (Metals)
STEP . . . . Solutions to Employment Problems (A program of National Association of Manufacturers)
SNL . . . . Somali National League
SNU . . . . Somali National Union
SYL . . . . Somali Youth League

SH . . . . Somatotrophic (Growth) Hormone (Endocrinology)
STH . . . . Somatotrophic (Growth) Hormone (Endocrinology)
SAA . . . . Some American Artists (An organization)
SRAM . . . . . . Some Remarks on Abstract Machines (Data processing)
SMR . . . . Somnolent Metabolic Rate (Medicine)
S . . . . Son(s)
SOB . . . . Son of a Bitch
SOT . . . . Son of Temperance (A heavy drinker) (Slang)
SONCM . . . . . SONAR Countermeasures and Deception
SEW . . . . SONAR Early Warning
SONAC . . . . . SONAR Nacelle (Sonacelle)
AG . . . . SONAR Research Ship (Navy symbol)
SSPMO . . . . . SONAR Systems Project Management Office
ST . . . . SONAR Technician (Navy rating)
SOM . . . . SONARman (Navy)
SOMH . . . . . . SONARman, Harbor Defense (Navy)
S & D . . . . Song and Dance Act (Slang)
SPA . . . . Songwriters Protective Association
SEFAR . . . . . . Sonic End Fire for Azimuth & Range
SONOAN . . . . Sonic Noise Analyzer
SOTIM . . . . . . Sonic Observation of the Trajectory and Impact of Missiles
S/T . . . . Sonic Telegraphy
SU . . . . Sonics and Ultrasonics
SBC . . . . Sonora-Baja California Railway (AAR code)
SAL . . . . Sons of the American Legion
SAR . . . . Sons of the American Revolution
SCV . . . . Sons of Confederate Veterans
SDM . . . . Sons and Daughters of Malta
SDPR . . . . . . Sons and Daughters of Pioneer Rivermen
SDS . . . . Sons and Daughters of the Soddies
SF . . . . Sons of the Holy Family
SISL . . . . Sons of Italy Supreme Lodge
SJWVUSA . . . . Sons of Jewish War Veterans of the United States of America
SM . . . . Sons of Malta
SNSL . . . . Sons of Norway Supreme Lodge
SR . . . . Sons of the Revolution
SSAWV . . . . . Sons of Spanish American War Veterans
S of T . . . . . . Sons of Temperance
ST . . . . Sons of Temperance
STNA . . . . . . Sons of Temperance of North America
SUVCW . . . . . Sons of Union Veterans of the Civil War
SV . . . . Sons of Veterans
SOO . . . . Soo Line Railroad Company (NYSE symbol)
SAP . . . . Soon As Possible
S . . . . Soprano (Music)
SA . . . . Soprano, Alto
SAB . . . . Soprano, Alto, Bass
SATB . . . . . . Soprano, Alto, Tenor, Bass (Music)
STB . . . . Soprano, Tenor, Bass
SKS . . . . Soren Kierkegaard Society
SFA . . . . Soroptimist Federation of the Americas
SIA . . . . Soroptimist International Association
SRI . . . . Sorry (Communications operator's procedural remark)
SKED . . . . . . Sort Key Edit (Library of Congress)
SURGE . . . . . Sorting, Updating, Report Generating, Etc. (Data processing)
S . . . . Sou (Monetary unit in France)
SAPP . . . . . . Soul Assurance Prayer Plan
SOB . . . . Souls on Board (Aviation slang)
SODAR . . . . . Sound Detecting and Ranging
SOF . . . . Sound on Film
SFAR . . . . . . Sound Fixing and Ranging
SOFAR . . . . . Sound Fixing and Ranging (Navy underground sound system)
SF . . . . Sound and Flash
S & F . . . . Sound and Flash (Battalion) (Military)
SIF . . . . Sound Intermediate Frequency
SL . . . . Sound Locator
S-L . . . . Sound Locator (Military)
SMPO . . . . . . Sound Motion Picture Operator (Navy)
SMP . . . . Sound Motion Picture Technician (Navy)
SONAR . . . . . Sound, Navigation and Ranging
SDOPR . . . . . Sound Operator (Navy)
SPL . . . . Sound Pressure Level
SORNG . . . . . Sound Ranging
SR . . . . Sound Ranging
SORC . . . . . . Sound Ranging Control
SRC . . . . Sound Ranging Control (Military)
SR . . . . Sound Report
SOSUS . . . . . Sound and Surveillance System
SOSVS . . . . . Sound Surveillance System
STC . . . . Sound Transmission Class (Followed by number, indicates FHA rating of sound insulating quality of a partition construction)

SVTP . . . . Sound, Velocity, Temperature, Pressure
ST . . . . Sounding Tube
SC . . . . Source Code
SDA . . . . Source Data Automation (Data processing)
SDAS . . . . . . Source Data Automation System
SDI . . . . Source Data Information
SEB . . . . Source Evaluation Board (NASA)
SODA . . . . . . Source Oriented Data Acquisition
SSAC . . . . . . Source Selection Advisory Council
SSA . . . . Source Selection Authority
SSEB . . . . Source Selection Evaluation Board
SS . . . . Source of Supply
S . . . . South; Southerly; or Southern
SA . . . . South Africa
SAAF . . . . . . South African Air Force
SA . . . . South African Airways
SAA . . . . South African Airways
SAAEB . . . . . . South African Atomic Energy Board
SACPO . . . . . South African Colored People's Organization
SACL . . . . . . South African Confederation of Labour
SACOD . . . . . South African Congress of Democrats
SACTU . . . . . South African Congress of Trade Unions
SACSIR . . . . . South African Council for Scientific and Industrial Research
SACTW . . . . . South African Council of Transport Workers
SADF . . . . . . South African Defence Forces
SAFTU . . . . . South African Federation of Trade Unions
SAIC . . . . South African Indian Congress
SAIMR . . . . . . South African Institute for Medical Research
SAIRR . . . . . . South African Institute of Racial Relations
SANB . . . . . . South African National Bibliography
SANS . . . . . . South African Naval Service
SAPA . . . . . . South African Press Agency
SARCCUS . . . . South African Regional Committee for Conservation and Utilization of
　　　　　　　　Soil
SAR . . . . South African Republic
SARLA . . . . . South African Rock Lobster Association (Defunct)
SATUC . . . . . . South African Trade Union Council
SATU . . . . . . South African Typographical Union
SA . . . . South America
SAIM . . . . . . South America Indian Mission
SAFE . . . . . . South American and Far East
SGP . . . . South American Gold & Platinum Company (NYSE symbol) (Delisted)
ISAP . . . . . . South American Petroleum Institute
SATO . . . . . . South American Travel Organization
SAAP . . . . . . South Atlantic Anomaly Probe (NASA-CNAE)
SOLANT . . . . . South Atlantic Force (Later, Command) (Navy) (World War II)
SOLANTFOR . . South Atlantic Force (Navy)
SAL . . . . South Atlantic League (Nickname: Sally) (Baseball)
SA . . . . South Australia
SBK . . . . South Brooklyn Railway Company (AAR code)
SB . . . . South Buffalo Railway Company (AAR code)
SC . . . . South Carolina
SCG . . . . South Carolina Electric & Gas Company (NYSE symbol)
SCEC . . . . . . South Central Electric Companies
SCREL . . . . . . South Central Regional Educational Laboratory Corporation
SOCHINAFOR . . South China Force (World War II)
SOPAT . . . . . South China Patrol (Navy) (World War II)
SD . . . . South Dakota
S DAK . . . . . . South Dakota
SEPL . . . . . . South European Pipeline (Oil)
SG . . . . South Georgia Railway Company (AAR code)
SJG . . . . South Jersey Gas Company (NYSE symbol)
SLR . . . . South Lancashire Regiment (British)
SOT . . . . South Omaha Terminal (AAR code)
SPATS . . . . . . South Pacific Air Transportation Service (Navy)
SPA . . . . South Pacific Area (World War II)
SOPAC . . . . . . South Pacific Area and Force (Later, South Pacific Command) (Navy)
　　　　　　　　(World War II)
SOPACBACOM . . South Pacific Base Command (Navy)
SCAT . . . . . . South Pacific Combat Air Transport (World War II)
SPC . . . . South Pacific Commission
SOPACCOMS . . South Pacific Communications (Navy)
PS . . . . South Pole
PSU . . . . South Puerto Rico Sugar Company (NYSE symbol)
SSH . . . . South Shore Line (AAR code)
SSBUS . . . . . . South Slavic Benevolent Union Sloga
SSSLF . . . . . . South Slavonian Socialist Labor Federation
SSE . . . . South-Southeast
SSW . . . . South-Southwest
SW . . . . South Wales
SUMPAC . . . . . Southampton University Man-Powered Aircraft (British)

SB . . . . Southbound
SE . . . . Southeast; Southeasterly; Southeastern
SEA . . . . Southeast Airlines, Inc.
SEA . . . . Southeast Asia
SEACDT . . . . . Southeast Asia Collective Defense Treaty
SEAC . . . . . . Southeast Asia Command
SEADAG . . . . . Southeast Asia Development Advisory Group (Department of State)
SEAIG . . . . . . Southeast Asia Information Group
SEALR . . . . . . Southeast Asia Logistic Requirement
SEAMIC . . . . . Southeast Asia Management Information Center (Navy)
SEAMORE . . . . Southeast Asia Mohawk Revision Program (Army aviation)
SEAOR . . . . . Southeast Asia Operational Requirements
SEATELCOM . . Southeast Asia Telecommunications System
SEATIC . . . . . Southeast Asia Translation and Interrogation Center (Navy)
SEATO . . . . . . Southeast Asia Treaty Organization
SEASTAG . . . . . Southeast Asia Treaty Organization Standardization Agreement
SEMCOG . . . . Southeast Michigan Council of Governments
SEPA . . . . . . Southeast Pacific Area
SEPACFOR . . . . Southeast Pacific Force (Navy)
SOEASTPAC . . . Southeast-Pacific Force (Later, Command) (Navy) (World War II)
SETINA . . . . . Southeast Texas Information Network Association
SAGFC . . . . . Southeastern Association of Game and Fish Commissioners
SEC . . . . South-Eastern Command
SCL . . . . Southeastern Composers' League
SCCA . . . . . . Southeastern Cottonseed Crushers Association
SEL . . . . Southeastern Educational Laboratory
SFA . . . . Southeastern Fisheries Association
SLMA . . . . . . Southeastern Lumber Manufacturers Association
SMTI . . . . . . Southeastern Massachusetts Technological Institute
SEPGA . . . . . Southeastern Pecan Growers Association
SPGA . . . . . . Southeastern Pecan Growers Association
SPEDCO . . . . . Southeastern Pennsylvania Development Corporation
SEPTA . . . . . . Southeastern Pennsylvania Transportation Authority
SEPA . . . . . . Southeastern Power Administration (Department of the Interior)
SEPA . . . . . . Southeastern Psychological Association
SPV . . . . Southeastern Public Service Company (NYSE symbol)
SER . . . . South-Eastern Railway (British)
SERAC . . . . . Southeastern Regional Arts Council
SAMAE . . . . . Southern Air Materiel Area, Europe
SAMAP . . . . . Southern Air Materiel Area, Pacific
SOAPD . . . . . Southern Air Procurement District
SRN . . . . Southern Air Transport, Inc.
SO . . . . Southern Airways, Inc.
SOU . . . . Southern Airways, Inc.
SACOA . . . . . Southern Appalachian Coal Operators Association
SAMS . . . . . . Southern Appalachian Migrants (Cincinnati slang)
SAS . . . . Southern Appalachian Studies
SACOM . . . . . Southern Area Command (Military)
SAA . . . . Southern Ash Association
SA . . . . Southern Association (Baseball league)
SACS . . . . . . Southern Association of Colleges and Schools
SASI . . . . Southern Association of Science and Industry
SAMLA . . . . . Southern Atlantic Modern Language Association
SAF . . . . Southern Attack Force (Navy)
SBC . . . . Southern Baptist Convention
SBF . . . . Southern Baptist Foundation
SCAN . . . . . . Southern California Answering Network (Electronic link of many libraries,
　　　　　　　　communities, etc.)
SCE . . . . Southern California Edison Company (NYSE symbol)
SPIN . . . . . . Southern California Police Information Network
SOCALSEC . . . Southern California Sector, Western Sea Frontier
SCTA . . . . . . Southern California Timing Association
SCLC . . . . . . Southern Christian Leadership Conference
SCPA . . . . . . Southern Coal Producers Association
SOUTHCOM . . Southern Command (Military)
SO . . . . Southern Company (NYSE symbol)
SC . . . . Southern Conference
SCEF . . . . . . Southern Conference Educational Fund
SCMA . . . . . . Southern Cypress Manufacturers Association
SDC . . . . Southern Defense Command (Army)
SEF . . . . Southern Education Foundation
SEP . . . . Southern Education Program
SERS . . . . . . Southern Education Reporting Service
SEATAF . . . . . Southern European Atomic Task Force
SETAF . . . . . . Southern European Task Force
SFA . . . . Southern Freight Association
SFMA . . . . . . Southern Furniture Manufacturers Association
SHP . . . . Southern Hardwood Producers
SHLMA . . . . . Southern Hardwood Lumber Manufacturers Association
SHA . . . . Southern Historical Association
SHC . . . . Southern Humanities Conference

SIU . . . . Southern Illinois University
SIG . . . . Southern Indiana Gas & Electric Company (NYSE symbol)
SOI . . . . Southern Indiana Railway (AAR code)
SINB . . . . Southern Interstate Nuclear Board
ISU . . . . Southern Iowa R. R. (AAR code)
SKILA . . . . . . Southern Korean Interim Legislative Assembly
SMU . . . . Southern Methodist University
SGA . . . . Southern Natural Gas Company (NYSE symbol)
SNY . . . . Southern New York Railway (AAR code)
SORC . . . . . . Southern Ocean Racing Conference
SP . . . . Southern Pacific Company (AAR code)
SPCO . . . . . . Southern Pacific Company
SX . . . . Southern Pacific Company (NYSE symbol) (Wall Street slang name: "Sopac")
SOPAC . . . . . . Southern Pacific Railroad Company
SPFL . . . . Southern Philippines Federation of Labor
SPA . . . . Southern Pine Association
SPIB . . . . Southern Pine Inspection Bureau
SPTA . . . . . . Southern Pressure Treaters Association
SPD . . . . Southern Procurement Division (Navy)
SPCA . . . . . . Southern Pulpwood Conservation Association
SOU . . . . Southern Railway Company (AAR code)
SR . . . . Southern Railway Company (NYSE symbol)
SRES . . . . Southern Railway Employees' Sangh (India)
SRC . . . . Southern Regional Council
SREB . . . . . . Southern Regional Educational Board
SRI . . . . Southern Research Institute
SRANC . . . . . Southern Rhodesia African National Congress
SRATUC . . . . Southern Rhodesian African Trade Union Congress
SRTUC . . . . . Southern Rhodesian Trade Unions Congress
SREC . . . . . . Southern Rice Export Corporation
SSLV . . . . . . Southern San Luis Valley R. R. (AAR code)
SSG . . . . Southern Society of Genealogists
SSIC . . . . Southern States Industrial Council
SSOC . . . . . . Southern Student Organizing Committee
STA . . . . Southern Textile Association
STDC . . . . . . Southern Travel Directors Council
STLF . . . . Southern Troops and Landing Force
SWA . . . . . . Southern Wholesalers Association
SWSA . . . . . . Southern Wood Seasoning Association
SWA . . . . . . Southern Woodwork Association
SW . . . . Southwest; Southwestern; or Southwesterly
SWA . . . . South-West Africa
SWAPO . . . . . South-West Africa People's Organization
SWANU . . . . South-West African National Union
SW . . . . Southwest Airways Company
SWA . . . . Southwest Airways Company
SAEA . . . . . . Southwest Atomic Energy Associates
SCAS . . . . . . Southwest Center for Advanced Studies
SWEDL . . . . . Southwest Educational Development Laboratory
SEFOR . . . . . Southwest Experimental Fast Oxide Reactor (for commercial atomic power)
SWLA . . . . . . Southwest Library Association
SWPA . . . . . . Southwest Pacific Area (World War II)
SOWESPAC . . . Southwest Pacific Command (Navy)
SWPF . . . . . . Southwest Pacific Force
SRC . . . . Southwest Radio Church (An organization)
SWRL . . . . . . Southwest Regional Laboratory for Educational Research and Development
SRC . . . . Southwest Research Corporation
SOWESSEAFRON . . Southwest Sea Frontier (Navy)
SWCEL . . . . . Southwestern Cooperative Educational Laboratory
SITL . . . . Southwestern Industrial Traffic League
SWIG . . . . . . Southwestern Irrigated Cotton Growers Association
SWMA . . . . . Southwestern Monuments Association
SPSA . . . . . . Southwestern Peanut Shellers Association
SPA . . . . Southwestern Power Administration (Department of the Interior)
SWPA . . . . . . Southwestern Power Administration (Department of the Interior)
SWPA . . . . . . Southwestern Psychological Association
SPS . . . . Southwestern Public Service Company (NYSE symbol)
SWRHL . . . . . Southwestern Radiological Health Laboratory (Las Vegas)
SWRI . . . . . . Southwestern Research Institute
SUSGR . . . . . Southwestern Union for the Study of Great Religions
SANTA . . . . . Souvenir and Novelty Trade Association
OSJ . . . . Sovereign Order of Saint John of Jerusalem
AEROFLOT . . . Soviet Air Line
SBI . . . . Soviet Bureau of Information
SMA . . . . Soviet Military Administration
SNB . . . . Soviet News Bureau
SSR . . . . Soviet Socialist Republic
SU . . . . Soviet Union (The USSR)
SAG . . . . Sowjetische Aktiengesellschaften (Soviet corporations in East Germany)

SKK . . . . Sowjetische Kontrollkommission
SMAD . . . . . . Sowjetische Militaeradministration
SMT . . . . Sowjetisches Militaertribunal
SBOM . . . . . . Soy Bean Oil Meal
SFRC . . . . . . Soya Food Research Council
SBCA . . . . . . Soybean Council of America
SCA . . . . Soybean Council of America
SPD . . . . Sozialdemokratische Partei Deutschlands (Social Democratic Party of Germany) (West Germany)
SPO . . . . Sozialdemokratische Partei Oesterreichs
SAP . . . . Sozialistische Arbeiterpartei
SAG . . . . Sozialistische Arbeitsgemeinschaft
SDS . . . . Sozialistische Deutsche Studentenbund (Student political organization) (Germany)
SED . . . . Sozialistische Einheitspartei Deutschlands (Socialist Union Party of the German Democratic Republic)
SPO . . . . Sozialistische Partei Oesterreichs
SRP . . . . Sozialistische Reichs-Partei
SPASCOMT . . . Space Assignment Committee
SAM . . . . Space Available Mail (Military)
SCRAM . . . . . Space Capsule Regulator and Monitor
SCHMOO . . . . Space Cargo Handler and Manipulator for Orbital Operations
SCALE . . . . . . Space Checkout and Launch Equipment
SPACECOM . . . Space Communications
SPAN . . . . . . Space Communications Network
SCAT . . . . . . Space Communications and Tracking
SACL . . . . . . Space and Component Log
SPACON . . . . . Space Control
SDC . . . . Space Defense Corporation
SDPO . . . . . . Space Defense Project Office (AMC)
SPADETS . . . . . Space Detection Network (Military)
SPADATS . . . . Space Detection and Tracking System (Air Force)
SPADATSC . . . Space Detection and Tracking System Center (Air Force)
SPADATSS . . . Space Detection and Tracking System Sensors (Air Force)
SDC . . . . Space Development Corporation
SDC . . . . Space Disturbance Center (Boulder, Colorado)
SDFC . . . . . . Space Disturbance Forecast Center (Environmental Science Services Administration)
SDMF . . . . . . Space Disturbance Monitoring Facility (Environmental Science Services Administration)
SDL . . . . Space Disturbances Laboratory (Environmental Science Services Administration)
SEF . . . . Space Education Foundation
SERT . . . . . . Space Electric Rocket Test
SEP . . . . Space Electronic Package
SET . . . . Space Electronics and Telemetry
SED . . . . Space Environment Division (of NASA)
SESL . . . . Space Environment Simulation Laboratory (NASA)
SES . . . . Space Environment Simulator (NASA)
SESP . . . . Space Experiment Support Program
SEPC . . . . . . Space Exploration Program Council (NASA)
SFAPS . . . . . . Space Flight Acceleration Profile Simulator (NASA)
SAFE . . . . . . Space and Flight Equipment Association
SAFEA . . . . . Space and Flight Equipment Association
SFO . . . . Space Flight Operations
SFOC . . . . . . Space Flight Operations Complex (NASA)
SFOD . . . . . . Space Flight Operations Director (NASA)
SFOF . . . . . . Space Flight Operations Facility (NASA)
SGLS . . . . . . Space-to-Ground Link Subsystem (NASA)
SPAMMER . . . . Space Hammer
SLC . . . . Space Launch Complex
SLOMAR . . . . Space Logistics, Maintenance and Rescue Spacecraft (Air Force)
SAMSO . . . . . Space and Missile Systems Organization (Merger of Ballistic Systems Division and Space Systems Division) (Air Force)
SNAP . . . . . . Space Nuclear Auxiliary Power
SNP . . . . Space Nuclear Propulsion
SNPO . . . . . . Space Nuclear Propulsion Office (AEC-NASA)
SOI . . . . Space Object Identification
SOC . . . . Space Operations Center
SPAD . . . . . . Space Patrol Active Defense (Air Force)
SPL . . . . Space Physics Laboratory (Aerospace corporation)
SPEPD . . . . . . Space Power and Electric Propulsion Division (Formerly Nuclear Systems and Space Power Division) (NASA)
SPS . . . . Space Power System
SPUR . . . . . . Space Power Unit Reactor (Air Force)
SPAD . . . . . . Space Principles, Applications and Doctrine (Air Force Systems Command)
SPARC . . . . . Space Program Analysis and Review Council (Air Force)
SPC . . . . Space Projects Center (NASA)
SREL . . . . Space Radiation Effects Laboratory (Langley, Virginia) (NASA)
SPANDAR . . . . Space and Range RADAR (NASA)
SPARC . . . . . Space Research Conic (NASA)

SRI . . . . Space Research Institute
SSAC . . . . Space Science Analysis and Command (Team) (NASA)
SSB . . . . Space Science Board (National Research Council)
SSDC . . . . Space Science Data Center (NASA)
SPASUR . . . . . Space Surveillance System (Navy)
SSS . . . . Space Surveillance System (Navy)
SSD . . . . Space Systems Division
STG . . . . Space Task Group (Later, Manned Spacecraft Center) (NASA)
STIC . . . . Space Technical Information Control
STAMP . . . . . . Space Technology Analysis and Mission Planning
STL . . . . Space Technology Laboratories (AEC)
STEP. . . . . Space Terminal Evaluation Program
STC . . . . Space Test Center (Air Force)
STAR . . . . Space Thermionic Auxiliary Reactor
START. . . . . . . Space Transport and Reentry Tests
STS . . . . Space Transportation System
SUPARCO . . . . Space & Upper Atmospheric Research Committee (Pakistan)
SV . . . . Space Vehicle
SVD . . . . Space Vehicles Division (NASA)
SWACS . . . . . . Space Warning and Control System (NORAD)
SWS . . . . Space Weapon Systems (Air Force)
SCEC . . . . Spaceborne Computer Engineering Conference
SC . . . . Spacecraft
SAF . . . . Spacecraft Assembly Facility (NASA)
SDAT . . . . Spacecraft Data Analysis Team (NASA)
SDHE . . . . Spacecraft Data Handling Equipment
SITE . . . . Spacecraft Instrumentation Test Equipment
SIPO . . . . Spacecraft Integration Project Office
SLA . . . . Spacecraft LM (Lunar Module) Adapter
SPOC . . . . Spacecraft Oceanography Project (Navy)
SOCS . . . . Spacecraft-Orientation-Control System
SPAC . . . . Spacecraft Performance Analysis and Command (NASA)
SPACE . . . . . . Spacecraft Prelaunch Automatic Checkout Equipment
START . . . . Spacecraft Technology and Advanced Reentry Tests (Air Force)
AGS. . . . . Spalding (A. G.) & Bros., Inc. (NYSE symbol)
SBS . . . . Spaniel Breeders Society
SPAMA . . . . . . Spanish Air Materiel Area
SBCP . . . . Spanish Base Construction Program
SBS . . . . Spanish Benevolent Society "La Nacional"
SPCM. . . . . . . Spanish Campaign Medal
SCR . . . . Spanish Communication Region (Air Force)
SIN . . . . Spanish International Network (Television)
SOPR . . . . Spanish Open Pool Reactor (Atomic energy)
SPI . . . . Spanish Paprika Institute
SRA . . . . Spanish Refugee Aid
SPWSM. . . . . . Spanish War Service Medal
S . . . . Spar (Buoy)
SP . . . . Spare Part
S/P . . . . Spare Parts
SPADE . . . . . . Spare Parts Analysis, Documentation and Evaluation
SPADL . . . . . . Spare Parts Application Data List
SPCR . . . . Spare Parts Change Request
SPDC . . . . Spare Parts Distributing Center (Navy)
SPL . . . . Spare Parts List
SPPC . . . . Spare Parts Provisioning Card
SPT . . . . Spare Parts Transfer
STPG . . . . Spare-Time Production for Gain (FAO)
SADL . . . . Spares Application Data List
SHE . . . . Spares Handling Expense
SIRC. . . . . Spares Integrated Reporting and Control (System)
SIIR . . . . Spares Item Inventory Record
SR . . . . Spares Requirement
SS . . . . Sparingly Soluble
SGM . . . . Spark Gap Modulation
SI . . . . Spark Ignition
SSM . . . . Spark Source Mass Spectrography
SPR . . . . Spartans Industries, Inc. (NYSE symbol)
SPA . . . . Sparton Corporation (NYSE symbol)
SPAC . . . . Spatial Computer
SPAYZ . . . . . . Spatial Property Analyzer
S . . . . Special
SA . . . . Special Action (Military)
SAF . . . . Special Action Force (Army)
S/A . . . . Special Activities (Air Force)
SAO. . . . . Special Activities Office (Air Force)
SA . . . . Special Agent
SAMBA . . . . . Special Agents Mutual Benefit Association (FBI)
S . . . . Special Air Mission (Military aircraft identification prefix)
SAM. . . . . Special Air Mission
SAS . . . . Special Air Service (British)

SATFOR . . . . . Special Air Task Force (Navy)
SAW . . . . Special Air Warfare
SAWC . . . . . . Special Air Warfare Center
SAWF . . . . . . Special Air Warfare Force(s)
SARD . . . . Special Airlift Requirement Directive (Air Force)
SARD . . . . Special Airlift Requirement Document (Army)
SAARF . . . . . . Special Allied Airborne Reconnaissance Force (Teams parachuted into POW areas to take supplies to prisoners or to help them get out) (World War II)
SAL . . . . Special Ammunition Load
SAS . . . . Special Ammunition Site
SAS . . . . Special Ammunition Stockage (Army)
SASP . . . . Special Ammunition Supply Point
SASCOM. . . . . Special Ammunition Support Command (Army)
SPARTA. . . . . . Special Antimissile Research Tests in Australia
SA . . . . Special Artificer (Navy)
SAITR . . . . . . Special Artificer, Instruments, Typewriter and Office Equipment Repairman (Navy)
SAIWR . . . . . . Special Artificer, Instruments, Watch Repairman (Navy)
SAO. . . . . Special Artificer, Optical (Navy)
SADMG . . . . . Special Artificer, Special Devices, Machine Gun Trainer (Navy)
SAD . . . . Special Artificer, Special Synthetic Training Devices (Navy)
SA . . . . Special Assignment
SAA . . . . Special Assignment Airlift (Air Force)
SPAST. . . . . . . Special Assistant (Navy)
SAC/SSW . . . . Special Assistant to the Chief of Staff for Special Warfare (Army)
SACA . . . . Special Assistant for Consumer Affairs (White House)
SACSA. . . . . . Special Assistant for Counterinsurgency and Special Activities
SAGE . . . . Special Assistant for Growing Enterprises (Division of National American Wholesale Grocers Association)
SASN . . . . Special Assistant to the Secretary of the Navy
SASM . . . . Special Assistant for Strategic Mobility (Air Force)
SAR . . . . Special Astronautical Requirement (Navy)
SADM . . . . Special Atomic Demolition Munitions
SB . . . . Special Bibliography
SCU . . . . Special Care Unit
SPECAT. . . . . . Special Category
SCARWAF . . . . Special Category Army Personnel with Air Force
SCNAWAF. . . . Special Category Navy with Air Force
SC . . . . Special Circular
SCWC. . . . . . . Special Commission on Weather Modification
SCAR . . . . Special Committee on Atlantic Research
SCIBP . . . . . . Special Committee for the International Biological Program (National Research Council)
SLAC . . . . Special Committee on Latin American Coordination
SCOR . . . . Special Committee on Oceanographic Research
SCOWR. . . . . . Special Committee on Water Research (International Council of Scientific Unions)
SPC . . . . Special Common (Projectile)
SCAAP . . . . . . Special Commonwealth African Assistance Plan
SC . . . . Special Constable
SCCS . . . . Special Consultative Committee on Security (OAS)
SCM . . . . Special Court-Martial (Army)
SPCM . . . . Special Court-Martial
SPCMO. . . . . . Special Court-Martial Order
SD . . . . Special Delivery
SDC . . . . Special Devices Center
SPECDEVCEN . . Special Devices Center
SPEDIAT . . . . . Special Diary Transcript (Military)
SDEG . . . . Special Doctrine Equipment Group (Army)
SDR . . . . Special Drawing Rights (of International Monetary Fund)
SD . . . . Special Duty
SDO. . . . . Special Duty Only (Military)
E . . . . Special electronics installation (Aviation designation used by all US military services)
SE . . . . Special Equipment
SEV . . . . Special Equipment Vehicle
SPECTRE . . . . . Special Executive for Counterintelligence, Terrorism, Revenge, and Extortion (Fictitious organization whose agents were characters in late Ian Fleming's "James Bond" mysteries)
SEODSE . . . . . Special Explosive Ordnance Disposal Supplies and Equipment
SF . . . . Special Facilities
SFC . . . . Special Flight Charts (Air Force)
SF . . . . Special Forces (Military)
SFOB . . . . Special Forces Operational Base
SFA . . . . Special Foreign Activities (Military)
SFCSIP . . . . . . Special Foreign Currency Science Information Program (National Science Foundation)
SIRSA . . . . Special Industrial Radio Service Association
SIR. . . . . Special Information Retrieval

SIO . . . . Special Inquiry Officer
SISTER . . . . . . Special Institution for Scientific and Technological Education and Research (In proposal stage, 1964, in Great Britain)
SIG . . . . Special Interest Group
SIG/AH . . . . . Special Interest Group/Arts and Humanities
SIG/ALP . . . . . Special Interest Group/Automated Language Processing
SIG/BSS . . . . . Special Interest Group/Behavioral and Social Sciences
SIG/BC . . . . . . Special Interest Group/Biomedical and Chemical Information Systems
SIG/CR . . . . . . Special Interest Group/Classification Research
SIG/ES . . . . . . Special Interest Group/Education for Information Science
SIG/IA . . . . . . Special Interest Group/Information Analysis Centers
SIGIR . . . . . . Special Interest Group on Information Retrieval
SIG/LA . . . . . . Special Interest Group/Library Automation and Networks
SIGPLAN . . . . Special Interest Group on Programming Languages (Association for Computing Machinery)
SIG/RT . . . . . . Special Interest Group/Reprographic Technology
SCAR . . . . . . Special International Committee on Antarctic Research
SIG . . . . Special Investigative Group (DOD)
SIR . . . . Special Investigative Requirement
SIOE . . . . Special Issue of Equipment
SLA . . . . Special Libraries Association
SLOE . . . . . . Special List of Equipment (Air Force)
SLAT . . . . . . Special Logistics Actions, Thailand
SM . . . . Special Memorandum
MSS . . . . . . Special Minesweeper (Navy symbol)
SMS . . . . Special Mint Set (Numismatics)
SMAC . . . . . . Special Mission Attack Computer
SMR . . . . . . Special Money Requisition
SNIE . . . . Special National Intelligence Estimates
SPENAVO . . . . Special Naval Observer
SNM . . . . Special Nuclear Material
SOA . . . . Special Open Allotment
SOA . . . . Special Operating Agency
SOFPAC . . . . . Special Operating Forces, Pacific
SPOPS . . . . . . Special Operations
SOC . . . . Special Operations Command (Military)
SOD . . . . Special Operations Detachment (Military)
SOG . . . . Special Operations Group (Navy)
SORO . . . . . . Special Operations Research Office
SOTFE . . . . . . Special Operations Task Force, Europe
SPEOPT . . . . . Special Optical Tracking System (NASA)
SOCMC . . . . . Special Order of the Commandant of the Marine Corps
SOD . . . . Special Order Discharge
SO . . . . Special Orders
SODTICIOAP . . Special Ordnance Depot Tool Identification, Classification, Inventory, and Obsolescence Analysis Program (Popularly called "Soda Cap")
SP . . . . Special Paper
SPHD . . . . . . Special Pay for Hostile Duty (Military)
SPRINT . . . . . Special Police Radio Inquiry Network (New York City)
SPERT . . . . . . Special Power Excursion Reactor Test (US reactor facilities)
SPC . . . . Special Program Code (Navy)
SPR . . . . Special Program Requirement
SPICE . . . . . . Special Programs Increasing Counseling Effectiveness (Pennsylvania State Department of Public Instruction)
SPR . . . . Special Project Report
SPO . . . . Special Projects Office (Navy)
SPSA . . . . . . Special Projects School for Air
SPISE . . . . . . Special Projects in Science Education
SP . . . . Special Propellants
SPA . . . . Special Public Assistance
SP . . . . Special Publication
SP . . . . Special Purpose
SPE . . . . Special Purpose Equipment
SPIW . . . . . . Special Purpose Individual Weapon (A rifle which fires flechettes or darts) (Pronounced "Spew")
SPV . . . . Special Purpose Vehicles
SRA . . . . Special Refractories Association
SR . . . . Special Regulations (Military)
SRR . . . . Special Reimbursement Rate
SRM . . . . . . Speed of Relative Movement
SR . . . . Special Report
SRPN . . . . . . Special Requisition Priority Number
SRCP . . . . . . Special Reserve Components Program
SSR . . . . Special Scientific Report
SSIR . . . . Special Security Investigation Requirement
SS . . . . Special Series
SS . . . . Special Service (Vessel load line mark)
SSF . . . . Special Service Force (Canadian and US troops under combined command) (World War II)
SSO . . . . Special Service Officer (Military)
SSU . . . . Special Service Unit (Military)

SPS . . . . Special Services (Military)
SS . . . . Special Session
SSCU . . . . . . Special Signal Conditioning Unit
SS . . . . Special Staff
SS . . . . Special Study
SSE . . . . Special Support Equipment
STAG . . . . . . Special Task Air Group
STAP . . . . . . Special Technical Assistance Program
STEM . . . . . . Special Technical and Economic Mission
STA . . . . Special Temporary Authorization (FCC)
STAD . . . . . . Special Temporary Aviation Duty
STS . . . . Special Test System (Air Force)
ST . . . . Special Text
STDP . . . . . . Special Training Devices Program
ST . . . . Special Translation
STS . . . . Special Treatment Steel
SUNFED . . . . Special United Nations Fund for Economic Development
SPWAR . . . . . Special Warfare
SWAT . . . . . . Special Warfare Armored Transporter (A vehicle)
SWAD . . . . . . Special Warfare Aviation Detachment (Army)
SWC . . . . Special Warfare Center (Army) (Later, J. F. Kennedy Center for Special Warfare)
SWM . . . . . . Special Warfare Mission
SWAC . . . . . . Special Warhead Arming Control
SW . . . . Special Weapon
SWS . . . . Special Weapon Systems (Military)
SWTC . . . . . . Special Weapon Technical Command (Navy)
SWC . . . . Special Weapons Command
SWDB . . . . . . Special Weapons Development Board
SWESS . . . . . Special Weapons Emergency Separation System
SWEL . . . . . . Special Weapons Equipment List
SWELSTRA . . . . Special Weapons Equipment List Single Theater Requisitioning Agency
SWETTU . . . . Special Weapons Experimental Tactical Test Unit
SWF . . . . Special Weapons Facility (Navy)
SWEFCO . . . . Special Weapons Ferry Control Office(r)
SWOD . . . . . . Special Weapons Ordnance Devices
SWOG . . . . . . Special Weapons Overflight Guide
SWP . . . . Special Weapons Project (Military)
SWAT . . . . . . Special Weapons and Tactics (Police)
SWTTEU . . . . . Special Weapons Test and Tactical Evaluation Unit
SWTA . . . . . . Special Weapons Training Allowance
SP(TR) . . . . . . Specialist (Transportation) (Coast Guard)
SPXTS . . . . . . Specialist, Air Stations Operations Desk – Time Shack (Navy rating)
SPXAC . . . . . . Specialist, Archivist (Navy rating)
SPXRS . . . . . . Specialist, Armed Forces Radio Service and Special Naval Radio Units (Navy rating)
SPXAR . . . . . . Specialist, Artist (Navy rating)
SPXBL . . . . . . Specialist, Ballistics (Navy rating)
SPXCC . . . . . . Specialist, Cable Censor (Navy rating)
SPXCT . . . . . . Specialist, Cartographer (Navy rating)
SPW . . . . Specialist, Chaplain's Assistant (Navy rating)
SPCW . . . . . . Specialist, Chemical Warfare (Navy rating)
SPC . . . . Specialist, Classification Interviewer (Navy rating)
SPQCR . . . . . . Specialist, Communications Specialist, Cryptographer (Navy rating)
SPQIN . . . . . . Specialist, Communications Specialist, Radio Intelligence (Navy rating)
SPQRP . . . . . . Specialist, Communications Specialist, Registered Publication Clerk (Navy rating)
SPQTE . . . . . . Specialist, Communications Specialist, Technician (Navy rating)
SPXCG . . . . . . Specialist, Crystal Grinder (Navy rating)
SPXDI . . . . . . Specialist, Discharge Interviewer (Navy rating)
SDO . . . . Specialist Duty Only (Navy personnel designation)
SPXED . . . . . . Specialist, Engineering Draftsman (Navy rating)
SPOEN . . . . . . Specialist, Engineering Inspector (Navy rating)
SPXFP . . . . . . Specialist, Fingerprint Expert (Navy rating)
SPF . . . . Specialist, Firefighter (Navy rating)
SPXGU . . . . . . Specialist, Gage Specialist (Navy rating)
SPG . . . . Specialist, Gunnery (Navy rating)
SPGN . . . . . . Specialist, Gunnery, Anti-Aircraft Gunnery Instructor (Navy rating)
SPGM . . . . . . Specialist, Gunnery, Aviation Free Gunnery Instructor (Navy rating)
SPOAV . . . . . . Specialist, Inspector of Aviation Material (Navy rating)
SPO . . . . Specialist, Inspector of Naval Material (Navy rating)
SPXID . . . . . . Specialist, Intelligence Duties (Navy rating)
SPXIR . . . . . . Specialist, Interpreter (Navy rating)
SPXJO . . . . . . Specialist, Journalist (Navy rating)
SPXKP . . . . . . Specialist, Key Punch Operator and Supervisor (Navy rating)
SPLT . . . . Specialist, Link Trainer Instructor (Navy rating)
SPTLT . . . . . . Specialist, Link Trainer Instructor (Navy rating)
SPM . . . . Specialist, Mail Clerk (Navy rating)
SPPMP . . . . . . Specialist, Motion Picture Production (Navy rating)
SPEPS . . . . . . Specialist, Motion Picture Service – Booker (Navy rating)
SPXNC . . . . . . Specialist, Naval Correspondent (Navy rating)

SPXQM....... Specialist, Operations – Plotting and Chart Work (Navy rating)
SPOOR...... Specialist, Ordnance Inspector (Navy rating)
SPS .... Specialist, Personnel Supervisor (Women's Reserve) (Navy rating)
SPSPS...... Specialist, Personnel Supervisor, V-10 (Navy rating)
SPOPE ...... Specialist, Petroleum Technician (Navy rating)
SPPPG ...... Specialist, Photogrammetry (Navy rating)
SPPLB....... Specialist, Photographer, Laboratory (Navy rating)
SPP......... Specialist, Photographic Specialist (Navy rating)
SPA .... Specialist, Physical Training Instructor (Navy rating)
SPXPI ...... Specialist, Pigeon Trainer (Navy rating)
SPXPL...... Specialist, Plastic Expert (Navy rating)
SPPS ...... Specialist, Port Security (Coast Guard)
SPXPC ...... Specialist, Position Classifier (Navy rating)
SPXPR ...... Specialist, Public Information (Navy rating)
SPPR....... Specialist, Public Relations (Coast Guard)
SPI......... Specialist, Punched Card Accounting Machine Operator (Navy rating)
SPERW ...... Specialist, Recreation and Welfare Assistant (Navy rating)
SPR .... Specialist, Recruiter (Navy rating)
SPXRL ...... Specialist, Research Laboratory (Navy rating)
SPS .... Specialist, Shore Patrol and Security (Navy rating)
SPXOP ...... Specialist, Special Project (Navy rating)
SPXST...... Specialist, Strategic Services (Navy rating)
SPT......... Specialist, Teacher (Navy rating)
SPXSB ...... Specialist, Telephone Switchboard Operator and Supervisor
SPXTD ...... Specialist, Topographic Draftsman (Navy rating)
SPV .... Specialist, Transport Airman (Navy rating)
SPU .... Specialist, Utility (Women's Reserve) (Navy rating)
SPPVM ...... Specialist, V-Mail (Navy rating)
SPXVA ...... Specialist, Visual Training Aids (Navy rating)
SRA .... Specialized Repair Activity
SSD .... Specialized Storage Depot
SSSO ...... Specialized Surplus Sales Office
STET........ Specialized Technique for Efficient Typesetting
STAR .... Specialized Training and Reassignment (Army)
STAR(S)..... Specialized Training and Reassignment (Student) (Military)
SD .... Specially Denatured
SDD........ Specially Designated Distributor (Liquor)
SMM .... Specially Meritorious Medal
SAA .... Specialty Advertising Association
SAGI .... Specialty Advertising Guild International
SANA....... Specialty Advertising National Association
SBOA....... Specialty Bakery Owners of America
SKT .... Specialty Knowledge Test (Military)
SPBA .... Specialty Paper and Board Affiliates
S .... Species
SA .... Specific Activity
SAT .... Specific Aptitude Test
SATB .... Specific Aptitude Test Battery
SDA .... Specific Dynamic Action (of foods) (Physiology)
SEA .... Specific Energy Absorption
S .... Specific Factor
SFT .... Specific Financial Transactions
SFC .... Specific Fuel Consumption
SPGR .... Specific Gravity
SG......... Specific Gravity
SIC .... Specific Inductive Capacity
SICR........ Specific Intelligence Collection Requirements
SLD .... Specific Language Disability (Education)
SLT .... Specific Launch Trajectory
SOI .... Specific Operating Instruction
SOR........ Specific Operational Requirement (Military)
SPF .... Specific-Pathogen Free
S-SRNA ..... Specific Soluble Ribonucleic Acid
SSS .... Specific Soluble Substance (Polysaccharide hapten)
SW......... Specific Weight
SDIP........ Specifically Designated Intelligence Position
S........... Specification
SD .... Specification for Design
SIR......... Specification Information Retrieval System (Data processing)
SPRINTER .... Specification of Profits with Interaction under Trial and Error Response
SR .... Specification Requirement
SSIA........ Specification Serial of Individual Assigned
SSN .... Specification Serial Number
SS .... Specification for Structure
SPECOMME ... Specified Command Middle East
SH .... Specified Hours
SPTC ...... Specified Period of Time Contract
SD .... Spectacle Dispenser (Navy technician)
SCEPTRON.... Spectral Comparative Pattern Recognizer
SED .... Spectral Energy Distribution
SSCR .... Spectral Shift Control Reactor (AEC)

SOAP ...... Spectrometric Oil Analysis Program
SA .... Spectrum Analyzer
SPA ...... Spectrum Analyzer
SAA .... Speech Association of America
SAID ...... Speech Auto-Instructional Device
SIL .... Speech Interference Level
SRT .... Speech Reception Thresholds (Audiometry)
SRI........ Speech Rehabilitation Institute
S.......... Speed
SOA ...... Speed of Advance (Military)
STAR ...... Speed Through Aerial Resupply (Air Force)
SOA ...... Speed of Approach
SCAT ...... Speed Control Approach/Takeoff
SR .... Speed Regulator
S/L .... Speedletter
SPDLTR..... Speedletter
SCH .... Spencer Chemical Company (NYSE symbol) (Delisted)
S-M-C ..... Sperm (or Spore) Mother-Cell
SPADE ..... Sperry Air Data Equipment
SPACE ..... Sperry Program for Advancing Careers through Education
SY .... Sperry Rand Corporation (NYSE symbol)
SUMS ...... Sperry UNIVAC Material System
S .... Sphere or Spherical
SCP .... Spherical Candlepower
SE .... Spherical Equivalent
SPE .... Spherical Probable Error
SM........ Spiegel, Inc. (NYSE symbol)
SOF .... Spillover Factor
SMRD ...... Spin Motor Rotation Detector
SSCC ...... Spin-Scan Cloud Camera (NASA)
SS .... Spin-Stabilized (Rockets)
SSAR ...... Spin-Stabilized Aircraft Rocket
SSR .... Spin Stabilized Rockets
STF .... Spin Test Facility (NASA)
SF .... Spinal Fluid (Medicine)
SFC .... Spinal Fluid Count (Medicine)
SCWEP ..... Spinnable Cotton Waste Equalization Program
SWAK ..... Spinners and Weavers Association of Korea
SERT ...... Spinning Satellite for Electric Rocket Test
SPURT...... Spinning Unguided Rocket Trajectory
SAE .... Spiral Aftereffect (Aerospace)
SFF .... Spiritual Frontiers Fellowship
SLIA .... Spiritual Life Institute of America
SRM .... Spiritual Regeneration Movement (Foundation of America)
SID .... Spiritus In Deo (Spirit Rests in God)
SVR .... Spiritus Vini Rectificatus (Rectified Spirit of Wine)
SVT .... Spiritus Vini Tenuis (Proof Spirit of Wine)
SAFARI .... Spiro Agnew Fans and Rooters, Incorporated
SB .... Splash Block
SR .... Split Ring (Technical drawings)
SST .... Split Second Timing
SA .... Splitting Amplifier
SEIOD ..... Spogli Elettronici dell'Italiano delle Origini e del Duecento (A lexical, morphological, and syntactical inventory of Old Italian texts)
SI .... Spokane International R. R. (AAR code)
SPS .... Spokane, Portland & Seattle Railway System (AAR code)
SFO .... Spoleczny Fundusz Oszczednosciowy
SCI .... Sponge and Chamois Institute
SPN .... Sponsor Program Number (Military)
SF .... Spontaneous Fission
SIT........ Spontaneous Ignition Temperature
SHR .... Spontaneously Hypertensive Rats
S .... Spool
SNL........ Spore Newsletter (A publication)
SBSUSA...... Sport Balloon Society of the United States
SFI......... Sport Fishing Institute
SAAMI ..... Sporting Arms and Ammunition Manufacturers Institute
SGJA ...... Sporting Goods Jobbers Association
SGMAA ..... Sporting Goods Manufacturers Agents Association
SGRA...... Sporting Goods Representatives Association
SCC....... Sports Car Club of America
SCCA ...... Sports Car Club of America
SSA .... Sportswear Salesmen's Association
SAP .... Spot Authorization Plan (WPB)
SF .... Spot Face
SI .... Spot Inspection (Military)
SW........ Spot Weld (Technical drawings)
SSR .... Spotted Swine Record
SAC .... Sprayed Acoustical Ceiling (Technical drawings)
SC .... Spread Correlation

SSMA . . . . . . Spread-Spectrum Multiple Access (Satellite communications)
SC . . . . Spreading Coefficient
SCD . . . . Spreading Cortical Depression
SOF . . . . Spreading Ocean Floor
SJCC . . . . . . Spring Joint Computer Conference
SMI . . . . Spring Manufacturers Institute
SRI . . . . Spring Research Institute
SA . . . . Springfield Armory (Army)
SPGT . . . . . . Springfield Terminal Railway Company (AAR code)
SIA . . . . Sprinkler Irrigation Association
SFPP . . . . . . Spruce Falls Power & Paper Company (AAR code)
SIS . . . . Spuria Iris Society
SGO . . . . Squadron Gunnery Officer
SL . . . . Squadron Leader (British Royal Air Force)
SMO . . . . Squadron Medical Officer
SOS . . . . Squadron Officers School (Air Force)
SOC . . . . Squadron Operations Center (Air Force)
SSM . . . . Squadron Sergeant Major
SSU . . . . Squadron Service Unit (Aircraft)
SSC . . . . Squadron Supervisory Console (Air Force)
Q . . . . Squall (Meteorology)
SQD . . . . Square D Company (NYSE symbol)
SF . . . . Square Foot
SMT . . . . Square Mesh Tracking (Air Force)
SP . . . . Square Punch
SQR . . . . Square Root (Data processing)
SY . . . . Square Yard
SMC . . . . Squared Multiple Correlation (Psychology)
SLFP . . . . Sri Lanka Freedom Party (Ceylon)
SLTUF . . . . . . Sri Lanka Trade Union Federation (Sri Lanka Vurthiya Samithi
       Sammelanaya) (Ceylon)
SAN . . . . Srpska Akademija Nauka i Umetnosti (Belgrade, Yugoslavia)
STFB . . . . Staatliche Forstwirtschaftsbetriebe
STEG . . . . . . Staatliche Gesellschaft zur Erfassung von Ruestungsgut (German Public
       Corporation for the Collection and Distribution of War Material)
SSD . . . . Staatssicherheitsdienst
SAS . . . . Stability Augmentation System (FAA)
SX . . . . Stability Index (Aviation)
SCS . . . . Stabilization & Control System
SBAE . . . . . . Stabilized Bombing Approach Equipment (Navy)
SFNA . . . . . . Stabilized Fuming Nitric Acid
STALO . . . . . . Stabilized Local Oscillator (RADAR)
SMO . . . . Stabilized Master Oscillator
SSD . . . . Stabilized Ship Detector (Navy)
SMF . . . . Stable Matrix Form
STOP . . . . . . Stable Ocean Platform
SPPS . . . . Stable Plasma Protein Solution (Medicine)
S . . . . Staff
SAO . . . . Staff Administrative Office (Military)
SCPD, OC of SA . . Staff Civilian Personnel Division, Office, Chief of Staff (Army)
SC . . . . Staff College (Military)
SCD, OC of SA . . Staff Communications Division, Office, Chief of Staff (Army)
SCO . . . . Staff Communications Office
CSSCO . . . . . . Staff Communications Office, Office of the Chief of Staff (Army)
SC . . . . Staff Corps
SDNCO . . . . . Staff Duty Noncommissioned Officer
SDO . . . . Staff Duty Officer
SI . . . . Staff Inspector
SJA . . . . Staff Judge Advocate (Air Force)
SMD, OC of SA . . Staff Management Division, Office, Chief of Staff (Army)
SM . . . . Staff Memorandum
SO . . . . Staff Officer
SOAA . . . . . . Staff Officers Association of America
SOD . . . . Staff Operations Division (NASA)
SORT . . . . . . Staff Organizations Round Table (American Library Association)
SPEC . . . . . . Staff of the Production Executive Committee (of the WPB)
SQMS . . . . . . Staff Quartermaster Sergeant
SR . . . . Staff Report
S/RS . . . . Staff Returns (Marine Corps)
SSG . . . . Staff Sergeant (Army)
SSGT . . . . . . Staff Sergeant
STFSGT . . . . . Staff Sergeant (Marine Corps)
SSM . . . . Staff Sergeant Major
SS . . . . Staff Specialist
SS . . . . Staff Surgeon
V . . . . Staff transport (When the first of two letters) (Designation for all
       US military aircraft)
SWO . . . . . . Staff Weather Officer
SWG . . . . . . Staff Working Group
SAILER . . . . . . Staffing of African Institutions for Legal Education and Research
       (An organization) (Later, International Legal Center)

STCA . . . . . . Staffordshire Terrier Club of America
SAGA . . . . . . Stage and Arena Guild of America
SC . . . . Stage Center (A stage direction)
SD . . . . Stage Direction
SD . . . . Stage Door (Theatrical slang)
SL . . . . Stage Left (A stage direction)
SM . . . . Stage Manager
SR . . . . Stage Right (A stage direction)
SIO . . . . Staged in Orbit
SSW . . . . Staggered Spondaic Word
STGAR . . . . . Staging Area (Military)
STGB . . . . . . Staging Base (Military)
SGAA . . . . . . Stained Glass Association of America
SLGA . . . . . . Stained and Leaded Glass Association
SS . . . . Stainless Steel
SST . . . . Stainless Steel
SSCr . . . . Stainless Steel Crown (Dentistry)
SSPFC . . . . . . Stainless Steel Plumbing Fixture Council
SSSC . . . . . . Stainless Steel Sink Council
S & P . . . . . . Stake and Platform (Technical drawings)
STA . . . . Staley (A. E.) Manufacturing Company (NYSE symbol)
STALAG . . . . . Stammlager (Prisoner-of-war camp) (German)
STALAGLUFT . . Stammlagerluft (Prisoner-of-war camp for airmen) (German)
SOS . . . . Stamp Out Sickness (Committee) (San Francisco, California)
SAE . . . . Stamped Addressed Envelope
SFTW . . . . . . Stamps for the Wounded
SOCM . . . . . . Stand-Off Cluster Munitions
S . . . . Standard
SAC . . . . Standard Aircraft Characteristics
SAE . . . . Standard Average European
SB . . . . Standard Bead
SBA . . . . Standard Beam Approach (British aircraft landing method)
SBN . . . . Standard Book Numbering
SB . . . . Standard Brands, Inc. (NYSE symbol)
SCE . . . . Standard Calomel Electrode
SCL . . . . Standard Classification List
SCC . . . . Standard Commodity Classification
SCFEL . . . . . . Standard COMSEC (Communications Security) Facility Equipment List
SCC . . . . Standard Community Classification
SCAMP . . . . . Standard Configuration and Modification Program
SCF . . . . Standard Cubic Foot
SD . . . . Standard Deviation
SESA . . . . . . Standard Electrica, SA (Brazilian affiliate of ITT)
SEP . . . . Standard Electronic Package
SEL . . . . Standard Elektrik Lorenz (Germany)
SENL . . . . . . Standard Equipment Nomenclature List
SE . . . . Standard Error
SEM . . . . Standard Error of the Mean
SFEC . . . . . . Standard Facility Equipment Card(s) (Electrical accounting machine)
SFEL . . . . . . Standard Facility Equipment List (Electronics)
SFML . . . . . . Standard Facility Material List (Electrical accounting machine)
SFY . . . . Standard Facility Years (FAA)
SFH . . . . Standard Fading Hour (National Bureau of Standards)
SF . . . . Standard Form (Military)
SS . . . . Standard Frequency Station
SGTR . . . . . . Standard Government Travel Request
SHIP . . . . Standard Hardware Interface Program
SP . . . . Standard Holding Pattern (Aviation)
SHP . . . . Standard Holding Procedure (Aviation)
SHE . . . . Standard Hydrogen Electrode
SIC . . . . Standard Industrial Classification (Code)
SIP . . . . Standard Inspection Procedure
SIA . . . . Standard Instrument Approach (RADAR) (Aviation)
SID . . . . Standard Instrument Departure (Aviation)
SITC . . . . . . Standard International Trade Classification (UN)
SJJRA . . . . . . Standard Jack and Jennet Registry of America
SJP . . . . Standard Jet Penetration (Aviation)
SKO . . . . Standard Kollsman Industries, Inc. (NYSE symbol)
SLCU . . . . . . Standard Landing Craft Unit
STANLANCRU . . Standard Landing Craft Unit (Military)
SLV . . . . Standard Launch Vehicle
SLA . . . . Standard Life Association
SLRAP . . . . . . Standard Low Frequency Range Approach
SM . . . . Standard Matched
SMOW . . . . . Standard Mean Ocean Water
SME . . . . Standard Medical Examination (Military)
SMSA . . . . . . Standard Metropolitan Statistical Area
SMS . . . . Standard Molecular System
SMR . . . . Standard Mortality Rate
SNL . . . . Standard Name Line
SNDL . . . . . . Standard Navy Distribution List

SNMMMIS.... Standard Navy Maintenance and Material Management Information System (Also known as 3M)
SNMMMS .... Standard Navy Maintenance and Material Management System
SNSL .... Standard Navy Stock List
STANINE .... Standard Nine Score (Military)
SNOW .... Standard Normal Ocean Water
SNDO ...... Standard Nomenclature of Diseases and Operations
SNL........ Standard Nomenclature List (Military)
SNPM ...... Standard and Nuclear Propulsion Module
ESSO .... Standard Oil
J.......... Standard Oil Company (NYSE symbol) (Wall Street slang name: "Jersey")
SN........ Standard Oil Company (Indiana) (NYSE symbol)
SOC....... Standard Oil Company
SOH....... Standard Oil Company (Ohio) (NYSE symbol)
SOHIO ..... Standard Oil Company (Ohio)
SD .... Standard Oil Company of California (NYSE symbol)
STANOLIND .. Standard Oil Company of Indiana
SOCONY .... Standard Oil Company of New York (Socony Mobile is now official name of firm)
SORAP ..... Standard Omni Range Approach
SOP....... Standard Operating Procedure
SOR ...... Standard Operating Report
SPK .... Standard Packaging Corporation (NYSE symbol) (Wall Street slang name: "Sputnik")
SPS ...... Standard Pipe Size
S & P..... Standard and Poor's Corporation
SP .... Standard Practice
SPI........ Standard Practice Instructions
SPS ...... Standard Press Steel Company
SDP ...... Standard Pressed Steel Company (NYSE symbol)
SPM ...... Standard Process Manual
SPC ...... Standard Products Committee (Navy)
SR .... Standard Range Approach (Aviation)
SRD ...... Standard Reference Data
SRM ...... Standard Reference Material
SRM ...... Standard Repair Manual
SRC ...... Standard Requirements Code (Military)
SSF....... Standard Saybolt Furol (Oil viscosity)
SSU ...... Standard Saybolt Universal (Oil viscosity)
SSCA ...... Standard Schnauzer Club of America
SS .... Standard Score (Psychology)
SSP ...... Standard Shop Practice
SSGS ...... Standard Space Guidance System
SSLS ...... Standard Space Launch System (BSD)
SSLV ...... Standard Space Launch Vehicle
STRIP ...... Standard Taped Routines for Image Processing (National Bureau of Standards)
STRIVE ..... Standard Techniques for Reporting Information on Value Engineering
STP ...... Standard Temperature and Pressure
STPD ...... Standard Temperature and Pressure, Dry
STP ...... Standard (Normal) Temperature and Pulse (Medicine)
STAR ...... Standard Terminal Arrival Route (Aviation)
STAR ...... Standard Test Authorization & Report System (Navy)
STD ...... Standard Test Dose
STS ...... Standard Test for Syphilis (Medicine)
STV ...... Standard Test Vehicle
ST .... Standard Time
STR ...... Standard Tool Request
STATRAFO ... Standard Transfer Order
STC ...... Standard Transmission Code (Data processing)
STCC ...... Standard Transportation Commodity Code
STANVAC.... Standard Vacuum Oil Company
SWG ...... Standard Wire Gauge
SWAG ...... Standard Written Agreement (Military)
SOLOG ..... Standardization of Certain Aspects of Operations and Logistics
S/E .... Standardization/Evaluation
SEG .... Standardization Evaluation Group
SR .... Standardization Report
STANAG..... Standardized Agreement (NATO)
SGTR ...... Standardized Government Travel Regulations
ST .... Standardized Test (Psychology)
SAA ...... Standards Association of Australia
SEAC ...... Standards Electronic Automatic Computer (National Bureau of Standards)
SES ...... Standards Engineers Society
SGA ...... Standards of Grade Authorization
SPARC ..... Standards Planning and Requirements Committee (ANSI)
SARP ...... Standards and Recommended Practices
SSC ...... Standards Steering Committee (ANSI)
STAG ...... Standards Technical Advisory Group
SWAC....... Standards Western Automatic Computer (National Bureau of Standards)

SFDS .... Standby Fighter Director Ship (Navy)
SBFC .... Standby for Further Clearance (Aviation)
SRAF ...... Standby Reserve of the Armed Forces
STADINAIR ... Standing Administrative Instruction for Air Attaches
SCOBA...... Standing Conference of the Canonical Orthodox Bishops in the Americas
SCOLMA..... Standing Conference on Library Materials on Africa (British)
SDW....... Standing Detonation Wave
SG........ Standing Group
SECAN...... Standing Group Communication Security and Evaluation Agency Washington
DACAN..... Standing Group Distribution and Accounting Agency, NATO
SGLO...... Standing Group Liaison Officer to the North Atlantic Council
SGN ...... Standing Group, North Atlantic Treaty Organization
SGREP ..... Standing Group Representative (NATO)
ACSL ...... Standing Lenticular Altocumulus (Meteorology)
SO........ Standing Order(s)
SRO .... Standing Room Only (Theater)
SSI .... Standing Signal Instructions
SWAMI ..... Standing Wave Area Monitor
SWIP ...... Standing Wave Impedance Probe (Geophysical instrument)
SWR ...... Standing-Wave Ratio (Voltage) (Electronics)
SP .... Standpipe
SB .... Stanford-Binet (Intelligence test)
SEL .... Stanford Electronic Laboratory (Stanford University)
SIDEC...... Stanford International Development Education Center (Stanford University)
SLAC ...... Stanford Linear Accelerator Center (AEC)
SPIRES ..... Stanford Physics Information Retrieval System
SRI........ Stanford Research Institute
SRILTA ...... Stanford Research Institute Lead Time Analysis
S4 .... Stanford School Scheduling System
SUDAER ..... Stanford University, Department of Aeronautics and Astronautics
SWAMI ...... Stanford Worldwide Acquisition of Meteorological Information (Weather prediction system)
STW....... Stanley Warner Corporation (NYSE symbol)
SRY .... Stanray Corporation (NYSE symbol) (Wall Street slang name: "Sorry")
SPL .... Staphylococcal Bacteriophage Lysate (Bacteriology)
SSMMA...... Staple and Stapling Machine Manufacturers Association (Defunct)
SFSD ...... Star Field Scanning Device
SR .... Star Route (A type of rural postal delivery route)
SSBFH ..... Star-Spangled Banner Flag House
STRAP....... Star Tracking Rocket Attitude Positioning (System) (NASA)
SE .... Starch Equivalent
STARAD ..... Starfish Radiation (Satellite) (NASA)
SCX .... Starrett (L. S.) Company (NYSE symbol)
S & S....... Stars & Stripes (Military newspaper)
SOM ...... Start-of-Message
SOMP....... Start-of-Message Priority
SOW ...... Start of Word
SP .... Starting Point
SP .... Starting Price
SDTP ...... Startover Data Transfer and Processing (Program)
SANA....... State, Army, Navy, Air
SOA....... State of the Art
SOTA...... State of the Art
SCM....... State-Certified Midwife
SCAD ...... State Commission Against Discrimination
SCUAE ..... State Committee on the Utilization of Atomic Energy (USSR)
SCC .... State Corporation Commission
SDC....... State Defense Council
SDLO...... State, Defense Liaison Office
S-DMICC .... State-Defense Military Information Control Committee
SD .... State Department
SDI .... State Disability Insurance
SDI/UC...... State Disability Insurance - Unemployment Compensation
SEA ...... State Economic Area
SEA ...... State Education Agency
SERS ...... State Employees Retirement System
SED ...... State Executive Director
SES ...... State Experiment Stations Division (of ARS, Department of Agriculture)
SEMIS....... State Extension Management Information System (Department of Agriculture)
SFCRS....... State-Federal Crop Reporting Service
SLA ...... State Liquor Authority
SM........ State Militia (e.g., NJSM - New Jersey State Militia)
SMA....... State Mutual of America (An insurance company)
SNL ...... State Narcotic Law
SARDA ..... State and Regional Defense Airlift Plan (FAA, Civil Defense)
SRN ...... State Registered Nurse
STC ...... State Teachers College
STSA ...... State Technical Services Act
SUA ...... State Universities Association
SUI .... State University of Iowa

SUNY . . . . . . State University of New York
SUNYA . . . . . . State University of New York at Albany
SUNY BCN . . State University of New York Biomedical Communication Network
SUY . . . . . . State University R. R. (AAR code)
SVEAD . . . . . . State Variable Estimation and Accuracy Determination
SWNCC . . . . . State, War, Navy Coordinating Committee
SB . . . . Statement of Billing
S/C . . . . Statement of Charges (Army)
SOCAR . . . . . Statement of Condition and Recommendation (Military)
SIT . . . . Statement of Inventory Transaction
SPH . . . . Statement of Personal History
S/S . . . . Statement of Service (Military)
SOW . . . . . . Statement of Work
SI . . . . Staten Island
SIR . . . . Staten Island Rapid Transit Railway Company (AAR code)
SIRT . . . . . . Staten Island Rapid Transit Railway Company
SOU . . . . . . Statens Offentlige Utredningar (Sweden)
SR . . . . Stateroom
SA . . . . State's Attorney
SUDS . . . . . . State's Urban Development Something-or-other (Slang for Urban
          Development Corporation, New York)
SAVES . . . . . . States Audiovisual Education Study
SML . . . . States Marine Lines
SISC . . . . Statewide Information Steering Committee (California)
SLEW . . . . . . Static Load Error Washout
SND . . . . Static No Delivery
SP . . . . Static Pressure
STS . . . . Static Test Stand
ST . . . . Static Thrust
S . . . . Station
SCAMA . . . . . Station Conferring and Monitoring Arrangement (NASA)
SDO . . . . Station Duty Officer (Navy)
SHQ . . . . Station Headquarters
SH . . . . Station Hospital (Military)
SI . . . . Station Identification
SKAMP . . . . . . Station-Keeping and Mobile Platform (Robot sailboat)
SP . . . . Station Pressure (Meteorology)
SQC . . . . Station Quality Control (RADAR)
SRA . . . . Station Representatives Association
SPBOT . . . . . Stationers and Publishers Board of Trade
SO . . . . Stationery Office (British)
SR . . . . Stationery Request
SCO . . . . Statistical Control Office(r)
SCORU . . . . . Statistical Control and Operations Records Unit (Air Force)
SCU . . . . Statistical Control Unit (Military)
SEI . . . . Statistical Engineering Institute
SPAN . . . . . . Statistical Processing and Analysis (Data processing)
SPON . . . . . . Statistical Profile of Old Norse
SQC . . . . Statistical Quality Control
STAQC . . . . . Statistical Quality Control System (Military)
SRS . . . . Statistical Reporting Service (Department of Agriculture)
SRG . . . . Statistical Research Group (Princeton University)
SSIM . . . . . . Statistical, Sampling Inventory Method
SSO . . . . Statistical Service Office(r) (Military)
SSU . . . . Statistical Service Unit (Military)
SS . . . . Statistical Standards
STEP . . . . . . Statistical Trajectory Estimation Program (NASA)
STAR . . . . . . Statistical Treatment of RADAR Returns
SONS . . . . . . Statistics of Naval Shipyards
SVN . . . . Statistiek van Nederland (Netherlands)
SQS . . . . Statistische Quellenwerke der Schweiz (Switzerland)
ST . . . . Statistisk Tabelvaerk (Denmark)
SM . . . . Statistiske Meddelelser (Denmark)
SBCS . . . . . . Statni Banka Ceskoslovenska
SR . . . . Statstjanstemannens Riksforbund (National Association of Salaried
          Employees in Government Service) (Sweden)
STLI . . . . Statue of Liberty National Monument
SOE . . . . Status of Equipment (Army)
SOF . . . . Status of Forces Agreement (International treaty)
SOFA . . . . . . Status of Forces Agreement (International treaty)
SOFT . . . . . . Status of Forces Treaty
SR . . . . Status Report
SOUSAFE . . . . Status of United States Air Force Equipment
S . . . . Statute
SM . . . . Statute Mile
SMI . . . . Statute Miles
SRO . . . . Statutory Rules and Orders
SR & O . . . . . Statutory Rules and Orders
STF . . . . . . Stauffer Chemical Company (NYSE symbol)
STEM . . . . . . Stay Time Extension Module (NASA)
SSFL . . . . Steady-State Fermi Level

SSO . . . . Steady-State Oscillation
SACA . . . . . . Steam Automobile Club of America
SCBR . . . . . . Steam-Cooled Breeder Reactor
SCDMR . . . . . . Steam-Cooled D$_2$O Moderated Reactor (AEC)
SCFBR . . . . . . Steam-Cooled Fast Breeder Reactor (AEC)
SE . . . . Steam Emulsion
SEN . . . . Steam Emulsion Number
SGHWR . . . . . Steam Generating Heavy Water Reactor (British)
SHEMA . . . . . . Steam Heating Equipment Manufacturers Association
ST . . . . Steam Trawler
ST . . . . Steam Tug
SY . . . . Steam Yacht
SB . . . . Steamboat
S . . . . Steamer
SPD . . . . Steamer Pays Dues (Shipping)
SS . . . . Steamship
SFBA . . . . . . Steamship Freight Brokers Association
SSHSA . . . . . . Steamship Historical Society of America
SMA . . . . Steatite Manufacturers Association
S . . . . Steel
SBMA . . . . . . Steel Bar Mills Association
SBW . . . . Steel Basement Window
SBI . . . . Steel Boiler Institute
SCOT . . . . . . Steel Car of Tomorrow
SC . . . . Steel Casting
SDI . . . . Steel Deck Institute
SDI . . . . Steel Door Institute
SFSA . . . . . . Steel Founders' Society of America
SG . . . . Steel Girder (Bridges)
SJI . . . . Steel Joist Institute
SKCMA . . . . . Steel Kitchen Cabinet Manufacturers Association
SMIA . . . . . . Steel Management in Action (Bethlehem Steel Company)
SPFA . . . . . . Steel Plate Fabricators Association
SPWA . . . . . . Steel Products Warehouse Association
SS . . . . Steel Sash
SSSI . . . . Steel Scaffolding and Shoring Institute
SSCI . . . . Steel Service Center Institute
SSCI . . . . Steel Shipping Container Institute
SSPC . . . . . . Steel Structures Painting Council
STI . . . . Steel Tank Institute
ST . . . . Steel Truss (Bridges)
SWI . . . . Steel Window Institute
SWR . . . . Steel Wire Rope
SW . . . . Steel Worker
SWOC . . . . . . Steel Workers Organizing Committee (Became United Steelworkers of
          America)
SH . . . . Steelton & Highspire R. R. (AAR code)
STAR . . . . . . Steerable Array RADAR
STARE . . . . . . Steerable Telemetry Antenna Receiving Equipment
STAFF . . . . . . Stellar Acquisition Flight Feasibility
STAR . . . . . . Stellar Attitude Reference
STARAN . . . . . Stellar Attitude Reference & Navigation
SIBS . . . . Stellar-Inertial Bombing System
SIDS . . . . Stellar Inertial Doppler System
STINGS . . . . . . Stellar Inertial Guidance System (BSD)
S . . . . Stem
STT . . . . Stenographer, Medical (Navy)
S & T . . . . . . Stenographer and Typist (Examination) (Civil Service Commission)
SIP . . . . Step in Place
SDT . . . . Step-Down Transformer
STC . . . . Stepchild
sr . . . . Steradian
SBI . . . . Sterchi Brothers Stores, Incorporated (NYSE symbol)
S . . . . Stere (Metric)
SAS . . . . Sterile Aqueous Suspension
SIS . . . . Sterile Injectable Suspension
SSS . . . . Sterile Saline Soak
SS . . . . Sterile Solution
SADL . . . . . . Sterilization Assembly Development Laboratory (NASA)
S & B . . . . . . Sterilization and Bath
STY . . . . Sterling Drug, Inc. (NYSE symbol)
SSGA . . . . . . Sterling Silversmiths Guild of America
SP . . . . Stern Post
JB . . . . Stetson Hat (After John Batterson Stetson, 19th-century American hat
          manufacturer) (Slang)
SSA . . . . Steuben Society of America
YS . . . . Stevedoring Barge (Navy symbol)
STN . . . . Stevens (J. P.) & Company, Inc. (NYSE symbol)
SIT . . . . Stevens Institute of Technology
SD . . . . Steward (Navy rating)
STET . . . . . . Steward, Technical (Marine Corps)

STDA . . . . Steward's Assistant (Navy)
STDB . . . . Steward's Branch (Marine Corps)
STM . . . . Steward's Mate (Navy rating)
STX . . . . Stewart-Warner Corporation (NYSE symbol)
STRT . . . . Stewartstown R. R. (AAR code)
NEN . . . . Stichting Nederlands Normalisatie-Instituut
SLATE . . . . . . Stimulated Learning by Automated Typewriter Environment
S . . . . Stimulus
SOI . . . . Stimulus Onset Interval
S-O-R . . . . . Stimulus–Organism-Response
SR . . . . Stimulus-Response
S-R . . . . Stimulus-Response
SM . . . . Stipendiary Magistrate
SP . . . . Stirrup Pump
SASIDS . . . . . Stochastic Adaptive Sequential Information Dissemination System
S . . . . Stock
SB & CR . . . . Stock Balance and Consumption Report
SCA . . . . Stock Company Association
SCC . . . . Stock Control Center (Army)
SC & D . . . . Stock Control and Distribution
SE . . . . Stock Exchange
SF . . . . Stock Fund
STKF . . . . . . Stock Fund
STKFA . . . . . Stock Fund Accounting
STKFS . . . . . Stock Fund Statement
SL . . . . Stock Length (Construction or manufacturing materials)
SL . . . . Stock Level
SL . . . . Stock List
SMR . . . . Stock Management Report
SCAN . . . . . . Stock Market Computer Answering Service
S/N . . . . Stock Number
SNAB . . . . . . Stock Number Action Bulletin
SNACS . . . . . Stock Number Assignment Control System (Air Force)
SNUD . . . . . . Stock Number User Directory (Air Force)
SPIRT . . . . . . Stock Point Interrogation/Requirements Technique
SRA . . . . Stock Record Account
SRAN . . . . . . Stock Record Account Number
SRC . . . . Stock Record Card (Military)
SRNR . . . . . . Stock Request Number
SSLT . . . . . . Stock Status Lag Time
ST . . . . Stock Transfer
SW . . . . Stock Width (Construction or manufacturing materials)
STL . . . . Stockage List
STLI . . . . Stockage List Item(s)
SO . . . . Stockage Objectives
S & I . . . . . . Stocked and Issued
SIPRI . . . . . . Stockholm International Peace Research Institute (Now, International Institute for Peace and Conflict Research)
STOT . . . . . . Stockpile-to-Target
STS . . . . Stockpile to Target Sequence
STE . . . . Stockton Terminal & Eastern R. R. (AAR code)
SBC . . . . Stokely-Van Camp, Inc. (NYSE symbol)
SMA . . . . . . Stoker Manufacturers Association
SB . . . . Stolen Base(s) (Baseball)
SA . . . . Stone Arch (Bridges)
STO . . . . Stone Container Corporation (NYSE symbol)
SW . . . . Stone & Webster, Inc. (NYSE symbol)
STRI . . . . . . Stones River National Battlefield
SO . . . . Stop Order
SP . . . . Stop Payment (Banking)
SFT . . . . Stop for Tea (British)
STOP . . . . . . Stop This Outrageous Purge (Group opposed to extremist measures used by segregationists in Arkansas; opposed by CROSS)
SUS . . . . Stop Unnecessary Spending
SWAT . . . . . . Stop Withholding All Taxes
SO . . . . Stopover (Slang)
SIT . . . . Stopping or Storage in Transit
STEM . . . . . . Storable Tubular Extendable Member
SCC . . . . Storage Connecting Circuit (Teletype)
SDP . . . . Storage and Distribution Point (Military)
SLR . . . . Storage Limits Register
SL . . . . Storage Location
SOF . . . . Storage Oscilloscope Fragments
SPAN . . . . . . Storage Planning and Allocation (Data processing)
SOCRATES . . . . Storage and Retrieval of Carrier Rates (Military shipments)
SR . . . . Storage Room
SAC . . . . Store and Clear Accumulator
SDD . . . . Store Door Delivery
S/F . . . . Store-and-Forward
SLW . . . . Store Logical Word
AF . . . . Store Ship (Navy symbol)

SC . . . . Stored Command
SEALS . . . . . . Stored Energy Actuated Lift System
SPAN . . . . . . Stored Program Alphanumerics (FAA)
SPC . . . . Stored Program Command (or Control) (Gemini) (NASA)
SPEC . . . . . . Stored Program Educational Computer
SPE . . . . Stored Program Element
SK . . . . Storekeeper
STO . . . . Storekeeper (Coast Guard)
SKV . . . . Storekeeper, Aviation (Navy)
SKCB . . . . . . Storekeeper, Construction Battalion, Stevedore (Navy)
SKD . . . . Storekeeper, Disbursing (Navy)
SKT . . . . Storekeeper, Technical (Navy)
SBK . . . . Storer Broadcasting Company (NYSE symbol)
SSC . . . . Stores Stock Catalog
SD . . . . Storm Detection
STRADAP . . . . . Storm RADAR Data Processor (ESD)
SFD . . . . Stouffer Foods Corporation (NYSE symbol)
SB . . . . Stove Bolt
SFAW . . . . . . Stove, Furnace and Allied Appliance Workers
SMIU . . . . . . Stove Mounters' International Union of North America (AFL-CIO)
SF . . . . Stowage Factor (Shipping)
STRAGL . . . . . Straggler Line (Military)
S . . . . Straight
SD . . . . Straight Duty
SFP . . . . Straight Fixed Price
S . . . . Straight-In (Aviation)
SI . . . . Straight-In Approach (Aviation)
STA . . . . Straight-In Approach (Aviation)
SL . . . . Straight Line (Statistics)
SLC . . . . Straight-Line Capacitance (or Capacity)
SLW . . . . Straight Line Wavelength
SS . . . . Straight Shank (Screw)
SS . . . . Straits Settlements (in Malaya)
SC & S . . . . . Strapped, Corded, and Sealed (as, of a package or bale)
SRC . . . . Strasburg R. R. (AAR code)
SAC . . . . Strategic Air Command
SACCEI . . . . . Strategic Air Command Communications-Electronics Instruction
SACCOMNET . . Strategic Air Command Communications Network
SACCS . . . . . Strategic Air Command Communications System
SACCS . . . . . Strategic Air Command Control System
SACLO . . . . . Strategic Air Command Liaison Officer
SAC/MEP . . . . Strategic Air Command/Minuteman Education Program
STN . . . . SAC (Strategic Air Command) Telephone Net (Air Force)
SACTTYNET . . . Strategic Air Command Teletype Network
SAF . . . . Strategic Air Force
STRAFPOA . . . . Strategic Air Force, Pacific Ocean Area
STRAIRPOA . . . Strategic Air Force, Pacific Ocean Areas
SALT . . . . . . Strategic Arms Limitation Talks
STRAC . . . . . Strategic Army Command
STARCOM . . . . Strategic Army Communications System (Military)
STRAC . . . . . Strategic Army Corps
STRAF . . . . . Strategic Army Force
SBS . . . . Strategic Balkan Services (World War II)
SBWG . . . . . . Strategic Bomb Wing (Military)
SBGP . . . . . . Strategic Bomber Group (Military)
SCC . . . . Strategic Communications Command (Army)
S & CM . . . . . Strategic and Critical Materials (Military)
S & C . . . . . . Strategic and Critical Raw Material
SES . . . . Strategic Engineering Survey (Navy)
SIA . . . . Strategic Industries Association
SID . . . . Strategic Intelligence Digests (Military)
SIRA . . . . . . Strategic Intelligence Research and Analysis
SIS . . . . Strategic Intelligence School (Military)
SLAM . . . . . . Strategic Low Altitude Missile
SM . . . . Strategic Missile
SMEC . . . . . . Strategic Missile Evaluation Committee (Air Force)
SMGP . . . . . . Strategic Missile Group (Air Force)
SMS . . . . Strategic Missile Squadron (Air Force)
SMSB . . . . . . Strategic Missile Support Base
SMW . . . . . . Strategic Missile Wing (Air Force)
SMWG . . . . . . Strategic Missile Wing (Air Force)
STOP . . . . . . Strategic Orbit Point
SO . . . . Strategic Outline Chart (Air Force)
SP . . . . Strategic Planning Chart (Air Force)
SRR . . . . Strategic Ready Reserve (Military)
SRM . . . . Strategic Reconnaissance Missile
SSU . . . . Strategic Services Unit (Formerly, OSS)
SSS . . . . Strategic Support Squadron (Air Force)
SSPO . . . . . . Strategic Systems Project Office (Navy)
STAG . . . . . . Strategy and Tactics Analysis Group (Army)

STF . . . . Stratiform (Meteorology)
SC . . . . Stratocumulus (Meteorology)
STRATWARM . . Stratospheric Warming
SSS . . . . Stratum Super Stratum (Layer Over Layer)
ST . . . . Stratus (Meteorology)
STFR . . . . Stratus Fractus (Meteorology)
SL . . . . Streamline
SCORE . . . . . . Street Corner Offense Reduction Experiment
SHSLB . . . . . . Street and Highway Safety Lighting Bureau
SDB . . . . Strength & Dynamics Branch (Air Force)
SM . . . . Streptomycin (A drug)
SCC . . . . Stress Corrosion Cracking (Metals)
SF . . . . Stress Formula
SMM . . . . . . Stress Memo Manual
STRAP . . . . . . Stretch Assembly Program (IBM)
SB . . . . Stretcher-Bearer
SP . . . . Stretcher Party
SM . . . . Stria Medullaris
SATK . . . . . . Strike Attack
SC . . . . Strike Command (Military)
STRICOM . . . . Strike Command (Military)
SRIB . . . . Strike Route Information Book (Strategic Air Command)
SO . . . . Strikeouts (Baseball)
SRCC . . . . . . Strikes, Riots, and Civil Commotions
STRIKFLTLANT . . Striking Fleet Atlantic
STRIKFORSOUTH . . Striking and Support Forces Southern Europe (Navy)
SNOBAL . . . . . String-Oriented Symbolic Language (Data processing)
SV . . . . Stroke Volume (Physiology)
SPM . . . . Strokes Per Minute
SCATE . . . . . . Stromberg-Carlson Automatic Test Equipment
SSS . . . . Strong Soap Solution
SVIB . . . . Strong Vocational Interest Blank (Testing)
SD . . . . Stronnictwo Demokratyczne (Democratic Party) (Poland)
Sr . . . . Strontium (Chemical element)
SU . . . . Strontium Units (Atomic energy)
SCM . . . . Strouds Creek & Muddlety R. R. (AAR code)
STAIR . . . . . . Structural Analysis Interpretive Routine
SCSH . . . . . . Structural Carbon Steel Hard
SCSM . . . . . . Structural Carbon Steel Medium
SCSS . . . . . . Structural Carbon Steel Soft
SCR . . . . Structural Ceramic Panel
SCPI . . . . Structural Clay Products Institute
SCPRF . . . . . . Structural Clay Products Research Foundation
SCT . . . . Structural Clay Tile (Technical drawings)
STRESS . . . . . Structural Engineering Systems Solver (Data processing)
SG . . . . Structural Glass
SIC . . . . Structural Influence Coefficient
SRS . . . . Structural Research Series
STM . . . . Structural Test Model
SWFPA . . . . . Structural Wood Fiber Products Association
SM . . . . Structures Memorandum
SMA . . . . Stucco Manufacturers Association
SK . . . . Studebaker Corporation (NYSE symbol) (Wall Street slang name: "Studie")
SDC . . . . Studebaker Driver's Club
SAMA . . . . . . Student American Medical Association
SCM . . . . Student Christian Movement
SCL . . . . Student of the Civil Law
SCC . . . . Student of Codrington College (Barbados)
SCEE . . . . . . Student Committee for Economic Education
SCUSA . . . . . Student Conference on United States Affairs
SCA . . . . Student Conservation Association
STEP . . . . . . Student Education Program
SFMF . . . . . . Student Foreign Missions Fellowship
SGIS . . . . . . Student Government Information Service
SHO . . . . . . Student Health Organizations
SHL . . . . Student Homophile League
SIP . . . . Student Insurance Producers Association
SIMS . . . . . . Student International Meditation Society
SIM . . . . Student Interracial Ministry
SLE . . . . Student Letter Exchange
SMC . . . . Student Mobilization Committee (to End the War in Vietnam)
SNCC . . . . . . Student National (formerly, Nonviolent) Coordinating Committee
SNEA . . . . . . Student National Education Association
SNAP . . . . . . Student Naval Aviation Pilot
SNAP(G) . . . . Student Naval Aviation Pilot (Glider)
SNA . . . . Student Naval Aviator
SNFO . . . . . . Student Naval Flight Officer
SNFS . . . . . . Student Naval Flight Surgeon
SPU . . . . Student Peace Union
SPATE . . . . . . Student Personnel Association for Teacher Education
SPIR . . . . Student Project for International Responsibility

SRL . . . . Student Religious Liberals
SSSJ . . . . . . Student Struggle for Soviet Jewry
STEP . . . . . . Student Transfer Education Plan (National Urban League)
SU . . . . Student Union
SWAP . . . . . . Student Woodlawn Area Project (Chicago, Illinois)
SWEAT . . . . . Student Work Experience and Training
SZO . . . . Student Zionist Organization
STELO . . . . . . Studenta Tutmonda Esperantista Liga (World League of Esperanto-Speaking Students)
SATC . . . . . . Students Army Training Corps
SCOHR . . . . . Students Committee on Human Rights
SCARE . . . . . . Students Concerned About a Ravaged Environment (Organization in Cloquet, Minnesota)
SDA . . . . Students for Democratic Action
SDS . . . . Students for a Democratic Society
STOP-NSA . . . Students to Oppose Participation in the National Student Association
SOUP . . . . . . Students Opposing Unfair Practices (in advertising)
SRBA . . . . . . Students for the Right to Bear Arms
SITA . . . . Students' International Travel Association
SKA . . . . Studienkommission for Atomenergie (Switzerland)
SSA . . . . Studio Suppliers Association
STL . . . . Studio-to-Transmitter Link
SNTS . . . . . . Studiorum Novi Testamenti Societas (Society for the Study of the New Testament)
SES . . . . Study of Education at Stanford (Stanford University)
SERB . . . . . . Study of the Enhanced Radiation Belt (NASA)
SOMISS . . . . . Study of Management Information Systems Support (Army)
SOAMUS . . . . . Study of One-Atmosphere Manned Underwater Structures
SPEED . . . . . . Study & Performance Efficiency in Entry Design
SRL . . . . Study Reference List
SR . . . . Study Regulation
SR . . . . Study Requirement (Air Force)
STMA . . . . . . Stuffed Toy Manufacturers Association
SB . . . . Stuffing Box
SAMP . . . . . . Stuntmen's Association of Motion Pictures
SA . . . . Sturmabteilung (Storm troopers) (NAZI Germany)
STUKA . . . . . . Sturzkampfflugzeug (German) (Dive bomber)
SMBJ . . . . . . Style Manual for Biological Journals
SBR . . . . Styrene-Butadiene Rubber
SMA . . . . Styrene and Maleic Anhydride (Copolymer)
SR . . . . Styrene Rubber
SA . . . . Sub Anno (Under the Year)
SCR . . . . Sub-Chief Ranger (Ancient Order of Foresters)
SCIT . . . . Sub-Committee on Interzonal Trade (Allied German Occupation Forces)
SDHIRS . . . . . Sub-District Headquarters Induction and Recruiting Station (Navy)
SF . . . . Sub Finem (Near the End)
SHV . . . . Sub Hoc Voce or Sub Verbo (Under This Word)
SJ . . . . Sub Judice (Under Consideration)
SL . . . . Sub-Lieutenant (British Navy)
SP . . . . Sub-Professional (Civil Service employees designation)
SUBRPIO . . . . Sub-Registered Publications Issuing Office
SV . . . . Sub Verbo (Under the Word)
SV . . . . Sub Voce (Under that Word)
SBE . . . . Subacute Bacterial Endocarditis
SSLE . . . . Subacute Sclerosing Leukoencephalitis (A disease)
SSPE . . . . Subacute Sclerosing Panencephalitis (A disease)
SAPO . . . . . . Subarea Petroleum Office
SCAR . . . . . . Subcaliber Aircraft Rocket
SCD . . . . Subcarrier Discriminator
SCO . . . . Subcarrier Oscillator
SFA . . . . Subcommittee on Frequency Allocations
SCOPT . . . . . . Subcommittee on (Computer) Programming Terminology (of ACM)
SCO . . . . Subcontract Consignment Order
SCD . . . . Subcontract Deviation
SMSO . . . . . . Subcontract Material Sales Order
SPC . . . . Subcontract Plans Committee
S/C . . . . Subcontractor(s)
SE . . . . Subcritical Experiment (AEC)
SFO . . . . Subfornical Organ
S . . . . Subito (Immediately; suddenly) (Music)
S . . . . Subject (Psychology)
S/A . . . . Subject to Approval
SANR . . . . . . Subject to Approval No Risk
SAL . . . . Subject Authority List
SCD . . . . Subject Captain's Discretion (Aviation)
SHAL . . . . . . Subject Heading Authority List (Data processing)
SMA . . . . Subject Matter Area
SMS . . . . Subject Matter Specialist
SPA . . . . Subject to Particular Average (Insurance)
SP . . . . Subject-Predicate
S . . . . Subject of a proposition in logic

SR . . . . Subject Ratio
STR . . . . Subject Terminal Control Release (Aviation)
SEU . . . . Subjective Expected Utility (Concept) (Psychology of union-management relations)
SMG . . . . Submachine Gun
SMD . . . . Submanubrial Dullness (Medicine)
S . . . . Submarine
S/M . . . . Submarine (British)
SS . . . . Submarine (Navy symbol)
SAR . . . . Submarine Advanced Reactor
SUBAD . . . . . . Submarine Air Defense
SAIP . . . . . . Submarine Antenna Improvement Program (Military)
SAFPLAN . . . . Submarine Area Frequency Plan (Navy)
SB . . . . Submarine Base (Navy)
SUBASE. . . . . Submarine Base
SCAR . . . . . . Submarine Celestial Altitude Recorder (Navy)
PC . . . . Submarine Chaser (173 feet) (Navy symbol)
SC . . . . Submarine Chaser (110 foot)
PC(C) . . . . . Submarine Chaser (Control) (173 feet) (Navy symbol)
SC(C) . . . . . Submarine Chaser (Control) (110 foot)
PCH . . . . Submarine Chaser (Hydrofoil) (Navy symbol)
SCTC . . . . . . Submarine Chaser Training Center
SCTRACEN . . . Submarine Chaser Training Center
SMSD . . . . . . Submarine Detector Ship's Magnet
SUBDIV. . . . . . Submarine Division (Navy)
SEBS . . . . Submarine Emergency Buoyancy System
SETT . . . . Submarine Escape Training Tank
SB . . . . Submarine Fog Bell (Mechanical) (Maps and charts)
SUB-BELL . . . . Submarine Fog Bell (Mechanical)
SFO . . . . Submarine Fog Oscillator (Maps and charts)
SUBLANT. . . . . Submarine Force, Atlantic Fleet
SUBEASTLANT . . Submarine Force, Eastern Atlantic
SUBPAC . . . . . Submarine Force, Pacific Fleet
SUBAD . . . . . . Submarine Force, Pacific Fleet Administration
SUBADMI . . . . Submarine Force, Pacific Fleet Administration, Mare Island
SUBPACAD . . . Submarine Force, Pacific Fleet, Administrative Command
SUBPACSUBORDCOM . . Submarine Force, Pacific Fleet, Subordinate Command
SUBIC . . . . . . Submarine Integrated Control Systems
SISS . . . . Submarine Integrated SONAR System
SIR . . . . Submarine Intermediate Reactor
SLAST . . . . . . Submarine-Launched Anti-Surface Ship Torpedo
SLBM . . . . . . Submarine-Launched Ballistic Missile(s) (Navy)
SLIM . . . . . . Submarine-Launched Inertial Missile
SUBMEDCEN . . Submarine Medical Center (Navy)
SMD . . . . Submarine Mine Depot
SM. . . . . Submarine, Mine Laying
SS(N) . . . . . . Submarine (Nuclear-Powered) (Navy symbol)
AO(SS) . . . . . Submarine Oiler (Navy ship symbol)
SSO . . . . Submarine Oiler (Navy symbol)
SORG . . . . . . Submarine Operations Research Group (Navy)
SORR . . . . . . Submarine Operations Research Report (Navy)
SUB-OSC . . . . . Submarine Oscillator
SP . . . . Submarine Patrol (Navy)
S/M . . . . Submarine Pay
SS . . . . Submarine Qualification (Navy)
SL . . . . Submarine Qualification Lapsed (Navy)
SQUIRE. . . . . . Submarine Quickened Response
SRS . . . . Submarine Reactor Small
YRB . . . . Submarine Repair and Berthing Barge (Navy symbol)
YRBM . . . . . . Submarine Repair, Berthing and Messing Barge (Navy symbol)
SRF . . . . Submarine Repair Facility
SRU . . . . Submarine Repair Unit
SUBRU . . . . . . Submarine Repair Unit
YRC . . . . Submarine Rescue Chamber (Navy symbol)
ASR . . . . Submarine Rescue Vessel (Navy symbol)
SUBROC . . . . . Submarine Rocket
SSTV . . . . . . Submarine Shock Test Vehicle
SUBRON . . . . . Submarine Squadron
SS . . . . Submarine Studies (by SORG)
SSC . . . . Submarine Supply Center
AS . . . . Submarine Tender (Navy symbol)
STAR . . . . . . Submarine Test and Research (Navy)
STR . . . . Submarine Thermal Reactor (AEC)
SSP . . . . Submarine Transport (Navy symbol)
SUBSLANT. . . . Submarines, Atlantic Fleet
SUBSPAC. . . . . Submarines, Pacific Fleet
SUBSCOFOR . . Submarines Scouting Force (Pacific Fleet)
SUBSSOWESPAC . . Submarines, Southwest Pacific Force
SOLARIS . . . . . Submerged Object Locating and Retrieving Identification System
SMRE . . . . . . Submerged Repeater Monitoring Equipment (RADAR)
X . . . . Submersible Craft (Navy ship symbol)

SDC . . . . Submersible Decompression Chamber (Underwater tank)
SPID . . . . Submersible Portable Inflatable Dwelling
STU . . . . Submersible Test Unit (Navy)
SIA . . . . Subminiature Integrated Antenna
SMX . . . . Submultiplexer Unit
SO . . . . Suboffice
SOS . . . . Suborbital Sequence (NASA)
SUBORCOM. . . Subordinate Command
SUBCOMNELM. . Subordinate Command, (US) Naval Forces, Eastern Atlantic and Mediterranean
SUBORCOMDSERVLANT. . Subordinate Command, Service Force, Atlantic Fleet
SUBCOM. . . . . Subordinate Command, Service Force, Pacific Fleet
SUBORCOMDSERVPAC. . Subordinate Command, Service Force, Pacific Fleet
SPE . . . . Subport of Embarkation
SCT . . . . Subroutine Call Table
STD . . . . Subscriber Trunk Dialing (Telephone communications)
SFMA . . . . . . Subscription Fulfillment Managers Association
STV . . . . Subscription Television
SA . . . . Subsistence Allowance
SPED . . . . . . Subsistence Preparation by Electronic Defusion (Army field kitchen)
SUBSELS . . . . Subsisting Elsewhere
SSD . . . . Subsoil Drain (Technical drawings)
SSP . . . . Subsolar Point (Aerospace)
SATA . . . . . . Subsonic Aerodynamic Testing Association
SCAD . . . . . . Subsonic Cruise Armed Decoy (Air Force)
SJT . . . . Subsonic Jet Transport
S . . . . Substantive
SAM . . . . Substitute Alloy Material (AEC)
SUBNO . . . . . Substitutes Not Desired
SUBOK . . . . . Substitution Acceptable
SSDR . . . . . . Subsystem Development Requirement
SNAP . . . . . . Subsystem for Nuclear Auxiliary Power
SSFVT . . . . . . Subsystems Functional Verification Test (NASA)
SEA . . . . Subterranean Exploration Agency
SUB . . . . Suburban Gas (NYSE symbol)
SPF . . . . Suburban Press Foundation
SPG . . . . Suburban Propane Gas Corporation (NYSE symbol)
SACB . . . . . . Subversive Activities Control Board
S . . . . Succeeded
SMI . . . . Success Motivation Institute
SP . . . . Successive Planometric (A discrimination task)
SPAN . . . . . . Successive, Proportionate, Additive Numeration (Decision making)
SS . . . . Successive Stereometric (A discrimination task)
SDH . . . . Succinic Dehydrogenase
SDA . . . . Succinic Dehydrogenase Activity (Medicine)
S . . . . Sucre (Monetary unit in Ecuador)
SUC . . . . SuCrest Corporation (NYSE symbol)
SDG . . . . Sucrose Density Gradients
SANU . . . . . . Sudan African National Union (Political party)
SDF . . . . Sudan Defence Force (British)
SRWU . . . . . . Sudan Railways Workers' (Trade) Union
SWFTU . . . . . Sudan Workers Federation of Trade Unions
SYU . . . . Sudanese Youth Union
SAI . . . . Sudden Auroral Intensity
SC . . . . Sudden Commencement
SCNA . . . . . . Sudden Cosmic-Noise Absorption
SDS . . . . Sudden Death Syndrome (in children)
SEA . . . . Sudden Enhancement of Atmospherics (NASA)
SID . . . . Sudden Ionospheric Disturbance (NASA)
SPA . . . . Sudden Phase Anomaly (NASA)
SUID . . . . . . Sudden Unexpected Infant Death
SGP . . . . Sudeten German Party
SLRA . . . . . . Suede and Leather Refinishers of America
SAD . . . . Sugar, Acetone, Diacetic Acid (Test)
SA . . . . Sugar Association
SAI . . . . Sugar Association, Incorporated
SC . . . . Sugar Coated
SCT . . . . Sugar-Coated Tablet
SHAVE . . . . . . Sugar Hotel Alpha Victor Echo (Apollo 10 astronauts' code for shaving operation)
SIT . . . . Sugar Industry Technologists
SII . . . . Sugar Information, Incorporated
SRA . . . . Sugar Rationing Administration (Department of Agriculture) (Ceased functions, 1948)
SRFI . . . . Sugar Research Foundation, Incorporated
SMA . . . . Suggested for Mature Audiences (Motion pictures)
SGD . . . . Sui Generis Degree
SWL . . . . Sulfite Waste Liquor
SE . . . . Sulfoethyl
SRA . . . . Sulfo-Ricinoleic Acid
S . . . . Sulfur (Chemical element)

SCU . . . . Sulfur-Coated Urea
SF . . . . Sulphation Factor (of blood serum)
SPMRL . . . . . Sulphite Pulp Manufacturers' Research League
SEC . . . . Sulphur Export Corporation
SI . . . . Sulphur Institute
SSR . . . . Sum of the Squared Residuals (Econometrics)
SYD . . . . Sum of the Year's Digits (Statistics)
SSA . . . . Sumi-E Society of America
SAEC . . . . . . Sumitomo Atomic Energy Commission (Japan)
SAEI . . . . Sumitomo Atomic Energy Industries, Ltd. (Japan)
S . . . . Summary
SALTI . . . . . . Summary Accounting for Low-Dollar Turnover Items (Army)
SBC . . . . Summary Billing Card
SCR . . . . Summary Control Report (Planning and Production) (Navy)
SCA . . . . Summary Cost Account
SC . . . . Summary Court (Navy)
SCM . . . . Summary Court-Martial
SUMCM . . . . . Summary Court-Martial
SCMO . . . . . . Summary Court-Martial Order
SUMCMO . . . . Summary Court-Martial Order
SM . . . . Summary Memorandum
SMEK . . . . . . Summary Message Enable Keyboard
SP . . . . Summary Plotter (RADAR)
SORTE . . . . . . Summary of Radiation Tolerant Electronics
SR . . . . Summary Report
SS . . . . Summary Sheet
STR . . . . Summary Technical Report
LS . . . . Summer (Vessel load line mark)
S . . . . Summer (Load line mark)
SCFMA . . . . . Summer and Casual Furniture Manufacturers Association
SCOPE . . . . . . Summer Community Organization and Political Education Program
SCOTCH . . . . . Summer Cultural Opportunities for Teams and Children (National
music program)
SEX . . . . Summer Experiment Group (Summer work for engineering undergraduates)
ST . . . . Summer Time (Daylight saving time)
SWP . . . . Summer Work Program
SP . . . . Summus Pontifex (Supreme Pontiff, Pope)
SPMA . . . . . . Sump Pump Manufacturers Association
SUV . . . . Sumpter Valley Railway (AAR code)
SC . . . . Sumter & Choctaw Railway (AAR code)
S . . . . Sun
SNL . . . . Sun Chemical Corporation (NYSE symbol)
SGIA . . . . . . Sun Glass Institute of America
SLOS . . . . . . Sun Line of Sight
SUN . . . . Sun Oil Company (NYSE symbol)
SUNOCO . . . . Sun Oil Company
SPM . . . . Sun Probe-Mars (NASA)
SVA . . . . Sun Valley Airlines
STB . . . . Sun's True Bearing (Navigation)
SMB . . . . Sunbeam Corporation (NYSE symbol)
S . . . . Sunday
SS . . . . Sunday School, or Sabbath School
SSU . . . . Sunday School Union
S & H . . . . . . Sundays and Holidays
SNS . . . . Sundstrand Corporation (NYSE symbol)
SPLIT . . . . . . Sundstrand Processing Languages Internally Translated
SFA . . . . Sunfinder Assembly
SUDAM . . . . . Sunk or Damaged (Navy)
SMRGC . . . . . Sun-Maid Raisin Growers of California
SDX . . . . Sunray DX Oil Company (NYSE symbol)
SR . . . . Sunrise (Meteorology)
SS . . . . Sunset (Meteorology)
SUCR . . . . . . Sunset Crater National Monument
SG . . . . Sunset Gun (Military ceremonial)
SUN . . . . Sunset Railway (AAR code)
SUS . . . . Sunshine Biscuits, Inc. (NYSE symbol)
SSC . . . . Sunshine Mining Company (NYSE symbol)
SL . . . . Suo Loco (In Its Place)
SAK . . . . Suomen Ammattiyhdistysten Keskusliitto (Confederation of Finnish Trade
Unions)
STTK . . . . Suomen Teknillisten Toimihenkilojarjestojen Keskusliitto (Federation of
Finnish Technical Functionary Organizations)
SVT . . . . Suomen Virallinen Tilasto (Finland)
SELL . . . . Suomi, Eesti, Latvija, Lietuva (Finland, Estonia, Latvia, Lithuania)
SCOTT-R . . . . . Super-Critical, Once-Thru Tube Reactor (Experiment) (General Electric
Company)
SFXR . . . . . . Super Flash X-Ray
SHF . . . . Super-High Frequency (Radio wave)
SULINAC . . . . Super Linear Accelerator (Space flight simulator)
SMI . . . . Super Market Institute
SPAR . . . . Super-Precision Approach RADAR

SS . . . . Super Sport (in automobile model name)
S . . . . Superb
SC . . . . Supercalendered (Paper)
SERJ . . . . Supercharged Ejector Ramjet (Aircraft engine)
SORTIE . . . . . Supercircular Orbital Reentry Test Integrated Environment
SUMMA . . . . . Superconducting Magnetic Mirror Apparatus
SQUID . . . . . . Superconducting Quantum Interference Detector
SFT . . . . Superfast Train
SADE . . . . Superheat Advanced Demonstration Experiment
SHC . . . . Superheat Control (Boilers)
SPX . . . . Superheat Power Experiment
SC . . . . Superimposed Current
SPVEA . . . . . . Superintendencia do Plano de Valorizacao Economica da Amazonia
(Brazil)
SCS . . . . Superintendent of Car Service
SD . . . . Superintendent of Documents (US Government Printing Office)
SOD . . . . Superintendent of Documents (US Government Printing Office)
SUPTNAVOBSY . . Superintendent, Naval Observatory
SRO . . . . Superintendent of Range Operations (NASA)
ST . . . . Superintendent of Transportation
SCE . . . . Superintending Civil Engineer (British)
SUPCON . . . . . Superintending Constructor
S . . . . Superior
SFC . . . . Superior Fine Cognac
SGC . . . . Superior Geocentric Conjunction
SHC . . . . Superior Heliocentric Conjunction
SOC . . . . Superior Oil Company (Nevada) (NYSE symbol)
SO . . . . Superior Old
SVC . . . . Superior Vena Cava (Anatomy)
SWC . . . . Superior White Crystal (Sugar)
SQ . . . . Superquick
SS & C . . . . . . Supersized and Calendered (Paper)
SCRAMJET . . . . Supersonic Combustion Ramjet
SCAT . . . . . . Supersonic Commercial Air Transport (NASA)
SIR . . . . Supersonic Infantry Rocket
SLAM . . . . . . Supersonic Low Altitude Missile
SMART . . . . . . Supersonic Military Air Research Track
SMART . . . . . . Supersonic Missile and Rocket Track
SNORT . . . . . . Supersonic Naval Ordnance Research Track
SST . . . . Supersonic Transport (Projected commercial aircraft)
STAB . . . . Supersonic Transport Advisory Board
STEG . . . . Supersonic Transport Evaluation Group
STOP . . . . Supersonic Transport Optimization Program (NASA)
STA . . . . Supersonic Tunnel Association
SWT . . . . Supersonic Wind Tunnel
SUPINSMAT . . . Supervising Inspector of Naval Material
SIOH . . . . Supervision, Inspection and Overhead
SPOOK . . . . . . Supervisor Program Over Other Kinds (Data processing)
SUPSHIP . . . . . Supervisor of Shipbuilding (Navy)
SATCO . . . . . . Supervisory Air Traffic Control Organizations (FAA)
SAP . . . . Supervisory Airplane Pilot
SC . . . . Supervisory Control
SCI . . . . Supervisory Cost Inspector (Navy)
SUPCOSTINS . . Supervisory Cost Inspector
SEER . . . . Supervisory Electronic Engineer Radio
SEIT . . . . Supervisory Electronic Installation Technician
SEMTR . . . . . . Supervisory Electronic Maintenance Technician (Relief)
SES . . . . Supervisory Electronics Specialist
SII . . . . Supervisory Immigrant Inspector (Immigration and Naturalization Service)
SIPI . . . . Supervisory Immigration Patrol Inspector (Immigration and Naturalization
Service)
STEP . . . . Supervisory Tape Executive Program (Data processing)
SAA . . . . Supima Association of America
SACC . . . . . . Supplemental Air Carrier Conference
SR . . . . Supplemental Report
SUB . . . . Supplemental Unemployment Benefit(s)
SVP . . . . Supplemental Vacation Plan
SA . . . . Supplementary Agreement
SAWRS . . . . . . Supplementary Airway Weather Reports
SAWRS . . . . . . Supplementary Aviation Weather Reporting Station
SUPINTREP . . . Supplementary Intelligence Report
SMO . . . . Supplementary Meteorological Office
SPR . . . . Supplementary Progress Report
SR . . . . Supplementary Regulation
SRR . . . . Supplementary Reserve Regulations (British Army)
SQR . . . . Supplier Quality Rating
SANDA . . . . . . Supplies and Accounts
S . . . . Supply (Department aboard a carrier) (Navy)
SAWBET . . . . . Supply Action Will Be Taken
SOK . . . . Supply Authorized (Supply OK)
SB . . . . Supply Bulletin

SC . . . . Supply Catalog (Military)
SUPCEN . . . . . Supply Center
SCD . . . . Supply, Commissary and Disbursing (Navy)
SC . . . . Supply Control (Military)
SCC . . . . Supply Control Center
SC . . . . Supply Corps
SCN . . . . Supply Corps, Navy
SDCP . . . . . . Supply Demand Control Points
SD . . . . Supply Department (Navy)
SD . . . . Supply Depot
SUPDEP . . . . . . Supply Depot
SEPORT . . . . . . Supply and Equipment Report (Army)
S & FO . . . . . . Supply and Fiscal Officer
SLA . . . . Supply Loading Airfield
S & L . . . . Supply and Logistics
S & M . . . . Supply and Maintenance (Army)
S & MA . . . . . Supply and Maintenance Agency (System) (Army)
SMC . . . . Supply & Maintenance Command (Army)
S & MMIS . . . . Supply and Maintenance Management Information System (Army)
SMIS . . . . Supply Management Information System
SMO . . . . Supply Management Office (Air Force)
SM . . . . Supply Manual
SO . . . . Supply Officer
SUPO . . . . Supply Officer
SOINC . . . . . . Supply Officer-in-Charge (Navy)
SOIC . . . . Supply Officer in Command
SOAP . . . . Supply Operations Assistance Program
SUPIER . . . . . . Supply Pier (Navy)
SUPPT . . . . . . Supply Point (Military)
SPAB . . . . Supply, Priorities and Allocations Board (World War II)
SRH . . . . Supply Railhead
SRS . . . . Supply Response Section (Navy)
SSS . . . . Supply Screening Section (Navy)
SUPSGT . . . . . Supply Sergeant (Marine Corps)
S & S . . . . Supply and Service (Army)
SUPOHDU . . . . Supply from Stock on Hand or Due in
SSC . . . . Supply Support Center (Navy)
SSR . . . . Supply Support Request (Military)
SSC . . . . Supply System Command (Navy)
S & T . . . . Supply and Transport
SAD . . . . Support Air Direction (Navy)
SAO . . . . Support Air Observation (Navy)
SAR . . . . Support Air Request (Net) (Navy communications)
SAMSOM . . . . Support Availability Multi-System Operational Model
SCF . . . . Support Carrier Force
SC . . . . Support Command (Army)
SUPCOM . . . . Support Command (Army)
SDC . . . . Support Design Change
SET-GO . . . . . Support and Encouragement for Talent - Gateway to Opportunity (Project)
SE . . . . Support Equipment (Military)
SPORTFOR . . . . Support Force
SIN . . . . Support Information Network
LES . . . . Support Landing Boat (Navy symbol)
LSSL . . . . Support Landing Ship (Large) MK III
SL . . . . Support Line (Military)
SPTL . . . . Support Line
SOS . . . . Support Our Soldiers (Network of antiwar-oriented coffee houses located near military bases)
SCOOP . . . . . Support Plan to Continuity of Operations Plan
SPUR . . . . Support for Promoting the Utilization of Resources (Esso Education Foundation)
SSMIS . . . . . . Support Services Management Information System (Army)
SS . . . . Support System (Air Force)
SURF . . . . Support of User Records and Files (Data processing)
SLPC . . . . Supported Liquid Phase Catalyst
SACC . . . . . . Supporting Arms Coordination Center (Air Force)
SF & S . . . . . Supporting Facilities and Services
APG . . . . Supporting Gunnery Ship (Navy symbol)
SR . . . . Supporting Research
SRT . . . . Supporting Research and Technology
SCOPE . . . . . Supportive Council on Preventive Effort (Ohio)
SCDSB . . . . . . Suppressed-Carrier Double Sideband
SS . . . . Supra Scriptum (Written Above)
SP . . . . Supraprotest
SIDE . . . . Suprathermal-Ion-Detector Experiment (Apollo) (NASA)
SAC . . . . Supreme Allied Command(er) (Headquarters in London) (World War II)
SACLANT . . . . Supreme Allied Commander, Atlantic (NATO)
SACLANTCEN . . Supreme Allied Commander, Atlantic, Anti-Submarine Warfare Research Center
SACLANTREPEUR . . Supreme Allied Commander, Atlantic, Representative in Europe
SACEUR . . . . . Supreme Allied Commander Europe (NATO)

SCARS . . . . . . SACEUR (Supreme Allied Commander Europe) Command Alerting Reporting System
SACMED . . . . . Supreme Allied Commander, Mediterranean
SACSEA . . . . . Supreme Allied Command(er), Southeast Asia
SAIORG . . . . . Supreme Assembly, International Order of Rainbow for Girls
D of M . . . . . . Supreme Caldron, Daughters of Mokanna
SCAW . . . . . . Supreme Camp of the American Woodmen
SCBA . . . . . . Supreme Circle Brotherhood of America
SUPCOM . . . . . Supreme Command
SCAEF . . . . . . Supreme Commander, Allied Expeditionary Force (World War II)
SCAP . . . . . . Supreme Commander of the Allied Powers in Japan
AASR-NMJ . . . Supreme Council, Ancient Accepted Scottish Rite of Freemasonry, Northern Masonic Jurisdiction
CBL . . . . Supreme Council Catholic Benevolent Legion
IAS . . . . Supreme Council of the Independent Associated Spiritualists
SCIAS . . . . . . Supreme Council of the Independent Associated Spiritualists
MOVPER . . . . . Supreme Council, Mystic Order Veiled Prophets of Enchanted Realm
SCNR . . . . . . Supreme Council for National Reconstruction (South Korea)
SCRA . . . . . . Supreme Council of the Royal Arcanum
SCSA . . . . . . Supreme Council for Sport in Africa
AASR-SMJ . . . . Supreme Council 33°, Ancient and Accepted Scottish Rite of Free-masonry, Southern Masonic Jurisdiction
SCWCU . . . . . Supreme Council of the Western Catholic Union
SC . . . . Supreme Court
SCUS . . . . . . Supreme Court of the United States
SECUS . . . . . . Supreme Emblem Club of the United States
SFWC . . . . . . Supreme Forest Woodmen Circle
SHAEF . . . . . . Supreme Headquarters, Allied Expeditionary Force (Europe) (World War II)
SHAPE . . . . . . Supreme Headquarters Allied Powers Europe (NATO)
STC . . . . SHAPE (Supreme Headquarters Allied Powers Europe) Technical Center (NATO)
SJC . . . . Supreme Judicial Court
DSA . . . . Supreme Lodge of the Danish Sisterhood of America
MOC . . . . Supreme Pup Tent, Military Order of the Cootie
SRZLO . . . . . . Supreme Royal Zuanna, Ladies of the Orient
OPS . . . . Supreme Temple Order Pythian Sisters
STOPS . . . . . . Supreme Temple Order Pythian Sisters
SWC . . . . Supreme War Council (World War I)
SOL . . . . Sure Out of Luck (Bowdlerized version)
SAA . . . . Surety Association of America
SAM . . . . Surface-to-Air Missile
SAMD . . . . . . Surface-to-Air Missile Development
SAMSAT . . . . . Surface-to-Air Missile Servicing, Assembly and Test
SA . . . . Surface Area
SAU . . . . Surface Attack Unit
SBT . . . . Surface Barrier Transistor
SCAT . . . . . . Surface-Controlled Avalanche Transistor
SCOUT . . . . . Surface-Controlled Oxide Unipolar Transistor
SEF . . . . Surface Effect Ship
SES . . . . Surface Effect Ship
SFM . . . . Surface Feet per Minute
SF . . . . Surface Foot
SM . . . . Surface Measure
SMS . . . . Surface Missile System
SURPIC . . . . . Surface Picture (AMVER) (Coast Guard)
SURANO . . . . . Surface RADAR and Navigation Operation
SURIC . . . . . . Surface Ship Integrated Control System (BUSHIPS; later, ESC)
SSM . . . . Surface-to-Surface Missile
SSMSN . . . . . . Surface-to-Surface Mission
STAM . . . . . . Surface Target Acquisition Model
ST . . . . Surface Tension
SUM . . . . Surface-to-Underwater Missile
S/V . . . . Surface Vessel
SWTL . . . . . . Surface-Wave Transmission Line
S . . . . Surfaced
S1S . . . . Surfaced or Dressed One Side
S1S1E . . . . . . Surfaced or Dressed One Side and One Edge (Technical drawings)
S4S . . . . Surfaced or Dressed Four Sides
S2S . . . . Surfaced or Dressed Two Sides
S & M . . . . . . Surfaced and Matched (Lumber)
SG . . . . Surgeon General (Army and Air Force)
SURGEN . . . . . Surgeon General
SGO . . . . Surgeon General's Office
SM . . . . Surgeon Major
SGH . . . . Surgical Hospital
SAPFU . . . . . . Surpassing All Previous Foul Ups (Military slang)
S . . . . Surplus
SMD . . . . Surplus Materials Division
SPB . . . . Surplus Property Board
SPO . . . . Surplus Property Office (Transferred to War Assets Administration, 1947)
SWPA . . . . . . Surplus War Property Administration (Terminated 1944)

SWPB	Surplus War Property Board (Terminated 1945)
SCD	Surrey Commercial Dock (British)
SURCAL	Surveillance Calibration Satellite
SD	Surveillance Drone (Air Force)
SURVM	Surveillance and Maintenance (Army)
SR	Surveillance RADAR (Air Force)
SRE	Surveillance RADAR Element
SSD	Surveillance Situation Display
SS	Surveillance Station (RADAR)
STAAS	Surveillance and Target Acquisition Aircraft System
STV	Surveillance Television
S	Survey
SCARF	Survey of Change and Residential Finance (Census Bureau)
SCP	Survey Control Point
SIC	Survey Information Center
SQ3R	Survey, Question, Read, Review, Recite (Psychology)
SURSAT	Survey Satellite (NASA)
AGS	Surveying Ship (Navy symbol)
SSHA	Survey of Study Habits and Attitudes (Education)
SLRV	Surveyor Lunar Roving Vehicle (Aerospace)
SSEAT	Surveyor Scientific Evaluation Advisory Team (NASA)
SD	Survival Dose
SEE	Survival, Evasion, and Escape (Military)
SERE	Survival, Evasion, Resistance and Escape (Military)
SRR	Survival, Recovery and Reconstitution (Military)
SCATA	Survival Sited Casualty Treatment Assemblage
ST	Survival Time
SIUFL	Suspend Issue and Use of Following Lots
SIUSM	Suspend from Issue and Use as Suspect Material
SAPC	Suspended Acoustical-Plaster Ceiling (Technical drawings)
SATC	Suspended Acoustical-Tile Ceiling (Technical drawings)
SPC	Suspended Plaster Ceiling (Technical drawings)
SSAC	Suspended Sprayed Acoustical Ceiling (Technical drawings)
SRU	Suspension and Release Units
SUU	Suspension Unit
SP	Suspicious Person
SA	Sustained Action (With reference to drugs)
SM	Sustained Medication (Pharmacy)
SOD	Sustained Operational Date
SSP	Sustained Superior Performance
SECO	Sustainer-Engine Cutoff
S	Suus (His)
SAF	Svenska Arbetsgivareforeningen (An employers' confederation) (Sweden)
SAAB	Svenska Aeroplan AB (Swedish automobile manufacturer; acronym used as name of its cars)
SKF	Svenska Kullagerfabriken AB (Swedish manufacturer, especially of ball bearings; active in many countries)
SSU	Sverges Socialdemokratiska Ungdomsforbund
SACO	Sveriges Akademikers Centralorganisation (Swedish Confederation of Professional Association)
SAC	Sveriges Arbetares Centralorganisation (Central Organization of Swedish Workers)
SG	Swamp Glider
SPP	Swaziland Progressive Party
SF	Swedenborg Foundation
SCCRI	Swedish Cement and Concrete Research Institute
SCCUS	Swedish Chamber of Commerce of the United States
SCS	Swedish Colonial Society
SIDA	Swedish International Development Agency
SJAA	Swedish Journalists Association of America
SLEEP	Swedish Low Energy Experimental Pile (Atomic energy)
SPHS	Swedish Pioneer Historical Society
SSRC	Swedish Space Research Committee
SSPB	Swedish State Power Board (Atomic energy)
SD	Sweep Driver
SYT	Sweet Young Thing (An attractive girl) (Slang)
SWA	Sweets Company of America, Inc. (NYSE symbol)
SVE	Swept Volume Efficiency (Air Force)
SWX	Swift & Company (NYSE symbol)
SC	Swimming Club
SWL	Swingline Inc. (NYSE symbol)
SWISSAIR	Swiss Air Transport Co., Ltd.
SAAU	Swiss Association of Autonomous Unions
SBS	Swiss Benevolent Society of New York
SFNCTU	Swiss Federation of National-Christian Trade Unions
SFPTU	Swiss Federation of Protestant Trade Unions
SFTU	Swiss Federation of Trade Unions
SFWM	Swiss Federation of Watch Manufacturers
SIN-ETH	Swiss Institute of Nuclear Research - Eidgenoessische Technische Hochschule
SMETC	Swiss Mouse Embryo Tissue Culture

SNB	Swiss National Bank
SRC	Swiss Red Cross
SSNY	Swiss Society of New York
SR	Swissair (Swiss Air Transport Co., Ltd.)
S	Switch
SWR	Switch Rails
SWS	Switch Stand
SWT	Switch Ties
SW	Switchband Wound (Relay)
SKA	Switchblade Knife Act
SB	Switchboard (Navy)
SB	Switchboard Operator (Navy)
SCAN	Switched Circuit Automatic Network (Army)
SSN	Switched Service Network
SWGR	Switchgear
SWCENT	Switching Central
STRAD	Switching, Transmitting, Receiving and Distribution
SUNA	Switchmen's Union of North America
SO	Switchover
SCA	Switzerland Cheese Association
SS	Sworn Statement
SL	Sydney & Louisburg Railway Company (AAR code)
SOMP	Sydney Ocean Meeting Point (Navy)
SCN	Sylvania-Corning Nuclear Corporation
SHIELD	Sylvania High Intelligence Electronic Defense
S	Symbol for Entropy
SG	Symbol Generator
SYMAN	Symbol Manipulation (Data processing)
SAP	Symbolic Address Program
SDA	Symbolic Disk Address
SIMM	Symbolic Integrated Maintenance Manual
SML	Symbolic Machine Language
SOAP	Symbolic Optimum Assembly Programming
SPAR	Symbolic Program Assembly Routine
SYMPAC	Symbolic Program for Automatic Control
SPACE	Symbolic Programming Anyone Can Enjoy
SPS	Symbolic Programming System (Data processing)
SSS	Symbolic Shorthand System
SURE	Symbolic Utilities Revenue Environment (IBM)
SZ	Symington Wayne Corporation (NYSE symbol)
SLIP	Symmetric List Processor (FORTRAN extension)
S	Symmetrical
SAD	Sympathetic Aerial Detonation (Air Force)
SNS	Sympathetic Nervous System (Physiology)
SFA	Symphony Foundation of America
SYCATE	Symptom-Cause-Test
SCA	Synagogue Council of America
SYMAP	Synagraphic Mapping System (Computer-made maps)
SS & D	Synchronization Separator and Digitizer
SPD	Synchronizer for Peripheral Devices
SAM	Synchronous Amplitude Modulation
SYNCOM	Synchronous Communication Satellite (GSFC)
SID	Synchronous Identification System
SMS	Synchronous Meteorological Satellite (NASA)
SOTS	Synchronous Orbiting Tracking Stations
SPAR	Synchronous Position Altitude Recorder
SAARDT	Syndicat Autonome des Agents de la Radiodiffusior du Togo (Autonomous Union of Radiobroadcasting Workers of Togo)
SAFOC	Syndicat Autonome des Fonctionnaires d'Oubangi-Chari (Autonomous Union of the Workers of Ubangi-Shari)
SATAM	Syndicat Autonome des Travailleurs de la Alimentation de Madagascar (Autonomous Union of Food Workers of Madagascar)
SYBEAUXARTS . .	Syndicat des Beaux Arts Africains (Union of African Fine Arts)
SCIMPEX	Syndicat des Commercants Importateurs et Exportateurs de l'Ouest African (Union of Commercial Importers and Exporters of West Africa)
SECIT	Syndicat des Employes Indigenes du Commerce du Togo (Union of Indigenous Employees of Commerce of Togo)
SEAN	Syndicat des Enseignants Africains du Niger (African Union of Teachers of Niger)
SEN	Syndicat des Enseignants du Niger (Union of Nigerian Teachers)
SET	Syndicat des Enseignants du Togo (Union of Togolese Teachers)
SELT	Syndicat des Enseignements Laics (Union of Public School Teachers) (Togo)
SEEN	Syndicat d'Etudes de l'Energie Nucleaire (Belgium)
SF	Syndicat des Fonctionnaires (Lao Civil Servants' Union)
SYMEVETOPHARSA	Syndicat des Medecins, Veterinaires, Pharmaciens, et Sages Femmes Africains du Mali (Union of African Doctors, Pharmacists, Midwives and Veterinarians of the Mali Federation)
SNEG	Syndicat National des Enseignants de Guinee (National Union of Guinean Teachers)

SNES . . . . Syndicat National de l'Enseignement Secondaire (National Union of Secondary Schoolteachers) (France)

SNET . . . . Syndicat National de l'Enseignement Technique (National Union of Technical Schoolteachers) (France)

SYNERCAU . . . Syndicat National d'Etudes et de Recherches pour les Cooperatives Agricoles et leur Unions

SNI . . . . Syndicat National des Instituteurs (National Union of Teachers) (France)

SNTC . . . . Syndicat National des Transporteurs de Cameroun (National Union of Cameroonese Transportation Workers)

SNTC . . . . Syndicat National des Travailleurs Congolais (National Union of Congolese Workers) (Leopoldville)

SPACG . . . . . . Syndicat du Personnel de l'Aeronautique Civile du Gabon (Union of Civil Aviation Employees of Gabon)

SPAAC . . . . . . Syndicat du Personnel Africain de l'Aeronautique Civile (African Union for Civil Aviation Employees)

STPM . . . . Syndicat Togolais du Personnel de la Meteorologie (Togolese Union of Meteorological Personnel)

STAGD . . . . . . Syndicat des Travailleurs de l'Administration Generale du Dahomey (Dahomean Union of General Administration Workers)

SYNTEEDISETO . . Syndicat des Travailleurs de l'Energie Electrique et de Distribution d'Eau du Togo (Union of Electrical Energy and Water Distribution Workers of Togo)

SENTRAB . . . . Syndicat des Travailleurs des Entreprises, Privees, Travaux Publics et Batiments (Union of Workers of Private Enterprises, Public Works and Buildings) (Togo)

SYNTIRT . . . . . Syndicat des Travailleurs des Industries Reunies du Togo (Union of Workers of United Industries of Togo)

STMD . . . . Syndicat des Travailleurs des Municipalites du Dahomey (Union of Municipal Workers of Dahomey)

STANAVITO . . Syndicat des Travailleurs de Transport et de la Navigation du Togo (Union of Transport and Navigation Workers of Togo)

SUEM . . . . Syndicat Unique des Enseignants de Mauritanie (Unitary Union of Mauritanian Teachers)

SNPL . . . . Syndicate National des Pilotes de Lignes (France)

SEK . . . . Synomospondia Ergaton Kyprou (Cyprus Workers' Confederation) ("Free Labour Syndicats")

SYNTOL . . . . . Syntagmatic Organization Language (Data processing)

SATO . . . . Synthetic Aircraft Turbine Oil

SYNDETS . . . . Synthetic Detergents

SDO . . . . Synthetic Drying Oil

SCOTT . . . . . . Synthetic Medium Older Tuberculin Trichloracetic Acid Precipitated

SOCMA . . . . . Synthetic Organic Chemical Manufacturers Association of the United States

SPI . . . . Synthetic Phase Isolation (Telemetry)

SU . . . . Syracuse University

SURC . . . . Syracuse University Research Corporation

SURI . . . . Syracuse University Research Institute

STARFIRE . . . . . System to Accumulate and Retrieve Financial Information with Random Extraction (Data processing)

SAB . . . . System Advisory Board

SAM . . . . System Analysis Machine (Data processing)

SAVE . . . . System for Automatic Value Exchange (Data processing)

SASI . . . . System on Automotive Safety Information

SCANS . . . . . System Checkout Automatic Network Simulator

SCOPE . . . . . System for Coordination of Peripheral Equipment

SD . . . . System Demonstration

SDC . . . . System Designator Code

SDC . . . . System Development Corporation

SDR . . . . System Development Requirement (Air Force)

SEI . . . . System/Equipment Inventory

SEPS . . . . System/Equipment Population Summary

SGDE . . . . . . System Ground Data Equipment (RADAR)

S-HI . . . . System-Human Interaction

SIXPAC . . . . . System for Inertial Experiment Pointing and Attitude Control

SISTRAN . . . . System for Information Storage and Retrieval and Analysis

SMD . . . . System Management Directive

SM . . . . System Mechanics

SNF . . . . System Noise Figure

SOLO . . . . . . System for Ordinary Life Operations

SOCRATES . . . System for Organizing Content to Review and Teach Educational Subjects (Data processing)

SOCRATES . . . . System for Organizing Current Reports to Aid Technology and Science

SOL . . . . System Oriented Language

SPP . . . . System Package Program

SPARTAN . . . . System for Personnel Automated Reports, Transactions, and Notices (Census Bureau, NASA)

SPEDE . . . . . . System for Processing Educational Data Electronically

SPD . . . . System Program Director (or Directive) (Air Force)

SPMS . . . . System Program Management Surveys (Air Force)

SPO . . . . System Program Office (Air Force)

SPO . . . . System Project Office

SRB . . . . System Review Board

SSE . . . . System Safety Engineering

SSEP . . . . System Safety Engineering Plan

S³Bᴾ . . . . System Source Selection Board Procedure (Air Force)

SSSBP . . . . System Source Selection Board Procedure (Air Force)

SSO . . . . System Staff Office

SSM . . . . System Support Management/Manager

SSP . . . . System Support Program

STOW . . . . . . System for Take-Off Weight

STAR . . . . System for Telephone Administrative Response (Data processing)

STO . . . . System Test Objectives

STP . . . . System Test Plan

STCW . . . . . . System Time Code Word

STU . . . . System Timing Unit

STM . . . . System Training Mission

STUFF . . . . System to Uncover Facts Fast

SDL . . . . Systematic Design Language

SNOP . . . . Systematized Nomenclature of Pathology (NCI)

SI . . . . Systeme International d'Unites (International System of Units)

SLE . . . . Systemic Lupus Erythematosus (Disease)

SAIM . . . . Systems Analysis and Integration Model

SARC . . . . Systems Analysis and Research Corporation

SYSTRAN . . . . Systems Analysis Translator (Data processing)

SAMBA . . . . . Systems Approach to Managing BUSHIPS (Bureau of Ships; later, ESC) Acquisitions (Navy)

SAP . . . . Systems Assurance Program (IBM)

SCP . . . . Systems Change Proposal

SC . . . . Systems Command (Air Force)

SYSCOM . . . . . Systems Command (Navy)

SCERT . . . . . . Systems and Computers Evaluation and Review Technique (Data processing)

SYSCON . . . . Systems Control

SDD . . . . Systems Definition Directive

SDAP . . . . . . Systems Development Analysis Program

SDL . . . . Systems Development Laboratories

SEE . . . . Systems Efficiency Expert

SE . . . . Systems Engineering

SEER . . . . Systems Engineering, Evaluation and Research

SEG . . . . Systems Engineering Group (Air Force)

SEMO . . . . . . Systems Engineering and Management Operations (Military)

SE/TD . . . . . . Systems Engineering and Technical Direction

SEDD . . . . . . Systems Evaluation and Development Division (NASA)

SHARE . . . . . Systems for Heat and Radiation Energy

SIL . . . . Systems Integration Laboratory

SLANG . . . . . Systems Language

SMS . . . . Systems Maintenance Sector

SMSE . . . . . . Systems Maintenance Sector (Electronics)

SMS . . . . Systems Maintenance Service

SMART . . . . . Systems Management Analysis, Research, and Testing

SMD . . . . Systems Manufacturing Division (IBM)

SNAP . . . . . . Systems for Nuclear Auxiliary Power

SDR . . . . SNAP (Systems for Nuclear Auxiliary Power) Development Reactor

SER . . . . SNAP (Systems for Nuclear Auxiliary Power) Experimental Reactor

SETF . . . . SNAP (Systems for Nuclear Auxiliary Power) Experimental Test Facility

SGCF . . . . . . SNAP (Systems for Nuclear Auxiliary Power) Generalized Critical Facility

STIR . . . . SNAP (Systems for Nuclear Auxiliary Power) Shield Test Irradiation Reactor

SPANAT . . . . Systems Planning Approach-North Atlantic (FAA)

S-P . . . . Systems and Procedures

SPA . . . . Systems and Procedures Association

SRC . . . . Systems Research Configuration

SRDS . . . . . . Systems Research and Development Service (FAA)

SSC . . . . Systems Science and Cybernetics

S3 . . . . Systems and Software Simulator

STL . . . . Systems Techniques Laboratory (Stanford University)

STC . . . . Systems Test Complex (NASA)

STP . . . . Systems Training Program (RADAR)

STPX . . . . . . Systems Training Program Exercise

SPEED . . . . . . Systemwide Project for Electronic Equipment at Depots (Military)

SD . . . . Systolic Discharge (Physiology)

SM . . . . Systolic Murmur (Physiology)

SZOT . . . . . . Szakszervezetek Orszagos Tanacsa (National Trade Union Council) (Hungary)

T

T . . . . T-Bar (Structural Metal Shape)
TTFN . . . . Ta Ta For Now
TCPC . . . . . . Tab Card Punch Control
TCR . . . . Tab Card Reader
TSF . . . . Tab Sequence Format
T . . . . Table
TA . . . . Table of Allowances
T/A . . . . Table of Allowances
TOA . . . . Table of Allowances
T/BA . . . . . . Table of Basic Allowances (Military)
TADOR . . . . . Table Data Organization and Reductions
TD . . . . Table of Distribution (Military)
TDA . . . . Table of Distribution and Allowances
TDA . . . . Table of Distribution-Augmentation (Military)
TE . . . . Table of Equipment
T/E . . . . Table of Equipment (Army)
TFI . . . . Table Fashion Institute
TIDOS . . . . . . Table and Item Documentation System
TLU . . . . Table Look Up (Data processing)
TO . . . . Table of Organization
T/O . . . . Table of Organization
T/OT . . . . . . Table of Organization (Tentative)
TBA . . . . Tables of Basic Allowances (Previously, Basic Tables of Commissioning
                        Allowances) (Navy)
TOE . . . . Tables of Organization and Equipment
T/O & E . . . . . Tables of Organization and Equipment (Army)
T . . . . Tablespoon (Measure)
TBSP . . . . Tablespoonful
TT . . . . Tablet Triturate (Pharmacy)
TFT . . . . Tabular Firing Tables (Military)
TPL . . . . Tabular Parts List
TABSOL . . . . . Tabular Systems-Oriented Language
TATDL . . . . . Tabulated Assembly Technical Data List
T . . . . Tabulated (or Charted) LORAN Reading
TNTDL . . . . . Tabulated Numerical Technical Data List
TCMA . . . . . . Tabulating Card Manufacturers Association
TABSIM . . . . . Tabulating Equipment Simulator
T . . . . Tace (Be Silent)
T . . . . Tackle (Football position)
TRA . . . . Tackle Representatives Association
TMBL . . . . . . Tacoma Municipal Belt Line (AAR code)
TAD . . . . Tactical Action Display (SAGE)
TAP . . . . Tactical Action Programs
TASD . . . . . . Tactical Action Situation Display
TAS . . . . Tactical Advisory Service (Department of Commerce)
TAB . . . . Tactical Air Base
TAC . . . . Tactical Air Command (Air Force)
TACC . . . . . . Tactical Air Command Central (Air Force)
TACLO . . . . . Tactical Air Command Liaison Officer
TACC . . . . . . Tactical Air Control Center
TACG . . . . . . Tactical Air Control Group (Air Force)
TACOC . . . . . Tactical Air Control Operation Center
TACP . . . . . . Tactical Air Control Party (Air Force)
TACRON . . . . Tactical Air Control Squadron
TACS . . . . . . Tactical Air Control System (Air Force)
TACA . . . . . . Tactical Air Coordinator, Airborne
TADAS . . . . . Tactical Air Defense Alerting System (Army)
TAD . . . . Tactical Air Direction
TADC . . . . . . Tactical Air Direction Center
TADP . . . . . . Tactical Air Direction Post (Military)
TAF . . . . Tactical Air Force
TAFHQ . . . . . Tactical Air Force Headquarters
TALO . . . . . . Tactical Air Liaison Officer (Air Force)

TAM . . . . Tactical Air Missile (Air Force)
TACAN . . . . . . Tactical Air Navigation (System)
TA . . . . TACAN (Tactical Air Navigation System) Approach
TAO . . . . TACAN (Tactical Air Navigation System) Only
TAN . . . . Tactical Air Navigational Aid
TACAN-DME . . Tactical Air Navigation Distance Measuring Equipment
TAOC . . . . . . Tactical Air Operations Center
TAPE . . . . . . Tactical Air Power Evaluation (Air Force)
TAR . . . . Tactical Air Reconnaissance
TARABS . . . . . Tactical Air Reconnaissance & Aerial Battlefield Surveillance System
TARC . . . . . . Tactical Air Reconnaissance Center (Shaw Air Force Base)
TARS . . . . . . Tactical Air Reconnaissance School (Air Force)
TARS . . . . . . Tactical Air Research and Survey Office (Air Force)
TASF . . . . . . Tactical Air Strike Force (Air Force)
TASE . . . . . . Tactical Air Support Element (Military)
TASS . . . . . . Tactical Air Support Section
TAWC . . . . . . Tactical Air Warfare Center (Air Force)
TAWCS . . . . . Tactical Air Weapons Control System
TABS . . . . . . Tactical Airborne Beacon System
TARP . . . . . . Tactical Airborne Recording Package
TAGS . . . . . . Tactical Aircraft Guidance System
TASMOL . . . . Tactical Aircraft Support Model
TAFDS . . . . . Tactical Airfield Fuel Distribution System
TALC . . . . . . Tactical Airlift Center
TADO . . . . . . Tactical Airlift Duty Officer
TAPS . . . . . . Tactical Area Positioning System
TAOR . . . . . . Tactical Area of Responsibility (Military)
TAS . . . . Tactical Area Switching
TAALS . . . . . Tactical Army Aircraft Landing Systems
TAW . . . . Tactical Assault Weapon
TAC . . . . Tactical Assignment Console
TADM . . . . . . Tactical Atomic Demolition Munitions (Military)
TARAN . . . . . Tactical Attack RADAR and Navigation
TSD . . . . TARAN (Tactical Attack RADAR and Navigation) System Data
TADS . . . . . . Tactical Automatic Digital Switch
TADSS . . . . . Tactical Automatic Digital Switching System
TBM . . . . Tactical Ballistic Missile (Air Force)
TBMX . . . . . . Tactical Ballistic Missile Experiment
TBX . . . . Tactical Ballistic Missile Experimental
TBGP . . . . . . Tactical Bomb Group (Air Force)
TBS . . . . Tactical Bomb Squadron (Air Force)
TBWG . . . . . . Tactical Bomb Wing (Air Force)
TCAP . . . . . . Tactical Channel Assignment Panel (Military radio)
CC . . . . Tactical Command Ship (Navy symbol)
CLC . . . . Tactical Command Ship (Navy symbol)
CBC . . . . Tactical Command Ship, Large (Navy symbol)
TACCTA . . . . . Tactical Commander's Terrain Analysis (Military)
TACOM . . . . . Tactical Communications
TACOMM . . . . Tactical Communications (Military)
TCC . . . . Tactical Control Center (Military)
TCO . . . . Tactical Control Officer (Army)
TACO . . . . . . Tactical Coordination Operator
TACCO . . . . . Tactical Coordinator
TDCC . . . . . . Tactical Data Communications Center
TDC . . . . Tactical Data Converter
TACDEN . . . . . Tactical Data Entry Unit (Army)
TDS . . . . Tactical Data System
TDPB . . . . . . Tactical Display Plotting Board
TD . . . . Tactical Division (Air Force)
TEW . . . . Tactical Early Warning
TEWS . . . . . . Tactical Electronic Warfare Support
T/E . . . . Tactical Emergency
TFDS . . . . . . Tactical Ferret Display System

TF . . . . Tactical Fighter
TFDM . . . . . . Tactical Fighter Dispensing Munition
TEX . . . . . . Tactical Fighter, Experimental (Airplane)
TFX . . . . . . Tactical Fighter, Experimental (Air Force)
TFX-N . . . . . Tactical Fighter Experimental - Navy
TFX-O . . . . . Tactical Fighter Experimental - Offensive
TFX-R . . . . . Tactical Fighter Experimental - Reconnaissance
TFGP . . . . . . Tactical Fighter Group (Air Force)
TFS . . . . Tactical Fighter Squadron (Air Force)
TFWC . . . . . . Tactical Fighter Weapons Center
TFWG . . . . . . Tactical Fighter Wing (Air Force)
TACFIRE . . . . . Tactical Fire Control System (of ADSAF)
TGSE . . . . . . Tactical Ground Support Equipment
TIIF . . . . Tactical Image Interpretation Facility
TID . . . . Tactical (or Target) Information Display
TIPI . . . . . . Tactical Information Processing and Interpretation (Military)
TICT . . . . Tactical Intelligence Collection Team (Military)
T/L . . . . Tactical Landing
TALAR . . . . . . Tactical Landing Approach Radio (Aviation)
TLS . . . . Tactical Landing System
TM . . . . Tactical Missile (Air Force)
TMG . . . . . . Tactical Missile Group (Air Force)
TMS . . . . Tactical Missile Squadron (Air Force)
TMW . . . . . . Tactical Missile Wing (Air Force)
TMD . . . . Tactical Mission Data (Military)
TMU . . . . Tactical Mobile Unit (Police)
TM . . . . Tale Monitor
TMMD . . . . . . Tactical Moving Mad Display
TACMAR . . . . . Tactical Multifunction Array RADAR (Air Force)
NAVTAC . . . . Tactical Navigation System
TACNAV . . . . Tactical Navigation System
TNDS . . . . . . Tactical Navigational Display System
TNW . . . . . . Tactical Nuclear Weapon
TOS . . . . Tactical Offense Subsystem
TOC . . . . . . Tactical Operations Center (Air Force)
TOR . . . . . . Tactical Operations Room (Air Force)
TOS . . . . . . Tactical Operations System (ADSAF)
TPF . . . . Tactical Patrol Force (Police)
TPE . . . . Tactical Performance Evaluation
TRS . . . . Tactical RADAR System
TRCE . . . . . . Tactical Radio Communications Equipment
TRS . . . . Tactical Radio Set
TRLFSW . . . . . Tactical Range Landing Force Support Weapon
TRR . . . . Tactical Range Recorder
TRSSGM . . . . . Tactical Range Surface-to-Surface Guided Missile
TRSSM . . . . . Tactical Range Surface-to-Surface Missile
TRR . . . . Tactical Reaction Reconnaissance
TRACE . . . . . Tactical Readiness and Checkout Equipment
TAC/R . . . . . Tactical Reconnaissance
TRDM . . . . . . Tactical Reconnaissance Data Marking
TRGP . . . . . . Tactical Reconnaissance Group (Air Force)
TRI . . . . Tactical Reconnaissance/Intelligence
TRS . . . . Tactical Reconnaissance Squadron (Air Force)
TRW . . . . Tactical Reconnaissance Wing
TRWG . . . . . Tactical Reconnaissance Wing (Air Force)
TACSATCOM . . Tactical Satellite Communications
TSD . . . . Tactical Situation Display
TSDI . . . . Tactical Situation Display Indicator
TSOP . . . . . . Tactical Standing Operating Procedure
TSF . . . . Tactical Strike Fighter
TSR . . . . Tactical Strike and Reconnaissance
TSS . . . . Tactical Strike System
TSC . . . . Tactical Support Center
TSE . . . . Tactical Support Element
TSM . . . . Tactical Survey Meter
TSSCS . . . . . . Tactical Synchronous Satellite Communication System
TTI . . . . Tactical Target Illustration
TTP . . . . Tactical Targeting Program
TTMP . . . . . . Tactical Targets Materials Program
TTF . . . . Tactical Task Force
TATTE . . . . . . Tactical Test Equipment
TUF . . . . Tactical Undercover Function (Chicago police operation)
TUOC . . . . . . Tactical Unit Operations Center
TWS . . . . Tactical Weather Station
TEAL . . . . . . Tactics, Equipment and Logistics Conference (between US, Great Britain, Australia, and Canada) (Developed "duck" designations for Mallard and Gander military communications systems)
TIPR . . . . . . Tactics Inspection Procedures Report
TIRR . . . . . . Tactics Inspection Results Report
TF . . . . Tactile Fremitus
TFB . . . . Taft Broadcasting Company (NYSE symbol)

THA . . . . Taft-Hartley Act
TSEC . . . . . . Taft Sanitary Engineering Center
TLMI . . . . . . Tag and Label Manufacturers Institute
TAVIP . . . . . . Tahun Vivere Pericoloso (The Year of Living Dangerously) (President Sukarno's national policy in 1964) (Indonesia)
TG . . . . Tail Gear
TLG . . . . Tail Landing Gear
TW . . . . Tail Wind
TEVROC . . . . Tailored Exhaust Velocity Rocket
TFL . . . . Taiwan Federation of Labor (Nationalist China)
TLDC . . . . . . Taiwan Land Development Corporation
TOPR . . . . . . Taiwan Open Pool Reactor (AEC)
TCB . . . . Take Care of Business (Teen slang)
TALF . . . . . . Take a Look Foundation
T . . . . Take Off (Aviation)
TO . . . . Take Off (Aviation)
TOB . . . . Take-Off Boost
TOG . . . . Take Off Gross (Weight) (Aviation)
TOGW . . . . . Take-Off Gross Weight
TOHP . . . . . . Take-Off Horsepower
TOLCAT . . . . Take-Off and Landing Critical Atmosphere Turbulence
TOPS . . . . . . Take Off Pounds Sensibly (Club)
PX Out . . . . . Take-off Time (Aviation)
TOW . . . . . . Take-Off Weight
T . . . . Taken
T & O . . . . . Taken and Offered (Sporting) (British)
TQ . . . . Tale Quale
TBS . . . . Talk-Between-Ships (which are tactically maneuvering; also, the VHF radio equipment used for this purpose)
TL . . . . Talk-Listen
TCI . . . . Tall Clubs International
TD & G . . . . . Tall, Dark and Gruesome (Teen slang)
TF . . . . Tallulah Falls Railway Company (AAR code)
TH . . . . Tally Ho (Air Force)
TLN . . . . Talon, Inc. (NYSE symbol) (Wall Street slang name: "Zipper")
TII . . . . Talos Integration Investigation
TAS . . . . Tampa Southern R. R. (AAR code)
TAB . . . . Tamper Attempt Board
TSA . . . . Tamworth Swine Association
TO . . . . Tandem Outlet
TPS . . . . Tandem Propeller Submarine
TRA . . . . Tandem Rotary Activator
TAN . . . . Tandy Corporation (NYSE symbol)
TANU . . . . . . Tanganyika African National Union (Political party)
TYL . . . . TANU (Tanganyika African National Union) Youth League (Tanganyika)
TAPU . . . . . . Tanganyika African Postal Union
TFL . . . . Tanganyika Federation of Labor
TPWU . . . . . . Tanganyika Plantation Workers Union
TRAU . . . . . . Tanganyika Railway African Union
TUPE . . . . . . Tanganyika Union of Public Employees
TAM . . . . . . Tangent Approximating Manifold
TANH . . . . . . Tangent, Hyperbolic
TLC . . . . Tangent Latitude Computer
TLCA . . . . . . Tangent Latitude Computer Amplifier
TM . . . . Tangent Mechanism
TB . . . . Tangential Bracket
TSS . . . . Tangential Signal Sensitivity
TROCA . . . . . Tangible Reinforcement Operant Conditioning Audiometry
TAEA . . . . . . Tangipahoa & Eastern R. R. (AAR code)
TATAWS . . . . Tank, Antitank and Assault Weapons System (Army)
TACOM . . . . . Tank Automotive Command (Army)
TB . . . . Tank Battalion (Army)
TANKBAT . . . . Tank Battalion (Army)
TABWAG . . . . Tank Battle War Game
TCS . . . . Tank Control System
TC . . . . Tank Corps
TCQC . . . . . . Tank Crew Qualification Course (Army)
TD . . . . Tank Destroyer (Military)
TDC . . . . Tank Destroyer Center (Army)
TDRTC . . . . . Tank Destroyer Replacement Training Center
TDT/FC . . . . . Tank Destroyer Tactical and Firing Center
TFCC . . . . . . Tank Fire Combat Computer
TFC . . . . Tank Fire Control
TFCS . . . . . . Tank Fire Control System
ATL . . . . Tank Landing Craft (Navy symbol)
TP . . . . Tank Piercing (Ammunition) (Military)
TRF . . . . Tank Range-Finder
TRK . . . . Tank Rangefinder Kit
TRV . . . . Tank Recovery Vehicle (Army)
TS . . . . Tank Steamer
K . . . . Tanker (Designation for all US military aircraft)

Y . . . . Tanker (Army symbol)
TOC . . . . Tanker Operational Circular
TOVALOP . . . . Tanker Owner Voluntary Agreement on Liability for Oil Pollution
TSC . . . . Tanker Service Committee
TTF . . . . Tanker Task Force
TCA . . . . Tanners' Council of America
Ta . . . . Tantalum (Chemical element)
TCB . . . . Tantalum Carbon Bond
TCR . . . . Tantalum-Controlled Rectifier
TFC . . . . Tantalum Foil Capacitor
TA . . . . Tape Adapter
TAPAC . . . . . Tape Automatic Positioning and Control
TAPE . . . . . . Tape Automatic Preparation Equipment
TBS . . . . Tape and Buffer System (Data processing)
TTC . . . . Tape to Card
TCU . . . . Tape Control Unit
TCVC . . . . . . Tape Control Via Console
TCAT . . . . . . Tape Controlled Automatic Testing
TRACE . . . . . . Tape-Controlled Recording Automatic Checkout Equipment (Component of automatic pilot) (Aviation)
TC . . . . Tape Core
TDHS . . . . . . Tape Data Handling System
TDS . . . . Tape Data Selector
TD . . . . Tape Degausser
TEE . . . . Tape Editing Equipment
TFOL . . . . . . Tape File Octal Load
TG . . . . Tape Gauge
THE . . . . Tape Handling Equipment
THOR . . . . . . Tape-Handling Option Routines
TIC . . . . Tape Identification Card
TIU . . . . Tape Identification Unit
TIPTOP . . . . . Tape Input/Tape Output (Data processing)
TIC . . . . Tape Intersystem Connection (Data processing)
TI . . . . Tape Inverter
TLR . . . . Tape Loop Recorder
TOTRAD . . . . Tape Output Test Rack Autonetics Diode
TPI . . . . Tape Phase Inverter
TPD . . . . Tape Playback Discriminator
TPDS . . . . . . Tape Playback Discriminator System
TPS . . . . Tape Plotting System
TPU . . . . Tape Preparation Unit
TPM . . . . Tape Preventive Maintenance
TTP . . . . Tape-to-Print
TAPAT . . . . . Tape Programmed Automatic Tester
TPR . . . . Tape Programmed Row (Data scanner)
TPA . . . . Tape Pulse Amplifier
TPS . . . . Tape Punch Subassembly
TPSP . . . . . . Tape Punch Subassembly Panel
TRAWL . . . . . Tape Read and Write Library
TR . . . . Tape Reader
TRC . . . . Tape Reader Calibrator
TRC . . . . Tape Reader Control
TR . . . . Tape Recorder
TR . . . . Tape Register
TRADIS . . . . . Tape Repeating Automatic Data Integration System
TSS . . . . Tape Search System
TU . . . . Tape Unit
TUFF-TUG . . . . Tape Update of Formatted Files-Format Table Tape Updater and Generator (Data processing)
T . . . . Taper
TS . . . . Taper Shank (Screw)
TAHA . . . . . . Tapered Aperture Horn Antenna
TLP . . . . Tapered Link Pin
TRB . . . . Tapered Roller Bearing
TAFX . . . . . . Tapping Fixture
TARMAC . . . . . Tar Macadam
T . . . . Tare
T . . . . Target
TAB . . . . Target Acquisition Battalion
TAD . . . . Target Acquisition Data
TACDACS . . . . Target Acquisition and Data Collection System
TAL . . . . Target Acquisition Laboratory
TAS . . . . Target Acquisition System
TAT . . . . Target Aircraft Transmitter
TA . . . . Target Area
TAAR . . . . . . Target Area Analysis-RADAR
TAD . . . . Target Area Designator (Air Force)
TAP . . . . Target Assignment Panel
TAG . . . . Target Attitude Group (Advertising)
TABSTONE . . . Target and Background Signal-to-Noise Evaluation
TBD . . . . Target Bearing Designator (Navy)

TBI . . . . Target Bearing Indicator (Military)
TARCAP . . . . . Target Combat Air Patrol (Navy)
TCS . . . . Target Control System
TCPTF . . . . . . Target Cost Plus Target Fee
TCS . . . . Target Cost System
TDC . . . . Target Data Collection
TDI . . . . Target Data Inventory
TDS . . . . Target Designation System (Navy)
TDT . . . . Target Designation Transmitter
TDD . . . . Target Detecting Device
TDCS . . . . . . Target Detection-Conversion Sensor
TDIL . . . . Target Detection, Identification, and Location
TDU . . . . Target Detection Unit
TDP . . . . Target Director Post (RADAR)
TDN . . . . Target Doppler Nullifier (RADAR)
TDRF . . . . . . Target Doppler Reference Frequency
TGS . . . . Target Generating System
THC . . . . Target Homing Correlator
THS . . . . Target Homing System
TI . . . . Target Identification
TIA . . . . Target Identification and Acquisition
TIAS . . . . . . Target Identification and Acquisition System
TINR . . . . . . Target Identification Navigation RADAR
TIR . . . . Target Illuminating RADAR (Air Force)
TIARA . . . . . Target Illumination & Recovery Aid
TIP . . . . Target Impact Point
TIO . . . . Target Indication Officer (Navy)
TIR . . . . Target Indication Room (Navy)
TIU . . . . Target Indication Unit (Navy)
TI . . . . Target Indicator
TIK . . . . Target Indicator Kit
TIS . . . . Target Information Sheet (Air Force)
TIS . . . . Target Information System
TIP . . . . Target Input Panel
TGI . . . . Target Intensifier
TIC . . . . Target Intercept Computer
TL . . . . Target Language
TLV . . . . Target Launch Vehicle (NASA)
TLS . . . . Target Location System
TMCL . . . . . . Target Map Coordinate Locator (Military)
TMS . . . . Target Marking System
TOG . . . . Target-Observer-Gun (Method) (Army)
T/O . . . . Target of Opportunity
TPI . . . . Target Position Indicator
TP . . . . Target Practice (Military)
TPT . . . . Target Practice (Ammunition) With Tracer
TP-T . . . . Target Practice (Ammunition) with Tracer
TRUMP . . . . . Target Radiometric Ultraviolet Measuring Program
TRR . . . . Target Ranging RADAR
TR . . . . Target Recognition
TRADEX . . . . . Target Resolution and Discrimination Experiment (ARPA)
TRESI . . . . . . Target Resolution Extraction of Statistical Invariances
T/S . . . . Target Seeker
TSAZ . . . . . . Target Seeker-Azimuth
TSA . . . . Target Signature Analysis
TSI . . . . Target Signature Investigation
TSM . . . . Target Signature Measurement
TSD . . . . Target Skin Distance
TS . . . . Target Strength
TSM . . . . Target-to-Surface-to-Missile Path
TSDF . . . . . . Target System Data File
TSDU . . . . . . Target System Data Update
TT . . . . Target Towing Aircraft (Navy)
TTC . . . . Target Track Central
TTR . . . . Target-Track RADAR (Air Force)
SST . . . . Target and Training Submarine (Navy symbol)
TSA . . . . Targhee Sheep Association
TEC . . . . Tarif Exterieur Commun (Common External Tariff) (for EEC countries)
TA . . . . Tariff Act
TB . . . . Tariff Bureau
TC . . . . Tariff Circular
TC . . . . Tariff Commission (US)
TN . . . . Tariff Number
TR . . . . Tariff Reform
TRICC . . . . . . Tariff Rules of the Interstate Commerce Commission
TSUS . . . . . . Tariff Schedule of the United States
TSC . . . . Tarleton State College (Texas)
TTTT . . . . Tartar-Talos-Terrier-Typhon
TE . . . . Task Element
CLC . . . . Task Fleet Command Ship (Navy symbol)
TASKFLOT . . . . Task Flotilla

TF	Task Force
TG	Task Group
TIP	Task Initiation and Prediction
TIPSY	Task Input Parameter Synthesizer
TMB	Task Maintenance Burden
TOC	Task Order Contract
TPI	Task Parameter Interpretation
TPS	Task Parameter Synthesizer
TRACE	Task Reporting and Current Evaluation
TU	Task Unit
TEAL	Tasman Empire Airways, Limited
TWU	Tata Workers' Union (India)
TCA	Tattoo Club of America
TEP	Tau Epsilon Phi (Fraternity)
TER	Tau Epsilon Rho (Fraternity)
TKE	Tau Kappa Epsilon (Fraternity) (Pronounced, "Teke")
TVG	Tavares & Gulf R. R. (AAR code)
TA	Tax Agent
TA	Tax Amortization (Plan)
TC	Tax Court (US)
TCUS	Tax Court of the United States
TEI	Tax Executives Institute
TEB	Tax-Exempt Bond
TF	Tax Foundation
TFI	Tax Foundation, Incorporated
TIP TOP	Tax Information Plan and Total Owed Purchase Accounting
TIA	Tax Institute of America
TPWBH	Tax Paid Wine Bottling House
TVA	Tax on Value Added (European manufacturing tax)
TRSR	Taxi and Runway Surveillance RADAR
TW	Taxiway
TRACE	Taxiway Routing and Coordination Equipment (Aviation)
TC	Tea Council of the United States of America
TPWU	Tea Plantation Workers' Union (Kenya)
TCA	Teach Cable Assembly (Robot technology)
TIPL	Teach Information Processing Language
TEAM	Teacher Education and Media (Project)
TET	Teacher of Electrotherapy
THT	Teacher of Hydrotherapy (British)
TS	Teacher Survey
TC	Teachers College (Columbia University)
TCC	Teachers College of Connecticut
TEC-NACS . . .	Teachers Educational Council - National Association Cosmetology Schools
TESOL	Teachers of English to Speakers of Other Languages
TFP	Teachers Freedom Party
TIAA	Teachers Insurance and Annuity Association
TA	Teaching Assistant (in a university)
TCM	Teaching Career Month
TCA	Teaching Curriculum Association (A generic term; not the name of a specific organization)
TEFL	Teaching English as a Foreign Language
TENES	Teaching English to the Non-English Speaking
TESL	Teaching English as a Second Language
TIPS	Teaching Information Processing System
TP	Teaching Practice
TRR	Teaching and Research Reactor
TD	Teachta Dala (Member of Parliament) (Ireland)
TL	Team Leader
TCWH(I)	Teamsters, Chauffeurs, Warehousemen and Helpers of America; International Brotherhood of (Indiana)
TC	Teardown Compliance
TDR	Teardown Deficiency Report
TDI	Tear-Down Inspection
TI	Teardown Inspection
t	Teaspoon (Measure)
TSP	Teaspoonful
TPI	Teatro Popolare Italiano (Italian theatrical troupe)
Tc	Technetium
T	Technical or Technician
TAB	Technical Abstract Bulletin (ASTIA)
TECHAD	Technical Adviser (Navy)
TAG	Technical Advisory Group
TAPE	Technical Advisory Panel for Electronics (Air Force)
TAIC	Technical Air Intelligence Center (Navy)
TAIU	Technical Aircraft Instrument Unit (Navy)
TAAG	Technical Analysis and Advisory Group (Navy)
TAC	Technical Applications Center (Air Force)
TAD	Technical Approach Demonstration
TAT	Technical Approval Team
TAC	Technical Area Coordinator

TAM	Technical Area Manager
TAP	Technical Area Plan (Navy)
TAG	Technical Art Group
TASS	Technical Assembly System
TAG	Technical Assessment Group (Navy)
TA	Technical Assistance
TAA	Technical Assistance Administration (UN)
TAB	Technical Assistance Board (of the United Nations)
TAC	Technical Assistance Committee (of the Economic and Social Council of the United Nations)
TAICH	Technical Assistance Information Clearing House
TAMA	Technical Assistance and Manufacturing Agreement
TAO	Technical Assistance Operations (UN)
TAP	Technical Assistance Program
TARS	Technical Assistance Recruitment Service (UN)
TAT	Technical Assistance Team (Air Force)
TAUN	Technical Assistance of the United Nations
TAFI	Technical Association of the Fur Industry
TAGA	Technical Association of the Graphic Arts
TAPPI	Technical Association of the Pulp and Paper Industry
TBRI	Technical Book Review Index
TB	Technical Bulletin
TABS	Technical and Business Service
TECSTAR	Technical Career Structure of the Army
TCP	Technical Change Proposal
TCR	Technical Change Request
TC	Technical Characteristics
TC	Technical Circular
TC	Technical College
TCIR	Technical Command Informal Reports (Army)
TCHEP	Technical Committee on High Energy Physics (of the Federal Council on Science and Technology)
TC	Technical Communication
TCTO	Technical Compliance Technical Order
TCD	Technical Contracts Department
TCC	Technical Control Center
TCF	Technical Control Facility
TCA	Technical Cooperation Administration (Transferred to Foreign Operations Administration, 1953)
TD	Technical Data
TDD	Technical Data Digest (Air Force)
TDP	Technical Data Package
TDR	Technical Data Report
TDR	Technical Data Requests
TDG	Technical Design Guide
TDC	Technical Development Center
TDD	Technical Development Division
TDEC	Technical Development Evaluation Center
TDO	Technical Development Objective
TDP	Technical Development Plan
TDR	Technical Development Requirement
TD	Technical Direction
TDCE	Technical Direction Contract Effort
TDB	Technical Directive Board
TDEC	Technical Division and Engineering Center (FAA)
TDC	Technical Document Center
TDL	Technical Document List
TDR	Technical Documentary Report
TE	Technical Engineer
TESTS	Technical-Engineering-Science Training for Secretaries
TEA	Technical Engineers Association
TENG	Technical Engineers Association
TECA	Technical Evaluation and Countermeasures Assignment
TE	Technical Exchange
TIMA	Technical Illustrators Management Association
TIIC	Technical Industrial Intelligence Committee (US Military Government, Germany)
TIID	Technical Industrial Intelligence Division (Allied Board set up to send experts into Germany to ferret out Germany's war-developed scientific secrets) (Post-World War II)
TIAC	Technical Information Advisory Committee (AEC)
TIB	Technical Information Bureau (British)
TIC	Technical Information Capability
TIC	Technical Information Center
TICA	Technical Information Center Administration (Conference)
TID	Technical Information Division (of Library of Congress)
TIE	Technical Information Exchange (National Bureau of Standards)
TIF	Technical Information File
TIL	Technical Information and Library Service
TIMI	Technical Information Maintenance Instruction
TIO	Technical Information Office

TIP........ Technical Information Panel (AEC)
TIP........ Technical Information Pilot (Announcement bulletin formerly
            published by Navy Research Section, Library of Congress)
TIP........ Technical Information Pool
TIPS....... Technical Information Processing System
TIPS....... Technical Information and Product Service
TIP........ Technical Information Program
TIP........ Technical Information Project (MIT)
TIR....... Technical Information Release
TIS........ Technical Information Section (Navy)
TIS........ Technical Information Service (AEC)
AIAA-TIS ... Technical Information Service (of American Institute of Aeronautics and
            Astronautics)
TISA....... Technical Information Support Activities (Army)
TISP....... Technical Information Support Personnel (Department of Labor)
TICLER..... Technical Input Check List/Evaluation Report
TI........ Technical Inspection
TIFO...... Technical Inspection Field Office, Office of the Inspector General
TIC....... Technical Institute Council
TI........ Technical Instruction
TIC....... Technical Instructors Course (Air Force)
TIE....... Technical Integration and Evaluation (Apollo) (NASA)
TI........ Technical Intelligence
TIC....... Technical Intelligence Center (Navy)
TIR....... Technical Intelligence Report
TKO....... Technical Knock Out (Boxing)
TL........ Technical Letter
TLM....... Technical Liaison Memo
TLO....... Technical Liaison Office (Military)
TL........ Technical Library
TLSS...... Technical Library Services Section
TM........ Technical Manual (Military)
TM........ Technical Materiel Corporation (NYSE symbol)
TMIS...... Technical Meetings Information Service
TM........ Technical Memorandum
TMR....... Technical Memorandum Report
TEMPO..... Technical Military Planning Operation
TM........ Technical Minutes
TM........ Technical Monograph
TNB....... Technical News Bulletin (National Bureau of Standards)
TN........ Technical Note
TOD....... Technical Objective Directive (or Document) (Air Force)
TO........ Technical Observer
TOR....... Technical Operating Report
TOD....... Technical Operations Department
TOI....... Technical Operations, Incorporated
TO........ Technical Order
TOCN...... Technical Order Change Notice (Air Force)
TOC....... Technical Order Compliance
TOFCN..... Technical Order Field Change Notice (Air Force)
TP........ Technical Pamphlet
TP........ Technical Paper
TPO....... Technical Planning Office
TPC....... Technical Prime Contractor
TP........ Technical Problem
TPI....... Technical Proficiency Inspection
TPPD...... Technical Program Planning Division (Air Force)
TPPD...... Technical Program Planning Document
TPR....... Technical Progress Report
TP........ Technical Proposal
TP........ Technical Publication
TPA....... Technical Publications Announcement
TPL....... Technical Publications Library
TPS....... Technical Publishing Society
TQE....... Technical Quality Evaluation (Polaris)
TRH....... Technical Reference Handbook
TR........ Technical Regulation
TR........ Technical Report
TECHREP ... Technical Representative (Military)
TR........ Technical Representative
TRG....... Technical Research Group, Inc.
TRI....... Technical Research Institute (Japan)
AG........ Technical Research Ship (Navy symbol)
AGTR...... Technical Research Ship (Navy symbol)
TRS....... Technical Research Ship
TRC....... Technical Resources Center (Syracuse University)
TRO....... Technical Reviewing Office
TSGT...... Technical Sergeant
TSGT(C) ... Technical Sergeant (Commissary) (Marine Corps)
TSB....... Technical Service Bulletin
TSCDP..... Technical Service Career Development Program

TSIT...... Technical Service Intelligence Team
TSO....... Technical Service Organization (A generic term)
TSU....... Technical Service Unit
TU....... Technical Service Unit (Military)
TECHSVS ... Technical Services (Army)
TSD....... Technical Services Division (National Library of Medicine)
TSG....... Technical Specialty Group (AIAA)
TSP....... Technical Specification
TSS....... Technical Specification Sheet
TSO....... Technical Standard Order
TSI....... Technical Standardization Inspection
TSR....... Technical Study Report
TSC....... Technical Subcommittee
TSR....... Technical Summary Report
TSMC...... Technical Supply Management Code
TSD....... Technical Support Directorate
TSRP...... Technical Support Real Property
TT....... Technical Test
TECHTAF ... Technical Training Air Force
TTAF...... Technical Training Air Force
TTC....... Technical Training Center (Air Force)
TTC....... Technical Training Command (Army Air Forces) (World War II)
TTD....... Technical Training Detachment
TT....... Technical Translations (CFSTI publication)
TWG....... Technical Working Group (of the Conference on the Discontinuance of
            Nuclear Weapon Tests)
TW....... Technical Works (Air Force)
TWIS...... Technically Workable Ideal System (Industrial engineering)
TE........ Technician (Communications) (Navy rating)
TEPPS..... Technique for Establishing Personnel Performance Standards (Navy)
TEAM...... Technique for Evaluation and Analysis of Maintainability
THERP..... Technique for Human Error Rate Prediction
TRIAL...... Technique to Retrieve Information from Abstracts of Literature
            (Data processing)
TIP........ Techniques in Product Selection (National Association of Manufacturers)
TIPS....... Techniques in Product Selection (National Association of Manufacturers)
TDCK...... Technisch Documentatie Centrum voor der Krijgsmacht (Netherland
            Armed Services Technical Documentation and Information Center)
TAL....... Technische Akademie der Luftwaffe (Germany)
TAN....... Technische Arbeitsnorm
TH........ Technische Hochschule
TKO....... Technische Kontrollorganisation
TP........ Technographic Publication
TAP....... Technological Adjustment Pay
TF........ Technological Forecasting
TWP....... Technological War Plan
TCI....... Technology Communications, Incorporated
TG........ Technology Gap
TORQUE.... Technology on Research Quantitative Utility Evaluation
TRACES..... Technology in Retrospect and Critical Events in Science (IITRI)
TUP....... Technology Utilization Program
THU....... Teck-Hughes Gold Mines (NYSE symbol)
T........ Tee (Piping Joint, etc.)
TEST...... Teen-Age Employment Skills Training, Inc.
TARS...... Teen Age Republicans
TRY....... Teens for Retarded Youth (Program in Fairfax County, Virginia)
T........ Teeth (Technical drawings)
TPI....... Teeth Per Inch (of cog wheels)
TT........ Teetotaler (Slang)
TBK....... TEFLON Bonding Kit
TCAF...... TEFLON Coated Aluminum Foil
TDC....... TEFLON Dielectric Capacitor
TIW....... TEFLON-Insulated Wire
TIM....... TEFLON Insulation Material
TEBROC..... Tehran Book Processing Centre
TEL....... TelAutograph Corporation (NYSE symbol)
TSS....... Telecommunication Switching System
TCWG...... Telecommunication Working Group
TAB....... Telecommunications Advisory Board
TCC....... Telecommunications Coordinating Committee (State Department)
TFU....... Telecommunications Flying Unit (British)
TPC....... Telecommunications Planning Committee (Civil defense)
TRE....... Telecommunications Research Establishment (British)
TELESAT..... Telecommunications Satellite
TDP....... Teledata Processing
TAGS...... Teledyne Airborne Geophysical Services
TSC....... Teledyne Systems Corporation
TDS....... Teleflora Delivery Service
TG....... Telegram
TG........ Telegraph
TARE...... Telegraph Automatic Routing Equipment

TB	Telegraph Bureau
TDO	Telegraph Delivery Order
TD	Telegraph Department
TDMS	Telegraph Distortion Measuring System
TELEFLORA	Telegraph Florists Delivery Service
TO	Telegraph Office
TSA	Telegraph System Analyzer
T	Telegrapher (Navy)
TA	Telegraphic Address
TT	Telegraphic Transfer (of funds)
TTS	Telegraphic Transfers (of Money) (Banking)
TSF	Telegraphie sans Fil (Wireless Telegraphy)
TASS	Telegraphnoye Agentstvo Sovyetskovo Soyuza (Telegraph Agency of the Soviet Union) (News agency)
T/M	Telemetering (or Telemetry)
MOE	Telemetering Mobile Station (ITU designation)
TELEPAK	Telemetering Package
TAMIS	Telemetric Automated Microbial Identification System
TDA	Telemetric Data Analyzer
TELEDAC	Telemetric Data Converter
TDM	Telemetric Data Monitor
TELUS	Telemetric Universal Sensor
TM	Telemetry
TADIC	Telemetry Analog-Digital Information Converter
TAP	Telemetry Antenna Pedestal
TARE	Telemetry Automatic Reduction Equipment
TCM	Telemetry Code Modulation
TCR	Telemetry Compression Routine
TMCOMP	Telemetry Computation
TD	Telemetry Data
TMD	Telemetry Data
TDD	Telemetry Data Digitizer
TEDES	Telemetry Data Evaluation System
TDS	Telemetry Decommutation System
TEU	Telemetry Equipment Unit
TES	Telemetry Evaluation Station
TGS	Telemetry Ground Station
TIPS	Telemetry Impact Prediction System (Air Force)
TLS	Telemetry Listing Submodule
TMS	Telemetry Modulation System
TMF	Telemetry Module Facility
TOMCAT	Telemetry On-Line Monitoring Compression & Transmission
TOPS	Telemetry On-Line Processing System (Data processing)
TPA	Telemetry Power Amplifier
TMPROC	Telemetry Processing
TPS	Telemetry Processing Station (NASA)
TP	Telemetry Processor
TPM	Telemetry Processor Module
TRIA	Telemetry Range Instrumentation Aircraft
TRANS	Telemetry Redundancy Analyzer System
TSIMS	Telemetry Simulation Submodule
TSCC	Telemetry Standards Coordination Committee
TSSA	Telemetry Subcarrier Spectrum Analyzer
TELSCOM	Telemetry-Surveillance-Communications
TWG	Telemetry Working Group
T	Telephone
TAS	Telephone Answering Service (or System)
TELB	Telephone Booth
TCM	Telephone Channel Monitor
FONECON	Telephone Conversation
TELECON	Telephone Conversation
TD	Telephone Department
TELFAD	Telephone Executive Leader for a Day (New England Telephone Company program for high school students)
TIF	Telephone Influence Factor
TDEC	Telephone Line Digital Error Checking
TN	Telephone Number
TO	Telephone Office
TELPAK	Telephone Package
TPC	Telephone Pickup Coil
TPUC	Telephone Pickup Coil
TPA	Telephone Pioneers of America
TTE	Telephone Terminal Equipment
TSX	Telephone Satellite, Experimental
TSF	Telephone Service Fitting
TPSF	Telephonie sans Fil (Wireless telephony)
TTMS	Telephoto Transmission Measuring Set
TP	Teleprinter
TECE	Teleprinter Error Correction Equipment
TRAIN	Telerail Automated Information Network (Association of American Railroads)

TOPS	Teleregister Omni Processing and Switching (Data processing)
TPR	Telescopic Photographic Recorder
T	Teletype
TT	Teletype
TIG	Teletype Input Generator
TIP	Teletype Input Processing
TPP	Teletype Page Printer
TSS	Teletype Switching Subsystem
TTL	Teletype Telling
TELETYPE	Teletypewriter
TT	Teletypewriter
TTY	Teletypewriter
TADS	Teletypewriter Automatic Dispatch System
TTC	Teletypewriter Center (Military)
TELECON	Teletypewriter Conference (Military)
TWX	Teletypewriter Exchange Service (of American Telephone and Telegraph Company) (Term also used generically for teletypewriter message)
TWPL	Teletypewriter, Private Line
TELSIM	Teletypewriter Simulation
TTEC	Teletypewriter Technician
TIGRIS	Televised Images of Gaseous Region in Interplanetary Space
TV	Television
TARC	Television Allocation Research Committee (or Council)
TASO	Television Allocations Study Organization
TAA	Television Appliance Association
TASCON	Television Automatic Sequence Control
TBC	Television Briefing Console
TvB	Television Bureau of Advertising
TBA	Television Bureau of Advertising
TVCAM	Television Camera and Control Equipment
TCS	Television Camera System
TCC	Television Control Center
TESA	Television and Electronics Service Association
TFR	Television Film Recorder
TIO	Television Information Office
TVIST	Television Information Storage Tube
TIROS	Television Infrared Observation Satellite (NASA)
TIREC	TIROS (Television Infrared Observation Satellite) Ice Reconnaissance
TOS	TIROS (Television Infrared Observation Satellite) Operational Satellite (or System) (NASA)
TOSS	TIROS (Television Infrared Observation Satellite) Operational Satellite System (NASA)
TVI	Television Interference (Communications)
TLL	Television LASER Link
TVM	Television Monitor (Video only)
TOC	Television Operating Center
TPEA	Television Program Export Association
TELERAN	Television, RADAR and Air Navigation
TRP	Television Remote Pickup
TSC	Television Scan Converter
TELSUN	Television Series for United Nations (A foundation formed to produce, and telecast on a commercial basis, dramatized descriptions of UN activities)
Te	Tellurium (Chemical element)
T	Telsa
TEM	Temiskaming & Northern Ontario Railway (AAR code)
TEF	Temperance Education Foundation
T	Temperature
TAVET	Temperature Acceleration Vibration Environmental Tester
TAC	Temperature Altitude Chamber
TA	Temperature, Axillary
TC	Temperature Capability
TC	Temperature Coefficient
TCBV	Temperature Coefficient of Breakdown Voltage
TCC	Temperature Coefficient of Capacitance
TCR	Temperature Coefficient of Resistance
TCRE	Temperature Compensated Reference Element
TCZD	Temperature-Compensated Zener Diode
TC	Temperature Control
TCI	Temperature Control Instrument
TCU	Temperature Control Unit
TDC	Temperature Density Computer
TDP	Temperature Density Plotter
TDR	Temperature Depth Recorder
TDS	Temperature, Depth, Salinity
TF	Temperature Factor
THI	Temperature Humidity Index
THIR	Temperature-Humidity Infrared Radiometer
TIL	Temperature Indicating Label
TIS	Temperature Indicating Switch
TI	Temperature Indicator

TIM . . . . Temperature Indicator Monitor
TLE . . . . Temperature-Limited Emission
TMS . . . . Temperature Management Station
TM . . . . Temperature, Mean
TMS . . . . Temperature Measurement Society
TM . . . . Temperature Meter
TPR . . . . Temperature, Pulse, Respiration (Medicine)
TR . . . . Temperature Range
TRFCS . . . . . . Temperature Rate Flight Control System
TR . . . . Temperature Recorder
TRC . . . . Temperature Recording Controller
TR . . . . Temperature, Rectal (Medicine)
TRPS . . . . . . Temperature Regulating Power Supply
TRAMPS . . . . . Temperature Regulator and Missile Power Supply
T-S . . . . Temperature-Salinity
TSD . . . . Temperature-Salinity-Density-Depth (Relationships) (Oceanography)
TST . . . . Temperature Sensing Transducer
TS . . . . Temperature Sensitive
TS . . . . Temperature Switch
TVR . . . . Temperature Variation of Resistance (Electricity)
TW . . . . Tempered Water
TJC . . . . Temple Junior College (Texas)
TOP . . . . Temple Opportunity Program (Temple University)
T . . . . Tempo
T . . . . Temporal
TBB . . . . Temporal Bone Banks (Otology)
TOP . . . . Temporarily Out of Print
TRLB . . . . Temporarily Replaced by Lighted Buoy Showing Same Characteristic (Maps and charts)
TRUB . . . . Temporarily Replaced by Unlighted Buoy (Maps and charts)
T . . . . Temporary
TEMAC . . . . . . Temporary Active Duty
TEMACINS . . . . Temporary Active Duty Under Instruction (Navy)
TAD . . . . Temporary Additional Duty
TEMADD . . . . . Temporary Additional Duty (Navy)
TEMADDCON . Temporary Additional Duty in Connection with (Specified activity) (Navy)
TEMADDINS . . Temporary Additional Duty Under Instruction (Navy)
TAPER . . . . . . Temporary Appointment Pending Establishment of a Register
TAD . . . . Temporary Attached Duty
TBM . . . . Temporary Bench Mark
TB . . . . Temporary Buoy (Maps and charts)
TCS . . . . Temporary Change of Station
TC . . . . Temporary Constable
TCH . . . . Temporary Construction Hole (Technical drawings)
TCC . . . . Temporary Council Committee (NATO)
TDF . . . . Temporary Detention Facility
TD . . . . Temporary Disability
TDRL . . . . Temporary Disability Retired List (Military)
TD . . . . Temporary Duty
TDY . . . . Temporary Duty
TEMDU . . . . . Temporary Duty (Navy)
TEMWAIT . . . . Temporary Duty Awaiting (Specified event) (Navy)
TEMDUINS . . . . Temporary Duty under Instruction (Navy)
TEMINS . . . . . Temporary Duty under Instruction (Navy)
TEMFLY . . . . . Temporary Duty Involving Flying (Navy)
TEMFLYINS . . Temporary Duty Involving Flying Under Instruction (Navy)
TDPFO . . . . . . Temporary Duty Pending Further Orders (Military)
TDS . . . . Temporary Duty Station (Air Force)
TEEL . . . . Temporary Expedient Equipment List (Army)
TEC . . . . Temporary Extended Compensation (Labor)
TEUC . . . . Temporary Extended Unemployment Compensation (Labor)
TG . . . . Temporary Gentleman (British slang term for officer for duration of the war) (World War I)
TGG . . . . Temporary Geographic Grid
TIN . . . . Temporary Instruction Notice
TIE . . . . Temporary/Intermittent Employee
TLB . . . . Temporary Lighted Buoy (Maps and charts)
TLA . . . . Temporary Lodging Allowance (Military)
TNEC . . . . Temporary National Economic Committee (Congressional committee which studied the American economic system) (World War II)
MEX . . . . "Temporary Rank" (Army slang)
TUC . . . . Temporary Unemployment Compensation (Labor)
TUB . . . . Temporary Unlighted Buoy (Maps and charts)
TW . . . . Temporary Warrant
T . . . . Tempore (In the Time Of)
TP . . . . Tempore Paschale (At Easter Time)
TR . . . . Tempore Regis (In the Time of the King)
TMJ . . . . Temporo-Mandibular Joint
TNCD . . . . Ten Nation Committee on Disarmament (Defunct, 1960)
X Yr Dev . . . . Ten Year Device (US Army badge)
TENOC . . . . . Ten-Year Oceanographic Program (Navy)

TE . . . . Tenants by the Entirety (Real estate)
TLC . . . . Tender Loving Care
T . . . . Tenero (Tender)
TN . . . . Tennessee
TAG . . . . Tennessee, Alabama & Georgia Railway Company (AAR code)
TC . . . . Tennessee Central Railway Company (AAR code)
TGT . . . . Tennessee Gas Transmission Company (NYSE symbol)
TPI . . . . Tennessee Polytechnic Institute
TENN . . . . Tennessee R. R. (AAR code)
TVA . . . . Tennessee Valley Authority
TVPPA . . . . . . Tennessee Valley Public Power Association
TWHBEAA . . . . Tennessee Walking Horse Breeders' & Exhibitors' Association of America
TWHTA . . . . . Tennessee Walking Horse Trainers' Association
TC . . . . Tennis Club
T . . . . Tenor
TBB . . . . Tenor, Baritone, Bass
T . . . . Tense
TS . . . . Tensile Strength
T . . . . Tension
TETRAC . . . . . Tension Truss Antenna Concept
T . . . . Tensor
TN . . . . Tentacular Nerve
TBOI . . . . Tentative Basis of Issue (Army)
TCR . . . . Tentative Cancellation Request
TCD . . . . Tentative Classification of Damage
TCD . . . . Tentative Classification of Documents
TOR . . . . Tentative Operational Requirement
TP . . . . Tentative Pamphlet
TSOR . . . . Tentative Specific Operational Requirement
TS . . . . Tentative Specification
TTE . . . . Tentative Tables of Equipment
T . . . . Tentative Target
TPW . . . . Tenth-Power Width
TID . . . . Ter in Die (Three Times Daily) (Medicine)
TDS . . . . Ter Die Sumendum (To Be Taken Three Times a Day) (Pharmacy)
TQD . . . . Ter Quaterve in Die (Four Times a Day) (Pharmacy)
T . . . . Tera (A prefix meaning multiplied by 10 to the 12th power)
TC . . . . Teracycle
THz . . . . Terahertz
Tb . . . . Terbium (Chemical element)
TBLC . . . . Term Birth, Living Child (Medicine)
TOE . . . . Term of Enlistment (Military)
TOI . . . . Term of Induction (Military)
TOS . . . . Term of Service
T . . . . Terminal or Termination
TAS . . . . Terminal Address Selector
TATC . . . . Terminal Air Traffic Control
TATCS . . . . . . Terminal Air Traffic Control System
TAD/P . . . . . . Terminal Area Distribution Processing
TANS . . . . Terminal Area Navigation System
TAPS . . . . Terminal Area Positive Separation (FAA)
TASC . . . . Terminal Area Sequencing and Control
TAR . . . . Terminal Area Surveillance RADAR
TASR . . . . Terminal Area Surveillance RADAR
TBT . . . . Terminal Ballistic Track
TBL . . . . Terminal Ballistics Laboratory (Army)
TB . . . . Terminal Block
TB . . . . Terminal Board
TCM . . . . Terminal-to-Computer Multiplexer
TCA . . . . Terminal Control Area
TMA . . . . Terminal Control Area (Aviation)
TDIS . . . . Terminal Data Input System
TEGMA . . . . . Terminal Elevator Grain Merchants Association
TES . . . . Terminal Encounter System
TE . . . . Terminal Equipment
TFE . . . . Terminal Flight Evaluation
TFM . . . . Terminal Forecast Manual
TG . . . . Terminal Guidance
TGS . . . . Terminal Guidance Sensor
TGSS . . . . Terminal Guidance Sensor System
TGS . . . . Terminal Guidance System
TERP . . . . Terminal Instrument Procedure (Aviation)
TI . . . . Terminal Island (San Pedro) (Navy base)
TLF . . . . Terminal Launch Facility
TL . . . . Terminal Limen
TNL . . . . Terminal Net Loss
TPL . . . . Terminal Per Line
TPS . . . . Terminal Performance Specification
TPI . . . . Terminal Phase Initiation
TERPS . . . . . . Terminal Planning System (Military)
TPLS . . . . Terminal Position Location System

REVERSE ACRONYMS AND INITIALISMS DICTIONARY

TRACON . . . . . Terminal RADAR Approach Control (FAA)
TRSA . . . . Terminal RADAR Service Area
TRAP . . . . Terminal Radiation Airborne Program
TRRA . . . . Terminal R. R. Association of St. Louis (AAR code)
TRR of ST L . . Terminal Railroad Association of St. Louis
TASD . . . . Terminal Railway, Alabama State Docks (AAR code)
TR . . . . Terminal Rendezvous
TRP . . . . Terminal Rendezvous Phase
TS . . . . Terminal (or Greater) Sensation
TS . . . . Terminal Service
TSV . . . . Terminal Stage Vehicle
TETRA . . . . . . Terminal Tracking Telescope
TVDP . . . . Terminal Vector Display Unit
TV . . . . Terminal Velocity (Navy)
TVOR . . . . . . Terminal VHF (Very High Frequency) Omnirange (Radio)
TPS . . . . Terminals Per Station
TWEP . . . . Terminate with Extreme Prejudice (To kill) (Counterintelligence)
TAG . . . . Terminating and Grounding
TAPO . . . . Termination Accountable Property Officer
TCO . . . . Termination Contracting Officers
TDC . . . . Termination Design Change
TI . . . . Termination Instruction
TCS . . . . Ternary Compound Semiconductor
TDM . . . . Ternary Delta Modulation
TC . . . . Terra Cotta (Technical drawings)
TARS . . . . Terrain Analog RADAR Simulator
TAAD . . . . Terrain Avoidance Accessory Device
TAO . . . . Terrain Avoidance Override
TAR . . . . Terrain-Avoidance RADAR
TCI . . . . Terrain-Clearance Indicator
TCM . . . . Terrain Clearance Measurement
TCR . . . . Terrain Clearance RADAR
TERCOM . . . . . Terrain Contour Matching (ASD)
TFD . . . . Terrain Following Display
TFE . . . . Terrain-Following Evaluator
TFF . . . . Terrain-Following Flight
TFFE . . . . Terrain-Following Flight Evaluator
TFR . . . . Terrain-Following RADAR
TFS . . . . Terrain-Following System
TOWA . . . . . . Terrain and Obstacle Warning and Avoidance
TERB . . . . Terrazzo Base
TDH . . . . Terre des Hommes (An international organization)
TAP . . . . Terrestrial Auxiliary Power
TURPS . . . . . . Terrestrial Unattended Reactor Power System
T . . . . Territorial or Territory
TA . . . . Territorial Army
TANS . . . . Territorial Army Nursing Service
TCG . . . . Territorial College of Guam
TD . . . . Territorial Decoration
TES . . . . Territorial Experiment Stations Division (of ARS, Department of
        Agriculture)
TF . . . . Territorial Force
TFNS . . . . Territorial Force Nursing Service
TERRES . . . . . Territorial Residents
TEP . . . . Territory Enterprises Proprietary
TH . . . . Territory of Hawaii (to 1959)
T . . . . Tertiary
TBA . . . . Tertiary Butyl Acetate
TOSF . . . . Tertiary of Third Order of St. Francis (Roman Catholic religious order)
T . . . . Tesla (Unit of magnetic flux density, one weber per square meter)
TAR . . . . Test Analysis Report
TADR . . . . Test Answer Document Reader
TAN . . . . Test Area North (AEC)
TAG . . . . Test Automation Growth
TBCA . . . . Test Boring Contractors Association
TB . . . . Test Bulletin
TC . . . . Test Console
TCNCO . . . . . Test Control Noncommissioned Officer
TCO . . . . Test Control Officer
TCU . . . . Test Control Unit
TC . . . . Test Controller
TCC . . . . Test Coordinating Center (Army)
TD . . . . Test Data
TDI . . . . Test Data Interpolation
TDR . . . . Test Data Recorder
TD . . . . Test Director
TDG . . . . Test Display Generator
TDT . . . . Test Dwell Time
TEU . . . . Test of Economic Understanding
TEG . . . . Test Element Group
TED . . . . Test Engineering Division (Navy)

TOEFL . . . . . . Test of English as a Foreign Language
TE . . . . Test Equipment
TECM . . . . Test Equipment Commodity Manager
TEE . . . . Test Equipment Engineer
TEK . . . . Test Equipment Kit
TEMS . . . . Test Equipment Maintenance Set
TEO . . . . Test Equipment Operator
TRACE . . . . . . Test Equipment for Rapid Automatic Checkout and Evaluation
        (Pan-American Airways)
TETA . . . . Test Equipment Technical Adviser
TED . . . . Test, Experiment and Development
TEA . . . . Test and Evaluation Agency
TEAM . . . . Test & Evaluation of Air Mobility
TEAM-UP . . . . Test Evaluation Analysis Management Uniformity Plan (Army)
T & EC . . . . . Test and Evaluation Command (Army)
TECOM . . . . . Test and Evaluation Command (Army)
TEAMS . . . . . . Test Evaluation and Monitoring System
TF . . . . Test Flight (Air Force)
TI . . . . Test Instrumentation
TIS . . . . Test Instrumentation System
TIM . . . . Test Instrumented Missile (Army)
TL . . . . Test Laboratory
TL . . . . Test Link
TLW . . . . Test Load Wire
TMPS . . . . Test and Maintenance Panel Subassembly
TM . . . . Test Manual
TMM . . . . Test Message Monitor
TMP . . . . Test Methods and Procedures
TMS . . . . Test Monitor System
TOSS . . . . Test Operation Support Segment
TOPSY . . . . . . Test Operations Planning System
TOL . . . . Test-Oriented Language
TOOL . . . . . . Test Oriented Operated Language (Data processing)
TPL . . . . Test Parts List
TPR . . . . Test Performance Recorder
TPS . . . . Test Pilot School (Navy)
TPTD . . . . Test Pilot Training Division
TPA . . . . Test Plans and Analysis
TPS . . . . Test Plotting System
TP . . . . Test Point
TPC . . . . Test Point Controller
TPD . . . . Test Point Data
TPL . . . . Test Point Logic
TPS . . . . Test Point Selector
TP . . . . Test Position
TARAN . . . . . . Test and Replace as Necessary
TR . . . . Test Report
TR . . . . Test Request
TRS . . . . Test Research Service
TRS . . . . Test Research Station
TRAMP . . . . . . Test Retrieval and Memory Print (Data processing)
TRIM . . . . Test Rules for Inventory Management
TR . . . . Test Run
TSR . . . . Test Schedule Request
TSSA . . . . Test Scorer and Statistical Analyzer (Data processing)
TSE . . . . Test Scoring (or Support) Equipment
TSC . . . . Test Set Computer
TSC . . . . Test Set Connection
TSE . . . . Test Set Electrical
TSL . . . . Test Set Logic
TSS . . . . Test Set Simulator
TSO . . . . Test Site Office
TS . . . . Test Solution (of a chemical) (Medicine)
TS . . . . Test Summary
TSO . . . . Test Support Office
TSP . . . . Test Support Program
TSW . . . . Test Switch
TTA . . . . Test Target Array
TTS . . . . Test and Training Satellite (NASA)
TESTRAN . . . . . Test Translator (Data processing)
TOUS . . . . Test on Understanding Science
TV . . . . Test Vehicle (Air Force)
TVDC . . . . Test Volts, Direct Current
T . . . . Testament
TA . . . . Testantibus Actis (As the Acts Show)
TD . . . . Testing and Development Division (Coast Guard)
TLS . . . . Testing the Limits for Sex (Psychology)
T & R . . . . . . Testing & Regulating Department (Especially, in a wire communications
        maintenance division)
TP . . . . Testosterone Propionate
TAT . . . . Tetanus Antitoxin (Medicine)

TT . . . . Tetanus Toxoid (Medicine)
TFW . . . . Tethered Free-Floating Worker
TRR . . . . Tethered RADAR Reflector
TADPO . . . . . . Tetraaminodiphenyl (Ether)
TBE . . . . Tetrabromoethane
TCAB . . . . . . Tetrachloroazobenzene
TDE . . . . Tetrachloro-Diphenyl-Ethane
TCNQ . . . . . . Tetracyanoquinodimethane
TC . . . . Tetracycline
TEA . . . . Tetraethylammonium (Biochemistry)
TEAB . . . . . . Tetraethylammonium Bromide (Biochemistry)
TEAC . . . . . . Tetraethylammonium Chloride (Biochemistry)
TEL . . . . Tetraethyl-Lead
TEPP . . . . . . Tetraethylpyrophosphate (Biochemistry)
TFE . . . . Tetrafluoroethylene
TEFLON . . . . . Tetrafluoroethylene Resin (Du Pont)
TC . . . . Tetrahedral Cubic (Metallography)
TRS . . . . Tetrahedral Research Satellite
THC . . . . Tetrahydracannabinol (Narcotic)
THF . . . . Tetrahydrofolic (Acid)
THF . . . . Tetrahydrofuran
THHP . . . . . . Tetrahydrohomopteroic (Acid)
THP . . . . Tetrahydropapaveroline
THT . . . . Tetrahydrothiophene
TPT . . . . Tetraisopropyl Titanate (Chemical)
TML . . . . Tetramethyl-Lead
TMTD . . . . . . Tetramethylthiuram Disulfide
TNA . . . . Tetranitroaniline
TNM . . . . Tetranitromethane
TPB . . . . Tetraphenylbutane (Chemical)
TV . . . . Tetrazolium Violet
TTX . . . . Tetrodotoxin
TJI . . . . Tex Johnston, Incorporated
THUMS . . . . . Texaco, Humble, Union, Mobil, and Shell (Petroleum companies)
TX . . . . Texaco Inc. (NYSE symbol)
TX . . . . Texas
TAGER . . . . . . Texas Association for Graduate Education and Research
TCU . . . . Texas Christian University
TCT . . . . Texas City Terminal Railway Company (AAR code)
TCAI . . . . Texas College of Arts and Industry
TEXACO . . . . Texas Company
TDMRA . . . . . Texas Delaine-Merino Record Association
TET . . . . Texas Eastern Transmission Corporation (NYSE symbol)
TEMP . . . . . . Texas Educational Microwave Project
TEA . . . . Texas Electronics Association
TXG . . . . Texas Gas Transmission Corporation (NYSE symbol)
TR . . . . Texas Gulf Producing Company (NYSE symbol) (Wall Street slang name: "Teddy Roosevelt")
TG . . . . Texas Gulf Sulphur Company (NYSE symbol) (Wall Street slang name: "Tough Guy")
TGCA . . . . . . Texas Gun Collectors Association
THD . . . . Texas Highway Department
TIPRO . . . . . . Texas Independent Producers and Royalty Owners Association
TIE . . . . Texas Information Exchange
TIAC . . . . Texas Instruments Automatic Computer
TIDAR . . . . . . Texas Instruments Digital Analog Readout
TI . . . . Texas Instruments, Inc.
TII . . . . Texas Instruments, Incorporated
TXN . . . . Texas Instruments, Inc. (NYSE symbol)
TIPACS . . . . . . Texas Instruments Planning and Control System
TL . . . . Texas League (Baseball)
TLC . . . . Texas Lutheran College
TEX MEX . . . . Texas Mexican Railway Company
TM . . . . Texas Mexican Railway Company (AAR code)
TNM . . . . Texas-New Mexico Railway Company (AAR code)
TNO . . . . Texas & New Orleans R. R. (AAR code)
TN . . . . Texas & Northern Railway Company (AAR code)
TOE . . . . Texas, Oklahoma & Eastern R. R. (AAR code)
TS . . . . Texas Pacific Coal & Oil Company (NYSE symbol)
TPL . . . . Texas Pacific Land Trust (NYSE symbol)
TPMP . . . . . . Texas Pacific-Missouri Pacific Terminal R. R. (AAR code)
TP . . . . Texas & Pacific Railway Company (AAR code)
T and P . . . . . Texas and Pacific Railway Company
TSL . . . . Texas Short Line Railway (AAR code)
TSE . . . . Texas South-Eastern R. R. (AAR code)
TSU . . . . Texas Southern University
TSC . . . . Texas Southmost College
TTI . . . . Texas Transportation Institute
TXU . . . . Texas Utilities Company (NYSE symbol)
TRAC . . . . . . Text Reckoning and Compiling (Data processing)
TALA . . . . . . Textile Association of Los Angeles

TBMA . . . . . . Textile Bag Manufacturers Association
TCMA . . . . . . Textile Chemical Manufacturers Association
TCA . . . . Textile Converters Association
TDPA . . . . . . Textile Data Processing Association
TEXDEALAM . . Textile Dealers Association of America
TDA . . . . Textile Distributors Association (Formerly, TFDA)
TDI . . . . Textile Dye Institute
TEB . . . . Textile Economics Bureau
TEA . . . . Textile Export Association of the US
TFDA . . . . . . Textile Fabric Distributors Association (Later, TDA)
TFA . . . . Textile Fabrics Association
TFI . . . . Textile Foundation, Incorporated
THS . . . . Textile History Society
TLA . . . . Textile Labor Association (India)
TRA . . . . Textile Refinishers Association
TRI . . . . Textile Research Institute
TSA . . . . Textile Salesmen's Association
TSCA . . . . . . Textile Supplies and Credit Association
TVA . . . . Textile Veterans Association
TWA . . . . Textile Waste Association
TWE . . . . Textile Waste Exchange
TWUA . . . . . . Textile Workers Union of America
TXT . . . . Textron Inc. (NYSE symbol)
THAI . . . . . . Thai Airways Company, Ltd.
TPF . . . . Thai Patriotic Front (Communist-directed activity outside Thailand) (Merged with TIM)
TAEC . . . . . . Thailand Atomic Energy Commission for Peace
TIM . . . . Thailand Independence Movement (Communist-directed activity outside Thailand) (Merged with TPF)
TRR . . . . Thailand Research Reactor (Atomic energy)
TUFEC . . . . . Thailand-UNESCO Fundamental Education Centre
TE . . . . Thalassia Extract
TI . . . . Thallium (Chemical element)
TBT . . . . Thallium Beam Tube
TGIF . . . . Thank God It's Friday (Meaning work-week is nearly over)
TGIF-OTMWDUM . . Thank God It's Friday - Only Two More Work Days Until Monday (Pentagon saying)
TU . . . . Thank You (Communications operator's procedural remark)
TNX . . . . Thanks (Communications operator's procedural remark)
TWTWTW . . . . That Was The Week That Was (Television program of English origin) (Also, TW3)
TW3 . . . . That Was The Week That Was (Television program of English origin) (Also, TWTWTW)
TMC . . . . Thatcher Glass Manufacturing Company, Inc. (NYSE symbol)
TAG . . . . The Acronym Generator (An RCA computer program)
TAG . . . . The Adjutant General (Army)
TAGBDUSA . . . The Adjutant General's Board, United States Army
TAGO . . . . . . The Adjutant General's Office
TAGRDCUSA . . The Adjutant General's Research and Development Command, United States Army
TAGSUSA . . . . The Adjutant General's School, Army
TASTA . . . . . . The Administrative Support, Theater Army
TASA . . . . . . The Aircraft Service Association
TAALS . . . . . . The American Association of Language Specialists
TAC . . . . The Architects Collaborative (Design firm)
TAADS . . . . . . The Army Authorization Document System
TAABS . . . . . . The Army Automated Budget System
TAERS . . . . . . The Army Equipment Record System
TAFFS . . . . . . The Army Functional Files System
TALS . . . . . . The Army Language School
TAMMS . . . . . The Army Maintenance Management System
TAOC . . . . . . The Army Operations Center
TARMOCS . . . . The Army Operations Center System
TAPER . . . . . . The Army Plan for Equipment Records
TARC . . . . . . The Army Research Council
TASAP . . . . . . The Army Scientific Advisory Panel
TASSA . . . . . . The Army Signal Supply Agency
TAS . . . . The Army Staff
TACFO . . . . . . TASAMS (The Army Supply and Maintenance System) Coordination Field Office
TASA . . . . . . The Assistant Secretary of the Army
TAG . . . . The Association for the Gifted
TDA . . . . The Disposables Association
TEAM . . . . . . The Electronic Association of Missouri
TEAM . . . . . . The European-Atlantic Movement
TEAM . . . . . . The Evangelical Alliance Mission
TFC . . . . The Felician College (Illinois)
THIS . . . . The Hospitality and Information Service
THIEF . . . . . . The Human Initiated Equipment Failures
TIS . . . . The Infantry School (Army)
TIG . . . . The Inspector General (Army)

TIOH . . . . The Institute of Heraldry (Army)
TIMS . . . . The Institute of Management Sciences
TIF . . . . The International Foundation
TIIAL . . . . The International Institute of Applied Linguistics
TJAG . . . . The Judge Advocate General (Army)
TJAGC . . . . . . The Judge Advocate General's Corps (Army)
TJAGSA . . . . . The Judge Advocate General's School, US Army
TKKTFSLB . . . . "The Kandy-Kolored Tangerine-Flake Streamline Baby" (Title of book by Tom Wolfe)
TM . . . . The Maccabees
TMHA . . . . . . The Military Housing Association
TNA . . . . The National Archives
TNSDUNSPHI . . The National Society to Discourage Use of the Name Smith for Purposes of Hypothetical Illustration
TNSA . . . . The National Spiritual Alliance of the United States of America
TNB . . . . The New Brood
TNYTI . . . . . . The New York Times Index
TOSCO . . . . . . The Oil Shale Corporation of America
TOM . . . . The Old Man
TOPS . . . . The Operational PERT System
TPMG . . . . The Provost Marshal General (Army)
TQMG . . . . . . The Quartermaster General (Army)
USSECMILCOMUN .. The Secretary, United States Delegation United Nations Staff Committee
TSG . . . . The Surgeon General (Army)
TTI . . . . The Teachers, Incorporated
TTCP . . . . The Technical Cooperative Program (US, UK, Canada, Australia) (Research)
TUIFU . . . . . . The Ultimate in Foul Ups (Military slang)
TUSAFG . . . . . The United States Air Force Group, American Mission for Aid to Turkey
TUSAB . . . . . . The United States Army Band
TUSAC . . . . . . The United States Army Chorus
TUSLOG . . . . . The United States Logistics Group (Military)
TUCOPS . . . . . The Universal Coterie of Pipe Smokers
TWHO . . . . . . The White House Office
TWITW . . . . . . "The Wind in the Willows," a book by Kenneth Grahame
TAFO . . . . Theater Accounting and Finance Office (Military)
TAZ . . . . Theater Administrative Zone (Military)
TABS . . . . Theater Air Base Survivability
TABV . . . . Theater Air Base Vulnerability
TATB . . . . Theater Air Transportation Board
TACS . . . . Theater Area Communications Systems (Military)
TAADC . . . . . . Theater Army Air Defense Command
TACAC . . . . . . Theater Army Civil Affairs Command
TAHQ . . . . . . Theater Army Headquarters
TALOG . . . . . . Theater Army Logistical Command
TARC . . . . Theater Army Replacement Command
TARS . . . . Theater Army Replacement System
TARTC . . . . . . Theater Army Replacement and Training Command
TASL . . . . Theater Authorized Stockage List (Military)
TCA . . . . Theater Commander's Approval (Military)
TGC . . . . Theater Ground Commander (Military)
THQ . . . . Theater Headquarters (Military)
TIS . . . . Theater Intelligence Section (Navy)
TICP . . . . Theater Inventory Control Point (Military)
TJADC . . . . . . Theater Joint Air Defense Command (Military)
TJOC . . . . Theater Joint Operations Center (Military)
TNC . . . . Theater Naval Commander
TNHQ . . . . . . Theater Navy Headquarters
TO . . . . Theater of Operations
TOPNS . . . . . . Theater of Operations
TOC . . . . Theater of Operations Command
TOMCAT . . . . . Theater of Operations Missile Continuous-Wave Anti-Tank Weapon
TOTEM . . . . . Theater Operations and Tactical Evaluation Model
TPWIC . . . . . . Theater Prisoner of War Information Center
TSD . . . . Theater Shipping Document
TTMCFC . . . . Theater Type Mobilization Corps Force Capabilities
TTMCFO . . . . Theater Type Mobilization Corps Force Objective
TCG . . . . Theatre Communications Group
TEDA . . . . Theatre Equipment Dealers Association
TESMA . . . . . . Theatre Equipment and Supply Manufacturers Association
TGATS . . . . . . Theatre Guild-American Theatre Society
TFI . . . . Theatre for Ideas (An organization)
TLA . . . . Theatre Library Association
TOA . . . . Theatre Owners of America
TSAB . . . . Theatre-Screen Advertising Bureau (Defunct)
TTA . . . . Theatre Television Authority
TMA . . . . Theatrical Mutual Association
T . . . . Theft
TIH . . . . Their Imperial Highnesses
TM . . . . Their Majesties

TRH . . . . Their Royal Highnesses
TSH . . . . Their Serene Highnesses
TAT . . . . Thematic Apperception Test (Psychology)
THI . . . . Theodor Herzl Institute
THART . . . . . . Theodore Army Terminal
TR . . . . Theodore (Teddy) Roosevelt
TRA . . . . Theodore Roosevelt Association
THRB . . . . Theodore Roosevelt Birthplace National Historic Site
TRCC . . . . . . Theodore Roosevelt Centennial Commission (Government agency)
THRO . . . . . . Theodore Roosevelt National Memorial Park
TAKC . . . . . . Theological Associate, King's College (London)
Theom L . . . . . Theomonistic Licensee
TIRH . . . . Theoretical Indoor Relative Humidity
TMD . . . . Theoretical Maximum Density
TRR . . . . Theoretical Research Report
TSD . . . . Theory of Signal Detection
TSDA . . . . . . Theory of Signal Detection Analysis
TS . . . . Theosophical Society
TS in A . . . . . Theosophical Society in America
TR . . . . Therapeutic Radiology
TWASPIT . . . . Therapeutic Work Aid Station for Physically Inactive Thinkers
TARGET . . . . . Thermal Advanced Reactor, Gas-Cooled, Exploiting Thorium
TAP . . . . Thermal Analysis Program
TAJ . . . . Thermal Arc Jet
TBO . . . . Thermal Bakeout
TBV . . . . Thermal Bypass Valve
TCB . . . . Thermal Compression Bond
K . . . . Thermal Conductivity (Symbol)
TC . . . . Thermal Conductivity
TCCM . . . . . . Thermal Control Coating Material
TCS . . . . Thermal Control Surface
TCS . . . . Thermal Control System
TCA . . . . Thermal Critical Assembly (Atomic energy)
TDP . . . . Thermal Death-Point
TDM . . . . Thermal Diffusion Method
TE . . . . Thermal Efficiency
TEC . . . . Thermal End Cover
TES . . . . Thermal Energy Storage
TEC . . . . Thermal Expansion Coefficient
TFT . . . . Thermal Fatigue Test
TINS . . . . Thermal Imaging Night Sight
TIS . . . . Thermal Insulation System
TKW . . . . Thermal Kilowatts
TMP . . . . Thermal Modeling Program
TNS . . . . Thermal Night Site
TPI . . . . Thermal Protection Investigation
TPS . . . . Thermal Protection System
TPSS . . . . . . Thermal Protection System Selection
TRF . . . . Thermal Radiation at Microwave Frequencies
TRM . . . . Thermal Resistance Measurement
TSC . . . . Thermal Surface Coating
TU . . . . Thermal Unit
TOPSY . . . . . . Thermally Operated Plasma System
TOS . . . . Thermally and Oxidatively Stable
TOSR . . . . . . Thermally and Oxidatively Stable Resin
TPC . . . . Thermally Protected Composite
TPP . . . . Thermally Protected Plastic
TRAC . . . . . . Thermally Regenerative Alloy Cell
TSR . . . . Thermally Stable Resin
TET . . . . Thermionic Emission Technique
TFE . . . . Thermionic Fuel Element
TIMM . . . . . . Thermionic Integrated Micro Modules
TDP . . . . Thermistor Detector Package
TMR . . . . Thermistor Micropower Resistor
TST . . . . Thermistor Sterilization Test
TSTP . . . . . . Thermistor Sterilization Test Program
TAJF . . . . Thermo-Acoustic Jet Facility (MSFC) (NASA)
TCD . . . . Thermochemical Deposition
TCK . . . . Thermo-Chemical-Kinetic
TCBE . . . . . . Thermo-Compression Bonding Equipment
TCC . . . . Thermo-Control Coating
TC . . . . Thermocouple
TDAS . . . . . . Thermocouple Data Acquisition System
TGC . . . . Thermocouple Gauge Control
TGT . . . . Thermocouple Gauge Tube
TCJ . . . . Thermocouple Junction
TCRJ . . . . . . Thermocouple Reference Junction
TRJ . . . . Thermocouple Reference Junction
TDA . . . . Thermodifferential Analysis
TDM . . . . Thermodynamic Molding
TSH . . . . Thermodynamic Suppression Head

TRC	Thermodynamics Research Center (Texas A & M University)
TRL	Thermodynamics Research Laboratory
T/E	Thermoelectric
TED	Thermoelectric Device
TECU	Thermoelectric Environmental Control Unit
TEG	Thermoelectric Generator
TOPS	Thermoelectric Outer Planet Spacecraft (NASA)
TEV	Thermoelectric Voltage
TGA	Thermogravimetric Analysis
TEGG	Thermogrip Electric Glue Gun
THR	Thermoid Company (NYSE symbol)
TIT	Thermo-Isolation Technique
THL	Thermoluminescence (Also TL)
TL	Thermoluminescence (Also THL)
TLD	Thermoluminescent Dosimeter
TMGE	Thermo-Magnetic-Galvanic Effect
TMA	Thermomechanical Analyzer
TML	Thermo-Mechanical Loading
TMP	Thermomechanical Processing
TN	Thermonuclear
TPV	Thermophotovoltaic
TPRC	Thermophysical Properties Research Center (Purdue University)
TFW	Thermoplastic Fan Wheel
TPFW	Thermoplastic Fan Wheel
TPS	Thermoplastic Storage
TRM	Thermoremanent Magnetism (or Magnetization)
TP	Thermosphere Probe
THS	Thermostat Switch
TCC	Therofor Catalytic Cracking
TEST	Thesaurus of Engineering and Scientific Terms
TKP	Theta Kappa Phi (Fraternity)
TPA	Theta Phi Alpha (Sorority)
TPP	Thiamine Pyrophosphate (Diphospho-Thiamine) (Biochemistry)
TFH	Thick-Film Hybrid
T	Thickness
TRM	Thickness Readout Module
T	Thief
TBL	Thin Base Laminate
TDF	Thin Dielectric Film
TES	Thin Elastic Shell
TF	Thin Film
TFB	Thin-Film Barrier
TFC	Thin-Film Capacitor
TFC	Thin-Film Cell
TFCA	Thin-Film Cell Array
TFC	Thin-Film Circuit
TFD	Thin-Film Distillation
TFIB	Thin-Film Interface Barrier
TFM	Thin-Film Microelectronics
TFPC	Thin-Film Photovoltaic Cell
TFPCA	Thin-Film Photovoltaic Cell Array
TFR	Thin-Film Resist
TFT	Thin-Film Technique (or Technology)
TFT	Thin-Film Transducer
TFT	Thin-Film Transistor
TGL	Thin Glass Laminate
TIF	Thin Iron Film
TLC	Thin Layer Chromatography (Chemistry)
TLE	Thin-Layer Electrophoresis
TLE	Thin Leading Edge
TNF	Thin Nickel Film
TNI	Thin Nickel Iron
TNIF	Thin Nickel Iron Film
TRIM	Thin Region Integral Method
TSL	Thin Shock Layer
TAFUBAR	Things Are Fouled Up Beyond All Recognition
TARFU	Things Are Really Fouled Up (Military slang)
TASFUIRA	Things Are So Fouled Up It's Really Amazing (Military slang)
TBA	Thiobarbituric Acid
TCH	Thiocarbohydrazide
THI	Thiokol Chemical Corporation (NYSE symbol)
TSC	Thiosemicarbazide
TMT	Thiram (Also TMTD)
TMTD	Thiram (Also TMT)
TAF	Third Air Force
TA	Third Attack (Men's lacrosse position, until 1933)
TAY	Third Avenue Transit Corporation (NYSE symbol)
TCPO	Third-Class Post Office
TD	Third Defense (Men's lacrosse position, until 1933)
THB	Third Harmonic Band
TODA	Third-Octave Digital Analyzer
TOR	Third Order Regular of St. Francis
TUSA	Third United States Army
TMDAG	This Mode of Transportation has been Determined to be More Advantageous to the Government
TSU	This Side Up
TUFI	This Umbrella Folds Itself (Trademark for type of umbrella)
TADF	Thomas A. Dooley Foundation
TNB	Thomas & Betts Company (NYSE symbol)
TED	Thomas Edmund Dewey (Republican candidate for President, 1948)
TAWS	Thomasville Aircraft Warning System
JWT	Thompson (J. Walter) Company (An advertising agency)
THCF	Thompson-Huston Company of France
THO	Thompson Products (NYSE symbol)
TAPCO	Thompson Products, Inc.
TSMG	Thompson Submachine Gun
THORAD	Thor Agena D (Rocket)
TAVE	Thor-Agena Vibration Experiment (NASA)
TD	Thor-Delta (Satellite)
TPT	Thor Power Tool Company (NYSE symbol)
TS	Thoreau Society
TD	Thoria Dispersed (Nickel)
Th	Thorium (Chemical element)
THUD	Thorium, Uranium, Deuterium
TUFCDF	Thorium-Uranium Fuel Cycle Development Facility (AEC)
TJC	Thornton Junior College (Illinois)
TCA	Thoroughbred Club of America
TRA	Thoroughbred Racing Associations of the United States
TRPB	Thoroughbred Racing Protective Bureau
THEN	Those Hags Encourage Neuterism (Organization opposed to NOW [National Organization for Women])
MBF	Thousand Board Feet (Lumber)
MBH	Thousands of BTU per Hour
MCM	Thousand Circular Mils
MCF	Thousand Cubic Feet
MBM	Thousand Feet Board Measure
MFBM	Thousand Feet Board Measure (Lumber)
MSM	Thousand Feet Surface Measure (Lumber)
KPSI	Thousands of Pounds Per Square Inch
T	Thread
THDI	Thread Die
THGA	Thread Gage
TI	Thread Institute
THTA	Thread Tap
TBI	Threaded Blind Insert
TS	Threaded Stud
TNOC	Threads No Couplings
TPI	Threads Per Inch
TEAS	Threat Evaluation and Action Selection (Civilian defense program)
TWI	Threat Warning Information (Air Force)
TAAP	Three-Axis Antenna Positioner
TAMAC	Three-Axis Manual Attitude Controller
TAP	Three-Axis Package
TARS	Three-Axis Reference System (Used in reference to Titan missile)
TARSCC	Three-Axis Reference System Checkout Console
3B	Three-base hits (Baseball)
TCD	Three-Channel Decoder
3/C	Three-Conductor (Wire or cable)
THFA	Three-Conductor, Heat and Flame Resistant, Armor Cable
THFR	Three-Conductor, Heat and Flame Resistant, Radio Cable
TSGA	Three Conductor, Shipboard, General Use, Armor Cable
3-D	Three Dimensional (Pictures or films)
TML	Three Mile Limit
3PH	Three-Phase
TPFW	Three-Phase Full Wave
TPHW	Three-Phase Half Wave
3P	Three-Pole, or Triple Pole (Switch)
THS	Three-Stage Least Squares (Econometrics)
TDL	Threshold Damage Level
TD	Threshold Detection
TDL	Threshold Detection Level
TED	Threshold Erythema Dose (Medicine)
TED	Threshold Extension Demodulator
TFT	Threshold Failure Temperatures
TLV	Threshold Limit Value
TLU	Threshold Logic Unit
TE	Thromboembolic (Medicine)
TCC	Thromboplastic Cell Component (Medicine)
TPC	Thromboplastic Plasma Component (Medicine)
TGT	Thromboplastin Generation (Test)
TTP	Thrombotic Thrombocytopenic Purpura
TGC	Throttle Governor Control

TBL	Through Bill of Lading
TGBL	Through Government Bill of Lading
THP	Through Hole Probe
TAM	Throw Away Maintenance
TMTC	Thru-Mode (or Tri-Mode) Tape Converter
TAD	Thrust-Augmented Delta (NASA)
TAID	Thrust-Augmented Improved Delta (Launch vehicle)
TAR	Thrust-Augmented Rocket
TAT	Thrust-Augmented Thor (NASA)
TC	Thrust Chamber (Air Force, NASA)
TCA	Thrust Chamber Assembly (Missile technology)
THP	Thrust Horsepower (Jet engines)
TL	Thrust Line
TMS	Thrust Measuring System
TME	Thrust Monopropellant Engine
TRV	Thrust Reduction Valve
TSFC	Thrust Specific Fuel Consumption
TSS	Thrust Stand System
TVC	Thrust Vector Control (Aerospace)
Tm	Thulium (Chemical element)
TERLS	Thumba Equatorial Launching Station (Indian rocket station)
T	Thunderstorm
TS	Thunderstorm (Meteorology)
TRP.	Thunderstorm Research Project (Environmental Science Services Administration)
T	Thymine
TB	Thymol Blue (An indicator)
TCD	Thyratron Core Driver
TH	Thyroid Hormone (Thyroxine) (Endocrinology)
T/S	Thyroid:Serum (Iodide ratio)
TSH	Thyroid-Stimulating (Thyrotrophic) Hormone (Endocrinology)
TSP	Thyroid-Stimulating Hormone of the Prepituitary Gland
TTH	Thyrotrophic Hormone (Endocrinology)
TRS	Ticket Reservation Systems, Inc.
TICUS	Tidal Current System
TES	Tidal Electric Station
H	Tide Correction
TGS	Tide Gage System
TMB	Tide Measuring Buoy
T	Tide Rips
TV	Tidewater Oil Company (NYSE symbol)
TRK	Tidewater-Raymond-Kiewit, Inc.
TS	Tidewater Southern Railway Company (AAR code)
TVDC	Tidewater Virginia Development Council
TFA	Tie Fabrics Association
TIH	Tie Line
TL	Tie Line
TP	Tie Plate (Technical drawings)
TP	Tie Point
T	Tied
TITE	Tijuana & Tecate Railway Company (AAR code)
TB	Tile Base (Technical drawings)
TCAA	Tile Contractors' Association of America
TCA	Tile Council of America
TD	Tile Drain (Technical drawings)
TF	Tile Floor (Technical drawings)
TMA	Tile Manufacturers Association
TSR	Tile-Shingle Roof (Technical drawings)
TW	Tile Wainscot (Technical drawings)
T	Tiler (Freemasonry)
TC	Till Countermanded
TF	Till Forbidden (i.e., repeat until forbidden to do so) (Advertising)
N	Tilt Correction
TIP.	Tilt Isolation Platform
L	Timber (Lumber) (Vessel load line mark)
TIAA	Timber Importers Association of America
TPA	Timber Producers Association of Michigan and Wisconsin
TPMA	Timber Products Manufacturers Association
T	Time
PX In	Time of Arrival (Aviation)
TOA	Time of Arrival
TASI.	Time Assignment Speech Interpolation (Telephone cables) (Bell System)
TA	Time and Attendance
T & A	Time and Attendance
TACCAR	Time Average Clutter Coherent Airborne RADAR
TB	Time Base
TBU	Time Base Unit
TBO	Time Between Overhaul
TCO	Time and Charges, Operate
T/C	Time Charter (Shipping)
TC	Time Check

TC	Time Closing
TCG	Time Code Generator
TCR	Time Code Reader
TCW	Time Code Word
TC	Time Compensation
TCTO	Time Compliance Technical Orders
TCC	Time Compression Coding
TICTAC.	Time Compression Tactical Communications
TC	Time to Computation
TCB	Time Correlation Buffer
TOD.	Time of Day
TIDDAC	Time in Deadband Digital Attitude Control
TD.	Time Delay
TDA	Time Delay Amplifier
TIDAR	Time Delay Array RADAR
TDC	Time Delay Closing
TDCN.	Time Delay Compression Network
TDG	Time-Delay Generator
TDO.	Time Delay Opening
TDR	Time Delay Relay
TDSQB	Time-Delay Squib (Navy)
TDS	Time Delay Switch
TOD.	Time of Delivery
TD	Time of Departure
T/D	Time Deposit (Banking)
TD	Time Difference
TDE	Time Displacement Error
TDIS	Time Distance (Military)
TDS	Time, Distance, Speed
TDDL	Time-Division Data Link (Radio)
TDMA	Time Division Multiple Access (Electronics)
TDM	Time-Division Multiplex (Radio)
TDMD.	Time Division Multiplex Device
TDS	Time-Division Switching
TDC	Time Domain Coding
TDCT	Time Domain Coding Technique
TDF	Time Domain Filter
TDR	Time Domain Reflectometry
TDE	Time Duration Error
TEMPO	Time and Effort Measurement through Periodic Observation
TFL	Time to Failure Location
TOF	Time of Filing
TFC	Time of First Call (Navy)
TOF	Time of Flight
TF	Time Frame
TTG	Time to Go (Air Force)
TIG	Time in Grade
TIMIG	Time in Grade (Military)
THI	Time Handed In (Navy)
TI	Time Index
TIMINT	Time Interval (Military)
TICE	Time Integral Cost Effectiveness
TIC	Time Interval Counter
TIM	Time Interval Measurement
TIM	Time Interval Meter
TJF	Time-to-Jitter Flag
TLU	Time of Last Update
TL	Time Lengths
TLI	Time-Life International
TLV	Time Like Vector
TL	Time Limit
TCP	Time-Limited Correlation Processing
TLS	Time Limited Signal
TLA	Time Line Analysis
T/L	Time Loan (Banking)
TMG	Time Mark Generator
TMF	Time Marker Frequency
T & M	Time and Materials
TMU.	Time Measurement Unit (Basic MTM unit)
TMR	Time Meter Reading
TM	Time, Mission
TMA	Time-Modulated Antenna
TM	Time Modulation
TM	Time Monitor
TMCC	Time-Multiplexer Communications Channels
TNA	Time of Nearest Approach
TO.	Time Opening
TORS	Time Order Reporting System
TOPIC	Time Ordered Programmer Integrated Circuit (NASA)
TOO	Time of Origin (Communications)
TPC	Time Polarity Control

TPT	Time Priority Table
TP	Time Pulse
TPD	Time Pulse Distributor
TQC	Time, Quality, Cost
TIR	Time in Range
TRM	Time Ratio Modulation
TOR	Time of Receipt
TOR	Time of Reception (Communications)
TRS	Time Reference System
TRUD	Time Remaining Until Dive (Air Force)
TRUT	Time Remaining Until Transition (Air Force)
TRP.	Time to Repair Part
TR	Time to Retrofire (Aerospace)
TSM	Time Scheduled Maintenance
TSA	Time Series Analysis
TSGS	Time Series Generation System
TS	Time Shack (NAS operations desk)
TSA	Time-Shared Amplifier
TSS	Time-Shared (or Sharing) System (Data processing)
TSK	Time Shift Keying
TSG	Time Signal Generator
TSO	Time Since Overhaul (of engine, or other equipment)
TSP	Time Sorting Program
TSU	Time Standard Unit
TSR	Time Status Register
TSQ	Time and Super Quick
TOT	Time on Tape (Military)
TOT	Time on Target (Artillery support)
TOT	Time over Target (Air support)
TOT	Time on Track
TOT	Time of Transmission (Communications)
TTT.	Time to Turn (Ship or aircraft)
TV	Time Variation of Gain
TVG	Time Variation of Gain
TVSM	Time-Varying Signal Measurement
TWX	Time Wire Transmission
TW	Time Word
TD	Timed Disintegration (Pharmacy)
TSAR	Timed Scanned Array RADAR
TB	Times at Bat (Baseball)
TLS	(The) Times Literary Supplement (London)
TBP	Timing Belt Pulley
TC	Timing Channel
TDIO	Timing and Data Input-Output
TD	Timing Device
TNF	Timing Negative Film
TOC	Timing Operation Center
TP	Timing Point
TPG	Timing Pulse Generator
TPI	Timing Pulse Idler
TRE	Timing Read Error
TRV	Timing Relay Valve
TRP.	Timing Release Pin
TS	Timing Selector
T/T	Timing and Telemetry
TU	Timing Unit
TDX	Timken-Detroit Axle (NYSE symbol)
TKR	Timken Roller Bearing Company (NYSE symbol)
TICA	Timpanogos Cave National Monument
Sn	Tin (Chemical element)
TCT	Tin Can Tourists of the World
TFS	Tin-Free Steel
TP	Tin Plate
TRI.	Tin Research Institute
TO	Tincture of Opium
TC	Tinned Copper
TDCU	Tinned Copper
TCW	Tinned Copper Weld
TS	Tip Speed
TMK	Tiravita Munnerrat Kalam
TISC	Tire Industry Safety Council
TRI.	Tire Retreading Institute
TRA	Tire and Rim Association
TBA	Tires, Batteries & Accessories
TEA	Tiselius Electrophoresis Apparatus
TIS.	Tishman Realty & Construction Company, Inc. (NYSE symbol)
TCA	Tissue Culture Association
TCID	Tissue Culture Infectious Dose
TCM	Tissue Culture Medium
TEIC	Tissue Equivalent Ionization Chamber
Ti	Titanium (Chemical element)

TBW	Titanium Butt Weld
TET	Titanium Elevon Track
TLZ	Titanium-Lead-Zinc
TML	Titanium Metallurgical Laboratory
TMCA	Titanium Metals Corporation of America
TCA	Tithe Commutation Act (British)
TRC	Tithe Rent-Charge
T.	Title (Bibliography)
TAN	Title Analytic (Bibliography)
T/B	Title Block (Technical drawings)
TL	Title List
TP	Title Page (Bibliography)
TPM	Title Page Mutilated
TPW	Title Page Wanting
TSAC	Title, Subtitle, and Caption
TCO	Tjanstemannens Centralorganisation (Central Organization of Salaried Employees) (Sweden)
TAT	To Accompany Troops
TBA	To Be Activated
TBA	To Be Announced
TBD	To Be Determined
TBD	To Be Disbanded
TBI	To Be Inactivated
TBW	To Be Withheld
TF	To Fill
TF	To Follow
TIP	To Insure Promptness
TTL	To Take Leave
TWIMC	To Whom It May Concern
TAUS	Tobacco Association of United States
TGIC	Tobacco Growers' Information Committee
TIRC	Tobacco Industry Research Committee (Later, Council for Tobacco Research, USA)
TI	Tobacco Institute
TMA	Tobacco Merchants Association of United States
TMV.	Tobacco Mosaic Virus (Biochemistry)
TRV	Tobacco Rattle Virus
TRSV	Tobacco Ring Spot Virus
TSAA	Tobacco Salesmen's Association of America
TTC	Tobacco Tax Council
TWIU	Tobacco Workers International Union
TOAD	Tobyhanna Army Depot
TFC	Toccoa Falls College (Georgia)
TEV	Today's English Version (of the Bible)
T.	Toe
X	A Toilet (Slang)
TGA	Toilet Goods Association
TP	Toilet Paper (Slang)
TMA	Toiletry Merchandisers Association
TVK	Toimihenkilo - ja Virkamiesjarjestojen Keskusliitto (Confederation of Intellectual and Government Workers) (Finland)
TAMS	Token and Medal Society
TOK	Toklan Royalty Corporation (NYSE symbol)
TKG.	Tokodynagraph
TKD.	Tokodynamometer
TAIC	Tokyo Atomic Industrial Consortium
TAW.	Toledo, Angola & Western Railway Company (AAR code)
TED	Toledo Edison Company (NYSE symbol)
TPW	Toledo, Peoria & Western R. R. (AAR code)
TP & W	Toledo, Peoria & Western Railroad
TT	Toledo Terminal R. R. (AAR code)
TSA	Tolkien Society of America
TC	Toll Center
TC	Toll Completing
TLR	Toll Line Release
TG	Tollgate (Maps and charts)
TF	Tolstoy Foundation
TDI	Toluene Diisocyanate (Chemical)
TADYL	Tom Dooley Youth League
TGC	Tomato Genetics Cooperative
T.	Tome
TRSL	Toms River Signal Laboratory (Army)
T.	Tomus (Volume)
TEB	Tone Encoded Burst
TGP	Tone Generator Panel
TM.	Tone Modulation
TONLAR	Tone-Operated Net Loss Adjusted Receiving
T & G	Tongue and Groove (Lumber)
TOTO	Tongue of the Ocean (Area of the Bahama Islands) (Navy)
TGB	Tongued, Grooved, and Beaded
T.	Tonnage (Shipping)

T	Ton(s)
TD	Tons per Day
TPD	Tons Per Day
TPH	Tons Per Hour
TPI	Tons Per Inch
TMH	Tons per Man-Hour
TM	Tons per Minute
TR	Tons Registered (Shipping)
T & A	Tonsillectomy and Adenoidectomy (Medicine)
TFO	Tonto Forest Observatory
TONT	Tonto National Monument
TLTP	Too Long to Print (Strip marking) (Aviation)
TNC	Too Numerous to Count
TS	Too Short (Symbol stamped in shoes which are not actually of the size marked)
TEAD	Tooele Army Depot
TOV	Tooele Valley Railway Company (AAR code)
TCT	Tool Change Time
TD	Tool Design
TDI	Tool and Die Institute
TD	Tool Disposition
TISTHR	Tool Inspection Small Tools Historical Record
TO	Tool Order
TRL	Tool Room Lathe
TS	Tool Sharpness
TS	Tool Steel
TS	Tool Storage
TCR	Tooling Change Request
TDC	Tooling Design Change
TOPA	Tooling Pattern
TOSE	Tooling Samples
TOTP	Tooling Template
TWA	Tooling Work Authorization
T	Tooth
TR	Toothed Ring (Technical drawings)
T	Top
TAD	Top Assembly Drawing
T & B	Top and Bottom (Technical drawings)
T & BB	Top and Bottom Bolt (Technical drawings)
TB & S	Top, Bottom, and Sides (Lumber)
TC	Top Center (Valve position)
TC	Top Chord
TC	Top of Column
TDC	Top Dead Center
TEG	Top Edge Gilt (Bibliography)
TEAM	Top European Advertising Media
TKD	Top Kit Drawing
TM	Top Management
TOVC	Top of Overcast (Aviation)
TP	Top Priority
TOPSEC	Top Secret
TS	Top Secret
TSCA	Top Secret Control Agency
TSCC	Top Secret Control Channels (Military)
TSCO	Top Secret Control Officer
TSCP	Top Secret Control Proceeding (Navy)
TSCS	Top Secret Control Section (Navy)
TIM	Topic Indexing Matrix
TD	Topographic Draftsman (Navy)
TE	Topographical Engineer
TOPSI	Topside Sounder, Ionosphere (NASA)
TU	Torah Umesorah-National Society for Hebrew Day Schools
TCC	Toroidal Combustion Chamber
TRC	Toroidal Propellant Container
TSS	Toroidal Space Station
TSS	Toroidal Support Submarine
TADP	Toronto Anti-Draft Programme
TBS	Toronto Baptist Seminary
THB	Toronto, Hamilton & Buffalo Railway Company (AAR code)
TNS	Toronto Normal School
TAT	Torpedo Attack Teacher (Navy)
TB	Torpedo Boat (Navy symbol)
E	Torpedo Boat (German symbol)
TB	Torpedo Bomber (or Bombing)
TBR	Torpedo Bomber Reconnaissance Aircraft (Navy)
VTB	Torpedo-Bombing Plane (Navy symbol)
TCU	Torpedo Control Unit
TORPCM	Torpedo Countermeasures and Deception
TDCO	Torpedo Data Computer Operator (Navy)
TDS	Torpedo Destruction System
TDM	Torpedo Detection Modification (SONAR)

TD	Torpedo Dive Bomber Aircraft
TERI	Torpedo Effective Range Indicator
TEE	Torpedo Experimental Establishment (British)
TF	Torpedo Fighter Aircraft (Navy)
TFCS	Torpedo Fire Control System
TG	Torpedo Group
TLP	Torpedo Landplane (Navy)
VT	Torpedo Plane (Navy symbol)
TR	Torpedo Reconnaissance Aircraft (Navy)
TRB	Torpedo Recovery Boat
TSP	Torpedo Seaplane (Navy)
TSR	Torpedo-Spotter Reconnaissance (Military)
TORPRON	Torpedo Squadron
YTT	Torpedo Testing Barge (Navy symbol)
YFT	Torpedo Transportation Lighter (Navy symbol)
TT	Torpedo Tube(s)
TM	Torpedoman's Mate
TMV	Torpedoman's Mate, Aviation (Navy rating)
TME	Torpedoman's Mate, Electrical (Navy rating)
T	Torque
TASR	Torque Arm Speed Reducer
T/I	Torque/Inertia
TLN	Torque Limiting Nut
TLSD	Torque Limiting Screw Driver
TOP	Torque Oil Pressure (Air Force)
TPSI	Torque Pressure in Pounds per Square Inch (Air Force)
TRSF	Torque-Regulated Speed Follower
TSD	Torque Screwdriver
TSDK	Torque Screwdriver Kit
TSK	Torque Screwdriver Kit
TBC	Torrey Botanical Club
TOR	Torrington Company (NYSE symbol)
THW	Torsion Head Wattmeter
TRI	Torsion Reaction Integrating
TOSBAC	Toshiba Scientific and Business Automatic Computer
TBC	Toss Bomb Computer
TA	Total Aboard (Aviation)
TAH	Total Abdominal Hysterectomy (Medicine)
TANC	Total Absorption Nuclear Cascade
TASC	Total Absorption Shower Cascade
TAP	Total Action Against Poverty (A federal government program)
TAFCSD	Total Active Federal Commissioned Service to Date
TAFMSD	Total Active Federal Military Service to Date
TAMS	Total Active Military Service
TAN	Total Ammonia Nitrogen
TAS-PAC	Total Analysis System for Production, Accounting, and Control (Data processing)
TVC	Total Annual Variable Cost
TASC	Total Avionic Support Capability
TBW	Total Bandwidth
TB	Total Bases
TB	Total Blank (Entertainment slang for poor show town)
TB	Total Bouts (Boxing)
TC	Total Chances
TCE	Total Composite Error
TCT	Total Composite Tolerance
TC	Total Cost
TD	Total Depth
TDE	Total Differential Equation
TDN	Total Digestible Nutrients
TDIP	Total Disability Income Provisions (Military)
TDS	Total Dissolved Solids
TDH	Total Dynamic Head
TEFA	Total Esterified Fatty Acid
TEC	Total Estimated Cost
TEMPO	Total Evaluation of Management and Production Output
TEN	Total Excretory (or Excreted) Nitrogen
TFA	Total Fatty Acids
TFN	Total Fecal Nitrogen
TFCSD	Total Federal Commissioned Service Date
TFF	Total Feedwater Flow
TFR	Total Final Reports (Air Force)
TFC	Total Fixed Cost
TGLC	Total Gate Leakage Current
THD	Total Harmonic Distortion
THD	Total Harmonic Distribution (Music)
THOMIS	Total Hospital and Medical Information System
TI	Total Immersion (Language study)
TIR	Total Indicated Runout
TIR	Total Indicator Reading
TIFS	Total In-Flight Simulation (or Simulator) (Air Force)

TILL	Total Initial Lamp Lumens
TIH	Total Installed Horsepower
TIHP	Total Installed Horsepower
TIMMS	Total Integrated Manpower Management System (Navy)
TIPS	Total Integrated Pneumatic System
TIR	Total Internal Reflecting
TIRP	Total Internal Reflection Prism
TIBC	Total Iron-Binding Capacity
TL	Total Length
TL	Total Load (Engineering)
TLS	Total Logic Solution
TL	Total Loss
TLO	Total Loss Only
TLP	Total Loss of Pay (Court-martial sentence) (Military)
TLC	Total Lung Capacity (Physiology)
TMIS	Total Management Information System
TMA	Total Materiel Assets (Military)
TMO	Total Materiel Objective
TMPO	Total Materiel Procurement Objective
TMR	Total Materiel Requirement (Military)
TMDT	Total Mean Down Time
TMSD	Total Military Service Date
TNV	Total Net Value
TNA	Total Nucleic Acid
TOA	Total Obligational Authority
TOP	Total Obscuring Power (Smoke cloud)
TOE	Total Operating Expense
TOAL	Total Ordnance Alteration Application List (Navy)
TOC	Total Organic Carbon
TPP	Total Package Procurement (Government contracting)
TPPC	Total Package Procurement Concept
TP	Total Parts
TPR	Total Peripheral Resistance
TP	Total Points
TP	Total Pressure
TPS	Total Product Support
TP	Total Protein
TQC	Total Quality Control
TRSD	Total Radiance Spectral Distribution
TRSP	Total Radiance Spectral Polarization
TRSD	Total Rated Service Date (Air Force)
TR	Total Regulation
TRQ	Total Requirement
TRI	Total Response Index (Psychology)
TR	Total Revenue
TRUMP	Total Revision and Upgrading of Marine Corps Programs
TSD	Total Spectral Density
TSC	Total System Control (Architecture)
TTP	Total Taxable Pay
TTPE	Total Taxable Pay Earned
TV	Total Volume
TVU	Total Volume Urine (in 24 hours)
TYSD	Total Years Service Date
TY	Total Yield
TEFC	Totally Enclosed - Fan Cooled
TP	Totally Positive
TRM	Totally Reflective Mirror
TGL	Touch and Go Landing (Aviation)
TD	Touchdown (Football)
TRODI	Touchdown Rate of Descent Indicator
TDV	Touchdown Velocity (Aviation)
TDZ	Touchdown Zone (Aviation)
TDZL	Touchdown Zone Lights (Aviation)
TS	Tough Situation (Bowdlerized version)
TC	Touring Club
THS	Tourist Hospitality Service (British)
TT	Tourist Trophy (Motorcycle racing) (British)
TSVP	Tournez s'il Vous Plait (Please Turn Over; PTO)
TTV	Tow Test Vehicle (Aerospace)
T	Toward (Altitude difference)
TAS	Towed Array SONAR
TASOS	Towed Array SONAR System
TASS	Towed Array SONAR System
TSR	Towed SONAR Response
TUG	Towed Universal Glider
TEC	Tower En Route Control (Aviation)
TECA	Tower En Route Control Area (Aviation)
TJM	Tower Jettison Motor
TLE	Tower Lighting Equipment
TSF	Tower Shielding Facility (AEC)
TSR	Tower Shielding Reactors (ORNL)

TS	Tower Station
TCU	Towering Cumulus (Meteorology)
T	Town
TC	Town Clerk or Town Councillor
TSO	Town Suboffice
T	Township
TOXREP	Toxic Incident Report
TU	Toxic Unit (Medicine)
TA	Toxin-Antitoxin (Medicine)
TAT	Toxin-Antitoxin
TAF	Toxoid-Antitoxin Floccules
TAM	Toxoid-Antitoxin Mixture (Medicine)
TKA	Toy Knights of America
TMUS	Toy Manufacturers of the United States
TOPPER	Toy Press Publishers, Editors, and Reporters
TWA	Toy Wholesalers Association of America
TAT	Trace Acceptance Tester
TCCS	Trace Contaminant Control System
TCA	Trace Contamination Analysis
TRADAD	Trace to Destination and Advise
TED	Trace Element Doping
TRFS	Trace Fuselage Station
TMGRS	Trace Material Generation Rate Simulator
TOU	Trace Operate Unit
T	Trace of Precipitation (Less than 0.005 inch of rain or 0.05 inch of snow)
TCCH	Tracer Control Chassis
TCN	Tracing Change Notice
TAR	Track Address Register
TCA	Track Crossing Angle
TD	Track Data
TDC	Track Data Central
TDS	Track Data Simulator
TDS	Track Data Storage
TD	Track Display
TFAA	Track and Field Athletes of America
TI	Track Identity
TIDY	Track Identity
TRID	Track Identity
TI	Track Imitation
TIP	Track Initiation and Prediction (RADAR)
TI	Track Initiator
TOJ	Track on Jamming
TLRP	Track Last Reference Position
TMG	Track Made Good (Aviation)
TNC	Track Navigation Computer
TNC	Track No Conversion
TN	Track Number
TPOS	Track Position
TPA	Track Production Area (Air Force)
TRPO	Track Reference Printout
TSD	Track Situation Display
TSA	Track Supply Association
TVEL	Track Velocity
TWS	Track-While-Scan (Communications)
TACV	Tracked Air Cushion Vehicle (High-speed ground transportation)
TRAP	Tracker Analysis Program
TAC	Tracking Accuracy Control
TAPRE	Tracking in an Active and Passive RADAR Environment
TALT	Tracking Altitude
TAS	Tracking Antenna System
TC	Tracking Camera
TRACE	Tracking and Communications, Extraterrestrial
TRACOMP	Tracking Comparison
TCC	Tracking and Control Center
TDA	Tracking and Data Acquisition
TDAS	Tracking and Data Acquisition System
TDEP	Tracking Data Editing Program (NASA)
TDH	Tracking Data Handling
TDP	Tracking Data Processor
TADS	Tracking and Display System
TDU	Tracking Display Unit
TERT	Tracking/Erosion Resistance Tester
TEASE	Tracking Errors and Simulation Evaluation (RADAR)
TF	Tracking Filter
TAGIS	Tracking and Ground Instrumentation System
TAGIU	Tracking and Ground Instrumentation Unit (NASA)
TG	Tracking and Guidance
TLTS	Tracking Loop Test Set
TMI	Tracking Merit Interception
TRANET	Tracking (Transit) Network (Navy)
TR	Tracking RADAR

TRAM . . . . . . Tracking RADAR Automatic Monitoring
TRCCC . . . . . . Tracking RADAR Central Control Console (BMEWS)
TRDTO . . . . . Tracking RADAR Data Takeoff
TREC . . . . . . Tracking RADAR Electronic Component
TRC . . . . Tracking, RADAR-Input, and Correlation
TSG . . . . Tracking (or Test) Signal Generator
TTC . . . . Tracking, Telemetry, and Command
TT . . . . Tracking Telescope
TB . . . . Tractor Biplane
TD . . . . Tractor-Drawn
TRACDR . . . . Tractor-Drawn
TM . . . . Tractor Monoplane
TSC . . . . Tractor Supply Company (NYSE symbol)
TA . . . . Trade Agreements Act (of US)
TAA . . . . Trade Agreements Act (of US)
TAC . . . . Trade Agreements Committee (An interagency committee of the
            executive branch of US government)
CT & C . . . . . . Trade and Commerce Committee (US Military Government)
TEA . . . . Trade Expansion Act
TL . . . . Trade-Last
TM . . . . Trade Mission
TOES . . . . . . Trade-Off Evaluation System
TPC . . . . Trade Policy Committee (Advisory to President)
TRA . . . . Trade Relations Association
TRC . . . . Trade Relations Council of the United States
TU . . . . Trade Union
TUC . . . . Trade(s) Union Council
TUCSA . . . . . Trade Union Council of South Africa
TUEL . . . . . . Trade Union Educational League
TULC . . . . . . Trade Union Leadership Council
TUUL . . . . . . Trade Union Unity League
TUIAFW . . . . Trade Unions International of Agricultural and Forestry Workers
UIBWM . . . . . Trade Unions International of Workers of Building, Wood and Building
            Materials Industries
TM . . . . Trademark
TTAB . . . . . . Trademark Trial and Appeal Board (of Patent Office)
TREND . . . . . Tradeoffs for Lifting Reentry Vehicle Evaluation and Nominal Design
TUC . . . . Trades Union Congress (Great Britain)
TUCN . . . . . . Trades Union Congress of Nigeria
TD . . . . Tradesman (Navy rating)
TA . . . . Trading As
T/A . . . . Trading As
TWEA . . . . . . Trading with the Enemy Act
TSIA . . . . Trading Stamp Institute of America
TO . . . . Traditional Orthography (Writing system)
TA . . . . Traffic Agent or Traffic Auditor
TAB . . . . Traffic Audit Bureau
TB . . . . Traffic Bureau
TC . . . . Traffic Collision
TC . . . . Traffic Commissioner or Traffic Consultant
TRACALS . . . . . Traffic Control Approach and Landing System (Aviation electronics)
TCC . . . . Traffic Control Center
TCP . . . . Traffic Control Post
TCR . . . . Traffic Control RADAR
TCS . . . . Traffic Control Station
TCT . . . . Traffic Control Transponder
TDP . . . . Traffic Data Processing
TD . . . . Traffic Director
TEA-ER . . . . . Traffic Executives Association, Eastern Railroads
TG . . . . Traffic Guidance (Aviation)
T . . . . Traffic Headquarters
TI . . . . Traffic Identification
TMO . . . . . . Traffic Management Office(r) (Air Force)
TM . . . . Traffic Manager
TMS . . . . Traffic Measurement System
TO . . . . Traffic Officer
TOPICS . . . . . Traffic Operations Program for Increasing Capacity and Safety
TORC . . . . . . Traffic Overload Reroute Control
TRP . . . . Traffic Regulation Point
TOR . . . . Traffic on Request (Aviation)
TSTP . . . . . . Traffic Safety Training Program
TSP . . . . Traffic Service Position (Telephone)
TSPS . . . . . . Traffic Service Position System
TSD . . . . Traffic Situation (Status) Display
TU . . . . Traffic Unit
TUR . . . . Traffic Usage Recorder
TPS . . . . Trail Pilot Sensor
TCA . . . . Trailer Coach Association
TCA . . . . Trailer Coaches Association of the West
TOFC . . . . . . Trailer on Flatcar (Railroad)
TICWAN . . . . . Trailerable Intracoastal Waterway Aids to Navigation (Boat)

TE . . . . Trailing Edge
TRIM . . . . . . Trails, Roads Interdiction Multisensor (Navy)
TAN . . . . Trainable Adaptive Network
TBP . . . . Trainable Bow Propeller
TMH . . . . . . Trainable Mentally Handicapped
TRBP . . . . . . Trainable Retractable Bow Propeller
TRP . . . . Trainable Retractable Propellers
TOE . . . . Trainborne Operational Equipment
TPR . . . . Trained Personnel Requirements (Air Force)
T . . . . Trainer (Designation for all US military aircraft)
TF . . . . Trainer Fighter
TFE . . . . Trainer Flight Equipment
TPCP . . . . . . Trainer Power Control Panel
TSCN . . . . . . Trainer Specification Change Notice
TAR . . . . Training and Administration of the Reserve
TAMCO . . . . . Training Aid for MOBIDIC Console Operations
TAD . . . . Training Aids Division (Navy)
TAG . . . . Training Aids Guide (Navy)
TAL . . . . Training Aids Library (Navy)
TARL . . . . . . Training Aids Research Laboratory (Air Force)
TAS . . . . Training Aids Section (Navy)
TAX . . . . Training Assessment Exercise
TRAINLANT . . . Training Atlantic Fleet (Navy)
ZKN . . . . Training Balloon (Navy symbol)
TRAINBASEFOR . . Training Base Force, Pacific Fleet (Navy)
TBS . . . . Training and Battle Simulation (SAGE)
TC . . . . Training Center
TRACEN . . . . . Training Center
TCEA . . . . . . Training Center for Experimental Aerodynamics (NATO)
TC . . . . Training Circular (Military)
PHIBTRA . . . . . Training Command Amphibious Forces
PHIBTRAINLANT . . Training Command Amphibious Forces, Atlantic Fleet
PHIBTRALANT . . Training Command Amphibious Forces, US Atlantic Fleet
PHIBSTRAPAC . . Training Command Amphibious Forces, US Pacific Fleet
PHIBTRAINPAC . . Training Command Amphibious Forces, US Pacific Fleet
PHIBTRAPAC . . Training Command Amphibious Forces, US Pacific Fleet
TRACOMDLANT . . Training Command, Atlantic Fleet (Navy)
TRACOMDPAC . . Training Command, Pacific Fleet (Navy)
TRACOMDSUBPAC . . Training Command, Submarines, Pacific Fleet (Navy)
TRACOMDWESTCOAST . . Training Command, West Coast (Navy)
TD . . . . Training Detachment
TRADET . . . . . Training Detachment (Navy)
TDO . . . . Training Development Officer (British)
TDC . . . . Training Device Center
T & DC . . . . . . Training and Distribution Center (Navy)
TADC . . . . . . Training and Distribution Center (Navy)
TD . . . . Training of Documentalists
TDS . . . . (Annual) Training Duty Status (Navy Reserve)
TED . . . . Training Equipment Development
TEL . . . . Training Equipment List
TEPI . . . . Training Equipment Planning Information (Military)
TEC . . . . Training Evaluation and Control
TRAEX . . . . . . Training and Experience (Military)
TF . . . . Training Film (Military)
VLN . . . . Training Glider (Navy symbol)
TWI . . . . Training with Industry
TI . . . . Training Instructor
T/L . . . . Training Literature
TNGLIT . . . . . Training Literature
TM . . . . Training Manual (Military)
TM . . . . Training Missions (Air Force)
TP . . . . Training Period (Military)
VN . . . . Training Plane (Navy symbol)
VSN(M) . . . . . Training Plane, 2-engine (Navy symbol)
TRIGA . . . . . . Training Reactor, Isotopes General Atomic
TRIM . . . . . . Training Records and Information Management System
TR . . . . Training Regulations (Military)
TRIM . . . . . . Training Relation and Instruction Mission (Military) (Vietnam, France,
            United States)
TRIGA . . . . . . Training, Research, Isotope, Production, General Atomic (AEC)
TRAPP . . . . . . Training and Retention as Permanent Party (Army)
TS . . . . Training Ship
TSED . . . . . . Training Simulators Engineering Department
TSA . . . . Training Situation Analysis (Navy)
TRAINRON . . . Training Squadron (Later, SERRON) (Navy)
TRASTA . . . . . Training Station (Navy)
TTF . . . . Training Task Force
TT & P . . . . . . Training, Transient and Patient
TTSFP . . . . . . Training Transition School (Squadron), Pacific Fleet (Navy)
TU . . . . Training Unit (Army)
TM . . . . Trainmaster (Railroading)

TJC . . . . Trajectory Chart	TNT . . . . Transient Nuclear Test (AEC)
TD . . . . Trajectory Diagram (Army)	TPRV . . . . . . Transient Peak Reverse Voltage
TJD . . . . Trajectory Diagram	TRE . . . . Transient Radiation Effect
TOLIP . . . . . . Trajectory Optimization and Linearized Pitch (Computer program)	TREAT . . . . . . Transient Radiation Effects Automated Tabulation
TPS . . . . Tramp Power Supply	TREES . . . . . . Transient Radiation Effects on Electronic Systems (Air Force)
TRA . . . . Trane Company (The) (NYSE symbol)	TREE . . . . Transient Radiation Effects on Electronics
TB . . . . Tranquility Base (Moon landing site)	TRADER . . . . . Transient Radiation Effects Recorder
TC . . . . Transaction Code (Military)	TREAT . . . . . . Transient Reactor Test Facility (AEC)
TIN . . . . Transaction Identification Number	TOSSA . . . . . . Transient or Steady-State Analysis (Data processing)
TL . . . . Transaction Listing	TINS . . . . Trans-Inertial Navigation System
TBO . . . . Transactions by Others	TIA . . . . Trans-International Airlines
TFO . . . . Transactions for Others	TRIN . . . . Trans-International Airlines, Incorporated
TAPS . . . . . . Trans-Alaska Pipeline System	TARE . . . . . . Transistor Analysis Recording Equipment
TAL . . . . Transalpine (Pipeline) (Western Europe)	TCD . . . . Transistor Chopper Driver
TAAN . . . . . . Trans-America Advertising Agency Network	TACT . . . . . . Transistor and Component Tester
TA . . . . Transamerica Corporation (NYSE symbol)	TCL . . . . Transistor Contact Land
TEST . . . . Transamerica Electronic Scoring Technique (Credit risk evaluation)	TCL . . . . Transistor Coupled Logic
TTT . . . . Transamerican Trailer Transport	TRADIC . . . . . Transistor-Digital Computer (Air Force)
TASSO . . . . . . Transatlantic Air Safety Service Organization	TDCM . . . . . . Transistor Driver Core Memory
TBPA . . . . . . Transatlantic Brides and Parents Association	TET . . . . Transistor Evaluation Test
TAPSC . . . . . . Trans-Atlantic Passenger Steamship Conference	TFA . . . . Transistor Feedback Amplifier
TAT . . . . Transatlantic Telephone (Cable)	TIM . . . . Transistor Information Microfile
TAA . . . . Trans-Australia Airlines	TMK . . . . Transistor Mounting Kit
TCA . . . . Trans-Canada Airlines	TMP . . . . Transistor Mounting Pad
TC . . . . Transceiver Code (Navy)	TOVD . . . . . . Transistor-Operated Voltage Divider
TCBM . . . . . . Transcontinental Ballistic Missile (Air Force)	TPC . . . . Transistor Photo Control
TCC . . . . Transcontinental Corps (Amateur radio)	TQP . . . . Transistor Qualification Program
TCFB . . . . . . Trans-Continental Freight Bureau	TQT . . . . Transistor Qualification Test
TCRPA . . . . . Trans-Continental Railroad Passenger Association	TQTP . . . . . . Transistor Qualification Test Program
TWEB . . . . . . Transcribed Weather Broadcast	TRACE . . . . . . Transistor Radio Automatic Circuit Evaluator
TAA . . . . Transcript of Absentee's Account	TRL . . . . Transistor Resistor Logic
T . . . . Transcription	TSR . . . . Transistor Saturable Reactor
TCS . . . . Transducer Calibration System	TSS . . . . Transistor Servo Simulator
TEU . . . . Transducer Excitation Unit	TTL . . . . Transistor-Transistor Logic
TIC . . . . Transducer Information Center	TRANSAC . . . . Transistorized Automatic Computer
TPP . . . . Transducer Power Programmer	TAC . . . . TRANSAC (Transistorized Automatic Computer) Assembler Compiler
TEC . . . . Transearth Coast (Aerospace)	TUG . . . . TRANSAC (Transistorized Automatic Computer) Users Group
TEI . . . . Transearth Injection (Aerospace)	TAC . . . . Transistorized Automatic Control
TE . . . . Transequatorial (Scatter)	TC . . . . Transistorized Carrier
TEEM . . . . . . Trans-Europ-Express-Marchandises (European express freight train service)	TDR . . . . Transistorized Digital Readout
TEE . . . . Trans-Europe Express (Continental high-speed train)	TFC . . . . Transistorized Frequency Converter
T/A . . . . Transfer of Accountability	THOR . . . . . . Transistorized High-Speed Operations Recorder
TCH . . . . Transfer in Channel	TIO . . . . Transistorized Image Orthicon
TOC . . . . Transfer of Control	TIPS . . . . Transistorized Inverter Power Supply
TOCC . . . . . . Transfer of Control Card	TPL . . . . Transistorized Portable Laboratory
TCR . . . . Transfer Control Register	TRICE . . . . . . Transistorized Realtime Incremental Computer
TED . . . . Transfer Effective Date (Military)	TRVM . . . . . . Transistorized Voltmeter
TEI . . . . Transfer on Error Indication	T . . . . Transit
TF . . . . Transfer Factor	TAA . . . . Transit-Advertising Association
T/F . . . . Transfer of Function (Military)	TA . . . . Transit Authority
TFA . . . . Transfer Function Analyzer	TRIPOLD . . . . . Transit Injected Polaris Derived
TFC . . . . Transfer Function Computer	TNR . . . . Transit Nuclear Radiation
TFC . . . . Transfer Function, Cumulative	TNRE . . . . . . Transit Nuclear Radiation Effect
TFH . . . . Transfer Function Hazard	TRAAC . . . . . Transit Research and Attitude Control (Navy satellite)
TFR . . . . Transfer Function Response	TS . . . . Transit Storage
THERMA . . . . . Transfer of Heat Reduced Magnetically	TT . . . . Transit Time (of blood through heart and lungs)
TLZ . . . . Transfer on Less Than Zero	TRWOV . . . . . Transit without Visa
TOMSI . . . . . . Transfer of Master Scheduled Item	T . . . . Transition or Transitional
TN . . . . Transfer on Negative	TTSP . . . . Transition Training Squadron, Pacific (Navy)
TNF . . . . Transfer on No Overflow	TTSA . . . . . . Transitional Training Squadron, Atlantic (Navy)
TNZ . . . . Transfer on Nonzero	TYP . . . . Transitional Year Program (Brandeis University)
TPA . . . . Transfer of Pay Account (Military)	T . . . . Transitive
TP . . . . Transfer on Positive	TRN . . . . Transitron Electronic Corporation (NYSE symbol)
TR . . . . Transfer Reset	T . . . . Translation
TRNA . . . . . . Transfer Ribonucleic Acid	TDT . . . . Translation and Docking Trainer
TS . . . . Transfer Set	TIP . . . . Translation Inhibitory Protein
TSW . . . . Transfer Switch	TR-I . . . . Translations Register - Index
TV . . . . Transfer Voucher	TAC . . . . Translator, Assembler, Compiler
TAP . . . . Transferrable Assets Program	TBS . . . . Translator Bail Switch
T . . . . Transferred (Navy)	TOM . . . . Translator Octal Mnemonic
TRIP . . . . . . Transformation-Induced Plasticity (Steel)	TLC . . . . Translunar Coast (Aerospace)
TR . . . . Transformation Ratio	TLI . . . . Translunar Injection (Aerospace)
T . . . . Transformer	TLX . . . . Trans-Lux Corporation (NYSE symbol)
TAC . . . . Transformer Analog Computer	TMI . . . . Trans-Mars Injection (Aerospace)
TASAS . . . . . Transformer Analogue Servo Analyzer cum Synthesizer	TGE . . . . Transmissible Gastro-Enteritis
TR . . . . Transformer-Rectifier	TCU . . . . Transmission Control Unit
TP . . . . Transforming Principle (Bacteriology)	TC . . . . Transmission Controller
TAQ . . . . Transient Airman Quarters (Air Force)	TDMS . . . . . . Transmission Distortion Measuring Set
TAG . . . . Transient Analysis Generator	T & D . . . . . . Transmission and Distribution
TRANC . . . . . Transient Center (Marine Corps)	TIES . . . . Transmission and Information Exchange System
TFL . . . . Transient Fault Locator	TIGR . . . . Transmission Integrated Rotor

XIC . . . . Transmission Interface Converter
TL . . . . Transmission Line (or Level)
TLA . . . . Transmission Line Assembly (or Adapter)
TPM . . . . Transmission and Processing Model
TSEM . . . . Transmission Secondary Emission Multiplier
TRANSEC . . . . Transmission Security (Communications)
TSAR . . . . . . Transmission Security Analysis Report
TS . . . . Transmission Set
TSTA . . . . . . Transmission, Signaling and Test Access
TU . . . . Transmission Unit
TELSCAR . . . . Transmit Electronically Location Shippers' Car Advice Reports
TFG . . . . Transmit Format Generator
TR . . . . Transmit(ter)-Receive(r)
TRU . . . . Transmit-Receive Unit
TEO . . . . . . Transmittal Engineering Order
TS . . . . Transmittal Sheet (Military)
TX . . . . Transmitter (General term)
XMTR . . . . Transmitter
TD . . . . Transmitter Distributor
TF . . . . Transmitter Frequency
TFM . . . . Transmitter Frequency Multiplier
TPR . . . . Transmitter Power Rating
TXRX . . . . . . Transmitter-Receiver
TS . . . . Transmitter Station
TTO . . . . Transmitter Turn-Off
T . . . . Transmitting
TSW . . . . Transmitting Slide Wire
TNC . . . . . . Trans-National Communications, Inc.
TAL . . . . Transocean Air Lines
TAC . . . . Transonic Aerodynamic Characteristics
TAN . . . . . . Transonic Aerodynamic Nozzle
TMT . . . . Transonic Model Tunnel
TRANSPAC . . . Trans-Pacific
TPA . . . . Trans-Pacific Airlines, Ltd.
TPPC . . . . . . Trans-Pacific Passenger Conference
TSS . . . . Transparent Semiconductor Shutter
TPP . . . . Trans-Pluto Probe
TCG . . . . Transponder Control Group
TINOP . . . . . . Transponder Inoperative (Aviation)
TIPE . . . . . . Transponder, Interrogator, Pinger and Echo Sounder
TIP . . . . Transponder Interrogator Processor
TMDI . . . . . . Transponder Miss Distance Indicator
TROO . . . . . . Transponder On-Off
TRI . . . . Transponder Receiver Isolation
AP . . . . Transport (Navy ship symbol)
APH . . . . Transport (Fitted to evacuate wounded) (Navy)
PS . . . . Transport (Russian aircraft symbol)
R . . . . Transport (Naval aircraft designation)
TAG . . . . Transport Air Group (Joint Army, Navy, and Marine Corps)
APV . . . . Transport and Aircraft Ferry (Navy symbol)
TAWU . . . . . Transport and Allied Workers' Union (Rhodesia and Nyasaland)
TALS . . . . . . Transport Approach and Landing Simulator
TCC . . . . Transport Control Center (Air Force)
TRANSDIV . . . Transport Division (Navy)
TDWU . . . . . Transport and Dock Workers' Union (India)
TE . . . . Transport Empty
TE . . . . Transport Erector (Air Force)
VR(HL) . . . . . Transport, 4-engine, Landplane (Navy symbol)
VR(HS) . . . . . Transport, 4-engine, Seaplane (Navy symbol)
TGPWU . . . . . Transport, General and Port Workers' Union (Aden)
VLR . . . . Transport Glider (Navy symbol)
TRANSGRPSOPAC . Transport Group, South Pacific Force (Navy)
TRLP . . . . Transport Landplane (Navy)
TL . . . . Transport Loaded
TM . . . . Transport Mechanism (Physiology)
TMC . . . . Transport Movement Control (Military)
TP . . . . Transport Pilot
G . . . . Transport Plane (Navy symbol)
VR . . . . Transport Plane (Multiengine) (Navy symbol)
TQM . . . . . . Transport Quartermaster
TRDC . . . . . . Transport Research and Development Command (Army)
TRSP . . . . . . Transport Seaplane (Navy)
TRANSRON . . . Transport Squadron (Navy)
VR . . . . Transport Squadron (Navy symbol)
AP(SS) . . . . . Transport Submarine (Navy symbol)
ASSP . . . . . . Transport Submarine (Navy symbol)
TS . . . . Transport and Supply
VR(ML) . . . . . Transport, 2-engine, Landplane (Navy symbol)
VR(MS) . . . . . Transport, 2-engine, Seaplane (Navy symbol)
TV . . . . Transport Vehicle
TWU . . . . Transport Workers' Union (British)

TWU . . . . Transport Workers' Union of America
TRACE . . . . . . Transportable Automated Control Environment
TCL . . . . Transportable Calibration Laboratory
TSC . . . . Transportable Communication System
TRANSCOM . . Transportable Communications
TCS . . . . Transportable Communications System
TGCS . . . . . . Transportable Ground Communications Station
TLT . . . . Transportable Link Terminal (AMC)
TMRBM . . . . Transportable Medium-Range Ballistic Missile
TRU . . . . Transportable Radio Unit (Military)
TRS . . . . Transportable Relay Station
TSCT . . . . . . Transportable Satellite Communication Terminal
TSCLT . . . . . . Transportable Satellite Communications Link Terminal
TRAVEL . . . . . Transportable Vertical Erectable Launcher
TARGET . . . . . Transportation Accident Research Graduate Education and Training
TAC . . . . Transportation Account Code
TRAC . . . . . . Transportation Account Code
TATSA . . . . . . Transportation Aircraft Test and Support Activity (Military)
TAAM . . . . . . Transportation Army Aviation Maintenance
TAA . . . . Transportation Association of America
TCPI . . . . Transportation Club of the Petroleum Industry
TCU . . . . Transportation-Communication Employees Union
TCS . . . . Transportation and Communications Service (of GSA)
TCU . . . . Transportation, Communications, and Utilities
TCO . . . . Transportation Company (Army)
TCC . . . . Transportation Control Card
TCC . . . . Transportation Control Committee (Navy)
TCMD . . . . . . Transportation Control and Movement Document
TCN . . . . Transportation Control Number (Air Force)
TCO . . . . Transportation Control Office(r) (Air Force)
TC . . . . Transportation Corps
TCR . . . . Transportation Corps Release
TRADCOM . . . . Transportation Corps Research and Development Command (Army)
TCSMC . . . . . . Transportation Corps Supply Maintenance Command (Army)
TCTC . . . . . . Transportation Corps Technical Committee
TDC . . . . Transportation Development Center (Cambridge, Massachusetts) (Department of Transportation) (Formerly, NASA Electronic Research Center)
TEMARS . . . . . Transportation Environmental Measurement and Recording System
TRANSGRPPHIBFOR . . Transportation Group Amphibious Forces (Navy)
TIRB . . . . Transportation Insurance Rating Bureau
TALUS . . . . . . Transportation and Land Use Study
TMC . . . . Transportation Materiel Command (AMC - Mobility)
TMP . . . . Transportation Motor Pool (Military)
TMT . . . . Transportation Motor Transport (Military)
TMO . . . . Transportation Movements Office(r)
TOT . . . . Transportation Office will Furnish the Necessary Transportation (Military)
TO . . . . Transportation Officer
TRO . . . . Transportation Officer
TP . . . . Transportation Priority
TPUS . . . . Transportation and Public Utilities Service (Later, part of Transportation and Communication Service, GSA)
T & RNP . . . . Transportation and Recruiting Naval Personnel (Budget appropriation title)
TR . . . . Transportation (or Travel) Request (Military)
T/R . . . . Transportation Request (Military)
TCREC . . . . . . Transportation Research Command (Army)
TRC . . . . Transportation Research Command
TRECOM . . . . . Transportation Research Command (AMC - Mobility)
TRF . . . . Transportation Research Foundation
TSA . . . . Transportation Service, Army
TSB . . . . Transportation Services Branch (Air Force)
TSA . . . . Transportation Standardization Agency (DOD)
TSMC . . . . . . Transportation Supply Maintenance Command
TSO . . . . Transportation Supply Officer
TEL . . . . Transporter-Erector-Launcher (Air Force)
TAP . . . . Transportes Aereos Portugueses, SARL
TAN . . . . Transportes Aereos Nacionales, SA (Tan Airlines)
TAI . . . . Transports Aeriens Intercontinentaux (Privately owned French airline)
TRANSPHIBLANT . . Transports, Amphibious Force, Atlantic Fleet (Navy)
TRANSPHIBPAC . . Transports, Amphibious Force, Pacific Fleet (Navy)
TRANSLANT . . . Transports, Atlantic Fleet (Navy)
TSP . . . . Transshipment Point
TSR . . . . Trans-Siberian Railway
TT . . . . Trans-Texas Airways
TTA . . . . Trans-Texas Airways
TRU . . . . Transuranium Processing Plant (AEC)
TRL . . . . Transuranium Research Laboratory (AEC)
TUR . . . . Transurethral Resection (of prostrate gland)
TUBE . . . . . . Trans-Urban Bicentennial Exposition
TAS . . . . Transverse Air Spring
TE . . . . Transverse Electric

TEW . . . . Transverse Electric Wave
TEM . . . . . . Transverse Electromagnetic (Wave) (Radio)
TEJ . . . . Transverse Expansion Joint (Technical drawings)
TFS . . . . Transverse Feed System
TFA . . . . Transverse Film Attenuator
TFF . . . . Transverse Flow Fan
TM . . . . Transverse Magnetic
TMW . . . . Transverse Magnetic Wave
TPV . . . . Transverse Pallial Vein
TS . . . . Transverse Section
TSF . . . . Transverse Shear Force
TVL . . . . Transverse Vertical Longitudinal
TWP . . . . Transwestern Pipeline Company (NYSE symbol)
TW . . . . Trans-World Airlines, Inc.
TWA . . . . Trans-World Airlines, Inc. (NYSE symbol)
TWF . . . . Trans-World Financial Company (NYSE symbol)
TWR . . . . Trans-World Radio
TRAPATT . . . . . Trapped Plasma Avalanche Triggered Transit (Bell Laboratories)
TRB . . . . Trapped Radiation Belt
TRD . . . . Trapped Radiation Detector
TP . . . . Travaux Publics (France)
TVLADVP . . . . Travel Advance Payment (TDY)
TAGA . . . . . . Travel Agents Guild of America
TA . . . . Travel Allowance
TVLALWADV . . Travel Allowance Advance (in PCS)
TAOS . . . . . . Travel Allowance on Separation (Military)
TVLALWS . . . Travel Allowance on Separation
TCI . . . . Travel Consultants, Incorporated
TDN . . . . Travel is Directed as Necessary in Military Service
T & E . . . . . . Travel and Entertainment (Internal Revenue)
TBGAA . . . . . . Travel By Government Automobile Authorized
TAGEX . . . . . Travel at Government Expense (Aviation)
TMI . . . . Travel Managers International
TBMAA . . . . . . Travel By Military Aircraft Authorized
TO . . . . Travel Order
TPA . . . . Travel by Personal Auto (or Travel by Privately Owned Conveyance Authorized) (Military)
TPC . . . . Travel by Privately Owned Conveyance Permitted for Convenience (Military)
TRA . . . . Travel Research Association
TTA . . . . Travel Time Authorized
T/T . . . . Travel/Tourism
TTO . . . . Travel and Transportation Order
TWT . . . . Travel With Troops
TW/OT . . . . . Travel Without Troops
TTG . . . . Travel with Troops Going
TTR . . . . Travel with Troops Returning
TPNEG . . . . . Travel Will Be Performed at No Expense to the Government (Military)
TETA . . . . . . Travelers Emergency Transportation Association (Sought to pool transportation of salesmen traveling similar routes) (World War II)
THI . . . . Travelers Health Institute
TPAA . . . . . . Travelers Protective Association of America
THSA . . . . . . Traveling Hat Salesmen's Association
TID . . . . Traveling Ionospheric Disturbance
TPO . . . . Traveling Post Office
TSR . . . . Traveling Stock Reserve
TW . . . . Traveling Wave
TWA . . . . Traveling-Wave Amplifier
TWM . . . . Traveling Wave MASER
TWT . . . . Traveling-Wave Tube (Radio)
TC . . . . Tre Corde (With three strings, or release the soft pedal) (Music)
T . . . . Tread (Stair details) (Technical drawings)
TI . . . . Treasure Island (San Francisco Bay) (Navy base)
TINSY . . . . . Treasure Island Naval Shipyard
TTC . . . . Treasure Trove Club
TUS . . . . Treasurer of the United States
TDS . . . . (US) Treasury Daily Statement
TD . . . . Treasury Decision
TD . . . . Treasury Department (in References to Rulings)
TD . . . . Treasury Division
TGF . . . . Treasury Guard Force
THPFB . . . . . . Treated Hard-Pressed Fiberboard (Technical drawings)
TIAS . . . . . . Treaties and Other International Acts Series (State Department)
TWGC . . . . . . Treatment of War Gas Casualties
TP . . . . Treaty Port
TRS . . . . Tree-Ring Society
TT . . . . Tree Tops
TJB . . . . Trench Junction Box
TM . . . . Trench Mortar
TPT . . . . Trenton-Princeton Traction Company (AAR code)
TP . . . . Treponema Pallidum

TPCF . . . . . . Treponema Pallidum Complement Fixation (Test)
TPI . . . . Treponema Pallidum Immobilizing (Test)
TPIA . . . . . . Treponema Pallidum-Immune Adherence (Test)
TNC . . . . Trevecca Nazarene College (Tennessee)
TB . . . . Trial Balance (Bookkeeping)
TB . . . . Trial Balloon
TC . . . . Trial Counsel
TE . . . . Trial (and) Error
TJA . . . . Trial Judge Advocate (Army)
TR . . . . Trial Report
TSP . . . . Trial Shot Point
TAC . . . . Triallylcyanurate
T . . . . Triangle
TGL . . . . Triangular Guide Line
TLR . . . . Triangulation-Listening-Ranging (SONAR)
TRA . . . . Triaxial Recording Accelerometer
TILRA . . . . . . Tribal Indian Land Rights Association
TBP . . . . Tributyl Phosphate (Chemical)
TBTO . . . . . . Tri-Butyl Tin Oxide
TCA . . . . Tricarboxylic Acid (Cycle) (Biochemistry)
TJ . . . . Triceps Jerk
TCESOM . . . . Trichlorethylene-Extracted-Soybean-Oil Meal
TF . . . . Trichlorethylene Finishing
TCA . . . . Trichloroacetate (Biochemistry)
TCA . . . . Trichloroacetic Acid
TCP . . . . Trichlorophenoxyacetic Acid (Weed killer)
TV . . . . Trichomonas Vaginalis
TY . . . . Tri-Continental Corporation (NYSE symbol)
TIA . . . . Tricot Institute of America
TCP . . . . Tricresyl Phosphate
TI . . . . Tricuspid Insufficiency (Medicine)
TCAP . . . . . . Tricyano-Amino-Propene
TC . . . . Tricycle Club (British)
TRCA . . . . . . Tricycle Racing Club of America
TRIDOP . . . . . Tri-Doppler
TRUST . . . . . Trieste United States Troops
TEA . . . . Triethyl-Aluminum
TEAE . . . . . . Triethylaminoethyl
TEB . . . . Triethylborane
TEM . . . . Triethylenemelamine (Textile finishing agent)
TEPA . . . . . . Triethylenephosphoramide (Biochemistry)
TTHA . . . . . . Triethylenetetraminehexaacetic Acid (Chemical)
TFM . . . . Trifluoromethylnitrophenol
TT . . . . Trigesimo-Secundo (Book from 10 to 12 1/2 centimeters in height) (Bibliography)
TDU . . . . Trigger Delay Unit
TGFA . . . . . . Triglyceride Fatty Acid (Biochemistry)
TGFB . . . . . . Triglycine Fluoberyllate
TGS . . . . Triglycine Sulfate
TFC . . . . Trigonometric Function Computer
TIBA . . . . . . Triiodobenzoic Acid
TRIAC . . . . . Tri-Iodothyroacetic Acid (Endocrinology)
TITH . . . . . . Tri-iodothyronine
TRIT . . . . . . Tri-Iodothyronine (Endocrinology)
T . . . . Trillo (Music)
TNT . . . . Trim, Neat and Terrific (Slang)
TPI . . . . Trim Position Indicator
TPA . . . . Trim Power Assembly
TRSH . . . . . . Trim Shell
TMB . . . . Tri-Methoxy-Boroxine
TMA . . . . Trimethyl Aluminum
TMAO . . . . . . Trimethylamine Oxide
TCAP . . . . . . Trimethyl-Cetyl-Ammonium Pentachlorphenate
TMS . . . . Trimethylsilyl (Reagents) (Chemistry)
TSJC . . . . . . Trinidad State Junior College (Colorado)
T & TEC . . . . Trinidad & Tobago Electricity Commission
T . . . . Trinitas (The Trinity)
TNA . . . . Trinitroaniline
TNB . . . . Trinitrobenzene (Explosive)
TNC . . . . Trinitro-Cellulose
TNP . . . . Trinitro-Phenol
TNT . . . . Trinitrotoluene (Explosive)
TNT . . . . Trinitrotoluol
TNX . . . . Trinitroxylene
TCD . . . . Trinity College, Dublin
TCL . . . . Trinity College, London
TT . . . . Trinity Term
TOPO . . . . . . Tri-n-Octylphosphineoxide
T . . . . Triode
TA . . . . Trip Authorization
TC . . . . Trip Coil

TR . . . . Trip Report
TEC . . . . Tripartite Engineering Committee (Allied German Occupation Forces)
TNC . . . . Tripartite Naval Commission (Allied German Occupation Forces)
TNCC . . . . . . Tripartite Nuclear Cross-Sections Committee (British, Canadian, and U.S.)
TTC . . . . Triphenyltetrazolium Chloride
TPN . . . . Triphosphopyridine Nucleotide (Biochemistry)
TPNH . . . . . Triphosphopyridine Nucleotide, Reduced Form (Biochemistry)
TPM . . . . Tri-Plate Module
T . . . . Triple
TER . . . . Triple Ejector Rack
TL . . . . Triple Lindy (Dance step)
TMR . . . . Triple Modular Redundancy (Aerospace data processing)
TMC . . . . Triple Molecular Collision
TP . . . . Triple Pole
TPDT . . . . . . Triple-Pole, Double-Throw
TPST . . . . . . Triple-Pole, Single-Throw
TSD . . . . Triple-Sequence Diffusion
TS . . . . Triple Strength
TSI . . . . Triple Sugar Iron (Chemical)
3T . . . . Triple Throw
TMHL . . . . . . Triplet Metastable Helium Level
TA . . . . Triplex Annealed
TAGC . . . . . . Tripped Automatic Gain Control
TSP . . . . Tri-Service Program (Military)
THAM . . . . . Tris-Hydroxy Methyl Aminomethane
TSP . . . . Trisodium Phosphate (Chemical)
H³ . . . . Tritium
T . . . . Tritium
TR . . . . Tritium Ratio (Measure of tritium activity) (AEC)
TU . . . . Tritium Unit (AEC)
TRC . . . . Trona Railway Company (AAR code)
TB . . . . Troop Basis
APP . . . . Troop Barge, Class A (Navy symbol)
APT . . . . Troop Barge, Class B (Navy symbol)
TC . . . . Troop Carrier (Air Force)
TCC . . . . Troop Carrier Command (World War II)
TCF . . . . Troop Carrier Forces
TCV . . . . Troop Carrying Vehicle
TET . . . . Troop Evaluation Tests (Army)
TI . . . . Troop Information
TID . . . . Troop Information Division
TI & E . . . . . Troop Information and Education
TIED . . . . . . Troop Information and Education Division
TIO . . . . Troop Information Officer
TIP . . . . Troop Information Program
TMAO . . . . . . Troop Movement Assignment Order
TPSN . . . . . . Troop Program Sequence Number
TT . . . . Troop Test
TUCR . . . . . . Troop Unit Change Request
HWQ . . . . . . Tropic High Water Inequality
TCHHW . . . . . Tropic Higher High Water
TCHHWI . . . . Tropic Higher High Water Interval
TCHLW . . . . . Tropic Higher Low Water
TCLHW . . . . . Tropic Lower High Water
TCLLW . . . . . Tropic Lower Low Water
TCLLWI . . . . . Tropic Lower Low Water Interval
TTC . . . . Tropic Test Center (Army)
T . . . . Tropical (Load line mark)
TABL . . . . . . Tropical Atlantic Biological Laboratory
TC . . . . Tropical Continental (American air mass)
TDAC . . . . . . Tropical Deterioration Administrative Committee (of NDRC) (World War II)
TF . . . . Tropical Fresh Water (Vessel load line mark)
TFW . . . . Tropical Fresh Water
TG . . . . Tropical Gulf (American air mass)
TM . . . . Tropical Medicine
TROMEX . . . . . Tropical Meteorological Experiment
TP . . . . Tropical Pacific (American air mass)
TRML . . . . . . Tropical Research Medical Laboratory (Army)
TSW . . . . Tropical Summer Winter (Vessel load line mark)
TCL . . . . Troposcatter Communications Link
TCS . . . . Troposcatter Communications System
TSS . . . . Tropospheric Scatter System
T . . . . Trotter
THM . . . . Trotting Horse Museum
TDM . . . . Trouble Detection and Monitoring
TFR . . . . Trouble and Failure Report
TR . . . . Trouble Report
TSL . . . . Trouble Shooting Loop
TBD . . . . Troubleshooting Block Diagram
TIA . . . . Trouser Institute of America (Absorbed by NOSA)
TU . . . . Trout, Unlimited (An organization)

T . . . . Troy (A system of weights for precious metals)
T . . . . Truce
TBEA . . . . . . Truck Body and Equipment Association
TRKDR . . . . . . Truck-Drawn
CTD (I) . . . . . . Truck Drivers, Chauffeurs and Helpers Union of Chicago and Vicinity
TRKHD . . . . . . Truck Head
THECC . . . . . . Truck and Heavy Equipment Claims Council
TMMB . . . . . . Truck Mixer Manufacturers Bureau
TAR . . . . Truck and Rail
TARVAN . . . . . Truck and Rail Van
TRO . . . . Truck Route Order (Army)
TSEI . . . . Truck Safety Equipment Institute
TTMA . . . . . . Truck Trailer Manufacturers Association
TEI . . . . Trucking Employers, Incorporated
TL . . . . Truckload
T . . . . True (Direction)
TAS . . . . True Air Speed
TAT . . . . True Air Temperature
TA . . . . True Altitude (Height) (Navigation)
TB . . . . True Bearing (Navigation)
TBP . . . . True Boiling Point
TCT . . . . True Centerline Tested
TC . . . . True Course
TDTG . . . . . . True Date-Time Group
TD . . . . True Depth (Diamond drilling)
TGT . . . . True Ground Track
TH . . . . True Heading
TIF . . . . True Involute Form
TM . . . . True Mean
TMV . . . . True Mean Value
TN . . . . True North
TP . . . . True Position
TP . . . . True Profile (Technical drawings)
TRE . . . . True Radiation Emittance
TRIPLTEE . . . . True Temperature Tunnel (Acronym pronounced, "Triple T")
TVP . . . . True Vapor Pressure
TVD . . . . True Vertical Depth (Diamonds)
TZD . . . . True Zenith Distance (Navigation)
TBC . . . . Trunk Block Connector
TCI . . . . Trunk Cut-In
TCO . . . . Trunk Cut-Off
TLCPC . . . . . Trunk Line-Central Passenger Committee
TPI . . . . Truss Plate Institute
TD . . . . Trust Deed
TEUN . . . . . . Trust for Education on the United Nations
TF . . . . Trust Fund
T/R . . . . Trust Receipt (Banking)
TERPACIS . . . . Trust Territory of the Pacific Islands
TFC . . . . Trustees for Conservation
TFDRL . . . . . . Trustees of the Franklin Delano Roosevelt Library
TC . . . . Trusteeship Council
TC(UN) . . . . . Trusteeship Council of the United Nations
TACT . . . . . . Truth About Civil Turmoil
TRW . . . . TRW, Inc. (Formerly, Thompson Ramo Wooldridge, Inc.) (NYSE symbol)
TPG . . . . Trypticase, Peptone, Glucose
TSA . . . . Trypticase Soy Agar
TGE . . . . Tryptone Glucose Extract (Milk agar)
TPB . . . . Tryptone Phosphate Broth
TPO . . . . Tryptophan Peroxidase (Biochemistry)
TP . . . . Tryptophan Pyrrolase
TPO . . . . Tryptophan Pyrrolase
TSSPS . . . . . . Tsentralniya Suvet na Profesionalnite Suyuzi (Central Council of Trade Unions) (Bulgaria)
TRASH . . . . . . Tsunami Research Advisory System of Hawaii
TS . . . . Tub-Sized
TCS . . . . Tube Cooling Supply
TDC . . . . Tube Deflection Coil
TBEX . . . . . . Tube Expander
TFA . . . . Tube Failure Alarm
TFD . . . . Tube Flood and Drain
TGX . . . . Tube-Generated X-Ray
THD . . . . Tube Heat Dissipator
THCC . . . . . . Tube Heating and Cooling Control
THS . . . . Tube Heating Supply
THC . . . . Tube Humidity Control
TOW . . . . . . Tube-Launched, Optically-Tracked, Wire-Guided (Anti-tank weapon)
TMC . . . . Tube Moisture Control
TPS . . . . Tube Pin Straightener
TPOM . . . . . . Tube Propagation d'Ondes Magnetron
TB . . . . Tubercle Bacillus (Bacteriology)
TA . . . . Tuberculin, Alkaline

TBE . . . . Tuberculin Bacillen Emulsion (Medicine)
TF . . . . Tuberculin Filtrate (Medicine)
TP . . . . Tuberculin Precipitation
TR . . . . Tuberculin R (New tuberculin)
TT . . . . Tuberculin Tested (Milk)
TB . . . . Tuberculosis
TWL . . . . Tuberculosis Welfare League
TDD . . . . Tuberculous Diseases Diploma (British)
TEMA . . . . . . Tubular Exchange Manufacturers Association
TFR . . . . Tubular Flow Reactor
TS . . . . Tubular (Tracheal) Sound
TSRC . . . . . . Tubular & Split Rivet Council
TCG . . . . Tucson, Cornelia & Gila Bend R. R. (AAR code)
TEL . . . . Tucson Engineering Laboratory
T . . . . Tuesday
TTMA . . . . . . Tufted Textile Manufacturers Association
T . . . . Tug (Navy)
AT . . . . Tug, Ocean-Going (Navy symbol)
TUS . . . . Tugboat Underwriting Syndicate
TSU . . . . Tulsa-Sapulpa Union Railway Company (AAR code)
TUMA . . . . . Tumacacori National Monument
TDV . . . . Tumbleweed Diagnostic Vehicle
TEX . . . . Tumbling Explorer
TIF . . . . Tumor-Inducing Factor (Medicine)
TIP . . . . Tumor Inhibitory Principle (A cancer-inhibiting substance)
T . . . . Tun (Unit of liquid capacity)
TBOA . . . . . . Tuna Boat Owners' Association
TRF . . . . Tuna Research Foundation
TCF . . . . Tunable Control Frequency
TNS . . . . Tunable Noise Source
TPA . . . . Tunable Parametric Amplifier
TCG . . . . Tune-Controlled Gain
TBWO . . . . . . Tuned Backward Wave Oscillator
TGO . . . . Tuned Grid Oscillator
TGTP . . . . . . Tuned Grid - Tuned Plate
THL . . . . Tuned Hybrid Lattice
TIC . . . . Tuned Integrated Circuit
TPO . . . . Tuned Plate Oscillator
TPTG . . . . . . Tuned Plate Tuned Grid (Electronic tube)
TRF . . . . Tuned Radio Frequency
TRT . . . . Tuned Receiver Tuner
TR & DL . . . . . Tung Research and Development League
TUW . . . . Tung-Sol Electric, Inc. (NYSE symbol)
W . . . . Tungsten (Chemical element)
TES . . . . Tungsten Electron Snatcher
TIG . . . . Tungsten-Inert-Gas (Underwater welding)
TI . . . . Tungsten Institute
TWMR . . . . . . Tungsten Water-Moderated Nuclear Rocket
TDIO . . . . Tuning Data Input-Output
TDA . . . . Tuning Device Assembly
TE . . . . Tuning Eye
TFF . . . . Tuning Fork Filter
TFO . . . . Tuning Fork Oscillator
TS . . . . Tuning Stability
TDS . . . . Tunnel Destruct System
TD . . . . Tunnel Diode
TDA . . . . Tunnel Diode Amplifier
TDAS . . . . . . Tunnel Diode Amplifier System
TDCT . . . . . . Tunnel Diode Charge Transformer
TDCTL . . . . . . Tunnel-Diode Charge-Transformer Logic
TDL . . . . Tunnel Diode Logic
TDM . . . . Tunnel Diode Mixer
TDT . . . . Tunnel Diode Transducer
TDTL . . . . . . Tunnel-Diode Transistor Logic
TR . . . . Tunnel Rectifier
TUPE . . . . . . Tupelo National Battlefield
TU . . . . Tupolev (Russian aircraft symbol; initialism taken from name of aircraft's designer)
TU . . . . Turbidity Unit
TD . . . . Turbine Direct Drive
TD . . . . Turbine Drive(n)
TDB . . . . Turbine-Driven Blower
TE . . . . Turbine Electric Drive
TERD . . . . . . Turbine Electric Reduction Drive
TECO . . . . . . Turbine Engine Checkout
TED . . . . Turbine Engine Division (Air Force)
TFS . . . . Turbine Flow Sensor
TGM . . . . Turbine Generator Management
TIT . . . . Turbine Inlet Temperature
TIGR . . . . . . Turbine-Integrated Geared Rotor
TMS . . . . Turbine Management Station

TOSS . . . . . . Turbine-Operated Suspension System (NASA)
TPCV . . . . . . Turbine Power Control Valve
TRD . . . . Turbine Reduction Drive
TFE . . . . Turbo-Fan Engine
TJ . . . . Turbojet
TJE . . . . Turbojet Engine
TJP . . . . Turbo-Jet Propulsion
TPE . . . . Turbo-Propeller Engine
TPC . . . . Turbo Pump Control
TSE . . . . Turbo-Shaft Engine
TA . . . . Turbulence Amplifier
TMS . . . . Turbulence Measuring System
TAPER . . . . . Turbulent Air Pilot Environment Research (NASA-FAA project)
TBL . . . . Turbulent Boundary Layer
TBJ . . . . Turbulent Bounded Jet
TCJ . . . . Turbulent Confined Jet
TFW . . . . Turbulent Far Wake
TRF . . . . Turf Research Foundation
THY . . . . Turk Haval Yollari AO (Turkish Airlines, Inc.)
TU . . . . Turkey (NATO)
T . . . . Turkish
TAA . . . . Turkish-American Associations
TAEC . . . . . . Turkish Atomic Energy Commission
TCTU . . . . . . Turkish Confederation of Trade Unions
TKP . . . . Turkiye Komunist Partisi
TOLEYIS . . . . Turkiye Otel, Lokanta ve Eglence Yerleri Isci Sendikalari Federasyonu (National Federation of Hotel, Restaurant and Amusement Places Workers' Unions) (Turkey)
TEKSIF . . . . . Turkiye Tekstil ve Orme Sanayii Iscileri Sendikalari Federasyonu (National Federation of Textile Unions) (Turkey)
TURCO . . . . . Turn Around Control (Navy)
TAT . . . . Turn-Around Time (Navy)
T & B . . . . . . Turn-and-Bank Indicators
T/S . . . . Turn-in-Slip (Military)
LT . . . . Turn Left After Takeoff (Aviation)
TOT . . . . Turn-On Time
TO . . . . A Turn Over (A prospective customer who cannot be sold by one clerk and is turned over to another) (Merchandising slang)
TOD . . . . Turn Over Device
TTP . . . . Turn Toward Peace (An organization; later, WWWCUS)
TO . . . . Turnover (Number) (With reference to enzyme activity)
TPI . . . . Turns Per Inch
TPL . . . . Turns Per Layer
TC . . . . Turret Captain (Navy)
TFC . . . . Turret Fire Control
THLS . . . . . . Turret Head Limit Switch
TLSG . . . . . . Turret Lathe Stop Gauge
TK . . . . Tuskegee R. R. (AAR code)
TEJO . . . . . . Tutmonda Esperantista Junulara Organizo (World Esperantist Youth Organization)
TEJA . . . . . . Tutmonda Esperantista Jurnalista Asocio (World Association of Esperantist Journalists)
T . . . . Tutti (Sing or play together) (Music)
TUZI . . . . . . Tuzigoot National Monument
CANAIRVAN . . 12th Air Defense Group Headquarters, Vancouver, British Columbia, Canada
TF . . . . Twentieth Century-Fox Film Corporation (NYSE symbol)
TCF . . . . Twentieth Century Fund
TAW . . . . . . Twice a Week (Advertising frequency)
TAN . . . . . . Twilight All Night
TBD . . . . Twin Boundary Diffusion
TB . . . . Twin Branch R. R. (AAR code)
TCM . . . . Twin-Cartridge Machine
TE . . . . Twin Engine
TFV . . . . Twin Falls Victory (Tracking ship) (NASA)
TWN . . . . . . Twin Industries Corporation (NYSE symbol) (Delisted)
TSS . . . . Twin-Screw Steamer (Nautical)
TSB . . . . Twin Sideband
TDG . . . . Twist Drill Gauge
TBP . . . . Twisted Bonded Pair
TJPOI . . . . . . Twisted Jute Packing and Oakum Institute
TM . . . . Twisting Moment
TAT . . . . Two-Axis Tracking
TATP . . . . . . Two-Axis Tracking Pedestal
2B . . . . Two-base hits (Baseball)
TBF . . . . Two-Body Force
TBP . . . . Two-Body Problem
TCK . . . . Two-Cavity Klystron
TCR . . . . Two-Color Radiometer
2/C . . . . Two-Conductor (Wire or cable)
TDF . . . . Two Degrees of Freedom

TFM . . . . Two-Fluid Manometer
TGRLSS . . . . . Two-Gas Regenerative Lift Support System
TGV . . . . Two Gentlemen of Verona (by Shakespeare)
TH . . . . Two Hands
2PH . . . . Two-Phase
TPF . . . . Two-Phase Flow
TPP . . . . Two-Phase Principle
TPBVP . . . . . . Two-Point Boundary Value Problem
2F . . . . Two-seater Fighter Aircraft (Navy)
TSDS . . . . Two-Speed Destroyer Sweeper (Military)
TS . . . . Two-Stage Least Squares (Econometrics)
TSLS . . . . Two-Stage Least Squares (Statistics)
TSA . . . . Two-Step Antenna
TTM . . . . Two-Tone Modulation
TFA . . . . Two-Way Finite Automata
TWT . . . . Two-Way-Traffic-in-Ideas Conference (of Labor Party) (British)
TYC . . . . Two-Year(-Old) Course (Horseracing)
TJC . . . . Tyler Junior College (Texas)
TVCS . . . . Tyler Vocational Card Sort (Guidance)
TAFB . . . . Tyndall Air Force Base

TA . . . . Type Availability
T/A . . . . Type Availability
TC . . . . Type Certificate
TYCOM . . . . . Type Commander
TG . . . . Type Genus
TMS . . . . Type, Model, and Series
TRC . . . . Type Requisition Code
TOS . . . . Type of Shipment
TS . . . . Type Specification
TS . . . . Typescript
TWK . . . . Typewriter Keyboard
TMEA . . . . . . Typewriter Manufacturers Export Association
T . . . . Typhlosole
TABU . . . . . . Typical Army Ball-Up (Slang for a military muddle)
TCCFU . . . . . Typical Coastal Command Foul Up (RAF slang) (World War II)
TYDAC . . . . . Typical Digital Automatic Computer
TEM . . . . Typical Egg Mass
TOM . . . . Typical Ocean Model (Oceanography)
TSAF . . . . . . Typical System Acquisition Flow
TD . . . . Typographic Draftsman (Navy)

U

UARCO . . . . . . UARCO, Inc. (Formerly, United Autographic Register Company)
US . . . . Ubi Supra (In the Place Above Mentioned)
UYT . . . . Udylite Corporation (NYSE symbol)
UIM . . . . Ufficio Informazioni Militare (Office of Military Information) (Italian)
UPC . . . . Uganda People's Congress
UPEU . . . . . . Uganda Public Employees' Union
UTUC . . . . . . Uganda Trades' Union Congress
UVPJU . . . . . . Uganda Vernacular, Primary and Junior Secondary Teachers' Union
UAAS . . . . Ukrainian Academy of Arts and Sciences in the US
UAL . . . . Ukrainian American League
UCSUS . . . . . . Ukrainian Catholic Students of the United States
UCCA . . . . . . Ukrainian Congress Committee of America
UESA . . . . Ukrainian Engineers' Society of America
UFSA . . . . Ukrainian Free Society of America
UKC . . . . Ukrainian Gold Cross
UIA . . . . Ukrainian Institute of America
ULCA . . . . . . Ukrainian Life Cooperative Association
UMANA . . . . . Ukrainian Medical Association of North America
UNAAA . . . . . Ukrainian National Aid Association of America
UNA . . . . Ukrainian National Association
UNWLA . . . . . Ukrainian National Women's League of America
UNYFA . . . . . Ukrainian National Youth Federation of America
UPSA . . . . Ukrainian Professional Society of America
URII . . . . Ukrainian Research and Information Institute
UWA . . . . Ukrainian Workingmen's Association
UYLNA . . . . . Ukrainian Youth League of North America
UHA . . . . Ukrains'ka Halyts'ka Armiia
UNR . . . . Ukrains'ka Natsional'na Rada
UPA . . . . Ukrains'ka Povstans'ka Armiia
URDP . . . . . . Ukrains'ka Revoliutsiino-Demokratychna Partiia
URZ . . . . Ulen Realization Corporation (NYSE symbol)
UIS . . . . Ulster-Irish Society
UAF . . . . Ultimate Asbestos Fibril
UOC . . . . Ultimate Operating Capability
URBM . . . . . . Ultimate Range Ballistic Missile (Air Force)
UTS . . . . Ultimate Tensile Strength
UU . . . . Ultimate User
UA . . . . Ultra-Audible
UF . . . . Ultra-Fine
UHA . . . . Ultra-High Altitude
UHF . . . . Ultra-High Frequency (Electricity of radio waves)
UDF . . . . UHF (Ultra-High Frequency) Direction Finder
UHFDF . . . . . Ultra-High-Frequency Direction Finder
UDOP . . . . . . UHF (Ultra-High Frequency) Doppler System
UHR . . . . Ultra-High Resistance
UHTREX . . . . . Ultra-High Temperature Reactor Experiment (AEC)
UHV . . . . Ultra-High Vacuum
UVC . . . . Ultra-High Vacuum Chamber
UVP . . . . Ultra-High Vacuum Pump
UVPS . . . . . . Ultra-High Vacuum Pumping Station
UL . . . . Ultra-Linear
ULR . . . . Ultra-Linear Rectifier
ULE . . . . Ultra-Low Expansion (Fused Silica)
ULF . . . . Ultra-Low Frequency
ULFJ . . . . Ultra-Low Frequency Jammer
ULFO . . . . . . Ultra-Low Frequency Oscillator
ULPR . . . . . . Ultra-Low-Pressure Rocket
UMF . . . . Ultra-Microfiche
UMW . . . . . . Ultra Microwaves
ULDMI . . . . . . Ultra-Precise LASER Distance Measuring Instrument
USMID . . . . . . Ultra-Sensitive Microwave Infrared Detector
USP . . . . Ultra-Sensitive Position
USW . . . . Ultra-Short Wave

USX . . . . Ultra-Soft X-Ray
UDC . . . . Ultrasonic Doppler Cardioscope (Heartbeat monitor)
UE . . . . Ultrasonic Engineering
UJT . . . . Ultrasonic Journal Tester
USK . . . . Ultrasonic Kit
ULD . . . . Ultrasonic Leak Detector
ULD . . . . Ultrasonic Light Diffraction
ULM . . . . Ultrasonic Light Modulator
USLD . . . . . . Ultrasonic Link Detector
ULLS . . . . Ultrasonic Liquid Level Sensor
UMA . . . . Ultrasonic Manufacturers Association
UMD . . . . Ultrasonic Material Dispersion
UMT . . . . Ultrasonic Material Testing
URW . . . . Ultrasonic Ring Welder
USD . . . . Ultrasonic Separation Detector
USSE . . . . Ultrasonic Soldering Equipment
USSI . . . . Ultrasonic Soldering Iron
USG . . . . Ultrasonic Space Grating
USC . . . . Ultrasonic Storage Cell
UT . . . . Ultrasonic Test
USTU . . . . . . Ultrasonic Test Unit
UTU . . . . Ultrasonic Test Unit
UTA . . . . Ultrasonic Thermal Action
UST . . . . Ultrasonic Transducer (Crystal) (Used in measuring human cardiac output)
UVD . . . . Ultrasonic Vapor Degresser
UW . . . . Ultrasonic Wave
UV . . . . Ultraviolet
UVASER . . . . . Ultraviolet Amplification by Stimulated Emission of Radiation
UBI . . . . Ultraviolet Blood Irradiation
ULTRACOM . . . Ultraviolet Communications
UVC . . . . Ultraviolet Communications System
UVD . . . . Ultraviolet Detector
UVIL . . . . Ultraviolet Inspection Light
UVIL . . . . Ultraviolet Ion LASER
UVL . . . . Ultraviolet Lamp
UVL . . . . Ultraviolet LASER
UVL . . . . Ultraviolet Light
ULS . . . . Ultraviolet Light Stabilizer
UVLS . . . . . . Ultraviolet Light Stabilizer
UVM . . . . Ultraviolet Meter
UPR . . . . Ultraviolet Proton Radiation
UVR . . . . Ultraviolet Radiation
UVR . . . . Ultraviolet Receiver
UVR . . . . Ultraviolet Rocket
USS . . . . Ultraviolet Scanning Spectrometer
USA . . . . Ultraviolet Spectral Analysis
UVSP . . . . . . Ultraviolet Spectral Photometer
USI . . . . Ultraviolet Spectroheliographic Instrument
UVS . . . . Ultraviolet Spectrometer
UVT . . . . Ultraviolet Transmission
UVT . . . . Ultraviolet Tube
UV . . . . Ultravisible
USGA . . . . . . Ulysses S. Grant Association
UMAD . . . . . . Umatilla Army Depot
UJB . . . . Umbilical Junction Box
UP . . . . Umbilical Pin
UTS . . . . Umbilical Test Set
UT . . . . Umbilical Tower (Aerospace)
UC . . . . Una Corda (With one string or with the soft pedal) (Music)
USPD . . . . . . Unabhaengige Sozialdemokratische Partei Deutschlands
UNAR . . . . . . Unable Approve Altitude Requested (Aviation)
UNRR . . . . . . Unable Approve Route Requested (Aviation)
UM . . . . Unable to Maintain (Aviation)

REVERSE ACRONYMS AND INITIALISMS DICTIONARY

UQL........ Unacceptable Quality Level
UCC .... Unadjusted Contractual Changes
UNR........ Unarco Industries, Inc. (NYSE symbol)
ULIA .... Unattached List, Indian Army
UPUC....... Unauthorized Publication or Use of Communications
UBHC .... Unburned Hydrocarbon
U .... Uncirculated
UMBR ...... Unclad-Metal Breeder Reactor (AEC)
U......... Unclassified
U/C .... Unclassified
IX .... Unclassified Miscellaneous (Navy ship symbol)
UWOA ..... Unclassified Without Attachment
U .... Uncle
US........ Uncle Sam
UTC........ "Uncle Tom's Cabin" (Title of book by Harriet Beecher Stowe)
US .... Unconditional Selection
US .... Unconditional Surrender
UCR....... Unconditioned Response
UR .... Unconditioned Response
UCS .... Unconditioned Stimulus
US .... Unconditioned Stimulus
UOT....... Uncontrollable Overtime
UCV .... Uncontrolled Variable
UW .... Unconventional Warfare
UPA....... Uncooled Parametric Amplifier
UCDP...... Uncorrected Data Processor
USW....... Und So Weiter (And So Forth) (German)
UZW ...... Und Zwar (That Is) (German)
UOS ...... Undelivered Order Schedule
UOO ...... Undelivered Orders Outstanding (Military)
UBA .... Undenatured Bacterial Antigen
U .... Under
UC........ Under Charge
UC .... Under Construction
UHC ...... Under Honorable Conditions
UM .... Under-Mentioned (i.e., mentioned later in a document)
UOHC ..... Under Other than Honorable Conditions (Military)
UP .... Under-Proof (Of spirituous liquors) (Distilling)
UP........ Under Provisions of
UPS .... Under Provisions of Section (Military)
US .... Under Secretary
SAFUS ..... Under Secretary of the Air Force
US of AF .... Under Secretary of the Air Force
USOFAF .... Under Secretary of the Air Force
US of A .... Under Secretary of the Army
USOFA ..... Under Secretary of the Army
UNDERSECNAV .. Under Secretary of the Navy
USO....... Under Secretary of the Navy's Office
US of S ..... Under Secretary of State
USW....... Under Secretary of War
USC .... Under Separate Cover
UUR .... Under Usual Reserves
UV .... Under Voltage
UVR .... Under Voltage Relay
UWR....... Under Weight Rejector
UC........ Undercarriage
UDT .... Underdeck Tonnage
UDC .... Underdeveloped Countries
UAA .... Undergarment Accessories Association
UGPA...... Undergraduate Grade-Point Average (Higher education)
UNT .... Undergraduate Navigator Training
UPT .... Undergraduate Pilot Training (Air Force)
UG .... Underground (Technical drawings)
UECA...... Underground Engineering Contractors Association
UGRR...... Underground Railroad (A smuggling system) (Criminal slang)
URD .... Underground Residential Distribution (Cable)
USSA ...... Underground Security Storage Association
USE .... Underground Service Entrance
ULM....... Undersea Long-Range Missile (Proposed)
ULMS ...... Undersea (or Underwater) Long-Range Missile System (Navy)
URIPS ...... Undersea Radioisotope Power Supply
URV .... Undersea Research Vehicle
USE .... Undersea Scientific Expedition
UST .... Undersea Technology
USW....... Undersea Warfare
UWDD ..... Undersea Warfare Development Division (Navy)
UWS....... Undersea Weapon System
UVD....... Undervoltage Device
UAM ...... Underwater-to-Air Missile (Air Force)
UAUM ..... Underwater-to-Air-to-Underwater Missile (Air Force)
UB .... Underwater Battery

UBFCS ..... Underwater Battery Fire Control System (Navy)
UBP .... Underwater Battery Plot (Antisubmarine warfare)
UCCRS ..... Underwater Coded Command Release System
UCWE ..... Underwater Countermeasures & Weapons Establishment (British)
UDT ...... Underwater Demolition Team (Navy)
UDTPHIBSPAC .. Underwater Demolition Teams, Amphibious Forces, Pacific Fleet (Navy)
UDU........ Underwater Demolition Unit
UDE .... Underwater Detection Establishment (British)
UERD ...... Underwater Explosives Research Division (Navy)
UERL ...... Underwater Explosives Research Laboratory
UFCS ...... Underwater Fire Control System
UWL ...... Underwater Launch
ULCER ..... Underwater Launch Control Energy Requirements
ULCER ..... Underwater Launch Current and Energy Recorder
ULM....... Underwater Launch Missile
UM .... Underwater Mechanic
UOL....... Underwater Object Locator
UOS ...... Underwater Ordnance Station (Navy)
UPC .... Underwater Pipe Cutter
USAW....... Underwater Security Advance Warnings (Navy)
USA .... Underwater Society of America
USL .... Underwater Sound Laboratory (Navy)
USP .... Underwater Sound Projection
USRL ...... Underwater Sound Reference Laboratory (Navy)
USS .... Underwater Sound Source
USM ...... Underwater-to-Surface Missile (Air Force)
UTRP ...... Underwater Tactical Range, Pacific
UTF .... Underwater Tank Facility
UWT....... Underwater Telephone
UTV .... Underwater Television
UTR .... Underwater Tracking Range
UUM ...... Underwater-to-Underwater Missile (Air Force)
UV........ Underwater Vehicle
UWAL...... Underwater Wide Angle Lens
URG ...... Underway Replenishment Group
URGR ..... Underway Replenishment Group (Military)
UTU .... Underway Training Unit
UWATU...... Underway Training Unit
UI .... Underwear Institute
UNA ...... Underwear-Negligee Associates
UNX ...... Underwood Corporation (NYSE symbol)
U/W .... Underwriter
UGA ...... Underwriters Grain Association
UL........ Underwriters' Laboratories (Inc.)
ULI .... Underwriters' Laboratories, Incorporated
U/A .... Underwriting Account (Business and trade)
UD .... Undesirable Discharge (Military)
UDDE...... Undesirable Discharge, Desertion without Trial (Navy)
UDFE ...... Undesirable Discharge, Fraudulent Enlistment (Navy)
UDCA ...... Undesirable Discharge, Trial by Civil Authorities (Navy)
UDUF ...... Undesirable Discharge, Unfitness (Navy)
UPO....... Undistorted Power Output
UBITRON .... Undulating Beam Interaction Electron Tube
UC .... Unemployment Compensation
UCX ...... Unemployment Compensation, Ex-Servicemen
UCFE ...... Unemployment Compensation, Federal Employees
UI .... Unemployment Insurance
UIA .... Unemployment Insurance Act (Canada)
UIS .... Unemployment Insurance Service (Labor)
UOC ...... Unequilibrated Ordinary Chondrites
UFA....... Unesterified Fatty Acids
UAO ...... Unexplained Aerial Object
UXB ...... Unexploded Bomb
UXO ...... Unexploded Ordnance
UXOI ...... Unexploded Ordnance Incident
ULP .... Unfair Labor Practice
UMS....... Unfederated Malay States
UPV....... Unfired Pressure Vessel
UCMT...... Unglazed Ceramic Mosaic Tile (Technical drawings)
USFU ...... Unglazed Structural Facing Units (Technical drawings)
USUB ..... Unglazed Structural Unit Base (Technical drawings)
UDC ...... Uniao Democratica Caboverdeana (Cape Verde Democratic Union)
UDN ...... Uniao Democratica Nacional (National Democratic Union) (Brazil)
UDENAMO ... Uniao Democratica Nacional de Mocambique (Mozambican National Democratic Union)
UPA........ Uniao das Populacoes de Angola (Angolan People's Union)
USF .... Uniaxial Stress Field
U/I .... Unidentified
UAP....... Unidentified Atmospheric Phenomena
UFO....... Unidentified Flying Object ("Flying saucers")
UGF....... Unidentified Growth Factor

UFC . . . . Unidirectional Filamentary Composite
UDP . . . . Unification du Droit Prive
U . . . . Unified
UNAAF . . . . . Unified Action Armed Forces (Military)
UNC . . . . Unified Coarse Thread
UCP . . . . Unified Command Plan
UNICOM . . . . Unified Communications (Radio station)
UNEF . . . . . . Unified Extra Fine (Thread)
UNF . . . . Unified Fine (Thread)
UFAS . . . . Unified Flight Analysis System (NASA)
UF . . . . Unified Forces (Military)
UNIFOR . . . . Unified Forces (Military)
ULSP . . . . . . Unified Legal Services Program
UNM . . . . . . Unified Miniature
URIR . . . . Unified Radioactive Isodromic Regulator
USBE . . . . . . Unified S-Band Equipment
USE . . . . Unified S-Band Equipment
USBS . . . . . . Unified S-Band System (Radio)
USS . . . . Unified S-Band System
USD . . . . Unified School District
USAM . . . . . . Unified Space Applications Mission
UNS . . . . Unified Special (Thread)
UTP . . . . Unified Test Plan
UTS . . . . Unified Transfer System (Computer to translate Russian to English)
U . . . . Uniform
UAR . . . . Uniform Airman Record
UA . . . . Uniform Allowance
UADPS . . . . . Uniform Automatic Data Processing System
UADPS, INAS . . Uniform Automatic Data Processing System/Industrial Naval Air Station
UBPVLS . . . . . Uniform Boiler and Pressure Vessel Laws Society
UCMJ . . . . . . Uniform Code of Military Justice
UCC . . . . Uniform Commercial Code
UCC . . . . Uniform Credit Code
UCR . . . . Uniform Crime Reports (Federal Bureau of Investigation)
UDL . . . . Uniform Data Link
UFA . . . . Uniform Firearms Act
UFC . . . . Uniform Freight Classification
UFCC . . . . . . Uniform Freight Classification Committee
ULT . . . . Uniform Low-Frequency Technique
UMF . . . . Uniform Magnetic Field
UME . . . . Uniform Manufacturers Exchange
UMIPS . . . . . Uniform Material Issue Priority System
UMMIPS . . . . Uniform Material Movement and Issue Priority System
UMPR . . . . . . Uniform Military Personnel Record
UMC . . . . Uniform Motion Coupling
UMC . . . . Uniform Moving Charge
UOR . . . . Uniform Officer Record
UPIR . . . . Uniform Photographic Interpretation Report (Military)
UQGS . . . . . . Uniform Quality Grading System (Tires)
UR . . . . Uniform Regulations
URS . . . . Uniform Reporting System
US . . . . Uniform System
UWM . . . . . . Uniform Wave Motion
UWT . . . . Uniform Wave Train
UWBS . . . . . . Uniform Work Breakdown Structure
USCA . . . . . . Uniformed Services Contingency Act
USCOA . . . . . Uniformed Services Contingency Option Act
USHB . . . . . . Uniformed Services Health Benefits
UJT . . . . Unijunction Transistor
UL . . . . Unilever Limited (NYSE symbol)
UN . . . . Unilever NV (NYSE symbol)
UPS . . . . Uninterruptable Power Supply
UTCD . . . . . . Uninunea Tineretului Comunist Dimitrovist
U . . . . Union(ist)
UAI . . . . Union Academique Internationale
UAJG . . . . . . Union d'Action des Jeunes de Guinee (Guinean Union of Youth Action)
UAT . . . . Union Aeromaritime de Transport (Privately owned French airline)
UAS . . . . Union of African States
UAM . . . . . . Union Africaine et Malagache (African and Malagasy Union) (Later, Common Afro-Malagasy Organization)
UAHC . . . . . . Union of American Hebrew Congregations
UAC . . . . Union Army of Commemoration
UAI . . . . Union des Associations Internationales
UATI . . . . . . Union des Associations Techniques Internationales
UNATRACAM . . Union des Associations Traditionelles du Cameroun (Union of Traditional Associations of Cameroon)
UAI . . . . Union Astronomique Internationale
BP . . . . Union Bag-Camp Paper Corporation (NYSE symbol)
UBA . . . . Union of Burma Airways
UBARI . . . . . . Union of Burma Applied Research Institute
UBAEC . . . . . Union of Burma Atomic Energy Centre

UC . . . . Union Camerounaise (Cameroonese Union)
UCTC . . . . . . Union Camerounaise des Travailleurs Croyants (Cameroonese Union of Believing Workers)
UCCE . . . . . . Union des Capitales de la Communaute Europeenne (Union of Capitals of the European Community)
UK . . . . Union Carbide Corporation (NYSE symbol) (Wall Street slang name: "Ukulele")
UCNC . . . . . . Union Carbide Nuclear Corporation
UCMP . . . . . . Union Catalog of Medical Periodicals
UCISS . . . . . Union Catholique Internationale de Service Social
UCPN . . . . . . Union des Chefs et des Populations du Nord (Union of Chiefs and Peoples of the North) (Togo)
UCB . . . . Union Chimique Belge (Belgium)
UCB . . . . Union Chemique-Chemische Bedrijven (Belgium)
UCEA . . . . . . Union Chimique Elf-Aquitane (France)
UCDEC . . . . . Union Chretienne Democrate d'Europe Centrale
UCN . . . . Union Civica Nacional (National Civic Union) (Dominican Republic)
UCRI . . . . . . Union Civica Radical Intransigente (Left wing radical political party) (Argentina)
UCRP . . . . . . Union Civica Radical del Pueblo (Moderate radical political party) (Argentina)
UNAKI . . . . . Union des Colons Agricoles du Kivu (Union of Agricultural Settlers of Kivu) (Congo - Leopoldville)
UCOL . . . . . . Union des Colons du Katanga (Settlers' Union of Katanga)
UNICOL . . . . Union des Colons de la Province Orientale (Union of Settlers in Orientale Province)
UCFA . . . . . . Union pour la Communaute Franco-Africaine (Union for the Franco-African Community) (Niger)
UCSL . . . . . . Union Congolaise des Syndicats Libres (Congolese Union of Free Syndicates) (Leopoldville)
UCAVJ . . . . . Union Continentale Africaine des Villes Jumelees (Continental African Union of Twin Cities)
UCPTE . . . . . Union pour la Coordination de la Production et du Transport de l'Electricite
UCM . . . . . . Union des Croyants Malagaches (Malagasy Christian Union)
UCK . . . . Union Culturelle Katangaise (Katangan Cultural Union)
UCI . . . . Union Cycliste Internationale (World governing body for amateur bicycle racing)
UDCA . . . . . . Union de Defense des Commercants et Artisans
UDIT . . . . . . Union pour la Defense des Interets du Tchad (Union for the Defense of Chadian Interests)
UDSM . . . . . Union des Democrates Sociaux de Madagascar (Union of Social Democrats of Madagascar)
UDA . . . . Union for Democratic Action
UDD . . . . Union Democratique Dahomeene (Dahomey Democratic Union)
UDDIA . . . . . Union Democratique pour la Defense des Interets Africains (Democratic Union to Defend African Interests)
UDEFEC . . . . Union Democratique des Femmes Camerounaises (Cameroonese Democratic Women's Union)
UDFT . . . . . . Union Democratique des Femmes Tunisiennes (Democratic Union of Tunisian Women)
UDJM . . . . . . Union Democratique de la Jeunesse Marocaine (Democratic Union of Moroccan Youth)
UDJV . . . . . . Union Democratique de la Jeunesse Voltaique (Voltaic Democratic Youth Union)
UDPT . . . . . . Union Democratique des Populations Togolaises (Democratic Union of Togolese People)
UDS . . . . Union Democratique Senegalaise (Senegalese Democratic Union)
UDSG . . . . . . Union Democratique et Sociale Gabonaise (Gabonese Democratic and Social Union)
UDSR . . . . . . Union Democratique et Socialiste de la Resistance (Democratic and Socialist Resistance Union)
UDETO . . . . . Union Democratique Togolaise (Togolese Democratic Union)
UDV . . . . Union Democratique Voltaique (Voltaic Democratic Union)
UDSM . . . . . . Union Departemental de Syndicats du Mungo (Departmental Union of the Trade Unions of Mungo) (Cameroon)
UDEAC . . . . . Union Douaniere et Economique de L'Afrique Centrale
UDE . . . . Union Douaniere Equatoriale (Equatorial Customs Unions)
UNECO . . . . . Union Economique du Congo (Economic Union of the Congo) (Usumbura)
FRITALUX . . . . Union Economique France, Italie, Benelux
UEP . . . . Union Electric Company (NYSE symbol)
UEM . . . . Union Electrica Madrilena (Spain)
UEBC . . . . . . Union Espanola Benefica de California
UNEASICO . . . Union des Etudiants et Anciens des Instituts Sociaux de Congo (Congolese Union of Students and Former Students of Social Institutes)
UEOA . . . . . . Union des Etudiants Ouest Africains (Union of West African Students)
UEFA . . . . . . Union of European Football Associations
UEA . . . . Union Europeenne de l'Ameublement
UEC . . . . Union Europeenne de la Carrosserie
UNECOLAIT . . Union Europeenne du Commerce Laitier
UECB . . . . . . Union Europeenne des Commerces du Betail

UECL . . . . Union Europeenne des Constructeurs de Logements
UEC . . . . Union Europeenne des Experts Comptables Economiques et Financiers
UEF . . . . Union Europeenne des Federalistes
UEF . . . . Union Europeenne Feminine
UEMS . . . . Union Europeenne de Medecine Sociale
EUROCOM . . . Union Europeenne des Negociants en Combustibles
UENDC . . . . . Union Europeenne des Negociants Detaillants en Combustibles
UEP . . . . Union Europeenne de Paiements
UEP . . . . Union Europeenne de Pedopsychiatres
UER . . . . Union Europeenne de Radiodiffusion
UEEB . . . . Union des Exploitations Electriques en Belgique
UFCE . . . . . . Union Federaliste des Communautes Ethniques Europeennes
UFEMAT . . . . . Union des Federations Nationales des Negociants en Materiaux de Construction de la CEE
UFA . . . . Union des Femmes d'Algerie (Union of Algerian Women)
UFOA . . . . . . Union des Femmes d l'Ouest Africain (West African Women's Union)
UFEMTO . . . . Union des Femmes du Togo (Togolese Women's Union)
UFIDA . . . . . . Union Financer Internationale pour le Developpement de l'Afrique (International Financial Union for the Development of Africa)
UFI . . . . Union des Foires Internationales
UFOD . . . . . . Union Francaise des Organismes de Documentation
UFN . . . . Union Franco-Nigerienne (French-Niger Union)
UNF . . . . Union Freight R. R. (AAR code)
UNG . . . . . . Union Gas Company of Canada (NYSE symbol)
UGS . . . . Union de la Gauche Socialiste
UGCAA . . . . . Union Generale des Cooperatives Agricoles d'Approvisionnement
UGEAO . . . . . Union General e des Etudiants d'Afrique Occidentale (General Union of West African Students)
UGT . . . . Union General de Trabajadores de Espana (General Union of Spanish Workers) (In exile)
UGTM . . . . . . Union General des Travailleurs de Mauritanie (General Union of Workers of Mauritania)
UGEC . . . . . . Union Generale des Etudiants Congolais (General Union of Congolese Students)
UGEED . . . . . Union Generale des Etudiants et Eleves Dahomeens
UGEG . . . . . Union Generale des Etudiants Guineens (General Union of Guinean Students)
UGEM . . . . . Union Generale des Etudiants du Maroc (General Union of Moroccan Students)
UGEMA . . . . Union Generale des Etudiants Musulmans d'Algerie (General Union of Moslem Students of Algeria)
UGET . . . . . . Union Generale des Etudiants Tunisiens (General Union of Tunisian Students)
UGSA . . . . . . Union Generale des Syndicats Algeriens (General Federation of Algerian Trade Unions)
UGTAN . . . . . Union Generale des Travailleurs d'Afrique Noire (General Union of Workers of Black Africa)
UGTA . . . . . . Union Generale des Travailleurs Algeriens (General Union of Algerian Workers)
UGTC . . . . . . Union Generale des Travailleurs du Cameroun (General Union of Workers of Cameroon)
UGTC . . . . . . Union Generale des Travailleurs Centrafricains (General Union of Central African Workers)
UGTCI . . . . . . Union Generale des Travailleurs de la Cote d'Ivoire (General Union of Workers of the Ivory Coast)
UGTD . . . . . . Union Generale des Travailleurs du Dahomey (General Union of Dahomey Workers)
UGTK . . . . . . Union Generale des Travailleurs du Kamerun (General Union of Workers of the Cameroon)
UGTM . . . . . . Union Generale des Travailleurs du Maroc (General Union of Workers of Morocco)
UGTS . . . . . . Union Generale des Travailleurs du Senegal (General Union of Workers of Senegal)
UGTT . . . . . . Union Generale Tunisienne du Travail (General Federation of Tunisian Workers)
UGGI . . . . . . Union Geodesique et Geophysique Internationale
UGI . . . . Union Geographique Internationale
UGB . . . . Union Giovantu Benadir (Benadir Youth Union) (Somalia)
UFE . . . . Union des Groupements Professionnels de l'Industrie de la Feculerie de Pommes de Terre
UNIDAHO . . . . Union des Independants du Dahomey (Independents Union of Dahomey)
UIT . . . . Union des Independants de Tananarive (Union of Independents of Tananarive)
UICA . . . . . . Union of Independent Colleges of Art
UNICE . . . . . . Union des Industries de la Communaute Europeenne
UNICO . . . . . Union pour les Interets du Peuple Congolais (Union for the Interests of the Congolese People)
UNISCO . . . . . Union des Interets Sociaux Congolais (Congolese Union of Social Interests)
UIA . . . . Union of International Associations
UIC . . . . Union of International Conventions
UIEO . . . . Union of International Engineering Organizations

UIM . . . . Union of International Motorboating (Belgium)
UISP . . . . Union International des Societes de la Paix (International Union of Peace Societies)
UIA . . . . Union Internationale contre l'Alcoolisme
UIA . . . . Union Internationale des Architectes
UIAPME . . . . . Union Internationale de l'Artisanat et des Petites et Moyennes Entreprises
UIAA . . . . Union Internationale des Association d'Annonceurs
UIAA . . . . Union Internationale des Associations d'Alpinisme
UNIADUSEC . . Union Internationale des Associations de Diplomes Universitaires en Sciences Economiques et Commerciales
UNIAPAC . . . . Union Internationale des Associations Patronales Catholiques
UIP . . . . Union Internationale d'Associations de Proprietaires de Wagons de Particuliers
UNIATEC . . . . Union Internationale des Associations Techniques Cinematographiques
UIAA . . . . Union Internationale des Assureurs Aeronautiques
UIACM . . . . . . Union Internationale des Automobile-Clubs Medicaux
UIA . . . . Union Internationale des Avocats
UICM . . . . . . Union Internationale Catholique des Classes Moyennes
UIC . . . . Union Internationale des Chemins de Fer
UICPA . . . . . . Union Internationale de Chimie Pure et Appliquee
UNICA . . . . . . Union Internationale du Cinema d'Amateurs
UICGF . . . . . . Union Internationale du Commerce en Gros de la Fleur
UICN . . . . Union Internationale pour la Conservation de la Nature et de Ses Ressources
UICC . . . . Union Internationale Contre le Cancer
UIPVT . . . . . . Union Internationale Contre le Peril Venerien et la Treponematose
UICT . . . . Union Internationale Contre la Tuberculose
UNO-CARA-PEN . . Union Internationale pour la Cooperation Culturelle (International Union for Cultural Co-operation)
UNICHAL . . . . Union Internationale des Distributeurs de Chaleur
UIES . . . . Union Internationale pour l'Education Sanitaire
UIE . . . . Union Internationale d'Electrothermie
UIEP . . . . Union Internationale des Entrepreneurs de Peinture
UIEIS . . . . Union Internationale pour l'Etude des Insectes Sociaux
UIES . . . . Union Internationale d'Etudes Sociales
UIE . . . . Union Internationale des Etudiants
UIEC . . . . Union Internationale de l'Exploitation Cinematographique
UIFI . . . . Union Internationale des Fabricants d'Impermeables
UIFL . . . . Union Internationale des Federations de Detaillants en Produits Laitiers
UFLC . . . . Union Internationale des Femmes Liberales Chretiennes
UNIMA . . . . . . Union Internationale de Grands Magasins
UIHPS . . . . . . Union Internationale d'Histoire et de Philosophie des Sciences
UIHE . . . . Union Internationale de l'Humanisme et de l'Ethique
UIIG . . . . Union Internationale de l'Industrie du Gaz
UIJDC . . . . . . Union Internationale de Jeunesse Democrate Chretienne
UIJS . . . . Union Internationale de la Jeunesse Socialiste
UILE . . . . Union Internationale pour la Liberte d'Enseignement
UIMJ . . . . Union Internationale des Maisons de Jeunesse (Service de la FIJC)
UIB . . . . Union Internationale des Maitres Boulangers
UITAM . . . . . . Union Internationale de Mecanique Theorique et Appliquee (International Union of Theoretical and Applied Mechanics)
UIM . . . . Union Internationale Motonautique
UINF . . . . Union Internationale de la Navigation Fluviale
UINL . . . . Union Internationale du Notariat Latin
UIDA . . . . Union Internationale des Organisations de Detaillants de la Branche Alimentaire
UIOF . . . . Union Internationale des Organismes Familiaux
UIOOT . . . . . . Union Internationale des Organismes Officiels de Tourisme
UTCPTT . . . . . . Union Internationale des Organismes Touristiques et Culturels des Postes et des Telecommunications (International Union of Tourist and Cultural Associations in the Postal and Telecommunications Services)
UIO . . . . Union Internationale des Orientalistes
UIP . . . . Union Internationale de Patinage
UIPCG . . . . . . Union Internationale de la Patisserie, Confiserie, Glacerie
UIPM . . . . Union Internationale de Pentathlon Moderne
UIP . . . . Union Internationale de Physique Pure et Appliquee
UIPC . . . . Union Internationale de la Presse Catholique
UIPM . . . . Union Internationale de la Presse Medicale
UNIPEDE . . . . Union Internationale de Producteurs et Distributeurs d'Energie Electrique
UIPE . . . . Union Internationale de Protection de l'Enfance
UIMP . . . . Union Internationale pour la Protection de la Moralite Publique
UIPPI . . . . Union Internationale pour la Protection de la Propriete Industrielle
UIP . . . . Union Internationale des Publicitaires
UIRD . . . . Union Internationale de la Resistance et de la Deportation
UISAE . . . . . . Union Internationale des Sciences Anthropologiques et Ethnologiques
UISB . . . . Union Internationale des Sciences Biologiques
UISN . . . . Union Internationale des Sciences de la Nutrition
UISPP . . . . . . Union Internationale des Sciences Prehistoriques et Protohistoriques
UIS . . . . Union Internationale de Secours
UISE . . . . Union Internationale de Secours aux Enfants

UIMC . . . . Union Internationale des Services Medicaux des Chemins de Fer
UIA . . . . Union Internationale des Syndicats des Industries Alimentaires
UIAT . . . . Union Internationale des Syndicats des Industries de l'Alimentation
et des Tabacs
UISSM . . . . . . Union Internationale des Syndicats des Industries Metallurgiques
et Mecaniques
UISM . . . . Union Internationale des Syndicats des Mineurs
UISTAF . . . . . . Union Internationale des Syndicats des Travailleurs Agricoles et
Forestiers et des Organisations des Paysans Travailleurs
UITBB . . . . Union Internationale des Syndicats des Travailleurs du Batiment, du
Bois et des Materiaux de Construction
UISTICPS . . . . Union Internationale des Syndicats des Travailleurs des Industries
Chimiques, du Petrole et Similaires
UIT . . . . Union Internationale des Telecommunications
UITP . . . . Union Internationale des Transports Publics
UIUSD . . . . . . Union Internationale Universitaire Socialiste et Democratique
UIV . . . . Union Internationale des Villes et Pouvoirs Locaux
UIP . . . . Union Interparlementaire
UNIGABON . . Union Interprofessionnelle du Gabon (Inter-Trade Union of Gabon)
UJ . . . . Union Jack
UJC . . . . Union de la Jeunesse Congolaise (Congolese Youth Union)
UJEKO . . . . . . Union de la Jeunesse Congolaise (Congolese Youth Union)
UJCD . . . . Union de la Jeunesse de la Cote d'Ivoire (Ivory Coast Youth Union)
UJDG . . . . Union de la Jeunesse Democratique Gabonaise (Union of Democratic Youth
of Gabon)
UJDK . . . . Union de la Jeunesse Democratique du Kongo (Union of Democratic Youth
of the Congo)
UJC . . . . Union Junior College (New Jersey)
UK . . . . Union Katangaise (Katanga Union)
ULI . . . . Union pour la Langue Internationale Ido
ULAJE . . . . . . Union Latino-Americaine des Jeunesses Evangeliques
ULAPC . . . . . . Union Latino-Americaine de la Presse Catholique
ULAST . . . . Union Latina Americana de Sociedades de Tisiologia (Latin American
Union of Societies of Phthisiology)
ULRSA . . . . . . Union and League of Romanian Societies of America
ULS . . . . Union List of Serials
UMT . . . . Union Marocaine du Travail (Moroccan Labor Union)
UMHK . . . . . . Union Miniere du Haut Katanga (Mining Company of Upper Katanga)
UMB . . . . Union Mondiale de Billard
UMEC . . . . Union Mondiale des Enseignants Catholiques
UMEJ . . . . Union Mondiale des Etudiants Juifs
UMJL . . . . Union Mondiale pour un Judaisme Liberal
UMOFC . . . . . . Union Mondiale des Organisations Feminines Catholiques
UMOSBESL . . . Union Mondiale des Organisations Syndicales sur Base Economique et
Sociale Liberale
UMOSEA . . . . . Union Mondiale des Organismes pour la Sauvegarde de l'Enfance et
de l'Adolescence
OSE . . . . Union Mondiale pour la Protection de la Sante des Populations Juives
et Oeuvres de Secours aux Enfants
UMHP . . . . . . Union Mondiale des Societes d'Histoire Pharmaceutique
UMC . . . . Union du Moyen-Congo (Union of the Middle Congo)
UMA . . . . Union de Mujeres Americanas (United Women of the Americas)
UNP . . . . Union Nacional Paraguaya (Political party in Paraguay)
UNEC . . . . Union National des Etudiants Camerounais (National Union of Cameroonese
Students)
UNARU . . . . . . Union Nationale Africaine du Ruanda-Urundi (African National Union of
Ruanda-Urundi)
UNAT . . . . Union Nationale des Agriculteurs Tunisiens (National Union of Tunisian
Farmers)
UNCC . . . . . . Union Nationale des Cheminots du Cameroun (National Union of
Railway Workers of Cameroon)
UNEM . . . . . . Union Nationale des Etudiants du Maroc (National Union of Moroccan
Students)
UNFT . . . . Union Nationale des Femmes de Tunisie (National Union of Tunisian
Workers)
UNFP . . . . Union Nationale des Forces Populaires (National Union of Popular
Forces) (Political party) (Morocco)
UNIUM . . . . . . Union Nationale des Intellectuels et Universitaires Malgaches (National
Union of Intellectuals and University People of Madagascar)
UNOC . . . . . . Union Nationale des Ouvriers Congolais (National Union of the
Congolese Workers)
UNAP . . . . Union Nationale Progressiste (National Progressive Union) (Burundi)
UNAR . . . . Union Nationale Ruandaise (Rwanda National Union)
UNASABEC . . . Union Nationale des Syndicats Agricoles Forestiers, des Bois, de l'Elevage,
et de la Peche du Cameroun (National Union of Farmers, Fishermen,
Forest Guards and Timber Workers of Cameroon)
UNSTD . . . . . . Union Nationale des Syndicats des Travailleurs du Dahomey (National
Union of Syndicates of Dahomey)
UNSTHV . . . . Union Nationale des Syndicats des Travailleurs de la Haute Volta
(National Federation of Workers' Union of the Upper Volta)

UNTA . . . . Union Nationale des Travailleurs Angolais (National Union of Angolan
Workers in Exile)
UNATRACO . . . Union Nationale des Travailleurs du Congo (National Union of Workers
of the Congo)
UNTC . . . . Union Nationale des Travailleurs Congolais (National Union of Congolese
Workers)
UNTCI . . . . . . Union Nationale des Travailleurs de Cote d'Ivoire (National Union of
Ivory Coast Workers)
UNTM . . . . . . Union Nationale des Travailleurs du Mali (National Union of Malian
Workers)
UNTN . . . . . . Union Nationale des Travailleurs Nigeriens (National Union of Nigerian
Workers)
UNTS . . . . Union Nationale des Travailleurs du Senegal (National Union of Workers
of Senegal)
UNTT . . . . Union Nationale des Travailleurs du Togo (National Union of Togolese
Workers)
UNR . . . . Union pour la Nouvelle Republique (Union for the New Republic)
(French political party)
UNRS . . . . Union pour la Nouvelle Republique Senegalaise (Union of the New
Senegalese Republic)
UOEF . . . . Union de Obreros Estivadores de Filipinos (Union of Longshoremen of the
Philippines)
UOCO . . . . . . Union Oil Company
UCL . . . . Union Oil Company of California (NYSE symbol)
UOMS . . . . Union des Originaires de Mauritanie du Sud (Union of Natives of South
Mauritania)
UOJCA . . . . . Union of Orthodox Jewish Congregations of America
UOC . . . . Union de l'Ouest Cameroun (Union of West Cameroon)
UOV . . . . Union Ouvriere du Viet-Nam (Vietnam Labor Union) (South Vietnam)
UNPAC . . . . . . Union Pacific Railroad
UPRR . . . . Union Pacific Railroad
UP . . . . Union Pacific R. R. Company (NYSE symbol and AAR code)
UPAJ . . . . Union Panafricaine des Journalistes
UPTC . . . . Union Panafricaine des Travailleurs Croyants (Pan-African Union of
Believing Workers)
UPADI . . . . . . Union Panamericana de Asociaciones de Ingenieros (Pan American
Federation of Engineering Societies)
UPRP . . . . Union des Paysans Ruraux et Progressistes (Union of Rural and Progressive
Farmers) (Congo – Kasai)
UPY . . . . Union of People's Youth (Bulgaria)
UPM . . . . Union du Peuple Malgache (Malagasy People's Union)
UPA . . . . Union of Poles in America
UPWA . . . . . . Union of Polish Women in America
UPC . . . . Union des Populations du Cameroun (Cameroon People's Union)
UPR . . . . Union des Populations Rurales (Union of Rural People) (Lomela-Kasai)
UNIPOCONGO . . Union des Populations Rurales du Congo (Union of Rural People of the
Congo)
UPAE . . . . Union Postal de las Americas y Espana
UPA . . . . Union Postale Arabe
UPIGO . . . . . . Union Professionnelle Internationale des Gynecologues et Obstetriciens
UPROCO . . . . Union Progressiste du Congo (Progressive Union of the Congo) (Niangara)
UPC . . . . Union Progressiste Congolaise (Congolese Progressive Union)
UPCO . . . . . . Union Progressiste Congolaise (Congolese Progressive Union)
UPECO . . . . . . Union Progressiste Congolaise (Congolese Progressive Union)
UPEQUA . . . . . Union Progressiste de l'Equateur (Progressive Union of Equateur Province)
(Congo – Leopoldville)
UPM . . . . Union Progressiste Mauritanienne (Mauritanian Progressive Union)
UPS . . . . Union Progressiste Senegalaise (Senegalese Progressive Union)
UPFM . . . . Union Progressive des Femmes Marocaines (Progressive Union of Moroccan
Women)
UPHPISEC . . . . Union for the Protection of the Human Person by International, Social
and Economic Cooperation
URSI . . . . Union Radio Scientifique Internationale (French-International Scientific
Radio Union) (Also, ISRI)
URTNA . . . . . . Union des Radio-Televisions Nationales Africaines (Union of African
National Radio and Television Stations)
URR . . . . Union R. R.-Pittsburgh (AAR code)
URB . . . . Union Regionale de Bamileke (Regional Union of Bamileke) (Cameroon)
URSNSC . . . . . Union Regionale des Syndicats du Nyong-et-Sanaga
URSW . . . . . . Union Regionale des Syndicats du Wouri (Regional Union of Wouri Unions)
URD . . . . Union Republicana Democratica (Democratic Republican Union) (Puerto
Rico, Venezuela)
URAC . . . . Union des Republiques de l'Afrique Centrale (Union of Central African
Republics)
URSS . . . . Union des Republiques Socialistes Sovietiques (French for Union of
Socialist Soviet Republics; USSR)
UREHE . . . . . . Union for Research and Experimentation in Higher Education
URPE . . . . Union des Resistants pour une Europe Unie
URCO . . . . . . Union des Ressortissants du Congo pour la Defense et la Promotion du
Congo (Union of Congolese for the Defense and Promotion of the Congo)

URBK . . . . Union Rheinische Braunkohlen Kraftstoff (West Germany)
URUCO . . . . . Union Rurale Congolaise – Buta-Province Orientale (Congolese Rural Union)
USCV . . . . Union Scientifique Continentale du Verre
USN . . . . Union des Scolaires Nigeriens (Union of Nigerian Scholars)
UST . . . . Union Senegalaise du Travail (Senegalese Labor Union)
URF . . . . Union des Services Routiers des Chemins de Fer Europeens
USC . . . . Union Sociale Camerounaise (Cameroonese Social Union)
USMM . . . . . . Union Socialiste des Musulmans Mauritaniens (Socialist Union of Mauritanian Moslems)
UST . . . . Union Socialiste Tchadienne (Chadien Socialist Union)
USA . . . . Union of South Africa
USSR . . . . Union of Soviet Socialist Republics
USSA . . . . Union Suisse des Syndicats Autonomes (Swiss Association of Autonomous Unions)
USA . . . . Union Syndicale de l'Agriculture (Union of Agricultural Workers) (Morocco)
USBA . . . . Union Syndicale des Bases Americaines (Union of American Base Workers) (Morocco)
USS . . . . Union Syndicale Suisse (Swiss Federation of Trade Unions)
USTG . . . . Union Syndicale des Travailleurs de Guinee (Guinean Federation of Workers)
USTS . . . . Union Syndicale des Travailleurs du Soudan (Federation of Sudanese Workers) (Mali)
USAC . . . . Union des Syndicats Autonomes Camerounais (Federation of Cameroonese Autonomous Unions)
USAM . . . . . . Union des Syndicats Autonomes de Madagascar (Federation of Malagasy Autonomous Unions)
USATT . . . . . . Union des Syndicats Autonomes des Travailleurs Tchadiens (Federation of Autonomous Workers Unions of Chad)
USCT . . . . Union des Syndicats Confederes du Togo (Federation of Confederated Unions of Togo)
USCC . . . . Union des Syndicats Croyants du Cameroun (Federation of Cameroonese Believers Unions)
USLD . . . . Union des Syndicats Libres du Dahomey (Federation of Free Unions of Dahomey)
USPC . . . . Union des Syndicats Professionels du Cameroun (Federation of Professional Trade Unions of Cameroon)
USTA . . . . Union des Syndicats des Travailleurs Algeriens (Federation of Unions of Algerian Workers)
USTD . . . . Union des Syndicats des Travailleurs du Dahomey (Federation of Workers Unions of Dahomey)
UTX . . . . Union Tank Car Company (NYSE symbol)
UTE . . . . Union Technique de l'Electricite (France)
UTICI . . . . Union Techniques des Ingenieurs Conseils (France)
UT . . . . Union Terminal Railway Company (AAR code)
UTTS . . . . Union Territoriale du Senegal des Travailleurs (Senegalese Workers Union)
UNISCAMTA . . Union Territoriale des Syndicats de Cadres, Agents de Maitrise, Techniciens et Assimiles du Senegal (Territorial Union of Leaders, Supervising Personnel and Related Workers of Senegal)
UTS-FO . . . . . Union Territoriale des Syndicats - Force Ouvrieres (Territorial Federation of Trade Unions Workers' Force) (French Somaliland)
UTS . . . . Union Theological Seminary
UTSV . . . . Union Theological Seminary in Virginia
UTR . . . . Union Transportation Company (AAR code)
UTA . . . . Union de Transports Aeriens (Privately owned international airline) (France)
UTC . . . . Union des Travailleurs Congolais (Union of Congolese Workers) (Leopoldville)
UTM . . . . Union des Travailleurs de Mauritanie (Union of Workers of Mauritania)
UTMCI . . . . . . Union des Travailleurs de la Moyenne Cote d'Ivoire (Union of Middle Ivory Coast Workers)
UTS . . . . Union des Travailleurs du Senegal (Senegalese Workers Union)
UTAC . . . . Union Tunisienne de l'Artisanat et du Commerce (Tunisian Union of Artisans and Merchants)
UDUAL . . . . . . Union de Universidades de America Latina
UU . . . . Union University (Tennessee)
UCIIM . . . . . . Unione Cattolica Italiana Insegnanti Medi
UIARVEP . . . . . Unione Italiana Agenti Rappresentati Viaggiatori e Piazzisti (Italian Union of Agents and Travelers)
UIB . . . . Unione Italiana Bancari (Italian Union of Bank Employees)
UIDAC . . . . . . Unione Italiana Dipendenti Aziende Commerciali ed Affini (Italian Union of Commercial and Allied Workers)
UILAM . . . . . . Unione Italiana Lavoratori Albergo e Mensa (Italian Union of Hotel and Restaurant Workers)
UILA . . . . Unione Italiana Lavoratori Assicurazioni (Italian Union of Insurance Workers)
UIL-GAS . . . . Unione Italiana Lavoratori Aziende Gas (Italian Union of Gas Workers)
UILC . . . . Unione Italiana Lavoratori Chimici (Italian Union of Chemical Workers)
UILIC . . . . Unione Italiana Lavoratori Imposte Consumo (Italian Union of Food Tax Levy Workers)

UILIA . . . . . . Unione Italiana Lavoratori Industrie Alimentari (Italian Union of Food-Processing Workers)
UILM . . . . Unione Italiana Lavoratori Metallurgici (Italian Metalworkers' Union)
UILPEM . . . . . Unione Italiana Lavoratori Petrolieri e Metanieri (Italian Union of Oil and Methane Gas Workers)
UILS . . . . Unione Italiana Lavoratori Saccariferi (Italian Union of Sugar Industry Workers)
UILT . . . . Unione Italiana Lavoratori delle Terra (National Union of Landworkers) (Italy)
UILT . . . . Unione Italiana Lavoratori Tessili (Italian Union of Textile Workers)
UILVECA . . . . Unione Italiana Lavoratori Vetro, Ceramica ed Abrasivi (Italian Union of Glass, Ceramics and Abrasive Workers)
UIL . . . . Unione Italiana del Lavoro (Italian Union of Labor)
UIM . . . . Unione Italiana Marittimi (Italian Union of Seamen)
UIP . . . . Unione Italiana Pescatori (Italian Union of Fishermen)
UILTRAS . . . . . Unione Italiana Trasporti ed Ausiliari del Traffico (Italian Union of Transport Workers and Auxiliary Services)
ULT . . . . Unione per la Lotta alla Tubercolosi (Union of Anti-Tuberculosis Association Workers) (Italy)
UM . . . . Unione Maniferro (Somalia)
UNDEL . . . . . . Unione Nazionale Dipendenti Enti Locali (National Union of Local Government Employees) (Italy)
UNLA . . . . . . Unione Nazionale per la Lotta contra l'Analfabetismo (Union for the Struggle Against Illiteracy) (Italy)
UPGS . . . . . . Unione Progressista della Gioventu Somala (Progressive Union of Somali Youth)
USFI . . . . Unione Sindacale Ferrovieri Italiani (National Union of Italian Railway Workers)
UNIFET . . . . . Unipolar Field-Effect Transistor
USP . . . . Unique Selling Proposition (Advertising)
UTM . . . . Uniunea Tineretului Muncitor
U . . . . Unit(s)
G . . . . Unit of Acceleration (Military)
UAS . . . . Unit Approval System (for approval of aircraft materials, parts, and appliances) (FAA)
UAL . . . . Unit Authorization List
UCI . . . . Unit Construction Index
UC . . . . Unit Cooler
UE . . . . Unit Equipment (as authorized to an Air Force unit)
UEAC . . . . Unit Equipment Aircraft
UET . . . . Unit Equipment Table (Military)
UEE . . . . Unit Essential Equipment
UESK . . . . Unit Essential Spares Kit (Military)
U/F . . . . Unit of Fire (Army)
UFAED . . . . . . Unit Forecast Authorization Equipment Data
UH . . . . Unit Heater (Technical drawings)
UIC . . . . Unit Identification Code (Army)
U/I . . . . Unit of Issue (Army)
ULD . . . . Unit Logic Device
UMC . . . . Unit Mail Clerk
UMR . . . . Unit Mail Room (Air Force)
UMD . . . . Unit Manning Document
U/M . . . . Unit of Measure
UME . . . . Unit Mobility Equipment
UMI . . . . Unit Movement Identifier (Army)
UNIPAC . . . . . Unit Packaging
UPO . . . . Unit Personnel Office(r)
UPS . . . . Unit Personnel Section (Military)
UPTT . . . . Unit Personnel and Tonnage Table (Military)
UP & T . . . . . Unit Personnel and Tonnage Tables
UP . . . . Unit Price
UPC . . . . Unit Processing Code
UPE . . . . Unit Proficiency Exercise
UPREAL . . . . . Unit Property Record and Equipment Authorization List
UPREL . . . . . . Unit Property Record and Equipment List
USE . . . . Unit Support Equipment
UTP . . . . Unit Territory Plan
UTP . . . . Unit Test Plan
UTC . . . . Unit Time Coding
UTA . . . . Unit Training Assembly (Military)
UTC . . . . Unit Training Center (Military)
UTS . . . . Unit Training Standard
UTL . . . . Unit Transmission Loss
UTS . . . . Unit Trouble Shooting
JT . . . . Unit Under Test
UFSJ . . . . Unitarian Fellowship for Social Justice
UHS . . . . Unitarian Historical Society
ULL . . . . Unitarian Laymen's League
USC . . . . Unitarian Service Committee (Post-World War II)
UUA . . . . Unitarian Universalist Association
UUFSJ . . . . . . Unitarian Universalist Fellowship for Social Justice

UUMA . . . . . . Unitarian Universalist Ministers Association
UUSC . . . . . . Unitarian Universalist Service Committee
UUWF . . . . . . Unitarian Universalist Women's Federation
UNIPRO . . . . . Unite et Progres du Burundi (Unity and Progress of Burundi)
UPRONA . . . . . Unite et Progres National (Unity and National Progress) (Burundi)
U . . . . United
UAA . . . . United Action for Animals
UAA . . . . United African Appeal
UAC . . . . United African Company
UANM . . . . . . United African Nationalist Movement
UA . . . . United Air Lines, Inc.
UAL . . . . United Air Lines (NYSE symbol) (Wall Street slang name: "You All")
UA . . . . United Aircraft Corporation (NYSE symbol)
UAC . . . . United Aircraft Corporation
UAP . . . . United Aircraft Products
UARL . . . . . . United Aircraft Research Laboratories
UAPA . . . . . . United Amateur Press Association
UAC . . . . United American Croats
UAM . . . . United American Mechanics
UAUOC . . . . . United American Ukrainian Organizations Committee
UAIM . . . . . . United Andean Indian Mission
UAR . . . . United Arab Republic
UNA . . . . United Artists Corporation (NYSE symbol)
PPF . . . . United Association of Journeymen and Apprentices of the Plumbing
                  and Pipe Fitting Industry of the United States and Canada
UAP . . . . United Australia Party
UBDMA . . . . . United Better Dress Manufacturers Association
UBS . . . . United Bible Societies
UBS . . . . United Biscuit Company of America (NYSE symbol)
PB . . . . United Board & Carton Corporation (NYSE symbol)
UBCHEA . . . . . United Board for Christian Higher Education in Asia
UBBA . . . . . . United Boys' Brigades of America
UB . . . . United Brethren in Christ
UBA . . . . United Breweries of America
UBCW . . . . . . United Brick and Clay Workers of America
UBCJ . . . . . . United Brotherhood of Carpenters and Joiners
CJA . . . . United Brotherhood of Carpenters and Joiners of America
UBEA . . . . . . United Business Education Association
UBSA . . . . . . United Business Schools Association
UCCF . . . . . . United Campus Christian Fellowship
UCC . . . . United Cancer Council
UCY . . . . United Caribbean Youth
UCF . . . . United-Carr Fastener Corporation (Later, United-Carr, Inc.) (NYSE
                  symbol)
UCF . . . . United Cat Federation
CLGW . . . . . . United Cement, Lime and Gypsum Workers International Union
UCLG . . . . . . United Cement, Lime and Gypsum Workers International Union
UCPA . . . . . . United Cerebral Palsy Associations
UCI . . . . United Charity Institutions of Jerusalem
UCMS . . . . . . United Christian Missionary Society
UCYM . . . . . . United Christian Youth Movement
UCC . . . . United Church of Christ
UCPF . . . . . . United Church Peace Fellowship
UCW . . . . United Church Women of the National Council of Churches
UCT . . . . United Commercial Travelers
UCFC . . . . . . United Community Funds and Councils of America
UCS . . . . United Community Services
UCS . . . . United Computing Systems
UCV . . . . United Confederate Veterans
UCF . . . . United Cooperative Farmers, Inc.
U . . . . United Corporation (NYSE symbol)
UCACEP . . . . . United Council of Associations of Civil Employees of Pakistan
UCP . . . . United Country Party (Australia)
UDC . . . . United Daughters of the Confederacy
UDEC . . . . . . United Digital Electronic Computer
UDSR . . . . . . United Duroc Swine Registry
UEIC . . . . . . United East India Company
UCC . . . . United Electric Coal Companies (NYSE symbol)
UE . . . . United Electrical, Radio and Machine Workers of America
UEF . . . . United Engineering & Foundry Company (NYSE symbol)
UET . . . . United Engineering Trustees
UEA . . . . United Epilepsy Association
UFP . . . . United Federal Party (Northern Rhodesia)
UFCT . . . . . . United Federation of College Teachers (AFL-CIO)
UFDC . . . . . . United Federation of Doll Clubs
UFPC . . . . . . United Federation of Postal Clerks (Formerly, NFPOC)
UFRWO . . . . . United Federation of Russian Workers' Organizations of USA and Canada
UFT . . . . United Federation of Teachers (New York)
UFCA . . . . . . United Film Carriers Association
UFL . . . . United Financial Corporation of California (NYSE symbol)
UFESA . . . . . . United Fire Equipment Service Association

UFC . . . . United Free Church (Scotland)
UFFVA . . . . . . United Fresh Fruit and Vegetable Association
UF . . . . United Fruit Company (NYSE symbol)
UFJC . . . . . . United Fund for Jewish Culture
UFMA . . . . . . United Fur Manufacturers Association
UFW . . . . United Furniture Workers of America
UGJA . . . . . . United Galician Jews of America
UGW . . . . United Garment Workers of America
GCCW . . . . . . United Gas, Coke and Chemical Workers of America
UGC . . . . United Gas Corporation (NYSE symbol)
UGI . . . . United Gas Improvement Company (NYSE symbol)
UGCW . . . . . . United Glass and Ceramic Workers of North America
UGOC . . . . . . United Greek Orthodox Charities
UDG . . . . United-Greenfield Corporation (NYSE symbol)
UHSA . . . . . . United Halsingian Society of America
HCMW . . . . . . United Hatters, Cap and Millinery Workers International Union
UHCMWIU . . . United Hatters, Cap and Millinery Workers International Union
UHF . . . . United Health Foundations
UHT . . . . United Hebrew Trades of the State of New York
UHAA . . . . . . United Horological Association of America
UHJA . . . . . . United Hungarian Jews of America
UHRA . . . . . . United Hunts Racing Association
UIWV . . . . . . United Indian War Veterans, USA
UICWA . . . . . . United Infants' and Children's Wear Association
UIBPIP . . . . . . United International Bureau for the Protection of Intellectual Property
UISA . . . . United Inventors and Scientists of America
UICANY . . . . . United Irish Counties Association of New York
UIW . . . . United Iron Workers
UIA . . . . United Israel Appeal
UIWU . . . . . . United Israel World Union
UIALC . . . . . . United-Italian American Labor Council
UIAL . . . . . . United Italian American League
UJA . . . . United Jewish Appeal
UKARC . . . . . . United Kingdom Agricultural Research Council
UKA . . . . United Kingdom Alliance
UKAEA . . . . . . United Kingdom Atomic Energy Authority
UKCIS . . . . . . United Kingdom Chemical Information Service
UKCR . . . . . . United Kingdom Communication Region (Air Force)
UK . . . . United Kingdom of Great Britain and Ireland
UKIP . . . . United Kingdom Import Plan
UKMRC . . . . . United Kingdom Medical Research Council
UKML . . . . . . United Knitwear Manufacturers League
ULC . . . . United Labor Congress (Nigeria)
ULZP . . . . . . United Labor Zionist Party
ULO . . . . United Labour Organization (Burma)
ULAA . . . . . . United Latin Americans of America
ULPA . . . . . . United Lightning Protection Association
ULRA . . . . . . United Lithuanian Relief Fund of America
ULT . . . . United Lodge of Theosophists
ULCM . . . . . . United Lutheran Church Men
ULS . . . . United Lutheran Society
UMNO . . . . . . United Malays National Organization
UMM . . . . United Merchants & Manufacturers, Inc. (NYSE symbol)
UMC . . . . United Methodist Church
UMFC . . . . . . United Methodist Free Churches
UKO . . . . United Milk Product Company (NYSE symbol)
UMW . . . . . . United Mine Workers of America
UMU . . . . United Mineworker's Union
UMS . . . . United Missionary Society
UMO . . . . United Molasses Company, Ltd.
                  (American Stock Exchange symbol)
UMBA . . . . . . United Mortgage Bankers of America
UMC . . . . United Motor Courts
NAPO . . . . . . United National Association of Post Office Craftsmen
UNAPOC . . . . . United National Association of Post Office Craftsmen
UNIP . . . . . . United National Independence Party (Northern Rhodesia)
UNLIS . . . . . . United National Life Insurance Society
UNP . . . . United National Party (Ceylon)
UN . . . . United Nations
UNAC . . . . . . United Nations Appeal for Children
UNAUS . . . . . United Nations Association of the United States
UNA-USA . . . . United Nations Association of the United States of America
UNAECC . . . . . United Nations Atomic Energy Control Commission
UNAEC . . . . . United Nations Atomic Energy Commission (Superseded by Disarmament
                  Commission, 1952)
UNCDF . . . . . United Nations Capital Development Fund
UNICEF . . . . . United Nations Children's Fund (Acronym taken from former name United
                  Nations International Children's Emergency Fund)
UNCACK . . . . United Nations Civil Assistance Command, Korea
UNC . . . . United Nations Command
UNCR . . . . . . United Nations Command (Rear)

UNCMAC . . . . United Nations Command Military Armistice Commission
UNCIP . . . . . . United Nations Commission for India and Pakistan
UNCITRAL . . . . United Nations Commission for International Trade Law
UNCURK . . . . . United Nations Commission for the Unification and Rehabilitation
        of Korea
UNCOK . . . . . United Nations Committee on Korea
UNCCP . . . . . United Nations Conciliation Commission for Palestine
UNCAST . . . . . United Nations Conference on Applications of Science and Technology
        (1963)
UNCIO . . . . . . United Nations Conference on International Organization
        (San Francisco, 1945)
UNCP . . . . . . United Nations Conference of Plenipotentiaries
UNCTAD . . . . United Nations Conference on Trade and Development
UNCA . . . . . . United Nations Correspondents Associated
UNDP . . . . . . United Nations Development Programme
UNDC . . . . . . United Nations Disarmament Commission (Also known as DC)
UNDI . . . . . . United Nations Document Index
UNEDA . . . . . . United Nations Economic Development Administration
UNESOB . . . . United Nations Economic and Social Office in Beirut
UNEC . . . . United Nations Education Conference
UNESCO . . . . United Nations Educational, Scientific and Cultural Organization
UNEF . . . . United Nations Emergency Force (to separate hostile forces of Israel and
        Egypt)
UNE . . . . . . United Nations European Headquarters (Geneva, Switzerland)
UNFB . . . . . . United Nations Film Board
UNFICYP . . . . United Nations Forces in Cyprus
UNGA . . . . . . United Nations General Assembly
UNHCR . . . . . United Nations High Commissioner for Refugees
UNIDO . . . . . . United Nations Industrial Development Organization
UNIC . . . . United Nations Information Centre
UNIO . . . . United Nations Information Organization
UNITAR . . . . . United Nations Institute for Training and Research
UNIS . . . . United Nations International School
UNJBS . . . . . . United Nations Joint Board of Strategy
UNKRA . . . . . United Nations Korean Reconstruction Agency
UNLL . . . . United Nations League of Lawyers
UNM . . . . United Nations Medal
UNMC . . . . . . United Nations Mediterranean Commission
UNMOGIP . . . . United Nations Military Observer Group in India and Pakistan
UNMAC . . . . United Nations Mixed Armistice Commission
UNOGIL . . . . United Nations Observer Group in Lebanon
UNO . . . . . . United Nations Organization
UNPC . . . . . . United Nations Palestine Commission
UNPIK . . . . . . United Nations Partisan Infantry Korea
UNPOC . . . . . United Nations Peace Observation Commission
UNPA . . . . . . United Nations Postal Administration
UNREF . . . . . . United Nations Refugee Fund
UNRPR . . . . . United Nations Relief for Palestine Refugees
UNRRA . . . . . . United Nations Relief and Rehabilitation Administration ("United Nations"
        in this body's name derives from the wartime alliance of this name,
        not from any affiliation with the postwar international organization)
UNRWA . . . . . United Nations Relief and Works Agency
UNRWAPRNE . . United Nations Relief and Works Agency for Palestine Refugees in the
        Near East (Pronounced: "Un wrap me")
UNRISD . . . . . United Nations Research Institute for Social Development
UNSS . . . . . . United Nations Sales Section (for UN documents)
UNSAC . . . . . United Nations Scientific Advisory Committee
UNSCEAR . . . . United Nations Scientific Committee on the Effects of Atomic Radiation
UNSCCUR . . . . United Nations Scientific Conference on the Conservation and
        Utilization of Resources
UNSG . . . . . . United Nations Secretary General
UNSC . . . . . . United Nations Security Council
UNSFH . . . . . United Nations Security Forces, Hollandia
UNSM . . . . . . United Nations Service Medal
UNSVM . . . . . United Nations Service Medal
UNSC . . . . . . United Nations Social Commission
UNSCOB . . . . United Nations Special Committee on the Balkans (Greece)
UNSCOP . . . . . United Nations Special Committee on Palestine
UNSF . . . . . . United Nations Special Fund
UNSCC . . . . . United Nations Standards Co-ordinating Committee
UNSU . . . . . . United Nations Study Unit (Philatelic organization)
UNTA . . . . . . United Nations Technical Assistance
UNTAA . . . . . United Nations Technical Assistance Administration
UNTCOK . . . . United Nations Temporary Committee on Korea
UNTEA . . . . . . United Nations Temporary Executive Authority (Administers territory of
        West Irian during transfer from the Netherlands to Indonesia)
UNTS . . . . . . United Nations Treaty Series (Project) (University of Washington)
UNTSO . . . . . United Nations Truce Supervision Organization (Works in Middle East
        between Israel and Arab nations)
UNTT . . . . . . United Nations Trust Territory
UNYOM . . . . . United Nations Yemen Observation Mission

UNWCC . . . . . United Nations War Crimes Commission ("United Nations" in this body's
        name derives from the wartime alliance of this name, not from any
        affiliation with the postwar international organization)
UNCF . . . . . . United Negro College Fund
UNCLE . . . . . . United Network Command for Law and Enforcement (Fictitious
        intelligence organization in various television series)
UNC . . . . United Network Company (New TV broadcasting network)
UVW . . . . United New Jersey Railroad and Canal (NYSE symbol)
UNC . . . . United Nuclear Corporation
UOIW . . . . . . United Optical and Instrument Workers of America
UOGC . . . . . . United Order of the Golden Cross
UOTS . . . . . . United Order True Sisters
UOMCA . . . . . United Orthodox Ministers & Cantors Association of America
        & Canada
UPFAW . . . . . . United Packinghouse Food and Allied Workers
UPWA . . . . . United Packinghouse Workers of America
UPNCA . . . . . United Pants and Novelties Contractors Association
UPP . . . . United Papermakers and Paperworkers
UPX . . . . United Paramount Theatres (NYSE symbol)
UPS . . . . United Parcel Service
UPTAJS . . . . . United Parent-Teachers Association of Jewish Schools
UPK . . . . United Park City Mines Company (NYSE symbol)
UPA . . . . United Patternmakers Association
UPP . . . . United People's Party (Sierra Leone)
UPPN . . . . . . United People's Party of Nigeria
PGW . . . . . . United Plant Guard Workers of America
UPGWA . . . . . United Plant Guard Workers of America
UPDA . . . . . . United Plastics Distributors Association
UPDMA . . . . . United Popular Dress Manufacturers Association
UPW . . . . United Port Workers' Union (Ceylon)
UPSS . . . . . . United Postal Stationery Society
UPC . . . . United Power Company (British)
UP . . . . United Presbyterian
UPC . . . . United Presbyterian Church
UPPF . . . . . . United Presbyterian Peace Fellowship
UP . . . . United Press (Merged with International News Service to form UPI)
UPI . . . . United Press International
UPIN . . . . . . United Press International Newspictures
UPG . . . . Union Progressiste Guineenne (Guinean Progressive Union)
UP . . . . United Provinces (India)
UPW . . . . United Public Workers of America
UROC . . . . . . **United Railroad Operating Crafts**
URWA . . . . . Ur ted Railroad Workers of America
URF . . . . **United Republican Fund**
URA . . . . United Republicans of America
URI . . . . United Research, Incorporated
URS . . . . United Research Service
URFDA-NYC . . United Retail Fish Dealers Association of New York City
URO . . . . United Rink Operators
URJA . . . . United Roumanian Jews of America
URW . . . . United Rubber, Cork, Linoleum and Plastic Workers of America
UROBA . . . . . . United Russian Orthodox Brotherhood of America
USSA . . . . . . United Saw Service Association
USA . . . . United Scenic Artists
USS . . . . United Scholarship Service
USS . . . . United Seamen's Service
US . . . . United Service
USO . . . . United Service Organizations
USA . . . . United Shareholders of America
USA . . . . United Shareowners of America
USH . . . . United Shoe Machinery Corporation
        (NYSE symbol)
USM . . . . United Shoe Machinery Corporation
USWA . . . . . . United Shoe Workers of America
RDWW . . . . . . **United Slate Tile and Composition Roofers, Damp and Waterproof**
        Workers Association
USA . . . . . . United Soccer Association
USUSA . . . . . . United Societies of the United States of America
USCL . . . . United Society for Christian Literature (British)
USI . . . . United Sons of Israel
USWV . . . . . . United Spanish War Veterans
US . . . . United States (of America)
USAN . . . . . . United States Adopted Name (Drugs)
USACIECA . . . . United States Advisory Commission on International Educational
        and Cultural Affairs
ACA . . . . United States Advisory Committee on the Arts
USAID . . . . . . United States Agency for International Development
USAIRA . . . . . United States Air Attache
USAC . . . . . . United States Air Corps
USACSR . . . . . United States Air Corps Specialist Reserve
USAF . . . . United States Air Force

USAFA . . . . . . United States Air Force Academy
USAFACS . . . . United States Air Force Air Crew School
USAFAPS . . . . United States Air Force Air Police School
USAFAPC . . . . United States Air Force Airframe Production Contract
USAFBMD . . . . United States Air Force Ballistic Missile Division
USAFBS . . . . . . United States Air Force Bandsman School
USAFBMS . . . . United States Air Force Basic Military School
USAFBS . . . . . United States Air Force Bombardment School
USAFD . . . . . . United States Air Force Dictionary
USAFETAC . . . . United States Air Force Environmental Technical Applications Center
USAFEL . . . . . . United States Air Force Epidemiological Laboratory
USAFE . . . . . . United States Air Force in Europe
USAFETPS . . . . United States Air Force Experimental Test Pilot School
USAFECI . . . . United States Air Force Extension Course Institute
USAFFGS . . . . United States Air Force Flexible Gunnery School
USAFFSR . . . . . United States Air Force Flight Safety Research
USAFHD . . . . . United States Air Force Historical Division
USAFIT . . . . . United States Air Force Institute of Technology
USAFMTC . . . . United States Air Force Marksmanship Training Center
USAFMEPCS . . . United States Air Force Mideast Postal and Courier Service
USAFNS . . . . United States Air Force Navigation School
USAFOCS . . . . United States Air Force Officer Candidate School
USAFPACPCS . . United States Air Force Pacific Postal and Courier Service
USAFPEB . . . . . United States Air Force Physical Evaluation Board
USAFPS . . . . . United States Air Force Pilot School
USAFRS . . . . . . United States Air Force Recruiting Service
USAFR . . . . . . United States Air Force Representative
USAIRMILCOMUN . . United States Air Force Representative, UN Military Staff
Committee
USAFR . . . . . . United States Air Force Reserve
USAFSAM . . . . United States Air Force School of Aerospace Medicine
USAFSS . . . . . . United States Air Force Security Service
USAFSAWC . . . . United States Air Force Special Air Warfare Center
USAFSRA . . . . . United States Air Force Special Reporting Agency
USAFSE . . . . . . United States Air Force Supervisory Examination
USAFTARC . . . . United States Air Force Tactical Air Reconnaissance Center
USAFTAWC . . . . United States Air Force Tactical Air Warfare Center
USAFTALC . . . . United States Air Force Tactical Airlift Center
USAFTFWC . . . United States Air Force Tactical Fighter Weapons Center
USAFTS . . . . . United States Air Force Technical School
USAFWPO . . . . United States Air Force Water Port Liaison Office(r)
USAFAGOS . . . United States Air Force's Air-Ground Operations School
USAFLANT . . . United States Air Forces, Atlantic
USAFI . . . . . . United States Air Forces Institute
USAFPAC . . . . United States Air Forces, Pacific
USAFSO . . . . . United States Air Forces Southern Command
USAFSTRIKE . . . United States Air Forces Strike Command
USAS . . . . United States Air Service
USACA . . . . . . United States Allied Commission Austria
USAC . . . . . . United States Alpine Club
USABF . . . . . . United States Amateur Baseball Federation
USALA . . . . . . United States Amateur Lacrosse Association
USARSA . . . . . United States Amateur Roller Skating Association
USAWF . . . . . . United States Amateur Wrestling Foundation
USA . . . . United States of America
USASCSOCR . . United States of America Standard Character Set for Optical Character
Recognition
USASCII . . . . . United States of America Standard Code for Information Interchange
USASI . . . . . . United States of America Standards Institute (Formerly, ASA; now ANSI)
USAPO . . . . . . United States Antarctic Projects Office
USARP . . . . . . United States Antarctic Research Program (National Science Foundation)
USAARC . . . . . United States Antiaircraft Replacement Center
USAFI . . . . . . United States Armed Forces Institute
USAFIME . . . . United States Armed Forces in Middle East
USASEXC . . . . United States Armed Services Exploitation Center
USAA . . . . United States Armor Association
USACDA . . . . United States Arms Control and Disarmament Agency
USA . . . . United States Army
USAAGDPSC . . United States Army Adjutant General Data Processing Service Center
USAAGPC . . . . United States Army Adjutant General Publications Centers
USAAGS . . . . . United States Army Adjutant General's School
USAAC . . . . . . United States Army Administration Center
USAADVCOM . . United States Army Advance Command
USAAGNG . . . United States Army Advisory Group (National Guard)
USAARU . . . . United States Army Aeromedical Research Unit
USAADB . . . . . United States Army Air Defense Board
USARADBD . . . . United States Army Air Defense Board
USAADCEN . . . United States Army Air Defense Center
USARADCOM . . United States Army Air Defense Command
USAADEA . . . . United States Army Air Defense Engineering Agency (AEC) (Formerly
USASADEA)

USAADS . . . . . United States Army Air Defense School
USARADSCH . . United States Army Air Defense School
USAAF . . . . . . United States Army Air Forces
USAAFIME . . . . United States Army Air Forces in the Middle East
USAAFUK . . . . United States Army Air Forces in the United Kingdom
USAASC . . . . . United States Army Air Service Command
USAATCO . . . . United States Army Air Traffic Coordinating Officer(s)
USAABELCTBD . . United States Army Airborne and Electronics Board
USAAESWBD . . United States Army Airborne, Electronics and Special Warfare Board
USAABMU . . . . United States Army Aircraft Base Maintenance Unit
USARAL . . . . . United States Army, Alaska
USARACS . . . . United States Army Alaska Communications Center
USAACS . . . . . United States Army Ambulance Service Association
USAAPSA . . . . United States Army Ammunition Procurement and Supply Agency
USAATBD . . . . United States Army Arctic Test Board
USAATC . . . . . United States Army Arctic Test Center
USAARMBD . . . United States Army Armor Board
USAARMC . . . . United States Army Armor Center
USAARENBD . . United States Army Armor and Engineer Board
USAARMHRU . . United States Army Armor Human Research Unit
USAARMS . . . . United States Army Armor School
USAARTYBD . . . United States Army Artillery Board
USAAMC . . . . United States Army Artillery and Missile Center
USAAMS . . . . United States Army Artillery and Missile School
USARMA . . . . United States Army Attache
USAAA . . . . . United States Army Audit Agency
USAAAWR . . . . United States Army Audit Agency, Washington Region
USAAB . . . . . . United States Army Aviation Board
USAAVNBD . . . United States Army Aviation Board
USAAVNC . . . . United States Army Aviation Center (CONARC)
USAACDA . . . . United States Army Aviation Combat Developments Agency (CDC)
USAFIB . . . . . . United States Army Aviation Flight Information Bulletin
USAAFIO . . . . United States Army Aviation Flight Information Office
USAAVNHRU . . United States Army Aviation Human Research Unit
USAAVCOM . . United States Army Aviation Materiel Command
USAAML . . . . United States Army Aviation Materiel Laboratories
USAAVLABS . . . United States Army Aviation Materiel Laboratories
USAAVNS . . . . United States Army Aviation School (CONARC)
USAASTA . . . . United States Army Aviation Systems Test Activity
USAAVNTA . . . United States Army Aviation Test Activity
USAAVNTBD . . United States Army Aviation Test Board
USAAFO . . . . . United States Army Avionics Field Office (Formerly USASAFO)
USABRL . . . . . United States Army Ballistic Research Laboratories
USABESRL . . . . United States Army Behavioral Science Research Laboratory
USAB . . . . United States Army, Berlin
USABIOLABS . . United States Army Biological Laboratories
USABAAR . . . . United States Army Board for Aviation Accident Research
USABVAPAC . . United States Army Broadcasting and Visual Activities, Pacific
CAR . . . . United States Army Caribbean
USARCARIB . . . United States Army, Caribbean
USACHB . . . . . United States Army Chaplain Board
USACHS . . . . . United States Army Chaplain School
USACBRWOC . . United States Army Chemical, Biological, and Radiological Weapons
Orientation Course
USACMLC . . . . United States Army Chemical Center
USACMLCS . . . United States Army Chemical Center and School
USACMLCB . . . United States Army Chemical Corps Board
ENCOM . . . . . United States Army Chemical Corps Engineering Command
USACCIA . . . . United States Army Chemical Corps Intelligence Agency
USACMLCSCH . . United States Army Chemical Corps School
USACCTC . . . . United States Army Chemical Corps Technical Committee
USACMLRDL . . United States Army Chemical Research & Development Laboratories
USACWL . . . . . United States Army Chemical Warfare Laboratory
USACSS . . . . . United States Army Chief of Support Services
USACAS . . . . . United States Army Civil Affairs School
USACTC . . . . . United States Army Clothing and Textile Center
USACTMC . . . . United States Army Clothing and Textile Materiel Center
USACCL . . . . . United States Army Coating and Chemical Laboratory
USACRREL . . . . United States Army Cold Regions Research and Engineering Laboratory
USACDC . . . . . United States Army Combat Developments Command
USACDCADA . . United States Army Combat Developments Command Air Defense Agency
USACDCARMA . . United States Army Combat Developments Command Armor Agency
USACDCARTYA . . United States Army Combat Developments Command Artillery Agency
USACDCAVNA . . United States Army Combat Developments Command Aviation Agency
USACDCCHA . . United States Army Combat Developments Command Chaplain Agency
USACDCCBRA . . United States Army Combat Developments Command Chemical-Biological-
Radiological Agency
USACDCCAA . . United States Army Combat Developments Command Civil Affairs Agency
USACDCCAG . . United States Army Combat Developments Command Combat Army Group
USACDCCSSG . . United States Army Combat Developments Command Combat Service
Support Group

USACDCCEA . . United States Army Combat Developments Command Communications-
         Electronics Agency
USACDCDPFO . . United States Army Combat Developments Command Data Processing
         Field Office
USACDCEA . . . United States Army Combat Developments Command Engineer Agency
USACDCFINA . . United States Army Combat Developments Command Finance Agency
USACDCIA . . . United States Army Combat Developments Command Infantry Agency
USACDCIAS . . United States Army Combat Developments Command Institute of Advanced
         Studies
USACDCICAS . . United States Army Combat Developments Command Institute of Combined
         Arms and Support
USACDCILC . . . United States Army Combat Developments Command Institute of Land
         Combat
USACDCINS . . United States Army Combat Developments Command Institute of Nuclear
         Studies
USACDCISS . . United States Army Combat Developments Command Institute of Special
         Studies
USACDCISA . . . United States Army Combat Developments Command Institute of Systems
         Analysis
USACDCINTA . . United States Army Combat Developments Command Intelligence Agency
USACDCIDDFO . . United States Army Combat Developments Command Internal Defense
         and Development Field Office
USACDCJAA . . United States Army Combat Developments Command Judge Advocate
         Agency
USACDCMA . . . United States Army Combat Developments Command Maintenance Agency
USACDCMSA . . United States Army Combat Developments Command Medical Service
         Agency
USACDCMPA . . United States Army Combat Developments Command Military Police
         Agency
USACDCPASA . . United States Army Combat Developments Command Personnel and
         Administrative Services Agency
USACDCSWA . . United States Army Combat Developments Command Special Warfare
         Agency
USACDCSA . . United States Army Combat Developments Command Supply Agency
USACDCTA . . United States Army Combat Developments Command Transportation Agency
USACDEC . . . . United States Army Combat Developments Experimentation Center
USACSA . . . . . United States Army Combat Surveillance Agency
USACSS . . . . . United States Army Combat Surveillance School
USACARMSCDA . . United States Army Combined Arms Combat Developments Agency
USACGSC . . . United States Army Command and General Staff College
USACIU . . . . . United States Army Command Information Unit
USACMS . . . . . United States Army Command Management School
USACRAPAC . . United States Army Command Reconnaissance Activities, Pacific Command
USACA . . . . . . United States Army Communications Agency
USACOMZEUR . . United States Army Communications Zone, Europe
USACSC . . . . United States Army Computer Systems Command
USACSSEC . . . United States Army Computer Systems Support and Evaluation Command
USACAF . . . . . United States Army Construction Agency, France
USACAK . . . . United States Army Construction Agency, Korea
USACAC . . . . . United States Army Continental Army Command (CONARC)
USAC . . . . United States Army Corps
USACE . . . . . . United States Army Corps of Engineers (Merged with General Equipment
         Command)
USACISO . . . . United States Army Counterinsurgency Support Office, Okinawa
USACRF . . . . . United States Army Counterintelligence Records Facility
USACS . . . . . United States Army Courier Service
USACSTA . . . . United States Army Courier Station
USADPC . . . . . United States Army Data Processing Center
USADSC . . . . United States Army Data Services and Administrative Systems Command
USADATCOM . . United States Army Data Support Command
USADC . . . . . . United States Army Data Support Command
USADEG . . . . . United States Army Dependents' Education Group
USADJ . . . . . . United States Army Depot, Japan
USADOFL . . . . United States Army Diamond Ordnance Fuze Laboratory
USADRB . . . . . United States Army Discharge Review Board
USAD . . . . United States Army Dispensary
USAEIS . . . . . United States Army Electronic Intelligence and Security
USAREPG . . . . United States Army Electronic Proving Ground
USAERDA . . . . United States Army Electronic Research & Development Agency
USAEC . . . . . . United States Army Electronics Command
USAECOM . . . . United States Army Electronics Command
USAECA . . . . . United States Army Electronics Command Computation Agency
USAEFMA . . . . United States Army Electronics Command Financial Management Agency
USAERA . . . . . United States Army Electronics Command Logistics Research Agency
USAEPA . . . . . United States Army Electronics Command Patent Agency
USAEMA . . . . . United States Army Electronics Materiel Agency (Formerly, USASSA)
USAEMSA . . . . United States Army Electronics Materiel Support Agency (Formerly,
         USASMSA)
USAEPG . . . . . United States Army Electronics Proving Ground
USAERDAW . . . United States Army Electronics Research and Development Activity,
         White Sands (New Mexico)

USAERDL . . . . . United States Army Electronics Research and Development Laboratory
         (Formerly, USASRDL)
USAESC . . . . . United States Army Electronics Support Command
USAEB . . . . . . United States Army Engineer Board
USAECFB . . . . United States Army Engineer Center and Fort Belvoir
USAECR . . . . . United States Army Engineer Center Regiment
USAEGD . . . . . United States Army Engineer Gulf District
USAES . . . . . . United States Army Engineer Shcool
USAETL . . . . . United States Army Engineer Topographic Laboratories
USAEWES . . . . United States Army Engineer Waterways Experiment Station
USAEEC . . . . . United States Army Enlisted Evaluation Center
USAEHL . . . . . United States Army Environmental Health Laboratory
USAEHA . . . . . United States Army Environmental Hygiene Agency
USAEARC . . . . United States Army Equipment Authorizations Review Center
USAREUR . . . . United States Army, Europe
USAEAGSC . . . United States Army, Europe, Adjutant General Support Center
USAREURORDCOM . . United States Army European Ordnance Command
USAEU . . . . . . United States Army Exhibit Unit
USAFS . . . . . . United States Army Finance School
USAF . . . . United States Army Forces
USARFANT . . . United States Army Forces, Antilles
USARLANT . . . United States Army Forces, Atlantic
USAFIA . . . . . United States Army Forces in Australia
USAFBI . . . . . . United States Army Forces in the British Isles
USAFICPA . . . . United States Army Forces in Central Pacific Area
USAFFE . . . . . . United States Army Forces, Far East (World War II)
USAFIK . . . . . United States Army Forces in Korea
AFMIDPAC . . . US Army Forces, Middle Pacific (Official name for the theater
         of war more commonly called MIDPAC) (World War II)
MIDPAC . . . . . US Army Forces, Middle Pacific (Name commonly used for AFMIDPAC)
USAFINZ . . . . United States Army Forces in New Zealand
AFPAC . . . . . . US Army Forces in the Pacific (World War II)
USAFSA . . . . . United States Army Forces in South America
USAFISPA . . . . United States Army Forces in the South Pacific Area
USARSO . . . . . United States Army Forces Southern Command
USARSOUTHCOM . . United States Army Forces Southern Command
USARSO-PR . . . United States Army Forces, Southern Command – Puerto Rico
USARSTRIKE . . . United States Army Forces Strike Command
USARFT . . . . . United States Army Forces, Taiwan
AFWESPAC . . . US Army Forces, Western Pacific
USAFSTC . . . . . United States Army Foreign Science and Technology Center
USAG . . . . United States Army Garrison
USAGSC . . . . . United States Army General Supplies Commodity Center
USAGIMRADA . . United States Army Geodesy Intelligence and Mapping Research and
         Development Agency
USAG . . . . . . United States Army in Greece
USAGG . . . . . United States Army Group, American Mission for Aid to Greece
USARHAW . . . United States Army, Hawaii
USAHOME . . . . United States Army Homes (Prefabricated houses, shipped overseas)
USAHTN . . . . . United States Army Hometown News Center
USAH . . . . United States Army Hospital
USAHEL . . . . . United States Army Human Engineering Laboratories
USAIPSG . . . . United States Army Industrial and Personnel Security Group
USAIB . . . . United States Army Infantry Board
USAIC . . . . . . United States Army Infantry Center
USAINFHRU . . . United States Army Infantry Human Research Unit
USAIS . . . . . . United States Army Infantry School
USAIDSC . . . . . United States Army Information and Data Systems Command
USAIDSCOM . . United States Army Information and Data Systems Command
USARIS . . . . . . United States Army Information School
USAIDR . . . . . United States Army Institute of Dental Research
USAINTB . . . . United States Army Intelligence Board
USAINTC . . . . United States Army Intelligence Center
USAINTC . . . . United States Army Intelligence Command
USAIC . . . . . . United States Army Intelligence Corps
USAINTELMDA . . United States Army Intelligence Materiel Developments Agency
USAINTS . . . . . United States Army Intelligence School
USAITFG . . . . . United States Army Intelligence Threats and Forecasts Group
USAICA . . . . . United States Army Interagency Communications Agency
USAIRR . . . . . . United States Army Investigative Records Repository
USAIRC . . . . . . United States Army Ionizing Radiation Center
USARJ . . . . . . United States Army, Japan
USAJFKCENSPWAR . . United States Army John F. Kennedy Center for Special Warfare
         (Airborne)
USAJSC . . . . . United States Army Joint Support Command
USALS . . . . . . United States Army Language School
USALDRHRU . . . United States Army Leadership Human Research Unit
USARMLO . . . . United States Army Liaison Officer
USALWL . . . . . United States Army Limited War Laboratory
USALCJ . . . . . United States Army Logistical Center, Japan
USALDJ . . . . . United States Army Logistics Depot, Japan

USALMC .... United States Army Logistics Management Center
USAMB...... United States Army Maintenance Board
USAMIDA .... United States Army Major Item Data Agency
USAMETA .... United States Army Management Engineering Training Agency
USAMS ..... United States Army Management School
USAMSSA .... United States Army Management Systems Support Agency
USAMC...... United States Army Materiel Command
USAMCFSA ... United States Army Materiel Command Field Safety Agency
USAM & TTC.. United States Army Mechanical & Technical Training Center (Also called MECHTECH)
USAMBRL .... United States Army Medical Biomechanical Research Laboratory
USAMC...... United States Army Medical Corps
USAMERDL ... United States Army Medical Equipment Research and Development Laboratory
USAMMA .... United States Army Medical Material Agency
USAMOAMA .. United States Army Medical Optical and Maintenance Activity
USAMRDC .... United States Army Medical Research and Development Command
USAMRL .... United States Army Medical Research Laboratory
USAMRN..... United States Army Medical Research and Nutrition
USAMRNL .... United States Army Medical Research and Nutrition Laboratory
USAMRU .... United States Army Medical Research Unit
USAMEDS .... United States Army Medical Service
USAMSMADHS .. United States Army Medical Service Meat and Dairy Hygiene School
USAMEDSVS .. United States Army Medical Service Veterinary School
USAMEDTC ... United States Army Medical Training Center
USAMUFD .... United States Army Medical Unit, Fort Detrick (Maryland)
USAMCC .... United States Army Metrology and Calibration Center
USAMAPLA ... United States Army Military Assistance Program Logistics Agency
USAMMT..... United States Army Military Mail Terminal
USAMPS ..... United States Army Military Police School
USAMP...... United States Army Mine Planter
USARMIS .... United States Army Mission
USAMC...... United States Army Missile Command
USAMICOM .. United States Army Missile Command
USAMC...... United States Army Mobility Command
USAMECOM .. United States Army Mobility Equipment Command
USAM ...... United States Army Mothers Organization, National
USAMC..... United States Army Munitions Command
USAMUCOM .. United States Army Munitions Command
USANAFBA ... United States Army, Navy and Air Force Bandsmen's Association
USANWTC ... United States Army Northern Warfare Training Center
USANWCG ... United States Army Nuclear Weapon Coordination Group
USANWSG ... United States Army Nuclear Weapon Systems Surety Group
USANC...... United States Army Nurse Corps
USAOAC..... United States Army Ordnance Ammunition Command (Merged with Munitions Command)
USAOC & S .. United States Army Ordnance Center and School
USAORDCORPS .. United States Army Ordnance Corps
USAOCBRL .. United States Army Ordnance Corps Ballistic Research Laboratory
USAOCCCL... United States Army Ordnance Corps Coating & Chemical Laboratory
USAOCDPS ... United States Army Ordnance Corps Development & Proof Services
USAOD...... United States Army Ordnance District
USAOGMS ... United States Army Ordnance Guided Missile School
USAOMC .... United States Army Ordnance Missile Command (Later, Missile Command)
USAORRF .... United States Army Ordnance Rocket Research Facility
USAOSWAC... United States Army Ordnance Special Weapons-Ammunition Command
USAOWC .... United States Army Ordnance Weapons Command (Merged with Missile Command)
USAOSREPLSTA .. United States Army Oversea Replacement Station
USAORP ..... United States Army Oversea Research Program
USAOSANO .. United States Army Oversea Supply Agency, New Orleans
USAOSANY... United States Army Oversea Supply Agency, New York
USAOSASF ... United States Army Oversea Supply Agency, San Francisco
USARPAC .... United States Army, Pacific
USAPT ...... United States Army Parachute Team
USAPG ..... United States Army Participation Group
USAPERSCEN .. United States Army Personnel Center
USAPRO .... United States Army Personnel Research Office
USAPSG ..... United States Army Personnel Security Group
USAPC ..... United States Army Petroleum Center
USAPA ..... United States Army Photographic Agency
USAPIC ..... United States Army Photointerpretation Center
USAPDA .... United States Army Physical Disability Agency
USAPRC .... United States Army Physical Review Council
USAPC ..... United States Army Pictorial Center
USAPRDC .... United States Army Polar Research and Development Center
USAPHS ..... United States Army Primary Helicopter School
USAPDC ..... United States Army Property Disposal Center (Merged with Defense Logistics Services Center)
USAQMCENFL .. United States Army Quartermaster Center and Fort Lee

USAQMC .... United States Army Quartermaster Corps (Merged with Supply & Maintenance Command)
USAQMS .... United States Army Quartermaster School
USAQMTC ... United States Army Quartermaster Training Command
USARPA .... United States Army Radio Propagation Agency
USARECSTA... United States Army Reception Station
USARCEN .... United States Army Records Center
USAREC ..... United States Army Recruiting Command
USARDA .... United States Army Regional Dental Activity
USARDL .... United States Army Research and Development Laboratories
USARDORAG .. United States Army Research and Development Operational Research Advisory Group
USARIEM..... United States Army Research Institute of Environmental Medicine
USARO ...... United States Army Research Office
USAR ...... United States Army Reserve
USARC ...... United States Army Reserve Center
USARET-RSGSTA.. United States Army Returnee – Reassignment Station
USARYIS ..... United States Army, Ryukyu Islands
USASCA .... United States Army Satellite Communications Agency
USASATCOMA .. United States Army Satellite Communications Agency
USASCHEUR... United States Army School, Europe
USASA ..... United States Army Security Agency
USASOS .... United States Army Services of Supply
USASADEA ... United States Army Signal Air Defense Engineering Agency (Now USAADEA)
USASATSA.... United States Army Signal Aviation Test Support Activity
USASAFO .... United States Army Signal Avionics Field Office (Now USAAFO)
USASCS .... United States Army Signal Center and School
USASCSA .... United States Army Signal Communications Security Agency
USASC ...... United States Army Signal Corps (Merged with Communications and Electronics Command)
USASIGC ..... United States Army Signal Corps (Merged with Communications & Electronics Command)
USASADEA ... United States Army Signal and Defense Electronic Agency
USASEA .... United States Army Signal Engineering Agency
USASESA.... United States Army Signal Equipment Support Agency
USASIMSA.... United States Army Signal Materiel Support Agency (Now USAEMSA)
USASMSA .... United States Army Signal Materiel Support Agency (Now USAEMSA)
USASRDL..... United States Army Signal Research and Development Laboratory (Later, USAERDL)
USASSA ..... United States Army Signal Supply Agency (Now USAEC)
USASSAFMPO . United States Army Signal Supply Agency, Fort Monmouth Procurement Office
USASSAMRO .. United States Army Signal Supply Agency, Midwestern Regional Office
USASSAUSAEPGPO .. United States Army Signal Supply Agency, United States Army Electronic Proving Ground Procurement Office
USASSAWPO .. United States Army Signal Supply Agency, Washington Procurement Office
USASSAWRO .. United States Army Signal Supply Agency, Western Regional Office
USASTC ..... United States Army Signal Training Center (Fort Gordon, Georgia)
USASTCFM ... United States Army Signal Training Command and Fort Monmouth
USASESS .... United States Army Southeastern Signal School
USASETAF.... United States Army Southern European Task Force
USASTAF..... United States Army Southern European Task Force
USASFV ..... United States Army Special Forces, Vietnam
USASSD ..... United States Army Special Security Detachment
USASWS .... United States Army Special Warfare School
USASTAF .... United States Army Strategic Air Forces in the Pacific
USASCC ..... United States Army Strategic Communications Command
USASTRATCOM .. United States Army Strategic Communications Command
USASTRATCOM-CONUS .. United States Army Strategic Communications Command – Continental United States
USASTRATCOM-EUR .. United States Army Strategic Communications Command – Europe
USASTRATCOM-PAC .. United States Army Strategic Communications Command – Pacific
USASTRATCOM-SO .. United States Army Strategic Communications Command – South
USASTRATCOM-V.. United States Army Strategic Communications Command – Vietnam
USASIS...... United States Army Strategic Intelligence School
USASC ...... United States Army Subsistence Center
USASMC..... United States Army Supply and Maintenance Command (AMC) (Formerly, QMC)
USASPTC..... United States Army Support Center
USASPTCM ... United States Army Support Center, Memphis
USASPTCP... United States Army Support Center, Philadelphia
USASPTCR.... United States Army Support Center, Richmond
USASUPCOM-CRB.. United States Army Support Command – Cam Ranh Bay
USASUPCOM-QN.. United States Army Support Command – Qui Nhon
USASUPCOM-SGN .. United States Army Support Command – Saigon
USASCV ..... United States Army Support Command, Vietnam
USASGV ..... United States Army Support Group, Vietnam
USASRU ..... United States Army Surgical Research Unit

USATACOM... United States Army Tank-Automotive Command
USATCA ..... United States Army Terminal Command/Atlantic
USATCEUR.... United States Army Terminal Command Europe
USATCG ..... United States Army Terminal Command, Gulf
USATCP ..... United States Army Terminal Command/Pacific
USATDGL .... United States Army Terminal Detachment, Great Lakes
USATUC ..... United States Army Terminal Unit, Canaveral
USATEC ..... United States Army Test and Evaluation Command (AMC)
USATECOM ... United States Army Test and Evaluation Command
USATC ...... United States Army Training Center
USATCD ..... United States Army Training Center, Air Defense
USATAC ..... United States Army Training Center, Engineer (Fort Leonard Wood, Missouri)
USATC FA.... United States Army Training Center, Field Artillery
USATCFLW ... United States Army Training Center and Fort Leonard Wood
USATRFSTA ... United States Army Transfer Station
USAT .... United States Army Transport
USATA(WH)... United States Army Transportation Agency (White House)
USATATSA ... United States Army Transportation Aircraft Test and Support Activity
USATAFO .... United States Army Transportation Aviation Field Office
USATCFE..... United States Army Transportation Center and Fort Eustis
USATCRTSA... United States Army Transportation Corps Road Test Support Activity
USATEA ..... United States Army Transportation Engineering Agency
USATREOG ... United States Army Transportation Environmental Operations Group
USATIA...... United States Army Transportation Intelligence Agency
USATMC ..... United States Army Transportation Materiel Command
USATRC ..... United States Army Transportation Research Command
USATRECOM .. United States Army Transportation Research and Engineering Command
USATSCH .... United States Army Transportation School
USATTB ..... United States Army Transportation Terminal, Brooklyn
USATTCARC... United States Army Transportation Terminal Command, Arctic
USATTCA .... United States Army Transportation Terminal Command, Atlantic
USATTCG .... United States Army Transportation Terminal Command, Gulf
USATTCP .... United States Army Transportation Terminal Command, Pacific
USATTAY .... United States Army Transportation Test Activity, Yuma (Arizona)
USATTC ..... United States Army Transportation Training Command
USATTC ..... United States Army Tropic Test Center
USARV ...... United States Army Vietnam
USAWC...... United States Army War College
USAWC ..... United States Army Weapons Command (AMC)
USAWECOM .. United States Army Weapons Command
USAARMA .... United States Assistant Army Attache
USLANT ..... United States Atlantic Subarea
USAEC ...... United States Atomic Energy Commission
USAC .... United States Auto Club
USBRO ...... United States Base Requirements Overseas
USBF .... United States Baseball Federation
USBWA ..... United States Basketball Writers Association
USBSA ...... United States Beet Sugar Association
USBMG...... United States Berlin Mission in Germany
USBGA ..... United States Blind Golfer's Association
USBTA ...... United States Board of Tax Appeals (Later, the Tax Court of the United States)
USBE .... United States Book Exchange
UBX........ US Borax & Chemical Corporation (NYSE symbol)
USBP .... United States Border Patrol (Treasury Department)
USBG ...... United States Botanic Garden
USBATU ..... United States – Brazil Aviation Training Unit
USBA .... United States Brewers Association
USBF .... United States Brewers Foundation
USBBS...... United States Bureau of Biological Survey
USBEP...... United States Bureau of Engraving and Printing
USBF .... United States Bureau of Fisheries
USBFDC ..... United States Bureau of Foreign and Domestic Commerce
USBGN...... United States Bureau of Geographical Names
USBIA...... United States Bureau of Insular Affairs
USBLS...... United States Bureau of Labor Statistics
USBL ...... United States Bureau of Lighthouses
USBM ...... United States Bureau of Mines
USBN ...... United States Bureau of Navigation
USBNP ..... United States Bureau of Navy Personnel
USBPR...... United States Bureau of Public Roads
USBR ...... United States Bureau of Reclamation (Department of the Interior)
USBS ...... United States Bureau of Standards
USCC ...... United States Cancellation Club
USCSRA ..... United States Cane Sugar Refiners' Association
USCSSB..... United States Cap Screw Service Bureau
USCHS ..... United States Capitol Historical Society
USCC ...... United States Catholic Conference (Formerly, NCWC)
USCHS ..... United States Catholic Historical Society
USCC ...... United States Chamber of Commerce

USCF ...... United States Chess Federation
USCF ...... United States Churchill Foundation
USCC ...... United States Circuit Court
CCA........ United States Circuit Court of Appeals (See CA)
USCCA ..... United States Circuit Court of Appeals
USC .... United States Citizen
USCRA ..... United States Citizens' Rights Association
USCAR ..... United States Civil Administration, Ryukyu Islands
USCAM...... United States Civil Aviation Mission
USCDC ..... United States Civil Defense Council
USCSC ..... United States Civil Service Commission
USCSE ...... United States Civil Service Examination
USCGS ..... United States Coast and Geodetic Survey
USC & GS.... United States Coast and Geodetic Survey
USCG...... United States Coast Guard
USCGA ..... United States Coast Guard Academy
USCGAD..... United States Coast Guard Air Detachment
USCGAS..... United States Coast Guard Air Station
USCGASB .... United States Coast Guard Aircraft and Supply Base
USCGAUX ... United States Coast Guard Auxiliary
USCGB...... United States Coast Guard Base
USCGC ..... United States Coast Guard Cutter
USCGD...... United States Coast Guard Depot
USCGRC ..... United States Coast Guard Receiving Center
USCGR ..... United States Coast Guard Reserve
USCGR(T) .... United States Coast Guard, Reserve (Temporary)
USCGR(W)... United States Coast Guard, Reserve (Women)
USCGSCF .... United States Coast Guard Shore Communication Facilities
USCGTS ..... United States Coast Guard Training Station
USCA .... United States Code (Law)
USCA .... United States Code Annotated (Based on official USC)
USCSC ..... United States Collegiate Sports Council
USC........ United States of Colombia
USCT .... United States Colored Troops (Civil War)
USCTA ..... United States Combined Training Association
USCOB ..... United States Commander, Berlin
USCINCEUR .. United States Commander-in-Chief Europe
USCINCSO ... United States Commander-in-Chief, Southern Command
USCC ...... United States Commercial Company
USCMI ..... United States Commission on Mathematical Instruction
CANLF...... United States Committee to Aid the National Liberation Front of South Vietnam
USCCEC ..... United States Committee for Care of European Children (Post-World War II)
USC-GARP ... United States Committee for the Global Atmospheric Research Program
USCOLD ..... United States Committee on Large Dams (of the International Commission on Large Dams)
USCPSHHM .. United States Committee to Promote Studies of the History of the Habsburg Monarchy
USCR .... United States Committee for Refugees
USCUN...... United States Committee for the United Nations (Later, UNAUS)
USCSB...... United States Communications Security Board
USCS .... United States Conciliation Service (Functions transferred to Federal Mediation and Conciliation Service, 1947)
USCCHO..... United States Conference of City Health Officers
USCM ...... United States Conference of Mayors
USCWCC ..... United States Conference for the World Council of Churches
USC........ United States Congress
USCG....... United States Consul General
USCAC...... United States Continental Army Command
USCONARC... United States Continental Army Command
USCA ...... United States Copper Association
USCC ...... United States Cotton Commission
USCICC ..... United States Council of the International Chamber of Commerce
CA .... United States Court of Appeals (Formerly, United States Circuit Court of Appeals)
USCC....... United States Court of Claims
USCCPA ..... United States Court of Customs and Patent Appeals
USCMA ..... United States Court of Military Appeals
USCA .... United States Courts of Appeals
USCC ...... United States Criminal Code
USCC ...... United States Criminal Court
USCMA ..... United States Crutch Manufacturers Association
USCSC ..... United States Cuban Sugar Council
USC ...... United States Customs
USCC ...... United States Customs Court
USCIA ...... United States Customs Inspectors' Association Port of New York
USDAO ..... United States Defense Attache Office
USDELIADB ... United States Delegation, Inter-American Defense Board
USMILCOMUN.. United States Delegation, United Nations Military Staff Committee
USDA .... United States Department of Agriculture

USDC . . . . United States Department of Commerce
USDOC . . . . . United States Department of Commerce
USDD . . . . United States Department of Defense
USDOD . . . . . United States Department of Defense
USDHE & W . . United States Department of Health, Education, and Welfare
USDI . . . . United States Department of the Interior
USDOI . . . . . . United States Department of the Interior
USDL . . . . United States Department of Labor
USDESEA . . . . . United States Dependent Schools, European Area
USDA . . . . United States Disarmament Administration (Transferred to US Arms
        Control and Disarmament Agency, 1961)
USDO . . . . United States Disbursing Officer
USDB . . . . United States Disciplinary Barracks
USD . . . . United States Dispensatory (Pharmacy)
USDC . . . . . . United States District Court
USDJ . . . . United States District Judge
USDR . . . . United States Divorce Reform
USDOCOLANDSOUTHEAST . . United States Document Office Allied Land Forces
        Southeastern Europe
USDOCO . . . . . United States Documents Officer
USEASA . . . . . United States Eastern Amateur Ski Association
USEFP . . . . United States Educational Foundation in Pakistan
USELMCENTO . . United States Element Central Treaty Organization
USE . . . . United States Embassy
USECC . . . . . . United States Employees' Compensation Commission (Functions transferred
        to Federal Security Agency, 1946)
USES . . . . United States Employment Service (Department of Labor)
USEO . . . . United States Engineer Office
USESSA . . . . . . United States Environmental Science Services Administration
USET . . . . United States Equestrian Team
USEP . . . . United States Escapee Program
USCINCEUR . . . United States European Command
USEUCOM . . . . United States European Command
USESF . . . . . . United States Exchange Stabilization Fund
USFARS . . . . . United States Federation of Amateur Roller Skaters
USFGC . . . . United States Feed Grains Council
USFHA . . . . . . United States Field Hockey Association
USFSA . . . . . . United States Figure Skating Association
USFCC . . . . . . United States Fire Companies Conference
USFWS . . . . . . United States Fish and Wildlife Service (Department of the Interior)
USFMIA . . . . . . United States Fishmeal Importers Association
USFF . . . . United States Flag Foundation
USF . . . . United States Fleet
USFADTC . . . . United States Fleet Air Defense Training Center
USFR . . . . United States Fleet Reserve
USRAD . . . . . . United States Fleet Shore Radio Station
USFSS . . . . United States Fleet SONAR School
USFTA . . . . . . United States Floor Tennis Association
USFC . . . . United States Foil Company
USFIA . . . . . . United States Forces in Australia
USFA . . . . United States Forces in Austria
USFORAZ . . . . United States Forces in Azores
USFET . . . . . . United States Forces, European Theater (American headquarters for
        occupation of Germany after SHAEF was dissolved) (World War II)
USFK . . . . United States Forces, Korea
USK . . . . United States Forces, Korea
USFIP . . . . United States Forces in the Philippines
UFO . . . . US & Foreign Securities Corporation (NYSE symbol)
USFS . . . . United States Foreign Service (Department of State)
USFS . . . . United States Forest Service
UFG . . . . US Freight Company (NYSE symbol)
USFS . . . . United States Frequency Standard
USFA . . . . United States Fuel Administration (Terminated)
USG . . . . United States Gage
USGS . . . . United States Geological Survey
USGA . . . . United States Golf Association
USG . . . . United States Government
USGLI . . . . . . United States Government Life Insurance
USGPO . . . . . . United States Government Printing Office
USGRDR . . . . . United States Government Research and Development Reports (National
        Bureau of Standards)
USGRDR-I . . . . United States Government Research and Development Reports Index
USGRR . . . . . . United States Government Research Reports (National Bureau of Standards
        publication)
USG . . . . United States Gypsum Company (NYSE symbol) (Wall Street slang name:
        "Gyp")
USHA . . . . . . United States Handball Association
USHWA . . . . . . United States Harness Writers' Association
USHMAC . . . . . United States Health Manpower Advisory Council
USHP . . . . United States Helium Plant (Amarillo, Texas)
HMY . . . . US Hoffman Machinery (NYSE symbol)

USHG . . . . . . United States Home Guard
USHGA . . . . . United States Hop Growers Association
USHA . . . . United States Housing Authority (Functions transferred to Public Housing
        Commissioner, 1947)
USHC . . . . United States Housing Corporation (Terminated, 1952)
USHO . . . . United States Hydrographic Office
USHL . . . . United States Hygienic Laboratory
USINOA . . . . . United States Immigration and Naturalization Officers' Association
USITA . . . . . . United States Independent Telephone Association
USI . . . . United States Industries, Incorporated (NYSE symbol)
USIA . . . . United States Information Agency
USIC . . . . United States Information Center (Department of State)
USIS . . . . United States Information Service (Name used abroad for USIA offices)
USITT . . . . . . United States Institute for Theatre Technology
USIB . . . . United States Intelligence Board (National Security Council)
USIAC . . . . . . United States Inter-American Council
USILA . . . . . . United States Intercollegiate Lacrosse Association
UNI . . . . United States International Airways
USISA . . . . . . United States International Sailing Association
USIU . . . . United States International University
US-JTC . . . . . . United States – Japan Trade Council
USJPRS . . . . . . United States Joint Publication Research Service
US JAYCEE . . . United States Junior Chamber of Commerce
USJCC . . . . . . United States Junior Chamber of Commerce (JAYCEES)
USKA . . . . United States Kart Association (Defunct)
USKBTC . . . . . United States Kerry Blue Terrier Club
USLCA . . . . . . United States Lacrosse Coaches' Association
USLTA . . . . . . United States Lawn Tennis Association
USL . . . . United States Legation
USLCMBA . . . . United States Letter Carriers Mutual Benefit Association
USLO . . . . . . United States Liaison Office(r)
USL . . . . United States Lines Company (NYSE symbol)
USLSA . . . . . . United States Livestock Sanitary Association
USLSO . . . . . . United States Logistics Support Office
USMSSB . . . . . United States Machine Screw Service Bureau
USM . . . . United States Mail
USMP . . . . United States Mallard Project (Army)
USM . . . . United States Marine(s)
USMAC . . . . . . United States Marine Air Corps
USMB . . . . United States Marine Barracks
USMC . . . . United States Marine Corps
USMCAS . . . . . United States Marine Corps Air Station
USMCR . . . . . . United States Marine Corps Reserve
USMCR(AF) . . . United States Marine Corps Reserve (Aviation Fleet)
USMCR(AO) . . . United States Marine Corps Reserve (Aviation, Organized)
USMCR(AV) . . . United States Marine Corps Reserve (Aviation, Volunteer)
USMCR(F) . . . . United States Marine Corps Reserve (Fleet)
USMCR(LS) . . . United States Marine Corps Reserve (Limited Service)
USMCR(O) . . . . United States Marine Corps Reserve (Organized)
USMCR(V) . . . . United States Marine Corps Reserve (Volunteer)
USMCR(VS) . . . United States Marine Corps Reserve (Volunteer Specialists)
USMCSS . . . . . United States Marine Corps Selective Service Selectee
USMCSSV . . . . United States Marine Corps Selective Service Volunteer
USMC(W) . . . . United States Marine Corps, Women
USMCR(W) . . . . United States Marine Corps Women's Reserve
USMCWR . . . . . United States Marine Corps Women's Reserve
USMH . . . . United States Marine Hospital
USMHS . . . . . . United States Marine Hospital Service
USMA . . . . United States Maritime Administration
USMC . . . . United States Maritime Commission (Functions transferred to Department
        of Commerce, 1950)
JSMS . . . . United States Maritime Service
JSMSGS . . . . . United States Maritime Service Graduate Station
JSMSOS . . . . . United States Maritime Service Officers School
JSMSTS . . . . . United States Maritime Service Training School
JSMSTS . . . . . United States Maritime Service Training Ship
USMSTS . . . . . United States Maritime Service Training Station
USMEMILCOMUN . . United States Members, United Nations Military Staff Committee
USMCA . . . . . . United States Men's Curling Association
USMM . . . . . . United States Merchant Marine
USMMA . . . . . United States Merchant Marine Academy
USMMCC . . . . United States Merchant Marine Cadet Corps
USNRM . . . . . United States Merchant Marine Reserve
USNRM2 . . . . . United States Merchant Marine Reserve Coastal Defense
USNRM1 . . . . . United States Merchant Marine Reserve Seagoing
USMA . . . . United States Military Academy
USMAPS . . . . . United States Military Academy Prep School
USMAPU . . . . . United States Military Academy Preparatory Unit
USMAG . . . . . United States Military Advisory Group
KMAG . . . . . . United States Military Advisory Group to the Republic of Korea
USMATS . . . . . United States Military Air Transport Service

REVERSE ACRONYMS AND INITIALISMS DICTIONARY

USMAC . . . . . . United States Military Assistance Command
USMACSV . . . . United States Military Assistance Command for South Vietnam
USMACTHAI . . United States Military Assistance Command Thailand
USMAC/V . . . . United States Military Assistance Command, Vietnam
USMA . . . . United States Military Attache
USMILATTACHE . . United States Military Attache
USMICC . . . . . United States Military Information Control Committee
USMLMCINCGSFG . . United States Military Liaison Mission to Commander-in-Chief,
　　　　　　　　　　 Group Soviet Forces, Germany
USMILLIAS . . . United States Military Liaison Office
GENMISH . . . . US Military Mission with the Iranian Gendarmerie
USMSMI . . . . . United States Military Supply Mission to India
USMILTAG . . . United States Military Technical Advisory Group
USMTMSA . . . . United States Military Training Mission to Saudi Arabia
USMT . . . . . . United States Military Transport
USM . . . . United States Mint
USM . . . . United States Minutemen
USMECBL . . . . United States Mission to the European Communities in Belgium and
　　　　　　　　　　 Luxembourg
USMEOUN . . . United States Mission to the European Office of the United Nations
USMIAEAA . . . United States Mission to the International Atomic Energy Agency in
　　　　　　　　　　 Austria
USMNATOEROF . . United States Mission to the North Atlantic Treaty Organization
　　　　　　　　　　 and European Regional Organizations in France
USMA . . . . United States Monopoly Association (For legal reasons, only the initialism
　　　　　　　　　　 is used by the group; it is never officially spelled out)
USNA . . . . . . United States National Army
USNC . . . . . . United States National Commission for UNESCO (of the Department of
　　　　　　　　　　 State)
USNC . . . . . . United States National Committee (IEC)
USNCFID . . . . United States National Committee for Federation Internationale de
　　　　　　　　　　 Documentation
USNC IBP . . . . United States National Committee for the International Biological Program
USICID . . . . . United States National Committee, International Commission on Irrigation
　　　　　　　　　　 and Drainage
USNC-IGY . . . United States National Committee for the International Geophysical Year
USNCPNM . . . United States National Committee for the Preservation of Nubian
　　　　　　　　　　 Monuments
USNCTAM . . . United States National Committee on Theoretical & Applied Mechanics
USNG . . . . . . United States National Guard
USNMR . . . . . United States National Military Representative
USNM . . . . . . United States National Museum (Smithsonian Institution)
USNSA . . . . . . United States National Student Association
USNA . . . . . . United States Naval Academy
USNAC . . . . . . United States Naval Administrative Command
USNAC . . . . . . United States Naval Air Corps
USNAMTC . . . . United States Naval Air Missile Test Center
USNAS . . . . . . United States Naval Air Service
USNAS . . . . . . United States Naval Air Station
USNATC . . . . . United States Naval Air Training Center
USNA . . . . . . United States Naval Aircraft
USNAAS . . . . . United States Naval Auxiliary Air Station
USNCEREL . . . United States Naval Civil Engineering Research and Evaluation Laboratory
USNCB . . . . . . United States Naval Construction Battalion (SEABEES) (BUDOCKS; later,
　　　　　　　　　　 FEC)
USNDD . . . . . United States Naval Drydocks
USNEL . . . . . . United States Naval Electronics Laboratory
USEES . . . . . . United States Naval Engineering Experiment Station (Annapolis, Maryland)
USNFR . . . . . . United States Naval Fleet Reserve
NAVFOR . . . . US Naval Forces
NAVFOREU . . . US Naval Forces Europe (Later, NAVEU)
NAVEU . . . . . . US Naval Forces in European Waters
NAVFORGER . . US Naval Forces Germany
NAVJAP . . . . . US Naval Forces, Japan
NAVMED . . . . US Naval Forces, Mediterranean (Formerly, NAVNAW)
NAVNAW . . . . US Naval Forces, Northwest African Waters (Later, NAVMED)
NAVWESPAC . . US Naval Forces Western Pacific
NAVHOME . . . US Naval Home (Philadelphia)
NAVHOSP . . . . US Naval Hospital
USNH . . . . . . United States Naval Hospital
USNI . . . . United States Naval Institute
USNIP . . . . . . United States Naval Institute Proceedings (Publication)
NID . . . . US Naval Intelligence Division (Usually, ONI)
USNLO . . . . . . United States Naval Liaison Officer
NAVMAG . . . . US Naval Magazine
USNACC . . . . . United States Naval Member of the Allied Control Commission (Germany)
USNMF . . . . . United States Naval Missile Facility
USNO . . . . . . United States Naval Observatory
USNOTS . . . . . United States Naval Ordnance Test Station
USNPS . . . . . . United States Naval Postgraduate School

USNP . . . . United States Naval Prison
USNPG . . . . . . United States Naval Proving Ground
USNRDL . . . . . United States Naval Radiological Defense Laboratory
NR . . . . US Naval Regulations
USNRB . . . . . . United States Naval Repair Base
USNAVYMILCOMUN . . United States Naval Representative, United Nations Military
　　　　　　　　　　 Staff Committee
USNRL . . . . . . United States Naval Research Laboratory
NR . . . . US Naval Reserve
USNR . . . . United States Naval Reserve
USNRF . . . . . . United States Naval Reserve Force
USNR(F) . . . . . United States Naval Reserve (Force)
USNRSV . . . . . United States Naval Reserve, Selective Volunteer
USNRV . . . . . . United States Naval Reserve, Volunteer
USNR(W) . . . . . United States Naval Reserve (Women's Reserve)
NAVSECSTA . . US Naval Security Station
USNS . . . . United States Naval Ship (Civilian manned)
NTX . . . . US Naval Teletypewriter Exchange (Formerly, NTE)
USNATRA . . . . United States Naval Training
USNTC . . . . . . United States Naval Training Center
USNTDC . . . . . United States Naval Training Device Center
USNTS . . . . . . United States Naval Training School
USS . . . . United States Naval Vessel
USNWC . . . . . United States Naval War College
USN . . . . United States Navy
USNEDS . . . . . United States Navy Experimental Diving Station
NFTSA . . . . . . US Navy Field Training Supervisors Association
USNAVSO . . . . United States Navy Forces Southern Command
USN(I)(SA) . . . United States Navy (Inductee) (Special Assignment)
USNMSC . . . . . United States Navy Medical Service Corps
USNR & SL . . . United States Navy Radio and Sound Laboratory (San Diego, California)
USNRS . . . . . . United States Navy Recruiting Station
USNR . . . . United States Navy Regulations
USREPOF . . . . . United States Navy Reporting Office(r)
USN(Ret) . . . . . United States Navy (Retired)
USRO . . . . United States Navy Routing Office
NAVSHIPLO . . US Navy Shipbuilding Office
NAVSHIPSA . . US Navy Shipbuilding Scheduling Activity
USNAVSOUTHCOM . . United States Navy Southern Command
USNTI . . . . . . United States Navy Travel Instructions
USNUSL . . . . . United States Navy Underwater Sound Laboratory (BUSHIPS; later, ESC)
USNWR . . . . . United States News & World Report (A publication)
USOE . . . . United States Office of Education
USOA . . . . . . United States Olympic Association
USOC . . . . . . United States Olympic Committee
USOM . . . . . . United States Operations Mission
USOMC . . . . . United States Ordnance Missile Command
USNRO . . . . . . United States Organized Naval Reserve
USNRO2 . . . . . United States Organized Naval Reserve Aviation
USNRO1 . . . . . United States Organized Naval Reserve Seagoing
USOA . . . . . . United States Overseas Airlines
USPTA . . . . . . United States Paddle Tennis Association
USPEC . . . . . . United States Paper Exporters Council
USPA . . . . United States Passport Agency (Department of State)
USP . . . . United States Patent
USPO . . . . United States Patent Office (Commerce Department)
USP . . . . United States Penitentiary
USP . . . . United States Pharmacopeia (Following name of a substance, signifies
　　　　　　　　　　 substance meets standards set by USP)
USPC . . . . United States Pharmacopoeial Convention
USPSF . . . . . . United States Pigeon Shooting Federation
CJ . . . . US Pipe & Foundry Company (NYSE symbol)
USP . . . . United States Playing Card Company (NYSE symbol)
PLY . . . . US Plywood Corporation (NYSE symbol)
USPA . . . . United States Polo Association
USPC . . . . United States Pony Clubs
USPTA . . . . . . United States Pony Trotting Association
USPO . . . . United States Post Office
USPA . . . . United States Potters' Association
USPEPA . . . . . United States Poultry and Egg Producers Association
USPS . . . . United States Power Squadrons
USPLTA . . . . . United States Professional Lawn Tennis Association
USPDO . . . . . . United States Property and Disbursing Officer
USP & DO . . . . United States Property and Disbursing Officer
USPFO . . . . . . United States Property and Fiscal Officer
USPHS . . . . . . United States Public Health Service
USPHSR . . . . . United States Public Health Service Reserve
USPPA . . . . . . United States Pulp Producers Association
USPC . . . . United States Purchasing Commission
USQBR . . . . . . United States Quarterly Book Review

USRPA . . . . . . United States Racing Pigeon Association
USRA . . . . United States Railroad Administration (Functions transferred to Department
    of the Treasury, 1939)
USRS . . . . . . United States Reclamation Service
USRCSI . . . . . . United States Red Cedar Shingle Industry
USN-I . . . . . . United States Regular Navy - Inductee
USN-I-CB . . . . United States Regular Navy - Inductee - Construction Battalion
USN-SV . . . . United States Regular Navy Selective Volunteer
USR . . . . United States (Supreme Court) Reports
USRNMC . . . . . United States Representative to NATO Military Committee
USRSG . . . . . . United States Representative, Standing Group (Military)
USREPMILCOMUN . . United States Representative, United Nations Military Staff
    Committee
USR . . . . United States Reserves
USRS . . . . . . United States Revised Statutes
USRA . . . . . . United States Revolver Association
USREDA . . . . . United States Rice Export Development Association
USRRC . . . . . . United States Road Racing Championship
USRS . . . . . . United States Rocket Society
USRS . . . . . . United States Rowing Society
R . . . . US Rubber Company (NYSE symbol)
USU . . . . United States Rubber Reclaiming Company (NYSE symbol)
USSA . . . . . . United States Salvage Association
USSBD . . . . . . United States Savings Bonds Division (Treasury Department)
USSLL . . . . . . United States Savings and Loan League
USSEA . . . . . . United States Scientific Export Association
USSS . . . . . . United States Secret Service
USSA . . . . . . United States Security Authority (for NATO affairs)
USSAC . . . . . . United States Security Authority for CENTO Affairs
USSAS . . . . . . United States Security Authority for SEATO Affairs
S . . . . United States Senate (When appended to legislative designations)
USS . . . . . . United States Senate
USSPG . . . . . . United States Senate Photographers Gallery
USSBA . . . . . . United States Seniors Bowling Association (Later, Seniors Division of the
    American Bowling Congress)
USSGA . . . . . . United States Seniors Golf Association
USSC . . . . . . United States Servas Committee
USSIA . . . . . . United States Shellac Importers Association
USS . . . . . . United States Ship
USSB . . . . . . United States Shipping Board (Terminated, 1933)
USR . . . . United States Shoe Corporation (NYSE symbol)
USSA . . . . . . United States Ski Association
USSEF . . . . . . United States Ski Educational Foundation
USSWA . . . . . United States Ski Writers Association
UV . . . . US Smelting, Refining & Mining Company (NYSE symbol)
USSFA . . . . . . United States Soccer Football Association
USEI . . . . . . United States Society of Esperanto Instructors
USSH . . . . . . United States Soldiers' Home
US-SALEP . . . . United States - South Africa Leader Exchange Program
USSOUTHCOM . . United States Southern Command (Air Force)
USSRA . . . . . . United States Squash Racquets Association
USS . . . . United States Standard
USG . . . . United States Standard Gage
USSG . . . . . . United States Standard Gage
USSGREP . . . . . United States Standing Group Representative (NATO)
USS . . . . United States Steamer
USSS . . . . . . United States Steamship
USS . . . . United States Steel Corporation
USSC . . . . . . United States Steel Corporation
X . . . . US Steel Corporation (NYSE symbol) (Wall Street slang name: "Steel")
USSF . . . . . . United States Steel Foundation
USSBIA . . . . . . United States Stone and Bead Importers Association
USSG . . . . . . United States Storekeeper-Gauger
USSAF . . . . . . United States Strategic Air Force (Later, Strategic Air Command)
USSTAF . . . . . . United States Strategic Air Forces
USSAFE . . . . . United States Strategic Air Forces in Europe
USSBS . . . . . . United States Strategic Bombing Survey
USSTAFE . . . . United States Strategic Tactical Air Force, Europe
USSTAF . . . . . United States Strategic and Tactical Air Forces
USSC . . . . . . United States Strike Command (Military combined Tactical Air Command
    and Strategic Army Command Force)
USSTRICOM . . United States Strike Command
USSPA . . . . . . United States Student Press Association
USSC . . . . . . United States Supreme Court
US . . . . US Supreme Court Reports
USTTA . . . . . . United States Table Tennis Association
USTSA . . . . . . United States Targhee Sheep Association
USTC . . . . . . United States Tariff Commission
USTS . . . . . . United States Time Standard (National Bureau of Standards)
UBO . . . . US Tobacco Company (NYSE symbol)
USTCA . . . . . . United States Track Coaches Association

USTFF . . . . . . United States Track and Field Federation
USTA . . . . . . United States Trademark Association
USTRC . . . . . United States Transportation Research Command (Army)
USTB . . . . . . United States Travel Bureau
USTS . . . . . . United States Travel Service (Department of Commerce)
USTA . . . . . United States Trotting Association (Governing body of harness racing in
    in US)
TFA . . . . US Trout Farmers Association
USTFA . . . . . United States Trout Farmers Association
USTDA . . . . . United States Truck Drivers Association
USTA . . . . . . United States Twirling Association
US/UK . . . . . . United States/United Kingdom
USVB . . . . . . United States Veterans Bureau
USVH . . . . . . United States Veterans Hospital
UVT . . . . United States Vitamin & Pharmaceutical Corporation (NYSE symbol)
USVBA . . . . . United States Volleyball Association
USV . . . . United States Volunteers (Civil War)
USWBC . . . . . United States War Ballot Commission (World War II)
USWB . . . . . . United States Weather Bureau
USWI . . . . . . United States West Indies
USWGA . . . . . United States Wholesale Grocers' Association
USWACC . . . . United States Women's Army Corps Center
USWACS . . . . United States Women's Army Corps School
USWCA . . . . . United States Women's Curling Association
USWLA . . . . . United States Women's Lacrosse Association
USWSRA . . . . United States Women's Squash Racquets Association
USWSSB . . . . United States Wood Screw Service Bureau
USYC . . . . . . United States Youth Council
USZI . . . . United States Zone of the Interior
USWAP . . . . . United Steel Workers' Association of the Philippines
USUCA . . . . . United Steel Workers' Union of Central Africa (Rhodesia and Nyasaland)
USW . . . . . . United Steelworkers of America
SAPW . . . . . . United Stone and Allied Products Workers of America
USAPWA . . . . . United Stone and Allied Products Workers of America
USC . . . . United Strasser Club
USKBA . . . . . United Strictly Kosher Butchers Association
USAF . . . . . . United Student Aid Fund
USCC . . . . . . United Student Christian Council in United States
USSA . . . . . . United Sugar Sampler's Association (Defunct)
USS . . . . United Swedish Societies
USA . . . . United Synagogue of America
USCJE . . . . . United Synagogue Commission on Jewish Education
USY . . . . United Synagogue Youth
UTC . . . . United Technology Center (A division of United Aircraft Corporation)
UTC . . . . United Technology Corporation
UTO . . . . United Telephone Organizations
UT . . . . United Territory
UTWA . . . . . . United Textile Workers of America
UTIRS . . . . . . United Tiberias Institutions Relief Society
UTUC . . . . . . United Trades Union Congress (India)
UTSE . . . . . . United Transport Service Employees
UTOA . . . . . . United Truck Owners of America
UTA . . . . United Typothetae of America
UUARC . . . . . United Ukrainian American Relief Committee
UUCA . . . . . . United Underwear Contractors Association
UUEW . . . . . . United Unions for Employees and Workers (Lebanon)
UUC . . . . United University Club (British)
UT . . . . United Utilities, Inc. (NYSE symbol)
UVMC . . . . . United Voluntary Motor Corps
UVS . . . . United Voluntary Services
UNW . . . . . . United Wallpaper, Inc. (NYSE symbol)
UWA . . . . . . United Weighers Association
UW . . . . United Weldors International Union
UWC . . . . . . United Whelan Corporation (NYSE symbol)
UWARC . . . . . United Whiteruthenian (Byelorussian) American Relief Committee
UWA . . . . . . United Women of the Americas
UWF . . . . . . United World Federalists
UWM . . . . . . United World Mission
UZRA . . . . . . United Zionist Revisionists of America
UTROAA . . . . Units to Round Out the Active Army
UOV . . . . Units of Variance
UCLM . . . . . . Unity of Czech Ladies and Men
UNI . . . . Unity Railways Company (AAR code)
UNADS . . . . . UNIVAC Automated Documentation System (Data processing)
USE . . . . UNIVAC Scientific Exchange (Data processing)
UNISTAR . . . . UNIVAC Storage and Retrieval System (Data processing)
UUA . . . . UNIVAC Users Association
U . . . . Universal
UANM . . . . . . Universal African Nationalist Movement
UATP . . . . . . Universal Air Travel Plan (Commercial airlines credit system)
UADW . . . . . . Universal Alliance of Diamond Workers

UNACOM . . . . Universal Army Communication System
UACC . . . . . . Universal Autograph Collector's Club (International)
UNIVAC . . . . . Universal Automatic Computer
UNAMACE . . . Universal Automatic Map Compilation Equipment
UBT . . . . Universal Book Tester (Measures performance of binding)
UBF . . . . Universal Buddhist Fellowship
UBC . . . . Universal Buffer Controller
UCCS . . . . . . Universal Camera Control System
UCS . . . . Universal Classification System
UCSD . . . . . . Universal Communications Switching Device
UNICOM . . . . Universal Components (Construction)
UNCOL . . . . . Universal Computer Oriented Language (Data processing)
UCC . . . . Universal Copyright Convention
UCCE . . . . . . Universal Craftsmen Council of Engineers
UCS . . . . Universal-Cyclops Steel Corporation (Later, CYL) (NYSE symbol)
UDT . . . . Universal Data Transcriber (Navy)
UDC . . . . Universal Decimal Classification
UDA . . . . Universal Detective Association
UDOFT . . . . . Universal Digital Operational Flight Trainer (Navy)
UDTI . . . . . . Universal Digital Transducer Indicator
UET . . . . Universal Engineer Tractor (Army)
UETA . . . . . . Universal Engineer Tractor, Armored (AMC - Mobility)
UETRT . . . . . . Universal Engineer Tractor, Rubber-Tired (AMC - Mobility)
UEA . . . . Universal Esperanto Association
UFD . . . . Universal Firing Device (Military)
UNI-FREDI . . . Universal Flight Range & Endurance Data Indicator
UNV . . . . Universal Insurance Company (American Stock Exchange symbol)
UNICOM . . . . Universal Integrated Communication System (Military)
UIRC . . . . . . Universal Interline Reservations Code
UJS . . . . Universal Jamming System
JNU . . . . Universal Jet Navigation Charts (Air Force)
ULTRA-X . . . . Universal Language for Typographic Reproduction Applications
UVV . . . . Universal Leaf Tobacco Company, Inc. (NYSE symbol)
UL . . . . Universal League
ULC . . . . Universal Load Cell
ULI . . . . Universal Logic Implementer
UMLER . . . . . Universal Machine Language Equipment Register (Railroads)
UMS . . . . Universal Maintenance Standards
UMC . . . . Universal Match Corporation
UMT . . . . Universal Match Corporation (NYSE symbol)
UMT . . . . Universal Microwave Trainer
UMS . . . . Universal Military Service
UMT . . . . Universal Military Training (Participants known as Umtees) (US Army)
(Post-World War II)
UMTS . . . . . . Universal Military Training Service (or System)
UMTSA . . . . . Universal Military Training and Service Act
UML . . . . Universal Mission Load (Military)
UNB . . . . Universal Navigation Beacon
UNC . . . . Universal Navigation Computer
UNIA . . . . . . Universal Negro Improvement Association (Organization led by Marcus
Aurelius Garvey)
UNE . . . . Universal Nonlinear Element
UNIT . . . . . . Universal Numerical Interchange Terminal
UOP . . . . Universal Oil Products Company (NYSE symbol)
UNOPAR . . . . . Universal Operator Performance Analyzer and Recorder
UPTP . . . . . . Universal Package Test Panel
UPCS . . . . . . Universal Philatelic Cover Society
UPPC . . . . . . Universal Pin Pack Connector
UPS . . . . Universal Polar Stereographic Grid
UPU . . . . Universal Postal Union (Post Office)
UNPS . . . . . . Universal Power Supply
UNIPOL . . . . . Universal Procedure Oriented Language
UNIPRO . . . . Universal Processor (Data processing)
URSP . . . . . . Universal RADAR Signal Processor
URT . . . . Universal RADAR Tracker
URG . . . . Universal Radio Group
UNIRAR . . . . Universal Radio Relay
URS . . . . Universal Reference System
URS . . . . Universal Regulating System
US . . . . Universal Service (News agency)
USCS . . . . . . Universal Ship Cancellation Society
USP . . . . Universal Signal Processor
USC . . . . Universal Specimen Chamber
USVT . . . . . . Universal Stray Voltage Tester
UTP . . . . Universal Tape Processor
UTTC . . . . . . Universal Tape-to-Tape Converter
UNITEL . . . . . Universal Teleservice (Satellite information service)
UTE . . . . Universal Test Equipment
UTM . . . . Universal Test Message
UTS . . . . Universal Test Station
UTM . . . . Universal Testing Machine

UTS . . . . Universal Thrust Stand
UT . . . . Universal Time (NASA)
UTC . . . . Universal Time Coordinated
UT . . . . Universal Trainer
UTM . . . . Universal Transverse Mercator (Grid)
UNUMO . . . . . Universal Underwater Mobile (Robot)
UVT . . . . Universal Voltage Tester
UWC . . . . Universal Water Charts (Air Force)
UCO . . . . Universal Weather Landing Code
UWC . . . . Universal Winding Company
UY . . . . Universal Youth
UHS . . . . Universalist Historical Society
UNAM . . . . . . Universidad Nacional Autonoma de Mexico
UVM . . . . Universitas Viridis Montis (University of the Green Mountains; i.e.,
University of Vermont)
UAREP . . . . . . Universities Associated for Research and Education in Pathology
UQP . . . . Universities and the Quest for Peace (An organization)
URA . . . . Universities Research Association
URAI . . . . . . Universities Research Association, Incorporated
USRA . . . . . . Universities Space Research Association
U . . . . University
UAA . . . . University Aviation Association
UBBR . . . . . . University Bureaus of Business Research
UC . . . . University of California
UCDWR . . . . . University of California Division of War Research
UCLJ . . . . . . University of California, La Jolla (AEC)
UCLRL . . . . . . University of California Lawrence Radiation Laboratory (AEC)
UCLA . . . . . . University of California, Los Angeles
UCRL . . . . . . University of California Radiation Laboratory
UCSD . . . . . . University of California, San Diego
UCSB . . . . . . University of California at Santa Barbara
UCM . . . . University Christian Movement (Formerly, NSCF)
UCD . . . . University College, Dublin
UCEMT . . . . . University Consortium in Educational Media and Technology
UCAR . . . . . . University Corporation for Atmospheric Research
UCEA . . . . . . University Council for Educational Administration
UD . . . . University of Denver
U-D . . . . University of Detroit
UE . . . . University Extension
UFF . . . . University Film Foundation
UFPA . . . . . . University Film Producers Association
UFTR . . . . . . University of Florida Teaching Reactor
UGC . . . . University Grants Commission (India)
UGC . . . . University Grants Committee (British)
UICSM . . . . . . University of Illinois Committee on School Mathematics
UNITEC . . . . . University Information Technology Corporation
UK . . . . University of Kansas
UKC . . . . University of Kansas City (Later, University of Missouri at Kansas City)
UKNR . . . . . . University of Kansas Nuclear Reactor
ULEA . . . . . . University Labor Education Association
UM . . . . University of Miami (Florida)
UMML . . . . . . University of Miami Marine Laboratory (Florida)
U of M . . . . . . University of Michigan
UMAP . . . . . . University of Michigan Assembly Program
UMMZ . . . . . . University of Michigan Museum of Zoology
UMKC . . . . . . University of Missouri - Kansas City
UMRR . . . . . . University of Missouri Research Reactor
UNTD . . . . . . University Naval Training Division (Canada)
UNB . . . . University of New Brunswick (Canada)
UNC . . . . University of North Carolina
UPA . . . . University Photographers Association of America
UPGRADE . . . . University of Pittsburgh Generalized Recording and Dissemination
Experiment
UP . . . . University Presses (General term applied to presses of various universities)
UPCHUK . . . . . University Program for the Comprehensive Handling and Utilization of
Knowledge (Humorous)
UPR . . . . University of Puerto Rico
URM . . . . University Reform Movement (in Latin America)
UR . . . . University Relations
URA . . . . University Research Associates
URI . . . . University of Rhode Island
URAEP . . . . . . University of Rochester Atomic Energy Project
UST . . . . University of Saint Thomas (Texas)
USF . . . . University of San Francisco (California)
USC . . . . University of Santa Clara (California)
USPP . . . . . . University Science Policy Planning (Program) (National Science
Foundation)
UNISA . . . . . . University of South Africa
USC . . . . University of South Carolina
USC . . . . University of Southern California
USCAL . . . . . . University of Southern California, Aeronautical Laboratory

USCEC . . . . . . University of Southern California, Engineering Center
USLO . . . . University Students for Law and Order
UTC . . . . University Teachers Certificate
UTR . . . . University Teaching Reactor
UTRR . . . . University of Teheran Research Reactor
UTSI . . . . University of Tennessee Space Institute
UTIA . . . . University of Toronto, Institute of Aerophysics
UTIAS . . . . . . University of Toronto, Institute of Aerospace Studies
UTR . . . . University Training Reactor (AEC)
UVAR . . . . University of Virginia Reactor
UVR . . . . University of Virginia Reactor
UW . . . . University of Washington (State)
UWAL . . . . . . University of Washington, Aeronautical Laboratory
UWTR . . . . . . University of Washington Training Reactor
UWI . . . . University of the West Indies (Jamaica)
UWO . . . . University of Western Ontario
UWRR . . . . . . University of Wyoming Research Reactor
UFA . . . . Universum-Film Aktien-Gesellschaft (German motion picture company)
U . . . . Unknown
UFAC . . . . Unlawful Flight to Avoid Custody
UFAP . . . . Unlawful Flight to Avoid Prosecution
UFAT . . . . Unlawful Flight to Avoid Testimony
UDAA . . . . . . Unlawfully Driving Away Auto
UNODIR . . . . Unless Otherwise Directed
UNOINDC . . . Unless Otherwise Indicated
U . . . . Unlimited (Aviation)
UMASS . . . . . Unlimited Machine Access from Scattered Sites (Data processing)
URM . . . . Unlimited Register Machine
UREKA . . . . . Unlimited Resources Ensure Keen Answers
UTP . . . . Unlisted Trading Privileges
ULLV . . . . . . Unmanned Lunar Logistics Vehicle (OMSF)
ULO . . . . Unmanned Lunar Orbiter (NASA)
UMS . . . . Unmanned Multifunction Satellite
UMOL . . . . . Unmanned Orbital Laboratory
UOMS . . . . . Unmanned Orbital Multifunction Satellite
UOS . . . . Unmanned Orbital Satellite
USO . . . . Unmanned Seismic Observatory (DOD)
USSS . . . . . . Unmanned Sensing Satellite System
USV . . . . Unmanned Strike Vehicle
UMSE . . . . . . Unmanned Surveillance Equipment
USE . . . . Unmanned Surveillance Equipment
UWS . . . . Unmanned Weather Station
U . . . . Unoccupied
UPF . . . . Unofficial Personnel Folder
UEO . . . . Unon de l'Europe Occidentale
UC . . . . Unoperated Control
UPVC . . . . . . Unplasticized Polyvinyl Chloride
U . . . . Unpleasant
USPL . . . . . . Unpriced Spare Parts List
UTR . . . . Unprogrammed Transfer Register
URI . . . . Unpublished Research Information (Conducted by National Science Foundation)
UISC . . . . . . Unreported Interstate Shipment of Cigarettes
U . . . . Unrestricted (Aviation)
UP . . . . Unrotated Projectile (Rocket)
UCR . . . . Unsatisfactory Condition Report
UEPR . . . . . . Unsatisfactory Equipment Performance Report (Military)
UER . . . . Unsatisfactory Equipment Report
UMR . . . . Unsatisfactory Material Reports (Military)
UR . . . . Unsatisfactory Report
URQ . . . . Unsatisfactory Report Questionnaire
UCJ . . . . Unsatisfied Claim and Judgment (State driver insurance)
UIBC . . . . . . Unsaturated Iron-Binding Capacity
UM . . . . Unscheduled Maintenance
US . . . . Unserviceable
UDMH . . . . . . Unsymmetrical Diemethylhydrazine
UUV . . . . Unter Ublicher Vorbehalt (Errors and Omissions Excepted) (German)
U-BOAT-S. . . . Unterseeboat (German submarine)
UAB . . . . Until Advised By
UAT . . . . Until Advised by the Tower (Aviation)
UCDWN . . . . . Until Cleared Down (Aviation)
UCLT . . . . . . Until Cleared to Land by the Tower (Aviation)
UE . . . . Until Exhausted
UFA . . . . Until Further Advised
UFN . . . . Until Further Notice
UNFURNOTE . . Until Further Notice
UHPFB . . . . . . Untreated Hard Pressed Fiber Board
UOC . . . . Unusual Occurrence Control
V . . . . Unusual Visibility
U . . . . Unwatched (with reference to a light) (Maps and charts)
U . . . . Up(per)

UDL . . . . Up Data Link
UDDF . . . . . . Up and Down Drafts (Meteorology)
UL . . . . Up Left (The rear left portion of a stage) (A stage direction)
UR . . . . Up Right (The rear right portion of a stage) (A stage direction)
US . . . . Up Stage (Away from audience) (A stage direction)
USC . . . . Up Stage Center (Away from audience) (A stage direction)
USL . . . . Up Stage Left (Away from audience) (A stage direction)
USR . . . . Up Stage Right (Away from audience) (A stage direction)
UTR . . . . Up Time Ratio
UGT . . . . Upgrade Training (Military)
UFMA . . . . . . Upholstered Furniture Manufacturers Association
UIU . . . . Upholsterers' International Union of North America
UDFAA . . . . . Upholstery and Decorative Fabrics Association of America
UDFMA . . . . . Upholstery & Drapery Fabric Manufacturers Association
UFMA . . . . . . Upholstery Fabric Manufacturers Association
ULG . . . . Upholstery Leather Group
UPJ . . . . Upjohn Company (NYSE symbol)
UCWR . . . . . Upon Completion Thereof Will Return to (Air Force)
UPREC . . . . . Upon Receipt
UC . . . . Upper Canada
UC . . . . Upper Case (i.e., capital letters) (Typography)
UCL . . . . Upper Control Limit (QCR)
UD . . . . Upper Deck (Naval)
UIR . . . . Upper Flight Information Region (Aviation)
UH . . . . Upper Half
ULC . . . . Upper Left Center (The rear left center portion of a stage) (A stage direction)
UL . . . . Upper Limb (Upper edge of sun, moon, etc.) (Navigation)
LU . . . . Upper Limen (Psychology)
UL . . . . Upper Limit
UMR . . . . Upper Maximum Range
UMP . . . . Upper Merion & Plymouth R. R. (AAR code)
UMREL . . . . . Upper Midwest Regional Educational Laboratory, Inc.
UM . . . . Upper Motor (Neurons)
UOT . . . . Upper Outer Tube
UP . . . . Upper Peninsula (Michigan)
UQ . . . . Upper Quadrile
URI . . . . Upper Respiratory Infection (Medicine)
USB . . . . Upper Sideband
UPSTAGE . . . . Upper Stage Guidance Experiment
URP . . . . Upper-Stage Reusable Payload
UTP . . . . Upper Trip Point
UCIS . . . . . . Uprange Computer Input System
UCOS . . . . . . Uprange Computer Output System
UMCA . . . . . . Uraba, Medellin and Central Airways, Inc.
U . . . . Uranium (Chemical element)
UIA . . . . Uranium Institute of America
UOPA . . . . . . Uranium Ore Processing Association
UPR . . . . Uranium Production Reactor
UNH . . . . Uranyl Nitrate Hexahydrate
UDDC . . . . . . Urban Design and Development Corporation
UD . . . . Urban District
UDC . . . . Urban District Council
UHG . . . . Urban History Group
UI . . . . Urban Institute
ULI . . . . Urban Land Institute
UMIS . . . . . . Urban Management Information System
UMTA . . . . . . Urban Mass Transportation Act
UMTA . . . . . . Urban Mass Transportation Administration (Department of Transportation)
UPAP . . . . . . Urban Planning Assistance Program
URA . . . . Urban Renewal Administration (of HHFA)
USA . . . . Urban Sanitary Authority (British)
UTC . . . . Urban Training Center
UTA . . . . Urban Transportation Administration (HUD)
UJC . . . . Urbana Junior College (Ohio)
UC . . . . Urbis Conditae (From the Foundation of the City; that is, of Rome)
UAL . . . . Urea-Ammonia Liquor
UAP . . . . Urea-Ammonium Phosphate
UCL . . . . Urea Clearance (Test) (Medicine)
UME . . . . Urethane Mixing Equipment
UD . . . . Urethral Discharge (Medicine)
UND . . . . Urgency of Need Designator
UAN . . . . Uric Acid Nitrogen
UDRP . . . . . . Uridina Diribose Phosphate
UD . . . . Uridine Diphosphate
UDP . . . . Uridine Diphosphate
UDPGA . . . . . Uridine Disphosphate Glucaronic Acid
UDPG . . . . . . Uridine Disphosphate Glucose
UTP . . . . Uridine Triphosphate (Biochemistry)
UT . . . . Urinary Tract (Medicine)
URB . . . . Uris Buildings Corporation (NYSE symbol)

UMa . . . . Ursa Major (IAU)
UMi . . . . Ursa Minor (IAU)
UTR . . . . Urticarial Transfusion Reaction
U & O . . . . . . Use and Occupancy (Real estate)
UUE . . . . Use Until Exhausted
UOA . . . . Used on Assembly
UCEA . . . . . . Used Clothing Exporters Association of America
U/W . . . . Used With
UT . . . . User Test
UTP . . . . User Test Program (Army)
UAIDE . . . . . . Users of Automatic Information Display Equipment
UMTD . . . . . . Using Mails to Defraud
URO . . . . Ustredni Rada Odboru (Central Council of Trade Unions) (Czechoslovakia)
UCHD . . . . . . Usual Childhood Diseases
UDC . . . . Usual Diseases of Childhood
UD . . . . Ut Dictum (As Directed)
UI . . . . Ut Infra (As Below)
US . . . . Ut Supra (As Above)
U . . . . Utah
UT . . . . Utah
UCR . . . . Utah Coal Route (AAR code)
UTOCO . . . . . Utah Oil Company
UTP . . . . Utah Power & Light Company (NYSE symbol)
UTAH . . . . . . Utah Railway Company (AAR code)
USAC . . . . . . Utah State Agricultural College
UTD . . . . UTD Corporation (Formerly, Union Twist Drill Company) (NYSE symbol)
UTJ . . . . Uterotubal Junction
UR . . . . Uti Rogas (Be It as You Desire) (Used by Romans to express assent to a proposition)
UT . . . . Utilities Man
URC . . . . Utilities Research Commission
U . . . . Utility (Designation for all US military aircraft)
CVU . . . . Utility Aircraft Carrier (Navy symbol)
UAC . . . . Utility Airplane Council
UAP . . . . Utility Amphibian Plane (Navy)

UBD . . . . Utility Binary Dump (Data processing)
UT . . . . Utility Boat
UCI . . . . Utility Card Input
UC . . . . Utility Cargo
UCEC . . . . . . Utility Commission Engineers Conference
UCO . . . . Utility Compiler
UCON . . . . . . Utility Control
UCP . . . . Utility Control Program
UD . . . . Utility Dog (Degree of obedience training)
UDT . . . . Utility Dog Tracker (Degree of obedience training)
UFU . . . . Utility Flight Unit (Navy)
LCU . . . . Utility Landing Craft (Navy symbol)
ULP . . . . Utility Landplane (Navy)
UTML . . . . . . Utility Motor Launch
UOL . . . . Utility Octal Load
UPP . . . . Utility Print Punch
URC . . . . Utility Radio Communication
URT . . . . Utility Radio Transmitter
USP . . . . Utility Seaplane (Navy, Coast Guard)
UTRON . . . . . . Utility Squadron (Navy)
UTRONFWDAREA . . Utility Squadron, Forward Area (Navy)
USP . . . . Utility Summary Program
UTT . . . . Utility Tactical Transport
UTTAS . . . . . . Utility Tactical Transport Aircraft System (Army)
UTP . . . . Utility Tape Processor
UTWING . . . . . Utility Wing (Navy)
UTWINGSERVLANT . . Utility Wing, Service Force, Atlantic (Navy)
UTWINGSERVPAC . . Utility Wing, Service Force, Pacific (Navy)
UWUA . . . . . . Utility Workers Union of America
UAFSC . . . . . . Utilization Air Force Specialty Code
UDS . . . . Utilization and Disposal Service (of General Services Administration)
UTELRAD . . . . Utilization of Enemy Electromagnetic Radiations
UJD . . . . Utriusque Juris Doctor (Doctor of Either Law; i.e., Canon Law or Civil Law)
U & P . . . . . . Uttering and Publishing

V

VAC . . . . V Amphibious Corps
V1S . . . . V-groove on One Side (Lumber)
V2S . . . . V-groove on Two Sides (Lumber)
VM . . . . V-Mail Specialists (Navy)
VIG . . . . Vaccinia Immune Globulin (Medicine)
VC . . . . Vacuolated Cell
VAR . . . . Vacuum Arc Remelting (Steel alloy)
VBP . . . . Vacuum Backing Pump
VBJ . . . . Vacuum Bell Jar
VBGQ . . . . . . Vacuum Brazed – Gas Quenched
VCMA . . . . . . Vacuum Cleaner Manufacturers Association
VCR . . . . Vacuum Contact Relay
VCS . . . . Vacuum Control Switch
VDE . . . . Vacuum Deposition Equipment
VDP . . . . Vacuum Diffusion Pump
VEBW . . . . . . Vacuum Electron Beam Welder
VEECO . . . . . Vacuum Electronics Engineering Company
VED . . . . Vacuum Energy Diverter
VES . . . . Vacuum Evaporator System
VFH . . . . Vacuum Film Handling
VFHT . . . . . . Vacuum Film Handling Technique
VFP . . . . Vacuum Fore Pump
VFM . . . . Vacuum Forming Machine
VFVC . . . . . . Vacuum Freezing, Vapor Compression (Desalination)
VFT . . . . Vacuum Friction Test
VGV . . . . Vacuum Gate Valve
VH . . . . Vacuum Housing
VHF . . . . Vacuum Hydrogen Furnace
VII . . . . Vacuum Impregnated Inductor
VLD . . . . Vacuum Leak Detector
VLB . . . . Vacuum Lens Blank
VLU . . . . Vacuum Lifting Unit
VLS . . . . Vacuum Loading System
VMF . . . . Vacuum Melting Furnace
VMM . . . . Vacuum Melting Module
VOB . . . . Vacuum Optical Bench
VPU . . . . Vacuum Penetration Unit
VP . . . . Vacuum Pickup
VPP . . . . Vacuum Pickup Pencil
VPS . . . . Vacuum Pickup System
VPOF . . . . . . Vacuum-Processed Oxide Free
VP . . . . Vacuum Pump
VPC . . . . Vacuum Pump Chamber
VPDF . . . . . . Vacuum Pump Discharge Filter
VPF . . . . Vacuum Pump Filter
VPS . . . . Vacuum Pump System
VPM . . . . Vacuum Pumping Module
VRT . . . . Vacuum Rectifying Tube
VS . . . . Vacuum Switch
VTF . . . . Vacuum Test Furnace
VTT . . . . Vacuum Thermal Testing
V . . . . Vacuum Tube
VT . . . . Vacuum Tube (Electronics)
VTA . . . . Vacuum Tube Amplifier
VTDC . . . . . . Vacuum Tube Development Committee (Columbia University)
VTM . . . . Vacuum Tube Module
VRD . . . . Vacuum Tube Relay Driver
VTT . . . . Vacuum Tube Transmitter
VTX . . . . Vacuum Tube Transmitter
VTV . . . . Vacuum Tube Voltmeter
VTVM . . . . . . Vacuum-Tube Voltmeter (Radio)
VUV . . . . Vacuum Ultraviolet
VV . . . . Vacuum Valve

VWA . . . . Vacuum Window Assembly
VWPI . . . . . . Vacuum Wood Preservers Institute
V . . . . Vagabond
VSO . . . . Valdosta Southern R. R. (AAR code)
VSC . . . . Valdosta State College (Georgia)
VWH . . . . Vale of White Horse (Hounds)
VFF . . . . Valence Force Field
VMT . . . . Validate Master Tape
VBWR . . . . . . Vallecitos Boiling Water Reactor (AEC)
VESR . . . . . . Vallecitos Experimental Superheat Reactor
VJC . . . . Vallejo Junior College (California)
VFGH . . . . . . Valley Forge General Hospital
VSL . . . . Valley & Siletz R. R. (AAR code)
VUA . . . . Valorous Unit Award (Army)
VTI . . . . Valparaiso Technical Institute (Indiana)
V and A . . . . . Valuable and Attractive (A marking used by RAF on such supplies as watches and cameras)
VC . . . . Valuable Cargo
VC . . . . Valuation Clause
V . . . . Value
VABA . . . . . . Value Added by Advertising
VAT . . . . Value-Added Tax
VAM . . . . Value Aluminizing Machine
VA . . . . Value Analysis
VE . . . . Value Effectiveness
VE . . . . Value Engineering
VEA . . . . Value Engineering Audit
VEC . . . . Value Engineering Change
VECP . . . . . . Value Engineering Change Proposals (Navy)
VEDR . . . . . . Value Engineering Design Review
VEFCA . . . . . . Value Engineering Functional Cost Analysis
VEG . . . . Value Engineering Guideline
VEGL . . . . . . Value Engineering Guideline
VEO . . . . Value Engineering Organization
VEP . . . . Value Engineering Program
VEPG . . . . . . Value Engineering Program Guideline
VESP . . . . . . Value Engineering Supplier Program
VETF . . . . . . Value Engineering Task Force
VET . . . . Value Engineering Training
VIP . . . . Value Improving Products
VNO . . . . Value Not Obtained
VPP . . . . Value Payable by Post
VIP . . . . Value in Performance
VTFT . . . . . . Value Task Force Team
VOP . . . . Valued as in Original Policy (Insurance)
V . . . . Valve (Technical drawings)
VB . . . . Valve Box
VMA . . . . Valve Manufacturers Association
VMS . . . . Valve Mounting System
VP . . . . Valve Positioner
VSL . . . . Valve Signal Light
VSD . . . . Valve Solenoid Driver
VPR . . . . Valveless Pulse Rocket
VDH . . . . Valvular Disease of the Heart (Medicine)
V . . . . Van
VASSS . . . . . . Van Allen Simplified Scoring System (Tennis)
VDL . . . . Van Diemen's Land (Former name of Tasmania)
DAF . . . . Van Doorn's Automobile Fabrieken (Dutch automobile manufacturer; acronym used as name of its cars)
V-L . . . . Van Langenhoven (Rifle)
VNT . . . . Van Norman Company (NYSE symbol)
VRT . . . . Van Raalte Company, Inc. (NYSE symbol)
V . . . . Vanadium (Chemical element)

VAS . . . . Vanadium-Alloys Steel Company (NYSE symbol)
VCA . . . . Vanadium Corporation of America (NYSE symbol)
VAAC . . . . . . Vanadyl Acetylacetonate
VSA . . . . Vancouver School of Art
VAFB . . . . . . Vandenberg Air Force Base (California)
VADE . . . . . . Vandenberg Automatic Data Evaluation (or Equipment)
VFO . . . . Vandenberg Field Office (Air Force)
VTP . . . . Vandenberg Test Program
VBA . . . . Vanilla Bean Association
VMA . . . . Vanilmandelic Acid
V . . . . Vapor
VCF . . . . Vapor Chamber Fin
VCS . . . . Vapor Coating System
VCD . . . . Vapor Compression Distillation
VCE . . . . Vapor Compression Evaporation
VCS . . . . Vapor Cooling System
VD . . . . Vapor Density
VDS . . . . Vapor Detection System
VFS . . . . Vapor Feed System
V/L . . . . Vapor-to-Liquid
VLS . . . . Vapor-Liquid-Solid
VPC . . . . Vapor Phase Chromatography
VPD . . . . Vapor-Phase Deacidification (of books and documents)
VP . . . . Vapor Pressure
VPO . . . . Vapor Pressure Osmometer
VRP . . . . Vapor Reheat Process
VS . . . . Vapor Seal (Technical drawings)
VLP . . . . Vaporizing Liquid Plenum
VDT . . . . Varactor Diode Test
VRH . . . . Var-Hour Meter
VL . . . . Varia Lectio (Variant Reading)
V . . . . Variable
VAC . . . . Variable Air Capacitor
VAMP . . . . . . Variable Anamorphic Motion Picture
VAL . . . . Variable Angle Launcher
VAN . . . . Variable Area Nozzle
VBPF . . . . . . Variable Band Pass Filter
VCD . . . . Variable-Capacitance Diode
VARICAP . . . . . Variable Capacitor
VCC . . . . Variable Ceramic Capacitor
VCR . . . . Variable Compression Ratio
VCS . . . . Variable Correlation Synchronization
VXO . . . . Variable Crystal Oscillator
VCO . . . . Variable Cycle Operation
VDL . . . . Variable Delay Line
VDT . . . . Variable Density Tunnel
VDS . . . . Variable-Depth SONAR
VDSS . . . . . . Variable Depth SONAR System
VDT . . . . Variable Differential Transformer
VDFG . . . . . . Variable Diode Function Generator
VDM . . . . . . Variable Direction Microphone
VDE . . . . Variable Display Equipment
VES . . . . Variable Elasticity of Substitution (Industrial production)
VEF . . . . Variable Electronic Filter
VEB . . . . Variable Elevation Beam (RADAR)
VFL . . . . Variable Focal Length
VFL . . . . Variable Focal-Length Lens
VFC . . . . Variable Frequency Control
VFO . . . . Variable Frequency Oscillator
VGA . . . . Variable Gain Amplifier
VGC . . . . Variable Gas Capacitor
VGW . . . . . . Variable Geometry Wing
VHP . . . . Variable Horse Power
VIT . . . . Variable Impedance Tube
ViP . . . . Variable Inductance Pickup
VIP . . . . Variable Information Processing (Navy)
VIPP . . . . Variable Information Processing Package
VIOC . . . . . . Variable Input-Output Code
VIC . . . . Variable Instruction Computer
VI . . . . Variable Interval
VLCR . . . . . . Variable Length Cavity Resonance
VLM . . . . Variable Length Multiply
VLFS . . . . . . Variable Low Frequency Standard
VMC . . . . Variable Message Cycle
VMC . . . . Variable Mica Capacitor
VMT . . . . Variable Mu Tube (Electronics)
VNL . . . . Variable Neodymium LASER
VNC . . . . Variable Neutralizing Capacitor
VOC . . . . Variable Oil Capacitor
VPC . . . . Variable Padder Capacitor
VPS . . . . Variable Parameter System

VPF . . . . Variable Parts Feeder
VPF . . . . Variable Phase Filter
VP . . . . Variable Pitch (as, an aircraft propeller)
VPP . . . . Variable Pitch Propeller
VPL . . . . Variable Pulse LASER
VPNL . . . . . . Variable Pulse Neodymium LASER
VQC . . . . Variable Quartz Capacitor
VRAM . . . . . . Variable Random Access Memory (Data processing)
VPG . . . . Variable-Rate Pulse Generator
VR . . . . Variable Ratio (Reinforcement)
VRB . . . . Variable Reenlistment Bonus (Military)
VRC . . . . Variable Reluctance Cartridge
VRM . . . . . . Variable Reluctance Microphone
VRP . . . . Variable Reluctance Pickup
VRT . . . . Variable Reluctance Transducer
VRCI . . . . . . Variable Resistive Components Institute
VARISTOR . . . . Variable Resistor
VSS . . . . Variable Slit Set
VSS . . . . Variable SONAR System
VSC . . . . Variable Speed Chopper
VSCF . . . . . . Variable-Speed Constant Frequency
VSD . . . . Variable-Speed Drive
VST . . . . Variable Stability Trainer
VSW . . . . Variable Sweep Wing
VTCC . . . . . . Variable Temperature Compensation Capacitor
VTCS . . . . . . Variable Thermal Control Surface
VTL . . . . Variable Threshold Logic
VT . . . . Variable Thrust
VTE . . . . Variable Thrust Engine
VTES . . . . . . Variable Thrust Engine System
VT . . . . Variable Time (Fuse) (Also known as a "proximity fuse")
VTS . . . . Variable Time Step
VTA . . . . Variable Transfer Address
VT . . . . Variable Transformer
VTW . . . . Variable Transmission Window
VTC . . . . Variable Trimmer Capacitor
VVC . . . . Variable Vacuum Capacitor
VVR . . . . Variable Voltage Rectifier
VVPP . . . . . . Variable Volume Piston Pump
VWP . . . . Variable Width Pulse
VWL . . . . Variable Word Length
VAR . . . . Varian Associates (NYSE symbol)
VR . . . . Variant Reading
V . . . . Variation
VFA . . . . Variation Flow Analysis
VPD . . . . Variation Per Day (Navigation)
VPH . . . . Variation Per Hour (Navigation)
VPM . . . . . . Variation Per Minute (Navigation)
VCI . . . . Variety Clubs International
VL . . . . Vario-Losser (Electronics)
VD . . . . Various Dates (Bibliography)
VP . . . . Various Paging, Various Places of Publication (Bibliography)
VP . . . . Various Places
VP . . . . Various Publications
VY . . . . Various Years (Bibliography)
ViC . . . . Varnish Insulating Compound
VM & P . . . . . Varnish Makers' and Painters' Naphtha
VCIM . . . . . . Varnished Cambric Insulation Material
VTA . . . . Varnished Tube Association
VDN . . . . Varudeklarationsnamnden (Labeling system) (Sweden)
VO of A . . . Vasa Order of America
VRF . . . . Vascular Research Foundation
VCC . . . . Vasoconstrictor Center (Physiology)
VCS . . . . Vasoconstrictor Substance (Physiology)
VDM . . . . . . Vasodepressor Material
VDC . . . . Vasodilator Center (Physiology)
VDS . . . . Vasodilator Substance
VEM . . . . Vasoexcitor Material (Physiology)
VIC . . . . Vasoinhibitory Center (Medicine)
VM . . . . Vasomotor
VMC . . . . Vasomotor Center (Physiology)
VDI . . . . Vat Dye Institute
VPS . . . . Vatican Philatelic Society
V . . . . Vector (Mathematics)
VAC . . . . Vector Analog Computer
VEEG . . . . . . Vector Electroencephalograph
VF . . . . Vector Field
ViLP . . . . . . Vector Impedance Locus Plotter
VM . . . . Vector Message
VVM . . . . Vector Voltmeter
VCG . . . . Vectorcardiogram (Medicine)

VS . . . . Vectoring Service
VOG . . . . Vectoroculogram
VSCNY . . . . . . Vedanta Society of the City of New York
VGAA . . . . . . Vegetable Growers Association of America
VOEC . . . . . . Vegetable Oil Export Corporation
VPMA . . . . . . Vegetable Parchment Manufacturers Association
VBA . . . . Vegetarian Brotherhood of America
VAB . . . . Vehicle Assembly Building
VAL . . . . Vehicle Authorization List (Military)
VATS . . . . . . Vehicle Automatic Test System
VECOS . . . . Vehicle Checkout Set
VCP . . . . Vehicle Collecting Point
VCG . . . . Vehicle Control Group
VCO . . . . Vehicle Control Officer (Air Force)
VDM . . . . Vehicle Deadlined for Maintenance
VDP . . . . Vehicle Deadlined for Parts
VDS . . . . Vehicle Design Section
VDPI . . . . . . Vehicle Direction and Position Indicator
VERC . . . . . . Vehicle Effectiveness Remaining Converter
VEA . . . . Vehicle Engineering Analysis
VESC . . . . . . Vehicle Equipment Safety Commission
VFCS . . . . . . Vehicle Flight Control System
VGS . . . . Vehicle Generating System
VMA . . . . Vehicle Maintenance Area
VMM . . . . Vehicle Model Movement
VOI . . . . Vehicle Ordnance Installation
VOCM . . . . . . Vehicle Out of Commission for Maintenance (Military)
VOCP . . . . . . Vehicle Out of Commission for Parts (Military)
VPD . . . . Vehicle Performance Data
VPLCC . . . . . Vehicle Propellant Loading Control Center
VRFWS . . . . . Vehicle Rapid Fire Weapon System (Army)
VR . . . . Vehicle Recovery
VRC . . . . Vehicle Research Corporation
VRB . . . . Vehicle Retaining Board
VSC . . . . Vehicle Sectoring Code
VSM . . . . Vehicle State Monitor
VSC . . . . Vehicle System Control
VT . . . . Vehicle Theft
VTR . . . . Vehicle Tracking Receiver
VWF . . . . Vehicle Work Flow
VTM . . . . Vehicles to the Mile (Military)
VPD . . . . Vehicles Per Day (Military)
VPH . . . . Vehicles Per Hour (Military)
VPM . . . . Vehicles Per Mile
VC . . . . Vehicular Communications
VCS . . . . Vehicular Communications System
VRS . . . . Vehicular RADIAC System
VTC . . . . Vehicular Traffic Control
V . . . . Vein
VESIAC . . . . . Vela Seismic Information Analysis Center (University of Michigan)
VUP . . . . Vela Uniform Platform
VL . . . . Velar Lobe
VEA . . . . Veliger Escape Aperture
V . . . . Velocity
VCP . . . . Velocity Control Programmer
VE . . . . Velocity Error
VF . . . . Velocity Failure
VG . . . . Velocity Gravity
V/H . . . . Velocity/Height
VIH . . . . Velocity Impact Hardening
VICI . . . . Velocity Indicating Coherent Integrator
VINS . . . . . . Velocity Inertia Navigation System
VIRNS . . . . . Velocity Inertia RADAR Navigation System
VMS . . . . Velocity Measurement System
VM . . . . Velocity Meter
VMO . . . . Velocity-Modulated Oscillator
VMT . . . . Velocity-Modulated Tube
VM . . . . Velocity Modulation
VNE . . . . Velocity Never to Exceed
VGH . . . . Velocity, Normal Gravity and Height
VP . . . . Velocity Pressure
VSS . . . . Velocity Sensor System
VTB . . . . Velocity Test Barrel
VVT . . . . Velocity Variation Tube
VVM . . . . Velocity Vector Measurement
VVMS . . . . . . Velocity Vector Measurement System
VV . . . . Velocity-Volume
VC . . . . Vender Contact
VEN . . . . Vendo Company (NYSE symbol)
VAF . . . . Vendor Approval Form
VCN . . . . Vendor Contract Notice

VCTD . . . . Vendor Contract Technical Data
VDRG . . . . Vendor Data Release Group
VDR . . . . Vendor Data Request
VDS . . . . Vendor Data Service
VDS . . . . Vendor Direct Shipment
VEM . . . . Vendor Engineering Memorandum
VIR . . . . Vendor Information Request
VIM . . . . Vendor Initial Measurement
VLD . . . . Vendor List of Drawings
VPN . . . . Vendor Part Number
VPI . . . . Vendor Parts Index
VQA . . . . Vendor Quality Assurance
VQC . . . . Vendor Quality Certification
VQD . . . . Vendor Quality Defect
VQZD . . . . Vendor Quality Zero Defects
VR . . . . Vendor Rating
VRM . . . . Vendor Receiving Memo
VSI . . . . Vendor Shipping Instruction
VTP . . . . Vendor Test Procedure
VTR . . . . Vendor Trouble Report
VVTC . . . . Vendor-Vendee Technical Committee
VWA . . . . Vendor Working Authority
VZD . . . . Vendor Zero Defect
VSD . . . . Vendor's Shipping Document
V . . . . Venerable
VC . . . . Venereal Case (Medical slang)
VD . . . . Venereal Disease
VDEL . . . . Venereal Disease Experimental Laboratory
VDG . . . . Venereal Disease Gonorrhea
VDRT . . . . Venereal Disease Reference Test (of Harris)
VDRL . . . . Venereal Disease Research Laboratory
VDS . . . . Venereal Disease Syphilis
VP . . . . Venereal Pamphlet (Navy)
VBI . . . . Venetian Blind Institute
VVBAA . . . . . . Venetian and Vertical Blind Association of America
VCCUS . . . . . . Venezuelan Chamber of Commerce of the United States
VEE . . . . Venezuelan Equine Encephalomyelitis (Veterinary medicine)
VZP . . . . Venezuelan Petroleum Company (NYSE symbol)
VDR . . . . Venous Diameter Ratio (Cancer detection)
VP . . . . Venous Pressure
V . . . . Vent
VH . . . . Vent Hole (Technical drawings)
VP . . . . Vent Pipe (Technical drawings)
VS . . . . Vent Stack (Technical drawings)
VSB . . . . Vent and Supply Bay
VV . . . . Vent Valve
VFS . . . . Ventilated Flight Suit
VD . . . . Ventilating Deadlight (Technical drawings)
VR . . . . Ventilation Rate
V . . . . Ventilator
V . . . . Ventral
VCS . . . . Ventral Collecting Sinus
VLCG . . . . Ventral Longitudinal Ciliated Groove
VML . . . . Ventral Mantle Lip
VPCF . . . . Ventral Peristomial Collar Fold
VPL . . . . Ventral(is) Posterolateral(is)
VS . . . . Ventral Sac
VNG . . . . Ventral Surface, Nephridial Gland
VK . . . . Ventral Wall, Kidney
VAT . . . . Ventricular Activation Time
VG . . . . Ventricular Gallop
VSD . . . . Ventricular Septal Defect (Medicine)
VMH . . . . Ventromedial Hypothalamic Nucleus
VMN . . . . Ventromedial Nucleus
VCY . . . . Ventura County Railway Company (AAR code)
V . . . . Venue
VDW . . . . Venus Departure Window
VEB . . . . Venus Entry Body
VFV . . . . Venus Flyby Vehicle
V . . . . Verb
VA . . . . Verb, Active
VI . . . . Verb Intransitive
VN . . . . Verb Neuter
VP . . . . Verb Passive
VR . . . . Verb Reflexive
VT . . . . Verb Transitive
VA . . . . Verbal Adjective
VASC . . . . Verbal Auditory Screen for Children
VISTA . . . . Verbal Information Storage and Text Analysis (in FORTRAN computer language)
VBN . . . . Verbal Noun

VOCG . . . . . . Verbal Order Commanding General
VOCO . . . . . . Verbal Order Commanding Officer
VO . . . . Verbal Orders
VOTAG . . . . . Verbal Orders of the Adjutant General
VOCS . . . . . . Verbal Orders Chief of Staff
VOC . . . . Verbal Orders of the Commander
VODP . . . . . . Verbal Orders by Direction of the President
VOGOV . . . . Verbal Orders of the Governor
VOSAF . . . . . . Verbal Orders Secretary of the Air Force
VOSA . . . . . . Verbal Orders of Secretary of the Army
VET . . . . Verbal Test
VDJ . . . . Verband der Deutschen Journalisten
VDDI . . . . . . Verband Deutscher Diplomingenieure (West Germany)
VDE . . . . Verband Deutscher Elektrotechniker (West Germany)
VFOI . . . . . . Verband Deutscher Feinmechanischer und Optischer Industrie (West Germany)
VDK . . . . Verband Deutscher Konsumgenossenschaften
VDPG . . . . . . Verband Deutscher Physikalischer Gesselschaften (West Germany)
VSK . . . . Verband Schweizerischer Konsumvereine
VWA . . . . Verband der Weiblichen Angestellten (Association of Female Employees) (West Germany)
VDM . . . . . . Verbi Die Minister (Minister, or Preacher, of the Word of God)
VG . . . . Verbi Gratia (For Example)
VCP . . . . Verdan Checkout Panel
VJB . . . . Verdan Junction Box
VMAVA . . . . . Verdun-Meuse-Argonne Veterans Association
VBI . . . . Verein Beratender Ingenieure
VDI . . . . Verein Deutscher Ingenieure (Society of German Engineers)
VFR . . . . Verein fuer Raumschiffahrt (Society for Space Travel) (Germany)
VAR . . . . Vereinigte Arabische Republik
VEBA . . . . . . Vereinigte Elektrizitaets und Bergwerks, AG (Holding company) (Germany)
VFW . . . . Vereinigte Flugtechnische Werke
VOB . . . . Vereinigung
VARA . . . . . . Vereinigung van Arbeiders Radio Amateurs
VSA . . . . Vereinigung Schweizerischer Angestelltenverbande (Federation of Swiss Employees' Societies)
VVN . . . . Vereinigung der Verfolgten des Naziregimes
VVB . . . . Vereinigung Volkseigener Betriebe
VVEAB . . . . . . Vereinigung Volkseigener Erfassungs und Aufkaufbetriebe
VVG . . . . Vereinigung Volkseigener Gueter
VVV . . . . Vereinigung Volkseigener Veriage
V (Bomb) . . . . Vergeltungswaffe Bomb (German "vengeance weapon")
VUTS . . . . . . Verification Unit Test Set
VAMOS . . . . . Verified Additional Military Occupational Specialty
VCF . . . . Verified Circulation Figure (Periodical publishing)
VPMOS . . . . . Verified Primary Military Occupational Specialty
VSMOS . . . . . Verified Secondary Military Occupational Specialty
VI . . . . Vermiculite Institute
VT . . . . Vermont
VJC . . . . Vermont Junior College
VMIC . . . . . . Vermont Maple Industry Council
VSTC . . . . . . Vermont State Teachers College
VCD . . . . Vernier Engine Cutoff (Air Force)
VECO . . . . . . Vernier-Engine Cutoff (NASA)
VSG . . . . Vernier Step Gage
VERNITRAC . . . Vernier Tracking by Automatic Correlation
VBOS . . . . . . Veronal Buffered Oxalated Saline
VO . . . . Verordnung
VAST . . . . . . Versatile Automatic Specification Tester
VATLS . . . . . . Versatile Automatic Target Locating System
VATE . . . . . . Versatile Automatic Test Equipment (Computers)
VAST . . . . . . Versatile Avionics Shop Tester
VATS . . . . . . Versatile Avionics Test Shop
VERDAN . . . . . Versatile Differential Analyzer
VET . . . . Versatile Engine Tester
VHS . . . . Versatile High Speed (Copier)
VIP . . . . Versatile Information Processor (Data processing)
VPM . . . . Versatile Packaging Machine
VRF . . . . Versatile Repair Facility
VSD . . . . Versatile Signal Device
VSG . . . . Versatile Symbol (or Signal) Generator
VC . . . . Versatility Code
V . . . . Verse
VV . . . . Verses
V . . . . Versicle
V . . . . Version
V . . . . Verso (Bibliography)
VAK . . . . Versuchs-Atomkraftwerk Kahl
VLB . . . . Versuchs-und Lehranstalt fuer Braverie
V . . . . Versus (Against)

V . . . . Verte (Turn over)
V . . . . Vertex
VAU . . . . Vertical Acceleration Unit
VAW . . . . Vertical Arc Welder
VAH . . . . Vertical Array Hydrophone
VAB . . . . Vertical Assembly Building (NASA)
VACTL . . . . . . Vertical Assembly Component Test Laboratory
VAB . . . . Vertical Axis Bearing
VAP . . . . Vertical Axis Pivots
VB . . . . Vertical Beam (of light)
VB . . . . Vertical Bomb (Air Force)
VCL . . . . Vertical Center Line
VCC . . . . Vertical Centering Control
VC . . . . Vertical Circle
Z . . . . Vertical component of the earth's magnetic field
VCO . . . . Vertical Control Operator (Military)
VCM . . . . Vertical Cutter Motion
VDA . . . . Vertical Danger Angle (Navigation)
VDP . . . . Vertical Data Processing
VDG . . . . Vertical and Direction Gyro
VD . . . . Vertical Drive
VER . . . . Vertical Earth Rate
VETS . . . . Vertical Engine Test Stand
VEP . . . . Vertical Extrusion Press
VF . . . . Vertical File
VFM . . . . Vertical Flight Maneuver
VG . . . . Vertical Grain
VGP . . . . Vertical Ground Point
VGA . . . . Vertical Gyro Alignment
VGI . . . . Vertical Gyro Indicator
VHC . . . . Vertical Hold Control
VIM . . . . Vertical Improved Mail (Post Office term for conveyorized handling of US mail in large modern buildings)
VIB . . . . Vertical Integration Building
VI . . . . Vertical Interval (Map-making)
VK . . . . Vertical Keel
VL . . . . Vertical Ladder (Technical drawings)
VLP . . . . Vertical Landing Point
VLF . . . . Vertical Launch Facility
VLAC . . . . . . Vertical Lift Aircraft Council
V . . . . Vertical in line (Aircraft engine)
VCB . . . . Vertical Location of the Center of Buoyancy
VCG . . . . Vertical Location of the Center of Gravity
VM . . . . Vertical Magnet
VMM . . . . Vertical Milling Machine
VERNAV . . . . . Vertical Navigation System
VPM . . . . Vertical Panel Mount
VPP . . . . Vertical Pinpoint
VPB . . . . Vertical Plot Board (Navy)
VP . . . . Vertical Polarization
VPM . . . . Vertical Polarization Mode
VPW . . . . Vertically Polarized Wave
VPP . . . . Vertical Pouch Packager
VRAH . . . . . . Vertical Receiving Array Hydrophone
VRH . . . . Vertical Receiving Hydrophone
VRA . . . . Vertical Reference Attitude
VRL . . . . Vertical Reference Line (Technical drawings)
V/STOL . . . . . Vertical/Short Takeoff and Landing (Air Force)
VSI . . . . Vertical Signal Indicator
VSD . . . . Vertical Situation Display
VSS . . . . Vertical Sounding System
VSP . . . . Vertical Speed (Aviation)
VSS . . . . Vertical Spike Soderberg (Pot) (Aluminum processing)
VS . . . . Vertical Stereoscopic (Photograph)
VS . . . . Vertical Stripes (on buoys, etc.) (Maps and charts)
VSS . . . . Vertical Support Structure
VT . . . . Vertical Tail
VTO . . . . Vertical Takeoff
VTOHL . . . . . . Vertical Take-Off and Horizontal Landing
VERTOL . . . . . Vertical Takeoff and Landing
VTOL . . . . . . Vertical Takeoff and Landing (Acronym used for a type of aircraft)
VERTIJET . . . . Vertical Take-Off and Landing Jet (Aircraft)
VTF . . . . Vertical Test Facility (NASA)
VTF . . . . Vertical Test Fixture
VTR . . . . Vertical Test Range
VTS . . . . Vertical Thrust Stand
VTE . . . . Vertical Tube Effects (Desalination)
VTPA . . . . . . Vertical Turbine Pump Association
VUF . . . . Vertical Upward Force
VVC . . . . Vertical Velocity Console
VVSS . . . . . . Vertical Volute Spring Suspension (Technical drawings)

VWH . . . . Vertical Weld Head
VWHA . . . . . . Vertical Weld Head Assembly
VRAD . . . . Vertically Referenced Attitude Display
VFW. . . . . Verwaltungsamt fuer Wirtschaft (Executive Committee for Economics)
                (German)
V . . . . Very
VDW . . . . Very Deep Water
VEWS . . . . . . Very Early Warning System
VF . . . . Very Fair
VF . . . . Very Fine
VFC . . . . Very Fine Cognac
VG . . . . Very Good (Condition) (Antiquarian book trade)
VH . . . . Very Heavy
VHB . . . . Very Heavy Bombardment (Air Force)
VH . . . . Very High
VHA . . . . Very High Altitude
VHF . . . . Very High Frequency (Electronics)
VDF . . . . Very-High-Frequency Direction Finding
VHF/DF . . . . Very High Frequency Direction-Finding
VHFF . . . . . . Very High Frequency Filter
VHFG . . . . . . Very High Frequency Generator
VHFI . . . . . . Very High Frequency Indeed (Ultra-high frequency) (British)
VHFJ . . . . . . Very High Frequency Jammer
VOR. . . . . . . Very-High-Frequency Omnidirectional Radio Range
VHFOR . . . . . Very High Frequency Omnirange
VOR. . . . . . . Very-High-Frequency Omnirange
VOR-DME . . . . Very-High-Frequency, Omnirange, Distance-Measuring Equipment
VOR/DMET . . . Very-High-Frequency Omnirange/Distance Measuring Equipment
                Compatible with TACAN
VORTAC . . . . . Very-High-Frequency Omnirange TACAN
VHFO . . . . . . Very High Frequency Oscillator
VHFR . . . . . . Very High Frequency Receiver
VHFT . . . . . . Very High Frequency Termination
VHO . . . . . . Very High Output
VHP . . . . Very High Performance
VHP . . . . Very High Pressure
VHC . . . . Very Highly Commended
VIC . . . . Very Important Customer
VIP . . . . Very Important Passenger
VIP . . . . Very Important Person
VIPI . . . . Very Important Person Indeed
VIP . . . . Very Important Poor
VLA . . . . Very Large Array
VLB . . . . Very Long Baseline
VLEASS . . . . . Very Long Endurance Acoustic Submarine Simulator
VLR . . . . Very Long Range
VERLORT . . . . . Very-Long-Range Tracking (NASA)
VLA . . . . Very Low Altitude
VLF . . . . Very Low Frequency (Electronics)
VLFJ . . . . Very Low Frequency Jammer
VLFR . . . . . . Very Low Frequency Receiver
VLR . . . . Very Low Range
VLS . . . . Very Low Speed
VMT . . . . Very Many Thanks
VO . . . . Very Old
VOP. . . . . . . Very Old Pale (Wines and spirits)
VOT. . . . . . . Very Old Tawny (Wines and spirits)
VOP. . . . . . . Very Oldest Procurable
V Rev . . . . . . Very Reverend
VSR . . . . Very Short Range
VSRBM . . . . . Very Short Range Ballistic Missile
VSW . . . . Very Short Wave
VSO . . . . Very Special Old
VSQ. . . . . . . Very Special Quality
VSO. . . . . . . Very Stable Oscillator
VS . . . . Very Superior
VSO . . . . Very Superior Old
VSOP . . . . . . Very Superior Old Pale (Wines and spirits)
VVO . . . . Very Very Old
VVS . . . . Very Very Superior
VW . . . . Very Worshipful
VE . . . . Vesicular Exanthema (Medicine)
VS . . . . Vesicular Sound (in auscultation of chest) (Medicine)
VS . . . . Vesicular Stomatitis (Medicine)
VSV . . . . Vesicular Stomatitis Virus
LEA/BZ . . . . . Vessel Leased to Brazil
LEA/CH . . . . . Vessel Leased to China
LEA/EC . . . . . Vessel Leased to Ecuador
LEA/FR . . . . . Vessel Leased to France
LEA/GR . . . . . Vessel Leased to Greece
LEA/MX . . . . . Vessel Leased to Mexico

LEA/NE . . . . . Vessel Leased to Netherlands
LEA/NO . . . . . Vessel Leased to Norway
LEA/PA . . . . . Vessel Leased to Panama
LEA/PG . . . . . Vessel Leased to Paraguay
LEA/PE . . . . . Vessel Leased to Peru
LEA/RU . . . . . Vessel Leased to Russia
LEA/UK . . . . . Vessel Leased to United Kingdom
LEA/UR . . . . . Vessel Leased to Uruguay
LOST/E . . . . . Vessel Lost Through Enemy Action (Navy)
VW . . . . Vessel Wall
VESCA(S) . . . . Vessels and Cargo
DI/SAL . . . . . Vessels Disposed of by Sale through Navy Material Redistribution Agency
DI/SCP . . . . . Vessels Disposed of by Scrapping (Navy)
DI/DES . . . . . Vessels Disposed of by Sinking, Burning, Abandoning or Other Means of
                Destruction
DI/TES . . . . . Vessels Disposed of by Using as Targets and Tests (Navy)
DI/FLC . . . . . Vessels in Forward Areas Transferred to State Dept. Foreign Liquidation
                Corp.
LOAN/A . . . . . Vessels Loaned to Army (Navy)
LOAN/C . . . . . Vessels Loaned to Coast Guard (Navy)
LOAN/M . . . . . Vessels Loaned to Miscellaneous Activities (US Maritime Academy, etc.)
                (Navy)
LOAN/S . . . . . Vessels Loaned to States (Navy)
LOAN/W . . . . . Vessels Loaned to War Shipping Administration (Navy)
LOST/A . . . . . Vessels Lost by Accident, Collision or Similar Methods (Navy)
LOST/P . . . . . Vessels Lost Due to Weather, Perils of the Sea or Similar Reasons (Navy)
DI/TRN. . . . . . Vessels Transferred to Other Government Agencies and Miscellaneous
                Activities (Navy)
DI/WSA . . . . . Vessels Transferred to War Shipping Administration–Maritime Commission
                for Disposition (Navy)
VP . . . . Vest Pocket
VPK . . . . Vest Pocket Kodak
VM . . . . Vestibular Membrane (Medicine)
VSB . . . . Vestigial Sideband (Radio)
VSBF . . . . . . Vestigial Sideband Filter
VSF . . . . Vestigial Sideband Filter
VSM. . . . . . . Vestigial Sideband Modulation
VMCCA . . . . . Veteran Motor Car Club of America
VWOA . . . . . . Veteran Wireless Operators Association
VALB . . . . . . Veterans of the Abraham Lincoln Brigade
VA . . . . Veterans Administration
VAH . . . . Veterans Administration Hospital
VARO. . . . . . . Veterans Administration Regional Office
VASRD . . . . . Veterans Administration Schedule for Rating Disabilities
VAVS . . . . . . Veterans Administration Voluntary Service
GI (Bill) . . . . . Veterans Benefits Act, Public Law 345, 1944
VCSFO . . . . . Veterans Canteen Service Field Office (Veterans Administration)
VES . . . . Veterans Employment Service (of USES)
VFER . . . . . . Veterans Federal Employment Representative (Civil Service Commission)
VFW . . . . Veterans of Foreign Wars of the USA
VFW . . . . Veterans of Future Wars (Facetious organization formed by Princeton
                students in 1930's)
VH . . . . Veterans Hospital
VHRTG . . . . . Veterans' Hospital Radio and Television Guild
VPSB . . . . . . Veterans Placement Service Board (Post-World War II)
VIPS. . . . . . . Veterans in Public Service Act
V of S . . . . . Veterans of Safety
VSLI . . . . Veterans Special Life Insurance (VA)
VWW . . . . . . Veterans of World War I of USA
VCH. . . . . . . Veterinary Convalescent Hospital
VC. . . . . Veterinary Corps
VEH . . . . Veterinary Evacuation Hospital
VGH . . . . Veterinary General Hospital
VetSci. . . . . . Veterinary Science
VS . . . . Veterinary Surgeon
VT . . . . Vetus Testamentum (The Old Testament) (Bible)
VAOR. . . . . . . VHF Aural Omnirange
VRB . . . . VHF Recovery Room
VFPR . . . . . . Via Flight Planned Route (Aviation)
VLFD. . . . . . . Via Low Frequency Direct
VNL. . . . . . . Via Net Loss
VOD . . . . Via Omni Direct
VASP . . . . . . Viacao Aeres Sao Paulo, SA (Brazil airline)
VBU . . . . Vibrating Bag Unloader
VCM . . . . Vibrating Coil Magnetometer
VRC . . . . Vibrating Reed Capacitor
VRE . . . . Vibrating Reed Electrometer
VRR . . . . Vibrating Reed Relay
VSM. . . . . . . Vibrating Sample Magnetometer
VSA . . . . Vibrating String Accelerometer
VAT . . . . Vibration Acceptance Test

VAS . . . . Vibration Analysis System
VCI . . . . Vibration Control Index
VDF . . . . Vibration Damping Fastener
VDM . . . . . . Vibration Damping Mount
VDP . . . . Vibration Diagnostic Program
VEC . . . . Vibration Exciter Control
VIM . . . . Vibration Isolation Module
VIS . . . . Vibration Isolation System
VMI . . . . Vibration Measurement Integrator
VMS . . . . Vibration Measuring System
VPA . . . . Vibration Pickup Amplifier
VPUA . . . . . . Vibration Pick-Up Amplifier
VRL . . . . Vibration Research Laboratory (Stanford University)
VS . . . . Vibration Seconds
VSR . . . . Vibration Sensitive Relay
VTE . . . . Vibration Test Equipment
VTPS . . . . . . Vibration Test Plotting System
VTS . . . . Vibration Test System (or Specification)
VT . . . . Vibration Testing
VVHR . . . . . . Vibration Velocity per Hour
VPM . . . . Vibrations Per Minute
VPS . . . . Vibrations Per Second
VPS . . . . Vibrator Power Supply
VBF . . . . Vibratory Bowl Feeder
VPF . . . . Vibratory Pan Feeder
VPT . . . . Vibratron Pressure Transducer
VA . . . . Vicar Apostolic
VC . . . . Vicar Choral
VR . . . . Vicar Rural
V . . . . Vicar, Vicarage
VIND . . . . Vicarious Interpolations Not Desired
VTE . . . . Vicarious Trial and Error (Psychology)
VF . . . . Vicarius Foraneus (Vicar-Forane)
VG . . . . Vicarius Generalis (Vicar-General)
V . . . . Vice (In place of, instead of)
V . . . . Vice (in a position or title)
VA . . . . Vice Admiral
VADM . . . . . . Vice Admiral
VABPF . . . . . . Vice Admiral British Pacific Fleet
VC . . . . Vice Chairman
VC . . . . Vice Chancellor
VCAS . . . . . . Vice-Chief of the Air Staff (British)
VCIGS . . . . . . Vice-Chief of the Imperial General Staff (British)
VCNO . . . . . . Vice Chief of Naval Operations
VOPNAV . . . . Vice Chief of Naval Operations
AFCVC . . . . . . Vice Chief of Staff (Air Force)
VCS . . . . Vice Chief of Staff
VC of S . . . . . Vice Chief of Staff (Army)
VC/SAF . . . . . Vice Chief of Staff, Air Force
VCSA . . . . . . Vice Chief of Staff, Army
VC of SA . . . . Vice Chief of Staff, Army
VC . . . . Vice Consul
VL . . . . Vice-Lieutenant (British)
VEEP . . . . Vice President
VP . . . . Vice President
VPGS . . . . . . Vice-President of the Geological Society (British)
VPLS . . . . . . Vice-President of the Linnaean Society (British)
VPRGS . . . . . . Vice-President of the Royal Geographical Society (British)
VPRI . . . . Vice-President of the Royal Institute (British)
VPRS . . . . . . Vice-President of the Royal Society (British)
VPSA . . . . . . Vice-President of the Society of Antiquaries (British)
VPZS . . . . . . Vice-President of the Zoological Society (British)
VV . . . . Vice Versa
V . . . . Vicinal (Local)
VIK . . . . Vick Chemical Company (NYSE symbol)
VA . . . . Vickers Armstrong Gun
V-A . . . . Vickers-Armstrong, Ltd.
VICK . . . . Vicksburg National Military Park
VKS . . . . Vicksburg, Shreveport and Pacific Railway (NYSE symbol)
VCW . . . . Victor Chemical Works (NYSE symbol)
VCR . . . . Victor Comptometer Corporation (NYSE symbol)
VESI . . . . Victor Educational Services Institute (Educational division of Victor Comptometer Corporation)
VERB . . . . . . Victor Electrowriter Remote Blackboard (Educational device of Victor Comptometer Corporation)
V . . . . Victoria
V & A . . . . . . Victoria and Albert Museum (London, England)
VA . . . . Victoria and Albert Order (British)
VC . . . . Victoria Cross (British)
VMH . . . . Victoria Medal of Honour
VR . . . . Victoria Regina (Queen Victoria)

VRI . . . . Victoria Regina Imperatrix (Victoria, Queen and Empress)
VR et I . . . . . Victoria Regina et Imperatrix (Victoria, Queen and Empress)
VHS . . . . Victorian House of Studies
V . . . . Victory (As in "the V campaign" in Europe, during World War II)
VE . . . . Victory in Europe (as in VE-Day)
V-J . . . . Victory-Japan (14 August 1945)
VMWWI . . . . Victory Medal World War I
VMWWII . . . . Victory Medal World War II
VOTE . . . . . . Victory Only Through Education (Program of Constructive Action, Inc.)
VIVA . . . . . . Victory in Vietnam Association
VI . . . . Vide Infra (See Below)
VS . . . . Vide Supra (See Above)
V . . . . Vide or Videte (See)
VIZ . . . . Videlicet (Namely)
VA . . . . Video Amplifier
VAC . . . . Video Amplifier Chain
VAR . . . . Video-Audio (or Visual-Aural) Range (Radio)
VBW . . . . Video Bandwidth
VCK . . . . Video Camera Kit
VCC . . . . Video Coaxial Connector
VCS . . . . Video Communications System
VICI . . . . Video Console Indexing
VCS . . . . Video Contrast Seeker
VC . . . . Video Correlator
VDCP . . . . . . Video Data Collection Program
VD . . . . Video Decoder
VDM . . . . Video Delta Modulation
VDMS . . . . . . Video Delta Modulation System
VDD . . . . Video Detector Diode
VDDP . . . . . . Video Digital Data Processing
VDS . . . . Video Display System
VDA . . . . Video Distribution Amplifier
VDF . . . . Video Frequency
VF . . . . Video Frequency
VFA . . . . Video Frequency Amplifier
VHR . . . . Video to Hardcopy Recorder
VIG . . . . Video Integrating Group
VI . . . . Video Integrator
VLI . . . . Video Load Impedance
VLA . . . . Video Logarithmic Amplifier
VMAP . . . . . . Video Map Equipment
VMM . . . . . . Video Map Module
VMG . . . . Video Mapping Group
VMG . . . . Video Mixer Group
VMS . . . . Video Modulation System
VOI . . . . Video Output Impedance
VOV . . . . Video Output Voltage
VPCA . . . . . . Video Prelaunch Command Amplifier
VPCDS . . . . . . Video Prelaunch Command Data System (Air Force)
VPE . . . . Video Processing Equipment
VPT . . . . Video Pulse Termination
VRS . . . . Video Reception System
VRK . . . . Video Recorder Kit
VRS . . . . Video Relay System
VS . . . . Video Selection
VSP . . . . Video Signal Processor
VSS . . . . Video Storage System
VSS . . . . Video Supervisory Signal
VSI . . . . Video Sweep Integrator
VSMS . . . . . . Video Switching Matrix System
VTRS . . . . . . Video Tape Recording System
VTRS . . . . . . Video Tape Response System
VVDS . . . . . . Video Verter Decision Storage
VDCU . . . . . . Videograph Display Control Unit
VTR . . . . Videotape Recording (or Recorder)
VAC . . . . Vidicon Alignment Coil
VET . . . . Vidicon Electron Tube
VTC . . . . Vidicon Television Camera
VPO . . . . Vienna Philharmonic Orchestra
VC . . . . Viet Cong
VCC . . . . Vietcong Captured
VCK . . . . Vietcong Killed
VCS . . . . Vietcong Suspects Detained
VSDR . . . . . . Vierteljahrsheft zur Statistik des Deutschen Reichs (Germany)
VN . . . . Vietnam
VNAF . . . . . . Vietnam Air Force
VAMP . . . . . . Vietnam Ammunition Program
VEWU . . . . . . Viet-Nam Educational Workers' Union (North Vietnam)
VGCL . . . . . . Vietnam General Confederation of Labor
VGFTU . . . . . . Viet-Nam General Federation of Trade Unions (North Vietnam)
VNMC . . . . . . Vietnam Marine Corps

VRIS . . . . Vietnam Refugee and Information Services
VSM . . . . Vietnam Service Medal (Military)
VAA . . . . Vietnamese American Association
VC . . . . Vietnamese Communists
VF . . . . View Factor
VL . . . . View Loss
VISTA . . . . . . Viewing Instantly Security Transactions Automatically (Wall Street)
VWDU . . . . . . Viewing Window Deicing Unit
VC . . . . Vigilance Committee
VIKA . . . . . . Viking Air Lines
VMC . . . . . . Villa Madonna College (Kentucky)
VMC . . . . . . Villa Maria College (Pennsylvania)
VWC . . . . . . Villa Walsh College (New Jersey)
V . . . . Village
VLW . . . . Village Level Workers (India)
VBL . . . . Vinblastine
VSC . . . . Vincentian Sisters of Charity (Roman Catholic religious order)
VAMP . . . . . . Vincristine Amethopterin (National Cancer Institute)
VI . . . . Vinegar Institute
VCCA . . . . . Vintage Chevrolet Club of America
VSCCA . . . . . Vintage Sports Car Club of America
VCZ . . . . Vinyl Carbazole
VFI . . . . Vinyl Fabrics Institute
VIM . . . . Vinyl Insulation Material
VL . . . . Violation of Lawful (Order) (Military)
VLRSN . . . . . Violation of Lawful Regulation Issued by the Secretary of the Navy
V . . . . Violet
V . . . . Violin
VB . . . . Vir Bonus (A Good Man)
VC . . . . Vir Clarissimus (A Most Illustrious Man)
VH . . . . Vir Honestus (A Worthy Man)
VM . . . . Vir Magnificus (Great Man)
VPP . . . . Viral Porcine Pneumonia (Veterinary medicine)
VP . . . . Viral Protein
VRI . . . . Viral Respiratory Infection (Illness)
V . . . . Virgin
VI . . . . Virgin Islands
VIC . . . . Virgin Islands Corporation (of the Department of the Interior, intended to promote VI economic development)
VIDC . . . . . . Virgin Islands Department of Commerce
ViIS . . . . Virgin Islands National Park
VM . . . . Virgin and Martyr (Church calendars)
VA . . . . Virginia
VARC . . . . . Virginia Associated Research Center
VBR . . . . Virginia Blue Ridge Railway (AAR code)
VC . . . . Virginia-Carolina Chemical Corporation (NYSE symbol)
VCPA . . . . . Virginia-Carolina Peanut Association
VCS . . . . Virginia & Carolina Southern R. R. (AAR code)
VC . . . . Virginia Central Railway (AAR code)
VCPA . . . . . Virginia Crab Packers Association
VEL . . . . Virginia Electric & Power Company (NYSE symbol)
VEPCO . . . . . Virginia Electric and Power Company
ViMS . . . . . . Virginia Institute of Marine Science
VISR . . . . Virginia Institute for Science Research
ViC . . . . Virginia Intermont College
VKE . . . . Virginia Iron, Coal and Coke Company (NYSE symbol)
VJC . . . . Virginia Junior College
VMC . . . . . . Virginia Medical College
VMI . . . . Virginia Military Institute
VPI . . . . Virginia Polytechnic Institute
VSC . . . . Virginia State College
VTSC . . . . . . Virginia Theological Seminary and College
VUU . . . . Virginia Union University
VGN . . . . . . Virginian Railway Company (AAR code)
VRY . . . . Virginian Railway Company (NYSE symbol)
VVCC . . . . . . Viri Clarissimi (Most Illustrious Men)
ViD . . . . Virtual Image Display
ViDS . . . . . . Virtual Image Display System
VPR . . . . Virtual PPI (Plan-Position Indicator) Reflectoscope (RADAR)
VPR-NMP . . . . Virtual PPI (Plan-Position Indicator) Reflectoscope with Navigational Microfilm Projector (RADAR)
VQ . . . . Virtual Quantum
VZ . . . . Virtual Zero
VIA . . . . Virus Inactivating Agent (Medicine)
VO . . . . Visa Office (Department of State)
VP . . . . Visa Petition
VE . . . . Visalia Electric R. R. (AAR code)
VS . . . . Visceral Sinus
VED . . . . Viscoelastic Damper
VEF . . . . Viscoelastic Fiber
VSA . . . . Viscoelastic Stress Analysis

VRC . . . . Viscometer Recorder-Controller
V . . . . Viscosity
VGC . . . . Viscosity Gravity Constant
VI . . . . Viscosity Index
VII . . . . Viscosity Index Improver
V . . . . Viscount
VRM . . . . Viscous Remnant Magnetization
V . . . . Visibility
VEDAR . . . . . Visible Energy Detection and Ranging
VIEW . . . . . . Visible, Informative, Emotionally Appealing, Workable (Package evaluation in marketing)
VLE . . . . Visible Light Emission
VRC . . . . Visible Record Computer
VS . . . . Visible Supply
VOS . . . . Visicoder Oscillograph System
V . . . . Vision
VERA . . . . . . Vision Electric Recording Apparatus (BBC)
VF . . . . Vision Frequency
VL . . . . Vision, Left
VOS . . . . Vision, Left Eye
VOD . . . . Vision, Right Eye
VR . . . . Vision, Right Eye
VTA . . . . Vision Test Apparatus
VIP . . . . Visit-Investigate-Purchase (Department of Commerce program)
VAQ . . . . . . Visiting Airmen's Quarters (Air Force)
VD . . . . Visiting Dignitary
VN . . . . Visiting Nurse
VNA . . . . Visiting Nurse Association
VOQ . . . . . . Visiting Officers' Quarters (Military)
VKG . . . . Visking Corporation (NYSE symbol)
VAMP . . . . . . Visual-Acoustic-Magnetic Program (NOO)
VAT . . . . Visual Acquisition Technique
VAT . . . . Visual Action Time
V . . . . Visual Acuity
VA . . . . Visual Acuity
VA . . . . Visual Aid
VAC . . . . Visual Aid Console
VATLS . . . . . Visual Airborne Target Locator System
VAS . . . . Visual Analysis System
VA . . . . Visual Approach (Aviation)
VAPI . . . . . . Visual Approach Path Indicator (Aviation)
VASI . . . . . . Visual Approach Slope Indicator (FAA)
VASIS . . . . . . Visual Approach Slope Indicator System
VAKT . . . . . . Visual, Association, Kinesthetic, Tactile (With reference to reading)
VAS . . . . Visual Attack System
VASCAR . . . . Visual Average Speed Computer and Recorder (Speed trap)
VCS . . . . Visual Call Sign (Communications)
VC . . . . Visual Capacity (Acuity)
VCC . . . . Visual Communications Congress
VICOED . . . . . Visual Communications Education
VCB . . . . Visual Control Board
VIDAT . . . . . Visual Data Acquisition
VDA . . . . Visual Discriminatory Acuity
VDD . . . . Visual Display Data
VDQ . . . . Visual Display of Quality
VDS . . . . Visual Docking Simulator
VE . . . . Visual Efficiency
VER . . . . Visual Evoked Response
VF . . . . Visual Field
VF . . . . Visual Flight (Aviation)
VFR . . . . Visual Flight Rules (Aviation)
VADA . . . . . . VFR (Visual Flight Rules) Arrival Delay Advisory (Aviation)
VCOT . . . . . . VFR (Visual Flight Rules) Conditions on Top (Aviation)
VFRSA . . . . . . VFR (Visual Flight Rules) Restrictions Still Apply (Aviation)
VGPI . . . . . . Visual Glide Path Indicator
VIGS . . . . . . Visual Glide Slope
VGSI . . . . . . Visual Glide Slope Indicator
VIP . . . . Visual Identification Point
VIDAC . . . . . Visual Information Display and Control
VIDIAC . . . . . Visual Information Display and Control
VIS . . . . Visual Information System
VI . . . . Visual Inspection
VIS . . . . Visual Instrumentation Subsystem
VIP . . . . Visual Integrated Presentation (Aviation)
VIG . . . . Visual Integrating Group
VIO . . . . Visual Intercept Officer (Navy)
VLA . . . . Visual Landing Aid
VLB . . . . Visual LASER Beam
VL . . . . Visual Laydown
VLD . . . . Visual Laydown Delivery
VLADD . . . . . Visual Low Angle Drogue Delivery

VMC . . . . Visual Meteorological Conditions (Aviation)	VIAS . . . . Voice Interference Analysis Set
VOIS . . . . Visual Observation Instrumentation Subsystem (Lunar space program)	VIPS . . . . Voice Interruption Priority System
VPC . . . . Visual Punch Card	VM . . . . Voice Modulation
VRR . . . . Visual Radio Range	VOC . . . . Voice-Operated Coder
VRG . . . . Visual Reference Gate (Aviation)	VODER . . . . . . Voice-Operated Demonstrator
VRS . . . . Visual Reference System	VODAT . . . . . . Voice-Operated Device for Automatic Transmission
VSTP . . . . Visual Satellite Tracking Program	VOGAD . . . . . . Voice-Operated Gain Adjusting Device
VSMF . . . . Visual Search Microfilm File (Data processing)	VOLCAS . . . . . Voice-Operated Loss Control and Suppressor
VS . . . . Visual Signaling (Military)	VOPR . . . . Voice Operated Relay
VSS . . . . Visual Simulation System	VOS . . . . Voice-Operated Switch
VTIP . . . . Visual Target Identification Point	VOX . . . . Voice-Operated Transmission
VT . . . . Visual Telegraphy	VRFI . . . . Voice Reporting Fault Indicator
VT . . . . Visual Toss	VRSA . . . . Voice Reporting Signal Assembly
VA . . . . Visual Training Aid Specialist (Navy)	VRSS . . . . Voice Reporting Signal System
VTO . . . . Visual Training Officer (Navy)	VRU . . . . Voice Response Unit
VTP . . . . Visual Transmitter Power	VSS . . . . Voice Signaling System
VC . . . . Vital Capacity	VT . . . . Voice Tube (Technical drawings)
VSF . . . . Vitreous Silica Fabric	VUNC . . . . . . Voice of United Nations Command
VCA . . . . Vitrified China Association	VV . . . . Voice Vocoder
VC . . . . Vitrified Clay (Technical drawings)	VPM . . . . Voix du Peuple Murundi (Voice of the Murundi People)
VCT . . . . Vitrified Clay Tile (Technical drawings)	VDA . . . . Volksbund fuer das Deutschtum in Ausland (NAZI Germany)
VIV . . . . Vivace (Lively) (Music)	VOMI . . . . Volksdeutsche Mittelstelle (NAZI Germany)
VX . . . . Vivas, Care (May You Live, Dear One)	VEB . . . . Volkseigene Betrieb
VYB . . . . Vivian, Younger and Bond, Ltd.	VEW . . . . Volkseigene Wirtschaft
VIV . . . . Vivid-Inventive-Vital (Spring fashions)	VEAB . . . . . . Volkseigener Erfassungs und Aufkaufbetrieb
VIL . . . . Vivisection Investigation League	VEH . . . . Volkseigener Handel
V . . . . Vixisti (You Lived)	VEG . . . . Volkseigenes Gut
V . . . . Vixit (He Lived)	VM . . . . Volksmarine
VC of A . . . . . Vizsla Club of America	VOPO . . . . . . Volkspolizei
VIV . . . . Vlaamse Ingenieurs-Vereiniging	VP . . . . Volkspolizei
VIBS . . . . Vocabulatory, Information, Block Design, Similarities (Psychology)	VPH . . . . Volkspolizeihelfer
VOICE . . . . . . Vocabulary of Intelligence Concept Expressions	VPKA . . . . . . Volkspolizeikreisamt
VC's . . . . Vocal Chords (Musical slang)	VW . . . . Volkswagen (German automobile)
VF . . . . Vocal Fremitus	VWCA . . . . . . Volkswagen Club of America
VR . . . . Vocal Resonance	VWR . . . . Volkswirtschaftsrat
VO-AG . . . . . . Vocational Agriculture (Education)	VA . . . . Volt-Ampere
VEA . . . . Vocational Education Act	VAR . . . . Volt-Ampere Reactive
VEPIS . . . . . . Vocational Education Program Information System	VOM . . . . Volt Ohm Meter
VFI . . . . Vocational Foundation, Incorporated	VOM . . . . Volt Ohm Milliameter
VICA . . . . Vocational Industrial Clubs of America	V/M . . . . Volt Per Meter
VOE . . . . Vocational Office Education (NASA employment program)	V/MIL . . . . . . Volt Per Mil
VRA . . . . Vocational Rehabilitation Administration (Became Social and Rehabilitation Service) (HEW)	VSTR . . . . Volt Second Transfer Ratio
VTO . . . . Vocational Training Officer (Navy)	V . . . . Volt, Volts, or Voltage
VTS . . . . Vocational Training Service	VBD . . . . Volta Bureau for the Deaf
VVI . . . . Vocational Values Inventory (Guidance in education)	VAR . . . . Voltage Adjusting Rheostat
VSC . . . . Vocations for Social Change (Employment clearinghouse)	VOLTAN . . . . . Voltage Amperage Normalizer
V . . . . Vocative	VAT . . . . Voltage Amplifier Tube
VVS . . . . Voenno-Vozdushnye Sily (Army Air Forces) (Part of the MO) (USSR)	VCS . . . . Voltage Calibration Set
VVS-VMF . . . Voenno-Vozdushnye Sily – Voenno-Morskogo Flota (Naval Air Force) (USSR)	VC . . . . Voltage Comparator
	VCT . . . . Voltage Control Transfer
VM . . . . Voennoe Ministerstvo (Ministry of War) (1950-53; merged into the MO) (USSR)	VCU . . . . Voltage Control Unit
	VCC . . . . Voltage-Controlled Capacitor
VAM . . . . Vogel's Approximation Method	VCXO . . . . . . Voltage-Controlled Crystal Oscillator
VP . . . . Voges-Proskauer Test (Bacteriology)	VCG . . . . Voltage-Controlled Generator
VOT . . . . Vogt Manufacturing Corporation (NYSE symbol)	VCLO . . . . . . Voltage-Controlled Local Oscillator
V . . . . Voice	VCM . . . . Voltage-Controlled Multivibrator
VA . . . . Voice of America	VCO . . . . Voltage-Controlled Oscillator
VOA . . . . Voice of America	VCSR . . . . . . Voltage-Controlled Shift Register
VAB . . . . Voice Answer Back	VCVS . . . . . . Voltage-Controlled Voltage Source
VCSL . . . . . . Voice Call Signs List	VCD . . . . Voltage Crossing Detector
VCSP . . . . . . Voice Call Signs Plan	VCT . . . . Voltage Curve Tracer
VOCODER . . . . Voice Coder	VD . . . . Voltage Detector
VODER . . . . . . Voice Coder	VDC . . . . Voltage to Digital Converter
VC . . . . Voice Coil	VDC . . . . Voltage Doubler Circuit
VOCOM . . . . . Voice Communications	VFC . . . . Voltage to Frequency Converter
VCL . . . . Voice Communications Laboratory	VG . . . . Voltage Gain
VCS . . . . Voice Communications System	VMFI . . . . . . Voltage Monitor and Fault Indicating
VODACOM . . . Voice Data Communications	VNIC . . . . . . Voltage Negative Immittance Converter
VDD . . . . Voice Digital Display	VPC . . . . Voltage to Pulse Converter
VDL . . . . Voice Direct Line	VRU . . . . Voltage Readout Unit
VEV . . . . Voice-Excited Vocoder	VRA . . . . Voltage Reference Amplifier
VF . . . . Voice Frequency (Communications)	VRT . . . . Voltage Reference Tube
VFC . . . . Voice Frequency Cable	VRPF . . . . . . Voltage-Regulated Plate Filament
VFC . . . . Voice Frequency Carrier (Channel)	VRPS . . . . . . Voltage-Regulated Power Supply
VFCT . . . . . . Voice Frequency Carrier Teletype	VRD . . . . Voltage Regulating Diode
VFF . . . . Voice Frequency Filter	VR . . . . Voltage Regulator
VFSS . . . . . . Voice Frequency Signaling System	VRA . . . . Voltage Regulator Alarm
VFTG . . . . . . Voice Frequency Telegraph	VRM . . . . Voltage Regulator Module
VFT . . . . Voice Frequency Terminal	VRT . . . . Voltage Regulator Tube
VIU . . . . Voice Intercommunications Unit	VR . . . . Voltage Relay
	VRMS . . . . . . Voltage Root Mean Square

VSC . . . . Voltage-Saturated Capacitor
VSR . . . . Voltage Sensing Relay
VSS . . . . Voltage Sensing Switch
VSA . . . . Voltage-Sensitive Amplifier
VSW . . . . . . Voltage Standing Wave
VSWR . . . . . . Voltage Standing-Wave Ratio (Electronics)
VTF . . . . Voltage Transfer Function
VTM . . . . Voltage Tunable Magnetron
VTNS . . . . . . Voltage Tunable Noise Source
VTO . . . . Voltage Tunable Oscillator
VVCD . . . . . . Voltage Variable Capacitance Diode
VVC . . . . Voltage Variable Capacitor (Electronics)
VVD . . . . Voltage Variable Diode
VA . . . . Voltaire Alternative
VS . . . . Voltaire Society
VAM . . . . . . Voltammeter
V . . . . Volti (Turn)
VS . . . . Volti Subito (Turn over quickly) (Music)
V . . . . Voltmeter
VM . . . . Voltmeter
VAD . . . . Voltmeter Analog-to-Digital Converter
VOCA . . . . . . Voltmeter-Calibrator
VDC . . . . Volts Direct Current
VPM . . . . Volts Per Meter
VPM . . . . Volts Per Mil
V . . . . Volume (Bibliography)
VAPS . . . . . . Volume, Article or chapter, Paragraph, Sentence (Numbers) (Indexing)
VC . . . . Volume of Compartment (Technical drawings)
VFLA . . . . . . Volume Folding and Limiting Amplifier
VFRA . . . . . . Volume Footwear Retailers Association
VI . . . . Volume Indicator (Radio equipment)
VLA . . . . Volume Limiting Amplifier
VPT . . . . Volume-Price Trend (Finance)
VPC . . . . Volume-Pulse-Charge
V & T . . . . . . Volume and Tension (of pulse)
VTI . . . . Volume Thickness Index
VU . . . . Volume Unit
V/V . . . . Volume/Volume (Concentration) (Chemistry)
VS . . . . Volumetric Solution
VAD . . . . Voluntary Aid Detachment
VDI . . . . Voluntary Data Inquiry
VHMCP . . . . . Voluntary Home Mortgage Credit Program (of HHFA)
VISA . . . . . . Voluntary International Service Assignments (of the Society of Friends)
VSO . . . . Voluntary Service Overseas (Military)
V . . . . Volunteer (US Naval Reserve)
VAC . . . . Volunteer Adviser Corps
VAR . . . . Volunteer Air Reserve
VART . . . . . . Volunteer Air Reserve Training (Air Force)
VARTU . . . . . Volunteer Air Reserve Training Unit (Air Force)
VB . . . . Volunteer Battalion (Military)
VC . . . . Volunteer Corps
VD . . . . Volunteer Decoration
VFD . . . . Volunteer Fire Department
VFON . . . . . . Volunteer Flight Officers Network
VMCR . . . . . . Volunteer Marine Corps Reserve
USMCR(NAVT) . . Volunteer Marine Corps Reserve, Aviation Specialist Transport Pilot
VOC . . . . Volunteer Officer Candidate (Army)
VOICE . . . . . . Volunteer Oil Industry Communications Effort

VPL . . . . Volunteer Prison League
VRD . . . . Volunteer Reserve Decoration (British)
VRS . . . . Volunteer Reserve Section
VTU . . . . Volunteer Reserve Training Unit (Coast Guard)
VDP . . . . Volunteer Reservists in Drill Pay Status (Navy)
VTU . . . . Volunteer Training Unit
VTU(MMS) . . . . Volunteer Training Unit (Merchant Marine Safety)
V of A . . . . . Volunteers of America
VOA . . . . Volunteers of America
VISION . . . . . Volunteers for Incommunity Service of Our Neighbors (Harvey, Illinois)
VID . . . . Volunteers for International Development
VITA . . . . . . Volunteers for International Technical Assistance
VISTA . . . . . . Volunteers in Service to America (Domestic "poverty corps," similar to Peace Corps)
VJ . . . . Vom Jahre (Of the year)
VKF . . . . Von Kármán Facility
VKIFD . . . . . . Von Kármán Institute for Fluid Dynamics
VON . . . . Von's Grocery Company (NYSE symbol)
VAN . . . . Vorlaeufige Arbeitsnormen
VNO . . . . Vornado, Inc. (NYSE symbol)
VAL . . . . Vortex Arc LASER
VALL . . . . . . Vortex Arc LASER Light
VALP . . . . . . Vortex Arc LASER Pump
VBP . . . . Vortex Breakdown Position
VRS . . . . Vortex Rate Sensor
VPA . . . . Vote Profile Analysis
VTS . . . . Vote Tally System
VP . . . . Voting Pool (Said of disposition of stocks)
VRA . . . . Voting Rights Act
VTC . . . . Voting Trust Certificates (A type of stock certificate)
VTC . . . . Voting Trust Company
V . . . . Vowel
VBL . . . . Voyager Biological Laboratory (NASA)
VSS . . . . Voyager Spacecraft Subsystem (NASA)
VDV . . . . Vozdushno-Desantnye Voiska (Airborne Troops) (An autonomous command) (USSR)
VFDM . . . . . . Vsemirnaia Federatsiia Demokraticheskoi Molodezhi (World Federation of Democratic Youth)
VOKS . . . . . . Vsesoiuznoe Obshchestvo Kul'turnoi Sviazi s Zagranitsei (All-Union Society for Cultural Relations with Foreign Countries) (USSR) (Initialism also used as title of periodical)
VNIIMP . . . . . Vsesoiuznyi Nauchno-Issledovatel'skii Institut Miasnoi Promyshlennosti
VINITI . . . . . . Vsesoyuznyy Institut Nauchnoy i Tekhnicheskoy Informatsii (All-Union Institute of Scientific and Technical Information) (USSR)
VTSPS . . . . . . Vsesoyuznyy Tsentral'nyy Sovet Professional'nykh Soyuzov (All Union Central Council of Trade Unions) (USSR)
VIFC . . . . VTOL (Vertical Takeoff and Landing) Integrated Flight Control
ViFCS . . . . . . VTOL (Vertical Takeoff and Landing) Integrated Flight Control System
VMC . . . . Vulcan Materials Company (NYSE symbol)
VF . . . . Vulcanized Fiber
VIR . . . . Vulcanized India Rubber
VR . . . . Vulcanized Rubber
VL . . . . Vulgar Latin
VP . . . . Vulnerable Point
VV . . . . Vulva and Vagina (Physiology)
VX . . . . Vxor Carissima (Most Dear Wife)
VUMS . . . . . . Vyzkumny Ustav pro Matematickych Stroju (Research Institute for Mathematical Machines) (Czechoslovakia)

W

WA .... Wabash R. R. Company (NYSE symbol)
WAB .... Wabash Railroad System (AAR code)
WOCT ...... WAC (Women's Army Corps) Officer Candidate Test
WBTS ...... Waco, Beaumont, Trinity & Sabine Railway Company (AAR code)
WAS .... Wadley Southern Railway Company (AAR code)
WAB....... Wage Adjustment Board (World War II)
WB .... Wage Board (Wage-earning federal workers' classification)
WB-S ...... Wage Board, Supervisor (Civil Service classification)
WC .... Wage Change
WHD .... Wage and Hour Division (Department of Labor)
WHPC ...... Wage Hour and Public Contracts Divisions (Department of Labor)
WHPCD..... Wage and Hour and Public Contracts Divisions (Department of Labor)
WAMPUM .... Wage and Manpower Process Utilizing Machines (Bureau of Indian Affairs)
W & PH..... Wage and Purchase Hire
WSB....... Wage Stabilization Board (Terminated, 1953)
WEB....... Wagner Earth Bridge
WEC....... Wagner Electric Corporation (NYSE symbol)
WL .... Wagons-Lits (Railroad sleeping or Pullman cars in Europe)
WR .... Wagons-Restaurants (Railroad dining cars)
WO .... Wait Order
WL .... Waiting List
WAT....... Waitt and Bond, Inc. (NYSE symbol)
WAC .... Wake Analysis and Control
WFC .... Wake Forest College (North Carolina)
WXY .... Waldorf System, Inc. (NYSE symbol)
WAG .... Walgreen Company (NYSE symbol)
WAI .... Walk Around Inspection
WKB .... Walker and Company (NYSE symbol)
WWCP ..... Walking Wounded Collecting Post (Military)
WO .... Walkover
W .... Wall
WEA ...... Wall Effect Amplifier
WMHS ..... Wall-Mounted Handling System (AEC)
WPI .... Wall Paper Institute
WSJ .... Wall Street Journal (A newspaper)
WV .... Wall Vent (Technical drawings)
WWV ...... Walla Walla Valley Railway Company (AAR code)
WBCO ..... Wallace Barnes Company
WLT....... Wallace & Tiernan, Inc. (NYSE symbol)
WB .... Wallboard
WWA ...... Wallcovering Wholesalers Association
WFC .... Walleye Filter Changer
WAM ...... Walleye Measurements Program
WI .... Wallops Island
WS........ Wallops Station (NASA)
WACA ..... Walnut Canyon National Monument
WESCO .... Walnut Export Sales Company
WWBA..... Walt Whitman Birthplace Association
WWSA...... Walt Whitman Society of America
WKNL ..... Walter Kidde Nuclear Laboratories, Inc.
WRAIN ..... Walter Reed Army Institute of Nursing
WRAMC .... Walter Reed Army Medical Center (Military)
WRGH ..... Walter Reed General Hospital
WRRR ..... Walter Reed Research Reactor
WRS ...... Walter Reed Society
WL .... Walther League
WW .... Walworth Company (NYSE symbol)
WHB....... The Wandering Hand Brigade (Men who are likely to take liberties with women)
W .... Wanting
W .... War
WAEPA ..... War Agencies Employees Protective Association
WASP ...... War Air Service Pattern (Department of Commerce)

WAA .... War Assets Administration (For disposal of US surplus war property) (Post-World War II) (Terminated after 1946)
WAC ...... War Assets Corporation (Post-World War II) (Succeeded by War Assests Administration)
WC .... War Cabinet
WCC ...... War Claims Commission (Abolished, 1954)
WC .... War College
WC-S ...... War Communications
WOCU ..... War on Community Ugliness (Program)
WCDO ..... War Consumable Distribution Objective
WCPAB ..... War Contracts Price Adjustment Board (All functions dispersed, 1951)
WCP....... War Control Planners (An organization)
WCPAB .... War Control Price Adjustment Board
WD .... War Damage
WDC ...... War Damage Commission (British)
WDC ...... War Damage Corporation (World War II)
WD........ War Department (Created, 1789; became Department of the Army, 1947)
WDCSA .... War Department Chief of Staff, US Army (Obsolete)
WARCAD.... War Department - Civil Affairs Division
WDGO ..... War Department General Order (Obsolete)
WDGS ..... War Department General Staff (Obsolete)
WDGF ..... War Department Ground Forces (Obsolete)
WDHCB .... War Department Hardship Claims Board (Obsolete)
WDI ...... War Department Intelligence (Obsolete)
WDMB ..... War Department Manpower Board (Obsolete)
WDPMG-ID ... War Department Provost Marshal General, Investigation Division (Obsolete)
WDSS...... War Department Special Staff (Obsolete)
WDV ...... War Department Vehicle (Obsolete)
WEF .... War Emergency Formula
WERS ...... War Emergency Radio Service
WEB....... War Engineering Board
WE........ War Establishment
WFC....... War Finance Committee
WFA .... War Food Administration (Determined military, civilian, and foreign requirements for human and animal food, and for food used industrially) (World War II) (Terminated 1945)
WFU....... War Frauds Unit
WOH ...... War on Hunger (Program)
WHO ...... War on Hunger Office (Department of State)
WMC ...... War Manpower Commission (Within the Office of Emergency Management) (World War II)
WMPCES(P) ... War Manpower Commission Employment Stabilization (Plan)
WMI ...... War Materials, Incorporated
WMV ...... War Munition Volunteers (British) (World War I)
WO .... War Office (British)
WOL ...... War-Office Letter (An order or an instruction) (British)
WO .... War Orientation (Navy)
WPL....... War Plan(s) (Navy)
WPNTS ..... War Plan Naval Transportation Service
WP........ War Plans
WPB ...... War Production Board (World War II)
WRM ...... War Readiness Materiel
WRSK ..... War Readiness Spares Kit
WRO ...... War Records Office
WRB....... War Refugee Board (Terminated 1945)
WRCB ..... War Relief Control Board (President's)
WRA ...... War Relocation Authority (Within Office of Emergency Management) (To provide for the relocation of persons whose removal seemed necessary for national security, and for their maintenance and supervision) (World War II)
WR .... War Reserve
WRPSM .... War Reserve Publication Shipment Memorandum

WR(W) . . . . . . War Reserve (Weapon)
WRI . . . . War Resisters' International
WRL . . . . War Resisters League
WRC . . . . War Resources Council (Terminated)
WR . . . . War Risk
WRI . . . . War Risks Insurance (British)
WRO . . . . War Risks Only
WASCO . . . . . War Safety Council
SAVBOND . . . War Savings Bonds (Allotment for purchase) (Navy)
WSS . . . . War Savings Staff
WSI . . . . War Service Indefinite
WSR . . . . War Service Regulation
WSA . . . . War Shipping Administration (Within Office of Emergency Management) (World War II)
WSATO . . . . . . War Shipping Administration Training Organization (Terminated)
WT . . . . War Tax
WTD . . . . War Trade Department (British) (World War I)
WTS . . . . War Training Service (of the Civil Aeronautics Administration) (Formerly Civilian Pilot Training) (World War II)
WD . . . . Ward Baking Company (NYSE symbol)
WIL . . . . Ward Indicator Light
W . . . . Warden
WAA . . . . Warden's Association of America
WR . . . . Wardroom (Navy)
WS . . . . Ware Shoals R. R. (AAR code)
W . . . . Warehouse
WB . . . . Warehouse Book
WR . . . . Warehouse Receipt (Often negotiable)
W/R . . . . Warehouse Receipt
WW . . . . Warehouse Warrant
WGPMS . . . . . Warehousing Gross Performance Measurement System
WAG . . . . Warfare Analysis Group (Navy)
WSS . . . . Warfare Systems School (Air Force)
WVL . . . . Warfare Vision Laboratory (Army)
WH . . . . Warhead
WHD . . . . Warhead
WEC . . . . Warhead Electrical Connector
WHDS . . . . . . Warhead Section (Military)
WSWL . . . . . . Warheads and Special Weapons Laboratory
W . . . . Warm
WA . . . . Warm Air
WFP . . . . Warm Front(al) Passage (Meteorology)
WGDS . . . . . . Warm Gas Distribution System
WBR . . . . Warner Brothers Company (NYSE symbol)
WB . . . . Warner Brothers Pictures, Inc. (NYSE symbol)
WAR . . . . Warner Company (NYSE symbol)
WHU . . . . Warner-Hudnut, Inc. (NYSE symbol)
WLA . . . . Warner-Lambert Pharmaceutical Company (NYSE symbol)
WRAMA . . . . . Warner Robins Air Material Area
WO . . . . Warning Order
W . . . . Warrant (A document entitling holder to purchase a given issue of stock)
W/A . . . . Warrant of Arrest
WAREX . . . . . Warrant Issued for Extradite
WLTE . . . . . . Warrant Loss to Enlisted Status (Revocation of appointment) (Navy)
WO . . . . Warrant Officer
WOHC . . . . . . Warrant Officer Hospital Corps
WOJG . . . . . . Warrant Officer Junior Grade
WOQT . . . . . . Warrant Officer Qualification Test
WOA . . . . Warrant Officers Association of the United States of America
WRN . . . . Warren (SD) Company (NYSE symbol)
WOV . . . . Warren & Ouachita Valley Railway Company (AAR code)
WSR . . . . Warren & Saline River R. R. (AAR code)
WRNT . . . . . . Warrenton Rail Road Company (AAR code)
WTO . . . . Warsaw Treaty Organization
WZT . . . . Wartegg-Zeichentest (Wartegg Test)
WT . . . . Wartime
WAA . . . . Wartime Aircraft Activity
WBP . . . . Wartime Basic Plan
WIAP . . . . . . Wartime Individual Augmentation Program (Military)
WIMS . . . . . . Wartime Instruction Manual for Merchant Ships (For deck officers of the United States Merchant Marine; popularly known as the "Convoy Bible") (World War II)
WPRI . . . . . . Wartime Pacific Routing Instructions (Navy)
WR . . . . Wartime Report
WR . . . . Wartime Requirements (Air Force document)
WUAA . . . . . . Wartime Unit Aircraft Activity
WRWK . . . . . . Warwick Railway Company (AAR code)
WFSA . . . . . . Wash Frock Salesmen's Association
WSNSCA . . . . Washable Suits, Novelties and Sportswear Contractors Association
W & M . . . . . Washburn and Moen (Wire Gage)
WOB . . . . Washed Overboard (Shipping)

WA . . . . Washington (State)
WAADS . . . . . . Washington Air Defense Sector (ADC)
WBA . . . . Washington Bar Association
WCFPR . . . . . . Washington Center of Foreign Policy Research
DCA . . . . Washington, DC (Airport symbol)
WDC . . . . Washington Document Center
WGMA . . . . . . Washington Gallery of Modern Art
WGL . . . . Washington Gas Light Company (NYSE symbol)
WHA . . . . Washington Headquarters Association
WHRC . . . . . . Washington Home Rule Committee
WIM . . . . Washington, Idaho & Montana Railway Company (AAR code)
WIT . . . . Washington Institute of Technology
WIC . . . . Washington International Center
WJC . . . . Washington and Jefferson College (Pennsylvania)
WLG . . . . Washington Liaison Group
WMA . . . . Washington Metropolitan Area
WMATA . . . . . Washington (DC) Metropolitan Area Transit Authority
WANAP . . . . . Washington National Airport
WNRC . . . . . . Washington National Records Center
WNY . . . . Washington (DC) Naval Yard
WOD . . . . Washington & Old Dominion R. R. (AAR code)
WORC . . . . . . Washington Operations Research Council
WPPSS . . . . . . Washington Public Power Supply System
WRNOA . . . . . Washington Reef Net Owners Association
WSO . . . . Washington Standardization Officers
WSEC . . . . . . Washington State Electronics Council
WSHGA . . . . . Washington State Holly Growers Association
WSU . . . . Washington State University
WSUOPR . . . . . Washington State University, Open Pool Reactor
WTA . . . . Washington Technological Association
WATC . . . . . . Washington Terminal Company (AAR code)
WWP . . . . Washington Water Power Company (NYSE symbol)
WR . . . . Washroom
WR . . . . Wassermann Reaction (Medicine)
W . . . . Waste
WCF . . . . Waste Calcination Facility (AEC)
WHR . . . . Waste Heat Removal
WPL . . . . Waste Pickle Liquor (Industrial waste)
WP . . . . Waste Pipe (Technical drawings)
WSEP . . . . . . Waste Solidification Engineering Prototype Plant (AEC)
WS . . . . Waste Stack (Technical drawings)
WP . . . . Wastepaper
WPB . . . . Waste-Paper Basket
WPUC . . . . . . Waste-Paper Utilization Council (Defunct)
WE . . . . Watch Error (Navigation)
WMDAA . . . . . Watch Material Distributors Association of America
W . . . . Watch Time
WTBTSP . . . . . Watch Tower Bible and Tract Society of Pennsylvania
WSIC . . . . . . Watchmakers of Switzerland Information Center
W . . . . Water
WAB . . . . Water-Activated Battery
WAK . . . . Water Analyzer Kit
WAAJ . . . . . . Water-Augmented Air Jet
WAJ . . . . Water-Augmented Jet
WB . . . . Water Ballast
YW . . . . Water Barge (Self-Propelled) (Navy symbol)
YWN . . . . Water Barge (Non-Self-Propelled) (Navy symbol)
WB . . . . Water Board
WBNS . . . . . . Water Boiler Neutron Source (Reactor) (AEC)
WBR . . . . Water Boiler Reactor
WBLC . . . . . . Water-Borne Logistics Craft
WB . . . . Water Box
WCV . . . . Water Check Valve
WC . . . . Water Closet (A toilet)
WCC . . . . Water-Cooled Copper
WCR . . . . Water-Cooled Reactor
WCR . . . . Water-Cooled Rod
WCDFMA . . . . Water Cooler and Drinking Fountain Manufacturers Association
WCAI . . . . . . Water Conditioning Association International
WCF . . . . Water Conditioning Foundation
WCRC . . . . . . Water Conditioning Research Council
WD . . . . Water Desurger
WEP . . . . Water Electrolysis Plenum
WER . . . . Water Electrolysis Rocket
WES . . . . Water Electrolysis System
WEWSA . . . . . Water Equipment Wholesalers and Suppliers Association
WEP . . . . Water-Extended Polyester
W & F . . . . . . Water and Feed
WF . . . . Water Filter
WF . . . . Water Finish
WFM . . . . Water Flow Meter

WG	Water Gage
WGR	Water Graphite Reactor Experiment (AEC)
WHE	Water Hammer Eliminator
WH	Water Heater
WHP	Water Horsepower
WHS	Water Hydraulic Section
WI	Water Injection
WIU	Water Injection Unit
WJP	Water Jet Pump
WL	Water Line
WM	Water Meter
W/O	Water-in-Oil
WP	Water Packed
WPO	Water for Peace Office (Department of State)
WPC	Water Pollution Control
WPCA	Water Pollution Control Administration (Department of the Interior)
WPCF	Water Pollution Control Federation
WPOD	Water Port of Debarkation
WPOE	Water Port of Embarkation
WPLO	Water Port Liaison Office(r) (Air Force)
WR	Water-Rail (Transportation)
W & R	Water and Rail
WRC	Water Resources Council
WRPA	Water Resources Planning Act (1965)
WRRA	Water Resources Research Act (1964)
WRSIC	Water Resources Scientific Information Center (Department of the Interior)
WRC	Water-Retention Coefficeint
WSWMA	Water and Sewage Works Manufacturers Association
WSGA	Water Soluble Gum Association
WS	Water Supply
WSP	Water Supply Point
WS	Water Surface (Elevation)
WSC	Water Systems Council
WT	Water Tank
WTV	Water Tank Vessel (Navy)
WT	Water Tender (Navy)
WTCB	Water Tender Construction Battalion (Navy)
WT	Water-Tube Boiler (Naval)
W	Water Vapor Content
E	Water Vapor Pressure
WVTR	Water Vapor Transmission Rate
WW	Water-White
WEDGE	Waterless Electrical Data Generating Effortless
WLO	Waterloo R. R. (AAR code)
WM	Watermark
WGDA	Watermelon Growers and Distributors Association
WP	Waterproof(ing)
WPMA	Waterproof Paper Manufacturers Association
WPP	Waterproof Paper Packing
WWF	Waterside Workers' Federation of Australia
WT	Watertight
WTD	Watertight Door
WAL	Watertown Arsenal Laboratory (Army)
WAML	Watertown Arsenal Medical Laboratory (Army)
WATR	Waterville R. R. (AAR code)
WVT	Watervliet Arsenal (Army)
WBTC	Waterways Bulk Transportation Council
WES	Waterways Experiment Station (of Army Corps of Engineers)
WESTAR	Waterways Experiment Station Terrain Analyzer RADAR
WW	Waterworks
WJ	Watkins-Johnson Company
W	Watt
WH	Watt-Hour(s)
WHR	Watt-Hour
WHDM	Watt Hour Demand Meter
WHM	Watt-Hour Meter
WM	Watt Meter
WLCAC	Watts Labor Community Action Committee (Los Angeles, California)
W/C	Watts Per Candle (Electricity)
WPC	Watts Per Candle
WKU	Waukesha Motor Company (NYSE symbol)
W/C	Wave Change
WA	Wave Form Analyzer
WFG	Wave Form Generator
WFM	Wave Form Monitor
WG	Wave-Guide
WGA	Wave-Guide Assembly
WGDL	Wave-Guide Delay Line
WDL	Wave-Guide Directional Localizer
WGF	Wave-Guide Filter
WFM	Wave-Guide Frequency Meter

WGS	Wave-Guide Glide Slope
WIMS	Wave-Guide Impedance Measuring Set
WGL	Wave-Guide Load
WGM	Wave-Guide Meter
WGNL	Wave-Guide Nitrogen Load
WGW	Wave-Guide Window
W	Wave Height Correction
WAMOSCOPE . .	Wave-Modulated Oscilloscope
WOQ	Wave Officers' Quarters
WL	Wavelength (Electronics)
WxB	Wax Bite (Dentistry)
WIC	Wax Insulating Compound
WxP	Wax Pattern (Dentistry)
WPI	Waxed Paper Institute
WPMC	Waxed Paper Merchandising Council
WP	Way-Point
WB	Waybill
WBC	Wayland Baptist College (Texas)
WGETS	Wayne George Encoder Test Set
WKT	Wayne Knitting Mills (NYSE symbol)
WSU	Wayne State University (Michigan)
WAW	Waynesburg & Washington R. R. (AAR code)
WOGS	We Old Girls Survive (A teachers' club in Michigan)
WTP	We, The People (An organization)
WWWTTUTWTU . .	We Won't Write to Them Until They Write to Us (A servicemen's club)
WDMF	Weak Disordered Magnetic Field
WS	Weak Signals (Radio)
WPJ	Weakened Plane Joint
WAC	Weapon Assignment Console
WAD	Weapon Assignment Display (Air Force)
WAX	Weapon Assignment and Target Extermination
WBTE	Weapon Battery Terminal Equipment (Air Force)
WC	Weapon Carrier
WCE	Weapon Control Equipment
WDI	Weapon Data Index (Navy)
WEDGE	Weapon Development Glide Entry
WD	Weapon Director (SAGE)
WRE	Weapon Research Establishment
WSM	Weapon Support Manager
WSSL	Weapon Support Stock List
WS	Weapon System
WSAD	Weapon System Analysis Division (Navy)
WSAO	Weapon System Analysis Office (Navy)
WSC	Weapon System Contractor
WSC	Weapon System Costing (Navy)
WSEIAC	Weapon System Effectiveness Industry Advisory Committee
WSECL	Weapon System Equipment Component List
WSEG	Weapon System Evaluation Group (DOD and Air Force)
WSEM	Weapon System Evaluation Missile
WSLO	Weapon System Logistics Officer
WSMAC	Weapon System Maintenance Action Center
WSM	Weapon System Manager
WSMO	Weapon System Materiel Officer (Air Force)
WSPOP	Weapon System Phase-Out Procedure
WSPG	Weapon System Phasing Group
WSPGL	Weapon System Program Guide List
WSPO	Weapon System Project Office (Air Force)
WSR	Weapon System Reliability
WSSS	Weapon System Storage Site
WESTT	Weapon System Tactical Tester
WST	Weapon System Test
WST	Weapon System Trainer (Navy)
WSTS	Weapon System Training Set
WSP	Weapon Systems Pouch
WSPACS	Weapon Systems Programming and Control System
WT	Weapon Test
WTRC	Weapon Test Reports Committee (AEC-DOD)
WALOPT	Weapons Allocation and Desired Ground-Zero Optimizer (Military)
WALP	Weapons Assignment Linear Program
WAO	Weapons Assignment Officer (Air Force)
WARM	Weapons Assignment Research Model (Military)
WAT	Weapons Assignment Technician
WC	Weapons Command (Army)
WECOM	Weapons Command (Army)
WCS	Weapons Control System
WCSS	Weapons Control System Simulator
WDA	Weapons Defended Area
WDS	Weapons Designation (or Delivery) Systems
WDE	Weapons Direction Evaluation
WDP	Weapons Direction Program
WDS	Weapons Direction System

WEBS . . . . Weapons Effectiveness Buoy System
WET . . . . Weapons Effectiveness Testing
WE-H . . . . Weapons Employment Handbook (DASA)
WEL . . . . Weapons/Equipment List
WECB . . . . . . Weapons Evaluation and Control Bureau (USACDA)
WGL . . . . Weapons Guidance Laboratory
WIN . . . . Weapons Interception (Military electronics)
WLB . . . . Weapons Logbook (Military)
WMC . . . . Weapons and Mobility Command (Army)
WMC . . . . Weapons Monitoring Center
WOSD . . . . . . Weapons Operational Systems Development (NORAD)
WOA . . . . Weapons Orientation Advanced
WPEC . . . . . . Weapons Production Engineering Center (Navy)
WPP . . . . Weapons Production Program
WRAP . . . . . . Weapons Readiness Analysis Program (BUWEPS)
WRESAT . . . . . Weapons Research Establishment Satellite (Australia)
WEPTU . . . . . Weapons Reserve Training Units (Navy)
WSR . . . . Weapons Spares Report (Navy)
WESCOM . . . . Weapons System Cost Model
WSDP . . . . . . Weapons System Development Plan
WESED . . . . . Weapons System Evaluation Division (DOD)
WSMC . . . . . . Weapons System Management Codes (Navy)
WSPD . . . . . . Weapons System Planning Data (Navy)
WESEG . . . . . Weapons Systems Evaluation Group (DOD)
WT . . . . Weapons Technician (Air Force)
WT . . . . Weapons Tight (Weapons will engage only objects identified as hostile)
WFP . . . . Wearout Failure Period
W . . . . Weather
WX . . . . Weather
W . . . . Weather aircraft equipped with meteorological gear (Designation for all US military aircraft)
WASP . . . . . . Weather-Atmospheric Sounding Projectile (Research rocket)
WB . . . . Weather Bomber (Air Force)
WBAWS . . . . . Weather, Briefing, Advisory and Warning Service
WBTV . . . . . . Weather Briefing Television
WEBROCK . . . Weather Buoy Rocket
WB . . . . Weather Bureau
WBAN . . . . . . Weather Bureau, Air Force, Navy (Manuals)
WBAS . . . . . . Weather Bureau Airport Station
WBC . . . . Weather Bureau Central Office (Washington, DC)
WBHO . . . . . . Weather Bureau Hurricane Forecast Office
WBO . . . . Weather Bureau Office
WBRH . . . . . . Weather Bureau, Regional Headquarters
WBRO . . . . . . Weather Bureau, Regional Office
WCRA . . . . . . Weather Control Research Association
WD . . . . Weather Division (Air Force)
WES . . . . Weather Editing Section (FAA)
WEFAX . . . . . Weather Facsimile (Environmental Science Services Administration)
WIB . . . . Weather Information Branch (Air Force)
WIND . . . . . . Weather Information Network and Display
WINDS . . . . . Weather Information Network & Display System
WIRDS . . . . . Weather Information Remoting and Display System
WIS . . . . Weather Information Service (Air Force)
WEARCON . . . Weather Observation and Forecasting Control System
WOSB . . . . . . Weather Observation Site Building
WP . . . . Weather Permitting
WRPC . . . . . . Weather Records Processing Centers
WRBC . . . . . . Weather Relay Broadcast Center
WRC . . . . Weather Relay Center
WSR . . . . Weather Surveillance RADAR
WSF . . . . Weather Support Force (Military)
WETM . . . . . . Weather Team (Air Force)
WWP . . . . Weather Wing Pamphlet (Air Force)
WWD . . . . Weather Working Days (Construction)
WCPC . . . . . . Weatherford College of Parker County (Texas)
WMWN . . . . . Weatherford, Mineral Wells & Northwestern Railway Company (AAR code)
WP . . . . Weatherproof
WRI . . . . Weatherstrip Research Institute
W . . . . Web
WD . . . . Web Depth
WDI . . . . Web Depth Index
WDO . . . . Web Depth Order
WGS . . . . Web Guide System
WINA . . . . . . Webb Institute of Naval Architecture
WINE . . . . . . Webb Institute of Naval Engineering
Wb . . . . Weber
WCJC . . . . . . Webster City Junior College (Iowa)
WIMSA . . . . . Webster Institute for Mathematics, Science and Arts (Webster College)
WAIS . . . . . . Wechsler's Adult Intelligence Scale
W . . . . Wednesday
WSSA . . . . . . Weed Science Society of America

WSA . . . . Weed Society of America
W . . . . Week
W/E . . . . Week Ending
WSF . . . . Week Second Feet
WHI . . . . Weekly Hospital Indemnity
WIR . . . . Weekly Intelligence Review
WENOA . . . . . Weekly Notice to Airmen (FAA)
WSR . . . . Weekly Summary Report
WFSt . . . . . . Wehrmachtfuehrungsstab (Armed Forces Operations Staff, German) (World War II)
W & I . . . . . . Weighing and Inspection
W . . . . Weight
WG . . . . Weight Guaranteed
W/V . . . . Weight/Volume (Concentration) (Chemistry)
WAGS . . . . . . Weighted Agreement Scores
WASP . . . . . . Weightless Analysis Sounding Probe (NASA)
WCA . . . . Weimaraner Club of America
WZO . . . . Wein Zollordnung (Germany)
WBL . . . . Welbilt Corporation (NYSE symbol)
WLS . . . . Welch Scientific Company (NYSE symbol)
WFC . . . . Weld Flange Connection
WHA . . . . Weld Head Assembly
WAA . . . . Welded Aluminum Alloy
WCM . . . . Welded Cordwood Module
WEPA . . . . . . Welded Electronic Packaging Association
WJD . . . . Welded Joint Design
WRMA . . . . . . Welded Ring Manufacturers Association
WSTI . . . . Welded Steel Tube Institute
WCP . . . . Welder Control Panel
WM . . . . Welding Memorandum
WRC . . . . Welding Research Council
WA . . . . Welfare Administration (Became Social and Rehabilitation Service) (HEW)
WARDS . . . . . Welfare of Animals Used for Research in Drugs and Therapy
WEM . . . . Welfare of Enlisted Men (Air Force)
WPPDA . . . . . Welfare and Pension Plans Disclosure Act (Department of Labor)
W & R . . . . . . Welfare and Recreation (Navy)
WBN . . . . Well Behaved Net
WD . . . . Well Deck
WFN . . . . Well Formed Net
WHU . . . . Well Head Unit
WK . . . . Well-Known
WKF . . . . Well Known Factor
WTR . . . . Well to Right (Aviation)
WRC . . . . Well to Right of Course (Aviation)
WAG . . . . Wellsville, Addison & Galeton R. R. Corporation (AAR code)
W . . . . Welsh (or Welch)
WBH . . . . Welsh Board of Health
WG . . . . Welsh Guards (British military)
WPSA . . . . . . Welsh Pony Society of America
WTCA . . . . . . Welsh Terrier Club of America
WBDJ . . . . . . Weltbund der Demokratischen Jugend
WGB . . . . Weltgewerkschaftsbund (World Federation of Trade Unions)
WTB . . . . Welttierschutzbund (World Federation for the Protection of Animals) (Also known as WFPA and FMPA)
WJC . . . . Wenatchee Junior College (Washington)
WDP . . . . Wenner Difference Potentiometer
WGFAR . . . . . Wenner-Gren Foundation for Anthropological Research
WKB . . . . Wentzel-Kramer-Brillouin (Method)
WSC . . . . Wesco Financial Corporation (NYSE symbol)
WLA . . . . Wescosa Lumber Association
W . . . . Wesleyan
WMS . . . . Wesleyan Missionary Society
WSG . . . . Wesleyan Service Guild
WU . . . . Wesleyan University
W . . . . West, Westerly, Western
WA . . . . West Africa
WAAC . . . . . . West African Airways Corporation
WACRI . . . . . . West African Cocoa Research Institution
WACU . . . . . . West African Customs Union
WAFC . . . . . . West African Fisheries Commission
WAFF . . . . . . West African Frontier Force
WC . . . . West Central (London postal district)
WC . . . . West Coast Airlines, Inc.
WCA . . . . West Coast Airlines, Inc.
WCBSU . . . . . . West Coast Base Service Unit (Navy)
WESCOBASESERVUNIT . . West Coast Base Service Unit (Navy)
WCCMORS . . . West Coast Classified Military Operations Research Symposium
WCCA . . . . . . West Coast Crossarm Association
WCDC . . . . . . West Coast (Naval Publications) Distribution Center
WCEMA . . . . . West Coast Electronic Manufacturers' Association
WCH . . . . West Coast Handling

WCLIB . . . . . . West Coast Lumber Inspection Bureau
WCLA . . . . . . West Coast Lumbermen's Association
WCMIA . . . . . West Coast Metal Importers Association
WCMA . . . . . . West Coast Mineral Association
WCSPA . . . . . West Coast Shrimp Producers Association
WCSS . . . . . . West Coast Sound School
WESCOSOUNDSCOL . . West Coast Sound School (Navy)
WCSA . . . . . . West Coast of South America
WCU . . . . West Coast University (California)
WEM . . . . West Essex Militia (British)
WGC . . . . West Georgia College
WG . . . . West German(ic)
WGAF . . . . . . West Germany Air Force
WHWTCA . . . . West Highland White Terrier Club of America
WI . . . . West India
WID . . . . West India Dock
WIF . . . . West India Fruit & Steamship Company, Inc. (AAR code)
WIR . . . . West India Regiment
WISA . . . . West Indian Students Association
WI . . . . West Indies or West Indian
WIF . . . . West Indies Federation
WID . . . . West Indies Sugar (NYSE symbol)
WKY . . . . West Kentucky Coal Company (NYSE symbol) (Wall Street slang name:
                "Whiskey")
WLD . . . . West Longitude Date
WBN . . . . West by North
WNW . . . . West-Northwest
WPBEF . . . . . . West Pakistan Bank Employees' Federation
WPFL . . . . West Pakistan Federation of Labor
WEP . . . . West Penn Electric Company (NYSE symbol)
WSP . . . . West Penn Power Company (NYSE symbol)
WPE . . . . West Pittston-Exeter R. R. (AAR code)
WS . . . . West Saxon
WSRR . . . . . . West Shore Railroad
WBS . . . . West by South
WSW . . . . West-Southwest
WV . . . . West Virginia
WCK . . . . West Virginia Coal and Coke Corporation (NYSE symbol)
WVN . . . . West Virginia Northern R. R. (AAR code)
WP . . . . West Virginia Pulp & Paper Company (NYSE symbol)
WVU . . . . West Virginia University
WWFS . . . . . . West Wales Field Society (British)
WYR . . . . The West Yorkshire Regiment (British Army)
WB . . . . Westbound
WCC . . . . Westchester Community College (New York)
WAB . . . . Western Actuarial Bureau
WACA . . . . . . Western Agricultural Chemicals Association
WADC . . . . . . Western Air Defense Command
WADF . . . . . . Western Air Defense Force
WSX . . . . Western Air Lines, Inc. (NYSE symbol)
WAPD . . . . . . Western Air Procurement District
WEAPD . . . . . Western Air Procurement District
WA . . . . Western Airlines, Inc.
WAL . . . . Western Airlines, Inc.
WAL . . . . Western Allegheny R. R. (AAR code)
WAA . . . . Western Amateur Astronomers
WA . . . . Western Approaches (to Great Britain and Ireland)
WATU . . . . . . Western Approaches Tactical Unit (Navy)
WAMTMTS . . . Western Area, Military Traffic Management and Terminal Service
WACM . . . . . . Western Association of Circuit Manufacturers
WASGFC . . . . . Western Association of State Game and Fish Commissioners
WASHO . . . . . Western Association of State Highway Officials
WESTLANT . . . . Western Atlantic Area
WA . . . . Western Australia
WBC . . . . Western Bancorporation (NYSE symbol)
WBSP . . . . . . Western Beet Sugar Producers (Defunct)
WBSI . . . . Western Behavioral Sciences Institute (La Jolla, California)
WBL . . . . Western Biological Laboratories
WBBA . . . . . . Western Bird Banding Association
WBFA . . . . . . Western Bohemian Fraternal Association
WCC . . . . Western Carolina College (North Carolina)
WESCAR . . . . . Western Carolinas (Navy)
WESCARSUBAREA . . Western Carolinas Subarea (Navy)
WCU . . . . Western Catholic Union
WCW . . . . Western College for Women (Ohio)
WC . . . . Western Command
WCR . . . . Western Communication Region (Air Force)
WESTCOMMRGN . . Western Communications Region
WCRSI . . . . . . Western Concrete Reinforcing Steel Institute
WCMR . . . . . . Western Contract Management Region (Air Force)
WCO . . . . Western Coordination Office (NASA) (Now, Western Operations Office)

WDPC . . . . . . Western Data Processing Center
WDC . . . . Western Defense Command (Army)
WDAF . . . . . . Western Desert Air Force
WDD . . . . Western Development Division (ARDC)
WDL . . . . Western Development Laboratories
WDA . . . . Western District Area (Air Force)
WEEF . . . . Western Electric Educational Fund
WEMA . . . . . . Western Electronic Manufacturers Association
WEW . . . . Western Electronic Week
WEMD . . . . . . Western Electronics Maintenance Depot
WESCON . . . . . Western Electronics Show and Convention (IEEE)
WEST . . . . Western Energy Supply & Transmission Associates
WEE . . . . Western Equine Encephalitis (Veterinary medicine)
WEU . . . . Western European Union (NATO)
WFA . . . . Western Falconry Association
WFM . . . . Western Federation of Miners
WFTC . . . . . . Western Flying Training Command (AAFWFTC)
WFIA . . . . Western Forest Industries Association
WFC . . . . Western Forestry Center
WFCA . . . . . . Western Forestry and Conservation Association
WFEX . . . . . . Western Fruit Express
WGC . . . . Western Gear Corporation
WGA . . . . Western Growers Association
WH . . . . Western Hemisphere
WHD . . . . Western Hemisphere Defense
WHR . . . . Western Hemisphere Reserve
WHI . . . . Western Highway Institute
WHA . . . . Western History Association
WIU . . . . Western Illinois University
WIN . . . . Western Information Network
WICHE . . . . . . Western Interstate Commission for Higher Education
WJCC . . . . . . Western Joint Computer Conference
WKSC . . . . . . Western Kentucky State College
WL . . . . Western League (Baseball)
WLA . . . . Western Literature Association
WLM . . . . Western Lumber Manufacturers
WM . . . . Western Maryland Railway Company (NYSE symbol and AAR code) (Wall
                Street slang name: "Wet Mary")
WMU . . . . Western Michigan University
WNTF . . . . . . Western Naval Task Force (Navy)
WNU . . . . Western Newspaper Union
WESTOMP . . . . Western Ocean Meeting Point
WODECO . . . . Western Offshore Drilling and Exploration Company
WOGA . . . . . . Western Oil and Gas Association
WO . . . . Western Operation
WOO . . . . Western Operations Office (Later, Western Support Office) (NASA)
WPBC . . . . . . Western Pacific Base Command (Marianas) (World War II)
WESTPACBACOM . . Western Pacific Base Command (Navy)
WESTPAC . . . . Western Pacific Railroad
WP . . . . Western Pacific R. R. (AAR code)
WRS . . . . Western Pacific R. R. Company (NYSE symbol)
WPA . . . . Western Pine Association
WPD . . . . Western Procurement Division (Marine Corps)
WPA . . . . Western Psychological Association
WRTA . . . . . . Western Railroad Traffic Association
WA . . . . Western Railway of Alabama (AAR code)
W of A . . . . . . Western Railway of Alabama
WREU . . . . . . Western Railway Employees' Union (India)
WRA . . . . Western Range Association
WRD . . . . Western Recruiting Division
WRCLA . . . . . Western Red Cedar Lumber Association
WRNWCA . . . . Western Red and Northern White Cedar Association
WRSFA . . . . . . Western Reinforcing Steel Fabricators Association
WESRAC . . . . . Western Research Application Center (University of Southern California)
WRU . . . . Western Reserve University (Later, Case-Western Reserve University)
WESSEAFRON . . Western Sea Frontier (Navy)
WSF . . . . Western Sea Frontier (Navy)
WSA . . . . Western Slavonic Association
WSBP . . . . . . Western Society of Business Publications
WSE . . . . Western Society of Engineers
WSGE . . . . . . Western Society of Gear Engineers
WSN . . . . Western Society of Naturalists
WSAAA . . . . . . Western States Advertising Agencies Association
WSMPA . . . . . Western States Meat Packers Association
WSO . . . . Western Support Office (Formerly, Western Operations Office) (NASA)
WTF . . . . Western Task Force (Navy)
WTN . . . . Western Technical Net (Air Force)
WTTC . . . . . . Western Technical Training Command (AAFWTTC)
WTR . . . . Western Test Range (Formerly, Pacific Missile Range)
WTOS . . . . . . Western Test Range Office of Safety (Air Force)
WESTAF . . . . . Western Transport Air Force

WEST	Western Transportation Company (AAR code)
WTLC	Western Trunk Line Committee
WUA	Western Underwriters Association
WUX	Western Union Exchange (Teleprinter)
WUI	Western Union International
WU	Western Union Telegraph Company (NYSE symbol)
WUTELCO	Western Union Telegraph Company
WYBL	Western Young Buddhist League
WWMP	Western Wood Moulding Producers
WWPA	Western Wood Products Association
WWBA	Western Wooden Box Association
WWA	Western Writers of America
WASP	Westinghouse Advanced Systems Planning Group
WAAD	Westinghouse Air Arm Division
WABCO	Westinghouse Air Brake Company
WK	Westinghouse Air Brake Company (NYSE symbol)
W-AL	Westinghouse–Astronuclear Laboratory
WAPD	Westinghouse Atomic Power Division (AEC)
WBC	Westinghouse Broadcasting Company
WCAP	Westinghouse Commercial Atomic Power
WESCO	Westinghouse Corporation
WDC	Westinghouse Defense Center
WEDAC	Westinghouse Digital Airborne Computer
WX	Westinghouse Electric Company (NYSE symbol) (Wall Street slang name: "Wex")
WEC	Westinghouse Electric Corporation
WECO	Westinghouse Electric Corporation
WETAC	Westinghouse Electronic Tubeless Analog Computer
WIAP	Westinghouse Industrial Atomic Power
WRDC	Westinghouse Research and Development Center
WTR	Westinghouse Test Reactor
WCC	Westminster Choir College (New Jersey)
W	Wet
WB	Wet Bulb (Thermometer, of a psychrometer) (Meteorology)
WBGT	Wet Bulb Globe Temperature
WBT	Wet Bulb Temperature
WD	Wet Dressing
WET	Wet Environment Trainer (Navy)
WGMA	Wet Ground Mica Association
WR	Wet Runway (Aviation)
WS	Wetted Surface
WEY	Weyenberg Shoe Manufacturing Company (NYSE symbol)
WB	Whale Boat
WOL	Wharf Owner's Liability (Insurance)
WCJC	Wharton County Junior College (Texas)
WNO	Wharton & Northern R. R. (AAR code)
WDYT	What Do You Think
WFI	Wheat Flour Institute
WRF	Wheat Ridge Foundation
WSB	Wheat-Soya Blend
WB	Wheel Base
WC	Wheel Chair
WHECON	Wheel Control
WDA	Wheel Drive Assembly
WP	Wheel of Progress
WFCMV	Wheeled Fuel Consuming Motor Vehicle
WL	Wheeler Laboratories, Inc.
WLE	Wheeling & Lake Erie Railway Company (NYSE symbol and AAR code)
WHX	Wheeling Steel Corporation (NYSE symbol)
WAE	When (or While) Actually Employed (Government short jobs)
WHAP	When (or Where) Applicable
WAB	When Authorized By
WABTOC	When Authorized by the Oversea Commander (Military)
WD	When Directed
DIRPRO	When Directed Proceed
WD	When Discovered
WD	When Distributed (NYSE symbol)
WI	When Issued (NYSE symbol)
RELBY	When Relieved By (Air Force)
WICA	While in Control Area (Aviation)
WICZ	While in Control Zone (Aviation)
W	Whip
WHR	Whirlpool Corporation (NYSE symbol)
WWI	Whirlwind I
WHIS	Whiskeytown-Shasta-Trinity National Recreation Area
W & S	Whisky and Soda
W	White (Light, buoy, beacon)
W	White (Maps and charts)
WASC	White, Anglo-Saxon Catholic
WASP	White, Anglo-Saxon Protestant
WASPS	White Appalachian Southern Protestants (Chicago slang)

WBC	White Blood Cell, or White Blood-Cell Count (Medicine)
WBC	White Blood Corpuscles
WCI	White Cast Iron
WCF	White Cathode Follower
WCP	White Combination Potentiometer
WDM	White (S. S.) Dental Manufacturing Company (NYSE symbol)
WF	White Fathers
WF	White Female
WFNA	White Fuming Nitric Acid
WH	White House
WHASA	White House Army Signal Agency
WHCA	White House Communications Agency
WHCA	White House Correspondents Association
WHHA	White House Historical Association
WHNPA	White House News Photographers Association
WHP	White House Police Force
WHO	White House Office
WHSS	White House Signal Support
WIL	White Indicating Light
WM	White Male
WH	White Motor Company (NYSE symbol)
WPY	White Pass & Yukon Route (AAR code)
WP	White Phosphorus (Military)
WPS	White Power Structure
WSMR	White Sands Missile Range (Air Force)
WESA	White Sands National Monument
WSPG	White Sands Proving Ground (Air Force)
WSSA	White Sands Signal Agency (Military)
WSTF	White Sands Test Facility (NASA)
WSW	White Sewing Machine Corporation (Later, White Consolidated Industries, Inc.) (NYSE symbol)
WSW	White Sidewall (Tires)
WS	White Sisters (Missionary Sisters of Our Lady of Africa) (Roman Catholic religious order)
WSC	White Sisters of Charity of St. Vincent de Paul (Roman Catholic religious order)
WSTA	White Slave Traffic Act
WEW	White Stores, Inc. (NYSE symbol)
WSYP	White Sulphur Springs & Yellowstone Park R. R. (AAR code)
WUMP	White, Urban, Middle Class, Protestant
WAR	Whiteruthenian American Relief
WCCA	Whiteruthenian (Byelorussian) Congress Committee of America
WIAS	Whiteruthenian Institute of Arts and Science
WRA	Whiteware Research Association
WHMI	Whitman Mission National Historic Site
WBR	Whole Body Radiation
WD	Whole Depth
WCFA	Wholesale Commission Florists of America
WDW	Wholesale Dealer in Wines
WDMA	Wholesale Druggists Merchandising Association
WDGI	Wholesale Dry Goods Institute
WPI	Wholesale Price Index
WSASSA	Wholesale School, Art & Stationery Supplies Association
WSA	Wholesale Stationers' Association
WSOEA	Wholesale Stationery and Office Equipment Association
WW	Wholesale Wine (License)
WISE	Wholesalers Institutional Service Extension (Division of National American Wholesale Grocers Association)
WIMC	Whom It May Concern
WCCA	Whooping Crane Conservation Association
WDYTYCIWSS . .	Why Don't You Take Your Change In War Savings Stamps (Cashier's sign) (World War II)
WALDO	Wichita Automatic Linear Data Output
WMSL	Wichita Mountains Seismological Laboratory (Military)
WIX	Wickes Corporation (NYSE symbol)
W	Wicket
W	Wide, Width
WADS	Wide Angle Display System
WAFFLE	Wide Angle Fixed Field Locating Equipment
WAL	Wide Angle Lens
WAOS	Wide Angle Optical System
WAS	Wide Angle Sensor
WARLA	Wide Aperture Radio Location Array
WADS	Wide Area Data Service
WATS	Wide Area Telephone (or Telecommunications) Service (American Telephone and Telegraph Company contract billing system)
WB	Wide Band (Radio)
WFOF	Wide Field Optical Filter
WFO	Wide Field Optics
WFA	Wide Frequency Antenna
WAT	Wideband Adapter Transformer

WBAT	Wideband Adapter Transformer
WBA	Wideband Amplifier
WAS	Wideband Antenna System
WCA	Wideband Cassegrain Antenna
WCAFS	Wideband Cassegrain Antenna Feed System
WBC	Wideband Coupler
WBCT	Wideband Current Transformer
WBD	Wideband Data
WBDL	Wideband Data Link
WDC	Wideband Directional Coupler
WHIP	Wideband High Intercept Probability
WBL	Wideband LASER
WBMCR	Wideband Multi-Channel Receiver
WBNL	Wideband Noise Limiting
WBNV	Wideband Noise Voltage
WBO	Wideband Oscilloscope
WBO	Wideband Overlap
WBR	Wideband Receiver
WBT	Wideband Transmitter (or Transformer)
WBV	Wideband Voltage
WBVCO	Wideband Voltage Controlled Oscillator
WQF	Wider Quaker Fellowship
W	Widow
WWWI	Widows of World War I
WIE	Wieboldt Stores, Inc. (NYSE symbol)
WEN	Wien Alaska Airlines
WBC	Wien Bridge Circuit
WBO	Wien Bridge Oscillator
WDL	Wien Displacement Law
W	Wife
YF (XYL)	Wife (Amateur radio slang)
WXC	Wilcox Oil Company (NYSE symbol)
WFPS	Wild Flower Preservation Society
WP	Wild Pitch (Baseball)
WDA	Wildlife Disease Association
WMI	Wildlife Management Institute
WR	Wildlife Restoration (Association)
WS	Wildlife Society
WS	Wilderness Society
WBC	Wilkes-Barre Connecting R. R. (AAR code)
WA	Will Adjust
WB	Will Be
W/B	Will Be
WBI	Will Be Issued
WIBIS	Will Be Issued
WBRBN	Will Be Reported by NOTAM (Notice to Airmen)
WC	Will Call
WILCO	Will Comply (Used after "Roger") (Radio term)
WN	Will Not
WNB	Will Not Be
WNP	Will Not Proceed
WP	Will Proceed to
WPWOD	Will Proceed Without Delay
WSB	Will Send Boat
WYAIO	Will You Accept, If Offered (the position of)
WJBU	William Jennings Bryan University (Tennessee)
WJC	William Jewel College (Missouri)
WPFA	William Penn Fraternal Association
WRAC	Willow Run Aeronautical Center (Michigan)
YIP	Willow Run Airport, Detroit, Michigan (Airport symbol)
WRRC	Willow Run Research Center (Air Force)
WAE	Wills and Administration of Estates (Law)
WSCOC	Wills Sainte Claire Owners Club
WCC	Wilson Cloud Chamber
WIL	Wilson & Company, Inc. (NYSE symbol)
WOS	Wilson Ornithological Society
WICR	Wilson's Creek Battlefield National Park
WW	Winchester & Western R. R. (AAR code)
W	Wind (Wind triangle problems)
WICA	Wind Cave National Park
WD	Wind Direction
WDI	Wind Direction Indicator (Aviation)
WL	Wind Load
WS	Wind Speed
WT	Wind Tunnel
WTD	Wind Tunnel Data
WTM	Wind Tunnel Memorandum
WTM	Wind Tunnel Model
WTN	Wind Tunnel Note
WV	Wind Velocity (Speed and direction) (Navigation)
WASP	Window Atmosphere Sounding Projectile (NASA)

WDU	Window Deicing Unit
WD	Window Detector
WD	Window Dimension (Technical drawings)
WGCL	Window Glass Cutters League of America
WSMA	Window Shade Manufacturers Association
WAGR	Windscale Advanced Gas-Cooled Reactor
WNS	Windsor Industries, Inc. (NYSE symbol)
WIC	Windsor Institute of Complementology
WAB	Wine Advisory Board
WG	Wine Gallon
WI	Wine Institute
WSWA	Wine and Spirits Wholesalers of America
WNF	Winfield R. R. (AAR code)
WCP	Wing Chord Plane
WCDB	Wing Control During Boost
WIG	Wing in Ground
WRL	Wing Reference Line
WSC	Wing Security Control (Air Force)
WWO	Wing Warrant Officer (British Royal Air Force)
WJC	Wingate Junior College (North Carolina)
WLTAS	Wingfoot Lighter-Than-Air Society
WEFT	Wings, Engines, Fuselage, Tail (System for identifying aircraft)
WNFR	Winifrede R. R. (AAR code)
WIN	Winn-Dixie Stores, Inc. (NYSE symbol)
WSS	Winston-Salem Southbound Railway (AAR code)
W	Winter (Vessel load line mark)
WNA	Winter, North Atlantic (Vessel load line mark)
W	Wire
WASSP	Wire Arc Seismic Section Profiler
WA	Wire Association
WCR	Wire Contact Relay
WG	Wire Gauge
WGP	Wire Grid Polarizer
WITNESS	Wire Installation Tester for Negating Errors by Sequencing and Standardization
WMBA	Wire Machinery Builders Association
WM	Wire Mesh
WNP	Wire Nonpayment
WP	Wire Payment
WRI	Wire Reinforcement Institute
WRRS	Wire Relay Radio System
WRI	Wire Rope Institute
WRTB	Wire Rope Technical Board
WW	Wire Way (Technical drawings)
WW	Wire-Wound
WBMA	Wirebound Box Manufacturers Association
WCM	Wired-Core Matrix
WCM	Wired-Core Memory
WX	Wireless (Communications)
WDL	Wireless Data Link
WO	Wireless Operator
WT	Wireless Telegraphy; Wireless Telephony; Wireless Telephone
WS	Wirtschaft und Statistik (Germany)
WI	Wisconsin
WATA	Wisconsin Automatic Test Apparatus
WBK	Wisconsin Bankshore's Corporation (NYSE symbol)
WPC	Wisconsin Electric Power Company (NYSE symbol)
WEP	Wisconsin Experiments Package
WIT	Wisconsin Institute of Technology
WPS	Wisconsin Public Service Corporation (NYSE symbol)
WTZ	Wissenschaftlich-Technische Zentren
WGL	Wissenschaftliche Gesellschaft fuer Luftschiffahrt
WR	Wissenschaftsrat (Science Council) (Germany)
WLN	Wiswesser Line Notation (Data processing)
WIT	Witco Chemical Company, Inc. (NYSE symbol)
W	With
W/	With (in conjunction with other abbreviations)
WAF	With All Faults
WA	With Average (Insurance)
WEF	With Effect From
W/E & SP	With Equipment and Spare Parts
WFE	With Food Element
WIE	With Immediate Effect
WMP	With Much Pleasure (Meaning, "We accept the invitation")
WOG	With Other Goods
WPA	With Particular Average
WPS	With Prior Service
WR	With Rights (Securities)
WW	With Warrants (NYSE symbol)
WWA	With the Will Annexed
WWN	With Winch

WDA . . . . Withdrawal of Availability (Military)
WOE . . . . . . Withdrawal of Enthusiasm (Airline pilots objection to
    "Welcome aboard" talks)
W/D . . . . Withdrawn
W/H . . . . Withholding
WE . . . . Withholding Exemptions
WI . . . . Within
WNL . . . . Within Normal Limits
W/O . . . . Without
WBS . . . . Without Benefit of Salvage
WC . . . . Without Charge
WOC . . . . (Government Official Serving) Without Compensation
WOD . . . . Without Dependents (Military)
WOE . . . . . . Without Equipment
W/OE & SP. . . Without Equipment and Spare Parts
WOP . . . . Without Payment
W/O/P . . . . . . Without Penalty
WOP . . . . Without Personnel
WOPE . . . . . . Without Personnel and Equipment
WOP . . . . Without Preference (Rating)
WP. . . . . Without Prejudice
WOP . . . . Without Priorities
XC. . . . . Without the Right to Coupons (Finance)
XR . . . . Without Rights (Stock brokerage)
W . . . . Without voice facilities on range or radiobeacon frequency
XW . . . . Without Warrants (NYSE symbol)
WOWN . . . . . Without Winch
WNLA . . . . . . Witswatersrand Native Labor Association (Nyasaland)
WINA . . . . . . Witton Network Analyzer
WAFE . . . . . . Wives of the Armed Forces, Emeritus
WFC. . . . . . . Wolf First Class (A philanderer) (Slang)
WOTR . . . . . . Wolf Trap Farm Park (National Park Service designation)
WPW . . . . . . Wolff-Parkinson-White (Syndrome)
W . . . . Wolframium (Tungsten) (A chemical element)
WOTT. . . . . . Wolves on the Track (A group of philanderers looking for girls) (Slang)
WOW . . . . . . Woman Ordnance Worker
WAAMA . . . . Woman's Auxiliary to the American Medical Association
WBA . . . . Woman's Benefit Association
WBM . . . . . . Woman's Board of Missions
WFL. . . . . . . Woman's Freedom League
WIBC . . . . . . Woman's International Bowling Congress
WNFGA . . . . . Woman's National Farm and Garden Association
WNSA. . . . . . Woman's National Sabbath Alliance
WUMS. . . . . . Woman's Union Missionary Society of America
WAVES . . . . . Women Accepted for Volunteer Emergency Service (US Navy Women's
    Reserve) (World War II and later)
WAF. . . . . . . Women in the Air Force
WAPS . . . . . . Women of the American Press Service (Accredited American women war
    correspondents) (World War II)
WAVES. . . . . . Women Appointed Volunteer Emergency Services (British) (World War II)
WICS . . . . . . Women in Community Service (An organization)
WM . . . . Women Marines
WMS . . . . . . Women in the Medical Service (Army)
WINS . . . . . . Women in National Service (Name given by Ladies' Home Journal to
    American housewives and their teen-age daughters, "the greatest
    reserve strength of America") (World War II)
WINKS . . . . . . Women in Numerous Kitchens (World War II)
WOWS . . . . . . Women Ordnance Workers (A national voluntary organization) (World
    War II)
WOW . . . . . . Women Our Wonders (Anti-feminist men's group)
WIPS . . . . Women in Production Service (A voluntary, semimilitary organization of
    women employees, primarily at the E.I. duPont de Nemours and
    Company, at Richmond, Va.) (World War II)
WPS . . . . Women in Public Service
WIRES . . . . . . Women in Radio and Electrical Service (World War II)
WISP . . . . . . Women Strike for Peace
WITS . . . . . . Women in Technical Service (World War II)
WUMPS . . . . . Women Umpires (World War II)
WUUN . . . . . . Women United for United Nations
WWWV . . . . . . Women World War Veterans
WAS . . . . Women's Addiction Service (National Institute of Mental Health)
WAIF . . . . . . Women's Adoption International Fund
WASP . . . . . . Women's Airforce Service Pilots (World War II)
WAO . . . . . . Women's American ORT
WACA . . . . . . Women's Apparel Chains Associations
WAAC . . . . . . Women's Army Auxiliary Corps (Name later changed to WAC) (World
    War II)
WACB . . . . . . Women's Army Classification Battery
WAC . . . . Women's Army Corps
WACRES . . . . . Women's Army Corps Reserve
WACSM . . . . . Women's Army Corps Service Medal

WACVA . . . . . Women's Army Corps-Veterans Association
WAMS. . . . . . Women's Automotive Maintenance Staff
WAAF. . . . . . Women's Auxiliary Air Force (Functioned under direct command of
    RAF) (World War II) (British)
WAAMMS . . . . Women's Auxiliary of the American Merchant Marine (World War II)
WAAS . . . . . . Women's Auxiliary Army Service
WAASC. . . . . . Women's Auxiliary Army Service Corps (British)
WAAAF. . . . . . Women's Auxiliary Australian Air Force
WAFS . . . . . . Women's Auxiliary Ferrying Squadron (Part of Air Transport Command)
    (World War II)
WAFS . . . . . . Women's Auxiliary Fire Service (British) (World War II)
WAPC . . . . . . Women's Auxiliary Police Corps (British) (World War II)
WASPS . . . . . Women's Auxiliary Service Platoon
WATS . . . . . . Women's Auxiliary Training Service
WB . . . . Women's Bureau (Department of Labor)
WCOF . . . . . . Women's Catholic Order of Foresters
WCA . . . . . . Women's Christian Association
WCTU . . . . . . Women's Christian Temperance Union
WCHI . . . . . . Women's Council for the Histadrut in Israel
WDCS . . . . . . Women's Division of Christian Service (of the Board of Missions, The
    Methodist Church)
WEIU . . . . . . Women's Educational and Industrial Union
WEST . . . . . . Women's Enlisted Screening Test
WEAL . . . . . . Women's Equity Action League
WFTD . . . . . . Women's Flying Training Detachment (World War II)
WHMA . . . . . . Women's Home Mission Association
WINS . . . . . . Women's Industrial and National Service Corps (British) (World War II)
WIDF . . . . . . Women's International Democratic Federation
WILPF . . . . . . Women's International League for Peace and Freedom
WIO . . . . Women's International ORT
WITCH . . . . . . Women's International Terrorist Conspiracy from Hell (Feminist group)
WIZO. . . . . . . Women's International Zionist Organization
WJCC . . . . . . Women's Joint Congressional Committee
WJLCER . . . . . Women's Joint Legislative Committee for Equal Rights
WLA . . . . . . Women's Land Army (British) (World War II)
WLA. . . . . . . Women's Land Army (Part of the United States Crop Corps) (World War II)
WLI . . . . Women's League for Israel
WMS . . . . . . Women's Medical Specialist
WMSC . . . . . . Women's Medical Specialists Corps
WNAAUS . . . . Women's National Aeronautical Association of the United States
WNAF . . . . . . Women's National Aquatic Forum
WNBA . . . . . . Women's National Book Association
WNDC . . . . . . Women's National Democratic Club
WNI. . . . . . . Women's National Institute
WNPC . . . . . . Women's National Press Club
WNRC . . . . . . Women's National Republican Club
WOHH . . . . . . Women's Organization of Hapoel Hamizrachi
WOSL. . . . . . . Women's Overseas Service League
WPCND . . . . . Women's Patriotic Conference on National Defense
WPSNY. . . . . . Women's Philatelic Society of New York
WRAP . . . . . . Women's Radical Action Project (Feminist group)
WRC . . . . Women's Relief Corps
WR . . . . Women's Reserve (Navy)
WA . . . . Women's Reserve, Aviation Nonflying Duties (USNR officer designation)
W-V(S) (CEC). . Women's Reserve, Civil Engineering Corps Duties (USNR commissioned
    officer designation)
WRCGR. . . . . . Women's Reserve of the Coast Guard Reserve
WC . . . . Women's Reserve, Communications Duties (USNR officer designation)
W-V(S) (DC) . . Women's Reserve, Dental Corps Duties (USNR commissioned officer
    designation)
W-V(S). . . . . . Women's Reserve, Emergency Duties (USNR commissioned officer
    designation)
WE. . . . . Women's Reserve, Engineering Duties (USNR officer designation)
W-V(S) (H) . . . Women's Reserve, Hospital Corps Duties (USNR commissioned officer
    designation)
WI . . . . Women's Reserve, Intelligence Duties (USNR officer designation)
WL . . . . Women's Reserve, Legal Specialist Duties (USNR officer designation)
W-V(S) (MC). . Women's Reserve, Medical Corps Duties (USNR commissioned officer
    designation)
WO . . . . Women's Reserve, Ordnance Duties (USNR officer designation)
W-V(S) (SC). . . Women's Reserve, Supply Corps Duties (USNR commissioned officer
    designation)
W . . . . Women's Reserve, Unlimited Service (USNR officer designation)
WRAF . . . . . . Women's Royal Air Force (British)
WRAC . . . . . . Women's Royal Army Corps (British)
WRCNS . . . . . Women's Royal Canadian Naval Service (World War II)
WRENS . . . . . Women's Royal Naval Service (WRNS) (Acronym is a phonetic reference
    to members of this British service branch)
WRNS. . . . . . Women's Royal Naval Service (A member is familiarly called a "Wren")
    (British) (World War II)
WSSI . . . . . . Women's Social Service for Israel

WTC	Women's Talent Corps
WTS	Women's Transport Service (British)
WUSL	Women's United Service League (British)
WVMA	Women's Veterinary Medical Association
WVS	Women's Voluntary Services (Coordinated work of women for national service) (British) (World War II)
WWSD	Women's War Savings Division
WWD	Women's Wear Daily
WWS	Women's Welfare Service
W	Won (Sports statistics)
WF	Won on Foul (Boxing)
W	Wood
WATW	Wood Awning Type Window
WB	Wood Base (Technical drawings)
WBF	Wood Block Floor (Technical drawings)
WBL	Wood Blocking
WCW	Wood Casement Window (Technical drawings)
WC	Wood Casing
WD	Wood Door (Technical drawings)
WDF	Wood Door and Frame (Technical drawings)
WDS	Wood Dye Stain
WFBI	Wood Fiber Blanket Institute
WFI	Wood Flooring Institute of America
WFS	Wood Furring Strips (Technical drawings)
WHBMA	Wood Hat Block Manufacturers Association
GWD	(Gar) Wood Industries, Inc. (NYSE symbol)
WJC	Wood Junior College (Mississippi)
WNSEA	Wood Naval Stores Export Association
WOFI	Wood Office Furniture Institute
WSR	Wood-Shingle Roof (Technical drawings)
WTSB	Wood Turners Service Bureau
WTSA	Wood Turners and Shapers Association
LIU	Wood, Wire and Metal Lathers International Union
WWML	Wood, Wire & Metal Lathers' International Union
WBI	Wooden Box Institute
WPTA	Wooden Pail and Tub Association
WOW	Woodmen of the World
WWLIS	Woodmen of the World Life Insurance Society
WHOI	Woods Hole Oceanographic Institution
WOD	Woodward Iron Company (NYSE symbol)
WMDA	Woodworking Machinery Distributors Association
WMMA	Woodworking Machinery Manufacturers Association
WHMAA	Wool Hat Manufacturers Association of America
WMC	Wool Manufacturers Council
WPCA	Wool Pullers Council of America
WTPBC	Wool Textiles Production Board of Control (British) (World War I)
WYJCA	Wool Yarn Jobbers Credit Association
WHIA	Woolen Hosiery Institute of America
WJA	Woolen Jobbers Association
WAWA	Woolens and Worsteds of America
WWA	Woolens and Worsteds of America (Association)
WA	Woolwich Armstrong Gun
Z	Woolworth (F. W.) Company (NYSE symbol) (Wall Street slang name: "Five & Dime")
WFEB	Worcester Foundation for Experimental Biology
WJC	Worcester Junior College (Massachusetts)
WPI	Worcester Polytechnic Institute
W	Word
WA	Word Add
WAF	Word Address Format
WA	Word After (Message handling)
WB	Word Before (Message handling)
WCM	Word Combine and Multiplexer
WCR	Word Control Register
WDS	Word Discrimination Score
WD	Word Display
WTS	Word Terminal Synchronous
WADEX	Words and Authors Index (Computer-produced index)
WAM	Words a Minute
WPM	Words Per Minute
WPS	Words Per Second
W	Work
WAP	Work Assignment Procedure
WA	Work Authorization
WAD	Work Authorization and Delegation
WB	Work Book
WBS	Work Breakdown Structure
WC	Work Center
WCD	Work Center Description
WD	Work(ing) Day
WETARFAC	Work Element Timer and Recorder for Automatic Computing

WFS	Work Function Surface
WGI	Work Glove Institute
WIN	Work Incentive Program (Department of Labor)
WMS	Work Measurement System (Post Office)
WO	Work Order
WOWAR	Work Order and Work Accomplishment Record
WIP	Work in Progress
WRO	Work Release Order
WR	Work Request
WU	Work Unit
WUC	Work Unit Code
WUTS	Work Unit Time Standard
WAC	Worked All Continents (Contacted at least one station on all continents) (Amateur radio)
WAS	Worked All States (Contacted at least one station in all states) (Amateur radio)
WA	Workers Anonymous (Mythical organization devoted to helping human beings overcome their desire to lead productive lives; created by columnist Arthur Hoppe in satirizing short work-week and early retirement schemes)
WDL	Workers' Defense League
WEA	Workers' Educational Association
WC	Working Capital
WC	Working Circle (Technical drawings)
WCAB	Working Committee of the Aeronautical Board
WC/WO	Working Committee on Weather Operations
WG	Working Group
WGER	Working Group on Extraterrestrial Resources (NASA)
WGR	Working Group Report
WP	Working Paper
WP	Working Party
WPR	Working Party on Rationing (Allied German Occupation Forces)
WP	Working Point
WP	Working Pressure
WSC	Working Security Committee (Navy)
WSP	Working Steam Pressure
WVDC	Working Voltage, Direct Current
WLCS	Workload and Cost Schedule (Military)
WLF	Workload Factor
WARES	Workload and Resources Evaluation System
WBF	Workmen's Benefit Fund of the USA
WC	Workmen's Compensation
WCA	Workmen's Compensation Act
WD	Works Department
WPA	Works Progress Administration (Created, 1935, to operate public works projects for unemployed persons; name changed to Work Projects Administration, 1939; later, absorbed by Federal Works Agency, which was terminated in 1942)
WA	Workshop Assembly (Torpedo)
WCD	Workshop for Cultural Democracy
WIN	Workshop in Nonviolence
WAAS	World Academy of Art and Science (Israel)
WARC	World Administrative Radio Conference
WAIF	World Adoption International Fund
WAC	World Aeronautical Charts (Air Force)
WAC	World Affairs Center for the United States
WAERSA	World Agricultural Economics and Rural Sociology Abstracts (A publication)
WAA	World American Airlift
WAY	World Assembly of Youth
WAAE	World Association for Adult Education
WADVBS	World Association of Daily Vacation Bible Schools
WAE	World Association of Estonians
WAGGGS	World Association of Girl Guides and Girl Scouts
WAJ	World Association of Judges
WAPOR	World Association for Public Opinion Research
WATA	World Association of Travel Agencies
WAWF	World Association of World Federalists
WB	World Bank
WBA	World Boxing Association
WB	World Brotherhood
WCA	World Campus Afloat (Cruise ship educational program)
WCSI	World Centre for Scientific Information
WCASS	World Conference of Ashkenazi and Sephardi Synagogues
WCGZ	World Confederation of General Zionists
WCOTP	World Confederation of Organizations of the Teaching Profession (Also known as CMOPE)
WCPT	World Confederation for Physical Therapy
WCF	World Congress of Faiths
WCF	World Congress of Flight
WCCESSA	World Council of Christian Education and Sunday School Association

WCC	World Council of Churches
WCJE	World Council on Jewish Education
WCWB	World Council for the Welfare of the Blind
WDC	World Data Center (National Academy of Sciences)
WDC-A	World Data Center A
WDC-B	World Data Center B
WDC	World Development Corporation
WEF	World Education Fellowship
WE	World Education, Inc.
WEI	World Education, Incorporated
WEF	World Evangelical Fellowship
WFCYWG	World Federation of Catholic Young Women and Girls
WFD	World Federation of the Deaf
WFDY	World Federation of Democratic Youth
WFEA	World Federation of Educational Associations
WFHJ	World Federation of Hungarian Jews
WFMH	World Federation for Mental Health
WFN	World Federation of Neurology
WFNS	World Federation of Neurosurgical Societies
WFOT	World Federation of Occupational Therapists
WFPT	World Federation for Physical Therapy
WFPA	World Federation for the Protection of Animals (Also known as FMPA and WTB)
WFSW	World Federation of Scientific Workers
WFSA	World Federation of Societies of Anesthesiologists
WFTU	World Federation of Trade Unions
WFUNA	World Federation of United Nations Associations
WFB	World Fellowship of Buddhists
WFSEC	World Fellowship of Slavic Evangelical Christians
WFP	World Food Program (UN)
WFA	World Friendship Association
WFF	World Friendship Federation
WFS	World Future Society
WGI	World Geophysical Interval
WGC	World Gospel Crusades
WGM	World Gospel Mission
WGS	World Government Sponsors
WHO	World Health Organization (The pronunciation "who" is not acceptable) (United Nations affiliate)
WHRC	World Health Research Center
WHBL	World Home Bible League
WHO	World Housing Organization
WIWP	World Institute for World Peace
WIPO	World Intellectual Property Organization (Proposed replacement for BIRPI)
WJC	World Jewish Congress
WJT	World Journal Tribune (Defunct New York City afternoon newspaper)
WLF	World Law Fund
WMS	World Magnetic Survey
WMA	World Medical Association
WMR	World Medical Relief
WMHY	World Mental Health Year (1960)
WMO	World Meteorological Organization
WMC	World Methodist Council
WMPL	World Mission Prayer League
WMC	World Missions to Children
WMM	World Movement of Mothers
WN	World Neighbors
WOMAN	World Organization of Mothers of All Nations
WPA	World Parliament Association
WPB	World Peace Brigade
WPC	World Peace Congress
WPF	World Peace Foundation
WPP	World Pen Pals
WPC	World Planning Chart (Aviation)
WPO	World Ploughing Organization
WPS	World Politics Simulation
WPC	World Power Conference
WPA	World Presbyterian Alliance
WPM	World Presbyterian Missions
WPF	World Prohibition Federation
WRY	World Refugee Year
WRF	World Rehabilitation Fund
WSRI	World Safety Research Institute
WSSA	World Secret Service Association
WSF	World Sephardi Federation
WSS	World Ship Society
WSC	World Spiritual Council
WSR	World Students Relief
WTP	World Tape Pals (An organization)
WTE	World Tapes for Education
WTCA	World Trade Centers Association
WTD	World Trade Directory (Department of Commerce)
WTWA	World Trade Writers Association
WUCT	World Union of Catholic Teachers
WUCWO	World Union of Catholic Women's Organizations
WUF	World Union of Free Thinkers
WUFTU	World Union of Free Trade Unions
WUJS	World Union of Jewish Students
WULTUO	World Union of Liberal Trade Union Organizations
WUPJ	World Union for Progressive Judaism
WUR	World University Roundtable
WUS	World University Service
WVA	World Veterinary Association
WVPA	World Veterinary Poultry Association
WVF	World Veterans Federation
WVF	World Veterans Fund
WV	World Vision
WWI	World War I
WWIVM	World War I Victory Medal
WWII	World War II
WWIIHSLB	World War II Honorable Service Lapel Button
WWIIVM	World War II Victory Medal
WWIII	World War III
WWTCA	World War Tank Corps Association
WWP	World Weather Program (National Science Foundation)
WWW	World Weather Watch
WWF	World Wildlife Fund
WWWCUS	World without War Council of the United States (Formerly, TTP)
WCEU	World's Christian Endeavor Union
WPSA	World's Poultry Science Association
WSCF	World's Student Christian Federation
WWCTU	World's Woman's Christian Temperance Union
WW	World-Wide
WWA	World Wide Airlines, Inc.
WWBPU	World Wide Baraca-Philathea Union
WEC	Worldwide Evangelization Crusade
WFP	Worldwide Fast for Peace
WWIS	World Wide Information Services
WWIO	Worldwide Inventory Objective
WWMCCS	World-Wide Military Command and Control System (Defense)
WORSAM	Worldwide Organizational Structure for Army Medical Support Study
WWPMU	World-Wide Prayer and Missionary Union
WWSN	World-Wide Seismology Net (National Bureau of Standards)
WWSSN	Worldwide Standardized Seismograph Network
STRATCOM . . .	Worldwide Strategic Communications System (Air Force)
WOSAC	Worldwide Synchronization of Atomic Clocks
WGJ	Worm Gear Jack
WGSJ	Worm Gear Screw Jack
WOIS	Worn Out in Service (Military)
WOW	Worn Out Wolf (An aging philanderer) (Slang)
WM	Worshipful Master (Masonry)
WCA	Worst Case Analysis
WCCA	Worst Case Circuit Analysis
WTH	Worthington Corporation (NYSE symbol)
WJC	Worthington Junior College (Minnesota)
WCT	Worthy Chief Templar
WGC	Worthy Grand Chaplain (Masonry)
WGG	Worthy Grand Guardian (Masonry)
WP	Worthy Patriarch
WGF	Wound Glass Fiber
WIA	Wounded in Action (Military)
WEMA	Woven Elastic Manufacturers Association
WFBMA	Woven Fabric Belting Manufacturers Association
WWPA	Woven Wire Products Association
WFL	Wredemann-Frang Law
WAML	Wright Aero Medical Laboratory (Air Force)
WAC	Wright Aeronautical Corporation
WAD	Wright Aeronautical Division
WADC	Wright Air Development Center (Air Force)
WADD	Wright Air Development Division
WAFB	Wright Air Force Base
WRBR	Wright Brothers National Memorial
WCL	Wright Center of Laboratories
WPAFB	Wright-Patterson Air Force Base
WTR	Wrightsville & Tennille R. R. (AAR code)
WWY	Wrigley (William Jr.) (Delaware) (NYSE symbol)
WAC	Write Address Counter
WB	Write Buffer
WC	Write and Compute
WDR	Write Drum
WF	Write Forward
WO	Write Out

WPB . . . . Write Printer Binary
WPD . . . . Write Printer Decimal
WPU . . . . Write Punch
WS . . . . Writer to the Signet (British)
WGAE . . . . . . Writers Guild of America, East
WGAW . . . . . . Writers Guild of America, West
WSA . . . . Writers' Sodality of America
WA . . . . Writing Ability
WIMA . . . . . . Writing Instrument Manufacturers Association
WPMA . . . . . . Writing Paper Manufacturers Association
WACO . . . . . . Written Advice of Contracting Officer (Military)

W . . . . Wrong
WF . . . . Wrong Font (Typesetting) (Proofreader's mark)
WI . . . . Wrought Iron
WUPA . . . . . Wupatki National Monument
WBCA . . . . . Wyandotte Bantam Club of America
WYS . . . . Wyandotte Southern R. R. (AAR code)
WYT . . . . Wyandotte Terminal R. R. (AAR code)
WYO . . . . Wyandotte Worsted Company (NYSE symbol)
WJLC . . . . Wye Junction Latching Circulator
WY . . . . Wyoming

X

XAFH . . . . X-Band Antenna Feed Horn
XAS . . . . X-Band Antenna System
XCT . . . . X-Band Communications Transponder
XDPS . . . . . . X-Band Diode Phase Shifter
XFH . . . . X-Band Feed Horn
XFM . . . . X-Band Ferrite Modulator
XFC . . . . X-Band Frequency Converter
XIA . . . . X-Band Interferometer Antenna
XK . . . . X-Band Klystron
XLA . . . . X-Band Limiter Attenuator
XMS . . . . X-Band Microwave Source
XMT . . . . X-Band Microwave Transmitter
XPA . . . . X-Band Parametric Amplifier
XPA . . . . X-Band Passive Array
XPS . . . . X-Band Phase Shifter
XPA . . . . X-Band Planar Array
XPAA . . . . . . X-Band Planar Array Antenna
XPA . . . . X-Band Power Amplifier
XPPA . . . . . . X-Band Pseudo-Passive Array
XPT . . . . X-Band Pulse Transmitter
XPPA . . . . . . X-Band Pulsed Power Amplifier
XRB . . . . X-Band RADAR Beacon
XSA . . . . X-Band Satellite Antenna
XSTA . . . . . . X-Band Satellite Tracking Antenna
XSR . . . . X-Band Scatterometer RADAR
XSTD . . . . . . X-Band Stripline Tunnel Diode
XSTDA . . . . . . X-Band Stripline Tunnel Diode Amplifier
XTA . . . . X-Band Tracking Antenna
XTWA . . . . . . X-Band Traveling Wave Amplifier
XTWM . . . . . . X-Band Traveling Wave MASER
XTO . . . . X-Band Triode Oscillator
XC . . . . X-Chromosome
XAT . . . . X-Ray Analysis Trial
XRCD . . . . . . X-Ray Crystal Density
XDP . . . . X-Ray Density Probe
XRD . . . . X-Ray Diffraction
XDP . . . . X-Ray Diffraction Powder
XDPC . . . . . . X-Ray Diffraction Powder Camera
XDS . . . . X-Ray Diffraction System
XEG . . . . X-Ray Emission Gauge
XES . . . . X-Ray Emission Spectra
XFD . . . . X-Ray Flow Detection

XRF . . . . X-Ray Fluorescence (Spectrometry)
XFA . . . . X-Ray Fluorescence Absorption
XHM . . . . . . X-Ray Hazard Meter
XIM . . . . . . X-Ray Intensity Meter
XRP . . . . X-Ray and Photofluorography Technician (Navy)
XSF . . . . X-Ray Scattering Facility
XRT . . . . X-Ray Technician (Navy)
XT . . . . X-Ray Tube
XVA . . . . X-Ray Vidicon Analysis
XECF . . . . . . XE Cold Flow Engine (NERVA)
XYA . . . . X-Y Axis
XYAT . . . . . . X-Y Axis Table
XYP . . . . X-Y Plotter
XYR . . . . X-Y Recorder
XDH . . . . Xanthine Dehydrogenase
XMS . . . . Xavier Mission Sisters (Catholic Mission Sisters of St. Francis Xavier) (Roman Catholic religious order)
XSB . . . . Xavier Society for the Blind
XU . . . . Xavier University (Louisiana; Ohio)
X . . . . Xenon (Chemical element)
Xe . . . . Xenon (Chemical element)
XAL . . . . Xenon Arc Lamp
XDT . . . . Xenon Discharge Tube
XFQH . . . . . . Xenon-Filled Quartz Helix
XFT . . . . Xenon Flash Tube
XIRS . . . . Xenon Infrared Searchlight
XIS . . . . Xenon Infrared Searchlight
XLC . . . . Xenon Lamp Collimator
XLPS . . . . . . Xenon Lamp Power Supply
XLDT . . . . . . Xenon LASER Discharge Tube
XLT . . . . Xenon LASER Tube
XLS . . . . Xenon Light Source
XLSS . . . . . . Xenon Light Source System
XOB . . . . Xenon Optical Beacon
XQH . . . . Xenon Quartz Helix
XSAL . . . . . . Xenon Short Arc Lamp
XRX . . . . Xerox Corporation (NYSE symbol)
XDS . . . . Xerox Data Systems (Formerly, SDS)
XPM . . . . Xerox Planning Model (A computerized representation of the Xerox Corporation's operations)
XPP . . . . Xi Psi Phi (Fraternity)
XSP . . . . Xi Sigma Pi (Fraternity)

Y

PY . . . . Yacht (Navy symbol)
YABA . . . . . . Yacht Architects and Brokers Association
YC. . . . . Yacht Club
YRA . . . . Yacht Racing Association (British)
YSB . . . . Yacht Safety Bureau
YCA . . . . Yachting Club of America
YAA . . . . Yachtsmen's Association of America
YPF . . . . Yacimientos Petroliferos Fiscales (Argentina) (Oil agency)
YVJC . . . . . . Yakima Valley Junior College (Washington)
YVT . . . . Yakima Valley Transportation Company (AAR code)
YAK . . . . Yakovlev (Russian aircraft symbol; initialism taken from name of aircraft's designer)
YLJ . . . . Yale Law Journal
YPM . . . . Yale Peabody Museum
YAT . . . . Yale & Towne Manufacturing Company (NYSE symbol)
YU . . . . Yale University
YUL . . . . Yale University Library
YAN . . . . Yancey R. R. (AAR code)
YANGPAT. . . Yangtze Patrol, Asiatic Fleet (Navy)
YSM . . . . Yangtze Service Medal
YAEC . . . . . . Yankee Atomic Electric Company
YCF . . . . Yankee Critical Facility (Atomic energy)
Y. . . . . Yard (Measure)
YB . . . . Yard Bird (Confined to camp) (Military slang)
YC. . . . . Yard Craft (Navy symbol)
YFD . . . . Yard Floating Dry Dock (Navy symbol)
YFU . . . . Yard Freight Unit
YP . . . . Yard Patrol
YS . . . . Yard Superintendent
YDSD . . . . . . Yards & Docks Supply Depot
YMA . . . . Yarn Merchants Association
YO . . . . Yarn Over
YAM . . . . Yates American Machine Company (NYSE symbol)
YAS . . . . Yaw Attitude Sensor
YA. . . . . Yaw Axis
YC. . . . . Yaw Channel
YC. . . . . Yaw Coupling
YCP . . . . Yaw Coupling Parameter
YDC. . . . . . . Yaw Damper Computer
YEA . . . . Yaw Error Amplifier
YPD . . . . Yaw Phase Detector
YAP . . . . Yaw and Pitch
YPA . . . . Yaw Precession Amplifier
YR . . . . Yaw Ring
YSE . . . . Yaw Steering Error
Y & MV . . . . . Yazoo and Mississippi Valley Railroad Company
Y . . . . Year
YOB . . . . Year of Birth
YOD . . . . Year of Death
YOM . . . . . . Year of Marriage
YO . . . . Year-Old
YB . . . . Yearbook
YSP . . . . Years Service for Severance Pay Purposes (Military)
YADH . . . . . . Yeast Alcohol Dehydrogenase
Y. . . . . Yellow (Buoy)
YL. . . . . Yellow (Maps and charts)
YDAA. . . . . . Yellow Dinitrophenyl Aspartic Acid
YE . . . . Yellow Edges
YE . . . . Yellow Enzyme
YG . . . . Yellow(ish) Green
YIL . . . . Yellow Indicator Lamp
YM . . . . Yellow Metal
YP . . . . Yellow Pine

YS . . . . Yellow Spot
YSI . . . . Yellow Springs Instrument Company
YVC. . . . . . . Yellow Varnish Cambric
YBRA . . . . . . Yellowstone-Bighorn Research Association
YELL . . . . . . Yellowstone National Park
Y. . . . . Yen (Japanese monetary unit)
Y. . . . . Yeoman
YN . . . . Yeoman (Navy rating)
YC. . . . . Yeomanry Cavalry (Military) (British)
YN . . . . Yes-No
YTHJ . . . . . . Yeshivath Torath Hayim in Jerusalem
YTA . . . . Yiddish Theatrical Alliance
YWU . . . . . . Yiddish Writers Union
YKUF . . . . . . Yiddisher Kultur Farband
YDB . . . . Yield Diffusion Bonding
YMS. . . . . . . Yield Measurement System
YP . . . . Yield Point (Ordinarily expressed in PSI)
YS . . . . Yield Strength (Ordinarily expressed in PSI)
YSB . . . . Yield Stress Bonding
YSDB . . . . . . Yield Stress Diffusion Bonding
YPE . . . . Yoho Pitch Extractor
YAR . . . . York-Antwerp Rules
YEB . . . . Yorkshire Electricity Board (British)
YLI . . . . The Yorkshire Light Infantry (British Army)
YTCA . . . . . . Yorkshire Terrier Club of America
YOSE . . . . . . Yosemite National Park
U . . . . You (Communications)
YAC . . . . Young Adult Council of National Social Welfare Assembly
YASD . . . . . . Young Adult Services Division (of ALA)
YAIC . . . . . . Young American Indian Council
YAAP . . . . . . Young Americans Against Pollution (Organization in Haverford, Pennsylvania)
YAF . . . . Young Americans for Freedom (An organization)
YCF . . . . Young Calvinist Federation
YCM . . . . Young Christian Movement
YCSM . . . . . . Young Christian Student Movement
YCS . . . . Young Christian Students (College, high school, or international)
YCW . . . . . . Young Christian Workers (Later, Young Christian Movement)
YCLA . . . . . . Young Circle League of America
YCI . . . . Young Communist International (Dissolved, 1943)
YCL . . . . Young Communist League
YDCA. . . . . . Young Democratic Clubs of America
YDL. . . . . . . Young Development Laboratories
YGS. . . . . . . Young Guard Society
YHT . . . . Young-Helmholtz Theory
YIE . . . . Young Interference Experiment
YIIJS . . . . . . Young Israel Institute for Jewish Studies
YLI . . . . Young Ladies Institute
YL. . . . . Young Lady (Amateur radio slang)
YLC. . . . . . . Young Life Campaign
Y. . . . . Young Men's (or Women's) Christian Association (Short form of reference, especially to the group's building or specific facility, as "the Y swimming pool")
YM . . . . Young Men's (Christian Association)
YMCA . . . . . . Young Men's Christian Association
YMCU . . . . . . Young Men's Christian Union
YMFS . . . . . . Young Men's Friendly Society (British)
YMHA . . . . . . Young Men's Hebrew Association
YMI . . . . Young Men's Institute
YM - YWHA . . Young Men's and Young Women's Hebrew Association
YMF . . . . Young Musicians Foundation
YP . . . . Young People
YPSL . . . . . . Young Peoples Socialist League

YPSCE	Young People's Society of Christian Endeavor
YPO	Young Presidents' Organization
YR	Young Republican
YRNF	Young Republican National Federation
YSA	Young Socialist Alliance
YS	Young Soldier(s)
YG	Young Spring & Wire Corporation (NYSE symbol)
YWS	Young Wales Society
YW	Young Women's (Christian Association)
YWCA	Young Women's Christian Association
YWCTU	Young Women's Christian Temperance Union
YWHA	Young Women's Hebrew Association
YWHS	Young Women's Help Society (British)
YWF	Young World Federalists
Y	Younger or Youngest
YME	Young's Modulus of Elasticity
YN	Youngstown & Northern R. R. (AAR code)
YB	Youngstown Sheet & Tube Company (NYSE symbol) (Wall Street slang name: "Yellow Belly")
YS	Youngstown & Southern Railway Company (AAR code)
YSD	Youngstown Steel Door Company (NYSE symbol)
Y	Your
URDIS	Your Dispatch (Military)
YIGIB	Your Improved Group Insurance Benefits
URLTR	(Reference) Your Letter (Military)
URMGM	Your Mailgram (Military)
URMSG	Your Message
YM	Your Message
YMD	Your Message Date
URAD	Your Radio (message) (Military)
URSER	(Reference) Your Serial (Military)
URTEL	Your Telegram
YAWF	Youth Against War and Fascism
YOAN	Youth of All Nations
YANK	Youth of America Needs to Know

YFC	Youth for Christ, International
YCAP	Youth Committee Against Poverty
YCD	Youth Correction Division (Department of Justice)
YDI	Youth Development, Incorporated
YES	Youth Employment Service
YH	Youth Hostel
YHA	Youth Hostels Association
YOB	Youth Opportunities Board
YOU	Youth Opportunities Unlimited (Project)
YOC	Youth Opportunity Campaign (Civil Service Commission)
YOC	Youth Opportunity Centers
YOC	Youth Opportunity Corps
YOU	Youth Organizations United
YTEP	Youth Training and Employment Project
YUK	Youth Uncovering Krud (Antipollution organization in Schenectady, New York)
YFU	Youth for Understanding
YW	Yreka Western R. R. (AAR code)
Yb	Ytterbium (Chemical element)
Y	Yttrium (A chemical element; also Yt)
Yt	Yttrium (A chemical element; also Y)
YAG	Yttrium Aluminum Garnet (LASER)
YAGL	Yttrium Aluminum Garnet LASER
YAL	Yttrium Aluminum LASER
YGL	Yttrium Garnet LASER
YIG	Yttrium Iron Garnet
YUBO	Yucca House National Monument
YRS	Yugoslav Relief Society
YFTU	Yugoslavia Federation of Trade Unions
Y	Yukon Standard Time (Aviation)
YT	Yukon Territory, Canada
YPG	Yuma Proving Ground (Arizona) (Army)
YTS	Yuma Test Station
YSL	Yves Saint Laurent (French couturier)

Z

ZAM . . . . Z-Axis Modulation
ZKD . . . . Zagreb Kajkavian Dialect XXX (of Serbo-Croatian)
ZZA . . . . Zamak Zinc Alloy
ZANC . . . . . . Zambia National Congress - Southern Rhodesia
ZAT . . . . Zantop Air Transport
ZNP . . . . Zanzibar Nationalist Party
ZPFL . . . . . . Zanzibar and Pemba Federation of Labour
ZPPP . . . . . . Zanzibar and Pemba People's Party
ZG . . . . Zap Gun
ZCZ . . . . Zavodi Crvena Zastava (Yugoslavia)
ZSD . . . . Zebra Stripe Display
ZISS . . . . . . Zebulun Israel Seafaring Society
ZYP . . . . Zefkrome Yarn Program (Dow Chemical Company)
ZLSM . . . . . Zeiss Light Section Microscope
ZAMP . . . . . . Zeitschrift fuer Angewandte Mathematic und Physik (Switzerland)
ZDMG . . . . . Zeitschrift der Deutschen Morgenlandischen Gesellschaft
ZD . . . . Zener Diode
ZVR . . . . Zener Voltage Regulator
ZVRD . . . . . . Zener Voltage Regulator Diode
Z . . . . Zenith
ZD . . . . Zenith Description
Z . . . . Zenith Distance (Astronomy)
ZD . . . . Zenith Distance (Navigation)
ZE . . . . Zenith Radio Corporation (NYSE symbol)
ZRC . . . . Zenith Radio Corporation
ZDC . . . . Zens Defense Center
ZKSK . . . . . . Zentrale Kommission fuer Staatliche Kontrolle
ZPKK . . . . . . Zentrale Parteikontrollkommission
ZRK . . . . Zentrale Revisionskommission
ZSGL . . . . . . Zentrale Schulgruppenleitungen
ZKD . . . . Zentraler Kurierdienst
ZR . . . . Zentralrat
ZAED . . . . . . Zentralstelle fuer Atomkernenergie-Dokumentation beim Gmelin-Institut
(Central Agency for Atomic Energy Documentation of the Gmelin
Institute) (Germany)
ZLDI . . . . . . Zentralstelle fuer Luftfahrtdokumentation und Inform
ZMD . . . . . . Zentralstelle fuer Maschinelle Dokumentation (West Germany)
ZVEI . . . . . . Zentralverband der Electro-technischen Industrie (West Germany)
ZV . . . . Zentralvorstand
Z . . . . Zero
ZAS . . . . Zero Access Storage
ZA . . . . Zero and Add
ZAP . . . . Zero and Add Packed
ZAI . . . . Zero Address Instruction
ZAAP . . . . . . Zero Antiaircraft Potential
ZAP . . . . Zero Antiaircraft Potential (Missile)
ZBL . . . . Zero-Based Linearity
ZB . . . . Zero Beat (Radio)
ZBR . . . . Zero Beat Reception
ZBR . . . . Zero Bend Radius
ZCD . . . . Zero Crossing Detector
ZD . . . . Zero Defects
ZDC . . . . Zero Defects Council
ZDP . . . . Zero Defects Program (or Proposal)
ZDPA . . . . . . Zero Defects Program Audit
ZDPG . . . . . . Zero Defects Program Guideline
ZDPO . . . . . . Zero Defects Program Objective
ZDPR . . . . . . Zero Defects Program Responsibility
ZE . . . . Zero Effusion
ZOE . . . . Zero-Energy
ZEA . . . . Zero Energy Assembly
ZEBRA . . . . . . Zero Energy Breeder Reactor Assembly (British)
ZEC . . . . Zero Energy Coefficient

ZEEP . . . . . . Zero Energy Experimental Pile (Nuclear reactor) (Canada)
ZER . . . . Zero Energy Reflection
ZERC . . . . . . Zero Energy Reflection Coefficient
ZES . . . . Zero Energy System
ZETR . . . . . . Zero-Energy Thermal Reactor (British)
ZETA . . . . . . Zero-Energy Thermonuclear Assembly (AEC)
ZEUS . . . . . . Zero-Energy Uranium System (British)
ZFS . . . . Zero Field Splitting
ZF . . . . Zero Frequency
ZGS . . . . Zero Gradient Synchrotron (AEC)
ZGE . . . . Zero-Gravity Expulsion (or Effect or Environment)
ZET . . . . Zero-Gravity Expulsion Technique
ZGET . . . . . . Zero-Gravity Expulsion Technique
ZGG . . . . Zero-Gravity Generator
ZGS . . . . Zero-Gravity Simulator
ZI . . . . Zero Input
ZIR . . . . Zero Internal Resistance
ZEL . . . . Zero-Length Launch (Air Force)
ZLL . . . . Zero Length Launcher
ZELL . . . . . . Zero Length Launching
ZLD . . . . Zero Level Drift
ZL . . . . Zero Lift
ZLC . . . . Zero Lift Cord
ZLD . . . . Zero Lift Drag
ZLG . . . . Zero Line Gap
ZOPI . . . . . . Zero Order Polynomial Interpolator
ZOPP . . . . . . Zero Order Polynomial Predictor
ZO . . . . Zero Output
ZPE . . . . Zero Point Energy
ZPG . . . . Zero Population Growth (An organization)
ZPPR . . . . . . Zero Power Plutonium Reactor (AEC)
ZPR . . . . Zero Power Reactor (AEC)
ZPRF . . . . . . Zero Power Reactor Facility
ZPT . . . . Zero Power Test
ZRP . . . . Zero Radial Play
ZERT . . . . . . Zero Reaction Tool
ZRT . . . . Zero Reaction Tool
ZS . . . . Zero Shift
ZSI . . . . Zero Size Image
ZSG . . . . Zero Speed Generator
ZSPG . . . . . . Zero-Speed Pulse Generator
ZSC . . . . Zero Subcarrier Chromaticity
ZS . . . . Zero and Subtract
ZS . . . . Zero Suppress
ZCR . . . . Zero-Temperature Coefficient Resistor
ZTP . . . . Zero Temperature Plasma
OTLP . . . . . . Zero Transmission Level Point
ZWL . . . . Zero Wave Length
ZWV . . . . Zero Wave Velocity
ZW . . . . Zero Wear
ZZC . . . . Zero-Zero Condition
ZZV . . . . Zero-Zero Visibility
ZIG . . . . Zester Immune Globulin
ZBT . . . . Zeta Beta Tau (Fraternity)
ZPE . . . . Zeta Phi Eta
ZTA . . . . Zeta Tau Alpha (Sorority)
ZAR . . . . Zeus Acquisition RADAR (Missile defense)
ZDR . . . . Zeus Discrimination RADAR (Missile defense)
ZMAR . . . . . . Zeus Multifunction Array RADAR
ZPAR . . . . . . Zeus Phased Array RADAR
ZPA . . . . Zeus Program Analysis
ZPEN . . . . . . Zeus Project Engineer Network
ZPO . . . . Zeus Project Office

ZZ . . . . Zig-Zag
ZZD . . . . Zig-Zag Diagram
ZZR . . . . Zig-Zag Rectifier
ZAPU . . . . . . Zimbabwe African People's Union (Southern Rhodesia)
Z . . . . Zinc
Zn . . . . Zinc (Chemical element)
ZAB . . . . Zinc-Air Battery
ZAPB . . . . . . Zinc/Air Primary Battery
ZAT . . . . Zinc Atmospheric Tracer
ZBE . . . . Zinc Battery Electrode
ZCB . . . . Zinc-Coated Bolt
ZCN . . . . Zinc-Coated Nut
ZCS . . . . Zinc-Coated Screw
ZCW . . . . Zinc-Coated Washer
ZDS . . . . Zinc Detection System
ZDA . . . . Zinc Development Association
ZDC . . . . Zinc Die Casting
ZDG . . . . Zinc-Doped Germanium
ZEC . . . . Zinc-Electrochemical Cell
ZECC . . . . . . Zinc-Electrochemical Cell
ZIP . . . . Zinc Impurity Photodetector
ZIX . . . . Zinc Isopropyl Xanthate
ZALIS . . . . . . Zinc and Lead International Service
ZMRI . . . . . . Zinc Metals Research Institute
ZnO . . . . Zinc Oxide
ZOE . . . . Zinc Oxide-Eugenol (Dental cement)
ZOP . . . . Zinc Oxide Pigment
ZOR . . . . Zinc Oxide Resistor
ZPB . . . . Zinc Primary Battery
ZNR . . . . Zinc Resistor
ZSC . . . . Zinc Silicate Coat
ZSB . . . . Zinc Storage Battery
ZSAT . . . . . . Zinc Sulfide Atmospheric Tracer
ZSDS . . . . . . Zinc Sulfide Detection System
ZSD . . . . Zinc Sulfide Detector
ZSS . . . . Zinc Sulfide System
ZST . . . . Zinc Sulfide Tracer
ZOA . . . . Zionist Organization of America
ZCMI . . . . . . Zion's Cooperative Mercantile Institution (Department store in Salt Lake City, Utah)
ZJ . . . . Zipper Jacket
ZT . . . . Zipper Tubing
ZCC . . . . Zirconia-Coated Crucible
ZCIC . . . . . . Zirconia-Coated Iridium Crucible
ZFC . . . . Zirconia Fuel Cell
ZIC . . . . Zirconia-Iridium Crucible
Zr . . . . Zirconium (Chemical element)

ZRC . . . . Zirconium Carbide
ZHR . . . . Zirconium Hydride Reactor
ZRN . . . . Zirconium Nitride
ZBS . . . . Zivena Beneficial Society
ZSL . . . . Zjednoczone Stronnictwo Ludowe (United Peasants' Party) (Poland)
Z . . . . Zloty (Monetary unit in Poland)
ZLD . . . . Zodiacal Light Device
ZG . . . . Zollgesetz (Germany)
ZGH . . . . Zonal Gravity Harmonic
ZH . . . . Zonal Harmonic
ZI . . . . Zonal Index
Z . . . . Zone
ZC . . . . Zone Capacity
ZD . . . . Zone Description
ZE . . . . Zone Effect
Z/F . . . . Zone of Fire (Military)
ZFO . . . . Zone Francaise d'Occupation
ZH . . . . Zone Heater
ZIP . . . . Zone Improvement Plan (Post Office code)
ZI . . . . Zone of Interior (Military)
Z of I . . . . . . Zone of Interior (Army)
ZIA . . . . Zone of Interior Armies
Z . . . . Zone Marker
Z . . . . Zone Meridian (Lower or upper branch)
ZR . . . . Zone Refined
ZST . . . . Zone Standard Time
ZT . . . . Zone Time (Navy)
ZTO . . . . Zone Transportation Office(r) (Military)
ZUP . . . . Zone a Urbaniser de Priorite (Priority Urbanization Zone) (France)
ZWC . . . . Zone Wind Computer
ZWP . . . . Zone Wind Plotter
Z of C . . . . . . Zones of Communications (Military)
ZI . . . . Zonta International
ZG . . . . Zoological Gardens
ZS . . . . Zoological Society (British)
ZSN . . . . Zoological Station of Naples
Z-M . . . . Zuckerman-Moloff (Sewage treatment method)
ZWO . . . . Zuiver Wentenschappelijk Orderzock (Netherlands)
ZMMD . . . . . . Zurich, Mainz, Munich, Darmstadt (A joint European university effort on ALGOL processors)
ZPRSN . . . . . Zurich Provisional Relative Sunspot Number (NASA)
ZLN . . . . Zwiazek Ludowo Narodowy (National Democrats) (Poland)
ZMK . . . . . . Zwiazek Mlodziezy Komunistyczne
ZMP . . . . Zwiazek Mlodziezy Polskiej
ZMWRP . . . . . Zwiazek Mlodziezy Wiejskiej Rzeczypospolitej Polskiej
ZFP . . . . Zyglo-Fluorescent Penetrant
ZFPT . . . . . . Zyglo-Fluorescent Penetrant Testing